Sporting News BOOKS

BASEBALL GUIDE

2004 EDITION

EXPLANATION OF STATISTICAL ABBREVIATIONS

A: assists. **AB:** at-bats. **Avg.:** batting average (hits divided by at-bats). **BB:** bases on balls. **Bk.:** balks. **CG:** complete games. **CS:** caught stealing. **E:** errors. **ER:** earned runs. **ERA:** earned-run average (earned runs times nine divided by innings pitched). **G:** games. **GB:** games behind. **GF:** games finished. **GDP:** grounding into double plays. **GS:** games started. **H:** hits. **HB:** hit batsmen. **HP:** hit by pitches. **HR:** home runs. **IBB:** intentional bases on balls. **IP:** innings pitched. **L:** losses. **LOB:** runners left on base. **OBP:** on-base percentage (hits plus bases on balls plus hit by pitches divided by at-bats plus bases on balls plus hit by pitches plus sacrifice flies). **Pct.:** winning percentage. **PO:** putouts. **Pos.:** position. **R:** runs. **RBI:** runs batted in. **Rel.:** relief appearances. **SB:** stolen bases. **SF:** sacrifice flies (run-scoring flyouts). **SH:** sacrifice hits (bunts that advance one or more runners but result in the batter being retired at first base or reaching first on an error). **ShO:** shutouts. **Slg.:** slugging percentage (total bases divided by at-bats). **SO:** strikeouts. **Sv.:** saves. **Sv. Op.:** save opportunities. **TB:** total bases (hits plus doubles plus two times the number of triples plus three times the number of home runs). **TBF:** total batters faced. **TC:** total chances (putouts plus assists plus errors). **TPA:** total plate appearances (at-bats plus bases on balls plus sacrifice hits plus sacrifice flies plus hit by pitches plus times reaching base on catcher's interference). **W:** wins. **WP:** wild pitches. **2B:** doubles. **3B:** triples.

Major league statistics compiled by STATS Inc., a News Corporation company, 8130 Lehigh Avenue, Morton Grove, IL 60053. STATS is a trademark of Sports Team Analysis and Tracking Systems, Inc.

Minor league statistics provided by SportsTicker.

ISBN: 0-89204-731-4

10 9 8 7 6 5 4 3 2 1

CONTENTS

ON THE COVER: Ichiro Suzuki photo by Dilip Vishwanat/THE SPORTING NEWS; bottom left to right: Todd Helton by Robert Seale/THE SPORTING NEWS; Dontrelle Willis by Bob Leverone/THE SPORTING NEWS; Esteban Loaiza by David Durochik for THE SPORTING NEWS.

2004 SEASON

Major League Baseball directories

Team by team

MAJOR LEAGUE BASEBALL

Address
245 Park Avenue
New York, NY 10167
Telephone
212-931-7800
FAX
212-949-5654
Website
www.mlb.com
Commissioner of baseball
Allan H. "Bud" Selig
President and chief operating officer
Robert DuPuy
Executive v.p., baseball operations
Richard "Sandy" Alderson
Executive vice president, business
Timothy J. Brosnan
Executive v.p,, labor relations and human resources
Robert D. Manfred
Executive v.p., administration
John McHale
Executive v.p., finance
Jonathan Mariner
Senior v.p., international business operations
Paul Archey
Senior v.p. and general counsel, labor relations
Frank Coonelly
Senior v.p., club relations and scheduling
Katy Feeney
Senior v.p., security and facilities
Kevin Hallinan
Senior v.p., public relations
Richard Levin
Senior v.p., club relations
Phyllis Merhige
Senior v.p., special events
Marla Miller
Senior v.p. and general counsel
Ethan Orlinsky
Senior v.p. and general counsel
Tom Ostertag
Senioe v.p., marketing and advertising
Jacqueline Parkes
Senior v.p., licensing
Howard Smith
Senior v.p., baseball operations
Jimmie Lee Solomon
Senior v.p., broadcasting
Chris Tully
V.p., domestic licensing
Steve Armus
V.p., community affairs
Tom Brasuell
V.p., baseball operations and admin.
Ed Burns
V.p., management information systems
Julio Carbonell
V.p., accounting and treasurer
Bob Clark
V.p., public relations operations
Patrick Courtney
V.p., MLB productions
Dave Gavant
V.p., domestic licensing-Cooperstown
Colin Hagen
V.p., publishing and photographs
Don Hintze
V.p., international licensing
Shawn Lawson-Cummings
V.p., strategic planning, recruiting and diversity
Wendy Lewis
V.p., broadcast operations
Bernadette McDonald
V.p., international baseball operations
Lou Melendez
V.p., design services
Anne Occi
V.p., human resources
Ray Scott
V.p., programming and business affairs
Elizabeth Scott
V.p., finance
Kathleen Torres
V.p., on-field operations
Bob Watson
Executive director, Baseball Tomorrow fund
Cathy Bradley
Executive producer, international TV and broadcast
Russell Gabay

OTHER ORGANIZATIONS

LABOR RELATIONS COMMITTEE

Address
245 Park Avenue
New York, NY 10167
Telephone
212-931-7401
212-949-5690 (FAX)
Exec. vice president, labor relations and human resources
Robert D. Manfred Jr.
Sr. v.p. & gen. counsel, labor relations
Francis Coonelly
Deputy general counsel
Jennifer Gefsky
Counsel
Paul Mifsud
Director, salary and contract admin.
John Ricco

BASEBALL ASSISTANCE TEAM INC.

Address
245 Park Avenue
New York, NY 10167
Telephone
212-931-7821
Chairman
Bobby Murcer
President
Earl Wilson
Vice presidents
Steve Garvey
Bob Gibson
Lou Gorman
Ed Stack
Executive director
James J. Martin
Secretary
Thomas J. Ostertag
Treasurer
Jonathan Mariner

ASSOCIATION OF PROFESSIONAL BASEBALL PLAYERS OF AMERICA

Address
1820 W. Orangewood Ave., Suite 206
Orange, CA 92868
Telephone
714-935-9993
714-935-0431 (FAX)
President
John J. McHale
Vice presidents
Roland Hemond
Robert Kennedy
Secretary/treasurer
Dick Beverage

NATIONAL BASEBALL HALL OF FAME AND MUSEUM

Address
P.O. Box 590
Cooperstown, NY 13326
Telephone
607-547-7200
607-547-2044 (FAX)
Hall of Fame board of directors chairman
Jane Forbes Clark
President
Dale Petroskey
V.p. of business and administration
Bill Haase
V.p. and chief curator
William T. Spencer Jr.
Curator of collections
Peter P. Clark
Executive director of retail marketing
Barbara Shinn
Controller
Frances L. Althiser

Librarian
James L. Gates
V.p. of communications and education
Jeff Idelson

MAJOR LEAGUE SCOUTING BUREAU

Address
3500 Porsche Way, Suite 100
Ontario, CA 91764
Telephone
909-980-1881
909-980-7794 (FAX)
Director
Frank Marcos

MAJOR LEAGUE BASEBALL PLAYERS ASSOCIATION

Address
12 E. 49th St., 24th Floor
New York, NY 10017
Telephone
212-826-0808
212-752-3649 (FAX)
Executive director and general counsel
Donald M. Fehr
Special assistants
Tony Bernazard
Phil Bradley
Steve Rogers
Associate general counsel
Eugene D. Orza
Assistant general counsel
Jeff Fannell
Doyle R. Pryor
Michael Weiner
Counsel
Robert Leneghan
Director of licensing
Judy Heeter
Director of communications
Greg Bouris

MINOR LEAGUE BASEBALL NATIONAL ASSOCIATION OF PROFESSIONAL BASEBALL LEAGUES

Address
P.O. Box A
St. Petersburg, FL 33731
Telephone
727-822-6937
727-821-5819 (FAX)
President/CEO
Mike Moore
Vice president
Stan Brand
Vice president, administration/COO
Pat O'Connor
General counsel
Scott Poley
Special counsel
George Yund
Exec. director/business operations
Misann Ellmaker
Executive director/Professional Baseball Umpire Corporation
Mike Fitzpatrick
Director/media relations
Jim Ferguson
Director/baseball operations
Tim Brunswick
Director of Professional Baseball Employment Opportunities
Ann Perkins

MAJOR LEAGUE BASEBALL PLAYERS ALUMNI ASSOC.

Address
1631 Mesa Ave., Suite B
Colorado Springs, CO 80906
Telephone
719-477-1870
719-477-1875 (FAX)
President
Brooks Robinson
Vice presidents
Bob Boone
George Brett
Mike Hegan
Chuck Hinton
Al Kaline
Carl Erskine
Rusty Staub
Robin Yount
Vice chairman
Fred Valentine

WORLD UMPIRES ASSOCIATION

Address
P.O. Box 760
Cocoa, FL 32923-0760
Telephone
321-637-3471
321-633-7018 (FAX)
President
John Hirschbeck
Vice president
Joe Brinkman
Secretary/treasurer
Tim Welke
Labor counsel
Joel Smith

BASEBALL WRITERS' ASSOCIATION OF AMERICA

President
Paul Hagen, Philadelphia Daily News
Vice president
Drew Olson, Milwaukee Journal Sentinel
Secretary/treasurer
Jack O'Connell, Hartford Courant

ELIAS SPORTS BUREAU

Address
500 Fifth Ave.
New York, NY 10110
Telephone
212-869-1530
212-354-0980 (FAX)
General manager
Seymour Siwoff

SPORTSTICKER ENTERPRISES, L.P.

Address
Harborside Financial Center
800 Plaza Two
Jersey City, NJ 07311
Boston office
Boston Fish Pier
West Building No. 1
Boston, MA 02210
Telephone
201-309-1200
201-860-9742 (FAX)
Boston office
617-951-1379
617-737-9960 (FAX)
General manager
Jim Morganthaler
Director, minor league operations
Jim Keller
Assistant dir., minor league operations
Michael Walczak

ANAHEIM ANGELS

AMERICAN LEAGUE WEST DIVISION

2004 SEASON

April

SUN	MON	TUE	WED	THU	FRI	SAT
4	5	6 SEA	7 SEA	8 SEA	9 TEX	10 TEX
11 TEX	12 TEX	13 SEA	14 SEA	15 SEA	16 OAK	17 OAK
18 OAK	19	20 TEX	21 TEX	22 TEX	23 OAK	24 OAK
25 OAK	26	27 DET	28 DET	29 DET	30 MIN	

May

SUN	MON	TUE	WED	THU	FRI	SAT
						1 MIN
2 MIN	3 DET	4 DET	5 DET	6 TB	7 TB	8 TB
9 TB	10	11 NYY	12 NYY	13 NYY	14 BAL	15 BAL
16 BAL	17	18 NYY	19 NYY	20 NYY	21 BAL	22 BAL
23 BAL	24 TOR	25	26 TOR	27 TOR	28 CHW	29 CHW
30 CHW	31					

June

SUN	MON	TUE	WED	THU	FRI	SAT
		1 BOS	2 BOS	3 CLE	4 CLE	5 CLE
6 CLE	7	8 MIL	9 MIL	10 MIL	11 CHC	12 CHC
13 CHC	14	15 PIT	16 PIT	17 PIT	18 HOU	19 HOU
20 HOU	21 OAK	22 OAK	23 OAK	24 OAK	25 LA	26 LA
27 LA	28	29 OAK	30 OAK			

Home games shaded. All-Star Game July 13 at Houston. Schedule subject to change.

July

SUN	MON	TUE	WED	THU	FRI	SAT
				1 OAK	2 LA	3 LA
4 LA	5	6 CHW	7 CHW	8 CHW	9 TOR	10 TOR
11 TOR	12	13 All-Star	14	15 BOS	16 BOS	17 BOS
18 BOS	19 CLE	20 CLE	21 TEX	22 TEX	23 SEA	24 SEA
25 SEA	26 TEX	27 TEX	28 TEX	29 SEA	30 SEA	31 SEA

August

SUN	MON	TUE	WED	THU	FRI	SAT
1 SEA	2	3 MIN	4 MIN	5 MIN	6 KC	7 KC
8 KC	9 KC	10 BAL	11 BAL	12 BAL	13 DET	14 DET
15 DET	16	17 TB	18 TB	19 TB	20 NYY	21 NYY
22 NYY	23 KC	24 KC	25 KC	26	27 MIN	28 MIN
29 MIN	30	31 BOS				

Sept./Oct.

SUN	MON	TUE	WED	THU	FRI	SAT
			1 BOS	2 BOS	3 CLE	4 CLE
5 CLE	6	7 TOR	8 TOR	9 TOR	10 CHW	11 CHW
12 CHW	13 SEA	14 SEA	15 SEA	16 SEA	17 TEX	18 TEX
19 TEX	20 SEA	21 SEA	22 SEA	23	24 OAK	25 OAK
26 OAK	27 TEX	28 TEX	29 TEX	30 TEX	1 OAK	2 OAK
3 OAK	4	5	6	7	8	9

CLUB DIRECTORY

Owner
Arturo Moreno
President
Dennis Kuhl
Vice president and general manager
Bill Stoneman
Vice president, communications
Tim Mead
Assistant general manager
Ken Forsch
Special assistants to the g.m.
Preston Gomez
Gary Sutherland
Director, scouting
Eddie Bane
Director, player development
Tony Reagins
Manager, baseball operations
Abe Flores
Manager, baseball information
Larry Babcock
Manager, media services
Nancy Mazmanian
Manager, community development
Matt Bennett

MINOR LEAGUE AFFILIATES

Class	Team	League	Manager
AAA	Salt Lake	Pacific Coast	Mike Brumley
AA	Arkansas	Texas	Tyrone Boykin
Advanced A	Rancho Cucamonga	California	Bobby Meacham
A	Cedar Rapids	Midwest	Bobby Magallanes
Advanced Rookie	Provo	Pioneer	Tom Kotchman
Rookie	Mesa	Arizona	Brian Harper

More on the Angels at www.foxsports.com/named/FS/MLB/teams

BROADCAST INFORMATION

Radio: ESPN-AM (710).
TV: KCAL-TV (Channel 9).
Cable TV: Fox Sports West.

SPRING TRAINING

Ballpark (city): Tempe Diablo Stadium (Tempe, Ariz.).
Ticket information: 714-940-2000.

SPRING TRAINING ROSTER

Manager—Mike Scioscia (14).
Coaches—Bud Black (24), Alfredo Griffin (4), Mickey Hatcher (7), Joe Maddon (70), Ron Roenicke (12), Steve Soliz (61).

No.	PITCHERS	B/T	Ht./Wt.	Age*	2003 Clubs
	Andrade, Steve	R/R	6-1/220	26	Arkansas, Rancho Cucamonga
	Bittner, Tim	L/L	6-2/265	23	Kannapolis, Winston-Salem, Rancho Cucamonga
51	Bootcheck, Chris	R/R	6-5/200	25	Salt Lake, Anaheim
	Colon, Bartolo	R/R	5-11/240	30	Chicago
53	Donnelly, Brendan	R/R	6-3/240	32	Anaheim
	Escobar, Kelvim	R/R	6-1/210	27	Toronto
	Fischer, Rich	R/R	6-3/180	23	Arkansas
	Green, Steve	R/R	6-2/200	26	Mesa, Salt Lake
	Gregg, Kevin	R/R	6-6/220	25	Arkansas, Salt Lake, Anaheim
	Jenks, Bobby	R/R	6-3/270	23	Mesa, Arkansas
58	Jones, Greg	R/R	6-2/195	27	Salt Lake, Anaheim
41	Lackey, John	R/R	6-6/235	25	Anaheim
45	Ortiz, Ramon	R/R	6-0/175	30	Anaheim
40	Percival, Troy	R/R	6-3/235	34	Anaheim
57	Rodriguez, Fran.	R/R	6-0/185	22	Anaheim
34	Sele, Aaron	R/R	6-5/230	33	R. Cucamonga, Salt Lake, Anaheim
62	Shields, Scot	R/R	6-1/170	28	Anaheim
54	Turnbow, Derrick	R/R	6-3/200	26	Arkansas, Salt Lake, Anaheim
56	Washburn, Jarrod	L/L	6-1/195	29	Anaheim
77	Weber, Ben	R/R	6-4/205	34	Anaheim
	Woods, Jake	L/L	6-1/195	22	R. Cucamonga

No.	CATCHERS	B/T	Ht./Wt.	Age*	2003 Clubs
3	Gregorio, Tom	R/R	6-2/215	26	Salt Lake, Anaheim
1	Molina, Bengie	R/R	5-11/220	29	Anaheim
28	Molina, Jose	R/R	6-2/220	28	Anaheim
19	Nieves, Wil	R/R	5-11/190	26	Salt Lake

No.	INFIELDERS	B/T	Ht./Wt.	Age*	2003 Clubs
5	Amezaga, Alfredo	B/R	5-10/165	26	Salt Lake, Anaheim
22	Eckstein, David	R/R	5-7/165	29	Anaheim
17	Erstad, Darin	L/L	6-2/210	29	Salt Lake, Anaheim
6	Figgins, Chone	B/R	5-7/160	26	Salt Lake, Anaheim
25	Glaus, Troy	R/R	6-5/240	27	Anaheim, R. Cucamonga
	Halter, Shane	R/R	6-0/195	34	Detroit
2	Kennedy, Adam	L/R	6-1/185	28	R. Cucamonga, Anaheim
	McPherson, Dallas	L/R	6-4/235	23	R. Cucamonga, Arkansas
39	Quinlan, Robb	R/R	6-1/195	27	Salt Lake, Anaheim

No.	OUTFIELDERS	B/T	Ht./Wt.	Age*	2003 Clubs
16	Anderson, Garret	L/L	6-3/225	31	Anaheim
55	DaVanon, Jeff	B/R	6-0/185	30	Salt Lake, Anaheim
	Guerrero, Vladimir	R/R	6-3/220	28	Montreal, Brevard County
	Guillen, Jose	R/R	5-11/190	27	Louisville, Cincinnati, Oakland
15	Salmon, Tim	R/R	6-3/235	35	Anaheim
64	Wesson, Barry	R/R	6-2/210	26	Salt Lake, Anaheim

*Age as of April 1, 2004.

BALLPARK INFORMATION

Ballpark (capacity, surface)
Angel Stadium of Anaheim
(45,050, grass)

Address
2000 Gene Autry Way
Anaheim, CA 92806

Official website
www.angelsbaseball.com

Business phone
714-940-2000

Ticket information
714-634-2000

Field dimensions (from home plate)
To left field at foul line, 330 feet
To center field, 400 feet
To right field at foul line, 330

First game played
April 19, 1966 (White Sox 3, Angels 1)

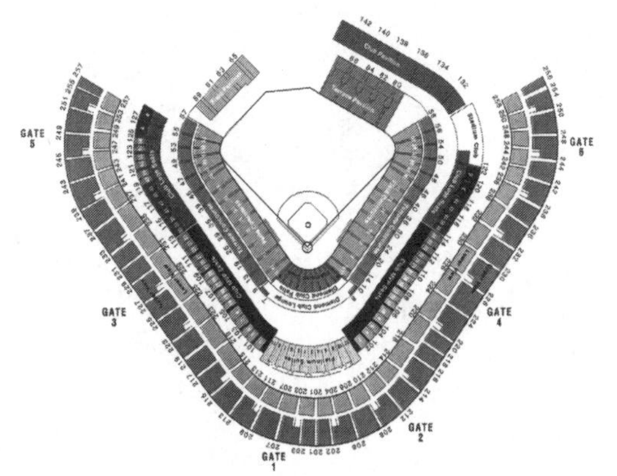

2003 REVIEW

DAY BY DAY

Date	Opp.	Res.	Score	(inn.*)	Hits	Opp. hits	Winning pitcher	Losing pitcher	Save	Record	Pos.	GB
3-30	Tex.	L	3-6		8	12	Valdes	Lackey	Urbina	0-1	4th	1.0
4-1	Tex.	W	10-0		13	5	Callaway	Park		1-1	T2nd	0.5
4-2	Tex.	W	11-5		14	10	Ortiz	Thomson		2-1	2nd	0.5
4-4	At Oak.	L	3-7		4	10	Lilly	Appier	Bradford	2-2	T2nd	1.0
4-5	At Oak.	L	2-4		7	8	Halama	Washburn	Foulke	2-3	T2nd	2.0
4-6	At Oak.	L	6-7		9	11	Bradford	Rodriguez	Foulke	2-4	T3rd	3.0
4-8	At Sea.	L	0-5		4	8	Moyer	Ortiz		2-5	T3rd	4.0
4-9	At Sea.	W	5-1		7	8	Appier	Pineiro		3-5	3rd	4.0
4-10	At Sea.	W	3-0		9	5	Washburn	Franklin	Percival	4-5	T2nd	3.0
4-11	Oak.	W	9-5		16	9	Lackey	Hudson	Rodriguez	5-5	2nd	2.0
4-12	Oak.	W	9-4		10	8	Weber	Halama		6-5	2nd	1.0
4-13	Oak.	W	8-2		9	5	Ortiz	Zito	Shields	7-5	T1st	...
4-14	At Tex.	L	0-4		6	7	Valdes	Appier		7-6	T1st	...
4-15	At Tex.	L	4-5		10	6	Lewis	Washburn	Urbina	7-7	T2nd	1.0
4-16	At Tex.	W	9-8		13	13	Rodriguez	Cordero	Percival	8-7	T1st	...
4-17	At Tex.	L	7-9		14	13	Drese	Callaway	Urbina	8-8	T2nd	1.0
4-18	Sea.	L	2-8		13	9	Moyer	Ortiz		8-9	3rd	2.0
4-19	Sea.	W	7-6		12	9	Rodriguez	Sasaki		9-9	3rd	1.0
4-20	Sea.	L	6-7		14	11	Hasegawa	Percival	Sasaki	9-10	3rd	2.0
4-22	N.Y.	L	3-8		10	9	Weaver	Lackey		9-11	3rd	3.0
4-23	N.Y.	L	2-9		6	18	Clemens	Callaway		9-12	T3rd	4.0
4-24	N.Y.	W	6-2		10	9	Ortiz	Pettitte		10-12	T3rd	4.0
4-25	Bos.	L	2-5		10	7	Fossum	Washburn	Fox	10-13	T3rd	5.0
4-26	Bos.	W	3-1		9	7	Shields	Burkett	Percival	11-13	3rd	4.0
4-27	Bos.	L	4-6	(14)	11	13	Mendoza	Callaway	Shiell	11-14	T3rd	5.0
4-29	At Cle.	W	10-1		13	7	Ortiz	Rodriguez		12-14	T3rd	5.0
4-30	At Cle.	W	6-2		13	5	Washburn	Anderson		13-14	T3rd	4.0
5-2	At Tor.	L	1-3		3	5	Lidle	Lackey		13-15	3rd	4.5
5-3	At Tor.	L	1-7		8	15	Davis	Shields		13-16	4th	5.5
5-4	At Tor.	L	2-8		4	14	Hendrickson	Ortiz	Escobar	13-17	4th	6.5
5-6	Cle.	W	6-1		5	6	Washburn	Rodriguez		14-17	3rd	6.5
5-7	Cle.	W	6-5		13	15	Shields	Elder	Percival	15-17	3rd	5.5
5-8	Cle.	W	7-1		10	3	Appier	Davis		16-17	3rd	4.5
5-9	Tor.	W	6-1		5	3	Sele	Davis		17-17	3rd	4.5
5-10	Tor.	L	4-7		9	10	Hendrickson	Ortiz		17-18	3rd	4.5
5-11	Tor.	L	2-4		6	7	Halladay	Washburn	Politte	17-19	3rd	5.5
5-13	At N.Y.	W	10-3		13	7	Lackey	Mussina		18-19	3rd	5.5
5-14	At N.Y.	W	5-3		12	8	Rodriguez	Wells	Percival	19-19	3rd	4.5
5-15	At N.Y.	L	4-10		10	14	Weaver	Sele		19-20	3rd	5.5
5-16	At Bos.	W	6-5		11	10	Rodriguez	Embree	Percival	20-20	3rd	5.5
5-17	At Bos.	W	6-2		12	9	Washburn	Timlin	Percival	21-20	3rd	5.5
5-18	At Bos.	L	3-5		11	11	Burkett	Lackey	Person	21-21	3rd	6.5
5-20	Bal.	W	7-6		8	15	Schoeneweis	Julio		22-21	3rd	6.5
5-21	Bal.	L	6-7		12	10	Ponson	Sele	Julio	22-22	3rd	6.5
5-22	Bal.	L	4-7		8	11	Roberts	Percival	Julio	22-23	3rd	7.5
5-23	T.B.	L	1-3		4	12	Gonzalez	Washburn	Carter	22-24	4th	8.5
5-24	T.B.	W	7-2		13	6	Lackey	Kennedy		23-24	3rd	7.5
5-25	T.B.	W	6-1		7	6	Appier	Brazelton		24-24	3rd	6.5
5-27	At Bal.	L	4-12		8	16	Ponson	Sele		24-25	3rd	7.5
5-28	At Bal.	L	2-6		9	13	Johnson	Ortiz		24-26	3rd	8.5
5-29	At T.B.	W	2-1		8	6	Washburn	Zambrano	Donnelly	25-26	3rd	8.5
5-30	At T.B.	L	6-8		6	12	Brazelton	Lackey	Carter	25-27	3rd	9.5
5-31	At T.B.	W	6-1		10	8	Appier	Kennedy		26-27	3rd	9.5
6-1	At T.B.	W	9-4		13	12	Sele	Reyes		27-27	3rd	9.5
6-3	At Mon.■	W	15-4		22	6	Ortiz	Ohka		28-27	3rd	9.5
6-4	At Mon.■	W	11-2		17	7	Washburn	Kim		29-27	3rd	9.5
6-5	At Mon.■	L	7-8	(14)	12	15	Eischen	Callaway		29-28	3rd	10.5
6-6	At Fla.	L	1-4		4	3	Pavano	Appier	Looper	29-29	3rd	10.5
6-7	At Fla.	W	9-2		11	5	Sele	Phelps		30-29	3rd	10.0
6-8	At Fla.	W	8-5		11	6	Ortiz	Penny	Percival	31-29	3rd	10.5
6-9	Phi.	L	0-3		6	8	Padilla	Washburn	Mesa	31-30	3rd	11.0
6-10	Phi.	W	2-1		4	6	Lackey	Duckworth	Percival	32-30	3rd	10.0
6-11	Phi.	W	5-3		9	8	Weber	Myers	Percival	33-30	3rd	9.0
6-13	N.Y. (NL)	L	3-7		8	13	Bacsik	Sele		33-31	3rd	10.5

Date	Opp.	Res.	Score	(inn.*)	Hits	Opp. hits	Winning pitcher	Losing pitcher	Save	Record	Pos.	GB
6-14	N.Y. (NL)	W	13-3		16	5	Ortiz	Roach		34-31	3rd	9.5
6-15	N.Y. (NL)	L	0-8		1	8	Trachsel	Washburn		34-32	3rd	10.5
6-16	At Sea.	L	3-6		5	11	Pineiro	Lackey	Rhodes	34-33	3rd	11.5
6-17	At Sea.	L	4-8		7	7	Franklin	Appier		34-34	3rd	12.5
6-18	At Sea.	L	0-2		5	7	Garcia	Sele	Rhodes	34-35	3rd	13.5
6-19	At Sea.	W	2-0		4	6	Ortiz	Moyer	Percival	35-35	3rd	12.5
6-20	At L.A.	L	2-5		7	9	Nomo	Washburn	Gagne	35-36	3rd	12.5
6-21	At L.A.	L	2-4		8	7	Ashby	Lackey	Gagne	35-37	3rd	13.5
6-22	At L.A.	W	6-3		12	9	Appier	Brown	Percival	36-37	3rd	12.5
6-24	Sea.	L	4-6		12	10	Garcia	Sele	Nelson	36-38	3rd	13.5
6-25	Sea.	W	6-3		10	10	Ortiz	Moyer	Percival	37-38	3rd	12.5
6-26	Sea.	L	6-10		10	13	Meche	Washburn	Hasegawa	37-39	3rd	13.5
6-27	L.A.	W	3-0		10	5	Lackey	Brown	Percival	38-39	3rd	13.5
6-28	L.A.	W	3-1		9	6	Appier	Ishii	Percival	39-39	3rd	12.5
6-29	L.A.	W	3-1		11	7	Sele	Perez	Percival	40-39	3rd	11.5
6-30	Tex.	L	3-6		6	12	Thomson	Ortiz	Urbina	40-40	3rd	12.5
7-1	Tex.	W	7-5		8	8	Washburn	Valdes	Percival	41-40	3rd	11.5
7-2	Tex.	W	5-0		6	4	Lackey	Benoit		42-40	3rd	11.5
7-3	Tex.	L	5-6		9	11	Mounce	Appier	Urbina	42-41	3rd	11.5
7-4	At Oak.	W	1-0		3	2	Sele	Mulder	Percival	43-41	3rd	10.5
7-5	At Oak.	W	6-3		11	6	Ortiz	Harang	Percival	44-41	3rd	10.5
7-6	At Oak.	L	5-6		8	9	Foulke	Schoeneweis		44-42	3rd	10.5
7-8	K.C.	L	0-4		4	7	May	Lackey		44-43	3rd	11.5
7-9	K.C.	W	5-3		9	10	Rodriguez	Affeldt	Percival	45-43	3rd	10.5
7-10	K.C.	W	7-1		10	5	Sele	George		46-43	3rd	9.5
7-11	Min.	W	5-0		6	4	Ortiz	Santana	Donnelly	47-43	3rd	9.5
7-12	Min.	W	6-1		11	5	Washburn	Radke		48-43	3rd	8.5
7-13	Min.	W	8-3		10	13	Lackey	Lohse		49-43	3rd	8.5
7-17	At Bal.	L	1-2		5	6	Lopez	Ortiz	Julio	49-44	3rd	8.5
7-18	At Bal.	L	5-6		11	8	Ligtenberg	Rodriguez	Julio	49-45	3rd	9.5
7-19	At Bal.	L	4-8		9	12	Ponson	Appier	Carrasco	49-46	3rd	9.5
7-20	At Bal.	L	6-7		12	14	Johnson	Lackey	Julio	49-47	3rd	9.5
7-21	At T.B.	L	2-3		7	9	Bell	Sele	Harper	49-48	3rd	9.5
7-22	At T.B.	W	3-1		6	3	Ortiz	Kennedy	Percival	50-48	3rd	9.5
7-23	At Tex.	L	9-12		16	13	Ramirez	Washburn	Cordero	50-49	3rd	10.5
7-24	At Tex.	W	10-6		13	10	Appier	Benoit	Percival	51-49	3rd	9.5
7-25	Oak.	L	2-3		8	10	Lilly	Donnelly	Foulke	51-50	3rd	10.5
7-26	Oak.	L	1-8		10	15	Harden	Sele		51-51	3rd	11.5
7-27	Oak.	L	1-10		4	13	Hudson	Ortiz		51-52	3rd	11.5
7-28	Oak.	W	2-1		7	6	Donnelly	Rincon	Percival	52-52	3rd	10.5
7-29	N.Y.	L	2-6		10	15	Pettitte	Appier		52-53	3rd	11.5
7-30	N.Y.	L	0-8		5	9	Clemens	Lackey		52-54	3rd	12.5
7-31	N.Y.	L	1-2	(10)	7	6	Benitez	Percival	Rivera	52-55	3rd	13.5
8-1	Tor.	W	5-0		10	4	Ortiz	Halladay		53-55	3rd	12.5
8-2	Tor.	L	1-6		7	12	Thurman	Washburn		53-56	3rd	13.5
8-3	Tor.	L	0-4		6	10	Escobar	Shields	Politte	53-57	3rd	14.5
8-5	At Bos.	L	9-10		11	11	Timlin	Donnelly	Kim	53-58	3rd	15.5
8-6	At Bos.	L	2-4		10	10	Martinez	Sele		53-59	3rd	15.5
8-7	At Bos.	L	3-9		8	14	Burkett	Ortiz		53-60	3rd	15.5
8-8	At Cle.	W	5-2		9	4	Washburn	Davis		54-60	3rd	14.5
8-9§	At Cle.	L	2-3	(13)	9	8	Cressend	Weber		54-61		
8-9∞	At Cle.	L	2-3		7	6	Boyd	Shields	Baez	54-62	3rd	16.0
8-10	At Cle.	L	1-3		8	4	Sabathia	Lackey	Betancourt	54-63	3rd	17.0
8-11	Chi.	W	10-8		14	15	Weber	Colon		55-63	3rd	16.0
8-12	Chi.	L	4-10		6	17	Wright	Ortiz		55-64	3rd	17.0
8-13	Chi.	W	2-1		10	6	Rodriguez	Buehrle	Percival	56-64	3rd	17.0
8-14	Chi.	W	5-1		9	5	Shields	Garland	Percival	57-64	3rd	16.0
8-15	Det.	W	3-1		9	7	Lackey	Cornejo	Percival	58-64	3rd	16.0
8-16	Det.	W	11-7		11	9	Glover	Ledezma		59-64	3rd	15.0
8-17	Det.	W	11-6		15	13	Ortiz	Bonderman		60-64	3rd	15.0
8-18	At Chi.	L	2-4		6	4	Gordon	Washburn		60-65	3rd	15.5
8-19	At Chi.	L	2-5		5	11	Garland	Shields	Gordon	60-66	3rd	16.5
8-20	At Chi.	L	3-5		10	11	Loaiza	Lackey	Marte	60-67	T3rd	16.5
8-21	At Det.	W	10-7		17	8	Sele	Roney		61-67	3rd	15.5
8-22	At Det.	W	6-5		8	10	Ortiz	Bonderman	Percival	62-67	3rd	14.5
8-23	At Det.	W	14-8	(10)	17	7	Donnelly	Spurling		63-67	3rd	13.5
8-24	At Det.	L	9-10		12	17	Walker	Percival		63-68	3rd	13.5
8-26	Min.	L	0-3		5	12	Radke	Lackey		63-69	3rd	14.0
8-27	Min.	W	5-4		12	11	Weber	Rincon	Percival	64-69	3rd	14.0
8-28	Min.	L	1-6		6	7	Lohse	Ortiz		64-70	3rd	15.0
8-29	At K.C.	W	10-3		15	8	Washburn	Gobble		65-70	3rd	15.0
8-31	At K.C.	W	7-4		10	10	Shields	Anderson	Percival	66-70		

Date	Opp.	Res.	Score	(inn.*)	Hits	Opp. hits	Winning pitcher	Losing pitcher	Save	Record	Pos.	GB
9-1	At Min.	W	10-2		10	7	Lackey	Rogers		67-70	3rd	15.0
9-2	At Min.	L	6-12		16	14	Lohse	Sele		67-71	3rd	16.0
9-3	At Min.	L	5-6		7	8	Guardado	Percival		67-72	3rd	16.0
9-5	K.C.	L	0-5		7	15	Anderson	Washburn		67-73	3rd	16.5
9-6†	K.C.	W	6-5		9	12	Weber	Grimsley	Percival	68-73		
9-6‡	K.C.	W	3-1		6	4	Gregg	Wright	Percival	69-73	3rd	15.0
9-7	K.C.	L	0-3		5	8	Abbott	Lackey	Affeldt	69-74	3rd	15.0
9-8	At Oak.	W	3-1		11	7	Rodriguez	Hudson	Percival	70-74	3rd	14.0
9-9	At Oak.	L	1-8		6	8	Duchscherer	Bootcheck		70-75	3rd	15.0
9-10	At Oak.	L	0-3		7	8	Lilly	Washburn	Foulke	70-76	3rd	16.0
9-11	At Oak.	L	4-14		9	11	Harden	Shields		70-77	3rd	17.0
9-12	At Sea.	L	4-7		10	8	Moyer	Lackey	Hasegawa	70-78	3rd	18.0
9-13	At Sea.	L	1-5		8	4	Garcia	Rodriguez		70-79	3rd	19.0
9-14	At Sea.	W	2-1		6	3	Gregg	Franklin	Percival	71-79	3rd	19.0
9-15	Oak.	L	4-7		8	11	Lilly	Ortiz	Foulke	71-80	3rd	20.0
9-16	Oak.	W	6-5		9	12	Turnbow	Mecir		72-80	3rd	19.0
9-17	Oak.	L	1-2		2	4	Zito	Shields	Mecir	72-81	3rd	20.0
9-19	At Tex.	L	2-3		7	7	Dickey	Lackey	Cordero	72-82	3rd	20.0
9-20	At Tex.	L	4-13		6	14	Lewis	Sele		72-83	3rd	20.0
9-21	At Tex.	W	11-6		18	8	Ortiz	Mahay		73-83	3rd	20.0
9-22	Sea.	L	1-5		6	13	Moyer	Washburn		73-84	3rd	21.0
9-23	Sea.	W	2-1	(11)	7	4	Rodriguez	Hasegawa		74-84	3rd	21.0
9-24	Sea.	W	4-0		8	5	Lackey	Meche		75-84	3rd	21.0
9-26	Tex.	W	5-3		7	6	Turnbow	Mahay	Rodriguez	76-84	3rd	20.0
9-27	Tex.	L	3-12		10	18	Lewis	Ortiz		76-85	3rd	20.0
9-28	Tex.	W	4-1		12	6	Shields	Thomson	Donnelly	77-85	3rd	19.0

Monthly records: March (0-1), April (13-13), May (13-13), June (14-13), July (12-15), August (14-15), September (11-15). *Innings, if other than nine. ■ At Hiram Bithorn Stadium, San Juan, Puerto Rico. † First game of a doubleheader. ‡ Second game of a doubleheader. § Day separate admission. ∞ Night separate admission.

RECORDS

2003 regular-season record: 77-85
Position: 3rd in A.L. West
Home: 45-37 **Road:** 32-48
A.L. East: 15-30 **A.L. Central:** 26-15
A.L. West: 25-33 N.L. 11-7
Vs. LH starters: 28-26
Vs. RH starters: 49-59
Grass: 70-77 **Artificial:** 7-8
Day: 21-24 **Night:** 56-61
1-Run: 16-20 **X-inn.:** 2-4
Doubleheaders: 1-0-0
Team record past five years: 403-407 (.498, ranks 8th in league in that span)

TEAM LEADERS

Batting average: Garret Anderson (.315).
At-bats: Garret Anderson (638).
Runs: Garret Anderson (80).
Hits: Garret Anderson (201).
Total Bases: Garret Anderson (345).
Doubles: Garret Anderson (49).
Triples: Scott Spiezio (7).
Home runs: Garret Anderson (29).
Runs batted in: Garret Anderson (116).
Stolen bases: Adam Kennedy (22).
Slugging percentage: Garret Anderson (.541).
On-base percentage: Tim Salmon (.374).
Wins: Ramon Ortiz (16).
Earned-run average: Scot Shields (2.85).
Complete games: John Lackey, Jarrod Washburn (2).
Shutouts: John Lackey (2).
Saves: Troy Percival (33).
Innings pitched: Jarrod Washburn (207.1).
Strikeouts: John Lackey (151).

GAMES BY POSITION

Catcher: Bengie Molina 117, Jose Molina 53, Shawn Wooten 19, Tom Gregorio 12.
First base: Scott Spiezio 114, Robb Quinlan 33, Shawn Wooten 32, Brad Fullmer 19, Adam Riggs 10, Benji Gil 5.
Second base: Adam Kennedy 140, Benji Gil 28, Chone Figgins 14, Trent Durrington 5, Adam Riggs 3, Wilson Delgado 1.
Third base: Troy Glaus 87, Scott Spiezio 52, Shawn Wooten 17, Alfredo Amezaga 13, Wilson Delgado 9, Trent Durrington 4, Benji Gil 4.
Shortstop: David Eckstein 116, Alfredo Amezaga 24, Benji Gil 20, Wilson Delgado 9, Chone Figgins 8.
Outfield: Garret Anderson 144, Jeff DaVanon 115, Eric Owens 97, Tim Salmon 78, Darin Erstad 66, Chone Figgins 47, Scott Spiezio 10, Barry Wesson 9, Adam Riggs 8, Julio Ramirez 5, Gary Johnson 4, Trent Durrington 1, Robb Quinlan 1.
Designated hitter: Tim Salmon 68, Brad Fullmer 41, Shawn Wooten 28, Garret Anderson 15, Troy Glaus 4, David Eckstein 3, Chone Figgins 3, Eric Owens 3, Robb Quinlan 3, Adam Riggs 3, Trent Durrington 2, Benji Gil 2, Alfredo Amezaga 1, Jeff DaVanon 1, Adam Kennedy 1, Julio Ramirez 1, Barry Wesson 1.

TOP DRAFT CHOICES

1. **Brandon Wood,** SS, Horizon H.S., Scottsdale, Ariz.
2. **Anthony Whittington,** LHP, Buffalo H.S., Putnam, W.Va.
3. **Sean Rodriguez,** SS, Braddock H.S., Miami.
4. **Bob Zimmerman** RHP, Southwest Missouri State.
5. **Blake Balkcom,** OF, Florida State.
6. **Jesse Smith,** RHP, Illinois Valley CC.
7. **Reggie Willits,** OF, Oklahoma.
8. **Josh Cowles,** RHP, East Valley H.S., Redlands, Calif.
9. **Von Stertzbach,** RHP, Central Florida.
10. **Patrice Lepage,** C, Edouard Montpetit College H.S., Montreal.

BALTIMORE ORIOLES

AMERICAN LEAGUE EAST DIVISION

2004 SEASON

April

SUN	MON	TUE	WED	THU	FRI	SAT
4 BOS	5	6 BOS	7 BOS	8 BOS	9 TB	10 TB
11 TB	12	13 BOS	14 BOS	15 BOS	16 TOR	17 TOR
18 TOR	19	20 TB	21 TB	22 TB	23 TOR	24 TOR
25 TOR	26 SEA	27 SEA	28 SEA	29 SEA	30 CLE	

May

SUN	MON	TUE	WED	THU	FRI	SAT
						1 CLE
2 CLE	3 CHW	4 CHW	5 CHW	6	7 CLE	8 CLE
9 CLE	10	11 CHW	12 CHW	13 CHW	14 ANA	15 ANA
16 ANA	17	18 SEA	19 SEA	20 SEA	21 ANA	22 ANA
23 ANA	24	25 NYY	26 NYY	27 NYY	28 DET	29 DET
30 DET	31					

June

SUN	MON	TUE	WED	THU	FRI	SAT
		1 NYY	2 NYY	3 NYY	4 TB	5 TB
6 TB	7	8 ARI	9 ARI	10 ARI	11 SF	12 SF
13 SF	14	15 LA	16 LA	17 LA	18 COL	19 COL
20 COL	21	22 NYY	23 NYY	24 NYY	25 ATL	26 ATL
27 ATL	28 KC	29 KC	30 KC			

July

SUN	MON	TUE	WED	THU	FRI	SAT
				1 KC	2 PHI	3 PHI
4 PHI	5 TB	6 TB	7 TB	8	9 KC	10 KC
11 KC	12	13 All-Star	14	15 TB	16 TB	17 TB
18 TB	19 KC	20 KC	21 BOS	22 BOS	23 MIN	24 MIN
25 MIN	26 BOS	27 BOS	28 BOS	29 NYY	30 NYY	31 NYY

August

SUN	MON	TUE	WED	THU	FRI	SAT
1 NYY	2	3 SEA	4 SEA	5	6 TEX	7 TEX
8 TEX	9 TEX	10 ANA	11 ANA	12 ANA	13 TOR	14 TOR
15 TOR	16 OAK	17 OAK	18 OAK	19	20 TOR	21 TOR
22 TOR	23 OAK	24 OAK	25 OAK	26 OAK	27 TEX	28 TEX
29 TEX	30	31 TB				

Sept./Oct.

SUN	MON	TUE	WED	THU	FRI	SAT
			1 TB	2 TB	3 NYY	4 NYY
5 NYY	6 MIN	7 MIN	8 MIN	9	10 NYY	11 NYY
12 NYY	13 TOR	14	15 TOR	16 TOR	17 MIN	18 MIN
19 MIN	20 BOS	21 BOS	22 BOS	23 BOS	24 DET	25 DET
26 DET	27 TOR	28 TOR	29 TOR	30 TOR	1 BOS	2 BOS
3 BOS	4	5	6	7	8	9

Home games shaded. All-Star Game July 13 at Houston. Schedule subject to change.

CLUB DIRECTORY

Chairman of the board/CEO
Peter G. Angelos
Vice chairman/chief operating officer
Joseph E. Foss
Executive vice president
John P. Angelos
Exec. v.p./baseball operations
Jim Beattie
V.p./baseball operations
Mike Flanagan
Assistant to v.p., baseball operations
Dave Ritterpusch
Director/baseball administration
Ed Kenney Jr.
Director/minor league operations
Darrell "Doc" Rodgers
Director/scouting
Tony DeMacio
Executive director/communications
Spiro Alafassos
Director/public relations
Bill Stetka
Manager, baseball information
Kevin Behan
Manager, communications
Monica Pence
Director/community relations
Julie Wagner

MINOR LEAGUE AFFILIATES

Class	Team	League	Manager
AAA	Ottawa	International	Tim Leiper
AA	Bowie	Eastern	Dave Trembley
Advanced A	Frederick	Carolina	Tom Lawless
A	Delmarva	South Atlantic	Bien Figueroa
Short-Season A	Aberdeen	New York-Pennsylvania	Don Buford
Advanced Rookie	Bluefield	Appalachian	Gary Kendall

More on the Orioles at www.foxsports.com/named/FS/MLB/teams

BROADCAST INFORMATION

Radio: WBAL-AM (1090).
TV: WJZ (Channel 13), WNUV (Channel 54), PAX (Channel 66).
Cable TV: Comcast SportsNet.

SPRING TRAINING

Ballpark (city): Fort Lauderdale Stadium (Fort Lauderdale, Fla.).
Ticket information: 954-776-1921.

SPRING TRAINING ROSTER

Manager—Lee Mazzilli (13).
Coaches—Terry Crowley (48), Rick Dempsey (24), Elrod Hendricks (44), Sam Perlozzo (2), Tom Trebelhorn (49), Mark Wiley (34).

No.	PITCHERS	B/T	Ht./Wt.	Age*	2003 Clubs
29	Ainsworth, Kurt	R/R	6-3/192	25	San Francisco, Fresno, Baltimore
30	Bauer, Rick	R/R	6-6/218	27	Ottawa, Baltimore
	Bautista, Denny	R/R	6-5/170	21	Jupiter, Carolina
79	Bedard, Erik	L/L	6-1/180	25	Frederick, G.C. Orioles, Aberdeen
	Cabrera, Danel	R/R	6-7/220	22	Delmarva
	Crouthers, Dave	R/R	6-3/205	24	Frederick, Bowie
14	Daal, Omar	L/L	6-3/193	32	Bowie, Baltimore
	DeJean, Mike	R/R	6-4/217	33	Milwaukee, St. Louis
59	DuBose, Eric	L/L	6-3/233	27	Ottawa, Baltimore
	Forystek, Brian	L/L	6-1/175	25	Bowie
27	Groom, Buddy	L/L	6-2/201	38	Baltimore
	Hannaman, Ryan	L/L	6-3/190	22	San Jose, Arizona Giants, Frederick
50	Julio, Jorge	R/R	6-1/223	25	Baltimore
	Loewen, Adam	L/L	6-6/230	19	Aberdeen
13	Lopez, Rodrigo	R/R	6-1/187	28	Bowie, Baltimore
36	Parrish, John	L/L	5-11/181	26	Bowie, Baltimore
	Ponson, Sidney	R/R	6-1/249	27	Baltimore, San Francisco
35	Riley, Matt	L/L	6-1/201	24	Bowie, Ottawa, Baltimore
	Rodriguez, Eddy	R/R	6-1/195	22	Bowie
52	Ryan, B.J.	L/L	6-6/247	28	Baltimore
28	Stephens, John	R/R	6-1/204	24	Ottawa

No.	CATCHERS	B/T	Ht./Wt.	Age*	2003 Clubs
17	Gil, Geronimo	R/R	6-2/227	28	Ottawa, Baltimore
18	Lopez, Javy	R/R	6-3/215	33	Atlanta

No.	INFIELDERS	B/T	Ht./Wt.	Age*	2003 Clubs
	Bautista, Jose	R/R	6-2/205	23	Lynchburg
21	Cust, Jack	L/R	6-1/225	25	Ottawa, Baltimore
15	Hairston Jr., Jerry	R/R	5-10/185	27	Bowie, Aberdeen, Baltimore
6	Mora, Melvin	R/R	5-11/198	32	Bowie, Baltimore
12	Morban, Jose	B/R	6-1/170	24	Baltimore
	Palmeiro, Rafael	L/L	6-0/190	39	Texas
1	Roberts, Brian	B/R	5-9/172	26	Ottawa, Baltimore
23	Segui, David	B/L	6-1/216	37	Frederick, Baltimore
4	Tejada, Miguel	R/R	5-9/200	27	Oakland
	Young, Walter	L/R	6-5/295	24	Lynchburg

No.	OUTFIELDERS	B/T	Ht./Wt.	Age*	2003 Clubs
3	Bigbie, Larry	L/L	6-4/215	26	G.C. Orioles, Ottawa, Baltimore
40	Cordova, Marty	R/R	6-0/213	34	Baltimore
25	Gibbons, Jay	L/L	6-0/193	27	Baltimore
32	Matos, Luis	R/R	6-0/208	25	Ottawa, Baltimore
	McDonald, Darnell	R/R	5-11/210	25	Ottawa
	Raines Jr., Tim	B/R	5-10/183	24	Bowie, Ottawa, Baltimore

Invited to spring training: RHP Tim Corcoran, RHP Darwin Cubillan, RHP Mike Paradis, RHP Willis Roberts, IF Napoleon Calzado, SS Felix Escalona, IF Eddy Garabito, 1B Chris Lemonis, 3B Jose Leon, IF Luis Lopez, IF/OF B.J. Surhoff, C Raul Casanova, C Bill Haselman, C Carlos Mendez, OF Cory Harris, OF Chad Mottola, OF Pedro Swann, C Keith Osik.

*Age as of April 1, 2004.

BALLPARK INFORMATION

Ballpark (capacity, surface)
Oriole Park at Camden Yards (48,190, grass)

Address
333 W. Camden St.
Baltimore, MD 21201

Official website
www.theorioles.com

Business phone
410-685-9800

Ticket information
410-481-SEAT

Field dimensions (from home plate)
To left field at foul line, 333 feet
To center field, 400 feet
To right field at foul line, 318

First game played
April 6, 1992 (Orioles 2, Indians 0)

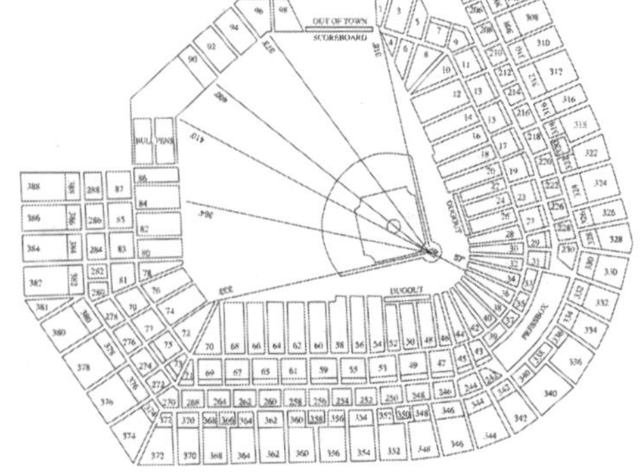

2003 REVIEW
DAY BY DAY

Date	Opp.	Res.	Score	(inn.*)	Hits	Opp. hits	Winning pitcher	Losing pitcher	Save	Record	Pos.	GB
3-31	Cle.	W	6-5	(13)	15	11	Ryan	Westbrook		1-0	T1st	...
4-2	Cle.	L	2-4		5	9	Rodriguez	Daal	Baez	1-1	3rd	1.5
4-3	Cle.	L	0-3		4	4	Anderson	Helling	Baez	1-2	3rd	2.0
4-4	Bos.	L	7-8		16	11	Burkett	Ponson		1-3	T3rd	3.0
4-5	Bos.	W	2-1		5	3	Ryan	Fox		2-3	T3rd	2.0
4-6	Bos.	L	2-12		5	12	Wakefield	Lopez		2-4	4th	3.0
4-8	At T.B.	L	7-8	(10)	12	16	Carter	Julio		2-5	5th	4.0
4-9	At T.B.	L	7-10		10	13	Levine	Roberts	Carter	2-6	5th	5.0
4-10	At T.B.	W	4-3		5	9	Ponson	Colome	Julio	3-6	5th	5.0
4-12	At Bos.	W	13-6		15	9	Johnson	Martinez		4-6	4th	5.0
4-13	At Bos.	L	0-2		6	6	Lowe	Lopez	Wakefield	4-7	5th	5.0
4-15	At Cle.	L	3-8		11	14	Davis	Daal		4-8	5th	6.5
4-16	At Cle.	W	4-3		6	8	Groom	Baez	Julio	5-8	4th	5.5
4-17	At Cle.	W	6-4	(12)	10	9	Roberts	Paronto	Julio	6-8	3rd	5.5
4-18	T.B.	W	9-7		8	10	Johnson	Zambrano	Julio	7-8	3rd	5.5
4-19	T.B.	L	7-8		14	11	Sosa	Lopez		7-9	3rd	6.5
4-20	T.B.	W	4-1		7	5	Daal	Bierbrodt	Julio	8-9	3rd	6.5
4-21	T.B.	W	4-0		9	5	Helling	Parris		9-9	3rd	6.5
4-22	Chi.	L	1-3		4	7	Loaiza	Ponson	Koch	9-10	3rd	7.5
4-23	Chi.	W	7-1		9	3	Johnson	Colon		10-10	3rd	7.5
4-24	Chi.	W	5-4		8	8	Roberts	Gordon	Julio	11-10	3rd	6.5
4-25	At T.B.	L	1-2		3	9	McClung	Daal	Carter	11-11	3rd	7.5
4-26	At T.B.	L	7-10		12	18	Zambrano	Helling	Carter	11-12	3rd	8.5
4-27	At T.B.	W	7-4		11	9	Ponson	Kennedy		12-12	3rd	7.5
4-29	At Det.	W	11-3		13	8	Johnson	Bonderman		13-12	3rd	6.5
5-1†	At Det.	W	5-2		11	7	Ryan	German	Julio	14-12		
5-1‡	At Det.	W	6-4		8	11	Daal	Maroth	Julio	15-12	3rd	6.5
5-2	K.C.	L	2-5		7	10	Asencio	Helling		15-13	3rd	7.5
5-3	K.C.	W	6-1		9	6	Ponson	Hernandez		16-13	3rd	6.5
5-4	K.C.	L	0-4		7	4	George	DuBose	Carrasco	16-14	3rd	6.5
5-5	Det.	L	1-6		6	10	Cornejo	Johnson	Sparks	16-15	3rd	7.0
5-6	Det.	L	6-7		7	12	German	Groom		16-16	3rd	7.0
5-7	Det.	L	4-9		7	12	Knotts	Daal		16-17	3rd	8.0
5-9†	At K.C.	W	15-5		17	11	Helling	Asencio		17-17		
5-9‡	At K.C.	W	5-4		8	11	Ponson	Hernandez	Julio	18-17	3rd	7.0
5-10	At K.C.	L	4-8		7	14	Carrasco	Groom		18-18	3rd	8.0
5-11	At K.C.	L	5-8		12	12	Lowe	Driskill		18-19	3rd	8.0
5-13	At Chi.	L	0-1		6	8	Loaiza	Daal	Koch	18-20	3rd	8.0
5-14	At Chi.	L	1-5		7	11	Gordon	Helling		18-21	4th	8.0
5-15	At Chi.	L	2-8		5	9	Colon	Ponson		18-22	4th	9.0
5-16	T.B.	L	1-5		7	8	McClung	Johnson		18-23	4th	9.0
5-17	T.B.	W	2-0		5	3	Hentgen	Gonzalez	Julio	19-23	4th	8.0
5-18	T.B.	L	8-9		14	16	Carter	Julio		19-24	4th	8.0
5-20	At Ana.	L	6-7		15	8	Schoeneweis	Julio		19-25	4th	8.5
5-21	At Ana.	W	7-6		10	12	Ponson	Sele	Julio	20-25	4th	8.5
5-22	At Ana.	W	7-4		11	8	Roberts	Percival	Julio	21-25	4th	7.5
5-23	At Tex.	L	3-5		10	11	Valdes	Hentgen	Urbina	21-26	4th	8.0
5-24	At Tex.	W	10-3		16	8	Daal	Thomson	Ligtenberg	22-26	4th	8.0
5-25	At Tex.	W	13-10		18	11	Driskill	Dickey	Julio	23-26	4th	7.0
5-27	Ana.	W	12-4		16	8	Ponson	Sele		24-26	4th	6.5
5-28	Ana.	W	6-2		13	9	Johnson	Ortiz		25-26	4th	5.5
5-29	Tex.	L	4-8		8	11	Valdes	Hentgen	Cordero	25-27	4th	6.0
5-30	Tex.	W	8-1		10	7	Daal	Thomson		26-27	4th	5.5
5-31	Tex.	W	7-1		11	8	Helling	Benoit		27-27	4th	4.5
6-1	Tex.	W	5-4		11	7	Ponson	Cordero	Julio	28-27	4th	4.5
6-3	At Hou.	L	6-11		14	14	Dotel	Groom		28-28	4th	4.5
6-4	At Hou.	L	4-6		6	11	Miller	Hentgen	Wagner	28-29	4th	5.0
6-5	At Hou.	L	1-11		9	14	Oswalt	Daal		28-30	4th	5.5
6-6	At StL.	L	6-8		12	11	Yan	Julio	Eldred	28-31	4th	6.5
6-7	At StL.	W	8-1		12	7	Ponson	Stephenson		29-31	4th	5.5
6-8	At StL.	L	10-11		16	18	Simontacchi	Driskill	Eldred	29-32	4th	6.0
6-10	Chi. (NL)	L	0-4		9	14	Estes	Hentgen		29-33	4th	6.5
6-11	Chi. (NL)	L	6-7		10	9	Clement	Daal	Borowski	29-34	4th	7.0
6-12	Chi. (NL)	W	6-1		11	6	Helling	Zambrano	Driskill	30-34	4th	6.5

Date	Opp.	Res.	Score	(inn.*)	Hits	Opp. hits	Winning pitcher	Losing pitcher	Save	Record	Pos.	GB
6-13	Mil.	W	7-2		10	8	Ponson	Rusch		31-34	4th	6.5
6-14	Mil.	L	3-8		9	14	Quevedo	Johnson		31-35	4th	7.5
6-15	Mil.	W	5-4		10	10	Lopez	Sheets	Julio	32-35	4th	7.5
6-18	Tor.	L	2-6		7	10	Halladay	Daal	Lopez	32-36	4th	8.5
6-19	Tor.	L	1-6		8	9	Escobar	Helling		32-37	4th	9.0
6-20	At Atl.	L	3-6		5	8	Maddux	Ponson	Smoltz	32-38	4th	10.0
6-21	At Atl.	L	2-10		7	11	Ramirez	Lopez		32-39	4th	10.5
6-22	At Atl.	W	9-3		11	7	Johnson	Reynolds	Hentgen	33-39	4th	10.5
6-23	At Tor.	L	4-13		11	20	Davis	Daal		33-40	4th	10.5
6-24	At Tor.	W	6-4		8	9	Helling	Escobar	Julio	34-40	4th	10.5
6-25	At Tor.	W	9-2		13	10	Ponson	Lidle		35-40	4th	10.5
6-26	At Tor.	L	8-13		11	15	Sturtze	Driskill	Lopez	35-41	4th	11.5
6-27	Phi.	L	2-4	(17)	10	15	Plesac	Daal	Mercado	35-42	4th	12.5
6-28	Phi.	L	5-9		12	14	Myers	Hentgen		35-43	4th	14.0
6-29	Phi.	L	3-4		9	7	Millwood	Helling	Mesa	35-44	4th	15.0
6-30	N.Y.	L	5-6		15	12	Pettitte	Ponson	Rivera	35-45	4th	16.0
7-1	N.Y.	W	7-3		11	14	Lopez	Mussina		36-45	4th	15.0
7-3	Tor.	W	6-5		11	12	Johnson	Davis	Julio	37-45	4th	14.5
7-4	Tor.	W	8-5		13	8	Driskill	Lopez	Julio	38-45	4th	13.5
7-5	Tor.	W	9-2		14	7	Ponson	Lidle		39-45	4th	12.5
7-6	Tor.	L	3-5	(10)	8	13	Acevedo	Ligtenberg		39-46	4th	13.5
7-8	At Sea.	L	5-6		11	16	Pineiro	Johnson	Hasegawa	39-47	4th	14.0
7-9	At Sea.	W	7-2		14	9	Helling	Franklin		40-47	4th	14.0
7-10	At Sea.	W	4-1		10	7	Ponson	Garcia		41-47	4th	13.0
7-11	At Oak.	L	0-2		3	5	Hudson	Lopez		41-48	4th	14.0
7-12	At Oak.	L	3-5		8	5	Mecir	Carrasco	Foulke	41-49	4th	14.0
7-13	At Oak.	L	0-1		4	6	Foulke	Carrasco		41-50	4th	15.0
7-17	Ana.	W	2-1		6	5	Lopez	Ortiz	Julio	42-50	4th	15.0
7-18	Ana.	W	6-5		8	11	Ligtenberg	Rodriguez	Julio	43-50	4th	15.0
7-19	Ana.	W	8-4		12	9	Ponson	Appier	Carrasco	44-50	4th	15.0
7-20	Ana.	W	7-6		14	12	Johnson	Lackey	Julio	45-50	4th	15.0
7-21	Tex.	W	3-2		7	7	Hentgen	Dickey	Julio	46-50	4th	14.0
7-22	Tex.	W	12-6		14	14	Driskill	Thomson		47-50	4th	13.5
7-23	At N.Y.	L	2-4		6	9	Pettitte	Helling	Rivera	47-51	4th	14.5
7-24	At N.Y.	W	5-3		13	6	Ponson	Clemens	Julio	48-51	4th	13.5
7-25	At Tor.	L	3-5		9	9	Lidle	Johnson	Miller	48-52	4th	14.5
7-26	At Tor.	W	7-2		14	7	Hentgen	Hendrickson		49-52	4th	13.5
7-27	At Tor.	L	1-10		3	15	Halladay	Lopez		49-53	4th	13.5
7-29	At Min.	W	7-5		11	10	Carrasco	Hawkins	Julio	50-53	4th	13.5
7-30	At Min.	L	1-5		6	8	Radke	Ponson		50-54	4th	14.5
7-31	At Min.	L	9-10	(10)	16	19	Hawkins	Driskill		50-55	4th	15.5
8-1	Bos.	W	2-1		9	4	Hentgen	Burkett	Julio	51-55	4th	14.5
8-2	Bos.	W	11-2		16	6	Lopez	Lowe		52-55	4th	14.5
8-3	Bos.	L	5-7		7	10	Wakefield	Helling	Kim	52-56	4th	14.5
8-4	Min.	L	2-3		10	6	Radke	Moss	Guardado	52-57	4th	15.0
8-5	Min.	W	3-2		9	6	Johnson	Rogers	Julio	53-57	4th	15.0
8-6	Min.	L	3-7		11	10	Lohse	Hentgen		53-58	4th	15.0
8-7	Min.	W	5-3		8	8	Lopez	Reed	Julio	54-58	4th	15.0
8-8§	At Bos.	W	10-4		13	12	Helling	Lowe		55-58		
8-8∞	At Bos.	W	4-2		7	7	DuBose	Fossum	Julio	56-58	4th	14.5
8-9	At Bos.	L	4-6		7	9	Embree	Driskill	Kim	56-59	4th	14.5
8-10	At Bos.	W	5-3		6	9	Johnson	Suppan	Julio	57-59	4th	13.5
8-11	At T.B.	L	3-4		6	11	Harper	Carrasco		57-60	4th	13.5
8-12	At T.B.	L	2-4		3	9	Bell	Lopez	Carter	57-61	4th	14.5
8-13	At T.B.	L	5-6	(10)	11	11	Carter	Ryan		57-62	4th	14.5
8-14	N.Y.	L	5-8		12	10	Pettitte	DuBose	Rivera	57-63	4th	15.5
8-15	N.Y.	L	4-6		11	11	Nelson	Julio	Rivera	57-64	4th	16.5
8-16	N.Y.	L	4-5	(12)	9	9	Hammond	Carrasco	Nelson	57-65	4th	17.5
8-17	N.Y.	L	0-8		3	10	Mussina	Lopez		57-66	4th	18.5
8-19	T.B.	L	2-9		6	16	Gonzalez	DuBose		57-67	4th	20.0
8-20	T.B.	W	9-5		7	13	Moss	Zambrano		58-67	4th	20.0
8-21	T.B.	W	5-4	(10)	12	9	Ryan	Colome		59-67	4th	19.5
8-22	At N.Y.	W	4-3		12	8	Hentgen	Wells	Groom	60-67	4th	18.5
8-23	At N.Y.	W	7-2		11	6	Lopez	Mussina		61-67	4th	17.5
8-24	At N.Y.	L	0-7		4	8	Contreras	DuBose		61-68	4th	18.5
8-25	At N.Y.	L	2-5		11	7	Pettitte	Moss	Rivera	61-69	4th	19.5
8-26	At Oak.	L	1-2	(12)	5	9	Wood	Parrish		61-70	4th	19.5
8-27	At Oak.	L	2-6		5	9	Zito	Hentgen		61-71	4th	19.5
8-28	At Oak.	L	4-6		9	8	Halama	Lopez	Foulke	61-72	4th	20.5
8-29	At Sea.	L	2-3		6	4	Soriano	Julio		61-73	4th	20.5
8-30	At Sea.	L	1-13		5	13	Meche	Moss		61-74	4th	21.5
8-31	At Sea.	L	0-3		5	10	Moyer	Johnson	Hasegawa	61-75	4th	22.5

Date	Opp.	Res.	Score	(inn.*)	Hits	Opp. hits	Winning pitcher	Losing pitcher	Save	Record	Pos.	GB
9-2	Oak.	L	0-2	(12)	7	5	Rincon	Julio	Foulke	61-76	4th	22.5
9-3	Oak.	W	9-0		13	7	Lopez	Hudson		62-76	4th	21.5
9-4	Oak.	W	7-5		10	10	Carrasco	Halama	Julio	63-76	4th	21.5
9-5	Sea.	L	4-6	(13)	21	14	Rhodes	Ligtenberg		63-77	4th	21.5
9-6	Sea.	W	3-1		10	7	DuBose	Moyer	Julio	64-77	4th	20.5
9-7	Sea.	W	2-1		4	5	Hentgen	Garcia	Julio	65-77	4th	20.5
9-8	Bos.	W	13-10		16	16	Ligtenberg	Kim		66-77	4th	20.5
9-9	Bos.	L	2-9		9	13	Lowe	Moss		66-78	4th	21.5
9-10	Bos.	L	0-5		3	11	Martinez	Johnson		66-79	4th	22.5
9-12	At Tor.	L	2-4		11	8	Towers	DuBose	Lopez	66-80	4th	24.0
9-13	At Tor.	L	1-6		9	6	Escobar	Hentgen		66-81	4th	25.5
9-14	At Tor.	W	5-3		7	7	Riley	Lidle	Julio	67-81	4th	24.5
9-15	N.Y.	L	1-13		10	15	Pettitte	Lopez		67-82	4th	25.5
9-16	N.Y.	L	3-6		7	9	Clemens	Johnson	Rivera	67-83	4th	26.5
9-17	N.Y.	W	5-3		7	11	DuBose	Wells	Julio	68-83	4th	25.5
9-18	N.Y.	T	1-1	(5)	5	5				68-83	4th	25.5
9-19	Tor.	L	2-5		4	11	Escobar	Carrasco	Lopez	68-84	4th	26.5
9-20	Tor.	W	2-1		9	6	Ligtenberg	Lidle	Julio	69-84	4th	26.5
9-21	Tor.	L	4-7		11	16	Walker	Carrasco	Lopez	69-85	4th	27.5
9-22	At Bos.	L	5-7		13	9	Suppan	Johnson	Kim	69-86	4th	27.5
9-23	At Bos.	L	5-6	(10)	11	7	Kim	Ainsworth		69-87	4th	28.5
9-24	At Bos.	W	7-3		13	8	Hentgen	Burkett		70-87	4th	27.5
9-25	At Bos.	L	3-14		4	18	Lowe	Daal		70-88	4th	28.0
9-26†	At N.Y.	L	2-11		8	14	Pettitte	Moss		70-89		
9-26‡	At N.Y.	W	3-2	(10)	5	8	Ligtenberg	Hammond	Julio	71-89	4th	28.0
9-27	At N.Y.	L	2-6		4	14	Clemens	Johnson		71-90	4th	29.0
9-28	At N.Y.	L	1-3		6	5	Wells	DuBose	Rivera	71-91	4th	30.0

Monthly records: March (1-0), April (12-12), May (14-15), June (8-18), July (15-10), August (11-20), September (10-16).
*Innings, if other than nine. † First game of a doubleheader. ‡ Second game of a doubleheader. § Day separate admission. ∞ Night separate admission.

RECORDS

2003 regular-season record: 71-91
Position: 4th in A.L. East
Home: 40-40 **Road:** 31-51
A.L. East: 31-45 **A.L. Central:** 14-18
A.L. West: 21-15 **N.L.** 5-13
Vs. LH starters: 17-30
Vs. RH starters: 54-61
Grass: 64-76 **Artificial:** 7-15
Day: 24-26 **Night:** 47-65
1-Run: 21-22 **X-inn.:** 4-10
Doubleheaders: 2-0-1
Team record past five years: 353-456 (.436, ranks 11th in league in that span)

TEAM LEADERS

Batting average: Melvin Mora (.317).
At-bats: Tony Batista (631).
Runs: Jay Gibbons (80).
Hits: Jay Gibbons (173).
Total Bases: Jay Gibbons (285).
Doubles: Jay Gibbons (39).
Triples: Brian Roberts (4).
Home runs: Tony Batista (26).
Runs batted in: Jay Gibbons (100).
Stolen bases: Brian Roberts (23).
Slugging percentage: Melvin Mora (.503).
On-base percentage: Melvin Mora (.418).
Wins: Sidney Ponson (14).
Earned-run average: Sidney Ponson (3.77).
Complete games: Sidney Ponson (4).
Shutouts: Rodrigo Lopez (1).
Saves: Jorge Julio (36).
Innings pitched: Jason Johnson (189.2).
Strikeouts: Jason Johnson (118).

GAMES BY POSITION

Catcher: Brook Fordyce 107, Geronimo Gil 53, Robert Machado 18.
First base: Jeff Conine 118, B.J. Surhoff 22, Jay Gibbons 13, Carlos Mendez 9, David Segui 8, Jose Leon 7, Melvin Mora 1.
Second base: Brian Roberts 107, Jerry Hairston Jr. 48, Jose Morban 12, Melvin Mora 6.
Third base: Tony Batista 154, Jose Leon 10, Jeff Conine 1, Jose Morban 1.
Shortstop: Deivi Cruz 147, Jose Morban 14, Melvin Mora 11, Brian Roberts 2.
Outfield: Jay Gibbons 144, Luis Matos 107, Larry Bigbie 80, Melvin Mora 79, Gary Matthews Jr. 40, B.J. Surhoff 27, Tim Raines Jr. 18, Jeff Conine 8, Pedro Swann 6, Marty Cordova 4, Jack Cust 1.
Designated hitter: David Segui 53, B.J. Surhoff 39, Jack Cust 23, Jose Morban 14, Jerry Hairston Jr. 9, Carlos Mendez 8, Tony Batista 7, Marty Cordova 5, Deivi Cruz 5, Jay Gibbons 5, Brian Roberts 4, Jose Leon 3, Luis Matos 2, Gary Matthews Jr. 1, Tim Raines Jr. 1, Pedro Swann 1.

TOP DRAFT CHOICES

1. **Nick Markakis,** OF, Young Harris (Ga.) JC.
2. **Brian Finch,** RHP, Texas A&M.
3. **Chris Ray,** RHP, William & Mary.
4. **Bob McCrory,** RHP, Southern Mississippi.
5. **Nate Spears,** SS, Charlotte H.S., Port Charlotte, Fla.
6. **Eric Sultemeier,** OF, Texas.
7. **Justin Azze,** LHP, Hawaii.
8. **Nathan Nery,** LHP, Moon Area H.S., Moon Township, Pa.
9. **Jarod Rine,** OF, West Virginia.
10. **Jacob Duncan,** OF, Texas Christian.

BOSTON RED SOX

AMERICAN LEAGUE EAST DIVISION

2004 SEASON

April

SUN	MON	TUE	WED	THU	FRI	SAT
4 BAL	5	6 BAL	7 BAL	8 BAL	9 TOR	10 TOR
11 TOR	12	13 BAL	14 BAL	15 BAL	16 NYY	17 NYY
18 NYY	19 NYY	20 TOR	21 TOR	22 TOR	23 NYY	24 NYY
25 NYY	26	27 TB	28 TB	29 TB	30 TEX	

May

SUN	MON	TUE	WED	THU	FRI	SAT
						1 TEX
2 TEX	3 CLE	4 CLE	5 CLE	6 CLE	7 KC	8 KC
9 KC	10 CLE	11 CLE	12 CLE	13 TOR	14 TOR	15 TOR
16 TOR	17	18 TB	19 TB	20 TB	21 TOR	22 TOR
23 TOR	24	25 OAK	26 OAK	27 OAK	28 SEA	29 SEA
30 SEA	31					

June

SUN	MON	TUE	WED	THU	FRI	SAT
		1 ANA	2 ANA	3	4 KC	5 KC
6 KC	7	8 SD	9 SD	10 SD	11 LA	12 LA
13 LA	14	15 COL	16 COL	17 COL	18 SF	19 SF
20 SF	21	22 MIN	23 MIN	24 MIN	25 PHI	26 PHI
27 PHI	28	29 NYY	30 NYY			

Home games shaded. All-Star Game July 13 at Houston. Schedule subject to change.

July

SUN	MON	TUE	WED	THU	FRI	SAT
				1 NYY	2 ATL	3 ATL
4 ATL	5	6 OAK	7 OAK	8 OAK	9 TEX	10 TEX
11 TEX	12	13 All-Star	14	15 ANA	16 ANA	17 ANA
18 ANA	19 SEA	20 SEA	21 BAL	22 BAL	23 NYY	24 NYY
25 NYY	26 BAL	27 BAL	28 BAL	29	30 MIN	31 MIN

August

SUN	MON	TUE	WED	THU	FRI	SAT
1 MIN	2 TB	3 TB	4 TB	5	6 DET	7 DET
8 DET	9 TB	10 TB	11 TB	12 TB	13 CHW	14 CHW
15 CHW	16 TOR	17 TOR	18 TOR	19	20 CHW	21 CHW
22 CHW	23 TOR	24 TOR	25 TOR	26 DET	27 DET	28 DET
29 DET	30	31 ANA				

Sept./Oct.

SUN	MON	TUE	WED	THU	FRI	SAT
			1 ANA	2 ANA	3 TEX	4 TEX
5 TEX	6 OAK	7 OAK	8 OAK	9 SEA	10 SEA	11 SEA
12 SEA	13	14 TB	15 TB	16 TB	17 NYY	18 NYY
19 NYY	20 BAL	21 BAL	22 BAL	23 BAL	24 NYY	25 NYY
26 NYY	27 TB	28 TB	29 TB	30	1 BAL	2 BAL
3 BAL	4	5	6	7	8	9

CLUB DIRECTORY

Principal owner
John W. Henry
President/chief executive officer
Larry Lucchino
General manager
Theo Epstein
Vice president/baseball operations
Michael D. Port
Assistant general manager
Joshua H. Byrnes
Director of baseball operations
Peter Woodfork
Director of player development
Benjamin P. Cherington
Director of amateur scouting
David Chadd
Vice president, publications and archives
Richard L. Bresciani
Vice president and club counsel
Elaine W. Steward
Dir. of media relations
Kevin J. Shea
Director of communications
Glenn Geffner
Community relations manager
Vanessa M. Leyvas

MINOR LEAGUE AFFILIATES

Class	Team	League	Manager
AAA	Pawtucket	International	Buddy Bailey
AA	Portland	Eastern	Ron Johnson
Advanced A	Sarasota	Florida State	Todd Claus
A	Augusta	South Atlantic	Chad Epperson
Short-Season A	Lowell	New York-Pennsylvania	Luis Alicea
Rookie	Gulf Coast Red Sox	Gulf Coast	Ralph Treuel

More on the Red Sox at www.foxsports.com/named/FS/MLB/teams

BROADCAST INFORMATION

Radio: WEEI-AM (680).
TV: WFXT-TV (Fox 25).
Cable TV: New England Sports Network.

SPRING TRAINING

Ballpark (city): City of Palms Park (Fort Myers, Fla.).
Ticket information: 941-334-4700.

SPRING TRAINING ROSTER

Manager—Terry Francona (16).
Coaches—Brad Mills, Ron Jackson (22), Lynn Jones, Euclides Rojas (54), Dave Wallace (37).

No.	PITCHERS	B/T	Ht./Wt.	Age*	2003 Clubs
61	Arroyo, Bronson	R/R	6-5/190	27	Pawtucket, Boston
	Bean, Colter	R/R	6-6/255	27	Trenton, Columbus
	Brown, Jamie	R/R	6-2/205	27	Buffalo, Pawtucket
	Dinardo, Lenny	L/L	6-4/195	24	Binghamton, St. Lucie
43	Embree, Alan	L/L	6-2/190	34	Sarasota, Boston
29	Foulke, Keith	R/R	6-0/210	31	Oakland
	Gamble, Jerome	R/R	6-2/200	23	Sarasota, Portland
	Hamulack, Tim	L/L	6-4/210	27	Tacoma
	Hebson, Bryan	R/R	6-5/210	28	Edmonton, Montreal, Pawtucket
51	Kim, Byung-Hyun	R/R	5-9/180	25	Tucson, Arizona, Boston
32	Lowe, Derek	R/R	6-6/214	30	Boston
	Malaska, Mark	L/L	6-3/191	26	Orlando, Durham, Tampa Bay
	Martinez, Anas.	R/R	6-2/180	25	Pawtucket, Portland
45	Martinez, Pedro	R/R	5-11/180	32	Boston
26	Mendoza, Ramiro	R/R	6-2/195	31	G.C. Red Sox, Sarasota, Pawtucket, Boston
38	Schilling, Curt	R/R	6-5/235	37	Tucson, Arizona
	Seibel, Phil	L/L	6-1/195	25	Norfolk, Binghamton
50	Timlin, Mike	R/R	6-4/210	38	Boston
49	Wakefield, Tim	R/R	6-2/214	37	Boston
48	Williamson, Scott	R/R	6-0/185	28	Cincinnati, Boston

No.	CATCHERS	B/T	Ht./Wt.	Age*	2003 Clubs
	Dominique, Andy	R/R	6-0/220	28	Portland, Pawtucket
	Hernandez, Michel	R/R	6-0/208	25	Columbus, New York
28	Mirabelli, Doug	R/R	6-1/227	33	Boston
33	Varitek, Jason	B/R	6-2/237	31	Boston

No.	INFIELDERS	B/T	Ht./Wt.	Age*	2003 Clubs
	Bellhorn, Mark	B/R	6-1/205	29	Chicago N.L., Colo. Springs, Colorado
5	Garciaparra, N.	R/R	6-0/190	30	Boston
15	Millar, Kevin	R/R	6-0/210	32	Boston
11	Mueller, Bill	B/R	5-10/180	33	Boston
34	Ortiz, David	L/L	6-4/230	28	Boston
	Reese, Pokey	R/R	5-11/180	30	Pittsburgh
	Youkilis, Kevin	R/R	6-1/220	25	Portland, Pawtucket

No.	OUTFIELDERS	B/T	Ht./Wt.	Age*	2003 Clubs
18	Damon, Johnny	L/L	6-2/190	30	Boston
28	Kapler, Gabe	R/R	6-2/208	28	Colorado, Colorado Springs, Lowell, Portland, Boston
7	Nixon, Trot	L/L	6-2/211	29	Boston
24	Ramirez, Manny	R/R	6-0/213	31	Boston

Invited to spring training: RHP, Edwin Almonte, RHP Jason Shiell, OF-1B Brian Daubach, OF-1B David McCarty.
*Age as of April 1, 2004.

BALLPARK INFORMATION

Ballpark (capacity, surface)
Fenway Park (36,298; grass)

Address
4 Yawkey Way
Boston, MA 02215-3496

Official website
www.redsox.com

Business phone
617-267-9440

Ticket information
617-482-4769

Field dimensions (from home plate)
To left field at foul line, 310 feet
To center field, 390 feet
To right field at foul line, 302 feet

First game played
April 20, 1912
(Red Sox 7, New York Highlanders 6)

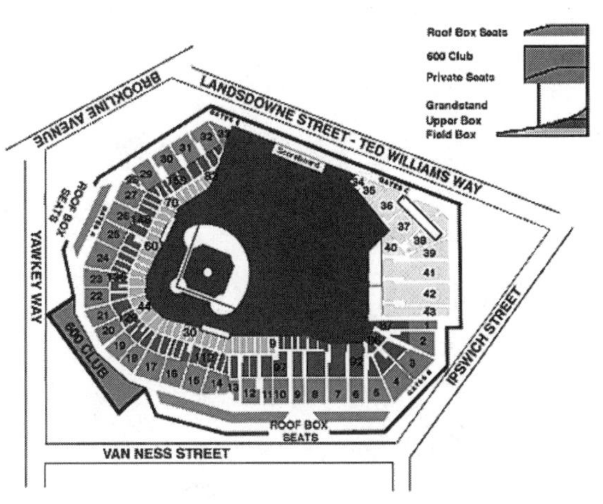

2003 REVIEW

DAY BY DAY

Date	Opp.	Res.	Score	(inn.*)	Hits	Opp. hits	Winning pitcher	Losing pitcher	Save	Record	Pos.	GB
3-31	At T.B.	L	4-6		8	7	McClung	Fox		0-1	T4th	1.0
4-1	At T.B.	W	9-8	(16)	13	19	Lyon	Sosa		1-1	T3rd	1.0
4-2	At T.B.	W	7-5		8	7	Lowe	Parque	Fox	2-1	2nd	1.0
4-3	At T.B.	W	14-5		16	11	Fossum	Bierbrodt		3-1	2nd	0.5
4-4	At Bal.	W	8-7		11	16	Burkett	Ponson		4-1	2nd	0.5
4-5	At Bal.	L	1-2		3	5	Ryan	Fox		4-2	2nd	0.5
4-6	At Bal.	W	12-2		12	5	Wakefield	Lopez		5-2	2nd	0.5
4-8	At Tor.	L	4-8		11	12	Hendrickson	Lowe		5-3	2nd	1.5
4-9	At Tor.	L	5-10		9	8	Sturtze	Fossum		5-4	3rd	2.5
4-10	At Tor.	W	8-7		11	10	Timlin	Politte		6-4	2nd	2.5
4-12	Bal.	L	6-13		9	15	Johnson	Martinez		6-5	2nd	3.5
4-13	Bal.	W	2-0		6	6	Lowe	Lopez	Wakefield	7-5	2nd	2.5
4-15	T.B.	W	6-5		15	11	Timlin	Levine		8-5	2nd	3.0
4-16	T.B.	W	6-4		10	7	Fox	Carter	Lyon	9-5	2nd	2.0
4-17	T.B.	W	6-0		12	4	Martinez	Kennedy		10-5	2nd	2.0
4-18	Tor.	W	7-3		11	8	Wakefield	Tam		11-5	2nd	2.0
4-19	Tor.	W	7-2		8	9	Lowe	Sturtze		12-5	2nd	2.0
4-20	Tor.	W	6-5		13	6	Timlin	Politte		13-5	2nd	2.0
4-21	Tor.	L	6-11		11	17	Lidle	Burkett		13-6	2nd	3.0
4-22	At Tex.	W	5-4		9	6	Martinez	Park	Fox	14-6	2nd	3.0
4-23	At Tex.	L	1-6		6	10	Thomson	Wakefield		14-7	2nd	4.0
4-24	At Tex.	L	5-16		9	19	Dickey	Lowe		14-8	2nd	4.0
4-25	At Ana.	W	5-2		7	10	Fossum	Washburn	Fox	15-8	2nd	4.0
4-26	At Ana.	L	1-3		7	9	Shields	Burkett	Percival	15-9	2nd	5.0
4-27	At Ana.	W	6-4	(14)	13	11	Mendoza	Callaway	Shiell	16-9	2nd	4.0
4-29	K.C.	W	7-2		12	8	Wakefield	George		17-9	2nd	3.0
4-30	K.C.	W	5-4		11	5	Embree	MacDougal		18-9	2nd	3.0
5-1	K.C.	W	6-5		11	8	Shiell	Grimsley	Lyon	19-9	2nd	3.0
5-2	Min.	L	7-11		12	15	Santana	Mendoza		19-10	2nd	4.0
5-3	Min.	W	9-1		13	5	Martinez	Fiore		20-10	2nd	3.0
5-4	Min.	L	4-9		9	14	Rogers	Timlin		20-11	2nd	3.0
5-5	At K.C.	L	6-7		10	11	Lopez	Lyon		20-12	2nd	3.5
5-6	At K.C.	W	7-3		13	7	Fossum	Affeldt		21-12	2nd	2.5
5-7	At K.C.	W	9-6		10	8	Woodard	Lopez	Lyon	22-12	2nd	2.5
5-9	At Min.	L	0-5		5	8	Santana	Martinez		22-13	2nd	3.0
5-10	At Min.	W	6-5		12	11	Wakefield	Rincon	Lyon	23-13	2nd	3.0
5-11	At Min.	L	8-9		15	15	Radke	Lowe	Guardado	23-14	2nd	3.0
5-13	Tex.	W	5-4		7	8	Embree	Cordero	Lyon	24-14	2nd	2.0
5-14	Tex.	W	7-1		8	6	Fossum	Benoit		25-14	2nd	1.0
5-15	Tex.	W	12-3		16	8	Martinez	Benes		26-14	2nd	1.0
5-16	Ana.	L	5-6		10	11	Rodriguez	Embree	Percival	26-15	2nd	1.0
5-17	Ana.	L	2-6		9	12	Washburn	Timlin	Percival	26-16	2nd	1.0
5-18	Ana.	W	5-3		11	11	Burkett	Lackey	Person	27-16	T1st	...
5-19	N.Y.	L	3-7		12	10	Wells	Fossum		27-17	2nd	1.0
5-20	N.Y.	W	10-7		11	11	Embree	Contreras	Lyon	28-17	T1st	...
5-21	N.Y.	L	2-4		9	6	Clemens	Wakefield	Rivera	28-18	2nd	1.0
5-23	Cle.	W	9-2		13	4	Lowe	Rodriguez		29-18	1st	+0.5
5-24	Cle.	W	12-3		15	8	Burkett	Anderson		30-18	1st	+1.5
5-25	Cle.	L	4-6		7	10	Davis	Fossum	Baez	30-19	1st	+1.5
5-26	At N.Y.	W	8-4		14	5	Wakefield	Clemens		31-19	1st	+2.5
5-27	At N.Y.	L	3-11		7	14	Pettitte	Chen		31-20	1st	+1.5
5-28	At N.Y.	L	5-6		9	11	Rivera	Lyon		31-21	1st	+0.5
5-30	At Tor.	L	2-13		9	12	Davis	Burkett		31-22	2nd	0.5
5-31	At Tor.	L	7-10		14	10	Sturtze	Fossum	Politte	31-23	2nd	0.5
6-1	At Tor.	L	8-11		14	19	Halladay	White		31-24	2nd	1.5
6-4†	At Pit.	W	11-4		16	7	Kim	Benson		32-24		
6-4‡	At Pit.	W	8-3		12	7	Lowe	D'Amico		33-24	1st	+0.5
6-5	At Pit.	L	4-5		7	11	Boehringer	Mendoza	Williams	33-25	2nd	0.5
6-6	At Mil.	L	3-9		5	12	Durocher	Almonte		33-26	2nd	1.5
6-7	At Mil.	W	11-10		14	12	Lyon	DeJean	Timlin	34-26	2nd	0.5
6-8	At Mil.	W	9-1		12	6	Lowe	Rusch		35-26	1st	+0.5
6-10	StL.	L	7-9		14	14	Kline	Lyon	Eldred	35-27	2nd	0.5
6-11	StL.	W	13-1		19	10	Burkett	Tomko		36-27	1st	+0.5
6-12	StL.	L	7-8	(13)	13	14	Yan	Mendoza		36-28	2nd	0.5

Date	Opp.	Res.	Score	(inn.*)	Hits	Opp. hits	Winning pitcher	Losing pitcher	Save	Record	Pos.	GB
6-13	Hou.	W	4-3		7	9	Rupe	Stone	Lyon	37-28	2nd	0.5
6-14	Hou.	W	8-4		12	9	Lowe	Redding		38-28	2nd	0.5
6-15	Hou.	W	3-2	(14)	14	13	Shiell	Bland		39-28	2nd	0.5
6-16	At Chi.	L	2-4		5	8	Buehrle	Rupe	Gordon	39-29	2nd	1.0
6-17	At Chi.	W	7-4		9	7	Burkett	Colon	Lyon	40-29	2nd	0.5
6-18	At Chi.	L	1-3		7	5	Loaiza	Wakefield	Koch	40-30	2nd	1.5
6-19	At Chi.	W	4-3	(10)	3	9	Lyon	Koch		41-30	2nd	1.0
6-21	At Phi.	L	5-6	(13)	15	11	Mesa	Seanez		41-31	2nd	2.0
6-22	At Phi.	L	0-5		3	7	Myers	Kim		41-32	3rd	3.0
6-23	Det.	W	3-1		10	6	Wakefield	Bonderman	Timlin	42-32	3rd	2.0
6-24	Det.	W	10-1		17	7	Lowe	Cornejo		43-32	2nd	2.0
6-25	Det.	W	11-2		14	8	Burkett	Maroth		44-32	2nd	2.0
6-26	Det.	W	6-4		10	8	Martinez	Roney	Lyon	45-32	2nd	2.0
6-27	Fla.	W	25-8		28	10	Kim	Pavano		46-32	2nd	2.0
6-28	Fla.	L	9-10		15	13	Bump	Lyon	Looper	46-33	2nd	3.5
6-29	Fla.	W	11-7		12	8	Lowe	Penny		47-33	2nd	3.5
7-1	At T.B.	L	3-4	(11)	10	10	Carter	Lyon		47-34	2nd	4.0
7-2	At T.B.	W	5-4		10	7	Martinez	Colome	Kim	48-34	2nd	3.5
7-3	At T.B.	L	5-6	(10)	6	9	Harper	Timlin		48-35	2nd	4.0
7-4	At N.Y.	W	10-3		15	11	Lowe	Wells		49-35	2nd	3.0
7-5	At N.Y.	W	10-2		10	11	Mendoza	Clemens		50-35	2nd	2.0
7-6	At N.Y.	L	1-7		6	14	Pettitte	Burkett		50-36	2nd	3.0
7-7	At N.Y.	L	1-2		3	7	Rivera	Kim		50-37	2nd	4.0
7-8	At Tor.	W	2-1	(12)	9	8	Jones	Tam	Kim	51-37	2nd	3.0
7-9	At Tor.	W	8-7		13	13	Lyon	Tam	Kim	52-37	2nd	3.0
7-10	At Tor.	W	7-1		13	8	Mendoza	Lidle		53-37	2nd	2.0
7-11	At Det.	W	5-3		12	4	Burkett	Maroth	Kim	54-37	2nd	2.0
7-12	At Det.	W	4-2	(11)	9	9	Jones	Rodney	Kim	55-37	2nd	1.0
7-13	At Det.	L	0-3		7	5	Ledezma	Wakefield	Mears	55-38	2nd	2.0
7-17	Tor.	L	2-5		9	9	Halladay	Lowe		55-39	2nd	3.0
7-18	Tor.	L	1-4		7	8	Escobar	Wakefield	Miller	55-40	2nd	4.0
7-19	Tor.	W	5-4	(10)	10	7	Kim	Lopez		56-40	2nd	4.0
7-20	Tor.	W	9-4		11	7	Martinez	Wasdin		57-40	2nd	4.0
7-21	Det.	W	14-5		18	12	Burkett	Bonderman	Fossum	58-40	2nd	3.0
7-22	Det.	W	7-4		11	7	Lowe	Maroth		59-40	2nd	2.5
7-23	T.B.	W	10-4		13	6	Wakefield	Harper		60-40	2nd	2.5
7-24	T.B.	L	9-15		9	21	Zambrano	Mendoza		60-41	2nd	2.5
7-25	N.Y.	L	3-4		10	8	Rivera	Kim		60-42	2nd	3.5
7-26	N.Y.	W	5-4		9	10	Kim	Benitez		61-42	2nd	2.5
7-27	N.Y.	W	6-4		7	11	Fossum	Hammond	Kim	62-42	2nd	1.5
7-29	At Tex.	W	14-7		14	9	Wakefield	Garcia		63-42	2nd	1.5
7-30	At Tex.	L	2-9		7	10	Ellis	Mendoza		63-43	2nd	2.5
7-31	At Tex.	L	3-7	(11)	12	9	Ramirez	Jones		63-44	2nd	3.5
8-1	At Bal.	L	1-2		4	9	Hentgen	Burkett	Julio	63-45	2nd	3.5
8-2	At Bal.	L	2-11		6	16	Lopez	Lowe		63-46	2nd	4.5
8-3	At Bal.	W	7-5		10	7	Wakefield	Helling	Kim	64-46	2nd	3.5
8-5	Ana.	W	10-9		11	11	Timlin	Donnelly	Kim	65-46	2nd	3.5
8-6	Ana.	W	4-2		10	10	Martinez	Sele		66-46	2nd	2.5
8-7	Ana.	W	9-3		14	8	Burkett	Ortiz		67-46	2nd	2.5
8-8§	Bal.	L	4-10		12	13	Helling	Lowe		67-47		
8-8∞	Bal.	L	2-4		7	7	DuBose	Fossum	Julio	67-48	2nd	4.0
8-9	Bal.	W	6-4		9	7	Embree	Driskill	Kim	68-48	2nd	3.0
8-10	Bal.	L	3-5		9	6	Johnson	Suppan	Julio	68-49	2nd	3.0
8-11	At Oak.	L	0-4		2	6	Hudson	Martinez		68-50	2nd	3.0
8-12	At Oak.	L	3-5		8	7	Zito	Burkett	Foulke	68-51	2nd	4.0
8-13	At Oak.	W	7-3		11	9	Lowe	Mulder		69-51	2nd	3.0
8-14	At Oak.	W	4-2	(10)	6	7	Kim	Mecir		70-51	2nd	3.0
8-15	At Sea.	L	5-10		8	13	Mateo	Timlin	Hasegawa	70-52	2nd	4.0
8-16	At Sea.	W	5-1		10	5	Martinez	Pineiro		71-52	2nd	4.0
8-17	At Sea.	L	1-3		4	6	Garcia	Burkett	Hasegawa	71-53	2nd	5.0
8-19	Oak.	L	2-3		7	3	Rincon	Williamson	Foulke	71-54	2nd	6.5
8-20	Oak.	L	6-8		17	11	Bradford	Kim	Foulke	71-55	2nd	7.5
8-21	Oak.	W	14-5		12	9	Fossum	Harden		72-55	2nd	7.0
8-22	Sea.	W	6-4		10	11	Suppan	Pineiro	Kim	73-55	2nd	6.0
8-23	Sea.	W	7-6	(10)	14	12	Timlin	Sasaki		74-55	2nd	5.0
8-24	Sea.	W	6-1		11	7	Lowe	Franklin		75-55	2nd	5.0
8-25	Sea.	W	8-1		12	8	Martinez	Meche	Arroyo	76-55	2nd	5.0
8-26	Tor.	L	9-12		15	16	Towers	Sauerbeck	Lopez	76-56	2nd	5.0
8-27	Tor.	W	6-3		11	10	Timlin	Halladay	Kim	77-56	2nd	4.0
8-29	N.Y.	W	10-5		14	6	Lowe	Contreras		78-56	2nd	3.5
8-30	N.Y.	L	7-10		10	15	Pettitte	Martinez	Rivera	78-57	2nd	4.5
8-31	N.Y.	L	4-8		9	10	Clemens	Wakefield	Rivera	78-58	2nd	5.5

Date	Opp.	Res.	Score	(inn.*)	Hits	Opp. hits	Winning pitcher	Losing pitcher	Save	Record	Pos.	GB
9-1	At Phi.	W	13-9		13	14	Kim	Mesa		79-58	2nd	4.5
9-2	At Chi.	W	2-1		2	4	Burkett	Colon	Kim	80-58	2nd	4.0
9-3	At Chi.	W	5-4	(10)	11	13	Kim	Gordon		81-58	2nd	3.0
9-5	At N.Y.	W	9-3		14	7	Martinez	Pettitte		82-58	2nd	2.5
9-6	At N.Y.	W	11-0		12	4	Wakefield	Clemens		83-58	2nd	1.5
9-7	At N.Y.	L	1-3		7	5	Wells	Suppan	Rivera	83-59	2nd	2.5
9-8	At Bal.	L	10-13		16	16	Ligtenberg	Kim		83-60	2nd	3.5
9-9	At Bal.	W	9-2		13	9	Lowe	Moss		84-60	2nd	3.5
9-10	At Bal.	W	5-0		11	3	Martinez	Johnson		85-60	2nd	3.5
9-12	Chi.	W	7-4		5	7	Suppan	Wright	Kim	86-60	2nd	4.0
9-13	Chi.	L	1-3		5	7	Colon	Wakefield		86-61	2nd	5.5
9-14	Chi.	L	2-7		9	10	Buehrle	Burkett	Marte	86-62	2nd	5.5
9-15	T.B.	W	8-2		14	4	Lowe	Sosa		87-62	2nd	5.5
9-16	T.B.	W	3-2		5	6	Martinez	Harper		88-62	2nd	5.5
9-17	T.B.	L	0-7		6	16	Zambrano	Suppan		88-63	2nd	5.5
9-18	T.B.	W	4-3		9	7	Wakefield	Bell	Kim	89-63	2nd	5.0
9-19	At Cle.	W	2-0		8	3	Burkett	Stanford	Embree	90-63	2nd	5.0
9-20	At Cle.	L	4-13		10	14	Lee	Lowe		90-64	2nd	6.0
9-21	At Cle.	W	2-0		4	4	Martinez	Lee	Kim	91-64	2nd	6.0
9-22	Bal.	W	7-5		9	13	Suppan	Johnson	Kim	92-64	2nd	5.0
9-23	Bal.	W	6-5	(10)	7	11	Kim	Ainsworth		93-64	2nd	5.0
9-24	Bal.	L	3-7		8	13	Hentgen	Burkett		93-65	2nd	5.0
9-25	Bal.	W	14-3		18	4	Lowe	Daal		94-65	2nd	4.5
9-26	At T.B.	W	7-2		12	8	Burkett	Gonzalez		95-65	2nd	4.0
9-27	At T.B.	L	4-5		10	9	Gaudin	Suppan	Carter	95-66	2nd	5.0
9-28	At T.B.	L	1-3		7	7	Zambrano	Lyon	Carter	95-67	2nd	6.0

Monthly records: March (0-1), April (18-8), May (13-14), June (16-10), July (16-11), August (15-14), September (17-9).
*Innings, if other than nine. † First game of a doubleheader. ‡ Second game of a doubleheader. § Day separate admission. ∞ Night separate admission.

RECORDS

2003 regular-season record: 95-67
Position: 2nd in A.L. East
Home: 53-28 **Road:** 42-39
A.L. East: 41-35 **A.L. Central:** 24-12
A.L. West: 19-13 N.L. 11-7
Vs. LH starters: 26-27
Vs. RH starters: 69-40
Grass: 84-53 **Artificial:** 11-14
Day: 28-22 **Night:** 67-45
1-Run: 26-16 **X-inn.:** 11-5
Doubleheaders: 1-0-0
Team record past five years: 449-360 (.555, ranks 4th in league in that span)

TEAM LEADERS

Batting average: Bill Mueller (.326).
At-bats: Nomar Garciaparra (658).
Runs: Nomar Garciaparra (120).
Hits: Nomar Garciaparra (198).
Total Bases: Nomar Garciaparra (345).
Doubles: Bill Mueller (45).
Triples: Nomar Garciaparra (13).
Home runs: Manny Ramirez (37).
Runs batted in: Nomar Garciaparra (105).
Stolen bases: Johnny Damon (30).
Slugging percentage: David Ortiz (.592).
On-base percentage: Manny Ramirez (.427).
Wins: Derek Lowe (17).
Earned-run average: Pedro Martinez (2.22).
Complete games: Pedro Martinez (3).
Shutouts: None.
Saves: Byung-Hyun Kim (16).
Innings pitched: Derek Lowe (203.1).
Strikeouts: Pedro Martinez (206).

GAMES BY POSITION

Catcher: Jason Varitek 137, Doug Mirabelli 55, Bill Haselman 2.
First base: Kevin Millar 101, David Ortiz 45, Shea Hillenbrand 28, Andy Abad 7, Dave McCarty 5, Damian Jackson 2, Doug Mirabelli 2, Gabe Kapler 1.
Second base: Todd Walker 139, Damian Jackson 38, Bill Mueller 10, Lou Merloni 7, Freddy Sanchez 3.
Third base: Bill Mueller 135, Shea Hillenbrand 29, Lou Merloni 7, Freddy Sanchez 7, Damian Jackson 3, Lou Collier 2.
Shortstop: Nomar Garciaparra 156, Damian Jackson 18, Freddy Sanchez 6, Bill Mueller 1.
Outfield: Johnny Damon 144, Trot Nixon 130, Manny Ramirez 128, Gabe Kapler 61, Damian Jackson 38, Kevin Millar 31, Jeremy Giambi 11, Adrian Brown 9, Dave McCarty 8, Lou Collier 2, Andy Abad 1, Lou Merloni 1.
Designated hitter: David Ortiz 74, Jeremy Giambi 30, Manny Ramirez 26, Kevin Millar 19, Damian Jackson 9, Doug Mirabelli 4, Jason Varitek 4, Bill Mueller 3, Bill Haselman 2, Shea Hillenbrand 2, Todd Walker 2, Johnny Damon 1, Gabe Kapler 1, Dave McCarty 1.

TOP DRAFT CHOICES

1a. **David Murphy,** OF, Baylor.
1b. **Matt Murton,** OF, Georgia Tech.
2a. **Abe Alvarez,** LHP, Long Beach State.
2b. **Mickey Hall,** OF, Walton H.S., Marietta, Ga.
3. **Beau Vaughan,** RHP, Arizona State.
4. **Jon Papelbon,** RHP, Mississippi State.
5. **Brian Marshall,** LHP, Virginia Commonwealth.
6. **Jessie Corn,** RHP, Jacksonville State.
7. **Jeremy West,** C, Arizona State.
8. **Lee Curtis,** 2B, College of Charleston.
9. **John Wilson,** RHP, Northeastern (Colo.) JC.
10. **Chris Durbin,** OF, Baylor.

CHICAGO WHITE SOX

AMERICAN LEAGUE CENTRAL DIVISION

2004 SEASON

April

SUN	MON	TUE	WED	THU	FRI	SAT
4	5 KC	6	7 KC	8 NYY	9 NYY	10 NYY
11 NYY	12	13 KC	14 KC	15 KC	16 TB	17 TB
18 TB	19	20 NYY	21 NYY	22 NYY	23 TB	24 TB
25 TB	26	27 CLE	28 CLE	29 TOR	30 TOR	

May

SUN	MON	TUE	WED	THU	FRI	SAT
						1 TOR
2 TOR	3 BAL	4 BAL	5 BAL	6	7 TOR	8 TOR
9 TOR	10	11 BAL	12 BAL	13 BAL	14 MIN	15 MIN
16 MIN	17 CLE	18 CLE	19 CLE	20 MIN	21 MIN	22 MIN
23 MIN	24	25 TEX	26 TEX	27 TEX	28 ANA	29 ANA
30 ANA	31					

June

SUN	MON	TUE	WED	THU	FRI	SAT
		1 OAK	2 OAK	3	4 SEA	5 SEA
6 SEA	7	8 PHI	9 PHI	10 PHI	11 ATL	12 ATL
13 ATL	14	15 FLA	16 FLA	17 FLA	18 MON	19 MON
20 MON	21 CLE	22 CLE	23 CLE	24 CLE	25 CHC	26 CHC
27 CHC	28	29 MIN	30 MIN			

Home games shaded. All-Star Game July 13 at Houston. Schedule subject to change.

July

SUN	MON	TUE	WED	THU	FRI	SAT
				1 MIN	2 CHC	3 CHC
4 CHC	5	6 ANA	7 ANA	8 ANA	9 SEA	10 SEA
11 SEA	12	13 All-Star	14	15 OAK	16 OAK	17 OAK
18 OAK	19 TEX	20 TEX	21 CLE	22 CLE	23 DET	24 DET
25 DET	26 MIN	27 MIN	28 MIN	29 DET	30 DET	31 DET

August

SUN	MON	TUE	WED	THU	FRI	SAT
1 DET	2	3 KC	4 KC	5 KC	6 CLE	7 CLE
8 CLE	9 CLE	10 KC	11 KC	12 KC	13 BOS	14 BOS
15 BOS	16	17 DET	18 DET	19 DET	20 BOS	21 BOS
22 BOS	23 DET	24 DET	25 DET	26 CLE	27 CLE	28 CLE
29 CLE	30	31 OAK				

Sept./Oct.

SUN	MON	TUE	WED	THU	FRI	SAT
			1 OAK	2 OAK	3 SEA	4 SEA
5 SEA	6 TEX	7 TEX	8 TEX	9 TEX	10 ANA	11 ANA
12 ANA	13	14 MIN	15 MIN	16 MIN	17 DET	18 DET
19 DET	20 MIN	21 MIN	22 MIN	23 KC	24 KC	25 KC
26 KC	27 DET	28 DET	29 DET	30 KC	1 KC	2 KC
3 KC	4	5	6	7	8	9

CLUB DIRECTORY

Chairman
Jerry Reinsdorf
Vice chairman
Eddie Einhorn
Executive vice president
Howard Pizer
Senior vice president, general manager
Ken Williams
Vice president, free agent and major league scouting
Larry Monroe
Executive advisor to Ken Williams
Roland Hemond
Assistant general manager
Rick Hahn
Senior director of scouting
Duane Shaffer
Director of scouting, special assignments
Doug Laumann
Director of player development
Dave Wilder
Director of community relations
Christine O'Reilly
Director of public relations
Scott Reifert

MINOR LEAGUE AFFILIATES

Class	Team	League	Manager
AAA	Charlotte	International	Nick Capra
AA	Birmingham	Southern	Razor Shines
Advanced A	Winston-Salem	Carolina	Ken Dominguez
A	Kannapolis	South Atlantic	Chris Cron
Advanced Rookie	Bristol	Appalachian	Jerry Hairston
Advanced Rookie	Great Falls	Pioneer	John Orton

BROADCAST INFORMATION

Radio: ESPN-AM (1000).
TV: WGN-TV (Channel 9).
Cable TV: Fox Sports Chicago.

SPRING TRAINING

Ballpark (city): Tucson Electric Park (Tucson, Ariz.).
Ticket information: 520-434-1111.

More on the White Sox at www.foxsports.com/named/FS/MLB/teams

SPRING TRAINING ROSTER

Manager—Ozzie Guillen (13).
Coaches—Don Cooper (34), Joey Cora, Art Kusnyer (53), Joe Nossek (23), Rafael Santana (1), Greg Walker (20).

No.	PITCHERS	B/T	Ht./Wt.	Age*	2003 Clubs
37	Adkins, Jon	L/R	6-0/200	26	Charlotte, Chicago A.L.
56	Buehrle, Mark	L/L	6-2/200	25	Chicago A.L.
38	Cotts, Neal	L/L	6-2/200	24	Chicago A.L., Birmingham
54	Diaz, Felix	R/R	6-1/180	23	Charlotte
20	Garland, Jon	R/R	6-6/205	24	Chicago A.L.
32	Ginter, Matt	R/R	6-1/220	26	Chicago A.L., Charlotte
	Grilli, Jason	R/R	6-4/205	27	Albuquerque, Jupiter
44	Koch, Billy	R/R	6-3/215	29	Charlotte, Chicago A.L.
21	Loaiza, Esteban	R/R	6-3/215	32	Chicago A.L.
	Majewski, Gary	R/R	6-2/206	24	Charlotte
	Malone, Corwin	R/L	6-3/200	23	Bristol, Kannapolis, Birmingham
43	Marte, Damaso	L/L	6-2/200	29	Chicago A.L.
	Meaux, Ryan	R/L	5-11/170	25	Winston-Salem, Birmingham
	Munoz, Arnaldo	L/L	5-9/170	21	Charlotte
	Pacheco, Enem.	R/R	6-1/170	25	Birmingham
	Politte, Cliff	R/R	5-11/185	30	Toronto, Syracuse
51	Rauch, Jon	R/R	6-10/230	25	Charlotte
52	Sanders, David	L/L	6-0/200	24	Chicago A.L., Charlotte
60	Schoeneweis, Scott	L/L	6-0/190	30	Anaheim, Chicago A.L.
	Wing, Ryan	L/L	6-2/170	22	Winston-Salem
46	Wright, Dan	R/R	6-5/225	26	Charlotte, Chicago A.L.
65	Wunsch, Kelly	L/L	6-5/225	31	Charlotte, Chicago A.L.

No.	CATCHERS	B/T	Ht./Wt.	Age*	2003 Clubs
15	Alomar Jr., Sandy	R/R	6-5/235	37	Charlotte, Chicago A.L.
27	Burke, Jamie	R/R	6-0/195	32	Charlotte, Chicago A.L.
8	Olivo, Miguel	R/R	6-0/220	25	Chicago A.L.
	Rivera, Michael	R/R	6-0/210	27	San Diego, Portland, Charlotte

No.	INFIELDERS	B/T	Ht./Wt.	Age*	2003 Clubs
24	Crede, Joe	R/R	6-2/195	25	Chicago A.L.
	Gload, Ross	L/L	6-0/180	27	Charlotte
14	Konerko, Paul	R/R	6-2/215	28	Chicago A.L.
35	Thomas, Frank	R/R	6-5/275	35	Chicago A.L.
	Uribe, Juan	R/R	5-11/173	24	Visalia, Tulsa, Colorado
22	Valentin, Jose	B/R	5-10/185	34	Chicago A.L.
	Yan, Ruddy	S/R	6-0/165	22	Winston-Salem

No.	OUTFIELDERS	B/T	Ht./Wt.	Age*	2003 Clubs
25	Borchard, Joe	B/R	6-5/220	25	Chicago A.L., Charlotte
12	Harris, Willie	L/R	5-9/175	25	Charlotte, Chicago A.L.
45	Lee, Carlos	R/R	6-2/235	27	Chicago A.L.
30	Ordonez, Magglio	R/R	6-0/210	30	Chicago A.L.
33	Rowand, Aaron	R/R	6-1/210	26	Charlotte, Chicago A.L.

Invited to spring training: RHP Robert Person, RHP Kris Honel, RHP Ryan Kohlmeier, LHP Josh Stewart, C Ryan Hankins, IF Mike Bell, IF Kelly Dransfeldt, OF Jeremy Reed.

*Age as of April 1, 2004.

BALLPARK INFORMATION

Ballpark (capacity, surface)
U.S. Cellular Field (to be announced, grass)

Address
333 W. 35th St.
Chicago, IL 60616

Official website
www.whitesox.com

Business phone
312-674-1000

Ticket information
312-674-1000

Field dimensions (from home plate)
To left field at foul line, 330 feet
To center field, 400 feet
To right field at foul line, 335 feet

First game played
April 18, 1991 (Tigers 16, White Sox 0)

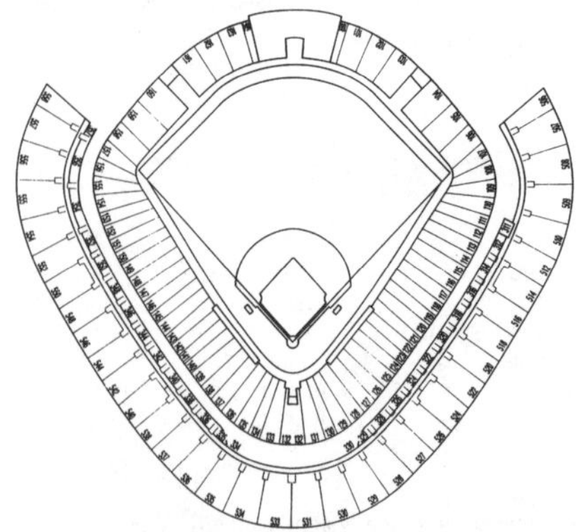

2003 REVIEW

DAY BY DAY

Date	Opp.	Res.	Score	(inn.*)	Hits	Opp. hits	Winning pitcher	Losing pitcher	Save	Record	Pos.	GB
3-31	At K.C.	L	0-3		3	7	Hernandez	Buehrle	MacDougal	0-1	T3rd	1.0
4-2	At K.C.	L	4-5		10	6	Lopez	White	MacDougal	0-2	T4th	2.0
4-3	At K.C.	L	6-12		8	16	Bukvich	Gordon		0-3	T4th	3.0
4-4	Det.	W	5-2		10	3	Loaiza	Cornejo	Koch	1-3	4th	3.0
4-5	Det.	W	7-0		13	3	Buehrle	Maroth		2-3	T3rd	3.0
4-6	Det.	W	10-2		9	8	Marte	German		3-3	T2nd	2.5
4-8	At Cle.	W	5-3	(10)	9	9	Koch	Paronto		4-3	2nd	2.0
4-9	At Cle.	L	2-5		8	7	Anderson	Garland	Baez	4-4	2nd	3.0
4-10	At Cle.	W	7-2		10	6	Buehrle	Davis		5-4	2nd	3.0
4-11	At Det.	W	5-0		10	2	Loaiza	Bernero		6-4	2nd	3.0
4-12	At Det.	L	3-4		11	8	Cornejo	Stewart	Anderson	6-5	2nd	4.0
4-13	At Det.	W	3-2		9	7	Colon	Knotts	Koch	7-5	2nd	3.0
4-15	K.C.	L	5-8		7	15	Lopez	Koch	MacDougal	7-6	T2nd	4.5
4-16	K.C.	W	4-3		5	5	Gordon	Grimsley		8-6	T2nd	3.5
4-17	K.C.	W	8-2		8	9	Loaiza	George		9-6	T2nd	2.5
4-18	Cle.	W	5-3		8	9	Colon	Traber		10-6	2nd	2.5
4-19	Cle.	W	12-3		16	6	Stewart	Anderson		11-6	2nd	2.5
4-20	Cle.	L	4-7		10	15	Davis	Buehrle		11-7	2nd	3.5
4-21	Cle.	L	2-9		8	13	Westbrook	Garland		11-8	2nd	4.0
4-22	At Bal.	W	3-1		7	4	Loaiza	Ponson	Koch	12-8	2nd	4.0
4-23	At Bal.	L	1-7		3	9	Johnson	Colon		12-9	2nd	4.5
4-24	At Bal.	L	4-5		8	8	Roberts	Gordon	Julio	12-10	2nd	5.5
4-25	Min.	L	1-6		5	9	Mays	Buehrle		12-11	2nd	5.5
4-26	Min.	W	7-4		10	6	Garland	Lohse		13-11	2nd	5.5
4-27	Min.	W	3-1		3	6	Loaiza	Reed	Marte	14-11	2nd	4.5
4-29	Oak.	L	2-3		5	6	Zito	Colon	Foulke	14-12	2nd	4.5
4-30	Oak.	L	1-4		4	9	Mulder	Buehrle		14-13	2nd	4.5
5-1	Oak.	W	7-5		13	7	Garland	Halama	Marte	15-13	2nd	3.5
5-2	Sea.	L	2-9		5	16	Franklin	Loaiza		15-14	2nd	4.5
5-3	Sea.	L	2-12		5	14	Garcia	Stewart		15-15	2nd	4.5
5-4	Sea.	L	1-5	(6)	4	9	Meche	Colon		15-16	3rd	5.5
5-6	At Oak.	L	0-6		5	7	Mulder	Buehrle		15-17	3rd	6.0
5-7	At Oak.	W	8-4		14	5	Loaiza	Lilly	Marte	16-17	3rd	5.0
5-8	At Oak.	L	5-8		11	14	Halama	Garland	Foulke	16-18	3rd	5.5
5-9	At Sea.	L	3-6		9	11	Franklin	Wright	Nelson	16-19	3rd	5.0
5-10	At Sea.	W	4-3		10	7	Colon	Meche	Marte	17-19	3rd	5.0
5-11	At Sea.	L	2-7		3	12	Moyer	Buehrle		17-20	3rd	6.0
5-13	Bal.	W	1-0		8	6	Loaiza	Daal	Koch	18-20	3rd	5.5
5-14	Bal.	W	5-1		11	7	Gordon	Helling		19-20	3rd	4.5
5-15	Bal.	W	8-2		9	5	Colon	Ponson		20-20	3rd	4.5
5-16	At Min.	L	3-18		9	20	Radke	Buehrle		20-21	3rd	4.5
5-17	At Min.	L	1-3		7	7	Mays	Garland	Guardado	20-22	3rd	4.5
5-18	At Min.	L	2-3		8	10	Hawkins	Gordon	Guardado	20-23	3rd	5.0
5-19	Tor.	L	2-12		7	15	Lidle	Wright		20-24	3rd	5.5
5-20	Tor.	W	4-1		8	9	Colon	Davis		21-24	3rd	4.5
5-21	Tor.	W	6-5		9	10	Marte	Politte	Koch	22-24	3rd	4.5
5-23	Det.	L	2-3		4	5	Maroth	Gordon	Spurling	22-25	3rd	5.0
5-24	Det.	L	0-1		3	5	Knotts	Loaiza	German	22-26	3rd	6.0
5-25	Det.	W	8-5	(12)	11	10	Glover	Sparks		23-26	3rd	6.0
5-26	At Tor.	L	5-11		9	11	Towers	Buehrle	Tam	23-27	3rd	6.5
5-27	At Tor.	L	1-5		7	9	Halladay	Colon		23-28	3rd	7.5
5-28	At Tor.	W	8-0		11	5	Garland	Escobar		24-28	3rd	7.5
5-29	At Tor.	W	3-2		7	5	Loaiza	Lidle	Koch	25-28	3rd	6.5
5-30	At Cle.	L	3-7		7	7	Sabathia	Wright		25-29	3rd	6.5
6-1	At Cle.	L	4-5	(10)	8	13	Boyd	Koch		25-30	3rd	6.0
6-2	At Cle.	L	2-5		6	7	Anderson	Colon	Baez	25-31	3rd	6.5
6-3	At Ari.	L	1-2		5	9	Villarreal	Gordon		25-32	3rd	7.5
6-4	At Ari.	L	6-8		10	15	Good	Garland	Valverde	25-33	3rd	7.5
6-5	At Ari.	W	3-2	(10)	11	3	Koch	Service		26-33	3rd	7.5
6-6	At L.A.	L	1-2		4	5	Ishii	Buehrle	Gagne	26-34	3rd	8.5
6-7	At L.A.	W	4-1		10	4	Colon	Ashby		27-34	3rd	8.5
6-8	At L.A.	W	10-3		11	8	Loaiza	Perez		28-34	3rd	7.5
6-10	S.F	W	5-3		9	7	Garland	Nathan		29-34	3rd	6.5
6-11	S.F	L	4-11		6	12	Foppert	Buehrle		29-35	3rd	7.5
6-12	S.F	L	4-8		9	8	Nathan	Colon		29-36	3rd	8.5
6-13	S.D.	W	5-3		9	10	Gordon	Linebrink	Koch	30-36	3rd	8.5

Date	Opp.	Res.	Score	(inn.*)	Hits	Opp. hits	Winning pitcher	Losing pitcher	Save	Record	Pos.	GB
6-14	S.D.	W	6-5		6	8	Gordon	Witasick	Koch	31-36	3rd	7.5
6-15	S.D.	L	0-1		7	3	Perez	Garland	Beck	31-37	3rd	7.5
6-16	Bos.	W	4-2		8	5	Buehrle	Rupe	Gordon	32-37	3rd	6.5
6-17	Bos.	L	4-7		7	9	Burkett	Colon	Lyon	32-38	3rd	6.5
6-18	Bos.	W	3-1		5	7	Loaiza	Wakefield	Koch	33-38	3rd	5.5
6-19	Bos.	L	3-4	(10)	9	3	Lyon	Koch		33-39	3rd	6.5
6-20	At Chi.	W	12-3		11	10	Garland	Estes		34-39	3rd	5.5
6-21	At Chi.	W	7-6		11	15	Buehrle	Clement	Koch	35-39	3rd	4.5
6-22	At Chi.	L	1-2		6	6	Zambrano	Marte	Borowski	35-40	3rd	5.5
6-24	At Min.	W	2-1		8	6	Loaiza	Reed	Koch	36-40	3rd	4.5
6-25	At Min.	L	5-6	(11)	13	12	Guardado	Koch		36-41	3rd	5.5
6-26	At Min.	W	5-1		8	5	Buehrle	Radke		37-41	3rd	5.5
6-27	Chi.	W	4-3		7	9	Koch	Alfonseca		38-41	3rd	5.5
6-28	Chi.	W	7-6		10	8	Koch	Cruz		39-41	3rd	4.5
6-29	Chi.	L	2-5		5	10	Wood	Loaiza		39-42	3rd	4.5
6-30	Min.	W	10-3		10	8	Garland	Mays		40-42	3rd	3.5
7-1	Min.	W	6-1		9	9	Buehrle	Radke		41-42	3rd	3.0
7-2	Min.	W	8-6	(12)	10	16	Koch	Guardado		42-42	3rd	3.0
7-4	At T.B.	L	3-4		5	10	Colome	Koch		42-43	3rd	4.5
7-5	At T.B.	L	2-3		11	8	Sosa	Loaiza	Carter	42-44	3rd	4.5
7-6	At T.B.	W	11-3		15	8	Buehrle	Standridge		43-44	3rd	4.5
7-8	At Det.	L	1-2		9	7	Spurling	Garland	Mears	43-45	3rd	5.5
7-9	At Det.	L	2-4		3	12	Bonderman	Colon	Mears	43-46	3rd	5.5
7-10	At Det.	L	0-1		8	6	Cornejo	Loaiza	Mears	43-47	3rd	5.5
7-11	At Cle.	L	5-12		10	11	Anderson	Wright		43-48	3rd	6.5
7-12§	At Cle.	W	7-4	(10)	9	8	Marte	Mulholland	Gordon	44-48		
7-12∞	At Cle.	L	2-4		6	9	Westbrook	Porzio	Baez	44-49	3rd	7.0
7-13	At Cle.	W	7-4		11	10	Marte	Betancourt	Gordon	45-49	2nd	7.0
7-17	Det.	L	9-10		13	16	Maroth	Colon		45-50	3rd	8.0
7-18	Det.	W	7-5		13	11	Buehrle	Roney	Gordon	46-50	3rd	7.0
7-19	Det.	W	6-2		8	6	Garland	Cornejo	Marte	47-50	3rd	7.0
7-20	Det.	W	10-1		16	5	Loaiza	Ledezma		48-50	3rd	7.0
7-21	Cle.	W	4-3		6	8	Porzio	Tallet	Gordon	49-50	3rd	6.0
7-22	Cle.	W	5-2		9	6	Colon	Davis	Marte	50-50	2nd	5.0
7-23	At Tor.	W	7-6		11	10	White	Acevedo	Marte	51-50	2nd	5.0
7-24	At Tor.	W	4-3	(13)	12	6	Gordon	Sturtze	White	52-50	2nd	4.0
7-25	T.B.	W	7-2		9	8	Loaiza	Sosa		53-50	2nd	4.0
7-26	T.B.	L	6-10		9	15	Malaska	White	Colome	53-51	2nd	4.0
7-27	T.B.	W	9-1		12	4	Colon	Kennedy		54-51	2nd	4.0
7-29	At K.C.	W	9-6		16	12	Buehrle	May	Gordon	55-51	2nd	3.0
7-30	At K.C.	W	15-4		19	10	Garland	Hernandez		56-51	2nd	2.0
7-31	At K.C.	W	8-6	(11)	12	15	Schoeneweis	Field		57-51	2nd	1.0
8-1	At Sea.	W	12-1		14	8	Colon	Garcia		58-51	2nd	...
8-2	At Sea.	L	0-10		3	10	Franklin	Wright		58-52	2nd	1.0
8-3	At Sea.	L	2-8		5	10	Meche	Buehrle		58-53	2nd	2.0
8-4	K.C.	L	9-13		11	13	Hernandez	Schoeneweis	Levine	58-54	2nd	3.0
8-5	K.C.	W	5-4		10	10	Loaiza	Snyder	Marte	59-54	2nd	2.0
8-6	K.C.	W	4-3		9	7	Colon	Wilson	Marte	60-54	2nd	1.0
8-8	Oak.	W	3-2		10	5	Buehrle	Mulder		61-54	1st	+0.5
8-9	Oak.	L	2-7		9	13	Bradford	Garland		61-55	2nd	0.5
8-10	Oak.	W	5-1		10	4	Loaiza	Harden		62-55	2nd	0.5
8-11	At Ana.	L	8-10		15	14	Weber	Colon		62-56	2nd	1.5
8-12	At Ana.	W	10-4		17	6	Wright	Ortiz		63-56	2nd	0.5
8-13	At Ana.	L	1-2		6	10	Rodriguez	Buehrle	Percival	63-57	2nd	1.5
8-14	At Ana.	L	1-5		5	9	Shields	Garland	Percival	63-58	2nd	2.0
8-15	At Tex.	L	5-11		9	12	Lewis	Loaiza		63-59	2nd	2.0
8-16	At Tex.	L	8-12		13	12	Benoit	Colon		63-60	T2nd	2.0
8-17	At Tex.	L	4-6		6	8	Powell	Marte	Cordero	63-61	T2nd	3.0
8-18	Ana.	W	4-2		4	6	Gordon	Washburn		64-61	2nd	2.0
8-19	Ana.	W	5-2		11	5	Garland	Shields	Gordon	65-61	2nd	1.0
8-20	Ana.	W	5-3		11	10	Loaiza	Lackey	Marte	66-61	2nd	...
8-21	Tex.	W	7-3		10	6	Colon	Lewis	Gordon	67-61	1st	+0.5
8-22	Tex.	W	7-1		5	6	Cotts	Dominguez		68-61	1st	+1.0
8-23	Tex.	W	13-2		17	8	Buehrle	Valdes	Wright	69-61	1st	+1.0
8-24	Tex.	L	0-5		4	6	Thomson	Garland		69-62	1st	+1.0
8-26	At N.Y.	W	13-2		11	5	Loaiza	Clemens		70-62	1st	+1.0
8-27	At N.Y.	W	11-2		15	9	Colon	Wells		71-62	1st	+1.0
8-28	At N.Y.	L	5-7		12	7	Mussina	Cotts	Rivera	71-63	2nd	...
8-29	At Det.	L	4-8		13	12	Robertson	Buehrle		71-64	2nd	...
8-30	At Det.	W	5-2		9	6	Garland	Maroth		72-64	1st	+0.5
8-31	At Det.	W	6-1		8	4	Loaiza	Cornejo		73-64	1st	+1.5

Date	Opp.	Res.	Score	(inn.*)	Hits	Opp. hits	Winning pitcher	Losing pitcher	Save	Record	Pos.	GB
9-2	Bos.	L	1-2		4	2	Burkett	Colon	Kim	73-65	1st	+1.0
9-3	Bos.	L	4-5	(10)	13	11	Kim	Gordon		73-66	T1st	...
9-5	Cle.	W	5-3		11	7	Garland	Traber	Gordon	74-66	T1st	...
9-6	Cle.	W	8-5		12	8	Loaiza	Cressend	Gordon	75-66	T1st	...
9-7	Cle.	W	7-3		8	7	Schoeneweis	Baez		76-66	T1st	...
9-8	Min.	W	5-2		9	10	Colon	Lohse		77-66	1st	+1.0
9-9	Min.	W	8-6		12	12	Buehrle	Pulido	Gordon	78-66	1st	+2.0
9-10	Min.	L	1-4		6	8	Santana	Garland	Guardado	78-67	1st	+1.0
9-11	Min.	L	2-5		9	9	Radke	Loaiza		78-68	T1st	...
9-12	At Bos.	L	4-7		7	5	Suppan	Wright	Kim	78-69	T1st	...
9-13	At Bos.	W	3-1		7	5	Colon	Wakefield		79-69	T1st	...
9-14	At Bos.	W	7-2		10	9	Buehrle	Burkett	Marte	80-69	T1st	...
9-16	At Min.	L	2-5		9	7	Radke	Loaiza		80-70	2nd	1.5
9-17	At Min.	L	2-4		6	6	Rogers	Garland	Guardado	80-71	2nd	2.5
9-18	At Min.	L	3-5		9	7	Lohse	Colon	Guardado	80-72	2nd	3.5
9-19	K.C.	W	8-5		12	7	Buehrle	Carrasco	Gordon	81-72	2nd	3.5
9-20	K.C.	L	1-7		5	14	Anderson	Loaiza		81-73	2nd	4.5
9-21	K.C.	L	4-10		6	10	May	Garland		81-74	T2nd	5.5
9-22	N.Y.	W	6-3	(10)	12	9	Gordon	White		82-74	T2nd	5.0
9-23	N.Y.	L	0-7		5	12	Contreras	Buehrle		82-75	T2nd	6.0
9-24	N.Y.	W	9-4		12	8	Loaiza	Mussina		83-75	2nd	6.0
9-25	At K.C.	L	3-7		8	8	Anderson	Wright		83-76	T2nd	6.0
9-26	At K.C.	W	11-2		11	4	Garland	May		84-76	2nd	6.0
9-27	At K.C.	W	19-3		21	5	Colon	Wright		85-76	2nd	5.0
9-28	At K.C.	W	5-1		8	3	Loaiza	Lima		86-76	2nd	4.0

Monthly records: March (0-1), April (14-12), May (11-16), June (15-13), July (17-9), August (16-13), September (13-12).
*Innings, if other than nine. § Day separate admission. ∞ Night separate admission.

RECORDS

2003 regular-season record: 86-76
Position: 2nd in A.L. Central
Home: 51-30 **Road:** 35-46
A.L. East: 21-15 **A.L. Central:** 42-34
A.L. West: 13-19 N.L. 10-8
Vs. LH starters: 26-25
Vs. RH starters: 60-51
Grass: 79-65 **Artificial:** 7-11
Day: 29-21 **Night:** 57-55
1-Run: 18-22 **X-inn.:** 8-4
Doubleheaders: 0-0-0
Team record past five years: 420-389 (.519, ranks 5th in league in that span)

TEAM LEADERS

Batting average: Magglio Ordonez (.317).
At-bats: Carlos Lee (623).
Runs: Carlos Lee (100).
Hits: Magglio Ordonez (192).
Total Bases: Magglio Ordonez (331).
Doubles: Magglio Ordonez (46).
Triples: D'Angelo Jimenez (5).
Home runs: Frank Thomas (42).
Runs batted in: Carlos Lee (113).
Stolen bases: Carlos Lee (18).
Slugging percentage: Frank Thomas (.562).
On-base percentage: Frank Thomas (.390).
Wins: Esteban Loaiza (21).
Earned-run average: Esteban Loaiza (2.90).
Complete games: Bartolo Colon (9).
Shutouts: None.
Saves: Tom Gordon (12).
Innings pitched: Bartolo Colon (242.0).
Strikeouts: Esteban Loaiza (207).

GAMES BY POSITION

Catcher: Miguel Olivo 113, Sandy Alomar Jr. 75, Josh Paul 11, Jamie Burke 4.
First base: Paul Konerko 119, Brian Daubach 45, Frank Thomas 27, Tony Graffanino 2, Jamie Burke 1.
Second base: D'Angelo Jimenez 68, Roberto Alomar 67, Tony Graffanino 29, Willie Harris 12, Aaron Miles 3.
Third base: Joe Crede 151, Tony Graffanino 20, D'Angelo Jimenez 2.
Shortstop: Jose Valentin 143, Tony Graffanino 36.
Outfield: Magglio Ordonez 157, Carlos Lee 156, Aaron Rowand 87, Carl Everett 68, Willie Harris 61, Armando Rios 32, Joe Borchard 16, Brian Daubach 12.
Designated hitter: Frank Thomas 124, Brian Daubach 15, Paul Konerko 14, Armando Rios 4, Carl Everett 3, Tony Graffanino 3, Aaron Miles 2, Magglio Ordonez 2, Jamie Burke 1, Carlos Lee 1, Josh Paul 1, Aaron Rowand 1.

TOP DRAFT CHOICES

1. **Brian Anderson,** OF, Arizona.
2. **Ryan Sweeney,** OF, Xavier H.S., Cedar Rapids, Iowa.
3. **Clint King,** OF, Southern Mississippi.
4. **Robert Valido,** SS, Coral Park H.S., Miami.
5. **Matt Nachreiner,** RHP, Rock Round (Texas) H.S.
6. **Chris Kelly,** OF, Pepperdine.
7. **James Casey,** RHP, Azle (Texas) H.S.
8. **John Russ,** RHP, Frank Phillips JC (Texas).
9. **David Cook,** OF, Miami (Ohio).
10. **Fraser Dizard,** LHP, Southern California.

CLEVELAND INDIANS

AMERICAN LEAGUE CENTRAL DIVISION

2004 SEASON

April

SUN	MON	TUE	WED	THU	FRI	SAT
4	5 MIN	6 MIN	7 MIN	8 KC	9 KC	10 KC
11 KC	12 MIN	13	14 MIN	15 MIN	16 DET	17 DET
18 DET	19 DET	20 KC	21 KC	22 KC	23 DET	24 DET
25 DET	26	27 CHW	28 CHW	29	30 BAL	

May

SUN	MON	TUE	WED	THU	FRI	SAT
						1 BAL
2 BAL	3 BOS	4 BOS	5 BOS	6 BOS	7 BAL	8 BAL
9 BAL	10 BOS	11 BOS	12 BOS	13	14 TB	15 TB
16 TB	17 CHW	18 CHW	19 CHW	20	21 TB	22 TB
23 TB	24	25 SEA	26 SEA	27 SEA	28 OAK	29 OAK
30 OAK	31					

June

SUN	MON	TUE	WED	THU	FRI	SAT
		1 TEX	2 TEX	3 ANA	4 ANA	5 ANA
6 ANA	7	8 FLA	9 FLA	10 FLA	11 CIN	12 CIN
13 CIN	14	15 NYM	16 NYM	17 NYM	18 ATL	19 ATL
20 ATL	21 CHW	22 CHW	23 CHW	24 CHW	25 COL	26 COL
27 COL	28	29 DET	30 DET			

Home games shaded. All-Star Game July 13 at Houston. Schedule subject to change.

July

SUN	MON	TUE	WED	THU	FRI	SAT
				1 DET	2 CIN	3 CIN
4 CIN	5 TEX	6 TEX	7 TEX	8 TEX	9 OAK	10 OAK
11 OAK	12	13 All-Star	14	15 SEA	16 SEA	17 SEA
18 SEA	19 ANA	20 ANA	21 CHW	22 CHW	23 KC	24 KC
25 KC	26 DET	27 DET	28 DET	29	30 KC	31 KC

August

SUN	MON	TUE	WED	THU	FRI	SAT
1 KC	2 TOR	3 TOR	4 TOR	5 TOR	6 CHW	7 CHW
8 CHW	9 CHW	10 TOR	11 TOR	12 TOR	13 MIN	14 MIN
15 MIN	16 TEX	17 TEX	18 TEX	19	20 MIN	21 MIN
22 MIN	23 NYY	24 NYY	25 NYY	26 CHW	27 CHW	28 CHW
29 CHW	30	31 NYY				

Sept./Oct.

SUN	MON	TUE	WED	THU	FRI	SAT
			1 NYY	2 NYY	3 ANA	4 ANA
5 ANA	6 SEA	7	8 SEA	9	10 OAK	11 OAK
12 OAK	13	14 DET	15 DET	16 DET	17 KC	18 KC
19 KC	20 DET	21 DET	22 DET	23 MIN	24 MIN	25 MIN
26 MIN	27 KC	28 KC	29 KC	30	1 MIN	2 MIN
3 MIN	4	5	6	7	8	9

CLUB DIRECTORY

President and chief executive officer
Lawrence J. Dolan

Executive vice president, general manager
Mark Shapiro

Vice president, public relations
Bob DiBiasio

Assistant g.m., scouting operations
John Mirabelli

Assistant general manager
Neal Huntington

Assistant general manager
Chris Antonetti

Director of player development
John Farrell

Director of player personnel
Steve Lubratich

Director of media relations
Bart Swain

MINOR LEAGUE AFFILIATES

Class	Team	League	Manager
AAA	Buffalo	International	Marty Brown
AA	Akron	Eastern	Brad Komminsk
Advanced A	Kinston	Carolina	Torey Lovullo
A	Lake County	South Atlantic	Luis Rivera
Short-Season A	Mahoning Valley	New York-Pennsylvania	Mike Sarbaugh
Advanced Rookie	Burlington	Appalachian	Rouglas Odor

BROADCAST INFORMATION

Radio: WTAM-AM (1100).
Cable TV: Fox Sports Net Ohio.

SPRING TRAINING

Ballpark (city): Chain Of Lakes (Winter Haven, Fla.).
Ticket information: 863-293-3900.

More on the Indians at www.foxsports.com/named/FS/MLB/teams

SPRING TRAINING ROSTER

Manager—Eric Wedge (22).
Coaches—Buddy Bell (6), Jeff Datz (29), Luis Isaac (4), Eddie Murray (33), Joel Skinner (35), Carl Willis (57).

No.	PITCHERS	B/T	Ht./Wt.	Age*	2003 Clubs
	Bartosh, Cliff	L/L	6-2/175	24	Portland
63	Betancourt, Rafael	R/R	6-2/176	28	Akron, Buffalo, Cleveland
	Cabrera, Fernando	R/R	6-4/170	22	Akron
27	Cressend, Jack	R/R	6-1/195	28	Kinston, Akron, Buffalo, Cleveland
	Cruceta, Francisco	R/R	6-2/180	22	Akron
50	Davis, Jason	R/R	6-6/210	23	Cleveland
49	Durbin, Chad	R/R	6-2/200	26	Mahoning Valley, Akron, Buffalo, Cleveland
	Gomez, Mariano	L/L	6-6/170	21	Kinston
	Guthrie, Jeremy	S/R	6-1/200	24	Akron, Buffalo
	Jimenez, Jose	R/R	6-3/230	30	Colorado
34	Lee, Cliff	L/L	6-3/190	25	Kinston, Akron, Buffalo, Cleveland
54	Riske, David	R/R	6-2/190	27	Cleveland
52	Sabathia, C.C.	L/L	6-7/290	23	Cleveland
61	Stanford, Jason	L/L	6-2/200	27	Buffalo, Cleveland
	Stewart, Scott	R/L	6-2/225	28	Brevard County, Montreal
30	Tallet, Brian	L/L	6-7/208	26	Cleveland, Buffalo
40	Traber, Billy	L/L	6-5/205	24	Cleveland
37	Westbrook, Jake	R/R	6-3/185	26	Buffalo, Cleveland
26	Wickman, Bob	R/R	6-1/240	35	Akron, Lake County

No.	CATCHERS	B/T	Ht./Wt.	Age*	2003 Clubs
44	Bard, Josh	B/R	6-3/215	26	Buffalo, Cleveland
15	Laker, Tim	R/R	6-3/225	34	Cleveland
20	Martinez, Victor	B/R	6-2/190	25	Buffalo, Akron, Cleveland

No.	INFIELDERS	B/T	Ht./Wt.	Age*	2003 Clubs
	Belliard, Ronnie	R/R	5-8/197	28	Colo. Springs, Colorado
1	Blake, Casey	R/R	6-2/210	30	Cleveland
28	Broussard, Ben	L/L	6-2/220	27	Buffalo, Cleveland
12	Gutierrez, Ricky	R/R	6-1/190	33	Buffalo, Cleveland
32	Hafner, Travis	L/R	6-3/240	26	Buffalo, Cleveland
8	McDonald, John	R/R	5-11/175	29	Mahoning Valley, Lake County, Cleveland
	Ochoa, Ivan	R/R	5-10/140	21	Kinston
	Peralta, Jhonny	R/R	6-1/180	21	Buffalo, Cleveland
7	Phillips, Brandon	R/R	5-11/185	22	Buffalo, Cleveland
	Smith, Corey	R/R	6-1/205	21	Akron
13	Vizquel, Omar	B/R	5-9/175	36	Lake County, Cleveland

No.	OUTFIELDERS	B/T	Ht./Wt.	Age*	2003 Clubs
24	Bradley, Milton	B/R	6-0/190	25	Cleveland
10	Crisp, Coco	B/R	6-0/185	24	Buffalo, Cleveland
6	Escobar, Alex	R/R	6-1/190	25	Buffalo, Cleveland
9	Gerut, Jody	L/L	6-0/190	26	Buffalo, Cleveland
11	Lawton, Matt	L/R	5-10/195	32	Akron, Cleveland
38	Ludwick, Ryan	R/L	6-3/203	25	Oklahoma, Texas, Cleveland
	Sizemore, Grady	L/L	6-2/200	21	Akron

Invited to spring training: RHP Jason Bere, RHP Giovanni Carrara, RHP Jeff D'Amico, RHP Luther Hackman, RHP Bob Howry, RHP Dave Lee, LHP Mike Porzio, LHP Carl Sadler, RHP Mark Wohlers, LHP Tim Young, IF Chris Clapinski, IF Kevin Orie, IF/OF Adam Piatt, OF Ernie Young, IF Lou Merloni.

*Age as of April 1, 2004.

BALLPARK INFORMATION

Ballpark (capacity, surface)
Jacobs Field (43,368, grass)

Address
2401 Ontario St.
Cleveland, OH 44115

Official website
www.indians.com

Business phone
216-420-4200

Ticket information
216-420-HITS, 1-866-48-TRIBE

Field dimensions (from home plate)
To left field at foul line, 325 feet
To center field, 405 feet
To right field at foul line, 325 feet

First game played
April 4, 1994
(Indians 4, Mariners 3, 11 innings)

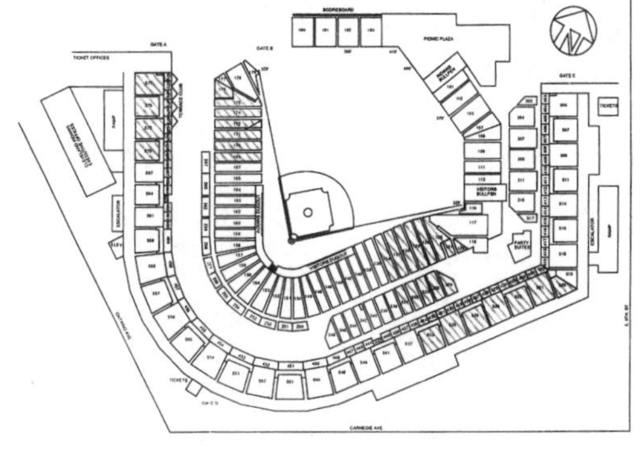

2003 REVIEW

DAY BY DAY

Date	Opp.	Res.	Score	(inn.*)	Hits	Opp. hits	Winning pitcher	Losing pitcher	Save	Record	Pos.	GB
3-31	At Bal.	L	5-6	(13)	11	15	Ryan	Westbrook		0-1	T3rd	1.0
4-2	At Bal.	W	4-2		9	5	Rodriguez	Daal	Baez	1-1	3rd	1.0
4-3	At Bal.	W	3-0		4	4	Anderson	Helling	Baez	2-1	3rd	1.0
4-4	At K.C.	L	1-5		6	8	George	Davis		2-2	3rd	2.0
4-5	At K.C.	L	1-3		2	12	Hernandez	Sabathia	MacDougal	2-3	T3rd	3.0
4-8	Chi.	L	3-5	(10)	9	9	Koch	Paronto		2-4	4th	3.5
4-9	Chi.	W	5-2		7	8	Anderson	Garland	Baez	3-4	3rd	3.5
4-10	Chi.	L	2-7		6	10	Buehrle	Davis		3-5	3rd	4.5
4-11	K.C.	L	0-1		8	4	Hernandez	Westbrook	MacDougal	3-6	4th	5.5
4-12	K.C.	L	2-5		9	9	George	Sabathia	Carrasco	3-7	4th	6.5
4-13	K.C.	W	6-1		13	9	Rodriguez	May		4-7	4th	5.5
4-14	K.C.	L	4-12		8	15	Affeldt	Anderson		4-8	4th	6.5
4-15	Bal.	W	8-3		14	11	Davis	Daal		5-8	4th	6.5
4-16	Bal.	L	3-4		8	6	Groom	Baez	Julio	5-9	4th	6.5
4-17	Bal.	L	4-6	(12)	9	10	Roberts	Paronto	Julio	5-10	4th	6.5
4-18	At Chi.	L	3-5		9	8	Colon	Traber		5-11	4th	7.5
4-19	At Chi.	L	3-12		6	16	Stewart	Anderson		5-12	4th	8.5
4-20	At Chi.	W	7-4		15	10	Davis	Buehrle		6-12	4th	8.5
4-21	At Chi.	W	9-2		13	8	Westbrook	Garland		7-12	4th	8.0
4-22	At Sea.	L	5-8		12	11	Carrara	Baez		7-13	4th	9.0
4-23	At Sea.	L	0-4		6	5	Meche	Rodriguez		7-14	4th	9.5
4-24	At Sea.	L	2-4		10	7	Moyer	Traber	Nelson	7-15	4th	10.5
4-25	At Oak.	L	2-5		6	11	Lilly	Davis	Foulke	7-16	4th	10.5
4-26	At Oak.	L	3-6		3	14	Bradford	Mulholland	Foulke	7-17	4th	11.5
4-27	At Oak.	L	3-4		8	8	Rincon	Baez		7-18	4th	11.5
4-29	Ana.	L	1-10		7	13	Ortiz	Rodriguez		7-19	4th	11.5
4-30	Ana.	L	2-6		5	13	Washburn	Anderson		7-20	4th	11.5
5-2	Tex.	W	6-5		6	6	Elder	Cordero	Baez	8-20	4th	11.0
5-3	Tex.	L	5-6		8	11	Powell	Santiago	Urbina	8-21	4th	11.0
5-4	Tex.	W	3-1		5	4	Sabathia	Thomson	Baez	9-21	4th	11.0
5-6	At Ana.	L	1-6		6	5	Washburn	Rodriguez		9-22	4th	11.5
5-7	At Ana.	L	5-6		15	13	Shields	Elder	Percival	9-23	4th	11.5
5-8	At Ana.	L	1-7		3	10	Appier	Davis		9-24	4th	12.0
5-9	At Tex.	W	9-5		16	11	Westbrook	Thomson		10-24	4th	10.5
5-10	At Tex.	W	6-4		10	8	Sabathia	Benes	Baez	11-24	4th	10.5
5-11	At Tex.	L	10-17		11	20	Benoit	Rodriguez		11-25	4th	11.5
5-13	Sea.	L	3-8		9	17	Pineiro	Anderson		11-26	4th	12.0
5-14	Sea.	W	7-2		9	4	Davis	Garcia		12-26	4th	11.0
5-15	Sea.	L	1-9		7	9	Carrara	Westbrook		12-27	4th	12.0
5-16	Oak.	W	3-2		7	4	Traber	Mulder	Baez	13-27	4th	11.0
5-17	Oak.	W	4-2		5	4	Mulholland	Rincon	Baez	14-27	4th	10.0
5-18	Oak.	L	5-8		6	13	Foulke	Baez		14-28	4th	10.5
5-19	Det.	W	10-9		14	10	Traber	Walker	Riske	15-28	4th	10.0
5-20	Det.	W	6-4		10	12	Riske	Roney		16-28	4th	9.0
5-21	Det.	W	4-0		7	7	Sabathia	Bonderman		17-28	4th	9.0
5-22	Det.	L	2-3	(11)	5	7	German	Phillips	Sparks	17-29	4th	10.0
5-23	At Bos.	L	2-9		4	13	Lowe	Rodriguez		17-30	4th	10.0
5-24	At Bos.	L	3-12		8	15	Burkett	Anderson		17-31	4th	11.0
5-25	At Bos.	W	6-4		10	7	Davis	Fossum	Baez	18-31	4th	11.0
5-26	At Det.	L	5-6		6	10	Avery	Boyd	German	18-32	4th	11.5
5-27	At Det.	W	5-2		8	4	Miceli	Walker	Baez	19-32	4th	11.5
5-28	At Det.	W	8-2		10	8	Rodriguez	Maroth		20-32	4th	11.5
5-30	Chi.	W	7-3		7	7	Sabathia	Wright		21-32	4th	10.0
6-1	Chi.	W	5-4	(10)	13	8	Boyd	Koch		22-32	4th	8.5
6-2	Chi.	W	5-2		7	6	Anderson	Colon	Baez	23-32	4th	8.0
6-3	At Col.	L	3-7		10	9	Elarton	Rodriguez		23-33	4th	9.0
6-4	At Col.	L	1-2		7	8	Oliver	Traber	Jimenez	23-34	4th	9.0
6-5	At Col.	L	4-7		4	10	Jennings	Sabathia	Jimenez	23-35	4th	10.0
6-6	At Ari.	W	6-3		12	7	Davis	Gonzalez	Baez	24-35	4th	10.0
6-7	At Ari.	L	3-5		7	11	Randolph	Anderson	Valverde	24-36	4th	11.0
6-8	At Ari.	L	3-13		6	18	Webb	Rodriguez		24-37	4th	11.0
6-10	S.D.	W	8-5		8	11	Westbrook	Tollberg	Baez	25-37	4th	10.0
6-11	S.D.	W	3-2		6	10	Sabathia	Eaton	Baez	26-37	4th	10.0
6-12	S.D.	L	4-9		8	10	Peavy	Davis		26-38	4th	11.0
6-13	L.A.	L	3-4	(10)	9	11	Quantrill	Westbrook	Gagne	26-39	4th	12.0
6-14	L.A.	L	2-5		6	10	Ashby	Tallet	Alvarez	26-40	4th	12.0

Date	Opp.	Res.	Score	(inn.*)	Hits	Opp. hits	Winning pitcher	Losing pitcher	Save	Record	Pos.	GB
6-15	L.A.	L	3-4		7	7	Nomo	Traber	Gagne	26-41	4th	12.0
6-17	At Det.	W	7-4		10	8	Sabathia	Bernero	Baez	27-41	4th	10.5
6-18	At Det.	W	4-1		10	7	Davis	Bonderman		28-41	4th	9.5
6-19	At Det.	W	10-3		14	8	Anderson	Cornejo		29-41	4th	9.5
6-20	At Pit.	L	4-5	(15)	18	10	Torres	Baez		29-42	4th	9.5
6-21	At Pit.	L	6-7	(15)	12	16	Sauerbeck	Miceli		29-43	4th	9.5
6-22	At Pit.	W	8-5		14	10	Sabathia	Vogelsong	Baez	30-43	4th	9.5
6-24	K.C.	L	1-3		8	11	George	Davis	MacDougal	30-44	4th	9.5
6-25	K.C.	L	1-3	(10)	6	11	Gilfillan	Riske	MacDougal	30-45	4th	10.5
6-26	K.C.	L	1-4		6	9	Lima	Rodriguez	MacDougal	30-46	4th	11.5
6-27	Cin.	W	3-0		7	6	Traber	Graves	Baez	31-46	4th	11.5
6-28	Cin.	L	4-5		7	8	Reitsma	Baez	Williamson	31-47	4th	11.5
6-29	Cin.	W	3-1		4	5	Davis	Haynes	Baez	32-47	4th	10.5
6-30†	At K.C.	W	10-5		17	6	Lee	Voyles		33-47		
6-30‡	At K.C.	W	8-5		14	10	Anderson	Walrond	Baez	34-47	4th	9.0
7-1	At K.C.	L	3-6		7	8	Lima	Rodriguez	MacDougal	34-48	4th	9.5
7-2	At K.C.	L	2-8		6	12	May	Traber		34-49	4th	10.5
7-3	At Min.	W	4-1		8	4	Sabathia	Rogers		35-49	4th	10.5
7-4	At Min.	L	2-9		8	10	Reed	Davis		35-50	4th	11.5
7-5	At Min.	W	13-2		16	6	Anderson	Mays		36-50	4th	10.5
7-6	At Min.	W	5-3	(10)	10	8	Riske	Guardado	Baez	37-50	4th	10.5
7-8	N.Y.	W	4-0		10	1	Traber	Weaver		38-50	4th	10.5
7-9	N.Y.	L	2-6		10	7	Wells	Sabathia		38-51	4th	10.5
7-10	N.Y.	W	3-2	(10)	10	7	Boyd	Hitchcock		39-51	4th	9.5
7-11	Chi.	W	12-5		11	10	Anderson	Wright		40-51	4th	9.5
7-12§	Chi.	L	4-7	(10)	8	9	Marte	Mulholland	Gordon	40-52		
7-12∞	Chi.	W	4-2		9	6	Westbrook	Porzio	Baez	41-52	4th	10.0
7-13	Chi.	L	4-7		10	11	Marte	Betancourt	Gordon	41-53	4th	11.0
7-17	At N.Y.	L	4-5		8	7	Rivera	Riske		41-54	4th	12.0
7-18	At N.Y.	L	4-10		9	11	Clemens	Anderson		41-55	4th	12.0
7-19	At N.Y.	L	4-7		9	8	Wells	Sabathia	Rivera	41-56	4th	13.0
7-20	At N.Y.	L	4-7		7	10	Mussina	Westbrook	Rivera	41-57	4th	14.0
7-21	At Chi.	L	3-4		8	6	Porzio	Tallet	Gordon	41-58	4th	14.0
7-22	At Chi.	L	2-5		6	9	Colon	Davis	Marte	41-59	4th	14.0
7-23	Det.	W	4-1		7	5	Anderson	Roney	Baez	42-59	4th	14.0
7-24	Det.	L	4-7		12	13	Cornejo	Sabathia	Mears	42-60	4th	14.0
7-25	Min.	L	5-6		10	11	Hawkins	Baez	Guardado	42-61	4th	15.0
7-26	Min.	W	9-2		17	6	Traber	Lohse		43-61	4th	14.0
7-27	Min.	W	3-2	(14)	12	12	Betancourt	Rincon		44-61	4th	14.0
7-29	At Oak.	L	2-6		8	9	Mulder	Anderson	Foulke	44-62	4th	14.0
7-30	At Oak.	W	4-2		8	11	Sabathia	Lilly	Baez	45-62	4th	13.0
7-31	At Oak.	L	1-3		6	5	Harden	Westbrook	Foulke	45-63	4th	13.0
8-1	At Tex.	L	3-10		5	11	Thomson	Traber		45-64	4th	13.0
8-2	At Tex.	L	7-9		10	10	Ramirez	Stanford	Cordero	45-65	4th	14.0
8-3	At Tex.	L	5-8		10	14	Dickey	Anderson	Cordero	45-66	4th	15.0
8-5	Sea.	L	1-2		3	10	Moyer	Sabathia	Hasegawa	45-67	4th	15.5
8-6	Sea.	W	10-6		15	8	Westbrook	Pineiro		46-67	4th	14.5
8-7	Sea.	W	3-0		8	7	Traber	Garcia	Baez	47-67	4th	13.5
8-8	Ana.	L	2-5		4	9	Washburn	Davis		47-68	4th	14.0
8-9§	Ana.	W	3-2	(13)	8	9	Cressend	Weber		48-68		
8-9∞	Ana.	W	3-2		6	7	Boyd	Shields	Baez	49-68	4th	13.0
8-10	Ana.	W	3-1		4	8	Sabathia	Lackey	Betancourt	50-68	4th	13.0
8-11	At Min.	L	3-5		8	10	Lohse	Westbrook	Hawkins	50-69	4th	14.0
8-12	At Min.	W	9-6		15	9	Betancourt	Baldwin		51-69	4th	13.0
8-13	At Min.	W	5-0	(14)	10	8	Mulholland	Rincon		52-69	4th	13.0
8-14	At Min.	W	8-3		14	9	Anderson	Radke		53-69	4th	12.5
8-15	T.B.	W	1-0		5	4	Sabathia	Harper		54-69	4th	11.5
8-16	T.B.	L	3-5		9	12	Malaska	Lee	Carter	54-70	4th	11.5
8-17	T.B.	W	5-4	(12)	11	9	Mulholland	Colome		55-70	4th	11.5
8-18	T.B.	L	4-7	(13)	11	15	Carter	Mulholland		55-71	4th	11.5
8-19	Min.	L	2-8		8	14	Santana	Davis		55-72	4th	11.5
8-20	Min.	L	3-4		9	6	Radke	Anderson	Guardado	55-73	4th	11.5
8-22	At T.B.	W	8-3		7	7	Lee	Kennedy		56-73	4th	12.0
8-23	At T.B.	W	7-5		10	9	Sabathia	Backe	Riske	57-73	4th	12.0
8-24	At T.B.	W	7-5		12	14	Westbrook	Gonzalez	Riske	58-73	4th	11.0
8-26	Det.	L	4-5		10	12	Cornejo	Traber	Walker	58-74	4th	12.0
8-27	Det.	W	9-7		12	10	Cressend	Spurling	Riske	59-74	4th	12.0
8-28	Det.	W	8-3		11	6	Lee	Bonderman		60-74	4th	11.0
8-29	Tor.	L	3-7		4	14	Escobar	Sabathia		60-75	4th	11.0
8-30	Tor.	L	3-9		6	15	Lidle	Westbrook	Towers	60-76	4th	12.0
8-31	Tor.	W	5-4		9	6	Baez	Kershner		61-76	4th	12.0

Date	Opp.	Res.	Score	(inn.*)	Hits	Opp. hits	Winning pitcher	Losing pitcher	Save	Record	Pos.	GB
9-1	At Det.	W	7-4		14	6	Santiago	Walker	Riske	62-76	4th	11.5
9-2	At Det.	L	6-8		11	9	Schmack	Durbin	Rodney	62-77	4th	11.5
9-3	At Det.	L	5-6	(11)	13	9	Walker	Santiago		62-78	4th	11.5
9-4	At Det.	L	1-2		6	5	Knotts	Westbrook	Patterson	62-79	4th	12.0
9-5	At Chi.	L	3-5		7	11	Garland	Traber	Gordon	62-80	4th	13.0
9-6	At Chi.	L	5-8		8	12	Loaiza	Cressend	Gordon	62-81	4th	14.0
9-7	At Chi.	L	3-7		7	8	Schoeneweis	Baez		62-82	4th	15.0
9-9	At K.C.	W	7-1		10	11	Davis	Gobble		63-82	4th	15.5
9-10	At K.C.	L	7-9		13	12	Wilson	Santiago	Affeldt	63-83	4th	15.5
9-11	At K.C.	W	6-5		13	11	Baez	Grimsley	Riske	64-83	4th	14.5
9-12	Min.	W	4-3		8	8	Sabathia	Rogers	Riske	65-83	4th	13.5
9-13	Min.	L	0-2		7	6	Lohse	Stanford	Guardado	65-84	4th	14.5
9-14	Min.	L	3-5		9	8	Rincon	Baez	Guardado	65-85	4th	15.5
9-15	Min.	L	6-13		7	12	Santana	Davis		65-86	4th	16.5
9-16	K.C.	L	8-12		10	15	May	Traber		65-87	4th	17.5
9-17	K.C.	W	9-1		12	5	Westbrook	Abbott		66-87	4th	17.5
9-18	K.C.	L	2-3		6	8	Lima	Sabathia	Leskanic	66-88	4th	18.5
9-19	Bos.	L	0-2		3	8	Burkett	Stanford	Embree	66-89	4th	19.5
9-20	Bos.	W	13-4		14	10	Lee	Lowe		67-89	4th	19.5
9-21	Bos.	L	0-2		4	4	Martinez	Lee	Kim	67-90	4th	20.5
9-23	At Min.	L	1-4		8	6	Rogers	Westbrook	Guardado	67-91	4th	21.5
9-24	At Min.	L	2-3		7	8	Orosco	Betancourt	Guardado	67-92	4th	22.5
9-26	At Tor.	W	2-1		4	6	Stanford	Lidle	Riske	68-92	4th	22.0
9-27	At Tor.	L	4-5		8	10	Halladay	Mulholland		68-93	4th	22.0
9-28	At Tor.	L	2-6		8	6	Towers	Lee		68-94	4th	22.0

Monthly records: March (0-1), April (7-19), May (14-12), June (13-15), July (11-16), August (16-13), September (7-18).
*Innings, if other than nine. † First game of a doubleheader. ‡ Second game of a doubleheader. § Day separate admission. ∞ Night separate admission.

RECORDS

2003 regular-season record: 68-94
Position: 4th in A.L. Central
Home: 38-43 **Road:** 30-51
A.L. East: 14-18 **A.L. Central:** 35-41
A.L. West: 13-23 N.L. 6-12
Vs. LH starters: 19-31
Vs. RH starters: 49-63
Grass: 58-88 **Artificial:** 10-6
Day: 21-31 **Night:** 47-63
1-Run: 15-25 **X-inn.:** 7-11
Doubleheaders: 1-0-0
Team record past five years: 420-390 (.519, ranks 6th in league in that span)

TEAM LEADERS

Batting average: Milton Bradley (.321).
At-bats: Casey Blake (557).
Runs: Casey Blake (80).
Hits: Casey Blake (143).
Total Bases: Jody Gerut (237).
Doubles: Casey Blake (35).
Triples: Coco Crisp (6).
Home runs: Jody Gerut (22).
Runs batted in: Jody Gerut (75).
Stolen bases: Milton Bradley (17).
Slugging percentage: Milton Bradley (.501).
On-base percentage: Milton Bradley (.421).
Wins: C.C. Sabathia (13).
Earned-run average: C.C. Sabathia (3.60).
Complete games: C.C. Sabathia (2).
Shutouts: C.C. Sabathia, Billy Traber (1).
Saves: Danys Baez (25).
Innings pitched: C.C. Sabathia (197.2).
Strikeouts: C.C. Sabathia (141).

GAMES BY POSITION

Catcher: Josh Bard 87, Tim Laker 50, Victor Martinez 40.
First base: Ben Broussard 114, Travis Hafner 42, Casey Blake 31, Shane Spencer 11, Bill Selby 1.
Second base: Brandon Phillips 109, John McDonald 37, Angel Santos 28, Zach Sorensen 14, Bill Selby 1.
Third base: Casey Blake 140, John McDonald 23, Bill Selby 10, Ricky Gutierrez 7, Jhonny Peralta 6, Angel Santos 4, Greg LaRocca 2, Zach Sorensen 1.
Shortstop: Jhonny Peralta 72, Omar Vizquel 64, John McDonald 27, Ricky Gutierrez 9, Zach Sorensen 3.
Outfield: Jody Gerut 113, Milton Bradley 93, Coco Crisp 90, Matt Lawton 74, Shane Spencer 43, Ryan Ludwick 32, Alex Escobar 25, Karim Garcia 23, Chris Magruder 8, Ellis Burks 2, Bill Selby 1, Zach Sorensen 1.
Designated hitter: Ellis Burks 51, Travis Hafner 43, Matt Lawton 21, Jody Gerut 11, Milton Bradley 8, Coco Crisp 7, Shane Spencer 7, Victor Martinez 5, Ryan Ludwick 4, Tim Laker 2, Bill Selby 2, Brian Anderson 1, Josh Bard 1, Karim Garcia 1, Greg LaRocca 1, Zach Sorensen 1.

TOP DRAFT CHOICES

1a. **Michael Aubrey,** 1B, Tulane.
1b. **Brad Snyder,** OF, Ball State.
1c. **Adam Miller,** RHP, McKinney (Texas) H.S.
2. **Javi Herrera,** C, Tennessee.
3. **Ryan Garko,** C, Stanford.
4. **Ben Harrison,** OF, Florida.
5. **Juan Valdes,** OF, Fernando Callejo H.S., Manati, Puerto Rico.
6. **Kevin Kouzmanoff,** 3B, Nevada.
7. **Matt Davis,** RHP, Ohio State.
8. **Bo Ashabraner,** RHP, Long Beach State.
9. **Anthony Lunetta,** SS, Southern California.
10. **Scott Roehl,** RHP, Arkansas.

DETROIT TIGERS

AMERICAN LEAGUE CENTRAL DIVISION

2004 SEASON

April

SUN	MON	TUE	WED	THU	FRI	SAT
4	5 TOR	6 TOR	7 TOR	8 MIN	9	10 MIN
11 MIN	12	13 TOR	14 TOR	15 TOR	16 CLE	17 CLE
18 CLE	19 CLE	20 MIN	21 MIN	22 MIN	23 CLE	24 CLE
25 CLE	26	27 ANA	28 ANA	29 ANA	30 SEA	

May

SUN	MON	TUE	WED	THU	FRI	SAT
						1 SEA
2 SEA	3 ANA	4 ANA	5 ANA	6	7 TEX	8 TEX
9 TEX	10	11 OAK	12 OAK	13 OAK	14 TEX	15 TEX
16 TEX	17	18 OAK	19 OAK	20 OAK	21 SEA	22 SEA
23 SEA	24	25 KC	26 KC	27 KC	28 BAL	29 BAL
30 BAL	31 KC					

June

SUN	MON	TUE	WED	THU	FRI	SAT
		1 KC	2 KC	3 KC	4 MIN	5 MIN
6 MIN	7	8 ATL	9 ATL	10 ATL	11 FLA	12 FLA
13 FLA	14	15 PHI	16 PHI	17 PHI	18 NYM	19 NYM
20 NYM	21	22 KC	23 KC	24 KC	25 ARI	26 ARI
27 ARI	28	29 CLE	30 CLE			

Home games shaded. All-Star Game July 13 at Houston. Schedule subject to change.

July

SUN	MON	TUE	WED	THU	FRI	SAT
				1 CLE	2 COL	3 COL
4 COL	5 NYY	6 NYY	7 NYY	8 MIN	9 MIN	10 MIN
11 MIN	12	13 All-Star	14	15 NYY	16 NYY	17 NYY
18 NYY	19 MIN	20 MIN	21 KC	22 KC	23 CHW	24 CHW
25 CHW	26 CLE	27 CLE	28 CLE	29 CHW	30 CHW	31 CHW

August

SUN	MON	TUE	WED	THU	FRI	SAT
1 CHW	2	3 TEX	4 TEX	5 TEX	6 BOS	7 BOS
8 BOS	9	10 OAK	11 OAK	12 OAK	13 ANA	14 ANA
15 ANA	16	17 CHW	18 CHW	19 CHW	20 SEA	21 SEA
22 SEA	23 CHW	24 CHW	25 CHW	26 BOS	27 BOS	28 BOS
29 BOS	30 KC	31 KC				

Sept./Oct.

SUN	MON	TUE	WED	THU	FRI	SAT
			1 KC	2	3 TB	4 TB
5 TB	6 KC	7 KC	8 KC	9 KC	10 MIN	11 MIN
12 MIN	13 MIN	14 CLE	15 CLE	16 CLE	17 CHW	18 CHW
19 CHW	20 CLE	21 CLE	22 CLE	23	24 BAL	25 BAL
26 BAL	27 CHW	28 CHW	29 CHW	30	1 TB	2 TB
3 TB	4	5	6	7	8	9

CLUB DIRECTORY

Owner/director
Michael Ilitch
President, CEO, general manager
David Dombrowski
Special assistants to the president
Al Kaline, Willie Horton
Special assistant to the g.m.
Steve Boros
Senior vice president
Jim Devellano
Vice president of player personnel
Scott Reid
V.p., assistant general manager
Al Avila
Director of scouting
Greg Smith
Director of minor league operations
Ricky Bennett
Senior director of communications
Cliff Russell
Media relations coordinator
Rick Thompson
Broadcasting and media relations mgr.
Molly Light
Director, community relations
Celia Bobrowsky

MINOR LEAGUE AFFILIATES

Class	Team	League	Manager
AAA	Toledo	International	Larry Parrish
AA	Erie	Eastern	Rick Sweet
Advanced A	Lakeland	Florida State	Gary Green
A	West Michigan	Midwest	Matt Walbeck
Short-Season A	Oneonta	New York-Pennsylvania	Mike Rojas
Rookie	Gulf Coast Tigers	Gulf Coast	Kevin Bradshaw

BROADCAST INFORMATION

Radio: WXYT-AM (1270).
Cable TV: Fox Sports Net Detroit.

SPRING TRAINING

Ballpark (city): Joker Marchant Stadium (Lakeland, Fla.).
Ticket information: 863-686-8075.

More on the Tigers at www.foxsports.com/named/FS/MLB/teams

SPRING TRAINING ROSTER

Manager—Alan Trammell (3).
Coaches—Bob Cluck (54), Bruce Fields (24), Kirk Gibson (22), Mick Kelleher (18), Lance Parrish (13), Juan Samuel (10).

No.	PITCHERS	B/T	Ht./Wt.	Age*	2003 Clubs
14	Anderson, Matt	R/R	6-4/200	27	Toledo, Detroit
	Baugh, Kenny	R/R	6-4/195	25	Lakeland, Erie
38	Bonderman, J.	R/R	6-2/210	21	Detroit
	Bumatay, Mike	L/L	6-0/170	24	Visalia, Tulsa
34	Cornejo, Nate	R/R	6-5/245	24	Detroit
36	Eckenstahler, Eric	L/L	6-7/220	27	Toledo, Detroit
62	German, Franklyn	R/R	6-7/270	24	Toledo, Detroit
	Henkel, Rob	R/L	6-2/210	25	Erie
	Johnson, Jason	R/R	6-6/217	30	Baltimore
35	Knotts, Gary	R/R	6-4/230	27	Toledo, Detroit
	Larrison, Preston	R/R	6-4/235	23	Toledo, Erie
	Ledezma, Wilfredo	L/L	6-3/150	23	Detroit
	Levine, Al	L/R	6-3/175	35	Tampa Bay, Kansas City
46	Maroth, Mike	L/L	6-0/190	26	Detroit
45	Mears, Chris	R/R	6-4/190	26	Toledo, Detroit
	Novoa, Roberto	R/R	6-5/200	24	Lakeland
28	Patterson, Danny	R/R	6-0/190	33	Toledo, Detroit
59	Robertson, Nate	R/L	6-2/215	26	Toledo, Detroit
56	Rodney, Fernando	R/R	5-11/208	27	Toledo, Detroit
52	Roney, Matt	R/R	6-3/230	24	Detroit
48	Spurling, Chris	R/R	6-5/228	26	Detroit
	Urdaneta, Lino	R/R	6-1/170	24	Jacksonville
32	Walker, Jamie	L/L	6-2/190	32	Detroit

No.	CATCHERS	B/T	Ht./Wt.	Age*	2003 Clubs
	DiFelice, Mike	R/R	6-2/205	34	Kansas City
15	Inge, Brandon	R/R	5-11/195	26	Toledo, Detroit
	Shelton, Chris	R/R	6-0/225	23	Lynchburg, Altoona

No.	INFIELDERS	B/T	Ht./Wt.	Age*	2003 Clubs
	Guillen, Carlos	B/R	6-1/205	28	Tacoma, Seattle
20	Infante, Omar	R/R	6-0/176	22	Toledo, Detroit
	Kelly, Donald	L/R	6-4/190	24	Lakeland, Erie
31	Munson, Eric	L/R	6-3/230	26	Detroit
12	Pena, Carlos	L/L	6-2/215	25	Toledo, Detroit
	Raburn, Ryan	R/R	6-0/185	22	Lakeland, West Michigan
	Vina, Fernando	L/R	5-9/180	34	Memphis, St. Louis

No.	OUTFIELDERS	B/T	Ht./Wt.	Age*	2003 Clubs
4	Higginson, Bobby	L/R	5-11/195	33	Detroit
	Logan, Nook	B/R	6-2/180	24	Erie
27	Monroe, Craig	R/R	6-1/215	27	Toledo, Detroit
26	Ross, Cody	R/L	5-11/180	23	Toledo, Detroit
19	Sanchez, Alex	L/L	5-10/159	27	Milwaukee, Detroit
	White, Rondell	R/R	6-1/220	32	San Diego, Kansas City
25	Young, Dmitri	B/R	6-2/245	30	Detroit

Invited to spring training: RHP Brian Schmack, RHP Esteban Yan, LHP Andy Van Hekken, IF Brent Abernathy, IF Danny Klassen, IF Warren Morris, IF Dean Palmer, IF Jason Smith, OF Marcus Thames.

*Age as of April 1, 2004.

BALLPARK INFORMATION

Ballpark (capacity, surface)
Comerica Park (40,120, grass)

Address
2100 Woodward
Detroit, MI 48201

Official website
www.detroittigers.com

Business phone
313-471-2000

Ticket information
313-471-2255

Field dimensions (from home plate)
To left field at foul line, 345 feet
To center field, 420 feet
To right field at foul line, 330 feet

First game played
April 11, 2000 (Tigers 5, Mariners 2)

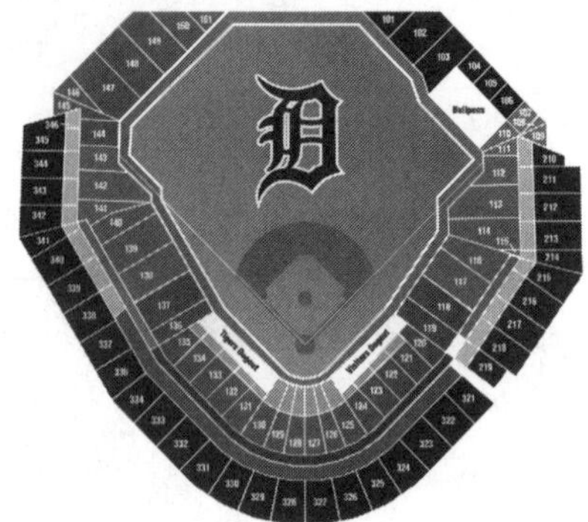

2003 REVIEW
DAY BY DAY

Date	Opp.	Res.	Score	(inn.*)	Hits	Opp. hits	Winning pitcher	Losing pitcher	Save	Record	Pos.	GB
3-31	Min.	L	1-3		4	8	Radke	Maroth	Guardado	0-1	T3rd	1.0
4-2	Min.	L	1-8		3	13	Mays	Bonderman		0-2	T4th	2.0
4-3	Min.	L	0-3		3	6	Lohse	Bernero	Guardado	0-3	T4th	3.0
4-4	At Chi.	L	2-5		3	10	Loaiza	Cornejo	Koch	0-4	5th	4.0
4-5	At Chi.	L	0-7		3	13	Buehrle	Maroth		0-5	5th	5.0
4-6	At Chi.	L	2-10		8	9	Marte	German		0-6	5th	5.5
4-9	K.C.	L	6-9		6	12	Affeldt	Bonderman	MacDougal	0-7	5th	6.5
4-10	K.C.	L	2-4		6	7	Asencio	Maroth	MacDougal	0-8	5th	7.5
4-11	Chi.	L	0-5		2	10	Loaiza	Bernero		0-9	5th	8.5
4-12	Chi.	W	4-3		8	11	Cornejo	Stewart	Anderson	1-9	5th	8.5
4-13	Chi.	L	2-3		7	9	Colon	Knotts	Koch	1-10	5th	8.5
4-15	At Min.	L	4-6		5	12	Lohse	Maroth	Guardado	1-11	5th	10.0
4-16	At Min.	L	2-4		6	10	Reed	Bernero	Guardado	1-12	5th	10.0
4-17	At Min.	L	0-6		7	13	Rogers	Bonderman		1-13	5th	10.0
4-18	At K.C.	L	3-4	(11)	11	10	Carrasco	Anderson		1-14	5th	11.0
4-19	At K.C.	L	2-9		5	12	Lopez	Knotts		1-15	5th	12.0
4-20	At K.C.	L	3-4		10	4	MacDougal	Maroth		1-16	5th	13.0
4-22	At Oak.	L	5-6	(11)	6	13	Rincon	Ledezma		1-17	5th	14.0
4-23	At Oak.	W	4-1		7	3	Bonderman	Zito	Anderson	2-17	5th	13.5
4-24	At Oak.	L	0-2		3	8	Mulder	Cornejo		2-18	5th	14.5
4-25	At Sea.	L	0-6		4	9	Pineiro	Maroth		2-19	5th	14.5
4-26	At Sea.	W	6-4		11	11	Walker	Franklin	Anderson	3-19	5th	14.5
4-27	At Sea.	L	3-4		4	5	Garcia	Bernero	Nelson	3-20	5th	14.5
4-29	Bal.	L	3-11		8	13	Johnson	Bonderman		3-21	5th	14.5
5-1†	Bal.	L	2-5		7	11	Ryan	German	Julio	3-22		
5-1‡	Bal.	L	4-6		11	8	Daal	Maroth	Julio	3-23	5th	14.5
5-2	T.B.	L	0-2		1	6	Kennedy	Knotts		3-24	5th	15.5
5-3	T.B.	L	6-8	(10)	12	10	Levine	Ledezma		3-25	5th	15.5
5-4	T.B.	W	7-3		11	6	Bonderman	Sosa	Spurling	4-25	5th	15.5
5-5	At Bal.	W	6-1		10	6	Cornejo	Johnson	Sparks	5-25	5th	15.5
5-6	At Bal.	W	7-6		12	7	German	Groom		6-25	5th	14.5
5-7	At Bal.	W	9-4		12	7	Knotts	Daal		7-25	5th	13.5
5-9	At T.B.	L	0-2		2	8	Parque	Bernero	Carter	7-26	5th	13.0
5-10	At T.B.	L	1-3		7	8	McClung	Bonderman	Carter	7-27	5th	14.0
5-11	At T.B.	W	9-2		15	8	Cornejo	Sosa		8-27	5th	14.0
5-13	Oak.	L	1-3		4	6	Lilly	Maroth	Foulke	8-28	5th	14.5
5-14	Oak.	W	2-1		8	6	Avery	Rincon		9-28	5th	13.5
5-15	Oak.	L	2-11		5	12	Zito	Bernero		9-29	5th	14.5
5-16	Sea.	L	3-6		7	10	Meche	Bonderman	Sasaki	9-30	5th	14.5
5-17	Sea.	L	3-6		11	12	Moyer	Cornejo	Sasaki	9-31	5th	14.5
5-18	Sea.	L	2-6		4	10	Pineiro	Maroth		9-32	5th	15.0
5-19	At Cle.	L	9-10		10	14	Traber	Walker	Riske	9-33	5th	15.5
5-20	At Cle.	L	4-6		12	10	Riske	Roney		9-34	5th	15.5
5-21	At Cle.	L	0-4		7	7	Sabathia	Bonderman		9-35	5th	16.5
5-22	At Cle.	W	3-2	(11)	7	5	German	Phillips	Sparks	10-35	5th	16.5
5-23	At Chi.	W	3-2		5	4	Maroth	Gordon	Spurling	11-35	5th	15.5
5-24	At Chi.	W	1-0		5	3	Knotts	Loaiza	German	12-35	5th	15.5
5-25	At Chi.	L	5-8	(12)	10	11	Glover	Sparks		12-36	5th	16.5
5-26	Cle.	W	6-5		10	6	Avery	Boyd	German	13-36	5th	16.0
5-27	Cle.	L	2-5		4	8	Miceli	Walker	Baez	13-37	5th	17.0
5-28	Cle.	L	2-8		8	10	Rodriguez	Maroth		13-38	5th	18.0
5-30	N.Y.	L	0-6		4	10	Contreras	Knotts		13-39	5th	17.5
5-31	N.Y.	W	4-2		12	3	Bernero	Weaver	German	14-39	5th	16.5
6-1	N.Y.	L	9-10	(17)	14	14	Wells	Sparks	Acevedo	14-40	5th	16.5
6-3	At S.D.	W	3-2		7	11	Walker	Lawrence	German	15-40	5th	16.5
6-4	At S.D.	W	5-3		10	9	Ledezma	Hackman	German	16-40	5th	15.5
6-5	At S.D.	L	1-5		4	9	Eaton	Bernero		16-41	5th	16.5
6-6	At S.F	L	3-5		8	8	Rueter	Bonderman	Worrell	16-42	5th	17.5
6-7	At S.F	L	5-7		11	11	Schmidt	Maroth		16-43	5th	18.5
6-8	At S.F	L	6-7		9	13	Nathan	German	Worrell	16-44	5th	18.5
6-10	L.A.	L	1-3	(12)	5	6	Shuey	Sparks	Gagne	16-45	5th	18.5
6-11	L.A.	L	1-3		6	4	Brown	Bernero	Gagne	16-46	5th	19.5
6-12	L.A.	L	2-3		6	10	Ishii	Bonderman	Gagne	16-47	5th	20.5
6-13	Col.	L	2-7		8	12	Chacon	Cornejo		16-48	5th	21.5

Date	Opp.	Res.	Score	(inn.*)	Hits	Opp. hits	Winning pitcher	Losing pitcher	Save	Record	Pos.	GB
6-14	Col.	W	9-7		15	9	Ledezma	Elarton	Spurling	17-48	5th	20.5
6-15	Col.	L	4-5		11	10	Jennings	Knotts	Jimenez	17-49	5th	20.5
6-17	Cle.	L	4-7		8	10	Sabathia	Bernero	Baez	17-50	5th	20.0
6-18	Cle.	L	1-4		7	10	Davis	Bonderman		17-51	5th	20.0
6-19	Cle.	L	3-10		8	14	Anderson	Cornejo		17-52	5th	21.0
6-20	At Col.	W	7-5		13	11	Maroth	Elarton		18-52	5th	20.0
6-21	At Col.	L	6-9		12	10	Jennings	Sparks		18-53	5th	20.0
6-22	At Col.	L	3-5		7	7	Neagle	Bernero	Jimenez	18-54	5th	21.0
6-23	At Bos.	L	1-3		6	10	Wakefield	Bonderman	Timlin	18-55	5th	21.5
6-24	At Bos.	L	1-10		7	17	Lowe	Cornejo		18-56	5th	21.5
6-25	At Bos.	L	2-11		8	14	Burkett	Maroth		18-57	5th	22.5
6-26	At Bos.	L	4-6		8	10	Martinez	Roney	Lyon	18-58	5th	23.5
6-27	Ari.	L	3-8		8	13	Randolph	Bernero		18-59	5th	24.5
6-28	Ari.	L	0-7		7	10	Webb	Bonderman		18-60	5th	24.5
6-29	Ari.	L	3-5	(10)	10	13	Oropesa	Spurling	Valverde	18-61	5th	24.5
6-30	Tor.	W	6-2		9	8	Maroth	Lidle		19-61	5th	23.5
7-1	Tor.	W	5-0		11	4	Roney	Hendrickson	Walker	20-61	5th	23.0
7-2	Tor.	L	2-8		9	11	Halladay	Bernero		20-62	5th	24.0
7-3	At K.C.	L	2-3		5	6	Affeldt	Bonderman	MacDougal	20-63	5th	25.0
7-4	At K.C.	L	8-9		11	13	Field	Cornejo	MacDougal	20-64	5th	26.0
7-5	At K.C.	W	9-5		12	9	Maroth	Voyles	Walker	21-64	5th	25.0
7-6	At K.C.	L	3-5		4	6	Lima	Roney	MacDougal	21-65	5th	26.0
7-8	Chi.	W	2-1		7	9	Spurling	Garland	Mears	22-65	5th	26.0
7-9	Chi.	W	4-2		12	3	Bonderman	Colon	Mears	23-65	5th	25.0
7-10	Chi.	W	1-0		6	8	Cornejo	Loaiza	Mears	24-65	5th	24.0
7-11	Bos.	L	3-5		4	12	Burkett	Maroth	Kim	24-66	5th	25.0
7-12	Bos.	L	2-4	(11)	9	9	Jones	Rodney	Kim	24-67	5th	26.0
7-13	Bos.	W	3-0		5	7	Ledezma	Wakefield	Mears	25-67	5th	26.0
7-17	At Chi.	W	10-9		16	13	Maroth	Colon		26-67	5th	26.0
7-18	At Chi.	L	5-7		11	13	Buehrle	Roney	Gordon	26-68	5th	26.0
7-19	At Chi.	L	2-6		6	8	Garland	Cornejo	Marte	26-69	5th	27.0
7-20	At Chi.	L	1-10		5	16	Loaiza	Ledezma		26-70	5th	28.0
7-21	At Bos.	L	5-14		12	18	Burkett	Bonderman	Fossum	26-71	5th	28.0
7-22	At Bos.	L	4-7		7	11	Lowe	Maroth		26-72	5th	28.0
7-23	At Cle.	L	1-4		5	7	Anderson	Roney	Baez	26-73	5th	29.0
7-24	At Cle.	W	7-4		13	12	Cornejo	Sabathia	Mears	27-73	5th	28.0
7-25	K.C.	L	3-8		13	15	Hernandez	Ledezma		27-74	5th	29.0
7-26	K.C.	W	5-1		10	3	Bonderman	Snyder		28-74	5th	28.0
7-27	K.C.	L	1-5		5	8	Lima	Maroth		28-75	5th	29.0
7-29	At Sea.	L	5-11		9	11	Meche	Roney		28-76	5th	29.0
7-30	At Sea.	L	3-13		8	17	Moyer	Cornejo		28-77	5th	29.0
7-31	At Sea.	L	0-4		3	6	Pineiro	Ledezma		28-78	5th	29.0
8-1	At Min.	L	4-10		11	15	Lohse	Bonderman	Baldwin	28-79	5th	29.0
8-2	At Min.	W	9-2		11	11	Maroth	Reed		29-79	5th	29.0
8-3	At Min.	L	2-7		8	13	Santana	Roney		29-80	5th	30.0
8-5	Oak.	L	2-7		10	9	Harden	Cornejo		29-81	5th	30.5
8-6	Oak.	L	3-9		7	14	Hudson	Ledezma		29-82	5th	30.5
8-7	Oak.	W	3-2		6	6	Bonderman	Zito	Patterson	30-82	5th	29.5
8-8	Min.	L	3-4		4	7	Santana	Maroth	Guardado	30-83	5th	30.0
8-9	Min.	L	4-8	(10)	11	11	Rincon	Mears		30-84	5th	30.5
8-10	Min.	L	3-4		7	9	Rogers	Cornejo	Guardado	30-85	5th	31.5
8-11	At Tex.	L	3-9		7	10	Benoit	Sparks		30-86	5th	32.5
8-12	At Tex.	W	7-4		11	5	Bonderman	Dominguez	Patterson	31-86	5th	31.5
8-13	At Tex.	L	3-7		9	10	Dickey	Maroth	Cordero	31-87	5th	32.5
8-14	At Tex.	L	3-6		11	11	Thomson	Roney	Cordero	31-88	5th	33.0
8-15	At Ana.	L	1-3		7	9	Lackey	Cornejo	Percival	31-89	5th	33.0
8-16	At Ana.	L	7-11		9	11	Glover	Ledezma		31-90	5th	33.0
8-17	At Ana.	L	6-11		13	15	Ortiz	Bonderman		31-91	5th	34.0
8-18	Tex.	L	2-4	(16)	10	13	Mahay	Sparks	Dickey	31-92	5th	34.0
8-19	Tex.	L	4-5		12	11	Thomson	Maroth	Shouse	31-93	5th	34.0
8-20	Tex.	L	0-6		6	9	Dickey	Cornejo		31-94	5th	34.0
8-21	Ana.	L	7-10		8	17	Sele	Roney		31-95	5th	35.0
8-22	Ana.	L	5-6		10	8	Ortiz	Bonderman	Percival	31-96	5th	36.0
8-23	Ana.	L	8-14	(10)	7	17	Donnelly	Spurling		31-97	5th	37.0
8-24	Ana.	W	10-9		17	12	Walker	Percival		32-97	5th	36.0
8-26	At Cle.	W	5-4		12	10	Cornejo	Traber	Walker	33-97	5th	36.0
8-27	At Cle.	L	7-9		10	12	Cressend	Spurling	Riske	33-98	5th	37.0
8-28	At Cle.	L	3-8		6	11	Lee	Bonderman		33-99	5th	37.0
8-29	Chi.	W	8-4		12	13	Robertson	Buehrle		34-99	5th	36.0
8-30	Chi.	L	2-5		6	9	Garland	Maroth		34-100	5th	37.0
8-31	Chi.	L	1-6		4	8	Loaiza	Cornejo		34-101	5th	38.0

Date	Opp.	Res.	Score	(inn.*)	Hits	Opp. hits	Winning pitcher	Losing pitcher	Save	Record	Pos.	GB
9-1	Cle.	L	4-7		6	14	Santiago	Walker	Riske	34-102	5th	38.5
9-2	Cle.	W	8-6		9	11	Schmack	Durbin	Rodney	35-102	5th	37.5
9-3	Cle.	W	6-5	(11)	9	13	Walker	Santiago		36-102	5th	36.5
9-4	Cle.	W	2-1		5	6	Knotts	Westbrook	Patterson	37-102	5th	36.0
9-5	At Tor.	L	6-8		10	12	Sturtze	Maroth	Lopez	37-103	5th	37.0
9-6	At Tor.	L	0-1	(10)	3	6	Halladay	Rodney		37-104	5th	38.0
9-7	At Tor.	L	0-8		4	14	Towers	Mears		37-105	5th	39.0
9-9	At N.Y.	L	2-4		8	8	White	Rodney	Rivera	37-106	5th	40.5
9-10	At N.Y.	L	5-15		5	12	Pettitte	Knotts		37-107	5th	40.5
9-11	At N.Y.	L	2-5		8	11	Clemens	Cornejo	Rivera	37-108	5th	40.5
9-12	K.C.	W	3-0		9	6	Maroth	Abbott	Rodney	38-108	5th	39.5
9-13	K.C.	L	0-7		7	12	Wright	Mears		38-109	5th	40.5
9-14	K.C.	L	2-7		5	11	Gobble	Robertson		38-110	5th	41.5
9-15	K.C.	L	4-10		10	13	Anderson	Knotts		38-111	5th	42.5
9-16	Tor.	L	6-9		9	14	Kershner	Cornejo		38-112	5th	43.5
9-17	Tor.	L	0-6		6	11	Halladay	Loux		38-113	5th	44.5
9-18	Tor.	L	6-10		6	12	Towers	Maroth		38-114	5th	45.5
9-19	At Min.	L	2-6		5	13	Milton	Bonderman		38-115	5th	46.5
9-20	At Min.	L	3-7		9	8	Santana	Robertson		38-116	5th	47.5
9-21	At Min.	L	4-6		11	12	Radke	Cornejo	Guardado	38-117	5th	48.5
9-22	At K.C.	L	6-12		10	16	Affeldt	Knotts		38-118	5th	49.0
9-23	At K.C.	W	15-6		18	12	Maroth	Lima		39-118	5th	49.0
9-24	At K.C.	W	4-3		5	7	Loux	Gobble	Rodney	40-118	5th	49.0
9-25	Min.	W	5-4	(11)	9	6	Mears	Thomas		41-118	5th	48.0
9-26	Min.	L	4-5	(11)	12	12	Guardado	German	Hawkins	41-119	5th	49.0
9-27	Min.	W	9-8		14	15	Rodney	Orosco		42-119	5th	48.0
9-28	Min.	W	9-4		15	12	Maroth	Johnson		43-119	5th	47.0

Monthly records: March (0-1), April (3-20), May (11-18), June (5-22), July (9-17), August (6-23), September (9-18).
*Innings, if other than nine. † First game of a doubleheader. ‡ Second game of a doubleheader.

RECORDS

2003 regular-season record: 43-119
Position: 5th in A.L. Central
Home: 23-58 **Road:** 20-61
A.L. East: 9-27 **A.L. Central:** 24-52
A.L. West: 6-26 N.L. 4-14
Vs. LH starters: 12-39
Vs. RH starters: 31-80
Grass: 41-106 **Artificial:** 2-13
Day: 12-43 **Night:** 31-76
1-Run: 19-18 **X-inn.:** 3-13
Doubleheaders: 0-1-0
Team record past five years: 312-496 (.386, ranks 14th in league in that span)

TEAM LEADERS

Batting average: Dmitri Young (.297).
At-bats: Dmitri Young (562).
Runs: Dmitri Young (78).
Hits: Dmitri Young (167).
Total Bases: Dmitri Young (302).
Doubles: Dmitri Young (34).
Triples: Dmitri Young (7).
Home runs: Dmitri Young (29).
Runs batted in: Dmitri Young (85).
Stolen bases: Alex Sanchez (44).
Slugging percentage: Dmitri Young (.537).
On-base percentage: Dmitri Young (.372).
Wins: Mike Maroth (9).
Earned-run average: Nate Cornejo (4.67).
Complete games: Nate Cornejo (2).
Shutouts: None.
Saves: Franklyn German, Chris Mears (5).
Innings pitched: Nate Cornejo (194.2).
Strikeouts: Jeremy Bonderman (108).

GAMES BY POSITION

Catcher: Brandon Inge 104, Matt Walbeck 55, A.J. Hinch 27, Ben Petrick 6.
First base: Carlos Pena 128, Kevin Witt 27, Shane Halter 12, Craig Paquette 5, Ben Petrick 2, Dean Palmer 1, Dmitri Young 1.
Second base: Warren Morris 89, Ramon Santiago 53, Shane Halter 24, Danny Klassen 4, Omar Infante 2.
Third base: Eric Munson 91, Shane Halter 50, Dmitri Young 16, Danny Klassen 13, Kevin Witt 5, Omar Infante 4, Dean Palmer 1.
Shortstop: Ramon Santiago 85, Omar Infante 63, Shane Halter 27, Danny Klassen 3.
Outfield: Bobby Higginson 118, Craig Monroe 108, Alex Sanchez 99, Dmitri Young 61, Andres Torres 50, Ben Petrick 32, Gene Kingsale 30, Kevin Witt 13, Hiram Bocachica 6, Cody Ross 6, Craig Paquette 5, Shane Halter 2.
Designated hitter: Dmitri Young 75, Kevin Witt 36, Dean Palmer 22, Craig Monroe 13, Bobby Higginson 8, Shane Halter 4, Gene Kingsale 4, Ernie Young 4, Eric Munson 3, Andres Torres 3, Carlos Pena 1, Matt Walbeck 1.

TOP DRAFT CHOICES

1. **Kyle Sleeth,** RHP, Wake Forest.
2. **Jay Sborz,** RHP, Langley H.S., Great Falls, Va.
3. **Tony Giarratano,** SS, Tulane.
4. **Josh Rainwater,** RHP, DeRidder (La.) H.S.
5. **Danny Zell,** LHP, Houston.
6. **Cody Collet,** C, Newbury Park (Calif.) H.S.
7. **Matt Vasquez,** RHP, UC Santa Barbara.
8. **Adam Trent,** RHP, Ooltewah (Tenn.) H.S.
9. **Eric Rodland,** 2B, Gonzaga.
10. **Sean Henry,** OF, Armijo H.S., Suisun City, Calif.

KANSAS CITY ROYALS

AMERICAN LEAGUE CENTRAL DIVISION

2004 SEASON

April

SUN	MON	TUE	WED	THU	FRI	SAT
4	5 CHW	6	7 CHW	8 CLE	9 CLE	10 CLE
11 CLE	12	13 CHW	14 CHW	15 CHW	16 MIN	17 MIN
18 MIN	19	20 CLE	21 CLE	22 CLE	23 MIN	24 MIN
25 MIN	26	27 TEX	28 TEX	29 TEX	30 NYY	

May

SUN	MON	TUE	WED	THU	FRI	SAT
						1 NYY
2 NYY	3 TOR	4 TOR	5 TOR	6	7 BOS	8 BOS
9 BOS	10 TOR	11 TOR	12 TOR	13	14 OAK	15 OAK
16 OAK	17	18 TEX	19 TEX	20 TEX	21 OAK	22 OAK
23 OAK	24	25 DET	26 DET	27 DET	28 MIN	29 MIN
30 MIN	31 DET					

June

SUN	MON	TUE	WED	THU	FRI	SAT
		1 DET	2 DET	3 DET	4 BOS	5 BOS
6 BOS	7	8 MON	9 MON	10 MON	11 NYM	12 NYM
13 NYM	14	15 ATL	16 ATL	17 ATL	18 PHI	19 PHI
20 PHI	21	22 DET	23 DET	24 DET	25 STL	26 STL
27 STL	28 BAL	29 BAL	30 BAL			

July

SUN	MON	TUE	WED	THU	FRI	SAT
				1 BAL	2 SD	3 SD
4 SD	5 MIN	6 MIN	7 MIN	8	9 BAL	10 BAL
11 BAL	12	13 All-Star	14	15 MIN	16 MIN	17 MIN
18 MIN	19 BAL	20 BAL	21 DET	22 DET	23 CLE	24 CLE
25 CLE	26	27 TB	28 TB	29 TB	30 CLE	31 CLE

August

SUN	MON	TUE	WED	THU	FRI	SAT
1 CLE	2	3 CHW	4 CHW	5 CHW	6 ANA	7 ANA
8 ANA	9 ANA	10 CHW	11 CHW	12 CHW	13 OAK	14 OAK
15 OAK	16	17 SEA	18 SEA	19 SEA	20 TEX	21 TEX
22 TEX	23 ANA	24 ANA	25 ANA	26 SEA	27 SEA	28 SEA
29 SEA	30 DET	31 DET				

Sept./Oct.

SUN	MON	TUE	WED	THU	FRI	SAT
			1 DET	2	3 MIN	4 MIN
5 MIN	6 DET	7 DET	8 DET	9 DET	10 TB	11 TB
12 TB	13 NYY	14 NYY	15 NYY	16	17 CLE	18 CLE
19 CLE	20 TB	21 TB	22 TB	23 CHW	24 CHW	25 CHW
26 CHW	27 CLE	28 CLE	29 CLE	30 CHW	1 CHW	2 CHW
3 CHW	4	5	6	7	8	9

Home games shaded. All-Star Game July 13 at Houston. Schedule subject to change.

CLUB DIRECTORY

Chairman/owner
David Glass
President
Dan Glass
Executive v.p. & chief operating officer
Herk Robinson
Sr. v.p. & g.m., baseball operations
Allard Baird
Vice president, baseball operations
George Brett
Vice president, broadcasting & p.r.
David Witty
Assistant g.m., player personnel
Muzzy Jackson
Senior advisor to the general manager
Art Stewart
Assistant to the general manager
Brian Murphy
Senior director, scouting
Deric Ladnier
Manager, baseball operations
Jim Wong
Director, minor league operations
Shaun McGinn
Director of media relations
Aaron Babcock
Manager, broadcast and media services
Chris Stathos
Manager, media relations
Lora Grosshans

MINOR LEAGUE AFFILIATES

Class	Team	League	Manager
AAA	Omaha	Pacific Coast	Mike Jirschele
AA	Wichita	Texas	Frank White
Advanced A	Wilmington	Carolina	Bill Gardner Jr.
A	Burlington	Midwest	Jim Gabella
Advanced Rookie	Idaho Falls	Pioneer	Brian Rupp
Rookie	Arizona Royals	Arizona	Lloyd Simmons

BROADCAST INFORMATION

Radio: WHB-AM (810).
Cable TV: Royals Television Network, LLC.

SPRING TRAINING

Ballpark (city): Surprise Stadium (Surprise, Ariz.).
Ticket information: 623-594-5600.

More on the Royals at www.foxsports.com/named/FS/MLB/teams

SPRING TRAINING ROSTER

Manager—Tony Pena (6).
Coaches—John Cumberland (47), John Mizerock (13), Jeff Pentland (22), Brian Poldberg, Bob Schaefer (44), Luis Silverio (17).

No.	PITCHERS	B/T	Ht./Wt.	Age*	2003 Clubs
48	Affeldt, Jeremy	L/L	6-4/215	24	Kansas City
19	Anderson, Brian	R/L	6-1/185	31	Cleveland, Kansas City
55	Appier, Kevin	R/R	6-2/215	36	Anaheim, Kansas City
53	Asencio, Miguel	R/R	6-2/190	23	Kansas City, G.C. Royals, Wichita
	Bass, Brian	R/R	6-0/190	22	Wilmington
35	Bukvich, Ryan	R/R	6-2/250	25	Kansas City, Omaha
59	Carrasco, D.J.	R/R	6-1/215	26	Kansas City
	Dawley, Joe	R/R	6-4/205	32	Atlanta, Richmond
	Field, Nate	R/R	6-2/200	28	Wichita, Omaha, Kansas City
32	George, Chris	L/L	6-2/200	24	Kansas City, Omaha
	Gobble, Jimmy	L/L	6-3/190	22	Wichita, Kansas City
38	Grimsley, Jason	R/R	6-3/205	36	Kansas City
40	Hernandez, Ru.	R/R	6-1/205	25	Omaha, Wichita, Kansas City
33	Leskanic, Curtis	R/R	6-0/196	35	Milwaukee, Kansas City
54	MacDougal, Mike	B/R	6-4/195	27	Kansas City
34	May, Darrell	L/L	6-2/185	31	Kansas City
	Snyder, Kyle	B/R	6-8/220	26	Omaha, G.C. Royals, Wichita, Kansas City
	Sullivan, Scott	R/R	6-3/210	33	Cincinnati, Chicago A.L.
	Vasquez, Jorge	R/R	6-1/165	25	Wilmington, Wichita
46	Voyles, Brad	R/R	6-0/195	27	Omaha, Kansas City

No.	CATCHERS	B/T	Ht./Wt.	Age*	2003 Clubs
	Santiago, Benito	R/R	6-1/200	39	San Francisco
	Stinnett, Kelly	R/R	5-11/225	34	Cincinnati, Philadelphia
	Tonis, Mike	R/R	6-3/220	25	Wichita

No.	INFIELDERS	B/T	Ht./Wt.	Age*	2003 Clubs
4	Berroa, Angel	R/R	6-0/175	26	Kansas City
	Graffanino, Tony	R/R	6-1/190	31	Chicago A.L.
28	Harvey, Ken	R/R	6-2/240	26	Kansas City
	Patterson, Jarrod	L/R	6-1/195	30	Omaha, Kansas City
16	Randa, Joe	R/R	5-11/190	34	Kansas City
12	Relaford, Desi	B/R	5-9/180	30	Kansas City
29	Sweeney, Mike	R/R	6-3/225	30	Kansas City, Omaha

No.	OUTFIELDERS	B/T	Ht./Wt.	Age*	2003 Clubs
15	Beltran, Carlos	B/R	6-1/190	26	Wichita, Kansas City
8	Brown, Dee	L/R	6-0/225	26	G.C. Royals, Omaha, Kansas City
	DeJesus, David	L/L	6-0/175	24	Wichita, Omaha, Kansas City
	Gettis, Byron	R/R	6-0/240	24	Wichita
	Gomez, Alexis	L/L	6-2/180	25	Omaha
	Gonzalez, Juan	R/R	6-3/220	34	Texas
45	Guiel, Aaron	L/R	5-10/200	31	Omaha, Kansas City
	Stairs, Matt	L/R	5-9/210	36	Nashville, Pittsburgh
	Thompson, Rich	L/R	6-3/180	24	New Haven, Syracuse, Nashville

Invited to spring training: RHP Donnie Bridges, RHP Shawn Camp, RHP Zack Greinke, RHP Erik Hiljus, LHP Dennys Reyes, RHP James Serrano, RHP Eric Thompson, LHP Mike Venafro, LHP Wes Walrond, RHP Kris Wilson, C Mitch Maier, IF Gookie Dawkins, IF Ruben Gotay, IF Wilton Guerrero, IF Mendy Lopez, IF Donald Murphy, IF Calvin Pickering, IF Rick Short, OF Brandon Berger, OF Shane Costa.

*Age as of April 1, 2004.

BALLPARK INFORMATION

Ballpark (capacity, surface)
Kauffman Stadium (40,793, grass)
Address
P.O. Box 419969
Kansas City, MO 64141-6969
Official website
www.kcroyals.com
Business phone
816-921-8000
Ticket information
816-504-4040, 800-6ROYALS
Field dimensions (from home plate)
To left field at foul line, 330 feet
To center field, 400 feet
To right field at foul line, 330 feet
First game played
April 10, 1973 (Royals 12, Rangers 1)

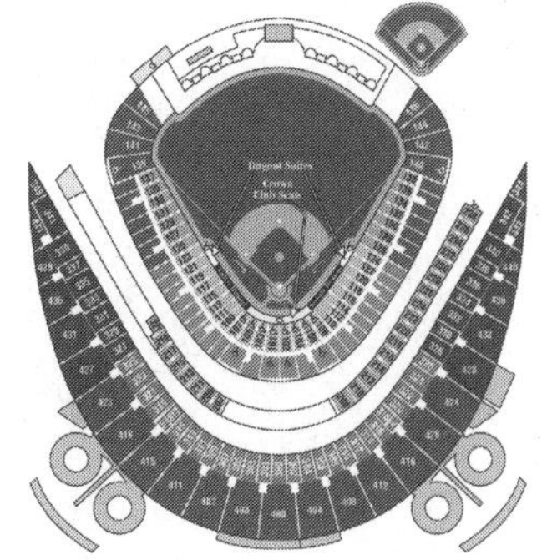

2003 REVIEW

DAY BY DAY

Date	Opp.	Res.	Score	(inn.*)	Hits	Opp. hits	Winning pitcher	Losing pitcher	Save	Record	Pos.	GB
3-31	Chi.	W	3-0		7	3	Hernandez	Buehrle	MacDougal	1-0	T1st	...
4-2	Chi.	W	5-4		6	10	Lopez	White	MacDougal	2-0	T1st	...
4-3	Chi.	W	12-6		16	8	Bukvich	Gordon		3-0	T1st	...
4-4	Cle.	W	5-1		8	6	George	Davis		4-0	1st	+1.0
4-5	Cle.	W	3-1		12	2	Hernandez	Sabathia	MacDougal	5-0	1st	+2.0
4-9	At Det.	W	9-6		12	6	Affeldt	Bonderman	MacDougal	6-0	1st	+3.0
4-10	At Det.	W	4-2		7	6	Asencio	Maroth	MacDougal	7-0	1st	+3.0
4-11	At Cle.	W	1-0		4	8	Hernandez	Westbrook	MacDougal	8-0	1st	+3.0
4-12	At Cle.	W	5-2		9	9	George	Sabathia	Carrasco	9-0	1st	+4.0
4-13	At Cle.	L	1-6		9	13	Rodriguez	May		9-1	1st	+3.0
4-14	At Cle.	W	12-4		15	8	Affeldt	Anderson		10-1	1st	+3.5
4-15	At Chi.	W	8-5		15	7	Lopez	Koch	MacDougal	11-1	1st	+4.5
4-16	At Chi.	L	3-4		5	5	Gordon	Grimsley		11-2	1st	+3.5
4-17	At Chi.	L	2-8		9	8	Loaiza	George		11-3	1st	+2.5
4-18	Det.	W	4-3	(11)	10	11	Carrasco	Anderson		12-3	1st	+2.5
4-19	Det.	W	9-2		12	5	Lopez	Knotts		13-3	1st	+2.5
4-20	Det.	W	4-3		4	10	MacDougal	Maroth		14-3	1st	+3.5
4-22	Min.	W	4-3		7	4	Hernandez	Rogers	MacDougal	15-3	1st	+4.0
4-24	Min.	W	2-1		4	7	George	Radke	MacDougal	16-3	1st	+5.5
4-25	At Tor.	L	5-6		9	10	Escobar	Carrasco		16-4	1st	+5.5
4-26	At Tor.	W	9-6		14	10	Grimsley	Tam	MacDougal	17-4	1st	+5.5
4-27	At Tor.	L	9-10		17	16	Politte	MacDougal		17-5	1st	+4.5
4-29	At Bos.	L	2-7		8	12	Wakefield	George		17-6	1st	+4.5
4-30	At Bos.	L	4-5		5	11	Embree	MacDougal		17-7	1st	+4.5
5-1	At Bos.	L	5-6		8	11	Shiell	Grimsley	Lyon	17-8	1st	+3.5
5-2	At Bal.	W	5-2		10	7	Asencio	Helling		18-8	1st	+4.5
5-3	At Bal.	L	1-6		6	9	Ponson	Hernandez		18-9	1st	+4.5
5-4	At Bal.	W	4-0		4	7	George	DuBose	Carrasco	19-9	1st	+5.0
5-5	Bos.	W	7-6		11	10	Lopez	Lyon		20-9	1st	+5.5
5-6	Bos.	L	3-7		7	13	Fossum	Affeldt		20-10	1st	+4.5
5-7	Bos.	L	6-9		8	10	Woodard	Lopez	Lyon	20-11	1st	+3.5
5-9†	Bal.	L	5-15		11	17	Helling	Asencio		20-12		
5-9‡	Bal.	L	4-5		11	8	Ponson	Hernandez	Julio	20-13	1st	+1.5
5-10	Bal.	W	8-4		14	7	Carrasco	Groom		21-13	1st	+2.5
5-11	Bal.	W	8-5		12	12	Lowe	Driskill		22-13	1st	+2.5
5-12	At Min.	W	3-2		8	9	Affeldt	Mays	MacDougal	23-13	1st	+3.5
5-13	At Min.	L	2-4	(10)	10	10	Hawkins	Lopez		23-14	1st	+2.5
5-14	At Min.	L	0-7		3	12	Reed	Hernandez		23-15	1st	+1.5
5-15	At Min.	W	9-5	(14)	14	12	Carrasco	Santana		24-15	1st	+2.5
5-16	Tor.	L	1-18		10	22	Hendrickson	George		24-16	1st	+1.5
5-17	Tor.	L	4-7		6	13	Halladay	Grimsley	Politte	24-17	1st	+0.5
5-18	Tor.	L	3-4		7	9	Sturtze	Snyder	Politte	24-18	2nd	0.5
5-20	At Sea.	L	4-7		6	11	Nelson	Carrasco		24-19	2nd	0.5
5-21	At Sea.	W	14-5		12	10	George	Garcia		25-19	2nd	0.5
5-22	At Sea.	L	1-5		6	11	Meche	Affeldt		25-20	2nd	1.5
5-23	At Oak.	L	1-4		8	12	Mulder	Snyder		25-21	2nd	1.5
5-24	At Oak.	W	3-1		3	7	Wilson	Lilly	MacDougal	26-21	2nd	1.5
5-25	At Oak.	L	3-4	(10)	8	7	Foulke	Carrasco		26-22	2nd	2.5
5-27	Sea.	L	7-15		10	20	Garcia	George		26-23	2nd	3.5
5-28	Sea.	L	2-5		5	8	Moyer	Affeldt	Sasaki	26-24	2nd	4.5
5-29	Oak.	L	1-6		9	10	Mulder	Snyder		26-25	2nd	4.5
5-30	Oak.	W	11-6		14	11	Wilson	Hudson		27-25	2nd	3.5
5-31	Oak.	L	6-7		10	7	Mecir	MacDougal	Foulke	27-26	2nd	3.5
6-1	Oak.	L	4-6		9	9	Bradford	DeHart	Foulke	27-27	2nd	3.5
6-3	At L.A.	L	3-4		8	10	Gagne	Carrasco		27-28	2nd	4.5
6-4	At L.A.	W	2-1		7	3	Snyder	Nomo	MacDougal	28-28	2nd	3.5
6-5	At L.A.	L	2-5		5	7	Brown	May	Gagne	28-29	2nd	4.5
6-7§	At Col.	W	13-11		14	12	George	Chacon	MacDougal	29-29		
6-7∞	At Col.	W	9-5		16	10	Gilfillan	Jones		30-29	2nd	4.5
6-8	At Col.	L	7-8		15	11	Elarton	DeHart	Jimenez	30-30	2nd	4.5
6-10	Ari.	W	7-3		13	8	Grimsley	Oropesa		31-30	2nd	3.5
6-11	Ari.	L	3-4		9	9	Good	May	Valverde	31-31	2nd	4.5
6-13	S.F	W	6-1		11	11	George	Schmidt		32-31	2nd	5.0
6-14	S.F	L	4-7		9	8	Moss	Walrond		32-32	2nd	5.0

Date	Opp.	Res.	Score	(inn.*)	Hits	Opp. hits	Winning pitcher	Losing pitcher	Save	Record	Pos.	GB
6-15	S.F	W	5-4		8	9	MacDougal	Worrell		33-32	2nd	4.0
6-16	Min.	W	9-8		12	15	MacDougal	Guardado		34-32	2nd	3.0
6-17	Min.	W	14-7		13	11	Wilson	Rogers		35-32	2nd	2.0
6-18	Min.	W	8-6		13	13	George	Reed	MacDougal	36-32	2nd	1.0
6-19	Min.	L	2-16		6	23	Mays	Snyder		36-33	2nd	2.0
6-20	At StL.	W	10-4		15	10	Lima	Morris		37-33	2nd	1.0
6-21	At StL.	L	1-8		6	14	Williams	May		37-34	2nd	1.0
6-22	At StL.	W	5-2		8	10	Affeldt	Stephenson	MacDougal	38-34	2nd	1.0
6-24	At Cle.	W	3-1		11	8	George	Davis	MacDougal	39-34	1st	...
6-25	At Cle.	W	3-1	(10)	11	6	Gilfillan	Riske	MacDougal	40-34	1st	...
6-26	At Cle.	W	4-1		9	6	Lima	Rodriguez	MacDougal	41-34	1st	+1.0
6-27	StL.	W	6-3		4	7	May	Stephenson	MacDougal	42-34	1st	+2.0
6-28	StL.	L	9-13		14	14	Fassero	Affeldt		42-35	1st	+1.0
6-29	StL.	L	6-13		10	14	Tomko	George		42-36	1st	...
6-30†	Cle.	L	5-10		6	17	Lee	Voyles		42-37		
6-30‡	Cle.	L	5-8		10	14	Anderson	Walrond	Baez	42-38	2nd	0.5
7-1	Cle.	W	6-3		8	7	Lima	Rodriguez	MacDougal	43-38	1st	+0.5
7-2	Cle.	W	8-2		12	6	May	Traber		44-38	1st	+1.5
7-3	Det.	W	3-2		6	5	Affeldt	Bonderman	MacDougal	45-38	1st	+2.5
7-4	Det.	W	9-8		13	11	Field	Cornejo	MacDougal	46-38	1st	+2.5
7-5	Det.	L	5-9		9	12	Maroth	Voyles	Walker	46-39	1st	+2.5
7-6	Det.	W	5-3		6	4	Lima	Roney	MacDougal	47-39	1st	+3.5
7-8	At Ana.	W	4-0		7	4	May	Lackey		48-39	1st	+4.5
7-9	At Ana.	L	3-5		10	9	Rodriguez	Affeldt	Percival	48-40	1st	+4.5
7-10	At Ana.	L	1-7		5	10	Sele	George		48-41	1st	+4.5
7-11	At Tex.	W	13-3		14	5	Wilson	Dickey		49-41	1st	+5.5
7-12	At Tex.	W	8-2		15	9	Lima	Valdes		50-41	1st	+6.5
7-13	At Tex.	W	8-2		11	12	May	Mounce		51-41	1st	+7.0
7-17	Sea.	W	7-1		12	8	Lima	Garcia		52-41	1st	+7.5
7-18	Sea.	L	3-6		10	8	Rhodes	MacDougal	Hasegawa	52-42	1st	+6.5
7-19	Sea.	W	5-1		10	3	May	Meche		53-42	1st	+6.5
7-20	Sea.	W	7-5	(10)	8	9	Wilson	Rhodes		54-42	1st	+6.5
7-21	Oak.	L	1-6		4	5	Rincon	Lowe		54-43	1st	+5.5
7-22	Oak.	L	0-10		3	13	Hudson	Wilson		54-44	1st	+5.0
7-23	At Min.	W	8-3		11	8	Affeldt	Santana		55-44	1st	+5.0
7-24	At Min.	L	2-6		6	6	Hawkins	Grimsley		55-45	1st	+4.0
7-25	At Det.	W	8-3		15	13	Hernandez	Ledezma		56-45	1st	+4.0
7-26	At Det.	L	1-5		3	10	Bonderman	Snyder		56-46	1st	+4.0
7-27	At Det.	W	5-1		8	5	Lima	Maroth		57-46	1st	+4.0
7-29	Chi.	L	6-9		12	16	Buehrle	May	Gordon	57-47	1st	+3.0
7-30	Chi.	L	4-15		10	19	Garland	Hernandez		57-48	1st	+2.0
7-31	Chi.	L	6-8	(11)	15	12	Schoeneweis	Field		57-49	1st	+1.0
8-1	T.B.	L	6-9		9	17	Backe	Lloyd	Carter	57-50	1st	...
8-2	T.B.	W	10-8		14	11	Leskanic	Malaska	MacDougal	58-50	1st	+1.0
8-3	T.B.	W	2-0		4	6	Gobble	Gonzalez	Affeldt	59-50	1st	+2.0
8-4	At Chi.	W	13-9		13	11	Hernandez	Schoeneweis	Levine	60-50	1st	+3.0
8-5	At Chi.	L	4-5		10	10	Loaiza	Snyder	Marte	60-51	1st	+2.0
8-6	At Chi.	L	3-4		7	9	Colon	Wilson	Marte	60-52	1st	+1.0
8-7	At T.B.	L	2-3		7	7	Gaudin	MacDougal		60-53	1st	+0.5
8-8	At T.B.	L	0-4		4	9	Gonzalez	Appier		60-54	2nd	0.5
8-9	At T.B.	W	6-2		10	10	Gobble	Zambrano		61-54	1st	+0.5
8-10	At T.B.	W	7-3		12	6	Hernandez	Sosa		62-54	1st	+0.5
8-11	N.Y.	W	12-9		14	15	Carrasco	Hitchcock		63-54	1st	+1.5
8-12	N.Y.	L	0-6		6	15	Mussina	May		63-55	1st	+0.5
8-13	N.Y.	W	11-0		16	4	Appier	Weaver		64-55	1st	+1.5
8-15	Min.	L	2-9		5	17	Rogers	Gobble		64-56	1st	+2.0
8-16	Min.	L	5-14		8	15	Lohse	Hernandez		64-57	1st	+2.0
8-17	Min.	W	5-4		12	8	May	Reed	Leskanic	65-57	1st	+3.0
8-18	At N.Y.	L	6-11		9	14	Weaver	Lima		65-58	1st	+2.0
8-19	At N.Y.	L	3-6		9	8	Pettitte	Appier	Rivera	65-59	1st	+1.0
8-20	At N.Y.	L	7-8		17	13	Clemens	Gobble	Rivera	65-60	1st	...
8-21	At Min.	L	3-4		9	5	Rogers	Levine	Guardado	65-61	3rd	1.0
8-22	At Min.	W	3-2		7	8	May	Lohse	Affeldt	66-61	2nd	1.0
8-23	At Min.	W	4-3		9	13	Carrasco	Mays	MacDougal	67-61	2nd	1.0
8-24	At Min.	L	1-8		8	10	Santana	Lloyd		67-62	2nd	1.0
8-26	Tex.	W	9-2		12	6	Anderson	Dickey		68-62	2nd	1.0
8-27	Tex.	W	9-0		13	5	May	Lewis		69-62	2nd	1.0
8-28	Tex.	W	6-5	(11)	13	9	Carrasco	Ramirez		70-62	1st	...
8-29	Ana.	L	3-10		8	15	Washburn	Gobble		70-63	1st	...
8-31	Ana.	L	4-7		10	10	Shields	Anderson	Percival	70-64		

Date	Opp.	Res.	Score	(inn.*)	Hits	Opp. hits	Winning pitcher	Losing pitcher	Save	Record	Pos.	GB
9-1	At Tex.	L	3-7		6	6	Lewis	May		70-65	2nd	2.0
9-2	At Tex.	L	7-8		10	8	Valdes	Affeldt	Cordero	70-66	3rd	2.0
9-3	At Tex.	W	3-1		4	7	Gobble	Thomson	MacDougal	71-66	3rd	1.0
9-4	Ari.	L	5-6	(10)	12	11	Mantei	Wilson		71-67	3rd	1.5
9-5	At Ana.	W	5-0		15	7	Anderson	Washburn		72-67	3rd	1.5
9-6†	At Ana.	L	5-6		12	9	Weber	Grimsley	Percival	72-68		
9-6‡	At Ana.	L	1-3		4	6	Gregg	Wright	Percival	72-69	3rd	3.0
9-7	At Ana.	W	3-0		8	5	Abbott	Lackey	Affeldt	73-69	3rd	3.0
9-9	Cle.	L	1-7		11	10	Davis	Gobble		73-70	3rd	4.5
9-10	Cle.	W	9-7		12	13	Wilson	Santiago	Affeldt	74-70	3rd	3.5
9-11	Cle.	L	5-6		11	13	Baez	Grimsley	Riske	74-71	3rd	3.5
9-12	At Det.	L	0-3		6	9	Maroth	Abbott	Rodney	74-72	3rd	3.5
9-13	At Det.	W	7-0		12	7	Wright	Mears		75-72	3rd	3.5
9-14	At Det.	W	7-2		11	5	Gobble	Robertson		76-72	3rd	3.5
9-15	At Det.	W	10-4		13	10	Anderson	Knotts		77-72	3rd	3.5
9-16	At Cle.	W	12-8		15	10	May	Traber		78-72	3rd	3.5
9-17	At Cle.	L	1-9		5	12	Westbrook	Abbott		78-73	3rd	4.5
9-18	At Cle.	W	3-2		8	6	Lima	Sabathia	Leskanic	79-73	3rd	4.5
9-19	At Chi.	L	5-8		7	12	Buehrle	Carrasco	Gordon	79-74	3rd	5.5
9-20	At Chi.	W	7-1		14	5	Anderson	Loaiza		80-74	3rd	5.5
9-21	At Chi.	W	10-4		10	6	May	Garland		81-74	T2nd	5.5
9-22	Det.	W	12-6		16	10	Affeldt	Knotts		82-74	T2nd	5.0
9-23	Det.	L	6-15		12	18	Maroth	Lima		82-75	T2nd	6.0
9-24	Det.	L	3-4		7	5	Loux	Gobble	Rodney	82-76	3rd	7.0
9-25	Chi.	W	7-3		8	8	Anderson	Wright		83-76	T2nd	6.0
9-26	Chi.	L	2-11		4	11	Garland	May		83-77	3rd	7.0
9-27	Chi.	L	3-19		5	21	Colon	Wright		83-78	3rd	7.0
9-28	Chi.	L	1-5		3	8	Loaiza	Lima		83-79	3rd	7.0

Monthly records: March (1-0), April (16-7), May (10-19), June (15-12), July (15-11), August (13-15), September (13-15).
*Innings, if other than nine. † First game of a doubleheader. ‡ Second game of a doubleheader. § Day separate admission. ∞ Night separate admission.

RECORDS

2003 regular-season record: 83-79
Position: 3rd in A.L. Central
Home: 40-40 **Road:** 43-39
A.L. East: 12-20 **A.L. Central:** 46-30
A.L. West: 16-20 N.L. 9-9
Vs. LH starters: 24-24
Vs. RH starters: 59-55
Grass: 75-70 **Artificial:** 8-9
Day: 27-26 **Night:** 56-53
1-Run: 18-22 **X-inn.:** 5-4
Doubleheaders: 0-3-0
Team record past five years: 351-458 (.434, ranks 12th in league in that span)

TEAM LEADERS

Batting average: Carlos Beltran (.307).
At-bats: Raul Ibanez (608).
Runs: Carlos Beltran (102).
Hits: Raul Ibanez (179).
Total Bases: Raul Ibanez (276).
Doubles: Raul Ibanez (33).
Triples: Carlos Beltran (10).
Home runs: Carlos Beltran (26).
Runs batted in: Carlos Beltran (100).
Stolen bases: Carlos Beltran (41).
Slugging percentage: Carlos Beltran (.522).
On-base percentage: Mike Sweeney (.391).
Wins: Darrell May (10).
Earned-run average: Darrell May (3.77).
Complete games: Brian Anderson, Darrell May, Jamey Wright (2).
Shutouts: Brian Anderson, Darrell May, Jamey Wright (1).
Saves: Mike MacDougal (27).
Innings pitched: Darrell May (210.0).
Strikeouts: Darrell May (115).

GAMES BY POSITION

Catcher: Brent Mayne 112, Mike DiFelice 58, Tom Prince 7.
First base: Ken Harvey 99, Mike Sweeney 45, Raul Ibanez 22, Mendy Lopez 17, Morgan Burkhart 2, Jarrod Patterson 2.
Second base: Desi Relaford 89, Carlos Febles 67, Mendy Lopez 11, Julius Matos 11, Brent Abernathy 9, Gookie Dawkins 3.
Third base: Joe Randa 129, Desi Relaford 33, Mendy Lopez 13, Julius Matos 13, Jarrod Patterson 4.
Shortstop: Angel Berroa 158, Desi Relaford 6, Mendy Lopez 4, Julius Matos 2, Carlos Febles 1.
Outfield: Raul Ibanez 131, Carlos Beltran 130, Aaron Guiel 89, Michael Tucker 85, Dee Brown 33, Desi Relaford 20, Rondell White 17, Brandon Berger 11, David DeJesus 9, Rontrez Johnson 6, Mendy Lopez 3, Julius Matos 1.
Designated hitter: Mike Sweeney 62, Ken Harvey 32, Michael Tucker 15, Raul Ibanez 12, Dee Brown 11, Carlos Beltran 8, Desi Relaford 5, Carlos Febles 4, Jarrod Patterson 4, Rondell White 4, Morgan Burkhart 2, Mike DiFelice 2, Aaron Guiel 2, Rontrez Johnson 2, Joe Randa 2, Brandon Berger 1, Julius Matos 1, Tom Prince 1.

TOP DRAFT CHOICES

1a. **Chris Lubanski,** OF, Kennedy-Kenrick H.S., Schwenksville, Pa.
1b. **Mitch Maier,** C, Toledo.
2. **Shane Costa,** OF, Cal State-Fullerton.
3. **Brian McFall,** 1B, Chandler-Gilbert (Ariz.) CC.
4. **Miguel Vega,** 3B, Carmen B. Huyke H.S., Arroyo, Puerto Rico.
5. **Chris Goodman,** RHP, Georgia Tech.
6. **Ryan Braun,** RHP, UNLV.
7. **Michael Aviles,** SS, Concordia (N.Y.) College.
8. **Brandon Powell,** 2B, Coastal Carolina.
9. **John Gragg,** LHP, Bethune-Cookman.
10. **Luis Cota,** RHP, Sunnyside H.S., Tucson.

MINNESOTA TWINS

AMERICAN LEAGUE CENTRAL DIVISION

2004 SEASON

April

SUN	MON	TUE	WED	THU	FRI	SAT
4	5 CLE	6 CLE	7 CLE	8 DET	9	10 DET
11 DET	12 CLE	13	14 CLE	15 CLE	16 KC	17 KC
18 KC	19	20 DET	21 DET	22 DET	23 KC	24 KC
25 KC	26 TOR	27 TOR	28 TOR	29	30 ANA	

May

SUN	MON	TUE	WED	THU	FRI	SAT
						1 ANA
2 ANA	3	4 SEA	5 SEA	6 SEA	7 OAK	8 OAK
9 OAK	10	11 SEA	12 SEA	13 SEA	14 CHW	15 CHW
16 CHW	17 TOR	18 TOR	19 TOR	20 CHW	21 CHW	22 CHW
23 CHW	24	25 TB	26 TB	27 TB	28 KC	29 KC
30 KC	31 TB					

June

SUN	MON	TUE	WED	THU	FRI	SAT
		1 TB	2 TB	3 TB	4 DET	5 DET
6 DET	7	8 NYM	9 NYM	10 NYM	11 PHI	12 PHI
13 PHI	14	15 MON	16 MON	17 MON	18 MIL	19 MIL
20 MIL	21	22 BOS	23 BOS	24 BOS	25 MIL	26 MIL
27 MIL	28	29 CHW	30 CHW			

July

SUN	MON	TUE	WED	THU	FRI	SAT
				1 CHW	2 ARI	3 ARI
4 ARI	5 KC	6 KC	7 KC	8 DET	9 DET	10 DET
11 DET	12	13 All-Star	14	15 KC	16 KC	17 KC
18 KC	19 DET	20 DET	21 TB	22 TB	23 BAL	24 BAL
25 BAL	26 CHW	27 CHW	28 CHW	29	30 BOS	31 BOS

August

SUN	MON	TUE	WED	THU	FRI	SAT
1 BOS	2	3 ANA	4 ANA	5 ANA	6 OAK	7 OAK
8 OAK	9 OAK	10 SEA	11 SEA	12 SEA	13 CLE	14 CLE
15 CLE	16	17 NYY	18 NYY	19 NYY	20 CLE	21 CLE
22 CLE	23 TEX	24 TEX	25 TEX	26 TEX	27 ANA	28 ANA
29 ANA	30	31 TEX				

Sept./Oct.

SUN	MON	TUE	WED	THU	FRI	SAT
			1 TEX	2 TEX	3 KC	4 KC
5 KC	6 BAL	7 BAL	8 BAL	9	10 DET	11 DET
12 DET	13 DET	14 CHW	15 CHW	16 CHW	17 BAL	18 BAL
19 BAL	20 CHW	21 CHW	22 CHW	23 CLE	24 CLE	25 CLE
26 CLE	27	28 NYY	29 NYY	30 NYY	1 CLE	2 CLE
3 CLE	4	5	6	7	8	9

Home games shaded. All-Star Game July 13 at Houston. Schedule subject to change.

CLUB DIRECTORY

Owner
Carl R. Pohlad
President, Twins Sports Inc.
T. Geron Bell
President, Minnesota Twins
Dave St. Peter
Vice president, general manager
Terry Ryan
Vice president, asst. general manager
Bill Smith
Vice president, operations
Matt Hoy
Assistant general manager
Wayne Krivsky
Director of minor leagues
Jim Rantz
Director of baseball operations
Rob Antony
Director of scouting
Mike Radcliff
Director of communications
Brad Ruiter
Media relations manager
Sean Harlin

MINOR LEAGUE AFFILIATES

Class	Team	League	Manager
AAA	Rochester	International	Phil Roof
AA	New Britain	Eastern	Stan Cliburn
Advanced A	Fort Myers	Florida State	Jose Marzan
A	Quad Cities	Midwest	Kevin Boles
Advanced Rookie	Elizabethton	Appalachian	Ray Smith
Rookie	Gulf Coast Twins	Gulf Coast	Riccardo Ingram

More on the Twins at www.foxsports.com/named/FS/MLB/teams

BROADCAST INFORMATION

Radio: WCCO-AM (830).
TV: KSTC-TV (Channel 45).
Cable TV: Victory Sports One.

SPRING TRAINING

Ballpark (city): Lee County Sports Complex (Fort Myers, Fla.).
Ticket information: 800-33-TWINS.

SPRING TRAINING ROSTER

Manager—Ron Gardenhire (35).
Coaches—Rick Anderson (40), Steve Liddle (9), Al Newman (62), Rick Stelmaszek (43), Scott Ullger (45), Jerry White (13).

No.	PITCHERS	B/T	Ht./Wt.	Age*	2003 Clubs
19	Balfour, Grant	R/R	6-2/185	26	Rochester, Minnesota
	Bonser, Boof	R/R	6-4/230	22	Norwich, Fresno
47	Douglass, Sean	R/R	6-6/218	24	Ottawa, Baltimore
	Durbin, J.D.	R/R	6-0/190	22	Fort Myers, New Britain
	Guerrier, Matt	R/R	6-3/185	25	Nashville
38	Johnson, Adam	R/R	6-2/210	24	Rochester, Minnesota
49	Lohse, Kyle	R/R	6-2/200	25	Minnesota
25	Mays, Joe	B/R	6-1/192	28	Minnesota
	Miller, Colby	R/R	6-2/190	22	Fort Myers
59	Nakamura, Mike	R/R	5-10/178	27	Minnesota, Rochester
36	Nathan, Joe	R/R	6-4/207	29	San Francisco
51	Pulido, Carlos	L/L	6-0/200	32	Rochester, Minnesota
22	Radke, Brad	R/R	6-2/188	31	Minnesota
39	Rincon, Juan	R/R	5-11/192	25	Rochester, Minnesota
33	Romero, J.C.	B/L	5-11/195	27	Minnesota
57	Santana, Johan	L/L	6-0/195	25	Minnesota
	Silva, Carlos	R/R	6-4/240	24	Philadelphia
56	Thomas, Brad	L/L	6-4/220	26	G.C. Twins, Rochester, Minnesota
	Wolfe, Brian	R/R	6-2/200	23	Fort Myers, New Britain

No.	CATCHERS	B/T	Ht./Wt.	Age*	2003 Clubs
	Blanco, Henry	R/R	5-11/224	32	Atlanta
	Bowen, Rob	B/R	6-3/225	23	New Britain, Rochester, Minnesota
24	LeCroy, Matt	R/R	6-2/225	28	Minnesota

No.	INFIELDERS	B/T	Ht./Wt.	Age*	2003 Clubs
	Bartlett, Jason	R/R	6-0/175	24	New Britain
15	Guzman, Cristian	B/R	6-0/195	26	Minnesota
47	Koskie, Corey	L/R	6-3/220	30	Minnesota
16	Mientkiewicz, D.	L/R	6-2/200	29	Minnesota
	Morneau, Justin	L/R	6-4/205	22	New Britain, Rochester, Minnesota
	Ojeda, Augie	B/R	5-8/175	29	Iowa, Chicago N.L.
34	Punto, Nick	B/R	5-9/175	26	Scranton/W.B., Philadelphia
2	Rivas, Luis	R/R	5-11/175	24	Minnesota
	Tiffee, Terry	B/R	6-3/210	24	New Britain

No.	OUTFIELDERS	B/T	Ht./Wt.	Age*	2003 Clubs
5	Cuddyer, Michael	R/R	6-2/225	25	G.C. Twins, Rochester, Minnesota
20	Ford, Lew	R/R	6-0/190	27	Rochester, Minnesota
	Garbe, B.J.	R/R	6-2/195	23	G.C. Twins, New Britain
48	Hunter, Torii	R/R	6-2/210	28	Minnesota
11	Jones, Jacque	L/L	5-10/200	28	Minnesota
	Kubel, Jason	L/R	5-11/195	21	Fort Myers
41	Restovich, Michael	R/R	6-4/245	25	Rochester, Minnesota
54	Ryan, Michael	L/R	6-0/185	26	Rochester, Minnesota
23	Stewart, Shannon	R/R	6-1/210	30	Syracuse, Toronto, Minnesota

Invited to spring training: RHP Jesse Crain, RHP Rick Helling, LHP Aaron Fultz, RHP Seth Greisinger, RHP Peter Munro, RHP Jeromy Palki, RHP Joe Roa, C Chris Heintz, C Brandon Marsters, C Joe Mauer, C Gabby Torres, IF Jake Mauer, IF Alex Prieto, IF Luis Rodriguez.

*Age as of April 1, 2004.

BALLPARK INFORMATION

Ballpark (capacity, surface)
Hubert H. Humphrey Metrodome (45,423, artificial)

Address
34 Kirby Puckett Place
Minneapolis, MN 55415

Official website
www.twinsbaseball.com

Business phone
612-375-1366

Ticket information
1-800-338-9467

Field dimensions (from home plate)
To left field at foul line, 343 feet
To center field, 408 feet
To right field at foul line, 327 feet

First game played
April 6, 1982 (Mariners 11, Twins 7)

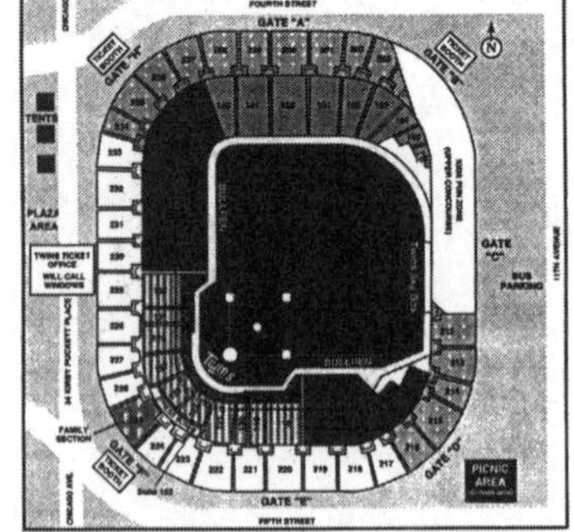

2003 REVIEW

DAY BY DAY

Date	Opp.	Res.	Score	(inn.*)	Hits	Opp. hits	Winning pitcher	Losing pitcher	Save	Record	Pos.	GB
3-31	At Det.	W	3-1		8	4	Radke	Maroth	Guardado	1-0	T1st	...
4-2	At Det.	W	8-1		13	3	Mays	Bonderman		2-0	T1st	...
4-3	At Det.	W	3-0		6	3	Lohse	Bernero	Guardado	3-0	T1st	...
4-4	Tor.	L	2-7		5	8	Sturtze	Reed		3-1	2nd	1.0
4-5	Tor.	L	3-4	(11)	10	10	Walker	Guardado	Escobar	3-2	2nd	2.0
4-6	Tor.	L	1-8		9	11	Lidle	Radke		3-3	T2nd	2.5
4-8	At N.Y.	L	3-7		5	9	Pettitte	Mays		3-4	3rd	3.0
4-9	At N.Y.	L	1-2		7	4	Mussina	Lohse	Acevedo	3-5	4th	4.0
4-10	At N.Y.	L	0-2		3	10	Wells	Reed		3-6	4th	5.0
4-11	At Tor.	W	6-4		12	8	Rogers	Lidle	Guardado	4-6	3rd	5.0
4-12	At Tor.	W	9-6		13	11	Hawkins	Escobar	Guardado	5-6	3rd	5.0
4-13	At Tor.	W	9-3		11	4	Mays	Hendrickson		6-6	3rd	4.0
4-15	Det.	W	6-4		12	5	Lohse	Maroth	Guardado	7-6	T2nd	4.5
4-16	Det.	W	4-2		10	6	Reed	Bernero	Guardado	8-6	T2nd	3.5
4-17	Det.	W	6-0		13	7	Rogers	Bonderman		9-6	T2nd	2.5
4-18	N.Y.	L	4-11		9	15	Clemens	Radke		9-7	3rd	3.5
4-19	N.Y.	L	2-4		9	6	Pettitte	Mays	Acevedo	9-8	3rd	4.5
4-20	N.Y.	L	2-8		6	14	Mussina	Lohse		9-9	3rd	5.5
4-21	N.Y.	L	1-15		7	14	Wells	Reed		9-10	3rd	6.0
4-22	At K.C.	L	3-4		4	7	Hernandez	Rogers	MacDougal	9-11	3rd	7.0
4-24	At K.C.	L	1-2		7	4	George	Radke	MacDougal	9-12	3rd	8.0
4-25	At Chi.	W	6-1		9	5	Mays	Buehrle		10-12	3rd	7.0
4-26	At Chi.	L	4-7		6	10	Garland	Lohse		10-13	3rd	8.0
4-27	At Chi.	L	1-3		6	3	Loaiza	Reed	Marte	10-14	3rd	8.0
4-29	T.B.	W	5-3		9	10	Rogers	Sosa	Guardado	11-14	3rd	7.0
4-30	T.B.	W	8-5		8	10	Radke	McClung		12-14	3rd	6.0
5-1	T.B.	W	6-5	(13)	15	9	Fiore	Harper		13-14	3rd	5.0
5-2	At Bos.	W	11-7		15	12	Santana	Mendoza		14-14	3rd	5.0
5-3	At Bos.	L	1-9		5	13	Martinez	Fiore		14-15	3rd	5.0
5-4	At Bos.	W	9-4		14	9	Rogers	Timlin		15-15	2nd	5.0
5-6	At T.B.	W	7-3		12	8	Radke	Parris		16-15	2nd	4.5
5-7	At T.B.	W	11-6		17	12	Rincon	Kennedy		17-15	2nd	3.5
5-8	At T.B.	W	5-0		8	5	Lohse	Brazelton		18-15	2nd	3.0
5-9	Bos.	W	5-0		8	5	Santana	Martinez		19-15	2nd	1.5
5-10	Bos.	L	5-6		11	12	Wakefield	Rincon	Lyon	19-16	2nd	2.5
5-11	Bos.	W	9-8		15	15	Radke	Lowe	Guardado	20-16	2nd	2.5
5-12	K.C.	L	2-3		9	8	Affeldt	Mays	MacDougal	20-17	2nd	3.5
5-13	K.C.	W	4-2	(10)	10	10	Hawkins	Lopez		21-17	2nd	2.5
5-14	K.C.	W	7-0		12	3	Reed	Hernandez		22-17	2nd	1.5
5-15	K.C.	L	5-9	(14)	12	14	Carrasco	Santana		22-18	2nd	2.5
5-16	Chi.	W	18-3		20	9	Radke	Buehrle		23-18	2nd	1.5
5-17	Chi.	W	3-1		7	7	Mays	Garland	Guardado	24-18	2nd	0.5
5-18	Chi.	W	3-2		10	8	Hawkins	Gordon	Guardado	25-18	1st	+0.5
5-20	At Oak.	L	1-4		6	13	Hudson	Reed	Foulke	25-19	1st	+0.5
5-21	At Oak.	W	4-3		9	10	Hawkins	Bradford	Guardado	26-19	1st	+0.5
5-22	At Oak.	W	6-5		14	6	Mays	Halama	Guardado	27-19	1st	+1.5
5-23	At Sea.	L	2-5		9	9	Moyer	Radke	Sasaki	27-20	1st	+1.5
5-24	At Sea.	W	7-2		14	6	Lohse	Pineiro		28-20	1st	+1.5
5-25	At Sea.	W	3-1		9	6	Reed	Franklin	Guardado	29-20	1st	+2.5
5-27	Oak.	W	4-3		3	8	Romero	Zito	Guardado	30-20	1st	+3.5
5-28	Oak.	W	6-5		6	13	Mays	Halama	Guardado	31-20	1st	+4.5
5-29	Sea.	L	6-10		10	18	Meche	Radke		31-21	1st	+4.5
5-30	Sea.	L	0-6		4	12	Pineiro	Lohse		31-22	1st	+3.5
5-31	Sea.	L	2-5		7	11	Franklin	Reed	Sasaki	31-23	1st	+3.5
6-1	Sea.	L	5-9		8	14	Garcia	Rogers		31-24	1st	+3.5
6-3	At S.F	W	6-4		13	11	Mays	Moss	Guardado	32-24	1st	+4.5
6-4	At S.F	L	3-4		5	9	Worrell	Rincon		32-25	1st	+3.5
6-5	At S.F	W	5-2		10	8	Lohse	Foppert	Guardado	33-25	1st	+4.5
6-6	At S.D.	W	7-5	(11)	14	14	Romero	Beck		34-25	1st	+5.0
6-7	At S.D.	W	6-2		12	5	Santana	Loewer	Nakamura	35-25	1st	+4.5
6-8	At S.D.	L	4-9		11	16	Lawrence	Hawkins		35-26	1st	+4.5
6-10	Col.	L	0-5		3	7	Jennings	Radke		35-27	1st	+3.5
6-11	Col.	W	7-4		15	12	Lohse	Cook	Guardado	36-27	1st	+4.5
6-12	Col.	W	15-3		18	10	Rogers	Oliver		37-27	1st	+5.0

Date	Opp.	Res.	Score	(inn.*)	Hits	Opp. hits	Winning pitcher	Losing pitcher	Save	Record	Pos.	GB
6-13	Ari.	W	3-1		6	4	Santana	Webb	Guardado	38-27	1st	+5.0
6-14	Ari.	L	2-9		8	12	Batista	Mays		38-28	1st	+5.0
6-15	Ari.	L	8-12		14	15	Koplove	Hawkins		38-29	1st	+4.0
6-16	At K.C.	L	8-9		15	12	MacDougal	Guardado		38-30	1st	+3.0
6-17	At K.C.	L	7-14		11	13	Wilson	Rogers		38-31	1st	+2.0
6-18	At K.C.	L	6-8		13	13	George	Reed	MacDougal	38-32	1st	+1.0
6-19	At K.C.	W	16-2		23	6	Mays	Snyder		39-32	1st	+2.0
6-20	At Mil.	L	2-3	(10)	5	7	Leskanic	Rincon		39-33	1st	+1.0
6-21	At Mil.	L	1-8		5	9	Franklin	Lohse		39-34	1st	+1.0
6-22	At Mil.	W	8-3		12	11	Rogers	Kinney		40-34	1st	+1.0
6-24	Chi.	L	1-2		6	8	Loaiza	Reed	Koch	40-35	2nd	...
6-25	Chi.	W	6-5	(11)	12	13	Guardado	Koch		41-35	2nd	...
6-26	Chi.	L	1-5		5	8	Buehrle	Radke		41-36	2nd	1.0
6-27	Mil.	L	1-13		8	19	Kinney	Lohse		41-37	2nd	2.0
6-28	Mil.	W	5-2		13	9	Rogers	Burba	Guardado	42-37	2nd	1.0
6-29	Mil.	W	5-4	(10)	14	9	Hawkins	DeJean		43-37	2nd	...
6-30	At Chi.	L	3-10		8	10	Garland	Mays		43-38	1st	+0.5
7-1	At Chi.	L	1-6		9	9	Buehrle	Radke		43-39	2nd	0.5
7-2	At Chi.	L	6-8	(12)	16	10	Koch	Guardado		43-40	2nd	1.5
7-3	Cle.	L	1-4		4	8	Sabathia	Rogers		43-41	2nd	2.5
7-4	Cle.	W	9-2		10	8	Reed	Davis		44-41	2nd	2.5
7-5	Cle.	L	2-13		6	16	Anderson	Mays		44-42	2nd	2.5
7-6	Cle.	L	3-5	(10)	8	10	Riske	Guardado	Baez	44-43	2nd	3.5
7-8	At Tex.	L	6-8		10	13	Powell	Lohse	Urbina	44-44	2nd	4.5
7-9	At Tex.	L	1-4		5	7	Benoit	Rogers	Urbina	44-45	2nd	4.5
7-10	At Tex.	L	4-9		11	11	Thomson	Reed		44-46	2nd	4.5
7-11	At Ana.	L	0-5		4	6	Ortiz	Santana	Donnelly	44-47	2nd	5.5
7-12	At Ana.	L	1-6		5	11	Washburn	Radke		44-48	2nd	6.5
7-13	At Ana.	L	3-8		13	10	Lackey	Lohse		44-49	3rd	7.5
7-17	Oak.	W	6-2		11	9	Reed	Hudson		45-49	2nd	7.5
7-18	Oak.	W	3-2		3	6	Hawkins	Zito	Guardado	46-49	2nd	6.5
7-19	Oak.	W	9-4		10	9	Radke	Mulder		47-49	2nd	6.5
7-20	Oak.	W	6-4		8	9	Rogers	Lilly	Guardado	48-49	2nd	6.5
7-21	Sea.	W	5-4		13	9	Rincon	Rhodes	Guardado	49-49	2nd	5.5
7-22	Sea.	L	8-10		11	11	Mateo	Mays	Hasegawa	49-50	3rd	5.5
7-23	K.C.	L	3-8		8	11	Affeldt	Santana		49-51	3rd	6.5
7-24	K.C.	W	6-2		6	6	Hawkins	Grimsley		50-51	3rd	5.5
7-25	At Cle.	W	6-5		11	10	Hawkins	Baez	Guardado	51-51	3rd	5.5
7-26	At Cle.	L	2-9		6	17	Traber	Lohse		51-52	3rd	5.5
7-27	At Cle.	L	2-3	(14)	12	12	Betancourt	Rincon		51-53	3rd	6.5
7-29	Bal.	L	5-7		10	11	Carrasco	Hawkins	Julio	51-54	3rd	6.5
7-30	Bal.	W	5-1		8	6	Radke	Ponson		52-54	3rd	5.5
7-31	Bal.	W	10-9	(10)	19	16	Hawkins	Driskill		53-54	3rd	4.5
8-1	Det.	W	10-4		15	11	Lohse	Bonderman	Baldwin	54-54	3rd	3.5
8-2	Det.	L	2-9		11	11	Maroth	Reed		54-55	3rd	4.5
8-3	Det.	W	7-2		13	8	Santana	Roney		55-55	3rd	4.5
8-4	At Bal.	W	3-2		6	10	Radke	Moss	Guardado	56-55	3rd	4.5
8-5	At Bal.	L	2-3		6	9	Johnson	Rogers	Julio	56-56	3rd	4.5
8-6	At Bal.	W	7-3		10	11	Lohse	Hentgen		57-56	3rd	3.5
8-7	At Bal.	L	3-5		8	8	Lopez	Reed	Julio	57-57	3rd	3.5
8-8	At Det.	W	4-3		7	4	Santana	Maroth	Guardado	58-57	3rd	3.0
8-9	At Det.	W	8-4	(10)	11	11	Rincon	Mears		59-57	3rd	2.5
8-10	At Det.	W	4-3		9	7	Rogers	Cornejo	Guardado	60-57	3rd	2.5
8-11	Cle.	W	5-3		10	8	Lohse	Westbrook	Hawkins	61-57	3rd	2.5
8-12	Cle.	L	6-9		9	15	Betancourt	Baldwin		61-58	3rd	2.5
8-13	Cle.	L	0-5	(14)	8	10	Mulholland	Rincon		61-59	3rd	3.5
8-14	Cle.	L	3-8		9	14	Anderson	Radke		61-60	3rd	4.0
8-15	At K.C.	W	9-2		17	5	Rogers	Gobble		62-60	3rd	3.0
8-16	At K.C.	W	14-5		15	8	Lohse	Hernandez		63-60	T2nd	2.0
8-17	At K.C.	L	4-5		8	12	May	Reed	Leskanic	63-61	T2nd	3.0
8-19	At Cle.	W	8-2		14	8	Santana	Davis		64-61	3rd	1.5
8-20	At Cle.	W	4-3		6	9	Radke	Anderson	Guardado	65-61	3rd	0.5
8-21	K.C.	W	4-3		5	9	Rogers	Levine	Guardado	66-61	2nd	0.5
8-22	K.C.	L	2-3		8	7	May	Lohse	Affeldt	66-62	3rd	1.5
8-23	K.C.	L	3-4		13	9	Carrasco	Mays	MacDougal	66-63	3rd	2.5
8-24	K.C.	W	8-1		10	8	Santana	Lloyd		67-63	3rd	1.5
8-26	At Ana.	W	3-0		12	5	Radke	Lackey		68-63	3rd	1.5
8-27	At Ana.	L	4-5		11	12	Weber	Rincon	Percival	68-64	3rd	2.5
8-28	At Ana.	W	6-1		7	6	Lohse	Ortiz		69-64	3rd	1.5
8-29	At Tex.	W	8-5		11	10	Balfour	Thomson	Guardado	70-64	3rd	0.5
8-30	At Tex.	W	2-0		8	6	Santana	Callaway	Guardado	71-64	3rd	0.5
8-31	At Tex.	L	10-11		15	18	Cordero	Guardado		71-65	3rd	1.5

Date	Opp.	Res.	Score	(inn.*)	Hits	Opp. hits	Winning pitcher	Losing pitcher	Save	Record	Pos.	GB
9-1	Ana.	L	2-10		7	10	Lackey	Rogers		71-66	3rd	2.0
9-2	Ana.	W	12-6		14	16	Lohse	Sele		72-66	2nd	1.0
9-3	Ana.	W	6-5		8	7	Guardado	Percival		73-66	T1st	...
9-5	Tex.	W	10-7		10	10	Rincon	Callaway	Guardado	74-66	T1st	...
9-6	Tex.	W	5-2		11	7	Radke	Dickey	Guardado	75-66	T1st	...
9-7	Tex.	W	5-4	(10)	8	9	Reed	Cordero		76-66	T1st	...
9-8	At Chi.	L	2-5		10	9	Colon	Lohse		76-67	2nd	1.0
9-9	At Chi.	L	6-8		12	12	Buehrle	Pulido	Gordon	76-68	2nd	2.0
9-10	At Chi.	W	4-1		8	6	Santana	Garland	Guardado	77-68	2nd	1.0
9-11	At Chi.	W	5-2		9	9	Radke	Loaiza		78-68	T1st	...
9-12	At Cle.	L	3-4		8	8	Sabathia	Rogers	Riske	78-69	T1st	...
9-13	At Cle.	W	2-0		6	7	Lohse	Stanford	Guardado	79-69	T1st	...
9-14	At Cle.	W	5-3		8	9	Rincon	Baez	Guardado	80-69	T1st	...
9-15	At Cle.	W	13-6		12	7	Santana	Davis		81-69	1st	+0.5
9-16	Chi.	W	5-2		7	9	Radke	Loaiza		82-69	1st	+1.5
9-17	Chi.	W	4-2		6	6	Rogers	Garland	Guardado	83-69	1st	+2.5
9-18	Chi.	W	5-3		7	9	Lohse	Colon	Guardado	84-69	1st	+3.5
9-19	Det.	W	6-2		13	5	Milton	Bonderman		85-69	1st	+3.5
9-20	Det.	W	7-3		8	9	Santana	Robertson		86-69	1st	+4.5
9-21	Det.	W	6-4		12	11	Radke	Cornejo	Guardado	87-69	1st	+5.5
9-23	Cle.	W	4-1		6	8	Rogers	Westbrook	Guardado	88-69	1st	+6.0
9-24	Cle.	W	3-2		8	7	Orosco	Betancourt	Guardado	89-69	1st	+6.0
9-25	At Det.	L	4-5	(11)	6	9	Mears	Thomas		89-70	1st	+6.0
9-26	At Det.	W	5-4	(11)	12	12	Guardado	German	Hawkins	90-70	1st	+6.0
9-27	At Det.	L	8-9		15	14	Rodney	Orosco		90-71	1st	+5.0
9-28	At Det.	L	4-9		12	15	Maroth	Johnson		90-72	1st	+4.0

Monthly records: March (1-0), April (11-14), May (19-9), June (12-15), July (10-16), August (18-11), September (19-7).
*Innings, if other than nine. † First game of a doubleheader. ‡ Second game of a doubleheader.

RECORDS

2003 regular-season record: 90-72
Position: 1st in A.L. Central
Home: 48-33 **Road:** 42-39
A.L. East: 17-15 **A.L. Central:** 43-33
A.L. West: 20-16 **N.L.** 10-8
Vs. LH starters: 25-29
Vs. RH starters: 65-43
Grass: 36-39 **Artificial:** 54-33
Day: 28-24 **Night:** 62-48
1-Run: 22-20 **X-inn.:** 9-8
Doubleheaders: 0-0-0
Team record past five years: 401-406 (.497, ranks 9th in league in that span)

TEAM LEADERS

Batting average: Shannon Stewart (.322).
At-bats: Torii Hunter (581).
Runs: Torii Hunter (83).
Hits: Jacque Jones (157).
Total Bases: Torii Hunter (262).
Doubles: Doug Mientkiewicz (38).
Triples: Cristian Guzman (14).
Home runs: Torii Hunter (26).
Runs batted in: Torii Hunter (102).
Stolen bases: Cristian Guzman (18).
Slugging percentage: Matthew LeCroy (.490).
On-base percentage: Doug Mientkiewicz (.393).
Wins: Kyle Lohse, Brad Radke (14).
Earned-run average: Johan Santana (3.07).
Complete games: Brad Radke (3).
Shutouts: Kyle Lohse, Brad Radke, Rick Reed (1).
Saves: Eddie Guardado (41).
Innings pitched: Brad Radke (212.1).
Strikeouts: Johan Santana (169).

GAMES BY POSITION

Catcher: A.J. Pierzynski 135, Matthew LeCroy 22, Tom Prince 22, Rob Bowen 7.
First base: Doug Mientkiewicz 139, Matthew LeCroy 17, Todd Sears 14, Denny Hocking 10, Justin Morneau 7, Michael Cuddyer 5.
Second base: Luis Rivas 134, Denny Hocking 26, Chris Gomez 23, Alex Prieto 5, Michael Cuddyer 1, Doug Mientkiewicz 1.
Third base: Corey Koskie 131, Denny Hocking 24, Chris Gomez 18, Michael Cuddyer 7, Doug Mientkiewicz 1.
Shortstop: Cristian Guzman 141, Chris Gomez 17, Denny Hocking 17, Alex Prieto 1.
Outfield: Torii Hunter 151, Dustan Mohr 110, Jacque Jones 101, Shannon Stewart 58, Bobby Kielty 36, Lew Ford 25, Michael Cuddyer 18, Michael Restovich 17, Michael Ryan 16, Denny Hocking 8, Doug Mientkiewicz 3.
Designated hitter: Matthew LeCroy 64, Bobby Kielty 32, Jacque Jones 29, Justin Morneau 23, Michael Restovich 7, Dustan Mohr 6, Todd Sears 6, Shannon Stewart 6, Lew Ford 4, Michael Ryan 4, Torii Hunter 3, Michael Cuddyer 2, Denny Hocking 2, Tom Prince 2, Chris Gomez 1, Doug Mientkiewicz 1, Luis Rivas 1.

TOP DRAFT CHOICES

1. **Matt Moses,** 3B, Mills Goodwin H.S., Richmond.
2. **Scott Baker,** RHP, Oklahoma State.
3. **Johnny Woodard,** 1B, Cosumnes River (Calif.) JC.
4. **David Shinskie,** RHP, Mt. Carmel Area H.S., Kulpmont, Pa.
5. **Brandon McArthur,** SS, Armwood H.S., Seffner, Fla.
6. **Errol Simonitsch,** LHP, Gonzaga.
7. **Chris Schutt,** RHP, Cornell.
8. **Brandon McConnell,** RHP, Foothill H.S., Red Bluff, Calif.
9. **Kevin Culpepper,** LHP, Georgia Southern.
10. **Chris Marini,** LHP, Glendale (Ariz.) CC.

NEW YORK YANKEES

AMERICAN LEAGUE EAST DIVISION

2004 SEASON

April

SUN	MON	TUE	WED	THU	FRI	SAT
28	29	30 † TB	31 † TB	1	2	3
4	5	6 TB	7 TB	8 CHW	9 CHW	10 CHW
11 CHW	12	13 TB	14 TB	15	16 BOS	17 BOS
18 BOS	19 BOS	20 CHW	21 CHW	22 CHW	23 BOS	24 BOS
25 BOS	26	27 OAK	28 OAK	29 OAK	30 KC	

May

SUN	MON	TUE	WED	THU	FRI	SAT
						1 KC
2 KC	3	4 OAK	5 OAK	6 OAK	7 SEA	8 SEA
9 SEA	10	11 ANA	12 ANA	13 ANA	14 SEA	15 SEA
16 SEA	17	18 ANA	19 ANA	20 ANA	21 TEX	22 TEX
23 TEX	24	25 BAL	26 BAL	27 BAL	28 TB	29 TB
30 TB	31					

June

SUN	MON	TUE	WED	THU	FRI	SAT
		1 BAL	2 BAL	3 BAL	4 TEX	5 TEX
6 TEX	7	8 COL	9 COL	10 COL	11 SD	12 SD
13 SD	14	15 ARI	16 ARI	17 ARI	18 LA	19 LA
20 LA	21	22 BAL	23 BAL	24 BAL	25 NYM	26 NYM
27 NYM	28	29 BOS	30 BOS			

July

SUN	MON	TUE	WED	THU	FRI	SAT
				1 BOS	2 NYM	3 NYM
4 NYM	5 DET	6 DET	7 DET	8 TB	9 TB	10 TB
11 TB	12	13 All-Star	14	15 DET	16 DET	17 DET
18 DET	19 TB	20 TB	21 TOR	22 TOR	23 BOS	24 BOS
25 BOS	26 TOR	27 TOR	28 TOR	29 BAL	30 BAL	31 BAL

August

SUN	MON	TUE	WED	THU	FRI	SAT
1 BAL	2	3 OAK	4 OAK	5 OAK	6 TOR	7 TOR
8 TOR	9 TOR	10 TEX	11 TEX	12 TEX	13 SEA	14 SEA
15 SEA	16	17 MIN	18 MIN	19 MIN	20 ANA	21 ANA
22 ANA	23 CLE	24 CLE	25 CLE	26 TOR	27 TOR	28 TOR
29 TOR	30	31 CLE				

Sept./Oct.

SUN	MON	TUE	WED	THU	FRI	SAT
			1 CLE	2 CLE	3 BAL	4 BAL
5 BAL	6 TB	7 TB	8 TB	9 TB	10 BAL	11 BAL
12 BAL	13 KC	14 KC	15 KC	16	17 BOS	18 BOS
19 BOS	20	21 TOR	22 TOR	23 TOR	24 BOS	25 BOS
26 BOS	27	28 MIN	29 MIN	30 MIN	1 TOR	2 TOR
3 TOR	4	5	6	7	8	9

Home games shaded. All-Star Game July 13 at Houston. Schedule subject to change.

CLUB DIRECTORY

Principal owner
George M. Steinbrenner III
President
Randy Levine
Special advisers
Yogi Berra, Reggie Jackson, Clyde King
Senior vice president, general manager
Brian Cashman
Sr. vice president, baseball operations
Mark Newman
Sr. vice president, player personnel
Gordon Blakeley
Vice president, assistant g.m.
Jean Afterman
Vice president and senior adviser
Gene Michael
Vice president, scouting
Lin Garrett
Vice president, player personnel
Billy Connors
V.p., corp. and community relations
Brian Smith
Vice president, major league scouting
Damon Oppenheimer
Coordinator of minor league instruction
Rick Down
Director of media relations and publicity
Rick Cerrone

MINOR LEAGUE AFFILIATES

Class	Team	League	Manager
AAA	Columbus	International	Bucky Dent
AA	Trenton	Eastern	Stump Merrill
Advanced A	Tampa	Florida State	Bill Masse
A	Battle Creek	Midwest	Mitch Seoane
Short-Season A	Staten Island	New York-Pennsylvania	Tommy John
Rookie	Gulf Coast Yankees	Gulf Coast	Oscar Acosta

More on the Yankees at www.foxsports.com/named/FS/MLB/teams

BROADCAST INFORMATION

Radio: WCBS-AM (880).
TV: WCBS-TV (Channel 2).
Cable TV: Yankee Entertainment and Sports Network.

SPRING TRAINING

Ballpark (city): Legends Field (Tampa, Fla.).
Ticket information: 813-879-2244, 813-287-8844.

SPRING TRAINING ROSTER

Manager—Joe Torre (6).
Coaches—Don Mattingly (23), Rich Monteleone (52), Willie Randolph (30), Luis Sojo, Mel Stottlemyre (34), Roy White.

No.	PITCHERS	B/T	Ht./Wt.	Age*	2003 Clubs
	Borrell, Danny	L/L	6-3/200	25	Columbus
	Brown, Kevin	R/R	6-4/200	39	Los Angeles
52	Contreras, Jose	R/R	6-4/224	32	Columbus, Trenton, Tampa, Staten Island, New York A.L.
	DePaula, Jorge	R/R	6-1/160	25	Columbus, New York A.L.
	Gordon, Tom	R/R	5-10/190	36	Chicago A.L.
76	Graman, Alex	L/L	6-4/200	26	Columbus
	Henn, Sean	R/L	6-5/200	22	G.C. Yankees, Tampa
45	Heredia, Felix	L/L	6-0/180	28	Cincinnati, New York A.L.
31	Karsay, Steve	R/R	6-3/215	32	Did Not Play
	Lieber, Jon	L/R	6-2/230	33	Tampa, G.C. Yankees
	Marsonek, Sam	R/R	6-6/225	25	Columbus
35	Mussina, Mike	L/R	6-2/185	35	New York A.L.
	Prinz, Bret	R/R	6-2/216	26	Arizona, Lancaster, El Paso, Tucson, New York A.L., Columbus
	Proctor, Scott	R/R	6-1/200	27	Jacksonville, Las Vegas, Columbus
	Quantrill, Paul	L/R	6-1/195	35	Los Angeles
	Ramirez, Ramon	R/R	5-11/170	22	Tampa, Trenton, Columbus
42	Rivera, Mariano	R/R	6-2/170	34	New York A.L.
	Sierra, Eduardo	R/R	6-3/185	21	Kane County
	Vazquez, Javier	R/R	6-2/205	27	Montreal
	Wang, Chien-ming	R/R	6-3/200	24	G.C. Yankees, Trenton
36	White, Gabe	L/L	6-2/204	32	Cincinnati, Louisville, G.C. Yankees, Tampa, Trenton, N.Y. A.L.

No.	CATCHERS	B/T	Ht./Wt.	Age*	2003 Clubs
17	Flaherty, John	R/R	6-1/200	36	New York A.L.
20	Posada, Jorge	B/R	6-2/205	32	New York A.L.

No.	INFIELDERS	B/T	Ht./Wt.	Age*	2003 Clubs
19	Boone, Aaron	R/R	6-2/200	31	Cincinnati, New York A.L.
	Cairo, Miguel	R/R	6-1/208	29	Memphis, St. Louis
	Clark, Tony	B/R	6-7/245	31	St. Lucie, New York N.L.
25	Giambi, Jason	L/R	6-3/230	33	New York A.L.
	Henson, Drew	R/R	6-5/220	24	Columbus, New York A.L.
2	Jeter, Derek	R/R	6-3/195	29	Trenton, New York A.L.
	Phillips, Andy	R/R	6-0/205	26	Columbus
12	Soriano, Alfonso	R/R	6-1/160	26	New York A.L.
	Tejeda, Ferdin	R/R	5-11/170	21	G.C. Yankees, Tampa
14	Wilson, Enrique	B/R	5-11/195	30	New York A.L.

No.	OUTFIELDERS	B/T	Ht./Wt.	Age*	2003 Clubs
	Crosby, Bubba	L/L	5-11/185	27	Las Vegas, Los Angeles, Columbus
	Lofton, Kenny	L/L	6-0/180	36	Pittsburgh, Chicago N.L.
55	Matsui, Hideki	L/R	6-2/210	29	New York A.L.
	Sheffield, Gary	R/R	6-0/205	35	Atlanta
	Vento, Mike	R/R	6-0/195	25	Trenton, Columbus
51	Williams, Bernie	B/R	6-2/205	35	Trenton, New York A.L.

*Age as of April 1, 2004.

BALLPARK INFORMATION

Ballpark (capacity, surface)
Yankee Stadium (57,478, grass)
Address
Yankee Stadium
E. 161 St. and River Ave.
Bronx, NY 10451
Official website
www.yankees.com
Business phone
718-293-4300
Ticket information
212-307-1212, 718-293-6013
Field dimensions (from home plate)
To left field at foul line, 318 feet
To center field, 408 feet
To right field at foul line, 314 feet
First game played
April 18, 1923 (Yankees 4, Red Sox 1)

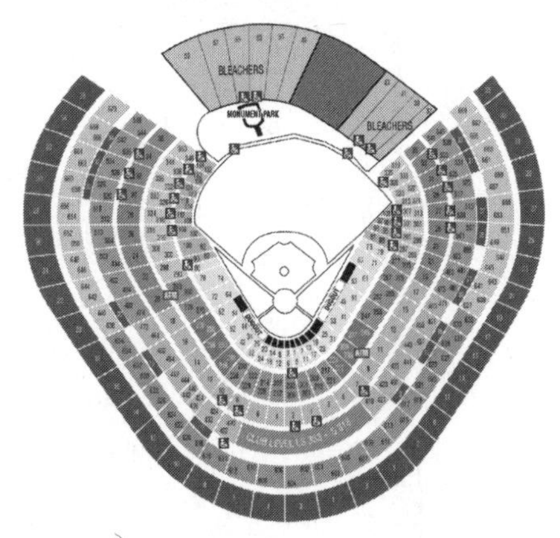

2003 REVIEW

DAY BY DAY

Date	Opp.	Res.	Score	(inn.*)	Hits	Opp. hits	Winning pitcher	Losing pitcher	Save	Record	Pos.	GB
3-31	At Tor.	W	8-4		7	9	Clemens	Halladay		1-0	T1st	...
4-1	At Tor.	W	10-1		13	8	Pettitte	Lidle		2-0	1st	+0.5
4-2	At Tor.	W	9-7		17	11	Mussina	Hendrickson	Acevedo	3-0	1st	+1.0
4-4	At T.B.	W	12-2		18	9	Wells	Parris		4-0	1st	+0.5
4-5	At T.B.	L	5-6		11	14	Carter	Osuna		4-1	1st	+0.5
4-6	At T.B.	W	10-5		15	11	Clemens	Zambrano		5-1	1st	+0.5
4-8	Min.	W	7-3		9	5	Pettitte	Mays		6-1	1st	+1.5
4-9	Min.	W	2-1		4	7	Mussina	Lohse	Acevedo	7-1	1st	+2.0
4-10	Min.	W	2-0		10	3	Wells	Reed		8-1	1st	+2.5
4-12	T.B.	W	5-4		12	9	Osuna	Harper		9-1	1st	+3.5
4-13	T.B.	L	1-2		5	10	Carter	Acevedo		9-2	1st	+2.5
4-14	Tor.	W	10-9		8	16	Contreras	Lopez	Hammond	10-2	1st	+3.0
4-15	Tor.	W	5-0		12	3	Mussina	Halladay		11-2	1st	+3.0
4-16	Tor.	L	6-7		11	17	Lidle	Hitchcock	Escobar	11-3	1st	+2.0
4-17	Tor.	W	4-0		4	5	Weaver	Walker		12-3	1st	+2.0
4-18	At Min.	W	11-4		15	9	Clemens	Radke		13-3	1st	+2.0
4-19	At Min.	W	4-2		6	9	Pettitte	Mays	Acevedo	14-3	1st	+2.0
4-20	At Min.	W	8-2		14	6	Mussina	Lohse		15-3	1st	+2.0
4-21	At Min.	W	15-1		14	7	Wells	Reed		16-3	1st	+3.0
4-22	At Ana.	W	8-3		9	10	Weaver	Lackey		17-3	1st	+3.0
4-23	At Ana.	W	9-2		18	6	Clemens	Callaway		18-3	1st	+4.0
4-24	At Ana.	L	2-6		9	10	Ortiz	Pettitte		18-4	1st	+4.0
4-25	At Tex.	W	3-2		6	7	Mussina	Lewis	Acevedo	19-4	1st	+4.0
4-26	At Tex.	W	7-5	(10)	9	8	Hammond	Urbina	Acevedo	20-4	1st	+5.0
4-27	At Tex.	L	7-10		12	15	Dickey	Weaver	Urbina	20-5	1st	+4.0
4-29	Sea.	L	0-6		7	13	Meche	Clemens		20-6	1st	+3.0
4-30	Sea.	W	8-5		9	8	Pettitte	Moyer		21-6	1st	+3.0
5-1	Sea.	W	2-1		9	6	Mussina	Pineiro	Rivera	22-6	1st	+3.0
5-2	Oak.	W	5-3		7	6	Wells	Lilly	Rivera	23-6	1st	+4.0
5-3	Oak.	L	3-5	(10)	5	14	Foulke	Acevedo		23-7	1st	+3.0
5-4	Oak.	L	0-2		4	4	Zito	Clemens	Foulke	23-8	1st	+3.0
5-6	At Sea.	L	7-12		14	15	Moyer	Pettitte		23-9	1st	+2.5
5-7	At Sea.	W	7-2		10	6	Mussina	Pineiro		24-9	1st	+2.5
5-8	At Sea.	W	16-5		17	12	Wells	Garcia		25-9	1st	+3.0
5-9	At Oak.	L	2-7		5	8	Hudson	Weaver		25-10	1st	+3.0
5-10	At Oak.	W	5-2		7	8	Clemens	Zito	Rivera	26-10	1st	+3.0
5-11	At Oak.	L	2-5		4	8	Mulder	Pettitte	Foulke	26-11	1st	+3.0
5-13	Ana.	L	3-10		7	13	Lackey	Mussina		26-12	1st	+2.0
5-14	Ana.	L	3-5		8	12	Rodriguez	Wells	Percival	26-13	1st	+1.0
5-15	Ana.	W	10-4		14	10	Weaver	Sele		27-13	1st	+1.0
5-16	Tex.	L	5-8	(12)	14	13	Dickey	Acevedo	Urbina	27-14	1st	+1.0
5-17	Tex.	L	2-5		5	8	Valdes	Pettitte	Urbina	27-15	1st	+1.0
5-18	Tex.	L	1-5		3	9	Thomson	Mussina		27-16	T1st	...
5-19	At Bos.	W	7-3		10	12	Wells	Fossum		28-16	1st	+1.0
5-20	At Bos.	L	7-10		11	11	Embree	Contreras	Lyon	28-17	T1st	...
5-21	At Bos.	W	4-2		6	9	Clemens	Wakefield	Rivera	29-17	1st	+1.0
5-22	Tor.	L	3-8		10	13	Halladay	Pettitte		29-18	1st	+0.5
5-23	Tor.	L	2-6		6	9	Escobar	Mussina		29-19	2nd	0.5
5-24	Tor.	L	2-5		6	10	Lidle	Wells	Politte	29-20	2nd	1.5
5-25	Tor.	L	3-5		12	8	Davis	Weaver	Politte	29-21	2nd	1.5
5-26	Bos.	L	4-8		5	14	Wakefield	Clemens		29-22	2nd	2.5
5-27	Bos.	W	11-3		14	7	Pettitte	Chen		30-22	2nd	1.5
5-28	Bos.	W	6-5		11	9	Rivera	Lyon		31-22	2nd	0.5
5-30	At Det.	W	6-0		10	4	Contreras	Knotts		32-22	1st	+0.5
5-31	At Det.	L	2-4		3	12	Bernero	Weaver	German	32-23	1st	+0.5
6-1	At Det.	W	10-9	(17)	14	14	Wells	Sparks	Acevedo	33-23	1st	+1.5
6-3	At Cin.	L	3-4		5	8	Reitsma	Osuna		33-24	1st	+1.0
6-4	At Cin.	L	2-6		7	9	Wilson	Mussina		33-25	2nd	0.5
6-5	At Cin.	W	10-2		16	6	Contreras	Graves		34-25	1st	+0.5
6-6	At Chi. (NL)	W	5-3		9	9	Wells	Zambrano	Rivera	35-25	1st	+1.5
6-7	At Chi. (NL)	L	2-5		6	7	Wood	Clemens		35-26	1st	+0.5
6-8	At Chi. (NL)	L	7-8		10	13	Prior	Pettitte	Borowski	35-27	2nd	0.5
6-10	Hou.	W	5-3		8	9	Mussina	Miller	Rivera	36-27	1st	+0.5
6-11	Hou.	L	0-8		0	14	Lidge	Weaver		36-28	2nd	0.5

Date	Opp.	Res.	Score	(inn.*)	Hits	Opp. hits	Winning pitcher	Losing pitcher	Save	Record	Pos.	GB
6-12	Hou.	W	6-5		12	11	Osuna	Dotel	Rivera	37-28	1st	+0.5
6-13	StL.	W	5-2		10	8	Clemens	Simontacchi	Rivera	38-28	1st	+0.5
6-14	StL.	W	13-4		15	8	Pettitte	Morris		39-28	1st	+0.5
6-15	StL.	W	5-2		7	4	Mussina	Williams	Rivera	40-28	1st	+0.5
6-17§	T.B.	L	2-11		4	18	Gonzalez	Weaver		40-29		
6-17∞	T.B.	W	10-2		14	7	Wells	Brazelton		41-29	1st	+0.5
6-18	T.B.	W	1-0	(12)	5	3	Hammond	Carter		42-29	1st	+1.5
6-20	At N.Y.	W	5-0		9	7	Pettitte	Trachsel		43-29	1st	+1.5
6-22	At N.Y.	W	7-3	(11)	10	11	Rivera	Lloyd		44-29	1st	+2.0
6-23	At T.B.	L	2-4		6	5	Zambrano	Clemens	Carter	44-30	1st	+1.0
6-24	At T.B.	W	10-9		16	13	Anderson	Carter	Rivera	45-30	1st	+2.0
6-25	At T.B.	W	8-5		7	10	Pettitte	Bell	Rivera	46-30	1st	+2.0
6-26	At T.B.	W	4-3		7	10	Mussina	Standridge	Rivera	47-30	1st	+2.0
6-27	N.Y.	W	6-4		11	12	Wells	Seo	Miceli	48-30	1st	+2.0
6-28§	N.Y.	W	7-1		11	6	Clemens	Griffiths		49-30		
6-28∞	At N.Y.	W	9-8		15	13	Claussen	Glavine	Rivera	50-30	1st	+3.5
6-29	N.Y.	W	5-3		9	4	Weaver	Leiter	Rivera	51-30	1st	+3.5
6-30	At Bal.	W	6-5		12	15	Pettitte	Ponson	Rivera	52-30	1st	+4.0
7-1	At Bal.	L	3-7		14	11	Lopez	Mussina		52-31	1st	+4.0
7-4	Bos.	L	3-10		11	15	Lowe	Wells		52-32	1st	+3.0
7-5	Bos.	L	2-10		11	10	Mendoza	Clemens		52-33	1st	+2.0
7-6	Bos.	W	7-1		14	6	Pettitte	Burkett		53-33	1st	+3.0
7-7	Bos.	W	2-1		7	3	Rivera	Kim		54-33	1st	+4.0
7-8	At Cle.	L	0-4		1	10	Traber	Weaver		54-34	1st	+3.0
7-9	At Cle.	W	6-2		7	10	Wells	Sabathia		55-34	1st	+3.0
7-10	At Cle.	L	2-3	(10)	7	10	Boyd	Hitchcock		55-35	1st	+2.0
7-11	At Tor.	W	8-5		14	9	Pettitte	Miller	Rivera	56-35	1st	+2.0
7-12	At Tor.	L	3-10		6	14	Halladay	Mussina		56-36	1st	+1.0
7-13	At Tor.	W	6-2		10	5	Weaver	Escobar		57-36	1st	+2.0
7-17	Cle.	W	5-4		7	8	Rivera	Riske		58-36	1st	+3.0
7-18	Cle.	W	10-4		11	9	Clemens	Anderson		59-36	1st	+4.0
7-19	Cle.	W	7-4		8	9	Wells	Sabathia	Rivera	60-36	1st	+4.0
7-20	Cle.	W	7-4		10	7	Mussina	Westbrook	Rivera	61-36	1st	+4.0
7-21	Tor.	L	0-8	(8)	5	15	Hendrickson	Weaver		61-37	1st	+3.0
7-23	Bal.	W	4-2		9	6	Pettitte	Helling	Rivera	62-37	1st	+2.5
7-24	Bal.	L	3-5		6	13	Ponson	Clemens	Julio	62-38	1st	+2.5
7-25	At Bos.	W	4-3		8	10	Rivera	Kim		63-38	1st	+3.5
7-26	At Bos.	L	4-5		10	9	Kim	Benitez		63-39	1st	+2.5
7-27	At Bos.	L	4-6		11	7	Fossum	Hammond	Kim	63-40	1st	+1.5
7-29	At Ana.	W	6-2		15	10	Pettitte	Appier		64-40	1st	+1.5
7-30	At Ana.	W	8-0		9	5	Clemens	Lackey		65-40	1st	+2.5
7-31	At Ana.	W	2-1	(10)	6	7	Benitez	Percival	Rivera	66-40	1st	+3.5
8-1	At Oak.	L	2-3	(10)	5	8	Foulke	Osuna		66-41	1st	+3.5
8-2	At Oak.	W	10-7		12	13	Weaver	Zito	Rivera	67-41	1st	+4.5
8-3	At Oak.	L	1-2		5	3	Mulder	Rivera		67-42	1st	+3.5
8-5	Tex.	W	6-2		9	7	Clemens	Lewis		68-42	1st	+3.5
8-6	Tex.	L	4-5		8	9	Mahay	Rivera	Cordero	68-43	1st	+2.5
8-7	Tex.	W	7-5		6	10	Mussina	Fultz	Rivera	69-43	1st	+2.5
8-8	Sea.	W	9-7		12	11	Hitchcock	Franklin	Rivera	70-43	1st	+4.0
8-9	Sea.	L	1-2		3	5	Meche	Pettitte	Hasegawa	70-44	1st	+3.0
8-10	Sea.	L	6-8		10	14	Soriano	Osuna	Hasegawa	70-45	1st	+3.0
8-11	At K.C.	L	9-12		15	14	Carrasco	Hitchcock		70-46	1st	+3.0
8-12	At K.C.	W	6-0		15	6	Mussina	May		71-46	1st	+4.0
8-13	At K.C.	L	0-11		4	16	Appier	Weaver		71-47	1st	+3.0
8-14	At Bal.	W	8-5		10	12	Pettitte	DuBose	Rivera	72-47	1st	+3.0
8-15	At Bal.	W	6-4		11	11	Nelson	Julio	Rivera	73-47	1st	+4.0
8-16	At Bal.	W	5-4	(12)	9	9	Hammond	Carrasco	Nelson	74-47	1st	+4.0
8-17	At Bal.	W	8-0		10	3	Mussina	Lopez		75-47	1st	+5.0
8-18	K.C.	W	11-6		14	9	Weaver	Lima		76-47	1st	+5.5
8-19	K.C.	W	6-3		8	9	Pettitte	Appier	Rivera	77-47	1st	+6.5
8-20	K.C.	W	8-7		13	17	Clemens	Gobble	Rivera	78-47	1st	+7.5
8-22	Bal.	L	3-4		8	12	Hentgen	Wells	Groom	78-48	1st	+6.0
8-23	Bal.	L	2-7		6	11	Lopez	Mussina		78-49	1st	+5.0
8-24	Bal.	W	7-0		8	4	Contreras	DuBose		79-49	1st	+5.0
8-25	Bal.	W	5-2		7	11	Pettitte	Moss	Rivera	80-49	1st	+5.0
8-26	Chi.	L	2-13		5	11	Loaiza	Clemens		80-50	1st	+5.0
8-27	Chi.	L	2-11		9	15	Colon	Wells		80-51	1st	+4.0
8-28	Chi.	W	7-5		7	12	Mussina	Cotts	Rivera	81-51	1st	+4.5
8-29	At Bos.	L	5-10		6	14	Lowe	Contreras		81-52	1st	+3.5
8-30	At Bos.	W	10-7		15	10	Pettitte	Martinez	Rivera	82-52	1st	+4.5
8-31	At Bos.	W	8-4		10	9	Clemens	Wakefield	Rivera	83-52	1st	+5.5

Date	Opp.	Res.	Score	(inn.*)	Hits	Opp. hits	Winning pitcher	Losing pitcher	Save	Record	Pos.	GB
9-1	At Tor.	L	1-8		4	13	Halladay	Wells		83-53	1st	+4.5
9-3	At Tor.	L	3-4		9	9	Kershner	Osuna	Lopez	83-54	1st	+3.0
9-4	At Tor.	W	3-2		7	4	Contreras	Walker	Rivera	84-54	1st	+3.5
9-5	Bos.	L	3-9		7	14	Martinez	Pettitte		84-55	1st	+2.5
9-6	Bos.	L	0-11		4	12	Wakefield	Clemens		84-56	1st	+1.5
9-7	Bos.	W	3-1		5	7	Wells	Suppan	Rivera	85-56	1st	+2.5
9-8	Tor.	W	9-3		16	8	Mussina	Escobar		86-56	1st	+3.5
9-9	Det.	W	4-2		8	8	White	Rodney	Rivera	87-56	1st	+3.5
9-10	Det.	W	15-5		12	5	Pettitte	Knotts		88-56	1st	+3.5
9-11	Det.	W	5-2		11	8	Clemens	Cornejo	Rivera	89-56	1st	+4.0
9-12	T.B.	W	10-4		17	13	Wells	Zambrano		90-56	1st	+4.0
9-13§	T.B.	W	6-5		10	14	White	Kennedy	Rivera	91-56		
9-13∞	T.B.	W	6-3		10	8	Mussina	Reyes	Rivera	92-56	1st	+5.5
9-14	T.B.	L	2-5		6	9	Harper	Heredia	Carter	92-57	1st	+5.5
9-15	At Bal.	W	13-1		15	10	Pettitte	Lopez		93-57	1st	+5.5
9-16	At Bal.	W	6-3		9	7	Clemens	Johnson	Rivera	94-57	1st	+5.5
9-17	At Bal.	L	3-5		11	7	DuBose	Wells	Julio	94-58	1st	+5.5
9-18	At Bal.	T	1-1	(5)	5	5				94-58	1st	+5.0
9-19	At T.B.	W	2-1		9	4	Contreras	Waechter	Rivera	95-58	1st	+5.0
9-20	At T.B.	W	7-1		10	9	Pettitte	Sosa		96-58	1st	+6.0
9-21	At T.B.	W	6-0		10	4	Clemens	Gonzalez		97-58	1st	+6.0
9-22	At Chi.	L	3-6	(10)	9	12	Gordon	White		97-59	1st	+5.0
9-23	At Chi.	W	7-0		12	5	Contreras	Buehrle		98-59	1st	+5.0
9-24	At Chi.	L	4-9		8	12	Loaiza	Mussina		98-60	1st	+5.0
9-26†	Bal.	W	11-2		14	8	Pettitte	Moss		99-60		
9-26‡	Bal.	L	2-3	(10)	8	5	Ligtenberg	Hammond	Julio	99-61	1st	+4.0
9-27	Bal.	W	6-2		14	4	Clemens	Johnson		100-61	1st	+5.0
9-28	Bal.	W	3-1		5	6	Wells	DuBose	Rivera	101-61	1st	+6.0

Monthly records: March (1-0), April (20-6), May (11-17), June (20-7), July (14-10), August (17-12), September (18-9).
*Innings, if other than nine. † First game of a doubleheader. ‡ Second game of a doubleheader. § Day separate admission. ∞ Night separate admission.

RECORDS

2003 regular-season record: 101-61
Position: 1st in A.L. East
Home: 50-32 **Road:** 51-29
A.L. East: 47-29 **A.L. Central:** 23-9
A.L. West: 18-18 N.L. 13-5
Vs. LH starters: 26-11
Vs. RH starters: 75-50
Grass: 83-56 **Artificial:** 18-5
Day: 35-26 **Night:** 66-35
1-Run: 22-14 **X-inn.:** 6-6
Doubleheaders: 0-0-1
Team record past five years: 484-322 (.600, ranks 1st in league in that span)

TEAM LEADERS

Batting average: Derek Jeter (.324).
At-bats: Alfonso Soriano (682).
Runs: Alfonso Soriano (114).
Hits: Alfonso Soriano (198).
Total Bases: Alfonso Soriano (358).
Doubles: Hideki Matsui (42).
Triples: Alfonso Soriano (5).
Home runs: Jason Giambi (41).
Runs batted in: Jason Giambi (107).
Stolen bases: Alfonso Soriano (35).
Slugging percentage: Jason Giambi (.527).
On-base percentage: Nick Johnson (.422).
Wins: Andy Pettitte (21).
Earned-run average: Mike Mussina (3.40).
Complete games: David Wells (4).
Shutouts: Roger Clemens, Mike Mussina, David Wells (1).
Saves: Mariano Rivera (40).
Innings pitched: Mike Mussina (214.2).
Strikeouts: Mike Mussina (195).

GAMES BY POSITION

Catcher: Jorge Posada 137, John Flaherty 40, Michel Hernandez 5.
First base: Jason Giambi 85, Nick Johnson 60, Todd Zeile 23, Fernando Seguignol 3, Luis Sojo 1.
Second base: Alfonso Soriano 155, Enrique Wilson 10, Luis Sojo 1, Robin Ventura 1.
Third base: Robin Ventura 80, Aaron Boone 54, Todd Zeile 30, Enrique Wilson 17, Drew Henson 3.
Shortstop: Derek Jeter 118, Enrique Wilson 33, Erick Almonte 31.
Outfield: Hideki Matsui 159, Bernie Williams 115, Raul Mondesi 97, Juan Rivera 56, Karim Garcia 50, David Dellucci 18, Ruben Sierra 17, Charles Gipson 8, Curtis Pride 3, Bubba Trammell 3, Chris Latham 2.
Designated hitter: Jason Giambi 69, Nick Johnson 34, Ruben Sierra 32, Bubba Trammell 15, Todd Zeile 8, Hideki Matsui 4, Robin Ventura 4, Bernie Williams 4, Charles Gipson 3, David Dellucci 2, Jorge Posada 2, Karim Garcia 1, Chris Latham 1, Raul Mondesi 1, Fernando Seguignol 1, Luis Sojo 1, Enrique Wilson 1.

TOP DRAFT CHOICES

1. **Eric Duncan,** 3B, Seton Hall Prep, Florham Park, N.J.
2. **Estee Harris,** OF, Islip H.S., Central Islip, N.Y.
3. **Tim Battle,** OF, McIntosh H.S., Peachtree City, Ga.
4. **Steven White,** RHP, Baylor.
5. **Cory Stuart,** RHP, U. of British Columbia.
6. **Jason Stephens,** RHP, Tallmadge (Ohio) H.S.
7. **Jose Perez,** OF, Oceanside (Calif.) H.S.
8. **Josh Smith,** RHP, Texas.
9. **Tyler Clippard,** RHP, J.W. Mitchell H.S., Trinity, Fla.
10. **T.J. Beam,** RHP, Mississippi.

OAKLAND ATHLETICS
AMERICAN LEAGUE WEST DIVISION

2004 SEASON

April

SUN	MON	TUE	WED	THU	FRI	SAT
4	5 TEX	6 TEX	7 TEX	8	9 SEA	10 SEA
11 SEA	12	13 TEX	14 TEX	15 TEX	16 ANA	17 ANA
18 ANA	19 SEA	20 SEA	21 SEA	22 SEA	23 ANA	24 ANA
25 ANA	26	27 NYY	28 NYY	29 NYY	30 TB	

May

SUN	MON	TUE	WED	THU	FRI	SAT
						1 TB
2 TB	3	4 NYY	5 NYY	6 NYY	7 MIN	8 MIN
9 MIN	10	11 DET	12 DET	13 DET	14 KC	15 KC
16 KC	17	18 DET	19 DET	20 DET	21 KC	22 KC
23 KC	24	25 BOS	26 BOS	27 BOS	28 CLE	29 CLE
30 CLE	31					

June

SUN	MON	TUE	WED	THU	FRI	SAT
		1 CHW	2 CHW	3 TOR	4 TOR	5 TOR
6 TOR	7 CIN	8 CIN	9 CIN	10	11 PIT	12 PIT
13 PIT	14	15 STL	16 STL	17 STL	18 CHC	19 CHC
20 CHC	21 ANA	22 ANA	23 ANA	24 ANA	25 SF	26 SF
27 SF	28	29 ANA	30 ANA			

July

SUN	MON	TUE	WED	THU	FRI	SAT
				1 ANA	2 SF	3 SF
4 SF	5	6 BOS	7 BOS	8 BOS	9 CLE	10 CLE
11 CLE	12	13 All-Star	14	15 CHW	16 CHW	17 CHW
18 CHW	19 TOR	20 TOR	21 SEA	22 SEA	23 TEX	24 TEX
25 TEX	26 SEA	27 SEA	28 SEA	29 TEX	30 TEX	31 TEX

August

SUN	MON	TUE	WED	THU	FRI	SAT
1 TEX	2	3 NYY	4 NYY	5 NYY	6 MIN	7 MIN
8 MIN	9 MIN	10 DET	11 DET	12 DET	13 KC	14 KC
15 KC	16 BAL	17 BAL	18 BAL	19	20 TB	21 TB
22 TB	23 BAL	24 BAL	25 BAL	26 BAL	27 TB	28 TB
29 TB	30	31 CHW				

Sept./Oct.

SUN	MON	TUE	WED	THU	FRI	SAT
			1 CHW	2 CHW	3 TOR	4 TOR
5 TOR	6 BOS	7 BOS	8 BOS	9	10 CLE	11 CLE
12 CLE	13 TEX	14 TEX	15 TEX	16 TEX	17 SEA	18 SEA
19 SEA	20	21 TEX	22 TEX	23 TEX	24 ANA	25 ANA
26 ANA	27 SEA	28 SEA	29 SEA	30 SEA	1 ANA	2 ANA
3 ANA	4	5	6	7	8	9

Home games shaded. All-Star Game July 13 at Houston. Schedule subject to change.

CLUB DIRECTORY

Owners
Stephen C. Schott
Ken Hofmann
President
Michael P. Crowley
Vice president and general manager
Billy Beane
Assistant general manager
Paul DePodesta
Special assistants to general manager
Randy Johnson
Matt Keough
Director of player development
Keith Lieppman
Director of scouting
Eric Kubota
Director of minor league operations
Ted Polakowski
V.p., broadcasting and communications
Ken Pries
Director of public relations
Jim Young
Baseball information manager
Mike Selleck

MINOR LEAGUE AFFILIATES

Class	Team	League	Manager
AAA	Sacramento	Pacific Coast	Tony DeFrancesco
AA	Midland	Texas	Webster Garrison
Advanced A	Modesto	California	Von Hayes
A	Kane County	Midwest	Dave Joppie
Short-Season A	Vancouver	Northwest	Dennis Rogers
Rookie	Scottsdale A's	Arizona	Ruben Escalera

BROADCAST INFORMATION

Radio: KFRC-AM (610).
TV: KICU-TV (Channel 36).
Cable TV: Fox Sports Bay Area.

SPRING TRAINING

Ballpark (city): Phoenix Stadium (Phoenix, Ariz.).
Ticket information: 602-392-0074.

More on the Athletics at www.foxsports.com/named/FS/MLB/teams

SPRING TRAINING ROSTER

Manager—Ken Macha (39).
Coaches—Brad Fischer (35), Bob Geren (52), Dave Hudgens (48), Chris Speier, Ron Washington (38), Curt Young.

No.	PITCHERS	B/T	Ht./Wt.	Age*	2003 Clubs
53	Bradford, Chad	R/R	6-5/203	29	Oakland
	Brooks, Frank	L/L	6-1/200	25	Reading, Altoona, Nashville
	Duchscherer, J.	R/R	6-3/190	26	Sacramento, Oakland
	Hammond, Chris	L/L	6-1/190	38	New York A.L.
40	Harden, Rich	L/R	6-1/180	22	Midland, Sacramento, Oakland
32	Harville, Chad	R/R	5-9/185	27	Sacramento, Oakland
15	Hudson, Tim	R/R	6-1/164	28	Oakland
	Lehr, Justin	R/R	6-1/200	26	Sacramento
45	Mecir, Jim	B/R	6-1/230	33	Sacramento, Oakland
20	Mulder, Mark	L/L	6-6/208	26	Oakland
	Ramos, Mario	L/L	5-11/180	26	Texas, Oklahoma, Frisco
	Redman, Mark	L/L	6-5/245	30	Florida
	Rheinecker, John	L/L	6-2/215	24	Sacramento, Midland
	Rhodes, Arthur	L/L	6-2/212	34	Seattle
73	Rincon, Ricardo	L/L	5-9/190	33	Oakland
	Wood, Mike	R/R	6-3/180	23	Sacramento, Oakland
75	Zito, Barry	L/L	6-4/215	25	Oakland

No.	CATCHERS	B/T	Ht./Wt.	Age*	2003 Clubs
	Melhuse, Adam	B/R	6-2/200	32	Sacramento, Oakland
	Miller, Damian	R/R	6-3/220	34	Chicago N.L.

No.	INFIELDERS	B/T	Ht./Wt.	Age*	2003 Clubs
	Bynum, Freddie	L/R	6-1/180	24	Midland
3	Chavez, Eric	L/R	6-1/206	26	Oakland
	Crosby, Bobby	R/R	6-3/195	24	Sacramento, Oakland
44	Durazo, Erubiel	L/L	6-3/240	29	Oakland
14	Ellis, Mark	R/R	5-11/180	26	Oakland
	German, Esteban	R/R	5-9/165	26	Sacramento, Oakland
10	Hatteberg, Scott	L/R	6-1/210	34	Oakland
	Johnson, Dan	L/R	6-2/220	24	Sacramento, Midland
	Koonce, Graham	L/L	6-4/225	28	Sacramento, Oakland
	Menechino, Frank	R/R	5-8/198	33	Oakland
	Rouse, Mike	L/R	5-11/185	23	Midland, Sacramento
	Scutaro, Marco	R/R	5-10/170	28	Norfolk, New York N.L.

No.	OUTFIELDERS	B/T	Ht./Wt.	Age*	2003 Clubs
22	Byrnes, Eric	R/R	6-2/210	28	Oakland
24	Dye, Jermaine	R/R	6-5/220	30	Sacramento, Oakland
	Edwards, Mike	R/R	6-1/185	27	Sacramento, Oakland
	Grabowski, Jason	L/R	6-3/200	27	Ariz. Athletics, Sacramento, Oakland
	Kielty, Bobby	B/R	6-1/225	27	Minnesota, Toronto
	Kotsay, Mark	L/L	6-0/201	28	San Diego
13	McMillon, Billy	L/L	5-11/195	32	Sacramento, Oakland
	Watson, Matt	L/R	5-11/200	25	St. Lucie, Binghamton, Norfolk, Brooklyn, New York N.L.

Invited to spring training: RHP Eric Cammack, RHP Wayne Gomes, IF Ramon Castro.

*Age as of April 1, 2004.

BALLPARK INFORMATION

Ballpark (capacity, surface)
The Network Associates Coliseum (43,662, grass)

Address
Oakland Athletics
7000 Coliseum Way
Oakland, CA 94621

Official website
www.oaklandathletics.com

Business phone
510-638-4900

Ticket information
510-638-4627

Field dimensions (from home plate)
To left field at foul line, 330 feet
To center field, 400 feet
To right field at foul line, 330 feet

First game played
April 17, 1968 (Orioles 4, Athletics 1)

2003 REVIEW
DAY BY DAY

Date	Opp.	Res.	Score	(inn.*)	Hits	Opp. hits	Winning pitcher	Losing pitcher	Save	Record	Pos.	GB
4-1	Sea.	W	5-0		8	5	Hudson	Garcia		1-0	1st	+0.5
4-2	Sea.	W	8-3		9	6	Zito	Moyer		2-0	1st	+0.5
4-3	Sea.	L	6-7	(11)	10	12	Nelson	Rincon		2-1	T1st	...
4-4	Ana.	W	7-3		10	4	Lilly	Appier	Bradford	3-1	1st	+1.0
4-5	Ana.	W	4-2		8	7	Halama	Washburn	Foulke	4-1	1st	+2.0
4-6	Ana.	W	7-6		11	9	Bradford	Rodriguez	Foulke	5-1	1st	+2.0
4-8	At Tex.	W	2-1		10	5	Zito	Yan	Foulke	6-1	1st	+2.0
4-9	At Tex.	W	13-5		13	11	Mulder	Valdes		7-1	1st	+3.0
4-10	At Tex.	L	4-5		6	11	Cordero	Bradford	Urbina	7-2	1st	+3.0
4-11	At Ana.	L	5-9		9	16	Lackey	Hudson	Rodriguez	7-3	1st	+2.0
4-12	At Ana.	L	4-9		8	10	Weber	Halama		7-4	1st	+1.0
4-13	At Ana.	L	2-8		5	9	Ortiz	Zito	Shields	7-5	T1st	...
4-14	At Sea.	L	3-4		7	9	Pineiro	Mulder	Sasaki	7-6	T1st	...
4-15	At Sea.	L	3-5		6	11	Rhodes	Bowie	Sasaki	7-7	T2nd	1.0
4-16	At Sea.	W	4-1		6	5	Hudson	Garcia	Foulke	8-7	T1st	...
4-17	At Sea.	L	3-4	(10)	8	10	Nelson	Fikac		8-8	T2nd	1.0
4-18	Tex.	W	9-0		12	6	Zito	Thomson		9-8	2nd	1.0
4-19	Tex.	W	12-2		15	5	Mulder	Valdes		10-8	T1st	...
4-20	Tex.	L	1-2		5	8	Lewis	Bradford	Urbina	10-9	2nd	1.0
4-22	Det.	W	6-5	(11)	13	6	Rincon	Ledezma		11-9	2nd	1.0
4-23	Det.	L	1-4		3	7	Bonderman	Zito	Anderson	11-10	2nd	2.0
4-24	Det.	W	2-0		8	3	Mulder	Cornejo		12-10	2nd	2.0
4-25	Cle.	W	5-2		11	6	Lilly	Davis	Foulke	13-10	2nd	2.0
4-26	Cle.	W	6-3		14	3	Bradford	Mulholland	Foulke	14-10	2nd	1.0
4-27	Cle.	W	4-3		8	8	Rincon	Baez		15-10	2nd	1.0
4-29	At Chi.	W	3-2		6	5	Zito	Colon	Foulke	16-10	2nd	1.0
4-30	At Chi.	W	4-1		9	4	Mulder	Buehrle		17-10	T1st	...
5-1	At Chi.	L	5-7		7	13	Garland	Halama	Marte	17-11	T1st	...
5-2	At N.Y.	L	3-5		6	7	Wells	Lilly	Rivera	17-12	2nd	1.0
5-3	At N.Y.	W	5-3	(10)	14	5	Foulke	Acevedo		18-12	2nd	1.0
5-4	At N.Y.	W	2-0		4	4	Zito	Clemens	Foulke	19-12	2nd	1.0
5-6	Chi.	W	6-0		7	5	Mulder	Buehrle		20-12	2nd	1.0
5-7	Chi.	L	4-8		5	14	Loaiza	Lilly	Marte	20-13	2nd	1.0
5-8	Chi.	W	8-5		14	11	Halama	Garland	Foulke	21-13	T1st	...
5-9	N.Y.	W	7-2		8	5	Hudson	Weaver		22-13	T1st	...
5-10	N.Y.	L	2-5		8	7	Clemens	Zito	Rivera	22-14	T1st	...
5-11	N.Y.	W	5-2		8	4	Mulder	Pettitte	Foulke	23-14	T1st	...
5-13	At Det.	W	3-1		6	4	Lilly	Maroth	Foulke	24-14	T1st	...
5-14	At Det.	L	1-2		6	8	Avery	Rincon		24-15	T1st	...
5-15	At Det.	W	11-2		12	5	Zito	Bernero		25-15	T1st	...
5-16	At Cle.	L	2-3		4	7	Traber	Mulder	Baez	25-16	2nd	1.0
5-17	At Cle.	L	2-4		4	5	Mulholland	Rincon	Baez	25-17	2nd	2.0
5-18	At Cle.	W	8-5		13	6	Foulke	Baez		26-17	2nd	2.0
5-20	Min.	W	4-1		13	6	Hudson	Reed	Foulke	27-17	2nd	2.0
5-21	Min.	L	3-4		10	9	Hawkins	Bradford	Guardado	27-18	2nd	2.0
5-22	Min.	L	5-6		6	14	Mays	Halama	Guardado	27-19	2nd	3.0
5-23	K.C.	W	4-1		12	8	Mulder	Snyder		28-19	2nd	3.0
5-24	K.C.	L	1-3		7	3	Wilson	Lilly	MacDougal	28-20	2nd	3.0
5-25	K.C.	W	4-3	(10)	7	8	Foulke	Carrasco		29-20	2nd	2.0
5-27	At Min.	L	3-4		8	3	Romero	Zito	Guardado	29-21	2nd	3.0
5-28	At Min.	L	5-6		13	6	Mays	Halama	Guardado	29-22	2nd	4.0
5-29	At K.C.	W	6-1		10	9	Mulder	Snyder		30-22	2nd	4.0
5-30	At K.C.	L	6-11		11	14	Wilson	Hudson		30-23	2nd	5.0
5-31	At K.C.	W	7-6		7	10	Mecir	MacDougal	Foulke	31-23	2nd	5.0
6-1	At K.C.	W	6-4		9	9	Bradford	DeHart	Foulke	32-23	2nd	5.0
6-3	At Fla.	L	2-13		8	18	Penny	Mulder		32-24	2nd	6.0
6-4	At Fla.	W	6-5		9	8	Bradford	Spooneybarger	Foulke	33-24	2nd	6.0
6-5	At Fla.	L	0-2		7	7	Willis	Lilly	Looper	33-25	2nd	7.0
6-6	At Phi.	W	7-4		7	10	Zito	Myers		34-25	2nd	6.0
6-8†	At Phi.	L	1-7		7	11	Millwood	Mulder		34-26		
6-8‡	At Phi.	L	3-8		5	9	Wolf	Harang		34-27	2nd	8.0
6-10	Atl.	W	4-3	(12)	9	7	Bradford	Bong		35-27	2nd	7.0
6-11	Atl.	L	6-11		12	13	Ramirez	Lilly		35-28	2nd	7.0
6-12	Atl.	L	2-4		6	7	Reynolds	Zito	Smoltz	35-29	2nd	8.0
6-13	Mon.	W	8-4		8	10	Mulder	Ohka		36-29	2nd	8.0

Date	Opp.	Res.	Score	(inn.*)	Hits	Opp. hits	Winning pitcher	Losing pitcher	Save	Record	Pos.	GB
6-14	Mon.	W	5-4		8	13	Rincon	Ayala	Foulke	37-29	2nd	7.0
6-15	Mon.	W	9-1		9	6	Hudson	Vazquez		38-29	2nd	7.0
6-17	Tex.	W	4-3		6	6	Lilly	Santos	Foulke	39-29	2nd	7.5
6-18	Tex.	W	4-3	(11)	11	9	Foulke	Dickey		40-29	2nd	7.5
6-19	Tex.	W	9-2		14	11	Mulder	Ramos		41-29	2nd	6.5
6-20	S.F	W	5-3		9	9	Harang	Moss	Foulke	42-29	2nd	5.5
6-21	S.F	L	4-6		8	11	Williams	Hudson	Worrell	42-30	2nd	6.5
6-22	S.F	W	6-5		7	9	Lilly	Zerbe	Foulke	43-30	2nd	5.5
6-23	At Tex.	W	3-1		6	5	Rincon	Urbina	Foulke	44-30	2nd	5.0
6-24	At Tex.	L	6-7		10	12	Ramos	Mulder	Urbina	44-31	2nd	6.0
6-25	At Tex.	L	8-9		16	15	Cordero	Mecir	Urbina	44-32	2nd	6.0
6-26	At Tex.	W	13-0		15	4	Hudson	Valdes		45-32	2nd	6.0
6-27	At S.F	L	0-6		7	9	Williams	Lilly		45-33	2nd	7.0
6-28	At S.F	L	7-8	(10)	13	17	Rodriguez	Foulke		45-34	2nd	7.0
6-29	At S.F	W	5-2		11	7	Mulder	Foppert	Foulke	46-34	2nd	6.0
6-30	Sea.	L	1-3		6	7	Moyer	Harang	Nelson	46-35	2nd	7.0
7-1	Sea.	W	3-2	(11)	9	8	Foulke	Nelson		47-35	2nd	6.0
7-2	Sea.	L	0-13		3	20	Pineiro	Lilly		47-36	2nd	7.0
7-3	Sea.	W	5-2		11	10	Zito	Franklin	Foulke	48-36	2nd	6.0
7-4	Ana.	L	0-1		2	3	Sele	Mulder	Percival	48-37	2nd	6.0
7-5	Ana.	L	3-6		6	11	Ortiz	Harang	Percival	48-38	2nd	7.0
7-6	Ana.	W	6-5		9	8	Foulke	Schoeneweis		49-38	2nd	6.0
7-8	T.B.	L	3-9		6	19	Bell	Zito		49-39	2nd	7.0
7-9	T.B.	W	6-3		11	9	Rincon	Colome	Foulke	50-39	2nd	6.0
7-10	T.B.	W	5-2		12	5	Mulder	Sosa		51-39	2nd	5.0
7-11	Bal.	W	2-0		5	3	Hudson	Lopez		52-39	2nd	5.0
7-12	Bal.	W	5-3		5	8	Mecir	Carrasco	Foulke	53-39	2nd	4.0
7-13	Bal.	W	1-0		6	4	Foulke	Carrasco		54-39	2nd	4.0
7-17	At Min.	L	2-6		9	11	Reed	Hudson		54-40	2nd	4.0
7-18	At Min.	L	2-3		6	3	Hawkins	Zito	Guardado	54-41	2nd	5.0
7-19	At Min.	L	4-9		9	10	Radke	Mulder		54-42	2nd	5.0
7-20	At Min.	L	4-6		9	8	Rogers	Lilly	Guardado	54-43	2nd	5.0
7-21	At K.C.	W	6-1		5	4	Rincon	Lowe		55-43	2nd	4.0
7-22	At K.C.	W	10-0		13	3	Hudson	Wilson		56-43	2nd	4.0
7-23	At Sea.	L	0-6		2	6	Franklin	Zito		56-44	2nd	5.0
7-24	At Sea.	W	3-0		6	7	Mulder	Meche	Foulke	57-44	2nd	4.0
7-25	At Ana.	W	3-2		10	8	Lilly	Donnelly	Foulke	58-44	2nd	4.0
7-26	At Ana.	W	8-1		15	10	Harden	Sele		59-44	2nd	4.0
7-27	At Ana.	W	10-1		13	4	Hudson	Ortiz		60-44	2nd	3.0
7-28	At Ana.	L	1-2		6	7	Donnelly	Rincon	Percival	60-45	2nd	3.0
7-29	Cle.	W	6-2		9	8	Mulder	Anderson	Foulke	61-45	2nd	3.0
7-30	Cle.	L	2-4		11	8	Sabathia	Lilly	Baez	61-46	2nd	4.0
7-31	Cle.	W	3-1		5	6	Harden	Westbrook	Foulke	62-46	2nd	4.0
8-1	N.Y.	W	3-2	(10)	8	5	Foulke	Osuna		63-46	2nd	3.0
8-2	N.Y.	L	7-10		13	12	Weaver	Zito	Rivera	63-47	2nd	4.0
8-3	N.Y.	W	2-1		3	5	Mulder	Rivera		64-47	2nd	4.0
8-5	At Det.	W	7-2		9	10	Harden	Cornejo		65-47	2nd	4.0
8-6	At Det.	W	9-3		14	7	Hudson	Ledezma		66-47	2nd	3.0
8-7	At Det.	L	2-3		6	6	Bonderman	Zito	Patterson	66-48	2nd	3.0
8-8	At Chi.	L	2-3		5	10	Buehrle	Mulder		66-49	2nd	3.0
8-9	At Chi.	W	7-2		13	9	Bradford	Garland		67-49	2nd	3.0
8-10	At Chi.	L	1-5		4	10	Loaiza	Harden		67-50	2nd	4.0
8-11	Bos.	W	4-0		6	2	Hudson	Martinez		68-50	2nd	3.0
8-12	Bos.	W	5-3		7	8	Zito	Burkett	Foulke	69-50	2nd	3.0
8-13	Bos.	L	3-7		9	11	Lowe	Mulder		69-51	2nd	4.0
8-14	Bos.	L	2-4	(10)	7	6	Kim	Mecir		69-52	2nd	4.0
8-15	Tor.	L	5-8		10	11	Towers	Harden	Miller	69-53	2nd	5.0
8-16	Tor.	W	6-4		8	7	Hudson	Hendrickson	Foulke	70-53	2nd	4.0
8-17	Tor.	W	7-3		12	5	Zito	Halladay	Foulke	71-53	2nd	4.0
8-19	At Bos.	W	3-2		3	7	Rincon	Williamson	Foulke	72-53	2nd	4.0
8-20	At Bos.	W	8-6		11	17	Bradford	Kim	Foulke	73-53	2nd	3.0
8-21	At Bos.	L	5-14		9	12	Fossum	Harden		73-54	2nd	3.0
8-22	At Tor.	L	3-6		9	10	Halladay	Zito	Lopez	73-55	2nd	3.0
8-23	At Tor.	W	11-5		13	8	Wood	Sturtze		74-55	2nd	2.0
8-24	At Tor.	W	17-2		19	7	Hudson	Escobar	Neu	75-55	2nd	1.0
8-25	At Tor.	W	8-6		14	11	Lilly	Lidle	Foulke	76-55	T1st	...
8-26	Bal.	W	2-1	(12)	9	5	Wood	Parrish		77-55	T1st	...
8-27	Bal.	W	6-2		9	5	Zito	Hentgen		78-55	1st	+1.0
8-28	Bal.	W	6-4		8	9	Halama	Lopez	Foulke	79-55	1st	+2.0
8-29	T.B.	W	5-2		7	7	Hudson	Kennedy	Foulke	80-55	1st	+2.0
8-30	T.B.	W	4-2		6	5	Lilly	Bell	Foulke	81-55	1st	+2.0
8-31	T.B.	W	4-3		4	6	Harden	Gonzalez	Bradford	82-55	1st	+2.0

Date	Opp.	Res.	Score	(inn.*)	Hits	Opp. hits	Winning pitcher	Losing pitcher	Save	Record	Pos.	GB
9-2	At Bal.	W	2-0	(12)	5	7	Rincon	Julio	Foulke	83-55	1st	+2.0
9-3	At Bal.	L	0-9		7	13	Lopez	Hudson		83-56	1st	+2.0
9-4	At Bal.	L	5-7		10	10	Carrasco	Halama	Julio	83-57	1st	+2.0
9-5	At T.B.	W	3-1		10	4	Lilly	Gonzalez	Foulke	84-57	1st	+2.0
9-6	At T.B.	L	4-7		9	11	Bell	Harden	Carter	84-58	1st	+2.0
9-7	At T.B.	L	2-11		9	9	Zambrano	Zito		84-59	1st	+2.0
9-8	Ana.	L	1-3		7	11	Rodriguez	Hudson	Percival	84-60	1st	+1.5
9-9	Ana.	W	8-1		8	6	Duchscherer	Bootcheck		85-60	1st	+2.5
9-10	Ana.	W	3-0		8	7	Lilly	Washburn	Foulke	86-60	1st	+2.5
9-11	Ana.	W	14-4		11	9	Harden	Shields		87-60	1st	+2.5
9-12	At Tex.	W	9-3		11	7	Zito	Drese	Foulke	88-60	1st	+2.5
9-13	At Tex.	W	9-3		13	11	Hudson	Dickey		89-60	1st	+2.5
9-14	At Tex.	W	6-5		7	12	Harville	Garcia	Foulke	90-60	1st	+3.5
9-15	At Ana.	W	7-4		11	8	Lilly	Ortiz	Foulke	91-60	1st	+4.5
9-16	At Ana.	L	5-6		12	9	Turnbow	Mecir		91-61	1st	+4.5
9-17	At Ana.	W	2-1		4	2	Zito	Shields	Mecir	92-61	1st	+4.5
9-19	Sea.	L	1-6		4	14	Franklin	Hudson		92-62	1st	+4.0
9-20	Sea.	L	3-9		6	17	Pineiro	Duchscherer		92-63	1st	+3.0
9-21	Sea.	W	12-0		15	4	Lilly	Meche		93-63	1st	+4.0
9-22	Tex.	W	7-3		11	6	Zito	Mounce		94-63	1st	+4.0
9-23	Tex.	W	4-3	(10)	12	9	Foulke	Cordero		95-63	1st	+5.0
9-24	Tex.	W	5-3		7	7	Hudson	Mahay	Harville	96-63	1st	+6.0
9-26	At Sea.	L	3-9		7	15	Pineiro	Wood	Mateo	96-64	1st	+5.0
9-27	At Sea.	L	4-7		7	12	Franklin	Bradford	Hasegawa	96-65	1st	+4.0
9-28	At Sea.	L	3-9		8	12	Moyer	Lilly		96-66	1st	+3.0

Monthly records: April (17-10), May (14-13), June (15-12), July (16-11), August (20-9), September (14-11).
*Innings, if other than nine. † First game of a doubleheader. ‡ Second game of a doubleheader.

RECORDS

2003 regular-season record: 96-66
Position: 1st in A.L. West
Home: 57-24 **Road:** 39-42
A.L. East: 28-13 **A.L. Central:** 25-20
A.L. West: 34-24 N.L. 9-9
Vs. LH starters: 26-19
Vs. RH starters: 70-47
Grass: 91-55 **Artificial:** 5-11
Day: 39-24 **Night:** 57-42
1-Run: 25-20 **X-inn.:** 10-4
Doubleheaders: 0-1-0
Team record past five years: 479-330 (.592, ranks 2nd in league in that span)

TEAM LEADERS

Batting average: Eric Chavez (.282).
At-bats: Miguel Tejada (636).
Runs: Miguel Tejada (98).
Hits: Miguel Tejada (177).
Total Bases: Eric Chavez (302).
Doubles: Miguel Tejada (42).
Triples: Eric Byrnes (9).
Home runs: Eric Chavez (29).
Runs batted in: Miguel Tejada (106).
Stolen bases: Eric Byrnes, Miguel Tejada (10).
Slugging percentage: Eric Chavez (.514).
On-base percentage: Erubiel Durazo (.374).
Wins: Tim Hudson (16).
Earned-run average: Tim Hudson (2.70).
Complete games: Mark Mulder (9).
Shutouts: Tim Hudson, Mark Mulder (2).
Saves: Keith Foulke (43).
Innings pitched: Tim Hudson (240.0).
Strikeouts: Tim Hudson (162).

GAMES BY POSITION

Catcher: Ramon Hernandez 139, Adam Melhuse 33, Mark Johnson 13.
First base: Scott Hatteberg 128, Erubiel Durazo 33, Graham Koonce 5, Dave McCarty 3, Billy McMillon 3, Adam Melhuse 1, Adam Piatt 1.
Second base: Mark Ellis 153, Frank Menechino 22, Esteban German 5.
Third base: Eric Chavez 154, Frank Menechino 19, Adam Melhuse 2, Jason Grabowski 1.
Shortstop: Miguel Tejada 162, Bobby Crosby 9, Frank Menechino 3.
Outfield: Terrence Long 137, Eric Byrnes 117, Chris Singleton 113, Jermaine Dye 61, Jose Guillen 44, Adam Piatt 38, Billy McMillon 36, Ron Gant 9, Dave McCarty 5, Jason Grabowski 3, Mike Edwards 2.
Designated hitter: Erubiel Durazo 121, Scott Hatteberg 15, Billy McMillon 9, Ron Gant 6, Jermaine Dye 3, Eric Byrnes 2, Bobby Crosby 2, Mike Edwards 2, Adam Piatt 2, Jason Grabowski 1, Jose Guillen 1, Terrence Long 1, Frank Menechino 1.

TOP DRAFT CHOICES

1a. **Brad Sullivan,** RHP, Houston.
1b. **Brian Snyder,** 3B, Stetson.
1c. **Omar Quintanilla,** SS, Texas.
2. **Andre Ethier,** OF, Arizona State.
3. **Dustin Majewski,** OF, Texas.
4. **Eddie Kim,** 1B, James Madison.
5. **Trent Peterson,** LHP, Florida State.
6. **Luke Appert ,** 2B, Minnesota.
7. **David Castillo,** C, Oral Roberts.
8. **Mike McGirr,** RHP, Richmond.
9. **Grant Reynolds,** RHP, Kennesaw State.
10. **Matt Lynch,** LHP, Florida State.

SEATTLE MARINERS
AMERICAN LEAGUE WEST DIVISION

2004 SEASON

April

SUN	MON	TUE	WED	THU	FRI	SAT
4	5	6 ANA	7 ANA	8 ANA	9 OAK	10 OAK
11 OAK	12	13 ANA	14 ANA	15 ANA	16 TEX	17 TEX
18 TEX	19 OAK	20 OAK	21 OAK	22 OAK	23 TEX	24 TEX
25 TEX	26 BAL	27 BAL	28 BAL	29 BAL	30 DET	

May

SUN	MON	TUE	WED	THU	FRI	SAT
						1 DET
2 DET	3	4 MIN	5 MIN	6 MIN	7 NYY	8 NYY
9 NYY	10	11 MIN	12 MIN	13 MIN	14 NYY	15 NYY
16 NYY	17	18 BAL	19 BAL	20 BAL	21 DET	22 DET
23 DET	24	25 CLE	26 CLE	27 CLE	28 BOS	29 BOS
30 BOS	31 TOR					

June

SUN	MON	TUE	WED	THU	FRI	SAT
		1 TOR	2 TOR	3	4 CHW	5 CHW
6 CHW	7 HOU	8 HOU	9 HOU	10	11 MON	12 MON
13 MON	14	15 MIL	16 MIL	17 MIL	18 PIT	19 PIT
20 PIT	21	22 TEX	23 TEX	24 TEX	25 SD	26 SD
27 SD	28 TEX	29 TEX	30 TEX			

July

SUN	MON	TUE	WED	THU	FRI	SAT
				1 TEX	2 STL	3 STL
4 STL	5	6 TOR	7 TOR	8 TOR	9 CHW	10 CHW
11 CHW	12	13 All-Star	14	15 CLE	16 CLE	17 CLE
18 CLE	19 BOS	20 BOS	21 OAK	22 OAK	23 ANA	24 ANA
25 ANA	26 OAK	27 OAK	28 OAK	29 ANA	30 ANA	31 ANA

August

SUN	MON	TUE	WED	THU	FRI	SAT
1 ANA	2	3 BAL	4 BAL	5 TB	6 TB	7 TB
8 TB	9	10 MIN	11 MIN	12 MIN	13 NYY	14 NYY
15 NYY	16	17 KC	18 KC	19 KC	20 DET	21 DET
22 DET	23 TB	24 TB	25 TB	26 KC	27 KC	28 KC
29 KC	30	31 TOR				

Sept./Oct.

SUN	MON	TUE	WED	THU	FRI	SAT
			1 TOR	2 TOR	3 CHW	4 CHW
5 CHW	6 CLE	7	8 CLE	9 BOS	10 BOS	11 BOS
12 BOS	13 ANA	14 ANA	15 ANA	16 ANA	17 OAK	18 OAK
19 OAK	20 ANA	21 ANA	22 ANA	23	24 TEX	25 TEX
26 TEX	27 OAK	28 OAK	29 OAK	30 OAK	1 TEX	2 TEX
3 TEX	4	5	6	7	8	9

Home games shaded. All-Star Game July 13 at Houston. Schedule subject to change.

CLUB DIRECTORY

Chairman & chief executive officer
Howard Lincoln
President and chief operating officer
Chuck Armstrong
Executive v.p., baseball operations
Bill Bavasi
Vice president, baseball administration
Lee Pelekoudas
Vice president, player development and scouting
Benny Looper
Director, player development
Frank Mattox
Vice president,scouting
Bob Fontaine
Director, professional scouting
Ken Compton
Director, baseball information
Tim Hevly
Vice president, communications
Randy Adamack
Director, public information
Rebecca Hale

MINOR LEAGUE AFFILIATES

Class	Team	League	Manager
AAA	Tacoma	Pacific Coast	Dan Rohn
AA	San Antonio	Texas	Dave Brundage
Advanced A	Inland Empire	California	Daren Brown
A	Wisconsin	Midwest	Steve Roadcap
Short-Season A	Everett	Northwest	Pedro Grifol
Rookie	Peoria Mariners	Arizona	Scott Steinmann

More on the Mariners at www.foxsports.com/named/FS/MLB/teams

BROADCAST INFORMATION

Radio: KOMO-AM (1000).
TV: KSTW (Channel 11).
Cable TV: Fox Sports Net Northwest.

SPRING TRAINING

Ballpark: Peoria Stadium (Peoria, Ariz.).
Ticket information: 480-784-4444.

SPRING TRAINING ROSTER

Manager—Bob Melvin (3).
Coaches—Mike Aldrete (25), Orlando Gomez (49), Rene Lachemann (15), Paul Molitor (4), Dave Myers (31), Bryan Price (32).

No.	PITCHERS	B/T	Ht./Wt.	Age*	2003 Clubs
	Baek, Cha Seung	R/R	6-4/190	23	San Antonio, Inland Empire
45	Franklin, Ryan	R/R	6-3/180	31	Seattle
34	Garcia, Freddy	R/R	6-4/240	27	Seattle
	Guardado, Eddie	R/L	6-0/194	33	Minnesota
17	Hasegawa, Shig.	R/R	5-11/180	35	Seattle
	Heaverlo, Jeff	R/R	6-1/215	26	Tacoma
	Jarvis, Kevin	L/R	6-2/200	34	Lake Elsinore, San Diego
	Johnson, Rett	R/R	6-2/210	24	Tacoma, San Antonio
	Looper, Aaron	R/R	6-2/185	27	Tacoma, Seattle
	Madritsch, Bobby	L/L	6-2/190	28	San Antonio
40	Mateo, Julio	R/R	6-0/177	26	Seattle
55	Meche, Gil	R/R	6-3/200	25	Seattle
50	Moyer, Jamie	L/L	6-0/175	41	Seattle
	Nageotte, Clint	R/R	6-3/200	23	San Antonio
38	Pineiro, Joel	R/R	6-1/200	25	Seattle
	Putz, J.J.	R/R	6-5/220	27	Tacoma, Seattle
22	Sasaki, Kazuhiro	R/R	6-4/220	36	Inland Empire, Everett, Tacoma, Seattle
39	Soriano, Rafael	R/R	6-1/175	24	Tacoma, Seattle
	Taylor, Aaron	R/R	6-8/245	26	Tacoma, Seattle
	Thornton, Matt	L/L	6-6/220	27	Inland Empire, Tacoma, San Antonio

No.	CATCHERS	B/T	Ht./Wt.	Age*	2003 Clubs
	Christianson, Ryan	R/R	6-2/210	22	Did Not Play
13	Davis, Ben	B/R	6-4/225	27	Seattle
6	Wilson, Dan	R/R	6-3/215	35	San Antonio, Seattle

No.	INFIELDERS	B/T	Ht./Wt.	Age*	2003 Clubs
	Aurilia, Rich	R/R	6-1/185	32	San Francisco
16	Bloomquist, Willie	R/R	5-11/185	26	Seattle
29	Boone, Bret	R/R	5-10/190	34	Seattle
	Dobbs, Greg	L/R	6-1/205	25	San Antonio
	Hansen, Dave	L/R	6-0/195	35	San Diego
	Leone, Justin	R/R	6-1/190	27	San Antonio
11	Martinez, Edgar	R/R	5-11/204	41	Seattle
5	Olerud, John	L/L	6-5/225	35	Seattle
39	Santiago, Ramon	B/R	5-11/167	24	Detroit
	Spiezio, Scott	B/R	6-2/225	31	Anaheim
23	Ugueto, Luis	B/R	5-11/170	25	Tacoma, San Antonio, Seattle

No.	OUTFIELDERS	B/T	Ht./Wt.	Age*	2003 Clubs
	Ibanez, Raul	L/R	6-2/200	31	Kansas City
	McCracken, Quin.	B/R	5-7/188	33	Arizona
32	Snelling, Chris	L/L	5-10/165	22	San Antonio, Tacoma
	Strong, Jamal	R/R	5-10/180	25	Ariz. Mariners, Tacoma, Seattle
51	Suzuki, Ichiro	L/R	5-9/172	30	Seattle
2	Winn, Randy	B/R	6-2/197	29	Seattle

Invited to spring training: C Pat Borders.

*Age as of April 1, 2004.

BALLPARK INFORMATION

Ballpark (capacity, surface)
Safeco Field (47,772, grass).

Address
1250 First Avenue South
Seattle, WA 98104

Official website
www.seattlemariners.com

Business phone
206-346-4000

Ticket information
206-346-4001

Field dimensions (from home plate)
To left field at foul line, 331 feet
To center field, 405 feet
To right field at foul line, 326 feet

First game played
July 15, 1999 (Padres 3, Mariners 2)

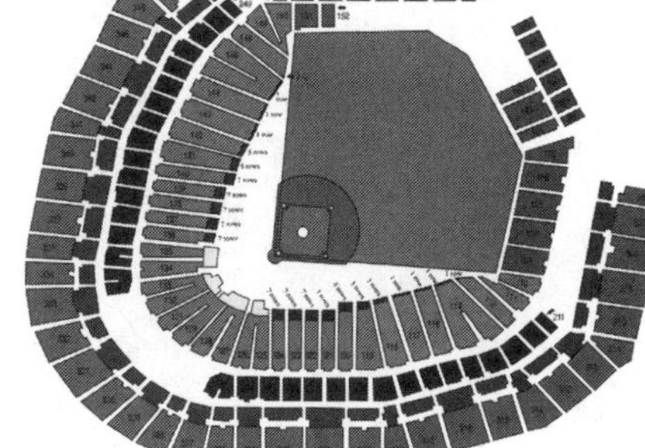

2003 REVIEW

DAY BY DAY

Date	Opp.	Res.	Score	(inn.*)	Hits	Opp. hits	Winning pitcher	Losing pitcher	Save	Record	Pos.	GB
4-1	At Oak.	L	0-5		5	8	Hudson	Garcia		0-1	4th	1.0
4-2	At Oak.	L	3-8		6	9	Zito	Moyer		0-2	4th	2.0
4-3	At Oak.	W	7-6	(11)	12	10	Nelson	Rincon		1-2	T3rd	1.0
4-4	At Tex.	W	6-4		9	7	Franklin	Cordero	Sasaki	2-2	T2nd	1.0
4-5	At Tex.	L	4-8		11	15	Lewis	Meche	Urbina	2-3	T2nd	2.0
4-6	At Tex.	W	11-2		14	4	Garcia	Park		3-3	2nd	2.0
4-8	Ana.	W	5-0		8	4	Moyer	Ortiz		4-3	2nd	2.0
4-9	Ana.	L	1-5		8	7	Appier	Pineiro		4-4	2nd	3.0
4-10	Ana.	L	0-3		5	9	Washburn	Franklin	Percival	4-5	T2nd	3.0
4-11	Tex.	L	2-4		5	8	Park	Garcia	Urbina	4-6	T3rd	3.0
4-12	Tex.	W	13-4		14	7	Meche	Drese		5-6	3rd	2.0
4-13	Tex.	W	4-3	(13)	9	12	Sasaki	Dickey		6-6	3rd	1.0
4-14	Oak.	W	4-3		9	7	Pineiro	Mulder	Sasaki	7-6	T1st	...
4-15	Oak.	W	5-3		11	6	Rhodes	Bowie	Sasaki	8-6	1st	+1.0
4-16	Oak.	L	1-4		5	6	Hudson	Garcia	Foulke	8-7	T1st	...
4-17	Oak.	W	4-3	(10)	10	8	Nelson	Fikac		9-7	1st	+1.0
4-18	At Ana.	W	8-2		9	13	Moyer	Ortiz		10-7	1st	+1.0
4-19	At Ana.	L	6-7		9	12	Rodriguez	Sasaki		10-8	T1st	...
4-20	At Ana.	W	7-6		11	14	Hasegawa	Percival	Sasaki	11-8	1st	+1.0
4-22	Cle.	W	8-5		11	12	Carrara	Baez		12-8	1st	+1.0
4-23	Cle.	W	4-0		5	6	Meche	Rodriguez		13-8	1st	+2.0
4-24	Cle.	W	4-2		7	10	Moyer	Traber	Nelson	14-8	1st	+2.0
4-25	Det.	W	6-0		9	4	Pineiro	Maroth		15-8	1st	+2.0
4-26	Det.	L	4-6		11	11	Walker	Franklin	Anderson	15-9	1st	+1.0
4-27	Det.	W	4-3		5	4	Garcia	Bernero	Nelson	16-9	1st	+1.0
4-29	At N.Y.	W	6-0		13	7	Meche	Clemens		17-9	1st	+1.0
4-30	At N.Y.	L	5-8		8	9	Pettitte	Moyer		17-10	T1st	...
5-1	At N.Y.	L	1-2		6	9	Mussina	Pineiro	Rivera	17-11	T1st	...
5-2	At Chi.	W	9-2		16	5	Franklin	Loaiza		18-11	1st	+1.0
5-3	At Chi.	W	12-2		14	5	Garcia	Stewart		19-11	1st	+1.0
5-4	At Chi.	W	5-1	(6)	9	4	Meche	Colon		20-11	1st	+1.0
5-6	N.Y.	W	12-7		15	14	Moyer	Pettitte		21-11	1st	+1.0
5-7	N.Y.	L	2-7		6	10	Mussina	Pineiro		21-12	1st	+1.0
5-8	N.Y.	L	5-16		12	17	Wells	Garcia		21-13	T1st	...
5-9	Chi.	W	6-3		11	9	Franklin	Wright	Nelson	22-13	T1st	...
5-10	Chi.	L	3-4		7	10	Colon	Meche	Marte	22-14	T1st	...
5-11	Chi.	W	7-2		12	3	Moyer	Buehrle		23-14	T1st	...
5-13	At Cle.	W	8-3		17	9	Pineiro	Anderson		24-14	T1st	...
5-14	At Cle.	L	2-7		4	9	Davis	Garcia		24-15	T1st	...
5-15	At Cle.	W	9-1		9	7	Carrara	Westbrook		25-15	T1st	...
5-16	At Det.	W	6-3		10	7	Meche	Bonderman	Sasaki	26-15	1st	+1.0
5-17	At Det.	W	6-3		12	11	Moyer	Cornejo	Sasaki	27-15	1st	+2.0
5-18	At Det.	W	6-2		10	4	Pineiro	Maroth		28-15	1st	+2.0
5-20	K.C.	W	7-4		11	6	Nelson	Carrasco		29-15	1st	+2.0
5-21	K.C.	L	5-14		10	12	George	Garcia		29-16	1st	+2.0
5-22	K.C.	W	5-1		11	6	Meche	Affeldt		30-16	1st	+3.0
5-23	Min.	W	5-2		9	9	Moyer	Radke	Sasaki	31-16	1st	+3.0
5-24	Min.	L	2-7		6	14	Lohse	Pineiro		31-17	1st	+3.0
5-25	Min.	L	1-3		6	9	Reed	Franklin	Guardado	31-18	1st	+2.0
5-27	At K.C.	W	15-7		20	10	Garcia	George		32-18	1st	+3.0
5-28	At K.C.	W	5-2		8	5	Moyer	Affeldt	Sasaki	33-18	1st	+4.0
5-29	At Min.	W	10-6		18	10	Meche	Radke		34-18	1st	+4.0
5-30	At Min.	W	6-0		12	4	Pineiro	Lohse		35-18	1st	+5.0
5-31	At Min.	W	5-2		11	7	Franklin	Reed	Sasaki	36-18	1st	+5.0
6-1	At Min.	W	9-5		14	8	Garcia	Rogers		37-18	1st	+5.0
6-3	At Phi.	W	4-0		10	6	Moyer	Millwood		38-18	1st	+6.0
6-4	At Phi.	W	7-2		14	5	Meche	Padilla		39-18	1st	+6.0
6-5	At Phi.	W	5-4		8	8	Mateo	Mesa	Sasaki	40-18	1st	+7.0
6-6	At N.Y. (NL)	L	2-3		9	5	Seo	Franklin	Benitez	40-19	1st	+6.0
6-8†	At N.Y. (NL)	W	13-1		17	6	Garcia	Leiter		41-19		
6-8‡	At N.Y. (NL)	W	7-0		14	3	Moyer	Bacsik		42-19	1st	+8.0
6-10	Mon.	L	3-7		9	11	Vazquez	Meche	Ayala	42-20	1st	+7.0
6-11	Mon.	L	1-3		8	9	Hernandez	Pineiro	Biddle	42-21	1st	+7.0
6-12	Mon.	W	1-0		5	5	Franklin	Vargas	Rhodes	43-21	1st	+8.0
6-13	Atl.	W	2-1		7	7	Garcia	Ortiz	Nelson	44-21	1st	+8.0

Date	Opp.	Res.	Score	(inn.*)	Hits	Opp. hits	Winning pitcher	Losing pitcher	Save	Record	Pos.	GB
6-14	Atl.	L	1-3		4	8	Hampton	Moyer	Smoltz	44-22	1st	+7.0
6-15	Atl.	W	2-1		5	5	Meche	Maddux	Nelson	45-22	1st	+7.0
6-16	Ana.	W	6-3		11	5	Pineiro	Lackey	Rhodes	46-22	1st	+7.5
6-17	Ana.	W	8-4		7	7	Franklin	Appier		47-22	1st	+7.5
6-18	Ana.	W	2-0		7	5	Garcia	Sele	Rhodes	48-22	1st	+7.5
6-19	Ana.	L	0-2		6	4	Ortiz	Moyer	Percival	48-23	1st	+6.5
6-20	At S.D.	L	3-5		7	9	Matthews	Nelson		48-24	1st	+5.5
6-21	At S.D.	W	4-2		10	5	Pineiro	Eaton	Hasegawa	49-24	1st	+6.5
6-22	At S.D.	L	1-3		5	5	Peavy	Franklin	Beck	49-25	1st	+5.5
6-24	At Ana.	W	6-4		10	12	Garcia	Sele	Nelson	50-25	1st	+6.0
6-25	At Ana.	L	3-6		10	10	Ortiz	Moyer	Percival	50-26	1st	+6.0
6-26	At Ana.	W	10-6		13	10	Meche	Washburn	Hasegawa	51-26	1st	+6.0
6-27	S.D.	W	8-2		10	4	Pineiro	Eaton		52-26	1st	+7.0
6-28	S.D.	L	0-6		3	12	Peavy	Franklin		52-27	1st	+7.0
6-29	S.D.	L	6-8		10	15	Beck	Rhodes	Witasick	52-28	1st	+6.0
6-30	At Oak.	W	3-1		7	6	Moyer	Harang	Nelson	53-28	1st	+7.0
7-1	At Oak.	L	2-3	(11)	8	9	Foulke	Nelson		53-29	1st	+6.0
7-2	At Oak.	W	13-0		20	3	Pineiro	Lilly		54-29	1st	+7.0
7-3	At Oak.	L	2-5		10	11	Zito	Franklin	Foulke	54-30	1st	+6.0
7-4	At Tex.	L	3-7		7	10	Dickey	Garcia	Urbina	54-31	1st	+6.0
7-5	At Tex.	W	3-2	(10)	10	9	Soriano	Urbina	Hasegawa	55-31	1st	+7.0
7-6	At Tex.	L	1-5		5	6	Valdes	Meche		55-32	1st	+6.0
7-8	Bal.	W	6-5		16	11	Pineiro	Johnson	Hasegawa	56-32	1st	+7.0
7-9	Bal.	L	2-7		9	14	Helling	Franklin		56-33	1st	+6.0
7-10	Bal.	L	1-4		7	10	Ponson	Garcia		56-34	1st	+5.0
7-11	T.B.	W	4-3		8	8	Moyer	Harper	Hasegawa	57-34	1st	+5.0
7-12	T.B.	L	5-6		6	11	Zambrano	Meche	Carter	57-35	1st	+4.0
7-13	T.B.	W	13-2		14	7	Pineiro	Standridge		58-35	1st	+4.0
7-17	At K.C.	L	1-7		8	12	Lima	Garcia		58-36	1st	+4.0
7-18	At K.C.	W	6-3		8	10	Rhodes	MacDougal	Hasegawa	59-36	1st	+5.0
7-19	At K.C.	L	1-5		3	10	May	Meche		59-37	1st	+5.0
7-20	At K.C.	L	5-7	(10)	9	8	Wilson	Rhodes		59-38	1st	+5.0
7-21	At Min.	L	4-5		9	13	Rincon	Rhodes	Guardado	59-39	1st	+4.0
7-22	At Min.	W	10-8		11	11	Mateo	Mays	Hasegawa	60-39	1st	+4.0
7-23	Oak.	W	6-0		6	2	Franklin	Zito		61-39	1st	+5.0
7-24	Oak.	L	0-3		7	6	Mulder	Meche	Foulke	61-40	1st	+4.0
7-25	Tex.	W	11-5		13	10	Moyer	Ellis	Soriano	62-40	1st	+4.0
7-26	Tex.	W	4-0		12	3	Pineiro	Lewis		63-40	1st	+4.0
7-27	Tex.	L	3-7		8	13	Thomson	Garcia		63-41	1st	+3.0
7-28	Tex.	L	1-10		5	15	Benoit	Franklin		63-42	1st	+3.0
7-29	Det.	W	11-5		11	9	Meche	Roney		64-42	1st	+3.0
7-30	Det.	W	13-3		17	8	Moyer	Cornejo		65-42	1st	+4.0
7-31	Det.	W	4-0		6	3	Pineiro	Ledezma		66-42	1st	+4.0
8-1	Chi.	L	1-12		8	14	Colon	Garcia		66-43	1st	+3.0
8-2	Chi.	W	10-0		10	3	Franklin	Wright		67-43	1st	+4.0
8-3	Chi.	W	8-2		10	5	Meche	Buehrle		68-43	1st	+4.0
8-5	At Cle.	W	2-1		10	3	Moyer	Sabathia	Hasegawa	69-43	1st	+4.0
8-6	At Cle.	L	6-10		8	15	Westbrook	Pineiro		69-44	1st	+3.0
8-7	At Cle.	L	0-3		7	8	Traber	Garcia	Baez	69-45	1st	+3.0
8-8	At N.Y.	L	7-9		11	12	Hitchcock	Franklin	Rivera	69-46	1st	+3.0
8-9	At N.Y.	W	2-1		5	3	Meche	Pettitte	Hasegawa	70-46	1st	+3.0
8-10	At N.Y.	W	8-6		14	10	Soriano	Osuna	Hasegawa	71-46	1st	+4.0
8-11	Tor.	L	3-5		11	7	Hendrickson	Pineiro	Lopez	71-47	1st	+3.0
8-12	Tor.	W	3-1		6	6	Garcia	Halladay	Hasegawa	72-47	1st	+3.0
8-13	Tor.	W	13-6		17	9	Mateo	Kershner		73-47	1st	+4.0
8-14	Tor.	L	2-5		9	10	Escobar	Meche	Lopez	73-48	1st	+4.0
8-15	Bos.	W	10-5		13	8	Mateo	Timlin	Hasegawa	74-48	1st	+5.0
8-16	Bos.	L	1-5		5	10	Martinez	Pineiro		74-49	1st	+4.0
8-17	Bos.	W	3-1		6	4	Garcia	Burkett	Hasegawa	75-49	1st	+4.0
8-19	At Tor.	W	9-1		16	6	Franklin	Escobar		76-49	1st	+4.0
8-20	At Tor.	L	2-5		6	6	Towers	Meche		76-50	1st	+3.0
8-21	At Tor.	L	3-7		7	11	Hendrickson	Moyer		76-51	1st	+3.0
8-22	At Bos.	L	4-6		11	10	Suppan	Pineiro	Kim	76-52	1st	+3.0
8-23	At Bos.	L	6-7	(10)	12	14	Timlin	Sasaki		76-53	1st	+2.0
8-24	At Bos.	L	1-6		7	11	Lowe	Franklin		76-54	1st	+1.0
8-25	At Bos.	L	1-8		8	12	Martinez	Meche	Arroyo	76-55	T1st	...
8-26	T.B.	W	9-3		12	7	Moyer	Zambrano		77-55	T1st	...
8-27	T.B.	L	4-8		5	11	Waechter	Pineiro		77-56	2nd	1.0
8-28	T.B.	L	2-3		7	6	Harper	Hasegawa	Carter	77-57	2nd	2.0
8-29	Bal.	W	3-2		4	6	Soriano	Julio		78-57	2nd	2.0
8-30	Bal.	W	13-1		13	5	Meche	Moss		79-57	2nd	2.0
8-31	Bal.	W	3-0		10	5	Moyer	Johnson	Hasegawa	80-57	2nd	2.0

Date	Opp.	Res.	Score	(inn.*)	Hits	Opp. hits	Winning pitcher	Losing pitcher	Save	Record	Pos.	GB
9-2	At T.B.	W	10-8	(11)	16	15	Hasegawa	Carter		81-57	2nd	2.0
9-3	At T.B.	L	0-7		2	11	Waechter	Garcia		81-58	2nd	2.0
9-4	At T.B.	L	0-1		4	6	Sosa	Franklin		81-59	2nd	2.0
9-5	At Bal.	W	6-4	(13)	14	21	Rhodes	Ligtenberg		82-59	2nd	2.0
9-6	At Bal.	L	1-3		7	10	DuBose	Moyer	Julio	82-60	2nd	2.0
9-7	At Bal.	L	1-2		5	4	Hentgen	Garcia	Julio	82-61	2nd	2.0
9-9	Tex.	L	4-5	(10)	8	11	Mahay	Hasegawa	Cordero	82-62	2nd	2.5
9-10	Tex.	W	3-1		4	4	Pineiro	Thomson		83-62	2nd	2.5
9-11	Tex.	W	8-2		10	5	Meche	Callaway		84-62	2nd	2.5
9-12	Ana.	W	7-4		8	10	Moyer	Lackey	Hasegawa	85-62	2nd	2.5
9-13	Ana.	W	5-1		4	8	Garcia	Rodriguez		86-62	2nd	2.5
9-14	Ana.	L	1-2		3	6	Gregg	Franklin	Percival	86-63	2nd	3.5
9-15	At Tex.	L	4-6		9	7	Lewis	Pineiro	Cordero	86-64	2nd	4.5
9-16	At Tex.	L	5-10		11	15	Thomson	Meche		86-65	2nd	4.5
9-17	At Tex.	W	5-1		11	5	Moyer	Drese		87-65	2nd	4.5
9-18	At Tex.	L	1-2	(10)	5	6	Cordero	Hasegawa		87-66	2nd	5.0
9-19	At Oak.	W	6-1		14	4	Franklin	Hudson		88-66	2nd	4.0
9-20	At Oak.	W	9-3		17	6	Pineiro	Duchscherer		89-66	2nd	3.0
9-21	At Oak.	L	0-12		4	15	Lilly	Meche		89-67	2nd	4.0
9-22	At Ana.	W	5-1		13	6	Moyer	Washburn		90-67	2nd	4.0
9-23	At Ana.	L	1-2	(11)	4	7	Rodriguez	Hasegawa		90-68	2nd	5.0
9-24	At Ana.	L	0-4		5	8	Lackey	Meche		90-69	2nd	6.0
9-26	Oak.	W	9-3		15	7	Pineiro	Wood	Mateo	91-69	2nd	5.0
9-27	Oak.	W	7-4		12	7	Franklin	Bradford	Hasegawa	92-69	2nd	4.0
9-28	Oak.	W	9-3		12	8	Moyer	Lilly		93-69	2nd	3.0

Monthly records: April (17-10), May (19-8), June (17-10), July (13-14), August (14-15), September (13-12).
*Innings, if other than nine. † First game of a doubleheader. ‡ Second game of a doubleheader.

RECORDS

2003 regular-season record: 93-69
Position: 2nd in A.L. West
Home: 50-31 **Road:** 43-38
A.L. East: 18-23 **A.L. Central:** 32-13
A.L. West: 33-25 N.L. 10-8
Vs. LH starters: 33-16
Vs. RH starters: 60-53
Grass: 83-64 **Artificial:** 10-5
Day: 29-16 **Night:** 64-53
1-Run: 16-15 **X-inn.:** 6-6
Doubleheaders: 1-0-0
Team record past five years: 472-338 (.583, ranks 3rd in league in that span)

TEAM LEADERS

Batting average: Ichiro Suzuki (.312).
At-bats: Ichiro Suzuki (679).
Runs: Bret Boone, Ichiro Suzuki (111).
Hits: Ichiro Suzuki (212).
Total Bases: Bret Boone (333).
Doubles: Randy Winn (37).
Triples: Ichiro Suzuki (8).
Home runs: Bret Boone (35).
Runs batted in: Bret Boone (117).
Stolen bases: Ichiro Suzuki (34).
Slugging percentage: Bret Boone (.535).
On-base percentage: Edgar Martinez (.406).
Wins: Jamie Moyer (21).
Earned-run average: Jamie Moyer (3.27).
Complete games: Joel Pineiro (3).
Shutouts: Joel Pineiro (2).
Saves: Shigetoshi Hasegawa (16).
Innings pitched: Jamie Moyer (215.0).
Strikeouts: Joel Pineiro (151).

GAMES BY POSITION

Catcher: Dan Wilson 96, Ben Davis 73, Pat Borders 7.
First base: John Olerud 152, Greg Colbrunn 14, John Mabry 9, Willie Bloomquist 3, Jeff Cirillo 1.
Second base: Bret Boone 158, Willie Bloomquist 7, Mark McLemore 6, Luis Ugueto 4.
Third base: Jeff Cirillo 85, Willie Bloomquist 37, Carlos Guillen 32, Mark McLemore 29, Pat Borders 2, Luis Ugueto 1.
Shortstop: Carlos Guillen 76, Rey Sanchez 46, Mark McLemore 38, Willie Bloomquist 18, Luis Ugueto 1.
Outfield: Ichiro Suzuki 159, Randy Winn 157, Mike Cameron 147, John Mabry 22, Mark McLemore 16, Willie Bloomquist 11, Chad Meyers 3, Jamal Strong 2.
Designated hitter: Edgar Martinez 140, Willie Bloomquist 12, John Mabry 12, Mark McLemore 11, Jamal Strong 7, Chad Meyers 6, Greg Colbrunn 4, Luis Ugueto 3, Pat Borders 1, Jeff Cirillo 1, Ben Davis 1, Carlos Guillen 1.

TOP DRAFT CHOICES

1. **Adam Jones,** SS/RHP, Morse H.S., San Diego.
2. **Jeff Flaig,** 3B, El Dorado H.S., Placentia, Calif.
3. **Ryan Feierabend,** LHP, Midview H.S., Grafton, Ohio.
4. **Paul Fagan,** LHP, Bartram Trail H.S., Jacksonville.
5. **Casey Abrams,** LHP, Wright State.
6. **Eric O'Flaherty,** LHP, Walla Walla (Wash.) H.S.
7. **Jeremy Dutton,** 3B, North Carolina State.
8. **Tom Oldham,** LHP, Creighton.
9. **Justin Ruchti,** C, Rice.
10. **Mike Cox,** 3B, Florida Atlantic.

TAMPA BAY DEVIL RAYS

AMERICAN LEAGUE EAST DIVISION

2004 SEASON

April

SUN	MON	TUE	WED	THU	FRI	SAT
28	29	30 † NYY	31 † NYY	1	2	3
4	5	6 NYY	7 NYY	8	9 BAL	10 BAL
11 BAL	12	13 NYY	14 NYY	15	16 CHW	17 CHW
18 CHW	19	20 BAL	21 BAL	22 BAL	23 CHW	24 CHW
25 CHW	26	27 BOS	28 BOS	29 BOS	30 OAK	

May

SUN	MON	TUE	WED	THU	FRI	SAT
						1 OAK
2 OAK	3 TEX	4 TEX	5 TEX	6 ANA	7 ANA	8 ANA
9 ANA	10	11 TEX	12 TEX	13 TEX	14 CLE	15 CLE
16 CLE	17	18 BOS	19 BOS	20 BOS	21 CLE	22 CLE
23 CLE	24	25 MIN	26 MIN	27 MIN	28 NYY	29 NYY
30 NYY	31 MIN					

June

SUN	MON	TUE	WED	THU	FRI	SAT
		1 MIN	2 MIN	3 MIN	4 BAL	5 BAL
6 BAL	7	8 SF	9 SF	10 SF	11 COL	12 COL
13 COL	14	15 SD	16 SD	17 SD	18 ARI	19 ARI
20 ARI	21	22 TOR	23 TOR	24 TOR	25 FLA	26 FLA
27 FLA	28 TOR	29 TOR	30 TOR			

July

SUN	MON	TUE	WED	THU	FRI	SAT
				1 TOR	2 FLA	3 FLA
4 FLA	5 BAL	6 BAL	7 BAL	8 NYY	9 NYY	10 NYY
11 NYY	12	13 All-Star	14	15 BAL	16 BAL	17 BAL
18 BAL	19 NYY	20 NYY	21 MIN	22 MIN	23 TOR	24 TOR
25 TOR	26	27 KC	28 KC	29 KC	30 TOR	31 TOR

August

SUN	MON	TUE	WED	THU	FRI	SAT
1 TOR	2 BOS	3 BOS	4 BOS	5 SEA	6 SEA	7 SEA
8 SEA	9 BOS	10 BOS	11 BOS	12 BOS	13 TEX	14 TEX
15 TEX	16	17 ANA	18 ANA	19 ANA	20 OAK	21 OAK
22 OAK	23 SEA	24 SEA	25 SEA	26	27 OAK	28 OAK
29 OAK	30	31 BAL				

Sept./Oct.

SUN	MON	TUE	WED	THU	FRI	SAT
			1 BAL	2 BAL	3 DET	4 DET
5 DET	6 NYY	7 NYY	8 NYY	9 NYY	10 KC	11 KC
12 KC	13	14 BOS	15 BOS	16 BOS	17 TOR	18 TOR
19 TOR	20 KC	21 KC	22 KC	23	24 TOR	25 TOR
26 TOR	27 BOS	28 BOS	29 BOS	30	1 DET	2 DET
3 DET	4	5	6	7	8	9

Home games shaded. All-Star Game July 13 at Houston. Schedule subject to change.

CLUB DIRECTORY

Managing general partner/CEO
Vincent J. Naimoli
Sr. v.p. baseball operations/g.m.
Chuck LaMar
Vice president of public relations
Rick Vaughn

Assistant general managers
Bart Braun
Scott Proefrock
Special assistants to the g.m.
Tim Wilken, Hal McRae
Director of scouting and player personnel
Cam Bonifay

Senior baseball adviser
Don Zimmer
Director of media relations
Chris Costello
Community relations director
Liz-Beth Lauck

MINOR LEAGUE AFFILIATES

Class	Team	League	Manager
AAA	Durham	International	Bill Evers
AA	Montgomery	Southern	Charlie Montoyo
Advanced A	Bakersfield	California	Mako Oliveras
A	Charleston (S.C.)	South Atlantic	Steve Livesey
Short-Season A	Hudson Valley	New York-Pennsylvania	Dave Howard
Advanced Rookie	Princeton	Appalachian	Jamie Nelson

BROADCAST INFORMATION

Radio: WFLA-AM (970).
Cable TV: Fox Sports Net.

SPRING TRAINING

Ballpark (city): Progress Energy Park Home of Al Lang Field (St. Petersburg, Fla.).
Ticket information: 727-825-3250.

More on the Devil Rays at www.foxsports.com/named/FS/MLB/teams

SPRING TRAINING ROSTER

Manager—Lou Piniella (14).
Coaches—Lee Elia (4), Tom Foley (16), Billy Hatcher (2), Chuck Hernandez (55), John McLaren (7), Matt Sinatro (15).

No.	PITCHERS	B/T	Ht./Wt.	Age*	2003 Clubs
34	Abbott, Paul	R/R	6-2/203	36	Tucson, Kansas City
28	Baez, Danys	R/R	6-3/225	26	Cleveland
41	Bell, Rob	R/R	6-5/225	27	Durham, Tampa Bay
45	Brazelton, Dewon	R/R	6-4/214	23	Durham, Tampa Bay, Bakersfield, Orlando
38	Carter, Lance	R/R	6-1/190	29	Tampa Bay
49	Colome, Jesus	R/R	6-4/205	26	Tampa Bay
68	Fortunato, Bart.	R/R	6-1/180	29	Durham, Orlando
50	Gaudin, Chad	R/R	5-11/165	21	Bakersfield, Orlando, Tampa Bay
54	Gonzalez, Jeremi	R/R	6-0/220	29	Durham, Tampa Bay
52	Halama, John	L/L	6-5/215	32	Oakland
58	Harper, Travis	R/R	6-4/192	27	Tampa Bay
30	Hendrickson, M.	L/L	6-9/230	29	Syracuse, Dunedin, Toronto
69	Hines, Carlos	R/R	6-3/190	23	Charleston-SC, Bakersfield, Orlando
37	McClung, Seth	L/R	6-6/235	23	Tampa Bay
	Miller, Trever	L/R	6-4/195	30	Toronto
27	Seay, Bobby	L/L	6-2/235	25	Tampa Bay, Durham
59	Sosa, Jorge	B/R	6-2/170	26	Durham, Tampa Bay
53	Standridge, Jason	R/R	6-4/230	25	Tampa Bay, Durham
43	Switzer, Jon	L/L	6-3/191	24	Orlando, Durham, Tampa Bay
40	Waechter, Doug	R/R	6-4/209	23	Orlando, Durham, Tampa Bay
21	White, Matt	R/R	6-5/235	25	Orlando
47	Zambrano, Victor	R/R	6-0/203	28	Durham, Tampa Bay
46	Zumwalt, Alec	R/R	6-2/205	23	Myrtle Beach, Greenville

No.	CATCHERS	B/T	Ht./Wt.	Age*	2003 Clubs
26	Fordyce, Brook	R/R	6-0/194	33	Baltimore
44	Hall, Toby	R/R	6-3/240	28	Tampa Bay
39	LaForest, Pete	L/R	6-2/208	26	Orlando, Durham, Tampa Bay

No.	INFIELDERS	B/T	Ht./Wt.	Age*	2003 Clubs
11	Blum, Geoff	B/R	6-3/200	30	Houston
	Fick, Robert	L/R	6-1/205	30	Atlanta
23	Lugo, Julio	R/R	6-1/170	28	Houston, Tampa Bay
24	Martinez, Tino	L/R	6-2/230	36	St. Louis
9	Perez, Antonio	R/R	5-11/170	24	Orlando, Durham, Tampa Bay
33	Perez, Eduardo	R/R	6-4/215	34	St. Louis
10	Rolls, Damian	R/R	6-2/215	26	Durham, Tampa Bay
1	Sanchez, Rey	R/R	5-9/170	36	Binghamton, New York N.L., Seattle

No.	OUTFIELDERS	B/T	Ht./Wt.	Age*	2003 Clubs
5	Baldelli, Rocco	R/R	6-4/190	22	Tampa Bay
13	Crawford, Carl	L/L	6-2/219	22	Tampa Bay
22	Cruz, Jose	B/R	6-0/210	29	San Francisco
60	Gomes, Jonny	R/R	6-1/205	23	Orlando, Durham, Tampa Bay
31	Hamilton, Josh	L/L	6-4/205	22	Did Not Play
19	Huff, Aubrey	L/R	6-4/231	27	Tampa Bay
	Young, Delmon	R/R	6-2/205	18	Did Not Play

Invited to spring training: RHP Ken Cloude, 3B Fernando Tatis, P William Glenn, RHP Dicky Gonzalez, SS Deivi Cruz, C-IF Edwards Guzman, IF Jason Maxwell, OF Anton French, OF Joey Gathright, RHP Mike Williams, RHP Todd Jones.

*Age as of April 1, 2004.

BALLPARK INFORMATION

Ballpark (capacity, surface)
Tropicana Field (44,445, artificial)

Address
One Tropicana Drive
St. Petersburg, FL 33705

Official website
www.devilrays.com

Business phone
727-825-3137

Ticket information
727-825-3250

Field dimensions (from home plate)
To left field at foul line, 315 feet
To center field, 404 feet
To right field at foul line, 322 feet

First game played
March 31, 1998 (Tigers 11, Devil Rays 6)

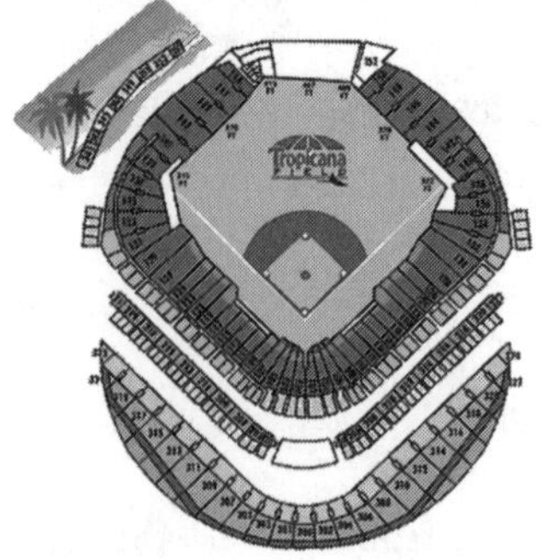

2003 REVIEW

DAY BY DAY

Date	Opp.	Res.	Score	(inn.*)	Hits	Opp. hits	Winning pitcher	Losing pitcher	Save	Record	Pos.	GB
3-31	Bos.	W	6-4		7	8	McClung	Fox		1-0	T1st	...
4-1	Bos.	L	8-9	(16)	19	13	Lyon	Sosa		1-1	T3rd	1.0
4-2	Bos.	L	5-7		7	8	Lowe	Parque	Fox	1-2	4th	2.0
4-3	Bos.	L	5-14		11	16	Fossum	Bierbrodt		1-3	4th	2.5
4-4	N.Y.	L	2-12		9	18	Wells	Parris		1-4	5th	3.5
4-5	N.Y.	W	6-5		14	11	Carter	Osuna		2-4	5th	2.5
4-6	N.Y.	L	5-10		11	15	Clemens	Zambrano		2-5	5th	3.5
4-8	Bal.	W	8-7	(10)	16	12	Carter	Julio		3-5	4th	3.5
4-9	Bal.	W	10-7		13	10	Levine	Roberts	Carter	4-5	4th	3.5
4-10	Bal.	L	3-4		9	5	Ponson	Colome	Julio	4-6	4th	4.5
4-12	At N.Y.	L	4-5		9	12	Osuna	Harper		4-7	5th	5.5
4-13	At N.Y.	W	2-1		10	5	Carter	Acevedo		5-7	T3rd	4.5
4-15	At Bos.	L	5-6		11	15	Timlin	Levine		5-8	3rd	6.0
4-16	At Bos.	L	4-6		7	10	Fox	Carter	Lyon	5-9	5th	6.0
4-17	At Bos.	L	0-6		4	12	Martinez	Kennedy		5-10	5th	7.0
4-18	At Bal.	L	7-9		10	8	Johnson	Zambrano	Julio	5-11	5th	8.0
4-19	At Bal.	W	8-7		11	14	Sosa	Lopez		6-11	4th	8.0
4-20	At Bal.	L	1-4		5	7	Daal	Bierbrodt	Julio	6-12	4th	9.0
4-21	At Bal.	L	0-4		5	9	Helling	Parris		6-13	5th	10.0
4-22	Tor.	W	4-3		11	5	Kennedy	Kershner	Carter	7-13	4th	10.0
4-23	Tor.	W	4-3		9	8	Venafro	Hendrickson	Carter	8-13	4th	10.0
4-24	Tor.	L	3-5		8	8	Sturtze	Sosa	Escobar	8-14	4th	10.0
4-25	Bal.	W	2-1		9	3	McClung	Daal	Carter	9-14	4th	10.0
4-26	Bal.	W	10-7		18	12	Zambrano	Helling	Carter	10-14	4th	10.0
4-27	Bal.	L	4-7		9	11	Ponson	Kennedy		10-15	4th	10.0
4-29	At Min.	L	3-5		10	9	Rogers	Sosa	Guardado	10-16	4th	10.0
4-30	At Min.	L	5-8		10	8	Radke	McClung		10-17	4th	11.0
5-1	At Min.	L	5-6	(13)	9	15	Fiore	Harper		10-18	5th	12.0
5-2	At Det.	W	2-0		6	1	Kennedy	Knotts		11-18	5th	12.0
5-3	At Det.	W	8-6	(10)	10	12	Levine	Ledezma		12-18	5th	11.0
5-4	At Det.	L	3-7		6	11	Bonderman	Sosa	Spurling	12-19	5th	11.0
5-6	Min.	L	3-7		8	12	Radke	Parris		12-20	5th	11.0
5-7	Min.	L	6-11		12	17	Rincon	Kennedy		12-21	5th	12.0
5-8	Min.	L	0-5		5	8	Lohse	Brazelton		12-22	5th	13.0
5-9	Det.	W	2-0		8	2	Parque	Bernero	Carter	13-22	5th	12.0
5-10	Det.	W	3-1		8	7	McClung	Bonderman	Carter	14-22	5th	12.0
5-11	Det.	L	2-9		8	15	Cornejo	Sosa		14-23	5th	12.0
5-13	At Tor.	W	7-5		12	10	Kennedy	Sturtze	Carter	15-23	5th	11.0
5-14	At Tor.	L	6-7		10	11	Lidle	Brazelton	Politte	15-24	5th	11.0
5-15	At Tor.	W	9-5		12	9	Colome	Davis		16-24	5th	11.0
5-16	At Bal.	W	5-1		8	7	McClung	Johnson		17-24	5th	10.0
5-17	At Bal.	L	0-2		3	5	Hentgen	Gonzalez	Julio	17-25	5th	10.0
5-18	At Bal.	W	9-8		16	14	Carter	Julio		18-25	5th	9.0
5-20	At Tex.	L	2-5		5	7	Benoit	Brazelton	Urbina	18-26	5th	9.5
5-21	At Tex.	L	7-8		14	13	Cordero	Colome	Urbina	18-27	5th	10.5
5-22	At Tex.	L	8-10		11	13	Van Poppel	Harper	Urbina	18-28	5th	10.5
5-23	At Ana.	W	3-1		12	4	Gonzalez	Washburn	Carter	19-28	5th	10.0
5-24	At Ana.	L	2-7		6	13	Lackey	Kennedy		19-29	5th	11.0
5-25	At Ana.	L	1-6		6	7	Appier	Brazelton		19-30	5th	11.0
5-27	Tex.	L	2-4		7	6	Lewis	Reyes	Urbina	19-31	5th	11.5
5-28	Tex.	W	6-4		12	4	Gonzalez	Benes	Carter	20-31	5th	10.5
5-29	Ana.	L	1-2		6	8	Washburn	Zambrano	Donnelly	20-32	5th	11.0
5-30	Ana.	W	8-6		12	6	Brazelton	Lackey	Carter	21-32	5th	10.5
5-31	Ana.	L	1-6		8	10	Appier	Kennedy		21-33	5th	10.5
6-1	Ana.	L	4-9		12	13	Sele	Reyes		21-34	5th	11.5
6-3	At Chi. (NL)	L	2-3		9	11	Remlinger	Levine		21-35	5th	11.5
6-4	At Chi. (NL)	W	5-2		11	5	Zambrano	Estes		22-35	5th	11.0
6-5	At Chi. (NL)	L	1-8		7	10	Clement	Brazelton		22-36	5th	11.5
6-6	At Hou.	L	8-11		11	11	Dotel	Harper	Wagner	22-37	5th	12.5
6-7	At Hou.	L	4-5		7	7	Saarloos	Levine	Wagner	22-38	5th	12.5
6-8	At Hou.	L	1-2		3	6	Redding	Zambrano	Wagner	22-39	5th	13.0
6-10	Cin.	L	2-4		12	6	Wilson	Standridge	Williamson	22-40	5th	13.5
6-11	Cin.	L	6-7		8	8	Reitsma	Colome	Williamson	22-41	5th	14.0
6-12	Cin.	L	1-2		4	6	Dempster	Gonzalez	Williamson	22-42	5th	14.5

Date	Opp.	Res.	Score	(inn.*)	Hits	Opp. hits	Winning pitcher	Losing pitcher	Save	Record	Pos.	GB
6-13	Pit.	W	7-1		8	1	Zambrano	Wells		23-42	5th	14.5
6-14	Pit.	L	9-12		14	17	Fogg	Bell	Williams	23-43	5th	15.5
6-15	Pit.	L	5-9		12	11	Sauerbeck	Levine	Williams	23-44	5th	16.5
6-17§	At N.Y.	W	11-2		18	4	Gonzalez	Weaver		24-44		
6-17∞	At N.Y.	L	2-10		7	14	Wells	Brazelton		24-45	5th	16.5
6-18	At N.Y.	L	0-1	(12)	3	5	Hammond	Carter		24-46	5th	17.5
6-20	At Fla.	L	1-3	(11)	6	6	Almanza	Levine		24-47	5th	18.5
6-21	At Fla.	L	0-2	(6)	2	5	Willis	Standridge		24-48	5th	19.0
6-22	At Fla.	L	2-3		9	2	Pavano	Gonzalez	Looper	24-49	5th	20.0
6-23	N.Y.	W	4-2		5	6	Zambrano	Clemens	Carter	25-49	5th	19.0
6-24	N.Y.	L	9-10		13	16	Anderson	Carter	Rivera	25-50	5th	20.0
6-25	N.Y.	L	5-8		10	7	Pettitte	Bell	Rivera	25-51	5th	21.0
6-26	N.Y.	L	3-4		10	7	Mussina	Standridge	Rivera	25-52	5th	22.0
6-27	Atl.	L	2-8		9	14	Ramirez	Gonzalez		25-53	5th	23.0
6-28	Atl.	W	9-7		13	10	Zambrano	Reynolds	Carter	26-53	5th	23.5
6-29	Atl.	L	0-2		3	7	Ortiz	Sosa	Smoltz	26-54	5th	24.5
7-1	Bos.	W	4-3	(11)	10	10	Carter	Lyon		27-54	5th	24.0
7-2	Bos.	L	4-5		7	10	Martinez	Colome	Kim	27-55	5th	24.5
7-3	Bos.	W	6-5	(10)	9	6	Harper	Timlin		28-55	5th	24.0
7-4	Chi.	W	4-3		10	5	Colome	Koch		29-55	5th	23.0
7-5	Chi.	W	3-2		8	11	Sosa	Loaiza	Carter	30-55	5th	22.0
7-6	Chi.	L	3-11		8	15	Buehrle	Standridge		30-56	5th	23.0
7-8	At Oak.	W	9-3		19	6	Bell	Zito		31-56	5th	22.5
7-9	At Oak.	L	3-6		9	11	Rincon	Colome	Foulke	31-57	5th	23.5
7-10	At Oak.	L	2-5		5	12	Mulder	Sosa		31-58	5th	23.5
7-11	At Sea.	L	3-4		8	8	Moyer	Harper	Hasegawa	31-59	5th	24.5
7-12	At Sea.	W	6-5		11	6	Zambrano	Meche	Carter	32-59	5th	23.5
7-13	At Sea.	L	2-13		7	14	Pineiro	Standridge		32-60	5th	24.5
7-17	Tex.	L	6-12		9	15	Thomson	Kennedy		32-61	5th	25.5
7-18	Tex.	W	2-0		8	7	Gonzalez	Valdes	Carter	33-61	5th	25.5
7-19	Tex.	L	3-7		7	11	Benoit	Zambrano		33-62	5th	26.5
7-20	Tex.	W	15-4		18	6	Sosa	Mounce		34-62	5th	26.5
7-21	Ana.	W	3-2		9	7	Bell	Sele	Harper	35-62	5th	25.5
7-22	Ana.	L	1-3		3	6	Ortiz	Kennedy	Percival	35-63	5th	26.0
7-23	At Bos.	L	4-10		6	13	Wakefield	Harper		35-64	5th	27.0
7-24	At Bos.	W	15-9		21	9	Zambrano	Mendoza		36-64	5th	26.0
7-25	At Chi.	L	2-7		8	9	Loaiza	Sosa		36-65	5th	27.0
7-26	At Chi.	W	10-6		15	9	Malaska	White	Colome	37-65	5th	26.0
7-27	At Chi.	L	1-9		4	12	Colon	Kennedy		37-66	5th	26.0
7-29	At Tor.	W	9-8		13	11	Levine	Miller	Carter	38-66	5th	26.0
7-30	At Tor.	W	5-3		7	7	Zambrano	Lidle	Colome	39-66	5th	26.0
7-31	At Tor.	W	7-6		13	8	Sosa	Hendrickson	Carter	40-66	5th	26.0
8-1	At K.C.	W	9-6		17	9	Backe	Lloyd	Carter	41-66	5th	25.0
8-2	At K.C.	L	8-10		11	14	Leskanic	Malaska	MacDougal	41-67	5th	26.0
8-3	At K.C.	L	0-2		6	4	Gobble	Gonzalez	Affeldt	41-68	5th	26.0
8-4	Tor.	W	10-1		10	7	Zambrano	Lidle		42-68	5th	25.5
8-5	Tor.	W	5-4	(10)	8	9	Colome	Acevedo		43-68	5th	25.5
8-6	Tor.	L	3-7		9	10	Halladay	Kennedy		43-69	5th	25.5
8-7	K.C.	W	3-2		7	7	Gaudin	MacDougal		44-69	5th	25.5
8-8	K.C.	W	4-0		9	4	Gonzalez	Appier		45-69	5th	25.5
8-9	K.C.	L	2-6		10	10	Gobble	Zambrano		45-70	5th	25.5
8-10	K.C.	L	3-7		6	12	Hernandez	Sosa		45-71	5th	25.5
8-11	Bal.	W	4-3		11	6	Harper	Carrasco		46-71	5th	24.5
8-12	Bal.	W	4-2		9	3	Bell	Lopez	Carter	47-71	5th	24.5
8-13	Bal.	W	6-5	(10)	11	11	Carter	Ryan		48-71	5th	23.5
8-15	At Cle.	L	0-1		4	5	Sabathia	Harper		48-72	5th	25.0
8-16	At Cle.	W	5-3		12	9	Malaska	Lee	Carter	49-72	5th	25.0
8-17	At Cle.	L	4-5	(12)	9	11	Mulholland	Colome		49-73	5th	26.0
8-18	At Cle.	W	7-4	(13)	15	11	Carter	Mulholland		50-73	5th	26.0
8-19	At Bal.	W	9-2		16	6	Gonzalez	DuBose		51-73	5th	26.0
8-20	At Bal.	L	5-9		13	7	Moss	Zambrano		51-74	5th	27.0
8-21	At Bal.	L	4-5	(10)	9	12	Ryan	Colome		51-75	5th	27.5
8-22	Cle.	L	3-8		7	7	Lee	Kennedy		51-76	5th	27.5
8-23	Cle.	L	5-7		9	10	Sabathia	Backe	Riske	51-77	5th	27.5
8-24	Cle.	L	5-7		14	12	Westbrook	Gonzalez	Riske	51-78	5th	28.5
8-26	At Sea.	L	3-9		7	12	Moyer	Zambrano		51-79	5th	29.0
8-27	At Sea.	W	8-4		11	5	Waechter	Pineiro		52-79	5th	28.0
8-28	At Sea.	W	3-2		6	7	Harper	Hasegawa	Carter	53-79	5th	28.0
8-29	At Oak.	L	2-5		7	7	Hudson	Kennedy	Foulke	53-80	5th	28.0
8-30	At Oak.	L	2-4		5	6	Lilly	Bell	Foulke	53-81	5th	29.0
8-31	At Oak.	L	3-4		6	4	Harden	Gonzalez	Bradford	53-82	5th	30.0

Date	Opp.	Res.	Score	(inn.*)	Hits	Opp. hits	Winning pitcher	Losing pitcher	Save	Record	Pos.	GB
9-2	Sea.	L	8-10	(11)	15	16	Hasegawa	Carter		53-83	5th	30.0
9-3	Sea.	W	7-0		11	2	Waechter	Garcia		54-83	5th	29.0
9-4	Sea.	W	1-0		6	4	Sosa	Franklin		55-83	5th	29.0
9-5	Oak.	L	1-3		4	10	Lilly	Gonzalez	Foulke	55-84	5th	29.0
9-6	Oak.	W	7-4		11	9	Bell	Harden	Carter	56-84	5th	28.0
9-7	Oak.	W	11-2		9	9	Zambrano	Zito		57-84	5th	28.0
9-9	Tor.	W	11-6		9	10	Waechter	Lidle	Kennedy	58-84	5th	28.5
9-10	Tor.	L	5-6		8	7	Hendrickson	Sosa	Lopez	58-85	5th	29.5
9-11	Tor.	L	1-3		5	6	Halladay	Gonzalez		58-86	5th	30.5
9-12	At N.Y.	L	4-10		13	17	Wells	Zambrano		58-87	5th	31.5
9-13§	At N.Y.	L	5-6		14	10	White	Kennedy	Rivera	58-88		
9-13∞	At N.Y.	L	3-6		8	10	Mussina	Reyes	Rivera	58-89	5th	33.5
9-14	At N.Y.	W	5-2		9	6	Harper	Heredia	Carter	59-89	5th	32.5
9-15	At Bos.	L	2-8		4	14	Lowe	Sosa		59-90	5th	33.5
9-16	At Bos.	L	2-3		6	5	Martinez	Harper		59-91	5th	34.5
9-17	At Bos.	W	7-0		16	6	Zambrano	Suppan		60-91	5th	33.5
9-18	At Bos.	L	3-4		7	9	Wakefield	Bell	Kim	60-92	5th	34.0
9-19	N.Y.	L	1-2		4	9	Contreras	Waechter	Rivera	60-93	5th	35.0
9-20	N.Y.	L	1-7		9	10	Pettitte	Sosa		60-94	5th	36.0
9-21	N.Y.	L	0-6		4	10	Clemens	Gonzalez		60-95	5th	37.0
9-22	At Tor.	W	5-2		9	4	Bell	Halladay		61-95	5th	36.0
9-23	At Tor.	L	5-8		11	10	Kershner	Zambrano	Miller	61-96	5th	37.0
9-24	At Tor.	L	3-5		9	6	Escobar	Waechter	Lopez	61-97	5th	37.0
9-25	At Tor.	L	8-10		12	11	Miller	Carter		61-98	5th	37.5
9-26	Bos.	L	2-7		8	12	Burkett	Gonzalez		61-99	5th	38.0
9-27	Bos.	W	5-4		9	10	Gaudin	Suppan	Carter	62-99	5th	38.0
9-28	Bos.	W	3-1		7	7	Zambrano	Lyon	Carter	63-99	5th	38.0

Monthly records: March (1-0), April (9-17), May (11-16), June (5-21), July (14-12), August (13-16), September (10-17).
*Innings, if other than nine. § Day separate admission. ∞ Night separate admission.

RECORDS

2003 regular-season record: 63-99
Position: 5th in A.L. East
Home: 36-45 **Road:** 27-54
A.L. East: 34-42 **A.L. Central:** 12-20
A.L. West: 14-22 N.L. 3-15
Vs. LH starters: 17-29
Vs. RH starters: 46-70
Grass: 21-47 **Artificial:** 42-52
Day: 14-34 **Night:** 49-65
1-Run: 23-28 **X-inn.:** 7-7
Doubleheaders: 0-0-0
Team record past five years: 318-490 (.394, ranks 13th in league in that span)

TEAM LEADERS

Batting average: Aubrey Huff (.311).
At-bats: Rocco Baldelli (637).
Runs: Aubrey Huff (91).
Hits: Aubrey Huff (198).
Total Bases: Aubrey Huff (353).
Doubles: Aubrey Huff (47).
Triples: Carl Crawford (9).
Home runs: Aubrey Huff (34).
Runs batted in: Aubrey Huff (107).
Stolen bases: Carl Crawford (55).
Slugging percentage: Aubrey Huff (.555).
On-base percentage: Aubrey Huff (.367).
Wins: Victor Zambrano (12).
Earned-run average: Jeremi Gonzalez (3.91).
Complete games: Jeremi Gonzalez (2).
Shutouts: Joe Kennedy, Jorge Sosa, Doug Waechter (1).
Saves: Lance Carter (26).
Innings pitched: Victor Zambrano (188.1).
Strikeouts: Victor Zambrano (132).

GAMES BY POSITION

Catcher: Toby Hall 130, Javier Valentin 42, Pete LaForest 4.
First base: Travis Lee 142, Aubrey Huff 22, Al Martin 1, Jared Sandberg 1.
Second base: Marlon Anderson 134, Antonio Perez 31, Terry Shumpert 14, Damion Easley 4, Brent Abernathy 2, Damian Rolls 2, Felix Escalona 1.
Third base: Damian Rolls 73, Jared Sandberg 50, Damion Easley 23, Chris Truby 13, Terry Shumpert 11, Aubrey Huff 8, Jeff Liefer 6, Antonio Perez 6, Felix Escalona 1, Jason Smith 1.
Shortstop: Julio Lugo 117, Rey Ordonez 34, Felix Escalona 8, Antonio Perez 6, Jared Sandberg 1, Terry Shumpert 1.
Outfield: Rocco Baldelli 154, Carl Crawford 146, Aubrey Huff 102, Damian Rolls 37, Jason Tyner 32, Terry Shumpert 14, George Lombard 13, Al Martin 13, Ben Grieve 10, Adam Piatt 7, Marlon Anderson 3, Matt Diaz 1, Jeff Liefer 1.
Designated hitter: Al Martin 57, Ben Grieve 37, Aubrey Huff 33, Terry Shumpert 17, Pete LaForest 12, Damion Easley 8, Jonny Gomes 8, Javier Valentin 6, Marlon Anderson 4, Adam Piatt 4, Jason Tyner 4, Antonio Perez 3, Rocco Baldelli 2, Matt Diaz 2, Travis Lee 2, Jeff Liefer 2, Carl Crawford 1.

TOP DRAFT CHOICES

1. **Delmon Young,** OF, Camarillo (Calif.) H.S.
2. **James Houser,** LHP, Sarasota (Fla.) H.S.
3. **Andrew Miller,** LHP, Buchholz H.S., Gainesville, Fla.
4. **Travis Schlichting,** 3B, Round Rock (Texas) H.S.
5. **Jon Barratt,** LHP, Hillcrest H.S., Springfield, Mo.
6. **Christian Lopez,** C, Hialeah H.S., Miami Lakes, Fla.
7. **Brian Henderson,** LHP, Houston.
8. **Matthew Maniscalco,** SS, Mississippi State.
9. **Billy Buckner,** RHP, Young Harris (Ga.) JC.
10. **Shaun Cumberland,** OF, Pace H.S., Milton, Fla.

TEXAS RANGERS

AMERICAN LEAGUE WEST DIVISION

2004 SEASON

April

SUN	MON	TUE	WED	THU	FRI	SAT
4	5 OAK	6 OAK	7 OAK	8	9 ANA	10 ANA
11 ANA	12 ANA	13 OAK	14 OAK	15 OAK	16 SEA	17 SEA
18 SEA	19	20 ANA	21 ANA	22 ANA	23 SEA	24 SEA
25 SEA	26	27 KC	28 KC	29 KC	30 BOS	

May

SUN	MON	TUE	WED	THU	FRI	SAT
						1 BOS
2 BOS	3 TB	4 TB	5 TB	6	7 DET	8 DET
9 DET	10	11 TB	12 TB	13 TB	14 DET	15 DET
16 DET	17	18 KC	19 KC	20 KC	21 NYY	22 NYY
23 NYY	24	25 CHW	26 CHW	27 CHW	28 TOR	29 TOR
30 TOR	31					

June

SUN	MON	TUE	WED	THU	FRI	SAT
		1 CLE	2 CLE	3	4 NYY	5 NYY
6 NYY	7 PIT	8 PIT	9 PIT	10	11 STL	12 STL
13 STL	14	15 CIN	16 CIN	17 CIN	18 FLA	19 FLA
20 FLA	21	22 SEA	23 SEA	24 SEA	25 HOU	26 HOU
27 HOU	28 SEA	29 SEA	30 SEA			

July

SUN	MON	TUE	WED	THU	FRI	SAT
				1 SEA	2 HOU	3 HOU
4 HOU	5 CLE	6 CLE	7 CLE	8 CLE	9 BOS	10 BOS
11 BOS	12	13 All-Star	14	15	16 TOR	17 TOR
18 TOR	19 CHW	20 CHW	21 ANA	22 ANA	23 OAK	24 OAK
25 OAK	26 ANA	27 ANA	28 ANA	29 OAK	30 OAK	31 OAK

August

SUN	MON	TUE	WED	THU	FRI	SAT
1 OAK	2	3 DET	4 DET	5 DET	6 BAL	7 BAL
8 BAL	9 BAL	10 NYY	11 NYY	12 NYY	13 TB	14 TB
15 TB	16 CLE	17 CLE	18 CLE	19	20 KC	21 KC
22 KC	23 MIN	24 MIN	25 MIN	26 MIN	27 BAL	28 BAL
29 BAL	30	31 MIN				

Sept./Oct.

SUN	MON	TUE	WED	THU	FRI	SAT
			1 MIN	2 MIN	3 BOS	4 BOS
5 BOS	6 CHW	7 CHW	8 CHW	9 CHW	10 TOR	11 TOR
12 TOR	13 OAK	14 OAK	15 OAK	16 OAK	17 ANA	18 ANA
19 ANA	20	21 OAK	22 OAK	23 OAK	24 SEA	25 SEA
26 SEA	27 ANA	28 ANA	29 ANA	30 ANA	1 SEA	2 SEA
3 SEA	4	5	6	7	8	9

Home games shaded. All-Star Game July 13 at Houston. Schedule subject to change.

CLUB DIRECTORY

Chairman of the board and owner
Thomas O. Hicks
President
Michael J. Cramer
Exec. vice president, general manager
John Hart
Senior vice president, communications
John Blake
Assistant general manager
Grady Fuson
Director of baseball operations
John Daniels
Director of minor league operations
John Lombardo
Director, community relations
Taunee Taylor
Media relations manager
Rich Rice

MINOR LEAGUE AFFILIATES

Class	Team	League	Manager
AAA	Oklahoma	Pacific Coast	Bobby Jones
AA	Frisco	Texas	Tim Ireland
Advanced A	Stockton	California	Arnie Beyeler
A	Clinton	Midwest	Carlos Subero
Short-Season A	Spokane	Northwest	Darryl Kennedy
Rookie	Arizona Rangers	Arizona	Pedro Lopez

More on the Rangers at www.foxsports.com/named/FS/MLB/teams

BROADCAST INFORMATION

Radio: KRLD-AM (1080); KESS (1270), Spanish.
TV: KDFW (Channel 4); KDFI (Channel 27).
Cable TV: Fox Sports Southwest.

SPRING TRAINING

Ballpark (city): Surprise Stadium (Surprise, Ariz.).
Ticket information: 623-594-5600.

SPRING TRAINING ROSTER

Manager—Buck Showalter (11).
Coaches—Mark Connor (52), DeMarlo Hale (20), Orel Hershiser (55), Rudy Jaramillo (8), Steve Smith (1), Don Wakamatsu (18).

No.	PITCHERS	B/T	Ht./Wt.	Age*	2003 Clubs
53	Benoit, Joaquin	R/R	6-3/205	26	Oklahoma, Texas
36	Callaway, Mickey	R/R	6-2/205	28	Salt Lake, Anaheim, Oklahoma, Texas
31	Cordero, Francisco	R/R	6-2/200	28	Texas
45	Dickey, R.A.	R/R	6-3/205	29	Oklahoma, Texas
	Dominguez, Juan	R/R	6-2/180	23	Stockton, Oklahoma, Frisco, Texas
37	Drese, Ryan	R/R	6-3/220	27	Frisco, Oklahoma, Texas
	Garcia, Rosman	R/R	6-2/160	25	Oklahoma, Texas
	Kozlowski, Ben	L/L	6-6/220	23	Frisco
48	Lewis, Colby	R/R	6-4/230	24	Oklahoma, Texas
	Mabeus, Chris	R/R	6-3/210	25	Modesto, Midland
32	Mahay, Ron	L/L	6-2/190	32	Oklahoma, Texas
	Moreno, Edwin	R/R	6-1/170	23	Frisco
	Nelson, Jeff	R/R	6-8/225	37	Seattle, New York A.L.
61	Park, Chan Ho	R/R	6-2/204	30	Frisco, Oklahoma, Texas
39	Powell, Jay	R/R	6-4/225	32	Frisco, Texas
54	Ramirez, Erasmo	L/L	6-0/180	27	Frisco, Oklahoma, Texas
	Regilio, Nick	R/R	6-2/185	25	Arizona Rangers, Frisco
	Rodriguez, Ricardo	R/R	6-3/190	25	Cleveland, Buffalo
	Rogers, Kenny	L/L	6-1/217	39	Minnesota
58	Shouse, Brian	L/L	5-11/180	35	Oklahoma, Texas
	Snare, Ryan	L/L	6-0/190	25	Frisco, Carolina
59	Zimmerman, Jeff	R/R	6-1/200	31	Arizona Rangers

No.	CATCHERS	B/T	Ht./Wt.	Age*	2003 Clubs
5	Diaz, Einar	R/R	5-10/195	31	Texas
	Laird, Gerald	R/R	6-2/195	24	Oklahoma, Texas

No.	INFIELDERS	B/T	Ht./Wt.	Age*	2003 Clubs
9	Blalock, Hank	L/R	6-1/192	23	Texas
	Bourgeios, Jason	B/R	5-9/170	22	Frisco, Stockton
	Fullmer, Brad	L/R	6-0/220	29	Anaheim
	Gonzalez, Adrian	L/L	6-2/190	21	Albuquerque, Carolina, Frisco
13	Lamb, Mike	L/R	6-1/195	28	Texas, Oklahoma
35	Perry, Herbert	R/R	6-2/235	34	Frisco, Texas
3	Rodriguez, Alex	R/R	6-3/210	28	Texas
23	Teixeira, Mark	B/R	6-2/215	23	Texas
	Young, Eric	R/R	5-8/186	36	Milwaukee, San Francisco
10	Young, Michael	R/R	6-1/190	27	Texas

No.	OUTFIELDERS	B/T	Ht./Wt.	Age*	2003 Clubs
	Dellucci, David	L/L	5-11/189	30	Arizona, New York A.L.
29	Greer, Rusty	L/L	6-0/195	35	Did Not Play
	Jordan, Brian	R/R	6-1/205	37	Los Angeles
28	Mench, Kevin	R/R	6-0/230	26	Frisco, Oklahoma, Texas
2	Nivar, Ramon	R/R	5-10/170	24	Frisco, Oklahoma, Texas
17	Nix, Laynce	L/L	6-0/190	23	Frisco, Texas

Invited to spring training: IF Manny Alexander, OF Chad Allen, RHP Carlos Almanzar, C Danny Ardoin, LHP Mike Bacsik, LHP Erick Burke, OF Jason Conti, C Ken Huckaby, LHP Glendon Rusch, RHP Erik Sabel, RHP Billy Sylvester, OF Jason Tyner, RHP John Wasdin, RHP Todd Williams.

*Age as of April 1, 2004.

BALLPARK INFORMATION

Ballpark (capacity, surface)
The Ballpark in Arlington (49,115, grass)

Address
1000 Ballpark Way
Arlington, TX 76011

Official website
www.texasrangers.com

Business phone
817-273-5222

Ticket information
817-273-5100

Field dimensions (from home plate)
To left field at foul line, 332 feet
To center field, 400 feet
To right field at foul line, 325 feet

First game played
April 11, 1994 (Brewers 4, Rangers 3)

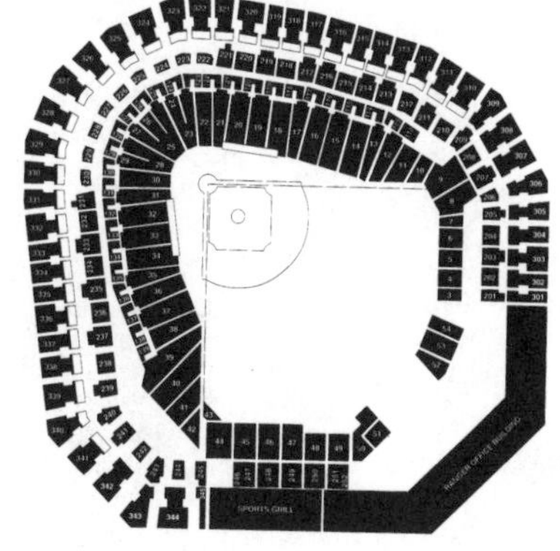

2003 REVIEW

DAY BY DAY

Date	Opp.	Res.	Score	(inn.*)	Hits	Opp. hits	Winning pitcher	Losing pitcher	Save	Record	Pos.	GB
3-30	At Ana.	W	6-3		12	8	Valdes	Lackey	Urbina	1-0	1st	+0.5
4-1	At Ana.	L	0-10		5	13	Callaway	Park		1-1	T2nd	0.5
4-2	At Ana.	L	5-11		10	14	Ortiz	Thomson		1-2	3rd	1.5
4-4	Sea.	L	4-6		7	9	Franklin	Cordero	Sasaki	1-3	4th	2.0
4-5	Sea.	W	8-4		15	11	Lewis	Meche	Urbina	2-3	T2nd	2.0
4-6	Sea.	L	2-11		4	14	Garcia	Park		2-4	T3rd	3.0
4-8	Oak.	L	1-2		5	10	Zito	Yan	Foulke	2-5	T3rd	4.0
4-9	Oak.	L	5-13		11	13	Mulder	Valdes		2-6	4th	5.0
4-10	Oak.	W	5-4		11	6	Cordero	Bradford	Urbina	3-6	4th	4.0
4-11	At Sea.	W	4-2		8	5	Park	Garcia	Urbina	4-6	T3rd	3.0
4-12	At Sea.	L	4-13		7	14	Meche	Drese		4-7	4th	3.0
4-13	At Sea.	L	3-4	(13)	12	9	Sasaki	Dickey		4-8	4th	3.0
4-14	Ana.	W	4-0		7	6	Valdes	Appier		5-8	4th	2.0
4-15	Ana.	W	5-4		6	10	Lewis	Washburn	Urbina	6-8	4th	2.0
4-16	Ana.	L	8-9		13	13	Rodriguez	Cordero	Percival	6-9	4th	2.0
4-17	Ana.	W	9-7		13	14	Drese	Callaway	Urbina	7-9	4th	2.0
4-18	At Oak.	L	0-9		6	12	Zito	Thomson		7-10	4th	3.0
4-19	At Oak.	L	2-12		5	15	Mulder	Valdes		7-11	4th	3.0
4-20	At Oak.	W	2-1		8	5	Lewis	Bradford	Urbina	8-11	4th	3.0
4-22	Bos.	L	4-5		6	9	Martinez	Park	Fox	8-12	4th	4.0
4-23	Bos.	W	6-1		10	6	Thomson	Wakefield		9-12	T3rd	4.0
4-24	Bos.	W	16-5		19	9	Dickey	Lowe		10-12	T3rd	4.0
4-25	N.Y.	L	2-3		7	6	Mussina	Lewis	Acevedo	10-13	T3rd	5.0
4-26	N.Y.	L	5-7	(10)	8	9	Hammond	Urbina	Acevedo	10-14	4th	5.0
4-27	N.Y.	W	10-7		15	12	Dickey	Weaver	Urbina	11-14	T3rd	5.0
4-29	At Tor.	W	16-11		17	18	Thomson	Hendrickson	Cordero	12-14	T3rd	5.0
4-30	At Tor.	W	11-3		18	10	Drese	Sturtze		13-14	T3rd	4.0
5-1	At Tor.	L	6-7		11	14	Halladay	Lewis	Politte	13-15	4th	4.0
5-2	At Cle.	L	5-6		6	6	Elder	Cordero	Baez	13-16	4th	5.0
5-3	At Cle.	W	6-5		11	8	Powell	Santiago	Urbina	14-16	3rd	5.0
5-4	At Cle.	L	1-3		4	5	Sabathia	Thomson	Baez	14-17	3rd	6.0
5-6	Tor.	L	5-15		7	17	Halladay	Lewis		14-18	4th	7.0
5-7	Tor.	W	5-4		9	8	Fultz	Sturtze	Urbina	15-18	4th	6.0
5-8	Tor.	L	6-8		13	10	Lidle	Drese	Politte	15-19	4th	6.0
5-9	Cle.	L	5-9		11	16	Westbrook	Thomson		15-20	4th	7.0
5-10	Cle.	L	4-6		8	10	Sabathia	Benes	Baez	15-21	4th	7.0
5-11	Cle.	W	17-10		20	11	Benoit	Rodriguez		16-21	4th	7.0
5-13	At Bos.	L	4-5		8	7	Embree	Cordero	Lyon	16-22	4th	8.0
5-14	At Bos.	L	1-7		6	8	Fossum	Benoit		16-23	4th	8.0
5-15	At Bos.	L	3-12		8	16	Martinez	Benes		16-24	4th	9.0
5-16	At N.Y.	W	8-5	(12)	13	14	Dickey	Acevedo	Urbina	17-24	4th	9.0
5-17	At N.Y.	W	5-2		8	5	Valdes	Pettitte	Urbina	18-24	4th	9.0
5-18	At N.Y.	W	5-1		9	3	Thomson	Mussina		19-24	4th	9.0
5-20	T.B.	W	5-2		7	5	Benoit	Brazelton	Urbina	20-24	4th	9.0
5-21	T.B.	W	8-7		13	14	Cordero	Colome	Urbina	21-24	4th	8.0
5-22	T.B.	W	10-8		13	11	Van Poppel	Harper	Urbina	22-24	4th	8.0
5-23	Bal.	W	5-3		11	10	Valdes	Hentgen	Urbina	23-24	3rd	8.0
5-24	Bal.	L	3-10		8	16	Daal	Thomson	Ligtenberg	23-25	4th	8.0
5-25	Bal.	L	10-13		11	18	Driskill	Dickey	Julio	23-26	4th	8.0
5-27	At T.B.	W	4-2		6	7	Lewis	Reyes	Urbina	24-26	4th	8.0
5-28	At T.B.	L	4-6		4	12	Gonzalez	Benes	Carter	24-27	4th	9.0
5-29	At Bal.	W	8-4		11	8	Valdes	Hentgen	Cordero	25-27	4th	9.0
5-30	At Bal.	L	1-8		7	10	Daal	Thomson		25-28	4th	10.0
5-31	At Bal.	L	1-7		8	11	Helling	Benoit		25-29	4th	11.0
6-1	At Bal.	L	4-5		7	11	Ponson	Cordero	Julio	25-30	4th	12.0
6-3	At Atl.	L	5-6		10	10	Gryboski	Urbina	Smoltz	25-31	4th	13.0
6-4	At Atl.	L	2-5		9	10	Maddux	Thomson	Smoltz	25-32	4th	14.0
6-5	At Atl.	L	4-8		8	10	Bong	Fultz		25-33	4th	15.0
6-6	At Mon.■	L	10-13		14	13	Hernandez	Lewis		25-34	4th	15.0
6-7	At Mon.■	L	4-5		8	4	Vargas	Shouse	Ayala	25-35	4th	15.5
6-8	At Mon.■	L	2-3		9	8	Stewart	Cordero	Biddle	25-36	4th	17.0
6-10	N.Y. (NL)	W	9-7		13	11	Thomson	Trachsel	Urbina	26-36	4th	16.0
6-11	N.Y. (NL)	L	2-8		9	10	Seo	Santos		26-37	4th	16.0
6-12	N.Y. (NL)	L	0-11		11	16	Leiter	Lewis		26-38	4th	17.0

Date	Opp.	Res.	Score	(inn.*)	Hits	Opp. hits	Winning pitcher	Losing pitcher	Save	Record	Pos.	GB
6-13	Fla.	L	0-8		5	16	Penny	Mounce		26-39	4th	18.0
6-14	Fla.	W	13-2		18	9	Valdes	Phelps		27-39	4th	17.0
6-15	Fla.	L	4-10		12	15	Redman	Thomson		27-40	4th	18.0
6-17	At Oak.	L	3-4		6	6	Lilly	Santos	Foulke	27-41	4th	19.5
6-18	At Oak.	L	3-4	(11)	9	11	Foulke	Dickey		27-42	4th	20.5
6-19	At Oak.	L	2-9		11	14	Mulder	Ramos		27-43	4th	20.5
6-20	Hou.	L	3-12		9	16	Miller	Thomson		27-44	4th	20.5
6-21	Hou.	L	5-9		7	12	Rosario	Valdes		27-45	4th	21.5
6-22	Hou.	L	1-3		7	7	Robertson	Benoit	Wagner	27-46	4th	21.5
6-23	Oak.	L	1-3		5	6	Rincon	Urbina	Foulke	27-47	4th	22.0
6-24	Oak.	W	7-6		12	10	Ramos	Mulder	Urbina	28-47	4th	22.0
6-25	Oak.	W	9-8		15	16	Cordero	Mecir	Urbina	29-47	4th	21.0
6-26	Oak.	L	0-13		4	15	Hudson	Valdes		29-48	4th	22.0
6-27	At Hou.	W	10-7		10	12	Benoit	Redding		30-48	4th	22.0
6-28	At Hou.	L	0-2		6	4	Robertson	Mounce	Wagner	30-49	4th	22.0
6-29	At Hou.	W	8-5		8	5	Garcia	Dotel	Urbina	31-49	4th	21.0
6-30	At Ana.	W	6-3		12	6	Thomson	Ortiz	Urbina	32-49	4th	21.0
7-1	At Ana.	L	5-7		8	8	Washburn	Valdes	Percival	32-50	4th	21.0
7-2	At Ana.	L	0-5		4	6	Lackey	Benoit		32-51	4th	22.0
7-3	At Ana.	W	6-5		11	9	Mounce	Appier	Urbina	33-51	4th	21.0
7-4	Sea.	W	7-3		10	7	Dickey	Garcia	Urbina	34-51	4th	20.0
7-5	Sea.	L	2-3	(10)	9	10	Soriano	Urbina	Hasegawa	34-52	4th	21.0
7-6	Sea.	W	5-1		6	5	Valdes	Meche		35-52	4th	20.0
7-8	Min.	W	8-6		13	10	Powell	Lohse	Urbina	36-52	4th	20.0
7-9	Min.	W	4-1		7	5	Benoit	Rogers	Urbina	37-52	4th	19.0
7-10	Min.	W	9-4		11	11	Thomson	Reed		38-52	4th	18.0
7-11	K.C.	L	3-13		5	14	Wilson	Dickey		38-53	4th	19.0
7-12	K.C.	L	2-8		9	15	Lima	Valdes		38-54	4th	19.0
7-13	K.C.	L	2-8		12	11	May	Mounce		38-55	4th	20.0
7-17	At T.B.	W	12-6		15	9	Thomson	Kennedy		39-55	4th	19.0
7-18	At T.B.	L	0-2		7	8	Gonzalez	Valdes	Carter	39-56	4th	20.0
7-19	At T.B.	W	7-3		11	7	Benoit	Zambrano		40-56	4th	19.0
7-20	At T.B.	L	4-15		6	18	Sosa	Mounce		40-57	4th	19.0
7-21	At Bal.	L	2-3		7	7	Hentgen	Dickey	Julio	40-58	4th	19.0
7-22	At Bal.	L	6-12		14	14	Driskill	Thomson		40-59	4th	20.0
7-23	Ana.	W	12-9		13	16	Ramirez	Washburn	Cordero	41-59	4th	20.0
7-24	Ana.	L	6-10		10	13	Appier	Benoit	Percival	41-60	4th	20.0
7-25	At Sea.	L	5-11		10	13	Moyer	Ellis	Soriano	41-61	4th	21.0
7-26	At Sea.	L	0-4		3	12	Pineiro	Lewis		41-62	4th	22.0
7-27	At Sea.	W	7-3		13	8	Thomson	Garcia		42-62	4th	21.0
7-28	At Sea.	W	10-1		15	5	Benoit	Franklin		43-62	4th	20.0
7-29	Bos.	L	7-14		9	14	Wakefield	Garcia		43-63	4th	21.0
7-30	Bos.	W	9-2		10	7	Ellis	Mendoza		44-63	4th	21.0
7-31	Bos.	W	7-3	(11)	9	12	Ramirez	Jones		45-63	4th	21.0
8-1	Cle.	W	10-3		11	5	Thomson	Traber		46-63	4th	20.0
8-2	Cle.	W	9-7		10	10	Ramirez	Stanford	Cordero	47-63	4th	20.0
8-3	Cle.	W	8-5		14	10	Dickey	Anderson	Cordero	48-63	4th	20.0
8-5	At N.Y.	L	2-6		7	9	Clemens	Lewis		48-64	4th	21.0
8-6	At N.Y.	W	5-4		9	8	Mahay	Rivera	Cordero	49-64	4th	20.0
8-7	At N.Y.	L	5-7		10	6	Mussina	Fultz	Rivera	49-65	4th	20.0
8-8	At Tor.	W	5-3		11	8	Dickey	Thurman	Cordero	50-65	4th	19.0
8-9	At Tor.	L	3-5		5	11	Escobar	Fultz	Lopez	50-66	4th	20.0
8-10	At Tor.	W	5-4		10	11	Lewis	Towers	Cordero	51-66	4th	20.0
8-11	Det.	W	9-3		10	7	Benoit	Sparks		52-66	4th	19.0
8-12	Det.	L	4-7		5	11	Bonderman	Dominguez	Patterson	52-67	4th	20.0
8-13	Det.	W	7-3		10	9	Dickey	Maroth	Cordero	53-67	4th	20.0
8-14	Det.	W	6-3		11	11	Thomson	Roney	Cordero	54-67	4th	19.0
8-15	Chi.	W	11-5		12	9	Lewis	Loaiza		55-67	4th	19.0
8-16	Chi.	W	12-8		12	13	Benoit	Colon		56-67	4th	18.0
8-17	Chi.	W	6-4		8	6	Powell	Marte	Cordero	57-67	4th	18.0
8-18	At Det.	W	4-2	(16)	13	10	Mahay	Sparks	Dickey	58-67	4th	17.5
8-19	At Det.	W	5-4		11	12	Thomson	Maroth	Shouse	59-67	4th	17.5
8-20	At Det.	W	6-0		9	6	Dickey	Cornejo		60-67	T3rd	16.5
8-21	At Chi.	L	3-7		6	10	Colon	Lewis	Gordon	60-68	4th	16.5
8-22	At Chi.	L	1-7		6	5	Cotts	Dominguez		60-69	4th	16.5
8-23	At Chi.	L	2-13		8	17	Buehrle	Valdes	Wright	60-70	4th	16.5
8-24	At Chi.	W	5-0		6	4	Thomson	Garland		61-70	4th	15.5
8-26	At K.C.	L	2-9		6	12	Anderson	Dickey		61-71	4th	16.0
8-27	At K.C.	L	0-9		5	13	May	Lewis		61-72	4th	17.0

Date	Opp.	Res.	Score	(inn.*)	Hits	Opp. hits	Winning pitcher	Losing pitcher	Save	Record	Pos.	GB
8-28	At K.C.	L	5-6	(11)	9	13	Carrasco	Ramirez		61-73	4th	18.0
8-29	Min.	L	5-8		10	11	Balfour	Thomson	Guardado	61-74	4th	19.0
8-30	Min.	L	0-2		6	8	Santana	Callaway	Guardado	61-75	4th	20.0
8-31	Min.	W	11-10		18	15	Cordero	Guardado		62-75	4th	20.0
9-1	K.C.	W	7-3		6	6	Lewis	May		63-75	4th	19.5
9-2	K.C.	W	8-7		8	10	Valdes	Affeldt	Cordero	64-75	4th	19.5
9-3	K.C.	L	1-3		7	4	Gobble	Thomson	MacDougal	64-76	4th	19.5
9-5	At Min.	L	7-10		10	10	Rincon	Callaway	Guardado	64-77	4th	20.0
9-6	At Min.	L	2-5		7	11	Radke	Dickey	Guardado	64-78	4th	20.0
9-7	At Min.	L	4-5	(10)	9	8	Reed	Cordero		64-79	4th	20.0
9-9	At Sea.	W	5-4	(10)	11	8	Mahay	Hasegawa	Cordero	65-79	4th	19.5
9-10	At Sea.	L	1-3		4	4	Pineiro	Thomson		65-80	4th	20.5
9-11	At Sea.	L	2-8		5	10	Meche	Callaway		65-81	4th	21.5
9-12	Oak.	L	3-9		7	11	Zito	Drese	Foulke	65-82	4th	22.5
9-13	Oak.	L	3-9		11	13	Hudson	Dickey		65-83	4th	23.5
9-14	Oak.	L	5-6		12	7	Harville	Garcia	Foulke	65-84	4th	24.5
9-15	Sea.	W	6-4		7	9	Lewis	Pineiro	Cordero	66-84	4th	24.5
9-16	Sea.	W	10-5		15	11	Thomson	Meche		67-84	4th	23.5
9-17	Sea.	L	1-5		5	11	Moyer	Drese		67-85	4th	24.5
9-18	Sea.	W	2-1	(10)	6	5	Cordero	Hasegawa		68-85	4th	24.0
9-19	Ana.	W	3-2		7	7	Dickey	Lackey	Cordero	69-85	4th	23.0
9-20	Ana.	W	13-4		14	6	Lewis	Sele		70-85	4th	22.0
9-21	Ana.	L	6-11		8	18	Ortiz	Mahay		70-86	4th	23.0
9-22	At Oak.	L	3-7		6	11	Zito	Mounce		70-87	4th	24.0
9-23	At Oak.	L	3-4	(10)	9	12	Foulke	Cordero		70-88	4th	25.0
9-24	At Oak.	L	3-5		7	7	Hudson	Mahay	Harville	70-89	4th	26.0
9-26	At Ana.	L	3-5		6	7	Turnbow	Mahay	Rodriguez	70-90	4th	26.0
9-27	At Ana.	W	12-3		18	10	Lewis	Ortiz		71-90	4th	25.0
9-28	At Ana.	L	1-4		6	12	Shields	Thomson	Donnelly	71-91	4th	25.0

Monthly records: March (1-0), April (12-14), May (12-15), June (7-20), July (13-14), August (17-12), September (9-16). *Innings, if other than nine. ■ At Hiram Bithorn Stadium, San Juan, Puerto Rico. † First game of a doubleheader. ‡ Second game of a doubleheader.

RECORDS

2003 regular-season record: 71-91
Position: 4th in A.L. West
Home: 43-38 **Road:** 28-53
A.L. East: 22-23 **A.L. Central:** 21-20
A.L. West: 24-34 N.L. 4-14
Vs. LH starters: 21-35
Vs. RH starters: 50-56
Grass: 64-80 **Artificial:** 7-11
Day: 17-22 **Night:** 54-69
1-Run: 17-20 **X-inn.:** 5-7
Doubleheaders: 0-0-0
Team record past five years: 382-428 (.472, ranks 10th in league in that span)

TEAM LEADERS

Batting average: Michael Young (.306).
At-bats: Michael Young (666).
Runs: Alex Rodriguez (124).
Hits: Michael Young (204).
Total Bases: Alex Rodriguez (364).
Doubles: Hank Blalock, Michael Young (33).
Triples: Michael Young (9).
Home runs: Alex Rodriguez (47).
Runs batted in: Alex Rodriguez (118).
Stolen bases: Alex Rodriguez (17).
Slugging percentage: Alex Rodriguez (.600).
On-base percentage: Alex Rodriguez (.396).
Wins: John Thomson (13).
Earned-run average: John Thomson (4.85).
Complete games: John Thomson (3).
Shutouts: R.A. Dickey, John Thomson (1).
Saves: Ugueth Urbina (26).
Innings pitched: John Thomson (217.0).
Strikeouts: John Thomson (136).

GAMES BY POSITION

Catcher: Einar Diaz 101, Todd Greene 51, Gerald Laird 16, Chad Kreuter 7.
First base: Mark Teixeira 116, Rafael Palmeiro 55, Mike Lamb 5, Herbert Perry 5, Jason Jones 3, Todd Greene 2.
Second base: Michael Young 159, Jermaine Clark 7, Hank Blalock 4, Donnie Sadler 1.
Third base: Hank Blalock 141, Donnie Sadler 23, Mark Teixeira 15, Herbert Perry 2, Mike Lamb 1.
Shortstop: Alex Rodriguez 158, Donnie Sadler 19, Michael Young 7.
Outfield: Carl Everett 72, Ryan Christenson 59, Juan Gonzalez 57, Shane Spencer 54, Doug Glanville 52, Laynce Nix 52, Donnie Sadler 41, Kevin Mench 35, Jason Jones 27, Ramon Nivar 26, Mark Teixeira 25, Marcus Thames 24, Ruben Sierra 23, Jermaine Clark 17, Ryan Ludwick 8, Mike Lamb 2.
Designated hitter: Rafael Palmeiro 97, Juan Gonzalez 24, Ruben Sierra 15, Jason Jones 6, Mike Lamb 6, Mark Teixeira 5, Marcus Thames 4, Todd Greene 3, Jermaine Clark 2, Carl Everett 1, Ramon Nivar 1, Laynce Nix 1, Alex Rodriguez 1, Shane Spencer 1.

TOP DRAFT CHOICES

1. **John Danks,** LHP, Round Rock (Texas) H.S.
2. **Vince Sinisi,** 1B, Rice.
3. **John Hudgins,** RHP, Stanford.
4. **Wes Littleton,** RHP, Cal State-Fullerton.
5. **Matt Lorenzo,** RHP, Kent State.
6. **Adam Bourassa,** OF, Wake Forest.
7. **Matt Farnum,** RHP, Texas A&M.
8. **Jeremy Cleveland,** OF, North Carolina.
9. **Tim Cunningham,** LHP, Stanford.
10. **Adam Fox,** 3B, Ohio.

TORONTO BLUE JAYS

AMERICAN LEAGUE EAST DIVISION

2004 SEASON

April

SUN	MON	TUE	WED	THU	FRI	SAT
4	5 DET	6 DET	7 DET	8	9 BOS	10 BOS
11 BOS	12	13 DET	14 DET	15 DET	16 BAL	17 BAL
18 BAL	19	20 BOS	21 BOS	22 BOS	23 BAL	24 BAL
25 BAL	26 MIN	27 MIN	28 MIN	29 CHW	30 CHW	

May

SUN	MON	TUE	WED	THU	FRI	SAT
						1 CHW
2 CHW	3 KC	4 KC	5 KC	6	7 CHW	8 CHW
9 CHW	10 KC	11 KC	12 KC	13 BOS	14 BOS	15 BOS
16 BOS	17 MIN	18 MIN	19 MIN	20	21 BOS	22 BOS
23 BOS	24 ANA	25	26 ANA	27 ANA	28 TEX	29 TEX
30 TEX	31 SEA					

June

SUN	MON	TUE	WED	THU	FRI	SAT
		1 SEA	2 SEA	3 OAK	4 OAK	5 OAK
6 OAK	7	8 LA	9 LA	10 LA	11 ARI	12 ARI
13 ARI	14	15 SF	16 SF	17 SF	18 SD	19 SD
20 SD	21	22 TB	23 TB	24 TB	25 MON	26 MON
27 MON	28 TB	29 TB	30 TB			

July

SUN	MON	TUE	WED	THU	FRI	SAT
				1 TB	2 * MON	3 * MON
4 * MON	5	6 SEA	7 SEA	8 SEA	9 ANA	10 ANA
11 ANA	12	13 All-Star	14	15	16 TEX	17 TEX
18 TEX	19 OAK	20 OAK	21 NYY	22 NYY	23 TB	24 TB
25 TB	26 NYY	27 NYY	28 NYY	29	30 TB	31 TB

August

SUN	MON	TUE	WED	THU	FRI	SAT
1 TB	2 CLE	3 CLE	4 CLE	5 CLE	6 NYY	7 NYY
8 NYY	9 NYY	10 CLE	11 CLE	12 CLE	13 BAL	14 BAL
15 BAL	16 BOS	17 BOS	18 BOS	19	20 BAL	21 BAL
22 BAL	23 BOS	24 BOS	25 BOS	26 NYY	27 NYY	28 NYY
29 NYY	30	31 SEA				

Sept./Oct.

SUN	MON	TUE	WED	THU	FRI	SAT
			1 SEA	2 SEA	3 OAK	4 OAK
5 OAK	6	7 ANA	8 ANA	9 ANA	10 TEX	11 TEX
12 TEX	13 BAL	14	15 BAL	16 BAL	17 TB	18 TB
19 TB	20	21 NYY	22 NYY	23 NYY	24 TB	25 TB
26 TB	27 BAL	28 BAL	29 BAL	30 BAL	1 NYY	2 NYY
3 NYY	4	5	6	7	8	9

Home games shaded. All-Star Game July 13 at Houston. Schedule subject to change. * San Juan, Puerto Rico.

CLUB DIRECTORY

President and CEO
Paul Godfrey
Senior v.p., baseball & general manager
J.P. Ricciardi
Senior vice president, communications and external affairs
Rob Godfrey
Vice president, baseball
Bob Mattick
V.p., baseball operations & asst. g.m.
Tim McCleary
Assistant to the general manager
Keith Law, Chris Buckley
Special assistant to general manager
Bill Livesey
Director of player personnel
Tony LaCava
Manager of minor league operations
Charlie Wilson
Vice president, special projects
Howard Starkman
Director, player development
Dick Scott
Director, scouting
Jon Lalonde
Director, communications
Jay Stenhouse
Director of public relations
Will Hill

MINOR LEAGUE AFFILIATES

Class	Team	League	Manager
AAA	Syracuse	International	Marty Pevey
AA	New Hampshire	Eastern	Mike Basso
Advanced A	Dunedin	Florida State	Omar Malave
A	Charleston (W.Va.)	South Atlantic	Ken Joyce
Short-Season A	Auburn	New York-Penn	Dennis Holmberg
Advanced Rookie	Pulaski	Appalachian	Gary Cathcart

More on the Blue Jays at www.foxsports.com/named/FS/MLB/teams

BROADCAST INFORMATION

Radio: The Fan (590).
Cable TV: Rogers SportsNet (RSN).

SPRING TRAINING

Ballpark (city): Dunedin Stadium at Grant Field (Dunedin, Fla.).
Ticket information: 800-707-8269; 727-733-0429.

SPRING TRAINING ROSTER

Manager—Carlos Tosca (14).
Coaches—Mike Barnett (56), Joe Breeden, Brian Butterfield (55), John Gibbons (58), Gil Patterson (47), Bruce Walton (52).

No.	PITCHERS	B/T	Ht./Wt.	Age*	2003 Clubs
	Adams, Terry	R/R	6-3/215	31	Philadelphia
	Arnold, Jason	R/R	6-3/210	24	New Haven, Syracuse
	Batista, Miguel	R/R	6-1/197	33	Arizona
	Chulk, Vinnie	R/R	6-2/195	25	Syracuse, Toronto
	de los Santos, V.	L/L	6-2/218	31	Milwaukee, Philadelphia
36	File, Bob	R/R	6-4/215	27	Dunedin, Syracuse
	Haines, Talley	R/R	6-3/205	27	Durham
32	Halladay, Roy	R/R	6-6/230	26	Toronto
	Hanson, D.J.	R/R	5-11/175	23	Charleston-WV
	Harper, Jesse	R/R	6-4/210	23	Dunedin
	Hentgen, Pat	R/R	6-2/195	35	Baltimore
46	Kershner, Jason	L/L	6-2/185	27	Syracuse, Toronto
	Ligtenberg, Kerry	R/R	6-2/222	32	Baltimore
	Lilly, Ted	L/L	6-1/190	28	Oakland
	Lopez, Aquilino	R/R	6-3/165	28	Toronto
	McGowan, Dustin	R/R	6-3/220	22	Dunedin, New Haven
34	Miller, Justin	R/R	6-2/195	26	Dunedin
	Rosario, Francisco	R/R	6-0/195	23	Did Not Play
	Speier, Justin	R/R	6-4/205	30	Colorado
	Towers, Josh	R/R	6-1/188	27	Syracuse, Toronto

No.	CATCHERS	B/T	Ht./Wt.	Age*	2003 Clubs
29	Cash, Kevin	R/R	6-0/185	26	Syracuse, Toronto
28	Myers, Greg	L/R	6-2/225	37	Toronto
	Quiroz, Guillermo	R/R	6-1/202	22	New Haven

No.	INFIELDERS	B/T	Ht./Wt.	Age*	2003 Clubs
2	Berg, Dave	R/R	5-11/185	33	Syracuse, Toronto
6	Clark, Howie	L/R	5-10/191	30	Syracuse, Toronto
25	Delgado, Carlos	L/R	6-3/230	31	Toronto
	Gomez, Chris	R/R	6-1/185	32	Minnesota
11	Hinske, Eric	L/R	6-2/225	26	Syracuse, Toronto
3	Hudson, Orlando	B/R	6-0/185	26	Toronto
17	Phelps, Josh	R/R	6-3/225	25	Syracuse, Toronto
	Pond, Simon	L/R	6-1/205	27	New Haven, Syracuse
	Sequea, Jorge	B/R	5-10/160	23	New Haven, Syracuse
5	Woodward, Chris	R/R	6-0/185	27	Toronto

No.	OUTFIELDERS	B/T	Ht./Wt.	Age*	2003 Clubs
27	Catalanotto, Frank	L/R	5-11/195	29	Toronto
	Griffin, John-Ford	L/L	6-2/215	24	New Haven
	Gross, Gabe	L/R	6-3/210	24	New Haven, Syracuse
37	Johnson, Reed	R/R	5-10/180	27	Syracuse, Toronto
15	Rios, Alexis	R/R	6-5/185	23	New Haven
10	Wells, Vernon	R/R	6-1/225	25	Toronto
13	Werth, Jayson	R/R	6-5/215	24	Dunedin, Toronto, Syracuse

Invited to spring training: LHP Bruce Chen, RHP Jayson Durocher, OF Chad Hermansen, LHP Chi-Hung Chen, RHP Pete Walker.

*Age as of April 1, 2004.

BALLPARK INFORMATION

Ballpark (capacity, surface)
SkyDome (50,516, artificial)

Address
One Blue Jays Way
Suite 3200
Toronto, Ontario M5V 1J1

Official website
www.bluejays.com

Business phone
416-341-1000

Ticket information
416-341-1234 and 1-888-OK GO JAY

Field dimensions (from home plate)
To left field at foul line, 330 feet
To center field, 400 feet
To right field at foul line, 330 feet

First game played
June 5, 1989 (Brewers 5, Blue Jays 3)

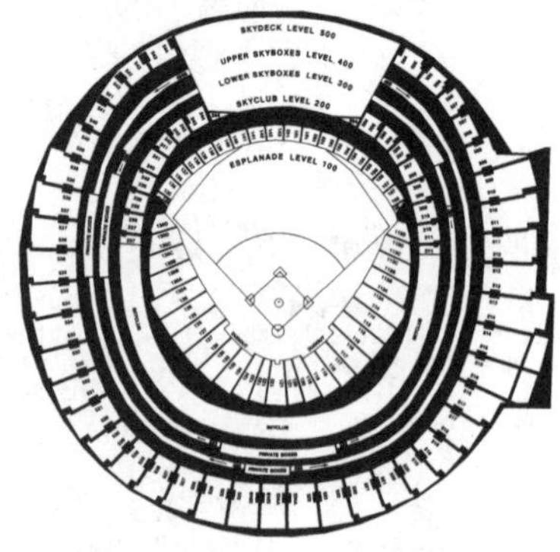

2003 REVIEW
DAY BY DAY

Date	Opp.	Res.	Score	(inn.*)	Hits	Opp. hits	Winning pitcher	Losing pitcher	Save	Record	Pos.	GB
3-31	N.Y.	L	4-8		9	7	Clemens	Halladay		0-1	T4th	1.0
4-1	N.Y.	L	1-10		8	13	Pettitte	Lidle		0-2	5th	2.0
4-2	N.Y.	L	7-9		11	17	Mussina	Hendrickson	Acevedo	0-3	5th	3.0
4-4	At Min.	W	7-2		8	5	Sturtze	Reed		1-3	T3rd	3.0
4-5	At Min.	W	4-3	(11)	10	10	Walker	Guardado	Escobar	2-3	T3rd	2.0
4-6	At Min.	W	8-1		11	9	Lidle	Radke		3-3	3rd	2.0
4-8	Bos.	W	8-4		12	11	Hendrickson	Lowe		4-3	3rd	2.0
4-9	Bos.	W	10-5		8	9	Sturtze	Fossum		5-3	2nd	2.0
4-10	Bos.	L	7-8		10	11	Timlin	Politte		5-4	3rd	3.0
4-11	Min.	L	4-6		8	12	Rogers	Lidle	Guardado	5-5	3rd	3.5
4-12	Min.	L	6-9		11	13	Hawkins	Escobar	Guardado	5-6	3rd	4.5
4-13	Min.	L	3-9		4	11	Mays	Hendrickson		5-7	T3rd	4.5
4-14	At N.Y.	L	9-10		16	8	Contreras	Lopez	Hammond	5-8	4th	5.5
4-15	At N.Y.	L	0-5		3	12	Mussina	Halladay		5-9	4th	6.5
4-16	At N.Y.	W	7-6		17	11	Lidle	Hitchcock	Escobar	6-9	3rd	5.5
4-17	At N.Y.	L	0-4		5	4	Weaver	Walker		6-10	4th	6.5
4-18	At Bos.	L	3-7		8	11	Wakefield	Tam		6-11	4th	7.5
4-19	At Bos.	L	2-7		9	8	Lowe	Sturtze		6-12	5th	8.5
4-20	At Bos.	L	5-6		6	13	Timlin	Politte		6-13	5th	9.5
4-21	At Bos.	W	11-6		17	11	Lidle	Burkett		7-13	4th	9.5
4-22	At T.B.	L	3-4		5	11	Kennedy	Kershner	Carter	7-14	5th	10.5
4-23	At T.B.	L	3-4		8	9	Venafro	Hendrickson	Carter	7-15	5th	11.5
4-24	At T.B.	W	5-3		8	8	Sturtze	Sosa	Escobar	8-15	5th	10.5
4-25	K.C.	W	6-5		10	9	Escobar	Carrasco		9-15	5th	10.5
4-26	K.C.	L	6-9		10	14	Grimsley	Tam	MacDougal	9-16	5th	11.5
4-27	K.C.	W	10-9		16	17	Politte	MacDougal		10-16	5th	10.5
4-29	Tex.	L	11-16		18	17	Thomson	Hendrickson	Cordero	10-17	5th	10.5
4-30	Tex.	L	3-11		10	18	Drese	Sturtze		10-18	5th	11.5
5-1	Tex.	W	7-6		14	11	Halladay	Lewis	Politte	11-18	4th	11.5
5-2	Ana.	W	3-1		5	3	Lidle	Lackey		12-18	4th	11.5
5-3	Ana.	W	7-1		15	8	Davis	Shields		13-18	4th	10.5
5-4	Ana.	W	8-2		14	4	Hendrickson	Ortiz	Escobar	14-18	4th	9.5
5-6	At Tex.	W	15-5		17	7	Halladay	Lewis		15-18	4th	8.5
5-7	At Tex.	L	4-5		8	9	Fultz	Sturtze	Urbina	15-19	4th	9.5
5-8	At Tex.	W	8-6		10	13	Lidle	Drese	Politte	16-19	4th	9.5
5-9	At Ana.	L	1-6		3	5	Sele	Davis		16-20	4th	9.5
5-10	At Ana.	W	7-4		10	9	Hendrickson	Ortiz		17-20	4th	9.5
5-11	At Ana.	W	4-2		7	6	Halladay	Washburn	Politte	18-20	4th	8.5
5-13	T.B.	L	5-7		10	12	Kennedy	Sturtze	Carter	18-21	4th	8.5
5-14	T.B.	W	7-6		11	10	Lidle	Brazelton	Politte	19-21	3rd	7.5
5-15	T.B.	L	5-9		9	12	Colome	Davis		19-22	3rd	8.5
5-16	At K.C.	W	18-1		22	10	Hendrickson	George		20-22	3rd	7.5
5-17	At K.C.	W	7-4		13	6	Halladay	Grimsley	Politte	21-22	3rd	6.5
5-18	At K.C.	W	4-3		9	7	Sturtze	Snyder	Politte	22-22	3rd	5.5
5-19	At Chi.	W	12-2		15	7	Lidle	Wright		23-22	3rd	5.5
5-20	At Chi.	L	1-4		9	8	Colon	Davis		23-23	3rd	5.5
5-21	At Chi.	L	5-6		10	9	Marte	Politte	Koch	23-24	3rd	6.5
5-22	At N.Y.	W	8-3		13	10	Halladay	Pettitte		24-24	3rd	5.5
5-23	At N.Y.	W	6-2		9	6	Escobar	Mussina		25-24	3rd	5.0
5-24	At N.Y.	W	5-2		10	6	Lidle	Wells	Politte	26-24	3rd	5.0
5-25	At N.Y.	W	5-3		8	12	Davis	Weaver	Politte	27-24	3rd	4.0
5-26	Chi.	W	11-5		11	9	Towers	Buehrle	Tam	28-24	3rd	4.0
5-27	Chi.	W	5-1		9	7	Halladay	Colon		29-24	3rd	3.0
5-28	Chi.	L	0-8		5	11	Garland	Escobar		29-25	3rd	3.0
5-29	Chi.	L	2-3		5	7	Loaiza	Lidle	Koch	29-26	3rd	3.5
5-30	Bos.	W	13-2		12	9	Davis	Burkett		30-26	3rd	3.0
5-31	Bos.	W	10-7		10	14	Sturtze	Fossum	Politte	31-26	3rd	2.0
6-1	Bos.	W	11-8		19	14	Halladay	White		32-26	3rd	2.0
6-3	At StL.	L	5-11		10	14	Morris	Escobar		32-27	3rd	2.0
6-4	At StL.	L	5-8		11	12	Simontacchi	Lidle	Eldred	32-28	3rd	2.5
6-5	At StL.	L	5-13		5	15	Williams	Hendrickson		32-29	3rd	3.0
6-6	At Cin.	W	9-2		15	9	Halladay	Riedling		33-29	3rd	3.0
6-7	At Cin.	L	8-9		10	14	Reitsma	Politte		33-30	3rd	3.0
6-8	At Cin.	W	5-0		12	4	Escobar	Haynes		34-30	3rd	2.5

Date	Opp.	Res.	Score	(inn.*)	Hits	Opp. hits	Winning pitcher	Losing pitcher	Save	Record	Pos.	GB
6-10	Pit.	W	13-8		19	14	Lidle	Benson		35-30	3rd	2.0
6-11	Pit.	W	8-5		11	12	Halladay	D'Amico		36-30	3rd	1.5
6-12	Pit.	W	5-4		7	6	Hendrickson	Suppan	Politte	37-30	3rd	1.0
6-13	Chi. (NL)	W	5-1		8	12	Escobar	Wood		38-30	3rd	1.0
6-14	Chi. (NL)	L	2-4		10	6	Prior	Davis	Borowski	38-31	3rd	2.0
6-15	Chi. (NL)	W	5-4	(10)	9	8	Lopez	Guthrie		39-31	3rd	2.0
6-18	At Bal.	W	6-2		10	7	Halladay	Daal	Lopez	40-31	3rd	2.0
6-19	At Bal.	W	6-1		9	8	Escobar	Helling		41-31	3rd	1.5
6-20	At Mon.	W	8-4		13	8	Lidle	Vazquez		42-31	3rd	1.5
6-21	At Mon.	L	5-8		13	9	Ayala	Politte	Biddle	42-32	3rd	2.0
6-22	At Mon.	W	4-2		11	5	Halladay	Hernandez	Politte	43-32	2nd	2.0
6-23	Bal.	W	13-4		20	11	Davis	Daal		44-32	2nd	1.0
6-24	Bal.	L	4-6		9	8	Helling	Escobar	Julio	44-33	3rd	2.0
6-25	Bal.	L	2-9		10	13	Ponson	Lidle		44-34	3rd	3.0
6-26	Bal.	W	13-8		15	11	Sturtze	Driskill	Lopez	45-34	3rd	3.0
6-27	Mon.	W	6-5		9	10	Miller	Manon		46-34	3rd	3.0
6-28	Mon.	L	2-4		5	11	Vargas	Davis	Biddle	46-35	3rd	4.5
6-29	Mon.	L	2-10		2	13	Ohka	Escobar		46-36	3rd	5.5
6-30	At Det.	L	2-6		8	9	Maroth	Lidle		46-37	3rd	6.5
7-1	At Det.	L	0-5		4	11	Roney	Hendrickson	Walker	46-38	3rd	6.5
7-2	At Det.	W	8-2		11	9	Halladay	Bernero		47-38	3rd	6.0
7-3	At Bal.	L	5-6		12	11	Johnson	Davis	Julio	47-39	3rd	6.5
7-4	At Bal.	L	5-8		8	13	Driskill	Lopez	Julio	47-40	3rd	6.5
7-5	At Bal.	L	2-9		7	14	Ponson	Lidle		47-41	3rd	6.5
7-6	At Bal.	W	5-3	(10)	13	8	Acevedo	Ligtenberg		48-41	3rd	6.5
7-8	Bos.	L	1-2	(12)	8	9	Jones	Tam	Kim	48-42	3rd	7.0
7-9	Bos.	L	7-8		13	13	Lyon	Tam	Kim	48-43	3rd	8.0
7-10	Bos.	L	1-7		8	13	Mendoza	Lidle		48-44	3rd	8.0
7-11	N.Y.	L	5-8		9	14	Pettitte	Miller	Rivera	48-45	3rd	9.0
7-12	N.Y.	W	10-3		14	6	Halladay	Mussina		49-45	3rd	8.0
7-13	N.Y.	L	2-6		5	10	Weaver	Escobar		49-46	3rd	9.0
7-17	At Bos.	W	5-2		9	9	Halladay	Lowe		50-46	3rd	9.0
7-18	At Bos.	W	4-1		8	7	Escobar	Wakefield	Miller	51-46	3rd	9.0
7-19	At Bos.	L	4-5	(10)	7	10	Kim	Lopez		51-47	3rd	10.0
7-20	At Bos.	L	4-9		7	11	Martinez	Wasdin		51-48	3rd	11.0
7-21	At N.Y.	W	8-0	(8)	15	5	Hendrickson	Weaver		52-48	3rd	10.0
7-23	Chi.	L	6-7		10	11	White	Acevedo	Marte	52-49	3rd	11.0
7-24	Chi.	L	3-4	(13)	6	12	Gordon	Sturtze	White	52-50	3rd	11.0
7-25	Bal.	W	5-3		9	9	Lidle	Johnson	Miller	53-50	3rd	11.0
7-26	Bal.	L	2-7		7	14	Hentgen	Hendrickson		53-51	3rd	11.0
7-27	Bal.	W	10-1		15	3	Halladay	Lopez		54-51	3rd	10.0
7-29	T.B.	L	8-9		11	13	Levine	Miller	Carter	54-52	3rd	11.0
7-30	T.B.	L	3-5		7	7	Zambrano	Lidle	Colome	54-53	3rd	12.0
7-31	T.B.	L	6-7		8	13	Sosa	Hendrickson	Carter	54-54	3rd	13.0
8-1	At Ana.	L	0-5		4	10	Ortiz	Halladay		54-55	3rd	13.0
8-2	At Ana.	W	6-1		12	7	Thurman	Washburn		55-55	3rd	13.0
8-3	At Ana.	W	4-0		10	6	Escobar	Shields	Politte	56-55	3rd	12.0
8-4	At T.B.	L	1-10		7	10	Zambrano	Lidle		56-56	3rd	12.5
8-5	At T.B.	L	4-5	(10)	9	8	Colome	Acevedo		56-57	3rd	13.5
8-6	At T.B.	W	7-3		10	9	Halladay	Kennedy		57-57	3rd	12.5
8-8	Tex.	L	3-5		8	11	Dickey	Thurman	Cordero	57-58	3rd	14.0
8-9	Tex.	W	5-3		11	5	Escobar	Fultz	Lopez	58-58	3rd	13.0
8-10	Tex.	L	4-5		11	10	Lewis	Towers	Cordero	58-59	3rd	13.0
8-11	At Sea.	W	5-3		7	11	Hendrickson	Pineiro	Lopez	59-59	3rd	12.0
8-12	At Sea.	L	1-3		6	6	Garcia	Halladay	Hasegawa	59-60	3rd	13.0
8-13	At Sea.	L	6-13		9	17	Mateo	Kershner		59-61	3rd	13.0
8-14	At Sea.	W	5-2		10	9	Escobar	Meche	Lopez	60-61	3rd	13.0
8-15	At Oak.	W	8-5		11	10	Towers	Harden	Miller	61-61	3rd	13.0
8-16	At Oak.	L	4-6		7	8	Hudson	Hendrickson	Foulke	61-62	3rd	14.0
8-17	At Oak.	L	3-7		5	12	Zito	Halladay	Foulke	61-63	3rd	15.0
8-19	Sea.	L	1-9		6	16	Franklin	Escobar		61-64	3rd	16.5
8-20	Sea.	W	5-2		6	6	Towers	Meche		62-64	3rd	16.5
8-21	Sea.	W	7-3		11	7	Hendrickson	Moyer		63-64	3rd	16.0
8-22	Oak.	W	6-3		10	9	Halladay	Zito	Lopez	64-64	3rd	15.0
8-23	Oak.	L	5-11		8	13	Wood	Sturtze		64-65	3rd	15.0
8-24	Oak.	L	2-17		7	19	Hudson	Escobar	Neu	64-66	3rd	16.0
8-25	Oak.	L	6-8		11	14	Lilly	Lidle	Foulke	64-67	3rd	17.0
8-26	At Bos.	W	12-9		16	15	Towers	Sauerbeck	Lopez	65-67	3rd	16.0
8-27	At Bos.	L	3-6		10	11	Timlin	Halladay	Kim	65-68	3rd	16.0
8-29	At Cle.	W	7-3		14	4	Escobar	Sabathia		66-68	3rd	15.5
8-30	At Cle.	W	9-3		15	6	Lidle	Westbrook	Towers	67-68	3rd	15.5
8-31	At Cle.	L	4-5		6	9	Baez	Kershner		67-69	3rd	16.5

Date	Opp.	Res.	Score	(inn.*)	Hits	Opp. hits	Winning pitcher	Losing pitcher	Save	Record	Pos.	GB
9-1	N.Y.	W	8-1		13	4	Halladay	Wells		68-69	3rd	15.5
9-3	N.Y.	W	4-3		9	9	Kershner	Osuna	Lopez	69-69	3rd	14.5
9-4	N.Y.	L	2-3		4	7	Contreras	Walker	Rivera	69-70	3rd	15.5
9-5	Det.	W	8-6		12	10	Sturtze	Maroth	Lopez	70-70	3rd	14.5
9-6	Det.	W	1-0	(10)	6	3	Halladay	Rodney		71-70	3rd	13.5
9-7	Det.	W	8-0		14	4	Towers	Mears		72-70	3rd	13.5
9-8	At N.Y.	L	3-9		8	16	Mussina	Escobar		72-71	3rd	14.5
9-9	At T.B.	L	6-11		10	9	Waechter	Lidle	Kennedy	72-72	3rd	15.5
9-10	At T.B.	W	6-5		7	8	Hendrickson	Sosa	Lopez	73-72	3rd	15.5
9-11	At T.B.	W	3-1		6	5	Halladay	Gonzalez		74-72	3rd	15.5
9-12	Bal.	W	4-2		8	11	Towers	DuBose	Lopez	75-72	3rd	15.5
9-13	Bal.	W	6-1		6	9	Escobar	Hentgen		76-72	3rd	16.0
9-14	Bal.	L	3-5		7	7	Riley	Lidle	Julio	76-73	3rd	16.0
9-16	At Det.	W	9-6		14	9	Kershner	Cornejo		77-73	3rd	16.5
9-17	At Det.	W	6-0		11	6	Halladay	Loux		78-73	3rd	15.5
9-18	At Det.	W	10-6		12	6	Towers	Maroth		79-73	3rd	15.0
9-19	At Bal.	W	5-2		11	4	Escobar	Carrasco	Lopez	80-73	3rd	15.0
9-20	At Bal.	L	1-2		6	9	Ligtenberg	Lidle	Julio	80-74	3rd	16.0
9-21	At Bal.	W	7-4		16	11	Walker	Carrasco	Lopez	81-74	3rd	16.0
9-22	T.B.	L	2-5		4	9	Bell	Halladay		81-75	3rd	16.0
9-23	T.B.	W	8-5		10	11	Kershner	Zambrano	Miller	82-75	3rd	16.0
9-24	T.B.	W	5-3		6	9	Escobar	Waechter	Lopez	83-75	3rd	15.0
9-25	T.B.	W	10-8		11	12	Miller	Carter		84-75	3rd	14.5
9-26	Cle.	L	1-2		6	4	Stanford	Lidle	Riske	84-76	3rd	15.0
9-27	Cle.	W	5-4		10	8	Halladay	Mulholland		85-76	3rd	15.0
9-28	Cle.	W	6-2		6	8	Towers	Lee		86-76	3rd	15.0

Monthly records: March (0-1), April (10-17), May (21-8), June (15-11), July (8-17), August (13-15), September (19-7).
*Innings, if other than nine. † First game of a doubleheader. ‡ Second game of a doubleheader.

RECORDS

2003 regular-season record: 86-76
Position: 3rd in A.L. East
Home: 41-40 **Road:** 45-36
A.L. East: 37-39 **A.L. Central:** 22-14
A.L. West: 17-15 N.L. 10-8
Vs. LH starters: 26-18
Vs. RH starters: 60-58
Grass: 36-30 **Artificial:** 50-46
Day: 30-23 **Night:** 56-53
1-Run: 14-23 **X-inn.:** 4-4
Doubleheaders: 0-0-0
Team record past five years: 411-399 (.507, ranks 7th in league in that span)

TEAM LEADERS

Batting average: Vernon Wells (.317).
At-bats: Vernon Wells (678).
Runs: Vernon Wells (118).
Hits: Vernon Wells (215).
Total Bases: Vernon Wells (373).
Doubles: Vernon Wells (49).
Triples: Frank Catalanotto, Orlando Hudson (6).
Home runs: Carlos Delgado (42).
Runs batted in: Carlos Delgado (145).
Stolen bases: Eric Hinske (12).
Slugging percentage: Carlos Delgado (.593).
On-base percentage: Carlos Delgado (.426).
Wins: Roy Halladay (22).
Earned-run average: Roy Halladay (3.25).
Complete games: Roy Halladay (9).
Shutouts: Roy Halladay (2).
Saves: Aquilino Lopez (14).
Innings pitched: Roy Halladay (266.0).
Strikeouts: Roy Halladay (204).

GAMES BY POSITION

Catcher: Greg Myers 81, Tom Wilson 76, Kevin Cash 34, Ken Huckaby 4.
First base: Carlos Delgado 147, Tom Wilson 14, Josh Phelps 8, Frank Catalanotto 5, Bobby Kielty 3, Dave Berg 2, Howie Clark 2.
Second base: Orlando Hudson 139, Dave Berg 24, Mike Bordick 13, Howie Clark 3.
Third base: Eric Hinske 124, Mike Bordick 22, Dave Berg 17, Howie Clark 13.
Shortstop: Chris Woodward 103, Mike Bordick 69, Dave Berg 1, Howie Clark 1.
Outfield: Vernon Wells 161, Reed Johnson 111, Frank Catalanotto 100, Shannon Stewart 69, Bobby Kielty 60, Jayson Werth 20, Dave Berg 6, Howie Clark 5, Tom Wilson 2.
Designated hitter: Josh Phelps 107, Greg Myers 22, Frank Catalanotto 21, Carlos Delgado 14, Dave Berg 7, Howie Clark 7, Jayson Werth 3, Reed Johnson 2, Shannon Stewart 2, Mike Bordick 1, Tom Wilson 1.

TOP DRAFT CHOICES

1. **Aaron Hill,** SS, Louisiana State.
2. **Josh Banks,** RHP, Florida International.
3. **Shaun Marcum,** RHP, Southwest Missouri State.
4. **Kurt Isenberg,** LHP, James Madison.
5. **Justin James,** RHP, Missouri.
6. **Christian Snavely,** OF, Ohio State.
7. **Danny Core,** RHP, Florida Atlantic.
8. **Chad Mulholland,** RHP, Southwest Missouri State.
9. **Jamie Vermilyea,** RHP, New Mexico.
10. **Jayce Tingler,** OF, Missouri.

ARIZONA DIAMONDBACKS

NATIONAL LEAGUE WEST DIVISION

2004 SEASON

April

SUN	MON	TUE	WED	THU	FRI	SAT
4	5	6 COL	7 COL	8 COL	9 STL	10 STL
11 STL	12 COL	13	14 COL	15 COL	16 SD	17 SD
18 SD	19	20 MIL	21 MIL	22 MIL	23 SD	24 SD
25 SD	26 CHC	27 CHC	28 CHC	29	30 PHI	

May

SUN	MON	TUE	WED	THU	FRI	SAT
						1 PHI
2 PHI	3	4 CHC	5 CHC	6 CHC	7 PHI	8 PHI
9 PHI	10 NYM	11 NYM	12 NYM	13 NYM	14 MON	15 MON
16 MON	17	18 ATL	19 ATL	20 ATL	21 FLA	22 FLA
23 FLA	24 FLA	25 SF	26 SF	27 SF	28 LA	29 LA
30 LA	31 SF					

June

SUN	MON	TUE	WED	THU	FRI	SAT
		1 SF	2 SF	3 SF	4 LA	5 LA
6 LA	7	8 BAL	9 BAL	10 BAL	11 TOR	12 TOR
13 TOR	14	15 NYY	16 NYY	17 NYY	18 TB	19 TB
20 TB	21 SD	22 SD	23 SD	24	25 DET	26 DET
27 DET	28 SD	29 SD	30 SD			

Home games shaded. All-Star Game July 13 at Houston. Schedule subject to change.

July

SUN	MON	TUE	WED	THU	FRI	SAT
				1 SD	2 MIN	3 MIN
4 MIN	5 LA	6 LA	7 LA	8 SF	9 SF	10 SF
11 SF	12	13 All-Star	14	15 LA	16 LA	17 LA
18 LA	19 SF	20 SF	21 HOU	22 HOU	23 COL	24 COL
25 COL	26 HOU	27 HOU	28 HOU	29 HOU	30 COL	31 COL

August

SUN	MON	TUE	WED	THU	FRI	SAT
1 COL	2	3 FLA	4 FLA	5 FLA	6 ATL	7 ATL
8 ATL	9	10 MON	11 MON	12 MON	13 NYM	14 NYM
15 NYM	16 PIT	17 PIT	18 PIT	19	20 CIN	21 CIN
22 CIN	23 PIT	24 PIT	25 PIT	26	27 CIN	28 CIN
29 CIN	30	31 LA				

Sept./Oct.

SUN	MON	TUE	WED	THU	FRI	SAT
			1 LA	2 LA	3 SF	4 SF
5 SF	6	7 LA	8 LA	9 LA	10 SF	11 SF
12 SF	13 COL	14 COL	15 COL	16 COL	17 STL	18 STL
19 STL	20	21 COL	22 COL	23 COL	24 SD	25 SD
26 SD	27 MIL	28 MIL	29 MIL	30	1 SD	2 SD
3 SD	4	5	6	7	8	9

CLUB DIRECTORY

Managing general partner
Jerry Colangelo
President
Richard Dozer
Sr. vice president and general manager
Joe Garagiola Jr.
Vice president, senior assistant g.m.
Sandy Johnson
Assistant general manager
Bob Miller
Assistant director of baseball operations
Fred Seymour
Director of player development
Tommy Jones
Director of scouting
Mike Rizzo
Director of public relations
Mike Swanson

MINOR LEAGUE AFFILIATES

Class	Team	League	Manager
AAA	Tucson	Pacific Coast	Chip Hale
AA	El Paso	Texas	Scott Coolbaugh
Advanced A	Lancaster	California	Eddie Rodriguez
A	South Bend	Midwest	Tony Perezchica
Short-Season A	Yakima	Northwest	Bill Plummer
Advanced Rookie	Missoula	Pioneer	Jim Presley

More on the Diamondbacks at www.foxsports.com/named/FS/MLB/teams

BROADCAST INFORMATION

Radio: KTAR-AM (620).
TV: KTVK (Channel 3)
Cable TV: Fox Sports Net Arizona.

SPRING TRAINING

Ballpark (city): Tucson Electric Park (Tucson, Ariz.).
Ticket information: 866-672-1343.

SPRING TRAINING ROSTER

Manager—Bob Brenly (15).
Coaches—Mark Davis (13), Chuck Kniffin (51), Al Pedrique, Rick Schu, Glenn Sherlock (53), Robin Yount (19).

No.	PITCHERS	B/T	Ht./Wt.	Age*	2003 Clubs
	Aquino, Greg	R/R	6-1/188	25	El Paso
	Bruney, Brian	R/R	6-3/226	22	Tucson, El Paso
	Daigle, Casey	R/R	6-5/217	22	El Paso
45	Dessens, Elmer	R/R	5-10/198	33	Arizona
	Fossum, Casey	B/L	6-1/165	26	Portland, Pawtucket, Boston
49	Gonzalez, Edgar	R/R	6-0/215	21	El Paso, Tucson, Arizona
52	Good, Andrew	R/R	6-1/209	24	Arizona, Tucson
	Gosling, Mike	L/L	6-2/210	23	Tucson
51	Johnson, Randy	R/L	6-10/231	40	Tucson, El Paso, Lancaster, Arizona
58	Koplove, Mike	R/R	5-10/178	27	Arizona, Tucson
	Lyon, Brandon	R/R	6-1/185	24	Pawtucket, Boston
31	Mantei, Matt	R/R	6-1/198	30	Tucson, Arizona
	Medders, Brandon	R/R	6-2/196	24	El Paso
	Nance, Shane	L/L	5-8/180	26	Indianapolis, Milwaukee
24	Patterson, John	R/R	6-5/208	26	Tucson, Arizona
34	Randolph, Steve	L/L	6-3/200	29	Tucson, Arizona
	Reynolds, Shane	R/R	6-3/215	36	Atlanta
	Sparks, Steve	R/R	6-0/195	38	Detroit, Oakland
	Stockman, Phil	R/R	6-6/200	24	El Paso, Tucson
47	Valverde, Jose	R/R	6-4/254	24	Tucson, Arizona
56	Villarreal, Oscar	L/R	6-0/177	22	Arizona
55	Webb, Brandon	R/R	6-2/228	24	Tucson, Arizona

No.	CATCHERS	B/T	Ht./Wt.	Age*	2003 Clubs
7	Hammock, Robby	R/R	5-11/180	26	Tucson, Arizona
	Mayne, Brent	L/R	6-1/190	35	Kansas City

No.	INFIELDERS	B/T	Ht./Wt.	Age*	2003 Clubs
	Alomar, Roberto	B/R	6-0/185	36	New York N.L., Chicago A.L.
3	Baerga, Carlos	B/R	5-11/215	35	Arizona
10	Cintron, Alex	B/R	6-2/199	25	Tucson, Arizona
	Colbrunn, Greg	R/R	6-0/215	34	Tacoma, Everett, Seattle
	Gil, Jerry	R/R	6-3/183	21	South Bend
	Hairston, Scott	R/R	6-0/188	23	El Paso, Tucson
28	Hillenbrand, Shea	R/R	6-1/211	28	Boston, Tucson, Arizona
11	Kata, Matt	B/R	6-1/185	26	Tucson, Arizona
66	Olson, Tim	R/R	6-2/200	25	El Paso, Tucson
	Sexson, Richie	R/R	6-8/236	29	Milwaukee
	Tracy, Chad	L/R	6-2/200	23	Tucson

No.	OUTFIELDERS	B/T	Ht./Wt.	Age*	2003 Clubs
29	Bautista, Danny	R/R	5-11/225	31	El Paso, Tucson, Arizona
12	Finley, Steve	L/L	6-2/194	39	Arizona
20	Gonzalez, Luis	L/R	6-2/200	36	Arizona
	Kroeger, Josh	L/L	6-2/200	21	Lancaster, El Paso
27	Terrero, Luis	R/R	6-2/206	23	Arizona, Tucson

Invited to spring training: LHP Jesse Orosco, RHP Brady Raggio, C Alan Zinter, OF Luis Garcia, OF Felix Jose, OF/IF Donnie Sadler.

*Age as of April 1, 2004.

BALLPARK INFORMATION

Ballpark (capacity, surface)
Bank One Ballpark (49,033, grass)
Address
401 East Jefferson
Phoenix, AZ 85004
Official website
www.azdiamondbacks.com
Business phone
602-462-6500
Ticket information
602-514-8400
Field dimensions (from home plate)
To left field at foul line, 330 feet
To center field, 407 feet
To right field at foul line, 334 feet
First game played
March 31, 1998 (Rockies 9, Diamondbacks 2)

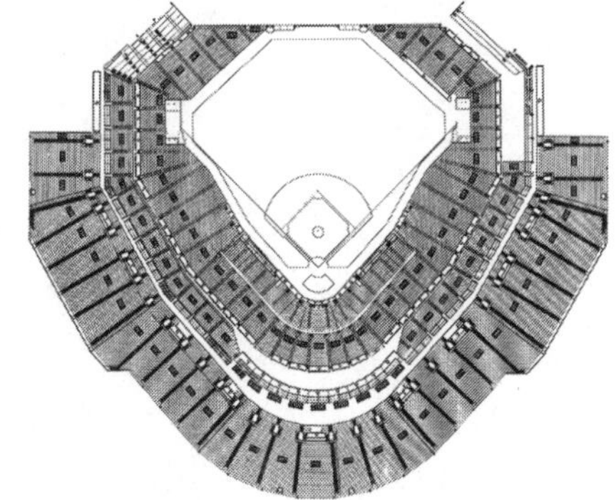

2003 REVIEW

DAY BY DAY

Date	Opp.	Res.	Score	(inn.*)	Hits	Opp. hits	Winning pitcher	Losing pitcher	Save	Record	Pos.	GB
3-31	L.A.	L	0-8		4	13	Nomo	Johnson		0-1	T4th	1.0
4-1	L.A.	W	5-4	(10)	9	8	Mantei	Shuey		1-1	T2nd	1.0
4-2	L.A.	L	0-5		3	12	Brown	Dessens		1-2	3rd	2.0
4-4	At Col.	L	1-2		3	5	Chacon	Kim	Jimenez	1-3	5th	3.0
4-5	At Col.	L	3-4	(10)	12	7	Reed	Batista		1-4	5th	4.0
4-6	At Col.	L	3-8		10	9	Jennings	Schilling		1-5	5th	5.0
4-7	At L.A.	W	6-4	(12)	12	11	Mantei	Ashby	Service	2-5	5th	5.0
4-8	At L.A.	L	3-5		5	9	Shuey	Batista	Gagne	2-6	5th	5.0
4-9	At L.A.	L	2-5		8	7	Dreifort	Kim	Gagne	2-7	5th	6.0
4-11	Mil.	L	7-11		10	16	Franklin	Johnson		2-8	5th	7.5
4-12	Mil.	L	2-3		7	6	Kinney	Schilling	DeJean	2-9	5th	8.0
4-13	Mil.	W	9-3		17	10	Dessens	Rusch		3-9	5th	8.0
4-14	Col.	L	3-5		10	10	Cruz	Kim	Jimenez	3-10	5th	9.0
4-15	Col.	L	1-12		6	14	Chacon	Patterson		3-11	5th	10.0
4-16	Col.	W	4-3		10	8	Mantei	Jimenez		4-11	5th	9.0
4-17	Col.	W	11-2		16	4	Schilling	Jennings		5-11	5th	8.5
4-18	At StL.	L	3-6		7	10	Williams	Dessens		5-12	5th	9.5
4-19	At StL.	W	4-3		8	6	Kim	Simontacchi	Mantei	6-12	5th	9.5
4-20	At StL.	W	1-0		9	5	Villarreal	Tomko	Mantei	7-12	T4th	8.5
4-22	At Mon.	L	0-4		9	7	Ohka	Good		7-13	T4th	8.5
4-23	At Mon.	W	6-2		12	6	Dessens	Hernandez		8-13	T4th	8.5
4-24	At Mon.	L	0-1		6	3	Vazquez	Kim	Biddle	8-14	5th	9.5
4-25	At N.Y.	L	3-4		9	7	Stanton	Villarreal	Benitez	8-15	5th	10.5
4-27†	At N.Y.	W	6-1		7	4	Webb	Glavine		9-15		
4-27‡	At N.Y.	W	7-3		11	10	Johnson	Seo	Mantei	10-15	T4th	8.5
4-28	Fla.	W	7-1		11	6	Dessens	Wayne		11-15	4th	8.0
4-29	Fla.	L	5-7		11	10	Redman	Kim		11-16	4th	8.0
4-30	Fla.	W	7-3		10	10	Batista	Pavano	Mantei	12-16	4th	8.0
5-1	Fla.	L	3-4		8	8	Almanza	Villarreal	Looper	12-17	4th	8.0
5-2	Atl.	L	2-4	(11)	13	8	Bong	Mantei		12-18	4th	8.0
5-3	Atl.	W	7-6		12	13	Villarreal	Gryboski	Mantei	13-18	4th	8.0
5-4	Atl.	L	4-7	(11)	10	9	Hodges	Capuano	Smoltz	13-19	4th	9.0
5-5	Phi.	W	10-1		11	7	Batista	Padilla		14-19	4th	8.5
5-6	Phi.	W	6-5		9	9	Villarreal	Adams		15-19	4th	8.5
5-7	Phi.	L	2-5		6	7	Millwood	Webb	Mesa	15-20	4th	9.5
5-9	At Pit.	W	5-0		12	4	Schilling	D'Amico		16-20	4th	10.0
5-10	At Pit.	L	4-5		10	7	Benson	Dessens	Williams	16-21	4th	10.0
5-11	At Pit.	W	2-1		5	6	Batista	Wells	Mantei	17-21	4th	9.0
5-13	At Phi.	W	6-1		11	6	Koplove	Mesa		18-21	T3rd	7.5
5-14	At Phi.	W	2-0		4	2	Schilling	Myers		19-21	T3rd	6.5
5-15	At Phi.	L	4-6		6	7	Cormier	Villarreal	Mesa	19-22	4th	7.5
5-16	Pit.	L	5-8	(12)	9	14	Boehringer	Mantei	Williams	19-23	4th	8.5
5-17	Pit.	L	5-8		10	9	Torres	Capuano	Williams	19-24	4th	8.5
5-18	Pit.	W	8-6		11	12	Webb	Suppan		20-24	4th	7.5
5-19	S.F	W	4-3		10	8	Mantei	Worrell		21-24	4th	6.5
5-20	S.F	L	5-6		11	11	Rueter	Dessens	Worrell	21-25	4th	7.5
5-21	S.F	L	0-6		4	9	Schmidt	Batista		21-26	4th	8.5
5-23	S.D.	W	5-3		10	8	Koplove	Matthews	Mantei	22-26	T3rd	7.5
5-24	S.D.	L	1-5		2	12	Lawrence	Schilling		22-27	T3rd	8.5
5-25	S.D.	W	9-5		10	9	Dessens	Nagy		23-27	T3rd	7.5
5-26	S.D.	W	8-4		11	8	Good	Eaton		24-27	T3rd	6.5
5-27	At S.F	L	3-4	(13)	6	9	Rodriguez	Mantei		24-28	4th	7.5
5-28	At S.F	L	2-10		5	12	Moss	Patterson		24-29	4th	8.5
5-30	At S.D.	W	8-3		13	8	Schilling	Tollberg		25-29	4th	8.5
5-31	At S.D.	L	7-8		14	16	Orosco	Service	Herges	25-30	4th	9.5
6-1	At S.D.	W	10-4		11	13	Gonzalez	Peavy		26-30	4th	9.5
6-2	At S.D.	L	1-4		8	9	Loewer	Patterson	Herges	26-31	4th	9.5
6-3	Chi. (AL)	W	2-1		9	5	Villarreal	Gordon		27-31	4th	8.5
6-4	Chi. (AL)	W	8-6		15	10	Good	Garland	Valverde	28-31	4th	8.5
6-5	Chi. (AL)	L	2-3	(10)	3	11	Koch	Service		28-32	4th	8.5
6-6	Cle.	L	3-6		7	12	Davis	Gonzalez	Baez	28-33	4th	9.5
6-7	Cle.	W	5-3		11	7	Randolph	Anderson	Valverde	29-33	4th	9.5
6-8	Cle.	W	13-3		18	6	Webb	Rodriguez		30-33	4th	9.5
6-10	At K.C.	L	3-7		8	13	Grimsley	Oropesa		30-34	4th	9.5

Date	Opp.	Res.	Score	(inn.*)	Hits	Opp. hits	Winning pitcher	Losing pitcher	Save	Record	Pos.	GB
6-11	At K.C.	W	4-3		9	9	Good	May	Valverde	31-34	4th	9.5
6-13	At Min.	L	1-3		4	6	Santana	Webb	Guardado	31-35	4th	10.0
6-14	At Min.	W	9-2		12	8	Batista	Mays		32-35	4th	10.0
6-15	At Min.	W	12-8		15	14	Koplove	Hawkins		33-35	4th	9.0
6-17	At Hou.	L	3-4		8	7	Dotel	Villarreal	Wagner	33-36	4th	9.0
6-18	At Hou.	W	2-1		8	5	Villarreal	Wagner	Valverde	34-36	4th	8.0
6-19	At Hou.	W	4-2		8	7	Batista	Redding	Valverde	35-36	4th	8.0
6-20	Cin.	W	6-5		11	11	Valverde	Williamson		36-36	3rd	7.0
6-21	Cin.	W	5-3		6	8	Patterson	Anderson	Valverde	37-36	3rd	7.0
6-22	Cin.	W	6-5		11	8	Oropesa	Mercker	Valverde	38-36	3rd	6.0
6-23	Hou.	W	7-6		9	6	Bottalico	Lidge	Raggio	39-36	3rd	6.0
6-24	Hou.	W	12-5		19	10	Batista	Redding		40-36	3rd	6.0
6-25	Hou.	W	3-2		6	6	Dessens	Miller	Valverde	41-36	3rd	5.0
6-27	At Det.	W	8-3		13	8	Randolph	Bernero		42-36	3rd	5.0
6-28	At Det.	W	7-0		10	7	Webb	Bonderman		43-36	3rd	5.0
6-29	At Det.	W	5-3	(10)	13	10	Oropesa	Spurling	Valverde	44-36	3rd	4.0
6-30	At Col.	W	8-7	(12)	15	7	Randolph	Jimenez		45-36	3rd	4.0
7-1	At Col.	L	4-7		10	14	Lopez	Good	Speier	45-37	3rd	5.0
7-2	At Col.	L	2-6		7	11	Jennings	Patterson	Fuentes	45-38	3rd	6.0
7-3	At Col.	W	8-4		14	12	Webb	Neagle		46-38	2nd	5.0
7-4	At L.A.	W	3-1	(10)	11	6	Villarreal	Martin	Mantei	47-38	2nd	5.0
7-5	At L.A.	L	0-2		4	5	Perez	Dessens	Gagne	47-39	2nd	5.0
7-6	At L.A.	W	2-1		6	4	Good	Nomo	Mantei	48-39	2nd	5.0
7-7	Col.	W	14-6		18	5	Randolph	Cruz		49-39	2nd	5.0
7-8	Col.	W	9-3		11	8	Webb	Reed		50-39	2nd	5.0
7-9	S.D.	W	8-3		8	7	Capuano	Peavy		51-39	2nd	4.0
7-10	S.D.	L	2-14		9	16	Jarvis	Dessens		51-40	2nd	4.0
7-11	S.F	L	7-10		10	12	Schmidt	Batista	Rodriguez	51-41	2nd	5.0
7-12	S.F	L	1-8		3	8	Williams	Schilling		51-42	2nd	6.0
7-13	S.F	W	7-4		8	6	Webb	Brower	Mantei	52-42	2nd	5.0
7-17	At S.D.	W	9-1		13	9	Schilling	Perez		53-42	2nd	5.0
7-18	At S.D.	W	6-0		9	5	Batista	Lawrence		54-42	2nd	5.0
7-19	At S.D.	L	0-2		8	4	Eaton	Webb	Beck	54-43	2nd	6.0
7-20	At S.D.	L	2-3		5	8	Jarvis	Johnson	Beck	54-44	2nd	7.0
7-21	At S.F	L	4-5		7	7	Zerbe	Dessens	Worrell	54-45	2nd	8.0
7-22	At S.F	L	1-3		9	10	Moss	Schilling	Worrell	54-46	2nd	9.0
7-23	At S.F	L	1-7		7	10	Brower	Batista		54-47	2nd	10.0
7-24	At S.F	L	2-3		12	5	Worrell	Myers		54-48	2nd	11.0
7-25	L.A.	W	2-1	(15)	12	3	Randolph	Quantrill		55-48	2nd	11.0
7-26	L.A.	W	1-0		5	6	Dessens	Ashby	Mantei	56-48	2nd	10.0
7-27	L.A.	L	0-1		4	9	Nomo	Schilling	Gagne	56-49	2nd	11.0
7-28	At Fla.	L	2-3		7	7	Redman	Batista	Looper	56-50	2nd	11.5
7-29	At Fla.	L	1-2		5	10	Penny	Webb	Looper	56-51	2nd	11.5
7-30	At Fla.	L	1-3		5	6	Willis	Johnson	Looper	56-52	2nd	12.5
8-1	At Chi.	L	3-4	(14)	15	13	Alfonseca	Oropesa		56-53	2nd	12.0
8-2	At Chi.	W	4-3		7	8	Villarreal	Borowski	Mantei	57-53	2nd	11.0
8-3	At Chi.	L	1-2		4	6	Clement	Villarreal	Veres	57-54	2nd	12.0
8-5	Mon.	W	8-5		11	10	Johnson	Vargas	Mantei	58-54	2nd	12.0
8-6	Mon.	W	3-2		12	4	Oropesa	Ayala	Mantei	59-54	2nd	11.0
8-7	Mon.	W	5-4	(10)	9	9	Valverde	Knott		60-54	2nd	11.0
8-8	N.Y.	L	1-3		7	8	Glavine	Webb	Stanton	60-55	2nd	12.0
8-9	N.Y.	W	2-1		7	8	Randolph	Franco		61-55	2nd	11.0
8-10	N.Y.	W	7-4		9	10	Johnson	Leiter	Mantei	62-55	2nd	11.0
8-12	At Cin.	W	2-0		4	6	Schilling	Wilson	Mantei	63-55	2nd	10.0
8-13	At Cin.	W	3-1		7	10	Randolph	Heredia	Mantei	64-55	2nd	9.0
8-14	At Cin.	L	2-3		4	7	Harang	Webb	Reitsma	64-56	2nd	9.5
8-15	At Atl.	L	4-10		11	11	Reynolds	Johnson		64-57	2nd	9.5
8-16	At Atl.	L	6-10		10	14	Gryboski	Oropesa		64-58	2nd	9.5
8-17	At Atl.	W	2-0		9	2	Schilling	Maddux	Mantei	65-58	2nd	8.5
8-18	At Atl.	L	1-6		4	8	Hampton	Batista		65-59	2nd	8.5
8-19	Cin.	W	6-1		11	6	Webb	Bale	Mantei	66-59	2nd	8.5
8-20	Cin.	L	0-2		6	7	Harang	Johnson	Reitsma	66-60	2nd	9.5
8-21	Cin.	W	9-3		10	7	Dessens	Graves		67-60	2nd	9.5
8-22	Chi.	L	1-4		3	6	Zambrano	Schilling		67-61	3rd	10.5
8-23	Chi.	W	13-2		16	8	Batista	Estes		68-61	2nd	10.5
8-24	Chi.	L	3-5		7	13	Clement	Randolph	Borowski	68-62	2nd	10.5
8-25	S.D.	W	11-8		14	14	Johnson	Peavy	Mantei	69-62	2nd	10.0
8-26	S.D.	L	4-5		4	10	Matthews	Valverde	Beck	69-63	2nd	11.0
8-27	S.D.	L	2-10		5	16	Lawrence	Schilling		69-64	2nd	12.0
8-29	S.F	W	5-4		11	7	Batista	Rueter	Mantei	70-64	2nd	10.5
8-30	S.F	L	1-2		6	6	Williams	Johnson	Worrell	70-65	3rd	11.5
8-31	S.F	L	1-3		7	6	Schmidt	Webb	Worrell	70-66	3rd	12.5

Date	Opp.	Res.	Score	(inn.*)	Hits	Opp. hits	Winning pitcher	Losing pitcher	Save	Record	Pos.	GB
9-1	S.F	L	0-2		6	8	Ponson	Villarreal	Worrell	70-67	3rd	13.5
9-2	At S.D.	L	3-6		8	13	Howard	Capuano		70-68	3rd	14.5
9-3	At S.D.	L	0-12		5	15	Lawrence	Batista		70-69	3rd	15.5
9-4	At K.C.	W	6-5	(10)	11	12	Mantei	Wilson		71-69	3rd	15.0
9-5	At S.F	W	8-1		13	4	Webb	Williams		72-69	3rd	14.0
9-6	At S.F	L	4-5	(11)	9	7	Eyre	Mantei		72-70	3rd	15.0
9-7	At S.F	W	9-6		13	13	Gonzalez	Nathan	Patterson	73-70	3rd	14.0
9-8	L.A.	L	3-10		5	14	Mota	Villarreal		73-71	3rd	14.5
9-9	L.A.	L	1-4		4	8	Jackson	Johnson	Gagne	73-72	3rd	15.5
9-10	L.A.	W	5-4		5	6	Villarreal	Quantrill	Mantei	74-72	3rd	15.5
9-11	L.A.	W	2-0		6	4	Capuano	Perez	Mantei	75-72	3rd	14.5
9-12	Col.	L	2-8		12	12	Jimenez	Dessens		75-73	3rd	15.5
9-13	Col.	W	16-6		15	10	Batista	Young		76-73	3rd	14.5
9-14	Col.	W	5-0		12	1	Johnson	Jennings		77-73	3rd	14.5
9-16	At L.A.	W	3-2		7	9	Schilling	Ishii	Mantei	78-73	3rd	15.0
9-17	At L.A.	W	2-0		5	3	Webb	Jackson	Mantei	79-73	3rd	15.0
9-18	At L.A.	L	0-2		7	4	Alvarez	Batista	Gagne	79-74	3rd	15.0
9-19	At Mil.	W	3-2		9	10	Villarreal	Nance	Mantei	80-74	3rd	15.0
9-20	At Mil.	W	10-4		14	10	Dessens	Franklin	Valverde	81-74	3rd	15.0
9-21	At Mil.	L	4-6		9	10	Obermueller	Schilling	Kolb	81-75	3rd	15.0
9-23	At Col.	L	9-20		12	17	Oliver	Webb		81-76	3rd	16.5
9-24	At Col.	W	6-3		11	9	Johnson	Jimenez	Mantei	82-76	3rd	15.5
9-25	At Col.	W	8-7		12	9	Villarreal	Fuentes	Mantei	83-76	3rd	15.0
9-26	StL.	W	7-6		13	9	Randolph	Tomko	Mantei	84-76	3rd	15.0
9-27	StL.	L	2-3		11	6	Hitchcock	Capuano	Isringhausen	84-77	3rd	15.5
9-28	StL.	L	5-9		14	9	Williams	Webb	Isringhausen	84-78	3rd	16.5

Monthly records: March (0-1), April (12-15), May (13-14), June (20-6), July (11-16), August (14-14), September (14-12).
*Innings, if other than nine. † First game of a doubleheader. ‡ Second game of a doubleheader.

RECORDS

2003 regular-season record: 84-78
Position: 3rd in N.L. West
Home: 45-36 **Road:** 39-42
N.L. East: 16-16 **N.L. Central:** 23-16
N.L. West: 34-42 A.L. 11-4
Vs. LH starters: 27-21
Vs. RH starters: 57-57
Grass: 79-74 **Artificial:** 5-4
Day: 29-25 **Night:** 55-53
1-Run: 30-25 **X-inn.:** 8-8
Doubleheaders: 1-0-0
Team record past five years: 459-351 (.567, ranks 3rd in league in that span)

TEAM LEADERS

Batting average: Alex Cintron (.317).
At-bats: Luis Gonzalez (579).
Runs: Luis Gonzalez (92).
Hits: Luis Gonzalez (176).
Total Bases: Luis Gonzalez (308).
Doubles: Luis Gonzalez (46).
Triples: Steve Finley (10).
Home runs: Luis Gonzalez (26).
Runs batted in: Luis Gonzalez (104).
Stolen bases: Steve Finley (15).
Slugging percentage: Luis Gonzalez (.532).
On-base percentage: Luis Gonzalez (.402).
Wins: Miguel Batista, Oscar Villarreal, Brandon Webb (10).
Earned-run average: Oscar Villarreal (2.57).
Complete games: Curt Schilling (3).
Shutouts: Curt Schilling (2).
Saves: Matt Mantei (29).
Innings pitched: Miguel Batista (193.1).
Strikeouts: Curt Schilling (194).

GAMES BY POSITION

Catcher: Rod Barajas 79, Chad Moeller 76, Robby Hammock 36.
First base: Lyle Overbay 75, Shea Hillenbrand 56, Mark Grace 39, Carlos Baerga 19, Craig Counsell 2.
Second base: Junior Spivey 98, Matt Kata 52, Carlos Baerga 15, Craig Counsell 10, Alex Cintron 9.
Third base: Craig Counsell 57, Matt Williams 42, Shea Hillenbrand 34, Matt Kata 23, Alex Cintron 16, Robby Hammock 16, Carlos Baerga 5.
Shortstop: Alex Cintron 93, Tony Womack 58, Craig Counsell 26, Matt Kata 6.
Outfield: Luis Gonzalez 154, Steve Finley 140, Danny Bautista 79, Quinton McCracken 55, David Dellucci 53, Raul Mondesi 43, Robby Hammock 17, Luis Terrero 3, Felix Jose 1, Junior Spivey 1.
Designated hitter: Carlos Baerga 6, Mark Grace 1, Robby Hammock 1, Felix Jose 1, Quinton McCracken 1.

TOP DRAFT CHOICES

1a. **Conor Jackson,** 3B, California.
1b. **Carlos Quentin,** OF, Stanford.
2. **Jamie D'Antona,** 3B, Wake Forest.
3. **Matt Chico,** LHP, Palomar (Calif.) JC.
4. **Chris Kinsey,** RHP, Sacramento State.
5. **Jeff Cook,** OF, Southern Mississippi.
6. **Orlando Mercado,** C, Antonio Luchetti H.S., Arecibo, Puerto Rico.
7. **Dustin Glant,** RHP, Purdue.
8. **Robbie Van,** LHP, UNLV.
9. **Steve Garrabrants,** 2B, Arizona State.
10. **Adam Bass,** RHP, Alabama-Huntsville.

ATLANTA BRAVES

NATIONAL LEAGUE EAST DIVISION

2004 SEASON

April

SUN	MON	TUE	WED	THU	FRI	SAT
4	5	6 NYM	7 NYM	8 NYM	9 CHC	10 CHC
11 CHC	12 NYM	13	14 NYM	15 NYM	16 FLA	17 FLA
18 FLA	19	20 CIN	21 CIN	22 CIN	23 FLA	24 FLA
25 FLA	26 SF	27 SF	28 SF	29	30 COL	

May

SUN	MON	TUE	WED	THU	FRI	SAT
						1 COL
2 COL	3	4 SD	5 SD	6 SD	7 HOU	8 HOU
9 HOU	10	11 STL	12 STL	13 STL	14 MIL	15 MIL
16 MIL	17	18 ARI	19 ARI	20 ARI	21 LA	22 LA
23 LA	24 MON	25 MON	26 MON	27 PHI	28 PHI	29 PHI
30 PHI	31 MON					

June

SUN	MON	TUE	WED	THU	FRI	SAT
		1 MON	2 MON	3 PHI	4 PHI	5 PHI
6 PHI	7	8 DET	9 DET	10 DET	11 CHW	12 CHW
13 CHW	14	15 KC	16 KC	17 KC	18 CLE	19 CLE
20 CLE	21	22 FLA	23 FLA	24 FLA	25 BAL	26 BAL
27 BAL	28 FLA	29 FLA	30 FLA			

Home games shaded. All-Star Game July 13 at Houston. Schedule subject to change. * San Juan, Puerto Rico.

July

SUN	MON	TUE	WED	THU	FRI	SAT
				1 FLA	2 BOS	3 BOS
4 BOS	5 * MON	6 * MON	7 * MON	8	9 PHI	10 PHI
11 PHI	12	13 All-Star	14	15 MON	16 MON	17 MON
18 MON	19 PHI	20 PHI	21 PIT	22 PIT	23 NYM	24 NYM
25 NYM	26 PIT	27 PIT	28 PIT	29 PIT	30 NYM	31 NYM

August

SUN	MON	TUE	WED	THU	FRI	SAT
1 NYM	2	3 HOU	4 HOU	5 HOU	6 ARI	7 ARI
8 ARI	9	10 MIL	11 MIL	12 MIL	13 STL	14 STL
15 STL	16 SD	17 SD	18 SD	19 LA	20 LA	21 LA
22 LA	23	24 COL	25 COL	26 COL	27 SF	28 SF
29 SF	30 SF	31 PHI				

Sept./Oct.

SUN	MON	TUE	WED	THU	FRI	SAT
			1 PHI	2	3 MON	4 MON
5 MON	6 PHI	7 PHI	8 PHI	9 PHI	10 MON	11 MON
12 MON	13 NYM	14 NYM	15 NYM	16 NYM	17 FLA	18 FLA
19 FLA	20	21 CIN	22 CIN	23 CIN	24 FLA	25 FLA
26 FLA	27 NYM	28 NYM	29 NYM	30	1 CHC	2 CHC
3 CHC	4	5	6	7	8	9

CLUB DIRECTORY

Chairman emeritus
William C. Bartholomay
Chairman and president
Terry McGuirk
Executive v.p. and general manager
John Schuerholz
Senior v.p. and asst. to the president
Henry L. Aaron
Vice president, assistant g.m.
Frank Wren
Executive v.p., business operations
Mike Plant
Special assistants to general manager
Dick Balderson, Jim Fregosi, Duane Larson, Jose Martinez, Chuck McMichael, Scott Nethery, Paul Snyder
Director of scouting
Roy Clark
Director of player personnel
Dayton Moore
Sr. v.p., public relations/communications
Greg Hughes

MINOR LEAGUE AFFILIATES

Class	Team	League	Manager
AAA	Richmond	International	Pat Kelly
AA	Greenville	Southern	Brian Snitker
Advanced A	Myrtle Beach	Carolina	Randy Ingle
A	Rome	South Atlantic	Rocket Wheeler
Advanced Rookie	Danville	Appalachian	Phil Wellman
Rookie	Gulf Coast Braves	Gulf Coast	Ralph Henriquez

More on the Braves at www.foxsports.com/named/FS/MLB/teams

BROADCAST INFORMATION

Radio: WSB-AM (750).
TV: TBS-TV (Channel 17).
Cable TV: Fox Sports Net South, Turner South.

SPRING TRAINING

Ballpark (city): Disney's Wide World of Sports Baseball Stadium (Kissimmee, Fla.).
Ticket information: 407-839-3900, 407-939-4263.

SPRING TRAINING ROSTER

Manager—Bobby Cox (6).
Coaches—Pat Corrales (39), Bobby Dews (52), Fredi Gonzalez (33), Glenn Hubbard (17), Leo Mazzone (54), Otis Nixon, Terry Pendleton (9).

No.	PITCHERS	B/T	Ht./Wt.	Age*	2003 Clubs
	Alfonseca, Antonio	R/R	6-5/250	31	Iowa, Chicago N.L.
	Almanza, Armando	L/L	6-3/240	31	Florida
51	Bong, Jung	L/L	6-3/175	23	Richmond, Atlanta
	Boyer, Blaine	R/R	6-3/190	22	Rome
36	Byrd, Paul	R/R	6-1/185	33	Greenville
	Capellan, Jose	R/R	6-3/170	23	G.C. Braves, Rome
	Colon, Roman	R/R	6-3/170	24	Greenville
26	Cunnane, Will	R/R	6-1/200	29	Iowa, Richmond, Atlanta
	Evert, Brett	L/L	6-6/200	23	Greenville
49	Gryboski, Kevin	R/R	6-5/235	30	Atlanta
32	Hampton, Mike	R/L	5-10/180	31	Atlanta
45	Hodges, Trey	R/R	6-3/187	25	Atlanta
	Nelson, Bubba	R/R	6-2/200	22	Greenville, Richmond
48	Ortiz, Russ	R/R	6-1/208	29	Atlanta
26	Pratt, Andy	L/L	5-11/160	24	Richmond
	Ramirez, Horacio	L/L	6-1/170	24	Atlanta
29	Smoltz, John	R/R	6-3/220	36	Atlanta
	Thomson, John	R/R	6-3/190	30	Texas
27	Wright, Jaret	R/R	6-2/230	28	Portland, San Diego, Atlanta

No.	CATCHERS	B/T	Ht./Wt.	Age*	2003 Clubs
23	Estrada, Johnny	B/R	5-11/209	27	Richmond, Atlanta
	Perez, Eddie	R/R	6-1/220	35	Milwaukee

No.	INFIELDERS	B/T	Ht./Wt.	Age*	2003 Clubs
	Betemit, Wilson	B/R	6-3/190	23	Richmond
16	DeRosa, Mark	R/R	6-1/205	29	Atlanta
1	Furcal, Rafael	B/R	5-10/165	26	Atlanta
2	Garcia, Jesse	R/R	5-10/171	30	Richmond, Atlanta
22	Giles, Marcus	R/R	5-8/180	25	Atlanta
	Green, Nick	R/R	6-0/180	25	Richmond
12	Hessman, Mike	R/R	6-5/215	26	Danville, Richmond, Atlanta
	Johnson, Kelly	L/R	6-1/205	22	G.C. Braves, Greenville
	LaRoche, Adam	L/L	6-3/180	24	Greenville, Richmond
	Lewis, Richard	R/R	6-1/190	23	Greenville
	Pena, Tony	R/R	6-1/160	23	Myrtle Beach
	Thorman, Scott	L/R	6-3/205	22	Myrtle Beach

No.	OUTFIELDERS	B/T	Ht./Wt.	Age*	2003 Clubs
	Drew, J.D.	L/R	6-1/200	28	Palm Beach, St. Louis
25	Jones, Andruw	R/R	6-1/210	26	Atlanta
10	Jones, Chipper	B/R	6-4/220	31	Atlanta
	Joseph, Onil	R/R	6-1/150	22	Rome
18	Langerhans, Ryan	L/L	6-3/195	24	Greenville, Richmond, Atlanta
	Marrero, Eli	R/R	6-1/180	30	Memphis, St. Louis
	Matthews, Gary	B/R	6-3/225	29	Baltimore, San Diego

Invited to spring training: 1B Julio Franco, LHP C.J. Nitkowski.

*Age as of April 1, 2004.

BALLPARK INFORMATION

Ballpark (capacity, surface)
Turner Field (50,091, grass)
Address
P.O. Box 4064
Atlanta, GA 30302
Official website
www.atlantabraves.com
Business phone
404-522-7630
Ticket information
404-249-6400 or 800-326-4000
Field dimensions (from home plate)
To left field at foul line, 335 feet
To center field, 401 feet
To right field at foul line, 330 feet
First game played
April 4, 1997 (Braves 5, Cubs 4)

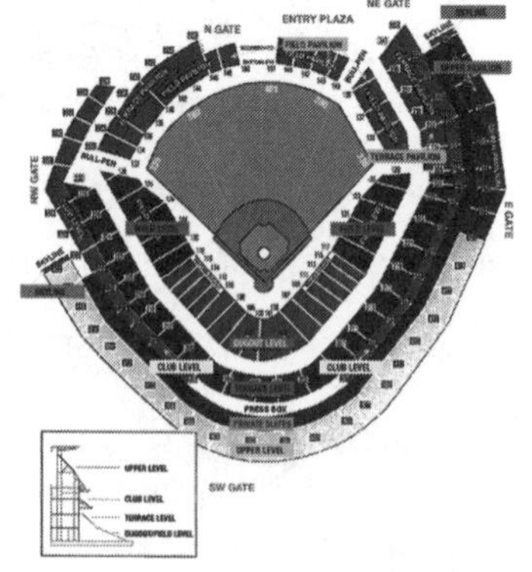

2003 REVIEW
DAY BY DAY

Date	Opp.	Res.	Score	(inn.*)	Hits	Opp. hits	Winning pitcher	Losing pitcher	Save	Record	Pos.	GB
3-31	Mon.	L	2-10		11	14	Armas	Maddux		0-1	T3rd	1.0
4-2	Mon.	L	0-3		3	9	Day	Ramirez	Biddle	0-2	T4th	2.0
4-3	Mon.	L	0-4		9	6	Vazquez	Ortiz		0-3	5th	3.0
4-4	Fla.	W	12-7		16	13	Hernandez	Nunez	Smoltz	1-3	T4th	2.0
4-5	Fla.	L	1-17		8	23	Beckett	Maddux		1-4	5th	2.0
4-6	Fla.	W	13-4		15	8	Ramirez	Penny		2-4	T4th	2.0
4-7	Fla.	W	3-0		5	5	Ortiz	Pavano	Smoltz	3-4	4th	1.5
4-8	At Phi.	L	3-4	(10)	9	4	Mesa	Gryboski		3-5	4th	1.5
4-9	At Phi.	L	2-16		10	18	Padilla	Maddux		3-6	T4th	2.5
4-10	At Phi.	W	6-2		13	4	Holmes	Roa		4-6	T4th	1.5
4-11	At Fla.	L	4-7		10	8	Penny	Ramirez	Looper	4-7	5th	2.5
4-12	At Fla.	L	5-12		12	15	Pavano	Ortiz		4-8	5th	3.5
4-13	At Fla.	W	7-1		12	4	Maddux	Redman	Smoltz	5-8	4th	3.5
4-15	At Mon.■	W	2-1	(10)	7	9	Bong	Smith	Smoltz	6-8	3rd	3.0
4-16	At Mon.■	W	3-2		11	7	Ramirez	Ohka	Smoltz	7-8	3rd	2.0
4-17	At Mon.■	W	14-8	(10)	13	9	Bong	Biddle		8-8	3rd	1.0
4-18	Phi.	W	5-4		6	8	Gryboski	Wolf	Smoltz	9-8	T2nd	0.5
4-19	Phi.	L	0-4		4	11	Padilla	Hampton		9-9	3rd	2.0
4-20	Phi.	W	8-1		12	5	Reynolds	Duckworth		10-9	T2nd	1.0
4-22	StL.	W	5-3		6	8	Ortiz	Stephenson	Smoltz	11-9	T2nd	1.0
4-23	StL.	W	4-2		7	6	Maddux	Morris	Smoltz	12-9	T1st	...
4-24	StL.	W	4-3		15	4	King	Kline		13-9	T1st	...
4-25	Mil.	L	5-12		13	12	Sheets	Reynolds		13-10	T2nd	1.0
4-26	Mil.	W	3-2		7	5	King	de los Santos	Smoltz	14-10	T2nd	1.0
4-27	Mil.	W	7-1		13	5	Ortiz	Rusch		15-10	T1st	...
4-29	At Hou.	W	3-1		6	6	Maddux	Oswalt	Smoltz	16-10	T1st	...
4-30	At Hou.	W	11-1		13	5	Hampton	Miller		17-10	T1st	...
5-1	At Hou.	W	8-7		11	14	Hernandez	Wagner	Smoltz	18-10	T1st	...
5-2	At Ari.	W	4-2	(11)	8	13	Bong	Mantei		19-10	1st	+1.0
5-3	At Ari.	L	6-7		13	12	Villarreal	Gryboski	Mantei	19-11	1st	+1.0
5-4	At Ari.	W	7-4	(11)	9	10	Hodges	Capuano	Smoltz	20-11	1st	+1.5
5-6	Col.	W	3-2		7	6	Hernandez	Jones	Smoltz	21-11	1st	+2.0
5-8†	Col.	W	12-6		9	7	Reynolds	Cruz	Smoltz	22-11		
5-8‡	Col.	W	5-2		8	6	Ortiz	Chacon	Smoltz	23-11	1st	+2.0
5-9	S.F	L	2-9		6	9	Foppert	Maddux	Brower	23-12	1st	+2.0
5-10	S.F	W	6-3		11	8	Gryboski	Nathan		24-12	1st	+2.0
5-11	S.F	W	7-3		10	9	Hampton	Schmidt		25-12	1st	+3.0
5-12	At L.A.	W	11-4		10	5	Bong	Gagne		26-12	1st	+3.0
5-13	At L.A.	W	3-1		7	5	Ortiz	Quantrill	Smoltz	27-12	1st	+3.0
5-14	At L.A.	L	1-5		5	8	Brown	Maddux		27-13	1st	+2.0
5-15	At S.D.	W	15-6		14	8	Ramirez	Deago		28-13	1st	+3.0
5-16	At S.D.	W	6-4		11	9	Gryboski	Nagy	Smoltz	29-13	1st	+3.0
5-17	At S.D.	W	12-2		16	7	Reynolds	Loewer		30-13	1st	+3.0
5-18	At S.D.	W	6-3		13	9	Ortiz	Lawrence	Smoltz	31-13	1st	+4.0
5-20	At Cin.	L	8-9		10	10	Sullivan	Hernandez	Williamson	31-14	1st	+3.0
5-21	At Cin.	L	3-9		8	9	Reitsma	Hampton		31-15	1st	+2.0
5-22	At Cin.	W	9-4		12	8	Reynolds	Dempster		32-15	1st	+2.0
5-23	N.Y.	L	5-6		10	8	Trachsel	Ortiz	Benitez	32-16	1st	+2.0
5-24	N.Y.	W	10-4		14	6	Ramirez	Glavine		33-16	1st	+2.0
5-25	N.Y.	W	3-1		6	5	Hernandez	Weathers	Smoltz	34-16	1st	+2.0
5-26	Cin.	L	6-7	(11)	12	12	White	Hernandez		34-17	1st	+2.0
5-27	Cin.	W	3-2	(10)	10	4	Hodges	Reitsma		35-17	1st	+2.5
5-28	Cin.	W	15-3		18	3	Ortiz	Austin	Bong	36-17	1st	+4.0
5-30	At N.Y.	W	5-2		11	7	Maddux	Glavine	Smoltz	37-17	1st	+4.5
5-31	At N.Y.	L	2-4		8	10	Seo	Hampton	Benitez	37-18	1st	+4.0
6-1	At N.Y.	L	4-10		7	13	Leiter	Gryboski		37-19	1st	+4.5
6-3	Tex.	W	6-5		10	10	Gryboski	Urbina	Smoltz	38-19	1st	+5.5
6-4	Tex.	W	5-2		10	9	Maddux	Thomson	Smoltz	39-19	1st	+6.5
6-5	Tex.	W	8-4		10	8	Bong	Fultz		40-19	1st	+6.5
6-7	Pit.	W	8-6		13	12	Hernandez	Boehringer	Smoltz	41-19	1st	+6.0
6-8	Pit.	W	6-5		12	9	Hodges	Fogg	Smoltz	42-19	1st	+6.0
6-10	At Oak.	L	3-4	(12)	7	9	Bradford	Bong		42-20	1st	+5.0
6-11	At Oak.	W	11-6		13	12	Ramirez	Lilly		43-20	1st	+5.0
6-12	At Oak.	W	4-2		7	6	Reynolds	Zito	Smoltz	44-20	1st	+6.0

Date	Opp.	Res.	Score	(inn.*)	Hits	Opp. hits	Winning pitcher	Losing pitcher	Save	Record	Pos.	GB
6-13	At Sea.	L	1-2		7	7	Garcia	Ortiz	Nelson	44-21	1st	+6.0
6-14	At Sea.	W	3-1		8	4	Hampton	Moyer	Smoltz	45-21	1st	+7.0
6-15	At Sea.	L	1-2		5	5	Meche	Maddux	Nelson	45-22	1st	+7.0
6-17	At Phi.	L	4-5		8	13	Wendell	Holmes		45-23	1st	+6.5
6-18	At Phi.	W	6-1		10	9	Ortiz	Millwood		46-23	1st	+8.0
6-19	At Phi.	L	2-3		7	5	Mesa	Smoltz		46-24	1st	+7.0
6-20	Bal.	W	6-3		8	5	Maddux	Ponson	Smoltz	47-24	1st	+8.0
6-21	Bal.	W	10-2		11	7	Ramirez	Lopez		48-24	1st	+8.0
6-22	Bal.	L	3-9		7	11	Johnson	Reynolds	Hentgen	48-25	1st	+8.0
6-24	Phi.	W	5-3		8	7	Ortiz	Millwood	Smoltz	49-25	1st	+7.5
6-25	Phi.	L	1-8		4	11	Padilla	Maddux		49-26	1st	+7.5
6-26	Phi.	L	1-8		5	15	Wolf	Hampton		49-27	1st	+7.0
6-27	At T.B.	W	8-2		14	9	Ramirez	Gonzalez		50-27	1st	+7.5
6-28	At T.B.	L	7-9		10	13	Zambrano	Reynolds	Carter	50-28	1st	+6.5
6-29	At T.B.	W	2-0		7	3	Ortiz	Sosa	Smoltz	51-28	1st	+6.5
6-30	At Fla.	L	1-8		5	7	Redman	Maddux		51-29	1st	+5.5
7-1	At Fla.	L	1-20		4	25	Beckett	Hampton		51-30	1st	+4.5
7-2	At Fla.	W	2-1	(13)	11	7	Gryboski	Almanza	Smoltz	52-30	1st	+5.5
7-3	Mon.	L	4-5		10	11	Vargas	Reynolds	Manon	52-31	1st	+4.5
7-4	Mon.	W	8-6		14	8	Ortiz	Ohka	Smoltz	53-31	1st	+5.5
7-5	Mon.	W	3-2		5	7	Bong	Biddle		54-31	1st	+6.5
7-6	Mon.	W	7-5		10	11	Hampton	Drew	Smoltz	55-31	1st	+7.5
7-7	At N.Y.	W	7-3		10	4	Ramirez	Seo		56-31	1st	+8.5
7-8	At N.Y.	W	5-3		11	10	Reynolds	Roach	Smoltz	57-31	1st	+8.5
7-9	At N.Y.	W	6-3		9	8	Ortiz	Glavine	Smoltz	58-31	1st	+8.5
7-10	At Chi.	W	13-3		13	9	Maddux	Estes		59-31	1st	+8.5
7-11	At Chi.	W	9-5		9	13	Hampton	Prior		60-31	1st	+8.5
7-12	At Chi.	L	3-7		6	11	Clement	Ramirez		60-32	1st	+7.5
7-13	At Chi.	W	7-2		13	10	Reynolds	Zambrano		61-32	1st	+8.5
7-17	N.Y.	W	3-2		12	8	Maddux	Franco		62-32	1st	+8.5
7-18	N.Y.	W	11-4		14	9	Hampton	Seo		63-32	1st	+9.5
7-19	N.Y.	W	7-4		10	7	Ortiz	Glavine	Smoltz	64-32	1st	+9.5
7-20	N.Y.	W	11-8		16	12	King	Stanton	Smoltz	65-32	1st	+9.5
7-21	Chi.	L	6-15		8	21	Veres	Reynolds		65-33	1st	+9.5
7-22	Chi.	W	8-4		12	8	Maddux	Mitre		66-33	1st	+10.5
7-23	Fla.	L	4-5	(12)	7	14	Bump	Hodges		66-34	1st	+9.5
7-24	Fla.	W	5-2		10	9	Ortiz	Penny	Smoltz	67-34	1st	+9.5
7-25	At Mon.	L	8-9	(11)	17	9	Ayala	Bong		67-35	1st	+9.5
7-26	At Mon.	W	15-4		18	12	Reynolds	Day		68-35	1st	+10.5
7-27	At Mon.	L	10-13		17	14	Manon	King	Biddle	68-36	1st	+10.5
7-28	At Mon.	W	10-8		14	13	Hampton	Vazquez	Smoltz	69-36	1st	+11.5
7-29	Hou.	W	6-3		18	6	Ortiz	Stone	Smoltz	70-36	1st	+11.5
7-30	Hou.	L	3-7		8	13	Villone	Ramirez		70-37	1st	+10.5
7-31	Hou.	W	7-4		12	6	Reynolds	Miller	Smoltz	71-37	1st	+10.5
8-1	L.A.	W	2-0		7	4	Maddux	Nomo	Smoltz	72-37	1st	+10.5
8-2	L.A.	W	6-4		10	7	Hampton	Ashby	Smoltz	73-37	1st	+11.0
8-3	L.A.	L	4-8		8	10	Mota	Ortiz		73-38	1st	+11.0
8-5	At Mil.	L	3-4		6	9	DeJean	Holmes	Kolb	73-39	1st	+10.0
8-6	At Mil.	W	10-2		12	12	Maddux	Franklin		74-39	1st	+11.0
8-7	At Mil.	W	7-1		8	5	Hampton	Obermueller		75-39	1st	+12.0
8-8	At StL.	W	7-2		10	5	Ortiz	Fassero		76-39	1st	+13.0
8-9	At StL.	L	1-3		7	6	Stephenson	Reynolds	Isringhausen	76-40	1st	+12.0
8-10	At StL.	L	2-3		8	6	Eldred	Smoltz	Isringhausen	76-41	1st	+12.0
8-12	S.D.	L	4-14		7	24	Eaton	Maddux		76-42	1st	+11.5
8-13	S.D.	W	7-1		14	4	Hampton	Jarvis		77-42	1st	+11.5
8-14	S.D.	W	7-4		8	9	Ortiz	Peavy	Smoltz	78-42	1st	+12.0
8-15	Ari.	W	10-4		11	11	Reynolds	Johnson		79-42	1st	+12.0
8-16	Ari.	W	10-6		14	10	Gryboski	Oropesa		80-42	1st	+12.0
8-17	Ari.	L	0-2		2	9	Schilling	Maddux	Mantei	80-43	1st	+11.0
8-18	Ari.	W	6-1		8	4	Hampton	Batista		81-43	1st	+11.5
8-19	At S.F	L	4-5	(10)	6	8	Worrell	King		81-44	1st	+11.5
8-20	At S.F	L	1-2		9	8	Nathan	Gryboski		81-45	1st	+11.5
8-21	At S.F	L	3-4	(10)	6	8	Rodriguez	Hodges		81-46	1st	+11.5
8-22	At Col.	W	9-3		16	4	Maddux	Jennings		82-46	1st	+11.5
8-23	At Col.	W	5-4		7	12	Hampton	Tsao	Smoltz	83-46	1st	+12.5
8-24	At Col.	W	12-6		17	11	Ortiz	Stark		84-46	1st	+13.5
8-26	N.Y.	L	5-6		8	7	Seo	Reynolds	Stanton	84-47	1st	+14.0
8-27	N.Y.	W	4-1		10	4	Maddux	Heilman	Mercker	85-47	1st	+15.0
8-28	N.Y.	L	1-3		3	6	Leiter	Hampton	Weathers	85-48	1st	+15.0
8-29	At Pit.	L	5-6		12	11	Tavarez	Cunnane		85-49	1st	+14.0
8-30	At Pit.	W	13-6		13	13	Ramirez	Perez		86-49	1st	+14.0
8-31	At Pit.	W	10-4		14	10	Reynolds	D'Amico		87-49	1st	+14.0

Date	Opp.	Res.	Score	(inn.*)	Hits	Opp. hits	Winning pitcher	Losing pitcher	Save	Record	Pos.	GB
9-1	At N.Y.	L	2-3		9	9	Wheeler	Hodges	Weathers	87-50	1st	+13.0
9-2	At N.Y.	L	1-3		6	7	Leiter	Hampton	Weathers	87-51	1st	+13.0
9-3	At N.Y.	L	3-9		7	10	Trachsel	Ortiz		87-52	1st	+12.0
9-5†	Pit.	W	3-2	(10)	9	3	Cunnane	Corey		88-52		
9-5‡	Pit.	L	3-5		10	8	Corey	Reynolds	Tavarez	88-53	1st	+11.0
9-6	Pit.	W	9-2		16	9	Maddux	D'Amico		89-53	1st	+11.0
9-7	Pit.	W	2-1		8	4	Hampton	Wells	Cunnane	90-53	1st	+11.0
9-8	Phi.	W	6-4		11	4	Ortiz	Millwood	Cunnane	91-53	1st	+12.0
9-9	Phi.	L	5-18		11	14	Wolf	Reynolds		91-54	1st	+11.0
9-10	Phi.	W	4-2		10	6	Ramirez	Padilla	Cunnane	92-54	1st	+11.0
9-11	Phi.	L	3-8		10	16	Myers	Maddux		92-55	1st	+10.5
9-12	At Fla.	L	4-5		7	10	Looper	King		92-56	1st	+9.5
9-13	At Fla.	L	3-8		10	9	Willis	Ortiz		92-57	1st	+8.5
9-14	At Fla.	W	8-4		12	10	Cunnane	Looper		93-57	1st	+9.5
9-15	At Mon.	W	10-6		13	10	Ramirez	Hernandez		94-57	1st	+10.0
9-16	At Mon.	L	4-5	(10)	11	9	Biddle	Hernandez		94-58	1st	+10.0
9-17	At Mon.	W	14-4		19	10	Hampton	Tucker		95-58	1st	+10.0
9-19	Fla.	W	1-0		6	3	Ortiz	Beckett		96-58	1st	+11.0
9-20	Fla.	L	5-6	(11)	11	10	Helling	Cunnane		96-59	1st	+10.5
9-21	Fla.	W	8-0		9	4	Maddux	Pavano		97-59	1st	+11.5
9-22	Fla.	L	3-6		6	11	Redman	Hampton	Urbina	97-60	1st	+10.5
9-23	Mon.	W	2-0		5	7	Wright	Vazquez	Smoltz	98-60	1st	+10.5
9-24	Mon.	W	9-1		12	6	Ortiz	Day		99-60	1st	+10.5
9-26	At Phi.	W	6-0		12	5	Ramirez	Padilla		100-60	1st	+10.0
9-27	At Phi.	L	6-7	(10)	10	14	Cormier	King		100-61	1st	+10.0
9-28	At Phi.	W	5-2		13	8	Maddux	Millwood	Marquis	101-61	1st	+10.0

Monthly records: March (0-1), April (17-9), May (20-8), June (14-11), July (20-8), August (16-12), September (14-12).
*Innings, if other than nine. ■ At Hiram Bithorn Stadium, San Juan, Puerto Rico. † First game of a doubleheader. ‡ Second game of a doubleheader.

RECORDS

2003 regular-season record: 101-61
Position: 1st in N.L. East
Home: 55-26 **Road:** 46-35
N.L. East: 41-35 **N.L. Central:** 27-12
N.L. West: 23-9 A.L. 10-5
Vs. LH starters: 24-13
Vs. RH starters: 77-48
Grass: 88-52 **Artificial:** 13-9
Day: 34-13 **Night:** 67-48
1-Run: 17-25 **X-inn.:** 7-10
Doubleheaders: 1-0-1
Team record past five years: 488-320 (.604, ranks 1st in league in that span)

TEAM LEADERS

Batting average: Gary Sheffield (.330).
At-bats: Rafael Furcal (664).
Runs: Rafael Furcal (130).
Hits: Rafael Furcal (194).
Total Bases: Gary Sheffield (348).
Doubles: Marcus Giles (49).
Triples: Rafael Furcal (10).
Home runs: Javy Lopez (43).
Runs batted in: Gary Sheffield (132).
Stolen bases: Rafael Furcal (25).
Slugging percentage: Javy Lopez (.687).
On-base percentage: Gary Sheffield (.419).
Wins: Russ Ortiz (21).
Earned-run average: Russ Ortiz (3.81).
Complete games: Mike Hampton, Greg Maddux, Russ Ortiz, Horacio Ramirez (1).
Shutouts: Russ Ortiz (1).
Saves: John Smoltz (45).
Innings pitched: Greg Maddux (218.1).
Strikeouts: Russ Ortiz (149).

GAMES BY POSITION

Catcher: Javy Lopez 120, Henry Blanco 52, Johnny Estrada 14.
First base: Robert Fick 115, Julio Franco 75, Matt Franco 15, Mike Hessman 4, Mark DeRosa 1.
Second base: Marcus Giles 139, Mark DeRosa 29, Jesse Garcia 6.
Third base: Vinny Castilla 147, Mark DeRosa 25, Mike Hessman 3, Jesse Garcia 2.
Shortstop: Rafael Furcal 155, Mark DeRosa 20, Jesse Garcia 3.
Outfield: Andruw Jones 155, Gary Sheffield 153, Chipper Jones 149, Darren Bragg 78, Ryan Langerhans 14, Mike Hessman 8, Matt Franco 3, Mark DeRosa 2.
Designated hitter: Matt Franco 3, Javy Lopez 3, Mark DeRosa 2, Chipper Jones 1.

TOP DRAFT CHOICES

1a. **Luis Atilano,** RHP, Gabriela Mistral H.S., San Juan, Puerto Rico.
1b. **Jarrod Saltalamacchia,** C, Royal Palm Beach H.S., West Palm Beach, Fla.
2a. **Jo Jo Reyes,** LHP, Riverside (Calif.) Poly H.S.
2b. **Paul Bacot,** RHP, Lakeside H.S., Atlanta.
3a. **Jacob Stevens,** LHP, Cape Coral (Fla.) H.S.
3b. **Matt Harrison,** LHP, South Granville H.S., Stem, N.C.
4. **Jamie Romak,** 3B, A.B. Lucas SS, London, Ont.
5. **Chris Vines,** RHP, Pelham (Ala.) H.S.
6. **Asher Demme,** RHP, South Lakes H.S., Reston, Va.
7. **Ryan Basner,** RHP, Western Carolina.
8. **Sean White,** RHP, Washington.
9. **Adam Stanley,** LHP, Garner (N.C.) H.S.
10. **Brad Nelson,** RHP, Lenoir (N.C.) CC.

CHICAGO CUBS

NATIONAL LEAGUE CENTRAL DIVISION

2004 SEASON

April

SUN	MON	TUE	WED	THU	FRI	SAT
4	5 CIN	6	7 CIN	8 CIN	9 ATL	10 ATL
11 ATL	12 PIT	13	14 PIT	15 PIT	16 CIN	17 CIN
18 CIN	19 CIN	20 PIT	21 PIT	22 PIT	23 NYM	24 NYM
25 NYM	26 ARI	27 ARI	28 ARI	29	30 STL	

July

SUN	MON	TUE	WED	THU	FRI	SAT
				1 HOU	2 CHW	3 CHW
4 CHW	5 MIL	6 MIL	7 MIL	8	9 STL	10 STL
11 STL	12	13 All-Star	14	15 MIL	16 MIL	17 MIL
18 MIL	19 STL	20 STL	21 CIN	22 CIN	23 PHI	24 PHI
25 PHI	26 MIL	27 MIL	28 MIL	29 MIL	30 PHI	31 PHI

May

SUN	MON	TUE	WED	THU	FRI	SAT
						1 STL
2 STL	3 STL	4 ARI	5 ARI	6 ARI	7 COL	8 COL
9 COL	10	11 LA	12 LA	13 LA	14 SD	15 SD
16 SD	17	18 SF	19 SF	20 SF	21 STL	22 STL
23 STL	24	25 HOU	26 HOU	27	28 PIT	29 PIT
30 PIT	31 HOU					

August

SUN	MON	TUE	WED	THU	FRI	SAT
1 PHI	2	3 COL	4 COL	5 COL	6 SF	7 SF
8 SF	9	10 SD	11 SD	12 SD	13 LA	14 LA
15 LA	16	17 MIL	18 MIL	19 MIL	20 HOU	21 HOU
22 HOU	23 MIL	24 MIL	25 MIL	26 HOU	27 HOU	28 HOU
29 HOU	30 MON	31 MON				

June

SUN	MON	TUE	WED	THU	FRI	SAT
		1 HOU	2 HOU	3	4 PIT	5 PIT
6 PIT	7 STL	8 STL	9 STL	10 STL	11 ANA	12 ANA
13 ANA	14 HOU	15 HOU	16 HOU	17 HOU	18 OAK	19 OAK
20 OAK	21	22 STL	23 STL	24 STL	25 CHW	26 CHW
27 CHW	28	29 HOU	30 HOU			

Sept./Oct.

SUN	MON	TUE	WED	THU	FRI	SAT
			1 MON	2	3 FLA	4 FLA
5 FLA	6 MON	7 MON	8 MON	9	10 FLA	11 FLA
12 FLA	13 PIT	14 PIT	15 PIT	16 CIN	17 CIN	18 CIN
19 CIN	20	21 PIT	22 PIT	23 PIT	24 NYM	25 NYM
26 NYM	27 CIN	28 CIN	29 CIN	30 CIN	1 ATL	2 ATL
3 ATL	4	5	6	7	8	9

Home games shaded. All-Star Game July 13 at Houston. Schedule subject to change.

CLUB DIRECTORY

President and chief executive officer
Andrew B. MacPhail

Vice president, general manager
Jim Hendry

Director, baseball operations
Scott Nelson

Special assistants to the g.m.
Keith Champion, Ken Kravec, Ed Lynch, Billy Williams

Assistant to g.m./scouting consultant
Grady Little

Director of scouting
John Stockstill

Dir of player dev./Latin American ops.
Oneri Fleita

Director of media relations
Sharon Pannozzo

Manager, baseball information
Chuck Wasserstrom

Manager, media relations
Samantha Newby

MINOR LEAGUE AFFILIATES

Class	Team	League	Manager
AAA	Iowa	Pacific Coast	Mike Quade
AA	West Tenn	Southern	Bobby Dickerson
Advanced A	Daytona	Florida State	Steve McFarland
A	Lansing	Midwest	Julio Garcia
Short-Season A	Boise	Northwest	Tom Beyers
Rookie	Mesa Cubs	Arizona	Trey Forkerway

More on the Cubs at www.foxsports.com/named/FS/MLB/teams

BROADCAST INFORMATION

Radio: WGN-AM (720).
TV: WGN-TV (Channel 9); WCIU-TV (Channel 26).
Cable TV: Fox Sports Net Chicago.

SPRING TRAINING

Ballpark (city): HoHoKam Park (Mesa, Ariz.).
Ticket information: 800-638-4253.

SPRING TRAINING ROSTER

Manager—Dusty Baker (12).
Coaches—Gene Clines (2), Wendell Kim (3), Juan Lopez (59), Gary Matthews (36), Dick Pole (46), Larry Rothschild (47).

No.	PITCHERS	B/T	Ht./Wt.	Age*	2003 Clubs
53	Beltran, Francis	R/R	6-5/220	24	Iowa
48	Borowski, Joe	R/R	6-2/225	32	Chicago N.L.
30	Clement, Matt	R/R	6-3/210	29	Chicago N.L.
51	Cruz, Juan	R/R	6-2/165	25	Iowa, Chicago N.L.
	Dempster, Ryan	R/R	6-3/215	26	Louisville, Cincinnati
44	Farnsworth, Kyle	R/R	6-4/235	27	Chicago N.L.
	Guzman, Angel	R/R	6-3/190	22	West Tenn
	Hawkins, LaTroy	R/R	6-5/214	31	Minnesota
	Leicester, Jon	R/R	6-2/220	25	West Tenn, Iowa
	Mercker, Kent	L/L	6-2/200	36	Cincinnati, Atlanta
	Mitre, Sergio	R/R	6-4/210	23	West Tenn, Chicago N.L.
	Pinto, Renyel	L/L	6-4/195	21	Daytona
22	Prior, Mark	R/R	6-5/230	23	Chicago N.L.
37	Remlinger, Mike	L/L	6-1/215	38	Chicago N.L.
	Sanchez, Felix	R/L	6-3/180	22	Arizona Cubs, West Tenn, Chicago N.L.
39	Smyth, Steve	L/L	6-1/195	25	Iowa
	Vasquez, Carlos	L/L	6-2/215	21	Lansing
	Webb, John	R/R	6-3/190	24	West Tenn
40	Wellemeyer, Todd	R/R	6-3/195	25	West Tenn, Iowa, Chicago N.L.
34	Wood, Kerry	R/R	6-5/225	26	Chicago N.L.
38	Zambrano, Carlos	B/R	6-5/245	22	Chicago N.L.

No.	CATCHERS	B/T	Ht./Wt.	Age*	2003 Clubs
9	Bako, Paul	L/R	6-2/215	31	Chicago N.L.
	Barrett, Michael	R/R	6-2/200	27	Edmonton, Montreal

No.	INFIELDERS	B/T	Ht./Wt.	Age*	2003 Clubs
	Cedeno, Ronny	R/R	6-1/180	21	Daytona
	Frese, Nate	R/R	6-3/205	26	Iowa
8	Gonzalez, Alex S.	R/R	6-0/200	30	Chicago N.L.
11	Grudzielanek, M.	R/R	6-1/190	33	Iowa, Chicago N.L.
	Harris, Brendan	R/R	6-1/195	23	West Tenn
	Lee, Derrek	R/R	6-5/248	28	Florida
	Martinez, Ramon	R/R	6-1/195	31	Chicago N.L.
16	Ramirez, Aramis	R/R	6-1/212	25	Pittsburgh, Chicago N.L.
	Walker, Todd	L/R	6-0/190	30	Boston

No.	OUTFIELDERS	B/T	Ht./Wt.	Age*	2003 Clubs
18	Alou, Moises	R/R	6-3/220	37	Chicago N.L.
	Dubois, Jason	R/R	6-4/200	25	West Tenn
24	Goodwin, Tom	L/R	6-0/185	35	Chicago N.L.
	Hollandsworth, T.	L/L	6-2/225	30	Florida
	Jackson, Nic	L/R	6-3/205	24	Iowa
28	Kelton, David	R/R	6-3/205	24	Iowa, Chicago N.L.
	Macias, Jose	B/R	5-8/190	32	Montreal
20	Patterson, Corey	L/R	5-9/180	24	Chicago N.L.
21	Sosa, Sammy	R/R	6-0/220	35	Chicago N.L.

Invited to spring training: RHP Gary Glover, RHP Jamey Wright, INF Bill Selby.
*Age as of April 1, 2004.

BALLPARK INFORMATION

Ballpark (capacity, surface)
Wrigley Field (39,241, grass)

Address
1060 W. Addison St.
Chicago, IL 60613-4397

Official website
www.cubs.com

Business phone
773-404-2827

Ticket information
773-404-2827

Field dimensions (from home plate)
To left field at foul line, 355 feet
To center field, 400 feet
To right field at foul line, 353 feet

First game played
April 20, 1916 (Cubs 7, Reds 6)

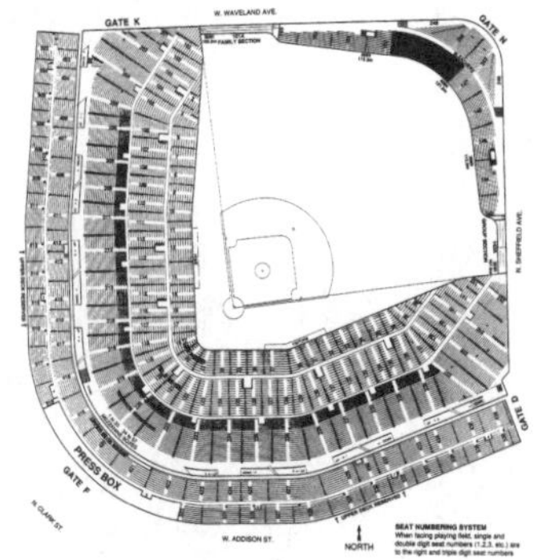

2003 REVIEW

DAY BY DAY

Date	Opp.	Res.	Score	(inn.*)	Hits	Opp. hits	Winning pitcher	Losing pitcher	Save	Record	Pos.	GB
3-31	At N.Y.	W	15-2		16	4	Wood	Glavine		1-0	T1st	...
4-2	At N.Y.	L	1-4		6	6	Leiter	Clement	Benitez	1-1	4th	1.0
4-3	At N.Y.	W	6-3		9	7	Prior	Trachsel		2-1	T3rd	1.0
4-4	At Cin.	L	9-10		13	11	Williamson	Veres		2-2	4th	2.0
4-5	At Cin.	W	9-7		14	7	Zambrano	Haynes	Borowski	3-2	T3rd	1.0
4-6	At Cin.	L	4-5		10	8	White	Guthrie	Williamson	3-3	4th	2.0
4-8	Mon.	W	6-1		7	4	Clement	Day		4-3	4th	1.0
4-9	Mon.	W	3-0		7	4	Prior	Vazquez		5-3	T2nd	0.5
4-10	Mon.	L	1-7		4	11	Armas	Estes		5-4	3rd	1.5
4-11	Pit.	L	2-3		8	8	D'Amico	Zambrano	Williams	5-5	3rd	2.5
4-12	Pit.	W	4-0		6	4	Wood	Benson	Borowski	6-5	3rd	1.5
4-13	Pit.	W	4-3		5	4	Farnsworth	Boehringer	Borowski	7-5	T2nd	0.5
4-14	Cin.	L	3-11		11	11	Anderson	Prior	Riedling	7-6	4th	0.5
4-15	Cin.	W	11-1		14	5	Estes	Graves		8-6	1st	+0.5
4-16	Cin.	W	10-4		11	10	Zambrano	Wilson		9-6	1st	+0.5
4-17	Cin.	W	16-3		16	6	Wood	Haynes	Benes	10-6	1st	+1.0
4-18	At Pit.	W	7-2		10	3	Clement	Benson		11-6	1st	+1.0
4-19	At Pit.	W	6-1	(10)	8	6	Prior	Sauerbeck		12-6	1st	+2.0
4-20	At Pit.	L	2-8		6	10	Torres	Estes		12-7	1st	+2.0
4-22	S.D.	W	7-2		4	7	Zambrano	Lawrence		13-7	1st	+2.5
4-23	S.D.	L	0-2		5	6	Eaton	Wood	Herges	13-8	1st	+2.5
4-24	S.D.	L	1-2		7	7	Perez	Clement	Wright	13-9	1st	+2.5
4-25	At Col.	W	11-7		16	11	Prior	Cruz		14-9	1st	+3.0
4-26	At Col.	L	5-8		5	17	Chacon	Estes	Jimenez	14-10	1st	+3.0
4-27	At Col.	L	3-6		6	7	Oliver	Zambrano	Jimenez	14-11	1st	+2.0
4-29	At S.F	W	4-2		9	9	Wood	Rueter	Borowski	15-11	1st	+2.0
4-30	At S.F	L	0-5		3	6	Schmidt	Clement		15-12	1st	+1.0
5-1	At S.F	W	5-1	(10)	12	8	Cruz	Worrell		16-12	1st	+1.0
5-2	Col.	W	7-4		10	10	Estes	Chacon	Borowski	17-12	1st	+1.0
5-3	Col.	L	4-6		8	10	Speier	Guthrie	Jimenez	17-13	2nd	...
5-4	Col.	W	5-4	(10)	6	10	Borowski	Reed		18-13	2nd	...
5-5	Mil.	L	3-5		6	7	Sheets	Clement	DeJean	18-14	2nd	...
5-6	Mil.	L	6-9		8	9	Leskanic	Cruz	DeJean	18-15	2nd	...
5-7	Mil.	W	2-1		10	5	Estes	Rusch	Borowski	19-15	1st	+1.0
5-9	StL.	L	3-6		10	10	Morris	Zambrano	Fassero	19-16	1st	+0.5
5-10	StL.	W	3-2	(10)	10	5	Remlinger	Eldred		20-16	1st	+1.5
5-12	At Mil.	W	11-5		19	10	Prior	Rusch		21-16	1st	+1.5
5-13	At Mil.	W	7-2		13	5	Estes	Quevedo		22-16	1st	+1.5
5-14	At Mil.	W	6-1		8	3	Zambrano	Kinney		23-16	1st	+2.5
5-15	At Mil.	W	4-2	(17)	12	9	Farnsworth	Kieschnick	Wellemeyer	24-16	1st	+2.5
5-16	At StL.	L	4-7		9	8	Williams	Clement	Eldred	24-17	1st	+1.5
5-17	At StL.	W	2-1		11	7	Remlinger	Kline	Borowski	25-17	1st	+2.5
5-18	At StL.	L	3-6		5	7	Hermanson	Cruz	Eldred	25-18	1st	+2.5
5-19	At StL.	L	0-2		4	7	Morris	Zambrano		25-19	1st	+2.0
5-21	At Pit.	L	2-5		7	8	D'Amico	Wood	Williams	25-20	1st	+1.5
5-22	At Pit.	W	3-2		12	7	Remlinger	Sauerbeck	Borowski	26-20	1st	+1.5
5-23	At Hou.	L	5-7		12	7	Linebrink	Prior	Wagner	26-21	1st	+0.5
5-24	At Hou.	W	3-2		10	8	Estes	Redding	Borowski	27-21	1st	+1.5
5-25	At Hou.	W	7-3		11	6	Zambrano	Miller		28-21	1st	+2.5
5-26	Pit.	L	0-10		5	8	Fogg	Wood		28-22	1st	+1.5
5-27	Pit.	L	4-9		7	14	Benson	Clement		28-23	1st	+1.5
5-28	Pit.	W	5-4		5	9	Prior	D'Amico	Borowski	29-23	1st	+1.5
5-30	Hou.	L	1-9		2	8	Miller	Estes		29-24	1st	+1.0
5-31	Hou.	W	1-0	(16)	10	6	Wellemeyer	Stone		30-24	1st	+2.0
6-1	Hou.	L	3-9		8	10	Robertson	Wood		30-25	1st	+1.0
6-3	T.B.	W	3-2		11	9	Remlinger	Levine		31-25	1st	+1.0
6-4	T.B.	L	2-5		5	11	Zambrano	Estes		31-26	1st	...
6-5	T.B.	W	8-1		10	7	Clement	Brazelton		32-26	1st	...
6-6	N.Y. (AL)	L	3-5		9	9	Wells	Zambrano	Rivera	32-27	T2nd	1.0
6-7	N.Y. (AL)	W	5-2		7	6	Wood	Clemens		33-27	2nd	1.0
6-8	N.Y. (AL)	W	8-7		13	10	Prior	Pettitte	Borowski	34-27	2nd	1.0
6-10	At Bal.	W	4-0		14	9	Estes	Hentgen		35-27	1st	...
6-11	At Bal.	W	7-6		9	10	Clement	Daal	Borowski	36-27	1st	...
6-12	At Bal.	L	1-6		6	11	Helling	Zambrano	Driskill	36-28	1st	...

Date	Opp.	Res.	Score	(inn.*)	Hits	Opp. hits	Winning pitcher	Losing pitcher	Save	Record	Pos.	GB
6-13	At Tor.	L	1-5		12	8	Escobar	Wood		36-29	1st	...
6-14	At Tor.	W	4-2		6	10	Prior	Davis	Borowski	37-29	1st	+1.0
6-15	At Tor.	L	4-5	(10)	8	9	Lopez	Guthrie		37-30	1st	+1.0
6-16	At Cin.	W	4-3		8	10	Clement	Anderson	Borowski	38-30	1st	+1.5
6-17	At Cin.	L	1-2	(10)	7	5	Williamson	Remlinger		38-31	1st	+0.5
6-18	At Cin.	W	4-1		11	3	Wood	Haynes		39-31	1st	+1.5
6-19	At Cin.	L	1-3		5	9	Wilson	Prior	Williamson	39-32	1st	+1.0
6-20	Chi.	L	3-12		10	11	Garland	Estes		39-33	1st	+0.5
6-21	Chi.	L	6-7		15	11	Buehrle	Clement	Koch	39-34	T2nd	0.5
6-22	Chi.	W	2-1		6	6	Zambrano	Marte	Borowski	40-34	2nd	0.5
6-24	Mil.	W	9-1		13	9	Wood	Quevedo		41-34	1st	+1.0
6-25	Mil.	L	6-12	(10)	7	16	Vizcaino	Wellemeyer		41-35	1st	+1.0
6-26	Mil.	L	3-5		6	6	Estrella	Borowski	DeJean	41-36	T1st	...
6-27	At Chi.	L	3-4		9	7	Koch	Alfonseca		41-37	T1st	...
6-28	At Chi.	L	6-7		8	10	Koch	Cruz		41-38	3rd	1.0
6-29	At Chi.	W	5-2		10	5	Wood	Loaiza		42-38	2nd	1.0
6-30	At Phi.	L	3-4		7	7	Padilla	Estes	Mesa	42-39	T2nd	1.0
7-1	At Phi.	L	3-4		10	11	Adams	Remlinger		42-40	3rd	1.0
7-2	At Phi.	W	1-0		7	1	Farnsworth	Wendell	Borowski	43-40	T1st	...
7-3	At Phi.	L	2-12		8	14	Myers	Zambrano		43-41	3rd	1.0
7-4	StL.	L	8-11		12	14	Tomko	Wood		43-42	3rd	2.0
7-5	StL.	W	6-5		12	9	Remlinger	Fassero		44-42	T2nd	1.0
7-6	StL.	L	1-4		8	6	Williams	Prior	Isringhausen	44-43	T2nd	2.0
7-7	Fla.	W	6-3		12	5	Clement	Beckett	Borowski	45-43	T2nd	1.0
7-8	Fla.	L	3-4		7	13	Bump	Remlinger	Looper	45-44	3rd	1.0
7-9	Fla.	W	5-1		8	3	Wood	Pavano		46-44	T2nd	1.0
7-10	Atl.	L	3-13		9	13	Maddux	Estes		46-45	T2nd	2.0
7-11	Atl.	L	5-9		13	9	Hampton	Prior		46-46	3rd	3.0
7-12	Atl.	W	7-3		11	6	Clement	Ramirez		47-46	3rd	2.0
7-13	Atl.	L	2-7		10	13	Reynolds	Zambrano		47-47	3rd	3.0
7-18	At Fla.	L	0-6		5	9	Redman	Clement		47-48	3rd	4.5
7-19	At Fla.	W	1-0		4	2	Wood	Penny		48-48	3rd	4.5
7-20	At Fla.	W	16-2		20	10	Zambrano	Willis		49-48	3rd	4.5
7-21	At Atl.	W	15-6		21	8	Veres	Reynolds		50-48	3rd	3.5
7-22	At Atl.	L	4-8		8	12	Maddux	Mitre		50-49	3rd	4.5
7-23	Phi.	L	0-3		4	4	Wolf	Clement		50-50	3rd	5.5
7-24	Phi.	L	6-14		9	14	Padilla	Wood		50-51	3rd	5.5
7-25	At Hou.	W	5-3		9	5	Zambrano	Dotel	Borowski	51-51	3rd	4.5
7-26	At Hou.	L	1-3		2	5	Redding	Cruz	Wagner	51-52	3rd	5.5
7-27	At Hou.	W	5-3		10	6	Estes	Robertson	Borowski	52-52	3rd	4.5
7-29	S.F	W	3-0		5	2	Clement	Moss		53-52	3rd	3.5
7-30	S.F	L	3-6		4	6	Schmidt	Wood		53-53	3rd	4.5
7-31	S.F	W	9-4		11	9	Zambrano	Brower		54-53	3rd	3.5
8-1	Ari.	W	4-3	(14)	13	15	Alfonseca	Oropesa		55-53	3rd	3.5
8-2	Ari.	L	3-4		8	7	Villarreal	Borowski	Mantei	55-54	3rd	3.5
8-3	Ari.	W	2-1		6	4	Clement	Villarreal	Veres	56-54	3rd	3.5
8-5	At S.D.	W	3-0		8	3	Prior	Lawrence	Borowski	57-54	3rd	2.5
8-6	At S.D.	W	3-2		7	5	Wood	Eaton	Borowski	58-54	2nd	2.5
8-7	At S.D.	W	9-3		13	13	Zambrano	Jarvis		59-54	2nd	1.5
8-8	At L.A.	L	1-3		3	8	Ashby	Estes	Gagne	59-55	2nd	2.5
8-9	At L.A.	L	1-6		5	8	Alvarez	Clement		59-56	3rd	2.5
8-10	At L.A.	W	3-1		5	5	Prior	Brown		60-56	3rd	2.5
8-11	Hou.	L	1-3		7	8	Miller	Wood	Wagner	60-57	3rd	3.5
8-12	Hou.	W	3-0		9	5	Zambrano	Redding		61-57	3rd	2.5
8-13	Hou.	W	6-4		8	8	Guthrie	Robertson	Borowski	62-57	3rd	1.5
8-14	Hou.	W	7-1		6	5	Clement	Fernandez		63-57	3rd	0.5
8-15	L.A.	W	2-1		6	7	Prior	Kida		64-57	1st	+0.5
8-16	L.A.	L	5-10		11	16	Perez	Remlinger		64-58	2nd	0.5
8-17	L.A.	L	0-3		6	7	Nomo	Zambrano	Gagne	64-59	2nd	0.5
8-19	At Hou.	L	8-12		11	15	Miceli	Clement		64-60	3rd	1.5
8-20	At Hou.	W	6-0		12	4	Prior	Fernandez		65-60	2nd	0.5
8-21	At Hou.	L	3-9		7	16	Villone	Wood		65-61	3rd	1.5
8-22	At Ari.	W	4-1		6	3	Zambrano	Schilling		66-61	2nd	0.5
8-23	At Ari.	L	2-13		8	16	Batista	Estes		66-62	3rd	0.5
8-24	At Ari.	W	5-3		13	7	Clement	Randolph	Borowski	67-62	3rd	0.5
8-26	At StL.	W	7-4		8	5	Prior	Stephenson		68-62	2nd	0.5
8-27	At StL.	L	2-4		8	7	Kline	Farnsworth	Isringhausen	68-63	3rd	1.5
8-28	At StL.	L	2-3		5	9	DeJean	Remlinger		68-64	3rd	1.5
8-29	Mil.	W	4-2		12	7	Clement	Sheets		69-64	3rd	0.5
8-30	Mil.	L	5-9		10	9	Kinney	Estes		69-65	3rd	1.5
8-31	Mil.	L	0-2		6	9	Davis	Cruz	Kolb	69-66	3rd	2.5

Date	Opp.	Res.	Score	(inn.*)	Hits	Opp. hits	Winning pitcher	Losing pitcher	Save	Record	Pos.	GB
9-1	StL.	W	7-0		17	6	Prior	Williams		70-66	3rd	1.5
9-2§	StL.	W	4-2	(15)	8	5	Guthrie	Fassero		71-66		
9-2∞	StL.	L	0-2		5	5	Morris	Wood	Isringhausen	71-67	3rd	1.5
9-3	StL.	W	8-7		13	13	Borowski	Williams		72-67	3rd	1.0
9-4	StL.	W	7-6		10	12	Remlinger	DeJean	Borowski	73-67	2nd	0.5
9-5	At Mil.	W	4-2		6	6	Cruz	Sheets	Borowski	74-67	2nd	0.5
9-6	At Mil.	W	8-4		9	11	Prior	Kinney		75-67	2nd	0.5
9-7	At Mil.	W	9-2		11	9	Wood	Davis		76-67	1st	+0.5
9-9	At Mon.■	W	4-3		11	7	Zambrano	Day	Borowski	77-67	T1st	...
9-10	At Mon.■	L	4-8		8	8	Ayala	Farnsworth		77-68	2nd	1.0
9-11	At Mon.■	L	2-3		7	11	Ohka	Prior	Eischen	77-69	2nd	1.0
9-12	Cin.	W	7-6		13	12	Alfonseca	Randall	Borowski	78-69	2nd	1.0
9-13	Cin.	W	9-6		14	13	Alfonseca	Belisle	Borowski	79-69	2nd	1.0
9-14	Cin.	L	0-1		7	4	Riedling	Zambrano	Reitsma	79-70	2nd	2.0
9-15	N.Y.	W	4-1		10	4	Clement	Griffiths	Borowski	80-70	2nd	1.5
9-16	N.Y.	W	3-2		7	8	Prior	Seo	Borowski	81-70	2nd	1.5
9-17	N.Y.	W	2-0		4	4	Wood	Leiter		82-70	2nd	0.5
9-19§	At Pit.	W	10-9		10	9	Veres	Figueroa	Borowski	83-70		
9-19∞	At Pit.	L	6-10		11	15	Torres	Cruz		83-71	2nd	1.5
9-20	At Pit.	L	2-8		7	11	Vogelsong	Clement		83-72	2nd	1.5
9-21	At Pit.	W	4-1		7	7	Prior	Perez	Borowski	84-72	2nd	0.5
9-23	At Cin.	W	6-0		8	2	Wood	Randall		85-72	1st	+1.0
9-24	At Cin.	W	8-0		10	4	Estes	Hall		86-72	1st	+1.0
9-25	At Cin.	L	7-9		11	11	Van Poppel	Zambrano	Reitsma	86-73	T1st	...
9-27†	Pit.	W	4-2		8	8	Prior	Fogg	Borowski	87-73		
9-27‡	Pit.	W	7-2		7	7	Clement	Vogelsong		88-73	1st	+2.0
9-28	Pit.	L	2-3		8	8	Wells	Cruz	Tavarez	88-74	1st	+1.0

Monthly records: March (1-0), April (14-12), May (15-12), June (12-15), July (12-14), August (15-13), September (19-8).
*Innings, if other than nine. ■ At Hiram Bithorn Stadium, San Juan, Puerto Rico. † First game of a doubleheader. ‡ Second game of a doubleheader. § Day separate admission. ∞ Night separate admission.

RECORDS

2003 regular-season record: 88-74
Position: 1st in N.L. Central
Home: 44-37 **Road:** 44-37
N.L. East: 15-15 **N.L. Central:** 47-37
N.L. West: 17-13 A.L. 9-9
Vs. LH starters: 18-20
Vs. RH starters: 70-54
Grass: 85-67 **Artificial:** 3-7
Day: 51-41 **Night:** 37-33
1-Run: 27-17 **X-inn.:** 8-3
Doubleheaders: 1-0-1
Team record past five years: 375-435 (.463, ranks 11th in league in that span)

TEAM LEADERS

Batting average: Mark Grudzielanek (.314).
At-bats: Moises Alou (565).
Runs: Sammy Sosa (99).
Hits: Moises Alou (158).
Total Bases: Sammy Sosa (286).
Doubles: Mark Grudzielanek (38).
Triples: Corey Patterson (7).
Home runs: Sammy Sosa (40).
Runs batted in: Sammy Sosa (103).
Stolen bases: Tom Goodwin (19).
Slugging percentage: Sammy Sosa (.553).
On-base percentage: Mark Grudzielanek (.366).
Wins: Mark Prior (18).
Earned-run average: Mark Prior (2.43).
Complete games: Kerry Wood (4).
Shutouts: Kerry Wood (2).
Saves: Joe Borowski (33).
Innings pitched: Carlos Zambrano (214.0).
Strikeouts: Kerry Wood (266).

GAMES BY POSITION

Catcher: Damian Miller 114, Paul Bako 69, Josh Paul 3.
First base: Eric Karros 97, Hee Seop Choi 69, Randall Simon 29, Lenny Harris 2, Ramon Martinez 2.
Second base: Mark Grudzielanek 121, Ramon Martinez 42, Tony Womack 14, Augie Ojeda 5, Bobby Hill 2, Jose Hernandez 1.
Third base: Aramis Ramirez 63, Mark Bellhorn 42, Ramon Martinez 37, Lenny Harris 35, Jose Hernandez 17, Augie Ojeda 1.
Shortstop: Alex S. Gonzalez 150, Ramon Martinez 32, Augie Ojeda 7, Jose Hernandez 5, Tony Womack 1.
Outfield: Moises Alou 142, Sammy Sosa 137, Corey Patterson 82, Tom Goodwin 57, Kenny Lofton 55, Troy O'Leary 51, Doug Glanville 18, Trenidad Hubbard 4, Lenny Harris 2, Jose Hernandez 2, David Kelton 2.
Designated hitter: Moises Alou 9.

TOP DRAFT CHOICES

1. **Ryan Harvey,** OF, Dunedin (Fla.) H.S.
3. **Jake Fox,** C, Michigan.
4. **Tony Richie,** C, Florida State.
5. **Darin Downs,** LHP, Santaluces H.S., Boynton Beach, Fla.
6. **Sean Marshall,** LHP, Virginia Commonwealth.
7. **Kyle Boyer,** OF, Cal State-Fullerton.
8. **Matt Lincoln,** LHP, Santa Ana (Calif.) JC.
9. **Drew Larsen,** SS, Salt Lake CC.
10. **Casey McGehee,** 3B, Fresno State.

CINCINNATI REDS
NATIONAL LEAGUE CENTRAL DIVISION

2004 SEASON

April

SUN	MON	TUE	WED	THU	FRI	SAT
4	5 CHC	6	7 CHC	8 CHC	9 PIT	10 PIT
11 PIT	12 PHI	13	14 PHI	15 PHI	16 CHC	17 CHC
18 CHC	19 CHC	20 ATL	21 ATL	22 ATL	23 PIT	24 PIT
25 PIT	26 PIT	27 MIL	28 MIL	29	30 HOU	

May

SUN	MON	TUE	WED	THU	FRI	SAT
						1 HOU
2 HOU	3 HOU	4 MIL	5 MIL	6 MIL	7 SF	8 SF
9 SF	10	11 SD	12 SD	13 SD	14 LA	15 LA
16 LA	17	18 COL	19 COL	20 COL	21 HOU	22 HOU
23 HOU	24 HOU	25 FLA	26 FLA	27 FLA	28 MON	29 MON
30 MON	31 FLA					

June

SUN	MON	TUE	WED	THU	FRI	SAT
		1 FLA	2 FLA	3	4 MON	5 MON
6 MON	7 OAK	8 OAK	9 OAK	10	11 CLE	12 CLE
13 CLE	14	15 TEX	16 TEX	17 TEX	18 STL	19 STL
20 STL	21	22 NYM	23 NYM	24 NYM	25 PIT	26 PIT
27 PIT	28	29 NYM	30 NYM			

Home games shaded. All-Star Game July 13 at Houston. Schedule subject to change.

July

SUN	MON	TUE	WED	THU	FRI	SAT
				1 NYM	2 CLE	3 CLE
4 CLE	5 STL	6 STL	7 STL	8 MIL	9 MIL	10 MIL
11 MIL	12	13 All-Star	14	15 STL	16 STL	17 STL
18 STL	19 MIL	20 MIL	21 CHC	22 CHC	23 PIT	24 PIT
25 PIT	26 STL	27 STL	28 STL	29	30 HOU	31 HOU

August

SUN	MON	TUE	WED	THU	FRI	SAT
1 HOU	2	3 SF	4 SF	5 SF	6 COL	7 COL
8 COL	9	10 LA	11 LA	12 LA	13 SD	14 SD
15 SD	16 STL	17 STL	18 STL	19	20 ARI	21 ARI
22 ARI	23	24 STL	25 STL	26 STL	27 ARI	28 ARI
29 ARI	30 HOU	31 HOU				

Sept./Oct.

SUN	MON	TUE	WED	THU	FRI	SAT
			1 HOU	2	3 MIL	4 MIL
5 MIL	6 HOU	7 HOU	8 HOU	9 MIL	10 MIL	11 MIL
12 MIL	13 PHI	14 PHI	15 PHI	16 CHC	17 CHC	18 CHC
19 CHC	20	21 ATL	22 ATL	23 ATL	24 PIT	25 PIT
26 PIT	27 CHC	28 CHC	29 CHC	30 CHC	1 PIT	2 PIT
3 PIT	4	5	6	7	8	9

CLUB DIRECTORY

General manager
Dan O'Brien
Assistant general manager
Dean Taylor
Director of amateur scouting
Terry Reynolds
Director of major league operations
Brad Kullman
Special assistants to the g.m.
Leland Maddox, Larry Barton Jr.
Director of international scouting/player development
Johnny Almaraz
Senior special assistant to the g.m. and advance scout
Gene Bennett
Special consultants to the g.m.
Johnny Bench, Ken Griffey Sr.
Director of player development
Tim Naehring
Director of media relations
Rob Butcher

MINOR LEAGUE AFFILIATES

Class	Team	League	Manager
AAA	Louisville	International	Rick Burleson
AA	Chattanooga	Southern	Jayhawk Owens
Advanced A	Potomac	Carolina	Edgar Caceres
A	Dayton	Midwest	Alonzo Powell
Advanced Rookie	Billings	Pioneer	Donnie Scott
Rookie	Gulf Coast Reds	Gulf Coast	Luis Aguayo

More on the Reds at www.foxsports.com/named/FS/MLB/teams

BROADCAST INFORMATION

Radio: WLW-AM (700).
Cable TV: Fox Sports Net.

SPRING TRAINING

Ballpark (city): Ed Smith Stadium (Sarasota, Fla.).
Ticket information: 941-954-4101.

SPRING TRAINING ROSTER

Manager—Dave Miley (12).
Coaches—Mark Berry (59), Chris Chambliss, Don Gullett (35), Tom Hume (47), Jerry Narron, Randy Whisler.

No.	PITCHERS	B/T	Ht./Wt.	Age*	2003 Clubs
29	Acevedo, Jose	R/R	6-0/185	26	Louisville, Cincinnati
	Belisle, Matt	B/R	6-3/195	23	Greenville, Richmond. Louisville, Cincinnati
	Cerros, Juan	R/R	6-1/200	27	Louisville, Cincinnati
77	Claussen, Brandon	R/L	6-2/175	24	Tampa, New York A.L., Columbus, Louisville
	Dumatrait, Phil	R/L	6-2/170	22	Potomac, Sasasota
32	Graves, Danny	R/R	6-0/185	30	Cincinnati
58	Hall, Josh	R/R	6-2/190	23	Chattanooga, Cincinnati
39	Harang, Aaron	R/R	6-7/240	25	Oakland, Sacramento, Louisville, Cincinnati
43	Haynes, Jimmy	R/R	6-4/219	31	Dayton, Louisville, Cincinnati
54	Hudson, Luke	R/R	6-3/195	26	Did Not Play
	Lidle, Cory	R/R	5-11/192	32	Syracuse, Toronto
	Mattox, David	R/R	6-2/195	23	Binghamton
51	Norton, Phil	R/L	6-1/190	28	Chicago N.L., Iowa, Cincinnati
	Reith, Brian	R/R	6-5/220	26	Louisville, Cincinnati
41	Reitsma, Chris	R/R	6-5/235	26	Louisville, Cincinnati
46	Riedling, John	R/R	5-11/190	28	Cincinnati
48	Valentine, Joe	R/R	6-2/195	24	Sacramento, Cincinnati, Louisville
38	Wagner, Ryan	R/R	6-4/210	21	Chattanooga, Louisville, Cin cinnati
40	Wilson, Paul	R/R	6-5/215	31	Cincinnati

No.	CATCHERS	B/T	Ht./Wt.	Age*	2003 Clubs
23	LaRue, Jason	R/R	5-11/200	30	Cincinnati
22	Miller, Corky	R/R	6-1/225	28	Louisville, Cincinnati

No.	INFIELDERS	B/T	Ht./Wt.	Age*	2003 Clubs
	Bergolla, William	R/R	6-0/175	21	Potomac
21	Casey, Sean	L/R	6-4/225	29	Cincinnati
7	Castro, Juan	R/R	5-11/195	31	Louisville, Cincinnati
	Encarnacion, Ed.	R/R	6-1/195	21	Potomac, Chattanooga
	Hummel, Tim	R/R	6-2/195	25	Charlotte, Cincinnati
3	Jimenez, D'Angelo	B/R	6-0/195	26	Chicago A.L., Cincinnati
11	Larkin, Barry	R/R	6-0/185	39	Cincinnati
16	Larson, Brandon	R/R	6-0/210	27	Louisville, Cincinnati
	Lopez, Felipe	B/R	6-0/185	23	Cincinnati, Louisville
4	Olmedo, Ray	B/R	5-11/155	22	Chattanooga, Louisville, Cincinnati

No.	OUTFIELDERS	B/T	Ht./Wt.	Age*	2003 Clubs
44	Dunn, Adam	L/R	6-6/240	24	Cincinnati
6	Freel, Ryan	R/R	5-10/178	28	Louisville, Cincinnati
30	Griffey Jr., Ken	L/L	6-3/205	34	Cincinnati
28	Kearns, Austin	R/R	6-3/220	23	Cincinnati, Chattanooga
26	Pena, Wily Mo	R/R	6-3/215	22	Louisville, Cincinnati
37	Smitherman, S.	R/R	6-4/235	25	Louisville, Chattanooga, Cincinnati
	Vander Wal, John	L/L	6-1/210	37	Milwaukee

Invited to spring training: RHP Todd Van Poppel, OF Reggie Taylor, LHP Mike Matthews.

*Age as of April 1, 2004.

BALLPARK INFORMATION

Ballpark (capacity, surface)
Great American Ball Park (42,271, grass)

Address
100 Main St.
Cincinnati, OH 45202

Official website
www.cincinnatireds.com

Business phone
513-765-7000

Ticket information
513-765-7400

Field dimensions (from home plate)
To left field at foul line, 328 feet
To center field, 404 feet
To right field at foul line, 325 feet

First game played
March 31, 2003 (Pirates 10, Reds 1)

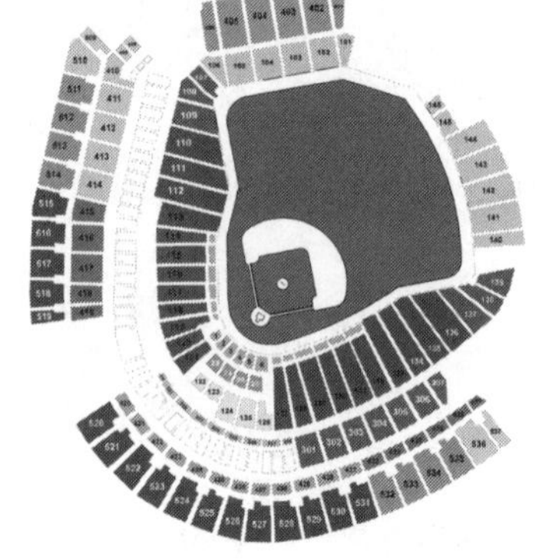

2003 REVIEW

DAY BY DAY

Date	Opp.	Res.	Score	(inn.*)	Hits	Opp. hits	Winning pitcher	Losing pitcher	Save	Record	Pos.	GB
3-31	Pit.	L	1-10		4	12	Benson	Haynes		0-1	T5th	1.0
4-2	Pit.	L	4-7		9	10	Torres	Manzanillo	Williams	0-2	T5th	2.0
4-3	Pit.	L	5-7		6	12	Fogg	Anderson	Williams	0-3	T5th	3.0
4-4	Chi.	W	10-9		11	13	Williamson	Veres		1-3	5th	3.0
4-5	Chi.	L	7-9		7	14	Zambrano	Haynes	Borowski	1-4	5th	3.0
4-6	Chi.	W	5-4		8	10	White	Guthrie	Williamson	2-4	5th	3.0
4-8	At Hou.	W	2-1	(10)	5	7	Dempster	Dotel	Williamson	3-4	5th	2.0
4-9	At Hou.	L	3-4		6	8	Lidge	Manzanillo	Wagner	3-5	5th	2.5
4-10	At Hou.	L	2-4		5	7	Robertson	Graves	Wagner	3-6	5th	3.5
4-11	Phi.	W	7-6		11	11	Williamson	Mesa		4-6	5th	3.5
4-12	Phi.	L	5-8		8	15	Millwood	Haynes		4-7	T5th	3.5
4-13	Phi.	L	1-13		6	9	Wolf	Dempster		4-8	T5th	3.5
4-14	At Chi.	W	11-3		11	11	Anderson	Prior	Riedling	5-8	5th	2.5
4-15	At Chi.	L	1-11		5	14	Estes	Graves		5-9	T5th	3.0
4-16	At Chi.	L	4-10		10	11	Zambrano	Wilson		5-10	T5th	4.0
4-17	At Chi.	L	3-16		6	16	Wood	Haynes	Benes	5-11	6th	5.0
4-19§	At Mon.■	L	7-8	(10)	12	11	Ayala	Williamson		5-12		
4-19∞	At Mon.■	L	5-9		8	11	Vazquez	Anderson		5-13	6th	7.0
4-20	At Mon.■	W	7-5		11	8	Sullivan	Ayala	Williamson	6-13	6th	6.0
4-22	L.A.	L	1-2		6	7	Shuey	Wilson	Gagne	6-14	6th	7.0
4-23	L.A.	W	3-0		8	9	Reitsma	Dreifort	Williamson	7-14	6th	6.0
4-24	L.A.	W	3-2	(11)	8	8	Heredia	Mota		8-14	T5th	5.0
4-25	S.D.	L	3-7		4	7	Peavy	Austin		8-15	6th	6.0
4-26	S.D.	W	7-6	(10)	10	8	Heredia	Wright		9-15	T5th	5.0
4-27	S.D.	W	7-5		8	11	Wilson	Lawrence	Williamson	10-15	5th	4.0
4-29	At Col.	L	5-10		7	13	Jennings	Reitsma		10-16	5th	5.0
4-30	At Col.	W	13-11		19	8	Sullivan	Miceli	Williamson	11-16	5th	4.0
5-1	At Col.	W	7-2		12	3	Austin	Cruz		12-16	4th	4.0
5-2	At S.F	W	5-1		9	10	Graves	Ainsworth		13-16	4th	4.0
5-3	At S.F	L	6-9		9	11	Foppert	Wilson	Worrell	13-17	5th	4.0
5-4	At S.F	L	1-6		6	9	Rueter	Dempster		13-18	5th	5.0
5-5	StL.	W	5-4		7	6	Williamson	Hermanson		14-18	5th	4.0
5-6	StL.	W	6-5		10	10	Reitsma	Calero		15-18	4th	3.0
5-7	StL.	W	4-2		5	6	Graves	Simontacchi	Williamson	16-18	4th	3.0
5-8	StL.	W	8-6		12	14	Sullivan	Crudale	Williamson	17-18	4th	2.5
5-9	Mil.	W	7-6	(10)	7	14	Reith	Vizcaino		18-18	4th	1.5
5-10	Mil.	L	3-9		13	10	Sheets	Riedling		18-19	4th	2.5
5-11	Mil.	W	7-5		8	9	Austin	Franklin	Williamson	19-19	4th	2.0
5-13	At StL.	W	7-2		12	9	Wilson	Simontacchi		20-19	3rd	2.5
5-14	At StL.	W	4-0		7	4	Graves	Morris		21-19	T2nd	2.5
5-15	At StL.	L	3-6		6	9	Stephenson	Riedling	Eldred	21-20	3rd	3.5
5-16	At Mil.	L	3-12		7	14	Franklin	Dempster		21-21	4th	3.5
5-17	At Mil.	L	6-8		12	8	DeJean	Williamson		21-22	4th	4.5
5-18	At Mil.	W	6-3	(10)	9	9	Sullivan	DeJean	Williamson	22-22	4th	3.5
5-20	Atl.	W	9-8		10	10	Sullivan	Hernandez	Williamson	23-22	4th	2.5
5-21	Atl.	W	9-3		9	8	Reitsma	Hampton		24-22	T3rd	1.5
5-22	Atl.	L	4-9		8	12	Reynolds	Dempster		24-23	4th	2.5
5-23	Fla.	L	4-8		9	12	Phelps	Austin		24-24	4th	2.5
5-24	Fla.	L	4-5		10	11	Penny	Wilson	Looper	24-25	4th	3.5
5-25	Fla.	L	2-6		9	15	Willis	Graves	Looper	24-26	4th	4.5
5-26	At Atl.	W	7-6	(11)	12	12	White	Hernandez		25-26	4th	3.5
5-27	At Atl.	L	2-3	(10)	4	10	Hodges	Reitsma		25-27	4th	3.5
5-28	At Atl.	L	3-15		3	18	Ortiz	Austin	Bong	25-28	4th	4.5
5-30	At Fla.	W	4-3	(11)	6	6	White	Almanza	Williamson	26-28	4th	3.5
5-31	At Fla.	L	2-3		6	9	Willis	Graves	Looper	26-29	4th	4.5
6-1	At Fla.	W	9-6		13	10	Sullivan	Pavano	Williamson	27-29	4th	3.5
6-3	N.Y. (AL)	W	4-3		8	5	Reitsma	Osuna		28-29	4th	3.5
6-4	N.Y. (AL)	W	6-2		9	7	Wilson	Mussina		29-29	4th	2.5
6-5	N.Y. (AL)	L	2-10		6	16	Contreras	Graves		29-30	4th	3.5
6-6	Tor.	L	2-9		9	15	Halladay	Riedling		29-31	4th	4.5
6-7	Tor.	W	9-8		14	10	Reitsma	Politte		30-31	4th	4.5
6-8	Tor.	L	0-5		4	12	Escobar	Haynes		30-32	4th	5.5
6-10	At T.B.	W	4-2		6	12	Wilson	Standridge	Williamson	31-32	4th	4.5
6-11	At T.B.	W	7-6		8	8	Reitsma	Colome	Williamson	32-32	4th	4.5

Date	Opp.	Res.	Score	(inn.*)	Hits	Opp. hits	Winning pitcher	Losing pitcher	Save	Record	Pos.	GB
6-12	At T.B.	W	2-1		6	4	Dempster	Gonzalez	Williamson	33-32	4th	3.5
6-13	Phi.	W	15-1		22	3	Haynes	Millwood		34-32	4th	2.5
6-14	Phi.	L	2-12		5	14	Wolf	Graves		34-33	4th	3.5
6-16	Chi.	L	3-4		10	8	Clement	Anderson	Borowski	34-34	4th	4.0
6-17	Chi.	W	2-1	(10)	5	7	Williamson	Remlinger		35-34	4th	3.0
6-18	Chi.	L	1-4		3	11	Wood	Haynes		35-35	4th	4.0
6-19	Chi.	W	3-1		9	5	Wilson	Prior	Williamson	36-35	4th	3.0
6-20	At Ari.	L	5-6		11	11	Valverde	Williamson		36-36	4th	3.0
6-21	At Ari.	L	3-5		8	6	Patterson	Anderson	Valverde	36-37	4th	3.5
6-22	At Ari.	L	5-6		8	11	Oropesa	Mercker	Valverde	36-38	4th	4.5
6-24	At StL.	W	7-4	(14)	12	19	Heredia	Fassero	Graves	37-38	4th	4.0
6-25	At StL.	L	6-9		9	13	Morris	Wilson	Isringhausen	37-39	4th	4.0
6-26	At StL.	L	7-11		12	17	Williams	Anderson		37-40	4th	4.0
6-27	At Cle.	L	0-3		6	7	Traber	Graves	Baez	37-41	4th	4.0
6-28	At Cle.	W	5-4		8	7	Reitsma	Baez	Williamson	38-41	4th	4.0
6-29	At Cle.	L	1-3		5	4	Davis	Haynes	Baez	38-42	4th	5.0
7-1	At Pit.	W	5-3		13	12	Graves	Tavarez	Williamson	39-42	4th	3.5
7-2	At Pit.	W	4-3		13	7	Heredia	Williams	Williamson	40-42	4th	2.5
7-3	At Pit.	L	7-8		11	12	Fogg	Dempster	Williams	40-43	4th	3.5
7-4	N.Y.	L	2-7		7	14	Glavine	Haynes	Benitez	40-44	4th	4.5
7-5	N.Y.	L	2-6		8	9	Trachsel	Graves	Weathers	40-45	4th	4.5
7-6	N.Y.	L	5-7		10	10	Cerda	Reith	Benitez	40-46	4th	5.5
7-7	At Hou.	L	1-7		4	11	Oswalt	Dempster		40-47	4th	5.5
7-8	At Hou.	L	3-6		7	7	Redding	Haynes	Wagner	40-48	4th	5.5
7-9	At Hou.	L	2-12		8	14	Robertson	Graves		40-49	4th	6.5
7-10	At Hou.	L	2-11		4	16	Villone	Wilson	Stone	40-50	5th	7.5
7-11	At Mil.	W	6-1		11	10	Dempster	Sheets		41-50	4th	7.5
7-12	At Mil.	W	5-1		8	5	Haynes	Franklin		42-50	4th	6.5
7-13	At Mil.	W	10-8	(12)	11	12	Heredia	Estrella		43-50	4th	6.5
7-17	Hou.	L	4-5		9	11	Robertson	Wilson	Wagner	43-51	4th	7.5
7-18	Hou.	L	3-5		6	10	Oswalt	Dempster	Wagner	43-52	4th	8.5
7-19	Hou.	L	8-9		14	10	Villone	Haynes	Dotel	43-53	4th	9.5
7-20	Hou.	L	3-6		5	9	Miller	Graves	Wagner	43-54	5th	10.5
7-21	Mil.	W	11-2		15	4	Acevedo	Kinney		44-54	5th	9.5
7-22	Mil.	L	4-6		11	10	Franklin	Wilson	Kolb	44-55	5th	10.5
7-23	Pit.	L	5-6		11	12	Boehringer	Mercker	Lincoln	44-56	5th	11.5
7-24	Pit.	L	5-7	(11)	9	10	Lincoln	Reitsma		44-57	5th	11.5
7-25	At N.Y.	L	1-3		7	11	Leiter	Graves	Stanton	44-58	5th	11.5
7-26	At N.Y.	W	8-3		12	5	Acevedo	Heilman		45-58	5th	11.5
7-27	At N.Y.	W	8-5		13	8	Wilson	Trachsel	Williamson	46-58	5th	10.5
7-28	Phi.	W	6-5	(10)	14	9	Williamson	Adams		47-58	5th	10.0
7-29	Col.	L	3-5		6	13	Oliver	Haynes	Speier	47-59	5th	10.0
7-30	Col.	W	3-2	(10)	7	7	Reitsma	Jimenez		48-59	5th	10.0
7-31	Col.	W	5-4	(10)	11	5	Riedling	Fuentes		49-59	5th	9.0
8-1	S.F	W	5-3		8	10	Reitsma	Rodriguez		50-59	5th	9.0
8-2	S.F	W	5-4		8	8	Wagner	Rodriguez	Heredia	51-59	5th	8.0
8-3	S.F	L	3-7		8	12	Hermanson	Haynes		51-60	5th	9.0
8-5	At L.A.	L	2-5		9	7	Brown	Graves	Gagne	51-61	5th	9.0
8-6	At L.A.	L	1-2		4	8	Perez	Heredia	Gagne	51-62	5th	10.0
8-7	At L.A.	L	3-4		6	9	Nomo	Wilson	Gagne	51-63	5th	10.0
8-8	At S.D.	L	0-1	(12)	7	7	Beck	Reith		51-64	5th	11.0
8-9	At S.D.	W	9-5		14	10	Harang	Perez		52-64	5th	10.0
8-10	At S.D.	L	0-2		7	13	Lawrence	Graves	Beck	52-65	5th	11.0
8-12	Ari.	L	0-2		6	4	Schilling	Wilson	Mantei	52-66	5th	11.5
8-13	Ari.	L	1-3		10	7	Randolph	Heredia	Mantei	52-67	5th	11.5
8-14	Ari.	W	3-2		7	4	Harang	Webb	Reitsma	53-67	5th	10.5
8-15	Hou.	W	9-7	(10)	10	11	Wagner	Lidge		54-67	5th	10.0
8-16	Hou.	L	2-5		5	6	Miller	Etherton	Wagner	54-68	5th	10.5
8-17	Hou.	W	4-3		6	6	Wilson	Redding	Reitsma	55-68	5th	9.5
8-19	At Ari.	L	1-6		6	11	Webb	Bale	Mantei	55-69	5th	10.5
8-20	At Ari.	W	2-0		7	6	Harang	Johnson	Reitsma	56-69	5th	9.5
8-21	At Ari.	L	3-9		7	10	Dessens	Graves		56-70	5th	10.5
8-22	At Hou.	W	4-3		8	9	Etherton	Miller	Reitsma	57-70	5th	9.5
8-23	At Hou.	W	3-1		6	5	Wilson	Redding	Reitsma	58-70	5th	8.5
8-24	At Hou.	L	3-6		5	11	Robertson	Reith	Wagner	58-71	5th	9.5
8-25	Mil.	L	6-10		9	12	Kinney	Harang	Kolb	58-72	5th	10.0
8-26	Mil.	L	1-7		4	9	Davis	Serafini		58-73	5th	11.0
8-27	Mil.	L	2-6		12	9	Franklin	Etherton		58-74	5th	12.0
8-28	Mil.	L	3-4	(10)	8	14	de los Santos	Reitsma	Kolb	58-75	T5th	12.0
8-29	StL.	W	8-5		10	13	Bale	Haren	Graves	59-75	5th	11.0
8-30	StL.	L	3-6		12	10	Tomko	Harang	Isringhausen	59-76	T5th	12.0
8-31	StL.	L	0-5		4	8	Hitchcock	Serafini		59-77	6th	13.0

Date	Opp.	Res.	Score	(inn.*)	Hits	Opp. hits	Winning pitcher	Losing pitcher	Save	Record	Pos.	GB
9-1	At Mil.	W	5-4		9	9	Etherton	Franklin	Reitsma	60-77	T5th	12.0
9-2	At Mil.	L	3-4		4	9	Vizcaino	Graves	Kolb	60-78	6th	12.5
9-3	At Mil.	L	6-9		10	9	Estrella	Randall	Kolb	60-79	6th	13.0
9-5	At StL.	W	4-2	(12)	9	6	Randall	Simontacchi	Reitsma	61-79	6th	13.0
9-6	At StL.	L	6-13		10	15	Williams	Serafini		61-80	6th	14.0
9-7	At StL.	L	0-9		3	16	Morris	Etherton		61-81	6th	14.5
9-8	Pit.	L	1-9		10	12	Fogg	Bale		61-82	6th	15.0
9-9	Pit.	W	10-6		13	14	Belisle	Boehringer		62-82	T5th	15.0
9-10	Pit.	L	2-3		4	10	Lincoln	Reitsma	Tavarez	62-83	T5th	16.0
9-11	Pit.	W	3-2		6	13	Randall	D'Amico	Reitsma	63-83	T5th	15.0
9-12	At Chi.	L	6-7		12	13	Alfonseca	Randall	Borowski	63-84	T5th	16.0
9-13	At Chi.	L	6-9		13	14	Alfonseca	Belisle	Borowski	63-85	6th	17.0
9-14	At Chi.	W	1-0		4	7	Riedling	Zambrano	Reitsma	64-85	T5th	17.0
9-15	At Pit.	L	3-6		8	7	Vogelsong	Van Poppel	Tavarez	64-86	T5th	17.5
9-16	At Pit.	W	12-4		17	9	Harang	Perez	Reith	65-86	5th	17.5
9-17	At Pit.	L	5-8		9	14	D'Amico	Etherton	Tavarez	65-87	T5th	17.5
9-18	At Pit.	L	0-7		4	12	Wells	Randall		65-88	T5th	18.5
9-19	At Phi.	L	3-7		5	7	Wolf	Hall		65-89	T5th	19.5
9-20	At Phi.	W	2-0		6	4	Van Poppel	Telemaco	Reitsma	66-89	5th	18.5
9-21	At Phi.	W	4-3		9	6	Serafini	Padilla	Reitsma	67-89	5th	17.5
9-23	Chi.	L	0-6		2	8	Wood	Randall		67-90	5th	18.0
9-24	Chi.	L	0-8		4	10	Estes	Hall		67-91	5th	19.0
9-25	Chi.	W	9-7		11	11	Van Poppel	Zambrano	Reitsma	68-91	5th	18.0
9-26	Mon.	L	1-5		5	9	Ohka	Harang		68-92	5th	18.5
9-27	Mon.	W	4-2		7	5	Reith	Hernandez		69-92	5th	19.0
9-28	Mon.	L	1-2		5	6	Tucker	Randall	Biddle	69-93	5th	19.0

Monthly records: March (0-1), April (11-15), May (15-13), June (12-13), July (11-17), August (10-18), September (10-16).
*Innings, if other than nine. ■ At Hiram Bithorn Stadium, San Juan, Puerto Rico. § Day separate admission. ∞ Night separate admission.

RECORDS

2003 regular-season record: 69-93
Position: 5th in N.L. Central
Home: 35-46 **Road:** 34-47
N.L. East: 14-19 **N.L. Central:** 34-50
N.L. West: 14-19 A.L. 7-5
Vs. LH starters: 16-29
Vs. RH starters: 53-64
Grass: 63-90 **Artificial:** 6-3
Day: 22-33 **Night:** 47-60
1-Run: 30-21 **X-inn.:** 15-5
Doubleheaders: 0-0-0
Team record past five years: 394-417 (.486, ranks 9th in league in that span)

TEAM LEADERS

Batting average: Jose Guillen (.337).
At-bats: Sean Casey (573).
Runs: Sean Casey (71).
Hits: Sean Casey (167).
Total Bases: Sean Casey (234).
Doubles: Jason LaRue (23).
Triples: Aaron Boone, Sean Casey (3).
Home runs: Adam Dunn (27).
Runs batted in: Sean Casey (80).
Stolen bases: Aaron Boone (15).
Slugging percentage: Jose Guillen (.629).
On-base percentage: Jose Guillen (.385).
Wins: Chris Reitsma (9).
Earned-run average: Paul Wilson (4.64).
Complete games: Danny Graves (2).
Shutouts: Danny Graves (1).
Saves: Scott Williamson (21).
Innings pitched: Danny Graves (169.0).
Strikeouts: Paul Wilson (93).

GAMES BY POSITION

Catcher: Jason LaRue 114, Kelly Stinnett 50, Corky Miller 11, Dane Sardinha 1.
First base: Sean Casey 144, Adam Dunn 19, Russell Branyan 14, Juan Castro 1, Jason LaRue 1, Dernell Stenson 1.
Second base: D'Angelo Jimenez 73, Juan Castro 56, Aaron Boone 19, Ray Olmedo 18, Ryan Freel 11, Felipe Lopez 3, Tim Hummel 1.
Third base: Aaron Boone 83, Juan Castro 30, Brandon Larson 24, Russell Branyan 20, Tim Hummel 20, Felipe Lopez 8, Ryan Freel 2, D'Angelo Jimenez 2, Jim Chamblee 1, Wily Mo Pena 1.
Shortstop: Barry Larkin 60, Ray Olmedo 51, Felipe Lopez 50, Juan Castro 24, Aaron Boone 5, Tim Hummel 2.
Outfield: Adam Dunn 102, Austin Kearns 80, Jose Guillen 78, Reggie Taylor 60, Ruben Mateo 54, Wily Mo Pena 47, Ken Griffey Jr. 43, Ryan Freel 24, Dernell Stenson 22, Russell Branyan 17, Stephen Smitherman 14, Eric Valent 8, Brandon Larson 3, Mark Budzinski 1, Jason LaRue 1.
Designated hitter: Ken Griffey Jr. 3, Adam Dunn 2, Russell Branyan 1.

TOP DRAFT CHOICES

1. **Ryan Wagner,** RHP, Houston.
2. **Thomas Pauly,** RHP, Princeton.
3. **Jose Ronda,** SS, Gabriela Mistral H.S., San Juan, Puerto Rico.
4. **Kenny Lewis,** OF, George Washington H.S., Danville, Va.
5. **Marc Cornell,** RHP, Ohio University.
6. **Richie Gardner,** RHP, Arizona.
7. **Carlos Guevara,** RHP, St. Mary's (Texas).
8. **Damian Ursin,** RHP, Southern University.
9. **Ben Himes,** OF, Oklahoma City U.
10. **Andy D'Alessio,** 1B, Barron Collier H.S., Naples, Fla.

COLORADO ROCKIES

NATIONAL LEAGUE WEST DIVISION

2004 SEASON

April

SUN	MON	TUE	WED	THU	FRI	SAT
4	5	6 ARI	7 ARI	8 ARI	9 LA	10 LA
11 LA	12 ARI	13	14 ARI	15 ARI	16 STL	17 STL
18 STL	19	20 LA	21 LA	22 LA	23 HOU	24 HOU
25 HOU	26 FLA	27 FLA	28 FLA	29	30 ATL	

May

SUN	MON	TUE	WED	THU	FRI	SAT
						1 ATL
2 ATL	3	4 MON	5 MON	6 MON	7 CHC	8 CHC
9 CHC	10	11 PIT	12 PIT	13 PIT	14 PHI	15 PHI
16 PHI	17 PHI	18 CIN	19 CIN	20 CIN	21 NYM	22 NYM
23 NYM	24	25 SD	26 SD	27 SD	28 SF	29 SF
30 SF	31 SD					

June

SUN	MON	TUE	WED	THU	FRI	SAT
		1 SD	2 SD	3	4 SF	5 SF
6 SF	7 SF	8 NYY	9 NYY	10 NYY	11 TB	12 TB
13 TB	14	15 BOS	16 BOS	17 BOS	18 BAL	19 BAL
20 BAL	21	22 MIL	23 MIL	24 MIL	25 CLE	26 CLE
27 CLE	28	29 MIL	30 MIL			

Home games shaded. All-Star Game July 13 at Houston. Schedule subject to change.

July

SUN	MON	TUE	WED	THU	FRI	SAT
				1 MIL	2 DET	3 DET
4 DET	5 SF	6 SF	7 SF	8 SD	9 SD	10 SD
11 SD	12	13 All-Star	14	15 SF	16 SF	17 SF
18 SF	19 SD	20 SD	21 LA	22 LA	23 ARI	24 ARI
25 ARI	26 LA	27 LA	28 LA	29 LA	30 ARI	31 ARI

August

SUN	MON	TUE	WED	THU	FRI	SAT
1 ARI	2	3 CHC	4 CHC	5 CHC	6 CIN	7 CIN
8 CIN	9 PHI	10 PHI	11 PHI	12 PHI	13 PIT	14 PIT
15 PIT	16	17 NYM	18 NYM	19 NYM	20 MON	21 MON
22 MON	23	24 ATL	25 ATL	26 ATL	27 FLA	28 FLA
29 FLA	30	31 SF				

Sept./Oct.

SUN	MON	TUE	WED	THU	FRI	SAT
			1 SF	2 SF	3 SD	4 SD
5 SD	6	7 SF	8 SF	9 SD	10 SD	11 SD
12 SD	13 ARI	14 ARI	15 ARI	16 ARI	17 LA	18 LA
19 LA	20	21 ARI	22 ARI	23 ARI	24 STL	25 STL
26 STL	27 LA	28 LA	29 LA	30 LA	1 HOU	2 HOU
3 HOU	4	5	6	7	8	9

CLUB DIRECTORY

Chairman
Charles K. Monfort
Vice chairman
Jerry D. McMorris, Richard L. Monfort
President
Keli S. McGregor
Executive vice president, g.m.
Daniel J. O'Dowd
Sr. director, communications/p.r.
Jay Alves
Sr. director, community & retail ops.
Jim Kellogg
Director, player personnel
Bill Geivett
Director, major league operations
Paul Egins
Director, scouting
Bill Schmidt

MINOR LEAGUE AFFILIATES

Class	Team	League	Manager
AAA	Colorado Springs	Pacific Coast	Marv Foley
AA	Tulsa	Texas	Tom Runnells
Advanced A	Visalia	California	Stu Cole
A	Asheville	South Atlantic	Joe Mikulik
Short-Season A	Tri-City	Northwest	Ron Gideon
Advanced Rookie	Casper	Pioneer	P.J. Carey

More on the Rockies at www.foxsports.com/named/FS/MLB/teams

BROADCAST INFORMATION

Radio: KOA-AM (850), KCUV-AM (1150).
TV: KWGN-TV (Channel 2).
Cable TV: Fox Sports Rocky Mountain.

SPRING TRAINING

Ballpark (city): Hi Corbett Field (Tucson, Ariz.).
Ticket information: 1-800-388-ROCK.

SPRING TRAINING ROSTER

Manager—Clint Hurdle (13).
Coaches—Sandy Alomar Sr. (2), Bob Apodaca (36), Dave Collins (29), Duane Espy (52), Rick Mathews (53), Jamie Quirk (9).

No.	PITCHERS	B/T	Ht./Wt.	Age*	2003 Clubs
43	Bernero, Adam	R/R	6-4/210	27	Detroit, Colorado
34	Chacon, Shawn	R/R	6-3/212	26	Colo. Springs, Colorado
28	Cook, Aaron	R/R	6-3/205	25	Colo. Springs, Colorado
	Dohmann, Scott	R/R	6-1/180	26	Tulsa
40	Fuentes, Brian	L/L	6-4/220	28	Colorado
	Hampson, Justin	L/L	6-1/180	23	Tulsa, Visalia
	Huisman, Justin	R/R	6-1/195	24	Tulsa
32	Jennings, Jason	L/R	6-2/245	25	Colorado
	Kennedy, Joe	R/L	6-4/237	24	Orlando, Durham, Tampa Bay
45	Lopez, Javier	L/L	6-4/200	26	Colorado
15	Neagle, Denny	L/L	6-3/225	35	Visalia, Colo. Springs, Colorado
39	Reed, Steve	R/R	6-2/212	38	Colorado
	Simpson, Allan	R/R	6-4/185	26	Tacoma
41	Stark, Denny	R/R	6-2/210	29	Visalia, Tulsa, Colo. Springs, Colorado
71	Tsao, Chin-hui	R/R	6-2/177	22	Tulsa, Colorado
	Vance, Cory	L/L	6-1/195	24	Colo. Springs, Colorado
	White, Matt	R/L	6-1/180	26	Sarasota, Portland, Pawtucket, Boston, Seattle, Buffalo
49	Young, Jason	R/R	6-5/210	24	Colo. Springs, Colorado

No.	CATCHERS	B/T	Ht./Wt.	Age*	2003 Clubs
	Closser, J.D.	B/R	5-10/175	24	Tulsa
	Greene, Todd	R/R	5-10/208	32	Frisco, Texas .
23	Johnson, Charles	R/R	6-3/250	32	Colorado

No.	INFIELDERS	B/T	Ht./Wt.	Age*	2003 Clubs
	Atkins, Garrett	R/R	6-3/210	24	Colo. Springs, Colorado
	Baker, Jeff	R/R	6-2/210	22	Asheville
	Barmes, Clint	R/R	6-0/175	25	Colo. Springs, Colorado
	Castilla, Vinny	R/R	6-1/205	36	Atlanta
	Gonzalez, Luis A.	R/R	5-11/170	24	Akron, Burlington
	Hawpe, Brad	L/L	6-3/200	24	Tulsa
17	Helton, Todd	L/L	6-2/204	30	Colorado
	Miles, Aaron	B/R	5-8/170	27	Charlotte, Chicago A.L.

No.	OUTFIELDERS	B/T	Ht./Wt.	Age*	2003 Clubs
	Burnitz, Jeromy	L/R	6-0/213	34	Binghamton, New Yotk N.L., Los Angeles
	Freeman, Choo	R/R	6-2/200	24	Colo. Springs
	Holliday, Matt	R/R	6-4/235	24	Tulsa
	Miller, Tony	R/R	5-9/180	23	Visalia
	Piedra, Jorge	L/L	6-0/190	24	Tulsa
	Reyes, Rene	B/R	5-11/213	26	Colo. Springs, Colorado
	Sullivan, Cory	L/L	6-0/180	24	Tulsa
33	Walker, Larry	L/R	6-3/235	37	Colorado
44	Wilson, Preston	R/R	6-2/213	29	Colorado

Invited to spring training: RHP Travis Driskill, RHP Jason Gilfillan, RHP Tim Harikkala, RHP Marc Kroon, RHP Turk Wendell, RHP Jeff Tam, RHP Brian Tollberg, SS Royce Clayton, IF Benji Gil, IF Damian Jackson, IF Andy Tracy, OF Mark Sweeney.

*Age as of April 1, 2004.

BALLPARK INFORMATION

Ballpark (capacity, surface)
Coors Field (50,449, grass)

Address
2001 Blake St.
Denver, CO 80205-2000

Official website
www.coloradorockies.com

Business phone
303-292-0200

Ticket information
800-388-7625

Field dimensions (from home plate)
To left field at foul line, 347 feet
To center field, 415 feet
To right field at foul line, 350

First game played
April 26, 1995 (Rockies 11, Mets 9, 14 innings)

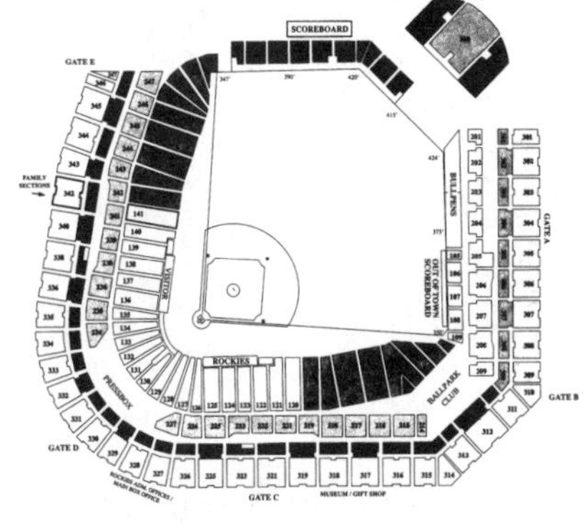

2003 REVIEW

DAY BY DAY

Date	Opp.	Res.	Score	(inn.*)	Hits	Opp. hits	Winning pitcher	Losing pitcher	Save	Record	Pos.	GB
4-1	At Hou.	L	4-10		8	14	Oswalt	Jennings		0-1	4th	1.5
4-2	At Hou.	L	7-8		13	15	Wagner	Jimenez		0-2	4th	2.5
4-3	At Hou.	W	10-5		14	9	Cruz	Robertson		1-2	T3rd	2.0
4-4	Ari.	W	2-1		5	3	Chacon	Kim	Jimenez	2-2	2nd	2.0
4-5	Ari.	W	4-3	(10)	7	12	Reed	Batista		3-2	2nd	2.0
4-6	Ari.	W	8-3		9	10	Jennings	Schilling		4-2	2nd	2.0
4-8	StL.	L	12-15	(13)	19	17	Eldred	Miceli		4-3	2nd	2.5
4-9	StL.	W	9-4		10	8	Cruz	Tomko		5-3	2nd	2.5
4-10	StL.	W	7-6		8	12	Lopez	Kline	Jimenez	6-3	2nd	2.5
4-11	At S.D.	L	4-6		9	12	Lawrence	Oliver	Villafuerte	6-4	2nd	3.5
4-12	At S.D.	W	3-2		8	8	Speier	Villafuerte	Jimenez	7-4	2nd	3.0
4-13	At S.D.	L	2-6		6	12	Wright	Cook		7-5	2nd	4.0
4-14	At Ari.	W	5-3		10	10	Cruz	Kim	Jimenez	8-5	2nd	4.0
4-15	At Ari.	W	12-1		14	6	Chacon	Patterson		9-5	2nd	4.0
4-16	At Ari.	L	3-4		8	10	Mantei	Jimenez		9-6	2nd	4.0
4-17	At Ari.	L	2-11		4	16	Schilling	Jennings		9-7	2nd	4.5
4-18	S.D.	W	12-1		17	5	Cook	Perez		10-7	2nd	4.5
4-19	S.D.	W	10-9		14	14	Reed	Villafuerte		11-7	2nd	4.5
4-20	S.D.	W	8-0		8	6	Chacon	Peavy		12-7	2nd	3.5
4-22	At Phi.	L	2-5		5	8	Millwood	Oliver	Mesa	12-8	2nd	3.5
4-23	At Phi.	L	4-6		6	9	Myers	Jennings	Mesa	12-9	2nd	4.5
4-24	At Phi.	L	1-9		4	14	Wolf	Cook		12-10	2nd	5.5
4-25	Chi.	L	7-11		11	16	Prior	Cruz		12-11	2nd	6.5
4-26	Chi.	W	8-5		17	5	Chacon	Estes	Jimenez	13-11	2nd	5.5
4-27	Chi.	W	6-3		7	6	Oliver	Zambrano	Jimenez	14-11	2nd	4.5
4-29	Cin.	W	10-5		13	7	Jennings	Reitsma		15-11	2nd	3.5
4-30	Cin.	L	11-13		8	19	Sullivan	Miceli	Williamson	15-12	2nd	4.5
5-1	Cin.	L	2-7		3	12	Austin	Cruz		15-13	2nd	4.5
5-2	At Chi.	L	4-7		10	10	Estes	Chacon	Borowski	15-14	2nd	4.5
5-3	At Chi.	W	6-4		10	8	Speier	Guthrie	Jimenez	16-14	2nd	4.5
5-4	At Chi.	L	4-5	(10)	10	6	Borowski	Reed		16-15	2nd	5.5
5-6	At Atl.	L	2-3		6	7	Hernandez	Jones	Smoltz	16-16	2nd	6.5
5-8†	At Atl.	L	6-12		7	9	Reynolds	Cruz	Smoltz	16-17		
5-8‡	At Atl.	L	2-5		6	8	Ortiz	Chacon	Smoltz	16-18	3rd	8.5
5-9	At Fla.	L	4-5		9	7	Looper	Speier		16-19	3rd	9.5
5-10	At Fla.	W	5-4		7	13	Jennings	Tejera	Jimenez	17-19	3rd	8.5
5-11	At Fla.	L	2-7		12	8	Pavano	Cook		17-20	3rd	8.5
5-12	N.Y.	L	6-9		11	11	Trachsel	Young	Benitez	17-21	T3rd	8.5
5-13	N.Y.	W	9-8		15	13	Reed	Cerda	Jimenez	18-21	T3rd	7.5
5-14	N.Y.	W	6-5		11	6	Reed	Stanton	Jimenez	19-21	T3rd	6.5
5-15	Mon.	W	4-2		10	8	Jones	Tucker	Jimenez	20-21	3rd	6.5
5-16	Mon.	L	1-4		6	10	Ayala	Cruz	Biddle	20-22	3rd	7.5
5-17	Mon.	L	4-6	(10)	9	11	Ayala	Jones	Biddle	20-23	3rd	7.5
5-18	Mon.	W	4-0		10	6	Chacon	Ohka		21-23	3rd	6.5
5-20	At L.A.	L	1-3		4	8	Brown	Oliver	Gagne	21-24	3rd	7.0
5-21	At L.A.	L	2-3		4	11	Ishii	Jennings	Gagne	21-25	3rd	8.0
5-22	At L.A.	L	3-4		2	7	Dreifort	Cook	Gagne	21-26	T3rd	8.5
5-23	S.F	W	10-7		11	16	Chacon	Moss		22-26	T3rd	7.5
5-24	S.F	L	1-5		4	11	Ainsworth	Elarton		22-27	T3rd	8.5
5-25	S.F	W	5-1		7	11	Oliver	Foppert		23-27	T3rd	7.5
5-26	S.F	W	12-7		18	9	Fuentes	Nathan		24-27	T3rd	6.5
5-27	L.A.	W	7-3		6	9	Cook	Ishii		25-27	3rd	6.5
5-28	L.A.	W	6-0		11	4	Chacon	Dreifort		26-27	3rd	6.5
5-29	L.A.	W	12-5		16	14	Elarton	Perez		27-27	3rd	6.0
5-30	At S.F	L	2-6		10	12	Ainsworth	Oliver		27-28	3rd	7.0
5-31	At S.F	L	1-2		3	8	Foppert	Jennings	Worrell	27-29	3rd	8.0
6-1	At S.F	L	0-4		8	6	Rueter	Cook		27-30	3rd	9.0
6-2	At S.F	W	4-1		9	6	Chacon	Schmidt	Jimenez	28-30	3rd	8.0
6-3	Cle.	W	7-3		9	10	Elarton	Rodriguez		29-30	3rd	7.0
6-4	Cle.	W	2-1		8	7	Oliver	Traber	Jimenez	30-30	3rd	7.0
6-5	Cle.	W	7-4		10	4	Jennings	Sabathia	Jimenez	31-30	3rd	6.0
6-7§	K.C.	L	11-13		12	14	George	Chacon	MacDougal	31-31		
6-7∞	K.C.	L	5-9		10	16	Gilfillan	Jones		31-32	3rd	8.0
6-8	K.C.	W	8-7		11	15	Elarton	DeHart	Jimenez	32-32	3rd	8.0
6-10	At Min.	W	5-0		7	3	Jennings	Radke		33-32	3rd	7.0

Date	Opp.	Res.	Score	(inn.*)	Hits	Opp. hits	Winning pitcher	Losing pitcher	Save	Record	Pos.	GB
6-11	At Min.	L	4-7		12	15	Lohse	Cook	Guardado	33-33	3rd	8.0
6-12	At Min.	L	3-15		10	18	Rogers	Oliver		33-34	3rd	9.0
6-13	At Det.	W	7-2		12	8	Chacon	Cornejo		34-34	3rd	8.0
6-14	At Det.	L	7-9		9	15	Ledezma	Elarton	Spurling	34-35	3rd	9.0
6-15	At Det.	W	5-4		10	11	Jennings	Knotts	Jimenez	35-35	3rd	8.0
6-16	S.D.	L	5-7		11	13	Witasick	Jimenez	Beck	35-36	3rd	8.5
6-17	S.D.	L	3-4		9	8	Peavy	Neagle	Witasick	35-37	3rd	8.5
6-18	S.D.	W	5-3		10	7	Chacon	Jarvis	Speier	36-37	3rd	7.5
6-19	S.D.	W	10-5		16	9	Oliver	Lawrence		37-37	3rd	7.5
6-20	Det.	L	5-7		11	13	Maroth	Elarton		37-38	4th	7.5
6-21	Det.	W	9-6		10	12	Jennings	Sparks		38-38	4th	7.5
6-22	Det.	W	5-3		7	7	Neagle	Bernero	Jimenez	39-38	4th	6.5
6-23	At S.D.	W	5-1		8	6	Chacon	Jarvis		40-38	4th	6.5
6-24	At S.D.	W	5-2		10	5	Oliver	Lawrence	Jimenez	41-38	4th	6.5
6-25	At S.D.	L	6-7		5	10	Hackman	Jones	Beck	41-39	4th	6.5
6-27	At Pit.	L	3-5		12	8	Fogg	Jennings	Williams	41-40	4th	7.5
6-28	At Pit.	W	5-4		7	11	Neagle	Benson	Jimenez	42-40	4th	7.5
6-29	At Pit.	L	0-9		4	11	Suppan	Chacon		42-41	4th	7.5
6-30	Ari.	L	7-8	(12)	7	15	Randolph	Jimenez		42-42	4th	8.5
7-1	Ari.	W	7-4		14	10	Lopez	Good	Speier	43-42	4th	8.5
7-2	Ari.	W	6-2		11	7	Jennings	Patterson	Fuentes	44-42	4th	8.5
7-3	Ari.	L	4-8		12	14	Webb	Neagle		44-43	4th	8.5
7-4	At Mil.	W	8-6		12	14	Reed	Estrella	Speier	45-43	4th	8.5
7-5	At Mil.	W	9-8		12	8	Oliver	Ford	Fuentes	46-43	4th	7.5
7-6	At Mil.	L	1-3		4	7	Sheets	Jimenez	DeJean	46-44	4th	8.5
7-7	At Ari.	L	6-14		5	18	Randolph	Cruz		46-45	4th	9.5
7-8	At Ari.	L	3-9		8	11	Webb	Reed		46-46	4th	10.5
7-9	S.F	W	11-7		12	10	Cook	Foppert		47-46	4th	9.5
7-10	S.F	W	11-3		13	9	Oliver	Powell		48-46	4th	8.5
7-11	L.A.	W	7-6		7	13	Fuentes	Shuey	Speier	49-46	4th	8.5
7-12	L.A.	W	5-3		10	7	Jennings	Ashby	Speier	50-46	4th	8.5
7-13	L.A.	L	3-9		7	12	Alvarez	Neagle		50-47	4th	8.5
7-17	At S.F	L	4-8		10	12	Moss	Jennings		50-48	4th	9.5
7-18	At S.F	L	0-7		5	12	Brower	Oliver		50-49	4th	10.5
7-19	At S.F	L	3-5		8	7	Schmidt	Chacon	Worrell	50-50	4th	11.5
7-20	At S.F	L	4-8		6	11	Foppert	Neagle		50-51	4th	12.5
7-21	At L.A.	W	4-1		9	6	Stark	Ashby		51-51	4th	12.5
7-22	At L.A.	L	2-5		7	10	Nomo	Jennings	Gagne	51-52	4th	13.5
7-23	At L.A.	W	8-3		11	6	Oliver	Ishii		52-52	4th	13.5
7-24	At L.A.	L	0-1	(11)	4	6	Shuey	Lopez		52-53	4th	14.5
7-25	Mil.	W	7-3		10	8	Tsao	Obermueller		53-53	4th	14.5
7-26	Mil.	W	13-8		16	14	Cook	de los Santos		54-53	4th	13.5
7-27	Mil.	W	6-1		7	7	Jennings	Franklin		55-53	4th	13.5
7-29	At Cin.	W	5-3		13	6	Oliver	Haynes	Speier	56-53	4th	12.5
7-30	At Cin.	L	2-3	(10)	7	7	Reitsma	Jimenez		56-54	4th	13.5
7-31	At Cin.	L	4-5	(10)	5	11	Riedling	Fuentes		56-55	4th	13.5
8-1	At Pit.	L	11-12		12	13	Sanchez	Bernero		56-56	T3rd	13.5
8-2	At Pit.	L	0-1		6	3	Meadows	Jennings	Lincoln	56-57	3rd	13.5
8-3	At Pit.	W	16-4		24	11	Oliver	D'Amico	Jimenez	57-57	T3rd	13.5
8-5	Phi.	L	2-7		9	8	Myers	Chacon		57-58	4th	14.5
8-6	Phi.	W	5-1		8	5	Tsao	Duckworth		58-58	4th	13.5
8-7	Phi.	W	4-3		6	8	Lopez	Millwood	Speier	59-58	4th	13.5
8-8	Pit.	W	13-6		16	10	Jimenez	Mahomes		60-58	4th	13.5
8-9	Pit.	L	4-10		6	11	D'Amico	Oliver		60-59	4th	13.5
8-10	Pit.	L	3-5		11	9	Figueroa	Chacon	Lincoln	60-60	4th	14.5
8-11	At Mon.	L	1-3		7	7	Day	Jennings	Biddle	60-61	4th	15.0
8-12	At Mon.	W	6-3	(11)	9	7	Fuentes	Biddle	Lopez	61-61	4th	14.0
8-13	At Mon.	L	5-6		10	9	Vazquez	Stark	Ayala	61-62	4th	14.0
8-15	At N.Y.	L	0-5		4	10	Glavine	Oliver		61-63	4th	14.0
8-16	At N.Y.	L	4-13		8	14	Seo	Chacon		61-64	4th	14.0
8-17	At N.Y.	L	4-6		8	11	Leiter	Jennings	Weathers	61-65	4th	14.0
8-18	At N.Y.	L	0-8		1	12	Trachsel	Tsao		61-66	4th	14.0
8-19	Fla.	W	10-2		13	6	Stark	Pavano		62-66	4th	14.0
8-20	Fla.	W	9-3		11	9	Vance	Redman		63-66	4th	14.0
8-21	Fla.	W	5-4		7	10	Speier	Looper		64-66	4th	14.0
8-22	Atl.	L	3-9		4	16	Maddux	Jennings		64-67	4th	15.0
8-23	Atl.	L	4-5		12	7	Hampton	Tsao	Smoltz	64-68	4th	16.0
8-24	Atl.	L	6-12		11	17	Ortiz	Stark		64-69	4th	16.0
8-26	S.F	L	1-3		5	9	Schmidt	Oliver	Worrell	64-70	4th	17.0

Date	Opp.	Res.	Score	(inn.*)	Hits	Opp. hits	Winning pitcher	Losing pitcher	Save	Record	Pos.	GB
8-27	S.F	L	4-6		8	12	Ponson	Jimenez	Worrell	64-71	4th	18.0
8-28	S.F	W	6-1		8	7	Jennings	Correia		65-71	4th	17.0
8-29	At L.A.	L	4-6		5	11	Brown	Vance	Gagne	65-72	4th	17.0
8-30	At L.A.	L	0-5		4	8	Mota	Stark		65-73	4th	18.0
8-31	At L.A.	L	0-3		6	4	Perez	Oliver	Gagne	65-74	4th	19.0
9-2	At S.F	L	1-2		5	7	Herges	Bernero	Worrell	65-75	4th	20.5
9-3	At S.F	L	6-7		7	14	Nathan	Fuentes		65-76	4th	21.5
9-5	L.A.	L	7-8		14	17	Mota	Reed	Gagne	65-77	4th	21.5
9-6	L.A.	L	2-10		6	13	Perez	Oliver		65-78	4th	22.5
9-7	L.A.	L	2-6		10	15	Alvarez	Jimenez	Gagne	65-79	4th	22.5
9-9	At StL.	W	8-1		9	9	Jennings	Haren		66-79	4th	22.5
9-10	At StL.	L	2-10		6	11	Tomko	Elarton		66-80	4th	23.5
9-11	At StL.	W	9-4		18	7	Oliver	Hitchcock		67-80	4th	22.5
9-12	At Ari.	W	8-2		12	12	Jimenez	Dessens		68-80	4th	22.5
9-13	At Ari.	L	6-16		10	15	Batista	Young		68-81	4th	22.5
9-14	At Ari.	L	0-5		1	12	Johnson	Jennings		68-82	4th	23.5
9-16	Hou.	L	4-14		9	12	Robertson	Tsao		68-83	4th	25.0
9-17	Hou.	W	7-5		12	12	Oliver	Villone	Speier	69-83	4th	25.0
9-18	Hou.	L	0-6		3	14	Miller	Jimenez		69-84	4th	25.0
9-19	S.D.	W	6-5		8	9	Elarton	Howard	Fuentes	70-84	4th	25.0
9-20	S.D.	L	3-11		8	15	Lawrence	Vance		70-85	4th	26.0
9-21	S.D.	W	5-3		8	9	Tsao	Eaton	Fuentes	71-85	4th	25.0
9-23	Ari.	W	20-9		17	12	Oliver	Webb		72-85	4th	25.5
9-24	Ari.	L	3-6		9	11	Johnson	Jimenez	Mantei	72-86	4th	25.5
9-25	Ari.	L	7-8		9	12	Villarreal	Fuentes	Mantei	72-87	4th	26.0
9-26	At S.D.	L	0-5		8	10	Eaton	Vance		72-88	4th	27.0
9-27	At S.D.	W	10-2		14	2	Stark	Bynum		73-88	4th	26.5
9-28	At S.D.	W	10-8		11	13	Lopez	Witasick	Speier	74-88	4th	26.5

Monthly records: April (15-12), May (12-17), June (15-13), July (14-13), August (9-19), September (9-14).
*Innings, if other than nine. † First game of a doubleheader. ‡ Second game of a doubleheader. § Day separate admission. ∞ Night separate admission.

RECORDS

2003 regular-season record: 74-88
Position: 4th in N.L. West
Home: 49-32 **Road:** 25-56
N.L. East: 11-21 **N.L. Central:** 19-20
N.L. West: 35-41 A.L. 9-6
Vs. LH starters: 20-26
Vs. RH starters: 54-62
Grass: 72-81 **Artificial:** 2-7
Day: 27-29 **Night:** 47-59
1-Run: 17-22 **X-inn.:** 2-7
Doubleheaders: 0-1-0
Team record past five years: 374-436 (.462, ranks 12th in league in that span)

TEAM LEADERS

Batting average: Todd Helton (.358).
At-bats: Jay Payton, Preston Wilson (600).
Runs: Todd Helton (135).
Hits: Todd Helton (209).
Total Bases: Todd Helton (367).
Doubles: Todd Helton (49).
Triples: Larry Walker (7).
Home runs: Preston Wilson (36).
Runs batted in: Preston Wilson (141).
Stolen bases: Preston Wilson (14).
Slugging percentage: Todd Helton (.630).
On-base percentage: Todd Helton (.458).
Wins: Darren Oliver (13).
Earned-run average: Shawn Chacon (4.60).
Complete games: Aaron Cook, Jason Jennings, Darren Oliver (1).
Shutouts: None.
Saves: Jose Jimenez (20).
Innings pitched: Jason Jennings (181.1).
Strikeouts: Jason Jennings (119).

GAMES BY POSITION

Catcher: Charles Johnson 107, Bobby Estalella 46, Gregg Zaun 14, Kit Pellow 7, Mandy Romero 2, Ben Petrick 1.
First base: Todd Helton 159, Greg Norton 9, Mark Sweeney 8, Mark Bellhorn 1, Jose Hernandez 1, Kit Pellow 1, Chris Richard 1.
Second base: Ronnie Belliard 113, Mark Bellhorn 20, Brent Butler 20, Juan Uribe 11, Pablo Ozuna 8, Tony Womack 7, Chris Stynes 5.
Third base: Chris Stynes 119, Greg Norton 34, Garrett Atkins 19, Mark Bellhorn 15, Brent Butler 8.
Shortstop: Juan Uribe 74, Jose Hernandez 69, Tony Womack 14, Clint Barmes 12, Mark Bellhorn 6, Brent Butler 4, Pablo Ozuna 3.
Outfield: Preston Wilson 155, Jay Payton 151, Larry Walker 131, Rene Reyes 36, Gabe Kapler 29, Mark Sweeney 17, Greg Vaughn 7, Mark Bellhorn 5, Pablo Ozuna 5, Greg Norton 3, Chris Richard 3, Ben Petrick 2, Kit Pellow 1, Juan Uribe 1, Tony Womack 1.
Designated hitter: Greg Vaughn 3, Larry Walker 2, Mark Sweeney 1.

TOP DRAFT CHOICES

1. **Ian Stewart,** 3B, La Quinta H.S., Garden Grove, Calif.
2. **Scott Beerer,** RHP, Texas A&M.
3. **Aaron Marsden,** LHP, Nebraska.
4. **Rick Guarno,** C, Arkansas-Little Rock.
5. **Christian Colonel,** SS, Texas Tech.
6. **Randy Blood,** 2B, UC Riverside.
7. **Larry Robles,** RHP, Cal State-Dominguez Hills.
8. **Darric Merrell,** RHP, Cal State-Fullerton.
9. **Gene Reynolds,** SS, Tampa.
10. **Marc Kaiser,** RHP, Lewis-Clark State (Idaho).

FLORIDA MARLINS

NATIONAL LEAGUE EAST DIVISION

2004 SEASON

April

SUN	MON	TUE	WED	THU	FRI	SAT
4	5	6 MON	7 MON	8 MON	9 PHI	10 PHI
11 PHI	12	13 * MON	14 * MON	15 * MON	16 ATL	17 ATL
18 ATL	19	20 PHI	21 PHI	22 PHI	23 ATL	24 ATL
25 ATL	26 COL	27 COL	28 COL	29 SF	30 SF	

May

SUN	MON	TUE	WED	THU	FRI	SAT
						1 SF
2 SF	3	4 LA	5 LA	6 LA	7 SD	8 SD
9 SD	10	11 HOU	12 HOU	13 HOU	14 STL	15 STL
16 STL	17	18 HOU	19 HOU	20 HOU	21 ARI	22 ARI
23 ARI	24 ARI	25 CIN	26 CIN	27 CIN	28 NYM	29 NYM
30 NYM	31 CIN					

June

SUN	MON	TUE	WED	THU	FRI	SAT
		1 CIN	2 CIN	3 NYM	4 NYM	5 NYM
6 NYM	7	8 CLE	9 CLE	10 CLE	11 DET	12 DET
13 DET	14	15 CHW	16 CHW	17 CHW	18 TEX	19 TEX
20 TEX	21	22 ATL	23 ATL	24 ATL	25 TB	26 TB
27 TB	28 ATL	29 ATL	30 ATL			

Home games shaded. All-Star Game July 13 at Houston. Schedule subject to change. * San Juan, Puerto Rico.

July

SUN	MON	TUE	WED	THU	FRI	SAT
				1 ATL	2 TB	3 TB
4 TB	5 PIT	6 PIT	7 PIT	8	9 NYM	10 NYM
11 NYM	12	13 All-Star	14	15	16 PIT	17 PIT
18 PIT	19 NYM	20 NYM	21 PHI	22 PHI	23 MON	24 MON
25 MON	26 PHI	27 PHI	28 PHI	29 PHI	30 MON	31 MON

August

SUN	MON	TUE	WED	THU	FRI	SAT
1 MON	2	3 ARI	4 ARI	5 ARI	6 MIL	7 MIL
8 MIL	9	10 STL	11 STL	12 STL	13 MIL	14 MIL
15 MIL	16 LA	17 LA	18 LA	19	20 SD	21 SD
22 SD	23	24 SF	25 SF	26 SF	27 COL	28 COL
29 COL	30 NYM	31 NYM				

Sept./Oct.

SUN	MON	TUE	WED	THU	FRI	SAT
			1 NYM	2 NYM	3 CHC	4 CHC
5 CHC	6	7 NYM	8 NYM	9 NYM	10 CHC	11 CHC
12 CHC	13 MON	14 MON	15 MON	16 MON	17 ATL	18 ATL
19 ATL	20	21 PHI	22 PHI	23 PHI	24 ATL	25 ATL
26 ATL	27 MON	28 MON	29 MON	30 PHI	1 PHI	2 PHI
3 PHI	4	5	6	7	8	9

CLUB DIRECTORY

Chairman, CEO and managing gen. partner
Jeffrey H. Loria
President
David P. Samson
Vice chairman
Joel A. Mael
Special assistants to president
Andre Dawson, Tony Perez
Senior v.p. and general manager
Larry Beinfest
Assistant general manager
Michael Hill
Vice president, player personnel
Dan Jennings
Special assistant to the g.m./pro scout
Orrin Freeman
Sr. v.p./dir. of international operations
Fred Ferreira
V.p., player development and scouting
Jim Fleming
Director of player development
Marc DelPiano
Director of minor league operations
Cheryl Evans
V.p., communications & broadcasting
P.J. Loyello
Director, media relations
Steve Copses
Manager, media relations
Andrew Feirstein
Manager, community affairs
Angela Smith

MINOR LEAGUE AFFILIATES

Class	Team	League	Manager
AAA	Albuquerque	Pacific Coast	Tracy Woodson
AA	Carolina	Southern	Ron Hassey
Advanced A	Jupiter	Florida State	Luis Dorante
A	Greensboro	South Atlantic	Steve Phillips
Short-Season A	Jamestown	New York-Pennsylvania	Benny Castillo
Rookie	Gulf Coast Marlins	Gulf Coast	Tim Cossins

More on the Marlins at www.foxsports.com/named/FS/MLB/teams

BROADCAST INFORMATION

Radio: WQAM-AM (560); WQBA-AM (1140, Spanish language).
TV: PAX-TV
Cable TV: Fox Sports Net.

SPRING TRAINING

Ballpark (city): Roger Dean Stadium (Jupiter, Fla.).
Ticket information: 561-775-1818.

SPRING TRAINING ROSTER

Manager—Jack McKeon (15).
Coaches—Pierre Arsenault (67), Jeff Cox (47), Doug Davis (23), Perry Hill (16), Bill Robinson (28), Wayne Rosenthal (26), Tony Taylor.

No.	PITCHERS	B/T	Ht./Wt.	Age*	2003 Clubs
21	Beckett, Josh	R/R	6-5/218	23	Jupiter, Carolina, Florida
	Belizario, Ronald	R/R	6-2/150	21	Greensboro, Jupiter
	Benitez, Armando	R/R	6-4/229	31	New York N.L., New York A.L., Seattle
	Bump, Nate	R/R	6-2/185	27	Albuquerque, Florida
34	Burnett, A.J.	R/R	6-4/232	27	Florida
	Cave, Kevin	R/R	6-2/220	23	Jupiter
	Flannery, Michael	R/R	6-1/195	24	Carolina
49	Fox, Chad	R/R	6-3/190	33	Sarasota, Pawtucket, Portland, Boston, Albuquerque, Florida
	Gracesqui, Franklyn	B/L	6-5/210	24	Carolina
	Holdzkom, Lincoln	R/R	6-4/240	22	Greensboro, Jupiter
39	Neal, Blaine	L/R	6-5/240	25	Albuquerque, Florida
	Neu, Mike	B/R	5-10/175	26	Oakland
45	Pavano, Carl	R/R	6-5/235	28	Florida
31	Penny, Brad	R/R	6-4/250	25	Florida
	Phelps, Tommy	L/L	6-3/192	30	Albuquerque, Florida, Jupiter
	Spooneybarger, T.	R/R	6-3/190	24	Florida
58	Tejera, Michael	L/L	5-9/190	27	Florida
48	Wayne, Justin	R/R	6-3/205	24	Jupiter, Florida, Albuquerque
35	Willis, Dontrelle	L/L	6-4/195	22	Carolina, Florida

No.	CATCHERS	B/T	Ht./Wt.	Age*	2003 Clubs
17	Castro, Ramon	R/R	6-3/235	28	Florida
52	Redmond, Mike	R/R	5-11/210	32	Florida
	Willingham, Josh	R/R	6-1/200	25	Jupiter, Gulf Coast Marlins, Carolina

No.	INFIELDERS	B/T	Ht./Wt.	Age*	2003 Clubs
1	Castillo, Luis	B/R	5-11/190	28	Florida
	Choi, Hee Seop	L/L	6-5/240	25	Iowa, Chicago N.L.
18	Conine, Jeff	R/R	6-1/220	37	Baltimore, Florida
11	Gonzalez, Alex	R/R	6-0/200	27	Florida
	Hooper, Kevin	R/R	5-10/160	27	Albuquerque
19	Lowell, Mike	R/R	6-3/215	30	Florida
12	Mordecai, Mike	R/R	5-10/185	36	Florida
	Valdez, Wilson	R/R	5-11/160	25	Albuquerque, Carolina
	Wilson, Josh	R/R	6-1/160	23	Carolina

No.	OUTFIELDERS	B/T	Ht./Wt.	Age*	2003 Clubs
	Aguila, Chris	R/R	5-11/180	25	Gulf Coast Marlins, Carolina
	Ambres, Chip	R/R	6-1/190	24	Carolina
22	Banks, Brian	B/R	6-3/218	33	Florida
20	Cabrera, Miguel	R/R	6-2/185	20	Carolina, Florida
27	Nunez, Abraham	B/R	6-2/186	27	Albuquerque, Jupiter
9	Pierre, Juan	L/L	6-0/180	26	Florida

Invited to spring training: RHP Toby Borland, LHP Cedric Bowers, RHP Bryce Florie, RHP Mike Fyhrie, RHP Delvin James, RHP David Manning, RHP Marty McLeary, LHP Matt Perisho, RHP; Scott Sanders, RHP; Aaron Small, C Matt Treanor, IF Felipe Crespo, IF Lenny Harris, IF Jason Wood, OF Ryan Christenson, OF Gerald Williams.

*Age as of April 1, 2004.

BALLPARK INFORMATION

Ballpark (capacity, surface)
Pro Player Stadium (36,331, grass)

Address
2267 Dan Marino Blvd.
Miami, Fla. 33056

Official website
www.floridamarlins.com

Business phone
305-626-7400

Ticket information
1-877-MARLINS

Field dimensions (from home plate)
To left field at foul line, 330 feet
To center field, 434 feet
To right field at foul line, 345 feet

First game played
April 5, 1993 (Marlins 6, Dodgers 3)

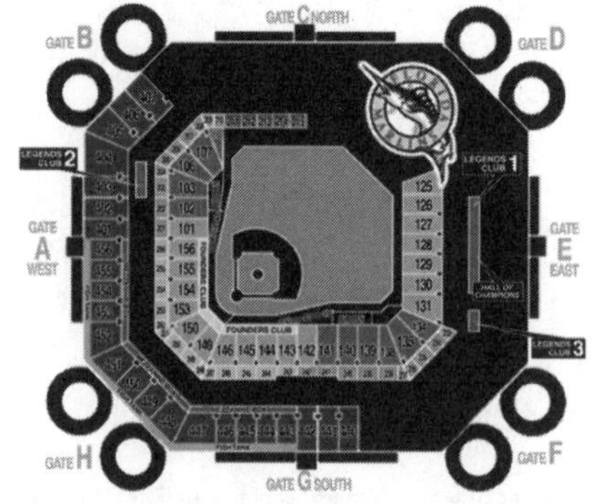

2003 REVIEW

DAY BY DAY

Date	Opp.	Res.	Score	(inn.*)	Hits	Opp. hits	Winning pitcher	Losing pitcher	Save	Record	Pos.	GB
3-31	Phi.	L	5-8		7	10	Millwood	Beckett	Mesa	0-1	T3rd	1.0
4-2	Phi.	L	2-8		5	12	Wolf	Pavano		0-2	T4th	2.0
4-3	Phi.	W	8-3		11	9	Redman	Padilla		1-2	T3rd	2.0
4-4	At Atl.	L	7-12		13	16	Hernandez	Nunez	Smoltz	1-3	T4th	2.0
4-5	At Atl.	W	17-1		23	8	Beckett	Maddux		2-3	4th	1.0
4-6	At Atl.	L	4-13		8	15	Ramirez	Penny		2-4	T4th	2.0
4-7	At Atl.	L	0-3		5	5	Ortiz	Pavano	Smoltz	2-5	5th	2.5
4-8	N.Y.	L	2-4		7	8	Leiter	Redman	Benitez	2-6	5th	2.5
4-9	N.Y.	W	3-2		11	5	Looper	Stanton		3-6	T4th	2.5
4-10	N.Y.	W	4-3		10	8	Spooneybarger	Benitez		4-6	T4th	1.5
4-11	Atl.	W	7-4		8	10	Penny	Ramirez	Looper	5-6	3rd	1.5
4-12	Atl.	W	12-5		15	12	Pavano	Ortiz		6-6	3rd	1.5
4-13	Atl.	L	1-7		4	12	Maddux	Redman	Smoltz	6-7	3rd	2.5
4-14	At Phi.	L	2-5		6	8	Padilla	Burnett	Mesa	6-8	3rd	3.5
4-15	At Phi.	L	3-4		10	6	Silva	Beckett	Mesa	6-9	4th	3.5
4-16	At Phi.	W	3-1		8	5	Penny	Myers	Looper	7-9	4th	2.5
4-17	At Phi.	W	7-3		8	6	Pavano	Millwood		8-9	4th	1.5
4-18	At N.Y.	L	3-6		9	12	Weathers	Nunez	Benitez	8-10	4th	2.0
4-19	At N.Y.	W	6-5		10	7	Looper	Benitez		9-10	4th	2.5
4-20	At N.Y.	L	4-7		10	7	Glavine	Nunez		9-11	4th	2.5
4-22	Mil.	W	4-2		6	10	Almanza	de los Santos	Looper	10-11	4th	2.5
4-23	Mil.	W	5-4	(12)	17	12	Almanza	Nance		11-11	4th	1.5
4-24	Mil.	W	4-2		9	4	Redman	Ritchie		12-11	4th	1.5
4-25	StL.	L	2-9		9	10	Tomko	Burnett		12-12	4th	2.5
4-26	StL.	W	5-3		9	8	Beckett	Kline	Looper	13-12	4th	2.5
4-27	StL.	L	6-7	(20)	13	22	Kline	Pavano		13-13	4th	2.5
4-28	At Ari.	L	1-7		6	11	Dessens	Wayne		13-14	4th	3.5
4-29	At Ari.	W	7-5		10	11	Redman	Kim		14-14	4th	3.0
4-30	At Ari.	L	3-7		10	10	Batista	Pavano	Mantei	14-15	4th	4.0
5-1	At Ari.	W	4-3		8	8	Almanza	Villarreal	Looper	15-15	4th	4.0
5-2	At Hou.	L	3-4		7	7	Stone	Penny	Wagner	15-16	4th	5.0
5-3	At Hou.	L	2-5		9	10	Redding	Wayne	Dotel	15-17	4th	5.0
5-4	At Hou.	L	2-5		10	9	Lidge	Spooneybarger	Wagner	15-18	4th	6.0
5-6	S.F	L	2-4		3	10	Nathan	Almanza	Worrell	15-19	4th	7.0
5-7	S.F	L	2-3		9	8	Moss	Beckett	Worrell	15-20	4th	7.5
5-8	S.F	L	2-3		6	7	Nathan	Looper	Worrell	15-21	4th	9.0
5-9	Col.	W	5-4		7	9	Looper	Speier		16-21	4th	8.0
5-10	Col.	L	4-5		13	7	Jennings	Tejera	Jimenez	16-22	4th	9.0
5-11	Col.	W	7-2		8	12	Pavano	Cook		17-22	4th	9.0
5-12	At S.D.	W	6-1		10	12	Levrault	Condrey		18-22	4th	9.0
5-13	At S.D.	L	5-6	(10)	9	10	Herges	Looper		18-23	4th	10.0
5-14	At S.D.	W	10-3		17	7	Willis	Bynum		19-23	4th	9.0
5-16	At L.A.	L	1-2		8	6	Dreifort	Almanza	Gagne	19-24	4th	10.5
5-17	At L.A.	L	1-4		3	11	Perez	Tejera	Gagne	19-25	4th	11.5
5-18	At L.A.	L	1-2		7	5	Nomo	Penny	Gagne	19-26	5th	12.5
5-20	At Mon.	L	4-6		8	13	Vazquez	Willis	Biddle	19-27	5th	12.5
5-21	At Mon.	L	2-7		8	11	Vargas	Pavano		19-28	5th	12.5
5-22	At Mon.	L	2-8		7	12	Hernandez	Tejera		19-29	5th	13.5
5-23	At Cin.	W	8-4		12	9	Phelps	Austin		20-29	5th	12.5
5-24	At Cin.	W	5-4		11	10	Penny	Wilson	Looper	21-29	5th	12.5
5-25	At Cin.	W	6-2		15	9	Willis	Graves	Looper	22-29	5th	12.5
5-26	Mon.	W	5-1		10	5	Pavano	Vargas		23-29	4th	11.5
5-28†	Mon.	W	4-3		12	4	Phelps	Hernandez	Looper	24-29		
5-28‡	Mon.	W	6-0		9	7	Tejera	Day		25-29	4th	11.5
5-29	Mon.	L	2-3		8	12	Ohka	Almanza	Biddle	25-30	4th	12.0
5-30	Cin.	L	3-4	(11)	6	6	White	Almanza	Williamson	25-31	4th	13.0
5-31	Cin.	W	3-2		9	6	Willis	Graves	Looper	26-31	4th	12.0
6-1	Cin.	L	6-9		10	13	Sullivan	Pavano	Williamson	26-32	5th	12.0
6-3	Oak.	W	13-2		18	8	Penny	Mulder		27-32	5th	12.0
6-4	Oak.	L	5-6		8	9	Bradford	Spooneybarger	Foulke	27-33	5th	13.0
6-5	Oak.	W	2-0		7	7	Willis	Lilly	Looper	28-33	4th	13.0
6-6	Ana.	W	4-1		3	4	Pavano	Appier	Looper	29-33	4th	12.5
6-7	Ana.	L	2-9		5	11	Sele	Phelps		29-34	4th	13.5
6-8	Ana.	L	5-8		6	11	Ortiz	Penny	Percival	29-35	4th	14.5

Date	Opp.	Res.	Score	(inn.*)	Hits	Opp. hits	Winning pitcher	Losing pitcher	Save	Record	Pos.	GB
6-10	At Mil.	W	12-4		13	11	Redman	Sheets		30-35	4th	13.5
6-11	At Mil.	W	6-5		9	13	Willis	Franklin	Looper	31-35	4th	13.5
6-12	At Mil.	L	5-6		12	6	Kinney	Pavano	DeJean	31-36	4th	14.5
6-13	At Tex.	W	8-0		16	5	Penny	Mounce		32-36	4th	13.5
6-14	At Tex.	L	2-13		9	18	Valdes	Phelps		32-37	4th	14.5
6-15	At Tex.	W	10-4		15	12	Redman	Thomson		33-37	4th	13.5
6-16	N.Y.	W	1-0		6	1	Willis	Glavine		34-37	4th	13.0
6-17	N.Y.	L	0-5		1	9	Seo	Pavano		34-38	4th	13.0
6-18	N.Y.	L	5-10		8	13	Leiter	Penny	Wheeler	34-39	5th	14.0
6-19	N.Y.	W	5-1		9	5	Phelps	Bacsik		35-39	4th	13.0
6-20	T.B.	W	3-1	(11)	6	6	Almanza	Levine		36-39	4th	13.0
6-21	T.B.	W	2-0	(6)	5	2	Willis	Standridge		37-39	4th	13.0
6-22	T.B.	W	3-2		2	9	Pavano	Gonzalez	Looper	38-39	4th	12.0
6-24	At N.Y.	W	8-4		13	8	Penny	Leiter	Tejera	39-39	4th	12.0
6-25	At N.Y.	L	3-6		10	10	Trachsel	Redman	Benitez	39-40	4th	12.0
6-26	At N.Y.	W	6-1		9	10	Willis	Heilman		40-40	4th	11.0
6-27	At Bos.	L	8-25		10	28	Kim	Pavano		40-41	4th	12.0
6-28	At Bos.	W	10-9		13	15	Bump	Lyon	Looper	41-41	4th	11.0
6-29	At Bos.	L	7-11		8	12	Lowe	Penny		41-42	4th	12.0
6-30	Atl.	W	8-1		7	5	Redman	Maddux		42-42	4th	11.0
7-1	Atl.	W	20-1		25	4	Beckett	Hampton		43-42	4th	10.0
7-2	Atl.	L	1-2	(13)	7	11	Gryboski	Almanza	Smoltz	43-43	4th	11.0
7-4	At Phi.	W	2-1		3	6	Looper	Mesa		44-43	4th	10.5
7-5	At Phi.	W	5-4		8	7	Penny	Padilla	Looper	45-43	4th	10.5
7-6	At Phi.	W	6-3		8	7	Redman	Wolf		46-43	4th	10.5
7-7	At Chi.	L	3-6		5	12	Clement	Beckett	Borowski	46-44	4th	11.5
7-8	At Chi.	W	4-3		13	7	Bump	Remlinger	Looper	47-44	4th	11.5
7-9	At Chi.	L	1-5		3	8	Wood	Pavano		47-45	4th	12.5
7-11	At Mon.	W	5-4		10	5	Penny	Biddle	Looper	48-45	4th	13.0
7-12	At Mon.	L	1-7		3	11	Hernandez	Redman		48-46	4th	13.0
7-13	At Mon.	W	11-4		14	8	Willis	Vargas		49-46	4th	13.0
7-18	Chi.	W	6-0		9	5	Redman	Clement		50-46	T3rd	13.5
7-19	Chi.	L	0-1		2	4	Wood	Penny		50-47	T3rd	14.5
7-20	Chi.	L	2-16		10	20	Zambrano	Willis		50-48	T3rd	15.5
7-21	Mon.	W	4-1		10	9	Beckett	Knott		51-48	3rd	14.5
7-22	Mon.	W	9-1		13	5	Pavano	Ohka		52-48	3rd	14.5
7-23	At Atl.	W	5-4	(12)	14	7	Bump	Hodges		53-48	3rd	13.5
7-24	At Atl.	L	2-5		9	10	Ortiz	Penny	Smoltz	53-49	3rd	14.5
7-25	Phi.	W	11-5		13	9	Urbina	Williams		54-49	3rd	13.5
7-26	Phi.	W	10-5		15	13	Beckett	Duckworth	Looper	55-49	3rd	13.5
7-27	Phi.	W	7-6		15	10	Urbina	Williams		56-49	3rd	12.5
7-28	Ari.	W	3-2		7	7	Redman	Batista	Looper	57-49	3rd	12.5
7-29	Ari.	W	2-1		10	5	Penny	Webb	Looper	58-49	3rd	12.5
7-30	Ari.	W	3-1		6	5	Willis	Johnson	Looper	59-49	3rd	11.5
8-1	Hou.	L	1-2		6	4	Redding	Beckett	Wagner	59-50	3rd	13.0
8-2	Hou.	W	5-2		8	3	Pavano	Robertson	Looper	60-50	3rd	13.0
8-3	Hou.	L	1-3		5	9	Fernandez	Redman	Wagner	60-51	3rd	13.0
8-5	At StL.	W	4-0		7	5	Penny	Williams		61-51	3rd	12.0
8-6	At StL.	W	7-3		13	6	Willis	Haren		62-51	3rd	12.0
8-7	At StL.	L	0-3		4	6	Tomko	Beckett	Isringhausen	62-52	3rd	13.0
8-8	At Mil.	W	5-3		7	9	Pavano	Sheets	Looper	63-52	T2nd	13.0
8-9	At Mil.	W	7-1		9	6	Redman	Manning		64-52	T2nd	12.0
8-10	At Mil.	L	4-5		10	10	de los Santos	Penny	Kolb	64-53	T2nd	12.0
8-11	L.A.	L	3-9		9	16	Perez	Willis		64-54	3rd	12.5
8-12	L.A.	W	5-4	(13)	11	10	Fox	Shuey		65-54	2nd	11.5
8-13	L.A.	W	2-1	(11)	6	7	Bump	Alvarez		66-54	2nd	11.5
8-14	L.A.	L	4-6		7	12	Brown	Redman	Gagne	66-55	3rd	12.5
8-15	S.D.	W	10-0		13	6	Penny	Perez		67-55	3rd	12.5
8-16	S.D.	W	6-3		10	10	Fox	Witasick	Looper	68-55	3rd	12.5
8-17	S.D.	W	11-7		15	8	Beckett	Eaton	Tejera	69-55	3rd	11.5
8-19	At Col.	L	2-10		6	13	Stark	Pavano		69-56	3rd	12.0
8-20	At Col.	L	3-9		9	11	Vance	Redman		69-57	3rd	12.0
8-21	At Col.	L	4-5		10	7	Speier	Looper		69-58	3rd	12.0
8-22	At S.F	L	4-6		11	10	Ponson	Willis	Worrell	69-59	3rd	13.0
8-23	At S.F	L	2-3		6	8	Brower	Beckett	Worrell	69-60	3rd	14.0
8-24	At S.F	W	7-4		11	10	Pavano	Rueter		70-60	3rd	14.0
8-26	At Pit.	L	3-4		4	10	Lincoln	Redman	Tavarez	70-61	T2nd	14.0
8-27	At Pit.	L	0-4		3	12	Wells	Penny		70-62	T2nd	15.0
8-28	At Pit.	L	0-5		5	10	Fogg	Willis		70-63	T2nd	15.0
8-29	Mon.	W	3-2		9	6	Looper	Biddle		71-63	T2nd	14.0
8-30	Mon.	W	4-3		7	9	Pavano	Hernandez	Looper	72-63	T2nd	14.0
8-31	Mon.	W	5-3		11	7	Redman	Day	Urbina	73-63	T2nd	14.0

Date	Opp.	Res.	Score	(inn.*)	Hits	Opp. hits	Winning pitcher	Losing pitcher	Save	Record	Pos.	GB
9-1	Mon.	W	5-2		12	3	Penny	Ohka	Looper	74-63	2nd	13.0
9-2	Pit.	L	2-3		6	7	Wells	Willis	Tavarez	74-64	T2nd	13.0
9-3	Pit.	W	3-0		7	5	Beckett	Fogg	Urbina	75-64	T2nd	12.0
9-4	Pit.	W	5-1		8	8	Tejera	Torres		76-64	T2nd	11.5
9-5	At Mon.■	L	2-6		9	7	Hernandez	Redman		76-65	3rd	12.0
9-6	At Mon.■	W	14-4		14	11	Penny	Ohka		77-65	3rd	12.0
9-7	At Mon.■	W	3-1		8	5	Willis	Vazquez	Looper	78-65	3rd	12.0
9-8	At N.Y.	W	5-0		9	6	Beckett	Trachsel		79-65	T2nd	12.0
9-9	At N.Y.	W	3-1		9	6	Urbina	Weathers	Looper	80-65	T2nd	11.0
9-10	At N.Y.	W	7-3		11	4	Redman	Seo		81-65	2nd	11.0
9-12	Atl.	W	5-4		10	7	Looper	King		82-65	2nd	9.5
9-13	Atl.	W	8-3		9	10	Willis	Ortiz		83-65	2nd	8.5
9-14	Atl.	L	4-8		10	12	Cunnane	Looper		83-66	2nd	9.5
9-16	At Phi.	L	0-14		6	17	Padilla	Pavano		83-67	2nd	10.0
9-17	At Phi.	W	11-4		14	8	Redman	Myers		84-67	2nd	10.0
9-18	At Phi.	L	4-5		8	8	Cormier	Fox		84-68	2nd	10.5
9-19	At Atl.	L	0-1		3	6	Ortiz	Beckett		84-69	3rd	11.5
9-20	At Atl.	W	6-5	(11)	10	11	Helling	Cunnane		85-69	2nd	10.5
9-21	At Atl.	L	0-8		4	9	Maddux	Pavano		85-70	2nd	11.5
9-22	At Atl.	W	6-3		11	6	Redman	Hampton	Urbina	86-70	2nd	10.5
9-23	Phi.	W	5-4		8	7	Tejera	Williams	Urbina	87-70	2nd	10.5
9-24	Phi.	W	6-5		9	7	Beckett	Myers	Urbina	88-70	2nd	10.5
9-25	Phi.	W	8-4		12	7	Penny	Wolf		89-70	2nd	10.0
9-26	N.Y.	W	4-3		11	6	Pavano	Heilman	Urbina	90-70	2nd	10.0
9-27	N.Y.	L	3-9		6	11	Seo	Tejera		90-71	2nd	10.0
9-28	N.Y.	W	4-0		7	4	Willis	Griffiths		91-71	2nd	10.0

Monthly records: March (0-1), April (14-14), May (12-16), June (16-11), July (17-7), August (14-14), September (18-8). *Innings, if other than nine. ■ At Hiram Bithorn Stadium, San Juan, Puerto Rico. † First game of a doubleheader. ‡ Second game of a doubleheader.

RECORDS

2003 regular-season record: 91-71
Position: 2nd in N.L. East
Home: 53-28 **Road:** 38-43
N.L. East: 48-28 **N.L. Central:** 19-20
N.L. West: 15-17 A.L. 9-6
Vs. LH starters: 27-11
Vs. RH starters: 64-60
Grass: 81-62 **Artificial:** 10-9
Day: 19-23 **Night:** 72-48
1-Run: 30-23 **X-inn.:** 6-4
Doubleheaders: 1-0-0
Team record past five years: 389-420 (.481, ranks 10th in league in that span)

TEAM LEADERS

Batting average: Luis Castillo (.314).
At-bats: Juan Pierre (668).
Runs: Juan Pierre (100).
Hits: Juan Pierre (204).
Total Bases: Derrek Lee (274).
Doubles: Juan Encarnacion (37).
Triples: Juan Pierre (7).
Home runs: Mike Lowell (32).
Runs batted in: Mike Lowell (105).
Stolen bases: Juan Pierre (65).
Slugging percentage: Mike Lowell (.530).
On-base percentage: Luis Castillo (.381).
Wins: Brad Penny, Mark Redman, Dontrelle Willis (14).
Earned-run average: Josh Beckett (3.04).
Complete games: Mark Redman (3).
Shutouts: Dontrelle Willis (2).
Saves: Braden Looper (28).
Innings pitched: Carl Pavano (201.0).
Strikeouts: Josh Beckett (152).

GAMES BY POSITION

Catcher: Ivan Rodriguez 138, Mike Redmond 37, Ramon Castro 18.
First base: Derrek Lee 155, Brian Banks 12, Andy Fox 2, Mike Mordecai 1, Mike Redmond 1.
Second base: Luis Castillo 152, Andy Fox 15, Mike Mordecai 12.
Third base: Mike Lowell 128, Miguel Cabrera 34, Mike Mordecai 12, Andy Fox 5, Mike Redmond 1.
Shortstop: Alex Gonzalez 150, Mike Mordecai 14, Andy Fox 9.
Outfield: Juan Pierre 161, Juan Encarnacion 155, Todd Hollandsworth 64, Miguel Cabrera 55, Brian Banks 33, Jeff Conine 25, Gerald Williams 16, Chad Allen 8, Lenny Harris 4, Andy Fox 2.
Designated hitter: Mike Lowell 2, Chad Allen 1, Brian Banks 1, Ramon Castro 1, Todd Hollandsworth 1, Ivan Rodriguez 1.

TOP DRAFT CHOICES

1. **Jeff Allison,** RHP, Veterans Memorial H.S., Peabody, Mass.
2. **Logan Kensing,** RHP, Texas A&M.
3. **Jonathan Fulton,** SS, George Washington H.S., Danville, Va.
4. **Jai Miller,** OF, Selma (Ala.) H.S.
5. **Cole Seifrig,** 3B, Heritage Hills H.S., Lincoln City, Ind.
6. **Lee Mitchell,** 3B, Georgia.
7. **David Marchbanks,** LHP, South Carolina.
8. **Tanner Rogers,** C, Columbine H.S., Littleton, Colo.
9. **David Humen,** RHP, Bethel College (Ind.).
10. **Jason Restko,** 3B, Marist H.S., Tingley Park, Ill.

HOUSTON ASTROS

NATIONAL LEAGUE CENTRAL DIVISION

2004 SEASON

April

SUN	MON	TUE	WED	THU	FRI	SAT
4	5 SF	6 SF	7 SF	8	9 MIL	10 MIL
11 MIL	12 STL	13 STL	14 STL	15 MIL	16 MIL	17 MIL
18 MIL	19	20 STL	21 STL	22 STL	23 COL	24 COL
25 COL	26	27 PIT	28 PIT	29 PIT	30 CIN	

May

SUN	MON	TUE	WED	THU	FRI	SAT
						1 CIN
2 CIN	3 CIN	4 PIT	5 PIT	6 PIT	7 ATL	8 ATL
9 ATL	10	11 FLA	12 FLA	13 FLA	14 NYM	15 NYM
16 NYM	17	18 FLA	19 FLA	20 FLA	21 CIN	22 CIN
23 CIN	24 CIN	25 CHC	26 CHC	27	28 STL	29 STL
30 STL	31 CHC					

June

SUN	MON	TUE	WED	THU	FRI	SAT
		1 CHC	2 CHC	3	4 STL	5 STL
6 STL	7 SEA	8 SEA	9 SEA	10	11 MIL	12 MIL
13 MIL	14 CHC	15 CHC	16 CHC	17 CHC	18 ANA	19 ANA
20 ANA	21 PIT	22 PIT	23 PIT	24 PIT	25 TEX	26 TEX
27 TEX	28	29 CHC	30 CHC			

July

SUN	MON	TUE	WED	THU	FRI	SAT
				1 CHC	2 TEX	3 TEX
4 TEX	5 SD	6 SD	7 SD	8 LA	9 LA	10 LA
11 LA	12	13 All-Star	14	15	16 SD	17 SD
18 SD	19 LA	20 LA	21 ARI	22 ARI	23 MIL	24 MIL
25 MIL	26 ARI	27 ARI	28 ARI	29 ARI	30 CIN	31 CIN

August

SUN	MON	TUE	WED	THU	FRI	SAT
1 CIN	2	3 ATL	4 ATL	5 ATL	6 MON	7 MON
8 MON	9	10 NYM	11 NYM	12 NYM	13 MON	14 MON
15 MON	16	17 PHI	18 PHI	19 PHI	20 CHC	21 CHC
22 CHC	23 PHI	24 PHI	25 PHI	26 CHC	27 CHC	28 CHC
29 CHC	30 CIN	31 CIN				

Sept./Oct.

SUN	MON	TUE	WED	THU	FRI	SAT
			1 CIN	2	3 PIT	4 PIT
5 PIT	6 CIN	7 CIN	8 CIN	9 PIT	10 PIT	11 PIT
12 PIT	13	14 STL	15 STL	16 STL	17 MIL	18 MIL
19 MIL	20	21 SF	22 SF	23 SF	24 MIL	25 MIL
26 MIL	27 STL	28 STL	29 STL	30	1 COL	2 COL
3 COL	4	5	6	7	8	9

Home games shaded. All-Star Game July 13 at Houston. Schedule subject to change.

CLUB DIRECTORY

Chairman and chief executive officer
Drayton McLane Jr.
President, baseball operations
Tal Smith
General manager
Gerry Hunsicker
Assistant general manager
Tim Purpura
Director of scouting
David Lakey
Special asst. to the g.m. for international scouting and development
Andres Reiner
Senior vice president, communications
Jay Lucas
Senior vice president, operations
Rob Matwick
Director of media relations
Jimmy Stanton

MINOR LEAGUE AFFILIATES

Class	Team	League	Manager
AAA	New Orleans	Pacific Coast	Chris Maloney
AA	Round Rock	Texas	Jackie Moore
Advanced A	Salem	Carolina	Russ Nixon
A	Lexington	South Atlantic	Ivan DeJesus
Short-Season A	Tri-City	New York-Pennsylvania	Gregg Langbehn
Advanced Rookie	Greeneville	Appalachian	Tim Bogar

More on the Astros at www.foxsports.com/named/FS/MLB/teams

BROADCAST INFORMATION

Radio: KTRH-AM (740); to be announced (Spanish language).
TV: To be announced.
Cable TV: Fox Sports Southwest.

SPRING TRAINING

Ballpark (city): Osceola County Stadium (Kissimmee, Fla.).
Ticket information: 321-697-3200.

SPRING TRAINING ROSTER

Manager—Jimy Williams (22).
Coaches—Mark Bailey (6), Jose Cruz (25), Burt Hooton (48), Gene Lamont (38), Harry Spilman (8), John Tamargo (30).

No.	PITCHERS	B/T	Ht./Wt.	Age*	2003 Clubs
	Astacio, Ezequiel	R/R	6-3/155	24	Clearwater
	Backe, Brandon	R/R	6-0/188	25	Durham, Tampa Bay
	Barrett, Jimmy	R/R	6-2/180	22	Salem
	Buchholz, Taylor	R/R	6-4/225	22	Reading
	Clemens, Roger	R/R	6-4/238	41	New York A.L.
29	Dotel, Octavio	R/R	6-0/200	30	Houston
	Duckworth, B.	R/R	6-2/195	28	Clearwater, Reading, Scranton/Wilkes-Barre, Philadelphia
	Gallo, Mike	L/L	6-0/175	26	Round Rock, New Orleans, Houston
55	Hernandez, Carlos	B/L	5-10/185	23	Did Not Play
54	Lidge, Brad	R/R	6-5/210	27	Houston
58	Miceli, Dan	R/R	6-0/225	33	Colorado, Buffalo, Cleveland, New York A.L., Houston
52	Miller, Wade	R/R	6-2/210	27	Houston
	Nieve, Fernando	R/R	6-0/195	21	Lexington
44	Oswalt, Roy	R/R	6-0/175	26	New Orleans, Houston
	Pettitte, Andy	L/L	6-5/225	31	New York A.L.
	Qualls, Chad	R/R	6-5/220	25	Round Rock
	Ramirez, Santiago	R/R	5-11/160	25	New Orleans, Round Rock
51	Redding, Tim	R/R	6-0/195	26	Houston
62	Robertson, J.	L/L	6-1/200	27	New Orleans, Houston
	Saarloos, Kirk	R/R	6-0/180	24	New Orleans, Houston
20	Stone, Ricky	R/R	6-1/170	29	Houston

No.	CATCHERS	B/T	Ht./Wt.	Age*	2003 Clubs
11	Ausmus, Brad	R/R	5-11/200	34	Houston
	Buck, John	R/R	6-3/220	23	New Orleans
46	Chavez, Raul	R/R	5-11/210	31	New Orleans, Houston
	Gimenez, Hector	B/R	5-10/200	21	Salem

No.	INFIELDERS	B/T	Ht./Wt.	Age*	2003 Clubs
5	Bagwell, Jeff	R/R	6-0/215	35	Houston
	Bruntlett, Eric	R/R	6-0/200	26	New Orleans, Houston
	Burke, Chris	R/R	5-11/190	24	Round Rock
14	Ensberg, Morgan	R/R	6-2/220	28	Houston
28	Everett, Adam	R/R	6-0/160	27	New Orleans, Houston
12	Kent, Jeff	R/R	6-1/215	36	Round Rock, Houston
10	Vizcaino, Jose	B/R	6-1/185	36	New Orleans, Houston
	Whiteman, Tommy	R/R	6-3/180	24	Round Rock

No.	OUTFIELDERS	B/T	Ht./Wt.	Age*	2003 Clubs
17	Berkman, Lance	B/L	6-1/220	28	Houston
7	Biggio, Craig	R/R	5-11/185	38	Houston
15	Hidalgo, Richard	R/R	6-3/220	28	Houston
	Jimerson, Charlton	R/R	6-3/210	24	Salem
24	Lane, Jason	R/L	6-2/215	27	New Orleans, Houston
	Palmeiro, Orlando	L/L	5-11/180	35	St. Louis
	Taveras, Willy	R/R	6-0/160	22	Kinston

Invited to spring training: LHP Nate Bland, RHP Kirk Bullinger, RHP Jared Fernandez, RHP Tony Fiore,.RHP Miguel Saladin, RHP Rodrigo Rosario, C Dax Norris, C Chris Tremie, IF Jason Alfaro, IF Mike Coolbaugh, IF Phil Hiatt.

*Age as of April 1, 2004.

BALLPARK INFORMATION

Ballpark (capacity, surface)
Minute Maid Park (40,950, grass)
Address
P.O. Box 288
Houston, TX 77001-0288
Official website
www.astros.com
Business phone
713-259-8000
Ticket information
713-259-8500, 1-800-ASTROS-2
Field dimensions (from home plate)
To left field at foul line, 315 feet
To center field, 435 feet
To right field at foul line, 326 feet
First game played
April 7, 2000 (Phillies 4, Astros 1)

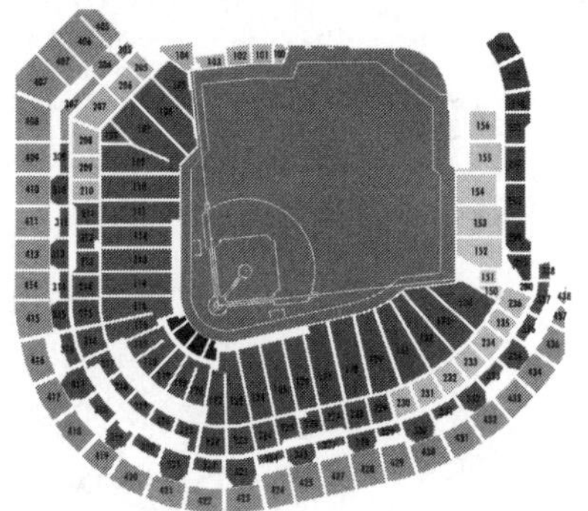

2003 REVIEW

DAY BY DAY

Date	Opp.	Res.	Score	(inn.*)	Hits	Opp. hits	Winning pitcher	Losing pitcher	Save	Record	Pos.	GB
4-1	Col.	W	10-4		14	8	Oswalt	Jennings		1-0	T1st	...
4-2	Col.	W	8-7		15	13	Wagner	Jimenez		2-0	T1st	...
4-3	Col.	L	5-10		9	14	Cruz	Robertson		2-1	T3rd	1.0
4-4	At StL.	W	6-5	(12)	7	13	Stone	Springer	Lidge	3-1	T2nd	1.0
4-5	At StL.	W	2-1		7	7	Munro	Fassero	Wagner	4-1	T1st	...
4-8	Cin.	L	1-2	(10)	7	5	Dempster	Dotel	Williamson	4-2	T2nd	0.5
4-9	Cin.	W	4-3		8	6	Lidge	Manzanillo	Wagner	5-2	1st	+0.5
4-10	Cin.	W	4-2		7	5	Robertson	Graves	Wagner	6-2	1st	+0.5
4-11	StL.	W	3-2		6	7	Dotel	Morris		7-2	1st	+0.5
4-12	StL.	L	0-3		6	10	Williams	Redding	Hermanson	7-3	1st	+0.5
4-13	StL.	L	8-11		10	11	Calero	Oswalt		7-4	1st	+0.5
4-14	At S.F	L	2-4		7	6	Moss	Miller	Worrell	7-5	T1st	...
4-15	At S.F	L	4-8		10	9	Ainsworth	Robertson	Rodriguez	7-6	T2nd	0.5
4-16	At S.F	W	8-5		15	11	Lidge	Brower	Wagner	8-6	T2nd	0.5
4-17	At Mil.	L	2-4		6	12	Kinney	Redding	de los Santos	8-7	T3rd	1.5
4-18	At Mil.	W	11-5		17	11	Oswalt	Rusch		9-7	3rd	1.5
4-19	At Mil.	L	2-3	(14)	13	12	Foster	Linebrink		9-8	3rd	2.5
4-20	At Mil.	L	4-5		8	9	Leskanic	Munro	DeJean	9-9	T3rd	2.5
4-22	At N.Y.	W	6-2		12	5	Redding	Cone		10-9	T2nd	2.5
4-23	At N.Y.	L	2-4		8	8	Leiter	Oswalt	Benitez	10-10	T2nd	2.5
4-24	At N.Y.	L	4-7		8	10	Astacio	Miller	Benitez	10-11	T2nd	2.5
4-25	At Mon.	L	2-10		6	14	Day	Robertson		10-12	T3rd	3.5
4-26	At Mon.	L	2-3	(10)	8	5	Biddle	Wagner		10-13	T3rd	3.5
4-27	At Mon.	W	6-3		10	7	Redding	Ohka	Dotel	11-13	3rd	2.5
4-29	Atl.	L	1-3		6	6	Maddux	Oswalt	Smoltz	11-14	T3rd	3.5
4-30	Atl.	L	1-11		5	13	Hampton	Miller		11-15	4th	3.5
5-1	Atl.	L	7-8		14	11	Hernandez	Wagner	Smoltz	11-16	5th	4.5
5-2	Fla.	W	4-3		7	7	Stone	Penny	Wagner	12-16	5th	4.5
5-3	Fla.	W	5-2		10	9	Redding	Wayne	Dotel	13-16	4th	3.5
5-4	Fla.	W	5-2		9	10	Lidge	Spooneybarger	Wagner	14-16	T3rd	3.5
5-5	Pit.	W	8-1		13	4	Miller	Benson		15-16	3rd	2.5
5-6	Pit.	W	10-9		9	12	Bland	Sauerbeck	Wagner	16-16	3rd	1.5
5-7	Pit.	W	13-4		13	9	Dotel	Tavarez		17-16	3rd	1.5
5-8	Pit.	W	6-2		10	6	Stone	Suppan		18-16	2nd	1.0
5-9	At Phi.	L	3-5		8	10	Myers	Oswalt	Mesa	18-17	3rd	1.0
5-10	At Phi.	L	0-2		5	6	Wolf	Miller		18-18	3rd	2.0
5-11	At Phi.	W	10-7		12	7	Munro	Padilla	Wagner	19-18	3rd	1.5
5-12	At Pit.	W	9-4		12	12	Stone	Torres		20-18	2nd	1.5
5-13	At Pit.	W	6-3		12	8	Munro	Williams	Wagner	21-18	2nd	1.5
5-14	At Pit.	L	2-3		7	7	D'Amico	Miller	Williams	21-19	T2nd	2.5
5-15	At Pit.	W	6-2		11	9	Oswalt	Benson		22-19	2nd	2.5
5-16	Phi.	W	4-2		11	11	Dotel	Wendell	Wagner	23-19	2nd	1.5
5-17	Phi.	L	4-9		8	10	Duckworth	Bland		23-20	2nd	2.5
5-18	Phi.	L	1-3		6	3	Millwood	Redding		23-21	2nd	2.5
5-20	StL.	W	3-2		6	5	Miller	Stephenson	Wagner	24-21	2nd	1.5
5-21	StL.	L	4-7		9	13	Williams	Munro	Eldred	24-22	T3rd	1.5
5-22	StL.	W	5-2		9	7	Robertson	Tomko	Wagner	25-22	2nd	1.5
5-23	Chi.	W	7-5		7	12	Linebrink	Prior	Wagner	26-22	2nd	0.5
5-24	Chi.	L	2-3		8	10	Estes	Redding	Borowski	26-23	3rd	1.5
5-25	Chi.	L	3-7		6	11	Zambrano	Miller		26-24	3rd	2.5
5-26	At StL.	L	5-10		11	14	Williams	Munro		26-25	3rd	2.5
5-27	At StL.	W	7-4		11	11	Robertson	Tomko	Wagner	27-25	3rd	1.5
5-28	At StL.	L	1-3		6	9	Simontacchi	Johnson		27-26	3rd	2.5
5-29	At StL.	W	7-4		9	11	Saarloos	Fassero	Wagner	28-26	3rd	2.0
5-30	At Chi.	W	9-1		8	2	Miller	Estes		29-26	2nd	1.0
5-31	At Chi.	L	0-1	(16)	6	10	Wellemeyer	Stone		29-27	2nd	2.0
6-1	At Chi.	W	9-3		10	8	Robertson	Wood		30-27	2nd	1.0
6-3	Bal.	W	11-6		14	14	Dotel	Groom		31-27	2nd	1.0
6-4	Bal.	W	6-4		11	6	Miller	Hentgen	Wagner	32-27	2nd	...
6-5	Bal.	W	11-1		14	9	Oswalt	Daal		33-27	2nd	...
6-6	T.B.	W	11-8		11	11	Dotel	Harper	Wagner	34-27	1st	+1.0
6-7	T.B.	W	5-4		7	7	Saarloos	Levine	Wagner	35-27	1st	+1.0
6-8	T.B.	W	2-1		6	3	Redding	Zambrano	Wagner	36-27	1st	+1.0
6-10	At N.Y. (AL)	L	3-5		9	8	Mussina	Miller	Rivera	36-28	2nd	...
6-11	At N.Y.(AL)	W	8-0		14	0	Lidge	Weaver		37-28	2nd	...

Date	Opp.	Res.	Score	(inn.*)	Hits	Opp. hits	Winning pitcher	Losing pitcher	Save	Record	Pos.	GB
6-12	At N.Y. (AL)	L	5-6		11	12	Osuna	Dotel	Rivera	37-29	2nd	...
6-13	At Bos.	L	3-4		9	7	Rupe	Stone	Lyon	37-30	2nd	...
6-14	At Bos.	L	4-8		9	12	Lowe	Redding		37-31	2nd	1.0
6-15	At Bos.	L	2-3	(14)	13	14	Shiell	Bland		37-32	2nd	1.0
6-17	Ari.	W	4-3		7	8	Dotel	Villarreal	Wagner	38-32	2nd	0.5
6-18	Ari.	L	1-2		5	8	Villarreal	Wagner	Valverde	38-33	2nd	1.5
6-19	Ari.	L	2-4		7	8	Batista	Redding	Valverde	38-34	3rd	1.5
6-20	At Tex.	W	12-3		16	9	Miller	Thomson		39-34	2nd	0.5
6-21	At Tex.	W	9-5		12	7	Rosario	Valdes		40-34	1st	+0.5
6-22	At Tex.	W	3-1		7	7	Robertson	Benoit	Wagner	41-34	1st	+0.5
6-23	At Ari.	L	6-7		6	9	Bottalico	Lidge	Raggio	41-35	2nd	...
6-24	At Ari.	L	5-12		10	19	Batista	Redding		41-36	2nd	1.0
6-25	At Ari.	L	2-3		6	6	Dessens	Miller	Valverde	41-37	3rd	1.0
6-27	Tex.	L	7-10		12	10	Benoit	Redding		41-38	3rd	0.5
6-28	Tex.	W	2-0		4	6	Robertson	Mounce	Wagner	42-38	2nd	0.5
6-29	Tex.	L	5-8		5	8	Garcia	Dotel	Urbina	42-39	3rd	1.5
7-1	Mil.	W	6-5	(10)	9	8	Stone	DeJean		43-39	T1st	...
7-2	Mil.	L	3-5	(11)	7	10	de los Santos	Stone	Estrella	43-40	T1st	...
7-3	Mil.	W	7-3		7	8	Robertson	Kinney	Dotel	44-40	T1st	...
7-4	At Pit.	L	2-3		6	5	Boehringer	Munro	Williams	44-41	2nd	1.0
7-5	At Pit.	L	3-4		10	9	Suppan	Saarloos	Williams	44-42	T2nd	1.0
7-6	At Pit.	L	3-8		4	14	D'Amico	Miller		44-43	T2nd	2.0
7-7	Cin.	W	7-1		11	4	Oswalt	Dempster		45-43	T2nd	1.0
7-8	Cin.	W	6-3		7	7	Redding	Haynes	Wagner	46-43	T1st	...
7-9	Cin.	W	12-2		14	8	Robertson	Graves		47-43	1st	+1.0
7-10	Cin.	W	11-2		16	4	Villone	Wilson	Stone	48-43	1st	+2.0
7-11	Pit.	W	4-2		10	6	Miller	D'Amico	Wagner	49-43	1st	+2.0
7-12	Pit.	L	2-5		6	10	Wells	Oswalt	Williams	49-44	1st	+1.0
7-13	Pit.	W	5-2		10	8	Redding	Fogg	Wagner	50-44	1st	+1.0
7-17	At Cin.	W	5-4		11	9	Robertson	Wilson	Wagner	51-44	1st	+2.0
7-18	At Cin.	W	5-3		10	6	Oswalt	Dempster	Wagner	52-44	1st	+3.0
7-19	At Cin.	W	9-8		10	14	Villone	Haynes	Dotel	53-44	1st	+3.0
7-20	At Cin.	W	6-3		9	5	Miller	Graves	Wagner	54-44	1st	+3.0
7-21	At Pit.	L	3-5		9	10	Fogg	Redding	Lincoln	54-45	1st	+3.0
7-22	At Pit.	W	2-0		8	3	Robertson	Torres	Wagner	55-45	1st	+4.0
7-23	At Mil.	W	3-2	(11)	7	7	Gallo	Kolb	Wagner	56-45	1st	+4.0
7-24	At Mil.	L	1-2		6	6	Sheets	Villone	Estrella	56-46	1st	+3.5
7-25	Chi.	L	3-5		5	9	Zambrano	Dotel	Borowski	56-47	1st	+3.5
7-26	Chi.	W	3-1		5	2	Redding	Cruz	Wagner	57-47	1st	+3.5
7-27	Chi.	L	3-5		6	10	Estes	Robertson	Borowski	57-48	1st	+2.5
7-29	At Atl.	L	3-6		6	18	Ortiz	Stone	Smoltz	57-49	1st	+2.0
7-30	At Atl.	W	7-3		13	8	Villone	Ramirez		58-49	1st	+2.0
7-31	At Atl.	L	4-7		6	12	Reynolds	Miller	Smoltz	58-50	1st	+2.0
8-1	At Fla.	W	2-1		4	6	Redding	Beckett	Wagner	59-50	1st	+2.0
8-2	At Fla.	L	2-5		3	8	Pavano	Robertson	Looper	59-51	1st	+1.0
8-3	At Fla.	W	3-1		9	5	Fernandez	Redman	Wagner	60-51	1st	+2.0
8-5	N.Y.	L	1-10		7	13	Leiter	Villone		60-52	1st	+2.0
8-6	N.Y.	W	11-1		15	8	Miller	Heilman		61-52	1st	+2.5
8-7	N.Y.	L	4-5		7	8	Trachsel	Lidge	Stanton	61-53	1st	+1.5
8-8	Mon.	W	5-1		8	5	Robertson	Vazquez		62-53	1st	+2.5
8-9	Mon.	L	1-3		6	11	Hernandez	Fernandez		62-54	1st	+2.0
8-10	Mon.	W	8-2		9	5	Villone	Downs		63-54	1st	+2.0
8-11	At Chi.	W	3-1		8	7	Miller	Wood	Wagner	64-54	1st	+2.0
8-12	At Chi.	L	0-3		5	9	Zambrano	Redding		64-55	1st	+1.0
8-13	At Chi.	L	4-6		8	8	Guthrie	Robertson	Borowski	64-56	1st	+1.0
8-14	At Chi.	L	1-7		5	6	Clement	Fernandez		64-57	T1st	...
8-15	At Cin.	L	7-9	(10)	11	10	Wagner	Lidge		64-58	T2nd	0.5
8-16	At Cin.	W	5-2		6	5	Miller	Etherton	Wagner	65-58	1st	+0.5
8-17	At Cin.	L	3-4		6	6	Wilson	Redding	Reitsma	65-59	1st	+0.5
8-19	Chi.	W	12-8		15	11	Miceli	Clement		66-59	1st	+1.0
8-20	Chi.	L	0-6		4	12	Prior	Fernandez		66-60	1st	+0.5
8-21	Chi.	W	9-3		16	7	Villone	Wood		67-60	1st	+1.0
8-22	Cin.	L	3-4		9	8	Etherton	Miller	Reitsma	67-61	1st	+0.5
8-23	Cin.	L	1-3		5	6	Wilson	Redding	Reitsma	67-62	T1st	...
8-24	Cin.	W	6-3		11	5	Robertson	Reith	Wagner	68-62	T1st	...
8-26	L.A.	W	18-4		17	8	Villone	Perez		69-62	1st	+0.5
8-27	L.A.	W	6-1		7	7	Miller	Nomo		70-62	1st	+1.0
8-28	L.A.	L	3-6		8	11	Shuey	Redding	Gagne	70-63	T1st	...
8-29	S.D.	L	1-7		6	14	Eaton	Robertson		70-64	T1st	...
8-30	S.D.	W	11-6		11	10	Fernandez	Jarvis	Wagner	71-64	T1st	...
8-31	S.D.	L	1-3		3	9	Peavy	Villone	Beck	71-65	2nd	1.0

Date	Opp.	Res.	Score	(inn.*)	Hits	Opp. hits	Winning pitcher	Losing pitcher	Save	Record	Pos.	GB
9-1	At L.A.	W	10-1		18	5	Miller	Nomo		72-65	T1st	...
9-2	At L.A.	L	1-4		8	6	Alvarez	Redding	Gagne	72-66	2nd	0.5
9-3	At L.A.	W	8-2		9	6	Robertson	Brown		73-66	1st	+0.5
9-5	At S.D.	W	5-4		9	8	Fernandez	Eaton	Wagner	74-66	1st	+0.5
9-6	At S.D.	W	10-4		13	5	Lidge	Witasick	Wagner	75-66	1st	+0.5
9-7	At S.D.	L	1-7		5	8	Peavy	Miller		75-67	2nd	0.5
9-8	At Mil.	W	8-4		12	5	Oswalt	Franklin		76-67	T1st	...
9-9	At Mil.	W	7-6		12	8	Lidge	Kolb	Wagner	77-67	T1st	...
9-10	At Mil.	W	3-1		9	7	Robertson	Martinez	Wagner	78-67	1st	+1.0
9-11	At Mil.	L	3-5		9	10	Sheets	Villone	Kolb	78-68	1st	+1.0
9-12	StL.	W	14-5		19	5	Miller	Williams		79-68	1st	+1.0
9-13	StL.	W	2-0		4	5	Oswalt	Morris	Wagner	80-68	1st	+1.0
9-14	StL.	W	4-1		6	3	Redding	Haren	Wagner	81-68	1st	+2.0
9-16	At Col.	W	14-4		12	9	Robertson	Tsao		82-68	1st	+1.5
9-17	At Col.	L	5-7		12	12	Oliver	Villone	Speier	82-69	1st	+0.5
9-18	At Col.	W	6-0		14	3	Miller	Jimenez		83-69	1st	+1.0
9-19	At StL.	W	8-1		13	6	Oswalt	Morris		84-69	1st	+1.5
9-20	At StL.	L	2-3	(13)	8	9	Simontacchi	Miceli		84-70	1st	+1.5
9-21	At StL.	L	4-6		12	7	Hitchcock	Robertson	Isringhausen	84-71	1st	+0.5
9-22	S.F	L	3-6		11	8	Nathan	Wagner	Worrell	84-72	T1st	...
9-23	S.F	L	3-10		4	10	Schmidt	Miller		84-73	2nd	1.0
9-24	S.F	W	2-1		4	3	Oswalt	Ponson	Wagner	85-73	2nd	1.0
9-25	Mil.	W	6-1		9	6	Redding	Davis		86-73	T1st	...
9-26	Mil.	L	5-12		14	12	Burba	Robertson	Rusch	86-74	2nd	0.5
9-27	Mil.	L	2-5		10	9	Obermueller	Villone	Kolb	86-75	2nd	2.0
9-28	Mil.	W	8-5		10	8	Stone	Martinez		87-75	2nd	1.0

Monthly records: April (11-15), May (18-12), June (13-12), July (16-11), August (13-15), September (16-10).
*Innings, if other than nine. † First game of a doubleheader. ‡ Second game of a doubleheader.

RECORDS

2003 regular-season record: 87-75
Position: 2nd in N.L. Central
Home: 48-33 **Road:** 39-42
N.L. East: 13-17 **N.L. Central:** 49-35
N.L. West: 14-16 A.L. 11-7
Vs. LH starters: 18-16
Vs. RH starters: 69-59
Grass: 85-71 **Artificial:** 2-4
Day: 23-25 **Night:** 64-50
1-Run: 19-21 **X-inn.:** 3-8
Doubleheaders: 0-0-0
Team record past five years: 433-377 (.535, ranks 5th in league in that span)

TEAM LEADERS

Batting average: Richard Hidalgo (.309).
At-bats: Craig Biggio (628).
Runs: Lance Berkman (110).
Hits: Jeff Bagwell (168).
Total Bases: Jeff Bagwell (317).
Doubles: Craig Biggio (44).
Triples: Lance Berkman (6).
Home runs: Jeff Bagwell (39).
Runs batted in: Jeff Bagwell (100).
Stolen bases: Jeff Bagwell (11).
Slugging percentage: Richard Hidalgo (.572).
On-base percentage: Lance Berkman (.412).
Wins: Jeriome Robertson (15).
Earned-run average: Roy Oswalt (2.97).
Complete games: Wade Miller (1).
Shutouts: None.
Saves: Billy Wagner (44).
Innings pitched: Wade Miller (187.1).
Strikeouts: Wade Miller (161).

GAMES BY POSITION

Catcher: Brad Ausmus 143, Gregg Zaun 31, Raul Chavez 16.
First base: Jeff Bagwell 158, Orlando Merced 12, Geoff Blum 6, Jose Vizcaino 1.
Second base: Jeff Kent 128, Geoff Blum 25, Jose Vizcaino 20, Eric Bruntlett 9, Dave Matranga 2, Tripp Cromer 1.
Third base: Morgan Ensberg 111, Geoff Blum 83, Orlando Merced 2, Jose Vizcaino 2, Eric Bruntlett 1.
Shortstop: Adam Everett 128, Jose Vizcaino 32, Julio Lugo 22, Geoff Blum 11, Eric Bruntlett 10.
Outfield: Lance Berkman 153, Craig Biggio 150, Richard Hidalgo 137, Brian L. Hunter 32, Orlando Merced 31, Colin Porter 14, Jason Lane 10, Geoff Blum 2, Eric Bruntlett 2.
Designated hitter: Orlando Merced 7, Morgan Ensberg 1, Richard Hidalgo 1.

TOP DRAFT CHOICES

2. **Jason Hirsh,** RHP, California Lutheran.
3. **Drew Stubbs,** OF, Atlanta (Texas) H.S.
4. **Josh Anderson,** OF, Eastern Kentucky.
5. **Josh Muecke,** LHP, Loyola Marymount.
6. **Cliff Davis,** RHP, Eupora (Miss) H.S.
7. **Jeff Jorgensen,** OF, Rice.
8. **Mike Collar,** RHP, Maine.
9. **Brock Koman,** 3B, Michigan.
10. **Beau Hearod,** OF, Alabama.

LOS ANGELES DODGERS

NATIONAL LEAGUE WEST DIVISION

2004 SEASON

April

SUN	MON	TUE	WED	THU	FRI	SAT
4	5 SD	6 SD	7 SD	8	9 COL	10 COL
11 COL	12	13 SD	14 SD	15 SD	16 SF	17 SF
18 SF	19	20 COL	21 COL	22 COL	23 SF	24 SF
25 SF	26	27 NYM	28 NYM	29 NYM	30 MON	

May

SUN	MON	TUE	WED	THU	FRI	SAT
						1 MON
2 MON	3	4 FLA	5 FLA	6 FLA	7 PIT	8 PIT
9 PIT	10	11 CHC	12 CHC	13 CHC	14 CIN	15 CIN
16 CIN	17	18 PHI	19 PHI	20 PHI	21 ATL	22 ATL
23 ATL	24	25 MIL	26 MIL	27 MIL	28 ARI	29 ARI
30 ARI	31 MIL					

June

SUN	MON	TUE	WED	THU	FRI	SAT
		1 MIL	2 MIL	3	4 ARI	5 ARI
6 ARI	7	8 TOR	9 TOR	10 TOR	11 BOS	12 BOS
13 BOS	14	15 BAL	16 BAL	17 BAL	18 NYY	19 NYY
20 NYY	21 SF	22 SF	23 SF	24 SF	25 ANA	26 ANA
27 ANA	28	29 SF	30 SF			

July

SUN	MON	TUE	WED	THU	FRI	SAT
				1 SF	2 ANA	3 ANA
4 ANA	5 ARI	6 ARI	7 ARI	8 HOU	9 HOU	10 HOU
11 HOU	12	13 All-Star	14	15 ARI	16 ARI	17 ARI
18 ARI	19 HOU	20 HOU	21 COL	22 COL	23 SD	24 SD
25 SD	26 COL	27 COL	28 COL	29 COL	30 SD	31 SD

August

SUN	MON	TUE	WED	THU	FRI	SAT
1 SD	2	3 PIT	4 PIT	5 PIT	6 PHI	7 PHI
8 PHI	9	10 CIN	11 CIN	12 CIN	13 CHC	14 CHC
15 CHC	16 FLA	17 FLA	18 FLA	19 ATL	20 ATL	21 ATL
22 ATL	23 MON	24 MON	25 MON	26 MON	27 NYM	28 NYM
29 NYM	30	31 ARI				

Sept./Oct.

SUN	MON	TUE	WED	THU	FRI	SAT
			1 ARI	2 ARI	3 STL	4 STL
5 STL	6	7 ARI	8 ARI	9 ARI	10 STL	11 STL
12 STL	13 SD	14 SD	15 SD	16 SD	17 COL	18 COL
19 COL	20	21 SD	22 SD	23 SD	24 SF	25 SF
26 SF	27 COL	28 COL	29 COL	30 COL	1 SF	2 SF
3 SF	4	5	6	7	8	9

Home games shaded. All-Star Game July 13 at Houston. Schedule subject to change.

CLUB DIRECTORY

Managing partner, chairman
Robert Daly
President and chief operating officer
Bob Graziano
Executive vice president and g.m.
Dan Evans
Vice president, assistant g.m.
Kim Ng
Senior vice president, communications
Derrick Hall
Senior vice president
Tommy Lasorda
Special assistant to general manager
Mark Weidemaier
Director, chief information officer
Mike Mularky
Director, public relations
John Olguin
Director, community affairs
Erikk Aldridge
Director, community relations
Don Newcombe
Director, professional scouting
Matt Slater
Director, amateur scouting
Logan White
Director, international scouting
Rene Francisco

MINOR LEAGUE AFFILIATES

Class	Team	League	Manager
AAA	Las Vegas	Pacific Coast	Terry Kennedy
AA	Jacksonville	Southern	Dino Ebel
Advanced A	Vero Beach	Florida State	Scott Little
A	South Georgia	South Atlantic	Dann Bilardello
Advanced Rookie	Ogden	Pioneer	Travis Barbary
Rookie	Gulf Coast Dodgers	Gulf Coast	Luis Salazar

More on the Dodgers at www.foxsports.com/named/FS/MLB/teams

BROADCAST INFORMATION

Radio: XTRA-AM (1150); KWKW-AM (1330, Spanish language).
TV: KCOP-TV (Channel 13)
Cable TV: Fox Sports Net 2.

SPRING TRAINING

Ballpark (city): Holman Stadium (Vero Beach, Fla.).
Ticket information: 772-569-4900.
General number: 772-569-4900.

SPRING TRAINING ROSTER

Manager—Jim Tracy (12).
Coaches—Jim Colborn (48), Glenn Hoffman (35), Jim Lett (18), Manny Mota (11), Jim Riggleman (56), John Shelby (31).

No.	PITCHERS	B/T	Ht./Wt.	Age*	2003 Clubs
47	Alvarez, Wilson	L/L	6-1/255	34	Las Vegas, Los Angeles
	Brazoban, Yhency	R/R	6-1/170	23	Trenton, Gulf Coast Yankees, Tampa
	Brown, Andrew	R/R	6-6/230	23	Jacksonville
	Colyer, Steve	L/L	6-4/205	25	Las Vegas, Los Angeles
37	Dreifort, Darren	R/R	6-2/211	31	Los Angeles
	Falkenborg, Brian	R/R	6-6/195	26	Tacoma
	Frasor, Jason	R/R	5-10/170	26	Vero Beach, Jacksonville
38	Gagne, Eric	R/R	6-2/195	28	Los Angeles
	Hanrahan, Joel	R/R	6-3/215	22	Las Vegas, Jacksonville
17	Ishii, Kazuhisa	L/L	6-0/200	30	Los Angeles
	Jackson, Edwin	R/R	6-3/190	20	Jacksonville, Los Angeles
	Kuo, Hong-Chih	L/L	6-4/200	22	Did Not Play
	Martin, Tom	L/L	6-1/206	33	Los Angeles
59	Mota, Guillermo	R/R	6-4/205	30	Los Angeles
10	Nomo, Hideo	R/R	6-2/210	35	Los Angeles
45	Perez, Odalis	L/L	6-0/150	26	Los Angeles
	Rodriguez, O.	L/L	5-10/155	23	Jacksonville
	Sanchez, Duaner	R/R	6-0/180	24	Nashville, Pittsburgh
44	Shuey, Paul	R/R	6-3/215	33	Las Vegas, Los Angeles
	Weaver, Jeff	R/R	6-5/200	27	New York A.L.

No.	CATCHERS	B/T	Ht./Wt.	Age*	2003 Clubs
	Hill, Koyie	B/R	6-0/190	25	Jacksonville, Las Vegas, Los Angeles
9	Hundley, Todd	B/R	5-11/200	34	Vero Beach, Los Angeles
16	Lo Duca, Paul	R/R	5-10/185	31	Los Angeles
40	Ross, Dave	R/R	6-2/205	27	Las Vegas, Los Angeles

No.	INFIELDERS	B/T	Ht./Wt.	Age*	2003 Clubs
	Aybar, Willy	S/R	6-0/175	21	Vero Beach
29	Beltre, Adrian	R/R	5-11/170	24	Los Angeles
13	Cora, Alex	L/R	6-0/180	28	Los Angeles
3	Izturis, Cesar	B/R	5-9/175	24	Los Angeles
49	Thurston, Joe	L/R	5-11/175	24	Las Vegas, Los Angeles
23	Ventura, Robin	L/R	6-1/190	36	New York A.L., Los Angeles

No.	OUTFIELDERS	B/T	Ht./Wt.	Age*	2003 Clubs
	Abercrombie, R.	R/R	6-3/210	23	Jacksonville
6	Cabrera, Jolbert	R/R	6-1/195	31	Los Angeles
52	Chen, Chin-Feng	R/R	6-1/189	26	Los Angeles, Las Vegas
	Encarnacion, Juan	R/R	6-3/215	28	Florida
15	Green, Shawn	L/L	6-4/200	31	Los Angeles
30	Roberts, Dave	L/L	5-10/180	31	Las Vegas, Ogden, Los Angeles
	Romano, Jason	R/R	6-0/185	24	Las Vegas, Los Angeles
26	Ruan, Wilkin	R/R	6-0/170	25	Las Vegas, Los Angeles
	Trammell, Bubba	R/R	6-2/220	32	New York A.L.

Invited to spring training: LHP Troy Brohawn, 1B/OF Jeremy Giambi, RHP Rick White, RHP Bill Simas.

*Age as of April 1, 2004.

BALLPARK INFORMATION

Ballpark (capacity, surface)
Dodger Stadium (56,000, grass)

Address
1000 Elysian Park Ave.
Los Angeles, CA 90012

Official website
www.dodgers.com

Business phone
323-224-1500

Ticket information
323-224-1448

Field dimensions (from home plate)
To left field at foul line, 330 feet
To center field, 395 feet
To right field at foul line, 330 feet

First game played
April 10, 1962 (Reds 6, Dodgers 3)

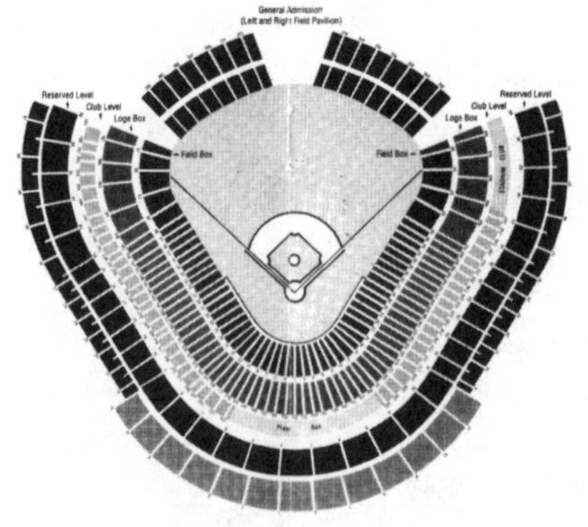

2003 REVIEW

DAY BY DAY

Date	Opp.	Res.	Score	(inn.*)	Hits	Opp. hits	Winning pitcher	Losing pitcher	Save	Record	Pos.	GB
3-31	At Ari.	W	8-0		13	4	Nomo	Johnson		1-0	T1st	...
4-1	At Ari.	L	4-5	(10)	8	9	Mantei	Shuey		1-1	T2nd	1.0
4-2	At Ari.	W	5-0		12	3	Brown	Dessens		2-1	2nd	1.0
4-3	At S.D.	L	1-6		2	12	Peavy	Ishii		2-2	2nd	1.5
4-4	At S.D.	L	2-4		7	8	Condrey	Dreifort	Villafuerte	2-3	T3rd	2.5
4-5	At S.D.	L	0-3		4	7	Lawrence	Nomo	Orosco	2-4	4th	3.5
4-6	At S.D.	W	4-3	(13)	8	9	Mota	Wright		3-4	T3rd	3.5
4-7	Ari.	L	4-6	(12)	11	12	Mantei	Ashby	Service	3-5	T3rd	4.5
4-8	Ari.	W	5-3		9	5	Shuey	Batista	Gagne	4-5	T3rd	3.5
4-9	Ari.	W	5-2		7	8	Dreifort	Kim	Gagne	5-5	3rd	3.5
4-10	At S.F	L	1-2		6	8	Ainsworth	Nomo	Worrell	5-6	3rd	4.5
4-11	At S.F	L	2-3		5	7	Rueter	Perez	Worrell	5-7	4th	5.5
4-13	At S.F	L	4-5	(12)	14	11	Brower	Ashby		5-8	4th	6.5
4-15	S.D.	L	2-3		8	9	Peavy	Nomo	Wright	5-9	4th	8.0
4-16	S.D.	W	3-0		8	5	Ishii	Lawrence	Gagne	6-9	4th	7.0
4-17	S.D.	W	4-3		9	5	Brohawn	Wright	Gagne	7-9	T3rd	6.5
4-18	S.F	L	1-5		4	11	Schmidt	Brown		7-10	T3rd	7.5
4-19	S.F	L	3-9		9	11	Moss	Ashby		7-11	T3rd	8.5
4-20	S.F	W	16-4		18	7	Nomo	Ainsworth		8-11	3rd	7.5
4-22	At Cin.	W	2-1		7	6	Shuey	Wilson	Gagne	9-11	3rd	6.5
4-23	At Cin.	L	0-3		9	8	Reitsma	Dreifort	Williamson	9-12	3rd	7.5
4-24	At Cin.	L	2-3	(11)	8	8	Heredia	Mota		9-13	T3rd	8.5
4-25	At Pit.	W	5-2		10	5	Brohawn	Williams	Gagne	10-13	T3rd	8.5
4-26	At Pit.	W	4-3		6	7	Nomo	Sauerbeck	Gagne	11-13	3rd	7.5
4-27	At Pit.	W	6-2		10	9	Ishii	Suppan		12-13	3rd	6.5
4-28	Phi.	L	0-3		8	8	Myers	Dreifort	Mesa	12-14	3rd	7.0
4-29	Phi.	W	6-2		12	8	Brown	Wolf		13-14	3rd	6.0
4-30	Phi.	W	4-0		6	7	Perez	Padilla	Gagne	14-14	3rd	6.0
5-1	Phi.	L	1-4		9	5	Duckworth	Nomo	Mesa	14-15	3rd	6.0
5-2	Pit.	L	3-5		10	7	Beimel	Quantrill	Williams	14-16	3rd	6.0
5-3	Pit.	W	4-1		12	6	Dreifort	Suppan	Gagne	15-16	3rd	6.0
5-4	Pit.	W	3-2		6	5	Brown	D'Amico	Gagne	16-16	3rd	6.0
5-6	At N.Y.	L	2-3		5	11	Astacio	Perez	Benitez	16-17	3rd	7.0
5-7	At N.Y.	W	2-1		5	3	Nomo	Trachsel	Gagne	17-17	T2nd	7.0
5-8	At N.Y.	W	6-1		12	6	Ishii	Glavine		18-17	2nd	7.0
5-9	At Mon.	W	9-5		15	10	Mota	Stewart		19-17	2nd	7.0
5-10	At Mon.	L	5-6		13	10	Ayala	Martin	Biddle	19-18	2nd	7.0
5-11	At Mon.	W	4-3		7	5	Perez	Hernandez	Gagne	20-18	2nd	6.0
5-12	Atl.	L	4-11		5	10	Bong	Gagne		20-19	2nd	6.0
5-13	Atl.	L	1-3		5	7	Ortiz	Quantrill	Smoltz	20-20	2nd	6.0
5-14	Atl.	W	5-1		8	5	Brown	Maddux		21-20	2nd	5.0
5-16	Fla.	W	2-1		6	8	Dreifort	Almanza	Gagne	22-20	2nd	5.5
5-17	Fla.	W	4-1		11	3	Perez	Tejera	Gagne	23-20	2nd	4.5
5-18	Fla.	W	2-1		5	7	Nomo	Penny	Gagne	24-20	2nd	3.5
5-20	Col.	W	3-1		8	4	Brown	Oliver	Gagne	25-20	2nd	3.0
5-21	Col.	W	3-2		11	4	Ishii	Jennings	Gagne	26-20	2nd	3.0
5-22	Col.	W	4-3		7	2	Dreifort	Cook	Gagne	27-20	2nd	2.5
5-23	At Mil.	W	6-4		11	10	Perez	Rusch	Mota	28-20	2nd	1.5
5-24	At Mil.	W	6-0		11	2	Nomo	Kinney		29-20	2nd	1.5
5-25	At Mil.	W	5-1		6	4	Brown	Sheets		30-20	2nd	0.5
5-27	At Col.	L	3-7		9	6	Cook	Ishii		30-21	2nd	1.0
5-28	At Col.	L	0-6		4	11	Chacon	Dreifort		30-22	2nd	2.0
5-29	At Col.	L	5-12		14	16	Elarton	Perez		30-23	2nd	2.5
5-30	Mil.	L	3-5		6	7	Sheets	Nomo	DeJean	30-24	2nd	3.5
5-31	Mil.	W	3-0		9	6	Brown	Quevedo	Gagne	31-24	2nd	3.5
6-1	Mil.	L	3-4		6	8	Durocher	Mota	DeJean	31-25	2nd	4.5
6-3	K.C.	W	4-3		10	8	Gagne	Carrasco		32-25	2nd	3.0
6-4	K.C.	L	1-2		3	7	Snyder	Nomo	MacDougal	32-26	2nd	4.0
6-5	K.C.	W	5-2		7	5	Brown	May	Gagne	33-26	2nd	3.0
6-6	Chi. (AL)	W	2-1		5	4	Ishii	Buehrle	Gagne	34-26	2nd	3.0
6-7	Chi. (AL)	L	1-4		4	10	Colon	Ashby		34-27	2nd	4.0
6-8	Chi. (AL)	L	3-10		8	11	Loaiza	Perez		34-28	2nd	5.0
6-10	At Det.	W	3-1	(12)	6	5	Shuey	Sparks	Gagne	35-28	2nd	4.0
6-11	At Det.	W	3-1		4	6	Brown	Bernero	Gagne	36-28	2nd	4.0

Date	Opp.	Res.	Score	(inn.*)	Hits	Opp. hits	Winning pitcher	Losing pitcher	Save	Record	Pos.	GB
6-12	At Det.	W	3-2		10	6	Ishii	Bonderman	Gagne	37-28	2nd	4.0
6-13	At Cle.	W	4-3	(10)	11	9	Quantrill	Westbrook	Gagne	38-28	2nd	3.0
6-14	At Cle.	W	5-2		10	6	Ashby	Tallet	Alvarez	39-28	2nd	3.0
6-15	At Cle.	W	4-3		7	7	Nomo	Traber	Gagne	40-28	2nd	2.0
6-17	S.F	W	4-1		9	8	Brown	Foppert	Gagne	41-28	2nd	1.0
6-18	S.F	W	8-2		11	6	Ishii	Rueter		42-28	T1st	...
6-19	S.F	L	0-2		3	6	Schmidt	Perez		42-29	2nd	1.0
6-20	Ana.	W	5-2		9	7	Nomo	Washburn	Gagne	43-29	T1st	...
6-21	Ana.	W	4-2		7	8	Ashby	Lackey	Gagne	44-29	T1st	...
6-22	Ana.	L	3-6		9	12	Appier	Brown	Percival	44-30	T1st	...
6-23	At S.F	L	2-3	(11)	10	9	Rodriguez	Gagne		44-31	2nd	1.0
6-24	At S.F	L	1-2		4	4	Schmidt	Perez		44-32	2nd	2.0
6-25	At S.F	W	6-0		16	3	Nomo	Moss		45-32	2nd	1.0
6-27	At Ana.	L	0-3		5	10	Lackey	Brown	Percival	45-33	2nd	2.0
6-28	At Ana.	L	1-3		6	9	Appier	Ishii	Percival	45-34	2nd	3.0
6-29	At Ana.	L	1-3		7	11	Sele	Perez	Percival	45-35	2nd	3.0
7-1	S.D.	L	1-7		8	13	Lawrence	Nomo		45-36	2nd	4.5
7-2	S.D.	L	3-4	(10)	6	8	Herges	Gagne	Beck	45-37	2nd	5.5
7-3	S.D.	L	4-7		9	9	Eaton	Brown	Beck	45-38	3rd	5.5
7-4	Ari.	L	1-3	(10)	6	11	Villarreal	Martin	Mantei	45-39	3rd	6.5
7-5	Ari.	W	2-0		5	4	Perez	Dessens	Gagne	46-39	3rd	5.5
7-6	Ari.	L	1-2		4	6	Good	Nomo	Mantei	46-40	3rd	6.5
7-7	At S.D.	L	1-7		5	12	Perez	Ashby		46-41	3rd	7.5
7-8	At S.D.	L	5-8		9	12	Eaton	Alvarez	Beck	46-42	3rd	8.5
7-9	At StL.	W	6-5		11	6	Ishii	Tomko	Gagne	47-42	3rd	7.5
7-10	At StL.	W	9-4		15	14	Perez	Morris	Quantrill	48-42	3rd	6.5
7-11	At Col.	L	6-7		13	7	Fuentes	Shuey	Speier	48-43	3rd	7.5
7-12	At Col.	L	3-5		7	10	Jennings	Ashby	Speier	48-44	3rd	8.5
7-13	At Col.	W	9-3		12	7	Alvarez	Neagle		49-44	3rd	7.5
7-17	StL.	W	6-3		8	5	Nomo	Stephenson	Gagne	50-44	3rd	7.5
7-18	StL.	W	8-5		11	9	Ishii	Eldred	Gagne	51-44	3rd	7.5
7-19	StL.	L	1-3		6	7	Haren	Brown	Isringhausen	51-45	3rd	8.5
7-20	StL.	L	7-10		12	10	Williams	Perez	Isringhausen	51-46	3rd	9.5
7-21	Col.	L	1-4		6	9	Stark	Ashby		51-47	3rd	10.5
7-22	Col.	W	5-2		10	7	Nomo	Jennings	Gagne	52-47	3rd	10.5
7-23	Col.	L	3-8		6	11	Oliver	Ishii		52-48	3rd	11.5
7-24	Col.	W	1-0	(11)	6	4	Shuey	Lopez		53-48	3rd	11.5
7-25	At Ari.	L	1-2	(15)	3	12	Randolph	Quantrill		53-49	3rd	12.5
7-26	At Ari.	L	0-1		6	5	Dessens	Ashby	Mantei	53-50	3rd	12.5
7-27	At Ari.	W	1-0		9	4	Nomo	Schilling	Gagne	54-50	3rd	12.5
7-29	At Phi.	L	0-2		3	5	Padilla	Ishii	Mesa	54-51	3rd	12.5
7-30	At Phi.	L	2-4		9	13	Wendell	Shuey	Mesa	54-52	3rd	13.5
7-31	At Phi.	L	3-7		7	8	Duckworth	Perez		54-53	3rd	13.5
8-1	At Atl.	L	0-2		4	7	Maddux	Nomo	Smoltz	54-54	T3rd	13.5
8-2	At Atl.	L	4-6		7	10	Hampton	Ashby	Smoltz	54-55	4th	13.5
8-3	At Atl.	W	8-4		10	8	Mota	Ortiz		55-55	T3rd	13.5
8-5	Cin.	W	5-2		7	9	Brown	Graves	Gagne	56-55	3rd	13.5
8-6	Cin.	W	2-1		8	4	Perez	Heredia	Gagne	57-55	3rd	12.5
8-7	Cin.	W	4-3		9	6	Nomo	Wilson	Gagne	58-55	3rd	12.5
8-8	Chi.	W	3-1		8	3	Ashby	Estes	Gagne	59-55	3rd	12.5
8-9	Chi.	W	6-1		8	5	Alvarez	Clement		60-55	3rd	11.5
8-10	Chi.	L	1-3		5	5	Prior	Brown		60-56	3rd	12.5
8-11	At Fla.	W	9-3		16	9	Perez	Willis		61-56	3rd	12.0
8-12	At Fla.	L	4-5	(13)	10	11	Fox	Shuey		61-57	3rd	12.0
8-13	At Fla.	L	1-2	(11)	7	6	Bump	Alvarez		61-58	3rd	12.0
8-14	At Fla.	W	6-4		12	7	Brown	Redman	Gagne	62-58	3rd	11.5
8-15	At Chi.	L	1-2		7	6	Prior	Kida		62-59	3rd	11.5
8-16	At Chi.	W	10-5		16	11	Perez	Remlinger		63-59	3rd	10.5
8-17	At Chi.	W	3-0		7	6	Nomo	Zambrano	Gagne	64-59	3rd	9.5
8-19	Mon.	L	5-7		9	13	Ayala	Quantrill	Biddle	64-60	3rd	10.0
8-20	Mon.	W	4-1	(10)	10	6	Gagne	Biddle		65-60	3rd	10.0
8-21	Mon.	W	2-1		5	9	Perez	Day	Gagne	66-60	3rd	10.0
8-22	N.Y.	W	2-1		6	7	Nomo	Leiter	Gagne	67-60	2nd	10.0
8-23	N.Y.	L	0-4		6	11	Trachsel	Ashby		67-61	3rd	11.0
8-24	N.Y.	L	1-2		2	8	Glavine	Brown	Franco	67-62	3rd	11.0
8-26	At Hou.	L	4-18		8	17	Villone	Perez		67-63	3rd	12.0
8-27	At Hou.	L	1-6		7	7	Miller	Nomo		67-64	3rd	13.0
8-28	At Hou.	W	6-3		11	8	Shuey	Redding	Gagne	68-64	3rd	12.0
8-29	Col.	W	6-4		11	5	Brown	Vance	Gagne	69-64	3rd	11.0
8-30	Col.	W	5-0		8	4	Mota	Stark		70-64	2nd	11.0
8-31	Col.	W	3-0		4	6	Perez	Oliver	Gagne	71-64	2nd	11.0

Date	Opp.	Res.	Score	(inn.*)	Hits	Opp. hits	Winning pitcher	Losing pitcher	Save	Record	Pos.	GB
9-1	Hou.	L	1-10		5	18	Miller	Nomo		71-65	2nd	12.0
9-2	Hou.	W	4-1		6	8	Alvarez	Redding	Gagne	72-65	2nd	12.0
9-3	Hou.	L	2-8		6	9	Robertson	Brown		72-66	2nd	13.0
9-5	At Col.	W	8-7		17	14	Mota	Reed	Gagne	73-66	2nd	12.0
9-6	At Col.	W	10-2		13	6	Perez	Oliver		74-66	2nd	12.0
9-7	At Col.	W	6-2		15	10	Alvarez	Jimenez	Gagne	75-66	2nd	11.0
9-8	At Ari.	W	10-3		14	5	Mota	Villarreal		76-66	2nd	10.5
9-9	At Ari.	W	4-1		8	4	Jackson	Johnson	Gagne	77-66	2nd	10.5
9-10	At Ari.	L	4-5		6	5	Villarreal	Quantrill	Mantei	77-67	2nd	11.5
9-11	At Ari.	L	0-2		4	6	Capuano	Perez	Mantei	77-68	2nd	11.5
9-12	S.D.	W	6-0		9	4	Alvarez	Jarvis		78-68	2nd	11.5
9-13	S.D.	W	4-0		10	6	Brown	Peavy		79-68	2nd	10.5
9-14	S.D.	W	5-2		12	5	Nomo	Howard	Gagne	80-68	2nd	10.5
9-16	Ari.	L	2-3		9	7	Schilling	Ishii	Mantei	80-69	2nd	12.0
9-17	Ari.	L	0-2		3	5	Webb	Jackson	Mantei	80-70	2nd	13.0
9-18	Ari.	W	2-0		4	7	Alvarez	Batista	Gagne	81-70	2nd	12.0
9-19	S.F	L	4-6		11	11	Hermanson	Brown	Worrell	81-71	2nd	13.0
9-20	S.F	L	0-6		7	13	Rueter	Nomo		81-72	2nd	14.0
9-21	S.F	W	7-5		10	9	Quantrill	Brower	Gagne	82-72	2nd	13.0
9-22	At S.D.	L	5-9		11	16	Bynum	Perez		82-73	2nd	14.0
9-23	At S.D.	W	2-1		9	5	Martin	Beck	Gagne	83-73	2nd	14.0
9-24	At S.D.	W	2-1	(11)	5	7	Shuey	Witasick	Gagne	84-73	2nd	13.0
9-25	At S.D.	L	1-6		9	8	Lawrence	Nomo		84-74	2nd	13.5
9-26	At S.F	L	1-10		7	13	Rueter	Ishii		84-75	2nd	14.5
9-27§	At S.F	W	5-0		7	2	Jackson	Williams		85-75		
9-27∞	At S.F	L	3-6		7	13	Nathan	Mota	Worrell	85-76	2nd	14.5
9-28	At S.F	L	3-12		9	14	Correia	Alvarez		85-77	2nd	15.5

Monthly records: March (1-0), April (13-14), May (17-10), June (14-11), July (9-18), August (17-11), September (14-13).
*Innings, if other than nine. § Day separate admission. ∞ Night separate admission.

RECORDS

2003 regular-season record: 85-77
Position: 2nd in N.L. West
Home: 46-35 **Road:** 39-42
N.L. East: 16-16 **N.L. Central:** 23-13
N.L. West: 35-41 A.L. 11-7
Vs. LH starters: 24-16
Vs. RH starters: 61-61
Grass: 83-73 **Artificial:** 2-4
Day: 26-14 **Night:** 59-63
1-Run: 26-23 **X-inn.:** 6-10
Doubleheaders: 0-0-0
Team record past five years: 426-384 (.526, ranks 6th in league in that span)

TEAM LEADERS

Batting average: Jolbert Cabrera (.282).
At-bats: Shawn Green (611).
Runs: Shawn Green (84).
Hits: Shawn Green (171).
Total Bases: Shawn Green (281).
Doubles: Shawn Green (49).
Triples: Cesar Izturis (6).
Home runs: Adrian Beltre (23).
Runs batted in: Shawn Green (85).
Stolen bases: Dave Roberts (40).
Slugging percentage: Shawn Green (.460).
On-base percentage: Shawn Green (.355).
Wins: Hideo Nomo (16).
Earned-run average: Guillermo Mota (1.97).
Complete games: Hideo Nomo (2).
Shutouts: Hideo Nomo (2).
Saves: Eric Gagne (55).
Innings pitched: Hideo Nomo (218.1).
Strikeouts: Kevin Brown (185).

GAMES BY POSITION

Catcher: Paul Lo Duca 123, Dave Ross 38, Todd Hundley 10.
First base: Fred McGriff 79, Robin Ventura 42, Ron Coomer 24, Paul Lo Duca 22, Mike Kinkade 13, Daryle Ward 13, Larry Barnes 8, Jolbert Cabrera 8.
Second base: Alex Cora 141, Jolbert Cabrera 59, Joe Thurston 3, Jason Romano 1.
Third base: Adrian Beltre 157, Ron Coomer 11, Jolbert Cabrera 5, Robin Ventura 3, Mike Kinkade 2.
Shortstop: Cesar Izturis 158, Alex Cora 15, Jolbert Cabrera 9, Adrian Beltre 1.
Outfield: Shawn Green 157, Dave Roberts 105, Jolbert Cabrera 63, Brian Jordan 62, Jeromy Burnitz 60, Mike Kinkade 36, Jason Romano 28, Wilkin Ruan 20, Rickey Henderson 18, Daryle Ward 11, Chad Hermansen 6, Paul Lo Duca 6, Larry Barnes 2, Bubba Crosby 1.
Designated hitter: Ron Coomer 4, Shawn Green 2, Brian Jordan 2, Larry Barnes 1, Mike Kinkade 1, Jason Romano 1.

TOP DRAFT CHOICES

1. **Chad Billingsley,** RHP, Defiance (Ohio) H.S.
2. **Chuck Tiffany,** LHP, Charter Oak H.S., Covina, Calif.
3. **Cory Van Allen,** LHP, Clements H.S., Sugar Land, Texas.
4. **Xavier Paul,** OF, Slidell (La.) H.S.
5. **Jordan Pratt,** RHP, Central H.S., Independence, Ore.
6. **Matthew Kemp,** OF, Midwest City (Okla.) H.S.
7. **Wesley Wright,** LHP, Goshen (Ala.) H.S.
8. **Lucas May,** 3B, Parkway West H.S., Chesterfield, Mo.
9. **Brett Dowdy,** 2B, Florida.
10. **Phil Sobkow,** RHP, Central Missouri State.

MILWAUKEE BREWERS

NATIONAL LEAGUE CENTRAL DIVISION

2004 SEASON

April

SUN	MON	TUE	WED	THU	FRI	SAT
4	5 STL	6 STL	7 STL	8 STL	9 HOU	10 HOU
11 HOU	12 SF	13 SF	14 SF	15 HOU	16 HOU	17 HOU
18 HOU	19	20 ARI	21 ARI	22 ARI	23 STL	24 STL
25 STL	26	27 CIN	28 CIN	29	30 PIT	

May

SUN	MON	TUE	WED	THU	FRI	SAT
						1 PIT
2 PIT	3	4 CIN	5 CIN	6 CIN	7 NYM	8 NYM
9 NYM	10	11 MON	12 MON	13 MON	14 ATL	15 ATL
16 ATL	17	18 * MON	19 * MON	20 * MON	21 PIT	22 PIT
23 PIT	24	25 LA	26 LA	27 LA	28 SD	29 SD
30 SD	31 LA					

June

SUN	MON	TUE	WED	THU	FRI	SAT
		1 LA	2 LA	3	4 SD	5 SD
6 SD	7	8 ANA	9 ANA	10 ANA	11 HOU	12 HOU
13 HOU	14	15 SEA	16 SEA	17 SEA	18 MIN	19 MIN
20 MIN	21	22 COL	23 COL	24 COL	25 MIN	26 MIN
27 MIN	28	29 COL	30 COL			

July

SUN	MON	TUE	WED	THU	FRI	SAT
				1 COL	2 PIT	3 PIT
4 PIT	5 CHC	6 CHC	7 CHC	8 CIN	9 CIN	10 CIN
11 CIN	12	13 All-Star	14	15 CHC	16 CHC	17 CHC
18 CHC	19 CIN	20 CIN	21 STL	22 STL	23 HOU	24 HOU
25 HOU	26 CHC	27 CHC	28 CHC	29 CHC	30 PIT	31 PIT

August

SUN	MON	TUE	WED	THU	FRI	SAT
1 PIT	2	3 NYM	4 NYM	5 NYM	6 FLA	7 FLA
8 FLA	9	10 ATL	11 ATL	12 ATL	13 FLA	14 FLA
15 FLA	16	17 CHC	18 CHC	19 CHC	20 PHI	21 PHI
22 PHI	23 CHC	24 CHC	25 CHC	26	27 PHI	28 PHI
29 PHI	30 PIT	31 PIT				

Sept./Oct.

SUN	MON	TUE	WED	THU	FRI	SAT
			1 PIT	2 PIT	3 CIN	4 CIN
5 CIN	6 PIT	7 PIT	8 PIT	9 CIN	10 CIN	11 CIN
12 CIN	13	14 SF	15 SF	16 SF	17 HOU	18 HOU
19 HOU	20 STL	21 STL	22 STL	23 STL	24 HOU	25 HOU
26 HOU	27 ARI	28 ARI	29 ARI	30 STL	1 STL	2 STL
3 STL	4	5	6	7	8	9

Home games shaded. All-Star Game July 13 at Houston. Schedule subject to change. * San Juan, Puerto Rico.

CLUB DIRECTORY

President and chief executive officer
To be announced
Executive vice president and g.m.
Doug Melvin
Executive v.p., business operations
Rick Schlesinger
Assistant general manager
Gord Ash
Director, community relations
Leonard Peace
Director, media relations
Jon Greenberg
Director, scouting
Jack Zduriencik
Special asst. to the g.m./player dev.
Reid Nichols
Special assistant to the g.m./scouting
Dick Groch

MINOR LEAGUE AFFILIATES

Class	Team	League	Manager
AAA	Indianapolis	International	Cecil Cooper
AA	Huntsville	Southern	Frank Kremblas
Advanced A	High Desert	California	Mel Queen
A	Beloit	Midwest	Don Money
Advanced Rookie	Helena	Pioneer	Johnny Narron
Rookie	Maryvale	Arizona	Mike Guerrero

More on the Brewers at www.foxsports.com/named/FS/MLB/teams

BROADCAST INFORMATION

Radio: WTMJ-AM (620).
TV: WCGV-TV (Channel 24).
Cable TV: Fox Sports North.

SPRING TRAINING

Ballpark (city): Maryvale Baseball Park (Phoenix, Ariz.).
Ticket information: 1-800-933-7890.

SPRING TRAINING ROSTER

Manager—Ned Yost (3).
Coaches—Bill Castro (35), Rich Dauer (25), Rich Donnelly (45), Mike Maddux (36), Dave Nelson (14), Butch Wynegar (16).

No.	PITCHERS	B/T	Ht./Wt.	Age*	2003 Clubs
	Adams, Mike	R/R	6-5/190	25	Huntsville
	Bausher, Tim	R/R	6-5/200	24	Beloit
	Bennett, Jeff	R/R	6-3/205	23	Altoona, Nashville
	Capuano, Chris	L/L	6-3/210	25	Tucson, Arizona
48	Crudale, Mike	R/R	6-0/220	27	St. Louis, Memphis, Indianapolis, Milwaukee
49	Davis, Doug	R/L	6-4/190	28	Oklahoma, Texas, Toronto, Huntsville, Indianapolis, Milwaukee
	De la Rosa, Jorge	L/L	6-1/190	22	Pawtucket, Portland
	Diggins, Ben	R/R	6-7/230	24	Huntsville
53	Estrella, Leo	R/R	6-1/185	29	Indianapolis, Milwaukee
52	Ford, Matt	B/L	6-1/170	22	Milwaukee
26	Franklin, Wayne	L/L	6-2/211	30	Milwaukee
	Hendrickson, Ben	R/R	6-4/190	23	Huntsville
55	Kieschnick, Brooks	L/R	6-4/230	31	Indianapolis, Milwaukee
50	Kinney, Matt	R/R	6-5/225	27	Milwaukee
41	Kolb, Danny	R/R	6-4/215	29	Indianapolis, Milwaukee
	Liriano, Pedro	R/R	6-2/170	23	Huntsville
31	Martinez, Luis	L/L	6-6/200	24	Huntsville, Indianapolis, Milwaukee
32	Neugebauer, Nick	R/R	6-3/235	23	Did Not Play
33	Obermueller, Wes	R/R	6-2/195	27	Omaha, Indianapolis, Milwaukee
	Phelps, Travis	R/R	6-2/166	26	Richmond
	Saenz, Chris	R/R	6-3/200	23	High Desert, Huntsville
	Sarfate, Dennis	R/R	6-4/210	22	Beloit
15	Sheets, Ben	R/R	6-1/200	25	Milwaukee
51	Vizcaino, Luis	R/R	5-11/180	29	Milwaukee

No.	CATCHERS	B/T	Ht./Wt.	Age*	2003 Clubs
	Bennett, Gary	R/R	6-0/208	31	San Diego
	Johnson, Kade	R/R	6-1/205	25	High Desert, Huntsville
	Moeller, Chad	R/R	6-3/215	29	Arizona

No.	INFIELDERS	B/T	Ht./Wt.	Age*	2003 Clubs
30	Counsell, Craig	L/R	6-0/184	33	Tucson, Arizona
6	Ginter, Keith	R/R	5-10/195	27	Milwaukee
2	Hall, Bill	R/R	6-0/198	24	Indianapolis, Milwaukee
	Hart, Corey	R/R	6-6/200	22	Huntsville
18	Helms, Wes	R/R	6-4/230	27	Indianapolis, Milwaukee
	Overbay, Lyle	L/L	6-2/222	27	Tucson, Arizona
10	Spivey, Junior	R/R	6-0/201	29	El Paso, Tucson, Arizona
23	Weeks, Rickie	R/R	6-0/195	21	Arizona Brewers, Beloit, Milwaukee

No.	OUTFIELDERS	B/T	Ht./Wt.	Age*	2003 Clubs
27	Clark, Brady	R/R	6-2/195	30	Indianapolis, Milwaukee
	Grieve, Ben	L/R	6-4/216	27	Tampa Bay
5	Jenkins, Geoff	L/R	6-1/213	29	Huntsville, Milwaukee
	Krynzel, Dave	L/L	6-1/180	22	Huntsville
20	Podsednik, Scott	L/L	6-0/170	28	Milwaukee

Invited to spring training: RHP Brian Bowles, RHP Dave Burba, RHP Matt Childers, RHP Adrian Hernandez, RHP Mike Kusiewicz, RHP Victor Santos, C Chris Coste, C Alex Delgado, C Mark Johnson, C John VandenBerg, IF Trent Durrington, IF Matt Erickson, 1B Prince Fielder, SS J.J. Hardy, IF/OF Jeff Liefer, OF Jon Nunnally, OF Chris Magruder.

*Age as of April 1, 2004.

BALLPARK INFORMATION

Ballpark (capacity, surface)
Miller Park (41,900, grass)
Address
One Brewers Way
Milwaukee, WI 53214-3652
Official website
www.milwaukeebrewers.com
Business phone
414-902-4400
Ticket information
414-902-4000, 800-933-7890
Field dimensions (from home plate)
To left field at foul line, 342 feet
To center field, 400 feet
To right field at foul line, 345 feet
First game played
April 6, 2001 (Brewers 5, Reds 4)

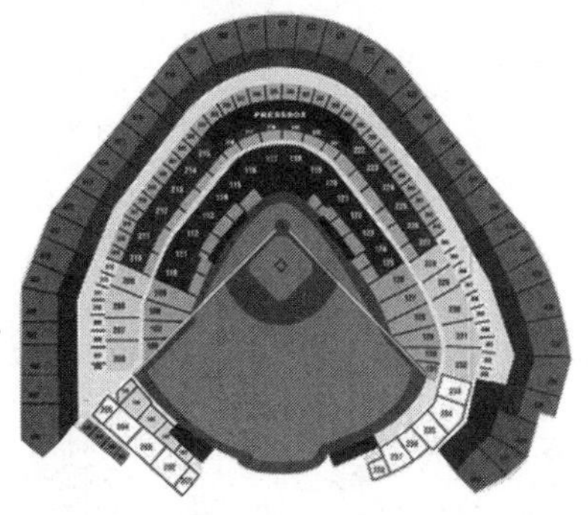

2003 REVIEW

DAY BY DAY

Date	Opp.	Res.	Score	(inn.*)	Hits	Opp. hits	Winning pitcher	Losing pitcher	Save	Record	Pos.	GB
3-31	At StL.	L	9-11		12	12	Springer	DeJean	Kline	0-1	T5th	1.0
4-2	At StL.	L	0-7		5	13	Williams	Rusch		0-2	T5th	2.0
4-3	At StL.	L	4-6		8	13	Stephenson	Kinney	Kline	0-3	T5th	3.0
4-4	S.F	L	5-7		10	12	Brower	Vizcaino	Worrell	0-4	6th	4.0
4-5	S.F	L	5-6		11	9	Ainsworth	Sheets	Eyre	0-5	6th	4.0
4-6	S.F	L	0-5		7	8	Rueter	Franklin	Brower	0-6	6th	5.0
4-8	At Pit.	W	5-3		8	5	Rusch	Wells	DeJean	1-6	6th	4.0
4-9	At Pit.	W	3-2		5	6	Ritchie	Fogg	DeJean	2-6	6th	3.5
4-10	At Pit.	L	1-3		7	7	Suppan	Sheets	Williams	2-7	6th	4.5
4-11	At Ari.	W	11-7		16	10	Franklin	Johnson		3-7	6th	4.5
4-12	At Ari.	W	3-2		6	7	Kinney	Schilling	DeJean	4-7	T5th	3.5
4-13	At Ari.	L	3-9		10	17	Dessens	Rusch		4-8	T5th	3.5
4-14	StL.	L	5-7		9	17	Tomko	Ritchie	Kline	4-9	6th	3.5
4-15	StL.	W	6-1		12	6	Sheets	Stephenson		5-9	T5th	3.0
4-16	StL.	L	2-15		6	16	Morris	Franklin		5-10	T5th	4.0
4-17	Hou.	W	4-2		12	6	Kinney	Redding	de los Santos	6-10	5th	4.0
4-18	Hou.	L	5-11		11	17	Oswalt	Rusch		6-11	5th	5.0
4-19	Hou.	W	3-2	(14)	12	13	Foster	Linebrink		7-11	5th	5.0
4-20	Hou.	W	5-4		9	8	Leskanic	Munro	DeJean	8-11	5th	4.0
4-22	At Fla.	L	2-4		10	6	Almanza	de los Santos	Looper	8-12	5th	5.0
4-23	At Fla.	L	4-5	(12)	12	17	Almanza	Nance		8-13	5th	5.0
4-24	At Fla.	L	2-4		4	9	Redman	Ritchie		8-14	T5th	5.0
4-25	At Atl.	W	12-5		12	13	Sheets	Reynolds		9-14	5th	5.0
4-26	At Atl.	L	2-3		5	7	King	de los Santos	Smoltz	9-15	T5th	5.0
4-27	At Atl.	L	1-7		5	13	Ortiz	Rusch		9-16	6th	5.0
4-29	Mon.	L	2-3		5	8	Stewart	DeJean	Biddle	9-17	6th	6.0
4-30	Mon.	L	5-9		9	13	Hernandez	Sheets		9-18	6th	6.0
5-1	Mon.	L	0-5		3	9	Day	Franklin		9-19	6th	7.0
5-2	N.Y.	L	3-9		8	15	Glavine	Rusch		9-20	6th	8.0
5-3	N.Y.	W	3-2		4	8	Foster	Weathers	DeJean	10-20	6th	7.0
5-4	N.Y.	L	3-5		5	5	Leiter	Kinney	Benitez	10-21	6th	8.0
5-5	At Chi.	W	5-3		7	6	Sheets	Clement	DeJean	11-21	6th	7.0
5-6	At Chi.	W	9-6		9	8	Leskanic	Cruz	DeJean	12-21	6th	6.0
5-7	At Chi.	L	1-2		5	10	Estes	Rusch	Borowski	12-22	6th	7.0
5-9	At Cin.	L	6-7	(10)	14	7	Reith	Vizcaino		12-23	6th	7.0
5-10	At Cin.	W	9-3		10	13	Sheets	Riedling		13-23	6th	7.0
5-11	At Cin.	L	5-7		9	8	Austin	Franklin	Williamson	13-24	6th	7.5
5-12	Chi.	L	5-11		10	19	Prior	Rusch		13-25	6th	8.5
5-13	Chi.	L	2-7		5	13	Estes	Quevedo		13-26	6th	9.5
5-14	Chi.	L	1-6		3	8	Zambrano	Kinney		13-27	6th	10.5
5-15	Chi.	L	2-4	(17)	9	12	Farnsworth	Kieschnick	Wellemeyer	13-28	6th	11.5
5-16	Cin.	W	12-3		14	7	Franklin	Dempster		14-28	6th	10.5
5-17	Cin.	W	8-6		8	12	DeJean	Williamson		15-28	6th	10.5
5-18	Cin.	L	3-6	(10)	9	9	Sullivan	DeJean	Williamson	15-29	6th	10.5
5-19	S.D.	W	6-5		9	10	Kinney	Keisler	DeJean	16-29	6th	9.5
5-20	S.D.	W	8-7		9	11	DeJean	Herges		17-29	6th	9.0
5-21	S.D.	W	10-0		12	2	Franklin	Peavy		18-29	6th	8.0
5-23	L.A.	L	4-6		10	11	Perez	Rusch	Mota	18-30	6th	8.5
5-24	L.A.	L	0-6		2	11	Nomo	Kinney		18-31	6th	9.5
5-25	L.A.	L	1-5		4	6	Brown	Sheets		18-32	6th	10.5
5-27	At S.D.	W	4-2		7	6	Vizcaino	Matthews	DeJean	19-32	6th	9.0
5-28	At S.D.	L	6-8		12	14	Matthews	Vizcaino		19-33	6th	10.0
5-29	At S.D.	W	3-2		8	5	Estrella	Lawrence	DeJean	20-33	6th	9.5
5-30	At L.A.	W	5-3		7	6	Sheets	Nomo	DeJean	21-33	6th	8.5
5-31	At L.A.	L	0-3		6	9	Brown	Quevedo	Gagne	21-34	6th	9.5
6-1	At L.A.	W	4-3		8	6	Durocher	Mota	DeJean	22-34	6th	8.5
6-5†	At N.Y.	W	8-7		13	10	Kinney	Trachsel	DeJean	23-34		
6-5‡	At N.Y.	W	5-3		9	8	Sheets	Glavine	DeJean	24-34	6th	8.0
6-6	Bos.	W	9-3		12	5	Durocher	Almonte		25-34	6th	8.0
6-7	Bos.	L	10-11		12	14	Lyon	DeJean	Timlin	25-35	6th	9.0
6-8	Bos.	L	1-9		6	12	Lowe	Rusch		25-36	6th	10.0
6-10	Fla.	L	4-12		11	13	Redman	Sheets		25-37	6th	10.0
6-11	Fla.	L	5-6		13	9	Willis	Franklin	Looper	25-38	6th	11.0
6-12	Fla.	W	6-5		6	12	Kinney	Pavano	DeJean	26-38	5th	10.0

Date	Opp.	Res.	Score	(inn.*)	Hits	Opp. hits	Winning pitcher	Losing pitcher	Save	Record	Pos.	GB
6-13	At Bal.	L	2-7		8	10	Ponson	Rusch		26-39	5th	10.0
6-14	At Bal.	W	8-3		14	9	Quevedo	Johnson		27-39	5th	10.0
6-15	At Bal.	L	4-5		10	10	Lopez	Sheets	Julio	27-40	6th	10.0
6-16	StL.	W	9-4		11	9	Leskanic	Eldred		28-40	5th	10.0
6-17	StL.	L	3-12		7	16	Stephenson	Kinney		28-41	6th	10.0
6-18	StL.	L	1-9		7	13	Simontacchi	Rusch		28-42	6th	11.0
6-19	StL.	L	4-8		12	11	Tomko	Quevedo	Isringhausen	28-43	6th	11.0
6-20	Min.	W	3-2	(10)	7	5	Leskanic	Rincon		29-43	6th	10.0
6-21	Min.	W	8-1		9	5	Franklin	Lohse		30-43	6th	9.5
6-22	Min.	L	3-8		11	12	Rogers	Kinney		30-44	6th	10.5
6-24	At Chi.	L	1-9		9	13	Wood	Quevedo		30-45	6th	11.0
6-25	At Chi.	W	12-6	(10)	16	7	Vizcaino	Wellemeyer		31-45	6th	10.0
6-26	At Chi.	W	5-3		6	6	Estrella	Borowski	DeJean	32-45	6th	9.0
6-27	At Min.	W	13-1		19	8	Kinney	Lohse		33-45	6th	8.0
6-28	At Min.	L	2-5		9	13	Rogers	Burba	Guardado	33-46	6th	9.0
6-29	At Min.	L	4-5	(10)	9	14	Hawkins	DeJean		33-47	6th	10.0
7-1	At Hou.	L	5-6	(10)	8	9	Stone	DeJean		33-48	6th	9.5
7-2	At Hou.	W	5-3	(11)	10	7	de los Santos	Stone	Estrella	34-48	6th	8.5
7-3	At Hou.	L	3-7		8	7	Robertson	Kinney	Dotel	34-49	6th	9.5
7-4	Col.	L	6-8		14	12	Reed	Estrella	Speier	34-50	6th	10.5
7-5	Col.	L	8-9		8	12	Oliver	Ford	Fuentes	34-51	6th	10.5
7-6	Col.	W	3-1		7	4	Sheets	Jimenez	DeJean	35-51	6th	10.5
7-7	Pit.	W	9-2		10	4	Franklin	Wells		36-51	6th	9.5
7-8	Pit.	L	7-8	(10)	9	12	Williams	DeJean	Torres	36-52	6th	9.5
7-9	Pit.	W	2-1	(12)	12	6	Kieschnick	Beimel		37-52	6th	9.5
7-10	Pit.	L	4-5		8	10	Suppan	Ford		37-53	6th	10.5
7-11	Cin.	L	1-6		10	11	Dempster	Sheets		37-54	6th	11.5
7-12	Cin.	L	1-5		5	8	Haynes	Franklin		37-55	6th	11.5
7-13	Cin.	L	8-10	(12)	12	11	Heredia	Estrella		37-56	6th	12.5
7-17	At Pit.	W	7-5		9	9	Franklin	Benson	Estrella	38-56	6th	12.5
7-18	At Pit.	L	2-7		11	13	Suppan	Rusch		38-57	6th	13.5
7-19	At Pit.	W	1-0		9	8	Sheets	D'Amico	Kolb	39-57	6th	13.5
7-20	At Pit.	L	3-6		12	10	Wells	Ford	Lincoln	39-58	6th	14.5
7-21	At Cin.	L	2-11		4	15	Acevedo	Kinney		39-59	6th	14.5
7-22	At Cin.	W	6-4		10	11	Franklin	Wilson	Kolb	40-59	6th	14.5
7-23	Hou.	L	2-3	(11)	7	7	Gallo	Kolb	Wagner	40-60	6th	15.5
7-24	Hou.	W	2-1		6	6	Sheets	Villone	Estrella	41-60	6th	14.5
7-25	At Col.	L	3-7		8	10	Tsao	Obermueller		41-61	6th	14.5
7-26	At Col.	L	8-13		14	16	Cook	de los Santos		41-62	6th	15.5
7-27	At Col.	L	1-6		7	7	Jennings	Franklin		41-63	6th	15.5
7-28	At N.Y.	W	4-2		7	5	Estrella	Weathers	Kolb	42-63	6th	15.0
7-29	At N.Y.	W	6-3		10	8	Sheets	Wheeler	DeJean	43-63	6th	14.0
7-30	At N.Y.	L	0-2		5	5	Leiter	Obermueller	Weathers	43-64	6th	15.0
7-31	At N.Y.	W	4-3		9	8	Kinney	Heilman	Kolb	44-64	6th	14.0
8-1	At Mon.	L	4-8		11	13	Ohka	Franklin		44-65	6th	15.0
8-2	At Mon.	L	1-7		8	6	Vazquez	Manning		44-66	6th	15.0
8-3	At Mon.	L	2-4		8	10	Hernandez	Sheets	Biddle	44-67	6th	16.0
8-5	Atl.	W	4-3		9	6	DeJean	Holmes	Kolb	45-67	6th	15.0
8-6	Atl.	L	2-10		12	12	Maddux	Franklin		45-68	6th	16.0
8-7	Atl.	L	1-7		5	8	Hampton	Obermueller		45-69	6th	16.0
8-8	Fla.	L	3-5		9	7	Pavano	Sheets	Looper	45-70	6th	17.0
8-9	Fla.	L	1-7		6	9	Redman	Manning		45-71	6th	17.0
8-10	Fla.	W	5-4		10	10	de los Santos	Penny	Kolb	46-71	6th	17.0
8-12	At Phi.	W	6-3		7	5	Franklin	Duckworth	Kolb	47-71	6th	16.5
8-13	At Phi.	L	4-11		9	14	Millwood	Sheets		47-72	6th	16.5
8-14	At Phi.	L	3-4		8	12	Wolf	Obermueller	Williams	47-73	6th	16.5
8-15	At Pit.	L	3-6		8	8	Figueroa	Kinney	Tavarez	47-74	6th	17.0
8-16	At Pit.	W	6-4		9	10	Vizcaino	Lincoln	Kolb	48-74	6th	16.5
8-17	At Pit.	L	2-5		8	12	Fogg	Franklin	Tavarez	48-75	6th	16.5
8-19	Phi.	W	6-4		8	10	DeJean	Wendell	Kolb	49-75	6th	16.5
8-20	Phi.	W	10-1		12	11	Kinney	Wolf		50-75	6th	15.5
8-21	Phi.	W	5-2		8	11	Estrella	Padilla	Kolb	51-75	6th	15.5
8-22	Pit.	W	3-2		7	4	Franklin	Wells	Kolb	52-75	6th	14.5
8-23	Pit.	W	7-6		12	14	Estrella	Corey		53-75	6th	13.5
8-24	Pit.	W	10-9		12	12	Kolb	Gonzalez		54-75	6th	13.5
8-25	At Cin.	W	10-6		12	9	Kinney	Harang	Kolb	55-75	6th	13.0
8-26	At Cin.	W	7-1		9	4	Davis	Serafini		56-75	6th	13.0
8-27	At Cin.	W	6-2		9	12	Franklin	Etherton		57-75	6th	13.0
8-28	At Cin.	W	4-3	(10)	14	8	de los Santos	Reitsma	Kolb	58-75	T5th	12.0
8-29	At Chi.	L	2-4		7	12	Clement	Sheets		58-76	6th	12.0
8-30	At Chi.	W	9-5		9	10	Kinney	Estes		59-76	T5th	12.0
8-31	At Chi.	W	2-0		9	6	Davis	Cruz	Kolb	60-76	5th	12.0

Date	Opp.	Res.	Score	(inn.*)	Hits	Opp. hits	Winning pitcher	Losing pitcher	Save	Record	Pos.	GB
9-1	Cin.	L	4-5		9	9	Etherton	Franklin	Reitsma	60-77	T5th	12.0
9-2	Cin.	W	4-3		9	4	Vizcaino	Graves	Kolb	61-77	5th	11.5
9-3	Cin.	W	9-6		9	10	Estrella	Randall	Kolb	62-77	5th	11.0
9-5	Chi.	L	2-4		6	6	Cruz	Sheets	Borowski	62-78	5th	12.0
9-6	Chi.	L	4-8		11	9	Prior	Kinney		62-79	5th	13.0
9-7	Chi.	L	2-9		9	11	Wood	Davis		62-80	5th	13.5
9-8	Hou.	L	4-8		5	12	Oswalt	Franklin		62-81	5th	14.0
9-9	Hou.	L	6-7		8	12	Lidge	Kolb	Wagner	62-82	T5th	15.0
9-10	Hou.	L	1-3		7	9	Robertson	Martinez	Wagner	62-83	T5th	16.0
9-11	Hou.	W	5-3		10	9	Sheets	Villone	Kolb	63-83	T5th	15.0
9-12	At S.F	L	2-8		9	10	Schmidt	Kinney		63-84	T5th	16.0
9-13	At S.F	W	5-4		7	12	Davis	Ponson	Kolb	64-84	5th	16.0
9-14	At S.F	L	4-5	(11)	9	11	Rodriguez	Estrella		64-85	T5th	17.0
9-15	At StL.	L	2-11		7	16	Tomko	Obermueller		64-86	T5th	17.5
9-16	At StL.	L	5-6		5	9	Hitchcock	Martinez	Isringhausen	64-87	6th	18.5
9-17	At StL.	W	7-6		10	13	Estrella	Isringhausen	Kolb	65-87	T5th	17.5
9-18	At StL.	L	0-13		3	16	Williams	Kinney		65-88	T5th	18.5
9-19	Ari.	L	2-3		10	9	Villarreal	Nance	Mantei	65-89	T5th	19.5
9-20	Ari.	L	4-10		10	14	Dessens	Franklin	Valverde	65-90	6th	19.5
9-21	Ari.	W	6-4		10	9	Obermueller	Schilling	Kolb	66-90	6th	18.5
9-23	StL.	L	1-5		3	10	Williams	Sheets		66-91	6th	19.0
9-24	StL.	L	4-8		8	13	Morris	Kinney	Isringhausen	66-92	6th	20.0
9-25	At Hou.	L	1-6		6	9	Redding	Davis		66-93	6th	20.0
9-26	At Hou.	W	12-5		12	14	Burba	Robertson	Rusch	67-93	6th	19.5
9-27	At Hou.	W	5-2		9	10	Obermueller	Villone	Kolb	68-93	6th	20.0
9-28	At Hou.	L	5-8		8	10	Stone	Martinez		68-94	6th	20.0

Monthly records: March (0-1), April (9-17), May (12-16), June (12-13), July (11-17), August (16-12), September (8-18).
*Innings, if other than nine. † First game of a doubleheader. ‡ Second game of a doubleheader.

RECORDS

2003 regular-season record: 68-94
Position: 6th in N.L. Central
Home: 31-50 **Road:** 37-44
N.L. East: 14-22 **N.L. Central:** 37-47
N.L. West: 12-18 A.L. 5-7
Vs. LH starters: 16-22
Vs. RH starters: 52-72
Grass: 66-87 **Artificial:** 2-7
Day: 22-34 **Night:** 46-60
1-Run: 25-21 **X-inn.:** 6-10
Doubleheaders: 1-0-0
Team record past five years: 339-470 (.419, ranks 16th in league in that span)

TEAM LEADERS

Batting average: Scott Podsednik (.314).
At-bats: Richie Sexson (606).
Runs: Scott Podsednik (100).
Hits: Scott Podsednik (175).
Total Bases: Richie Sexson (332).
Doubles: Geoff Jenkins (30).
Triples: Scott Podsednik (8).
Home runs: Richie Sexson (45).
Runs batted in: Richie Sexson (124).
Stolen bases: Scott Podsednik (43).
Slugging percentage: Richie Sexson (.548).
On-base percentage: Scott Podsednik (.379).
Wins: Ben Sheets (11).
Earned-run average: Ben Sheets (4.45).
Complete games: Doug Davis, Wayne Franklin, Matt Kinney, Glendon Rusch, Ben Sheets (1).
Shutouts: Wayne Franklin (1).
Saves: Danny Kolb (21).
Innings pitched: Ben Sheets (220.2).
Strikeouts: Ben Sheets (157).

GAMES BY POSITION

Catcher: Eddie Perez 102, Keith Osik 78.
First base: Richie Sexson 162.
Second base: Eric Young 99, Keith Ginter 53, Bill Hall 18, Enrique Cruz 6, Rickie Weeks 4.
Third base: Wes Helms 130, Keith Ginter 40, Enrique Cruz 2, Bill Hall 1.
Shortstop: Royce Clayton 141, Bill Hall 18, Enrique Cruz 13, Keith Ginter 2.
Outfield: Scott Podsednik 139, Geoff Jenkins 123, Brady Clark 105, John Vander Wal 89, Alex Sanchez 36, Jason Conti 20, Mark Smith 15, Jeffrey Hammonds 10, Pete Zoccolillo 7, Brooks Kieschnick 3, Keith Ginter 2.
Designated hitter: Brooks Kieschnick 4, Geoff Jenkins 1, Eric Young 1.

TOP DRAFT CHOICES

1. **Rickie Weeks,** 2B, Southern University.
2. **Anthony Gwynn,** OF, San Diego State.
3. **Lou Palmisano,** C, Broward (Fla.) CC.
4. **Charlie Fermaint,** OF, Jose S. Alegria H.S., Dorado, Puerto Rico.
5. **Bryan Opdyke,** C, Catalina Foothills H.S., Tucson.
6. **Robbie Wooley,** RHP, Taylor H.S., Kokomo, Ind.
7. **Brian Montalbo,** RHP, California.
8. **Ryan Marion,** RHP, Glenn H.S., Kernersville, N.C.
9. **Greg Kloosterman,** LHP, Bethel College (Ind.).
10. **Tyler Morrison,** RHP, Glendora (Calif.) H.S.

MONTREAL EXPOS

NATIONAL LEAGUE EAST DIVISION

2004 SEASON

April

SUN	MON	TUE	WED	THU	FRI	SAT
4	5	6 FLA	7 FLA	8 FLA	9 * NYM	10 * NYM
11 * NYM	12	13 * FLA	14 * FLA	15 * FLA	16 PHI	17 PHI
18 PHI	19 NYM	20 NYM	21 NYM	22 NYM	23 PHI	24 PHI
25 PHI	26 SD	27 SD	28 SD	29 SD	30 LA	

May

SUN	MON	TUE	WED	THU	FRI	SAT
						1 LA
2 LA	3	4 COL	5 COL	6 COL	7 STL	8 STL
9 STL	10	11 MIL	12 MIL	13 MIL	14 ARI	15 ARI
16 ARI	17	18 * MIL	19 * MIL	20 * MIL	21 * SF	22* SF
23 * SF	24 ATL	25 ATL	26 ATL	27	28 CIN	29 CIN
30 CIN	31 ATL					

June

SUN	MON	TUE	WED	THU	FRI	SAT
		1 ATL	2 ATL	3	4 CIN	5 CIN
6 CIN	7	8 KC	9 KC	10 KC	11 SEA	12 SEA
13 SEA	14	15 MIN	16 MIN	17 MIN	18 CHW	19 CHW
20 CHW	21	22 PHI	23 PHI	24 PHI	25 TOR	26 TOR
27 TOR	28 PHI	29 PHI	30 PHI			

July

SUN	MON	TUE	WED	THU	FRI	SAT
				1 PHI	2 * TOR	3 * TOR
4 * TOR	5 * ATL	6 * ATL	7 * ATL	8 * PIT	9 * PIT	10 * PIT
11 * PIT	12	13 All-Star	14	15 ATL	16 ATL	17 ATL
18 ATL	19 PIT	20 PIT	21 NYM	22 NYM	23 FLA	24 FLA
25 FLA	26 NYM	27 NYM	28 NYM	29 NYM	30 FLA	31 FLA

August

SUN	MON	TUE	WED	THU	FRI	SAT
1 FLA	2	3 STL	4 STL	5 STL	6 HOU	7 HOU
8 HOU	9	10 ARI	11 ARI	12 ARI	13 HOU	14 HOU
15 HOU	16 SF	17 SF	18 SF	19	20 COL	21 COL
22 COL	23 LA	24 LA	25 LA	26 LA	27 SD	28 SD
29 SD	30 CHC	31 CHC				

Sept./Oct.

SUN	MON	TUE	WED	THU	FRI	SAT
			1 CHC	2	3 ATL	4 ATL
5 ATL	6 CHC	7 CHC	8 CHC	9	10 ATL	11 ATL
12 ATL	13 FLA	14 FLA	15 FLA	16 FLA	17 PHI	18 PHI
19 PHI	20	21 NYM	22 NYM	23 NYM	24 PHI	25 PHI
26 PHI	27 FLA	28 FLA	29 FLA	30	1 NYM	2 NYM
3 NYM	4	5	6	7	8	9

Home games shaded. All-Star Game July 13 at Houston. Schedule subject to change. * San Juan, Puerto Rico.

CLUB DIRECTORY

President
Tony Tavares
Vice president & general manager
Omar Minaya
Assistant general manager
Tony Siegle

Director, player development
Adam Wogan
Director, scouting
Dana Brown
Director, pro scouting
Lee MacPhail

Director, media services
Monique Giroux
Director, baseball information
John Dever

MINOR LEAGUE AFFILIATES

Class	Team	League	Manager
AAA	Edmonton	Pacific Coast	Dave Huppert
AA	Harrisburg	Eastern	Dave Machemer
Advanced A	Brevard County	Florida State	Tim Raines
A	Savannah	South Atlantic	Bob Henley
Short-Season A	Vermont	New York-Pennsylvania	Joe Marchese
Rookie	Melbourne	Gulf Coast	Arturo Defreites

BROADCAST INFORMATION

Radio: To be announced.
TV: To be announced.

SPRING TRAINING

Ballpark (city): Space Coast Stadium (Melbourne, Fla.).
Ticket information: 321-633-8119.

More on the Expos at www.foxsports.com/named/FS/MLB/teams

SPRING TRAINING ROSTER

Manager—Frank Robinson (20).
Coaches—Manny Acta (14), Tom McCraw (17), Jerry Morales (28), Bob Natal (13), Randy St. Claire (49).

No.	PITCHERS	B/T	Ht./Wt.	Age*	2003 Clubs
36	Armas, Tony	R/R	6-3/225	25	Montreal
56	Ayala, Luis	R/R	6-2/170	26	Gulf Coast Expos, Montreal
	Bentz, Chad	R/L	6-2/215	23	Harrisburg
60	Biddle, Rocky	R/R	6-3/230	27	Montreal
	Choate, Randy	L/L	6-2/190	28	New York A.L., Columbus
53	Corcoran, Roy	R/R	5-10/170	23	Brevard County, Harrisburg, Montreal, Edmonton
62	Cordero, Chad	R/R	6-0/195	22	Brevard County, Montreal
54	Day, Zach	R/R	6-4/210	25	Gulf Coast Expos, Brevard County, Montreal
58	Eischen, Joey	L/L	6-0/215	33	Montreal
61	Hernandez, Livan	R/R	6-2/240	29	Montreal
	Hill, Shawn	R/R	6-2/185	22	Brevard County, Harrisburg
31	Kim, Sun-Woo	R/R	6-1/185	26	Montreal, Edmonton
24	Ohka, Tomo	R/R	6-1/180	28	Montreal
43	Smith, Dan	R/R	6-3/225	28	Montreal
	Song, Seung	R/R	6-1/190	23	Harrisburg, Edmonton
52	Tucker, T.J.	R/R	6-3/265	25	Edmonton, Montreal
33	Vargas, Claudio	R/R	6-3/225	24	Edmonton, Harrisburg, Montreal

No.	CATCHERS	B/T	Ht./Wt.	Age*	2003 Clubs
39	Schneider, Brian	L/R	6-1/200	27	Montreal

No.	INFIELDERS	B/T	Ht./Wt.	Age*	2003 Clubs
	Batista, Tony	R/R	6-0/208	30	Baltimore
18	Cabrera, Orlando	R/R	5-9/180	29	Montreal
2	Carroll, Jamey	R/R	5-9/175	30	Montreal
	Fox, Andy	L/R	6-4/200	33	Florida
58	Hodges, Scott	L/R	6-0/190	25	Edmonton
	Johnson, Nick	L/L	6-3/195	25	Columbus, Trenton, New York A.L.
	Labandeira, Josh	R/R	5-7/180	25	Harrisburg, Brevard County
4	Mateo, Henry	B/R	6-0/180	27	Montreal
3	Vidro, Jose	B/R	5-11/195	29	Montreal

No.	OUTFIELDERS	B/T	Ht./Wt.	Age*	2003 Clubs
11	Bergeron, Peter	L/R	6-0/190	26	Edmonton
22	Calloway, Ron	L/L	6-1/210	27	Montreal
29	Cepicky, Matt	L/R	6-2/225	26	Montreal, Edmonton
19	Chavez, Endy	L/L	5-9/170	26	Montreal
	Church, Ryan	L/L	6-1/190	25	Akron
	Everett, Carl	B/R	6-0/215	32	Texas, Chicago A.L.
	Pascucci, Val	R/R	6-6/235	25	Edmonton
	Rivera, Juan	R/R	6-2/170	25	Columbus, New York A.L.
48	Sledge, Terrmel	L/L	6-0/180	27	Edmonton
	Watson, Brandon	L/R	6-1/170	22	Harrisburg
6	Wilkerson, Brad	L/L	6-0/205	26	Montreal

Invited to spring training: RHP Jeremy Fikac, C Gregg Zaun.

*Age as of April 1, 2004.

BALLPARK INFORMATION

Ballpark (capacity, surface)
Olympic Stadium (46,620, artificial)

Address
P.O. Box 500, Station M
Montreal, Que. H1V 3P2

Official website
www.montrealexpos.com

Business phone
514-253-3434

Ticket information
800-GO-EXPOS

Field dimensions (from home plate)
To left field at foul line, 325 feet
To center field, 404 feet
To right field at foul line, 325 feet

First game played
April 15, 1977 (Phillies 7, Expos 2)

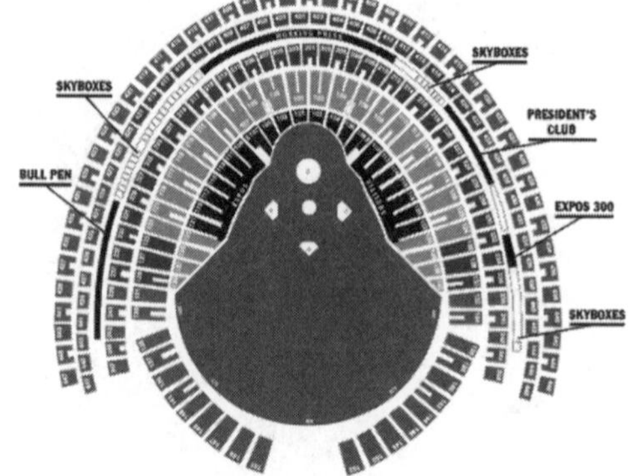

2003 REVIEW

DAY BY DAY

Date	Opp.	Res.	Score	(inn.*)	Hits	Opp. hits	Winning pitcher	Losing pitcher	Save	Record	Pos.	GB
3-31	At Atl.	W	10-2		14	11	Armas	Maddux		1-0	T1st	...
4-2	At Atl.	W	3-0		9	3	Day	Ramirez	Biddle	2-0	T1st	...
4-3	At Atl.	W	4-0		6	9	Vazquez	Ortiz		3-0	1st	+1.0
4-4	At N.Y.	L	0-4		5	13	Cone	Ohka		3-1	1st	+1.0
4-5	At N.Y.	L	1-3		6	8	Glavine	Armas	Benitez	3-2	T1st	...
4-6	At N.Y.	W	8-5		17	7	Stewart	Benitez	Biddle	4-2	1st	+1.0
4-8	At Chi.	L	1-6		4	7	Clement	Day		4-3	T1st	...
4-9	At Chi.	L	0-3		4	7	Prior	Vazquez		4-4	T2nd	1.0
4-10	At Chi.	W	7-1		11	4	Armas	Estes		5-4	T1st	...
4-11	N.Y.■	W	10-0		11	2	Ohka	Cone		6-4	1st	+1.0
4-12	N.Y.■	W	5-4		11	10	Hernandez	Seo	Biddle	7-4	1st	+1.0
4-13	N.Y.■	W	2-1	(10)	6	6	Biddle	Stanton		8-4	1st	+1.0
4-14	N.Y.■	W	5-3		6	7	Smith	Strickland	Biddle	9-4	1st	+1.0
4-15	Atl.■	L	1-2	(10)	9	7	Bong	Smith	Smoltz	9-5	T1st	...
4-16	Atl.■	L	2-3		7	11	Ramirez	Ohka	Smoltz	9-6	T1st	...
4-17	Atl.■	L	8-14	(10)	9	13	Bong	Biddle		9-7	T1st	...
4-19§	Cin.■	W	8-7	(10)	11	12	Ayala	Williamson		10-7		
4-19∞	Cin.■	W	9-5		11	8	Vazquez	Anderson		11-7	1st	+1.0
4-20	Cin.■	L	5-7		8	11	Sullivan	Ayala	Williamson	11-8	1st	+1.0
4-22	Ari.	W	4-0		7	9	Ohka	Good		12-8	1st	+1.0
4-23	Ari.	L	2-6		6	12	Dessens	Hernandez		12-9	T1st	...
4-24	Ari.	W	1-0		3	6	Vazquez	Kim	Biddle	13-9	T1st	...
4-25	Hou.	W	10-2		14	6	Day	Robertson		14-9	1st	+1.0
4-26	Hou.	W	3-2	(10)	5	8	Biddle	Wagner		15-9	1st	+1.0
4-27	Hou.	L	3-6		7	10	Redding	Ohka	Dotel	15-10	T1st	...
4-29	At Mil.	W	3-2		8	5	Stewart	DeJean	Biddle	16-10	T1st	...
4-30	At Mil.	W	9-5		13	9	Hernandez	Sheets		17-10	T1st	...
5-1	At Mil.	W	5-0		9	3	Day	Franklin		18-10	T1st	...
5-2	At StL.	L	1-8		6	13	Simontacchi	Ohka		18-11	2nd	1.0
5-3	At StL.	L	1-3		9	6	Stephenson	Vargas	Calero	18-12	2nd	1.0
5-4	At StL.	L	2-6		6	6	Morris	Vazquez		18-13	3rd	2.0
5-6	S.D.	W	4-2		9	7	Hernandez	Peavy	Biddle	19-13	2nd	2.0
5-7	S.D.	W	12-9	(10)	16	11	Biddle	Orosco		20-13	2nd	1.5
5-8	S.D.	W	12-5		14	10	Ohka	Lawrence		21-13	2nd	2.0
5-9	L.A.	L	5-9		10	15	Mota	Stewart		21-14	2nd	2.0
5-10	L.A.	W	6-5		10	13	Ayala	Martin	Biddle	22-14	2nd	2.0
5-11	L.A.	L	3-4		5	7	Perez	Hernandez	Gagne	22-15	2nd	3.0
5-12	At S.F	W	4-3		9	12	Day	Moss	Biddle	23-15	2nd	3.0
5-13	At S.F	W	6-4		9	10	Smith	Ainsworth	Biddle	24-15	2nd	3.0
5-14	At S.F	W	6-3		8	6	Vargas	Foppert		25-15	2nd	2.0
5-15	At Col.	L	2-4		8	10	Jones	Tucker	Jimenez	25-16	2nd	3.0
5-16	At Col.	W	4-1		10	6	Ayala	Cruz	Biddle	26-16	2nd	3.0
5-17	At Col.	W	6-4	(10)	11	9	Ayala	Jones	Biddle	27-16	2nd	3.0
5-18	At Col.	L	0-4		6	10	Chacon	Ohka		27-17	2nd	4.0
5-20	Fla.	W	6-4		13	8	Vazquez	Willis	Biddle	28-17	2nd	3.0
5-21	Fla.	W	7-2		11	8	Vargas	Pavano		29-17	2nd	2.0
5-22	Fla.	W	8-2		12	7	Hernandez	Tejera		30-17	2nd	2.0
5-23	Phi.	L	2-4		7	11	Millwood	Day	Mesa	30-18	2nd	2.0
5-24	Phi.	W	3-2		7	4	Ayala	Silva		31-18	2nd	2.0
5-25	Phi.	W	5-3		6	8	Vazquez	Myers	Biddle	32-18	2nd	2.0
5-26	At Fla.	L	1-5		5	10	Pavano	Vargas		32-19	2nd	2.0
5-28†	At Fla.	L	3-4		4	12	Phelps	Hernandez	Looper	32-20		
5-28‡	At Fla.	L	0-6		7	9	Tejera	Day		32-21	2nd	4.0
5-29	At Fla.	W	3-2		12	8	Ohka	Almanza	Biddle	33-21	2nd	3.5
5-30	At Phi.	L	5-12		9	12	Cormier	Vazquez		33-22	2nd	4.5
6-1†	At Phi.	L	3-4		3	9	Wolf	Hernandez	Mesa	33-23		
6-1‡	At Phi.	L	1-4		5	8	Myers	Smith	Mesa	33-24	2nd	4.5
6-3	Ana.■	L	4-15		6	22	Ortiz	Ohka		33-25	2nd	5.5
6-4	Ana.■	L	2-11		7	17	Washburn	Kim		33-26	2nd	6.5
6-5	Ana.■	W	8-7	(14)	15	12	Eischen	Callaway		34-26	2nd	6.5
6-6	Tex.■	W	13-10		13	14	Hernandez	Lewis		35-26	2nd	6.0
6-7	Tex.■	W	5-4		4	8	Vargas	Shouse	Ayala	36-26	2nd	6.0
6-8	Tex.■	W	3-2		8	9	Stewart	Cordero	Biddle	37-26	2nd	6.0
6-10	At Sea.	W	7-3		11	9	Vazquez	Meche	Ayala	38-26	2nd	5.0

Date	Opp.	Res.	Score	(inn.*)	Hits	Opp. hits	Winning pitcher	Losing pitcher	Save	Record	Pos.	GB
6-11	At Sea.	W	3-1		9	8	Hernandez	Pineiro	Biddle	39-26	2nd	5.0
6-12	At Sea.	L	0-1		5	5	Franklin	Vargas	Rhodes	39-27	2nd	6.0
6-13	At Oak.	L	4-8		10	8	Mulder	Ohka		39-28	2nd	6.0
6-14	At Oak.	L	4-5		13	8	Rincon	Ayala	Foulke	39-29	2nd	7.0
6-15	At Oak.	L	1-9		6	9	Hudson	Vazquez		39-30	2nd	7.0
6-18†	At Pit.	L	3-7		8	13	D'Amico	Hernandez	Williams	39-31		
6-18‡	At Pit.	L	3-4		8	11	Torres	Biddle		39-32	2nd	8.0
6-19	At Pit.	W	5-2		15	9	Ohka	Torres	Biddle	40-32	2nd	7.0
6-20	Tor.	L	4-8		8	13	Lidle	Vazquez		40-33	2nd	8.0
6-21	Tor.	W	8-5		9	13	Ayala	Politte	Biddle	41-33	2nd	8.0
6-22	Tor.	L	2-4		5	11	Halladay	Hernandez	Politte	41-34	2nd	8.0
6-23	Pit.	W	3-0		8	3	Vargas	Suppan	Biddle	42-34	2nd	7.5
6-24	Pit.	W	6-4		9	8	Ohka	D'Amico	Biddle	43-34	2nd	7.5
6-25	Pit.	L	5-6		9	9	Sauerbeck	Eischen	Williams	43-35	2nd	7.5
6-27	At Tor.	L	5-6		10	9	Miller	Manon		43-36	3rd	8.0
6-28	At Tor.	W	4-2		11	5	Vargas	Davis	Biddle	44-36	3rd	7.0
6-29	At Tor.	W	10-2		13	2	Ohka	Escobar		45-36	3rd	7.0
6-30	At N.Y.	L	1-3		7	8	Trachsel	Vazquez	Benitez	45-37	3rd	7.0
7-1	At N.Y.	L	6-7		8	13	Benitez	Manon		45-38	3rd	7.0
7-2	At N.Y.	W	11-4		15	6	Hernandez	Seo		46-38	3rd	7.0
7-3	At Atl.	W	5-4		11	10	Vargas	Reynolds	Manon	47-38	3rd	6.0
7-4	At Atl.	L	6-8		8	14	Ortiz	Ohka	Smoltz	47-39	3rd	7.0
7-5	At Atl.	L	2-3		7	5	Bong	Biddle		47-40	3rd	8.0
7-6	At Atl.	L	5-7		11	10	Hampton	Drew	Smoltz	47-41	3rd	9.0
7-7	Phi.	W	8-1		10	7	Hernandez	Duckworth		48-41	3rd	9.0
7-8	Phi.	L	6-13		13	16	Myers	Vargas		48-42	3rd	10.0
7-9	Phi.	L	0-2		3	3	Millwood	Ohka		48-43	3rd	11.0
7-11	Fla.	L	4-5		5	10	Penny	Biddle	Looper	48-44	3rd	12.5
7-12	Fla.	W	7-1		11	3	Hernandez	Redman		49-44	3rd	11.5
7-13	Fla.	L	4-11		8	14	Willis	Vargas		49-45	3rd	12.5
7-17	At Phi.	L	2-5	(11)	10	11	Plesac	Drew		49-46	T3rd	13.5
7-18	At Phi.	W	3-1		11	9	Vazquez	Wolf		50-46	T3rd	13.5
7-19	At Phi.	L	3-4	(11)	7	9	Mesa	Almonte		50-47	T3rd	14.5
7-20	At Phi.	L	2-3		7	9	Myers	Vargas	Mesa	50-48	T3rd	15.5
7-21	At Fla.	L	1-4		9	10	Beckett	Knott		50-49	4th	15.5
7-22	At Fla.	L	1-9		5	13	Pavano	Ohka		50-50	4th	16.5
7-23	N.Y.	W	5-2		9	7	Vazquez	Seo	Biddle	51-50	4th	15.5
7-24	N.Y.	W	5-1		11	7	Hernandez	Glavine	Biddle	52-50	4th	15.5
7-25	Atl.	W	9-8	(11)	9	17	Ayala	Bong		53-50	4th	14.5
7-26	Atl.	L	4-15		12	18	Reynolds	Day		53-51	4th	15.5
7-27	Atl.	W	13-10		14	17	Manon	King	Biddle	54-51	4th	14.5
7-28	Atl.	L	8-10		13	14	Hampton	Vazquez	Smoltz	54-52	4th	15.5
7-29	StL.	L	1-2		4	5	Stephenson	Hernandez		54-53	4th	16.5
7-30	StL.	L	1-11		7	11	Haren	Vargas		54-54	4th	16.5
7-31	StL.	W	3-2		8	7	Day	Williams	Biddle	55-54	4th	16.5
8-1	Mil.	W	8-4		13	11	Ohka	Franklin		56-54	4th	16.5
8-2	Mil.	W	7-1		6	8	Vazquez	Manning		57-54	4th	16.5
8-3	Mil.	W	4-2		10	8	Hernandez	Sheets	Biddle	58-54	4th	15.5
8-5	At Ari.	L	5-8		10	11	Johnson	Vargas	Mantei	58-55	4th	15.5
8-6	At Ari.	L	2-3		4	12	Oropesa	Ayala	Mantei	58-56	4th	16.5
8-7	At Ari.	L	4-5	(10)	9	9	Valverde	Knott		58-57	4th	17.5
8-8	At Hou.	L	1-5		5	8	Robertson	Vazquez		58-58	4th	18.5
8-9	At Hou.	W	3-1		11	6	Hernandez	Fernandez		59-58	4th	17.5
8-10	At Hou.	L	2-8		5	9	Villone	Downs		59-59	4th	17.5
8-11	Col.	W	3-1		7	7	Day	Jennings	Biddle	60-59	4th	17.0
8-12	Col.	L	3-6	(11)	7	9	Fuentes	Biddle	Lopez	60-60	4th	17.0
8-13	Col.	W	6-5		9	10	Vazquez	Stark	Ayala	61-60	4th	17.0
8-15	S.F	W	4-1		6	5	Hernandez	Foppert		62-60	4th	17.5
8-16	S.F	W	4-1		10	7	Day	Schmidt	Biddle	63-60	4th	17.5
8-17	S.F	W	4-2		5	9	Biddle	Ponson		64-60	4th	16.5
8-18	S.F	W	4-0		9	3	Vazquez	Hermanson		65-60	4th	16.5
8-19	At L.A.	W	7-5		13	9	Ayala	Quantrill	Biddle	66-60	4th	15.5
8-20	At L.A.	L	1-4	(10)	6	10	Gagne	Biddle		66-61	4th	15.5
8-21	At L.A.	L	1-2		9	5	Perez	Day	Gagne	66-62	4th	15.5
8-22	At S.D.	L	3-5		7	12	Linebrink	Eischen	Beck	66-63	4th	16.5
8-23	At S.D.	L	0-1	(10)	4	5	Matthews	Biddle		66-64	4th	17.5
8-24	At S.D.	W	8-4		13	9	Knott	Jarvis		67-64	4th	17.5
8-25	Phi.	W	12-1		15	8	Hernandez	Wolf		68-64	4th	17.0
8-26	Phi.	W	14-10		16	14	Eischen	Williams	Ayala	69-64	4th	16.0

Date	Opp.	Res.	Score	(inn.*)	Hits	Opp. hits	Winning pitcher	Losing pitcher	Save	Record	Pos.	GB
8-27	Phi.	W	9-6		14	7	Almonte	Plesac	Biddle	70-64	4th	16.0
8-28	Phi.	W	4-0		7	4	Vazquez	Telemaco		71-64	4th	15.0
8-29	At Fla.	L	2-3		6	9	Looper	Biddle		71-65	4th	15.0
8-30	At Fla.	L	3-4		9	7	Pavano	Hernandez	Looper	71-66	4th	16.0
8-31	At Fla.	L	3-5		7	11	Redman	Day	Urbina	71-67	4th	17.0
9-1	At Fla.	L	2-5		3	12	Penny	Ohka	Looper	71-68	4th	17.0
9-2	At Phi.	L	3-5		7	8	Cormier	Vazquez	Plesac	71-69	4th	17.0
9-3	At Phi.	L	3-8		7	11	Millwood	Tucker		71-70	4th	17.0
9-5	Fla.■	W	6-2		7	9	Hernandez	Redman		72-70	4th	16.5
9-6	Fla.■	L	4-14		11	14	Penny	Ohka		72-71	4th	17.5
9-7	Fla.■	L	1-3		5	8	Willis	Vazquez	Looper	72-72	4th	18.5
9-9	Chi.■	L	3-4		7	11	Zambrano	Day	Borowski	72-73	4th	19.0
9-10	Chi.■	W	8-4		8	8	Ayala	Farnsworth		73-73	4th	19.0
9-11	Chi.■	W	3-2		11	7	Ohka	Prior	Eischen	74-73	4th	18.0
9-12	N.Y.	W	7-4		13	9	Tucker	Leiter	Ayala	75-73	4th	17.0
9-13	N.Y.	L	4-5		10	7	Trachsel	Vazquez	Roberts	75-74	4th	17.0
9-14	N.Y.	W	7-3		9	6	Day	Glavine		76-74	4th	17.0
9-15	Atl.	L	6-10		10	13	Ramirez	Hernandez		76-75	4th	18.0
9-16	Atl.	W	5-4	(10)	9	11	Biddle	Hernandez		77-75	4th	17.0
9-17	Atl.	L	4-14		10	19	Hampton	Tucker		77-76	4th	18.0
9-18	At N.Y.	W	1-0		7	3	Vazquez	Trachsel	Cordero	78-76	4th	17.5
9-19	At N.Y.	W	7-1		10	9	Day	Glavine		79-76	4th	17.5
9-20	At N.Y.	W	4-3	(10)	8	11	Cordero	Stanton	Biddle	80-76	4th	16.5
9-21	At N.Y.	W	4-2		10	8	Ayala	Roberts	Biddle	81-76	4th	16.5
9-23	At Atl.	L	0-2		7	5	Wright	Vazquez	Smoltz	81-77	4th	17.0
9-24	At Atl.	L	1-9		6	12	Ortiz	Day		81-78	4th	18.0
9-26	At Cin.	W	5-1		9	5	Ohka	Harang		82-78	4th	18.0
9-27	At Cin.	L	2-4		5	7	Reith	Hernandez		82-79	4th	18.0
9-28	At Cin.	W	2-1		6	5	Tucker	Randall	Biddle	83-79	4th	18.0

Monthly records: March (1-0), April (16-10), May (16-12), June (12-15), July (10-17), August (16-13), September (12-12). *Innings, if other than nine. ■ At Hiram Bithorn Stadium, San Juan, Puerto Rico. † First game of a doubleheader. ‡ Second game of a doubleheader. § Day separate admission. ∞ Night separate admission.

RECORDS

2003 regular-season record: 83-79
Position: 4th in N.L. East
Home: 52-29 **Road:** 31-50
N.L. East: 35-41 **N.L. Central:** 20-16
N.L. West: 19-13 A.L. 9-9
Vs. LH starters: 21-20
Vs. RH starters: 62-59
Grass: 28-41 **Artificial:** 55-38
Day: 29-27 **Night:** 54-52
1-Run: 22-24 **X-inn.:** 9-8
Doubleheaders: 0-3-0
Team record past five years: 369-441 (.456, ranks 13th in league in that span)

TEAM LEADERS

Batting average: Vladimir Guerrero (.330).
At-bats: Orlando Cabrera (626).
Runs: Orlando Cabrera (95).
Hits: Orlando Cabrera (186).
Total Bases: Orlando Cabrera (288).
Doubles: Orlando Cabrera (47).
Triples: Endy Chavez (5).
Home runs: Vladimir Guerrero (25).
Runs batted in: Orlando Cabrera (80).
Stolen bases: Orlando Cabrera (24).
Slugging percentage: Vladimir Guerrero (.586).
On-base percentage: Vladimir Guerrero (.426).
Wins: Livan Hernandez (15).
Earned-run average: Livan Hernandez (3.20).
Complete games: Livan Hernandez (8).
Shutouts: Zach Day, Javier Vazquez (1).
Saves: Rocky Biddle (34).
Innings pitched: Livan Hernandez (233.1).
Strikeouts: Javier Vazquez (241).

GAMES BY POSITION

Catcher: Brian Schneider 98, Michael Barrett 68, Edwards Guzman 4.
First base: Wil Cordero 123, Brad Wilkerson 27, Jeff Liefer 21, Edwards Guzman 13, Joe Vitiello 12.
Second base: Jose Vidro 137, Henry Mateo 43, Jamey Carroll 11, Jose Macias 4.
Third base: Jamey Carroll 67, Fernando Tatis 49, Todd Zeile 34, Edwards Guzman 28, Jose Macias 25.
Shortstop: Orlando Cabrera 162, Jamey Carroll 14, Henry Mateo 2.
Outfield: Endy Chavez 135, Brad Wilkerson 135, Vladimir Guerrero 112, Ron Calloway 97, Jose Macias 62, Joe Vitiello 15, Henry Mateo 10, Matt Cepicky 4, Wil Cordero 1.
Designated hitter: Edwards Guzman 3, Henry Mateo 3, Wil Cordero 2, Brian Schneider 2, Jamey Carroll 1, Jose Macias 1, Joe Vitiello 1.

TOP DRAFT CHOICES

1. **Chad Cordero,** RHP, Cal State-Fullerton.
2. **Jerry Owens,** OF, The Masters (Calif.) College.
3. **Kory Casto,** OF, Portland.
4. **Edgardo Baez,** OF, Jose S. Alegria H.S., Dorado, Puerto Rico.
5. **Trey Webb,** SS, Baylor.
6. **Josh Whitesell,** 1B, Loyola Marymount.
7. **Devin Perrin,** RHP, Grand Canyon.
8. **Daryl Thompson,** RHP, La Plata H.S., Mechanicsville, Md.
9. **Gabriel Sosa,** LHP, Lino Padron Rivera H.S., Vega Baja, Puerto Rico.
10. **Victor Hamisevicz,** 1B, Gonzaga College H.S., Dunn Loring, Va.

NEW YORK METS

NATIONAL LEAGUE EAST DIVISION

2004 SEASON

April

SUN	MON	TUE	WED	THU	FRI	SAT
4	5	6 ATL	7 ATL	8 ATL	9 * MON	10 * MON
11 * MON	12 ATL	13	14 ATL	15 ATL	16 PIT	17 PIT
18 PIT	19 MON	20 MON	21 MON	22 MON	23 CHC	24 CHC
25 CHC	26	27 LA	28 LA	29 LA	30 SD	

May

SUN	MON	TUE	WED	THU	FRI	SAT
						1 SD
2 SD	3	4 SF	5 SF	6 SF	7 MIL	8 MIL
9 MIL	10 ARI	11 ARI	12 ARI	13 ARI	14 HOU	15 HOU
16 HOU	17	18 STL	19 STL	20 STL	21 COL	22 COL
23 COL	24	25 PHI	26 PHI	27	28 FLA	29 FLA
30 FLA	31 PHI					

June

SUN	MON	TUE	WED	THU	FRI	SAT
		1 PHI	2 PHI	3 FLA	4 FLA	5 FLA
6 FLA	7	8 MIN	9 MIN	10 MIN	11 KC	12 KC
13 KC	14	15 CLE	16 CLE	17 CLE	18 DET	19 DET
20 DET	21	22 CIN	23 CIN	24 CIN	25 NYY	26 NYY
27 NYY	28	29 CIN	30 CIN			

Home games shaded. All-Star Game July 13 at Houston. Schedule subject to change. * San Juan, Puerto Rico.

July

SUN	MON	TUE	WED	THU	FRI	SAT
				1 CIN	2 NYY	3 NYY
4 NYY	5 PHI	6 PHI	7 PHI	8 PHI	9 FLA	10 FLA
11 FLA	12	13 All-Star	14	15 PHI	16 PHI	17 PHI
18 PHI	19 FLA	20 FLA	21 MON	22 MON	23 ATL	24 ATL
25 ATL	26 MON	27 MON	28 MON	29 MON	30 ATL	31 ATL

August

SUN	MON	TUE	WED	THU	FRI	SAT
1 ATL	2	3 MIL	4 MIL	5 MIL	6 STL	7 STL
8 STL	9	10 HOU	11 HOU	12 HOU	13 ARI	14 ARI
15 ARI	16	17 COL	18 COL	19 COL	20 SF	21 SF
22 SF	23 SD	24 SD	25 SD	26 SD	27 LA	28 LA
29 LA	30 FLA	31 FLA				

Sept./Oct.

SUN	MON	TUE	WED	THU	FRI	SAT
			1 FLA	2 FLA	3 PHI	4 PHI
5 PHI	6	7 FLA	8 FLA	9 FLA	10 PHI	11 PHI
12 PHI	13 ATL	14 ATL	15 ATL	16 ATL	17 PIT	18 PIT
19 PIT	20	21 MON	22 MON	23 MON	24 CHC	25 CHC
26 CHC	27 ATL	28 ATL	29 ATL	30	1 MON	2 MON
3 MON	4	5	6	7	8	9

CLUB DIRECTORY

Chairman and chief executive officer
Fred Wilpon
President
Saul B. Katz
General manager
Jim Duquette
Special assistants to the g.m.
Al Goldis, Bill Livesey
Assistant g.m./dir. of baseball operations
Gary LaRocque
Director, amateur scouting
Jack Bowen
Vice president, media relations
Jay Horwitz
Executive v.p., business operations
Dave Howard
Director of minor league operations
Kevin Morgan

MINOR LEAGUE AFFILIATES

Class	Team	League	Manager
AAA	Norfolk	International	John Stearns
AA	Binghamton	Eastern	Ken Oberkfell
Advanced A	St. Lucie	Florida State	Tim Teufel
A	Capital City	South Atlantic	To be announced
Short-Season A	Brooklyn	New York-Pennsylvania	To be announced
Advanced Rookie	Kingsport	Appalachian	Mookie Wilson
Rookie	Gulf Coast Mets	Gulf Coast	To be announced

More on the Mets at www.foxsports.com/named/FS/MLB/teams

BROADCAST INFORMATION

Radio: WFAN-AM (660).
TV: WPIX-TV (Channel 11).
Cable TV: Fox Sports New York, MSG Network.

SPRING TRAINING

Ballpark (city): Thomas J. White Stadium (Port St. Lucie, Fla.).
Ticket information: 772-871-2115.

SPRING TRAINING ROSTER

Manager—Art Howe (18).
Coaches—Don Baylor (25), Bobby Floyd, Matt Galante (4), Rick Peterson, Gary Pettis (2), Nelson Silverio (54), Denny Walling (15).

No.	PITCHERS	B/T	Ht./Wt.	Age*	2003 Clubs
17	Anderson, Jason	L/R	6-0/170	24	Columbus, New York A.L., Norfolk, New York N.L.
	Bevis, P.J.	R/R	6-3/175	23	Binghamton, Norfolk
43	Cerda, Jaime	L/L	6-0/175	25	Norfolk, New York N.L.
	Diaz, Joselo	R/R	6-0/175	23	Vero Beach, Jacksonville, St. Lucie
45	Franco, John	L/L	5-10/185	43	St. Lucie, Norfolk, New York N.L.
47	Glavine, Tom	L/L	6-0/185	38	New York N.L.
46	Griffiths, Jeremy	R/R	6-6/240	26	Norfolk, New York N.L.
48	Heilman, Aaron	R/R	6-5/220	25	Norfolk, New York N.L.
	Keppel, Bob	R/R	6-5/205	21	Brooklyn, Binghamton
22	Leiter, Al	L/L	6-3/220	38	New York N.L.
46	Looper, Braden	R/R	6-3/220	29	Florida
	Moreno, Orber	R/R	6-3/200	26	Binghamton, Norfolk, New York N.L.
36	Roberts, Grant	R/R	6-3/205	26	St. Lucie, Norfolk, New York N.L.
40	Seo, Jae Weong	R/R	6-1/210	26	New York N.L.
	Stanton, Mike	L/L	6-1/215	36	Binghamton, Brooklyn, New York N.L.
38	Strange, Pat	R/R	6-5/243	23	New York N.L., Norfolk
28	Strickland, Scott	R/R	5-11/180	27	New York N.L.
29	Trachsel, Steve	R/R	6-4/205	33	New York N.L.
35	Weathers, Dave	R/R	6-3/230	34	New York N.L.
39	Wheeler, Dan	R/R	6-3/222	26	Norfolk, New York N.L.
	Yates, Tyler	R/R	6-4/220	26	St. Lucie, Binghamton, Norfolk

No.	CATCHERS	B/T	Ht./Wt.	Age*	2003 Clubs
	Jacobs, Mike	L/R	6-2/200	23	Binghamton
31	Piazza, Mike	R/R	6-3/215	35	Norfolk, New York N.L.
3	Wilson, Vance	R/R	5-11/190	31	New York N.L.

No.	INFIELDERS	B/T	Ht./Wt.	Age*	2003 Clubs
	Baldiris, Aaron	R/R	6-2/195	21	Capital City, Brooklyn
	Brazell, Craig	L/R	6-3/210	23	Binghamton, Norfolk
12	Garcia, Danny	R/R	6-1/174	23	Binghamton, Norfolk, New York N.L.
25	Matsui, Kazuo	B/R	5-9/180	28	Played in Japan
11	McEwing, Joe	R/R	5-11/170	31	Norfolk, New York N.L.
23	Phillips, Jason	R/R	6-1/177	27	Norfolk, New York N.L.
7	Reyes, Jose	B/R	6-0/160	20	Norfolk, New York N.L.
42	Vaughn, Mo	L/R	6-1/275	36	New York N.L.
9	Wigginton, Ty	R/R	6-0/200	26	New York N.L.

No.	OUTFIELDERS	B/T	Ht./Wt.	Age*	2003 Clubs
	Cameron, Mike	R/R	6-2/200	31	Seattle
19	Cedeno, Roger	B/R	6-1/205	29	New York N.L.
61	Duncan, Jeff	L/L	6-2/188	25	Binghamton, Norfolk, New York N.L.
30	Floyd, Cliff	L/R	6-4/230	31	New York N.L.
	Garcia, Karim	L/L	6-0/195	28	Cleveland, Buffalo, New York A.L.
21	Gonzalez, Raul	R/R	5-9/190	30	Norfolk, New York N.L.
	Lydon, Wayne	R/R	6-2/190	22	St. Lucie
6	Perez, Timo	L/L	5-9/167	28	Norfolk, New York N.L.
20	Redman, Prentice	R/R	6-3/185	24	Norfolk, New York N.L.

Invited to spring training: RHP Pete Zamora, C Joe Hieptas, C Justin Huber, C Brett Kay, OF Esix Snead.

*Age as of April 1, 2004.

BALLPARK INFORMATION

Ballpark (capacity, surface)
Shea Stadium (57,393, grass)

Address
123-01 Roosevelt Ave.
Flushing, NY 11368

Official website
www.mets.com

Business phone
718-507-METS

Ticket information
718-507-TIXX

Field dimensions (from home plate)
To left field at foul line, 338 feet
To center field, 410 feet
To right field at foul line, 338 feet

First game played
April 17, 1964 (Pirates 4, Mets 3)

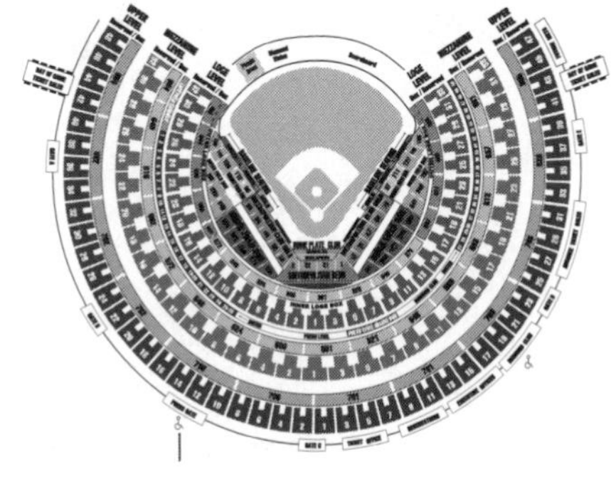

2003 REVIEW

DAY BY DAY

Date	Opp.	Res.	Score	(inn.*)	Hits	Opp. hits	Winning pitcher	Losing pitcher	Save	Record	Pos.	GB
3-31	Chi.	L	2-15		4	16	Wood	Glavine		0-1	T3rd	1.0
4-2	Chi.	W	4-1		6	6	Leiter	Clement	Benitez	1-1	3rd	1.0
4-3	Chi.	L	3-6		7	9	Prior	Trachsel		1-2	T3rd	2.0
4-4	Mon.	W	4-0		13	5	Cone	Ohka		2-2	T2nd	1.0
4-5	Mon.	W	3-1		8	6	Glavine	Armas	Benitez	3-2	T1st	...
4-6	Mon.	L	5-8		7	17	Stewart	Benitez	Biddle	3-3	T2nd	1.0
4-8	At Fla.	W	4-2		8	7	Leiter	Redman	Benitez	4-3	T1st	...
4-9	At Fla.	L	2-3		5	11	Looper	Stanton		4-4	T2nd	1.0
4-10	At Fla.	L	3-4		8	10	Spooneybarger	Benitez		4-5	3rd	1.0
4-11	At Mon.■	L	0-10		2	11	Ohka	Cone		4-6	4th	2.0
4-12	At Mon.■	L	4-5		10	11	Hernandez	Seo	Biddle	4-7	4th	3.0
4-13	At Mon.■	L	1-2	(10)	6	6	Biddle	Stanton		4-8	5th	4.0
4-14	At Mon.■	L	3-5		7	6	Smith	Strickland	Biddle	4-9	5th	5.0
4-15	At Pit.	W	3-1		6	5	Glavine	Fogg	Benitez	5-9	5th	4.0
4-16	At Pit.	L	3-6		6	12	Suppan	Cone		5-10	5th	4.0
4-17	At Pit.	W	7-2		13	9	Seo	D'Amico		6-10	5th	3.0
4-18	Fla.	W	6-3		12	9	Weathers	Nunez	Benitez	7-10	5th	2.5
4-19	Fla.	L	5-6		7	10	Looper	Benitez		7-11	5th	4.0
4-20	Fla.	W	7-4		7	10	Glavine	Nunez		8-11	5th	3.0
4-22	Hou.	L	2-6		5	12	Redding	Cone		8-12	5th	4.0
4-23	Hou.	W	4-2		8	8	Leiter	Oswalt	Benitez	9-12	5th	3.0
4-24	Hou.	W	7-4		10	8	Astacio	Miller	Benitez	10-12	5th	3.0
4-25	Ari.	W	4-3		7	9	Stanton	Villarreal	Benitez	11-12	5th	3.0
4-27†	Ari.	L	1-6		4	7	Webb	Glavine		11-13		
4-27‡	Ari.	L	3-7		10	11	Johnson	Seo	Mantei	11-14	5th	4.0
4-29	At StL.	L	3-13		7	17	Morris	Leiter		11-15	5th	5.0
4-30	At StL.	L	4-13		7	16	Williams	Astacio		11-16	5th	6.0
5-1	At StL.	L	5-6	(10)	11	12	Eldred	Strickland		11-17	5th	7.0
5-2	At Mil.	W	9-3		15	8	Glavine	Rusch		12-17	5th	7.0
5-3	At Mil.	L	2-3		8	4	Foster	Weathers	DeJean	12-18	5th	7.0
5-4	At Mil.	W	5-3		5	5	Leiter	Kinney	Benitez	13-18	5th	7.0
5-6	L.A.	W	3-2		11	5	Astacio	Perez	Benitez	14-18	5th	7.0
5-7	L.A.	L	1-2		3	5	Nomo	Trachsel	Gagne	14-19	5th	7.5
5-8	L.A.	L	1-6		6	12	Ishii	Glavine		14-20	5th	9.0
5-9	S.D.	L	4-5		7	10	Hackman	Weathers	Orosco	14-21	5th	9.0
5-10	S.D.	W	4-2	(10)	11	6	Stanton	Wright		15-21	5th	9.0
5-11	S.D.	W	3-2		8	7	Lloyd	Matthews	Benitez	16-21	5th	9.0
5-12	At Col.	W	9-6		11	11	Trachsel	Young	Benitez	17-21	5th	9.0
5-13	At Col.	L	8-9		13	15	Reed	Cerda	Jimenez	17-22	5th	10.0
5-14	At Col.	L	5-6		6	11	Reed	Stanton	Jimenez	17-23	5th	10.0
5-15	At S.F	L	3-11		6	17	Rueter	Leiter		17-24	5th	11.0
5-16	At S.F	L	5-7		8	15	Nathan	Weathers	Worrell	17-25	5th	12.0
5-17	At S.F	W	5-1		6	5	Trachsel	Moss		18-25	5th	12.0
5-18	At S.F	W	5-1		8	6	Glavine	Ainsworth		19-25	4th	12.0
5-20	Phi.	L	7-11		9	14	Myers	Lloyd		19-26	4th	12.0
5-21	Phi.	W	5-4		12	8	Benitez	Adams		20-26	4th	11.0
5-22	Phi.	W	6-3		12	5	Astacio	Padilla	Benitez	21-26	4th	11.0
5-23	At Atl.	W	6-5		8	10	Trachsel	Ortiz	Benitez	22-26	4th	10.0
5-24	At Atl.	L	4-10		6	14	Ramirez	Glavine		22-27	4th	11.0
5-25	At Atl.	L	1-3		5	6	Hernandez	Weathers	Smoltz	22-28	4th	12.0
5-27	At Phi.	W	4-2		10	7	Leiter	Wolf	Benitez	23-28	4th	11.5
5-28	At Phi.	L	3-11		8	13	Padilla	Astacio		23-29	5th	12.5
5-29	At Phi.	W	5-0		9	6	Trachsel	Millwood		24-29	5th	12.0
5-30	Atl.	L	2-5		7	11	Maddux	Glavine	Smoltz	24-30	5th	13.0
5-31	Atl.	W	4-2		10	8	Seo	Hampton	Benitez	25-30	5th	12.0
6-1	Atl.	W	10-4		13	7	Leiter	Gryboski		26-30	4th	11.0
6-5†	Mil.	L	7-8		10	13	Kinney	Trachsel	DeJean	26-31		
6-5‡	Mil.	L	3-5		8	9	Sheets	Glavine	DeJean	26-32	5th	13.5
6-6	Sea.	W	3-2		5	9	Seo	Franklin	Benitez	27-32	5th	13.0
6-8†	Sea.	L	1-13		6	17	Garcia	Leiter		27-33		
6-8‡	Sea.	L	0-7		3	14	Moyer	Bacsik		27-34	5th	15.0
6-10	At Tex.	L	7-9		11	13	Thomson	Trachsel	Urbina	27-35	5th	15.0
6-11	At Tex.	W	8-2		10	9	Seo	Santos		28-35	5th	15.0
6-12	At Tex.	W	11-0		16	11	Leiter	Lewis		29-35	5th	15.0

Date	Opp.	Res.	Score	(inn.*)	Hits	Opp. hits	Winning pitcher	Losing pitcher	Save	Record	Pos.	GB
6-13	At Ana.	W	7-3		13	8	Bacsik	Sele		30-35	5th	14.0
6-14	At Ana.	L	3-13		5	16	Ortiz	Roach		30-36	5th	15.0
6-15	At Ana.	W	8-0		8	1	Trachsel	Washburn		31-36	5th	14.0
6-16	At Fla.	L	0-1		1	6	Willis	Glavine		31-37	5th	14.5
6-17	At Fla.	W	5-0		9	1	Seo	Pavano		32-37	5th	13.5
6-18	At Fla.	W	10-5		13	8	Leiter	Penny	Wheeler	33-37	4th	13.5
6-19	At Fla.	L	1-5		5	9	Phelps	Bacsik		33-38	5th	13.5
6-20	N.Y.	L	0-5		7	9	Pettitte	Trachsel		33-39	5th	14.5
6-22	N.Y.	L	3-7	(11)	11	10	Rivera	Lloyd		33-40	5th	15.0
6-24	Fla.	L	4-8		8	13	Penny	Leiter	Tejera	33-41	5th	16.0
6-25	Fla.	W	6-3		10	10	Trachsel	Redman	Benitez	34-41	5th	15.0
6-26	Fla.	L	1-6		10	9	Willis	Heilman		34-42	5th	15.0
6-27	At N.Y.	L	4-6		12	11	Wells	Seo	Miceli	34-43	5th	16.0
6-28†	At N.Y.	L	1-7		6	11	Clemens	Griffiths		34-44		
6-28‡	N.Y.	L	8-9		13	15	Claussen	Glavine	Rivera	34-45	5th	16.5
6-29	At N.Y.	L	3-5		4	9	Weaver	Leiter	Rivera	34-46	5th	17.5
6-30	Mon.	W	3-1		8	7	Trachsel	Vazquez	Benitez	35-46	5th	16.5
7-1	Mon.	W	7-6		13	8	Benitez	Manon		36-46	5th	15.5
7-2	Mon.	L	4-11		6	15	Hernandez	Seo		36-47	5th	16.5
7-4	At Cin.	W	7-2		14	7	Glavine	Haynes	Benitez	37-47	5th	16.0
7-5	At Cin.	W	6-2		9	8	Trachsel	Graves	Weathers	38-47	5th	16.0
7-6	At Cin.	W	7-5		10	10	Cerda	Reith	Benitez	39-47	5th	16.0
7-7	Atl.	L	3-7		4	10	Ramirez	Seo		39-48	5th	17.0
7-8	Atl.	L	3-5		10	11	Reynolds	Roach	Smoltz	39-49	5th	18.0
7-9	Atl.	L	3-6		8	9	Ortiz	Glavine	Smoltz	39-50	5th	19.0
7-10	Phi.	L	2-7		7	15	Padilla	Trachsel		39-51	5th	20.0
7-11	Phi.	L	3-10		7	14	Wolf	Heilman		39-52	5th	21.0
7-12	Phi.	L	2-4	(11)	8	13	Mesa	Franco		39-53	5th	21.0
7-13	Phi.	W	4-3		11	12	Benitez	Adams		40-53	5th	21.0
7-17	At Atl.	L	2-3		8	12	Maddux	Franco		40-54	5th	22.0
7-18	At Atl.	L	4-11		9	14	Hampton	Seo		40-55	5th	23.0
7-19	At Atl.	L	4-7		7	10	Ortiz	Glavine	Smoltz	40-56	5th	24.0
7-20	At Atl.	L	8-11		12	16	King	Stanton	Smoltz	40-57	5th	25.0
7-21	At Phi.	W	8-6		13	12	Heilman	Duckworth	Franco	41-57	5th	24.0
7-22	At Phi.	W	7-5		11	12	Trachsel	Millwood	Wheeler	42-57	5th	24.0
7-23	At Mon.	L	2-5		7	9	Vazquez	Seo	Biddle	42-58	5th	24.0
7-24	At Mon.	L	1-5		7	11	Hernandez	Glavine	Biddle	42-59	5th	25.0
7-25	Cin.	W	3-1		11	7	Leiter	Graves	Stanton	43-59	5th	24.0
7-26	Cin.	L	3-8		5	12	Acevedo	Heilman		43-60	5th	25.0
7-27	Cin.	L	5-8		8	13	Wilson	Trachsel	Williamson	43-61	5th	25.0
7-28	Mil.	L	2-4		5	7	Estrella	Weathers	Kolb	43-62	5th	26.0
7-29	Mil.	L	3-6		8	10	Sheets	Wheeler	DeJean	43-63	5th	27.0
7-30	Mil.	W	2-0		5	5	Leiter	Obermueller	Weathers	44-63	5th	26.0
7-31	Mil.	L	3-4		8	9	Kinney	Heilman	Kolb	44-64	5th	27.0
8-1	StL.	L	2-8		6	12	Kline	Wheeler		44-65	5th	28.0
8-2	StL.	L	9-10		17	10	Tomko	Seo	Yan	44-66	5th	29.0
8-3	StL.	W	13-5		19	10	Griffiths	Stephenson		45-66	5th	28.0
8-5	At Hou.	W	10-1		13	7	Leiter	Villone		46-66	5th	27.0
8-6	At Hou.	L	1-11		8	15	Miller	Heilman		46-67	5th	28.0
8-7	At Hou.	W	5-4		8	7	Trachsel	Lidge	Stanton	47-67	5th	28.0
8-8	At Ari.	W	3-1		8	7	Glavine	Webb	Stanton	48-67	5th	28.0
8-9	At Ari.	L	1-2		8	7	Randolph	Franco		48-68	5th	28.0
8-10	At Ari.	L	4-7		10	9	Johnson	Leiter	Mantei	48-69	5th	28.0
8-12	S.F	W	5-4		8	11	Heilman	Ponson	Weathers	49-69	5th	27.0
8-13	S.F	W	9-2		13	9	Trachsel	Williams		50-69	5th	27.0
8-15	Col.	W	5-0		10	4	Glavine	Oliver		51-69	5th	27.5
8-16	Col.	W	13-4		14	8	Seo	Chacon		52-69	5th	27.5
8-17	Col.	W	6-4		11	8	Leiter	Jennings	Weathers	53-69	5th	26.5
8-18	Col.	W	8-0		12	1	Trachsel	Tsao		54-69	5th	26.5
8-19	At S.D.	L	2-3		7	7	Linebrink	Stanton	Beck	54-70	5th	26.5
8-20	At S.D.	L	1-2		8	4	Beck	Roberts		54-71	5th	26.5
8-21	At S.D.	W	5-1		4	7	Seo	Perez		55-71	5th	25.5
8-22	At L.A.	L	1-2		7	6	Nomo	Leiter	Gagne	55-72	5th	26.5
8-23	At L.A.	W	4-0		11	6	Trachsel	Ashby		56-72	5th	26.5
8-24	At L.A.	W	2-1		8	2	Glavine	Brown	Franco	57-72	5th	26.5
8-26	At Atl.	W	6-5		7	8	Seo	Reynolds	Stanton	58-72	5th	25.5
8-27	At Atl.	L	1-4		4	10	Maddux	Heilman	Mercker	58-73	5th	26.5
8-28	At Atl.	W	3-1		6	3	Leiter	Hampton	Weathers	59-73	5th	25.5
8-29	Phi.	L	0-7		3	9	Millwood	Trachsel		59-74	5th	25.5
8-30	Phi.	L	2-4		6	11	Wolf	Glavine	Mesa	59-75	5th	26.5
8-31	Phi.	L	1-4		2	4	Padilla	Seo	Mesa	59-76	5th	27.5

Date	Opp.	Res.	Score	(inn.*)	Hits	Opp. hits	Winning pitcher	Losing pitcher	Save	Record	Pos.	GB
9-1	Atl.	W	3-2		9	9	Wheeler	Hodges	Weathers	60-76	5th	26.5
9-2	Atl.	W	3-1		7	6	Leiter	Hampton	Weathers	61-76	5th	25.5
9-3	Atl.	W	9-3		10	7	Trachsel	Ortiz		62-76	5th	24.5
9-4	At Phi.	L	5-6		7	12	de los Santos	Stanton		62-77	5th	25.0
9-5	At Phi.	L	0-1		6	3	Padilla	Seo	Cormier	62-78	5th	25.5
9-6	At Phi.	L	6-9		9	12	Myers	Griffiths	Wendell	62-79	5th	26.5
9-7	At Phi.	L	4-5	(11)	8	11	Cormier	Wheeler		62-80	5th	27.5
9-8	Fla.	L	0-5		6	9	Beckett	Trachsel		62-81	5th	28.5
9-9	Fla.	L	1-3		6	9	Urbina	Weathers	Looper	62-82	5th	28.5
9-10	Fla.	L	3-7		4	11	Redman	Seo		62-83	5th	29.5
9-12	At Mon.	L	4-7		9	13	Tucker	Leiter	Ayala	62-84	5th	29.0
9-13	At Mon.	W	5-4		7	10	Trachsel	Vazquez	Roberts	63-84	5th	28.0
9-14	At Mon.	L	3-7		6	9	Day	Glavine		63-85	5th	29.0
9-15	At Chi.	L	1-4		4	10	Clement	Griffiths	Borowski	63-86	5th	30.0
9-16	At Chi.	L	2-3		8	7	Prior	Seo	Borowski	63-87	5th	30.0
9-17	At Chi.	L	0-2		4	4	Wood	Leiter		63-88	5th	31.0
9-18	Mon.	L	0-1		3	7	Vazquez	Trachsel	Cordero	63-89	5th	31.5
9-19	Mon.	L	1-7		9	10	Day	Glavine		63-90	5th	32.5
9-20	Mon.	L	3-4	(10)	11	8	Cordero	Stanton	Biddle	63-91	5th	32.5
9-21	Mon.	L	2-4		8	10	Ayala	Roberts	Biddle	63-92	5th	33.5
9-23	Pit.	W	1-0		8	8	Leiter	Wells		64-92	5th	33.0
9-24	Pit.	W	5-3		10	10	Trachsel	D'Amico	Stanton	65-92	5th	33.0
9-25	Pit.	L	1-3		4	10	Torres	Roberts	Tavarez	65-93	5th	33.5
9-26	At Fla.	L	3-4		6	11	Pavano	Heilman	Urbina	65-94	5th	34.5
9-27	At Fla.	W	9-3		11	6	Seo	Tejera		66-94	5th	33.5
9-28	At Fla.	L	0-4		4	7	Willis	Griffiths		66-95	5th	34.5

Monthly records: March (0-1), April (11-15), May (14-14), June (10-16), July (9-18), August (15-12), September (7-19).
*Innings, if other than nine. ■ At Hiram Bithorn Stadium, San Juan, Puerto Rico. † First game of a doubleheader. ‡ Second game of a doubleheader.

RECORDS

2003 regular-season record: 66-95
Position: 5th in N.L. East
Home: 34-46 **Road:** 32-49
N.L. East: 27-49 **N.L. Central:** 17-22
N.L. West: 17-14 A.L. 5-10
Vs. LH starters: 18-25
Vs. RH starters: 48-70
Grass: 61-82 **Artificial:** 5-13
Day: 21-30 **Night:** 45-65
1-Run: 15-28 **X-inn.:** 1-6
Doubleheaders: 0-3-0
Team record past five years: 414-395 (.512, ranks 7th in league in that span)

TEAM LEADERS

Batting average: Jose Reyes (.307).
At-bats: Ty Wigginton (573).
Runs: Ty Wigginton (73).
Hits: Ty Wigginton (146).
Total Bases: Ty Wigginton (227).
Doubles: Ty Wigginton (36).
Triples: Ty Wigginton (6).
Home runs: Jeromy Burnitz, Cliff Floyd (18).
Runs batted in: Ty Wigginton (71).
Stolen bases: Roger Cedeno (14).
Slugging percentage: Cliff Floyd (.518).
On-base percentage: Cliff Floyd (.376).
Wins: Steve Trachsel (16).
Earned-run average: Steve Trachsel (3.78).
Complete games: Steve Trachsel (2).
Shutouts: Steve Trachsel (2).
Saves: Armando Benitez (21).
Innings pitched: Steve Trachsel (204.2).
Strikeouts: Al Leiter (139).

GAMES BY POSITION

Catcher: Vance Wilson 89, Mike Piazza 64, Jason Phillips 29, Joe DePastino 1.
First base: Jason Phillips 84, Tony Clark 80, Mo Vaughn 24, Jay Bell 13, Joe McEwing 5, Mike Glavine 3, Mike Piazza 1.
Second base: Roberto Alomar 72, Joe McEwing 55, Marco Scutaro 39, Danny Garcia 17, Jay Bell 14, Rey Sanchez 12.
Third base: Ty Wigginton 155, Jay Bell 14, Joe McEwing 2.
Shortstop: Jose Reyes 69, Joe McEwing 42, Rey Sanchez 42, Jorge Velandia 23, Jay Bell 12, Marco Scutaro 1.
Outfield: Roger Cedeno 128, Timo Perez 104, Cliff Floyd 95, Raul Gonzalez 88, Jeromy Burnitz 65, Tsuyoshi Shinjo 54, Jeff Duncan 52, Joe McEwing 18, Prentice Redman 10, Matt Watson 5, Tony Clark 1, Danny Garcia 1.
Designated hitter: Cliff Floyd 9, Jay Bell 1.

TOP DRAFT CHOICES

1. **Lastings Milledge,** OF, Lakewood Ranch H.S., Palmetto, Fla.
4. **Shane Hawk,** LHP, Oklahoma State.
5. **Corey Coles,** OF, Louisiana-Lafayette.
6. **Mateo Miramontes,** RHP, Nevada-Reno.
7. **Brian Bannister,** RHP, Southern California.
8. **Seth Pietsch,** OF, Oregon State.
9. **Vince Cordova,** RHP, Loyola Marymount.
10. **David Reaver,** SS, Richmond.

PHILADELPHIA PHILLIES

NATIONAL LEAGUE EAST DIVISION

2004 SEASON

April

SUN	MON	TUE	WED	THU	FRI	SAT
4	5 PIT	6	7 PIT	8 PIT	9 FLA	10 FLA
11 FLA	12 CIN	13	14 CIN	15 CIN	16 MON	17 MON
18 MON	19	20 FLA	21 FLA	22 FLA	23 MON	24 MON
25 MON	26	27 STL	28 STL	29 STL	30 ARI	

May

SUN	MON	TUE	WED	THU	FRI	SAT
						1 ARI
2 ARI	3	4 STL	5 STL	6 STL	7 ARI	8 ARI
9 ARI	10	11 SF	12 SF	13 SF	14 COL	15 COL
16 COL	17 COL	18 LA	19 LA	20 LA	21 SD	22 SD
23 SD	24	25 NYM	26 NYM	27 ATL	28 ATL	29 ATL
30 ATL	31 NYM					

June

SUN	MON	TUE	WED	THU	FRI	SAT
		1 NYM	2 NYM	3 ATL	4 ATL	5 ATL
6 ATL	7	8 CHW	9 CHW	10 CHW	11 MIN	12 MIN
13 MIN	14	15 DET	16 DET	17 DET	18 KC	19 KC
20 KC	21	22 MON	23 MON	24 MON	25 BOS	26 BOS
27 BOS	28 MON	29 MON	30 MON			

July

SUN	MON	TUE	WED	THU	FRI	SAT
				1 MON	2 BAL	3 BAL
4 BAL	5 NYM	6 NYM	7 NYM	8 NYM	9 ATL	10 ATL
11 ATL	12	13 All-Star	14	15 NYM	16 NYM	17 NYM
18 NYM	19 ATL	20 ATL	21 FLA	22 FLA	23 CHC	24 CHC
25 CHC	26 FLA	27 FLA	28 FLA	29 FLA	30 CHC	31 CHC

August

SUN	MON	TUE	WED	THU	FRI	SAT
1 CHC	2	3 SD	4 SD	5 SD	6 LA	7 LA
8 LA	9 COL	10 COL	11 COL	12 COL	13 SF	14 SF
15 SF	16	17 HOU	18 HOU	19 HOU	20 MIL	21 MIL
22 MIL	23 HOU	24 HOU	25 HOU	26	27 MIL	28 MIL
29 MIL	30	31 ATL				

Sept./Oct.

SUN	MON	TUE	WED	THU	FRI	SAT
			1 ATL	2	3 NYM	4 NYM
5 NYM	6 ATL	7 ATL	8 ATL	9 ATL	10 NYM	11 NYM
12 NYM	13 CIN	14 CIN	15 CIN	16	17 MON	18 MON
19 MON	20	21 FLA	22 FLA	23 FLA	24 MON	25 MON
26 MON	27 PIT	28 PIT	29 PIT	30 FLA	1 FLA	2 FLA
3 FLA	4	5	6	7	8	9

Home games shaded. All-Star Game July 13 at Houston. Schedule subject to change.

CLUB DIRECTORY

General partner, president and CEO
David Montgomery
Chairman
Bill Giles
Vice president & general manager
Ed Wade

Vice president, public relations
Larry Shenk
Assistant general manager
Ruben Amaro Jr.
Asst. g.m., scouting & player dev.
Mike Arbuckle

Director, minor league operations
Steve Noworyta
Director, media relations
Leigh Tobin
Director, community relations
Gene Dias

MINOR LEAGUE AFFILIATES

Class	Team	League	Manager
AAA	Scranton/Wilkes-Barre	International	Marc Bombard
AA	Reading	Eastern	Greg Legg
Advanced A	Clearwater	Florida State	Mike Schmidt
A	Lakewood	South Atlantic	P.J. Forbes
Short-Season A	Batavia	New York-Penn	Luis Melendez
Rookie	Gulf Coast Phillies	Gulf Coast	Roly deArmas

More on the Phillies at www.foxsports.com/named/FS/MLB/teams

BROADCAST INFORMATION

Radio: WPEN-AM (950).
TV: UPN 57.
Cable TV: Comcast SportsNet.

SPRING TRAINING

Ballpark (city): Clearwater Community Sports Complex (Clearwater, Fla.).
Ticket information: 215-463-1000, 727-442-8496.

SPRING TRAINING ROSTER

Manager—Larry Bowa (10).

Coaches—Mick Billmeyer, Greg Gross (21), Ramon Henderson (59), Joe Kerrigan (16), Milt Thompson, Gary Varsho (25), John Vukovich (18).

No.	PITCHERS	B/T	Ht./Wt.	Age*	2003 Clubs
	Alvarez, Victor	L/L	5-10/150	27	Los Angeles, Las Vegas
	Bucktrot, Keith	L/R	6-2/180	23	Clearwater, Reading
48	Coggin, Dave	R/R	6-4/205	27	Scranton/Wilkes-Barre, Clearwater
37	Cormier, Rheal	L/L	5-10/195	36	Philadelphia
56	Geary, Geoff	R/R	6-0/170	27	Scranton/Wilkes-Barre, Philadelphia
50	Hancock, Josh	R/R	6-3/217	25	Scranton/Wilkes-Barre, Philadelphia
	Hernandez, Roberto	R/R	6-4/250	39	Richmond, Atlanta
28	Junge, Eric	R/R	6-5/215	27	Philadelphia, Scranton/Wilkes-Barre
57	Madson, Ryan	L/R	6-6/180	23	Clearwater, Scranton/Wilkes-Barre, Philadelphia
34	Millwood, Kevin	R/R	6-4/220	29	Philadelphia
	Milton, Eric	L/L	6-3/225	28	Fort Myers, Minnesota
39	Myers, Brett	R/R	6-4/215	23	Philadelphia
44	Padilla, Vicente	R/R	6-2/215	26	Philadelphia
	Perez, Franklin	R/R	6-2/175	25	Did Not Play
	Ramirez, Elizardo	R/R	6-0/145	21	Clearwater
	Simon, Alfredo	R/R	6-4/175	22	Lakewood
	Smith, Bud	L/L	6-0/170	24	Reading, Clearwater
47	Telemaco, Amaury	R/R	6-3/222	30	Scranton/Wilkes-Barre, Philadelphia
13	Wagner, Billy	L/L	5-11/195	32	Houston
43	Wolf, Randy	L/L	6-0/194	27	Philadelphia
	Worrell, Tim	R/R	6-4/230	36	San Francisco

No.	CATCHERS	B/T	Ht./Wt.	Age*	2003 Clubs
24	Lieberthal, Mike	R/R	6-0/195	32	Philadelphia
3	Pratt, Todd	R/R	6-3/235	37	Philadelphia

No.	INFIELDERS	B/T	Ht./Wt.	Age*	2003 Clubs
4	Bell, David	R/R	5-10/195	31	Philadelphia
	Howard, Ryan	L/L	6-4/230	24	Clearwater
65	Machado, And.	B/R	5-11/165	23	Reading, Philadelphia
9	Perez, Tomas	B/R	5-11/177	30	Philadelphia
23	Polanco, Placido	R/R	5-10/185	28	Philadelphia
	Richardson, Juan	R/R	6-1/175	25	Reading
6	Rollins, Jimmy	B/R	5-8/165	25	Philadelphia
25	Thome, Jim	L/R	6-4/240	33	Philadelphia
	Utley, Chase	L/R	6-1/170	25	Scranton/Wilkes-Barre, Philadelphia
	Wooten, Shawn	R/R	5-10/230	31	Anaheim

No.	OUTFIELDERS	B/T	Ht./Wt.	Age*	2003 Clubs
53	Abreu, Bobby	L/R	6-0/200	30	Philadelphia
5	Burrell, Pat	R/R	6-4/222	27	Philadelphia
29	Byrd, Marlon	R/R	6-0/230	26	Scranton/Wilkes-Barre, Reading, Philadelphia
	Glanville, Doug	R/R	6-2/174	33	Oklahoma, Frisco, Texas, Chicago N.L.
33	Ledee, Ricky	L/L	6-1/200	30	Philadelphia
22	Michaels, Jason	R/R	6-0/204	27	Clearwater, Philadelphia
66	Padilla, Jorge	R/R	6-2/200	24	Reading

Invited to spring training: LHP Jim Crowell, RHP Gavin Floyd, LHP Cole Hamels, RHP Adam Roller, LHP Mike Spiegel, C John Castellano, C Casey Martinez, C Jeremy Salazar, C Nick Tempesta, IF Jim Deschaine, IF J.P. Roberge, OF Mark Budzinski, OF Lou Collier, OF Kevin Gibbs, OF Jim Rushford, OF Mark Smith.

*Age as of April 1, 2004.

BALLPARK INFORMATION

Ballpark (capacity, surface)
Citizens Bank Park (43,500, grass)

Address
One Citizens Bank Way
Philadelphia, PA 19148

Official website
www.phillies.com

Business phone
215-463-6000

Ticket information
215-463-1000

Field dimensions (from home plate)
To left field at foul line, 329 feet
To center field, 401 feet
To right field at foul line, 330 feet

First game played
Scheduled for April 12, 2004, vs. Cincinnati

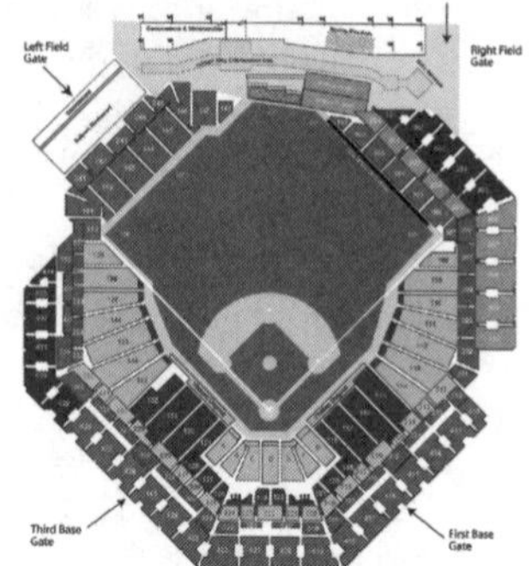

2003 REVIEW
DAY BY DAY

Date	Opp.	Res.	Score	(inn.*)	Hits	Opp. hits	Winning pitcher	Losing pitcher	Save	Record	Pos.	GB
3-31	At Fla.	W	8-5		10	7	Millwood	Beckett	Mesa	1-0	T1st	...
4-2	At Fla.	W	8-2		12	5	Wolf	Pavano		2-0	T1st	...
4-3	At Fla.	L	3-8		9	11	Redman	Padilla		2-1	2nd	1.0
4-4	Pit.	L	1-9		3	12	Suppan	Roa	Torres	2-2	T2nd	1.0
4-5	Pit.	W	16-1		19	10	Silva	D'Amico		3-2	T1st	...
4-6	Pit.	L	0-2		8	8	Benson	Myers	Williams	3-3	T2nd	1.0
4-8	Atl.	W	4-3	(10)	4	9	Mesa	Gryboski		4-3	T1st	...
4-9	Atl.	W	16-2		18	10	Padilla	Maddux		5-3	1st	+1.0
4-10	Atl.	L	2-6		4	13	Holmes	Roa		5-4	T1st	...
4-11	At Cin.	L	6-7		11	11	Williamson	Mesa		5-5	2nd	1.0
4-12	At Cin.	W	8-5		15	8	Millwood	Haynes		6-5	2nd	1.0
4-13	At Cin.	W	13-1		9	6	Wolf	Dempster		7-5	2nd	1.0
4-14	Fla.	W	5-2		8	6	Padilla	Burnett	Mesa	8-5	2nd	1.0
4-15	Fla.	W	4-3		6	10	Silva	Beckett	Mesa	9-5	T1st	...
4-16	Fla.	L	1-3		5	8	Penny	Myers	Looper	9-6	T1st	...
4-17	Fla.	L	3-7		6	8	Pavano	Millwood		9-7	T1st	...
4-18	At Atl.	L	4-5		8	6	Gryboski	Wolf	Smoltz	9-8	T2nd	0.5
4-19	At Atl.	W	4-0		11	4	Padilla	Hampton		10-8	2nd	1.0
4-20	At Atl.	L	1-8		5	12	Reynolds	Duckworth		10-9	T2nd	1.0
4-22	Col.	W	5-2		8	5	Millwood	Oliver	Mesa	11-9	T2nd	1.0
4-23	Col.	W	6-4		9	6	Myers	Jennings	Mesa	12-9	T1st	...
4-24	Col.	W	9-1		14	4	Wolf	Cook		13-9	T1st	...
4-25	S.F	L	4-7		10	9	Nathan	Padilla		13-10	T2nd	1.0
4-26	S.F	W	10-2		12	9	Duckworth	Williams	Silva	14-10	T2nd	1.0
4-27	S.F	W	1-0		4	0	Millwood	Foppert		15-10	T1st	...
4-28	At L.A.	W	3-0		8	8	Myers	Dreifort	Mesa	16-10	1st	+0.5
4-29	At L.A.	L	2-6		8	12	Brown	Wolf		16-11	3rd	0.5
4-30	At L.A.	L	0-4		7	6	Perez	Padilla	Gagne	16-12	3rd	1.5
5-1	At L.A.	W	4-1		5	9	Duckworth	Nomo	Mesa	17-12	3rd	1.5
5-2	At S.D.	L	4-5	(10)	7	11	Matthews	Mesa		17-13	3rd	2.5
5-3	At S.D.	W	5-4	(10)	8	10	Silva	Wright	Mesa	18-13	3rd	1.5
5-4	At S.D.	W	3-1		5	3	Wolf	Eaton	Mesa	19-13	2nd	1.5
5-5	At Ari.	L	1-10		7	11	Batista	Padilla		19-14	3rd	2.0
5-6	At Ari.	L	5-6		9	9	Villarreal	Adams		19-15	3rd	3.0
5-7	At Ari.	W	5-2		7	6	Millwood	Webb	Mesa	20-15	3rd	2.5
5-9	Hou.	W	5-3		10	8	Myers	Oswalt	Mesa	21-15	3rd	2.5
5-10	Hou.	W	2-0		6	5	Wolf	Miller		22-15	3rd	2.5
5-11	Hou.	L	7-10		7	12	Munro	Padilla	Wagner	22-16	3rd	3.5
5-13	Ari.	L	1-6		6	11	Koplove	Mesa		22-17	3rd	5.0
5-14	Ari.	L	0-2		2	4	Schilling	Myers		22-18	3rd	5.0
5-15	Ari.	W	6-4		7	6	Cormier	Villarreal	Mesa	23-18	3rd	5.0
5-16	At Hou.	L	2-4		11	11	Dotel	Wendell	Wagner	23-19	3rd	6.0
5-17	At Hou.	W	9-4		10	8	Duckworth	Bland		24-19	3rd	6.0
5-18	At Hou.	W	3-1		3	6	Millwood	Redding		25-19	3rd	6.0
5-20	At N.Y.	W	11-7		14	9	Myers	Lloyd		26-19	3rd	5.0
5-21	At N.Y.	L	4-5		8	12	Benitez	Adams		26-20	3rd	5.0
5-22	At N.Y.	L	3-6		5	12	Astacio	Padilla	Benitez	26-21	3rd	6.0
5-23	At Mon.	W	4-2		11	7	Millwood	Day	Mesa	27-21	3rd	5.0
5-24	At Mon.	L	2-3		4	7	Ayala	Silva		27-22	3rd	6.0
5-25	At Mon.	L	3-5		8	6	Vazquez	Myers	Biddle	27-23	3rd	7.0
5-27	N.Y.	L	2-4		7	10	Leiter	Wolf	Benitez	27-24	3rd	7.5
5-28	N.Y.	W	11-3		13	8	Padilla	Astacio		28-24	3rd	7.5
5-29	N.Y.	L	0-5		6	9	Trachsel	Millwood		28-25	3rd	8.0
5-30	Mon.	W	12-5		12	9	Cormier	Vazquez		29-25	3rd	8.0
6-1†	Mon.	W	4-3		9	3	Wolf	Hernandez	Mesa	30-25		
6-1‡	Mon.	W	4-1		8	5	Myers	Smith	Mesa	31-25	3rd	6.0
6-3	Sea.	L	0-4		6	10	Moyer	Millwood		31-26	3rd	7.0
6-4	Sea.	L	2-7		5	14	Meche	Padilla		31-27	3rd	8.0
6-5	Sea.	L	4-5		8	8	Mateo	Mesa	Sasaki	31-28	3rd	9.0
6-6	Oak.	L	4-7		10	7	Zito	Myers		31-29	3rd	9.5
6-8†	Oak.	W	7-1		11	7	Millwood	Mulder		32-29		
6-8‡	Oak.	W	8-3		9	5	Wolf	Harang		33-29	3rd	9.5
6-9	At Ana.	W	3-0		8	6	Padilla	Washburn	Mesa	34-29	3rd	9.0
6-10	At Ana.	L	1-2		6	4	Lackey	Duckworth	Percival	34-30	3rd	9.0

Date	Opp.	Res.	Score	(inn.*)	Hits	Opp. hits	Winning pitcher	Losing pitcher	Save	Record	Pos.	GB
6-11	At Ana.	L	3-5		8	9	Weber	Myers	Percival	34-31	3rd	10.0
6-13	At Cin.	L	1-15		3	22	Haynes	Millwood		34-32	3rd	10.5
6-14	At Cin.	W	12-2		14	5	Wolf	Graves		35-32	3rd	10.5
6-17	Atl.	W	5-4		13	8	Wendell	Holmes		36-32	3rd	9.0
6-18	Atl.	L	1-6		9	10	Ortiz	Millwood		36-33	3rd	10.0
6-19	Atl.	W	3-2		5	7	Mesa	Smoltz		37-33	3rd	9.0
6-21	Bos.	W	6-5	(13)	11	15	Mesa	Seanez		38-33	3rd	9.5
6-22	Bos.	W	5-0		7	3	Myers	Kim		39-33	3rd	8.5
6-24	At Atl.	L	3-5		7	8	Ortiz	Millwood	Smoltz	39-34	3rd	9.5
6-25	At Atl.	W	8-1		11	4	Padilla	Maddux		40-34	3rd	8.5
6-26	At Atl.	W	8-1		15	5	Wolf	Hampton		41-34	3rd	7.5
6-27	At Bal.	W	4-2	(17)	15	10	Plesac	Daal	Mercado	42-34	2nd	7.5
6-28	At Bal.	W	9-5		14	12	Myers	Hentgen		43-34	2nd	6.5
6-29	At Bal.	W	4-3		7	9	Millwood	Helling	Mesa	44-34	2nd	6.5
6-30	Chi.	W	4-3		7	7	Padilla	Estes	Mesa	45-34	2nd	5.5
7-1	Chi.	W	4-3		11	10	Adams	Remlinger		46-34	2nd	4.5
7-2	Chi.	L	0-1		1	7	Farnsworth	Wendell	Borowski	46-35	2nd	5.5
7-3	Chi.	W	12-2		14	8	Myers	Zambrano		47-35	2nd	4.5
7-4	Fla.	L	1-2		6	3	Looper	Mesa		47-36	2nd	5.5
7-5	Fla.	L	4-5		7	8	Penny	Padilla	Looper	47-37	2nd	6.5
7-6	Fla.	L	3-6		7	8	Redman	Wolf		47-38	2nd	7.5
7-7	At Mon.	L	1-8		7	10	Hernandez	Duckworth		47-39	2nd	8.5
7-8	At Mon.	W	13-6		16	13	Myers	Vargas		48-39	2nd	8.5
7-9	At Mon.	W	2-0		3	3	Millwood	Ohka		49-39	2nd	8.5
7-10	At N.Y.	W	7-2		15	7	Padilla	Trachsel		50-39	2nd	8.5
7-11	At N.Y.	W	10-3		14	7	Wolf	Heilman		51-39	2nd	8.5
7-12	At N.Y.	W	4-2	(11)	13	8	Mesa	Franco		52-39	2nd	7.5
7-13	At N.Y.	L	3-4		12	11	Benitez	Adams		52-40	2nd	8.5
7-17	Mon.	W	5-2	(11)	11	10	Plesac	Drew		53-40	2nd	8.5
7-18	Mon.	L	1-3		9	11	Vazquez	Wolf		53-41	2nd	9.5
7-19	Mon.	W	4-3	(11)	9	7	Mesa	Almonte		54-41	2nd	9.5
7-20	Mon.	W	3-2		9	7	Myers	Vargas	Mesa	55-41	2nd	9.5
7-21	N.Y.	L	6-8		12	13	Heilman	Duckworth	Franco	55-42	2nd	9.5
7-22	N.Y.	L	5-7		12	11	Trachsel	Millwood	Wheeler	55-43	2nd	10.5
7-23	At Chi.	W	3-0		4	4	Wolf	Clement		56-43	2nd	9.5
7-24	At Chi.	W	14-6		14	9	Padilla	Wood		57-43	2nd	9.5
7-25	At Fla.	L	5-11		9	13	Urbina	Williams		57-44	2nd	9.5
7-26	At Fla.	L	5-10		13	15	Beckett	Duckworth	Looper	57-45	2nd	10.5
7-27	At Fla.	L	6-7		10	15	Urbina	Williams		57-46	2nd	10.5
7-28	At Cin.	L	5-6	(10)	9	14	Williamson	Adams		57-47	2nd	11.5
7-29	L.A.	W	2-0		5	3	Padilla	Ishii	Mesa	58-47	2nd	11.5
7-30	L.A.	W	4-2		13	9	Wendell	Shuey	Mesa	59-47	2nd	10.5
7-31	L.A.	W	7-3		8	7	Duckworth	Perez		60-47	2nd	10.5
8-1	S.D.	W	6-0		10	3	Millwood	Jarvis		61-47	2nd	10.5
8-2†	S.D.	L	4-6		7	7	Peavy	Wolf		61-48		
8-2‡	S.D.	W	10-4		14	10	Cormier	Roa		62-48	2nd	11.0
8-3	S.D.	L	2-5	(10)	5	9	Witasick	Mesa	Beck	62-49	2nd	11.0
8-5	At Col.	W	7-2		8	9	Myers	Chacon		63-49	2nd	10.0
8-6	At Col.	L	1-5		5	8	Tsao	Duckworth		63-50	2nd	11.0
8-7	At Col.	L	3-4		8	6	Lopez	Millwood	Speier	63-51	2nd	12.0
8-8	At S.F	L	1-9		3	11	Foppert	Wolf		63-52	T2nd	13.0
8-9	At S.F	W	8-6	(10)	11	10	Wendell	Brower		64-52	T2nd	12.0
8-10	At S.F	L	2-5		11	9	Correia	Myers		64-53	T2nd	12.0
8-12	Mil.	L	3-6		5	7	Franklin	Duckworth	Kolb	64-54	3rd	12.0
8-13	Mil.	W	11-4		14	9	Millwood	Sheets		65-54	3rd	12.0
8-14	Mil.	W	4-3		12	8	Wolf	Obermueller	Williams	66-54	2nd	12.0
8-15	StL.	W	7-4		12	12	Padilla	Williams	Plesac	67-54	2nd	12.0
8-16	StL.	W	5-4		9	7	Myers	Haren	Mesa	68-54	2nd	12.0
8-17	StL.	W	6-4		7	6	Telemaco	Tomko	Williams	69-54	2nd	11.0
8-19	At Mil.	L	4-6		10	8	DeJean	Wendell	Kolb	69-55	2nd	11.5
8-20	At Mil.	L	1-10		11	12	Kinney	Wolf		69-56	2nd	11.5
8-21	At Mil.	L	2-5		11	8	Estrella	Padilla	Kolb	69-57	2nd	11.5
8-22	At StL.	W	9-4		14	9	Cormier	Kline		70-57	2nd	11.5
8-23	At StL.	L	3-5		12	10	Hitchcock	Telemaco	Isringhausen	70-58	2nd	12.5
8-24	At StL.	L	0-3		6	8	Tomko	Millwood	DeJean	70-59	2nd	13.5
8-25	At Mon.	L	1-12		8	15	Hernandez	Wolf		70-60	T2nd	14.0
8-26	At Mon.	L	10-14		14	16	Eischen	Williams	Ayala	70-61	T2nd	14.0
8-27	At Mon.	L	6-9		7	14	Almonte	Plesac	Biddle	70-62	T2nd	15.0
8-28	At Mon.	L	0-4		4	7	Vazquez	Telemaco		70-63	T2nd	15.0
8-29	At N.Y.	W	7-0		9	3	Millwood	Trachsel		71-63	T2nd	14.0
8-30	At N.Y.	W	4-2		11	6	Wolf	Glavine	Mesa	72-63	T2nd	14.0
8-31	At N.Y.	W	4-1		4	2	Padilla	Seo	Mesa	73-63	T2nd	14.0

Date	Opp.	Res.	Score	(inn.*)	Hits	Opp. hits	Winning pitcher	Losing pitcher	Save	Record	Pos.	GB
9-1	Bos.	L	9-13		14	13	Kim	Mesa		73-64	3rd	14.0
9-2	Mon.	W	5-3		8	7	Cormier	Vazquez	Plesac	74-64	T2nd	13.0
9-3	Mon.	W	8-3		11	7	Millwood	Tucker		75-64	T2nd	12.0
9-4	N.Y.	W	6-5		12	7	de los Santos	Stanton		76-64	T2nd	11.5
9-5	N.Y.	W	1-0		3	6	Padilla	Seo	Cormier	77-64	2nd	11.0
9-6	N.Y.	W	9-6		12	9	Myers	Griffiths	Wendell	78-64	2nd	11.0
9-7	N.Y.	W	5-4	(11)	11	8	Cormier	Wheeler		79-64	2nd	11.0
9-8	At Atl.	L	4-6		4	11	Ortiz	Millwood	Cunnane	79-65	T2nd	12.0
9-9	At Atl.	W	18-5		14	11	Wolf	Reynolds		80-65	T2nd	11.0
9-10	At Atl.	L	2-4		6	10	Ramirez	Padilla	Cunnane	80-66	3rd	12.0
9-11	At Atl.	W	8-3		16	10	Myers	Maddux		81-66	3rd	11.0
9-12	At Pit.	L	4-8		7	12	Wells	Telemaco		81-67	3rd	11.0
9-13	At Pit.	L	3-5		8	8	Fogg	Millwood	Tavarez	81-68	3rd	11.0
9-14	At Pit.	W	10-7		14	10	Wolf	Torres	Williams	82-68	3rd	11.0
9-16	Fla.	W	14-0		17	6	Padilla	Pavano		83-68	3rd	10.5
9-17	Fla.	L	4-11		8	14	Redman	Myers		83-69	3rd	11.5
9-18	Fla.	W	5-4		8	8	Cormier	Fox		84-69	3rd	11.0
9-19	Cin.	W	7-3		7	5	Wolf	Hall		85-69	2nd	11.0
9-20	Cin.	L	0-2		4	6	Van Poppel	Telemaco	Reitsma	85-70	3rd	11.0
9-21	Cin.	L	3-4		6	9	Serafini	Padilla	Reitsma	85-71	3rd	12.0
9-23	At Fla.	L	4-5		7	8	Tejera	Williams	Urbina	85-72	3rd	12.5
9-24	At Fla.	L	5-6		7	9	Beckett	Myers	Urbina	85-73	3rd	13.5
9-25	At Fla.	L	4-8		7	12	Penny	Wolf		85-74	3rd	14.0
9-26	Atl.	L	0-6		5	12	Ramirez	Padilla		85-75	3rd	15.0
9-27	Atl.	W	7-6	(10)	14	10	Cormier	King		86-75	3rd	14.0
9-28	Atl.	L	2-5		8	13	Maddux	Millwood	Marquis	86-76	3rd	15.0

Monthly records: March (1-0), April (15-12), May (13-13), June (16-9), July (15-13), August (13-16), September (13-13).
*Innings, if other than nine. † First game of a doubleheader. ‡ Second game of a doubleheader.

RECORDS

2003 regular-season record: 86-76
Position: 3rd in N.L. East
Home: 49-32 **Road:** 37-44
N.L. East: 39-37 **N.L. Central:** 21-18
N.L. West: 18-14 A.L. 8-7
Vs. LH starters: 14-17
Vs. RH starters: 72-59
Grass: 34-37 **Artificial:** 52-39
Day: 27-23 **Night:** 59-53
1-Run: 20-18 **X-inn.:** 10-3
Doubleheaders: 2-0-1
Team record past five years: 394-415 (.487, ranks 8th in league in that span)

TEAM LEADERS

Batting average: Mike Lieberthal (.313).
At-bats: Jimmy Rollins (628).
Runs: Jim Thome (111).
Hits: Bobby Abreu (173).
Total Bases: Jim Thome (331).
Doubles: Jimmy Rollins (42).
Triples: Jimmy Rollins (6).
Home runs: Jim Thome (47).
Runs batted in: Jim Thome (131).
Stolen bases: Bobby Abreu (22).
Slugging percentage: Jim Thome (.573).
On-base percentage: Bobby Abreu (.409).
Wins: Randy Wolf (16).
Earned-run average: Vicente Padilla (3.62).
Complete games: Kevin Millwood (5).
Shutouts: Kevin Millwood (3).
Saves: Jose Mesa (24).
Innings pitched: Kevin Millwood (222.0).
Strikeouts: Randy Wolf (177).

GAMES BY POSITION

Catcher: Mike Lieberthal 131, Todd Pratt 35, Kelly Stinnett 1.
First base: Jim Thome 156, Tomas Perez 9, Todd Pratt 6, Tyler Houston 1.
Second base: Placido Polanco 99, Chase Utley 37, Tomas Perez 26, Nick Punto 16, David Bell 3.
Third base: David Bell 85, Tomas Perez 58, Tyler Houston 21, Placido Polanco 21, Nick Punto 9, Travis Chapman 1.
Shortstop: Jimmy Rollins 154, Nick Punto 7, Tomas Perez 4.
Outfield: Bobby Abreu 158, Pat Burrell 140, Marlon Byrd 131, Ricky Ledee 71, Jason Michaels 38.
Designated hitter: Pat Burrell 2, Ricky Ledee 2, Jim Thome 2.

TOP DRAFT CHOICES

3. **Tim Moss,** 2B, Texas.
4. **Michael Bourn,** OF, Houston.
5. **Javon Moran,** OF, Auburn.
6. **Jordan Parraz,** RHP, Green Valley H.S., Henderson, Nev.
7. **Kyle Kendrick,** RHP, Mount Vernon (Wash.) H.S.
8. **Matt Linder,** RHP, Winston Churchill H.S., Thunder Bay, Ont.
9. **Jason Crosland,** 3B, Lamar (Colo.) CC.
10. **Matt Hopper,** 1B, Nebraska.

PITTSBURGH PIRATES

NATIONAL LEAGUE CENTRAL DIVISION

2004 SEASON

April

SUN	MON	TUE	WED	THU	FRI	SAT
4	5 PHI	6	7 PHI	8 PHI	9 CIN	10 CIN
11 CIN	12 CHC	13	14 CHC	15 CHC	16 NYM	17 NYM
18 NYM	19	20 CHC	21 CHC	22 CHC	23 CIN	24 CIN
25 CIN	26 CIN	27 HOU	28 HOU	29 HOU	30 MIL	

May

SUN	MON	TUE	WED	THU	FRI	SAT
						1 MIL
2 MIL	3	4 HOU	5 HOU	6 HOU	7 LA	8 LA
9 LA	10	11 COL	12 COL	13 COL	14 SF	15 SF
16 SF	17	18 SD	19 SD	20 SD	21 MIL	22 MIL
23 MIL	24	25 STL	26 STL	27 STL	28 CHC	29 CHC
30 CHC	31 STL					

June

SUN	MON	TUE	WED	THU	FRI	SAT
		1 STL	2 STL	3 STL	4 CHC	5 CHC
6 CHC	7 TEX	8 TEX	9 TEX	10	11 OAK	12 OAK
13 OAK	14	15 ANA	16 ANA	17 ANA	18 SEA	19 SEA
20 SEA	21 HOU	22 HOU	23 HOU	24 HOU	25 CIN	26 CIN
27 CIN	28 STL	29 STL	30 STL			

July

SUN	MON	TUE	WED	THU	FRI	SAT
				1	2 MIL	3 MIL
4 MIL	5 FLA	6 FLA	7 FLA	8 * MON	9 * MON	10 * MON
11 * MON	12	13 All-Star	14	15	16 FLA	17 FLA
18 FLA	19 MON	20 MON	21 ATL	22 ATL	23 CIN	24 CIN
25 CIN	26 ATL	27 ATL	28 ATL	29 ATL	30 MIL	31 MIL

August

SUN	MON	TUE	WED	THU	FRI	SAT
1 MIL	2	3 LA	4 LA	5 LA	6 SD	7 SD
8 SD	9	10 SF	11 SF	12 SF	13 COL	14 COL
15 COL	16 ARI	17 ARI	18 ARI	19 STL	20 STL	21 STL
22 STL	23 ARI	24 ARI	25 ARI	26	27 STL	28 STL
29 STL	30 MIL	31 MIL				

Sept./Oct.

SUN	MON	TUE	WED	THU	FRI	SAT
			1 MIL	2 MIL	3 HOU	4 HOU
5 HOU	6 MIL	7 MIL	8 MIL	9 HOU	10 HOU	11 HOU
12 HOU	13 CHC	14 CHC	15 CHC	16	17 NYM	18 NYM
19 NYM	20	21 CHC	22 CHC	23 CHC	24 CIN	25 CIN
26 CIN	27 PHI	28 PHI	29 PHI	30	1 CIN	2 CIN
3 CIN	4	5	6	7	8	9

Home games shaded. All-Star Game July 13 at Houston. Schedule subject to change. * San Juan, Puerto Rico.

CLUB DIRECTORY

General partner
Kevin S. McClatchy
Sr. v.p. and general manager
Dave Littlefield
Assistant g.m./player personnel
Roy Smith

Special assistants to the g.m.
John Flores, Jax Robertson, Doug Strange, Pete Vuckovich, Louie Eljaua
Vice president, communications
Patty Paytas
Director of media relations
Jim Trdinich

Director of player development
To be announced
Director of business development
Bob Derda

MINOR LEAGUE AFFILIATES

Class	Team	League	Manager
AAA	Nashville	Pacific Coast	Trent Jewett
AA	Altoona	Eastern	Dale Sveum
Advanced A	Lynchburg	Carolina	Tony Beasley
A	Hickory	South Atlantic	Dave Clark
Short-Season A	Williamsport	New York-Pennsylvania	Jeff Branson
Rookie	Gulf Coast Pirates	Gulf Coast	Woody Huyke

BROADCAST INFORMATION

Radio: KDKA-AM (1020).
Cable TV: Fox Sports Pittsburgh.

SPRING TRAINING

Ballpark (city): McKechnie Field (Bradenton, Fla.).
Ticket information: 941-748-4610.

More on the Pirates at www.foxsports.com/named/FS/MLB/teams

SPRING TRAINING ROSTER

Manager— Lloyd McClendon (23).
Coaches—Rusty Kuntz (48), Pete Mackanin (25), Gerald Perry (28), John Russell (13), Bruce Tanner (52), Spin Williams (54).

No.	PITCHERS	B/T	Ht./Wt.	Age*	2003 Clubs
53	Beimel, Joe	L/L	6-3/220	26	Pittsburgh
34	Benson, Kris	R/R	6-4/195	29	Pittsburgh
71	Boehringer, Brian	B/R	6-2/192	34	Pittsburgh
	Boyd, Jason	R/R	6-3/180	31	Buffalo, Cleveland
	Bradley, Bobby	R/R	6-1/180	23	Gulf Coast Pirates, Lynchburg
	Burnett, Sean	L/L	6-1/180	21	Altoona
44	Corey, Mark	R/R	6-3/220	29	Nashville, Pittsburgh
27	Fogg, Josh	R/R	6-0/202	27	Nashville, Pittsburgh
51	Gonzalez, Mike	R/L	6-2/213	25	Lynchburg, Altoona, Pawtucket, Nashville, Pittsburgh
39	Grabow, John	L/L	6-2/185	25	Altoona, Nashville, Pittsburgh
	Johnston, Mike	L/L	6-3/200	25	Altoona
46	Meadows, Brian	R/R	6-3/236	28	Nashville, Pittsburgh
	Oquendo, Ian	R/R	5-11/165	22	Lynchburg, Altoona
48	Perez, Oliver	L/L	6-3/160	22	Portland, San Diego, Pittsburgh
	Stewart, Cory	L/L	6-4/180	24	Mobile
31	Torres, Salomon	R/R	5-11/210	32	Nashville, Pittsburgh
	VanBenschoten, J.	R/R	6-4/215	23	Lynchburg, Altoona
22	Vogelsong, Ryan	R/R	6-3/205	26	Nashville, Pittsburgh
32	Wells, Kip	R/R	6-3/205	26	Pittsburgh
58	Williams, David	L/L	6-2/213	25	Nashville

No.	CATCHERS	B/T	Ht./Wt.	Age*	2003 Clubs
11	Cota, Humberto	R/R	6-0/210	25	Pittsburgh, Nashville
	Doumit, Ryan	B/R	6-0/200	22	Lynchburg
30	House, J.R.	R/R	5-10/202	24	Gulf Coast Pirates, Altoona, Pittsburgh
18	Kendall, Jason	R/R	6-0/197	29	Pittsburgh

No.	INFIELDERS	B/T	Ht./Wt.	Age*	2003 Clubs
	Castillo, Jose	R/R	5-11/185	23	Altoona
17	Hill, Bobby	B/R	5-10/190	25	Chicago N.L., Iowa, Nashville, Pittsburgh
10	Nunez, A.O.	B/R	5-11/186	28	Pittsburgh
55	Rivera, Carlos	L/L	6-1/245	25	Nashville, Pittsburgh
	Sanchez, Freddy	R/R	5-11/185	26	Boston, Pawtucket, Nashville
	Stynes, Chris	R/R	5-10/205	31	Colorado
2	Wilson, Jack	R/R	6-0/193	26	Pittsburgh

No.	OUTFIELDERS	B/T	Ht./Wt.	Age*	2003 Clubs
56	Alvarez, Tony	R/R	6-1/200	24	Nashville
38	Bay, Jason	R/R	6-2/200	25	San Diego, Portland, Pittsburgh
26	Davis, J.J.	R/R	6-5/240	25	Nashville, Pittsburgh
59	Mackowiak, Rob	L/R	5-10/192	27	Nashville, Pittsburgh
5	Redman, Tike	L/L	5-11/166	27	Nashville, Pittsburgh
36	Wilson, Craig	R/R	6-2/218	27	Pittsburgh

Invited to spring training: RHP Juan Acevedo, 1B/OF Daryle Ward.

*Age as of April 1, 2004.

BALLPARK INFORMATION

Ballpark (capacity, surface)
PNC Park (38,496, grass)
Address
PNC Park at North Shore
115 Federal Street
Pittsburgh, PA 15212
Official website
www.pittsburghpirates.com
Business phone
412-323-5000
Ticket information
800-BUY-BUCS
Field dimensions (from home plate)
To left field at foul line, 325 feet
To center field, 399 feet
To right field at foul line, 320 feet
First game played
April 9, 2001 (Reds 8, Pirates 2)

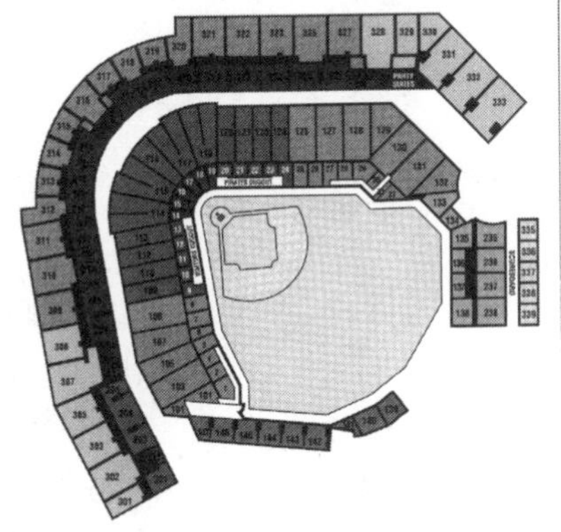

2003 REVIEW

DAY BY DAY

Date	Opp.	Res.	Score	(inn.*)	Hits	Opp. hits	Winning pitcher	Losing pitcher	Save	Record	Pos.	GB
3-31	At Cin.	W	10-1		12	4	Benson	Haynes		1-0	T1st	...
4-2	At Cin.	W	7-4		10	9	Torres	Manzanillo	Williams	2-0	T1st	...
4-3	At Cin.	W	7-5		12	6	Fogg	Anderson	Williams	3-0	T1st	...
4-4	At Phi.	W	9-1		12	3	Suppan	Roa	Torres	4-0	1st	+1.0
4-5	At Phi.	L	1-16		10	19	Silva	D'Amico		4-1	T1st	...
4-6	At Phi.	W	2-0		8	8	Benson	Myers	Williams	5-1	1st	+0.5
4-8	Mil.	L	3-5		5	8	Rusch	Wells	DeJean	5-2	1st	+0.5
4-9	Mil.	L	2-3		6	5	Ritchie	Fogg	DeJean	5-3	T2nd	0.5
4-10	Mil.	W	3-1		7	7	Suppan	Sheets	Williams	6-3	2nd	0.5
4-11	At Chi.	W	3-2		8	8	D'Amico	Zambrano	Williams	7-3	2nd	0.5
4-12	At Chi.	L	0-4		4	6	Wood	Benson	Borowski	7-4	2nd	0.5
4-13	At Chi.	L	3-4		4	5	Farnsworth	Boehringer	Borowski	7-5	T2nd	0.5
4-15	N.Y.	L	1-3		5	6	Glavine	Fogg	Benitez	7-6	T2nd	0.5
4-16	N.Y.	W	6-3		12	6	Suppan	Cone		8-6	T2nd	0.5
4-17	N.Y.	L	2-7		9	13	Seo	D'Amico		8-7	T3rd	1.5
4-18	Chi.	L	2-7		3	10	Clement	Benson		8-8	4th	2.5
4-19	Chi.	L	1-6	(10)	6	8	Prior	Sauerbeck		8-9	4th	3.5
4-20	Chi.	W	8-2		10	6	Torres	Estes		9-9	T3rd	2.5
4-22	S.F	W	5-2		6	9	Suppan	Foppert		10-9	T2nd	2.5
4-23	S.F	L	3-4	(13)	16	10	Brower	Tavarez		10-10	T2nd	2.5
4-24	S.F	L	1-3		7	9	Moss	Benson	Worrell	10-11	T2nd	2.5
4-25	L.A.	L	2-5		5	10	Brohawn	Williams	Gagne	10-12	T3rd	3.5
4-26	L.A.	L	3-4		7	6	Nomo	Sauerbeck	Gagne	10-13	T3rd	3.5
4-27	L.A.	L	2-6		9	10	Ishii	Suppan		10-14	4th	3.5
4-29	At S.D.	W	7-2		13	9	D'Amico	Eaton		11-14	T3rd	3.5
4-30	At S.D.	W	8-5		9	10	Benson	Perez	Williams	12-14	3rd	2.5
5-1	At S.D.	W	5-2		9	4	Wells	Peavy	Williams	13-14	3rd	2.5
5-2	At L.A.	W	5-3		7	10	Beimel	Quantrill	Williams	14-14	3rd	2.5
5-3	At L.A.	L	1-4		6	12	Dreifort	Suppan	Gagne	14-15	3rd	2.5
5-4	At L.A.	L	2-3		5	6	Brown	D'Amico	Gagne	14-16	T3rd	3.5
5-5	At Hou.	L	1-8		4	13	Miller	Benson		14-17	4th	3.5
5-6	At Hou.	L	9-10		12	9	Bland	Sauerbeck	Wagner	14-18	5th	3.5
5-7	At Hou.	L	4-13		9	13	Dotel	Tavarez		14-19	5th	4.5
5-8	At Hou.	L	2-6		6	10	Stone	Suppan		14-20	5th	5.0
5-9	Ari.	L	0-5		4	12	Schilling	D'Amico		14-21	5th	5.0
5-10	Ari.	W	5-4		7	10	Benson	Dessens	Williams	15-21	5th	5.0
5-11	Ari.	L	1-2		6	5	Batista	Wells	Mantei	15-22	5th	5.5
5-12	Hou.	L	4-9		12	12	Stone	Torres		15-23	5th	6.5
5-13	Hou.	L	3-6		8	12	Munro	Williams	Wagner	15-24	5th	7.5
5-14	Hou.	W	3-2		7	7	D'Amico	Miller	Williams	16-24	5th	7.5
5-15	Hou.	L	2-6		9	11	Oswalt	Benson		16-25	5th	8.5
5-16	At Ari.	W	8-5	(12)	14	9	Boehringer	Mantei	Williams	17-25	5th	7.5
5-17	At Ari.	W	8-5		9	10	Torres	Capuano	Williams	18-25	5th	7.5
5-18	At Ari.	L	6-8		12	11	Webb	Suppan		18-26	5th	7.5
5-21	Chi.	W	5-2		8	7	D'Amico	Wood	Williams	19-26	5th	6.0
5-22	Chi.	L	2-3		7	12	Remlinger	Sauerbeck	Borowski	19-27	5th	7.0
5-23	StL.	L	8-10	(10)	15	17	Eldred	Meadows	Fassero	19-28	5th	7.0
5-24	StL.	L	0-6		9	10	Morris	Suppan		19-29	5th	8.0
5-25	StL.	W	8-7		10	10	Boehringer	Hermanson	Williams	20-29	5th	8.0
5-26	At Chi.	W	10-0		8	5	Fogg	Wood		21-29	5th	7.0
5-27	At Chi.	W	9-4		14	7	Benson	Clement		22-29	5th	6.0
5-28	At Chi.	L	4-5		9	5	Prior	D'Amico	Borowski	22-30	5th	7.0
5-30	At StL.	W	7-3		12	8	Suppan	Stephenson		23-30	5th	6.0
5-31	At StL.	W	4-3		9	6	Wells	Williams	Williams	24-30	5th	6.0
6-1	At StL.	L	4-5		8	7	Kline	Beimel	Fassero	24-31	5th	6.0
6-4†	Bos.	L	4-11		7	16	Kim	Benson		24-32		
6-4‡	Bos.	L	3-8		7	12	Lowe	D'Amico		24-33	5th	7.0
6-5	Bos.	W	5-4		11	7	Boehringer	Mendoza	Williams	25-33	5th	7.0
6-7	At Atl.	L	6-8		12	13	Hernandez	Boehringer	Smoltz	25-34	5th	8.5
6-8	At Atl.	L	5-6		9	12	Hodges	Fogg	Smoltz	25-35	5th	9.5
6-10	At Tor.	L	8-13		14	19	Lidle	Benson		25-36	5th	9.5
6-11	At Tor.	L	5-8		12	11	Halladay	D'Amico		25-37	5th	10.5
6-12	At Tor.	L	4-5		6	7	Hendrickson	Suppan	Politte	25-38	6th	10.5
6-13	At T.B.	L	1-7		1	8	Zambrano	Wells		25-39	6th	10.5

Date	Opp.	Res.	Score	(inn.*)	Hits	Opp. hits	Winning pitcher	Losing pitcher	Save	Record	Pos.	GB
6-14	At T.B.	W	12-9		17	14	Fogg	Bell	Williams	26-39	6th	10.5
6-15	At T.B.	W	9-5		11	12	Sauerbeck	Levine	Williams	27-39	5th	9.5
6-18†	Mon.	W	7-3		13	8	D'Amico	Hernandez	Williams	28-39		
6-18‡	Mon.	W	4-3		11	8	Torres	Biddle		29-39	5th	9.0
6-19	Mon.	L	2-5		9	15	Ohka	Torres	Biddle	29-40	5th	9.0
6-20	Cle.	W	5-4	(15)	10	18	Torres	Baez		30-40	5th	8.0
6-21	Cle.	W	7-6	(15)	16	12	Sauerbeck	Miceli		31-40	5th	7.5
6-22	Cle.	L	5-8		10	14	Sabathia	Vogelsong	Baez	31-41	5th	8.5
6-23	At Mon.	L	0-3		3	8	Vargas	Suppan	Biddle	31-42	5th	8.5
6-24	At Mon.	L	4-6		8	9	Ohka	D'Amico	Biddle	31-43	5th	9.5
6-25	At Mon.	W	6-5		9	9	Sauerbeck	Eischen	Williams	32-43	5th	8.5
6-27	Col.	W	5-3		8	12	Fogg	Jennings	Williams	33-43	5th	7.0
6-28	Col.	L	4-5		11	7	Neagle	Benson	Jimenez	33-44	5th	8.0
6-29	Col.	W	9-0		11	4	Suppan	Chacon		34-44	5th	8.0
7-1	Cin.	L	3-5		12	13	Graves	Tavarez	Williamson	34-45	5th	7.5
7-2	Cin.	L	3-4		7	13	Heredia	Williams	Williamson	34-46	5th	7.5
7-3	Cin.	W	8-7		12	11	Fogg	Dempster	Williams	35-46	5th	7.5
7-4	Hou.	W	3-2		5	6	Boehringer	Munro	Williams	36-46	5th	7.5
7-5	Hou.	W	4-3		9	10	Suppan	Saarloos	Williams	37-46	5th	6.5
7-6	Hou.	W	8-3		14	4	D'Amico	Miller		38-46	5th	6.5
7-7	At Mil.	L	2-9		4	10	Franklin	Wells		38-47	5th	6.5
7-8	At Mil.	W	8-7	(10)	12	9	Williams	DeJean	Torres	39-47	5th	5.5
7-9	At Mil.	L	1-2	(12)	6	12	Kieschnick	Beimel		39-48	5th	6.5
7-10	At Mil.	W	5-4		10	8	Suppan	Ford		40-48	4th	6.5
7-11	At Hou.	L	2-4		6	10	Miller	D'Amico	Wagner	40-49	5th	7.5
7-12	At Hou.	W	5-2		10	6	Wells	Oswalt	Williams	41-49	5th	6.5
7-13	At Hou.	L	2-5		8	10	Redding	Fogg	Wagner	41-50	5th	7.5
7-17	Mil.	L	5-7		9	9	Franklin	Benson	Estrella	41-51	5th	8.5
7-18	Mil.	W	7-2		13	11	Suppan	Rusch		42-51	5th	8.5
7-19	Mil.	L	0-1		8	9	Sheets	D'Amico	Kolb	42-52	5th	9.5
7-20	Mil.	W	6-3		10	12	Wells	Ford	Lincoln	43-52	4th	9.5
7-21	Hou.	W	5-3		10	9	Fogg	Redding	Lincoln	44-52	4th	8.5
7-22	Hou.	L	0-2		3	8	Robertson	Torres	Wagner	44-53	4th	9.5
7-23	At Cin.	W	6-5		12	11	Boehringer	Mercker	Lincoln	45-53	4th	9.5
7-24	At Cin.	W	7-5	(11)	10	9	Lincoln	Reitsma		46-53	4th	8.5
7-25	At StL.	W	10-5		10	8	Meadows	Eldred		47-53	4th	7.5
7-26	At StL.	L	8-13		12	19	Williams	Fogg	Isringhausen	47-54	4th	8.5
7-27	At StL.	L	3-4		6	12	Eldred	Lincoln		47-55	4th	8.5
7-28	At StL.	W	3-0		11	7	Suppan	Tomko		48-55	4th	8.0
7-29	S.D.	L	7-8		7	11	Roa	Lincoln	Beck	48-56	4th	8.0
7-30	S.D.	W	7-2		8	6	Wells	Lawrence	Meadows	49-56	4th	8.0
7-31	S.D.	L	7-10		8	16	Eaton	Fogg	Beck	49-57	4th	8.0
8-1	Col.	W	12-11		13	12	Sanchez	Bernero		50-57	4th	8.0
8-2	Col.	W	1-0		3	6	Meadows	Jennings	Lincoln	51-57	4th	7.0
8-3	Col.	L	4-16		11	24	Oliver	D'Amico	Jimenez	51-58	4th	8.0
8-5	At S.F	L	0-3		6	6	Schmidt	Wells	Worrell	51-59	4th	8.0
8-6	At S.F	W	2-0		7	3	Tavarez	Ponson		52-59	4th	8.0
8-7	At S.F	L	5-7		7	7	Eyre	Boehringer	Worrell	52-60	4th	8.0
8-8	At Col.	L	6-13		10	16	Jimenez	Mahomes		52-61	4th	9.0
8-9	At Col.	W	10-4		11	6	D'Amico	Oliver		53-61	4th	8.0
8-10	At Col.	W	5-3		9	11	Figueroa	Chacon	Lincoln	54-61	4th	8.0
8-11	StL.	L	4-6		17	10	Haren	Wells	Isringhausen	54-62	4th	9.0
8-12	StL.	L	6-10		12	12	Tomko	Fogg	Simontacchi	54-63	4th	9.0
8-13	StL.	W	6-5		13	11	Tavarez	Borbon		55-63	4th	8.0
8-14	StL.	L	3-4		7	11	Stephenson	D'Amico	Isringhausen	55-64	4th	8.0
8-15	Mil.	W	6-3		8	8	Figueroa	Kinney	Tavarez	56-64	4th	7.5
8-16	Mil.	L	4-6		10	9	Vizcaino	Lincoln	Kolb	56-65	4th	8.0
8-17	Mil.	W	5-2		12	8	Fogg	Franklin	Tavarez	57-65	4th	7.0
8-19	At StL.	L	5-13		9	13	Eldred	Beimel		57-66	4th	8.0
8-20	At StL.	W	14-0		15	3	D'Amico	Stephenson		58-66	4th	7.0
8-21	At StL.	L	3-6		10	11	Eldred	Lincoln		58-67	4th	8.0
8-22	At Mil.	L	2-3		4	7	Franklin	Wells	Kolb	58-68	4th	8.0
8-23	At Mil.	L	6-7		14	12	Estrella	Corey		58-69	4th	8.0
8-24	At Mil.	L	9-10		12	12	Kolb	Gonzalez		58-70	4th	9.0
8-26	Fla.	W	4-3		10	4	Lincoln	Redman	Tavarez	59-70	4th	9.0
8-27	Fla.	W	4-0		12	3	Wells	Penny		60-70	4th	9.0
8-28	Fla.	W	5-0		10	5	Fogg	Willis		61-70	4th	8.0
8-29	Atl.	W	6-5		11	12	Tavarez	Cunnane		62-70	4th	7.0
8-30	Atl.	L	6-13		13	13	Ramirez	Perez		62-71	4th	8.0
8-31	Atl.	L	4-10		10	14	Reynolds	D'Amico		62-72	4th	9.0

Date	Opp.	Res.	Score	(inn.*)	Hits	Opp. hits	Winning pitcher	Losing pitcher	Save	Record	Pos.	GB
9-2	At Fla.	W	3-2		7	6	Wells	Willis	Tavarez	63-72	4th	8.0
9-3	At Fla.	L	0-3		5	7	Beckett	Fogg	Urbina	63-73	4th	8.5
9-4	At Fla.	L	1-5		8	8	Tejera	Torres		63-74	4th	9.0
9-5†	At Atl.	L	2-3	(10)	3	9	Cunnane	Corey		63-75		
9-5‡	At Atl.	W	5-3		8	10	Corey	Reynolds	Tavarez	64-75	4th	9.5
9-6	At Atl.	L	2-9		9	16	Maddux	D'Amico		64-76	4th	10.5
9-7	At Atl.	L	1-2		4	8	Hampton	Wells	Cunnane	64-77	4th	11.0
9-8	At Cin.	W	9-1		12	10	Fogg	Bale		65-77	4th	10.5
9-9	At Cin.	L	6-10		14	13	Belisle	Boehringer		65-78	4th	11.5
9-10	At Cin.	W	3-2		10	4	Lincoln	Reitsma	Tavarez	66-78	4th	11.5
9-11	At Cin.	L	2-3		13	6	Randall	D'Amico	Reitsma	66-79	4th	11.5
9-12	Phi.	W	8-4		12	7	Wells	Telemaco		67-79	4th	11.5
9-13	Phi.	W	5-3		8	8	Fogg	Millwood	Tavarez	68-79	4th	11.5
9-14	Phi.	L	7-10		10	14	Wolf	Torres	Williams	68-80	4th	12.5
9-15	Cin.	W	6-3		7	8	Vogelsong	Van Poppel	Tavarez	69-80	4th	12.0
9-16	Cin.	L	4-12		9	17	Harang	Perez	Reith	69-81	4th	13.0
9-17	Cin.	W	8-5		14	9	D'Amico	Etherton	Tavarez	70-81	4th	12.0
9-18	Cin.	W	7-0		12	4	Wells	Randall		71-81	4th	12.0
9-19§	Chi.	L	9-10		9	10	Veres	Figueroa	Borowski	71-82		
9-19∞	Chi.	W	10-6		15	11	Torres	Cruz		72-82	4th	12.5
9-20	Chi.	W	8-2		11	7	Vogelsong	Clement		73-82	4th	11.5
9-21	Chi.	L	1-4		7	7	Prior	Perez	Borowski	73-83	4th	11.5
9-23	At N.Y.	L	0-1		8	8	Leiter	Wells		73-84	4th	12.0
9-24	At N.Y.	L	3-5		10	10	Trachsel	D'Amico	Stanton	73-85	4th	13.0
9-25	At N.Y.	W	3-1		10	4	Torres	Roberts	Tavarez	74-85	4th	12.0
9-27†	At Chi.	L	2-4		8	8	Prior	Fogg	Borowski	74-86		
9-27‡	At Chi.	L	2-7		7	7	Clement	Vogelsong		74-87	4th	14.0
9-28	At Chi.	W	3-2		8	8	Wells	Cruz	Tavarez	75-87	4th	13.0

Monthly records: March (1-0), April (11-14), May (12-16), June (10-14), July (15-13), August (13-15), September (13-15).
*Innings, if other than nine. † First game of a doubleheader. ‡ Second game of a doubleheader. § Day separate admission. ∞ Night separate admission.

RECORDS

2003 regular-season record: 75-87
Position: 4th in N.L. Central
Home: 39-42 **Road:** 36-45
N.L. East: 15-18 **N.L. Central:** 39-45
N.L. West: 16-17 A.L. 5-7
Vs. LH starters: 20-25
Vs. RH starters: 55-62
Grass: 70-80 **Artificial:** 5-7
Day: 24-34 **Night:** 51-53
1-Run: 24-27 **X-inn.:** 5-5
Doubleheaders: 1-2-2
Team record past five years: 356-452 (.441, ranks 15th in league in that span)

TEAM LEADERS

Batting average: Jason Kendall (.325).
At-bats: Jason Kendall (587).
Runs: Jason Kendall (84).
Hits: Jason Kendall (191).
Total Bases: Reggie Sanders (257).
Doubles: Brian Giles (30).
Triples: Abraham O. Nunez (7).
Home runs: Reggie Sanders (31).
Runs batted in: Reggie Sanders (87).
Stolen bases: Kenny Lofton (18).
Slugging percentage: Reggie Sanders (.567).
On-base percentage: Brian Giles (.430).
Wins: Josh Fogg, Jeff Suppan, Kip Wells (10).
Earned-run average: Kip Wells (3.28).
Complete games: Jeff Suppan (3).
Shutouts: Jeff Suppan (2).
Saves: Mike Williams (25).
Innings pitched: Kip Wells (197.1).
Strikeouts: Kip Wells (147).

GAMES BY POSITION

Catcher: Jason Kendall 146, Craig Wilson 21, Humberto Cota 4.
First base: Randall Simon 80, Carlos Rivera 60, Kevin Young 44, Craig Wilson 36, Matt Stairs 31.
Second base: Jeff Reboulet 76, Abraham O. Nunez 71, Pokey Reese 33, Rob Mackowiak 15, Bobby Hill 1.
Third base: Aramis Ramirez 96, Jose Hernandez 58, Rob Mackowiak 19, Jeff Reboulet 7, Abraham O. Nunez 1.
Shortstop: Jack Wilson 149, Abraham O. Nunez 23.
Outfield: Reggie Sanders 120, Brian Giles 105, Kenny Lofton 81, Matt Stairs 55, Tike Redman 54, Craig Wilson 46, Adam Hyzdu 34, Rob Mackowiak 30, Jason Bay 26, J.J. Davis 10, Kevin Young 1.
Designated hitter: Craig Wilson 3, Reggie Sanders 2, Matt Stairs 2.

TOP DRAFT CHOICES

1. **Paul Maholm,** LHP, Mississippi State.
2. **Tom Gorzelanny,** LHP, Triton JC (Ill.).
3. **Steve Lerud,** C, Galena H.S., Reno, Nev.
4. **Kyle Pearson,** RHP, Mosley H.S., Panama City, Fla.
5. **Craig Stansberry,** 3B, Rice.
6. **C.J. Smith,** 1B, Florida.
7. **Russell Johnson,** RHP, Benjamin Russell H.S., Alexander City, Ala.
8. **Sergio Silva,** RHP, Pacific.
9. **Kent Wulf,** 2B, Quartz Hill H.S., Lancaster, Calif.
10. **John Peabody,** OF, Rancho Bernardo H.S., San Diego.

ST. LOUIS CARDINALS

NATIONAL LEAGUE CENTRAL DIVISION

2004 SEASON

April

SUN	MON	TUE	WED	THU	FRI	SAT
4	5 MIL	6 MIL	7 MIL	8 MIL	9 ARI	10 ARI
11 ARI	12 HOU	13 HOU	14 HOU	15	16 COL	17 COL
18 COL	19	20 HOU	21 HOU	22 HOU	23 MIL	24 MIL
25 MIL	26	27 PHI	28 PHI	29 PHI	30 CHC	

May

SUN	MON	TUE	WED	THU	FRI	SAT
						1 CHC
2 CHC	3 CHC	4 PHI	5 PHI	6 PHI	7 MON	8 MON
9 MON	10	11 ATL	12 ATL	13 ATL	14 FLA	15 FLA
16 FLA	17	18 NYM	19 NYM	20 NYM	21 CHC	22 CHC
23 CHC	24	25 PIT	26 PIT	27 PIT	28 HOU	29 HOU
30 HOU	31 PIT					

June

SUN	MON	TUE	WED	THU	FRI	SAT
		1 PIT	2 PIT	3 PIT	4 HOU	5 HOU
6 HOU	7 CHC	8 CHC	9 CHC	10 CHC	11 TEX	12 TEX
13 TEX	14	15 OAK	16 OAK	17 OAK	18 CIN	19 CIN
20 CIN	21	22 CHC	23 CHC	24 CHC	25 KC	26 KC
27 KC	28 PIT	29 PIT	30 PIT			

July

SUN	MON	TUE	WED	THU	FRI	SAT
				1	2 SEA	3 SEA
4 SEA	5 CIN	6 CIN	7 CIN	8	9 CHC	10 CHC
11 CHC	12	13 All-Star	14	15 CIN	16 CIN	17 CIN
18 CIN	19 CHC	20 CHC	21 MIL	22 MIL	23 SF	24 SF
25 SF	26 CIN	27 CIN	28 CIN	29	30 SF	31 SF

August

SUN	MON	TUE	WED	THU	FRI	SAT
1 SF	2	3 MON	4 MON	5 MON	6 NYM	7 NYM
8 NYM	9	10 FLA	11 FLA	12 FLA	13 ATL	14 ATL
15 ATL	16 CIN	17 CIN	18 CIN	19 PIT	20 PIT	21 PIT
22 PIT	23	24 CIN	25 CIN	26 CIN	27 PIT	28 PIT
29 PIT	30	31 SD				

Sept./Oct.

SUN	MON	TUE	WED	THU	FRI	SAT
			1 SD	2 SD	3 LA	4 LA
5 LA	6 SD	7 SD	8 SD	9	10 LA	11 LA
12 LA	13	14 HOU	15 HOU	16 HOU	17 ARI	18 ARI
19 ARI	20 MIL	21 MIL	22 MIL	23 MIL	24 COL	25 COL
26 COL	27 HOU	28 HOU	29 HOU	30 MIL	1 MIL	2 MIL
3 MIL	4	5	6	7	8	9

Home games shaded. All-Star Game July 13 at Houston. Schedule subject to change.

CLUB DIRECTORY

Chairman of the board/general partner
William O. DeWitt Jr.
Vice chairman
Frederick O. Hanser
President
Mark C. Lamping
Vice president, general manager
Walt Jocketty
Vice president/player personnel
Jerry Walker
Vice president/baseball development
Jeff Luhnow
V.p., special asst. to the g.m.
Bob Gebhard
Special assistant to the general manager
Mike Jorgensen
Vice president, community relations
Marty Hendin
Director, media relations
Brian Bartow
Assistant general manager
John Mozeliak
Director, player development
Bruce Manno
Director, professional scouting
Marteese Robinson
Director, baseball operations
Scott Smulczenski

MINOR LEAGUE AFFILIATES

Class	Team	League	Manager
AAA	Memphis	Pacific Coast	Danny Sheaffer
AA	Tennessee	Southern	Mark DeJohn
Advanced A	Palm Beach	Florida State	Tom Nieto
A	Peoria	Midwest	Joe Cunningham
Short-Season A	New Jersey	New York-Pennsylvania	Tommy Shields
Advanced Rookie	Johnson City	Appalachian	Tommy Kidwell

More on the Cardinals at www.foxsports.com/named/FS/MLB/teams

BROADCAST INFORMATION

Radio: KMOX-AM (1120).
TV: KPLR-TV (Channel 11).
Cable TV: Fox Sports Midwest.

SPRING TRAINING

Ballpark (city): Roger Dean Stadium (Jupiter, Fla.).
Ticket information: 561-966-3309.

SPRING TRAINING ROSTER

Manager—Tony La Russa (10).
Coaches—Dave Duncan (18), Marty Mason (38), Dave McKay (39), Jose Oquendo (11), Mitchell Page (12), Joe Pettini (24).

No.	PITCHERS	B/T	Ht./Wt.	Age*	2003 Clubs
66	Ankiel, Rick	L/L	6-1/210	24	Tennessee
40	Calero, Kiko	R/R	6-1/180	29	St. Louis
29	Carpenter, Chris	R/R	6-6/215	28	Palm Beach, Tennessee, Memphis
23	Eldred, Cal	R/R	6-4/235	36	St. Louis
50	Haren, Danny	R/R	6-5/220	23	Tennessee, Memphis, St. Louis
44	Isringhausen, J.	R/R	6-3/230	31	Tennessee, St. Louis
77	Journell, Jimmy	R/R	6-4/205	26	Memphis, St. Louis
	King, Ray	L/L	6-1/247	30	Atlanta
49	Kline, Steve	B/L	6-1/215	31	St. Louis
	Lincoln, Mike	R/R	6-2/213	28	Nashville, Pittsburgh
	Marquis, Jason	L/R	6-1/210	25	Richmond, Atlanta
35	Morris, Matt	R/R	6-5/220	29	St. Louis
	Narveson, Chris	L/L	6-3/180	22	Palm Beach, Tennessee
	Parrott, Rhett	R/R	6-2/190	24	Tennessee, Memphis
60	Pearce, Josh	R/R	6-3/220	26	Palm Beach, Tennessee, Memphis, St. Louis
	Rust, Evan	R/R	6-1/210	25	Orlando, Durham
	Ryan, Jason	B/R	6-3/195	28	Memphis
46	Simontacchi, J.	R/R	6-2/190	30	St. Louis
37	Suppan, Jeff	R/R	6-2/220	29	Pittsburgh, Boston
	Tavarez, Julian	R/L	6-2/195	30	Pittsburgh
	Wainwright, Adam	R/R	6-8/205	22	Greenville
19	Williams, Woody	R/R	6-0/200	37	St. Louis

No.	CATCHERS	B/T	Ht./Wt.	Age*	2003 Clubs
22	Matheny, Mike	R/R	6-3/220	33	St. Louis
32	Widger, Chris	R/R	6-2/210	32	Memphis, St. Louis

No.	INFIELDERS	B/T	Ht./Wt.	Age*	2003 Clubs
	Anderson, Marlon	L/R	5-11/200	30	Tampa Bay
	Butler, Brent	R/R	6-0/180	26	Colorado, Colo. Springs
	Cox, Steve	L/L	6-4/225	29	Played in Japan
	Gall, John	R/R	6-0/195	25	Tennessee, Memphis
31	Hart, Bo	R/R	5-11/170	27	Memphis, St. Louis
	Luna, Hector	R/R	6-1/170	24	Akron
5	Pujols, Albert	R/R	6-3/225	24	St. Louis
3	Renteria, Edgar	R/R	6-1/200	28	St. Louis
27	Rolen, Scott	R/R	6-4/240	28	St. Louis

No.	OUTFIELDERS	B/T	Ht./Wt.	Age*	2003 Clubs
15	Edmonds, Jim	L/L	6-1/212	33	St. Louis
0	Robinson, Kerry	L/L	6-0/175	30	Memphis, St. Louis
	Sanders, Reggie	R/R	6-1/205	36	Pittsburgh
99	Taguchi, So	R/R	5-10/163	34	Memphis, St. Louis

Invited to spring training: RHP Alan Benes, OF Emil Brown, RHP Matt Duff, IF Wilson Delgado, OF Ray Lankford, 1B Luis Ortiz, OF Chris Prieto, OF Mark Quinn, OF Greg Vaughn.

*Age as of April 1, 2004.

BALLPARK INFORMATION

Ballpark (capacity, surface)
Busch Stadium (50,354, grass)
Address
250 Stadium Plaza
St. Louis, MO 63102
Official website
www.stlcardinals.com
Business phone
314-421-3060
Ticket information
314-421-2400
Field dimensions (from home plate)
To left field at foul line, 330 feet
To center field, 402 feet
To right field at foul line, 330 feet
First game played
May 12, 1966 (Cardinals 4, Braves 3)

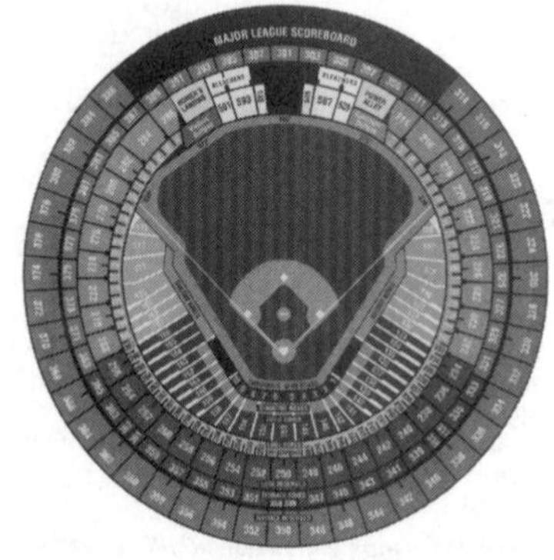

2003 REVIEW

DAY BY DAY

Date	Opp.	Res.	Score	(inn.*)	Hits	Opp. hits	Winning pitcher	Losing pitcher	Save	Record	Pos.	GB
3-31	Mil.	W	11-9		12	12	Springer	DeJean	Kline	1-0	T1st	...
4-2	Mil.	W	7-0		13	5	Williams	Rusch		2-0	T1st	...
4-3	Mil.	W	6-4		13	8	Stephenson	Kinney	Kline	3-0	T1st	...
4-4	Hou.	L	5-6	(12)	13	7	Stone	Springer	Lidge	3-1	T2nd	1.0
4-5	Hou.	L	1-2		7	7	Munro	Fassero	Wagner	3-2	T3rd	1.0
4-8	At Col.	W	15-12	(13)	17	19	Eldred	Miceli		4-2	T2nd	0.5
4-9	At Col.	L	4-9		8	10	Cruz	Tomko		4-3	4th	1.0
4-10	At Col.	L	6-7		12	8	Lopez	Kline	Jimenez	4-4	4th	2.0
4-11	At Hou.	L	2-3		7	6	Dotel	Morris		4-5	4th	3.0
4-12	At Hou.	W	3-0		10	6	Williams	Redding	Hermanson	5-5	4th	2.0
4-13	At Hou.	W	11-8		11	10	Calero	Oswalt		6-5	4th	1.0
4-14	At Mil.	W	7-5		17	9	Tomko	Ritchie	Kline	7-5	T1st	...
4-15	At Mil.	L	1-6		6	12	Sheets	Stephenson		7-6	T2nd	0.5
4-16	At Mil.	W	15-2		16	6	Morris	Franklin		8-6	T2nd	0.5
4-18	Ari.	W	6-3		10	7	Williams	Dessens		9-6	2nd	1.0
4-19	Ari.	L	3-4		6	8	Kim	Simontacchi	Mantei	9-7	2nd	2.0
4-20	Ari.	L	0-1		5	9	Villarreal	Tomko	Mantei	9-8	2nd	2.0
4-22	At Atl.	L	3-5		8	6	Ortiz	Stephenson	Smoltz	9-9	4th	3.0
4-23	At Atl.	L	2-4		6	7	Maddux	Morris	Smoltz	9-10	4th	3.0
4-24	At Atl.	L	3-4		4	15	King	Kline		9-11	4th	3.0
4-25	At Fla.	W	9-2		10	9	Tomko	Burnett		10-11	2nd	3.0
4-26	At Fla.	L	3-5		8	9	Beckett	Kline	Looper	10-12	2nd	3.0
4-27	At Fla.	W	7-6	(20)	22	13	Kline	Pavano		11-12	2nd	2.0
4-29	N.Y.	W	13-3		17	7	Morris	Leiter		12-12	2nd	2.0
4-30	N.Y.	W	13-4		16	7	Williams	Astacio		13-12	2nd	1.0
5-1	N.Y.	W	6-5	(10)	12	11	Eldred	Strickland		14-12	2nd	1.0
5-2	Mon.	W	8-1		13	6	Simontacchi	Ohka		15-12	2nd	1.0
5-3	Mon.	W	3-1		6	9	Stephenson	Vargas	Calero	16-12	1st	...
5-4	Mon.	W	6-2		6	6	Morris	Vazquez		17-12	1st	...
5-5	At Cin.	L	4-5		6	7	Williamson	Hermanson		17-13	1st	...
5-6	At Cin.	L	5-6		10	10	Reitsma	Calero		17-14	1st	...
5-7	At Cin.	L	2-4		6	5	Graves	Simontacchi	Williamson	17-15	2nd	1.0
5-8	At Cin.	L	6-8		14	12	Sullivan	Crudale	Williamson	17-16	3rd	1.5
5-9	At Chi.	W	6-3		10	10	Morris	Zambrano	Fassero	18-16	2nd	0.5
5-10	At Chi.	L	2-3	(10)	5	10	Remlinger	Eldred		18-17	2nd	1.5
5-13	Cin.	L	2-7		9	12	Wilson	Simontacchi		18-18	4th	3.0
5-14	Cin.	L	0-4		4	7	Graves	Morris		18-19	4th	4.0
5-15	Cin.	W	6-3		9	6	Stephenson	Riedling	Eldred	19-19	4th	4.0
5-16	Chi.	W	7-4		8	9	Williams	Clement	Eldred	20-19	3rd	3.0
5-17	Chi.	L	1-2		7	11	Remlinger	Kline	Borowski	20-20	3rd	4.0
5-18	Chi.	W	6-3		7	5	Hermanson	Cruz	Eldred	21-20	3rd	3.0
5-19	Chi.	W	2-0		7	4	Morris	Zambrano		22-20	2nd	2.0
5-20	At Hou.	L	2-3		5	6	Miller	Stephenson	Wagner	22-21	3rd	2.5
5-21	At Hou.	W	7-4		13	9	Williams	Munro	Eldred	23-21	2nd	1.5
5-22	At Hou.	L	2-5		7	9	Robertson	Tomko	Wagner	23-22	3rd	2.5
5-23	At Pit.	W	10-8	(10)	17	15	Eldred	Meadows	Fassero	24-22	3rd	1.5
5-24	At Pit.	W	6-0		10	9	Morris	Suppan		25-22	2nd	1.5
5-25	At Pit.	L	7-8		10	10	Boehringer	Hermanson	Williams	25-23	2nd	2.5
5-26	Hou.	W	10-5		14	11	Williams	Munro		26-23	2nd	1.5
5-27	Hou.	L	4-7		11	11	Robertson	Tomko	Wagner	26-24	2nd	1.5
5-28	Hou.	W	3-1		9	6	Simontacchi	Johnson		27-24	2nd	1.5
5-29	Hou.	L	4-7		11	9	Saarloos	Fassero	Wagner	27-25	2nd	2.0
5-30	Pit.	L	3-7		8	12	Suppan	Stephenson		27-26	3rd	2.0
5-31	Pit.	L	3-4		6	9	Wells	Williams	Williams	27-27	3rd	3.0
6-1	Pit.	W	5-4		7	8	Kline	Beimel	Fassero	28-27	3rd	2.0
6-3	Tor.	W	11-5		14	10	Morris	Escobar		29-27	3rd	2.0
6-4	Tor.	W	8-5		12	11	Simontacchi	Lidle	Eldred	30-27	3rd	1.0
6-5	Tor.	W	13-5		15	5	Williams	Hendrickson		31-27	3rd	1.0
6-6	Bal.	W	8-6		11	12	Yan	Julio	Eldred	32-27	T2nd	1.0
6-7	Bal.	L	1-8		7	12	Ponson	Stephenson		32-28	3rd	2.0
6-8	Bal.	W	11-10		18	16	Simontacchi	Driskill	Eldred	33-28	3rd	2.0
6-10	At Bos.	W	9-7		14	14	Kline	Lyon	Eldred	34-28	3rd	1.0
6-11	At Bos.	L	1-13		10	19	Burkett	Tomko		34-29	3rd	2.0
6-12	At Bos.	W	8-7	(13)	14	13	Yan	Mendoza		35-29	3rd	1.0

Date	Opp.	Res.	Score	(inn.*)	Hits	Opp. hits	Winning pitcher	Losing pitcher	Save	Record	Pos.	GB
6-13	At N.Y. (AL)	L	2-5		8	10	Clemens	Simontacchi	Rivera	35-30	3rd	1.0
6-14	At N.Y. (AL)	L	4-13		8	15	Pettitte	Morris		35-31	3rd	2.0
6-15	At N.Y. (AL)	L	2-5		4	7	Mussina	Williams	Rivera	35-32	3rd	2.0
6-16	At Mil.	L	4-9		9	11	Leskanic	Eldred		35-33	3rd	3.0
6-17	At Mil.	W	12-3		16	7	Stephenson	Kinney		36-33	3rd	2.0
6-18	At Mil.	W	9-1		13	7	Simontacchi	Rusch		37-33	3rd	2.0
6-19	At Mil.	W	8-4		11	12	Tomko	Quevedo	Isringhausen	38-33	2nd	1.0
6-20	K.C.	L	4-10		10	15	Lima	Morris		38-34	3rd	1.0
6-21	K.C.	W	8-1		14	6	Williams	May		39-34	T2nd	0.5
6-22	K.C.	L	2-5		10	8	Affeldt	Stephenson	MacDougal	39-35	3rd	1.5
6-24	Cin.	L	4-7	(14)	19	12	Heredia	Fassero	Graves	39-36	3rd	2.0
6-25	Cin.	W	9-6		13	9	Morris	Wilson	Isringhausen	40-36	2nd	1.0
6-26	Cin.	W	11-7		17	12	Williams	Anderson		41-36	T1st	...
6-27	At K.C.	L	3-6		7	4	May	Stephenson	MacDougal	41-37	T1st	...
6-28	At K.C.	W	13-9		14	14	Fassero	Affeldt		42-37	1st	+0.5
6-29	At K.C.	W	13-6		14	10	Tomko	George		43-37	1st	+1.0
6-30	S.F	L	1-5		7	10	Schmidt	Haren		43-38	1st	+1.0
7-1	S.F	L	1-5		6	8	Brower	Williams		43-39	T1st	...
7-2	S.F	L	1-4		6	5	Williams	Stephenson	Worrell	43-40	T1st	...
7-3	S.F	W	9-5		14	10	Simontacchi	Rueter		44-40	T1st	...
7-4	At Chi.	W	11-8		14	12	Tomko	Wood		45-40	1st	+1.0
7-5	At Chi.	L	5-6		9	12	Remlinger	Fassero		45-41	1st	+1.0
7-6	At Chi.	W	4-1		6	8	Williams	Prior	Isringhausen	46-41	1st	+2.0
7-7	At S.F	L	1-5		7	10	Williams	Stephenson		46-42	1st	+1.0
7-8	At S.F	L	3-8		7	12	Brower	Haren		46-43	T1st	...
7-9	L.A.	L	5-6		6	11	Ishii	Tomko	Gagne	46-44	T2nd	1.0
7-10	L.A.	L	4-9		14	15	Perez	Morris	Quantrill	46-45	T2nd	2.0
7-11	S.D.	W	4-2		8	3	Williams	Lawrence	Isringhausen	47-45	2nd	2.0
7-12	S.D.	W	9-7	(11)	13	14	Simontacchi	Herges		48-45	2nd	1.0
7-13	S.D.	W	3-1		4	8	Simontacchi	Matthews	Isringhausen	49-45	2nd	1.0
7-17	At L.A.	L	3-6		5	8	Nomo	Stephenson	Gagne	49-46	2nd	2.0
7-18	At L.A.	L	5-8		9	11	Ishii	Eldred	Gagne	49-47	2nd	3.0
7-19	At L.A.	W	3-1		7	6	Haren	Brown	Isringhausen	50-47	2nd	3.0
7-20	At L.A.	W	10-7		10	12	Williams	Perez	Isringhausen	51-47	2nd	3.0
7-21	At S.D.	L	4-5	(10)	8	11	Witasick	Painter		51-48	2nd	3.0
7-22	At S.D.	L	2-3		9	6	Perez	Fassero	Beck	51-49	2nd	4.0
7-23	At S.D.	W	8-4		17	12	Tomko	Lawrence		52-49	2nd	4.0
7-25	Pit.	L	5-10		8	10	Meadows	Eldred		52-50	2nd	3.5
7-26	Pit.	W	13-8		19	12	Williams	Fogg	Isringhausen	53-50	2nd	3.5
7-27	Pit.	W	4-3		12	6	Eldred	Lincoln		54-50	2nd	2.5
7-28	Pit.	L	0-3		7	11	Suppan	Tomko		54-51	2nd	3.0
7-29	At Mon.	W	2-1		5	4	Stephenson	Hernandez		55-51	2nd	2.0
7-30	At Mon.	W	11-1		11	7	Haren	Vargas		56-51	2nd	2.0
7-31	At Mon.	L	2-3		7	8	Day	Williams	Biddle	56-52	2nd	2.0
8-1	At N.Y.	W	8-2		12	6	Kline	Wheeler		57-52	2nd	2.0
8-2	At N.Y.	W	10-9		10	17	Tomko	Seo	Yan	58-52	2nd	1.0
8-3	At N.Y.	L	5-13		10	19	Griffiths	Stephenson		58-53	2nd	2.0
8-5	Fla.	L	0-4		5	7	Penny	Williams		58-54	2nd	2.0
8-6	Fla.	L	3-7		6	13	Willis	Haren		58-55	3rd	3.0
8-7	Fla.	W	3-0		6	4	Tomko	Beckett	Isringhausen	59-55	3rd	2.0
8-8	Atl.	L	2-7		5	10	Ortiz	Fassero		59-56	3rd	3.0
8-9	Atl.	W	3-1		6	7	Stephenson	Reynolds	Isringhausen	60-56	2nd	2.0
8-10	Atl.	W	3-2		6	8	Eldred	Smoltz	Isringhausen	61-56	2nd	2.0
8-11	At Pit.	W	6-4		10	17	Haren	Wells	Isringhausen	62-56	2nd	2.0
8-12	At Pit.	W	10-6		12	12	Tomko	Fogg	Simontacchi	63-56	2nd	1.0
8-13	At Pit.	L	5-6		11	13	Tavarez	Borbon		63-57	2nd	1.0
8-14	At Pit.	W	4-3		11	7	Stephenson	D'Amico	Isringhausen	64-57	T1st	...
8-15	At Phi.	L	4-7		12	12	Padilla	Williams	Plesac	64-58	T2nd	0.5
8-16	At Phi.	L	4-5		7	9	Myers	Haren	Mesa	64-59	3rd	1.0
8-17	At Phi.	L	4-6		6	7	Telemaco	Tomko	Williams	64-60	3rd	1.0
8-19	Pit.	W	13-5		13	9	Eldred	Beimel		65-60	2nd	1.0
8-20	Pit.	L	0-14		3	15	D'Amico	Stephenson		65-61	3rd	1.0
8-21	Pit.	W	6-3		11	10	Eldred	Lincoln		66-61	2nd	1.0
8-22	Phi.	L	4-9		9	14	Cormier	Kline		66-62	3rd	1.0
8-23	Phi.	W	5-3		10	12	Hitchcock	Telemaco	Isringhausen	67-62	T1st	...
8-24	Phi.	W	3-0		8	6	Tomko	Millwood	DeJean	68-62	T1st	...
8-26	Chi.	L	4-7		5	8	Prior	Stephenson		68-63	3rd	1.0
8-27	Chi.	W	4-2		7	8	Kline	Farnsworth	Isringhausen	69-63	2nd	1.0
8-28	Chi.	W	3-2		9	5	DeJean	Remlinger		70-63	T1st	...
8-29	At Cin.	L	5-8		13	10	Bale	Haren	Graves	70-64	T1st	...
8-30	At Cin.	W	6-3		10	12	Tomko	Harang	Isringhausen	71-64	T1st	...
8-31	At Cin.	W	5-0		8	4	Hitchcock	Serafini		72-64	1st	+1.0

Date	Opp.	Res.	Score	(inn.*)	Hits	Opp. hits	Winning pitcher	Losing pitcher	Save	Record	Pos.	GB
9-1	At Chi.	L	0-7		6	17	Prior	Williams		72-65	T1st	...
9-2§	At Chi.	L	2-4	(15)	5	8	Guthrie	Fassero		72-66		
9-2∞	At Chi.	W	2-0		5	5	Morris	Wood	Isringhausen	73-66	1st	+0.5
9-3	At Chi.	L	7-8		13	13	Borowski	Williams		73-67	2nd	0.5
9-4	At Chi.	L	6-7		12	10	Remlinger	DeJean	Borowski	73-68	3rd	1.0
9-5	Cin.	L	2-4	(12)	6	9	Randall	Simontacchi	Reitsma	73-69	3rd	2.0
9-6	Cin.	W	13-6		15	10	Williams	Serafini		74-69	3rd	2.0
9-7	Cin.	W	9-0		16	3	Morris	Etherton		75-69	3rd	1.5
9-9	Col.	L	1-8		9	9	Jennings	Haren		75-70	3rd	2.5
9-10	Col.	W	10-2		11	6	Tomko	Elarton		76-70	3rd	2.5
9-11	Col.	L	4-9		7	18	Oliver	Hitchcock		76-71	3rd	2.5
9-12	At Hou.	L	5-14		5	19	Miller	Williams		76-72	3rd	3.5
9-13	At Hou.	L	0-2		5	4	Oswalt	Morris	Wagner	76-73	3rd	4.5
9-14	At Hou.	L	1-4		3	6	Redding	Haren	Wagner	76-74	3rd	5.5
9-15	Mil.	W	11-2		16	7	Tomko	Obermueller		77-74	3rd	5.0
9-16	Mil.	W	6-5		9	5	Hitchcock	Martinez	Isringhausen	78-74	3rd	5.0
9-17	Mil.	L	6-7		13	10	Estrella	Isringhausen	Kolb	78-75	3rd	5.0
9-18	Mil.	W	13-0		16	3	Williams	Kinney		79-75	3rd	5.0
9-19	Hou.	L	1-8		6	13	Oswalt	Morris		79-76	3rd	6.0
9-20	Hou.	W	3-2	(13)	9	8	Simontacchi	Miceli		80-76	3rd	5.0
9-21	Hou.	W	6-4		7	12	Hitchcock	Robertson	Isringhausen	81-76	3rd	4.0
9-23	At Mil.	W	5-1		10	3	Williams	Sheets		82-76	3rd	3.5
9-24	At Mil.	W	8-4		13	8	Morris	Kinney	Isringhausen	83-76	3rd	3.5
9-26	At Ari.	L	6-7		9	13	Randolph	Tomko	Mantei	83-77	3rd	3.5
9-27	At Ari.	W	3-2		6	11	Hitchcock	Capuano	Isringhausen	84-77	3rd	4.0
9-28	At Ari.	W	9-5		9	14	Williams	Webb	Isringhausen	85-77	3rd	3.0

Monthly records: March (1-0), April (12-12), May (14-15), June (16-11), July (13-14), August (16-12), September (13-13).
*Innings, if other than nine. § Day separate admission. ∞ Night separate admission.

RECORDS

2003 regular-season record: 85-77
Position: 3rd in N.L. Central
Home: 48-33 **Road:** 37-44
N.L. East: 17-13 **N.L. Central:** 46-38
N.L. West: 12-18 A.L. 10-8
Vs. LH starters: 19-17
Vs. RH starters: 66-60
Grass: 83-73 **Artificial:** 2-4
Day: 37-24 **Night:** 48-53
1-Run: 14-25 **X-inn.:** 7-6
Doubleheaders: 0-0-0
Team record past five years: 445-364 (.550, ranks 4th in league in that span)

TEAM LEADERS

Batting average: Albert Pujols (.359).
At-bats: Albert Pujols (591).
Runs: Albert Pujols (137).
Hits: Albert Pujols (212).
Total Bases: Albert Pujols (394).
Doubles: Albert Pujols (51).
Triples: Bo Hart (5).
Home runs: Albert Pujols (43).
Runs batted in: Albert Pujols (124).
Stolen bases: Edgar Renteria (34).
Slugging percentage: Albert Pujols (.667).
On-base percentage: Albert Pujols (.439).
Wins: Woody Williams (18).
Earned-run average: Matt Morris (3.76).
Complete games: Matt Morris (5).
Shutouts: Matt Morris (3).
Saves: Jason Isringhausen (22).
Innings pitched: Woody Williams (220.2).
Strikeouts: Woody Williams (153).

GAMES BY POSITION

Catcher: Mike Matheny 138, Chris Widger 41, Joe Girardi 13, Eli Marrero 6.
First base: Tino Martinez 126, Albert Pujols 62, Eduardo Perez 5, Mike Matheny 4, Miguel Cairo 3, Eli Marrero 2, Chris Widger 1.
Second base: Bo Hart 69, Fernando Vina 60, Miguel Cairo 40, Wilson Delgado 12, So Taguchi 1.
Third base: Scott Rolen 153, Miguel Cairo 12, Eduardo Perez 12, Wilson Delgado 11.
Shortstop: Edgar Renteria 156, Wilson Delgado 11, Miguel Cairo 7, Bo Hart 3.
Outfield: Jim Edmonds 129, Albert Pujols 113, Orlando Palmeiro 112, Kerry Robinson 88, J.D. Drew 75, Eduardo Perez 71, So Taguchi 38, Eli Marrero 31, Miguel Cairo 27, Chris Widger 1.
Designated hitter: Tino Martinez 5, Jim Edmonds 2, Eduardo Perez 1, Albert Pujols 1, Jason Simontacchi 1.

TOP DRAFT CHOICES

1. **Daric Barton,** C, Marina H.S., Huntington Beach, Calif.
2. **Stuart Pomeranz,** RHP, Houston H.S., Collierville, Tenn.
3. **Dennis Dove,** RHP, Georgia Southern.
4. **Mark Michael,** RHP, Delaware.
5. **Brandon Yarbrough,** C, Richmond H.S., Ellerbe, N.C.
6. **Matt Weagle,** RHP, Franklin Pierce (N.H.).
7. **Brendan Ryan,** SS, Lewis-Clark State (Idaho).
8. **Matt Pagnozzi,** C, Central Arizona JC.
9. **Justin Garza,** RHP, Seminole State JC (Okla).
10. **Buddy Blair,** LHP, Oklahoma.

SAN DIEGO PADRES

NATIONAL LEAGUE WEST DIVISION

2004 SEASON

April

SUN	MON	TUE	WED	THU	FRI	SAT
4	5 LA	6 LA	7 LA	8 SF	9	10 SF
11 SF	12	13 LA	14 LA	15 LA	16 ARI	17 ARI
18 ARI	19 SF	20 SF	21 SF	22 SF	23 ARI	24 ARI
25 ARI	26 MON	27 MON	28 MON	29 MON	30 NYM	

May

SUN	MON	TUE	WED	THU	FRI	SAT
						1 NYM
2 NYM	3	4 ATL	5 ATL	6 ATL	7 FLA	8 FLA
9 FLA	10	11 CIN	12 CIN	13 CIN	14 CHC	15 CHC
16 CHC	17	18 PIT	19 PIT	20 PIT	21 PHI	22 PHI
23 PHI	24	25 COL	26 COL	27 COL	28 MIL	29 MIL
30 MIL	31 COL					

June

SUN	MON	TUE	WED	THU	FRI	SAT
		1 COL	2 COL	3	4 MIL	5 MIL
6 MIL	7	8 BOS	9 BOS	10 BOS	11 NYY	12 NYY
13 NYY	14	15 TB	16 TB	17 TB	18 TOR	19 TOR
20 TOR	21 ARI	22 ARI	23 ARI	24	25 SEA	26 SEA
27 SEA	28 ARI	29 ARI	30 ARI			

Home games shaded. All-Star Game July 13 at Houston. Schedule subject to change.

July

SUN	MON	TUE	WED	THU	FRI	SAT
				1 ARI	2 KC	3 KC
4 KC	5 HOU	6 HOU	7 HOU	8 COL	9 COL	10 COL
11 COL	12	13 All-Star	14	15	16 HOU	17 HOU
18 HOU	19 COL	20 COL	21 SF	22 SF	23 LA	24 LA
25 LA	26 SF	27 SF	28 SF	29 SF	30 LA	31 LA

August

SUN	MON	TUE	WED	THU	FRI	SAT
1 LA	2	3 PHI	4 PHI	5 PHI	6 PIT	7 PIT
8 PIT	9	10 CHC	11 CHC	12 CHC	13 CIN	14 CIN
15 CIN	16 ATL	17 ATL	18 ATL	19	20 FLA	21 FLA
22 FLA	23 NYM	24 NYM	25 NYM	26 NYM	27 MON	28 MON
29 MON	30	31 STL				

Sept./Oct.

SUN	MON	TUE	WED	THU	FRI	SAT
			1 STL	2 STL	3 COL	4 COL
5 COL	6 STL	7 STL	8 STL	9 COL	10 COL	11 COL
12 COL	13 LA	14 LA	15 LA	16 LA	17 SF	18 SF
19 SF	20	21 LA	22 LA	23 LA	24 ARI	25 ARI
26 ARI	27	28 SF	29 SF	30 SF	1 ARI	2 ARI
3 ARI	4	5	6	7	8	9

CLUB DIRECTORY

Chairman
John Moores
President and chief operating officer
Dick Freeman
Exec. v.p., baseball operations and g.m.
Kevin Towers
Vice president, community relations
Michele Anderson
Assistant general manager
Fred Uhlman Jr.
Director, scouting
Bill Gayton
Director, minor league operations
Priscilla Oppenheimer
Director, player development
Tye Waller

MINOR LEAGUE AFFILIATES

Class	Team	League	Manager
AAA	Portland	Pacific Coast	Craig Colbert
AA	Mobile	Southern	Gary Jones
Advanced A	Lake Elsinore	California	Rick Renteria
A	Fort Wayne	Midwest	Randy Ready
Short-Season A	Eugene	Northwest	Roy Howell
Rookie	Arizona	Arizona	Carlos Lezcano

More on the Padres at www.foxsports.com/named/FS/MLB/teams

BROADCAST INFORMATION

Radio: MIGHTY 1090, KURS-AM (1040, Spanish).
TV: KUSI (Channel 9/51).
Cable TV: Channel 4 Padres.

SPRING TRAINING

Ballpark (city): Peoria Stadium (Peoria, Ariz.).
Ticket information: 623-878-4337, 800-409-1511.

SPRING TRAINING ROSTER

Manager—Bruce Bochy (15).
Coaches—Darrel Akerfelds (48), Darren Balsley, Davey Lopes (24), Dave Magadan (12), Tony Muser (40), Rob Picciolo (5).

No.	PITCHERS	B/T	Ht./Wt.	Age*	2003 Clubs
47	Beck, Rod	R/R	6-1/235	35	Iowa, San Diego
	Bruback, Matt	R/R	6-7/215	25	Iowa, Nashville, Portland
53	Eaton, Adam	R/R	6-2/190	26	San Diego
	Germano, Justin	R/R	6-2/190	21	Lake Elsinore, Mobile
	Hitchcock, Sterling	L/L	6-0/200	32	New York A.L., St. Louis
51	Hoffman, Trevor	R/R	6-0/205	36	Lake Elsinore, San Diego
39	Howard, Ben	R/R	6-2/190	25	Portland, San Diego
50	Lawrence, Brian	R/R	6-0/195	27	San Diego
38	Linebrink, Scott	R/R	6-2/200	27	New Orleans, Houston, San Diego
	Otsuka, Akinori	R/R	5-11/200	32	Played in Japan
	Oxspring, Chris	L/R	6-1/180	26	Mobile
44	Peavy, Jake	R/R	6-1/180	22	San Diego
	Sweeney, Brian	R/R	6-2/185	29	Tacoma, Seattle
	Szuminski, Jason	R/R	6-5/225	25	Daytona. West Tenn, Iowa
45	Tankersley, Dennis	R/R	6-2/185	25	San Diego, Portland
	Tucker, Rusty	R/L	6-1/190	23	Mobile
	Valdes, Ismael	R/R	6-4/225	30	Frisco, Texas
56	Walker, Kevin	L/L	6-4/190	27	Lake Elsinore, Portland, San Diego
	Wells, David	L/L	6-4/230	40	New York A.L.
46	Witasick, Jay	R/R	6-4/235	31	Lake Elsinore, Portland, San Diego

No.	CATCHERS	B/T	Ht./Wt.	Age*	2003 Clubs
	Hernandez, Ra.	R/R	6-0/210	27	Oakland
20	Ojeda, Miguel	R/R	6-2/190	29	San Diego
11	Quintero, Hum.	R/R	6-1/190	24	Mobile, San Diego
	Wilson, Tom	R/R	6-3/220	33	Toronto

No.	INFIELDERS	B/T	Ht./Wt.	Age*	2003 Clubs
33	Burroughs, Sean	L/R	6-2/200	23	San Diego
	Castro, Bernie	B/R	5-10/165	24	Portland
	Cirillo, Jeff	R/R	6-1/200	34	Arizona Mariners, Inland Empire, Tacoma, Seattle
3	Greene, Khalil	R/R	5-11/210	24	Mobile, Portland, San Diego
8	Loretta, Mark	R/R	6-0/186	32	San Diego
23	Nevin, Phil	R/R	6-2/231	33	Lake Elsinore, Portland, San Diego
9	Sears, Todd	L/R	6-5/215	28	Minnesota, Rochester, San Diego
1	Vazquez, Ramon	L/R	5-11/170	27	Lake Elsinore, San Diego

No.	OUTFIELDERS	B/T	Ht./Wt.	Age*	2003 Clubs
34	Buchanan, Brian	R/R	6-4/230	30	San Diego
24	Giles, Brian	L/L	5-10/205	33	Pittsburgh, San Diego
	Guzman, Freddy	B/R	5-10/165	23	Lake Elsinore, Mobile, Portland
30	Klesko, Ryan	L/L	6-3/220	32	San Diego
	Long, Terrence	L/L	6-1/202	28	Oakland
22	Nady, Xavier	R/R	6-0/180	25	Portland, San Diego
	Payton, Jay	R/R	5-10/185	31	Colorado
	Stanley, Henri	L/L	5-10/185	26	New Orleans

Invited to spring training: SS Rey Ordonez.

*Age as of April 1, 2004.

BALLPARK INFORMATION

Ballpark (capacity, surface)
Petco Park (42,000, grass)

Address
100 Park Blvd.
San Diego, CA 92101

Official website
www.padres.com

Business phone
619-795-5000

Ticket information
1-877-FRIAR-TIX

Field dimensions (from home plate)
To left field at foul line, 334 feet
To center field, 396 feet
To right field at foul line, 322 feet

First game played
Scheduled for April 8, 2004, vs. San Francisco

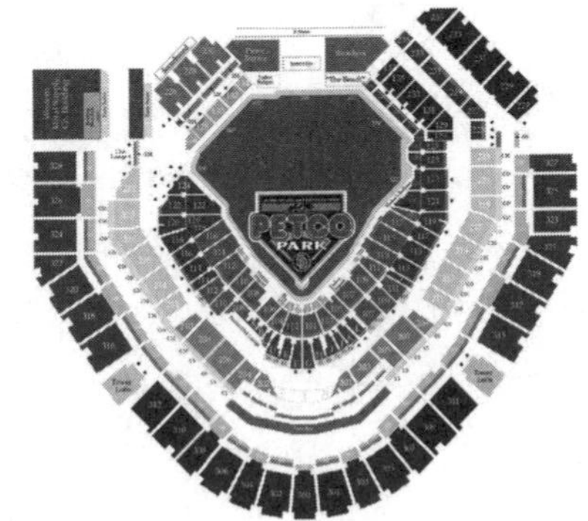

2003 REVIEW

DAY BY DAY

Date	Opp.	Res.	Score	(inn.*)	Hits	Opp. hits	Winning pitcher	Losing pitcher	Save	Record	Pos.	GB
3-31	S.F	L	2-5		7	9	Rodriguez	Condrey	Worrell	0-1	T4th	1.0
4-1	S.F	L	1-8		4	10	Schmidt	Eaton		0-2	5th	2.0
4-2	S.F	L	3-5		6	5	Moss	Perez	Worrell	0-3	5th	3.0
4-3	L.A.	W	6-1		12	2	Peavy	Ishii		1-3	5th	2.5
4-4	L.A.	W	4-2		8	7	Condrey	Dreifort	Villafuerte	2-3	T3rd	2.5
4-5	L.A.	W	3-0		7	4	Lawrence	Nomo	Orosco	3-3	3rd	2.5
4-6	L.A.	L	3-4	(13)	9	8	Mota	Wright		3-4	T3rd	3.5
4-7	At S.F	L	4-7		11	9	Worrell	Bynum		3-5	T3rd	4.5
4-8	At S.F	W	9-4		15	10	Peavy	Eyre		4-5	T3rd	3.5
4-9	At S.F	L	11-15		15	16	Nathan	Tankersley		4-6	4th	4.5
4-11	Col.	W	6-4		12	9	Lawrence	Oliver	Villafuerte	5-6	3rd	5.0
4-12	Col.	L	2-3		8	8	Speier	Villafuerte	Jimenez	5-7	T3rd	5.5
4-13	Col.	W	6-2		12	6	Wright	Cook		6-7	3rd	5.5
4-15	At L.A.	W	3-2		9	8	Peavy	Nomo	Wright	7-7	3rd	6.0
4-16	At L.A.	L	0-3		5	8	Ishii	Lawrence	Gagne	7-8	3rd	6.0
4-17	At L.A.	L	3-4		5	9	Brohawn	Wright	Gagne	7-9	T3rd	6.5
4-18	At Col.	L	1-12		5	17	Cook	Perez		7-10	T3rd	7.5
4-19	At Col.	L	9-10		14	14	Reed	Villafuerte		7-11	T3rd	8.5
4-20	At Col.	L	0-8		6	8	Chacon	Peavy		7-12	T4th	8.5
4-22	At Chi.	L	2-7		7	4	Zambrano	Lawrence		7-13	T4th	8.5
4-23	At Chi.	W	2-0		6	5	Eaton	Wood	Herges	8-13	T4th	8.5
4-24	At Chi.	W	2-1		7	7	Perez	Clement	Wright	9-13	T3rd	8.5
4-25	At Cin.	W	7-3		7	4	Peavy	Austin		10-13	T3rd	8.5
4-26	At Cin.	L	6-7	(10)	8	10	Heredia	Wright		10-14	4th	8.5
4-27	At Cin.	L	5-7		11	8	Wilson	Lawrence	Williamson	10-15	T4th	8.5
4-29	Pit.	L	2-7		9	13	D'Amico	Eaton		10-16	5th	8.5
4-30	Pit.	L	5-8		10	9	Benson	Perez	Williams	10-17	5th	9.5
5-1	Pit.	L	2-5		4	9	Wells	Peavy	Williams	10-18	5th	9.5
5-2	Phi.	W	5-4	(10)	11	7	Matthews	Mesa		11-18	5th	8.5
5-3	Phi.	L	4-5	(10)	10	8	Silva	Wright	Mesa	11-19	5th	9.5
5-4	Phi.	L	1-3		3	5	Wolf	Eaton	Mesa	11-20	5th	10.5
5-6	At Mon.	L	2-4		7	9	Hernandez	Peavy	Biddle	11-21	5th	11.5
5-7	At Mon.	L	9-12	(10)	11	16	Biddle	Orosco		11-22	5th	12.5
5-8	At Mon.	L	5-12		10	14	Ohka	Lawrence		11-23	5th	13.5
5-9	At N.Y.	W	5-4		10	7	Hackman	Weathers	Orosco	12-23	5th	13.5
5-10	At N.Y.	L	2-4	(10)	6	11	Stanton	Wright		12-24	5th	13.5
5-11	At N.Y.	L	2-3		7	8	Lloyd	Matthews	Benitez	12-25	5th	13.5
5-12	Fla.	L	1-6		12	10	Levrault	Condrey		12-26	5th	13.5
5-13	Fla.	W	6-5	(10)	10	9	Herges	Looper		13-26	5th	12.5
5-14	Fla.	L	3-10		7	17	Willis	Bynum		13-27	5th	12.5
5-15	Atl.	L	6-15		8	14	Ramirez	Deago		13-28	5th	13.5
5-16	Atl.	L	4-6		9	11	Gryboski	Nagy	Smoltz	13-29	5th	14.5
5-17	Atl.	L	2-12		7	16	Reynolds	Loewer		13-30	5th	14.5
5-18	Atl.	L	3-6		9	13	Ortiz	Lawrence	Smoltz	13-31	5th	14.5
5-19	At Mil.	L	5-6		10	9	Kinney	Keisler	DeJean	13-32	5th	14.5
5-20	At Mil.	L	7-8		11	9	DeJean	Herges		13-33	5th	15.5
5-21	At Mil.	L	0-10		2	12	Franklin	Peavy		13-34	5th	16.5
5-23	At Ari.	L	3-5		8	10	Koplove	Matthews	Mantei	13-35	5th	16.5
5-24	At Ari.	W	5-1		12	2	Lawrence	Schilling		14-35	5th	16.5
5-25	At Ari.	L	5-9		9	10	Dessens	Nagy		14-36	5th	16.5
5-26	At Ari.	L	4-8		8	11	Good	Eaton		14-37	5th	16.5
5-27	Mil.	L	2-4		6	7	Vizcaino	Matthews	DeJean	14-38	5th	17.5
5-28	Mil.	W	8-6		14	12	Matthews	Vizcaino		15-38	5th	17.5
5-29	Mil.	L	2-3		5	8	Estrella	Lawrence	DeJean	15-39	5th	18.0
5-30	Ari.	L	3-8		8	13	Schilling	Tollberg		15-40	5th	19.0
5-31	Ari.	W	8-7		16	14	Orosco	Service	Herges	16-40	5th	19.0
6-1	Ari.	L	4-10		13	11	Gonzalez	Peavy		16-41	5th	20.0
6-2	Ari.	W	4-1		9	8	Loewer	Patterson	Herges	17-41	5th	19.0
6-3	Det.	L	2-3		11	7	Walker	Lawrence	German	17-42	5th	19.0
6-4	Det.	L	3-5		9	10	Ledezma	Hackman	German	17-43	5th	20.0
6-5	Det.	W	5-1		9	4	Eaton	Bernero		18-43	5th	19.0
6-6	Min.	L	5-7	(11)	14	14	Romero	Beck		18-44	5th	20.0
6-7	Min.	L	2-6		5	12	Santana	Loewer	Nakamura	18-45	5th	21.0
6-8	Min.	W	9-4		16	11	Lawrence	Hawkins		19-45	5th	21.0

Date	Opp.	Res.	Score	(inn.*)	Hits	Opp. hits	Winning pitcher	Losing pitcher	Save	Record	Pos.	GB
6-10	At Cle.	L	5-8		11	8	Westbrook	Tollberg	Baez	19-46	5th	21.0
6-11	At Cle.	L	2-3		10	6	Sabathia	Eaton	Baez	19-47	5th	22.0
6-12	At Cle.	W	9-4		10	8	Peavy	Davis		20-47	5th	22.0
6-13	At Chi. (AL)	L	3-5		10	9	Gordon	Linebrink	Koch	20-48	5th	22.0
6-14	At Chi. (AL)	L	5-6		8	6	Gordon	Witasick	Koch	20-49	5th	23.0
6-15	At Chi. (AL)	W	1-0		3	7	Perez	Garland	Beck	21-49	5th	22.0
6-16	At Col.	W	7-5		13	11	Witasick	Jimenez	Beck	22-49	5th	21.5
6-17	At Col.	W	4-3		8	9	Peavy	Neagle	Witasick	23-49	5th	20.5
6-18	At Col.	L	3-5		7	10	Chacon	Jarvis	Speier	23-50	5th	20.5
6-19	At Col.	L	5-10		9	16	Oliver	Lawrence		23-51	5th	21.5
6-20	Sea.	W	5-3		9	7	Matthews	Nelson		24-51	5th	20.5
6-21	Sea.	L	2-4		5	10	Pineiro	Eaton	Hasegawa	24-52	5th	21.5
6-22	Sea.	W	3-1		5	5	Peavy	Franklin	Beck	25-52	5th	20.5
6-23	Col.	L	1-5		6	8	Chacon	Jarvis		25-53	5th	21.5
6-24	Col.	L	2-5		5	10	Oliver	Lawrence	Jimenez	25-54	5th	22.5
6-25	Col.	W	7-6		10	5	Hackman	Jones	Beck	26-54	5th	21.5
6-27	At Sea.	L	2-8		4	10	Pineiro	Eaton		26-55	5th	22.5
6-28	At Sea.	W	6-0		12	3	Peavy	Franklin		27-55	5th	22.5
6-29	At Sea.	W	8-6		15	10	Beck	Rhodes	Witasick	28-55	5th	21.5
7-1	At L.A.	W	7-1		13	8	Lawrence	Nomo		29-55	5th	22.0
7-2	At L.A.	W	4-3	(10)	8	6	Herges	Gagne	Beck	30-55	5th	22.0
7-3	At L.A.	W	7-4		9	9	Eaton	Brown	Beck	31-55	5th	21.0
7-4	S.F	L	6-8		7	12	Foppert	Peavy	Worrell	31-56	5th	22.0
7-5	S.F	W	5-2		8	5	Jarvis	Schmidt	Beck	32-56	5th	21.0
7-6	S.F	L	2-3		5	9	Rodriguez	Hackman	Worrell	32-57	5th	22.0
7-7	L.A.	W	7-1		12	5	Perez	Ashby		33-57	5th	22.0
7-8	L.A.	W	8-5		12	9	Eaton	Alvarez	Beck	34-57	5th	22.0
7-9	At Ari.	L	3-8		7	8	Capuano	Peavy		34-58	5th	22.0
7-10	At Ari.	W	14-2		16	9	Jarvis	Dessens		35-58	5th	21.0
7-11	At StL.	L	2-4		3	8	Williams	Lawrence	Isringhausen	35-59	5th	22.0
7-12	At StL.	L	7-9	(11)	14	13	Simontacchi	Herges		35-60	5th	23.0
7-13	At StL.	L	1-3		8	4	Simontacchi	Matthews	Isringhausen	35-61	5th	23.0
7-17	Ari.	L	1-9		9	13	Schilling	Perez		35-62	5th	24.0
7-18	Ari.	L	0-6		5	9	Batista	Lawrence		35-63	5th	25.0
7-19	Ari.	W	2-0		4	8	Eaton	Webb	Beck	36-63	5th	25.0
7-20	Ari.	W	3-2		8	5	Jarvis	Johnson	Beck	37-63	5th	25.0
7-21	StL.	W	5-4	(10)	11	8	Witasick	Painter		38-63	5th	25.0
7-22	StL.	W	3-2		6	9	Perez	Fassero	Beck	39-63	5th	25.0
7-23	StL.	L	4-8		12	17	Tomko	Lawrence		39-64	5th	26.0
7-25	At S.F	L	2-5		6	5	Rodriguez	Witasick		39-65	5th	27.5
7-26	At S.F	W	2-1		7	9	Jarvis	Williams	Beck	40-65	5th	26.5
7-27	At S.F	L	2-6		7	10	Foppert	Peavy		40-66	5th	27.5
7-29	At Pit.	W	8-7		11	7	Roa	Lincoln	Beck	41-66	5th	26.5
7-30	At Pit.	L	2-7		6	8	Wells	Lawrence	Meadows	41-67	5th	27.5
7-31	At Pit.	W	10-7		16	8	Eaton	Fogg	Beck	42-67	5th	26.5
8-1	At Phi.	L	0-6		3	10	Millwood	Jarvis		42-68	5th	26.5
8-2†	At Phi.	W	6-4		7	7	Peavy	Wolf		43-68		
8-2‡	At Phi.	L	4-10		10	14	Cormier	Roa		43-69	5th	26.0
8-3	At Phi.	W	5-2	(10)	9	5	Witasick	Mesa	Beck	44-69	5th	26.0
8-5	Chi.	L	0-3		3	8	Prior	Lawrence	Borowski	44-70	5th	27.0
8-6	Chi.	L	2-3		5	7	Wood	Eaton	Borowski	44-71	5th	27.0
8-7	Chi.	L	3-9		13	13	Zambrano	Jarvis		44-72	5th	28.0
8-8	Cin.	W	1-0	(12)	7	7	Beck	Reith		45-72	5th	28.0
8-9	Cin.	L	5-9		10	14	Harang	Perez		45-73	5th	28.0
8-10	Cin.	W	2-0		13	7	Lawrence	Graves	Beck	46-73	5th	28.0
8-12	At Atl.	W	14-4		24	7	Eaton	Maddux		47-73	5th	27.0
8-13	At Atl.	L	1-7		4	14	Hampton	Jarvis		47-74	5th	27.0
8-14	At Atl.	L	4-7		9	8	Ortiz	Peavy	Smoltz	47-75	5th	27.5
8-15	At Fla.	L	0-10		6	13	Penny	Perez		47-76	5th	27.5
8-16	At Fla.	L	3-6		10	10	Fox	Witasick	Looper	47-77	5th	27.5
8-17	At Fla.	L	7-11		8	15	Beckett	Eaton	Tejera	47-78	5th	27.5
8-19	N.Y.	W	3-2		7	7	Linebrink	Stanton	Beck	48-78	5th	27.0
8-20	N.Y.	W	2-1		4	8	Beck	Roberts		49-78	5th	27.0
8-21	N.Y.	L	1-5		7	4	Seo	Perez		49-79	5th	28.0
8-22	Mon.	W	5-3		12	7	Linebrink	Eischen	Beck	50-79	5th	28.0
8-23	Mon.	W	1-0	(10)	5	4	Matthews	Biddle		51-79	5th	28.0
8-24	Mon.	L	4-8		9	13	Knott	Jarvis		51-80	5th	28.0
8-25	At Ari.	L	8-11		14	14	Johnson	Peavy	Mantei	51-81	5th	28.5
8-26	At Ari.	W	5-4		10	4	Matthews	Valverde	Beck	52-81	5th	28.5

Date	Opp.	Res.	Score	(inn.*)	Hits	Opp. hits	Winning pitcher	Losing pitcher	Save	Record	Pos.	GB
8-27	At Ari.	W	10-2		16	5	Lawrence	Schilling		53-81	5th	28.5
8-29	At Hou.	W	7-1		14	6	Eaton	Robertson		54-81	5th	27.0
8-30	At Hou.	L	6-11		10	11	Fernandez	Jarvis	Wagner	54-82	5th	28.0
8-31	At Hou.	W	3-1		9	3	Peavy	Villone	Beck	55-82	5th	28.0
9-2	Ari.	W	6-3		13	8	Howard	Capuano		56-82	5th	28.5
9-3	Ari.	W	12-0		15	5	Lawrence	Batista		57-82	5th	28.5
9-5	Hou.	L	4-5		8	9	Fernandez	Eaton	Wagner	57-83	5th	28.5
9-6	Hou.	L	4-10		5	13	Lidge	Witasick	Wagner	57-84	5th	29.5
9-7	Hou.	W	7-1		8	5	Peavy	Miller		58-84	5th	28.5
9-9	S.F	L	3-8		9	11	Correia	Howard		58-85	5th	29.5
9-10	S.F	L	1-7		5	10	Rueter	Lawrence		58-86	5th	30.5
9-11	S.F	W	5-4	(10)	11	6	Matthews	Worrell		59-86	5th	29.5
9-12	At L.A.	L	0-6		4	9	Alvarez	Jarvis		59-87	5th	30.5
9-13	At L.A.	L	0-4		6	10	Brown	Peavy		59-88	5th	30.5
9-14	At L.A.	L	2-5		5	12	Nomo	Howard	Gagne	59-89	5th	31.5
9-15	At S.F	L	7-8		13	13	Nathan	Witasick	Worrell	59-90	5th	32.5
9-16	At S.F	L	2-4		7	7	Williams	Eaton	Worrell	59-91	5th	33.5
9-17	At S.F	L	3-8		7	12	Schmidt	Bynum		59-92	5th	34.5
9-18	At S.F	W	7-3		13	8	Peavy	Ponson		60-92	5th	33.5
9-19	At Col.	L	5-6		9	8	Elarton	Howard	Fuentes	60-93	5th	34.5
9-20	At Col.	W	11-3		15	8	Lawrence	Vance		61-93	5th	34.5
9-21	At Col.	L	3-5		9	8	Tsao	Eaton	Fuentes	61-94	5th	34.5
9-22	L.A.	W	9-5		16	11	Bynum	Perez		62-94	5th	34.5
9-23	L.A.	L	1-2		5	9	Martin	Beck	Gagne	62-95	5th	35.5
9-24	L.A.	L	1-2	(11)	7	5	Shuey	Witasick	Gagne	62-96	5th	35.5
9-25	L.A.	W	6-1		8	9	Lawrence	Nomo		63-96	5th	35.0
9-26	Col.	W	5-0		10	8	Eaton	Vance		64-96	5th	35.0
9-27	Col.	L	2-10		2	14	Stark	Bynum		64-97	5th	35.5
9-28	Col.	L	8-10		13	11	Lopez	Witasick	Speier	64-98	5th	36.5

Monthly records: March (0-1), April (10-16), May (6-23), June (12-15), July (14-12), August (13-15), September (9-16).
*Innings, if other than nine. † First game of a doubleheader. ‡ Second game of a doubleheader.

RECORDS

2003 regular-season record: 64-98
Position: 5th in N.L. West
Home: 35-46 **Road:** 29-52
N.L. East: 10-22 **N.L. Central:** 13-23
N.L. West: 33-43 A.L. 8-10
Vs. LH starters: 17-30
Vs. RH starters: 47-68
Grass: 62-93 **Artificial:** 2-5
Day: 19-31 **Night:** 45-67
1-Run: 21-20 **X-inn.:** 8-8
Doubleheaders: 0-0-1
Team record past five years: 359-451 (.443, ranks 14th in league in that span)

TEAM LEADERS

Batting average: Mark Loretta (.314).
At-bats: Mark Loretta (589).
Runs: Mark Loretta (74).
Hits: Mark Loretta (185).
Total Bases: Mark Loretta (260).
Doubles: Mark Kotsay, Mark Loretta (28).
Triples: Sean Burroughs (6).
Home runs: Ryan Klesko (21).
Runs batted in: Mark Loretta (72).
Stolen bases: Gary Matthews Jr. (12).
Slugging percentage: Rondell White (.465).
On-base percentage: Mark Loretta (.372).
Wins: Jake Peavy (12).
Earned-run average: Adam Eaton (4.08).
Complete games: Adam Eaton, Brian Lawrence (1).
Shutouts: None.
Saves: Rod Beck (20).
Innings pitched: Brian Lawrence (210.2).
Strikeouts: Jake Peavy (156).

GAMES BY POSITION

Catcher: Gary Bennett 91, Miguel Ojeda 48, Wiki Gonzalez 23, Michael Rivera 19, Humberto Quintero 11.
First base: Ryan Klesko 111, Phil Nevin 31, Brian Buchanan 24, Dave Hansen 20, Lou Merloni 2, Miguel Ojeda 2, Michael Rivera 1, Todd Sears 1.
Second base: Mark Loretta 150, Keith Lockhart 27, Lou Merloni 10, Ramon Vazquez 3, Dave Hansen 1.
Third base: Sean Burroughs 137, Lou Merloni 25, Dave Hansen 11, Ramon Vazquez 4, Keith Lockhart 3.
Shortstop: Ramon Vazquez 108, Donaldo Mendez 26, Lou Merloni 23, Khalil Greene 20, Mark Loretta 3.
Outfield: Mark Kotsay 126, Xavier Nady 105, Rondell White 104, Gary Matthews Jr. 92, Brian Buchanan 43, Shane Victorino 32, Brian Giles 29, Phil Nevin 29, Jason Bay 3, Lou Merloni 2, Jermaine Clark 1.
Designated hitter: Brian Buchanan 5, Dave Hansen 3, Rondell White 3, Ryan Klesko 1.

TOP DRAFT CHOICES

1. **Tim Stauffer,** RHP, Richmond.
2. **Daniel Moore,** LHP, North Carolina.
3. **Colt Morton,** C, North Carolina State.
4. **Peter Stonard,** SS, San Diego State.
5. **Billy Hogan,** SS, Chandler-Gilbert JC (Ariz.).
6. **Cory Patton,** OF, Texas A&M.
7. **Clark Girardeau,** RHP, South Alabama.
8. **Dirk Hayhurst,** RHP, Kent State.
9. **Matt Lauderdale,** C, College of Charleston.
10. **Fernando Valenzuela Jr.,** 1B, UNLV.

SAN FRANCISCO GIANTS

NATIONAL LEAGUE WEST DIVISION

2004 SEASON

April

SUN	MON	TUE	WED	THU	FRI	SAT
4	5 HOU	6 HOU	7 HOU	8 SD	9	10 SD
11 SD	12 MIL	13 MIL	14 MIL	15	16 LA	17 LA
18 LA	19 SD	20 SD	21 SD	22 SD	23 LA	24 LA
25 LA	26 ATL	27 ATL	28 ATL	29 FLA	30 FLA	

May

SUN	MON	TUE	WED	THU	FRI	SAT
						1 FLA
2 FLA	3	4 NYM	5 NYM	6 NYM	7 CIN	8 CIN
9 CIN	10	11 PHI	12 PHI	13 PHI	14 PIT	15 PIT
16 PIT	17	18 CHC	19 CHC	20 CHC	21 * MON	22 * MON
23 * MON	24	25 ARI	26 ARI	27 ARI	28 COL	29 COL
30 COL	31 ARI					

June

SUN	MON	TUE	WED	THU	FRI	SAT
		1 ARI	2 ARI	3 ARI	4 COL	5 COL
6 COL	7 COL	8 TB	9 TB	10 TB	11 BAL	12 BAL
13 BAL	14	15 TOR	16 TOR	17 TOR	18 BOS	19 BOS
20 BOS	21 LA	22 LA	23 LA	24 LA	25 OAK	26 OAK
27 OAK	28	29 LA	30 LA			

July

SUN	MON	TUE	WED	THU	FRI	SAT
				1 LA	2 OAK	3 OAK
4 OAK	5 COL	6 COL	7 COL	8 ARI	9 ARI	10 ARI
11 ARI	12	13 All-Star	14	15 COL	16 COL	17 COL
18 COL	19 ARI	20 ARI	21 SD	22 SD	23 STL	24 STL
25 STL	26 SD	27 SD	28 SD	29 SD	30 STL	31 STL

August

SUN	MON	TUE	WED	THU	FRI	SAT
1 STL	2	3 CIN	4 CIN	5 CIN	6 CHC	7 CHC
8 CHC	9	10 PIT	11 PIT	12 PIT	13 PHI	14 PHI
15 PHI	16 MON	17 MON	18 MON	19	20 NYM	21 NYM
22 NYM	23	24 FLA	25 FLA	26 FLA	27 ATL	28 ATL
29 ATL	30 ATL	31 COL				

Sept./Oct.

SUN	MON	TUE	WED	THU	FRI	SAT
			1 COL	2 COL	3 ARI	4 ARI
5 ARI	6	7 COL	8 COL	9	10 ARI	11 ARI
12 ARI	13	14 MIL	15 MIL	16 MIL	17 SD	18 SD
19 SD	20	21 HOU	22 HOU	23 HOU	24 LA	25 LA
26 LA	27	28 SD	29 SD	30 SD	1 LA	2 LA
3 LA	4	5	6	7	8	9

Home games shaded. All-Star Game July 13 at Houston. Schedule subject to change. * San Juan, Puerto Rico.

CLUB DIRECTORY

President and managing general partner
Peter A. Magowan

Executive vice president/COO
Larry Baer

Senior v.p. and general manager
Brian Sabean

Vice president and assistant g.m.
Ned Colletti

Vice president of player personnel
Dick Tidrow

Special assistant to the general manager
Ron Perranoski

Director of player development
Jack Hiatt

Coordinator of minor league instruction
Fred Stanley

Media relations manager
Jim Moorehead

Baseball information manager
Blake Rhodes

Director, broadcasting & media services
Maria Jacinto

MINOR LEAGUE AFFILIATES

Class	Team	League	Manager
AAA	Fresno	Pacific Coast	Bill Hayes
AA	Norwich	Eastern	Shane Turner
Advanced A	San Jose	California	Lenn Sakata
A	Hagerstown	South Atlantic	Mike Ramsey
Short-Season A	Salem-Keizer	Northwest	Joe Strain
Rookie	Arizona Giants	Arizona	Bert Hunter

More on the Giants at www.foxsports.com/named/FS/MLB/teams

BROADCAST INFORMATION

Radio: KNBR-AM (680).
TV: KTVU-TV (Channel 2).
Cable TV: Fox Sports Net.

SPRING TRAINING

Ballpark (city): Scottsdale Stadium (Scottsdale, Ariz.).
Ticket information: 602-990-7972.

SPRING TRAINING ROSTER

Manager—Felipe Alou (23).
Coaches—Carlos Alfonso (17), Mark Gardner (26), Gene Glynn (15), Joe Lefebvre (18), Luis Pujols (65), Dave Righetti (19), Ron Wotus (10).

No.	PITCHERS	B/T	Ht./Wt.	Age*	2003 Clubs
38	Brower, Jim	R/R	6-3/215	31	San Francisco
40	Christiansen, J.	R/L	6-5/241	34	San Jose, Fresno, San Francisco
53	Correia, Kevin	R/R	6-3/200	23	Norwich, Fresno, San Francisco
48	Eyre, Scott	L/L	6-1/210	31	San Francisco
34	Foppert, Jesse	R/R	6-6/210	23	Fresno, San Jose, San Francisco
48	Herges, Matt	L/R	6-0/205	34	Portland, San Diego, San Francisco
32	Hermanson, D.	R/R	6-2/200	31	St. Louis, Fresno, San Francisco
43	Jensen, Ryan	R/R	6-0/205	28	San Francisco, Fresno
60	Lowry, Noah	L/L	6-2/190	23	Norwich, Fresno, San Francisco
31	Nen, Robb	R/R	6-5/222	34	Did Not Play
47	Rodriguez, Felix	R/R	6-1/198	31	San Francisco
46	Rueter, Kirk	L/L	6-3/212	33	Fresno, San Francisco
29	Schmidt, Jason	R/R	6-5/205	31	San Francisco
	Tomko, Brett	R/R	6-4/215	30	St. Louis
	Valdez, Merkin	R/R	6-3/170	22	Hagerstown
57	Williams, Jerome	R/R	6-3/180	22	Fresno, San Francisco
41	Zerbe, Chad	L/L	6-0/200	31	San Jose, Fresno, San Francisco

No.	CATCHERS	B/T	Ht./Wt.	Age*	2003 Clubs
37	Castillo, Alberto	R/R	6-0/200	34	Fresno, San Francisco
	Knoedler, Justin	R/R	6-2/210	23	San Jose
52	Lunsford, Trey	R/R	6-1/195	24	San Francisco, Arizona Giants, Salem-Keizer, San Jose, Fresno
26	Pierzynski, A.J.	L/R	6-3/220	27	Minnesota
8	Torrealba, Yorvit	R/R	5-11/180	25	San Francisco

No.	INFIELDERS	B/T	Ht./Wt.	Age*	2003 Clubs
13	Alfonzo, Edgardo	R/R	5-11/187	30	San Francisco
	Athas, Jamie	L/R	6-2/190	24	Norwich
	Chavez, Angel	R/R	6-1/180	22	San Jose
5	Durham, Ray	B/R	5-8/180	32	San Francisco
39	Feliz, Pedro	R/R	6-1/205	28	San Francisco
28	Niekro, Lance	R/R	6-3/210	25	Fresno, San Francisco
1	Perez, Neifi	B/R	6-0/175	30	San Francisco
2	Ransom, Cody	R/R	6-2/190	28	Fresno, San Francisco
6	Snow, J.T.	L/L	6-2/209	36	San Francisco

No.	OUTFIELDERS	B/T	Ht./Wt.	Age*	2003 Clubs
25	Bonds, Barry	L/L	6-2/228	39	San Francisco
56	Ellison, Jason	R/R	5-10/180	25	San Francisco, Fresno
9	Grissom, Marquis	R/R	5-11/180	36	San Francisco
41	Hammonds, J.	R/R	6-0/207	33	Milwaukee, Arizona Giants, Fresno, San Francisco
50	Linden, Todd	B/R	6-3/210	23	Fresno, San Francisco
	Mohr, Dustan	R/R	6-1/210	27	Minnesota
20	Torcato, Tony	L/R	6-1/195	24	Fresno, San Francisco
	Tucker, Michael	L/R	6-2/195	32	Kansas City
21	Valderrama, C.	R/R	5-11/175	26	Norwich, San Francisco, Fresno

Invited to spring training: RHP Brian Cooper, RHP Chris Gissell, RHP Matt Montgomery, LHP Adam Pettyjohn, LHP Kevin Pickford, RHP Tyler Walker, IF Brian Dallimore, IF Francisco Santos, OF Nathan Haynes, OF Robert Stratton.

*Age as of April 1, 2004.

BALLPARK INFORMATION

Ballpark (capacity, surface)
SBC Park (41,584, grass)

Address
24 Willie Mays Plaza
San Francisco, CA 94107

Official website
www.sfgiants.com

Business phone
415-972-2000

Ticket information
415-972-2000

Field dimensions (from home plate)
To left field at foul line, 339 feet
To center field, 399 feet
To right field at foul line, 309 feet

First game played
April 11, 2000 (Dodgers 6, Giants 5)

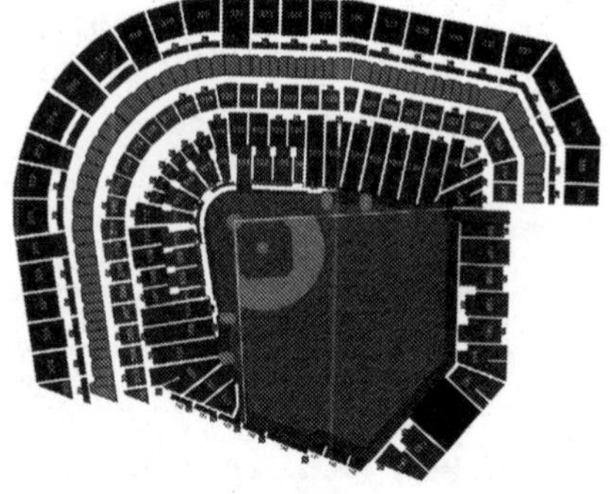

2003 REVIEW

DAY BY DAY

Date	Opp.	Res.	Score	(inn.*)	Hits	Opp. hits	Winning pitcher	Losing pitcher	Save	Record	Pos.	GB
3-31	At S.D.	W	5-2		9	7	Rodriguez	Condrey	Worrell	1-0	T1st	...
4-1	At S.D.	W	8-1		10	4	Schmidt	Eaton		2-0	1st	+1.0
4-2	At S.D.	W	5-3		5	6	Moss	Perez	Worrell	3-0	1st	+1.0
4-4	At Mil.	W	7-5		12	10	Brower	Vizcaino	Worrell	4-0	1st	+2.0
4-5	At Mil.	W	6-5		9	11	Ainsworth	Sheets	Eyre	5-0	1st	+2.0
4-6	At Mil.	W	5-0		8	7	Rueter	Franklin	Brower	6-0	1st	+2.0
4-7	S.D.	W	7-4		9	11	Worrell	Bynum		7-0	1st	+2.5
4-8	S.D.	L	4-9		10	15	Peavy	Eyre		7-1	1st	+2.5
4-9	S.D.	W	15-11		16	15	Nathan	Tankersley		8-1	1st	+2.5
4-10	L.A.	W	2-1		8	6	Ainsworth	Nomo	Worrell	9-1	1st	+2.5
4-11	L.A.	W	3-2		7	5	Rueter	Perez	Worrell	10-1	1st	+3.5
4-13	L.A.	W	5-4	(12)	11	14	Brower	Ashby		11-1	1st	+4.0
4-14	Hou.	W	4-2		6	7	Moss	Miller	Worrell	12-1	1st	+4.0
4-15	Hou.	W	8-4		9	10	Ainsworth	Robertson	Rodriguez	13-1	1st	+4.0
4-16	Hou.	L	5-8		11	15	Lidge	Brower	Wagner	13-2	1st	+4.0
4-18	At L.A.	W	5-1		11	4	Schmidt	Brown		14-2	1st	+4.5
4-19	At L.A.	W	9-3		11	9	Moss	Ashby		15-2	1st	+4.5
4-20	At L.A.	L	4-16		7	18	Nomo	Ainsworth		15-3	1st	+3.5
4-22	At Pit.	L	2-5		9	6	Suppan	Foppert		15-4	1st	+3.5
4-23	At Pit.	W	4-3	(13)	10	16	Brower	Tavarez		16-4	1st	+4.5
4-24	At Pit.	W	3-1		9	7	Moss	Benson	Worrell	17-4	1st	+5.5
4-25	At Phi.	W	7-4		9	10	Nathan	Padilla		18-4	1st	+6.5
4-26	At Phi.	L	2-10		9	12	Duckworth	Williams	Silva	18-5	1st	+5.5
4-27	At Phi.	L	0-1		0	4	Millwood	Foppert		18-6	1st	+4.5
4-29	Chi.	L	2-4		9	9	Wood	Rueter	Borowski	18-7	1st	+3.5
4-30	Chi.	W	5-0		6	3	Schmidt	Clement		19-7	1st	+4.5
5-1	Chi.	L	1-5	(10)	8	12	Cruz	Worrell		19-8	1st	+4.5
5-2	Cin.	L	1-5		10	9	Graves	Ainsworth		19-9	1st	+4.5
5-3	Cin.	W	9-6		11	9	Foppert	Wilson	Worrell	20-9	1st	+4.5
5-4	Cin.	W	6-1		9	6	Rueter	Dempster		21-9	1st	+5.5
5-6	At Fla.	W	4-2		10	3	Nathan	Almanza	Worrell	22-9	1st	+6.5
5-7	At Fla.	W	3-2		8	9	Moss	Beckett	Worrell	23-9	1st	+7.0
5-8	At Fla.	W	3-2		7	6	Nathan	Looper	Worrell	24-9	1st	+7.0
5-9	At Atl.	W	9-2		9	6	Foppert	Maddux	Brower	25-9	1st	+7.0
5-10	At Atl.	L	3-6		8	11	Gryboski	Nathan		25-10	1st	+7.0
5-11	At Atl.	L	3-7		9	10	Hampton	Schmidt		25-11	1st	+6.0
5-12	Mon.	L	3-4		12	9	Day	Moss	Biddle	25-12	1st	+6.0
5-13	Mon.	L	4-6		10	9	Smith	Ainsworth	Biddle	25-13	1st	+6.0
5-14	Mon.	L	3-6		6	8	Vargas	Foppert		25-14	1st	+5.0
5-15	N.Y.	W	11-3		17	6	Rueter	Leiter		26-14	1st	+5.5
5-16	N.Y.	W	7-5		15	8	Nathan	Weathers	Worrell	27-14	1st	+5.5
5-17	N.Y.	L	1-5		5	6	Trachsel	Moss		27-15	1st	+4.5
5-18	N.Y.	L	1-5		6	8	Glavine	Ainsworth		27-16	1st	+3.5
5-19	At Ari.	L	3-4		8	10	Mantei	Worrell		27-17	1st	+3.0
5-20	At Ari.	W	6-5		11	11	Rueter	Dessens	Worrell	28-17	1st	+3.0
5-21	At Ari.	W	6-0		9	4	Schmidt	Batista		29-17	1st	+3.0
5-23	At Col.	L	7-10		16	11	Chacon	Moss		29-18	1st	+1.5
5-24	At Col.	W	5-1		11	4	Ainsworth	Elarton		30-18	1st	+1.5
5-25	At Col.	L	1-5		11	7	Oliver	Foppert		30-19	1st	+0.5
5-26	At Col.	L	7-12		9	18	Fuentes	Nathan		30-20	T1st	...
5-27	Ari.	W	4-3	(13)	9	6	Rodriguez	Mantei		31-20	1st	+1.0
5-28	Ari.	W	10-2		12	5	Moss	Patterson		32-20	1st	+2.0
5-30	Col.	W	6-2		12	10	Ainsworth	Oliver		33-20	1st	+3.5
5-31	Col.	W	2-1		8	3	Foppert	Jennings	Worrell	34-20	1st	+3.5
6-1	Col.	W	4-0		6	8	Rueter	Cook		35-20	1st	+4.5
6-2	Col.	L	1-4		6	9	Chacon	Schmidt	Jimenez	35-21	1st	+4.0
6-3	Min.	L	4-6		11	13	Mays	Moss	Guardado	35-22	1st	+3.0
6-4	Min.	W	4-3		9	5	Worrell	Rincon		36-22	1st	+4.0
6-5	Min.	L	2-5		8	10	Lohse	Foppert	Guardado	36-23	1st	+3.0
6-6	Det.	W	5-3		8	8	Rueter	Bonderman	Worrell	37-23	1st	+3.0
6-7	Det.	W	7-5		11	11	Schmidt	Maroth		38-23	1st	+4.0
6-8	Det.	W	7-6		13	9	Nathan	German	Worrell	39-23	1st	+5.0
6-10	At Chi. (AL)	L	3-5		7	9	Garland	Nathan		39-24	1st	+4.0
6-11	At Chi. (AL)	W	11-4		12	6	Foppert	Buehrle		40-24	1st	+4.0

Date	Opp.	Res.	Score	(inn.*)	Hits	Opp. hits	Winning pitcher	Losing pitcher	Save	Record	Pos.	GB
6-12	At Chi. (AL)	W	8-4		8	9	Nathan	Colon		41-24	1st	+4.0
6-13	At K.C.	L	1-6		11	11	George	Schmidt		41-25	1st	+3.0
6-14	At K.C.	W	7-4		8	9	Moss	Walrond		42-25	1st	+3.0
6-15	At K.C.	L	4-5		9	8	MacDougal	Worrell		42-26	1st	+2.0
6-17	At L.A.	L	1-4		8	9	Brown	Foppert	Gagne	42-27	1st	+1.0
6-18	At L.A.	L	2-8		6	11	Ishii	Rueter		42-28	T1st	...
6-19	At L.A.	W	2-0		6	3	Schmidt	Perez		43-28	1st	+1.0
6-20	At Oak.	L	3-5		9	9	Harang	Moss	Foulke	43-29	T1st	...
6-21	At Oak.	W	6-4		11	8	Williams	Hudson	Worrell	44-29	T1st	...
6-22	At Oak.	L	5-6		9	7	Lilly	Zerbe	Foulke	44-30	T1st	...
6-23	L.A.	W	3-2	(11)	9	10	Rodriguez	Gagne		45-30	1st	+1.0
6-24	L.A.	W	2-1		4	4	Schmidt	Perez		46-30	1st	+2.0
6-25	L.A.	L	0-6		3	16	Nomo	Moss		46-31	1st	+1.0
6-27	Oak.	W	6-0		9	7	Williams	Lilly		47-31	1st	+2.0
6-28	Oak.	W	8-7	(10)	17	13	Rodriguez	Foulke		48-31	1st	+3.0
6-29	Oak.	L	2-5		7	11	Mulder	Foppert	Foulke	48-32	1st	+3.0
6-30	At StL.	W	5-1		10	7	Schmidt	Haren		49-32	1st	+3.5
7-1	At StL.	W	5-1		8	6	Brower	Williams		50-32	1st	+4.5
7-2	At StL.	W	4-1		5	6	Williams	Stephenson	Worrell	51-32	1st	+5.5
7-3	At StL.	L	5-9		10	14	Simontacchi	Rueter		51-33	1st	+5.0
7-4	At S.D.	W	8-6		12	7	Foppert	Peavy	Worrell	52-33	1st	+5.0
7-5	At S.D.	L	2-5		5	8	Jarvis	Schmidt	Beck	52-34	1st	+5.0
7-6	At S.D.	W	3-2		9	5	Rodriguez	Hackman	Worrell	53-34	1st	+5.0
7-7	StL.	W	5-1		10	7	Williams	Stephenson		54-34	1st	+5.0
7-8	StL.	W	8-3		12	7	Brower	Haren		55-34	1st	+5.0
7-9	At Col.	L	7-11		10	12	Cook	Foppert		55-35	1st	+4.0
7-10	At Col.	L	3-11		9	13	Oliver	Powell		55-36	1st	+4.0
7-11	At Ari.	W	10-7		12	10	Schmidt	Batista	Rodriguez	56-36	1st	+5.0
7-12	At Ari.	W	8-1		8	3	Williams	Schilling		57-36	1st	+6.0
7-13	At Ari.	L	4-7		6	8	Webb	Brower	Mantei	57-37	1st	+5.0
7-17	Col.	W	8-4		12	10	Moss	Jennings		58-37	1st	+5.0
7-18	Col.	W	7-0		12	5	Brower	Oliver		59-37	1st	+5.0
7-19	Col.	W	5-3		7	8	Schmidt	Chacon	Worrell	60-37	1st	+6.0
7-20	Col.	W	8-4		11	6	Foppert	Neagle		61-37	1st	+7.0
7-21	Ari.	W	5-4		7	7	Zerbe	Dessens	Worrell	62-37	1st	+8.0
7-22	Ari.	W	3-1		10	9	Moss	Schilling	Worrell	63-37	1st	+9.0
7-23	Ari.	W	7-1		10	7	Brower	Batista		64-37	1st	+10.0
7-24	Ari.	W	3-2		5	12	Worrell	Myers		65-37	1st	+11.0
7-25	S.D.	W	5-2		5	6	Rodriguez	Witasick		66-37	1st	+11.0
7-26	S.D.	L	1-2		9	7	Jarvis	Williams	Beck	66-38	1st	+10.0
7-27	S.D.	W	6-2		10	7	Foppert	Peavy		67-38	1st	+11.0
7-29	At Chi.	L	0-3		2	5	Clement	Moss		67-39	1st	+11.5
7-30	At Chi.	W	6-3		6	4	Schmidt	Wood		68-39	1st	+12.5
7-31	At Chi.	L	4-9		9	11	Zambrano	Brower		68-40	1st	+12.0
8-1	At Cin.	L	3-5		10	8	Reitsma	Rodriguez		68-41	1st	+12.0
8-2	At Cin.	L	4-5		8	8	Wagner	Rodriguez	Heredia	68-42	1st	+11.0
8-3	At Cin.	W	7-3		12	8	Hermanson	Haynes		69-42	1st	+12.0
8-5	Pit.	W	3-0		6	6	Schmidt	Wells	Worrell	70-42	1st	+12.0
8-6	Pit.	L	0-2		3	7	Tavarez	Ponson		70-43	1st	+11.0
8-7	Pit.	W	7-5		7	7	Eyre	Boehringer	Worrell	71-43	1st	+11.0
8-8	Phi.	W	9-1		11	3	Foppert	Wolf		72-43	1st	+12.0
8-9	Phi.	L	6-8	(10)	10	11	Wendell	Brower		72-44	1st	+11.0
8-10	Phi.	W	5-2		9	11	Correia	Myers		73-44	1st	+11.0
8-12	At N.Y.	L	4-5		11	8	Heilman	Ponson	Weathers	73-45	1st	+10.0
8-13	At N.Y.	L	2-9		9	13	Trachsel	Williams		73-46	1st	+9.0
8-15	At Mon.	L	1-4		5	6	Hernandez	Foppert		73-47	1st	+9.5
8-16	At Mon.	L	1-4		7	10	Day	Schmidt	Biddle	73-48	1st	+9.5
8-17	At Mon.	L	2-4		9	5	Biddle	Ponson		73-49	1st	+8.5
8-18	At Mon.	L	0-4		3	9	Vazquez	Hermanson		73-50	1st	+8.5
8-19	Atl.	W	5-4	(10)	8	6	Worrell	King		74-50	1st	+8.5
8-20	Atl.	W	2-1		8	9	Nathan	Gryboski		75-50	1st	+9.5
8-21	Atl.	W	4-3	(10)	8	6	Rodriguez	Hodges		76-50	1st	+9.5
8-22	Fla.	W	6-4		10	11	Ponson	Willis	Worrell	77-50	1st	+10.0
8-23	Fla.	W	3-2		8	6	Brower	Beckett	Worrell	78-50	1st	+10.5
8-24	Fla.	L	4-7		10	11	Pavano	Rueter		78-51	1st	+10.5
8-26	At Col.	W	3-1		9	5	Schmidt	Oliver	Worrell	79-51	1st	+11.0
8-27	At Col.	W	6-4		12	8	Ponson	Jimenez	Worrell	80-51	1st	+12.0
8-28	At Col.	L	1-6		7	8	Jennings	Correia		80-52	1st	+11.5
8-29	At Ari.	L	4-5		7	11	Batista	Rueter	Mantei	80-53	1st	+10.5
8-30	At Ari.	W	2-1		6	6	Williams	Johnson	Worrell	81-53	1st	+11.0
8-31	At Ari.	W	3-1		6	7	Schmidt	Webb	Worrell	82-53	1st	+11.0

Date	Opp.	Res.	Score	(inn.*)	Hits	Opp. hits	Winning pitcher	Losing pitcher	Save	Record	Pos.	GB
9-1	At Ari.	W	2-0		8	6	Ponson	Villarreal	Worrell	83-53	1st	+12.0
9-2	Col.	W	2-1		7	5	Herges	Bernero	Worrell	84-53	1st	+12.0
9-3	Col.	W	7-6		14	7	Nathan	Fuentes		85-53	1st	+13.0
9-5	Ari.	L	1-8		4	13	Webb	Williams		85-54	1st	+12.0
9-6	Ari.	W	5-4	(11)	7	9	Eyre	Mantei		86-54	1st	+12.0
9-7	Ari.	L	6-9		13	13	Gonzalez	Nathan	Patterson	86-55	1st	+11.0
9-9	At S.D.	W	8-3		11	9	Correia	Howard		87-55	1st	+10.5
9-10	At S.D.	W	7-1		10	5	Rueter	Lawrence		88-55	1st	+11.5
9-11	At S.D.	L	4-5	(10)	6	11	Matthews	Worrell		88-56	1st	+11.5
9-12	Mil.	W	8-2		10	9	Schmidt	Kinney		89-56	1st	+11.5
9-13	Mil.	L	4-5		12	7	Davis	Ponson	Kolb	89-57	1st	+10.5
9-14	Mil.	W	5-4	(11)	11	9	Rodriguez	Estrella		90-57	1st	+10.5
9-15	S.D.	W	8-7		13	13	Nathan	Witasick	Worrell	91-57	1st	+11.0
9-16	S.D.	W	4-2		7	7	Williams	Eaton	Worrell	92-57	1st	+12.0
9-17	S.D.	W	8-3		12	7	Schmidt	Bynum		93-57	1st	+13.0
9-18	S.D.	L	3-7		8	13	Peavy	Ponson		93-58	1st	+12.0
9-19	At L.A.	W	6-4		11	11	Hermanson	Brown	Worrell	94-58	1st	+13.0
9-20	At L.A.	W	6-0		13	7	Rueter	Nomo		95-58	1st	+14.0
9-21	At L.A.	L	5-7		9	10	Quantrill	Brower	Gagne	95-59	1st	+13.0
9-22	At Hou.	W	6-3		8	11	Nathan	Wagner	Worrell	96-59	1st	+14.0
9-23	At Hou.	W	10-3		10	4	Schmidt	Miller		97-59	1st	+14.0
9-24	At Hou.	L	1-2		3	4	Oswalt	Ponson	Wagner	97-60	1st	+13.0
9-26	L.A.	W	10-1		13	7	Rueter	Ishii		98-60	1st	+14.5
9-27§	L.A.	L	0-5		2	7	Jackson	Williams		98-61		
9-27∞	L.A.	W	6-3		13	7	Nathan	Mota	Worrell	99-61	1st	+14.5
9-28	L.A.	W	12-3		14	9	Correia	Alvarez		100-61	1st	+15.5

Monthly records: March (1-0), April (18-7), May (15-13), June (15-12), July (19-8), August (14-13), September (18-8).
*Innings, if other than nine. § Day separate admission. ∞ Night separate admission.

RECORDS

2003 regular-season record: 100-61
Position: 1st in N.L. West
Home: 57-24 **Road:** 43-37
N.L. East: 14-17 **N.L. Central:** 23-13
N.L. West: 53-23 A.L. 10-8
Vs. LH starters: 26-11
Vs. RH starters: 74-50
Grass: 99-55 **Artificial:** 1-6
Day: 31-27 **Night:** 69-34
1-Run: 28-12 **X-inn.:** 9-3
Doubleheaders: 0-0-0
Team record past five years: 468-340 (.579, ranks 2nd in league in that span)

TEAM LEADERS

Batting average: Barry Bonds (.341).
At-bats: Marquis Grissom (587).
Runs: Barry Bonds (111).
Hits: Marquis Grissom (176).
Total Bases: Barry Bonds (292).
Doubles: Marquis Grissom (33).
Triples: Ray Durham (5).
Home runs: Barry Bonds (45).
Runs batted in: Barry Bonds (90).
Stolen bases: Marquis Grissom (11).
Slugging percentage: Barry Bonds (.749).
On-base percentage: Barry Bonds (.529).
Wins: Jason Schmidt (17).
Earned-run average: Jason Schmidt (2.34).
Complete games: Jason Schmidt (5).
Shutouts: Jason Schmidt (3).
Saves: Tim Worrell (38).
Innings pitched: Jason Schmidt (207.2).
Strikeouts: Jason Schmidt (208).

GAMES BY POSITION

Catcher: Benito Santiago 106, Yorvit Torrealba 66, Alberto Castillo 10, Trey Lunsford 1.
First base: J.T. Snow 97, Andres Galarraga 69, Pedro Feliz 12, Lance Niekro 3, Francisco Santos 1.
Second base: Ray Durham 105, Neifi Perez 57, Eric Young 18, Edgardo Alfonzo 6.
Third base: Edgardo Alfonzo 133, Pedro Feliz 49, Neifi Perez 2.
Shortstop: Rich Aurilia 123, Neifi Perez 45, Cody Ransom 12.
Outfield: Jose Cruz 158, Marquis Grissom 148, Barry Bonds 123, Jeffrey Hammonds 30, Ruben Rivera 27, Marvin Benard 21, Pedro Feliz 15, Todd Linden 13, Tony Torcato 6, Carlos Valderrama 5, Jason Ellison 4, Francisco Santos 3, Eric Young 2, Yorvit Torrealba 1.
Designated hitter: Barry Bonds 6, Andres Galarraga 2, Rich Aurilia 1, Carlos Valderrama 1.

TOP DRAFT CHOICES

1a. **David Aardsma,** RHP, Rice.
1b. **Craig Whitaker,** RHP, Lufkin (Texas) H.S.
2a. **Todd Jennings,** C, Long Beach State.
2b. **Nate Schierholtz,** 3B, Chabot JC (Calif.).
3. **Brian Buscher,** 3B, South Carolina.
4. **Brooks McNiven,** RHP, U. of British Columbia.
5. **Mike Wagner,** OF, Washington.
6. **Billy Sadler,** RHP, Louisiana State.
7. **Pat Misch,** LHP, Western Michigan.
8. **Tim Hutting,** SS, Long Beach State.
9. **Kellen Ludwig,** RHP, Chipola J.C. (Fla.).
10. **Jesse Schmidt,** OF, Sacramento State.

2003 REVIEW

Year in review

American League Division Series

National League Division Series

American League Championship Series

National League Championship Series

World Series

All-Star Game

Notable Performances

Transactions

Award Winners

Miscellaneous

Necrology

YEAR IN REVIEW

THE TOP STORIES OF THE PAST YEAR

By STEVE GIETSCHIER
TSN Senior Managing Editor

As the 2003 regular season moved toward its conclusion, baseball romantics were savoring the possibility that one of the sport's longest-held dreams would finally be realized. These students of history were hoping that either the Chicago Cubs or the Boston Red Sox (or both) would qualify for postseason play and that one of these teams would overcome decades of futility and win the World Series. The Cubs, burdened, some have said, by the "Curse of the Billy Goat," had not made an appearance in the Series since 1945 and had not won one since 1908. Shackled just as firmly by the "Curse of the Bambino," Boston had not captured a World Series since 1918, but the Red Sox had wound up as Series losers four times since then, in 1946, 1967, 1975 and 1986. Players and managers of these teams denied the weight of their teams' past, but supporters were not so sure. Cub fans had for years endured a number of inferior teams and suffered with some that seemed better on paper than on the field. Red Sox fans, many of whom have waxed eloquent in print about their plight, were additionally afflicted by the peculiar thorn in their sides that is the persistent success of the New York Yankees.

T.S. Eliot wrote that "April is the cruelest month," but baseball fans know that the most important dreams die in the fall. For these two teams, such was the case again. The Cubs squandered a 3-1 lead in the National League Championship Series and saw their World Series hopes dashed by a most unfortunate string of events. The Red Sox played the Yankees even into the 11th inning of the seventh game of the American League Championship Series only to see a home run send them home in shock. That the Yankees were themselves upstaged in the Series by the Florida Marlins, an improbable aggregate of overachieving youngsters led by their 72-year-old manager, Jack McKeon (TSN's Co-Sportsman of the Year), salved the wounds of many fans around Baseball Nation who had pulled temporarily for Chicago and Boston. But for the loyalists who have plunked their money down for decades to attend games at Wrigley Field and Fenway Park, the pain continues unabated.

Overall, the contrast between the 2003 season and its most recent predecessors was remarkable for the absence of labor-management strife and a marked decrease in the public argument about the game's alleged economic difficulties. "One year's experience is not sufficient to make a judgment," said Robert DuPuy, Major League Baseball's president and chief operating officer, "but we are pleased with the increase in competitive balance on the field." Perhaps the collective bargaining agreement finalized late in 2002 really did alleviate some of the problems that caused such rancor for so long. At any rate, baseball in 2003 seemed to get it mostly right, glorying in the achievements of its players and concluding the season with an emotional and thrilling October. Only after the games were done did two sources of ugliness emerge: the specter of a new collusion grievance and the possibility of widespread use of performance-enhancing drugs.

ANGELS CHANGE HANDS

On May 15, MLB owners approved the sale of the Anaheim Angels from the Walt Disney Company to advertising businessman Arturo Moreno for $184 million. Moreno, a Mexican-American, became the first Hispanic owner to hold a majority stake in a major league club. Disney had taken control of the team and bought a 25 percent stake in the Angels from Gene Autry in 1996, then bought the rest of the club in 1998 following Autry's death.

Frank McCourt, a Boston real estate developer, reached an agreement in October to buy the Los Angeles Dodgers from News Corp. for a price estimated at $430 million. McCourt submitted supporting paperwork in late December with the hope that the owners might approve the sale in January 2004. News Corp. bought the Dodgers from Peter O'Malley in 1998 for $311 million and claimed to have lost money every year since.

OTHER ECONOMIC NEWS

MLB documents that became public in March revealed that the four clubs targeted as potential candidates for contraction in July 2001 were the Angels, Minnesota Twins, Montreal Expos and Tampa Bay Devil Rays. Under an early contraction plan, the Oakland A's would have been moved to Anaheim to replace the Angels. Pursuant to the collective bargaining agreement signed in 2002, MLB agreed to maintain the current number of clubs through the 2006 season.

In November, the Milwaukee Brewers' board of directors instructed general manager Doug Melvin to cut the team's payroll for 2004 to $30 million, far below the average. The board also forced the resignation of president and CEO Ulice Payne Jr. Angry members of the Wisconsin legislature, which approved a sales-tax increase to finance construction of Miller Park, demanded an audit of the Brewers and urged commissioner Allan H. "Bud" Selig, who owns the club in a trust, to sell his interests.

The Associated Press announced late in December that only one club, the Yankees, had exceeded 2003's salary threshold of $117 million, above which teams owe a luxury tax of 17.5 percent. As a result, the Yankees paid a tax of $11.82 million, in addition to approximately $50 million to baseball's expanded revenue-sharing plan under which a total of about $225 million moved from richer clubs to poorer ones.

POSSIBLE COLLUSION GRIEVANCE

The Major League Baseball Players Association began a process in January that might lead to a grievance charging owners with salary collusion. Lawyers requested documents "that would reflect inter-club communications and communications between the commissioner's office and clubs about free-agent negotiations." Some agents had told the union previously that their clients had received similar offers from several teams. In addition, catcher Ivan Rodriguez, one of the game's premier players and a free agent after the 2002 season, had received only two offers. One called for a 33 percent pay cut, and the other was for $10 million, a slight raise, but with $7 million deferred without interest over three years.

Concerns about collusion were renewed after the season when an inordinately large number of players were released by their current teams as free agents, and yet bidding for the services of these players seemed somewhat restrained. The number of players earning more than a million dollars decreased from 413 in 2002 to 385 in 2003, and the median salary dropped from roughly $900,000 to $800,000. Teams pointed to the weak national economy and the threat of the luxury tax as reasons for this slowdown, but the union was not so sure.

INCREASED DRUG TESTING

On November 14, MLB announced that 5 percent to 7 percent of the 1,438 anonymous drug tests for steroids conducted during the 2003 season had produced positive results. The new collective bargaining agreement sanctioned this testing but did not provide for any penalties for positive results. Instead, since the percentage of positives exceeded 5 percent, testing will continue in 2004, and players who test positive will be identified to the commissioner's office and the players association and will be given treatment and counseling. Additional positive tests will result in more severe penalties, with a one-year suspension coming after the fifth positive test. Dick Pound, head of the World Anti-Doping Agency, a creation of the Olympic movement, called baseball's policy on steroids a "complete joke," in part because tests won't be conducted during the offseason.

Concerns about players taking other drugs, including nutritional supplements and diet pills, arose after the death from heatstroke of Baltimore Orioles pitcher Steve Bechler on February 17. Toxicology tests confirmed significant amounts of an over-the-counter dietary supplement containing ephedra in Bechler's body.

The 2003 tests for steroids did not seek to detect the presence of THG, the newest so-called designer steroid, but THG was added to the list of banned substances for 2004. Late in the year, a grand jury in San Francisco began investigating the Bay Area Laboratory Co-Operative, or BALCO, a nutritional supplement lab whose activities might be linked to THG. Several prominent players, including Barry Bonds and Jason Giambi, were subpoenaed to testify.

UMPIRES AND QUESTEC

The relationship between MLB and its umpires continued to cause sparks. On January 29, U.S. District judge Lewis A. Kaplan granted MLB a summary judgment in its lawsuit filed July 18, 2002, against the World Umpires Association, successor union to the Major League Umpires Association. The commissioner's office had sent umpire John Hirschbeck a warning letter about his conduct in a game on April 28, 2002. The letter alleged that Hirschbeck, a crew chief, had told the plate umpire that day to refrain from issuing warnings if pitchers threw brushback pitches. It also accused him of a poor performance behind the plate during a game on May 4, 2002, and ordered him to appear before Sandy Alderson, MLB's executive vice president for baseball operations, for a disciplinary hearing. The WUA attempted to file a grievance over this matter on May 29, 2002, but MLB sued, arguing that the matter was a disciplinary procedure not subject to arbitration.

Hirschbeck was suspended for 10 days on February 5, 2003, pursuant to a telephone conversation with Rob Manfred, executive vice president for labor relations. Hirschbeck allegedly made personal threats against Manfred after he learned that an acquaintance was among 26 employees MLB laid off on January 22.

MLB suspended umpire Bruce Froemming for 10 days on January 31 and removed him from the crew scheduled to umpire the season-opening series in Tokyo for using an anti-Semitic slur to describe Cathy Davis, an administrator in MLB's umpiring office. MLB had told Froemming to let the umpiring office make his travel arrangements for Japan, but he made them himself. That prompted a telephone conversation with Davis, during which Froemming made the remark. He later apologized.

On February 19, MLB proposed evaluating umpires with QuesTec Inc.'s Umpire Information System, already being challenged by the WUA in an unfair labor charge filed September 23, 2002. The QuesTec system uses computers and cameras and an operator to analyze the accuracy of umpires' calls of balls and strikes. It was installed on an experimental basis in some ballparks in 2002 and was used in at least 10 parks in 2003. QuesTec's proprietary technology puts cameras in both dugouts and on both sides of the infield to track the flight of each pitched ball as it travels to the plate. The system then determines if the pitch traveled through the strike zone. The WUA opposed this system, arguing that MLB did not provide sufficient information on how it works, and individual umpires admitted that the thought of a computerized "Big Brother" looking over their shoulders affected their work. Players, too, complained that experienced umpires were reacting to the system by altering the way they called balls and strikes. On May 24, Arizona Diamondbacks pitcher Curt Schilling became so enraged at QuesTec that he destroyed one of the cameras at Bank One Ballpark. He was later fined $15,000.

In November, Alderson voiced strong support for the system as "absolutely critical" to getting strikes called according to the rule book in every game.

NEW VETERANS COMMITTEE

The National Baseball Hall of Fame's redesigned Veterans Committee conducted its first election, the results of which were announced on February 26. No one was elected.

The Veterans Committee was reconstituted in 2001 to replace the 15-member committee that had often been accused of cronyism and inconsistent standards. The new committee consists of all living members of the Hall of Fame, all recipients of the J.G. Taylor Spink Award and the Ford C. Frick Award and members of the old committee whose terms had not expired. The committee will consider former players every two years (with the next ballot to be cast in 2005) and former managers, umpires and executives every four years (with the next ballot to be cast in 2007). Still to be decided, pending conclusion of a comprehensive study of African-American baseball, is whether and how to induct any additional players from the Negro leagues.

ALL-STAR GAME EXPERIMENT

On January 16, owners approved Selig's proposal to have the league whose team wins the All-Star Game get home-field advantage in the World Series. The 2002 All-Star Game, played in Milwaukee, was called after 11 innings with the score tied, 7-7, much to the chagrin of fans. Selig said of his proposed two-year experiment raising the stakes of the All-Star Game: "This energizes it. This gives them something to really play for ... It was not and should not be a meaningless exhibition game." The change was strongly backed by FOX television and approved by the players association on May 1. The American League won the 2003 game, 7-6, at U.S. Cellular Field in Chicago, but television ratings were roughly the same as in 2002 despite the new stakes.

SEASON OPENER IN JAPAN CANCELED

On March 18, MLB, bowing to the imminent threat of the United States' entry into war in Iraq, canceled plans for Mariners and the A's to open the season with games on March 25 and 26 in the Tokyo Dome. This trip would have marked the return of Seattle players Ichiro Suzuki, Shigetoshi Hasegawa and Kazuhiro Sasaki to their native land. The games were rescheduled for April 3 and June 30 in Oakland.

The Expos, owned by MLB, played 59 home games in Montreal in 2003 and 22 at Hiram Bithorn Stadium in San Juan, Puerto Rico. MLB continued to seek a buyer for the Expos and to examine moving the team to another city, but officials announced late in the year that the team would remain in Montreal and split its 2004 home games between that city and San Juan.

ONE PARK OPENS; TWO CLOSE

The Reds opened Great American Ball Park on March 31, losing to the Pittsburgh Pirates, 10-1, before a capacity crowd of 42,343. The Philadelphia Phillies closed Veterans Stadium with four consecutive sellouts, culminating with their final game on September 28 when they lost to the Braves, 5-2, before a crowd of 58,554. The San Diego Padres closed Qualcomm Stadium on the same date, losing to the Colorado Rockies, 10-8, before 60,988. The Phillies will open Citizens Bank Park on April 12, 2004, playing against the Reds. The Padres will open Petco Park on April 8, 2004, with a game against the Giants.

SEVENTH YEAR OF INTERLEAGUE PLAY

Regular-season games between A.L. and N.L. clubs continued for the seventh consecutive season. Overall, N.L. teams won 137 games and lost 115, increasing their lead to 863-833 in total interleague play. The Yankees complied the best interleague mark (13-5) among A.L. teams while the Devil Rays won only three games. In the N.L., the Diamondbacks finished with the best record (11-4), and the Mets finished worst (5-10, including six losses to the Yankees). Attendance during the interleague period averaged 31,034, down from 2002's 31,962, but 20.1 percent higher than the average for intraleague games played to that point in the season.

ATLANTA WINS DIVISION AGAIN

The Braves won the N.L. East title for the ninth year in a row. Leaving aside the incomplete 1994 season, Atlanta has now won an unprecedented 12 consecutive division crowns. The Braves enjoyed a relatively easy run to the title. They led the Expos by four games at the end of May, the Phillies by 5½ games at the end of June and the Phillies by 10½ games at the end of July. The Braves clinched the title on September 18, even though idle, when the Phillies beat the Marlins, 5-4. Bobby Cox was named TSN's N.L. Manager of the Year for the second straight season and for a record sixth time overall.

The Braves' offense led the league in batting average, hits, runs and home runs. Gary Sheffield hit .330 (fifth in the league) with 39 homers (tied for seventh) and 132 RBIs (second). Javy Lopez, TSN's N.L. Comeback Player of the Year, batted .328, drove in 109 runs (eighth) and hit 43 home runs (tied for fourth), a record for a catcher. Andruw Jones added 36 homers and 116 RBIs (seventh), Marcus Giles batted .316 (seventh) and Chipper Jones hit .305 with 106 RBIs (tied for ninth).

Newcomer Russ Ortiz led the team and the league with 21 wins against only seven losses and paced the team in ERA (3.81). Greg Maddux won 16 games and set a major league record with 15 or more wins in 16 straight seasons. Mike Hampton won 14 games, Horacio Ramirez 12 and Shane Reynolds 11. John Smoltz finished second in the league in saves with 45.

MARLINS TAKE WILD CARD

Florida became the wild card in the playoffs by going 75-49 after McKeon succeeded Jeff Torborg as manager. The Marlins reached second place briefly in early August and again later in the month. They took over second place for good on September 20 and clinched the wild card on September 26 when they beat the Mets, 4-3. They won 18 games in the season's last month and six of their last seven. Mike Lowell led Florida's offense with 32 homers and 105 RBIs. Derrek Lee added 31 homers and 92 RBIs. Miguel Cabrera joined the team on June 20 from the minors and hit 12 homers with 62 RBIs. Juan Pierre batted .305 and led the league with 65 stolen bases. Brad Penny, Mark Redman and Dontrelle Willis, TSN's N.L. Rookie Pitcher of the Year, each won 14 games. Carl Pavano added 12 victories. Braden Looper had 28 saves.

CUBS CAPTURE N.L. CENTRAL TITLE

Just one season after going 67-95, the Cubs won their first division title since 1989. Chicago battled the Houston Astros and the St. Louis Cardinals all season long and were in third place as late as September 3. The Cubs reached first place on

September 7 but didn't grab the lead for good until September 23. Chicago clinched the pennant four days later by sweeping a doubleheader from Pittsburgh as Houston lost to the Brewers.

The Cubs hit only .259 as a team (11th in the N.L.), and only one regular, Mark Grudzielanek, batted over .300. Sammy Sosa hit 40 home runs (sixth in the league) and drove in 103 runs. Moises Alou added 22 homers and 91 RBIs.

Chicago pitchers struck out a major league record 1,404 batters, led by Kerry Wood (266) and Mark Prior (245), first and second in the league. Prior won 18 games. Wood and Matt Clement won 14, and Carlos Zambrano added 13. Joe Borowski recorded 33 saves, sixth in the N.L.

GIANTS GRAB N.L. WEST FLAG

After winning the wild-card slot in 2002, San Francisco, under new manager Felipe Alou, won the N.L. West title by 15½ games over the Dodgers. The Giants coasted to the pennant, becoming the ninth team to hold first place for the entire season. Winning 19 games in April, they built a 4½-game lead and never were challenged. They led the division by 12 games at the end of July and clinched the title on September 17 by beating the Padres as the Dodgers lost to the Diamondbacks.

San Francisco won despite a sputtering offense. The Giants finished sixth in the N.L. in batting average, fifth in slugging percentage and on-base percentage, seventh in home runs and 10th in hits. Bonds led the Giants' offense. He batted .341 (third in the league) and hit 45 homers (tied for second).

Jason Schmidt won 17 games, fourth in the league. Joe Nathan won 12 games, and Kirk Rueter added 10. Schmidt led the N.L. in ERA (2.34), and Tim Worrell finished with 38 saves, fourth in the league.

YANKEES WIN SIXTH STRAIGHT

The Yankees won their sixth consecutive A.L. East title and their seventh in eight seasons. Unlike the previous two years, when New York trailed the Red Sox for most of the first half, this time the team occupied first place most of the way. The Yankees fell into second briefly in late May and then again in early June, but held the division lead from June 12 to the end of the season. The Yankees built a 7½-game lead on August 20 and won the division by six games. They clinched the title on September 23 by beating the Chicago White Sox, 7-0.

Giambi led the New York offense with 41 home runs (fourth in the A.L.), 107 RBIs (tied for eighth) and a .412 on-base percentage (third in the league). Alfonso Soriano hit 38 homers (tied for fifth) and drove in 91 runs, and Jorge Posada added 30 homers and 101 RBIs. Derek Jeter hit .324 (third in the league), and Hideki Matsui, an experienced Japanese player but technically a rookie, drove in 106 runs (tied for 10th).

Andy Pettitte led New York in wins with 21 (tied for second), and Mike Mussina and Roger Clemens each won 17 games. David Wells added 15. Mariano Rivera had 40 saves, good for third in the league.

BOSTON TAKES WILD CARD

The Red Sox won the wild-card spot in the playoffs by putting together one of the great offensive seasons in major league history. Boston finished first in the league in batting average, slugging average, on-base percentage, runs, hits, doubles, total bases and runs batted in. The Red Sox set major league records for most extra-base hits in a season (649), most total bases in a season (2,832), highest slugging average (.491) and most runs scored before the first out in a game (10 against the Marlins on June 27). Derek Lowe won 17 games, Pedro Martinez 14, John Burkett 12 and Tim Wakefield 11. Martinez led the league in ERA (2.22). The Red Sox led the wild-card race most of the season and held off the Mariners. They clinched a playoff spot on September 25 by beating Baltimore, 14-3.

TWINS SECURE CENTRAL CROWN AGAIN

Minnesota overcame a surprising start by the Kansas City Royals and a late charge by the White Sox to win its second consecutive Central Division title. The Twins spent the second half of May in first place but fell back to second and then third for most of July and August. They regained a share of first place on September 3 and clinched the division on September 23 by beating the Cleveland Indians, 4-1, and then watching New York beat Chicago and the Detroit Tigers defeat Kansas City. Minnesota's record after the All-Star break, 45-20, was the best in baseball.

Minnesota finished third in the league in batting average, third in hits and sixth in runs. The Twins' offensive leaders were catcher A.J. Pierzynski, who batted .312 (tied for seventh in the league), and outfielder Torii Hunter, who hit 26 home runs and drove in 102 runs.

Kyle Lohse and Brad Radke each won 14 games. Veteran Kenny Rogers won 13, and Johan Santana added 12 against only three losses. Eddie Guardado saved 41 games, second highest in the league.

OAKLAND REPEATS AS WEST WINNER

Oakland won its second straight A.L. West title by three games over the Mariners. The A's trailed Seattle for most of the year, sometimes by as much as seven games. Oakland reached a tie for first place on August 25 and then built a solid lead as the Mariners slowed down the stretch. The A's clinched the crown on September 23 by beating Texas, 4-3, in 10 innings, as Anaheim was edging Seattle, 2-1, in 11 innings.

The importance of on-base percentage to Oakland's success was much discussed throughout the season, in part because of Michael Lewis' book, *Moneyball*, but the 2003 A's finished 10th in the league in on-base percentage. Offensive leaders were Eric Chavez (29 home runs and 101 RBIs) and Miguel Tejada (27 homers and 106 RBIs).

Tim Hudson won 16 games (tied for eighth in the league), Mark Mulder added 15 wins and Barry Zito had 14. Keith Foulke, TSN's A.L. Reliever of the Year, led the league in saves with 43.

Last year's World Series champions, the Angels, finished in third place (77-85) in the A.L. West, 22 games worse than their 2002 record.

DIVISION SERIES WINNERS

Two division series went four games, and the other two went the maximum five games. The Yankees and the Marlins each dropped the first game of their series to the Twins and the Giants, respectively, before winning three straight. The Red Sox became the fourth team to win a division series after dropping the first two games, defeating Oakland by winning one game in extra innings and two by one run. The Cubs and Braves alternated wins, with the Cubs taking the deciding game, 5-1.

MARLINS DEFEAT CUBS IN SEVEN

In the N.L. Championship Series, the Marlins and the Cubs split the first two games in Chicago. Florida won Game 1, 9-8, on a pinch-hit home run by Lowell in the 11th inning. The Cubs rebounded in Game 2, winning 12-3 behind Prior. Home runs by Sosa, Aramis Ramirez and two by Alex S. Gonzalez turned the game into a rout.

When the series shifted to Pro Player Stadium, the Cubs won Game 3 on a pinch-hit triple by Doug Glanville in the 11th inning. They won Game 4, too, 8-3, scoring four runs in the first and two more in the third. But Florida's Josh Beckett struck out 11 and pitched a two-hitter in Game 5, and his teammates hit three homers in a 4-0 Marlins victory. Back in Chicago, the Cubs came within five outs of advancing to the World Series before losing Game 6, 8-3. Prior took a three-run lead into the eighth inning when the Marlins sent 12 batters to the plate, getting eight runs, five hits, three walks, one error and an inadvertent assist from fan Steve Bartman, who quite possibly prevented Alou from catching a foul ball hit by Luis Castillo that would have been the second out. The next night, Florida won again, 9-6, with Beckett entering the game in the fifth and pitching four innings of one-hit relief. The Marlins thus earned a trip to the World Series for the first time since 1997 when they also qualified as the wild card.

YANKEES EDGE RED SOX IN SEVEN

New York and Boston split the first two games of the A.L. Championship Series. The Red Sox won Game 1 on the road, 5-2, getting home runs from David Ortiz, Todd Walker and Manny Ramirez and two-hit pitching over six innings from Tim Wakefield. New York took Game 2, 6-2, with Pettitte outpitching Lowe.

When the series moved to Boston, the Yankees won Game 3, 4-3, in a pitching duel between Clemens and Martinez. An altercation erupted on the field, and Martinez tossed Yankees coach Don Zimmer to the ground. That was followed by another scuffle in the Yankees bullpen. After a rainout, the Red Sox bounced back to win Game 4, 3-2, as Wakefield outpitched Mussina, but the Yankees came right back to win Game 5, 4-2, behind Wells' pitching and three second-inning runs. Back in New York, the Red Sox forced Game 7 by winning Game 6, 9-6, with three runs in the seventh and two in the ninth. The Yankees won the series the following night in a tense, dramatic game. New York scored three runs in the eighth, tying the score at 5-5, and won the game in the 11th inning on a home run by Aaron Boone. The Yankees thus advanced to the World Series for the sixth time in eight years.

FLORIDA WINS SECOND WORLD SERIES

Because the A.L. won the 2003 All-Star Game, the Series opened in New York. Penny opposed Wells in Game 1, and Florida came away with a 3-2 win. The Marlins manufactured a run in the first inning on a drag-bunt single, a flare single and a sacrifice fly, and they scored two more in the fifth when Pierre's single scored Jeff Conine and Juan Encarnacion. Pettitte won Game 2 for New York, 6-1, giving up only six hits in 8⅔ innings. The Yankees scored three runs in the first on a Matsui home run.

As the series moved to Miami, the Yankees won Game 3, again by a 6-1 score. Beckett struck out 10 and gave up only three hits and two runs in 7⅓ innings for the Marlins, but he was matched by Mussina, who struck out nine and surrendered only one run in seven innings. The Yankees took a 2-1 lead in the eighth inning when Matsui singled to score Jeter, and they added four more runs in the ninth off Chad Fox and Looper. Game 4 matched Clemens, in what was billed as the last start of his illustrious career, against Pavano. Seemingly overmatched, the Marlins scored three runs in the first inning on a two-run homer by Cabrera and a single by Lee. New York countered with one run in the second and two in the ninth on a pinch-hit triple by Ruben Sierra to tie the score. Florida won the game in the 12th on a leadoff homer by Alex Gonzalez.

The Marlins won Game 5 as well, 6-4, after back spasms forced Wells to leave the game after only one inning. Florida spotted the Yankees a run in the first, but came back to score three in the second on a double by Gonzalez and a single by Penny. The Marlins added another run in the fourth on a double by Pierre and two more in the fifth on a single by Lowell. New York countered with one run in the seventh inning and two in the ninth, but it wasn't enough. Pitching on three days' rest, Beckett closed down New York in Game 6, pitching a five-hit shutout and defeating Pettitte, 2-0. The Marlins scored their first run in the fifth. Gonzalez singled, went to second on a Pierre single and scored when Castillo doubled. They added a second run in the sixth. Conine reached on Jeter's error, and Lowell walked. Conine went to third on a fielder's choice and scored on Encarnacion's sacrifice fly. Beckett struck out nine and allowed more than one baserunner in only one inning, the third. Florida thus became the third wild-card team to win the Series, duplicating their 1997 accomplishment.

The Marlins voted 37 full World Series shares, each worth $306,149.92 ($34,002.45 more than 2002), 29 partial shares and 11 cash awards. The Yankees voted 39 full shares, each worth $180,889.71, and 45 partial shares.

OTHER FEATS AND EVENTS

Bonds continued his dominating march through the batting section of the record book. He hit 45 home runs to bring his career total to 658, two behind Willie Mays, who is third on the all-time list, and 97 behind leader Henry Aaron. Bonds hit his 650th homer on August 12 against the Mets' David Weathers. He led the N.L. in on-base percentage (.529), slugging percentage (.749), walks (148) and intentional walks (61). He now holds N.L. records for most career home runs by a lefthanded batter, most times hitting two or more home runs in a game (64), most consecutive seasons with 30 or more home runs (12), highest career slugging average

(.602), most seasons with 100 or more runs batted in (12), most career bases on balls (2,070), most career intentional bases on balls (484), most seasons leading the league in bases on balls (9), most seasons leading the league in intentional bases on balls (9), most seasons with 100 or more bases on balls (11) and most consecutive games with one or more bases on balls (20).

Sosa became the 18th player and Rafael Palmeiro of the Rangers the 19th to reach the 500-home run mark. Sosa hit No. 500 on April 4 in the seventh inning of a game against the Reds in Cincinnati. The pitcher was Scott Sullivan. Palmeiro reached 500 on May 11, connecting in the seventh inning off David Elder of the Indians. Sosa, who missed seven games after a suspension for using a corked bat against Tampa Bay on June 3, finished the year with 539 career homers, and Palmeiro stood at 528. Clemens won the 300th game of his career on June 13, defeating the Cardinals, 5-2, and also recorded his 4,000th strikeout in the same game, striking out Edgar Renteria in the second inning. He ended the season with 310 wins and 4,099 strikeouts. Kevin Millwood of the Phillies pitched a no-hitter on April 27 against the Giants, winning, 1-0. Six Astros pitchers combined to no-hit the Yankees in an 8-0 Houston victory June 11. The Braves' Rafael Furcal made an unassisted triple play on August 10 in St. Louis. Rickey Henderson, who signed with the Dodgers on July 14, added to his major league career records for most stolen bases (1,406), walks (2,190) and runs (2,295).

Albert Pujols of the Cardinals led the N.L. in batting average (.359), Jim Thome of the Phillies led the league in home runs with 47 and Colorado's Preston Wilson led in RBIs with 141. Pujols had the longest hitting streak, 30 games. The Dodgers' Eric Gagne saved 55 games in 55 chances and was named TSN's N.L. Pitcher of the Year and N.L. Reliever of the Year. Bill Mueller of the Red Sox led the A.L. in batting average (.326) and became the first player to hit grand slams from both sides of the plate in the same game, doing so on July 29 at Texas. Alex Rodriguez of the Rangers led the league in home runs for the third straight year (47) and became the youngest player (four months shy of his 28th birthday) to reach the 300-home run mark. The Toronto Blue Jays' Carlos Delgado led the majors in RBIs with 145. He also became the 15th player to hit four homers in a game, doing so on September 25 against Tampa Bay. Carl Crawford of Tampa Bay led the league in stolen bases with 55, and Nomar Garciaparra of the Red Sox, who got six hits in a game on June 21, had the league's longest batting streak, 26 games. Roy Halladay of Toronto led the A.L. in wins with 22 and was named TSN's A.L. Pitcher of the Year. Esteban Loaiza of the White Sox, Andy Pettitte of the Yankees and Jamie Moyer of the Mariners each won 21 games, and Loaiza led the league in strikeouts with 207.

The Tigers threatened to set a modern record for most losses in a season. Their 119 defeats did establish an A.L. mark, surpassing the 1916 Philadelphia Athletics, who lost 117, but a Tigers win on the season's final day enabled them to avoid tying the 1962 Mets, who hold the modern big-league record.

The average length of a nine-inning game fell significantly in both leagues, to 2:44 in the A.L. and 2:48 in the N.L.

LITTLE CHANGE IN ATTENDANCE

Major league baseball games drew 67,568,397 fans, down slightly from the figure of 67,859,176 for 2002. Average attendance, 28,013, stayed below the 30,000-mark for the second year in a row and fell from 28,134. N.L. teams drew 36,660,559 to their home games while A.L. teams attracted 30,907,838 to theirs.

For the first time ever, all 30 teams drew over one million fans. Five teams drew more than three million: the Yankees (who led both leagues with 3,465,585), Seattle and Anaheim in the A.L., and San Francisco and Los Angeles in the N.L. Fourteen other teams exceeded the two-million mark while four clubs (the Yankees, Angels, Red Sox and Cubs) set all-time franchise records.

Fourteen teams (seven A.L. and seven N.L.) saw attendance rise. The Indians' attendance declined the most, down 886,939 to 1,730,001.

FIVE MANAGERIAL CHANGES

Two teams replaced managers during the season, and three more made changes immediately after it ended. The Marlins fired Torborg following their game on May 10 with the team mired in fourth place in the N.L. East with a 16-22 record. Torborg had come to the Marlins in February 2002, with owner Jeffrey Loria, from Montreal. Torborg's replacement, McKeon, was a former manager of the Royals, A's, Padres and Reds. Cincinnati fired Bob Boone, manager since the start of the 2001 season, on July 28, replacing him on an interim basis with Dave Miley, a manager in their minor league system. The Reds were 46-58 (.442) and fifth in the N.L. Central at the time of Boone's dismissal, and they finished even worse, 23-35 (.397), and still in fifth.

On September 29, the White Sox fired Jerry Manuel, and the Orioles decided not to offer Mike Hargrove a new contract. Manuel's teams had won 500 games in six seasons, fourth-most for any White Sox manager, and had finished in second place in the A.L. Central with an 86-76 record. But the team missed the playoffs for the third season in a row. The White Sox hired their former shortstop, Ozzie Guillen, to replace Manuel on November 3. Guillen, without managerial experience, was the Marlins' third base coach. Baltimore endured four losing seasons under Hargrove and finished fourth in the A.L. East (71-91). The Orioles hired Lee Mazzilli, the Yankees' first base coach, on November 7 to replace him. Following the World Series, the Red Sox announced that they would not renew Grady Little's contract, despite consecutive 90-win seasons and nearly making the World Series. In the popular mind, Little was being blamed for his controversial decision in Game 7 of the ALCS, keeping Martinez in the game in the eighth inning when the Yankees rallied to tie the score, but team officials denied this. They hired former Phillies manager Terry Francona on December 4. The Reds decided on the same day to removed the "interim" tag from Miley's job title.

SEVEN ARBITRATION CASES

Seventy-two players filed for salary arbitration,

but only seven cases proceeded through the hearing and decision stages. Before exchanging figures, Hunter signed a four-year contract for $32 million with the Twins, and Millwood and the Phillies agreed on a one-year contract worth $9.9 million. Teams exchanged figures with 35 players, led by Maddux, who asked the Braves for $16 million against the team's offer of $13.5 million. After exchanging figures, Danny Graves and the Reds agreed on a three-year contract for $17.25 million, and Billy Koch and the White Sox signed a two-year contract for $10.625 million. Maddux settled for $14.75 million, the largest arbitration contract ever.

Pitchers Freddy Garcia of the Mariners and Redman of the Marlins were the only players to win their cases. Garcia won $6.875 million and Redman won $2.15 million. Carlos Beltran, A.J. Burnett, Bruce Chen, Vladimir Nunez and Javier Vasquez

FINAL STANDINGS

AMERICAN LEAGUE

EAST DIVISION

Team	N.Y.	Bos.	Tor.	Bal.	TB.	Min.	Chi.	K.C.	Cle.	Det.	Oak.	Sea.	Ana.	Tex.	N.L.	W	L	Pct.	GB	LD1st	DIF	Lead
New York.....	...	10	10	13	14	7	2	4	5	5	3	5	6	4	13-5	101	61	.623	.....	9/28	171	7.5
Boston.........	9	...	10	10	12	2	5	5	4	8	3	5	6	5	11-7	95	67	.586	6.0	6/11	13	2.5
Toronto........	9	9	...	11	8	3	3	5	4	7	2	4	7	4	10-8	86	76	.531	15.0	...	...	...
Baltimore.....	6	9	8	...	8	3	2	3	3	3	2	4	8	7	5-13	71	91	.438	30.0	3/31	1	0.0
Tampa Bay...	5	7	11	11	...	0	3	3	2	4	3	5	3	3	3-15	63	99	.389	38.0	3/31	1	0.0

CENTRAL DIVISION

Team	Min.	Chi.	K.C.	Cle.	Det.	N.Y.	Bos.	Tor.	Bal.	TB.	Oak.	Sea.	Ana.	Tex.	N.L.	W	L	Pct.	GB	LD1st	DIF	Lead
Minnesota....	...	10	8	10	15	0	4	3	4	6	8	3	4	5	10-8	90	72	.556	.....	9/28	65	6.0
Chicago.......	9	...	11	11	11	4	4	6	4	3	4	2	4	3	10-8	86	76	.531	4.0	9/14	24	2.0
Kansas City..	11	8	...	13	14	2	1	1	4	4	2	4	3	7	9-9	83	79	.512	7.0	8/29	106	7.5
Cleveland.....	9	8	6	...	12	2	2	2	3	5	3	3	3	4	6-12	68	94	.420	22.0	...	...	...
Detroit.........	4	8	5	7	...	1	1	2	3	2	3	1	1	1	4-14	43	119	.265	47.0	...	...	...

WEST DIVISION

Team	Oak.	Sea.	Ana.	Tex.	N.Y.	Bos.	Tor.	Bal.	TB.	Min.	Chi.	K.C.	Cle.	Det.	N.L.	W	L	Pct.	GB	LD1st	DIF	Lead
Oakland.......	...	7	12	15	6	4	5	7	6	1	5	7	6	6	9-9	96	66	.593	.....	9/28	61	6.0
Seattle.........	12	...	11	10	4	2	3	5	4	6	7	5	6	8	10-8	93	69	.574	3.0	8/26	135	8.0
Anaheim......	8	8	...	9	3	3	2	1	6	5	3	6	6	6	11-7	77	85	.475	19.0	4/16	4	0.0
Texas..........	4	10	10	...	5	4	5	2	6	4	4	2	5	6	4-14	71	91	.438	25.0	3/31	2	0.5

NOTE: Read across for wins, down for losses; final standings are shaded.

Abbreviations: LD1st denotes last date in 1st place; DIF denotes days in first place; Lead denotes largest lead.

Clinching dates: New York (East)—September 23; Minnesota (Central)—September 23; Oakland (West)—September 23; Boston (wild card)—September 25.

NATIONAL LEAGUE

EAST DIVISION

Team	Atl.	Fla.	Phi.	Mon.	N.Y.	Chi.	Hou.	St.L.	Pit.	Cin.	Mil.	S.F.	L.A.	Ari.	Col.	S.D.	A.L.	W	L	Pct.	GB	LD1st	DIF	Lead
Atlanta.........	...	9	9	12	11	4	5	4	7	3	4	2	4	5	6	6	10-5	101	61	.623	.....	9/28	156	15.0
Florida..........	10	...	13	13	12	2	1	3	2	4	7	1	2	5	2	5	9-6	91	71	.562	10.0	...	...	...
Philadelphia.	10	6	...	11	12	5	4	4	2	4	2	3	5	2	4	4	8-7	86	76	.531	15.0	4/28	14	1.0
Montreal......	7	6	8	...	14	3	3	1	3	4	6	7	2	2	4	4	9-9	83	79	.512	18.0	5/1	30	1.0
New York.....	8	7	7	5	...	1	4	1	4	4	3	4	3	2	5	3	5-10	66	95	.410	34.5	4/8	2	0.0

CENTRAL DIVISION

Team	Chi.	Hou.	St.L.	Pit.	Cin.	Mil.	Atl.	Fla.	Phi.	Mon.	N.Y.	S.F.	L.A.	Ari.	Col.	S.D.	A.L.	W	L	Pct.	GB	LD1st	DIF	Lead
Chicago.......	...	9	8	10	10	10	2	4	1	3	5	4	2	4	3	4	9-9	88	74	.543	.....	9/28	78	3.0
Houston.......	7	...	11	10	12	9	1	5	2	3	2	2	4	1	4	3	11-7	87	75	.537	1.0	9/25	92	4.0
St. Louis......	9	7	...	10	7	13	2	3	2	5	5	1	2	3	2	4	10-8	85	77	.525	3.0	9/2	32	2.0
Pittsburgh....	8	6	7	...	11	7	2	4	4	3	2	2	1	3	6	4	5-7	75	87	.463	13.0	4/14	10	1.0
Cincinnati.....	7	5	9	5	...	8	3	2	5	2	2	3	2	2	4	3	7-5	69	93	.426	19.0	...	...	...
Milwaukee...	6	8	3	10	10	...	2	2	4	0	6	1	2	3	1	5	5-7	68	94	.420	20.0	...	...	...

WEST DIVISION

Team	S.F.	L.A.	Ari.	Col.	S.D.	Atl.	Fla.	Phi.	Mon.	N.Y.	Chi.	Hou.	St.L.	Pit.	Cin.	Mil.	A.L.	W	L	Pct.	GB	LD1st	DIF	Lead
San Fran......	...	13	14	12	14	4	5	3	0	2	2	4	5	4	3	5	10-8	100	61	.621	.....	9/28	182	15.5
Los Angeles.	6	...	9	12	8	2	5	2	4	3	4	2	4	5	4	4	11-7	85	77	.525	15.5	6/22	6	0.0
Arizona........	5	10	...	10	9	2	2	4	4	4	2	5	3	3	7	3	11-4	84	78	.519	16.5	...	...	...
Colorado......	7	7	9	...	12	0	4	2	3	2	3	2	4	3	2	5	9-6	74	88	.457	26.5	...	...	...
San Diego....	5	11	10	7	...	1	1	3	2	3	2	3	2	2	3	1	8-10	64	98	.395	36.5	...	...	...

NOTE: Read across for wins, down for losses; final standings are shaded.

Abbreviations: LD1st denotes last date in 1st place; DIF denotes days in first place; Lead denotes largest lead.

Clinching dates: Atlanta (East)—September 18; Chicago (Central)—September 27; San Francisco (West)—September 17; Florida (wild card)—September 26.

lost their cases, with the Royals' Beltran still getting $6.0 million, the second-highest salary ever for a player losing a case.

The 72 players who filed earned an average increase of 92 percent, according to the Associated Press, down from 130 percent in 2002 and the lowest rise since 1996. The 72 received an average salary of $2,758,542, breaking the previous mark of $2,717,661, set in 2002.

SALARIES RISE SLOWLY

According to figures compiled by the players association and released by the Associated Press in December, the average major league salary rose just 3.3 percent to $2,372,189, the smallest increase since 1996, the year after the 1994-95 labor stoppage. The Yankees had the highest average for the fifth consecutive year, $4,687,002, and the Devil Rays had the lowest, $776,775.

CONCLUSION

After the Marlins won the World Series, commissioner Selig, who announced in April that he would not seek re-election after his term expires in 2006, commented on baseball's general popularity. "I've had many people since say to me, 'There was a buzz again.' ... I had said before that I thought we were in the middle of a great renaissance. I think this confirms it. And we're going to do everything possible to continue it." However perceptive this view proves to be, here (starting on page 166) is how the game on the field ended up in 2003:

INTERLEAGUE RECORDS

AMERICAN LEAGUE

EAST DIVISION

A.L. team vs.	Ari.	Atl.	Chi.	Cin.	Col.	Fla.	Hou.	L.A.	Mil.	Mon.	N.Y.	Phi.	Pit.	St.L.	S.D.	S.F.	W	L	Pct.
New York........	0-0	0-0	1-2	1-2	0-0	0-0	2-1	0-0	0-0	0-0	6-0	0-0	0-0	3-0	0-0	0-0	13	5	.722
Boston............	0-0	0-0	0-0	0-0	0-0	2-1	3-0	0-0	2-1	0-0	0-0	1-2	2-1	1-2	0-0	0-0	11	7	.611
Toronto	0-0	0-0	2-1	2-1	0-0	0-0	0-0	0-0	0-0	3-3	0-0	0-0	3-0	0-3	0-0	0-0	10	8	.556
Baltimore........	0-0	1-2	1-2	0-0	0-0	0-0	0-3	0-0	2-1	0-0	0-0	0-3	0-0	1-2	0-0	0-0	5	13	.278
Tampa Bay	0-0	1-2	1-2	0-3	0-0	0-3	0-3	0-0	0-0	0-0	0-0	0-0	1-2	0-0	0-0	0-0	3	15	.167

CENTRAL DIVISION

A.L. team vs.	Ari.	Atl.	Chi.	Cin.	Col.	Fla.	Hou.	L.A.	Mil.	Mon.	N.Y.	Phi.	Pit.	St.L.	S.D.	S.F.	W	L	Pct.
Minnesota	1-2	0-0	0-0	0-0	2-1	0-0	0-0	0-0	3-3	0-0	0-0	0-0	0-0	0-0	2-1	2-1	10	8	.556
Chicago..........	1-2	0-0	4-2	0-0	0-0	0-0	0-0	2-1	0-0	0-0	0-0	0-0	0-0	0-0	2-1	1-2	10	8	.556
Kansas City	1-2	0-0	0-0	0-0	2-1	0-0	0-0	1-2	0-0	0-0	0-0	0-0	0-0	3-3	0-0	2-1	9	9	.500
Cleveland........	1-2	0-0	0-0	2-1	0-3	0-0	0-0	0-3	0-0	0-0	0-0	0-0	1-2	0-0	2-1	0-0	6	12	.333
Detroit...........	0-3	0-0	0-0	0-0	2-4	0-0	0-0	0-3	0-0	0-0	0-0	0-0	0-0	0-0	2-1	0-3	4	14	.222

WEST DIVISION

A.L. team vs.	Ari.	Atl.	Chi.	Cin.	Col.	Fla.	Hou.	L.A.	Mil.	Mon.	N.Y.	Phi.	Pit.	St.L.	S.D.	S.F.	W	L	Pct.
Oakland..........	0-0	1-2	0-0	0-0	0-0	1-2	0-0	0-0	0-0	3-0	0-0	1-2	0-0	0-0	0-0	3-3	9	9	.500
Seattle............	0-0	2-1	0-0	0-0	0-0	0-0	0-0	0-0	0-0	1-2	2-1	3-0	0-0	0-0	2-4	0-0	10	8	.556
Anaheim	0-0	0-0	0-0	0-0	0-0	2-1	0-0	4-2	0-0	2-1	1-2	2-1	0-0	0-0	0-0	0-0	11	7	.611
Texas..............	0-0	0-3	0-0	0-0	0-0	1-2	2-4	0-0	0-0	0-3	1-2	0-0	0-0	0-0	0-0	0-0	4	14	.222

NOTE: Teams are listed in order of their final standings, not by their interleague records.

NATIONAL LEAGUE

EAST DIVISION

N.L. team vs.	Ana.	Bal.	Bos.	Chi.	Cle.	Det.	K.C.	Min.	N.Y.	Oak.	Sea.	T.B.	Tex.	Tor.	W	L	Pct.
Atlanta	0-0	2-1	0-0	0-0	0-0	0-0	0-0	0-0	0-0	2-1	1-2	2-1	3-0	0-0	10	5	.667
Florida	1-2	0-0	1-2	0-0	0-0	0-0	0-0	0-0	0-0	2-1	0-0	3-0	2-1	0-0	9	6	.600
Philadelphia	1-2	3-0	2-1	0-0	0-0	0-0	0-0	0-0	0-0	2-1	0-3	0-0	0-0	0-0	8	7	.533
Montreal....................	1-2	0-0	0-0	0-0	0-0	0-0	0-0	0-0	0-0	0-3	2-1	0-0	3-0	3-3	9	9	.500
New York	2-1	0-0	0-0	0-0	0-0	0-0	0-0	0-0	0-6	0-0	1-2	0-0	2-1	0-0	5	10	.333

CENTRAL DIVISION

N.L. team vs.	Ana.	Bal.	Bos.	Chi.	Cle.	Det.	K.C.	Min.	N.Y.	Oak.	Sea.	T.B.	Tex.	Tor.	W	L	Pct.
Chicago	0-0	2-1	0-0	2-4	0-0	0-0	0-0	0-0	2-1	0-0	0-0	2-1	0-0	1-2	9	9	.500
Houston	0-0	3-0	0-3	0-0	0-0	0-0	0-0	0-0	1-2	0-0	0-0	3-0	4-2	0-0	11	7	.611
St. Louis....................	0-0	2-1	2-1	0-0	0-0	0-0	3-3	0-0	0-3	0-0	0-0	0-0	0-0	3-0	10	8	.556
Pittsburgh	0-0	0-0	1-2	0-0	2-1	0-0	0-0	0-0	0-0	0-0	0-0	2-1	0-0	0-3	5	7	.417
Cincinnati	0-0	0-0	0-0	0-0	1-2	0-0	0-0	0-0	2-1	0-0	0-0	3-0	0-0	1-2	7	5	.583
Milwaukee	0-0	1-2	1-2	0-0	0-0	0-0	0-0	3-3	0-0	0-0	0-0	0-0	0-0	0-0	5	7	.417

WEST DIVISION

N.L. team vs.	Ana.	Bal.	Bos.	Chi.	Cle.	Det.	K.C.	Min.	N.Y.	Oak.	Sea.	T.B.	Tex.	Tor.	W	L	Pct.
San Francisco...........	0-0	0-0	0-0	2-1	0-0	3-0	1-2	1-2	0-0	3-3	0-0	0-0	0-0	0-0	10	8	.556
Los Angeles	2-4	0-0	0-0	1-2	3-0	3-0	2-1	0-0	0-0	0-0	0-0	0-0	0-0	0-0	11	7	.611
Arizona......................	0-0	0-0	0-0	2-1	2-1	3-0	2-1	2-1	0-0	0-0	0-0	0-0	0-0	0-0	11	4	.733
Colorado....................	0-0	0-0	0-0	0-0	3-0	4-2	1-2	1-2	0-0	0-0	0-0	0-0	0-0	0-0	9	6	.600
San Diego.................	0-0	0-0	0-0	1-2	1-2	1-2	0-0	1-2	0-0	0-0	4-2	0-0	0-0	0-0	8	10	.444

NOTE: Teams are listed in order of their final standings, not by their interleague records.

A.L. DIVISION SERIES

BOSTON VS. OAKLAND

RESULTS

Day	Date	Place	Score
Wed.	Oct. 1	Oakland	Oakland 5, Boston 4
Thur.	Oct. 2	Oakland	Oakland 5, Boston 1
Sat.	Oct. 4	Boston	Boston 3, Oakland 1
Sun.	Oct. 5	Boston	Boston 5, Oakland 4
Mon.	Oct. 6	Oakland	Boston 4, Oakland 3

BOX SCORES

GAME 1

OAKLAND 5, BOSTON 4

WEDNESDAY, OCTOBER 1, AT OAKLAND

Boston	AB	R	H	BI	BB	SO	PO	A
Damon, cf	5	0	1	0	1	0	4	1
Garciaparra, ss	5	1	2	0	1	1	3	3
To.Walker, 2b	5	2	4	3	0	0	3	1
D.Jackson, 2b	1	0	0	0	0	1	0	1
M.Ramirez, lf	5	0	0	0	1	1	3	0
D.Ortiz, dh	5	0	0	0	1	2	0	0
Millar, 1b	6	0	2	0	0	1	5	3
Mueller, 3b	5	0	1	0	1	1	1	4
Nixon, rf	3	0	0	0	0	1	2	0
McCarty, ph	0	0	0	0	0	0	0	0
A.Brown, ph-rf	1	0	0	0	0	1	0	0
Kapler, ph-rf	2	0	0	0	0	1	0	0
Varitek, c	3	1	2	1	2	1	13	0
P.Martinez, p	0	0	0	0	0	0	1	2
Timlin, p	0	0	0	0	0	0	0	0
B.Kim, p	0	0	0	0	0	0	0	0
Embree, p	0	0	0	0	0	0	0	0
Williamson, p	0	0	0	0	0	0	0	0
Lowe, p	0	0	0	0	0	0	0	0
TOTALS	46	4	12	4	7	11	35	15

Oakland	AB	R	H	BI	BB	SO	PO	A
M.Ellis, 2b	4	1	1	0	2	2	1	4
Durazo, dh	4	1	2	3	2	0	0	0
E.Chavez, 3b	6	1	0	0	0	1	5	0
Tejada, ss	6	0	1	1	0	1	2	4
Hatteberg, 1b	4	0	0	0	2	1	8	0
J.Guillen, lf	3	0	1	0	0	2	1	0
Long, ph-lf-rf	2	0	0	0	1	2	0	0
Ra.Hernandez, c	4	0	2	1	2	0	11	1
Dye, rf	3	0	0	0	0	0	2	0
McMillon, ph	0	0	0	0	1	0	0	0
Byrnes, pr-lf	1	1	0	0	0	1	0	0
Singleton, cf	4	1	1	0	0	0	6	0
T.Hudson, p	0	0	0	0	0	0	0	0
R.Rincon, p	0	0	0	0	0	0	0	0
Bradford, p	0	0	0	0	0	0	0	0
Foulke, p	0	0	0	0	0	0	0	0
Harden, p	0	0	0	0	0	0	0	0
TOTALS	41	5	8	5	10	10	36	9

Boston ....1 0 0 0 1 0 2 0 0 0 0 0—4 12 2
Oakland ....0 0 3 0 0 0 0 0 1 0 0 1—5 8 0

Boston	IP	H	R	ER	HR	BB	SO
P.Martinez	7.0	6	3	3	0	4	3
Timlin (HOLD)	1.0	0	0	0	0	0	2
B.Kim (HOLD)	0.2	0	1	1	0	1	1
Embree (BS)	0.1	1	0	0	0	0	0
Williamson	1.0	0	0	0	0	1	2
Lowe (L)	1.2	1	1	1	0	4	2

Oakland	IP	H	R	ER	HR	BB	SO
T.Hudson	6.2	10	3	3	2	1	5
R.Rincon (BS)	0.2	2	1	1	1	1	1
Bradford	0.2	0	0	0	0	1	1
Foulke	3.0	0	0	0	0	2	3
Harden (W)	1.0	0	0	0	0	2	1

E—P.Martinez, To.Walker. DP—Boston 1, Oakland 1. LOB—Boston 13, Oakland 12. Scoring Position—Boston 1 for 10, Oakland 4 for 11. 2B—Mueller, Durazo, Singleton. HR—To.Walker (1st inning, 2 out, 0 on) off T.Hudson, Varitek (5th inning, 1 out, 0 on) off T.Hudson, To.Walker (7th inning, 2 out, 1 on) off R.Rincon. SB—Damon, E.Chavez, Singleton. WP—Harden. HBP—Singleton by B.Kim. T—4:37. A—50,606. U—HP-Marsh, 1B-Cooper, 2B-Bell, 3B-Darling, LF-Welke, RF-Gibson.

HOW THEY SCORED

FIRST INNING

Red Sox—Damon grounded out, second baseman Ellis to first baseman Hatteberg. Garciaparra struck out. Walker homered to right on a 3-1 count. Ramirez struck out. One run. Red Sox 1, Athletics 0.

THIRD INNING

Athletics—Dye flied out to right fielder Nixon. Singleton doubled to right. Ellis walked on four pitches. Durazo doubled to center, Singleton scored, Ellis scored. Chavez flied out to left fielder Ramirez. Tejada singled to center, Durazo scored. Tejada was out advancing, center fielder Damon to third baseman Mueller to second baseman Walker to first baseman Millar to shortstop Garciaparra to second baseman Walker, Tejada out. Three runs. Athletics 3, Red Sox 1.

FIFTH INNING

Red Sox—Nixon flied out to center fielder Singleton. Varitek homered to right on a 1-0 count. Damon grounded out, first baseman Hatteberg unassisted. Garciaparra singled to left. Walker singled to center, Garciaparra to third. Ramirez grounded into fielder's choice, shortstop Tejada to second baseman Ellis, Walker out. One run. Athletics 3, Red Sox 2.

SEVENTH INNING

Red Sox—Varitek walked. Damon grounded into a double play, second baseman Ellis to shortstop Tejada to first baseman Hatteberg, Varitek out. Garciaparra singled to left. Rincon pitching. Walker homered to right on a 2-0 count, Garciaparra scored. Ramirez flied out to right fielder Dye. Two runs. Red Sox 4, Athletics 3.

NINTH INNING

Athletics—Jackson in as second baseman. Kim pitching. Hernandez flied out to center fielder Damon. McMillon pinch-hitting for Dye. McMillon walked on four pitches. Byrnes pinch-running for McMillon. Singleton was hit by a pitch, Byrnes to second. Ellis struck out. Embree pitching. Durazo singled to left, Byrnes scored, Singleton to third. Chavez grounded out, shortstop Garciaparra to first baseman Millar. One run. Athletics 4, Red Sox 4.

TWELFTH INNING

Athletics—Durazo walked on a full count. Chavez grounded into fielder's choice, second baseman Jackson to shortstop Garciaparra, Durazo out. Tejada grounded out, third baseman Mueller to first baseman Millar, Chavez to second. Hatteberg walked on a full count. Chavez stole third. On defensive indifference, Hatteberg to second. Long was intentionally walked. Hernandez bunt single to third, Chavez scored, Hatteberg to third, Long to second. One run. Athletics 5, Red Sox 4.

GAME 2

OAKLAND 5, BOSTON 1

THURSDAY, OCTOBER 2, AT OAKLAND

Boston	AB	R	H	BI	BB	SO	PO	A
Damon, cf	4	0	2	1	0	0	4	0
Garciaparra, ss	3	0	1	0	1	0	0	5
To.Walker, 2b	4	0	0	0	0	0	3	1
M.Ramirez, lf	3	0	1	0	1	1	0	0
D.Ortiz, dh	4	0	0	0	0	2	0	0
Millar, 1b	4	0	0	0	0	2	5	1
Mueller, 3b	4	0	1	0	0	1	0	0
Kapler, rf	3	0	0	0	0	2	2	0
Varitek, ph	1	0	0	0	0	0	0	0
Mirabelli, c	3	1	1	0	0	2	9	0
Wakefield, p	0	0	0	0	0	0	1	0
Embree, p	0	0	0	0	0	0	0	0
Williamson, p	0	0	0	0	0	0	0	0
TOTALS	33	1	6	1	2	10	24	7

Oakland	AB	R	H	BI	BB	SO	PO	A
M.Ellis, 2b	2	1	0	0	1	2	0	2
Durazo, dh	4	0	1	0	0	1	0	0
E.Chavez, 3b	4	0	0	0	0	1	0	1
Tejada, ss	4	0	0	0	0	0	2	1
Hatteberg, 1b	4	0	1	0	0	1	8	0
J.Guillen, lf	1	1	0	0	2	0	2	0
Long, lf	1	0	1	0	0	0	3	0
Ra.Hernandez, c	4	1	1	1	0	0	10	0
Dye, rf	3	1	0	0	0	1	1	0
Byrnes, cf	4	1	2	2	0	2	1	0
Zito, p	0	0	0	0	0	0	0	1
Bradford, p	0	0	0	0	0	0	0	0
Foulke, p	0	0	0	0	0	0	0	1
TOTALS	31	5	6	3	3	8	27	6

Boston ....0 0 1 0 0 0 0 0 0—1 6 1
Oakland ....0 5 0 0 0 0 0 0 x—5 6 0

Boston	IP	H	R	ER	HR	BB	SO
Wakefield (L)	6.0	4	5	3	0	3	7
Embree	1.0	0	0	0	0	0	0
Williamson	1.0	2	0	0	0	0	1

Oakland	IP	H	R	ER	HR	BB	SO
Zito (W)	7.0	5	1	1	0	2	9
Bradford	1.0	0	0	0	0	0	1
Foulke	1.0	1	0	0	0	0	0

E—To.Walker. LOB—Boston 7, Oakland 7. Scoring Position—Boston 1 for 5, Oakland 2 for 12. 2B—Damon, Mirabelli, Byrnes. PB—Mirabelli. HBP—Dye by Wakefield, M.Ellis by Wakefield. T—2:37. A—36,305. U—HP-Cooper, 1B-Bell, 2B-Darling, 3B-Welke, LF-Gibson, RF-Marsh.

HOW THEY SCORED

SECOND INNING

Athletics—Hatteberg grounded out, first baseman Millar unassisted. Guillen walked on a full count. On Mirabelli's passed ball, Guillen to second. Hernandez singled to right, Guillen scored. Dye was hit by a pitch, Hernandez to second. Byrnes doubled to left, Hernandez scored, Dye scored. Ellis walked on a full count. Durazo grounded out, first baseman Millar to pitcher Wakefield, Byrnes to third, Ellis to second. Chavez safe at second on Walker's error, Byrnes scored, Ellis scored. Tejada flied out to center fielder Damon. Five runs. Athletics 5, Red Sox 0.

THIRD INNING

Red Sox—Kapler flied out to center fielder Byrnes. Mirabelli doubled to left. Damon doubled to center, Mirabelli scored. Garciaparra walked. Walker grounded out, first baseman Hatteberg unassisted, Damon to third, Garciaparra to second. Ramirez flied out to left fielder Guillen. One run. Athletics 5, Red Sox 1.

GAME 3

BOSTON 3, OAKLAND 1

SATURDAY, OCTOBER 4, AT BOSTON

Oakland	AB	R	H	BI	BB	SO	PO	A
McMillon, lf	5	0	0	0	0	1	1	0
Durazo, dh	4	1	0	0	1	2	0	0
Tejada, ss	5	0	0	0	0	1	4	2
E.Chavez, 3b	4	0	0	0	1	0	2	3
Ra.Hernandez, c	5	0	0	0	0	1	8	0
Hatteberg, 1b	4	0	1	0	0	0	7	0
M.Ellis, 2b	4	0	1	0	0	1	6	3
Long, rf	4	0	1	0	0	0	2	0
Byrnes, cf	4	0	3	0	0	1	1	0
Lilly, p	0	0	0	0	0	0	0	1
Bradford, p	0	0	0	0	0	0	0	0
R.Rincon, p	0	0	0	0	0	0	0	0
Mecir, p	0	0	0	0	0	0	0	0
Harden, p	0	0	0	0	0	0	0	0
TOTALS	39	1	6	0	2	7	31	9

Boston	AB	R	H	BI	BB	SO	PO	A
Damon, cf	4	0	1	0	0	1	2	0
Garciaparra, ss	4	0	2	0	1	0	1	1
Mueller, 3b	5	0	0	0	0	2	0	1
M.Ramirez, lf	4	0	0	0	1	2	1	1
D.Ortiz, dh	4	0	0	0	1	1	0	0
Millar, 1b	4	0	1	0	1	1	9	5
Varitek, c	4	1	1	0	0	0	5	0
A.Brown, pr	0	0	0	0	0	0	0	0
Mirabelli, c	1	1	1	0	0	0	4	0
Kapler, rf	4	0	0	0	0	0	2	0
Nixon, ph	1	1	1	2	0	0	0	0
D.Jackson, 2b	3	0	0	0	0	1	3	3
To.Walker, ph-2b	1	0	0	0	0	0	0	0
Lowe, p	0	0	0	0	0	0	6	2
Timlin, p	0	0	0	0	0	0	0	2
Williamson, p	0	0	0	0	0	0	0	0
TOTALS	39	3	7	2	4	8	33	15

Oakland ....0 0 0 0 0 1 0 0 0 0 0—1 6 4
Boston ....0 1 0 0 0 0 0 0 0 0 2—3 7 2

Oakland	IP	H	R	ER	HR	BB	SO
Lilly	7.0	2	1	0	0	2	5
Bradford	1.2	2	0	0	0	1	2
R.Rincon	0.2	0	0	0	0	0	1
Mecir	0.2	1	0	0	0	1	0
Harden (L)	0.1	2	2	2	1	0	0

Boston	IP	H	R	ER	HR	BB	SO
Lowe	7.0	6	1	0	0	2	2
Timlin	3.0	0	0	0	0	0	3
Williamson (W)	1.0	0	0	0	0	0	2

E—Ra.Hernandez, E.Chavez 2, Tejada, Lowe, Garciaparra. DP—Oakland 2. LOB—Oakland 7, Boston 10. Scoring Position—Oakland 1 for 6, Boston 0 for 10. 2B—Damon. HR—Nixon (11th inning, 1 out, 1 on) off Harden. SB—Byrnes, Garciaparra. HBP—Damon by Lilly. T—3:42. A—35,460. U—HP-Emmel, 1B-Davis, 2B-Joyce, 3B-Welke, LF-Montague, RF-Barrett.

HOW THEY SCORED

SECOND INNING

Red Sox—Millar infield single to short. Varitek safe on fielder's choice and Tejada's error, Millar to second. Kapler grounded into fielder's choice, third baseman Chavez unassisted, Millar out, Varitek to second. On Chavez's error, Varitek to third. Jackson safe on failed fielder's choice, Kapler to second. Jackson to first on obstruction. Damon flied out to left fielder McMillon. Garciaparra popped out to second baseman Ellis. One run. Red Sox 1, Athletics 0.

SIXTH INNING

Athletics—Byrnes singled to center. Byrnes stole second. McMillon grounded out, second baseman Jackson to first baseman Millar, Byrnes to third. Durazo walked. Tejada grounded into fielder's choice, pitcher Lowe to catcher Varitek, Byrnes out, Durazo to second. On Lowe's error, Durazo to third, Tejada to second. Chavez was intentionally walked. Hernandez safe on Garciaparra's error, Durazo scored, Tejada to third, Chavez to second. Tejada was out advancing, left fielder Ramirez to catcher Varitek, Tejada out. One run. Red Sox 1, Athletics 1.

ELEVENTH INNING

Red Sox—Harden pitching. Millar popped out to shortstop Tejada. Mirabelli singled to right. Nixon pinch-hitting for Kapler. Nixon homered to center on a 1-1 count, Mirabelli scored. Two runs. Red Sox 3, Athletics 1.

GAME 4

BOSTON 5, OAKLAND 4

SUNDAY, OCTOBER 5, AT BOSTON

Oakland	AB	R	H	BI	BB	SO	PO	A
M.Ellis, 2b	4	0	0	0	1	1	2	4
Durazo, dh	5	0	1	0	0	0	0	0
E.Chavez, 3b	4	0	1	0	0	0	0	2
Tejada, ss	4	0	0	0	0	0	1	4
Hatteberg, 1b	3	2	1	0	1	1	11	1
J.Guillen, lf	4	0	2	0	0	0	1	0
Melhuse, c	4	1	3	1	0	0	2	0
Dye, rf	4	1	2	3	0	1	4	0
Byrnes, cf	4	0	1	0	0	1	2	0
T.Hudson, p	0	0	0	0	0	0	0	0
Sparks, p	0	0	0	0	0	0	1	0
R.Rincon, p	0	0	0	0	0	0	0	1
Foulke, p	0	0	0	0	0	0	0	0
TOTALS	36	4	11	4	2	4	24	12

Boston	AB	R	H	BI	BB	SO	PO	A
Damon, cf	4	1	1	2	0	0	5	1
Garciaparra, ss	4	1	1	0	0	1	0	0
To.Walker, 2b	4	1	1	1	0	0	2	1
D.Jackson, 2b	0	0	0	0	0	0	0	0
M.Ramirez, lf	4	1	2	0	0	0	0	0
D.Ortiz, dh	4	0	1	2	0	1	0	0
A.Brown, pr-dh	0	0	0	0	0	0	0	0
Millar, 1b	3	0	0	0	1	0	8	1
Nixon, rf	2	0	1	0	1	0	1	0
Mueller, 3b	2	0	0	0	1	0	5	2
Varitek, c	3	1	0	0	0	0	5	0
Burkett, p	0	0	0	0	0	0	1	0
Wakefield, p	0	0	0	0	0	0	0	0
Williamson, p	0	0	0	0	0	0	0	0
TOTALS	30	5	7	5	3	2	27	5

Oakland ..... 0 1 0 0 0 3 0 0 0—4 11 1
Boston ..... 0 0 2 0 0 1 0 2 x—5 7 0

Oakland	IP	H	R	ER	HR	BB	SO
T.Hudson	1.0	0	0	0	0	0	1
Sparks	4.0	2	2	2	1	3	1
R.Rincon (HOLD)	2.0	2	1	1	1	0	0
Foulke (BS, L)	1.0	3	2	2	0	0	0

Boston	IP	H	R	ER	HR	BB	SO
Burkett	5.1	9	4	4	1	2	1
Wakefield	1.2	2	0	0	0	0	0
Williamson (W)	2.0	0	0	0	0	0	3

E—M.Ellis. DP—Oakland 1, Boston 1. LOB—Oakland 7, Boston 4. Scoring Position—Oakland 3 for 12, Boston 3 for 8. 2B—E.Chavez, Garciaparra, D.Ortiz. 3B—Melhuse. HR—Damon (3rd inning, 1 out, 1 on) off Sparks, Dye (6th inning, 1 out, 1 on) off Burkett, To.Walker (6th inning, 0 out, 0 on) off R.Rincon. T—3:02. A—35,048. U—HP-Davis, 1B-Joyce, 2B-Welke, 3B-Montague, LF-Barrett, RF-Emmel.

HOW THEY SCORED

SECOND INNING

Athletics—Hatteberg walked. Guillen singled to center, Hatteberg to second. Melhuse singled to center, Hatteberg to third, Guillen to second. Dye singled to left, Hatteberg scored, Guillen to third, Melhuse to second. Byrnes popped out to second baseman Walker. Ellis fouled out to first baseman Millar. Durazo popped out to third baseman Mueller. One run. Athletics 1, Red Sox 0.

THIRD INNING

Red Sox—Mueller walked on a full count. Varitek grounded into fielder's choice, shortstop Tejada to second baseman Ellis, Mueller out. On Ellis' error, Varitek to third. Damon homered to right on a 0-1 count, Varitek scored. Garciaparra flied out to right fielder Dye. Walker grounded out, shortstop Tejada to first baseman Hatteberg. Two runs. Red Sox 2, Athletics 1.

SIXTH INNING

Athletics—Hatteberg infield single, fielded by pitcher Burkett. Guillen lined out to third baseman Mueller. Melhuse tripled to right, Hatteberg scored. Dye homered to left on a 1-1 count, Melhuse scored. Wakefield pitching. Byrnes singled to center. Ellis lined into a double play, first baseman Millar unassisted, Byrnes out. Three runs. Athletics 4, Red Sox 2.

Red Sox—Rincon pitching. Walker homered to right on a full count. Ramirez flied out to center fielder Byrnes. Ortiz lined out to right fielder Dye. Millar flied out to left fielder Guillen. One run. Athletics 4, Red Sox 3.

EIGHTH INNING

Red Sox—Foulke pitching. Damon grounded out, shortstop Tejada to first baseman Hatteberg. Garciaparra doubled to center. Walker lined out to center fielder Byrnes. Ramirez singled to left, Garciaparra to third. Ortiz doubled to right, Garciaparra scored, Ramirez scored. Brown pinch-running for Ortiz. Millar flied out to right fielder Dye. Two runs. Red Sox 5, Athletics 4.

GAME 5

BOSTON 4, OAKLAND 3

MONDAY, OCTOBER 6, AT OAKLAND

Boston	AB	R	H	BI	BB	SO	PO	A
Damon, cf	2	1	1	0	1	0	1	0
A.Brown, ph-cf	1	0	0	0	0	0	0	0
Garciaparra, ss	4	0	0	0	0	0	1	9
To.Walker, 2b	2	1	0	0	0	1	1	0
D.Jackson, 2b	1	0	0	0	0	0	2	0
M.Ramirez, lf	4	1	1	3	0	3	1	0
D.Ortiz, dh	4	0	1	0	0	1	0	0
Kapler, pr-dh	0	0	0	0	0	0	0	0
Millar, 1b	4	0	2	0	0	0	10	0
Mueller, 3b	3	0	0	0	1	0	3	3
Nixon, rf	4	0	0	0	0	2	0	1
Varitek, c	3	1	1	1	0	1	8	0
P.Martinez, p	0	0	0	0	0	0	0	1
Embree, p	0	0	0	0	0	0	0	0
Timlin, p	0	0	0	0	0	0	0	0
Williamson, p	0	0	0	0	0	0	0	0
Lowe, p	0	0	0	0	0	0	0	0
TOTALS	32	4	6	4	2	8	27	14

Oakland	AB	R	H	BI	BB	SO	PO	A
M.Ellis, 2b	3	0	0	0	0	1	2	3
McMillon, ph	1	0	1	1	0	0	0	0
Menechino, pr-2b	0	0	0	0	0	0	0	0
Long, ph	1	0	0	0	0	1	0	0
Durazo, dh	4	1	1	0	0	1	0	0
E.Chavez, 3b	4	0	0	0	0	1	0	0
Tejada, ss	4	0	1	1	0	2	0	2
Hatteberg, 1b	2	1	0	0	2	0	10	0
Byrnes, pr	0	0	0	0	0	0	0	0
J.Guillen, lf	3	0	2	1	1	0	4	0
Ra.Hernandez, c	2	0	0	0	0	0	6	2
Dye, rf	3	0	1	0	0	0	2	0
Melhuse, ph	1	0	0	0	0	1	0	0
Singleton, cf	3	1	1	0	1	1	3	1
Zito, p	0	0	0	0	0	0	0	0
Lilly, p	0	0	0	0	0	0	0	0
Bradford, p	0	0	0	0	0	0	0	0
R.Rincon, p	0	0	0	0	0	0	0	0
TOTALS	31	3	7	3	4	8	27	8

Boston ..... 0 0 0 0 0 4 0 0 0—4 6 0
Oakland ..... 0 0 0 1 0 1 0 1 0—3 7 0

Boston	IP	H	R	ER	HR	BB	SO
P.Martinez (W)	7.0	7	3	3	0	1	6
Embree (HOLD)	0.2	0	0	0	0	0	0
Timlin (HOLD)	0.1	0	0	0	0	0	0
Williamson	0.0	0	0	0	0	2	0
Lowe (S)	1.0	0	0	0	0	1	2
Oakland	**IP**	**H**	**R**	**ER**	**HR**	**BB**	**SO**
Zito (L)	6.0	4	4	4	2	2	4
Lilly	2.0	0	0	0	0	0	2
Bradford	0.1	2	0	0	0	0	1
R.Rincon	0.2	0	0	0	0	0	1

P.Martinez pitched to 2 batters in the 8th. Williamson pitched to 2 batters in the 9th.

LOB—Boston 4, Oakland 7. Scoring Position—Boston 1 for 5, Oakland 2 for 7. 2B—Durazo, Tejada, J.Guillen, Singleton. HR—Varitek (6th inning, 0 out, 0 on) off Zito, M.Ramirez (6th inning, 1 out, 2 on) off Zito. SB—Damon. SH—Ra.Hernandez. HBP—To.Walker by Zito, Ra.Hernandez by P.Martinez. T—3:05. A—49,397. U—HP-Welke, 1B-Gibson, 2B-Marsh, 3B-Cooper, LF-Bell, RF-Darling.

HOW THEY SCORED

FOURTH INNING

Athletics—Chavez grounded out, shortstop Garciaparra to first baseman Millar. Tejada struck out. Hatteberg walked. Guillen doubled to center, Hatteberg scored. Guillen was out advancing, right fielder Nixon to shortstop Garciaparra to third baseman Mueller, Guillen out. One run. Athletics 1, Red Sox 0.

SIXTH INNING

Red Sox—Varitek homered to left on a full count. Damon walked on a full count. Garciaparra fouled out to first baseman Hatteberg. Walker was hit by a pitch, Damon to second. Ramirez homered to left on a full count, Damon scored, Walker scored. Ortiz struck out. Millar popped out to second baseman Ellis. Four runs. Red Sox 4, Athletics 1.

Athletics—Jackson in as second baseman. Ellis struck out. Durazo doubled to center. Chavez popped out to shortstop Garciaparra. Tejada doubled to center, Durazo scored. Hatteberg grounded out, shortstop Garciaparra to first baseman Millar. One run. Red Sox 4, Athletics 2.

EIGHTH INNING

Athletics—Brown in as center fielder. Singleton doubled to right. McMillon pinch-hitting for Ellis. McMillon singled to right, Singleton scored. Menechino pinch-running for McMillon. Embree pitching. Durazo popped out to third baseman Mueller. Chavez flied out to left fielder Ramirez. Timlin pitching. Tejada grounded into fielder's choice, shortstop Garciaparra to second baseman Jackson, Menechino out. One run. Red Sox 4, Athletics 3.

STATISTICS

BOSTON RED SOX' BATTING AND FIELDING AVERAGES

		BATTING														FIELDING			
Player, position	G	AB	R	H	TB	2B	3B	HR	RBI	BB	IBB	SO	Avg.	OBP	Slg.	PO	A	E	Avg.
Mirabelli,c	2	4	2	2	3	1	0	0	0	0	0	2	.500	.500	.750	13	0	0	1.000
Damon,cf	5	19	2	6	11	2	0	1	3	2	0	1	.316	.409	.579	16	2	0	1.000
Walker,2b-ph	5	16	4	5	14	0	0	3	4	0	0	1	.313	.353	.875	9	3	2	.857
Garciaparra,ss	5	20	2	6	7	1	0	0	0	3	1	2	.300	.391	.350	5	18	1	.958
Varitek,c-ph	5	14	4	4	10	0	0	2	2	2	1	2	.286	.375	.714	31	0	0	1.000
Millar,1b	5	21	0	5	5	0	0	0	0	2	0	4	.238	.304	.238	37	10	0	1.000
Ramirez,lf	5	20	2	4	7	0	0	1	3	3	1	7	.200	.304	.350	5	1	0	1.000
Nixon,rf-ph	4	10	1	2	5	0	0	1	2	1	0	3	.200	.273	.500	3	1	0	1.000
Mueller,3b	5	19	0	2	3	1	0	0	0	3	1	4	.105	.227	.158	9	10	0	1.000
Ortiz,dh	5	21	0	2	3	1	0	0	2	2	1	7	.095	.174	.143	0	0	0	.000
Burkett,p	1	0	0	0	0	0	0	0	0	0	0	0	.000	.000	.000	1	0	0	1.000
Embree,p	3	0	0	0	0	0	0	0	0	0	0	0	.000	.000	.000	0	0	0	.000
Kim,p	1	0	0	0	0	0	0	0	0	0	0	0	.000	.000	.000	0	0	0	.000
Lowe,p	3	0	0	0	0	0	0	0	0	0	0	0	.000	.000	.000	6	2	1	.889
Martinez,p	2	0	0	0	0	0	0	0	0	0	0	0	.000	.000	.000	1	3	1	.800
McCarty,ph	1	0	0	0	0	0	0	0	0	0	0	0	.000	.000	.000	0	0	0	.000
Timlin,p	3	0	0	0	0	0	0	0	0	0	0	0	.000	.000	.000	0	2	0	1.000
Wakefield,p	2	0	0	0	0	0	0	0	0	0	0	0	.000	.000	.000	1	0	0	1.000
Williamson,p	5	0	0	0	0	0	0	0	0	0	0	0	.000	.000	.000	0	0	0	.000
Brown,rf-ph-pr-dh-cf	4	2	0	0	0	0	0	0	0	0	0	1	.000	.000	.000	0	0	0	.000
Jackson,2b	4	5	0	0	0	0	0	0	0	0	0	2	.000	.000	.000	5	4	0	1.000
Kapler,rf-ph-dh-pr	4	9	0	0	0	0	0	0	0	0	0	3	.000	.000	.000	4	0	0	1.000
Totals	5	180	17	38	68	6	0	8	16	18	5	39	.211	.290	.378	146	56	5	.976

OAKLAND ATHLETICS' BATTING AND FIELDING AVERAGES

		BATTING														FIELDING			
Player, position	G	AB	R	H	TB	2B	3B	HR	RBI	BB	IBB	SO	Avg.	OBP	Slg.	PO	A	E	Avg.
Melhuse,c-ph	2	5	1	3	5	0	1	0	1	0	0	1	.600	.600	1.000	2	0	0	1.000
Byrnes,lf-pr-cf	5	13	2	6	7	1	0	0	2	0	0	5	.462	.462	.538	4	0	0	1.000
Guillen,lf	4	11	1	5	6	1	0	0	1	3	0	2	.455	.571	.545	8	0	0	1.000
Singleton,cf	2	7	2	2	4	2	0	0	0	1	0	1	.286	.444	.571	9	1	0	1.000
Long,lf-rf-ph	4	8	0	2	2	0	0	0	0	1	1	3	.250	.333	.250	5	0	0	1.000
Durazo,dh	5	21	3	5	7	2	0	0	3	3	0	4	.238	.333	.333	0	0	0	.000
Dye,rf	4	13	2	3	6	0	0	1	3	0	0	2	.231	.286	.462	9	0	0	1.000
Hernandez,c	4	15	1	3	3	0	0	0	2	2	0	1	.200	.333	.200	35	3	1	.974
Hatteberg,1b	5	17	3	3	3	0	0	0	0	5	0	3	.176	.364	.176	44	1	0	1.000
McMillon,ph-lf	3	6	0	1	1	0	0	0	1	1	0	1	.167	.286	.167	1	0	0	1.000
Ellis,2b	5	17	2	2	2	0	0	0	0	4	0	7	.118	.318	.118	11	16	1	.964
Tejada,ss	5	23	0	2	3	1	0	0	2	0	0	4	.087	.087	.130	9	13	1	.957
Chavez,3b	5	22	1	1	2	1	0	0	0	1	1	3	.045	.087	.091	7	6	2	.867

Player, position	G	AB	R	H	TB	2B	3B	HR	RBI	BB	IBB	SO	Avg.	OBP	Slg.	PO	A	E	Avg.
	BATTING															FIELDING			
Bradford,p	4	0	0	0	0	0	0	0	0	0	0	0	.000	.000	.000	0	0	0	.000
Foulke,p	3	0	0	0	0	0	0	0	0	0	0	0	.000	.000	.000	0	1	0	1.000
Harden,p	2	0	0	0	0	0	0	0	0	0	0	0	.000	.000	.000	0	0	0	.000
Hudson,p	2	0	0	0	0	0	0	0	0	0	0	0	.000	.000	.000	0	0	0	.000
Lilly,p	2	0	0	0	0	0	0	0	0	0	0	0	.000	.000	.000	0	1	0	1.000
Mecir,p	1	0	0	0	0	0	0	0	0	0	0	0	.000	.000	.000	0	0	0	.000
Menechino,2b-pr	1	0	0	0	0	0	0	0	0	0	0	0	.000	.000	.000	0	0	0	.000
Rincon,p	4	0	0	0	0	0	0	0	0	0	0	0	.000	.000	.000	0	1	0	1.000
Sparks,p	1	0	0	0	0	0	0	0	0	0	0	0	.000	.000	.000	1	0	0	1.000
Zito,p	2	0	0	0	0	0	0	0	0	0	0	0	.000	.000	.000	0	1	0	1.000
Totals	5	178	18	38	51	8	1	1	15	21	2	37	.213	.310	.287	145	44	5	.974

BOSTON RED SOX' PITCHING RECORDS

Pitcher	G	GS	CG	IP	H	R	ER	HR	BB	IBB	SO	HB	WP	W	L	Pct.	ERA
Williamson	5	0	0	5.0	2	0	0	0	3	0	8	0	0	2	0	1.000	0.00
Timlin	3	0	0	4.1	0	0	0	0	0	0	5	0	0	0	0	.000	0.00
Embree	3	0	0	2.0	1	0	0	0	0	0	0	0	0	0	0	.000	0.00
Lowe	3	1	0	9.2	7	2	1	0	7	2	6	0	0	0	1	.000	0.93
Wakefield	2	1	0	7.2	6	5	3	0	3	0	7	2	0	0	1	.000	3.52
Martinez	2	2	0	14.0	13	6	6	0	5	0	9	1	0	1	0	1.000	3.86
Burkett	1	1	0	5.1	9	4	4	1	2	0	1	0	0	0	0	.000	6.75
Kim	1	0	0	0.2	0	1	1	0	1	0	1	1	0	0	0	.000	13.50
Totals	5	5	0	48.2	38	18	15	1	21	2	37	4	0	3	2	.600	2.77

No shutouts. Saves—Lowe.

OAKLAND ATHLETICS' PITCHING RECORDS

Pitcher	G	GS	CG	IP	H	R	ER	HR	BB	IBB	SO	HB	WP	W	L	Pct.	ERA
Lilly	2	1	0	9.0	2	1	0	0	2	0	7	1	0	0	0	.000	0.00
Bradford	4	0	0	3.2	4	0	0	0	2	2	5	0	0	0	0	.000	0.00
Mecir	1	0	0	0.2	1	0	0	0	1	1	0	0	0	0	0	.000	0.00
Zito	2	2	0	13.0	9	5	5	2	4	0	13	1	0	1	1	.500	3.46
Hudson	2	2	0	7.2	10	3	3	2	1	0	6	0	0	0	0	.000	3.52
Foulke	3	0	0	5.0	4	2	2	0	2	1	3	0	0	0	1	.000	3.60
Rincon	4	0	0	4.0	4	2	2	2	1	0	3	0	0	0	0	.000	4.50
Sparks	1	0	0	4.0	2	2	2	1	3	0	1	0	0	0	0	.000	4.50
Harden	2	0	0	1.1	2	2	2	1	2	1	1	0	1	1	1	.500	13.50
Totals	5	5	0	48.1	38	17	16	8	18	5	39	2	1	2	3	.400	2.98

No shutouts or saves.

SCORE BY INNINGS

Boston	1	1	3	0	1	5	2	2	0	0	2	0	—17
Oakland	0	6	3	1	0	5	0	1	1	0	0	1	—18

MISCELLANEOUS STATISTICS

Sacrifice hits—Hernandez.
Sacrifice flies—None.
Stolen bases—Damon 2, Byrnes, Chavez, Garciaparra, Singleton.
Caught stealing—None.
Double plays—Chavez, Ellis and Hatteberg 3; Ellis, Tejada and Hatteberg; Millar (unassisted).
Left on bases—Boston 13, 7, 10, 4, 4—38; Oakland 12, 7, 7, 7, 7—40.
Scoring position—Boston 1 for 10, 1 for 5, 0 for 10, 3 for 8, 1 for 5—6 for 38; Oakland 4 for 11, 2 for 12, 1 for 6, 3 for 12, 2 for 7—12 for 48.
Hit by pitcher—by Wakefield 2 (Dye, Ellis), by Martinez (Hernandez), by Lilly (Damon), by Kim (Singleton), by Zito (Walker).
Passed balls—Mirabelli.
Balks—None.
Time of games—4:37, 2:37, 3:42, 3:02, 3:05—Avg.: 3:24.
Attendance—50,606, 36,305, 35,460, 35,048, 49,397—206,816.
Umpires—Marsh, Randy; Cooper, Eric; Bell, Wally; Darling, Gary; Welke, Tim; Emmel, Paul; Davis, Gerry; Joyce, Jim; Welke, Bill; Montague, Ed; Gibson, Greg.

MINNESOTA VS. NEW YORK

RESULTS

Day	Date	Place	Score
Tue.	Sep. 30	New York	Minnesota 3, New York 1
Thur.	Oct. 2	New York	New York 4, Minnesota 1
Sat.	Oct. 4	Minnesota	New York 3, Minnesota 1
Sun.	Oct. 5	Minnesota	New York 8, Minnesota 1

BOX SCORES

GAME 1

MINNESOTA 3, NEW YORK 1

TUESDAY, SEPTEMBER 30, AT NEW YORK

Minnesota	AB	R	H	BI	BB	SO	PO	A
Sh.Stewart, lf	5	0	2	0	0	2	2	0
Rivas, 2b	3	0	0	1	0	1	0	5
Mientkiewicz, 1b	4	0	0	0	0	0	11	1
LeCroy, dh	3	1	1	0	1	1	0	0
J.Jones, rf	4	0	1	0	0	2	2	0
Hunter, cf	2	1	1	1	2	0	0	0
Koskie, 3b	4	0	2	0	0	0	0	2
Pierzynski, c	2	0	0	0	2	0	8	0
C.Guzman, ss	4	1	1	0	0	1	3	5
J.Santana, p	0	0	0	0	0	0	0	0
R.Reed, p	0	0	0	0	0	0	0	0
J.Romero, p	0	0	0	0	0	0	1	0
Hawkins, p	0	0	0	0	0	0	0	1
Guardado, p	0	0	0	0	0	0	0	0
TOTALS	31	3	8	2	5	7	27	14

NY Yankees	AB	R	H	BI	BB	SO	PO	A
A.Soriano, 2b	5	0	2	1	0	2	2	3
N.Johnson, 1b	4	0	0	0	1	1	11	1
Jeter, ss	3	0	2	0	1	0	1	4
Ja.Giambi, dh	4	0	0	0	0	2	0	0
Posada, c	4	0	0	0	0	2	7	2
B.Williams, cf	4	1	2	0	0	1	2	0
Matsui, lf	3	0	1	0	1	0	1	0
A.Boone, 3b	4	0	2	0	0	0	2	1
J.Rivera, rf	2	0	0	0	0	0	0	0
Sierra, ph-rf	2	0	0	0	0	0	0	0
Mussina, p	0	0	0	0	0	0	1	3
J.Nelson, p	0	0	0	0	0	0	0	0
F.Heredia, p	0	0	0	0	0	0	0	2
TOTALS	35	1	9	1	3	8	27	16

Minnesota ....0 0 1 0 0 2 0 0 0—3 8 0
NY Yankees ....0 0 0 0 0 0 0 0 1—1 9 1

Minnesota	IP	H	R	ER	HR	BB	SO
J.Santana	4.0	3	0	0	0	2	3
R.Reed	0.2	1	0	0	0	0	0
J.Romero	1.1	1	0	0	0	1	1
Hawkins (W)	2.0	1	0	0	0	0	4
Guardado (S)	1.0	3	1	1	0	0	0

NY Yankees	IP	H	R	ER	HR	BB	SO
Mussina (L)	7.0	7	3	3	0	3	6
J.Nelson	0.0	0	0	0	0	1	0
F.Heredia	2.0	1	0	0	0	1	1

J.Romero pitched to 1 batter in the 7th. J.Nelson pitched to 1 batter in the 8th.

E—A.Soriano. DP—Minnesota 1, NY Yankees 2. LOB—Minnesota 8, NY Yankees 10. Scoring Position—Minnesota 1 for 6, NY Yankees 1 for 10. 2B—Sh.Stewart, Koskie, A.Soriano, A.Boone. 3B—Hunter. SB—A.Soriano. CS—Koskie. S—Rivas. SH—Rivas. WP—F.Heredia. T—3:18. A—56,292. U—HP-Montague, 1B-Barrett, 2B-Emmel, 3B-Davis, LF-Joyce, RF-Welke.

HOW THEY SCORED

THIRD INNING

Twins—Pierzynski grounded out, second baseman Soriano to first baseman Johnson. Guzman infield single to second. Stewart singled to left, Guzman to third. Rivas hit a sacrifice fly to center fielder Williams, Guzman scored. Mientkiewicz grounded out, pitcher Mussina to first baseman Johnson. One run. Twins 1, Yankees 0.

SIXTH INNING

Twins—LeCroy singled to left. Jones struck out. Hunter tripled to center, LeCroy scored. On Soriano's error, Hunter scored. Koskie doubled to left. Koskie was caught stealing, catcher Posada to third baseman Boone, Koskie out. Pierzynski walked on a full count. Guzman struck out. Two runs. Twins 3, Yankees 0.

NINTH INNING

Yankees—Guardado pitching. Williams singled to right. Matsui flied out to left fielder Stewart. Boone doubled to left, Williams to third. Sierra flied out to right fielder Jones. Soriano infield single to second, Williams scored, Boone to third. Johnson grounded out, third baseman Koskie to first baseman Mientkiewicz. One run. Twins 3, Yankees 1.

GAME 2

NEW YORK 4, MINNESOTA 1

THURSDAY, OCTOBER 2, AT NEW YORK

Minnesota	AB	R	H	BI	BB	SO	PO	A
Sh.Stewart, lf	3	0	2	0	1	1	1	0
Rivas, 2b	4	0	0	0	0	2	2	5
Mientkiewicz, 1b	3	0	0	0	1	1	10	1
LeCroy, dh	4	0	0	0	0	1	0	0
J.Jones, rf	4	0	0	0	0	1	1	0
Hunter, cf	4	1	2	1	0	1	3	0
Koskie, 3b	4	0	0	0	0	3	2	0
Pierzynski, c	4	0	0	0	0	0	4	0
C.Guzman, ss	2	0	0	0	1	1	0	1
Radke, p	0	0	0	0	0	0	1	2
Hawkins, p	0	0	0	0	0	0	0	0
J.Romero, p	0	0	0	0	0	0	0	1
J.Rincon, p	0	0	0	0	0	0	0	1
TOTALS	32	1	4	1	3	11	24	11

NY Yankees	AB	R	H	BI	BB	SO	PO	A
A.Soriano, 2b	4	2	3	1	0	0	0	4
Jeter, ss	3	1	1	0	1	0	1	1
Ja.Giambi, dh	4	0	2	2	0	1	0	0
B.Williams, cf	3	0	1	1	0	0	2	0
Posada, c	4	0	1	0	0	1	11	1
Matsui, lf	3	0	0	0	1	1	0	0
A.Boone, 3b	4	0	0	0	0	1	0	2
N.Johnson, 1b	2	1	0	0	1	0	10	0
J.Rivera, rf	3	0	0	0	0	0	1	0
Pettitte, p	0	0	0	0	0	0	1	2
M.Rivera, p	0	0	0	0	0	0	1	1
TOTALS	30	4	8	4	3	4	27	11

Minnesota ....0 0 0 0 1 0 0 0 0—1 4 1
NY Yankees ....1 0 0 0 0 0 3 0 x—4 8 1

Minnesota	IP	H	R	ER	HR	BB	SO
Radke (L)	6.1	5	2	2	0	2	4
Hawkins	0.0	2	2	1	0	0	0
J.Romero	0.2	1	0	0	0	0	0
J.Rincon	1.0	0	0	0	0	1	0

NY Yankees	IP	H	R	ER	HR	BB	SO
Pettitte (W)	7.0	4	1	1	1	3	10
M.Rivera (S)	2.0	0	0	0	0	0	1

Hawkins pitched to 3 batters in the 7th.

E—Hawkins, Jeter. DP—Minnesota 1. LOB—Minnesota 7, NY Yankees 8. Scoring Position—Minnesota 0 for 3, NY Yankees 3 for 10. 2B—Posada. HR—Hunter (5th inning, 0 out, 0 on) off Pettitte. SB—A.Soriano, Jeter. S—B.Williams. SH—J.Rivera. WP—Pettitte. HBP—N.Johnson by Radke. T—3:07. A—56,479. U—HP-Barrett, 1B-Emmel, 2B-Davis, 3B-Joyce, LF-Welke, RF-Montague.

HOW THEY SCORED

FIRST INNING

Yankees—Soriano singled to left. Jeter singled to center, Soriano to second. Giambi singled to right, Soriano to third, Jeter to second. Williams hit a sacrifice fly to center fielder Hunter, Soriano scored. Posada struck out. Jeter stole third. Matsui struck out. One run. Yankees 1, Twins 0.

FIFTH INNING

Twins—Hunter homered to center on a 1-1 count. Koskie struck out. Pierzynski grounded out, catcher Posada to first baseman Johnson. Guzman safe on Jeter's error. Stewart singled to center, Guzman to third. Rivas grounded out, third baseman Boone to first baseman Johnson. One run. Yankees 1, Twins 1.

SEVENTH INNING

Yankees—Johnson was hit by a pitch. J.Rivera sacrificed, pitcher Radke to first baseman Mientkiewicz, Johnson to second. Hawkins pitching. Soriano singled to left, Johnson scored. Jeter safe at second on Hawkins' error, Soriano to third. Giambi singled to center, Soriano scored, Jeter scored. Romero pitching. Williams singled to center, Giambi to second. Posada grounded out, pitcher Romero to first baseman Mientkiewicz, Giambi to third, Williams to second. Matsui grounded out, second baseman Rivas to first baseman Mientkiewicz. Three runs. Yankees 4, Twins 1.

GAME 3

NEW YORK 3, MINNESOTA 1

SATURDAY, OCTOBER 4, AT MINNESOTA

NY Yankees	AB	R	H	BI	BB	SO	PO	A
A.Soriano, 2b	5	0	0	0	0	1	1	3
Jeter, ss	4	0	1	0	1	1	0	2
Ja.Giambi, dh	4	0	0	0	1	1	0	0
Dellucci, pr-dh	0	0	0	0	0	0	0	0
B.Williams, cf	3	1	2	1	2	1	1	0
Posada, c	4	0	0	0	0	1	9	0
Matsui, lf	4	1	2	2	0	1	1	0
A.Boone, 3b	3	0	0	0	0	2	0	2
N.Johnson, 1b	3	0	0	0	1	1	10	0
J.Rivera, rf	4	1	3	0	0	0	3	0
Clemens, p	0	0	0	0	0	0	1	0
M.Rivera, p	0	0	0	0	0	0	1	0
TOTALS	34	3	8	3	5	9	27	7

Minnesota	AB	R	H	BI	BB	SO	PO	A
Sh.Stewart, lf	3	0	1	0	1	0	1	0
Rivas, 2b	2	0	0	0	0	0	0	2
M.Ryan, ph	1	0	0	0	0	1	0	0
Hocking, 2b	0	0	0	0	0	0	0	0
L.Ford, ph	1	0	0	0	0	1	0	0
C.Gomez, 2b	0	0	0	0	0	0	0	0
Mientkiewicz, 1b	4	0	1	0	0	0	10	1
LeCroy, dh	4	0	0	0	0	2	0	0
J.Jones, rf	4	0	1	0	0	2	2	0
Hunter, cf	4	0	0	0	0	1	2	0
Koskie, 3b	3	0	0	0	0	2	2	0
Pierzynski, c	3	1	1	1	0	0	9	0
C.Guzman, ss	3	0	1	0	0	0	0	4
Lohse, p	0	0	0	0	0	0	1	1
K.Rogers, p	0	0	0	0	0	0	0	0
J.Romero, p	0	0	0	0	0	0	0	1
J.Rincon, p	0	0	0	0	0	0	0	0
TOTALS	32	1	5	1	1	9	27	9

NY Yankees ....0 2 1 0 0 0 0 0 0—3 8 1
Minnesota ....0 0 1 0 0 0 0 0 0—1 5 0

NY Yankees	IP	H	R	ER	HR	BB	SO
Clemens (W)	7.0	5	1	1	1	1	6
M.Rivera (S)	2.0	0	0	0	0	0	3

Minnesota	IP	H	R	ER	HR	BB	SO
Lohse (L)	5.0	6	3	3	1	2	5
K.Rogers	1.1	1	0	0	0	1	3
J.Romero	1.1	1	0	0	0	1	0
J.Rincon	1.1	0	0	0	0	1	1

E—B.Williams. LOB—NY Yankees 10, Minnesota 5. Scoring Position—NY Yankees 2 for 10, Minnesota 0 for 6. 2B—B.Williams. HR—Matsui (2nd inning, 1 out, 1 on) off Lohse, Pierzynski (3rd inning, 0 out, 0 on) off Clemens. SB—Sh.Stewart. SH—A.Boone. T—3:02. A—55,915. U—HP-Bell, 1B-Darling, 2B-Welke, 3B-Gibson, LF-Marsh, RF-Cooper.

HOW THEY SCORED

SECOND INNING

Yankees—Williams doubled to right. Posada grounded out, first baseman Mientkiewicz unassisted, Williams to third. Matsui homered to right on the first pitch, Williams scored. Boone struck out. Johnson grounded out, first baseman Mientkiewicz to pitcher Lohse. Two runs. Yankees 2, Twins 0.

THIRD INNING

Yankees—J.Rivera infield single to third. Soriano struck out. Jeter singled to center, J.Rivera to second. Giambi flied out to center fielder Hunter. Williams singled to center, J.Rivera scored, Jeter to second. Posada struck out. One run. Yankees 3, Twins 0.
Twins—Pierzynski homered to right on a full count. Guzman flied out to center fielder Williams. Stewart flied out to left fielder Matsui. Rivas popped out to second baseman Soriano. One run. Yankees 3, Twins 1.

GAME 4

NEW YORK 8, MINNESOTA 1

SUNDAY, OCTOBER 5, AT MINNESOTA

New York	AB	R	H	RBI	BB	SO	PO	A
A.Soriano, 2b	5	0	2	2	0	3	0	2
Jeter, ss	4	1	2	1	1	1	1	2
Ja.Giambi, dh	4	1	2	0	1	1	0	0
B.Williams, cf	5	1	1	1	0	0	4	0
Posada, c	5	1	2	0	0	2	5	1
Matsui, lf	5	1	1	1	0	1	3	0
A.Boone, 3b	4	1	1	0	0	0	1	4
J.Rivera, rf	3	1	1	0	1	0	2	0
N.Johnson, 1b	4	1	1	2	0	0	11	0
D.Wells, p	0	0	0	0	0	0	0	0
G.White, p	0	0	0	0	0	0	0	1
TOTALS	39	8	13	7	3	8	27	10

Minnesota	AB	R	H	BI	BB	SO	PO	A
Sh.Stewart, lf	4	0	1	0	0	1	3	1
Rivas, 2b	4	0	0	0	0	1	2	1
Mientkiewicz, 1b	4	0	1	0	0	1	4	1
Hunter, cf	4	1	3	0	0	0	6	0
Pierzynski, c	4	0	2	0	0	0	8	0
Cuddyer, dh	4	0	1	1	0	3	0	0
J.Jones, rf	4	0	0	0	0	0	2	0
Koskie, 3b	4	0	1	0	0	0	0	0
C.Guzman, ss	4	0	0	0	0	0	1	3
J.Santana, p	0	0	0	0	0	0	1	0
J.Rincon, p	0	0	0	0	0	0	0	0
Milton, p	0	0	0	0	0	0	0	0
Hawkins, p	0	0	0	0	0	0	0	0
Guardado, p	0	0	0	0	0	0	0	0
TOTALS	36	1	9	1	0	6	27	6

NY Yankees ....0 0 0 6 0 0 0 1 1—8 13 0
Minnesota ....0 0 0 1 0 0 0 0 0—1 9 1

New York	IP	H	R	ER	HR	BB	SO
D.Wells (W)	7.2	8	1	1	0	0	5
G.White	1.1	1	0	0	0	0	1

Minnesota	IP	H	R	ER	HR	BB	SO
J.Santana (L)	3.2	6	6	6	0	1	3
J.Rincon	0.0	1	0	0	0	2	0
Milton	3.1	2	0	0	0	0	2
Hawkins	1.0	2	1	1	0	0	1
Guardado	1.0	2	1	1	1	0	2

J. Rincon pitched to 3 batters in the 4th.

E—Hawkins. DP—Minnesota 1. LOB—NY Yankees 7, Minnesota 8. Scoring Position—NY Yankees 6 for 13, Minnesota 1 for 7. 2B—Ja.Giambi 2, B.Williams, Matsui, N.Johnson, Sh.Stewart. HR—Jeter (9th inning, 0 out, 0 on) off Guardado. SB—A.Boone. PB—Pierzynski. T—2:49. A—55,875. U—HP-Darling, 1B-Welke, 2B-Gibson, 3B-Marsh, LF-Cooper, RF-Bell.

HOW THEY SCORED

FOURTH INNING

Yankees—Jeter struck out. Giambi doubled to left. Williams doubled to left, Giambi scored. Posada singled to left, Williams to third. Matsui doubled to center, Williams scored, Posada to third. Boone lined out to shortstop Guzman. J.Rivera was intentionally walked. Johnson doubled to center, Posada scored, Matsui scored, J.Rivera to third. Rincon pitching. Soriano singled to left, J.Rivera scored, Johnson scored. Jeter walked on a full count, Soriano to second. On Pierzynski's passed ball, Soriano to third, Jeter to second. Giambi walked on four pitches. Milton pitching. Williams grounded into fielder's choice, shortstop Guzman to second baseman Rivas, Giambi out. Six runs. Yankees 6, Twins 0.

Twins—Mientkiewicz grounded out, second baseman Soriano to first baseman Johnson. Hunter singled to left. Pierzynski infield single to first, Hunter to third. Cuddyer singled to center, Hunter scored, Pierzynski to second. Jones fouled out to left fielder Matsui. Koskie flied out to center fielder Williams. One run. Yankees 6, Twins 1.

EIGHTH INNING

Yankees—Hawkins pitching. Boone singled to left. Boone stole second. J.Rivera bunt single to third, Boone to third. On Hawkins' error, Boone scored, J.Rivera to second. Johnson flied into a double play, left fielder Stewart to shortstop Guzman to second baseman Rivas, J.Rivera out. Soriano struck out. One run. Yankees 7, Twins 1.

NINTH INNING

Yankees—Guardado pitching. Jeter homered to left on the first pitch. Giambi struck out. Williams flied out to center fielder Hunter. Posada singled to center. Matsui struck out. One run. Yankees 8, Twins 1.

STATISTICS

NEW YORK YANKEES' BATTING AND FIELDING AVERAGES

	BATTING															FIELDING			
Player, position	**G**	**AB**	**R**	**H**	**TB**	**2B**	**3B**	**HR**	**RBI**	**BB**	**IBB**	**SO**	**Avg.**	**OBP**	**Slg.**	**PO**	**A**	**E**	**Avg.**
Jeter,ss	4	14	2	6	9	0	0	1	1	4	1	2	.429	.556	.643	3	9	1	.923
Williams,cf	4	15	3	6	8	2	0	0	3	2	1	2	.400	.444	.533	9	0	1	.900
Soriano,2b	4	19	2	7	8	1	0	0	4	0	0	6	.368	.368	.421	3	12	1	.938
Rivera,rf	4	12	2	4	4	0	0	0	0	1	1	0	.333	.385	.333	6	0	0	1.000
Matsui,lf	4	15	2	4	8	1	0	1	3	2	0	3	.267	.353	.533	5	0	0	1.000
Giambi,dh	4	16	1	4	6	2	0	0	2	2	0	5	.250	.333	.375	0	0	0	.000
Boone,3b	4	15	1	3	4	1	0	0	0	0	0	3	.200	.200	.267	3	9	0	1.000
Posada,c	4	17	1	3	4	1	0	0	0	0	0	6	.176	.176	.235	32	4	0	1.000
Johnson,1b	4	13	2	1	2	1	0	0	2	3	0	2	.077	.294	.154	42	1	0	1.000
Clemens,p	1	0	0	0	0	0	0	0	0	0	0	0	.000	.000	.000	1	0	0	1.000
Dellucci,dh-pr	1	0	0	0	0	0	0	0	0	0	0	0	.000	.000	.000	0	0	0	.000
Heredia,p	1	0	0	0	0	0	0	0	0	0	0	0	.000	.000	.000	0	2	0	1.000
Mussina,p	1	0	0	0	0	0	0	0	0	0	0	0	.000	.000	.000	1	3	0	1.000
Nelson,p	1	0	0	0	0	0	0	0	0	0	0	0	.000	.000	.000	0	0	0	.000
Pettitte,p	1	0	0	0	0	0	0	0	0	0	0	0	.000	.000	.000	1	2	0	1.000
Rivera,p	2	0	0	0	0	0	0	0	0	0	0	0	.000	.000	.000	2	1	0	1.000
Wells,p	1	0	0	0	0	0	0	0	0	0	0	0	.000	.000	.000	0	0	0	.000
White,p	1	0	0	0	0	0	0	0	0	0	0	0	.000	.000	.000	0	1	0	1.000
Sierra,rf-ph	1	2	0	0	0	0	0	0	0	0	0	0	.000	.000	.000	0	0	0	.000
Totals	4	138	16	38	53	9	0	2	15	14	3	29	.275	.344	.384	108	44	3	.981

MINNESOTA TWINS' BATTING AND FIELDING AVERAGES

	BATTING															FIELDING			
Player, position	**G**	**AB**	**R**	**H**	**TB**	**2B**	**3B**	**HR**	**RBI**	**BB**	**IBB**	**SO**	**Avg.**	**OBP**	**Slg.**	**PO**	**A**	**E**	**Avg.**
Hunter,cf	4	14	3	6	11	0	1	1	2	2	1	2	.429	.500	.786	11	0	0	1.000
Stewart,lf	4	15	0	6	8	2	0	0	0	2	0	4	.400	.471	.533	7	1	0	1.000
Cuddyer,dh	1	4	0	1	1	0	0	0	1	0	0	3	.250	.250	.250	0	0	0	.000
Pierzynski,c	4	13	1	3	6	0	0	1	1	2	1	0	.231	.333	.462	29	0	0	1.000
Koskie,3b	4	15	0	3	4	1	0	0	0	0	0	5	.200	.200	.267	4	2	0	1.000
Guzman,ss	4	13	1	2	2	0	0	0	0	1	0	2	.154	.214	.154	4	13	0	1.000
Mientkiewicz,1b	4	15	0	2	2	0	0	0	0	1	0	2	.133	.188	.133	35	4	0	1.000
Jones,rf	4	16	0	2	2	0	0	0	0	0	0	5	.125	.125	.125	7	0	0	1.000
LeCroy,dh	3	11	1	1	1	0	0	0	0	1	0	4	.091	.167	.091	0	0	0	.000
Gomez,2b	1	0	0	0	0	0	0	0	0	0	0	0	.000	.000	.000	0	0	0	.000
Guardado,p	2	0	0	0	0	0	0	0	0	0	0	0	.000	.000	.000	0	0	0	.000
Hawkins,p	3	0	0	0	0	0	0	0	0	0	0	0	.000	.000	.000	0	1	2	.333
Hocking,2b	1	0	0	0	0	0	0	0	0	0	0	0	.000	.000	.000	0	0	0	.000
Lohse,p	1	0	0	0	0	0	0	0	0	0	0	0	.000	.000	.000	1	1	0	1.000
Milton,p	1	0	0	0	0	0	0	0	0	0	0	0	.000	.000	.000	0	0	0	.000
Radke,p	1	0	0	0	0	0	0	0	0	0	0	0	.000	.000	.000	1	2	0	1.000
Reed,p	1	0	0	0	0	0	0	0	0	0	0	0	.000	.000	.000	0	0	0	.000
Rincon,p	3	0	0	0	0	0	0	0	0	0	0	0	.000	.000	.000	0	1	0	1.000
Rogers,p	1	0	0	0	0	0	0	0	0	0	0	0	.000	.000	.000	0	0	0	.000
Romero,p	3	0	0	0	0	0	0	0	0	0	0	0	.000	.000	.000	1	2	0	1.000
Santana,p	2	0	0	0	0	0	0	0	0	0	0	0	.000	.000	.000	1	0	0	1.000
Ford,ph	1	1	0	0	0	0	0	0	0	0	0	1	.000	.000	.000	0	0	0	.000
Ryan,ph	1	1	0	0	0	0	0	0	0	0	0	1	.000	.000	.000	0	0	0	.000
Rivas,2b	4	13	0	0	0	0	0	0	1	0	0	4	.000	.000	.000	4	13	0	1.000
Totals	4	131	6	26	37	3	1	2	5	9	2	33	.198	.248	.282	105	40	2	.986

NEW YORK YANKEES' PITCHING RECORDS

Pitcher	G	GS	CG	IP	H	R	ER	HR	BB	IBB	SO	HB	WP	W	L	Pct.	ERA
Rivera	2	0	0	4.0	0	0	0	0	0	0	4	0	0	0	0	.000	0.00
Heredia	1	0	0	2.0	1	0	0	0	1	1	1	0	1	0	0	.000	0.00
White	1	0	0	1.1	1	0	0	0	0	0	1	0	0	0	0	.000	0.00
Wells	1	1	0	7.2	8	1	1	0	0	0	5	0	0	1	0	1.000	1.17
Clemens	1	1	0	7.0	5	1	1	1	1	0	6	0	0	1	0	1.000	1.29
Pettitte	1	1	0	7.0	4	1	1	1	3	0	10	0	1	1	0	1.000	1.29
Mussina	1	1	0	7.0	7	3	3	0	3	1	6	0	0	0	1	.000	3.86
Nelson	1	0	0	0.0	0	0	0	0	1	0	0	0	0	0	0	.000	-
Totals	4	4	0	36.0	26	6	6	2	9	2	33	0	2	3	1	.750	1.50

No shutouts. Saves—Rivera 2.

MINNESOTA TWINS' PITCHING RECORDS

Pitcher	G	GS	CG	IP	H	R	ER	HR	BB	IBB	SO	HB	WP	W	L	Pct.	ERA
Milton	1	0	0	3.1	2	0	0	0	0	0	2	0	0	0	0	.000	0.00
Romero	3	0	0	3.1	3	0	0	0	2	1	1	0	0	0	0	.000	0.00
Rincon	3	0	0	2.1	1	0	0	0	4	0	1	0	0	0	0	.000	0.00
Rogers	1	0	0	1.1	1	0	0	0	1	1	3	0	0	0	0	.000	0.00
Reed	1	0	0	0.2	1	0	0	0	0	0	0	0	0	0	0	.000	0.00
Radke	1	1	0	6.1	5	2	2	0	2	0	4	1	0	0	1	.000	2.84
Lohse	1	1	0	5.0	6	3	3	1	2	0	5	0	0	0	1	.000	5.40
Hawkins	3	0	0	3.0	5	3	2	0	0	0	5	0	0	1	0	1.000	6.00
Santana	2	2	0	7.2	9	6	6	0	3	1	6	0	0	0	1	.000	7.04
Guardado	2	0	0	2.0	5	2	2	1	0	0	2	0	0	0	0	.000	9.00
Totals	4	4	0	35.0	38	16	15	2	14	3	29	1	0	1	3	.250	3.86

No shutouts. Saves—Guardado.

SCORE BY INNINGS

New York	1	2	1	6	0	0	3	1	2—16
Minnesota	0	0	2	1	1	2	0	0	0— 6

MISCELLANEOUS STATISTICS

Sacrifice hits—Boone, Rivas, Rivera.
Sacrifice flies—Rivas, Williams.
Stolen bases—Soriano 2, Boone, Jeter, Stewart.
Caught stealing—Koskie.
Double plays—Guzman, Rivas and Mientkiewicz; Heredia, Posada and Johnson; Jeter, Soriano and Johnson; Rivas, Guzman and Mientkiewicz; Stewart, Guzman and Rivas.
Left on bases—New York 10, 8, 10, 7—35; Minnesota 8, 7, 5, 8—28.
Scoring position—New York 1 for 10, 3 for 10, 2 for 10, 6 for 13—12 for 43; Minnesota 1 for 6, 0 for 3, 0 for 6, 1 for 7—2 for 22.
Hit by pitcher—by Radke (Johnson).
Passed balls—Pierzynski.
Balks—None.
Time of games—3:18, 3:07, 3:02, 2:49—Avg.: 3:04.
Attendance—56,292, 56,479, 55,915, 55,875—224,561.
Umpires—Montague, Ed; Barrett, Ted; Emmel, Paul; Davis, Gerry; Joyce, Jim; Bell, Wally; Darling, Gary; Welke, Tim; Gibson, Greg; Marsh, Randy.

N.L. DIVISION SERIES

SAN FRANCISCO VS. FLORIDA

RESULTS

Day	Date	Place	Score
Tue.	Sep. 30	San Francisco	San Francisco 2, Florida 0
Wed.	Oct. 1	San Francisco	Florida 9, San Francisco 5
Fri.	Oct. 3	Florida	Florida 4, San Francisco 3
Sat.	Oct. 4	Florida	Florida 7, San Francisco 6

BOX SCORES

GAME 1

SAN FRANCISCO 2, FLORIDA 0

TUESDAY, SEPTEMBER 30, AT SAN FRANCISCO

Florida	AB	R	H	BI	BB	SO	PO	A
Pierre, cf	4	0	0	0	0	1	3	0
L.Castillo, 2b	4	0	0	0	0	0	0	0
I.Rodriguez, c	4	0	1	0	0	0	9	0
D.Lee, 1b	4	0	0	0	0	0	8	0
M.Cabrera, 3b	3	0	0	0	0	1	0	2
Encarnacion, rf	3	0	1	0	0	0	3	0
Conine, lf	3	0	1	0	0	0	1	0
A.Gonzalez, ss	3	0	0	0	0	1	0	1
Beckett, p	1	0	0	0	0	1	0	2
Hollandsworth, ph	1	0	0	0	0	1	0	0
C.Fox, p	0	0	0	0	0	0	0	0
TOTALS	30	0	3	0	0	5	24	5

San Francisco	AB	R	H	BI	BB	SO	PO	A
Durham, 2b	4	0	1	0	0	1	1	1
J.Snow, 1b	4	0	0	0	0	1	8	1
Aurilia, ss	3	1	0	0	1	0	1	3
Bonds, lf	1	1	0	0	3	0	0	0
Alfonzo, 3b	4	0	2	1	0	1	1	2
B.Santiago, c	4	0	0	0	0	0	5	0
Grissom, cf	2	0	0	0	1	2	2	0
J.Cruz, rf	2	0	0	0	1	2	8	0
Schmidt, p	3	0	0	0	0	2	1	1
TOTALS	27	2	3	1	6	9	27	8

Florida	0 0 0	0 0 0	0 0 0—0	3 1
San Francisco	0 0 0	1 0 0	0 1 x—2	3 2

Florida	IP	H	R	ER	HR	BB	SO
Beckett (L)	7.0	2	1	1	0	5	9
C.Fox	1.0	1	1	1	0	1	0

San Francisco	IP	H	R	ER	HR	BB	SO
Schmidt (W)	9.0	3	0	0	0	0	5

E—M.Cabrera, J.Snow, Aurilia. LOB—Florida 4, San Francisco 7. Scoring Position—Florida 0 for 2, San Francisco 2 for 9. 2B—Alfonzo. SB—Bonds. SH—Beckett. WP—Beckett. T—2:33. A—43,704. U—HP-Hirschbeck, 1B-Miller, 2B-Gorman, 3B-Young, LF-Rapuano, RF-Wegner.

HOW THEY SCORED

FOURTH INNING

Giants—Aurilia walked on a full count. Bonds walked on a full count, Aurilia to second. Alfonzo bunt single to third, Aurilia to third, Bonds to second. On Cabrera's error, Aurilia scored, Bonds to third, Alfonzo to second. Santiago grounded out, third baseman Cabrera to first baseman Lee. Grissom walked on a full count. Cruz struck out. Schmidt struck out. One run. Giants 1, Marlins 0.

EIGHTH INNING

Giants—C.Fox pitching. Snow flied out to left fielder Conine. Aurilia flied out to center fielder Pierre. Bonds was intentionally walked. Bonds stole second. Alfonzo doubled to center, Bonds scored. Santiago grounded out, third baseman Cabrera to first baseman Lee. One run. Giants 2, Marlins 0.

GAME 2

FLORIDA 9, SAN FRANCISCO 5

WEDNESDAY, OCTOBER 1, AT SAN FRANCISCO

Florida	AB	R	H	BI	BB	SO	PO	A
Pierre, cf	5	3	4	3	0	0	3	0
L.Castillo, 2b	5	0	1	1	0	1	0	1
I.Rodriguez, c	4	0	1	1	1	0	6	1
D.Lee, 1b	5	1	1	1	0	0	9	1
M.Cabrera, 3b	5	0	0	0	0	3	1	1
B.Looper, p	0	0	0	0	0	0	0	0
Urbina, p	0	0	0	0	0	0	1	0
Encarnacion, rf	4	1	1	1	1	0	3	0
Conine, lf	5	2	2	1	0	0	1	0
A.Gonzalez, ss	5	1	1	0	0	1	2	2
Penny, p	1	0	1	0	0	0	1	0
Hollandsworth, ph	1	1	1	0	0	0	0	0
Helling, p	0	0	0	0	0	0	0	0
Pavano, p	0	0	0	0	0	0	0	0
L.Harris, ph	1	0	1	0	0	0	0	0
C.Fox, p	0	0	0	0	0	0	0	1
B.Banks, ph	1	0	0	0	0	0	0	0
Willis, p	0	0	0	0	0	0	0	0
Lowell, 3b	0	0	0	0	0	0	0	1
TOTALS	42	9	14	8	2	5	27	8

San Francisco	AB	R	H	BI	BB	SO	PO	A
Durham, 2b	4	1	1	0	1	1	0	1
J.Snow, 1b	5	0	1	1	0	2	8	1
Aurilia, ss	4	1	1	0	0	0	3	5
Bonds, lf	2	1	1	1	2	0	1	0
Alfonzo, 3b	4	1	2	2	0	0	0	1
B.Santiago, c	3	0	1	0	0	1	6	1
Grissom, cf	4	0	0	1	0	1	3	1
J.Cruz, rf	4	0	0	0	0	2	6	0
Ponson, p	1	0	0	0	0	0	0	0
Feliz, ph	1	1	1	0	0	0	0	0
Nathan, p	0	0	0	0	0	0	0	0
Christiansen, p	0	0	0	0	0	0	0	0
Herges, p	0	0	0	0	0	0	0	0
Hammonds, ph	1	0	0	0	0	0	0	0
F.Rodriguez, p	0	0	0	0	0	0	0	0
Brower, p	0	0	0	0	0	0	0	0
Worrell, p	0	0	0	0	0	0	0	0
N.Perez, ph	1	0	0	0	0	0	0	0
TOTALS	34	5	8	5	3	7	27	10

Florida	1 0 0	0 3 3	1 1 0—9	14 0
San Francisco	1 0 0	3 1 0	0 0 0—5	8 2

Florida	IP	H	R	ER	HR	BB	SO
Penny	4.0	4	4	4	0	1	5
Helling	0.1	2	1	1	0	2	0
Pavano (W)	0.2	0	0	0	0	0	0
C.Fox (HOLD)	2.0	0	0	0	0	0	2
Willis	0.1	2	0	0	0	0	0
B.Looper (HOLD)	0.2	0	0	0	0	0	0
Urbina	1.0	0	0	0	0	0	0

San Francisco	IP	H	R	ER	HR	BB	SO
Ponson	5.0	7	4	4	0	0	3
Nathan (BS, L)	0.1	4	3	3	1	0	1
Christiansen	0.0	1	0	0	0	0	0
Herges	0.2	0	0	0	0	0	0
F.Rodriguez	1.0	1	1	0	0	1	0
Brower	1.0	1	1	0	0	1	1
Worrell	1.0	0	0	0	0	0	0

Christiansen pitched to 1 batter in the 6th.

E—J.Snow, Grissom. DP—San Francisco 1. LOB—Florida 8, San Francisco 6. Scoring Position—Florida 4 for 13, San Francisco 2 for 9. 2B—Pierre, Bonds, Alfonzo. 3B—Feliz. HR—Encarnacion (6th inning, 1 out, 0 on) off Nathan. SB—Pierre. SH—B.Santiago. WP—Ponson. T—3:06. A—43,766. U—HP-Miller, 1B-Gorman, 2B-Young, 3B-Rapuano, LF-Wegner, RF-Hirschbeck.

HOW THEY SCORED

FIRST INNING

Marlins—Pierre singled to right. Castillo singled to center, Pierre to second. Rodriguez flied out to center fielder Grissom. On Ponson's wild pitch, Pierre to third, Castillo to second. Lee grounded out, shortstop Aurilia to first baseman Snow, Pierre scored, Castillo to third. Cabrera flied out to right fielder Cruz. One run. Marlins 1, Giants 0.

Giants—Durham singled to right. Snow struck out. Aurilia flied out to right fielder Encarnacion. Bonds doubled to right, Durham scored. Alfonzo flied out to right fielder Encarnacion. One run. Marlins 1, Giants 1.

FOURTH INNING

Giants—Aurilia bunt single to second. Bonds walked on four pitches, Aurilia to second. Alfonzo doubled to center, Aurilia scored, Bonds scored. Santiago sacrificed, pitcher Penny unassisted, Alfonzo to third. Grissom grounded out, third baseman Cabrera to first baseman Lee, Alfonzo scored. Cruz struck out. Three runs. Giants 4, Marlins 1.

FIFTH INNING

Marlins—Conine infield single to second. Gonzalez struck out. Hollandsworth pinch-hitting for Penny. Hollandsworth singled to left, Conine to second. Pierre singled to right, Conine scored, Hollandsworth to third. Castillo grounded out, shortstop Aurilia to first baseman Snow, Hollandsworth scored, Pierre to second. Pierre stole third. Rodriguez singled to right, Pierre scored. Lee lined out to right fielder Cruz. Three runs. Marlins 4, Giants 4.

Giants—Helling pitching. Feliz pinch-hitting for Ponson. Feliz tripled to center. Durham walked on four pitches. Snow singled to right, Feliz scored, Durham to third. Aurilia fouled out to first baseman Lee. Bonds was intentionally walked, Snow to second. Pavano pitching. Alfonzo popped out to shortstop Gonzalez. Santiago popped out to first baseman Lee. One run. Giants 5, Marlins 4.

SIXTH INNING

Marlins—Nathan pitching. Cabrera struck out. Encarnacion homered to left on a 2-1 count. Conine singled to left. Gonzalez singled to center, Conine to second. Harris pinch-hitting for Pavano. Harris singled to center, Conine to third, Gonzalez to second. Christiansen pitching. Pierre doubled to right, Conine scored, Gonzalez scored, Harris to third. Herges pitching. Castillo flied out to center fielder Grissom. Harris was out advancing, center fielder Grissom to catcher Santiago, Harris out. Three runs. Marlins 7, Giants 5.

SEVENTH INNING

Marlins—Rodriguez pitching. Rodriguez lined out to right fielder Cruz. Lee singled to left. Cabrera safe at second on Snow's error, Lee to third. Encarnacion was intentionally walked. Conine grounded into fielder's choice, first baseman Snow to shortstop Aurilia, Lee scored, Cabrera to third, Encarnacion out. Gonzalez lined out to center fielder Grissom. One run. Marlins 8, Giants 5.

EIGHTH INNING

Marlins—Brower pitching. Banks pinch-hitting for C.Fox. Banks flied out to right fielder Cruz. Pierre singled to center. Castillo grounded out, second baseman Durham to first baseman Snow, Pierre to second. Rodriguez walked. Lee safe on Grissom's error, Pierre scored, Rodriguez to third. Cabrera struck out. One run. Marlins 9, Giants 5.

GAME 3

FLORIDA 4, SAN FRANCISCO 3

FRIDAY, OCTOBER 3, AT FLORIDA

San Francisco	AB	R	H	BI	BB	SO	PO	A
Durham, 2b	5	0	1	0	0	1	1	1
Nathan, p	0	0	0	0	0	0	0	0
F.Rodriguez, p	0	0	0	0	0	0	0	1
Hammonds, ph	0	0	0	0	0	0	0	0
Worrell, p	0	0	0	0	0	0	0	2
Grissom, cf	6	0	2	0	0	2	2	0
Aurilia, ss	4	1	0	0	2	1	1	6
Bonds, lf	4	1	1	0	2	0	1	0
Alfonzo, 3b	5	1	4	1	1	0	1	3
Galarraga, 1b	4	0	0	0	0	1	10	1
Eyre, p	0	0	0	0	0	0	0	0
Y.Torrealba, c	1	0	0	0	0	0	5	0
B.Santiago, c	3	0	1	0	1	1	6	0
N.Perez, pr-2b	1	0	0	0	1	0	2	0
J.Cruz, rf	4	0	0	1	1	0	1	0
Rueter, p	2	0	1	0	0	0	2	0
Feliz, ph	1	0	1	1	0	0	0	0
Herges, p	0	0	0	0	0	0	0	0
J.Snow, 1b	3	0	1	0	0	0	0	0
TOTALS	43	3	12	3	8	6	32	14

Florida	AB	R	H	BI	BB	SO	PO	A
Pierre, cf	5	1	0	0	1	0	4	0
L.Castillo, 2b	5	1	3	0	1	0	6	4
I.Rodriguez, c	5	1	2	4	1	1	8	1
D.Lee, 1b	5	0	2	0	0	1	5	1
Encarnacion, rf	4	0	0	0	1	2	3	0
Lowell, 3b	3	0	0	0	0	1	1	1
C.Fox, p	0	0	0	0	0	0	0	0
Urbina, p	0	0	0	0	0	0	0	0
Hollandsworth, ph	1	0	0	0	0	1	0	0
Pavano, p	0	0	0	0	0	0	0	0
L.Harris, ph	1	0	0	0	0	0	0	0
B.Looper, p	0	0	0	0	0	0	0	0
Conine, lf	4	0	1	0	1	1	2	0
A.Gonzalez, ss	4	1	0	0	1	1	3	1
M.Redman, p	2	0	0	0	0	1	0	2
M.Cabrera, 3b	1	0	0	0	1	1	1	2
TOTALS	40	4	8	4	7	10	33	12

San Francisco ....0 0 0 0 0 2 0 0 0 0 1—3 12 1
Florida ....2 0 0 0 0 0 0 0 0 0 2—4 8 1

San Francisco	IP	H	R	ER	HR	BB	SO
Rueter	5.0	3	2	2	1	2	2
Herges	1.2	1	0	0	0	1	4
Eyre	0.1	0	0	0	0	0	0
Nathan	0.0	0	0	0	0	1	0
F.Rodriguez	2.0	1	0	0	0	0	4
Worrell (L)	1.2	3	2	0	0	3	0

Florida	IP	H	R	ER	HR	BB	SO
M.Redman	6.0	7	2	2	0	3	4
C.Fox	2.0	2	0	0	0	2	1
Urbina	1.0	1	0	0	0	1	1
Pavano	1.0	1	0	0	0	0	0
B.Looper (W)	1.0	1	1	0	0	2	0

Nathan pitched to 1 batter in the 8th.

E—J.Cruz, A.Gonzalez. LOB—San Francisco 18, Florida 12. Scoring Position—San Francisco 2 for 16, Florida 2 for 7. 2B—Alfonzo, L.Castillo 2, D.Lee. HR—I.Rodriguez (1st inning, 1 out, 1 on) off Rueter. SB—D.Lee. CS—Grissom. SH—J.Cruz, Y.Torrealba, M.Cabrera. HBP—Hammonds by Pavano. T—4:11. A—61,488. U—HP-Scott, 1B-Cederstrom,2B-Kellogg, 3B-Cuzzi, LF-Froemming, RF-Wendelstedt.

HOW THEY SCORED

FIRST INNING

Marlins—Pierre grounded out, third baseman Alfonzo to first baseman Galarraga. Castillo doubled to left. Rodriguez homered to left on a 0-2 count, Castillo scored. Lee lined out to first baseman Galarraga. Encarnacion grounded out, shortstop Aurilia to first baseman Galarraga. Two runs. Marlins 2, Giants 0.

SIXTH INNING

Giants—Bonds infield single to pitcher Redman. Alfonzo singled to left, Bonds to second. Galarraga grounded out, pitcher Redman to second baseman Castillo to first baseman Lee, Bonds to third, Alfonzo to second. Santiago walked on a full count. Cruz grounded into fielder's choice, third baseman Lowell to second baseman Castillo, Bonds scored, Alfonzo to third, Santiago out. Feliz pinch-hitting for Rueter. Feliz singled to left, Alfonzo scored, Cruz to second. Durham struck out. Two runs. Marlins 2, Giants 2.

ELEVENTH INNING

Giants—Looper pitching. Aurilia walked. Bonds safe on Gonzalez's error, Aurilia to third. Alfonzo singled to right, Aurilia scored, Bonds to second. Torrealba sacrificed, third baseman Cabrera to second baseman Castillo, Bonds to third, Alfonzo to second. Perez was intentionally walked. Cruz grounded into fielder's choice, first baseman Lee to catcher Rodriguez, Bonds out, Alfonzo to third, Perez to second. Snow grounded out, second baseman Castillo to first baseman Lee. One run. Giants 3, Marlins 2.

Marlins—Conine safe on Cruz's error. Gonzalez walked, Conine to second. Cabrera sacrificed, pitcher Worrell to second baseman Perez, Conine to third, Gonzalez to second. Pierre was intentionally walked. Castillo grounded into fielder's choice, pitcher Worrell to catcher Torrealba, Conine out, Gonzalez to third, Pierre to second. Rodriguez singled to right, Gonzalez scored, Pierre scored, Castillo to second. Two runs. Marlins 4, Giants 3.

GAME 4

FLORIDA 7, SAN FRANCISCO 6

SATURDAY, OCTOBER 4, AT FLORIDA

San Francisco	AB	R	H	BI	BB	SO	PO	A
Durham, 2b	4	1	1	0	0	2	2	1
Hammonds, rf-cf	4	1	2	0	1	0	2	0
Aurilia, ss	4	1	1	1	0	2	3	3
Bonds, lf	2	0	0	1	1	0	2	0
Alfonzo, 3b	4	1	1	1	0	0	2	2
Grissom, cf	2	1	0	0	1	0	0	0
Herges, p	0	0	0	0	0	0	1	0
F.Rodriguez, p	0	0	0	0	0	0	0	0
N.Perez, ph	1	1	1	0	0	0	0	0
J.Snow, 1b	4	0	3	2	0	0	7	1
Y.Torrealba, c	2	0	0	1	0	0	5	0
Feliz, ph	1	0	0	0	0	1	0	0
J.Williams, p	1	0	0	0	0	1	0	1
Brower, p	0	0	0	0	0	0	0	0
Galarraga, ph	1	0	0	0	0	0	0	0
Hermanson, p	0	0	0	0	0	0	0	0
J.Cruz, rf	1	0	0	0	0	0	0	0
B.Santiago, ph	1	0	0	0	0	0	0	0
TOTALS	32	6	9	6	3	6	24	8

Florida	AB	R	H	BI	BB	SO	PO	A
Pierre, cf	5	1	1	0	0	0	4	0
L.Castillo, 2b	3	1	1	0	2	2	1	2
I.Rodriguez, c	4	2	2	1	1	0	7	1
D.Lee, 1b	2	1	1	1	1	1	7	0
M.Cabrera, 3b	5	1	4	3	0	1	1	1
Encarnacion, rf	4	0	0	0	0	1	2	0
Conine, lf	3	0	0	1	1	0	4	1
A.Gonzalez, ss	4	0	0	0	0	0	1	3
Willis, p	3	1	3	0	0	0	0	0
Penny, p	0	0	0	0	0	0	0	0
B.Banks, ph	1	0	0	0	0	0	0	0
Pavano, p	0	0	0	0	0	0	0	0
Urbina, p	0	0	0	0	0	0	0	0
TOTALS	34	7	12	6	5	5	27	8

San Francisco	0 1 0	0 0 4	0 0 1—6	9	2
Florida	0 1 2	2 0 0	0 2 x—7	12	0

San Francisco	IP	H	R	ER	HR	BB	SO
J.Williams	2.0	5	3	3	0	1	1
Brower	2.0	4	2	2	0	2	2
Hermanson	1.0	1	0	0	0	1	0
Herges	2.0	0	0	0	0	1	1
F.Rodriguez (L)	1.0	2	2	1	0	0	1

Florida	IP	H	R	ER	HR	BB	SO
Willis	5.1	5	5	5	0	2	3
Penny (BS)	1.2	1	0	0	0	0	1
Pavano (W)	1.0	0	0	0	0	1	1
Urbina (S)	1.0	3	1	1	0	0	1

J.Williams pitched to 3 batters in the 3rd. Hermanson pitched to 1 batter in the 6th.

E—Y.Torrealba, Aurilia. DP—San Francisco 2. LOB—San Francisco 5, Florida 11. Scoring Position—San Francisco 5 for 6, Florida 3 for 16. 2B—Aurilia, Alfonzo, N.Perez, L.Castillo, I.Rodriguez, M.Cabrera 2. 3B—Willis. S—Bonds, Y.Torrealba. SH—Encarnacion. HBP—Durham by Urbina, D.Lee by Herges; by F.Rodriguez. T—3:19. A—65,464. U—HP-Cederstrom, 1B-Kellogg, 2B-Cuzzi, 3B-Froemming, LF-Wendelstedt, RF-Scott.

HOW THEY SCORED

SECOND INNING

Giants—Alfonzo grounded out, third baseman Cabrera to first baseman Lee. Grissom walked on four pitches. Snow singled to center, Grissom to third. Torrealba hit a sacrifice fly to left fielder Conine, Grissom scored. Williams struck out. One run. Giants 1, Marlins 0.

Marlins—Cabrera doubled to left. Encarnacion sacrificed, pitcher Williams to first baseman Snow, Cabrera to third. Conine safe on Aurilia's error, Cabrera scored. Gonzalez popped out to shortstop Aurilia. Willis singled to center, Conine to second. Pierre lined out to third baseman Alfonzo. One run. Marlins 1, Giants 1.

THIRD INNING

Marlins—Castillo walked on a full count. Rodriguez doubled to center, Castillo scored. Lee singled to left, Rodriguez scored. Brower pitching. Cabrera doubled to left, Lee to third. Encarnacion grounded out, third baseman Alfonzo to first baseman Snow. Conine was intentionally walked. Gonzalez grounded into a double play, third baseman Alfonzo to first baseman Snow, Cabrera out, Conine to second. Two runs. Marlins 3, Giants 1.

FOURTH INNING

Marlins—Willis singled to left. Pierre singled to center, Willis to second. Castillo struck out. Rodriguez grounded out, first baseman Snow unassisted, Willis to third, Pierre to second. Lee walked on a full count. Cabrera singled to left, Willis scored, Pierre scored, Lee to second. Lee to third, Cabrera to second. Encarnacion struck out. Two runs. Marlins 5, Giants 1.

SIXTH INNING

Giants—Durham singled to left. Hammonds infield single to third, Durham to third. Aurilia doubled to left, Durham scored, Hammonds to third. Bonds hit a sacrifice fly to left fielder Conine, Hammonds scored. Alfonzo doubled to center, Aurilia scored. Penny pitching. Grissom grounded out, shortstop Gonzalez to first baseman Lee, Alfonzo to third. Snow singled to center, Alfonzo scored. Snow was picked off, catcher Rodriguez to first baseman Lee, Snow out. Four runs. Marlins 5, Giants 5.

EIGHTH INNING

Marlins—Rodriguez pitching. Pierre flied out to left fielder Bonds. Castillo struck out. Rodriguez singled to left. Lee was hit by a pitch, Rodriguez to second. Cabrera singled to right, Rodriguez scored, Lee to third. On Torrealba's error, Lee scored, Cabrera to third. Encarnacion popped out to shortstop Aurilia. Two runs. Marlins 7, Giants 5.

NINTH INNING

Giants—Urbina pitching. Perez pinch-hitting for Rodriguez. Perez doubled to right. Snow singled to right, Perez scored. Feliz pinch-hitting for Torrealba. Feliz struck out. Santiago pinch-hitting for Cruz. Santiago flied out to right fielder Encarnacion. Durham was hit by a pitch, Snow to second. Hammonds singled to left, Snow to third, Durham to second. Snow was out advancing, left fielder Conine to catcher Rodriguez, Snow out. One run. Marlins 7, Giants 6.

FLORIDA MARLINS' BATTING AND FIELDING AVERAGES

Player, position	G	AB	R	H	TB	2B	3B	HR	RBI	BB	IBB	SO	Avg.	OBP	Slg.	PO	A	E	Avg.
	BATTING															FIELDING			
Willis,p	2	3	1	3	5	0	1	0	0	0	0	0	1.000	1.000	1.667	0	0	0	.000
Penny,p	2	1	0	1	1	0	0	0	0	0	0	0	1.000	1.000	1.000	1	0	0	1.000
Harris,ph	2	2	0	1	1	0	0	0	0	0	0	0	.500	.500	.500	0	0	0	.000
Rodriguez,c	4	17	3	6	10	1	0	1	6	3	0	1	.353	.450	.588	30	3	0	1.000
Hollandsworth,ph	3	3	1	1	1	0	0	0	0	0	0	2	.333	.333	.333	0	0	0	.000
Castillo,2b	4	17	2	5	8	3	0	0	1	3	0	3	.294	.400	.471	7	7	0	1.000
Cabrera,3b	4	14	1	4	6	2	0	0	3	1	0	6	.286	.333	.429	3	6	1	.900
Conine,lf	4	15	2	4	4	0	0	0	2	2	1	1	.267	.353	.267	8	1	0	1.000
Pierre,cf	4	19	5	5	6	1	0	0	3	1	1	1	.263	.300	.316	14	0	0	1.000
Lee,1b	4	16	2	4	5	1	0	0	2	1	0	2	.250	.368	.313	29	2	0	1.000
Encarnacion,rf	4	15	1	2	5	0	0	1	1	2	1	3	.133	.235	.333	11	0	0	1.000
Gonzalez,ss	4	16	2	1	1	0	0	0	0	1	0	3	.063	.118	.063	6	7	1	.929
Fox,p	3	0	0	0	0	0	0	0	0	0	0	0	.000	.000	.000	0	1	0	1.000
Helling,p	1	0	0	0	0	0	0	0	0	0	0	0	.000	.000	.000	0	0	0	.000
Looper,p	2	0	0	0	0	0	0	0	0	0	0	0	.000	.000	.000	0	0	0	.000
Pavano,p	3	0	0	0	0	0	0	0	0	0	0	0	.000	.000	.000	0	0	0	.000
Urbina,p	3	0	0	0	0	0	0	0	0	0	0	0	.000	.000	.000	1	0	0	1.000
Beckett,p	1	1	0	0	0	0	0	0	0	0	0	1	.000	.000	.000	0	2	0	1.000
Banks,ph	2	2	0	0	0	0	0	0	0	0	0	0	.000	.000	.000	0	0	0	.000
Redman,p	1	2	0	0	0	0	0	0	0	0	0	1	.000	.000	.000	0	2	0	1.000
Lowell,3b	2	3	0	0	0	0	0	0	0	0	0	1	.000	.000	.000	1	2	0	1.000
Totals	4	146	20	37	53	8	1	2	18	14	3	25	.253	.327	.363	111	33	2	.986

SAN FRANCISCO GIANTS' BATTING AND FIELDING AVERAGES

Player, position	G	AB	R	H	TB	2B	3B	HR	RBI	BB	IBB	SO	Avg.	OBP	Slg.	PO	A	E	Avg.
	BATTING															FIELDING			
Feliz,ph	3	3	1	2	4	0	1	0	1	0	0	1	.667	.667	1.333	0	0	0	.000
Alfonzo,3b	4	17	3	9	13	4	0	0	5	1	0	1	.529	.556	.765	4	8	0	1.000
Rueter,p	1	2	0	1	1	0	0	0	0	0	0	0	.500	.500	.500	2	0	0	1.000
Hammonds,ph-cf-rf	3	5	1	2	2	0	0	0	0	1	0	0	.400	.571	.400	2	0	0	1.000
Perez,ph-2b-pr	3	3	1	1	2	1	0	0	0	1	1	0	.333	.500	.667	2	0	0	1.000
Snow,1b	4	16	0	5	5	0	0	0	3	0	0	3	.313	.313	.313	23	3	2	.929
Durham,2b	4	17	2	4	4	0	0	0	0	1	0	5	.235	.316	.235	4	4	0	1.000
Bonds,lf	4	9	3	2	3	1	0	0	2	8	6	0	.222	.556	.333	4	0	0	1.000
Santiago,c-ph	4	11	0	2	2	0	0	0	0	1	0	2	.182	.250	.182	17	1	0	1.000
Grissom,cf	4	14	1	2	2	0	0	0	1	2	0	5	.143	.250	.143	7	1	1	.889
Aurilia,ss	4	15	4	2	3	1	0	0	1	3	0	3	.133	.278	.200	8	17	2	.926
Brower,p	2	0	0	0	0	0	0	0	0	0	0	0	.000	.000	.000	0	0	0	.000
Christiansen,p	1	0	0	0	0	0	0	0	0	0	0	0	.000	.000	.000	0	0	0	.000
Eyre,p	1	0	0	0	0	0	0	0	0	0	0	0	.000	.000	.000	0	0	0	.000
Herges,p	3	0	0	0	0	0	0	0	0	0	0	0	.000	.000	.000	1	0	0	1.000
Hermanson,p	1	0	0	0	0	0	0	0	0	0	0	0	.000	.000	.000	0	0	0	.000
Nathan,p	2	0	0	0	0	0	0	0	0	0	0	0	.000	.000	.000	0	0	0	.000
Rodriguez,p	3	0	0	0	0	0	0	0	0	0	0	0	.000	.000	.000	0	1	0	1.000
Worrell,p	2	0	0	0	0	0	0	0	0	0	0	0	.000	.000	.000	0	2	0	1.000
Ponson,p	1	1	0	0	0	0	0	0	0	0	0	0	.000	.000	.000	0	0	0	.000
Williams,p	1	1	0	0	0	0	0	0	0	0	0	1	.000	.000	.000	0	1	0	1.000
Schmidt,p	1	3	0	0	0	0	0	0	0	0	0	2	.000	.000	.000	1	1	0	1.000
Torrealba,c	2	3	0	0	0	0	0	0	1	0	0	0	.000	.000	.000	10	0	1	.909
Galarraga,1b-ph	2	5	0	0	0	0	0	0	0	0	0	1	.000	.000	.000	10	1	0	1.000
Cruz,rf	4	11	0	0	0	0	0	0	1	2	1	4	.000	.154	.000	15	0	1	.938
Totals	4	136	16	32	41	7	1	0	15	20	8	28	.235	.338	.301	110	40	7	.955

FLORIDA MARLINS' PITCHING RECORDS

Pitcher	G	GS	CG	IP	H	R	ER	HR	BB	IBB	SO	HB	WP	W	L	Pct.	ERA
Pavano	3	0	0	2.2	1	0	0	0	1	1	1	1	0	2	0	1.000	0.00
Looper	2	0	0	1.2	1	1	0	0	2	1	0	0	0	1	0	1.000	0.00
Beckett	1	1	0	7.0	2	1	1	0	5	1	9	0	1	0	1	.000	1.29
Fox	3	0	0	5.0	3	1	1	0	3	2	3	0	0	0	0	.000	1.80
Redman	1	1	0	6.0	7	2	2	0	3	1	4	0	0	0	0	.000	3.00
Urbina	3	0	0	3.0	4	1	1	0	1	1	2	1	0	0	0	.000	3.00
Penny	2	1	0	5.2	5	4	4	0	1	0	6	0	0	0	0	.000	6.35
Willis	2	1	0	5.2	7	5	5	0	2	0	3	0	0	0	0	.000	7.94
Helling	1	0	0	0.1	2	1	1	0	2	1	0	0	0	0	0	.000	27.00
Totals	4	4	0	37.0	32	16	15	0	20	8	28	2	1	3	1	.750	3.65

No shutouts. Saves—Urbina.

SAN FRANCISCO GIANTS' PITCHING RECORDS

Pitcher	G	GS	CG	IP	H	R	ER	HR	BB	IBB	SO	HB	WP	W	L	Pct.	ERA
Schmidt	1	1	1	9.0	3	0	0	0	0	0	5	0	0	1	0	1.000	0.00
Herges	3	0	0	4.1	1	0	0	0	2	0	5	1	0	0	0	.000	0.00
Worrell	2	0	0	2.2	3	2	0	0	3	1	0	0	0	0	1	.000	0.00
Hermanson	1	0	0	1.0	1	0	0	0	1	0	0	0	0	0	0	.000	0.00
Eyre	1	0	0	0.1	0	0	0	0	0	0	0	0	0	0	0	.000	0.00
Rodriguez	3	0	0	4.0	4	3	1	0	1	1	5	1	0	0	1	.000	2.25
Rueter	1	1	0	5.0	3	2	2	1	2	0	2	0	0	0	0	.000	3.60
Brower	2	0	0	3.0	5	3	2	0	3	1	3	0	0	0	0	.000	6.00
Ponson	1	1	0	5.0	7	4	4	0	0	0	3	0	1	0	0	.000	7.20
Williams	1	1	0	2.0	5	3	3	0	1	0	1	0	0	0	0	.000	13.50
Nathan	2	0	0	0.1	4	3	3	1	1	0	1	0	0	0	1	.000	81.00
Christiansen	1	0	0	0.0	1	0	0	0	0	0	0	0	0	0	0	.000	-
Totals	4	4	1	36.2	37	20	15	2	14	3	25	2	1	1	3	.250	3.68

No saves. Shutouts—Schmidt.

SCORE BY INNINGS

Florida	3	1	2	2	3	3	1	3	0	0	2—20
San Francisco	1	1	0	4	1	6	0	1	1	0	1—16

MISCELLANEOUS STATISTICS

Sacrifice hits—Beckett, Cabrera, Cruz, Encarnacion, Santiago, Torrealba.
Sacrifice flies—Bonds, Torrealba.
Stolen bases—Bonds, Lee, Pierre.
Caught stealing—Grissom.
Double plays—Alfonzo and Snow; Durham, Aurilia and Snow.
Left on bases—Florida 4, 8, 12, 11—35; San Francisco 7, 6, 18, 5—36.
Scoring position—Florida 0 for 2, 4 for 13, 2 for 7, 3 for 16—9 for 38; San Francisco 2 for 9, 2 for 9, 2 for 16, 5 for 6—11 for 40.
Hit by pitcher—by Urbina (Durham), by Rodriguez (Lee), by Pavano (Hammonds), by Herges (Lee).
Passed balls—None.
Balks—None.
Time of games—2:33, 3:06, 4:11, 3:19-Avg.: 3:17.
Attendance—43,704, 43,766, 61,488, 65,464—214,422.
Umpires—Hirschbeck, John; Miller, Bill; Gorman, Brian; Young, Larry; Rapuano, Ed; Scott, Dale; Cederstrom, Gary; Kellogg, Jeff; Cuzzi, Phil; Froemming, Bruce.

CHICAGO VS. ATLANTA

RESULTS

Day	Date	Place	Score
Tue.	Sep. 30	Atlanta	Chicago 4, Atlanta 2
Wed.	Oct. 1	Atlanta	Atlanta 5, Chicago 3
Fri.	Oct. 3	Chicago	Chicago 3, Atlanta 1
Sat.	Oct. 4	Chicago	Atlanta 6, Chicago 4
Sun.	Oct. 5	Atlanta	Chicago 5, Atlanta 1

BOX SCORES

GAME 1

CHICAGO 4, ATLANTA 2

TUESDAY, SEPTEMBER 30, AT ATLANTA

Chi Cubs	AB	R	H	BI	BB	SO	PO	A
K.Lofton, cf	5	0	2	1	0	0	2	0
Grudzielanek, 2b	4	0	0	0	1	2	2	1
S.Sosa, rf	3	0	1	0	2	1	2	0
Alou, lf	5	1	2	0	0	1	1	0
A.Ramirez, 3b	2	1	1	0	2	0	0	1
Karros, 1b	4	1	2	0	0	1	3	1
A.Gonzalez, ss	2	0	0	0	0	1	1	0
Simon, ph	1	0	0	0	0	1	0	0
R.Martinez, ss	1	0	0	0	0	1	1	2
Bako, c	3	0	0	1	1	2	14	0
K.Wood, p	4	1	2	2	0	1	1	1
Remlinger, p	0	0	0	0	0	0	0	0
K.Farnsworth, p	0	0	0	0	0	0	0	0
Borowski, p	0	0	0	0	0	0	0	0
TOTALS	34	4	10	4	6	11	27	6

Atlanta	AB	R	H	RBI	BB	SO	PO	A
Furcal, ss	5	0	0	0	0	3	1	4
M.Giles, 2b	2	1	1	1	1	0	2	4
J.Garcia, 2b	0	0	0	0	0	0	1	1
DeRosa, ph-2b	0	0	0	0	1	0	1	0
Sheffield, rf	3	0	0	0	1	0	0	1
C.Jones, lf	4	0	0	1	0	2	0	0
A.Jones, cf	3	0	0	0	1	1	2	0
J.Lopez, c	4	0	1	0	0	1	12	0
Fick, 1b	3	0	0	0	1	2	6	1
Castilla, 3b	3	0	1	0	1	1	1	1
Ru.Ortiz, p	2	0	0	0	0	2	1	0
King, p	0	0	0	0	0	0	0	0
Gryboski, p	0	0	0	0	0	0	0	0
J.Wright, p	0	0	0	0	0	0	0	0
Mercker, p	0	0	0	0	0	0	0	0
M.Franco, ph	1	1	0	0	0	1	0	0
Ro.Hernandez, p	0	0	0	0	0	0	0	0
Ju.Franco, ph	1	0	0	0	0	1	0	0
TOTALS	31	2	3	2	6	14	27	12

Chi Cubs	0 0 0	0 0 4	0 0 0—4	10	0
Atlanta	0 0 1	0 0 0	0 1 0—2	3	1

Chi Cubs	IP	H	R	ER	HR	BB	SO
K.Wood (W)	7.1	2	2	2	1	5	11
Remlinger (HOLD)	0.1	0	0	0	0	0	0
K.Farnsworth (HOLD)	0.1	0	0	0	0	1	0
Borowski (S)	1.0	1	0	0	0	0	3

Atlanta	IP	H	R	ER	HR	BB	SO
Ru.Ortiz (L)	5.2	8	4	4	0	3	7
King	0.0	1	0	0	0	0	0
Gryboski	0.1	0	0	0	0	0	0
J.Wright	1.0	0	0	0	0	2	3
Mercker	1.0	0	0	0	0	1	1
Ro.Hernandez	1.0	1	0	0	0	0	0

King pitched to 1 batter in the 6th.

E—M.Giles. DP—Atlanta 3. LOB—Chi Cubs 9, Atlanta 8. Scoring Position—Chi Cubs 4 for 15, Atlanta 0 for 2. 2B—K.Wood. HR—M.Giles (3rd inning, 2 out, 0 on) off K.Wood. SB—K.Lofton, S.Sosa. WP—K.Wood. T—3:21. A—52,043. U—HP-Froemming, 1B-Wendelstedt, 2B-Scott, 3B-Cederstrom, LF-Kellogg, RF-Cuzzi.

HOW THEY SCORED

THIRD INNING

Braves—Ortiz struck out. Furcal grounded out, first baseman Karros to pitcher Wood. Giles homered to left on a 1-0 count. Sheffield lined out to center fielder Lofton. One run. Braves 1, Cubs 0.

SIXTH INNING

Cubs—Alou singled to center. Ramirez singled to center, Alou to second. Karros singled to left, Alou to third, Ramirez to second. Simon pinch-hitting for Gonzalez. Simon struck out. Bako grounded out, first baseman Fick to second baseman Giles to pitcher Ortiz, Alou scored, Ramirez to third, Karros to second. Wood doubled to center, Ramirez scored, Karros scored. King pitching. Lofton singled to center, Wood scored. Gryboski pitching. Grudzielanek grounded out, shortstop Furcal to first baseman Fick. Four runs. Cubs 4, Braves 1.

EIGHTH INNING

Braves—M.Franco pinch-hitting for Mercker. M.Franco struck out, safe on Wood wild pitch. Furcal struck out. DeRosa pinch-hitting for Garcia. DeRosa walked on a full count, M.Franco to second. Sheffield walked on a full count, M.Franco to third, DeRosa to second. Remlinger pitching. C.Jones grounded into fielder's choice, shortstop Martinez to second baseman Grudzielanek, M.Franco scored, DeRosa to third, Sheffield out. Farnsworth pitching. A.Jones walked, C.Jones to second. Lopez grounded into fielder's choice, shortstop Martinez to second baseman Grudzielanek, A.Jones out. One run. Cubs 4, Braves 2.

GAME 2

ATLANTA 5, CHICAGO 3

WEDNESDAY, OCTOBER 1, AT ATLANTA

Chi Cubs	AB	R	H	BI	BB	SO	PO	A
K.Lofton, cf	3	1	0	0	2	1	0	0
Grudzielanek, 2b	4	1	0	0	1	1	3	1
S.Sosa, rf	2	0	2	1	2	0	0	0
Alou, lf	3	0	1	1	1	1	4	0
A.Ramirez, 3b	4	0	1	0	0	1	3	4
Karros, 1b	4	0	1	0	0	1	5	0
Glanville, pr	0	1	0	0	0	0	0	0
A.Gonzalez, ss	0	0	0	0	0	0	1	0
R.Martinez, ss	3	0	0	0	0	1	1	2
Simon, ph-1b	1	0	1	0	0	0	1	1
D.Miller, c	2	0	0	0	1	2	6	1
Goodwin, ph	0	0	0	1	0	0	0	0
Bako, c	0	0	0	0	0	0	0	0
C.Zambrano, p	3	0	0	0	0	2	0	1
K.Farnsworth, p	0	0	0	0	0	0	0	0
Veres, p	0	0	0	0	0	0	0	0
O'Leary, ph	1	0	0	0	0	0	0	0
TOTALS	30	3	6	3	7	10	24	10

Atlanta	AB	R	H	BI	BB	SO	PO	A
Furcal, ss	3	2	2	0	1	0	4	2
DeRosa, 2b-3b	5	0	2	2	0	2	2	1
Sheffield, rf	5	0	1	0	0	0	2	0
C.Jones, lf	4	1	1	1	0	0	1	0
J.Lopez, c	4	1	3	0	0	1	10	1
A.Jones, cf	4	0	1	1	0	0	1	1
Fick, 1b	3	0	0	0	0	0	5	2
Ju.Franco, 1b	1	0	0	0	0	0	1	0
Castilla, 3b	3	0	1	0	1	2	0	3
J.Garcia, pr-2b	0	1	0	0	0	0	0	1
Hampton, p	2	0	1	0	0	0	1	2
M.Giles, ph	1	0	1	1	0	0	0	0
Bragg, pr	0	0	0	0	0	0	0	0

Atlanta	AB	R	H	BI	BB	SO	PO	A
King, p	0	0	0	0	0	0	0	0
Gryboski, p	0	0	0	0	0	0	0	0
Smoltz, p	0	0	0	0	0	0	0	0
TOTALS	35	5	13	5	2	5	27	13

Chi Cubs .... 2 0 0 0 0 0 0 1 0—3 6 0
Atlanta .... 1 0 0 1 0 1 0 2 x—5 13 0

Chi Cubs	IP	H	R	ER	HR	BB	SO
C.Zambrano	5.2	11	3	3	0	0	4
K.Farnsworth	1.1	1	0	0	0	0	1
Veres (L)	1.0	1	2	2	0	2	0

Atlanta	IP	H	R	ER	HR	BB	SO
Hampton	6.0	4	2	2	0	5	9
King	0.0	0	0	0	0	1	0
Gryboski (HOLD)	1.0	0	0	0	0	1	1
Smoltz (BS, W)	2.0	2	1	1	0	0	0

King pitched to 1 batter in the 7th.

DP—Atlanta 3. LOB—Chi Cubs 8, Atlanta 10. Scoring Position—Chi Cubs 2 for 10, Atlanta 5 for 13. 2B—S.Sosa, DeRosa. S—Goodwin. SH—Furcal, Smoltz. T—3:07. A—52,743. U—HP-Wendelstedt, 1B-Scott, 2B-Cederstrom, 3B-Kellogg, LF-Cuzzi, RF-Froemming.

HOW THEY SCORED

FIRST INNING

Cubs—Lofton walked. Grudzielanek walked on four pitches, Lofton to second. Sosa doubled to center, Lofton scored, Grudzielanek to third. Alou safe on failed fielder's choice, Grudzielanek scored. Ramirez singled to center, Sosa to third, Alou to second. Karros struck out. Martinez struck out. Miller struck out. Two runs. Cubs 2, Braves 0.

Braves—Furcal singled to center. DeRosa singled to right, Furcal to third. Sheffield fouled out to third baseman Ramirez. C.Jones grounded into fielder's choice, second baseman Grudzielanek to shortstop Martinez, Furcal scored, DeRosa out. Lopez struck out. One run. Cubs 2, Braves 1.

FOURTH INNING

Braves—Sheffield grounded out, third baseman Ramirez to first baseman Karros. C.Jones singled to center. Lopez singled to right, C.Jones to third. A.Jones singled to right, C.Jones scored, Lopez to second. Fick flied out to left fielder Alou. Castilla struck out. One run. Braves 2, Cubs 2.

SIXTH INNING

Braves—Lopez singled to center. A.Jones popped out to third baseman Ramirez. Fick fouled out to catcher Miller. Castilla singled to center, Lopez to second. Giles pinch-hitting for Hampton. Giles singled to left, Lopez scored, Castilla to second. Bragg pinch-running for Giles. Furcal infield single to pitcher Zambrano, Castilla to third, Bragg to second. Farnsworth pitching. DeRosa struck out. One run. Braves 3, Cubs 2.

EIGHTH INNNING

Cubs—J.Franco in as first baseman. Smoltz pitching. Ramirez flied out to right fielder Sheffield. Karros singled to center. Glanville pinch-running for Karros. Simon pinch-hitting for Martinez. Simon infield single to second, Glanville to third. Goodwin pinch-hitting for Miller. Goodwin hit a sacrifice fly to center fielder A.Jones, Glanville scored. Simon was out advancing, center fielder A.Jones to third baseman Castilla to second baseman DeRosa, Simon out. One run. Braves 3, Cubs 3.

Braves—Gonzalez in as shortstop. Simon in as first baseman. Bako in as catcher. Veres pitching. J.Franco grounded out, third baseman Ramirez to first baseman Simon. Castilla walked on a full count. Garcia pinch-running for Castilla. Smoltz sacrificed, first baseman Simon to second baseman Grudzielanek, Garcia to second. Furcal was intentionally walked. DeRosa doubled to center, Garcia scored, Furcal scored. Sheffield fouled out to shortstop Gonzalez. Two runs. Braves 5, Cubs 3.

GAME 3

CHICAGO 3, ATLANTA 1

FRIDAY, OCTOBER 3, AT CHICAGO

Atlanta	AB	R	H	BI	BB	SO	PO	A
Furcal, ss	4	0	0	0	0	1	1	6
M.Giles, 2b	3	0	1	1	0	1	1	3
Sheffield, rf	2	0	0	0	1	0	1	0
C.Jones, lf	3	0	0	0	1	0	2	0
J.Lopez, c	4	0	0	0	0	2	3	1
A.Jones, cf	2	0	0	0	2	2	3	0
Fick, 1b	4	0	0	0	0	0	11	1
Castilla, 3b	3	0	0	0	0	1	1	2
Maddux, p	2	0	0	0	0	0	0	0
J.Wright, p	0	0	0	0	0	0	0	1
DeRosa, ph	1	1	1	0	0	0	0	0
Gryboski, p	0	0	0	0	0	0	1	0
TOTALS	28	1	2	1	4	7	24	14

Chi Cubs	AB	R	H	BI	BB	SO	PO	A
K.Lofton, cf	4	1	2	0	0	0	3	0
Grudzielanek, 2b	4	1	1	0	0	0	4	4
S.Sosa, rf	4	0	0	0	0	1	1	0
Alou, lf	4	1	2	0	0	0	2	0
Simon, 1b	4	0	1	2	0	1	8	0
A.Ramirez, 3b	4	0	2	1	0	0	1	1
A.Gonzalez, ss	3	0	0	0	1	0	2	7
D.Miller, c	3	0	0	0	1	1	6	0
Prior, p	3	0	0	0	0	0	0	0
TOTALS	33	3	8	3	2	3	27	12

Atlanta .... 0 0 0 0 0 0 0 1 0—1 2 4
Chi Cubs .... 2 0 0 0 0 0 0 1 x—3 8 0

Atlanta	IP	H	R	ER	HR	BB	SO
Maddux (L)	6.0	6	2	2	0	1	1
J.Wright	1.0	0	0	0	0	0	0
Gryboski	1.0	2	1	1	0	1	2

Chi Cubs	IP	H	R	ER	HR	BB	SO
Prior (W)	9.0	2	1	1	0	4	7

E—J.Lopez, Castilla, Furcal, A.Jones. DP—Chi Cubs 1. LOB—Atlanta 6, Chi Cubs 8. Scoring Position—Atlanta 0 for 2, Chi Cubs 2 for 8. 2B—DeRosa, A.Ramirez. SB—K.Lofton 2, Alou. CS—A.Gonzalez. S—M.Giles. WP—Maddux, Prior. HBP—Sheffield by Prior. T—2:43. A—39,982. U—HP-Gorman, 1B-Young, 2B-Rapuano, 3B-Welke, LF-Hirschbeck, RF-Miller.

HOW THEY SCORED

FIRST INNING

Cubs—Lofton singled to right. Grudzielanek bunt single to first, Lofton to second. Sosa struck out. Alou flied out to center fielder A.Jones. Lofton stole third. On Maddux's wild pitch, Grudzielanek to second. Simon singled to right, Lofton scored, Grudzielanek scored. Ramirez singled to right, Simon to second. Gonzalez grounded into fielder's choice, shortstop Furcal to second baseman Giles, Ramirez out. Two runs. Cubs 2, Braves 0

EIGHTH INNING

Braves—DeRosa pinch-hitting for Wright. DeRosa doubled to center. Furcal grounded out, second baseman Grudzielanek to first baseman Simon, DeRosa to third. Giles hit a sacrifice fly to center fielder Lofton, DeRosa scored. Sheffield fouled out to third baseman Ramirez. One run. Cubs 2, Braves 1.

Cubs—Gryboski pitching. Sosa grounded out, first baseman Fick to pitcher Gryboski. Alou infield single to short. Simon struck out. Alou stole second. Ramirez doubled to right, Alou scored. Gonzalez was intentionally walked. Miller struck out. One run. Cubs 3, Braves 1.

GAME 4

ATLANTA 6, CHICAGO 4

SATURDAY, OCTOBER 4, AT CHICAGO

Atlanta	AB	R	H	RBI	BB	SO	PO	A
Furcal, ss	4	0	1	0	1	1	1	6
M.Giles, 2b	4	2	1	0	1	0	4	4
C.Jones, lf	3	2	2	4	2	0	0	0
J.Lopez, c	5	0	2	0	0	1	5	0
A.Jones, cf	4	1	0	0	1	2	2	0
Ju.Franco, 1b	4	1	3	0	1	1	12	1
Castilla, 3b	4	0	2	1	1	1	1	1
Bragg, rf	5	0	0	1	0	1	1	0
Ru.Ortiz, p	3	0	1	0	0	0	0	2
King, p	0	0	0	0	0	0	0	0
Gryboski, p	0	0	0	0	0	0	0	0
J.Wright, p	0	0	0	0	0	0	1	0
Fick, ph	1	0	0	0	0	0	0	0
Cunnane, p	0	0	0	0	0	0	0	0
M.Franco, ph	1	0	0	0	0	0	0	0
Smoltz, p	0	0	0	0	0	0	0	0
TOTALS	38	6	12	6	7	7	27	14

Chi Cubs	AB	R	H	BI	BB	SO	PO	A
K.Lofton, cf	5	0	0	0	0	1	1	0
Grudzielanek, 2b	4	0	1	0	1	0	2	4
S.Sosa, rf	4	1	0	0	1	0	4	0
Alou, lf	4	0	3	1	0	0	1	0
A.Ramirez, 3b	4	0	0	0	0	1	0	2
Karros, 1b	4	2	3	2	0	0	11	0
J.Cruz, p	0	0	0	0	0	0	0	0
A.Gonzalez, ss	3	0	1	0	1	1	1	4
Bako, c	1	0	0	0	1	0	4	1
Glanville, ph	1	0	0	0	0	0	0	0
Veres, p	0	0	0	0	0	0	0	0
K.Farnsworth, p	0	0	0	0	0	0	0	1
M.Guthrie, p	0	0	0	0	0	0	0	0
Simon, 1b	1	1	1	0	0	0	0	0
Clement, p	2	0	0	0	0	1	0	0
Alfonseca, p	0	0	0	0	0	0	0	0
Remlinger, p	0	0	0	0	0	0	0	0
D.Miller, ph-c	2	0	1	1	0	1	3	0
TOTALS	35	4	10	4	4	5	27	12

Atlanta	0 0 0	1 3 0	0 2 0—6	12	0
Chi Cubs	0 0 1	0 0 1	0 1 1—4	10	0

Atlanta	IP	H	R	ER	HR	BB	SO
Ru.Ortiz (W)	5.0	7	2	2	1	4	2
King (HOLD)	0.2	0	0	0	0	0	0
Gryboski (HOLD)	0.1	0	0	0	0	0	1
J.Wright (HOLD)	1.0	0	0	0	0	0	0
Cunnane	1.0	1	1	1	1	0	1
Smoltz (S)	1.0	2	1	1	0	0	1

Chi Cubs	IP	H	R	ER	HR	BB	SO
Clement (L)	4.2	8	4	4	1	4	3
Alfonseca	1.0	1	0	0	0	0	0
Remlinger	0.1	0	0	0	0	1	1
Veres	0.1	1	0	0	0	0	0
K.Farnsworth	1.0	0	0	0	0	0	1
M.Guthrie	0.2	2	2	2	1	1	0
J.Cruz	1.0	0	0	0	0	1	2

Ru.Ortiz pitched to 2 batters in the 6th.

DP—Atlanta 2. LOB—Atlanta 12, Chi Cubs 8. Scoring Position—Atlanta 2 for 9, Chi Cubs 1 for 10. 2B—J.Lopez, Alou, D.Miller, Simon. HR—C.Jones (5th inning, 1 out, 1 on) off Clement, Karros (6th inning, 0 out, 0 on) off Ru.Ortiz, C.Jones (8th inning, 2 out, 1 on) off M.Guthrie, Karros (8th inning, 2 out, 0 on) off Cunnane. SB—Furcal. WP—Clement, M.Guthrie. T—3:40. A—39,983. U—HP-Young, 1B-Rapuano, 2B-Welke, 3B-Hirschbeck, LF-Miller, RF-Gorman.

HOW THEY SCORED

THIRD INNING

Cubs—Lofton grounded out, third baseman Castilla to first baseman J.Franco. Grudzielanek grounded out, pitcher Ortiz to first baseman J.Franco. Sosa walked on a full count. Alou doubled to left, Sosa scored. Ramirez popped out to first baseman J.Franco. One run. Cubs 1, Braves 0.

FOURTH INNING

Braves—A.Jones struck out. J.Franco walked on a full count. Castilla singled to center, J.Franco to third. Bragg grounded into fielder's choice, shortstop Gonzalez to second baseman Grudzielanek, J.Franco scored, Castilla out. Ortiz grounded out, third baseman Ramirez to first baseman Karros. One run. Braves 1, Cubs 1.

FIFTH INNING

Braves—Furcal singled to right. Giles grounded into fielder's choice, shortstop Gonzalez to second baseman Grudzielanek, Furcal out. C.Jones homered to center on a 1-0 count, Giles scored. Lopez grounded out, shortstop Gonzalez to first baseman Karros. A.Jones walked on a full count. J.Franco singled to center, A.Jones to third. Castilla singled to left, A.Jones scored, J.Franco to second. Alfonseca pitching. Bragg grounded out, second baseman Grudzielanek to first baseman Karros. Three runs. Braves 4, Cubs 1.

SIXTH INNING

Cubs—Karros homered to left on a 1-0 count. Gonzalez walked on four pitches. King pitching. Glanville pinch-hitting for Bako. Glanville grounded into a double play, shortstop Furcal to second baseman Giles to first baseman J.Franco, Gonzalez out. Miller pinch-hitting for Remlinger. Gryboski pitching. Miller struck out. One run. Braves 4, Cubs 2.

EIGHTH INNING

Braves—Fick pinch-hitting for Wright. Fick was out bunting, pitcher Farnsworth to first baseman Karros. Guthrie pitching. Furcal flied out to right fielder Sosa. Giles walked. On Guthrie's wild pitch, Giles to second. C.Jones homered to left on a full count, Giles scored. Lopez doubled to right. A.Jones grounded out, second baseman Grudzielanek to first baseman Karros. Two runs. Braves 6, Cubs 2.

Cubs—Cunnane pitching. Alou popped out to second baseman Giles. Ramirez struck out. Karros homered to center on a 3-1 count. Gonzalez grounded out, shortstop Furcal to first baseman J.Franco. One run. Braves 6, Cubs 3.

NINTH INNING

Cubs—Smoltz pitching. Simon doubled to left. Miller doubled to right, Simon scored. Lofton struck out. Grudzielanek popped out to second baseman Giles. Sosa flied out to center fielder A.Jones. One run. Braves 6, Cubs 4.

GAME 5

CHICAGO 5, ATLANTA 1

SUNDAY, OCTOBER 5, AT ATLANTA

Chi Cubs	AB	R	H	BI	BB	SO	PO	A
K.Lofton, cf	4	1	2	0	0	0	2	1
Grudzielanek, 2b	4	0	1	0	0	1	4	3
S.Sosa, rf	3	0	0	0	1	2	1	0
Alou, lf	4	1	2	1	0	2	2	0
A.Ramirez, 3b	4	1	1	2	0	0	0	2
Karros, 1b	4	1	0	0	0	1	8	0
A.Gonzalez, ss	4	1	2	1	0	1	1	6
D.Miller, c	4	0	0	0	0	1	9	0
K.Wood, p	3	0	0	0	0	1	0	0
Goodwin, ph	1	0	1	1	0	0	0	0
Borowski, p	0	0	0	0	0	0	0	0
TOTALS	35	5	9	5	1	9	27	12

Atlanta	AB	R	H	BI	BB	SO	PO	A
Furcal, ss	3	1	1	0	1	0	1	4
M.Giles, 2b	4	0	1	0	0	1	3	0
Sheffield, rf	4	0	1	1	0	0	1	0

Atlanta	AB	R	H	BI	BB	SO	PO	A
C.Jones, lf	4	0	0	0	0	2	1	0
J.Lopez, c	4	0	1	0	0	1	9	2
A.Jones, cf	4	0	0	0	0	2	0	0
Ju.Franco, 1b	2	0	1	0	1	0	11	0
Castilla, 3b	3	0	0	0	0	1	0	7
Hampton, p	2	0	0	0	0	2	0	2
Gryboski, p	0	0	0	0	0	0	0	0
J.Wright, p	0	0	0	0	0	0	0	0
DeRosa, ph	1	0	0	0	0	0	0	0
Cunnane, p	0	0	0	0	0	0	0	0
King, p	0	0	0	0	0	0	1	0
TOTALS	31	1	5	1	2	9	27	15

Chi Cubs .... 1 1 0 0 0 2 0 0 1—5 9 0
Atlanta .... 0 0 0 0 0 1 0 0 0—1 5 1

Chi Cubs	IP	H	R	ER	HR	BB	SO
K.Wood (W)	8.0	5	1	1	0	2	7
Borowski	1.0	0	0	0	0	0	2

Atlanta	IP	H	R	ER	HR	BB	SO
Hampton (L)	6.2	7	4	4	2	1	7
Gryboski	0.1	0	0	0	0	0	0
J.Wright	1.0	0	0	0	0	0	1
Cunnane	0.2	2	1	0	0	0	1
King	0.1	0	0	0	0	0	0

E—Castilla. DP—Chi Cubs 1. LOB—Chi Cubs 4, Atlanta 5. Scoring Position—Chi Cubs 2 for 6, Atlanta 0 for 3. 2B—K.Lofton, Goodwin, J.Lopez, Ju.Franco. HR—A.Gonzalez (2nd inning, 0 out, 0 on) off Hampton, A.Ramirez (6th inning, 1 out, 1 on) off Hampton. CS—K.Lofton. WP—Hampton. T—2:50. A—54,357. U—HP-Kellogg, 1B-Cuzzi, 2B-Froemming, 3B-Wendelstedt, LF-Scott, RF-Cederstrom.

HOW THEY SCORED

FIRST INNING

Cubs—Lofton doubled to right. Grudzielanek struck out. On Hampton's wild pitch, Lofton to third. Sosa walked. Alou singled to left, Lofton scored, Sosa to second. Ramirez grounded into fielder's choice, third baseman Castilla to second baseman Giles, Sosa to third, Alou out. Karros struck out. One run. Cubs 1, Braves 0.

SECOND INNING

Cubs—Gonzalez homered to center on a 1-0 count. Miller grounded out, shortstop Furcal to first baseman J.Franco. Wood struck out. Lofton grounded out, third baseman Castilla to first baseman J.Franco. One run. Cubs 2, Braves 0.

SIXTH INNING

Cubs—Sosa struck out. Alou infield single to second. Ramirez homered to center on a 1-0 count, Alou scored. Karros grounded out, third baseman Castilla to first baseman J.Franco. Gonzalez flied out to left fielder C.Jones. Two runs. Cubs 4, Braves 0.

Braves—Furcal walked. Giles singled to left, Furcal to second. Sheffield grounded into fielder's choice, center fielder Lofton to second baseman Grudzielanek, Furcal scored, Giles out. C.Jones grounded into a double play, shortstop Gonzalez to second baseman Grudzielanek to first baseman Karros, Sheffield out. One run. Cubs 4, Braves 1.

NINTH INNING

Cubs—Cunnane pitching. Ramirez popped out to second baseman Giles. Karros safe on Castilla's error. Gonzalez singled to left, Karros to third. Miller struck out. Goodwin pinch-hitting for Wood. Goodwin doubled to right, Karros scored, Gonzalez to third. King pitching. Gonzalez was out advancing, catcher Lopez to pitcher King, Gonzalez out. One run. Cubs 5, Braves 1.

STATISTICS

CHICAGO CUBS' BATTING AND FIELDING AVERAGES

	BATTING														FIELDING			
Player, position	G	AB	R	H	TB	2B	3B	HR	RBI	BB	IBB	SO	Avg.	OBP	Slg.	PO	A	E	Avg.
Goodwin,ph	2	1	0	1	2	1	0	0	2	0	0	0	1.000	.500	2.000	0	0	0	.000
Alou,lf	5	20	3	10	11	1	0	0	3	1	0	4	.500	.524	.550	10	0	0	1.000
Simon,ph-1b	4	7	1	3	4	1	0	0	2	0	0	2	.429	.429	.571	9	1	0	1.000
Karros,1b	4	16	4	6	12	0	0	2	2	0	0	3	.375	.375	.750	27	1	0	1.000
Lofton,cf	5	21	3	6	7	1	0	0	1	2	0	2	.286	.348	.333	8	1	0	1.000
Wood,p	2	7	1	2	3	1	0	0	2	0	0	2	.286	.286	.429	1	1	0	1.000
Ramirez,3b	5	18	2	5	9	1	0	1	3	2	0	2	.278	.350	.500	4	10	0	1.000
Gonzalez,ss	5	12	1	3	6	0	0	1	1	2	1	3	.250	.357	.500	6	17	0	1.000
Sosa,rf	5	16	1	3	4	1	0	0	1	6	1	4	.188	.409	.250	8	0	0	1.000
Grudzielanek,2b	5	20	2	3	3	0	0	0	0	3	0	4	.150	.261	.150	15	13	0	1.000
Miller,c-ph	4	11	0	1	2	1	0	0	1	2	0	5	.091	.231	.182	24	1	0	1.000
Alfonseca,p	1	0	0	0	0	0	0	0	0	0	0	0	.000	.000	.000	0	0	0	.000
Borowski,p	2	0	0	0	0	0	0	0	0	0	0	0	.000	.000	.000	0	0	0	.000
Cruz,p	1	0	0	0	0	0	0	0	0	0	0	0	.000	.000	.000	0	0	0	.000
Farnsworth,p	3	0	0	0	0	0	0	0	0	0	0	0	.000	.000	.000	0	1	0	1.000
Guthrie,p	1	0	0	0	0	0	0	0	0	0	0	0	.000	.000	.000	0	0	0	.000
Remlinger,p	2	0	0	0	0	0	0	0	0	0	0	0	.000	.000	.000	0	0	0	.000
Veres,p	2	0	0	0	0	0	0	0	0	0	0	0	.000	.000	.000	0	0	0	.000
Glanville,pr-ph	2	1	1	0	0	0	0	0	0	0	0	0	.000	.000	.000	0	0	0	.000
O'Leary,ph	1	1	0	0	0	0	0	0	0	0	0	0	.000	.000	.000	0	0	0	.000
Clement,p	1	2	0	0	0	0	0	0	0	0	0	1	.000	.000	.000	0	0	0	.000
Prior,p	1	3	0	0	0	0	0	0	0	0	0	0	.000	.000	.000	0	0	0	.000
Zambrano,p	1	3	0	0	0	0	0	0	0	0	0	2	.000	.000	.000	0	1	0	1.000
Bako,c	3	4	0	0	0	0	0	0	1	2	0	2	.000	.333	.000	18	1	0	1.000
Martinez,ss	2	4	0	0	0	0	0	0	0	0	0	2	.000	.000	.000	2	4	0	1.000
Totals	5	167	19	43	63	8	0	4	19	20	2	38	.257	.335	.377	132	52	0	1.000

ATLANTA BRAVES' BATTING AND FIELDING AVERAGES

	BATTING														FIELDING			
Player, position	G	AB	R	H	TB	2B	3B	HR	RBI	BB	IBB	SO	Avg.	OBP	Slg.	PO	A	E	Avg.
Franco,ph-1b	4	8	1	4	5	1	0	0	0	2	0	2	.500	.600	.625	24	1	0	1.000
DeRosa,2b-ph-3b	4	7	1	3	5	2	0	0	2	1	0	2	.429	.500	.714	3	1	0	1.000
Giles,2b-ph	5	14	3	5	8	0	0	1	3	2	0	2	.357	.412	.571	10	11	1	.955

Player, position	G	AB	R	H	TB	2B	3B	HR	RBI	BB	IBB	SO	Avg.	OBP	Slg.	PO	A	E	Avg.
	BATTING															FIELDING			
Lopez,c	5	21	1	7	9	2	0	0	0	0	0	6	.333	.333	.429	39	4	1	.977
Castilla,3b	5	16	0	4	4	0	0	0	1	3	0	6	.250	.368	.250	3	14	2	.895
Hampton,p	2	4	0	1	1	0	0	0	0	0	0	2	.250	.250	.250	1	4	0	1.000
Furcal,ss	5	19	3	4	4	0	0	0	0	3	1	5	.211	.318	.211	8	22	1	.968
Ortiz,p	2	5	0	1	1	0	0	0	0	0	0	2	.200	.200	.200	1	2	0	1.000
Jones,lf	5	18	3	3	9	0	0	2	6	3	0	4	.167	.286	.500	4	0	0	1.000
Sheffield,rf	4	14	0	2	2	0	0	0	1	2	0	0	.143	.294	.143	4	1	0	1.000
Jones,cf	5	17	1	1	1	0	0	0	1	4	0	7	.059	.238	.059	8	1	1	.900
Cunnane,p	2	0	0	0	0	0	0	0	0	0	0	0	.000	.000	.000	0	0	0	.000
Garcia,2b-pr	2	0	1	0	0	0	0	0	0	0	0	0	.000	.000	.000	1	2	0	1.000
Gryboski,p	5	0	0	0	0	0	0	0	0	0	0	0	.000	.000	.000	1	0	0	1.000
Hernandez,p	1	0	0	0	0	0	0	0	0	0	0	0	.000	.000	.000	0	0	0	.000
King,p	4	0	0	0	0	0	0	0	0	0	0	0	.000	.000	.000	1	0	0	1.000
Mercker,p	1	0	0	0	0	0	0	0	0	0	0	0	.000	.000	.000	0	0	0	.000
Smoltz,p	2	0	0	0	0	0	0	0	0	0	0	0	.000	.000	.000	0	0	0	.000
Wright,p	4	0	0	0	0	0	0	0	0	0	0	0	.000	.000	.000	1	1	0	1.000
Franco,ph	2	2	1	0	0	0	0	0	0	0	0	1	.000	.000	.000	0	0	0	.000
Maddux,p	1	2	0	0	0	0	0	0	0	0	0	0	.000	.000	.000	0	0	0	.000
Bragg,pr-rf	2	5	0	0	0	0	0	0	1	0	0	1	.000	.000	.000	1	0	0	1.000
Fick,1b-ph	4	11	0	0	0	0	0	0	0	1	0	2	.000	.083	.000	22	4	0	1.000
Totals	5	163	15	35	49	5	0	3	15	21	1	42	.215	.306	.301	132	68	6	.971

CHICAGO CUBS' PITCHING RECORDS

Pitcher	G	GS	CG	IP	H	R	ER	HR	BB	IBB	SO	HB	WP	W	L	Pct.	ERA
Farnsworth	3	0	0	2.2	1	0	0	0	1	0	2	0	0	0	0	.000	0.00
Borowski	2	0	0	2.0	1	0	0	0	0	0	5	0	0	0	0	.000	0.00
Alfonseca	1	0	0	1.0	1	0	0	0	0	0	0	0	0	0	0	.000	0.00
Cruz	1	0	0	1.0	0	0	0	0	1	0	2	0	0	0	0	.000	0.00
Remlinger	2	0	0	0.2	0	0	0	0	1	0	1	0	0	0	0	.000	0.00
Prior	1	1	1	9.0	2	1	1	0	4	0	7	1	1	1	0	1.000	1.00
Wood	2	2	0	15.1	7	3	3	1	7	0	18	0	1	2	0	1.000	1.76
Zambrano	1	1	0	5.2	11	3	3	0	0	0	4	0	0	0	0	.000	4.76
Clement	1	1	0	4.2	8	4	4	1	4	0	3	0	1	0	1	.000	7.71
Veres	2	0	0	1.1	2	2	2	0	2	1	0	0	0	0	1	.000	13.50
Guthrie	1	0	0	0.2	2	2	2	1	1	0	0	0	1	0	0	.000	27.00
Totals	5	5	1	44.0	35	15	15	3	21	1	42	1	4	3	2	.600	3.07

No shutouts. Saves—Borowski.

ATLANTA BRAVES' PITCHING RECORDS

Pitcher	G	GS	CG	IP	H	R	ER	HR	BB	IBB	SO	HB	WP	W	L	Pct.	ERA
Wright	4	0	0	4.0	0	0	0	0	2	0	4	0	0	0	0	.000	0.00
Hernandez	1	0	0	1.0	1	0	0	0	0	0	0	0	0	0	0	.000	0.00
King	4	0	0	1.0	1	0	0	0	1	0	0	0	0	0	0	.000	0.00
Mercker	1	0	0	1.0	0	0	0	0	1	0	1	0	0	0	0	.000	0.00
Maddux	1	1	0	6.0	6	2	2	0	1	0	1	0	1	0	1	.000	3.00
Gryboski	5	0	0	3.0	2	1	1	0	2	1	4	0	0	0	0	.000	3.00
Hampton	2	2	0	12.2	11	6	6	2	6	0	16	0	1	0	1	.000	4.26
Ortiz	2	2	0	10.2	15	6	6	1	7	1	9	0	0	1	1	.500	5.06
Cunnane	2	0	0	1.2	3	2	1	1	0	0	2	0	0	0	0	.000	5.40
Smoltz	2	0	0	3.0	4	2	2	0	0	0	1	0	0	1	0	1.000	6.00
Totals	5	5	0	44.0	43	19	18	4	20	2	38	0	2	2	3	.400	3.68

No shutouts. Saves—Smoltz.

SCORE BY INNINGS

Chicago	5	1	1	0	0	7	0	3	2	—19
Atlanta	1	0	1	2	3	2	0	6	0	—15

MISCELLANEOUS STATISTICS

Sacrifice hits—Furcal, Smoltz.
Sacrifice flies—Giles, Goodwin.
Stolen bases—Lofton 3, Alou, Furcal, Sosa.
Caught stealing—Gonzalez, Lofton.
Double plays—Furcal, Giles and Franco 2; Castilla, DeRosa and Fick; Castilla, Giles and Fick; Furcal, Garcia and Fick; Furcal, Giles and Fick; Gonzalez, Grudzielanek and Karros; Grudzielanek, Gonzalez and Simon; Hampton, Furcal and Fick.
Left on bases—Chicago 9, 8, 8, 8, 4—37; Atlanta 8, 10, 6, 12, 5—41.
Scoring position—Chicago 4 for 15, 2 for 10, 2 for 8, 1 for 10, 2 for 6—11 for 49; Atlanta 0 for 2, 5 for 13, 0 for 2, 2 for 9, 0 for 3—7 for 29.
Hit by pitcher—by Prior (Sheffield).
Passed balls—None.
Balks—None.
Time of games—3:21, 3:07, 2:43, 3:40, 2:50-Avg.: 3:08.
Attendance—52,043, 52,743, 39,982, 39,983, 54,357—239,108.
Umpires—Froemming, Bruce; Wendelstedt, Hunter; Scott, Dale; Cederstrom, Gary; Kellogg, Jeff; Gorman, Brian; Young, Larry; Rapuano, Ed; Welke, Bill; Hirschbeck, John; Cuzzi, Phil.

A.L. CHAMPIONSHIP SERIES

BOSTON VS. NEW YORK

RESULTS

Day	Date	Place	Score
Wed.	Oct. 8	New York	Boston 5, New York 2
Thur.	Oct. 9	New York	New York 6, Boston 2
Sat.	Oct. 11	Boston	New York 4, Boston 3
Mon.	Oct. 13	Boston	Boston 3, New York 2
Tue.	Oct 14	Boston	New York 4, Boston 2
Wed.	Oct. 15	New York	Boston 9, New York 6
Thur.	Oct 16	New York	New York 6, Boston 5

BOX SCORES

GAME 1

BOSTON 5, NEW YORK 2

WEDNESDAY, OCTOBER 8, AT NEW YORK

Boston	AB	R	H	BI	BB	SO	PO	A
To.Walker, 2b	5	1	2	1	0	0	1	4
D.Jackson, pr-2b	0	0	0	0	0	0	0	0
Mueller, 3b	5	0	1	0	0	0	2	0
Garciaparra, ss	5	0	0	0	0	2	1	0
M.Ramirez, lf	5	3	4	1	0	0	2	0
D.Ortiz, dh	3	1	1	2	1	1	0	0
Millar, 1b	5	0	2	1	0	2	8	0
Nixon, rf	3	0	2	0	1	0	2	0
Mirabelli, c	4	0	1	0	0	1	6	0
Kapler, cf	4	0	0	0	0	1	5	0
Wakefield, p	0	0	0	0	0	0	0	0
Embree, p	0	0	0	0	0	0	0	0
Timlin, p	0	0	0	0	0	0	0	0
Williamson, p	0	0	0	0	0	0	0	0
TOTALS	39	5	13	5	2	7	27	4

NY Yankees	AB	R	H	BI	BB	SO	PO	A
A.Soriano, 2b	4	0	0	0	0	2	1	2
Jeter, ss	4	0	0	0	0	0	3	2
Ja.Giambi, dh	3	1	0	0	1	1	0	0
B.Williams, cf	3	1	0	0	1	0	4	0
Posada, c	4	0	2	1	0	1	7	2
Matsui, lf	2	0	1	1	0	0	1	0
A.Boone, 3b	3	0	0	0	0	0	0	0
N.Johnson, 1b	3	0	0	0	0	0	8	1
J.Rivera, rf	2	0	0	0	0	1	3	0
Sierra, ph-rf	1	0	0	0	0	0	0	0
Mussina, p	0	0	0	0	0	0	0	1
F.Heredia, p	0	0	0	0	0	0	0	0
J.Nelson, p	0	0	0	0	0	0	0	0
G.White, p	0	0	0	0	0	0	0	1
Contreras, p	0	0	0	0	0	0	0	0
TOTALS	29	2	3	2	2	5	27	9

Boston	0 0 0	2 2 0	1 0 0—5	13 0
NY Yankees	0 0 0	0 0 0	2 0 0—2	3 0

Boston	IP	H	R	ER	HR	BB	SO
Wakefield (W)	6.0	2	2	2	0	2	2
Embree	1.0	1	0	0	0	0	0
Timlin (HOLD)	1.0	0	0	0	0	0	1
Williamson (S)	1.0	0	0	0	0	0	2

NY Yankees	IP	H	R	ER	HR	BB	SO
Mussina (L)	5.2	8	4	4	3	2	4
F.Heredia	0.2	0	0	0	0	0	0
J.Nelson	0.1	2	1	1	0	0	0
G.White	1.1	2	0	0	0	0	0
Contreras	1.0	1	0	0	0	0	3

Wakefield pitched to 2 batters in the 7th.

LOB—Boston 10, NY Yankees 3. Scoring Position—Boston 2 for 8, NY Yankees 1 for 5. 2B—Posada. HR—D.Ortiz (4th inning, 0 out, 1 on) off Mussina, To.Walker (5th inning, 0 out, 0 on) off Mussina, M.Ramirez (5th inning, 2 out, 0 on) off Mussina. CS—D.Jackson. S—Matsui. WP—Contreras. HBP—D.Ortiz by J.Nelson. T—3:20. A—56,281. U—HP-McClelland, 1B-Craft, 2B-Marquez, 3B-Cousins, LF-West, RF-Hernandez.

HOW THEY SCORED

FOURTH INNING

Red Sox—Ramirez infield single to pitcher Mussina. Ortiz homered to right on a full count, Ramirez scored. Millar struck out. Nixon singled to center. Mirabelli struck out. Kapler struck out. Two runs. Red Sox 2, Yankees 0.

FIFTH INNING

Red Sox—Walker homered to right on a 2-0 count. Mueller flied out to center fielder Williams. Garciaparra struck out. Ramirez homered to right on a 1-1 count. Ortiz grounded out, catcher Posada to first baseman Johnson. Two runs. Red Sox 4, Yankees 0.

SEVENTH INNING

Red Sox—Mueller grounded out, shortstop Jeter to first baseman Johnson. Nelson pitching. Garciaparra grounded out, catcher Posada to first baseman Johnson. Ramirez singled to right. Ortiz was hit by a pitch, Ramirez to second. Millar singled to left, Ramirez scored, Ortiz to second. White pitching. Nixon singled to right, Ortiz to third, Millar to second. Mirabelli grounded into fielder's choice, second baseman Soriano to shortstop Jeter, Nixon out. Two runs. Red Sox 5, Yankees 0.

Yankees—Giambi walked. Williams walked on four pitches, Giambi to second. Embree pitching. Posada doubled to center, Giambi scored, Williams to third. Matsui hit a sacrifice fly to left fielder Ramirez, Williams scored. Boone flied out to center fielder Kapler. Johnson lined out to center fielder Kapler. Two runs. Red Sox 5, Yankees 2.

GAME 2

NEW YORK 6, BOSTON 2

THURSDAY, OCTOBER 9, AT NEW YORK

Boston	AB	R	H	BI	BB	SO	PO	A
Kapler, cf	4	0	1	0	0	2	0	0
McCarty, ph	1	0	0	0	0	1	0	0
Mueller, 3b	4	0	1	0	0	1	0	2
Garciaparra, ss	4	0	2	0	0	0	1	7
M.Ramirez, lf	4	0	1	0	0	1	2	0
D.Ortiz, dh	3	0	0	0	1	0	0	0
Millar, 1b	4	0	0	0	0	1	12	4
Varitek, c	4	2	2	1	0	0	5	0
Nixon, rf	3	0	1	0	1	1	0	1
D.Jackson, 2b	3	0	1	1	0	1	2	4
To.Walker, ph	1	0	1	0	0	0	0	0
Lowe, p	0	0	0	0	0	0	1	1
Sauerbeck, p	0	0	0	0	0	0	0	0
Arroyo, p	0	0	0	0	0	0	1	0
TOTALS	35	2	10	2	2	8	24	19

NY Yankees	AB	R	H	BI	BB	SO	PO	A
A.Soriano, 2b	4	0	0	0	0	2	2	2
Jeter, ss	5	1	1	0	0	1	4	3
Ja.Giambi, dh	3	0	2	0	1	0	0	0
Dellucci, pr-dh	0	1	0	0	0	0	0	0
B.Williams, cf	3	2	2	1	1	0	1	0
Posada, c	3	0	1	2	1	0	8	1
Matsui, lf	3	1	1	1	1	0	1	0
N.Johnson, 1b	4	1	1	2	0	0	8	0
A.Boone, 3b	3	0	0	0	0	1	1	1

NY Yankees	AB	R	H	BI	BB	SO	PO	A
K.Garcia, rf	4	0	0	0	0	0	2	0
Pettitte, p	0	0	0	0	0	0	0	0
Contreras, p	0	0	0	0	0	0	0	0
M.Rivera, p	0	0	0	0	0	0	0	0
TOTALS	32	6	8	6	4	4	27	7

Boston .... 0 1 0 0 0 1 0 0 0—2 10 1
NY Yankees .... 0 2 1 0 1 0 2 0 x—6 8 0

Boston	IP	H	R	ER	HR	BB	SO
Lowe (L)	6.2	7	6	6	1	3	2
Sauerbeck	0.1	1	0	0	0	1	0
Arroyo	1.0	0	0	0	0	0	2

NY Yankees	IP	H	R	ER	HR	BB	SO
Pettitte (W)	6.2	9	2	2	1	2	5
Contreras (HOLD)	1.1	0	0	0	0	0	1
M.Rivera	1.0	1	0	0	0	0	2

E—D.Jackson. DP—NY Yankees 2. LOB—Boston 8, NY Yankees 8. Scoring Position—Boston 2 for 7, NY Yankees 3 for 11. 2B—Varitek, B.Williams, Posada. HR—N.Johnson (2nd inning, 1 out, 1 on) off Lowe, Varitek (6th inning, 2 out, 0 on) off Pettitte. SB—Nixon, A.Boone. CS—Kapler. PB—Varitek. HBP—A.Boone by Lowe, A.Soriano by Arroyo. T—3:05. A—56,295. U—HP-Craft, 1B-Marquez, 2B-Cousins, 3B-West, LF-Hernandez, RF-McClelland.

HOW THEY SCORED

SECOND INNING

Red Sox—Varitek doubled to right. Nixon singled to center, Varitek to third. Jackson singled to center, Varitek scored, Nixon to second. Kapler grounded into a double play, shortstop Jeter to first baseman Johnson, Nixon to third, Jackson out. Mueller grounded out, third baseman Boone to first baseman Johnson. One run. Red Sox 1, Yankees 0.

Yankees—Posada walked. Matsui grounded into fielder's choice, second baseman Jackson to shortstop Garciaparra, Posada out. Johnson homered to right on a 0-1 count, Matsui scored. Boone grounded out, third baseman Mueller to first baseman Millar. Garcia grounded out, shortstop Garciaparra to first baseman Millar. Two runs. Yankees 2, Red Sox 1.

THIRD INNING

Yankees—Soriano flied out to left fielder Ramirez. Jeter infield single to third. Giambi singled to left, Jeter to second. Williams singled to right, Jeter scored, Giambi to second. Posada safe on Jackson's error, Giambi to third, Williams to second. Matsui grounded into fielder's choice, first baseman Millar to catcher Varitek, Giambi out, Williams to third, Posada to second. Johnson grounded out, shortstop Garciaparra to first baseman Millar. One run. Yankees 3, Red Sox 1.

FIFTH INNING

Yankees—Giambi grounded out, pitcher Lowe to first baseman Millar. Williams doubled to center. Posada flied out to left fielder Ramirez. Matsui singled to right, Williams scored. Matsui was out advancing, right fielder Nixon to first baseman Millar to shortstop Garciaparra to second baseman Jackson, Matsui out. One run. Yankees 4, Red Sox 1.

SIXTH INNING

Red Sox—Ortiz flied out to left fielder Matsui. Millar struck out. Varitek homered to left on a 1-0 count. Nixon flied out to center fielder Williams. One run. Yankees 4, Red Sox 2.

SEVENTH INNING

Yankees—Soriano grounded out, first baseman Millar unassisted. Jeter grounded out, third baseman Mueller to first baseman Millar. Giambi singled to right. Williams walked on four pitches, Giambi to second. Sauerbeck pitching. Dellucci pinch-running for Giambi. Posada doubled to center, Dellucci scored, Williams scored. On Varitek's passed ball, Posada to third. Matsui walked on a full count. Johnson grounded out, second baseman Jackson to first baseman Millar. Two runs. Yankees 6, Red Sox 2.

GAME 3

NEW YORK 4, BOSTON 3

SATURDAY, OCTOBER 11, AT BOSTON

NY Yankees	AB	R	H	BI	BB	SO	PO	A
E.Wilson, 3b	4	0	0	0	0	1	0	1
A.Boone, 3b	0	0	0	0	0	0	1	0
Jeter, ss	4	1	2	1	0	1	2	4
Ja.Giambi, dh	4	0	0	0	0	1	0	0
B.Williams, cf	4	0	0	0	0	2	3	0
Posada, c	3	2	1	0	1	1	7	1
N.Johnson, 1b	4	1	2	0	0	1	9	1
Matsui, lf	4	0	1	1	0	0	1	0
K.Garcia, rf	2	0	1	1	0	0	1	0
J.Rivera, rf	0	0	0	0	0	0	0	0
A.Soriano, 2b	3	0	0	0	0	1	2	4
Clemens, p	0	0	0	0	0	0	0	0
F.Heredia, p	0	0	0	0	0	0	0	0
Contreras, p	0	0	0	0	0	0	0	0
M.Rivera, p	0	0	0	0	0	0	1	1
TOTALS	32	4	7	3	1	8	27	12

Boston	AB	R	H	BI	BB	SO	PO	A
Damon, cf	4	1	3	0	0	0	1	0
To.Walker, 2b	3	1	1	0	1	0	4	5
Garciaparra, ss	4	0	0	0	0	2	1	2
M.Ramirez, lf	4	0	1	2	0	1	2	0
D.Ortiz, dh	3	1	0	0	1	1	0	0
Millar, 1b	4	0	1	0	0	1	10	0
Nixon, rf	3	0	0	0	0	0	1	0
Mueller, 3b	2	0	0	0	1	1	0	2
Varitek, c	3	0	0	0	0	1	8	0
P.Martinez, p	0	0	0	0	0	0	0	1
Timlin, p	0	0	0	0	0	0	0	0
Embree, p	0	0	0	0	0	0	0	0
TOTALS	30	3	6	2	3	7	27	10

NY Yankees .... 0 1 1 2 0 0 0 0 0—4 7 0
Boston .... 2 0 0 0 0 0 1 0 0—3 6 0

NY Yankees	IP	H	R	ER	HR	BB	SO
Clemens (W)	6.0	5	2	2	0	1	7
F.Heredia	0.0	0	1	1	0	1	0
Contreras (HOLD)	1.0	1	0	0	0	1	0
M.Rivera (S)	2.0	0	0	0	0	0	0

Boston	IP	H	R	ER	HR	BB	SO
P.Martinez (L)	7.0	6	4	4	1	1	6
Timlin	1.0	0	0	0	0	0	2
Embree	1.0	1	0	0	0	0	0

F.Heredia pitched to 1 batter in the 7th.

DP—NY Yankees 3, Boston 2. LOB—NY Yankees 3, Boston 3. Scoring Position—NY Yankees 2 for 6, Boston 1 for 5. 2B—Posada, Matsui, To.Walker. HR—Jeter (3rd inning, 1 out, 0 on) off P.Martinez. CS—M.Ramirez. HBP—K.Garcia by P.Martinez. T—3:09. A—34,209. U—HP-Marquez, 1B-Cousins, 2B-West, 3B-Hernandez, LF-McClelland, RF-Craft.

HOW THEY SCORED

FIRST INNING

Red Sox—Damon infield single to third. Walker doubled to left, Damon to third. Garciaparra struck out. Ramirez singled to center, Damon scored, Walker scored. Ortiz struck out. Ramirez was caught stealing, catcher Posada to shortstop Jeter, Ramirez out. Two runs. Red Sox 2, Yankees 0.

SECOND INNING

Yankees—Posada doubled to center. Johnson grounded out, pitcher Martinez to first baseman Millar. Matsui popped out to second baseman Walker. Garcia singled to right, Posada scored. Soriano flied out to left fielder Ramirez. One run. Red Sox 2, Yankees 1.

THIRD INNING

Yankees—Wilson struck out. Jeter homered to left on the first pitch. Giambi struck out. Williams struck out. One run. Yankees 2, Red Sox 2.

FOURTH INNING

Yankees—Posada walked on a full count. Johnson singled to left, Posada to third. Matsui doubled to right, Posada scored, Johnson to third. Garcia was hit by a pitch. Soriano grounded into a double play, shortstop Garciaparra to second baseman Walker to first baseman Millar, Johnson scored, Matsui to third, Garcia out. Wilson popped out to second baseman Walker. Two runs. Yankees 4, Red Sox 2.

SEVENTH INNING

Red Sox—Boone in as third baseman. Heredia pitching. Ortiz walked on a full count. Contreras pitching. Millar singled to center, Ortiz to third. Nixon grounded into a double play, second baseman Soriano to shortstop Jeter to first baseman Johnson, Ortiz scored, Millar out. Mueller walked on a full count. Varitek fouled out to third baseman Boone. One run. Yankees 4, Red Sox 3.

GAME 4

BOSTON 3, NEW YORK 2

MONDAY, OCTOBER 13, AT BOSTON

NY Yankees	AB	R	H	BI	BB	SO	PO	A
A.Soriano, 2b	4	0	1	0	1	1	3	3
Jeter, ss	4	0	2	1	0	0	2	5
Ja.Giambi, dh	3	0	0	0	1	0	0	0
B.Williams, cf	2	0	1	0	2	0	1	0
Posada, c	4	0	0	0	0	2	10	2
Matsui, lf	4	0	0	0	0	3	2	0
N.Johnson, 1b	4	0	0	0	0	3	5	0
A.Boone, 3b	3	0	0	0	0	2	1	1
Sierra, ph	1	1	1	1	0	0	0	0
Dellucci, rf	3	1	1	0	0	1	0	0
Mussina, p	0	0	0	0	0	0	0	0
F.Heredia, p	0	0	0	0	0	0	0	0
J.Nelson, p	0	0	0	0	0	0	0	0
TOTALS	32	2	6	2	4	12	24	11

Boston	AB	R	H	BI	BB	SO	PO	A
Damon, cf	4	0	0	0	0	2	4	0
To.Walker, 2b	3	1	2	1	0	0	0	1
D.Jackson, pr-2b	0	0	0	0	0	0	0	0
Garciaparra, ss	4	0	0	0	0	1	1	0
M.Ramirez, lf	3	0	0	0	0	1	3	0
D.Ortiz, dh	3	0	0	0	0	2	0	0
Millar, 1b	2	1	0	0	1	2	4	1
Nixon, rf	3	1	3	1	0	0	0	0
Mueller, 3b	2	0	0	0	1	2	2	0
Mirabelli, c	2	0	1	0	0	0	8	0
Varitek, ph-c	1	0	0	1	0	0	4	0
Wakefield, p	0	0	0	0	0	0	0	0
Timlin, p	0	0	0	0	0	0	1	0
Williamson, p	0	0	0	0	0	0	0	0
TOTALS	27	3	6	3	2	10	27	2

NY Yankees ....0 0 0 0 1 0 0 0 1—2 6 1
Boston ....0 0 0 1 1 0 1 0 x—3 6 0

NY Yankees	IP	H	R	ER	HR	BB	SO
Clemens (W)	6.0	5	2	2	0	1	7
Mussina (L)	6.2	6	3	3	2	2	10
F.Heredia	0.2	0	0	0	0	0	0
J.Nelson	0.2	0	0	0	0	0	0

Boston	IP	H	R	ER	HR	BB	SO
Wakefield (W)	7.0	5	1	1	0	4	8
Timlin (HOLD)	1.0	0	0	0	0	0	1
Williamson (S)	1.0	1	1	1	1	0	3

Wakefield pitched to 1 batter in the 8th.

E—A.Boone. DP—NY Yankees 3, Boston 1. LOB—NY Yankees 8, Boston 3. Scoring Position—NY Yankees 1 for 9, Boston 0 for 1. 2B—Jeter, Nixon. HR—To.Walker (4th inning, 0 out, 0 on) off Mussina, Nixon (5th inning, 1 out, 0 on) off Mussina, Sierra (9th inning, 1 out, 0 on) off Williamson. SB—Dellucci. CS—Nixon 2. PB—Mirabelli. HBP—To.Walker by F.Heredia, Dellucci by Wakefield. T—2:49. A—34,599. U—HP-Cousins, 1B-West, 2B-Hernandez, 3B-McClelland, LF-Craft, RF-Marquez.

HOW THEY SCORED

FOURTH INNING

Red Sox—Walker homered to right on a 2-2 count. Garciaparra popped out to shortstop Jeter. Ramirez safe on Boone's error. Ortiz grounded into a double play, second baseman Soriano to shortstop Jeter to first baseman Johnson, Ramirez out. One run. Red Sox 1, Yankees 0.

FIFTH INNING

Yankees—Boone struck out. Dellucci singled to right. Soriano singled to left, Dellucci to second. Jeter doubled past third, Dellucci scored, Soriano to third. Giambi flied out to center fielder Damon. Williams walked. Posada lined out to left fielder Ramirez. One run. Red Sox 1, Yankees 1.

Red Sox—Millar struck out. Nixon homered to center on the first pitch. Mueller struck out. Mirabelli grounded out, shortstop Jeter to first baseman Johnson. One run. Red Sox 2, Yankees 1.

SEVENTH INNING

Red Sox—Ortiz struck out. Millar walked. Nixon doubled to left, Millar to third. Mueller was intentionally walked. Varitek pinch-hitting for Mirabelli. Varitek grounded into fielder's choice, shortstop Jeter to second baseman Soriano, Millar scored, Nixon to third, Mueller out. Heredia pitching. Nixon was caught stealing, catcher Posada to second baseman Soriano to catcher Posada to third baseman Boone, Nixon out. One run. Red Sox 3, Yankees 1.

NINTH INNING

Yankees—Jackson in as second baseman. Williamson pitching. Johnson struck out. Sierra pinch-hitting for Boone. Sierra homered to right on a 1-2 count. Dellucci struck out. Soriano struck out. One run. Red Sox 3, Yankees 2.

GAME 5

NEW YORK 4, BOSTON 2

TUESDAY, OCTOBER 14, AT BOSTON

NY Yankees	AB	R	H	BI	BB	SO	PO	A
A.Soriano, 2b	5	0	1	1	0	1	3	4
Jeter, ss	5	0	0	0	0	0	4	5
Ja.Giambi, dh	3	0	1	0	1	1	0	0
Dellucci, pr-dh	0	0	0	0	0	0	0	0
B.Williams, cf	4	1	0	0	0	0	0	0
Posada, c	3	1	1	0	1	0	6	0
Matsui, lf	4	0	1	1	0	0	1	0
N.Johnson, 1b	3	1	0	0	1	0	10	1
A.Boone, 3b	3	1	2	0	1	1	1	3
K.Garcia, rf	3	0	1	2	1	1	1	0
D.Wells, p	0	0	0	0	0	0	0	0
M.Rivera, p	0	0	0	0	0	0	1	0
TOTALS	33	4	7	4	5	4	27	13

Boston	AB	R	H	BI	BB	SO	PO	A
Damon, cf	4	0	0	0	0	0	1	0
To.Walker, 2b	4	1	2	0	0	0	1	5
Garciaparra, ss	2	0	0	1	2	1	3	4
M.Ramirez, lf	4	1	1	1	0	1	3	0
D.Ortiz, dh	4	0	2	0	0	0	0	0
Millar, 1b	4	0	0	0	0	1	14	1
Mueller, 3b	4	0	0	0	0	1	0	3
Nixon, rf	3	0	0	0	0	1	1	0
Varitek, c	4	0	1	0	0	1	4	1
Lowe, p	0	0	0	0	0	0	0	1
Embree, p	0	0	0	0	0	0	0	1
Arroyo, p	0	0	0	0	0	0	0	0
TOTALS	33	2	6	2	2	6	27	16

NY Yankees ....0 3 0 0 0 0 0 1 0—4 7 1
Boston ....0 0 0 1 0 0 0 1 0—2 6 1

NY Yankees	IP	H	R	ER	HR	BB	SO
D.Wells (W)	7.0	4	1	1	1	2	5
M.Rivera (S)	2.0	2	1	1	0	0	1

Boston	IP	H	R	ER	HR	BB	SO
Lowe (L)	7.1	7	4	4	0	4	3
Embree	0.2	0	0	0	0	0	0
Arroyo	1.0	0	0	0	0	1	1

E—A.Soriano, Millar. DP—NY Yankees 1, Boston 1. LOB—NY Yankees 7, Boston 7. Scoring Position—NY Yankees 4 for 10, Boston 0 for 5. 3B—To.Walker. HR—M.Ramirez (4th inning, 0 out, 0 on) off D.Wells. CS—A.Boone. HBP—Nixon by D.Wells. T—3:04. A—34,619. U—HP-West, 1B-Hernandez, 2B-McClelland, 3B-Craft, LF-Marquez, RF-Cousins.

HOW THEY SCORED

SECOND INNING

Yankees—Williams grounded out, first baseman Millar unassisted. Posada walked. Matsui grounded out, third baseman Mueller to first baseman Millar, Posada to second. Johnson was intentionally walked. Boone infield single to third, Posada to third, Johnson to second. Garcia singled to center, Posada scored, Johnson scored, Boone to second. Soriano singled to right, Boone scored, Garcia to third. Jeter grounded out, second baseman Walker to first baseman Millar. Three runs. Yankees 3, Red Sox 0.

FOURTH INNING

Red Sox—Ramirez homered to left on the first pitch. Ortiz singled to center. Millar grounded into a double play, second baseman Soriano to shortstop Jeter to first baseman Johnson, Ortiz out. Mueller struck out. One run. Yankees 3, Red Sox 1.

EIGHTH INNING

Yankees—Giambi walked on a full count. Dellucci pinch-running for Giambi. Williams grounded into fielder's choice, first baseman Millar to shortstop Garciaparra, Dellucci out. Posada singled to right, Williams to third. Embree pitching. Matsui grounded out, pitcher Embree to third baseman Mueller to first baseman Millar, Williams scored, Posada to second. Johnson flied out to left fielder Ramirez. One run. Yankees 4, Red Sox 1.

Red Sox—Dellucci in as designated hitter. M.Rivera pitching. Walker tripled to right. Garciaparra grounded out, first baseman Johnson to pitcher M.Rivera, Walker scored. Ramirez struck out. Ortiz singled to center. Millar grounded into fielder's choice, shortstop Jeter to second baseman Soriano, Ortiz out. One run. Yankees 4, Red Sox 2.

GAME 6

BOSTON 9, NEW YORK 6

WEDNESDAY, OCTOBER 15, AT NEW YORK

Boston	AB	R	H	BI	BB	SO	PO	A
Damon, cf	3	0	1	1	3	0	6	0
To.Walker, 2b	6	1	1	0	0	2	2	3
D.Jackson, 2b	0	0	0	0	0	0	0	0
Garciaparra, ss	5	2	4	0	0	0	1	4
M.Ramirez, lf	4	2	1	0	1	0	0	0
D.Ortiz, dh	5	1	2	3	0	3	0	0
Millar, 1b	5	0	2	1	0	2	8	1
Mueller, 3b	5	1	3	0	0	1	0	3
Nixon, rf	5	1	1	2	0	3	2	0
Varitek, c	4	1	1	1	1	2	7	0
Burkett, p	0	0	0	0	0	0	1	0
Arroyo, p	0	0	0	0	0	0	0	0
T.Jones, p	0	0	0	0	0	0	0	0
Embree, p	0	0	0	0	0	0	0	0
Timlin, p	0	0	0	0	0	0	0	0
Williamson, p	0	0	0	0	0	0	0	0
TOTALS	42	9	16	8	5	13	27	11

NY Yankees	AB	R	H	BI	BB	SO	PO	A
A.Soriano, 2b	5	0	2	2	0	0	1	4
Jeter, ss	3	0	1	0	2	0	1	2
Ja.Giambi, dh	5	1	1	1	0	3	0	0
B.Williams, cf	5	0	0	0	0	0	2	0
Posada, c	5	2	2	1	0	0	13	0
Matsui, lf	4	1	2	0	0	0	1	0
N.Johnson, 1b	4	1	3	1	0	0	7	0
A.Boone, 3b	4	0	0	1	0	2	1	1
K.Garcia, rf	4	1	1	0	0	2	1	0
Pettitte, p	0	0	0	0	0	0	0	2
Contreras, p	0	0	0	0	0	0	0	0
F.Heredia, p	0	0	0	0	0	0	0	0
J.Nelson, p	0	0	0	0	0	0	0	0
G.White, p	0	0	0	0	0	0	0	1
TOTALS	39	6	12	6	2	7	27	10

Boston	0 0 4	0 0 0	3 0 2—9	16	1
NY Yankees	1 0 0	4 1 0	0 0 0—6	12	2

Boston	IP	H	R	ER	HR	BB	SO
Burkett	3.2	7	5	3	1	0	1
Arroyo	1.1	2	1	1	1	1	2
T.Jones	0.1	1	0	0	0	1	1
Embree (W)	1.2	1	0	0	0	0	1
Timlin (HOLD)	1.0	1	0	0	0	0	1
Williamson (S)	1.0	0	0	0	0	0	1

NY Yankees	IP	H	R	ER	HR	BB	SO
Pettitte	5.0	8	4	4	1	2	5
Contreras (BS, L)	1.1	4	3	3	0	1	3
F.Heredia	0.2	0	0	0	0	2	2
J.Nelson	1.1	2	1	1	0	0	2
G.White	0.2	2	1	1	1	0	1

E—Garciaparra, A.Boone, Matsui. DP—Boston 1, NY Yankees 2. LOB—Boston 11, NY Yankees 8. Scoring Position—Boston 4 for 12, NY Yankees 2 for 8. 2B—Damon, M.Ramirez, Mueller 2, A.Soriano, N.Johnson. 3B—Garciaparra. HR—Ja.Giambi (1st inning, 2 out, 0 on) off Burkett, Varitek (3rd inning, 0 out, 0 on) off Pettitte, Posada (5th inning, 1 out, 0 on) off Arroyo, Nixon (9th inning, 1 out, 1 on) off G.White. SB—Damon, A.Soriano 2, Jeter. WP—Contreras, F.Heredia. PB—Varitek. T—3:57. A—56,277. U—HP-Hernandez, 1B-McClelland, 2B-Craft, 3B-Marquez, LF-Cousins, RF-West.

HOW THEY SCORED

FIRST INNING

Yankees—Soriano flied out to center fielder Damon. Jeter grounded out, third baseman Mueller to first baseman Millar. Giambi homered to center on the first pitch. Williams grounded out, second baseman Walker to first baseman Millar. One run. Yankees 1, Red Sox 0.

THIRD INNING

Red Sox—Varitek homered to left on a 0-1 count. Damon walked on a full count. Walker singled to right, Damon to second. Garciaparra grounded into fielder's choice, shortstop Jeter to third baseman Boone, Damon out, Walker to second. Ramirez walked on four pitches, Walker to third, Garciaparra to second. Ortiz singled to center, Walker scored, Garciaparra scored, Ramirez to second. Millar singled to center, Ramirez scored, Ortiz to second. Mueller grounded into a double play, third baseman Boone to second baseman Soriano to first baseman Johnson, Millar out. Four runs. Red Sox 4, Yankees 1.

FOURTH INNING

Yankees—Williams grounded out, first baseman Millar to pitcher Burkett. Posada singled to right. Matsui singled to center, Posada to third. Johnson doubled to right, Posada scored, Matsui to third. Boone grounded out, shortstop Garciaparra to first baseman Millar, Matsui scored. Garcia safe on Garciaparra's error, Johnson to third. Soriano doubled to center, Johnson scored, Garcia scored. Arroyo pitching. Jeter walked. Giambi struck out. Four runs. Yankees 5, Red Sox 4.

FIFTH INNING

Yankees—Williams flied out to right fielder Nixon. Posada homered to left on a 3-1 count. Matsui flied out to center fielder Damon. Johnson singled to center. Boone struck out. One run. Yankees 6, Red Sox 4.

SEVENTH INNING

Red Sox—Garciaparra tripled to center. On Matsui's error, Garciaparra scored. Ramirez doubled to center. On Contreras' wild pitch, Ramirez to third. Ortiz infield single to first, Ramirez scored. Millar flied out to right fielder Garcia. Mueller singled to center, Ortiz to second. Heredia pitching. On Heredia's wild pitch, Ortiz to third, Mueller to second. Nixon struck out. Varitek was intentionally walked. Damon walked on four pitches, Ortiz scored, Mueller to third, Varitek to second. Walker struck out. Three runs. Red Sox 7, Yankees 6.

NINTH INNING

Red Sox—Millar struck out. Mueller doubled to center. White pitching. Nixon homered to right on a 1-2 count, Mueller scored. Varitek struck out. Damon doubled to left. Walker grounded out, pitcher White to first baseman Johnson. Two runs. Red Sox 9, Yankees 6.

GAME 7

NEW YORK 6, BOSTON 5

THURSDAY, OCTOBER 16, AT NEW YORK

Boston	AB	R	H	BI	BB	SO	PO	A
Damon, cf	5	0	0	0	0	1	7	0
To.Walker, 2b	5	0	1	0	0	0	0	3
Garciaparra, ss	5	0	1	0	0	2	3	0
M.Ramirez, lf	5	0	1	0	0	0	3	0
D.Ortiz, dh	5	1	2	1	0	1	0	0
Kapler, pr-dh	0	0	0	0	0	0	0	0
Millar, 1b	5	2	2	1	0	0	6	1
Nixon, rf	4	1	1	2	1	2	1	0

Boston	AB	R	H	BI	BB	SO	PO	A
Mueller, 3b	5	0	1	0	0	1	0	1
Varitek, c	4	1	2	0	0	1	8	0
D.Jackson, pr	0	0	0	0	0	0	0	0
Mirabelli, c	1	0	0	0	0	1	1	0
P.Martinez, p	0	0	0	0	0	0	1	0
Embree, p	0	0	0	0	0	0	0	0
Timlin, p	0	0	0	0	0	0	0	0
Wakefield, p	0	0	0	0	0	0	0	0
TOTALS	44	5	11	4	1	9	30	5

NY Yankees	AB	R	H	BI	BB	SO	PO	A
A.Soriano, 2b	5	0	0	0	0	4	1	4
N.Johnson, 1b	4	0	0	0	1	0	14	0
Jeter, ss	5	1	1	0	0	2	3	4
B.Williams, cf	5	1	2	1	0	1	1	0
Matsui, lf	5	1	2	0	0	0	1	0
Posada, c	5	0	1	2	0	0	9	0
Ja.Giambi, dh	5	2	2	2	0	1	0	0
E.Wilson, 3b	3	0	1	0	0	0	1	2
Sierra, ph	0	0	0	0	1	0	0	0
A.Boone, pr-3b	1	1	1	1	0	0	0	1
K.Garcia, rf	3	0	1	0	1	1	3	0
Clemens, p	0	0	0	0	0	0	0	0
Mussina, p	0	0	0	0	0	0	0	0
F.Heredia, p	0	0	0	0	0	0	0	0
J.Nelson, p	0	0	0	0	0	0	0	0
D.Wells, p	0	0	0	0	0	0	0	0
M.Rivera, p	0	0	0	0	0	0	0	0
TOTALS	41	6	11	6	3	9	33	11

Boston	0 3 0	1 0 0	0 1 0	0 0—5	11	0
NY Yankees	0 0 0	0 1 0	1 3 0	0 1—6	11	1

Boston	IP	H	R	ER	HR	BB	SO
P.Martinez	7.1	10	5	5	2	1	8
Embree	0.1	0	0	0	0	0	0
Timlin	1.1	0	0	0	0	2	1
Wakefield (L)	1.0	1	1	1	1	0	0

NY Yankees	IP	H	R	ER	HR	BB	SO
Clemens	3.0	6	4	3	2	1	1
Mussina	3.0	2	0	0	0	0	3
F.Heredia	0.2	0	0	0	0	0	1
J.Nelson	0.2	0	0	0	0	0	1
D.Wells	0.2	1	1	1	1	0	0
M.Rivera (W)	3.0	2	0	0	0	0	3

Wakefield pitched to 1 batter in the 11th. Clemens pitched to 3 batters in the 4th.

E—E.Wilson. DP—NY Yankees 1. LOB—Boston 7, NY Yankees 8. Scoring Position—Boston 0 for 9, NY Yankees 2 for 7. 2B—D.Ortiz, Varitek, Jeter, Matsui 2, Posada. HR—Nixon (2nd inning, 1 out, 1 on) off Clemens, Millar (4th inning, 0 out, 0 on) off Clemens, Ja.Giambi (5th inning, 0 out, 0 on) off P.Martinez, Ja.Giambi (7th inning, 2 out, 0 on) off P.Martinez, D.Ortiz (8th inning, 1 out, 0 on) off D.Wells, A.Boone (11th inning, 0 out, 0 on) off Wakefield. T—3:56. A—56,279. U—HP-McClelland, 1B-Craft, 2B-Marquez, 3B-Cousins, LF-West, RF-Hernandez.

HOW THEY SCORED

SECOND INNING

Red Sox—Ortiz lined out to center fielder Williams. Millar singled to center. Nixon homered to right on a 2-0 count, Millar scored. Mueller struck out. Varitek doubled to right. Damon safe at second on Wilson's error, Varitek scored. Walker grounded out, first baseman Johnson unassisted. Three runs. Red Sox 3, Yankees 0.

FOURTH INNING

Red Sox—Millar homered to left on the first pitch. Nixon walked on a full count. Mueller singled to center, Nixon to third. Mussina pitching. Varitek struck out. Damon grounded into a double play, shortstop Jeter to first baseman Johnson, Mueller out. One run. Red Sox 4, Yankees 0.

FIFTH INNING

Yankees—Giambi homered to center on the first pitch. Wilson flied out to left fielder Ramirez. Garcia struck out. Soriano struck out. One run. Red Sox 4, Yankees 1.

SEVENTH INNING

Yankees—Matsui grounded out, second baseman Walker to first baseman Millar. Posada lined out to center fielder Damon. Giambi homered to center on a 2-2 count. Wilson infield single to first. Garcia singled to right, Wilson to second. Soriano struck out. One run. Red Sox 4, Yankees 2.

EIGHTH INNING

Red Sox—Ramirez grounded out, third baseman Wilson to first baseman Johnson. Wells pitching. Ortiz homered to right on the first pitch. Millar grounded out, shortstop Jeter to first baseman Johnson. Nixon popped out to shortstop Jeter. One run. Red Sox 5, Yankees 2.

Yankees—Johnson popped out to shortstop Garciaparra. Jeter doubled to center. Williams singled to center, Jeter scored. Matsui doubled to right, Williams to third. Posada doubled to center, Williams scored, Matsui scored. Embree pitching. Giambi flied out to center fielder Damon. Timlin pitching. Sierra pinch-hitting for Wilson. Sierra was intentionally walked. Boone pinch-running for Sierra. Garcia walked on four pitches, Posada to third, Boone to second. Soriano grounded into fielder's choice, second baseman Walker to shortstop Garciaparra, Garcia out. Three runs. Yankees 5, Red Sox 5.

ELEVENTH INNING

Yankees—Boone homered to left on the first pitch. One run. Yankees 6, Red Sox 5.

STATISTICS

NEW YORK YANKEES' BATTING AND FIELDING AVERAGES

	BATTING															FIELDING			
Player, position	G	AB	R	H	TB	2B	3B	HR	RBI	BB	IBB	SO	Avg.	OBP	Slg.	PO	A	E	Avg.
Sierra,rf-ph	3	2	1	1	4	0	0	1	1	1	1	0	.500	.667	2.000	0	0	0	.000
Dellucci,dh-pr-rf	3	3	2	1	1	0	0	0	0	0	0	1	.333	.500	.333	0	0	0	.000
Matsui,lf	7	26	3	8	11	3	0	0	4	1	0	3	.308	.321	.423	8	0	1	.889
Posada,c	7	27	5	8	15	4	0	1	6	3	0	4	.296	.367	.556	60	6	0	1.000
Garcia,rf	5	16	1	4	4	0	0	0	3	2	0	4	.250	.368	.250	8	0	0	1.000
Jeter,ss	7	30	3	7	12	2	0	1	2	2	0	4	.233	.281	.400	19	25	0	1.000
Giambi,dh	7	26	4	6	15	0	0	3	3	4	0	7	.231	.333	.577	0	0	0	.000
Johnson,1b	7	26	4	6	10	1	0	1	3	2	1	4	.231	.286	.385	61	3	0	1.000
Williams,cf	7	26	5	5	6	1	0	0	2	4	0	3	.192	.300	.231	12	0	0	1.000
Boone,3b-pr	7	17	2	3	6	0	0	1	2	1	0	6	.176	.263	.353	5	7	2	.857
Wilson,3b	2	7	0	1	1	0	0	0	0	0	0	1	.143	.143	.143	1	3	1	.800
Soriano,2b	7	30	0	4	5	1	0	0	3	1	0	11	.133	.188	.167	13	23	1	.973
Clemens,p	2	0	0	0	0	0	0	0	0	0	0	0	.000	.000	.000	0	0	0	.000
Contreras,p	4	0	0	0	0	0	0	0	0	0	0	0	.000	.000	.000	0	0	0	.000
Heredia,p	5	0	0	0	0	0	0	0	0	0	0	0	.000	.000	.000	0	0	0	.000
Mussina,p	3	0	0	0	0	0	0	0	0	0	0	0	.000	.000	.000	0	1	0	1.000
Nelson,p	4	0	0	0	0	0	0	0	0	0	0	0	.000	.000	.000	0	0	0	.000
Pettitte,p	2	0	0	0	0	0	0	0	0	0	0	0	.000	.000	.000	0	2	0	1.000
Rivera,p	4	0	0	0	0	0	0	0	0	0	0	0	.000	.000	.000	2	1	0	1.000
Wells,p	2	0	0	0	0	0	0	0	0	0	0	0	.000	.000	.000	0	0	0	.000
White,p	2	0	0	0	0	0	0	0	0	0	0	0	.000	.000	.000	0	2	0	1.000
Rivera,rf	2	2	0	0	0	0	0	0	0	0	0	1	.000	.000	.000	3	0	0	1.000
Totals	7	238	30	54	90	12	0	8	29	21	2	49	.227	.299	.378	192	73	5	.981

BOSTON RED SOX' BATTING AND FIELDING AVERAGES

Player, position	G	AB	R	H	TB	2B	3B	HR	RBI	BB	IBB	SO	Avg.	OBP	Slg.	PO	A	E	Avg.
	BATTING															FIELDING			
Walker,2b-ph	7	27	5	10	19	1	1	2	2	1	0	2	.370	.414	.704	8	21	0	1.000
Nixon,rf	7	24	3	8	18	1	0	3	5	3	0	7	.333	.429	.750	7	1	0	1.000
Jackson,2b-pr	5	3	0	1	1	0	0	0	1	0	0	1	.333	.333	.333	2	4	1	.857
Ramirez,lf	7	29	6	9	16	1	0	2	4	1	0	4	.310	.333	.552	15	0	0	1.000
Varitek,c-ph	6	20	4	6	14	2	0	2	3	1	1	5	.300	.333	.700	36	1	0	1.000
Mirabelli,c	3	7	0	2	2	0	0	0	0	0	0	2	.286	.286	.286	15	0	0	1.000
Ortiz,dh	7	26	4	7	14	1	0	2	6	3	0	8	.269	.367	.538	0	0	0	.000
Garciaparra,ss	7	29	2	7	9	0	1	0	1	2	0	8	.241	.290	.310	11	17	1	.966
Millar,1b	7	29	3	7	10	0	0	1	3	1	0	9	.241	.267	.345	62	8	1	.986
Mueller,3b	7	27	1	6	8	2	0	0	0	2	1	7	.222	.276	.296	4	11	0	1.000
Damon,cf	5	20	1	4	5	1	0	0	1	3	0	3	.200	.304	.250	19	0	0	1.000
Kapler,cf-dh-pr	3	8	0	1	1	0	0	0	0	0	0	3	.125	.125	.125	5	0	0	1.000
Arroyo,p	3	0	0	0	0	0	0	0	0	0	0	0	.000	.000	.000	1	0	0	1.000
Burkett,p	1	0	0	0	0	0	0	0	0	0	0	0	.000	.000	.000	1	0	0	1.000
Embree,p	5	0	0	0	0	0	0	0	0	0	0	0	.000	.000	.000	0	1	0	1.000
Jones,p	1	0	0	0	0	0	0	0	0	0	0	0	.000	.000	.000	0	0	0	.000
Lowe,p	2	0	0	0	0	0	0	0	0	0	0	0	.000	.000	.000	1	2	0	1.000
Martinez,p	2	0	0	0	0	0	0	0	0	0	0	0	.000	.000	.000	1	1	0	1.000
Sauerbeck,p	1	0	0	0	0	0	0	0	0	0	0	0	.000	.000	.000	0	0	0	.000
Timlin,p	5	0	0	0	0	0	0	0	0	0	0	0	.000	.000	.000	1	0	0	1.000
Wakefield,p	3	0	0	0	0	0	0	0	0	0	0	0	.000	.000	.000	0	0	0	.000
Williamson,p	3	0	0	0	0	0	0	0	0	0	0	0	.000	.000	.000	0	0	0	.000
McCarty,ph	1	1	0	0	0	0	0	0	0	0	0	1	.000	.000	.000	0	0	0	.000
Totals	7	250	29	68	117	9	2	12	26	17	2	60	.272	.326	.468	189	67	3	.988

NEW YORK YANKEES' PITCHING RECORDS

Pitcher	G	GS	CG	IP	H	R	ER	HR	BB	IBB	SO	HB	WP	W	L	Pct.	ERA
Rivera	4	0	0	8.0	5	1	1	0	0	0	6	0	0	1	0	1.000	1.13
Wells	2	1	0	7.2	5	2	2	2	2	0	5	1	0	1	0	1.000	2.35
Heredia	5	0	0	2.2	0	1	1	0	3	1	3	1	1	0	0	.000	3.38
Mussina	3	2	0	15.1	16	7	7	5	4	1	17	0	0	0	2	.000	4.11
White	2	0	0	2.0	4	1	1	1	0	0	1	0	0	0	0	.000	4.50
Pettitte	2	2	0	11.2	17	6	6	2	4	0	10	0	0	1	0	1.000	4.63
Clemens	2	2	0	9.0	11	6	5	2	2	0	8	0	0	1	0	1.000	5.00
Contreras	4	0	0	4.2	6	3	3	0	2	0	7	0	2	0	1	.000	5.79
Nelson	4	0	0	3.0	4	2	2	0	0	0	3	1	0	0	0	.000	6.00
Totals	7	7	0	64.0	68	29	28	12	17	2	60	3	3	4	3	.571	3.94

No shutouts. Saves—Rivera 2.

BOSTON RED SOX' PITCHING RECORDS

Pitcher	G	GS	CG	IP	H	R	ER	HR	BB	IBB	SO	HB	WP	W	L	Pct.	ERA
Timlin	5	0	0	5.1	1	0	0	0	2	1	6	0	0	0	0	.000	0.00
Embree	5	0	0	4.2	3	0	0	0	0	0	1	0	0	1	0	1.000	0.00
Jones	1	0	0	0.1	1	0	0	0	1	0	1	0	0	0	0	.000	0.00
Sauerbeck	1	0	0	0.1	1	0	0	0	1	0	0	0	0	0	0	.000	0.00
Wakefield	3	2	0	14.0	8	4	4	1	6	0	10	1	0	2	1	.667	2.57
Arroyo	3	0	0	3.1	2	1	1	1	2	0	5	1	0	0	0	.000	2.70
Williamson	3	0	0	3.0	1	1	1	1	0	0	6	0	0	0	0	.000	3.00
Martinez	2	2	0	14.1	16	9	9	3	2	0	14	1	0	0	1	.000	5.65
Lowe	2	2	0	14.0	14	10	10	1	7	1	5	1	0	0	2	.000	6.43
Burkett	1	1	0	3.2	7	5	3	1	0	0	1	0	0	0	0	.000	7.36
Totals	7	7	0	63.0	54	30	28	8	21	2	49	4	0	3	4	.429	4.00

No shutouts. Saves—Williamson 3.

SCORE BY INNINGS

New York	1	6	2	6	4	0	5	4	1	0	1—30
Boston	2	4	4	5	3	1	6	2	2	0	0—29

MISCELLANEOUS STATISTICS

Sacrifice hits—None.
Sacrifice flies—Matsui.
Stolen bases—Soriano 2, Boone, Damon, Dellucci, Jeter, Nixon.
Caught stealing—Nixon 2, Boone, Jackson, Kapler, Ramirez.
Double plays—Soriano, Jeter and Johnson 4; Jeter and Johnson 2; Jeter, Soriano and Johnson 2; Boone, Soriano and Johnson; Garciaparra and Millar; Garciaparra, Walker and Millar; Millar (unassisted); Mueller, Walker and Millar; Walker, Garciaparra and Millar.
Left on bases—New York 3, 8, 3, 8, 7, 8, 8—45; Boston 10, 8, 3, 3, 7, 11, 7—49.
Scoring position—New York 1 for 5, 3 for 11, 2 for 6, 1 for 9, 4 for 10, 2 for 8, 2 for 7—15 for 56; Boston 2 for 8, 2 for 7, 1 for 5, 0 for 1, 0 for 5, 4 for 12, 0 for 9—9 for 47.
Hit by pitcher—by Wells (Nixon), by Nelson (Ortiz), by Martinez (Garcia), by Wakefield (Dellucci), by Heredia (Walker), by Lowe (Boone), by Arroyo (Soriano).
Passed balls—Varitek 2, Mirabelli.
Balks—None.
Time of games—3:20, 3:05, 3:09, 2:49, 3:04, 3:57, 3:56—Avg.: 3:20.
Attendance—56,281, 56,295, 34,209, 34,599, 34,619, 56,277, 56,279—328,559.
Umpires-McClelland, Tim; Craft, Terry; Marquez, Alfonso; Cousins, Derryl; West, Joe; Hernandez, Angel.

N.L. CHAMPIONSHIP SERIES

FLORIDA VS. CHICAGO

RESULTS

Day	Date	Place	Score
Tue.	Oct. 7	Chicago	Florida 9, Chicago 8
Wed.	Oct. 8	Chicago	Chicago 12, Florida 3
Fri.	Oct. 10	Florida	Chicago 5, Florida 4
Sat.	Oct. 11	Florida	Chicago 8, Florida 3
Sun.	Oct. 12	Florida	Florida 4, Chicago 0
Tue.	Oct 14	Chicago	Florida 8, Chicago 3
Wed.	Oct. 15	Chicago	Florida 9, Chicago 6

BOX SCORES

GAME 1

FLORIDA 9, CHICAGO 8

TUESDAY, OCTOBER 7, AT CHICAGO

Florida	AB	R	H	BI	BB	SO	PO	A
Pierre, cf	5	2	1	0	1	0	1	0
L.Castillo, 2b	5	1	3	0	1	0	4	5
I.Rodriguez, c	5	1	2	5	1	1	9	0
D.Lee, 1b	5	0	0	0	1	3	15	1
M.Cabrera, 3b	6	2	2	1	0	1	1	2
B.Looper, p	0	0	0	0	0	0	0	0
Encarnacion, rf	5	1	2	1	0	1	1	0
Conine, lf	4	0	1	1	0	0	1	0
A.Gonzalez, ss	5	0	0	0	0	0	0	7
Beckett, p	3	0	1	0	0	1	1	0
C.Fox, p	0	0	0	0	0	0	0	0
Hollandsworth, ph	1	1	1	0	0	0	0	0
Urbina, p	0	0	0	0	0	0	0	0
Lowell, ph-3b	1	1	1	1	0	0	0	1
TOTALS	45	9	14	9	4	7	33	16

Chi Cubs	AB	R	H	BI	BB	SO	PO	A
K.Lofton, cf	4	2	1	0	1	0	3	0
Grudzielanek, 2b	5	1	2	1	0	0	5	3
S.Sosa, rf	5	1	1	2	0	1	3	0
Alou, lf	4	1	1	2	1	0	1	0
A.Ramirez, 3b	5	1	1	0	0	0	1	2
Simon, 1b	5	1	1	0	0	2	8	0
A.Gonzalez, ss	5	1	3	3	0	1	3	2
M.Guthrie, p	0	0	0	0	0	0	0	0
Alfonseca, p	0	0	0	0	0	0	0	0
Bako, c	3	0	0	0	0	1	4	1
K.Farnsworth, p	0	0	0	0	0	0	0	1
Goodwin, ph	1	0	0	0	0	1	0	0
Borowski, p	0	0	0	0	0	0	0	0
R.Martinez, ss	1	0	0	0	0	0	1	1
C.Zambrano, p	2	0	0	0	0	2	0	1
Remlinger, p	0	0	0	0	0	0	0	0
D.Miller, c	3	0	1	0	0	1	4	0
TOTALS	43	8	11	8	2	9	33	11

Florida	0 0 5	0 0 1	0 0 2	0 1—9	14 1
Chi Cubs	4 0 0	0 0 2	0 0 2	0 0—8	11 1

Florida	IP	H	R	ER	HR	BB	SO
Beckett	6.1	8	6	6	2	1	5
C.Fox	1.2	1	0	0	0	1	1
Urbina (BS, W)	2.0	2	2	2	1	0	2
B.Looper (S)	1.0	0	0	0	0	0	1

Chi Cubs	IP	H	R	ER	HR	BB	SO
C.Zambrano	6.0	9	6	5	3	1	3
Remlinger	0.1	1	0	0	0	0	0
K.Farnsworth	1.2	0	0	0	0	0	3
Borowski	2.0	2	2	1	0	1	1
M.Guthrie (L)	0.1	1	1	1	1	0	0
Alfonseca	0.2	1	0	0	0	2	0

E—A.Gonzalez, Grudzielanek. DP—Florida 1, Chi Cubs 1. LOB—Florida 8, Chi Cubs 5. Scoring Position—Florida 2 for 13, Chi Cubs 4 for 11. 2B—L.Castillo, Hollandsworth, K.Lofton, Simon, A.Gonzalez, D.Miller. 3B—Pierre, Conine, Grudzielanek, A.Ramirez. HR—Alou (1st inning, 1 out, 1 on) off Beckett, I.Rodriguez (3rd inning, 1 out, 2 on) off C.Zambrano, M.Cabrera (3rd inning, 2 out, 0 on) off C.Zambrano, Encarnacion (3rd inning, 2 out, 0 on) off C.Zambrano, A.Gonzalez (6th inning, 2 out, 1 on) off Beckett, S.Sosa (9th inning, 2 out, 1 on) off Urbina, Lowell (11th inning, 0 out, 0 on) off M.Guthrie. SB—L.Castillo 2. CS—Pierre. S—Conine. SH—K.Lofton. PB—Bako. T—3:44. A—39,567. U—HP-Crawford, 1B-Meriwether, 2B-Culbreth, 3B-Everitt, LF-Poncino, RF-Reilly.

HOW THEY SCORED

FIRST INNING

Cubs—Lofton walked on four pitches. Grudzielanek tripled to center, Lofton scored. Sosa popped out to third baseman Cabrera. Alou homered to left on a 1-0 count, Grudzielanek scored. Ramirez tripled to center. Simon struck out. Gonzalez doubled to left, Ramirez scored. Bako flied out to left fielder Conine. Four runs. Cubs 4, Marlins 0.

THIRD INNING

Marlins—Beckett lined out to right fielder Sosa. Pierre tripled to right. Castillo walked. Rodriguez homered to left on a 1-0 count, Pierre scored, Castillo scored. Lee struck out. Cabrera homered to left on a 3-1 count. Encarnacion homered to left on a 1-0 count. Conine flied out to right fielder Sosa. Five runs. Marlins 5, Cubs 4.

SIXTH INNING

Marlins—Cabrera infield single to short. Encarnacion singled to center, Cabrera to second. On Bako's passed ball, Cabrera to third, Encarnacion to second. Conine hit a sacrifice fly to center fielder Lofton, Cabrera scored, Encarnacion to third. Gonzalez fouled out to third baseman Ramirez. Beckett struck out. One run. Marlins 6, Cubs 4.

Cubs—Alou grounded out, shortstop Gonzalez to first baseman Lee. Ramirez popped out to first baseman Lee. Simon doubled to right.Gonzalez homered to right on a 2-1 count, Simon scored. Bako struck out. Two runs. Marlins 6, Cubs 6.

NINTH INNING

Marlins—Borowski pitching. Gonzalez flied out to center fielder Lofton. Hollandsworth pinch-hitting for C.Fox. Hollandsworth doubled to center. Pierre walked. Castillo safe on fielder's choice and Grudzielanek's error, Hollandsworth to third, Pierre to second. Rodriguez singled to right, Hollandsworth scored, Pierre scored, Castillo to third. Lee popped out to second baseman Grudzielanek. Cabrera grounded into fielder's choice, second baseman Grudzielanek to shortstop Gonzalez, Rodriguez out. Two runs. Marlins 8, Cubs 6.

Cubs—Urbina pitching. Miller grounded out, second baseman Castillo to first baseman Lee. Lofton doubled to right. Grudzielanek grounded out, third baseman Cabrera to first baseman Lee. Sosa homered to left on a 1-1 count, Lofton scored. Alou flied out to right fielder Encarnacion. Two runs. Marlins 8, Cubs 8.

ELEVENTH INNING

Marlins—Guthrie pitching. Martinez in as shortstop. Lowell pinch-hitting for Urbina. Lowell homered to center on a full count. Pierre grounded out, second baseman Grudzielanek to first baseman Simon. Alfonseca pitching. Castillo infield single to short. Castillo stole second. Rodriguez was intentionally walked. Lee walked on a full count, Castillo to third, Rodriguez to second. Cabrera lined into a double play, shortstop Martinez to second baseman Grudzielanek, Rodriguez out. One run. Marlins 9, Cubs 8.

GAME 2

CHICAGO 12, FLORIDA 3

WEDNESDAY, OCTOBER 8, AT CHICAGO

Florida	AB	R	H	BI	BB	SO	PO	A
Pierre, cf	5	0	0	0	0	0	1	0
L.Castillo, 2b	3	0	0	0	1	0	3	2
Pavano, p	0	0	0	0	0	0	0	0
Tejera, p	0	0	0	0	0	0	0	0
L.Harris, ph	1	0	0	0	0	0	0	0
I.Rodriguez, c	3	0	1	0	0	1	3	0
Redmond, c	0	1	0	0	1	0	2	0
D.Lee, 1b	4	1	2	1	0	0	8	1
M.Cabrera, 3b-ss	4	1	2	1	0	1	0	1
Encarnacion, rf	4	0	1	0	0	1	5	0
Conine, lf	3	0	3	0	1	0	1	0
A.Gonzalez, ss	2	0	0	0	0	1	0	3
Lowell, ph-3b	2	0	0	0	0	0	1	1
Penny, p	1	0	0	0	0	1	0	1
Bump, p	0	0	0	0	0	0	0	0
B.Banks, ph	1	0	0	0	0	0	0	0
Helling, p	0	0	0	0	0	0	0	1
Mordecai, ph-2b	2	0	0	0	0	0	0	0
TOTALS	35	3	9	2	3	5	24	10

Chi Cubs	AB	R	H	BI	BB	SO	PO	A
K.Lofton, cf	5	1	4	2	0	0	2	0
Grudzielanek, 2b	5	1	2	1	0	1	4	8
S.Sosa, rf	3	2	1	2	2	1	1	0
Goodwin, rf	0	0	0	0	0	0	0	0
Alou, lf	4	0	0	0	0	0	1	1
O'Leary, ph-lf	1	0	0	0	0	0	0	0
A.Ramirez, 3b	4	1	1	1	1	0	0	2
Simon, 1b	4	1	3	2	0	0	9	0
Karros, ph-1b	1	0	1	0	0	0	1	1
A.Gonzalez, ss	4	3	2	3	0	0	2	2
R.Martinez, ph-ss	1	0	0	0	0	0	0	0
Bako, c	4	3	2	1	1	2	6	0
Prior, p	2	0	0	0	0	0	0	0
Veres, p	0	0	0	0	0	0	0	0
M.Guthrie, p	0	0	0	0	0	0	1	0
TOTALS	38	12	16	12	4	4	27	14

Florida	0 0 0	0 0 2	0 1 0—	3	9	1
Chi Cubs	2 3 3	0 3 1	0 0 x—	12	16	1

Florida	IP	H	R	ER	HR	BB	SO
Penny (L)	2.0	7	7	7	2	2	0
Bump	1.0	2	1	1	0	0	1
Helling	3.0	5	4	3	2	2	1
Pavano	1.0	1	0	0	0	0	1
Tejera	1.0	1	0	0	0	0	1

Chi Cubs	IP	H	R	ER	HR	BB	SO
Prior (W)	7.0	8	3	2	2	2	5
Veres	1.1	1	0	0	0	1	0
M.Guthrie	0.2	0	0	0	0	0	0

Penny pitched to 2 batters in the 3rd. Prior pitched to 2 batters in the 8th.

E—Conine, Simon. DP—Chi Cubs 2. LOB—Florida 8, Chi Cubs 8. Scoring Position—Florida 2 for 10, Chi Cubs 7 for 16. 2B—Encarnacion, Conine, Grudzielanek, Simon, Bako. HR—S.Sosa (2nd inning, 2 out, 1 on) off Penny, A.Ramirez (3rd inning, 0 out, 0 on) off Penny, A.Gonzalez (5th inning, 0 out, 1 on) off Helling, D.Lee (6th inning, 0 out, 0 on) off Prior, M.Cabrera (6th inning, 0 out, 0 on) off Prior, A.Gonzalez (6th inning, 1 out, 0 on) off Helling. SB—K.Lofton. SH—Prior 2. WP—Bump, Helling. T—3:02. A—39,562. U—HP-Meriwether, 1B-Culbreth, 2B-Vanover, 3B-Everitt, LF-Poncino, RF-Reilly.

HOW THEY SCORED

FIRST INNING

Cubs—Lofton grounded out, pitcher Penny to first baseman Lee. Grudzielanek infield single to short. Sosa walked on four pitches, Grudzielanek to second. Alou flied out to right fielder Encarnacion, Grudzielanek to third. Ramirez walked, Sosa to second. Simon singled to left, Grudzielanek scored, Sosa scored, Ramirez to second. Gonzalez flied out to left fielder Conine. Two runs. Cubs 2, Marlins 0.

SECOND INNING

Cubs—Bako infield single to second. Prior sacrificed, third baseman Cabrera to second baseman Castillo, Bako to second. Lofton infield single to short, Bako scored. Lofton stole second. Grudzielanek grounded out, second baseman Castillo to first baseman Lee, Lofton to third. Sosa homered to center on a 1-1 count, Lofton scored. Alou lined out to right fielder Encarnacion. Three runs. Cubs 5, Marlins 0.

THIRD INNING

Cubs—Ramirez homered to left on a full count. Simon singled to right. Bump pitching. Gonzalez grounded into fielder's choice, shortstop Gonzalez to second baseman Castillo, Simon out. Bako doubled to center, Gonzalez scored. Prior grounded out, second baseman Castillo to first baseman Lee, Bako to third. Lofton singled to left, Bako scored. On Bump's wild pitch, Lofton to second. Grudzielanek struck out. Three runs. Cubs 8, Marlins 0.

FIFTH INNING

Cubs—Simon doubled to left. On Helling's wild pitch, Simon to third. Gonzalez homered to left on a full count, Simon scored. Bako remained at bat on Conine's fielding error, Bako walked on a full count. Prior sacrificed, first baseman Lee to second baseman Castillo, Bako to second. Lofton singled to right, Bako to third. Grudzielanek doubled to left, Bako scored, Lofton to third. Sosa was intentionally walked. Alou grounded into fielder's choice, pitcher Helling to catcher Rodriguez, Lofton out, Grudzielanek to third, Sosa to second. Ramirez flied out to right fielder Encarnacion. Three runs. Cubs 11, Marlins 0.

SIXTH INNING

Marlins—Lee homered to left on a 1-1 count. Cabrera homered to center on a 1-2 count. Encarnacion struck out. Conine singled to center. Lowell pinch-hitting for Gonzalez. Lowell flied into a double play, left fielder Alou to second baseman Grudzielanek to first baseman Simon, Conine out. Two runs. Cubs 11, Marlins 2.

Cubs—Cabrera in as shortstop. Lowell in as third baseman. Simon grounded out, first baseman Lee unassisted. Gonzalez homered to center on a 2-2 count. Bako struck out. Prior flied out to right fielder Encarnacion. One run. Cubs 12, Marlins 2.

EIGHTH INNING

Marlins—O'Leary in as left fielder. Redmond walked on a full count. Lee safe on Simon's error, Redmond to second. Veres pitching. Cabrera infield single to third, Redmond to third, Lee to second. Encarnacion grounded into a double play, second baseman Grudzielanek to shortstop Gonzalez to first baseman Simon, Redmond scored, Lee to third, Cabrera out. Conine walked on a full count. Lowell popped out to second baseman Grudzielanek. One run. Cubs 12, Marlins 3.

GAME 3

CHICAGO 5, FLORIDA 4

FRIDAY, OCTOBER 10, AT FLORIDA

Chi Cubs	AB	R	H	BI	BB	SO	PO	A
K.Lofton, cf	6	2	3	0	0	0	5	0
Grudzielanek, 2b	4	0	0	0	0	0	2	2
Borowski, p	0	0	0	0	0	0	0	0
Glanville, ph-lf	1	0	1	1	0	0	0	0
S.Sosa, rf	5	0	3	1	1	2	4	0
Alou, lf	6	0	2	0	0	0	0	0
Remlinger, p	0	0	0	0	0	0	0	1
A.Ramirez, 3b	4	0	0	0	2	2	1	5
Karros, 1b	4	1	1	0	0	1	9	0
K.Farnsworth, p	0	0	0	0	0	0	0	1
R.Martinez, 2b	1	0	0	0	0	1	0	2
A.Gonzalez, ss	4	0	0	0	1	1	0	3
D.Miller, c	1	0	0	0	2	0	8	0
Goodwin, ph	1	1	1	0	0	0	0	0
Bako, c	1	0	0	0	0	1	0	0
K.Wood, p	1	0	0	1	0	0	0	3
Simon, 1b	2	1	1	2	0	0	4	0
TOTALS	41	5	12	5	6	8	33	17

Florida	AB	R	H	BI	BB	SO	PO	A
Pierre, cf	5	0	2	0	0	1	4	0
L.Castillo, 2b	4	0	0	1	1	1	3	3
I.Rodriguez, c	5	0	1	1	1	2	10	0

Florida	AB	R	H	BI	BB	SO	PO	A
D.Lee, 1b	6	0	1	0	0	1	12	1
M.Cabrera, 3b-rf	4	2	2	0	1	1	0	2
Encarnacion, rf	3	0	0	0	0	2	0	0
C.Fox, p	0	0	0	0	0	0	0	0
Mordecai, ph-ss	1	0	0	0	0	0	0	0
Conine, lf	5	0	1	0	0	0	1	0
A.Gonzalez, ss	3	1	2	1	0	1	3	3
Hollandsworth, ph	1	0	1	1	0	0	0	0
Urbina, p	0	0	0	0	0	0	0	0
L.Harris, ph	1	0	0	0	0	0	0	0
Tejera, p	0	0	0	0	0	0	0	0
B.Looper, p	0	0	0	0	0	0	0	0
M.Redman, p	1	0	0	0	1	0	0	1
Lowell, 3b	2	1	0	0	1	0	0	1
TOTALS	41	4	10	4	5	9	33	11

Chi Cubs	1 1 0	0 0 0	0 2 0	0 1—5	12 0
Florida	0 1 0	0 0 0	2 1 0	0 0—4	10 0

Chi Cubs	IP	H	R	ER	HR	BB	SO
K.Wood	6.2	7	3	3	0	3	7
K.Farnsworth	1.0	1	1	1	0	0	1
Borowski (BS, W)	2.1	2	0	0	0	2	0
Remlinger (S)	1.0	0	0	0	0	0	1

Florida	IP	H	R	ER	HR	BB	SO
M.Redman	6.2	8	2	2	0	4	3
C.Fox	1.1	2	2	2	1	1	1
Urbina	2.0	0	0	0	0	0	4
Tejera (L)	0.1	1	1	1	0	0	0
B.Looper	0.2	1	0	0	0	1	0

DP—Florida 1. LOB—Chi Cubs 12, Florida 12. Scoring Position—Chi Cubs 3 for 11, Florida 3 for 11. 2B—Alou, A.Gonzalez. 3B—Goodwin, Glanville. HR—Simon (8th inning, 1 out, 1 on) off C.Fox. SB—Pierre. S—K.Wood. SH—Grudzielanek, K.Wood, Pierre, L.Castillo, Mordecai. WP—Remlinger. T—4:16. A—65,115. U—HP-Culbreth, 1B-Everitt, 2B-Poncino, 3B-Reilly, LF-Crawford, RF-Meriwether.

HOW THEY SCORED

FIRST INNING

Cubs—Lofton infield single to first. Grudzielanek sacrificed, pitcher Redman to first baseman Lee, Lofton to second. Sosa singled to left, Lofton scored. Alou grounded into a double play, second baseman Castillo to shortstop Gonzalez to first baseman Lee, Sosa out. One run. Cubs 1, Marlins 0.

SECOND INNING

Cubs—Ramirez grounded out, third baseman Cabrera to first baseman Lee. Karros singled to right. Gonzalez walked on a full count, Karros to second. Miller walked, Karros to third, Gonzalez to second. Wood hit a sacrifice fly to center fielder Pierre, Karros scored. Lofton singled to left, Gonzalez to third, Miller to second. Grudzielanek flied out to left fielder Conine. One run. Cubs 2, Marlins 0.

Marlins—Lee flied out to center fielder Lofton. Cabrera singled to left. Encarnacion struck out. Conine singled to right, Cabrera to second. Gonzalez doubled to left, Cabrera scored, Conine to third. Redman grounded out, pitcher Wood to first baseman Karros. One run. Cubs 2, Marlins 1.

SEVENTH INNING

Marlins—Gonzalez singled to center. Lowell walked on a full count, Gonzalez to second. Pierre sacrificed, pitcher Wood to first baseman Karros, Gonzalez to third, Lowell to second. Castillo grounded out, second baseman Grudzielanek to first baseman Karros, Gonzalez scored, Lowell to third. Rodriguez singled to right, Lowell scored. Farnsworth pitching. Simon in as first baseman. Lee struck out. Two runs. Marlins 3, Cubs 2.

EIGHTH INNING

Cubs—Gonzalez flied out to center fielder Pierre. Goodwin pinch-hitting for Miller. Goodwin tripled to center. Simon homered to center on the first pitch, Goodwin scored. Lofton grounded out, first baseman Lee unassisted. Grudzielanek grounded out, shortstop Gonzalez to first baseman Lee. Two runs. Cubs 4, Marlins 3.

Marlins—Bako in as catcher. Cabrera singled to center. Mordecai pinch-hitting for C.Fox. Mordecai sacrificed, pitcher Farnsworth to second baseman Grudzielanek, Cabrera to second. Conine lined out to center fielder Lofton. Borowski pitching. Martinez in as second baseman. Hollandsworth pinch-hitting for Gonzalez. Hollandsworth singled to left, Cabrera scored. Hollandsworth to second. Lowell flied out to right fielder Sosa. One run. Cubs 4, Marlins 4.

ELEVENTH INNING

Cubs—Tejera pitching. Simon lined out to second baseman Castillo. Lofton singled to left. Glanville pinch-hitting for Borowski. Looper pitching. Glanville tripled to center, Lofton scored. Sosa was intentionally walked. Alou popped out to first baseman Lee. Ramirez popped out to second baseman Castillo. One run. Cubs 5, Marlins 4.

GAME 4

CHICAGO 8, FLORIDA 3

SATURDAY, OCTOBER 11, AT FLORIDA

Chi Cubs	AB	R	H	BI	BB	SO	PO	A
K.Lofton, cf	3	2	1	0	2	0	2	0
Grudzielanek, 2b	5	0	0	0	0	2	3	3
S.Sosa, rf	2	2	0	0	3	2	3	0
Alou, lf	4	2	2	1	1	0	2	0
A.Ramirez, 3b	4	2	3	6	1	1	0	4
Karros, 1b	4	0	0	0	1	1	12	0
A.Gonzalez, ss	5	0	1	1	0	2	1	5
D.Miller, c	4	0	1	0	0	1	4	1
Clement, p	4	0	0	0	0	1	0	1
K.Farnsworth, p	0	0	0	0	0	0	0	0
TOTALS	35	8	8	8	8	10	27	14

Florida	AB	R	H	BI	BB	SO	PO	A
Pierre, cf	4	1	1	0	0	0	0	0
L.Castillo, 2b	4	0	0	0	0	0	2	2
I.Rodriguez, c	4	0	2	1	0	0	10	0
D.Lee, 1b	3	0	0	0	0	0	8	1
M.Cabrera, rf	4	1	1	0	0	0	4	0
Lowell, 3b	3	0	0	0	1	1	0	2
Conine, lf	4	1	1	0	0	1	1	0
A.Gonzalez, ss	3	0	0	1	0	2	1	1
Willis, p	0	0	0	0	0	0	1	0
Helling, p	1	0	0	0	0	0	0	0
Hollandsworth, ph	1	0	1	1	0	0	0	0
Bump, p	0	0	0	0	0	0	0	1
Penny, p	0	0	0	0	0	0	0	1
L.Harris, ph	0	0	0	0	1	0	0	0
Pavano, p	0	0	0	0	0	0	0	0
TOTALS	31	3	6	3	2	4	27	8

Chi Cubs	4 0 2	1 0 0	1 0 0—8	8 0
Florida	0 0 0	0 2 0	0 1 0—3	6 1

Chi Cubs	IP	H	R	ER	HR	BB	SO
Clement (W)	7.2	5	3	3	0	2	3
K.Farnsworth	1.1	1	0	0	0	0	1

Florida	IP	H	R	ER	HR	BB	SO
Willis (L)	2.1	3	6	6	1	5	2
Helling	2.2	2	1	1	0	2	4
Bump	2.0	1	1	1	1	0	2
Penny	1.0	2	0	0	0	1	0
Pavano	1.0	0	0	0	0	0	2

E—I.Rodriguez. DP—Chi Cubs 1. LOB—Chi Cubs 8, Florida 4. Scoring Position—Chi Cubs 4 for 10, Florida 3 for 5. 2B—I.Rodriguez. HR—A.Ramirez (1st inning, 1 out, 3 on) off Willis, A.Ramirez (7th inning, 1 out, 0 on) off Bump. CS—Pierre. WP—Helling. HBP—D.Lee by Clement. T—2:58. A—65,829. U—HP-Everitt, 1B-Poncino, 2B-Reilly, 3B-Crawford, LF-Meriwether, RF-Culbreth.

HOW THEY SCORED

FIRST INNING

Cubs—Lofton walked on a full count. Grudzielanek struck out. Sosa walked on four pitches, Lofton to second. Alou walked on four pitches, Lofton to third, Sosa to second. Ramirez homered to left on a 2-2 count, Lofton scored, Sosa scored, Alou scored. Karros flied out to right fielder Cabrera. Gonzalez struck out. Four runs. Cubs 4, Marlins 0.

THIRD INNING

Cubs—Grudzielanek flied out to right fielder Cabrera. Sosa walked on a full count. Alou singled to left, Sosa to second. Ramirez singled to right, Sosa scored, Alou to third. On Rodriguez's error, Ramirez to second. Karros walked on a full count. Helling pitching. Gonzalez singled to left, Alou scored, Ramirez to third, Karros to second. Miller struck out. Clement grounded out, second baseman Castillo to first baseman Lee. Two runs. Cubs 6, Marlins 0.

FOURTH INNING

Cubs—Lofton walked on a full count. Grudzielanek struck out. On Helling's wild pitch, Lofton to second. Sosa struck out. Alou singled to right, Lofton scored. Ramirez walked on a full count, Alou to second. Karros flied out to left fielder Conine. One run. Cubs 7, Marlins 0.

FIFTH INNING

Marlins—Cabrera singled to right. Lowell grounded out, first baseman Karros unassisted, Cabrera to second. Conine infield single to short, Cabrera to third. Gonzalez grounded out, shortstop Gonzalez to first baseman Karros, Cabrera scored, Conine to second. Hollandsworth pinch-hitting for Helling. Hollandsworth singled to center, Conine scored. Pierre flied out to left fielder Alou. Two runs. Cubs 7, Marlins 2.

SEVENTH INNING

Cubs—Alou grounded out, shortstop Gonzalez to first baseman Lee. Ramirez homered to left on a 0-1 count. Karros struck out. Gonzalez lined out to shortstop Gonzalez. One run. Cubs 8, Marlins 2.

EIGHTH INNING

Marlins—Harris pinch-hitting for Penny. Harris walked on a full count. Pierre grounded into fielder's choice, third baseman Ramirez to second baseman Grudzielanek, Harris out. Castillo grounded out, pitcher Clement to first baseman Karros, Pierre to second. Farnsworth pitching. Rodriguez doubled to right, Pierre scored. Lee lined out to second baseman Grudzielanek. One run. Cubs 8, Marlins 3.

GAME 5

FLORIDA 4, CHICAGO 0

SUNDAY, OCTOBER 12, AT FLORIDA

Chi Cubs	AB	R	H	BI	BB	SO	PO	A
K.Lofton, cf	4	0	0	0	0	1	3	0
Grudzielanek, 2b	4	0	0	0	0	1	3	3
S.Sosa, rf	4	0	0	0	0	1	2	0
Alou, lf	3	0	1	0	0	1	1	0
A.Ramirez, 3b	2	0	0	0	1	2	0	2
Simon, 1b	3	0	0	0	0	0	9	0
A.Gonzalez, ss	3	0	1	0	0	1	1	3
Bako, c	3	0	0	0	0	2	5	1
C.Zambrano, p	1	0	0	0	0	1	0	2
Goodwin, ph	1	0	0	0	0	1	0	0
Veres, p	0	0	0	0	0	0	0	1
Alfonseca, p	0	0	0	0	0	0	0	0
O'Leary, ph	1	0	0	0	0	0	0	0
Remlinger, p	0	0	0	0	0	0	0	0
TOTALS	29	0	2	0	1	11	24	12

Florida	AB	R	H	BI	BB	SO	PO	A
Pierre, cf	4	0	1	0	1	0	2	0
L.Castillo, 2b	4	0	1	0	0	1	0	4
I.Rodriguez, c	3	1	1	1	1	0	11	0
M.Cabrera, rf	2	1	1	0	1	1	1	0
D.Lee, 1b	4	0	0	0	0	1	10	1
Lowell, 3b	4	1	2	2	0	0	2	1
Conine, lf	3	1	1	1	1	1	0	0
A.Gonzalez, ss	4	0	0	0	0	1	0	5
Beckett, p	3	0	1	0	1	0	1	0
TOTALS	31	4	8	4	5	5	27	11

Chi Cubs	0 0 0	0 0 0	0 0 0—0 2 0
Florida	0 0 0	0 2 0	1 1 x—4 8 0

Chi Cubs	IP	H	R	ER	HR	BB	SO
C.Zambrano (L)	5.0	5	2	2	1	4	5
Veres	1.1	2	1	1	1	0	0
Alfonseca	0.2	0	0	0	0	0	0
Remlinger	1.0	1	1	1	1	1	0
Florida	**IP**	**H**	**R**	**ER**	**HR**	**BB**	**SO**
Beckett (W)	9.0	2	0	0	0	1	11

DP—Chi Cubs 1. LOB—Chi Cubs 3, Florida 9. Scoring Position—Chi Cubs 0 for 0, Florida 0 for 2. HR—Lowell (5th inning, 2 out, 1 on) off C.Zambrano, I.Rodriguez (7th inning, 1 out, 0 on) off Veres, Conine (8th inning, 1 out, 0 on) off Remlinger. WP—C.Zambrano. HBP—M.Cabrera by C.Zambrano. T—2:42. A—65,279. U—HP-Poncino, 1B-Reilly, 2B-Crawford, 3B-Meriwether, LF-Culbreth, RF-Everitt.

HOW THEY SCORED

FIFTH INNING

Marlins—Rodriguez grounded out, pitcher Zambrano to second baseman Grudzielanek to first baseman Simon. Cabrera walked. Lee flied out to center fielder Lofton. Lowell homered to left on a 1-0 count, Cabrera scored. Conine flied out to center fielder Lofton. Two runs. Marlins 2, Cubs 0.

SEVENTH INNING

Marlins—Castillo grounded out, second baseman Grudzielanek to first baseman Simon. Rodriguez homered to left on a 0-1 count. Cabrera singled to center. Alfonseca pitching. Lee grounded into a double play, third baseman Ramirez to second baseman Grudzielanek to first baseman Simon, Cabrera out. One run. Marlins 3, Cubs 0.

EIGHTH INNING

Marlins—Remlinger pitching. Lowell flied out to right fielder Sosa. Conine homered to left on the first pitch. Gonzalez flied out to center fielder Lofton. Beckett walked. Pierre lined out to shortstop Gonzalez. One run. Marlins 4, Cubs 0.

GAME 6

FLORIDA 8, CHICAGO 3

TUESDAY, OCTOBER 14, AT CHICAGO

Florida	AB	R	H	BI	BB	SO	PO	A
Pierre, cf	5	1	3	1	0	0	0	0
L.Castillo, 2b	4	1	1	0	1	0	3	1
I.Rodriguez, c	4	1	1	1	1	1	9	0
M.Cabrera, rf	5	1	1	0	0	1	3	0
Encarnacion, rf	0	0	0	0	0	0	1	0
D.Lee, 1b	5	1	1	2	0	1	6	1
Lowell, 3b	3	1	0	0	1	1	1	0
Conine, lf	2	0	1	1	1	0	2	0
A.Gonzalez, ss	3	0	0	0	0	1	2	4
C.Fox, p	0	0	0	0	0	0	0	0
Hollandsworth, ph	0	1	0	0	1	0	0	0
Urbina, p	0	0	0	0	0	0	0	0
Pavano, p	2	0	0	0	0	1	0	0
Willis, p	0	0	0	0	0	0	0	1
Mordecai, ss	2	1	1	3	0	0	0	0
TOTALS	35	8	9	8	5	6	27	7

Chi Cubs	AB	R	H	BI	BB	SO	PO	A
K.Lofton, cf	5	1	1	0	0	2	6	0
Grudzielanek, 2b	3	0	1	1	0	1	3	3
S.Sosa, rf	4	1	3	1	0	1	3	0
Alou, lf	4	0	2	0	0	0	2	0
A.Ramirez, 3b	4	0	1	0	0	1	1	2
Simon, 1b	2	0	0	0	0	0	2	0
Karros, ph-1b	1	0	0	0	1	0	1	0
A.Gonzalez, ss	3	0	0	0	1	1	3	0
Alfonseca, p	0	0	0	0	0	0	0	0
Bako, c	4	1	2	0	0	1	6	1
Prior, p	2	0	0	0	0	2	0	0
K.Farnsworth, p	0	0	0	0	0	0	0	0
Remlinger, p	0	0	0	0	0	0	0	0
R.Martinez, ss	1	0	0	0	0	0	0	0
TOTALS	33	3	10	2	2	9	27	6

				R	H	E
Florida	0 0 0	0 0 0	0 8 0	8	9	0
Chi Cubs	1 0 0	0 0 1	1 0 0	3	10	2

Florida	IP	H	R	ER	HR	BB	SO
Pavano	5.2	7	2	2	0	1	5
Willis	1.0	1	1	1	0	1	2
C.Fox (W)	0.1	2	0	0	0	0	0
Urbina	2.0	0	0	0	0	0	2

Chi Cubs	IP	H	R	ER	HR	BB	SO
Prior (L)	7.1	6	5	3	0	3	6
K.Farnsworth	0.1	1	3	3	0	2	0
Remlinger	0.1	1	0	0	0	0	0
Alfonseca	1.0	1	0	0	0	0	0

E—A.Gonzalez, Grudzielanek. DP—Florida 2, Chi Cubs 1. LOB—Florida 6, Chi Cubs 7. Scoring Position—Florida 4 for 10, Chi Cubs 3 for 8. 2B—Pierre, D.Lee, Mordecai, S.Sosa. CS—Pierre. S—Conine. SH—Grudzielanek, Prior. WP—Willis, Prior. PB—Bako. T—3:00. A—39,577. U—HP-Reilly, 1B-Crawford, 2B-Meriwether, 3B-Culbreth, LF-Everitt, RF-Poncino.

HOW THEY SCORED

FIRST INNING

Cubs—Lofton singled to right. Grudzielanek sacrificed, first baseman Lee to second baseman Castillo, Lofton to second. Sosa doubled to right, Lofton scored. Alou infield single to short. Ramirez lined out to left fielder Conine. Simon lined out to right fielder Cabrera. One run. Cubs 1, Marlins 0.

SIXTH INNING

Cubs—Sosa infield single to third. Alou singled to left, Sosa to second. Ramirez grounded into a double play, shortstop Gonzalez to first baseman Lee, Sosa to third, Alou out. Willis pitching. Karros pinch-hitting for Simon. Karros walked. On Willis' wild pitch, Sosa scored. Gonzalez struck out. One run. Cubs 2, Marlins 0.

SEVENTH INNING

Cubs—Bako singled to center. Prior sacrificed, pitcher Willis to second baseman Castillo, Bako to second. Lofton struck out. C.Fox pitching. Mordecai in as shortstop. Grudzielanek singled to center, Bako scored. Sosa singled to right, Grudzielanek to third. Alou flied out to right fielder Cabrera. One run. Cubs 3, Marlins 0.

EIGHTH INNING

Marlins—Mordecai flied out to left fielder Alou. Pierre doubled to left. Castillo walked on a full count. On Prior's wild pitch, Pierre to third. Rodriguez singled to left, Pierre scored, Castillo to second. Cabrera safe on Gonzalez's error, Castillo to third, Rodriguez to second. Lee doubled to left, Castillo scored, Rodriguez scored, Cabrera to third. Farnsworth pitching. Lowell was intentionally walked. Conine hit a sacrifice fly to right fielder Sosa, Cabrera scored, Lee to third. Lowell to second. Hollandsworth pinch-hitting for C.Fox. Hollandsworth was intentionally walked. Mordecai doubled to center, Lee scored, Lowell scored, Hollandsworth scored. Remlinger pitching. Pierre singled to right, Mordecai scored. Castillo popped out to second baseman Grudzielanek. Eight runs. Marlins 8, Cubs 3.

GAME 7

FLORIDA 9, CHICAGO 6

WEDNESDAY, OCTOBER 15, AT CHICAGO

Florida	AB	R	H	BI	BB	SO	PO	A
Pierre, cf	5	1	2	0	0	0	5	0
L.Castillo, 2b	4	1	1	1	1	0	1	2
I.Rodriguez, c	4	2	1	1	1	2	6	0
M.Cabrera, rf	5	1	1	4	0	1	7	0
Urbina, p	0	0	0	0	0	0	0	0
D.Lee, 1b	5	0	2	1	0	2	7	0
Lowell, 3b	5	1	1	0	0	2	0	2
Conine, lf	3	2	3	0	1	0	1	0
A.Gonzalez, ss	4	0	1	2	0	0	0	3
M.Redman, p	1	0	0	0	0	0	0	0
Penny, p	0	0	0	0	0	0	0	0
B.Banks, ph	0	1	0	0	1	0	0	0
Beckett, p	2	0	0	0	0	2	0	0
Encarnacion, rf	0	0	0	0	0	0	0	0
TOTALS	38	9	12	9	4	9	27	7

Chi Cubs	AB	R	H	BI	BB	SO	PO	A
K.Lofton, cf	4	0	0	0	0	1	5	1
Grudzielanek, 2b	4	0	1	0	0	0	0	1
S.Sosa, rf	3	1	0	0	0	1	1	0
Alou, lf	4	1	1	2	0	0	2	0
A.Ramirez, 3b	3	0	0	0	0	0	1	1
Karros, 1b	3	1	1	0	0	1	6	0
Simon, ph	1	0	0	0	0	1	0	0
A.Gonzalez, ss	4	1	1	0	0	1	2	3
D.Miller, c	2	0	0	1	0	0	9	1
Goodwin, ph	1	0	0	0	0	1	0	0
Bako, c	1	0	0	0	0	0	1	0
K.Wood, p	2	1	1	2	0	0	0	0
K.Farnsworth, p	0	0	0	0	0	0	0	0
Veres, p	0	0	0	0	0	0	0	0
O'Leary, ph	1	1	1	1	0	0	0	0
Remlinger, p	0	0	0	0	0	0	0	0
Borowski, p	0	0	0	0	0	0	0	0
TOTALS	33	6	6	6	0	6	27	7

				R	H	E
Florida	3 0 0	0 3 1	2 0 0	9	12	0
Chi Cubs	0 3 2	0 0 0	1 0 0	6	6	0

Florida	IP	H	R	ER	HR	BB	SO
M.Redman	3.0	5	5	5	2	0	1
Penny (W)	1.0	0	0	0	0	0	0
Beckett	4.0	1	1	1	1	0	3
Urbina (S)	1.0	0	0	0	0	0	2

Chi Cubs	IP	H	R	ER	HR	BB	SO
K.Wood (L)	5.2	7	7	7	1	4	6
K.Farnsworth	1.0	3	2	2	0	0	2
Veres	0.1	1	0	0	0	0	0
Remlinger	0.2	0	0	0	0	0	1
Borowski	1.1	1	0	0	0	0	0

LOB—Florida 6, Chi Cubs 2. Scoring Position—Florida 5 for 10, Chi Cubs 1 for 2. 2B—I.Rodriguez, D.Lee, A.Gonzalez, A.Gonzalez. 3B—Pierre. HR—M.Cabrera (1st inning, 1 out, 2 on) off K.Wood, K.Wood (2nd inning, 2 out, 1 on) off M.Redman, Alou (3rd inning, 1 out, 1 on) off M.Redman, O'Leary (7th inning, 2 out, 0 on) off Beckett. SB—D.Lee. HBP—S.Sosa by M.Redman, A.Ramirez by Urbina. T—3:11. A—39,574. U—HP-Crawford, 1B-Meriwether, 2B-Culbreth, 3B-Everitt, LF-Poncino, RF-Reilly.

HOW THEY SCORED

FIRST INNING

Marlins—Pierre tripled to right. Castillo lined out to left fielder Alou. Rodriguez walked on a full count. Cabrera homered to center on a 1-2 count, Pierre scored, Rodriguez scored. Lee struck out. Lowell struck out. Three runs. Marlins 3, Cubs 0.

SECOND INNING

Cubs—Ramirez popped out to second baseman Castillo. Karros singled to right. Gonzalez doubled to center, Karros to third. Miller grounded out, third baseman Lowell to first baseman Lee, Karros scored, Gonzalez to third. Wood homered to center on a full count, Gonzalez scored. Lofton struck out. Three runs. Marlins 3, Cubs 3.

THIRD INNING

Cubs—Grudzielanek grounded out, shortstop Gonzalez to first baseman Lee. Sosa was hit by a pitch. Alou homered to left on a full count, Sosa scored. Ramirez lined out to right fielder Cabrera. Karros flied out to center fielder Pierre. Two runs. Cubs 5, Marlins 3.

FIFTH INNING

Marlins—Banks pinch-hitting for Penny. Banks walked. Pierre flied out to center fielder Lofton. Castillo walked on a full count, Banks to second. Rodriguez doubled to left, Banks scored, Castillo to third. Cabrera grounded out, first baseman Karros unassisted, Castillo scored, Rodriguez to third. Lee singled to right, Rodriguez scored. Lee stole second. Lowell struck out. Three runs. Marlins 6, Cubs 5.

SIXTH INNING

Marlins—Conine singled to center. Gonzalez flied out to center fielder Lofton. Beckett struck out. Pierre singled to right, Conine to third. Farnsworth pitching. Castillo infield single to pitcher Farnsworth, Conine scored, Pierre to second. Rodriguez struck out. One run. Marlins 7, Cubs 5.

SEVENTH INNING

Marlins—Cabrera grounded out, shortstop Gonzalez to first baseman Karros. Lee struck out. Lowell singled to right. Conine singled to center, Lowell to second. Veres pitching. Gonzalez doubled to center, Lowell scored, Conine scored. Gonzalez was out advancing, center fielder Lofton to catcher Miller to third baseman Ramirez, Gonzalez out. Two runs. Marlins 9, Cubs 5.

Cubs—Gonzalez flied out to center fielder Pierre. Goodwin pinch-hitting for Miller. Goodwin struck out. O'Leary pinch-hitting for Veres. O'Leary homered to right on a full count. Lofton flied out to right fielder Cabrera. One run. Marlins 9, Cubs 6.

STATISTICS

FLORIDA MARLINS' BATTING AND FIELDING AVERAGES

	BATTING															FIELDING			
Player, position	**G**	**AB**	**R**	**H**	**TB**	**2B**	**3B**	**HR**	**RBI**	**BB**	**IBB**	**SO**	**Avg.**	**OBP**	**Slg.**	**PO**	**A**	**E**	**Avg.**
Hollandsworth,ph	4	3	2	3	4	1	0	0	2	1	1	0	1.000	1.000	1.333	0	0	0	.000
Conine,lf	7	24	4	11	17	1	1	1	3	4	0	2	.458	.500	.708	7	0	1	.875
Cabrera,3b-ss-rf	7	30	9	10	19	0	0	3	6	2	0	6	.333	.394	.633	16	5	0	1.000
Rodriguez,c	7	28	5	9	17	2	0	2	10	5	2	7	.321	.424	.607	58	0	1	.983
Pierre,cf	7	33	5	10	15	1	2	0	1	2	0	1	.303	.343	.455	13	0	0	1.000
Encarnacion,rf	5	12	1	3	7	1	0	1	1	0	0	4	.250	.250	.583	7	0	0	1.000
Beckett,p	3	8	0	2	2	0	0	0	0	1	0	3	.250	.333	.250	2	0	0	1.000
Castillo,2b	7	28	3	6	7	1	0	0	2	5	0	2	.214	.333	.250	16	19	0	1.000
Lowell,3b-ph	7	20	5	4	10	0	0	2	3	3	1	4	.200	.304	.500	4	8	0	1.000
Mordecai,2b-ph-ss	3	5	1	1	2	1	0	0	3	0	0	0	.200	.200	.400	0	0	0	.000
Lee,1b	7	32	2	6	11	2	0	1	4	1	0	8	.188	.235	.344	66	6	0	1.000
Gonzalez,ss	7	24	1	3	5	2	0	0	4	0	0	6	.125	.125	.208	6	26	1	.970
Bump,p	2	0	0	0	0	0	0	0	0	0	0	0	.000	.000	.000	0	1	0	1.000
Fox,p	3	0	0	0	0	0	0	0	0	0	0	0	.000	.000	.000	0	0	0	.000
Looper,p	2	0	0	0	0	0	0	0	0	0	0	0	.000	.000	.000	0	0	0	.000
Redmond,c	1	0	1	0	0	0	0	0	0	1	0	0	.000	1.000	.000	2	0	0	1.000
Tejera,p	2	0	0	0	0	0	0	0	0	0	0	0	.000	.000	.000	0	0	0	.000
Urbina,p	4	0	0	0	0	0	0	0	0	0	0	0	.000	.000	.000	0	0	0	.000
Willis,p	2	0	0	0	0	0	0	0	0	0	0	0	.000	.000	.000	1	1	0	1.000
Banks,ph	2	1	1	0	0	0	0	0	0	1	0	0	.000	.500	.000	0	0	0	.000
Helling,p	2	1	0	0	0	0	0	0	0	0	0	0	.000	.000	.000	0	1	0	1.000
Penny,p	3	1	0	0	0	0	0	0	0	0	0	1	.000	.000	.000	0	2	0	1.000
Harris,ph	3	2	0	0	0	0	0	0	0	1	0	0	.000	.333	.000	0	0	0	.000
Pavano,p	3	2	0	0	0	0	0	0	0	0	0	1	.000	.000	.000	0	0	0	.000
Redman,p	2	2	0	0	0	0	0	0	0	1	0	0	.000	.333	.000	0	1	0	1.000
Totals	7	256	40	68	116	12	3	10	39	28	4	45	.266	.340	.453	198	70	3	.989

CHICAGO CUBS' BATTING AND FIELDING AVERAGES

	BATTING															FIELDING			
Player, position	**G**	**AB**	**R**	**H**	**TB**	**2B**	**3B**	**HR**	**RBI**	**BB**	**IBB**	**SO**	**Avg.**	**OBP**	**Slg.**	**PO**	**A**	**E**	**Avg.**
Glanville,lf-ph	1	1	0	1	3	0	1	0	1	0	0	0	1.000	1.000	3.000	0	0	0	.000
O'Leary,lf-ph	3	3	1	1	4	0	0	1	1	0	0	0	.333	.333	1.333	0	0	0	.000
Wood,p	2	3	1	1	4	0	0	1	3	0	0	0	.333	.250	1.333	0	3	0	1.000
Lofton,cf	7	31	8	10	11	1	0	0	2	3	0	4	.323	.382	.355	26	1	0	1.000
Alou,lf	7	29	4	9	16	1	0	2	5	2	0	1	.310	.355	.552	9	1	0	1.000
Sosa,rf	7	26	7	8	15	1	0	2	6	6	3	9	.308	.455	.577	17	0	0	1.000
Simon,1b-ph	6	17	3	5	10	2	0	1	4	0	0	3	.294	.294	.588	32	0	1	.970
Gonzalez,ss	7	28	5	8	19	2	0	3	7	2	0	7	.286	.333	.679	12	18	1	.968
Bako,c	6	16	4	4	5	1	0	0	1	1	0	7	.250	.294	.313	22	3	0	1.000
Goodwin,ph-rf	5	4	1	1	3	0	1	0	0	0	0	3	.250	.250	.750	0	0	0	.000
Ramirez,3b	7	26	4	6	17	0	1	3	7	5	0	6	.231	.375	.654	4	18	0	1.000
Karros,1b-ph	5	13	2	3	3	0	0	0	0	2	0	3	.231	.333	.231	29	1	0	1.000
Grudzielanek,2b	7	30	2	6	9	1	1	0	3	0	0	5	.200	.200	.300	20	23	2	.956
Miller,c	4	10	0	2	3	1	0	0	1	2	0	2	.200	.333	.300	25	2	0	1.000
Alfonseca,p	3	0	0	0	0	0	0	0	0	0	0	0	.000	.000	.000	0	0	0	.000
Borowski,p	3	0	0	0	0	0	0	0	0	0	0	0	.000	.000	.000	0	0	0	.000
Farnsworth,p	5	0	0	0	0	0	0	0	0	0	0	0	.000	.000	.000	0	2	0	1.000
Guthrie,p	2	0	0	0	0	0	0	0	0	0	0	0	.000	.000	.000	1	0	0	1.000
Remlinger,p	5	0	0	0	0	0	0	0	0	0	0	0	.000	.000	.000	0	1	0	1.000
Veres,p	3	0	0	0	0	0	0	0	0	0	0	0	.000	.000	.000	0	1	0	1.000
Zambrano,p	2	3	0	0	0	0	0	0	0	0	0	3	.000	.000	.000	0	3	0	1.000
Clement,p	1	4	0	0	0	0	0	0	0	0	0	1	.000	.000	.000	0	1	0	1.000
Martinez,ss-ph-2b	4	4	0	0	0	0	0	0	0	0	0	1	.000	.000	.000	1	3	0	1.000
Prior,p	2	4	0	0	0	0	0	0	0	0	0	2	.000	.000	.000	0	0	0	.000
Totals	7	252	42	65	122	10	4	13	41	23	3	57	.258	.324	.484	198	81	4	.986

FLORIDA MARLINS' PITCHING RECORDS

Pitcher	G	GS	CG	IP	H	R	ER	HR	BB	IBB	SO	HB	WP	W	L	Pct.	ERA
Looper	2	0	0	1.2	1	0	0	0	1	1	1	0	0	0	0	.000	0.00
Pavano	3	1	0	7.2	8	2	2	0	1	0	8	0	0	0	0	.000	2.35
Urbina	4	0	0	7.0	2	2	2	1	0	0	10	1	0	1	0	1.000	2.57
Beckett	3	2	1	19.1	11	7	7	3	2	0	19	0	0	1	0	1.000	3.26
Fox	3	0	0	3.1	5	2	2	1	2	0	2	0	0	1	0	1.000	5.40
Bump	2	0	0	3.0	3	2	2	1	0	0	3	0	1	0	0	.000	6.00
Helling	2	0	0	5.2	7	5	4	2	4	1	5	0	2	0	0	.000	6.35
Redman	2	2	0	9.2	13	7	7	2	4	0	4	1	0	0	0	.000	6.52
Tejera	2	0	0	1.1	2	1	1	0	0	0	1	0	0	0	1	.000	6.75
Penny	3	1	0	4.0	9	7	7	2	3	1	0	0	0	1	1	.500	15.75
Willis	2	1	0	3.1	4	7	7	1	6	0	4	0	1	0	1	.000	18.90
Totals	7	7	1	66.0	65	42	41	13	23	3	57	2	4	4	3	.571	5.59

Shutouts—Beckett. Saves—Looper, Urbina.

CHICAGO CUBS' PITCHING RECORDS

Pitcher	G	GS	CG	IP	H	R	ER	HR	BB	IBB	SO	HB	WP	W	L	Pct.	ERA
Alfonseca	3	0	0	2.1	2	0	0	0	2	1	0	0	0	0	0	.000	0.00
Borowski	3	0	0	5.2	5	2	1	0	3	1	1	0	0	1	0	1.000	1.59
Remlinger	5	0	0	3.1	3	1	1	1	1	0	2	0	1	0	0	.000	2.70
Veres	3	0	0	3.0	4	1	1	1	1	0	0	0	0	0	0	.000	3.00
Prior	2	2	0	14.1	14	8	5	2	5	0	11	0	1	1	1	.500	3.14
Clement	1	1	0	7.2	5	3	3	0	2	0	3	1	0	1	0	1.000	3.52
Zambrano	2	2	0	11.0	14	8	7	4	5	0	8	1	1	0	1	.000	5.73
Wood	2	2	0	12.1	14	10	10	1	7	0	13	0	0	0	1	.000	7.30
Guthrie	2	0	0	1.0	1	1	1	1	0	0	0	0	0	0	1	.000	9.00
Farnsworth	5	0	0	5.1	6	6	6	0	2	2	7	0	0	0	0	.000	10.13
Totals	7	7	0	66.0	68	40	32	10	28	4	45	2	3	3	4	.429	4.36

No shutouts. Saves—Remlinger.

SCORE BY INNINGS

Florida	3 1 5			0 7 4			5 12 2			0 1	—40
Chicago	12 7 7			1 3 4			3 2 2			0 1	—42

MISCELLANEOUS STATISTICS

Sacrifice hits—Prior 3, Grudzielanek 2, Castillo, Lofton, Mordecai, Pierre, Wood.
Sacrifice flies—Conine 2, Wood.
Stolen bases—Castillo 2, Lee, Lofton, Pierre.
Caught stealing—Pierre 3.
Double plays—Gonzalez and Lee 2; Alou, Grudzielanek and Simon; Castillo, Gonzalez and Lee; Gonzalez, Castillo and Lee; Gonzalez, Grudzielanek and Karros; Grudzielanek, Gonzalez and Simon; Martinez and Grudzielanek; Ramirez, Grudzielanek and Karros; Ramirez, Grudzielanek and Simon.
Left on bases—Florida 8, 8, 12, 4, 9, 6, 6—53; Chicago 5, 8, 12, 8, 3, 7, 2—45.
Scoring position—Florida 2 for 13, 2 for 10, 3 for 11, 3 for 5, 0 for 2, 4 for 10, 5 for 10—19 for 61; Chicago 4 for 11, 7 for 16, 3 for 11, 4 for 10, 0 for 0, 3 for 8, 1 for 2—22 for 58.
Hit by pitcher—by Urbina (Ramirez), by Clement (Lee), by Redman (Sosa), by Zambrano (Cabrera).
Passed balls—Bako 2.
Balks—None.
Time of games—3:44, 3:02, 4:16, 2:58, 2:42, 3:00, 3:11—Avg.: 3:16.
Attendance—39,567, 39,562, 65,115, 65,829, 65,279, 39,577, 39,574—354,503.
Umpires—Crawford, Jerry; Meriwether, Chuck; Culbreth, Fieldin; Everitt, Mike; Vanover, Larry; Poncino, Larry; Reilly, Mike.

WORLD SERIES

FLORIDA VS. NEW YORK

RESULTS

Day	Date	Place	Score
Sat.	Oct. 18	New York	Florida 3, New York 2
Sun.	Oct. 19	New York	New York 6, Florida 1
Tue.	Oct. 21	Florida	New York 6, Forida 1
Wed.	Oct. 22	Florida	Florida 4, New York 3
Thur.	Oct. 23	Florida	Florida 6, New York 4
Sat.	Oct. 25	New York	Florida, 2 New York 0

BOX SCORES

GAME 1

FLORIDA 3, NEW YORK 2

SATURDAY, OCTOBER 18, AT NEW YORK

Florida	AB	R	H	BI	BB	SO	PO	A
Pierre, cf	3	1	2	2	1	0	3	0
L.Castillo, 2b	5	0	1	0	0	0	2	1
I.Rodriguez, c	3	0	0	1	0	0	7	1
M.Cabrera, lf	3	0	0	0	1	0	4	0
D.Lee, 1b	4	0	1	0	0	1	7	0
Lowell, 3b	4	0	0	0	0	0	1	3
Conine, dh	2	1	1	0	2	0	0	0
Encarnacion, rf	4	1	2	0	0	1	2	0
A.Gonzalez, ss	3	0	0	0	0	1	1	4
Penny, p	0	0	0	0	0	0	0	0
Willis, p	0	0	0	0	0	0	0	1
Urbina, p	0	0	0	0	0	0	0	0
TOTALS	31	3	7	3	4	3	27	10

NY Yankees	AB	R	H	BI	BB	SO	PO	A
A.Soriano, 2b	5	0	1	0	0	1	3	2
N.Johnson, 1b	4	0	0	0	1	1	9	0
Jeter, ss	4	0	1	1	0	1	1	4
B.Williams, cf	4	1	2	1	0	0	5	0
Matsui, lf	4	0	3	0	0	0	2	0
Posada, c	2	0	0	0	2	1	3	0
Ja.Giambi, dh	3	0	0	0	1	1	0	0
Dellucci, pr	0	0	0	0	0	0	0	0
A.Boone, 3b	4	0	0	0	0	1	2	3
K.Garcia, rf	2	1	2	0	0	0	0	0
J.Rivera, ph-rf	1	0	0	0	0	1	2	0
Sierra, ph	0	0	0	0	1	0	0	0
D.Wells, p	0	0	0	0	0	0	0	1
J.Nelson, p	0	0	0	0	0	0	0	0
Contreras, p	0	0	0	0	0	0	0	0
TOTALS	33	2	9	2	5	7	27	10

Florida....................................1 0 0 0 2 0 0 0 0—3 7 1
NY Yankees...........................0 0 1 0 0 1 0 0 0—2 9 0

Florida	IP	H	R	ER	HR	BB	SO
Penny (W)	5.1	7	2	2	1	3	3
Willis (HOLD)	2.1	2	0	0	0	0	2
Urbina (S)	1.1	0	0	0	0	2	2

NY Yankees	IP	H	R	ER	HR	BB	SO
D.Wells (L)	7.0	6	3	3	0	2	1
J.Nelson	1.0	1	0	0	0	1	0
Contreras	1.0	0	0	0	0	1	2

Bases on balls—Off Penny 3 (Posada 2, N.Johnson), off Urbina 2 (Sierra, Ja.Giambi), off D.Wells 2 (Conine 2), off J.Nelson 1 (M.Cabrera), off Contreras 1 (Pierre).

Strikeouts—By Penny 3 (Ja.Giambi, A.Boone, N.Johnson), by Willis 2 (Jeter, J.Rivera), by Urbina 2 (Posada, A.Soriano), by D.Wells 1 (D.Lee), by Contreras 2 (Encarnacion, A.Gonzalez).

E—M.Cabrera. DP—Florida 2, NY Yankees 1. LOB—Florida 8, NY Yankees 9. Scoring Position—Florida 1 for 7, NY Yankees 1 for 12. HR—B.Williams (6th inning, 1 out, 0 on) off Penny. SB—Pierre, L.Castillo, A.Soriano, Posada. S—I.Rodriguez. SH—A.Gonzalez. HBP—Pierre by D.Wells. T—3:43. A—55,769. U—HP-Marsh, 1B-Young, 2B-Darling, 3B-Kellogg, LF-Rapuano, RF-Welke.

PLAY BY PLAY

FIRST INNING

Marlins—Pierre bunt single to first. Castillo singled to right, Pierre to third. Rodriguez hit a sacrifice fly to center fielder Williams, Pierre scored. Cabrera popped out to shortstop Jeter. Castillo stole second. Lee struck out. One run. Marlins 1, Yankees 0.

Yankees—Soriano infield single to short. Soriano stole second. Johnson struck out. Jeter flied out to right fielder Encarnacion. Williams flied out to center fielder Pierre.

SECOND INNING

Marlins—Lowell grounded out, third baseman Boone to first baseman Johnson. Conine singled to right. Encarnacion singled to center, Conine to second. Gonzalez grounded into a double play, third baseman Boone to first baseman Johnson, Conine out.

Yankees—Matsui flied out to left fielder Cabrera. Posada walked on four pitches. Giambi struck out. Boone struck out.

THIRD INNING

Marlins—Pierre grounded out, second baseman Soriano to first baseman Johnson. Castillo grounded out, shortstop Jeter to first baseman Johnson. Rodriguez flied out to left fielder Matsui.

Yankees—Garcia singled to left. On Cabrera's error, Garcia to second. Soriano grounded out, shortstop Gonzalez to first baseman Lee. Johnson walked. Jeter singled to center, Garcia scored, Johnson to third. Williams popped out to left fielder Cabrera. Johnson was picked off, catcher Rodriguez to third baseman Lowell, Johnson out. One run. Marlins 1, Yankees 1.

FOURTH INNING

Marlins—Cabrera flied out to center fielder Williams. Lee flied out to center fielder Williams. Lowell flied out to left fielder Matsui.

Yankees—Matsui singled to right. Posada walked on a full count, Matsui to second. Giambi grounded into a double play, shortstop Gonzalez to first baseman Lee, Matsui to third, Posada out. Boone grounded out, third baseman Lowell to first baseman Lee.

FIFTH INNING

Marlins—Conine walked on a full count. Encarnacion singled to center, Conine to second. Gonzalez sacrificed, third baseman Boone to second baseman Soriano, Conine to third, Encarnacion to second. Pierre singled to left, Conine scored, Encarnacion scored. Castillo flied out to center fielder Williams. Rodriguez grounded out, shortstop Jeter to first baseman Johnson. 2 runs. Marlins 3, Yankees 1.

Yankees—Garcia singled to right. Soriano grounded into a double play, shortstop Gonzalez to second baseman Castillo to first baseman Lee, Garcia out. Johnson flied out to left fielder Cabrera.

SIXTH INNING

Marlins—Cabrera grounded out, shortstop Jeter to first baseman Johnson. Lee grounded out, pitcher Wells to first baseman Johnson. Lowell popped out to second baseman Soriano.

Yankees—Jeter grounded out, third baseman Lowell to first baseman Lee. Williams homered to center on a 1-0 count. Matsui singled to right. Willis pitching. Posada grounded into fielder's choice, third baseman Lowell to second baseman Castillo, Matsui out. Posada stole second. Giambi grounded out, shortstop Gonzalez to first baseman Lee. One run. Marlins 3, Yankees 2.

SEVENTH INNING

Marlins—Conine walked on a full count. Encarnacion flied out to center fielder Williams. Gonzalez popped out to third baseman Boone. Pierre was hit by a pitch, Conine to second. Castillo grounded into fielder's choice, shortstop Jeter to second baseman Soriano, Pierre out.

Yankees—Boone lined out to center fielder Pierre. J.Rivera pinch-hitting for Garcia. J.Rivera struck out. Soriano grounded out, pitcher Willis to first baseman Lee.

EIGHTH INNING

Marlins—J.Rivera in as right fielder. Nelson pitching. Rodriguez flied out to right fielder J.Rivera. Cabrera walked on a full count. Lee singled to right, Cabrera to third. Lowell flied out to right fielder J.Rivera. Conine fouled out to first baseman Johnson.

Yankees—Johnson flied out to left fielder Cabrera. Jeter struck out. Williams singled to left. Matsui singled to center, Williams to third. Urbina pitching. Posada struck out.

NINTH INNING

Marlins—Contreras pitching. Encarnacion struck out. Gonzalez struck out. Pierre walked. Pierre stole second. Castillo grounded out, second baseman Soriano to first baseman Johnson.

Yankees—Giambi walked. Dellucci pinch-running for Giambi. Boone flied out to right fielder Encarnacion. Sierra pinch-hitting for J.Rivera. Sierra walked on a full count, Dellucci to second. Soriano struck out. Johnson flied out to center fielder Pierre.

GAME 2

NEW YORK 6, FLORIDA 1

SUNDAY, OCTOBER 19, AT NEW YORK

Florida	**AB**	**R**	**H**	**BI**	**BB**	**SO**	**PO**	**A**
Pierre, cf	4	0	1	0	0	0	2	0
L.Castillo, 2b	4	1	2	0	0	0	2	3
I.Rodriguez, c	3	0	1	0	0	1	8	2
Redmond, c	1	0	0	0	0	0	2	0
M.Cabrera, lf	4	0	0	0	0	0	0	1
D.Lee, 1b	4	0	1	1	0	1	4	1
Lowell, 3b	4	0	1	0	0	0	1	1
Conine, dh	3	0	0	0	0	2	0	0
Encarnacion, rf	2	0	0	0	1	1	3	0
A.Gonzalez, ss	3	0	0	0	0	2	2	3
M.Redman, p	0	0	0	0	0	0	0	1
Helling, p	0	0	0	0	0	0	0	0
C.Fox, p	0	0	0	0	0	0	0	0
Pavano, p	0	0	0	0	0	0	0	0
B.Looper, p	0	0	0	0	0	0	0	0
TOTALS	32	1	6	1	1	7	24	12

NY Yankees	**AB**	**R**	**H**	**BI**	**BB**	**SO**	**PO**	**A**
A.Soriano, 2b	3	1	1	2	1	2	5	4
Jeter, ss	4	0	1	0	0	2	0	5
Ja.Giambi, dh	3	1	1	0	0	0	0	0
B.Williams, cf	2	1	1	0	2	0	3	0
Matsui, lf	4	1	1	3	0	0	0	0
Posada, c	3	0	0	0	1	2	7	1
A.Boone, 3b	4	0	1	0	0	2	0	3
N.Johnson, 1b	4	2	3	0	0	1	9	0
J.Rivera, rf	4	0	1	1	0	0	3	0
Pettitte, p	0	0	0	0	0	0	0	0
Contreras, p	0	0	0	0	0	0	0	0
TOTALS	31	6	10	6	4	9	27	13

Florida .... 0 0 0 0 0 0 0 0 1—1 6 0
NY Yankees .... 3 1 0 2 0 0 0 0 x—6 10 2

Florida	**IP**	**H**	**R**	**ER**	**HR**	**BB**	**SO**
M.Redman (L)	2.1	5	4	4	1	2	2
Helling	2.2	2	2	2	1	0	2
C.Fox	1.0	1	0	0	0	1	1
Pavano	1.0	1	0	0	0	1	2
B.Looper	1.0	1	0	0	0	0	2

NY Yankees	**IP**	**H**	**R**	**ER**	**HR**	**BB**	**SO**
Pettitte (W)	8.2	6	1	0	0	1	7
Contreras	0.1	0	0	0	0	0	0

Bases on balls—Off M.Redman 2 (B.Williams, A.Soriano), off C.Fox 1 (Posada), off Pavano 1 (B.Williams), off Pettitte 1 (Encarnacion).

Strikeouts—By M.Redman 2 (Jeter, A.Soriano), by Helling 2 (Posada, A.Boone), by C.Fox 1 (A.Boone), by Pavano 2 (Jeter, A.Soriano), by B.Looper 2 (Posada, N.Johnson), by Pettitte 7 (Conine 2, I.Rodriguez, D.Lee, Encarnacion, A.Gonzalez 2).

E—A.Boone 2. DP—Florida 1, NY Yankees 3. LOB—Florida 5, NY Yankees 6. Scoring Position—Florida 1 for 5, NY Yankees 1 for 5. 2B—Ja.Giambi, N.Johnson, J.Rivera. HR—Matsui (1st inning, 2 out, 2 on) off M.Redman, A.Soriano (4th inning, 2 out, 1 on) off Helling. CS—L.Castillo, A.Soriano, Posada. WP—M.Redman. HBP—Ja.Giambi by M.Redman. T—2:56. A—55,750. U—HP-Young, 1B-Darling, 2B-Kellogg, 3B-Rapuano, LF-Welke, RF-Marsh.

PLAY BY PLAY

FIRST INNING

Marlins—Pierre grounded out, second baseman Soriano to first baseman Johnson. Castillo infield single to short. Rodriguez struck out. Castillo was caught stealing, catcher Posada to second baseman Soriano, Castillo out.

Yankees—Soriano walked. Jeter struck out. Soriano was caught stealing, pitcher Redman to first baseman Lee to shortstop Gonzalez, Soriano out. Giambi was hit by a pitch. Williams singled to center, Giambi to third. Matsui homered to center on a 3-0 count, Giambi scored, Williams scored. Posada grounded out, second baseman Castillo to first baseman Lee. Three runs. Yankees 3, Marlins 0.

SECOND INNING

Marlins—Cabrera lined out to center fielder Williams. Lee flied out to right fielder J.Rivera. Lowell flied out to center fielder Williams.

Yankees—Boone flied out to right fielder Encarnacion. Johnson bunt single to third. J.Rivera doubled to left, Johnson scored. J.Rivera was out advancing, left fielder Cabrera to shortstop Gonzalez to catcher Rodriguez to third baseman Lowell, J.Rivera out. Soriano struck out. One run. Yankees 4, Marlins 0.

THIRD INNING

Marlins—Conine struck out. Encarnacion struck out. Gonzalez struck out.

Yankees—Jeter singled to left. Giambi lined out to center fielder Pierre. On Redman's wild pitch, Jeter to second. Williams walked on a full count. Helling pitching. Matsui grounded into fielder's choice, second baseman Castillo to shortstop Gonzalez, Jeter to third, Williams out. Posada struck out.

FOURTH INNING

Marlins—Pierre bunt single to first. Castillo grounded into fielder's choice, third baseman Boone to second baseman Soriano, Pierre out. Rodriguez grounded into a double play, shortstop Jeter to second baseman Soriano to first baseman Johnson, Castillo out.

Yankees—Boone struck out. Johnson singled to center. J.Rivera fouled out to catcher Rodriguez. Soriano homered to left on a 1-2 count, Johnson scored. Jeter grounded out, shortstop Gonzalez to first baseman Lee. Two runs. Yankees 6, Marlins 0.

FIFTH INNING

Marlins—Cabrera safe on Boone's error. Lee struck out. Lowell grounded out, shortstop Jeter to first baseman Johnson, Cabrera to second. Conine flied out to center fielder Williams.

Yankees—Giambi flied out to right fielder Encarnacion. Williams grounded out, third baseman Lowell to first baseman Lee. Matsui flied out to right fielder Encarnacion.

SIXTH INNING

Marlins—Encarnacion walked. Gonzalez struck out. Pierre grounded out, first baseman Johnson unassisted, Encarnacion to second. Castillo grounded out, shortstop Jeter to first baseman Johnson.

Yankees—C.Fox pitching. Posada walked. Boone struck out. Posada was caught stealing, catcher Rodriguez to second baseman Castillo, Posada out. Johnson doubled to right. J.Rivera flied out to center fielder Pierre.

SEVENTH INNING

Marlins—Rodriguez singled to center. Cabrera grounded into a double play, third baseman Boone to second baseman Soriano to first baseman Johnson, Rodriguez out. Lee flied out to right fielder J.Rivera.

Yankees—Pavano pitching. Soriano struck out. Jeter struck out. Giambi doubled to left. Williams walked on four pitches. Matsui grounded out, second baseman Castillo to first baseman Lee.

EIGHTH INNING

Marlins—Lowell singled to right. Conine struck out. Encarnacion grounded out, second baseman Soriano to first baseman Johnson, Lowell to second. Gonzalez grounded out, shortstop Jeter to first baseman Johnson.

Yankees—Redmond in as catcher. Looper pitching. Posada struck out. Boone singled to center. Johnson struck out. J.Rivera grounded into fielder's choice, shortstop Gonzalez to second baseman Castillo, Boone out.

NINTH INNING

Marlins—Pierre grounded out, shortstop Jeter to first baseman Johnson. Castillo singled to center. Redmond flied out to right fielder J.Rivera. Cabrera safe on Boone's error, Castillo to second. Lee singled to right, Castillo scored, Cabrera to second. Contreras pitching. Lowell grounded into fielder's choice, third baseman Boone to second baseman Soriano, Lee out. One run. Yankees 6, Marlins 1.

GAME 3

NEW YORK 6, FLORIDA 1

TUESDAY, OCTOBER 21, AT FLORIDA

NY Yankees	AB	R	H	BI	BB	SO	PO	A
A.Soriano, 2b	4	1	0	0	1	3	1	2
Jeter, ss	4	3	3	0	0	1	2	3
Ja.Giambi, 1b	2	0	0	0	2	1	7	1
Dellucci, pr-rf	1	0	0	0	0	0	1	0
B.Williams, cf	5	1	1	3	0	1	0	0
Matsui, lf	3	0	1	1	1	1	0	0
Posada, c	2	0	0	1	2	0	11	2
K.Garcia, rf	3	0	0	0	0	0	2	0
Sierra, ph	1	0	0	0	0	1	0	0
M.Rivera, p	0	0	0	0	0	0	0	0
A.Boone, 3b	4	1	1	1	0	1	0	1
Mussina, p	3	0	0	0	0	3	1	1
N.Johnson, 1b	1	0	0	0	0	0	2	0
TOTALS	33	6	6	6	6	12	27	10

Florida	AB	R	H	BI	BB	SO	PO	A
Pierre, cf	3	1	2	0	1	0	2	0
L.Castillo, 2b	4	0	0	0	0	3	1	0
I.Rodriguez, c	4	0	1	0	0	0	12	0
M.Cabrera, rf	4	0	2	1	0	2	3	0
D.Lee, 1b	4	0	0	0	0	0	4	1
Lowell, 3b	4	0	0	0	0	2	1	0
Conine, lf	4	0	2	0	0	0	1	0
A.Gonzalez, ss	3	0	1	0	0	1	2	1
Encarnacion, ph	1	0	0	0	0	1	0	0
Beckett, p	2	0	0	0	0	2	0	2
Willis, p	0	0	0	0	0	0	0	0
C.Fox, p	0	0	0	0	0	0	1	0
B.Looper, p	0	0	0	0	0	0	0	0
Hollandsworth, ph	1	0	0	0	0	0	0	0
TOTALS	34	1	8	1	1	11	27	4

NY Yankees.....0 0 0 1 0 0 0 1 4—6 6 1
Florida.....1 0 0 0 0 0 0 0 0—1 8 0

NY Yankees	IP	H	R	ER	HR	BB	SO
Mussina (W)	7.0	7	1	1	0	1	9
M.Rivera (S)	2.0	1	0	0	0	0	2

Florida	IP	H	R	ER	HR	BB	SO
Beckett (L)	7.1	3	2	2	0	3	10
Willis	0.1	1	0	0	0	2	0
C.Fox	0.2	1	2	2	1	1	1
B.Looper	0.2	1	2	2	1	0	1

Bases on balls—Off Mussina 1 (Pierre), off Beckett 3 (Ja.Giambi, Posada, Matsui), off Willis 2 (Ja.Giambi, Posada), off C.Fox 1 (A.Soriano).

Strikeouts—By Mussina 9 (L.Castillo 2 2, A.Gonzalez, Lowell 2, Beckett 2, M.Cabrera), by M.Rivera 2 (Encarnacion, M.Cabrera), by Beckett 10 (B.Williams, Mussina 2 2, Ja.Giambi, Jeter, A.Boone, A.Soriano 2 2), by C.Fox 1 (Sierra), by B.Looper 1 (Matsui).

E—A.Boone. LOB—NY Yankees 8, Florida 8. Scoring Position—NY Yankees 2 for 8, Florida 2 for 9. 2B—Jeter 2, Pierre, I.Rodriguez, A.Gonzalez. HR—A.Boone (9th inning, 0 out, 0 on) off C.Fox, B.Williams (9th inning, 2 out, 2 on) off B.Looper. CS—Pierre. SH—Beckett. PB—Posada. HBP—Jeter by B.Looper, Matsui by Beckett. T—3:21. A—65,731. U—HP-Darling, 1B-Kellogg, 2B-Rapuano, 3B-Welke, LF-Marsh, RF-Young.

PLAY BY PLAY

FIRST INNING

Yankees—Soriano struck out. Jeter struck out. Giambi popped out to third baseman Lowell.

Marlins—Pierre doubled to center. Castillo struck out. Rodriguez flied out to right fielder Garcia. Cabrera singled to right, Pierre scored. Lee grounded out, first baseman Giambi to pitcher Mussina. One run. Marlins 1, Yankees 0.

SECOND INNING

Yankees—Williams flied out to right fielder Cabrera. Matsui grounded out, pitcher Beckett to first baseman Lee. Posada grounded out, first baseman Lee unassisted.

Marlins—Lowell popped out to second baseman Soriano. Conine grounded out, shortstop Jeter to first baseman Giambi. Gonzalez doubled to left. Beckett struck out.

THIRD INNING

Yankees—Garcia flied out to right fielder Cabrera. Boone lined out to right fielder Cabrera. Mussina struck out.

Marlins—Pierre grounded out, shortstop Jeter to first baseman Giambi. Castillo struck out. Rodriguez safe on Boone's error. Cabrera struck out.

FOURTH INNING

Yankees—Soriano struck out. Jeter doubled to left. Giambi walked on a full count. Williams popped out to shortstop Gonzalez. Matsui was hit by a pitch, Jeter to third, Giambi to second. Posada walked on a full count, Jeter scored, Giambi to third, Matsui to second. Garcia grounded out, first baseman Lee unassisted. One run. Yankees 1, Marlins 1.

Marlins—Lee grounded out, third baseman Boone to first baseman Giambi. Lowell struck out. Conine flied out to right fielder Garcia.

FIFTH INNING

Yankees—Boone popped out to shortstop Gonzalez. Mussina struck out. Soriano grounded out, pitcher Beckett to first baseman Lee.

Marlins—Gonzalez struck out. Beckett struck out. Pierre singled to left. Pierre was caught stealing, catcher Posada to shortstop Jeter, Pierre out.

SIXTH INNING

Yankees—Jeter singled to center. Giambi struck out. Williams struck out. Matsui walked on four pitches, Jeter to second. Posada grounded into fielder's choice, shortstop Gonzalez to second baseman Castillo, Matsui out.

Marlins—Castillo grounded out, second baseman Soriano to first baseman Giambi. Rodriguez doubled to left. Cabrera singled to right, Rodriguez to third. Lee grounded into fielder's choice, pitcher Mussina to catcher Posada, Rodriguez out, Cabrera to second. Lowell struck out.

SEVENTH INNING

Yankees—Garcia lined out to center fielder Pierre. Boone struck out. Mussina struck out.

Marlins—Conine singled to left. Gonzalez fouled out to first baseman Giambi. Beckett sacrificed, first baseman Giambi unassisted, Conine to second. Pierre was intentionally walked. Castillo struck out.

EIGHTH INNING

Yankees—Soriano struck out. Jeter doubled to right. Willis pitching. Giambi walked. Williams flied out to center fielder Pierre, Jeter to third. Matsui singled to left, Jeter scored, Giambi to second. Dellucci pinch-running for Giambi. Posada walked on four pitches, Dellucci to third, Matsui to second. Sierra pinch-hitting for Garcia. C.Fox pitching. Sierra struck out. One run. Yankees 2, Marlins 1.

Marlins—Dellucci in as right fielder. M.Rivera pitching. Johnson in as first baseman. Rodriguez fouled out to right fielder Dellucci. Cabrera struck out. Lee popped out to shortstop Jeter.

NINTH INNING

Yankees—Boone homered to left on a 0-1 count. Johnson grounded out, first baseman Lee to pitcher C.Fox. Soriano walked on a full count. Looper pitching. Jeter was hit by a pitch, Soriano to second. Dellucci flied out to left fielder Conine. Williams homered to center on a 2-1 count, Soriano scored, Jeter scored. Matsui struck out. Four runs. Yankees 6, Marlins 1.

Marlins—Lowell grounded out, shortstop Jeter to first baseman Johnson. Conine singled to right. Encarnacion pinch-hitting for Gonzalez. Encarnacion struck out. Hollandsworth pinch-hitting for Looper. On Posada's passed ball, Conine to second. Hollandsworth grounded out, second baseman Soriano to first baseman Johnson.

GAME 4

FLORIDA 4, NEW YORK 3

WEDNESDAY, OCTOBER 22, AT FLORIDA

NY Yankees	AB	R	H	BI	BB	SO	PO	A
A.Soriano, 2b	6	0	1	0	0	2	3	3
Jeter, ss	6	0	1	0	0	1	0	6
Ja.Giambi, 1b	6	0	2	0	0	1	11	1
B.Williams, cf	6	2	4	0	0	0	4	0
Matsui, lf	3	0	1	0	2	0	2	0
Posada, c	4	0	1	0	0	1	6	1
Dellucci, pr-rf	0	1	0	0	0	0	0	0
K.Garcia, rf	3	0	0	0	0	1	1	0
Sierra, ph	1	0	1	2	0	0	0	0
Contreras, p	0	0	0	0	0	0	0	1
J.Rivera, ph	0	0	0	0	1	0	0	0
Weaver, p	0	0	0	0	0	0	1	0
A.Boone, 3b	4	0	0	1	0	1	0	1
Clemens, p	2	0	1	0	0	0	1	1
N.Johnson, ph	1	0	0	0	0	0	0	0
J.Nelson, p	0	0	0	0	0	0	0	0
Flaherty, c	2	0	0	0	0	0	4	0
TOTALS	44	3	12	3	3	7	33	14

Florida	AB	R	H	BI	BB	SO	PO	A
Pierre, cf	4	0	0	0	1	0	8	0
L.Castillo, 2b	4	0	0	0	0	2	2	7
I.Rodriguez, c	5	1	2	0	0	1	7	0
M.Cabrera, rf	5	1	1	2	0	2	0	0
B.Looper, p	0	0	0	0	0	0	1	0
Conine, lf	5	1	3	0	0	0	3	0
Lowell, 3b	5	0	1	0	0	0	1	3
D.Lee, 1b	5	0	2	1	0	1	11	1
A.Gonzalez, ss	5	1	1	1	0	2	3	3
Pavano, p	2	0	0	0	0	1	0	0
Urbina, p	0	0	0	0	0	0	0	0
Hollandsworth, ph	1	0	0	0	0	1	0	0
C.Fox, p	0	0	0	0	0	0	0	0
Encarnacion, rf	0	0	0	0	0	0	0	0
TOTALS	41	4	10	4	1	10	36	14

NY Yankees..........0 1 0 0 0 0 0 0 2 0 0 0—3 12 0
Florida..........3 0 0 0 0 0 0 0 0 0 0 1—4 10 0

NY Yankees	IP	H	R	ER	HR	BB	SO
Clemens	7.0	8	3	3	1	0	5
J.Nelson	1.0	1	0	0	0	0	1
Contreras	2.0	0	0	0	0	1	4
Weaver (L)	1.0	1	1	1	1	0	0

Florida	IP	H	R	ER	HR	BB	SO
Pavano	8.0	7	1	1	0	0	4
Urbina (BS)	1.0	2	2	2	0	1	0
C.Fox	1.1	2	0	0	0	2	2
B.Looper (W)	1.2	1	0	0	0	0	1

Weaver pitched to 1 batter in the 12th.

Bases on balls—Off Contreras 1 (Pierre), off Urbina 1 (Matsui), off C.Fox 2 (J.Rivera, Matsui).

Strikeouts—By Clemens 5 (L.Castillo 2, Pavano, A.Gonzalez 2), by J.Nelson 1 (M.Cabrera), by Contreras 4 (I.Rodriguez, Hollandsworth, D.Lee, M.Cabrera), by Pavano 4 (Jeter, K.Garcia, Posada, A.Soriano), by C.Fox 2 (Ja.Giambi, A.Soriano), by B.Looper 1 (A.Boone).

DP—Florida 2. LOB—NY Yankees 10, Florida 7. Scoring Position—NY Yankees 2 for 10, Florida 1 for 7. 2B—Jeter, B.Williams, I.Rodriguez. 3B—Sierra. HR—M.Cabrera (1st inning, 2 out, 1 on) off Clemens, A.Gonzalez (12th inning, 0 out, 0 on) off Weaver. S—A.Boone. SH—Dellucci, L.Castillo, Pavano. T—4:03. A—65,934. U—HP-Kellogg, 1B-Rapuano, 2B-Welke, 3B-Marsh, LF-Young, RF-Darling.

PLAY BY PLAY

FIRST INNING

Yankees—Soriano singled to center. Jeter grounded into a double play, second baseman Castillo to shortstop Gonzalez to first baseman Lee, Soriano out. Giambi flied out to center fielder Pierre.

Marlins—Pierre grounded out, second baseman Soriano to first baseman Giambi. Castillo grounded out, shortstop Jeter to first baseman Giambi. Rodriguez singled to right. Cabrera homered to right on a 2-2 count, Rodriguez scored. Conine singled to left. Lowell singled to right, Conine to third. Lee singled to left, Conine scored, Lowell to second. Gonzalez flied out to right fielder Garcia. Three runs. Marlins 3, Yankees 0.

SECOND INNING

Yankees—Williams singled to left. Matsui infield single to third, Williams to second. Posada infield single to pitcher Pavano, Williams to third, Matsui to second. Garcia struck out. Boone hit a sacrifice fly to center fielder Pierre, Williams scored, Matsui to third, Posada to second. Clemens grounded out, first baseman Lee unassisted. One run. Marlins 3, Yankees 1.

Marlins—Pavano grounded out, first baseman Giambi to pitcher Clemens. Pierre grounded out, shortstop Jeter to first baseman Giambi. Castillo struck out.

THIRD INNING

Yankees—Soriano flied out to center fielder Pierre. Jeter grounded out, third baseman Lowell to first baseman Lee. Giambi singled to right. Williams singled to right, Giambi to second. Matsui flied out to left fielder Conine.

Marlins—Rodriguez grounded out, shortstop Jeter to first baseman Giambi. Cabrera grounded out, shortstop Jeter to first baseman Giambi. Conine singled to right. Lowell lined out to second baseman Soriano.

FOURTH INNING

Yankees—Posada grounded out, second baseman Castillo to first baseman Lee. Garcia grounded out, second baseman Castillo to first baseman Lee. Boone flied out to center fielder Pierre.

Marlins—Lee singled to center. Gonzalez struck out. Pavano sacrificed, catcher Posada to second baseman Soriano, Lee to second. Pierre grounded out, second baseman Soriano to first baseman Giambi.

FIFTH INNING

Yankees—Clemens singled to center. Soriano struck out. Jeter grounded into a double play, second baseman Castillo to shortstop Gonzalez to first baseman Lee, Clemens out.

Marlins—Castillo grounded out, pitcher Clemens to first baseman Giambi. Rodriguez doubled to center. Cabrera grounded out, shortstop Jeter to first baseman Giambi. Conine flied out to center fielder Williams.

SIXTH INNING

Yankees—Giambi flied out to left fielder Conine. Williams flied out to center fielder Pierre. Matsui flied out to center fielder Pierre.

Marlins—Lowell flied out to center fielder Williams. Lee grounded out, third baseman Boone to first baseman Giambi. Gonzalez struck out.

SEVENTH INNING

Yankees—Posada struck out. Garcia grounded out, first baseman Lee unassisted. Boone grounded out, third baseman Lowell to first baseman Lee. Marlins seventh. Pavano struck out. Pierre flied out to left fielder Matsui. Castillo struck out.

EIGHTH INNING

Yankees—Johnson pinch-hitting for Clemens. Johnson grounded out, second baseman Castillo to first baseman Lee. Soriano flied out to center fielder Pierre. Jeter struck out.

Marlins—Nelson pitching. Rodriguez grounded out, second baseman Soriano to first baseman Giambi. Cabrera struck out. Conine singled to right. Lowell flied out to left fielder Matsui.

NINTH INNING

Yankees—Urbina pitching. Giambi flied out to left fielder Conine. Williams singled to center. Matsui walked on a full count, Williams to second. Posada grounded into fielder's choice, second baseman Castillo to shortstop Gonzalez, Williams to third,

Matsui out. Sierra pinch-hitting for Garcia. Dellucci pinch-running for Posada. Sierra tripled to right, Williams scored, Dellucci scored. Boone grounded out, shortstop Gonzalez to first baseman Lee. Two runs. Marlins 3, Yankees 3.

Marlins—Dellucci in as right fielder. Contreras pitching. Flaherty in as catcher. Lee struck out. Gonzalez flied out to center fielder Williams. Hollandsworth pinch-hitting for Urbina. Hollandsworth struck out.

TENTH INNING

Yankees—C.Fox pitching. Flaherty flied out to center fielder Pierre. Soriano struck out. Jeter doubled to right. Giambi struck out.

Marlins—Pierre walked on four pitches. Castillo sacrificed, pitcher Contreras to second baseman Soriano, Pierre to second. Rodriguez struck out. Cabrera struck out.

ELEVENTH INNING

Yankees—Williams doubled to right. Matsui walked. Dellucci sacrificed, third baseman Lowell to second baseman Castillo, Williams to third, Matsui to second. J.Rivera pinch-hitting for Contreras. J.Rivera was intentionally walked. Looper pitching. Encarnacion in as right fielder. Boone struck out. Flaherty popped out to third baseman Lowell.

Marlins—Weaver pitching. Conine flied out to center fielder Williams. Lowell popped out to pitcher Weaver. Lee grounded out, shortstop Jeter to first baseman Giambi.

TWELFTH INNING

Yankees—Soriano grounded out, first baseman Lee to pitcher Looper. Jeter popped out to second baseman Castillo. Giambi singled to right. Williams grounded out, second baseman Castillo to first baseman Lee.

Marlins—Gonzalez homered to left on a full count. One run. Marlins 4, Yankees 3.

GAME 5

FLORIDA 6, NEW YORK 4

THURSDAY, OCTOBER 23, AT FLORIDA

NY Yankees	AB	R	H	BI	BB	SO	PO	A
Jeter, ss	4	2	3	1	1	0	2	3
E.Wilson, 2b	4	0	2	1	1	0	5	1
B.Williams, cf	4	0	1	1	0	0	2	0
Matsui, lf	5	0	0	0	0	0	0	0
Posada, c	4	0	1	0	0	1	8	1
N.Johnson, 1b	4	1	2	0	0	1	5	1
K.Garcia, rf	3	0	1	0	0	1	1	0
A.Soriano, ph-rf	1	0	0	0	0	1	0	0
A.Boone, 3b	4	0	1	0	0	0	1	2
D.Wells, p	0	0	0	0	0	0	0	1
Dellucci, ph	1	0	0	0	0	0	0	0
Contreras, p	0	0	0	0	0	0	0	0
J.Rivera, ph	1	0	0	0	0	0	0	0
Hammond, p	0	0	0	0	0	0	0	1
Sierra, ph	1	0	0	0	0	1	0	0
J.Nelson, p	0	0	0	0	0	0	0	0
Ja.Giambi, ph	1	1	1	1	0	0	0	0
TOTALS	37	4	12	4	2	5	24	10

Florida	AB	R	H	BI	BB	SO	PO	A
Pierre, cf	3	0	1	1	1	0	1	0
L.Castillo, 2b	4	0	0	0	0	1	2	6
I.Rodriguez, c	4	1	1	0	0	2	6	0
M.Cabrera, rf	4	0	1	0	0	1	4	0
Willis, p	0	0	0	0	0	0	0	0
B.Looper, p	0	0	0	0	0	0	0	0
Urbina, p	0	0	0	0	0	0	0	0
Conine, lf	3	1	1	0	1	0	1	0
Lowell, 3b	3	1	1	2	1	1	0	3
D.Lee, 1b	3	2	1	0	1	1	10	0
A.Gonzalez, ss	4	1	2	1	0	1	0	0
Penny, p	2	0	1	2	0	0	1	0
Encarnacion, rf	1	0	0	0	0	1	2	0
TOTALS	31	6	9	6	4	8	27	9

NY Yankees	1 0 0	0 0 0	1 0 2—4	12	1
Florida	0 3 0	1 2 0	0 0 x—6	9	1

NY Yankees	IP	H	R	ER	HR	BB	SO
D.Wells	1.0	0	0	0	0	0	0
Contreras (L)	3.0	5	4	4	0	3	4
Hammond	2.0	2	2	0	0	0	0
J.Nelson	2.0	2	0	0	0	1	4

Florida	IP	H	R	ER	HR	BB	SO
Penny (W)	7.0	8	2	1	0	2	4
Willis	1.0	1	0	0	0	0	1
B.Looper	0.1	3	2	2	1	0	0
Urbina (S)	0.2	0	0	0	0	0	0

Bases on balls—Off Contreras 3 (D.Lee, Lowell, Pierre), off J.Nelson 1 (Conine), off Penny 2 (Jeter, E.Wilson).

Strikeouts—By Contreras 4 (I.Rodriguez, L.Castillo, A.Gonzalez, M.Cabrera), by J.Nelson 4 (I.Rodriguez, D.Lee, Encarnacion, Lowell), by Penny 4 (Sierra, K.Garcia, Posada, N.Johnson), by Willis 1 (A.Soriano).

E—E.Wilson, D.Lee. DP—NY Yankees 2, Florida 1. LOB—NY Yankees 9, Florida 6. Scoring Position—NY Yankees 1 for 8, Florida 4 for 9. 2B—E.Wilson, Pierre, Conine, A.Gonzalez. HR—Ja.Giambi (9th inning, 1 out, 0 on) off B.Looper. CS—A.Gonzalez. S—B.Williams. SH—Penny. T—3:05. A—65,975. U—HP-Rapuano, 1B-Welke, 2B-Marsh, 3B-Young, LF-Darling, RF-Kellogg.

PLAY BY PLAY

FIRST INNING

Yankees—Jeter singled to right. Wilson bunt single to first, Jeter to second. On Lee's error, Jeter to third. Williams hit a sacrifice fly to right fielder Cabrera, Jeter scored. Matsui grounded out, second baseman Castillo to first baseman Lee, Wilson to second. Posada struck out. One run. Yankees 1, Marlins 0.

Marlins—Pierre was out bunting, first baseman Johnson to second baseman Wilson. Castillo grounded out, shortstop Jeter to first baseman Johnson. Rodriguez grounded out, pitcher Wells to first baseman Johnson.

SECOND INNING

Yankees—Johnson struck out. Garcia struck out. Boone singled to left. Dellucci pinch-hitting for Wells. Dellucci grounded out, pitcher Penny unassisted.

Marlins—Contreras pitching. Cabrera lined out to second baseman Wilson. Conine flied out to center fielder Williams. Lowell walked on four pitches. Lee walked on a full count, Lowell to second. Gonzalez doubled to center, Lowell scored, Lee to third. Penny singled to center, Lee scored, Gonzalez scored. Pierre walked on four pitches, Penny to second. Castillo struck out. Three runs. Marlins 3, Yankees 1.

THIRD INNING

Yankees—Jeter walked on a full count. Wilson grounded into a double play, third baseman Lowell to second baseman Castillo to first baseman Lee, Jeter out. Williams grounded out, second baseman Castillo to first baseman Lee.

Marlins—Rodriguez struck out. Cabrera struck out. Conine doubled to left. Lowell grounded out, shortstop Jeter to first baseman Johnson.

FOURTH INNING

Yankees—Matsui grounded out, second baseman Castillo to first baseman Lee. Posada singled to left. Johnson grounded out, first baseman Lee unassisted, Posada to second. Garcia grounded out, second baseman Castillo to first baseman Lee.

Marlins—Lee singled to left. Gonzalez struck out. Penny sacrificed, third baseman Boone to second baseman Wilson, Lee to second. Pierre doubled to center, Lee scored. Castillo fouled out to third baseman Boone. One run. Marlins 4, Yankees 1.

FIFTH INNING

Yankees—Boone flied out to right fielder Cabrera. J.Rivera pinch-hitting for Contreras. J.Rivera grounded out, third baseman Lowell to first baseman Lee. Jeter grounded out, third baseman Lowell to first baseman Lee.

Marlins—Hammond pitching. Rodriguez singled to center. Cabrera flied out to right fielder Garcia, Rodriguez to second. Conine safe on fielder's choice and Wilson's error, Rodriguez to third. Lowell singled to center, Rodriguez scored, Conine scored. Lee grounded into a double play, second baseman Wilson to shortstop Jeter to first baseman Johnson, Lowell out. Two runs. Marlins 6, Yankees 1.

SIXTH INNING

Yankees—Wilson flied out to center fielder Pierre. Williams singled to right. Matsui flied out to left fielder Conine. Posada grounded out, second baseman Castillo to first baseman Lee.

Marlins—Gonzalez grounded out, pitcher Hammond to first baseman Johnson. Penny popped out to second baseman Wilson. Pierre popped out to shortstop Jeter.

SEVENTH INNING

Yankees—Johnson singled to center. Garcia singled to center, Johnson to third. Boone popped out to right fielder Cabrera. Sierra pinch-hitting for Hammond. Sierra struck out. Jeter singled to center, Johnson scored, Garcia to third. Wilson walked on a full count, Jeter to second. Williams flied out to right fielder Cabrera. One run. Marlins 6, Yankees 2.

Marlins—Nelson pitching. Castillo lined out to center fielder Williams. Rodriguez struck out. Cabrera singled to center. Conine walked on a full count, Cabrera to second. Lowell struck out.

EIGHTH INNING

Yankees—Willis pitching. Encarnacion in as right fielder. Matsui flied out to right fielder Encarnacion. Posada popped out to second baseman Castillo. Johnson singled to right. Soriano pinch-hitting for Garcia. Soriano struck out.

Marlins—Soriano in as right fielder. Lee struck out. Gonzalez singled to right. Encarnacion struck out. Gonzalez was caught stealing, catcher Posada to second baseman Wilson, Gonzalez out.

NINTH INNING

Yankees—Looper pitching. Boone fouled out to catcher Rodriguez. Giambi pinch-hitting for Nelson. Giambi homered to center on a 2-2 count. Jeter singled to right. Wilson doubled to right, Jeter scored. Urbina pitching. Williams flied out to right fielder Encarnacion, Wilson to third. Matsui grounded out, first baseman Lee unassisted. Two runs. Marlins 6, Yankees 4.

GAME 6

FLORIDA 2, NEW YORK 0

SATURDAY, OCTOBER 25, AT NEW YORK

Florida	AB	R	H	BI	BB	SO	PO	A
Pierre, cf	4	0	1	0	1	2	2	0
L.Castillo, 2b	5	0	1	1	0	1	1	4
I.Rodriguez, c	3	0	1	0	1	0	9	1
M.Cabrera, lf	4	0	0	0	0	2	3	0
Conine, dh	4	1	0	0	0	0	0	0
Lowell, 3b	3	0	2	0	1	0	1	1
D.Lee, 1b	4	0	0	0	0	3	4	0
Encarnacion, rf	3	0	0	1	0	1	3	0
A.Gonzalez, ss	4	1	2	0	0	0	3	2
Beckett, p	0	0	0	0	0	0	1	0
TOTALS	34	2	7	2	3	9	27	8

NY Yankees	AB	R	H	BI	BB	SO	PO	A
Jeter, ss	4	0	0	0	0	2	3	2
N.Johnson, 1b	3	0	0	0	1	0	6	0
B.Williams, cf	4	0	1	0	0	1	2	0
Matsui, lf	4	0	0	0	0	1	1	0
Posada, c	4	0	1	0	0	2	9	0
Ja.Giambi, dh	2	0	0	0	1	0	0	0
K.Garcia, rf	3	0	1	0	0	1	3	0
E.Wilson, 3b	0	0	0	0	0	0	0	0
A.Boone, 3b	1	0	0	0	0	1	1	3
Sierra, ph-rf	1	0	0	0	0	1	0	0
A.Soriano, 2b	3	0	2	0	0	0	2	0
Pettitte, p	0	0	0	0	0	0	0	3
M.Rivera, p	0	0	0	0	0	0	0	1
TOTALS	29	0	5	0	2	9	27	9

Florida.................................0 0 0 0 1 1 0 0 0—2 7 0
NY Yankees..........................0 0 0 0 0 0 0 0 0—0 5 1

Florida	IP	H	R	ER	HR	BB	SO
Beckett (W)	9.0	5	0	0	0	2	9

NY Yankees	IP	H	R	ER	HR	BB	SO
Pettitte (L)	7.0	6	2	1	0	3	7
M.Rivera	2.0	1	0	0	0	0	2

Bases on balls—Off Beckett 2 (Ja.Giambi, N.Johnson), off Pettitte 3 (I.Rodriguez, Lowell, Pierre).

Strikeouts—By Beckett 9 (Sierra, B.Williams, Jeter 2, K.Garcia, Posada 2, A.Boone, Matsui), by Pettitte 7 (L.Castillo, D.Lee 2, Encarnacion, Pierre, M.Cabrera 2), by M.Rivera 2 (D.Lee, Pierre).

E—Jeter. DP—Florida 2. LOB—Florida 9, NY Yankees 5. Scoring Position—Florida 1 for 6, NY Yankees 0 for 7. 2B—Lowell, B.Williams, Posada. S—Encarnacion. SH—A.Boone. T—2:57. A—55,773. U—HP-Welke, 1B-Marsh, 2B-Young, 3B-Darling, LF-Kellogg, RF-Rapuano.

PLAY BY PLAY

FIRST INNING

Marlins—Pierre popped out to shortstop Jeter. Castillo struck out. Rodriguez singled to center. Cabrera grounded out, pitcher Pettitte to first baseman Johnson.

Yankees—Jeter struck out. Johnson flied out to right fielder Encarnacion. Williams doubled to left. Matsui flied out to right fielder Encarnacion.

SECOND INNING

Marlins—Conine flied out to left fielder Matsui. Lowell doubled to right. Lee struck out. Encarnacion struck out.

Yankees—Posada struck out. Giambi walked on four pitches. Garcia grounded into fielder's choice, second baseman Castillo to shortstop Gonzalez, Giambi out. Boone struck out.

THIRD INNING

Marlins—Gonzalez grounded out, third baseman Boone to first baseman Johnson. Pierre walked on a full count. Castillo grounded into fielder's choice, third baseman Boone to second baseman Soriano, Pierre out. Rodriguez flied out to right fielder Garcia.

Yankees—Soriano singled to center. Jeter grounded out, second baseman Castillo to first baseman Lee, Soriano to second. Johnson walked. Williams grounded into a double play, second baseman Castillo to shortstop Gonzalez to first baseman Lee, Johnson out.

FOURTH INNING

Marlins—Cabrera struck out. Conine flied out to center fielder Williams. Lowell grounded out, shortstop Jeter to first baseman Johnson.

Yankees—Matsui flied out to center fielder Pierre. Posada struck out. Giambi flied out to left fielder Cabrera.

FIFTH INNING

Marlins—Lee struck out. Encarnacion grounded out, third baseman Boone to first baseman Johnson. Gonzalez singled to center. Pierre singled to center, Gonzalez to second. Castillo singled to right, Gonzalez scored, Pierre to third. Castillo to second. Rodriguez was intentionally walked. Cabrera struck out. One run. Marlins 1, Yankees 0.

Yankees—Garcia singled to right. Boone sacrificed, catcher Rodriguez to second baseman Castillo, Garcia to second. Soriano popped out to third baseman Lowell. Jeter struck out.

SIXTH INNING

Marlins—Conine safe on Jeter's error. Lowell walked on four pitches, Conine to second. Lee grounded into fielder's choice, pitcher Pettitte to shortstop Jeter, Conine to third, Lowell out. Encarnacion hit a sacrifice fly to right fielder Garcia, Conine scored. Gonzalez bunt single to third, Lee to second. Pierre struck out. One run. Marlins 2, Yankees 0.

Yankees—Johnson flied out to right fielder Encarnacion. Williams struck out. Matsui struck out.

SEVENTH INNING

Marlins—Castillo lined out to third baseman Boone. Rodriguez grounded out, pitcher Pettitte to first baseman Johnson. Cabrera flied out to right fielder Garcia.

Yankees—Posada doubled to left. Giambi grounded out, third baseman Lowell to first baseman Lee. Garcia struck out. Sierra pinch-hitting for Boone. Sierra struck out.

EIGHTH INNING

Marlins—Wilson in as third baseman. Sierra in as right fielder. M.Rivera pitching. Conine grounded out, pitcher M.Rivera to first baseman Johnson. Lowell infield single to third. Lee struck out. Encarnacion grounded into fielder's choice, shortstop Jeter to second baseman Soriano, Lowell out.

Yankees—Soriano singled to left. Jeter flied out to center fielder Pierre. Johnson grounded into a double play, second baseman Castillo to shortstop Gonzalez to first baseman Lee, Soriano out.

NINTH INNING

Marlins—Gonzalez flied out to center fielder Williams. Pierre struck out. Castillo lined out to shortstop Jeter.

Yankees—Williams flied out to left fielder Cabrera. Matsui flied out to left fielder Cabrera. Posada grounded out, pitcher Beckett unassisted.

STATISTICS

FLORIDA MARLINS' BATTING AND FIELDING AVERAGES

	BATTING															FIELDING			
Player, position	G	AB	R	H	TB	2B	3B	HR	RBI	BB	IBB	SO	Avg.	OBP	Slg.	PO	A	E	Avg.
Penny,p	2	2	0	1	1	0	0	0	2	0	0	0	.500	.500	.500	1	0	0	1.000
Conine,dh-lf	6	21	4	7	8	1	0	0	0	3	0	2	.333	.417	.381	5	0	0	1.000
Pierre,cf	6	21	2	7	9	2	0	0	3	5	1	2	.333	.481	.429	18	0	0	1.000
Gonzalez,ss	6	22	3	6	11	2	0	1	2	0	0	7	.273	.273	.500	11	13	0	1.000
Rodriguez,c	6	22	2	6	8	2	0	0	1	1	1	4	.273	.292	.364	49	4	0	1.000
Lowell,3b	6	23	1	5	6	1	0	0	2	2	0	3	.217	.280	.261	5	11	0	1.000
Lee,1b	6	24	2	5	5	0	0	0	2	1	0	7	.208	.240	.208	40	3	1	.977
Encarnacion,rf-ph	6	11	1	2	2	0	0	0	1	1	0	5	.182	.231	.182	10	0	0	1.000
Cabrera,lf-rf	6	24	1	4	7	0	0	1	3	1	0	7	.167	.200	.292	14	1	1	.938
Castillo,2b	6	26	1	4	4	0	0	0	1	0	0	7	.154	.154	.154	10	21	0	1.000
Fox,p	3	0	0	0	0	0	0	0	0	0	0	0	.000	.000	.000	1	0	0	1.000
Helling,p	1	0	0	0	0	0	0	0	0	0	0	0	.000	.000	.000	0	0	0	.000
Looper,p	4	0	0	0	0	0	0	0	0	0	0	0	.000	.000	.000	1	0	0	1.000
Redman,p	1	0	0	0	0	0	0	0	0	0	0	0	.000	.000	.000	0	1	0	1.000
Urbina,p	3	0	0	0	0	0	0	0	0	0	0	0	.000	.000	.000	0	0	0	.000
Willis,p	3	0	0	0	0	0	0	0	0	0	0	0	.000	.000	.000	0	1	0	1.000
Redmond,c	1	1	0	0	0	0	0	0	0	0	0	0	.000	.000	.000	2	0	0	1.000
Beckett,p	2	2	0	0	0	0	0	0	0	0	0	2	.000	.000	.000	1	2	0	1.000
Hollandsworth,ph	2	2	0	0	0	0	0	0	0	0	0	1	.000	.000	.000	0	0	0	.000
Pavano,p	2	2	0	0	0	0	0	0	0	0	0	1	.000	.000	.000	0	0	0	.000
Totals	6	203	17	47	61	8	0	2	17	14	2	48	.232	.282	.300	168	57	2	.991

NEW YORK YANKEES' BATTING AND FIELDING AVERAGES

	BATTING															FIELDING			
Player, position	G	AB	R	H	TB	2B	3B	HR	RBI	BB	IBB	SO	Avg.	OBP	Slg.	PO	A	E	Avg.
Wilson,2b-3b	2	4	0	2	3	1	0	0	1	1	0	0	.500	.600	.750	5	1	1	.857
Clemens,p	1	2	0	1	1	0	0	0	0	0	0	0	.500	.500	.500	1	1	0	1.000
Williams,cf	6	25	5	10	18	2	0	2	5	2	0	2	.400	.429	.720	16	0	0	1.000
Jeter,ss	6	26	5	9	12	3	0	0	2	1	0	7	.346	.393	.462	8	23	1	.969
Johnson,1b-ph	6	17	3	5	6	1	0	0	0	2	0	3	.294	.368	.353	31	1	0	1.000
Garcia,rf	5	14	1	4	4	0	0	0	0	0	0	3	.286	.286	.286	7	0	0	1.000
Matsui,lf	6	23	1	6	9	0	0	1	4	3	0	2	.261	.370	.391	5	0	0	1.000
Sierra,ph-rf	5	4	0	1	3	0	1	0	2	1	0	3	.250	.400	.750	0	0	0	.000
Giambi,dh-1b-ph	6	17	2	4	8	1	0	1	1	4	0	3	.235	.409	.471	18	2	0	1.000
Soriano,2b-rf-ph	6	22	2	5	8	0	0	1	2	2	0	9	.227	.292	.364	14	11	0	1.000
Rivera,rf-ph	4	6	0	1	2	1	0	0	1	1	1	1	.167	.286	.333	5	0	0	1.000
Posada,c	6	19	0	3	4	1	0	0	1	5	0	7	.158	.333	.211	44	5	0	1.000
Boone,3b	6	21	1	3	6	0	0	1	2	0	0	6	.143	.136	.286	4	13	3	.850
Contreras,p	4	0	0	0	0	0	0	0	0	0	0	0	.000	.000	.000	0	1	0	1.000
Hammond,p	1	0	0	0	0	0	0	0	0	0	0	0	.000	.000	.000	0	1	0	1.000
Nelson,p	3	0	0	0	0	0	0	0	0	0	0	0	.000	.000	.000	0	0	0	.000
Pettitte,p	2	0	0	0	0	0	0	0	0	0	0	0	.000	.000	.000	0	3	0	1.000
Rivera,p	2	0	0	0	0	0	0	0	0	0	0	0	.000	.000	.000	0	1	0	1.000
Weaver,p	1	0	0	0	0	0	0	0	0	0	0	0	.000	.000	.000	1	0	0	1.000
Wells,p	2	0	0	0	0	0	0	0	0	0	0	0	.000	.000	.000	0	2	0	1.000
Dellucci,pr-rf-ph	4	2	1	0	0	0	0	0	0	0	0	0	.000	.000	.000	1	0	0	1.000
Flaherty,c	1	2	0	0	0	0	0	0	0	0	0	0	.000	.000	.000	4	0	0	1.000
Mussina,p	1	3	0	0	0	0	0	0	0	0	0	3	.000	.000	.000	1	1	0	1.000
Totals	6	207	21	54	84	10	1	6	21	22	1	49	.261	.338	.406	165	66	5	.979

FLORIDA MARLINS' PITCHING RECORDS

Pitcher	G	GS	CG	IP	H	R	ER	HR	BB	IBB	SO	HB	WP	W	L	Pct.	ERA
Willis	3	0	0	3.2	4	0	0	0	2	0	3	0	0	0	0	.000	0.00
Pavano	2	1	0	9.0	8	1	1	0	1	0	6	0	0	0	0	.000	1.00
Beckett	2	2	1	16.1	8	2	2	0	5	0	19	1	0	1	1	.500	1.10
Penny	2	2	0	12.1	15	4	3	1	5	0	7	0	0	2	0	1.000	2.19
Fox	3	0	0	3.0	4	2	2	1	4	1	4	0	0	0	0	.000	6.00

Pitcher	G	GS	CG	IP	H	R	ER	HR	BB	IBB	SO	HB	WP	W	L	Pct.	ERA
Urbina	3	0	0	3.0	2	2	2	0	3	0	2	0	0	0	0	.000	6.00
Helling	1	0	0	2.2	2	2	2	1	0	0	2	0	0	0	0	.000	6.75
Looper	4	0	0	3.2	6	4	4	2	0	0	4	1	0	1	0	1.000	9.82
Redman	1	1	0	2.1	5	4	4	1	2	0	2	1	1	0	1	.000	15.43
Totals	6	6	1	56.0	54	21	20	6	22	1	49	3	1	4	2	.667	3.21

Shutouts—Beckett. Saves—Urbina 2.

NEW YORK YANKEES' PITCHING RECORDS

Pitcher	G	GS	CG	IP	H	R	ER	HR	BB	IBB	SO	HB	WP	W	L	Pct.	ERA
Nelson	3	0	0	4.0	4	0	0	0	2	0	5	0	0	0	0	.000	0.00
Rivera	2	0	0	4.0	2	0	0	0	0	0	4	0	0	0	0	.000	0.00
Hammond	1	0	0	2.0	2	2	0	0	0	0	0	0	0	0	0	.000	0.00
Pettitte	2	2	0	15.2	12	3	1	0	4	1	14	0	0	1	1	.500	0.57
Mussina	1	1	0	7.0	7	1	1	0	1	1	9	0	0	1	0	1.000	1.29
Wells	2	2	0	8.0	6	3	3	0	2	0	1	1	0	0	1	.000	3.38
Clemens	1	1	0	7.0	8	3	3	1	0	0	5	0	0	0	0	.000	3.86
Contreras	4	0	0	6.1	5	4	4	0	5	0	10	0	0	0	1	.000	5.68
Weaver	1	0	0	1.0	1	1	1	1	0	0	0	0	0	0	1	.000	9.00
Totals	6	6	0	55.0	47	17	13	2	14	2	48	1	0	2	4	.333	2.13

No shutouts. Saves—Rivera.

SCORE BY INNINGS

Florida	5	3	0	1	5	1	0	0	1	0	0	1—17
New York	4	2	1	3	0	1	1	1	8	0	0	0—21

MISCELLANEOUS STATISTICS

Sacrifice hits—Beckett, Boone, Castillo, Dellucci, Gonzalez, Pavano, Penny.
Sacrifice flies—Boone, Encarnacion, Rodriguez, Williams.
Stolen bases—Castillo, Pierre, Posada, Soriano.
Caught stealing—Castillo, Gonzalez, Pierre, Posada, Soriano.
Double plays—Castillo, Gonzalez and Lee 4; Boone and Johnson; Boone, Soriano and Johnson; Gonzalez and Lee; Gonzalez, Castillo and Lee; Jeter, Soriano and Johnson; Lowell, Castillo and Lee; Wilson, Jeter and Johnson.
Left on bases—Florida 8, 5, 8, 7, 6, 9—43; New York 9, 6, 8, 10, 9, 5—47.
Scoring position—Florida 1 for 7, 1 for 5, 2 for 9, 1 for 7, 4 for 9, 1 for 6—10 for 43; New York 1 for 12, 1 for 5, 2 for 8, 2 for 10, 1 for 8, 0 for 7—7 for 50.
Hit by pitcher—by Wells (Pierre), by Looper (Jeter), by Redman (Giambi), by Beckett (Matsui).
Passed balls—Posada.
Balks—None.
Time of games—3:43, 2:56, 3:21, 4:03, 3:05, 2:57—Avg.: 3:20.
Attendance—55,769, 55,750, 65,731, 65,934, 65,975, 55,773—364,932.
Umpires—Marsh, Randy; Young, Larry; Darling, Gary; Kellogg, Jeff; Rapuano, Ed; Welke, Tim.

ALL-STAR GAME

BOX SCORE

AMERICAN 7, NATIONAL 6

TUESDAY, JULY 15, AT U.S. CELLULAR FIELD, CHICAGO

National League	AB	R	H	BI	BB	SO	PO	A
Renteria, ss (Cardinals)	2	0	0	0	0	1	0	0
Furcal, ph-ss (Braves)	3	1	1	0	0	1	0	1
Edmonds, cf (Cardinals)	2	0	1	0	0	1	1	0
A.Jones, ph-cf (Braves)	2	2	2	3	0	0	1	0
Pujols, lf (Cardinals)	3	0	1	1	0	0	1	0
L.Gonzalez, lf (D'backs)	1	0	1	0	0	0	0	0
Bonds, dh (Giants)	3	0	0	0	0	0	0	0
Ro.White, ph-dh (Padres)	1	0	0	0	0	0	0	0
Sheffield, rf (Braves)	1	1	0	0	1	0	0	0
P.Wilson, rf (Rockies)	2	0	1	0	0	1	2	0
Helton, 1b (Rockies)	2	1	1	2	0	1	2	0
Sexson, 1b (Brewers)	2	0	0	0	0	0	5	0
Rolen, 3b (Cardinals)	2	1	1	0	0	0	0	1
Lowell, 3b (Marlins)	1	0	1	0	0	0	0	1
A.Boone, ph-3b (Reds)	1	0	0	0	0	0	0	0
J.Lopez, c (Braves)	2	0	0	0	0	0	9	0
Lo Duca, ph-c (Dodgers)	2	0	1	0	0	0	2	0
Vidro, 2b (Expos)	2	0	0	0	0	2	1	0
L.Castillo, 2b (Marlins)	2	0	0	0	0	0	0	0
Schmidt, p (Giants)	0	0	0	0	0	0	0	0
Wolf, p (Phillies)	0	0	0	0	0	0	0	0
K.Wood, p (Cubs)	0	0	0	0	0	0	0	0
Ru.Ortiz, p (Braves)	0	0	0	0	0	0	0	0
W.Williams, p (Cardinals)	0	0	0	0	0	0	0	0
B.Wagner, p (Astros)	0	0	0	0	0	0	0	0
Gagne, p (Dodgers)	0	0	0	0	0	0	0	0
TOTALS	36	6	11	6	1	7	24	3

American League	AB	R	H	RBI	BB	SO	PO	A
Suzuki, rf (Mariners)	1	1	0	0	2	0	2	0
M.Ordonez, ph-rf (W. Sox)	1	0	0	0	0	0	3	0
A.Soriano, 2b (Yankees)	3	0	0	0	0	1	0	0
Ja.Giambi, 1b (Yankees)	1	1	1	1	0	0	3	0
C.Delgado, 1b (Blue Jays)	3	0	1	1	0	1	5	0
Ra.Hernandez, c (Athletics)	1	0	0	0	0	0	2	0
A.Rodriguez, ss (Rangers)	3	1	1	0	0	1	0	2
Garciaparra, ss (Red Sox)	1	0	0	0	0	0	1	1
G.Anderson, lf (Angels)	4	1	3	2	0	1	0	0
Mora, pr-lf (Orioles)	0	1	0	0	0	0	0	0
E.Martinez, dh (Mariners)	2	0	0	0	0	2	0	0
C.Everett, ph-dh (White Sox)	1	0	0	0	0	0	0	0
Matsui, cf (Yankees)	2	0	1	0	0	0	2	0
V.Wells, pr-cf (Blue Jays)	2	1	1	1	0	0	3	0
Glaus, 3b (Angels)	3	0	0	0	0	2	0	1
Blalock, ph-3b (Rangers)	1	1	1	2	0	0	0	0
Posada, c (Yankees)	2	0	0	0	0	2	5	0
B.Boone, 2b (Mariners)	2	0	0	0	0	1	1	1
Loaiza, p (White Sox)	0	0	0	0	0	0	0	0
Clemens, p (Yankees)	0	0	0	0	0	0	0	0
Moyer, p (Mariners)	0	0	0	0	0	0	0	0
Hasegawa, p (Mariners)	0	0	0	0	0	0	0	0
Guardado, p (Twins)	0	0	0	0	0	0	0	0
Mulder, p (Athletics)	0	0	0	0	0	0	0	1
Donnelly, p (Angels)	0	0	0	0	0	0	0	0
Foulke, p (Athletics)	0	0	0	0	0	0	0	0
TOTALS	33	7	9	7	2	11	27	6

National League	0 0 0	0 5 0	1 0 0	—6
American League	0 0 1	0 0 2	1 3 x	—7

National League	IP	H	R	ER	HR	BB	SO
Schmidt (Giants)	2.0	1	0	0	0	0	3
Wolf (Phillies)	1.0	1	1	1	0	1	2
K.Wood (Cubs)	1.0	1	0	0	0	0	2
Ru.Ortiz (Braves)	1.0	0	0	0	0	1	2
W.Williams (Cardinals)	1.0	2	2	2	1	0	1
B.Wagner (Astros) (HOLD)	1.0	1	1	1	1	0	0
Gagne (Dodgers) (L)	1.0	3	3	3	1	0	1

American League	IP	H	R	ER	HR	BB	SO
Loaiza (White Sox)	2.0	1	0	0	0	0	1
Clemens (Yankees)	1.0	0	0	0	0	0	2
Moyer (Mariners)	1.0	0	0	0	0	0	1
Hasegawa (Mariners)	0.2	3	4	4	1	1	1
Guardado (Twins)	0.1	2	1	1	0	0	0
Mulder (Athletics)	2.0	5	1	1	1	0	1
Donnelly (Angels) (W)	1.0	0	0	0	0	0	1
Foulke (Athletics) (S)	1.0	0	0	0	0	0	0

E—Furcal. DP—A.L. 2. LOB—N.L. 4, A.L. 5. Hitting with runners in scoring position—N.L. 3 for 4, A.L. 4 for 7. 2B—A.Jones, Lowell, G.Anderson, V.Wells. HR—Helton (5th inning, 0 out, 1 on) off Hasegawa, G.Anderson (6th inning, 0 out, 1 on) off W.Williams, A.Jones (7th inning, 1 out, 0 on) off Mulder, Ja.Giambi (7th inning, 2 out, 0 on) off B.Wagner, Blalock (8th inning, 2 out, 1 on) off Gagne. WP—Wolf. HBP—E.Martinez by Schmidt. T—2:38. A—47,609. U—HP-McClelland, 1B-Young, 2B-Darling, 3B-Cederstrom, LF-Carlson, RF-Welke.

PLAY BY PLAY

FIRST INNING

N.L.—Renteria grounded out, shortstop Rodriguez to first baseman Delgado. Edmonds singled to right. Pujols lined out to center fielder Matsui. Bonds flied out to right fielder Suzuki.

A.L.—Suzuki grounded out, first baseman Helton unassisted. Soriano flied out to center fielder Edmonds. Delgado flied out to left fielder Pujols.

SECOND INNING

N.L.—Sheffield fouled out to first baseman Delgado. Helton struck out. Rolen fouled out to first baseman Delgado.

A.L.—Rodriguez struck out. Anderson struck out. Martinez was hit by a pitch. Matsui singled to left, Martinez to second. Glaus struck out.

THIRD INNING

N.L.—Clemens pitching. Lopez grounded out, third baseman Glaus to first baseman Delgado. Vidro struck out. Renteria struck out.

A.L.—Wolf pitching. Posada struck out. Suzuki walked. On Wolf's wild pitch, Suzuki to second. Soriano struck out. Delgado singled to left, Suzuki scored. Rodriguez grounded out, third baseman Rolen to first baseman Helton. One run. A.L. 1, N.L. 0.

FOURTH INNING

N.L.—Moyer pitching. Edmonds struck out. Pujols flied out to right fielder Suzuki. Bonds flied out to center fielder Matsui.

A.L.—Wood pitching. Anderson singled to right. Martinez struck out. Matsui grounded into fielder's choice, second baseman Vidro unassisted, Anderson out. Wells pinch-running for Matsui. Glaus struck out.

FIFTH INNING

N.L.—Wells in as center fielder. Hasegawa pitching. Sheffield walked. Helton homered to center on the first pitch, Sheffield scored. Rolen singled to right. Lopez flied out to center fielder Wells. Vidro struck out. Furcal pinch-hitting for Renteria. Furcal singled to center, Rolen to second. Guardado pitching. Jones pinch-hitting for Edmonds. Jones doubled to left, Rolen scored, Furcal scored. Pujols singled to left, Jones scored. Bonds grounded out, first baseman Delgado unassisted. Five runs. N.L. 5, A.L. 1.

A.L.—Furcal in as shortstop. Jones in as center fielder. Gonzalez in as left fielder. Wilson in as right fielder. Sexson in as first baseman. Lowell in as third baseman. Castillo in as second baseman. Ortiz pitching. Posada struck out. Suzuki walked on a full count. Soriano flied out to right fielder Wilson. Delgado struck out.

SIXTH INNING

N.L.—Giambi in as first baseman. Hernandez in as catcher. Boone in as second baseman. Mulder pitching. Wilson singled to center. Sexson grounded into a double play, shortstop Rodriguez to second baseman Boone to first baseman Giambi, Wilson out. Lowell doubled to right. Lo Duca pinch-hitting for Lopez. Lo Duca infield single to short, Lowell to third. Castillo grounded out, pitcher Mulder to first baseman Giambi.

A.L.—Lo Duca in as catcher. W.Williams pitching. Rodriguez infield single to short. On Furcal's error, Rodriguez to second. Anderson homered to center on a 0-1 count, Rodriguez scored. Martinez struck out. Wells flied out to center fielder Jones. Glaus popped out to first baseman Sexson. Two runs. N.L. 5, A.L. 3.

SEVENTH INNING

N.L.—Garciaparra in as shortstop. Furcal struck out. Jones homered to center on a 2-2 count. Gonzalez singled to right. White pinch-hitting for Bonds. White grounded into a double play, shortstop Garciaparra to first baseman Giambi, Gonzalez out. One run. N.L. 6, A.L. 3.

A.L.—White in as designated hitter. Wagner pitching. Boone flied out to right fielder Wilson. Ordonez pinch-hitting for Suzuki. Ordonez fouled out to first baseman Sexson. Giambi homered to right on the first pitch. Hernandez grounded out, third baseman Lowell to first baseman Sexson. One run. N.L. 6, A.L. 4.

EIGHTH INNING

N.L.—Ordonez in as right fielder. Donnelly pitching. Wilson struck out. Sexson flied out to right fielder Ordonez. Boone pinch-hitting for Lowell. Boone lined out to right fielder Ordonez.

A.L.—Boone in as third baseman. Gagne pitching. Garciaparra grounded out, shortstop Furcal to first baseman Sexson. Anderson doubled to center. Mora pinch-running for Anderson. Everett pinch-hitting for Martinez. Everett grounded out, first baseman Sexson unassisted, Mora to third. Wells doubled to center, Mora scored. Blalock pinch-hitting for Glaus. Blalock homered to right on a 3-1 count, Wells scored. Boone struck out. Three runs. A.L. 7, N.L. 6.

NINTH INNING

N.L.—Mora in as left fielder. Everett in as designated hitter. Blalock in as third baseman. Foulke pitching. Lo Duca flied out to center fielder Wells. Castillo lined out to center fielder Wells. Furcal flied out to right fielder Ordonez. Final score: A.L. 7, N.L. 6.

NOTABLE PERFORMANCES

BOX SCORES OF NO-HIT GAMES

KEVIN MILLWOOD

SUNDAY, APRIL 27, AT PHILADELPHIA

GIANTS	AB	R	H	BI	PHILLIES	AB	R	H	BI
Durham, 2b	2	0	0	0	Rollins, ss	4	0	1	0
Grissom, cf	4	0	0	0	Ledee, cf	3	1	2	1
Aurilia, ss	2	0	0	0	Abreu, rf	3	0	1	0
Bonds, lf	3	0	0	0	Burrell, lf	3	0	0	0
Cruz, rf	3	0	0	0	Thome, 1b	2	0	0	0
Snow, 1b	3	0	0	0	Lieberthal, c	2	0	0	0
Torrealba, c	3	0	0	0	Bell, 3b	3	0	0	0
Feliz, 3b	2	0	0	0	Utley, 2b	2	0	0	0
Perez, ph	1	0	0	0	Perez, 2b	1	0	0	0
Foppert, p	2	0	0	0	Millwood, p	3	0	0	0
Nathan, p	0	0	0	0					
Rodriguez, p	0	0	0	0					
Benard, ph	1	0	0	0					
TOTALS	26	0	0	0	**TOTALS**	26	1	4	1

San Francisco ..	0	0	0	0	0	0	0	0	0—0	0	0
Philadelphia	1	0	0	0	0	0	0	0	x—1	4	0

San Francisco	IP	H	R	ER	BB	K	#Pit
Foppert (L, 0-2)	6	3	1	1	4	5	115
Nathan	1	0	0	0	0	1	15
Rodriguez	1	1	0	0	0	1	16

Philadelphia	IP	H	R	ER	BB	K	#Pit
Millwood (W, 4-1)	9	0	0	0	3	10	108

E—None. DP—San Francisco 2 (Durham to Aurilia to Snow; Feliz to Durham to Snow). LOB—San Francisco 2, Philadelphia 6. Scoring Position—San Francisco, 0 for 0; Philadelphia, 0 for 6. 3B—Rollins (1). HR—Ledee (3). Runners Moved Up—Abreu. GDP—Abreu, Burrell. CS—Durham (1). HBP—Abreu by F.Rodriguez. T—2:35. A—40,016. Umpires—HP, Mike Everitt; 1B, Hunter Wendelstedt; 2B, Larry Young; 3B, Charlie Reliford.

ASTROS TEAM

WEDNESDAY, JUNE 11, AT NEW YORK

ASTROS	AB	R	H	BI	YANKEES	AB	R	H	BI
Biggio, cf	5	1	2	0	Soriano, 2b	4	0	0	0
Blum, 3b	5	1	1	0	Jeter, ss	3	0	0	0
Bagwell, 1b	5	1	2	0	Giambi, dh	3	0	0	0
Kent, 2b	4	0	1	0	Posada, c	3	0	0	0
Berkman, lf	4	2	1	2	Ventura, 3b	3	0	0	0
Hidalgo, rf	5	1	2	2	Trammell, ph	1	0	0	0
Merced, dh	5	1	1	0	Matsui, cf	4	0	0	0
Vizcaino, ss	2	0	1	1	Zeile, 1b	2	0	0	0
Everett, ss	1	0	0	0	Mondesi, rf	3	0	0	0
Ausmus, c	4	1	3	1	J.Rivera, lf	3	0	0	0
TOTALS	40	8	14	6	**TOTALS**	29	0	0	0

Houston	1	1	2	0	0	0	1	1	2—8	14	1
New York	0	0	0	0	0	0	0	0	0—0	0	1

Houston	IP	H	R	ER	BB	K	#Pit
Oswalt	1	0	0	0	0	2	23
Munro	2.2	0	0	0	3	2	55
Saarloos	1.1	0	0	0	0	1	16
Lidge (W, 4-0)	2	0	0	0	0	2	23
Dotel	1	0	0	0	0	4	20
Wagner	1	0	0	0	0	2	14

New York	IP	H	R	ER	BB	K	#Pit
Weaver (L, 3-5)	6.1	10	5	5	1	2	85
Hammond	0.2	0	0	0	0	1	6
Anderson	1	2	1	1	0	1	16
Reyes	1	2	2	2	1	0	18

E—Blum (3), Jeter (4). LOB—Houston 8, New York 6. Scoring Position—Houston, 2 for 14; New York, 0 for 2. 2B—Biggio (20), Bagwell (13), Hidalgo 2 (13), J.Vizcaino (5). 3B—Merced (2). HR—Berkman (12). SF—J.Vizcaino. Runners Moved Up—Blum, J.Kent. SB—A.Soriano (18). HBP—Ja.Giambi by Munro. WP—Dotel, Weaver, Anderson. T—2:52. A—29,905. Umpires—HP, Mike Fichter; 1B, Jerry Layne; 2B, Dana DeMuth; 3B, Marvin Hudson.

LOW-HIT GAMES

AMERICAN LEAGUE

ONE-HIT GAMES

Date	Pitcher(s), Team, Opponent, Result—Player with hit
5-2	Joe Kennedy, Tampa Bay at Detroit, W 2-0—Andres Torres (single in first)
6-13	Victor Zambrano (7 inn.), Travis Harper (0.0 inn.), Jesus Colome (1 inn.) and Al Levine (1 inn.), Tampa Bay vs. Pittsburgh, W 7-1—Jack Wilson (single in fifth)
7-8	Billy Traber, Cleveland vs. New York, W 4-0—John Flaherty (single in third)

TWO-HIT GAMES

Date	Pitcher(s), Team, Opponent, Result—Player(s) with hit(s)
4-5	Runelvys Hernandez (7 inn.), Jason Grimsley (1 inn.) and Mike MacDougal (1 inn.), Kansas City vs. Cleveland, W 3-1—John McDonald (double in third), Milton Bradley (double in third)
4-11	Esteban Loaiza (8 inn.) and Billy Koch (1 inn.), Chicago at Detroit, W 5-0—Shane Halter (single in fourth), Ramon Santiago (single in sixth)
5-9	Jim Parque (6 inn.), Travis Harper (1.2 inn.), John Rocker (0.0 inn.) and Lance Carter (1.1 inn.), Tampa Bay vs. Detroit, W 2-0—Dean Palmer (single in seventh), Shane Halter (single in seventh)
6-22	Jeremi Gonzalez (7 inn.) and Jesus Colome (1 inn.), Tampa Bay at Florida, L 2-3—Miguel Cabrera (triple in third), Mike Lowell (home run in seventh)
7-4	Aaron Sele (5 inn.), Francisco Rodriguez (2 inn.), Brendan Donnelly (1 inn.) and Troy Percival (1 inn.), Anaheim at Oakland, W 1-0—Scott Hatteberg (single in first), Miguel Tejada (double in sixth)
7-23	Ryan Franklin, Seattle vs. Oakland, W 6-0—Miguel Tejada (double in fourth), Scott Hatteberg (single in ninth)
8-11	Tim Hudson, Oakland vs. Boston, W 4-0—Manny Ramirez (single in second), Nomar Garciaparra (single in seventh)
9-2	Bartolo Colon, Chicago vs. Boston, L 1-2—Trot Nixon (home run in second), Gabe Kapler (home run in sixth)
9-3	Doug Waechter, Tampa Bay vs. Seattle, W 7-0—Rey Sanchez (single in third), Dan Wilson (single in sixth)
9-17	Barry Zito (8.1 inn.), Chad Bradford (0.1 inn.) and Jim Mecir (0.1 inn.), Oakland at Anaheim, W 2-1—Alfredo Amezaga (single in sixth), Garret Anderson (single in seventh)

NATIONAL LEAGUE

NO-HIT GAMES

Date	Pitcher(s), Team, Opponent
4-27	Kevin Millwood, Philadelphia vs. San Francisco, W 1-0
6-11	Roy Oswalt (1 inn.), Pete Munro (2.2 inn.), Kirk Saarloos (1.1 inn.), Brad Lidge (2 inn.), Octavio Dotel (1 inn.) and Billy Wagner (1 inn.), Houston at New York, W 8-0

ONE-HIT GAMES

Date	Pitcher(s), Team, Opponent, Result—Player with hit
6-15	Steve Trachsel, New York at Anaheim, W 8-0—David Eckstein (single in sixth)
6-16	Dontrelle Willis, Florida vs. New York, W 1-0—Ty Wigginton (single in fourth)
6-17	Jae Weong Seo (6.2 inn.), Dave Weathers (1.1 inn.) and Armando Benitez (1 inn.), New York at Florida, W 5-0—Juan Encarnacion (single in fifth)
7-2	Matt Clement (7 inn.), Mark Guthrie (0.2 inn.), Kyle Farnsworth (0.1 inn.) and Joe Borowski (1 inn.), Chicago at Philadelphia, W 1-0—David Bell (single in fifth)
8-18	Steve Trachsel, New York vs. Colorado, W 8-0—Chin-hui Tsao (double in sixth)
9-14	Randy Johnson, Arizona vs. Colorado, W 5-0—Rene Reyes (single in fifth)

TWO-HIT GAMES

Date	Pitcher(s), Team, Opponent, Result—Player(s) with hit(s)
4-3	Jake Peavy (5 inn.), Mike Bynum (2 inn.) and Brandon Villafuerte (2 inn.), San Diego vs. Los Angeles, W 6-1—Brian Jordan (home run in second), Shawn Green (single in seventh)
4-11	Tomo Ohka (8 inn.) and Scott Stewart (1 inn.), Montreal vs. New York, W 10-0—Cliff Floyd (single in fourth), Roger Cedeno (single in ninth)
5-14	Curt Schilling, Arizona at Philadelphia, W 2-0—David Bell (double in third), Bobby Abreu (single in fifth)
5-21	Wayne Franklin, Milwaukee vs. San Diego, W 10-0—Rondell White (single in second), Ramon Vazquez (single in ninth)
5-22	Darren Dreifort (6 inn.), Paul Shuey (1 inn.), Tom Martin (0.2 inn.), Paul Quantrill (0.1 inn.) and Eric Gagne (1 inn.), Los Angeles vs. Colorado, W 4-3—Mark Sweeney (double in first and double in third)
5-24	Hideo Nomo, Los Angeles at Milwaukee, W 6-0—John Vander Wal (single in seventh), Wes Helms (single in seventh)
5-24	Brian Lawrence, San Diego at Arizona, W 5-1—Steve Finley (single in second), Tony Womack (single in third)
5-30	Wade Miller, Houston at Chicago, W 9-1—Damian Miller (single in third), Corey Patterson (home run in fifth)
6-21	Dontrelle Willis, Florida vs. Tampa Bay, W 2-0—Damian Rolls (single in first), Aubrey Huff (single in first)
6-29	Tomo Ohka, Montreal at Toronto, W 10-2—Carlos Delgado (double in seventh), Mike Bordick (single in eighth)
7-19	Kerry Wood, Chicago at Florida, W 1-0—Ivan Rodriguez (double in first), Juan Pierre (single in sixth)
7-26	Tim Redding (7 inn.), Brad Lidge (0.2 inn.) and Billy Wagner (1.1 inn.), Houston vs. Chicago, W 3-1—Aramis Ramirez (triple in fifth and single in seventh)
7-29	Matt Clement, Chicago vs. San Francisco, W 3-0—Marquis Grissom (single in fourth), Andres Galarraga (single in seventh)
8-17	Curt Schilling (8 inn.) and Matt Mantei (1 inn.), Arizona at Atlanta, W 2-0—Marcus Giles (double in first), Gary Sheffield (single in ninth)
8-24	Tom Glavine (7 inn.), Grant Roberts (1.2 inn.) and John Franco (0.1 inn.), New York at Los Angeles, W 2-1—Jolbert Cabrera (double in fifth), Cesar Izturis (triple in fifth)
8-31	Vicente Padilla (8 inn.) and Jose Mesa (1 inn.), Philadelphia at New York, W 4-1—Jose Reyes (single in seventh), Tony Clark (double in seventh)
9-23	Kerry Wood (7 inn.), Kyle Farnsworth (1 inn.) and Mike Remlinger (1 inn.), Chicago at Cincinnati, W 6-0—Wily Mo Pena (single in seventh), Sean Casey (single in ninth)
9-27	Edwin Jackson (6 inn.), Guillermo Mota (1 inn.), Tom Martin (0.1 inn.), Paul Quantrill (0.2 inn.) and Eric Gagne (1 inn.), Los Angeles at San Francisco, W 5-0—Jeffrey Hammonds (double in third), Benito Santiago (single in sixth)
9-27	Denny Stark (6 inn.), Aaron Cook (1 inn.), Jason Young (1 inn.) and Chin-hui Tsao (1 inn.), Colorado at San Diego, W 10-2—Sean Burroughs (single in third), Brian Giles (home run in sixth)

15-STRIKEOUT GAMES

AMERICAN LEAGUE

No occurrences

NATIONAL LEAGUE

Date	Pitcher, Team, Opponent	IP	H	R	ER	BB	SO	Result
6-26	Mark Prior, Chicago vs. Milwaukee	8	4	2	2	0	16	L 3-5

10-STRIKEOUT GAMES

AMERICAN LEAGUE

Team	No.	Pitchers
Boston	6	Pedro Martinez 6.
Oakland	5	Mark Mulder 2, Ted Lilly 1, Barry Zito 1, Rich Harden 1.
Toronto	5	Kelvim Escobar 2, Roy Halladay 2, Cory Lidle 1.
Chicago	4	Esteban Loaiza 2, Bartolo Colon 1, Jon Garland 1.
New York	4	Roger Clemens 2, Mike Mussina 1, Andy Pettitte 1.
Minnesota	2	Johan Santana 2.
Baltimore	1	Rodrigo Lopez 1.
Seattle	1	Joel Pineiro 1.
Texas	1	Colby Lewis 1.
Anaheim	0	None.
Cleveland	0	None.
Detroit	0	None.
Kansas City	0	None.
Tampa Bay	0	None.

NATIONAL LEAGUE

Team	No.	Pitchers
Chicago	21	Kerry Wood 11, Mark Prior 8, Matt Clement 1, Carlos Zambrano 1.
Arizona	19	Curt Schilling 9, Randy Johnson 5, Brandon Webb 4, Miguel Batista 1.
Montreal	11	Javier Vazquez 9, Livan Hernandez 1, Tony Armas 1.
San Francisco	7	Jason Schmidt 5, Jesse Foppert 2.
Florida	6	Mark Redman 3, Carl Pavano 1, Brad Penny 1, Josh Beckett 1.
Philadelphia	5	Kevin Millwood 2, Brett Myers 2, Vicente Padilla 1.
San Diego	5	Jake Peavy 2, Oliver Perez 2, Adam Eaton 1.
Los Angeles	4	Darren Dreifort 2, Kevin Brown 1, Odalis Perez 1.
Cincinnati	2	Ryan Dempster 1, Jose Acevedo 1.
Houston	2	Wade Miller 1, Roy Oswalt 1.
Pittsburgh	2	Jeff D'Amico 1, Oliver Perez 1.
Atlanta	1	Greg Maddux 1.
New York	1	Al Leiter 1.
St. Louis	1	Matt Morris 1.
Colorado	1	Jason Jennings 1.
Milwaukee	0	None.

1-0 GAMES

AMERICAN LEAGUE

Date	Winner	Loser	Inn.*	Site
4-11	†Runelvys Hernandez, Kansas City	†Jake Westbrook, Cleveland	5	Cleveland
5-13	†Esteban Loaiza, Chicago	†Omar Daal, Baltimore	4	Chicago
5-24	†Gary Knotts, Detroit	†Esteban Loaiza, Chicago	3	Chicago
6-12	†Ryan Franklin, Seattle	†Claudio Vargas, Montreal	4	Seattle
6-18	†Chris Hammond, New York	†Lance Carter, Tampa Bay	12	New York
7-4	†Aaron Sele, Anaheim	Mark Mulder, Oakland	6	Oakland
7-10	†Nate Cornejo, Detroit	Esteban Loaiza, Chicago	1	Detroit
7-13	†Keith Foulke, Oakland	†Hector Carrasco, Baltimore	9	Oakland
8-15	C.C. Sabathia, Cleveland	†Travis Harper, Tampa Bay	9	Cleveland
9-4	Jorge Sosa, Tampa Bay	Ryan Franklin, Seattle	2	Tampa Bay
9-6	Roy Halladay, Toronto	†Fernando Rodney, Detroit	10	Toronto

PLAYERS HITTING HOME RUNS IN 1-0 GAMES: 6-12—Bret Boone, Seattle.

*Inning in which run scored. †Did not pitch complete game.

NATIONAL LEAGUE

Date	Winner	Loser	Inn.*	Site
4-20	†Oscar Villarreal, Arizona	†Brett Tomko, St. Louis	5	St. Louis
4-24	†Javier Vazquez, Montreal	†Byung-Hyun Kim, Arizona	7	Montreal
4-27	Kevin Millwood, Philadelphia	†Jesse Foppert, San Francisco	1	Philadelphia
5-31	†Todd Wellemeyer, Chicago	†Ricky Stone, Houston	16	Chicago
6-15	†Oliver Perez, San Diego	†Jon Garland, Chicago	3	Chicago
6-16	Dontrelle Willis, Florida	†Tom Glavine, New York	4	Florida
7-2	†Kyle Farnsworth, Chicago	†Turk Wendell, Philadelphia	9	Philadelphia
7-19	†Ben Sheets, Milwaukee	†Jeff D'Amico, Pittsburgh	4	Pittsburgh
7-19	Kerry Wood, Chicago	†Brad Penny, Florida	5	Florida
7-24	†Paul Shuey, Los Angeles	†Javier Lopez, Colorado	11	Los Angeles
7-26	†Elmer Dessens, Arizona	†Andy Ashby, Los Angeles	5	Arizona
7-27	†Hideo Nomo, Los Angeles	†Curt Schilling, Arizona	2	Arizona
8-2	†Brian Meadows, Pittsburgh	†Jason Jennings, Colorado	2	Pittsburgh
8-8	†Rod Beck, San Diego	†Brian Reith, Cincinnati	12	San Diego
8-23	†Mike Matthews, San Diego	†Rocky Biddle, Montreal	10	San Diego
9-5	†Vicente Padilla, Philadelphia	†Jae Weong Seo, New York	8	Philadelphia
9-14	†John Riedling, Cincinnati	Carlos Zambrano, Chicago	9	Chicago
9-18	†Javier Vazquez, Montreal	†Steve Trachsel, New York	3	New York

Date	Winner	Loser	Inn.*	Site
9-19	Russ Ortiz, Atlanta	†Josh Beckett, Florida	2	Atlanta
9-23	Al Leiter, New York	†Kip Wells, Pittsburgh	4	New York

PLAYERS HITTING HOME RUNS IN 1-0 GAMES: 4-24—Vladimir Guerrero, Montreal; 4-27—Ricky Ledee, Philadelphia; 6-16—Ivan Rodriguez, Florida; 7-2—Sammy Sosa, Chicago; 9-18—Todd Zeile, Montreal.

*Inning in which run scored. †Did not pitch complete game.

FOUR OR MORE HITS IN ONE GAME

AMERICAN LEAGUE

Team	No.	Hitters
Boston	18	Manny Ramirez 3, Bill Mueller 3, Nomar Garciaparra 3, Johnny Damon 2, Doug Mirabelli 1, Todd Walker 1, Jason Varitek 1, Kevin Millar 1, Jeremy Giambi 1, Gabe Kapler 1, Shea Hillenbrand 1.
New York	17	Alfonso Soriano 3, Bernie Williams 2, Jason Giambi 2, Nick Johnson 2, Hideki Matsui 2, Robin Ventura 1, Raul Mondesi 1, Derek Jeter 1, Jorge Posada 1, Bubba Trammell 1, Juan Rivera 1.
Seattle	16	Ichiro Suzuki 5, Edgar Martinez 3, Mark McLemore 1, John Olerud 1, Bret Boone 1, Dan Wilson 1, Jeff Cirillo 1, Randy Winn 1, Carlos Guillen 1, Willie Bloomquist 1.
Toronto	16	Frank Catalanotto 3, Vernon Wells 3, Greg Myers 2, Carlos Delgado 2, Eric Hinske 2, Reed Johnson 2, Tom Wilson 1, Howie Clark 1.
Minnesota	14	A.J. Pierzynski 3, Corey Koskie 2, Cristian Guzman 2, Denny Hocking 1, Shannon Stewart 1, Doug Mientkiewicz 1, Jacque Jones 1, Bobby Kielty 1, Michael Ryan 1, Lew Ford 1.
Texas	14	Hank Blalock 4, Alex Rodriguez 3, Michael Young 3, Doug Glanville 2, Juan Gonzalez 1, Carl Everett 1.
Baltimore	13	Jay Gibbons 3, Melvin Mora 2, Luis Matos 2, Brian Roberts 2, B.J. Surhoff 1, Tony Batista 1, Robert Machado 1, Larry Bigbie 1.
Anaheim	12	Garret Anderson 3, David Eckstein 3, Eric Owens 1, Scott Spiezio 1, Bengie Molina 1, Troy Glaus 1, Jeff DaVanon 1, Chone Figgins 1.
Kansas City	11	Brent Mayne 2, Aaron Guiel 2, Rondell White 1, Michael Tucker 1, Raul Ibanez 1, Dee Brown 1, Carlos Beltran 1, Angel Berroa 1, Ken Harvey 1.
Oakland	11	Miguel Tejada 4, Eric Chavez 2, Terrence Long 1, Ramon Hernandez 1, Erubiel Durazo 1, Eric Byrnes 1, Mark Ellis 1.
Tampa Bay	11	Aubrey Huff 3, Travis Lee 2, Damion Easley 1, Marlon Anderson 1, Julio Lugo 1, Toby Hall 1, Carl Crawford 1, Rocco Baldelli 1.
Cleveland	10	Omar Vizquel 2, Casey Blake 2, Milton Bradley 2, Ben Broussard 1, Chris Magruder 1, Travis Hafner 1, Coco Crisp 1.
Chicago	7	Carl Everett 2, Roberto Alomar 1, Frank Thomas 1, Magglio Ordonez 1, D'Angelo Jimenez 1, Miguel Olivo 1.
Detroit	6	Dmitri Young 2, Kevin Witt 1, Warren Morris 1, Craig Monroe 1, Omar Infante 1.

NATIONAL LEAGUE

Team	No.	Hitters
St. Louis	23	Albert Pujols 6, Jim Edmonds 4, Edgar Renteria 4, Tino Martinez 3, Bo Hart 3, Fernando Vina 1, Mike Matheny 1, Scott Rolen 1.
Atlanta	21	Marcus Giles 6, Rafael Furcal 5, Vinny Castilla 3, Gary Sheffield 2, Chipper Jones 2, Andruw Jones 2, Robert Fick 1.
Colorado	17	Todd Helton 5, Ronnie Belliard 4, Jay Payton 3, Preston Wilson 3, Juan Uribe 1, Kit Pellow 1.
Chicago	16	Moises Alou 3, Mark Grudzielanek 3, Corey Patterson 2, Sammy Sosa 1, Tom Goodwin 1, Eric Karros 1, Kenny Lofton 1, Alex S. Gonzalez 1, Trenidad Hubbard 1, Paul Bako 1, Ramon Martinez 1.
Pittsburgh	16	Jason Kendall 3, Aramis Ramirez 3, Jack Wilson 3, Reggie Sanders 2, Tike Redman 2, Jeff Reboulet 1, Brian Giles 1, Rob Mackowiak 1.
Arizona	14	Steve Finley 4, Tony Womack 2, Alex Cintron 2, Matt Kata 2, David Dellucci 1, Shea Hillenbrand 1, Rod Barajas 1, Robby Hammock 1.
Florida	13	Juan Pierre 4, Luis Castillo 3, Ivan Rodriguez 2, Todd Hollandsworth 1, Derrek Lee 1, Juan Encarnacion 1, Miguel Cabrera 1.
Milwaukee	12	Geoff Jenkins 4, Richie Sexson 3, Royce Clayton 1, Wes Helms 1, Scott Podsednik 1, Brady Clark 1, Bill Hall 1.
Houston	12	Craig Biggio 3, Richard Hidalgo 2, Lance Berkman 2, Jeff Bagwell 1, Jeff Kent 1, Brian L. Hunter 1, Geoff Blum 1, Morgan Ensberg 1.
Los Angeles	11	Shawn Green 3, Paul Lo Duca 2, Adrian Beltre 2, Fred McGriff 1, Alex Cora 1, Dave Roberts 1, Cesar Izturis 1.
Philadelphia	11	Placido Polanco 3, Marlon Byrd 3, Jimmy Rollins 2, Mike Lieberthal 1, Tomas Perez 1, Bobby Abreu 1.
San Diego	11	Mark Loretta 5, Rondell White 2, Phil Nevin 1, Brian Buchanan 1, Sean Burroughs 1, Ramon Vazquez 1.
San Francisco	10	Marquis Grissom 4, Rich Aurilia 3, Jeffrey Hammonds 1, Neifi Perez 1, Pedro Feliz 1.
New York	9	Ty Wigginton 3, Mo Vaughn 1, Rey Sanchez 1, Cliff Floyd 1, Roger Cedeno 1, Vance Wilson 1, Jason Phillips 1.
Cincinnati	5	Sean Casey 2, Ken Griffey Jr. 1, Reggie Taylor 1, Ryan Freel 1.
Montreal	4	Vladimir Guerrero 1, Orlando Cabrera 1, Brad Wilkerson 1, Henry Mateo 1.

FIVE OR MORE HITS IN ONE GAME

AMERICAN LEAGUE

Date	Player, Team, Opponent	AB	R	H	2B	3B	HR	RBI	Result
4-27	Alex Rodriguez, Texas vs. New York	5	1	5	2	0	0	6	W 10-7
5-6	Dmitri Young, Detroit at Baltimore	5	2	5	0	2	2	5	W 7-6
5-6	Jacque Jones, Minnesota at Tampa Bay	5	3	5	1	0	2	2	W 7-3
5-25	Melvin Mora, Baltimore at Texas	5	2	5	2	0	0	2	W 13-10
5-27	Randy Winn, Seattle at Kansas City	5	2	5	1	0	0	0	W 15-7
6-19	Miguel Tejada, Oakland vs. Texas	5	2	5	1	0	1	2	W 9-2
6-21	Nomar Garciaparra, Boston at Philadelphia	6	1	6	0	0	0	1	L 5-6
6-24	Nomar Garciaparra, Boston vs. Detroit	5	3	5	0	0	0	0	W 10-1
6-27	Johnny Damon, Boston vs. Florida	7	3	5	1	1	0	3	W 25-8
6-29	Eric Byrnes, Oakland at San Francisco	5	2	5	2	1	1	2	W 5-2
7-5	Casey Blake, Cleveland at Minnesota	5	3	5	2	0	2	7	W 13-2
7-9	Frank Catalanotto, Toronto vs. Boston	5	3	5	1	0	1	2	L 7-8
8-23	Eric Owens, Anaheim at Detroit	6	2	5	0	0	0	2	W 14-8
9-16	Angel Berroa, Kansas City at Cleveland	5	3	5	0	1	0	1	W 12-8

NATIONAL LEAGUE

Date	Player, Team, Opponent	AB	R	H	2B	3B	HR	RBI	Result
4-5	Jimmy Rollins, Philadelphia vs. Pittsburgh	6	4	5	3	0	0	3	W 16-1
4-11	Geoff Jenkins, Milwaukee at Arizona	5	3	5	1	0	0	3	W 11-7
4-19	Geoff Blum, Houston at Milwaukee	7	0	5	1	0	0	0	L 2-3
4-27	Tino Martinez, St. Louis at Florida	8	2	5	0	1	0	0	W 7-6
5-23	Albert Pujols, St. Louis at Pittsburgh	6	2	5	2	0	0	2	W 10-8
5-29	Ronnie Belliard, Colorado vs. Los Angeles	5	4	5	2	0	0	0	W 12-5
6-12	Edgar Renteria, St. Louis at Boston	6	2	5	1	0	0	0	W 8-7
6-30	Matt Kata, Arizona at Colorado	6	3	5	1	0	1	2	W 8-7
7-7	Shea Hillenbrand, Arizona vs. Colorado	5	4	5	1	0	3	7	W 14-6
7-18	Gary Sheffield, Atlanta vs. New York	5	4	5	0	0	2	4	W 11-4
7-21	Tom Goodwin, Chicago at Atlanta	6	4	5	1	0	0	0	W 15-6
7-29	Marcus Giles, Atlanta vs. Houston	5	1	5	0	0	0	1	W 6-3
9-3	Moises Alou, Chicago vs. St. Louis	5	2	5	0	0	1	4	W 8-7
9-8	Cesar Izturis, Los Angeles at Arizona	5	3	5	0	1	1	2	W 10-3

HITTING STREAKS OF 15 OR MORE GAMES

AMERICAN LEAGUE

G	Player, Team	Span of streak
26	Nomar Garciaparra, Boston	Apr. 27-May 26
23	Melvin Mora, Baltimore	May 17-June 12
22	Eric Byrnes, Oakland	May 8-June 1
20	Tim Salmon, Anaheim	Apr. 11-May 3
	Todd Walker, Boston	May 10-June 5
	Vernon Wells, Toronto	June 6-June 28
	Mike Bordick, Toronto	July 18-Aug. 13
	Reed Johnson, Toronto	Aug. 29-Sept. 23
19	Ichiro Suzuki, Seattle	June 4-June 24
18	Magglio Ordonez, Chicago	Apr. 3-Apr. 22
16	Rondell White, San Diego	May 19-June 6
	Vernon Wells, Toronto	July 9-July 30
	Dmitri Young, Detroit	Aug. 14-Aug. 30
	Joe Randa, Kansas City	Aug. 17-Sept. 3
15	Alfonso Soriano, New York	Apr. 13-Apr. 27
	Luis Matos, Baltimore	May 23-June 10
	Bret Boone, Seattle	May 24-June 10
	Garret Anderson, Anaheim	July 5-July 23
	D'Angelo Jimenez, Cincinnati	July 8-July 25
	Jay Gibbons, Baltimore	July 29-Aug. 11
	Manny Ramirez, Boston	Aug. 20-Sept. 10

NATIONAL LEAGUE

G	Player, Team	Span of streak
30	Albert Pujols, St. Louis	July 12-Aug. 16
26	Kenny Lofton, Pittsburgh	Apr. 29-May 30
25	Paul Lo Duca, Los Angeles	May 17-June 18
24	Gary Sheffield, Atlanta	July 26-Aug. 20
23	Jason Kendall, Pittsburgh	June 24-July 21
22	Aramis Ramirez, Pittsburgh	May 14-June 11
18	Lance Berkman, Houston	May 24-June 12
17	Todd Helton, Colorado	June 15-July 2
	Jose Reyes, New York	July 30-Aug. 18
	Jack Wilson, Pittsburgh	Aug. 10-Aug. 30
16	Gary Sheffield, Atlanta	Apr. 3-Apr. 19
	Luis Castillo, Florida	Apr. 17-May 4
	Austin Kearns, Cincinnati	May 4-May 23
	Rondell White, San Diego	May 19-June 6
	Ray Durham, San Francisco	May 27-June 14
	Geoff Blum, Houston	June 25-July 17
15	Steve Finley, Arizona	June 19-July 4
	Richie Sexson, Milwaukee	July 1-July 18
	Orlando Cabrera, Montreal	July 2-July 20
	D'Angelo Jimenez, Cincinnati	July 8-July 25
	Marlon Byrd, Philadelphia	July 20-Aug. 2
	Luis Castillo, Florida	Aug. 14-Aug. 31
	Sean Burroughs, San Diego	Aug. 19-Sept. 5

MULTI-HOMER GAMES

AMERICAN LEAGUE

Team	No.	Hitters
Boston	17	David Ortiz 6, Bill Mueller 2, Todd Walker 2, Manny Ramirez 1, Johnny Damon 1, Trot Nixon 1, Jason Varitek 1, Kevin Millar 1, Jeremy Giambi 1, Gabe Kapler 1.
Texas	17	Juan Gonzalez 4, Alex Rodriguez 3, Rafael Palmeiro 2, Carl Everett 2, Mark Teixeira 2, Todd Greene 1, Michael Young 1, Hank Blalock 1, Laynce Nix 1.
New York	14	Jason Giambi 4, Alfonso Soriano 2, Robin Ventura 1, Bernie Williams 1, John Flaherty 1, Derek Jeter 1, Jorge Posada 1, Aaron Boone 1, Nick Johnson 1, Juan Rivera 1.
Toronto	14	Carlos Delgado 5, Vernon Wells 3, Greg Myers 2, Eric Hinske 2, Frank Catalanotto 1, Reed Johnson 1.
Chicago	12	Frank Thomas 4, Jose Valentin 3, Magglio Ordonez 3, Paul Konerko 1, Carlos Lee 1.
Anaheim	10	Garret Anderson 3, Jeff DaVanon 3, Tim Salmon 2, Scott Spiezio 1, Troy Glaus 1.
Cleveland	9	Ben Broussard 2, Ellis Burks 1, Karim Garcia 1, Matt Lawton 1, Casey Blake 1, Jody Gerut 1, Ryan Ludwick 1, Travis Hafner 1.
Minnesota	8	Jacque Jones 3, Matthew LeCroy 2, A.J. Pierzynski 1, Corey Koskie 1, Bobby Kielty 1.
Oakland	8	Eric Chavez 2, Erubiel Durazo 2, Scott Hatteberg 1, Jose Guillen 1, Miguel Tejada 1, Ramon Hernandez 1.
Seattle	8	Bret Boone 3, Edgar Martinez 1, John Olerud 1, Mike Cameron 1, Randy Winn 1, Ichiro Suzuki 1.
Baltimore	5	Tony Batista 2, Jeff Conine 1, Deivi Cruz 1, Jay Gibbons 1.
Detroit	5	Dmitri Young 2, Carlos Pena 1, Brandon Inge 1, Craig Monroe 1.
Kansas City	5	Carlos Beltran 2, Raul Ibanez 1, Ken Harvey 1, Aaron Guiel 1.
Tampa Bay	5	Ben Grieve 1, Adam Piatt 1, Damian Rolls 1, Julio Lugo 1, Aubrey Huff 1.

NATIONAL LEAGUE

Team	No.	Hitters
Atlanta	19	Javy Lopez 8, Gary Sheffield 2, Vinny Castilla 2, Chipper Jones 2, Marcus Giles 2, Andruw Jones 1, Robert Fick 1, Rafael Furcal 1.
St. Louis	13	Jim Edmonds 5, Albert Pujols 4, Tino Martinez 2, Edgar Renteria 1, Scott Rolen 1.
Colorado	13	Preston Wilson 4, Jay Payton 3, Todd Helton 2, Larry Walker 1, Bobby Estalella 1, Ronnie Belliard 1, Juan Uribe 1.
Cincinnati	12	Aaron Boone 3, Ken Griffey Jr. 2, Jose Guillen 2, Adam Dunn 2, Sean Casey 1, Jason LaRue 1, Austin Kearns 1.
Houston	12	Jeff Bagwell 5, Richard Hidalgo 3, Brad Ausmus 1, Lance Berkman 1, Morgan Ensberg 1, Jason Lane 1.
Philadelphia	12	Jim Thome 6, Pat Burrell 4, Mike Lieberthal 1, Ricky Ledee 1.
Chicago	11	Sammy Sosa 5, Aramis Ramirez 2, Moises Alou 1, Alex S. Gonzalez 1, Randall Simon 1, Corey Patterson 1.
Milwaukee	9	Richie Sexson 4, John Vander Wal 1, Geoff Jenkins 1, Wes Helms 1, Scott Podsednik 1, Keith Ginter 1.
Pittsburgh	9	Reggie Sanders 3, Craig Wilson 2, Matt Stairs 1, Brian Giles 1, Rob Mackowiak 1, Jason Bay 1.
San Francisco	9	Barry Bonds 3, Benito Santiago 1, Marquis Grissom 1, Ray Durham 1, Rich Aurilia 1, Jose Cruz 1, Pedro Feliz 1.
Florida	8	Derrek Lee 3, Mike Lowell 3, Alex Gonzalez 1, Miguel Cabrera 1.
Los Angeles	7	Adrian Beltre 2, Fred McGriff 1, Jeromy Burnitz 1, Ron Coomer 1, Jolbert Cabrera 1, Dave Ross 1.
Montreal	7	Jose Vidro 2, Todd Zeile 1, Vladimir Guerrero 1, Orlando Cabrera 1, Brian Schneider 1, Brad Wilkerson 1.
Arizona	6	Luis Gonzalez 2, Steve Finley 1, Carlos Baerga 1, Danny Bautista 1, Shea Hillenbrand 1.
New York	4	Mike Piazza 1, Jeromy Burnitz 1, Tony Clark 1, Jose Reyes 1.
San Diego	3	Ryan Klesko 3.

THREE-HOMER GAMES

Date	Player, Team, Opponent	AB	R	H	2B	3B	HR	RBI	Result
4-25	Richie Sexson, Milwaukee at Atlanta	5	4	4	1	0	3	5	W 12-5
5-8	Aaron Boone, Cincinnati vs. St. Louis	4	3	3	0	0	3	3	W 8-6
5-19	Carlos Pena, Detroit at Cleveland	4	3	3	0	0	3	7	L 9-10
5-21	Geoff Jenkins, Milwaukee vs. San Diego	5	3	3	0	0	3	4	W 10-0
5-29	Todd Helton, Colorado vs. Los Angeles	5	4	4	0	0	3	6	W 12-5
6-4	Garret Anderson, Anaheim at Montreal (P.R.)	5	3	3	0	0	3	5	W 11-2
7-4	Moises Alou, Chicago vs. St. Louis	5	3	3	0	0	3	5	L 8-11
7-7	Shea Hillenbrand, Arizona vs. Colorado	5	4	5	1	0	3	7	W 14-6
7-29	Bill Mueller, Boston at Texas	5	3	3	0	0	3	9	W 14-7
7-30	Jose Valentin, Chicago at Kansas City	4	3	3	0	0	3	5	W 15-4
9-16	Richard Hidalgo, Houston at Colorado	4	4	3	0	0	3	5	W 14-4
9-25	Carlos Delgado, Toronto vs. Tampa Bay	4	4	4	0	0	4	6	W 10-8

GRAND SLAMS

AMERICAN LEAGUE

Date	Batter, Team	Pitcher, Team	Inn.*	Site
3-31	Alfonso Soriano, New York	Roy Halladay, Toronto	6	Toronto
4-8	Hideki Matsui, New York	Joe Mays, Minnesota	5	New York
4-9	Dee Brown, Kansas City	Wilfredo Ledezma, Detroit	3	Detroit
4-9	Vernon Wells, Toronto	Ramiro Mendoza, Boston	5	Toronto
4-17	Carlos Lee, Chicago	Chris George, Kansas City	5	Chicago
4-21	Alfonso Soriano, New York	Rick Reed, Minnesota	4	Minnesota
4-22	Mike Cameron, Seattle	Danys Baez, Cleveland	9	Seattle
4-30	Raul Mondesi, New York	Jamie Moyer, Seattle	1	New York
5-3	Vernon Wells, Toronto	Ben Weber, Anaheim	7	Toronto
5-7	A.J. Pierzynski, Minnesota	Joe Kennedy, Tampa Bay	5	Tampa Bay
5-8	Garret Anderson, Anaheim	Jason Davis, Cleveland	5	Anaheim
5-13	Scott Spiezio, Anaheim	Juan Acevedo, New York	9	New York
5-19	Carlos Pena, Detroit	Jason Davis, Cleveland	3	Cleveland
5-22	Brian Roberts, Baltimore	Troy Percival, Anaheim	9	Anaheim
5-25	Carlos Lee, Chicago	Adam Bernero, Detroit	5	Chicago
5-25	Mark Teixeira, Texas	Rick Helling, Baltimore	3	Texas
5-28	Brian Roberts, Baltimore	Ramon Ortiz, Anaheim	2	Baltimore
6-6	Carlos Delgado, Toronto	John Riedling, Cincinnati	2	Cincinnati
6-7	Kevin Millar, Boston	Jayson Durocher, Milwaukee	7	Milwaukee
6-7§	Mike Sweeney, Kansas City	Shawn Chacon, Colorado	2	Colorado
6-12	A.J. Pierzynski, Minnesota	Darren Oliver, Colorado	1	Minnesota
6-13	Jay Gibbons, Baltimore	Jayson Durocher, Milwaukee	5	Baltimore
6-13	Julio Lugo, Tampa Bay	Brian Boehringer, Pittsburgh	8	Tampa Bay
6-14	Brad Fullmer, Anaheim	Jason Roach, New York	3	Anaheim
6-17	Bret Boone, Seattle	Kevin Appier, Anaheim	5	Seattle
6-20	Miguel Olivo, Chicago	Shawn Estes, Chicago	1	Chicago
6-24	Marlon Anderson, Tampa Bay	Al Reyes, New York	7	Tampa Bay
6-28§	Hideki Matsui, New York	Jeremy Griffiths, New York	3	New York
6-30†	Casey Blake, Cleveland	Kris Wilson, Kansas City	8	Kansas City
7-4	Eric Hinske, Toronto	Travis Driskill, Baltimore	6	Baltimore
7-13	Willie Bloomquist, Seattle	Rob Bell, Tampa Bay	1	Seattle
7-18	Tony Batista, Baltimore	Jarrod Washburn, Anaheim	1	Baltimore
7-18	Ichiro Suzuki, Seattle	Mike MacDougal, Kansas City	9	Kansas City
7-20	David Segui, Baltimore	Francisco Rodriguez, Anaheim	6	Baltimore
7-23	Trot Nixon, Boston	Al Levine, Tampa Bay	7	Boston
7-24	Damian Rolls, Tampa Bay	Chad Fox, Boston	5	Boston
7-26	Jody Gerut, Cleveland	Kyle Lohse, Minnesota	2	Cleveland
7-28	Rafael Palmeiro, Texas	Arthur Rhodes, Seattle	7	Seattle
7-29	Bill Mueller, Boston	Aaron Fultz, Texas	7	Texas
7-29	Bill Mueller, Boston	Jay Powell, Texas	8	Texas
7-30	Paul Konerko, Chicago	Sean Lowe, Kansas City	7	Kansas City
7-30	Randy Winn, Seattle	Nate Cornejo, Detroit	1	Seattle
7-31	Alex Rodriguez, Texas	Todd Jones, Boston	11	Texas
8-2	John Olerud, Seattle	Matt Ginter, Chicago	7	Seattle
8-7	Enrique Wilson, New York	Joaquin Benoit, Texas	2	New York
8-8	Nick Johnson, New York	Ryan Franklin, Seattle	6	New York
8-15	Ichiro Suzuki, Seattle	Mike Timlin, Boston	6	Seattle
8-24	Miguel Tejada, Oakland	Josh Towers, Toronto	6	Toronto
8-24	Ramon Hernandez, Oakland	Kelvim Escobar, Toronto	1	Toronto
8-26	Frank Thomas, Chicago	Roger Clemens, New York	5	New York
9-1	Scott Spiezio, Anaheim	Kenny Rogers, Minnesota	3	Minnesota
9-1	Trot Nixon, Boston	Turk Wendell, Philadelphia	9	Philadelphia
9-2	Cody Ross, Detroit	Cliff Lee, Cleveland	3	Detroit
9-5	Michael Young, Texas	Johan Santana, Minnesota	4	Minnesota
9-10	Jorge Posada, New York	Brian Schmack, Detroit	8	New York
9-13	Randy Winn, Seattle	Francisco Rodriguez, Anaheim	8	Seattle
9-15	Miguel Tejada, Oakland	Ramon Ortiz, Anaheim	4	Anaheim
9-20	Hank Blalock, Texas	Aaron Sele, Anaheim	2	Texas
9-21	Mark Ellis, Oakland	Kazuhiro Sasaki, Seattle	5	Oakland
9-23	Jason Giambi, New York	Kelly Wunsch, Chicago	9	Chicago
9-24	Tony Batista, Baltimore	John Burkett, Boston	1	Boston
9-26	Jose Valentin, Chicago	D.J. Carrasco, Kansas City	8	Kansas City
9-28	Carlos Delgado, Toronto	Cliff Lee, Cleveland	1	Toronto

*Inning in which grand slam was hit. †First game of doubleheader. §Day game separate admission.

NATIONAL LEAGUE

Date	Batter, Team	Pitcher, Team	Inn.*	Site
4-4	Reggie Sanders, Pittsburgh	Joe Roa, Philadelphia	1	Philadelphia
4-4	Brad Ausmus, Houston	Brett Tomko, St. Louis	1	St. Louis
4-11	Brad Wilkerson, Montreal	David Cone, New York	3	San Juan
4-17	Javy Lopez, Atlanta	Rocky Biddle, Montreal	10	San Juan
4-17	Carlos Baerga, Arizona	Jason Jennings, Colorado	2	Arizona
4-24	Chase Utley, Philadelphia	Aaron Cook, Colorado	3	Philadelphia
4-25	John Vander Wal, Milwaukee	Trey Hodges, Atlanta	4	Atlanta
4-30	Adam Hyzdu, Pittsburgh	Oliver Perez, San Diego	3	San Diego
5-4	Cliff Floyd, New York	Matt Kinney, Milwaukee	6	Milwaukee
5-5	Matt Williams, Arizona	Vicente Padilla, Philadelphia	1	Arizona
5-8†	Robert Fick, Atlanta	Nelson Cruz, Colorado	1	Atlanta
5-9	Fernando Vina, St. Louis	Carlos Zambrano, Chicago	2	Chicago
5-16	Wes Helms, Milwaukee	Scott Sullivan, Cincinnati	6	Milwaukee
5-17	Gary Sheffield, Atlanta	Mike Bynum, San Diego	8	San Diego
5-23	Jeromy Burnitz, New York	Russ Ortiz, Atlanta	6	Atlanta
5-24	Fred McGriff, Los Angeles	Matt Kinney, Milwaukee	5	Milwaukee
5-26	Adam Dunn, Cincinnati	Roberto Hernandez, Atlanta	11	Atlanta
5-28	Eddie Perez, Milwaukee	Carlton Loewer, San Diego	1	San Diego
6-3	Morgan Ensberg, Houston	Kerry Ligtenberg, Baltimore	8	Houston
6-7§	Charles Johnson, Colorado	Jason Grimsley, Kansas City	8	Colorado
6-8	Scott Rolen, St. Louis	Rick Bauer, Baltimore	6	St. Louis
6-11	Pedro Feliz, San Francisco	Mark Buehrle, Chicago	1	Chicago
6-11	Kelly Stinnett, Cincinnati	Dewon Brazelton, Tampa Bay	3	Tampa Bay
6-12	Rich Aurilia, San Francisco	Damaso Marte, Chicago	9	Chicago
6-15	Jose Reyes, New York	Jarrod Washburn, Anaheim	2	Anaheim
6-15	Troy O'Leary, Chicago	Cory Lidle, Toronto	6	Toronto
6-19	Chris Stynes, Colorado	Brian Lawrence, San Diego	1	Colorado
6-20	Robert Fick, Atlanta	Sidney Ponson, Baltimore	4	Atlanta
6-20	Rondell White, San Diego	Jeff Nelson, Seattle	9	San Diego
6-29	Rondell White, San Diego	Arthur Rhodes, Seattle	9	Seattle
7-4	John Vander Wal, Milwaukee	Aaron Cook, Colorado	1	Milwaukee
7-5	Geoff Jenkins, Milwaukee	Nelson Cruz, Colorado	7	Milwaukee
7-9	Adam Everett, Houston	Danny Graves, Cincinnati	1	Houston
7-11	Wil Cordero, Montreal	Brad Penny, Florida	4	Montreal
7-17	John Vander Wal, Milwaukee	Kris Benson, Pittsburgh	1	Pittsburgh
7-17	Craig Wilson, Pittsburgh	Wayne Franklin, Milwaukee	5	Pittsburgh
7-20	Alberto Castillo, San Francisco	Denny Neagle, Colorado	4	San Francisco
7-21	Russell Branyan, Cincinnati	Brooks Kieschnick, Milwaukee	7	Cincinnati
7-24	Bobby Abreu, Philadelphia	Kerry Wood, Chicago	6	Chicago
7-28	Marcus Giles, Atlanta	Javier Vazquez, Montreal	6	Montreal
7-30	Edgardo Alfonzo, San Francisco	Kerry Wood, Chicago	2	Chicago
8-2	Bo Hart, St. Louis	Jae Weong Seo, New York	4	New York
8-9	Reggie Taylor, Cincinnati	Mike Matthews, San Diego	8	San Diego
8-17	Brad Wilkerson, Montreal	Tim Worrell, San Francisco	9	Montreal
8-20	Reggie Sanders, Pittsburgh	Esteban Yan, St. Louis	5	St. Louis
8-27	Marlon Byrd, Philadelphia	Hector Almonte, Montreal	7	Montreal
8-27	Phil Nevin, San Diego	Stephen Randolph, Arizona	8	Arizona
8-28	Preston Wilson, Colorado	Jim Brower, San Francisco	7	Colorado
9-1	Jeff Kent, Houston	Rodney Myers, Los Angeles	9	Los Angeles
9-3	J.D. Drew, St. Louis	Felix Sanchez, Chicago	6	Chicago
9-3	Rich Aurilia, San Francisco	Jason Jennings, Colorado	1	San Francisco
9-8	Shawn Green, Los Angeles	Stephen Randolph, Arizona	9	Arizona
9-9	Tomas Perez, Philadelphia	Trey Hodges, Atlanta	2	Atlanta
9-9	Jason Michaels, Philadelphia	Jung Bong, Atlanta	6	Atlanta
9-15	Brian Schneider, Montreal	Trey Hodges, Atlanta	9	Montreal
9-16	Mike Lieberthal, Philadelphia	Blaine Neal, Florida	8	Philadelphia
9-19	Jose Vidro, Montreal	Tom Glavine, New York	4	New York
9-19†	Jason Bay, Pittsburgh	Carlos Zambrano, Chicago	2	Pittsburgh
9-23	Edgardo Alfonzo, San Francisco	Ricky Stone, Houston	2	Houston
9-23	Larry Walker, Colorado	Brandon Webb, Arizona	1	Colorado

*Inning in which grand slam was hit. †First game of doubleheader. §Day game separate admission.

TRANSACTIONS

JANUARY 1, 2003-DECEMBER 31, 2003

JANUARY 2

Padres traded RHP Jeremy Fikac to **Athletics**.
Rangers signed RHP John Thomson.
Cubs signed INF Ramon Martinez.
Twins organization signed INF Chris Gomez.

JANUARY 3

Cubs signed RHP Dave Veres.
Mariners signed INF Greg Colbrunn.

JANUARY 6

Devil Rays organization signed 3B Chris Truby.
Cardinals signed RHPs Joey Hamilton and Al Levine.
Royals organization signed INFs Luis Ordaz and Elvis Pena and RHP Buddy Carlyle.
Braves signed 1B Rob Fick.

JANUARY 7

Reds organization signed LHPs Kent Mercker and Felix Heredia.
Rockies signed 3B Chris Stynes.
Royals signed RHP Albie Lopez.
Rangers organization signed C Chad Kreuter.

JANUARY 8

Cubs organization signed INF/OF Lenny Harris.
Indians organization signed RHP Dave Burba.
Marlins signed OF Todd Hollandsworth.

JANUARY 9

Diamondbacks signed RHP Elmer Dessens.
Rangers organization signed OF Jim Rushford.

JANUARY 10

Royals signed INF Desi Relaford.
Brewers signed RHP Dave Mlicki.
Brewers organization signed RHP Mike Buddie.

JANUARY 11

Tigers traded LHP Mark Redman and RHP Jerrod Fuell to **Marlins** for RHP Gary Knotts and LHPs Nate Robertson and Rob Henkel.
Mets signed OF Tsuyoshi Shinjo.

JANUARY 12

Marlins signed OF Gerald Williams.
Reds signed RHP Paul Wilson.

JANUARY 13

Braves signed LHP Mike Venafro.
Dodgers organization signed LHP Pedro Borbon.
Mets organization signed LHP Pedro Feliciano.

JANUARY 14

Yankees signed OF Hideki Matsui.
Red Sox claimed 1B/OF Kevin Millar off waivers from **Marlins**.
Red Sox signed 3B Bill Mueller.
Brewers organization signed C Keith Osik.
Brewers signed RHP Todd Ritchie.

JANUARY 15

White Sox traded RHPs Antonio Osuna and Deivi Lantigua to **Yankees** for RHP Orlando Hernandez and cash.
White Sox signed OF Armando Rios.
White Sox traded RHPs Rocky Biddle and Orlando Hernandez and OF Jeff Liefer and cash to **Expos** for RHP Bartolo Colon and INF Jorge Nunez.
Cubs signed LHP Mark Guthrie.
Reds organization signed LHP Jimmy Anderson.
Mariners signed OF John Mabry.
Rangers signed RHP Ismael Valdes.

JANUARY 16

Cubs organization signed OF Tom Goodwin.
Marlins signed OF Juan Encarnacion.
Royals organization signed RHP Sean Lowe.
Dodgers organization signed LHP Wilson Alvarez.
Yankees organization signed C John Flaherty.
Phillies signed 3B Tyler Houston.
Cardinals signed RHP Brett Tomko.
Rangers organization signed OF Ryan Christenson.

JANUARY 17

Red Sox claimed INF Earl Snyder off waivers from **Indians**.
Dodgers organization signed INF Terry Shumpert.

JANUARY 20

Devil Rays organization signed LHP Jim Parque and OF Ryan Thompson.
White Sox signed RHP Tom Gordon.
Cardinals signed RHP Dustin Hermanson.

JANUARY 21

Brewers claimed OF Brady Clark off waivers from **Mets**.
Brewers organization signed RHP Chuck Smith.

JANUARY 22

Red Sox signed 1B/DH David Ortiz.
White Sox signed RHP Rick White.
Rockies organization signed RHP Rich Garces.
Marlins signed C Ivan Rodriguez.

JANUARY 23

Braves signed RHP Roberto Hernandez.
Red Sox organization signed C/1B Dave Nilsson.
Royals organization signed RHP James Baldwin.

JANUARY 24

Diamondbacks organization signed RHP Manny Aybar.
Rockies signed INF Jose Hernandez and RHP Steve Reed.
Yankees signed RHP Jon Lieber.
Mets organization signed LHP Graeme Lloyd.
Mariners organization signed RHP Jamey Wright.
Giants organization signed OF Ruben Rivera.

JANUARY 25

Astros traded OF Daryle Ward to **Dodgers** for RHP Ruddy Lugo.

JANUARY 27

White Sox organization signed RHPs Esteban Loaiza, Gil Heredia and Brian Cooper, INF/OF Brian Daubach, Cs Jamie Burke and Steven Morales and OF Cliff Brumbaugh.
Rockies traded OF/INF Jason Romano to **Dodgers** for OF Luke Allen.
Yankees signed RHP Juan Acevedo.
Mets signed RHP Dan Wheeler.
Rangers organization signed OF/DH Ruben Sierra.

JANUARY 28

Brewers organization signed OF John Vander Wal.
Giants signed OF Jose Cruz Jr.

JANUARY 29

Diamondbacks organization signed LHP Ron Villone and RHP Mike Jackson.

Rockies organization signed LHP Darren Oliver.
Phillies organization signed RHP Mike Fyhrie.
Giants organization signed 1B Andres Galarraga.

JANUARY 30

Diamondbacks organization signed RHP Ricky Bottalico.
Dodgers organization signed INF Ron Coomer.

JANUARY 31

Pirates signed RHP Jeff Suppan.
Diamondbacks organization signed INF Carlos Baerga.

FEBRUARY 1

Cardinals signed OF Orlando Palmeiro.

FEBRUARY 3

Padres signed 2B Keith Lockhart.

FEBRUARY 4

Red Sox claimed RHP Bronson Arroyo off waivers from **Pirates**.

FEBRUARY 5

Mariners signed LHPs Ryan Anderson, Steve Kent, Bobby Madritsch and Matt Thornton, RHP Julio Mateo and OF Jamal Strong.

FEBRUARY 6

Devil Rays signed 1B Travis Lee.
Yankees signed RHP Jose Contreras.

FEBRUARY 7

Astros organization signed RHP Anthony Telford.

FEBRUARY 12

Mets organization signed INF Jay Bell.

FEBRUARY 13

Mets organization signed RHP David Cone.

FEBRUARY 14

Dodgers organization signed RHP Bill Simas.

FEBRUARY 15

Red Sox obtained 1B/OF Kevin Millar from **Marlins** for cash. (Millar earlier had rejected a waiver claim by Boston. Also, a Japanese team relinquished its claim on Millar.)

FEBRUARY 20

Mets organization signed 1B/OF Tony Clark.

FEBRUARY 21

Athletics organization signed OF Ron Gant.

FEBRUARY 22

Red Sox organization signed RHP Robert Person.
Mets organization signed RHP T.J. Mathews.

FEBRUARY 25

Pirates signed OF Reggie Sanders.
Expos organization signed INF Jose Offerman.
Reds claimed 1B/OF Dernell Stenson off waivers from **Red Sox**.
Dodgers organization signed LHP Tom Martin.

FEBRUARY 27

Dodgers organization signed INF Chin-Ling Hu.

MARCH 11

Rockies traded OF Jack Cust to **Orioles** for 1B/OF Chris Richard.

MARCH 17

Devil Rays organization signed RHP Rob Bell.

MARCH 19

Yankees traded OF Rondell White to **Padres** for OF Bubba Trammell and LHP Mark Phillips.

MARCH 24

Devil Rays traded OF Jason Conti to **Brewers** for C Javier Valentin.

MARCH 26

Padres claimed LHP Mike Matthews off waivers from **Brewers**.

MARCH 27

Cardinals released RHPs Al Levine and Joey Hamilton.
Astros released RHP Shane Reynolds.

MARCH 28

Red Sox claimed RHP Dicky Gonzalez off waivers from **Expos**.
Tigers released 2B Damion Easley.
Marlins released OF Al Martin.

MARCH 29

Devil Rays signed OF Al Martin.
Indians traded catcher A.J. Hinch to **Tigers** for a player to be named.

APRIL 2

Devil Rays signed 2B Damion Easley.

APRIL 4

Royals claimed 2B Brent Abernathy off waivers from **Devil Rays**.
Diamondbacks released LHP Greg Swindell.

APRIL 8

Red Sox organization signed C Bill Haselman.

APRIL 10

Braves signed RHP Shane Reynolds.

APRIL 11

Reds organization signed RHP Joey Hamilton.

APRIL 12

Royals organization signed C Sandy Martinez.

APRIL 18

Cardinals organization signed C Chris Widger.
Indians organization signed RHP Blake Stein.

APRIL 23

Rockies organization signed OF Greg Vaughn.

MAY 1

Astros released SS Julio Lugo.

MAY 7

Red Sox claimed LHP Bruce Chen off waivers from **Astros**.

MAY 15

Devil Rays signed SS Julio Lugo.

MAY 23

Padres claimed OF Gary Matthews Jr. off waivers from **Orioles**.

MAY 27

Cardinals traded minor league OF Rick Asadoorian and cash to **Rangers** for RHP Esteban Yan.
Brewers traded OF Alex Sanchez to **Tigers** for minor league LHP Chad Petty and minor league OF Gary Varner.

MAY 29

Red Sox traded INF Shea Hillenbrand to **Diamondbacks** for RHP Byung-Hyun Kim.

MAY 30

Mets announced retirement of RHP David Cone.

JUNE 4

Devil Rays released INF Damion Easley.
Brewers released OF Jeffrey Hammonds.
Indians traded INF Bill Selby to **Cardinals** organization for minor league C Clint Chauncey.

JUNE 6

Devil Rays claimed INF/OF Jeff Lieber off waivers from **Expos**.
Mariners acquired LHP Matt White from **Red Sox** for minor league OF Sheldon Fulse.
Yankees traded minor league OF Marcus Thames to **Rangers** for OF/DH Ruben Sierra.
Reds released RHPs Pete Harnisch and Jaime Navarro.

JUNE 11

Yankees released RHP Juan Acevedo.
Royals organization signed RHP Jose Lima.

JUNE 12

Diamondbacks organization signed LHP Dennys Reyes.

JUNE 17

Blue Jays signed RHP Juan Acevedo.

JUNE 19

Royals released RHP Albie Lopez.
Rockies released OF Gabe Kapler.
Cubs traded INF Mark Bellhorn and minor league RHP Travis Anderson to **Rockies** for INF Jose Hernandez.

JUNE 24

Red Sox organization signed OF Gabe Kapler.

JUNE 25

Yankees obtained RHP Dan Miceli and OF Karim Garcia from **Indians** for a player to be named.
Yankees released RHP Mike Thurman and OF Charles Gipson.

JUNE 30

Rockies released RHP Todd Jones.

JULY 1

Rangers traded OF Carl Everett to **White Sox** for players to be named.
Mets traded 2B Roberto Alomar to **White Sox** for minor league LHP Royce Ring, minor league RHP Edwin Almonte and minor league INF Andrew Salvo.
Rockies traded INF Luis Lopez to **Orioles**.
Giants signed OF Jeffrey Hammonds.

JULY 2

Brewers traded RHP Curtis Leskanic to **Royals** for RHP Wes Obermueller and minor league INF Alejandro Machado.
Red Sox signed RHP Todd Jones.

JULY 3

Orioles organization signed OF Ruben Rivera.

JULY 6

Reds acquired INF D'Angelo Jimenez from **White Sox** for minor league RHP Scott Dunn.

JULY 11

Rangers traded RHP Ugueth Urbina to **Marlins** for minor league OF Will Smith, minor league LHP Ryan Snare and minor league 1B Adrian Gonzalez.

JULY 13

Giants acquired RHP Matt Herges from **Padres** for minor league RHP Clay Hensley and future considerations.
Rockies traded C Ben Petrick to the **Tigers** for RHP Adam Bernero.
Brewers organization signed LHP Doug Davis.
Rockies released OF Greg Vaughn.

JULY 14

Mets traded OF Jeromy Burnitz to **Dodgers** for minor league INF Victor Diaz and minor league RHPs Joselo Diaz and Kole Strayhorn.
Dodgers signed OF Rickey Henderson.

JULY 16

Twins traded OF Bobby Kielty to **Blue Jays** for OF Shannon Stewart.
Mets traded RHP Armando Benitez to **Yankees** for RHP Jason Anderson and minor league RHPs Anderson Garcia and Ryan Bicondoa.

JULY 18

Rockies acquired INF Tony Womack from **Diamondbacks** for minor league P Mike Watson.
Indians traded OF Shane Spencer and RHP Ricardo Rodriguez to **Rangers** for OF Ryan Ludwick.

JULY 20

Pirates traded RHP Mike Williams to **Phillies** for minor league LHP Frank Brooks.

JULY 22

Cubs obtained 3B Aramis Ramirez, OF Kenny Lofton and cash considerations from **Pirates** for INF Jose Hernandez, minor league RHP Matt Bruback and a player to be named.
Pirates traded LHPs Scott Sauerbeck and Mike Gonzalez to **Red Sox** for RHP Brandon Lyon and minor league RHP Anastacio Martinez.
Yankees acquired LHP Jesse Orosco from **Padres**.

JULY 23

Padres claimed RHP Joe Roa off waivers from **Rockies**.

JULY 25

Rangers acquired minor league RHPs Frank Francisco and Josh Rupe and minor league OF Anthony Webster from **White Sox** to complete July 1 deal that sent OF Carl Everett to Chicago.

JULY 28

Mets traded LHP Graeme Lloyd to **Royals** for minor league RHP Jeremy Hill.

JULY 29

Mets traded INF Rey Sanchez to **Mariners** for minor league OF Kenny Kelly.
Yankees traded OF Raul Mondesi to **Diamondbacks** for OF David Dellucci, RHP Bret Prinz and minor league C Jon Sprowl.
Yankees traded RHP Dan Miceli to **Astros** for a player to be named.
Rockies traded LHP Chris Michalak to **Reds** for a player to be named.
Reds traded RHP Scott Williamson to **Red Sox** for minor league LHP Phillip Dumatrait and other considerations.
White Sox traded RHP Gary Glover and minor league RHP Scott Dunn and minor league LHP Tim Bittner to **Angels** for LHP Scott Schoeneweis and minor league RHP Doug Nickle.

JULY 30

Cubs traded minor league OF Jason Fransz and cash to **Rangers** for OF Doug Glanville.
Athletics traded minor league RHPs Aaron Harang, Joe Valentine and Jeffrey Bruksch to **Reds** for OF Jose Guillen.
Angels released RHP Kevin Appier.

JULY 31

Orioles traded RHP Sidney Ponson to **Giants** for LHP Damian Moss, RHP Kurt Ainsworth and minor league LHP Ryan Hannaman.
Red Sox traded INF Freddy Sanchez, LHP Mike Gonzalez and cash to **Pirates** for RHPs Jeff Suppan, Brandon Lyon and Anastacio Martinez.
Reds traded 3B Aaron Boone to **Yankees** for minor league LHPs Brandon Claussen and Charlie Manning and cash.
Yankees acquired LHP Gabe White from **Reds** for a player to be named.
Yankees traded 3B Robin Ventura to **Dodgers** for minor league OF Bubba Crosby and minor league RHP Scott Proctor.
Devil Rays sold RHP Al Levine to **Royals**.

AUGUST 5

Red Sox claimed OF/1B David McCarty off waivers from **Athletics**.

AUGUST 6

Mariners traded RHP Jeff Nelson to the **Yankees** for RHP Armando Benitez and cash.
Royals signed RHP Kevin Appier.

AUGUST 8

Royals traded minor league LHP Aric Leclair to **Diamondbacks** for RHP Paul Abbott.

AUGUST 9

Blue Jays released RHP Juan Acevedo.

AUGUST 11

White Sox released RHP Rick White.

AUGUST 12

Reds traded LHP Kent Mercker to **Braves** for a player to be named.

AUGUST 14

Astros signed RHP Rick White.
Reds acquired minor league RHP Matt Belisle from **Braves** to complete August 12 trade that sent LHP Kent Mercker to Atlanta.

AUGUST 16

Cubs traded minor league OF Ray Sadler to **Pirates** for 1B Randall Simon.

AUGUST 17

Yankees released INF Todd Zeile.

AUGUST 18

Angels released INF Benji Gil.
Orioles released RHP Rick Helling.
Reds acquired minor league LHP Tyler Pelland from **Red Sox** to complete July 29 trade that sent RHP Scott Williamson to Boston.

AUGUST 19

Devil Rays claimed OF Adam Piatt off waivers from **Athletics**.
Brewers traded INF Eric Young to **Giants** for minor league RHP **Greg Bruso.**
Cubs traded minor league RHP Enmanuel Ramires and cash to the **Rockies** for INF Tony Womack.

AUGUST 20

Expos signed INF Todd Zeile.

AUGUST 22

Marlins signed RHP Rick Helling.
Brewers traded RHP Mike DeJean to **Cardinals** for players to be named.
Cardinals traded minor league RHP Justin Pope and minor league LHP Ben Julianel to the **Yankees** for LHP Sterling Hitchcock.
Reds traded RHP Scott Sullivan to **White Sox** for a player to be named.

AUGUST 25

Reds traded minor league LHP John Koronka to **Cubs** for LHP Phil Norton.
Indians traded LHP Brian Anderson to **Royals** for minor league OF Trey Dyson and minor league RHP Kieran Mattison and cash.
Yankees claimed LHP Felix Heredia off waivers from **Reds**.

AUGUST 26

Rockies signed C Gregg Zaun.
Royals acquired OF Rondell White from **Padres** for minor league LHP Chris Tierney and minor league RHP Brian Sanches.
Pirates traded OF Brian Giles to **Padres** for LHP Oliver Perez, OF Jason Bay and a player to be named.

AUGUST 27

Reds claimed INF Tim Hummel off waivers from **White Sox** to complete August 22 trade that sent RHP Scott Sullivan to Chicago.

AUGUST 28

Red Sox acquired INF Lou Merloni from **Padres** for minor league RHP Rene Miniel.

AUGUST 31

Yankees traded LHP Jesse Orosco to **Twins** for RHP Juan Padilla.
Yankees activated INF Luis Sojo.
Orioles traded OF/INF Jeff Conine to **Marlins** for minor league RHPs Denny Bautista and Don Levinski.
Reds traded catcher Kelly Stinnett to **Phillies** for a player to be named.

SEPTEMBER 4

Royals released RHP Sean Lowe.

SEPTEMBER 7

Phillies released 3B Tyler Houston.

SEPTEMBER 10

White Sox released RHP Jose Paniagua.

SEPTEMBER 12

Devil Rays released LHP Jim Parque.

OCTOBER 2

Rockies claimed LHP Alex Herrera off waivers from **Indians**.

OCTOBER 27

Yankees released INF Luis Sojo.

NOVEMBER 3

Phillies traded RHP Brandon Duckworth and minor league RHPs Taylor Buchholz and Ezequiel Astacio to **Astros** for LHP Billy Wagner.

NOVEMBER 4

Rangers organization signed INF David Newhan.

NOVEMBER 5

White Sox released RHP Scott Randall.

NOVEMBER 7

Brewers organization signed RHPs Jason Childers and Ben Ford and INF Trent Durrington.
Braves released 1B Rob Fick.

NOVEMBER 8

Padres organization signed OF Gene Kingsale.

NOVEMBER 10

Rockies organization signed RHP Jason Gilfillan.
Marlins organization signed OF Ryan Christenson.
Dodgers organization signed OF John Barnes and INF Nelson Castro.
Phillies organization signed OFs Mark Budzinski and Kevin Gibbs.
Braves organization signed RHP Chad Ricketts.

NOVEMBER 12

Diamondbacks organization signed C/1B Alan Zinter.
Brewers organization signed RHP Brian Bowles, C Chris Coster and OF Chris Magruder.

NOVEMBER 13

Royals released INF Brent Abernathy.
Rangers organization signed C Ken Huckaby.

NOVEMBER 14

Red Sox organization signed OF Adam Hyzdu.
Marlins organization signed RHPs Delvin James and Bryce Florie and INF Felipe Crespo.
Twins traded C A.J. Pierzynski to **Giants** for RHP Joe Nathan and minor league RHP Boof Bonser and minor league LHP Francisco Liriano.
Padres claimed OF Henri Stanley off waivers from **Astros**.
Padres organization signed RHP Joey Hamilton.
Devil Rays signed RHP Paul Abbott and LHP John Halama.

NOVEMBER 16

Pirates organization signed C Keith McDonald.
Brewers organization signed OF Jacob Cruz.

NOVEMBER 17

Rangers organization signed INF Andy Fox.

NOVEMBER 18

Cardinals organization signed C Cody McKay.
Blue Jays signed RHP Pat Hentgen.
Blue Jays traded OF Bobby Kielty and a player to be named to **Athletics** for LHP Ted Lilly.
Athletics organization signed RHP Eric Cammack.
Indians organization signed LHP Tim Young.
Braves organization signed OF Dewayne Wise.

NOVEMBER 19

Athletics claimed LHP Mario Ramos off waivers from **Rangers**.
Mariners signed OF Raul Ibanez.

NOVEMBER 20

Cardinals traded 1B Tino Martinez and cash considerations to **Devil Rays** for minor league RHP Evan Rust and a player to be named.
Twins claimed RHP Matt Guerrier off waivers from **Pirates**.
Rockies released 2B Ronnie Belliard.
Red Sox claimed minor league RHP Edwin Almonte and minor league LHP Phil Seibel off waivers from **Mets**.
Red Sox signed LHP Tim Hamulack.
Orioles claimed 1B Walter Young off waivers from **Pirates**.

NOVEMBER 21

Phillies organization signed OF Mark Smith.

NOVEMBER 24

Angels signed RHP Kelvim Escobar.
Braves claimed OF Gary Matthews Jr. off waivers from **Padres.**
Marlins organization signed LHP Cedrick Bowers and RHP Scott Sanders.
Twins organization signed RHP Seth Greisinger.

NOVEMBER 25

Diamondbacks organization signed LHP Jesse Orosco.
Athletics traded C Ramon Hernandez and OF Terrence Long to **Padres** for OF Mark Kotsay.

NOVEMBER 26

Cubs traded 1B Hee Seop Choi and a player to be named to the **Marlins** for 1B Derrek Lee.

NOVEMBER 28

Diamondbacks traded RHP Curt Schilling to **Red Sox** for LHP Casey Fossum, RHP Brandon Lyon, minor league LHP Jorge de la Rosa and a player to be named.

DECEMBER 1

Diamondbacks traded INFs Junior Spivey and Craig Counsell, C Chad Moeller, minor league 1B Lyle Overbay and minor league LHPs Jorge de la Rosa and Chris Capuano to **Brewers** for 1B Richie Sexson, minor league LHP Shane Nance and a player to be named.
Yankees signed RHP Tom Gordon.

DECEMBER 2

Rockies traded shortstop Juan Uribe to **White Sox** for minor league INF Aaron Miles.

DECEMBER 3

Blue Jays organization signed LHP Chi-Hung Cheng.
Cubs signed RHP LaTroy Hawkins.
Brewers organization signed RHP Victor Santos, C Mark Johnson and OF Jon Nunnally.
Twins traded LHP Eric Milton to **Phillies** for RHP Carlos Silva, INF Nick Punto and a player to be named.

DECEMBER 4

Yankees traded 1B Nick Johnson, LHP Randy Choate and OF Juan Rivera to **Expos** for RHP Javier Vazquez.
Rangers organization signed RHP Todd Williams.

DECEMBER 6

Giants singed OF Michael Tucker.

DECEMBER 8

Red Sox claimed LHP Mark Malaska off waivers from **Devil Rays.**
Indians claimed LHP Cliff Bartosh off waivers from **Tigers**.
Devil Rays signed OF/INF Eduardo Perez.
Rangers claimed OF Jason Tyner off waivers from **Devil Rays**.
Blue Jays signed RHP Kerry Ligtenberg.

DECEMBER 9

Angels signed RHP Bartolo Colon.
Red Sox organization signed INF Luis Soto.
Royals signed OF Matt Stairs and RHP Scott Sullivan.
Mariners signed LHP Eddie Guardado.
Braves signed RHP John Thomson.
Phillies signed RHP Tim Worrell.
Padres signed RHP Akinori Otsuka.
Cardinals signed INF Brent Butler and 1B/OF Steve Cox.

DECEMBER 10

Tigers signed 2B Fernando Vina.
Rangers signed 1B Brad Fullmer.
Rockies signed 3B Vinny Castilla.
Mets signed SS Kazuo Matsui.

DECEMBER 11

Astros signed LHP Andy Pettitte.
Royals signed C Benito Santiago.
Padres released INF Donaldo Mendez.

DECEMBER 12

Blue Jays signed RHP Miguel Batista.

DECEMBER 13

Cardinals traded OF J.D. Drew and OF/C Eli Marrero to **Braves** for RHP Jason Marquis, LHP Ray King and minor league RHP Adam Wainwright.

Dodgers traded RHP Kevin Brown to **Yankees** for RHP Jeff Weaver, minor league RHP Yhency Brazoban, a player to be named and cash.
Marlins traded OF Juan Encarnacion to **Dodgers** for a player to be named.
Red Sox signed RHP Kevin Foulke.

DECEMBER 14

Orioles signed SS Miguel Tejada.
Devil Rays traded RHP Brandon Backe to **Astros** for 3B Geoff Blum.
Blue Jays traded LHP Mark Hendrickson and a player to be named to **Rockies** for RHP Justin Speier.
Royals signed INF Tony Graffanino.
Devil Rays acquired LHP Mark Hendrickson from **Rockies** for LHP Joe Kennedy.
Tigers signed OF Rondell White.
Mets signed OF Mike Cameron.

DECEMBER 15

Athletics obtained C Michael Barrett from **Expos** and LHP Frank Brooks from **Mets** for players to be named.
Diamondbacks traded OF Quinton McCracken to **Mariners** for INF Greg Colbrunn and signed C Brent Mayne.
Diamondbacks acquired OF Gary Varner from **Brewers** and OF Michael Goss from **Red Sox** to complete earlier trades.
Rockies traded RHP Chris Buglovsky to **Mariners** for RHP Allan Simpson and waived OF Luke Allen and INF Pablo Ozuna.
Marlins acquired minor league RHP Mike Nannini from **Cubs** and minor league OF Travis Ezi from **Dodgers** to complete earlier trades.
Dodgers acquired minor league RHP Brandon Weeden from **Yankees** to complete an earlier trade.
Expos signed OF Carl Everett.
Phillies signed RHP Roberto Hernandez.
Padres traded OF Rich Thompson to **Royals** for RHP Jason Szuminski and cash considerations.
Blue Jays sent RHP Sandy Nin to **Rockies** to complete an earlier trade.
Rockies signed C Todd Greene.
Twins traded OF Dustan Mohr to **Giants** for a player to be named.

DECEMBER 16

Rockies traded INF Mark Bellhorn to **Red Sox** for a player to be named.
Marlins traded LHP Mark Redman to **Athletics** for RHP Mike Neu.
Athletics traded C Mike Barrett to **Cubs** for a player to be named.
Devil Rays signed OF Jose Cruz Jr. and SS Rey Sanchez.
Cardinals signed OF Reggie Sanders and RHP Jeff Suppan.
Cardinals organization signed OF Greg Vaughn and RHP Alan Benes.
Rockies organization signed INF Benji Gil.

DECEMBER 17

Yankees signed OF Gary Sheffield.
Indians organization signed RHP Bobby Howry.
Tigers signed RHP Al Levine.
Royals signed C Kelly Stinnett.
Mariners signed 1B/3B Scott Spiezio.
Braves signed C Eddie Perez.
Twins obtained minor league LHPs David Gassner from **Blue Jays** and J.T. Thomas from **Giants** and RHP Bobby Korecky from **Phillies** to complete earlier trades.
Phillies organization signed INF Lou Collier.

DECEMBER 18

Tigers signed C Mike DiFelice.
Twins signed C Henry Blanco.
Yankees signed RHP Paul Quantrill.
Yankees traded LHP Chris Hammond and cash to **Athletics** for minor league RHP Eduardo Sierra and INF J.T. Stotts.
Cubs signed OF Todd Hollandswortth and LHP Kent Mercker.
Padres signed LHP Sterling Hitchcock and RHP Ismael Valdes.
Indians organization signed OF/INF Adam Piatt.
Cubs organization signed INF/OF Bill Selby and RHPs Gary Glover and Jamey Wright.

DECEMBER 19

Angels signed OF Jose Guillen.
Yankees signed INF Miguel Cairo.
Braves signed RHP Antonio Alfonseca.
Cubs traded minor league RHP Wilton Chavez to **Expos** for INF/OF Jose Macias.
Phillies claimed LHP Victor Alvarez off waivers from **Dodgers**.

DECEMBER 20

Rockies signed OF Jeromy Burnitz.

DECEMBER 21

Athletics acquired C Damian Miller and cash from **Cubs** to complete December 16 trade that sent Michael Barrett to Chicago.

DECEMBER 22

Orioles signed C Javy Lopez.
Brewers signed OF Ben Grieve and C Gary Bennett.
Rangers organization signed OF Jason Tyner and LHP Mike Bacsik.
Athletics signed LHP Arthur Rhodes.
Braves signed LHP Armando Almanza.
Brewers organization signed RHP Adrian Hernandez.

DECEMBER 23

Yankees signed OF Kenny Lofton.
Red Sox signed 2B Pokey Reese
Athletics sent minor league LHP Bill Murphy to **Marlins** to complete an earlier trade.
Diamondbacks signed RHPs Shane Reynolds and Steve Sparks.
Cubs signed INF Todd Walker.
Astros organization signed RHP Tony Fiore and OF Phil Hiatt.
Phillies signed INF-OF Shawn Wooten.
Red Sox organizatiion signed RHP Edwin Almonte.
Pirates signed 3B Chris Stynes.

DECEMBER 26

Indians signed 2B Ron Belliard.
Expos signed 3B Tony Batista.

DECEMBER 27

Rangers signed OF Brian Jordan.
Blue Jays signed LHP Valerio de los Santos.
Blue Jays organization signed OF Chad Hermansen and RHP Jayson Durocher.

DECEMBER 28

Red Sox organization signed 1B Brian Daubach.

DECEMBER 29

Reds signed RHP Cory Lidle.
Rangers signed OF David Dellucci.
Devil Rays signed C Brook Fordyce.

DECEMBER 30

Tigers signed RHP Jason Johnson.
Orioles signed RHP Mike DeJean.

DECEMBER 31

Padres signed LHP David Wells.

AWARD WINNERS

THE SPORTING NEWS

AMERICAN LEAGUE

Pitcher of the Year: Roy Halladay, Toronto
Rookie Player of the Year: Jody Gerut, Cleveland, OF
Rookie Pitcher of the Year: Rafael Soriano, Seattle
Fireman of the Year: Keith Foulke, Oakland
Comeback Player of the Year: Gil Meche, Seattle
Manager of the Year: Tony Pena, Kansas City

NATIONAL LEAGUE

Pitcher of the Year: Eric Gagne, Los Angeles
Rookie Player of the Year: Scott Podsednik, Milwaukee, OF
Rookie Pitcher of the Year: Dontrelle Willis, Florida
Fireman of the Year: Eric Gagne, Los Angeles
Comeback Player of the Year: Javy Lopez, Atlanta
Manager of the Year: Bobby Cox, Atlanta

MAJOR LEAGUE

Player of the Year: Albert Pujols, St. Louis
Executive of the Year: Brian Sabean, San Francisco

MINOR LEAGUE

Player of the Year: Zack Greinke, Wilmington, Carolina; Wichita,Texas

Manager of the Year: Tony DeFrancesco, Sacramento, Pacific Coast

Executive of the Year: Jay Miller, Round Rock, Texas

BASEBALL WRITERS' ASSOCIATION OF AMERICA

AMERICAN LEAGUE

MOST VALUABLE PLAYER

Player, Team	1	2	3	4	5	6	7	8	9	10	Pts.
Alex Rodriguez, Texas	6	5	6	6	2	1	1	-	1	-	242
Carlos Delgado, Toronto	5	8	3	1	1	2	4	2	1	-	213
Jorge Posada, New York	5	4	4	3	4	1	1	-	1	-	194
Shannon Stewart, Minnesota	3	2	2	3	2	3	2	1	2	1	140
David Ortiz, Boston	4	3	2	2	-	3	-	-	1	-	130
Manny Ramirez, Boston	1	3	3	1	1	1	2	2	1	1	100
Nomar Garciaparra, Boston	1	2	1	-	6	2	2	1	-	2	99
Vernon Wells, Toronto	1	-	1	3	1	1	4	3	2	1	84
Carlos Beltran, Kansas City	-	-	1	4	2	2	1	2	3	3	77
Bret Boone, Seattle	-	-	1	1	3	2	-	4	4	2	65
Miguel Tejada, Oakland	1	-	1	1	1	-	2	-	2	2	49
Bill Mueller, Boston	-	-	2	-	1	2	3	-	-	1	45
Jason Giambi, New York	1	-	-	1	-	1	1	1	-	3	36
Garret Anderson, Anaheim	-	-	-	1	2	1	-	3	1	-	35
Keith Foulke, Oakland	-	-	1	-	-	-	-	1	3	3	20
Frank Thomas, Chicago	-	-	-	1	-	-	1	2	1	1	20
Eric Chavez, Oakland	-	-	-	-	1	1	-	2	-	1	18
Carlos Lee, Chicago	-	-	-	-	-	1	1	1	2	-	16
Magglio Ordonez, Chicago	-	-	-	-	-	1	1	1	1	2	16
Alfonso Soriano, New York	-	-	-	-	1	1	-	1	-	1	15
Derek Jeter, New York	-	1	-	-	-	-	-	-	-	1	10
Pedro Martinez, Boston	-	-	-	-	-	1	-	-	1	-	7
Ichiro Suzuki, Seattle	-	-	-	-	-	1	-	-	-	1	6
Esteban Loaiza, Chicago	-	-	-	-	-	-	1	-	-	-	4
Jason Varitez, Boston	-	-	-	-	-	-	1	-	-	-	4
Aubrey Huff, Tampa Bay	-	-	-	-	-	-	-	-	1	2	4
Mariano Rivera, New York	-	-	-	-	-	-	-	1	-	-	3

Fourteen points awarded for a first-place vote, nine for second and down to one for 10th.

CY YOUNG AWARD

Pitcher, Team	1	2	3	Pts.
Roy Halladay, Toronto	26	2	-	136
Esteban Loaiza, Chicago	2	16	5	63
Pedro Martinez, Boston	-	3	11	20
Tim Hudson, Oakland	-	4	3	15
Jamie Moyer, Seattle	-	2	6	12
Andy Pettitte, New York	-	1	1	4
Keith Foulke, Oakland	-	-	1	1
Johan Santana, Minnesota	-	-	1	1

Five points awarded for a first-place vote, three for second and one for third.

MANAGER OF THE YEAR

Manager, Team	1	2	3	Pts.
Tony Pena, Kansas City	24	3	1	130
Ron Gardenhire, Minnesota	4	7	3	44
Ken Macha, Oakland	-	7	5	26
Grady Little, Boston	-	4	7	19
Joe Torre, New York	-	2	8	14
Lou Piniella, Tampa Bay	-	4	1	13
Carlos Tosca, Toronto	-	1	-	3
Edge Wedge, Cleveland	-	-	2	2
Alan Trammell, Detroit	-	-	1	1

Five points awarded for a first-place vote, three for second and one for third.

ROOKIE OF THE YEAR

Player, Team	1	2	3	Pts.
Angel Berroa, Kansas City	12	7	7	88
Hideki Matsui, New York	10	9	7	84
Rocco Baldelli, Tampa Bay	5	5	11	51
Jody Gerut, Cleveland	-	6	2	20
Mark Teixeira, Texas	1	1	1	9

Five points awarded for a first-place vote, three for second and one for third.

NATIONAL LEAGUE

MOST VALUABLE PLAYER

Player, Team	1	2	3	4	5	6	7	8	9	10	Pts.
Barry Bonds, San Francisco	28	2	2	-	-	-	-	-	-	-	426
Albert Pujols, St. Louis	3	29	-	-	-	-	-	-	-	-	303
Gary Sheffield, Atlanta	1	1	18	9	2	1	-	-	-	-	247
Jim Thome, Philadelphia	-	-	5	12	9	5	-	-	-	-	203
Javy Lopez, Atlanta	-	-	4	3	5	8	8	1	-	1	159
Eric Gagne, Los Angeles	-	-	3	6	5	4	4	2	2	1	143
Todd Helton, Colorado	-	-	-	2	3	2	2	6	2	3	75
Sammy Sosa, Chicago	-	-	-	-	1	4	2	2	6	1	53
Mark Prior, Chicago	-	-	-	-	2	3	1	1	4	2	44
Juan Pierre, Florida	-	-	-	-	1	-	5	3	1	2	39
Mike Lowell, Florida	-	-	-	-	-	2	2	3	1	1	30
Richie Sexson, Milwaukee	-	-	-	-	1	1	-	1	1	5	21
Andruw Jones, Atlanta	-	-	-	-	-	1	1	1	1	1	15
Jeff Bagwell, Houston	-	-	-	-	-	1	-	2	1	1	14
Edgar Renteria, St. Louis	-	-	-	-	1	-	-	-	1	5	13
Preston Wilson, Colorado	-	-	-	-	-	-	1	1	2	1	12
Vladimir Guerrero, Montreal	-	-	-	-	-	-	2	-	1	-	10
John Smoltz, Atlanta	-	-	-	-	1	-	-	1	-	-	9
Marcus Giles, Atlanta	-	-	-	-	1	-	-	-	1	1	9
Richard Hidalgo, Houston	-	-	-	-	-	-	-	1	2	2	9
Luis Castillo, Florida	-	-	-	-	-	-	2	-	-	-	8
Jason Schmidt, San Francisco	-	-	-	-	-	-	-	1	1	2	7
Ivan Rodriguez, Florida	-	-	-	-	-	-	1	-	-	1	5
Billy Wagner, Houston	-	-	-	-	-	-	-	-	2	1	5
Luis Gonzalez, Arizona	-	-	-	-	-	-	-	-	2	-	4
Chipper Jones Atlanta	-	-	-	-	-	-	1	-	-	-	4
Bobby Abreu, Philadelphia	-	-	-	-	-	-	-	1	-	-	3
Miguel Cabrera, Florida	-	-	-	-	-	-	-	1	-	-	3
Jim Edmonds, St. Louis	-	-	-	-	-	-	-	1	-	-	3
Mark Grudzielanek, Chicago	-	-	-	-	-	-	-	1	-	-	3
Derrek Lee, Florida	-	-	-	-	-	-	-	1	-	-	3
Russ Ortiz, Atlanta	-	-	-	-	-	-	-	1	-	-	3
Rafael Furcal, Atlanta	-	-	-	-	-	-	-	-	1	-	2
Dontrelle Willis, Florida	-	-	-	-	-	-	-	-	-	1	1

Fourteen points awarded for a first-place vote, nine for second and down to one for 10th.

CY YOUNG AWARD

Pitcher, Team	1	2	3	Pts.
Eric Gagne, Los Angeles	28	2	-	146
Jason Schmidt, San Francisco	2	17	12	73
Mark Prior, Chicago	2	11	17	60
Russ Ortiz, Atlanta	-	2	3	9

Five points awarded for a first-place vote, three for second and one for third.

MANAGER OF THE YEAR

Manager, Team	1	2	3	Pts.
Jack McKeon, Florida	19	6	3	116
Dusty Baker, Chicago	2	15	7	62
Bobby Cox, Atlanta	6	5	11	56
Felipe Alou, San Francisco	5	6	8	51
Frank Robinson, Montreal	-	-	3	3

Five points awarded for a first-place vote, three for second and one for third.

ROOKIE OF THE YEAR

Player, Team	1	2	3	Pts.
Dontrelle Willis, Florida	17	9	6	118
Scott Podsednik, Milwaukee	8	10	11	81
Brandon Webb, Arizona	7	10	8	73
Marlon Byrd, Philadelphia	-	1	3	6
Miguel Cabrera, Florida	-	1	-	3
Brad Lidge, Houston	-	1	-	3
Jeriome Robertson, Houston	-	-	2	2
Jose Reyes, New York	-	-	1	1
Ty Wigginton, New York	-	-	1	1

Five points awarded for a first-place vote, three for second and one for third.

MISCELLANEOUS

ATTENDANCE

AMERICAN LEAGUE

	2003 Home	2003 Road	2003 Dates	2003 Home Avg.	2002 Home	2002 Dates	2002 Average	*Pct. Change
New York	3,465,585	2,792,669	81	42,785	3,461,644	80	43,271	-1.1
Seattle	3,268,864	2,197,903	81	40,356	3,540,482	81	43,710	-7.7
Anaheim	3,061,090	2,177,196	81	37,791	2,305,565	81	28,464	+32.8
Boston	2,724,165	2,443,539	81	33,632	2,650,063	81	32,717	+2.8
Baltimore	2,454,523	2,184,536	81	30,303	2,682,917	81	33,122	-8.5
Oakland	2,216,596	2,151,375	81	27,365	2,169,811	81	26,788	+2.2
Texas	2,095,132	2,343,754	81	25,866	2,352,447	80	29,406	-12.0
Minnesota	1,946,011	2,027,421	81	24,025	1,924,473	81	23,759	+1.1
Chicago	1,939,611	2,187,616	81	23,946	1,676,804	81	20,701	+15.7
Toronto	1,799,458	2,120,472	81	22,216	1,636,904	81	20,209	+9.9
Kansas City	1,779,895	2,118,583	78	22,819	1,323,034	77	17,182	+32.8
Cleveland	1,730,001	1,959,760	81	21,358	2,616,940	81	32,308	-33.9
Detroit	1,368,285	1,960,254	80	17,104	1,503,623	80	18,795	-9.0
Tampa Bay	1,058,622	2,189,670	81	13,069	1,065,762	81	13,158	-0.7
Totals	30,907,838	30,854,748	1130	27,352	30,910,469	1127	27,427	-0.3

*Percentage change refers to the change in average home attendance between 2003 and 2002.

NATIONAL LEAGUE

	2003 Home	2003 Road	2003 Dates	2003 Home Avg.	2002 Home	2002 Dates	2002 Average	*Pct. Change
San Francisco	3,264,903	2,671,937	81	40,307	3,253,205	81	40,163	+0.4
Los Angeles	3,138,626	2,308,118	81	38,748	3,131,077	81	38,655	+0.2
Chicago	2,962,630	2,672,454	80	37,033	2,693,071	78	34,527	+7.3
St. Louis	2,910,371	2,356,937	81	35,931	3,011,756	81	37,182	-3.4
Arizona	2,805,202	2,362,681	81	34,632	3,200,725	81	39,515	-12.4
Houston	2,454,038	2,233,775	81	30,297	2,517,407	81	31,079	-2.5
Atlanta	2,401,082	2,292,455	79	30,393	2,603,482	81	32,142	-5.4
Cincinnati	2,355,160	2,168,529	81	29,076	1,855,973	80	23,200	+25.3
Colorado	2,334,085	2,229,517	81	28,816	2,737,918	81	33,801	-14.7
Philadelphia	2,223,353	2,188,704	78	28,505	1,618,141	79	20,483	+39.2
New York	2,132,341	2,293,679	77	27,693	2,804,838	78	35,959	-23.0
San Diego	2,030,064	2,354,016	81	25,063	2,220,416	81	27,413	-8.6
Milwaukee	1,685,049	2,205,068	81	20,803	1,969,693	81	24,317	-14.5
Pittsburgh	1,636,761	2,229,336	78	20,984	1,784,993	79	22,595	-7.1
Florida	1,303,214	2,079,475	80	16,290	813,111	81	10,038	+62.3
Montreal	1,023,680	2,066,968	81	12,638	732,901	81	9,048	+39.7
Totals	36,660,559	36,713,649	1282	28,596	36,948,707	1285	28,754	-0.5
Major League totals	67,568,397	67,568,397	2412	28,013	67,859,176	2412	28,134	-0.4

*Percentage change refers to the change in average home attendance between 2003 and 2002.

DEBUTS

Player	Pos.	Team	Birth date	Birthplace	Debut	*Age
Adkins, Jonathan Scott	P	Chicago A.L.	8-30-77	Huntington, West Virginia	8-14	25
Almonte, Edwin	P	New York N.L.	12-17-76	Santiago, Dominican Republic	7-7	26
Anderson, Jason R.	P	New York A.L.	6-9-79	Danville, Illinois	3-31	23
Atkins, Garrett Bernard	3B	Colorado	12-12-79	Orange, California	8-3	23
Ayala, Luis Ignacio	P	Montreal	1-12-78	Los Mochis, Mexico	3-31	25
Baldelli, Rocco Daniel	CF	Tampa Bay	9-25-81	Woonsocket, Rhode Island	3-31	21
Barmes, Clint Harold	SS	Colorado	3-6-79	Vincennes, Indiana	9-5	24
Bay, Jason Raymond	CF	San Diego	9-20-78	Trail, Canada	5-23	24
Belisle, Matthew Thomas	P	Cincinnati	6-6-80	McCallum, Texas	9-7	23
Betancourt, Rafael Jose	P	Cleveland	4-29-75	Cumana, Venezuela	7-13	28
Bland, Nathan Garrett	P	Houston	12-27-74	Birmingham, Alabama	5-5	28
Bonderman, Jeremy Allen	P	Detroit	10-28-82	Kennewick, Washington	4-2	20
Bootcheck, Christopher Brandon	P	Anaheim	10-24-78	LaPorte, Indiana	9-9	24
Bowen, Robert McClure	C	Minnesota	2-24-81	Bedford, Texas	9-1	22
Bruntlett, Eric Kevin	PH	Houston	3-29-78	Lafayette, Indiana	6-27	25
Budzinski, Mark Joseph	PH	Cincinnati	8-26-73	Baltimore, Maryland	8-3	29
Bump, Nathan Louis	P	Florida	7-24-76	Towanda, Pennsylvania	6-28	26
Cabrera, Jose Miguel Torres	LF	Florida	4-18-83	Maracay, Venezuela	6-20	20

Player	Pos.	Team	Birth date	Birthplace	Debut	*Age
Calero, Enrique Nomar	P	St. Louis	1-9-75	Santurce, Puerto Rico	4-2	28
Calloway, Ronald Isiah	RF	Montreal	9-4-76	San Jose, California	3-31	26
Capuano, Christopher Frank	P	Arizona	8-19-78	Springfield, Massachusetts	5-4	24
Carrasco, Daniel	P	Kansas City	4-12-77	Safford, Arizona	4-2	25
Cerros, R. Juan	P	Cincinnati	9-25-76	Monterrey, Mexico	9-8	26
Chamblee, James Nathaniel	3B	Cincinnati	5-6-75	Denton, Texas	8-24	28
Chapman, Travis A.	PH	Philadelphia	6-5-78	Jacksonville, Florida	9-9	25
Chulk, Charles Vincent	P	Toronto	12-19-78	Miami, Florida	9-8	24
Claussen, Brandon	P	New York A.L.	5-1-79	Rapid City, South Dakota	6-28	24
Colyer, Stephen Edward	P	Los Angeles	2-22-79	St. Louis, Missouri	4-3	24
Contreras, Jose	P	New York A.L.	12-12-71	Havana, Cuba	3-31	31
Corcoran, Roy Elliot	P	Montreal	5-11-80	Baton Rouge, Louisiana	7-30	23
Cordero, Chad P.	P	Montreal	3-18-82	Upland, California	8-30	21
Correia, Kevin John	P	San Francisco	8-24-80	San Diego, California	7-10	22
Cotts, Neal James	P	Chicago A.L.	3-25-80	Belleville, Illinois	8-12	23
Crosby, Richard Stephen	PH	Los Angeles	8-11-76	Houston, Texas	5-29	26
Crosby, Robert Edward	PH	Oakland	1-12-80	Lakewood, California	9-2	23
Cruz, Enrique Manuel	PH	Milwaukee	11-21-81	Santo Domingo, Dominican Republic	4-2	21
Deago, Roger I. Villarreal	P	San Diego	6-21-77	Monagrillo, Panama	5-10	25
DeJesus, David Christopher	CF	Kansas City	12-20-79	Brooklyn, New York	9-2	23
DePastino, Joseph Bernard	PH	New York N.L.	9-4-73	Philadelphia, Pennsylvania	8-5	29
DePaula, Jorge	P	New York A.L.	11-10-78	Sabana Grande, Dominican Republic	9-5	24
Diaz, Matthew E.	PH	Tampa Bay	3-3-78	Portland, Oregon	7-19	25
Dominguez, Juan Ramon	P	Texas	5-18-80	Ensanchez Ramirez, Dominican Republic	8-12	23
Duncan, Jeffrey Matthew	PH	New York N.L.	12-9-78	Harvey, Illinois	5-20	24
Edwards, Michael Donald	PH	Oakland	11-24-76	Goshen, New York	9-20	26
Ellison, Jason Jerome	LF	San Francisco	4-4-78	Quincy, California	5-9	25
Ferrari, Anthony Michael	P	Montreal	6-22-78	San Francisco, California	6-7	24
Foppert, Jesse W.	P	San Francisco	7-10-80	Reading, Pennsylvania	4-14	22
Ford, Jon Lewis	CF	Minnesota	8-12-76	Beaumont, Texas	5-29	26
Ford, Matthew Lee	P	Milwaukee	4-8-81	Plantation, Florida	4-2	21
Gallo, Michael Dwain	P	Houston	3-18-78	Long Beach, California	7-2	25
Garcia, Daniel Joseph	2B	New York N.L.	4-12-80	Riverside, California	9-2	23
Garcia, Rosman J.	P	Texas	1-3-79	Maracay, Venezuela	4-19	24
Gaudin, Chad Edward	P	Tampa Bay	3-24-83	New Orleans, Louisiana	8-1	20
Geary, Geoffrey Michael	P	Philadelphia	8-26-76	Buffalo, New York	8-27	27
Gerut, Joseph	CF	Cleveland	9-18-77	Elmhurst, Illinois	4-26	25
Gilfillan, Jason Edward	P	Kansas City	8-31-76	Shelby, North Carolina	5-16	26
Glavine, Michael Patrick	PH	New York N.L.	1-24-73	Concord, Massachusetts	9-14	30
Gobble, Billy James	P	Kansas City	7-19-81	Bristol, Tennessee	8-3	22
Gomes, Jonny Johnson	DH	Tampa Bay	11-22-80	Petaluma, California	9-12	22
Gonzalez, Edgar Gerardo	P	Arizona	2-23-83	Monterrey, Mexico	6-1	20
Gonzalez, Michael Vela	P	Pittsburgh	5-23-78	Corpus Christi, Texas	8-11	25
Good, Andrew Richard	P	Arizona	9-19-79	San Diego, California	4-18	23
Grabow, John	P	Pittsburgh	11-4-78	Arcadia, California	9-14	24
Greene, Khalil Thabit	PH	San Diego	10-21-79	Butler, Pennsylvania	9-3	23
Gregg, Kevin Marschall	P	Anaheim	6-20-78	Corvallis, Oregon	8-9	25
Gregorio, Thomas Andrew	C	Anaheim	5-5-77	Brooklyn, New York	9-5	26
Griffiths, Jeremy Richard	P	New York N.L.	3-22-78	Fairview, Ohio	6-5	25
Hall, Joshua Alan	P	Cincinnati	12-16-80	Lynchburg, Virginia	8-2	22
Hammock, Robert Wade	3B	Arizona	5-13-77	Macon, Georgia	4-11	25
Harden, James Richard	P	Oakland	11-30-81	Victoria, Canada	7-21	21
Haren, Daniel John	P	St. Louis	9-17-80	Monterey Park, California	6-30	22
Hart, Bodhi J. Hart	2B	St. Louis	9-27-76	Creswell, Oregon	6-19	26
Hebson, Bryan McCall	P	Montreal	3-12-76	Columbus, Georgia	7-6	27
Heilman, Aaron Michael	P	New York N.L.	11-12-78	Logansport, Indiana	6-26	24
Hernandez, Michel	C	New York A.L.	8-12-78	La Habana, Cuba	9-6	25
Hessman, Michael Steven	PH	Atlanta	3-5-78	Fountain Valley, California	8-22	25
Hill, Koyie Dolan	PH	Los Angeles	3-9-79	Tulsa, Oklahoma	9-5	24
House, James Rodger	PH	Pittsburgh	11-11-79	Charleston, West Virginia	9-27	23
Hummel, Timothy Robert	PH	Cincinnati	11-18-78	Goshen, New York	8-26	24
Jackson, Edwin	P	Los Angeles	9-9-83	Neu-Ulm, West Germany	9-9	20
Johnson, Gerald Clyde	RF	Anaheim	10-29-75	Palo Alto, California	4-26	27
Johnson, Reed Cameron	PR	Toronto	12-8-76	Riverside, California	4-17	26
Johnson, Rontrez DeMon	CF	Kansas City	12-8-76	Marshall, Texas	3-31	26
Jones, Greg Alan	P	Anaheim	11-15-76	Clearwater, Florida	7-30	26
Jones, Jason D.	DH	Texas	10-17-76	Marietta, Georgia	7-23	26
Journell, James Richard	P	St. Louis	12-29-77	Springfield, Ohio	6-29	25
Kata, Matthew John	PR	Arizona	3-14-78	Avon Lakes, Ohio	6-15	25

Player	Pos.	Team	Birth date	Birthplace	Debut	*Age
Kelton, David Wayne	PH	Chicago N.L.	12-17-79	Dothan, Alabama	6-8	23
Koonce, Graham CLinton	PH	Oakland	5-15-75	El Cajon, California	9-20	28
LaForest, Pierre-Luc	DH	Tampa Bay	1-17-78	Hull, Canada	9-2	25
Laird, Gerald Lee	C	Texas	11-13-79	Westminster, California	4-30	23
Ledezma, Wilfredo J.	P	Detroit	1-21-81	Guarico, Venezuela	4-2	22
Linden, Todd A.	LF	San Francisco	6-30-80	Edmonds, Washington	8-18	23
Looper, Aaron Joseph	P	Seattle	9-7-76	Ada, Oklahoma	8-2	26
Lopez, Aquilino	P	Toronto	4-21-75	Villa Altagracia, Dominican Republic	4-2	27
Lopez, Javier Alfonso	P	Colorado	7-11-77	San Juan, Puerto Rico	4-1	25
Lowry, Noah Ryan	P	San Francisco	10-10-80	Ventura, California	9-5	22
Machado, Anderson Javier	PR	Philadelphia	1-25-81	Caracas, Venezuela	9-27	22
Madson, Ryan Michael	P	Philadelphia	8-28-80	Long Beach, California	9-27	23
Malaska, Dennis Mark	P	Tampa Bay	1-17-78	Youngstown, Ohio	7-17	25
Manning, David Anthony	P	Milwaukee	8-14-72	Buffalo, New York	8-2	30
Manon, Julio Alberto	P	Montreal	7-10-73	Guerra Distrito, Dominican Republic	6-5	29
Martinez, Luis	P	Milwaukee	1-20-80	Santo Domingo, Dominican Republic	9-3	23
Matranga, David Michael	PH	Houston	1-8-77	Orange, California	6-27	26
Matsui, Hideki	LF	New York A.L.	6-12-74	Kanazawa, Japan	3-31	28
McClung, Michael Seth	P	Tampa Bay	2-7-81	Lewisburg, West Virginia	3-31	22
Mears, Christopher Peter	P	Detroit	1-20-78	Ottawa, Canada	6-29	25
Mendez, Carlos Alberto Castillo	PH	Baltimore	6-18-74	Caracas, Venezuela	5-22	28
Miles, Aaron Wade	PH	Chicago A.L.	12-15-76	Pittsburg, California	9-11	26
Miller, Matt Jacob	P	Colorado	11-23-71	Greenwood, Mississippi	6-27	31
Mitre, Sergio Armando	P	Chicago N.L.	2-16-81	Los Angeles, California	7-22	22
Morban, Jose	SS	Baltimore	12-2-79	Santiago, Dominican Republic	4-6	23
Morneau, Justin Ernest	DH	Minnesota	5-15-81	New Westminster, Canada	6-10	22
Mounce, Anthony David	P	Texas	2-8-75	Sacramento, California	6-13	28
Nakamura, Micheal Yoshihide	P	Minnesota	9-6-76	Nara, Japan	6-7	26
Neu, Michael	P	Oakland	3-9-78	Napa, California	4-9	25
Niekro, Lance Joseph	1B	San Francisco	1-29-79	Winter Haven, Florida	9-5	24
Nivar, Ramon A.	CF	Texas	2-22-80	San Cristobal, Dominican Republic	7-30	23
Nix, Layne Michael	CF	Texas	10-30-80	Houston, Texas	7-10	22
Ohme, Kevin Arthur	P	St. Louis	4-13-71	Palm Beach, Florida	4-14	32
Ojeda, Miguel Arturo	C	San Diego	1-29-75	Sonora, Mexico	5-17	28
Olmedo, Rainer Gustavo	PH	Cincinnati	5-31-81	Maracay, Venezuela	5-25	21
Peralta, Jhonny Antonio	3B	Cleveland	5-28-82	Santiago, Dominican Republic	6-12	21
Perez, Antonio Miguel	PR	Tampa Bay	1-26-80	Bani, Dominican Republic	5-14	23
Phelps, Thomas Allen	P	Florida	3-4-74	Seoul, South Korea	3-31	29
Porter, Colin F.	PH	Houston	11-23-75	Tucson, Arizona	5-30	27
Prieto, Alejandro Antonio	PH	Minnesota	6-19-76	Caracas, Venezuela	7-26	27
Putz, Joseph Jason	P	Seattle	2-22-77	Trenton, Michigan	8-11	26
Quinlan, Robb William	1B	Anaheim	3-17-77	Maplewood, Minnesota	7-28	26
Quintero, Humberto	PH	San Diego	8-8-79	Maracaibo, Venezuela	9-3	24
Ramirez, Erasmo	P	Texas	4-29-76	Santa Ana, California	4-30	27
Ramirez, Horacio	P	Atlanta	11-24-79	Carson, California	4-2	23
Ramos, Mario Martin	P	Texas	10-19-77	Aurora, Illinois	6-19	25
Randall, Scott Phillip	P	Cincinnati	10-29-75	Fullerton, California	8-26	27
Randolph, Stephen LeCharles	P	Arizona	5-1-74	Okinawa, Japan	3-31	28
Redman, Prentice Montezz	PR	New York N.L.	8-23-79	Tuscaloosa, Alabama	8-24	24
Reyes, Jose Bernabe	SS	New York N.L.	6-11-83	Villa Gonzalez, Dominican Republic	6-10	19
Reyes, Rene	RF	Colorado	2-21-78	Margarita, Venezuela	7-22	25
Rivera, Carlos Alberto	PH	Pittsburgh	6-10-78	Fajardo, Puerto Rico	6-22	25
Roach, Jason Glenn	P	New York N.L.	4-20-76	Kinston, North Carolina	6-14	27
Roney, Matthew S.	P	Detroit	1-10-80	Tulsa, Oklahoma	4-2	23
Rosario, Rodrigo	P	Houston	12-14-77	La Romana, Dominican Republic	6-21	25
Ross, Cody J.	RF	Detroit	12-23-80	Portales, New Mexico	7-4	22
Sanchez, Felix Antonio	P	Chicago N.L.	8-3-81	Puerto Plata, Dominican Republic	9-3	22
Sanders, David Andrew	P	Chicago A.L.	8-29-79	Oklahoma City, Oklahoma	4-23	23
Santos, Francisco Alejandro	RF	San Francisco	3-9-74	Santo Domingo, Dominican Republic	6-18	29
Sardinha, Dane K.A.A.	PH	Cincinnati	4-8-79	Honolulu, Hawaii	9-6	24
Schmack, Brian Robert	P	Detroit	12-7-73	Chicago, Illinois	8-24	29
Smitherman, Stephen Lydell	PH	Cincinnati	9-1-78	McAlester, Oklahoma	7-1	24
Snyder, Kyle Ehren	P	Kansas City	9-9-77	Houston, Texas	5-1	25
Sorensen, Zach Hart	PH	Cleveland	1-3-77	Salt Lake City, Utah	6-3	26
Spurling, Christopher Michael	P	Detroit	6-28-77	Dayton, Ohio	4-2	25
Stanford, Jason John	P	Cleveland	1-27-77	Tucson, Arizona	7-6	26
Stenson, Dernell Renuald	PH	Cincinnati	6-17-78	LaGrange, Georgia	8-13	25
Stewart, Joshua Craig	P	Chicago A.L.	12-5-78	Paducah, Kentucky	4-6	24
Strong, Jamal Najar	PR	Seattle	8-5-78	Pasadena, California	9-2	25
Sweeney, Brian Edward	P	Seattle	6-13-74	Yonkers, New York	8-16	29

Player	Pos.	Team	Birth date	Birthplace	Debut	*Age
Switzer, Jon Michael	P	Tampa Bay	8-13-79	Houston, Texas	8-2	23
Teixeira, Mark Charles	DH	Texas	4-11-80	Severna Park, Maryland	4-1	22
Terrero, Luis Enrique	CF	Arizona	5-18-80	Barahona, Dominican Republic	7-10	23
Traber, William Henry, Jr.	P	Cleveland	9-18-79	Torrance, California	4-4	23
Tsao, Chin-hui	P	Colorado	6-2-81	Hua-Lien, Taiwan	7-25	22
Utley, Chase Cameron	PH	Philadelphia	12-17-78	Pasadena, California	4-4	24
Valderrama, Carlos Alberto	CF	San Francisco	11-30-77	Bachaquero, Venezuela	6-21	25
Valentine, Joseph John	P	Cincinnati	12-24-79	Las Vegas, Nevada	8-24	23
Valverde, Jose Rafael	P	Arizona	7-24-79	San Pedro de Macoris, Dominican Republic	6-1	23
Vargas, Claudio Almonte	P	Montreal	6-19-78	Valverde Mao, Dominican Republic	4-26	24
Victorino, Shane Patrick	PR	San Diego	11-30-80	Wailuku, Hawaii	4-2	22
Villarreal, Oscar Eduardo	P	Arizona	11-22-81	Nuevo Leon, Mexico	3-31	21
Waechter, Douglas Michael	P	Tampa Bay	1-28-81	St. Petersburg, Florida	8-27	22
Wagner, Ryan	P	Cincinnati	7-15-82	Yoakum, Texas	7-19	21
Walrond, Leslie Dale	P	Kansas City	11-7-76	Muskogee, Oklahoma	6-8	26
Watson, Matthew Kyle	PH	New York N.L.	11-5-78	Lancaster, Pennsylvania	9-12	24
Webb, Brandon T.	P	Arizona	5-9-79	Ashland, Kentucky	4-22	23
Weeks, Rickie	2B	Milwaukee	9-13-82	Daytona Beach, Florida	9-15	21
Wellemeyer, Todd Allen	P	Chicago N.L.	8-30-78	Louisville, Kentucky	5-15	24
White, Matthew J.	P	Boston	8-19-77	Pittsfield, Massachusetts	5-27	25
Williams, Jerome Lee	P	San Francisco	12-4-81	Honolulu, Hawaii	4-26	21
Willis, Dontrelle Wayne	P	Florida	1-12-82	Oakland, California	5-9	21
Wood, Michael Burton	P	Oakland	4-26-80	West Palm Beach, Florida	8-21	23
Young, Jason Kariya	P	Colorado	9-28-79	Oakland, California	5-12	23
Zoccolillo, Peter G.	PH	Milwaukee	2-6-77	Bronx, New York	9-5	26

*Denotes age on date of debut.

2003 FREE-AGENT FILINGS

AMERICAN LEAGUE

Anaheim: Eric Owens, Scott Spiezio.
Baltimore: Tony Batista, Albert Belle, Hector Carrasco, Deivi Cruz, Scott Erickson, Brook Fordyce, Pat Hentgen, Kerry Ligtenberg, B.J. Surhoff.
Boston: John Burkett, Bill Haselman, Todd Jones, Dave McCarty, Robert Person, Jeff Suppan, Mike Timlin, Todd Walker.
Chicago: Roberto Alomar, Sandy Alomar Jr., Bartolo Colon, Carl Everett, Tom Gordon, Tony Graffanino, Scott Sullivan.
Cleveland: Jason Bere, Ellis Burks, Terry Mulholland, Mark Wohlers.
Detroit: Shane Halter, Dean Palmer, Matt Walbeck.
Kansas City: Brian Anderson, Kevin Appier, Mike DiFelice, Jason Grimsley, Raul Ibanez, Curtis Leskanic, Alan Levine, Jose Lima, Graeme Lloyd, Brent Mayne, Tom Prince, Joe Randa, Michael Tucker, Rondell White, Jamey Wright.
Minnesota: Chris Gomez, Eddie Guardado, LaTroy Hawkins, Denny Hocking, Jesse Orosco, Rick Reed, Kenny Rogers, Shannon Stewart.
New York: Roger Clemens, John Flaherty, Felix Heredia, Jeff Nelson, Antonio Osuna, Andy Pettitte, Ruben Sierra, David Wells, Gabe White.
Oakland: Keith Foulke, Jose Guillen, Ricardo Rincon, Steve Sparks, Miguel Tejada.
Seattle: Armando Benitez, Pat Borders, Mike Cameron, Shigetoshi Hasegawa, John Mabry, Mark McLemore, Arthur Rhodes, Rey Sanchez.
Tampa Bay: Ben Grieve, Travis Lee, Al Martin, Rey Ordonez, Terry Shumpert.
Texas: Juan Gonzalez, Rafael Palmeiro, John Thomson, Ismael Valdes.
Toronto: Mike Bordick, Kelvim Escobar, Cory Lidle.

NATIONAL LEAGUE

Arizona: Carlos Baerga, Miguel Batista, Mark Grace, Felix Jose, Raul Mondesi, Mike Myers.
Atlanta: Darren Bragg, Vinny Castilla, Julio Franco, Matt Franco, Roberto Hernandez, Darren Holmes, Javy Lopez, Greg Maddux, Kent Mercker, Shane Reynolds, Gary Sheffield.
Chicago: Antonio Alfonseca, Shawn Estes, Doug Glanville, Tom Goodwin, Mark Grudzielanek, Mark Guthrie, Eric Karros, Kenny Lofton, Troy O'Leary, Dave Veres, Tony Womack.
Cincinnati: Todd Van Poppel.
Colorado: Greg Norton, Darren Oliver, Steve Reed, Chris Stynes, Mark Sweeney, Gregg Zaun.
Florida: Luis Castillo, Andy Fox, Chad Fox, Lenny Harris, Rick Helling, Todd Hollandsworth, Mike Mordecai, Ivan Rodriguez, Ugueth Urbina, Gerald Williams.
Houston: Brad Ausmus, Orlando Merced, Dan Miceli, Brian Moehler, Ron Villone, Jose Vizcaino, Rick White.
Los Angeles: Wilson Alvarez, Andy Ashby, Jeromy Burnitz, Ron Coomer, Rickey Henderson, Brian Jordan, Tom Martin, Fred McGriff, Paul Quantrill, Robin Ventura.
Milwaukee: Dave Burba, Royce Clayton, Keith Osik, Eduardo Perez, Todd Ritchie, Glendon Rusch, John Vander Wal.
Montreal: Wil Cordero, Vladimir Guerrero, Jose Mercedes, Fernando Tatis, Todd Zeile.
New York: Pedro Astacio, Jay Bell, Tony Clark, John Franco,
Philadelphia: Terry Adams, Jose Mesa, Kevin Millwood, Dan Plesac, Todd Pratt, Kelly Stinnett, Turk Wendell, Mike Williams.
Pittsburgh: Pat Meares, Jeff Reboulet, Pokey Reese, Reggie Sanders, Matt Stairs, Julian Tavarez.
St. Louis: Miguel Cairo, Chris Carpenter, Mike DeJean, Cal Eldred, Jeff Fassero, Joe Girardi, Sterling Hitchcock, Steve Kline, Lance Painter, Orlando Palmeiro, Eduardo A. Perez, Russ Springer, Garrett Stephenson, Brett Tomko, Fernando Vina, Chris Widger.
San Diego: Rod Beck.
San Francisco: Rich Aurilia, Marvin Benard, Jose Cruz Jr., Andres Galarraga, Jeffrey Hammonds, Dustin Hermanson, Sidney Ponson, Benito Santiago, J.T. Snow, Tim Worrell, Eric Young.

MAJOR LEAGUE RULE 5 DRAFT

(Listed in order of selection)

Player	Pos.	Drafted by	Drafted from (major league organization)
Christopher Shelton	C	Detroit	Nashville, Pacific Coast League (Pirates)
Richard Thompson	OF	San Diego	Nashville, Pacific Coast League (Pirates)
Alec Zumwalt	RHP	Tampa Bay	Richmond, International League (Braves)
Frank Brooks	LHP	New York Mets	Nashville, Pacific Coast League (Pirates)
Jeff Bennett	RHP	Milwaukee	Nashville, Pacific Coast League (Pirates)
Jose Bautista	3B	Baltimore	Nashville, Pacific Coast League (Pirates)
David Mattox	RHP	Cincinnati	Norfolk. International League (Mets)
Christopher Mabeus	RHP	Texas	Sacramento, Pacific Coast League (Athletics)
Matthew White	LHP	Colorado	Buffalo, Internatiional League (Indians)
Jason Szuminski	RHP	Kansas City	Iowa, Pacific Coast League (Cubs)
Andrew Fox	2B-3B	Montreal	Oklahoma, Pacific Coast League (Rangers)
Talley Haines	RHP	Toronto	Durham, International League (Devil Rays)
Jason Grilli	RHP	Chicago White Sox	Albuquerque, Pacific Coast League (Marlins)
Hector Luna	SS	St. Louis	Buffalo, International League (Indians)
Leonard Dinardo	LHP	Boston	Norfolk, International League (Mets)
Willy Taveras	OF	Houston	Buffalo, International League (Indians)
Michael Bumatay	LHP	Detroit	Colorado Springs, Pacific Coast League (Rockies)
Luis Gonzalez	INF	Colorado	Buffalo, International League (Indians)
Colter Bean	RHP	Boston	Columbus, Internatiional League (Yankees)
Lino Urdaneta	RHP	Detroit	Buffalo, Internatiional League (Indians)

NECROLOGY

DEATHS

Ed Albosta, 84, at Saginaw, Mich., on January 7. Righthander Albosta lost all eight of his major league decisions, going 0-2 for the 1941 Dodgers and 0-6 for the 1946 Pirates.

Chuck Aleno, 85, at DeLand, Fla., on February 10. Aleno was a reserve infielder for the Reds from 1941 through 1944, appearing in a total of 118 games.

Toby Atwell, 78, at Purcellville, Va., on January 25. Atwell, a catcher, broke into the majors in 1952, a season in which he batted .290 for the Cubs in 362 at-bats and was named a reserve on the National League All-Star team. Atwell later played for the Pirates and Braves, finishing a five-season major league career with a .260 average.

Red Barbary, 83, at Simpsonville, S.C., on September 27. Barbary made one appearance as a pinch hitter for the 1943 Senators.

Earl Battey, 68, at Ocala, Fla., on November 15. Battey, a three-time Gold Glove catcher, hit .302 for the Twins in 1961 (the club's first season in Minnesota after relocating from Washington) and batted .297 for Minnesota's 1965 pennant-winning team. A 13-season major leaguer who broke in with the White Sox, he played in five All-Star Games and had a career .270 batting average.

Ralph Beard, 73, at West Palm Beach, Fla., on February 10. Beard, a righthander, lost all four of his decisions for the 1954 Cardinals.

Steve Bechler, 23, of heatstroke-related problems, during spring training at the Orioles' camp in Fort Lauderdale, Fla., on February 17. The righthander made three relief appearances for Baltimore in 2002.

Greg Biagini, 51, at Oklahoma City on October 3. Biagini managed Rochester to the 1990 International League pennant and Oklahoma City to the 1996 American Association playoffs championship.

Dick Bogard, 66, at La Palma, Calif., on August 29. Bogard was scouting director for the Athletics from 1984 to 1994.

Bobby Bonds, 57, at San Carlos, Calif., on August 23. Bonds possessed a rare blend of power and speed. Five times a 30-30 man, he hit 25 or more home runs in nine seasons and exceeded 40 steals seven times in a 14-year major league career that began in 1968. Bonds, who spent his first seven seasons with the Giants and went on to play for the Yankees, Angels, White Sox, Rangers, Indians, Cardinals and Cubs, hit 332 homers and drove in 1,024 runs. The outfielder also won three Gold Gloves. The father of current Giants superstar Barry Bonds, he set a still-standing record when he struck out 189 times in 1970.

Sam Bowens, 64, at Wilmington, N.C., on March 28. Outfielder Bowens was a regular in one big-league season, 1964, when he played 139 games and hit 22 home runs for an Orioles team that finished just two games behind the pennant-winning Yankees. In seven years overall in the majors (five with Baltimore, two with Washington), Bowens batted .223.

Ken Brett, 55, at Spokane, Wash., on November 18. Brett compiled an 83-85 record over 14 major league seasons. The lefthander, who pitched for the Red Sox, Brewers, Phillies, Pirates, Yankees, White Sox, Angels, Twins, Dodgers and Royals, became the youngest pitcher in World Series history when, at 19 years and 20 days, he made a relief appearance for Boston against St. Louis in Game 4 of the 1967 Series. Brett, a career .262 hitter, set a major league record for pitchers in 1973 by homering in four consecutive games while a member of the Phillies. A brother of Hall of Famer George Brett, he was the winning pitcher—as a representative of the Pirates—in the 1974 All-Star Game.

Jack Brewer, 84, at Sun City, Calif., on November 30. Brewer, a righthander, compiled a 9-10 record while pitching for the Giants from 1944 through 1946.

Jack Bruner, 78, at Lincoln, Neb., on June 24. Lefthander Bruner was 2-4 overall in 1949 and 1950 in duty with the White Sox and the Browns.

Bill Buhler, 75, at Long Beach, Calif., on May 17. Buhler was the assistant trainer for the Brooklyn and Los Angeles Dodgers from 1957 through 1959 and the head trainer for the Dodgers from 1960 through 1995.

Wally Burnette, 73, at Danville, Va., on February 12. Pitching for the Kansas City A's from 1956 through 1958, the righthander was 14-21 with a 3.56 ERA.

Dick Butler, 92, at Fort Worth, Texas, on December 20. A baseball executive for nearly a half-century, Butler served in such capacities as president of both the South Atlantic League and the Texas League and supervisor of umpires for the American League.

Joe Buzas, 83, at Salt Lake City on March 19. Buzas, owner of the Salt Lake City club of the Pacific Coast League and a longtime owner of minor league teams, was a shortstop who batted .262 in 30 games as a member of the 1945 Yankees.

Ivan Calderon, 41, in a shooting at Loiza, Puerto Rico, on December 27. Outfielder Calderon batted .272 over 10 major league seasons. He hit 28 home runs for the White Sox in 1987, had 87 RBIs for the Chicago club in 1989 and batted .300 with 19 homers for the Expos in 1991. He also played for the Mariners and Red Sox.

Ed Chandler, 81, at Las Vegas, Nev., on July 6. Chandler pitched in 15 games for the 1947 Dodgers and was 0-1.

George "Slick" Coffman, 92, at Birmingham, Ala., on May 8. Brother of longtime major league pitcher Dick Coffman, he compiled a 15-12 record while pitching for the Tigers and the Browns in a four-season big-league career that ended in 1940.

Alta Cohen, 94, at Maplewood, N.J., on March 11. Outfielder Cohen played a total of 29 games in the majors. He appeared in one game for Brooklyn in 1931 and in nine games for the Dodgers in 1932 before winding up his big-league career with a 19-game stint with the Phillies in 1933. He batted .194 overall.

Ken Coleman, 78, at Plymouth, Mass., on August 21. Coleman broadcast Red Sox games on radio and television for 20 years (1966-1974 and 1979-1989). He also was an Indians and Reds broadcaster.

Al Corwin, 76, at Geneva, Ill., on October 23. Called up from the minors by the Giants in July 1951, Corwin made eight starts and seven relief appearances and helped the N.L. club make its miracle run to the pennant by compiling a 5-1 record. Corwin relieved in Game 5 of the '51 World Series, then spent four more years in the majors. Working largely out of the bullpen, the righthander posted a 6-1 mark in 1952 and was 7-8 overall from 1953 through 1955.

Dave DeBusschere, 62, at New York on May 14. A star player on two NBA championship teams with the New York Knicks in the early 1970s, DeBusschere pitched in a total of 36 big-league games in 1962 and 1963. The righthander was 0-0 in 12 relief appearances with the White Sox in '62 and compiled a 3-4 record in 24 games as a starter/reliever for the American League club in '63. One of his victories was a six-hit shutout against Cleveland.

Joe Decker, 55, at Fraser, Mich., on March 2. Decker's best season in a nine-year major league career came in 1974 when he posted a 16-14 record for Minnesota. He was 36-44 overall while pitching for the Cubs, Twins and Mariners.

Charlie Devens, 93, at Milton, Mass., on August 13. Former Harvard star Devens made his professional baseball debut as a Yankee in 1932, breaking in with a complete-game six-hitter against the Red Sox. He pitched in 16 games overall in the majors, going 5-3 for the Yanks from '32 through 1934.

Larry Doby, 78, at Montclair, N.J., on June 18. The first black player in American League history, Doby broke into the big leagues with the Indians on July 5, 1947—nearly three months after Jackie Robinson had shattered the majors' modern color barrier with the Brooklyn Dodgers. Doby helped Cleveland win the A.L. pennant and the World Series in 1948, batting .301 with 14 home runs in the regular season and hitting .318 in the Series with a key homer in Game 4. He was the A.L. home run champion in 1952 and 1954 and drove in a league-high 126 runs in '54, a year in which the Indians established an A.L. record (since broken) with 111 victories. Doby, who hit 253 homers in a 13-season major league career that included two stints with both the Indians and the White Sox and a short stay with the Tigers, batted .283 overall. The Hall of Famer became the majors' second black manager—after Frank Robinson—when he took over the White Sox midway through the 1978 season.

Harry Eisenstat, 87, at Beachwood, Ohio, on March 21. Eisenstat, a lefthander who pitched eight seasons in the majors and compiled a 25-27 record, won a career-high nine games for Detroit in 1938. He capped that season by pitching the Tigers to a 4-1 victory over Cleveland in a game in which the Indians' Bob Feller set a then-major league record with 18 strikeouts. In addition to pitching for the Tigers in '38 and part of 1939, Eisenstat also saw duty with Brooklyn (1935-37) and Cleveland (1939-42).

Al Epperly, 84, at McFarland, Wis., on April 14. Epperly's two stints in the majors came 12 years apart. The righthander broke in with the Cubs in 1938, posting a 2-0 record in nine games. He returned to the big leagues in 1950, appearing in five games for Brooklyn without a decision.

Hilly Flitcraft, 79, at Boulder, Colo., on April 2. Flitcraft made three relief appearances for the 1942 Phillies.

Jim Fridley, 78, at Port Charlotte, Fla., on February 28. Playing in his 13th major league game, Cleveland outfielder Fridley went 6-for-6 against the Athletics on April 29, 1952, at Philadelphia. All six of Fridley's hits were singles. Fridley wound up batting .251 in 62 games for the Indians in '52. His other big-league service consisted of 85 games with the Orioles in 1954 and a five-game stint with the Reds in 1958.

Greg Garrett, 55, at Newhall, Calif., on June 7. Lefthander Garrett was 5-6 for the Angels in 1970 and 0-1 for the Reds in 1971.

Earl Gillespie, 81, at West Allis, Wis., on December 12. Gillespie was the longtime radio voice of the Milwaukee Braves, calling the team's games from 1953 (the Braves' first season in Wisconsin after relocating from Boston) through 1963. The first half of that time frame featured record-breaking N.L. attendance in Milwaukee and two pennants and a World Series championship for the Braves.

Al Gionfriddo, 81, at Solvang, Calif., on March 14. Brooklyn outfielder Gionfriddo's sensational catch of Joe DiMaggio's long drive in the sixth inning of Game 6 of the 1947 World Series robbed DiMaggio of a potential game-tying, three-run homer. The Dodgers held on to win that game, but they lost to the Yankees in Game 7. Game 6 marked the last major league appearance for Gionfriddo, whose career consisted of 191 games with the Pirates and 37 with Brooklyn. In his lone season of regular duty, he batted .284 for the Pirates in 1945.

Francis "Red" Hardy, 80, at Phoenix on August 15. Hardy made two relief appearances for the 1951 Giants.

Johnny Hopp, 86, at Scottsbluff, Neb., on June 1. Outfielder/first baseman Hopp played for four World Series championship teams—the 1942 and 1944 Cardinals and the 1950 and 1951 Yankees—and also was a member of the 1943 pennant-winning Cards. He batted .336 for the '44 Cardinals and .333 for the 1946 Braves. In '50, he hit .340 for the Pirates in 318 at-bats before being sold to the Yankees in September. His batting average over 14 major league seasons was .296.

Art Houtteman, 75, at Rochester Hills, Mich., on May 6. Houtteman was a 19-game winner for the Tigers in 1950, a year in which he tossed a league-leading four shutouts. In 1954, the righthander compiled a 15-7 record for the A.L. champion Indians. Houtteman, who had two other double-figure win totals and also experienced a 20-loss season, was 87-91 over 12 years in the big leagues.

John "Spider" Jorgensen, 84, at Rancho Cucamonga, Calif., on November 6. He was a regular in one of his five major league seasons—his rookie year, 1947, with the Dodgers. Jorgensen broke into the majors in the same game that marked Jackie Robinson's debut—he played third base for Brooklyn on opening day in '47 and Robinson was at first base—and he went on to hit .274 in his first season. Jorgensen, who also played for the Giants, had a career .266 batting average. He started 10 World Series games for Brooklyn.

Joe Just, 87, at Franklin, Wis., on November 22. Just, a catcher, appeared in a total of 25 games for the Reds in 1944 and 1945.

Bob Kammeyer, 52, at Sacramento on January 27. Kammeyer made seven relief appearances for the Yankees in 1978 and one for the Yanks in 1979.

Harry Kinzy, 92, at Fort Worth, Texas, on June 22. Kinzy lost his only decision while making 11 relief appearances and two starts for the 1934 White Sox.

Johnny Klippstein, 75, at Elgin, Ill., on October 10. Klippstein worked almost exclusively in relief over the last 10 seasons of an 18-year major league career that began in 1950. He went 4-0 in 28 games as a reliever for the 1959 World Series champion Los Angeles Dodgers and was a standout for the 1965 A.L. pennant-winning Twins, going 9-3 with a 2.24 ERA for Minnesota in 56 appearances out of the bullpen. The righthander broke into the majors with the Cubs and won a total of 19 games for Chicago in 1952 and 1953. He started a career-high 29 games for the 1956 Reds and was 12-11 overall that season.

Leonard Koppett, 79, at San Francisco on June 22. A member of the writers wing of the Baseball Hall of Fame, Koppett was an erudite journalist and author who covered the Yankees, Giants, Dodgers and Mets while with the *New York Herald Tribune*, *New York Post* and *New York Times*. He also worked on the West Coast and wrote a column for the Sporting News.

Al "Mickey" Kreitner, 80, at Nashville on March 6. Kreitner, a catcher, appeared in a total of 42 games for the Cubs in 1943 and 1944.

Joan B. Kroc, 75, at Rancho Santa Fe, Calif., on October 12. Kroc was former owner of the Padres. Having taking over management of the San Diego club when her husband died in 1984, she sold the N.L. franchise in 1990.

Sam Lacy, 99, at Washington, D.C., on May 8. Longtime sports editor of the *Baltimore Afro American* newspaper, Lacy championed black athletes' fight for equal rights in a newspaper career that extended over 70-plus years. He fought for the integration of modern major league baseball, then chronicled the hardships that Jackie Robinson—and Lacy himself, as a reporter—encountered when Robinson broke in with the Dodgers. Lacy wrote with authority and conviction on a wide range of topics, gaining enshrinement in the writers wing of the Baseball Hall of Fame.

Don Landrum, 66, at Pittsburg, Calif., on January 9. A reserve outfielder for most of his eight seasons in the majors, Landrum was the Cubs' No. 1 center fielder in 1965. He stole 14 bases and hit 20 doubles in '65 but finished with a .226 batting average. Landrum was a .234 career hitter who also played for the Phillies, Cardinals and Giants.

Earl Lawson, 79, at Sacramento on January 14. Lawson covered the Reds for Cincinnati newspapers for 3½ decades and was voted into the writers wing of the Baseball Hall of Fame.

Allen Lewis, 86, at Clearwater, Fla., on September 14. A longtime baseball writer for the *Philadelphia Inquirer*, Lewis was a Phillies beat writer from 1946 to 1972. He is a member of the writers wing of the Baseball Hall of Fame.

Al Libke, 84, at Wenatchee, Wash., on March 7. Libke was a regular Reds outfielder in 1945 and 1946, batting .283 and .253. He also pitched in a total of five games for Cincinnati in those seasons.

Vince Lloyd, 86, at Green Valley, Ariz., on July 3. Lloyd spent nearly four decades at WGN radio and television in Chicago, working alongside Jack Brickhouse while covering both the Cubs and the White Sox and with Lou Bourdreau on Cubs games. Beginning in 1965, he was a radio voice of the Cubs for more than two decades.

George Maloney, 75, at Barstow, Calif., on July 29. Maloney was an American League umpire from 1969 through 1983.

Phil McCullough, 85, at Decatur, Ga., on January 16. Righthander McCullough's major league career consisted of a three-inning stint for the Washington Senators in 1942.

Mickey McDermott, 74, at Phoenix on August 7. McDermott had a standout season for the Red Sox in 1953, a year in which he compiled an 18-10 record, tossed four shutouts and had a 3.01 ERA. A little more than two months after season's end, though, the lefthander was traded to Washington in a deal that sent Jackie Jensen to Boston. He won a total of 17 games for the Senators in 1954 and 1955 but posted only four victories in his final four big-league seasons (1956 through 1958, 1961). In 12 years in the majors, McDermott was 69-69. Besides the Red Sox and Senators, he also pitched for the Yankees (for whom he made a relief appearance in the 1956 World Series), Athletics (two stints), Tigers and Cardinals.

Mickey McGowan, 81, at Waycross, Ga., on March 8. McGowan made three relief appearances for the 1948 Giants.

Norm McRae, 55, at Garland, Texas, on July 25. McRae made 22 relief appearances for the Tigers over the 1969 and 1970 seasons. He was 0-0 with a 3.15 ERA.

Bill Merrill, 79, at Arlington, Texas, on March 29. Merrill did play-by-play and color commentary for the Rangers from 1974 to 1981.

Durwood Merrill, 64, at Texarkana, Texas, on January 11. Merrill was an American League umpire from 1977 through 1999.

Jim Mertz, 86, at Waycross, Ga., on February 4. Mertz spent one season in the majors—1943, a year in which the righthander compiled a 5-7 record for Washington.

Bud Metheny, 87, at Virginia Beach, Va., on January 2. Metheny was the Yankees' primary right fielder during the war years of 1943, 1944 and 1945. In '43, he hit .261 in 360 at-bats and started two games in the Yanks' five-game World Series triumph over the Cardinals. He had more than 500 at-bats in each of the next two seasons and batted .239 and .248. Metheny hit 14 homers in '44.

Dutch Meyer, 87, at Fort Worth, Texas, on January 19. He was the Indians' regular second baseman in 1945, batting .292 in 130 games. Meyer, who had broken into the majors by appearing in one game for the 1937 Cubs, played for the Tigers from 1940 through 1942 and wound up his big-league career with a 72-game stint for Cleveland in 1946.

Bill Miller, 76, at Lititz, Pa., on July 1. Lefthander Miller was a member of the Yankees' 1952 and 1953 World Series championship teams and also pitched for the Yanks in 1954 before winding up his big-league career with the Orioles in 1955. A starter and a reliever, he tossed two shutouts in '52 and was 6-9 overall in the majors.

Ray Murray, 85, at Fort Worth, Texas, on April 9. Murray was a backup catcher who played for the Indians, Athletics and Orioles in a six-season major league career that ended in 1954. In 1953, he appeared in 84 games with the A's and batted .284.

Joe Ostrowski, 86, at Wilkes-Barre, Pa., on January 3. Primarily a relief pitcher, Ostrowski made a total of 50 appearances out of the bullpen for the Yankees' 1951 and 1952 World Series champions. The lefthander also pitched for the St. Louis Browns during a five-year major league career in which he compiled a 23-25 record.

Paul Owens, 79, at Woodbury, N.J., on December 26. Owens was the general manager of the 1980 World Series champion Phillies and guided the Phils to the N.L. pennant in 1983 after taking over as manager just past the midpoint of the season.

Billy Parker, 56, at Sun City West, Ariz., on February 9. Parker was a reserve infielder for the Angels from 1971 through 1973. He appeared in 94 games.

Claude Passeau, 94, at Lucedale, Miss., on August 30. Passeau, a righthander, was a double-figure winner in the National League for 10 consecutive seasons—the last seven years in that streak as a member of the Cubs. Traded by the Phillies to Chicago in 1939, he was a 20-game winner for Cubs in 1940, won 19 games in 1942 and posted 15 victories in 1943 and again in 1944 before helping Chicago to the World Series in 1945 with a 17-9 record. In '45, he posted a career-low 2.46 ERA, hurled five regular-season shutouts and pitched a one-hit, 3-0 triumph over Detroit in the Series. In 13 big-league seasons, he was 162-150.

Rusty Peters, 88, at Harrisonburg, Va., on February 21. Infielder Peters' most extensive duty in a 10-year major league career came in 1937 when he appeared in 116 games with the Athletics and batted .260 with 43 RBIs. He also played for the Indians (six seasons) and the Browns.

Jim Pruett, 85, at Waukesha, Wis., on July 29. Pruett, a catcher, appeared in a total of nine games for the Athletics in 1944 and 1945.

Frank "Ribs" Raney, 80, at Warren, Mich., on July 7. Raney pitched in a total of four games for the Browns in 1949 and 1950 and had decisions in all four. His record: 1-3.

Billy Rogell, 98, at Sterling Heights, Mich., on August 9. Rogell was the shortstop for the Tigers' first World Series champions, the 1935 team, batting .275 in the regular season and .292 in the Series. In 1934, he drove in 100 runs for the A.L. pennant-winning Tigers despite hitting only three home runs. A .303 hitter for Detroit in 1931, Rogell finished at .295 in 1933 and .296 in '34. He spent 10 seasons with the Tigers, three with the Red Sox (with whom he broke into the majors in 1925) and one year with the Cubs (for whom he wound up his big-league career in 1940).

Ernie Rudolph, 92, at Black River Falls, Wis., on January 13. Rudolph made seven relief appearances for the 1945 Dodgers.

Sonny Senerchia, 72, at Freehold, N.J., on November 1. Senerchia saw action at third base for the 1952 Pirates and batted .220 in 29 games. Three of his 22 major league hits were home runs.

Pete Sivess, 89, at Candler, N.C., on June 1. Primarily a reliever, righthander Sivess compiled a 7-11 record while a member of the Phillies from 1936 through 1938.

Jim Sheehan, 90, at New Haven, Conn., on December 2. In his only big-league game, catcher Sheehan was hitless in four at-bats for the 1936 Giants.

Dwain "Lefty" Sloat, 84, at St. Paul, Minn., on April 18. Lefthander Sloat pitched in four games for the 1948 Dodgers and in five games for the 1949 Cubs. He lost his only major league decision.

Bob "Riverboat" Smith, 75, at Clarence, Mo., on June 23. Smith pitched in a total of 30 big-league games in 1958 and 1959, appearing with the Red Sox, Cubs and Indians and going 4-4.

Warren Spahn, 82, at Broken Arrow, Okla., on November 24. Spahn was the winningest lefthander in big-league history. Pitching 20 years for the Boston and Milwaukee Braves and 21 seasons overall in the majors, he won 363 games and equaled Christy Mathewson's National League record by posting 20 or more victories in a season 13 times. The Hall of Famer, who did not win his first major league game until he was 25 years old, tossed 63 shutouts and threw two no-hitters (the first in the final month of the 1960 season, the second in the first month of the 1961 season). Spahn captured the Cy Young Award in 1957, a year in which he went 21-11 with a 2.69 ERA for the World Series-winning Braves. He won 22 games for Milwaukee's 1958 N.L. champions and 15 for Boston's 1948 N.L. pennant-winning club. At age 42, Spahn went 23-7 in 1963 and fashioned a 2.60 ERA. He also is in the record books as a hitter—his 35 home runs are a career record for an N.L. pitcher.

Dernell Stenson, 25, in a shooting in the Phoenix area on November 5. Stenson, an outfielder/first baseman, made his major league debut in 2003, batting .247 for the Reds with three home runs and 13 RBIs in 37 games. He was playing in the Arizona Fall League at the time of his death.

Haywood Sullivan, 72, at Fort Myers, Fla., on February 12. A former reserve catcher for the Red Sox (1955, 1957, 1959-60) and Kansas City's No. 1 receiver in 1961, Sullivan rose through the ranks of Boston's front office as player-personnel director, general manager and part owner and helped oversee Sox teams that won A.L. pennants in 1967, 1975 and 1986. He was part of the Red Sox's ownership group from 1978 to 1993.

Jarvis Tatum, 56, at Los Angeles on January 6. Outfielder Tatum appeared in a total of 102 games for the Angels from 1968 through 1970 and hit .232.

Pete Taylor, 75, at Annapolis, Md., on November 17. Taylor's major league career consisted of a two-inning relief stint for the 1952 Browns.

C. Carlisle Tippit, 83, at Chagrin Falls, Ohio, on June 7. Tippit was part owner of the Indians from 1972 to 1986.

John Welaj, 89, at Arlington, Texas, on September 13. Welaj was a part-time outfielder for Washington from 1939 through 1941 and for the Philadelphia A's in 1943.

Max West, 87, at Sierra Madre, Calif., on December 31. West spent seven seasons in the majors. The outfielder/first baseman's best year was 1939, when hit .285 with 19 home runs and 82 RBIs for the Braves. In 1940, he started for the National League in the All-Star Game and smashed a three-run homer in the first inning. Overall, he batted .254 in the big leagues and hit 77 homers.

Jim Westlake, 72, at Sacramento on January 3. His big-league career consisted of one pinch-hitting appearance for the Phillies in 1955. He struck out.

Don Wheeler, 81, at Bloomington, Minn., on December 10. Wheeler was a catcher for the 1949 White Sox, appearing in 67 games and batting .240.

Dick Whitman, 82, at Peoria, Ariz., on February 12. A reserve outfielder who played in only 285 big-league games, Whitman nonetheless played in two World Series. He made one pinch-hitting appearance for Brooklyn in the 1949 Series and three for the Phillies in the 1950 Fall Classic. Whitman saw his most extensive duty in the majors in his rookie season of 1946, playing in 104 games for the Dodgers and batting .260.

Chris Zachary, 59, at Knoxville, Tenn., on April 19. Zachary managed only a 10-29 record over nine big-league seasons—he broke in with Houston in 1963 at age 19—but contributed to Detroit's A.L. East Division championship in 1972. Making 24 relief appearances and one start for the Tigers, the righthander had a 1.41 ERA. He pitched in one game in the '72 ALCS against Oakland.

2003 A.L. STATISTICS

Batting

Designated hitting

Pinch-hitting

Pitching

Fielding

Miscellaneous

BATTING

TEAM

Team	G	TPA	AB	R	H	TB	2B	3B	HR	RBI	SH	SF	HP	BB	IBB	SO	SB	CS	GDP	LOB	ShO	Avg.	OBP	Slg.
Boston	162	6530	5769	961	1667	2832	371	40	238	932	24	64	53	620	61	943	88	35	126	1224	5	.289	.360	.491
Toronto	162	6364	5661	894	1580	2573	357	33	190	853	11	56	90	546	40	1081	37	25	146	1175	5	.279	.349	.455
Minnesota	162	6324	5655	801	1567	2440	318	45	155	755	42	52	63	512	36	1027	94	44	139	1166	5	.277	.341	.431
Kansas City	162	6239	5568	836	1526	2378	288	39	162	781	63	57	75	476	32	926	120	42	128	1096	5	.274	.336	.427
Seattle	162	6281	5561	795	1509	2282	290	33	139	759	35	46	53	586	34	989	108	37	130	1202	10	.271	.344	.410
New York	163	6431	5605	877	1518	2540	304	14	230	845	25	35	81	684	54	1042	98	33	154	1239	7	.271	.356	.453
Anaheim	162	6119	5487	736	1473	2265	276	33	150	687	50	50	56	476	42	838	129	61	125	1086	12	.268	.330	.413
Baltimore	163	6241	5665	743	1516	2297	277	24	152	695	51	40	54	431	32	902	89	36	123	1121	12	.268	.323	.405
Texas	162	6293	5664	826	1506	2569	274	36	239	799	24	42	75	488	31	1052	65	25	115	1141	11	.266	.330	.454
Tampa Bay	162	6212	5654	715	1501	2286	298	38	137	678	32	50	56	420	46	1030	142	42	108	1129	10	.265	.320	.404
Chicago	162	6148	5487	791	1445	2446	303	19	220	766	43	41	58	519	27	916	77	29	132	1074	8	.263	.331	.446
Oakland	162	6189	5497	768	1398	2291	317	24	176	742	22	53	59	556	52	898	48	14	118	1130	6	.254	.327	.417
Cleveland	162	6188	5572	699	1413	2235	296	26	158	660	46	41	62	466	25	1062	86	61	128	1068	5	.254	.316	.401
Detroit	162	6071	5466	591	1312	2050	201	39	153	553	65	49	47	443	24	1099	98	63	114	1047	17	.240	.300	.375
Totals	1135	87630	78311	11033	20931	33484	4170	443	2499	10505	533	676	882	7223	536	13805	1279	547	1786	15898	118	.267	.333	.428

INDIVIDUAL

TOP QUALIFIERS FOR BATTING CHAMPIONSHIP

Minimum 502 plate appearances. *Lefthanded batter. †Switch-hitter.

Player, Team	G	TPA	AB	R	H	TB	2B	3B	HR	RBI	SH	SF	HP	BB	IBB	SO	SB	CS	GDP	Avg.	OBP	Slg.
Mueller, Bill, Bos.+	146	600	524	85	171	283	45	5	19	85	4	6	7	59	2	77	1	4	11	.326	.398	.540
Ramirez, Manny, Bos.	154	679	569	117	185	334	36	1	37	104	0	5	8	97	28	94	3	1	22	.325	.427	.587
Jeter, Derek, N.Y.	119	542	482	87	156	217	25	3	10	52	3	1	13	43	2	88	11	5	10	.324	.393	.450
Wells, Vernon, Tor.	161	735	678	118	215	373	49	5	33	117	0	8	7	42	2	80	4	1	21	.317	.359	.550
Ordonez, Magglio, Chi.	160	674	606	95	192	331	46	3	29	99	0	4	7	57	1	73	9	5	20	.317	.380	.546
Anderson, Garret, Ana.*	159	673	638	80	201	345	49	4	29	116	0	4	0	31	10	83	6	3	15	.315	.345	.541
Suzuki, Ichiro, Sea.*	159	725	679	111	212	296	29	8	13	62	3	1	6	36	7	69	34	8	3	.312	.352	.436
Pierzynski, A.J., Min.*	137	533	487	63	152	226	35	3	11	74	2	5	15	24	12	55	3	1	13	.312	.360	.464
Huff, Aubrey, TB.*	162	706	636	91	198	353	47	3	34	107	0	9	8	53	17	80	2	3	19	.311	.367	.555
Stewart, Shannon, Tor.-Min.	136	644	573	90	176	263	44	2	13	73	2	11	6	52	3	66	4	6	10	.307	.364	.459
Beltran, Carlos, K.C.+	141	602	521	102	160	272	14	10	26	100	0	7	2	72	4	81	41	4	8	.307	.389	.522
Young, Michael, Tex.	160	713	666	106	204	297	33	9	14	72	3	7	1	36	1	103	13	2	14	.306	.339	.446
Nixon, Trot, Bos.*	134	513	441	81	135	255	24	6	28	87	1	3	3	65	4	96	4	2	3	.306	.396	.578
Jones, Jacque, Min.*	136	548	517	76	157	240	33	1	16	69	1	5	4	21	2	105	13	1	10	.304	.333	.464
Delgado, Carlos, Tor.*	161	705	570	117	172	338	38	1	42	145	0	7	19	109	23	137	0	0	9	.302	.426	.593

DEPARTMENTAL LEADERS: G—Matsui, N.Y., 163 ;AB—Soriano, N.Y., 682; R—Rodriguez, Tex., 124; H—Wells, Tor., 215; TB—Wells, Tor., 373; 1B—Suzuki, Sea., 162; 2B—Anderson, Ana., Wells, Tor., 49; 3B—Guzman, Min., 14; HR—Rodriguez, Tex., 47; RBI—Delgado, Tor., 145; SH—Santiago, Det., 18; SF—Conine, Bal., 12; HP—Giambi, N.Y., 21; BB—Giambi, N.Y., 129; IBB—Ramirez, Bos., 28; SO—Giambi, N.Y., 140; SB—Crawford, TB., 55; CS—Sanchez, Det., 18; GDP—Konerko, Chi., 28; Slg.—Rodriguez, Tex., .600; OBP—Ramirez, Bos., .427.

ALL PLAYERS

*Lefthanded batter. †Switch-hitter.

Player, Team	G	TPA	AB	R	H	TB	2B	3B	HR	RBI	SH	SF	HP	BB	IBB	SO	SB	CS	GDP	Avg.	OBP	Slg.
Abad, Andy, Bos.*	9	19	17	1	2	2	0	0	0	0	0	0	0	2	0	5	0	1	1	.118	.211	.118
Abernathy, Brent, TB.-K.C.	12	37	34	3	2	2	0	0	0	0	2	0	0	1	0	3	1	0	2	.059	.086	.059
Affeldt, Jeremy, K.C.*	36	7	6	0	2	2	0	0	0	2	0	0	0	1	0	1	0	0	0	.333	.429	.333
Almonte, Erick, N.Y.	31	111	100	17	26	35	6	0	1	11	2	0	1	8	0	24	1	0	3	.260	.321	.350
Alomar Jr., Sandy, Chi.	75	204	194	22	52	79	12	0	5	26	5	1	0	4	0	17	0	0	4	.268	.281	.407
Alomar, Roberto, Chi.†	67	296	253	42	64	86	11	1	3	17	8	4	1	30	1	37	6	2	9	.253	.330	.340
Amezaga, Alfredo, Ana.†	37	120	105	15	22	35	3	2	2	7	5	0	1	9	0	23	2	2	2	.210	.278	.333
Anderson, Brian, Cle.-K.C.	34	2	1	0	0	0	0	0	0	0	0	0	0	1	0	0	0	0	0	.000	.500	.000
Anderson, Garret, Ana.*	159	673	638	80	201	345	49	4	29	116	0	4	0	31	10	83	6	3	15	.315	.345	.541
Anderson, Marlon, TB.*	145	535	482	59	130	181	27	3	6	67	4	5	3	41	5	60	19	3	6	.270	.328	.376
Appier, Kevin, Ana.-K.C.	23	5	5	0	0	0	0	0	0	0	0	0	0	0	0	4	0	0	0	.000	.000	.000
Avery, Steve, Det.*	19	1	1	1	1	1	0	0	0	0	0	0	0	0	0	0	0	0	0	1.000	1.000	1.000
Backe, Brandon, TB.	29	0	0	1	0	0	0	0	0	0	0	0	0	0	0	0	0	0	0	.000	.000	.000
Baez, Danys, Cle.	73	1	1	0	0	0	0	0	0	0	0	0	0	0	0	0	0	0	0	.000	.000	.000
Baldelli, Rocco, TB.	156	684	637	89	184	265	32	8	11	78	3	6	8	30	4	128	27	10	10	.289	.326	.416
Bard, Josh, Cle.†	91	330	303	25	74	113	13	1	8	36	1	3	0	22	1	53	0	2	9	.244	.293	.373
Batista, Tony, Bal.	161	670	631	76	148	248	20	1	26	99	0	6	5	28	4	102	4	3	20	.235	.270	.393
Bell, Rob, TB.	19	2	2	0	0	0	0	0	0	0	0	0	0	0	0	1	0	0	0	.000	.000	.000
Beltran, Carlos, K.C.†	141	602	521	102	160	272	14	10	26	100	0	7	2	72	4	81	41	4	8	.307	.389	.522
Benoit, Joaquin, Tex.	25	2	2	0	0	0	0	0	0	0	0	0	0	0	0	0	0	0	0	.000	.000	.000
Berg, Dave, Tor.	61	174	161	26	41	61	6	1	4	18	1	1	0	11	0	34	0	1	7	.255	.301	.379
Berger, Brandon, K.C.	13	38	32	3	7	7	0	0	0	3	1	0	0	5	0	4	0	0	0	.219	.324	.219
Bernero, Adam, Det.	19	4	4	0	0	0	0	0	0	0	0	0	0	0	0	1	0	0	0	.000	.000	.000
Berroa, Angel, K.C.	158	635	567	92	163	256	28	7	17	73	13	8	18	29	3	100	21	5	13	.287	.338	.451
Bigbie, Larry, Bal.*	83	319	287	43	87	131	15	1	9	31	1	2	0	29	3	60	7	1	2	.303	.365	.456
Blake, Casey, Cle.	152	621	557	80	143	229	35	0	17	67	8	8	10	38	1	109	7	9	11	.257	.312	.411
Blalock, Hank, Tex.*	143	615	567	89	170	296	33	3	29	90	0	3	1	44	1	97	2	3	16	.300	.350	.522
Bloomquist, Willie, Sea.	89	220	196	30	49	63	7	2	1	14	2	2	1	19	1	39	4	1	6	.250	.317	.321

Player, Team	G	TPA	AB	R	H	TB	2B	3B	HR	RBI	SH	SF	HP	BB	IBB	SO	SB	CS	GDP	Avg.	OBP	Slg.
Bocachica, Hiram, Det.	6	22	22	1	1	2	1	0	0	0	0	0	0	0	0	7	0	0	0	.045	.045	.091
Bonderman, Jeremy, Det.	33	2	2	0	0	0	0	0	0	0	0	0	0	0	0	2	0	0	0	.000	.000	.000
Boone, Aaron, N.Y.	54	209	189	31	48	79	13	0	6	31	3	2	3	11	0	30	8	0	7	.254	.302	.418
Boone, Bret, Sea.	159	705	622	111	183	333	35	5	35	117	1	7	7	68	3	125	16	3	17	.294	.366	.535
Borchard, Joe, Chi.†	16	57	49	5	9	13	1	0	1	5	0	3	0	5	0	18	0	1	0	.184	.246	.265
Borders, Pat, Sea.	12	15	14	1	2	3	1	0	0	1	0	0	0	1	0	5	0	0	0	.143	.200	.214
Bordick, Mike, Tor.	102	379	343	39	94	131	18	2	5	54	0	1	2	33	0	60	3	1	8	.274	.340	.382
Bowen, Rob, Min.†	7	11	10	0	1	1	0	0	0	1	0	1	0	0	0	4	0	0	1	.100	.091	.100
Bradley, Milton, Cle.†	101	451	377	61	121	189	34	2	10	56	0	5	5	64	8	73	17	7	10	.321	.421	.501
Brazelton, Dewon, TB.	10	1	1	0	0	0	0	0	0	0	0	0	0	0	0	0	0	0	0	.000	.000	.000
Broussard, Ben, Cle.*	116	429	386	53	96	171	21	3	16	55	3	3	5	32	2	75	5	2	6	.249	.312	.443
Brown, Adrian, Bos.†	9	16	15	2	3	3	0	0	0	1	0	0	0	1	0	4	2	0	0	.200	.250	.200
Brown, Dee, K.C.*	50	143	132	16	30	43	7	0	2	14	0	1	2	8	1	37	1	1	0	.227	.280	.326
Buehrle, Mark, Chi.*	35	6	6	0	1	1	0	0	0	1	0	0	0	0	0	3	0	0	0	.167	.167	.167
Burke, Jamie, Chi.	6	8	8	0	3	3	0	0	0	2	0	0	0	0	0	0	0	0	0	.375	.375	.375
Burkett, John, Bos.	32	2	1	0	0	0	0	0	0	0	1	0	0	0	0	0	0	0	0	.000	.000	.000
Burkhart, Morgan, K.C.†	6	16	15	1	3	3	0	0	0	1	0	0	0	1	0	2	0	0	0	.200	.250	.200
Burks, Ellis, Cle.	55	228	198	27	52	83	11	1	6	28	0	0	3	27	2	46	1	1	4	.263	.360	.419
Byrnes, Eric, Oak.	121	461	414	64	109	190	27	9	12	51	0	2	2	42	4	71	10	2	3	.263	.333	.459
Cameron, Mike, Sea.	147	612	534	74	135	230	31	5	18	76	1	2	5	70	1	137	17	7	13	.253	.344	.431
Carrasco, D.J., K.C.	50	2	2	0	0	0	0	0	0	0	0	0	0	0	0	1	0	0	1	.000	.000	.000
Cash, Kevin, Tor.	34	117	106	10	15	21	3	0	1	8	5	1	1	4	0	22	0	0	6	.142	.179	.198
Catalanotto, Frank, Tor.*	133	535	489	83	146	231	34	6	13	59	2	3	6	35	1	62	2	2	9	.299	.351	.472
Chavez, Eric, Oak.*	156	654	588	94	166	302	39	5	29	101	0	3	1	62	10	89	8	3	14	.282	.350	.514
Christenson, Ryan, Tex.	60	186	165	22	29	42	7	0	2	16	2	1	3	15	0	44	2	2	3	.176	.255	.255
Cirillo, Jeff, Sea.	87	293	258	24	53	70	11	0	2	23	4	2	5	24	1	32	1	1	6	.205	.284	.271
Clark, Howie, Tor.*	38	77	70	9	25	30	3	1	0	7	2	0	2	3	0	6	0	1	3	.357	.400	.429
Clark, Jermaine, Tex.*	24	54	46	2	8	10	2	0	0	6	1	1	0	6	0	4	2	1	1	.174	.264	.217
Claussen, Brandon, N.Y.	1	4	4	0	1	1	0	0	0	1	0	0	0	0	0	1	0	0	0	.250	.250	.250
Clemens, Roger, N.Y.	33	2	1	0	0	0	0	0	0	0	1	0	0	0	0	1	0	0	0	.000	.000	.000
Colbrunn, Greg, Sea.	22	62	58	7	16	28	1	1	3	7	0	0	0	4	0	16	0	1	3	.276	.323	.483
Collier, Lou, Bos.	4	1	1	0	0	0	0	0	0	0	0	0	0	0	0	0	0	1	0	.000	.000	.000
Colon, Bartolo, Chi.	34	7	6	0	0	0	0	0	0	0	1	0	0	0	0	3	0	0	0	.000	.000	.000
Conine, Jeff, Bal.	124	547	493	75	143	227	33	3	15	80	0	12	5	37	5	60	5	0	14	.290	.338	.460
Contreras, Jose, N.Y.	18	3	3	0	0	0	0	0	0	0	0	0	0	0	0	2	0	0	0	.000	.000	.000
Cordova, Marty, Bal.	9	39	30	5	7	11	1	0	1	4	0	0	1	8	1	5	1	0	1	.233	.410	.367
Cornejo, Nate, Det.	32	5	4	0	0	0	0	0	0	0	1	0	0	0	0	4	0	0	0	.000	.000	.000
Crawford, Carl, TB.*	151	661	630	80	177	228	18	9	5	54	1	3	1	26	4	102	55	10	5	.281	.309	.362
Crede, Joe, Chi.	151	580	536	68	140	232	31	2	19	75	2	4	6	32	1	75	1	1	11	.261	.308	.433
Crisp, Coco, Cle.†	99	447	414	55	110	146	15	6	3	27	7	3	0	23	1	51	15	9	4	.266	.302	.353
Crosby, Bobby, Oak.	11	14	12	1	0	0	0	0	0	0	0	0	1	1	0	5	0	0	0	.000	.143	.000
Cruz, Deivi, Bal.	152	572	548	61	137	207	24	2	14	65	7	2	2	13	1	49	1	2	13	.250	.269	.378
Cuddyer, Michael, Min.	35	114	102	14	25	44	1	3	4	8	0	0	0	12	0	19	1	1	6	.245	.325	.431
Cust, Jack, Bal.*	27	84	73	7	19	38	7	0	4	11	0	0	1	10	0	25	0	0	0	.260	.357	.521
Damon, Johnny, Bos.*	145	690	608	103	166	246	32	6	12	67	6	6	2	68	4	74	30	6	5	.273	.345	.405
Daubach, Brian, Chi.*	95	219	183	26	42	71	11	0	6	21	0	1	1	34	1	54	1	0	3	.230	.352	.388
DaVanon, Jeff, Ana.†	123	382	330	56	93	147	16	1	12	43	4	5	1	42	0	59	17	5	6	.282	.360	.445
Davis, Ben, Sea.†	80	269	246	25	58	94	18	0	6	42	1	4	0	18	2	61	0	0	5	.236	.284	.382
Davis, Doug, Tex.-Tor.	13	1	1	0	0	0	0	0	0	0	0	0	0	0	0	1	0	0	0	.000	.000	.000
Davis, Jason, Cle.	28	3	2	0	0	0	0	0	0	0	1	0	0	0	0	1	0	0	0	.000	.000	.000
Dawkins, Gookie, K.C.	3	3	2	0	0	0	0	0	0	0	0	0	0	1	0	2	0	0	0	.000	.333	.000
DeHart, Rick, K.C.*	4	1	1	0	0	0	0	0	0	0	0	0	0	0	0	1	0	0	0	.000	.000	.000
DeJesus, David, K.C.*	12	10	7	0	2	4	0	1	0	0	1	0	1	1	0	2	0	0	0	.286	.444	.571
Delgado, Carlos, Tor.*	161	705	570	117	172	338	38	1	42	145	0	7	19	109	23	137	0	0	9	.302	.426	.593
Delgado, Wilson, Ana.†	19	58	50	4	16	16	0	0	0	4	0	0	0	8	0	8	0	0	1	.320	.414	.320
Dellucci, David, N.Y.*	21	58	51	8	9	13	1	0	1	4	1	0	2	4	0	13	3	0	2	.176	.263	.255
Diaz, Einar, Tex.	101	361	334	30	86	114	14	1	4	35	4	4	10	9	0	32	3	1	12	.257	.294	.341
Diaz, Matt, TB.	4	10	9	2	1	1	0	0	0	0	0	0	0	1	0	3	0	0	0	.111	.200	.111
Dickey, R.A., Tex.	38	1	1	0	1	1	0	0	0	0	0	0	0	0	0	0	0	0	0	1.000	1.000	1.000
DiFelice, Mike, K.C.	62	205	189	29	48	75	16	1	3	25	1	2	4	9	0	30	1	0	6	.254	.299	.397
Driskill, Travis, Bal.	20	1	1	0	0	0	0	0	0	0	0	0	0	0	0	0	0	0	0	.000	.000	.000
Durazo, Erubiel, Oak.*	154	645	537	92	139	231	29	0	21	77	0	6	2	100	12	105	1	1	11	.259	.374	.430
Durrington, Trent, Ana.	12	17	14	5	2	2	0	0	0	1	0	0	0	3	0	0	1	1	0	.143	.294	.143
Dye, Jermaine, Oak.	65	253	221	28	38	56	6	0	4	20	0	4	3	25	2	42	1	0	11	.172	.261	.253
Easley, Damion, TB.	36	110	107	8	20	28	3	1	1	7	1	0	0	2	0	18	0	0	3	.187	.202	.262
Eckstein, David, Ana.	120	517	452	59	114	147	22	1	3	31	10	4	15	36	0	45	16	5	9	.252	.325	.325
Edwards, Mike, Oak.	4	6	4	0	1	1	0	0	0	0	0	0	0	2	0	1	0	0	0	.250	.500	.250
Ellis, Mark, Oak.	154	622	553	78	137	205	31	5	9	52	9	5	7	48	4	94	6	2	7	.248	.313	.371
Erstad, Darin, Ana.*	67	284	258	35	65	86	7	1	4	17	2	2	4	18	1	40	9	1	8	.252	.309	.333
Escalona, Felix, TB.	10	29	27	2	5	7	2	0	0	2	0	0	0	2	0	6	1	0	0	.185	.241	.259
Escobar, Alex, Cle.	28	108	99	16	27	44	2	0	5	14	0	1	1	7	1	33	1	0	0	.273	.324	.444
Escobar, Kelvim, Tor.	41	6	6	1	1	1	0	0	0	1	0	0	0	0	0	3	0	0	0	.167	.167	.167
Everett, Carl, Tex.-Chi.†	147	602	526	93	151	268	27	3	28	92	4	4	15	53	6	84	8	4	7	.287	.366	.510
Febles, Carlos, K.C.	74	219	196	31	46	51	5	0	0	11	5	0	5	13	0	30	8	2	8	.235	.299	.260
Figgins, Chone, Ana.†	71	270	240	34	71	88	9	4	0	27	6	4	0	20	0	38	13	7	1	.296	.345	.367
Fiore, Tony, Min.	21	1	1	0	0	0	0	0	0	0	0	0	0	0	0	1	0	0	0	.000	.000	.000
Flaherty, John, N.Y.	40	116	105	16	28	48	8	0	4	14	5	1	1	4	1	19	0	0	6	.267	.297	.457
Ford, Lew, Min.	34	83	73	16	24	42	7	1	3	15	1	0	1	8	0	9	2	0	1	.329	.402	.575
Fordyce, Brook, Bal.	108	376	348	28	95	129	12	2	6	31	6	2	1	19	1	44	2	3	10	.273	.311	.371
Franklin, Ryan, Sea.	32	5	4	1	1	1	0	0	0	0	1	0	0	0	0	1	0	0	0	.250	.250	.250
Fullmer, Brad, Ana.*	63	235	206	32	63	103	9	2	9	35	0	1	2	26	4	31	5	4	4	.306	.387	.500
Gant, Ron, Oak.	17	44	41	4	6	9	0	0	1	4	0	1	0	2	0	9	0	0	1	.146	.182	.220

Player, Team	G	TPA	AB	R	H	TB	2B	3B	HR	RBI	SH	SF	HP	BB	IBB	SO	SB	CS	GDP	Avg.	OBP	Slg.
Garcia, Freddy, Sea.	33	5	5	0	1	1	0	0	0	1	0	0	0	0	0	0	0	0	1	.200	.200	.200
Garcia, Karim, Cle.-N.Y.*	76	262	244	25	64	103	6	0	11	35	0	3	1	14	2	52	0	2	8	.262	.302	.422
Garciaparra, Nomar, Bos.	156	719	658	120	198	345	37	13	28	105	1	10	11	39	1	61	19	5	10	.301	.345	.524
Garland, Jon, Chi.	32	4	2	0	0	0	0	0	0	0	1	0	0	1	0	0	0	0	0	.000	.333	.000
George, Chris, K.C.*	18	3	1	0	1	1	0	0	0	1	2	0	0	0	0	0	0	0	0	1.000	1.000	1.000
German, Esteban, Oak.	5	4	4	0	1	1	0	0	0	1	0	0	0	0	0	1	0	0	1	.250	.250	.250
Gerut, Jody, Cle.*	127	525	480	66	134	237	33	2	22	75	1	2	7	35	4	70	4	5	13	.279	.336	.494
Giambi, Jason, N.Y.*	156	690	535	97	134	282	25	0	41	107	0	5	21	129	9	140	2	1	9	.250	.412	.527
Giambi, Jeremy, Bos.*	50	156	127	15	25	45	5	0	5	15	1	0	2	26	0	42	1	0	3	.197	.342	.354
Gibbons, Jay, Bal.*	160	682	625	80	173	285	39	2	23	100	0	5	3	49	11	89	0	1	12	.277	.330	.456
Gil, Benji, Ana.	62	135	125	12	24	34	5	1	1	9	4	2	0	4	1	33	5	1	5	.192	.214	.272
Gil, Geronimo, Bal.	54	186	169	22	40	53	4	0	3	16	2	0	3	12	0	34	0	0	2	.237	.299	.314
Gipson, Charles, N.Y.	18	12	10	3	2	2	0	0	0	2	1	0	0	1	0	2	2	1	0	.200	.273	.200
Glanville, Doug, Tex.	52	203	195	22	53	70	5	0	4	14	2	0	0	6	1	25	4	0	2	.272	.294	.359
Glaus, Troy, Ana.	91	367	319	53	79	148	17	2	16	50	0	1	1	46	4	73	7	2	8	.248	.343	.464
Gomes, Jonny, TB.	8	16	15	1	2	3	1	0	0	0	0	0	1	0	0	6	0	0	0	.133	.188	.200
Gomez, Chris, Min.	58	185	175	14	44	62	9	3	1	15	2	1	0	7	1	13	2	1	10	.251	.279	.354
Gonzalez, Jeremi, TB.	25	6	6	0	0	0	0	0	0	0	0	0	0	0	0	3	0	0	0	.000	.000	.000
Gonzalez, Juan, Tex.	82	346	327	49	96	187	17	1	24	70	0	1	4	14	1	73	1	1	10	.294	.329	.572
Grabowski, Jason, Oak.*	8	9	8	0	0	0	0	0	0	0	0	0	0	1	0	5	0	0	0	.000	.111	.000
Graffanino, Tony, Chi.	90	281	250	51	65	107	15	3	7	23	3	1	3	24	1	37	8	0	1	.260	.331	.428
Greene, Todd, Tex.	62	210	205	25	47	89	10	1	10	20	0	1	2	2	0	47	0	0	2	.229	.243	.434
Gregorio, Tom, Ana.	12	21	19	1	3	3	0	0	0	2	0	0	1	1	0	8	0	0	0	.158	.238	.158
Grieve, Ben, TB.*	55	205	165	28	38	57	7	0	4	17	0	2	6	32	1	41	0	0	3	.230	.371	.345
Guiel, Aaron, K.C.*	99	401	354	63	98	173	30	0	15	52	2	5	13	27	0	63	3	5	3	.277	.346	.489
Guillen, Carlos, Sea.†	109	451	388	63	107	153	19	3	7	52	5	5	1	52	2	64	4	4	12	.276	.359	.394
Guillen, Jose, Oak.	45	186	170	25	45	78	7	1	8	23	2	1	5	7	1	32	0	0	8	.265	.311	.459
Gutierrez, Ricky, Cle.	16	56	50	2	13	16	3	0	0	3	1	1	1	3	0	5	0	0	1	.260	.309	.320
Guzman, Cristian, Min.†	143	585	534	78	143	195	15	14	3	53	12	4	5	30	0	79	18	9	4	.268	.311	.365
Hafner, Travis, Cle.*	91	324	291	35	74	141	19	3	14	40	0	1	10	22	2	81	2	1	7	.254	.327	.485
Hairston Jr., Jerry, Bal.	58	259	218	25	59	81	12	2	2	21	10	2	6	23	0	25	14	5	8	.271	.353	.372
Hall, Toby, TB.	130	498	463	50	117	176	23	0	12	47	0	5	7	23	4	40	0	1	14	.253	.295	.380
Halladay, Roy, Tor.	36	9	9	2	1	1	0	0	0	0	0	0	0	0	0	3	0	0	0	.111	.111	.111
Halter, Shane, Det.	114	393	360	33	78	123	5	2	12	30	3	3	0	27	0	77	2	3	11	.217	.269	.342
Harang, Aaron, Oak.	7	1	1	0	0	0	0	0	0	0	0	0	0	0	0	1	0	0	0	.000	.000	.000
Harris, Willie, Chi.*	79	150	137	19	28	33	3	1	0	5	3	0	0	10	0	28	12	2	1	.204	.259	.241
Harvey, Ken, K.C.	135	524	485	50	129	198	30	0	13	64	3	2	5	29	4	94	2	3	15	.266	.313	.408
Haselman, Bill, Bos.	4	3	3	0	0	0	0	0	0	0	0	0	0	0	0	1	0	0	0	.000	.000	.000
Hatteberg, Scott, Oak.*	147	622	541	63	137	207	34	0	12	61	3	3	9	66	0	53	0	1	14	.253	.342	.383
Hawkins, LaTroy, Min.	74	1	0	0	0	0	0	0	0	0	1	0	0	0	0	0	0	0	0	.000	.000	.000
Helling, Rick, Bal.	24	1	1	0	0	0	0	0	0	0	0	0	0	0	0	1	0	0	0	.000	.000	.000
Hendrickson, Mark, Tor.*	30	4	4	1	1	4	0	0	1	1	0	0	0	0	0	1	0	0	1	.250	.250	1.000
Henson, Drew, N.Y.	5	8	8	2	1	1	0	0	0	0	0	0	0	0	0	2	0	0	0	.125	.125	.125
Hentgen, Pat, Bal.	28	5	5	0	0	0	0	0	0	0	0	0	0	0	0	0	0	0	0	.000	.000	.000
Hernandez, Michel, N.Y.	5	5	4	0	1	1	0	0	0	0	0	0	0	1	0	1	0	0	0	.250	.400	.250
Hernandez, Ramon, Oak.	140	536	483	70	132	221	24	1	21	78	2	6	12	33	2	79	0	0	14	.273	.331	.458
Higginson, Bobby, Det.*	130	539	469	61	110	173	13	4	14	52	1	6	3	59	3	73	8	8	12	.235	.320	.369
Hillenbrand, Shea, Bos.	49	200	185	20	56	82	17	0	3	38	0	4	4	7	1	26	1	0	9	.303	.335	.443
Hinch, A.J., Det.	27	82	74	7	15	29	3	1	3	11	1	2	2	3	0	18	0	0	3	.203	.247	.392
Hinske, Eric, Tor.*	124	514	449	74	109	196	45	3	12	63	0	5	1	59	1	104	12	2	11	.243	.329	.437
Hocking, Denny, Min.†	83	209	188	22	45	68	10	2	3	22	3	3	0	15	0	37	0	1	3	.239	.291	.362
Huckaby, Ken, Tor.	5	11	11	1	2	3	1	0	0	2	0	0	0	0	0	2	0	0	0	.182	.182	.273
Hudson, Orlando, Tor.†	142	521	474	54	127	187	21	6	9	57	0	3	5	39	1	87	5	4	13	.268	.328	.395
Hudson, Tim, Oak.	34	3	3	0	1	1	0	0	0	1	0	0	0	0	0	1	0	0	1	.333	.333	.333
Huff, Aubrey, TB.*	162	706	636	91	198	353	47	3	34	107	0	9	8	53	17	80	2	3	19	.311	.367	.555
Hunter, Torii, Min.	154	642	581	83	145	262	31	4	26	102	0	6	5	50	7	106	6	7	15	.250	.312	.451
Ibanez, Raul, K.C.*	157	671	608	95	179	276	33	5	18	90	1	10	3	49	5	81	8	4	10	.294	.345	.454
Infante, Omar, Det.	69	244	221	24	49	57	6	1	0	8	3	2	0	18	0	37	6	3	1	.222	.278	.258
Inge, Brandon, Det.	104	366	330	32	67	112	15	3	8	30	4	3	5	24	0	79	4	4	8	.203	.265	.339
Jackson, Damian, Bos.	109	172	161	34	42	52	7	0	1	13	2	1	0	8	0	28	16	8	4	.261	.294	.323
Jeter, Derek, N.Y.	119	542	482	87	156	217	25	3	10	52	3	1	13	43	2	88	11	5	10	.324	.393	.450
Jimenez, D'Angelo, Chi.†	73	308	271	35	69	111	11	5	7	26	4	1	0	32	1	46	4	3	3	.255	.332	.410
Johnson, Gary, Ana.*	5	9	8	1	3	4	1	0	0	0	0	0	0	1	0	1	0	1	0	.375	.444	.500
Johnson, Jason, Bal.	32	6	5	1	1	1	0	0	0	0	0	0	0	1	0	3	0	0	0	.200	.333	.200
Johnson, Mark, Oak.*	13	33	27	3	3	4	1	0	0	3	1	1	1	3	0	4	0	0	0	.111	.219	.148
Johnson, Nick, N.Y.*	96	406	324	60	92	153	19	0	14	47	3	1	8	70	4	57	5	2	9	.284	.422	.472
Johnson, Reed, Tor.	114	457	412	79	121	176	21	2	10	52	1	4	20	20	1	67	5	3	10	.294	.353	.427
Johnson, Rontrez, K.C.	8	3	3	3	1	1	0	0	0	0	0	0	0	0	0	2	0	0	0	.333	.333	.333
Jones, Jacque, Min.*	136	548	517	76	157	240	33	1	16	69	1	5	4	21	2	105	13	1	10	.304	.333	.464
Jones, Jason, Tex.†	40	121	107	11	23	38	6	0	3	11	0	1	3	10	0	21	0	1	1	.215	.298	.355
Kapler, Gabe, Bos.	68	172	158	29	46	71	11	1	4	23	0	0	0	14	0	23	4	2	5	.291	.349	.449
Kennedy, Adam, Ana.*	143	510	449	71	121	179	17	1	13	49	2	5	9	45	4	73	22	9	7	.269	.344	.399
Kielty, Bobby, Min.-Tor.†	137	509	427	71	104	171	26	1	13	57	0	4	7	71	6	92	8	3	11	.244	.358	.400
Kim, Byung-Hyun, Bos.	49	7	7	0	2	2	0	0	0	0	0	0	0	0	0	0	0	0	0	.286	.286	.286
Kingsale, Gene, Det.†	39	140	120	11	25	33	3	1	1	8	8	2	0	10	0	17	1	3	2	.208	.265	.275
Klassen, Danny, Det.	22	78	73	9	18	26	3	1	1	7	1	0	0	4	0	26	0	1	1	.247	.286	.356
Knotts, Gary, Det.	20	1	1	0	0	0	0	0	0	0	0	0	0	0	0	0	0	0	0	.000	.000	.000
Konerko, Paul, Chi.	137	495	444	49	104	177	19	0	18	65	0	4	4	43	7	50	0	0	28	.234	.305	.399
Koonce, Graham, Oak.*	6	8	8	0	1	2	1	0	0	0	0	0	0	0	0	6	0	0	0	.125	.125	.250
Koskie, Corey, Min.*	131	562	469	76	137	212	29	2	14	69	0	9	7	77	5	113	11	5	5	.292	.393	.452
Kreuter, Chad, Tex.†	7	21	18	0	2	3	1	0	0	0	0	0	0	3	0	2	0	0	0	.111	.238	.167
Lackey, John, Ana.	33	3	3	0	0	0	0	0	0	0	0	0	0	0	0	2	0	0	0	.000	.000	.000

Player, Team	G	TPA	AB	R	H	TB	2B	3B	HR	RBI	SH	SF	HP	BB	IBB	SO	SB	CS	GDP	Avg.	OBP	Slg.
LaForest, Pete, TB.*	19	51	48	0	8	10	2	0	0	6	0	1	1	1	0	14	0	0	1	.167	.196	.208
Laird, Gerald, Tex.	19	50	44	9	12	19	2	1	1	4	0	0	1	5	0	11	0	0	2	.273	.360	.432
Laker, Tim, Cle.	52	176	162	17	39	59	11	0	3	21	5	0	0	9	1	38	2	2	4	.241	.281	.364
Lamb, Mike, Tex.*	28	42	38	3	5	5	0	0	0	2	0	1	1	2	0	7	1	0	1	.132	.190	.132
LaRocca, Greg, Cle.	5	10	9	3	3	4	1	0	0	0	0	0	0	1	0	1	0	0	0	.333	.400	.444
Latham, Chris, N.Y.†	4	2	2	3	2	2	0	0	0	0	0	0	0	0	0	0	1	0	0	1.000	1.000	1.000
Lawton, Matt, Cle.*	99	429	374	57	93	157	19	0	15	53	0	1	7	47	0	47	10	3	8	.249	.343	.420
LeCroy, Matthew, Min.	107	374	345	39	99	169	19	0	17	64	0	0	4	25	1	82	0	1	8	.287	.342	.490
Lee, Carlos, Chi.	158	671	623	100	181	311	35	1	31	113	0	7	4	37	2	91	18	4	20	.291	.331	.499
Lee, Travis, TB.*	145	613	542	75	149	249	37	3	19	70	1	6	0	64	4	97	6	2	13	.275	.348	.459
Leon, Jose, Bal.	21	59	54	6	13	14	1	0	0	0	0	0	2	3	0	18	0	0	1	.241	.305	.259
Lewis, Colby, Tex.	26	1	1	0	0	0	0	0	0	0	0	0	0	0	0	1	0	0	0	.000	.000	.000
Lidle, Cory, Tor.	31	6	6	1	2	2	0	0	0	0	0	0	0	0	0	0	0	0	0	.333	.333	.333
Liefer, Jeff, TB.*	9	28	25	4	3	7	1	0	1	3	0	0	0	3	1	13	0	0	0	.120	.214	.280
Lilly, Ted, Oak.*	32	5	5	0	0	0	0	0	0	0	0	0	0	0	0	1	0	0	0	.000	.000	.000
Lima, Jose, K.C.	14	3	2	1	1	1	0	0	0	0	1	0	0	0	0	0	0	0	0	.500	.500	.500
Loaiza, Esteban, Chi.	34	6	5	1	1	1	0	0	0	0	1	0	0	0	0	2	0	0	0	.200	.200	.200
Lohse, Kyle, Min.	33	6	3	0	1	1	0	0	0	0	3	0	0	0	0	1	0	0	0	.333	.333	.333
Lombard, George, TB.*	13	38	37	8	8	12	1	0	1	4	0	0	1	0	0	6	1	0	0	.216	.237	.324
Long, Terrence, Oak.*	140	522	486	64	119	187	22	2	14	61	0	2	3	31	4	67	4	1	9	.245	.293	.385
Lopez, Mendy, K.C.	52	100	94	13	26	42	5	1	3	11	2	0	0	4	0	28	2	0	3	.277	.306	.447
Lopez, Rodrigo, Bal.	26	2	2	0	0	0	0	0	0	0	0	0	0	0	0	2	0	0	0	.000	.000	.000
Lowe, Derek, Bos.	33	5	4	0	0	0	0	0	0	0	1	0	0	0	0	0	0	0	0	.000	.000	.000
Ludwick, Ryan, Tex.-Cle.	47	175	162	17	40	71	8	1	7	26	1	0	0	12	1	48	2	0	1	.247	.299	.438
Lugo, Julio, TB.	117	482	433	58	119	185	13	4	15	53	7	3	4	35	0	88	10	3	5	.275	.333	.427
Mabry, John, Sea.*	64	122	104	12	22	37	6	0	3	16	0	0	3	15	2	21	0	0	3	.212	.328	.356
Machado, Robert, Bal.	18	55	49	8	13	17	1	0	1	3	0	0	0	6	0	12	0	0	0	.265	.345	.347
Magruder, Chris, Cle.†	9	30	26	3	9	16	2	1	1	3	0	0	1	3	0	6	0	1	0	.346	.433	.615
Maroth, Mike, Det.*	33	4	2	0	1	1	0	0	0	0	1	0	0	1	0	0	0	0	0	.500	.667	.500
Martin, Al, TB.*	100	258	238	19	60	85	12	2	3	26	0	1	2	17	4	51	2	2	8	.252	.306	.357
Martinez, Edgar, Sea.	145	603	497	72	146	243	25	0	24	98	0	7	7	92	7	95	0	1	17	.294	.406	.489
Martinez, Pedro, Bos.	29	3	3	0	0	0	0	0	0	0	0	0	0	0	0	0	0	0	0	.000	.000	.000
Martinez, Victor, Cle.†	49	174	159	15	46	53	4	0	1	16	0	1	1	13	0	21	1	1	8	.289	.345	.333
Matos, Julius, K.C.	28	59	57	7	15	22	1	0	2	7	1	0	0	1	0	12	1	0	2	.263	.276	.386
Matos, Luis, Bal.	109	486	439	70	133	201	23	3	13	45	10	2	7	28	0	90	15	7	9	.303	.353	.458
Matsui, Hideki, N.Y.*	163	695	623	82	179	271	42	1	16	106	0	6	3	63	5	86	2	2	25	.287	.353	.435
Matthews Jr., Gary, Bal.†	41	172	162	21	33	53	12	1	2	20	0	0	1	9	0	29	0	3	4	.204	.250	.327
May, Darrell, K.C.*	35	5	4	0	0	0	0	0	0	0	1	0	0	0	0	2	0	0	0	.000	.000	.000
Mayne, Brent, K.C.*	113	414	372	39	91	128	17	1	6	36	4	3	3	32	5	59	0	2	10	.245	.307	.344
Mays, Joe, Min.†	31	5	3	0	1	1	0	0	0	0	1	0	0	1	0	1	0	0	0	.333	.500	.333
McCarty, Dave, Oak.-Bos.	24	57	53	6	18	26	5	0	1	8	0	1	0	3	0	14	0	0	0	.340	.368	.491
McDonald, John, Cle.	82	233	214	21	46	60	9	1	1	14	4	2	2	11	0	31	3	3	4	.215	.258	.280
McLemore, Mark, Sea.†	99	352	309	34	72	97	15	2	2	37	0	3	2	38	0	71	5	5	4	.233	.318	.314
McMillon, Billy, Oak.*	66	175	153	15	41	70	11	0	6	26	0	1	2	19	1	36	0	0	3	.268	.354	.458
Meche, Gil, Sea.	32	5	5	0	1	1	0	0	0	0	0	0	0	0	0	1	0	0	0	.200	.200	.200
Melhuse, Adam, Oak.†	40	86	77	13	23	45	7	0	5	14	0	0	0	9	0	19	0	0	2	.299	.372	.584
Mench, Kevin, Tex.	38	139	125	15	40	58	12	0	2	11	0	1	3	10	0	17	1	1	2	.320	.381	.464
Mendez, Carlos, Bal.	26	46	45	3	10	12	2	0	0	5	0	1	0	0	0	12	0	0	0	.222	.217	.267
Menechino, Frank, Oak.	43	109	83	10	16	22	0	0	2	9	2	1	4	19	1	16	0	0	2	.193	.364	.265
Merloni, Lou, Bos.	15	34	30	4	7	8	1	0	0	1	0	0	0	4	0	8	0	0	0	.233	.324	.267
Meyers, Chad, Sea.	9	1	1	1	0	0	0	0	0	0	0	0	0	0	0	0	1	0	0	.000	.000	.000
Mientkiewicz, Doug, Min.*	142	574	487	67	146	219	38	1	11	65	2	6	5	74	4	55	4	1	9	.300	.393	.450
Miles, Aaron, Chi.†	8	12	12	3	4	7	3	0	0	2	0	0	0	0	0	0	0	0	0	.333	.333	.583
Millar, Kevin, Bos.	148	618	544	83	150	257	30	1	25	96	0	9	5	60	5	108	3	2	14	.276	.348	.472
Mirabelli, Doug, Bos.	62	176	163	23	42	73	13	0	6	18	0	1	1	11	0	36	0	0	3	.258	.307	.448
Mohr, Dustan, Min.	121	387	348	50	87	139	22	0	10	36	2	3	1	33	0	106	5	2	10	.250	.314	.399
Molina, Bengie, Ana.	119	430	409	37	115	181	24	0	14	71	2	4	2	13	2	31	1	1	17	.281	.304	.443
Molina, Jose, Ana.	53	123	114	12	21	25	4	0	0	6	4	1	3	1	0	26	0	0	1	.184	.210	.219
Mondesi, Raul, N.Y.	98	403	361	56	93	170	23	3	16	49	0	2	2	38	6	66	17	7	6	.258	.330	.471
Monroe, Craig, Det.	128	458	425	51	102	191	18	1	23	70	1	3	2	27	2	89	4	2	10	.240	.287	.449
Mora, Melvin, Bal.	96	413	344	68	109	173	17	1	15	48	6	2	12	49	0	71	6	3	3	.317	.418	.503
Morban, Jose, Bal.†	61	77	71	14	10	16	0	0	2	5	2	0	1	3	0	21	8	0	0	.141	.187	.225
Morneau, Justin, Min.*	40	115	106	14	24	40	4	0	4	16	0	0	0	9	1	30	0	0	4	.226	.287	.377
Morris, Warren, Det.*	97	377	346	37	94	129	13	2	6	37	4	3	1	23	1	42	4	2	6	.272	.316	.373
Mounce, Tony, Tex.*	11	2	2	0	0	0	0	0	0	0	0	0	0	0	0	1	0	0	1	.000	.000	.000
Moyer, Jamie, Sea.*	33	6	5	1	2	2	0	0	0	0	1	0	0	0	0	1	0	0	0	.400	.400	.400
Mueller, Bill, Bos.†	146	600	524	85	171	283	45	5	19	85	4	6	7	59	2	77	1	4	11	.326	.398	.540
Mulder, Mark, Oak.*	26	6	4	0	0	0	0	0	0	1	1	1	0	0	0	3	0	0	1	.000	.000	.000
Mulholland, Terry, Cle.	45	1	1	0	0	0	0	0	0	0	0	0	0	0	0	1	0	0	0	.000	.000	.000
Munson, Eric, Det.*	99	357	313	28	75	138	9	0	18	50	1	7	1	35	1	61	3	0	4	.240	.312	.441
Mussina, Mike, N.Y.*	31	2	2	0	0	0	0	0	0	0	0	0	0	0	0	0	0	0	0	.000	.000	.000
Myers, Greg, Tor.*	121	369	329	51	101	165	19	0	15	52	0	3	0	37	2	57	0	3	14	.307	.374	.502
Nivar, Ramon, Tex.	28	97	90	9	19	24	1	2	0	7	2	0	1	4	0	10	4	2	1	.211	.253	.267
Nix, Laynce, Tex.*	53	195	184	25	47	81	10	0	8	30	1	1	0	9	0	53	3	0	1	.255	.289	.440
Nixon, Trot, Bos.*	134	513	441	81	135	255	24	6	28	87	1	3	3	65	4	96	4	2	3	.306	.396	.578
Olerud, John, Sea.*	152	634	539	64	145	210	35	0	10	83	2	3	6	84	7	67	0	1	20	.269	.372	.390
Olivo, Miguel, Chi.	114	346	317	37	75	114	19	1	6	27	4	2	4	19	0	80	6	4	3	.237	.287	.360
Ordonez, Magglio, Chi.	160	674	606	95	192	331	46	3	29	99	0	4	7	57	1	73	9	5	20	.317	.380	.546
Ordonez, Rey, TB.	34	124	117	14	37	57	11	0	3	22	2	2	1	2	0	12	0	2	3	.316	.328	.487
Ortiz, David, Bos.*	128	509	448	79	129	265	39	2	31	101	0	2	1	58	8	83	0	0	9	.288	.369	.592
Ortiz, Ramon, Ana.	32	6	5	1	0	0	0	0	0	0	1	0	0	0	0	2	0	0	0	.000	.000	.000
Owens, Eric, Ana.	111	257	241	29	65	74	6	0	1	20	4	1	1	10	0	24	11	8	4	.270	.300	.307

Player, Team	G	TPA	AB	R	H	TB	2B	3B	HR	RBI	SH	SF	HP	BB	IBB	SO	SB	CS	GDP	Avg.	OBP	Slg.
Palmeiro, Rafael, Tex.*	154	654	561	92	146	285	21	2	38	112	0	4	5	84	9	77	2	0	7	.260	.359	.508
Palmer, Dean, Det.	26	98	86	3	12	14	2	0	0	6	0	1	2	9	0	28	0	0	2	.140	.235	.163
Paquette, Craig, Det.	11	33	33	2	5	5	0	0	0	0	0	0	0	0	0	5	0	0	2	.152	.152	.152
Park, Chan Ho, Tex.	7	1	0	1	0	0	0	0	0	0	0	0	0	1	0	0	0	0	0	.000	1.000	.000
Parris, Steve, TB.	10	1	1	0	0	0	0	0	0	0	0	0	0	0	0	0	0	0	0	.000	.000	.000
Patterson, Jarrod, K.C.*	13	25	22	3	4	4	0	0	0	0	0	0	0	3	1	6	0	0	0	.182	.280	.182
Paul, Josh, Chi.	13	20	17	6	6	6	0	0	0	4	0	0	0	3	0	3	0	0	0	.353	.450	.353
Pena, Carlos, Det.*	131	516	452	51	112	199	21	6	18	50	1	4	6	53	1	123	4	5	6	.248	.332	.440
Peralta, Jhonny, Cle.	77	270	242	24	55	79	10	1	4	21	2	2	4	20	0	65	1	3	5	.227	.295	.326
Perez, Antonio, TB.	48	147	125	19	31	45	6	1	2	12	2	1	1	18	0	34	4	1	1	.248	.345	.360
Perry, Herbert, Tex.	11	24	24	1	4	5	1	0	0	2	0	0	0	0	0	3	0	0	0	.167	.167	.208
Person, Robert, Bos.	7	1	1	0	0	0	0	0	0	0	0	0	0	0	0	1	0	0	0	.000	.000	.000
Petrick, Ben, Det.	43	129	120	18	27	45	6	0	4	12	1	0	0	8	0	30	0	0	3	.225	.273	.375
Pettitte, Andy, N.Y.*	33	7	7	0	1	1	0	0	0	1	0	0	0	0	0	2	0	0	0	.143	.143	.143
Phelps, Josh, Tor.	119	453	396	57	106	186	18	1	20	66	0	1	17	39	3	115	1	2	12	.268	.358	.470
Phillips, Brandon, Cle.	112	393	370	36	77	115	18	1	6	33	5	1	3	14	0	77	4	5	12	.208	.242	.311
Piatt, Adam, Oak.-TB.	61	143	132	11	30	61	13	0	6	18	0	2	0	9	0	46	1	2	2	.227	.273	.462
Pierzynski, A.J., Min.*	137	533	487	63	152	226	35	3	11	74	2	5	15	24	12	55	3	1	13	.312	.360	.464
Pineiro, Joel, Sea.	32	5	4	1	0	0	0	0	0	0	1	0	0	0	0	3	0	0	0	.000	.000	.000
Ponson, Sidney, Bal.	21	5	5	0	0	0	0	0	0	0	0	0	0	0	0	0	0	0	0	.000	.000	.000
Posada, Jorge, N.Y.†	142	588	481	83	135	249	24	0	30	101	0	4	10	93	6	110	2	4	13	.281	.405	.518
Pride, Curtis, N.Y.*	4	12	12	1	1	4	0	0	1	1	0	0	0	0	0	2	0	0	1	.083	.083	.333
Prieto, Alex, Min.	8	11	11	1	1	1	0	0	0	0	0	0	0	0	0	4	0	0	0	.091	.091	.091
Prince, Tom, Min.-K.C.	32	57	48	5	10	18	2	0	2	6	2	0	2	5	0	7	1	0	2	.208	.309	.375
Quinlan, Robb, Ana.	38	101	94	13	27	35	4	2	0	4	1	0	0	6	0	16	1	2	3	.287	.330	.372
Radke, Brad, Min.	33	5	5	0	1	1	0	0	0	0	0	0	0	0	0	1	0	0	0	.200	.200	.200
Raines Jr., Tim, Bal.†	20	46	43	4	6	9	1	1	0	2	0	0	1	2	0	12	0	0	2	.140	.196	.209
Ramirez, Julio, Ana.	6	3	2	1	0	0	0	0	0	0	1	0	0	0	0	0	0	0	0	.000	.000	.000
Ramirez, Manny, Bos.	154	679	569	117	185	334	36	1	37	104	0	5	8	97	28	94	3	1	22	.325	.427	.587
Ramos, Mario, Tex.*	3	1	1	0	0	0	0	0	0	0	0	0	0	0	0	1	0	0	0	.000	.000	.000
Randa, Joe, K.C.	131	566	502	80	146	227	31	1	16	72	9	7	7	41	0	61	1	0	12	.291	.348	.452
Relaford, Desi, K.C.†	141	557	500	70	127	188	27	5	8	59	8	3	6	40	1	70	20	4	10	.254	.315	.376
Restovich, Michael, Min.	24	64	53	10	15	22	3	2	0	4	0	0	1	10	0	12	0	0	3	.283	.406	.415
Reyes, Carlos, TB.†	10	2	1	0	0	0	0	0	0	0	0	0	0	1	0	0	0	0	0	.000	.500	.000
Riggs, Adam, Ana.	24	72	61	11	15	30	4	1	3	5	2	0	0	9	0	9	3	1	2	.246	.343	.492
Rios, Armando, Chi.*	49	112	104	4	22	31	3	0	2	11	2	1	0	5	0	13	0	1	6	.212	.245	.298
Rivas, Luis, Min.	135	521	475	69	123	181	16	9	8	43	8	3	5	30	0	65	17	7	20	.259	.308	.381
Rivera, Juan, N.Y.	57	185	173	22	46	81	14	0	7	26	1	1	0	10	1	27	0	0	8	.266	.304	.468
Roberts, Brian, Bal.†	112	512	460	65	124	169	22	4	5	41	4	1	1	46	1	58	23	6	9	.270	.337	.367
Rodriguez, Alex, Tex.	161	715	607	124	181	364	30	6	47	118	0	6	15	87	10	126	17	3	16	.298	.396	.600
Rodriguez, Ricardo, Cle.	15	3	3	0	0	0	0	0	0	0	0	0	0	0	0	1	0	0	0	.000	.000	.000
Rogers, Kenny, Min.*	33	5	4	1	0	0	0	0	0	0	0	0	0	1	0	1	0	0	0	.000	.200	.000
Rolls, Damian, TB.	107	404	373	43	95	136	20	0	7	46	2	3	7	19	1	84	11	3	5	.255	.301	.365
Romero, J.C., Min.†	73	1	1	0	0	0	0	0	0	0	0	0	0	0	0	1	0	0	0	.000	.000	.000
Roney, Matt, Det.	45	2	2	0	1	1	0	0	0	0	0	0	0	0	0	1	0	0	0	.500	.500	.500
Ross, Cody, Det.	6	22	19	1	4	8	1	0	1	5	1	0	1	1	0	3	0	0	0	.211	.286	.421
Rowand, Aaron, Chi.	93	170	157	22	45	71	8	0	6	24	2	1	3	7	0	21	0	0	1	.287	.327	.452
Ryan, Michael, Min.*	27	68	61	13	24	46	7	0	5	13	0	1	0	6	0	12	2	1	4	.393	.441	.754
Sabathia, C.C., Cle.*	31	6	6	1	3	3	0	0	0	0	0	0	0	0	0	1	0	0	0	.500	.500	.500
Sadler, Donnie, Tex.	77	150	131	27	26	38	5	2	1	5	2	2	2	13	0	34	4	3	1	.198	.277	.290
Salmon, Tim, Ana.	148	621	528	78	145	245	35	4	19	72	0	6	10	77	3	93	3	1	12	.275	.374	.464
Sanchez, Alex, Det.*	101	423	394	43	114	140	13	5	1	22	7	3	1	18	0	46	44	18	4	.289	.320	.355
Sanchez, Freddy, Bos.	20	34	34	6	8	10	2	0	0	2	0	0	0	0	0	8	0	0	0	.235	.235	.294
Sanchez, Rey, Sea.	46	186	170	22	50	57	5	1	0	11	4	2	2	8	1	21	1	0	3	.294	.330	.335
Sandberg, Jared, TB.	55	156	136	15	29	59	10	1	6	23	2	0	2	16	1	52	0	0	3	.213	.305	.434
Santana, Johan, Min.*	45	3	3	0	1	1	0	0	0	0	0	0	0	0	0	1	0	0	0	.333	.333	.333
Santiago, Ramon, Det.†	141	507	444	41	100	126	18	1	2	29	18	2	10	33	0	66	10	4	9	.225	.292	.284
Santos, Angel, Cle.†	32	80	76	9	17	31	3	1	3	6	1	0	0	3	0	18	1	1	0	.224	.253	.408
Santos, Victor, Tex.	8	3	2	0	0	0	0	0	0	0	1	0	0	0	0	1	0	0	0	.000	.000	.000
Sears, Todd, Min.*	24	74	65	7	16	24	2	0	2	11	0	1	1	7	0	15	0	0	4	.246	.324	.369
Segui, David, Bal.†	67	252	224	26	59	86	10	1	5	25	0	1	1	26	2	47	1	0	8	.263	.341	.384
Seguignol, Fernando, N.Y.†	5	8	7	0	1	1	0	0	0	0	0	0	0	1	0	3	0	0	0	.143	.250	.143
Selby, Bill, Cle.*	27	44	39	3	4	5	1	0	0	5	1	1	0	3	0	11	0	0	0	.103	.163	.128
Sele, Aaron, Ana.	25	3	3	0	1	1	0	0	0	0	0	0	0	0	0	0	0	0	1	.333	.333	.333
Shumpert, Terry, TB.	59	99	84	14	16	31	5	2	2	7	2	1	2	10	0	17	1	0	0	.190	.289	.369
Sierra, Ruben, Tex.-N.Y.†	106	336	307	33	83	129	17	1	9	43	0	2	0	27	3	47	2	1	9	.270	.327	.420
Singleton, Chris, Oak.*	120	341	306	38	75	104	24	1	1	36	2	6	1	26	4	55	7	2	2	.245	.301	.340
Smith, Jason, TB.*	1	4	4	0	1	1	0	0	0	0	0	0	0	0	0	0	0	0	0	.250	.250	.250
Snyder, Kyle, K.C.†	15	2	2	0	0	0	0	0	0	0	0	0	0	0	0	1	0	0	0	.000	.000	.000
Sojo, Luis, N.Y.	3	4	4	0	0	0	0	0	0	0	0	0	0	0	0	0	0	0	0	.000	.000	.000
Sorensen, Zach, Cle.†	36	44	37	2	5	9	1	0	1	2	0	0	0	7	0	13	0	3	0	.135	.273	.243
Soriano, Alfonso, N.Y.	156	734	682	114	198	358	36	5	38	91	0	2	12	38	7	130	35	8	8	.290	.338	.525
Spencer, Shane, Cle.-Tex.	119	448	395	39	99	155	20	0	12	49	0	5	3	45	0	92	2	0	8	.251	.328	.392
Spiezio, Scott, Ana.†	158	581	521	69	138	236	36	7	16	83	2	7	5	46	8	66	6	3	12	.265	.326	.453
Standridge, Jason, TB.	8	1	0	0	0	0	0	0	0	0	0	0	0	1	0	0	0	1	0	.000	1.000	.000
Stewart, Shannon, Tor.-Min.	136	644	573	90	176	263	44	2	13	73	2	11	6	52	3	66	4	6	10	.307	.364	.459
Strong, Jamal, Sea.	12	2	2	2	0	0	0	0	0	0	0	0	0	0	0	0	0	0	0	.000	.000	.000
Suppan, Jeff, Bos.	11	3	2	0	0	0	0	0	0	0	1	0	0	0	0	1	0	0	0	.000	.000	.000
Surhoff, B.J., Bal.*	93	354	319	32	94	129	20	0	5	41	3	2	1	29	3	29	2	2	4	.295	.353	.404
Suzuki, Ichiro, Sea.*	159	725	679	111	212	296	29	8	13	62	3	1	6	36	7	69	34	8	3	.312	.352	.436
Swann, Pedro, Bal.*	8	15	14	3	3	7	1	0	1	2	0	0	0	1	0	4	0	0	1	.214	.267	.500
Sweeney, Mike, K.C.	108	463	392	62	115	183	18	1	16	83	0	5	2	64	5	56	3	2	13	.293	.391	.467

Player, Team	G	TPA	AB	R	H	TB	2B	3B	HR	RBI	SH	SF	HP	BB	IBB	SO	SB	CS	GDP	Avg.	OBP	Slg.
Tallet, Brian, Cle.*	5	2	2	0	0	0	0	0	0	0	0	0	0	0	0	1	0	0	0	.000	.000	.000
Tam, Jeff, Tor.	44	1	1	0	1	2	1	0	0	1	0	0	0	0	0	0	0	0	0	1.000	1.000	2.000
Teixeira, Mark, Tex.†	146	589	529	66	137	254	29	5	26	84	0	2	14	44	5	120	1	2	14	.259	.331	.480
Tejada, Miguel, Oak.	162	703	636	98	177	300	42	0	27	106	0	8	6	53	7	65	10	0	12	.278	.336	.472
Thames, Marcus, Tex.	30	84	73	12	15	20	2	0	1	4	0	1	2	8	0	18	0	1	2	.205	.298	.274
Thomas, Frank, Chi.	153	662	546	87	146	307	35	0	42	105	0	4	12	100	4	115	0	0	11	.267	.390	.562
Thomson, John, Tex.	35	1	1	0	0	0	0	0	0	0	0	0	0	0	0	0	0	0	0	.000	.000	.000
Torres, Andres, Det.†	59	185	168	23	37	50	4	3	1	9	6	1	0	10	0	35	5	5	5	.220	.263	.298
Towers, Josh, Tor.	14	1	1	0	0	0	0	0	0	0	0	0	0	0	0	0	0	0	0	.000	.000	.000
Traber, Billy, Cle.*	33	4	4	0	0	0	0	0	0	0	0	0	0	0	0	2	0	0	0	.000	.000	.000
Trammell, Bubba, N.Y.	22	61	55	4	11	16	5	0	0	5	0	0	0	6	0	10	0	0	1	.200	.279	.291
Truby, Chris, TB.	13	49	43	4	12	15	3	0	0	3	1	0	0	5	0	13	0	0	1	.279	.354	.349
Tucker, Michael, K.C.*	104	438	389	61	102	171	20	5	13	55	6	2	2	39	3	88	8	10	8	.262	.331	.440
Tyner, Jason, TB.*	46	102	90	12	25	32	7	0	0	6	2	0	0	10	0	12	2	1	1	.278	.350	.356
Ugueto, Luis, Sea.†	12	6	5	4	1	1	0	0	0	1	0	0	0	1	0	0	2	0	0	.200	.333	.200
Valdes, Ismael, Tex.	22	6	4	0	0	0	0	0	0	0	2	0	0	0	0	0	0	0	0	.000	.000	.000
Valentin, Javier, TB.†	49	142	135	13	30	48	7	1	3	15	0	1	1	5	0	31	0	0	7	.222	.254	.356
Valentin, Jose, Chi.†	144	569	503	79	119	233	26	2	28	74	7	2	3	54	4	114	8	3	6	.237	.313	.463
Varitek, Jason, Bos.†	142	521	451	63	123	231	31	1	25	85	5	7	7	51	8	106	3	2	10	.273	.351	.512
Ventura, Robin, N.Y.*	89	326	283	31	71	111	13	0	9	42	3	0	0	40	2	62	0	0	8	.251	.344	.392
Vizquel, Omar, Cle.†	64	285	250	43	61	84	13	2	2	19	5	1	0	29	0	20	8	3	11	.244	.321	.336
Voyles, Brad, K.C.	11	1	1	0	0	0	0	0	0	0	0	0	0	0	0	1	0	0	0	.000	.000	.000
Wakefield, Tim, Bos.	35	1	0	0	0	0	0	0	0	0	0	0	1	0	0	0	0	0	0	.000	1.000	.000
Walbeck, Matt, Det.†	59	144	138	11	24	33	4	1	1	6	2	0	1	3	0	26	0	1	3	.174	.197	.239
Walker, Todd, Bos.*	144	647	587	92	166	251	38	4	13	85	1	10	1	48	0	54	1	1	17	.283	.333	.428
Washburn, Jarrod, Ana.*	32	5	5	0	1	1	0	0	0	0	0	0	0	0	0	1	0	0	0	.200	.200	.200
Wells, David, N.Y.*	31	6	6	0	1	2	1	0	0	0	0	0	0	0	0	1	0	0	0	.167	.167	.333
Wells, Vernon, Tor.	161	735	678	118	215	373	49	5	33	117	0	8	7	42	2	80	4	1	21	.317	.359	.550
Werth, Jayson, Tor.	26	51	48	7	10	20	4	0	2	10	0	0	0	3	0	22	1	0	0	.208	.255	.417
Wesson, Barry, Ana.	10	11	11	2	2	5	0	0	1	3	0	0	0	0	0	4	1	0	0	.182	.182	.455
Westbrook, Jake, Cle.	34	1	0	0	0	0	0	0	0	0	0	0	0	1	0	0	0	0	0	.000	1.000	.000
White, Rondell, K.C.	22	85	75	13	26	46	6	1	4	21	0	2	2	6	0	8	0	0	2	.347	.400	.613
Williams, Bernie, N.Y.†	119	521	445	77	117	183	19	1	15	64	0	2	3	71	8	61	5	0	21	.263	.367	.411
Wilson, Dan, Sea.	96	337	316	32	76	107	15	2	4	43	3	3	0	15	0	52	0	0	8	.241	.272	.339
Wilson, Enrique, N.Y.†	63	147	135	18	31	49	9	0	3	15	2	1	2	7	0	14	3	1	3	.230	.276	.363
Wilson, Tom, Tor.	96	287	256	37	66	100	19	0	5	35	0	2	1	28	0	80	0	0	4	.258	.331	.391
Winn, Randy, Sea.†	157	660	600	103	177	255	37	4	11	75	6	5	8	41	0	108	23	5	9	.295	.346	.425
Witt, Kevin, Det.*	93	289	270	25	71	110	9	0	10	26	0	3	1	15	0	68	1	1	5	.263	.301	.407
Woodward, Chris, Tor.	104	386	349	49	91	138	22	2	7	45	0	6	3	28	0	72	1	2	6	.261	.316	.395
Wooten, Shawn, Ana.	98	300	272	25	66	95	8	0	7	32	0	3	1	24	5	45	0	4	7	.243	.303	.349
Wright, Dan, Chi.	20	2	2	0	0	0	0	0	0	0	0	0	0	0	0	0	0	0	0	.000	.000	.000
Young, Dmitri, Det.†	155	635	562	78	167	302	34	7	29	85	0	4	11	58	16	130	2	1	16	.297	.372	.537
Young, Ernie, Det.	5	15	11	0	2	2	0	0	0	0	0	0	0	4	0	5	0	2	1	.182	.400	.182
Young, Michael, Tex.	160	713	666	106	204	297	33	9	14	72	3	7	1	36	1	103	13	2	14	.306	.339	.446
Zambrano, Victor, TB.	34	5	3	0	0	0	0	0	0	0	2	0	0	0	0	2	0	0	0	.000	.000	.000
Zeile, Todd, N.Y.	66	214	186	29	39	65	8	0	6	23	0	4	0	24	0	36	0	0	3	.210	.294	.349
Zito, Barry, Oak.*	35	6	6	0	0	0	0	0	0	0	0	0	0	0	0	1	0	0	0	.000	.000	.000

PLAYERS WITH TWO OR MORE TEAMS

Player, Team	G	TPA	AB	R	H	TB	2B	3B	HR	RBI	SH	SF	HP	BB	IBB	SO	SB	CS	GDP	Avg.	OBP	Slg.
Abernathy, Brent, TB.	2	7	7	1	0	0	0	0	0	0	0	0	0	0	0	0	1	0	0	.000	.000	.000
Abernathy, Brent, K.C.	10	30	27	2	2	2	0	0	0	0	2	0	0	1	0	3	0	0	2	.074	.107	.074
Anderson, Brian, Cle.	27	2	1	0	0	0	0	0	0	0	0	0	0	1	0	0	0	0	0	.000	.500	.000
Anderson, Brian, K.C.	7	0	0	0	0	0	0	0	0	0	0	0	0	0	0	0	0	0	0	...	...	...
Appier, Kevin, Ana.	19	5	5	0	0	0	0	0	0	0	0	0	0	0	0	4	0	0	0	.000	.000	.000
Appier, Kevin, K.C.	4	0	0	0	0	0	0	0	0	0	0	0	0	0	0	0	0	0	0	...	...	...
Davis, Doug, Tex.	1	0	0	0	0	0	0	0	0	0	0	0	0	0	0	0	0	0	0	...	...	...
Davis, Doug, Tor.	12	1	1	0	0	0	0	0	0	0	0	0	0	0	0	1	0	0	0	.000	.000	.000
Everett, Carl, Tex.†	74	313	270	53	74	147	13	3	18	51	4	3	5	31	2	48	4	1	2	.274	.356	.544
Everett, Carl, Chi.†	73	289	256	40	77	121	14	0	10	41	0	1	10	22	4	36	4	3	5	.301	.377	.473
Garcia, Karim, Cle.*	24	101	93	8	18	34	1	0	5	14	0	2	1	5	1	20	0	0	4	.194	.238	.366
Garcia, Karim, N.Y.*	52	161	151	17	46	69	5	0	6	21	0	1	0	9	1	32	0	2	4	.305	.342	.457
Kielty, Bobby, Min.†	75	284	238	40	60	100	13	0	9	32	0	1	3	42	2	56	6	2	5	.252	.370	.420
Kielty, Bobby, Tor.†	62	225	189	31	44	71	13	1	4	25	0	3	4	29	4	36	2	1	6	.233	.342	.376
Ludwick, Ryan, Tex.	8	30	26	3	4	5	1	0	0	0	0	0	0	4	0	9	0	0	0	.154	.267	.192
Ludwick, Ryan, Cle.	39	145	136	14	36	66	7	1	7	26	1	0	0	8	1	39	2	0	1	.265	.306	.485
McCarty, Dave, Oak.	8	28	26	2	7	9	2	0	0	2	0	1	0	1	0	7	0	0	0	.269	.286	.346
McCarty, Dave, Bos.	16	29	27	4	11	17	3	0	1	6	0	0	0	2	0	7	0	0	0	.407	.448	.630
Piatt, Adam, Oak.	47	107	100	6	24	46	10	0	4	15	0	1	0	6	0	30	1	2	2	.240	.280	.460
Piatt, Adam, TB.	14	36	32	5	6	15	3	0	2	3	0	1	0	3	0	16	0	0	0	.188	.250	.469
Prince, Tom, Min.	24	49	40	5	8	16	2	0	2	5	2	0	2	5	0	7	1	0	0	.200	.319	.400
Prince, Tom, K.C.	8	8	8	0	2	2	0	0	0	1	0	0	0	0	0	0	0	0	2	.250	.250	.250
Sierra, Ruben, Tex.†	43	147	133	14	35	53	9	0	3	12	0	0	0	14	1	27	1	1	2	.263	.333	.398
Sierra, Ruben, N.Y.†	63	189	174	19	48	76	8	1	6	31	0	2	0	13	2	20	1	0	7	.276	.323	.437
Spencer, Shane, Cle.	64	232	210	23	57	91	10	0	8	26	0	3	1	18	0	52	2	0	6	.271	.328	.433
Spencer, Shane, Tex.	55	216	185	16	42	64	10	0	4	23	0	2	2	27	0	40	0	0	2	.227	.329	.346
Stewart, Shannon, Tor.	71	340	303	47	89	136	22	2	7	35	0	8	2	27	2	30	1	2	6	.294	.347	.449
Stewart, Shannon, Min.	65	304	270	43	87	127	22	0	6	38	2	3	4	25	1	36	3	4	4	.322	.384	.470

AWARDED FIRST BASE ON OBSTRUCTION OR CATCHER'S INTERFERENCE: Bard, Cleveland (Bennett); Boone, New York (Wilson, Diaz); Byrnes, Oakland (Diaz); Guillen, Oakland (Wilson); Higginson, Detroit (Olivo).

DESIGNATED HITTING

TEAM

Team	G	TPA	AB	R	H	TB	2B	3B	HR	RBI	SH	SF	HP	BB	IBB	SO	SB	CS	GDP	Avg.	OBP	Slg.
Seattle	153	673	553	93	161	263	30	0	24	107	0	7	9	104	8	108	5	1	17	.291	.407	.476
Minnesota	153	664	600	83	164	261	40	0	19	96	0	1	6	57	5	146	6	0	18	.273	.342	.435
Detroit	153	645	575	68	157	256	23	5	22	69	0	4	8	58	8	144	6	4	15	.273	.346	.445
Boston	153	678	574	109	155	307	37	2	37	117	1	6	6	91	11	120	4	3	12	.270	.372	.535
Kansas City	153	664	590	86	158	238	28	2	16	85	4	3	6	61	6	109	4	3	19	.268	.341	.403
Cleveland	153	662	579	88	155	262	33	4	22	88	3	2	7	71	7	132	12	6	10	.268	.354	.453
Toronto	153	668	589	88	155	265	30	1	26	85	0	3	15	61	5	146	1	6	19	.263	.346	.450
Anaheim	153	649	574	65	147	239	30	1	20	86	1	4	4	66	5	99	6	6	14	.256	.335	.416
Chicago	153	674	566	86	143	276	31	0	34	91	0	5	11	92	4	108	0	2	13	.253	.365	.488
Texas	153	667	590	86	149	280	28	2	33	101	0	2	5	70	8	105	3	1	11	.253	.336	.475
Baltimore	154	652	583	67	144	220	30	2	14	61	5	1	3	60	5	116	3	1	14	.247	.320	.377
Tampa Bay	153	659	588	67	144	227	32	3	15	67	1	4	10	56	8	126	2	3	16	.245	.319	.386
Oakland	153	662	565	89	135	229	31	0	21	74	0	5	3	89	8	117	1	1	10	.239	.343	.405
New York	154	682	568	77	135	232	23	1	24	86	3	5	14	92	2	119	2	2	17	.238	.355	.408
Totals	2517	9299	8094	1152	2102	3555	426	23	327	1213	18	52	107	1028	90	1695	55	39	205	.260	.349	.439

TOP DESIGNATED HITTERS

Minimum 100 at-bats. *Lefthanded batter. †Switch-hitter.

Player, Team	G	TPA	AB	R	H	TB	2B	3B	HR	RBI	SH	SF	HP	BB	IBB	SO	SB	CS	GDP	Avg.	OBP	Slg.
Young, Dmitri, Det.†	75	316	282	39	93	153	17	5	11	40	0	1	6	27	6	64	1	1	9	.330	.399	.543
Huff, Aubrey, TB.*	33	147	136	17	43	75	9	1	7	19	0	0	0	11	3	12	0	0	4	.316	.367	.551
Ortiz, David, Bos.*	74	314	277	60	86	194	23	2	27	73	0	1	1	35	6	46	0	0	6	.310	.389	.700
Jones, Jacque, Min.*	29	119	110	16	34	55	9	0	4	23	0	1	0	8	2	19	3	0	5	.309	.353	.500
Witt, Kevin, Det.*	36	137	124	15	38	62	3	0	7	15	0	2	0	11	0	29	0	1	1	.306	.358	.500
Martinez, Edgar, Sea.	140	598	492	72	145	242	25	0	24	98	0	7	7	92	7	93	0	1	17	.295	.408	.492
Surhoff, B.J., Bal.*	39	159	143	16	41	60	7	0	4	17	1	0	0	15	3	19	0	1	1	.287	.354	.420
Johnson, Nick, N.Y.*	34	138	109	19	31	49	6	0	4	17	3	0	3	23	0	21	1	1	5	.284	.422	.450
Fullmer, Brad, Ana.*	41	159	141	19	39	63	6	0	6	26	0	1	1	16	1	24	2	3	3	.277	.352	.447
Sweeney, Mike, K.C.	62	270	239	32	65	92	7	1	6	41	0	3	1	27	3	37	2	0	8	.272	.344	.385
Gonzalez, Juan, Tex.	24	109	103	16	28	61	9	0	8	20	0	0	1	5	1	24	0	0	5	.272	.312	.592
Hafner, Travis, Cle.*	43	167	149	21	40	78	11	3	7	23	0	1	3	14	2	45	1	0	2	.268	.341	.523
Phelps, Josh, Tor.	107	421	370	52	99	173	18	1	18	58	0	1	15	35	3	107	1	2	11	.268	.354	.468
LeCroy, Matthew, Min.	64	238	220	24	58	97	12	0	9	35	0	0	4	14	1	63	0	0	5	.264	.319	.441
Burks, Ellis, Cle.	51	218	190	26	50	81	11	1	6	27	0	0	2	26	2	45	1	1	2	.263	.358	.426

ALL DESIGNATED HITTERS

*Lefthanded batter. †Switch-hitter.

Player, Team	G	TPA	AB	R	H	TB	2B	3B	HR	RBI	SH	SF	HP	BB	IBB	SO	SB	CS	GDP	Avg.	OBP	Slg.
Anderson, Garret, Ana.*	15	65	61	7	22	37	3	0	4	17	0	0	0	4	1	7	2	0	3	.361	.400	.607
Anderson, Marlon, TB.*	4	15	13	0	4	5	1	0	0	2	0	0	1	1	0	2	0	1	0	.308	.400	.385
Baldelli, Rocco, TB.	2	9	8	2	2	3	1	0	0	0	0	0	0	1	0	1	0	1	0	.250	.333	.375
Bard, Josh, Cle.†	1	1	0	0	0	0	0	0	0	0	0	0	0	1	0	0	0	0	0	.000	1.000	.000
Batista, Tony, Bal.	7	29	27	1	3	3	0	0	0	0	0	0	0	2	0	6	0	0	3	.111	.172	.111
Beltran, Carlos, K.C.†	8	36	31	5	9	12	0	0	1	3	0	0	0	5	0	3	0	2	3	.290	.389	.387
Berg, Dave, Tor.	7	5	4	2	2	5	0	0	1	1	0	0	0	1	0	1	0	0	0	.500	.600	1.250
Berger, Brandon, K.C.	1	4	2	0	0	0	0	0	0	0	1	0	0	1	0	0	0	0	0	.000	.333	.000
Bloomquist, Willie, Sea.	12	1	1	3	0	0	0	0	0	0	0	0	0	0	0	0	1	0	0	.000	.000	.000
Bordick, Mike, Tor.	1	1	1	0	0	0	0	0	0	0	0	0	0	0	0	1	0	0	0	.000	.000	.000
Bradley, Milton, Cle.†	8	35	27	6	11	20	3	0	2	4	0	0	1	7	1	6	3	2	1	.407	.543	.741
Brown, Dee, K.C.*	11	35	32	4	7	7	0	0	0	4	0	0	0	3	0	11	0	0	0	.219	.286	.219
Burke, Jamie, Chi.	1	1	1	0	0	0	0	0	0	0	0	0	0	0	0	0	0	0	0	.000	.000	.000
Burkhart, Morgan, K.C.†	2	8	8	0	0	0	0	0	0	0	0	0	0	0	0	2	0	0	0	.000	.000	.000
Burks, Ellis, Cle.	51	218	190	26	50	81	11	1	6	27	0	0	2	26	2	45	1	1	2	.263	.358	.426
Byrnes, Eric, Oak.	2	2	2	0	0	0	0	0	0	0	0	0	0	0	0	1	0	0	0	.000	.000	.000
Catalanotto, Frank, Tor.*	21	86	82	11	20	29	6	0	1	6	0	0	0	4	0	13	0	1	2	.244	.279	.354
Clark, Howie, Tor.*	7	11	11	1	2	2	0	0	0	1	0	0	0	0	0	1	0	1	0	.182	.182	.182
Clark, Jermaine, Tex.*	2	0	0	0	0	0	0	0	0	0	0	0	0	0	0	0	1	0	0	.000	.000	.000
Colbrunn, Greg, Sea.	4	12	10	1	2	2	0	0	0	0	0	0	0	2	0	3	0	0	0	.200	.333	.200
Cordova, Marty, Bal.	5	22	19	3	4	8	1	0	1	4	0	0	0	3	0	4	0	0	1	.211	.318	.421
Crawford, Carl, TB.*	1	4	4	0	0	0	0	0	0	0	0	0	0	0	0	2	0	0	0	.000	.000	.000
Crisp, Coco, Cle.†	7	31	27	3	5	6	1	0	0	2	1	0	0	3	0	4	2	1	0	.185	.267	.222
Crosby, Bobby, Oak.	2	6	5	0	0	0	0	0	0	0	0	0	0	1	0	2	0	0	0	.000	.167	.000
Cruz, Deivi, Bal.	5	18	14	2	1	1	0	0	0	0	2	0	0	2	0	2	0	0	0	.071	.188	.071
Cuddyer, Michael, Min.	2	5	4	0	0	0	0	0	0	0	0	0	0	1	0	0	0	0	0	.000	.200	.000
Cust, Jack, Bal.*	23	79	69	7	17	35	6	0	4	11	0	0	1	9	0	24	0	0	0	.246	.342	.507
Damon, Johnny, Bos.*	1	2	0	0	0	0	0	0	0	0	0	0	1	1	1	0	0	0	0	.000	1.000	.000
Daubach, Brian, Chi.*	15	41	35	7	11	14	3	0	0	2	0	0	0	6	0	8	0	0	0	.314	.415	.400
DaVanon, Jeff, Ana.†	1	1	0	0	0	0	0	0	0	0	0	0	0	1	0	0	0	0	0	.000	1.000	.000
Davis, Ben, Sea.†	1	1	1	0	0	0	0	0	0	0	0	0	0	0	0	1	0	0	0	.000	.000	.000
Delgado, Carlos, Tor.*	14	60	46	10	14	24	4	0	2	9	0	1	0	13	2	8	0	0	1	.304	.450	.522
Dellucci, David, N.Y.*	2	2	1	1	0	0	0	0	0	0	0	0	0	1	0	0	0	0	0	.000	.500	.000
Diaz, Matt, TB.	2	4	4	1	1	1	0	0	0	0	0	0	0	0	0	1	0	0	0	.250	.250	.250
DiFelice, Mike, K.C.	2	2	2	2	2	5	0	0	1	1	0	0	0	0	0	0	0	0	0	1.000	1.000	2.500
Durazo, Erubiel, Oak.*	121	506	424	77	107	183	25	0	17	56	0	4	1	77	8	82	1	1	7	.252	.366	.432

Player, Team	G	TPA	AB	R	H	TB	2B	3B	HR	RBI	SH	SF	HP	BB	IBB	SO	SB	CS	GDP	Avg.	OBP	Slg.
Durrington, Trent, Ana.	2	0	0	0	0	0	0	0	0	0	0	0	0	0	0	0	0	1	0	.000	.000	.000
Dye, Jermaine, Oak.	3	12	10	2	1	1	0	0	0	1	0	1	0	1	0	0	0	0	0	.100	.167	.100
Easley, Damion, TB.	8	14	14	1	2	4	0	1	0	1	0	0	0	0	0	4	0	0	0	.143	.143	.286
Eckstein, David, Ana.	3	12	11	0	2	2	0	0	0	0	0	0	0	1	0	1	2	0	0	.182	.250	.182
Edwards, Mike, Oak.	2	4	2	0	1	1	0	0	0	0	0	0	0	2	0	0	0	0	0	.500	.750	.500
Everett, Carl, Tex.-Chi.†	4	17	14	1	6	7	1	0	0	0	0	0	1	2	0	2	0	2	0	.429	.529	.500
Febles, Carlos, K.C.	4	1	1	2	1	1	0	0	0	0	0	0	0	0	0	0	0	0	0	1.000	1.000	1.000
Figgins, Chone, Ana.†	3	4	4	0	0	0	0	0	0	0	0	0	0	0	0	1	0	1	0	.000	.000	.000
Ford, Lew, Min.	4	1	1	1	0	0	0	0	0	0	0	0	0	0	0	0	1	0	0	.000	.000	.000
Fullmer, Brad, Ana.*	41	159	141	19	39	63	6	0	6	26	0	1	1	16	1	24	2	3	3	.277	.352	.447
Gant, Ron, Oak.	6	20	20	2	2	5	0	0	1	1	0	0	0	0	0	6	0	0	0	.100	.100	.250
Garcia, Karim, Cle.*	1	5	4	0	1	1	0	0	0	1	0	0	0	1	1	1	0	0	0	.250	.400	.250
Gerut, Jody, Cle.*	11	46	43	6	14	20	3	0	1	12	1	0	0	2	0	6	0	0	0	.326	.356	.465
Giambi, Jason, N.Y.*	69	305	241	36	53	109	8	0	16	41	0	2	11	51	1	60	1	1	3	.220	.377	.452
Giambi, Jeremy, Bos.*	30	115	90	10	15	24	3	0	2	11	1	0	2	22	0	29	1	0	1	.167	.342	.267
Gibbons, Jay, Bal.*	5	17	16	3	4	8	1	0	1	1	0	0	0	1	0	3	0	0	0	.250	.294	.500
Gil, Benji, Ana.	2	1	1	1	0	0	0	0	0	0	0	0	0	0	0	0	0	0	0	.000	.000	.000
Gipson, Charles, N.Y.	3	0	0	1	0	0	0	0	0	0	0	0	0	0	0	0	0	0	0	.000	.000	.000
Glaus, Troy, Ana.	4	16	14	3	4	8	1	0	1	4	0	0	0	2	0	3	0	0	1	.286	.375	.571
Gomes, Jonny, TB.	8	16	15	1	2	3	1	0	0	0	0	0	1	0	0	6	0	0	0	.133	.188	.200
Gonzalez, Juan, Tex.	24	109	103	16	28	61	9	0	8	20	0	0	1	5	1	24	0	0	5	.272	.312	.592
Grabowski, Jason, Oak.*	1	2	1	0	0	0	0	0	0	0	0	0	0	1	0	0	0	0	0	.000	.500	.000
Graffanino, Tony, Chi.	3	2	2	2	0	0	0	0	0	0	0	0	0	0	0	0	0	0	0	.000	.000	.000
Greene, Todd, Tex.	3	9	8	2	2	3	1	0	0	0	0	0	1	0	0	2	0	0	0	.250	.333	.375
Grieve, Ben, TB.*	37	157	128	20	29	43	5	0	3	14	0	1	4	24	1	30	0	0	2	.227	.363	.336
Guiel, Aaron, K.C.*	2	10	8	4	4	11	1	0	2	2	0	0	2	0	0	0	0	0	0	.500	.600	1.375
Guillen, Carlos, Sea.†	1	5	2	3	1	1	0	0	0	0	0	0	0	3	0	1	0	0	0	.500	.800	.500
Guillen, Jose, Oak.	1	1	1	0	0	0	0	0	0	0	0	0	0	0	0	0	0	0	1	.000	.000	.000
Hafner, Travis, Cle.*	43	167	149	21	40	78	11	3	7	23	0	1	3	14	2	45	1	0	2	.268	.341	.523
Hairston Jr., Jerry, Bal.	9	36	33	2	7	9	2	0	0	2	2	0	0	1	0	4	0	0	2	.212	.235	.273
Halter, Shane, Det.	4	14	14	2	2	5	0	0	1	3	0	0	0	0	0	4	0	0	0	.143	.143	.357
Harvey, Ken, K.C.	32	132	123	13	28	45	11	0	2	15	0	0	2	7	1	31	0	0	4	.228	.280	.366
Haselman, Bill, Bos.	2	3	3	0	0	0	0	0	0	0	0	0	0	0	0	1	0	0	0	.000	.000	.000
Hatteberg, Scott, Oak.*	15	58	53	2	12	17	5	0	0	3	0	0	1	4	0	7	0	0	1	.226	.293	.321
Higginson, Bobby, Det.*	8	33	26	4	4	7	0	0	1	3	0	1	0	6	1	8	2	0	0	.154	.303	.269
Hillenbrand, Shea, Bos.	2	6	6	2	3	7	1	0	1	4	0	0	0	0	0	0	0	0	0	.500	.500	1.167
Hocking, Denny, Min.†	2	2	1	0	0	0	0	0	0	0	0	0	0	1	0	0	0	0	0	.000	.500	.000
Huff, Aubrey, TB.*	33	147	136	17	43	75	9	1	7	19	0	0	0	11	3	12	0	0	4	.316	.367	.551
Hunter, Torii, Min.	3	12	10	0	3	5	2	0	0	1	0	0	0	2	0	2	0	0	0	.300	.417	.500
Ibanez, Raul, K.C.*	12	51	48	7	17	25	3	1	1	7	0	0	0	3	1	7	0	0	1	.354	.392	.521
Jackson, Damian, Bos.	9	2	2	5	0	0	0	0	0	0	0	0	0	0	0	2	2	2	0	.000	.000	.000
Johnson, Nick, N.Y.*	34	138	109	19	31	49	6	0	4	17	3	0	3	23	0	21	1	1	5	.284	.422	.450
Johnson, Rontrez, K.C.	2	1	1	3	1	1	0	0	0	0	0	0	0	0	0	0	0	0	0	1.000	1.000	1.000
Jones, Jacque, Min.*	29	119	110	16	34	55	9	0	4	23	0	1	0	8	2	19	3	0	5	.309	.353	.500
Jones, Jason, Tex.†	6	19	15	3	4	5	1	0	0	0	0	0	0	4	0	2	0	0	0	.267	.421	.333
Kennedy, Adam, Ana.*	1	1	0	0	0	0	0	0	0	0	0	0	0	1	0	0	0	0	0	.000	1.000	.000
Kielty, Bobby, Min.†	32	128	106	22	26	44	6	0	4	16	0	0	1	21	1	29	2	0	4	.245	.375	.415
Kingsale, Gene, Det.†	4	8	8	1	0	0	0	0	0	0	0	0	0	0	0	1	0	0	1	.000	.000	.000
Konerko, Paul, Chi.	14	45	39	2	5	5	0	0	0	2	0	1	0	5	0	5	0	0	3	.128	.222	.128
LaForest, Pete, TB.*	12	37	36	0	6	7	1	0	0	1	0	0	1	0	0	12	0	0	1	.167	.189	.194
Laker, Tim, Cle.	2	4	3	0	0	0	0	0	0	0	0	0	0	1	0	3	0	1	0	.000	.250	.000
Lamb, Mike, Tex.*	6	21	19	1	2	2	0	0	0	1	0	1	0	1	0	2	0	0	1	.105	.143	.105
Lawton, Matt, Cle.*	21	96	84	14	21	33	3	0	3	13	0	0	1	11	0	7	5	1	3	.250	.344	.393
LeCroy, Matthew, Min.	64	238	220	24	58	97	12	0	9	35	0	0	4	14	1	63	0	0	5	.264	.319	.441
Lee, Carlos, Chi.	1	3	3	1	2	2	0	0	0	2	0	0	0	0	0	0	0	0	0	.667	.667	.667
Lee, Travis, TB.*	2	8	7	2	2	6	1	0	1	2	0	1	0	0	0	1	0	0	1	.286	.250	.857
Leon, Jose, Bal.	3	6	4	0	1	1	0	0	0	0	0	0	0	2	0	3	0	0	0	.250	.500	.250
Liefer, Jeff, TB.*	2	9	8	2	1	2	1	0	0	0	0	0	0	1	1	4	0	0	0	.125	.222	.250
Long, Terrence, Oak.*	1	5	5	1	1	1	0	0	0	1	0	0	0	0	0	3	0	0	0	.200	.200	.200
Ludwick, Ryan, Cle.	4	12	10	0	0	0	0	0	0	0	1	0	0	1	1	6	0	0	0	.000	.091	.000
Mabry, John, Sea.*	12	34	28	3	7	10	3	0	0	5	0	0	1	5	1	7	0	0	0	.250	.382	.357
Martin, Al, TB.*	57	190	175	14	45	66	10	1	3	20	0	1	2	12	3	40	2	1	7	.257	.311	.377
Martinez, Edgar, Sea.	140	598	492	72	145	242	25	0	24	98	0	7	7	92	7	93	0	1	17	.295	.408	.492
Martinez, Victor, Cle.†	5	15	13	5	4	4	0	0	0	0	0	0	0	2	0	0	0	0	1	.308	.400	.308
Matos, Julius, K.C.	1	1	1	0	0	0	0	0	0	0	0	0	0	0	0	0	0	0	0	.000	.000	.000
Matos, Luis, Bal.	2	10	10	0	2	3	1	0	0	1	0	0	0	0	0	1	0	0	1	.200	.200	.300
Matsui, Hideki, N.Y.*	4	8	8	0	2	3	1	0	0	0	0	0	0	0	0	2	0	0	1	.250	.250	.375
Matthews Jr., Gary, Bal.†	1	4	4	1	2	4	2	0	0	2	0	0	0	0	0	0	0	0	0	.500	.500	1.000
McCarty, Dave, Bos.	1	1	1	0	0	0	0	0	0	0	0	0	0	0	0	0	0	0	0	.000	.000	.000
McLemore, Mark, Sea.†	11	21	18	7	6	8	2	0	0	4	0	0	1	2	0	3	2	0	0	.333	.429	.444
McMillon, Billy, Oak.*	9	39	35	5	11	21	1	0	3	12	0	0	1	3	0	12	0	0	0	.314	.385	.600
Mendez, Carlos, Bal.	8	23	22	3	4	5	1	0	0	2	0	1	0	0	0	4	0	0	0	.182	.174	.227
Menechino, Frank, Oak.	1	1	1	0	0	0	0	0	0	0	0	0	0	0	0	0	0	0	0	.000	.000	.000
Meyers, Chad, Sea.	6	0	0	1	0	0	0	0	0	0	0	0	0	0	0	0	1	0	0	.000	.000	.000
Mientkiewicz, Doug, Min.*	1	0	0	1	0	0	0	0	0	0	0	0	0	0	0	0	0	0	0	.000	.000	.000
Miles, Aaron, Chi.†	2	3	3	1	1	2	1	0	0	0	0	0	0	0	0	0	0	0	0	.333	.333	.667
Millar, Kevin, Bos.	19	77	67	9	18	29	5	0	2	12	0	3	0	7	0	15	1	0	2	.269	.325	.433
Mirabelli, Doug, Bos.	4	10	8	2	2	5	0	0	1	2	0	1	0	1	0	3	0	0	0	.250	.300	.625
Mohr, Dustan, Min.	6	3	3	3	1	2	1	0	0	0	0	0	0	0	0	0	0	0	0	.333	.333	.667
Mondesi, Raul, N.Y.	1	4	4	1	0	0	0	0	0	0	0	0	0	0	0	2	0	0	0	.000	.000	.000
Monroe, Craig, Det.	13	28	26	1	3	6	0	0	1	2	0	0	0	2	1	7	0	0	0	.115	.179	.231
Morban, Jose, Bal.†	14	15	14	4	4	4	0	0	0	3	0	0	1	0	0	3	2	0	0	.286	.333	.286
Morneau, Justin, Min.*	23	88	82	7	18	24	3	0	1	11	0	0	0	6	1	23	0	0	4	.220	.273	.293
Mueller, Bill, Bos.†	3	3	3	0	0	0	0	0	0	0	0	0	0	0	0	1	0	0	0	.000	.000	.000
Munson, Eric, Det.*	3	3	2	1	2	5	0	0	1	2	0	0	0	1	0	0	0	0	0	1.000	1.000	2.500
Myers, Greg, Tor.*	22	70	63	9	16	27	2	0	3	8	0	1	0	6	0	14	0	2	5	.254	.314	.429

Player, Team	G	TPA	AB	R	H	TB	2B	3B	HR	RBI	SH	SF	HP	BB	IBB	SO	SB	CS	GDP	Avg.	OBP	Slg.
Nivar, Ramon, Tex.	1	1	1	0	0	0	0	0	0	0	0	0	0	0	0	0	0	0	0	.000	.000	.000
Nix, Laynce, Tex.*	1	0	0	1	0	0	0	0	0	0	0	0	0	0	0	0	0	0	0	.000	.000	.000
Ordonez, Magglio, Chi.	2	7	6	1	3	4	1	0	0	0	0	0	0	1	0	0	0	0	0	.500	.571	.667
Ortiz, David, Bos.*	74	314	277	60	86	194	23	2	27	73	0	1	1	35	6	46	0	0	6	.310	.389	.700
Owens, Eric, Ana.	3	2	2	1	1	1	0	0	0	0	0	0	0	0	0	1	0	0	0	.500	.500	.500
Palmeiro, Rafael, Tex.*	97	411	359	52	90	172	12	2	22	68	0	1	3	48	6	51	1	0	4	.251	.343	.479
Palmer, Dean, Det.	22	87	78	2	11	13	2	0	0	4	0	0	2	7	0	27	0	0	2	.141	.230	.167
Patterson, Jarrod, K.C.*	4	14	11	1	0	0	0	0	0	0	0	0	0	3	1	3	0	0	0	.000	.214	.000
Paul, Josh, Chi.	1	1	1	2	1	1	0	0	0	2	0	0	0	0	0	0	0	0	0	1.000	1.000	1.000
Pena, Carlos, Det.*	1	4	4	1	2	3	1	0	0	0	0	0	0	0	0	0	0	0	0	.500	.500	.750
Perez, Antonio, TB.	3	1	1	0	0	0	0	0	0	0	0	0	0	0	0	0	0	0	0	.000	.000	.000
Phelps, Josh, Tor.	107	421	370	52	99	173	18	1	18	58	0	1	15	35	3	107	1	2	11	.268	.354	.468
Piatt, Adam, Oak.-TB.	7	17	14	1	1	1	0	0	0	0	0	0	0	3	0	7	0	0	1	.071	.235	.071
Posada, Jorge, N.Y.†	2	9	8	0	2	2	0	0	0	1	0	0	0	1	0	2	0	0	0	.250	.333	.250
Prince, Tom, Min.-K.C.	3	1	1	1	0	0	0	0	0	0	0	0	0	0	0	0	0	0	0	.000	.000	.000
Quinlan, Robb, Ana.	3	12	12	1	4	5	1	0	0	1	0	0	0	0	0	3	0	0	0	.333	.333	.417
Raines Jr., Tim, Bal.†	1	1	0	1	0	0	0	0	0	0	0	0	0	1	0	0	0	0	0	.000	1.000	.000
Ramirez, Julio, Ana.	1	1	0	1	0	0	0	0	0	0	1	0	0	0	0	0	0	0	0	.000	.000	.000
Ramirez, Manny, Bos.	26	120	96	17	24	40	4	0	4	13	0	1	2	21	4	20	0	1	3	.250	.392	.417
Randa, Joe, K.C.	2	9	6	0	2	2	0	0	0	0	1	0	1	1	0	0	0	0	0	.333	.500	.333
Relaford, Desi, K.C.†	5	14	12	2	6	10	1	0	1	3	0	0	0	2	0	0	2	0	0	.500	.571	.833
Restovich, Michael, Min.	7	7	6	1	4	4	0	0	0	1	0	0	1	0	0	2	0	0	0	.667	.714	.667
Riggs, Adam, Ana.	3	6	4	0	0	0	0	0	0	0	0	0	0	2	0	0	0	0	0	.000	.333	.000
Rios, Armando, Chi.*	4	13	13	0	0	0	0	0	0	0	0	0	0	0	0	3	0	0	1	.000	.000	.000
Rivas, Luis, Min.	1	0	0	1	0	0	0	0	0	0	0	0	0	0	0	0	0	0	0	.000	.000	.000
Roberts, Brian, Bal.†	4	13	12	2	5	8	1	1	0	0	0	0	0	1	0	1	0	0	0	.417	.462	.667
Rodriguez, Alex, Tex	1	5	3	3	3	6	0	0	1	2	0	0	0	2	0	0	0	0	0	1.000	1.000	2.000
Ryan, Michael, Min.*	4	12	11	0	4	7	3	0	0	0	0	0	0	1	0	3	0	0	0	.364	.417	.636
Salmon, Tim, Ana.	68	291	248	26	62	102	17	1	7	30	0	3	3	37	2	48	0	0	7	.250	.351	.411
Sears, Todd, Min.*	6	22	21	2	7	12	2	0	1	7	0	0	0	1	0	3	0	0	0	.333	.364	.571
Segui, David, Bal.†	53	217	193	22	49	71	8	1	4	18	0	0	1	23	2	40	1	0	6	.254	.336	.368
Seguignol, Fernando, N.Y.†	1	1	1	0	0	0	0	0	0	0	0	0	0	0	0	1	0	0	0	.000	.000	.000
Selby, Bill, Cle.*	2	4	4	1	1	1	0	0	0	0	0	0	0	0	0	2	0	0	0	.250	.250	.250
Shumpert, Terry, TB.	17	20	14	3	1	4	0	0	1	3	1	1	1	3	0	4	0	0	0	.071	.263	.286
Sierra, Ruben, Tex.-N.Y.†	47	179	163	19	42	68	6	1	6	28	0	2	0	14	1	24	1	0	6	.258	.313	.417
Sojo, Luis, N.Y.	1	1	1	0	0	0	0	0	0	0	0	0	0	0	0	0	0	0	0	.000	.000	.000
Sorensen, Zach, Cle.†	1	0	0	1	0	0	0	0	0	0	0	0	0	0	0	0	0	0	0	.000	.000	.000
Spencer, Shane, Cle.-Tex.	8	33	30	5	8	18	1	0	3	6	0	1	0	2	0	10	0	0	1	.267	.303	.600
Stewart, Shannon, Tor.-Min.	8	36	34	5	11	16	2	0	1	4	0	0	0	2	0	2	0	0	0	.324	.361	.471
Strong, Jamal, Sea.	7	1	1	2	0	0	0	0	0	0	0	0	0	0	0	0	0	0	0	.000	.000	.000
Surhoff, B.J., Bal.*	39	159	143	16	41	60	7	0	4	17	1	0	0	15	3	19	0	1	1	.287	.354	.420
Swann, Pedro, Bal.*	1	3	3	0	0	0	0	0	0	0	0	0	0	0	0	2	0	0	0	.000	.000	.000
Sweeney, Mike, K.C.	62	270	239	32	65	92	7	1	6	41	0	3	1	27	3	37	2	0	8	.272	.344	.385
Teixeira, Mark, Tex.†	5	21	17	2	4	5	1	0	0	3	0	0	0	4	1	7	0	0	1	.235	.381	.294
Thames, Marcus, Tex.	4	1	1	0	1	1	0	0	0	0	0	0	0	0	0	0	0	1	0	1.000	1.000	1.000
Thomas, Frank, Chi.	124	545	453	69	114	241	25	0	34	83	0	4	10	78	4	92	0	0	9	.252	.371	.532
Torres, Andres, Det.†	3	0	0	2	0	0	0	0	0	0	0	0	0	0	0	0	3	0	0	.000	.000	.000
Trammell, Bubba, N.Y.	15	48	44	4	10	14	4	0	0	4	0	0	0	4	0	8	0	0	1	.227	.292	.318
Tucker, Michael, K.C.*	15	59	50	8	11	18	4	0	1	6	2	0	0	7	0	13	0	1	3	.220	.316	.360
Tyner, Jason, TB.*	4	3	3	2	2	3	1	0	0	3	0	0	0	0	0	0	0	0	0	.667	.667	1.000
Ugueto, Luis, Sea.†	3	0	0	1	0	0	0	0	0	0	0	0	0	0	0	0	1	0	0	.000	.000	.000
Valentin, Javier, TB.†	6	14	14	1	3	4	1	0	0	2	0	0	0	0	0	4	0	0	1	.214	.214	.286
Varitek, Jason, Bos.†	4	15	13	1	4	5	1	0	0	1	0	0	0	2	0	2	0	0	0	.308	.400	.385
Ventura, Robin, N.Y.*	4	6	6	0	1	1	0	0	0	0	0	0	0	0	0	2	0	0	0	.167	.167	.167
Walbeck, Matt, Det.†	1	1	1	0	0	0	0	0	0	0	0	0	0	0	0	0	0	0	1	.000	.000	.000
Walker, Todd, Bos.*	2	10	8	3	3	3	0	0	0	1	0	0	0	2	0	1	0	0	0	.375	.500	.375
Werth, Jayson, Tor.	3	2	1	1	0	0	0	0	0	0	0	0	0	1	0	1	0	0	0	.000	.500	.000
Wesson, Barry, Ana.	1	0	0	1	0	0	0	0	0	0	0	0	0	0	0	0	0	0	0	.000	.000	.000
White, Rondell, K.C.	4	16	14	3	5	9	1	0	1	3	0	0	0	2	0	2	0	0	0	.357	.438	.643
Williams, Bernie, N.Y.†	4	14	11	1	1	2	1	0	0	0	0	0	0	3	0	4	0	0	1	.091	.286	.182
Wilson, Enrique, N.Y.†	1	1	1	0	0	0	0	0	0	0	0	0	0	0	0	0	0	0	0	.000	.000	.000
Wilson, Tom, Tor.	1	3	2	1	0	0	0	0	0	0	0	0	0	1	0	0	0	0	0	.000	.333	.000
Witt, Kevin, Det.*	36	137	124	15	38	62	3	0	7	15	0	2	0	11	0	29	0	1	1	.306	.358	.500
Wooten, Shawn, Ana.	28	78	76	5	13	21	2	0	2	8	0	0	0	2	1	11	0	1	0	.171	.192	.276
Young, Dmitri, Det.†	75	316	282	39	93	153	17	5	11	40	0	1	6	27	6	64	1	1	9	.330	.399	.543
Young, Ernie, Det.	4	14	10	0	2	2	0	0	0	0	0	0	0	4	0	4	0	2	1	.200	.429	.200
Zeile, Todd, N.Y.	8	27	25	1	8	9	1	0	0	2	0	1	0	1	0	5	0	0	0	.320	.333	.360

DESIGNATED HITTERS WITH TWO OR MORE TEAMS

Player, Team	G	TPA	AB	R	H	TB	2B	3B	HR	RBI	SH	SF	HP	BB	IBB	SO	SB	CS	GDP	Avg.	OBP	Slg.
Everett, Carl, Tex.†	1	4	4	0	0	0	0	0	0	0	0	0	0	0	0	2	0	0	0	.000	.000	.000
Everett, Carl, Chi.†	3	13	10	1	6	7	1	0	0	0	0	0	1	2	0	0	0	2	0	.600	.692	.700
Piatt, Adam, Oak.	2	6	6	0	0	0	0	0	0	0	0	0	0	0	0	4	0	0	1	.000	.000	.000
Piatt, Adam, TB.	5	11	8	1	1	1	0	0	0	0	0	0	0	3	0	3	0	0	0	.125	.364	.125
Prince, Tom, Min.	2	0	0	1	0	0	0	0	0	0	0	0	0	0	0	0	0	0	0	.000	.000	.000
Prince, Tom, K.C.	1	1	1	0	0	0	0	0	0	0	0	0	0	0	0	0	0	0	0	.000	.000	.000
Sierra, Ruben, Tex.†	15	61	55	6	15	25	4	0	2	7	0	0	0	6	0	12	1	0	0	.273	.344	.455
Sierra, Ruben, N.Y.†	32	118	108	13	27	43	2	1	4	21	0	2	0	8	1	12	0	0	6	.250	.297	.398
Spencer, Shane, Cle.	7	28	25	5	8	18	1	0	3	6	0	1	0	2	0	7	0	0	1	.320	.357	.720
Spencer, Shane, Tex.	1	5	5	0	0	0	0	0	0	0	0	0	0	0	0	3	0	0	0	.000	.000	.000
Stewart, Shannon, Tor.	2	9	9	1	2	5	0	0	1	2	0	0	0	0	0	0	0	0	0	.222	.222	.556
Stewart, Shannon, Min.	6	27	25	4	9	11	2	0	0	2	0	0	0	2	0	2	0	0	0	.360	.407	.440

The following designated hitters, each of whom appeared in at least one game, had no plate appearances, runs scored or stolen base attempts: Johnson, Reed, Toronto (2); Amezaga, Alfredo, Anaheim; Anderson, Brian, Cleveland; Borders, Pat, Seattle; Cirillo, Jeff, Seattle; Garcia, Karim, New York; Gomez, Chris, Minnesota; Kapler, Gabe, Boston; LaRocca, Greg, Cleveland; Latham, Chris, New York; Rowand, Aaron, Chicago.

PINCH-HITTING

TEAM

Team	G	TPA	AB	R	H	TB	2B	3B	HR	RBI	SH	SF	HP	BB	IBB	SO	SB	CS	GDP	Avg.	OBP	Slg.
Minnesota	75	119	105	15	34	55	6	0	5	19	0	1	0	13	3	29	0	0	6	.324	.395	.524
Anaheim	77	113	99	14	31	43	9	0	1	18	0	0	2	12	2	25	2	0	4	.313	.398	.434
Detroit	86	119	103	11	31	40	3	0	2	14	0	0	3	13	3	25	1	0	3	.301	.395	.388
Kansas City	67	83	73	14	20	32	1	1	3	5	1	0	1	8	1	21	2	0	5	.274	.354	.438
Baltimore	50	68	60	4	16	23	4	0	1	6	0	1	0	7	0	21	2	1	2	.267	.338	.383
Boston	73	109	91	7	22	41	7	0	4	19	1	3	1	13	3	25	0	0	0	.242	.333	.451
Toronto	86	125	108	12	25	32	5	1	0	20	1	2	2	12	3	32	0	0	4	.231	.315	.296
Tampa Bay	98	148	124	10	28	47	6	2	3	30	2	2	3	17	3	35	2	1	1	.226	.329	.379
Oakland	72	114	102	9	23	35	6	0	2	18	1	1	0	10	1	33	1	0	6	.225	.292	.343
New York	72	98	83	5	17	24	4	0	1	12	1	0	1	13	2	21	0	1	4	.205	.320	.289
Texas	60	79	68	3	13	16	3	0	0	7	0	0	1	10	1	14	0	0	2	.191	.304	.235
Chicago	86	118	105	12	20	34	5	0	3	16	0	1	0	12	1	28	1	0	2	.190	.271	.324
Seattle	63	72	60	4	10	16	0	0	2	8	2	1	1	8	2	17	0	0	3	.167	.271	.267
Cleveland	74	102	82	4	13	13	0	0	0	11	1	4	1	14	1	25	1	0	2	.159	.277	.159
Totals	1039	1467	1263	124	303	451	59	4	27	203	10	16	16	162	26	351	12	3	44	.240	.330	.357

TOP PINCH-HITTERS

Minimum 20 at-bats. *Lefthanded batter. †Switch-hitter.

Player, Team	G	TPA	AB	R	H	TB	2B	3B	HR	RBI	SH	SF	HP	BB	IBB	SO	SB	CS	GDP	Avg.	OBP	Slg.
McMillon, Billy, Oak.*	29	29	26	2	10	17	4	0	1	7	0	0	0	3	0	5	0	0	2	.385	.448	.654
Wooten, Shawn, Ana.	23	23	20	1	7	8	1	0	0	3	0	0	0	3	2	5	0	0	1	.350	.435	.400
Sierra, Ruben, Tex.-N.Y.†	30	30	28	0	7	8	1	0	0	3	0	0	0	2	1	2	0	0	2	.250	.300	.286
Martin, Al, TB.*	40	38	31	3	6	11	0	1	1	11	0	1	0	6	2	5	0	0	1	.194	.316	.355
Myers, Greg, Tor.*	33	33	28	4	5	5	0	0	0	5	0	0	0	5	1	10	0	0	1	.179	.303	.179
Mabry, John, Sea.*	28	27	23	1	2	2	0	0	0	3	0	0	1	3	1	8	0	0	1	.087	.222	.087

NOTE: Only six batters (rather than the usual 15) are listed above since they are the only players to have the minimum 20 pinch-hit at-bats during the 2003 A.L. season.

ALL PINCH-HITTERS

*Lefthanded batter. †Switch-hitter.

Player, Team	G	TPA	AB	R	H	TB	2B	3B	HR	RBI	SH	SF	HP	BB	IBB	SO	SB	CS	GDP	Avg.	OBP	Slg.
Abad, Andy, Bos.*	1	1	1	0	0	0	0	0	0	0	0	0	0	0	0	0	0	0	0	.000	.000	.000
Abernathy, Brent, TB.-K.C.	2	2	2	0	0	0	0	0	0	0	0	0	0	0	0	0	0	0	0	.000	.000	.000
Alomar Jr., Sandy, Chi.	3	3	3	2	1	2	1	0	0	2	0	0	0	0	0	0	0	0	0	.333	.333	.667
Alomar, Roberto, Chi.†	2	2	2	1	1	1	0	0	0	0	0	0	0	0	0	1	0	0	0	.500	.500	.500
Anderson, Marlon, TB.*	18	18	17	3	6	10	1	0	1	6	0	0	0	1	0	2	1	0	0	.353	.389	.588
Avery, Steve, Det.*	1	1	1	1	1	1	0	0	0	0	0	0	0	0	0	0	0	0	0	1.000	1.000	1.000
Baldelli, Rocco, TB.	2	2	1	0	0	0	0	0	0	0	0	0	0	1	0	1	0	0	0	.000	.500	.000
Bard, Josh, Cle.†	8	8	4	0	1	1	0	0	0	1	0	1	0	3	0	1	0	0	1	.250	.500	.250
Beltran, Carlos, K.C.†	4	4	4	1	3	6	0	0	1	1	0	0	0	0	0	1	0	0	0	.750	.750	1.500
Berg, Dave, Tor.	11	10	10	0	0	0	0	0	0	0	0	0	0	0	0	5	0	0	0	.000	.000	.000
Berger, Brandon, K.C.	2	2	2	0	1	1	0	0	0	0	0	0	0	0	0	0	0	0	0	.500	.500	.500
Bigbie, Larry, Bal.*	4	4	3	0	1	1	0	0	0	1	0	1	0	0	0	1	0	0	0	.333	.250	.333
Blake, Casey, Cle.	1	1	0	0	0	0	0	0	0	1	0	1	0	0	0	0	0	0	0	.000	.000	.000
Blalock, Hank, Tex.*	7	7	7	0	2	3	1	0	0	3	0	0	0	0	0	1	0	0	1	.286	.286	.429
Bloomquist, Willie, Sea.	9	9	6	0	1	1	0	0	0	1	2	1	0	0	0	2	0	0	1	.167	.143	.167
Borders, Pat, Sea.	2	2	2	1	1	1	0	0	0	0	0	0	0	0	0	1	0	0	0	.500	.500	.500
Bordick, Mike, Tor.	3	3	3	0	1	1	0	0	0	2	0	0	0	0	0	1	0	0	0	.333	.333	.333
Bowen, Rob, Min.†	1	1	1	0	0	0	0	0	0	0	0	0	0	0	0	0	0	0	1	.000	.000	.000
Broussard, Ben, Cle.*	4	4	4	0	1	1	0	0	0	1	0	0	0	0	0	2	0	0	0	.250	.250	.250
Brown, Dee, K.C.*	10	10	10	1	1	1	0	0	0	0	0	0	0	0	0	5	0	0	0	.100	.100	.100
Burke, Jamie, Chi.	1	1	1	0	0	0	0	0	0	0	0	0	0	0	0	0	0	0	0	.000	.000	.000
Burkhart, Morgan, K.C.†	2	2	2	0	0	0	0	0	0	0	0	0	0	0	0	0	0	0	0	.000	.000	.000
Burks, Ellis, Cle.	2	2	1	0	0	0	0	0	0	0	0	0	1	0	0	0	0	0	0	.000	.500	.000
Byrnes, Eric, Oak.	5	5	5	0	0	0	0	0	0	0	0	0	0	0	0	2	0	0	0	.000	.000	.000
Cameron, Mike, Sea.	1	1	1	1	1	4	0	0	1	2	0	0	0	0	0	0	0	0	0	1.000	1.000	4.000
Catalanotto, Frank, Tor.*	16	15	14	1	3	5	0	1	0	3	0	0	0	1	0	4	0	0	1	.214	.267	.357
Chavez, Eric, Oak.*	2	2	2	0	1	1	0	0	0	0	0	0	0	0	0	0	0	0	0	.500	.500	.500
Clark, Howie, Tor.*	9	8	6	0	2	2	0	0	0	1	1	0	1	0	0	1	0	0	0	.333	.429	.333
Clark, Jermaine, Tex.*	2	2	1	0	0	0	0	0	0	0	0	0	0	1	0	0	0	0	0	.000	.500	.000
Colbrunn, Greg, Sea.	5	5	4	1	2	5	0	0	1	1	0	0	0	1	0	1	0	0	0	.500	.600	1.250
Crawford, Carl, TB.*	5	5	4	1	0	0	0	0	0	0	0	0	0	1	0	1	0	0	0	.000	.200	.000
Crede, Joe, Chi.	1	1	1	0	1	1	0	0	0	2	0	0	0	0	0	0	0	0	0	1.000	1.000	1.000
Crisp, Coco, Cle.†	3	3	2	0	0	0	0	0	0	0	1	0	0	0	0	0	0	0	0	.000	.000	.000
Crosby, Bobby, Oak.	3	3	3	0	0	0	0	0	0	0	0	0	0	0	0	2	0	0	0	.000	.000	.000
Cruz, Deivi, Bal.	1	1	1	0	0	0	0	0	0	0	0	0	0	0	0	0	0	0	0	.000	.000	.000
Cuddyer, Michael, Min.	8	8	8	2	4	7	0	0	1	3	0	0	0	0	0	1	0	0	0	.500	.500	.875
Cust, Jack, Bal.*	6	6	4	0	0	0	0	0	0	0	0	0	0	2	0	1	0	0	0	.000	.333	.000
Damon, Johnny, Bos.*	3	3	3	0	0	0	0	0	0	0	0	0	0	0	0	0	0	0	0	.000	.000	.000
Daubach, Brian, Chi.*	33	26	19	4	2	4	2	0	0	4	0	1	0	6	0	10	0	0	0	.105	.308	.211
DaVanon, Jeff, Ana.†	18	18	16	2	6	8	2	0	0	6	0	0	0	2	0	5	0	0	0	.375	.444	.500
Davis, Ben, Sea.†	7	7	7	0	1	1	0	0	0	0	0	0	0	0	0	2	0	0	0	.143	.143	.143

Player, Team	G	TPA	AB	R	H	TB	2B	3B	HR	RBI	SH	SF	HP	BB	IBB	SO	SB	CS	GDP	Avg.	OBP	Slg.
DeJesus, David, K.C.*	2	2	1	0	0	0	0	0	0	0	1	0	0	0	0	1	0	0	0	.000	.000	.000
Delgado, Wilson, Ana.†	4	4	3	0	1	1	0	0	0	1	0	0	0	1	0	2	0	0	0	.333	.500	.333
Dellucci, David, N.Y.*	1	1	1	0	0	0	0	0	0	0	0	0	0	0	0	0	0	0	0	.000	.000	.000
Diaz, Matt, TB.	2	1	1	0	0	0	0	0	0	0	0	0	0	0	0	0	0	0	0	.000	.000	.000
DiFelice, Mike, K.C.	6	5	4	2	3	6	0	0	1	1	0	0	0	1	0	1	0	0	0	.750	.800	1.500
Durazo, Erubiel, Oak.*	1	1	1	0	0	0	0	0	0	0	0	0	0	0	0	1	0	0	0	.000	.000	.000
Durrington, Trent, Ana.	3	3	2	2	1	1	0	0	0	1	0	0	0	1	0	0	0	0	0	.500	.667	.500
Dye, Jermaine, Oak.	1	1	1	0	0	0	0	0	0	0	0	0	0	0	0	1	0	0	0	.000	.000	.000
Easley, Damion, TB.	8	7	7	0	1	3	0	1	0	1	0	0	0	0	0	3	0	0	0	.143	.143	.429
Eckstein, David, Ana.	1	1	1	0	0	0	0	0	0	0	0	0	0	0	0	1	0	0	0	.000	.000	.000
Edwards, Mike, Oak.	3	3	2	0	0	0	0	0	0	0	0	0	0	1	0	1	0	0	0	.000	.333	.000
Ellis, Mark, Oak.	2	2	2	0	0	0	0	0	0	0	0	0	0	0	0	2	0	0	0	.000	.000	.000
Erstad, Darin, Ana.*	1	1	1	0	1	1	0	0	0	0	0	0	0	0	0	0	0	0	0	1.000	1.000	1.000
Escobar, Alex, Cle.	3	3	3	0	1	1	0	0	0	0	0	0	0	0	0	2	0	0	0	.333	.333	.333
Everett, Carl, Tex.-Chi.†	9	8	6	1	1	1	0	0	0	0	0	0	0	2	2	1	1	0	0	.167	.375	.167
Febles, Carlos, K.C.	2	2	2	1	1	1	0	0	0	0	0	0	0	0	0	0	0	0	0	.500	.500	.500
Figgins, Chone, Ana.†	1	1	1	1	0	0	0	0	0	0	0	0	0	0	0	0	0	0	0	.000	.000	.000
Flaherty, John, N.Y.	1	1	1	1	1	1	0	0	0	0	0	0	0	0	0	0	0	0	0	1.000	1.000	1.000
Ford, Lew, Min.	8	7	6	3	3	8	2	0	1	1	0	0	0	1	0	2	0	0	0	.500	.571	1.333
Fordyce, Brook, Bal.	1	1	1	0	0	0	0	0	0	0	0	0	0	0	0	0	0	0	0	.000	.000	.000
Fullmer, Brad, Ana.*	5	4	3	2	1	2	1	0	0	0	0	0	0	1	0	1	0	0	0	.333	.500	.667
Gant, Ron, Oak.	6	6	5	0	1	1	0	0	0	1	0	1	0	0	0	3	0	0	0	.200	.167	.200
Garcia, Karim, N.Y.*	2	2	2	0	1	1	0	0	0	1	0	0	0	0	0	1	0	0	0	.500	.500	.500
Garciaparra, Nomar, Bos.	1	1	0	0	0	0	0	0	0	1	0	1	0	0	0	0	0	0	0	.000	.000	.000
German, Esteban, Oak.	1	1	1	0	0	0	0	0	0	0	0	0	0	0	0	0	0	0	1	.000	.000	.000
Gerut, Jody, Cle.*	4	4	4	0	1	1	0	0	0	1	0	0	0	0	0	2	0	0	0	.250	.250	.250
Giambi, Jason, N.Y.*	2	2	2	0	0	0	0	0	0	0	0	0	0	0	0	1	0	0	1	.000	.000	.000
Giambi, Jeremy, Bos.*	13	13	12	0	4	5	1	0	0	0	0	0	0	1	0	3	0	0	0	.333	.385	.417
Gil, Benji, Ana.	7	7	7	0	1	1	0	0	0	0	0	0	0	0	0	4	0	0	0	.143	.143	.143
Gil, Geronimo, Bal.	1	1	1	0	0	0	0	0	0	0	0	0	0	0	0	0	0	0	1	.000	.000	.000
Gipson, Charles, N.Y.	3	3	1	0	0	0	0	0	0	1	1	0	0	1	0	0	0	1	0	.000	.500	.000
Gomes, Jonny, TB.	4	3	2	1	0	0	0	0	0	0	0	0	1	0	0	0	0	0	0	.000	.333	.000
Gomez, Chris, Min.	6	6	5	0	1	1	0	0	0	0	0	0	0	1	0	1	0	0	1	.200	.333	.200
Gonzalez, Juan, Tex.	1	1	0	0	0	0	0	0	0	0	0	0	0	1	0	0	0	0	0	.000	1.000	.000
Grabowski, Jason, Oak.*	5	5	5	0	0	0	0	0	0	0	0	0	0	0	0	4	0	0	0	.000	.000	.000
Graffanino, Tony, Chi.	15	15	15	2	3	6	0	0	1	3	0	0	0	0	0	4	0	0	0	.200	.200	.400
Greene, Todd, Tex.	8	8	8	0	0	0	0	0	0	0	0	0	0	0	0	3	0	0	0	.000	.000	.000
Gregorio, Tom, Ana.	1	1	1	0	0	0	0	0	0	0	0	0	0	0	0	1	0	0	0	.000	.000	.000
Grieve, Ben, TB.*	9	9	7	1	2	3	1	0	0	0	0	0	0	2	1	4	0	0	0	.286	.444	.429
Guiel, Aaron, K.C.*	10	9	9	0	1	1	0	0	0	0	0	0	0	0	0	5	0	0	0	.111	.111	.111
Guillen, Jose, Oak.	2	2	2	0	0	0	0	0	0	0	0	0	0	0	0	0	0	0	1	.000	.000	.000
Gutierrez, Ricky, Cle.	2	2	2	0	0	0	0	0	0	0	0	0	0	0	0	0	0	0	0	.000	.000	.000
Guzman, Cristian, Min.†	2	2	2	0	0	0	0	0	0	0	0	0	0	0	0	1	0	0	0	.000	.000	.000
Hafner, Travis, Cle.*	8	7	5	0	0	0	0	0	0	1	0	1	0	1	0	2	0	0	0	.000	.143	.000
Hairston Jr., Jerry, Bal.	1	1	1	0	0	0	0	0	0	0	0	0	0	0	0	1	0	0	0	.000	.000	.000
Halter, Shane, Det.	10	10	8	1	2	2	0	0	0	1	0	0	0	2	0	2	0	0	0	.250	.400	.250
Harris, Willie, Chi.*	8	8	5	0	0	0	0	0	0	0	0	0	0	3	0	0	0	0	0	.000	.375	.000
Harvey, Ken, K.C.	5	5	3	1	1	1	0	0	0	1	0	0	1	1	0	0	0	0	0	.333	.600	.333
Haselman, Bill, Bos.	1	1	1	0	0	0	0	0	0	0	0	0	0	0	0	0	0	0	0	.000	.000	.000
Hatteberg, Scott, Oak.*	7	7	6	0	1	1	0	0	0	1	0	0	0	1	0	1	0	0	0	.167	.286	.167
Henson, Drew, N.Y.	1	1	1	0	0	0	0	0	0	0	0	0	0	0	0	1	0	0	0	.000	.000	.000
Hernandez, Michel, N.Y.	1	1	1	0	0	0	0	0	0	0	0	0	0	0	0	0	0	0	0	.000	.000	.000
Hernandez, Ramon, Oak.	5	5	5	0	0	0	0	0	0	0	0	0	0	0	0	1	0	0	1	.000	.000	.000
Higginson, Bobby, Det.*	6	6	4	0	2	2	0	0	0	1	0	0	0	2	0	0	0	0	0	.500	.667	.500
Hillenbrand, Shea, Bos.	2	2	2	0	1	2	1	0	0	1	0	0	0	0	0	1	0	0	0	.500	.500	1.000
Hinch, A.J., Det.	1	1	1	1	1	4	0	0	1	2	0	0	0	0	0	0	0	0	0	1.000	1.000	4.000
Hinske, Eric, Tor.*	3	3	3	0	0	0	0	0	0	0	0	0	0	0	0	1	0	0	0	.000	.000	.000
Hocking, Denny, Min.†	8	8	8	0	4	4	0	0	0	1	0	0	0	0	0	1	0	0	0	.500	.500	.500
Huckaby, Ken, Tor.	1	1	1	1	1	2	1	0	0	1	0	0	0	0	0	0	0	0	0	1.000	1.000	2.000
Hudson, Orlando, Tor.†	4	4	3	0	0	0	0	0	0	0	0	0	0	1	0	2	0	0	0	.000	.250	.000
Hunter, Torii, Min.	1	1	1	0	0	0	0	0	0	0	0	0	0	0	0	1	0	0	0	.000	.000	.000
Ibanez, Raul, K.C.*	1	1	1	0	0	0	0	0	0	0	0	0	0	0	0	0	0	0	0	.000	.000	.000
Jackson, Damian, Bos.	4	4	3	0	1	1	0	0	0	2	0	0	0	1	0	0	0	0	0	.333	.500	.333
Jeter, Derek, N.Y.	1	1	1	0	0	0	0	0	0	0	0	0	0	0	0	0	0	0	0	.000	.000	.000
Jimenez, D'Angelo, Chi.†	5	5	5	0	0	0	0	0	0	0	0	0	0	0	0	1	0	0	0	.000	.000	.000
Johnson, Gary, Ana.*	2	2	2	0	0	0	0	0	0	0	0	0	0	0	0	1	0	0	0	.000	.000	.000
Johnson, Mark, Oak.*	1	1	1	0	0	0	0	0	0	0	0	0	0	0	0	0	0	0	0	.000	.000	.000
Johnson, Nick, N.Y.*	6	6	4	0	1	1	0	0	0	2	0	0	0	2	0	0	0	0	0	.250	.500	.250
Johnson, Reed, Tor.	7	7	5	1	1	2	1	0	0	1	0	1	0	1	0	0	0	0	1	.200	.286	.400
Johnson, Rontrez, K.C.	1	1	1	0	0	0	0	0	0	0	0	0	0	0	0	1	0	0	0	.000	.000	.000
Jones, Jacque, Min.*	9	9	7	0	2	2	0	0	0	2	0	1	0	1	0	1	0	0	1	.286	.333	.286
Jones, Jason, Tex.†	8	8	7	0	1	1	0	0	0	1	0	0	0	1	0	3	0	0	0	.143	.250	.143
Kapler, Gabe, Bos.	9	9	8	0	0	0	0	0	0	0	0	0	0	1	0	3	0	0	0	.000	.111	.000
Kennedy, Adam, Ana.*	10	10	8	2	2	6	1	0	1	3	0	0	1	1	0	2	0	0	1	.250	.400	.750
Kielty, Bobby, Min.-Tor.†	17	17	14	3	5	8	0	0	1	7	0	1	0	2	1	2	0	0	1	.357	.412	.571
Kingsale, Gene, Det.†	4	4	3	0	1	1	0	0	0	0	0	0	0	1	0	0	0	0	0	.333	.500	.333
Klassen, Danny, Det.	4	2	2	1	1	1	0	0	0	0	0	0	0	0	0	0	0	0	0	.500	.500	.500
Konerko, Paul, Chi.	15	15	14	1	2	5	0	0	1	2	0	0	0	1	0	2	0	0	1	.143	.200	.357
Koonce, Graham, Oak.*	1	1	1	0	0	0	0	0	0	0	0	0	0	0	0	1	0	0	0	.000	.000	.000
LaForest, Pete, TB.*	6	6	5	0	1	1	0	0	0	1	0	0	1	0	0	2	0	0	0	.200	.333	.200
Laird, Gerald, Tex.	1	1	0	0	0	0	0	0	0	0	0	0	0	1	0	0	0	0	0	.000	1.000	.000
Laker, Tim, Cle.	2	2	2	0	0	0	0	0	0	1	0	0	0	0	0	1	0	0	0	.000	.000	.000

Player, Team	G	TPA	AB	R	H	TB	2B	3B	HR	RBI	SH	SF	HP	BB	IBB	SO	SB	CS	GDP	Avg.	OBP	Slg.
Lamb, Mike, Tex.*	17	16	15	1	2	2	0	0	0	1	0	0	1	0	0	4	0	0	0	.133	.188	.133
LaRocca, Greg, Cle.	2	2	1	0	0	0	0	0	0	0	0	0	0	1	0	0	0	0	0	.000	.500	.000
Lawton, Matt, Cle.*	4	4	4	0	1	1	0	0	0	0	0	0	0	0	0	2	1	0	0	.250	.250	.250
LeCroy, Matthew, Min.	15	14	14	0	4	5	1	0	0	0	0	0	0	0	0	5	0	0	0	.286	.286	.357
Lee, Carlos, Chi.	2	2	2	0	0	0	0	0	0	0	0	0	0	0	0	0	0	0	0	.000	.000	.000
Lee, Travis, TB.*	2	2	2	0	0	0	0	0	0	0	0	0	0	0	0	1	0	0	0	.000	.000	.000
Leon, Jose, Bal.	3	3	3	0	1	1	0	0	0	0	0	0	0	0	0	1	0	0	0	.333	.333	.333
Long, Terrence, Oak.*	5	5	5	2	3	6	0	0	1	5	0	0	0	0	0	2	0	0	0	.600	.600	1.200
Lopez, Mendy, K.C.	6	6	6	1	1	4	0	0	1	2	0	0	0	0	0	2	0	0	0	.167	.167	.667
Ludwick, Ryan, Cle.	5	5	4	0	0	0	0	0	0	0	0	0	0	1	1	0	0	0	0	.000	.200	.000
Mabry, John, Sea.*	28	27	23	1	2	2	0	0	0	3	0	0	1	3	1	8	0	0	1	.087	.222	.087
Machado, Robert, Bal.	1	1	1	0	0	0	0	0	0	0	0	0	0	0	0	1	0	0	0	.000	.000	.000
Magruder, Chris, Cle.†	1	1	1	0	0	0	0	0	0	0	0	0	0	0	0	0	0	0	0	.000	.000	.000
Martin, Al, TB.*	40	38	31	3	6	11	0	1	1	11	0	1	0	6	2	5	0	0	1	.194	.316	.355
Martinez, Edgar, Sea.	7	7	6	0	1	1	0	0	0	0	0	0	0	1	0	2	0	0	1	.167	.286	.167
Martinez, Victor, Cle.†	6	6	3	1	1	1	0	0	0	1	0	1	0	2	0	0	0	0	0	.333	.500	.333
Matos, Julius, K.C.	5	5	5	1	2	2	0	0	0	0	0	0	0	0	0	1	0	0	1	.400	.400	.400
Matsui, Hideki, N.Y.*	2	2	2	0	0	0	0	0	0	0	0	0	0	0	0	0	0	0	0	.000	.000	.000
Matthews Jr., Gary, Bal.†	2	2	1	0	1	2	1	0	0	2	0	0	0	1	0	0	0	1	0	1.000	1.000	2.000
Mayne, Brent, K.C.*	2	2	2	0	0	0	0	0	0	0	0	0	0	0	0	1	0	0	0	.000	.000	.000
McCarty, Dave, Bos.	4	4	3	0	2	3	1	0	0	2	0	0	0	1	0	0	0	0	0	.667	.750	1.000
McDonald, John, Cle.	1	1	1	0	0	0	0	0	0	0	0	0	0	0	0	0	0	0	0	.000	.000	.000
McLemore, Mark, Sea.†	7	7	6	0	1	1	0	0	0	0	0	0	0	1	0	1	0	0	0	.167	.286	.167
McMillon, Billy, Oak.*	29	29	26	2	10	17	4	0	1	7	0	0	0	3	0	5	0	0	2	.385	.448	.654
Melhuse, Adam, Oak.†	6	6	6	0	2	3	1	0	0	2	0	0	0	0	0	1	0	0	0	.333	.333	.500
Mench, Kevin, Tex.	3	3	2	0	0	0	0	0	0	0	0	0	0	1	0	0	0	0	0	.000	.333	.000
Mendez, Carlos, Bal.	11	10	10	1	3	5	2	0	0	0	0	0	0	0	0	3	0	0	0	.300	.300	.500
Menechino, Frank, Oak.	12	11	8	2	1	1	0	0	0	0	0	0	0	3	0	2	0	0	0	.125	.364	.125
Merloni, Lou, Bos.	2	2	2	0	1	1	0	0	0	0	0	0	0	0	0	1	0	0	0	.500	.500	.500
Mientkiewicz, Doug, Min.*	1	1	1	1	1	2	1	0	0	0	0	0	0	0	0	0	0	0	0	1.000	1.000	2.000
Miles, Aaron, Chi.†	4	4	4	0	1	2	1	0	0	1	0	0	0	0	0	0	0	0	0	.250	.250	.500
Millar, Kevin, Bos.	7	7	3	1	1	4	0	0	1	5	0	1	0	3	1	2	0	0	0	.333	.571	1.333
Mirabelli, Doug, Bos.	6	6	5	0	1	2	1	0	0	2	0	1	0	0	0	2	0	0	0	.200	.167	.400
Mohr, Dustan, Min.	6	6	6	0	0	0	0	0	0	0	0	0	0	0	0	6	0	0	0	.000	.000	.000
Molina, Bengie, Ana.	4	4	4	0	1	1	0	0	0	1	0	0	0	0	0	0	0	0	1	.250	.250	.250
Molina, Jose, Ana.	2	2	2	0	1	1	0	0	0	0	0	0	0	0	0	0	0	0	0	.500	.500	.500
Mondesi, Raul, N.Y.	1	1	0	0	0	0	0	0	0	0	0	0	0	1	0	0	0	0	0	.000	1.000	.000
Monroe, Craig, Det.	18	16	13	0	3	3	0	0	0	0	0	0	0	3	2	4	0	0	0	.231	.375	.231
Mora, Melvin, Bal.	2	2	2	0	1	2	1	0	0	1	0	0	0	0	0	1	0	0	0	.500	.500	1.000
Morban, Jose, Bal.†	11	11	10	1	2	5	0	0	1	1	0	0	0	1	0	5	2	0	0	.200	.273	.500
Morneau, Justin, Min.*	16	16	14	4	5	11	0	0	2	4	0	0	0	2	0	4	0	0	0	.357	.438	.786
Morris, Warren, Det.*	11	11	10	0	3	3	0	0	0	2	0	0	0	1	1	2	0	0	1	.300	.364	.300
Mueller, Bill, Bos.†	7	7	7	1	1	4	0	0	1	1	0	0	0	0	0	3	0	0	0	.143	.143	.571
Munson, Eric, Det.*	8	8	5	1	3	6	0	0	1	4	0	0	0	3	0	0	0	0	0	.600	.750	1.200
Myers, Greg, Tor.*	33	33	28	4	5	5	0	0	0	5	0	0	0	5	1	10	0	0	1	.179	.303	.179
Nivar, Ramon, Tex.	1	1	1	0	0	0	0	0	0	0	0	0	0	0	0	0	0	0	0	.000	.000	.000
Nix, Laynce, Tex.*	3	3	3	0	0	0	0	0	0	0	0	0	0	0	0	1	0	0	0	.000	.000	.000
Nixon, Trot, Bos.*	11	10	8	0	1	1	0	0	0	0	0	0	0	2	0	2	0	0	0	.125	.300	.125
Olerud, John, Sea.*	2	2	1	0	0	0	0	0	0	0	0	0	0	1	1	0	0	0	0	.000	.500	.000
Olivo, Miguel, Chi.	1	1	1	0	0	0	0	0	0	0	0	0	0	0	0	1	0	0	0	.000	.000	.000
Ordonez, Magglio, Chi.	2	2	2	1	2	5	0	0	1	1	0	0	0	0	0	0	0	0	0	1.000	1.000	2.500
Ortiz, David, Bos.*	11	11	11	1	3	7	1	0	1	3	0	0	0	0	0	4	0	0	0	.273	.273	.636
Owens, Eric, Ana.	12	12	11	2	3	4	1	0	0	2	0	0	0	1	0	2	1	0	0	.273	.333	.364
Palmeiro, Rafael, Tex.*	4	4	3	0	2	2	0	0	0	1	0	0	0	1	0	0	0	0	0	.667	.750	.667
Palmer, Dean, Det.	2	2	2	0	0	0	0	0	0	0	0	0	0	0	0	1	0	0	0	.000	.000	.000
Paquette, Craig, Det.	3	3	3	0	0	0	0	0	0	0	0	0	0	0	0	0	0	0	0	.000	.000	.000
Patterson, Jarrod, K.C.*	4	4	4	1	1	1	0	0	0	0	0	0	0	0	0	1	0	0	0	.250	.250	.250
Pena, Carlos, Det.*	3	3	3	0	1	1	0	0	0	1	0	0	0	0	0	2	0	0	0	.333	.333	.333
Peralta, Jhonny, Cle.	1	1	0	0	0	0	0	0	0	0	0	0	0	1	0	0	0	0	0	.000	1.000	.000
Perez, Antonio, TB.	3	2	2	0	0	0	0	0	0	0	0	0	0	0	0	1	0	0	0	.000	.000	.000
Perry, Herbert, Tex.	4	4	4	0	1	1	0	0	0	0	0	0	0	0	0	0	0	0	0	.250	.250	.250
Petrick, Ben, Det.	5	5	5	0	0	0	0	0	0	0	0	0	0	0	0	2	0	0	0	.000	.000	.000
Phelps, Josh, Tor.	14	14	11	2	3	3	0	0	0	1	0	0	1	2	2	3	0	0	0	.273	.429	.273
Phillips, Brandon, Cle.	4	3	1	2	0	0	0	0	0	0	0	0	0	2	0	1	0	0	0	.000	.667	.000
Piatt, Adam, Oak.-TB.	17	15	14	0	2	3	1	0	0	0	0	0	0	1	0	6	0	0	1	.143	.200	.214
Pierzynski, A.J., Min.*	6	6	5	1	2	3	1	0	0	2	0	0	0	1	1	1	0	0	0	.400	.500	.600
Posada, Jorge, N.Y.†	9	9	6	1	2	3	1	0	0	2	0	0	1	2	0	4	0	0	0	.333	.556	.500
Pride, Curtis, N.Y.*	1	1	1	0	0	0	0	0	0	0	0	0	0	0	0	0	0	0	1	.000	.000	.000
Prieto, Alex, Min.	3	3	3	0	0	0	0	0	0	0	0	0	0	0	0	2	0	0	0	.000	.000	.000
Prince, Tom, Min.-K.C.	5	5	3	0	0	0	0	0	0	0	0	0	0	2	0	0	0	0	1	.000	.400	.000
Quinlan, Robb, Ana.	2	2	2	0	1	1	0	0	0	0	0	0	0	0	0	0	0	0	0	.500	.500	.500
Raines Jr., Tim, Bal.†	4	3	3	0	0	0	0	0	0	0	0	0	0	0	0	2	0	0	0	.000	.000	.000
Ramirez, Manny, Bos.	2	2	0	0	0	0	0	0	0	0	0	0	0	2	1	0	0	0	0	.000	1.000	.000
Randa, Joe, K.C.	2	2	2	0	0	0	0	0	0	0	0	0	0	0	0	0	0	0	1	.000	.000	.000
Relaford, Desi, K.C.†	12	11	8	4	4	7	1	1	0	0	0	0	0	3	0	1	2	0	0	.500	.636	.875
Restovich, Michael, Min.	2	2	2	0	2	2	0	0	0	1	0	0	0	0	0	0	0	0	0	1.000	1.000	1.000
Riggs, Adam, Ana.	4	4	3	1	2	3	1	0	0	1	0	0	0	1	0	0	1	0	0	.667	.750	1.000
Rios, Armando, Chi.*	15	15	14	0	2	2	0	0	0	1	0	0	0	1	0	4	0	0	1	.143	.200	.143
Rivera, Juan, N.Y.	6	6	6	0	2	3	1	0	0	1	0	0	0	0	0	1	0	0	0	.333	.333	.500
Roberts, Brian, Bal.†	1	1	1	0	1	1	0	0	0	0	0	0	0	0	0	0	0	0	0	1.000	1.000	1.000
Rodriguez, Alex, Tex.	2	2	2	0	0	0	0	0	0	0	0	0	0	0	0	1	0	0	0	.000	.000	.000
Rolls, Damian, TB.	4	4	4	0	1	1	0	0	0	0	0	0	0	0	0	2	0	1	0	.250	.250	.250

Player, Team	G	TPA	AB	R	H	TB	2B	3B	HR	RBI	SH	SF	HP	BB	IBB	SO	SB	CS	GDP	Avg.	OBP	Slg.
Rowand, Aaron, Chi.	5	4	4	0	1	1	0	0	0	0	0	0	0	0	0	1	0	0	0	.250	.250	.250
Ryan, Michael, Min.*	10	10	9	2	3	4	1	0	0	0	0	0	0	1	0	1	0	0	0	.333	.400	.444
Sabathia, C.C., Cle.*	1	1	1	0	1	1	0	0	0	0	0	0	0	0	0	0	0	0	0	1.000	1.000	1.000
Sadler, Donnie, Tex.	3	3	2	1	1	2	1	0	0	0	0	0	0	1	0	0	0	0	0	.500	.667	1.000
Salmon, Tim, Ana.	3	3	3	0	0	0	0	0	0	0	0	0	0	0	0	0	0	0	0	.000	.000	.000
Sanchez, Alex, Det.*	5	5	5	1	3	4	1	0	0	0	0	0	0	0	0	0	0	0	0	.600	.600	.800
Sanchez, Freddy, Bos.	4	4	4	2	3	4	1	0	0	0	0	0	0	0	0	0	0	0	0	.750	.750	1.000
Sandberg, Jared, TB.	6	6	6	0	2	3	1	0	0	1	0	0	0	0	0	3	0	0	0	.333	.333	.500
Santiago, Ramon, Det.†	4	4	2	3	2	3	1	0	0	0	0	0	1	1	0	0	1	0	0	1.000	1.000	1.500
Santos, Angel, Cle.†	2	2	2	0	0	0	0	0	0	0	0	0	0	0	0	1	0	0	0	.000	.000	.000
Sears, Todd, Min.*	6	5	4	0	0	0	0	0	0	0	0	0	0	1	0	0	0	0	2	.000	.200	.000
Segui, David, Bal.†	9	9	8	1	3	3	0	0	0	1	0	0	0	1	0	3	0	0	0	.375	.444	.375
Seguignol, Fernando, N.Y.†	3	3	3	0	0	0	0	0	0	0	0	0	0	0	0	3	0	0	0	.000	.000	.000
Selby, Bill, Cle.*	18	18	16	1	3	3	0	0	0	3	0	0	0	2	0	4	0	0	0	.188	.278	.188
Shumpert, Terry, TB.	23	19	12	1	2	5	0	0	1	3	1	1	1	4	0	2	0	0	0	.167	.389	.417
Sierra, Ruben, Tex.-N.Y.†	30	30	28	0	7	8	1	0	0	3	0	0	0	2	1	2	0	0	2	.250	.300	.286
Singleton, Chris, Oak.*	10	10	7	3	4	5	1	0	0	2	1	0	0	2	1	1	1	0	0	.571	.667	.714
Sojo, Luis, N.Y.	1	1	1	0	0	0	0	0	0	0	0	0	0	0	0	0	0	0	0	.000	.000	.000
Sorensen, Zach, Cle.†	11	11	10	0	1	1	0	0	0	0	0	0	0	1	0	3	0	0	0	.100	.182	.100
Spencer, Shane, Cle.	10	10	10	0	2	2	0	0	0	1	0	0	0	0	0	4	0	0	1	.200	.200	.200
Spiezio, Scott, Ana.†	11	11	9	1	3	5	2	0	0	0	0	0	1	1	0	1	0	0	1	.333	.455	.556
Stewart, Shannon, Min.	1	1	0	0	0	0	0	0	0	0	0	0	0	1	1	0	0	0	0	.000	1.000	.000
Strong, Jamal, Sea.	1	1	1	0	0	0	0	0	0	0	0	0	0	0	0	0	0	0	0	.000	.000	.000
Surhoff, B.J., Bal.*	10	10	9	0	3	3	0	0	0	0	0	0	0	1	0	1	0	0	1	.333	.400	.333
Suzuki, Ichiro, Sea.*	2	2	2	0	0	0	0	0	0	0	0	0	0	0	0	0	0	0	0	.000	.000	.000
Swann, Pedro, Bal.*	2	2	1	1	0	0	0	0	0	0	0	0	0	1	0	1	0	0	0	.000	.500	.000
Sweeney, Mike, K.C.	1	1	1	0	0	0	0	0	0	0	0	0	0	0	0	0	0	0	1	.000	.000	.000
Teixeira, Mark, Tex.†	3	3	2	1	0	0	0	0	0	0	0	0	0	1	0	0	0	0	0	.000	.333	.000
Thames, Marcus, Tex.	3	3	2	0	2	2	0	0	0	0	0	0	0	1	0	0	0	0	0	1.000	1.000	1.000
Thomas, Frank, Chi.	2	2	2	0	0	0	0	0	0	0	0	0	0	0	0	1	0	0	0	.000	.000	.000
Torres, Andres, Det.†	7	7	7	0	2	2	0	0	0	1	0	0	0	0	0	2	0	0	0	.286	.286	.286
Trammell, Bubba, N.Y.	7	7	7	0	1	2	1	0	0	0	0	0	0	0	0	2	0	0	0	.143	.143	.286
Tucker, Michael, K.C.*	5	5	2	1	0	0	0	0	0	0	0	0	0	3	1	1	0	0	1	.000	.600	.000
Tyner, Jason, TB.*	14	13	11	0	4	5	1	0	0	5	1	0	0	1	0	3	1	0	0	.364	.417	.455
Ugueto, Luis, Sea.†	2	2	1	0	0	0	0	0	0	1	0	0	0	1	0	0	0	0	0	.000	.500	.000
Valentin, Javier, TB.†	5	5	5	0	1	2	1	0	0	2	0	0	0	0	0	2	0	0	0	.200	.200	.400
Valentin, Jose, Chi.†	7	7	7	0	3	4	1	0	0	0	0	0	0	0	0	3	0	0	0	.429	.429	.571
Varitek, Jason, Bos.†	15	15	12	2	3	7	1	0	1	2	1	0	1	1	1	3	0	0	0	.250	.357	.583
Ventura, Robin, N.Y.*	12	12	9	1	2	2	0	0	0	2	0	0	0	3	1	3	0	0	0	.222	.417	.222
Vizquel, Omar, Cle.†	1	1	1	0	0	0	0	0	0	0	0	0	0	0	0	0	0	0	0	.000	.000	.000
Walbeck, Matt, Det.†	5	5	5	2	2	2	0	0	0	0	0	0	0	0	0	1	0	0	1	.400	.400	.400
Walker, Todd, Bos.*	7	7	6	0	0	0	0	0	0	0	0	0	0	1	0	1	0	0	0	.000	.143	.000
Werth, Jayson, Tor.	3	3	2	0	0	0	0	0	0	0	0	0	0	1	0	2	0	0	0	.000	.333	.000
White, Rondell, K.C.	1	1	1	0	1	1	0	0	0	0	0	0	0	0	0	0	0	0	0	1.000	1.000	1.000
Williams, Bernie, N.Y.†	2	2	1	1	1	2	1	0	0	0	0	0	0	1	0	0	0	0	0	1.000	1.000	2.000
Wilson, Enrique, N.Y.†	3	3	2	1	1	4	0	0	1	1	0	0	0	1	0	0	0	0	0	.500	.667	2.000
Wilson, Tom, Tor.	17	17	16	2	7	10	3	0	0	4	0	0	0	1	0	3	0	0	1	.438	.471	.625
Witt, Kevin, Det.*	20	18	18	0	2	3	1	0	0	0	0	0	0	0	0	7	0	0	1	.111	.111	.167
Wooten, Shawn, Ana.	23	23	20	1	7	8	1	0	0	3	0	0	0	3	2	5	0	0	1	.350	.435	.400
Young, Dmitri, Det.†	7	7	5	0	2	2	0	0	0	2	0	0	2	0	0	1	0	0	0	.400	.571	.400
Young, Ernie, Det.	1	1	1	0	0	0	0	0	0	0	0	0	0	0	0	1	0	0	0	.000	.000	.000
Zeile, Todd, N.Y.	12	10	10	0	0	0	0	0	0	0	0	0	0	0	0	3	0	0	1	.000	.000	.000

PINCH-HITTERS WITH TWO OR MORE TEAMS

Player, Team	G	TPA	AB	R	H	TB	2B	3B	HR	RBI	SH	SF	HP	BB	IBB	SO	SB	CS	GDP	Avg.	OBP	Slg.
Abernathy, Brent, TB.	1	1	1	0	0	0	0	0	0	0	0	0	0	0	0	0	0	0	0	.000	.000	.000
Abernathy, Brent, K.C.	1	1	1	0	0	0	0	0	0	0	0	0	0	0	0	0	0	0	0	.000	.000	.000
Everett, Carl, Tex.†	4	3	2	0	0	0	0	0	0	0	0	0	0	1	1	1	0	0	0	.000	.333	.000
Everett, Carl, Chi.†	5	5	4	1	1	1	0	0	0	0	0	0	0	1	1	0	1	0	0	.250	.400	.250
Kielty, Bobby, Min.†	10	10	8	2	3	6	0	0	1	5	0	0	0	2	1	2	0	0	1	.375	.500	.750
Kielty, Bobby, Tor.†	7	7	6	1	2	2	0	0	0	2	0	1	0	0	0	0	0	0	0	.333	.286	.333
Piatt, Adam, Oak.	10	8	8	0	0	0	0	0	0	0	0	0	0	0	0	3	0	0	1	.000	.000	.000
Piatt, Adam, TB.	7	7	6	0	2	3	1	0	0	0	0	0	0	1	0	3	0	0	0	.333	.429	.500
Prince, Tom, Min.	3	3	1	0	0	0	0	0	0	0	0	0	0	2	0	0	0	0	0	.000	.667	.000
Prince, Tom, K.C.	2	2	2	0	0	0	0	0	0	0	0	0	0	0	0	0	0	0	1	.000	.000	.000
Sierra, Ruben, Tex.†	7	7	7	0	2	3	1	0	0	1	0	0	0	0	0	0	0	0	1	.286	.286	.429
Sierra, Ruben, N.Y.†	23	23	21	0	5	5	0	0	0	2	0	0	0	2	1	2	0	0	1	.238	.304	.238

PITCHING

TEAM

Team	W	L	Pct.	ERA	G	CG	ShO	Rel.	Sv.-Op.	IP	H	TBF	R	ER	HR	SH	SF	HB	BB	IBB	SO	WP	Bk.
Oakland	96	66	.593	3.63	162	16	14	364	48-60	1441.2	1336	6078	643	582	140	55	29	54	499	42	1018	41	10
Seattle	93	69	.574	3.76	162	8	15	366	38-52	1441.0	1340	6025	637	602	173	35	43	54	466	24	1001	35	4
New York	101	61	.623	4.02	163	8	12	367	49-67	1462.0	1512	6209	716	653	145	37	48	49	375	36	1119	33	0
Chicago	86	76	.531	4.17	162	12	4	361	36-53	1431.0	1364	6067	715	663	162	48	57	53	518	30	1056	39	4
Cleveland	68	94	.420	4.21	162	5	7	428	34-59	1459.1	1477	6254	778	682	179	51	46	64	501	37	943	49	7
Anaheim	77	85	.475	4.28	162	5	9	375	39-52	1431.1	1444	6161	743	680	190	25	42	76	486	38	980	53	3
Minnesota	90	72	.556	4.41	162	7	8	399	45-64	1462.0	1526	6246	758	716	187	54	41	50	402	35	997	62	9
Boston	95	67	.586	4.48	162	5	6	437	36-57	1464.2	1503	6355	809	729	153	28	52	76	488	41	1141	44	0
Toronto	86	76	.531	4.69	162	14	6	443	36-53	1435.0	1560	6270	826	748	184	29	38	57	485	46	984	56	2
Baltimore	71	91	.438	4.76	163	9	3	425	41-62	1449.2	1579	6366	820	767	198	42	35	80	526	43	981	42	4
Tampa Bay	63	99	.389	4.93	162	7	7	372	30-55	1436.2	1454	6340	852	787	196	39	65	95	639	37	877	65	9
Kansas City	83	79	.512	5.05	162	7	10	407	36-64	1438.2	1569	6366	867	808	190	36	65	66	566	33	865	60	9
Detroit	43	119	.265	5.30	162	3	5	451	27-46	1438.2	1616	6376	928	847	195	47	60	56	557	35	764	52	5
Texas	71	91	.438	5.67	162	4	3	494	43-63	1433.1	1625	6413	969	903	208	41	56	63	603	45	1009	51	8
Totals	1123	1145	.495	4.52	1135	110	109	5689	538-807	20225.0	20905	87526	11061	10167	2500	567	677	893	7111	522	13735	682	74

NOTE: Totals for earned runs for several clubs do not agree with composite total for all pitchers of each respective club due to instances in which provisions of Section 10.18(i) of the Scoring Rules were applied. The following differences are to be noted: New York pitchers add to 655; Anaheim pitchers add to 681; Boston pitchers add to 731: Kansas Citv pitchers add to 809; Detroit pitchers add to 850; Texas pitchers add to 906.

TOP QUALIFIERS FOR EARNED-RUN AVERAGE TITLE

Minimum 162 innings. *Throws lefthanded.

Pitcher, Team	W	L	Pct.	ERA	G	GS	CG	ShO	GF	Sv.-Op.	IP	H	TBF	R	ER	HR	SH	SF	HB	BB	IBB	SO	WP	Bk.
Martinez, Pedro, Bos.	14	4	.778	2.22	29	29	3	0	0	0-0	186.2	147	749	52	46	7	4	4	9	47	0	206	5	0
Hudson, Tim, Oak.	16	7	.696	2.70	34	34	3	2	0	0-0	240.0	197	967	84	72	15	11	2	10	61	9	162	6	0
Loaiza, Esteban, Chi.	21	9	.700	2.90	34	34	1	0	0	0-0	226.1	196	922	75	73	17	7	6	10	56	2	207	3	1
Mulder, Mark, Oak.*	15	9	.625	3.13	26	26	9	2	0	0-0	186.2	180	747	66	65	15	7	2	2	40	2	128	7	0
Halladay, Roy, Tor.	22	7	.759	3.25	36	36	9	2	0	0-0	266.0	253	1071	111	96	26	3	2	9	32	1	204	6	1
Moyer, Jamie, Sea.*	21	7	.750	3.27	33	33	1	0	0	0-0	215.0	199	897	83	78	19	7	6	8	66	3	129	0	0
Zito, Barry, Oak.*	14	12	.538	3.30	35	35	4	1	0	0-0	231.2	186	957	98	85	19	7	7	6	88	3	146	4	0
Mussina, Mike, N.Y.	17	8	.680	3.40	31	31	2	1	0	0-0	214.2	192	855	86	81	21	1	4	3	40	4	195	4	0
Franklin, Ryan, Sea.	11	13	.458	3.57	32	32	2	1	0	0-0	212.0	199	877	93	84	34	8	5	9	61	3	99	1	2
Sabathia, C.C., Cle.*	13	9	.591	3.60	30	30	2	1	0	0-0	197.2	190	832	85	79	19	10	4	6	66	3	141	4	2
May, Darrell, K.C.*	10	8	.556	3.77	35	32	2	1	1	0-1	210.0	197	868	98	88	31	5	6	2	53	1	115	5	0
Anderson, Brian, Cle.-K.C.*	14	11	.560	3.78	32	31	2	1	0	0-0	197.2	212	821	110	83	27	3	12	4	43	3	87	3	1
Pineiro, Joel, Sea.	16	11	.593	3.78	32	32	3	2	0	0-0	211.2	192	890	94	89	19	3	9	6	76	3	151	5	0
Colon, Bartolo, Chi.	15	13	.536	3.87	34	34	9	0	0	0-0	242.0	223	984	107	104	30	5	8	5	67	3	173	8	3
Clemens, Roger, N.Y.	17	9	.654	3.91	33	33	1	1	0	0-0	211.2	199	878	99	92	24	3	6	5	58	1	190	5	0

DEPARTMENTAL LEADERS: W—Halladay, Tor., 22; L—Maroth, Det., 21; G—Miller, Tor., 79; GS—Halladay, Tor., 36; CG—Colon, Chi., Halladay, Tor., Mulder, Oak., 9; ShO—Halladay, Tor., Hudson, Oak., Lackey, Ana., Mulder, Oak., Pineiro, Sea., 2; GF—Foulke, Oak., 67; Sv.—Foulke, Oak., 43; IP—Halladay, Tor., 266.0; H—Halladay, Tor., 253; TBF—Halladay, Tor., 1071 ;R—Lidle, Tor., 133; ER—Lidle, Tor., Maroth, Det., 123; HR—Franklin, Sea., Maroth, Det., Washburn, Ana., 34; SH—Radke, Min., 12; SF—Anderson, Cle.-K.C., 12; HB—Zambrano, TB., 20; TBB—Zambrano, TB., 106; IBB—Bradford, Oak., Hudson, Oak., 9; SO—Loaiza, Chi., 207; WP—Zambrano, TB., 15; Bk.—Lilly, Oak., Rogers, Min., 4

ALL PITCHERS

*Throws lefthanded.

Pitcher, Team	W	L	Pct.	ERA	G	GS	CG	ShO	GF	Sv.-Op.	IP	H	TBF	R	ER	HR	SH	SF	HB	BB	IBB	SO	WP	Bk.
Abbott, Paul, K.C.	1	2	.333	5.29	10	8	0	0	0	0-0	47.2	47	214	29	28	8	2	1	2	26	2	32	2	0
Acevedo, Juan, N.Y.-Tor.	1	5	.167	6.57	39	0	0	0	25	6-8	38.1	52	188	32	28	6	2	3	2	18	4	28	4	0
Adkins, Jon, Chi.	0	0	.000	4.82	4	0	0	0	2	0-0	9.1	8	42	5	5	1	1	1	1	7	0	3	0	0
Affeldt, Jeremy, K.C.*	7	6	.538	3.93	36	18	0	0	5	4-4	126.0	126	533	58	55	12	2	5	5	38	1	98	2	2
Ainsworth, Kurt, Bal.	0	1	.000	11.57	3	0	0	0	2	0-0	2.1	6	15	3	3	1	0	0	0	1	0	4	0	0
Almonte, Hector, Bos.	0	1	.000	8.22	7	0	0	0	4	0-0	7.2	9	39	7	7	1	1	2	0	7	1	6	1	0
Anderson, Brian, Cle.-K.C.*	14	11	.560	3.78	32	31	2	1	0	0-0	197.2	212	821	110	83	27	3	12	4	43	3	87	3	1
Anderson, Jason, N.Y.	1	0	1.000	4.79	22	0	0	0	12	0-0	20.2	23	100	13	11	3	0	2	2	14	4	9	3	0
Anderson, Matt, Det.	0	1	.000	5.40	23	0	0	0	10	3-4	23.1	25	105	17	14	5	2	1	1	9	1	13	1	0
Appier, Kevin, Ana.-K.C.	8	9	.471	5.40	23	23	0	0	0	0-0	111.2	120	499	69	67	21	1	1	8	43	4	55	6	1
Arroyo, Bronson, Bos.	0	0	.000	2.08	6	0	0	0	2	1-1	17.1	10	66	5	4	0	0	0	1	4	2	14	0	0
Asencio, Miguel, K.C.	2	1	.667	5.21	8	8	1	0	0	0-0	48.1	54	215	29	28	4	3	5	3	21	0	27	1	0
Avery, Steve, Det.*	2	0	1.000	5.63	19	0	0	0	5	0-1	16.0	19	71	11	10	5	1	0	0	7	1	6	0	0
Backe, Brandon, TB.	1	1	.500	5.44	28	0	0	0	8	0-0	44.2	40	192	28	27	6	2	1	2	25	1	36	3	0
Baez, Danys, Cle.	2	9	.182	3.81	73	0	0	0	46	25-35	75.2	65	318	36	32	9	6	1	4	23	0	66	5	0
Baldwin, James, Min.	0	1	.000	5.40	10	0	0	0	3	1-2	15.0	21	69	10	9	6	0	2	0	4	1	7	0	0
Balfour, Grant, Min.	1	0	1.000	4.15	17	1	0	0	6	0-1	26.0	23	115	12	12	4	2	1	0	14	2	30	0	0
Bauer, Rick, Bal.	0	0	.000	4.55	35	0	0	0	10	0-1	61.1	58	259	36	31	5	1	3	4	24	3	43	6	0
Bell, Rob, TB.	5	4	.556	5.52	19	18	0	0	0	0-0	101.0	103	440	64	62	15	2	2	5	39	1	44	0	0
Benes, Alan, Tex.	0	3	.000	11.40	4	4	0	0	0	0-0	15.0	29	79	20	19	2	0	1	0	8	0	11	0	1
Benitez, Armando, N.Y.-Sea.	1	1	.500	2.66	24	0	0	0	9	0-1	23.2	18	104	9	7	1	0	0	0	17	2	25	0	0
Benoit, Joaquin, Tex.	8	5	.615	5.49	25	17	0	0	1	0-0	105.0	99	462	67	64	23	1	4	3	51	0	87	3	1
Bere, Jason, Cle.	0	0	.000	4.05	2	2	0	0	0	0-0	6.2	5	28	3	3	0	1	1	0	2	0	1	0	0
Bernero, Adam, Det.	1	12	.077	6.08	18	17	0	0	0	0-0	100.2	104	447	68	68	14	3	6	7	41	0	54	1	0
Betancourt, Rafael, Cle.	2	2	.500	2.13	33	0	0	0	13	1-3	38.0	27	154	11	9	5	1	1	1	13	2	36	1	0
Bierbrodt, Nick, TB.-Cle.*	0	2	.000	9.14	18	5	0	0	4	0-0	43.1	64	223	47	44	9	2	5	5	27	3	29	4	1

Pitcher, Team	W	L	Pct.	ERA	G	GS	CG	ShO	GF	Sv.-Op.	IP	H	TBF	R	ER	HR	SH	SF	HB	BB	IBB	SO	WP	Bk.
Bonderman, Jeremy, Det.	6	19	.240	5.56	33	28	0	0	0	0-0	162.0	193	727	118	100	23	3	6	4	58	2	108	12	2
Bootcheck, Chris, Ana.	0	1	.000	9.58	4	1	0	0	2	0-0	10.1	16	53	13	11	5	0	0	0	6	0	7	0	0
Bowie, Micah, Oak.*	0	1	.000	7.56	6	0	0	0	3	0-0	8.1	13	38	7	7	1	0	0	0	2	0	4	0	0
Bowles, Brian, Tor.	0	0	.000	2.57	5	0	0	0	2	0-0	7.0	8	34	4	2	1	0	0	2	2	0	2	0	0
Boyd, Jason, Cle.	3	1	.750	4.30	44	0	0	0	13	0-1	52.1	38	221	25	25	4	0	2	3	26	1	31	2	0
Bradford, Chad, Oak.	7	4	.636	3.04	72	0	0	0	12	2-5	77.0	67	322	28	26	7	1	0	7	30	9	62	0	1
Brazelton, Dewon, TB.	1	6	.143	6.89	10	10	0	0	0	0-0	48.1	57	225	49	37	9	2	2	3	23	1	24	1	0
Buehrle, Mark, Chi.*	14	14	.500	4.14	35	35	2	0	0	0-0	230.1	250	978	124	106	22	7	7	5	61	2	119	1	0
Bukvich, Ryan, K.C.	1	0	1.000	9.58	9	0	0	0	6	0-0	10.1	12	52	11	11	2	1	1	0	9	0	8	1	0
Burkett, John, Bos.	12	9	.571	5.15	32	30	1	0	1	0-0	181.2	202	785	108	104	20	4	6	9	47	1	107	3	0
Callaway, Mickey, Ana.-Tex.	1	7	.125	6.68	23	7	0	0	8	0-0	60.2	84	284	50	45	7	2	5	2	24	1	41	2	0
Carrara, Giovanni, Sea.	2	0	1.000	6.83	23	0	0	0	7	0-0	29.0	40	137	22	22	6	1	0	2	14	0	13	0	0
Carrasco, D.J., K.C.	6	5	.545	4.82	50	2	0	0	21	2-5	80.1	82	355	44	43	8	1	4	7	40	4	57	6	0
Carrasco, Hector, Bal.	2	6	.250	4.93	40	0	0	0	10	1-3	38.1	40	174	22	21	5	4	0	2	20	3	27	0	0
Carter, Lance, TB.	7	5	.583	4.33	62	0	0	0	55	26-33	79.0	72	328	39	38	12	1	6	4	19	6	47	0	0
Chen, Bruce, Bos.*	0	1	.000	5.11	5	2	0	0	2	0-0	12.1	12	50	8	7	4	0	1	0	2	0	12	0	0
Choate, Randy, N.Y.*	0	0	.000	7.36	5	0	0	0	2	0-0	3.2	7	16	3	3	0	0	0	0	1	0	0	0	0
Chulk, Vinnie, Tor.	0	0	.000	5.06	3	0	0	0	2	0-1	5.1	6	25	3	3	0	0	0	0	3	0	2	0	0
Claussen, Brandon, N.Y.*	1	0	1.000	1.42	1	1	0	0	0	0-0	6.1	8	28	2	1	1	0	0	0	1	0	5	0	0
Clemens, Roger, N.Y.	17	9	.654	3.91	33	33	1	1	0	0-0	211.2	199	878	99	92	24	3	6	5	58	1	190	5	0
Colome, Jesus, TB.	3	7	.300	4.50	54	0	0	0	24	2-8	74.0	69	334	37	37	9	2	4	3	46	5	69	7	0
Colon, Bartolo, Chi.	15	13	.536	3.87	34	34	9	0	0	0-0	242.0	223	984	107	104	30	5	8	5	67	3	173	8	3
Contreras, Jose, N.Y.	7	2	.778	3.30	18	9	0	0	2	0-1	71.0	52	293	27	26	4	0	1	5	30	1	72	2	0
Cordero, Francisco, Tex.	5	8	.385	2.94	73	0	0	0	36	15-25	82.2	70	352	33	27	4	3	4	2	38	6	90	1	0
Cornejo, Nate, Det.	6	17	.261	4.67	32	32	2	0	0	0-0	194.2	236	842	111	101	18	7	6	3	58	8	46	1	0
Cortes, David, Cle.	0	0	.000	12.00	2	0	0	0	2	0-0	3.0	8	18	5	4	1	0	1	0	0	0	1	0	0
Cotts, Neal, Chi.*	1	1	.500	8.10	4	4	0	0	0	0-0	13.1	15	69	12	12	1	1	0	0	17	0	10	0	0
Creek, Doug, Tor.*	0	0	.000	3.29	21	0	0	0	3	0-1	13.2	14	69	6	5	2	0	2	2	12	3	11	2	0
Cressend, Jack, Cle.	2	1	.667	2.51	33	0	0	0	8	0-1	43.0	40	174	12	12	1	4	0	2	9	1	28	1	0
Daal, Omar, Bal.*	4	11	.267	6.34	19	17	0	0	1	0-0	93.2	134	434	69	66	11	8	3	2	30	1	53	2	0
Davis, Doug, Tex.-Tor.*	4	6	.400	5.37	13	12	0	0	0	0-0	57.0	74	267	37	34	8	3	0	1	30	1	27	6	0
Davis, Jason, Cle.	8	11	.421	4.68	27	27	1	0	0	0-0	165.1	172	696	101	86	25	7	3	8	47	4	85	9	2
DeHart, Rick, K.C.*	0	2	.000	13.50	4	0	0	0	2	0-0	4.0	8	21	6	6	1	0	0	0	2	0	1	0	0
DePaula, Jorge, N.Y.	0	0	.000	0.79	4	1	0	0	3	0-0	11.1	3	38	1	1	1	0	0	1	1	0	7	0	0
Dickey, R.A., Tex.	9	8	.529	5.09	38	13	1	1	6	1-1	116.2	135	513	68	66	16	4	3	5	38	5	94	5	2
Dominguez, Juan, Tex.	0	2	.000	7.16	6	3	0	0	1	0-0	16.1	16	73	14	13	5	1	1	0	12	0	13	1	0
Donnelly, Brendan, Ana.	2	2	.500	1.58	63	0	0	0	15	3-5	74.0	55	307	14	13	2	3	1	4	24	1	79	1	0
Douglass, Sean, Bal.	0	0	.000	13.50	3	0	0	0	0	0-0	8.0	14	44	12	12	2	0	0	1	6	0	3	0	0
Drese, Ryan, Tex.	2	4	.333	6.85	11	8	0	0	0	0-0	46.0	61	223	42	35	8	0	0	5	24	1	26	2	0
Driskill, Travis, Bal.	3	5	.375	6.00	20	0	0	0	6	1-1	48.0	62	215	35	32	8	3	2	1	9	2	33	3	0
DuBose, Eric, Bal.*	3	6	.333	3.79	17	10	1	0	3	0-1	73.2	60	305	33	31	6	2	3	5	25	2	44	0	1
Duchscherer, Justin, Oak.	1	1	.500	3.31	4	3	0	0	0	0-0	16.1	17	71	7	6	1	1	0	2	3	0	15	0	0
Durbin, Chad, Cle.	0	1	.000	7.27	3	1	0	0	0	0-0	8.2	18	45	12	7	2	0	0	0	3	0	8	2	0
Eckenstahler, Eric, Det.*	0	0	.000	2.87	20	0	0	0	5	0-0	15.2	9	71	6	5	0	0	0	2	15	1	12	1	0
Elder, Dave, Cle.	1	1	.500	19.29	4	0	0	0	1	0-1	2.1	5	16	5	5	2	0	0	0	4	0	3	1	0
Ellis, Robert, Tex.	1	1	.500	8.35	4	4	0	0	0	0-0	18.1	26	89	17	17	7	0	2	1	10	0	8	0	0
Embree, Alan, Bos.*	4	1	.800	4.25	65	0	0	0	15	1-2	55.0	49	221	26	26	5	0	2	0	16	3	45	0	0
Escobar, Kelvim, Tor.	13	9	.591	4.29	41	26	1	1	12	4-5	180.1	189	797	94	86	15	5	5	9	78	3	159	9	0
Fetters, Mike, Min.	0	0	.000	0.00	5	0	0	0	2	0-0	6.0	2	22	0	0	0	0	0	1	1	0	1	0	0
Field, Nate, K.C.	1	1	.500	4.15	19	0	0	0	7	0-0	21.2	19	97	10	10	3	0	1	1	14	1	19	0	0
Fikac, Jeremy, Oak.	0	1	.000	4.50	14	0	0	0	1	0-0	16.0	14	71	8	8	4	0	0	3	11	1	9	0	0
Fiore, Tony, Min.	1	1	.500	5.50	21	0	0	0	10	0-0	36.0	32	161	25	22	5	2	3	3	21	1	23	3	0
Fossum, Casey, Bos.*	6	5	.545	5.47	19	14	0	0	2	1-1	79.0	82	346	55	48	9	1	3	4	34	0	63	4	0
Foulke, Keith, Oak.	9	1	.900	2.08	72	0	0	0	67	43-48	86.2	57	338	21	20	10	1	1	7	20	2	88	0	1
Fox, Chad, Bos.	1	2	.333	4.50	17	0	0	0	10	3-5	18.0	19	93	10	9	2	2	1	1	17	2	19	1	0
Franklin, Ryan, Sea.	11	13	.458	3.57	32	32	2	1	0	0-0	212.0	199	877	93	84	34	8	5	9	61	3	99	1	2
Fultz, Aaron, Tex.*	1	3	.250	5.21	64	0	0	0	10	0-0	67.1	75	296	43	39	9	4	2	2	27	7	53	1	1
Garcia, Freddy, Sea.	12	14	.462	4.51	33	33	1	0	0	0-0	201.1	196	862	109	101	31	2	8	11	71	2	144	11	0
Garcia, Reynaldo, Tex.	0	0	.000	9.00	17	0	0	0	4	0-0	18.0	19	87	18	18	6	1	1	2	14	0	15	3	0
Garcia, Rosman, Tex.	1	2	.333	6.02	46	0	0	0	7	0-2	46.1	63	224	33	31	4	1	1	2	23	0	25	1	1
Garland, Jon, Chi.	12	13	.480	4.51	32	32	0	0	0	0-0	191.2	188	813	103	96	28	4	8	4	74	1	108	8	0
Gaudin, Chad, TB.	2	0	1.000	3.60	15	3	0	0	5	0-0	40.0	37	173	18	16	4	0	2	1	16	0	23	1	0
George, Chris, K.C.*	9	6	.600	7.11	18	18	0	0	0	0-0	93.2	120	441	75	74	22	2	4	3	44	2	39	5	3
German, Franklyn, Det.	2	4	.333	6.04	45	0	0	0	15	5-7	44.2	47	222	32	30	5	2	1	2	45	3	41	8	1
Gilfillan, Jason, K.C.	2	0	1.000	7.71	13	0	0	0	4	0-1	16.1	22	83	14	14	3	1	0	1	10	1	12	5	0
Ginter, Matt, Chi.	0	0	.000	13.50	3	0	0	0	0	0-0	3.1	2	15	5	5	1	1	0	2	1	0	0	0	0
Glover, Gary, Chi.-Ana.	2	0	1.000	4.74	42	0	0	0	15	0-0	62.2	77	279	33	33	6	0	5	3	22	3	37	2	0
Gobble, Jimmy, K.C.*	4	5	.444	4.61	9	9	0	0	0	0-0	52.2	56	230	32	27	8	1	3	4	15	0	31	1	0
Gonzalez, Jeremi, TB.	6	11	.353	3.91	25	25	2	0	0	0-0	156.1	131	668	71	68	18	3	9	12	69	1	97	3	2
Gordon, Tom, Chi.	7	6	.538	3.16	66	0	0	0	35	12-17	74.0	57	310	29	26	4	4	3	4	31	3	91	5	0
Gregg, Kevin, Ana.	2	0	1.000	3.28	5	3	0	0	0	0-0	24.2	18	97	9	9	3	0	0	1	8	0	14	0	0
Grimsley, Jason, K.C.	2	6	.250	5.16	76	0	0	0	5	0-7	75.0	88	346	47	43	6	6	5	5	36	5	58	4	0
Groom, Buddy, Bal.*	1	3	.250	5.36	60	0	0	0	20	1-3	45.1	58	207	27	27	7	1	1	3	14	2	34	1	0
Guardado, Eddie, Min.*	3	5	.375	2.89	66	0	0	0	60	41-45	65.1	50	260	22	21	7	3	2	0	14	2	60	5	0
Halama, John, Oak.*	3	5	.375	4.22	35	13	0	0	4	0-0	108.2	117	484	68	51	18	7	3	2	36	2	51	3	3
Halladay, Roy, Tor.	22	7	.759	3.25	36	36	9	2	0	0-0	266.0	253	1071	111	96	26	3	2	9	32	1	204	6	1
Hammond, Chris, N.Y.*	3	2	.600	2.86	62	0	0	0	16	1-4	63.0	65	262	23	20	5	5	3	2	11	0	45	1	0
Harang, Aaron, Oak.	1	3	.250	5.34	7	6	0	0	1	0-0	30.1	41	136	19	18	5	2	1	0	9	0	16	0	1
Harden, Rich, Oak.	5	4	.556	4.46	15	13	0	0	0	0-0	74.2	72	324	38	37	5	2	3	1	40	1	67	6	0
Harper, Travis, TB.	4	8	.333	3.77	61	0	0	0	14	1-6	93.0	86	388	45	39	9	7	3	6	31	8	64	6	0
Harville, Chad, Oak.	1	0	1.000	5.82	21	0	0	0	5	1-1	21.2	25	104	15	14	3	0	1	1	17	1	18	3	0
Hasegawa, Shigetoshi, Sea.	2	4	.333	1.48	63	0	0	0	36	16-17	73.0	62	283	12	12	5	1	0	0	18	3	32	0	0

Pitcher, Team	W	L	Pct.	ERA	G	GS	CG	ShO	GF	Sv.-Op.	IP	H	TBF	R	ER	HR	SH	SF	HB	BB	IBB	SO	WP	Bk.
Hawkins, LaTroy, Min.	9	3	.750	1.86	74	0	0	0	12	2-8	77.1	69	310	20	16	4	4	1	1	15	1	75	5	0
Helling, Rick, Bal.	7	8	.467	5.71	24	24	0	0	0	0-0	138.2	156	603	90	88	30	4	2	12	40	0	86	4	1
Hendrickson, Mark, Tor.*	9	9	.500	5.51	30	30	1	1	0	0-0	158.1	207	703	111	97	24	1	8	0	40	3	76	4	0
Hentgen, Pat, Bal.	7	8	.467	4.09	28	22	1	0	2	1-1	160.2	150	676	74	73	25	3	2	5	58	1	100	4	1
Heredia, Felix, N.Y.*	0	1	.000	1.20	12	0	0	0	4	0-1	15.0	13	62	5	2	1	0	0	0	5	2	4	0	0
Hernandez, Runelvys, K.C.	7	5	.583	4.61	16	16	0	0	0	0-0	91.2	87	397	51	47	9	1	4	6	37	0	48	2	1
Herrera, Alex, Cle.*	0	0	.000	9.00	10	0	0	0	3	0-0	7.0	7	36	7	7	3	0	0	0	8	1	6	1	0
Hill, Jeremy, K.C.	0	0	.000	0.00	1	0	0	0	1	0-0	1.0	1	4	0	0	0	0	0	0	0	0	0	0	0
Hitchcock, Sterling, N.Y.*	1	3	.250	5.44	27	1	0	0	8	0-0	49.2	57	221	33	30	6	1	2	0	18	3	36	1	0
Howry, Bob, Bos.	0	0	.000	12.46	4	0	0	0	3	0-1	4.1	11	27	6	6	1	0	1	0	3	1	4	0	0
Hudson, Tim, Oak.	16	7	.696	2.70	34	34	3	2	0	0-0	240.0	197	967	84	72	15	11	2	10	61	9	162	6	0
Johnson, Adam, Min.	0	1	.000	47.25	2	0	0	0	1	0-0	1.1	8	13	8	7	1	0	0	0	1	0	0	1	0
Johnson, Jason, Bal.	10	10	.500	4.18	32	32	0	0	0	0-0	189.2	216	858	100	88	22	3	1	10	80	8	118	7	0
Jones, Greg, Ana.	0	0	.000	4.88	18	0	0	0	7	0-0	27.2	29	127	15	15	3	0	0	2	14	0	28	5	0
Jones, Todd, Bos.	2	1	.667	5.52	26	0	0	0	7	0-0	29.1	32	133	19	18	2	0	1	0	13	2	31	0	0
Julio, Jorge, Bal.	0	7	.000	4.38	64	0	0	0	51	36-44	61.2	60	273	36	30	10	2	1	2	34	4	52	0	0
Kennedy, Joe, TB.*	3	12	.200	6.13	32	22	1	1	7	1-2	133.2	167	619	101	91	19	1	8	11	47	1	77	3	1
Kershner, Jason, Tor.*	3	3	.500	3.17	40	0	0	0	8	0-1	54.0	43	220	21	19	5	2	3	2	15	2	32	2	0
Kim, Byung-Hyun, Bos.	8	5	.615	3.18	49	5	0	0	35	16-19	79.1	70	336	38	28	6	3	2	8	18	3	69	1	0
Knotts, Gary, Det.	3	8	.273	6.04	20	18	0	0	0	0-0	95.1	111	442	70	64	14	1	4	4	47	0	51	4	0
Koch, Billy, Chi.	5	5	.500	5.77	55	0	0	0	45	11-15	53.0	59	244	36	34	10	2	3	1	28	1	42	3	0
Lackey, John, Ana.	10	16	.385	4.63	33	33	2	2	0	0-0	204.0	223	885	117	105	31	2	6	10	66	4	151	11	1
Ledezma, Wilfredo, Det.*	3	7	.300	5.79	34	8	0	0	13	0-1	84.0	99	376	55	54	12	1	4	3	35	3	49	2	0
Lee, Cliff, Cle.*	3	3	.500	3.61	9	9	0	0	0	0-0	52.1	41	210	28	21	7	1	1	2	20	1	44	3	0
Lee, David, Cle.	1	0	1.000	4.70	8	0	0	0	2	0-0	7.2	4	34	4	4	1	0	0	0	6	1	7	1	0
Leskanic, Curtis, K.C.	1	0	1.000	1.73	27	0	0	0	9	2-3	26.0	16	101	7	5	1	0	1	0	11	1	22	1	0
Levine, Al, TB.-K.C.	3	6	.333	2.79	54	0	0	0	21	1-4	71.0	67	303	29	22	9	4	0	3	29	1	30	3	0
Lewis, Colby, Tex.	10	9	.526	7.30	26	26	0	0	0	0-0	127.0	163	594	104	103	23	2	2	5	70	1	88	5	0
Lidle, Cory, Tor.	12	15	.444	5.75	31	31	2	0	0	0-0	192.2	216	840	133	123	24	5	5	5	60	3	112	9	0
Ligtenberg, Kerry, Bal.	4	2	.667	3.34	68	0	0	0	21	1-4	59.1	60	247	23	22	9	2	1	2	14	3	47	0	0
Lilly, Ted, Oak.*	12	10	.545	4.34	32	31	0	0	0	0-0	178.1	179	773	92	86	24	3	4	5	58	3	147	5	4
Lima, Jose, K.C.	8	3	.727	4.91	14	14	0	0	0	0-0	73.1	80	321	40	40	7	1	3	5	26	0	32	2	2
Linton, Doug, Tor.	0	0	.000	3.00	7	0	0	0	7	0-0	9.0	7	35	3	3	2	0	0	0	4	0	7	0	0
Lloyd, Graeme, K.C.*	0	2	.000	10.95	16	0	0	0	4	0-1	12.1	29	74	18	15	0	0	2	1	7	0	8	0	0
Loaiza, Esteban, Chi.	21	9	.700	2.90	34	34	1	0	0	0-0	226.1	196	922	75	73	17	7	6	10	56	2	207	3	1
Lohse, Kyle, Min.	14	11	.560	4.61	33	33	2	1	0	0-0	201.0	211	850	107	103	28	8	5	5	45	1	130	10	1
Looper, Aaron, Sea.	0	0	.000	5.14	6	0	0	0	3	0-0	7.0	7	29	4	4	1	0	0	1	2	0	6	0	0
Lopez, Albie, K.C.	4	2	.667	12.71	15	0	0	0	3	0-3	22.2	41	125	32	32	7	1	0	0	17	1	15	3	0
Lopez, Aquilino, Tor.	1	3	.250	3.42	72	0	0	0	34	14-16	73.2	58	316	31	28	5	2	2	5	34	5	64	2	1
Lopez, Rodrigo, Bal.	7	10	.412	5.82	26	26	3	1	0	0-0	147.0	188	663	101	95	24	3	7	10	43	6	103	2	1
Loux, Shane, Det.	1	1	.500	7.12	11	4	0	0	1	0-0	30.1	37	140	24	24	4	1	1	4	12	1	8	1	0
Lowe, Derek, Bos.	17	7	.708	4.47	33	33	1	0	0	0-0	203.1	216	886	113	101	17	3	5	11	72	4	110	3	0
Lowe, Sean, K.C.	1	1	.500	6.25	28	0	0	0	6	0-1	44.2	55	208	32	31	7	1	1	2	21	5	28	2	0
Lyon, Brandon, Bos.	4	6	.400	4.12	49	0	0	0	31	9-12	59.0	73	273	33	27	6	1	4	2	19	5	50	0	0
MacDougal, Mike, K.C.	3	5	.375	4.08	68	0	0	0	61	27-35	64.0	64	285	36	29	4	3	2	8	32	0	57	6	0
Mahay, Ron, Tex.*	3	3	.500	3.18	35	0	0	0	5	0-3	45.1	33	189	19	16	3	0	0	0	20	7	38	4	0
Malaska, Mark, TB.*	2	1	.667	2.81	22	0	0	0	3	0-3	16.0	13	70	7	5	0	1	0	1	12	3	17	0	0
Maroth, Mike, Det.*	9	21	.300	5.73	33	33	1	0	0	0-0	193.1	231	847	131	123	34	8	8	8	50	2	87	7	0
Marte, Damaso, Chi.*	4	2	.667	1.58	71	0	0	0	25	11-18	79.2	50	314	16	14	3	3	3	3	34	6	87	1	0
Martinez, Pedro, Bos.	14	4	.778	2.22	29	29	3	0	0	0-0	186.2	147	749	52	46	7	4	4	9	47	0	206	5	0
Mateo, Julio, Sea.	4	0	1.000	3.15	50	0	0	0	17	1-1	85.2	69	338	32	30	14	2	4	5	13	1	71	1	1
May, Darrell, K.C.*	10	8	.556	3.77	35	32	2	1	1	0-1	210.0	197	868	98	88	31	5	6	2	53	1	115	5	0
Mays, Joe, Min.	8	8	.500	6.30	31	21	0	0	4	0-1	130.0	159	576	92	91	21	3	3	4	39	2	50	3	0
McClung, Seth, TB.	4	1	.800	5.35	12	5	0	0	2	0-0	38.2	33	167	23	23	6	1	1	3	25	1	25	2	0
Mears, Chris, Det.	1	3	.250	5.44	29	3	0	0	16	5-5	41.1	50	178	28	25	5	0	1	3	11	0	21	2	0
Meche, Gil, Sea.	15	13	.536	4.59	32	32	1	0	0	0-0	186.1	187	785	97	95	30	3	5	3	63	2	130	7	0
Mecir, Jim, Oak.	2	3	.400	5.59	41	0	0	0	7	1-2	37.0	40	165	25	23	4	3	2	1	16	1	25	1	0
Mendoza, Ramiro, Bos.	3	5	.375	6.75	37	5	0	0	8	0-1	66.2	98	311	51	50	10	1	4	5	20	4	36	1	0
Miadich, Bart, Ana.	0	0	.000	18.00	1	0	0	0	0	0-0	2.0	5	12	4	4	0	0	0	1	1	0	3	1	0
Miceli, Dan, Cle.-N.Y.	1	1	.500	2.29	20	0	0	0	7	1-2	19.2	13	83	7	5	3	0	0	0	9	1	20	1	0
Miller, Trever, Tor.*	2	2	.500	4.61	79	0	0	0	18	4-5	52.2	46	233	30	27	7	1	0	5	28	3	44	2	0
Milton, Eric, Min.*	1	0	1.000	2.65	3	3	0	0	0	0-0	17.0	15	66	5	5	2	0	1	0	1	0	7	0	0
Moss, Damian, Bal.*	1	5	.167	6.22	10	9	0	0	0	0-0	50.2	63	244	40	35	12	2	2	6	29	2	22	1	0
Mounce, Tony, Tex.*	1	5	.167	7.11	11	11	0	0	0	0-0	50.2	65	238	42	40	9	2	1	5	25	0	30	1	0
Moyer, Jamie, Sea.*	21	7	.750	3.27	33	33	1	0	0	0-0	215.0	199	897	83	78	19	7	6	8	66	3	129	0	0
Mulder, Mark, Oak.*	15	9	.625	3.13	26	26	9	2	0	0-0	186.2	180	747	66	65	15	7	2	2	40	2	128	7	0
Mulholland, Terry, Cle.*	3	4	.429	4.91	45	3	0	0	14	0-2	99.0	117	445	60	54	17	0	6	6	37	6	42	1	0
Mullen, Scott, K.C.*	0	0	.000	16.62	2	0	0	0	0	0-0	4.1	11	29	8	8	2	0	0	0	5	0	3	1	0
Mussina, Mike, N.Y.	17	8	.680	3.40	31	31	2	1	0	0-0	214.2	192	855	86	81	21	1	4	3	40	4	195	4	0
Myette, Aaron, Cle.	0	0	.000	23.63	2	0	0	0	1	0-0	2.2	7	18	7	7	1	0	0	1	2	0	1	0	0
Nakamura, Mike, Min.	0	0	.000	7.82	12	0	0	0	7	1-1	12.2	20	62	11	11	4	0	0	1	2	0	14	0	0
Nelson, Jeff, Sea.-N.Y.	4	2	.667	3.74	70	0	0	0	28	8-14	55.1	51	240	25	23	4	4	2	4	24	3	68	3	1
Neu, Mike, Oak.	0	0	.000	3.64	32	0	0	0	26	1-1	42.0	43	194	18	17	2	1	0	2	26	2	20	4	0
Nitkowski, C.J., Tex.*	0	0	.000	7.45	6	0	0	0	0	0-0	9.2	17	52	8	8	0	1	2	0	8	1	5	0	0
Orosco, Jesse, N.Y.-Min.*	1	1	.500	8.00	23	0	0	0	3	0-1	9.0	8	48	9	8	0	1	2	1	11	3	7	3	0
Ortiz, Ramon, Ana.	16	13	.552	5.20	32	32	1	0	0	0-0	180.0	209	814	121	104	28	3	7	12	63	0	94	4	0
Osuna, Antonio, N.Y.	2	5	.286	3.73	48	0	0	0	16	0-1	50.2	58	232	22	21	3	2	2	2	20	3	47	3	0
Paniagua, Jose, Chi.	0	0	.000	108.00	1	0	0	0	0	0-0	0.1	3	5	4	4	0	0	0	0	1	0	0	0	0
Park, Chan Ho, Tex.	1	3	.250	7.58	7	7	0	0	0	0-0	29.2	34	146	26	25	5	1	3	6	25	0	16	1	1
Paronto, Chad, Cle.	0	2	.000	9.45	6	0	0	0	5	0-0	6.2	7	29	8	7	1	1	1	0	3	0	6	0	0
Parque, Jim, TB.*	1	1	.500	11.94	5	5	0	0	0	0-0	17.1	27	95	23	23	2	1	0	1	16	0	8	0	0
Parris, Steve, TB.	0	3	.000	6.18	10	7	0	0	1	0-0	43.2	60	200	32	30	12	2	2	0	13	0	14	2	0

Pitcher, Team	W	L	Pct.	ERA	G	GS	CG	ShO	GF	Sv.-Op.	IP	H	TBF	R	ER	HR	SH	SF	HB	BB	IBB	SO	WP	Bk.
Parrish, John, Bal.*	0	1	.000	1.90	14	0	0	0	2	0-2	23.2	17	93	7	5	2	0	1	1	8	2	15	2	0
Patterson, Danny, Det.	0	0	.000	4.08	19	0	0	0	9	3-3	17.2	15	73	8	8	1	2	0	1	4	0	19	0	0
Percival, Troy, Ana.	0	5	.000	3.47	52	0	0	0	49	33-37	49.1	33	206	22	19	7	0	1	3	23	1	48	1	0
Person, Robert, Bos.	0	0	.000	7.71	7	0	0	0	3	1-1	11.2	11	55	10	10	0	0	2	1	8	0	10	2	0
Pettitte, Andy, N.Y.*	21	8	.724	4.02	33	33	1	0	0	0-0	208.1	227	896	109	93	21	5	5	1	50	3	180	5	0
Phillips, Jason C., Cle.	0	1	.000	9.00	3	0	0	0	2	0-0	5.0	9	25	5	5	1	0	1	0	2	0	2	0	0
Pineiro, Joel, Sea.	16	11	.593	3.78	32	32	3	2	0	0-0	211.2	192	890	94	89	19	3	9	6	76	3	151	5	0
Politte, Cliff, Tor.	1	5	.167	5.66	54	0	0	0	30	12-18	49.1	52	216	32	31	11	1	3	1	17	4	40	1	0
Ponson, Sidney, Bal.	14	6	.700	3.77	21	21	4	0	0	0-0	148.0	147	622	65	62	10	2	3	4	43	2	100	6	0
Porzio, Mike, Chi.*	1	1	.500	6.43	3	3	0	0	0	0-0	14.0	18	62	10	10	2	2	1	2	1	0	9	0	0
Powell, Jay, Tex.	3	0	1.000	7.82	51	0	0	0	20	0-0	58.2	75	279	58	51	7	1	6	2	34	3	40	6	0
Prinz, Bret, N.Y.	0	0	.000	18.00	2	0	0	0	2	0-0	2.0	6	15	4	4	1	0	0	0	3	1	2	0	0
Pulido, Carlos, Min.*	0	1	.000	4.02	7	1	0	0	1	0-0	15.2	15	65	9	7	0	1	2	0	3	0	6	1	0
Putz, J.J., Sea.	0	0	.000	4.91	3	0	0	0	0	0-0	3.2	4	18	2	2	0	0	0	0	3	0	3	0	0
Radke, Brad, Min.	14	10	.583	4.49	33	33	3	1	0	0-0	212.1	242	888	111	106	32	12	4	5	28	2	120	0	0
Ramirez, Erasmo, Tex.*	3	1	.750	3.86	34	0	0	0	9	0-1	49.0	46	200	21	21	4	2	2	4	9	0	28	1	0
Ramos, Mario, Tex.*	1	1	.500	6.23	3	3	0	0	0	0-0	13.0	11	65	9	9	3	1	0	2	13	0	8	0	0
Reed, Rick, Min.	6	12	.333	5.07	27	21	2	1	1	0-1	135.0	155	583	80	76	21	2	4	5	29	2	71	3	0
Reichert, Dan, Tor.	0	0	.000	6.06	15	0	0	0	2	0-1	16.1	28	82	12	11	2	0	0	2	8	3	13	0	0
Reyes, Al, N.Y.	0	0	.000	3.18	13	0	0	0	2	0-1	17.0	13	73	7	6	1	0	0	0	9	1	9	1	0
Reyes, Carlos, TB.	0	3	.000	5.22	10	3	0	0	5	0-0	39.2	40	161	23	23	10	1	2	2	5	0	13	1	1
Rhodes, Arthur, Sea.*	3	3	.500	4.17	67	0	0	0	14	3-6	54.0	53	228	25	25	4	2	0	1	18	2	48	2	0
Riggan, Jerrod, Cle.	0	0	.000	9.00	2	0	0	0	1	0-0	4.0	7	19	4	4	0	0	1	0	1	0	2	0	1
Riley, Matt, Bal.*	1	0	1.000	1.80	2	2	0	0	0	0-0	10.0	7	41	2	2	1	0	0	0	5	0	8	0	0
Rincon, Juan, Min.	5	6	.455	3.68	58	0	0	0	20	0-1	85.2	74	370	38	35	5	2	5	4	38	7	63	7	0
Rincon, Ricardo, Oak.*	8	4	.667	3.25	64	0	0	0	16	0-3	55.1	45	241	21	20	4	8	2	3	32	4	40	0	0
Riske, David, Cle.	2	2	.500	2.29	68	0	0	0	24	8-13	74.2	52	293	21	19	9	4	1	3	20	3	82	1	0
Rivera, Mariano, N.Y.	5	2	.714	1.66	64	0	0	0	57	40-46	70.2	61	277	15	13	3	1	2	4	10	1	63	0	0
Roberts, Willis, Bal.	3	1	.750	5.72	26	0	0	0	9	0-0	39.1	41	174	26	25	7	1	0	7	16	2	26	2	0
Robertson, Nate, Det.*	1	2	.333	5.44	8	8	0	0	0	0-0	44.2	55	203	27	27	6	0	0	0	23	2	33	3	0
Rocker, John, TB.*	0	0	.000	9.00	2	0	0	0	0	0-0	1.0	2	8	1	1	0	0	0	1	3	0	0	0	0
Rodney, Fernando, Det.	1	3	.250	6.07	27	0	0	0	11	3-6	29.2	35	143	20	20	2	3	3	1	17	1	33	0	0
Rodriguez, Francisco, Ana.	8	3	.727	3.03	59	0	0	0	23	2-6	86.0	50	334	30	29	12	2	4	2	35	5	95	7	0
Rodriguez, Ricardo, Cle.	3	9	.250	5.73	15	15	0	0	0	0-0	81.2	89	360	57	52	16	3	2	3	28	1	41	4	1
Rodriguez, Rich, Ana.*	0	0	.000	2.45	3	0	0	0	2	0-0	3.2	4	15	1	1	0	0	1	0	1	0	3	0	0
Rogers, Kenny, Min.*	13	8	.619	4.57	33	31	0	0	0	0-0	195.0	227	851	108	99	22	9	3	11	50	5	116	6	4
Romero, J.C., Min.*	2	0	1.000	5.00	73	0	0	0	17	0-4	63.0	66	295	37	35	7	4	0	6	42	7	50	9	2
Roney, Matt, Det.	1	9	.100	5.45	45	11	0	0	12	0-2	100.2	102	449	67	61	17	4	4	4	48	4	47	2	2
Rupe, Ryan, Bos.	1	1	.500	6.30	4	1	0	0	0	0-1	10.0	13	45	9	7	4	1	0	0	1	0	7	0	0
Ryan, B.J., Bal.*	4	1	.800	3.40	76	0	0	0	17	0-2	50.1	42	219	19	19	1	1	3	3	27	0	63	2	0
Sabathia, C.C., Cle.*	13	9	.591	3.60	30	30	2	1	0	0-0	197.2	190	832	85	79	19	10	4	6	66	3	141	4	2
Sadler, Carl, Cle.*	0	0	.000	1.86	18	0	0	0	5	0-0	9.2	11	45	2	2	0	1	1	2	5	0	10	1	0
Sanders, David, Chi.*	0	0	.000	6.14	20	0	0	0	7	0-0	22.0	25	102	16	15	5	0	1	1	11	0	14	0	0
Santana, Johan, Min.*	12	3	.800	3.07	45	18	0	0	7	0-0	158.1	127	644	56	54	17	2	4	3	47	1	169	6	2
Santiago, Jose, Cle.	1	3	.250	2.84	25	0	0	0	4	0-2	31.2	37	138	11	10	2	0	0	0	14	3	15	0	0
Santos, Victor, Tex.	0	2	.000	7.01	8	4	0	0	2	0-0	25.2	29	117	21	20	5	1	1	1	16	1	15	0	0
Sasaki, Kazuhiro, Sea.	1	2	.333	4.05	35	0	0	0	25	10-14	33.1	31	150	17	15	2	2	2	1	15	2	29	4	0
Sauerbeck, Scott, Bos.*	0	1	.000	6.48	26	0	0	0	2	0-1	16.2	17	87	14	12	1	0	1	4	18	3	18	1	0
Schmack, Brian, Det.	1	0	1.000	3.46	11	0	0	0	1	0-0	13.0	14	55	6	5	1	0	2	1	4	0	4	1	0
Schoeneweis, Scott, Ana.-Chi.*	3	2	.600	4.18	59	0	0	0	19	0-2	64.2	63	276	35	30	3	2	1	4	19	5	56	3	0
Seanez, Rudy, Bos.	0	1	.000	6.23	9	0	0	0	4	0-1	8.2	11	44	7	6	2	0	1	0	6	1	9	3	0
Seay, Bobby, TB.*	0	0	.000	3.00	12	0	0	0	2	0-1	9.0	7	39	3	3	0	0	2	0	6	0	5	0	0
Sele, Aaron, Ana.	7	11	.389	5.77	25	25	0	0	0	0-0	121.2	135	553	82	78	17	2	5	12	58	1	53	5	0
Service, Scott, Tor.	0	0	.000	4.50	15	0	0	0	4	0-1	16.0	17	69	8	8	3	0	1	0	6	0	17	0	0
Shields, Scot, Ana.	5	6	.455	2.85	44	13	0	0	5	1-1	148.1	138	609	56	47	12	3	4	5	38	6	111	4	0
Shiell, Jason, Bos.	2	0	1.000	4.63	17	0	0	0	6	1-2	23.1	23	110	13	12	4	0	0	2	17	2	23	2	0
Shouse, Brian, Tex.*	0	1	.000	3.10	62	0	0	0	14	1-1	61.0	62	253	24	21	1	3	0	4	14	6	40	0	0
Snyder, Kyle, K.C.	1	6	.143	5.17	15	15	0	0	0	0-0	85.1	94	364	52	49	11	0	9	2	21	3	39	4	0
Soriano, Rafael, Sea.	3	0	1.000	1.53	40	0	0	0	12	1-2	53.0	30	201	9	9	2	0	1	3	12	1	68	0	0
Sosa, Jorge, TB.	5	12	.294	4.62	29	19	1	1	4	0-0	128.2	137	566	71	66	14	4	5	4	60	4	72	8	1
Sparks, Steve, Det.-Oak.	0	6	.000	4.88	51	0	0	0	26	2-4	107.0	114	460	68	58	13	1	7	3	37	4	54	3	0
Spurling, Chris, Det.	1	3	.250	4.68	66	0	0	0	18	3-6	77.0	78	326	42	40	9	3	5	3	22	1	38	2	0
Standridge, Jason, TB.	0	5	.000	6.37	8	7	1	0	1	0-0	35.1	38	157	25	25	7	1	1	1	16	0	20	4	0
Stanford, Jason, Cle.*	1	3	.250	3.60	13	8	0	0	1	0-0	50.0	48	213	20	20	5	0	1	1	16	1	30	0	0
Stewart, Josh, Chi.*	1	2	.333	5.96	5	5	0	0	0	0-0	25.2	28	121	18	17	4	1	1	0	16	0	13	0	0
Sturtze, Tanyon, Tor.	7	6	.538	5.94	40	8	0	0	7	0-0	89.1	107	415	67	59	14	2	2	7	43	3	54	6	0
Sullivan, Scott, Chi.	0	0	.000	3.77	15	0	0	0	2	0-0	14.1	9	58	6	6	2	1	1	1	6	0	13	0	0
Suppan, Jeff, Bos.	3	4	.429	5.57	11	10	0	0	0	0-0	63.0	70	276	41	39	12	1	4	2	20	0	32	4	0
Sweeney, Brian, Sea.	0	0	.000	1.93	5	0	0	0	2	0-0	9.1	7	35	2	2	0	0	0	1	1	0	7	0	0
Switzer, Jon, TB.*	0	0	.000	7.45	5	0	0	0	1	0-0	9.2	13	46	8	8	2	0	1	4	3	0	7	1	0
Tallet, Brian, Cle.*	0	2	.000	4.74	5	3	0	0	1	0-0	19.0	23	87	14	10	2	2	0	1	8	0	9	0	0
Tam, Jeff, Tor.	0	4	.000	5.64	44	0	0	0	9	1-2	44.2	58	214	30	28	5	2	1	1	25	7	26	2	0
Taylor, Aaron, Sea.	0	0	.000	8.53	10	0	0	0	4	0-0	12.2	17	62	12	12	0	0	1	1	6	0	9	2	0
Thomas, Brad, Min.*	0	1	.000	7.71	3	0	0	0	1	0-0	4.2	6	22	4	4	1	0	0	0	3	1	2	0	0
Thomson, John, Tex.	13	14	.481	4.85	35	35	3	1	0	0-0	217.0	234	910	125	117	27	2	7	4	49	2	136	5	0
Thurman, Corey, Tor.	1	1	.500	6.46	6	3	0	0	0	0-0	15.1	21	76	11	11	3	0	0	0	9	1	11	0	0
Timlin, Mike, Bos.	6	4	.600	3.55	72	0	0	0	13	2-6	83.2	77	340	37	33	11	4	1	4	9	3	65	0	0
Tolar, Kevin, Bos.*	0	0	.000	9.00	6	0	0	0	0	0-0	4.0	5	18	5	4	1	0	0	0	2	0	3	0	0
Towers, Josh, Tor.	8	1	.889	4.48	14	8	1	0	2	1-1	64.1	67	265	34	32	15	0	2	4	7	1	42	1	0
Traber, Billy, Cle.*	6	9	.400	5.24	33	18	1	1	0	0-0	111.2	132	503	67	65	15	4	3	5	40	4	88	6	0
Turnbow, Derrick, Ana.	2	0	1.000	0.59	11	0	0	0	7	0-0	15.1	7	53	1	1	0	0	0	0	3	0	15	0	0
Urbina, Ugueth, Tex.	0	4	.000	4.19	39	0	0	0	37	26-30	38.2	33	167	19	18	6	4	3	0	18	2	41	2	1

Pitcher, Team	W	L	Pct.	ERA	G	GS	CG	ShO	GF	Sv.-Op.	IP	H	TBF	R	ER	HR	SH	SF	HB	BB	IBB	SO	WP	Bk.
Valdes, Ismael, Tex.	8	8	.500	6.10	22	22	0	0	0	0-0	115.0	148	511	83	78	23	4	7	5	29	0	47	2	0
Van Poppel, Todd, Tex.	1	0	1.000	8.53	7	1	0	0	0	0-0	12.2	20	67	14	12	1	0	0	0	9	2	9	0	0
Venafro, Mike, TB.*	1	0	1.000	4.74	24	0	0	0	6	0-0	19.0	24	85	10	10	1	0	1	3	3	0	9	1	0
Voyles, Brad, K.C.	0	2	.000	7.18	11	3	0	0	4	0-0	31.1	47	158	29	25	6	2	2	1	18	1	24	3	0
Waechter, Doug, TB.	3	2	.600	3.31	6	5	1	1	0	0-0	35.1	29	145	13	13	4	0	0	1	15	0	29	0	0
Wakefield, Tim, Bos.	11	7	.611	4.09	35	33	0	0	2	1-1	202.1	193	872	106	92	23	2	4	12	71	0	169	8	0
Walker, Jamie, Det.*	4	3	.571	3.32	78	0	0	0	19	3-7	65.0	61	273	30	24	9	5	2	2	17	1	45	1	0
Walker, Pete, Tor.	2	2	.500	4.88	23	7	0	0	2	0-0	55.1	59	242	31	30	11	2	1	2	24	2	29	2	0
Walrond, Les, K.C.*	0	2	.000	10.13	7	0	0	0	2	0-0	8.0	11	41	9	9	2	0	0	0	7	1	6	1	0
Wasdin, John, Tor.	0	1	.000	23.40	3	2	0	0	0	0-0	5.0	16	35	13	13	2	0	1	0	4	0	5	0	0
Washburn, Jarrod, Ana.*	10	15	.400	4.43	32	32	2	0	0	0-0	207.1	205	876	106	102	34	5	6	11	54	4	118	4	1
Weaver, Jeff, N.Y.	7	9	.438	5.99	32	24	0	0	3	0-0	159.1	211	735	113	106	16	9	9	11	47	2	93	2	0
Weber, Ben, Ana.	5	1	.833	2.69	62	0	0	0	20	0-2	80.1	84	332	26	24	7	4	1	0	22	7	46	4	0
Wells, David, N.Y.*	15	7	.682	4.14	31	30	4	1	0	0-0	213.0	242	887	101	98	24	6	7	8	20	0	101	3	0
Westbrook, Jake, Cle.	7	10	.412	4.33	34	22	1	0	4	0-0	133.0	142	580	70	64	9	4	3	12	56	1	58	3	0
White, Gabe, N.Y.*	2	1	.667	4.38	12	0	0	0	1	0-1	12.1	8	49	7	6	2	1	1	1	2	1	6	0	0
White, Matt, Bos.-Sea.*	0	1	.000	22.24	6	0	0	0	3	0-0	5.2	13	33	14	14	3	0	1	0	5	0	0	0	0
White, Rick, Chi.	1	2	.333	6.61	34	0	0	0	12	1-1	47.2	56	207	39	35	11	1	2	1	13	2	37	0	0
Williamson, Scott, Bos.	0	1	.000	6.20	24	0	0	0	6	0-2	20.1	20	89	15	14	1	0	1	0	9	2	21	4	0
Wilson, Kris, K.C.	6	3	.667	5.33	29	4	0	0	7	0-1	72.2	92	328	49	43	13	0	4	6	16	3	42	0	1
Wood, Mike, Oak.	2	1	.667	10.54	7	1	0	0	2	0-0	13.2	24	72	17	16	1	1	0	2	7	2	15	2	0
Woodard, Steve, Bos.	1	0	1.000	5.09	7	0	0	0	0	0-0	17.2	23	81	10	10	3	0	1	1	5	2	12	1	0
Wright, Dan, Chi.	1	7	.125	6.15	20	15	0	0	1	1-1	86.1	91	388	63	59	16	6	4	3	46	2	47	6	0
Wright, Jamey, K.C.	1	2	.333	4.26	4	4	2	1	0	0-0	25.1	23	106	14	12	1	0	0	1	11	0	19	0	0
Wunsch, Kelly, Chi.*	0	0	.000	2.75	43	0	0	0	6	0-0	36.0	17	160	13	11	1	1	5	7	25	4	33	1	0
Yan, Esteban, Tex.	0	1	.000	6.94	15	0	0	0	6	0-0	23.1	31	110	19	18	5	0	0	2	7	1	25	5	0
Zambrano, Victor, TB.	12	10	.545	4.21	34	28	1	0	2	0-0	188.1	165	836	97	88	21	3	10	20	106	2	132	15	3
Zito, Barry, Oak.*	14	12	.538	3.30	35	35	4	1	0	0-0	231.2	186	957	98	85	19	7	7	6	88	3	146	4	0

PITCHERS WITH TWO OR MORE TEAMS

Pitcher, Team	W	L	Pct.	ERA	G	GS	CG	ShO	GF	Sv.-Op.	IP	H	TBF	R	ER	HR	SH	SF	HB	BB	IBB	SO	WP	Bk.
Acevedo, Juan, N.Y.	0	3	.000	7.71	25	0	0	0	19	6-7	25.2	34	125	24	22	5	2	3	2	10	3	19	2	0
Acevedo, Juan, Tor.	1	2	.333	4.26	14	0	0	0	6	0-1	12.2	18	63	8	6	1	0	0	0	8	1	9	2	0
Anderson, Brian, Cle.*	9	10	.474	3.71	25	24	0	0	0	0-0	148.0	162	623	88	61	21	2	10	4	32	3	72	2	1
Anderson, Brian, K.C.*	5	1	.833	3.99	7	7	2	1	0	0-0	49.2	50	198	22	22	6	1	2	0	11	0	15	1	0
Appier, Kevin, Ana.	7	7	.500	5.63	19	19	0	0	0	0-0	92.2	105	422	60	58	17	0	1	8	36	4	50	4	1
Appier, Kevin, K.C.	1	2	.333	4.26	4	4	0	0	0	0-0	19.0	15	77	9	9	4	1	0	0	7	0	5	2	0
Benitez, Armando, N.Y.	1	1	.500	1.93	9	0	0	0	2	0-0	9.1	8	40	4	2	0	0	0	0	6	1	10	0	0
Benitez, Armando, Sea.	0	0	.000	3.14	15	0	0	0	7	0-1	14.1	10	64	5	5	1	0	0	0	11	1	15	0	0
Bierbrodt, Nick, TB.*	0	2	.000	9.68	13	5	0	0	1	0-0	35.1	59	190	41	38	9	2	3	5	23	3	20	4	1
Bierbrodt, Nick, Cle.*	0	0	.000	6.75	5	0	0	0	3	0-0	8.0	5	33	6	6	0	0	2	0	4	0	9	0	0
Callaway, Mickey, Ana.	1	4	.200	6.81	17	4	0	0	8	0-0	38.1	57	184	32	29	7	0	2	1	16	1	22	0	0
Callaway, Mickey, Tex.	0	3	.000	6.45	6	3	0	0	0	0-0	22.1	27	100	18	16	0	2	3	1	8	0	19	2	0
Davis, Doug, Tex.*	0	0	.000	12.00	1	1	0	0	0	0-0	3.0	4	17	4	4	2	0	0	0	4	0	2	0	0
Davis, Doug, Tor.*	4	6	.400	5.00	12	11	0	0	0	0-0	54.0	70	250	33	30	6	3	0	1	26	1	25	6	0
Glover, Gary, Chi.	1	0	1.000	4.54	24	0	0	0	8	0-0	35.2	43	160	18	18	3	0	3	2	14	2	23	1	0
Glover, Gary, Ana.	1	0	1.000	5.00	18	0	0	0	7	0-0	27.0	34	119	15	15	3	0	2	1	8	1	14	1	0
Levine, Al, TB.	3	5	.375	2.90	36	0	0	0	14	0-2	49.2	45	208	23	16	7	3	0	2	18	0	25	3	0
Levine, Al, K.C.	0	1	.000	2.53	18	0	0	0	7	1-2	21.1	22	95	6	6	2	1	0	1	11	1	5	0	0
Miceli, Dan, Cle.	1	1	.500	1.20	13	0	0	0	4	0-1	15.0	9	61	4	2	1	0	0	0	6	1	19	1	0
Miceli, Dan, N.Y.	0	0	.000	5.79	7	0	0	0	3	1-1	4.2	4	22	3	3	2	0	0	0	3	0	1	0	0
Nelson, Jeff, Sea.	3	2	.600	3.35	46	0	0	0	25	7-11	37.2	34	159	16	14	3	4	2	2	14	1	47	2	1
Nelson, Jeff, N.Y.	1	0	1.000	4.58	24	0	0	0	3	1-3	17.2	17	81	9	9	1	0	0	2	10	2	21	1	0
Orosco, Jesse, N.Y.*	0	0	.000	10.38	15	0	0	0	0	0-1	4.1	4	24	6	5	0	1	1	0	6	3	4	0	0
Orosco, Jesse, Min.*	1	1	.500	5.79	8	0	0	0	3	0-0	4.2	4	24	3	3	0	0	1	1	5	0	3	3	0
Schoeneweis, Scott, Ana.*	1	1	.500	3.96	39	0	0	0	12	0-1	38.2	37	163	19	17	2	1	1	3	10	3	29	1	0
Schoeneweis, Scott, Chi.*	2	1	.667	4.50	20	0	0	0	7	0-1	26.0	26	113	16	13	1	1	0	1	9	2	27	2	0
Sparks, Steve, Det.	0	6	.000	4.72	42	0	0	0	24	2-4	89.2	95	386	57	47	11	1	6	3	34	4	49	3	0
Sparks, Steve, Oak.	0	0	.000	5.71	9	0	0	0	2	0-0	17.1	19	74	11	11	2	0	1	0	3	0	5	0	0
White, Matt, Bos.*	0	1	.000	27.00	3	0	0	0	1	0-0	3.2	10	23	11	11	1	0	1	0	3	0	0	0	0
White, Matt, Sea.*	0	0	.000	13.50	3	0	0	0	2	0-0	2.0	3	10	3	3	2	0	0	0	2	0	0	0	0

NOTE: The following pitchers combined to pitch shutout games: Anaheim (7)—Callaway, Shields and Weber; Washburn and Percival; Ortiz, Donnelly and Percival; Lackey, Donnelly and Percival; Sele, F. Rodriguez, Donnelly and Percival; Ortiz, Shields and Donnelly; Ortiz and Weber; Baltimore (2)—Helling and Groom; Hentgen, Groom and Julio; Boston (6)—Lowe and Wakefield; Martinez and Timlin; Wakefield, Timlin and Fossum; Martinez and Embree; Martinez, Timlin and Kim; Burkett, Timlin, Kim and Embree; Chicago (4)—Buehrle and White; Loaiza and Koch; Loaiza, Gordon and Koch; Garland and Koch; Cleveland (5)—Anderson and Baez; Sabathia, Traber, Boyd and Baez; Traber, Riske and Baez; Traber, Riske and Baez; Davis, Cressend, Betancourt, Mulholland and Riske; Detroit (5)—Knotts and German; Roney, Rodney and Walker; Cornejo, Walker and Mears; Ledezma, Walker and Mears; Maroth, Anderson, Walker and Rodney; Kansas City (7)—Hernandez, Grimsley and MacDougal; Hernandez, Grimsley and MacDougal; George, Grimsley and Carrasco; May, Grimsley and Carrasco; Gobble, Leskanic and Affeldt; Appier, Affeldt and Leskanic; Abbott and Affeldt; Minnesota (5)—Lohse and Guardado; Rogers and Fiore; Santana, Hawkins, Romero and Guardado; Santana, Rincon, Hawkins and Guardado; Lohse, Hawkins and Guardado; New York (9)—Mussina and Anderson; Weaver and Hammond; Contreras, Osuna and Hammond; Clemens, Rivera and Hammond; Pettitte, Hammond, Anderson and Rivera; Mussina and Rivera; Contreras, Osuna and Hammond; Clemens, Heredia and Osuna; Contreras and Rivera; Oakland (9)—Hudson and Rincon; Zito and Foulke; Hudson, Halama and Neu; Zito and Foulke; Hudson and Halama; Mulder, Rincon and Foulke; Lilly, Bradford, Halama, Mecir and Foulke; Zito, Bradford, Mecir, Rincon and Foulke; Lilly, Bradford, Rincon and Foulke; Seattle (12)—Moyer, Nelson and Rhodes; Meche, Hasegawa, Rhodes and Nelson; Pineiro, Mateo and Soriano; Meche, Rhodes and Hasegawa; Moyer, Hasegawa and Rhodes; Moyer, Hasegawa and Nelson; Franklin and Rhodes; Garcia and Rhodes; Pineiro and Mateo; Pineiro, Rhodes and Nelson; Franklin, Soriano and Looper; Moyer, Benitez and Hasegawa; Tampa Bay (4)—Parque, Harper, Rocker and Carter; Gonzalez and Carter; Gonzalez and Colome; Zambrano and Carter; Texas (1)—Valdes and Cordero; Toronto (3)—Hendrickson and Service; Escobar, Miller and Politte; Towers and Walker.

FIELDING

TEAM

Team	G	PO	A	E	TC	DP	TP	PB	Pct.
Seattle	162	4323	1450	65	5838	159	0	12	.989
Minnesota	162	4386	1481	87	5954	114	0	10	.985
Texas	162	4300	1703	94	6097	168	0	11	.985
Chicago	162	4293	1588	93	5974	154	0	13	.984
Baltimore	163	4349	1683	105	6137	164	0	12	.983
Tampa Bay	162	4310	1580	103	5993	158	0	9	.983
Oakland	162	4325	1779	107	6211	145	0	9	.983
Kansas City	162	4316	1705	108	6129	143	0	8	.982
Anaheim	162	4294	1517	105	5916	138	0	11	.982
Boston	162	4394	1679	113	6186	130	0	20	.982
New York	163	4386	1578	114	6078	126	0	13	.981
Toronto	162	4305	1742	117	6164	161	0	10	.981
Cleveland	162	4378	1780	126	6284	178	0	11	.980
Detroit	162	4316	1813	138	6267	194	0	11	.978
Totals	1135	60675	23078	1475	85228	2132	0	160	.983

INDIVIDUAL

FIRST BASEMEN

NOTE: All caps denotes fielding-percentage leader based on 81 games for catchers, 108 for all other non-pitchers and 162 innings for pitchers. *Throws lefthanded.

Player, Team	G	GS	PO	A	E	TC	DP	Pct.
Abad, Andy, Bos.*	7	3	35	1	1	37	2	.973
Berg, Dave, Tor.	2	1	15	1	0	16	2	1.000
Blake, Casey, Cle.	31	12	131	12	0	143	22	1.000
Bloomquist, Willie, Sea.	3	0	6	1	0	7	0	1.000
Broussard, Ben, Cle.*	114	101	957	63	9	1029	85	.991
Burke, Jamie, Chi.	1	0	1	1	0	2	0	1.000
Burkhart, Morgan, K.C.*	2	1	10	0	0	10	2	1.000
Catalanotto, Frank, Tor.	5	2	20	3	2	25	3	.920
Cirillo, Jeff, Sea.	1	0	2	0	0	2	1	1.000
Clark, Howie, Tor.	2	0	4	0	0	4	1	1.000
Colbrunn, Greg, Sea.	14	13	83	5	1	89	5	.989
Conine, Jeff, Bal.	118	118	1060	80	9	1149	106	.992
Cuddyer, Michael, Min.	5	3	30	1	1	32	2	.969
Daubach, Brian, Chi.	45	30	245	21	1	267	21	.996
Delgado, Carlos, Tor.	147	147	1355	103	10	1468	137	.993
Durazo, Erubiel, Oak.*	33	33	298	9	6	313	26	.981
Fullmer, Brad, Ana.	19	17	142	11	0	153	17	1.000
Giambi, Jason, N.Y.	85	85	748	19	4	771	63	.995
Gibbons, Jay, Bal.*	13	11	91	7	1	99	16	.990
Gil, Benji, Ana.	5	1	15	4	0	19	2	1.000
Graffanino, Tony, Chi.	2	0	6	0	0	6	0	1.000
Greene, Todd, Tex.	2	0	5	3	0	8	0	1.000
Hafner, Travis, Cle.	42	40	369	18	6	393	47	.985
Halter, Shane, Det.	12	7	84	4	2	90	13	.978
Harvey, Ken, K.C.	99	94	805	80	11	896	78	.988
Hatteberg, Scott, Oak.	128	126	1177	81	10	1268	101	.992
Hillenbrand, Shea, Bos.	28	17	193	13	0	206	13	1.000
Hocking, Denny, Min.	10	1	44	4	1	49	3	.980
Huff, Aubrey, TB.	22	20	166	12	0	178	23	1.000
Ibanez, Raul, K.C.	22	18	164	19	1	184	15	.995
Jackson, Damian, Bos.	2	0	4	0	0	4	0	1.000
Johnson, Nick, N.Y.*	60	60	512	34	5	551	44	.991
Jones, Jason, Tex.	3	0	3	0	0	3	0	1.000
Kapler, Gabe, Bos.	1	0	3	0	0	3	0	1.000
Kielty, Bobby, Tor.	3	2	19	2	0	21	2	1.000
KONERKO, Paul, Chi.	119	105	889	80	2	971	102	.998
Koonce, Graham, Oak.*	5	1	22	3	0	25	3	1.000
Lamb, Mike, Tex.	5	0	6	1	0	7	0	1.000
LeCroy, Matthew, Min.	17	12	99	3	1	103	7	.990
Lee, Travis, TB.*	142	141	1223	100	3	1326	117	.998
Leon, Jose, Bal.	7	5	44	2	1	47	7	.979
Lopez, Mendy, K.C.	17	4	59	9	0	68	3	1.000
Mabry, John, Sea.	9	6	44	8	0	52	7	1.000
Martin, Al, TB.*	1	0	2	0	0	2	0	1.000
McCarty, Dave, Oak.-Bos.*	8	4	49	3	2	54	4	.963
McMillon, Billy, Oak.*	3	0	5	0	0	5	0	1.000
Melhuse, Adam, Oak.	1	0	2	0	0	2	0	1.000
Mendez, Carlos, Bal.	9	3	28	3	2	33	1	.939
Mientkiewicz, Doug, Min.	139	133	1091	68	4	1163	86	.997
Millar, Kevin, Bos.	101	96	858	81	4	943	80	.996
Mirabelli, Doug, Bos.	2	0	5	1	1	7	0	.857
Mora, Melvin, Bal.	1	0	2	0	0	2	0	1.000
Morneau, Justin, Min.	7	2	29	4	1	34	1	.971
Olerud, John, Sea.*	152	143	1096	125	3	1224	126	.998
Ortiz, David, Bos.*	45	44	342	30	3	375	20	.992
Palmeiro, Rafael, Tex.*	55	55	445	49	2	496	53	.996
Palmer, Dean, Det.	1	1	9	1	0	10	0	1.000
Paquette, Craig, Det.	5	4	42	1	0	43	4	1.000
Patterson, Jarrod, K.C.	2	0	9	1	0	10	0	1.000
Pena, Carlos, Det.*	128	124	1135	91	13	1239	130	.990
Perry, Herbert, Tex.	5	3	18	3	0	21	2	1.000
Petrick, Ben, Det.	2	0	3	0	0	3	0	1.000
Phelps, Josh, Tor.	8	8	55	4	2	61	2	.967
Piatt, Adam, Oak.	1	0	6	0	0	6	1	1.000
Quinlan, Robb, Ana.	33	19	146	13	2	161	15	.988
Riggs, Adam, Ana.	10	9	71	10	2	83	5	.976
Sandberg, Jared, TB.	1	1	7	0	0	7	0	1.000
Sears, Todd, Min.	14	11	93	7	1	101	7	.990
Segui, David, Bal.*	8	6	52	6	0	58	7	1.000
Seguignol, Fernando, N.Y.	3	1	9	3	0	12	0	1.000
Selby, Bill, Cle.	1	0	0	0	0	0	0	.000
Sojo, Luis, N.Y.	1	0	0	0	0	0	0	.000
Spencer, Shane, Cle.	11	9	66	1	0	67	3	1.000
Spiezio, Scott, Ana.	114	89	722	57	5	784	61	.994
Surhoff, B.J., Bal.	22	20	157	11	1	169	14	.994
Sweeney, Mike, K.C.	45	45	379	35	4	418	30	.990
Teixeira, Mark, Tex.	116	104	931	71	4	1006	95	.996
Thomas, Frank, Chi.	27	27	206	9	1	216	19	.995
Wilson, Tom, Tor.	14	2	46	4	1	51	4	.980
Witt, Kevin, Det.	27	26	214	20	0	234	31	1.000
Wooten, Shawn, Ana.	32	27	207	14	1	222	21	.995
Young, Dmitri, Det.	1	0	5	0	0	5	0	1.000
Zeile, Todd, N.Y.	23	17	181	15	1	197	11	.995

FIRST BASEMEN WITH TWO OR MORE TEAMS

Player, Team	G	GS	PO	A	E	TC	DP	Pct.
McCarty, Dave, Oak.*	3	2	26	1	1	28	2	.964
McCarty, Dave, Bos.*	5	2	23	2	1	26	2	.962

SECOND BASEMEN

Player, Team	G	GS	PO	A	E	TC	DP	Pct.
Abernathy, Brent, TB.-K.C.	11	7	13	28	1	42	4	.976
Alomar, Roberto, Chi.	67	65	119	171	3	293	37	.990
Anderson, Marlon, TB.	134	117	194	350	15	559	91	.973
Berg, Dave, Tor.	24	20	38	53	2	93	8	.978
Blalock, Hank, Tex.	4	1	2	7	1	10	1	.900
Bloomquist, Willie, Sea.	7	0	3	3	0	6	0	1.000
Boone, Bret, Sea.	158	158	268	426	7	701	107	.990
Bordick, Mike, Tor.	13	10	30	37	0	67	6	1.000
Clark, Howie, Tor.	3	3	4	13	1	18	1	.944
Clark, Jermaine, Tex.	7	2	5	6	0	11	2	1.000
Cuddyer, Michael, Min.	1	0	0	0	0	0	0	.000
Dawkins, Gookie, K.C.	3	1	3	4	0	7	0	1.000
Delgado, Wilson, Ana.	1	1	4	3	0	7	1	1.000
Durrington, Trent, Ana.	5	1	1	5	0	6	0	1.000
Easley, Damion, TB.	4	3	4	7	0	11	1	1.000
Ellis, Mark, Oak.	153	147	324	455	14	793	95	.982
Escalona, Felix, TB.	1	1	3	4	0	7	3	1.000
Febles, Carlos, K.C.	67	57	98	162	3	263	34	.989
Figgins, Chone, Ana.	14	12	23	27	1	51	6	.980
German, Esteban, Oak.	5	0	5	6	0	11	1	1.000
Gil, Benji, Ana.	28	22	32	62	2	96	14	.979
Gomez, Chris, Min.	23	16	37	50	1	88	10	.989
Graffanino, Tony, Chi.	29	22	53	77	3	133	22	.977
Hairston Jr., Jerry, Bal.	48	48	103	136	5	244	34	.980
Halter, Shane, Det.	24	22	40	74	0	114	12	1.000
Harris, Willie, Chi.	12	7	13	24	0	37	5	1.000
Hocking, Denny, Min.	26	14	31	36	0	67	9	1.000
Hudson, Orlando, Tor.	139	129	268	477	12	757	99	.984

Player, Team	G	GS	PO	A	E	TC	DP	Pct.
Infante, Omar, Det.	2	1	3	3	0	6	2	1.000
Jackson, Damian, Bos.	38	14	18	54	3	75	6	.960
Jimenez, D'Angelo, Chi.	68	67	118	174	7	299	41	.977
KENNEDY, Adam, Ana.	140	125	235	371	6	612	78	.990
Klassen, Danny, Det.	4	4	12	16	1	29	4	.966
Lopez, Mendy, K.C.	11	10	22	15	0	37	5	1.000
Matos, Julius, K.C.	11	5	10	24	1	35	4	.971
McDonald, John, Cle.	37	31	49	95	3	147	27	.980
McLemore, Mark, Sea.	6	3	9	11	1	21	3	.952
Menechino, Frank, Oak.	22	15	30	42	1	73	11	.986
Merloni, Lou, Bos.	7	2	5	5	0	10	3	1.000
Mientkiewicz, Doug, Min.	1	0	0	0	0	0	0	.000
Miles, Aaron, Chi.	3	1	1	6	0	7	0	1.000
Mora, Melvin, Bal.	6	5	14	16	0	30	6	1.000
Morban, Jose, Bal.	12	5	14	23	1	38	4	.974
Morris, Warren, Det.	89	85	182	271	6	459	83	.987
Mueller, Bill, Bos.	10	10	22	17	0	39	7	1.000
Perez, Antonio, TB.	31	30	35	65	1	101	11	.990
Phillips, Brandon, Cle.	109	104	236	325	11	572	76	.981
Prieto, Alex, Min.	5	1	5	6	0	11	1	1.000
Relaford, Desi, K.C.	89	83	183	223	8	414	50	.981
Riggs, Adam, Ana.	3	1	3	3	0	6	0	1.000
Rivas, Luis, Min.	134	131	218	325	10	553	64	.982
Roberts, Brian, Bal.	107	105	198	324	7	529	68	.987
Rolls, Damian, TB.	2	0	0	0	0	0	0	.000
Sadler, Donnie, Tex.	1	1	1	0	0	1	0	1.000
Sanchez, Freddy, Bos.	3	2	9	2	0	11	1	1.000
Santiago, Ramon, Det.	53	50	105	153	10	268	45	.963
Santos, Angel, Cle.	28	21	39	64	2	105	17	.981
Selby, Bill, Cle.	1	0	0	1	0	1	0	1.000
Shumpert, Terry, TB.	14	10	21	24	1	46	3	.978
Sojo, Luis, N.Y.	1	1	0	3	0	3	0	1.000
Sorensen, Zach, Cle.	14	6	14	20	2	36	5	.944
Soriano, Alfonso, N.Y.	155	154	293	445	19	757	88	.975
Ugueto, Luis, Sea.	4	0	2	3	0	5	2	1.000
Ventura, Robin, N.Y.	1	0	0	2	0	2	0	1.000
Walker, Todd, Bos.	139	134	235	391	16	642	78	.975
Wilson, Enrique, N.Y.	10	8	14	20	0	34	2	1.000
Young, Michael, Tex.	159	158	305	471	10	786	117	.987

SECOND BASEMEN WITH TWO OR MORE TEAMS

Player, Team	G	GS	PO	A	E	TC	DP	Pct.
Abernathy, Brent, TB.	2	1	1	8	1	10	0	.900
Abernathy, Brent, K.C.	9	6	12	20	0	32	4	1.000

THIRD BASEMEN

Player, Team	G	GS	PO	A	E	TC	DP	Pct.
Amezaga, Alfredo, Ana.	13	11	12	20	2	34	1	.941
Batista, Tony, Bal.	154	154	91	292	20	403	33	.950
Berg, Dave, Tor.	17	15	8	24	2	34	0	.941
Blake, Casey, Cle.	140	136	91	289	19	399	29	.952
Blalock, Hank, Tex.	141	131	110	238	15	363	32	.959
Bloomquist, Willie, Sea.	37	29	21	44	2	67	3	.970
Boone, Aaron, N.Y.	54	52	36	111	6	153	7	.961
Borders, Pat, Sea.	2	0	0	1	0	1	0	1.000
Bordick, Mike, Tor.	22	17	20	32	1	53	4	.981
Chavez, Eric, Oak.	154	153	125	343	14	482	33	.971
Cirillo, Jeff, Sea.	85	76	65	108	4	177	7	.977
Clark, Howie, Tor.	13	10	2	20	1	23	4	.957
Collier, Lou, Bos.	2	0	1	1	0	2	0	1.000
Conine, Jeff, Bal.	1	1	0	4	0	4	0	1.000
Crede, Joe, Chi.	151	149	107	264	14	385	29	.964
Cuddyer, Michael, Min.	7	5	2	7	0	9	0	1.000
Delgado, Wilson, Ana.	9	4	3	10	2	15	2	.867
Durrington, Trent, Ana.	4	1	1	1	0	2	0	1.000
Easley, Damion, TB.	23	22	12	35	4	51	2	.922
Escalona, Felix, TB.	1	0	0	0	0	0	0	.000
Gil, Benji, Ana.	4	1	2	2	0	4	1	1.000
Glaus, Troy, Ana.	87	86	56	136	16	208	11	.923
Gomez, Chris, Min.	18	15	14	31	1	46	3	.978
Grabowski, Jason, Oak.	1	0	0	0	0	0	0	.000
Graffanino, Tony, Chi.	20	12	5	18	1	24	2	.958
Guillen, Carlos, Sea.	32	32	38	45	3	86	3	.965
Gutierrez, Ricky, Cle.	7	5	5	5	0	10	0	1.000
Halter, Shane, Det.	50	42	36	98	2	136	12	.985
Henson, Drew, N.Y.	3	2	4	3	0	7	0	1.000
Hillenbrand, Shea, Bos.	29	28	26	42	3	71	3	.958
Hinske, Eric, Tor.	124	120	80	214	22	316	13	.930
Hocking, Denny, Min.	24	12	19	33	2	54	1	.963
Huff, Aubrey, TB.	8	7	7	8	3	18	2	.833
Infante, Omar, Det.	4	3	1	8	1	10	1	.900
Jackson, Damian, Bos.	3	2	1	7	1	9	0	.889
Jimenez, D'Angelo, Chi.	2	1	0	4	2	6	0	.667
Klassen, Danny, Det.	13	12	15	24	0	39	3	1.000
Koskie, Corey, Min.	131	130	91	234	9	334	15	.973
Lamb, Mike, Tex.	1	0	0	0	0	0	0	.000
LaRocca, Greg, Cle.	2	2	0	6	0	6	0	1.000
Leon, Jose, Bal.	10	8	10	16	1	27	3	.963
Liefer, Jeff, TB.	6	6	5	8	1	14	0	.929
Lopez, Mendy, K.C.	13	5	3	15	0	18	0	1.000
Matos, Julius, K.C.	13	7	3	9	0	12	0	1.000
McDonald, John, Cle.	23	9	10	17	3	30	2	.900
McLemore, Mark, Sea.	29	25	16	48	2	66	8	.970
Melhuse, Adam, Oak.	2	0	0	1	1	2	0	.500
Menechino, Frank, Oak.	19	9	6	21	2	29	2	.931
Merloni, Lou, Bos.	7	4	6	14	0	20	1	1.000
Mientkiewicz, Doug, Min.	1	0	0	0	0	0	0	.000
Morban, Jose, Bal.	1	0	0	0	0	0	0	.000
Mueller, Bill, Bos.	135	124	76	235	16	327	22	.951
Munson, Eric, Det.	91	88	68	150	19	237	13	.920
Palmer, Dean, Det.	1	1	0	4	0	4	0	1.000
Patterson, Jarrod, K.C.	4	0	0	0	1	1	0	.000
Peralta, Jhonny, Cle.	6	3	2	6	0	8	1	1.000
Perez, Antonio, TB.	6	3	1	7	1	9	0	.889
Perry, Herbert, Tex.	2	2	2	2	0	4	1	1.000
RANDA, Joe, K.C.	129	127	102	238	7	347	12	.980
Relaford, Desi, K.C.	33	23	11	60	6	77	5	.922
Rolls, Damian, TB.	73	68	75	135	6	216	16	.972
Sadler, Donnie, Tex.	23	18	15	30	2	47	3	.957
Sanchez, Freddy, Bos.	7	4	4	12	0	16	0	1.000
Sandberg, Jared, TB.	50	41	34	75	5	114	4	.956
Santos, Angel, Cle.	4	1	0	3	0	3	0	1.000
Selby, Bill, Cle.	10	6	6	19	2	27	2	.926
Shumpert, Terry, TB.	11	1	1	1	0	2	0	1.000
Smith, Jason, TB.	1	1	0	2	2	4	1	.500
Sorensen, Zach, Cle.	1	0	0	0	0	0	0	.000
Spiezio, Scott, Ana.	52	43	31	61	6	98	10	.939
Teixeira, Mark, Tex.	15	11	10	20	7	37	0	.811
Truby, Chris, TB.	13	13	9	32	1	42	4	.976
Ugueto, Luis, Sea.	1	0	0	0	0	0	0	.000
Ventura, Robin, N.Y.	80	76	44	146	5	195	9	.974
Wilson, Enrique, N.Y.	17	9	6	26	2	34	4	.941
Witt, Kevin, Det.	5	0	1	4	0	5	0	1.000
Wooten, Shawn, Ana.	17	16	12	26	1	39	1	.974
Young, Dmitri, Det.	16	16	8	37	8	53	5	.849
Zeile, Todd, N.Y.	30	24	17	49	6	72	8	.917

SHORTSTOPS

Player, Team	G	GS	PO	A	E	TC	DP	Pct.
Alicea, Luis, K.C.	1	0	0	0	0	0	0	.000
Almonte, Erick, N.Y.	31	29	49	67	12	128	13	.906
Amezaga, Alfredo, Ana.	24	21	39	57	3	99	11	.970
Berg, Dave, Tor.	1	0	0	0	0	0	0	.000
Berroa, Angel, K.C.	158	158	264	473	24	761	108	.968
Bloomquist, Willie, Sea.	18	14	24	37	2	63	8	.968
Bordick, Mike, Tor.	69	64	113	180	4	297	53	.987
Clark, Howie, Tor.	1	0	0	0	0	0	0	.000
Crosby, Bobby, Oak.	9	0	5	11	2	18	2	.889
Cruz, Deivi, Bal.	147	144	222	409	16	647	96	.975
Delgado, Wilson, Ana.	9	8	20	18	1	39	6	.974
Eckstein, David, Ana.	116	114	193	293	8	494	67	.984
Escalona, Felix, TB.	8	8	15	21	0	36	8	1.000
Febles, Carlos, K.C.	1	0	0	0	0	0	0	.000
Figgins, Chone, Ana.	8	6	11	18	2	31	4	.935
Garciaparra, Nomar, Bos.	156	155	216	456	20	692	83	.971
Gil, Benji, Ana.	20	13	25	35	4	64	12	.938
Gomez, Chris, Min.	17	11	13	21	1	35	3	.971
Graffanino, Tony, Chi.	36	26	42	79	4	125	17	.968
Guillen, Carlos, Sea.	76	70	122	162	11	295	56	.963
Gutierrez, Ricky, Cle.	9	9	13	26	3	42	4	.929
Guzman, Cristian, Min.	141	137	195	352	11	558	67	.980
Halter, Shane, Det.	27	18	33	62	5	100	14	.950
Hocking, Denny, Min.	17	14	23	41	0	64	8	1.000
Infante, Omar, Det.	63	59	117	211	13	341	53	.962
Jackson, Damian, Bos.	18	6	19	18	5	42	4	.881
Jeter, Derek, N.Y.	118	118	159	271	14	444	51	.968
Klassen, Danny, Det.	3	1	5	8	2	15	0	.867
Lopez, Mendy, K.C.	4	0	2	7	1	10	1	.900
Lugo, Julio, TB.	117	116	211	336	17	564	75	.970
Matos, Julius, K.C.	2	0	0	1	0	1	0	1.000
McDonald, John, Cle.	27	20	39	54	4	97	17	.959

Player, Team	G	GS	PO	A	E	TC	DP	Pct.
McLemore, Mark, Sea.	38	34	46	95	4	145	26	.972
Menechino, Frank, Oak.	3	0	1	1	1	3	1	.667
Mora, Melvin, Bal.	11	10	19	30	1	50	5	.980
Morban, Jose, Bal.	14	7	13	12	0	25	7	1.000
Mueller, Bill, Bos.	1	0	1	0	0	1	0	1.000
Ordonez, Rey, TB.	34	32	61	102	5	168	31	.970
Peralta, Jhonny, Cle.	72	69	104	222	8	334	43	.976
Perez, Antonio, TB.	6	5	13	13	0	26	2	1.000
Prieto, Alex, Min.	1	0	1	1	0	2	0	1.000
Relaford, Desi, K.C.	6	4	6	11	0	17	2	1.000
Roberts, Brian, Bal.	2	2	1	8	2	11	1	.818
RODRIGUEZ, Alex, Tex.	158	158	227	464	8	699	111	.989
Sadler, Donnie, Tex.	19	3	7	15	2	24	3	.917
Sanchez, Freddy, Bos.	6	1	2	9	0	11	1	1.000
Sanchez, Rey, Sea.	46	44	77	109	4	190	33	.979
Sandberg, Jared, TB.	1	0	1	1	0	2	0	1.000
Santiago, Ramon, Det.	85	84	141	248	10	399	68	.975
Shumpert, Terry, TB.	1	1	0	3	0	3	0	1.000
Sorensen, Zach, Cle.	3	1	2	6	0	8	1	1.000
Tejada, Miguel, Oak.	162	162	240	490	21	751	95	.972
Ugueto, Luis, Sea.	1	0	0	0	0	0	0	.000
Valentin, Jose, Chi.	143	136	225	396	20	641	96	.969
Vizquel, Omar, Cle.	64	63	114	203	7	324	59	.978
Wilson, Enrique, N.Y.	33	16	32	45	1	78	8	.987
Woodward, Chris, Tor.	103	98	159	300	17	476	69	.964
Young, Michael, Tex.	7	1	4	5	0	9	1	1.000

OUTFIELDERS

Player, Team	G	GS	PO	A	E	TC	DP	Pct.
Abad, Andy, Bos.*	1	1	0	0	0	0	0	.000
Anderson, Garret, Ana.*	144	144	326	13	1	340	2	.997
Anderson, Marlon, TB.	3	3	4	0	0	4	0	1.000
Baldelli, Rocco, TB.	154	149	437	14	5	456	4	.989
Beltran, Carlos, K.C.	130	129	371	10	5	386	3	.987
Berg, Dave, Tor.	6	4	5	0	1	6	0	.833
Berger, Brandon, K.C.	11	8	16	1	0	17	0	1.000
Bigbie, Larry, Bal.*	80	78	165	5	1	171	0	.994
Bloomquist, Willie, Sea.	11	7	18	0	0	18	0	1.000
Bocachica, Hiram, Det.	6	5	11	1	0	12	0	1.000
Borchard, Joe, Chi.	16	15	32	0	0	32	0	1.000
Bradley, Milton, Cle.	93	93	245	6	2	253	3	.992
Brown, Adrian, Bos.	9	2	9	0	0	9	0	1.000
Brown, Dee, K.C.	33	23	62	2	1	65	1	.985
Burks, Ellis, Cle.	2	2	5	0	0	5	0	1.000
Byrnes, Eric, Oak.	117	108	212	5	2	219	1	.991
Cameron, Mike, Sea.	147	145	485	3	4	492	2	.992
Catalanotto, Frank, Tor.	100	95	146	4	1	151	0	.993
Christenson, Ryan, Tex.	59	46	134	0	0	134	0	1.000
Clark, Howie, Tor.	5	3	4	0	0	4	0	1.000
Clark, Jermaine, Tex.	17	11	29	2	0	31	0	1.000
Collier, Lou, Bos.	2	0	0	0	0	0	0	.000
Conine, Jeff, Bal.	8	5	8	0	0	8	0	1.000
Cordova, Marty, Bal.	4	4	7	2	0	9	0	1.000
Crawford, Carl, TB.*	146	143	352	10	3	365	1	.992
Crisp, Coco, Cle.	90	89	213	5	1	219	2	.995
Cuddyer, Michael, Min.	18	16	24	1	0	25	0	1.000
Cust, Jack, Bal.	1	0	3	0	0	3	0	1.000
DAMON, Johnny, Bos.*	144	141	362	7	1	370	2	.997
Daubach, Brian, Chi.	12	9	13	0	1	14	0	.929
DaVanon, Jeff, Ana.	115	82	229	2	4	235	0	.983
DeJesus, David, K.C.*	9	0	2	0	0	2	0	1.000
Dellucci, David, N.Y.*	18	15	31	1	0	32	1	1.000
Diaz, Matt, TB.	1	1	6	0	1	7	0	.857
Durrington, Trent, Ana.	1	0	0	0	0	0	0	.000
Dye, Jermaine, Oak.	61	60	106	1	0	107	0	1.000
Edwards, Mike, Oak.	2	0	0	0	0	0	0	.000
Erstad, Darin, Ana.*	66	66	190	2	0	192	1	1.000
Escobar, Alex, Cle.	25	25	59	3	2	64	2	.969
Everett, Carl, Tex.-Chi.	140	132	282	9	4	295	2	.986
Figgins, Chone, Ana.	47	41	113	1	0	114	0	1.000
Ford, Lew, Min.	25	12	35	1	3	39	1	.923
Gant, Ron, Oak.	9	5	9	0	0	9	0	1.000
Garcia, Karim, Cle.-N.Y.*	73	68	135	7	6	148	0	.959
Gerut, Jody, Cle.*	113	108	234	9	4	247	2	.984
Giambi, Jeremy, Bos.*	11	7	17	0	1	18	0	.944
Gibbons, Jay, Bal.*	144	144	283	8	5	296	1	.983
Gipson, Charles, N.Y.	8	2	8	0	0	8	0	1.000
Glanville, Doug, Tex.	52	47	117	1	0	118	0	1.000
Gonzalez, Juan, Tex.	57	57	98	10	0	108	2	1.000
Grabowski, Jason, Oak.	3	0	3	0	0	3	0	1.000
Grieve, Ben, TB.	10	10	17	1	1	19	1	.947
Guiel, Aaron, K.C.	89	84	190	9	3	202	2	.985
Guillen, Jose, Oak.	44	43	65	0	4	69	0	.942
Halter, Shane, Det.	2	0	0	0	0	0	0	.000
Harris, Willie, Chi.	61	23	83	3	2	88	0	.977
Higginson, Bobby, Det.	118	116	249	4	5	258	0	.981
Hocking, Denny, Min.	8	4	10	0	0	10	0	1.000
Huff, Aubrey, TB.	102	102	190	5	6	201	1	.970
Hunter, Torii, Min.	151	149	425	5	4	434	1	.991
Ibanez, Raul, K.C.	131	124	243	9	3	255	2	.988
Jackson, Damian, Bos.	38	19	51	4	0	55	1	1.000
Johnson, Gary, Ana.*	4	2	6	0	0	6	0	1.000
Johnson, Reed, Tor.	111	94	163	6	4	173	1	.977
Johnson, Rontrez, K.C.	6	0	0	0	1	1	0	.000
Jones, Jacque, Min.*	101	97	211	2	5	218	0	.977
Jones, Jason, Tex.	27	25	41	3	1	45	0	.978
Kapler, Gabe, Bos.	61	41	77	5	6	88	1	.932
Kielty, Bobby, Min.-Tor.	96	82	155	3	3	161	0	.981
Kingsale, Gene, Det.	30	29	66	0	1	67	0	.985
Lamb, Mike, Tex.	2	1	1	0	0	1	0	1.000
Latham, Chris, N.Y.	2	0	3	0	0	3	0	1.000
Lawton, Matt, Cle.	74	73	133	4	1	138	0	.993
Lee, Carlos, Chi.	156	155	307	8	7	322	1	.978
Liefer, Jeff, TB.	1	0	2	0	0	2	0	1.000
Lombard, George, TB.	13	9	26	1	1	28	0	.964
Long, Terrence, Oak.*	137	124	239	3	4	246	0	.984
Lopez, Mendy, K.C.	3	2	5	0	0	5	0	1.000
Ludwick, Ryan, Tex.-Cle.*	40	38	86	2	0	88	0	1.000
Mabry, John, Sea.	22	10	21	1	1	23	0	.957
Magruder, Chris, Cle.	8	7	11	0	0	11	0	1.000
Martin, Al, TB.*	13	10	23	0	0	23	0	1.000
Matos, Julius, K.C.	1	0	0	0	0	0	0	.000
Matos, Luis, Bal.	107	106	304	5	4	313	1	.987
Matsui, Hideki, N.Y.	159	156	320	13	8	341	4	.977
Matthews Jr., Gary, Bal.	40	38	99	2	0	101	0	1.000
McCarty, Dave, Oak.-Bos.*	13	9	12	0	0	12	0	1.000
McLemore, Mark, Sea.	16	14	28	1	0	29	0	1.000
McMillon, Billy, Oak.*	36	26	47	0	1	48	0	.979
Mench, Kevin, Tex.	35	33	59	1	1	61	0	.984
Merloni, Lou, Bos.	1	0	0	0	0	0	0	.000
Meyers, Chad, Sea.	3	0	0	0	0	0	0	.000
Mientkiewicz, Doug, Min.	3	2	3	0	0	3	0	1.000
Millar, Kevin, Bos.	31	26	50	3	1	54	0	.981
Mohr, Dustan, Min.	110	90	239	2	6	247	0	.976
Mondesi, Raul, N.Y.	97	95	198	7	3	208	1	.986
Monroe, Craig, Det.	108	102	221	8	7	236	1	.970
Mora, Melvin, Bal.	79	77	162	9	1	172	2	.994
Nivar, Ramon, Tex.	26	23	70	3	3	76	1	.961
Nix, Laynce, Tex.*	52	47	130	1	5	136	0	.963
Nixon, Trot, Bos.*	130	119	231	4	4	239	0	.983
Ordonez, Magglio, Chi.	157	157	321	7	2	330	1	.994
Owens, Eric, Ana.	97	60	164	3	5	172	2	.971
Paquette, Craig, Det.	5	4	10	0	0	10	0	1.000
Petrick, Ben, Det.	32	25	61	2	2	65	1	.969
Piatt, Adam, Oak.-TB.	45	34	50	2	1	53	1	.981
Pride, Curtis, N.Y.	3	3	5	0	0	5	0	1.000
Quinlan, Robb, Ana.	1	1	5	0	0	5	0	1.000
Raines Jr., Tim, Bal.	18	9	37	1	1	39	1	.974
Ramirez, Julio, Ana.	5	0	3	0	1	4	0	.750
Ramirez, Manny, Bos.	128	126	207	11	4	222	1	.982
Relaford, Desi, K.C.	20	14	37	4	2	43	2	.953
Restovich, Michael, Min.	17	13	29	1	0	30	0	1.000
Riggs, Adam, Ana.	8	7	13	1	0	14	1	1.000
Rios, Armando, Chi.*	32	23	51	1	1	53	0	.981
Rivera, Juan, N.Y.	56	43	90	3	2	95	0	.979
Rolls, Damian, TB.	37	28	63	0	1	64	0	.984
Ross, Cody, Det.*	6	6	15	0	2	17	0	.882
Rowand, Aaron, Chi.	87	39	114	6	0	120	0	1.000
Ryan, Michael, Min.	16	11	33	2	0	35	1	1.000
Sadler, Donnie, Tex.	41	13	43	2	0	45	0	1.000
Salmon, Tim, Ana.	78	78	133	4	6	143	1	.958
Sanchez, Alex, Det.*	99	92	278	1	6	285	0	.979
Selby, Bill, Cle.	1	0	1	0	0	1	0	1.000
Shumpert, Terry, TB.	14	7	17	0	1	18	0	.944
Sierra, Ruben, Tex.-N.Y.	40	33	44	1	1	46	0	.978
Singleton, Chris, Oak.*	113	86	187	1	6	194	1	.969
Sorensen, Zach, Cle.	1	0	0	0	0	0	0	.000
Spencer, Shane, Cle.-Tex.	97	86	180	4	3	187	2	.984
Spiezio, Scott, Ana.	10	3	6	0	0	6	0	1.000
Stewart, Shannon, Tor.-Min.	127	127	281	7	5	293	0	.983
Strong, Jamal, Sea.	2	0	0	0	0	0	0	.000
Surhoff, B.J., Bal.	27	25	44	0	1	45	0	.978

Player, Team	G	GS	PO	A	E	TC	DP	Pct.
Suzuki, Ichiro, Sea.	159	156	337	12	2	351	4	.994
Swann, Pedro, Bal.	6	3	6	0	0	6	0	1.000
Teixeira, Mark, Tex.	25	18	29	0	1	30	0	.967
Thames, Marcus, Tex.	24	21	37	1	0	38	0	1.000
Torres, Andres, Det.	50	39	102	4	1	107	1	.991
Trammell, Bubba, N.Y.	3	3	9	0	0	9	0	1.000
Tucker, Michael, K.C.	85	85	173	7	2	182	0	.989
Tyner, Jason, TB.*	32	18	49	1	2	52	1	.962
Wells, Vernon, Tor.	161	161	383	3	4	390	0	.990
Werth, Jayson, Tor.	20	11	27	1	0	28	0	1.000
Wesson, Barry, Ana.	9	2	9	0	0	9	0	1.000
White, Rondell, K.C.	17	17	45	0	1	46	0	.978
Williams, Bernie, N.Y.	115	113	290	3	1	294	1	.997
Wilson, Tom, Tor.	2	1	1	0	0	1	0	1.000
Winn, Randy, Sea.	157	154	363	3	3	369	1	.992
Witt, Kevin, Det.	13	9	20	0	0	20	0	1.000
Young, Dmitri, Det.	61	59	125	5	2	132	2	.985

OUTFIELDERS WITH TWO OR MORE TEAMS

Player, Team	G	GS	PO	A	E	TC	DP	Pct.
Everett, Carl, Tex.	72	67	137	6	2	145	2	.986
Everett, Carl, Chi.	68	65	145	3	2	150	0	.987
Garcia, Karim, Cle.*	23	22	36	2	4	42	0	.905
Garcia, Karim, N.Y.*	50	46	99	5	2	106	0	.981
Kielty, Bobby, Min.	36	34	68	1	2	71	0	.972
Kielty, Bobby, Tor.	60	48	87	2	1	90	0	.989
Ludwick, Ryan, Tex.*	8	8	16	0	0	16	0	1.000
Ludwick, Ryan, Cle.*	32	30	70	2	0	72	0	1.000
McCarty, Dave, Oak.*	5	5	5	0	0	5	0	1.000
McCarty, Dave, Bos.*	8	4	7	0	0	7	0	1.000
Piatt, Adam, Oak.	38	28	43	2	1	46	1	.978
Piatt, Adam, TB.	7	6	7	0	0	7	0	1.000
Sierra, Ruben, Tex.	23	20	24	1	1	26	0	.962
Sierra, Ruben, N.Y.	17	13	20	0	0	20	0	1.000
Spencer, Shane, Cle.	43	37	75	2	1	78	1	.987
Spencer, Shane, Tex.	54	49	105	2	2	109	1	.982
Stewart, Shannon, Tor.	69	69	145	3	4	152	0	.974
Stewart, Shannon, Min.	58	58	136	4	1	141	0	.993

CATCHERS

Player, Team	G	GS	PO	A	E	TC	DP	PB	Pct.
Alomar Jr., Sandy, Chi.	75	57	371	16	1	388	3	3	.997
Bard, Josh, Cle.	87	80	486	55	5	546	7	4	.991
Borders, Pat, Sea.	7	4	29	1	0	30	0	0	1.000
Bowen, Rob, Min.	7	0	15	2	1	18	0	1	.944
Burke, Jamie, Chi.	4	2	7	1	0	8	0	1	1.000
Cash, Kevin, Tor.	34	31	179	13	1	193	0	1	.995
Davis, Ben, Sea.	73	66	421	24	4	449	9	8	.991
Diaz, Einar, Tex.	101	95	650	50	8	708	9	4	.989
DiFelice, Mike, K.C.	58	54	304	35	2	341	1	2	.994
Flaherty, John, N.Y.	40	31	200	10	2	212	0	0	.991
Fordyce, Brook, Bal.	107	100	624	41	3	668	5	6	.996
Gil, Geronimo, Bal.	53	49	326	34	6	366	3	3	.984
Greene, Todd, Tex.	51	49	287	26	4	317	4	6	.987
Gregorio, Tom, Ana.	12	6	44	2	1	47	0	3	.979
Hall, Toby, TB.	130	126	685	60	9	754	10	7	.988
Haselman, Bill, Bos.	2	0	2	0	0	2	0	0	1.000
Hernandez, Michel, N.Y.	5	1	10	0	0	10	0	0	1.000
Hernandez, Ramon, Oak.	139	133	864	53	8	925	10	8	.991
Hinch, A.J., Det.	27	23	110	6	2	118	0	2	.983
Huckaby, Ken, Tor.	4	3	17	3	0	20	1	0	1.000
Inge, Brandon, Det.	104	98	500	67	2	569	11	5	.996
Johnson, Mark, Oak.	13	10	65	4	0	69	0	0	1.000
Kreuter, Chad, Tex.	7	6	31	3	0	34	0	0	1.000
LaForest, Pete, TB.	4	3	16	1	0	17	0	1	1.000
Laird, Gerald, Tex.	16	12	65	8	1	74	2	1	.986
Laker, Tim, Cle.	50	42	265	19	5	289	6	4	.983
LeCroy, Matthew, Min.	22	20	95	4	2	101	0	2	.980
Machado, Robert, Bal.	18	14	83	14	1	98	3	3	.990
Martinez, Victor, Cle.	40	40	231	23	1	255	2	3	.996
Mayne, Brent, K.C.	112	108	593	43	4	640	5	5	.994
Melhuse, Adam, Oak.	33	19	129	10	1	140	1	1	.993
Mirabelli, Doug, Bos.	55	43	319	21	4	344	3	14	.988
Molina, Bengie, Ana.	117	109	672	63	5	740	10	4	.993
Molina, Jose, Ana.	53	39	221	17	1	239	0	3	.996
Myers, Greg, Tor.	81	67	404	22	8	434	4	2	.982
Olivo, Miguel, Chi.	113	98	692	39	9	740	5	8	.988
Paul, Josh, Chi.	11	5	27	4	0	31	0	1	1.000
Petrick, Ben, Det.	6	3	25	0	0	25	0	0	1.000
Pierzynski, A.J., Min.	135	131	843	45	6	894	6	5	.993
Posada, Jorge, N.Y.	137	131	933	75	6	1014	4	13	.994
Prince, Tom, Min.-K.C.	29	12	91	6	0	97	0	3	1.000
Valentin, Javier, TB.	42	33	212	13	0	225	1	1	1.000
Varitek, Jason, Bos.	137	119	854	43	9	906	8	6	.990
Walbeck, Matt, Det.	55	38	172	16	4	192	1	4	.979
WILSON, Dan, Sea.	96	92	587	20	1	608	4	4	.998
Wilson, Tom, Tor.	76	61	401	26	4	431	4	7	.991
Wooten, Shawn, Ana.	19	8	65	4	0	69	0	1	1.000

CATCHERS WITH TWO OR MORE TEAMS

Player, Team	G	GS	PO	A	E	TC	DP	PB	Pct.
Prince, Tom, Min.	22	11	83	5	0	88	0	2	1.000
Prince, Tom, K.C.	7	1	8	1	0	9	0	1	1.000

CATCHERS—SPECIAL STATS*

Player, Team	G	Inn.	SBA	CCS	PCS	CS%	ER	CERA
Alomar Jr.,Sandy, CWS	75	511.0	26	4	2	.17	267	4.70
Bard,Josh, Cle	87	715.2	64	19	4	.32	344	4.33
Borders,Pat, Sea	7	36.0	5	1	2	.33	5	1.25
Bowen,Rob, Min	7	23.1	8	0	0	0	17	6.56
Burke,Jamie, CWS	4	18.0	2	0	0	0	14	7.00
Cash,Kevin, Tor	34	278.0	20	5	1	.26	129	4.18
Davis,Ben, Sea	73	587.2	49	15	2	.32	253	3.87
Diaz,Einar, Tex	101	842.0	72	22	1	.31	512	5.47
DiFelice,Mike, KC	58	469.2	53	15	1	.29	304	5.83
Flaherty,John, NYY	40	284.0	28	6	3	.24	117	3.71
Fordyce,Brook, Bal	107	884.2	90	14	6	.17	471	4.79
Gil,Geronimo, Bal	53	435.2	48	10	0	.21	235	4.85
Greene,Todd, Tex	51	430.1	57	16	3	.30	283	5.92
Gregorio,Tom, Ana	12	60.0	5	1	1	.25	37	5.55
Hall,Toby, TB	130	1107.0	78	31	3	.41	614	4.99
Haselman,Bill, Bos	2	2.0	1	0	0	0	0	0.00
Hernandez,Michel, NYY	5	13.0	1	0	0	0	3	2.08
Hernandez,Ramon, Oak	139	1172.2	109	23	13	.24	453	3.48
Hinch,A.J., Det	27	197.2	26	2	1	.08	109	4.96
Huckaby,Ken, Tor	4	27.0	5	0	0	0	11	3.67
Inge,Brandon, Det	104	867.1	110	30	10	.30	496	5.15
Johnson,Mark, Oak	13	83.0	7	1	1	.17	32	3.47
Kreuter,Chad, Tex	7	50.0	5	0	0	0	37	6.66
LaForest,Pete, TB	4	24.0	5	0	0	0	11	4.13
Laird,Gerald, Tex	16	111.0	7	3	0	.43	71	5.76
Laker,Tim, Cle	50	401.2	34	8	3	.26	179	4.01
LeCroy,Matthew, Min	22	158.0	18	3	1	.18	87	4.96
Machado,Robert, Bal	18	129.1	20	6	1	.32	61	4.24
Martinez,Victor, Cle	40	342.0	29	8	1	.29	159	4.18
Mayne,Brent, KC	112	948.0	82	22	4	.28	493	4.68
Melhuse,Adam, Oak	33	186.0	18	4	1	.24	97	4.69
Mirabelli,Doug, Bos	55	387.1	51	9	3	.19	196	4.55
Molina,Bengie, Ana	117	949.2	81	31	5	.41	456	4.32
Molina,Jose, Ana	53	332.0	25	6	1	.25	149	4.04
Myers,Greg, Tor	81	583.2	62	10	2	.17	274	4.23
Olivo,Miguel, CWS	113	848.0	53	19	0	.36	359	3.81
Paul,Josh, CWS	11	54.0	6	3	1	.60	23	3.83
Petrick,Ben, Det	6	35.0	4	1	0	.25	20	5.14
Pierzynski,A.J., Min	135	1165.2	66	17	3	.27	537	4.15
Posada,Jorge, NYY	137	1165.0	100	26	2	.27	533	4.12
Prince,Tom, TOT	29	136.0	7	3	0	.43	86	5.69
Prince,Tom, Min	22	115.0	5	3	0	.60	75	5.87
Prince,Tom, KC	7	21.0	2	0	0	0	11	4.71
Valentin,Javier, TB	42	305.2	23	6	1	.27	162	4.77
Varitek,Jason, Bos	137	1075.1	84	19	4	.24	533	4.46
Walbeck,Matt, Det	55	338.2	42	6	4	.16	222	5.90
Wilson,Dan, Sea	96	817.1	40	8	4	.22	344	3.79
Wilson,Tom, Tor	76	546.1	71	12	2	.17	334	5.50
Wooten,Shawn, Ana	19	89.2	17	2	1	.13	38	3.81
Average	55	430.1	39	10	2	.31	216	4.52

***Inn.** denotes the number of innings the catcher was behind the plate. **SBA** denotes stolen bases attempted. **CCS** denotes number of runners caught stealing by the catcher. **PCS** denotes number of runners caught stealing by the pitcher. **CS%** denotes the catcher's caught stealing percentage, figured by subtracting PCS from SBA and dividing this number into CCS. **ER** denotes number of earned runs scored when catcher was behind plate. **CERA** denotes catcher's ERA when he was behind the plate, figured the same way a pitcher's ERA is computed (ER*9/IP).

PITCHERS

Player, Team	G	GS	PO	A	E	TC	DP	Pct.
Abbott, Paul, K.C.	10	8	8	6	1	15	0	.933
Acevedo, Juan, N.Y.-Tor.	39	0	6	2	1	9	0	.889
Adkins, Jon, Chi.	4	0	2	1	0	3	0	1.000
Affeldt, Jeremy, K.C.*	36	18	4	19	1	24	2	.958

Player, Team	G	GS	PO	A	E	TC	DP	Pct.
Ainsworth, Kurt, Bal.	3	0	1	0	0	1	0	1.000
Almonte, Hector, Bos.	7	0	1	0	0	1	0	1.000
Anderson, Brian, Cle.-K.C.*	32	31	8	37	2	47	2	.957
Anderson, Jason, N.Y.	22	0	1	0	0	1	0	1.000
Anderson, Matt, Det.	23	0	1	2	1	4	0	.750
Appier, Kevin, Ana.-K.C.	23	23	4	6	0	10	0	1.000
Arroyo, Bronson, Bos.	6	0	2	0	0	2	0	1.000
Asencio, Miguel, K.C.	8	8	2	7	1	10	1	.900
Avery, Steve, Det.*	19	0	4	3	0	7	1	1.000
Backe, Brandon, TB.	28	0	3	3	0	6	1	1.000
Baez, Danys, Cle.	73	0	5	11	1	17	0	.941
Baldwin, James, Min.	10	0	3	3	1	7	0	.857
Balfour, Grant, Min.	17	1	0	4	0	4	0	1.000
Bauer, Rick, Bal.	35	0	2	9	0	11	1	1.000
Bell, Rob, TB.	19	18	9	10	1	20	0	.950
Benes, Alan, Tex.	4	4	2	1	0	3	0	1.000
Benitez, Armando, N.Y.-Sea.	24	0	3	0	0	3	0	1.000
Benoit, Joaquin, Tex.	25	17	8	15	1	24	0	.958
Bere, Jason, Cle.	2	2	0	2	0	2	0	1.000
Bernero, Adam, Det.	18	17	6	14	0	20	1	1.000
Betancourt, Rafael, Cle.	33	0	1	2	0	3	0	1.000
Bierbrodt, Nick, TB.-Cle.*	18	5	1	2	0	3	1	1.000
Bonderman, Jeremy, Det.	33	28	14	25	1	40	2	.975
Bootcheck, Chris, Ana.	4	1	0	0	0	0	0	.000
Bowie, Micah, Oak.*	6	0	0	2	0	2	0	1.000
Bowles, Brian, Tor.	5	0	0	0	1	1	0	.000
Boyd, Jason, Cle.	44	0	2	11	1	14	1	.929
Bradford, Chad, Oak.	72	0	2	20	1	23	0	.957
Brazelton, Dewon, TB.	10	10	3	7	1	11	1	.909
Buehrle, Mark, Chi.*	35	35	15	38	0	53	3	1.000
Bukvich, Ryan, K.C.	9	0	0	4	0	4	0	1.000
Burkett, John, Bos.	32	30	7	19	1	27	4	.963
Callaway, Mickey, Ana.-Tex.	23	7	8	5	1	14	1	.929
Carrara, Giovanni, Sea.	23	0	4	4	0	8	1	1.000
Carrasco, D.J., K.C.	50	2	4	9	1	14	1	.929
Carrasco, Hector, Bal.	40	0	5	4	0	9	0	1.000
Carter, Lance, TB.	62	0	4	5	0	9	0	1.000
Chen, Bruce, Bos.*	5	2	0	0	0	0	0	.000
Choate, Randy, N.Y.*	5	0	0	1	0	1	0	1.000
Chulk, Vinnie, Tor.	3	0	0	3	0	3	0	1.000
Claussen, Brandon, N.Y.*	1	1	0	1	0	1	0	1.000
Clemens, Roger, N.Y.	33	33	7	32	1	40	2	.975
Colome, Jesus, TB.	54	0	6	10	1	17	0	.941
Colon, Bartolo, Chi.	34	34	12	17	3	32	3	.906
Contreras, Jose, N.Y.	18	9	1	9	1	11	1	.909
Cordero, Francisco, Tex.	73	0	8	10	1	19	0	.947
Cornejo, Nate, Det.	32	32	15	34	2	51	4	.961
Cortes, David, Cle.	2	0	0	0	0	0	0	.000
Cotts, Neal, Chi.*	4	4	1	1	0	2	1	1.000
Creek, Doug, Tor.*	21	0	2	1	1	4	1	.750
Cressend, Jack, Cle.	33	0	2	0	2	4	0	.500
Daal, Omar, Bal.*	19	17	8	25	1	34	3	.971
Davis, Doug, Tex.-Tor.*	13	12	3	7	0	10	0	1.000
Davis, Jason, Cle.	27	27	10	26	6	42	4	.857
DeHart, Rick, K.C.*	4	0	0	3	0	3	0	1.000
DePaula, Jorge, N.Y.	4	1	2	0	0	2	0	1.000
Dickey, R.A., Tex.	38	13	5	14	0	19	1	1.000
Dominguez, Juan, Tex.	6	3	0	1	0	1	0	1.000
Donnelly, Brendan, Ana.	63	0	4	3	2	9	0	.778
Douglass, Sean, Bal.	3	0	0	0	0	0	0	.000
Drese, Ryan, Tex.	11	8	1	4	0	5	2	1.000
Driskill, Travis, Bal.	20	0	3	6	0	9	1	1.000
DuBose, Eric, Bal.*	17	10	4	11	0	15	1	1.000
Duchscherer, Justin, Oak.	4	3	0	3	0	3	0	1.000
Durbin, Chad, Cle.	3	1	0	1	1	2	1	.500
Eckenstahler, Eric, Det.*	20	0	0	0	1	1	0	.000
Elder, Dave, Cle.	4	0	0	1	0	1	0	1.000
Ellis, Robert, Tex.	4	4	0	2	0	2	0	1.000
Embree, Alan, Bos.*	65	0	4	8	0	12	0	1.000
Escobar, Kelvim, Tor.	41	26	15	18	2	35	2	.943
Fetters, Mike, Min.	5	0	0	0	0	0	0	.000
Field, Nate, K.C.	19	0	2	7	0	9	0	1.000
Fikac, Jeremy, Oak.	14	0	0	2	0	2	0	1.000
Fiore, Tony, Min.	21	0	3	6	0	9	3	1.000
Fossum, Casey, Bos.*	19	14	1	8	0	9	0	1.000
Foulke, Keith, Oak.	72	0	3	12	0	15	1	1.000
Fox, Chad, Bos.	17	0	0	2	1	3	0	.667
Franklin, Ryan, Sea.	32	32	10	18	0	28	2	1.000
Fultz, Aaron, Tex.*	64	0	7	11	0	18	3	1.000
Garcia, Freddy, Sea.	33	33	20	22	1	43	3	.977
Garcia, Reynaldo, Tex.	17	0	2	1	0	3	0	1.000
Garcia, Rosman, Tex.	46	0	5	4	0	9	0	1.000
Garland, Jon, Chi.	32	32	16	30	0	46	1	1.000
Gaudin, Chad, TB.	15	3	4	2	0	6	0	1.000
George, Chris, K.C.*	18	18	10	12	1	23	1	.957
German, Franklyn, Det.	45	0	1	5	0	6	1	1.000
Gilfillan, Jason, K.C.	13	0	2	0	0	2	0	1.000
Ginter, Matt, Chi.	3	0	1	0	0	1	0	1.000
Glover, Gary, Chi.-Ana.	42	0	2	6	1	9	2	.889
Gobble, Jimmy, K.C.*	9	9	3	4	0	7	0	1.000
Gonzalez, Jeremi, TB.	25	25	15	11	1	27	0	.963
Gordon, Tom, Chi.	66	0	6	10	0	16	1	1.000
Gregg, Kevin, Ana.	5	3	1	1	0	2	0	1.000
Grimsley, Jason, K.C.	76	0	17	14	1	32	2	.969
Groom, Buddy, Bal.*	60	0	2	6	0	8	0	1.000
Guardado, Eddie, Min.*	66	0	3	2	1	6	0	.833
Halama, John, Oak.*	35	13	9	19	1	29	1	.966
Halladay, Roy, Tor.	36	36	23	50	1	74	5	.986
Hammond, Chris, N.Y.*	62	0	2	6	0	8	1	1.000
Harang, Aaron, Oak.	7	6	0	3	0	3	0	1.000
Harden, Rich, Oak.	15	13	5	11	1	17	3	.941
Harper, Travis, TB.	61	0	11	6	0	17	0	1.000
Harville, Chad, Oak.	21	0	0	0	0	0	0	.000
Hasegawa, Shigetoshi, Sea.	63	0	10	12	0	22	2	1.000
Hawkins, LaTroy, Min.	74	0	1	9	0	10	0	1.000
Helling, Rick, Bal.	24	24	4	12	3	19	0	.842
Hendrickson, Mark, Tor.*	30	30	8	22	2	32	2	.938
Hentgen, Pat, Bal.	28	22	7	19	1	27	1	.963
Heredia, Felix, N.Y.*	12	0	1	5	0	6	0	1.000
Hernandez, Runelvys, K.C.	16	16	6	10	0	16	2	1.000
Herrera, Alex, Cle.*	10	0	0	1	0	1	0	1.000
Hill, Jeremy, K.C.	1	0	0	0	0	0	0	.000
Hitchcock, Sterling, N.Y.*	27	1	2	4	1	7	1	.857
Howry, Bob, Bos.	4	0	0	0	0	0	0	.000
Hudson, Tim, Oak.	34	34	20	54	2	76	1	.974
Johnson, Adam, Min.	2	0	0	0	0	0	0	.000
Johnson, Jason, Bal.	32	32	8	24	3	35	0	.914
Jones, Greg, Ana.	18	0	0	1	0	1	0	1.000
Jones, Todd, Bos.	26	0	4	3	0	7	0	1.000
Julio, Jorge, Bal.	64	0	4	4	0	8	0	1.000
Kennedy, Joe, TB.*	32	22	13	20	1	34	1	.971
Kershner, Jason, Tor.*	40	0	7	5	0	12	1	1.000
Kim, Byung-Hyun, Bos.	49	5	11	11	1	23	0	.957
Knotts, Gary, Det.	20	18	8	15	0	23	1	1.000
Koch, Billy, Chi.	55	0	6	3	0	9	0	1.000
Lackey, John, Ana.	33	33	14	22	3	39	2	.923
Ledezma, Wilfredo, Det.*	34	8	4	7	0	11	0	1.000
Lee, Cliff, Cle.*	9	9	1	5	1	7	0	.857
Lee, David, Cle.	8	0	0	0	0	0	0	.000
Leskanic, Curtis, K.C.	27	0	9	2	0	11	2	1.000
Levine, Al, TB.-K.C.	54	0	4	11	0	15	0	1.000
Lewis, Colby, Tex.	26	26	8	13	0	21	1	1.000
Lidle, Cory, Tor.	31	31	15	31	0	46	4	1.000
Ligtenberg, Kerry, Bal.	68	0	1	7	0	8	0	1.000
Lilly, Ted, Oak.*	32	31	5	15	0	20	1	1.000
Lima, Jose, K.C.	14	14	7	4	0	11	1	1.000
Linton, Doug, Tor.	7	0	1	2	0	3	1	1.000
Lloyd, Graeme, K.C.*	16	0	1	1	0	2	0	1.000
Loaiza, Esteban, Chi.	34	34	16	31	2	49	2	.959
Lohse, Kyle, Min.	33	33	16	21	1	38	1	.974
Looper, Aaron, Sea.	6	0	0	1	0	1	0	1.000
Lopez, Albie, K.C.	15	0	1	3	0	4	0	1.000
Lopez, Aquilino, Tor.	72	0	2	7	2	11	0	.818
Lopez, Rodrigo, Bal.	26	26	8	15	2	25	1	.920
Loux, Shane, Det.	11	4	3	5	0	8	0	1.000
LOWE, Derek, Bos.	33	33	20	45	0	65	0	1.000
Lowe, Sean, K.C.	28	0	3	5	1	9	0	.889
Lyon, Brandon, Bos.	49	0	3	7	1	11	0	.909
MacDougal, Mike, K.C.	68	0	5	8	3	16	0	.813
Mahay, Ron, Tex.*	35	0	4	5	2	11	0	.818
Malaska, Mark, TB.*	22	0	1	3	0	4	2	1.000
Maroth, Mike, Det.*	33	33	9	42	2	53	2	.962
Marte, Damaso, Chi.*	71	0	2	9	0	11	1	1.000
Martinez, Pedro, Bos.	29	29	14	20	0	34	0	1.000
Mateo, Julio, Sea.	50	0	5	4	2	11	0	.818
May, Darrell, K.C.*	35	32	9	18	2	29	1	.931
Mays, Joe, Min.	31	21	7	20	1	28	3	.964
McClung, Seth, TB.	12	5	2	3	0	5	1	1.000
Mears, Chris, Det.	29	3	3	5	0	8	2	1.000
Meche, Gil, Sea.	32	32	15	20	1	36	2	.972
Mecir, Jim, Oak.	41	0	2	8	0	10	0	1.000
Mendoza, Ramiro, Bos.	37	5	4	9	0	13	1	1.000
Miadich, Bart, Ana.	1	0	1	0	0	1	0	1.000
Miceli, Dan, Cle.-N.Y.	20	0	0	5	1	6	0	.833
Miller, Trever, Tor.*	79	0	5	2	0	7	0	1.000
Milton, Eric, Min.*	3	3	0	0	0	0	0	.000
Moss, Damian, Bal.*	10	9	1	10	1	12	0	.917
Mounce, Tony, Tex.*	11	11	2	8	0	10	0	1.000

Player, Team	G	GS	PO	A	E	TC	DP	Pct.
Moyer, Jamie, Sea.*	33	33	19	31	1	51	2	.980
Mulder, Mark, Oak.*	26	26	14	31	0	45	2	1.000
Mulholland, Terry, Cle.*	45	3	4	13	0	17	1	1.000
Mullen, Scott, K.C.*	2	0	0	0	0	0	0	.000
Mussina, Mike, N.Y.	31	31	14	35	0	49	2	1.000
Myette, Aaron, Cle.	2	0	0	0	0	0	0	.000
Nakamura, Mike, Min.	12	0	0	2	0	2	0	1.000
Nelson, Jeff, Sea.-N.Y.	70	0	0	4	0	4	0	1.000
Neu, Mike, Oak.	32	0	3	11	0	14	0	1.000
Nitkowski, C.J., Tex.*	6	0	0	5	0	5	1	1.000
Orosco, Jesse, N.Y.-Min.*	23	0	1	1	0	2	0	1.000
Ortiz, Ramon, Ana.	32	32	12	18	4	34	1	.882
Osuna, Antonio, N.Y.	48	0	2	7	0	9	0	1.000
Paniagua, Jose, Chi.	1	0	0	0	0	0	0	.000
Park, Chan Ho, Tex.	7	7	3	6	1	10	2	.900
Paronto, Chad, Cle.	6	0	0	0	0	0	0	.000
Parque, Jim, TB.*	5	5	0	2	0	2	0	1.000
Parris, Steve, TB.	10	7	6	2	0	8	0	1.000
Parrish, John, Bal.*	14	0	1	3	2	6	0	.667
Patterson, Danny, Det.	19	0	3	3	1	7	0	.857
Percival, Troy, Ana.	52	0	2	0	0	2	0	1.000
Person, Robert, Bos.	7	0	0	2	0	2	0	1.000
Pettitte, Andy, N.Y.*	33	33	7	29	6	42	1	.857
Phillips, Jason C., Cle.	3	0	2	1	0	3	0	1.000
Pineiro, Joel, Sea.	32	32	20	24	1	45	2	.978
Politte, Cliff, Tor.	54	0	2	1	0	3	0	1.000
Ponson, Sidney, Bal.	21	21	12	18	1	31	2	.968
Porzio, Mike, Chi.*	3	3	0	4	0	4	0	1.000
Powell, Jay, Tex.	51	0	6	5	0	11	0	1.000
Prinz, Bret, N.Y.	2	0	0	0	0	0	0	.000
Pulido, Carlos, Min.*	7	1	0	2	0	2	0	1.000
Putz, J.J., Sea.	3	0	1	0	0	1	0	1.000
Radke, Brad, Min.	33	33	17	32	1	50	0	.980
Ramirez, Erasmo, Tex.*	34	0	2	8	0	10	0	1.000
Ramos, Mario, Tex.*	3	3	1	1	0	2	0	1.000
Reed, Rick, Min.	27	21	5	11	1	17	0	.941
Reichert, Dan, Tor.	15	0	1	1	0	2	0	1.000
Reyes, Al, N.Y.	13	0	1	0	0	1	0	1.000
Reyes, Carlos, TB.	10	3	3	3	0	6	1	1.000
Rhodes, Arthur, Sea.*	67	0	1	6	0	7	0	1.000
Riggan, Jerrod, Cle.	2	0	0	2	0	2	0	1.000
Riley, Matt, Bal.*	2	2	1	0	0	1	0	1.000
Rincon, Juan, Min.	58	0	15	10	0	25	0	1.000
Rincon, Ricardo, Oak.*	64	0	2	9	0	11	0	1.000
Riske, David, Cle.	68	0	2	5	0	7	2	1.000
Rivera, Mariano, N.Y.	64	0	4	15	2	21	0	.905
Roberts, Willis, Bal.	26	0	4	4	0	8	0	1.000
Robertson, Nate, Det.*	8	8	2	6	0	8	0	1.000
Rocker, John, TB.*	2	0	0	0	0	0	0	.000
Rodney, Fernando, Det.	27	0	0	3	0	3	0	1.000
Rodriguez, Francisco, Ana.	59	0	6	9	0	15	2	1.000
Rodriguez, Ricardo, Cle.	15	15	7	15	2	24	0	.917
Rodriguez, Rich, Ana.*	3	0	0	0	0	0	0	.000
Rogers, Kenny, Min.*	33	31	20	36	2	58	4	.966
Romero, J.C., Min.*	73	0	8	12	2	22	1	.909
Roney, Matt, Det.	45	11	7	11	2	20	0	.900
Rupe, Ryan, Bos.	4	1	3	1	0	4	0	1.000
Ryan, B.J., Bal.*	76	0	3	6	1	10	2	.900
Sabathia, C.C., Cle.*	30	30	7	19	2	28	2	.929
Sadler, Carl, Cle.*	18	0	0	2	0	2	0	1.000
Sanders, David, Chi.*	20	0	0	0	0	0	0	.000
Santana, Johan, Min.*	45	18	3	11	3	17	1	.824
Santiago, Jose, Cle.	25	0	1	3	2	6	0	.667
Santos, Victor, Tex.	8	4	1	3	1	5	0	.800
Sasaki, Kazuhiro, Sea.	35	0	0	2	0	2	0	1.000
Sauerbeck, Scott, Bos.*	26	0	1	2	1	4	0	.750
Schmack, Brian, Det.	11	0	1	1	0	2	0	1.000
Schoeneweis, Scott, Ana.-Chi.*	59	0	3	8	2	13	1	.846
Seanez, Rudy, Bos.	9	0	1	1	0	2	0	1.000
Seay, Bobby, TB.*	12	0	0	1	0	1	0	1.000
Sele, Aaron, Ana.	25	25	6	14	1	21	0	.952
Service, Scott, Tor.	15	0	1	1	0	2	0	1.000
Shields, Scot, Ana.	44	13	18	26	1	45	0	.978
Shiell, Jason, Bos.	17	0	1	2	1	4	0	.750
Shouse, Brian, Tex.*	62	0	6	18	0	24	1	1.000
Snyder, Kyle, K.C.	15	15	10	13	0	23	2	1.000
Soriano, Rafael, Sea.	40	0	2	4	0	6	0	1.000
Sosa, Jorge, TB.	29	19	4	9	0	13	0	1.000
Sparks, Steve, Det.-Oak.	51	0	8	16	1	25	6	.960
Spurling, Chris, Det.	66	0	1	7	0	8	0	1.000
Standridge, Jason, TB.	8	7	2	2	0	4	0	1.000
Stanford, Jason, Cle.*	13	8	4	1	0	5	1	1.000
Stewart, Josh, Chi.*	5	5	1	8	1	10	0	.900
Sturtze, Tanyon, Tor.	40	8	6	14	0	20	1	1.000
Sullivan, Scott, Chi.	15	0	1	1	1	3	0	.667
Suppan, Jeff, Bos.	11	10	3	11	0	14	0	1.000
Sweeney, Brian, Sea.	5	0	3	0	0	3	0	1.000
Switzer, Jon, TB.*	5	0	0	0	0	0	0	.000
Tallet, Brian, Cle.*	5	3	0	5	1	6	0	.833
Tam, Jeff, Tor.	44	0	3	8	1	12	3	.917
Taylor, Aaron, Sea.	10	0	0	2	0	2	0	1.000
Thomas, Brad, Min.*	3	0	1	1	0	2	0	1.000
Thomson, John, Tex.	35	35	17	36	2	55	2	.964
Thurman, Corey, Tor.	6	3	0	0	0	0	0	.000
Timlin, Mike, Bos.	72	0	8	15	2	25	0	.920
Tolar, Kevin, Bos.*	6	0	0	1	0	1	0	1.000
Towers, Josh, Tor.	14	8	9	10	1	20	0	.950
Traber, Billy, Cle.*	33	18	7	13	0	20	2	1.000
Turnbow, Derrick, Ana.	11	0	3	1	0	4	1	1.000
Urbina, Ugueth, Tex.	39	0	3	2	0	5	0	1.000
Valdes, Ismael, Tex.	22	22	4	21	4	29	1	.862
Van Poppel, Todd, Tex.	7	1	2	1	0	3	0	1.000
Venafro, Mike, TB.*	24	0	2	0	0	2	0	1.000
Voyles, Brad, K.C.	11	3	1	4	0	5	0	1.000
Waechter, Doug, TB.	6	5	2	1	0	3	0	1.000
Wakefield, Tim, Bos.	35	33	16	19	1	36	0	.972
Walker, Jamie, Det.*	78	0	4	11	1	16	1	.938
Walker, Pete, Tor.	23	7	2	9	1	12	0	.917
Walrond, Les, K.C.*	7	0	1	2	0	3	0	1.000
Wasdin, John, Tor.	3	2	0	0	0	0	0	.000
Washburn, Jarrod, Ana.*	32	32	6	17	1	24	1	.958
Weaver, Jeff, N.Y.	32	24	9	17	1	27	1	.963
Weber, Ben, Ana.	62	0	5	17	2	24	0	.917
Wells, David, N.Y.*	31	30	7	32	0	39	2	1.000
Westbrook, Jake, Cle.	34	22	6	24	1	31	3	.968
White, Gabe, N.Y.*	12	0	0	2	1	3	0	.667
White, Matt, Bos.-Sea.*	6	0	0	1	0	1	0	1.000
White, Rick, Chi.	34	0	3	8	0	11	2	1.000
Williamson, Scott, Bos.	24	0	0	3	0	3	0	1.000
Wilson, Kris, K.C.	29	4	12	8	4	24	0	.833
Wood, Mike, Oak.	7	1	0	4	1	5	0	.800
Woodard, Steve, Bos.	7	0	0	1	0	1	0	1.000
Wright, Dan, Chi.	20	15	12	8	1	21	0	.952
Wright, Jamey, K.C.	4	4	1	3	0	4	0	1.000
Wunsch, Kelly, Chi.*	43	0	4	2	1	7	0	.857
Yan, Esteban, Tex.	15	0	1	2	2	5	0	.600
Zambrano, Victor, TB.	34	28	10	16	2	28	2	.929
Zito, Barry, Oak.*	35	35	12	28	1	41	1	.976

PITCHERS WITH TWO OR MORE TEAMS

Player, Team	G	GS	PO	A	E	TC	DP	Pct.
Acevedo, Juan, N.Y.	25	0	4	2	1	7	0	.857
Acevedo, Juan, Tor.	14	0	2	0	0	2	0	1.000
Anderson, Brian, Cle.*	25	24	6	30	1	37	2	.973
Anderson, Brian, K.C.*	7	7	2	7	1	10	0	.900
Appier, Kevin, Ana.	19	19	3	6	0	9	0	1.000
Appier, Kevin, K.C.	4	4	1	0	0	1	0	1.000
Benitez, Armando, N.Y.	9	0	1	0	0	1	0	1.000
Benitez, Armando, Sea.	15	0	2	0	0	2	0	1.000
Bierbrodt, Nick, TB.*	13	5	1	2	0	3	1	1.000
Bierbrodt, Nick, Cle.*	5	0	0	0	0	0	0	.000
Callaway, Mickey, Ana.	17	4	5	4	1	10	0	.900
Callaway, Mickey, Tex.	6	3	3	1	0	4	1	1.000
Davis, Doug, Tex.*	1	1	0	0	0	0	0	.000
Davis, Doug, Tor.*	12	11	3	7	0	10	0	1.000
Glover, Gary, Chi.	24	0	1	3	1	5	1	.800
Glover, Gary, Ana.	18	0	1	3	0	4	1	1.000
Levine, Al, TB.	36	0	2	7	0	9	0	1.000
Levine, Al, K.C.	18	0	2	4	0	6	0	1.000
Miceli, Dan, Cle.	13	0	0	2	0	2	0	1.000
Miceli, Dan, N.Y.	7	0	0	3	1	4	0	.750
Nelson, Jeff, Sea.	46	0	0	3	0	3	0	1.000
Nelson, Jeff, N.Y.	24	0	0	1	0	1	0	1.000
Orosco, Jesse, N.Y.*	15	0	1	1	0	2	0	1.000
Orosco, Jesse, Min.*	8	0	0	0	0	0	0	.000
Schoeneweis, Scott, Ana.*	39	0	2	6	2	10	1	.800
Schoeneweis, Scott, Chi.*	20	0	1	2	0	3	0	1.000
Sparks, Steve, Det.	42	0	6	12	1	19	5	.947
Sparks, Steve, Oak.	9	0	2	4	0	6	1	1.000
White, Matt, Bos.*	3	0	0	0	0	0	0	.000
White, Matt, Sea.*	3	0	0	1	0	1	0	1.000

MISCELLANEOUS

SHUTOUT GAMES

Read across for wins, down for losses.

Team	Oak.	K.C.	N.Y.	Min.	Sea.	Cle.	Bos.	Tor.	Ana.	TB.	Chi.	Det.	Tex.	Bal.	N.L.	W	L	Pct.
Oakland	..	1	1	0	3	0	1	0	1	0	1	1	2	3	0	14	6	.700
Kansas City	0	..	1	0	0	1	0	0	3	1	1	1	1	1	0	10	5	.667
New York	0	1	..	1	0	0	0	2	1	2	1	1	0	2	1	12	7	.632
Minnesota	0	1	0	..	0	1	1	0	1	1	0	2	1	0	0	8	5	.615
Seattle	2	0	1	1	..	1	0	0	2	0	1	2	1	1	3	15	10	.600
Cleveland	0	0	1	1	1	..	0	0	0	1	0	1	0	1	1	7	5	.583
Boston	0	0	1	0	0	2	..	0	0	1	0	0	0	2	0	6	5	.545
Toronto	0	0	1	0	0	0	0	..	1	0	0	3	0	0	1	6	5	.545
Anaheim	1	0	0	1	3	0	0	1	..	0	0	0	2	0	1	9	12	.429
Tampa Bay	0	1	0	0	2	0	1	0	0	..	0	2	1	0	0	7	10	.412
Chicago	0	0	0	0	0	0	0	1	0	0	..	2	0	1	0	4	8	.333
Detroit	0	1	0	0	0	0	1	1	0	0	2	..	0	0	0	5	17	.227
Texas	0	0	0	0	0	0	0	0	1	0	1	1	..	0	0	3	11	.214
Baltimore	1	0	0	0	0	0	0	0	0	2	0	0	0	..	0	3	12	.200
N.L. Clubs	2	0	1	1	1	0	1	0	2	2	1	1	3	1	..	..	..	..
Lost	6	5	7	5	10	5	5	5	12	10	8	17	11	12	7	109	118	.480

A.L. shutouts vs N.L. clubs (7): Anaheim vs Los Angeles, Cleveland vs Cincinnati, New York vs New York, Seattle vs Montreal, Seattle vs New York, Seattle vs Philadelphia, Toronto vs Cincinnati.

HOME RECORD

Read across for home wins, down for road losses.

Team	Oak.	Bos.	Chi.	Sea.	N.Y.	Min.	Ana.	Tex.	Tor.	Bal.	K.C.	Cle.	TB.	Det.	N.L.	W	L	Pct.
Oakland	..	2	2	5	4	1	7	8	2	6	2	5	5	2	6	57	24	.704
Boston	1	..	1	4	4	1	4	3	6	5	3	2	7	6	6	53	28	.654
Chicago	3	2	..	0	2	7	3	3	2	3	5	7	2	7	5	51	30	.630
Seattle	7	2	4	..	1	1	6	6	2	4	2	3	3	5	4	50	31	.617
New York	1	5	1	3	..	3	1	2	4	6	3	4	6	3	8	50	32	.610
Minnesota	6	2	7	1	0	..	2	3	0	2	5	4	3	8	5	48	33	.593
Anaheim	5	1	3	4	1	4	..	6	2	1	4	3	2	3	6	45	37	.549
Texas	3	4	3	6	1	4	6	..	1	1	2	4	3	3	2	43	38	.531
Toronto	1	5	2	2	3	0	3	2	..	6	2	2	4	3	6	41	40	.506
Baltimore	2	4	2	2	2	2	6	5	4	..	1	1	6	0	3	40	40	.500
Kansas City	1	1	4	3	2	6	0	3	0	2	..	5	2	7	4	40	40	.500
Cleveland	2	1	6	3	2	3	3	2	1	1	2	..	2	6	4	38	43	.469
Tampa Bay	2	5	2	2	2	0	2	3	5	7	2	0	..	2	2	36	45	.444
Detroit	2	1	5	0	1	3	1	0	2	0	2	4	1	..	1	23	58	.284
N.L. Clubs	6	4	4	3	4	4	4	7	5	7	4	7	8	6	..	..	..	..
Lost on Road	42	39	46	38	29	39	48	53	36	51	39	51	54	61	62	615	519	.542

HOME RECORDS IN INTERLEAGUE GAMES

Team				Total	Team				Total
Anaheim	3-0 vs. L.A.	1-2 vs. N.Y.	2-1 vs. Phi.	6-3	Minnesota	2-1 vs. Mil.	2-1 vs. Col.	1-2 vs. Ari.	5-4
Baltimore	2-1 vs. Mil.	1-2 vs. Chi.	0-3 vs. Phi.	3-6	New York	2-1 vs. Hou.	3-0 vs. N.Y.	3-0 vs. St.L.	8-1
Boston	3-0 vs. Hou.	1-2 vs. St.L.	2-1 vs. Fla.	6-3	Oakland	1-2 vs. Atl.	3-0 vs. Mon.	2-1 vs. S.F.	6-3
Chicago	2-1 vs. Chi.	2-1 vs. S.D.	1-2 vs. S.F.	5-4	Seattle	2-1 vs. Atl.	1-2 vs. Mon.	1-2 vs. S.D.	4-5
Cleveland	2-1 vs. Cin.	0-3 vs. L.A.	2-1 vs. S.D.	4-5	Tampa Bay	1-2 vs. Atl.	0-3 vs. Cin.	1-2 vs. Pit.	2-7
Detroit	0-3 vs. L.A.	1-2 vs. Col.	0-3 vs. Ari.	1-8	Texas	0-3 vs. Hou.	1-2 vs. N.Y.	1-2 vs. Fla.	2-7
Kansas City	1-2 vs. St.L.	2-1 vs. S.F.	1-2 vs. Ari.	4-5	Toronto	2-1 vs. Chi.	1-2 vs. Mon.	3-0 vs. Pit.	6-3

ROAD RECORD

Read across for road wins, down for home losses.

Team	N.Y.	Tor.	Sea.	K.C.	Bos.	Min.	Oak.	Chi.	Ana.	Bal.	Cle.	Tex.	TB.	Det.	N.L.	W	L	Pct.
New York	..	6	2	1	5	4	2	1	5	7	1	2	8	2	5	51	29	.638
Toronto	6	..	2	3	4	3	1	1	4	5	2	2	4	4	4	45	36	.556
Seattle	3	1	..	3	0	5	5	3	5	1	3	4	1	3	6	43	38	.531
Kansas City	0	1	1	..	0	5	1	4	3	2	8	4	2	7	5	43	39	.524
Boston	5	4	1	2	..	1	2	4	2	5	2	2	5	2	5	42	39	.519
Minnesota	0	3	2	3	2	..	2	3	2	2	6	2	3	7	5	42	39	.519
Oakland	2	3	2	5	2	0	..	3	5	1	1	7	1	4	3	39	42	.481
Chicago	2	4	2	6	2	2	1	..	1	1	4	0	1	4	5	35	46	.432
Anaheim	2	0	4	2	2	1	3	0	..	0	3	3	4	3	5	32	48	.400
Baltimore	4	4	2	2	5	1	0	0	2	..	2	2	2	3	2	31	51	.378
Cleveland	0	1	0	4	1	6	1	2	0	2	..	2	3	6	2	30	51	.370
Texas	4	4	4	0	0	0	1	1	4	1	1	..	3	3	2	28	53	.346
Tampa Bay	3	6	3	1	2	0	1	1	1	4	2	0	..	2	1	27	54	.333
Detroit	0	0	1	3	0	1	1	3	0	3	3	1	1	..	3	20	61	.247
N.L. Clubs	1	3	5	5	3	4	3	4	3	6	5	7	7	8	..	..	..	..
Lost at home	32	40	31	40	28	33	24	30	37	40	43	38	45	58	53	508	626	.448

PITCHING AGAINST EACH CLUB

ANAHEIM—77-85

Pitcher	Bal. W-L	Bos. W-L	Chi. W-L	Cle. W-L	Det. W-L	K.C. W-L	Min. W-L	N.Y. W-L	Oak. W-L	Sea. W-L	T.B. W-L	Tex. W-L	Tor. W-L	N.L. W-L	Total W-L
Appier, Kevin	0-1	0-0	0-0	1-0	0-0	0-0	0-0	0-1	0-1	1-1	2-0	1-2	0-0	2-1	7-7
Bootcheck, Chris	0-0	0-0	0-0	0-0	0-0	0-0	0-0	0-0	0-1	0-0	0-0	0-0	0-0	0-0	0-1
Callaway, Mickey	0-0	0-1	0-0	0-0	0-0	0-0	0-0	0-1	0-0	0-0	0-0	1-1	0-0	0-1	1-4
Donnelly, Brendan	0-0	0-1	0-0	0-0	1-0	0-0	0-0	0-0	1-1	0-0	0-0	0-0	0-0	0-0	2-2
Glover, Gary	0-0	0-0	0-0	0-0	1-0	0-0	0-0	0-0	0-0	0-0	0-0	0-0	0-0	0-0	1-0
Gregg, Kevin	0-0	0-0	0-0	0-0	0-0	1-0	0-0	0-0	0-0	1-0	0-0	0-0	0-0	0-0	2-0
Lackey, John	0-1	0-1	0-1	0-1	1-0	0-2	2-1	1-2	1-0	1-2	1-1	1-2	0-1	2-1	10-16
Ortiz, Ramon	0-2	0-1	0-1	1-0	2-0	0-0	1-1	1-0	2-2	2-2	1-0	2-2	1-2	3-0	16-13
Percival, Troy	0-1	0-0	0-0	0-0	0-1	0-0	0-1	0-1	0-0	0-1	0-0	0-0	0-0	0-0	0-5
Rodriguez, Francisco	0-1	1-0	1-0	0-0	0-0	1-0	0-0	1-0	1-1	2-1	0-0	1-0	0-0	0-0	8-3
Schoeneweis, Scott	1-0	0-0	0-0	0-0	0-0	0-0	0-0	0-0	0-1	0-0	0-0	0-0	0-0	0-0	1-1
Sele, Aaron	0-2	0-1	0-0	0-0	1-0	1-0	0-1	0-1	1-1	0-2	1-1	0-1	1-0	2-1	7-11
Shields, Scot	0-0	1-0	1-1	1-1	0-0	1-0	0-0	0-0	0-2	0-0	0-0	1-0	0-2	0-0	5-6
Turnbow, Derrick	0-0	0-0	0-0	0-0	0-0	0-0	0-0	0-0	1-0	0-0	0-0	1-0	0-0	0-0	2-0
Washburn, Jarrod	0-0	1-1	0-1	3-0	0-0	1-1	1-0	0-0	0-2	1-2	1-1	1-2	0-2	1-3	10-15
Weber, Ben	0-0	0-0	1-0	0-1	0-0	1-0	1-0	0-0	1-0	0-0	0-0	0-0	0-0	1-0	5-1
Totals	1-8	3-6	3-4	6-3	6-1	6-3	5-4	3-6	8-12	8-11	6-3	9-10	2-7	11-7	77-85

NO-DECESIONS: Greg Jones, Bart Miadich, Rich Rodriguez.

INTERLEAGUE: Kevin Appier 0-1, Aaron Sele 1-0, Ramon Ortiz 1-0 vs. Marlins; Jarrod Washburn 0-1, John Lackey 1-1, Kevin Appier 2-0, Aaron Sele 1-0 vs. Dodgers; Ramon Ortiz 1-0, Mickey Callaway 0-1, Jarrod Washburn 1-0 vs. Expos; Aaron Sele 0-1, Ramon Ortiz 1-0, Jarrod Washburn 0-1 vs. Mets; Jarrod Washburn 0-1, John Lackey 1-0, Ben Weber 1-0 vs. Phillies. Total: 11-7.

BALTIMORE—71-91

Pitcher	Ana. W-L	Bos. W-L	Chi. W-L	Cle. W-L	Det. W-L	K.C. W-L	Min. W-L	N.Y. W-L	Oak. W-L	Sea. W-L	TB. W-L	Tex. W-L	Tor. W-L	N.L. W-L	Totals W-L
Ainsworth, Kurt	0-0	0-1	0-0	0-0	0-0	0-0	0-0	0-0	0-0	0-0	0-0	0-0	0-0	0-0	0-1
Carrasco, Hector	0-0	0-0	0-0	0-0	0-0	0-0	1-0	0-1	1-2	0-0	0-1	0-0	0-2	0-0	2-6
Daal, Omar	0-0	0-1	0-1	0-2	1-1	0-0	0-0	0-0	0-0	0-0	1-1	2-0	0-2	0-3	4-11
Driskill, Travis	0-0	0-1	0-0	0-0	0-0	0-1	0-1	0-0	0-0	0-0	0-0	2-0	1-1	0-1	3-5
DuBose, Eric	0-0	1-0	0-0	0-0	0-0	0-1	0-0	1-3	0-0	1-0	0-1	0-0	0-1	0-0	3-6
Groom, Buddy	0-0	0-0	0-0	1-0	0-1	0-1	0-0	0-0	0-0	0-0	0-0	0-0	0-0	0-1	1-3
Helling, Rick	0-0	1-1	0-1	0-1	0-0	1-1	0-0	0-1	0-0	1-0	1-1	1-0	1-1	1-1	7-8
Hentgen, Pat	0-0	2-0	0-0	0-0	0-0	0-0	0-1	1-0	0-1	1-0	1-0	1-2	1-1	0-3	7-8
Johnson, Jason	2-0	2-2	1-0	0-0	1-1	0-0	1-0	0-2	0-0	0-2	1-1	0-0	1-1	1-1	10-10
Julio, Jorge	0-1	0-0	0-0	0-0	0-0	0-0	0-0	0-1	0-1	0-1	0-2	0-0	0-0	0-1	0-7
Ligtenberg, Kerry	1-0	1-0	0-0	0-0	0-0	0-0	0-0	1-0	0-0	0-1	0-0	0-0	1-1	0-0	4-2
Lopez, Rodrigo	1-0	1-2	0-0	0-0	0-0	0-0	1-0	2-2	1-2	0-0	0-2	0-0	0-1	1-1	7-10
Moss, Damian	0-0	0-1	0-0	0-0	0-0	0-0	0-1	0-2	0-0	0-1	1-0	0-0	0-0	0-0	1-5
Parrish, John	0-0	0-0	0-0	0-0	0-0	0-0	0-0	0-0	0-1	0-0	0-0	0-0	0-0	0-0	0-1
Ponson, Sidney	3-0	0-1	0-2	0-0	0-0	2-0	0-1	1-1	0-0	1-0	2-0	1-0	2-0	2-1	14-6
Riley, Matt	0-0	0-0	0-0	0-0	0-0	0-0	0-0	0-0	0-0	0-0	0-0	0-0	1-0	0-0	1-0
Roberts, Willis	1-0	0-0	1-0	1-0	0-0	0-0	0-0	0-0	0-0	0-0	0-1	0-0	0-0	0-0	3-1
Ryan, B.J.	0-0	1-0	0-0	1-0	1-0	0-0	0-0	0-0	0-0	0-0	1-1	0-0	0-0	0-0	4-1
Totals	8-1	9-10	2-4	3-3	3-3	3-4	3-4	6-13	2-7	4-5	8-11	7-2	8-11	5-13	71-91

NO-DECESIONS: Rick Bauer, Sean Douglass.

INTERLEAGUE: Sidney Ponson 0-1, Rodrigo Lopez 0-1, Jason Johnson 1-0 vs. Braves; Pat Hentgen 0-1, Omar Daal 0-1, Rick Helling 1-0 vs. Cubs; Buddy Groom 0-1, Pat Hentgen 0-1, Omar Daal 0-1 vs. Astros; Sidney Ponson 1-0, Jason Johnson 0-1, Rodrigo Lopez 1-0 vs. Brewers; Omar Daal 0-1, Pat Hentgen 0-1, Rick Helling 0-1 vs. Phillies; Travis Driskill 0-1, Jorge Julio 0-1, Sidney Ponson 1-0 vs. Cardinals. Total: 5-13.

BOSTON—95-67

Pitcher	Ana. W-L	Bal. W-L	Chi. W-L	Cle. W-L	Det. W-L	K.C. W-L	Min. W-L	N.Y. W-L	Oak. W-L	Sea. W-L	TB. W-L	Tex. W-L	Tor. W-L	N.L. W-L	Totals W-L
Almonte, Hector	0-0	0-0	0-0	0-0	0-0	0-0	0-0	0-0	0-0	0-0	0-0	0-0	0-0	0-1	0-1
Burkett, John	2-1	1-2	2-1	2-0	3-0	0-0	0-0	0-1	0-1	0-1	1-0	0-0	0-2	1-0	12-9
Chen, Bruce	0-0	0-0	0-0	0-0	0-0	0-0	0-0	0-1	0-0	0-0	0-0	0-0	0-0	0-0	0-1
Embree, Alan	0-1	1-0	0-0	0-0	0-0	1-0	0-0	1-0	0-0	0-0	0-0	1-0	0-0	0-0	4-1
Fossum, Casey	1-0	0-1	0-0	0-1	0-0	1-0	0-0	1-1	1-0	0-0	1-0	1-0	0-2	0-0	6-5
Fox, Chad	0-0	0-1	0-0	0-0	0-0	0-0	0-0	0-0	0-0	0-0	1-1	0-0	0-0	0-0	1-2
Jones, Todd	0-0	0-0	0-0	0-0	1-0	0-0	0-0	0-0	0-0	0-0	0-0	0-1	1-0	0-0	2-1
Kim, Byung-Hyun	0-0	1-1	1-0	0-0	0-0	0-0	0-0	1-2	1-1	0-0	0-0	0-0	1-0	3-1	8-5
Lowe, Derek	0-0	3-2	0-0	1-1	2-0	0-0	0-1	2-0	1-0	1-0	2-0	0-1	1-2	4-0	17-7
Lyon, Brandon	0-0	0-0	1-0	0-0	0-0	0-1	0-0	0-1	0-0	0-0	1-2	0-0	1-0	1-2	4-6
Martinez, Pedro	1-0	1-1	0-0	1-0	1-0	0-0	1-1	1-1	0-1	2-0	3-0	2-0	1-0	0-0	14-4
Mendoza, Ramiro	1-0	0-0	0-0	0-0	0-0	0-0	0-1	1-0	0-0	0-0	0-1	0-1	1-0	0-2	3-5
Rupe, Ryan	0-0	0-0	0-1	0-0	0-0	0-0	0-0	0-0	0-0	0-0	0-0	0-0	0-0	1-0	1-1
Sauerbeck, Scott	0-0	0-0	0-0	0-0	0-0	0-0	0-0	0-0	0-0	0-0	0-0	0-0	0-1	0-0	0-1
Seanez, Rudy	0-0	0-0	0-0	0-0	0-0	0-0	0-0	0-0	0-0	0-0	0-0	0-0	0-0	0-1	0-1
Shiell, Jason	0-0	0-0	0-0	0-0	0-0	1-0	0-0	0-0	0-0	0-0	0-0	0-0	0-0	1-0	2-0
Suppan, Jeff	0-0	1-1	1-0	0-0	0-0	0-0	0-0	0-1	0-0	1-0	0-2	0-0	0-0	0-0	3-4
Timlin, Mike	1-1	0-0	0-0	0-0	0-0	0-0	0-1	0-0	0-0	1-1	1-1	0-0	3-0	0-0	6-4
Wakefield, Tim	0-0	2-0	0-2	0-0	1-1	1-0	1-0	2-2	0-0	0-0	2-0	1-1	1-1	0-0	11-7
White, Matt	0-0	0-0	0-0	0-0	0-0	0-0	0-0	0-0	0-0	0-0	0-0	0-0	0-1	0-0	0-1
Williamson, Scott	0-0	0-0	0-0	0-0	0-0	0-0	0-0	0-0	0-1	0-0	0-0	0-0	0-0	0-0	0-1
Woodard, Steve	0-0	0-0	0-0	0-0	0-0	1-0	0-0	0-0	0-0	0-0	0-0	0-0	0-0	0-0	1-0
Totals	6-3	10-9	5-4	4-2	8-1	5-1	2-4	9-10	3-4	5-2	12-7	5-4	10-9	11-7	95-67

NO-DECESIONS: Bronson Arroyo, Bob Howry, Robert Person, Kevin Tolar.

INTERLEAGUE: Byung-Hyun Kim 1-0, Brandon Lyon 0-1, Derek Lowe 1-0 vs. Marlins; Ryan Rupe 1-0, Derek Lowe 1-0, Jason Shiell 1-0 vs. Astros; Hector Almonte 0-1, Brandon Lyon 1-0, Derek Lowe 1-0 vs. Brewers; Rudy Seanez 0-1, Byung-Hyun Kim 1-1 vs. Phillies; Byung-Hyun Kim 1-0, Derek Lowe 1-0, Ramiro Mendoza 0-1 vs. Pirates; Ramiro Mendoza 0-1, Brandon Lyon 0-1, John Burkett 1-0 vs. Cardinals. Total: 11-7.

CHICAGO—86-76

Pitcher	Ana. W-L	Bal. W-L	Bos. W-L	Cle. W-L	Det. W-L	K.C. W-L	Min. W-L	N.Y. W-L	Oak. W-L	Sea. W-L	TB. W-L	Tex. W-L	Tor. W-L	N.L. W-L	Totals W-L
Buehrle, Mark	0-1	0-0	2-0	1-1	2-1	2-1	3-2	0-1	1-2	0-2	1-0	1-0	0-1	1-2	14-14
Colon, Bartolo	0-1	1-1	1-2	2-1	1-2	2-0	1-1	1-0	0-1	2-1	1-0	1-1	1-1	1-1	15-13
Cotts, Neal	0-0	0-0	0-0	0-0	0-0	0-0	0-0	0-1	0-0	0-0	0-0	1-0	0-0	0-0	1-1
Garland, Jon	1-1	0-0	0-0	1-2	2-1	2-1	2-3	0-0	1-2	0-0	0-0	0-1	1-0	2-2	12-13
Glover, Gary	0-0	0-0	0-0	0-0	1-0	0-0	0-0	0-0	0-0	0-0	0-0	0-0	0-0	0-0	1-0
Gordon, Tom	1-0	1-1	0-1	0-0	0-1	1-1	0-1	1-0	0-0	0-0	0-0	0-0	1-0	2-1	7-6
Koch, Billy	0-0	0-0	0-1	1-1	0-0	0-1	1-1	0-0	0-0	0-0	0-1	0-0	0-0	3-0	5-5
Loaiza, Esteban	1-0	2-0	1-0	1-0	4-2	3-1	2-2	2-0	2-0	0-1	1-1	0-1	1-0	1-1	21-9
Marte, Damaso	0-0	0-0	0-0	2-0	1-0	0-0	0-0	0-0	0-0	0-0	0-0	0-1	1-0	0-1	4-2
Porzio, Mike	0-0	0-0	0-0	1-1	0-0	0-0	0-0	0-0	0-0	0-0	0-0	0-0	0-0	0-0	1-1
Schoeneweis, Scott	0-0	0-0	0-0	1-0	0-0	1-1	0-0	0-0	0-0	0-0	0-0	0-0	0-0	0-0	2-1
Stewart, Josh	0-0	0-0	0-0	1-0	0-1	0-0	0-0	0-0	0-0	0-1	0-0	0-0	0-0	0-0	1-2
White, Rick	0-0	0-0	0-0	0-0	0-0	0-1	0-0	0-0	0-0	0-0	0-1	0-0	1-0	0-0	1-2
Wright, Dan	1-0	0-0	0-1	0-2	0-0	0-1	0-0	0-0	0-0	0-2	0-0	0-0	0-1	0-0	1-7
Totals	4-3	4-2	4-5	11-8	11-8	11-8	9-10	4-2	4-5	2-7	3-3	3-4	6-3	10-8	86-76

NO-DECESIONS: Jon Adkins, Matt Ginter, Jose Paniagua, David Sanders, Scott Sullivan, Kelly Wunsch.

INTERLEAGUE: Tom Gordon 0-1, Jon Garland 0-1, Billy Koch 1-0 vs. Diamondbacks; Jon Garland 1-0, Mark Buehrle 1-0, Billy Koch 2-0, Damaso Marte 0-1, Esteban Loaiza 0-1 vs. Cubs; Mark Buehrle 0-1, Bartolo Colon 1-0, Esteban Loaiza 1-0 vs. Dodgers; Tom Gordon 2-0, Jon Garland 0-1 vs. Padres; Jon Garland 1-0, Mark Buehrle 0-1, Bartolo Colon 0-1 vs. Giants. Total: 10-8.

CLEVELAND—68-94

Pitcher	Ana. W-L	Bal. W-L	Bos. W-L	Chi. W-L	Det. W-L	K.C. W-L	Min. W-L	N.Y. W-L	Oak. W-L	Sea. W-L	TB. W-L	Tex. W-L	Tor. W-L	N.L. W-L	Totals W-L
Anderson, Brian	0-1	1-0	0-1	3-1	2-0	1-1	2-1	0-1	0-1	0-1	0-0	0-1	0-0	0-1	9-10
Baez, Danys	0-0	0-1	0-0	0-1	0-0	1-0	0-2	0-0	0-2	0-1	0-0	0-0	1-0	0-2	2-9
Betancourt, Rafael	0-0	0-0	0-0	0-1	0-0	0-0	2-1	0-0	0-0	0-0	0-0	0-0	0-0	0-0	2-2
Boyd, Jason	1-0	0-0	0-0	1-0	0-1	0-0	0-0	1-0	0-0	0-0	0-0	0-0	0-0	0-0	3-1
Cressend, Jack	1-0	0-0	0-0	0-1	1-0	0-0	0-0	0-0	0-0	0-0	0-0	0-0	0-0	0-0	2-1
Davis, Jason	0-2	1-0	1-0	1-2	1-0	1-2	0-3	0-0	0-1	1-0	0-0	0-0	0-0	2-1	8-11
Durbin, Chad	0-0	0-0	0-0	0-0	0-1	0-0	0-0	0-0	0-0	0-0	0-0	0-0	0-0	0-0	0-1
Elder, Dave	0-1	0-0	0-0	0-0	0-0	0-0	0-0	0-0	0-0	0-0	0-0	1-0	0-0	0-0	1-1
Lee, Cliff	0-0	0-0	0-1	0-0	1-0	1-0	0-0	0-0	0-0	0-0	1-1	0-0	0-1	0-0	3-3
Lee, David	0-0	0-0	1-0	0-0	0-0	0-0	0-0	0-0	0-0	0-0	0-0	0-0	0-0	0-0	1-0
Miceli, Dan	0-0	0-0	0-0	0-0	1-0	0-0	0-0	0-0	0-0	0-0	0-0	0-0	0-0	0-1	1-1
Mulholland, Terry	0-0	0-0	0-0	0-1	0-0	0-0	1-0	0-0	1-1	0-0	1-1	0-0	0-1	0-0	3-4
Paronto, Chad	0-0	0-1	0-0	0-1	0-0	0-0	0-0	0-0	0-0	0-0	0-0	0-0	0-0	0-0	0-2
Phillips, Jason C.	0-0	0-0	0-0	0-0	0-1	0-0	0-0	0-0	0-0	0-0	0-0	0-0	0-0	0-0	0-1
Riske, David	0-0	0-0	0-0	0-0	1-0	0-1	1-0	0-1	0-0	0-0	0-0	0-0	0-0	0-0	2-2
Rodriguez, Ricardo	0-2	1-0	0-1	0-0	1-0	1-2	0-0	0-0	0-0	0-1	0-0	0-1	0-0	0-2	3-9
Sabathia, C.C.	1-0	0-0	0-0	1-0	2-1	0-3	2-0	0-2	1-0	0-1	2-0	2-0	0-1	2-1	13-9
Santiago, Jose	0-0	0-0	0-0	0-0	1-1	0-1	0-0	0-0	0-0	0-0	0-0	0-1	0-0	0-0	1-3
Stanford, Jason	0-0	0-0	0-1	0-0	0-0	0-0	0-1	0-0	0-0	0-0	0-0	0-1	1-0	0-0	1-3
Tallet, Brian	0-0	0-0	0-0	0-1	0-0	0-0	0-0	0-0	0-0	0-0	0-0	0-0	0-0	0-1	0-2
Traber, Billy	0-0	0-0	0-0	0-2	1-1	0-2	1-0	1-0	1-0	1-1	0-0	0-1	0-0	1-2	6-9
Westbrook, Jake	0-0	0-1	0-0	2-0	0-1	1-1	0-2	0-1	0-1	1-1	1-0	1-0	0-1	1-1	7-10
Totals	3-6	3-3	2-4	8-11	12-7	6-13	9-10	2-5	3-6	3-6	5-2	4-5	2-4	6-12	68-94

NO-DECESIONS: Jason Bere, Nick Bierbrodt, David Cortes, Alex Herrera, Aaron Myette, Jerrod Riggan, Carl Sadler.

INTERLEAGUE: Jason Davis 1-0, Brian Anderson 0-1, Ricardo Rodriguez 0-1 vs. Diamondbacks; Billy Traber 1-0, Danys Baez 0-1, Jason Davis 1-0 vs. Reds; Ricardo Rodriguez 0-1, Billy Traber 0-1, C.C. Sabathia 0-1 vs. Rockies; Jake Westbrook 0-1, Brian Tallet 0-1, Billy Traber 0-1 vs. Dodgers; Dan Miceli 0-1, Danys Baez 0-1, C.C. Sabathia 1-0 vs. Pirates; Jake Westbrook 1-0, C.C. Sabathia 1-0, Jason Davis 0-1 vs. Padres. Total: 6-12.

DETROIT—43-119

Pitcher	Ana. W-L	Bal. W-L	Bos. W-L	Chi. W-L	Cle. W-L	K.C. W-L	Min. W-L	N.Y. W-L	Oak. W-L	Sea. W-L	TB. W-L	Tex. W-L	Tor. W-L	N.L. W-L	Totals W-L
Anderson, Matt	0-0	0-0	0-0	0-0	0-0	0-1	0-0	0-0	0-0	0-0	0-0	0-0	0-0	0-0	0-1
Avery, Steve	0-0	0-0	0-0	0-0	1-0	0-0	0-0	0-0	1-0	0-0	0-0	0-0	0-0	0-0	2-0
Bernero, Adam	0-0	0-0	0-0	0-1	0-1	0-0	0-2	1-0	0-1	0-1	0-1	0-0	0-1	0-4	1-12
Bonderman, Jeremy	0-2	0-1	0-2	1-0	0-3	1-2	0-4	0-0	2-0	0-1	1-1	1-0	0-0	0-3	6-19
Cornejo, Nate	0-1	1-0	0-1	2-3	2-1	0-1	0-2	0-1	0-2	0-2	1-0	0-1	0-1	0-1	6-17
German, Franklyn	0-0	1-1	0-0	0-1	1-0	0-0	0-1	0-0	0-0	0-0	0-0	0-0	0-0	0-1	2-4
Knotts, Gary	0-0	1-0	0-0	1-1	1-0	0-3	0-0	0-2	0-0	0-0	0-1	0-0	0-0	0-1	3-8
Ledezma, Wilfredo	0-1	0-0	1-0	0-1	0-0	0-1	0-0	0-0	0-2	0-1	0-1	0-0	0-0	2-0	3-7
Loux, Shane	0-0	0-0	0-0	0-0	0-0	1-0	0-0	0-0	0-0	0-0	0-0	0-0	0-1	0-0	1-1
Maroth, Mike	0-0	0-1	0-3	2-2	0-1	3-3	2-3	0-0	0-1	0-2	0-0	0-2	1-2	1-1	9-21
Mears, Chris	0-0	0-0	0-0	0-0	0-0	0-1	1-1	0-0	0-0	0-0	0-0	0-0	0-1	0-0	1-3
Robertson, Nate	0-0	0-0	0-0	1-0	0-0	0-1	0-1	0-0	0-0	0-0	0-0	0-0	0-0	0-0	1-2
Rodney, Fernando	0-0	0-0	0-1	0-0	0-0	0-0	1-0	0-1	0-0	0-0	0-0	0-0	0-1	0-0	1-3
Roney, Matt	0-1	0-0	0-1	0-1	0-2	0-1	0-1	0-0	0-0	0-1	0-0	0-1	1-0	0-0	1-9
Schmack, Brian	0-0	0-0	0-0	0-0	1-0	0-0	0-0	0-0	0-0	0-0	0-0	0-0	0-0	0-0	1-0
Sparks, Steve	0-0	0-0	0-0	0-1	0-0	0-0	0-0	0-1	0-0	0-0	0-0	0-2	0-0	0-2	0-6
Spurling, Chris	0-1	0-0	0-0	1-0	0-1	0-0	0-0	0-0	0-0	0-0	0-0	0-0	0-0	0-1	1-3
Walker, Jamie	1-0	0-0	0-0	0-0	1-3	0-0	0-0	0-0	0-0	1-0	0-0	0-0	0-0	1-0	4-3
Totals	1-6	3-3	1-8	8-11	7-12	5-14	4-15	1-5	3-6	1-8	2-4	1-6	2-7	4-14	43-119

NO-DECESIONS: Eric Eckenstahler, Danny Patterson.

INTERLEAGUE: Adam Bernero 0-1, Chris Spurling 0-1, Jeremy Bonderman 0-1 vs. Diamondbacks; Nate Cornejo 0-1, Mike Maroth 1-0, Wilfredo Ledezma 1-0, Gary Knotts 0-1, Steve Sparks 0-1, Adam Bernero 0-1 vs. Rockies; Steve Sparks 0-1, Adam Bernero 0-1, Jeremy Bonderman 0-1 vs. Dodgers; Jamie Walker 1-0, Wilfredo Ledezma 1-0, Adam Bernero 0-1 vs. Padres; Jeremy Bonderman 0-1, Mike Maroth 0-1, Franklyn German 0-1 vs. Giants. Total: 4-14.

KANSAS CITY—83-79

Pitcher	Ana. W-L	Bal. W-L	Bos. W-L	Chi. W-L	Cle. W-L	Det. W-L	Min. W-L	N.Y. W-L	Oak. W-L	Sea. W-L	TB. W-L	Tex. W-L	Tor. W-L	N.L. W-L	Totals W-L
Abbott, Paul	1-0	0-0	0-0	0-0	0-1	0-1	0-0	0-0	0-0	0-0	0-0	0-0	0-0	0-0	1-2
Affeldt, Jeremy	0-1	0-0	0-1	0-0	1-0	3-0	2-0	0-0	0-0	0-2	0-0	0-1	0-0	1-1	7-6
Anderson, Brian	1-1	0-0	0-0	2-0	0-0	1-0	0-0	0-0	0-0	0-0	0-0	1-0	0-0	0-0	5-1
Appier, Kevin	0-0	0-0	0-0	0-0	0-0	0-0	0-0	1-1	0-0	0-0	0-1	0-0	0-0	0-0	1-2
Asencio, Miguel	0-0	1-1	0-0	0-0	0-0	1-0	0-0	0-0	0-0	0-0	0-0	0-0	0-0	0-0	2-1
Bukvich, Ryan	0-0	0-0	0-0	1-0	0-0	0-0	0-0	0-0	0-0	0-0	0-0	0-0	0-0	0-0	1-0
Carrasco, D.J.	0-0	1-0	0-0	0-1	0-0	1-0	2-0	1-0	0-1	0-1	0-0	1-0	0-1	0-1	6-5
DeHart, Rick	0-0	0-0	0-0	0-0	0-0	0-0	0-0	0-0	0-1	0-0	0-0	0-0	0-0	0-1	0-2
Field, Nate	0-0	0-0	0-0	0-1	0-0	1-0	0-0	0-0	0-0	0-0	0-0	0-0	0-0	0-0	1-1
George, Chris	0-1	1-0	0-1	0-1	3-0	0-0	2-0	0-0	0-0	1-1	0-0	0-0	0-1	2-1	9-6
Gilfillan, Jason	0-0	0-0	0-0	0-0	1-0	0-0	0-0	0-0	0-0	0-0	0-0	0-0	0-0	1-0	2-0
Gobble, Jimmy	0-1	0-0	0-0	0-0	0-1	1-1	0-1	0-1	0-0	0-0	2-0	1-0	0-0	0-0	4-5
Grimsley, Jason	0-1	0-0	0-1	0-1	0-1	0-0	0-1	0-0	0-0	0-0	0-0	0-0	1-1	1-0	2-6
Hernandez, Runelvys	0-0	0-2	0-0	2-1	2-0	1-0	1-2	0-0	0-0	0-0	1-0	0-0	0-0	0-0	7-5
Leskanic, Curtis	0-0	0-0	0-0	0-0	0-0	0-0	0-0	0-0	0-0	0-0	1-0	0-0	0-0	0-0	1-0
Levine, Al	0-0	0-0	0-0	0-0	0-0	0-0	0-1	0-0	0-0	0-0	0-0	0-0	0-0	0-0	0-1
Lima, Jose	0-0	0-0	0-0	0-1	3-0	2-1	0-0	0-1	0-0	1-0	0-0	1-0	0-0	1-0	8-3
Lloyd, Graeme	0-0	0-0	0-0	0-0	0-0	0-0	0-1	0-0	0-0	0-0	0-1	0-0	0-0	0-0	0-2
Lopez, Albie	0-0	0-0	1-1	2-0	0-0	1-0	0-1	0-0	0-0	0-0	0-0	0-0	0-0	0-0	4-2
Lowe, Sean	0-0	1-0	0-0	0-0	0-0	0-0	0-0	0-0	0-1	0-0	0-0	0-0	0-0	0-0	1-1
MacDougal, Mike	0-0	0-0	0-1	0-0	0-0	1-0	1-0	0-0	0-1	0-1	0-1	0-0	0-1	1-0	3-5
May, Darrell	1-0	0-0	0-0	1-2	2-1	0-0	2-0	0-1	0-0	1-0	0-0	2-1	0-0	1-3	10-8
Snyder, Kyle	0-0	0-0	0-0	0-1	0-0	0-1	0-1	0-0	0-2	0-0	0-0	0-0	0-1	1-0	1-6
Voyles, Brad	0-0	0-0	0-0	0-0	0-1	0-1	0-0	0-0	0-0	0-0	0-0	0-0	0-0	0-0	0-2
Walrond, Les	0-0	0-0	0-0	0-0	0-1	0-0	0-0	0-0	0-0	0-0	0-0	0-0	0-0	0-1	0-2
Wilson, Kris	0-0	0-0	0-0	0-1	1-0	0-0	1-0	0-0	2-1	1-0	0-0	1-0	0-0	0-1	6-3
Wright, Jamey	0-1	0-0	0-0	0-1	0-0	1-0	0-0	0-0	0-0	0-0	0-0	0-0	0-0	0-0	1-2
Totals	3-6	4-3	1-5	8-11	13-6	14-5	11-8	2-4	2-7	4-5	4-3	7-2	1-5	9-9	83-79

NO-DECESIONS: Jeremy Hill, Scott Mullen.

INTERLEAGUE: Jason Grimsley 1-0, Darrell May 0-1, Kris Wilson 0-1 vs. Diamondbacks; Chris George 1-0, Jason Gilfillan 1-0, Rick DeHart 0-1 vs. Rockies; D.J. Carrasco 0-1, Kyle Snyder 1-0, Darrell May 0-1 vs. Dodgers; Chris George 1-0, Mike MacDougal 1-0, Les Walrond 0-1 vs. Giants; Jose Lima 1-0, Darrell May 1-1, Jeremy Affeldt 1-1, Chris George 0-1 vs. Cardinals. Total: 9-9.

MINNESOTA—90-72

Pitcher	Ana. W-L	Bal. W-L	Bos. W-L	Chi. W-L	Cle. W-L	Det. W-L	K.C. W-L	N.Y. W-L	Oak. W-L	Sea. W-L	TB. W-L	Tex. W-L	Tor. W-L	N.L. W-L	Totals W-L
Baldwin, James	0-0	0-0	0-0	0-0	0-1	0-0	0-0	0-0	0-0	0-0	0-0	0-0	0-0	0-0	0-1
Balfour, Grant	0-0	0-0	0-0	0-0	0-0	0-0	0-0	0-0	0-0	0-0	0-0	1-0	0-0	0-0	1-0
Fiore, Tony	0-0	0-0	0-1	0-0	0-0	0-0	0-0	0-0	0-0	0-0	1-0	0-0	0-0	0-0	1-1
Guardado, Eddie	1-0	0-0	0-0	1-1	0-1	1-0	0-1	0-0	0-0	0-0	0-0	0-1	0-1	0-0	3-5
Hawkins, LaTroy	0-0	1-1	0-0	1-0	1-0	0-0	2-0	0-0	2-0	0-0	0-0	0-0	1-0	1-2	9-3
Johnson, Adam	0-0	0-0	0-0	0-0	0-0	0-1	0-0	0-0	0-0	0-0	0-0	0-0	0-0	0-0	0-1
Lohse, Kyle	2-1	1-0	0-0	1-2	2-1	3-0	1-1	0-2	0-0	1-1	1-0	0-1	0-0	2-2	14-11
Mays, Joe	0-0	0-0	0-0	2-1	0-1	1-0	1-2	0-2	2-0	0-1	0-0	0-0	1-0	1-1	8-8
Milton, Eric	0-0	0-0	0-0	0-0	0-0	1-0	0-0	0-0	0-0	0-0	0-0	0-0	0-0	0-0	1-0
Orosco, Jesse	0-0	0-0	0-0	0-0	1-0	0-1	0-0	0-0	0-0	0-0	0-0	0-0	0-0	0-0	1-1
Pulido, Carlos	0-0	0-0	0-0	0-1	0-0	0-0	0-0	0-0	0-0	0-0	0-0	0-0	0-0	0-0	0-1
Radke, Brad	1-1	2-0	1-0	3-2	1-1	2-0	0-1	0-1	1-0	0-2	2-0	1-0	0-1	0-1	14-10
Reed, Rick	0-0	0-1	0-0	0-2	1-0	1-1	1-2	0-2	1-1	1-1	0-0	1-1	0-1	0-0	6-12
Rincon, Juan	0-1	0-0	0-1	0-0	1-2	1-0	0-0	0-0	0-0	1-0	1-0	1-0	0-0	0-2	5-6
Rogers, Kenny	0-1	0-1	1-0	1-0	1-2	2-0	2-2	0-0	1-0	0-1	1-0	0-1	1-0	3-0	13-8
Romero, J.C.	0-0	0-0	0-0	0-0	0-0	0-0	0-0	0-0	1-0	0-0	0-0	0-0	0-0	1-0	2-0
Santana, Johan	0-1	0-0	2-0	1-0	2-0	3-0	1-2	0-0	0-0	0-0	0-0	1-0	0-0	2-0	12-3
Thomas, Brad	0-0	0-0	0-0	0-0	0-0	0-1	0-0	0-0	0-0	0-0	0-0	0-0	0-0	0-0	0-1
Totals	4-5	4-3	4-2	10-9	10-9	15-4	8-11	0-7	8-1	3-6	6-0	5-4	3-3	10-8	90-72

NO-DECESIONS: Mike Fetters, Mike Nakamura.

INTERLEAGUE: Johan Santana 1-0, LaTroy Hawkins 0-1, Joe Mays 0-1 vs. Diamondbacks; Brad Radke 0-1, Kyle Lohse 1-0, Kenny Rogers 1-0 vs. Rockies; LaTroy Hawkins 1-0, Juan Rincon 0-1, Kyle Lohse 0-2, Kenny Rogers 2-0 vs. Brewers; LaTroy Hawkins 0-1, J.C. Romero 1-0, Johan Santana 1-0 vs. Padres; Joe Mays 1-0, Juan Rincon 0-1, Kyle Lohse 1-0 vs. Giants. Total: 10-8.

NEW YORK—101-61

Pitcher	Ana. W-L	Bal. W-L	Bos. W-L	Chi. W-L	Cle. W-L	Det. W-L	K.C. W-L	Min. W-L	Oak. W-L	Sea. W-L	TB. W-L	Tex. W-L	Tor. W-L	N.L. W-L	Totals W-L
Acevedo, Juan	0-0	0-0	0-0	0-0	0-0	0-0	0-0	0-0	0-1	0-0	0-1	0-1	0-0	0-0	0-3
Anderson, Jason	0-0	0-0	0-0	0-0	0-0	0-0	0-0	0-0	0-0	0-0	1-0	0-0	0-0	0-0	1-0
Benitez, Armando	1-0	0-0	0-1	0-0	0-0	0-0	0-0	0-0	0-0	0-0	0-0	0-0	0-0	0-0	1-1
Claussen, Brandon	0-0	0-0	0-0	0-0	0-0	0-0	0-0	0-0	0-0	0-0	0-0	0-0	0-0	1-0	1-0
Clemens, Roger	2-0	2-1	2-3	0-1	1-0	1-0	1-0	1-0	1-1	0-1	2-1	1-0	1-0	2-1	17-9
Contreras, Jose	0-0	1-0	0-2	1-0	0-0	1-0	0-0	0-0	0-0	0-0	1-0	0-0	2-0	1-0	7-2
Hammond, Chris	0-0	1-1	0-1	0-0	0-0	0-0	0-0	0-0	0-0	0-0	1-0	1-0	0-0	0-0	3-2
Heredia, Felix	0-0	0-0	0-0	0-0	0-0	0-0	0-0	0-0	0-0	0-0	0-1	0-0	0-0	0-0	0-1
Hitchcock, Sterling	0-0	0-0	0-0	0-0	0-1	0-0	0-1	0-0	0-0	1-0	0-0	0-0	0-1	0-0	1-3
Mussina, Mike	0-1	1-2	0-0	1-1	1-0	0-0	1-0	2-0	0-0	2-0	2-0	2-1	3-2	2-1	17-8
Nelson, Jeff	0-0	1-0	0-0	0-0	0-0	0-0	0-0	0-0	0-0	0-0	0-0	0-0	0-0	0-0	1-0
Osuna, Antonio	0-0	0-0	0-0	0-0	0-0	0-0	0-0	0-0	0-1	0-1	1-1	0-0	0-1	1-1	2-5
Pettitte, Andy	1-1	6-0	3-1	0-0	0-0	1-0	1-0	2-0	0-1	1-2	2-0	0-1	2-1	2-1	21-8
Rivera, Mariano	0-0	0-0	3-0	0-0	1-0	0-0	0-0	0-0	0-1	0-0	0-0	0-1	0-0	1-0	5-2
Weaver, Jeff	2-0	0-0	0-0	0-0	0-1	0-1	1-1	0-0	1-1	0-0	0-1	0-1	2-2	1-1	7-9
Wells, David	0-1	1-2	2-1	0-1	2-0	1-0	0-0	2-0	1-0	1-0	3-0	0-0	0-2	2-0	15-7
White, Gabe	0-0	0-0	0-0	0-1	0-0	1-0	0-0	0-0	0-0	0-0	1-0	0-0	0-0	0-0	2-1
Totals	6-3	13-6	10-9	2-4	5-2	5-1	4-2	7-0	3-6	5-4	14-5	4-5	10-9	13-5	101-61

NO-DECESIONS: Randy Choate, Jorge DePaula, Dan Miceli, Jesse Orosco, Bret Prinz, Al Reyes.

INTERLEAGUE: David Wells 1-0, Roger Clemens 0-1, Andy Pettitte 0-1 vs. Cubs; Antonio Osuna 0-1, Mike Mussina 0-1, Jose Contreras 1-0 vs. Reds; Mike Mussina 1-0, Antonio Osuna 1-0, Jeff Weaver 0-1 vs. Astros; Andy Pettitte 1-0, Mariano Rivera 1-0, David Wells 1-0, Roger Clemens 1-0, Brandon Claussen 1-0, Jeff Weaver 1-0 vs. Mets; Roger Clemens 1-0, Andy Pettitte 1-0, Mike Mussina 1-0 vs. Cardinals. Total: 13-5.

OAKLAND—96-66

Pitcher	Ana. W-L	Bal. W-L	Bos. W-L	Chi. W-L	Cle. W-L	Det. W-L	K.C. W-L	Min. W-L	N.Y. W-L	Sea. W-L	TB. W-L	Tex. W-L	Tor. W-L	N.L. W-L	Totals W-L
Bowie, Micah	0-0	0-0	0-0	0-0	0-0	0-0	0-0	0-0	0-0	0-1	0-0	0-0	0-0	0-0	0-1
Bradford, Chad	1-0	0-0	1-0	1-0	1-0	0-0	1-0	0-1	0-0	0-1	0-0	0-2	0-0	2-0	7-4
Duchscherer, Justin	1-0	0-0	0-0	0-0	0-0	0-0	0-0	0-0	0-0	0-1	0-0	0-0	0-0	0-0	1-1
Fikac, Jeremy	0-0	0-0	0-0	0-0	0-0	0-0	0-0	0-0	0-0	0-1	0-0	0-0	0-0	0-0	0-1
Foulke, Keith	1-0	1-0	0-0	0-0	1-0	0-0	1-0	0-0	2-0	1-0	0-0	2-0	0-0	0-1	9-1
Halama, John	1-1	1-1	0-0	1-1	0-0	0-0	0-0	0-2	0-0	0-0	0-0	0-0	0-0	0-0	3-5
Harang, Aaron	0-1	0-0	0-0	0-0	0-0	0-0	0-0	0-0	0-0	0-1	0-0	0-0	0-0	1-1	1-3
Harden, Rich	2-0	0-0	0-1	0-1	1-0	1-0	0-0	0-0	0-0	0-0	1-1	0-0	0-1	0-0	5-4
Harville, Chad	0-0	0-0	0-0	0-0	0-0	0-0	0-0	0-0	0-0	0-0	0-0	1-0	0-0	0-0	1-0
Hudson, Tim	1-2	1-1	1-0	0-0	0-0	1-0	1-1	1-1	1-0	2-1	1-0	3-0	2-0	1-1	16-7
Lilly, Ted	4-0	0-0	0-0	0-1	1-1	1-0	0-1	0-1	0-1	1-2	2-0	1-0	1-0	1-3	12-10
Mecir, Jim	0-1	1-0	0-1	0-0	0-0	0-0	1-0	0-0	0-0	0-0	0-0	0-1	0-0	0-0	2-3
Mulder, Mark	0-1	0-0	0-1	2-1	1-1	1-0	2-0	0-1	2-0	1-1	1-0	3-1	0-0	2-2	15-9
Rincon, Ricardo	0-1	1-0	1-0	0-0	1-1	1-1	1-0	0-0	0-0	0-1	1-0	1-0	0-0	1-0	8-4
Wood, Mike	0-0	1-0	0-0	0-0	0-0	0-0	0-0	0-0	0-0	0-1	0-0	0-0	1-0	0-0	2-1
Zito, Barry	1-1	1-0	1-0	1-0	0-0	1-2	0-0	0-2	1-2	2-1	0-2	4-0	1-1	1-1	14-12
Totals	12-8	7-2	4-3	5-4	6-3	6-3	7-2	1-8	6-3	7-12	6-3	15-4	5-2	9-9	96-66

NO-DECESIONS: Mike Neu, Steve Sparks.

INTERLEAGUE: Chad Bradford 1-0, Ted Lilly 0-1, Barry Zito 0-1 vs. Braves; Mark Mulder 0-1, Chad Bradford 1-0, Ted Lilly 0-1 vs. Marlins; Mark Mulder 1-0, Ricardo Rincon 1-0, Tim Hudson 1-0 vs. Expos; Barry Zito 1-0, Mark Mulder 0-1, Aaron Harang 0-1 vs. Phillies; Aaron Harang 1-0, Keith Foulke 0-1, Tim Hudson 0-1, Ted Lilly 1-1, Mark Mulder 1-0 vs. Giants. Total: 9-9.

SEATTLE—93-69

Pitcher	Ana. W-L	Bal. W-L	Bos. W-L	Chi. W-L	Cle. W-L	Det. W-L	K.C. W-L	Min. W-L	N.Y. W-L	Oak. W-L	TB. W-L	Tex. W-L	Tor. W-L	N.L. W-L	Totals W-L
Carrara, Giovanni	0-0	0-0	0-0	0-0	2-0	0-0	0-0	0-0	0-0	0-0	0-0	0-0	0-0	0-0	2-0
Franklin, Ryan	1-2	0-1	0-1	3-0	0-0	0-1	0-0	1-1	0-1	3-1	0-1	1-1	1-0	1-3	11-13
Garcia, Freddy	3-0	0-2	1-0	1-1	0-2	1-0	1-2	1-0	0-1	0-2	0-1	1-3	1-0	2-0	12-14
Hasegawa, Shigetoshi	1-1	0-0	0-0	0-0	0-0	0-0	0-0	0-0	0-0	0-0	1-1	0-2	0-0	0-0	2-4
Mateo, Julio	0-0	0-0	1-0	0-0	0-0	0-0	0-0	1-0	0-0	0-0	0-0	0-0	1-0	1-0	4-0
Meche, Gil	1-1	1-0	0-1	2-1	1-0	2-0	1-1	1-0	2-0	0-2	0-1	2-3	0-2	2-1	15-13
Moyer, Jamie	4-2	1-1	0-0	1-0	2-0	2-0	1-0	1-0	1-1	2-1	2-0	2-0	0-1	2-1	21-7
Nelson, Jeff	0-0	0-0	0-0	0-0	0-0	0-0	1-0	0-0	0-0	2-1	0-0	0-0	0-0	0-1	3-2
Pineiro, Joel	1-1	1-0	0-2	0-0	1-1	3-0	0-0	1-1	0-2	4-0	1-1	2-1	0-1	2-1	16-11
Rhodes, Arthur	0-0	1-0	0-0	0-0	0-0	0-0	1-1	0-1	0-0	1-0	0-0	0-0	0-0	0-1	3-3
Sasaki, Kazuhiro	0-1	0-0	0-1	0-0	0-0	0-0	0-0	0-0	0-0	0-0	0-0	1-0	0-0	0-0	1-2
Soriano, Rafael	0-0	1-0	0-0	0-0	0-0	0-0	0-0	0-0	1-0	0-0	0-0	1-0	0-0	0-0	3-0
Totals	11-8	5-4	2-5	7-2	6-3	8-1	5-4	6-3	4-5	12-7	4-5	10-10	3-4	10-8	93-69

NO-DECESIONS: Armando Benitez, Aaron Looper, J.J. Putz, Brian Sweeney, Aaron Taylor, Matt White.

INTERLEAGUE: Freddy Garcia 1-0, Jamie Moyer 0-1, Gil Meche 1-0 vs. Braves; Gil Meche 0-1, Joel Pineiro 0-1, Ryan Franklin 1-0 vs. Expos; Ryan Franklin 0-1, Freddy Garcia 1-0, Jamie Moyer 1-0 vs. Mets; Jamie Moyer 1-0, Gil Meche 1-0, Julio Mateo 1-0 vs. Phillies; Arthur Rhodes 0-1, Jeff Nelson 0-1, Joel Pineiro 2-0, Ryan Franklin 0-2 vs. Padres. Total: 10-8.

TAMPA BAY—63-99

Pitcher	Ana. W-L	Bal. W-L	Bos. W-L	Chi. W-L	Cle. W-L	Det. W-L	K.C. W-L	Min. W-L	N.Y. W-L	Oak. W-L	Sea. W-L	Tex. W-L	Tor. W-L	N.L. W-L	Totals W-L
Backe, Brandon	0-0	0-0	0-0	0-0	0-1	0-0	1-0	0-0	0-0	0-0	0-0	0-0	0-0	0-0	1-1
Bell, Rob	1-0	1-0	0-1	0-0	0-0	0-0	0-0	0-0	0-1	2-1	0-0	0-0	1-0	0-1	5-4
Bierbrodt, Nick	0-0	0-1	0-1	0-0	0-0	0-0	0-0	0-0	0-0	0-0	0-0	0-0	0-0	0-0	0-2
Brazelton, Dewon	1-1	0-0	0-0	0-0	0-0	0-0	0-0	0-1	0-1	0-0	0-0	0-1	0-1	0-1	1-6
Carter, Lance	0-0	3-0	1-1	0-0	1-0	0-0	0-0	0-0	2-2	0-0	0-1	0-0	0-1	0-0	7-5
Colome, Jesus	0-0	0-2	0-1	1-0	0-1	0-0	0-0	0-0	0-0	0-1	0-0	0-1	2-0	0-1	3-7
Gaudin, Chad	0-0	0-0	1-0	0-0	0-0	0-0	1-0	0-0	0-0	0-0	0-0	0-0	0-0	0-0	2-0
Gonzalez, Jeremi	1-0	1-1	0-1	0-0	0-1	0-0	1-1	0-0	1-1	0-2	0-0	2-0	0-1	0-3	6-11
Harper, Travis	0-0	1-0	1-2	0-0	0-1	0-0	0-0	0-1	1-1	0-0	1-1	0-1	0-0	0-1	4-8
Kennedy, Joe	0-3	0-1	0-1	0-1	0-1	1-0	0-0	0-1	0-1	0-1	0-0	0-1	2-1	0-0	3-12
Levine, Al	0-0	1-0	0-1	0-0	0-0	1-0	0-0	0-0	0-0	0-0	0-0	0-0	1-0	0-4	3-5
Malaska, Mark	0-0	0-0	0-0	1-0	1-0	0-0	0-1	0-0	0-0	0-0	0-0	0-0	0-0	0-0	2-1
McClung, Seth	0-0	2-0	1-0	0-0	0-0	1-0	0-0	0-1	0-0	0-0	0-0	0-0	0-0	0-0	4-1
Parque, Jim	0-0	0-0	0-1	0-0	0-0	1-0	0-0	0-0	0-0	0-0	0-0	0-0	0-0	0-0	1-1
Parris, Steve	0-0	0-1	0-0	0-0	0-0	0-0	0-0	0-1	0-1	0-0	0-0	0-0	0-0	0-0	0-3
Reyes, Carlos	0-1	0-0	0-0	0-0	0-0	0-0	0-0	0-0	0-1	0-0	0-0	0-1	0-0	0-0	0-3
Sosa, Jorge	0-0	1-0	0-2	1-1	0-0	0-2	0-1	0-1	0-1	0-1	1-0	1-0	1-2	0-1	5-12
Standridge, Jason	0-0	0-0	0-0	0-1	0-0	0-0	0-0	0-0	0-1	0-0	0-1	0-0	0-0	0-2	0-5
Venafro, Mike	0-0	0-0	0-0	0-0	0-0	0-0	0-0	0-0	0-0	0-0	0-0	0-0	1-0	0-0	1-0
Waechter, Doug	0-0	0-0	0-0	0-0	0-0	0-0	0-0	0-0	0-1	0-0	2-0	0-0	1-1	0-0	3-2
Zambrano, Victor	0-1	1-2	3-0	0-0	0-0	0-0	0-1	0-0	1-2	1-0	1-1	0-1	2-1	3-1	12-10
Totals	3-6	11-8	7-12	3-3	2-5	4-2	3-4	0-6	5-14	3-6	5-4	3-6	11-8	3-15	63-99

NO-DECESIONS: John Rocker, Bobby Seay, Jon Switzer.

INTERLEAGUE: Jeremi Gonzalez 0-1, Victor Zambrano 1-0, Jorge Sosa 0-1 vs. Braves; Al Levine 0-1, Victor Zambrano 1-0, Dewon Brazelton 0-1 vs. Cubs; Jason Standridge 0-1, Jesus Colome 0-1, Jeremi Gonzalez 0-1 vs. Reds; Al Levine 0-1, Jason Standridge 0-1, Jeremi Gonzalez 0-1 vs. Marlins; Travis Harper 0-1, Al Levine 0-1, Victor Zambrano 0-1 vs. Astros; Victor Zambrano 1-0, Al Levine 0-1, Rob Bell 0-1 vs. Pirates. Total: 3-15.

TEXAS—71-91

Pitcher	Ana. W-L	Bal. W-L	Bos. W-L	Chi. W-L	Cle. W-L	Det. W-L	K.C. W-L	Min. W-L	N.Y. W-L	Oak. W-L	Sea. W-L	TB. W-L	Tor. W-L	N.L. W-L	Totals W-L
Benes, Alan	0-0	0-0	0-1	0-0	0-1	0-0	0-0	0-0	0-0	0-0	0-0	0-1	0-0	0-0	0-3
Benoit, Joaquin	0-2	0-1	0-1	1-0	1-0	1-0	0-0	1-0	0-0	0-0	1-0	2-0	0-0	1-1	8-5
Callaway, Mickey	0-0	0-0	0-0	0-0	0-0	0-0	0-0	0-2	0-0	0-0	0-1	0-0	0-0	0-0	0-3
Cordero, Francisco	0-1	0-1	0-1	0-0	0-1	0-0	0-0	1-1	0-0	2-1	1-1	1-0	0-0	0-1	5-8
Dickey, R.A.	1-0	0-2	1-0	0-0	1-0	2-0	0-2	0-1	2-0	0-2	1-1	0-0	1-0	0-0	9-8
Dominguez, Juan	0-0	0-0	0-0	0-1	0-0	0-1	0-0	0-0	0-0	0-0	0-0	0-0	0-0	0-0	0-2
Drese, Ryan	1-0	0-0	0-0	0-0	0-0	0-0	0-0	0-0	0-0	0-1	0-2	0-0	1-1	0-0	2-4
Ellis, Robert	0-0	0-0	1-0	0-0	0-0	0-0	0-0	0-0	0-0	0-0	0-1	0-0	0-0	0-0	1-1
Fultz, Aaron	0-0	0-0	0-0	0-0	0-0	0-0	0-0	0-0	0-1	0-0	0-0	0-0	1-1	0-1	1-3
Garcia, Rosman	0-0	0-0	0-1	0-0	0-0	0-0	0-0	0-0	0-0	0-1	0-0	0-0	0-0	1-0	1-2
Lewis, Colby	3-0	0-0	0-0	1-1	0-0	0-0	1-1	0-0	0-2	1-0	2-1	1-0	1-2	0-2	10-9
Mahay, Ron	0-2	0-0	0-0	0-0	0-0	1-0	0-0	0-0	1-0	0-1	1-0	0-0	0-0	0-0	3-3
Mounce, Tony	1-0	0-0	0-0	0-0	0-0	0-0	0-1	0-0	0-0	0-1	0-0	0-1	0-0	0-2	1-5
Park, Chan Ho	0-1	0-0	0-1	0-0	0-0	0-0	0-0	0-0	0-0	0-0	1-1	0-0	0-0	0-0	1-3
Powell, Jay	0-0	0-0	0-0	1-0	1-0	0-0	0-0	1-0	0-0	0-0	0-0	0-0	0-0	0-0	3-0
Ramirez, Erasmo	1-0	0-0	1-0	0-0	1-0	0-0	0-1	0-0	0-0	0-0	0-0	0-0	0-0	0-0	3-1
Ramos, Mario	0-0	0-0	0-0	0-0	0-0	0-0	0-0	0-0	0-0	1-1	0-0	0-0	0-0	0-0	1-1
Santos, Victor	0-0	0-0	0-0	0-0	0-0	0-0	0-0	0-0	0-0	0-1	0-0	0-0	0-0	0-1	0-2
Shouse, Brian	0-0	0-0	0-0	0-0	0-0	0-0	0-0	0-0	0-0	0-0	0-0	0-0	0-0	0-1	0-1
Thomson, John	1-2	0-3	1-0	1-0	1-2	2-0	0-1	1-1	1-0	0-1	2-1	1-0	1-0	1-3	13-14
Urbina, Ugueth	0-0	0-0	0-0	0-0	0-0	0-0	0-0	0-0	0-1	0-1	0-1	0-0	0-0	0-1	0-4
Valdes, Ismael	2-1	2-0	0-0	0-1	0-0	0-0	1-1	0-0	1-0	0-3	1-0	0-1	0-0	1-1	8-8
Van Poppel, Todd	0-0	0-0	0-0	0-0	0-0	0-0	0-0	0-0	0-0	0-0	0-0	1-0	0-0	0-0	1-0
Yan, Esteban	0-0	0-0	0-0	0-0	0-0	0-0	0-0	0-0	0-0	0-1	0-0	0-0	0-0	0-0	0-1
Totals	10-9	2-7	4-5	4-3	5-4	6-1	2-7	4-5	5-4	4-15	10-10	6-3	5-4	4-14	71-91

NO-DECESIONS: Doug Davis, Reynaldo Garcia, C.J. Nitkowski.

INTERLEAGUE: Aaron Fultz 0-1, Ugueth Urbina 0-1, John Thomson 0-1 vs. Braves; Tony Mounce 0-1, Ismael Valdes 1-0, John Thomson 0-1 vs. Marlins; John Thomson 0-1, Rosman Garcia 1-0, Ismael Valdes 0-1, Joaquin Benoit 1-1, Tony Mounce 0-1 vs. Astros; Colby Lewis 0-1, Brian Shouse 0-1, Francisco Cordero 0-1 vs. Expos; John Thomson 1-0, Victor Santos 0-1, Colby Lewis 0-1 vs. Mets. Total: 4-14.

TORONTO—86-76

Pitcher	Ana. W-L	Bal. W-L	Bos. W-L	Chi. W-L	Cle. W-L	Det. W-L	K.C. W-L	Min. W-L	N.Y. W-L	Oak. W-L	Sea. W-L	TB. W-L	Tex. W-L	N.L. W-L	Totals W-L
Acevedo, Juan	0-0	1-0	0-0	0-1	0-0	0-0	0-0	0-0	0-0	0-0	0-0	0-1	0-0	0-0	1-2
Davis, Doug	1-1	1-1	1-0	0-1	0-0	0-0	0-0	0-0	1-0	0-0	0-0	0-1	0-0	0-2	4-6
Escobar, Kelvim	1-0	3-1	1-0	0-1	1-0	0-0	1-0	0-1	1-2	0-1	1-1	1-0	1-0	2-2	13-9
Halladay, Roy	1-1	2-0	2-1	1-0	1-0	3-0	1-0	0-0	3-2	1-1	0-1	2-1	2-0	3-0	22-7
Hendrickson, Mark	2-0	0-1	1-0	0-0	0-0	0-1	1-0	0-1	1-1	0-1	2-0	1-2	0-1	1-1	9-9
Kershner, Jason	0-0	0-0	0-0	0-0	0-1	1-0	0-0	0-0	1-0	0-0	0-1	1-1	0-0	0-0	3-3
Lidle, Cory	1-0	1-4	1-1	1-1	1-1	0-1	0-0	1-1	2-1	0-1	0-0	1-3	1-0	2-1	12-15
Lopez, Aquilino	0-0	0-1	0-1	0-0	0-0	0-0	0-0	0-0	0-1	0-0	0-0	0-0	0-0	1-0	1-3
Miller, Trever	0-0	0-0	0-0	0-0	0-0	0-0	0-0	0-0	0-1	0-0	0-0	1-1	0-0	1-0	2-2
Politte, Cliff	0-0	0-0	0-2	0-1	0-0	0-0	1-0	0-0	0-0	0-0	0-0	0-0	0-0	0-2	1-5
Sturtze, Tanyon	0-0	1-0	2-1	0-1	0-0	1-0	1-0	1-0	0-0	0-1	0-0	1-1	0-2	0-0	7-6
Tam, Jeff	0-0	0-0	0-3	0-0	0-0	0-0	0-1	0-0	0-0	0-0	0-0	0-0	0-0	0-0	0-4
Thurman, Corey	1-0	0-0	0-0	0-0	0-0	0-0	0-0	0-0	0-0	0-0	0-0	0-0	0-1	0-0	1-1
Towers, Josh	0-0	1-0	1-0	1-0	1-0	2-0	0-0	0-0	0-0	1-0	1-0	0-0	0-1	0-0	8-1
Walker, Pete	0-0	1-0	0-0	0-0	0-0	0-0	0-0	1-0	0-2	0-0	0-0	0-0	0-0	0-0	2-2
Wasdin, John	0-0	0-0	0-1	0-0	0-0	0-0	0-0	0-0	0-0	0-0	0-0	0-0	0-0	0-0	0-1
Totals	7-2	11-8	9-10	3-6	4-2	7-2	5-1	3-3	9-10	2-5	4-3	8-11	4-5	10-8	86-76

NO-DECESIONS: Brian Bowles, Vinnie Chulk, Doug Creek, Doug Linton, Dan Reichert, Scott Service.

INTERLEAGUE: Kelvim Escobar 1-0, Aquilino Lopez 1-0, Doug Davis 0-1 vs. Cubs; Roy Halladay 1-0, Cliff Politte 0-1, Kelvim Escobar 1-0 vs. Reds; Cory Lidle 1-0, Trever Miller 1-0, Cliff Politte 0-1, Roy Halladay 1-0, Doug Davis 0-1, Kelvim Escobar 0-1 vs. Expos; Cory Lidle 1-0, Roy Halladay 1-0, Mark Hendrickson 1-0 vs. Pirates; Kelvim Escobar 0-1, Cory Lidle 0-1, Mark Hendrickson 0-1 vs. Cardinals. Total: 10-8..

HOME RUNS BY PARKS

	At Ana.	At Bal.	At Bos.	At CWS.	At Cle.	At Det.	At KC.	At Min.	At NYY.	At Oak.	At Sea.	At TB.	At Tex.	At Tor.	At N.L. Parks	Totals 2003	Totals 2002	HR Allow.
Anaheim	68	3	6	3	4	4	3	4	4	8	7	3	11	2	20	150	152	190
Baltimore	3	79	7	1	3	0	7	4	6	3	5	8	4	12	10	152	165	198
Boston	4	19	111	9	2	3	4	5	16	4	3	18	10	11	19	238	177	153
Chicago	1	2	5	130	8	9	18	5	10	3	7	5	4	5	8	220	217	162
Cleveland	3	2	1	14	69	16	11	14	3	5	2	5	9	1	3	158	192	179
Detroit	6	6	4	7	15	67	14	6	1	2	6	2	4	1	12	153	124	195
Kansas City	5	3	5	6	10	11	69	11	1	2	8	2	9	7	13	162	140	190
Minnesota	5	4	3	8	8	10	13	76	0	2	3	6	3	4	10	155	167	187
New York	7	19	7	7	0	7	3	12	106	8	4	16	4	13	17	230	223	145
Oakland	11	2	3	7	3	4	11	4	3	88	9	1	18	8	4	176	205	140
Seattle	10	1	0	6	4	7	10	8	5	5	69	1	6	3	4	139	152	173
Tampa Bay	2	12	8	4	4	4	1	3	5	4	12	56	2	15	5	137	133	196
Texas	15	6	4	4	1	5	3	3	5	8	11	7	140	17	10	239	230	208
Toronto	4	11	8	3	4	7	4	6	7	3	4	12	8	94	15	190	187	184
N.L. clubs	8	8	13	9	6	8	11	10	10	14	8	10	13	8	....	136	137	....
2003 Totals	152	177	185	218	141	162	182	171	182	159	158	152	245	201	150	2499	....	2500
2002 Totals	141	204	145	222	171	122	209	150	186	182	146	163	245	191	....	....	2464	....

AT ANAHEIM (152):

Anaheim (68)—Anderson 12, Salmon 10, Glaus 9, Kennedy 8, B. Molina 7, Spiezio 7, Wooten 5, DaVanon 3, Fullmer 3, Eckstein 1, Erstad 1, Gil 1, Wesson 1. **Baltimore (3)**—Batista 1, Gibbons 1, B. Roberts 1. **Boston (4)**—Hillenbrand 1, Ortiz 1, Ramirez 1, Varitek 1. **Chicago (1)**—Thomas 1. **Cleveland (3)**—Burks 1, McDonald 1, Spencer 1. **Detroit (6)**—Higginson 3, D. Young 2, Petrick 1. **Kansas City (5)**—Guiel 2, Beltran 1, Berroa 1, Harvey 1. **Los Angeles (1)**—Kinkade 1. **Minnesota (5)**—Jones 2, Hocking 1, Hunter 1, Rivas 1. **New York (5)**—Burnitz 3, Perez 1, Reyes 1. **New York (7)**—Posada 2, Giambi 1, Matsui 1, Mondesi 1, Soriano 1, Williams 1. **Oakland (11)**—Durazo 2, Hatteberg 2, Long 2, McMillon 2, Tejada 2, Hernandez 1. Philadelphia (2)—Rollins 1, Thome 1. **Seattle (10)**—Boone 5, Cameron 1, Martinez 1, McLemore 1, Wilson 1, Winn 1. **Tampa Bay (2)**—Baldelli 1, Grieve 1. **Texas (15)**—Rodriguez 4, Young 3, Blalock 2, Palmeiro 2, Glanville 1, Gonzalez 1, Laird 1, Teixeira 1. **Toronto (4)**—Myers 1, Wells 1, Werth 1, Wilson 1.

AT BALTIMORE (177):

Anaheim (3)—Anderson 1, Glaus 1, Spiezio 1. **Baltimore (79)**—Gibbons 12, Batista 10, Conine 8, Mora 8, Cruz 7, Matos 6, Bigbie 4, Surhoff 4, Fordyce 3, B. Roberts 3, Cust 2, Gil 2, Matthews Jr. 2, Morban 2, Segui 2, Cordova 1, Hairston Jr. 1, Machado 1, Swann 1. **Boston (19)**—Damon 3, Garciaparra 3, Mueller 3, Ortiz 3, Varitek 2, Hillenbrand 1, Mirabelli 1, Nixon 1, Ramirez 1, Walker 1. **Chicago (1)**—Gonzalez 1. **Chicago (2)**—Thomas 1, Valentin 1. **Cleveland (2)**—Garcia 1, Lawton 1. **Detroit (6)**—Inge 2, D. Young 2, Halter 1, Monroe 1. **Kansas City (3)**—DiFelice 1, Harvey 1, Sweeney 1. **Milwaukee (2)**—Kieschnick 1, Sexson 1. **Minnesota (4)**—Hunter 2, Mientkiewicz 1, Stewart 1. **New York (19)**—Soriano 4, Boone 3, Garcia 3, Flaherty 2, Giambi 2, Posada 1, J. Rivera 1, Sierra 1, Williams 1, Wilson 1. **Oakland (2)**—Chavez 1, McMillon 1. **Philadelphia (5)**—Thome 2, Ledee 1, Michaels 1, Perez 1. **Seattle (1)**—Suzuki 1. **Tampa Bay (12)**—Sandberg 3, Huff 2, Lugo 2, Anderson 1, Easley 1, Hall 1, Lombard 1, Ordonez 1. **Texas (6)**—Diaz 2, Blalock 1, Gonzalez 1, Rodriguez 1, Sierra 1. **Toronto (11)**—Hinske 4, Myers 2, Wells 2, Delgado 1, Phelps 1, Stewart 1.

AT BOSTON (185):

Anaheim (6)—Anderson 1, Glaus 1, Kennedy 1, B. Molina 1, Salmon 1, Spiezio 1. **Baltimore (7)**—Batista 2, Cust 2, Matos 2, Fordyce 1. **Boston (111)**—Garciaparra 18, Ramirez 18, Ortiz 17, Varitek 13, Millar 10, Nixon 10, Mueller 6, Walker 6, Damon 5, Mirabelli 3, Giambi 2, Kapler 2, McCarty 1. **Chicago (5)**—Lee 2, Alomar Jr. 1, Everett 1, Valentin 1. **Cleveland (1)**—Lawton 1. **Detroit (4)**—D. Young 2, Munson 1, Pena 1. **Florida (4)**—Lee 2, Encarnacion 1, Lowell 1. **Houston (4)**—Bagwell 1, Blum 1, Ensberg 1, Hidalgo 1. **Kansas City (5)**—Beltran 2, DiFelice 1, Ibanez 1, Sweeney 1. **Minnesota (3)**—LeCroy 2, Mohr 1. **New York (7)**—Posada 4, Giambi 2, Soriano 1. **Oakland (3)**—Durazo 1, Hernandez 1, Tejada 1. **St. Louis (5)**—Drew 2, Edmonds 2, Pujols 1. **Tampa Bay (8)**—Baldelli 1, Hall 1, Huff 1, Lee 1, Ordonez 1, Perez 1, Rolls 1, Shumpert 1. **Texas (4)**—Blalock 1, Everett 1, Gonzalez 1, Greene 1. **Toronto (8)**—Berg 1, Bordick 1, Catalanotto 1, Delgado 1, Kielty 1, Myers 1, Wells 1, Woodward 1.

AT CHICAGO (218):

Anaheim (3)—Riggs 2, Amezaga 1. **Baltimore (1)**—Bigbie 1. **Boston (9)**—Nixon 2, Ortiz 2, Ramirez 2, Kapler 1, Millar 1, Varitek 1. **Chicago (3)**—Alou 1, Gonzalez 1, Hernandez 1. **Chicago (130)**—Thomas 29, Lee 18, Ordonez 17, Valentin 14, Crede 11, Konerko 9, Everett 5, Rowand 5, Daubach 4, Graffanino 4, Olivo 4, Alomar Jr. 3, Jimenez 3, Alomar 2, Rios 2. **Cleveland (14)**—Burks 3, Garcia 3, Blake 2, Bard 1, Broussard 1, Gerut 1, Hafner 1, B. Phillips 1, Spencer 1. **Detroit (7)**—Munson 4, Pena 1, Witt 1, D. Young 1. **Kansas City (6)**—Sweeney 2, Beltran 1, Berroa 1, Randa 1, White 1. **Minnesota (8)**—Kielty 2, Pierzynski 2, Cuddyer 1, Hunter 1, Koskie 1, LeCroy 1. **New York (7)**—Giambi 2, Soriano 2, Johnson 1, J. Rivera 1, Williams 1. **Oakland (7)**—Chavez 2, Hernandez 2, Durazo 1, Melhuse 1, Tejada 1. **San Francisco (6)**—Bonds 3, Aurilia 1, Cruz 1, Feliz 1. **Seattle (6)**—Cameron 2, Cirillo 1, Martinez 1, Suzuki 1, Winn 1. **Tampa Bay (4)**—Baldelli 2, Hall 1, Lugo 1. **Texas (4)**—Blalock 2, Palmeiro 1, Rodriguez 1. **Toronto (3)**—Catalanotto 1, Hinske 1, Stewart 1.

AT CLEVELAND (141):

Anaheim (4)—Anderson 2, Fullmer 1, B. Molina 1. **Baltimore (3)**—Conine 1, Hairston Jr. 1, Mora 1. **Boston (2)**—Garciaparra 1, Nixon 1. **Chicago (8)**—Jimenez 2, Konerko 2, Ordonez 2, Graffanino 1, Thomas 1. **Cincinnati (1)**—Dunn 1. **Cleveland (69)**—Gerut 13, Broussard 7, Hafner 7, Lawton 6, Bard 5, Bradley 4, Escobar 4, Crisp 3, Peralta 3, B. Phillips 3, Blake 2, Burks 2, Ludwick 2, Spencer 2, Vizquel 2, Garcia 1, Laker 1, Magruder 1, Santos 1. **Detroit (15)**—Pena 5, Monroe 3, D. Young 3, Halter 1, Inge 1, Klassen 1, Witt 1. **Kansas City (10)**—Ibanez 2, Tucker 2, Guiel 1, Harvey 1, Mayne 1, Randa 1, Sweeney 1, White 1. **Los Angeles (1)**—Ross 1. **Minnesota (8)**—Hunter 3, Guzman 2, LeCroy 1, Mientkiewicz 1, Mohr 1. **Oakland (3)**—Durazo 1, Hernandez 1, Tejada 1. **San Diego (4)**—Buchanan 2, Klesko 1, White 1. **Seattle (4)**—Martinez 2, Boone 1, Olerud 1. **Tampa Bay (4)**—Lugo 2, Lee 1, Sandberg 1. **Texas (1)**—Rodriguez 1. **Toronto (4)**—Phelps 2, Bordick 1, Catalanotto 1.

AT DETROIT (162):

Anaheim (4)—Anderson 1, DaVanon 1, Kennedy 1, Riggs 1. **Arizona (2)**—Finley 1, Hammock 1. **Boston (3)**—Damon 1, Nixon 1, Varitek 1. **Chicago (9)**—Crede 2, Lee 2, Thomas 2, Graffanino 1, Jimenez 1, Valentin 1. **Cleveland (16)**—Broussard 5, Blake 2, Bradley 2, Gerut 2, B. Phillips 2, Escobar 1, Hafner 1, Lawton 1. **Colorado (6)**—Hernandez 1, Johnson 1, Payton 1, Sweeney 1, Uribe 1, Vaughn 1. **Detroit (67)**—Monroe 10, D. Young 10, Pena 8, Munson 7, Halter 6, Higginson 6, Inge 4, Morris 4, Witt 4, Petrick 2, Hinch 1, Kingsale 1, Ross 1, Santiago 1, Torres 1, Walbeck 1. **Kansas City (11)**—Guiel 2, Mayne 2, Beltran 1, Berroa 1, Brown 1, Ibanez 1, Randa 1, Relaford 1, White 1. **Minnesota (10)**—Jones 2, Cuddyer 1, Gomez 1, Hunter 1, LeCroy 1, Mohr 1, Morneau 1, Pierzynski 1, Ryan 1. **New York (7)**—Giambi 2, Jeter 1, Mondesi 1, Posada 1, Soriano 1, Zeile 1. **Oakland (4)**—Chavez 2, Guillen 1, Piatt 1. **Seattle (7)**—Boone 3, Colbrunn 1, Guillen 1, Martinez 1, Suzuki 1. **Tampa Bay (4)**—Huff 3, Hall 1. **Texas (5)**—Rodriguez 3, Spencer 1, Teixeira 1. **Toronto (7)**—Wells 3, Delgado 2, Hudson 1, Johnson 1.

AT KANSAS CITY (182):

Anaheim (3)—Anderson 1, B. Molina 1, Spiezio 1. **Arizona (1)**—L. Gonzalez 1. **Baltimore (7)**—Gibbons 3, Segui 2, Batista 1, Cruz 1. **Boston (4)**—Damon 1, Garciaparra 1, Mueller 1, Varitek 1. **Chicago (18)**—Valentin 6, Lee 4, Konerko 3, Ordonez 2, Crede 1, Graffanino 1, Thomas 1. **Cleveland (11)**—Blake 2, Gerut 2, Lawton 2, Bard 1, Laker 1, Martinez 1, Peralta 1, Spencer 1. **Detroit (14)**—Monroe 3, Hinch 2, Munson 2, D. Young 2, Halter 1, Higginson 1, Morris 1, Sanchez 1, Witt 1. **Kansas City (69)**—Beltran 10, Randa 9, Ibanez 8, Tucker 8, Sweeney 7, Berroa 6, Harvey 5, Relaford 5, Guiel 4, M. Lopez 3, Brown 1, DiFelice 1, Mayne 1, White 1. **Minnesota (13)**—Rivas 3, Koskie 2, Ford 1, Hunter 1, Jones 1, LeCroy 1, Mohr 1, Morneau 1, Prince 1, Stewart 1. **New York (3)**—Giambi 1, Matsui 1, Posada 1. **Oakland (11)**—Byrnes 2, Chavez 2, Durazo 2, Hernandez 1, Long 1, Menechino 1, Piatt 1, Tejada 1. **St. Louis (8)**—Edmonds 3, Pujols 2, Rolen 2, Renteria 1. **San Francisco (2)**—Bonds 1, Cruz 1. **Seattle (10)**—Mabry 2, Martinez 2, Boone 1, Cameron 1, Davis 1, Suzuki 1, Wilson 1, Winn 1. **Tampa Bay (1)**—Lee 1. **Texas (3)**—Rodriguez 2, Palmeiro 1. **Toronto (4)**—Delgado 1, Johnson 1, Phelps 1, Wells 1.

AT MINNESOTA (171):

Anaheim (4)—Anderson 1, B. Molina 1, Spiezio 1, Wooten 1. **Arizona (1)**—Hammock 1. **Baltimore (4)**—Gibbons 2, Batista 1, Cruz 1. **Boston (5)**—Giambi 2, Mueller 1, Varitek 1, Walker 1. **Chicago (5)**—Valentin 3, Crede 1, Everett 1. **Cleveland (14)**—Blake 4, Lawton 2, Ludwick 2, Bradley 1, Broussard 1, Gerut 1, Hafner 1, Santos 1, Spencer 1. **Colorado (5)**—Johnson 1, Payton 1, Vaughn 1, Walker 1, Wilson 1. **Detroit (6)**—Monroe 2, Higginson 1, Pena 1, Petrick 1, Santiago 1. **Kansas City (11)**—Beltran 3, Guiel 3, Ibanez 2, Berroa 1, Mayne 1, Relaford 1. **Milwaukee (4)**—Kieschnick 1, Perez 1, Sexson 1, Vander Wal 1. **Minnesota (76)**—Hunter 12, LeCroy 9, Koskie 8, Jones 7, Mientkiewicz 6, Pierzynski 6, Kielty 4, Mohr 4, Rivas 4, Ryan 4, Stewart 4, Ford 2, Sears 2, Cuddyer 1, Guzman 1, Morneau 1, Prince 1. **New York (12)**—Williams 3, Johnson 2, Mondesi 2, Soriano 2, Ventura 2, Giambi 1. **Oakland (4)**—Hernandez 2, Long 1, Singleton 1. **Seattle (8)**—Boone 3, Martinez 2, Cameron 1, Suzuki 1, Winn 1. **Tampa Bay (3)**—Huff 2, Baldelli 1. **Texas (3)**—Rodriguez 2, Young 1. **Toronto (6)**—Phelps 2, Wells 2, Catalanotto 1, Delgado 1.

AT NEW YORK (182):

Anaheim (4)—Spiezio 2, Anderson 1, DaVanon 1. **Baltimore (6)**—Bigbie 1, Conine 1, Cruz 1, Fordyce 1, Gibbons 1, Surhoff 1. **Boston (16)**—Ortiz 4, Mueller 3, Millar 2, Varitek 2, Garciaparra 1, Hillenbrand 1, Nixon 1, Ramirez 1, Walker 1. **Chicago (10)**—Konerko 3, Ordonez 2, Thomas 2, Alomar 1, Crede 1, Everett 1. **Cleveland (3)**—Bradley 1, Gerut 1, Spencer 1. **Detroit (1)**—Halter 1. **Houston (3)**—Berkman 1, Biggio 1, Ensberg 1. **Kansas City (1)**—Beltran 1. **New York (3)**—Burnitz 2, Clark 1. **New York (106)**—Posada 15, Soriano 15, Giambi 12, Matsui 9, Mondesi 9, Johnson 8, Jeter 7, Sierra 5, Williams 5, J. Rivera 4, Ventura 4, Zeile 4, Boone 3, Garcia 3, Dellucci 1, Pride 1, Wilson 1. **Oakland (3)**—Byrnes 1, Chavez 1, Hatteberg 1. **St. Louis (4)**—Martinez 2, Edmonds 1,

Pujols 1. **Seattle (5)**—Boone 2, Davis 1, Martinez 1, Winn 1. **Tampa Bay (5)**—Lee 2, Anderson 1, Baldelli 1, Grieve 1. **Texas (5)**—Rodriguez 2, Blalock 1, Gonzalez 1, Palmeiro 1. **Toronto (7)**—Delgado 3, Wells 2, Stewart 1, Wilson 1.

AT OAKLAND (159):

Anaheim (8)—Salmon 4, Glaus 1, B. Molina 1, Spiezio 1, Wooten 1. **Atlanta (8)**—A. Jones 2, Castilla 1, Fick 1, Furcal 1, Giles 1, Lopez 1, Sheffield 1. **Baltimore (3)**—Bigbie 1, Cruz 1, B. Roberts 1. **Boston (4)**—Ramirez 2, Millar 1, Mueller 1. **Chicago (3)**—Olivo 1, Ordonez 1, Thomas 1. **Cleveland (5)**—Blake 1, Bradley 1, Ludwick 1, Santos 1, Spencer 1. **Detroit (2)**—Monroe 1, D. Young 1. **Kansas City (2)**—Randa 1, Sweeney 1. **Minnesota (2)**—Hunter 1, Kielty 1. **Montreal (2)**—Cabrera 1, Vidro 1. **New York (8)**—Giambi 2, Williams 2, Flaherty 1, Matsui 1, Posada 1, Wilson 1. **Oakland (88)**—Tejada 15, Chavez 12, Durazo 10, Hernandez 9, Long 8, Byrnes 7, Ellis 7, Hatteberg 6, Guillen 4, Dye 3, McMillon 2, Melhuse 2, Gant 1, Menechino 1, Piatt 1. **San Francisco (4)**—Feliz 3, Bonds 1. **Seattle (5)**—Martinez 2, Colbrunn 1, Davis 1, Olerud 1. **Tampa Bay (4)**—Anderson 1, Baldelli 1, Hall 1, Huff 1. **Texas (8)**—Everett 2, Palmeiro 2, Blalock 1, Greene 1, Rodriguez 1, Teixeira 1. **Toronto (3)**—Hinske 2, Woodward 1.

AT SEATTLE (158):

Anaheim (7)—Fullmer 2, Anderson 1, Erstad 1, Owens 1, Salmon 1, Spiezio 1. **Baltimore (5)**—Batista 2, Gibbons 1, Matos 1, Segui 1. **Boston (3)**—Millar 1, Nixon 1, Ramirez 1. **Chicago (7)**—Lee 2, Everett 1, Konerko 1, Rowand 1, Thomas 1, Valentin 1. **Cleveland (2)**—Blake 1, Hafner 1. **Detroit (6)**—Higginson 2, D. Young 2, Halter 1, Witt 1. **Kansas City (8)**—Ibanez 3, Beltran 2, Berroa 1, Randa 1, Tucker 1. **Minnesota (3)**—Koskie 1, Mohr 1, Pierzynski 1. **Montreal (2)**—Cabrera 1, Chavez 1. **New York (4)**—Giambi 1, Johnson 1, Matsui 1, Soriano 1. **Oakland (9)**—Chavez 5, Durazo 1, Ellis 1, Hatteberg 1, Hernandez 1. **San Diego (6)**—White 3, Burroughs 1, Kotsay 1, Mendez 1. **Seattle (69)**—Boone 16, Cameron 11, Martinez 8, Olerud 8, Suzuki 8, Winn 6, Guillen 4, Davis 2, Bloomquist 1, Cirillo 1, Colbrunn 1, Mabry 1, McLemore 1, Wilson 1. **Tampa Bay (12)**—Huff 3, Hall 2, Lee 2, Lugo 1, Martin 1, Perez 1, Rolls 1, Valentin 1. **Texas (11)**—Palmeiro 6, Rodriguez 2, Blalock 1, Glanville 1, Greene 1. **Toronto (4)**—Catalanotto 1, Delgado 1, Johnson 1, Wells 1.

AT TAMPA BAY (152):

Anaheim (3)—DaVanon 2, Kennedy 1. **Atlanta (4)**—Castilla 1, A. Jones 1, C. Jones 1, Sheffield 1. **Baltimore (8)**—Batista 3, Bigbie 1, Fordyce 1, Gibbons 1, Gil 1, Mora 1. **Boston (18)**—Millar 4, Garciaparra 3, Ramirez 3, Nixon 2, Giambi 1, Kapler 1, Mirabelli 1, Ortiz 1, Varitek 1, Walker 1. **Chicago (5)**—Ordonez 2, Crede 1, Daubach 1, Valentin 1. **Cincinnati (5)**—Kearns 2, Boone 1, Guillen 1, Stinnett 1. **Cleveland (5)**—Hafner 2, Blake 1, Gerut 1, Ludwick 1. **Detroit (2)**—Munson 2. **Kansas City (2)**—Beltran 1, Matos 1. **Minnesota (6)**—Jones 2, Hunter 1, Kielty 1, Mohr 1, Pierzynski 1. **New York (16)**—Soriano 5, Giambi 2, Posada 2, Williams 2, Flaherty 1, Johnson 1, Mondesi 1, J. Rivera 1, Ventura 1. **Oakland (1)**—Guillen 1. **Pittsburgh (1)**—Ramirez 1. **Seattle (1)**—Davis 1. **Tampa Bay (56)**—Huff 15, Lee 9, Crawford 5, Lugo 5, Hall 4, Rolls 4, Anderson 2, Baldelli 2, Grieve 2, Martin 2, Piatt 2, Valentin 2, Ordonez 1, Shumpert 1. **Texas (7)**—Gonzalez 2, Greene 1, Palmeiro 1, Sadler 1, Teixeira 1, Thames 1. **Toronto (12)**—Phelps 3, Delgado 2, Berg 1, Hinske 1, Hudson 1, Kielty 1, Myers 1, Wells 1, Wilson 1.

AT TEXAS (245):

Anaheim (11)—Erstad 2, Kennedy 2, Amezaga 1, DaVanon 1, Eckstein 1, Glaus 1, B. Molina 1, Salmon 1, Spiezio 1. **Baltimore (4)**—Matos 2, Conine 1, Mora 1. **Boston (10)**—Mueller 3, Nixon 3, Garciaparra 1, Jackson 1, Ortiz 1, Ramirez 1. **Chicago (4)**—Alomar Jr. 1, Crede 1, Everett 1, Lee 1. **Cleveland (9)**—Blake 2, Broussard 2, Lawton 2, Bradley 1, Laker 1, Ludwick 1. **Detroit (4)**—Pena 2, Monroe 1, Munson 1. **Florida (3)**—Lowell 3. **Houston (5)**—Bagwell 1, Berkman 1, Biggio 1, Everett 1, Hidalgo 1. **Kansas City (9)**—Guiel 2, Harvey 2, Beltran 1, Berroa 1, Ibanez 1, Matos 1, Sweeney 1. **Minnesota (3)**—Hocking 1, Hunter 1, LeCroy 1. **New York (5)**—Wilson 2, Clark 1, Floyd 1, Phillips 1. **New York (4)**—Giambi 1, Johnson 1, Mondesi 1, Soriano 1. **Oakland (18)**—Chavez 3, Tejada 3, Durazo 2, Hatteberg 2, Hernandez 2, Long 2, Byrnes 1, Dye 1, Ellis 1, Guillen 1. **Seattle (6)**—Martinez 3, Guillen 2, Cameron 1. **Tampa Bay (2)**—Huff 2. **Texas (140)**—Rodriguez 26, Palmeiro 21, Teixeira 19, Blalock 18, Gonzalez 11, Everett 10, Young 9, Nix 7, Greene 4, Jones 3, Spencer 3, Christenson 2, Diaz 2, Glanville 2, Sierra 2, Mench 1. **Toronto (8)**—Delgado 3, Hudson 1, Myers 1, Stewart 1, Wells 1, Werth 1.

AT TORONTO (201):

Anaheim (2)—Eckstein 1, Salmon 1. **Baltimore (12)**—Batista 4, Mora 3, Conine 2, Bigbie 1, Gibbons 1, Matos 1. **Boston (11)**—Millar 3, Ramirez 3, Damon 2, Mirabelli 1, Nixon 1, Ortiz 1. **Chicago (1)**—O'Leary 1. **Chicago (5)**—Ordonez 2, Borchard 1, Jimenez 1, Lee 1. **Cleveland (1)**—Hafner 1. **Detroit (1)**—Monroe 1. **Kansas City (7)**—Beltran 1, Berroa 1, Harvey 1, Mayne 1, Randa 1, Sweeney 1, Tucker 1. Minnesota (4)—Cuddyer 1, Kielty 1, LeCroy 1, Mientkiewicz 1. **Montreal (2)**—W. Cordero 1, Vidro 1. **New York (13)**—Giambi 6, Posada 2, Soriano 2, Almonte 1, Ventura 1, Zeile 1. **Oakland (8)**—Tejada 3, Durazo 1, Guillen 1, Hernandez 1, McMillon 1, Melhuse 1. **Pittsburgh (5)**—Giles 2, Stairs 2, Ramirez 1. **Seattle (3)**—Boone 1, Martinez 1, Wilson 1. **Tampa Bay (15)**—Huff 5, Lugo 4, Lee 2, Baldelli 1, Liefer 1, Rolls 1, Sandberg 1. **Texas (17)**—Gonzalez 5, Everett 3, Greene 2, Rodriguez 2, Blalock 1, Nix 1, Palmeiro 1, Teixeira 1, Young 1. **Toronto (94)**—Delgado 24, Wells 13, Phelps 11, Myers 8, Catalanotto 7, Johnson 6, Hudson 5, Hinske 4, Woodward 4, Stewart 3, Berg 2, Bordick 2, Kielty 2, Wilson 2, Cash 1.

PARK DATA (SELECTED BATTING CATEGORIES AT EACH STADIUM)

This section contains selected batting statistics for all American League parks for 2003. A key component of this section is an index number for each category, which is used to determine how a given park influences a particular statistic. For example, Chicago's U.S. Cellular Field may not have a reputation as a home-run haven, but last year's park index of 134 actually was the highest in the A.L. And the park has boosted the long-ball power of both left- and righthanded batters over the past few years.

For each A.L. park, we show how the home team and its opponents performed, both at home and on the road, with the exception being that we do not include data from interleague games. The differences in interleague opponents and ballparks would skew the data.

By comparing the per-game averages at the home park and on the road, we can evaluate the park's impact. This is done by simply dividing the home average by the road average and multiplying the result by 100, generating a park index. If the home and road per-game averages are equal, the index equals 100, and it can be concluded that the park had no impact. An index above 100 means that the park favors that particular statistic. The indexes for at-bats, runs, hits, errors and infield errors are determined on a per-game basis; all other stats are calculated on a per-at-bat basis. "E-infield" denotes infield *fielding* errors. "Alt." is the approximate elevation of the ballpark.

For most parks, data is presented both for 2003 and for the last three years overall. If the park's dimensions have changed over that time, however, the data from the old and new configurations will not be combined. Following all the teams' charts is a ranking section that shows which parks most inflate runs, home runs and batting average.

ANAHEIM **Home park:** Angel Stadium of Anaheim **Alt.:** 160 feet **Surface:** Grass

	2003 Season							2001-03 Seasons						
	Home Games			Road Games				Home Games			Road Games			
Category	**Ana.**	**Opp.**	**Total**	**Ana.**	**Opp.**	**Total**	**Index**	**Ana.**	**Opp.**	**Total**	**Ana.**	**Opp.**	**Total**	**Index**
G	73	73	146	71	71	142		217	217	434	215	215	430	
Avg	.268	.264	.266	.266	.269	.268	99	.270	.258	.264	.268	.257	.263	100
AB	2398	2565	4963	2451	2355	4806	100	7296	7618	14914	7545	7069	14614	101
R	320	312	632	323	367	690	89	997	949	1946	1012	950	1962	98
H	643	677	1320	652	634	1286	100	1971	1965	3936	2023	1816	3839	102
2B	122	132	254	131	111	242	102	372	397	769	426	317	743	101
3B	12	8	20	14	17	31	62	40	18	58	37	40	77	74
HR	59	76	135	62	94	156	84	199	218	417	192	248	440	93
BB	203	224	427	224	222	446	93	630	688	1318	645	685	1330	97
SO	348	472	820	392	398	790	101	1113	1368	2481	1224	1240	2464	99
E	44	32	76	44	36	80	92	137	127	264	128	153	281	93
E-Infield	37	26	63	36	27	63	97	119	101	220	114	121	235	93
LHB-Avg	.281	.245	.262	.286	.272	.279	94	.278	.249	.264	.274	.255	.265	99
LHB-HR	28	36	64	34	46	80	75	85	96	181	95	108	203	86
RHB-Avg	.257	.282	.270	.250	.267	.258	105	.262	.265	.264	.262	.259	.260	101
RHB-HR	31	40	71	28	48	76	93	114	122	236	97	140	237	99

BALTIMORE **Home park:** Oriole Park at Camden Yards **Alt.:** 20 feet **Surface:** Grass

	2003 Season							2002-03 Seasons						
	Home Games			Road Games				Home Games			Road Games			
Category	**Bal.**	**Opp.**	**Total**	**Bal.**	**Opp.**	**Total**	**Index**	**Bal.**	**Opp.**	**Total**	**Bal.**	**Opp.**	**Total**	**Index**
G	72	72	144	73	73	146		144	144	288	145	145	290	
Avg	.276	.262	.269	.258	.287	.272	99	.261	.261	.261	.253	.283	.268	97
AB	2431	2523	4954	2566	2507	5073	99	4837	5066	9903	5049	4968	10017	100
R	325	330	655	332	380	712	93	617	661	1278	632	754	1386	93
H	671	662	1333	663	719	1382	98	1263	1323	2586	1277	1407	2684	97
2B	130	124	254	115	146	261	100	241	233	474	275	275	550	87
3B	6	8	14	13	17	30	48	16	13	29	25	36	61	48
HR	68	90	158	63	85	148	109	149	191	340	129	176	305	113
BB	199	236	435	189	223	412	108	406	477	883	384	465	849	105
SO	368	440	808	415	432	847	98	793	866	1659	847	880	1727	97
E	36	56	92	54	50	104	90	78	110	188	90	88	178	106
E-Infield	31	42	73	47	45	92	80	64	88	152	76	77	153	100
LHB-Avg	.267	.282	.276	.266	.272	.269	102	.260	.265	.263	.263	.276	.271	97
LHB-HR	23	45	68	22	44	66	103	53	92	145	42	93	135	106
RHB-Avg	.281	.244	.264	.254	.300	.275	96	.261	.258	.260	.248	.289	.266	98
RHB-HR	45	45	90	41	41	82	114	96	99	195	87	83	170	118

BOSTON

Home park: Fenway Park **Alt.:** 21 feet **Surface:** Grass

	2003 Season							2001-03 Seasons						
	Home Games			Road Games				Home Games			Road Games			
Category	Bos.	Opp.	Total	Bos.	Opp.	Total	Index	Bos.	Opp.	Total	Bos.	Opp.	Total	Index
G	72	72	144	72	72	144		216	216	432	215	215	430	
Avg	.308	.259	.284	.259	.263	.261	109	.288	.255	.271	.269	.252	.261	104
AB	2480	2530	5010	2587	2507	5094	98	7379	7550	14929	7745	7287	15032	99
R	445	343	788	365	362	727	108	1171	997	2168	1138	968	2106	102
H	765	656	1421	671	660	1331	107	2128	1922	4050	2083	1834	3917	103
2B	178	146	324	138	150	288	114	487	429	916	436	361	797	116
3B	17	17	34	9	20	29	119	49	32	81	31	52	83	98
HR	95	61	156	108	64	172	92	253	185	438	292	201	493	89
BB	288	191	479	230	241	471	103	782	597	1379	702	686	1388	100
SO	359	479	838	481	536	1017	84	1254	1624	2878	1404	1559	2963	98
E	49	44	93	48	35	83	112	150	137	287	137	128	265	108
E-Infield	42	36	78	40	29	69	113	125	117	242	114	112	226	107
LHB-Avg	.301	.258	.279	.251	.267	.259	108	.287	.249	.267	.260	.251	.256	105
LHB-HR	41	28	69	53	38	91	73	112	77	189	143	112	255	75
RHB-Avg	.317	.261	.288	.267	.260	.264	109	.290	.260	.275	.277	.252	.265	104
RHB-HR	54	33	87	55	26	81	115	141	108	249	149	89	238	105

CHICAGO

Home park: U.S. Cellular Field **Alt.:** 595 feet **Surface:** Grass

	2003 Season							2001-03 Seasons						
	Home Games			Road Games				Home Games			Road Games			
Category	Chi.	Opp.	Total	Chi.	Opp.	Total	Index	Chi.	Opp.	Total	Chi.	Opp.	Total	Index
G	72	72	144	72	72	144		216	216	432	216	216	432	
Avg	.266	.249	.257	.264	.258	.261	98	.273	.258	.265	.266	.264	.265	100
AB	2358	2448	4806	2535	2341	4876	99	7153	7429	14582	7526	7106	14632	100
R	363	297	660	346	344	690	96	1156	1005	2161	1035	1057	2092	103
H	628	609	1237	670	605	1275	97	1952	1913	3865	2002	1874	3876	100
2B	132	122	254	143	126	269	96	381	383	764	428	377	805	95
3B	9	12	21	10	11	21	101	31	29	60	38	37	75	80
HR	115	79	194	82	65	147	134	333	259	592	244	212	456	130
BB	219	217	436	228	247	475	93	717	690	1407	666	694	1360	104
SO	373	511	884	425	429	854	105	1193	1349	2542	1306	1223	2529	101
E	30	46	76	52	38	90	84	114	147	261	153	131	284	92
E-Infield	25	40	65	44	31	75	87	103	126	229	128	105	233	98
LHB-Avg	.256	.256	.256	.259	.275	.269	95	.275	.262	.267	.252	.279	.268	99
LHB-HR	25	40	65	22	30	52	126	86	134	220	76	100	176	128
RHB-Avg	.270	.241	.258	.266	.242	.257	101	.272	.253	.264	.272	.249	.263	100
RHB-HR	90	39	129	60	35	95	138	247	125	372	168	112	280	132

CLEVELAND

Home park: Jacobs Field **Alt.:** 660 feet **Surface:** Grass

	2003 Season							2001-03 Seasons						
	Home Games			Road Games				Home Games			Road Games			
Category	Cle.	Opp.	Total	Cle.	Opp.	Total	Index	Cle.	Opp.	Total	Cle.	Opp.	Total	Index
G	72	72	144	72	72	144		215	215	430	217	217	434	
Avg	.251	.253	.252	.260	.274	.267	95	.260	.266	.263	.265	.273	.269	98
AB	2420	2526	4946	2519	2410	4929	100	7197	7577	14774	7572	7264	14836	101
R	297	315	612	331	374	705	87	1024	1074	2098	1082	1115	2197	96
H	607	640	1247	654	660	1314	95	1870	2018	3888	2005	1983	3988	98
2B	132	125	257	133	135	268	96	382	424	806	379	412	791	102
3B	7	11	18	16	12	28	64	25	32	57	53	54	107	53
HR	63	66	129	86	94	180	71	249	212	461	265	213	478	97
BB	204	223	427	193	224	417	102	668	764	1432	709	739	1448	99
SO	457	461	918	474	370	844	108	1366	1551	2917	1408	1290	2698	109
E	50	60	110	61	38	99	111	139	163	302	167	127	294	104
E-Infield	44	53	97	53	33	86	113	123	143	266	137	108	245	110
LHB-Avg	.251	.248	.249	.263	.284	.271	92	.260	.271	.265	.263	.285	.273	97
LHB-HR	41	24	65	42	34	76	87	149	88	237	145	83	228	102
RHB-Avg	.251	.257	.254	.257	.268	.263	97	.260	.263	.261	.266	.265	.265	99
RHB-HR	22	42	64	44	60	104	60	100	124	224	120	130	250	92

DETROIT

Home park: Comerica Park **Alt.:** 585 feet **Surface:** Grass

	2003 Season							2001-02 Season						
	Home Games			Road Games				Home Games			Road Games			
Category	**Det.**	**Opp.**	**Total**	**Det.**	**Opp.**	**Total**	**Index**	**Det.**	**Opp.**	**Total**	**Det.**	**Opp.**	**Total**	**Index**
G	72	72	144	72	72	144		143	143	286	144	144	288	
Avg	.237	.271	.255	.239	.302	.270	94	.255	.278	.267	.252	.295	.273	98
AB	2409	2612	5021	2448	2422	4870	103	4741	5053	9794	4985	4943	9928	99
R	252	391	643	275	441	716	90	558	713	1271	603	850	1453	88
H	571	709	1280	584	731	1315	97	1208	1405	2613	1258	1456	2714	97
2B	84	123	207	96	155	251	80	210	277	487	294	326	620	80
3B	18	26	44	14	20	34	126	66	58	124	21	39	60	209
HR	62	87	149	74	90	164	88	107	115	222	125	191	316	71
BB	178	256	434	219	243	462	91	372	447	819	368	457	825	101
SO	464	370	834	510	313	823	98	771	722	1493	980	740	1720	88
E	55	57	112	65	36	101	111	129	90	219	128	94	222	99
E-Infield	46	46	92	52	31	83	111	104	76	180	94	82	176	103
LHB-Avg	.257	.292	.273	.246	.314	.275	99	.272	.289	.280	.264	.290	.277	101
LHB-HR	33	45	78	45	44	89	89	70	77	147	60	87	147	100
RHB-Avg	.209	.256	.237	.229	.292	.265	90	.238	.270	.255	.242	.298	.270	94
RHB-HR	29	42	71	29	46	75	88	37	38	75	65	104	169	45

KANSAS CITY

Home park: Ewing M. Kauffman Stadium **Alt.:** 750 feet **Surface:** Grass

	2003 Season							2001-03 Seasons						
	Home Games			Road Games				Home Games			Road Games			
Category	**K.C.**	**Opp.**	**Total**	**K.C.**	**Opp.**	**Total**	**Index**	**K.C.**	**Opp.**	**Total**	**K.C.**	**Opp.**	**Total**	**Index**
G	71	71	142	73	73	146		215	215	430	217	217	434	
Avg	.281	.292	.286	.264	.264	.264	108	.275	.291	.283	.255	.264	.259	109
AB	2388	2583	4971	2542	2414	4956	103	7334	7808	15142	7533	7173	14706	104
R	382	458	840	351	307	658	131	1094	1312	2406	948	1001	1949	125
H	671	753	1424	671	638	1309	112	2017	2272	4289	1918	1895	3813	114
2B	135	142	277	111	135	246	112	384	435	819	356	368	724	110
3B	15	16	31	18	14	32	97	58	52	110	50	45	95	112
HR	60	102	162	80	70	150	108	200	309	509	197	244	441	112
BB	215	248	463	203	242	445	104	631	734	1365	611	761	1372	97
SO	350	373	723	464	401	865	83	1059	1197	2256	1367	1207	2574	85
E	36	59	95	54	55	109	90	145	171	316	162	157	319	100
E-Infield	28	53	81	46	46	92	91	118	146	264	134	138	272	98
LHB-Avg	.276	.297	.286	.256	.279	.266	107	.274	.295	.285	.249	.269	.259	110
LHB-HR	28	41	69	43	29	72	94	77	139	216	99	111	210	100
RHB-Avg	.286	.288	.287	.272	.253	.262	109	.276	.287	.282	.259	.260	.259	109
RHB-HR	32	61	93	37	41	78	120	123	170	293	98	133	231	123

MINNESOTA

Home park: Hubert H. Humphrey Metrodome **Alt.:** 815 feet **Surface:** Turf

	2003 Season							2001-03 Seasons						
	Home Games			Road Games				Home Games			Road Games			
Category	**Min.**	**Opp.**	**Total**	**Min.**	**Opp.**	**Total**	**Index**	**Min.**	**Opp.**	**Total**	**Min.**	**Opp.**	**Total**	**Index**
G	72	72	144	72	72	144		216	216	432	215	215	430	
Avg	.274	.266	.270	.277	.264	.270	100	.274	.263	.268	.273	.267	.270	99
AB	2436	2624	5060	2577	2425	5002	101	7274	7693	14967	7649	7297	14946	100
R	353	341	694	360	324	684	101	1052	972	2024	1036	1007	2043	99
H	668	699	1367	713	640	1353	101	1994	2024	4018	2090	1946	4036	99
2B	139	142	281	143	122	265	105	459	427	886	427	367	794	111
3B	24	13	37	16	8	24	152	60	50	110	45	32	77	143
HR	71	85	156	69	81	150	103	200	228	428	231	262	493	87
BB	245	178	423	210	178	388	108	692	556	1248	637	592	1229	101
SO	452	485	937	444	389	833	111	1382	1449	2831	1445	1166	2611	108
E	32	55	87	46	56	102	85	109	165	274	141	151	292	93
E-Infield	24	44	68	36	44	80	85	83	134	217	119	128	247	87
LHB-Avg	.286	.267	.276	.294	.258	.278	100	.282	.271	.277	.282	.272	.277	100
LHB-HR	34	44	78	25	31	56	134	103	113	216	126	114	240	90
RHB-Avg	.262	.266	.264	.260	.268	.264	100	.264	.257	.260	.262	.263	.263	99
RHB-HR	37	41	78	44	50	94	84	97	115	212	105	148	253	83

NEW YORK

Home park: Yankee Stadium **Alt.:** 55 feet **Surface:** Grass

	2003 Season							2001-03 Seasons						
	Home Games			Road Games				Home Games			Road Games			
Category	**N.Y.**	**Opp.**	**Total**	**N.Y.**	**Opp.**	**Total**	**Index**	**N.Y.**	**Opp.**	**Total**	**N.Y.**	**Opp.**	**Total**	**Index**
G	73	73	146	72	72	144		215	215	430	216	216	432	
Avg	.263	.265	.264	.277	.267	.272	97	.271	.253	.262	.273	.265	.269	97
AB	2410	2585	4995	2583	2500	5083	97	7200	7559	14759	7727	7439	15166	98
R	349	336	685	426	309	735	92	1113	929	2042	1182	946	2128	96
H	633	686	1319	715	667	1382	94	1950	1912	3862	2106	1969	4075	95
2B	120	132	252	143	163	306	84	383	373	756	420	432	852	91
3B	5	10	15	9	13	22	69	17	25	42	23	42	65	66
HR	94	66	160	107	56	163	100	292	205	497	292	178	470	109
BB	277	177	454	321	172	493	94	775	539	1314	835	566	1401	96
SO	443	509	952	473	475	948	102	1343	1623	2966	1513	1514	3027	101
E	54	50	104	49	41	90	114	153	166	319	157	126	283	113
E-Infield	47	37	84	41	35	76	109	133	121	254	135	110	245	104
LHB-Avg	.254	.273	.263	.274	.265	.270	97	.272	.250	.261	.269	.253	.261	100
LHB-HR	49	29	78	58	23	81	105	164	92	256	157	77	234	115
RHB-Avg	.272	.260	.265	.280	.269	.274	97	.270	.255	.262	.276	.273	.275	95
RHB-HR	45	37	82	49	33	82	96	128	113	241	135	101	236	103

OAKLAND

Home park: Network Associates Coliseum **Alt.:** 25 feet **Surface:** Grass

	2003 Season							2001-03 Seasons						
	Home Games			Road Games				Home Games			Road Games			
Category	**Oak.**	**Opp.**	**Total**	**Oak.**	**Opp.**	**Total**	**Index**	**Oak.**	**Opp.**	**Total**	**Oak.**	**Opp.**	**Total**	**Index**
G	72	72	144	72	72	144		216	216	432	216	216	432	
Avg	.257	.226	.241	.253	.255	.254	95	.259	.239	.249	.260	.261	.261	95
AB	2378	2439	4817	2518	2366	4884	99	7180	7448	14628	7628	7240	14868	98
R	333	234	567	355	313	668	85	1072	820	1892	1123	928	2051	92
H	612	551	1163	636	604	1240	94	1861	1779	3640	1985	1892	3877	94
2B	141	112	253	141	106	247	104	391	338	729	434	328	762	97
3B	8	7	15	13	9	22	69	30	25	55	36	37	73	77
HR	75	57	132	84	57	141	95	267	187	454	253	191	444	104
BB	227	214	441	263	228	491	91	817	594	1411	799	669	1468	98
SO	380	472	852	416	434	850	102	1265	1464	2729	1312	1341	2653	105
E	36	55	91	57	38	95	96	137	148	285	158	121	279	102
E-Infield	33	47	80	46	34	80	100	115	118	233	131	103	234	100
LHB-Avg	.264	.224	.247	.252	.250	.251	98	.272	.240	.258	.263	.256	.260	99
LHB-HR	36	15	51	46	25	71	75	143	62	205	141	79	220	97
RHB-Avg	.251	.227	.237	.253	.258	.256	93	.246	.238	.241	.257	.265	.261	92
RHB-HR	39	42	81	38	32	70	114	124	125	249	112	112	224	111

SEATTLE

Home park: Safeco Field **Alt.:** -2 feet **Surface:** Grass

	2003 Season							2001-03 Seasons						
	Home Games			Road Games				Home Games			Road Games			
Category	**Sea.**	**Opp.**	**Total**	**Sea.**	**Opp.**	**Total**	**Index**	**Sea.**	**Opp.**	**Total**	**Sea.**	**Opp.**	**Total**	**Index**
G	72	72	144	72	72	144		216	216	432	216	216	432	
Avg	.271	.235	.253	.275	.265	.270	93	.274	.238	.256	.285	.260	.273	94
AB	2387	2437	4824	2570	2411	4981	97	7192	7399	14591	7763	7283	15046	97
R	370	271	641	355	315	670	96	1092	830	1922	1179	974	2153	89
H	646	573	1219	708	639	1347	90	1969	1764	3733	2214	1892	4106	91
2B	109	84	193	153	116	269	74	352	322	674	444	382	826	84
3B	16	10	26	15	4	19	141	46	19	65	44	31	75	89
HR	64	81	145	66	78	144	104	185	214	399	217	251	468	88
BB	278	208	486	245	209	454	111	863	617	1480	779	622	1401	109
SO	422	455	877	462	429	891	102	1279	1424	2703	1368	1337	2705	103
E	28	45	73	34	33	67	109	95	162	257	114	149	263	98
E-Infield	21	39	60	31	25	56	107	77	138	215	94	129	223	96
LHB-Avg	.269	.247	.257	.277	.277	.277	93	.280	.248	.264	.294	.273	.284	93
LHB-HR	26	50	76	16	47	63	124	69	122	191	72	121	193	102
RHB-Avg	.272	.224	.249	.274	.252	.264	94	.268	.229	.249	.278	.248	.263	94
RHB-HR	38	31	69	50	31	81	88	116	92	208	145	130	275	78

TAMPA BAY

Home park: Tropicana Field **Alt.:** 15 feet **Surface:** Turf

	2003 Season							2001-03 Seasons						
	Home Games			Road Games				Home Games			Road Games			
Category	T.B.	Opp.	Total	T.B.	Opp.	Total	Index	T.B.	Opp.	Total	T.B.	Opp.	Total	Index
G	72	72	144	72	72	144		216	216	432	215	215	430	
Avg	.269	.259	.264	.266	.274	.270	98	.267	.266	.267	.252	.281	.266	100
AB	2486	2533	5019	2570	2391	4961	101	7411	7666	15077	7495	7164	14659	102
R	319	370	689	331	391	722	95	933	1164	2097	905	1220	2125	98
H	669	655	1324	684	656	1340	99	1977	2042	4019	1891	2011	3902	103
2B	133	136	269	128	147	275	97	415	438	853	377	429	806	103
3B	17	13	30	15	12	27	110	45	42	87	32	30	62	136
HR	53	86	139	76	93	169	81	157	262	419	193	296	489	83
BB	195	275	470	165	289	454	102	607	799	1406	564	845	1409	97
SO	450	420	870	450	364	814	106	1413	1368	2781	1460	1150	2610	104
E	51	57	108	40	41	81	133	149	139	288	168	126	294	98
E-Infield	42	55	97	31	39	70	139	129	127	256	137	112	249	102
LHB-Avg	.274	.255	.265	.277	.269	.273	97	.272	.272	.272	.266	.285	.275	99
LHB-HR	35	35	70	37	44	81	86	90	121	211	93	132	225	91
RHB-Avg	.263	.262	.262	.254	.280	.267	98	.262	.262	.262	.239	.277	.258	101
RHB-HR	18	51	69	39	49	88	77	67	141	208	100	164	264	77

TEXAS

Home park: The Ballpark in Arlington **Alt.:** 551 feet **Surface:** Grass

	2003 Season							2001-03 Seasons						
	Home Games			Road Games				Home Games			Road Games			
Category	Tex.	Opp.	Total	Tex.	Opp.	Total	Index	Tex.	Opp.	Total	Tex.	Opp.	Total	Index
G	72	72	144	72	72	144		217	217	434	214	214	428	
Avg	.287	.287	.287	.244	.285	.264	109	.283	.286	.285	.255	.280	.267	106
AB	2465	2591	5056	2570	2439	5009	101	7402	7853	15255	7632	7228	14860	101
R	443	435	878	301	410	711	123	1260	1302	2562	1016	1189	2205	115
H	707	743	1450	626	694	1320	110	2097	2248	4345	1948	2027	3975	108
2B	125	168	293	119	138	257	113	404	526	930	403	442	845	107
3B	22	17	39	10	16	26	149	50	61	111	26	52	78	139
HR	129	92	221	89	89	178	123	361	290	651	283	258	541	117
BB	223	262	485	201	278	479	100	736	810	1546	672	848	1520	99
SO	450	480	930	486	425	911	101	1350	1393	2743	1460	1250	2710	99
E	39	49	88	50	45	95	93	135	148	283	143	140	283	99
E-Infield	31	40	71	42	37	79	90	112	122	234	115	117	232	99
LHB-Avg	.287	.288	.288	.238	.290	.267	108	.284	.284	.284	.259	.287	.274	104
LHB-HR	62	44	106	36	44	80	128	149	137	286	110	121	231	116
RHB-Avg	.287	.285	.286	.247	.279	.261	109	.283	.288	.286	.253	.275	.263	109
RHB-HR	67	48	115	53	45	98	118	212	153	365	173	137	310	118

TORONTO

Home park: SkyDome **Alt.:** 300 feet **Surface:** Turf

	2003 Season							2001-03 Seasons						
	Home Games			Road Games				Home Games			Road Games			
Category	Tor.	Opp.	Total	Tor.	Opp.	Total	Index	Tor.	Opp.	Total	Tor.	Opp.	Total	Index
G	72	72	144	72	72	144		216	216	432	215	215	430	
Avg	.283	.282	.282	.273	.265	.269	105	.273	.274	.273	.262	.272	.267	102
AB	2471	2608	5079	2568	2429	4997	102	7362	7693	15055	7665	7326	14991	100
R	406	404	810	386	320	706	115	1124	1136	2260	1091	1009	2100	107
H	699	735	1434	701	643	1344	107	2008	2105	4113	2008	1990	3998	102
2B	182	157	339	151	112	263	127	453	481	934	400	379	779	119
3B	14	17	31	13	17	30	102	43	40	83	47	41	88	94
HR	76	99	175	81	68	149	116	252	253	505	252	222	474	106
BB	255	218	473	236	210	446	104	699	703	1402	663	685	1348	104
SO	461	486	947	521	382	903	103	1421	1420	2841	1565	1268	2833	100
E	44	46	90	57	42	99	91	134	143	277	154	127	281	98
E-Infield	39	36	75	49	34	83	90	121	114	235	129	101	230	102
LHB-Avg	.294	.273	.283	.271	.249	.260	109	.267	.279	.274	.269	.277	.273	100
LHB-HR	42	40	82	37	24	61	135	122	120	242	128	101	229	108
RHB-Avg	.275	.290	.282	.275	.280	.277	102	.276	.268	.273	.257	.266	.261	104
RHB-HR	34	59	93	44	44	88	103	130	133	263	124	121	245	105

2001-2003 A.L. BALLPARK INDEX RANKINGS

RUNS PER GAME

Team	Home Games				Road Games				Index
	Games	Team	Opp.	Total	Games	Team	Opp.	Total	
KC	215	1094	1312	2406	217	948	1001	1949	125
Tex	217	1260	1302	2562	214	1016	1189	2205	115
Tor	216	1124	1136	2260	215	1091	1009	2100	107
CWS	216	1156	1005	2161	216	1035	1057	2092	103
Bos	216	1171	997	2168	215	1138	968	2106	102
Min	216	1052	972	2024	215	1036	1007	2043	99
Ana	217	997	949	1946	215	1012	950	1962	98
TB	216	933	1164	2097	215	905	1220	2125	98
Cle	215	1024	1074	2098	217	1082	1115	2197	96
NYY	215	1113	929	2042	216	1182	946	2128	96
Bal*	144	617	661	1278	145	632	754	1386	93
Oak	216	1072	820	1892	216	1123	928	2051	92
Det**	72	252	391	643	72	275	441	716	90
Sea	216	1092	830	1922	216	1179	974	2153	89

*Current dimensions began 2002; **Current dimensions began 2003

HOME RUNS PER AT-BAT

Team	Home Games				Road Games				Index
	Games	Team	Opp.	Total	Games	Team	Opp.	Total	
CWS	216	333	259	592	216	244	212	456	130
Tex	217	361	290	651	214	283	258	541	117
Bal*	144	149	191	340	145	129	176	305	113
KC	215	200	309	509	217	197	244	441	112
NYY	215	292	205	497	216	292	178	470	109
Tor	216	252	253	505	215	252	222	474	106
Oak	216	267	187	454	216	253	191	444	104
Cle	215	249	212	461	217	265	213	478	97
Ana	217	199	218	417	215	192	248	440	93
Bos	216	253	185	438	215	292	201	493	89
Det**	72	62	87	149	72	74	90	164	88
Sea	216	185	214	399	216	217	251	468	88
Min	216	200	228	428	215	231	262	493	87
TB	216	157	262	419	215	193	296	489	83

*Current dimensions began 2002; **Current dimensions began 2003

BATTING AVERAGE

Team	Home Games				Road Games				Index
	Games	Team	Opp.	Total	Games	Team	Opp.	Total	
KC	215	.275	.291	.283	217	.255	.264	.259	109
Tex	217	.283	.286	.285	214	.255	.280	.267	106
Bos	216	.288	.255	.271	215	.269	.252	.261	104
Tor	216	.273	.274	.273	215	.262	.272	.267	102
Ana	217	.270	.258	.264	215	.268	.257	.263	100
TB	216	.267	.266	.267	215	.252	.281	.266	100
CWS	216	.273	.258	.265	216	.266	.264	.265	100
Min	216	.274	.263	.268	215	.273	.267	.270	99
Cle	215	.260	.266	.263	217	.265	.273	.269	98
Bal*	144	.261	.261	.261	145	.253	.283	.268	97
NYY	215	.271	.253	.262	216	.273	.265	.269	97
Oak	216	.259	.239	.249	216	.260	.261	.261	95
Det**	72	.237	.271	.255	72	.239	.302	.270	94
Sea	216	.274	.238	.256	216	.285	.260	.273	94

*Current dimensions began 2002; **Current dimensions began 2003

2003 N.L. STATISTICS

Batting

Designated hitting

Pinch-hitting

Pitching

Fielding

Miscellaneous

BATTING

TEAM

Team	G	TPA	AB	R	H	TB	2B	3B	HR	RBI	SH	SF	HP	BB	IBB	SO	SB	CS	GDP	LOB	ShO	Avg.	OBP	Slg.
Atlanta	162	6378	5670	907	1608	2696	321	31	235	872	65	49	49	545	46	933	68	22	124	1170	4	.284	.349	.475
St. Louis	162	6466	5672	876	1580	2574	342	32	196	827	87	54	73	580	68	952	82	32	136	1217	7	.279	.350	.454
Pittsburgh	162	6315	5581	753	1492	2346	275	45	163	711	79	38	87	529	42	1049	86	37	112	1214	9	.267	.338	.420
Colorado	162	6283	5518	853	1472	2458	330	31	198	814	55	38	52	619	46	1134	63	37	140	1156	12	.267	.344	.445
Florida	162	6186	5490	751	1459	2310	292	44	157	709	82	41	57	515	44	978	150	74	114	1114	9	.266	.333	.421
San Fran.	161	6204	5456	755	1440	2319	281	29	180	713	76	39	40	593	79	980	53	37	130	1188	6	.264	.338	.425
Arizona	162	6261	5570	717	1467	2320	303	47	152	696	63	52	45	531	63	1006	76	38	126	1185	12	.263	.330	.417
Houston	162	6320	5583	805	1466	2407	308	30	191	763	61	38	81	557	44	1021	66	30	125	1185	5	.263	.336	.431
Philadelphia	162	6333	5543	791	1448	2325	325	27	166	757	46	38	55	651	56	1155	72	29	120	1220	10	.261	.343	.419
San Diego	162	6246	5531	678	1442	2147	257	32	128	641	50	42	57	565	34	1073	76	39	142	1219	9	.261	.333	.388
Chicago	162	6187	5519	724	1431	2297	302	24	172	691	80	46	50	492	40	1158	73	31	135	1114	10	.259	.323	.416
Montreal	162	6116	5437	711	1404	2180	294	25	144	682	72	40	45	522	58	990	100	39	143	1102	8	.258	.326	.401
Milwaukee	162	6270	5548	714	1423	2325	266	24	196	685	62	40	71	547	41	1221	99	39	158	1155	7	.256	.329	.419
New York	161	6007	5341	642	1317	1999	262	24	124	607	78	45	54	489	42	1035	70	31	136	1086	10	.247	.314	.374
Cincinnati	162	6211	5509	694	1349	2176	239	21	182	669	66	32	79	524	34	1326	80	34	102	1134	10	.245	.318	.395
Los Angeles	162	6036	5458	574	1328	2010	260	25	124	544	71	28	72	407	43	985	80	36	121	1108	13	.243	.303	.368
Totals	1295	99819	88426	11945	23126	36889	4657	491	2708	11381	1093	660	967	8666	780	16996	1294	585	2064	18567	141	.262	.332	.417

INDIVIDUAL

TOP QUALIFIERS FOR BATTING CHAMPIONSHIP

Minimum 502 plate appearances. *Lefthanded batter. †Switch-hitter.

Player, Team	G	TPA	AB	R	H	TB	2B	3B	HR	RBI	SH	SF	HP	BB	IBB	SO	SB	CS	GDP	Avg.	OBP	Slg.
Pujols, Albert, St.L.	157	685	591	137	212	394	51	1	43	124	0	5	10	79	12	65	5	1	13	.359	.439	.667
Helton, Todd, Col.*	160	703	583	135	209	367	49	5	33	117	0	7	2	111	21	72	0	4	19	.358	.458	.630
Bonds, Barry, S.F.*	130	550	390	111	133	292	22	1	45	90	0	2	10	148	61	58	7	0	7	.341	.529	.749
Renteria, Edgar, St.L.	157	663	587	96	194	282	47	1	13	100	3	7	1	65	12	54	34	7	21	.330	.394	.480
Sheffield, Gary, Atl.	155	678	576	126	190	348	37	2	39	132	0	8	8	86	6	55	18	4	16	.330	.419	.604
Kendall, Jason, Pit.	150	666	587	84	191	244	29	3	6	58	1	3	25	49	3	40	8	7	9	.325	.399	.416
Giles, Marcus, Atl.	145	635	551	101	174	290	49	2	21	69	10	4	11	59	2	80	14	4	7	.316	.390	.526
Castillo, Luis, Fla.+	152	676	595	99	187	236	19	6	6	39	15	1	2	63	0	60	21	19	7	.314	.381	.397
Loretta, Mark, S.D.	154	653	589	74	185	260	28	4	13	72	3	4	3	54	2	62	5	4	17	.314	.372	.441
Grudzielanek, Mark, Chi.	121	531	481	73	151	200	38	1	3	38	7	2	11	30	0	64	6	2	12	.314	.366	.416
Podsednik, Scott, Mil.*	154	628	558	100	175	247	29	8	9	58	8	2	4	56	2	91	43	10	11	.314	.379	.443
Lieberthal, Mike, Phi.	131	561	508	68	159	230	30	1	13	81	0	3	12	38	2	59	0	0	14	.313	.373	.453
Vidro, Jose, Mon.+	144	592	509	77	158	239	36	0	15	65	2	5	7	69	6	50	3	2	16	.310	.397	.470
Hidalgo, Richard, Hou.	141	585	514	91	159	294	43	4	28	88	0	5	8	58	8	104	9	7	10	.309	.385	.572
Pierre, Juan, Fla.*	162	747	668	100	204	249	28	7	1	41	15	3	5	55	1	35	65	20	9	.305	.361	.373

DEPARTMENTAL LEADERS: G—Cabrera, Mon., Pierre, Fla., Sexson, Mil., 162; AB—Pierre, Fla., 668; R—Pujols, St.L., 137; H—Pujols, St.L., 212; TB—Pujols, St.L., 394; 1B—Pierre, Fla., 168; 2B—Pujols, St.L., 51; 3B—Finley, Ari., Furcal, Atl., 10; HR—Thome, Phi., 47; RBI—Wilson, Col., 141; SH—Castillo, Fla., Pierre, Fla., Schmidt, S.F., 15; SF—Ramirez, Pit.-Chi., 11; HP—Biggio, Hou., 27; BB—Bonds, S.F., 148; IBB—Bonds, S.F., 61; SO—Thome, Phi., 182; SB—Pierre, Fla., 65; CS—Pierre, Fla., 20; GDP—Payton, Col., 27; Slg.—Bonds, S.F., .749; OBP—Bonds, S.F., .529.

ALL PLAYERS

*Lefthanded batter. †Switch-hitter.

Player, Team	G	TPA	AB	R	H	TB	2B	3B	HR	RBI	SH	SF	HP	BB	IBB	SO	SB	CS	GDP	Avg.	OBP	Slg.
Abreu, Bobby, Phi.*	158	695	577	99	173	270	35	1	20	101	0	7	2	109	13	126	22	9	13	.300	.409	.468
Acevedo, Jose, Cin.	5	11	9	0	0	0	0	0	0	0	2	0	0	0	0	5	0	0	1	.000	.000	.000
Adams, Terry, Phi.	66	1	1	0	0	0	0	0	0	0	0	0	0	0	0	1	0	0	0	.000	.000	.000
Ainsworth, Kurt, S.F.	12	26	22	0	1	1	0	0	0	0	4	0	0	0	0	7	0	0	0	.045	.045	.045
Alfonseca, Antonio, Chi.	60	1	0	0	0	0	0	0	0	0	1	0	0	0	0	0	0	0	0	.000	.000	.000
Alfonzo, Edgardo, S.F.	142	586	514	56	133	201	25	2	13	81	3	7	4	58	4	41	5	2	14	.259	.334	.391
Allen, Chad, Fla.	12	25	24	2	5	8	1	1	0	0	0	0	1	0	0	5	0	0	1	.208	.240	.333
Allen, Luke, Col.*	2	2	2	0	0	0	0	0	0	0	0	0	0	0	0	0	0	0	1	.000	.000	.000
Almonte, Edwin, N.Y.	12	1	1	0	0	0	0	0	0	0	0	0	0	0	0	0	0	0	1	.000	.000	.000
Almonte, Hector, Mon.	28	1	1	0	0	0	0	0	0	0	0	0	0	0	0	1	0	0	0	.000	.000	.000
Alomar, Roberto, N.Y.†	73	302	263	34	69	94	17	1	2	22	4	4	2	29	2	40	6	0	8	.262	.336	.357
Alou, Moises, Chi.	151	638	565	83	158	261	35	1	22	91	0	3	7	63	7	67	3	1	16	.280	.357	.462
Alvarez, Wilson, L.A.*	21	31	29	1	5	5	0	0	0	0	1	0	0	1	0	9	0	0	2	.172	.200	.172
Anderson, Jimmy, Cin.*	8	13	9	1	1	1	0	0	0	0	2	0	0	2	0	4	0	0	0	.111	.273	.111
Armas, Tony, Mon.	5	10	10	0	2	2	0	0	0	0	0	0	0	0	0	2	0	0	0	.200	.200	.200
Ashby, Andy, L.A.	21	17	14	0	0	0	0	0	0	0	3	0	0	0	0	8	0	0	0	.000	.000	.000
Astacio, Pedro, N.Y.	7	14	11	1	1	1	0	0	0	0	3	0	0	0	0	2	0	0	0	.091	.091	.091
Atkins, Garrett, Col.	25	73	69	6	11	13	2	0	0	4	0	0	1	3	0	14	0	0	1	.159	.205	.188
Aurilia, Rich, S.F.	129	545	505	65	140	207	26	1	13	58	0	3	1	36	0	82	2	2	18	.277	.325	.410
Ausmus, Brad, Hou.	143	509	450	43	103	131	12	2	4	47	4	5	4	46	1	66	5	3	8	.229	.303	.291
Austin, Jeff, Cin.	7	10	8	0	1	1	0	0	0	0	2	0	0	0	0	5	0	0	0	.125	.125	.125
Ayala, Luis, Mon.	65	1	1	0	0	0	0	0	0	0	0	0	0	0	0	0	0	0	0	.000	.000	.000
Bacsik, Mike, N.Y.*	5	3	3	0	0	0	0	0	0	0	0	0	0	0	0	1	0	0	0	.000	.000	.000
Baerga, Carlos, Ari.†	105	231	207	31	71	96	13	0	4	39	1	3	2	18	1	20	1	1	6	.343	.396	.464
Bagwell, Jeff, Hou.	160	702	605	109	168	317	28	2	39	100	0	3	6	88	3	119	11	4	25	.278	.373	.524
Bako, Paul, Chi.*	70	213	188	19	43	62	13	3	0	17	1	1	1	22	3	47	0	1	2	.229	.311	.330
Bale, John, Cin.*	10	17	17	0	2	2	0	0	0	0	0	0	0	0	0	8	0	0	0	.118	.118	.118
Banks, Brian, Fla.†	92	180	149	14	35	57	6	2	4	23	2	2	2	25	1	38	2	1	4	.235	.348	.383

Player, Team	G	TPA	AB	R	H	TB	2B	3B	HR	RBI	SH	SF	HP	BB	IBB	SO	SB	CS	GDP	Avg.	OBP	Slg.
Barajas, Rod, Ari.	80	239	220	19	48	72	15	0	3	28	1	3	1	14	7	43	0	0	6	.218	.265	.327
Barmes, Clint, Col.	12	28	25	2	8	10	2	0	0	2	0	1	2	0	0	10	0	0	0	.320	.357	.400
Barnes, Larry, L.A.*	30	39	38	2	8	10	2	0	0	2	0	0	0	1	0	9	0	0	0	.211	.231	.263
Barrett, Michael, Mon.	70	252	226	33	47	90	9	2	10	30	2	1	2	21	7	37	0	0	6	.208	.280	.398
Batista, Miguel, Ari.	36	62	57	3	4	5	1	0	0	0	4	0	0	1	0	33	0	0	2	.070	.086	.088
Bautista, Danny, Ari.	88	314	284	29	78	112	16	3	4	36	2	3	4	21	2	50	3	2	7	.275	.330	.394
Bay, Jason, S.D.-Pit.	30	107	87	15	25	46	7	1	4	14	0	0	1	19	0	29	3	1	0	.287	.421	.529
Beckett, Josh, Fla.	24	52	46	3	7	9	2	0	0	3	5	0	0	1	0	14	0	0	1	.152	.170	.196
Beimel, Joe, Pit.*	70	5	5	0	0	0	0	0	0	0	0	0	0	0	0	2	0	0	0	.000	.000	.000
Belisle, Matt, Cin.†	6	1	1	0	0	0	0	0	0	0	0	0	0	0	0	1	0	0	0	.000	.000	.000
Bell, David, Phi.	85	348	297	32	58	84	14	0	4	37	0	6	4	41	1	40	0	0	7	.195	.296	.283
Bell, Jay, N.Y.	72	142	116	11	21	22	1	0	0	3	1	1	2	22	1	38	0	0	4	.181	.319	.190
Bellhorn, Mark, Chi.-Col.†	99	307	249	27	55	73	10	1	2	26	1	4	3	50	1	78	5	6	3	.221	.353	.293
Belliard, Ronnie, Col.	116	505	447	73	124	183	31	2	8	50	6	1	2	49	0	71	7	2	7	.277	.351	.409
Beltre, Adrian, L.A.	158	608	559	50	134	237	30	2	23	80	1	6	5	37	4	103	2	2	13	.240	.290	.424
Benard, Marvin, S.F.*	46	77	71	5	14	19	3	1	0	4	1	1	0	4	0	9	1	0	3	.197	.237	.268
Benes, Alan, Chi.	3	1	1	0	0	0	0	0	0	0	0	0	0	0	0	0	0	0	0	.000	.000	.000
Benitez, Armando, N.Y.	45	1	1	0	0	0	0	0	0	0	0	0	0	0	0	1	0	0	0	.000	.000	.000
Bennett, Gary, S.D.	96	338	307	26	73	94	15	0	2	42	3	2	2	24	3	48	3	0	8	.238	.296	.306
Benson, Kris, Pit.	18	37	30	2	0	0	0	0	0	0	6	0	0	1	0	11	0	0	1	.000	.032	.000
Berkman, Lance, Hou.†	153	658	538	110	155	277	35	6	25	93	1	3	9	107	13	108	5	3	10	.288	.412	.515
Bernero, Adam, Col.	31	2	2	1	0	0	0	0	0	0	0	0	0	0	0	1	0	0	0	.000	.000	.000
Biddle, Rocky, Mon.	73	1	1	0	0	0	0	0	0	0	0	0	0	0	0	1	0	0	0	.000	.000	.000
Biggio, Craig, Hou.	153	717	628	102	166	259	44	2	15	62	3	2	27	57	3	116	8	4	4	.264	.350	.412
Blanco, Henry, Atl.	55	166	151	11	30	41	8	0	1	13	3	1	1	10	2	21	0	0	3	.199	.252	.272
Blum, Geoff, Hou.†	123	449	420	51	110	159	19	0	10	52	2	5	2	20	1	50	0	0	15	.262	.295	.379
Bonds, Barry, S.F.*	130	550	390	111	133	292	22	1	45	90	0	2	10	148	61	58	7	0	7	.341	.529	.749
Bong, Jung, Atl.*	44	7	5	0	0	0	0	0	0	0	1	0	0	1	0	2	0	0	0	.000	.167	.000
Boone, Aaron, Cin.	106	447	403	61	110	189	19	3	18	65	3	0	5	35	2	74	15	3	6	.273	.339	.469
Bragg, Darren, Atl.*	104	181	162	21	39	46	5	1	0	9	4	0	2	13	1	38	2	1	1	.241	.305	.284
Branyan, Russell, Cin.*	74	205	176	22	38	77	12	0	9	26	0	1	1	27	0	69	0	0	1	.216	.322	.438
Brohawn, Troy, L.A.*	12	1	1	0	1	1	0	0	0	0	0	0	0	0	0	0	0	0	0	1.000	1.000	1.000
Brower, Jim, S.F.	51	19	17	2	3	3	0	0	0	1	1	0	1	0	0	5	0	0	0	.176	.222	.176
Brown, Kevin, L.A.	32	70	63	4	10	13	3	0	0	2	6	1	0	0	0	28	0	0	1	.159	.156	.206
Bruntlett, Eric, Hou.	31	56	54	3	14	20	3	0	1	4	1	1	0	0	0	10	0	0	1	.259	.255	.370
Buchanan, Brian, S.D.	115	229	198	29	52	90	10	2	8	29	0	3	3	24	1	51	6	2	8	.263	.346	.455
Budzinski, Mark, Cin.*	4	7	7	0	0	0	0	0	0	0	0	0	0	0	0	4	0	0	0	.000	.000	.000
Bump, Nate, Fla.	32	1	0	0	0	0	0	0	0	0	1	0	0	0	0	0	0	0	0	.000	.000	.000
Burba, Dave, Mil.	17	11	10	0	0	0	0	0	0	0	1	0	0	0	0	7	0	0	1	.000	.000	.000
Burnett, A.J., Fla.	4	9	7	0	1	1	0	0	0	0	0	0	0	2	0	3	0	0	0	.143	.333	.143
Burnitz, Jeromy, N.Y.-L.A.*	126	505	464	63	111	226	22	0	31	77	0	1	5	35	9	112	5	4	5	.239	.299	.487
Burrell, Pat, Phi.	146	599	522	57	109	211	31	4	21	64	0	1	4	72	2	142	0	0	18	.209	.309	.404
Burroughs, Sean, S.D.*	146	578	517	62	148	208	27	6	7	58	2	4	11	44	4	75	7	2	13	.286	.352	.402
Butler, Brent, Col.	37	99	90	13	19	27	3	1	1	4	1	0	1	7	2	13	1	0	2	.211	.276	.300
Bynum, Mike, S.D.*	13	11	10	0	3	3	0	0	0	0	1	0	0	0	0	4	0	0	0	.300	.300	.300
Byrd, Marlon, Phi.	135	553	495	86	150	207	28	4	7	45	4	3	7	44	3	94	11	1	8	.303	.366	.418
Cabrera, Jolbert, L.A.	128	380	347	43	98	152	32	2	6	37	3	3	10	17	3	62	6	4	10	.282	.332	.438
Cabrera, Miguel, Fla.	87	346	314	39	84	147	21	3	12	62	4	1	2	25	3	84	0	2	12	.268	.325	.468
Cabrera, Orlando, Mon.	162	691	626	95	186	288	47	2	17	80	3	9	1	52	3	64	24	2	18	.297	.347	.460
Cairo, Miguel, St.L.	92	290	261	41	64	98	15	2	5	32	3	7	6	13	1	30	4	1	6	.245	.289	.375
Calero, Kiko, St.L.	26	4	4	1	1	1	0	0	0	1	0	0	0	0	0	0	0	0	0	.250	.250	.250
Calloway, Ron, Mon.*	126	369	340	36	81	127	17	1	9	52	4	3	2	20	1	80	9	2	13	.238	.282	.374
Capuano, Chris, Ari.*	9	8	8	0	0	0	0	0	0	0	0	0	0	0	0	5	0	0	0	.000	.000	.000
Carroll, Jamey, Mon.	105	260	227	31	59	74	10	1	1	10	9	2	3	19	0	39	5	2	10	.260	.323	.326
Casey, Sean, Cin.*	147	629	573	71	167	234	19	3	14	80	0	3	2	51	4	58	4	0	19	.291	.350	.408
Castilla, Vinny, Atl.	147	578	542	65	150	250	28	3	22	76	1	6	3	26	3	86	1	2	22	.277	.310	.461
Castillo, Alberto, S.F.	11	15	15	2	3	7	1	0	1	4	0	0	0	0	0	5	0	0	0	.200	.200	.467
Castillo, Luis, Fla.†	152	676	595	99	187	236	19	6	6	39	15	1	2	63	0	60	21	19	7	.314	.381	.397
Castro, Juan, Cin.	113	348	320	28	81	124	14	1	9	33	7	3	0	18	1	58	2	3	7	.253	.290	.388
Castro, Ramon, Fla.	40	57	53	6	15	32	2	0	5	8	0	0	0	4	0	11	0	0	0	.283	.333	.604
Cedeno, Roger, N.Y.†	148	527	484	70	129	183	25	4	7	37	2	2	1	38	3	86	14	9	8	.267	.320	.378
Cepicky, Matt, Mon.*	5	8	8	0	2	3	1	0	0	0	0	0	0	0	0	2	0	0	0	.250	.250	.375
Cerda, Jaime, N.Y.*	27	1	1	0	0	0	0	0	0	0	0	0	0	0	0	1	0	0	0	.000	.000	.000
Chacon, Shawn, Col.	23	48	46	4	9	14	2	0	1	5	2	0	0	0	0	16	0	0	0	.196	.196	.304
Chamblee, Jim, Cin.	2	2	2	0	0	0	0	0	0	0	0	0	0	0	0	2	0	0	0	.000	.000	.000
Chapman, Travis, Phi.	1	1	1	0	0	0	0	0	0	0	0	0	0	0	0	0	0	0	0	.000	.000	.000
Chavez, Endy, Mon.*	141	526	483	66	121	171	25	5	5	47	9	3	0	31	3	59	18	7	7	.251	.294	.354
Chavez, Raul, Hou.	19	38	37	5	10	16	1	1	1	4	0	0	0	1	0	6	0	0	3	.270	.289	.432
Chen, Bruce, Hou.*	11	1	1	0	0	0	0	0	0	0	0	0	0	0	0	0	0	0	0	.000	.000	.000
Chen, Chin-Feng, L.A.	1	1	1	0	0	0	0	0	0	0	0	0	0	0	0	0	0	0	0	.000	.000	.000
Choi, Hee Seop, Chi.*	80	245	202	31	44	85	17	0	8	28	2	0	4	37	1	71	1	1	2	.218	.350	.421
Cintron, Alex, Ari.†	117	487	448	70	142	219	26	6	13	51	5	3	2	29	0	33	2	3	7	.317	.359	.489
Clark, Brady, Mil.	128	356	315	33	86	127	21	1	6	40	2	7	9	21	0	40	13	2	12	.273	.330	.403
Clark, Jermaine, S.D.*	1	3	2	0	0	0	0	0	0	1	0	1	0	0	0	1	0	1	0	.000	.000	.000
Clark, Tony, N.Y.†	125	280	254	29	59	120	13	0	16	43	0	1	1	24	2	73	0	0	8	.232	.300	.472
Clayton, Royce, Mil.	146	543	483	49	110	161	16	1	11	39	4	4	3	49	10	92	5	2	25	.228	.301	.333
Clement, Matt, Chi.	32	71	62	3	9	11	2	0	0	3	8	0	1	0	0	26	0	0	0	.145	.159	.177
Colyer, Steve, L.A.*	13	1	0	0	0	0	0	0	0	0	0	0	0	1	0	0	0	0	0	.000	1.000	.000
Condrey, Clay, S.D.	9	10	10	1	2	2	0	0	0	0	0	0	0	0	0	6	0	0	0	.200	.200	.200
Cone, David, N.Y.*	5	4	4	0	1	1	0	0	0	0	0	0	0	0	0	1	0	0	0	.250	.250	.250
Conine, Jeff, Fla.	25	99	84	13	20	38	3	0	5	15	1	1	0	13	0	10	0	0	2	.238	.337	.452
Conti, Jason, Mil.*	30	52	48	3	11	19	2	0	2	7	1	1	0	2	0	18	0	1	1	.229	.255	.396
Cook, Aaron, Col.	43	37	29	3	5	5	0	0	0	3	6	0	0	2	0	10	0	0	1	.172	.226	.172
Coomer, Ron, L.A.	69	137	125	11	30	46	4	0	4	15	0	1	1	10	2	19	0	0	7	.240	.299	.368
Cora, Alex, L.A.*	148	514	477	39	119	161	24	3	4	34	9	2	10	16	3	59	4	2	5	.249	.287	.338

Player, Team	G	TPA	AB	R	H	TB	2B	3B	HR	RBI	SH	SF	HP	BB	IBB	SO	SB	CS	GDP	Avg.	OBP	Slg.
Corcoran, Roy, Mon.	5	1	1	0	0	0	0	0	0	0	0	0	0	0	0	1	0	0	0	.000	.000	.000
Cordero, Chad, Mon.	12	1	0	0	0	0	0	0	0	0	1	0	0	0	0	0	0	0	0	.000	.000	.000
Cordero, Wil, Mon.	130	492	436	57	121	196	27	0	16	71	0	3	4	49	5	90	1	1	11	.278	.354	.450
Cormier, Rheal, Phi.*	65	3	2	1	1	1	0	0	0	0	0	0	0	1	0	0	0	0	0	.500	.667	.500
Correia, Kevin, S.F.	10	14	13	1	2	2	0	0	0	2	1	0	0	0	0	6	0	0	0	.154	.154	.154
Cota, Humberto, Pit.	10	17	16	1	4	5	1	0	0	1	0	0	0	1	0	5	0	0	0	.250	.294	.313
Counsell, Craig, Ari.*	89	351	303	40	71	92	6	3	3	21	3	2	2	41	0	32	11	4	4	.234	.328	.304
Cromer, Tripp, Hou.	3	4	4	0	1	3	0	1	0	1	0	0	0	0	0	0	0	0	0	.250	.250	.750
Crosby, Bubba, L.A.*	9	12	12	0	1	1	0	0	0	1	0	0	0	0	0	3	0	0	0	.083	.083	.083
Cruz, Enrique, Mil.	60	76	71	6	6	7	1	0	0	2	0	0	1	4	0	30	0	0	2	.085	.145	.099
Cruz, Jose, S.F.†	158	650	539	90	135	223	26	1	20	68	2	7	0	102	6	121	5	8	14	.250	.366	.414
Cruz, Juan, Chi.	25	13	12	1	3	5	0	1	0	1	1	0	0	0	0	5	0	0	0	.250	.250	.417
Cruz, Nelson, Col.	20	15	13	1	2	3	1	0	0	1	2	0	0	0	0	2	0	0	0	.154	.154	.231
D'Amico, Jeff, Pit.	29	63	48	3	6	10	1	0	1	3	9	0	0	6	0	23	0	0	2	.125	.222	.208
Darensbourg, Vic, Col.-Mon.*	10	1	1	0	0	0	0	0	0	0	0	0	0	0	0	1	0	0	0	.000	.000	.000
Davis, Doug, Mil.	8	21	20	0	2	2	0	0	0	0	1	0	0	0	0	9	0	0	0	.100	.100	.100
Davis, J.J., Pit.	19	38	35	1	7	10	0	0	1	4	0	0	0	3	0	13	0	1	0	.200	.263	.286
Dawley, Joe, Atl.	5	1	1	0	0	0	0	0	0	0	0	0	0	0	0	1	0	0	0	.000	.000	.000
Day, Zach, Mon.	23	49	47	2	2	2	0	0	0	2	1	0	0	1	0	22	0	0	0	.043	.063	.043
de los Santos, Valerio, Mil.-Phi.*	51	1	1	0	0	0	0	0	0	0	0	0	0	0	0	1	0	0	0	.000	.000	.000
Deago, Roger, S.D.	2	4	4	0	0	0	0	0	0	0	0	0	0	0	0	3	0	0	0	.000	.000	.000
Delgado, Wilson, St.L.†	43	82	77	8	13	16	3	0	0	3	0	1	1	3	0	10	0	0	4	.169	.207	.208
Dellucci, David, Ari.*	70	190	165	18	40	63	11	3	2	19	1	2	3	19	1	45	9	0	4	.242	.328	.382
Dempster, Ryan, Cin.	24	35	33	1	1	1	0	0	0	0	1	0	0	1	0	19	0	0	0	.030	.059	.030
DePastino, Joe, N.Y.	2	2	2	0	0	0	0	0	0	0	0	0	0	0	0	1	0	0	0	.000	.000	.000
DeRosa, Mark, Atl.	103	288	266	40	70	102	14	0	6	22	0	1	5	16	0	49	1	0	6	.263	.316	.383
Dessens, Elmer, Ari.	36	59	46	1	9	12	1	1	0	6	10	0	0	3	0	11	0	0	0	.196	.245	.261
Dotel, Octavio, Hou.	76	6	6	0	0	0	0	0	0	0	0	0	0	0	0	4	0	0	0	.000	.000	.000
Downs, Scott, Mon.*	1	1	1	0	0	0	0	0	0	0	0	0	0	0	0	0	0	0	0	.000	.000	.000
Dreifort, Darren, L.A.	10	19	15	0	2	3	1	0	0	1	3	0	0	1	0	9	0	0	0	.133	.188	.200
Drew, J.D., St.L.*	100	328	287	60	83	147	13	3	15	42	2	0	3	36	0	48	2	2	6	.289	.374	.512
Drew, Tim, Mon.	6	2	1	0	0	0	0	0	0	0	1	0	0	0	0	0	0	0	0	.000	.000	.000
Duckworth, Brandon, Phi.	24	30	27	1	5	5	0	0	0	2	1	0	0	2	0	5	0	0	1	.185	.241	.185
Duncan, Jeff, N.Y.*	56	166	139	13	27	34	0	2	1	10	8	0	2	17	3	41	4	2	1	.194	.291	.245
Dunn, Adam, Cin.*	116	469	381	70	82	177	12	1	27	57	0	4	10	74	8	126	8	2	4	.215	.354	.465
Durham, Ray, S.F.†	110	469	410	61	117	181	30	5	8	33	4	2	3	50	2	82	7	7	4	.285	.366	.441
Eaton, Adam, S.D.	39	68	56	4	11	20	3	0	2	3	7	0	1	4	0	25	0	0	1	.196	.262	.357
Edmonds, Jim, St.L.*	137	531	447	89	123	276	32	2	39	89	1	2	4	77	6	127	1	3	11	.275	.385	.617
Eischen, Joey, Mon.*	71	4	4	1	1	1	0	0	0	0	0	0	0	0	0	2	0	0	0	.250	.250	.250
Elarton, Scott, Col.	11	17	14	2	1	1	0	0	0	0	1	0	0	2	0	4	0	0	0	.071	.188	.071
Eldred, Cal, St.L.	63	2	2	0	1	1	0	0	0	0	0	0	0	0	0	1	0	0	0	.500	.500	.500
Ellison, Jason, S.F.	7	10	10	1	1	1	0	0	0	0	0	0	0	0	0	1	0	0	0	.100	.100	.100
Encarnacion, Juan, Fla.	156	653	601	80	162	268	37	6	19	94	5	6	4	37	0	82	19	8	17	.270	.313	.446
Ensberg, Morgan, Hou.	127	441	385	69	112	204	15	1	25	60	1	1	6	48	1	60	7	2	10	.291	.377	.530
Estalella, Bobby, Col.	46	165	140	17	28	56	7	0	7	21	2	3	1	19	0	55	2	0	4	.200	.294	.400
Estes, Shawn, Chi.	30	51	39	4	7	11	1	0	1	3	9	1	0	2	0	17	0	0	0	.179	.214	.282
Estrada, Johnny, Atl.†	16	39	36	2	11	11	0	0	0	2	0	0	3	0	0	3	0	0	1	.306	.359	.306
Etherton, Seth, Cin.	7	10	7	0	1	1	0	0	0	0	3	0	0	0	0	2	0	0	0	.143	.143	.143
Everett, Adam, Hou.	128	436	387	51	99	147	18	3	8	51	11	1	9	28	6	66	8	1	7	.256	.320	.380
Eyre, Scott, S.F.*	74	2	2	0	1	1	0	0	0	0	0	0	0	0	0	0	0	0	0	.500	.500	.500
Farnsworth, Kyle, Chi.	77	1	1	0	0	0	0	0	0	0	0	0	0	0	0	0	0	0	0	.000	.000	.000
Fassero, Jeff, St.L.*	62	10	9	0	0	0	0	0	0	0	1	0	0	0	0	4	0	0	0	.000	.000	.000
Feliciano, Pedro, N.Y.*	23	5	3	0	0	0	0	0	0	0	1	0	0	1	0	1	0	0	0	.000	.250	.000
Feliz, Pedro, S.F.	95	249	235	31	58	121	9	3	16	48	1	2	1	10	0	53	2	2	7	.247	.278	.515
Fernandez, Jared, Hou.	12	10	9	1	0	0	0	0	0	0	1	0	0	0	0	3	0	0	0	.000	.000	.000
Fick, Robert, Atl.*	126	460	409	52	110	171	26	1	11	80	0	7	2	42	4	47	1	0	9	.269	.335	.418
Figueroa, Nelson, Pit.	12	7	7	0	0	0	0	0	0	0	0	0	0	0	0	4	0	0	0	.000	.000	.000
Finley, Steve, Ari.*	147	582	516	82	148	258	24	10	22	70	0	3	6	57	4	94	15	8	6	.287	.363	.500
Floyd, Cliff, N.Y.*	108	425	365	57	106	189	25	2	18	68	0	6	3	51	2	66	3	0	10	.290	.376	.518
Fogg, Josh, Pit.	26	51	42	4	8	8	0	0	0	1	7	0	0	2	0	15	1	0	0	.190	.227	.190
Foppert, Jesse, S.F.	23	38	37	3	3	6	1	1	0	1	0	0	1	0	0	19	0	0	1	.081	.105	.162
Ford, Matt, Mil.†	25	8	7	0	1	2	1	0	0	1	0	0	0	1	0	3	0	0	0	.143	.250	.286
Fox, Andy, Fla.*	70	120	108	12	21	28	5	1	0	8	1	0	4	7	0	29	1	2	2	.194	.269	.259
Franco, Julio, Atl.	103	223	197	28	58	89	12	2	5	31	0	1	0	25	5	43	0	1	8	.294	.372	.452
Franco, Matt, Atl.*	112	148	134	11	33	47	5	0	3	15	1	2	0	11	0	26	0	1	4	.246	.299	.351
Franklin, Wayne, Mil.*	36	71	59	1	10	11	1	0	0	3	12	0	0	0	0	18	0	0	2	.169	.169	.186
Freel, Ryan, Cin.	43	153	137	23	39	59	6	1	4	12	2	1	4	9	1	13	9	4	2	.285	.344	.431
Fuentes, Brian, Col.*	75	1	1	0	0	0	0	0	0	0	0	0	0	0	0	0	0	0	0	.000	.000	.000
Furcal, Rafael, Atl.†	156	734	664	130	194	294	35	10	15	61	3	4	3	60	2	76	25	2	1	.292	.352	.443
Galarraga, Andres, S.F.	110	293	272	36	82	133	15	0	12	42	0	0	2	19	1	61	1	3	9	.301	.352	.489
Gallo, Mike, Hou.*	32	2	2	0	0	0	0	0	0	0	0	0	0	0	0	0	0	0	0	.000	.000	.000
Garcia, Danny, N.Y.	19	63	56	5	12	20	2	0	2	6	1	1	3	2	0	11	0	0	2	.214	.274	.357
Garcia, Jesse, Atl.	13	10	10	6	4	6	0	1	0	2	0	0	0	0	0	1	0	1	0	.400	.400	.600
Giles, Brian, Pit.-S.D.*	134	609	492	93	147	253	34	6	20	88	0	4	8	105	12	58	4	3	12	.299	.427	.514
Giles, Marcus, Atl.	145	635	551	101	174	290	49	2	21	69	10	4	11	59	2	80	14	4	7	.316	.390	.526
Ginter, Keith, Mil.	127	415	358	51	92	153	15	2	14	44	0	3	17	37	1	87	1	1	8	.257	.352	.427
Girardi, Joe, St.L.	16	26	23	1	3	3	0	0	0	1	0	0	0	3	0	4	0	0	2	.130	.231	.130
Glanville, Doug, Chi.	28	55	51	2	12	15	0	0	1	2	1	1	0	2	0	4	0	1	0	.235	.259	.294
Glavine, Mike, N.Y.*	6	7	7	0	1	1	0	0	0	0	0	0	0	0	0	2	0	0	0	.143	.143	.143
Glavine, Tom, N.Y.*	33	67	53	4	8	9	1	0	0	3	10	0	0	4	0	13	0	0	0	.151	.211	.170
Gonzalez, Alex, Fla.	150	582	528	52	135	234	33	6	18	77	3	5	13	33	13	106	0	4	8	.256	.313	.443
Gonzalez, Alex S., Chi.	152	601	536	71	122	219	37	0	20	59	8	4	6	47	1	123	3	3	17	.228	.295	.409
Gonzalez, Edgar, Ari.	9	5	4	1	1	1	0	0	0	0	1	0	0	0	0	0	0	0	0	.250	.250	.250
Gonzalez, Luis, Ari.*	156	679	579	92	176	308	46	4	26	104	0	3	3	94	17	67	5	3	19	.304	.402	.532
Gonzalez, Raul, N.Y.	107	246	217	28	50	72	12	2	2	21	0	1	1	27	1	34	3	0	8	.230	.317	.332

Player, Team	G	TPA	AB	R	H	TB	2B	3B	HR	RBI	SH	SF	HP	BB	IBB	SO	SB	CS	GDP	Avg.	OBP	Slg.
Gonzalez, Wiki, S.D.	24	73	65	1	13	18	5	0	0	10	1	1	1	5	1	13	0	0	3	.200	.264	.277
Good, Andrew, Ari.	16	20	16	0	2	2	0	0	0	1	4	0	0	0	0	5	0	0	0	.125	.125	.125
Goodwin, Tom, Chi.*	87	184	171	26	49	62	10	0	1	12	1	1	0	11	0	33	19	5	3	.287	.328	.363
Grace, Mark, Ari.*	66	155	135	13	27	41	5	0	3	16	1	3	0	16	2	15	0	0	6	.200	.279	.304
Graves, Danny, Cin.	31	57	54	2	6	6	0	0	0	0	3	0	0	0	0	15	1	0	0	.111	.111	.111
Green, Shawn, L.A.*	160	691	611	84	171	281	49	2	19	85	0	6	6	68	2	112	6	2	18	.280	.355	.460
Greene, Khalil, S.D.	20	70	65	8	14	26	4	1	2	6	0	0	1	4	0	19	0	1	3	.215	.271	.400
Griffey Jr., Ken, Cin.*	53	201	166	34	41	94	12	1	13	26	1	1	6	27	5	44	1	0	3	.247	.370	.566
Griffiths, Jeremy, N.Y.	9	11	9	0	0	0	0	0	0	0	1	0	0	1	0	3	0	0	0	.000	.100	.000
Grissom, Marquis, S.F.	149	618	587	82	176	275	33	3	20	79	3	6	2	20	0	82	11	3	14	.300	.322	.468
Grudzielanek, Mark, Chi.	121	531	481	73	151	200	38	1	3	38	7	2	11	30	0	64	6	2	12	.314	.366	.416
Gryboski, Kevin, Atl.	64	1	1	0	0	0	0	0	0	0	0	0	0	0	0	1	0	0	0	.000	.000	.000
Guerrero, Vladimir, Mon.	112	467	394	71	130	231	20	3	25	79	0	4	6	63	22	53	9	5	18	.330	.426	.586
Guillen, Jose, Cin.	91	349	315	52	106	198	21	1	23	63	6	2	9	17	1	63	1	3	8	.337	.385	.629
Guthrie, Mark, Chi.	65	1	1	0	0	0	0	0	0	0	0	0	0	0	0	1	0	0	0	.000	.000	.000
Guzman, Edwards, Mon.*	52	155	146	15	35	43	5	0	1	14	3	1	0	5	2	17	0	0	6	.240	.263	.295
Hackman, Luther, S.D.	65	2	2	0	0	0	0	0	0	0	0	0	0	0	0	2	0	0	0	.000	.000	.000
Hall, Bill, Mil.	52	155	142	23	37	65	9	2	5	20	4	1	1	7	0	28	1	2	5	.261	.298	.458
Hall, Josh, Cin.	6	7	6	2	1	1	0	0	0	0	1	0	0	0	0	2	0	0	0	.167	.167	.167
Hamilton, Joey, Cin.	3	3	3	0	0	0	0	0	0	0	0	0	0	0	0	3	0	0	0	.000	.000	.000
Hammock, Robby, Ari.	65	216	195	30	55	93	10	2	8	28	0	2	2	17	3	44	3	2	5	.282	.343	.477
Hammonds, Jeffrey, Mil.-S.F.	46	149	132	22	32	56	12	0	4	13	0	0	1	16	0	28	1	0	3	.242	.329	.424
Hampton, Mike, Atl.	32	74	60	6	11	21	2	1	2	8	9	0	0	5	0	13	0	0	2	.183	.246	.350
Hansen, Dave, S.D.*	110	159	135	13	33	45	4	1	2	15	0	0	1	23	3	25	1	0	4	.244	.358	.333
Harang, Aaron, Cin.	9	17	17	0	1	1	0	0	0	0	0	0	0	0	0	11	0	0	0	.059	.059	.059
Haren, Danny, St.L.	15	28	25	0	2	4	2	0	0	1	1	0	1	1	0	10	0	0	1	.080	.148	.160
Harris, Lenny, Chi.-Fla.*	88	163	145	14	28	34	3	0	1	8	1	1	0	16	3	21	1	0	2	.193	.272	.234
Hart, Bo, St.L.	77	321	296	46	82	117	13	5	4	28	6	1	6	12	0	64	3	1	3	.277	.317	.395
Haynes, Jimmy, Cin.	18	30	23	2	6	7	1	0	0	3	7	0	0	0	0	4	0	0	0	.261	.261	.304
Heilman, Aaron, N.Y.	14	23	22	1	1	1	0	0	0	1	0	0	0	1	0	13	0	0	0	.045	.087	.045
Helling, Rick, Fla.	11	2	2	0	1	2	1	0	0	0	0	0	0	0	0	0	0	0	0	.500	.500	1.000
Helms, Wes, Mil.	134	536	476	56	124	214	21	0	23	67	0	7	10	43	3	131	0	1	10	.261	.330	.450
Helton, Todd, Col.*	160	703	583	135	209	367	49	5	33	117	0	7	2	111	21	72	0	4	19	.358	.458	.630
Henderson, Rickey, L.A.	30	84	72	7	15	22	1	0	2	5	0	0	1	11	0	16	3	0	0	.208	.321	.306
Heredia, Felix, Cin.*	57	3	3	0	1	1	0	0	0	0	0	0	0	0	0	0	0	0	0	.333	.333	.333
Herges, Matt, S.D.-S.F.*	67	3	3	0	1	1	0	0	0	0	0	0	0	0	0	1	0	0	0	.333	.333	.333
Hermansen, Chad, L.A.	11	27	25	2	4	5	1	0	0	2	0	0	0	2	0	9	0	0	0	.160	.222	.200
Hermanson, Dustin, St.L.-S.F.	32	15	11	0	0	0	0	0	0	0	3	0	0	1	0	6	0	0	0	.000	.083	.000
Hernandez, Jose, Col.-Chi.-Pit.	150	571	519	58	117	180	18	3	13	57	0	5	1	46	0	177	2	1	16	.225	.287	.347
Hernandez, Livan, Mon.	33	82	74	2	14	15	1	0	0	6	6	0	1	1	0	14	0	0	2	.189	.211	.203
Hessman, Mike, Atl.	19	26	21	2	6	14	2	0	2	3	0	0	0	5	1	6	0	0	2	.286	.423	.667
Hidalgo, Richard, Hou.	141	585	514	91	159	294	43	4	28	88	0	5	8	58	8	104	9	7	10	.309	.385	.572
Hill, Bobby, Chi.-Pit.†	6	9	7	1	2	2	0	0	0	0	0	0	0	2	0	2	0	0	1	.286	.444	.286
Hill, Koyie, L.A.†	3	3	3	0	1	2	1	0	0	0	0	0	0	0	0	2	0	0	0	.333	.333	.667
Hillenbrand, Shea, Ari.	85	354	330	40	88	159	18	1	17	59	0	5	2	17	3	44	0	0	13	.267	.302	.482
Hitchcock, Sterling, St.L.*	8	14	12	0	1	1	0	0	0	0	2	0	0	0	0	5	0	0	0	.083	.083	.083
Hodges, Trey, Atl.	52	6	5	0	0	0	0	0	0	0	1	0	0	0	0	4	0	0	0	.000	.000	.000
Hollandsworth, Todd, Fla.*	93	254	228	32	58	96	23	3	3	20	2	2	0	22	4	55	2	3	2	.254	.317	.421
House, J.R., Pit.	1	1	1	0	1	1	0	0	0	0	0	0	0	0	0	0	0	0	0	1.000	1.000	1.000
Houston, Tyler, Phi.*	54	103	97	7	27	39	6	0	2	14	0	0	0	6	1	19	0	0	2	.278	.320	.402
Howard, Ben, S.D.	6	11	11	1	1	1	0	0	0	0	0	0	0	0	0	5	0	0	0	.091	.091	.091
Hubbard, Trenidad, Chi.	10	21	16	2	4	5	1	0	0	2	0	0	1	4	0	3	1	0	0	.250	.429	.313
Hummel, Tim, Cin.	26	94	84	9	19	30	5	0	2	10	1	1	0	8	0	13	0	0	1	.226	.290	.357
Hundley, Todd, L.A.†	21	41	33	2	6	13	1	0	2	11	0	0	0	8	0	13	0	1	0	.182	.341	.394
Hunter, Brian L., Hou.	56	108	98	13	23	31	6	1	0	13	0	3	1	6	0	21	0	0	1	.235	.278	.316
Hyzdu, Adam, Pit.	51	75	63	16	13	21	5	0	1	8	0	1	1	10	0	21	0	0	2	.206	.320	.333
Ishii, Kazuhisa, L.A.*	27	43	34	1	1	3	0	1	0	0	9	0	0	0	0	16	0	0	1	.029	.029	.088
Isringhausen, Jason, St.L.	40	2	2	0	1	3	0	1	0	3	0	0	0	0	0	0	0	0	0	.500	.500	1.500
Izturis, Cesar, L.A.†	158	593	558	47	140	176	21	6	1	40	7	3	0	25	8	70	10	5	8	.251	.282	.315
Jackson, Edwin, L.A.	4	8	6	0	0	0	0	0	0	0	1	0	0	1	0	2	0	0	0	.000	.143	.000
Jarvis, Kevin, S.D.*	17	29	22	3	3	3	0	0	0	2	3	0	0	4	0	7	0	0	1	.136	.269	.136
Jenkins, Geoff, Mil.*	124	554	487	81	144	262	30	2	28	95	0	3	6	58	10	120	0	0	12	.296	.375	.538
Jennings, Jason, Col.*	33	65	54	3	12	15	3	0	0	3	5	1	0	5	0	16	0	0	0	.222	.283	.278
Jensen, Ryan, S.F.	6	5	5	0	2	2	0	0	0	2	0	0	0	0	0	0	0	0	0	.400	.400	.400
Jimenez, D'Angelo, Cin.†	73	331	290	34	84	122	13	2	7	31	2	3	2	34	0	43	7	4	4	.290	.365	.421
Jimenez, Jose, Col.	63	19	17	3	3	3	0	0	0	0	2	0	0	0	0	10	0	0	0	.176	.176	.176
Johnson, Charles, Col.	108	414	356	49	82	162	20	0	20	61	1	7	1	49	2	84	1	3	8	.230	.320	.455
Johnson, Jonathan, Hou.	4	4	4	0	0	0	0	0	0	0	0	0	0	0	0	2	0	0	0	.000	.000	.000
Johnson, Randy, Ari.	18	38	36	2	7	10	0	0	1	3	2	0	0	0	0	17	0	0	0	.194	.194	.278
Jones, Andruw, Atl.	156	659	595	101	165	305	28	2	36	116	0	6	5	53	2	125	4	3	18	.277	.338	.513
Jones, Chipper, Atl.†	153	656	555	103	169	287	33	2	27	106	0	6	1	94	13	83	2	2	10	.305	.402	.517
Jones, Todd, Col.†	33	2	2	0	0	0	0	0	0	0	0	0	0	0	0	1	0	0	1	.000	.000	.000
Jordan, Brian, L.A.	66	253	224	28	67	94	9	0	6	28	0	2	4	23	3	30	1	1	3	.299	.372	.420
Jose, Felix, Ari.†	18	24	18	1	6	10	1	0	1	6	0	0	0	6	1	3	0	0	1	.333	.500	.556
Kapler, Gabe, Col.	39	76	67	10	15	17	2	0	0	4	0	0	0	8	1	18	2	0	3	.224	.307	.254
Karros, Eric, Chi.	114	365	336	37	96	150	16	1	12	40	0	1	0	28	1	46	1	1	14	.286	.340	.446
Kata, Matt, Ari.†	78	322	288	42	74	121	16	5	7	29	5	3	1	25	0	53	3	2	4	.257	.315	.420
Kearns, Austin, Cin.	82	338	292	39	77	133	11	0	15	58	0	0	5	41	1	68	5	2	7	.264	.364	.455
Keisler, Randy, S.D.*	3	2	2	0	0	0	0	0	0	0	0	0	0	0	0	1	0	0	0	.000	.000	.000
Kelton, David, Chi.	10	12	12	1	2	3	1	0	0	1	0	0	0	0	0	5	0	0	0	.167	.167	.250
Kendall, Jason, Pit.	150	666	587	84	191	244	29	3	6	58	1	3	25	49	3	40	8	7	9	.325	.399	.416
Kent, Jeff, Hou.	130	552	505	77	150	257	39	1	22	93	0	3	5	39	2	85	6	2	13	.297	.351	.509
Kida, Masao, L.A.	3	4	4	0	1	1	0	0	0	0	0	0	0	0	0	2	0	0	0	.250	.250	.250
Kieschnick, Brooks, Mil.*	70	76	70	12	21	43	1	0	7	12	0	0	0	6	0	13	0	0	2	.300	.355	.614
Kim, Byung-Hyun, Ari.	7	15	13	0	2	3	1	0	0	1	2	0	0	0	0	2	0	0	0	.154	.154	.231

Player, Team	G	TPA	AB	R	H	TB	2B	3B	HR	RBI	SH	SF	HP	BB	IBB	SO	SB	CS	GDP	Avg.	OBP	Slg.
Kim, Sun-Woo, Mon.	4	3	3	0	0	0	0	0	0	0	0	0	0	0	0	1	0	0	0	.000	.000	.000
Kinkade, Mike, L.A.	88	191	162	25	35	57	7	0	5	14	0	0	16	13	2	38	1	3	8	.216	.335	.352
Kinney, Matt, Mil.	33	62	55	3	2	3	1	0	0	0	5	0	0	2	0	27	0	0	1	.036	.070	.055
Klesko, Ryan, S.D.*	121	474	397	47	100	181	18	0	21	67	0	9	3	65	5	83	2	5	11	.252	.354	.456
Kline, Steve, St.L.†	78	3	2	0	1	2	1	0	0	2	1	0	0	0	0	0	0	0	0	.500	.500	1.000
Knott, Eric, Mon.*	13	5	5	0	0	0	0	0	0	0	0	0	0	0	0	2	0	0	0	.000	.000	.000
Kotsay, Mark, S.D.*	128	541	482	64	128	185	28	4	7	38	1	1	1	56	3	82	6	3	8	.266	.343	.384
Lane, Jason, Hou.	18	27	27	5	8	22	2	0	4	10	0	0	0	0	0	2	0	0	0	.296	.296	.815
Langerhans, Ryan, Atl.*	16	15	15	2	4	4	0	0	0	0	0	0	0	0	0	6	0	0	1	.267	.267	.267
Larkin, Barry, Cin.	70	265	241	39	68	92	16	1	2	18	1	0	1	22	0	32	2	0	7	.282	.345	.382
Larson, Brandon, Cin.	32	104	89	6	9	13	1	0	1	9	0	2	0	13	0	31	2	2	2	.101	.212	.146
LaRue, Jason, Cin.	118	437	379	52	87	160	23	1	16	50	1	4	20	33	4	111	3	3	9	.230	.321	.422
Lawrence, Brian, S.D.	33	72	67	7	15	20	2	0	1	5	2	0	0	3	0	18	0	0	1	.224	.257	.299
Ledee, Ricky, Phi.*	121	291	255	37	63	121	15	2	13	46	1	1	0	34	5	59	0	0	4	.247	.334	.475
Lee, Derrek, Fla.	155	643	539	91	146	274	31	2	31	92	0	6	10	88	7	131	21	8	9	.271	.379	.508
Leiter, Al, N.Y.*	30	60	53	2	1	1	0	0	0	0	5	0	0	2	0	28	0	0	2	.019	.055	.019
Levrault, Allen, Fla.	19	2	2	0	0	0	0	0	0	0	0	0	0	0	0	1	0	0	0	.000	.000	.000
Lidge, Brad, Hou.	78	4	4	0	0	0	0	0	0	0	0	0	0	0	0	4	0	0	0	.000	.000	.000
Lieberthal, Mike, Phi.	131	561	508	68	159	230	30	1	13	81	0	3	12	38	2	59	0	0	14	.313	.373	.453
Liefer, Jeff, Mon.*	35	92	88	6	17	29	3	0	3	18	0	1	0	3	0	26	0	1	2	.193	.217	.330
Linden, Todd, S.F.†	18	39	38	2	8	12	1	0	1	6	0	0	0	1	0	8	0	0	2	.211	.231	.316
Linebrink, Scott, Hou.-S.D.	52	13	12	0	2	3	1	0	0	0	1	0	0	0	0	7	0	0	0	.167	.167	.250
Lo Duca, Paul, L.A.	147	630	568	64	155	214	34	2	7	52	7	1	10	44	6	54	0	2	21	.273	.335	.377
Lockhart, Keith, S.D.*	62	111	95	18	23	39	5	1	3	8	2	0	1	13	0	19	0	1	2	.242	.339	.411
Loewer, Carlton, S.D.	5	7	5	0	0	0	0	0	0	1	1	0	0	1	0	3	0	0	1	.000	.167	.000
Lofton, Kenny, Pit.-Chi.*	140	610	547	97	162	246	32	8	12	46	7	6	4	46	3	51	30	9	6	.296	.352	.450
Looper, Braden, Fla.	74	2	1	1	1	1	0	0	0	0	1	0	0	0	0	0	0	0	0	1.000	1.000	1.000
Lopez, Felipe, Cin.†	59	229	197	28	42	59	7	2	2	13	2	1	1	28	1	59	8	5	2	.213	.313	.299
Lopez, Javier, Col.*	75	5	5	1	1	1	0	0	0	1	0	0	0	0	0	1	0	0	0	.200	.200	.200
Lopez, Javy, Atl.	129	495	457	89	150	314	29	3	43	109	0	1	4	33	5	90	0	1	10	.328	.378	.687
Loretta, Mark, S.D.	154	653	589	74	185	260	28	4	13	72	3	4	3	54	2	62	5	4	17	.314	.372	.441
Lowell, Mike, Fla.	130	557	492	76	136	261	27	1	32	105	0	6	3	56	6	78	3	1	14	.276	.350	.530
Lowry, Noah, S.F.*	4	2	2	1	1	1	0	0	0	0	0	0	0	0	0	1	0	0	0	.500	.500	.500
Lugo, Julio, Hou.	22	74	65	6	16	19	3	0	0	2	0	0	0	9	1	12	2	1	2	.246	.338	.292
Lunsford, Trey, S.F.	1	1	1	0	0	0	0	0	0	0	0	0	0	0	0	0	0	0	0	.000	.000	.000
Machado, Andy, Phi.†	1	0	0	0	0	0	0	0	0	0	0	0	0	0	0	0	1	0	0	.000	.000	.000
Macias, Jose, Mon.†	111	288	272	31	65	96	15	2	4	22	2	1	2	11	1	45	4	3	5	.239	.273	.353
Mackowiak, Rob, Pit.*	77	193	174	20	47	77	4	4	6	19	0	0	4	15	2	53	6	0	1	.270	.342	.443
Maddux, Greg, Atl.	37	78	68	2	10	13	3	0	0	2	8	1	0	1	0	21	0	0	0	.147	.157	.191
Mahomes, Pat, Pit.	9	4	4	0	1	1	0	0	0	0	0	0	0	0	0	2	0	0	0	.250	.250	.250
Manning, David, Mil.	2	1	1	0	0	0	0	0	0	0	0	0	0	0	0	1	0	0	0	.000	.000	.000
Manon, Julio, Mon.	23	1	1	0	0	0	0	0	0	0	0	0	0	0	0	1	0	0	0	.000	.000	.000
Marquis, Jason, Atl.*	21	4	2	0	1	2	1	0	0	1	2	0	0	0	0	0	0	0	0	.500	.500	1.000
Marrero, Eli, St.L.	41	116	107	10	24	38	4	2	2	20	0	2	0	7	0	18	0	1	0	.224	.267	.355
Martin, Tom, L.A.*	80	1	1	0	0	0	0	0	0	0	0	0	0	0	0	1	0	0	0	.000	.000	.000
Martinez, Luis, Mil.*	4	4	4	0	0	0	0	0	0	0	0	0	0	0	0	3	0	0	0	.000	.000	.000
Martinez, Ramon, Chi.	108	333	293	30	83	110	16	1	3	34	6	8	2	24	1	50	0	1	8	.283	.333	.375
Martinez, Tino, St.L.*	138	547	476	66	130	204	25	2	15	69	2	7	9	53	7	71	1	1	14	.273	.352	.429
Mateo, Henry, Mon.†	100	169	154	29	37	42	3	1	0	7	1	0	3	11	0	38	11	1	0	.240	.304	.273
Mateo, Ruben, Cin.	74	224	207	16	50	68	9	0	3	18	0	2	3	12	1	53	0	0	4	.242	.290	.329
Matheny, Mike, St.L.	141	498	441	43	111	157	18	2	8	47	8	3	2	44	16	81	1	1	11	.252	.320	.356
Matranga, Dave, Hou.	6	5	5	1	1	4	0	0	1	1	0	0	0	0	0	2	0	0	0	.200	.200	.800
Matthews Jr., Gary, S.D.†	103	341	306	50	83	116	19	1	4	22	0	0	1	34	0	66	12	5	4	.271	.346	.379
Matthews, Mike, S.D.*	77	3	2	0	0	0	0	0	0	0	1	0	0	0	0	1	0	0	0	.000	.000	.000
McCracken, Quinton, Ari.†	115	226	203	17	46	55	5	2	0	18	5	3	0	15	2	34	5	1	4	.227	.276	.271
McEwing, Joe, N.Y.	119	313	278	31	67	81	11	0	1	16	6	1	3	25	4	57	3	0	6	.241	.309	.291
McGriff, Fred, L.A.*	86	329	297	32	74	127	14	0	13	40	0	0	1	31	4	66	0	0	7	.249	.322	.428
Meadows, Brian, Pit.	34	18	14	0	1	1	0	0	0	0	3	0	0	1	0	6	0	0	0	.071	.133	.071
Meluskey, Mitch, Hou.†	12	12	9	1	1	2	1	0	0	2	0	1	0	2	0	2	0	0	0	.111	.250	.222
Mendez, Donaldo, S.D.	26	94	84	10	19	31	6	0	2	9	0	1	2	7	1	32	1	0	0	.226	.298	.369
Mercado, Hector, Phi.*	13	2	2	0	0	0	0	0	0	0	0	0	0	0	0	0	0	0	1	.000	.000	.000
Merced, Orlando, Hou.*	123	230	212	20	49	79	17	2	3	26	0	2	1	15	2	33	3	2	3	.231	.283	.373
Mercker, Kent, Cin.-Atl.*	67	1	1	0	0	0	0	0	0	0	0	0	0	0	0	1	0	0	0	.000	.000	.000
Merloni, Lou, S.D.	65	179	151	20	41	55	7	2	1	17	2	3	1	22	2	33	2	3	3	.272	.362	.364
Miceli, Dan, Col.-Hou.	37	1	1	0	0	0	0	0	0	0	0	0	0	0	0	1	0	0	0	.000	.000	.000
Michaels, Jason, Phi.	76	125	109	20	36	62	11	0	5	17	0	0	1	15	1	22	0	0	3	.330	.416	.569
Miller, Corky, Cin.	14	38	30	4	8	8	0	0	0	1	0	1	2	5	0	7	0	0	1	.267	.395	.267
Miller, Damian, Chi.	114	400	352	34	82	130	19	1	9	36	7	1	1	39	6	91	1	0	15	.233	.310	.369
Miller, Wade, Hou.	36	70	63	4	10	13	3	0	0	6	5	0	0	2	0	16	0	0	0	.159	.185	.206
Millwood, Kevin, Phi.	35	79	68	4	4	6	2	0	0	1	6	0	0	5	0	34	0	0	2	.059	.123	.088
Mitre, Sergio, Chi.	3	2	2	1	1	1	0	0	0	0	0	0	0	0	0	1	0	0	0	.500	.500	.500
Moehler, Brian, Hou.	3	4	4	0	0	0	0	0	0	0	0	0	0	0	0	2	0	0	0	.000	.000	.000
Moeller, Chad, Ari.	78	269	239	29	64	104	17	1	7	29	3	2	2	23	11	59	1	2	7	.268	.335	.435
Mondesi, Raul, Ari.	45	183	162	27	49	83	8	1	8	22	0	2	1	18	0	31	5	4	3	.302	.372	.512
Mordecai, Mike, Fla.	65	101	89	11	19	29	4	0	2	8	3	1	0	8	3	21	3	0	0	.213	.276	.326
Moreno, Orber, N.Y.	7	1	1	0	0	0	0	0	0	0	0	0	0	0	0	1	0	0	0	.000	.000	.000
Morris, Matt, St.L.	27	66	52	5	10	15	2	0	1	3	12	0	0	2	0	16	0	0	1	.192	.222	.288
Moss, Damian, S.F.	21	37	29	1	7	7	0	0	0	1	7	0	0	1	0	12	0	0	0	.241	.267	.241
Mota, Guillermo, L.A.	76	9	9	1	2	5	0	0	1	2	0	0	0	0	0	4	0	0	0	.222	.222	.556
Mullen, Scott, L.A.	1	1	1	0	0	0	0	0	0	0	0	0	0	0	0	1	0	0	0	.000	.000	.000
Munro, Pete, Hou.	40	4	1	0	0	0	0	0	0	0	2	0	0	1	0	0	0	0	0	.000	.500	.000
Myers, Brett, Phi.	33	69	62	3	9	10	1	0	0	1	5	0	0	2	0	18	0	0	1	.145	.172	.161
Myers, Rodney, L.A.	4	2	2	0	0	0	0	0	0	0	0	0	0	0	0	2	0	0	0	.000	.000	.000
Nady, Xavier, S.D.	110	404	371	50	99	145	17	1	9	39	2	1	6	24	0	74	6	2	14	.267	.321	.391
Nagy, Charles, S.D.*	5	2	2	0	0	0	0	0	0	0	0	0	0	0	0	0	0	0	0	.000	.000	.000

Player, Team	G	TPA	AB	R	H	TB	2B	3B	HR	RBI	SH	SF	HP	BB	IBB	SO	SB	CS	GDP	Avg.	OBP	Slg.
Nathan, Joe, S.F.	78	2	1	0	0	0	0	0	0	0	1	0	0	0	0	1	0	0	0	.000	.000	.000
Neagle, Denny, Col.*	7	13	11	0	0	0	0	0	0	0	2	0	0	0	0	4	0	0	1	.000	.000	.000
Nevin, Phil, S.D.	59	248	226	30	63	110	8	0	13	46	0	1	0	21	1	44	2	0	9	.279	.339	.487
Niekro, Lance, S.F.	5	5	5	2	1	2	1	0	0	2	0	0	0	0	0	1	0	0	0	.200	.200	.400
Nomo, Hideo, L.A.	33	74	65	4	9	13	1	0	1	3	6	0	0	3	0	25	0	0	1	.138	.176	.200
Norton, Greg, Col.†	114	197	179	19	47	80	15	0	6	31	0	1	1	16	0	47	2	1	4	.263	.325	.447
Norton, Phil, Chi.-Cin.	21	1	1	0	0	0	0	0	0	0	0	0	0	0	0	1	0	0	0	.000	.000	.000
Nunez, Abraham O., Pit.†	118	351	311	37	77	111	8	7	4	35	9	2	3	26	1	53	9	3	8	.248	.310	.357
O'Leary, Troy, Chi.*	93	194	174	18	38	62	9	0	5	28	1	4	1	14	1	31	3	0	8	.218	.275	.356
Obermueller, Wes, Mil.	12	25	23	1	3	3	0	0	0	1	2	0	0	0	0	6	0	0	0	.130	.130	.130
Ohka, Tomo, Mon.	35	65	55	2	10	10	0	0	0	3	8	0	0	2	0	10	0	0	1	.182	.211	.182
Ohme, Kevin, St.L.*	2	1	1	0	1	1	0	0	0	0	0	0	0	0	0	0	0	0	0	1.000	1.000	1.000
Ojeda, Augie, Chi.†	12	27	25	2	3	3	0	0	0	0	0	0	1	1	1	5	0	0	1	.120	.185	.120
Ojeda, Miguel, S.D.	61	163	141	13	33	51	6	0	4	22	0	1	3	18	2	26	1	1	2	.234	.331	.362
Oliver, Darren, Col.	35	73	67	6	17	23	3	0	1	8	2	0	1	3	0	17	0	0	1	.254	.296	.343
Olmedo, Ray, Cin.†	79	250	230	24	55	63	6	1	0	17	7	0	0	13	0	46	1	1	4	.239	.280	.274
Ortiz, Russ, Atl.	35	82	70	6	18	28	4	0	2	10	6	1	1	4	0	17	0	0	1	.257	.303	.400
Osik, Keith, Mil.	80	275	241	22	60	78	12	0	2	21	0	0	3	31	0	44	0	1	7	.249	.342	.324
Oswalt, Roy, Hou.	21	48	39	4	7	8	1	0	0	0	7	0	0	2	0	15	0	0	0	.179	.220	.205
Overbay, Lyle, Ari.*	86	293	254	23	70	102	20	0	4	28	0	2	2	35	7	67	1	0	8	.276	.365	.402
Ozuna, Pablo, Col.	17	45	40	5	8	9	1	0	0	2	1	0	2	2	0	6	3	0	1	.200	.273	.225
Padilla, Vicente, Phi.	32	77	67	1	4	4	0	0	0	1	3	0	1	6	0	34	0	0	1	.060	.149	.060
Painter, Lance, St.L.*	22	1	1	0	0	0	0	0	0	0	0	0	0	0	0	0	0	0	0	.000	.000	.000
Palmeiro, Orlando, St.L.*	141	364	317	37	86	110	13	1	3	33	7	6	2	32	3	31	3	3	1	.271	.336	.347
Patterson, Corey, Chi.*	83	347	329	49	98	168	17	7	13	55	0	2	1	15	2	77	16	5	5	.298	.329	.511
Patterson, John, Ari.	16	13	13	1	1	1	0	0	0	1	0	0	0	0	0	4	0	0	0	.077	.077	.077
Paul, Josh, Chi.	3	7	6	0	0	0	0	0	0	0	1	0	0	0	0	3	0	0	0	.000	.000	.000
Pavano, Carl, Fla.	33	68	61	4	6	10	2	1	0	1	5	0	0	2	0	27	0	0	0	.098	.127	.164
Payton, Jay, Col.	157	658	600	93	181	307	32	5	28	89	5	3	7	43	3	77	6	4	27	.302	.354	.512
Peavy, Jake, S.D.	32	68	55	4	4	4	0	0	0	1	8	0	2	3	0	21	0	0	0	.073	.150	.073
Pellow, Kit, Col.	11	21	18	6	8	16	3	1	1	4	0	1	2	0	0	4	0	0	0	.444	.476	.889
Pena, Wily Mo, Cin.	80	181	165	20	36	59	6	1	5	16	1	0	3	12	2	53	3	2	2	.218	.283	.358
Penny, Brad, Fla.	33	73	68	3	9	18	1	1	2	8	5	0	0	0	0	27	0	0	2	.132	.132	.265
Perez, Eddie, Mil.	107	375	350	26	95	147	17	1	11	45	6	2	0	17	3	47	0	1	16	.271	.304	.420
Perez, Eduardo, St.L.	105	289	253	47	72	121	16	0	11	41	1	2	4	29	1	53	5	2	7	.285	.365	.478
Perez, Neifi, S.F.†	120	353	328	27	84	114	19	4	1	31	9	2	0	14	3	23	3	2	9	.256	.285	.348
Perez, Odalis, L.A.*	30	63	52	3	5	5	0	0	0	0	10	0	0	1	0	14	0	0	2	.096	.113	.096
Perez, Oliver, S.D.-Pit.*	24	44	39	0	7	7	0	0	0	4	3	1	0	1	0	11	0	0	1	.179	.195	.179
Perez, Timo, N.Y.*	127	382	346	32	93	126	21	0	4	42	7	9	2	18	1	29	5	6	5	.269	.301	.364
Perez, Tomas, Phi.†	125	327	298	39	79	114	18	1	5	33	4	2	0	23	11	54	0	1	7	.265	.316	.383
Petrick, Ben, Col.	3	2	2	0	0	0	0	0	0	0	0	0	0	0	0	1	0	0	0	.000	.000	.000
Phelps, Tommy, Fla.*	27	14	11	1	1	1	0	0	0	0	1	0	0	2	0	3	0	0	1	.091	.231	.091
Phillips, Jason, N.Y.	119	453	403	45	120	178	25	0	11	58	0	1	10	39	3	50	0	1	21	.298	.373	.442
Piazza, Mike, N.Y.	68	273	234	37	67	113	13	0	11	34	0	3	1	35	3	40	0	0	11	.286	.377	.483
Pierre, Juan, Fla.*	162	747	668	100	204	249	28	7	1	41	15	3	5	55	1	35	65	20	9	.305	.361	.373
Podsednik, Scott, Mil.*	154	628	558	100	175	247	29	8	9	58	8	2	4	56	2	91	43	10	11	.314	.379	.443
Polanco, Placido, Phi.	122	554	492	87	142	220	30	3	14	63	8	4	8	42	1	38	14	2	16	.289	.352	.447
Ponson, Sidney, S.F.	10	25	22	1	2	3	1	0	0	0	3	0	0	0	0	5	0	0	1	.091	.091	.136
Porter, Colin, Hou.*	24	33	32	5	6	6	0	0	0	0	0	0	0	1	0	17	1	0	1	.188	.212	.188
Powell, Brian, S.F.	1	2	2	0	0	0	0	0	0	0	0	0	0	0	0	0	0	0	0	.000	.000	.000
Pratt, Todd, Phi.	43	156	125	16	34	58	10	1	4	20	1	2	6	22	0	38	0	0	3	.272	.400	.464
Prior, Mark, Chi.	32	81	72	6	18	25	4	0	1	6	7	0	0	2	0	27	0	0	1	.250	.270	.347
Puffer, Brandon, Hou.	13	3	3	0	0	0	0	0	0	0	0	0	0	0	0	2	0	0	0	.000	.000	.000
Pujols, Albert, St.L.	157	685	591	137	212	394	51	1	43	124	0	5	10	79	12	65	5	1	13	.359	.439	.667
Punto, Nick, Phi.†	64	99	92	14	20	25	2	0	1	4	0	0	0	7	1	22	2	1	0	.217	.273	.272
Quantrill, Paul, L.A.*	89	1	1	0	0	0	0	0	0	0	0	0	0	0	0	1	0	0	0	.000	.000	.000
Quevedo, Ruben, Mil.	9	11	10	1	3	3	0	0	0	0	1	0	0	0	0	5	0	0	0	.300	.300	.300
Quintero, Humberto, S.D.	12	24	23	1	5	5	0	0	0	2	0	0	0	1	1	6	0	0	0	.217	.250	.217
Ramirez, Aramis, Pit.-Chi.	159	670	607	75	165	282	32	2	27	106	0	11	10	42	3	99	2	2	21	.272	.324	.465
Ramirez, Horacio, Atl.*	29	67	61	3	6	8	0	1	0	2	6	0	0	0	0	12	0	0	1	.098	.098	.131
Randall, Scott, Cin.	15	4	4	0	1	1	0	0	0	0	0	0	0	0	0	1	0	0	0	.250	.250	.250
Randolph, Stephen, Ari.*	50	4	3	0	0	0	0	0	0	0	1	0	0	0	0	2	0	0	0	.000	.000	.000
Ransom, Cody, S.F.	20	28	27	7	6	10	1	0	1	1	0	0	0	1	0	11	0	0	0	.222	.250	.370
Reames, Britt, Mon.	2	1	1	0	0	0	0	0	0	0	0	0	0	0	0	0	0	0	0	.000	.000	.000
Reboulet, Jeff, Pit.	93	299	261	37	63	86	10	2	3	25	6	1	4	27	3	47	2	1	6	.241	.321	.330
Redding, Tim, Hou.	33	60	50	4	10	13	3	0	0	2	8	0	0	2	0	19	0	0	0	.200	.231	.260
Redman, Mark, Fla.*	29	66	61	0	1	1	0	0	0	1	4	0	0	1	0	31	0	0	1	.016	.032	.016
Redman, Prentice, N.Y.	15	27	24	3	3	7	1	0	1	2	1	0	1	1	0	9	2	0	1	.125	.192	.292
Redman, Tike, Pit.*	56	248	230	36	76	111	16	5	3	19	2	0	2	14	0	18	7	3	1	.330	.374	.483
Redmond, Mike, Fla.	59	141	125	12	30	39	7	1	0	11	2	2	5	7	0	16	0	0	2	.240	.302	.312
Reed, Steve, Col.	67	1	0	0	0	0	0	0	0	1	0	1	0	0	0	0	0	0	0	.000	.000	.000
Reese, Pokey, Pit.	37	120	107	9	23	28	2	0	1	12	2	2	0	9	1	31	6	0	2	.215	.271	.262
Reith, Brian, Cin.	42	7	7	0	0	0	0	0	0	0	0	0	0	0	0	4	0	0	0	.000	.000	.000
Reitsma, Chris, Cin.	57	8	8	0	1	1	0	0	0	2	0	0	0	0	0	6	0	0	0	.125	.125	.125
Remlinger, Mike, Chi.*	73	1	1	0	0	0	0	0	0	0	0	0	0	0	0	1	0	0	0	.000	.000	.000
Renteria, Edgar, St.L.	157	663	587	96	194	282	47	1	13	100	3	7	1	65	12	54	34	7	21	.330	.394	.480
Reyes, Jose, N.Y.†	69	292	274	47	84	119	12	4	5	32	2	3	0	13	0	36	13	3	1	.307	.334	.434
Reyes, Rene, Col.†	53	123	116	13	30	45	7	1	2	7	1	1	0	5	0	19	2	1	3	.259	.287	.388
Reynolds, Shane, Atl.	30	65	54	0	5	5	0	0	0	3	10	0	0	1	0	26	0	0	1	.093	.109	.093
Richard, Chris, Col.*	19	30	27	3	6	12	1	1	1	3	0	0	0	3	0	6	0	1	1	.222	.300	.444
Riedling, John, Cin.	55	19	18	2	4	4	0	0	0	2	1	0	0	0	0	10	0	0	0	.222	.222	.222
Ritchie, Todd, Mil.	5	11	9	0	2	2	0	0	0	0	2	0	0	0	0	2	0	0	0	.222	.222	.222
Rivera, Carlos, Pit.*	78	107	95	12	21	35	5	0	3	10	1	2	1	8	2	28	0	0	2	.221	.283	.368
Rivera, Michael, S.D.	19	58	53	2	9	13	1	0	1	2	0	0	0	5	0	11	0	0	4	.170	.241	.245
Rivera, Ruben, S.F.	31	55	50	6	9	17	2	0	2	4	0	0	0	5	1	14	1	0	0	.180	.255	.340

Player, Team	G	TPA	AB	R	H	TB	2B	3B	HR	RBI	SH	SF	HP	BB	IBB	SO	SB	CS	GDP	Avg.	OBP	Slg.
Roa, Joe, Phi.-Col.-S.D.	28	7	7	0	2	2	0	0	0	1	0	0	0	0	0	3	0	0	0	.286	.286	.286
Roach, Jason, N.Y.	2	2	2	0	2	2	0	0	0	0	0	0	0	0	0	0	0	0	0	1.000	1.000	1.000
Roberts, Dave, L.A.*	107	440	388	56	97	119	6	5	2	16	5	0	4	43	1	39	40	14	0	.250	.331	.307
Robertson, Jeriome, Hou.*	33	58	52	4	8	10	0	1	0	3	5	0	0	1	0	14	0	0	2	.154	.170	.192
Robinson, Kerry, St.L.*	116	221	208	19	52	67	6	3	1	16	4	0	1	8	3	27	6	1	3	.250	.281	.322
Rodriguez, Felix, S.F.	68	1	1	0	1	1	0	0	0	0	0	0	0	0	0	0	0	0	0	1.000	1.000	1.000
Rodriguez, Ivan, Fla.	144	578	511	90	152	242	36	3	16	85	1	5	6	55	6	92	10	6	18	.297	.369	.474
Rolen, Scott, St.L.	154	657	559	98	160	295	49	1	28	104	0	7	9	82	5	104	13	3	19	.286	.382	.528
Rollins, Jimmy, Phi.†	156	689	628	85	165	243	42	6	8	62	5	2	0	54	4	113	20	12	9	.263	.320	.387
Romano, Jason, L.A.	37	37	36	3	3	3	0	0	0	0	0	0	0	1	0	8	2	0	2	.083	.108	.083
Romero, Mandy, Col.†	3	9	7	2	3	4	1	0	0	0	0	0	2	0	0	1	0	0	1	.429	.556	.571
Ross, Dave, L.A.	40	140	124	19	32	69	7	0	10	18	0	1	2	13	0	42	0	0	4	.258	.336	.556
Ruan, Wilkin, L.A.	21	41	41	2	9	13	2	1	0	2	0	0	0	0	0	7	1	0	0	.220	.220	.317
Rueter, Kirk, S.F.*	27	61	53	5	7	7	0	0	0	3	6	0	0	2	0	8	1	0	0	.132	.164	.132
Rusch, Glendon, Mil.*	33	41	34	2	7	7	0	0	0	2	4	0	0	3	0	7	0	0	2	.206	.270	.206
Saarloos, Kirk, Hou.	36	9	5	0	0	0	0	0	0	1	3	0	0	1	0	0	0	0	0	.000	.167	.000
Sanchez, Alex, Mil.*	43	176	163	15	46	62	10	3	0	10	2	2	2	7	0	28	8	6	1	.282	.316	.380
Sanchez, Rey, N.Y.	56	183	174	11	36	41	3	1	0	12	0	1	0	8	2	18	1	1	7	.207	.240	.236
Sanders, Reggie, Pit.	130	498	453	74	129	257	27	4	31	87	0	2	5	38	4	110	15	5	10	.285	.345	.567
Santiago, Benito, S.F.	108	434	401	53	112	170	21	2	11	56	0	2	2	29	0	69	0	1	13	.279	.329	.424
Santos, Francisco, S.F.*	8	15	15	2	3	8	2	0	1	1	0	0	0	0	0	3	0	0	0	.200	.200	.533
Sardinha, Dane, Cin.	1	2	2	0	0	0	0	0	0	0	0	0	0	0	0	1	0	0	0	.000	.000	.000
Sauerbeck, Scott, Pit.	53	1	1	0	0	0	0	0	0	0	0	0	0	0	0	1	0	0	0	.000	.000	.000
Schilling, Curt, Ari.	24	59	52	4	3	3	0	0	0	0	4	0	0	3	0	21	0	0	0	.058	.109	.058
Schmidt, Jason, S.F.	29	78	61	2	4	4	0	0	0	0	15	0	0	2	0	30	0	0	0	.066	.095	.066
Schneider, Brian, Mon.*	108	377	335	34	77	132	26	1	9	46	1	2	2	37	8	75	0	2	12	.230	.309	.394
Scutaro, Marco, N.Y.	48	91	75	10	16	26	4	0	2	6	1	1	1	13	2	14	2	0	1	.213	.333	.347
Sears, Todd, S.D.*	9	8	8	2	2	3	1	0	0	0	0	0	0	0	0	3	0	0	0	.250	.250	.375
Seo, Jae Weong, N.Y.	35	58	51	3	5	6	1	0	0	0	4	0	0	3	0	19	0	0	0	.098	.148	.118
Serafini, Dan, Cin.†	11	7	6	0	0	0	0	0	0	0	1	0	0	0	0	2	0	0	0	.000	.000	.000
Sexson, Richie, Mil.	162	718	606	97	165	332	28	2	45	124	0	5	9	98	7	151	2	3	18	.272	.379	.548
Sheets, Ben, Mil.	34	72	66	0	5	5	0	0	0	2	5	0	0	1	0	35	0	0	0	.076	.090	.076
Sheffield, Gary, Atl.	155	678	576	126	190	348	37	2	39	132	0	8	8	86	6	55	18	4	16	.330	.419	.604
Shinjo, Tsuyoshi, N.Y.	62	124	114	10	22	28	3	0	1	7	2	1	1	6	1	12	0	1	0	.193	.238	.246
Shuey, Paul, L.A.	62	2	2	0	0	0	0	0	0	0	0	0	0	0	0	0	0	0	0	.000	.000	.000
Silva, Carlos, Phi.	62	10	9	0	2	3	1	0	0	1	1	0	0	0	0	2	0	0	1	.222	.222	.333
Simon, Randall, Pit.-Chi.*	124	431	410	47	113	178	17	0	16	72	0	1	4	16	2	37	0	0	7	.276	.309	.434
Simontacchi, Jason, St.L.	48	38	38	3	5	6	1	0	0	0	0	0	0	0	0	14	0	0	0	.132	.132	.158
Smith, Dan, Mon.	32	2	2	0	0	0	0	0	0	0	0	0	0	0	0	0	0	0	0	.000	.000	.000
Smith, Mark, Mil.	33	69	63	8	15	28	4	0	3	10	0	2	0	4	0	13	0	0	5	.238	.275	.444
Smitherman, Stephen, Cin.	21	47	44	3	7	12	2	0	1	6	0	0	0	3	0	9	1	0	0	.159	.213	.273
Smoltz, John, Atl.	62	1	1	0	0	0	0	0	0	0	0	0	0	0	0	0	0	0	0	.000	.000	.000
Snow, J.T., S.F.*	103	396	330	48	90	138	18	3	8	51	1	2	8	55	0	55	1	2	7	.273	.387	.418
Sosa, Sammy, Chi.	137	589	517	99	144	286	22	0	40	103	0	5	5	62	9	143	0	1	14	.279	.358	.553
Speier, Justin, Col.	72	1	1	0	0	0	0	0	0	0	0	0	0	0	0	0	0	0	0	.000	.000	.000
Spivey, Junior, Ari.	106	408	365	52	93	158	22	2	13	50	0	3	7	33	1	95	4	3	7	.255	.326	.433
Spooneybarger, Tim, Fla.	33	3	3	0	0	0	0	0	0	0	0	0	0	0	0	3	0	0	0	.000	.000	.000
Springer, Russ, St.L.	17	2	1	0	0	0	0	0	0	0	1	0	0	0	0	1	0	0	0	.000	.000	.000
Stairs, Matt, Pit.*	121	357	305	49	89	171	20	1	20	57	0	2	5	45	3	64	0	1	7	.292	.389	.561
Stanton, Mike, N.Y.*	50	1	1	0	0	0	0	0	0	0	0	0	0	0	0	0	0	0	1	.000	.000	.000
Stark, Denny, Col.	17	28	22	1	0	0	0	0	0	4	1	1	0	4	0	6	0	0	1	.000	.148	.000
Stenson, Dernell, Cin.*	37	93	81	14	20	34	5	0	3	13	0	1	0	11	0	24	0	0	0	.247	.333	.420
Stephenson, Garrett, St.L.	32	55	44	0	9	9	0	0	0	2	7	0	1	3	0	18	0	0	0	.205	.271	.205
Stewart, Scott, Mon.	51	2	2	0	0	0	0	0	0	0	0	0	0	0	0	1	0	0	0	.000	.000	.000
Stinnett, Kelly, Cin.-Phi.	67	207	186	14	44	66	13	0	3	19	2	1	4	14	3	52	0	0	3	.237	.302	.355
Stone, Ricky, Hou.	65	3	3	0	0	0	0	0	0	0	0	0	0	0	0	2	0	0	0	.000	.000	.000
Strange, Pat, N.Y.	6	1	1	0	0	0	0	0	0	0	0	0	0	0	0	0	0	0	0	.000	.000	.000
Strickland, Scott, N.Y.	19	2	1	0	0	0	0	0	0	0	1	0	0	0	0	0	0	0	0	.000	.000	.000
Stynes, Chris, Col.	138	502	443	71	113	183	31	3	11	73	3	2	6	48	1	76	3	1	8	.255	.335	.413
Suppan, Jeff, Pit.	21	52	41	3	12	13	1	0	0	2	8	0	1	2	0	11	0	0	0	.293	.341	.317
Sweeney, Mark, Col.*	67	106	97	13	25	40	9	0	2	14	0	0	0	9	1	27	0	1	2	.258	.321	.412
Taguchi, So, St.L.	43	59	54	9	14	28	3	1	3	13	1	0	0	4	1	11	0	0	2	.259	.310	.519
Tatis, Fernando, Mon.	53	196	175	15	34	46	6	0	2	15	0	0	3	18	0	40	2	1	7	.194	.281	.263
Tavarez, Julian, Pit.*	64	5	4	0	0	0	0	0	0	0	0	0	0	1	0	2	0	0	0	.000	.200	.000
Taylor, Reggie, Cin.*	100	194	180	17	39	63	5	2	5	19	2	0	1	11	0	68	7	0	4	.217	.266	.350
Tejera, Michael, Fla.*	50	16	15	0	1	1	0	0	0	0	1	0	0	0	0	1	0	0	1	.067	.067	.067
Telemaco, Amaury, Phi.	8	15	14	1	4	7	3	0	0	0	1	0	0	0	0	4	0	0	0	.286	.286	.500
Terrero, Luis, Ari.	5	5	4	0	1	1	0	0	0	0	0	0	1	0	0	1	0	0	0	.250	.400	.250
Thome, Jim, Phi.*	159	698	578	111	154	331	30	3	47	131	0	5	4	111	11	182	0	3	5	.266	.385	.573
Thurston, Joe, L.A.*	12	11	10	2	2	2	0	0	0	0	0	0	0	1	0	1	0	0	0	.200	.273	.200
Tollberg, Brian, S.D.	3	3	2	0	0	0	0	0	0	0	1	0	0	0	0	0	0	0	0	.000	.000	.000
Tomko, Brett, St.L.	35	78	63	4	18	19	1	0	0	9	11	0	0	4	0	15	0	1	1	.286	.328	.302
Torcato, Tony, S.F.*	14	18	16	0	3	4	1	0	0	1	1	0	1	0	0	4	0	0	0	.188	.235	.250
Torrealba, Yorvit, S.F.	66	221	200	22	52	78	10	2	4	29	3	2	2	14	1	39	1	0	3	.260	.312	.390
Torres, Salomon, Pit.	43	41	32	3	2	4	0	1	0	1	6	0	1	2	0	16	0	0	1	.063	.143	.125
Trachsel, Steve, N.Y.	36	72	58	3	11	13	2	0	0	4	11	1	0	2	0	16	0	0	1	.190	.213	.224
Tsao, Chin-hui, Col.	9	15	13	2	2	3	1	0	0	0	2	0	0	0	0	1	0	0	0	.154	.154	.231
Tucker, T.J., Mon.	46	20	19	1	5	6	1	0	0	0	1	0	0	0	0	6	0	0	0	.263	.263	.316
Urbina, Ugueth, Fla.	33	2	0	0	0	0	0	0	0	0	1	0	0	1	0	0	0	0	0	.000	1.000	.000
Uribe, Juan, Col.	87	343	316	45	80	135	19	3	10	33	6	1	3	17	0	60	7	2	3	.253	.297	.427
Utley, Chase, Phi.*	43	152	134	13	32	50	10	1	2	21	0	1	6	11	0	22	2	0	3	.239	.322	.373
Valderrama, Carlos, S.F.	7	7	7	0	1	1	0	0	0	0	0	0	0	0	0	3	1	0	0	.143	.143	.143
Valent, Eric, Cin.*	18	44	42	3	9	9	0	0	0	1	0	0	0	2	0	9	0	0	0	.214	.250	.214
Valverde, Jose, Ari.	54	1	1	1	1	2	1	0	0	0	0	0	0	0	0	0	0	0	0	1.000	1.000	2.000
Van Poppel, Todd, Cin.	9	10	9	0	1	1	0	0	0	0	1	0	0	0	0	4	0	0	0	.111	.111	.111

Player, Team	G	TPA	AB	R	H	TB	2B	3B	HR	RBI	SH	SF	HP	BB	IBB	SO	SB	CS	GDP	Avg.	OBP	Slg.
Vance, Cory, Col.*	9	9	7	2	2	3	1	0	0	0	2	0	0	0	0	1	0	0	0	.286	.286	.429
Vander Wal, John, Mil.*	117	374	327	50	84	153	25	1	14	45	0	0	1	46	3	104	1	2	5	.257	.350	.468
Vargas, Claudio, Mon.	23	35	30	1	0	0	0	0	0	0	4	0	0	1	0	15	0	0	0	.000	.032	.000
Vaughn, Greg, Col.	22	46	37	8	7	19	3	0	3	5	0	1	0	8	0	13	0	0	0	.189	.326	.514
Vaughn, Mo, N.Y.*	27	96	79	10	15	26	2	0	3	15	0	1	2	14	2	22	0	0	2	.190	.323	.329
Vazquez, Javier, Mon.	34	79	65	5	10	12	0	1	0	6	12	0	0	2	0	8	0	0	0	.154	.179	.185
Vazquez, Ramon, S.D.*	116	484	422	56	110	144	17	4	3	30	5	3	2	52	2	88	10	3	4	.261	.342	.341
Velandia, Jorge, N.Y.	23	72	58	6	11	16	3	1	0	8	3	1	0	10	1	15	0	0	1	.190	.304	.276
Ventura, Robin, L.A.*	49	127	109	11	24	46	5	1	5	13	0	0	0	18	2	25	0	0	3	.220	.331	.422
Victorino, Shane, S.D.†	36	83	73	8	11	13	2	0	0	4	1	1	1	7	0	17	7	2	5	.151	.232	.178
Vidro, Jose, Mon.†	144	592	509	77	158	239	36	0	15	65	2	5	7	69	6	50	3	2	16	.310	.397	.470
Villafuerte, Brandon, S.D.	31	1	1	0	0	0	0	0	0	0	0	0	0	0	0	1	0	0	0	.000	.000	.000
Villarreal, Oscar, Ari.*	86	3	3	0	0	0	0	0	0	0	0	0	0	0	0	2	0	0	0	.000	.000	.000
Villone, Ron, Hou.*	19	44	42	2	7	11	1	0	1	2	1	0	1	0	0	17	0	0	0	.167	.186	.262
Vina, Fernando, St.L.*	61	285	259	35	65	99	14	4	4	23	3	1	11	11	0	24	4	4	5	.251	.309	.382
Vitiello, Joe, Mon.	38	86	76	12	26	41	6	0	3	13	0	1	2	7	0	14	0	0	1	.342	.407	.539
Vizcaino, Jose, Hou.†	91	203	189	14	47	69	7	3	3	26	4	1	1	8	3	22	0	1	5	.249	.281	.365
Vogelsong, Ryan, Pit.	6	8	6	0	1	1	0	0	0	0	2	0	0	0	0	2	0	0	0	.167	.167	.167
Wagner, Billy, Hou.*	78	3	2	1	0	0	0	0	0	1	0	0	0	1	0	0	0	0	0	.000	.333	.000
Walker, Larry, Col.*	143	564	454	86	129	216	25	7	16	79	0	1	11	98	14	87	7	4	9	.284	.422	.476
Ward, Daryle, L.A.*	52	114	109	6	20	21	1	0	0	9	0	1	1	3	0	19	0	0	4	.183	.211	.193
Watson, Matt, N.Y.*	15	25	23	0	4	6	2	0	0	2	1	0	0	1	0	5	0	0	1	.174	.208	.261
Wayne, Justin, Fla.	2	2	2	0	0	0	0	0	0	0	0	0	0	0	0	1	0	0	0	.000	.000	.000
Weathers, Dave, N.Y.	77	3	3	0	0	0	0	0	0	0	0	0	0	0	0	1	0	0	0	.000	.000	.000
Webb, Brandon, Ari.	29	59	50	2	5	6	1	0	0	0	7	0	0	2	0	21	0	0	0	.100	.135	.120
Weeks, Rickie, Mil.	7	14	12	1	2	3	1	0	0	0	0	0	1	1	0	6	0	0	0	.167	.286	.250
Wellemeyer, Todd, Chi.	15	3	1	0	0	0	0	0	0	0	1	0	0	1	0	0	0	0	0	.000	.500	.000
Wells, Kip, Pit.	34	73	68	8	13	19	3	0	1	5	4	0	0	1	0	23	0	0	0	.191	.203	.279
Wendell, Turk, Phi.*	56	2	2	0	0	0	0	0	0	0	0	0	0	0	0	2	0	0	0	.000	.000	.000
Wheeler, Dan, N.Y.	35	2	2	0	0	0	0	0	0	0	0	0	0	0	0	0	0	0	0	.000	.000	.000
White, Gabe, Cin.*	34	2	2	0	0	0	0	0	0	0	0	0	0	0	0	2	0	0	0	.000	.000	.000
White, Rondell, S.D.	115	449	413	49	115	192	17	3	18	66	0	3	8	25	2	71	1	4	11	.278	.330	.465
Widger, Chris, St.L.	44	112	102	9	24	33	9	0	0	14	1	2	1	6	1	20	0	0	5	.235	.279	.324
Wigginton, Ty, N.Y.	156	633	573	73	146	227	36	6	11	71	1	4	9	46	2	124	12	2	15	.255	.318	.396
Wilkerson, Brad, Mon.*	146	602	504	78	135	234	34	4	19	77	2	3	4	89	0	155	13	10	5	.268	.380	.464
Williams, Gerald, Fla.	27	35	31	5	4	5	1	0	0	3	2	0	0	2	0	5	3	0	0	.129	.182	.161
Williams, Jerome, S.F.	21	43	37	1	4	5	1	0	0	1	6	0	0	0	0	19	0	0	0	.108	.108	.135
Williams, Matt, Ari.	44	156	134	17	33	54	9	0	4	16	0	4	2	16	1	26	0	0	1	.246	.327	.403
Williams, Woody, St.L.	34	86	70	12	17	26	4	1	1	7	9	1	1	5	0	26	0	0	0	.243	.299	.371
Willis, Dontrelle, Fla.*	27	63	58	2	14	19	2	0	1	4	2	0	0	3	0	8	0	0	0	.241	.279	.328
Wilson, Craig, Pit.	116	358	309	49	81	158	15	4	18	48	0	1	13	35	4	89	3	1	6	.262	.360	.511
Wilson, Jack, Pit.	150	615	558	58	143	197	21	3	9	62	11	6	4	36	3	74	5	5	11	.256	.303	.353
Wilson, Paul, Cin.	29	59	52	1	6	7	1	0	0	1	4	1	0	2	0	28	0	0	1	.115	.145	.135
Wilson, Preston, Col.	155	661	600	94	169	322	43	1	36	141	0	3	4	54	1	139	14	7	23	.282	.343	.537
Wilson, Vance, N.Y.	96	292	268	28	65	100	9	1	8	39	2	2	5	15	1	56	1	2	6	.243	.293	.373
Wolf, Randy, Phi.*	33	82	70	9	14	20	6	0	0	11	6	1	0	5	0	22	0	0	1	.200	.250	.286
Womack, Tony, Ari.-Col.-Chi.*	103	364	349	43	79	107	14	4	2	22	2	1	3	9	0	47	13	5	7	.226	.251	.307
Wood, Kerry, Chi.	32	70	61	4	10	17	1	0	2	6	8	0	0	1	0	26	0	0	1	.164	.177	.279
Worrell, Tim, S.F.	76	3	3	0	0	0	0	0	0	0	0	0	0	0	0	3	0	0	0	.000	.000	.000
Wright, Jaret, S.D.-Atl.	50	5	4	0	1	2	1	0	0	0	1	0	0	0	0	2	0	0	0	.250	.250	.500
Yan, Esteban, St.L.	39	1	1	0	1	1	0	0	0	0	0	0	0	0	0	0	0	0	0	1.000	1.000	1.000
Young, Eric, Mil.-S.F.	135	541	475	80	119	186	20	1	15	34	2	2	5	57	2	44	28	12	12	.251	.336	.392
Young, Jason, Col.	8	8	7	1	2	3	1	0	0	0	0	0	0	1	0	1	0	0	0	.286	.375	.429
Young, Kevin, Pit.	52	96	84	8	17	27	4	0	2	7	0	0	0	12	0	25	1	0	1	.202	.302	.321
Zambrano, Carlos, Chi.†	32	80	75	9	18	29	5	0	2	6	4	0	0	1	0	26	0	0	2	.240	.250	.387
Zaun, Gregg, Hou.-Col.†	74	189	166	15	38	58	8	0	4	21	1	2	1	19	0	21	1	1	5	.229	.309	.349
Zeile, Todd, Mon.	34	127	113	11	29	50	2	2	5	19	0	1	3	10	0	18	1	0	3	.257	.331	.442
Zerbe, Chad, S.F.*	33	6	5	0	0	0	0	0	0	0	1	0	0	0	0	2	0	0	0	.000	.000	.000
Zoccolillo, Pete, Mil.*	20	39	37	0	4	5	1	0	0	3	0	0	0	2	0	13	0	0	1	.108	.154	.135

PLAYERS WITH TWO OR MORE TEAMS

Player, Team	G	TPA	AB	R	H	TB	2B	3B	HR	RBI	SH	SF	HP	BB	IBB	SO	SB	CS	GDP	Avg.	OBP	Slg.
Bay, Jason, S.D.	3	10	8	2	2	6	1	0	1	2	0	0	1	1	0	1	0	0	0	.250	.400	.750
Bay, Jason, Pit.	27	97	79	13	23	40	6	1	3	12	0	0	0	18	0	28	3	1	0	.291	.423	.506
Bellhorn, Mark, Chi.†	51	173	139	15	29	44	7	1	2	22	0	4	1	29	1	46	3	3	2	.209	.341	.317
Bellhorn, Mark, Col.†	48	134	110	12	26	29	3	0	0	4	1	0	2	21	0	32	2	3	1	.236	.368	.264
Burnitz, Jeromy, N.Y.*	65	259	234	38	64	136	18	0	18	45	0	0	4	21	6	55	1	4	4	.274	.344	.581
Burnitz, Jeromy, L.A.*	61	246	230	25	47	90	4	0	13	32	0	1	1	14	3	57	4	0	1	.204	.252	.391
Darensbourg, Vic, Col.*	3	0	0	0	0	0	0	0	0	0	0	0	0	0	0	0	0	0	0	...	...	...
Darensbourg, Vic, Mon.*	7	1	1	0	0	0	0	0	0	0	0	0	0	0	0	1	0	0	0	.000	.000	.000
de los Santos, Valerio, Mil.*	45	1	1	0	0	0	0	0	0	0	0	0	0	0	0	1	0	0	0	.000	.000	.000
de los Santos, Valerio, Phi.*	6	0	0	0	0	0	0	0	0	0	0	0	0	0	0	0	0	0	0	...	...	...
Giles, Brian, Pit.*	105	481	388	70	116	202	30	4	16	70	0	2	6	85	11	48	0	3	8	.299	.430	.521
Giles, Brian, S.D.*	29	128	104	23	31	51	4	2	4	18	0	2	2	20	1	10	4	0	4	.298	.414	.490
Hammonds, Jeffrey, Mil.	10	41	38	2	6	11	2	0	1	3	0	0	0	3	0	7	0	0	2	.158	.220	.289
Hammonds, Jeffrey, S.F.	36	108	94	20	26	45	10	0	3	10	0	0	1	13	0	21	1	0	1	.277	.370	.479
Harris, Lenny, Chi.*	75	146	131	11	24	30	3	0	1	7	1	1	0	13	3	20	1	0	1	.183	.255	.229
Harris, Lenny, Fla.*	13	17	14	3	4	4	0	0	0	1	0	0	0	3	0	1	0	0	1	.286	.412	.286
Herges, Matt, S.D.*	40	1	1	0	0	0	0	0	0	0	0	0	0	0	0	1	0	0	0	.000	.000	.000
Herges, Matt, S.F.*	27	2	2	0	1	1	0	0	0	0	0	0	0	0	0	0	0	0	0	.500	.500	.500
Hermanson, Dustin, St.L.	23	1	0	0	0	0	0	0	0	0	0	0	0	1	0	0	0	0	0	.000	1.000	.000
Hermanson, Dustin, S.F.	9	14	11	0	0	0	0	0	0	0	3	0	0	0	0	6	0	0	0	.000	.000	.000
Hernandez, Jose, Col.	69	286	257	33	61	93	6	1	8	27	0	2	0	27	0	95	1	1	6	.237	.308	.362
Hernandez, Jose, Chi.	23	72	69	6	13	24	3	1	2	9	0	0	0	3	0	26	0	0	1	.188	.222	.348

Player, Team	G	TPA	AB	R	H	TB	2B	3B	HR	RBI	SH	SF	HP	BB	IBB	SO	SB	CS	GDP	Avg.	OBP	Slg.
Hernandez, Jose, Pit.	58	213	193	19	43	63	9	1	3	21	0	3	1	16	0	56	1	0	9	.223	.282	.326
Hill, Bobby, Chi.†	5	5	4	0	1	1	0	0	0	0	0	0	0	1	0	2	0	0	1	.250	.400	.250
Hill, Bobby, Pit.†	1	4	3	1	1	1	0	0	0	0	0	0	0	1	0	0	0	0	0	.333	.500	.333
Linebrink, Scott, Hou.	9	9	8	0	0	0	0	0	0	0	1	0	0	0	0	5	0	0	0	.000	.000	.000
Linebrink, Scott, S.D.	43	4	4	0	2	3	1	0	0	0	0	0	0	0	0	2	0	0	0	.500	.500	.750
Lofton, Kenny, Pit.*	84	374	339	58	94	148	19	4	9	26	2	3	2	28	1	29	18	5	2	.277	.333	.437
Lofton, Kenny, Chi.*	56	236	208	39	68	98	13	4	3	20	5	3	2	18	2	22	12	4	4	.327	.381	.471
Mercker, Kent, Cin.*	49	0	0	0	0	0	0	0	0	0	0	0	0	0	0	0	0	0	0	...	...	...
Mercker, Kent, Atl.*	18	1	1	0	0	0	0	0	0	0	0	0	0	0	0	1	0	0	0	.000	.000	.000
Miceli, Dan, Col.	14	0	0	0	0	0	0	0	0	0	0	0	0	0	0	0	0	0	0	...	...	...
Miceli, Dan, Hou.	23	1	1	0	0	0	0	0	0	0	0	0	0	0	0	1	0	0	0	.000	.000	.000
Norton, Phil, Chi.	4	0	0	0	0	0	0	0	0	0	0	0	0	0	0	0	0	0	0	...	...	...
Norton, Phil, Cin.	17	1	1	0	0	0	0	0	0	0	0	0	0	0	0	1	0	0	0	.000	.000	.000
Perez, Oliver, S.D.*	19	38	33	0	7	7	0	0	0	4	3	1	0	1	0	10	0	0	1	.212	.229	.212
Perez, Oliver, Pit.*	5	6	6	0	0	0	0	0	0	0	0	0	0	0	0	1	0	0	0	.000	.000	.000
Ramirez, Aramis, Pit.	96	415	375	44	105	168	25	1	12	67	0	8	7	25	3	68	1	1	17	.280	.330	.448
Ramirez, Aramis, Chi.	63	255	232	31	60	114	7	1	15	39	0	3	3	17	0	31	1	1	4	.259	.314	.491
Roa, Joe, Phi	6	4	4	0	1	1	0	0	0	1	0	0	0	0	0	2	0	0	0	.250	.250	.250
Roa, Joe, Col	4	0	0	0	0	0	0	0	0	0	0	0	0	0	0	0	0	0	0	...	...	...
Roa, Joe, S.D.	18	3	3	0	1	1	0	0	0	0	0	0	0	0	0	1	0	0	0	.333	.333	.333
Simon, Randall, Pit.*	91	321	307	34	84	128	14	0	10	51	0	0	2	12	1	30	0	0	6	.274	.305	.417
Simon, Randall, Chi.*	33	110	103	13	29	50	3	0	6	21	0	1	2	4	1	7	0	0	1	.282	.318	.485
Stinnett, Kelly, Cin.	60	199	179	14	41	63	13	0	3	19	2	1	4	13	3	51	0	0	3	.229	.294	.352
Stinnett, Kelly, Phi.	7	8	7	0	3	3	0	0	0	0	0	0	0	1	0	1	0	0	0	.429	.500	.429
Womack, Tony, Ari.*	61	231	219	30	52	74	10	3	2	15	1	1	2	8	0	27	8	3	6	.237	.270	.338
Womack, Tony, Col.*	21	81	79	9	15	17	2	0	0	5	1	0	1	0	0	9	3	1	1	.190	.200	.215
Womack, Tony, Chi.*	21	52	51	4	12	16	2	1	0	2	0	0	0	1	0	11	2	1	0	.235	.250	.314
Wright, Jaret, S.D.	39	5	4	0	1	2	1	0	0	0	1	0	0	0	0	2	0	0	0	.250	.250	.500
Wright, Jaret, Atl.	11	0	0	0	0	0	0	0	0	0	0	0	0	0	0	0	0	0	0	...	...	...
Young, Eric, Mil.	109	459	404	71	105	170	18	1	15	31	2	1	4	48	2	34	25	7	9	.260	.344	.421
Young, Eric, S.F.	26	82	71	9	14	16	2	0	0	3	0	1	1	9	0	10	3	5	3	.197	.293	.225
Zaun, Gregg, Hou.†	59	138	120	9	26	36	7	0	1	13	1	2	1	14	0	14	1	0	5	.217	.299	.300
Zaun, Gregg, Col.†	15	51	46	6	12	22	1	0	3	8	0	0	0	5	0	7	0	1	0	.261	.333	.478

AWARDED FIRST BASE ON OBSTRUCTION OR CATCHER'S INTERFERENCE: Clark, Milwaukee 2 (Girardi, Wilson); Boone, Cincinnati (Wilson, Diaz); Buchanan, San Diego (Capuano); Kapler, Colorado (Moeller); Kendall, Pittsburgh (Rodriguez); Pierre, Florida (Moeller).

DESIGNATED HITTING

TEAM

Team	G	TPA	AB	R	H	TB	2B	3B	HR	RBI	SH	SF	HP	BB	IBB	SO	SB	CS	GDP	Avg.	OBP	Slg.
St. Louis	9	39	33	7	14	27	1	0	4	10	0	1	0	5	0	4	0	1	1	.424	.487	.818
Montreal	9	38	35	5	14	19	2	0	1	4	0	0	0	3	0	6	2	1	0	.400	.447	.543
Arizona	9	39	34	5	12	15	3	0	0	6	1	1	0	3	0	4	0	0	0	.353	.395	.441
San Francisco	9	40	32	8	11	22	2	0	3	7	0	0	0	8	4	10	2	0	0	.344	.475	.688
Milwaukee	6	27	26	4	8	15	1	0	2	5	0	0	0	1	0	1	0	0	1	.308	.333	.577
Colorado	6	24	23	6	7	21	2	0	4	8	0	0	0	1	0	5	0	0	0	.304	.333	.913
Pittsburgh	6	28	23	4	7	11	1	0	1	1	0	0	0	5	0	9	0	0	0	.304	.429	.478
Atlanta	9	38	35	4	10	13	0	0	1	5	0	0	0	3	0	8	0	1	2	.286	.342	.371
Chicago	9	41	35	7	10	16	1	1	1	8	0	1	0	5	1	4	0	0	2	.286	.366	.457
Florida	6	27	25	4	7	15	3	1	1	4	0	0	1	1	0	5	0	0	0	.280	.333	.600
Houston	9	41	36	3	10	14	2	1	0	4	0	1	0	4	1	7	0	0	1	.278	.341	.389
New York	9	40	37	5	9	16	2	1	1	5	0	0	0	3	0	11	0	0	0	.243	.300	.432
Los Angeles	9	37	32	2	7	11	1	0	1	3	0	1	0	4	0	6	1	0	1	.219	.297	.344
Philadelphia	6	30	28	3	6	12	0	0	2	3	0	0	0	2	0	11	0	0	1	.214	.267	.429
Cincinnati	6	26	20	4	4	8	1	0	1	1	0	0	2	4	0	8	0	0	0	.200	.385	.400
San Diego	9	38	31	6	6	15	0	0	3	11	0	1	0	6	0	7	1	0	0	.194	.316	.484
Totals	144	553	485	77	142	250	22	4	26	85	1	6	3	58	6	106	6	3	9	.293	.368	.515

TOP DESIGNATED HITTERS

Minimum 15 at-bats. *Lefthanded batter. †Switch-hitter.

Player, Team	G	TPA	AB	R	H	TB	2B	3B	HR	RBI	SH	SF	HP	BB	IBB	SO	SB	CS	GDP	Avg.	OBP	Slg.
Baerga, Carlos, Ari.†	6	26	23	4	9	12	3	0	0	6	0	1	0	2	0	1	0	0	0	.391	.423	.522
Bonds, Barry, S.F.*	6	27	19	8	7	16	0	0	3	6	0	0	0	8	4	5	1	0	0	.368	.556	.842
Martinez, Tino, St.L.*	5	21	16	3	5	12	1	0	2	6	0	1	0	4	0	3	0	0	1	.313	.429	.750
Alou, Moises, Chi.	9	40	35	7	10	16	1	1	1	8	0	1	0	4	0	4	0	0	2	.286	.350	.457
Merced, Orlando, Hou.*	7	32	30	2	8	12	2	1	0	3	0	0	0	2	1	5	0	0	1	.267	.313	.400
Floyd, Cliff, N.Y.*	9	39	36	5	9	16	2	1	1	5	0	0	0	3	0	10	0	0	0	.250	.308	.444
Kieschnick, Brooks, Mil.*	4	17	17	2	4	10	0	0	2	3	0	0	0	0	0	1	0	0	1	.235	.235	.588
Coomer, Ron, L.A.	4	16	16	0	2	2	0	0	0	0	0	0	0	0	0	3	0	0	1	.125	.125	.125

NOTE: Only eight batters are listed above since they are the only players to have the minimum 15 DH at-bats during the 2003 N.L. season.

ALL DESIGNATED HITTERS

*Lefthanded batter. †Switch-hitter.

Player, Team	G	TPA	AB	R	H	TB	2B	3B	HR	RBI	SH	SF	HP	BB	IBB	SO	SB	CS	GDP	Avg.	OBP	Slg.
Allen, Chad, Fla.	1	1	1	1	1	3	0	1	0	0	0	0	0	0	0	0	0	0	0	1.000	1.000	3.000
Alou, Moises, Chi.	9	40	35	7	10	16	1	1	1	8	0	1	0	4	0	4	0	0	2	.286	.350	.457
Aurilia, Rich, S.F.	1	5	5	0	1	1	0	0	0	0	0	0	0	0	0	1	0	0	0	.200	.200	.200
Baerga, Carlos, Ari.†	6	26	23	4	9	12	3	0	0	6	0	1	0	2	0	1	0	0	0	.391	.423	.522
Banks, Brian, Fla.†	1	4	4	1	1	2	1	0	0	0	0	0	0	0	0	0	0	0	0	.250	.250	.500
Barnes, Larry, L.A.*	1	1	1	0	0	0	0	0	0	0	0	0	0	0	0	1	0	0	0	.000	.000	.000
Bell, Jay, N.Y.	1	1	1	0	0	0	0	0	0	0	0	0	0	0	0	1	0	0	0	.000	.000	.000
Bonds, Barry, S.F.*	6	27	19	8	7	16	0	0	3	6	0	0	0	8	4	5	1	0	0	.368	.556	.842
Branyan, Russell, Cin.*	1	4	2	0	0	0	0	0	0	0	0	0	0	2	0	0	0	0	0	.000	.500	.000
Buchanan, Brian, S.D.	5	11	7	1	2	5	0	0	1	3	0	1	0	3	0	2	1	0	0	.286	.455	.714
Burrell, Pat, Phi.	2	12	12	0	2	2	0	0	0	0	0	0	0	0	0	3	0	0	1	.167	.167	.167
Carroll, Jamey, Mon.	1	1	0	0	0	0	0	0	0	0	0	0	0	1	0	0	0	0	0	.000	1.000	.000
Castro, Ramon, Fla.	1	4	3	0	1	1	0	0	0	0	0	0	0	1	0	0	0	0	0	.333	.500	.333
Coomer, Ron, L.A.	4	16	16	0	2	2	0	0	0	0	0	0	0	0	0	3	0	0	1	.125	.125	.125
Cordero, Wil, Mon.	2	8	6	1	3	7	1	0	1	2	0	0	0	2	0	1	0	0	0	.500	.625	1.167
DeRosa, Mark, Atl.	2	9	7	1	1	1	0	0	0	1	0	0	0	2	0	2	0	0	0	.143	.333	.143
Dunn, Adam, Cin.*	2	8	6	3	2	6	1	0	1	1	0	0	1	1	0	2	0	0	0	.333	.500	1.000
Edmonds, Jim, St.L.*	2	8	8	1	5	8	0	0	1	2	0	0	0	0	0	1	0	1	0	.625	.625	1.000
Ensberg, Morgan, Hou.	1	5	3	0	0	0	0	0	0	0	0	0	0	2	0	1	0	0	0	.000	.400	.000
Floyd, Cliff, N.Y.*	9	39	36	5	9	16	2	1	1	5	0	0	0	3	0	10	0	0	0	.250	.308	.444
Franco, Matt, Atl.*	3	12	11	1	4	4	0	0	0	1	0	0	0	1	0	3	0	1	1	.364	.417	.364
Galarraga, Andres, S.F.	2	8	8	0	3	5	2	0	0	1	0	0	0	0	0	4	0	0	0	.375	.375	.625
Grace, Mark, Ari.*	1	5	3	1	0	0	0	0	0	0	1	0	0	1	0	1	0	0	0	.000	.250	.000
Green, Shawn, L.A.*	2	8	6	0	1	1	0	0	0	1	0	1	0	1	0	1	0	0	0	.167	.250	.167
Griffey Jr., Ken, Cin.*	3	13	12	1	2	2	0	0	0	0	0	0	1	0	0	6	0	0	0	.167	.231	.167
Guzman, Edwards, Mon.*	3	9	9	0	2	2	0	0	0	0	0	0	0	0	0	1	0	0	0	.222	.222	.222
Hammock, Robby, Ari.	1	3	3	0	1	1	0	0	0	0	0	0	0	0	0	1	0	0	0	.333	.333	.333
Hansen, Dave, S.D.*	3	9	7	2	0	0	0	0	0	0	0	0	0	2	0	2	0	0	0	.000	.222	.000
Hidalgo, Richard, Hou.	1	4	3	1	2	2	0	0	0	1	0	1	0	0	0	1	0	0	0	.667	.500	.667
Hollandsworth, Todd, Fla.*	1	4	4	0	1	1	0	0	0	0	0	0	0	0	0	1	0	0	0	.250	.250	.250
Jenkins, Geoff, Mil.*	1	5	4	1	3	3	0	0	0	2	0	0	0	1	0	0	0	0	0	.750	.800	.750
Jones, Chipper, Atl.†	1	5	5	2	4	7	0	0	1	2	0	0	0	0	0	0	0	0	0	.800	.800	1.400
Jordan, Brian, L.A.	2	8	5	1	3	4	1	0	0	1	0	0	0	3	0	0	1	0	0	.600	.750	.800
Jose, Felix, Ari.†	1	4	4	0	2	2	0	0	0	0	0	0	0	0	0	1	0	0	0	.500	.500	.500
Karros, Eric, Chi.	1	1	0	0	0	0	0	0	0	0	0	0	0	1	1	0	0	0	0	.000	1.000	.000
Kieschnick, Brooks, Mil.*	4	17	17	2	4	10	0	0	2	3	0	0	0	0	0	1	0	0	1	.235	.235	.588
Kinkade, Mike, L.A.	1	4	4	1	1	4	0	0	1	1	0	0	0	0	0	1	0	0	0	.250	.250	1.000
Klesko, Ryan, S.D.*	1	4	3	0	0	0	0	0	0	0	0	0	0	1	0	1	0	0	0	.000	.250	.000
Ledee, Ricky, Phi.*	2	9	9	2	3	6	0	0	1	2	0	0	0	0	0	3	0	0	0	.333	.333	.667
Lopez, Javy, Atl.	3	12	12	0	1	1	0	0	0	1	0	0	0	0	0	3	0	0	1	.083	.083	.083

Player, Team	G	TPA	AB	R	H	TB	2B	3B	HR	RBI	SH	SF	HP	BB	IBB	SO	SB	CS	GDP	Avg.	OBP	Slg.
Lowell, Mike, Fla.	2	9	9	1	2	6	1	0	1	3	0	0	0	0	0	1	0	0	0	.222	.222	.667
Macias, Jose, Mon.†	1	5	5	0	2	2	0	0	0	1	0	0	0	0	0	0	0	1	0	.400	.400	.400
Martinez, Tino, St.L.*	5	21	16	3	5	12	1	0	2	6	0	1	0	4	0	3	0	0	1	.313	.429	.750
Mateo, Henry, Mon.†	3	6	6	3	3	3	0	0	0	0	0	0	0	0	0	1	2	0	0	.500	.500	.500
McCracken, Quinton, Ari.†	1	1	1	0	0	0	0	0	0	0	0	0	0	0	0	0	0	0	0	.000	.000	.000
Merced, Orlando, Hou.*	7	32	30	2	8	12	2	1	0	3	0	0	0	2	1	5	0	0	1	.267	.313	.400
Pena, Wily Mo, Cin.	1	1	0	0	0	0	0	0	0	0	0	0	0	1	0	0	0	0	0	.000	1.000	.000
Perez, Eduardo, St.L.	1	5	4	2	2	2	0	0	0	0	0	0	0	1	0	0	0	0	0	.500	.600	.500
Pujols, Albert, St.L.	1	5	5	1	2	5	0	0	1	2	0	0	0	0	0	0	0	0	0	.400	.400	1.000
Rodriguez, Ivan, Fla.	1	5	4	1	1	2	1	0	0	1	0	0	1	0	0	3	0	0	0	.250	.400	.500
Sanders, Reggie, Pit.	2	10	10	2	3	4	1	0	0	0	0	0	0	0	0	3	0	0	0	.300	.300	.400
Schneider, Brian, Mon.*	2	7	7	1	2	2	0	0	0	0	0	0	0	0	0	3	0	0	0	.286	.286	.286
Stairs, Matt, Pit.*	3	8	4	2	2	5	0	0	1	1	0	0	0	4	0	0	0	0	0	.500	.750	1.250
Sweeney, Mark, Col.*	1	4	4	1	1	4	0	0	1	3	0	0	0	0	0	1	0	0	0	.250	.250	1.000
Thome, Jim, Phi.*	2	9	7	1	1	4	0	0	1	1	0	0	0	2	0	5	0	0	0	.143	.333	.571
Valderrama, Carlos, S.F.	1	0	0	0	0	0	0	0	0	0	0	0	0	0	0	0	1	0	0	.000	.000	.000
Vaughn, Greg, Col.	3	12	11	3	4	11	1	0	2	3	0	0	0	1	0	3	0	0	0	.364	.417	1.000
Vitiello, Joe, Mon.	1	2	2	0	2	3	1	0	0	1	0	0	0	0	0	0	0	0	0	1.000	1.000	1.500
Walker, Larry, Col.*	2	8	8	2	2	6	1	0	1	2	0	0	0	0	0	1	0	0	0	.250	.250	.750
White, Rondell, S.D.	3	14	14	3	4	10	0	0	2	8	0	0	0	0	0	2	0	0	0	.286	.286	.714
Wilson, Craig, Pit.	3	10	9	0	2	2	0	0	0	0	0	0	0	1	0	6	0	0	0	.222	.300	.222
Young, Eric, Mil.	1	5	5	1	1	2	1	0	0	0	0	0	0	0	0	0	0	0	0	.200	.200	.400

The following designated hitters, each of whom appeared in at least one game, had no plate appearances, runs scored or stolen base attempts: Romano, Jason, Los Angeles; Simontacchi, Jason, St. Louis.

PINCH-HITTING

TEAM

Team	G	TPA	AB	R	H	TB	2B	3B	HR	RBI	SH	SF	HP	BB	IBB	SO	SB	CS	GDP	Avg.	OBP	Slg.
Montreal	129	226	206	27	56	74	6	0	4	27	2	2	4	12	3	50	6	3	4	.272	.321	.359
Arizona	132	266	236	25	62	92	10	1	6	41	2	4	1	23	4	49	2	2	6	.263	.326	.390
Colorado	140	285	254	29	66	104	19	2	5	37	0	1	4	26	0	76	2	1	8	.260	.337	.409
San Francisco	130	193	177	18	45	70	8	1	5	26	3	1	1	11	1	36	2	2	6	.254	.300	.395
Florida	125	223	196	18	49	73	7	4	3	20	3	0	2	22	1	49	1	1	5	.250	.332	.372
Philadelphia	135	238	213	28	52	76	7	1	5	23	3	1	1	20	1	59	1	0	2	.244	.311	.357
St. Louis	142	292	254	23	59	77	6	3	2	30	2	4	2	30	1	54	2	2	4	.232	.314	.303
Los Angeles	125	237	215	20	48	67	10	0	3	24	2	1	3	16	2	63	1	0	4	.223	.285	.312
San Diego	144	291	243	31	54	80	12	1	4	30	2	5	1	39	3	58	1	2	11	.222	.329	.329
Atlanta	135	236	212	20	47	68	3	0	6	35	2	2	3	17	4	46	0	0	5	.222	.286	.321
Milwaukee	148	282	254	23	56	86	10	1	6	32	0	4	5	19	0	67	3	2	5	.220	.284	.339
Pittsburgh	139	281	243	27	53	90	10	0	9	42	2	4	3	29	0	81	1	3	2	.218	.305	.370
Cincinnati	142	272	239	23	51	97	12	2	10	52	3	1	1	28	0	87	3	0	7	.213	.297	.406
Houston	147	286	257	22	54	85	13	0	6	38	2	3	3	21	2	52	1	0	3	.210	.275	.331
Chicago	123	236	206	14	32	46	8	0	2	16	2	3	0	25	4	58	3	0	9	.155	.244	.223
New York	136	267	236	11	36	53	6	1	3	25	2	6	3	20	1	62	0	1	1	.153	.223	.225
Totals	2172	4111	3641	359	820	1238	147	17	79	498	32	42	37	358	27	947	29	19	82	.225	.298	.340

TOP PINCH-HITTERS

Minimum 20 at-bats. *Lefthanded batter. †Switch-hitter.

Player, Team	G	TPA	AB	R	H	TB	2B	3B	HR	RBI	SH	SF	HP	BB	IBB	SO	SB	CS	GDP	Avg.	OBP	Slg.
Houston, Tyler, Phi.*	32	31	29	3	13	17	4	0	0	8	0	0	0	2	1	6	0	0	0	.448	.484	.586
Kieschnick, Brooks, Mil.*	24	24	21	5	8	14	0	0	2	3	0	0	0	3	0	6	0	0	0	.381	.458	.667
Hollandsworth, Todd, Fla.*	28	26	20	3	7	12	0	1	1	2	0	0	0	6	1	3	0	0	0	.350	.500	.600
Castro, Ramon, Fla.	27	27	26	3	9	17	2	0	2	4	0	0	0	1	0	6	0	0	0	.346	.370	.654
Baerga, Carlos, Ari.†	63	63	55	9	19	24	2	0	1	10	0	0	0	8	0	7	0	1	1	.345	.429	.436
Goodwin, Tom, Chi.*	32	32	29	4	10	13	3	0	0	4	0	0	0	3	0	5	2	0	0	.345	.406	.448
Norton, Greg, Col.†	78	78	71	9	23	43	8	0	4	17	0	0	1	6	0	21	2	0	2	.324	.385	.606
Drew, J.D., St.L.*	29	28	25	4	8	14	0	0	2	5	0	0	0	3	0	5	1	0	0	.320	.393	.560
Ginter, Keith, Mil.	32	32	29	5	9	16	1	0	2	6	0	1	1	1	0	7	0	0	0	.310	.344	.552
Galarraga, Andres, S.F.	44	44	40	4	12	19	1	0	2	6	0	0	0	4	1	8	0	1	3	.300	.364	.475
Perez, Neifi, S.F.†	29	29	27	1	8	9	1	0	0	5	1	1	0	0	0	2	0	0	0	.296	.286	.333
Palmeiro, Orlando, St.L.*	56	54	44	6	13	17	2	1	0	6	1	2	0	7	0	4	0	0	1	.295	.377	.386
Sweeney, Mark, Col.*	47	47	44	6	13	17	4	0	0	3	0	0	0	3	0	12	0	0	1	.295	.340	.386
Macias, Jose, Mon.†	35	35	34	4	10	14	1	0	1	4	0	0	1	0	0	9	0	1	0	.294	.314	.412
Mordecai, Mike, Fla.	25	25	21	3	6	7	1	0	0	1	2	0	0	2	0	5	0	0	0	.286	.348	.333
Coomer, Ron, L.A.	33	31	28	2	8	10	2	0	0	3	0	0	0	3	2	8	0	0	0	.286	.355	.357
Clark, Brady, Mil.	40	40	35	1	10	12	2	0	0	7	0	1	2	2	0	3	2	0	1	.286	.350	.343

ALL PINCH-HITTERS

*Lefthanded batter. †Switch-hitter.

Player, Team	G	TPA	AB	R	H	TB	2B	3B	HR	RBI	SH	SF	HP	BB	IBB	SO	SB	CS	GDP	Avg.	OBP	Slg.
Alfonzo, Edgardo, S.F.	3	3	3	1	2	3	1	0	0	2	0	0	0	0	0	1	0	0	0	.667	.667	1.000
Allen, Chad, Fla.	4	4	4	0	1	1	0	0	0	0	0	0	0	0	0	1	0	0	0	.250	.250	.250
Allen, Luke, Col.*	2	2	2	0	0	0	0	0	0	0	0	0	0	0	0	0	0	0	1	.000	.000	.000
Alomar, Roberto, N.Y.†	4	4	1	0	1	1	0	0	0	3	0	3	0	0	0	0	0	0	0	1.000	.250	1.000
Alou, Moises, Chi.	1	1	1	0	0	0	0	0	0	0	0	0	0	0	0	0	0	0	0	.000	.000	.000
Atkins, Garrett, Col.	8	8	8	0	1	1	0	0	0	0	0	0	0	0	0	2	0	0	0	.125	.125	.125
Aurilia, Rich, S.F.	5	5	4	2	2	5	0	0	1	5	0	0	0	1	0	0	0	0	0	.500	.600	1.250
Baerga, Carlos, Ari.†	63	63	55	9	19	24	2	0	1	10	0	0	0	8	0	7	0	1	1	.345	.429	.436
Bagwell, Jeff, Hou.	2	2	2	0	0	0	0	0	0	0	0	0	0	0	0	0	0	0	0	.000	.000	.000
Bako, Paul, Chi.*	2	2	2	0	0	0	0	0	0	0	0	0	0	0	0	1	0	0	0	.000	.000	.000
Banks, Brian, Fla.†	53	53	45	4	8	11	1	1	0	6	0	0	1	7	0	15	0	0	1	.178	.302	.244
Barnes, Larry, L.A.*	19	17	17	1	4	5	1	0	0	0	0	0	0	0	0	5	0	0	0	.235	.235	.294
Barrett, Michael, Mon.	5	5	5	0	1	2	1	0	0	0	0	0	0	0	0	1	0	0	0	.200	.200	.400
Bautista, Danny, Ari.	10	10	8	2	3	4	1	0	0	2	0	0	0	2	2	2	0	0	0	.375	.500	.500
Bay, Jason, Pit.	2	2	2	0	1	1	0	0	0	0	0	0	0	0	0	0	0	0	0	.500	.500	.500
Beimel, Joe, Pit.*	1	1	1	0	0	0	0	0	0	0	0	0	0	0	0	1	0	0	0	.000	.000	.000
Bell, Jay, N.Y.	27	27	19	0	1	2	1	0	0	1	1	1	1	5	0	6	0	0	0	.053	.269	.105
Bellhorn, Mark, Chi.-Col.†	28	28	22	1	3	7	1	0	1	2	0	0	0	6	0	11	0	1	0	.136	.321	.318
Belliard, Ronnie, Col.	7	7	7	0	2	2	0	0	0	0	0	0	0	0	0	4	0	0	1	.286	.286	.286
Beltre, Adrian, L.A.	1	1	1	0	0	0	0	0	0	0	0	0	0	0	0	1	0	0	0	.000	.000	.000
Benard, Marvin, S.F.*	26	25	24	2	4	6	0	1	0	1	1	0	0	0	0	4	0	0	1	.167	.167	.250
Bennett, Gary, S.D.	7	7	7	0	0	0	0	0	0	0	0	0	0	0	0	0	0	0	1	.000	.000	.000
Biggio, Craig, Hou.	3	3	3	0	1	1	0	0	0	0	0	0	0	0	0	1	0	0	0	.333	.333	.333
Blanco, Henry, Atl.	4	3	3	0	0	0	0	0	0	0	0	0	0	0	0	0	0	0	0	.000	.000	.000
Blum, Geoff, Hou.†	19	19	16	2	3	3	0	0	0	2	0	0	0	3	1	5	0	0	0	.188	.316	.188
Bonds, Barry, S.F.*	2	2	1	0	0	0	0	0	0	0	0	0	0	1	0	1	0	0	0	.000	.500	.000
Bong, Jung, Atl.*	1	1	1	0	0	0	0	0	0	0	0	0	0	0	0	1	0	0	0	.000	.000	.000
Boone, Aaron, Cin.	2	2	2	0	1	3	0	1	0	1	0	0	0	0	0	0	0	0	0	.500	.500	1.500
Bragg, Darren, Atl.*	21	19	18	1	5	5	0	0	0	2	0	0	0	1	0	5	0	0	1	.278	.316	.278
Branyan, Russell, Cin.*	27	27	20	2	3	7	1	0	1	5	0	0	0	7	0	10	0	0	0	.150	.370	.350
Bruntlett, Eric, Hou.	12	12	12	1	4	5	1	0	0	0	0	0	0	0	0	1	0	0	0	.333	.333	.417
Buchanan, Brian, S.D.	54	54	44	7	10	15	2	0	1	3	0	1	0	9	0	10	1	0	3	.227	.352	.341

Player, Team	G	TPA	AB	R	H	TB	2B	3B	HR	RBI	SH	SF	HP	BB	IBB	SO	SB	CS	GDP	Avg.	OBP	Slg.
Budzinski, Mark, Cin.*	3	3	3	0	0	0	0	0	0	0	0	0	0	0	0	2	0	0	0	.000	.000	.000
Burnitz, Jeromy, L.A.*	1	1	1	0	0	0	0	0	0	0	0	0	0	0	0	1	0	0	0	.000	.000	.000
Burrell, Pat, Phi.	6	6	4	1	1	1	0	0	0	0	0	0	0	2	0	1	0	0	0	.250	.500	.250
Burroughs, Sean, S.D.*	10	10	8	2	2	2	0	0	0	0	0	0	0	2	0	2	0	0	0	.250	.400	.250
Butler, Brent, Col.	9	8	8	2	2	3	1	0	0	0	0	0	0	0	0	0	0	0	0	.250	.250	.375
Byrd, Marlon, Phi.	7	7	7	1	1	2	1	0	0	1	0	0	0	0	0	1	0	0	0	.143	.143	.286
Cabrera, Jolbert, L.A.	23	23	22	1	5	6	1	0	0	2	1	0	0	0	0	7	0	0	1	.227	.227	.273
Cabrera, Miguel, Fla.	1	1	1	0	0	0	0	0	0	0	0	0	0	0	0	1	0	0	0	.000	.000	.000
Cairo, Miguel, St.L.	22	22	20	1	2	2	0	0	0	1	0	0	0	2	0	4	0	0	0	.100	.182	.100
Calloway, Ron, Mon.*	34	34	29	4	7	12	2	0	1	7	0	2	1	2	0	5	1	0	1	.241	.294	.414
Carroll, Jamey, Mon.	18	18	17	3	6	6	0	0	0	0	0	0	0	1	0	5	0	1	1	.353	.389	.353
Casey, Sean, Cin.*	3	3	2	0	1	1	0	0	0	1	0	0	0	1	0	0	0	0	0	.500	.667	.500
Castillo, Alberto, S.F.	2	2	2	1	1	2	1	0	0	0	0	0	0	0	0	0	0	0	0	.500	.500	1.000
Castillo, Luis, Fla.†	1	1	1	0	0	0	0	0	0	0	0	0	0	0	0	0	0	0	0	.000	.000	.000
Castro, Juan, Cin.	10	10	8	0	3	3	0	0	0	0	2	0	0	0	0	1	0	0	0	.375	.375	.375
Castro, Ramon, Fla.	27	27	26	3	9	17	2	0	2	4	0	0	0	1	0	6	0	0	0	.346	.370	.654
Cedeno, Roger, N.Y.†	26	26	26	1	4	7	0	0	1	4	0	0	0	0	0	4	0	1	1	.154	.154	.269
Cepicky, Matt, Mon.*	3	3	3	0	0	0	0	0	0	0	0	0	0	0	0	0	0	0	0	.000	.000	.000
Chamblee, Jim, Cin.	1	1	1	0	0	0	0	0	0	0	0	0	0	0	0	1	0	0	0	.000	.000	.000
Chapman, Travis, Phi.	1	1	1	0	0	0	0	0	0	0	0	0	0	0	0	0	0	0	0	.000	.000	.000
Chavez, Endy, Mon.*	10	10	9	1	2	2	0	0	0	1	1	0	0	0	0	0	1	0	0	.222	.222	.222
Chavez, Raul, Hou.	3	3	2	2	1	4	0	0	1	2	0	0	0	1	0	0	0	0	0	.500	.667	2.000
Chen, Chin-Feng, L.A.	1	1	1	0	0	0	0	0	0	0	0	0	0	0	0	0	0	0	0	.000	.000	.000
Choi, Hee Seop, Chi.*	13	11	10	0	0	0	0	0	0	0	0	0	0	1	0	8	0	0	0	.000	.091	.000
Cintron, Alex, Ari.†	8	8	8	0	2	4	0	1	0	2	0	0	0	0	0	1	0	0	0	.250	.250	.500
Clark, Brady, Mil.	40	40	35	1	10	12	2	0	0	7	0	1	2	2	0	3	2	0	1	.286	.350	.343
Clark, Tony, N.Y.†	53	53	46	3	9	17	2	0	2	9	0	0	1	6	0	14	0	0	0	.196	.302	.370
Clayton, Royce, Mil.	5	5	4	0	0	0	0	0	0	1	0	0	0	1	0	1	0	0	0	.000	.200	.000
Conti, Jason, Mil.*	13	13	12	1	4	5	1	0	0	0	0	0	0	1	0	3	0	0	0	.333	.385	.417
Coomer, Ron, L.A.	33	31	28	2	8	10	2	0	0	3	0	0	0	3	2	8	0	0	0	.286	.355	.357
Cora, Alex, L.A.*	6	6	6	0	0	0	0	0	0	0	0	0	0	0	0	0	0	0	0	.000	.000	.000
Cordero, Wil, Mon.	10	10	8	1	1	2	1	0	0	2	0	0	0	2	1	1	0	0	0	.125	.300	.250
Cota, Humberto, Pit.	7	7	7	0	3	4	1	0	0	0	0	0	0	0	0	0	0	0	0	.429	.429	.571
Counsell, Craig, Ari.*	8	8	8	0	0	0	0	0	0	0	0	0	0	0	0	1	0	0	0	.000	.000	.000
Cromer, Tripp, Hou.	2	2	2	0	0	0	0	0	0	0	0	0	0	0	0	0	0	0	0	.000	.000	.000
Crosby, Bubba, L.A.*	8	8	8	0	1	1	0	0	0	1	0	0	0	0	0	1	0	0	0	.125	.125	.125
Cruz, Enrique, Mil.	36	36	34	1	2	2	0	0	0	0	0	0	1	1	0	13	0	0	1	.059	.111	.059
Cruz, Jose, S.F.†	2	2	1	1	1	1	0	0	0	0	0	0	0	1	0	0	0	0	0	1.000	1.000	1.000
Darensbourg, Vic, Mon.*	1	1	1	0	0	0	0	0	0	0	0	0	0	0	0	1	0	0	0	.000	.000	.000
Davis, J.J., Pit.	9	9	9	0	1	1	0	0	0	2	0	0	0	0	0	4	0	0	0	.111	.111	.111
Delgado, Wilson, St.L.†	24	24	20	1	4	4	0	0	0	1	0	1	1	2	0	2	0	0	1	.200	.292	.200
Dellucci, David, Ari.*	20	19	17	2	2	2	0	0	0	0	0	0	0	2	0	10	1	0	0	.118	.211	.118
DePastino, Joe, N.Y.	2	2	2	0	0	0	0	0	0	0	0	0	0	0	0	1	0	0	0	.000	.000	.000
DeRosa, Mark, Atl.	33	33	31	3	6	9	0	0	1	4	0	0	1	1	0	5	0	0	0	.194	.242	.290
Dessens, Elmer, Ari.	2	2	1	0	0	0	0	0	0	0	1	0	0	0	0	1	0	0	0	.000	.000	.000
Drew, J.D., St.L.*	29	28	25	4	8	14	0	0	2	5	0	0	0	3	0	5	1	0	0	.320	.393	.560
Duncan, Jeff, N.Y.*	7	7	6	1	2	4	0	1	0	0	1	0	0	0	0	2	0	0	0	.333	.333	.667
Dunn, Adam, Cin.*	6	6	4	3	3	12	0	0	3	8	0	0	0	2	0	0	0	0	0	.750	.833	3.000
Durham, Ray, S.F.†	7	7	6	0	0	0	0	0	0	0	0	0	0	1	0	2	0	0	0	.000	.143	.000
Eaton, Adam, S.D.	6	6	5	0	2	3	1	0	0	0	1	0	0	0	0	3	0	0	0	.400	.400	.600
Edmonds, Jim, St.L.*	9	9	8	0	0	0	0	0	0	0	0	0	0	1	0	5	0	0	0	.000	.111	.000
Eischen, Joey, Mon.*	2	2	2	0	1	1	0	0	0	0	0	0	0	0	0	1	0	0	0	.500	.500	.500
Ellison, Jason, S.F.	1	1	1	0	0	0	0	0	0	0	0	0	0	0	0	1	0	0	0	.000	.000	.000
Encarnacion, Juan, Fla.	1	1	1	0	0	0	0	0	0	0	0	0	0	0	0	1	0	0	0	.000	.000	.000
Ensberg, Morgan, Hou.	23	21	16	3	6	13	1	0	2	8	0	0	1	4	0	2	0	0	0	.375	.524	.813
Estes, Shawn, Chi.	1	1	0	0	0	0	0	0	0	0	1	0	0	0	0	0	0	0	0	.000	.000	.000
Estrada, Johnny, Atl.†	3	3	2	1	1	1	0	0	0	0	0	0	1	0	0	0	0	0	0	.500	.667	.500
Everett, Adam, Hou.	1	1	0	0	0	0	0	0	0	0	1	0	0	0	0	0	0	0	0	.000	.000	.000
Feliz, Pedro, S.F.	25	25	24	1	4	9	2	0	1	3	0	0	0	1	0	8	0	0	1	.167	.200	.375
Fick, Robert, Atl.*	13	13	11	0	2	2	0	0	0	3	0	0	1	1	0	3	0	0	0	.182	.308	.182
Finley, Steve, Ari.*	9	9	8	2	2	5	0	0	1	3	0	0	0	1	0	3	0	0	0	.250	.333	.625
Floyd, Cliff, N.Y.*	5	4	3	0	0	0	0	0	0	0	0	0	0	1	0	2	0	0	0	.000	.250	.000
Fox, Andy, Fla.*	37	36	32	1	6	9	1	1	0	0	1	0	0	3	0	7	0	1	2	.188	.257	.281
Franco, Julio, Atl.	41	41	38	1	9	10	1	0	0	7	0	0	0	3	2	9	0	0	2	.237	.293	.263
Franco, Matt, Atl.*	92	84	78	6	15	22	1	0	2	10	0	1	0	5	0	18	0	0	1	.192	.238	.282
Freel, Ryan, Cin.	5	5	5	1	1	4	0	0	1	1	0	0	0	0	0	1	0	0	0	.200	.200	.800
Furcal, Rafael, Atl.†	2	2	2	0	0	0	0	0	0	0	0	0	0	0	0	0	0	0	0	.000	.000	.000
Galarraga, Andres, S.F.	44	44	40	4	12	19	1	0	2	6	0	0	0	4	1	8	0	1	3	.300	.364	.475
Garcia, Jesse, Atl.	3	2	2	2	1	1	0	0	0	1	0	0	0	0	0	0	0	0	0	.500	.500	.500
Giles, Marcus, Atl.	7	7	5	2	2	3	1	0	0	2	0	1	0	1	0	1	0	0	0	.400	.429	.600
Ginter, Keith, Mil.	32	32	29	5	9	16	1	0	2	6	0	1	1	1	0	7	0	0	0	.310	.344	.552
Girardi, Joe, St.L.	4	4	3	0	1	1	0	0	0	1	0	0	0	1	0	1	0	0	0	.333	.500	.333
Glanville, Doug, Chi.	14	14	13	0	2	2	0	0	0	0	0	0	0	1	0	1	0	0	0	.154	.214	.154
Glavine, Mike, N.Y.*	4	4	4	0	0	0	0	0	0	0	0	0	0	0	0	2	0	0	0	.000	.000	.000
Glavine, Tom, N.Y.*	1	1	1	0	0	0	0	0	0	0	0	0	0	0	0	0	0	0	0	.000	.000	.000
Gonzalez, Alex S., Chi.	4	4	3	0	0	0	0	0	0	0	0	0	0	1	0	2	0	0	0	.000	.250	.000
Gonzalez, Luis, Ari.*	2	2	2	0	1	1	0	0	0	0	0	0	0	0	0	0	0	0	0	.500	.500	.500
Gonzalez, Raul, N.Y.	36	36	31	3	5	5	0	0	0	3	0	0	0	5	1	10	0	0	0	.161	.278	.161
Gonzalez, Wiki, S.D.	2	2	1	0	0	0	0	0	0	1	0	1	0	0	0	0	0	0	0	.000	.000	.000
Goodwin, Tom, Chi.*	32	32	29	4	10	13	3	0	0	4	0	0	0	3	0	5	2	0	0	.345	.406	.448
Grace, Mark, Ari.*	28	27	24	0	3	3	0	0	0	2	0	1	0	2	1	5	0	0	2	.125	.185	.125
Green, Shawn, L.A.*	1	1	0	0	0	0	0	0	0	0	0	0	0	1	0	0	0	0	0	.000	1.000	.000
Greene, Khalil, S.D.	1	1	1	0	0	0	0	0	0	0	0	0	0	0	0	0	0	0	0	.000	.000	.000
Griffey Jr., Ken, Cin.*	7	7	5	0	1	1	0	0	0	2	0	1	0	1	0	2	0	0	0	.200	.286	.200
Grissom, Marquis, S.F.	2	2	2	0	0	0	0	0	0	0	0	0	0	0	0	0	0	0	1	.000	.000	.000

Player, Team	G	TPA	AB	R	H	TB	2B	3B	HR	RBI	SH	SF	HP	BB	IBB	SO	SB	CS	GDP	Avg.	OBP	Slg.
Grudzielanek, Mark, Chi.	2	2	2	0	0	0	0	0	0	0	0	0	0	0	0	0	0	0	0	.000	.000	.000
Guillen, Jose, Cin.	18	18	17	2	5	5	0	0	0	3	0	0	0	1	0	5	0	0	2	.294	.333	.294
Guzman, Edwards, Mon.*	10	10	9	3	4	4	0	0	0	0	0	0	0	1	1	2	0	0	0	.444	.500	.444
Hall, Bill, Mil.	18	18	16	1	3	4	1	0	0	1	0	1	0	1	0	5	0	0	0	.188	.222	.250
Hammock, Robby, Ari.	3	3	3	0	1	1	0	0	0	0	0	0	0	0	0	1	0	0	0	.333	.333	.333
Hammonds, Jeffrey, S.F.	8	8	7	2	1	1	0	0	0	0	0	0	0	1	0	1	0	0	0	.143	.250	.143
Hampton, Mike, Atl.	1	1	0	0	0	0	0	0	0	0	1	0	0	0	0	0	0	0	0	.000	.000	.000
Hansen, Dave, S.D.*	78	65	55	3	9	11	0	1	0	3	0	0	0	10	3	14	0	0	2	.164	.292	.200
Harris, Lenny, Chi.-Fla.*	47	46	40	5	8	8	0	0	0	2	1	0	0	5	2	6	0	0	2	.200	.289	.200
Hart, Bo, St.L.	7	7	6	1	1	1	0	0	0	1	0	1	0	0	0	2	0	0	0	.167	.143	.167
Helms, Wes, Mil.	4	3	2	0	0	0	0	0	0	0	0	0	0	1	0	0	0	0	0	.000	.333	.000
Helton, Todd, Col.*	1	1	1	0	0	0	0	0	0	0	0	0	0	0	0	0	0	0	0	.000	.000	.000
Henderson, Rickey, L.A.	13	13	10	1	3	3	0	0	0	0	0	0	1	2	0	2	1	0	0	.300	.462	.300
Hermansen, Chad, L.A.	5	5	4	0	0	0	0	0	0	0	0	0	0	1	0	3	0	0	0	.000	.200	.000
Hernandez, Jose, Col.-Chi.-Pit.	6	6	6	0	1	1	0	0	0	2	0	0	0	0	0	3	0	0	0	.167	.167	.167
Hessman, Mike, Atl.	6	6	5	1	1	4	0	0	1	1	0	0	0	1	0	1	0	0	1	.200	.333	.800
Hidalgo, Richard, Hou.	4	4	3	1	0	0	0	0	0	0	0	0	0	1	0	3	0	0	0	.000	.250	.000
Hill, Bobby, Chi.-Pit.†	4	4	3	0	0	0	0	0	0	0	0	0	0	1	0	1	0	0	1	.000	.250	.000
Hill, Koyie, L.A.†	3	3	3	0	1	2	1	0	0	0	0	0	0	0	0	2	0	0	0	.333	.333	.667
Hillenbrand, Shea, Ari.	2	2	2	1	1	4	0	0	1	2	0	0	0	0	0	1	0	0	0	.500	.500	2.000
Hollandsworth, Todd, Fla.*	28	26	20	3	7	12	0	1	1	2	0	0	0	6	1	3	0	0	0	.350	.500	.600
House, J.R., Pit.	1	1	1	0	1	1	0	0	0	0	0	0	0	0	0	0	0	0	0	1.000	1.000	1.000
Houston, Tyler, Phi.*	32	31	29	3	13	17	4	0	0	8	0	0	0	2	1	6	0	0	0	.448	.484	.586
Hubbard, Trenidad, Chi.	6	6	4	0	0	0	0	0	0	0	0	0	0	2	0	2	0	0	0	.000	.333	.000
Hummel, Tim, Cin.	6	6	6	1	3	4	1	0	0	2	0	0	0	0	0	1	0	0	0	.500	.500	.667
Hundley, Todd, L.A.†	13	13	13	2	3	9	0	0	2	7	0	0	0	0	0	6	0	0	0	.231	.231	.692
Hunter, Brian L., Hou.	27	27	25	2	4	4	0	0	0	2	0	0	1	1	0	7	0	0	0	.160	.222	.160
Hyzdu, Adam, Pit.	21	21	17	2	2	3	1	0	0	2	0	1	0	3	0	9	0	0	0	.118	.238	.176
Izturis, Cesar, L.A.†	2	2	1	2	1	1	0	0	0	0	0	0	0	1	0	0	0	0	0	1.000	1.000	1.000
Jennings, Jason, Col.*	1	1	1	0	1	1	0	0	0	0	0	0	0	0	0	0	0	0	0	1.000	1.000	1.000
Jones, Andruw, Atl.	3	3	3	1	1	4	0	0	1	2	0	0	0	0	0	1	0	0	0	.333	.333	1.333
Jones, Chipper, Atl.†	3	3	2	0	1	1	0	0	0	0	0	0	0	1	0	0	0	0	0	.500	.667	.500
Jordan, Brian, L.A.	2	2	2	0	0	0	0	0	0	0	0	0	0	0	0	0	0	0	1	.000	.000	.000
Jose, Felix, Ari.†	16	16	11	1	4	8	1	0	1	6	0	0	0	5	1	1	0	0	0	.364	.563	.727
Kapler, Gabe, Col.	17	17	15	3	7	9	2	0	0	1	0	0	0	2	0	4	0	0	0	.467	.529	.600
Karros, Eric, Chi.	26	26	21	1	2	2	0	0	0	1	0	0	0	5	1	6	0	0	4	.095	.269	.095
Kata, Matt, Ari.†	4	4	2	1	0	0	0	0	0	2	1	1	0	0	0	1	1	0	0	.000	.000	.000
Kearns, Austin, Cin.	4	4	2	0	1	1	0	0	0	0	0	0	0	2	0	0	0	0	0	.500	.750	.500
Kelton, David, Chi.	5	5	5	0	0	0	0	0	0	0	0	0	0	0	0	2	0	0	0	.000	.000	.000
Kendall, Jason, Pit.	4	4	4	0	1	2	1	0	0	2	0	0	0	0	0	0	0	0	0	.250	.250	.500
Kent, Jeff, Hou.	3	3	2	0	0	0	0	0	0	0	0	0	0	1	0	1	0	0	0	.000	.333	.000
Kieschnick, Brooks, Mil.*	24	24	21	5	8	14	0	0	2	3	0	0	0	3	0	6	0	0	0	.381	.458	.667
Kinkade, Mike, L.A.	41	41	37	5	10	14	4	0	0	5	0	0	2	2	0	12	0	0	1	.270	.341	.378
Klesko, Ryan, S.D.*	17	17	12	1	3	7	1	0	1	3	0	1	0	4	0	0	0	0	0	.250	.412	.583
Kotsay, Mark, S.D.*	1	1	1	0	1	2	1	0	0	2	0	0	0	0	0	0	0	0	0	1.000	1.000	2.000
Lane, Jason, Hou.	9	8	8	1	2	3	1	0	0	3	0	0	0	0	0	0	0	0	0	.250	.250	.375
Larkin, Barry, Cin.	10	10	8	1	2	6	1	0	1	4	0	0	0	2	0	1	0	0	0	.250	.400	.750
Larson, Brandon, Cin.	7	7	7	0	0	0	0	0	0	0	0	0	0	0	0	1	0	0	2	.000	.000	.000
LaRue, Jason, Cin.	3	3	3	1	2	6	1	0	1	3	0	0	0	0	0	0	0	0	0	.667	.667	2.000
Ledee, Ricky, Phi.*	58	54	49	6	11	18	1	0	2	7	0	1	0	4	0	14	0	0	1	.224	.278	.367
Lieberthal, Mike, Phi.	2	2	2	0	1	1	0	0	0	0	0	0	0	0	0	0	0	0	0	.500	.500	.500
Liefer, Jeff, Mon.*	15	15	15	1	4	4	0	0	0	3	0	0	0	0	0	7	0	0	1	.267	.267	.267
Linden, Todd, S.F.†	4	4	4	0	2	2	0	0	0	1	0	0	0	0	0	1	0	0	0	.500	.500	.500
Lo Duca, Paul, L.A.	2	2	2	0	1	2	1	0	0	1	0	0	0	0	0	0	0	0	0	.500	.500	1.000
Lockhart, Keith, S.D.*	42	41	34	6	6	9	0	0	1	5	1	0	1	5	0	9	0	0	1	.176	.300	.265
Lofton, Kenny, Pit.-Chi.*	7	7	6	1	1	2	1	0	0	1	0	1	0	0	0	1	0	0	0	.167	.143	.333
Lopez, Felipe, Cin.†	4	4	3	0	0	0	0	0	0	1	0	0	0	1	0	1	1	0	0	.000	.250	.000
Lopez, Javy, Atl.	12	12	10	2	3	6	0	0	1	3	0	0	0	2	1	2	0	0	0	.300	.417	.600
Loretta, Mark, S.D.	9	9	9	1	5	9	1	0	1	3	0	0	0	0	0	2	0	1	0	.556	.556	1.000
Macias, Jose, Mon.†	35	35	34	4	10	14	1	0	1	4	0	0	1	0	0	9	0	1	0	.294	.314	.412
Mackowiak, Rob, Pit.*	29	27	23	1	4	7	0	0	1	3	0	0	1	3	0	12	1	0	0	.174	.296	.304
Maddux, Greg, Atl.	1	1	0	0	0	0	0	0	0	0	1	0	0	0	0	0	0	0	0	.000	.000	.000
Marrero, Eli, St.L.	12	12	11	1	4	5	1	0	0	2	0	0	0	1	0	1	0	0	0	.364	.417	.455
Martinez, Ramon, Chi.	10	10	6	1	2	3	1	0	0	2	0	2	0	2	0	0	0	0	0	.333	.400	.500
Martinez, Tino, St.L.*	7	7	5	0	0	0	0	0	0	0	0	0	0	2	1	2	0	0	0	.000	.286	.000
Mateo, Henry, Mon.†	49	49	43	8	11	12	1	0	0	3	1	0	2	3	0	13	4	1	0	.256	.333	.279
Mateo, Ruben, Cin.	20	20	17	1	1	4	0	0	1	2	0	0	0	3	0	7	0	0	0	.059	.200	.235
Matheny, Mike, St.L.	5	5	5	0	3	3	0	0	0	1	0	0	0	0	0	0	0	0	1	.600	.600	.600
Matranga, Dave, Hou.	5	5	5	1	1	4	0	0	1	1	0	0	0	0	0	2	0	0	0	.200	.200	.800
Matthews Jr., Gary, S.D.†	17	17	16	3	2	3	1	0	0	2	0	0	0	1	0	7	0	0	2	.125	.176	.188
McCracken, Quinton, Ari.†	57	57	54	2	12	14	2	0	0	3	0	0	0	3	0	10	0	1	2	.222	.263	.259
McEwing, Joe, N.Y.	14	14	14	1	3	3	0	0	0	0	0	0	0	0	0	4	0	0	0	.214	.214	.214
McGriff, Fred, L.A.*	7	7	6	1	2	2	0	0	0	0	0	0	0	1	0	4	0	0	0	.333	.429	.333
Meluskey, Mitch, Hou.†	12	12	9	1	1	2	1	0	0	2	0	1	0	2	0	2	0	0	0	.111	.250	.222
Merced, Orlando, Hou.*	78	76	69	3	13	22	6	0	1	8	0	1	1	5	0	12	0	0	1	.188	.250	.319
Merloni, Lou, S.D.	14	14	10	5	4	6	2	0	0	3	0	1	0	3	0	1	0	0	0	.400	.500	.600
Michaels, Jason, Phi.	45	44	39	7	10	17	1	0	2	4	0	0	0	5	0	9	0	0	1	.256	.341	.436
Miller, Corky, Cin.	3	3	3	0	0	0	0	0	0	0	0	0	0	0	0	2	0	0	0	.000	.000	.000
Miller, Damian, Chi.	3	3	3	0	1	2	1	0	0	0	0	0	0	0	0	1	0	0	0	.333	.333	.667
Miller, Wade, Hou.	3	3	2	0	0	0	0	0	0	0	0	0	0	1	0	2	0	0	0	.000	.333	.000
Moeller, Chad, Ari.	2	2	2	0	0	0	0	0	0	0	0	0	0	0	0	1	0	0	0	.000	.000	.000
Mondesi, Raul, Ari.	2	2	2	0	0	0	0	0	0	0	0	0	0	0	0	1	0	0	0	.000	.000	.000
Mordecai, Mike, Fla.	25	25	21	3	6	7	1	0	0	1	2	0	0	2	0	5	0	0	0	.286	.348	.333
Myers, Brett, Phi.	1	1	0	0	0	0	0	0	0	0	1	0	0	0	0	0	0	0	0	.000	.000	.000
Nady, Xavier, S.D.	8	7	6	0	1	1	0	0	0	0	0	0	0	1	0	1	0	0	0	.167	.286	.167

Player, Team	G	TPA	AB	R	H	TB	2B	3B	HR	RBI	SH	SF	HP	BB	IBB	SO	SB	CS	GDP	Avg.	OBP	Slg.
Niekro, Lance, S.F.	1	1	1	0	0	0	0	0	0	0	0	0	0	0	0	0	0	0	0	.000	.000	.000
Norton, Greg, Col.†	78	78	71	9	23	43	8	0	4	17	0	0	1	6	0	21	2	0	2	.324	.385	.606
Nunez, Abraham O., Pit.†	32	32	26	3	1	1	0	0	0	1	1	1	0	4	0	8	0	2	1	.038	.161	.038
O'Leary, Troy, Chi.*	46	45	39	2	5	9	1	0	1	7	0	1	0	5	1	12	0	0	3	.128	.222	.231
Ojeda, Miguel, S.D.	14	14	10	2	3	4	1	0	0	2	0	1	0	3	0	1	0	0	0	.300	.429	.400
Oliver, Darren, Col.	2	2	2	0	0	0	0	0	0	0	0	0	0	0	0	0	0	0	0	.000	.000	.000
Olmedo, Ray, Cin.†	13	13	13	0	2	3	1	0	0	0	0	0	0	0	0	4	0	0	1	.154	.154	.231
Ortiz, Russ, Atl.	1	1	1	0	0	0	0	0	0	0	0	0	0	0	0	0	0	0	0	.000	.000	.000
Osik, Keith, Mil.	2	2	2	0	0	0	0	0	0	0	0	0	0	0	0	0	0	0	0	.000	.000	.000
Overbay, Lyle, Ari.*	11	11	10	1	4	8	1	0	1	4	0	1	0	0	0	0	0	0	1	.400	.364	.800
Ozuna, Pablo, Col.	3	3	2	0	0	0	0	0	0	0	0	0	1	0	0	0	0	0	0	.000	.333	.000
Palmeiro, Orlando, St.L.*	56	54	44	6	13	17	2	1	0	6	1	2	0	7	0	4	0	0	1	.295	.377	.386
Patterson, Corey, Chi.*	4	4	4	1	3	3	0	0	0	0	0	0	0	0	0	0	1	0	0	.750	.750	.750
Payton, Jay, Col.	7	7	5	2	1	2	1	0	0	2	0	0	1	1	0	0	0	0	1	.200	.429	.400
Pellow, Kit, Col.	2	2	2	0	0	0	0	0	0	0	0	0	0	0	0	2	0	0	0	.000	.000	.000
Pena, Wily Mo, Cin.	27	27	26	1	4	5	1	0	0	3	0	0	0	1	0	11	0	0	1	.154	.185	.192
Penny, Brad, Fla.	1	1	1	0	0	0	0	0	0	0	0	0	0	0	0	1	0	0	0	.000	.000	.000
Perez, Eddie, Mil.	9	9	8	1	2	5	1	1	0	3	0	0	0	1	0	2	0	1	0	.250	.333	.625
Perez, Eduardo, St.L.	42	42	37	4	8	10	2	0	0	6	0	0	0	5	0	7	0	2	0	.216	.310	.270
Perez, Neifi, S.F.†	29	29	27	1	8	9	1	0	0	5	1	1	0	0	0	2	0	0	0	.296	.286	.333
Perez, Timo, N.Y.*	27	27	25	0	4	5	1	0	0	4	0	1	0	1	0	4	0	0	0	.160	.185	.200
Perez, Tomas, Phi.†	41	41	37	6	6	8	0	1	0	1	2	0	0	2	0	13	0	0	0	.162	.205	.216
Phillips, Jason, N.Y.	10	10	9	0	2	3	1	0	0	0	0	0	1	0	0	2	0	0	0	.222	.300	.333
Piazza, Mike, N.Y.	4	4	3	0	1	1	0	0	0	0	0	0	0	1	0	1	0	0	0	.333	.500	.333
Pierre, Juan, Fla.*	1	1	1	0	0	0	0	0	0	0	0	0	0	0	0	1	0	0	0	.000	.000	.000
Podsednik, Scott, Mil.*	19	18	14	1	3	3	0	0	0	0	0	0	1	3	0	2	0	0	1	.214	.389	.214
Polanco, Placido, Phi.	2	2	2	0	0	0	0	0	0	0	0	0	0	0	0	1	0	0	0	.000	.000	.000
Porter, Colin, Hou.*	5	5	5	0	2	2	0	0	0	0	0	0	0	0	0	2	1	0	0	.400	.400	.400
Pratt, Todd, Phi.	5	5	5	1	1	4	0	0	1	2	0	0	0	0	0	2	0	0	0	.200	.200	.800
Prior, Mark, Chi.	2	2	2	0	0	0	0	0	0	0	0	0	0	0	0	2	0	0	0	.000	.000	.000
Pujols, Albert, St.L.	7	7	6	0	1	1	0	0	0	0	0	0	0	1	0	1	0	0	0	.167	.286	.167
Punto, Nick, Phi.†	28	28	27	3	5	5	0	0	0	0	0	0	0	1	0	8	0	0	0	.185	.214	.185
Quintero, Humberto, S.D.	2	2	2	0	2	2	0	0	0	0	0	0	0	0	0	0	0	0	0	1.000	1.000	1.000
Ramirez, Aramis, Chi.	1	1	0	0	0	0	0	0	0	0	0	0	0	1	0	0	0	0	0	.000	1.000	.000
Randolph, Stephen, Ari.*	1	1	1	0	0	0	0	0	0	0	0	0	0	0	0	1	0	0	0	.000	.000	.000
Ransom, Cody, S.F.	4	4	4	0	1	1	0	0	0	0	0	0	0	0	0	2	0	0	0	.250	.250	.250
Reboulet, Jeff, Pit.	18	18	15	4	4	7	0	0	1	1	1	0	0	2	0	3	0	0	0	.267	.353	.467
Redman, Prentice, N.Y.	2	2	2	0	0	0	0	0	0	0	0	0	0	0	0	1	0	0	0	.000	.000	.000
Redman, Tike, Pit.*	4	4	4	1	2	3	1	0	0	0	0	0	0	0	0	2	0	0	0	.500	.500	.750
Redmond, Mike, Fla.	24	23	22	2	6	10	2	1	0	3	0	0	1	0	0	5	0	0	0	.273	.304	.455
Reese, Pokey, Pit.	5	5	3	0	0	0	0	0	0	0	0	0	0	2	0	2	0	0	0	.000	.400	.000
Renteria, Edgar, St.L.	1	1	1	0	0	0	0	0	0	0	0	0	0	0	0	0	0	0	0	.000	.000	.000
Reyes, Rene, Col.†	18	18	16	2	4	8	2	1	0	1	0	1	0	1	0	4	0	0	0	.250	.278	.500
Richard, Chris, Col.*	15	15	13	1	2	4	0	1	0	1	0	0	0	2	0	5	0	0	1	.154	.267	.308
Rivera, Carlos, Pit.*	29	29	27	3	6	10	1	0	1	3	0	0	0	2	0	9	0	0	0	.222	.276	.370
Rivera, Michael, S.D.	1	1	1	0	0	0	0	0	0	0	0	0	0	0	0	0	0	0	1	.000	.000	.000
Rivera, Ruben, S.F.	4	4	4	0	1	1	0	0	0	0	0	0	0	0	0	0	1	0	0	.250	.250	.250
Roberts, Dave, L.A.*	3	3	2	0	0	0	0	0	0	0	1	0	0	0	0	0	0	0	0	.000	.000	.000
Robinson, Kerry, St.L.*	51	50	46	3	10	12	0	1	0	4	1	0	0	3	0	14	1	0	1	.217	.265	.261
Rodriguez, Ivan, Fla.	8	8	7	0	1	1	0	0	0	2	0	0	0	1	0	0	0	0	1	.143	.250	.143
Rolen, Scott, St.L.	1	1	1	0	0	0	0	0	0	0	0	0	0	0	0	1	0	0	0	.000	.000	.000
Rollins, Jimmy, Phi.†	2	2	2	0	0	0	0	0	0	0	0	0	0	0	0	1	0	0	0	.000	.000	.000
Romano, Jason, L.A.	8	8	8	0	1	1	0	0	0	0	0	0	0	0	0	2	0	0	0	.125	.125	.125
Romero, Mandy, Col.†	1	1	1	0	0	0	0	0	0	0	0	0	0	0	0	0	0	0	1	.000	.000	.000
Ross, Dave, L.A.	3	3	3	1	1	4	0	0	1	1	0	0	0	0	0	0	0	0	1	.333	.333	1.333
Ruan, Wilkin, L.A.	1	1	1	0	0	0	0	0	0	0	0	0	0	0	0	0	0	0	0	.000	.000	.000
Rusch, Glendon, Mil.*	1	1	1	0	1	1	0	0	0	1	0	0	0	0	0	0	0	0	0	1.000	1.000	1.000
Sanchez, Alex, Mil.*	7	7	7	1	2	2	0	0	0	1	0	0	0	0	0	1	1	0	0	.286	.286	.286
Sanchez, Rey, N.Y.	2	2	2	0	1	1	0	0	0	0	0	0	0	0	0	1	0	0	0	.500	.500	.500
Sanders, Reggie, Pit.	15	15	12	4	4	10	0	0	2	5	0	0	0	3	0	4	0	1	0	.333	.467	.833
Santiago, Benito, S.F.	2	2	2	1	1	1	0	0	0	1	0	0	0	0	0	0	0	0	0	.500	.500	.500
Santos, Francisco, S.F.*	5	5	5	1	2	6	1	0	1	1	0	0	0	0	0	0	0	0	0	.400	.400	1.200
Sardinha, Dane, Cin.	1	1	1	0	0	0	0	0	0	0	0	0	0	0	0	1	0	0	0	.000	.000	.000
Schneider, Brian, Mon.*	9	9	9	1	2	5	0	0	1	5	0	0	0	0	0	4	0	0	0	.222	.222	.556
Scutaro, Marco, N.Y.	8	8	7	1	1	1	0	0	0	0	0	0	0	1	0	1	0	0	0	.143	.250	.143
Sears, Todd, S.D.*	9	8	8	2	2	3	1	0	0	0	0	0	0	0	0	3	0	0	0	.250	.250	.375
Sheffield, Gary, Atl.	1	1	0	0	0	0	0	0	0	0	0	0	0	1	1	0	0	0	0	.000	1.000	.000
Shinjo, Tsuyoshi, N.Y.	15	15	15	0	1	1	0	0	0	0	0	0	0	0	0	1	0	0	0	.067	.067	.067
Simon, Randall, Pit.-Chi.*	20	20	20	1	3	3	0	0	0	3	0	0	0	0	0	5	0	0	0	.150	.150	.150
Smith, Mark, Mil.	19	19	17	3	3	10	1	0	2	6	0	1	0	1	0	6	0	0	1	.176	.211	.588
Smitherman, Stephen, Cin.	8	8	8	3	2	5	0	0	1	3	0	0	0	0	0	3	1	0	0	.250	.250	.625
Snow, J.T., S.F.*	5	4	3	0	0	0	0	0	0	0	0	0	0	1	0	1	0	0	0	.000	.250	.000
Spivey, Junior, Ari.	9	9	9	1	3	6	0	0	1	2	0	0	0	0	0	0	0	0	0	.333	.333	.667
Stairs, Matt, Pit.*	42	42	35	3	8	16	2	0	2	9	0	1	1	5	0	6	0	0	1	.229	.333	.457
Stenson, Dernell, Cin.*	14	14	12	2	4	7	3	0	0	5	0	0	0	2	0	5	0	0	0	.333	.429	.583
Stinnett, Kelly, Cin.-Phi.	18	18	16	0	5	6	1	0	0	2	0	0	1	1	0	8	0	0	0	.313	.389	.375
Stynes, Chris, Col.	17	17	14	1	6	9	0	0	1	10	0	0	1	2	0	4	0	0	0	.429	.529	.643
Sweeney, Mark, Col.*	47	47	44	6	13	17	4	0	0	3	0	0	0	3	0	12	0	0	1	.295	.340	.386
Taguchi, So, St.L.	13	13	11	1	3	6	1	1	0	2	0	0	0	2	0	3	0	0	0	.273	.385	.545
Tatis, Fernando, Mon.	4	4	3	0	1	1	0	0	0	0	0	0	0	1	0	0	0	0	0	.333	.500	.333
Taylor, Reggie, Cin.*	49	48	43	5	9	16	2	1	1	6	1	0	0	4	0	18	1	0	1	.209	.277	.372
Terrero, Luis, Ari.	3	3	2	0	1	1	0	0	0	0	0	0	1	0	0	0	0	0	0	.500	.667	.500
Thome, Jim, Phi.*	2	2	0	0	0	0	0	0	0	0	0	0	0	2	0	0	0	0	0	.000	1.000	.000
Thurston, Joe, L.A.*	9	9	8	2	2	2	0	0	0	0	0	0	0	1	0	1	0	0	0	.250	.333	.250
Tomko, Brett, St.L.	2	2	2	1	1	1	0	0	0	0	0	0	0	0	0	0	0	0	0	.500	.500	.500

Player, Team	G	TPA	AB	R	H	TB	2B	3B	HR	RBI	SH	SF	HP	BB	IBB	SO	SB	CS	GDP	Avg.	OBP	Slg.
Torcato, Tony, S.F.*	9	9	7	0	2	3	1	0	0	1	1	0	1	0	0	2	0	0	0	.286	.375	.429
Torrealba, Yorvit, S.F.	1	1	1	0	0	0	0	0	0	0	0	0	0	0	0	1	0	0	0	.000	.000	.000
Torres, Salomon, Pit.	1	1	1	0	0	0	0	0	0	0	0	0	0	0	0	1	0	0	0	.000	.000	.000
Tucker, T.J., Mon.	2	2	2	0	1	1	0	0	0	0	0	0	0	0	0	0	0	0	0	.500	.500	.500
Uribe, Juan, Col.	3	3	3	0	0	0	0	0	0	0	0	0	0	0	0	0	0	0	0	.000	.000	.000
Utley, Chase, Phi.*	6	6	4	0	0	0	0	0	0	0	0	0	1	1	0	2	1	0	0	.000	.333	.000
Valderrama, Carlos, S.F.	1	1	1	0	0	0	0	0	0	0	0	0	0	0	0	1	0	0	0	.000	.000	.000
Valent, Eric, Cin.*	9	9	8	0	1	1	0	0	0	0	0	0	0	1	0	3	0	0	0	.125	.222	.125
Vander Wal, John, Mil.*	30	29	29	0	6	8	2	0	0	2	0	0	0	0	0	10	0	0	0	.207	.207	.276
Vaughn, Greg, Col.	14	14	11	2	0	0	0	0	0	0	0	0	0	3	0	6	0	0	0	.000	.214	.000
Vaughn, Mo, N.Y.*	2	2	2	0	0	0	0	0	0	0	0	0	0	0	0	0	0	0	0	.000	.000	.000
Vazquez, Ramon, S.D.*	5	5	4	0	0	0	0	0	0	0	0	0	0	1	0	2	0	0	0	.000	.200	.000
Ventura, Robin, L.A.*	8	8	6	0	1	1	0	0	0	0	0	0	0	2	0	2	0	0	0	.167	.375	.167
Victorino, Shane, S.D.†	2	2	2	0	1	1	0	0	0	0	0	0	0	0	0	0	0	0	1	.500	.500	.500
Vidro, Jose, Mon.†	7	7	5	0	3	3	0	0	0	0	0	0	0	2	1	0	0	0	0	.600	.714	.600
Vina, Fernando, St.L.*	1	1	0	0	0	0	0	0	0	0	0	0	1	0	0	0	0	0	0	.000	1.000	.000
Vitiello, Joe, Mon.	11	10	10	1	2	5	0	0	1	2	0	0	0	0	0	1	0	0	1	.200	.200	.500
Vizcaino, Jose, Hou.†	48	48	46	3	11	14	0	0	1	7	1	0	0	1	1	7	0	0	1	.239	.255	.304
Walker, Larry, Col.*	12	11	11	1	3	4	1	0	0	1	0	0	0	0	0	3	0	0	0	.273	.273	.364
Ward, Daryle, L.A.*	29	28	25	2	4	4	0	0	0	4	0	1	0	2	0	6	0	0	0	.160	.214	.160
Watson, Matt, N.Y.*	11	11	11	0	1	2	1	0	0	0	0	0	0	0	0	3	0	0	0	.091	.091	.182
Weeks, Rickie, Mil.	3	3	2	0	0	0	0	0	0	0	0	0	0	1	0	2	0	0	0	.000	.333	.000
Wells, Kip, Pit.	2	2	2	1	2	3	1	0	0	0	0	0	0	0	0	0	0	0	0	1.000	1.000	1.500
White, Rondell, S.D.	8	8	7	0	1	2	1	0	0	3	0	0	0	1	0	3	0	1	0	.143	.250	.286
Widger, Chris, St.L.	3	3	3	0	0	0	0	0	0	0	0	0	0	0	0	2	0	0	0	.000	.000	.000
Wigginton, Ty, N.Y.	1	1	1	0	0	0	0	0	0	0	0	0	0	0	0	0	0	0	0	.000	.000	.000
Wilkerson, Brad, Mon.*	2	2	2	0	0	0	0	0	0	0	0	0	0	0	0	0	0	0	0	.000	.000	.000
Williams, Gerald, Fla.	6	6	6	0	1	1	0	0	0	1	0	0	0	0	0	2	1	0	0	.167	.167	.167
Williams, Matt, Ari.	6	6	5	2	3	5	2	0	0	3	0	1	0	0	0	1	0	0	0	.600	.500	1.000
Wilson, Craig, Pit.	26	26	23	2	5	11	0	0	2	7	0	0	1	2	0	11	0	0	0	.217	.308	.478
Wilson, Jack, Pit.	2	2	2	1	1	2	1	0	0	0	0	0	0	0	0	1	0	0	0	.500	.500	1.000
Wilson, Paul, Cin.	1	1	1	0	0	0	0	0	0	0	0	0	0	0	0	0	0	0	0	.000	.000	.000
Wilson, Preston, Col.	1	1	1	0	0	0	0	0	0	0	0	0	0	0	0	1	0	0	0	.000	.000	.000
Wilson, Vance, N.Y.	8	7	6	1	0	0	0	0	0	1	0	1	0	0	0	3	0	0	0	.000	.000	.000
Womack, Tony, Ari.-Col.-Chi.*	10	10	10	1	1	2	1	0	0	0	0	0	0	0	0	3	0	0	0	.100	.100	.200
Young, Eric, Mil.-S.F.	14	14	13	4	2	3	1	0	0	0	0	0	0	1	0	1	1	2	0	.154	.214	.231
Young, Kevin, Pit.	13	12	9	1	3	4	1	0	0	1	0	0	0	3	0	3	0	0	0	.333	.500	.444
Zaun, Gregg, Hou.-Col.†	33	33	31	2	5	8	3	0	0	3	0	1	0	1	0	6	0	0	1	.161	.182	.258
Zoccolillo, Pete, Mil.*	13	12	11	0	2	2	0	0	0	1	0	0	0	1	0	5	0	0	1	.182	.250	.182

PINCH-HITTERS WITH TWO OR MORE TEAMS

Player, Team	G	TPA	AB	R	H	TB	2B	3B	HR	RBI	SH	SF	HP	BB	IBB	SO	SB	CS	GDP	Avg.	OBP	Slg.
Bellhorn, Mark, Chi.†	10	10	10	1	2	6	1	0	1	1	0	0	0	0	0	4	0	0	0	.200	.200	.600
Bellhorn, Mark, Col.†	18	18	12	0	1	1	0	0	0	1	0	0	0	6	0	7	0	1	0	.083	.389	.083
Harris, Lenny, Chi.*	36	36	32	3	4	4	0	0	0	1	1	0	0	3	2	5	0	0	1	.125	.200	.125
Harris, Lenny, Fla.*	11	10	8	2	4	4	0	0	0	1	0	0	0	2	0	1	0	0	1	.500	.600	.500
Hernandez, Jose, Col.	1	1	1	0	0	0	0	0	0	0	0	0	0	0	0	0	0	0	0	.000	.000	.000
Hernandez, Jose, Chi.	3	3	3	0	0	0	0	0	0	0	0	0	0	0	0	2	0	0	0	.000	.000	.000
Hernandez, Jose, Pit.	2	2	2	0	1	1	0	0	0	2	0	0	0	0	0	1	0	0	0	.500	.500	.500
Hill, Bobby, Chi.†	3	3	2	0	0	0	0	0	0	0	0	0	0	1	0	1	0	0	1	.000	.333	.000
Hill, Bobby, Pit.†	1	1	1	0	0	0	0	0	0	0	0	0	0	0	0	0	0	0	0	.000	.000	.000
Lofton, Kenny, Pit.*	3	3	2	0	0	0	0	0	0	1	0	1	0	0	0	0	0	0	0	.000	.000	.000
Lofton, Kenny, Chi.*	4	4	4	1	1	2	1	0	0	0	0	0	0	0	0	1	0	0	0	.250	.250	.500
Simon, Randall, Pit.*	15	15	15	1	3	3	0	0	0	3	0	0	0	0	0	4	0	0	0	.200	.200	.200
Simon, Randall, Chi.*	5	5	5	0	0	0	0	0	0	0	0	0	0	0	0	1	0	0	0	.000	.000	.000
Stinnett, Kelly, Cin.	12	12	11	0	2	3	1	0	0	2	0	0	1	0	0	7	0	0	0	.182	.250	.273
Stinnett, Kelly, Phi.	6	6	5	0	3	3	0	0	0	0	0	0	0	1	0	1	0	0	0	.600	.667	.600
Womack, Tony, Ari.*	2	2	2	1	1	2	1	0	0	0	0	0	0	0	0	1	0	0	0	.500	.500	1.000
Womack, Tony, Col.*	2	2	2	0	0	0	0	0	0	0	0	0	0	0	0	0	0	0	0	.000	.000	.000
Womack, Tony, Chi.*	6	6	6	0	0	0	0	0	0	0	0	0	0	0	0	2	0	0	0	.000	.000	.000
Young, Eric, Mil.	11	11	10	3	1	2	1	0	0	0	0	0	0	1	0	1	0	1	0	.100	.182	.200
Young, Eric, S.F.	3	3	3	1	1	1	0	0	0	0	0	0	0	0	0	0	1	1	0	.333	.333	.333
Zaun, Gregg, Hou.†	32	32	30	2	5	8	3	0	0	3	0	1	0	1	0	5	0	0	1	.167	.188	.267
Zaun, Gregg, Col.†	1	1	1	0	0	0	0	0	0	0	0	0	0	0	0	1	0	0	0	.000	.000	.000

PITCHING

TEAM

Team	W	L	Pct.	ERA	G	CG	ShO	Rel.	Sv.-Op.	IP	H	TBF	R	ER	HR	SH	SF	HB	BB	IBB	SO	WP	Bk.
Los Angeles	85	77	.525	3.16	162	3	17	438	58-66	1457.2	1254	6001	556	511	127	62	19	40	526	35	1289	50	5
San Francisco	100	61	.621	3.73	161	7	10	461	43-60	1437.1	1349	6090	638	595	136	61	53	43	546	34	1006	68	8
Chicago	88	74	.543	3.83	162	13	14	420	36-51	1456.1	1304	6227	683	619	143	82	36	71	617	36	1404	63	3
Arizona	84	78	.519	3.84	162	7	11	452	42-55	1455.0	1379	6230	685	621	150	81	31	72	526	53	1291	52	9
Houston	87	75	.537	3.86	162	1	5	502	50-64	1450.0	1350	6176	677	622	161	66	36	74	565	53	1139	40	4
Montreal	83	79	.512	4.01	162	15	10	437	42-60	1437.2	1467	6171	716	640	181	46	35	71	463	51	1028	71	4
Florida	91	71	.562	4.04	162	7	11	395	36-50	1445.1	1415	6165	692	648	128	60	53	40	530	40	1132	51	11
Philadelphia	86	76	.531	4.04	162	9	13	437	33-51	1443.2	1386	6195	697	648	142	79	29	77	536	51	1060	53	4
Atlanta	101	61	.623	4.10	162	4	7	489	51-71	1456.1	1425	6247	740	663	147	63	39	42	555	69	992	53	4
New York	66	95	.410	4.48	161	3	10	412	38-53	1413.1	1497	6204	754	704	168	63	43	45	576	71	907	45	7
St. Louis	85	77	.525	4.60	162	9	10	460	41-71	1463.2	1544	6375	796	748	210	68	45	65	508	36	969	53	1
Pittsburgh	75	87	.463	4.64	162	7	10	457	44-68	1444.1	1527	6293	801	744	178	81	44	61	502	58	926	50	2
San Diego	64	98	.395	4.87	162	2	10	473	31-49	1431.1	1458	6303	831	774	208	54	53	62	611	52	1091	64	3
Milwaukee	68	94	.420	5.02	162	5	3	460	44-71	1452.0	1590	6459	873	810	219	69	47	61	575	43	1034	57	8
Cincinnati	69	93	.426	5.09	162	4	5	475	38-64	1446.1	1578	6423	886	818	209	70	43	48	590	61	932	46	3
Colorado	74	88	.457	5.20	162	3	4	500	34-54	1420.0	1629	6364	892	821	200	54	53	84	552	51	866	48	8
Totals	1306	1284	.504	4.28	1295	99	150	7268	661-958	23110.1	23152	99923	11917	10986	2707	1059	659	956	8778	794	17066	864	84

NOTE: Totals for earned runs for several clubs do not agree with composite total for all pitchers of each respective club due to instances in which provisions of Section 10.18(i) of the Scoring Rules were applied. The following differences are to be noted: Houston pitchers add to 623; Montreal pitchers add to 641; Florida pitchers add to 649; Philadelphia pitchers add to 651; New York pitchers add to 706; St. Louis pitchers add to 751; Pittsburgh pitchers add to 746; San Diego pitchers add to 775; Milwaukee pitchers add to 811; Colorado pitchers add to 826.

INDIVIDUAL

TOP QUALIFIERS FOR EARNED-RUN AVERAGE TITLE

Minimum 162 innings. *Throws lefthanded.

Pitcher, Team	W	L	Pct.	ERA	G	GS	CG	ShO	GF	Sv.-Op.	IP	H	TBF	R	ER	HR	SH	SF	HB	BB	IBB	SO	WP	Bk.
Schmidt, Jason, S.F.	17	5	.773	2.34	29	29	5	3	0	0-0	207.2	152	819	56	54	14	6	3	5	46	1	208	7	1
Brown, Kevin, L.A.	14	9	.609	2.39	32	32	0	0	0	0-0	211.0	184	856	67	56	11	12	2	5	56	2	185	5	1
Prior, Mark, Chi.	18	6	.750	2.43	30	30	3	1	0	0-0	211.1	183	863	67	57	15	9	2	9	50	4	245	9	0
Webb, Brandon, Ari.	10	9	.526	2.84	29	28	1	1	1	0-0	180.2	140	750	65	57	12	9	1	13	68	4	172	9	1
Schilling, Curt, Ari.	8	9	.471	2.95	24	24	3	2	0	0-0	168.0	144	673	58	55	17	11	1	3	32	2	194	4	0
Nomo, Hideo, L.A.	16	13	.552	3.09	33	33	2	2	0	0-0	218.1	175	897	82	75	24	11	3	1	98	6	177	11	0
Zambrano, Carlos, Chi.	13	11	.542	3.11	32	32	3	1	0	0-0	214.0	188	907	88	74	9	11	6	10	94	12	168	6	1
Wood, Kerry, Chi.	14	11	.560	3.20	32	32	4	2	0	0-0	211.0	152	887	77	75	24	11	6	21	100	2	266	10	0
Hernandez, Livan, Mon.	15	10	.600	3.20	33	33	8	0	0	0-0	233.1	225	967	92	83	27	6	4	10	57	3	178	6	1
Vazquez, Javier, Mon.	13	12	.520	3.24	34	34	4	1	0	0-0	230.2	198	938	93	83	28	6	6	4	57	5	241	11	1
Wells, Kip, Pit.	10	9	.526	3.28	31	31	1	0	0	0-0	197.1	171	835	77	72	24	15	2	7	76	7	147	7	0
Batista, Miguel, Ari.	10	9	.526	3.54	36	29	2	1	5	0-0	193.1	197	822	85	76	13	10	6	8	60	3	142	7	0
Redman, Mark, Fla.*	14	9	.609	3.59	29	29	3	0	0	0-0	190.2	172	802	82	76	16	10	5	5	61	3	151	8	2
Padilla, Vicente, Phi.	14	12	.538	3.62	32	32	1	1	0	0-0	208.2	196	876	94	84	22	11	7	16	62	4	133	3	2
Redding, Tim, Hou.	10	14	.417	3.68	33	32	0	0	0	0-0	176.0	179	769	85	72	16	7	3	7	65	4	116	3	0

DEPARTMENTAL LEADERS: W—Ortiz, Atl., 21; L—D'Amico, Pit., 16; G—Quantrill, L.A., 89; GS—Maddux, Atl., 36; CG—Hernandez, Mon., 8; ShO—Millwood, Phi., Morris, St.L., Schmidt, S.F., 3; GF—Gagne, L.A., Wagner, Hou., 67; Sv.—Gagne, L.A., 55; IP—Hernandez, Mon., 233.1; H—Tomko, St.L., 252; TBF—Hernandez, Mon., 967; R—Franklin, Mil., 129; ER—Franklin, Mil., Tomko, St.L., 119; HR—Franklin, Mil., 36; SH—Wells, Pit., 15; SF—Kinney, Mil., 11; HB—Wood, Chi., 21; TBB—Ortiz, Atl., 102; IBB—Zambrano, Chi., 12; SO—Wood, Chi., 266; WP—Clement, Chi., Day, Mon., 13; Bk.—Franklin, Mil., Penny, Fla., 4.

ALL PITCHERS

*Throws lefthanded.

Pitcher, Team	W	L	Pct.	ERA	G	GS	CG	ShO	GF	Sv.-Op.	IP	H	TBF	R	ER	HR	SH	SF	HB	BB	IBB	SO	WP	Bk.
Acevedo, Jose, Cin.	2	0	1.000	2.67	5	4	1	0	1	0-0	27.0	17	103	8	8	3	1	2	1	6	1	23	1	0
Adams, Terry, Phi.	1	4	.200	2.65	66	0	0	0	16	0-0	68.0	68	284	22	20	1	3	2	2	23	4	51	4	0
Ainsworth, Kurt, S.F.	5	4	.556	3.82	11	11	0	0	0	0-0	66.0	66	283	31	28	7	2	2	1	26	0	48	2	0
Alfonseca, Antonio, Chi.	3	1	.750	5.83	60	0	0	0	17	0-4	66.1	76	296	43	43	7	4	1	2	27	3	51	0	0
Almanza, Armando, Fla.*	4	5	.444	6.08	51	0	0	0	15	0-2	50.1	59	230	37	34	10	1	3	2	25	2	49	2	1
Almonte, Edwin, N.Y.	0	0	.000	11.12	12	0	0	0	3	0-0	11.1	21	57	15	14	3	1	0	0	5	1	7	1	0
Almonte, Hector, Mon.	1	1	.500	6.83	28	0	0	0	5	0-1	29.0	34	137	22	22	4	1	0	2	17	2	26	5	0
Alvarez, Juan, Fla.*	0	0	.000	3.09	9	0	0	0	3	0-0	11.2	8	46	4	4	2	0	0	1	8	1	6	0	0
Alvarez, Victor, L.A.*	0	1	.000	12.71	5	0	0	0	3	0-0	5.2	9	31	8	8	1	1	0	1	6	0	3	0	0
Alvarez, Wilson, L.A.*	6	2	.750	2.37	21	12	1	1	2	1-1	95.0	80	377	27	25	5	2	1	5	23	1	82	1	0
Anderson, Jason, N.Y.	0	0	.000	5.06	6	0	0	0	2	0-0	10.2	10	47	6	6	2	0	2	1	5	1	7	0	0
Anderson, Jimmy, Cin.*	1	5	.167	8.84	8	7	0	0	1	0-0	38.2	60	184	39	38	8	0	3	0	14	1	13	0	0
Armas, Tony, Mon.	2	1	.667	2.61	5	5	0	0	0	0-0	31.0	25	124	9	9	4	2	2	1	8	0	23	0	0
Ashby, Andy, L.A.	3	10	.231	5.18	21	12	0	0	5	0-0	73.0	90	318	42	42	8	7	2	3	17	2	41	5	0
Astacio, Pedro, N.Y.	3	2	.600	7.36	7	7	0	0	0	0-0	36.2	47	174	30	30	8	1	1	3	18	1	20	4	0
Austin, Jeff, Cin.	2	3	.400	8.58	7	7	0	0	0	0-0	28.1	28	132	27	27	9	1	0	0	21	0	22	1	0
Ayala, Luis, Mon.	10	3	.769	2.92	65	0	0	0	24	5-8	71.0	65	288	27	23	8	3	1	5	13	3	46	1	0
Aybar, Manny, S.F.	0	0	.000	6.00	3	0	0	0	1	0-0	3.0	4	16	2	2	1	0	1	0	3	0	2	0	0
Bacsik, Mike, N.Y.*	1	2	.333	10.19	5	3	0	0	1	0-0	17.2	28	85	21	20	5	0	1	0	8	0	12	0	0
Bale, John, Cin.*	1	2	.333	4.47	10	9	0	0	0	0-0	46.1	50	195	24	23	7	1	2	2	12	2	37	1	0
Batista, Miguel, Ari.	10	9	.526	3.54	36	29	2	1	5	0-0	193.1	197	822	85	76	13	10	6	8	60	3	142	7	0
Beck, Rod, S.D.	3	2	.600	1.78	36	0	0	0	30	20-20	35.1	25	140	7	7	4	1	0	1	11	2	32	0	0
Beckett, Josh, Fla.	9	8	.529	3.04	24	23	0	0	1	0-0	142.0	132	601	54	48	9	5	1	2	56	4	152	6	1
Beimel, Joe, Pit.*	1	3	.250	5.05	69	0	0	0	11	0-5	62.1	69	276	35	35	7	3	5	4	33	6	42	0	1

Pitcher, Team	W	L	Pct.	ERA	G	GS	CG	ShO	GF	Sv.-Op.	IP	H	TBF	R	ER	HR	SH	SF	HB	BB	IBB	SO	WP	Bk.
Belisle, Matt, Cin.	1	1	.500	5.19	6	0	0	0	2	0-1	8.2	10	39	5	5	1	2	1	1	2	0	6	0	0
Benes, Alan, Chi.	0	0	.000	2.16	3	0	0	0	1	1-1	8.1	8	36	2	2	0	0	0	0	6	0	9	0	1
Benitez, Armando, N.Y.	3	3	.500	3.10	45	0	0	0	40	21-28	49.1	41	209	18	17	5	0	1	0	24	1	50	3	1
Benson, Kris, Pit.	5	9	.357	4.97	18	18	0	0	0	0-0	105.0	127	475	67	58	14	3	4	1	36	4	68	7	0
Bernero, Adam, Col.	0	2	.000	5.23	31	0	0	0	5	0-2	32.2	33	142	22	19	5	2	2	1	13	1	26	2	0
Biddle, Rocky, Mon.	5	8	.385	4.65	73	0	0	0	58	34-41	71.2	71	330	43	37	10	4	1	6	40	5	54	8	0
Bland, Nate, Hou.*	1	2	.333	5.75	22	0	0	0	2	0-1	20.1	22	96	13	13	3	4	1	2	12	2	18	3	0
Boehringer, Brian, Pit.	5	4	.556	5.49	62	0	0	0	18	0-3	62.1	64	278	39	38	11	3	2	3	30	3	47	0	1
Bong, Jung, Atl.*	6	2	.750	5.05	44	0	0	0	14	1-3	57.0	56	247	32	32	8	3	1	2	31	6	47	6	1
Borbon, Pedro, St.L.*	0	1	.000	20.25	7	0	0	0	3	0-0	4.0	14	28	9	9	2	0	0	1	2	2	0	0	0
Borland, Toby, Fla.	0	0	.000	1.86	7	0	0	0	1	0-0	9.2	3	40	3	2	0	0	1	0	8	1	4	0	0
Borowski, Joe, Chi.	2	2	.500	2.63	68	0	0	0	59	33-37	68.1	53	280	23	20	5	4	0	1	19	1	66	0	0
Bottalico, Ricky, Ari.	1	0	1.000	5.40	2	0	0	0	0	0-0	1.2	3	10	1	1	0	0	0	0	2	1	2	0	0
Brohawn, Troy, L.A.*	2	0	1.000	3.86	12	0	0	0	5	0-0	11.2	10	48	6	5	2	0	0	0	4	0	13	0	0
Brower, Jim, S.F.	8	5	.615	3.96	51	5	0	0	13	2-3	100.0	90	411	48	44	8	5	4	1	39	2	65	4	0
Brown, Kevin, L.A.	14	9	.609	2.39	32	32	0	0	0	0-0	211.0	184	856	67	56	11	12	2	5	56	2	185	5	1
Bullinger, Kirk, Hou.	0	0	.000	6.75	7	0	0	0	3	0-0	8.0	7	33	6	6	2	0	0	0	1	0	5	0	0
Bump, Nate, Fla.	4	0	1.000	4.71	32	0	0	0	8	0-0	36.1	34	167	21	19	3	1	1	7	20	0	17	0	0
Burba, Dave, Mil.	1	1	.500	3.53	17	2	0	0	2	0-0	43.1	42	193	19	17	5	2	0	4	19	2	35	2	0
Burnett, A.J., Fla.	0	2	.000	4.70	4	4	0	0	0	0-0	23.0	18	106	13	12	2	2	1	2	18	2	21	2	0
Bynum, Mike, S.D.*	1	4	.200	8.75	13	5	0	0	3	0-0	36.0	44	165	35	35	14	1	0	1	15	0	35	0	0
Calero, Kiko, St.L.	1	1	.500	2.82	26	1	0	0	7	1-4	38.1	29	162	12	12	5	1	3	1	20	2	51	3	1
Capuano, Chris, Ari.*	2	4	.333	4.64	9	5	0	0	2	0-0	33.0	27	139	19	17	3	4	1	6	11	1	23	3	0
Cerda, Jaime, N.Y.*	1	1	.500	5.85	27	0	0	0	9	0-1	32.1	32	144	21	21	4	2	2	0	20	1	19	3	1
Cerros, Juan, Cin.	0	0	.000	4.85	11	0	0	0	2	0-0	13.0	11	57	7	7	1	0	1	2	5	2	9	0	0
Chacon, Shawn, Col.	11	8	.579	4.60	23	23	0	0	0	0-0	137.0	124	596	73	70	12	10	5	12	58	4	93	8	0
Chen, Bruce, Hou.*	0	0	.000	6.00	11	0	0	0	2	0-0	12.0	14	60	8	8	2	3	2	2	8	1	8	0	0
Christiansen, Jason, S.F.*	0	0	.000	5.19	40	0	0	0	7	0-1	26.0	25	115	15	15	3	0	0	1	11	0	22	2	0
Clement, Matt, Chi.	14	12	.538	4.11	32	32	2	1	0	0-0	201.2	169	851	100	92	22	10	2	14	79	2	171	13	0
Colyer, Steve, L.A.*	0	0	.000	2.75	13	0	0	0	3	0-0	19.2	22	84	6	6	0	1	0	0	9	0	16	1	0
Condrey, Clay, S.D.	1	2	.333	8.47	9	6	0	0	0	0-0	34.0	43	168	32	32	7	3	0	3	21	4	25	0	0
Cone, David, N.Y.	1	3	.250	6.50	5	4	0	0	0	0-0	18.0	20	85	13	13	4	1	0	0	13	1	13	0	0
Cook, Aaron, Col.	4	6	.400	6.02	43	16	1	0	4	0-0	124.0	160	579	89	83	8	4	6	8	57	7	43	10	0
Corcoran, Roy, Mon.	0	0	.000	1.23	5	0	0	0	2	0-0	7.1	7	31	2	1	0	0	0	0	3	0	2	1	0
Cordero, Chad, Mon.	1	0	1.000	1.64	12	0	0	0	4	1-1	11.0	4	40	2	2	1	1	0	0	3	1	12	1	0
Corey, Mark, Pit.	1	2	.333	5.34	22	0	0	0	10	0-0	30.1	29	131	19	18	2	1	3	1	11	1	27	2	0
Cormier, Rheal, Phi.*	8	0	1.000	1.70	65	0	0	0	21	1-4	84.2	54	327	18	16	4	4	0	1	25	2	67	0	1
Correia, Kevin, S.F.	3	1	.750	3.66	10	7	0	0	1	0-0	39.1	41	173	16	16	6	1	1	4	18	1	28	2	0
Crudale, Mike, St.L.-Mil.	0	1	.000	2.61	22	0	0	0	6	0-1	20.2	12	93	8	6	1	1	1	1	18	1	13	1	0
Cruz, Juan, Chi.	2	7	.222	6.05	25	6	0	0	3	0-1	61.0	66	284	44	41	7	7	2	7	28	0	65	4	0
Cruz, Nelson, Col.	3	5	.375	7.21	20	7	0	0	1	0-1	53.2	65	233	43	43	15	1	2	3	11	2	38	3	0
Cunnane, Will, Atl.	2	2	.500	2.70	20	0	0	0	8	3-3	20.0	14	80	6	6	2	0	0	0	6	2	20	1	0
D'Amico, Jeff, Pit.	9	16	.360	4.77	29	29	2	1	0	0-0	175.1	204	765	104	93	23	11	5	7	42	6	100	6	0
Darensbourg, Vic, Col.-Mon.*	0	0	.000	8.00	9	0	0	0	3	0-0	9.0	17	46	9	8	2	1	0	0	1	0	4	0	0
Davis, Doug, Mil.*	3	2	.600	2.58	8	8	1	0	0	0-0	52.1	49	224	18	15	8	3	2	0	21	0	35	1	0
Dawley, Joe, Atl.	0	0	.000	18.00	5	0	0	0	4	0-0	7.0	15	41	14	14	3	0	0	1	3	0	8	1	0
Day, Zach, Mon.	9	8	.529	4.18	23	23	1	1	0	0-0	131.1	132	580	64	61	8	2	5	10	59	3	61	13	0
de los Santos, Valerio, Mil.-Phi.*	4	3	.571	4.50	51	0	0	0	6	1-4	52.0	45	228	31	26	8	7	4	5	25	0	39	2	0
Deago, Roger, S.D.*	0	1	.000	7.84	2	2	0	0	0	0-0	10.1	11	49	9	9	0	1	1	0	8	0	10	3	0
DeJean, Mike, Mil.-St.L.	5	8	.385	4.68	76	0	0	0	45	19-27	82.2	86	365	46	43	13	1	3	2	39	7	71	3	0
Dempster, Ryan, Cin.	3	7	.300	6.54	22	20	0	0	1	0-0	115.2	134	545	89	84	14	9	4	5	70	4	84	3	0
Dessens, Elmer, Ari.	8	8	.500	5.07	34	30	0	0	1	0-0	175.2	212	781	107	99	22	9	3	4	57	6	113	3	2
Dotel, Octavio, Hou.	6	4	.600	2.48	76	0	0	0	13	4-6	87.0	53	346	25	24	9	2	1	3	31	2	97	2	0
Downs, Scott, Mon.*	0	1	.000	15.00	1	1	0	0	0	0-0	3.0	5	17	5	5	2	0	0	0	3	2	4	0	1
Dreifort, Darren, L.A.	4	4	.500	4.03	10	10	0	0	0	0-0	60.1	58	261	29	27	6	3	1	0	25	0	67	3	1
Drew, Tim, Mon.	0	2	.000	12.46	6	1	0	0	3	0-0	8.2	12	46	12	12	3	1	2	0	8	1	3	3	0
Duckworth, Brandon, Phi.	4	7	.364	4.94	24	18	0	0	2	0-0	93.0	98	424	58	51	12	9	1	10	44	3	68	5	0
Durocher, Jayson, Mil.	2	0	1.000	11.05	6	0	0	0	0	0-0	7.1	9	33	9	9	4	0	0	1	2	0	7	2	0
Eaton, Adam, S.D.	9	12	.429	4.08	31	31	1	0	0	0-0	183.0	173	789	91	83	20	5	5	7	68	6	146	7	1
Eischen, Joey, Mon.*	2	2	.500	3.06	70	0	0	0	15	1-4	53.0	57	221	27	18	7	3	0	3	13	1	40	3	0
Elarton, Scott, Col.	4	4	.500	6.27	11	10	0	0	0	0-0	51.2	73	253	46	36	13	3	4	4	20	3	20	3	0
Eldred, Cal, St.L.	7	4	.636	3.74	62	0	0	0	18	8-14	67.1	62	293	32	28	9	5	3	4	31	4	67	4	0
Estes, Shawn, Chi.*	8	11	.421	5.73	29	28	1	1	0	0-0	152.1	182	699	113	97	20	11	7	1	83	1	103	6	0
Estrella, Leo, Mil.	7	3	.700	4.36	58	0	0	0	18	3-8	66.0	75	290	32	32	10	4	3	3	21	5	25	2	1
Etherton, Seth, Cin.	2	4	.333	6.90	7	7	0	0	0	0-0	30.0	39	145	23	23	4	3	3	3	15	1	17	0	0
Eyre, Scott, S.F.*	2	1	.667	3.32	74	0	0	0	10	1-3	57.0	60	256	23	21	4	2	3	1	26	0	35	6	0
Farnsworth, Kyle, Chi.	3	2	.600	3.30	77	0	0	0	13	0-3	76.1	53	312	31	28	6	4	1	0	36	1	92	6	0
Fassero, Jeff, St.L.*	1	7	.125	5.68	62	6	0	0	15	3-6	77.2	93	354	51	49	17	3	1	2	34	4	55	2	0
Feliciano, Pedro, N.Y.*	0	0	.000	3.35	23	0	0	0	8	0-0	48.1	52	218	21	18	5	0	1	3	21	3	43	3	1
Fernandez, Jared, Hou.	3	3	.500	3.99	12	6	0	0	3	0-0	38.1	37	161	17	17	2	3	1	2	12	2	19	3	0
Ferrari, Anthony, Mon.*	0	0	.000	6.75	4	0	0	0	1	0-0	4.0	4	21	3	3	1	0	0	1	5	1	1	1	0
Figueroa, Nelson, Pit.	2	1	.667	3.31	12	3	0	0	1	0-0	35.1	28	146	13	13	8	2	2	2	13	2	23	2	0
Fogg, Josh, Pit.	10	9	.526	5.26	26	26	1	0	0	0-0	142.0	166	625	90	83	22	6	4	9	40	0	71	2	0
Foppert, Jesse, S.F.	8	9	.471	5.03	23	21	0	0	0	0-0	111.0	103	500	69	62	16	5	9	3	69	4	101	12	0
Ford, Matt, Mil.*	0	3	.000	4.33	25	4	0	0	12	0-0	43.2	46	197	23	21	5	0	1	1	21	0	26	0	0
Foster, John, Mil.*	2	0	1.000	4.71	23	0	0	0	3	0-2	21.0	30	99	11	11	5	1	1	1	8	2	16	1	0
Fox, Chad, Fla.	2	1	.667	2.13	21	0	0	0	3	0-0	25.1	16	105	6	6	1	3	4	0	14	2	27	5	0
Franco, John, N.Y.*	0	3	.000	2.62	38	0	0	0	13	2-3	34.1	35	148	11	10	5	1	1	1	13	2	16	2	0
Franklin, Wayne, Mil.*	10	13	.435	5.50	36	34	1	1	1	0-0	194.2	201	870	129	119	36	12	3	10	94	2	116	3	4
Fuentes, Brian, Col.*	3	3	.500	2.75	75	0	0	0	23	4-6	75.1	64	320	24	23	7	0	3	6	34	2	82	2	1
Gagne, Eric, L.A.	2	3	.400	1.20	77	0	0	0	67	55-55	82.1	37	306	12	11	2	4	0	3	20	2	137	2	0
Gallo, Mike, Hou.*	1	0	1.000	3.00	32	0	0	0	6	0-1	30.0	28	121	10	10	3	2	3	1	10	2	16	0	0
Geary, Geoff, Phi.	0	0	.000	4.50	5	0	0	0	2	0-0	6.0	8	28	3	3	0	1	0	0	3	0	3	0	0
Glavine, Tom, N.Y.*	9	14	.391	4.52	32	32	0	0	0	0-0	183.1	205	791	94	92	21	7	4	2	66	7	82	2	0
Gonzalez, Edgar, Ari.	2	1	.667	4.91	9	2	0	0	1	0-1	18.1	28	85	10	10	3	1	1	0	7	2	14	2	0

Pitcher, Team	W	L	Pct.	ERA	G	GS	CG	ShO	GF	Sv.-Op.	IP	H	TBF	R	ER	HR	SH	SF	HB	BB	IBB	SO	WP	Bk.
Gonzalez, Mike, Pit.*	0	1	.000	7.56	16	0	0	0	2	0-0	8.1	7	38	7	7	4	1	1	0	6	0	6	1	0
Gonzalez, Wiki, S.D.	0	0	.000	0.00	1	0	0	0	1	0-0	1.0	0	4	0	0	0	0	0	0	1	0	0	0	0
Good, Andrew, Ari.	4	2	.667	5.29	16	10	0	0	0	0-0	66.1	74	289	42	39	15	3	4	3	16	3	42	3	0
Grabow, John, Pit.*	0	0	.000	3.60	5	0	0	0	1	0-0	5.0	6	22	3	2	0	0	0	0	0	0	9	0	0
Graves, Danny, Cin.	4	15	.211	5.33	30	26	2	1	3	2-2	169.0	204	741	108	100	30	6	3	7	41	6	60	2	0
Griffiths, Jeremy, N.Y.	1	4	.200	7.02	9	6	0	0	1	0-0	41.0	57	199	34	32	5	4	0	2	19	2	25	1	0
Gryboski, Kevin, Atl.	6	4	.600	3.86	64	0	0	0	9	0-4	44.1	44	191	22	19	3	4	0	2	23	6	32	2	0
Guthrie, Mark, Chi.*	2	3	.400	2.74	65	0	0	0	10	0-1	42.2	40	187	14	13	6	6	2	3	22	4	24	3	0
Hackman, Luther, S.D.	2	2	.500	5.17	65	0	0	0	16	0-2	76.2	78	347	51	44	7	2	2	8	36	2	48	6	0
Hall, Josh, Cin.	0	2	.000	6.57	6	5	0	0	1	0-0	24.2	33	121	22	18	4	0	1	0	15	1	18	0	0
Hamilton, Joey, Cin.	0	0	.000	12.66	3	0	0	0	1	0-0	10.2	21	57	15	15	3	0	0	0	5	0	7	0	0
Hampton, Mike, Atl.*	14	8	.636	3.84	31	31	1	0	0	0-0	190.0	186	823	91	81	14	10	5	1	78	4	110	10	1
Hancock, Josh, Phi.	0	0	.000	3.00	2	0	0	0	0	0-0	3.0	2	11	1	1	0	0	0	0	0	0	4	0	0
Harang, Aaron, Cin.	4	3	.571	5.28	9	9	0	0	0	0-0	46.0	48	191	28	27	6	3	0	1	10	0	26	3	0
Haren, Danny, St.L.	3	7	.300	5.08	14	14	0	0	0	0-0	72.2	84	320	44	41	9	4	2	5	22	0	43	3	0
Haynes, Jimmy, Cin.	2	12	.143	6.30	18	18	1	0	0	0-0	94.1	118	448	74	66	14	7	2	3	57	3	49	2	0
Hebson, Bryan, Mon.	0	0	.000	13.50	2	0	0	0	1	0-0	2.0	4	12	3	3	1	0	1	1	1	0	1	0	0
Heilman, Aaron, N.Y.	2	7	.222	6.75	14	13	0	0	0	0-0	65.1	79	315	53	49	13	5	3	3	41	2	51	5	0
Helling, Rick, Fla.	1	0	1.000	0.55	11	0	0	0	5	0-0	16.1	11	62	1	1	1	0	0	0	5	0	12	1	0
Heredia, Felix, Cin.*	5	2	.714	3.00	57	0	0	0	18	1-4	72.0	61	303	27	24	9	4	2	2	28	5	41	5	0
Herges, Matt, S.D.-S.F.	3	2	.600	2.62	67	0	0	0	24	3-6	79.0	68	332	27	23	3	2	6	3	29	2	68	1	1
Hermanson, Dustin, St.L.-S.F.	3	3	.500	4.06	32	6	0	0	12	1-6	68.2	70	291	32	31	9	4	2	3	24	4	39	3	0
Hernandez, Livan, Mon.	15	10	.600	3.20	33	33	8	0	0	0-0	233.1	225	967	92	83	27	6	4	10	57	3	178	6	1
Hernandez, Roberto, Atl.	5	3	.625	4.35	66	0	0	0	12	0-4	60.0	61	282	36	29	10	4	0	3	43	7	45	0	0
Hitchcock, Sterling, St.L.*	5	1	.833	3.79	8	6	0	0	0	0-0	38.0	34	162	17	16	8	3	1	1	14	1	32	2	0
Hodges, Trey, Atl.	3	3	.500	4.66	52	1	0	0	15	0-2	65.2	69	296	38	34	11	2	3	3	31	7	66	7	0
Hoffman, Trevor, S.D.	0	0	.000	2.00	9	0	0	0	7	0-0	9.0	7	36	2	2	1	0	0	0	3	0	11	0	0
Holmes, Darren, Atl.	1	2	.333	4.29	48	0	0	0	12	0-1	42.0	47	180	22	20	5	0	1	0	11	0	46	1	0
Howard, Ben, S.D.	1	3	.250	3.63	6	6	0	0	0	0-0	34.2	31	148	17	14	10	1	0	0	15	1	24	1	0
Ishii, Kazuhisa, L.A.*	9	7	.563	3.86	27	27	0	0	0	0-0	147.0	129	656	72	63	16	6	2	6	101	4	140	10	2
Isringhausen, Jason, St.L.	0	1	.000	2.36	40	0	0	0	31	22-25	42.0	31	174	14	11	2	1	0	0	18	1	41	6	0
Jackson, Edwin, L.A.	2	1	.667	2.45	4	3	0	0	0	0-0	22.0	17	91	6	6	2	1	1	1	11	1	19	3	0
Jarvis, Kevin, S.D.	4	8	.333	5.87	16	16	0	0	0	0-0	92.0	113	413	65	60	15	2	5	2	32	5	49	2	0
Jennings, Jason, Col.	12	13	.480	5.11	32	32	1	0	0	0-0	181.1	212	820	115	103	20	11	6	5	88	7	119	7	0
Jensen, Ryan, S.F.	0	0	.000	10.80	6	2	0	0	3	0-0	13.1	21	64	16	16	6	4	2	1	5	0	3	0	0
Jimenez, Jose, Col.	2	10	.167	5.22	63	7	0	0	40	20-23	101.2	137	471	62	59	7	4	3	6	32	5	45	4	0
Johnson, Jonathan, Hou.	0	1	.000	5.87	4	3	0	0	0	0-0	15.1	20	78	11	10	2	0	1	0	15	3	7	1	0
Johnson, Randy, Ari.*	6	8	.429	4.26	18	18	1	1	0	0-0	114.0	125	489	61	54	16	4	3	8	27	3	125	1	1
Jones, Todd, Col.	1	4	.200	8.24	33	1	0	0	7	0-5	39.1	61	193	39	36	8	3	2	1	18	0	28	0	0
Journell, Jimmy, St.L.	0	0	.000	6.00	7	0	0	0	2	0-0	9.0	10	48	7	6	0	0	1	0	11	0	8	1	0
Junge, Eric, Phi.	0	0	.000	3.52	6	0	0	0	1	0-0	7.2	5	28	3	3	1	0	0	0	1	0	5	0	0
Keisler, Randy, S.D.*	0	1	.000	12.00	2	2	0	0	0	0-0	6.0	7	33	9	8	3	0	1	1	7	0	5	0	1
Kida, Masao, L.A.	0	1	.000	3.00	3	2	0	0	1	0-0	12.0	15	53	5	4	0	0	0	0	3	0	8	3	0
Kieschnick, Brooks, Mil.	1	1	.500	5.26	42	0	0	0	15	0-0	53.0	66	242	32	31	5	2	0	6	13	4	39	2	0
Kim, Byung-Hyun, Ari.	1	5	.167	3.56	7	7	0	0	0	0-0	43.0	34	181	17	17	6	3	0	4	15	0	33	0	0
Kim, Sun-Woo, Mon.	0	1	.000	8.36	4	3	0	0	1	0-0	14.0	24	72	13	13	6	0	1	4	8	0	5	0	0
King, Ray, Atl.*	3	4	.429	3.51	80	0	0	0	9	0-1	59.0	46	247	30	23	3	1	2	1	27	2	43	4	0
Kinney, Matt, Mil.	10	13	.435	5.19	33	31	1	0	1	0-0	190.2	201	847	121	110	27	10	11	6	80	4	152	10	2
Kline, Steve, St.L.*	5	5	.500	3.82	78	0	0	0	22	3-7	63.2	56	274	29	27	5	3	2	3	30	5	31	2	0
Knott, Eric, Mon.*	1	2	.333	5.12	13	1	0	0	1	0-0	19.1	23	86	12	11	2	1	1	0	6	0	17	0	0
Kolb, Danny, Mil.	1	2	.333	1.96	37	0	0	0	25	21-23	41.1	34	175	10	9	2	1	0	1	19	3	39	1	0
Koplove, Mike, Ari.	3	0	1.000	2.15	31	0	0	0	5	0-1	37.2	31	157	11	9	3	2	2	5	10	1	27	1	0
Lawrence, Brian, S.D.	10	15	.400	4.19	33	33	1	0	0	0-0	210.2	206	884	106	98	27	11	6	11	57	8	116	4	0
Leiter, Al, N.Y.*	15	9	.625	3.99	30	30	1	1	0	0-0	180.2	176	798	83	80	15	11	6	9	94	11	139	5	1
Leskanic, Curtis, Mil.	4	0	1.000	2.70	26	0	0	0	5	0-0	26.2	22	116	8	8	1	0	0	1	18	0	28	2	0
Levrault, Allen, Fla.	1	0	1.000	3.86	19	0	0	0	4	0-0	28.0	38	133	12	12	3	1	2	1	15	2	21	1	0
Lidge, Brad, Hou.	6	3	.667	3.60	78	0	0	0	9	1-6	85.0	60	349	36	34	6	2	3	5	42	7	97	4	1
Lincoln, Mike, Pit.	3	4	.429	5.20	36	0	0	0	14	5-8	36.1	38	153	22	21	5	1	1	1	13	0	28	1	0
Linebrink, Scott, Hou.-S.D.	3	2	.600	3.31	52	6	0	0	8	0-0	92.1	93	397	37	34	9	4	6	6	36	4	68	11	0
Lloyd, Graeme, N.Y.*	1	2	.333	3.31	36	0	0	0	12	0-0	35.1	39	149	16	13	2	1	2	0	7	2	17	1	0
Loewer, Carlton, S.D.	1	2	.333	6.65	5	5	0	0	0	0-0	21.2	35	105	17	16	3	0	1	1	8	1	11	1	0
Looper, Braden, Fla.	6	4	.600	3.68	74	0	0	0	64	28-34	80.2	82	347	34	33	4	3	3	1	29	1	56	2	0
Lopez, Javier, Col.*	4	1	.800	3.70	75	0	0	0	11	1-2	58.1	58	242	25	24	5	1	0	4	12	2	40	1	3
Lowry, Noah, S.F.*	0	0	.000	0.00	4	0	0	0	3	0-0	6.1	1	24	0	0	0	0	0	1	2	0	5	0	0
Maddux, Greg, Atl.	16	11	.593	3.96	36	36	1	0	0	0-0	218.1	225	901	112	96	24	10	9	8	33	7	124	3	0
Madson, Ryan, Phi.	0	0	.000	0.00	1	0	0	0	0	0-0	2.0	0	6	0	0	0	0	0	0	0	0	0	0	0
Mahomes, Pat, Pit.	0	1	.000	4.84	9	1	0	0	1	0-0	22.1	19	97	13	12	2	2	4	0	12	1	13	1	0
Mann, Jim, Pit.	0	0	.000	10.80	2	0	0	0	0	0-0	1.2	5	12	4	2	1	0	0	0	1	0	1	0	0
Manning, David, Mil.	0	2	.000	16.20	2	2	0	0	0	0-0	6.2	11	38	13	12	1	1	1	0	8	0	2	2	0
Manon, Julio, Mon.	1	2	.333	4.13	23	0	0	0	7	1-1	28.1	26	125	13	13	3	2	2	1	17	1	15	0	0
Mantei, Matt, Ari.	5	4	.556	2.62	50	0	0	0	44	29-32	55.0	37	220	17	16	6	4	2	2	18	1	68	1	0
Manzanillo, Josias, Cin.	0	2	.000	12.66	9	0	0	0	1	0-1	10.2	21	59	20	15	7	1	0	0	4	0	12	0	0
Marquis, Jason, Atl.	0	0	.000	5.53	21	2	0	0	10	1-1	40.2	43	182	27	25	3	0	3	2	18	2	19	2	0
Martin, Tom, L.A.*	1	2	.333	3.53	80	0	0	0	13	0-1	51.0	36	210	21	20	6	0	2	2	24	4	51	1	0
Martinez, Luis, Mil.*	0	3	.000	9.92	4	4	0	0	0	0-0	16.1	25	86	18	18	3	4	0	0	15	2	10	3	1
Matthews, Mike, S.D.*	6	4	.600	4.45	77	0	0	0	20	0-3	64.2	65	281	34	32	4	3	5	4	29	5	44	4	0
Meadows, Brian, Pit.	2	1	.667	4.72	34	7	0	0	11	1-1	76.1	91	329	45	40	8	2	1	1	11	2	38	4	0
Mercado, Hector, Phi.*	0	0	.000	5.79	13	0	0	0	4	1-2	18.2	18	86	12	12	5	0	2	1	12	0	15	1	0
Mercedes, Jose, Mon.	0	0	.000	0.00	5	0	0	0	0	0-0	7.1	6	31	3	0	0	0	0	0	5	0	3	1	0
Mercker, Kent, Cin.-Atl.*	0	2	.000	1.95	67	0	0	0	15	1-5	55.1	46	242	16	12	6	6	1	0	32	4	48	4	1
Mesa, Jose, Phi.	5	7	.417	6.52	61	0	0	0	47	24-28	58.0	71	273	44	42	7	1	0	1	31	2	45	3	0
Miceli, Dan, Col.-Hou.	1	3	.250	3.55	37	0	0	0	9	0-0	50.2	46	211	20	20	10	3	0	2	16	2	38	3	1
Middlebrook, Jason, N.Y.	0	0	.000	10.29	5	0	0	0	2	0-0	7.0	13	36	8	8	0	1	1	0	4	0	3	1	0
Miller, Matt, Col.	0	0	.000	2.08	4	0	0	0	2	0-0	4.1	5	18	1	1	0	0	0	0	2	0	5	0	0
Miller, Wade, Hou.	14	13	.519	4.13	33	33	1	0	0	0-0	187.1	168	797	96	86	17	8	7	10	77	1	161	4	0

Pitcher, Team	W	L	Pct.	ERA	G	GS	CG	ShO	GF	Sv.-Op.	IP	H	TBF	R	ER	HR	SH	SF	HB	BB	IBB	SO	WP	Bk.
Millwood, Kevin, Phi.	14	12	.538	4.01	35	35	5	3	0	0-0	222.0	210	930	103	99	19	12	5	4	68	6	169	2	0
Mitre, Sergio, Chi.	0	1	.000	8.31	3	2	0	0	1	0-0	8.2	15	43	8	8	1	0	1	0	4	1	3	0	0
Moehler, Brian, Hou.	0	0	.000	7.90	3	3	0	0	0	0-0	13.2	22	66	12	12	4	1	1	0	6	0	5	0	0
Molina, Gabe, St.L.	0	0	.000	13.50	3	0	0	0	1	0-0	2.2	5	14	4	4	1	0	0	0	1	0	1	0	0
Moreno, Orber, N.Y.	0	0	.000	7.88	7	0	0	0	4	0-0	8.0	10	36	7	7	1	1	0	0	3	0	5	0	0
Morris, Matt, St.L.	11	8	.579	3.76	27	27	5	3	0	0-0	172.1	164	703	76	72	20	5	3	4	39	1	120	3	0
Moss, Damian, S.F.*	9	7	.563	4.70	21	20	0	0	0	0-0	115.0	121	518	62	60	12	3	4	5	63	3	57	11	3
Mota, Guillermo, L.A.	6	3	.667	1.97	76	0	0	0	18	1-3	105.0	78	410	23	23	7	3	1	1	26	4	99	0	0
Mullen, Scott, L.A.*	0	0	.000	9.00	1	1	0	0	0	0-0	3.0	2	17	3	3	0	0	1	1	5	0	1	0	0
Munro, Pete, Hou.	3	4	.429	4.67	40	2	0	0	8	0-1	54.0	63	249	30	28	7	3	1	5	26	2	27	1	0
Myers, Brett, Phi.	14	9	.609	4.43	32	32	1	1	0	0-0	193.0	205	848	99	95	20	6	3	9	76	8	143	9	0
Myers, Mike, Ari.*	0	1	.000	5.70	64	0	0	0	17	0-3	36.1	38	172	23	23	4	1	0	5	21	1	21	1	0
Myers, Rodney, L.A.	0	0	.000	6.00	4	0	0	0	3	0-0	9.0	10	42	7	6	1	0	0	1	4	0	5	0	0
Nagy, Charles, S.D.	0	2	.000	4.38	5	0	0	0	0	0-0	12.1	15	52	7	6	0	1	0	0	3	0	7	0	0
Nance, Shane, Mil.*	0	2	.000	4.81	26	0	0	0	6	0-1	24.1	34	118	16	13	5	1	2	1	10	1	25	1	0
Nathan, Joe, S.F.	12	4	.750	2.96	78	0	0	0	9	0-3	79.0	51	316	26	26	7	2	4	3	33	3	83	4	1
Neagle, Denny, Col.*	2	4	.333	7.90	7	7	0	0	0	0-0	35.1	47	161	31	31	12	1	0	1	12	0	21	1	0
Neal, Blaine, Fla.	0	0	.000	8.14	18	0	0	0	6	0-0	21.0	38	108	20	19	2	1	5	1	9	1	10	1	0
Nomo, Hideo, L.A.	16	13	.552	3.09	33	33	2	2	0	0-0	218.1	175	897	82	75	24	11	3	1	98	6	177	11	0
Norton, Phil, Chi.-Cin.*	0	0	.000	3.00	21	0	0	0	4	0-0	18.0	9	68	6	6	0	1	0	0	9	0	7	1	0
Nunez, Vladimir, Fla.	0	3	.000	16.03	14	0	0	0	4	0-3	10.2	21	63	21	19	7	1	2	0	7	0	10	0	0
Obermueller, Wes, Mil.	2	5	.286	5.07	12	11	0	0	0	0-0	65.2	81	303	40	37	10	1	2	6	25	2	34	5	0
Ohka, Tomo, Mon.	10	12	.455	4.16	34	34	2	0	0	0-0	199.0	233	864	106	92	24	8	3	9	45	11	118	8	0
Ohme, Kevin, St.L.*	0	0	.000	0.00	2	0	0	0	0	0-0	4.1	3	17	0	0	0	0	1	0	1	1	2	1	0
Oliver, Darren, Col.*	13	11	.542	5.04	33	32	1	0	0	0-0	180.1	201	786	108	101	21	4	5	8	61	3	88	0	0
Olsen, Kevin, Fla.	0	0	.000	12.75	7	0	0	0	2	0-0	12.0	25	62	18	17	2	0	0	0	4	1	12	1	0
Oropesa, Eddie, Ari.*	3	3	.500	5.82	47	0	0	0	9	0-0	38.2	38	180	27	25	3	3	0	2	27	2	39	3	1
Orosco, Jesse, S.D.*	1	1	.500	7.56	42	0	0	0	10	2-3	25.0	33	118	22	21	4	0	2	2	10	0	22	4	0
Ortiz, Russ, Atl.	21	7	.750	3.81	34	34	1	1	0	0-0	212.1	177	912	101	90	17	6	7	4	102	7	149	5	0
Oswalt, Roy, Hou.	10	5	.667	2.97	21	21	0	0	0	0-0	127.1	116	514	48	42	15	7	1	5	29	0	108	1	0
Padilla, Vicente, Phi.	14	12	.538	3.62	32	32	1	1	0	0-0	208.2	196	876	94	84	22	11	7	16	62	4	133	3	2
Painter, Lance, St.L.*	0	1	.000	5.50	22	0	0	0	1	0-1	18.0	17	77	12	11	3	1	0	0	7	1	11	0	0
Patterson, John, Ari.	1	4	.200	6.05	16	8	0	0	3	1-1	55.0	61	252	39	37	7	1	2	2	30	5	43	4	0
Pavano, Carl, Fla.	12	13	.480	4.30	33	32	2	0	1	0-0	201.0	204	846	99	96	19	9	10	7	49	10	133	3	2
Pearce, Josh, St.L.	0	0	.000	3.00	7	0	0	0	2	0-0	9.0	11	39	3	3	0	0	0	1	2	0	4	1	0
Pearson, Jason, St.L.*	0	0	.000	63.00	2	0	0	0	0	0-0	1.0	4	10	7	7	1	0	0	0	3	0	1	0	0
Peavy, Jake, S.D.	12	11	.522	4.11	32	32	0	0	0	0-0	194.2	173	827	94	89	33	7	5	6	82	3	156	2	0
Penny, Brad, Fla.	14	10	.583	4.13	32	32	0	0	0	0-0	196.1	195	811	96	90	21	7	5	3	56	6	138	3	4
Perez, Odalis, L.A.*	12	12	.500	4.52	30	30	0	0	0	0-0	185.1	191	772	98	93	28	5	3	3	46	4	141	2	1
Perez, Oliver, S.D.-Pit.*	4	10	.286	5.47	24	24	0	0	0	0-0	126.2	129	579	80	77	22	5	2	4	77	3	141	7	1
Phelps, Tommy, Fla.*	3	2	.600	4.00	27	7	0	0	8	0-0	63.0	70	276	32	28	3	1	2	2	23	1	43	1	0
Plesac, Dan, Phi.*	2	1	.667	2.70	58	0	0	0	9	2-4	33.1	29	141	12	10	3	2	0	1	11	1	37	1	0
Ponson, Sidney, S.F.	3	6	.333	3.71	10	10	0	0	0	0-0	68.0	64	276	29	28	6	4	2	1	18	3	34	3	0
Powell, Brian, S.F.	0	1	.000	13.50	1	1	0	0	0	0-0	4.2	8	22	7	7	3	0	0	0	1	0	3	0	0
Prinz, Bret, Ari.	0	0	.000	0.00	1	0	0	0	0	0-0	1.0	1	5	0	0	0	0	0	0	1	1	1	0	0
Prior, Mark, Chi.	18	6	.750	2.43	30	30	3	1	0	0-0	211.1	183	863	67	57	15	9	2	9	50	4	245	9	0
Puffer, Brandon, Hou.	0	0	.000	5.14	13	0	0	0	4	0-1	21.0	24	99	13	12	2	2	0	1	16	3	10	1	0
Quantrill, Paul, L.A.	2	5	.286	1.75	89	0	0	0	21	1-5	77.1	61	291	18	15	2	4	0	3	15	2	44	0	0
Quevedo, Ruben, Mil.	1	4	.200	6.75	9	8	0	0	0	0-0	42.2	53	196	32	32	12	1	3	0	23	1	19	0	0
Raggio, Brady, Ari.	0	0	.000	6.48	10	0	0	0	4	1-1	8.1	9	38	6	6	1	1	0	0	6	1	8	0	0
Ramirez, Horacio, Atl.*	12	4	.750	4.00	29	29	1	0	0	0-0	182.1	181	781	91	81	21	12	3	6	72	10	100	5	1
Randall, Scott, Cin.	2	5	.286	6.51	15	2	0	0	2	0-1	27.2	34	127	20	20	1	2	0	2	11	3	25	1	0
Randolph, Stephen, Ari.*	8	1	.889	4.05	50	0	0	0	9	0-0	60.0	50	271	28	27	7	5	0	2	43	3	50	4	2
Reames, Britt, Mon.	0	0	.000	27.00	2	0	0	0	0	0-0	1.1	4	10	4	4	0	0	0	0	2	0	1	0	0
Redding, Tim, Hou.	10	14	.417	3.68	33	32	0	0	0	0-0	176.0	179	769	85	72	16	7	3	7	65	4	116	3	0
Redman, Mark, Fla.*	14	9	.609	3.59	29	29	3	0	0	0-0	190.2	172	802	82	76	16	10	5	5	61	3	151	8	2
Reed, Steve, Col.	5	3	.625	3.27	67	0	0	0	22	0-2	63.1	59	269	24	23	9	2	1	8	26	3	39	1	2
Reith, Brian, Cin.	2	3	.400	4.11	42	1	0	0	15	1-1	61.1	61	277	32	28	8	3	5	1	36	6	39	1	0
Reitsma, Chris, Cin.	9	5	.643	4.29	57	3	0	0	36	12-18	84.0	92	351	41	40	14	4	1	0	19	6	53	2	0
Remlinger, Mike, Chi.*	6	5	.545	3.65	73	0	0	0	26	0-1	69.0	54	301	30	28	11	2	2	2	39	4	83	2	0
Reyes, Dennys, Pit.-Ari.*	0	0	.000	10.66	15	0	0	0	4	0-0	12.2	15	63	16	15	2	1	2	0	10	1	16	5	0
Reynolds, Shane, Atl.	11	9	.550	5.43	30	29	0	0	0	0-0	167.1	191	731	104	101	20	10	3	8	59	6	94	0	1
Riedling, John, Cin.	2	3	.400	4.90	55	8	0	0	11	1-4	101.0	107	455	61	55	7	2	6	3	47	0	65	7	1
Ritchie, Todd, Mil.	1	2	.333	5.08	5	5	0	0	0	0-0	28.1	36	131	17	16	4	2	2	4	10	0	15	3	0
Roa, Joe, Phi.-Col.-S.D.	1	3	.250	6.14	28	4	0	0	9	0-0	51.1	69	232	36	35	10	3	1	2	10	0	38	1	0
Roach, Jason, N.Y.	0	2	.000	12.00	2	2	0	0	0	0-0	9.0	14	46	12	12	3	1	0	1	4	0	2	2	0
Roberts, Grant, N.Y.	0	3	.000	3.79	18	0	0	0	5	1-1	19.0	19	79	9	8	0	1	0	1	3	1	10	0	0
Robertson, Jeriome, Hou.*	15	9	.625	5.10	32	31	0	0	0	0-0	160.2	180	711	98	91	23	8	5	6	64	8	99	1	2
Rodriguez, Felix, S.F.	8	2	.800	3.10	68	0	0	0	24	2-3	61.0	59	265	21	21	5	3	1	4	29	2	46	5	1
Rosario, Rodrigo, Hou.	1	0	1.000	1.13	2	2	0	0	0	0-0	8.0	5	33	2	1	0	0	0	1	3	1	6	1	0
Rueter, Kirk, S.F.*	10	5	.667	4.53	27	27	0	0	0	0-0	147.0	170	632	77	74	14	9	2	1	47	2	41	0	0
Rusch, Glendon, Mil.*	1	12	.077	6.42	32	19	1	0	1	1-1	123.1	171	573	93	88	11	5	2	4	45	3	93	3	0
Saarloos, Kirk, Hou.	2	1	.667	4.93	36	4	0	0	11	0-0	49.1	55	218	31	27	4	1	1	3	17	3	43	0	0
Sanchez, Duaner, Pit.	1	0	1.000	16.50	6	0	0	0	2	0-0	6.0	15	34	11	11	2	0	1	2	1	0	3	0	0
Sanchez, Felix, Chi.*	0	0	.000	10.80	3	0	0	0	0	0-0	1.2	2	9	2	2	1	0	0	0	3	0	2	0	0
Sanchez, Jesus, Col.*	0	0	.000	9.00	9	0	0	0	4	0-0	8.0	11	38	8	8	1	0	0	0	4	2	2	1	0
Sauerbeck, Scott, Pit.*	3	4	.429	4.05	53	0	0	0	11	0-4	40.0	30	173	20	18	5	2	0	1	25	2	32	0	0
Schilling, Curt, Ari.	8	9	.471	2.95	24	24	3	2	0	0-0	168.0	144	673	58	55	17	11	1	3	32	2	194	4	0
Schmidt, Jason, S.F.	17	5	.773	2.34	29	29	5	3	0	0-0	207.2	152	819	56	54	14	6	3	5	46	1	208	7	1
Seo, Jae Weong, N.Y.	9	12	.429	3.82	32	31	0	0	0	0-0	188.1	193	806	94	80	18	8	4	6	46	11	110	2	0
Serafini, Dan, Cin.*	1	3	.250	5.40	10	4	0	0	2	0-0	30.0	41	141	23	18	5	3	2	0	14	1	13	1	0
Service, Scott, Ari.	0	2	.000	4.91	18	0	0	0	7	1-1	18.1	21	77	10	10	1	1	1	0	2	1	18	1	0
Sheets, Ben, Mil.	11	13	.458	4.45	34	34	1	0	0	0-0	220.2	232	931	122	109	29	11	6	6	43	2	157	7	0
Shuey, Paul, L.A.	6	4	.600	3.00	62	0	0	0	18	0-1	69.0	50	281	24	23	6	2	0	4	33	3	60	3	0
Silva, Carlos, Phi.	3	1	.750	4.43	62	1	0	0	15	1-3	87.1	92	381	43	43	7	6	1	8	37	5	48	12	1

Pitcher, Team	W	L	Pct.	ERA	G	GS	CG	ShO	GF	Sv.-Op.	IP	H	TBF	R	ER	HR	SH	SF	HB	BB	IBB	SO	WP	Bk.
Simontacchi, Jason, St.L.	9	5	.643	5.56	46	16	1	0	7	1-3	126.1	153	563	82	78	21	2	4	5	41	0	74	4	0
Smith, Dan, Mon.	2	2	.500	5.26	32	0	0	0	8	0-1	37.2	42	170	23	22	11	0	0	2	18	2	35	5	0
Smoltz, John, Atl.	0	2	.000	1.12	62	0	0	0	55	45-49	64.1	48	244	9	8	2	0	1	0	8	1	73	2	0
Speier, Justin, Col.	3	1	.750	4.05	72	0	0	0	31	9-12	73.1	73	319	37	33	11	1	4	7	23	6	66	0	0
Spooneybarger, Tim, Fla.	1	2	.333	4.07	33	0	0	0	9	0-1	42.0	27	159	21	19	1	2	3	1	11	0	32	5	0
Springer, Russ, St.L.	1	1	.500	8.31	17	0	0	0	4	0-1	17.1	19	77	16	16	8	0	0	1	6	0	11	1	0
Stanton, Mike, N.Y.*	2	7	.222	4.57	50	0	0	0	24	5-7	45.1	37	194	25	23	6	1	3	2	19	4	34	2	1
Stark, Denny, Col.	3	3	.500	5.83	17	13	0	0	0	0-0	78.2	98	366	57	51	12	2	7	3	33	2	30	2	1
Stephenson, Garrett, St.L.	7	13	.350	4.59	32	27	1	0	3	0-0	174.1	167	747	94	89	30	11	9	13	60	3	91	5	0
Stewart, Scott, Mon.*	3	1	.750	3.98	51	0	0	0	9	0-1	43.0	52	186	22	19	5	1	1	1	13	4	29	1	1
Stone, Ricky, Hou.	6	4	.600	3.69	65	0	0	0	20	1-1	83.0	76	350	36	34	11	4	1	6	31	4	47	1	0
Strange, Pat, N.Y.	0	0	.000	11.00	6	0	0	0	1	0-0	9.0	13	48	11	11	4	0	0	0	11	0	5	0	0
Strickland, Scott, N.Y.	0	2	.000	2.25	19	0	0	0	3	0-1	20.0	16	84	6	5	1	0	0	1	10	1	16	1	0
Sullivan, Scott, Cin.	6	0	1.000	3.62	50	0	0	0	6	0-1	49.2	39	218	22	20	4	0	2	5	26	4	43	1	0
Suppan, Jeff, Pit.	10	7	.588	3.57	21	21	3	2	0	0-0	141.0	147	597	57	56	11	10	2	6	31	5	78	3	0
Tankersley, Dennis, S.D.	0	1	.000	0.00	1	1	0	0	0	0-0	0.0	3	7	7	7	0	0	0	0	4	0	0	0	0
Tavarez, Julian, Pit.	3	3	.500	3.66	64	0	0	0	29	11-14	83.2	75	350	37	34	1	9	1	5	27	8	39	3	0
Tejera, Michael, Fla.*	3	4	.429	4.67	50	6	0	0	10	2-2	81.0	82	353	44	42	6	8	1	1	36	3	58	0	0
Telemaco, Amaury, Phi.	1	4	.200	3.97	8	8	0	0	0	0-0	45.1	41	194	22	20	5	3	1	7	11	2	29	3	0
Tollberg, Brian, S.D.	0	2	.000	6.97	3	3	0	0	0	0-0	10.1	9	45	11	8	1	1	1	0	4	0	2	0	0
Tomko, Brett, St.L.	13	9	.591	5.28	33	32	2	0	0	0-0	202.2	252	903	126	119	35	12	3	5	57	2	114	6	0
Torres, Salomon, Pit.	7	5	.583	4.76	41	16	0	0	7	2-3	121.0	128	518	65	64	19	4	1	7	42	5	84	3	0
Trachsel, Steve, N.Y.	16	10	.615	3.78	33	33	2	2	0	0-0	204.2	204	857	90	86	26	8	8	3	65	9	111	5	2
Tsao, Chin-hui, Col.	3	3	.500	6.02	9	8	0	0	1	0-0	43.1	48	196	30	29	11	3	0	4	20	1	29	0	0
Tucker, T.J., Mon.	2	3	.400	4.73	45	7	0	0	7	0-2	80.0	90	349	49	42	8	0	1	4	20	1	47	1	0
Urbina, Ugueth, Fla.	3	0	1.000	1.41	33	0	0	0	11	6-8	38.1	23	149	6	6	2	2	2	0	13	0	37	2	0
Valentine, Joe, Cin.	0	0	.000	18.00	2	0	0	0	1	0-0	2.0	5	12	4	4	1	0	0	0	1	0	1	0	0
Valverde, Jose, Ari.	2	1	.667	2.15	54	0	0	0	33	10-11	50.1	24	204	16	12	4	0	1	2	26	2	71	2	0
Van Poppel, Todd, Cin.	2	1	.667	4.54	9	4	0	0	1	0-0	35.2	31	144	18	18	7	1	0	1	6	0	25	0	1
Vance, Cory, Col.*	1	3	.250	5.60	9	3	0	0	1	0-1	27.1	31	121	19	17	6	0	2	1	10	0	12	0	1
Vargas, Claudio, Mon.	6	8	.429	4.34	23	20	0	0	0	0-0	114.0	111	492	59	55	16	4	4	7	41	5	62	2	0
Vazquez, Javier, Mon.	13	12	.520	3.24	34	34	4	1	0	0-0	230.2	198	938	93	83	28	6	6	4	57	5	241	11	1
Veres, Dave, Chi.	2	1	.667	4.68	31	0	0	0	9	1-2	32.2	36	136	17	17	4	2	4	1	5	0	26	3	1
Villafuerte, Brandon, S.D.	0	2	.000	4.20	31	0	0	0	11	2-5	40.2	39	187	20	19	7	2	1	3	26	2	34	2	0
Villarreal, Oscar, Ari.	10	7	.588	2.57	86	1	0	0	14	0-4	98.0	80	422	40	28	6	9	3	3	46	10	80	3	2
Villone, Ron, Hou.*	6	6	.500	4.13	19	19	0	0	0	0-0	106.2	91	449	51	49	16	3	3	5	48	1	91	1	0
Vizcaino, Luis, Mil.	4	3	.571	6.39	75	0	0	0	21	0-6	62.0	64	272	45	44	16	2	1	1	25	3	61	3	0
Vogelsong, Ryan, Pit.	2	2	.500	6.55	6	5	0	0	0	0-0	22.0	30	108	19	16	1	3	1	2	9	3	15	1	0
Wagner, Billy, Hou.*	1	4	.200	1.78	78	0	0	0	67	44-47	86.0	52	335	18	17	8	1	0	3	23	5	105	4	0
Wagner, Ryan, Cin.	2	0	1.000	1.66	17	0	0	0	3	0-1	21.2	13	88	4	4	2	0	1	0	12	1	25	4	0
Walker, Kevin, S.D.*	0	0	.000	5.40	11	0	0	0	2	0-0	6.2	5	30	4	4	1	0	0	0	5	0	5	0	0
Watson, Mark, Cin.*	0	0	.000	4.50	2	0	0	0	2	0-0	2.0	2	9	1	1	0	0	0	0	1	0	2	0	0
Wayne, Justin, Fla.	0	2	.000	11.81	2	2	0	0	0	0-0	5.1	9	31	7	7	1	0	1	1	5	0	1	1	0
Weathers, Dave, N.Y.	1	6	.143	3.08	77	0	0	0	20	7-9	87.2	87	384	33	30	6	8	0	6	40	6	75	1	0
Webb, Brandon, Ari.	10	9	.526	2.84	29	28	1	1	1	0-0	180.2	140	750	65	57	12	9	1	13	68	4	172	9	1
Wellemeyer, Todd, Chi.	1	1	.500	6.51	15	0	0	0	8	1-1	27.2	25	122	22	20	5	1	0	0	19	1	30	0	0
Wells, Kip, Pit.	10	9	.526	3.28	31	31	1	0	0	0-0	197.1	171	835	77	72	24	15	2	7	76	7	147	7	0
Wendell, Turk, Phi.	3	3	.500	3.38	56	0	0	0	20	1-5	64.0	54	273	24	24	6	6	3	6	28	5	27	1	0
Wheeler, Dan, N.Y.	1	3	.250	3.71	35	0	0	0	10	2-3	51.0	49	215	23	21	6	0	3	1	17	4	35	1	0
White, Gabe, Cin.*	3	0	1.000	3.93	34	0	0	0	4	0-1	34.1	36	141	15	15	5	1	2	1	6	3	23	0	0
White, Rick, Hou.	0	0	.000	3.72	15	0	0	0	3	0-0	19.1	18	86	9	8	2	1	0	3	8	0	17	2	0
Williams, Jerome, S.F.	7	5	.583	3.30	21	21	2	1	0	0-0	131.0	116	545	54	48	10	6	3	7	49	3	88	2	1
Williams, Mike, Pit.-Phi.	1	7	.125	6.14	68	0	0	0	47	28-35	63.0	66	299	44	43	5	6	2	4	41	6	39	2	0
Williams, Woody, St.L.	18	9	.667	3.87	34	33	0	0	1	0-1	220.2	220	944	101	95	20	11	6	11	55	2	153	3	0
Williamson, Scott, Cin.	5	3	.625	3.19	42	0	0	0	34	21-26	42.1	34	187	15	15	6	2	0	1	25	4	53	8	0
Willis, Dontrelle, Fla.*	14	6	.700	3.30	27	27	2	2	0	0-0	160.2	148	668	61	59	13	3	1	3	58	0	142	7	1
Wilson, Paul, Cin.	8	10	.444	4.64	28	28	0	0	0	0-0	166.2	190	730	97	86	24	7	0	7	50	5	93	1	0
Witasick, Jay, S.D.	3	7	.300	4.53	46	0	0	0	14	2-7	45.2	42	202	24	23	6	3	1	1	25	4	42	5	0
Wolf, Randy, Phi.*	16	10	.615	4.23	33	33	2	2	0	0-0	200.0	176	850	101	94	27	8	4	6	78	4	177	6	0
Wood, Kerry, Chi.	14	11	.560	3.20	32	32	4	2	0	0-0	211.0	152	887	77	75	24	11	6	21	100	2	266	10	0
Worrell, Tim, S.F.	4	4	.500	2.87	76	0	0	0	64	38-45	78.1	74	335	35	25	5	3	3	0	28	6	65	5	0
Wright, Jaret, S.D.-Atl.	2	5	.286	7.35	50	0	0	0	17	2-5	56.1	76	269	46	46	9	2	4	3	31	2	50	12	0
Yan, Esteban, St.L.	2	0	1.000	6.02	39	0	0	0	17	1-1	43.1	53	199	29	29	8	2	4	5	16	4	28	4	0
Young, Jason, Col.	0	2	.000	8.44	8	3	0	0	1	0-0	21.1	34	108	22	20	8	1	1	1	9	0	18	2	0
Zambrano, Carlos, Chi.	13	11	.542	3.11	32	32	3	1	0	0-0	214.0	188	907	88	74	9	11	6	10	94	12	168	6	1
Zerbe, Chad, S.F.*	1	1	.500	4.71	33	1	0	0	14	0-1	49.2	60	218	26	26	3	3	7	1	14	2	17	1	0

PITCHERS WITH TWO OR MORE TEAMS

Pitcher, Team	W	L	Pct.	ERA	G	GS	CG	ShO	GF	Sv.-Op.	IP	H	TBF	R	ER	HR	SH	SF	HB	BB	IBB	SO	WP	Bk.
Crudale, Mike, St.L.	0	1	.000	2.38	13	0	0	0	4	0-1	11.1	11	59	5	3	1	1	1	1	12	1	6	1	0
Crudale, Mike, Mil.	0	0	.000	2.89	9	0	0	0	2	0-0	9.1	1	34	3	3	0	0	0	0	6	0	7	0	0
Darensbourg, Vic, Col.*	0	0	.000	0.00	3	0	0	0	2	0-0	2.1	4	12	1	0	0	0	0	0	0	0	0	0	0
Darensbourg, Vic, Mon.*	0	0	.000	10.80	6	0	0	0	1	0-0	6.2	13	34	8	8	2	1	0	0	1	0	4	0	0
de los Santos, Valerio, Mil.*	3	3	.500	4.13	45	0	0	0	5	1-4	48.0	38	205	24	22	8	6	4	4	22	0	35	1	0
de los Santos, Valerio, Phi.*	1	0	1.000	9.00	6	0	0	0	1	0-0	4.0	7	23	7	4	0	1	0	1	3	0	4	1	0
DeJean, Mike, Mil.	4	7	.364	4.87	58	0	0	0	40	18-26	64.2	69	286	38	35	12	0	3	1	27	7	58	3	0
DeJean, Mike, St.L.	1	1	.500	4.00	18	0	0	0	5	1-1	18.0	17	79	8	8	1	1	0	1	12	0	13	0	0
Herges, Matt, S.D.	2	2	.500	2.86	40	0	0	0	21	3-5	44.0	40	192	16	14	2	1	5	2	20	2	40	1	0
Herges, Matt, S.F.	1	0	1.000	2.31	27	0	0	0	3	0-1	35.0	28	140	11	9	1	1	1	1	9	0	28	0	1
Hermanson, Dustin, St.L.	1	2	.333	5.46	23	0	0	0	10	1-6	29.2	35	129	18	18	4	2	1	1	14	2	12	1	0
Hermanson, Dustin, S.F.	2	1	.667	3.00	9	6	0	0	2	0-0	39.0	35	162	14	13	5	2	1	2	10	2	27	2	0
Linebrink, Scott, Hou.	1	1	.500	4.26	9	6	0	0	2	0-0	31.2	38	140	15	15	4	2	1	3	14	1	17	5	0
Linebrink, Scott, S.D.	2	1	.667	2.82	43	0	0	0	6	0-0	60.2	55	257	22	19	5	2	5	3	22	3	51	6	0

Pitcher, Team	W	L	Pct.	ERA	G	GS	CG	ShO	GF	Sv.-Op.	IP	H	TBF	R	ER	HR	SH	SF	HB	BB	IBB	SO	WP	Bk.
Mercker, Kent, Cin.*	0	2	.000	2.35	49	0	0	0	8	0-3	38.1	31	169	13	10	5	6	0	0	25	2	41	2	1
Mercker, Kent, Atl.*	0	0	.000	1.06	18	0	0	0	7	1-2	17.0	15	73	3	2	1	0	1	0	7	2	7	2	0
Miceli, Dan, Col.	0	2	.000	5.66	14	0	0	0	1	0-0	20.2	24	95	13	13	7	1	0	1	9	1	18	1	0
Miceli, Dan, Hou.	1	1	.500	2.10	23	0	0	0	8	0-0	30.0	22	116	7	7	3	2	0	1	7	1	20	2	1
Norton, Phil, Chi.*	0	0	.000	5.40	4	0	0	0	2	0-0	3.1	2	14	2	2	0	0	0	0	3	0	0	1	0
Norton, Phil, Cin.*	0	0	.000	2.45	17	0	0	0	2	0-0	14.2	7	54	4	4	0	1	0	0	6	0	7	0	0
Perez, Oliver, S.D.*	4	7	.364	5.38	19	19	0	0	0	0-0	103.2	103	473	65	62	20	4	2	3	65	2	117	6	1
Perez, Oliver, Pit.*	0	3	.000	5.87	5	5	0	0	0	0-0	23.0	26	106	15	15	2	1	0	1	12	1	24	1	0
Reyes, Dennys, Pit.*	0	0	.000	10.45	12	0	0	0	4	0-0	10.1	10	50	13	12	1	1	2	0	9	1	11	5	0
Reyes, Dennys, Ari.*	0	0	.000	11.57	3	0	0	0	0	0-0	2.1	5	13	3	3	1	0	0	0	1	0	5	0	0
Roa, Joe, Phi.	0	2	.000	6.05	6	3	0	0	1	0-0	19.1	28	88	13	13	3	1	0	1	4	0	16	1	0
Roa, Joe, Col.	0	0	.000	4.05	4	0	0	0	3	0-0	6.2	7	26	3	3	2	0	0	0	0	0	4	0	0
Roa, Joe, S.D.	1	1	.500	6.75	18	1	0	0	5	0-0	25.1	34	118	20	19	5	2	1	1	6	0	18	0	0
Williams, Mike, Pit.	1	3	.250	6.27	40	0	0	0	33	25-30	37.1	42	175	26	26	5	1	2	1	22	1	20	1	0
Williams, Mike, Phi.	0	4	.000	5.96	28	0	0	0	14	3-5	25.2	24	124	18	17	0	5	0	3	19	5	19	1	0
Wright, Jaret, S.D.	1	5	.167	8.37	39	0	0	0	14	2-4	47.1	69	233	44	44	9	1	4	2	28	2	41	10	0
Wright, Jaret, Atl.	1	0	1.000	2.00	11	0	0	0	3	0-1	9.0	7	36	2	2	0	1	0	1	3	0	9	2	0

NOTE: The following pitchers combined to pitch shutout games: Arizona (6)—Batista, Villarreal, Myers and Mantei; Dessens, Oropesa, Valverde and Mantei; Schilling, Oropesa, Valverde and Mantei; Schilling and Mantei; Capuano, Valverde and Mantei; Webb and Mantei; Atlanta (6)—Ortiz, Hernandez, Gryboski and Smoltz; Ortiz and Smoltz; Maddux, King, Hernandez, Gryboski and Smoltz; Maddux, King, Holmes, Hernandez and Mercker; Reynolds, Wright and Smoltz; Ramirez, Wright, King, Cunnane and Mercker; Chicago (8)—Wood, Remlinger and Borowski; Zambrano, Remlinger, Alfonseca, Borowski, Farnsworth and Wellemeyer; Estes, Alfonseca and Borowski; Clement, Guthrie, Farnsworth and Borowski; Prior, Farnsworth, Guthrie, Remlinger and Borowski; Prior, Farnsworth and Borowski; Prior and Farnsworth; Wood, Farnsworth and Remlinger; Cincinnati (4)—Reitsma and Williamson; Harang, Wagner and Reitsma; Hall, Riedling and Reitsma; Van Poppel, Norton and Reitsma; Colorado (4)—Chacon, Fuentes and Jimenez; Chacon, Fuentes, Speier, Lopez, Reed and Jimenez; Chacon and Darensbourg; Jennings and Fuentes; Florida (9)—Tejera, Almanza and Levrault; Willis, Nunez and Looper; Penny and Almanza; Redman, Urbina and Looper; Penny and Urbina; Penny, Urbina and Looper; Beckett and Urbina; Beckett, Bump, Urbina and Looper; Willis, Helling, Tejera and Looper; Houston (5)—Oswalt, Munro, Saarloos, Lidge, Dotel and Wagner; Robertson, Lidge, Dotel and Wagner; Robertson, Lidge and Wagner; Oswalt, Dotel and Wagner; Miller, Dotel and Gallo; Los Angeles (14)—Ishii, Martin, Quantrill and Gagne; Perez and Gagne; Brown, Martin, Shuey and Gagne; Brown and Gagne; Nomo and W. Alvarez; Perez and Gagne; Brown, Gagne, Quantrill, Martin and Shuey; Nomo and Gagne; Nomo, Quantrill and Gagne; Ishii, Mota, Martin and Shuey; Perez, Martin and Gagne; Brown, Martin and Gagne; W. Alvarez and Gagne; Jackson, Mota, Martin, Quantrill and Gagne; Milwaukee (2)—Sheets and Kolb; Davis and Kolb; Montreal (8)—Vazquez, Stewart, Tucker and Eischen; Ohka and Stewart; Ohka, Eischen, Smith and Stewart; Vazquez, Eischen and Biddle; Vargas and Biddle; Day, Eischen, Ayala and Biddle; Vazquez and Ayala; Vazquez, Stewart and Cordero; New York (7)—Cone, Weathers, Stanton and Benitez; Trachsel, Lloyd and Benitez; Leiter, Lloyd and Franco; Seo, Weathers and Benitez; Leiter and Weathers; Glavine, Roberts and Stanton; Trachsel, Weathers and Stanton; Philadelphia (6)—Myers, Plesac and Mesa; Padilla, Cormier and Mesa; Padilla, Plesac and Mesa; Millwood and Cormier; Padilla and Cormier; Padilla and Silva; Pittsburgh (7)—Benson, Sauerbeck, Boehringer and Williams; Fogg and Tavarez; Meadows, Boehringer and Lincoln; Fogg and Tavarez; Wells, Meadows and Corey; Fogg, Lincoln and Tavarez; Wells and Meadows; San Diego (10)—Eaton and Herges; Lawrence and Orosco; Perez, Hackman and Beck; Peavy, Orosco and Witasick; Eaton, Matthews, Witasick, Orosco and Beck; Peavy, Witasick and Beck; Lawrence, Hackman, Witasick and Beck; Eaton, Witasick and Matthews; Lawrence, Villafuerte and Roa; Eaton, Linebrink, Matthews, Witasick and Villafuerte; San Francisco (6)—Rueter and Brower; Rueter, Nathan, Eyre and Rodriguez; Brower, Christiansen, Nathan and Rodriguez; Schmidt, Christiansen and Worrell; Ponson and Worrell; Rueter, Herges and Rodriguez; St. Louis (7)—Williams, Painter, Calero, Fassero and Hermanson; Williams, Springer, Fassero and Hermanson; Tomko and Isringhausen; Tomko, Kline, Simontacchi and DeJean; Hitchcock, Eldred, Kline and Springer; Morris, Kline, DeJean and Isringhausen; Williams, Kline and Pearce.

FIELDING

TEAM

Team	G	PO	A	E	TC	DP	TP	PB	Pct.
St. Louis	162	4391	1644	77	6112	138	0	7	.987
Florida	162	4336	1590	78	6004	162	0	11	.987
San Francisco	161	4312	1675	80	6067	163	0	8	.987
Houston	162	4350	1710	95	6155	149	0	4	.985
Philadelphia	162	4331	1694	97	6122	146	0	16	.984
Montreal	162	4313	1732	102	6147	152	0	11	.983
San Diego	162	4294	1634	102	6030	141	0	15	.983
Chicago	162	4369	1681	106	6156	157	0	12	.983
Arizona	162	4365	1693	107	6165	132	0	15	.983
Milwaukee	162	4356	1617	114	6087	142	0	14	.981
Colorado	162	4260	1785	116	6161	165	1	11	.981
Los Angeles	162	4373	1810	119	6302	164	0	8	.981
Atlanta	162	4369	1884	121	6374	166	1	7	.981
Pittsburgh	162	4333	1844	123	6300	159	0	10	.980
New York	161	4240	1655	118	6013	158	0	5	.980
Cincinnati	162	4339	1700	141	6180	152	0	9	.977
Totals	1295	69331	27348	1696	98375	2446	2	163	.983

INDIVIDUAL

FIRST BASEMEN

NOTE: All caps denotes fielding-percentage leader based on 81 games for catchers, 108 for all other non-pitchers and 162 innings for pitchers. *Throws lefthanded.

Player, Team	G	GS	PO	A	E	TC	DP	Pct.
Baerga, Carlos, Ari.	19	13	123	8	2	133	12	.985
Bagwell, Jeff, Hou.	158	158	1290	112	9	1411	125	.994
Banks, Brian, Fla.	12	6	72	2	0	74	11	1.000
Barnes, Larry, L.A.*	8	5	43	2	0	45	4	1.000
Bell, Jay, N.Y.	13	2	33	0	1	34	3	.971
Bellhorn, Mark, Col.	1	0	1	1	0	2	0	1.000
Blum, Geoff, Hou.	6	0	11	0	0	11	1	1.000
Branyan, Russell, Cin.	14	10	98	7	1	106	13	.991
Buchanan, Brian, S.D.	24	19	137	9	2	148	19	.986
Cabrera, Jolbert, L.A.	8	4	25	2	0	27	2	1.000
Cairo, Miguel, St.L.	3	0	9	0	0	9	1	1.000
Casey, Sean, Cin.	144	144	1257	75	6	1338	112	.996
Castro, Juan, Cin.	1	0	0	0	0	0	0	.000
Choi, Hee Seop, Chi.*	69	55	523	40	5	568	46	.991
Clark, Tony, N.Y.	80	50	465	25	4	494	42	.992
Coomer, Ron, L.A.	24	15	106	10	0	116	10	1.000
Cordero, Wil, Mon.	123	117	1065	66	5	1136	90	.996
Counsell, Craig, Ari.	2	0	3	0	0	3	1	1.000
DeRosa, Mark, Atl.	1	0	1	0	0	1	1	1.000
Dunn, Adam, Cin.	19	7	81	8	1	90	10	.989
Feliz, Pedro, S.F.	12	9	82	4	0	86	9	1.000
Fick, Robert, Atl.	115	111	1004	52	14	1070	89	.987
Fox, Andy, Fla.	2	2	14	1	0	15	3	1.000
Franco, Julio, Atl.	75	38	432	32	1	465	47	.998
Franco, Matt, Atl.	15	10	122	6	3	131	13	.977
Galarraga, Andres, S.F.	69	57	503	29	3	535	56	.994
Glavine, Mike, N.Y.*	3	1	10	1	0	11	1	1.000
Grace, Mark, Ari.*	39	28	258	19	2	279	24	.993
Guzman, Edwards, Mon.	13	9	68	3	2	73	7	.973
Hansen, Dave, S.D.	20	9	105	10	0	115	14	1.000
Harris, Lenny, Chi.	2	0	5	1	0	6	0	1.000
Helton, Todd, Col.*	159	159	1418	156	11	1585	149	.993
Hernandez, Jose, Col.	1	1	8	1	0	9	0	1.000
Hessman, Mike, Atl.	4	3	30	1	0	31	3	1.000
Hillenbrand, Shea, Ari.	56	52	439	27	5	471	32	.989
Houston, Tyler, Phi.	1	0	6	0	0	6	1	1.000
Karros, Eric, Chi.	97	84	675	47	6	728	80	.992
Kinkade, Mike, L.A.	13	6	72	10	0	82	7	1.000
Klesko, Ryan, S.D.*	111	103	849	84	6	939	67	.994
LaRue, Jason, Cin.	1	1	7	1	0	8	0	1.000
Lee, Derrek, Fla.	155	153	1279	97	5	1381	132	.996
Liefer, Jeff, Mon.	21	19	142	7	3	152	18	.980
Lo Duca, Paul, L.A.	22	17	158	11	1	170	14	.994
Marrero, Eli, St.L.	2	0	6	0	0	6	0	1.000
Martinez, Ramon, Chi.	2	0	1	0	0	1	0	1.000
MARTINEZ, Tino, St.L.	126	126	1026	85	3	1114	92	.997
Matheny, Mike, St.L.	4	0	7	0	0	7	1	1.000
McEwing, Joe, N.Y.	5	0	8	0	0	8	1	1.000
McGriff, Fred, L.A.*	79	79	667	41	8	716	66	.989
Merced, Orlando, Hou.	12	4	50	4	1	55	6	.982
Merloni, Lou, S.D.	2	0	5	0	0	5	1	1.000
Mordecai, Mike, Fla.	1	1	10	0	0	10	1	1.000
Nevin, Phil, S.D.	31	30	239	21	1	261	26	.996
Niekro, Lance, S.F.	3	0	4	0	0	4	1	1.000
Norton, Greg, Col.	9	0	20	2	0	22	0	1.000
Ojeda, Miguel, S.D.	2	1	12	0	0	12	1	1.000
Overbay, Lyle, Ari.*	75	69	643	58	2	703	48	.997
Pellow, Kit, Col.	1	1	9	0	0	9	0	1.000
Perez, Eduardo, St.L.	5	0	9	2	0	11	1	1.000
Perez, Tomas, Phi.	9	3	35	3	0	38	5	1.000
Phillips, Jason, N.Y.	84	82	667	44	7	718	72	.990
Piazza, Mike, N.Y.	1	0	3	0	0	3	0	1.000
Pratt, Todd, Phi.	6	4	44	2	0	46	3	1.000
Pujols, Albert, St.L.	62	36	340	33	1	374	34	.997
Redmond, Mike, Fla.	1	0	1	0	0	1	1	1.000
Richard, Chris, Col.*	1	0	3	1	0	4	1	1.000
Rivera, Carlos, Pit.*	60	14	229	15	4	248	22	.984
Rivera, Michael, S.D.	1	0	2	0	0	2	0	1.000
Santos, Francisco, S.F.*	1	1	5	0	0	5	2	1.000
Sears, Todd, S.D.	1	0	1	0	0	1	1	1.000
Sexson, Richie, Mil.	162	162	1363	130	11	1504	131	.993
Simon, Randall, Pit.-Chi.*	109	99	852	72	6	930	71	.994
Snow, J.T., S.F.*	97	93	814	74	5	893	82	.994
Stairs, Matt, Pit.	31	27	212	10	2	224	16	.991
Stenson, Dernell, Cin.*	1	0	1	0	0	1	0	1.000
Sweeney, Mark, Col.*	8	1	12	0	0	12	2	1.000
Thome, Jim, Phi.	156	155	1372	86	5	1463	132	.997
Vaughn, Mo, N.Y.	24	24	179	8	5	192	21	.974
Ventura, Robin, L.A.	42	25	252	17	2	271	26	.993
Vitiello, Joe, Mon.	12	6	74	8	2	84	7	.976
Vizcaino, Jose, Hou.	1	0	6	0	0	6	0	1.000
Ward, Daryle, L.A.*	13	11	108	10	1	119	14	.992
Widger, Chris, St.L.	1	0	2	1	0	3	0	1.000
Wilkerson, Brad, Mon.*	27	11	148	9	0	157	8	1.000
Wilson, Craig, Pit.	36	29	229	20	3	252	31	.988
Young, Kevin, Pit.	44	16	202	18	1	221	25	.995

TRIPLE PLAY: Helton, Col.

FIRST BASEMEN WITH TWO OR MORE TEAMS

Player, Team	G	GS	PO	A	E	TC	DP	Pct.
Simon, Randall, Pit.*	80	76	655	52	4	711	55	.994
Simon, Randall, Chi.*	29	23	197	20	2	219	16	.991

SECOND BASEMEN

Player, Team	G	GS	PO	A	E	TC	DP	Pct.
Alfonzo, Edgardo, S.F.	6	6	11	14	0	25	3	1.000
Alomar, Roberto, N.Y.	72	69	138	171	6	315	50	.981
Baerga, Carlos, Ari.	15	15	21	40	1	62	11	.984
Bell, David, Phi.	3	3	3	8	0	11	1	1.000
Bell, Jay, N.Y.	14	10	15	25	2	42	7	.952
Bellhorn, Mark, Col.	20	12	31	41	2	74	6	.973
Belliard, Ronnie, Col.	113	105	224	311	15	550	79	.973
Blum, Geoff, Hou.	25	18	34	42	1	77	8	.987
Boone, Aaron, Cin.	19	19	43	63	0	106	14	1.000
Bruntlett, Eric, Hou.	9	3	13	14	0	27	4	1.000
Butler, Brent, Col.	20	18	32	51	1	84	10	.988
Cabrera, Jolbert, L.A.	59	40	93	95	1	189	24	.995
Cairo, Miguel, St.L.	40	33	58	88	2	148	17	.986
Carroll, Jamey, Mon.	11	5	12	15	0	27	5	1.000
Castillo, Luis, Fla.	152	151	286	433	10	729	99	.986
Castro, Juan, Cin.	56	45	100	154	4	258	33	.984
Cintron, Alex, Ari.	9	5	14	17	0	31	5	1.000
Cora, Alex, L.A.	141	122	286	377	15	678	112	.978
Counsell, Craig, Ari.	10	7	9	22	0	31	5	1.000
Cromer, Tripp, Hou.	1	0	1	2	0	3	1	1.000
Cruz, Enrique, Mil.	6	1	3	7	0	10	0	1.000

Player, Team	G	GS	PO	A	E	TC	DP	Pct.
Delgado, Wilson, St.L.	12	6	12	20	0	32	3	1.000
DeRosa, Mark, Atl.	29	25	49	78	2	129	21	.984
Durham, Ray, S.F.	105	101	185	309	5	499	66	.990
Fox, Andy, Fla.	15	8	14	22	3	39	6	.923
Freel, Ryan, Cin.	11	10	14	20	1	35	2	.971
Garcia, Danny, N.Y.	17	16	36	40	4	80	9	.950
Garcia, Jesse, Atl.	6	0	6	4	0	10	1	1.000
Giles, Marcus, Atl.	139	136	278	471	14	763	85	.982
Ginter, Keith, Mil.	53	49	103	128	2	233	35	.991
Grudzielanek, Mark, Chi.	121	115	231	331	8	570	94	.986
Hall, Bill, Mil.	18	14	41	46	4	91	14	.956
Hansen, Dave, S.D.	1	0	0	0	0	0	0	.000
Hart, Bo, St.L.	69	65	167	180	4	351	35	.989
Hernandez, Jose, Chi.	1	0	0	0	0	0	0	.000
Hill, Bobby, Chi.-Pit.	3	0	1	2	0	3	0	1.000
Hummel, Tim, Cin.	1	1	2	3	0	5	1	1.000
Jimenez, D'Angelo, Cin.	73	72	164	214	4	382	56	.990
Kata, Matt, Ari.	52	45	106	131	3	240	27	.988
Kent, Jeff, Hou.	128	127	278	354	11	643	83	.983
Lockhart, Keith, S.D.	27	14	37	33	1	71	8	.986
Lopez, Felipe, Cin.	3	3	3	4	1	8	1	.875
LORETTA, Mark, S.D.	150	144	273	412	7	692	84	.990
Macias, Jose, Mon.	4	0	0	2	0	2	0	1.000
Mackowiak, Rob, Pit.	15	11	21	30	0	51	3	1.000
Martinez, Ramon, Chi.	42	33	56	84	3	143	26	.979
Mateo, Henry, Mon.	43	20	49	82	4	135	23	.970
Matranga, Dave, Hou.	2	0	2	0	0	2	0	1.000
McEwing, Joe, N.Y.	55	42	100	101	1	202	26	.995
Merloni, Lou, S.D.	10	2	9	10	1	20	1	.950
Mordecai, Mike, Fla.	12	3	5	10	1	16	4	.938
Nunez, Abraham O., Pit.	71	60	125	198	7	330	42	.979
Ojeda, Augie, Chi.	5	4	8	9	0	17	2	1.000
Olmedo, Ray, Cin.	18	12	35	36	0	71	9	1.000
Ozuna, Pablo, Col.	8	8	22	31	1	54	9	.981
Perez, Neifi, S.F.	57	37	97	134	3	234	36	.987
Perez, Tomas, Phi.	26	17	52	54	2	108	11	.981
Polanco, Placido, Phi.	99	99	213	301	4	518	69	.992
Punto, Nick, Phi.	16	7	36	28	1	65	6	.985
Reboulet, Jeff, Pit.	76	62	134	215	4	353	51	.989
Reese, Pokey, Pit.	33	29	66	119	6	191	24	.969
Romano, Jason, L.A.	1	0	0	0	0	0	0	.000
Sanchez, Rey, N.Y.	12	6	16	23	2	41	8	.951
Scutaro, Marco, N.Y.	39	18	52	52	2	106	13	.981
Spivey, Junior, Ari.	98	90	169	269	8	446	54	.982
Stynes, Chris, Col.	5	4	7	10	0	17	3	1.000
Taguchi, So, St.L.	1	0	0	0	0	0	0	.000
Thurston, Joe, L.A.	3	0	2	4	1	7	2	.857
Uribe, Juan, Col.	11	10	25	40	1	66	10	.985
Utley, Chase, Phi.	37	36	65	107	3	175	31	.983
Vazquez, Ramon, S.D.	3	2	6	9	0	15	5	1.000
Vidro, Jose, Mon.	137	137	199	396	10	605	76	.983
Vina, Fernando, St.L.	60	58	147	158	8	313	44	.974
Vizcaino, Jose, Hou.	20	14	35	44	2	81	9	.975
Weeks, Rickie, Mil.	4	2	1	1	1	3	0	.667
Womack, Tony, Col.-Chi.	21	15	32	39	0	71	8	1.000
Young, Eric, Mil.-S.F.	117	113	230	306	16	552	67	.971

SECOND BASEMEN WITH TWO OR MORE TEAMS

Player, Team	G	GS	PO	A	E	TC	DP	Pct.
Hill, Bobby, Chi.	2	0	1	0	0	1	0	1.000
Hill, Bobby, Pit.	1	0	0	2	0	2	0	1.000
Womack, Tony, Col.	7	5	12	14	0	26	4	1.000
Womack, Tony, Chi.	14	10	20	25	0	45	4	1.000
Young, Eric, Mil.	99	96	196	251	15	462	55	.968
Young, Eric, S.F.	18	17	34	55	1	90	12	.989

THIRD BASEMEN

Player, Team	G	GS	PO	A	E	TC	DP	Pct.
Alfonzo, Edgardo, S.F.	133	133	79	233	11	323	17	.966
Atkins, Garrett, Col.	19	16	9	25	6	40	0	.850
Baerga, Carlos, Ari.	5	4	6	7	0	13	0	1.000
Bell, David, Phi.	85	81	62	168	8	238	17	.966
Bell, Jay, N.Y.	14	7	7	13	1	21	2	.952
Bellhorn, Mark, Chi.-Col.	57	47	24	94	7	125	5	.944
Beltre, Adrian, L.A.	157	150	112	309	19	440	33	.957
Blum, Geoff, Hou.	83	72	32	135	5	172	18	.971
Boone, Aaron, Cin.	83	81	62	180	14	256	20	.945
Branyan, Russell, Cin.	20	18	12	49	2	63	5	.968
Bruntlett, Eric, Hou.	1	0	0	0	0	0	0	.000
Burroughs, Sean, S.D.	137	132	105	239	12	356	26	.966
Butler, Brent, Col.	8	0	1	4	2	7	0	.714
Cabrera, Jolbert, L.A.	5	3	1	7	0	8	2	1.000
Cabrera, Miguel, Fla.	34	30	17	53	1	71	2	.986
Cairo, Miguel, St.L.	12	2	3	6	2	11	1	.818
Carroll, Jamey, Mon.	67	46	43	115	5	163	8	.969
Castilla, Vinny, Atl.	147	144	98	307	19	424	28	.955
Castro, Juan, Cin.	30	20	17	42	1	60	7	.983
Chamblee, Jim, Cin.	1	0	0	0	0	0	0	.000
Chapman, Travis, Phi.	1	0	0	0	0	0	0	.000
Cintron, Alex, Ari.	16	14	14	22	3	39	0	.923
Coomer, Ron, L.A.	11	6	4	10	0	14	2	1.000
Counsell, Craig, Ari.	57	49	32	105	2	139	9	.986
Cruz, Enrique, Mil.	2	0	0	2	1	3	0	.667
Delgado, Wilson, St.L.	11	2	2	6	0	8	0	1.000
DeRosa, Mark, Atl.	25	18	12	44	4	60	4	.933
Ensberg, Morgan, Hou.	111	89	77	184	9	270	18	.967
Feliz, Pedro, S.F.	49	28	24	82	3	109	8	.972
Fox, Andy, Fla.	5	3	4	5	1	10	1	.900
Freel, Ryan, Cin.	2	1	0	2	0	2	2	1.000
Garcia, Jesse, Atl.	2	0	2	1	0	3	1	1.000
Ginter, Keith, Mil.	40	32	19	51	6	76	6	.921
Guzman, Edwards, Mon.	28	18	6	37	2	45	3	.956
Hall, Bill, Mil.	1	0	0	0	1	1	0	.000
Hammock, Robby, Ari.	16	11	8	45	4	57	4	.930
Hansen, Dave, S.D.	11	8	6	16	1	23	0	.957
Harris, Lenny, Chi.	35	26	10	45	3	58	4	.948
Helms, Wes, Mil.	130	130	88	236	19	343	20	.945
Hernandez, Jose, Chi.-Pit.	75	64	40	158	9	207	19	.957
Hessman, Mike, Atl.	3	0	0	3	0	3	0	1.000
Hillenbrand, Shea, Ari.	34	30	15	54	7	76	5	.908
Houston, Tyler, Phi.	21	21	15	29	3	47	0	.936
Hummel, Tim, Cin.	20	18	10	32	5	47	0	.894
Jimenez, D'Angelo, Cin.	2	0	0	2	0	2	0	1.000
Kata, Matt, Ari.	23	19	10	41	1	52	3	.981
Kinkade, Mike, L.A.	2	1	0	0	1	1	0	.000
Larson, Brandon, Cin.	24	22	18	48	4	70	7	.943
Lockhart, Keith, S.D.	3	2	2	6	1	9	0	.889
Lopez, Felipe, Cin.	8	2	3	4	0	7	0	1.000
LOWELL, Mike, Fla.	128	128	84	243	9	336	27	.973
Macias, Jose, Mon.	25	16	9	35	3	47	1	.936
Mackowiak, Rob, Pit.	19	17	11	24	2	37	4	.946
Martinez, Ramon, Chi.	37	22	12	48	5	65	6	.923
McEwing, Joe, N.Y.	2	1	2	5	0	7	1	1.000
Merced, Orlando, Hou.	2	0	0	1	0	1	0	1.000
Merloni, Lou, S.D.	25	17	12	37	4	53	3	.925
Mordecai, Mike, Fla.	12	1	5	3	1	9	0	.889
Norton, Greg, Col.	34	27	24	49	6	79	3	.924
Nunez, Abraham O., Pit.	1	0	0	1	0	1	0	1.000
Ojeda, Augie, Chi.	1	0	0	0	0	0	0	.000
Pena, Wily Mo, Cin.	1	0	0	1	0	1	0	1.000
Perez, Eduardo, St.L.	12	6	3	7	3	13	1	.769
Perez, Neifi, S.F.	2	0	0	0	0	0	0	.000
Perez, Tomas, Phi.	58	36	37	86	6	129	12	.953
Polanco, Placido, Phi.	21	21	10	37	2	49	5	.959
Punto, Nick, Phi.	9	3	5	6	1	12	0	.917
Ramirez, Aramis, Pit.-Chi.	159	156	97	336	33	466	24	.929
Reboulet, Jeff, Pit.	7	0	3	3	0	6	1	1.000
Redmond, Mike, Fla.	1	0	0	0	0	0	0	.000
Rolen, Scott, St.L.	153	152	109	298	13	420	23	.969
Stynes, Chris, Col.	119	111	92	225	9	326	22	.972
Tatis, Fernando, Mon.	49	48	32	88	4	124	9	.968
Vazquez, Ramon, S.D.	4	3	2	3	1	6	0	.833
Ventura, Robin, L.A.	3	2	1	1	1	3	0	.667
Vizcaino, Jose, Hou.	2	1	0	0	0	0	0	.000
Wigginton, Ty, N.Y.	155	153	117	293	16	426	27	.962
Williams, Matt, Ari.	42	35	21	72	4	97	5	.959
Zeile, Todd, Mon.	34	34	22	67	5	94	4	.947

THIRD BASEMEN WITH TWO OR MORE TEAMS

Player, Team	G	GS	PO	A	E	TC	DP	Pct.
Bellhorn, Mark, Chi.	42	39	18	72	6	96	4	.938
Bellhorn, Mark, Col.	15	8	6	22	1	29	1	.966
Hernandez, Jose, Chi.	17	13	5	25	1	31	5	.968
Hernandez, Jose, Pit.	58	51	35	133	8	176	14	.955
Ramirez, Aramis, Pit.	96	94	62	216	23	301	10	.924
Ramirez, Aramis, Chi.	63	62	35	120	10	165	14	.939

SHORTSTOPS

Player, Team	G	GS	PO	A	E	TC	DP	Pct.
Aurilia, Rich, S.F.	123	123	173	316	13	502	80	.974
Barmes, Clint, Col.	12	8	19	27	2	48	6	.958

Player, Team	G	GS	PO	A	E	TC	DP	Pct.
Bell, Jay, N.Y.	12	6	11	19	1	31	6	.968
Bellhorn, Mark, Col.	6	2	1	9	0	10	1	1.000
Beltre, Adrian, L.A.	1	0	0	0	0	0	0	.000
Blum, Geoff, Hou.	11	3	3	18	1	22	6	.955
Boone, Aaron, Cin.	5	3	3	15	3	21	1	.857
Bruntlett, Eric, Hou.	10	5	12	14	1	27	3	.963
Butler, Brent, Col.	4	2	4	7	0	11	2	1.000
Cabrera, Jolbert, L.A.	9	3	7	11	2	20	4	.900
Cabrera, Orlando, Mon.	162	160	258	456	18	732	101	.975
Cairo, Miguel, St.L.	7	4	5	10	1	16	2	.938
Carroll, Jamey, Mon.	14	2	7	15	0	22	4	1.000
Castro, Juan, Cin.	24	18	28	43	0	71	14	1.000
Cintron, Alex, Ari.	93	90	138	235	8	381	56	.979
Clayton, Royce, Mil.	141	137	193	396	14	603	76	.977
Cora, Alex, L.A.	15	5	10	18	0	28	4	1.000
Counsell, Craig, Ari.	26	18	23	66	1	90	9	.989
Cruz, Enrique, Mil.	13	6	8	20	0	28	3	1.000
Delgado, Wilson, St.L.	11	3	5	13	1	19	1	.947
DeRosa, Mark, Atl.	20	8	21	42	0	63	9	1.000
Everett, Adam, Hou.	128	116	207	344	17	568	71	.970
Fox, Andy, Fla.	9	3	5	10	0	15	3	1.000
Furcal, Rafael, Atl.	155	154	237	481	31	749	108	.959
Garcia, Jesse, Atl.	3	0	0	1	0	1	0	1.000
Ginter, Keith, Mil.	2	1	4	3	0	7	1	1.000
Gonzalez, Alex, Fla.	150	150	237	426	16	679	109	.976
GONZALEZ, Alex S., Chi.	150	141	193	422	10	625	95	.984
Greene, Khalil, S.D.	20	18	27	51	3	81	11	.963
Hall, Bill, Mil.	18	18	30	48	4	82	10	.951
Hart, Bo, St.L.	3	1	2	5	0	7	1	1.000
Hernandez, Jose, Col.-Chi.	74	68	118	191	5	314	50	.984
Hummel, Tim, Cin.	2	1	1	4	0	5	0	1.000
Izturis, Cesar, L.A.	158	154	198	481	16	695	94	.977
Kata, Matt, Ari.	6	4	7	5	0	12	1	1.000
Larkin, Barry, Cin.	60	58	71	159	9	239	36	.962
Lopez, Felipe, Cin.	50	42	60	132	15	207	20	.928
Loretta, Mark, S.D.	3	0	2	0	0	2	0	1.000
Lugo, Julio, Hou.	22	21	30	55	3	88	10	.966
Martinez, Ramon, Chi.	32	18	29	57	2	88	15	.977
Mateo, Henry, Mon.	2	0	1	1	0	2	1	1.000
McEwing, Joe, N.Y.	42	24	51	92	5	148	26	.966
Mendez, Donaldo, S.D.	26	26	26	71	5	102	10	.951
Merloni, Lou, S.D.	23	16	35	43	1	79	11	.987
Mordecai, Mike, Fla.	14	9	14	26	1	41	7	.976
Nunez, Abraham O., Pit.	23	14	29	44	1	74	9	.986
Ojeda, Augie, Chi.	7	2	8	9	0	17	2	1.000
Olmedo, Ray, Cin.	51	40	60	122	14	196	21	.929
Ozuna, Pablo, Col.	3	2	3	6	1	10	0	.900
Perez, Neifi, S.F.	45	33	71	129	2	202	33	.990
Perez, Tomas, Phi.	4	4	4	7	1	12	3	.917
Punto, Nick, Phi.	7	5	5	17	0	22	2	1.000
Ransom, Cody, S.F.	12	5	9	17	1	27	7	.963
Renteria, Edgar, St.L.	156	154	191	439	16	646	83	.975
Reyes, Jose, N.Y.	69	69	107	215	9	331	42	.973
Rollins, Jimmy, Phi.	154	153	203	463	14	680	92	.979
Sanchez, Rey, N.Y.	42	40	57	116	2	175	23	.989
Scutaro, Marco, N.Y.	1	0	1	1	0	2	0	1.000
Uribe, Juan, Col.	74	69	143	242	11	396	57	.972
Vazquez, Ramon, S.D.	108	102	131	274	13	418	57	.969
Velandia, Jorge, N.Y.	23	22	39	66	3	108	13	.972
Vizcaino, Jose, Hou.	32	17	31	48	3	82	12	.963
Wilson, Jack, Pit.	149	148	218	454	17	689	104	.975
Womack, Tony, Ari.-Col.-Chi.	73	62	86	161	9	256	33	.965

TRIPLE PLAYS: Hernandez, Col.; Furcal, Atl. (unassited).

SHORTSTOPS WITH TWO OR MORE TEAMS

Player, Team	G	GS	PO	A	E	TC	DP	Pct.
Hernandez, Jose, Col.	69	67	116	181	5	302	49	.983
Hernandez, Jose, Chi.	5	1	2	10	0	12	1	1.000
Womack, Tony, Ari.	58	50	70	130	7	207	28	.966
Womack, Tony, Col.	14	12	16	31	2	49	5	.959
Womack, Tony, Chi.	1	0	0	0	0	0	0	.000

OUTFIELDERS

Player, Team	G	GS	PO	A	E	TC	DP	Pct.
Abreu, Bobby, Phi.	158	156	304	6	6	316	0	.981
Allen, Chad, Fla.	8	4	13	1	0	14	0	1.000
Alou, Moises, Chi.	142	140	203	4	6	213	1	.972
Banks, Brian, Fla.	33	22	38	1	1	40	0	.975
Barnes, Larry, L.A.*	2	0	2	0	0	2	0	1.000
Bautista, Danny, Ari.	79	72	123	1	5	129	0	.961

Player, Team	G	GS	PO	A	E	TC	DP	Pct.
Bay, Jason, S.D.-Pit.	29	26	48	1	1	50	0	.980
Bellhorn, Mark, Col.	5	0	2	0	0	2	0	1.000
Benard, Marvin, S.F.*	21	13	37	2	0	39	0	1.000
Berkman, Lance, Hou.*	153	153	254	10	3	267	0	.989
Biggio, Craig, Hou.	150	150	326	9	1	336	1	.997
Blum, Geoff, Hou.	2	0	0	1	0	1	0	1.000
Bonds, Barry, S.F.*	123	122	236	5	2	243	2	.992
Bragg, Darren, Atl.	78	28	79	1	1	81	0	.988
Branyan, Russell, Cin.	17	13	30	0	0	30	0	1.000
Bruntlett, Eric, Hou.	2	0	0	0	0	0	0	.000
Buchanan, Brian, S.D.	43	17	47	2	0	49	1	1.000
Budzinski, Mark, Cin.*	1	1	3	0	0	3	0	1.000
Burnitz, Jeromy, N.Y.-L.A.	125	124	222	5	7	234	0	.970
Burrell, Pat, Phi.	140	138	234	7	6	247	0	.976
Byrd, Marlon, Phi.	131	124	295	5	5	305	1	.984
Cabrera, Jolbert, L.A.	63	32	55	3	2	60	0	.967
Cabrera, Miguel, Fla.	55	55	99	5	3	107	1	.972
Cairo, Miguel, St.L.	27	15	31	1	1	33	1	.970
Calloway, Ron, Mon.*	97	79	166	4	3	173	0	.983
Cedeno, Roger, N.Y.	128	115	231	5	3	239	0	.987
Cepicky, Matt, Mon.	4	1	1	0	0	1	0	1.000
Chavez, Endy, Mon.*	135	112	279	9	3	291	2	.990
Clark, Brady, Mil.	105	69	174	5	5	184	3	.973
Clark, Jermaine, S.D.	1	1	2	0	0	2	0	1.000
Clark, Tony, N.Y.	1	0	1	0	0	1	0	1.000
Conine, Jeff, Fla.	25	25	44	3	0	47	3	1.000
Conti, Jason, Mil.	20	7	29	1	3	33	0	.909
Cordero, Wil, Mon.	1	0	0	0	0	0	0	.000
Crosby, Bubba, L.A.*	1	1	2	0	1	3	0	.667
Cruz, Jose, S.F.	158	152	340	18	2	360	7	.994
Davis, J.J., Pit.	10	8	13	1	0	14	0	1.000
Dellucci, David, Ari.*	53	38	79	1	2	82	0	.976
DeRosa, Mark, Atl.	2	1	2	0	0	2	0	1.000
Drew, J.D., St.L.	75	70	154	7	1	162	1	.994
Duncan, Jeff, N.Y.*	52	41	136	0	0	136	0	1.000
Dunn, Adam, Cin.	102	100	208	5	10	223	2	.955
Edmonds, Jim, St.L.*	129	118	335	12	5	352	5	.986
Ellison, Jason, S.F.	4	2	3	0	0	3	0	1.000
ENCARNACION, Juan, Fla.	155	155	329	7	0	336	3	1.000
Feliz, Pedro, S.F.	15	11	22	0	1	23	0	.957
Finley, Steve, Ari.*	140	130	258	9	5	272	2	.982
Floyd, Cliff, N.Y.	95	94	159	8	5	172	4	.971
Fox, Andy, Fla.	2	1	1	0	0	1	0	1.000
Franco, Matt, Atl.	3	0	1	0	0	1	0	1.000
Freel, Ryan, Cin.	24	22	58	2	0	60	0	1.000
Garcia, Danny, N.Y.	1	0	0	0	0	0	0	.000
Giles, Brian, Pit.-S.D.*	134	134	288	6	4	298	0	.987
Ginter, Keith, Mil.	2	2	1	0	0	1	0	1.000
Glanville, Doug, Chi.	18	9	30	1	0	31	1	1.000
Gonzalez, Luis, Ari.	154	154	249	9	3	261	1	.989
Gonzalez, Raul, N.Y.	88	45	134	4	1	139	1	.993
Goodwin, Tom, Chi.	57	32	66	0	0	66	0	1.000
Green, Shawn, L.A.*	157	157	261	9	5	275	1	.982
Griffey Jr., Ken, Cin.*	43	43	89	3	1	93	0	.989
Grissom, Marquis, S.F.	148	141	343	3	8	354	1	.977
Guerrero, Vladimir, Mon.	112	112	217	10	7	234	1	.970
Guillen, Jose, Cin.	78	72	169	9	8	186	1	.957
Hammock, Robby, Ari.	17	9	14	0	1	15	0	.933
Hammonds, Jeffrey, Mil.-S.F.	40	34	66	1	0	67	0	1.000
Harris, Lenny, Chi.-Fla.	6	1	5	0	0	5	0	1.000
Henderson, Rickey, L.A.*	18	17	20	1	1	22	1	.955
Hermansen, Chad, L.A.	6	5	8	0	0	8	0	1.000
Hernandez, Jose, Chi.	2	2	1	0	0	1	0	1.000
Hessman, Mike, Atl.	8	0	4	0	1	5	0	.800
Hidalgo, Richard, Hou.	137	136	277	22	4	303	5	.987
Hollandsworth, Todd, Fla.*	64	57	114	5	2	121	0	.983
Hubbard, Trenidad, Chi.	4	3	5	0	0	5	0	1.000
Hunter, Brian L., Hou.	32	16	33	1	2	36	0	.944
Hyzdu, Adam, Pit.	34	12	37	1	0	38	0	1.000
JENKINS, Geoff, Mil.	123	122	222	11	0	233	1	1.000
Jones, Andruw, Atl.	155	153	390	8	3	401	1	.993
Jones, Chipper, Atl.	149	149	202	9	7	218	2	.968
Jordan, Brian, L.A.	62	59	98	2	1	101	0	.990
Jose, Felix, Ari.	1	1	0	0	0	0	0	.000
Kapler, Gabe, Col.	29	12	29	3	1	33	1	.970
Kearns, Austin, Cin.	80	77	199	5	2	206	0	.990
Kelton, David, Chi.	2	2	4	0	0	4	0	1.000
Kieschnick, Brooks, Mil.	3	3	2	0	1	3	0	.667
Kinkade, Mike, L.A.	36	28	32	0	3	35	0	.914
Kotsay, Mark, S.D.*	126	120	324	13	3	340	4	.991
Lane, Jason, Hou.*	10	3	7	0	0	7	0	1.000

Player, Team	G	GS	PO	A	E	TC	DP	Pct.
Langerhans, Ryan, Atl.*	14	1	12	1	0	13	0	1.000
Larson, Brandon, Cin.	3	3	9	1	0	10	0	1.000
LaRue, Jason, Cin.	1	0	0	0	0	0	0	.000
Ledee, Ricky, Phi.*	71	54	98	5	0	103	0	1.000
Linden, Todd, S.F.	13	7	13	0	1	14	0	.929
Lo Duca, Paul, L.A.	6	6	10	1	0	11	0	1.000
Lofton, Kenny, Pit.-Chi.*	136	132	314	8	3	325	2	.991
Macias, Jose, Mon.	62	37	82	4	2	88	2	.977
Mackowiak, Rob, Pit.	30	11	30	0	0	30	0	1.000
Marrero, Eli, St.L.	31	17	49	1	1	51	0	.980
Mateo, Henry, Mon.	10	3	9	0	0	9	0	1.000
Mateo, Ruben, Cin.	54	49	106	2	2	110	1	.982
Matthews Jr., Gary, S.D.	92	69	150	2	1	153	0	.993
McCracken, Quinton, Ari.	55	39	58	1	1	60	1	.983
McEwing, Joe, N.Y.	18	5	21	0	0	21	0	1.000
Merced, Orlando, Hou.	31	22	43	4	2	49	1	.959
Merloni, Lou, S.D.	2	0	2	0	0	2	0	1.000
Michaels, Jason, Phi.	38	14	37	3	1	41	0	.976
Mondesi, Raul, Ari.	43	43	80	1	3	84	1	.964
Nady, Xavier, S.D.	105	98	170	12	6	188	2	.968
Nevin, Phil, S.D.	29	29	47	1	1	49	0	.980
Norton, Greg, Col.	3	0	0	0	0	0	0	.000
O'Leary, Troy, Chi.*	51	31	58	3	0	61	0	1.000
Ozuna, Pablo, Col.	5	0	1	0	0	1	0	1.000
PALMEIRO, Orlando, St.L.*	112	65	165	6	0	171	1	1.000
Patterson, Corey, Chi.	82	79	152	3	4	159	1	.975
Payton, Jay, Col.	151	148	306	6	4	316	1	.987
Pellow, Kit, Col.	1	1	1	0	0	1	0	1.000
Pena, Wily Mo, Cin.	47	39	85	1	2	88	1	.977
Perez, Eduardo, St.L.	71	51	113	1	4	118	0	.966
Perez, Timo, N.Y.*	104	85	180	6	2	188	1	.989
Petrick, Ben, Col.	2	0	2	1	0	3	0	1.000
Pierre, Juan, Fla.*	161	161	402	6	3	411	5	.993
Podsednik, Scott, Mil.*	139	130	345	5	3	353	1	.992
Porter, Colin, Hou.*	14	6	17	0	0	17	0	1.000
Pujols, Albert, St.L.	113	113	198	7	3	208	0	.986
Redman, Prentice, N.Y.	10	5	16	0	0	16	0	1.000
Redman, Tike, Pit.*	54	51	127	1	2	130	0	.985
Reyes, Rene, Col.	36	23	50	3	2	55	0	.964
Richard, Chris, Col.*	3	3	5	0	0	5	0	1.000
Rivera, Ruben, S.F.	27	8	42	0	0	42	0	1.000
Roberts, Dave, L.A.*	105	98	202	4	5	211	1	.976
Robinson, Kerry, St.L.*	88	29	93	0	0	93	0	1.000
Romano, Jason, L.A.	28	4	18	0	0	18	0	1.000
Ruan, Wilkin, L.A.	20	8	22	1	0	23	0	1.000
Sanchez, Alex, Mil.*	36	36	99	3	1	103	1	.990
Sanders, Reggie, Pit.	120	112	222	6	4	232	2	.983
Santos, Francisco, S.F.*	3	1	3	0	0	3	0	1.000
Sheffield, Gary, Atl.	153	153	283	7	4	294	2	.986
Shinjo, Tsuyoshi, N.Y.	54	27	98	5	3	106	1	.972
Smith, Mark, Mil.	15	13	24	0	1	25	0	.960
Smitherman, Stephen, Cin.	14	9	17	0	0	17	0	1.000
Sosa, Sammy, Chi.	137	136	212	2	5	219	1	.977
Spivey, Junior, Ari.	1	0	0	0	0	0	0	.000
Stairs, Matt, Pit.	55	50	73	4	1	78	0	.987
Stenson, Dernell, Cin.*	22	20	44	2	1	47	0	.979
Sweeney, Mark, Col.*	17	13	18	0	0	18	0	1.000
Taguchi, So, St.L.	38	8	30	2	0	32	1	1.000
Taylor, Reggie, Cin.	60	30	98	2	1	101	0	.990
Terrero, Luis, Ari.	3	0	1	0	0	1	0	1.000
Torcato, Tony, S.F.	6	1	5	0	1	6	0	.833
Torrealba, Yorvit, S.F.	1	0	0	0	0	0	0	.000
Uribe, Juan, Col.	1	1	3	0	0	3	0	1.000
Valderrama, Carlos, S.F.	5	1	6	0	0	6	0	1.000
Valent, Eric, Cin.*	8	8	20	1	0	21	0	1.000
Vander Wal, John, Mil.*	89	87	176	4	3	183	2	.984
Vaughn, Greg, Col.	7	4	12	0	0	12	0	1.000
Victorino, Shane, S.D.	32	17	42	3	0	45	0	1.000
Vitiello, Joe, Mon.	15	13	14	0	0	14	0	1.000
Walker, Larry, Col.	131	128	229	8	4	241	2	.983
Ward, Daryle, L.A.*	11	11	10	0	0	10	0	1.000
Watson, Matt, N.Y.	5	2	11	0	2	13	0	.846
White, Rondell, S.D.	104	102	173	6	4	183	2	.978
Widger, Chris, St.L.	1	0	1	0	0	1	0	1.000
Wilkerson, Brad, Mon.*	135	129	257	11	5	273	1	.982
Williams, Gerald, Fla.	16	5	16	0	1	17	0	.941
Wilson, Craig, Pit.	46	32	87	3	2	92	0	.978
Wilson, Preston, Col.	155	153	331	8	7	346	1	.980
Womack, Tony, Col.	1	0	1	0	0	1	0	1.000
Young, Eric, S.F.	2	0	2	0	0	2	0	1.000
Young, Kevin, Pit.	1	1	1	0	1	2	0	.500
Zoccolillo, Pete, Mil.	7	7	16	0	0	16	0	1.000

OUTFIELDERS WITH TWO OR MORE TEAMS

Player, Team	G	GS	PO	A	E	TC	DP	Pct.
Bay, Jason, S.D.	3	3	8	0	0	8	0	1.000
Bay, Jason, Pit.	26	23	40	1	1	42	0	.976
Burnitz, Jeromy, N.Y.	65	64	138	2	2	142	0	.986
Burnitz, Jeromy, L.A.	60	60	84	3	5	92	0	.946
Giles, Brian, Pit.*	105	105	233	4	2	239	0	.992
Giles, Brian, S.D.*	29	29	55	2	2	59	0	.966
Hammonds, Jeffrey, Mil.	10	10	17	0	0	17	0	1.000
Hammonds, Jeffrey, S.F.	30	24	49	1	0	50	0	1.000
Harris, Lenny, Chi.	2	0	0	0	0	0	0	.000
Harris, Lenny, Fla.	4	1	5	0	0	5	0	1.000
Lofton, Kenny, Pit.*	81	80	203	5	0	208	2	1.000
Lofton, Kenny, Chi.*	55	52	111	3	3	117	0	.974

CATCHERS

Player, Team	G	GS	PO	A	E	TC	DP	PB	Pct.
Ausmus, Brad, Hou.	143	129	982	76	3	1061	13	3	.997
Bako, Paul, Chi.	69	57	440	33	6	479	2	4	.987
Barajas, Rod, Ari.	79	65	543	40	0	583	6	8	1.000
Barrett, Michael, Mon.	68	63	391	21	1	413	5	7	.998
Bennett, Gary, S.D.	91	87	535	25	2	562	5	6	.996
Blanco, Henry, Atl.	52	42	255	25	1	281	4	1	.996
Castillo, Alberto, S.F.	10	3	37	2	1	40	0	0	.975
Castro, Ramon, Fla.	18	2	51	3	1	55	0	1	.982
Chavez, Raul, Hou.	16	7	55	3	0	58	0	0	1.000
Cota, Humberto, Pit.	4	2	18	0	0	18	0	0	1.000
DePastino, Joe, N.Y.	1	0	1	0	0	1	0	0	1.000
Estalella, Bobby, Col.	46	43	248	19	4	271	2	3	.985
Estrada, Johnny, Atl.	14	6	47	1	0	48	0	0	1.000
Girardi, Joe, St.L.	13	5	23	0	1	24	0	0	.958
Gonzalez, Wiki, S.D.	23	17	128	7	1	136	0	1	.993
Guzman, Edwards, Mon.	4	4	23	0	0	23	0	1	1.000
Hammock, Robby, Ari.	36	28	263	18	2	283	2	4	.993
Hundley, Todd, L.A.	10	7	49	3	1	53	0	0	.981
Johnson, Charles, Col.	107	103	561	34	4	599	5	6	.993
Kendall, Jason, Pit.	146	145	841	48	10	899	3	9	.989
LaRue, Jason, Cin.	114	109	649	46	11	706	8	6	.984
Lieberthal, Mike, Phi.	131	129	868	44	9	921	2	11	.990
Lo Duca, Paul, L.A.	123	120	1014	100	15	1129	14	6	.987
Lopez, Javy, Atl.	120	114	718	53	5	776	6	6	.994
Lunsford, Trey, S.F.	1	0	0	0	0	0	0	0	.000
Marrero, Eli, St.L.	6	4	29	4	0	33	0	0	1.000
MATHENY, Mike, St.L.	138	121	774	49	0	823	7	5	1.000
Miller, Corky, Cin.	11	9	60	5	0	65	0	0	1.000
Miller, Damian, Chi.	114	103	940	73	3	1016	6	8	.997
Moeller, Chad, Ari.	76	69	490	37	7	534	3	3	.987
Ojeda, Miguel, S.D.	48	35	293	14	6	313	1	4	.981
Osik, Keith, Mil.	78	71	479	44	5	528	5	6	.991
Paul, Josh, Chi.	3	2	20	2	0	22	1	0	1.000
Pellow, Kit, Col.	7	2	14	0	0	14	0	1	1.000
Perez, Eddie, Mil.	102	91	613	32	6	651	6	8	.991
Petrick, Ben, Col.	1	0	0	0	0	0	0	0	.000
Phillips, Jason, N.Y.	29	26	148	6	1	155	0	0	.994
Piazza, Mike, N.Y.	64	63	346	31	7	384	7	1	.982
Pratt, Todd, Phi.	35	33	231	9	1	241	4	5	.996
Quintero, Humberto, S.D.	11	7	52	2	1	55	1	2	.982
Redmond, Mike, Fla.	37	26	195	10	1	206	2	0	.995
Rivera, Michael, S.D.	19	16	133	7	2	142	0	2	.986
Rodriguez, Ivan, Fla.	138	134	915	47	8	970	9	10	.992
Romero, Mandy, Col.	2	2	13	2	1	16	0	0	.938
Ross, Dave, L.A.	38	35	259	26	4	289	2	2	.986
Santiago, Benito, S.F.	106	106	629	34	5	668	3	8	.993
Sardinha, Dane, Cin.	1	0	2	0	0	2	0	0	1.000
Schneider, Brian, Mon.	98	95	661	45	3	709	12	3	.996
Stinnett, Kelly, Cin.-Phi.	51	44	268	21	2	291	3	3	.993
Torrealba, Yorvit, S.F.	66	52	365	29	1	395	3	0	.997
Widger, Chris, St.L.	41	32	185	14	1	200	1	2	.995
Wilson, Craig, Pit.	21	15	87	11	1	99	1	1	.990
Wilson, Vance, N.Y.	89	71	442	43	5	490	5	4	.990
Zaun, Gregg, Hou.-Col.	45	38	223	10	6	239	0	2	.975

CATCHERS WITH TWO OR MORE TEAMS

Player, Team	G	GS	PO	A	E	TC	DP	PB	Pct.
Stinnett, Kelly, Cin.	50	44	262	21	2	285	3	3	.993
Stinnett, Kelly, Phi.	1	0	6	0	0	6	0	0	1.000
Zaun, Gregg, Hou.	31	26	152	8	4	164	0	1	.976
Zaun, Gregg, Col.	14	12	71	2	2	75	0	1	.973

CATCHERS—SPECIAL STATS*

Player, Team	G	Inn.	SBA	CCS	PCS	CS%	ER	CERA
Ausmus,Brad, Hou	143	1158.0	105	31	6	.31	471	3.66
Bako,Paul, ChC	69	507.2	40	11	2	.29	215	3.81
Barajas,Rod, Ari	79	595.0	43	16	1	.38	239	3.62
Barrett,Michael, Mon	68	562.2	26	10	0	.38	266	4.25
Bennett,Gary, SD	91	747.0	60	11	1	.19	319	3.84
Blanco,Henry, Atl	52	388.0	44	10	1	.23	193	4.48
Castillo,Alberto, SF	10	38.0	1	0	0	0	13	3.08
Castro,Ramon, Fla	18	65.2	2	0	0	0	24	3.29
Chavez,Raul, Hou	16	77.2	5	2	1	.50	38	4.40
Cota,Humberto, Pit	4	23.0	2	0	1	0	15	5.87
DePastino,Joe, NYM	1	1.0	0	0	0	0	0	0.00
Estalella,Bobby, Col	46	374.1	37	10	2	.29	197	4.74
Estrada,Johnny, Atl	14	76.1	6	0	0	0	34	4.01
Girardi,Joe, StL	13	52.0	3	0	0	0	32	5.54
Gonzalez,Wiki, SD	23	151.0	18	2	2	.13	120	7.15
Guzman,Edwards, Mon	4	34.0	1	0	1	0	24	6.35
Hammock,Robby, Ari	36	264.0	25	6	1	.25	120	4.09
Hundley,Todd, LA	10	63.2	7	1	1	.17	23	3.25
Johnson,Charles, Col	107	897.2	62	15	11	.29	523	5.24
Kendall,Jason, Pit	146	1278.1	86	16	7	.20	633	4.46
LaRue,Jason, Cin	114	954.1	64	16	1	.25	539	5.08
Lieberthal,Mike, Phi	131	1143.2	103	18	1	.18	519	4.08
Lo Duca,Paul, LA	123	1080.0	140	43	14	.34	328	2.73
Lopez,Javy, Atl	120	992.0	75	20	3	.28	436	3.96
Lunsford,Trey, SF	1	1.0	0	0	0	0	0	0.00
Marrero,Eli, StL	6	36.1	3	2	1	1.00	22	5.45
Matheny,Mike, StL	138	1096.2	55	12	3	.23	558	4.58
Miller,Corky, Cin	11	78.2	12	1	1	.09	40	4.58
Miller,Damian, ChC	114	929.2	69	26	1	.38	401	3.88
Moeller,Chad, Ari	76	596.0	54	12	2	.23	262	3.96
Ojeda,Miguel, SD	48	336.0	26	4	1	.16	205	5.49
Osik,Keith, Mil	78	630.1	57	14	4	.26	322	4.60
Paul,Josh, ChC	3	19.0	3	1	1	.50	3	1.42
Pellow,Kit, Col	7	24.0	2	0	0	0	16	6.00
Perez,Eddie, Mil	102	821.2	80	16	3	.21	488	5.35
Petrick,Ben, Col	1	1.0	1	0	0	0	4	36.00
Phillips,Jason, NYM	29	229.1	12	4	0	.33	128	5.02
Piazza,Mike, NYM	64	532.1	82	17	6	.22	235	3.97
Pratt,Todd, Phi	35	296.0	33	4	1	.13	126	3.83
Quintero,Humberto, SD	11	58.1	3	0	1	0	42	6.48
Redmond,Mike, Fla	37	247.1	33	4	1	.13	143	5.20
Rivera,Michael, SD	19	139.0	13	2	1	.17	88	5.70
Rodriguez,Ivan, Fla	138	1132.1	60	19	1	.32	481	3.82
Romero,Mandy, Col	2	17.0	3	1	0	.33	16	8.47
Ross,Dave, LA	38	314.0	45	13	3	.31	160	4.59
Santiago,Benito, SF	106	902.2	54	8	2	.15	354	3.53
Sardinha,Dane, Cin	1	4.0	0	0	0	0	3	6.75
Schneider,Brian, Mon	98	841.0	51	21	6	.47	350	3.75
Stinnett,Kelly, TOT	51	413.1	29	7	2	.26	239	5.20
Stinnett,Kelly, Cin	50	409.1	29	7	2	.26	236	5.19
Stinnett,Kelly, Phi	1	4.0	0	0	0	0	3	6.75
Torrealba,Yorvit, SF	66	495.2	41	14	5	.39	228	4.14
Widger,Chris, StL	41	278.2	18	5	1	.29	136	4.39
Wilson,Craig, Pit	21	143.0	7	2	0	.29	96	6.04
Wilson,Vance, NYM	89	650.2	56	15	10	.33	341	4.72
Zaun,Gregg, TOT	45	320.1	34	4	7	.15	178	5.00
Zaun,Gregg, Hou	31	214.1	24	3	5	.16	113	4.74
Zaun,Gregg, Col	14	106.0	10	1	2	.13	65	5.52
Average	54	428.0	35	9	2	.31	203	4.27

***Inn.** denotes the number of innings the catcher was behind the plate. **SBA** denotes stolen bases attempted. **CCS** denotes number of runners caught stealing by the catcher. **PCS** denotes number of runners caught stealing by the pitcher. **CS%** denotes the catcher's caught stealing percentage, figured by subtracting PCS from SBA and dividing this number into CCS. **ER** denotes number of earned runs scored when catcher was behind plate. **CERA** denotes catcher's ERA when he was behind the plate, figured the same way a pitcher's ERA is computed (ER*9/IP).

PITCHERS

Player, Team	G	GS	PO	A	E	TC	DP	Pct.
Acevedo, Jose, Cin.	5	4	1	3	0	4	1	1.000
Adams, Terry, Phi.	66	0	10	9	1	20	1	.950
Ainsworth, Kurt, S.F.	11	11	4	6	0	10	0	1.000
Alfonseca, Antonio, Chi.	60	0	2	8	1	11	0	.909
Almanza, Armando, Fla.*	51	0	1	5	1	7	0	.857
Almonte, Edwin, N.Y.	12	0	0	3	0	3	0	1.000
Almonte, Hector, Mon.	28	0	1	3	0	4	0	1.000
Alvarez, Juan, Fla.*	9	0	1	2	0	3	0	1.000
Alvarez, Victor, L.A.*	5	0	0	0	0	0	0	.000
Alvarez, Wilson, L.A.*	21	12	4	16	0	20	2	1.000
Anderson, Jason, N.Y.	6	0	0	2	0	2	0	1.000
Anderson, Jimmy, Cin.*	8	7	0	10	0	10	0	1.000
Armas, Tony, Mon.	5	5	0	4	0	4	0	1.000
Ashby, Andy, L.A.	21	12	4	11	0	15	1	1.000
Astacio, Pedro, N.Y.	7	7	2	2	0	4	0	1.000
Austin, Jeff, Cin.	7	7	2	5	0	7	1	1.000
Ayala, Luis, Mon.	65	0	8	19	1	28	0	.964
Aybar, Manny, S.F.	3	0	0	0	0	0	0	.000
Bacsik, Mike, N.Y.*	5	3	0	3	0	3	0	1.000
Bale, John, Cin.*	10	9	1	7	0	8	0	1.000
Batista, Miguel, Ari.	36	29	10	31	3	44	2	.932
Beck, Rod, S.D.	36	0	1	6	0	7	0	1.000
Beckett, Josh, Fla.	24	23	6	19	1	26	0	.962
Beimel, Joe, Pit.*	69	0	2	12	0	14	0	1.000
Belisle, Matt, Cin.	6	0	0	2	0	2	0	1.000
Benes, Alan, Chi.	3	0	1	0	0	1	0	1.000
Benitez, Armando, N.Y.	45	0	3	1	0	4	0	1.000
Benson, Kris, Pit.	18	18	6	10	1	17	2	.941
Bernero, Adam, Col.	31	0	3	5	0	8	1	1.000
Biddle, Rocky, Mon.	73	0	0	4	0	4	0	1.000
Bland, Nate, Hou.*	22	0	0	4	2	6	0	.667
Boehringer, Brian, Pit.	62	0	3	3	0	6	0	1.000
Bong, Jung, Atl.*	44	0	2	13	0	15	4	1.000
Borbon, Pedro, St.L.*	7	0	1	1	0	2	0	1.000
Borland, Toby, Fla.	7	0	2	1	0	3	0	1.000
Borowski, Joe, Chi.	68	0	5	11	0	16	0	1.000
Bottalico, Ricky, Ari.	2	0	0	0	0	0	0	.000
Brohawn, Troy, L.A.*	12	0	0	2	0	2	0	1.000
Brower, Jim, S.F.	51	5	5	14	0	19	2	1.000
Brown, Kevin, L.A.	32	32	14	43	3	60	2	.950
Bullinger, Kirk, Hou.	7	0	1	1	0	2	0	1.000
Bump, Nate, Fla.	32	0	2	7	0	9	0	1.000
Burba, Dave, Mil.	17	2	5	7	0	12	0	1.000
Burnett, A.J., Fla.	4	4	3	4	0	7	0	1.000
Bynum, Mike, S.D.*	13	5	4	4	1	9	0	.889
Calero, Kiko, St.L.	26	1	2	3	0	5	0	1.000
Capuano, Chris, Ari.*	9	5	1	8	1	10	1	.900
Cerda, Jaime, N.Y.*	27	0	0	6	0	6	0	1.000
Cerros, Juan, Cin.	11	0	2	1	0	3	0	1.000
Chacon, Shawn, Col.	23	23	14	18	1	33	1	.970
Chen, Bruce, Hou.*	11	0	0	1	0	1	0	1.000
Christiansen, Jason, S.F.*	40	0	3	3	0	6	0	1.000
Clement, Matt, Chi.	32	32	20	23	4	47	0	.915
Colyer, Steve, L.A.*	13	0	1	2	0	3	1	1.000
Condrey, Clay, S.D.	9	6	1	8	1	10	0	.900
Cone, David, N.Y.	5	4	0	3	0	3	0	1.000
Cook, Aaron, Col.	43	16	14	23	1	38	3	.974
Corcoran, Roy, Mon.	5	0	2	1	0	3	1	1.000
Cordero, Chad, Mon.	12	0	2	0	0	2	0	1.000
Corey, Mark, Pit.	22	0	1	3	1	5	0	.800
Cormier, Rheal, Phi.*	65	0	2	29	0	31	0	1.000
Correia, Kevin, S.F.	10	7	3	4	0	7	0	1.000
Crudale, Mike, St.L.-Mil.	22	0	1	2	0	3	0	1.000
Cruz, Juan, Chi.	25	6	2	9	2	13	0	.846
Cruz, Nelson, Col.	20	7	6	6	0	12	2	1.000
Cunnane, Will, Atl.	20	0	1	2	0	3	0	1.000
D'Amico, Jeff, Pit.	29	29	5	16	1	22	2	.955
Darensbourg, Vic, Col.-Mon.*	9	0	3	3	1	7	0	.857
Davis, Doug, Mil.*	8	8	3	3	0	6	0	1.000
Dawley, Joe, Atl.	5	0	0	0	0	0	0	.000
Day, Zach, Mon.	23	23	9	22	1	32	1	.969
de los Santos, Valerio, Mil.-Phi.*	51	0	1	13	2	16	1	.875
Deago, Roger, S.D.*	2	2	0	4	0	4	0	1.000
DeJean, Mike, Mil.-St.L.	76	0	9	14	0	23	2	1.000
Dempster, Ryan, Cin.	22	20	4	14	3	21	2	.857
Dessens, Elmer, Ari.	34	30	9	18	0	27	2	1.000
Dotel, Octavio, Hou.	76	0	0	6	0	6	0	1.000
Downs, Scott, Mon.*	1	1	0	0	0	0	0	.000
Dreifort, Darren, L.A.	10	10	9	15	1	25	1	.960
Drew, Tim, Mon.	6	1	1	1	0	2	0	1.000
Duckworth, Brandon, Phi.	24	18	7	11	2	20	0	.900
Durocher, Jayson, Mil.	6	0	0	2	0	2	0	1.000
Eaton, Adam, S.D.	31	31	19	27	3	49	1	.939
Eischen, Joey, Mon.*	70	0	1	13	2	16	1	.875
Elarton, Scott, Col.	11	10	3	11	0	14	1	1.000
Eldred, Cal, St.L.	62	0	3	10	0	13	0	1.000
Estes, Shawn, Chi.*	29	28	10	30	3	43	6	.930
Estrella, Leo, Mil.	58	0	8	14	1	23	1	.957
Etherton, Seth, Cin.	7	7	1	2	0	3	0	1.000

Player, Team	G	GS	PO	A	E	TC	DP	Pct.
Eyre, Scott, S.F.*	74	0	2	11	2	15	1	.867
Farnsworth, Kyle, Chi.	77	0	5	12	0	17	0	1.000
Fassero, Jeff, St.L.*	62	6	5	12	1	18	1	.944
Feliciano, Pedro, N.Y.*	23	0	3	6	1	10	0	.900
Fernandez, Jared, Hou.	12	6	2	11	0	13	1	1.000
Ferrari, Anthony, Mon.*	4	0	0	1	0	1	0	1.000
Figueroa, Nelson, Pit.	12	3	1	6	1	8	0	.875
Fogg, Josh, Pit.	26	26	13	16	1	30	1	.967
Foppert, Jesse, S.F.	23	21	3	13	1	17	0	.941
Ford, Matt, Mil.*	25	4	2	5	1	8	1	.875
Foster, John, Mil.*	23	0	1	1	0	2	0	1.000
Fox, Chad, Fla.	21	0	0	3	0	3	0	1.000
Franco, John, N.Y.*	38	0	1	9	0	10	0	1.000
Franklin, Wayne, Mil.*	36	34	8	24	0	32	2	1.000
Fuentes, Brian, Col.*	75	0	3	9	1	13	1	.923
Gagne, Eric, L.A.	77	0	4	11	0	15	0	1.000
Gallo, Mike, Hou.*	32	0	3	7	1	11	1	.909
Geary, Geoff, Phi.	5	0	0	0	0	0	0	.000
Glavine, Tom, N.Y.*	32	32	6	42	2	50	5	.960
Gonzalez, Edgar, Ari.	9	2	1	3	0	4	0	1.000
Gonzalez, Mike, Pit.*	16	0	0	3	0	3	0	1.000
Gonzalez, Wiki, S.D.	1	0	0	1	0	1	0	1.000
Good, Andrew, Ari.	16	10	4	10	1	15	0	.933
Grabow, John, Pit.*	5	0	0	0	0	0	0	.000
Graves, Danny, Cin.	30	26	12	35	0	47	2	1.000
Griffiths, Jeremy, N.Y.	9	6	2	7	1	10	1	.900
Gryboski, Kevin, Atl.	64	0	3	6	1	10	0	.900
Guthrie, Mark, Chi.*	65	0	2	12	0	14	1	1.000
Hackman, Luther, S.D.	65	0	7	11	1	19	1	.947
Hall, Josh, Cin.	6	5	4	1	0	5	0	1.000
Hamilton, Joey, Cin.	3	0	0	0	0	0	0	.000
Hampton, Mike, Atl.*	31	31	15	52	1	68	4	.985
Hancock, Josh, Phi.	2	0	0	0	0	0	0	.000
Harang, Aaron, Cin.	9	9	2	4	0	6	0	1.000
Haren, Danny, St.L.	14	14	3	5	0	8	0	1.000
Haynes, Jimmy, Cin.	18	18	11	15	1	27	4	.963
Hebson, Bryan, Mon.	2	0	0	0	0	0	0	.000
Heilman, Aaron, N.Y.	14	13	3	12	2	17	0	.882
Helling, Rick, Fla.	11	0	1	2	0	3	0	1.000
Heredia, Felix, Cin.*	57	0	3	3	1	7	0	.857
Herges, Matt, S.D.-S.F.	67	0	2	9	1	12	2	.917
Hermanson, Dustin, St.L.-S.F.	32	6	8	8	0	16	1	1.000
Hernandez, Livan, Mon.	33	33	16	47	1	64	6	.984
Hernandez, Roberto, Atl.	66	0	3	11	1	15	1	.933
Hitchcock, Sterling, St.L.*	8	6	1	1	1	3	0	.667
Hodges, Trey, Atl.	52	1	8	7	0	15	1	1.000
Hoffman, Trevor, S.D.	9	0	2	1	0	3	1	1.000
Holmes, Darren, Atl.	48	0	2	2	1	5	1	.800
Howard, Ben, S.D.	6	6	3	3	0	6	0	1.000
Ishii, Kazuhisa, L.A.*	27	27	4	14	0	18	0	1.000
Isringhausen, Jason, St.L.	40	0	0	6	0	6	0	1.000
Jackson, Edwin, L.A.	4	3	0	3	0	3	0	1.000
Jarvis, Kevin, S.D.	16	16	13	15	0	28	0	1.000
Jennings, Jason, Col.	32	32	9	25	2	36	2	.944
Jensen, Ryan, S.F.	6	2	0	2	0	2	0	1.000
Jimenez, Jose, Col.	63	7	9	16	3	28	1	.893
Johnson, Jonathan, Hou.	4	3	4	2	0	6	0	1.000
Johnson, Randy, Ari.*	18	18	2	14	0	16	0	1.000
Jones, Todd, Col.	33	1	5	4	1	10	1	.900
Journell, Jimmy, St.L.	7	0	0	1	1	2	0	.500
Junge, Eric, Phi.	6	0	1	0	0	1	0	1.000
Keisler, Randy, S.D.*	2	2	0	1	0	1	0	1.000
Kida, Masao, L.A.	3	2	0	1	0	1	0	1.000
Kieschnick, Brooks, Mil.	42	0	8	11	0	19	2	1.000
Kim, Byung-Hyun, Ari.	7	7	3	14	1	18	0	.944
Kim, Sun-Woo, Mon.	4	3	1	1	0	2	0	1.000
King, Ray, Atl.*	80	0	3	12	0	15	0	1.000
Kinney, Matt, Mil.	33	31	13	22	1	36	4	.972
Kline, Steve, St.L.*	78	0	1	16	0	17	3	1.000
Knott, Eric, Mon.*	13	1	0	2	1	3	0	.667
Kolb, Danny, Mil.	37	0	2	4	0	6	0	1.000
Koplove, Mike, Ari.	31	0	0	10	0	10	0	1.000
Lawrence, Brian, S.D.	33	33	14	42	3	59	2	.949
Leiter, Al, N.Y.*	30	30	4	27	0	31	4	1.000
Leskanic, Curtis, Mil.	26	0	2	2	0	4	0	1.000
Levrault, Allen, Fla.	19	0	0	2	0	2	1	1.000
Lidge, Brad, Hou.	78	0	2	4	0	6	0	1.000
Lincoln, Mike, Pit.	36	0	1	4	1	6	0	.833
Linebrink, Scott, Hou.-S.D.	52	6	6	4	0	10	0	1.000
Lloyd, Graeme, N.Y.*	36	0	3	5	0	8	0	1.000
Loewer, Carlton, S.D.	5	5	0	1	1	2	0	.500

Player, Team	G	GS	PO	A	E	TC	DP	Pct.
Looper, Braden, Fla.	74	0	1	10	0	11	0	1.000
Lopez, Javier, Col.*	75	0	5	13	0	18	0	1.000
Lowry, Noah, S.F.*	4	0	0	1	0	1	0	1.000
Maddux, Greg, Atl.	36	36	13	58	2	73	5	.973
Madson, Ryan, Phi.	1	0	0	0	0	0	0	.000
Mahomes, Pat, Pit.	9	1	4	4	0	8	0	1.000
Mann, Jim, Pit.	2	0	0	0	0	0	0	.000
Manning, David, Mil.	2	2	0	1	0	1	0	1.000
Manon, Julio, Mon.	23	0	1	2	1	4	0	.750
Mantei, Matt, Ari.	50	0	1	4	0	5	0	1.000
Manzanillo, Josias, Cin.	9	0	0	1	1	2	0	.500
Marquis, Jason, Atl.	21	2	3	8	1	12	0	.917
Martin, Tom, L.A.*	80	0	3	7	0	10	2	1.000
Martinez, Luis, Mil.*	4	4	0	3	0	3	0	1.000
Matthews, Mike, S.D.*	77	0	2	12	0	14	1	1.000
Meadows, Brian, Pit.	34	7	5	10	2	17	0	.882
Mercado, Hector, Phi.*	13	0	0	3	0	3	0	1.000
Mercedes, Jose, Mon.	5	0	0	1	0	1	0	1.000
Mercker, Kent, Cin.-Atl.*	67	0	6	6	1	13	0	.923
Mesa, Jose, Phi.	61	0	4	2	1	7	0	.857
Miceli, Dan, Col.-Hou.	37	0	7	4	0	11	0	1.000
Middlebrook, Jason, N.Y.	5	0	1	0	0	1	0	1.000
Miller, Matt, Col.	4	0	1	1	0	2	0	1.000
Miller, Wade, Hou.	33	33	13	21	1	35	1	.971
Millwood, Kevin, Phi.	35	35	11	23	2	36	0	.944
Mitre, Sergio, Chi.	3	2	0	3	0	3	0	1.000
Moehler, Brian, Hou.	3	3	0	5	0	5	0	1.000
Molina, Gabe, St.L.	3	0	0	0	0	0	0	.000
Moreno, Orber, N.Y.	7	0	0	2	0	2	0	1.000
Morris, Matt, St.L.	27	27	15	17	0	32	0	1.000
Moss, Damian, S.F.*	21	20	5	15	0	20	0	1.000
Mota, Guillermo, L.A.	76	0	6	14	2	22	0	.909
Mullen, Scott, L.A.*	1	1	0	0	0	0	0	.000
Munro, Pete, Hou.	40	2	4	10	0	14	2	1.000
Myers, Brett, Phi.	32	32	12	28	2	42	1	.952
Myers, Mike, Ari.*	64	0	4	8	0	12	0	1.000
Myers, Rodney, L.A.	4	0	0	1	0	1	1	1.000
Nagy, Charles, S.D.	5	0	1	2	0	3	0	1.000
Nance, Shane, Mil.*	26	0	4	3	1	8	1	.875
Nathan, Joe, S.F.	78	0	4	5	0	9	1	1.000
Neagle, Denny, Col.*	7	7	1	3	0	4	1	1.000
Neal, Blaine, Fla.	18	0	1	1	0	2	0	1.000
Nomo, Hideo, L.A.	33	33	14	28	1	43	4	.977
Norton, Phil, Chi.-Cin.*	21	0	1	2	0	3	0	1.000
Nunez, Vladimir, Fla.	14	0	1	0	1	2	0	.500
Obermueller, Wes, Mil.	12	11	13	12	0	25	1	1.000
Ohka, Tomo, Mon.	34	34	10	35	4	49	2	.918
Ohme, Kevin, St.L.*	2	0	1	0	0	1	0	1.000
Oliver, Darren, Col.*	33	32	6	28	0	34	3	1.000
Olsen, Kevin, Fla.	7	0	0	0	0	0	0	.000
Oropesa, Eddie, Ari.*	47	0	2	11	1	14	1	.929
Orosco, Jesse, S.D.*	42	0	4	4	0	8	1	1.000
Ortiz, Russ, Atl.	34	34	13	25	1	39	5	.974
Oswalt, Roy, Hou.	21	21	10	13	0	23	1	1.000
Padilla, Vicente, Phi.	32	32	12	35	4	51	1	.922
Painter, Lance, St.L.*	22	0	2	5	0	7	1	1.000
Patterson, John, Ari.	16	8	3	2	0	5	0	1.000
Pavano, Carl, Fla.	33	32	11	28	0	39	2	1.000
Pearce, Josh, St.L.	7	0	1	1	0	2	0	1.000
Pearson, Jason, St.L.*	2	0	0	0	0	0	0	.000
Peavy, Jake, S.D.	32	32	17	20	3	40	3	.925
Penny, Brad, Fla.	32	32	19	12	1	32	1	.969
Perez, Odalis, L.A.*	30	30	5	42	1	48	3	.979
Perez, Oliver, S.D.-Pit.*	24	24	1	15	1	17	0	.941
Phelps, Tommy, Fla.*	27	7	3	6	0	9	0	1.000
Plesac, Dan, Phi.*	58	0	0	5	0	5	0	1.000
Ponson, Sidney, S.F.	10	10	9	10	0	19	3	1.000
Powell, Brian, S.F.	1	1	3	2	0	5	0	1.000
Prinz, Bret, Ari.	1	0	0	1	0	1	0	1.000
Prior, Mark, Chi.	30	30	8	12	3	23	0	.870
Puffer, Brandon, Hou.	13	0	0	8	0	8	0	1.000
Quantrill, Paul, L.A.	89	0	2	19	0	21	3	1.000
Quevedo, Ruben, Mil.	9	8	2	8	0	10	0	1.000
Raggio, Brady, Ari.	10	0	0	0	0	0	0	.000
Ramirez, Horacio, Atl.*	29	29	7	32	3	42	5	.929
Randall, Scott, Cin.	15	2	2	4	0	6	0	1.000
Randolph, Stephen, Ari.*	50	0	4	5	0	9	1	1.000
Reames, Britt, Mon.	2	0	0	0	0	0	0	.000
Redding, Tim, Hou.	33	32	6	30	2	38	2	.947
Redman, Mark, Fla.*	29	29	5	24	1	30	0	.967
Reed, Steve, Col.	67	0	4	14	0	18	2	1.000

Player, Team	G	GS	PO	A	E	TC	DP	Pct.
Reith, Brian, Cin.	42	1	1	6	1	8	0	.875
Reitsma, Chris, Cin.	57	3	1	9	2	12	0	.833
Remlinger, Mike, Chi.*	73	0	3	4	0	7	0	1.000
Reyes, Dennys, Pit.-Ari.*	15	0	1	2	1	4	0	.750
Reynolds, Shane, Atl.	30	29	7	20	0	27	3	1.000
Riedling, John, Cin.	55	8	11	12	1	24	1	.958
Ritchie, Todd, Mil.	5	5	1	5	1	7	0	.857
Roa, Joe, Phi.-Col.-S.D.	28	4	4	9	0	13	2	1.000
Roach, Jason, N.Y.	2	2	0	3	0	3	0	1.000
Roberts, Grant, N.Y.	18	0	1	6	0	7	0	1.000
Robertson, Jeriome, Hou.*	32	31	11	35	4	50	2	.920
Rodriguez, Felix, S.F.	68	0	0	9	1	10	2	.900
Rosario, Rodrigo, Hou.	2	2	0	2	0	2	0	1.000
Rueter, Kirk, S.F.*	27	27	10	33	0	43	5	1.000
Rusch, Glendon, Mil.*	32	19	3	16	0	19	1	1.000
Saarloos, Kirk, Hou.	36	4	2	6	2	10	1	.800
Sanchez, Duaner, Pit.	6	0	0	0	0	0	0	.000
Sanchez, Felix, Chi.*	3	0	0	0	0	0	0	.000
Sanchez, Jesus, Col.*	9	0	0	2	0	2	0	1.000
Sauerbeck, Scott, Pit.*	53	0	3	10	0	13	2	1.000
Schilling, Curt, Ari.	24	24	8	13	5	26	1	.808
Schmidt, Jason, S.F.	29	29	13	15	2	30	1	.933
Seo, Jae Weong, N.Y.	32	31	11	35	1	47	0	.979
Serafini, Dan, Cin.*	10	4	1	4	1	6	0	.833
Service, Scott, Ari.	18	0	2	1	0	3	0	1.000
Sheets, Ben, Mil.	34	34	22	19	2	43	0	.953
Shuey, Paul, L.A.	62	0	12	12	0	24	0	1.000
Silva, Carlos, Phi.	62	1	3	18	1	22	2	.955
Simontacchi, Jason, St.L.	46	16	13	15	2	30	1	.933
Smith, Dan, Mon.	32	0	1	1	0	2	0	1.000
Smoltz, John, Atl.	62	0	4	6	0	10	1	1.000
Speier, Justin, Col.	72	0	4	5	0	9	0	1.000
Spooneybarger, Tim, Fla.	33	0	6	5	0	11	0	1.000
Springer, Russ, St.L.	17	0	3	3	0	6	1	1.000
Stanton, Mike, N.Y.*	50	0	2	8	3	13	0	.769
Stark, Denny, Col.	17	13	5	9	0	14	0	1.000
Stephenson, Garrett, St.L.	32	27	7	21	0	28	3	1.000
Stewart, Scott, Mon.*	51	0	0	7	0	7	0	1.000
Stone, Ricky, Hou.	65	0	9	8	0	17	0	1.000
Strange, Pat, N.Y.	6	0	0	2	0	2	0	1.000
Strickland, Scott, N.Y.	19	0	2	2	0	4	0	1.000
Sullivan, Scott, Cin.	50	0	2	5	0	7	0	1.000
Suppan, Jeff, Pit.	21	21	15	19	1	35	1	.971
Tankersley, Dennis, S.D.	1	1	0	0	0	0	0	.000
Tavarez, Julian, Pit.	64	0	6	20	0	26	3	1.000
Tejera, Michael, Fla.*	50	6	2	19	1	22	2	.955
Telemaco, Amaury, Phi.	8	8	7	5	0	12	0	1.000
Tollberg, Brian, S.D.	3	3	4	2	0	6	0	1.000
TOMKO, Brett, St.L.	33	32	18	30	0	48	0	1.000
Torres, Salomon, Pit.	41	16	11	18	0	29	1	1.000
Trachsel, Steve, N.Y.	33	33	16	30	2	48	2	.958
Tsao, Chin-hui, Col.	9	8	3	9	0	12	2	1.000
Tucker, T.J., Mon.	45	7	9	13	1	23	0	.957
Urbina, Ugueth, Fla.	33	0	0	3	0	3	0	1.000
Valentine, Joe, Cin.	2	0	0	0	0	0	0	.000
Valverde, Jose, Ari.	54	0	3	1	0	4	0	1.000
Van Poppel, Todd, Cin.	9	4	1	2	1	4	0	.750
Vance, Cory, Col.*	9	3	3	5	1	9	0	.889
Vargas, Claudio, Mon.	23	20	5	13	1	19	1	.947
Vazquez, Javier, Mon.	34	34	10	34	2	46	3	.957
Veres, Dave, Chi.	31	0	1	2	0	3	0	1.000
Villafuerte, Brandon, S.D.	31	0	6	7	0	13	0	1.000
Villarreal, Oscar, Ari.	86	1	5	17	3	25	1	.880
Villone, Ron, Hou.*	19	19	14	16	0	30	0	1.000
Vizcaino, Luis, Mil.	75	0	5	6	0	11	0	1.000
Vogelsong, Ryan, Pit.	6	5	2	5	1	8	1	.875
Wagner, Billy, Hou.*	78	0	5	11	0	16	0	1.000
Wagner, Ryan, Cin.	17	0	3	0	1	4	0	.750
Walker, Kevin, S.D.*	11	0	0	2	0	2	0	1.000
Watson, Mark, Cin.*	2	0	0	0	0	0	0	.000
Wayne, Justin, Fla.	2	2	0	1	0	1	0	1.000
Weathers, Dave, N.Y.	77	0	2	15	4	21	2	.810
Webb, Brandon, Ari.	29	28	15	32	3	50	0	.940
Wellemeyer, Todd, Chi.	15	0	1	2	0	3	0	1.000
Wells, Kip, Pit.	31	31	7	31	5	43	0	.884
Wendell, Turk, Phi.	56	0	3	11	0	14	1	1.000
Wheeler, Dan, N.Y.	35	0	1	4	0	5	0	1.000
White, Gabe, Cin.*	34	0	1	3	0	4	1	1.000
White, Rick, Hou.	15	0	0	1	1	2	1	.500
Williams, Jerome, S.F.	21	21	11	14	3	28	3	.893
Williams, Mike, Pit.-Phi.	68	0	8	14	2	24	1	.917
Williams, Woody, St.L.	34	33	16	33	1	50	1	.980
Williamson, Scott, Cin.	42	0	1	1	1	3	0	.667
Willis, Dontrelle, Fla.*	27	27	2	17	4	23	2	.826
Wilson, Paul, Cin.	28	28	8	18	1	27	1	.963
Witasick, Jay, S.D.	46	0	0	7	1	8	0	.875
Wolf, Randy, Phi.*	33	33	14	24	3	41	0	.927
Wood, Kerry, Chi.	32	32	18	18	1	37	3	.973
Worrell, Tim, S.F.	76	0	6	8	1	15	0	.933
Wright, Jaret, S.D.-Atl.	50	0	7	9	0	16	3	1.000
Yan, Esteban, St.L.	39	0	8	1	0	9	0	1.000
Young, Jason, Col.	8	3	0	3	0	3	0	1.000
Zambrano, Carlos, Chi.	32	32	19	46	4	69	2	.942
Zerbe, Chad, S.F.*	33	1	3	13	0	16	1	1.000

PITCHERS WITH TWO OR MORE TEAMS

Player, Team	G	GS	PO	A	E	TC	DP	Pct.
Crudale, Mike, St.L.	13	0	1	1	0	2	0	1.000
Crudale, Mike, Mil.	9	0	0	1	0	1	0	1.000
Darensbourg, Vic, Col.*	3	0	2	0	1	3	0	.667
Darensbourg, Vic, Mon.*	6	0	1	3	0	4	0	1.000
de los Santos, Valerio, Mil.*	45	0	1	12	1	14	1	.929
de los Santos, Valerio, Phi.*	6	0	0	1	1	2	0	.500
DeJean, Mike, Mil.	58	0	7	12	0	19	2	1.000
DeJean, Mike, St.L.	18	0	2	2	0	4	0	1.000
Herges, Matt, S.D.	40	0	0	5	0	5	1	1.000
Herges, Matt, S.F.	27	0	2	4	1	7	1	.857
Hermanson, Dustin, St.L.	23	0	5	5	0	10	1	1.000
Hermanson, Dustin, S.F.	9	6	3	3	0	6	0	1.000
Linebrink, Scott, Hou.	9	6	3	1	0	4	0	1.000
Linebrink, Scott, S.D.	43	0	3	3	0	6	0	1.000
Mercker, Kent, Cin.*	49	0	6	6	1	13	0	.923
Mercker, Kent, Atl.*	18	0	0	0	0	0	0	.000
Miceli, Dan, Col.	14	0	4	2	0	6	0	1.000
Miceli, Dan, Hou.	23	0	3	2	0	5	0	1.000
Norton, Phil, Chi.*	4	0	1	0	0	1	0	1.000
Norton, Phil, Cin.*	17	0	0	2	0	2	0	1.000
Perez, Oliver, S.D.*	19	19	0	11	0	11	0	1.000
Perez, Oliver, Pit.*	5	5	1	4	1	6	0	.833
Reyes, Dennys, Pit.*	12	0	0	2	1	3	0	.667
Reyes, Dennys, Ari.*	3	0	1	0	0	1	0	1.000
Roa, Joe, Phi.	6	3	1	4	0	5	2	1.000
Roa, Joe, Col.	4	0	1	1	0	2	0	1.000
Roa, Joe, S.D.	18	1	2	4	0	6	0	1.000
Williams, Mike, Pit.	40	0	4	9	0	13	1	1.000
Williams, Mike, Phi.	28	0	4	5	2	11	0	.818
Wright, Jaret, S.D.	39	0	7	7	0	14	3	1.000
Wright, Jaret, Atl.	11	0	0	2	0	2	0	1.000

MISCELLANEOUS

SHUTOUT GAMES

Read across for wins, down for losses.

Team	Atl.	S.F.	St.L.	Chi.	L.A.	Phi.	Mon.	Fla.	Pit.	S.D.	N.Y.	Hou.	Ari.	Cin.	Mil.	Col.	A.L.	W	L	Pct.
Atlanta	..	0	0	0	1	1	1	3	0	0	0	0	0	0	0	0	1	7	4	.636
San Francisco	0	..	0	1	2	0	0	0	1	0	0	0	2	0	1	2	1	10	6	.625
St. Louis	0	0	..	2	0	1	0	1	1	0	0	1	0	2	2	0	0	10	7	.588
Chicago	0	1	1	..	0	1	1	1	1	1	1	3	0	2	0	0	1	14	10	.583
Los Angeles	0	2	0	1	..	1	0	0	0	3	0	0	5	0	2	3	0	17	13	.567
Philadelphia	1	1	0	1	2	..	1	1	0	1	2	1	0	0	0	0	2	13	10	.565
Montreal	2	1	0	0	0	1	..	0	1	0	2	0	2	0	1	0	0	10	8	.556
Florida	0	0	1	1	0	0	1	..	1	1	3	0	0	0	0	0	3	11	9	.550
Pittsburgh	0	1	2	1	0	1	0	2	..	0	0	0	0	1	0	2	0	10	9	.526
San Diego	0	0	0	1	1	0	1	0	0	..	0	0	2	2	0	1	2	10	9	.526
New York	0	0	0	0	1	1	1	1	1	0	..	0	0	0	1	2	2	10	10	.500
Houston	0	0	1	0	0	0	0	0	1	0	0	..	0	0	0	1	2	5	5	.500
Arizona	1	0	1	0	3	1	0	0	1	1	0	0	..	1	0	1	1	11	12	.478
Cincinnati	0	0	1	1	1	1	0	0	0	0	0	0	1	..	0	0	0	5	10	.333
Milwaukee	0	0	0	1	0	0	0	0	1	1	0	0	0	0	..	0	0	3	7	.300
Colorado	0	0	0	0	1	0	1	0	0	1	0	0	0	0	0	..	1	4	12	.250
A.L. Clubs	0	0	0	0	1	1	1	0	0	0	2	0	0	2	0	0	..	..	..	..
Lost	4	6	7	10	13	10	8	9	9	9	10	5	12	10	7	12	16	150	141	.515

N.L. shutouts vs A.L. clubs (16): Atlanta vs Tampa Bay, Chicago vs Baltimore, Houston vs New York, Houston vs Texas, New York vs Anaheim, New York vs Texas, Philadelphia vs Boston, Philadelphia vs Anaheim, San Diego vs Chicago, San Diego vs Seattle, San Francisco vs Oakland, Colorado vs Minnesota, Florida vs Oakland, Florida vs Texas, Florida vs Tampa Bay, Arizona vs Detroit.

HOME RECORD

Read across for home wins, down for road losses.

Team	S.F.	Atl.	Fla.	Mon.	Phi.	Col.	Hou.	St.L.	L.A.	Ari.	Chi.	Pit.	Cin.	S.D.	N.Y.	Mil.	A.L.	W	L	Pct.
San Francisco	..	3	2	0	2	9	2	2	8	7	1	2	2	7	2	2	6	57	24	.704
Atlanta	2	..	6	5	5	3	2	3	2	3	1	5	2	2	7	2	5	55	26	.679
Florida	0	6	..	9	7	2	1	1	2	3	1	2	1	3	6	3	6	53	28	.654
Montreal	4	3	5	..	7	2	2	1	1	2	2	2	2	3	8	3	5	52	29	.642
Philadelphia	2	5	4	8	..	3	2	3	3	1	3	1	1	2	5	2	4	49	32	.605
Colorado	6	0	3	2	2	..	1	2	5	6	2	1	1	7	2	3	6	49	32	.605
Houston	1	0	3	2	1	2	..	6	2	1	4	6	7	1	1	4	7	48	33	.593
St. Louis	1	2	1	3	2	1	4	..	0	1	5	5	5	3	3	6	6	48	33	.593
Los Angeles	4	1	3	2	2	8	1	2	..	4	2	2	3	5	1	1	5	46	35	.568
Arizona	3	1	2	3	2	6	3	1	5	..	1	1	5	5	2	1	4	45	36	.556
Chicago	2	1	2	2	0	2	4	6	1	2	..	5	5	1	3	3	5	44	37	.543
Pittsburgh	1	1	3	2	2	4	5	2	0	1	4	..	4	1	1	5	3	39	42	.481
Cincinnati	2	2	0	1	3	2	2	5	2	1	5	2	..	2	0	3	3	35	46	.432
San Diego	2	0	1	2	1	4	1	2	7	6	0	0	2	..	2	1	4	35	46	.432
New York	2	5	3	4	3	4	2	1	1	1	1	2	1	2	..	1	1	34	46	.425
Milwaukee	0	1	2	0	3	1	5	2	0	1	0	5	4	3	1	..	3	31	50	.383
A.L. Clubs	5	4	3	5	2	3	5	5	3	2	5	4	2	5	5	4	..	..	..	..
Lost on Road	37	35	43	50	44	56	42	44	42	42	37	45	47	52	49	44	73	720	575	.556

HOME RECORDS IN INTERLEAGUE GAMES

Team				Total	Team				Total
Arizona	2-1 vs. Chi.	2-1 vs. Cle.		4-2	Milwaukee	1-2 vs. Bos.	2-1 vs. Min.		3-3
Atlanta	2-1 vs. Bal.	3-0 vs. Tex.		5-1	Montreal	1-2 vs. Ana.	3-0 vs. Tex.	1-2 vs. Tor.	5-4
Chicago	1-2 vs. Chi.	2-1 vs. N.Y.	2-1 vs. TB.	5-4	New York	0-3 vs. N.Y.	1-2 vs. Sea.		1-5
Cincinnati	2-1 vs. N.Y.	1-2 vs. Tor.		3-3	Philadelphia	2-1 vs. Bos.	2-1 vs. Oak.	0-3 vs. Sea.	4-5
Colorado	3-0 vs. Cle.	2-1 vs. Det.	1-2 vs. K.C.	6-3	Pittsburgh	1-2 vs. Bos.	2-1 vs. Cle.		3-3
Florida	1-2 vs. Ana.	2-1 vs. Oak.	3-0 vs. TB.	6-3	St. Louis	2-1 vs. Bal.	1-2 vs. K.C.	3-0 vs. Tor.	6-3
Houston	3-0 vs. Bal.	1-2 vs. Tex.	3-0 vs. TB.	7-2	San Diego	1-2 vs. Det.	1-2 vs. Min.	2-1 vs. Sea.	4-5
Los Angeles	2-1 vs. Ana.	1-2 vs. Chi.	2-1 vs. K.C.	5-4	San Francisco	3-0 vs. Det.	1-2 vs. Min.	2-1 vs. Oak.	6-3

ROAD RECORD

Read across for road wins, down for home losses.

Team	Atl.	Chi.	S.F.	Hou.	L.A.	Ari.	Fla.	Mil.	Phi.	St.L.	Pit.	Cin.	N.Y.	Mon.	S.D.	Col.	A.L.	W	L	Pct.
Atlanta	..	3	0	3	2	2	3	2	4	1	2	1	4	7	4	3	5	46	35	.568
Chicago	1	..	2	5	1	2	2	7	1	2	5	5	2	1	3	1	4	44	37	.543
San Francisco	1	1	..	2	5	7	3	3	1	3	2	1	0	0	7	3	4	43	37	.538
Houston	1	3	1	..	2	0	2	5	1	5	4	5	1	1	2	2	4	39	42	.481
Los Angeles	1	2	2	1	..	5	2	3	0	2	3	1	2	2	3	4	6	39	42	.481
Arizona	1	1	2	2	5	..	0	2	2	2	2	2	2	1	4	4	7	39	42	.481
Florida	4	1	1	0	0	2	..	4	6	2	0	3	6	4	2	0	3	38	43	.469
Milwaukee	1	6	1	3	2	2	0	..	1	1	5	6	5	0	2	0	2	37	44	.457
Philadelphia	5	2	1	2	2	1	2	0	..	1	1	3	7	3	2	1	4	37	44	.457
St. Louis	0	4	0	3	2	2	2	7	0	..	5	2	2	2	1	1	4	37	44	.457
Pittsburgh	1	4	1	1	1	2	1	2	2	5	..	7	1	1	3	2	2	36	45	.444
Cincinnati	1	2	1	3	0	1	2	5	2	4	3	..	2	1	1	2	4	34	47	.420
New York	3	0	2	2	2	1	4	2	4	0	2	3	..	1	1	1	4	32	49	.395
Montreal	4	1	3	1	1	0	1	3	1	0	1	2	6	..	1	2	4	31	50	.383
San Diego	1	2	3	2	4	4	0	0	2	0	2	1	1	0	..	3	4	29	52	.358
Colorado	0	1	1	1	2	3	1	2	0	2	2	1	0	1	5	..	3	25	56	.309
A.L. Clubs	1	4	3	2	4	2	3	3	5	3	3	3	5	4	5	3	..	..	..	..
Lost at home	26	37	24	33	35	36	28	50	32	33	42	46	46	29	46	32	64	586	709	.453

PITCHING AGAINST EACH CLUB

ARIZONA—84-78

Pitcher	Atl. W-L	Chi. W-L	Cin. W-L	Col. W-L	Fla. W-L	Hou. W-L	L.A. W-L	Mil. W-L	Mon. W-L	N.Y. W-L	Phi. W-L	Pit. W-L	S.D. W-L	S.F. W-L	St.L. W-L	A.L. W-L	Totals W-L
Batista, Miguel	0-1	1-0	0-0	1-1	1-1	2-0	0-2	0-0	0-0	0-0	1-0	1-0	1-1	1-3	0-0	1-0	10-9
Bottalico, Ricky	0-0	0-0	0-0	0-0	0-0	1-0	0-0	0-0	0-0	0-0	0-0	0-0	0-0	0-0	0-0	0-0	1-0
Capuano, Chris	0-1	0-0	0-0	0-0	0-0	0-0	1-0	0-0	0-0	0-0	0-0	0-1	1-1	0-0	0-1	0-0	2-4
Dessens, Elmer	0-0	0-0	1-0	0-1	1-0	1-0	1-2	2-0	1-0	0-0	0-0	0-1	1-1	0-2	0-1	0-0	8-8
Gonzalez, Edgar	0-0	0-0	0-0	0-0	0-0	0-0	0-0	0-0	0-0	0-0	0-0	0-0	1-0	1-0	0-0	0-1	2-1
Good, Andrew	0-0	0-0	0-0	0-1	0-0	0-0	1-0	0-0	0-1	0-0	0-0	0-0	1-0	0-0	0-0	2-0	4-2
Johnson, Randy	0-1	0-0	0-1	2-0	0-1	0-0	0-2	0-1	1-0	2-0	0-0	0-0	1-1	0-1	0-0	0-0	6-8
Kim, Byung-Hyun	0-0	0-0	0-0	0-2	0-1	0-0	0-1	0-0	0-1	0-0	0-0	0-0	0-0	0-0	1-0	0-0	1-5
Koplove, Mike	0-0	0-0	0-0	0-0	0-0	0-0	0-0	0-0	0-0	0-0	1-0	0-0	1-0	0-0	0-0	1-0	3-0
Mantei, Matt	0-1	0-0	0-0	1-0	0-0	0-0	2-0	0-0	0-0	0-0	0-0	0-1	0-0	1-2	0-0	1-0	5-4
Myers, Mike	0-0	0-0	0-0	0-0	0-0	0-0	0-0	0-0	0-0	0-0	0-0	0-0	0-0	0-1	0-0	0-0	0-1
Oropesa, Eddie	0-1	0-1	1-0	0-0	0-0	0-0	0-0	0-0	1-0	0-0	0-0	0-0	0-0	0-0	0-0	1-1	3-3
Patterson, John	0-0	0-0	1-0	0-2	0-0	0-0	0-0	0-0	0-0	0-0	0-0	0-0	0-1	0-1	0-0	0-0	1-4
Randolph, Stephen	0-0	0-1	1-0	2-0	0-0	0-0	1-0	0-0	0-0	1-0	0-0	0-0	0-0	0-0	1-0	2-0	8-1
Schilling, Curt	1-0	0-1	1-0	1-1	0-0	0-0	1-1	0-2	0-0	0-0	1-0	1-0	2-2	0-2	0-0	0-0	8-9
Service, Scott	0-0	0-0	0-0	0-0	0-0	0-0	0-0	0-0	0-0	0-0	0-0	0-0	0-1	0-0	0-0	0-1	0-2
Valverde, Jose	0-0	0-0	1-0	0-0	0-0	0-0	0-0	0-0	1-0	0-0	0-0	0-0	0-1	0-0	0-0	0-1	2-1
Villarreal, Oscar	1-0	1-1	0-0	1-0	0-1	1-1	2-1	1-0	0-0	0-1	1-1	0-0	0-0	0-1	1-0	1-0	10-7
Webb, Brandon	0-0	0-0	1-1	2-1	0-1	0-0	1-0	0-0	0-0	1-1	0-1	1-0	0-1	2-1	0-1	2-1	10-9
Totals	2-5	2-4	7-2	10-9	2-5	5-1	10-9	3-3	4-2	4-2	4-2	3-3	9-10	5-14	3-3	11-4	84-78

NO-DECISIONS: Bret Prinz, Brady Raggio, Dennys Reyes.

INTERLEAGUE: Oscar Villarreal 1-0, Andrew Good 1-0, Scott Service 0-1 vs. White Sox; Edgar Gonzalez 0-1, Stephen Randolph 1-0, Brandon Webb 1-0 vs. Indians; Stephen Randolph 1-0, Eddie Oropesa 1-0, Brandon Webb 1-0 vs. Tigers; Eddie Oropesa 0-1, Andrew Good 1-0, Matt Mantei 1-0 vs. Royals; Brandon Webb 0-1, Miguel Batista 1-0, Mike Koplove 1-0 vs. Twins. Total: 11-4.

ATLANTA—101-61

Pitcher	Ari. W-L	Chi. W-L	Cin. W-L	Col. W-L	Fla. W-L	Hou. W-L	L.A. W-L	Mil. W-L	Mon. W-L	N.Y. W-L	Phi. W-L	Pit. W-L	S.D. W-L	S.F. W-L	St.L. W-L	A.L. W-L	Totals W-L
Bong, Jung	1-0	0-0	0-0	0-0	0-0	0-0	1-0	0-0	3-1	0-0	0-0	0-0	0-0	0-0	0-0	1-1	6-2
Cunnane, Will	0-0	0-0	0-0	0-0	1-1	0-0	0-0	0-0	0-0	0-0	0-0	1-1	0-0	0-0	0-0	0-0	2-2
Gryboski, Kevin	1-1	0-0	0-0	0-0	1-0	0-0	0-0	0-0	0-0	0-1	1-1	0-0	1-0	1-1	0-0	1-0	6-4
Hampton, Mike	1-0	1-0	0-1	1-0	0-2	1-0	1-0	1-0	3-0	1-3	0-2	1-0	1-0	1-0	0-0	1-0	14-8
Hernandez, Ro.	0-0	0-0	0-2	1-0	1-0	1-0	0-0	0-0	0-1	1-0	0-0	1-0	0-0	0-0	0-0	0-0	5-3
Hodges, Trey	1-0	0-0	1-0	0-0	0-1	0-0	0-0	0-0	0-0	0-1	0-0	1-0	0-0	0-1	0-0	0-0	3-3
Holmes, Darren	0-0	0-0	0-0	0-0	0-0	0-0	0-0	0-1	0-0	0-0	1-1	0-0	0-0	0-0	0-0	0-0	1-2
King, Ray	0-0	0-0	0-0	0-0	0-1	0-0	0-0	1-0	0-1	1-0	0-1	0-0	0-0	0-1	1-0	0-0	3-4
Maddux, Greg	0-1	2-0	0-0	1-0	2-2	1-0	1-1	1-0	0-1	3-0	1-3	1-0	0-1	0-1	1-0	2-1	16-11
Ortiz, Russ	0-0	0-0	1-0	2-0	3-2	1-0	1-1	1-0	2-1	2-2	3-0	0-0	2-0	0-0	2-0	1-1	21-7
Ramirez, Horacio	0-0	0-1	0-0	0-0	1-1	0-1	0-0	0-0	2-1	2-0	2-0	1-0	1-0	0-0	0-0	3-0	12-4
Reynolds, Shane	1-0	1-1	1-0	1-0	0-0	1-0	0-0	0-1	1-1	1-1	1-1	1-1	1-0	0-0	0-1	1-2	11-9
Smoltz, John	0-0	0-0	0-0	0-0	0-0	0-0	0-0	0-0	0-0	0-0	0-1	0-0	0-0	0-0	0-1	0-0	0-2
Wright, Jaret	0-0	0-0	0-0	0-0	0-0	0-0	0-0	0-0	1-0	0-0	0-0	0-0	0-0	0-0	0-0	0-0	1-0
Totals	5-2	4-2	3-3	6-0	9-10	5-1	4-2	4-2	12-7	11-8	9-10	7-2	6-1	2-4	4-2	10-5	101-61

NO-DECISIONS: Joe Dawley, Jason Marquis, Kent Mercker.

INTERLEAGUE: Greg Maddux 1-0, Horacio Ramirez 1-0, Shane Reynolds 0-1 vs. Orioles; Jung Bong 0-1, Horacio Ramirez 1-0, Shane Reynolds 1-0 vs. Athletics; Russ Ortiz 0-1, Mike Hampton 1-0, Greg Maddux 0-1 vs. Mariners; Horacio Ramirez 1-0, Shane Reynolds 0-1, Russ Ortiz 1-0 vs. Devil Rays; Kevin Gryboski 1-0, Greg Maddux 1-0, Jung Bong 1-0 vs. Rangers. Total: 10-5.

CHICAGO—88-74

Pitcher	Ari. W-L	Atl. W-L	Cin. W-L	Col. W-L	Fla. W-L	Hou. W-L	L.A. W-L	Mil. W-L	Mon. W-L	N.Y. W-L	Phi. W-L	Pit. W-L	S.D. W-L	S.F. W-L	St.L. W-L	A.L. W-L	Totals W-L
Alfonseca, Antonio	1-0	0-0	2-0	0-0	0-0	0-0	0-0	0-0	0-0	0-0	0-0	0-0	0-0	0-0	0-0	0-1	3-1
Borowski, Joe	0-1	0-0	0-0	1-0	0-0	0-0	0-0	0-1	0-0	0-0	0-0	0-0	0-0	0-0	1-0	0-0	2-2
Clement, Matt	2-0	1-0	1-0	0-0	1-1	1-1	0-1	1-1	1-0	1-1	0-1	2-2	0-1	1-1	0-1	2-1	14-12
Cruz, Juan	0-0	0-0	0-0	0-0	0-0	0-1	0-0	1-2	0-0	0-0	0-0	0-2	0-0	1-0	0-1	0-1	2-7
Estes, Shawn	0-1	0-1	2-0	1-1	0-0	2-1	0-1	2-1	0-1	0-0	0-1	0-1	0-0	0-0	0-0	1-2	8-11
Farnsworth, Kyle	0-0	0-0	0-0	0-0	0-0	0-0	0-0	1-0	0-1	0-0	1-0	1-0	0-0	0-0	0-1	0-0	3-2
Guthrie, Mark	0-0	0-0	0-1	0-1	0-0	1-0	0-0	0-0	0-0	0-0	0-0	0-0	0-0	0-0	1-0	0-1	2-3
Mitre, Sergio	0-0	0-1	0-0	0-0	0-0	0-0	0-0	0-0	0-0	0-0	0-0	0-0	0-0	0-0	0-0	0-0	0-1
Prior, Mark	0-0	0-1	0-2	1-0	0-0	1-1	2-0	2-0	1-1	2-0	0-0	4-0	1-0	0-0	2-1	2-0	18-6
Remlinger, Mike	0-0	0-0	0-1	0-0	0-1	0-0	0-1	0-0	0-0	0-0	0-1	1-0	0-0	0-0	4-1	1-0	6-5
Veres, Dave	0-0	1-0	0-1	0-0	0-0	0-0	0-0	0-0	0-0	0-0	0-0	1-0	0-0	0-0	0-0	0-0	2-1
Wellemeyer, Todd	0-0	0-0	0-0	0-0	0-0	1-0	0-0	0-1	0-0	0-0	0-0	0-0	0-0	0-0	0-0	0-0	1-1
Wood, Kerry	0-0	0-0	3-0	0-0	2-0	0-3	0-0	2-0	0-0	2-0	0-1	1-2	1-1	1-1	0-2	2-1	14-11
Zambrano, Carlos	1-0	0-1	2-2	0-1	1-0	3-0	0-1	1-0	1-0	0-0	0-1	0-1	2-0	1-0	0-2	1-2	13-11
Totals	4-2	2-4	10-7	3-3	4-2	9-7	2-4	10-6	3-3	5-1	1-5	10-8	4-2	4-2	8-9	9-9	88-74

NO-DECISIONS: Alan Benes, Phil Norton, Felix Sanchez.

INTERLEAGUE: Shawn Estes 1-0, Matt Clement 1-0, Carlos Zambrano 0-1 vs. Orioles; Shawn Estes 0-1, Matt Clement 0-1, Antonio Alfonseca 0-1, Carlos Zambrano 1-0, Juan Cruz 0-1, Kerry Wood 1-0 vs. White Sox; Carlos Zambrano 0-1, Kerry Wood 1-0, Mark Prior 1-0 vs. Yankees; Mike Remlinger 1-0, Shawn Estes 0-1, Matt Clement 1-0 vs. Devil Rays; Kerry Wood 0-1, Mark Prior 1-0, Mark Guthrie 0-1 vs. Blue Jays. Total: 9-9.

CINCINNATI—69-93

Pitcher	Ari. W-L	Atl. W-L	Chi. W-L	Col. W-L	Fla. W-L	Hou. W-L	L.A. W-L	Mil. W-L	Mon. W-L	N.Y. W-L	Phi. W-L	Pit. W-L	S.D. W-L	S.F. W-L	St.L. W-L	A.L. W-L	Totals W-L
Acevedo, Jose	0-0	0-0	0-0	0-0	0-0	0-0	0-0	1-0	0-0	1-0	0-0	0-0	0-0	0-0	0-0	0-0	2-0
Anderson, Jimmy	0-1	0-0	1-1	0-0	0-0	0-0	0-0	0-0	0-1	0-0	0-0	0-1	0-0	0-0	0-1	0-0	1-5
Austin, Jeff	0-0	0-1	0-0	1-0	0-1	0-0	0-0	1-0	0-0	0-0	0-0	0-0	0-1	0-0	0-0	0-0	2-3
Bale, John	0-1	0-0	0-0	0-0	0-0	0-0	0-0	0-0	0-0	0-0	0-0	0-1	0-0	0-0	1-0	0-0	1-2
Belisle, Matt	0-0	0-0	0-1	0-0	0-0	0-0	0-0	0-0	0-0	0-0	0-0	1-0	0-0	0-0	0-0	0-0	1-1
Dempster, Ryan	0-0	0-1	0-0	0-0	0-0	1-2	0-0	1-1	0-0	0-0	0-1	0-1	0-0	0-1	0-0	1-0	3-7
Etherton, Seth	0-0	0-0	0-0	0-0	0-0	1-1	0-0	1-1	0-0	0-0	0-0	0-1	0-0	0-0	0-1	0-0	2-4
Graves, Danny	0-1	0-0	0-1	0-0	0-2	0-3	0-1	0-1	0-0	0-2	0-1	1-0	0-1	1-0	2-0	0-2	4-15
Hall, Josh	0-0	0-0	0-1	0-0	0-0	0-0	0-0	0-0	0-0	0-0	0-1	0-0	0-0	0-0	0-0	0-0	0-2
Harang, Aaron	2-0	0-0	0-0	0-0	0-0	0-0	0-0	0-1	0-1	0-0	0-0	1-0	1-0	0-0	0-1	0-0	4-3
Haynes, Jimmy	0-0	0-0	0-3	0-1	0-0	0-2	0-0	1-0	0-0	0-1	1-1	0-1	0-0	0-1	0-0	0-2	2-12
Heredia, Felix	0-1	0-0	0-0	0-0	0-0	0-0	1-1	1-0	0-0	0-0	0-0	1-0	1-0	0-0	1-0	0-0	5-2
Manzanillo, Josias	0-0	0-0	0-0	0-0	0-0	0-1	0-0	0-0	0-0	0-0	0-0	0-1	0-0	0-0	0-0	0-0	0-2
Mercker, Kent	0-1	0-0	0-0	0-0	0-0	0-0	0-0	0-0	0-0	0-0	0-0	0-1	0-0	0-0	0-0	0-0	0-2
Randall, Scott	0-0	0-0	0-2	0-0	0-0	0-0	0-0	0-1	0-1	0-0	0-0	1-1	0-0	0-0	1-0	0-0	2-5
Reith, Brian	0-0	0-0	0-0	0-0	0-0	0-1	0-0	1-0	1-0	0-1	0-0	0-0	0-1	0-0	0-0	0-0	2-3
Reitsma, Chris	0-0	1-1	0-0	1-1	0-0	0-0	1-0	0-1	0-0	0-0	0-0	0-2	0-0	1-0	1-0	4-0	9-5
Riedling, John	0-0	0-0	1-0	1-0	0-0	0-0	0-0	0-1	0-0	0-0	0-0	0-0	0-0	0-0	0-1	0-1	2-3
Serafini, Dan	0-0	0-0	0-0	0-0	0-0	0-0	0-0	0-1	0-0	0-0	1-0	0-0	0-0	0-0	0-2	0-0	1-3
Sullivan, Scott	0-0	1-0	0-0	1-0	1-0	0-0	0-0	1-0	1-0	0-0	0-0	0-0	0-0	0-0	1-0	0-0	6-0
Van Poppel, Todd	0-0	0-0	1-0	0-0	0-0	0-0	0-0	0-0	0-0	0-0	1-0	0-1	0-0	0-0	0-0	0-0	2-1
Wagner, Ryan	0-0	0-0	0-0	0-0	0-0	1-0	0-0	0-0	0-0	0-0	0-0	0-0	0-0	1-0	0-0	0-0	2-0
White, Gabe	0-0	1-0	1-0	0-0	1-0	0-0	0-0	0-0	0-0	0-0	0-0	0-0	0-0	0-0	0-0	0-0	3-0
Williamson, Scott	0-1	0-0	2-0	0-0	0-0	0-0	0-0	0-1	0-1	0-0	2-0	0-0	0-0	0-0	1-0	0-0	5-3
Wilson, Paul	0-1	0-0	1-1	0-0	0-1	2-2	0-2	0-1	0-0	1-0	0-0	0-0	1-0	0-1	1-1	2-0	8-10
Totals	2-7	3-3	7-10	4-2	2-4	5-12	2-4	8-10	2-4	2-4	5-4	5-11	3-3	3-3	9-7	7-5	69-93

NO-DECISIONS: Juan Cerros, Joey Hamilton, Phil Norton, Joe Valentine, Mark Watson.

INTERLEAGUE: Danny Graves 0-1, Chris Reitsma 1-0, Jimmy Haynes 0-1 vs. Indians; Chris Reitsma 1-0, Paul Wilson 1-0, Danny Graves 0-1 vs. Yankees; Paul Wilson 1-0, Chris Reitsma 1-0, Ryan Dempster 1-0 vs. Devil Rays; John Riedling 0-1, Chris Reitsma 1-0, Jimmy Haynes 0-1 vs. Blue Jays. Total: 7-5.

COLORADO—74-88

Pitcher	Ari. W-L	Atl. W-L	Chi. W-L	Cin. W-L	Fla. W-L	Hou. W-L	L.A. W-L	Mil. W-L	Mon. W-L	N.Y. W-L	Phi. W-L	Pit. W-L	S.D. W-L	S.F. W-L	St.L. W-L	A.L. W-L	Totals W-L
Bernero, Adam	0-0	0-0	0-0	0-0	0-0	0-0	0-0	0-0	0-0	0-0	0-0	0-1	0-0	0-1	0-0	0-0	0-2
Chacon, Shawn	2-0	0-1	1-1	0-0	0-0	0-0	1-0	0-0	1-0	0-1	0-1	0-2	3-0	2-1	0-0	1-1	11-8
Cook, Aaron	0-0	0-0	0-0	0-0	0-1	0-0	1-1	1-0	0-0	0-0	0-1	0-0	1-1	1-1	0-0	0-1	4-6
Cruz, Nelson	1-1	0-1	0-1	0-1	0-0	1-0	0-0	0-0	0-1	0-0	0-0	0-0	0-0	0-0	1-0	0-0	3-5
Elarton, Scott	0-0	0-0	0-0	0-0	0-0	0-0	1-0	0-0	0-0	0-0	0-0	0-0	1-0	0-1	0-1	2-2	4-4
Fuentes, Brian	0-1	0-0	0-0	0-1	0-0	0-0	1-0	0-0	1-0	0-0	0-0	0-0	0-0	1-1	0-0	0-0	3-3
Jennings, Jason	2-2	0-1	0-0	1-0	1-0	0-1	1-2	1-0	0-1	0-1	0-1	0-2	0-0	1-2	1-0	4-0	12-13
Jimenez, Jose	1-3	0-0	0-0	0-1	0-0	0-2	0-1	0-1	0-0	0-0	0-0	1-0	0-1	0-1	0-0	0-0	2-10
Jones, Todd	0-0	0-1	0-0	0-0	0-0	0-0	0-0	0-0	1-1	0-0	0-0	0-0	0-1	0-0	0-0	0-1	1-4
Lopez, Javier	1-0	0-0	0-0	0-0	0-0	0-0	0-1	0-0	0-0	0-0	1-0	0-0	1-0	0-0	1-0	0-0	4-1
Miceli, Dan	0-0	0-0	0-0	0-1	0-0	0-0	0-0	0-0	0-0	0-0	0-0	0-0	0-0	0-0	0-1	0-0	0-2
Neagle, Denny	0-1	0-0	0-0	0-0	0-0	0-0	0-1	0-0	0-0	0-0	0-0	1-0	0-1	0-1	0-0	1-0	2-4
Oliver, Darren	1-0	0-0	1-0	1-0	0-0	1-0	1-3	1-0	0-0	0-1	0-1	1-1	2-1	2-3	1-0	1-1	13-11
Reed, Steve	1-1	0-0	0-1	0-0	0-0	0-0	0-1	1-0	0-0	2-0	0-0	0-0	1-0	0-0	0-0	0-0	5-3
Speier, Justin	0-0	0-0	1-0	0-0	1-1	0-0	0-0	0-0	0-0	0-0	0-0	0-0	1-0	0-0	0-0	0-0	3-1
Stark, Denny	0-0	0-1	0-0	0-0	1-0	0-0	1-1	0-0	0-1	0-0	0-0	0-0	1-0	0-0	0-0	0-0	3-3
Tsao, Chin-hui	0-0	0-1	0-0	0-0	0-0	0-1	0-0	1-0	0-0	0-1	1-0	0-0	1-0	0-0	0-0	0-0	3-3
Vance, Cory	0-0	0-0	0-0	0-0	1-0	0-0	0-1	0-0	0-0	0-0	0-0	0-0	0-2	0-0	0-0	0-0	1-3
Young, Jason	0-1	0-0	0-0	0-0	0-0	0-0	0-0	0-0	0-0	0-1	0-0	0-0	0-0	0-0	0-0	0-0	0-2
Totals	9-10	0-6	3-3	2-4	4-2	2-4	7-12	5-1	3-4	2-5	2-4	3-6	12-7	7-12	4-2	9-6	74-88

NO-DECISIONS: Vic Darensbourg, Matt Miller, Joe Roa, Jesus Sanchez.

INTERLEAGUE: Scott Elarton 1-0, Darren Oliver 1-0, Jason Jennings 1-0 vs. Indians; Shawn Chacon 1-0, Scott Elarton 0-2, Jason Jennings 2-0, Denny Neagle 1-0 vs. Tigers; Shawn Chacon 0-1, Todd Jones 0-1, Scott Elarton 1-0 vs. Royals; Jason Jennings 1-0, Aaron Cook 0-1, Darren Oliver 0-1 vs. Twins. Total: 9-6.

FLORIDA—91-71

Pitcher	Ari. W-L	Atl. W-L	Chi. W-L	Cin. W-L	Col. W-L	Hou. W-L	L.A. W-L	Mil. W-L	Mon. W-L	N.Y. W-L	Phi. W-L	Pit. W-L	S.D. W-L	S.F. W-L	St.L. W-L	A.L. W-L	Totals W-L
Almanza, Armando	1-0	0-1	0-0	0-1	0-0	0-0	0-1	2-0	0-1	0-0	0-0	0-0	0-0	0-1	0-0	1-0	4-5
Beckett, Josh	0-0	2-1	0-1	0-0	0-0	0-1	0-0	0-0	1-0	1-0	2-2	1-0	1-0	0-2	1-1	0-0	9-8
Bump, Nate	0-0	1-0	1-0	0-0	0-0	0-0	1-0	0-0	0-0	0-0	0-0	0-0	0-0	0-0	0-0	1-0	4-0
Burnett, A.J.	0-0	0-0	0-0	0-0	0-0	0-0	0-0	0-0	0-0	0-0	0-1	0-0	0-0	0-0	0-1	0-0	0-2
Fox, Chad	0-0	0-0	0-0	0-0	0-0	0-0	1-0	0-0	0-0	0-0	0-1	0-0	1-0	0-0	0-0	0-0	2-1
Helling, Rick	0-0	1-0	0-0	0-0	0-0	0-0	0-0	0-0	0-0	0-0	0-0	0-0	0-0	0-0	0-0	0-0	1-0
Levrault, Allen	0-0	0-0	0-0	0-0	0-0	0-0	0-0	0-0	0-0	0-0	0-0	0-0	1-0	0-0	0-0	0-0	1-0
Looper, Braden	0-0	1-1	0-0	0-0	1-1	0-0	0-0	0-0	1-0	2-0	1-0	0-0	0-1	0-1	0-0	0-0	6-4
Nunez, Vladimir	0-0	0-1	0-0	0-0	0-0	0-0	0-0	0-0	0-0	0-2	0-0	0-0	0-0	0-0	0-0	0-0	0-3
Pavano, Carl	0-1	1-2	0-1	0-1	1-1	1-0	0-0	1-1	3-1	1-1	1-2	0-0	0-0	1-0	0-1	2-1	12-13
Penny, Brad	1-0	1-2	0-1	1-0	0-0	0-1	0-1	0-1	3-0	1-1	3-0	0-1	1-0	0-0	1-0	2-2	14-10
Phelps, Tommy	0-0	0-0	0-0	1-0	0-0	0-0	0-0	0-0	1-0	1-0	0-0	0-0	0-0	0-0	0-0	0-2	3-2
Redman, Mark	2-0	2-1	1-0	0-0	0-1	0-1	0-1	3-0	1-2	1-2	3-0	0-1	0-0	0-0	0-0	1-0	14-9
Spooneybarger, T.	0-0	0-0	0-0	0-0	0-0	0-1	0-0	0-0	0-0	1-0	0-0	0-0	0-0	0-0	0-0	0-1	1-2
Tejera, Michael	0-0	0-0	0-0	0-0	0-1	0-0	0-1	0-0	1-1	0-1	1-0	1-0	0-0	0-0	0-0	0-0	3-4
Urbina, Ugueth	0-0	0-0	0-0	0-0	0-0	0-0	0-0	0-0	0-0	1-0	2-0	0-0	0-0	0-0	0-0	0-0	3-0
Wayne, Justin	0-1	0-0	0-0	0-0	0-0	0-1	0-0	0-0	0-0	0-0	0-0	0-0	0-0	0-0	0-0	0-0	0-2
Willis, Dontrelle	1-0	1-0	0-1	2-0	0-0	0-0	0-1	1-0	2-1	3-0	0-0	0-2	1-0	0-1	1-0	2-0	14-6
Totals	5-2	10-9	2-4	4-2	2-4	1-5	2-5	7-2	13-6	12-7	13-6	2-4	5-1	1-5	3-3	9-6	91-71

NO-DECISIONS: Juan Alvarez, Toby Borland, Blaine Neal, Kevin Olsen.

INTERLEAGUE: Carl Pavano 1-0, Tommy Phelps 0-1, Brad Penny 0-1 vs. Angels; Carl Pavano 0-1, Nate Bump 1-0, Brad Penny 0-1 vs. Red Sox; Brad Penny 1-0, Tim Spooneybarger 0-1, Dontrelle Willis 1-0 vs. Athletics; Armando Almanza 1-0, Dontrelle Willis 1-0, Carl Pavano 1-0 vs. Devil Rays; Brad Penny 1-0, Tommy Phelps 0-1, Mark Redman 1-0 vs. Rangers. Total: 9-6.

HOUSTON—87-75

Pitcher	Ari. W-L	Atl. W-L	Chi. W-L	Cin. W-L	Col. W-L	Fla. W-L	L.A. W-L	Mil. W-L	Mon. W-L	N.Y. W-L	Phi. W-L	Pit. W-L	S.D. W-L	S.F. W-L	St.L. W-L	A.L. W-L	Totals W-L
Bland, Nate	0-0	0-0	0-0	0-0	0-0	0-0	0-0	0-0	0-0	0-0	0-1	1-0	0-0	0-0	0-0	0-1	1-2
Dotel, Octavio	1-0	0-0	0-1	0-1	0-0	0-0	0-0	0-0	0-0	0-0	1-0	1-0	0-0	0-0	1-0	2-2	6-4
Fernandez, Jared	0-0	0-0	0-2	0-0	0-0	1-0	0-0	0-0	0-1	0-0	0-0	0-0	2-0	0-0	0-0	0-0	3-3
Gallo, Mike	0-0	0-0	0-0	0-0	0-0	0-0	0-0	1-0	0-0	0-0	0-0	0-0	0-0	0-0	0-0	0-0	1-0
Johnson, Jonathan	0-0	0-0	0-0	0-0	0-0	0-0	0-0	0-0	0-0	0-0	0-0	0-0	0-0	0-0	0-1	0-0	0-1
Lidge, Brad	0-1	0-0	0-0	1-1	0-0	1-0	0-0	1-0	0-0	0-1	0-0	0-0	1-0	1-0	0-0	1-0	6-3
Linebrink, Scott	0-0	0-0	1-0	0-0	0-0	0-0	0-0	0-1	0-0	0-0	0-0	0-0	0-0	0-0	0-0	0-0	1-1
Miceli, Dan	0-0	0-0	1-0	0-0	0-0	0-0	0-0	0-0	0-0	0-0	0-0	0-0	0-0	0-0	0-1	0-0	1-1
Miller, Wade	0-1	0-2	2-1	2-1	1-0	0-0	2-0	0-0	0-0	1-1	0-1	2-2	0-1	0-2	2-0	2-1	14-13
Munro, Pete	0-0	0-0	0-0	0-0	0-0	0-0	0-0	0-1	0-0	0-0	1-0	1-1	0-0	0-0	1-2	0-0	3-4
Oswalt, Roy	0-0	0-1	0-0	2-0	1-0	0-0	0-0	2-0	0-0	0-1	0-1	1-1	0-0	1-0	2-1	1-0	10-5
Redding, Tim	0-2	0-0	1-2	1-2	0-0	2-0	0-2	1-1	1-0	1-0	0-1	1-1	0-0	0-0	1-1	1-2	10-14
Robertson, J.	0-0	0-0	1-2	4-0	1-1	0-1	1-0	2-1	1-1	0-0	0-0	1-0	0-1	0-1	2-1	2-0	15-9
Rosario, Rodrigo	0-0	0-0	0-0	0-0	0-0	0-0	0-0	0-0	0-0	0-0	0-0	0-0	0-0	0-0	0-0	1-0	1-0
Saarloos, Kirk	0-0	0-0	0-0	0-0	0-0	0-0	0-0	0-0	0-0	0-0	0-0	0-1	0-0	0-0	1-0	1-0	2-1
Stone, Ricky	0-0	0-1	0-1	0-0	0-0	1-0	0-0	2-1	0-0	0-0	0-0	2-0	0-0	0-0	1-0	0-1	6-4
Villone, Ron	0-0	1-0	1-0	2-0	0-1	0-0	1-0	0-3	1-0	0-1	0-0	0-0	0-1	0-0	0-0	0-0	6-6
Wagner, Billy	0-1	0-1	0-0	0-0	1-0	0-0	0-0	0-0	0-1	0-0	0-0	0-0	0-0	0-1	0-0	0-0	1-4
Totals	1-5	1-5	7-9	12-5	4-2	5-1	4-2	9-8	3-3	2-4	2-4	10-6	3-3	2-4	11-7	11-7	87-75

NO-DECISIONS: Kirk Bullinger, Bruce Chen, Brian Moehler, Brandon Puffer, Rick White.

INTERLEAGUE: Octavio Dotel 1-0, Wade Miller 1-0, Roy Oswalt 1-0 vs. Orioles; Ricky Stone 0-1, Nate Bland 0-1, Tim Redding 0-1 vs. Red Sox; Wade Miller 0-1, Brad Lidge 1-0, Octavio Dotel 0-1 vs. Yankees; Octavio Dotel 1-0, Kirk Saarloos 1-0, Tim Redding 1-0 vs. Devil Rays; Wade Miller 1-0, Octavio Dotel 0-1, Rodrigo Rosario 1-0, Jeriome Robertson 2-0, Tim Redding 0-1 vs. Rangers. Total: 11-7.

LOS ANGELES—85-77

Pitcher	Ari. W-L	Atl. W-L	Chi. W-L	Cin. W-L	Col. W-L	Fla. W-L	Hou. W-L	Mil. W-L	Mon. W-L	N.Y. W-L	Phi. W-L	Pit. W-L	S.D. W-L	S.F. W-L	St.L. W-L	A.L. W-L	Totals W-L
Alvarez, Victor	0-0	0-0	0-0	0-0	0-0	0-1	0-0	0-0	0-0	0-0	0-0	0-0	0-0	0-0	0-0	0-0	0-1
Alvarez, Wilson	1-0	0-0	1-0	0-0	2-0	0-0	1-0	0-0	0-0	0-0	0-0	0-0	1-1	0-1	0-0	0-0	6-2
Ashby, Andy	0-2	0-1	1-0	0-0	0-2	0-0	0-0	0-0	0-0	0-1	0-0	0-0	0-1	0-2	0-0	2-1	3-10
Brohawn, Troy	0-0	0-0	0-0	0-0	0-0	0-0	0-0	0-0	0-0	0-0	0-0	1-0	1-0	0-0	0-0	0-0	2-0
Brown, Kevin	1-0	1-0	0-1	1-0	2-0	1-0	0-1	2-0	0-0	0-1	1-0	1-0	1-1	1-2	0-1	2-2	14-9
Dreifort, Darren	1-0	0-0	0-0	0-1	1-1	1-0	0-0	0-0	0-0	0-0	0-1	1-0	0-1	0-0	0-0	0-0	4-4
Gagne, Eric	0-0	0-1	0-0	0-0	0-0	0-0	0-0	0-0	1-0	0-0	0-0	0-0	0-1	0-1	0-0	1-0	2-3
Ishii, Kazuhisa	0-1	0-0	0-0	0-0	1-2	0-0	0-0	0-0	0-0	1-0	0-1	1-0	1-1	1-1	2-0	2-1	9-7
Jackson, Edwin	1-1	0-0	0-0	0-0	0-0	0-0	0-0	0-0	0-0	0-0	0-0	0-0	0-0	1-0	0-0	0-0	2-1
Kida, Masao	0-0	0-0	0-1	0-0	0-0	0-0	0-0	0-0	0-0	0-0	0-0	0-0	0-0	0-0	0-0	0-0	0-1
Martin, Tom	0-1	0-0	0-0	0-0	0-0	0-0	0-0	0-0	0-1	0-0	0-0	0-0	1-0	0-0	0-0	0-0	1-2
Mota, Guillermo	1-0	1-0	0-0	0-1	2-0	0-0	0-0	0-1	1-0	0-0	0-0	0-0	1-0	0-1	0-0	0-0	6-3
Nomo, Hideo	2-1	0-1	1-0	1-0	1-0	1-0	0-2	1-1	0-0	2-0	0-1	1-0	1-4	2-2	1-0	2-1	16-13
Perez, Odalis	1-1	0-0	1-0	1-0	2-1	2-0	0-1	1-0	2-0	0-1	1-1	0-0	0-1	0-3	1-1	0-2	12-12
Quantrill, Paul	0-2	0-1	0-0	0-0	0-0	0-0	0-0	0-0	0-1	0-0	0-0	0-1	0-0	1-0	0-0	1-0	2-5
Shuey, Paul	1-1	0-0	0-0	1-0	1-1	0-1	1-0	0-0	0-0	0-0	0-1	0-0	1-0	0-0	0-0	1-0	6-4
Totals	9-10	2-4	4-2	4-2	12-7	5-2	2-4	4-2	4-2	3-3	2-5	5-1	8-11	6-13	4-2	11-7	85-77

NO-DECISIONS: Steve Colyer, Scott Mullen, Rodney Myers.

INTERLEAGUE: Hideo Nomo 1-0, Andy Ashby 1-0, Kevin Brown 0-2, Kazuhisa Ishii 0-1, Odalis Perez 0-1 vs. Angels; Kazuhisa Ishii 1-0, Andy Ashby 0-1, Odalis Perez 0-1 vs. White Sox; Paul Quantrill 1-0, Andy Ashby 1-0, Hideo Nomo 1-0 vs. Indians; Paul Shuey 1-0, Kevin Brown 1-0, Kazuhisa Ishii 1-0 vs. Tigers; Eric Gagne 1-0, Hideo Nomo 0-1, Kevin Brown 1-0 vs. Royals. Total: 11-7.

MILWAUKEE—68-94

Pitcher	Ari. W-L	Atl. W-L	Chi. W-L	Cin. W-L	Col. W-L	Fla. W-L	Hou. W-L	L.A. W-L	Mon. W-L	N.Y. W-L	Phi. W-L	Pit. W-L	S.D. W-L	S.F. W-L	St.L. W-L	A.L. W-L	Totals W-L
Burba, Dave	0-0	0-0	0-0	0-0	0-0	0-0	1-0	0-0	0-0	0-0	0-0	0-0	0-0	0-0	0-0	0-1	1-1
Davis, Doug	0-0	0-0	1-1	1-0	0-0	0-0	0-1	0-0	0-0	0-0	0-0	0-0	0-0	1-0	0-0	0-0	3-2
de los Santos, V.	0-0	0-1	0-0	1-0	0-1	1-1	1-0	0-0	0-0	0-0	0-0	0-0	0-0	0-0	0-0	0-0	3-3
DeJean, Mike	0-0	1-0	0-0	1-1	0-0	0-0	0-1	0-0	0-1	0-0	1-0	0-1	1-0	0-0	0-1	0-2	4-7
Durocher, Jayson	0-0	0-0	0-0	0-0	0-0	0-0	0-0	1-0	0-0	0-0	0-0	0-0	0-0	0-0	0-0	1-0	2-0
Estrella, Leo	0-0	0-0	1-0	1-1	0-1	0-0	0-0	0-0	0-0	1-0	1-0	1-0	1-0	0-1	1-0	0-0	7-3
Ford, Matt	0-0	0-0	0-0	0-0	0-1	0-0	0-0	0-0	0-0	0-0	0-0	0-2	0-0	0-0	0-0	0-0	0-3
Foster, John	0-0	0-0	0-0	0-0	0-0	0-0	1-0	0-0	0-0	1-0	0-0	0-0	0-0	0-0	0-0	0-0	2-0
Franklin, Wayne	1-1	0-1	0-0	3-3	0-1	0-1	0-1	0-0	0-2	0-0	1-0	3-1	1-0	0-1	0-1	1-0	10-13
Kieschnick, Brooks	0-0	0-0	0-1	0-0	0-0	0-0	0-0	0-0	0-0	0-0	0-0	1-0	0-0	0-0	0-0	0-0	1-1
Kinney, Matt	1-0	0-0	1-2	1-1	0-0	1-0	1-1	0-1	0-0	2-1	1-0	0-1	1-0	0-1	0-4	1-1	10-13
Kolb, Danny	0-0	0-0	0-0	0-0	0-0	0-0	0-2	0-0	0-0	0-0	0-0	1-0	0-0	0-0	0-0	0-0	1-2
Leskanic, Curtis	0-0	0-0	1-0	0-0	0-0	0-0	1-0	0-0	0-0	0-0	0-0	0-0	0-0	0-0	1-0	1-0	4-0
Manning, David	0-0	0-0	0-0	0-0	0-0	0-1	0-0	0-0	0-1	0-0	0-0	0-0	0-0	0-0	0-0	0-0	0-2
Martinez, Luis	0-0	0-0	0-0	0-0	0-0	0-0	0-2	0-0	0-0	0-0	0-0	0-0	0-0	0-0	0-1	0-0	0-3
Nance, Shane	0-1	0-0	0-0	0-0	0-0	0-1	0-0	0-0	0-0	0-0	0-0	0-0	0-0	0-0	0-0	0-0	0-2
Obermueller, Wes	1-0	0-1	0-0	0-0	0-1	0-0	1-0	0-0	0-0	0-1	0-1	0-0	0-0	0-0	0-1	0-0	2-5
Quevedo, Ruben	0-0	0-0	0-2	0-0	0-0	0-0	0-0	0-1	0-0	0-0	0-0	0-0	0-0	0-0	0-1	1-0	1-4
Ritchie, Todd	0-0	0-0	0-0	0-0	0-0	0-1	0-0	0-0	0-0	0-0	0-0	1-0	0-0	0-0	0-1	0-0	1-2
Rusch, Glendon	0-1	0-1	0-2	0-0	0-0	0-0	0-1	0-1	0-0	0-1	0-0	1-1	0-0	0-0	0-2	0-2	1-12
Sheets, Ben	0-0	1-0	1-2	1-1	1-0	0-2	2-0	1-1	0-2	2-0	0-1	1-1	0-0	0-1	1-1	0-1	11-13
Vizcaino, Luis	0-0	0-0	1-0	1-1	0-0	0-0	0-0	0-0	0-0	0-0	0-0	1-0	1-1	0-1	0-0	0-0	4-3
Totals	3-3	2-4	6-10	10-8	1-5	2-7	8-9	2-4	0-6	6-3	4-2	10-7	5-1	1-5	3-13	5-7	68-94

NO-DECISIONS: Mike Crudale.

INTERLEAGUE: Glendon Rusch 0-1, Ruben Quevedo 1-0, Ben Sheets 0-1 vs. Orioles; Jayson Durocher 1-0, Mike DeJean 0-1, Glendon Rusch 0-1 vs. Red Sox; Mike DeJean 0-1, Curtis Leskanic 1-0, Wayne Franklin 1-0, Matt Kinney 1-1, Dave Burba 0-1 vs. Twins. Total: 5-7.

MONTREAL—83-79

Pitcher	Ari. W-L	Atl. W-L	Chi. W-L	Cin. W-L	Col. W-L	Fla. W-L	Hou. W-L	L.A. W-L	Mil. W-L	N.Y. W-L	Phi. W-L	Pit. W-L	S.D. W-L	S.F. W-L	St.L. W-L	A.L. W-L	Totals W-L
Almonte, Hector	0-0	0-0	0-0	0-0	0-0	0-0	0-0	0-0	0-0	0-0	1-1	0-0	0-0	0-0	0-0	0-0	1-1
Armas, Tony	0-0	1-0	1-0	0-0	0-0	0-0	0-0	0-0	0-0	0-1	0-0	0-0	0-0	0-0	0-0	0-0	2-1
Ayala, Luis	0-1	1-0	1-0	1-1	2-0	0-0	0-0	2-0	0-0	1-0	1-0	0-0	0-0	0-0	0-0	1-1	10-3
Biddle, Rocky	0-0	1-2	0-0	0-0	0-1	0-2	1-0	0-1	0-0	1-0	0-0	0-1	1-1	1-0	0-0	0-0	5-8
Cordero, Chad	0-0	0-0	0-0	0-0	0-0	0-0	0-0	0-0	0-0	1-0	0-0	0-0	0-0	0-0	0-0	0-0	1-0
Day, Zach	0-0	1-2	0-2	0-0	1-0	0-2	1-0	0-1	1-0	2-0	0-1	0-0	0-0	2-0	1-0	0-0	9-8
Downs, Scott	0-0	0-0	0-0	0-0	0-0	0-0	0-1	0-0	0-0	0-0	0-0	0-0	0-0	0-0	0-0	0-0	0-1
Drew, Tim	0-0	0-1	0-0	0-0	0-0	0-0	0-0	0-0	0-0	0-0	0-1	0-0	0-0	0-0	0-0	0-0	0-2
Eischen, Joey	0-0	0-0	0-0	0-0	0-0	0-0	0-0	0-0	0-0	0-0	1-0	0-1	0-1	0-0	0-0	1-0	2-2
Hernandez, Livan	0-1	0-1	0-0	0-1	0-0	3-2	1-0	0-1	2-0	3-0	2-1	0-1	1-0	1-0	0-1	2-1	15-10
Kim, Sun-Woo	0-0	0-0	0-0	0-0	0-0	0-0	0-0	0-0	0-0	0-0	0-0	0-0	0-0	0-0	0-0	0-1	0-1
Knott, Eric	0-1	0-0	0-0	0-0	0-0	0-1	0-0	0-0	0-0	0-0	0-0	0-0	1-0	0-0	0-0	0-0	1-2
Manon, Julio	0-0	1-0	0-0	0-0	0-0	0-0	0-0	0-0	0-0	0-1	0-0	0-0	0-0	0-0	0-0	0-1	1-2
Ohka, Tomo	1-0	0-2	1-0	1-0	0-1	1-3	0-1	0-0	1-0	1-1	0-1	2-0	1-0	0-0	0-1	1-2	10-12
Smith, Dan	0-0	0-1	0-0	0-0	0-0	0-0	0-0	0-0	0-0	1-0	0-1	0-0	0-0	1-0	0-0	0-0	2-2
Stewart, Scott	0-0	0-0	0-0	0-0	0-0	0-0	0-0	0-1	1-0	1-0	0-0	0-0	0-0	0-0	0-0	1-0	3-1
Tucker, T.J.	0-0	0-1	0-0	1-0	0-1	0-0	0-0	0-0	0-0	1-0	0-1	0-0	0-0	0-0	0-0	0-0	2-3
Vargas, Claudio	0-1	1-0	0-0	0-0	0-0	1-2	0-0	0-0	0-0	0-0	0-2	1-0	0-0	1-0	0-2	2-1	6-8
Vazquez, Javier	1-0	1-2	0-1	1-0	1-0	1-1	0-1	0-0	1-0	2-2	3-2	0-0	0-0	1-0	0-1	1-2	13-12
Totals	2-4	7-12	3-3	4-2	4-3	6-13	3-3	2-4	6-0	14-5	8-11	3-3	4-2	7-0	1-5	9-9	83-79

NO-DECISIONS: Roy Corcoran, Vic Darensbourg, Anthony Ferrari, Bryan Hebson, Jose Mercedes, Britt Reames.

INTERLEAGUE: Tomo Ohka 0-1, Joey Eischen 1-0, Sun-Woo Kim 0-1 vs. Angels; Tomo Ohka 0-1, Luis Ayala 0-1, Javier Vazquez 0-1 vs. Athletics; Javier Vazquez 1-0, Livan Hernandez 1-0, Claudio Vargas 0-1 vs. Mariners; Livan Hernandez 1-0, Claudio Vargas 1-0, Scott Stewart 1-0 vs. Rangers; Javier Vazquez 0-1, Julio Manon 0-1, Luis Ayala 1-0, Livan Hernandez 0-1, Claudio Vargas 1-0, Tomo Ohka 1-0 vs. Blue Jays. Total: 9-9.

NEW YORK—66-95

Pitcher	Ari. W-L	Atl. W-L	Chi. W-L	Cin. W-L	Col. W-L	Fla. W-L	Hou. W-L	L.A. W-L	Mil. W-L	Mon. W-L	Phi. W-L	Pit. W-L	S.D. W-L	S.F. W-L	St.L. W-L	A.L. W-L	Totals W-L
Astacio, Pedro	0-0	0-0	0-0	0-0	0-0	0-0	1-0	1-0	0-0	0-0	1-1	0-0	0-0	0-0	0-1	0-0	3-2
Bacsik, Mike	0-0	0-0	0-0	0-0	0-0	0-1	0-0	0-0	0-0	0-0	0-0	0-0	0-0	0-0	0-0	1-1	1-2
Benitez, Armando	0-0	0-0	0-0	0-0	0-0	0-2	0-0	0-0	0-0	1-1	2-0	0-0	0-0	0-0	0-0	0-0	3-3
Cerda, Jaime	0-0	0-0	0-0	1-0	0-1	0-0	0-0	0-0	0-0	0-0	0-0	0-0	0-0	0-0	0-0	0-0	1-1
Cone, David	0-0	0-0	0-0	0-0	0-0	0-0	0-1	0-0	0-0	1-1	0-0	0-1	0-0	0-0	0-0	0-0	1-3
Franco, John	0-1	0-1	0-0	0-0	0-0	0-0	0-0	0-0	0-0	0-0	0-1	0-0	0-0	0-0	0-0	0-0	0-3
Glavine, Tom	1-1	0-4	0-1	1-0	1-0	1-1	0-0	1-1	1-1	1-3	0-1	1-0	0-0	1-0	0-0	0-1	9-14
Griffiths, Jeremy	0-0	0-0	0-1	0-0	0-0	0-1	0-0	0-0	0-0	0-0	0-1	0-0	0-0	0-0	1-0	0-1	1-4
Heilman, Aaron	0-0	0-1	0-0	0-1	0-0	0-2	0-1	0-0	0-1	0-0	1-1	0-0	0-0	1-0	0-0	0-0	2-7
Leiter, Al	0-1	3-0	1-1	1-0	1-0	2-1	2-0	0-1	2-0	0-1	1-0	1-0	0-0	0-1	0-1	1-2	15-9
Lloyd, Graeme	0-0	0-0	0-0	0-0	0-0	0-0	0-0	0-0	0-0	0-0	0-1	0-0	1-0	0-0	0-0	0-1	1-2
Roach, Jason	0-0	0-1	0-0	0-0	0-0	0-0	0-0	0-0	0-0	0-0	0-0	0-0	0-0	0-0	0-0	0-1	0-2
Roberts, Grant	0-0	0-0	0-0	0-0	0-0	0-0	0-0	0-0	0-0	0-1	0-0	0-1	0-1	0-0	0-0	0-0	0-3
Seo, Jae Weong	0-1	2-2	0-1	0-0	1-0	2-1	0-0	0-0	0-0	0-3	0-2	1-0	1-0	0-0	0-1	2-1	9-12
Stanton, Mike	1-0	0-1	0-0	0-0	0-1	0-1	0-0	0-0	0-0	0-2	0-1	0-0	1-1	0-0	0-0	0-0	2-7
Strickland, Scott	0-0	0-0	0-0	0-0	0-0	0-0	0-0	0-0	0-0	0-1	0-0	0-0	0-0	0-0	0-1	0-0	0-2
Trachsel, Steve	0-0	2-0	0-1	1-1	2-0	1-1	1-0	1-1	0-1	2-1	2-2	1-0	0-0	2-0	0-0	1-2	16-10
Weathers, Dave	0-0	0-1	0-0	0-0	0-0	1-1	0-0	0-0	0-2	0-0	0-0	0-0	0-1	0-1	0-0	0-0	1-6
Wheeler, Dan	0-0	1-0	0-0	0-0	0-0	0-0	0-0	0-0	0-1	0-0	0-1	0-0	0-0	0-0	0-1	0-0	1-3
Totals	2-4	8-11	1-5	4-2	5-2	7-12	4-2	3-3	3-6	5-14	7-12	4-2	3-3	4-2	1-5	5-10	66-95

NO-DECISIONS: Edwin Almonte, Jason Anderson, Pedro Feliciano, Jason Middlebrook, Orber Moreno, Pat Strange.

INTERLEAGUE: Mike Bacsik 1-0, Jason Roach 0-1, Steve Trachsel 1-0 vs. Angels; Steve Trachsel 0-1, Graeme Lloyd 0-1, Tom Glavine 0-1, Jae Weong Seo 0-1, Jeremy Griffiths 0-1, Al Leiter 0-1 vs. Yankees; Jae Weong Seo 1-0, Al Leiter 0-1, Mike Bacsik 0-1 vs. Mariners; Steve Trachsel 0-1, Jae Weong Seo 1-0, Al Leiter 1-0 vs. Rangers. Total: 5-10.

PHILADELPHIA—86-76

Pitcher	Ari. W-L	Atl. W-L	Chi. W-L	Cin. W-L	Col. W-L	Fla. W-L	Hou. W-L	L.A. W-L	Mil. W-L	Mon. W-L	N.Y. W-L	Pit. W-L	S.D. W-L	S.F. W-L	St.L. W-L	A.L. W-L	Totals W-L
Adams, Terry	0-1	0-0	1-0	0-1	0-0	0-0	0-0	0-0	0-0	0-0	0-2	0-0	0-0	0-0	0-0	0-0	1-4
Cormier, Rheal	1-0	1-0	0-0	0-0	0-0	1-0	0-0	0-0	0-0	2-0	1-0	0-0	1-0	0-0	1-0	0-0	8-0
de los Santos, V.	0-0	0-0	0-0	0-0	0-0	0-0	0-0	0-0	0-0	0-0	1-0	0-0	0-0	0-0	0-0	0-0	1-0
Duckworth, B.	0-0	0-1	0-0	0-0	0-1	0-1	1-0	2-0	0-1	0-1	0-1	0-0	0-0	1-0	0-0	0-1	4-7
Mesa, Jose	0-1	2-0	0-0	0-1	0-0	0-1	0-0	0-0	0-0	1-0	1-0	0-0	0-2	0-0	0-0	1-2	5-7
Millwood, Kevin	1-0	0-4	0-0	1-1	1-1	1-1	1-0	0-0	1-0	3-0	1-2	0-1	1-0	1-0	0-1	2-1	14-12
Myers, Brett	0-1	1-0	1-0	0-0	2-0	0-3	1-0	1-0	0-0	3-1	2-0	0-1	0-0	0-1	1-0	2-2	14-9
Padilla, Vicente	0-1	3-2	2-0	0-1	0-0	2-2	0-1	1-1	0-1	0-0	4-1	0-0	0-0	0-1	1-0	1-1	14-12
Plesac, Dan	0-0	0-0	0-0	0-0	0-0	0-0	0-0	0-0	0-0	1-1	0-0	0-0	0-0	0-0	0-0	1-0	2-1
Roa, Joe	0-0	0-1	0-0	0-0	0-0	0-0	0-0	0-0	0-0	0-0	0-0	0-1	0-0	0-0	0-0	0-0	0-2
Silva, Carlos	0-0	0-0	0-0	0-0	0-0	1-0	0-0	0-0	0-0	0-1	0-0	1-0	1-0	0-0	0-0	0-0	3-1
Telemaco, Amaury	0-0	0-0	0-0	0-1	0-0	0-0	0-0	0-0	0-0	0-1	0-0	0-1	0-0	0-0	1-1	0-0	1-4
Wendell, Turk	0-0	1-0	0-1	0-0	0-0	0-0	0-1	1-0	0-1	0-0	0-0	0-0	0-0	1-0	0-0	0-0	3-3
Williams, Mike	0-0	0-0	0-0	0-0	0-0	0-3	0-0	0-0	0-0	0-1	0-0	0-0	0-0	0-0	0-0	0-0	0-4
Wolf, Randy	0-0	2-1	1-0	3-0	1-0	1-2	1-0	0-1	1-1	1-2	2-1	1-0	1-1	0-1	0-0	1-0	16-10
Totals	2-4	10-9	5-1	4-5	4-2	6-13	4-2	5-2	2-4	11-8	12-7	2-4	4-3	3-3	4-2	8-7	86-76

NO-DECISIONS: Geoff Geary, Josh Hancock, Eric Junge, Ryan Madson, Hector Mercado.

INTERLEAGUE: Vicente Padilla 1-0, Brandon Duckworth 0-1, Brett Myers 0-1 vs. Angels; Dan Plesac 1-0, Brett Myers 1-0, Kevin Millwood 1-0 vs. Orioles; Jose Mesa 1-1, Brett Myers 1-0 vs. Red Sox; Brett Myers 0-1, Kevin Millwood 1-0, Randy Wolf 1-0 vs. Athletics; Kevin Millwood 0-1, Vicente Padilla 0-1, Jose Mesa 0-1 vs. Mariners. Total: 8-7.

PITTSBURGH—75-87

Pitcher	Ari. W-L	Atl. W-L	Chi. W-L	Cin. W-L	Col. W-L	Fla. W-L	Hou. W-L	L.A. W-L	Mil. W-L	Mon. W-L	N.Y. W-L	Phi. W-L	S.D. W-L	S.F. W-L	St.L. W-L	A.L. W-L	Totals W-L
Beimel, Joe	0-0	0-0	0-0	0-0	0-0	0-0	0-0	1-0	0-1	0-0	0-0	0-0	0-0	0-0	0-2	0-0	1-3
Benson, Kris	1-0	0-0	1-2	1-0	0-1	0-0	0-2	0-0	0-1	0-0	0-0	1-0	1-0	0-1	0-0	0-2	5-9
Boehringer, Brian	1-0	0-1	0-1	1-1	0-0	0-0	1-0	0-0	0-0	0-0	0-0	0-0	0-0	0-1	1-0	1-0	5-4
Corey, Mark	0-0	1-1	0-0	0-0	0-0	0-0	0-0	0-0	0-1	0-0	0-0	0-0	0-0	0-0	0-0	0-0	1-2
D'Amico, Jeff	0-1	0-2	2-1	1-1	1-1	0-0	2-1	0-1	0-1	1-1	0-2	0-1	1-0	0-0	1-1	0-2	9-16
Figueroa, Nelson	0-0	0-0	0-1	0-0	1-0	0-0	0-0	0-0	1-0	0-0	0-0	0-0	0-0	0-0	0-0	0-0	2-1
Fogg, Josh	0-0	0-1	1-1	3-0	1-0	1-1	1-1	0-0	1-1	0-0	0-1	1-0	0-1	0-0	0-2	1-0	10-9
Gonzalez, Mike	0-0	0-0	0-0	0-0	0-0	0-0	0-0	0-0	0-1	0-0	0-0	0-0	0-0	0-0	0-0	0-0	0-1
Lincoln, Mike	0-0	0-0	0-0	2-0	0-0	1-0	0-0	0-0	0-1	0-0	0-0	0-0	0-1	0-0	0-2	0-0	3-4
Mahomes, Pat	0-0	0-0	0-0	0-0	0-1	0-0	0-0	0-0	0-0	0-0	0-0	0-0	0-0	0-0	0-0	0-0	0-1
Meadows, Brian	0-0	0-0	0-0	0-0	1-0	0-0	0-0	0-0	0-0	0-0	0-0	0-0	0-0	0-0	1-1	0-0	2-1
Perez, Oliver	0-0	0-1	0-1	0-1	0-0	0-0	0-0	0-0	0-0	0-0	0-0	0-0	0-0	0-0	0-0	0-0	0-3
Sanchez, Duaner	0-0	0-0	0-0	0-0	1-0	0-0	0-0	0-0	0-0	0-0	0-0	0-0	0-0	0-0	0-0	0-0	1-0
Sauerbeck, Scott	0-0	0-0	0-2	0-0	0-0	0-0	0-1	0-1	0-0	1-0	0-0	0-0	0-0	0-0	0-0	2-0	3-4
Suppan, Jeff	0-1	0-0	0-0	0-0	1-0	0-0	1-1	0-2	3-0	0-1	1-0	1-0	0-0	1-0	2-1	0-1	10-7
Tavarez, Julian	0-0	1-0	0-0	0-1	0-0	0-0	0-1	0-0	0-0	0-0	0-0	0-0	0-0	1-1	1-0	0-0	3-3
Torres, Salomon	1-0	0-0	2-0	1-0	0-0	0-1	0-2	0-0	0-0	1-1	1-0	0-1	0-0	0-0	0-0	1-0	7-5
Vogelsong, Ryan	0-0	0-0	1-1	1-0	0-0	0-0	0-0	0-0	0-0	0-0	0-0	0-0	0-0	0-0	0-0	0-1	2-2
Wells, Kip	0-1	0-1	1-0	1-0	0-0	2-0	1-0	0-0	1-3	0-0	0-1	1-0	2-0	0-1	1-1	0-1	10-9
Williams, Mike	0-0	0-0	0-0	0-1	0-0	0-0	0-1	0-1	1-0	0-0	0-0	0-0	0-0	0-0	0-0	0-0	1-3
Totals	3-3	2-7	8-10	11-5	6-3	4-2	6-10	1-5	7-10	3-3	2-4	4-2	4-2	2-4	7-10	5-7	75-87

NO-DECISIONS: John Grabow, Jim Mann, Dennys Reyes.

INTERLEAGUE: Kris Benson 0-1, Jeff D'Amico 0-1, Brian Boehringer 1-0 vs. Red Sox; Scott Sauerbeck 1-0, Salomon Torres 1-0, Ryan Vogelsong 0-1 vs. Indians; Kip Wells 0-1, Scott Sauerbeck 1-0, Josh Fogg 1-0 vs. Devil Rays; Kris Benson 0-1, Jeff D'Amico 0-1, Jeff Suppan 0-1 vs. Blue Jays. Total: 5-7.

SAN DIEGO—64-98

Pitcher	Ari. W-L	Atl. W-L	Chi. W-L	Cin. W-L	Col. W-L	Fla. W-L	Hou. W-L	L.A. W-L	Mil. W-L	Mon. W-L	N.Y. W-L	Phi. W-L	Pit. W-L	S.F. W-L	St.L. W-L	A.L. W-L	Totals W-L
Beck, Rod	0-0	0-0	0-0	1-0	0-0	0-0	0-0	0-1	0-0	0-0	1-0	0-0	0-0	0-0	0-0	1-1	3-2
Bynum, Mike	0-0	0-0	0-0	0-0	0-1	0-1	0-0	1-0	0-0	0-0	0-0	0-0	0-0	0-2	0-0	0-0	1-4
Condrey, Clay	0-0	0-0	0-0	0-0	0-0	0-1	0-0	1-0	0-0	0-0	0-0	0-0	0-0	0-1	0-0	0-0	1-2
Deago, Roger	0-0	0-1	0-0	0-0	0-0	0-0	0-0	0-0	0-0	0-0	0-0	0-0	0-0	0-0	0-0	0-0	0-1
Eaton, Adam	1-1	1-0	1-1	0-0	1-1	0-1	1-1	2-0	0-0	0-0	0-0	0-1	1-1	0-2	0-0	1-3	9-12
Hackman, Luther	0-0	0-0	0-0	0-0	1-0	0-0	0-0	0-0	0-0	0-0	1-0	0-0	0-0	0-1	0-0	0-1	2-2
Herges, Matt	0-0	0-0	0-0	0-0	0-0	1-0	0-0	1-0	0-1	0-0	0-0	0-0	0-0	0-0	0-1	0-0	2-2
Howard, Ben	1-0	0-0	0-0	0-0	0-1	0-0	0-0	0-1	0-0	0-0	0-0	0-0	0-0	0-1	0-0	0-0	1-3
Jarvis, Kevin	2-0	0-1	0-1	0-0	0-2	0-0	0-1	0-1	0-0	0-1	0-0	0-1	0-0	2-0	0-0	0-0	4-8
Keisler, Randy	0-0	0-0	0-0	0-0	0-0	0-0	0-0	0-0	0-1	0-0	0-0	0-0	0-0	0-0	0-0	0-0	0-1
Lawrence, Brian	3-1	0-1	0-2	1-1	2-2	0-0	0-0	3-1	0-1	0-1	0-0	0-0	0-1	0-1	0-2	1-1	10-15
Linebrink, Scott	0-0	0-0	0-0	0-0	0-0	0-0	0-0	0-0	0-0	1-0	1-0	0-0	0-0	0-0	0-0	0-1	2-1
Loewer, Carlton	1-0	0-1	0-0	0-0	0-0	0-0	0-0	0-0	0-0	0-0	0-0	0-0	0-0	0-0	0-0	0-1	1-2
Matthews, Mike	1-1	0-0	0-0	0-0	0-0	0-0	0-0	0-0	1-1	1-0	0-1	1-0	0-0	1-0	0-1	1-0	6-4
Nagy, Charles	0-1	0-1	0-0	0-0	0-0	0-0	0-0	0-0	0-0	0-0	0-0	0-0	0-0	0-0	0-0	0-0	0-2
Orosco, Jesse	1-0	0-0	0-0	0-0	0-0	0-0	0-0	0-0	0-0	0-1	0-0	0-0	0-0	0-0	0-0	0-0	1-1
Peavy, Jake	0-3	0-1	0-0	1-0	1-1	0-0	2-0	2-1	0-1	0-1	0-0	1-0	0-1	2-2	0-0	3-0	12-11
Perez, Oliver	0-1	0-0	1-0	0-1	0-1	0-1	0-0	1-0	0-0	0-0	0-1	0-0	0-1	0-1	1-0	1-0	4-7
Roa, Joe	0-0	0-0	0-0	0-0	0-0	0-0	0-0	0-0	0-0	0-0	0-0	0-1	1-0	0-0	0-0	0-0	1-1
Tankersley, Dennis	0-0	0-0	0-0	0-0	0-0	0-0	0-0	0-0	0-0	0-0	0-0	0-0	0-0	0-1	0-0	0-0	0-1
Tollberg, Brian	0-1	0-0	0-0	0-0	0-0	0-0	0-0	0-0	0-0	0-0	0-0	0-0	0-0	0-0	0-0	0-1	0-2
Villafuerte, B.	0-0	0-0	0-0	0-0	0-2	0-0	0-0	0-0	0-0	0-0	0-0	0-0	0-0	0-0	0-0	0-0	0-2
Witasick, Jay	0-0	0-0	0-0	0-0	1-1	0-1	0-1	0-1	0-0	0-0	0-0	1-0	0-0	0-2	1-0	0-1	3-7
Wright, Jaret	0-0	0-0	0-0	0-1	1-0	0-0	0-0	0-2	0-0	0-0	0-1	0-1	0-0	0-0	0-0	0-0	1-5
Totals	10-9	1-6	2-4	3-3	7-12	1-5	3-3	11-8	1-5	2-4	3-3	3-4	2-4	5-14	2-4	8-10	64-98

NO-DECISIONS: Wiki Gonzalez, Trevor Hoffman, Kevin Walker.

INTERLEAGUE: Scott Linebrink 0-1, Jay Witasick 0-1, Oliver Perez 1-0 vs. White Sox; Brian Tollberg 0-1, Adam Eaton 0-1, Jake Peavy 1-0 vs. Indians; Brian Lawrence 0-1, Luther Hackman 0-1, Adam Eaton 1-0 vs. Tigers; Rod Beck 0-1, Carlton Loewer 0-1, Brian Lawrence 1-0 vs. Twins; Mike Matthews 1-0, Adam Eaton 0-2, Jake Peavy 2-0, Rod Beck 1-0 vs. Mariners. Total: 8-10.

SAN FRANCISCO—100-61

Pitcher	Ari. W-L	Atl. W-L	Chi. W-L	Cin. W-L	Col. W-L	Fla. W-L	Hou. W-L	L.A. W-L	Mil. W-L	Mon. W-L	N.Y. W-L	Phi. W-L	Pit. W-L	S.D. W-L	St.L. W-L	A.L. W-L	Totals W-L
Ainsworth, Kurt	0-0	0-0	0-0	0-1	2-0	0-0	1-0	1-1	1-0	0-1	0-1	0-0	0-0	0-0	0-0	0-0	5-4
Brower, Jim	1-1	0-0	0-1	0-0	1-0	1-0	0-1	1-1	1-0	0-0	0-0	0-1	1-0	0-0	2-0	0-0	8-5
Correia, Kevin	0-0	0-0	0-0	0-0	0-1	0-0	0-0	1-0	0-0	0-0	0-0	1-0	0-0	1-0	0-0	0-0	3-1
Eyre, Scott	1-0	0-0	0-0	0-0	0-0	0-0	0-0	0-0	0-0	0-0	0-0	0-0	1-0	0-1	0-0	0-0	2-1
Foppert, Jesse	0-0	1-0	0-0	1-0	2-2	0-0	0-0	0-1	0-0	0-2	0-0	1-1	0-1	2-0	0-0	1-2	8-9
Herges, Matt	0-0	0-0	0-0	0-0	1-0	0-0	0-0	0-0	0-0	0-0	0-0	0-0	0-0	0-0	0-0	0-0	1-0
Hermanson, D.	0-0	0-0	0-0	1-0	0-0	0-0	0-0	1-0	0-0	0-1	0-0	0-0	0-0	0-0	0-0	0-0	2-1
Moss, Damian	2-0	0-0	0-1	0-0	1-1	1-0	1-0	1-1	0-0	0-1	0-1	0-0	1-0	1-0	0-0	1-2	9-7
Nathan, Joe	0-1	1-1	0-0	0-0	1-1	2-0	1-0	1-0	0-0	0-0	1-0	1-0	0-0	2-0	0-0	2-1	12-4
Ponson, Sidney	1-0	0-0	0-0	0-0	1-0	1-0	0-1	0-0	0-1	0-1	0-1	0-0	0-1	0-1	0-0	0-0	3-6
Powell, Brian	0-0	0-0	0-0	0-0	0-1	0-0	0-0	0-0	0-0	0-0	0-0	0-0	0-0	0-0	0-0	0-0	0-1
Rodriguez, Felix	1-0	1-0	0-0	0-2	0-0	0-0	0-0	1-0	1-0	0-0	0-0	0-0	0-0	3-0	0-0	1-0	8-2
Rueter, Kirk	1-1	0-0	0-1	1-0	1-0	0-1	0-0	3-1	1-0	0-0	1-0	0-0	0-0	1-0	0-1	1-0	10-5
Schmidt, Jason	3-0	0-1	2-0	0-0	2-1	0-0	1-0	3-0	1-0	0-1	0-0	0-0	1-0	2-1	1-0	1-1	17-5
Williams, Jerome	2-1	0-0	0-0	0-0	0-0	0-0	0-0	0-1	0-0	0-0	0-1	0-1	0-0	1-1	2-0	2-0	7-5
Worrell, Tim	1-1	1-0	0-1	0-0	0-0	0-0	0-0	0-0	0-0	0-0	0-0	0-0	0-0	1-1	0-0	1-1	4-4
Zerbe, Chad	1-0	0-0	0-0	0-0	0-0	0-0	0-0	0-0	0-0	0-0	0-0	0-0	0-0	0-0	0-0	0-1	1-1
Totals	14-5	4-2	2-4	3-3	12-7	5-1	4-2	13-6	5-1	0-7	2-4	3-3	4-2	14-5	5-1	10-8	100-61

NO-DECISIONS: Manny Aybar, Jason Christiansen, Ryan Jensen, Noah Lowry.

INTERLEAGUE: Joe Nathan 1-1, Jesse Foppert 1-0 vs. White Sox; Kirk Rueter 1-0, Jason Schmidt 1-0, Joe Nathan 1-0 vs. Tigers; Jason Schmidt 0-1, Damian Moss 1-0, Tim Worrell 0-1 vs. Royals; Damian Moss 0-1, Tim Worrell 1-0, Jesse Foppert 0-1 vs. Twins; Damian Moss 0-1, Felix Rodriguez 1-0, Jerome Williams 2-0, Jesse Foppert 0-1, Chad Zerbe 0-1 vs. Athletics. Total: 10-8.

ST. LOUIS—85-77

.....................Ari.	Atl.	Chi.	Cin.	Col.	Fla.	Hou.	L.A.	Mil.	Mon.	N.Y.	Phi.	Pit.	S.D.	S.F.	A.L.		Totals
Pitcher	W-L	W-L	W-L	W-L	W-L	W-L	W-L	W-L	W-L	W-L	W-L	W-L	W-L	W-L	W-L	W-L	W-L
Borbon, Pedro	0-0	0-0	0-0	0-0	0-0	0-0	0-0	0-0	0-0	0-0	0-0	0-0	0-1	0-0	0-0	0-0	0-1
Calero, Kiko	0-0	0-0	0-0	0-1	0-0	0-0	1-0	0-0	0-0	0-0	0-0	0-0	0-0	0-0	0-0	0-0	1-1
Crudale, Mike	0-0	0-0	0-0	0-1	0-0	0-0	0-0	0-0	0-0	0-0	0-0	0-0	0-0	0-0	0-0	0-0	0-1
DeJean, Mike	0-0	0-0	1-1	0-0	0-0	0-0	0-0	0-0	0-0	0-0	0-0	0-0	0-0	0-0	0-0	0-0	1-1
Eldred, Cal	0-0	1-0	0-1	0-0	1-0	0-0	0-0	0-1	0-1	0-0	1-0	0-0	4-1	0-0	0-0	0-0	7-4
Fassero, Jeff	0-0	0-1	0-2	0-1	0-0	0-0	0-2	0-0	0-0	0-0	0-0	0-0	0-0	0-1	0-0	1-0	1-7
Haren, Danny	0-0	0-0	0-0	0-1	0-1	0-1	0-1	1-0	0-0	1-0	0-0	0-1	1-0	0-0	0-2	0-0	3-7
Hermanson, D.	0-0	0-0	1-0	0-1	0-0	0-0	0-0	0-0	0-0	0-0	0-0	0-0	0-1	0-0	0-0	0-0	1-2
Hitchcock, Sterling	1-0	0-0	0-0	1-0	0-1	0-0	1-0	0-0	1-0	0-0	0-0	1-0	0-0	0-0	0-0	0-0	5-1
Isringhausen, J.	0-0	0-0	0-0	0-0	0-0	0-0	0-0	0-0	0-1	0-0	0-0	0-0	0-0	0-0	0-0	0-0	0-1
Kline, Steve	0-0	0-1	1-1	0-0	0-1	1-1	0-0	0-0	0-0	0-0	1-0	0-1	1-0	0-0	0-0	1-0	5-5
Morris, Matt	0-0	0-1	3-0	2-1	0-0	0-0	0-3	0-1	2-0	1-0	1-0	0-0	1-0	0-0	0-0	1-2	11-8
Painter, Lance	0-0	0-0	0-0	0-0	0-0	0-0	0-0	0-0	0-0	0-0	0-0	0-0	0-0	0-1	0-0	0-0	0-1
Simontacchi, J.	0-1	0-0	0-0	0-3	0-0	0-0	2-0	0-0	1-0	1-0	0-0	0-0	0-0	2-0	1-0	2-1	9-5
Springer, Russ	0-0	0-0	0-0	0-0	0-0	0-0	0-1	0-0	1-0	0-0	0-0	0-0	0-0	0-0	0-0	0-0	1-1
Stephenson, G.	0-0	1-1	0-1	1-0	0-0	0-0	0-1	0-1	2-1	2-0	0-1	0-0	1-2	0-0	0-2	0-3	7-13
Tomko, Brett	0-2	0-0	1-0	1-0	1-1	2-0	0-2	0-1	3-0	0-0	1-0	1-1	1-1	1-0	0-0	1-1	13-9
Williams, Woody	2-0	0-0	2-2	2-0	0-0	0-1	3-1	1-0	3-0	0-1	1-0	0-1	1-1	1-0	0-1	2-1	18-9
Yan, Esteban	0-0	0-0	0-0	0-0	0-0	0-0	0-0	0-0	0-0	0-0	0-0	0-0	0-0	0-0	0-0	2-0	2-0
Totals	3-3	2-4	9-8	7-9	2-4	3-3	7-11	2-4	13-3	5-1	5-1	2-4	10-7	4-2	1-5	10-8	85-77

NO-DECISIONS: Jimmy Journell, Gabe Molina, Kevin Ohme, Josh Pearce, Jason Pearson.

INTERLEAGUE: Esteban Yan 1-0, Garrett Stephenson 0-1, Jason Simontacchi 1-0 vs. Orioles; Steve Kline 1-0, Brett Tomko 0-1, Esteban Yan 1-0 vs. Red Sox; Matt Morris 0-1, Jeff Fassero 1-0, Woody Williams 1-0, Garrett Stephenson 0-2, Brett Tomko 1-0 vs. Royals; Jason Simontacchi 0-1, Matt Morris 0-1, Woody Williams 0-1 vs. Yankees; Matt Morris 1-0, Jason Simontacchi 1-0, Woody Williams 1-0 vs. Blue Jays. Total: 10-8.

HOME RUNS BY PARKS

	At Ari.	At Atl.	At Chi.	At Cin.	At Col.	At Fla.	At Hou.	At L.A.	At Mil.	At Mon.	At N.Y.	At Phi.	At Pit.	At St.L.	At S.D.	At S.F.	At A.L. Parks	Totals 2003	Totals 2002	HR Allow.
Arizona	79	3	4	2	16	2	4	9	4	3	3	3	2	2	8	4	4	152	165	150
Atlanta	4	111	6	6	6	8	4	3	6	23	12	10	6	5	10	3	12	235	164	147
Chicago	3	2	86	12	5	2	11	4	13	3	2	4	7	4	5	4	5	172	200	143
Cincinnati	3	2	3	97	8	3	9	2	16	10	5	1	4	10	1	2	6	182	169	209
Colorado	14	1	1	2	113	2	2	5	5	3	1	2	7	7	14	8	11	198	152	200
Florida	5	11	4	5	1	72	5	1	8	12	8	5	1	1	7	4	7	157	146	128
Houston	1	1	5	16	7	2	97	2	13	4	3	2	10	9	4	3	12	191	167	161
Los Angeles	8	2	2	0	11	4	3	68	4	4	0	2	2	1	7	4	2	124	155	127
Milwaukee	1	5	12	17	4	0	7	4	108	2	7	2	5	11	1	4	6	196	139	219
Montreal	2	9	2	1	2	5	2	3	5	81	11	7	3	0	2	3	6	144	162	181
New York	1	8	1	5	5	6	5	2	3	2	54	5	5	2	3	4	13	124	160	168
Philadelphia	5	10	4	5	5	5	2	4	1	15	10	83	1	4	1	4	7	166	165	142
Pittsburgh	5	3	2	18	5	1	6	0	9	2	0	2	81	18	4	1	6	163	142	178
St. Louis	5	2	12	10	3	2	10	8	16	2	5	4	15	85	0	0	17	196	175	210
San Diego	7	2	0	7	16	1	2	6	3	3	2	3	3	1	55	7	10	128	136	208
San Francisco	15	3	2	4	10	2	7	9	4	0	2	2	2	4	20	82	12	180	198	136
A.L. clubs	4	4	7	8	13	3	10	10	14	28	7	7	7	14	8	6	....	150	124	....
2003 Totals	162	179	153	215	230	120	186	140	232	*197	132	144	161	178	150	143	136	2708	....	2707
2002 Totals	167	146	204	197	232	126	158	159	164	163	162	153	148	154	135	114	....	....	2595	....

*There were actually 122 home runs hit at Montreal in 2003. The total also includes 75 home runs hit by teams when Montreal played its 22 "home" games at Hiram Bithorn Stadium in San Juan, Puerto Rico.

AT ARIZONA (162):

Arizona (79)—Hillenbrand 11, Finley 10, Spivey 10, Cintron 6, L. Gonzalez 6, Hammock 5, Mondesi 5, Baerga 4, Barajas 3, Counsell 3, Kata 3, Bautista 2, Dellucci 2, Grace 2, Moeller 2, Overbay 2, Womack 2, Williams 1. **Atlanta (4)**—A. Jones 2, Fick 1, Furcal 1. **Chicago (3)**—Sosa 2, Ramirez 1. **Chicago (3)**—Daubach 1, Ordonez 1, Thomas 1. **Cincinnati (3)**—Freel 1, Guillen 1, Taylor 1. **Cleveland (1)**—Sorensen 1. Colorado (14)—Wilson 4, Helton 3, Payton 2, Walker 2, Chacon 1, Richard 1, Zaun 1. **Florida (5)**—Lowell 2, Banks 1, Gonzalez 1, Hollandsworth 1. **Houston (1)**—Everett 1. **Los Angeles (8)**—Burnitz 2, Green 2, Jordan 2, Izturis 1, Roberts 1. **Milwaukee (1)**—Clayton 1. **Montreal (2)**—Cabrera 1, Guerrero 1. **New York (1)**—Wigginton 1. **Philadelphia (5)**—Thome 2, Abreu 1, Burrell 1, Houston 1. **Pittsburgh (5)**—Lofton 1, Ramirez 1, Sanders 1, Simon 1, Young 1. **St. Louis (5)**—Edmonds 2, Martinez 1, Perez 1, Taguchi 1. **San Diego (7)**—Bay 1, Burroughs 1, Eaton 1, Klesko 1, Matthews Jr. 1, Nevin 1, White 1. **San Francisco (15)**—Bonds 4, Grissom 3, Aurilia 2, Snow 2, Cruz 1, Durham 1, Galarraga 1, Santiago 1.

AT ATLANTA (179):

Arizona (3)—Cintron 1, L. Gonzalez 1, Spivey 1. **Atlanta (111)**—Lopez 26, Sheffield 20, A. Jones 16, C. Jones 16, Giles 9, Castilla 6, Fick 4, Furcal 4, DeRosa 3, M. Franco 3, J. Franco 1, Hampton 1, Hessman 1, Ortiz 1. **Baltimore (2)**—Conine 1, Matos 1. **Chicago (2)**—Gonzalez 1, Sosa 1. **Cincinnati (2)**—Dunn 1, Guillen 1. **Colorado (1)**—Wilson 1. **Florida (11)**—Gonzalez 3, Cabrera 2, Lowell 2, Encarnacion 1, Lee 1, Mordecai 1, Rodriguez 1. **Houston (1)**—Bagwell 1. **Los Angeles (2)**—Beltre 1, Ventura 1. **Milwaukee (5)**—Sexson 3, Vander Wal 2. **Montreal (9)**—Barrett 3, Cabrera 2, Wilkerson 2, W. Cordero 1, Vidro 1. **New York (8)**—Burnitz 2, Piazza 2, Reyes 2, Phillips 1, Wigginton 1. **Philadelphia (10)**—Lieberthal 3, Perez 2, Burrell 1, Ledee 1, Michaels 1, Thome 1, Utley 1. **Pittsburgh (3)**—Reboulet 1, Sanders 1, C. Wilson 1. **St. Louis (2)**—Edmonds 1, Martinez 1. **San Diego (2)**—Matthews Jr. 1, White 1. **San Francisco (3)**—Cruz 1, Galarraga 1, Santiago 1. **Texas (2)**—Gonzalez 1, Teixeira 1.

AT CHICAGO (153):

Arizona (4)—L. Gonzalez 2, Cintron 1, Spivey 1. **Atlanta (6)**—Castilla 2, Furcal 2, Blanco 1, A. Jones 1. **Chicago (86)**—Sosa 19, Alou 14, Gonzalez 11, Karros 7, Patterson 7, Miller 6, Choi 5, Ramirez 4, Martinez 3, Grudzielanek 2, Wood 2, Bellhorn 1, Glanville 1, Hernandez 1, Lofton 1, O'Leary 1, Zambrano 1. **Chicago (1)**—Olivo 1. **Cincinnati (3)**—Dunn 1, Guillen 1, Jimenez 1. **Colorado (1)**—Wilson 1. **Florida (4)**—Rodriguez 2, Castillo 1, Lee 1. **Houston (5)**—Ensberg 2, Berkman 1, Biggio 1, Hidalgo 1. **Los Angeles (2)**—Beltre 1, Burnitz 1. **Milwaukee (12)**—Jenkins 3, Ginter 2, Helms 2, Sexson 2, Kieschnick 1, Perez 1, Smith 1. **Montreal (2)**—Guerrero 2. **New York (1)**—Cedeno 1. **New York (6)**—Giambi 2, Matsui 1, Mondesi 1, Posada 1, Ventura 1. **Philadelphia (4)**—Abreu 1, Ledee 1, Pratt 1, Thome 1. **Pittsburgh (2)**—C. Wilson 1, J. Wilson 1. **St. Louis (12)**—Edmonds 4, Drew 2, Pujols 2, Martinez 1, Perez 1, Rolen 1, Vina 1. **San Francisco (2)**—Alfonzo 2.

AT CINCINNATI (215):

Arizona (2)—Finley 1, L. Gonzalez 1. **Atlanta (6)**—Castilla 2, Lopez 2, Furcal 1, A. Jones 1. **Chicago (12)**—Sosa 5, Alou 1, Choi 1, Harris 1, Karros 1, Lofton 1, Ramirez 1, Simon 1. **Cincinnati (97)**—Dunn 16, LaRue 12, Boone 10, Guillen 10, Casey 8, Kearns 8, Branyan 7, Griffey Jr. 5, Castro 4, Jimenez 3, Stenson 3, Taylor 3, Larkin 2, Mateo 2, Stinnett 2, Pena 1, Smitherman 1. **Colorado (2)**—Johnson 1, Wilson 1. **Florida (5)**—Lowell 2, Banks 1, Encarnacion 1, Lee 1. **Houston (16)**—Bagwell 4, Berkman 3, Hidalgo 3, Kent 3, Biggio 1, Ensberg 1, Villone 1. **Milwaukee (17)**—Jenkins 6, Hall 2, Helms 2, Sexson 2, Ginter 1, Perez 1, Smith 1, Vander Wal 1, Young 1. **Montreal (1)**—Wilkerson 1. **New York (5)**—Burnitz 2, Clark 1, Floyd 1, Perez 1. **New York (4)**—Giambi 2, Matsui 1, Soriano 1. **Philadelphia (5)**—Abreu 1, Bell 1, Ledee 1, Michaels 1, Polanco 1. **Pittsburgh (18)**—C. Wilson 4, Sanders 3, Kendall 2, Simon 2, Bay 1, Hernandez 1, Lofton 1, Mackowiak 1, Nunez 1, Stairs 1, Young 1. **St. Louis (10)**—Pujols 4, Renteria 2, Rolen 2, Drew 1, Edmonds 1. **San Diego (7)**—Klesko 3, White 2, Nady 1, Vazquez 1. **San Francisco (4)**—Bonds 1, Feliz 1, Galarraga 1, Santiago 1. **Toronto (4)**—Delgado 2, Wells 2.

AT COLORADO (230):

Arizona (16)—Finley 4, Bautista 2, L. Gonzalez 2, Hillenbrand 2, Moeller 2, Cintron 1, Hammock 1, Kata 1, Mondesi 1. **Atlanta (6)**—Furcal 2, Castilla 1, A. Jones 1, C. Jones 1, Sheffield 1. **Chicago (5)**—Patterson 2, Choi 1, Karros 1, Prior 1. **Cincinnati (8)**—Casey 2, Guillen 2, Boone 1, Dunn 1, LaRue 1, Lopez 1. **Cleveland (2)**—Bard 1, Gerut 1. **Colorado (113)**—Helton 23, Wilson 21, Payton 13, Johnson 12, Stynes 10, Walker 8, Belliard 6, Uribe 6, Hernandez 4, Estalella 2, Norton 2, Reyes 2, Butler 1, Oliver 1, Sweeney 1, Vaughn 1. **Detroit (6)**—Halter 1, Higginson 1, Morris 1, Munson 1, Witt 1, D. Young 1. **Florida (1)**—Gonzalez 1. **Houston (7)**—Hidalgo 3, Bagwell 1, Ensberg 1, Everett 1, Kent 1. **Kansas City (5)**—Beltran 1, Berroa 1, Guiel 1, Sweeney 1, Tucker 1. **Los Angeles (11)**—Beltre 2, Cabrera 2, Coomer 2, Green 2, Cora 1, Hundley 1, Mota 1. **Milwaukee (4)**—Vander Wal 2, Sexson 1, Young 1. **Montreal (2)**—Barrett 1, Guerrero 1. **New York (5)**—Piazza 3, Alomar 1, Floyd 1. **Philadelphia (5)**—Abreu 2, Byrd 1, Ledee 1, Polanco 1. **Pittsburgh (5)**—Simon 2, Giles 1, Rivera 1, Sanders 1. **St. Louis (3)**—Edmonds 1, Matheny 1, Rolen 1. **San Diego (16)**—Klesko 4, Kotsay 3, Burroughs 2, Nevin 2, Buchanan 1, Giles 1, Greene 1, Loretta 1, Mendez 1. **San Francisco (10)**—Feliz 3, Bonds 2, Aurilia 1, Grissom 1, Hammonds 1, Rivera 1, Santiago 1.

AT FLORIDA (120):

Anaheim (2)—Anderson 1, Glaus 1. **Arizona (2)**—Cintron 1, Hillenbrand 1. **Atlanta (8)**—Lopez 2, Castilla 1, Furcal 1, A. Jones 1, C. Jones 1, Ortiz 1, Sheffield 1. **Chicago (2)**—Gonzalez 1, Sosa 1. **Cincinnati (3)**—Griffey Jr. 2, Casey 1. **Colorado (2)**—Wilson 2. **Florida (72)**—Lowell 14, Lee 11, Encarnacion 9, Rodriguez 8, Cabrera 7, Gonzalez 7, Castro 4, Conine 3, Castillo 2, Penny 2, Banks 1, Hollandsworth 1, Mordecai 1, Pierre 1, Willis 1. **Houston (2)**—Kent 1, Merced 1. **Los Angeles (4)**—Beltre 2, Burnitz 2. **Montreal (5)**—Guerrero 3, Wilkerson 2. **New York (6)**—Wigginton 3, Burnitz 2, Floyd 1. **Oakland (1)**—Melhuse 1. **Philadelphia (5)**—Thome 2, Bell 1, Byrd 1, Polanco 1. **Pittsburgh (1)**—Stairs 1. **St. Louis (2)**—Marrero 1, Pujols 1. **San Diego (1)**—Bennett 1. **San Francisco (2)**—Bonds 1, Santiago 1.

AT HOUSTON (186):

Arizona (4)—L. Gonzalez 2, Cintron 1, Kata 1. **Atlanta (4)**—Sheffield 2, DeRosa 1, A. Jones 1. **Baltimore (2)**—Batista 1, Gibbons 1. **Chicago (11)**—Alou 2, Ramirez 2, Gonzalez 1, Grudzielanek 1, Karros 1, Patterson 1, Simon 1, Sosa 1, Zambrano 1. **Cincinnati (9)**—Griffey Jr. 3, Casey 1, Castro 1, Dunn 1, Freel 1, Jimenez 1, LaRue 1. **Colorado (2)**—Estalella 2. **Florida (5)**—Gonzalez 2, Lee 2, Encarnacion 1. **Houston (97)**—Bagwell 22, Ensberg 16, Berkman 11, Hidalgo 11, Kent 9, Biggio 6, Blum 6, Everett 5, Lane 4, Vizcaino 2, Ausmus 1, Bruntlett 1, Matranga 1, Merced 1, Zaun 1. **Los Angeles (3)**—Burnitz 1, McGriff 1, Ross 1. **Milwaukee (7)**—Sexson 4, Helms 1, Podsednik 1, Young 1. **Montreal (2)**—Cabrera 1, W. Cordero 1. **New York (5)**—Clark 2, Perez 1, Scutaro 1, Wilson 1. **Philadelphia (2)**—Polanco 1, Thome 1. **Pittsburgh (6)**—Ramirez 2, Lofton 1, Nunez 1, Sanders 1, Stairs 1. **St. Louis (10)**—Pujols 3, Renteria 3, Cairo 1, Edmonds 1, Matheny 1, Taguchi 1. **San Diego (2)**—Loretta 1, Nevin 1. **San Francisco (7)**—Feliz 2, Grissom 2, Alfonzo 1, Durham 1, Galarraga 1. **Tampa Bay (5)**—Anderson 1, Baldelli 1, Hall 1, Lee 1, Sandberg 1. **Texas (3)**—Palmeiro 2, Mench 1.

AT LOS ANGELES (140):

Anaheim (3)—Anderson 2, Fullmer 1. **Arizona (9)**—L. Gonzalez 5, Kata 1, Moeller 1, Overbay 1, Williams 1. **Atlanta (3)**—Castilla 1, Lopez 1, Sheffield 1. **Chicago (4)**—Sosa 2, Miller 1, Ramirez 1. **Chicago (4)**—Thomas 2, Crede 1, Lee 1. **Cincinnati (2)**—Jimenez 1, Larson 1. **Colorado (5)**—Hernandez 2, Payton 2, Estalella 1. **Florida (1)**—Castillo 1. **Houston (2)**—Ausmus 1, Kent 1. **Kansas City (3)**—Berroa 2, Beltran 1. **Los Angeles (68)**—Beltre 13, Green 10, McGriff 7, Burnitz 6, Ross 5, Cabrera 4, Lo Duca 4, Ventura 4, Cora 3, Jordan 3, Coomer 2, Henderson 2, Kinkade 2, Hundley 1, Nomo 1, Roberts 1. **Milwaukee (4)**—Sexson 2, Helms 1, Young 1. **Montreal (3)**—Guerrero 2, Wilkerson 1. **New York (2)**—Reyes 1, Wigginton 1. **Philadelphia (4)**—Lieberthal 2, Abreu 1, Thome 1. **St. Louis (8)**—Pujols 2, Rolen 2, Edmonds 1, Perez 1, Renteria 1, Williams 1. **San Diego (6)**—Klesko 2, White 2, Burroughs 1, Giles 1. **San Francisco (9)**—Bonds 2, Galarraga 2, Grissom 2, Linden 1, Rivera 1, Santiago 1.

AT MILWAUKEE (232):

Arizona (4)—Finley 1, Hillenbrand 1, Johnson 1, Kata 1. **Atlanta (6)**—Giles 2, A. Jones 2, Castilla 1, J. Franco 1. **Boston (9)**—Millar 3, Ramirez 2, Mueller 1, Nixon 1, Ortiz 1, Varitek 1. **Chicago (13)**—O'Leary 3, Simon 3, Sosa 2, Alou 1, Choi 1, Karros 1, Miller 1, Patterson 1. **Cincinnati (16)**—Boone 4, Dunn 2, Griffey Jr. 2, Pena 2, Branyan 1, Casey 1, Freel 1, Guillen 1, Hummel 1, LaRue 1. **Colorado (5)**—Helton 1, Johnson 1, Norton 1, Payton 1, Wilson 1. **Florida (8)**—Encarnacion 3, Lee 3, Castillo 1, Lowell 1. **Houston (13)**—Bagwell 4, Hidalgo 4, Biggio 2, Berkman 1, Ensberg 1, Vizcaino 1. **Los Angeles (4)**—McGriff 2, Green 1, Lo Duca 1. **Milwaukee (108)**—Sexson 23, Helms 16, Jenkins 16, Ginter 9, Podsednik 7, Vander Wal 7, Young 7, Clark 5, Clayton 5, Perez 5, Hall 2, Kieschnick 2, Conti 1, Hammonds 1, Osik 1, Smith 1. **Minnesota (5)**—Koskie 2, Hocking 1, Hunter 1, Morneau 1. **Montreal (5)**—Wilkerson 2, Barrett 1, Cabrera 1, Liefer 1. **New York (3)**—Floyd 2, Clark 1. **Philadelphia (1)**—Thome 1. **Pittsburgh (9)**—Stairs 2, Lofton 1, Mackowiak 1, Ramirez 1, Redman 1, Sanders 1, C. Wilson 1, J. Wilson 1. **St. Louis (16)**—Perez 3, Rolen 3, Drew 2, Matheny 2, Pujols 2, Cairo 1, Edmonds 1, Morris 1, Palmeiro 1. **San Diego (3)**—Nady 2, Vazquez 1. **San Francisco (4)**—Aurilia 1, Bonds 1, Cruz 1, Santiago 1.

AT MONTREAL (197):

Anaheim (15)—Anderson 5, DaVanon 4, Fullmer 2, Glaus 2, B. Molina 1, Salmon 1. **Arizona (3)**—Finley 1, L. Gonzalez 1, Moeller 1. **Atlanta (23)**—Lopez 5, Giles 4, Fick 3, A. Jones 3, Sheffield 3, C. Jones 2, Castilla 1, Furcal 1, Hampton 1. **Chicago (3)**—Alou 1, Lofton 1, Ramirez 1. **Cincinnati (10)**—Kearns 3, Boone 2, Castro 1, Dunn 1, Guillen 1, Lopez 1, Mateo 1. **Colorado (3)**—Helton 1, Norton 1, Wilson 1. **Florida (12)**—Lee 5, Lowell 3, Castro 1, Encarnacion 1, Gonzalez 1, Hollandsworth 1. **Houston (4)**—Bagwell 2, Hidalgo 1, Kent 1. **Los Angeles (4)**—McGriff 2, Green 1, Ross 1. **Milwaukee (2)**—Clayton 1, Young 1. **Montreal (81)**—Guerrero 15, Schneider 9, Wilkerson 9, Cabrera 8, W. Cordero 8, Vidro 7, Barrett 5, Calloway 5, Chavez 4, Macias 3, Zeile 3, Vitiello 2, Carroll 1, Guzman 1, Tatis 1. **New York (2)**—Clark 1, Garcia 1. **Philadelphia (15)**—Abreu 3, Polanco 3, Byrd 2, Ledee 2, Bell 1, Burrell 1, Lieberthal 1, Michaels

1, Rollins 1. **Pittsburgh (2)**—Reboulet 1, Sanders 1. **St. Louis (2)**—Renteria 1, Rolen 1. **San Diego (3)**—Klesko 1, Rivera 1, White 1. **Texas (5)**—Everett 2, Blalock 1, Gonzalez 1, Teixeira 1. **Toronto (8)**—Wells 3, Bordick 1, Catalanotto 1, Hendrickson 1, Hudson 1, Myers 1.

AT NEW YORK (132):

Arizona (3)—L. Gonzalez 1, Grace 1, Williams 1. **Atlanta (12)**—C. Jones 4, DeRosa 2, J. Franco 2, Castilla 1, Fick 1, Lopez 1, Sheffield 1. **Chicago (2)**—Patterson 2. **Cincinnati (5)**—Castro 2, Guillen 2, Dunn 1. **Colorado (1)**—Walker 1. **Florida (8)**—Gonzalez 2, Rodriguez 2, Castillo 1, Conine 1, Lee 1, Lowell 1. **Houston (3)**—Berkman 1, Hidalgo 1, Kent 1. **Milwaukee (7)**—Clayton 2, Sexson 2, Jenkins 1, Osik 1, Young 1. **Montreal (11)**—Vidro 4, W. Cordero 2, Zeile 2, Calloway 1, Liefer 1, Vitiello 1. **New York (54)**—Floyd 10, Clark 9, Phillips 7, Cedeno 5, Burnitz 4, Piazza 4, Wigginton 4, Wilson 3, Alomar 1, Duncan 1, Garcia 1, Gonzalez 1, Perez 1, Reyes 1, Shinjo 1, Vaughn 1. **New York (7)**—Giambi 2, Jeter 2, Soriano 2, Matsui 1. **Philadelphia (10)**—Burrell 4, Thome 3, Houston 1, Lieberthal 1, Punto 1. **St. Louis (5)**—Hart 2, Drew 1, Pujols 1, Renteria 1. **San Diego (2)**—Buchanan 1, Nady 1. **San Francisco (2)**—Bonds 2.

AT PHILADELPHIA (144):

Arizona (3)—Cintron 1, Moeller 1, Williams 1. **Atlanta (10)**—Sheffield 4, Fick 1, J. Franco 1, Giles 1, A. Jones 1, C. Jones 1, Lopez 1. **Boston (3)**—Walker 2, Nixon 1. **Chicago (4)**—Estes 1, Gonzalez 1, Miller 1, Sosa 1. **Cincinnati (1)**—Pena 1. **Colorado (2)**—Estalella 1, Payton 1. **Florida (5)**—Cabrera 2, Conine 1, Encarnacion 1, Rodriguez 1. **Houston (2)**—Berkman 1, Blum 1. **Los Angeles (2)**—Beltre 1, Lo Duca 1. **Milwaukee (2)**—Ginter 1, Young 1. **Montreal (7)**—Cabrera 2, W. Cordero 2, Calloway 1, Tatis 1, Wilkerson 1. **New York (5)**—Burnitz 1, Floyd 1, McEwing 1, Phillips 1, Redman 1. **Oakland (1)**—Chavez 1. **Philadelphia (83)**—Thome 28, Abreu 11, Burrell 9, Polanco 7, Ledee 6, Lieberthal 6, Rollins 5, Byrd 3, Pratt 3, Perez 2, Bell 1, Michaels 1, Utley 1. **Pittsburgh (2)**—Reese 1, Sanders 1. **St. Louis (4)**—Edmonds 1, Martinez 1, Palmeiro 1, Rolen 1. **San Diego (3)**—Buchanan 1, Nevin 1, Ojeda 1. **San Francisco (2)**—Cruz 1, Grissom 1. **Seattle (3)**—Boone 2, Cameron 1.

AT PITTSBURGH (161):

Arizona (2)—Overbay 1, Spivey 1. **Atlanta (6)**—A. Jones 2, Castilla 1, Giles 1, Hessman 1, Lopez 1. **Boston (7)**—Nixon 3, Ramirez 2, Varitek 1, Walker 1. **Chicago (7)**—Ramirez 3, Sosa 2, Gonzalez 1, Goodwin 1. **Cincinnati (4)**—Branyan 1, Freel 1, Guillen 1, Pena 1. **Colorado (7)**—Johnson 2, Payton 2, Estalella 1, Helton 1, Uribe 1. **Florida (1)**—Lee 1. **Houston (10)**—Kent 3, Berkman 2, Ensberg 2, Bagwell 1, Blum 1, Hidalgo 1. **Los Angeles (2)**—Green 1, Kinkade 1. **Milwaukee (5)**—Jenkins 2, Podsednik 1, Sexson 1, Vander Wal 1. **Montreal (3)**—Calloway 1, W. Cordero 1, Macias 1. **New York (5)**—Burnitz 2, Piazza 2, Vaughn 1. **Philadelphia (1)**—Thome 1. **Pittsburgh (81)**—Sanders 17, Stairs 13, Giles 10, C. Wilson 9, Ramirez 6, Lofton 4, Simon 4, Kendall 3, Bay 2, Hernandez 2, Nunez 2, Redman 2, Rivera 2, J. Wilson 2, Davis 1, Mackowiak 1, Wells 1. **St. Louis (15)**—Edmonds 3, Martinez 3, Pujols 3, Rolen 3, Cairo 1, Hart 1, Vina 1. **San Diego (3)**—Matthews Jr. 1, Nevin 1, White 1. **San Francisco (2)**—Alfonzo 1, Cruz 1.

AT SAN DIEGO (150):

Arizona (8)—Finley 3, L. Gonzalez 2, Hillenbrand 2, Jose 1. **Atlanta (10)**—Castilla 3, Furcal 2, Giles 1, A. Jones 1, C. Jones 1, Lopez 1, Sheffield 1. **Chicago (5)**—Sosa 2, Alou 1, Karros 1, Ramirez 1. **Cincinnati (1)**—Taylor 1. **Colorado (14)**—Walker 3, Payton 2, Wilson 2, Belliard 1, Helton 1, Hernandez 1, Johnson 1, Norton 1, Uribe 1, Zaun 1. **Detroit (3)**—D. Young 2, Witt 1. **Florida (7)**—Lowell 3, Lee 2, Banks 1, Rodriguez 1. **Houston (4)**—Biggio 2, Bagwell 1, Kent 1. **Los Angeles (7)**—Green 2, Beltre 1, Burnitz 1, Jordan 1, Lo Duca 1, McGriff 1. **Milwaukee (1)**—Perez 1. Minnesota (4)—Jones 2, Hunter 1, Mientkiewicz 1. **Montreal (2)**—Vidro 1, Wilkerson 1. **New York (3)**—Cedeno 1, Scutaro 1, Wigginton 1. **Philadelphia (1)**—Burrell 1. **Pittsburgh (4)**—J. Wilson 2, Hyzdu 1, Mackowiak 1. **San Diego (55)**—Loretta 10, Klesko 8, Nevin 6, Nady 5, White 4, Buchanan 3, Lockhart 3, Ojeda 3, Burroughs 2, Giles 2, Hansen 2, Bennett 1, Eaton 1, Kotsay 1, Lawrence 1, Matthews Jr. 1, Merloni 1, Vazquez 1. **San Francisco (20)**—Snow 4, Alfonzo 3, Durham 3, Aurilia 2, Bonds 2, Cruz 2, Santiago 2, Grissom 1, Torrealba 1. **Seattle (1)**—Boone 1.

AT SAN FRANCISCO (143):

Arizona (4)—Mondesi 2, Cintron 1, L. Gonzalez 1. **Atlanta (3)**—Giles 1, Lopez 1, Sheffield 1. **Chicago (4)**—Gonzalez 2, Alou 1, Sosa 1. **Cincinnati (2)**—Guillen 1, LaRue 1. **Colorado (8)**—Helton 2, Payton 2, Norton 1, Stynes 1, Walker 1, Wilson 1. **Detroit (3)**—Inge 1, Monroe 1, D. Young 1. **Florida (4)**—Cabrera 1, Encarnacion 1, Gonzalez 1, Lee 1. **Houston (3)**—Biggio 1, Chavez 1, Merced 1. **Los Angeles (4)**—Beltre 2, Kinkade 1, Ross 1. **Milwaukee (4)**—Sexson 2, Clark 1, Kieschnick 1. **Minnesota (1)**—Mientkiewicz 1. **Montreal (3)**—Calloway 1, Guerrero 1, Liefer 1. **New York (4)**—Floyd 1, Gonzalez 1, Phillips 1, Wilson 1. **Oakland (2)**—Byrnes 1, Piatt 1. **Philadelphia (4)**—Burrell 2, Rollins 1, Thome 1. **Pittsburgh (1)**—J. Wilson 1. **San Diego (7)**—White 2, Greene 1, Klesko 1, Kotsay 1, Loretta 1, Nevin 1. **San Francisco (82)**—Bonds 23, Grissom 10, Cruz 9, Alfonzo 6, Aurilia 6, Feliz 6, Galarraga 6, Durham 3, Torrealba 3, Hammonds 2, Santiago 2, Snow 2, Castillo 1, Perez 1, Ransom 1, Santos 1.

AT ST. LOUIS (178):

Arizona (2)—Finley 1, L. Gonzalez 1. **Atlanta (5)**—Sheffield 2, Giles 1, A. Jones 1, Lopez 1. **Baltimore (6)**—Cruz 3, Batista 1, Conine 1, Mora 1. **Chicago (4)**—Bellhorn 1, Ramirez 1, Simon 1, Sosa 1. **Cincinnati (10)**—Dunn 2, Kearns 2, Casey 1, Castro 1, Griffey Jr. 1, Guillen 1, Hummel 1, Jimenez 1. **Colorado (7)**—Belliard 1, Helton 1, Johnson 1, Payton 1, Pellow 1, Uribe 1, Zaun 1. **Florida (1)**—Rodriguez 1. **Houston (9)**—Berkman 3, Ausmus 2, Bagwell 1, Blum 1, Hidalgo 1, Kent 1. **Kansas City (5)**—Harvey 2, Berroa 1, Randa 1, Relaford 1. **Los Angeles (1)**—Ross 1. **Milwaukee (11)**—Clayton 2, Perez 2, Conti 1, Ginter 1, Hall 1, Helms 1, Kieschnick 1, Sexson 1, Young 1. **New York (2)**—Vaughn 1, Wilson 1. **Philadelphia (4)**—Burrell 2, Thome 2. **Pittsburgh (18)**—Sanders 4, Giles 3, Mackowiak 2, C. Wilson 2, J. Wilson 2, D'Amico 1, Kendall 1, Lofton 1, Reboulet 1, Simon 1. **St. Louis (85)**—Pujols 21, Edmonds 17, Rolen 12, Drew 7, Martinez 6, Perez 5, Matheny 4, Renteria 4, Cairo 2, Vina 2, Hart 1, Marrero 1, Palmeiro 1, Robinson 1, Taguchi 1. **San Diego (1)**—Kotsay 1. **San Francisco (4)**—Bonds 2, Cruz 2. Toronto (3)—Delgado 1, Johnson 1, Woodward 1.

PARK DATA (SELECTED BATTING CATEGORIES AT EACH STADIUM)

This section contains selected batting statistics for all National League parks for 2003. A key component of this section is an index number for each category, which is used to determine how a given park influences a particular statistic. To illustrate, the Dodgers had all sorts of problems scoring runs last season, and their park index of 83 indicates that Dodger Stadium certainly didn't help. Most of their other offensive indexes suffered as well, with the lone exception being home runs (121).

For each N.L. park, we show how the home team and its opponents performed, both at home and on the road, with the exception being that we do not include data from interleague games. The differences in interleague opponents and ballparks would skew the data.

By comparing the per-game averages at the home park and on the road, we can evaluate the park's impact. This is done by simply dividing the home average by the road average and multiplying the result by 100, generating a park index. If the home and road per-game averages are equal, the index equals 100, and it can be concluded that the park had no impact. An index above 100 means that the park favors that particular statistic. The indexes for at-bats, runs, hits, errors and infield errors are determined on a per-game basis; all other stats are calculated on a per-at-bat basis. "E-infield" denotes infield *fielding* errors. "Alt." is the approximate elevation of the ballpark.

For most parks, data is presented both for 2003 and for the last three years overall. If the park's dimensions have changed over that time, however, the data from the old and new configurations will not be combined. Following all the teams' charts is a ranking section that shows which parks most inflate runs, home runs and batting average.

ARIZONA

Home park: Bank One Ballpark **Alt.:** 1,090 feet **Surface:** Grass

	2003 Season							2001-03 Seasons						
	Home Games			Road Games				Home Games			Road Games			
Category	**Ari.**	**Opp.**	**Total**	**Ari.**	**Opp.**	**Total**	**Index**	**Ari.**	**Opp.**	**Total**	**Ari.**	**Opp.**	**Total**	**Index**
G	75	75	150	72	72	144		222	222	444	216	216	432	
Avg	.273	.253	.263	.247	.244	.245	107	.280	.253	.266	.249	.242	.246	108
AB	2521	2608	5129	2514	2383	4897	101	7453	7762	15215	7577	7103	14680	101
R	365	349	714	264	280	544	126	1188	1011	2199	933	833	1766	121
H	689	659	1348	620	582	1202	108	2088	1963	4051	1889	1716	3605	109
2B	150	144	294	113	100	213	132	416	385	801	357	297	654	118
3B	27	15	42	16	7	23	174	69	51	120	47	21	68	170
HR	73	79	152	69	65	134	108	254	265	519	228	198	426	118
BB	276	241	517	217	239	456	108	875	647	1522	746	640	1386	106
SO	448	605	1053	479	578	1057	95	1325	1817	3142	1470	1712	3182	95
E	44	41	85	52	44	96	85	126	136	262	128	147	275	93
E-Infield	33	37	70	45	36	81	83	109	112	221	113	126	239	90
LHB-Avg	.281	.288	.284	.256	.245	.251	113	.290	.273	.283	.262	.252	.258	110
LHB-HR	32	38	70	40	25	65	104	128	110	238	132	82	214	110
RHB-Avg	.265	.230	.244	.236	.244	.240	102	.269	.242	.253	.234	.235	.235	108
RHB-HR	41	41	82	29	40	69	113	126	155	281	96	116	212	125

ATLANTA

Home park: Turner Field **Alt.:** 1,050 feet **Surface:** Grass

	2003 Season							2001-03 Seasons						
	Home Games			Road Games				Home Games			Road Games			
Category	**Atl.**	**Opp.**	**Total**	**Atl.**	**Opp.**	**Total**	**Index**	**Atl.**	**Opp.**	**Total**	**Atl.**	**Opp.**	**Total**	**Index**
G	75	75	150	69	69	138		219	219	438	212	212	424	
Avg	.286	.249	.267	.286	.271	.279	96	.270	.249	.259	.264	.253	.259	100
AB	2530	2586	5116	2517	2357	4874	97	7275	7533	14808	7512	7083	14595	98
R	392	340	732	418	336	754	89	1027	899	1926	1034	854	1888	99
H	723	643	1366	720	639	1359	92	1965	1877	3842	1985	1794	3779	98
2B	138	122	260	153	150	303	82	373	335	708	392	344	736	95
3B	15	11	26	14	10	24	103	38	29	67	34	39	73	90
HR	101	64	165	104	72	176	89	254	190	444	249	194	443	99
BB	254	264	518	226	231	457	108	687	734	1421	715	697	1412	99
SO	413	443	856	432	432	864	94	1287	1394	2681	1418	1397	2815	94
E	58	54	112	53	43	96	107	161	155	316	140	136	276	111
E-Infield	46	41	87	49	37	86	93	139	127	266	120	109	229	112
LHB-Avg	.285	.245	.263	.273	.250	.261	101	.264	.258	.261	.265	.245	.255	102
LHB-HR	23	19	42	20	24	44	89	68	72	140	62	65	127	108
RHB-Avg	.286	.251	.269	.292	.282	.288	94	.274	.244	.259	.264	.258	.261	99
RHB-HR	78	45	123	84	48	132	90	186	118	304	187	129	316	95

CHICAGO

Home park: Wrigley Field **Alt.:** 595 feet **Surface:** Grass

	2003 Season							2001-03 Seasons						
	Home Games			Road Games				Home Games			Road Games			
Category	**Chi.**	**Opp.**	**Total**	**Chi.**	**Opp.**	**Total**	**Index**	**Chi.**	**Opp.**	**Total**	**Chi.**	**Opp.**	**Total**	**Index**
G	72	72	144	69	69	138		219	219	438	219	219	438	
Avg	.255	.236	.245	.261	.238	.250	98	.253	.237	.245	.255	.256	.255	96
AB	2392	2464	4856	2405	2261	4666	100	7192	7464	14656	7596	7246	14842	99
R	306	305	611	333	285	618	95	964	935	1899	1014	988	2002	95
H	610	581	1191	627	538	1165	98	1819	1772	3591	1935	1855	3790	95
2B	126	106	232	136	104	240	93	343	348	691	395	369	764	92
3B	8	9	17	11	8	19	86	36	26	62	42	44	86	73
HR	79	60	139	78	62	140	95	250	222	472	261	204	465	103
BB	241	283	524	202	241	443	114	792	794	1586	714	787	1501	107
SO	560	664	1224	478	577	1055	111	1618	1984	3602	1572	1722	3294	111
E	51	52	103	48	47	95	104	144	151	295	155	148	303	97
E-Infield	44	39	83	38	41	79	101	120	127	247	129	127	256	96
LHB-Avg	.241	.238	.239	.261	.238	.249	96	.245	.241	.243	.243	.270	.256	95
LHB-HR	14	23	37	22	27	49	74	82	84	166	101	100	201	82
RHB-Avg	.261	.234	.248	.261	.238	.250	99	.258	.235	.246	.262	.246	.255	97
RHB-HR	65	37	102	56	35	91	107	168	138	306	160	104	264	118

CINCINNATI

Home park: Great American Ball Park **Alt.:** 550 feet **Surface:** Grass

	2003 Season							2001-02 Seasons (Cinergy Field)						
	Home Games			Road Games				Home Games			Road Games			
Category	**Cin.**	**Opp.**	**Total**	**Cin.**	**Opp.**	**Total**	**Index**	**Cin.**	**Opp.**	**Total**	**Cin.**	**Opp.**	**Total**	**Index**
G	75	75	150	72	72	144		150	150	300	147	147	294	
Avg	.248	.271	.260	.242	.289	.265	98	.266	.279	.273	.254	.266	.260	105
AB	2505	2675	5180	2504	2481	4985	100	5047	5374	10421	5105	4936	10041	102
R	322	405	727	311	403	714	98	697	792	1489	654	681	1335	109
H	622	725	1347	607	716	1323	98	1342	1502	2844	1295	1312	2607	107
2B	117	154	271	105	151	256	102	318	319	637	238	266	504	122
3B	5	6	11	15	27	42	25	8	21	29	34	28	62	45
HR	88	110	198	69	84	153	125	159	201	360	166	133	299	116
BB	241	255	496	240	272	512	93	525	483	1008	451	506	957	101
SO	586	449	1035	612	386	998	100	1021	936	1957	1156	852	2008	94
E	72	52	124	57	49	106	112	113	102	215	128	106	234	90
E-Infield	59	47	106	47	45	92	111	89	86	175	101	91	192	89
LHB-Avg	.255	.264	.260	.248	.283	.265	98	.287	.282	.284	.275	.274	.274	104
LHB-HR	39	39	78	32	35	67	116	73	87	160	87	70	157	100
RHB-Avg	.244	.275	.260	.239	.292	.266	98	.251	.278	.265	.237	.260	.249	107
RHB-HR	49	71	120	37	49	86	132	86	114	200	79	63	142	134

COLORADO

Home park: Coors Field **Alt.:** 5,280 feet **Surface:** Grass

	2003 Season							2001-03 Seasons						
	Home Games			Road Games				Home Games			Road Games			
Category	**Col.**	**Opp.**	**Total**	**Col.**	**Opp.**	**Total**	**Index**	**Col.**	**Opp.**	**Total**	**Col.**	**Opp.**	**Total**	**Index**
G	72	72	144	75	75	150		219	219	438	222	222	444	
Avg	.294	.288	.291	.236	.287	.261	112	.314	.285	.299	.242	.271	.256	117
AB	2450	2600	5050	2558	2485	5043	104	7560	7809	15369	7624	7346	14970	104
R	458	397	855	305	405	710	125	1418	1303	2721	911	1109	2020	137
H	721	749	1470	603	712	1315	116	2375	2224	4599	1847	1991	3838	121
2B	169	142	311	137	150	287	108	491	458	949	369	432	801	115
3B	23	21	44	5	14	19	231	87	54	141	33	47	80	172
HR	98	104	202	74	77	151	134	299	349	648	210	243	453	139
BB	291	218	509	277	288	565	90	747	766	1513	733	807	1540	96
SO	439	416	855	608	360	968	88	1279	1335	2614	1672	1232	2904	88
E	48	54	102	59	53	112	95	145	160	305	144	144	288	107
E-Infield	40	42	82	50	46	96	89	114	122	236	121	127	248	96
LHB-Avg	.336	.301	.316	.247	.312	.285	111	.346	.289	.319	.265	.289	.276	115
LHB-HR	30	44	74	25	27	52	150	140	135	275	105	87	192	139
RHB-Avg	.277	.279	.278	.230	.267	.247	113	.291	.282	.287	.227	.260	.243	118
RHB-HR	68	60	128	49	50	99	125	159	214	373	105	156	261	139

FLORIDA

Home park: Pro Player Stadium **Alt.:** 10 feet **Surface:** Grass

	2003 Season							2001-03 Seasons						
	Home Games			Road Games				Home Games			Road Games			
Category	**Fla.**	**Opp.**	**Total**	**Fla.**	**Opp.**	**Total**	**Index**	**Fla.**	**Opp.**	**Total**	**Fla.**	**Opp.**	**Total**	**Index**
G	72	72	144	72	72	144		215	215	430	217	217	434	
Avg	.273	.240	.256	.259	.268	.263	97	.268	.247	.257	.257	.272	.264	97
AB	2403	2501	4904	2479	2369	4848	101	7143	7442	14585	7537	7185	14722	100
R	340	264	604	308	326	634	95	994	890	1884	907	1086	1993	95
H	656	599	1255	641	636	1277	98	1915	1835	3750	1934	1957	3891	97
2B	113	122	235	145	145	290	80	375	380	755	416	407	823	93
3B	23	21	44	16	10	26	167	63	65	128	30	46	76	170
HR	64	45	109	74	63	137	79	199	170	369	216	223	439	85
BB	240	237	477	219	237	456	103	754	804	1558	642	813	1455	108
SO	425	571	996	451	451	902	109	1404	1691	3095	1508	1315	2823	111
E	33	46	79	41	56	97	81	117	132	249	145	154	299	84
E-Infield	28	37	65	37	48	85	76	93	108	201	124	130	254	80
LHB-Avg	.303	.231	.262	.260	.267	.263	100	.277	.247	.258	.260	.284	.275	94
LHB-HR	4	16	20	3	20	23	83	33	62	95	32	89	121	75
RHB-Avg	.260	.245	.253	.258	.269	.263	96	.265	.246	.257	.255	.264	.259	99
RHB-HR	60	29	89	71	43	114	79	166	108	274	184	134	318	89

HOUSTON

Home park: Minute Maid Park **Alt.:** 22 feet **Surface:** Grass

	2003 Season							2001-03 Seasons						
	Home Games			Road Games				Home Games			Road Games			
Category	**Hou.**	**Opp.**	**Total**	**Hou.**	**Opp.**	**Total**	**Index**	**Hou.**	**Opp.**	**Total**	**Hou.**	**Opp.**	**Total**	**Index**
G	72	72	144	72	72	144		222	222	444	219	219	438	
Avg	.266	.244	.255	.253	.254	.253	101	.275	.252	.264	.250	.258	.254	104
AB	2388	2432	4820	2560	2388	4948	97	7427	7652	15079	7612	7270	14882	100
R	365	301	666	331	299	630	106	1153	979	2132	1000	922	1922	109
H	635	593	1228	647	607	1254	98	2046	1932	3978	1906	1875	3781	104
2B	131	103	234	137	123	260	92	421	365	786	404	386	790	98
3B	18	18	36	6	7	13	284	55	41	96	29	40	69	137
HR	82	79	161	82	66	148	112	266	254	520	241	221	462	111
BB	251	222	473	250	273	523	93	804	659	1463	770	765	1535	94
SO	417	507	924	493	500	993	96	1414	1702	3116	1548	1550	3098	99
E	40	45	85	39	54	93	91	128	152	280	129	145	274	101
E-Infield	37	38	75	31	48	79	95	112	124	236	110	123	233	100
LHB-Avg	.255	.251	.253	.241	.272	.259	98	.289	.267	.276	.256	.266	.262	105
LHB-HR	16	21	37	16	26	42	89	78	101	179	64	88	152	118
RHB-Avg	.269	.239	.256	.257	.243	.251	102	.271	.243	.258	.248	.252	.250	103
RHB-HR	66	58	124	66	40	106	121	188	153	341	177	133	310	108

LOS ANGELES

Home park: Dodger Stadium **Alt.:** 340 feet **Surface:** Grass

	2003 Season							2001-03 Seasons						
	Home Games			Road Games				Home Games			Road Games			
Category	**L.A.**	**Opp.**	**Total**	**L.A.**	**Opp.**	**Total**	**Index**	**L.A.**	**Opp.**	**Total**	**L.A.**	**Opp.**	**Total**	**Index**
G	72	72	144	72	72	144		216	216	432	219	219	438	
Avg	.241	.222	.231	.252	.247	.250	93	.247	.231	.239	.265	.252	.259	92
AB	2316	2373	4689	2551	2378	4929	95	7034	7313	14347	7774	7212	14986	97
R	243	222	465	279	281	560	83	812	779	1591	1043	949	1992	81
H	557	526	1083	643	587	1230	88	1734	1692	3426	2060	1818	3878	90
2B	114	74	188	119	111	230	86	329	279	608	403	373	776	82
3B	8	4	12	14	20	34	37	30	16	46	45	48	93	52
HR	59	62	121	54	51	105	121	205	212	417	235	206	441	99
BB	170	230	400	201	246	447	94	613	719	1332	618	737	1355	103
SO	425	607	1032	450	534	984	110	1299	1699	2998	1392	1562	2954	106
E	56	46	102	52	52	104	98	152	146	298	140	163	303	100
E-Infield	44	43	87	41	41	82	106	125	126	251	117	128	245	104
LHB-Avg	.249	.215	.235	.245	.238	.242	97	.242	.228	.235	.257	.247	.253	93
LHB-HR	29	19	48	27	15	42	117	71	83	154	91	79	170	95
RHB-Avg	.231	.226	.228	.259	.252	.255	89	.249	.234	.241	.270	.255	.263	92
RHB-HR	30	43	73	27	36	63	124	134	129	263	144	127	271	101

MILWAUKEE

Home park: Miller Park **Alt.:** 635 feet **Surface:** Grass

	2003 Season							2001-03 Seasons						
	Home Games			Road Games				Home Games			Road Games			
Category	**Mil.**	**Opp.**	**Total**	**Mil.**	**Opp.**	**Total**	**Index**	**Mil.**	**Opp.**	**Total**	**Mil.**	**Opp.**	**Total**	**Index**
G	75	75	150	75	75	150		222	222	444	225	225	450	
Avg	.255	.273	.264	.252	.285	.268	98	.254	.265	.260	.249	.275	.262	99
AB	2531	2741	5272	2585	2546	5131	103	7339	7815	15154	7749	7492	15241	101
R	318	426	744	329	387	716	104	936	1137	2073	968	1147	2115	99
H	646	747	1393	651	726	1377	101	1864	2071	3935	1928	2062	3990	100
2B	120	144	264	126	141	267	96	359	417	776	389	406	795	98
3B	8	20	28	13	20	33	83	33	48	81	43	54	97	84
HR	100	110	210	82	87	169	121	250	299	549	246	251	497	111
BB	260	282	542	257	254	511	103	715	873	1588	733	900	1633	98
SO	545	497	1042	583	461	1044	97	1644	1481	3125	1791	1380	3171	99
E	58	38	96	49	60	109	88	145	120	265	150	137	287	94
E-Infield	51	35	86	40	53	93	92	129	102	231	123	113	236	99
LHB-Avg	.280	.284	.283	.271	.260	.266	106	.266	.277	.272	.258	.263	.260	104
LHB-HR	30	41	71	24	24	48	138	91	132	223	85	95	180	124
RHB-Avg	.244	.266	.255	.242	.298	.270	94	.247	.258	.253	.244	.283	.263	96
RHB-HR	70	69	139	58	63	121	114	159	167	326	161	156	317	104

MONTREAL

Home park: Olympic Stadium **Alt.:** 90 feet **Surface:** Turf

	2003 Season							2001-03 Seasons						
	Home Games			Road Games				Home Games			Road Games			
Category	**Mon.**	**Opp.**	**Total**	**Mon.**	**Opp.**	**Total**	**Index**	**Mon.**	**Opp.**	**Total**	**Mon.**	**Opp.**	**Total**	**Index**
G	56	56	112	72	72	144		200	200	400	216	216	432	
Avg	.280	.260	.270	.239	.265	.252	107	.269	.263	.266	.244	.270	.257	103
AB	1856	1963	3819	2441	2373	4814	102	6607	7026	13633	7350	7160	14510	101
R	307	251	558	237	287	524	137	956	944	1900	825	955	1780	115
H	520	511	1031	583	630	1213	109	1776	1846	3622	1796	1931	3727	105
2B	135	121	256	99	127	226	143	445	423	868	349	371	720	128
3B	14	6	20	8	12	20	126	37	28	65	41	44	85	81
HR	50	62	112	57	54	111	127	180	225	405	181	207	388	111
BB	179	149	328	223	214	437	95	660	575	1235	679	702	1381	95
SO	306	366	672	477	439	916	92	1236	1369	2605	1506	1392	2898	96
E	31	33	64	42	46	88	94	148	140	288	149	150	299	104
E-Infield	24	29	53	36	33	69	99	116	118	234	127	121	248	102
LHB-Avg	.267	.254	.261	.231	.289	.258	101	.263	.272	.268	.238	.281	.258	104
LHB-HR	17	20	37	21	21	42	117	69	83	152	73	90	163	102
RHB-Avg	.291	.264	.277	.246	.248	.247	112	.273	.256	.264	.250	.262	.256	103
RHB-HR	33	42	75	36	33	69	131	111	142	253	108	117	225	117

NEW YORK

Home park: Shea Stadium **Alt.:** 20 feet **Surface:** Grass

	2003 Season							2001-03 Seasons						
	Home Games			Road Games				Home Games			Road Games			
Category	**N.Y.**	**Opp.**	**Total**	**N.Y.**	**Opp.**	**Total**	**Index**	**N.Y.**	**Opp.**	**Total**	**N.Y.**	**Opp.**	**Total**	**Index**
G	74	74	148	68	68	136		218	218	436	211	211	422	
Avg	.256	.266	.261	.239	.275	.257	102	.248	.258	.253	.253	.269	.261	97
AB	2415	2564	4979	2279	2244	4523	101	7177	7649	14826	7255	7000	14255	101
R	291	336	627	276	308	584	99	848	961	1809	904	961	1865	94
H	618	683	1301	544	617	1161	103	1779	1972	3751	1839	1881	3720	98
2B	128	155	283	107	120	227	113	340	378	718	356	373	729	95
3B	9	14	23	14	25	39	54	29	44	73	30	54	84	84
HR	48	71	119	56	70	126	86	177	230	407	194	225	419	93
BB	229	266	495	219	231	450	100	689	693	1382	685	666	1351	98
SO	447	458	905	463	353	816	101	1365	1548	2913	1430	1292	2722	103
E	59	50	109	40	52	92	109	175	156	331	144	153	297	108
E-Infield	49	45	94	35	42	77	112	146	133	279	122	125	247	109
LHB-Avg	.270	.255	.263	.257	.250	.254	103	.256	.255	.256	.250	.255	.253	101
LHB-HR	24	23	47	27	15	42	96	79	81	160	70	67	137	112
RHB-Avg	.246	.273	.260	.226	.287	.258	101	.242	.259	.252	.256	.276	.266	95
RHB-HR	24	48	72	29	55	84	81	98	149	247	124	158	282	84

PHILADELPHIA

Home park: Citizens Bank Park **Alt.:** 20 feet **Surface:** Grass

	2003 Season (Veterans Stadium)							2001-03 Seasons (Veterans Stadium)						
	Home Games			Road Games				Home Games			Road Games			
Category	**Phi.**	**Opp.**	**Total**	**Phi.**	**Opp.**	**Total**	**Index**	**Phi.**	**Opp.**	**Total**	**Phi.**	**Opp.**	**Total**	**Index**
G	72	72	144	75	75	150		215	215	430	219	219	438	
Avg	.264	.235	.250	.259	.273	.266	94	.256	.239	.248	.266	.273	.269	92
AB	2379	2446	4825	2625	2482	5107	98	7059	7321	14380	7709	7316	15025	97
R	349	266	615	373	369	742	86	963	848	1811	1057	1074	2131	87
H	628	576	1204	681	678	1359	92	1809	1752	3561	2049	1995	4044	90
2B	148	135	283	145	157	302	99	409	394	803	435	448	883	95
3B	15	11	26	12	15	27	102	50	38	88	40	51	91	101
HR	68	54	122	76	76	152	85	212	190	402	225	224	449	94
BB	302	233	535	282	247	529	107	822	708	1530	816	742	1558	103
SO	496	555	1051	539	403	942	118	1470	1598	3068	1538	1282	2820	114
E	38	34	72	54	42	96	78	101	117	218	151	152	303	73
E-Infield	33	32	65	42	32	74	91	88	99	187	117	120	237	80
LHB-Avg	.270	.231	.252	.262	.282	.271	93	.251	.242	.247	.274	.281	.277	89
LHB-HR	40	13	53	38	27	65	83	107	63	170	102	76	178	97
RHB-Avg	.259	.238	.248	.257	.268	.263	94	.261	.238	.248	.259	.268	.264	94
RHB-HR	28	41	69	38	49	87	86	105	127	232	123	148	271	92

PITTSBURGH

Home park: PNC Park **Alt.:** 730 feet **Surface:** Grass

	2003 Season							2001-03 Seasons						
	Home Games			Road Games				Home Games			Road Games			
Category	**Pit.**	**Opp.**	**Total**	**Pit.**	**Opp.**	**Total**	**Index**	**Pit.**	**Opp.**	**Total**	**Pit.**	**Opp.**	**Total**	**Index**
G	75	75	150	75	75	150		224	224	448	222	222	444	
Avg	.278	.269	.274	.257	.267	.262	105	.262	.269	.266	.242	.270	.256	104
AB	2510	2655	5165	2615	2482	5097	101	7388	7857	15245	7546	7275	14821	102
R	342	357	699	343	356	699	100	981	1119	2100	892	1068	1960	106
H	699	714	1413	671	663	1334	106	1936	2112	4048	1828	1965	3793	106
2B	135	139	274	111	138	249	109	390	433	823	335	403	738	108
3B	17	10	27	23	12	35	76	33	38	71	49	43	92	75
HR	74	73	147	76	86	162	90	201	227	428	230	236	466	89
BB	231	224	455	248	234	482	93	715	743	1458	699	756	1455	97
SO	442	436	878	534	426	960	90	1360	1313	2673	1677	1248	2925	89
E	66	43	109	47	52	99	110	194	160	354	152	147	299	117
E-Infield	60	37	97	40	47	87	111	163	140	303	129	129	258	116
LHB-Avg	.298	.294	.296	.273	.276	.274	108	.275	.284	.280	.255	.283	.270	104
LHB-HR	34	26	60	29	32	61	98	88	88	176	85	96	181	93
RHB-Avg	.267	.251	.259	.246	.261	.253	102	.255	.259	.257	.236	.262	.248	104
RHB-HR	40	47	87	47	54	101	84	113	139	252	145	140	285	87

ST. LOUIS

Home park: Busch Stadium **Alt.:** 535 feet **Surface:** Grass

	2003 Season							2001-03 Seasons						
	Home Games			Road Games				Home Games			Road Games			
Category	**St.L.**	**Opp.**	**Total**	**St.L.**	**Opp.**	**Total**	**Index**	**St.L.**	**Opp.**	**Total**	**St.L.**	**Opp.**	**Total**	**Index**
G	72	72	144	72	72	144		220	220	440	221	221	442	
Avg	.283	.251	.267	.267	.284	.276	97	.276	.246	.261	.264	.272	.268	97
AB	2433	2525	4958	2572	2497	5069	98	7317	7552	14869	7748	7382	15130	99
R	368	314	682	387	356	743	92	1125	867	1992	1104	1027	2131	94
H	688	634	1322	688	709	1397	95	2022	1856	3878	2049	2009	4058	96
2B	161	133	294	138	148	286	105	415	379	794	401	415	816	99
3B	5	13	18	21	12	33	56	31	23	54	50	33	83	66
HR	77	79	156	94	102	196	81	245	228	473	269	263	532	90
BB	253	219	472	270	229	499	97	768	723	1491	748	720	1468	103
SO	373	449	822	462	429	891	94	1269	1480	2749	1444	1327	2771	101
E	33	49	82	34	49	83	99	123	162	285	135	149	284	101
E-Infield	28	38	66	27	38	65	102	99	128	227	105	124	229	100
LHB-Avg	.256	.257	.256	.264	.296	.280	92	.272	.249	.260	.271	.272	.271	96
LHB-HR	30	30	60	33	30	63	100	110	90	200	103	99	202	104
RHB-Avg	.297	.247	.273	.270	.277	.273	100	.279	.244	.261	.260	.272	.266	98
RHB-HR	47	49	96	61	72	133	73	135	138	273	166	164	330	82

SAN DIEGO

Home park: Petco Park **Alt.:** 0 feet **Surface:** Grass

	2003 Season (Qualcomm Stadium)							2001-03 Seasons (Qualcomm Stadium)						
	Home Games			Road Games				Home Games			Road Games			
Category	**S.D.**	**Opp.**	**Total**	**S.D.**	**Opp.**	**Total**	**Index**	**S.D.**	**Opp.**	**Total**	**S.D.**	**Opp.**	**Total**	**Index**
G	72	72	144	72	72	144		216	216	432	219	219	438	
Avg	.256	.256	.256	.264	.277	.270	95	.251	.257	.254	.258	.283	.270	94
AB	2404	2527	4931	2508	2394	4902	101	7178	7593	14771	7632	7382	15014	100
R	270	342	612	331	415	746	82	855	998	1853	1045	1218	2263	83
H	615	647	1262	661	664	1325	95	1803	1949	3752	1969	2091	4060	94
2B	96	115	211	126	125	251	84	300	345	645	391	438	829	79
3B	18	17	35	12	20	32	109	48	48	96	33	56	89	110
HR	48	87	135	63	101	164	82	161	258	419	216	294	510	84
BB	265	272	537	238	281	519	103	806	716	1522	790	786	1576	98
SO	484	513	997	482	473	955	104	1492	1551	3043	1597	1408	3005	103
E	46	47	93	41	39	80	116	176	137	313	154	149	303	105
E-Infield	37	37	74	38	28	66	112	156	108	264	128	118	246	109
LHB-Avg	.243	.264	.253	.277	.293	.284	89	.263	.267	.265	.267	.293	.278	95
LHB-HR	17	33	50	28	38	66	74	74	111	185	97	129	226	82
RHB-Avg	.267	.251	.258	.252	.267	.260	99	.240	.249	.245	.250	.277	.264	93
RHB-HR	31	54	85	35	63	98	87	87	147	234	119	165	284	85

SAN FRANCISCO

Home park: SBC Park **Alt.:** 0 feet **Surface:** Grass

	2003 Season							2001-03 Seasons						
	Home Games			Road Games				Home Games			Road Games			
Category	**S.F.**	**Opp.**	**Total**	**S.F.**	**Opp.**	**Total**	**Index**	**S.F.**	**Opp.**	**Total**	**S.F.**	**Opp.**	**Total**	**Index**
G	72	72	144	71	71	142		219	219	438	215	215	430	
Avg	.275	.243	.259	.249	.252	.250	103	.263	.247	.255	.269	.259	.264	97
AB	2391	2487	4878	2434	2304	4738	102	7243	7572	14815	7579	7075	14654	99
R	353	259	612	309	296	605	100	1003	844	1847	1109	967	2076	87
H	658	605	1263	605	581	1186	105	1906	1873	3779	2037	1833	3870	96
2B	120	116	236	128	111	239	96	381	361	742	418	343	761	96
3B	17	13	30	9	11	20	146	62	54	116	35	39	74	155
HR	70	55	125	86	63	149	81	222	137	359	331	216	547	65
BB	278	233	511	259	244	503	99	856	709	1565	822	773	1595	97
SO	412	481	893	474	416	890	97	1283	1445	2728	1461	1295	2756	98
E	42	53	95	29	37	66	142	138	147	285	124	129	253	111
E-Infield	33	44	77	25	31	56	136	109	120	229	94	110	204	110
LHB-Avg	.264	.230	.246	.255	.263	.260	95	.254	.246	.250	.284	.274	.279	90
LHB-HR	27	15	42	35	20	55	75	98	39	137	139	81	220	61
RHB-Avg	.281	.252	.267	.245	.244	.245	109	.267	.248	.258	.262	.248	.256	101
RHB-HR	43	40	83	51	43	94	85	124	98	222	192	135	327	68

2001-2003 N.L. BALLPARK INDEX RANKINGS

RUNS PER GAME

Team	Home Games				Road Games				Index
	Games	Team	Opp.	Total	Games	Team	Opp.	Total	
Col	219	1418	1303	2721	222	911	1109	2020	137
Ari	222	1188	1011	2199	216	933	833	1766	121
Mon	200	956	944	1900	216	825	955	1780	115
Hou	222	1153	979	2132	219	1000	922	1922	109
Pit	224	981	1119	2100	222	892	1068	1960	106
Mil	222	936	1137	2073	225	968	1147	2115	99
Atl	219	1027	899	1926	212	1034	854	1888	99
Cin*	75	322	405	727	72	311	403	714	98
ChC	219	964	935	1899	219	1014	988	2002	95
Fla	215	994	890	1884	217	907	1086	1993	95
NYM	218	848	961	1809	211	904	961	1865	94
StL	220	1125	867	1992	221	1104	1027	2131	94
Phi	215	963	848	1811	219	1057	1074	2131	87
SF	219	1003	844	1847	215	1109	967	2076	87
SD	216	855	998	1853	219	1045	1218	2263	83
LA	216	812	779	1591	219	1043	949	1992	81

*Current dimensions began 2003.

HOME RUNS PER AT-BAT

Team	Home Games				Road Games				Index
	Games	Team	Opp.	Total	Games	Team	Opp.	Total	
Col	219	299	349	648	222	210	243	453	139
Cin*	75	88	110	198	72	69	84	153	125
Ari	222	254	265	519	216	228	198	426	118
Mil	222	250	299	549	225	246	251	497	111
Mon	200	180	225	405	216	181	207	388	111
Hou	222	266	254	520	219	241	221	462	111
ChC	219	250	222	472	219	261	204	465	103
Atl	219	254	190	444	212	249	194	443	99
LA	216	205	212	417	219	235	206	441	99
Phi	215	212	190	402	219	225	224	449	94
NYM	218	177	230	407	211	194	225	419	93
StL	220	245	228	473	221	269	263	532	90
Pit	224	201	227	428	222	230	236	466	89
Fla	215	199	170	369	217	216	223	439	85
SD	216	161	258	419	219	216	294	510	84
SF	219	222	137	359	215	331	216	547	65

*Current dimensions began 2003.

BATTING AVERAGE

Team	Home Games				Road Games				Index
	Games	Team	Opp.	Total	Games	Team	Opp.	Total	
Col	219	.314	.285	.299	222	.242	.271	.256	117
Ari	222	.280	.253	.266	216	.249	.242	.246	108
Hou	222	.275	.252	.264	219	.250	.258	.254	104
Pit	224	.262	.269	.266	222	.242	.270	.256	104
Mon	200	.269	.263	.266	216	.244	.270	.257	103
Atl	219	.270	.249	.259	212	.264	.253	.259	100
Mil	222	.254	.265	.260	225	.249	.275	.262	99
Cin*	75	.248	.271	.260	72	.242	.289	.265	98
Fla	215	.268	.247	.257	217	.257	.272	.264	97
StL	220	.276	.246	.261	221	.264	.272	.268	97
NYM	218	.248	.258	.253	211	.253	.269	.261	97
SF	219	.263	.247	.255	215	.269	.259	.264	97
ChC	219	.253	.237	.245	219	.255	.256	.255	96
SD	216	.251	.257	.254	219	.258	.283	.270	94
LA	216	.247	.231	.239	219	.265	.252	.259	92
Phi	215	.256	.239	.248	219	.266	.273	.269	92

*Current dimensions began 2003.

2003 STATISTICAL LEADERS

2003 AMERICAN LEAGUE LEADERS

BATTING

Batting Average

(minimum 502 PA)

Player, Team	AB	H	Avg.
B Mueller, Bos.	524	171	.326
M Ramirez, Bos.	569	185	.325
D Jeter, N.Y.	482	156	.324
V Wells, Tor.	678	215	.317
M Ordonez, Chi.	606	192	.317
G Anderson, Ana.	638	201	.315
I Suzuki, Sea.	679	212	.312
A Pierzynski, Min.	487	152	.312
A Huff, T.B.	636	198	.311
S Stewart, Tor.-Min.	573	176	.307

On-Base Percentage

(minimum 502 PA; *AB+BB+HBP+SF)

Player, Team	*PA	OB	OBP
M Ramirez, Bos.	679	290	.427
C Delgado, Tor.	705	300	.426
J Giambi, N.Y.	690	284	.412
E Martinez, Sea.	603	245	.406
J Posada, N.Y.	588	238	.405
B Mueller, Bos.	596	237	.398
T Nixon, Bos.	512	203	.396
A Rodriguez, Tex.	715	283	.396
D Mientkiewicz, Min.	572	225	.393
D Jeter, N.Y.	539	212	.393

Slugging Percentage

(minimum 502 PA)

Player, Team	AB	TB	Slg.
A Rodriguez, Tex.	607	364	.600
C Delgado, Tor.	570	338	.593
D Ortiz, Bos.	448	265	.592
M Ramirez, Bos.	569	334	.587
T Nixon, Bos.	441	255	.578
F Thomas, Chi.	546	307	.562
A Huff, T.B.	636	353	.555
V Wells, Tor.	678	373	.550
M Ordonez, Chi.	606	331	.546
G Anderson, Ana.	638	345	.541

Games

H Matsui, N.Y. 163
A Huff, T.B. 162
M Tejada, Oak. 162
4 tied with 161

Plate Appearances

V Wells, Tor. 735
A Soriano, N.Y. 734
I Suzuki, Sea. 725
N Garciaparra, Bos. 719
A Rodriguez, Tex. 715

At-Bats

A Soriano, N.Y. 682
I Suzuki, Sea. 679
V Wells, Tor. 678
M Young, Tex. 666
N Garciaparra, Bos. 658

Hits

V Wells, Tor. 215
I Suzuki, Sea. 212
M Young, Tex. 204
G Anderson, Ana. 201
3 tied with 198

Singles

I Suzuki, Sea. 162
M Young, Tex. 148
C Crawford, T.B. 145
R Baldelli, T.B. 133
V Wells, Tor. 128

Doubles

G Anderson, Ana. 49
V Wells, Tor. 49
A Huff, T.B. 47
M Ordonez, Chi. 46
2 tied with 45

Triples

C Guzman, Min. 14
N Garciaparra, Bos. 13
C Beltran, K.C. 10
4 tied with 9

Home Runs

A Rodriguez, Tex. 47
C Delgado, Tor. 42
F Thomas, Chi. 42
J Giambi, N.Y. 41
2 tied with 38

Total Bases

V Wells, Tor. 373
A Rodriguez, Tex. 364
A Soriano, N.Y. 358
A Huff, T.B. 353
2 tied with 345

Runs Scored

A Rodriguez, Tex. 124
N Garciaparra, Bos. 120
V Wells, Tor. 118
C Delgado, Tor. 117
M Ramirez, Bos. 117

Runs Batted In

C Delgado, Tor. 145
A Rodriguez, Tex. 118
B Boone, Sea. 117
V Wells, Tor. 117
G Anderson, Ana. 116

GDP

P Konerko, Chi. 28
H Matsui, N.Y. 25
M Ramirez, Bos. 22
V Wells, Tor. 21
B Williams, N.Y. 21

Sacrifice Hits

R Santiago, Det. 18
A Berroa, K.C. 13
C Guzman, Min. 12
3 tied with 10

Sacrifice Flies

J Conine, Bal. 12
S Stewart, Tor.-Min. 11
N Garciaparra, Bos. 10
R Ibanez, K.C. 10
T Walker, Bos. 10

Stolen Bases

C Crawford, T.B. 55
A Sanchez, Det. 44
C Beltran, K.C. 41
A Soriano, N.Y. 35
I Suzuki, Sea. 34

Caught Stealing

A Sanchez, Det. 18
R Baldelli, T.B. 10
C Crawford, T.B. 10
M Tucker, K.C. 10
4 tied with 9

Walks

J Giambi, N.Y. 129
C Delgado, Tor. 109
E Durazo, Oak. 100
F Thomas, Chi. 100
M Ramirez, Bos. 97

Intentional Walks

M Ramirez, Bos. 28
C Delgado, Tor. 23
A Huff, T.B. 17
D Young, Det. 16
2 tied with 12

Hit by Pitch

J Giambi, N.Y. 21
R Johnson, Tor. 20
C Delgado, Tor. 19
A Berroa, K.C. 18
J Phelps, Tor. 17

Strikeouts

J Giambi, N.Y. 140
M Cameron, Sea. 137
C Delgado, Tor. 137
A Soriano, N.Y. 130
D Young, Det. 130

2003 NATIONAL LEAGUE LEADERS

BATTING

Batting Average
(minimum 502 PA)

Player, Team	AB	H	Avg.
A Pujols, St.L.	591	212	.359
T Helton, Col.	583	209	.358
B Bonds, S.F.	390	133	.341
E Renteria, St.L.	587	194	.330
G Sheffield, Atl.	576	190	.330
J Kendall, Pit.	587	191	.325
M Giles, Atl.	551	174	.316
L Castillo, Fla.	595	187	.314
M Loretta, S.D.	589	185	.314
M Grudzielanek, Chi.	481	151	.314

On-Base Percentage
(minimum 502 PA; *AB+BB+HBP+SF)

Player, Team	*PA	OB	OBP
B Bonds, S.F.	550	291	.529
T Helton, Col.	703	322	.458
A Pujols, St.L.	685	301	.439
B Giles, Pit.-S.D.	609	260	.427
L Walker, Col.	564	238	.422
G Sheffield, Atl.	678	284	.419
L Berkman, Hou.	657	271	.412
B Abreu, Phi.	695	284	.409
C Jones, Atl.	656	264	.402
L Gonzalez, Ari.	679	273	.402

Slugging Percentage
(minimum 502 PA)

Player, Team	AB	TB	Slg.
B Bonds, S.F.	390	292	.749
A Pujols, St.L.	591	394	.667
T Helton, Col.	583	367	.630
J Edmonds, St.L.	447	276	.617
G Sheffield, Atl.	576	348	.604
J Thome, Phi.	578	331	.573
R Hidalgo, Hou.	514	294	.572
S Sosa, Chi.	517	286	.553
R Sexson, Mil.	606	332	.548
G Jenkins, Mil.	487	262	.538

Games
O Cabrera, Mon. 162
J Pierre, Fla. 162
R Sexson, Mil. 162
3 tied with 160

Plate Appearances
J Pierre, Fla. 747
R Furcal, Atl. 734
R Sexson, Mil. 718
C Biggio, Hou. 717
T Helton, Col. 703

At-Bats
J Pierre, Fla. 668
R Furcal, Atl. 664
C Biggio, Hou. 628
J Rollins, Phi. 628
O Cabrera, Mon. 626

Hits
A Pujols, St.L. 212
T Helton, Col. 209
J Pierre, Fla. 204
R Furcal, Atl. 194
E Renteria, St.L. 194

Singles
J Pierre, Fla. 168
L Castillo, Fla. 156
J Kendall, Pit. 153
M Loretta, S.D. 140
R Furcal, Atl. 134

Doubles
A Pujols, St.L. 51
M Giles, Atl. 49
S Green, L.A. 49
T Helton, Col. 49
S Rolen, St.L. 49

Triples
S Finley, Ari. 10
R Furcal, Atl. 10
K Lofton, Pit.-Chi. 8
S Podsednik, Mil. 8
4 tied with 7

Home Runs
J Thome, Phi. 47
B Bonds, S.F. 45
R Sexson, Mil. 45
J Lopez, Atl. 43
A Pujols, St.L. 43

Total Bases
A Pujols, St.L. 394
T Helton, Col. 367
G Sheffield, Atl. 348
R Sexson, Mil. 332
J Thome, Phi. 331

Runs Scored
A Pujols, St.L. 137
T Helton, Col. 135
R Furcal, Atl. 130
G Sheffield, Atl. 126
2 tied with 111

Runs Batted In
P Wilson, Col. 141
G Sheffield, Atl. 132
J Thome, Phi. 131
A Pujols, St.L. 124
R Sexson, Mil. 124

GDP
J Payton, Col. 27
J Bagwell, Hou. 25
R Clayton, Mil. 25
P Wilson, Col. 23
V Castilla, Atl. 22

Sacrifice Hits
L Castillo, Fla. 15
J Pierre, Fla. 15
J Schmidt, S.F. 15
3 tied with 12

Sacrifice Flies
A Ramirez, Pit.-Chi. 11
O Cabrera, Mon. 9
R Klesko, S.D. 9
T Perez, N.Y. 9
2 tied with 8

Stolen Bases
J Pierre, Fla. 65
S Podsednik, Mil. 43
D Roberts, L.A. 40
E Renteria, St.L. 34
K Lofton, Pit.-Chi. 30

Caught Stealing
J Pierre, Fla. 20
L Castillo, Fla. 19
D Roberts, L.A. 14
J Rollins, Phi. 12
E Young, Mil.-S.F. 12

Walks
B Bonds, S.F. 148
T Helton, Col. 111
J Thome, Phi. 111
B Abreu, Phi. 109
L Berkman, Hou. 107

Intentional Walks
B Bonds, S.F. 61
V Guerrero, Mon. 22
T Helton, Col. 21
L Gonzalez, Ari. 17
M Matheny, St.L. 16

Hit by Pitch
C Biggio, Hou. 27
J Kendall, Pit. 25
J LaRue, Cin. 20
K Ginter, Mil. 17
M Kinkade, L.A. 16

Strikeouts
J Thome, Phi. 182
J Hernandez, Co.-Chi.-Pit. 177
B Wilkerson, Mon. 155
R Sexson, Mil. 151
S Sosa, Chi. 143

AMERICAN LEAGUE PITCHING LEADERS

Earned Run Average

(minimum 162 IP)

Pitcher, Team	IP	ER	ERA
P Martinez, Bos.	186.2	46	2.22
T Hudson, Oak.	240.0	72	2.70
E Loaiza, Chi.	226.1	73	2.90
M Mulder, Oak.	186.2	65	3.13
R Halladay, Tor.	266.0	96	3.25
J Moyer, Sea.	215.0	78	3.27
B Zito, Oak.	231.2	85	3.30
M Mussina, N.Y.	214.2	81	3.40
R Franklin, Sea.	212.0	84	3.57
C Sabathia, Cle.	197.2	79	3.60

Won-Lost Percentage

(minimum 15 decisions)

Pitcher, Team	W	L	Pct.
J Santana, Min.	12	3	.800
P Martinez, Bos.	14	4	.778
R Halladay, Tor.	22	7	.759
J Moyer, Sea.	21	7	.750
A Pettitte, N.Y.	21	8	.724
D Lowe, Bos.	17	7	.708
E Loaiza, Chi.	21	9	.700
S Ponson, Bal.	14	6	.700
T Hudson, Oak.	16	7	.696
D Wells, N.Y.	15	7	.682

Opponents' Batting Average

(minimum 162 IP)

Pitcher, Team	AB	H	Avg.
P Martinez, Bos.	685	147	.215
B Zito, Oak.	849	186	.219
T Hudson, Oak.	883	197	.223
E Loaiza, Chi.	843	196	.233
V Zambrano, T.B.	697	165	.237
M Mussina, N.Y.	807	192	.238
J Pineiro, Sea.	796	192	.241
D May, K.C.	802	197	.246
J Moyer, Sea.	810	199	.246
T Wakefield, Bos.	783	193	.246

Games

T Miller, Tor. 79
J Walker, Det. 78
J Grimsley, K.C. 76
B Ryan, Bal. 76
L Hawkins, Min. 74

Wins

R Halladay, Tor. 22
E Loaiza, Chi. 21
J Moyer, Sea. 21
A Pettitte, N.Y. 21
3 tied with 17

Hits Allowed

R Halladay, Tor. 253
M Buehrle, Chi. 250
B Radke, Min. 242
D Wells, N.Y. 242
N Cornejo, Det. 236

Batters Faced

R Halladay, Tor. 1071
B Colon, Chi. 984
M Buehrle, Chi. 978
T Hudson, Oak. 967
B Zito, Oak. 957

Walks Allowed

V Zambrano, T.B. 106
B Zito, Oak. 88
J Johnson, Bal. 80
K Escobar, Tor. 78
J Pineiro, Sea. 76

Games Started

R Halladay, Tor. 36
M Buehrle, Chi. 35
J Thomson, Tex. 35
B Zito, Oak. 35
3 tied with 34

Losses

M Maroth, Det. 21
J Bonderman, Det. 19
N Cornejo, Det. 17
J Lackey, Ana. 16
2 tied with 15

Doubles Allowed

R Halladay, Tor. 54
D Wells, N.Y. 54
J Burkett, Bos. 53
J Thomson, Tex. 51
M Buehrle, Chi. 48

Innings Pitched

R Halladay, Tor. 266.0
B Colon, Chi. 242.0
T Hudson, Oak. 240.0
B Zito, Oak. 231.2
M Buehrle, Chi. 230.1

Hit Batsmen

V Zambrano, T.B. 20
6 tied with 12

Complete Games

B Colon, Chi. 9
R Halladay, Tor. 9
M Mulder, Oak. 9
3 tied with 4

Saves

K Foulke, Oak. 43
E Guardado, Min. 41
M Rivera, N.Y. 40
J Julio, Bal. 36
T Percival, Ana. 33

Triples Allowed

C Lidle, Tor. 11
M Maroth, Det. 9
B Anderson, Cle.-K.C. 8
J Benoit, Tex. 8
5 tied with 7

Runs Allowed

C Lidle, Tor. 133
M Maroth, Det. 131
J Thomson, Tex. 125
M Buehrle, Chi. 124
R Ortiz, Ana. 121

Wild Pitches

V Zambrano, T.B. 15
J Bonderman, Det. 12
F Garcia, Sea. 11
J Lackey, Ana. 11
K Lohse, Min. 10

Games Finished

K Foulke, Oak. 67
M MacDougal, K.C. 61
E Guardado, Min. 60
M Rivera, N.Y. 57
L Carter, T.B. 55

Shutouts

R Halladay, Tor. 2
T Hudson, Oak. 2
J Lackey, Ana. 2
M Mulder, Oak. 2
J Pineiro, Sea. 2

Home Runs Allowed

R Franklin, Sea. 34
M Maroth, Det. 34
J Washburn, Ana. 34
B Radke, Min. 32
3 tied with 31

Strikeouts

E Loaiza, Chi. 207
P Martinez, Bos. 206
R Halladay, Tor. 204
M Mussina, N.Y. 195
R Clemens, N.Y. 190

Balks

T Lilly, Oak. 4
K Rogers, Min. 4
4 tied with 3

NATIONAL LEAGUE PITCHING LEADERS

Earned-Run Average

(minimum 162 IP)

Pitcher, Team	IP	ER	ERA
J Schmidt, S.F.	207.2	54	2.34
K Brown, L.A.	211.0	56	2.39
M Prior, Chi.	211.1	57	2.43
B Webb, Ari.	180.2	57	2.84
C Schilling, Ari.	168.0	55	2.95
H Nomo, L.A.	218.1	75	3.09
C Zambrano, Chi.	214.0	74	3.11
K Wood, Chi.	211.0	75	3.20
L Hernandez, Mon.	233.1	83	3.20
J Vazquez, Mon.	230.2	83	3.24

Won-Lost Percentage

(minimum 15 decisions)

Pitcher, Team	W	L	Pct.
J Schmidt, S.F.	17	5	.773
R Ortiz, Atl.	21	7	.750
M Prior, Chi.	18	6	.750
J Nathan, S.F.	12	4	.750
H Ramirez, Atl.	12	4	.750
D Willis, Fla.	14	6	.700
W Williams, St.L.	18	9	.667
R Oswalt, Hou.	10	5	.667
K Rueter, S.F.	10	5	.667
M Hampton, Atl.	14	8	.636

Opponents' Batting Average

(minimum 162 IP)

Pitcher, Team	AB	H	Avg.
J Schmidt, S.F.	759	152	.200
K Wood, Chi.	749	152	.203
B Webb, Ari.	659	140	.212
R Ortiz, Atl.	793	177	.223
H Nomo, L.A.	784	175	.223
M Clement, Chi.	746	169	.227
J Vazquez, Mon.	865	198	.229
C Schilling, Ari.	626	144	.230
M Prior, Chi.	793	183	.231
K Wells, Pit.	735	171	.233

Games

P Quantrill, L.A. 89
O Villarreal, Ari. 86
R King, Atl. 80
T Martin, L.A. 80
4 tied with 78

Wins

R Ortiz, Atl. 21
M Prior, Chi. 18
W Williams, St.L. 18
J Schmidt, S.F. 17
4 tied with 16

Hits Allowed

B Tomko, St.L. 252
T Ohka, Mon. 233
B Sheets, Mil. 232
L Hernandez, Mon. 225
G Maddux, Atl. 225

Batters Faced

L Hernandez, Mon. 967
W Williams, St.L. 944
J Vazquez, Mon. 938
B Sheets, Mil. 931
K Millwood, Phi. 930

Walks Allowed

R Ortiz, Atl. 102
K Ishii, L.A. 101
K Wood, Chi. 100
H Nomo, L.A. 98
3 tied with 94

Games Started

G Maddux, Atl. 36
K Millwood, Phi. 35
5 tied with 34

Losses

J D'Amico, Pit. 16
D Graves, Cin. 15
B Lawrence, S.D. 15
T Glavine, N.Y. 14
T Redding, Hou. 14

Doubles Allowed

J Seo, N.Y. 61
D Graves, Cin. 56
C Pavano, Fla. 54
B Tomko, St.L. 54
2 tied with 52

Innings Pitched

L Hernandez, Mon. 233.1
J Vazquez, Mon. 230.2
K Millwood, Phi. 222.0
B Sheets, Mil. 220.2
W Williams, St.L. 220.2

Hit Batsmen

K Wood, Chi. 21
V Padilla, Phi. 16
M Clement, Chi. 14
G Stephenson, St.L. 13
B Webb, Ari. 13

Complete Games

L Hernandez, Mon. 8
K Millwood, Phi. 5
M Morris, St.L. 5
J Schmidt, S.F. 5
2 tied with 4

Saves

E Gagne, L.A. 55
J Smoltz, Atl. 45
B Wagner, Hou. 44
T Worrell, S.F. 38
R Biddle, Mon. 34

Triples Allowed

T Glavine, N.Y. 10
W Franklin, Mil. 8
8 tied with 7

Runs Allowed

W Franklin, Mil. 129
B Tomko, St.L. 126
B Sheets, Mil. 122
M Kinney, Mil. 121
J Jennings, Col. 115

Wild Pitches

M Clement, Chi. 13
Z Day, Mon. 13
J Foppert, S.F. 12
C Silva, Phi. 12
J Wright, S.D.-Atl. 12

Games Finished

E Gagne, L.A. 67
B Wagner, Hou. 67
B Looper, Fla. 64
T Worrell, S.F. 64
J Borowski, Chi. 59

Shutouts

K Millwood, Phi. 3
M Morris, St.L. 3
J Schmidt, S.F. 3
7 tied with 2

Home Runs Allowed

W Franklin, Mil. 36
B Tomko, St.L. 35
J Peavy, S.D. 33
D Graves, Cin. 30
G Stephenson, St.L. 30

Strikeouts

K Wood, Chi. 266
M Prior, Chi. 245
J Vazquez, Mon. 241
J Schmidt, S.F. 208
C Schilling, Ari. 194

Balks

W Franklin, Mil. 4
B Penny, Fla. 4
J Lopez, Col. 3
D Moss, S.F. 3
11 tied with 2

AMERICAN LEAGUE SPECIAL BATTING LEADERS

Scoring-Position Average†
(minimum 100 PA)

Player, Team	AB	H	Avg.
M Sweeney, K.C.	108	43	.398
C Delgado, Tor.	157	56	.357
E Martinez, Sea.	142	50	.352
R Winn, Sea.	169	59	.349
C Beltran, K.C.	150	52	.347
C Lee, Chi.	153	53	.346
B Molina, Ana.	107	37	.346
F Catalanotto, Tor.	96	33	.344
I Suzuki, Sea.	105	36	.343
M Anderson, T.B.	126	43	.341

Leadoff OBP†
(minimum 150 PA; *AB+BB+HBP+SF)

Player, Team	*PA	OB	OBP
J Hairston Jr., Bal.	203	79	.389
A Guiel, K.C.	282	109	.387
S Stewart, Tor.-Min.	641	233	.363
R Johnson, Tor.	365	129	.353
I Suzuki, Sea.	718	253	.352
T Graffanino, Chi.	165	58	.352
C Figgins, Ana.	151	53	.351
D Jimenez, Chi.	244	84	.344
A Soriano, N.Y.	675	231	.342
M Lawton, Cle.	181	61	.337

Cleanup Slugging†
(minimum 150 PA)

Player, Team	AB	TB	Slg.
C Delgado, Tor.	570	338	.593
M Ramirez, Bos.	569	334	.587
G Anderson, Ana.	456	266	.583
M Bradley, Cle.	179	101	.564
M Tejada, Oak.	305	166	.544
M Ordonez, Chi.	563	306	.544
D Young, Det.	448	240	.536
J Giambi, N.Y.	152	80	.526
E Chavez, Oak.	154	79	.513
M LeCroy, Min.	212	108	.509

Avg. vs. LHP
(minimum 125 PA)

M Bradley, Cle.	.402
M Ramirez, Bos.	.385
I Suzuki, Sea.	.359
N Garciaparra, Bos.	.357
V Wells, Tor.	.347

OBP vs. LHP
(minimum 125 PA)

M Bradley, Cle.	.500
M Ramirez, Bos.	.476
E Martinez, Sea.	.457
F Thomas, Chi.	.446
B Kielty, Min.-Tor.	.417

Slg. vs. LHP
(minimum 125 PA)

F Thomas, Chi.	.732
A Rodriguez, Tex.	.652
M Bradley, Cle.	.634
C Monroe, Det.	.631
M Ramirez, Bos.	.629

Pitches Seen

J Giambi, N.Y.	2916
J Damon, Bos.	2850
F Thomas, Chi.	2824
C Delgado, Tor.	2807
M Young, Tex.	2788

GDP/GDP Opp.†
(minimum 50 PA)

C Singleton, Oak.	0.03
I Suzuki, Sea.	0.03
T Nixon, Bos.	0.03
L Bigbie, Bal.	0.04
M Mora, Bal.	0.04

Avg. vs. RHP
(minimum 377 PA)

B Mueller, Bos.	.342
T Nixon, Bos.	.330
H Blalock, Tex.	.329
A Pierzynski, Min.	.324
R Ibanez, K.C.	.319

OBP vs. RHP
(minimum 377 PA)

C Delgado, Tor.	.439
J Giambi, N.Y.	.430
T Nixon, Bos.	.423
M Ramirez, Bos.	.411
B Mueller, Bos.	.409

Slg. vs. RHP
(minimum 377 PA)

D Ortiz, Bos.	.654
C Delgado, Tor.	.649
T Nixon, Bos.	.635
A Huff, T.B.	.596
H Blalock, Tex.	.596

Pitches per PA
(minimum 502 PA)

E Martinez, Sea.	4.32
F Thomas, Chi.	4.27
J Giambi, N.Y.	4.23
J Damon, Bos.	4.13
E Hinske, Tor.	4.08

SB Success Pct.
(minimum 20 SB attempts)

C Beltran, K.C.	91.1
M Anderson, T.B.	86.4
A Rodriguez, Tex.	85.0
C Crawford, T.B.	84.6
2 tied with	83.3

Avg. at Home
(minimum 251 PA)

N Garciaparra, Bos.	.359
M Young, Tex.	.353
L Matos, Bal.	.350
H Blalock, Tex.	.342
B Mueller, Bos.	.342

Late & Close Avg.†
(minimum 50 PA)

L Bigbie, Bal.	.426
M Ordonez, Chi.	.425
D Mientkiewicz, Min.	.397
G Anderson, Ana.	.370
S Hatteberg, Oak.	.361

AB per Home Run
(minimum 502 PA)

A Rodriguez, Tex.	12.9
F Thomas, Chi.	13.0
J Giambi, N.Y.	13.0
C Delgado, Tor.	13.6
D Ortiz, Bos.	14.5

Pct. of Pitches Taken
(minimum 1500 pitches)

S Hatteberg, Oak.	67.1
E Martinez, Sea.	65.0
N Johnson, N.Y.	64.3
J Olerud, Sea.	64.2
F Thomas, Chi.	63.4

Steals of Third

I Suzuki, Sea.	12
C Crawford, T.B.	9
A Sanchez, Det.	7
C Beltran, K.C.	6
A Berroa, K.C.	6

Avg. on Road
(minimum 251 PA)

E Martinez, Sea.	.339
G Anderson, Ana.	.339
D Jeter, N.Y.	.330
V Wells, Tor.	.329
A Pierzynski, Min.	.328

Bases Loaded Avg.
(minimum 10 PA)

M Sweeney, K.C.	.667
R Baldelli, T.B.	.600
M Bordick, Tor.	.600
C Delgado, Tor.	.588
D Jeter, N.Y.	.533

Times on Base*
(*H+BB+HBP)

C Delgado, Tor.	300
M Ramirez, Bos.	290
J Giambi, N.Y.	284
A Rodriguez, Tex.	283
V Wells, Tor.	264

Ground/Fly Ratio†
(minimum 502 PA)

J Jones, Min.	2.58
K Harvey, K.C.	2.49
D Jeter, N.Y.	2.41
H Matsui, N.Y.	2.17
L Rivas, Min.	2.16

Pct. CS by Catchers
(minimum 50 SB attempts)

T Hall, T.B.	41.3
B Molina, Ana.	40.8
M Olivo, Chi.	35.8
J Bard, Cle.	31.7
E Diaz, Tex.	31.0

†**Scoring-Position Average** denotes batting average when a runner is at second and/or third base. **Leadoff OBP** denotes OBP for a player batting in the first position of the batting order. **Cleanup Slugging** denotes slugging percentage for a player batting in the fourth position of the batting order. **Late & Close Avg.** refers to batting average when the game is in the seventh inning or later and the batting team is either leading by one run, tied, or has the potential tying run on base, at bat or on deck (a batting situation coming close to a pitcher's save situation). **Ground/Fly Ratio** denotes ground balls hit divided by fly balls hit. All batted balls except line drives and bunts are included. **GDP/GDP Opp.** denotes the ratio of times grounding into double plays per opportunities to do so (any situation with a runner on first and less than two out).

NATIONAL LEAGUE SPECIAL BATTING LEADERS

Scoring-Position Average†
(minimum 100 PA)

Player, Team	AB	H	Avg.
T Helton, Col.	133	55	.414
S Podsednik, Mil.	105	40	.381
G Sheffield, Atl.	153	58	.379
I Rodriguez, Fla.	144	54	.375
M Cabrera, Fla.	96	36	.375
A Pujols, St.L.	131	49	.374
B Abreu, Phi.	155	56	.361
J Kent, Hou.	134	48	.358
M Loretta, S.D.	136	47	.346
2 tied with			.342

Leadoff OBP†
(minimum 150 PA; *AB+BB+HBP+SF)

Player, Team	*PA	OB	OBP
M Grissom, S.F.	170	70	.412
S Podsednik, Mil.	276	110	.399
M Byrd, Phi.	356	133	.374
T Redman, Pit.	218	80	.367
C Counsell, Ari.	225	81	.360
R Durham, S.F.	370	133	.359
J Pierre, Fla.	675	242	.359
M Grudzielanek, Chi.	321	115	.358
K Lofton, Pit.-Chi.	593	210	.354
R Furcal, Atl.	729	257	.353

Cleanup Slugging†
(minimum 150 PA)

Player, Team	AB	TB	Slg.
B Bonds, S.F.	324	249	.769
R Sanders, Pit.	140	95	.679
J Thome, Phi.	220	144	.655
J Edmonds, St.L.	250	156	.624
V Guerrero, Mon.	262	159	.607
B Abreu, Phi.	165	98	.594
S Rolen, St.L.	133	77	.579
C Floyd, N.Y.	244	140	.574
L Gonzalez, Ari.	184	105	.571
R Sexson, Mil.	336	191	.568

Avg. vs. LHP
(minimum 125 PA)

Player, Team	Avg.
E Renteria, St.L.	.391
A Pujols, St.L.	.387
T Helton, Col.	.387
I Rodriguez, Fla.	.376
E Karros, Chi.	.366

OBP vs. LHP
(minimum 125 PA)

Player, Team	OBP
B Bonds, S.F.	.509
E Renteria, St.L.	.503
T Helton, Col.	.470
D Lee, Fla.	.462
I Rodriguez, Fla.	.460

Slg. vs. LHP
(minimum 125 PA)

Player, Team	Slg.
B Bonds, S.F.	.790
A Pujols, St.L.	.732
C Wilson, Pit.	.692
G Sheffield, Atl.	.675
E Renteria, St.L.	.670

Pitches Seen

B Abreu, Phi.	2994
J Thome, Phi.	2870
R Furcal, Atl.	2845
R Sexson, Mil.	2838
T Helton, Col.	2830

GDP/GDP Opp.†
(minimum 50 PA)

Player, Team	Ratio
R Furcal, Atl.	0.01
O Palmeiro, St.L.	0.02
J Reyes, N.Y.	0.02
J Thome, Phi.	0.03
J Burnitz, N.Y.-L.A.	0.05

Avg. vs. RHP
(minimum 377 PA)

Player, Team	Avg.
L Gonzalez, Ari.	.354
A Pujols, St.L.	.350
T Helton, Col.	.344
J Kendall, Pit.	.331
B Bonds, S.F.	.331

OBP vs. RHP
(minimum 377 PA)

Player, Team	OBP
B Bonds, S.F.	.537
L Gonzalez, Ari.	.459
T Helton, Col.	.452
B Abreu, Phi.	.440
A Pujols, St.L.	.434

Slg. vs. RHP
(minimum 377 PA)

Player, Team	Slg.
B Bonds, S.F.	.729
J Lopez, Atl.	.677
A Pujols, St.L.	.646
J Edmonds, St.L.	.631
J Thome, Phi.	.623

Pitches per PA
(minimum 502 PA)

Player, Team	P/PA
B Wilkerson, Mon.	4.37
B Abreu, Phi.	4.31
S Rolen, St.L.	4.15
P Burrell, Phi.	4.14
J Edmonds, St.L.	4.13

SB Success Pct.
(minimum 20 SB attempts)

Player, Team	Pct.
R Furcal, Atl.	92.6
O Cabrera, Mon.	92.3
E Renteria, St.L.	82.9
G Sheffield, Atl.	81.8
S Podsednik, Mil.	81.1

Avg. at Home
(minimum 251 PA)

Player, Team	Avg.
T Helton, Col.	.391
A Pujols, St.L.	.388
B Bonds, S.F.	.369
E Renteria, St.L.	.356
B Abreu, Phi.	.349

Late & Close Avg.†
(minimum 50 PA)

Player, Team	Avg.
C Baerga, Ari.	.407
S Podsednik, Mil.	.398
A Pujols, St.L.	.390
D Jimenez, Cin.	.377
J Kendall, Pit.	.374

AB per Home Run
(minimum 502 PA)

Player, Team	AB/HR
B Bonds, S.F.	8.7
J Edmonds, St.L.	11.5
J Thome, Phi.	12.3
S Sosa, Chi.	12.9
R Sexson, Mil.	13.5

Pct. of Pitches Taken
(minimum 1500 pitches)

Player, Team	Pct.
B Bonds, S.F.	65.9
B Abreu, Phi.	65.6
C Counsell, Ari.	64.3
D Roberts, L.A.	64.1
J Kendall, Pit.	63.0

Steals of Third

Player, Team	SB
J Pierre, Fla.	11
E Renteria, St.L.	8
R Sanders, Pit.	7
O Cabrera, Mon.	6
2 tied with	5

Avg. on Road
(minimum 251 PA)

Player, Team	Avg.
G Sheffield, Atl.	.343
L Gonzalez, Ari.	.342
M Giles, Atl.	.342
J Kendall, Pit.	.336
A Pujols, St.L.	.331

Bases Loaded Avg.
(minimum 10 PA)

Player, Team	Avg.
R Belliard, Col.	.625
C Stynes, Col.	.615
J Kent, Hou.	.600
M Lieberthal, Phi.	.563
3 tied with	.556

Times on Base*
(*H+BB+HBP)

Player, Team	TOB
T Helton, Col.	322
A Pujols, St.L.	301
B Bonds, S.F.	291
B Abreu, Phi.	284
G Sheffield, Atl.	284

Ground/Fly Ratio†
(minimum 502 PA)

Player, Team	Ratio
L Castillo, Fla.	2.81
J Pierre, Fla.	2.67
E Chavez, Mon.	2.17
R Cedeno, N.Y.	2.10
C Izturis, L.A.	1.98

Pct. CS by Catchers
(minimum 50 SB attempts)

Player, Team	Pct.
D Miller, Chi.	38.2
P Lo Duca, L.A.	34.1
I Rodriguez, Fla.	32.2
B Ausmus, Hou.	31.3
C Johnson, Col.	29.4

†**Scoring-Position Average** denotes batting average when a runner is at second and/or third base. **Leadoff OBP** denotes OBP for a player batting in the first position of the batting order. **Cleanup Slugging** denotes slugging percentage for a player batting in the fourth position of the batting order. **Late & Close Avg.** refers to batting average when the game is in the seventh inning or later and the batting team is either leading by one run, tied, or has the potential tying run on base, at bat or on deck (a batting situation coming close to a pitcher's save situation). **Ground/Fly Ratio** denotes ground balls hit divided by fly balls hit. All batted balls except line drives and bunts are included. **GDP/GDP Opp.** denotes the ratio of times grounding into double plays per opportunities to do so (any situation with a runner on first and less than two out).

AMERICAN LEAGUE SPECIAL PITCHING LEADERS

Baserunners per 9 IP
(minimum 162 IP)

Pitcher, Team	IP	BR	BR/9
P Martinez, Bos.	186.2	203	9.79
M Mussina, N.Y.	214.2	235	9.85
R Halladay, Tor.	266.0	294	9.95
T Hudson, Oak.	240.0	268	10.05
E Loaiza, Chi.	226.1	262	10.42
M Mulder, Oak.	186.2	222	10.70
D May, K.C.	210.0	252	10.80
B Zito, Oak.	231.2	280	10.88
B Colon, Chi.	242.0	295	10.97
R Clemens, N.Y.	211.2	262	11.14

Strikeouts per 9 IP
(minimum 162 IP)

Pitcher, Team	IP	SO	SO/9
P Martinez, Bos.	186.2	206	9.93
E Loaiza, Chi.	226.1	207	8.23
M Mussina, N.Y.	214.2	195	8.18
R Clemens, N.Y.	211.2	190	8.08
K Escobar, Tor.	180.1	159	7.94
A Pettitte, N.Y.	208.1	180	7.78
T Wakefield, Bos.	202.1	169	7.52
T Lilly, Oak.	178.1	147	7.42
R Halladay, Tor.	266.0	204	6.90
J Lackey, Ana.	204.0	151	6.66

Run Support per 9 IP†
(minimum 162 IP)

Pitcher, Team	IP	R	R/9
D Lowe, Bos.	203.1	164	7.26
A Pettitte, N.Y.	208.1	163	7.04
B Anderson, Cle.-K.C.	197.2	141	6.42
R Ortiz, Ana.	180.0	127	6.35
D Wells, N.Y.	213.0	150	6.34
J Garland, Chi.	191.2	129	6.06
R Halladay, Tor.	266.0	179	6.06
P Martinez, Bos.	186.2	125	6.03
J Pineiro, Sea.	211.2	141	6.00
G Meche, Sea.	186.1	124	5.99

Opposition OBP
(minimum 162 IP)

P Martinez, Bos. .272
M Mussina, N.Y. .275
R Halladay, Tor. .275
T Hudson, Oak. .280
E Loaiza, Chi. .286

Opposition SLG
(minimum 162 IP)

T Hudson, Oak. .308
P Martinez, Bos. .314
B Zito, Oak. .324
E Loaiza, Chi. .350
J Pineiro, Sea. .359

Hits per 9 IP
(minimum 162 IP)

P Martinez, Bos. 7.09
B Zito, Oak. 7.23
T Hudson, Oak. 7.39
E Loaiza, Chi. 7.79
V Zambrano, T.B. 7.88

Home Runs per 9 IP
(minimum 162 IP)

P Martinez, Bos. 0.34
T Hudson, Oak. 0.56
E Loaiza, Chi. 0.68
M Mulder, Oak. 0.72
B Zito, Oak. 0.74

Avg. vs. LHB
(minimum 125 BFP)

D Riske, Cle. .145
K Foulke, Oak. .158
D Marte, Chi. .168
F Rodriguez, Ana. .186
J Santana, Min. .191

Avg. vs. RHB
(minimum 225 BFP)

P Martinez, Bos. .179
E Loaiza, Chi. .191
V Zambrano, T.B. .206
T Hudson, Oak. .214
B Zito, Oak. .218

Avg. Allowed Sc. Pos.†
(minimum 125 BFP)

J Santana, Min. .165
R Clemens, N.Y. .186
E Loaiza, Chi. .192
P Martinez, Bos. .200
J Gonzalez, T.B. .209

OBP Leading off Inn.
(minimum 150 BFP)

R Clemens, N.Y. .243
P Martinez, Bos. .245
B Zito, Oak. .253
R Halladay, Tor. .261
M Mussina, N.Y. .264

SO/BB Ratio
(minimum 162 IP)

R Halladay, Tor. 6.38
D Wells, N.Y. 5.05
M Mussina, N.Y. 4.88
P Martinez, Bos. 4.38
B Radke, Min. 4.29

Grd/Fly Ratio Off†
(minimum 162 IP)

D Lowe, Bos. 3.92
R Halladay, Tor. 2.70
T Hudson, Oak. 2.26
M Mulder, Oak. 2.01
A Pettitte, N.Y. 1.76

Pitches per Start
(minimum 30 games started)

J Pineiro, Sea. 109.3
B Zito, Oak. 107.1
C Sabathia, Cle. 104.9
R Clemens, N.Y. 104.8
M Mussina, N.Y. 104.6

Pitches per Batter
(minimum 162 IP)

D Wells, N.Y. 3.39
R Halladay, Tor. 3.39
M Mulder, Oak. 3.51
C Lidle, Tor. 3.52
B Radke, Min. 3.52

Stolen Bases Allowed

J Johnson, Bal. 32
J Bonderman, Det. 25
K Escobar, Tor. 24
T Lilly, Oak. 24
2 tied with 23

Caught Stealing Off

M Maroth, Det. 11
M Mulder, Oak. 10
M Mussina, N.Y. 10
3 tied with 9

SB Pct. Allowed
(minimum 162 IP)

B Anderson, Cle.-K.C. 11.1
B Colon, Chi. 14.3
M Buehrle, Chi. 20.0
J Davis, Cle. 27.3
C Sabathia, Cle. 35.7

Pickoffs

M Maroth, Det. 8
M Mulder, Oak. 7
B Anderson, Cle.-K.C. 6
N Cornejo, Det. 6
R Franklin, Sea. 6

PkOf Throw/Runner†
(minimum 162 IP)

M Maroth, Det. 0.87
B Colon, Chi. 0.84
R Clemens, N.Y. 0.82
A Pettitte, N.Y. 0.76
T Lilly, Oak. 0.63

GDP Induced

B Colon, Chi. 31
N Cornejo, Det. 30
J Westbrook, Cle. 26
B Anderson, Cle.-K.C. 25
2 tied with 24

GDP per 9 IP
(minimum 162 IP)

N Cornejo, Det. 1.4
B Colon, Chi. 1.2
B Anderson, Cle.-K.C. 1.1
J Thomson, Tex. 1.0
J Davis, Cle. 1.0

Quality Starts†

T Hudson, Oak. 27
E Loaiza, Chi. 27
M Buehrle, Chi. 24
R Halladay, Tor. 23
B Zito, Oak. 23

†**Run Support per 9 IP** denotes the number of runs scored by a pitcher's team while he was still in the game times nine divided by his innings pitched. **Avg. Allowed Sc. Pos.** denotes batting average allowed when a runner is at second and/or third base. **Grd/Fly Ratio Off** denotes ground balls allowed divided by fly balls allowed. All batted balls except line drives and bunts are included. **PkOf Throw/Runner** denotes the number of pickoff throws made by a pitcher divided by the number of runners on first base. **Quality Starts** denote the number of outings in which a starting pitcher works at least six innings and allows three or fewer earned runs.

NATIONAL LEAGUE SPECIAL PITCHING LEADERS

Baserunners per 9 IP

(minimum 162 IP)

Pitcher, Team	IP	BR	BR/9
J Schmidt, S.F.	207.2	203	8.80
C Schilling, Ari.	168.0	179	9.59
J Vazquez, Mon.	230.2	259	10.11
M Prior, Chi.	211.1	242	10.31
K Brown, L.A.	211.0	245	10.45
M Morris, St.L.	172.1	207	10.81
G Maddux, Atl.	218.1	266	10.96
B Webb, Ari.	180.2	221	11.01
M Redman, Fla.	190.2	238	11.23
L Hernandez, Mon.	233.1	292	11.26

Strikeouts per 9 IP

(minimum 162 IP)

Pitcher, Team	IP	SO	SO/9
K Wood, Chi.	211.0	266	11.35
M Prior, Chi.	211.1	245	10.43
C Schilling, Ari.	168.0	194	10.39
J Vazquez, Mon.	230.2	241	9.40
J Schmidt, S.F.	207.2	208	9.01
B Webb, Ari.	180.2	172	8.57
R Wolf, Phi.	200.0	177	7.97
K Brown, L.A.	211.0	185	7.89
W Miller, Hou	187.1	161	7.73
M Clement, Chi.	201.2	171	7.63

Run Support per 9 IP†

(minimum 162 IP)

Pitcher, Team	IP	R	R/9
W Williams, St.L.	220.2	171	6.97
B Tomko, St.L.	202.2	152	6.75
R Wolf, Phi.	200.0	149	6.70
R Ortiz, Atl.	212.1	153	6.49
S Reynolds, Atl.	167.1	120	6.45
D Oliver, Col.	180.1	123	6.14
B Penny, Fla.	196.1	132	6.05
H Ramirez, Atl.	182.1	121	5.97
M Hampton, Atl.	190.0	118	5.59
W Miller, Hou	187.1	114	5.48

Opposition OBP

(minimum 162 IP)

J Schmidt, S.F.	.250
C Schilling, Ari.	.270
J Vazquez, Mon.	.278
M Prior, Chi.	.283
K Brown, L.A.	.290

Avg. vs. LHB

(minimum 125 BFP)

Pitcher, Team	Avg.
E Gagne, L.A.	.130
O Dotel, Hou.	.152
M Hampton, Atl.	.164
G Mota, L.A.	.181
K Ishii, L.A.	.192

SO/BB Ratio

(minimum 162 IP)

Pitcher, Team	Ratio
C Schilling, Ari.	6.06
M Prior, Chi.	4.90
J Schmidt, S.F.	4.52
J Vazquez, Mon.	4.23
G Maddux, Atl.	3.76

Stolen Bases Allowed

Pitcher, Team	SB
K Millwood, Phi.	41
G Maddux, Atl.	26
O Perez, L.A.	25
M Kinney, Mil.	24
R Ortiz, Atl.	22

PkOf Throw/Runner†

(minimum 162 IP)

Pitcher, Team	Ratio
S Trachsel, N.Y.	0.99
G Maddux, Atl.	0.85
J Seo, N.Y.	0.82
A Leiter, N.Y.	0.80
D Oliver, Col.	0.64

Opposition SLG

(minimum 162 IP)

Pitcher, Team	SLG
B Webb, Ari.	.307
J Schmidt, S.F.	.316
K Brown, L.A.	.318
C Zambrano, Chi.	.331
K Wood, Chi.	.344

Avg. vs. RHB

(minimum 225 BFP)

Pitcher, Team	Avg.
B Wagner, Hou.	.154
B Webb, Ari.	.167
R Ortiz, Atl.	.187
O Villarreal, Ari.	.204
J Schmidt, S.F.	.204

Grd/Fly Ratio Off†

(minimum 162 IP)

Pitcher, Team	Ratio
B Webb, Ari.	3.44
K Brown, L.A.	3.37
C Zambrano, Chi.	2.28
M Clement, Chi.	2.04
M Batista, Ari.	2.04

Caught Stealing Off

Pitcher, Team	CS
H Nomo, L.A.	14
K Ishii, L.A.	13
A Leiter, N.Y.	11
3 tied with	9

GDP Induced

Pitcher, Team	GDP
H Ramirez, Atl.	29
S Estes, Chi.	27
B Penny, Fla.	26
K Rueter, S.F.	24
C Zambrano, Chi.	24

Hits per 9 IP

(minimum 162 IP)

Pitcher, Team	H/9
K Wood, Chi.	6.48
J Schmidt, S.F.	6.59
B Webb, Ari.	6.97
H Nomo, L.A.	7.21
R Ortiz, Atl.	7.50

Avg. Allowed Sc. Pos.†

(minimum 125 BFP)

Pitcher, Team	Avg.
K Wood, Chi.	.157
K Ishii, L.A.	.166
K Wells, Pit.	.169
K Brown, L.A.	.178
M Prior, Chi.	.183

Pitches per Start

(minimum 30 games started)

Pitcher, Team	Pitches
M Prior, Chi.	113.4
K Wood, Chi.	110.8
W Williams, St.L.	110.2
J Vazquez, Mon.	110.0
L Hernandez, Mon.	108.5

SB Pct. Allowed

(minimum 162 IP)

Pitcher, Team	Pct.
T Ohka, Mon.	20.0
M Hampton, Atl.	33.3
J Seo, N.Y.	36.4
C Zambrano, Chi.	37.5
K Wood, Chi.	38.5

GDP per 9 IP

(minimum 162 IP)

Pitcher, Team	GDP/9
H Ramirez, Atl.	1.4
B Penny, Fla.	1.2
T Glavine, N.Y.	1.1
D Oliver, Col.	1.1
J Jennings, Col.	1.1

Home Runs per 9 IP

(minimum 162 IP)

Pitcher, Team	HR/9
C Zambrano, Chi.	0.38
K Brown, L.A.	0.47
B Webb, Ari.	0.60
M Batista, Ari.	0.61
J Schmidt, S.F.	0.61

OBP Leading off Inn.

(minimum 150 BFP)

J Seo, N.Y.	.227
D Willis, Fla.	.251
C Schilling, Ari.	.254
J Schmidt, S.F.	.258
W Williams, St.L.	.272

Pitches per Batter

(minimum 162 IP)

Pitcher, Team	Pitches
G Maddux, Atl.	3.26
D Graves, Cin.	3.35
T Ohka, Mon.	3.44
J D'Amico, Pit.	3.47
D Oliver, Col.	3.50

Pickoffs

Pitcher, Team	PK
J Beimel, Pit.	7
O Perez, L.A.	7
J Robertson, Hou.	7
3 tied with	5

Quality Starts†

Pitcher, Team	QS
K Brown, L.A.	25
K Millwood, Phi.	23
M Prior, Chi.	23
4 tied with	22

†**Run Support per 9 IP** denotes the number of runs scored by a pitcher's team while he was still in the game times nine divided by his innings pitched. **Avg. Allowed Sc. Pos.** denotes batting average allowed when a runner is at second and/or third base. **Grd/Fly Ratio Off** denotes ground balls allowed divided by fly balls allowed. All batted balls except line drives and bunts are included. **PkOf Throw/Runner** denotes the number of pickoff throws made by a pitcher divided by the number of runners on first base. **Quality Starts** denote the number of outings in which a starting pitcher works at least six innings and allows three or fewer earned runs.

AMERICAN LEAGUE RELIEF PITCHING LEADERS

Saves

Pitcher, Team	Saves
K Foulke, Oak.	43
E Guardado, Min.	41
M Rivera, N.Y.	40
J Julio, Bal.	36
T Percival, Ana.	33
M MacDougal, K.C.	27
L Carter, T.B.	26
U Urbina, Tex.	26
D Baez, Cle.	25
2 tied with	16

Save Percentage

(minimum 20 save opportunities)

Pitcher, Team	Opp.	Sv.	Pct.
E Guardado, Min.	45	41	91.1
K Foulke, Oak.	48	43	89.6
T Percival, Ana.	37	33	89.2
M Rivera, N.Y.	46	40	87.0
U Urbina, Tex.	30	26	86.7
J Julio, Bal.	44	36	81.8
L Carter, T.B.	33	26	78.8
M MacDougal, K.C.	35	27	77.1
D Baez, Cle.	35	25	71.4
F Cordero, Tex.	25	15	60.0

Relief ERA

(minimum 50 relief IP)

Pitcher, Team	IP	ER	ERA
S Hasegawa, Sea.	73.0	12	1.48
R Soriano, Sea.	53.0	9	1.53
B Donnelly, Ana.	74.0	13	1.58
D Marte, Chi.	79.2	14	1.58
M Rivera, N.Y.	70.2	13	1.66
S Shields, Ana.	69.2	13	1.68
L Hawkins, Min.	77.1	16	1.86
K Foulke, Oak.	86.2	20	2.08
D Riske, Cle.	74.2	19	2.29
B Weber, Ana.	80.1	24	2.69

Relief Wins

K Foulke, Oak.	9
L Hawkins, Min.	9
R Rincon, Oak.	8
F Rodriguez, Ana.	8
3 tied with	7

Relief Losses

D Baez, Cle.	9
F Cordero, Tex.	8
T Harper, T.B.	8
J Colome, T.B.	7
J Julio, Bal.	7

Holds†

B Donnelly, Ana.	29
J Grimsley, K.C.	28
L Hawkins, Min.	28
C Bradford, Oak.	23
J Romero, Min.	22

Blown Saves†

D Baez, Cle.	10
F Cordero, Tex.	10
J Julio, Bal.	8
M MacDougal, K.C.	8
3 tied with	7

Relief Games

T Miller, Tor.	79
J Walker, Det.	78
J Grimsley, K.C.	76
B Ryan, Bal.	76
L Hawkins, Min.	74

Games Finished

K Foulke, Oak.	67
M MacDougal, K.C.	61
E Guardado, Min.	60
M Rivera, N.Y.	57
L Carter, T.B.	55

Relief Innings

S Sparks, Det.-Oak.	107.0
T Harper, T.B.	93.0
K Foulke, Oak.	86.2
F Rodriguez, Ana.	86.0
2 tied with	85.2

Pct. Inherited Scored†

(minimum 30 inherited runners)

B Groom, Bal.	14.6
C Bradford, Oak.	16.4
S Hasegawa, Sea.	16.7
T Gordon, Chi.	18.9
R Rincon, Oak.	20.0

Opposition Avg.

(minimum 50 relief IP)

R Soriano, Sea.	.162
F Rodriguez, Ana.	.172
K Foulke, Oak.	.184
D Marte, Chi.	.185
D Riske, Cle.	.196

Opposition OBP

(minimum 50 relief IP)

R Soriano, Sea.	.224
E Guardado, Min.	.249
K Foulke, Oak.	.249
J Mateo, Sea.	.259
D Riske, Cle.	.260

Opposition SLG

(minimum 50 relief IP)

R Soriano, Sea.	.238
D Marte, Chi.	.266
B Ryan, Bal.	.286
B Donnelly, Ana.	.287
T Gordon, Chi.	.291

First Batter Avg.

(minimum 40 first BFP)

J Kershner, Tor.	.114
T Gordon, Chi.	.133
E Guardado, Min.	.136
R Soriano, Sea.	.139
S Sparks, Det.-Oak.	.143

Avg. vs. LHB

(minimum 50 relief IP)

D Riske, Cle.	.145
K Foulke, Oak.	.158
D Marte, Chi.	.168
E Guardado, Min.	.175
J Kershner, Tor.	.178

Avg. vs. RHB

(minimum 50 relief IP)

R Soriano, Sea.	.132
F Rodriguez, Ana.	.156
D Baez, Cle.	.165
J Boyd, Cle.	.176
A Lopez, Tor.	.186

Avg., Runners On†

(minimum 50 relief IP)

S Hasegawa, Sea.	.134
K Foulke, Oak.	.138
A Lopez, Tor.	.162
R Soriano, Sea.	.164
B Donnelly, Ana.	.176

Avg., Scoring Pos.†

(minimum 50 relief IP)

R Soriano, Sea.	.111
M Roney, Det.	.114
B Donnelly, Ana.	.134
T Miller, Tor.	.150
A Lopez, Tor.	.164

Easy Saves†

K Foulke, Oak.	28
E Guardado, Min.	28
T Percival, Ana.	24
M Rivera, N.Y.	23
2 tied with	19

Regular Saves†

J Julio, Bal.	16
E Guardado, Min.	13
M Rivera, N.Y.	12
K Foulke, Oak.	11
4 tied with	9

Tough Saves†

M Rivera, N.Y.	5
K Foulke, Oak.	4
D Marte, Chi.	4
7 tied with	2

Pitches per Batter

(minimum 50 relief IP)

C Hammond, N.Y.	3.47
J Kershner, Tor.	3.50
K Wilson, K.C.	3.50
M Timlin, Bos.	3.51
B Lyon, Bos.	3.53

†Holds denote the number of times a relief pitcher enters the game in a save situation, records at least one out and leaves the game never having relinquished the lead. A pitcher cannot finish the game and receive credit for a hold, nor can he earn a hold and a save in the same game. **Blown Saves** denote the number of times a relief pitcher enters a game in a save situation and allows the tying or go-ahead run to score. **Pct. Inherited Scored** denotes the percent of interited runners (those on base when a reliever enters the game) that score. **Avg., Runners On** denotes batting average allowed when runners are on base. **Avg., Scoring Pos.** denotes batting average allowed when a runner is at second and/or third base. **Easy Saves** denote saves in which the first batter faced doesn't represent the tying run and the reliever pitches one inning or less. **Regular Saves** denote those saves that are not Easy Saves or Tough Saves. **Tough Saves** denote saves which occur after the reliever enters with the tying run anywhere on base.

NATIONAL LEAGUE RELIEF PITCHING LEADERS

Saves

Pitcher, Team	Saves
E Gagne, L.A.	55
J Smoltz, Atl.	45
B Wagner, Hou.	44
T Worrell, S.F.	38
R Biddle, Mon.	34
J Borowski, Chi.	33
M Mantei, Ari.	29
B Looper, Fla.	28
M Williams, Pit.-Phi.	28
J Mesa, Phi.	24

Save Percentage

(minimum 20 save opportunities)

Pitcher, Team	Opp.	Sv.	Pct.
R Beck, S.D.	20	20	100.0
E Gagne, L.A.	55	55	100.0
B Wagner, Hou.	47	44	93.6
J Smoltz, Atl.	49	45	91.8
D Kolb, Mil.	23	21	91.3
M Mantei, Ari.	32	29	90.6
J Borowski, Chi.	37	33	89.2
J Isringhausen, St.L.	25	22	88.0
J Jimenez, Col.	23	20	87.0
J Mesa, Phi.	28	24	85.7

Relief ERA

(minimum 50 relief IP)

Pitcher, Team	IP	ER	ERA
J Smoltz, Atl.	64.1	8	1.12
E Gagne, L.A.	82.1	11	1.20
R Cormier, Phi.	84.2	16	1.70
P Quantrill, L.A.	77.1	15	1.75
B Wagner, Hou.	86.0	17	1.78
K Mercker, Cin.-Atl.	55.1	12	1.95
G Mota, L.A.	105.0	23	1.97
J Valverde, Ari.	50.1	12	2.15
O Villarreal, Ari.	95.0	26	2.46
O Dotel, Hou.	87.0	24	2.48

Relief Wins

J Nathan, S.F.	12
L Ayala, Mon.	10
O Villarreal, Ari.	10
4 tied with	8

Relief Losses

R Biddle, Mon.	8
M DeJean, Mil.-St.L.	8
5 tied with	7

Holds†

O Dotel, Hou.	33
B Lidge, Hou.	28
T Martin, L.A.	28
P Quantrill, L.A.	28
D Weathers, N.Y.	26

Blown Saves†

M DeJean, Mil.-St.L.	8
A Benitez, N.Y.	7
R Biddle, Mon.	7
M Williams, Pit.-Phi.	7
T Worrell, S.F.	7

Relief Games

P Quantrill, L.A.	89
O Villarreal, Ari.	85
R King, Atl.	80
T Martin, L.A.	80
4 tied with	78

Games Finished

E Gagne, L.A.	67
B Wagner, Hou.	67
B Looper, Fla.	64
T Worrell, S.F.	64
J Borowski, Chi.	59

Relief Innings

G Mota, L.A.	105.0
O Villarreal, Ari.	95.0
D Weathers, N.Y.	87.2
O Dotel, Hou.	87.0
B Wagner, Hou.	86.0

Pct. Inherited Scored†

(minimum 30 inherited runners)

T Martin, L.A.	11.9
R Cormier, Phi.	13.9
L Ayala, Mon.	16.7
J Lopez, Col.	18.6
S Reed, Col.	20.5

Opposition Avg.

(minimum 50 relief IP)

E Gagne, L.A.	.133
J Valverde, Ari.	.137
B Wagner, Hou.	.169
O Dotel, Hou.	.172
R Cormier, Phi.	.182

Opposition OBP

(minimum 50 relief IP)

E Gagne, L.A.	.199
J Smoltz, Atl.	.230
B Wagner, Hou.	.234
R Cormier, Phi.	.248
O Dotel, Hou.	.253

Opposition SLG

(minimum 50 relief IP)

E Gagne, L.A.	.176
J Valverde, Ari.	.234
B Wagner, Hou.	.266
R Cormier, Phi.	.269
J Smoltz, Atl.	.281

First Batter Avg.

(minimum 40 first BFP)

T Martin, L.A.	.100
J Valverde, Ari.	.114
L Hackman, S.D.	.143
R Cormier, Phi.	.145
J Riedling, Cin.	.163

Avg. vs. LHB

(minimum 50 relief IP)

R Cormier, Phi.	.119
E Gagne, L.A.	.130
O Dotel, Hou.	.152
M Mantei, Ari.	.155
J Valverde, Ari.	.169

Avg. vs. RHB

(minimum 50 relief IP)

J Valverde, Ari.	.112
E Gagne, L.A.	.135
J Nathan, S.F.	.136
B Wagner, Hou.	.154
S Reed, Col.	.165

Avg., Runners On†

(minimum 50 relief IP)

E Gagne, L.A.	.121
M Mantei, Ari.	.132
K Mercker, Cin.-Atl.	.157
B Wagner, Hou.	.167
J Smoltz, Atl.	.169

Avg., Scoring Pos.†

(minimum 50 relief IP)

M Mantei, Ari.	.088
B Wagner, Hou.	.094
E Gagne, L.A.	.118
P Shuey, L.A.	.149
J Smoltz, Atl.	.152

Easy Saves†

E Gagne, L.A.	28
J Smoltz, Atl	27
B Wagner, Hou.	24
T Worrell, S.F.	22
R Biddle, Mon.	21

Regular Saves†

E Gagne, L.A.	25
B Wagner, Hou.	16
J Borowski, Chi.	15
J Smoltz, Atl	15
T Worrell, S.F.	14

Tough Saves†

J Tavarez, Pit.	4
B Wagner, Hou.	4
J Smoltz, Atl	3
7 tied with	2

Pitches per Batter

(minimum 50 relief IP)

L Estrella, Mil.	3.38
F Heredia, Cin.	3.39
D Wheeler, N.Y.	3.41
J Tavarez, Pit.	3.42
B Kieschnick, Mil.	3.43

†**Holds** denote the number of times a relief pitcher enters the game in a save situation, records at least one out and leaves the game never having relinquished the lead. A pitcher cannot finish the game and receive credit for a hold, nor can he earn a hold and a save in the same game. **Blown Saves** denote the number of times a relief pitcher enters a game in a save situation and allows the tying or go-ahead run to score. **Pct. Inherited Scored** denotes the percent of interited runners (those on base when a reliever enters the game) that score. **Avg., Runners On** denotes batting average allowed when runners are on base. **Avg., Scoring Pos.** denotes batting average allowed when a runner is at second and/or third base. **Easy Saves** denote saves in which the first batter faced doesn't represent the tying run and the reliever pitches one inning or less. **Regular Saves** denote those saves that are not Easy Saves or Tough Saves. **Tough Saves** denote saves which occur after the reliever enters with the tying run anywhere on base.

2003 ACTIVE CAREER LEADERS

BATTING

Batting Average

(minimum 1000 PA)

Rk.	Player	AB	H	Avg.
1.	Todd Helton	3504	1182	.337
2.	Albert Pujols	1771	591	.334
3.	Ichiro Suzuki	2018	662	.328
4.	Nomar Garciaparra	3812	1231	.323
5.	Vladimir Guerrero	3763	1215	.323
6.	Mike Piazza	5350	1708	.319
7.	Derek Jeter	4870	1546	.317
8.	Manny Ramirez	5004	1585	.317
9.	Edgar Martinez	6727	2119	.315
10.	Larry Walker	6334	1992	.314
11.	Frank Thomas	6611	2048	.310
12.	Chipper Jones	5144	1588	.309
13.	Alex Rodriguez	4989	1535	.308
14.	Magglio Ordonez	3605	1108	.307
15.	Juan Pierre	2077	638	.307
16.	Mike Sweeney	3306	1014	.307
17.	Bobby Abreu	3566	1091	.306
18.	Jose Vidro	3073	940	.306
19.	Bernie Williams	6403	1950	.305
20.	Jason Kendall	4032	1226	.304
21.	Ivan Rodriguez	6167	1875	.304
22.	Mark Grace	8065	2445	.303
23.	Shannon Stewart	3720	1127	.303
24.	Jason Giambi	4493	1358	.302
25.	Brian Giles	3502	1056	.302

On-Base Percentage

(minimum 1000 PA; *AB+BB+HBP+SF)

Rk.	Player	*PA	OB	OBP
1.	Barry Bonds	10963	4749	.433
2.	Frank Thomas	8167	3499	.428
3.	Todd Helton	4113	1750	.425
4.	Edgar Martinez	8113	3431	.423
5.	Brian Giles	4271	1783	.417
6.	Jason Giambi	5460	2266	.415
7.	Manny Ramirez	5910	2438	.413
8.	Albert Pujols	2035	839	.412
9.	Jim Thome	6420	2640	.411
10.	Jeff Bagwell	8626	3543	.411
11.	Bobby Abreu	4245	1737	.409
12.	Lance Berkman	2560	1043	.407
13.	Chipper Jones	6064	2451	.404
14.	John Olerud	8360	3357	.402
15.	Rickey Henderson	13316	5343	.401
16.	Gary Sheffield	8026	3218	.401
17.	Larry Walker	7340	2936	.400
18.	Carlos Delgado	5467	2157	.395
19.	Bernie Williams	7385	2882	.390
20.	Vladimir Guerrero	4220	1646	.390
21.	Derek Jeter	5489	2137	.389
22.	Tim Salmon	6589	2560	.389
23.	Mike Piazza	6007	2328	.388
24.	Jason Kendall	4616	1778	.385
25.	Mark Grace	9273	3554	.383

Slugging Percentage

(minimum 1000 PA)

Rk.	Player	AB	TB	SLG
1.	Todd Helton	3504	2158	.616
2.	Albert Pujols	1771	1085	.613
3.	Barry Bonds	8725	5253	.602
4.	Manny Ramirez	5004	2991	.598
5.	Vladimir Guerrero	3763	2211	.588
6.	Alex Rodriguez	4989	2899	.581
7.	Mike Piazza	5350	3058	.572
8.	Jim Thome	5218	2964	.568
9.	Frank Thomas	6611	3752	.568
10.	Larry Walker	6334	3594	.567
11.	Juan Gonzalez	6428	3620	.563
12.	Brian Giles	3502	1970	.563
13.	Lance Berkman	2139	1203	.562
14.	Ken Griffey Jr.	7079	3977	.562
15.	Carlos Delgado	4550	2541	.558
16.	Nomar Garciaparra	3812	2116	.555
17.	Jason Giambi	4493	2468	.549
18.	Jeff Bagwell	7125	3909	.549
19.	Sammy Sosa	7543	4121	.546
20.	Chipper Jones	5144	2785	.541
21.	Jim Edmonds	4592	2447	.533
22.	Gary Sheffield	6729	3548	.527
23.	Magglio Ordonez	3605	1900	.527
24.	Richie Sexson	2975	1566	.526
25.	Edgar Martinez	6727	3531	.525

Hits

Rickey Henderson	3055
Rafael Palmeiro	2780
Roberto Alomar	2679
Barry Bonds	2595
Fred McGriff	2477
Craig Biggio	2461
Mark Grace	2445
Julio Franco	2358
Andres Galarraga	2330
Barry Larkin	2240
Steve Finley	2166
B.J. Surhoff	2142
Jeff Bagwell	2137
Edgar Martinez	2119
Ellis Burks	2101
Sammy Sosa	2099
Ken Griffey Jr.	2080
John Olerud	2079
Marquis Grissom	2065
Frank Thomas	2048

Home Runs

Player	Home Runs
Barry Bonds	658
Sammy Sosa	539
Rafael Palmeiro	528
Fred McGriff	491
Ken Griffey Jr.	481
Juan Gonzalez	429
Jeff Bagwell	419
Frank Thomas	418
Andres Galarraga	398
Jim Thome	381
Gary Sheffield	379
Matt Williams	378
Mike Piazza	358
Greg Vaughn	355
Ellis Burks	351
Larry Walker	351
Manny Ramirez	347
Alex Rodriguez	345
Mo Vaughn	328
Ron Gant	321

Runs Batted In

Player	Runs Batted In
Barry Bonds	1742
Rafael Palmeiro	1687
Fred McGriff	1543
Sammy Sosa	1450
Andres Galarraga	1423
Jeff Bagwell	1421
Frank Thomas	1390
Juan Gonzalez	1387
Ken Griffey Jr.	1384
Gary Sheffield	1232
Ruben Sierra	1224
Matt Williams	1218
Larry Walker	1212
Ellis Burks	1205
Edgar Martinez	1198
Robin Ventura	1154
Mark Grace	1146
Tino Martinez	1146
John Olerud	1145
Manny Ramirez	1140

Stolen Bases

Player	Stolen Bases
Rickey Henderson	1406
Kenny Lofton	538
Barry Bonds	500
Roberto Alomar	474
Eric Young	436
Marquis Grissom	425
Craig Biggio	389
Barry Larkin	377
Tom Goodwin	364
Tony Womack	309
Omar Vizquel	299
Steve Finley	296
Mark McLemore	272
Julio Franco	265
Reggie Sanders	262
Brian L. Hunter	260
Luis Castillo	250
Johnny Damon	244
Ron Gant	243
Sammy Sosa	233

Seasons Played

Rickey Henderson	25
Jesse Orosco	24
Roger Clemens	20
Julio Franco	19
John Franco	19
Fred McGriff	18
Mark McLemore	18
Andres Galarraga	18
Dan Plesac	18
Rafael Palmeiro	18

Doubles

Rafael Palmeiro	543
Barry Bonds	536
Craig Biggio	517
Mark Grace	511
Rickey Henderson	510
Roberto Alomar	498
Edgar Martinez	491
John Olerud	473
Jeff Bagwell	455
Andres Galarraga	444

Total Bases

Barry Bonds	5253
Rafael Palmeiro	4983
Rickey Henderson	4588
Fred McGriff	4436
Sammy Sosa	4121
Andres Galarraga	4032
Ken Griffey Jr.	3977
Roberto Alomar	3951
Jeff Bagwell	3909
Frank Thomas	3752

Strikeouts

Andres Galarraga	2000
Sammy Sosa	1977
Fred McGriff	1863
Rickey Henderson	1694
Jim Thome	1559
Greg Vaughn	1513
Jay Bell	1443
Mo Vaughn	1429
Ron Gant	1411
Jeff Bagwell	1406

SB Success Pct.
(minimum 100 SB attempts)

Carlos Beltran	88.2
Pokey Reese	85.2
Tony Womack	83.1
Barry Larkin	83.0
Doug Glanville	81.6
Brian L. Hunter	81.0
Roberto Alomar	80.9
Rickey Henderson	80.8
Aaron Boone	80.5
Alex Rodriguez	79.4

Games

Rickey Henderson	3081
Barry Bonds	2569
Rafael Palmeiro	2567
Fred McGriff	2433
Roberto Alomar	2323
Craig Biggio	2253
Andres Galarraga	2250
Mark Grace	2245
Julio Franco	2144
Steve Finley	2127

Triples

Steve Finley	108
Kenny Lofton	86
Roberto Alomar	78
Barry Bonds	74
Barry Larkin	73
Johnny Damon	68
Jay Bell	67
Rickey Henderson	66
Ellis Burks	63
Ray Durham	62

Walks

Rickey Henderson	2190
Barry Bonds	2070
Frank Thomas	1386
Fred McGriff	1296
Jeff Bagwell	1287
Edgar Martinez	1225
Rafael Palmeiro	1224
John Olerud	1198
Gary Sheffield	1110
Jim Thome	1108

SO/BB Ratio
(minimum 1000 AB)

Mark Grace	.597
Barry Bonds	.670
Eric Young	.692
Brian Giles	.702
Gary Sheffield	.717
Rickey Henderson	.774
Orlando Palmeiro	.776
Frank Thomas	.777
John Olerud	.780
Matt Lawton	.840

Caught Stealing

Rickey Henderson	335
Eric Young	151
Kenny Lofton	142
Barry Bonds	140
Omar Vizquel	123
Tom Goodwin	118
Mark McLemore	117
Craig Biggio	116
Marquis Grissom	114
Roberto Alomar	112

At-Bats

Rickey Henderson	10961
Rafael Palmeiro	9553
Roberto Alomar	8902
Barry Bonds	8725
Fred McGriff	8685
Craig Biggio	8588
Andres Galarraga	8086
Mark Grace	8065
Julio Franco	7869
Steve Finley	7843

AB per HR
(minimum 1000 AB)

Barry Bonds	13.3
Jim Thome	13.7
Sammy Sosa	14.0
Manny Ramirez	14.4
Alex Rodriguez	14.5
Ken Griffey Jr.	14.7
Mike Piazza	14.9
Carlos Delgado	15.0
Juan Gonzalez	15.0
Albert Pujols	15.5

Intentional Walks

Barry Bonds	484
Ken Griffey Jr.	204
Fred McGriff	169
Frank Thomas	159
Rafael Palmeiro	153
John Olerud	151
Jeff Bagwell	148
Sammy Sosa	144
Mo Vaughn	144
Robin Ventura	131

Sacrifice Hits

Tom Glavine	178
Omar Vizquel	165
Jay Bell	159
Roberto Alomar	145
Greg Maddux	143
Mark McLemore	103
Curt Schilling	102
Jose Vizcaino	99
Mike Bordick	97
Shane Reynolds	97

GDP

Julio Franco	279
Fred McGriff	225
John Olerud	215
Todd Zeile	210
Rafael Palmeiro	208
Jeff Bagwell	207
Ivan Rodriguez	205
Roberto Alomar	202
Benito Santiago	194
Mark Grace	192

Runs Scored

Rickey Henderson	2295
Barry Bonds	1941
Rafael Palmeiro	1548
Craig Biggio	1503
Roberto Alomar	1490
Jeff Bagwell	1402
Fred McGriff	1342
Sammy Sosa	1314
Barry Larkin	1274
Ken Griffey Jr.	1271

AB per RBI
(minimum 1000 AB)

Manny Ramirez	4.4
Juan Gonzalez	4.6
Albert Pujols	4.6
Todd Helton	4.7
Carlos Delgado	4.7
Frank Thomas	4.8
Mike Piazza	4.8
Jim Thome	4.9
Jason Giambi	5.0
Lance Berkman	5.0

Hit by Pitch

Craig Biggio	241
Andres Galarraga	177
Jason Kendall	158
Fernando Vina	152
Larry Walker	121
Jeff Bagwell	119
Carlos Delgado	109
Mo Vaughn	108
Damion Easley	103
Gary Sheffield	99

Sacrifice Flies

Ruben Sierra	111
Frank Thomas	105
Rafael Palmeiro	102
Mark Grace	99
B.J. Surhoff	99
Roberto Alomar	96
Jeff Bagwell	95
John Olerud	88
Gary Sheffield	88
Barry Bonds	84

AB per GDP
(minimum 1000 AB)

Greg Maddux	180.1
Ichiro Suzuki	144.1
Rafael Furcal	129.9
Alex Sanchez	113.2
Joe McEwing	111.0
Russell Branyan	110.4
Tom Glavine	107.7
Johnny Damon	100.7
Tony Womack	100.3
Brad Wilkerson	94.0

PITCHING

Wins

Roger Clemens	310
Greg Maddux	289
Tom Glavine	251
Randy Johnson	230
David Wells	200
Mike Mussina	199
Kevin Brown	197
David Cone	194
Jamie Moyer	185
Kevin Appier	169

Losses

Greg Maddux	163
Roger Clemens	160
Tom Glavine	157
Kevin Appier	136
John Burkett	136
Jamie Moyer	132
Kevin Brown	131
Terry Mulholland	131
David Wells	128
David Cone	126

Won-Lost Percentage

(minimum 100 decisions)

Pedro Martinez	.712
Tim Hudson	.708
Randy Johnson	.669
Roger Clemens	.660
Andy Pettitte	.656
Mike Mussina	.644
Greg Maddux	.639
Russ Ortiz	.633
Matt Morris	.632
Freddy Garcia	.626

ERA

(minimum 750 IP)

Pedro Martinez	2.58
John Franco	2.74
Greg Maddux	2.89
Randy Johnson	3.10
Barry Zito	3.12
Jesse Orosco	3.16
Kevin Brown	3.16
Roger Clemens	3.19
Tim Hudson	3.26
Matt Morris	3.28

Games

Jesse Orosco	1252
Dan Plesac	1064
John Franco	1036
Mike Stanton	885
Mark Guthrie	765
Roberto Hernandez	762
Jose Mesa	762
Steve Reed	738
Mike Timlin	736
Jeff Nelson	714

Games Started

Roger Clemens	606
Greg Maddux	571
Tom Glavine	537
Randy Johnson	444
Kevin Brown	441
John Burkett	423
Jamie Moyer	420
David Cone	419
Kevin Appier	400
2 tied with	386

Innings Pitched

Roger Clemens	4278.2
Greg Maddux	3968.2
Tom Glavine	3528.0
Randy Johnson	3122.1
Kevin Brown	3051.0
David Cone	2898.2
David Wells	2826.2
Jamie Moyer	2737.2
Mike Mussina	2668.2
John Burkett	2648.1

Batters Faced

Roger Clemens	17653
Greg Maddux	16117
Tom Glavine	14821
Randy Johnson	12900
Kevin Brown	12645
David Cone	12184
David Wells	11811
Jamie Moyer	11585
John Burkett	11324
Kevin Appier	10936

Complete Games

Roger Clemens	117
Greg Maddux	103
Randy Johnson	88
Curt Schilling	79
Kevin Brown	72
David Cone	56
Mike Mussina	53
Tom Glavine	52
David Wells	52
John Smoltz	47

Complete Game Pct.

(minimum 100 games started)

Curt Schilling	0.23
Randy Johnson	0.20
Roger Clemens	0.19
Greg Maddux	0.18
Kevin Brown	0.16
Livan Hernandez	0.15
Mark Mulder	0.15
Terry Mulholland	0.15
Pedro Martinez	0.14
Mike Mussina	0.14

Shutouts

Roger Clemens	46
Randy Johnson	35
Greg Maddux	34
David Cone	22
Tom Glavine	22
Mike Mussina	21
Curt Schilling	19
Kevin Brown	17
Pedro Martinez	15
John Smoltz	14

Quality Start Pct.†

(minimum 100 games started)

Barry Zito	71.4
Pedro Martinez	70.8
Randy Johnson	70.0
Greg Maddux	68.3
Curt Schilling	68.0
Tim Hudson	67.9
Kevin Brown	67.8
Kerry Wood	66.9
Matt Morris	65.7
Mark Buehrle	65.4

Strikeouts

Roger Clemens	4099
Randy Johnson	3871
Greg Maddux	2765
David Cone	2668
Curt Schilling	2542
Pedro Martinez	2426
John Smoltz	2313
Kevin Brown	2264
Tom Glavine	2136
Mike Mussina	2126

Walks Allowed

Roger Clemens	1379
Randy Johnson	1258
Tom Glavine	1206
David Cone	1137
Al Leiter	968
Kevin Appier	930
Kenny Rogers	898
Tom Gordon	870
Kevin Brown	847
Greg Maddux	838

Strikeouts per 9 IP

(minimum 750 IP)

Randy Johnson	11.16
Kerry Wood	10.62
Pedro Martinez	10.50
Hideo Nomo	9.07
Curt Schilling	8.85
Arthur Rhodes	8.84
Mike Remlinger	8.82
Dan Plesac	8.74
Roger Clemens	8.62
David Cone	8.28

Walks per 9 IP

(minimum 750 IP)

Rick Reed	1.66
Brad Radke	1.75
Brian Anderson	1.87
Greg Maddux	1.90
David Wells	1.99
Mike Mussina	2.01
Ramiro Mendoza	2.05
Shane Reynolds	2.10
Curt Schilling	2.10
Jose Lima	2.14

***Quality Starts** denote the number of outings in which a starting pitcher works at least six innings and allows three or fewer earned runs.

SO/BB Ratio
(minimum 750 IP)

Pedro Martinez................4.38
Curt Schilling..................4.22
Mike Mussina..................3.56
Rick Reed........................3.40
Shane Reynolds..............3.36
Greg Maddux..................3.30
Javier Vazquez................3.25
Brad Radke.....................3.09
Randy Johnson 3.08
David Wells.....................3.00

Opposition Avg.
(minimum 750 IP)

Pedro Martinez.............. .206
Kerry Wood .... .209
Randy Johnson .... .215
Barry Zito...................... .219
Jesse Orosco .... .223
Roger Clemens .... .231
Hideo Nomo.................. .231
John Smoltz.................. .232
David Cone.................... .232
Mike Remlinger .... .235

Hit Batsmen

Randy Johnson................146
Roger Clemens 141
Kevin Brown 129
Greg Maddux 109
Tim Wakefield..................109
Pedro Astacio 108
David Cone 106
Pedro Martinez 99
Aaron Sele..........................98
Al Leiter.............................94

Saves

John Franco 424
Trevor Hoffman................352
Roberto Hernandez..........320
Rod Beck..........................286
Troy Percival 283
Mariano Rivera 283
Jose Mesa........................249
Billy Wagner 225
Ugueth Urbina..................206
Armando Benitez.............197

Hits per 9 IP
(minimum 750 IP)

Pedro Martinez................6.72
Kerry Wood 6.75
Randy Johnson 7.02
Barry Zito........................7.22
Jesse Orosco 7.33
Hideo Nomo....................7.68
Roger Clemens 7.73
John Smoltz....................7.74
David Cone......................7.77
Mike Remlinger 7.82

Opposition OBP
(minimum 750 IP)

Pedro Martinez.............. .268
Curt Schilling .... .282
Greg Maddux .... .287
Mike Mussina................ .290
John Smoltz.................. .292
Roger Clemens .... .296
Barry Zito...................... .297
Randy Johnson .... .300
Kevin Millwood .... .301
Rick Reed...................... .303

Wild Pitches

David Cone 149
Roger Clemens 125
John Smoltz 122
Kevin Appier 104
Hideo Nomo 102
Tom Gordon 98
Kevin Brown 96
David Wells........................94
Randy Johnson 92
Jason Grimsley 88

Save Percentage
(minimum 50 save opportunities)

Eric Gagne 96.4
John Smoltz....................92.4
Trevor Hoffman 88.9
Mariano Rivera................86.5
Troy Percival 86.3
Keith Foulke 85.6
Billy Wagner....................85.6
Kazuhiro Sasaki 85.4
Jose Mesa 85.3
Mike Williams 85.2

Baserunners per 9 IP
(minimum 750 IP)

Pedro Martinez................9.55
Curt Schilling 10.19
Greg Maddux 10.37
Mike Mussina................10.55
John Smoltz..................10.68
Roger Clemens 10.93
Barry Zito......................10.98
Randy Johnson 11.07
Kevin Millwood 11.18
Tim Hudson 11.23

Opposition Slg.
(minimum 750 IP)

Pedro Martinez.............. .315
Barry Zito...................... .333
Jesse Orosco .... .335
Randy Johnson .... .338
John Franco .... .339
Greg Maddux .... .339
Kevin Brown.................. .343
Roger Clemens .... .344
Kerry Wood .... .345
John Smoltz.................. .351

GDP Induced

Greg Maddux 338
Tom Glavine 336
Kevin Brown 309
Roger Clemens 283
Kenny Rogers 248
Terry Mulholland..............239
Mike Hampton..................231
Jamie Moyer....................227
John Burkett 224
Andy Pettitte 212

Games Finished

John Franco 754
Roberto Hernandez..........597
Trevor Hoffman................527
Rod Beck..........................509
Jesse Orosco 501
Jose Mesa........................473
Dan Plesac 422
Troy Percival 418
Mariano Rivera 405
Todd Jones 401

Home Runs per 9 IP
(minimum 750 IP)

Greg Maddux 0.53
Kevin Brown....................0.56
John Franco 0.57
Terry Adams....................0.57
Derek Lowe 0.64
Pedro Martinez................0.65
Matt Morris 0.66
Roger Clemens 0.68
Tom Glavine 0.68
John Smoltz....................0.72

Home Runs Allowed

David Wells......................330
Roger Clemens 321
Jamie Moyer....................314
Randy Johnson................283
Mike Mussina 278
Terry Mulholland..............269
Tom Glavine 268
Steve Trachsel..................265
Curt Schilling 263
2 tied with........................258

GDP per 9 IP
(minimum 750 IP)

Shawn Estes 1.24
Jamey Wright..................1.23
Julian Tavarez..................1.20
Mike Hampton 1.13
Andy Pettitte 1.06
Paul Quantrill 1.03
Jason Grimsley 1.03
Kirk Rueter......................1.02
Derek Lowe 1.01
Terry Adams....................1.01

SB Pct. Allowed
(minimum 750 IP)

Kirk Rueter......................35.6
Terry Mulholland 42.1
Omar Daal 42.2
Kenny Rogers 42.5
Jeff Weaver 48.4
Chan Ho Park..................49.5
Wilson Alvarez 49.7
Brian Anderson 50.5
Chris Hammond..............50.8
Ryan Dempster 51.9

HISTORY

All-time results

Award winners

Hall of Fame

ALL-TIME RESULTS

AMERICAN LEAGUE CHAMPIONS

Year	Team	Manager
1901	Chicago	Clark Griffith
1902	Philadelphia	Connie Mack
1903	Boston	Jimmy Collins
1904	Boston	Jimmy Collins
1905	Philadelphia	Connie Mack
1906	Chicago	Fielder Jones
1907	Detroit	Hugh Jennings
1908	Detroit	Hugh Jennings
1909	Detroit	Hugh Jennings
1910	Philadelphia	Connie Mack
1911	Philadelphia	Connie Mack
1912	Boston	Jake Stahl
1913	Philadelphia	Connie Mack
1914	Philadelphia	Connie Mack
1915	Boston	Bill Carrigan
1916	Boston	Bill Carrigan
1917	Chicago	Pants Rowland
1918	Boston	Ed Barrow
1919	Chicago	Kid Gleason
1920	Cleveland	Tris Speaker
1921	New York	Miller Huggins
1922	New York	Miller Huggins
1923	New York	Miller Huggins
1924	Washington	Bucky Harris
1925	Washington	Bucky Harris
1926	New York	Miller Huggins
1927	New York	Miller Huggins
1928	New York	Miller Huggins
1929	Philadelphia	Connie Mack
1930	Philadelphia	Connie Mack
1931	Philadelphia	Connie Mack
1932	New York	Joe McCarthy
1933	Washington	Joe Cronin
1934	Detroit	Mickey Cochrane
1935	Detroit	Mickey Cochrane
1936	New York	Joe McCarthy
1937	New York	Joe McCarthy
1938	New York	Joe McCarthy
1939	New York	Joe McCarthy
1940	Detroit	Del Baker
1941	New York	Joe McCarthy
1942	New York	Joe McCarthy
1943	New York	Joe McCarthy
1944	St. Louis	Luke Sewell
1945	Detroit	Steve O'Neill
1946	Boston	Joe Cronin
1947	New York	Bucky Harris
1948	Cleveland*	Lou Boudreau
1949	New York	Casey Stengel
1950	New York	Casey Stengel
1951	New York	Casey Stengel
1952	New York	Casey Stengel
1953	New York	Casey Stengel
1954	Cleveland	Al Lopez
1955	New York	Casey Stengel
1956	New York	Casey Stengel
1957	New York	Casey Stengel
1958	New York	Casey Stengel
1959	Chicago	Al Lopez
1960	New York	Casey Stengel
1961	New York	Ralph Houk
1962	New York	Ralph Houk
1963	New York	Ralph Houk
1964	New York	Yogi Berra
1965	Minnesota	Sam Mele
1966	Baltimore	Hank Bauer
1967	Boston	Dick Williams
1968	Detroit	Mayo Smith
1969	Baltimore (East Division)	Earl Weaver
1970	Baltimore (East Division)	Earl Weaver
1971	Baltimore (East Division)	Earl Weaver
1972	Oakland (West Division)	Dick Williams
1973	Oakland (West Division)	Dick Williams
1974	Oakland (West Division)	Al Dark
1975	Boston (East Division)	Darrell Johnson
1976	New York (East Division)	Billy Martin
1977	New York (East Division)	Billy Martin
1978	New York (East Division)	Billy Martin, Bob Lemon
1979	Baltimore (East Division)	Earl Weaver
1980	Kansas City (West Division)	Jim Frey
1981	New York (East Division)	Gene Michael, Bob Lemon
1982	Milwaukee (East Division)	Buck Rodgers, Harvey Kuenn
1983	Baltimore (East Division)	Joe Altobelli
1984	Detroit (East Division)	Sparky Anderson
1985	Kansas City (West Division)	Dick Howser
1986	Boston (East Division)	John McNamara
1987	Minnesota (West Division)	Tom Kelly
1988	Oakland (West Division)	Tony La Russa
1989	Oakland (West Division)	Tony La Russa
1990	Oakland (West Division)	Tony La Russa
1991	Minnesota (West Division)	Tom Kelly
1992	Toronto (East Division)	Cito Gaston
1993	Toronto (East Division)	Cito Gaston
1994	None†	
1995	Cleveland (Central Division)	Mike Hargrove
1996	New York (East Division)	Joe Torre
1997	Cleveland (Central Division)	Mike Hargrove
1998	New York (East Division)	Joe Torre
1999	New York (East Division)	Joe Torre
2000	New York (East Division)	Joe Torre
2001	New York (East Division)	Joe Torre
2002	Anaheim (West Division)	Mike Scioscia
2003	New York (East Division)	Joe Torre

*Defeated Boston in one-game playoff. †New York finished the strike-shortened season with the league's best record.

NATIONAL LEAGUE CHAMPIONS

Year	Team	Manager
1876	Chicago	Albert Spalding
1877	Boston	Harry Wright
1878	Boston	Harry Wright
1879	Providence	George Wright
1880	Chicago	Cap Anson
1881	Chicago	Cap Anson
1882	Chicago	Cap Anson
1883	Boston	Jack Burdock, John Morrill
1884	Providence	Frank Bancroft
1885	Chicago	Cap Anson
1886	Chicago	Cap Anson
1887	Detroit	William Watkins
1888	New York	James Mutrie
1889	New York	James Mutrie
1890	Brooklyn	William McGunnigle
1891	Boston	Frank Selee
1892	Boston	Frank Selee
1893	Boston	Frank Selee
1894	Baltimore	Ned Hanlon
1895	Baltimore	Ned Hanlon
1896	Baltimore	Ned Hanlon
1897	Boston	Frank Selee
1898	Boston	Frank Selee
1899	Brooklyn	Ned Hanlon

Year	Team	Manager
1900	Brooklyn	Ned Hanlon
1901	Pittsburgh	Fred Clarke
1902	Pittsburgh	Fred Clarke
1903	Pittsburgh	Fred Clarke
1904	New York	John McGraw
1905	New York	John McGraw
1906	Chicago	Frank Chance
1907	Chicago	Frank Chance
1908	Chicago	Frank Chance
1909	Pittsburgh	Fred Clarke
1910	Chicago	Frank Chance
1911	New York	John McGraw
1912	New York	John McGraw
1913	New York	John McGraw
1914	Boston	George Stallings
1915	Philadelphia	Pat Moran
1916	Brooklyn	Wilbert Robinson
1917	New York	John McGraw
1918	Chicago	Fred Mitchell
1919	Cincinnati	Pat Moran
1920	Brooklyn	Wilbert Robinson
1921	New York	John McGraw
1922	New York	John McGraw
1923	New York	John McGraw
1924	New York	John McGraw
1925	Pittsburgh	Bill McKechnie
1926	St. Louis	Rogers Hornsby
1927	Pittsburgh	Donie Bush
1928	St. Louis	Bill McKechnie
1929	Chicago	Joe McCarthy
1930	St. Louis	Gabby Street
1931	St. Louis	Gabby Street
1932	Chicago	Rogers Hornsby, Charlie Grimm
1933	New York	Bill Terry
1934	St. Louis	Frank Frisch
1935	Chicago	Charlie Grimm
1936	New York	Bill Terry
1937	New York	Bill Terry
1938	Chicago	Charlie Grimm, Gabby Hartnett
1939	Cincinnati	Bill McKechnie
1940	Cincinnati	Bill McKechnie
1941	Brooklyn	Leo Durocher
1942	St. Louis	Billy Southworth
1943	St. Louis	Billy Southworth
1944	St. Louis	Billy Southworth
1945	Chicago	Charlie Grimm
1946	St. Louis*	Eddie Dyer
1947	Brooklyn	Clyde Sukeforth, Burt Shotton
1948	Boston	Billy Southworth
1949	Brooklyn	Burt Shotton
1950	Philadelphia	Eddie Sawyer
1951	New York†	Leo Durocher
1952	Brooklyn	Charlie Dressen
1953	Brooklyn	Charlie Dressen
1954	New York	Leo Durocher
1955	Brooklyn	Walter Alston
1956	Brooklyn	Walter Alston
1957	Milwaukee	Fred Haney
1958	Milwaukee	Fred Haney
1959	Los Angeles‡	Walter Alston
1960	Pittsburgh	Danny Murtaugh
1961	Cincinnati	Fred Hutchinson
1962	San Francisco§	Al Dark
1963	Los Angeles	Walter Alston
1964	St. Louis	Johnny Keane
1965	Los Angeles	Walter Alston
1966	Los Angeles	Walter Alston
1967	St. Louis	Red Schoendienst
1968	St. Louis	Red Schoendienst
1969	New York (East Division)	Gil Hodges
1970	Cincinnati (West Division)	Sparky Anderson
1971	Pittsburgh (East Division)	Danny Murtaugh
1972	Cincinnati (West Division)	Sparky Anderson
1973	New York (East Division)	Yogi Berra
1974	Los Angeles (West Division)	Walter Alston
1975	Cincinnati (West Division)	Sparky Anderson
1976	Cincinnati (West Division)	Sparky Anderson
1977	Los Angeles (West Division)	Tommy Lasorda
1978	Los Angeles (West Division)	Tommy Lasorda
1979	Pittsburgh (East Division)	Chuck Tanner
1980	Philadelphia (East Division)	Dallas Green
1981	Los Angeles (West Division)	Tommy Lasorda
1982	St. Louis (East Division)	Whitey Herzog
1983	Philadelphia (East Division)	Pat Corrales, Paul Owens
1984	San Diego (West Division)	Dick Williams
1985	St. Louis (East Division)	Whitey Herzog
1986	New York (East Division)	Dave Johnson
1987	St. Louis (East Division)	Whitey Herzog
1988	Los Angeles (West Division)	Tommy Lasorda
1989	San Francisco (West Division)	Roger Craig
1990	Cincinnati (West Division)	Lou Piniella
1991	Atlanta (West Division)	Bobby Cox
1992	Atlanta (West Division)	Bobby Cox
1993	Philadelphia (East Division)	Jim Fregosi
1994	None∞	
1995	Atlanta (East Division)	Bobby Cox
1996	Atlanta (East Division)	Bobby Cox
1997	Florida (East Division)	Jim Leyland
1998	San Diego (West Division)	Bruce Bochy
1999	Atlanta (East Division)	Bobby Cox
2000	New York (East Division)	Bobby Valentine
2001	Arizona (West Division)	Bob Brenly
2002	San Francisco (West Division)	Dusty Baker
2003	Florida (East Division)	Jeff Torborg, Jack McKeon

*Defeated Brooklyn, two games to none, in playoff for pennant.
†Defeated Brooklyn, two games to one, in playoff for pennant.
‡Defeated Milwaukee, two games to none, in playoff for pennant.
§Defeated Los Angeles, two games to one, in playoff for pennant.
∞Montreal finished the strike-shortened season with the league's best record.

WORLD SERIES

Year	Winner	Loser	Games
1903	Boston A.L.	Pittsburgh N.L.	5-3
1904	No Series		
1905	New York N.L.	Philadelphia A.L.	4-1
1906	Chicago A.L.	Chicago N.L.	4-2
1907	Chicago N.L.	Detroit A.L.	*4-0
1908	Chicago N.L.	Detroit A.L.	4-1
1909	Pittsburgh N.L.	Detroit A.L.	4-3
1910	Philadelphia A.L.	Chicago N.L.	4-1
1911	Philadelphia A.L.	New York N.L.	4-2
1912	Boston A.L.	New York N.L.	*4-3
1913	Philadelphia A.L.	New York N.L.	4-1
1914	Boston N.L.	Philadelphia A.L.	4-0
1915	Boston A.L.	Philadelphia N.L.	4-1
1916	Boston A.L.	Brooklyn N.L.	4-1
1917	Chicago A.L.	New York N.L.	4-2
1918	Boston A.L.	Chicago N.L.	4-2
1919	Cincinnati N.L.	Chicago A.L.	5-3
1920	Cleveland A.L.	Brooklyn N.L.	5-2
1921	New York N.L.	New York A.L.	5-3
1922	New York N.L.	New York A.L.	*4-0
1923	New York A.L.	New York N.L.	4-2
1924	Washington A.L.	New York N.L.	4-3
1925	Pittsburgh N.L.	Washington A.L.	4-3
1926	St. Louis N.L.	New York A.L.	4-3
1927	New York A.L.	Pittsburgh, N.L.	4-0
1928	New York A.L.	St. Louis N.L.	4-0
1929	Philadelphia A.L.	Chicago N.L.	4-1
1930	Philadelphia A.L.	St. Louis N.L.	4-2

Year	Winner	Loser	Games
1931—	St. Louis N.L.	Philadelphia A.L.	4-3
1932—	New York A.L.	Chicago N.L.	4-0
1933—	New York N.L.	Washington A.L.	4-1
1934—	St. Louis N.L.	Detroit A.L.	4-3
1935—	Detroit A.L.	Chicago N.L.	4-2
1936—	New York A.L.	New York N.L.	4-2
1937—	New York A.L.	New York N.L.	4-1
1938—	New York A.L.	Chicago N.L.	4-0
1939—	New York A.L.	Cincinnati N.L.	4-0
1940—	Cincinnati N.L.	Detroit A.L.	4-3
1941—	New York A.L.	Brooklyn N.L.	4-1
1942—	St. Louis N.L.	New York A.L.	4-1
1943—	New York A.L.	St. Louis N.L.	4-1
1944—	St. Louis N.L.	St. Louis A.L.	4-2
1945—	Detroit A.L.	Chicago N.L.	4-3
1946—	St. Louis N.L.	Boston A.L.	4-3
1947—	New York A.L.	Brooklyn, N.L.	4-3
1948—	Cleveland A.L.	Boston N.L.	4-2
1949—	New York A.L.	Brooklyn N.L.	4-1
1950—	New York A.L.	Philadelphia N.L.	4-0
1951—	New York A.L.	New York N.L.	4-2
1952—	New York A.L.	Brooklyn N.L.	4-3
1953—	New York A.L.	Brooklyn N.L.	4-2
1954—	New York N.L.	Cleveland A.L.	4-0
1955—	Brooklyn N.L.	New York A.L.	4-3
1956—	New York A.L.	Brooklyn N.L.	4-3
1957—	Milwaukee N.L.	New York A.L.	4-3
1958—	New York A.L.	Milwaukee N.L.	4-3
1959—	Los Angeles N.L.	Chicago A.L.	4-2
1960—	Pittsburgh N.L.	New York A.L.	4-3
1961—	New York A.L.	Cincinnati N.L.	4-1
1962—	New York A.L.	San Francisco N.L.	4-3
1963—	Los Angeles N.L.	New York A.L.	4-0
1964—	St. Louis N.L.	New York A.L.	4-3
1965—	Los Angeles N.L.	Minnesota A.L.	4-3
1966—	Baltimore A.L.	Los Angeles N.L.	4-0
1967—	St. Louis N.L.	Boston A.L.	4-3
1968—	Detroit A.L.	St. Louis N.L.	4-3
1969—	New York N.L.	Baltimore A.L.	4-1
1970—	Baltimore A.L.	Cincinnati N.L.	4-1
1971—	Pittsburgh N.L.	Baltimore A.L.	4-3
1972—	Oakland A.L.	Cincinnati N.L.	4-3
1973—	Oakland A.L.	New York N.L.	4-3
1974—	Oakland A.L.	Los Angeles N.L.	4-1
1975—	Cincinnati N.L.	Boston A.L.	4-3
1976—	Cincinnati N.L.	New York A.L.	4-0
1977—	New York A.L.	Los Angeles N.L.	4-2
1978—	New York A.L.	Los Angeles N.L.	4-2
1979—	Pittsburgh N.L.	Baltimore A.L.	4-3
1980—	Philadelphia N.L.	Kansas City A.L.	4-2
1981—	Los Angeles N.L.	New York A.L.	4-2
1982—	St. Louis N.L.	Milwaukee A.L.	4-3
1983—	Baltimore A.L.	Philadelphia N.L.	4-1
1984—	Detroit A.L.	San Diego N.L.	4-1
1985—	Kansas City A.L.	St. Louis N.L.	4-3
1986—	New York N.L.	Boston A.L.	4-3
1987—	Minnesota A.L.	St. Louis N.L.	4-3
1988—	Los Angeles N.L.	Oakland A.L.	4-1
1989—	Oakland A.L.	San Francisco N.L.	4-0
1990—	Cincinnati N.L.	Oakland A.L.	4-0
1991—	Minnesota A.L.	Atlanta N.L.	4-3
1992—	Toronto A.L.	Atlanta N.L.	4-2
1993—	Toronto A.L.	Philadelphia N.L.	4-2
1994—	No Series		
1995—	Atlanta N.L.	Cleveland A.L.	4-2
1996—	New York A.L.	Atlanta N.L.	4-2
1997—	Florida N.L.	Cleveland A.L.	4-3
1998—	New York A.L.	San Diego N.L.	4-0
1999—	New York A.L.	Atlanta N.L.	4-0
2000—	New York A.L.	New York N.L.	4-1
2001—	Arizona N.L.	New York A.L.	4-3
2002—	Anaheim A.L.	San Francisco N.L.	4-3
2003—	Florida N.L.	New York A.L.	4-2

*Includes tie game.

DIVISION SERIES

AMERICAN LEAGUE

Year	Winner (Division)	Loser (Division)	Games
1981—	New York (East)	Milwaukee (East)	3-2
	Oakland (West)	Kansas City (West)	3-0
1995—	Cleveland (Central)	Boston (East)	3-0
	Seattle (West)	New York* (East)	3-2
1996—	New York (East)	Texas (West)	3-1
	Baltimore (East)*	Cleveland (Central)	3-1
1997—	Baltimore (East)	Seattle (West)	3-1
	Cleveland (Central)	New York (East)*	3-2
1998—	New York (East)	Texas (West)	3-0
	Cleveland (Central)	Boston (East)*	3-1
1999—	New York (East)	Texas (West)	3-0
	Boston (East)*	Cleveland (Central)	3-2
2000—	New York (East)	Oakland (West)	3-2
	Seattle (West)*	Chicago (Central)	3-0
2001—	New York (East)	Oakland (West)*	3-2
	Seattle (West)	Cleveland (Central)	3-2
2002—	Anaheim (West)*	New York (East)	3-1
	Minnesota (Central)	Oakland (West)	3-2
2003—	Boston (East)*	Oakland (West)	3-2
	New York (East)	Minnesota (Central)	3-1

NATIONAL LEAGUE

Year	Winner (Division)	Loser (Division)	Games
1981—	Montreal (East)	Philadelphia (East)	3-2
	Los Angeles (West)	Houston (West)	3-2
1995—	Atlanta (East)	Colorado* (West)	3-1
	Cincinnati (Central)	Los Angeles (West)	3-0
1996—	Atlanta (East)	Los Angeles (West)*	3-0
	St. Louis (Central)	San Diego (West)	3-0
1997—	Atlanta (East)	Houston (Central)	3-0
	Florida (East)*	San Francisco (West)	3-0
1998—	Atlanta (East)	Chicago (Central)*	3-0
	San Diego (West)	Houston (Central)	3-1
1999—	Atlanta (East)	Houston (Central)	3-1
	New York (East)*	Arizona (West)	3-1
2000—	St. Louis (Central)	Atlanta (East)	3-0
	New York (East)*	San Francisco (West)	3-1
2001—	Arizona (West)	St. Louis (Central)*	3-2
	Atlanta (East)	Houston (Central)	3-0
2002—	St. Louis (Central)	Arizona (West)	3-0
	San Francisco (West)*	Atlanta (East)	3-2
2003—	Chicago (Central)	Atlanta (East)	3-2
	Florida (East)*	San Francisco (West)	3-1

*Wild-card team.

CHAMPIONSHIP SERIES

AMERICAN LEAGUE

Year	Winner (Division)	Loser (Division)	Games
1969—	Baltimore (East)	Minnesota (West)	3-0
1970—	Baltimore (East)	Minnesota (West)	3-0
1971—	Baltimore (East)	Oakland (West)	3-0
1972—	Oakland (West)	Detroit (East)	3-2
1973—	Oakland (West)	Baltimore (East)	3-2
1974—	Oakland (West)	Baltimore (East)	3-1
1975—	Boston (East)	Oakland (West)	3-0
1976—	New York (East)	Kansas City (West)	3-2
1977—	New York (East)	Kansas City (West)	3-2
1978—	New York (East)	Kansas City (West)	3-1
1979—	Baltimore (East)	California (West)	3-1
1980—	Kansas City (West)	New York (East)	3-0

Year	Winner (Division)	Loser (Division)	Games
1981—	New York (East)	Oakland (West)	3-0
1982—	Milwaukee (East)	California (West)	3-2
1983—	Baltimore (East)	Chicago (West)	3-1
1984—	Detroit (East)	Kansas City (West)	3-0
1985—	Kansas City (West)	Toronto (East)	4-3
1986—	Boston (East)	California (West)	4-3
1987—	Minnesota (West)	Detroit (East)	4-1
1988—	Oakland (West)	Boston (East)	4-0
1989—	Oakland (West)	Toronto (East)	4-1
1990—	Oakland (West)	Boston (East)	4-0
1991—	Minnesota (West)	Toronto (East)	4-1
1992—	Toronto (East)	Oakland (West)	4-2
1993—	Toronto (East)	Chicago (West)	4-2
1994—	No series		
1995—	Cleveland (Central)	Seattle (West)	4-2
1996—	New York (East)	Baltimore (East)*	4-1
1997—	Cleveland (Central)	Baltimore (East)	4-2
1998—	New York (East)	Cleveland (Central)	4-2
1999—	New York (East)	Boston (East)*	4-1
2000—	New York (East)	Seattle (West)	4-2
2001—	New York (East)	Seattle (West)	4-1
2002—	Anaheim (West)*	Minnesota (Central)	4-1
2003—	New York (East)	Boston (East)*	4-3

NATIONAL LEAGUE

Year	Winner (Division)	Loser (Division)	Games
1969—	New York (East)	Atlanta (West)	3-0
1970—	Cincinnati (West)	Pittsburgh (East)	3-0
1971—	Pittsburgh (East)	San Francisco (West)	3-1
1972—	Cincinnati (West)	Pittsburgh (East)	3-2
1973—	New York (East)	Cincinnati (West)	3-2
1974—	Los Angeles (West)	Pittsburgh (East)	3-1
1975—	Cincinnati (West)	Pittsburgh (East)	3-0
1976—	Cincinnati (West)	Philadelphia (East)	3-0
1977—	Los Angeles (West)	Philadelphia (East)	3-1
1978—	Los Angeles (West)	Philadelphia (East)	3-1
1979—	Pittsburgh (East)	Cincinnati (West)	3-0
1980—	Philadelphia (East)	Houston (West)	3-2
1981—	Los Angeles (West)	Montreal (East)	3-2
1982—	St. Louis (East)	Atlanta (West)	3-0
1983—	Philadelphia (East)	Los Angeles (West)	3-1
1984—	San Diego (West)	Chicago (East)	3-2
1985—	St. Louis (East)	Los Angeles (West)	4-2
1986—	New York (East)	Houston (West)	4-2
1987—	St. Louis (East)	San Francisco (West)	4-3
1988—	Los Angeles (West)	New York (East)	4-3
1989—	San Francisco (West)	Chicago (East)	4-1
1990—	Cincinnati (West)	Pittsburgh (East)	4-2
1991—	Atlanta (West)	Pittsburgh (East)	4-3
1992—	Atlanta (West)	Pittsburgh (East)	4-3
1993—	Philadelphia (East)	Atlanta (West)	4-2
1994—	No series		
1995—	Atlanta (East)	Cincinnati (Central)	4-0
1996—	Atlanta (East)	St. Louis (Central)	4-3
1997—	Florida (East)*	Atlanta (East)	4-2
1998—	San Diego (West)	Atlanta (East)	4-2
1999—	Atlanta (East)	New York (East)*	4-2
2000—	New York (East)*	St. Louis (Central)	4-1
2001—	Arizona (West)	Atlanta (East)	4-1
2002—	San Francisco (West)*	St. Louis (Central)	4-1
2003—	Florida (East)*	Chicago (Central)	4-3

*Wild-card team.

ALL-STAR GAME

Date	Site	Score (Winner)	Winning pitcher (Losing pitcher)	Winning manager (Losing manager)	Att.
7-6-33	Comiskey Park Chicago	4-2 (A.L.)	Lefty Gomez, Yankees (Bill Hallahan, Cardinals)	Connie Mack, Athletics (John McGraw, Giants)	47,595
7-10-34	Polo Grounds New York	9-7 (A.L.)	Mel Harder, Indians (Van Mungo, Dodgers)	Joe Cronin, Senators (Bill Terry, Giants)	48,363
7-8-35	Municipal Stadium Cleveland	4-1 (A.L.)	Lefty Gomez, Yankees (Bill Walker, Cardinals)	Mickey Cochrane, Tigers (Frankie Frisch, Cardinals)	69,831
7-7-36	Braves Field Boston	4-3 (N.L.)	Dizzy Dean, Cardinals (Lefty Grove, Red Sox)	Charlie Grimm, Cubs (Joe McCarthy, Yankees)	25,556
7-7-37	Griffith Stadium Washington	8-3 (A.L.)	Lefty Gomez, Yankees (Dizzy Dean, Cardinals)	Joe McCarthy, Yankees (Bill Terry, Giants)	31,391
7-6-38	Crosley Field Cincinnati	4-1 (N.L.)	Johnny Vander Meer, Reds (Lefty Gomez, Yankees)	Bill Terry, Giants (Joe McCarthy, Yankees)	27,067
7-11-39	Yankee Stadium New York	3-1 (A.L.)	Tommy Bridges, Tigers (Bill Lee, Cubs)	Joe McCarthy, Yankees (Gabby Hartnett, Cubs)	62,892
7-9-40	Sportsman's Park St. Louis	4-0 (N.L.)	Paul Derringer, Reds (Red Ruffing, Yankees)	Bill McKechnie, Reds (Joe Cronin, Red Sox)	32,373
7-8-41	Briggs Stadium Detroit	7-5 (A.L.)	Ed Smith, White Sox (Claude Passeau, Cubs)	Del Baker, Tigers (Bill McKechnie, Reds)	54,674
7-6-42	Polo Grounds New York	3-1 (A.L.)	Spud Chandler, Yankees (Mort Cooper, Cardinals)	Joe McCarthy, Yankees (Leo Durocher, Dodgers)	33,694
7-13-43	Shibe Park Philadelphia	5-3 (A.L.)	Dutch Leonard, Senators (Mort Cooper, Cardinals)	Joe McCarthy, Yankees (Billy Southworth, Cardinals)	31,938
7-11-44	Forbes Field Pittsburgh	7-1 (N.L.)	Ken Raffensberger, Phillies (Tex Hughson, Red Sox)	Billy Southworth, Cardinals (Joe McCarthy, Yankees)	29,589
1945	No game played.				
7-9-46	Fenway Park Boston	12-0 (A.L.)	Bob Feller, Indians (Claude Passeau, Cubs)	Steve O'Neill, Tigers (Charlie Grimm, Cubs)	34,906
7-8-47	Wrigley Field Chicago	2-1 (A.L.)	Frank Shea, Yankees (Johnny Sain, Braves)	Joe Cronin, Red Sox (Eddie Dyer, Cardinals)	41,123
7-13-48	Sportsman's Park St. Louis	5-2 (A.L.)	Vic Raschi, Yankees (Johnny Schmitz, Cubs)	Bucky Harris, Yankees (Leo Durocher, Dodgers)	34,009
7-12-49	Ebbets Field Brooklyn	11-7 (A.L.)	Virgil Trucks, Tigers (Don Newcombe, Dodgers)	Lou Boudreau, Indians (Billy Southworth, Braves)	32,577
7-11-50	Comiskey Park Chicago	4-3* (N.L.)	Ewell Blackwell, Reds (Ted Gray, Tigers)	Burt Shotton, Dodgers (Casey Stengel, Yankees)	46,127
7-10-51	Briggs Stadium Detroit	8-3 (N.L.)	Sal Maglie, Giants (Ed Lopat, Yankees)	Eddie Sawyer, Phillies (Casey Stengel, Yankees)	52,075

Date	Site	Score (Winner)	Winning pitcher (Losing pitcher)	Winning manager (Losing manager)	Att.
7-8-52	Shibe Park Philadelphia	3-2† (N.L.)	Bob Rush, Cubs (Bob Lemon, Indians)	Leo Durocher, Giants (Casey Stengel, Yankees)	32,785
7-14-53	Crosley Field Cincinnati	5-1 (N.L.)	Warren Spahn, Braves (Allie Reynolds, Yankees)	Chuck Dressen, Dodgers (Casey Stengel, Yankees)	30,846
7-13-54	Municipal Stadium Cleveland	11-9 (A.L.)	Dean Stone, Senators (Gene Conley, Braves)	Casey Stengel, Yankees (Walter Alston, Dodgers)	68,751
7-12-55	Milwaukee Co. Stadium Milwaukee	6-5‡ (N.L.)	Gene Conley, Braves (Frank Sullivan, Red Sox)	Leo Durocher, Giants (Al Lopez, Indians)	45,314
7-10-56	Griffith Stadium Washington	7-3 (N.L.)	Bob Friend, Pirates (Billy Pierce, White Sox)	Walter Alston, Dodgers (Casey Stengel, Yankees)	28,843
7-9-57	Busch Stadium St. Louis	6-5 (A.L.)	Jim Bunning, Tigers (Curt Simmons, Phillies)	Casey Stengel, Yankees (Walter Alston, Dodgers)	30,693
7-8-58	Memorial Stadium Baltimore	4-3 (A.L.)	Early Wynn, White Sox (Bob Friend, Pirates)	Casey Stengel, Yankees (Fred Haney, Braves)	48,829
7-7-59	Forbes Field Pittsburgh	5-4 (N.L.)	Johnny Antonelli, Giants (Whitey Ford, Yankees)	Fred Haney, Braves (Casey Stengel, Yankees)	35,277
8-3-59	Memorial Coliseum Los Angeles	5-3 (A.L.)	Jerry Walker, Orioles (Don Drysdale, Dodgers)	Casey Stengel, Yankees (Fred Haney, Braves)	55,105
7-11-60	Municipal Stadium Kansas City	5-3 (N.L.)	Bob Friend, Pirates (Bill Monbouquette, Red Sox)	Walter Alston, Dodgers (Al Lopez, White Sox)	30,619
7-13-60	Yankee Stadium New York	6-0 (N.L.)	Vernon Law, Pirates (Whitey Ford, Yankees)	Walter Alston, Dodgers (Al Lopez, White Sox)	38,362
7-11-61	Candlestick Park San Francisco	5-4§ (N.L.)	Stu Miller, Giants (Hoyt Wilhelm, Orioles)	Danny Murtaugh, Pirates (Paul Richards, Orioles)	44,115
7-31-61	Fenway Park Boston	1-1 (tie)		Paul Richards, Orioles (A.L.) Danny Murtaugh, Pirates (N.L.)	31,851
7-10-62	District of Col. Stad. Washington	3-1 (N.L.)	Juan Marichal, Giants (Camilo Pascual, Twins)	Fred Hutchinson, Reds (Ralph Houk, Yankees)	45,480
7-30-62	Wrigley Field Chicago	9-4 (A.L.)	Ray Herbert, White Sox (Art Mahaffey, Phillies)	Ralph Houk, Yankees (Fred Hutchinson, Reds)	38,359
7-9-63	Municipal Stadium Cleveland	5-3 (N.L.)	Larry Jackson, Cubs (Jim Bunning, Tigers)	Alvin Dark, Giants (Ralph Houk, Yankees)	44,160
7-7-64	Shea Stadium New York	7-4 (N.L.)	Juan Marichal, Giants (Dick Radatz, Red Sox)	Walter Alston, Dodgers (Al Lopez, White Sox)	50,850
7-13-65	Metropolitan Stadium Bloomington, Minn.	6-5 (N.L.)	Sandy Koufax, Dodgers (Sam McDowell, Indians)	Gene Mauch, Phillies (Al Lopez, White Sox)	46,706
7-12-66	Busch Stadium St. Louis	2-1§ (N.L.)	Gaylord Perry, Giants (Pete Richert, Senators)	Walter Alston, Dodgers (Sam Mele, Twins)	49,936
7-11-67	Anaheim Stadium Anaheim, Calif.	2-1∞ (N.L.)	Don Drysdale, Dodgers (Jim Hunter, Athletics)	Walter Alston, Dodgers (Hank Bauer, Orioles)	46,309
7-9-68	Astrodome Houston	1-0 (N.L.)	Don Drysdale, Dodgers (Luis Tiant, Indians)	Red Schoendienst, Cardinals (Dick Williams, Red Sox)	48,321
7-23-69	R.F.K. Stadium Washington	9-3 (N.L.)	Steve Carlton, Cardinals (Mel Stottlemyre, Yankees)	Red Schoendienst, Cardinals (Mayo Smith, Tigers)	45,259
7-14-70	Riverfront Stadium Cincinnati	5-4‡ (N.L.)	Claude Osteen, Dodgers (Clyde Wright, Angels)	Gil Hodges, Mets (Earl Weaver, Orioles)	51,838
7-13-71	Tiger Stadium Detroit	6-4 (A.L.)	Vida Blue, Athletics (Dock Ellis, Pirates)	Earl Weaver, Orioles (Sparky Anderson, Reds)	53,559
7-25-72	Atlanta Stadium Atlanta	4-3§ (N.L.)	Tug McGraw, Mets (Dave McNally, Orioles)	Danny Murtaugh, Pirates (Earl Weaver, Orioles)	53,107
7-24-73	Royals Stadium Kansas City	7-1 (N.L.)	Rick Wise, Cardinals (Bert Blyleven, Twins)	Sparky Anderson, Reds (Dick Williams, Athletics)	40,849
7-23-74	Three Rivers Stadium Pittsburgh	7-2 (N.L.)	Ken Brett, Pirates (Luis Tiant, Red Sox)	Yogi Berra, Mets (Dick Williams, Athletics)	50,706
7-15-75	Milwaukee Co. Stadium Milwaukee	6-3 (N.L.)	Jon Matlack, Mets (Jim Hunter, Yankees)	Walter Alston, Dodgers (Alvin Dark, Athletics)	51,480
7-13-76	Veterans Stadium Philadelphia	7-1 (N.L)	Randy Jones, Padres (Mark Fidrych, Tigers)	Sparky Anderson, Reds (Darrell Johnson, Red Sox)	63,974
7-19-77	Yankee Stadium New York	7-5 (N.L.)	Don Sutton, Dodgers (Jim Palmer, Orioles)	Sparky Anderson, Reds (Billy Martin, Yankees)	56,683
7-11-78	San Diego Stadium San Diego	7-3 (N.L.)	Bruce Sutter, Cubs (Rich Gossage, Yankees)	Tommy Lasorda, Dodgers (Billy Martin, Yankees)	51,549
7-17-79	Kingdome Seattle	7-6 (N.L.)	Bruce Sutter, Cubs (Jim Kern, Rangers)	Tommy Lasorda, Dodgers (Bob Lemon, Yankees)	58,905
7-8-80	Dodger Stadium Los Angeles	4-2 (N.L.)	Jerry Reuss, Dodgers (Tommy John, Yankees)	Chuck Tanner, Pirates (Earl Weaver, Orioles)	56,088
8-9-81	Municipal Stadium Cleveland	5-4 (N.L.)	Vida Blue, Giants (Rollie Fingers, Brewers)	Dallas Green, Phillies (Jim Frey, Royals)	72,086
7-13-82	Olympic Stadium Montreal	4-1 (N.L.)	Steve Rogers, Expos (Dennis Eckersley, Red Sox)	Tommy Lasorda, Dodgers (Billy Martin, Athletics)	59,057
7-6-83	Comiskey Park Chicago	13-3 (A.L.)	Dave Stieb, Blue Jays (Mario Soto, Reds)	Harvey Kuenn, Brewers (Whitey Herzog, Cardinals)	43,801

Date	Site	Score (Winner)	Winning pitcher (Losing pitcher)	Winning manager (Losing manager)	Att.
7-10-84	Candlestick Park San Francisco	3-1 (N.L.)	Charlie Lea, Expos (Dave Stieb, Blue Jays)	Paul Owens, Phillies (Joe Altobelli, Orioles)	57,756
7-16-85	Metrodome Minneapolis	6-1 (N.L.)	LaMarr Hoyt, Padres (Jack Morris, Tigers)	Dick Williams, Padres (Sparky Anderson, Tigers)	54,960
7-15-86	Astrodome Houston	3-2 (A.L.)	Roger Clemens, Red Sox (Dwight Gooden, Mets)	Dick Howser, Royals (Whitey Herzog, Cardinals)	45,774
7-14-87	Oak.-Alameda Co. Col. Oakland	2-0▲ (N.L.)	Lee Smith, Cubs (Jay Howell, Athletics)	Dave Johnson, Mets (John McNamara, Red Sox)	49,671
7-12-88	Riverfront Stadium Cincinnati	2-1 (A.L.)	Frank Viola, Twins (Dwight Gooden, Mets)	Tom Kelly, Twins (Whitey Herzog, Cardinals)	55,837
7-11-89	Anaheim Stadium Anaheim, Calif.	5-3 (A.L.)	Nolan Ryan, Rangers (John Smoltz, Braves)	Tony La Russa, Athletics (Tommy Lasorda, Dodgers)	64,036
7-10-90	Wrigley Field Chicago	2-0 (A.L.)	Bret Saberhagen, Royals (Jeff Brantley, Giants)	Tony La Russa, Athletics (Roger Craig, Giants)	39,071
7-9-91	SkyDome Toronto	4-2 (A.L.)	Jimmy Key, Blue Jays (Dennis Martinez, Expos)	Tony La Russa, Athletics (Lou Piniella, Reds)	52,383
7-14-92	Jack Murphy Stadium San Diego	13-6 (A.L.)	Kevin Brown, Rangers (Tom Glavine, Braves)	Tom Kelly, Twins (Bobby Cox, Braves)	59,372
7-13-93	Oriole Park at Camden Yards, Baltimore	9-3 (A.L.)	Jack McDowell, White Sox (John Burkett, Giants)	Cito Gaston, Blue Jays (Bobby Cox, Braves)	48,147
7-12-94	Three Rivers Stadium Pittsburgh	8-7§ (N.L.)	Doug Jones, Phillies (Jason Bere, White Sox)	Jim Fregosi, Phillies (Cito Gaston, Blue Jays)	59,568
7-11-95	Ballpark in Arlington Arlington, Texas	3-2 (N.L.)	Heathcliff Slocumb, Phillies (Steve Ontiveros, A's)	Felipe Alou, Expos (Buck Showalter, Yankees)	50,920
7-9-96	Veterans Stadium Philadelphia	6-0 (N.L.)	John Smoltz, Braves (Charles Nagy, Indians)	Bobby Cox, Braves (Mike Hargrove, Indians)	62,670
7-8-97	Jacobs Field Cleveland	3-1 (A.L.)	Jose Rosado, Royals (Shawn Estes, Giants)	Joe Torre, Yankees (Bobby Cox, Braves)	44,916
7-7-98	Coors Field Colorado	13-8 (A.L.)	Bartolo Colon, Indians (Ugueth Urbina, Expos)	Mike Hargrove, Indians (Jim Leyland, Marlins)	51,267
7-13-99	Fenway Park Boston	4-1 (A.L.)	Pedro Martinez, Red Sox (Curt Schilling, Phillies)	Joe Torre, Yankees (Bruce Bochy, Padres)	34,187
7-11-00	Turner Field Atlanta	6-3 (A.L.)	James Baldwin, White Sox (Al Leiter, Mets)	Joe Torre, Yankees (Bobby Cox, Braves)	51,323
7-10-01	Safeco Field Seattle	4-1 (A.L.)	Freddy Garcia, Mariners (Chan Ho Park, Dodgers)	Joe Torre, Yankees (Bobby Valentine, Mets)	47,364
7-9-02	Miller Park Milwaukee	7-7■ (tie)		Joe Torre, Yankees Bob Brenly, Diamondbacks	41,871
7-15-03	U.S. Cellular Field Chicago	7-6 (A.L.)	Brendan Donnelly, Angels (Eric Gagne, Dodgers)	Mike Scioscia, Angels (Dusty Baker, Cubs)	47,609

*14 innings. †5 innings (rain). ‡12 innings. §10 innings. ∞15 innings. ▲13 innings. ■11 innings.

AWARD WINNERS

THE SPORTING NEWS

MOST VALUABLE PLAYER

AMERICAN LEAGUE

Year	Player	Team	Pos.	Points
1929	Al Simmons	Philadelphia	OF	40
1930	Joe Cronin	Washington	SS	52
1931	Lou Gehrig	New York	1B	40
1932	Jimmie Foxx	Philadelphia	1B	46
1933	Jimmie Foxx	Philadelphia	1B	49
1934	Lou Gehrig	New York	1B	51
1935	Hank Greenberg	Detroit	1B	64
1936	Lou Gehrig	New York	1B	55
1937	Charlie Gehringer	Detroit	2B	78
1938	Jimmie Foxx	Boston	1B	304
1939	Joe DiMaggio	New York	OF	280
1940	Hank Greenberg	Detroit	OF	292
1941	Joe DiMaggio	New York	OF	291
1942	Joe Gordon	New York	2B	270
1943	Spud Chandler	New York	P	246
1944	Bobby Doerr	Boston	2B	
1945	Eddie Mayo	Detroit	2B	

NATIONAL LEAGUE

Year	Player	Team	Pos.	Points
1929	No selection			
1930	Bill Terry	New York	1B	47
1931	Chuck Klein	Philadelphia	OF	40
1932	Chuck Klein	Philadelphia	OF	46
1933	Carl Hubbell	New York	P	64
1934	Dizzy Dean	St. Louis	P	57
1935	Arky Vaughan	Pittsburgh	SS	42
1936	Carl Hubbell	New York	P	61
1937	Joe Medwick	St. Louis	OF	70
1938	Ernie Lombardi	Cincinnati	C	229
1939	Bucky Walters	Cincinnati	P	303
1940	Frank McCormick	Cincinnati	1B	274
1941	Dolf Camilli	Brooklyn	1B	300
1942	Mort Cooper	St. Louis	P	263
1943	Stan Musial	St. Louis	OF	267
1944	Marty Marion	St. Louis	SS	
1945	Tommy Holmes	Boston	OF	

PLAYER AND PITCHER OF THE YEAR

AMERICAN LEAGUE

Year	Player	Team	Pos.
1944	Bobby Doerr	Boston	2B
	Hal Newhouser	Detroit	P
1945	Eddie Mayo	Detroit	2B
	Hal Newhouser	Detroit	P
1946	No selections		
1947	No selections		
1948	Lou Boudreau	Cleveland	SS
	Bob Lemon	Cleveland	P
1949	Ted Williams	Boston	OF
	Ellis Kinder	Boston	P
1950	Phil Rizzuto	New York	SS
	Bob Lemon	Cleveland	P
1951	Ferris Fain	Philadelphia	1B
	Bob Feller	Cleveland	P
1952	Luke Easter	Cleveland	1B
	Bobby Shantz	Philadelphia	P
1953	Al Rosen	Cleveland	3B
	Bob Porterfield	Washington	P
1954	Bobby Avila	Cleveland	2B
	Bob Lemon	Cleveland	P
1955	Al Kaline	Detroit	OF
	Whitey Ford	New York	P
1956	Mickey Mantle	New York	OF
	Billy Pierce	Chicago	P
1957	Ted Williams	Boston	OF
	Billy Pierce	Chicago	P
1958	Jackie Jensen	Boston	OF
	Bob Turley	New York	P
1959	Nellie Fox	Chicago	2B
	Early Wynn	Chicago	P
1960	Roger Maris	New York	OF
	Chuck Estrada	Baltimore	P
1961	Roger Maris	New York	OF
	Whitey Ford	New York	P
1962	Mickey Mantle	New York	OF
	Dick Donovan	Cleveland	P
1963	Al Kaline	Detroit	OF
	Whitey Ford	New York	P
1964	Brooks Robinson	Baltimore	3B
	Dean Chance	Los Angeles	P
1965	Tony Oliva	Minnesota	OF
	Jim Grant	Minnesota	P
1966	Frank Robinson	Baltimore	OF
	Jim Kaat	Minnesota	P

NATIONAL LEAGUE

Year	Player	Team	Pos.
1944	Marty Marion	St. Louis	SS
	Bill Voiselle	New York	P
1945	Tommy Holmes	Boston	OF
	Hank Borowy	Chicago	P
1946	No selections		
1947	No selections		
1948	Stan Musial	St. Louis	OF-1B
	Johnny Sain	Boston	P
1949	Enos Slaughter	St. Louis	OF
	Howard Pollet	St. Louis	P
1950	Ralph Kiner	Pittsburgh	OF
	Jim Konstanty	Philadelphia	P
1951	Stan Musial	St. Louis	OF
	Preacher Roe	Brooklyn	P
1952	Hank Sauer	Chicago	OF
	Robin Roberts	Philadelphia	P
1953	Roy Campanella	Brooklyn	C
	Warren Spahn	Milwaukee	P
1954	Willie Mays	New York	OF
	Johnny Antonelli	New York	P
1955	Duke Snider	Brooklyn	OF
	Robin Roberts	Philadelphia	P
1956	Hank Aaron	Milwaukee	OF
	Don Newcombe	Brooklyn	P
1957	Stan Musial	St. Louis	1B
	Warren Spahn	Milwaukee	P
1958	Ernie Banks	Chicago	SS
	Warren Spahn	Milwaukee	P
1959	Ernie Banks	Chicago	SS
	Sam Jones	San Francisco	P
1960	Dick Groat	Pittsburgh	SS
	Vern Law	Pittsburgh	P
1961	Frank Robinson	Cincinnati	OF
	Warren Spahn	Milwaukee	P
1962	Maury Wills	Los Angeles	SS
	Don Drysdale	Los Angeles	P
1963	Hank Aaron	Milwaukee	OF
	Sandy Koufax	Los Angeles	P
1964	Ken Boyer	St. Louis	3B
	Sandy Koufax	Los Angeles	P
1965	Willie Mays	San Francisco	OF
	Sandy Koufax	Los Angeles	P
1966	Roberto Clemente	Pittsburgh	OF
	Sandy Koufax	Los Angeles	P

Year	Player	Team	Pos.
1967—	Carl Yastrzemski	Boston	OF
	Jim Lonborg	Boston	P
1968—	Ken Harrelson	Boston	OF
	Denny McLain	Detroit	P
1969—	Harmon Killebrew	Minnesota	1B-3B
	Denny McLain	Detroit	P
1970—	Harmon Killebrew	Minnesota	3B
	Sam McDowell	Cleveland	P
1971—	Tony Oliva	Minnesota	OF
	Vida Blue	Oakland	P
1972—	Dick Allen	Chicago	1B
	Wilbur Wood	Chicago	P
1973—	Reggie Jackson	Oakland	OF
	Jim Palmer	Baltimore	P
1974—	Jeff Burroughs	Texas	OF
	Jim Hunter	Oakland	P
1975—	Fred Lynn	Boston	OF
	Jim Palmer	Baltimore	P
1976—	Thurman Munson	New York	C
	Jim Palmer	Baltimore	P
1977—	Rod Carew	Minnesota	1B
	Nolan Ryan	California	P
1978—	Jim Rice	Boston	OF
	Ron Guidry	New York	P
1979—	Don Baylor	California	OF
	Mike Flanagan	Baltimore	P
1980—	George Brett	Kansas City	3B
	Steve Stone	Baltimore	P
1981—	Tony Armas	Oakland	OF
	Jack Morris	Detroit	P
1982—	Robin Yount	Milwaukee	SS
	Dave Stieb	Toronto	P
1983—	Cal Ripken Jr.	Baltimore	SS
	LaMarr Hoyt	Chicago	P
1984—	Don Mattingly	New York	1B
	Willie Hernandez	Detroit	P
1985—	Don Mattingly	New York	1B
	Bret Saberhagen	Kansas City	P
1986—	Don Mattingly	New York	1B
	Roger Clemens	Boston	P
1987—	George Bell	Toronto	OF
	Jimmy Key	Toronto	P
1988—	Jose Canseco	Oakland	OF
	Frank Viola	Minnesota	P
1989—	Ruben Sierra	Texas	OF
	Bret Saberhagen	Kansas City	P
1990—	Cecil Fielder	Detroit	1B
	Bob Welch	Oakland	P
1991—	Cal Ripken Jr.	Baltimore	SS
	Roger Clemens	Boston	P

Year	Player	Team	Pos.
1967—	Orlando Cepeda	St. Louis	1B
	Mike McCormick	San Francisco	P
1968—	Pete Rose	Cincinnati	OF
	Bob Gibson	St. Louis	P
1969—	Willie McCovey	San Francisco	1B
	Tom Seaver	New York	P
1970—	Johnny Bench	Cincinnati	C
	Bob Gibson	St. Louis	P
1971—	Joe Torre	St. Louis	3B
	Ferguson Jenkins	Chicago	P
1972—	Billy Williams	Chicago	OF
	Steve Carlton	Philadelphia	P
1973—	Bobby Bonds	San Francisco	OF
	Ron Bryant	San Francisco	P
1974—	Lou Brock	St. Louis	OF
	Mike Marshall	Los Angeles	P
1975—	Joe Morgan	Cincinnati	2B
	Tom Seaver	New York	P
1976—	George Foster	Cincinnati	OF
	Randy Jones	San Diego	P
1977—	George Foster	Cincinnati	OF
	Steve Carlton	Philadelphia	P
1978—	Dave Parker	Pittsburgh	OF
	Vida Blue	San Francisco	P
1979—	Keith Hernandez	St. Louis	1B
	Joe Niekro	Houston	P
1980—	Mike Schmidt	Philadelphia	3B
	Steve Carlton	Philadelphia	P
1981—	Andre Dawson	Montreal	OF
	Fernando Valenzuela	Los Angeles	P
1982—	Dale Murphy	Atlanta	OF
	Steve Carlton	Philadelphia	P
1983—	Dale Murphy	Atlanta	OF
	John Denny	Philadelphia	P
1984—	Ryne Sandberg	Chicago	2B
	Rick Sutcliffe	Chicago	P
1985—	Willie McGee	St. Louis	OF
	Dwight Gooden	New York	P
1986—	Mike Schmidt	Philadelphia	3B
	Mike Scott	Houston	P
1987—	Andre Dawson	Chicago	OF
	Rick Sutcliffe	Chicago	P
1988—	Andy Van Slyke	Pittsburgh	OF
	Orel Hershiser	Los Angeles	P
1989—	Kevin Mitchell	San Francisco	OF
	Mark Davis	San Diego	P
1990—	Barry Bonds	Pittsburgh	OF
	Doug Drabek	Pittsburgh	P
1991—	Barry Bonds	Pittsburgh	OF
	Tom Glavine	Atlanta	P

PITCHER OF THE YEAR

AMERICAN LEAGUE

Year	Pitcher	Team
1992—	Dennis Eckersley	Oakland
1993—	Jack McDowell	Chicago
1994—	Jimmy Key	New York
1995—	Randy Johnson	Seattle
1996—	Pat Hentgen	Toronto
1997—	Roger Clemens	Toronto
1998—	Roger Clemens	Toronto
1999—	Pedro Martinez	Boston
2000—	Pedro Martinez	Boston
2001—	Roger Clemens	New York
2002—	Barry Zito	Oakland
2003—	Roy Halladay	Toronto

NATIONAL LEAGUE

Year	Pitcher	Team
1992—	Greg Maddux	Chicago
1993—	Greg Maddux	Atlanta
1994—	Greg Maddux	Atlanta
1995—	Greg Maddux	Atlanta
1996—	John Smoltz	Atlanta
1997—	Pedro Martinez	Montreal
1998—	Kevin Brown	San Diego
1999—	Mike Hampton	Houston
2000—	Tom Glavine	Atlanta
2001—	Curt Schilling	Arizona
2002—	Curt Schilling	Arizona
2003—	Eric Gagne	Los Angeles

ROOKIE OF THE YEAR

1946—Combined selection—Del Ennis, Philadelphia N.L., OF
1947—Combined selection—Jackie Robinson, Brooklyn N.L., 1B
1948—Combined selection—Richie Ashburn, Philadelphia N.L., OF

AMERICAN LEAGUE

Year	Player	Team	Pos.
1949—	Roy Sievers	St. Louis	OF
1950—	Whitey Ford	New York	P
1951—	Minnie Minoso	Chicago	OF
1952—	Clint Courtney	St. Louis	C
1953—	Harvey Kuenn	Detroit	SS
1954—	Bob Grim	New York	P
1955—	Herb Score	Cleveland	P
1956—	Luis Aparicio	Chicago	SS
1957—	Tony Kubek	New York	IF-OF
	(No pitcher named)		
1958—	Albie Pearson	Washington	OF
	Ryne Duren	New York	P
1959—	Bob Allison	Washington	OF
1960—	Ron Hansen	Baltimore	SS
1961—	Dick Howser	Kansas City	SS
	Don Schwall	Boston	P
1962—	Tom Tresh	New York	OF-SS
1963—	Pete Ward	Chicago	3B
	Gary Peters	Chicago	P
1964—	Tony Oliva	Minnesota	OF
	Wally Bunker	Baltimore	P
1965—	Curt Blefary	Baltimore	OF
	Marcelino Lopez	California	P
1966—	Tommie Agee	Chicago	OF
	Jim Nash	Kansas City	P
1967—	Rod Carew	Minnesota	2B
	Tom Phoebus	Baltimore	P
1968—	Del Unser	Washington	OF
	Stan Bahnsen	New York	P
1969—	Carlos May	Chicago	OF
	Mike Nagy	Boston	P
1970—	Roy Foster	Cleveland	OF
	Bert Blyleven	Minnesota	P
1971—	Chris Chambliss	Cleveland	1B
	Bill Parsons	Milwaukee	P
1972—	Carlton Fisk	Boston	C
	Dick Tidrow	Cleveland	P
1973—	Al Bumbry	Baltimore	OF
	Steve Busby	Kansas City	P
1974—	Mike Hargrove	Texas	1B
	Frank Tanana	California	P
1975—	Fred Lynn	Boston	OF
	Dennis Eckersley	Cleveland	P
1976—	Butch Wynegar	Minnesota	C
	Mark Fidrych	Detroit	P
1977—	Mitchell Page	Oakland	OF
	Dave Rozema	Detroit	P
1978—	Paul Molitor	Milwaukee	2B
	Rich Gale	Kansas City	P
1979—	Pat Putnam	Texas	1B
	Mark Clear	California	P
1980—	Joe Charboneau	Cleveland	OF
	Britt Burns	Chicago	P
1981—	Rich Gedman	Boston	C
	Dave Righetti	New York	P
1982—	Cal Ripken Jr.	Baltimore	SS-3B
	Ed Vande Berg	Seattle	P
1983—	Ron Kittle	Chicago	OF
	Mike Boddicker	Baltimore	P
1984—	Alvin Davis	Seattle	1B
	Mark Langston	Seattle	P
1985	Ozzie Gullen	Chicago	SS
	Teddy Higuera	Milwaukee	P
1986—	Jose Canseco	Oakland	OF
	Mark Eichhorn	Toronto	P
1987—	Mark McGwire	Oakland	1B
	Mike Henneman	Detroit	P
1988—	Walt Weiss	Oakland	SS
	Bryan Harvey	California	P

NATIONAL LEAGUE

Year	Player	Team	Pos.
1949—	Don Newcombe	Brooklyn	P
1950—	Combined A.L.-N.L. selection		
1951—	Willie Mays	New York	OF
1952—	Joe Black	Brooklyn	P
1953—	Jim Gilliam	Brooklyn	2B
1954—	Wally Moon	St. Louis	OF
1955—	Bill Virdon	St. Louis	OF
1956—	Frank Robinson	Cincinnati	OF
1957—	Ed Bouchee	Philadelphia	1B
	Jack Sanford	Philadelphia	P
1958—	Orlando Cepeda	San Francisco	1B
	Carlton Willey	Milwaukee	P
1959—	Willie McCovey	San Francisco	1B
1960—	Frank Howard	Los Angeles	OF
1961—	Billy Williams	Chicago	OF
	Ken Hunt	Cincinnati	P
1962—	Ken Hubbs	Chicago	2B
1963—	Pete Rose	Cincinnati	2B
	Ray Culp	Philadelphia	P
1964—	Dick Allen	Philadelphia	3B
	Billy McCool	Cincinnati	P
1965—	Joe Morgan	Houston	2B
	Frank Linzy	San Francisco	P
1966—	Tommy Helms	Cincinnati	3B
	Don Sutton	Los Angeles	P
1967—	Lee May	Cincinnati	1B
	Dick Hughes	St. Louis	P
1968—	Johnny Bench	Cincinnati	C
	Jerry Koosman	New York	P
1969—	Coco Laboy	Montreal	3B
	Tom Griffin	Houston	P
1970—	Bernie Carbo	Cincinnati	OF
	Carl Morton	Montreal	P
1971—	Earl Williams	Atlanta	C
	Reggie Cleveland	St. Louis	P
1972—	Dave Rader	San Francisco	C
	Jon Matlack	New York	P
1973—	Gary Matthews	San Francisco	OF
	Steve Rogers	Montreal	P
1974—	Greg Gross	Houston	OF
	John D'Acquisto	San Francisco	P
1975—	Gary Carter	Montreal	OF-C
	John Montefusco	San Francisco	P
1976—	Larry Herndon	San Francisco	OF
	Butch Metzger	San Diego	P
1977—	Andre Dawson	Montreal	OF
	Bob Owchinko	San Diego	P
1978—	Bob Horner	Atlanta	3B
	Don Robinson	Pittsburgh	P
1979—	Jeff Leonard	Houston	OF
	Rick Sutcliffe	Los Angeles	P
1980—	Lonnie Smith	Philadelphia	OF
	Bill Gullickson	Montreal	P
1981—	Tim Raines	Montreal	OF
	Fernando Valenzuela	Los Angeles	P
1982—	Johnny Ray	Pittsburgh	2B
	Steve Bedrosian	Atlanta	P
1983—	Darryl Strawberry	New York	OF
	Craig McMurtry	Atlanta	P
1984—	Juan Samuel	Philadelphia	2B
	Dwight Gooden	New York	P
1985—	Vince Coleman	St. Louis	OF
	Tom Browning	Cincinnati	P
1986—	Robby Thompson	San Francisco	2B
	Todd Worrell	St. Louis	P
1987—	Benito Santiago	San Diego	C
	Mike Dunne	Pittsburgh	P
1988—	Mark Grace	Chicago	1B
	Tim Belcher	Los Angeles	P

Year	Player	Team	Pos.
1989—	Craig Worthington	Baltimore	3B
	Tom Gordon	Kansas City	P
1990—	Sandy Alomar Jr.	Cleveland	C
	Kevin Appier	Kansas City	P
1991—	Chuck Knoblauch	Minnesota	2B
	Juan Guzman	Toronto	P
1992—	Pat Listach	Milwaukee	SS
	Cal Eldred	Milwaukee	P
1993—	Tim Salmon	California	OF
	Aaron Sele	Boston	P
1994—	Bob Hamelin	Kansas City	DH
	Brian Anderson	California	P
1995—	Garret Anderson	California	OF
	Julian Tavarez	Cleveland	P
1996—	Derek Jeter	New York	SS
	James Baldwin	Chicago	P
1997—	Nomar Garciaparra	Boston	SS
	Jason Dickson	Anaheim	P
1998—	Ben Grieve	Oakland	OF
	Rolando Arrojo	Tampa Bay	P
1999—	Carlos Beltran	Kansas City	OF
	Tim Hudson	Oakland	P
2000—	Mark Quinn	Kansas City	OF-DH
	Kazuhiro Sasaki	Seattle	P
2001—	Ichiro Suzuki	Seattle	OF
	C.C. Sabathia	Cleveland	P
2002—	Eric Hinske	Toronto	3B
	Rodrigo Lopez	Baltimore	P
2003—	Jody Gerut	Cleveland	OF
	Rafael Soriano	Seattle	P

Year	Player	Team	Pos.
1989—	Jerome Walton	Chicago	OF
	Andy Benes	San Diego	P
1990—	David Justice	Atlanta	OF
	Mike Harkey	Chicago	P
1991—	Jeff Bagwell	Houston	1B
	Al Osuna	Houston	P
1992—	Eric Karros	Los Angeles	1B
	Tim Wakefield	Pittsburgh	P
1993—	Mike Piazza	Los Angeles	C
	Kirk Rueter	Montreal	P
1994—	Raul Mondesi	Los Angeles	OF
	Steve Trachsel	Chicago	P
1995—	Chipper Jones	Atlanta	3B
	Hideo Nomo	Los Angeles	P
1996—	Jason Kendall	Pittsburgh	C
	Alan Benes	St. Louis	P
1997—	Scott Rolen	Philadelphia	3B
	Matt Morris	St. Louis	P
1998—	Todd Helton	Colorado	1B
	Kerry Wood	Chicago	P
1999—	Preston Wilson	Florida	OF
	Scott Williamson	Cincinnati	P
2000—	Rafael Furcal	Atlanta	2B-SS
	Rick Ankiel	St. Louis	P
2001—	Albert Pujols	St. Louis	O-3-1B
	Roy Oswalt	Houston	P
2002—	Brad Wilkerson	Montreal	OF-1B
	Jason Jennings	Colorado	P
2003—	Scott Podsednik	Milwaukee	OF
	Dontrelle Willis	Florida	P

FIREMAN OF THE YEAR

AMERICAN LEAGUE

Year	Pitcher	Team
1960—	Mike Fornieles	Boston
1961—	Luis Arroyo	New York
1962—	Dick Radatz	Boston
1963—	Stu Miller	Baltimore
1964—	Dick Radatz	Boston
1965—	Eddie Fisher	Chicago
1966—	Jack Aker	Kansas City
1967—	Minnie Rojas	California
1968—	Wilbur Wood	Chicago
1969—	Ron Perranoski	Minnesota
1970—	Ron Perranoski	Minnesota
1971—	Ken Sanders	Milwaukee
1972—	Sparky Lyle	New York
1973—	John Hiller	Detroit
1974—	Terry Forster	Chicago
1975—	Rich Gossage	Chicago
1976—	Bill Campbell	Minnesota
1977—	Bill Campbell	Boston
1978—	Rich Gossage	New York
1979—	Mike Marshall	Minnesota
	Jim Kern	Texas
1980—	Dan Quisenberry	Kansas City
1981—	Rollie Fingers	Milwaukee
1982—	Dan Quisenberry	Kansas City
1983—	Dan Quisenberry	Kansas City
1984—	Dan Quisenberry	Kansas City
1985—	Dan Quisenberry	Kansas City
1986—	Dave Righetti	New York
1987—	Dave Righetti	New York
	Jeff Reardon	Minnesota
1988—	Dennis Eckersley	Oakland
1989—	Jeff Russell	Texas
1990—	Bobby Thigpen	Chicago
1991—	Dennis Eckersley	Oakland
	Bryan Harvey	California
1992—	Dennis Eckersley	Oakland
1993—	Jeff Montgomery	Kansas City

NATIONAL LEAGUE

Year	Pitcher	Team
1960—	Lindy McDaniel	St. Louis
1961—	Stu Miller	San Francisco
1962—	Roy Face	Pittsburgh
1963—	Lindy McDaniel	Chicago
1964—	Al McBean	Pittsburgh
1965—	Ted Abernathy	Chicago
1966—	Phil Regan	Los Angeles
1967—	Ted Abernathy	Cincinnati
1968—	Phil Regan	L.A.-Chicago
1969—	Wayne Granger	Cincinnati
1970—	Wayne Granger	Cincinnati
1971—	Dave Giusti	Pittsburgh
1972—	Clay Carroll	Cincinnati
1973—	Mike Marshall	Montreal
1974—	Mike Marshall	Los Angeles
1975—	Al Hrabosky	St. Louis
1976—	Rawly Eastwick	Cincinnati
1977—	Rollie Fingers	San Diego
1978—	Rollie Fingers	San Diego
1979—	Bruce Sutter	Chicago
1980—	Rollie Fingers	San Diego
	Tom Hume	Cincinnati
1981—	Bruce Sutter	St. Louis
1982—	Bruce Sutter	St. Louis
1983—	Al Holland	Philadelphia
	Lee Smith	Chicago
1984—	Bruce Sutter	St. Louis
1985—	Jeff Reardon	Montreal
1986—	Todd Worrell	St. Louis
1987—	Steve Bedrosian	Philadelphia
1988—	John Franco	Cincinnati
1989—	Mark Davis	San Diego
1990—	John Franco	New York
1991—	Lee Smith	St. Louis
1992—	Doug Jones	Houston
	Lee Smith	St. Louis
1993—	Randy Myers	Chicago

AMERICAN LEAGUE

Year	Pitcher	Team
1994—	Lee Smith	Baltimore
1995—	Jose Mesa	Cleveland
1996—	John Wetteland	New York
1997—	Mariano Rivera	New York
1998—	Tom Gordon	Boston
1999—	Mariano Rivera	New York
2000—	Todd Jones	Detroit
2001—	Mariano Rivera	New York
2002—	Billy Koch	Oakland
2003—	Keith Foulke	Oakland

NATIONAL LEAGUE

Year	Pitcher	Team
1994—	John Franco	New York
1995—	Randy Myers	Chicago
1996—	Trevor Hoffman	San Diego
1997—	Jeff Shaw	Cincinnati
1998—	Trevor Hoffman	San Diego
1999—	Ugueth Urbina	Montreal
2000—	Antonio Alfonseca	Florida
2001—	Armando Benitez	New York
	Robb Nen	San Francisco
2002—	John Smoltz	Atlanta
2003—	Eric Gagne	Los Angeles

COMEBACK PLAYER OF THE YEAR

AMERICAN LEAGUE

Year	Pitcher	Team
1965—	Norm Cash	Detroit
1966—	Boog Powell	Baltimore
1967—	Dean Chance	Minnesota
1968—	Ken Harrelson	Boston
1969—	Tony Conigliaro	Boston
1970—	Clyde Wright	California
1971—	Norm Cash	Detroit
1972—	Luis Tiant	Boston
1973—	John Hiller	Detroit
1974—	Ferguson Jenkins	Texas
1975—	Boog Powell	Cleveland
1976—	Dock Ellis	New York
1977—	Eric Soderholm	Chicago
1978—	Mike Caldwell	Milwaukee
1979—	Willie Horton	Seattle
1980—	Matt Keough	Oakland
1981—	Richie Zisk	Seattle
1982—	Andre Thornton	Cleveland
1983—	Alan Trammell	Detroit
1984—	Dave Kingman	Oakland
1985—	Gorman Thomas	Seattle
1986—	John Candelaria	California
1987—	Bret Saberhagen	Kansas City
1988—	Storm Davis	Oakland
1989—	Bert Blyleven	California
1990—	Dave Winfield	California
1991—	Jose Guzman	Texas
1992—	Rick Sutcliffe	Baltimore
1993—	Bo Jackson	Chicago
1994—	Jose Canseco	Texas
1995—	Tim Wakefield	Boston
1996—	Kevin Elster	Texas
1997—	David Justice	Cleveland
1998—	Bret Saberhagen	Boston
1999—	John Jaha	Oakland
2000—	Frank Thomas	Chicago
2001—	Ruben Sierra	Texas
2002—	Tim Salmon	Anaheim
2003—	Gil Meche	Seattle

NATIONAL LEAGUE

Year	Pitcher	Team
1965—	Vernon Law	Pittsburgh
1966—	Phil Regan	Los Angeles
1967—	Mike McCormick	San Francisco
1968—	Alex Johnson	Cincinnati
1969—	Tommie Agee	New York
1970—	Jim Hickman	Chicago
1971—	Al Downing	Los Angeles
1972—	Bobby Tolan	Cincinnati
1973—	Dave Johnson	Atlanta
1974—	Jim Wynn	Los Angeles
1975—	Randy Jones	San Diego
1976—	Tommy John	Los Angeles
1977—	Willie McCovey	San Francisco
1978—	Willie Stargell	Pittsburgh
1979—	Lou Brock	St. Louis
1980—	Jerry Reuss	Los Angeles
1981—	Bob Knepper	Houston
1982—	Joe Morgan	San Francisco
1983—	John Denny	Philadelphia
1984—	Joaquin Andujar	St. Louis
1985—	Rick Reuschel	Pittsburgh
1986—	Ray Knight	New York
1987—	Rick Sutcliffe	Chicago
1988—	Tim Leary	Los Angeles
1989—	Lonnie Smith	Atlanta
1990—	John Tudor	St. Louis
1991—	Terry Pendleton	Atlanta
1992—	Gary Sheffield	San Diego
1993—	Andres Galarraga	Colorado
1994—	Tim Wallach	Los Angeles
1995—	Ron Gant	Cincinnati
1996—	Eric Davis	Cincinnati
1997—	Darren Daulton	Phi.-Fla.
1998—	Greg Vaughn	San Diego
1999—	Rickey Henderson	New York
2000—	Andres Galarraga	Atlanta
2001—	Matt Morris	St. Louis
2002—	Mike Lieberthal	Philadelphia
2003—	Javy Lopez	Atlanta

MAJOR LEAGUE PLAYER OF THE YEAR

Year	Player	Team
1936—	Carl Hubbell	New York N.L.
1937—	Johnny Allen	Cleveland A.L.
1938—	Johnny Vander Meer	Cincinnati N.L.
1939—	Joe DiMaggio	New York A.L.
1940—	Bob Feller	Cleveland A.L.
1941—	Ted Williams	Boston A.L.
1942—	Ted Williams	Boston A.L.
1943—	Spud Chandler	New York A.L.
1944—	Marty Marion	St. Louis N.L.
1945—	Hal Newhouser	Detroit A.L.
1946—	Stan Musial	St. Louis N.L.
1947—	Ted Williams	Boston A.L.
1948—	Lou Boudreau	Cleveland A.L.
1949—	Ted Williams	Boston A.L.
1950—	Phil Rizzuto	New York A.L.
1951—	Stan Musial	St. Louis N.L.
1952—	Robin Roberts	Philadelphia N.L.
1953—	Al Rosen	Cleveland A.L.
1954—	Willie Mays	New York N.L.
1955—	Duke Snider	Brooklyn N.L.
1956—	Mickey Mantle	New York A.L.
1957—	Ted Williams	Boston A.L.
1958—	Bob Turley	New York A.L.
1959—	Early Wynn	Chicago A.L.
1960—	Bill Mazeroski	Pittsburgh N.L.
1961—	Roger Maris	New York A.L.
1962—	Maury Wills	Los Angeles N.L.
	Don Drysdale	Los Angeles N.L.
1963—	Sandy Koufax	Los Angeles N.L.
1964—	Ken Boyer	St. Louis N.L.
1965—	Sandy Koufax	Los Angeles N.L.
1966—	Frank Robinson	Baltimore A.L.
1967—	Carl Yastrzemski	Boston A.L.
1968—	Denny McLain	Detroit A.L.
1969—	Willie McCovey	San Francisco N.L.
1970—	Johnny Bench	Cincinnati N.L.
1971—	Joe Torre	St. Louis N.L.
1972—	Billy Williams	Chicago N.L.
1973—	Reggie Jackson	Oakland A.L.
1974—	Lou Brock	St. Louis N.L.
1975—	Joe Morgan	Cincinnati N.L.
1976—	Joe Morgan	Cincinnati N.L.

Year	Player	Team
1977	Rod Carew	Minnesota A.L.
1978	Ron Guidry	New York A.L.
1979	Willie Stargell	Pittsburgh N.L.
1980	George Brett	Kansas City A.L.
1981	Fernando Valenzuela	Los Angeles N.L.
1982	Robin Yount	Milwaukee A.L.
1983	Cal Ripken Jr.	Baltimore A.L.
1984	Ryne Sandberg	Chicago N.L.
1985	Don Mattingly	New York A.L.
1986	Roger Clemens	Boston A.L.
1987	George Bell	Toronto A.L.
1988	Orel Hershiser	Los Angeles N.L.
1989	Kevin Mitchell	San Francisco N.L.
1990	Barry Bonds	Pittsburgh N.L.
1991	Cal Ripken Jr.	Baltimore A.L.
1992	Gary Sheffield	San Diego N.L.
1993	Frank Thomas	Chicago A.L.
1994	Jeff Bagwell	Houston N.L.
1995	Albert Belle	Cleveland A.L.
1996	Alex Rodriguez	Seattle A.L.
1997	Ken Griffey Jr.	Seattle A.L.
1998	Sammy Sosa	Chicago N.L.
1999	Rafael Palmeiro	Texas A.L.
2000	Carlos Delgado	Toronto A.L.
2001	Barry Bonds	San Francisco N.L.
2002	Alex Rodriguez	Texas A.L
2003	Albert Pujols	St. Louis N.L.

MAJOR LEAGUE MANAGER OF THE YEAR

Year	Manager	Team
1936	Joe McCarthy	New York A.L.
1937	Bill McKechnie	Boston N.L.
1938	Joe McCarthy	New York A.L.
1939	Leo Durocher	Brooklyn N.L.
1940	Bill McKechnie	Cincinnati N.L.
1941	Billy Southworth	St. Louis N.L.
1942	Billy Southworth	St. Louis N.L.
1943	Joe McCarthy	New York A.L.
1944	Luke Sewell	St. Louis A.L.
1945	Ossie Bluege	Washington A.L.
1946	Eddie Dyer	St. Louis N.L.
1947	Bucky Harris	New York A.L.
1948	Bill Meyer	Pittsburgh N.L.
1949	Casey Stengel	New York A.L.
1950	Red Rolfe	Detroit A.L.
1951	Leo Durocher	New York N.L.
1952	Eddie Stanky	St. Louis N.L.
1953	Casey Stengel	New York A.L.
1954	Leo Durocher	New York N.L.
1955	Walter Alston	Brooklyn N.L.
1956	Birdie Tebbetts	Cincinnati N.L.
1957	Fred Hutchinson	St. Louis N.L.
1958	Casey Stengel	New York A.L.
1959	Walter Alston	Los Angeles N.L.
1960	Danny Murtaugh	Pittsburgh N.L.
1961	Ralph Houk	New York A.L.
1962	Bill Rigney	Los Angeles A.L.
1963	Walter Alston	Los Angeles N.L.
1964	Johnny Keane	St. Louis N.L.
1965	Sam Mele	Minnesota A.L.
1966	Hank Bauer	Baltimore A.L.
1967	Dick Williams	Boston A.L.
1968	Mayo Smith	Detroit A.L.
1969	Gil Hodges	New York N.L.
1970	Danny Murtaugh	Pittsburgh N.L.
1971	Charlie Fox	San Francisco N.L.
1972	Chuck Tanner	Chicago A.L.
1973	Gene Mauch	Montreal N.L.
1974	Bill Virdon	New York A.L.
1975	Darrell Johnson	Boston A.L.
1976	Danny Ozark	Philadelphia N.L.
1977	Earl Weaver	Baltimore A.L.
1978	George Bamberger	Milwaukee A.L.
1979	Earl Weaver	Baltimore A.L.
1980	Bill Virdon	Houston N.L.
1981	Billy Martin	Oakland A.L.
1982	Whitey Herzog	St. Louis N.L.
1983	Tony La Russa	Chicago A.L.
1984	Jim Frey	Chicago N.L.
1985	Bobby Cox	Toronto A.L.
1986	John McNamara	Boston A.L.
	Hal Lanier	Houston N.L.
1987	Sparky Anderson	Detroit A.L.
	Buck Rodgers	Montreal N.L.
1988	Tony La Russa	Oakland A.L.
	Tommy Lasorda	L.A. N.L. (tie)
	Jim Leyland	Pit. N.L. (tie)
1989	Frank Robinson	Baltimore A.L.
	Don Zimmer	Chicago N.L.
1990	Jeff Torborg	Chicago A.L.
	Jim Leyland	Pittsburgh N.L.
1991	Tom Kelly	Minnesota A.L.
	Bobby Cox	Atlanta N.L.
1992	Tony La Russa	Oakland A.L.
	Jim Leyland	Pittsburgh N.L.
1993	Johnny Oates	Baltimore A.L.
	Bobby Cox	Atlanta N.L.
1994	Buck Showalter	New York A.L.
	Felipe Alou	Montreal N.L.
1995	Mike Hargrove	Cleveland A.L.
	Don Baylor	Colorado N.L.
1996	Johnny Oates	Texas A.L.
	Bruce Bochy	San Diego N.L.
1997	Dave Johnson	Baltimore A.L.
	Dusty Baker	San Fran. N.L.
1998	Joe Torre	New York A.L.
	Bruce Bochy	San Diego N.L.
1999	Jimy Williams	Boston A.L.
	Bobby Cox	Atlanta N.L.
2000	Jerry Manuel	Chicago A.L.
	Dusty Baker	San Fran. N.L.
2001	Lou Piniella	Seattle A.L.
	Larry Bowa	Philadelphia N.L.
2002	Mike Scioscia	Anaheim A.L.
	Bobby Cox	Atlanta N.L.
2003	Tony Pena	Kansas City A.L.
	Bobby Cox	Atlanta N.L.

MAJOR LEAGUE EXECUTIVE OF THE YEAR

Year	Executive	Team
1936	Branch Rickey	St. Louis N.L.
1937	Ed Barrow	New York A.L.
1938	Warren Giles	Cincinnati N.L.
1939	Larry MacPhail	Brooklyn N.L.
1940	Walter Briggs Sr.	Detroit A.L.
1941	Ed Barrow	New York A.L.
1942	Branch Rickey	St. Louis N.L.
1943	Clark Griffith	Washington A.L.
1944	Billy DeWitt	St. Louis A.L.
1945	Phil Wrigley	Chicago N.L.
1946	Tom Yawkey	Boston A.L.
1947	Branch Rickey	Brooklyn N.L.
1948	Bill Veeck	Cleveland A.L.
1949	Bob Carpenter	Philadelphia N.L.
1950	George Weiss	New York A.L.
1951	George Weiss	New York A.L.
1952	George Weiss	New York A.L.
1953	Lou Perini	Milwaukee N.L.
1954	Horace Stoneham	New York N.L.
1955	Walter O'Malley	Brooklyn N.L.
1956	Gabe Paul	Cincinnati N.L.
1957	Frank Lane	St. Louis N.L.
1958	Joe Brown	Pittsburgh N.L.
1959	Buzzie Bavasi	Los Angeles N.L.
1960	George Weiss	New York A.L.
1961	Dan Topping	New York A.L.
1962	Fred Haney	Los Angeles A.L.
1963	Bing Devine	St. Louis N.L.
1964	Bing Devine	St. Louis N.L.
1965	Cal Griffith	Minnesota A.L.
1966	Lee MacPhail	Commissioner's Off.
1967	Dick O'Connell	Boston A.L.
1968	Jim Campbell	Detroit A.L.
1969	John Murphy	New York N.L.
1970	Harry Dalton	Baltimore A.L.
1971	Cedric Tallis	Kansas City A.L.
1972	Roland Hemond	Chicago A.L.
1973	Bob Howsam	Cincinnati N.L.
1974	Gabe Paul	New York A.L.
1975	Dick O'Connell	Boston A.L.
1976	Joe Burke	Kansas City A.L.
1977	Bill Veeck	Chicago A.L.
1978	Spec Richardson	San Francisco N.L.
1979	Hank Peters	Baltimore A.L.
1980	Tal Smith	Houston N.L.
1981	John McHale	Montreal N.L.
1982	Harry Dalton	Milwaukee A.L.
1983	Hank Peters	Baltimore A.L.
1984	Dallas Green	Chicago N.L.
1985	John Schuerholz	Kansas City A.L.
1986	Frank Cashen	New York N.L.
1987	Al Rosen	San Francisco N.L.
1988	Fred Claire	Los Angeles N.L.
1989	Roland Hemond	Baltimore A.L.
1990	Bob Quinn	Cincinnati N.L.
1991	Andy MacPhail	Minnesota A.L.
1992	Dan Duquette	Montreal N.L.
1993	Lee Thomas	Philadelphia N.L.
1994	John Hart	Cleveland A.L.
1995	John Hart	Cleveland A.L.
1996	Doug Melvin	Texas A.L.
1997	Cam Bonifay	Pittsburgh N.L.
1998	Gerry Hunsicker	Houston N.L.
1999	Billy Beane	Oakland A.L.
2000	Walt Jocketty	St. Louis N.L.
2001	Pat Gillick	Seattle A.L.
2002	Terry Ryan	Minnesota A.L.
2003	Brian Sabean	San Francisco N.L.

1925
1B— Jim Bottomley, St. Louis N.L.
2B— Rogers Hornsby, St. Louis N.L.
SS— Glenn Wright, Pittsburgh N.L.
3B— Pie Traynor, Pittsburgh N.L.
OF— Kiki Cuyler, Pittsburgh N.L.
OF— Max Carey, Pittsburgh N.L.
OF— Goose Goslin, Washington A.L.
C— Mickey Cochrane, Phil. A.L.
P— Walter Johnson, Washington A.L.
P— Ed Rommel, Philadelphia A.L.
P— Dazzy Vance, Brooklyn N.L.

1926
1B— George Burns, Cleveland A.L.
2B— Rogers Hornsby, St. Louis N.L.
SS— Joe Sewell, Cleveland A.L.
3B— Pie Traynor, Pittsburgh N.L.
OF— Goose Goslin, Washington A.L.
OF— John Mostil, Chicago A.L.
OF— Babe Ruth, New York A.L.
C— Bob O'Farrell, St. Louis N.L.
P— Herb Pennock, New York A.L.
P— George Uhle, Cleveland A.L.
P— Grover Alexander, St. Louis N.L.

1927
1B— Lou Gehrig, New York A.L.
2B— Rogers Hornsby, New York N.L.
SS— Travis Jackson, New York N.L.
3B— Pie Traynor, Pittsburgh N.L.
OF— Babe Ruth, New York A.L.
OF— Al Simmons, Philadelphia A.L.
OF— Paul Waner, Pittsburgh N.L.
C— Gabby Hartnett, Chicago N.L.
P— Charley Root, Chicago N.L.
P— Ted Lyons, Chicago A.L.

1928
1B— Lou Gehrig, New York A.L.
2B— Rogers Hornsby, Boston N.L.
SS— Travis Jackson, New York N.L.
3B— Fred Lindstrom, New York N.L.
OF— Babe Ruth, New York A.L.
OF— Heinie Manush, St. Louis A.L.
OF— Paul Waner, Pittsburgh N.L.
C— Mickey Cochrane, Phil. A.L.
P— Lefty Grove, Philadelphia A.L.
P— Waite Hoyt, New York A.L.

1929
1B— Jimmie Foxx, Philadelphia A.L.
2B— Rogers Hornsby, Chicago N.L.
SS— Travis Jackson, New York N.L.
3B— Pie Traynor, Pittsburgh, N.L.
OF— Al Simmons, Philadelphia A.L.
OF— Hack Wilson, Chicago N.L.
OF— Babe Ruth, New York A.L.
C— Mickey Cochrane, Phil. A.L.
P— Lefty Grove, Philadelphia A.L.
P— Burleigh Grimes, Pittsburgh N.L.

1930
1B— Bill Terry, New York N.L.
2B— Frank Frisch, St. Louis N.L.
SS— Joe Cronin, Washington A.L.
3B— Fred Lindstrom, New York N.L.
OF— Al Simmons, Philadelphia A.L.
OF— Hack Wilson, Chicago N.L.
OF— Babe Ruth, New York A.L.
C— Mickey Cochrane, Phil. A.L.
P— Lefty Grove, Philadelphia A.L.
P— Wes Ferrell, Cleveland A.L.

1931
1B— Lou Gehrig, New York A.L.
2B— Frank Frisch, St. Louis N.L.
SS— Joe Cronin, Washington A.L.
3B— Pie Traynor, Pittsburgh N.L.
OF— Al Simmons, Philadelphia A.L.
OF— Earl Averill, Cleveland A.L.
OF— Babe Ruth, New York A.L.
C— Mickey Cochrane, Phil. A.L.
P— Lefty Grove, Philadelphia A.L.
P— George Earnshaw, Phil. A.L.

1932
1B— Jimmie Foxx, Philadelphia A.L.
2B— Tony Lazzeri, New York A.L.
SS— Joe Cronin, Washington A.L.
3B— Pie Traynor, Pittsburgh N.L.
OF— Lefty O'Doul, Brooklyn N.L.
OF— Earl Averill, Cleveland A.L.
OF— Chuck Klein, Philadelphia N.L.
C— Bill Dickey, New York A.L.
P— Lefty Grove, Philadelphia A.L.
P— Lon Warneke, Chicago N.L.

1933
1B— Jimmie Foxx, Philadelphia A.L.
2B— Charley Gehringer, Detroit A.L.
SS— Joe Cronin, Washington A.L.
3B— Pie Traynor, Pittsburgh N.L.
OF— Al Simmons, Chicago A.L.
OF— Wally Berger, Boston N.L.
OF— Chuck Klein, Philadelphia N.L.
C— Bill Dickey, New York A.L.
P— Alvin Crowder, Washington A.L.
P— Carl Hubbell, New York N.L.

1934
1B— Lou Gehrig, New York A.L.
2B— Charley Gehringer, Detroit A.L.
SS— Joe Cronin, Washington A.L.
3B— Mike Higgins, Philadelphia A.L.
OF— Al Simmons, Chicago A.L.
OF— Earl Averill, Cleveland A.L.
OF— Mel Ott, New York N.L.
C— Mickey Cochrane, Detroit A.L.
P— Lefty Gomez, New York A.L.
P— Schoolboy Rowe, Detroit A.L.
P— Dizzy Dean, St. Louis N.L.

1935
1B— Hank Greenberg, Detroit A.L.
2B— Charley Gehringer, Detroit A.L.
SS— Arky Vaughan, Pittsburgh N.L.
3B— Pepper Martin, St. Louis N.L.
OF— Joe Medwick, St. Louis N.L.
OF— Doc Cramer, Philadelphia A.L.
OF— Mel Ott, New York N.L.
C— Mickey Cochrane, Detroit A.L.
P— Carl Hubbell, New York N.L.
P— Dizzy Dean, St. Louis N.L.

1936
1B— Lou Gehrig, New York A.L.
2B— Charley Gehringer, Detroit A.L.
SS— Luke Appling, Chicago A.L.
3B— Mike Higgins, Philadelphia A.L.
OF— Joe Medwick, St. Louis N.L.
OF— Earl Averill, Cleveland A.L.
OF— Mel Ott, New York N.L.
C— Bill Dickey, New York A.L.
P— Carl Hubbell, New York N.L.
P— Dizzy Dean, St. Louis N.L.

1937
1B— Lou Gehrig, New York A.L.
2B— Charley Gehringer, Detroit A.L.
SS— Dick Bartell, New York N.L.
3B— Red Rolfe, New York A.L.
OF— Joe Medwick, St. Louis N.L.
OF— Joe DiMaggio, New York A.L.
OF— Paul Waner, Pittsburgh N.L.
C— Gabby Hartnett, Chicago N.L.
P— Carl Hubbell, New York N.L.
P— Red Ruffing, New York A.L.

1938
1B— Jimmie Foxx, Boston A.L.
2B— Charley Gehringer, Detroit A.L.
SS— Joe Cronin, Boston A.L.
3B— Red Rolfe, New York A.L.
OF— Joe Medwick, St. Louis N.L.
OF— Joe DiMaggio, New York A.L.
OF— Mel Ott, New York N.L.
C— Bill Dickey, New York A.L.
P— Red Ruffing, New York A.L.
P— Lefty Gomez, New York A.L.
P— Johnny Vander Meer, Cin. N.L.

1939
1B— Jimmie Foxx, Boston A.L.
2B— Joe Gordon, New York A.L.
SS— Joe Cronin, Boston A.L.
3B— Red Rolfe, New York A.L.
OF— Joe Medwick, St. Louis N.L.
OF— Joe DiMaggio, New York A.L.
OF— Ted Williams, Boston A.L.
C— Bill Dickey, New York A.L.
P— Red Ruffing, New York A.L.
P— Bob Feller, Cleveland A.L.
P— Bucky Walters, Cincinnati N.L.

1940
1B— Frank McCormick, Cincinnati N.L.
2B— Joe Gordon, New York A.L.
SS— Luke Appling, Chicago A.L.
3B— Stan Hack, Chicago N.L.
OF— Hank Greenberg, Detroit A.L.
OF— Joe DiMaggio, New York A.L.
OF— Ted Williams, Boston A.L.
C— Harry Danning, New York N.L.
P— Bob Feller, Cleveland A.L.
P— Bucky Walters, Cincinnati N.L.
P— Paul Derringer, Cincinnati N.L.

1941
1B— Dolf Camilli, Brooklyn N.L.
2B— Joe Gordon, New York A.L.
SS— Cecil Travis, Washington A.L.
3B— Stan Hack, Chicago N.L.
OF— Ted Williams, Boston A.L.
OF— Joe DiMaggio, New York A.L.
OF— Pete Reiser, Brooklyn N.L.
C— Bill Dickey, New York A.L.
P— Bob Feller, Cleveland A.L.
P— Whitlow Wyatt, Brooklyn N.L.
P— Thornton Lee, Chicago A.L.

1942
1B— Johnny Mize, New York N.L.
2B— Joe Gordon, New York A.L.
SS— Johnny Pesky, Boston A.L.
3B— Stan Hack, Chicago N.L.
OF— Ted Williams, Boston A.L.
OF— Joe DiMaggio, New York A.L.
OF— Enos Slaughter, St. Louis N.L.
C— Mickey Owen, Brooklyn N.L.
P— Mort Cooper, St. Louis N.L.
P— Tiny Bonham, New York A.L.
P— Tex Hughson, Boston A.L.

1943
1B— Rudy York, Detroit A.L.
2B— Billy Herman, Brooklyn N.L.
SS— Luke Appling, Chicago A.L.
3B— Billy Johnson, New York A.L.
OF— Dick Wakefield, Detroit A.L.
OF— Stan Musial, St. Louis N.L.
OF— Bill Nicholson, Chicago N.L.
C— Walker Cooper, St. Louis N.L.
P— Spud Chandler, New York A.L.
P— Mort Cooper, St. Louis N.L.
P— Rip Sewell, Pittsburgh N.L.

1944
1B— Ray Sanders, St. Louis N.L.
2B— Bobby Doerr, Boston A.L.
SS— Marty Marion, St. Louis N.L.
3B— Bob Elliott, Pittsburgh N.L.
OF— Stan Musial, St. Louis N.L.
OF— Dick Wakefield, Detroit A.L.
OF— Dixie Walker, Brooklyn, N.L.
C— Walker Cooper, St. Louis N.L.
P— Hal Newhouser, Detroit A.L.
P— Mort Cooper, St. Louis N.L.
P— Dizzy Trout, Detroit A.L.

1945
1B— Phil Cavarretta, Chicago N.L.
2B— George Stirnweiss, N.Y. A.L.
SS— Marty Marion, St. Louis N.L.
3B— Whitey Kurowski, St. Louis N.L.
OF— Tommy Holmes, Boston N.L.
OF— Andy Pafko, Chicago N.L.
OF— Goody Rosen, Brooklyn N.L.
C— Paul Richards, Detroit A.L.
P— Hal Newhouser, Detroit A.L.
P— Boo Ferriss, Boston A.L.
P— Hank Borowy, Chicago N.L.

1946
1B— Stan Musial, St. Louis N.L.
2B— Bobby Doerr, Boston A.L.
SS— Johnny Pesky, Boston A.L.
3B— George Kell, Detroit A.L.
OF— Ted Williams, Boston A.L.
OF— Dom DiMaggio, Boston A.L.
OF— Enos Slaughter, St. Louis N.L.
C— Aaron Robinson, New York A.L.
P— Hal Newhouser, Detroit A.L.
P— Bob Feller, Cleveland A.L.
P— Boo Ferriss, Boston A.L.

1947
1B— Johnny Mize, New York N.L.
2B— Joe Gordon, Cleveland A.L.
SS— Lou Boudreau, Cleveland A.L.
3B— George Kell, Detroit A.L.
OF— Ted Williams, Boston A.L.
OF— Joe DiMaggio, New York A.L.
OF— Ralph Kiner, Pittsburgh N.L.
C— Walker Cooper, New York N.L.
P— Ewell Blackwell, Cincinnati N.L.
P— Bob Feller, Cleveland A.L.
P— Ralph Branca, Brooklyn N.L.

1948
1B— Johnny Mize, New York N.L.
2B— Joe Gordon, Cleveland A.L.
SS— Lou Boudreau, Cleveland A.L.
3B— Bob Elliott, Boston N.L.
OF— Ted Williams, Boston A.L.
OF— Joe DiMaggio, New York A.L.
OF— Stan Musial, St. Louis N.L.
C— Birdie Tebbetts, Boston A.L.
P— Johnny Sain, Boston N.L.
P— Bob Lemon, Cleveland A.L.
P— Harry Brecheen, St. Louis N.L.

1949
1B— Tommy Henrich, New York A.L.
2B— Jackie Robinson, Brooklyn N.L.
SS— Phil Rizzuto, New York A.L.
3B— George Kell, Detroit A.L.
OF— Ted Williams, Boston A.L.
OF— Stan Musial, St. Louis N.L.
OF— Ralph Kiner, Pittsburgh N.L.
C— Roy Campanella, Brooklyn N.L.
P— Mel Parnell, Boston A.L.
P— Ellis Kinder, Boston A.L.
P— Joe Page, New York A.L.

1950
1B— Walt Dropo, Boston A.L.
2B— Jackie Robinson, Brooklyn N.L.
SS— Phil Rizzuto, New York A.L.
3B— George Kell, Detroit A.L.
OF— Stan Musial, St. Louis N.L.
OF— Ralph Kiner, Pittsburgh N.L.
OF— Larry Doby, Cleveland A.L.
C— Yogi Berra, New York A.L.
P— Vic Raschi, New York A.L.
P— Bob Lemon, Cleveland A.L.
P— Jim Konstanty, Phil. N.L.

1951
1B— Ferris Fain, Philadelphia A.L.
2B— Jackie Robinson, Brooklyn N.L.
SS— Phil Rizzuto, New York A.L.
3B— George Kell, Detroit A.L.
OF— Stan Musial, St. Louis N.L.
OF— Ted Williams, Boston A.L.
OF— Ralph Kiner, Pittsburgh N.L.
C— Roy Campanella, Brooklyn N.L.
P— Sal Maglie, New York N.L.
P— Preacher Roe, Brooklyn N.L.
P— Allie Reynolds, New York A.L.

1952
1B— Ferris Fain, Philadelphia A.L.
2B— Jackie Robinson, Brooklyn N.L.
SS— Phil Rizzuto, New York A.L.
3B— George Kell, Boston A.L.
OF— Stan Musial, St. Louis N.L.
OF— Hank Sauer, Chicago N.L.
OF— Mickey Mantle, New York A.L.
C— Yogi Berra, New York A.L.
P— Robin Roberts, Philadelphia N.L.
P— Bobby Shantz, Philadelphia A.L.
P— Allie Reynolds, New York A.L.

1953
1B— Mickey Vernon, Washington A.L.
2B— Red Schoendienst, St. Louis N.L.
SS— Pee Wee Reese, Brooklyn N.L.
3B— Al Rosen, Cleveland A.L.
OF— Stan Musial, St. Louis N.L.
OF— Duke Snider, Brooklyn N.L.
OF— Carl Furillo, Brooklyn N.L.
C— Roy Campanella, Brooklyn N.L.
P— Robin Roberts, Philadelphia N.L.
P— Warren Spahn, Milwaukee N.L.
P— Bob Porterfield, Washington A.L.

1954
1B— Ted Kluszewski, Cincinnati N.L.
2B— Bobby Avila, Cleveland A.L.
SS— Alvin Dark, New York N.L.
3B— Al Rosen, Cleveland A.L.
OF— Willie Mays, New York N.L.
OF— Stan Musial, St. Louis N.L.
OF— Duke Snider, Brooklyn N.L.
C— Yogi Berra, New York A.L.
P— Bob Lemon, Cleveland A.L.
P— Johnny Antonelli, New York N.L.
P— Robin Roberts, Philadelphia N.L.

1955
1B— Ted Kluszewski, Cincinnati N.L.
2B— Nellie Fox, Chicago A.L.
SS— Ernie Banks, Chicago N.L.
3B— Ed Mathews, Milwaukee N.L.
OF— Duke Snider, Brooklyn N.L.
OF— Ted Williams, Boston A.L.
OF— Al Kaline, Detroit A.L.
C— Roy Campanella, Brooklyn N.L.
P— Robin Roberts, Philadelphia N.L.
P— Don Newcombe, Brooklyn N.L.
P— Whitey Ford, New York A.L.

1956
1B— Ted Kluszewski, Cincinnati N.L.
2B— Nellie Fox, Chicago A.L.
SS— Harvey Kuenn, Detroit A.L.
3B— Ken Boyer, St. Louis N.L.
OF— Mickey Mantle, New York A.L.
OF— Hank Aaron, Milwaukee N.L.
OF— Ted Williams, Boston A.L.
C— Yogi Berra, New York A.L.
P— Don Newcombe, Brooklyn N.L.
P— Whitey Ford, New York A.L.
P— Billy Pierce, Chicago A.L.

1957
1B— Stan Musial, St. Louis N.L.
2B— Red Schoendienst, N.Y.-Mil. N.L.
SS— Gil McDougald, New York A.L.
3B— Ed Mathews, Milwaukee N.L.
OF— Mickey Mantle, New York A.L.
OF— Ted Williams, Boston A.L.
OF— Willie Mays, New York N.L.
C— Yogi Berra, New York A.L.
P— Warren Spahn, Milwaukee N.L.
P— Billy Pierce, Chicago N.L.
P— Jim Bunning, Detroit A.L.

1958
1B— Stan Musial, St. Louis N.L.
2B— Nellie Fox, Chicago A.L.
SS— Ernie Banks, Chicago N.L.
3B— Frank Thomas, Pittsburgh N.L.
OF— Ted Williams, Boston A.L.
OF— Willie Mays, San Francisco N.L.
OF— Hank Aaron, Milwaukee N.L.
C— Del Crandall, Milwaukee N.L.
P— Bob Turley, New York A.L.
P— Warren Spahn, Milwaukee N.L.
P— Bob Friend, Pittsburgh N.L.

1959
1B— Orlando Cepeda, S.F. N.L.
2B— Nellie Fox, Chicago A.L.
SS— Ernie Banks, Chicago N.L.
3B— Ed Mathews, Milwaukee N.L.
OF— Minnie Minoso, Cleveland A.L.
OF— Willie Mays, San Francisco N.L.
OF— Hank Aaron, Milwaukee N.L.
C— Sherm Lollar, Chicago A.L.
P— Early Wynn, Chicago A.L.
P— Sam Jones, San Francisco N.L.
P— Johnny Antonelli, S.F. N.L.

1960
1B— Bill Skowron, New York A.L.
2B— Bill Mazeroski, Pittsburgh N.L.
SS— Ernie Banks, Chicago N.L.
3B— Ed Mathews, Milwaukee N.L.
OF— Minnie Minoso, Chicago A.L.
OF— Willie Mays, San Francisco N.L.
OF— Roger Maris, New York A.L.
C— Del Crandall, Milwaukee N.L.
P— Vernon Law, Pittsburgh N.L.
P— Warren Spahn, Milwaukee N.L.
P— Ernie Broglio, St. Louis N.L.

1961

AMERICAN LEAGUE

1B— Norm Cash, Detroit
2B— Bobby Richardson, New York
SS— Tony Kubek, New York
3B— Brooks Robinson, Baltimore
OF— Mickey Mantle, New York
OF— Roger Maris, New York
OF— Rocky Colavito, Detroit
C— Elston Howard, New York
P— Whitey Ford, New York
P— Frank Lary, Detroit

NATIONAL LEAGUE

1B— Orlando Cepeda, San Francisco
2B— Frank Bolling, Milwaukee
SS— Maury Wills, Los Angeles
3B— Ken Boyer, St. Louis
OF— Willie Mays, San Francisco
OF— Frank Robinson, Cincinnati
OF— Roberto Clemente, Pittsburgh
C— Smoky Burgess, Pittsburgh
P— Joey Jay, Cincinnati
P— Warren Spahn, Milwaukee

1962

AMERICAN LEAGUE

1B— Norm Siebern, Kansas City
2B— Bobby Richardson, New York
SS— Tom Tresh, New York
3B— Brooks Robinson, Baltimore
OF— Leon Wagner, Los Angeles
OF— Mickey Mantle, New York
OF— Al Kaline, Detroit
C— Earl Battey, Minnesota
P— Ralph Terry, New York
P— Dick Donovan, Cleveland

NATIONAL LEAGUE

1B— Orlando Cepeda, San Francisco
2B— Bill Mazeroski, Pittsburgh
SS— Maury Wills, Los Angeles
3B— Ken Boyer, St. Louis
OF— Tommy Davis, Los Angeles
OF— Willie Mays, San Francisco
OF— Frank Robinson, Cincinnati
C— Del Crandall, Milwaukee
P— Don Drysdale, Los Angeles
P— Bob Purkey, Cincinnati

1963

AMERICAN LEAGUE

1B— Joe Pepitone, New York
2B— Bobby Richardson, New York
SS— Luis Aparicio, Baltimore
3B— Frank Malzone, Boston
OF— Carl Yastrzemski, Boston
OF— Albie Pearson, Los Angeles
OF— Al Kaline, Detroit
C— Elston Howard, New York
P— Whitey Ford, New York
P— Gary Peters, Chicago

NATIONAL LEAGUE

1B— Bill White, St. Louis
2B— Jim Gilliam, Los Angeles
SS— Dick Groat, St. Louis
3B— Ken Boyer, St. Louis
OF— Tommy Davis, Los Angeles
OF— Willie Mays, San Francisco
OF— Hank Aaron, Milwaukee
C— John Edwards, Cincinnati
P— Sandy Koufax, Los Angeles
P— Juan Marichal, San Francisco

1964

AMERICAN LEAGUE

1B— Dick Stuart, Boston
2B— Bobby Richardson, New York
SS— Jim Fregosi, Los Angeles
3B— Brooks Robinson, Baltimore
OF— Harmon Killebrew, Minnesota
OF— Mickey Mantle, New York
OF— Tony Oliva, Minnesota
C— Elston Howard, New York
P— Dean Chance, Los Angeles
P— Gary Peters, Chicago

NATIONAL LEAGUE

1B— Bill White, St. Louis
2B— Ron Hunt, New York
SS— Dick Groat, St. Louis
3B— Ken Boyer, St. Louis
OF— Billy Williams, Chicago
OF— Willie Mays, San Francisco
OF— Roberto Clemente, Pittsburgh
C— Joe Torre, Milwaukee
P— Sandy Koufax, Los Angeles
P— Jim Bunning, Philadelphia

1965

AMERICAN LEAGUE

1B— Fred Whitfield, Cleveland
2B— Bobby Richardson, New York
SS— Zoilo Versalles, Minnesota
3B— Brooks Robinson, Baltimore
OF— Carl Yastrzemski, Boston
OF— Jimmie Hall, Minnesota
OF— Tony Oliva, Minnesota
C— Earl Battey, Minnesota
P— Jim Grant, Minnesota
P— Mel Stottlemyre, New York

NATIONAL LEAGUE

1B— Willie McCovey, San Francisco
2B— Pete Rose, Cincinnati
SS— Maury Wills, Los Angeles
3B— Deron Johnson, Cincinnati
OF— Willie Stargell, Pittsburgh
OF— Willie Mays, San Francisco
OF— Hank Aaron, Milwaukee
C— Joe Torre, Milwaukee
P— Sandy Koufax, Los Angeles
P— Juan Marichal, San Francisco

1966

AMERICAN LEAGUE

1B— Boog Powell, Baltimore
2B— Bobby Richardson, New York
SS— Luis Aparicio, Baltimore
3B— Brooks Robinson, Baltimore
OF— Frank Robinson, Baltimore
OF— Al Kaline, Detroit
OF— Tony Oliva, Minnesota
C— Paul Casanova, Washington
P— Jim Kaat, Minnesota
P— Earl Wilson, Detroit

NATIONAL LEAGUE

1B— Felipe Alou, Atlanta
2B— Pete Rose, Cincinnati
SS— Gene Alley, Pittsburgh
3B— Ron Santo, Chicago
OF— Willie Stargell, Pittsburgh
OF— Willie Mays, San Francisco
OF— Roberto Clemente, Pittsburgh
C— Joe Torre, Atlanta
P— Sandy Koufax, Los Angeles
P— Juan Marichal, San Francisco

1967

AMERICAN LEAGUE

1B— Harmon Killebrew, Minnesota
2B— Rod Carew, Minnesota
SS— Jim Fregosi, California
3B— Brooks Robinson, Baltimore
OF— Carl Yastrzemski, Boston
OF— Al Kaline, Detroit
OF— Frank Robinson, Baltimore
C— Bill Freehan, Detroit
P— Jim Lonborg, Boston
P— Earl Wilson, Detroit

NATIONAL LEAGUE

1B— Orlando Cepeda, St. Louis
2B— Bill Mazeroski, Pittsburgh
SS— Gene Alley, Pittsburgh
3B— Ron Santo, Chicago
OF— Hank Aaron, Atlanta
OF— Jim Wynn, Houston
OF— Roberto Clemente, Pittsburgh
C— Tim McCarver, St. Louis
P— Mike McCormick, San Francisco
P— Ferguson Jenkins, Chicago

1968

AMERICAN LEAGUE

1B— Boog Powell, Baltimore
2B— Rod Carew, Minnesota
SS— Luis Aparicio, Chicago
3B— Brooks Robinson, Baltimore
OF— Ken Harrelson, Boston
OF— Willie Horton, Detroit
OF— Frank Howard, Washington
C— Bill Freehan, Detroit
P— Dave McNally, Baltimore
P— Denny McLain, Detroit

NATIONAL LEAGUE

1B— Willie McCovey, San Francisco
2B— Tommy Helms, Cincinnati
SS— Don Kessinger, Chicago
3B— Ron Santo, Chicago
OF— Billy Williams, Chicago
OF— Curt Flood, St. Louis
OF— Pete Rose, Cincinnati
C— Johnny Bench, Cincinnati
P— Bob Gibson, St. Louis
P— Juan Marichal, San Francisco

1969

AMERICAN LEAGUE

1B— Boog Powell, Baltimore
2B— Rod Carew, Minnesota
SS— Rico Petrocelli, Boston
3B— Harmon Killebrew, Minnesota
OF— Frank Howard, Washington
OF— Paul Blair, Baltimore
OF— Reggie Jackson, Oakland
C— Bill Freehan, Detroit
RHP— Denny McLain, Detroit
LHP— Mike Cuellar, Baltimore

NATIONAL LEAGUE

1B— Willie McCovey, San Francisco
2B— Glenn Beckert, Chicago
SS— Don Kessinger, Chicago
3B— Ron Santo, Chicago
OF— Cleon Jones, New York
OF— Matty Alou, Pittsburgh
OF— Hank Aaron, Atlanta
C— Johnny Bench, Cincinnati
RHP— Tom Seaver, New York
LHP— Steve Carlton, St. Louis

1970

AMERICAN LEAGUE

1B— Boog Powell, Baltimore
2B— Dave Johnson, Baltimore
SS— Luis Aparicio, Chicago
3B— Harmon Killebrew, Minnesota
OF— Frank Howard, Washington
OF— Reggie Smith, Boston
OF— Tony Oliva, Minnesota
C— Ray Fosse, Cleveland
RHP— Jim Perry, Minnesota
LHP— Sam McDowell, Cleveland

NATIONAL LEAGUE

1B— Willie McCovey, San Francisco
2B— Glenn Beckert, Chicago
SS— Don Kessinger, Chicago
3B— Tony Perez, Cincinnati
OF— Billy Williams, Chicago
OF— Bobby Tolan, Cincinnati
OF— Hank Aaron, Atlanta
C— Johnny Bench, Cincinnati
RHP— Bob Gibson, St. Louis
LHP— Jim Merritt, Cincinnati

1971

AMERICAN LEAGUE

1B— Norm Cash, Detroit
2B— Cookie Rojas, Kansas City
SS— Leo Cardenas, Minnesota
3B— Brooks Robinson, Baltimore
OF— Merv Rettenmund, Baltimore
OF— Bobby Murcer, New York
OF— Tony Oliva, Minnesota
C— Bill Freehan, Detroit
RHP— Jim Palmer, Baltimore
LHP— Vida Blue, Oakland

NATIONAL LEAGUE

1B— Lee May, Cincinnati
2B— Glenn Beckett, Chicago
SS— Bud Harrelson, New York
3B— Joe Torre, St. Louis
OF— Willie Stargell, Pittsburgh
OF— Willie Davis, Los Angeles
OF— Hank Aaron, Atlanta
C— Manny Sanguillen, Pittsburgh
RHP— Ferguson Jenkins, Chicago
LHP— Steve Carlton, St. Louis

1972

AMERICAN LEAGUE

1B— Dick Allen, Chicago
2B— Rod Carew, Minnesota
SS— Luis Aparicio, Boston
3B— Brooks Robinson, Baltimore
OF— Joe Rudi, Oakland
OF— Bobby Murcer, New York
OF— Richie Scheinblum, Kansas City
C— Carlton Fisk, Boston
RHP— Gaylord Perry, Cleveland
LHP— Wilbur Wood, Chicago

NATIONAL LEAGUE

1B— Willie Stargell, Pittsburgh
2B— Joe Morgan, Cincinnati
SS— Chris Speier, San Francisco
3B— Ron Santo, Chicago
OF— Billy Williams, Chicago
OF— Cesar Cedeno, Houston
OF— Roberto Clemente, Pittsburgh
C— Johnny Bench, Cincinnati
RHP— Ferguson Jenkins, Chicago
LHP— Steve Carlton, Philadelphia

1973

AMERICAN LEAGUE

1B— John Mayberry, Kansas City
2B— Rod Carew, Minnesota
SS— Bert Campaneris, Oakland
3B— Sal Bando, Oakland
OF— Reggie Jackson, Oakland
OF— Amos Otis, Kansas City
OF— Bobby Murcer, New York
C— Thurman Munson, New York
RHP— Jim Palmer, Baltimore
LHP— Ken Holtzman, Oakland

NATIONAL LEAGUE

1B— Tony Perez, Cincinnati
2B— Dave Johnson, Atlanta
SS— Bill Russell, Los Angeles
3B— Darrell Evans, Atlanta
OF— Bobby Bonds, San Francisco
OF— Cesar Cedeno, Houston
OF— Pete Rose, Cincinnati
C— Johnny Bench, Cincinnati
RHP— Tom Seaver, New York
LHP— Ron Bryant, San Francisco

1974

AMERICAN LEAGUE

1B— Dick Allen, Chicago
2B— Rod Carew, Minnesota
SS— Bert Campaneris, Oakland
3B— Sal Bando, Oakland
OF— Joe Rudi, Oakland
OF— Paul Blair, Baltimore
OF— Jeff Burroughs, Texas
C— Thurman Munson, New York
DH— Tommy Davis, Baltimore
RHP— Jim Hunter, Oakland
LHP— Mike Cuellar, Baltimore

NATIONAL LEAGUE

1B— Steve Garvey, Los Angeles
2B— Joe Morgan, Cincinnati
SS— Dave Concepcion, Cincinnati
3B— Mike Schmidt, Philadelphia
OF— Lou Brock, St. Louis
OF— Jim Wynn, Los Angeles
OF— Richie Zisk, Pittsburgh
C— Johnny Bench, Cincinnati
RHP— Andy Messersmith, Los Angeles
LHP— Don Gullett, Cincinnati

1975

AMERICAN LEAGUE

1B— John Mayberry, Kansas City
2B— Rod Carew, Minnesota
SS— Toby Harrah, Texas
3B— Graig Nettles, New York
OF— Jim Rice, Boston
OF— Fred Lynn, Boston
OF— Reggie Jackson, Oakland
C— Thurman Munson, New York
DH— Willie Horton, Detroit
RHP— Jim Palmer, Baltimore
LHP— Jim Kaat, Chicago

NATIONAL LEAGUE

1B— Steve Garvey, Los Angeles
2B— Joe Morgan, Cincinnati
SS— Larry Bowa, Philadelphia
3B— Bill Madlock, Chicago
OF— Greg Luzinski, Philadelphia
OF— Al Oliver, Pittsburgh
OF— Dave Parker, Pittsburgh
C— Johnny Bench, Cincinnati
RHP— Tom Seaver, New York
LHP— Randy Jones, San Diego

1976

AMERICAN LEAGUE

1B— Chris Chambliss, New York
2B— Bobby Grich, Baltimore
3B— George Brett, Kansas City
SS— Mark Belanger, Baltimore
OF— Joe Rudi, Oakland
OF— Mickey Rivers, New York
OF— Reggie Jackson, Baltimore
C— Thurman Munson, New York
DH— Hal McRae, Kansas City
RHP— Jim Palmer, Baltimore
LHP— Frank Tanana, California

NATIONAL LEAGUE

1B— Willie Montanez, S.F.-Atl.
2B— Joe Morgan, Cincinnati
3B— Mike Schmidt, Philadelphia
SS— Dave Concepcion, Cincinnati
OF— George Foster, Cincinnati
OF— Cesar Cedeno, Houston
OF— Ken Griffey, Cincinnati
C— Bob Boone, Philadelphia
RHP— Don Sutton, Los Angeles
LHP— Randy Jones, San Diego

1977

AMERICAN LEAGUE

1B— Rod Carew, Minnesota
2B— Willie Randolph, New York
3B— Graig Nettles, New York
SS— Rick Burleson, Boston
OF— Jim Rice, Boston
OF— Larry Hisle, Minnesota
OF— Bobby Bonds, California
C— Carlton Fisk, Boston
DH— Hal McRae, Kansas City
RHP— Nolan Ryan, California
LHP— Frank Tanana, California

NATIONAL LEAGUE

1B— Steve Garvey, Los Angeles
2B— Joe Morgan, Cincinnati
3B— Mike Schmidt, Philadelphia
SS— Garry Templeton, St. Louis
OF— George Foster, Cincinnati
OF— Dave Parker, Pittsburgh
OF— Greg Luzinski, Philadelphia
C— Ted Simmons, St. Louis
RHP— Rick Reuschel, Chicago
LHP— Steve Carlton, Philadelphia

1978

AMERICAN LEAGUE

1B— Rod Carew, Minnesota
2B— Frank White, Kansas City
3B— Graig Nettles, New York
SS— Robin Yount, Milwaukee
OF— Jim Rice, Boston
OF— Larry Hisle, Milwaukee
OF— Fred Lynn, Boston
C— Jim Sundberg, Texas
DH— Rusty Staub, Detroit
RHP— Jim Palmer, Baltimore
LHP— Ron Guidry, New York

NATIONAL LEAGUE

1B— Steve Garvey, Los Angeles
2B— Dave Lopes, Los Angeles
3B— Pete Rose, Cincinnati
SS— Larry Bowa, Philadelphia
OF— George Foster, Cincinnati
OF— Dave Parker, Pittsburgh
OF— Jack Clark, San Francisco
C— Ted Simmons, St. Louis
RHP— Gaylord Perry, San Diego
LHP— Vida Blue, San Francisco

1979

AMERICAN LEAGUE

1B— Cecil Cooper, Milwaukee
2B— Bobby Grich, California
3B— George Brett, Kansas City
SS— Roy Smalley, Minnesota
OF— Jim Rice, Boston
OF— Fred Lynn, Boston
OF— Ken Singleton, Baltimore
C— Darrell Porter, Kansas City
DH— Don Baylor, California
RHP— Jim Kern, Texas
LHP— Mike Flanagan, Baltimore

NATIONAL LEAGUE

1B— Keith Hernandez, St. Louis
2B— Dave Lopes, Los Angeles
3B— Mike Schmidt, Philadelphia
SS— Garry Templeton, St. Louis
OF— Dave Kingman, Chicago
OF— Omar Moreno, Pittsburgh
OF— Dave Winfield, San Diego
C— Ted Simmons, St. Louis
RHP— Joe Niekro, Houston
LHP— Steve Carlton, Philadelphia

1980

AMERICAN LEAGUE

1B— Cecil Cooper, Milwaukee
2B— Willie Randolph, New York
3B— George Brett, Kansas City
SS— Robin Yount, Milwaukee
OF— Ben Oglivie, Milwaukee
OF— Al Bumbry, Baltimore
OF— Reggie Jackson, New York
DH— Reggie Jackson, New York
C— Rick Cerone, New York
RHP— Steve Stone, Baltimore
LHP— Tommy John, New York

NATIONAL LEAGUE

1B— Keith Hernandez, St. Louis
2B— Manny Trillo, Philadelphia
3B— Mike Schmidt, Philadelphia
SS— Garry Templeton, St. Louis
OF— Dusty Baker, Los Angeles
OF— Cesar Cedeno, Houston
OF— George Hendrick, St. Louis
C— Gary Carter, Montreal
RHP— Jim Bibby, Pittsburgh
LHP— Steve Carlton, Philadelphia

1981

AMERICAN LEAGUE

1B— Cecil Cooper, Milwaukee
2B— Bobby Grich, California
3B— Buddy Bell, Texas
SS— Rick Burleson, California
OF— Rickey Henderson, Oakland
OF— Dwayne Murphy, Oakland
OF— Tony Armas, Oakland
C— Jim Sundberg, Texas
DH— Richie Zisk, Seattle
RHP— Jack Morris, Detroit
LHP— Ron Guidry, New York

NATIONAL LEAGUE

1B— Pete Rose, Philadelphia
2B— Manny Trillo, Philadelphia
3B— Mike Schmidt, Philadelphia
SS— Dave Concepcion, Cincinnati
OF— George Foster, Cincinnati
OF— Andre Dawson, Montreal
OF— Pedro Guerrero, Los Angeles
C— Gary Carter, Montreal
RHP— Tom Seaver, Cincinnati
LHP— Fernando Valenzuela, Los Angeles

1982

AMERICAN LEAGUE

1B— Cecil Cooper, Milwaukee
2B— Damaso Garcia, Toronto
3B— Doug DeCinces, California
SS— Robin Yount, Milwaukee
OF— Dave Winfield, New York
OF— Gorman Thomas, Milwaukee
OF— Dwight Evans, Boston
C— Lance Parrish, Detroit
DH— Hal McRae, Kansas City
RHP— Dave Stieb, Toronto
LHP— Geoff Zahn, California

NATIONAL LEAGUE

1B— Al Oliver, Montreal
2B— Manny Trillo, Philadelphia
3B— Mike Schmidt, Philadelphia
SS— Ozzie Smith, St. Louis
OF— Lonnie Smith, St. Louis
OF— Dale Murphy, Atlanta
OF— Pedro Guerrero, Los Angeles
C— Gary Carter, Montreal
RHP— Steve Rogers, Montreal
LHP— Steve Carlton, Philadelphia

1983

AMERICAN LEAGUE

1B— Eddie Murray, Baltimore
2B— Lou Whitaker, Detroit
3B— Wade Boggs, Boston
SS— Cal Ripken, Baltimore
OF— Jim Rice, Boston
OF— Dave Winfield, New York
OF— Lloyd Moseby, Toronto
C— Carlton Fisk, Chicago
DH— Greg Luzinski, Chicago
RHP— LaMarr Hoyt, Chicago
LHP— Ron Guidry, New York

NATIONAL LEAGUE

1B— George Hendrick, St. Louis
2B— Glenn Hubbard, Atlanta
3B— Mike Schmidt, Philadelphia
SS— Dickie Thon, Houston
OF— Dale Murphy, Atlanta
OF— Andre Dawson, Montreal
OF— Tim Raines, Montreal
C— Tony Pena, Pittsburgh
RHP— John Denny, Philadelphia
LHP— Larry McWilliams, Pittsburgh

1984

AMERICAN LEAGUE

1B— Don Mattingly, New York
2B— Lou Whitaker, Detroit
3B— Buddy Bell, Texas
SS— Cal Ripken, Baltimore
OF— Tony Armas, Boston
OF— Dwight Evans, Boston
OF— Dave Winfield, New York
C— Lance Parrish, Detroit
DH— Dave Kingman, Oakland
RHP— Mike Boddicker, Baltimore
LHP— Willie Hernandez, Detroit

NATIONAL LEAGUE

1B— Keith Hernandez, New York
2B— Ryne Sandberg, Chicago
3B— Mike Schmidt, Philadelphia
SS— Ozzie Smith, St. Louis
OF— Dale Murphy, Atlanta
OF— Jose Cruz, Houston
OF— Tony Gwynn, San Diego
C— Gary Carter, Montreal
RHP— Rick Sutcliffe, Chicago
LHP— Mark Thurmond, San Diego

1985

AMERICAN LEAGUE

1B— Don Mattingly, New York
2B— Damaso Garcia, Toronto
3B— Wade Boggs, Boston
SS— Cal Ripken, Baltimore
OF— Rickey Henderson, New York
OF— Harold Baines, Chicago
OF— Phil Bradley, Seattle
C— Carlton Fisk, Chicago
DH— Don Baylor, New York
RHP— Bret Saberhagen, Kansas City
LHP— Ron Guidry, New York

NATIONAL LEAGUE

1B— Keith Hernandez, New York
2B— Tom Herr, St. Louis
3B— Tim Wallach, Montreal
SS— Ozzie Smith, St. Louis
OF— Dave Parker, Cincinnati
OF— Willie McGee, St. Louis
OF— Dale Murphy, Atlanta
C— Gary Carter, New York
RHP— Dwight Gooden, New York
LHP— John Tudor, St. Louis

1986

AMERICAN LEAGUE

1B— Don Mattingly, New York
2B— Tony Bernazard, Cleveland
3B— Wade Boggs, Boston
SS— Tony Fernandez, Toronto
OF— Jim Rice, Boston
OF— George Bell, Toronto
OF— Kirby Puckett, Minnesota
C— Rich Gedman, Boston
DH— Don Baylor, Boston
RHP— Roger Clemens, Boston
LHP— Teddy Higuera, Milwaukee

NATIONAL LEAGUE

1B— Keith Hernandez, New York
2B— Steve Sax, Los Angeles
3B— Mike Schmidt, Philadelphia
SS— Ozzie Smith, St. Louis
OF— Tim Raines, Montreal
OF— Tony Gwynn, San Diego
OF— Dave Parker, Cincinnati
C— Gary Carter, New York
RHP— Mike Scott, Houston
LHP— Fernando Valenzuela, Los Angeles

1987

AMERICAN LEAGUE

1B— Don Mattingly, New York
2B— Willie Randolph, New York
3B— Wade Boggs, Boston
SS— Alan Trammell, Detroit
OF— George Bell, Toronto
OF— Kirby Puckett, Minnesota
OF— Dwight Evans, Boston
C— Matt Nokes, Detroit
DH— Paul Molitor, Milwaukee
RHP— Roger Clemens, Boston
LHP— Jimmy Key, Toronto

NATIONAL LEAGUE

1B— Jack Clark, St. Louis
2B— Juan Samuel, Philadelphia
3B— Tim Wallach, Montreal
SS— Ozzie Smith, St. Louis
OF— Andre Dawson, Chicago
OF— Tony Gwynn, San Diego
OF— Eric Davis, Cincinnati
C— Benito Santiago, San Diego
RHP— Rick Sutcliffe, Chicago
LHP— Zane Smith, Atlanta

1988

AMERICAN LEAGUE

1B— George Brett, Kansas City
2B— Johnny Ray, California
3B— Wade Boggs, Boston
SS— Alan Trammell, Detroit
OF— Kirby Puckett, Minnesota
OF— Mike Greenwell, Boston
OF— Jose Canseco, Oakland
C— Ernie Whitt, Toronto
DH— Harold Baines, Chicago
RHP— Dave Stewart, Oakland
LHP— Frank Viola, Minnesota

NATIONAL LEAGUE

1B— Will Clark, San Francisco
2B— Ryne Sandberg, Chicago
3B— Bobby Bonilla, Pittsburgh
SS— Barry Larkin, Cincinnati
OF— Darryl Strawberry, New York
OF— Andy Van Slyke, Pittsburgh
OF— Kevin McReynolds, New York
C— Mike LaValliere, Pittsburgh
RHP— Orel Hershiser, Los Angeles
LHP— Danny Jackson, Cincinnati

1989

AMERICAN LEAGUE

1B— Fred McGriff, Toronto
2B— Julio Franco, Texas
3B— Carney Lansford, Oakland
SS— Cal Ripken, Baltimore
OF— Ruben Sierra, Texas
OF— Kirby Puckett, Minnesota
OF— Robin Yount, Milwaukee
C— Mickey Tettleton, Baltimore
DH— Harold Baines, Chi.-Tex.
RHP— Bret Saberhagen, Kansas City
LHP— Chuck Finley, California

NATIONAL LEAGUE

1B— Will Clark, San Francisco
2B— Ryne Sandberg, Chicago
3B— Howard Johnson, New York
SS— Shawon Dunston, Chicago
OF— Tony Gwynn, San Diego
OF— Kevin Mitchell, San Francisco
OF— Eric Davis, Cincinnati
C— Benito Santiago, San Diego
RHP— Mike Scott, Houston
LHP— Mark Davis, San Diego

1990

AMERICAN LEAGUE

1B— Cecil Fielder, Detroit
2B— Julio Franco, Texas
3B— Kelly Gruber, Toronto
SS— Alan Trammell, Detroit
OF— Rickey Henderson, Oakland
OF— Jose Canseco, Oakland
OF— Ellis Burks, Boston
C— Carlton Fisk, Chicago
DH— Dave Parker, Milwaukee
RHP— Bob Welch, Oakland
LHP— Chuck Finley, California

NATIONAL LEAGUE

1B— Eddie Murray, Los Angeles
2B— Ryne Sandberg, Chicago
3B— Matt Williams, San Francisco
SS— Barry Larkin, Cincinnati
OF— Barry Bonds, Pittsburgh
OF— Bobby Bonilla, Pittsburgh
OF— Darryl Strawberry, New York
C— Mike Scioscia, Los Angeles
RHP— Doug Drabek, Pittsburgh
LHP— Frank Viola, New York

1991

AMERICAN LEAGUE

1B— Cecil Fielder, Detroit
2B— Julio Franco, Texas
3B— Wade Boggs, Boston
SS— Cal Ripken, Baltimore
OF— Jose Canseco, Oakland
OF— Joe Carter, Toronto
OF— Ken Griffey Jr., Seattle
C— Mickey Tettleton, Detroit
RHP— Roger Clemens, Boston
LHP— Jim Abbott, California

NATIONAL LEAGUE

1B— Will Clark, San Francisco
2B— Ryne Sandberg, Chicago
3B— Terry Pendleton, Atlanta
SS— Barry Larkin, Cincinnati
OF— Barry Bonds, Pittsburgh
OF— Bobby Bonilla, Pittsburgh
OF— Ron Gant, Atlanta
C— Benito Santiago, San Diego
RHP— Jose Rijo, Cincinnati
LHP— Tom Glavine, Atlanta

1992

AMERICAN LEAGUE

1B— Mark McGwire, Oakland
2B— Roberto Alomar, Toronto
3B— Edgar Martinez, Seattle
SS— Travis Fryman, Detroit
OF— Joe Carter, Toronto
OF— Mike Devereaux, Baltimore
OF— Kirby Puckett, Minnesota
C— Mickey Tettleton, Detroit
RHP— Jack McDowell, Chicago
LHP— Dave Fleming, Seattle

NATIONAL LEAGUE

1B— Fred McGriff, San Diego
2B— Ryne Sandberg, Chicago
3B— Gary Sheffield, San Diego
SS— Barry Larkin, Cincinnati
OF— Barry Bonds, Pittsburgh
OF— Andy Van Slyke, Pittsburgh
OF— Larry Walker, Montreal
C— Darren Daulton, Philadelphia
RHP— Greg Maddux, Chicago
LHP— Tom Glavine, Atlanta

1993

AMERICAN LEAGUE

1B— Frank Thomas, Chicago
2B— Carlos Baerga, Cleveland
3B— Travis Fryman, Detroit
SS— Cal Ripken Jr., Baltimore
OF— Albert Belle, Cleveland
OF— Juan Gonzalez, Texas
OF— Ken Griffey Jr., Seattle
C— Mike Stanley, New York
DH— Paul Molitor, Toronto
RHP— Jack McDowell, Chicago
LHP— Jimmy Key, New York

NATIONAL LEAGUE

1B— Fred McGriff, S.D.-Atl.
2B— Robby Thompson, San Francisco
3B— Matt Williams, San Francisco
SS— Jay Bell, Pittsburgh
OF— Barry Bonds, San Francisco
OF— Lenny Dykstra, Philadelphia
OF— David Justice, Atlanta
C— Mike Piazza, Los Angeles
RHP— Greg Maddux, Atlanta
LHP— Steve Avery, Atlanta

1994

AMERICAN LEAGUE

1B— Frank Thomas, Chicago
2B— Chuck Knoblauch, Minnesota
3B— Wade Boggs, New York
SS— Cal Ripken Jr., Baltimore
OF— Albert Belle, Cleveland
OF— Ken Griffey Jr., Seattle
OF— Kirby Puckett, Minnesota
C— Ivan Rodriguez, Texas
DH— Paul Molitor, Toronto
RHP— David Cone, Kansas City
LHP— Jimmy Key, New York

NATIONAL LEAGUE

1B— Jeff Bagwell, Houston
2B— Craig Biggio, Houston
3B— Matt Williams, San Francisco
SS— Barry Larkin, Cincinnati
OF— Moises Alou, Montreal
OF— Barry Bonds, San Francisco
OF— Tony Gwynn, San Diego
C— Mike Piazza, Los Angeles
RHP— Greg Maddux, Atlanta
LHP— Danny Jackson, Philadelphia

1995

AMERICAN LEAGUE

1B— Mo Vaughn, Boston
2B— Carlos Baerga, Cleveland
3B— Jim Thome, Cleveland
SS— Cal Ripken Jr., Baltimore
OF— Albert Belle, Cleveland
OF— Tim Salmon, California
OF— Jim Edmonds, California
Manny Ramirez, Cleveland
C— Ivan Rodriguez, Texas
DH— Edgar Martinez, Seattle
RHP— Mike Mussina, Baltimore
LHP— Randy Johnson, Seattle

NATIONAL LEAGUE

1B— Eric Karros, Los Angeles
2B— Craig Biggio, Houston
3B— Vinny Castilla, Colorado
SS— Barry Larkin, Cincinnati
OF— Reggie Sanders, Cincinnati
OF— Dante Bichette, Colorado
OF— Sammy Sosa, Chicago
C— Mike Piazza, Los Angeles
RHP— Greg Maddux, Atlanta
LHP— Pete Schourek, Cincinnati

1996

AMERICAN LEAGUE

1B— Mark McGwire, Oakland
2B— Roberto Alomar, Baltimore
3B— Jim Thome, Cleveland
SS— Alex Rodriguez, Seattle
OF— Albert Belle, Cleveland
OF— Juan Gonzalez, Texas
OF— Ken Griffey Jr., Seattle
C— Ivan Rodriguez, Texas
DH— Paul Molitor, Minnesota
RHP— Pat Hentgen, Toronto
LHP— Andy Pettitte, New York

NATIONAL LEAGUE

1B— Jeff Bagwell, Houston
2B— Eric Young, Colorado
3B— Ken Caminiti, San Diego
SS— Barry Larkin, Cincinnati
OF— Barry Bonds, San Francisco
OF— Ellis Burks, Colorado
OF— Gary Sheffield, Florida
C— Mike Piazza, Los Angeles
RHP— John Smoltz, Atlanta
LHP— Al Leiter, Florida

1997

AMERICAN LEAGUE

1B— Tino Martinez, New York
2B— Chuck Knoblauch, Minnesota
3B— Matt Williams, Cleveland
SS— Nomar Garciaparra, Boston
OF— Ken Griffey Jr., Seattle
OF— David Justice, Cleveland
OF— Tim Salmon, Anaheim
C— Ivan Rodriguez, Texas
DH— Edgar Martinez, Seattle
RHP— Roger Clemens, Toronto
LHP— Randy Johnson, Seattle

NATIONAL LEAGUE

1B— Jeff Bagwell, Houston
2B— Craig Biggio, Houston
3B— Vinny Castillo, Colorado
SS— Jeff Blauser, Atlanta
OF— Barry Bonds, San Francisco
OF— Tony Gwynn, San Diego
OF— Larry Walker, Colorado
C— Mike Piazza, Los Angeles
RHP— Pedro Martinez, Montreal
LHP— Denny Neagle, Atlanta

1998

AMERICAN LEAGUE

1B— Rafael Palmeiro, Baltimore
2B— Roberto Alomar, Baltimore
3B— Scott Brosius, New York
SS— Alex Rodriguez, Seattle
OF— Ken Griffey Jr., Seattle
OF— Juan Gonzalez, Texas
OF— Albert Belle, Chicago
C— Ivan Rodriguez, Texas
DH— Jose Canseco, Toronto
RHP— Pedro Martinez, Boston
LHP— David Wells, New York

NATIONAL LEAGUE

1B— Mark McGwire, St. Louis
2B— Craig Biggio, Houston
3B— Vinny Castillo, Colorado
SS— Barry Larkin, Cincinnati
OF— Sammy Sosa, Chicago
OF— Moises Alou, Houston
OF— Greg Vaughn, San Diego
C— Mike Piazza, L.A.-Fla.-N.Y.
RHP— Kevin Brown, San Diego
LHP— Tom Glavine, Atlanta

1999

AMERICAN LEAGUE

1B— Rafael Palmeiro, Texas
2B— Roberto Alomar, Cleveland
3B— Dean Palmer, Detroit
SS— Nomar Garciaparra, Boston
OF— Shawn Green, Toronto
OF— Ken Griffey Jr., Seattle
OF— Manny Ramirez, Cleveland
C— Ivan Rodriguez, Texas
RHP— Pedro Martinez, Boston
LHP— Jamie Moyer, Seattle

NATIONAL LEAGUE

1B— Jeff Bagwell, Houston
2B— Edgardo Alfonzo, New York
3B— Chipper Jones, Atlanta
SS— Barry Larkin, Cincinnati
OF— Sammy Sosa, Chicago
OF— Vladimir Guerrero, Montreal
OF— Larry Walker, Colorado
C— Mike Piazza, New York
RHP— Jose Lima, Houston
LHP— Mike Hampton, Houston

2000

AMERICAN LEAGUE

1B— Carlos Delgado, Toronto
2B— Roberto Alomar, Cleveland
3B— Travis Fryman, Cleveland
SS— Alex Rodriguez, Seattle
OF— Darin Erstad, Anaheim
OF— Magglio Ordonez, Chicago
OF— Bernie Williams, New York
C— Jorge Posada, New York
RHP— Pedro Martinez, Boston
LHP— David Wells, Toronto

NATIONAL LEAGUE

1B— Todd Helton, Colorado
2B— Jeff Kent, San Francisco
3B— Chipper Jones, Atlanta
SS— Edgar Renteria, St. Louis
OF— Barry Bonds, San Francisco
OF— Vladimir Guerrero, Montreal
OF— Sammy Sosa, Chicago
C— Mike Piazza, New York
RHP— Greg Maddux, Atlanta
LHP— Tom Glavine, Atlanta

2001

AMERICAN LEAGUE

1B— Jim Thome, Cleveland
2B— Bret Boone, Seattle
3B— Troy Glaus, Anaheim
SS— Alex Rodriguez, Texas
OF— Juan Gonzalez, Cleveland
OF— Manny Ramirez, Boston
OF— Ichiro Suzuki, Seattle
C— Jorge Posada, New York
RHP— Roger Clemens, New York
LHP— Mark Mulder, Oakland
DH— Edgar Martinez, Seattle

NATIONAL LEAGUE

1B— Todd Helton, Colorado
2B— Craig Biggio, Houston
3B— Chipper Jones, Atlanta
SS— Rich Aurilia, San Francisco
OF— Barry Bonds, San Francisco
OF— Luis Gonzalez, Arizona
OF— Sammy Sosa, Chicago
C— Mike Piazza, New York
RHP— Curt Schilling, Arizona
LHP— Randy Johnson, Arizona

2002

AMERICAN LEAGUE

1B— Jason Giambi, New York
2B— Alfonso Soriano, New York
3B— Eric Chavez, Oakland
SS— Alex Rodriguez, Texas
OF— Garret Anderson, Anaheim
OF— Torii Hunter, Minnesota
OF— Bernie Williams, New York
C— Jorge Posada, New York
RHP— Derek Lowe, Boston
LHP— Barry Zito, Oakland
DH— Manny Ramirez, Boston

NATIONAL LEAGUE

1B— Todd Helton, Colorado
2B— Jeff Kent, San Francisco
3B— Scott Rolen, Phil.-St.L.
SS— Edgar Renteria, St. Louis
OF— Barry Bonds, San Francisco
OF— Vladimir Guerrero, Montreal
OF— Sammy Sosa, Chicago
C— Mike Piazza, New York
RHP— Curt Schilling, Arizona
LHP— Randy Johnson, Arizona

2003

AMERICAN LEAGUE

1B— Carlos Delgado, Toronto
2B— Bret Boone, Seattle
3B— Bill Mueller, Boston
SS— Alex Rodriguez, Texas
OF— Garret Anderson, Anaheim
OF— Vernon Wells, Toronto
OF— Magglio Ordonez, White Sox
C— Jorge Posada, New York
RHP— Roy Halladay, Toronto
LHP— Andy Pettitte, New York
DH— Frank Thomas, Chicago

NATIONAL LEAGUE

1B— Todd Helton, Colorado
2B— Marcus Giles, Atlanta
3B— Scott Rolen, St. Louis
SS— Edgar Renteria, St. Louis
OF— Barry Bonds, San Francisco
OF— Albert Pujols, St. Louis
OF— Gary Sheffield, Atlanta
C— Javy Lopez, Atlanta
RHP— Eric Gagne, Los Angeles
LHP— Randy Wolf, Philadelphia

MINOR LEAGUE PLAYER OF THE YEAR

Year Player, Team, League
1936—John Vander Meer, Durham, Piedmont
1937—Charlie Keller, Newark, International
1938—Fred Hutchinson, Seattle, Pacific Coast
1939—Lou Novikoff, Tulsa, Texas; Los Angeles, Pacific Coast
1940—Phil Rizzuto, Kansas City, American Association
1941—John Lindell, Newark, International
1942—Dick Barrett, Seattle, Pacific Coast
1943—Chet Covington, Scranton, Eastern
1944—Rip Collins, Albany, Eastern
1945—Gil Coan, Chattanooga, Southern
1946—Sibby Sisti, Indianapolis, American Association

Year Player, Team, League
1947—Hank Sauer, Syracuse, International
1948—Gene Woodling, San Francisco, Pacific Coast
1949—Orie Arntzen, Albany, Eastern
1950—Frank Saucier, San Antonio, Texas
1951—Gene Conley, Hartford, Eastern
1952—Bill Skowron, Kansas City, American Association
1953—Gene Conley, Toledo, American Association
1954—Herb Score, Indianapolis, American Association
1955—John Murff, Dallas, Texas
1956—Steve Bilko, Los Angeles, Pacific Coast
1957—Norm Siebern, Denver, American Association

Year Player, Team, League
1958—Jim O'Toole, Nashville, Southern
1959—Frank Howard, Victoria-Spokane
1960—Willie Davis, Spokane, Pacific Coast
1961—Howie Koplitz, Birmingham, Southern
1962—Bob Bailey, Columbus, International
1963—Don Buford, Indianapolis, International
1964—Mel Stottlemyre, Richmond, International
1965—Joe Foy, Toronto, International
1966—Mike Epstein, Rochester, International
1967—Johnny Bench, Buffalo, International
1968—Merv Rettenmund, Rochester, International
1969—Danny Walton, Oklahoma City, American Association
1970—Don Baylor, Rochester, International
1971—Bobby Grich, Rochester, International
1972—Tom Paciorek, Albuquerque, Pacific Coast
1973—Steve Ontiveros, Phoenix, Pacific Coast
1974—Jim Rice, Pawtucket, International
1975—Hector Cruz, Tulsa, American Association
1976—Pat Putnam, Asheville, Western Carolina
1977—Ken Landreaux, S.L.C., Pacific Coast; El Paso, Texas
1978—Champ Summers, Indianapolis, American Association
1979—Mark Bomback, Vancouver, Pacific Coast
1980—Tim Raines, Denver, American Association
1981—Mike Marshall, Albuquerque, Pacific Coast
1982—Ron Kittle, Edmonton, Pacific Coast

Year Player, Team, League
1983—Kevin McReynolds, Las Vegas, Pacific Coast
1984—Alan Knicely, Wichita, American Association
1985—Jose Canseco, Hunt., Southern-Tac., Pacific Coast
1986—Tim Pyznarski, Las Vegas, Pacific Coast
1987—Randy Milligan, Tidewater, International
1988—Sandy Alomar Jr., Las Vegas, Pacific Coast
Gary Sheffield, Denver, American Association (tie)
1989—Sandy Alomar Jr., Las Vegas, Pacific Coast
1990—Jose Offerman, Albuquerque, Pacific Coast
1991—Pedro Martinez, Albuquerque, Pacific Coast
1992—Tim Salmon, Edmonton, Pacific Coast
1993—Cliff Floyd, Harrisburg, Eastern
1994—Derek Jeter, Tampa, Florida State; Albany, Eastern; Columbus, International
1995—Karim Garcia, Albuquerque, Pacific Coast
1996—Vladimir Guerrero, West Palm Beach, Florida State; Harrisburg, Eastern
1997—Ben Grieve, Huntsville, Southern; Edmonton, Pacific Coast
1998—Gabe Kapler, Jacksonville, Southern
1999—Rick Ankiel, Arkansas, Texas; Memphis, Pacific Coast
2000—Jon Rauch, Win.-Salem, Carolina; Birmingham, Southern
2001—Josh Beckett, Brevard County, Fla. State; Portland, Eastern
2002—Jason Stokes, Kane County, Midwest
2003—Zack Greinke, Wilmington, Carolina; Wichita, Texas

MINOR LEAGUE MANAGER OF THE YEAR

Year Manager, Team, League
1936—Al Sothoron, Milwaukee, American Association
1937—Jake Flowers, Salisbury, Eastern Shore
1938—Paul Richards, Atlanta, Southern
1939—Bill Meyer, Kansas City, American Association
1940—Larry Gilbert, Nashville, Southern
1941—Burt Shotton, Columbus, American Association
1942—Eddie Dyer, Columbus, American Association
1943—Nick Cullop, Columbus, American Association
1944—Al Thomas, Baltimore, International
1945—Lefty O'Doul, San Francisco, Pacific Coast
1946—Clay Hopper, Montreal, International
1947—Nick Cullop, Milwaukee, American Association
1948—Casey Stengel, Oakland, Pacific Coast
1949—Fred Haney, Hollywood, Pacific Coast
1950—Rollie Hemsley, Columbus, American Association
1951—Charlie Grimm, Milwaukee, American Association
1952—Luke Appling, Memphis, Southern
1953—Bobby Bragan, Hollywood, Pacific Coast
1954—Kerby Farrell, Indianapolis, American Association
1955—Bill Rigney, Minneapolis, American Association
1956—Kerby Farrell, Indianapolis, American Association
1957—Ben Geraghty, Wichita, American Association
1958—Cal Ermer, Birmingham, Southern
1959—Pete Reiser, Victoria, Texas
1960—Mel McGaha, Toronto, International
1961—Kerby Farrell, Buffalo, International
1962—Ben Geraghty, Jacksonville, International
1963—Rollie Hemsley, Indianapolis, International
1964—Harry Walker, Jacksonville, International
1965—Grady Hatton, Oklahoma City, Pacific Coast
1966—Bob Lemon, Seattle, Pacific Coast
1967—Bob Skinner, San Diego, Pacific Coast
1968—Jack Tighe, Toledo, International
1969—Clyde McCullough, Tidewater, International

Year Manager, Team, League
1970—Tommy Lasorda, Spokane, Pacific Coast
1971—Del Rice, Salt Lake City, Pacific Coast
1972—Hank Bauer, Tidewater, International
1973—Joe Morgan, Charleston, International
1974—Joe Altobelli, Rochester, International
1975—Joe Frazier, Tidewater, International
1976—Vern Rapp, Denver, American Association
1977—Tommy Thompson, Arkan., Texas
1978—Les Moss, Evansville, American Association
1979—Vern Benson, Syracuse, International
1980—Hal Lanier, Springfield, American Association
1981—Del Crandall, Albuquerque, Pacific Coast
1982—George Scherger, Indianapolis, American Association
1983—Bill Dancy, Reading, Eastern
1984—Bob Rodgers, Indianapolis, American Association
1985—Jim Fregosi, Louisville, American Association
1986—Joe Sparks, Indianapolis, American Association
1987—Terry Collins, Albuquerque, Pacific Coast
1988—Joe Sparks, Indianapolis, American Association
1989—Bob Bailor, Syracuse, International
1990—Sal Rende, Omaha, American Association
1991—Chris Chambliss, Greenville, Southern
1992—Grady Little, Greenville, Southern
1993—Jim Tracy, Harrisburg, Eastern
1994—Mike Jirschele, Wilmington, Carolina
1995—Pete Mackanin, Ottawa, International
1996—John Mizerock, Wilmington, Carolina
1997—Marv Foley, Rochester, International
1998—Doug Davis, Columbia, South Atlantic
1999—DeMarlo Hale, Trenton, Eastern
2000—Joel Skinner, Buffalo, International
2001—Tony Pena, New Orleans, Pacific Coast
2002—Eric Wedge, Buffalo, International
2003—Tony DeFrancesco, Sacramento, Pacific Coast

MINOR LEAGUE EXECUTIVE OF THE YEAR (HIGHER CLASSIFICATIONS, 1936-1992)

(Restricted to Class AAA starting in 1963)

Year Executive, Team, League
1936—Earl Mann, Atlanta, Southern
1937—Robert LaMotte, Savannah, Sally
1938—Louis McKenna, St. Paul, American Association
1939—Bruce Dudley, Louisville, American Association
1940—Roy Hamey, Kansas City, American Association
1941—Emil Sick, Seattle, Pacific Coast

Year Executive, Team, League
1942—Bill Veeck, Milwaukee, American Association
1943—Clarence Rowland, Los Angeles, Pacific Coast
1944—William Mulligan, Seattle, Pacific Coast
1945—Bruce Dudley, Louisville, American Association
1946—Earl Mann, Atlanta, Southern
1947—William Purnhage, Waterloo, I.I.I.

Year	Executive, Team, League
1948	Edward Glennon, Birmingham, Southern
1949	Ted Sullivan, Indianapolis, American Association
1950	Clearnce (Brick) Laws, Oakland, Pacific Coast
1951	Robert Howsam, Denver, West
1952	Jack Cooke, Toronto, International
1953	Richard Burnett, Dallas, Texas
1954	Edward Stumpf, Indianapolis, American Association
1955	Dewey Soriano, Seattle, Pacific Coast
1956	Robert Howsam, Denver American Association
1957	John Stiglmeier, Buffalo, International
1958	Edward Glennon, Birmingham, Southern
1959	Edward Leishman, Salt Lake City, Pacific Coast
1960	Ray Winder, Little Rock, Southern
1961	Elten Schiller, Omaha, American Association
1962	George Sisler Jr., Rochester, International
1963	Lewis Matlin, Hawaii, Pacific Coast
1964	Edward Leishman, San Diego, Pacific Coast
1965	Harold Cooper, Columbus, International
1966	John Quinn Jr., Hawaii, Pacific Coast
1967	Hillman Lyons, Richmond, International
1968	Gabe Paul Jr., Tulsa, Pacific Coast
1969	Bill Gardner, Louisville, International
1970	Dick King, Wichita, American Association
1971	Carl Steinfeldt Jr., Rochester, International
1972	Don Labbruzzo, Evansville, American Association
1973	Merle Miller, Tucson, Pacific Coast
1974	John Carbray, Sacramento, Pacific Coast
1975	Stan Naccarato, Tacoma, Pacific Coast
1976	Art Teece, Salt Lake City, Pacific Coast
1977	George Sisler Jr., Columbus, International
1978	Willie Sanchez, Albuquerque, Pacific Coast
1979	George Sisler Jr., Columbus, International
1980	Jim Burris, Denver, American Association
1981	Pat McKernan, Albuquerque, Pacific Coast
1982	A. Ray Smith, Louisville, American Association
1983	A. Ray Smith, Louisville, American Association
1984	Mike Tamburro, Pawtucket, International
1985	Patty Cox Hampton, Oklahoma City, American Association
1986	Bob Goughan, Rochester, International
1987	Stu Kehoe, Vancouver, Pacific Coast
1988	Bob Rich, Buffalo, American Association
1989	Larry Schmittou, Nashville, American Association
1990	Greg Corns, Phoenix, Pacific Coast
1991	Tom Maloney, Denver, American Association
1992	Lou Schwechheimer, Pawtucket, International

MINOR LEAGUE EXECUTIVE OF THE YEAR (LOWER CLASSIFICATIONS, 1950-1990)

(Separate awards for Class AA and Class A started in 1963; for Short Class A in 1988)

Year	Executive, Team, League
1950	H. Cooper, Hutchinson, Western Association
1951	O. W. (Bill) Hayes, Triple, B.S.
1952	Hillman Lyons, Danville, MOV
1953	Carl Roth, Peoria, I.I.I.
1954	James Meagham, Cedar Rapids, I.I.I.
1955	John Petrakis, Dubuque, MOV
1956	Marvin Milkes, Fresno, California
1957	Richard Wagner, Lincoln, West.
1958	Gerald Waring, Macon, Sally
1959	Clay Dennis, Des Moines, I.I.I.
1960	Hubert Kittle, Yakima, Northwest
1961	David Steele, Fresno, California
1962	John Quinn Jr., San Jose, California
1963	Hugh Finnerty, Tulsa, Texas
	Ben Jewell, M. Valley, Pioneer
1964	Glynn West, Birmingham, Southern
	James Bayens, Rock Hill, W. Carolina
1965	Dick Butler, Dallas-Ft. Worth, Texas
	Ken. Blackman, Quad Cities, Midwest
1966	Tom Fleming, Evansville, Southern
	Cappy Harada, Lodi, California
1967	Robert Quinn, Reading, Eastern
	Pat Williams, Spar'burg, W.C.
1968	Phil Howser, Charlotte, Southern
	Merle Miller, Burlington, Midwest
1969	Charlie Blaney, Albuquerque, Texas
	Bill Gorman, Visalia, California
1970	Carl Sawatski, Arkansas, Texas
	Bob Williams, Bakersfield, California
1971	Miles Wolff, Savannah, Dixie Association
	Ed Holtz, Appleton, Midwest
1972	John Begzos, S. Antonio, Texas
	Bob Piccinini, Modesto, California
1973	Dick Kravitz, Jacksonville, Southern
	Fritz Colschen, Clinton, Midwest
1974	Jim Paul, El Paso, Texas
	Bing Russell, Portland, Northwest
1975	Jim Paul, El Paso, Texas
	Cordy Jensen, Eugene, Northwest
1976	Woodrow Reid, Chattanooga, Southern
	Don Buchheister, Cedar Rapids, Midwest
1977	Jim Paul, El Paso, Texas
	Harry Pells, Quad Cities, Midwest
1978	Larry Schmittou, Nashville, Southern
	Dave Hersh, Appleton, Midwest
1979	Bill Rigney Jr., Midland, Texas
	Tom Romenesko, Greensboro, W.C.
1980	Frances Crockett, Charlotte, Southern
	Tom Romenesko, Greensboro, W.C.
1981	Allie Prescott, Memphis, Southern
	Dan Overstreet, Hagerstown, Caro.
1982	Art Clarkson, Birmingham, Southern
	Bob Carruesco, Stockton, California
1983	Edward Kenney, New Britain, Eastern
	Terry Reynolds, Vero Beach, Florida State
1984	Bruce Baldwin, Greenville, Southern
	Dave Tarrolly, Beloit, Midwest
1985	Ben Bernard, Albany-Colonie, Eastern
	Pete Vonachen, Peoria, Midwest
1986	Bill Davidson, Midland, Texas
	Rob Dlugozima, Durham, Carolina
1987	Joe Preseren, Tulsa, Texas
	Skip Weisman, Greensboro, South Atlantic
1988	Bill Valentine, Arkansas, Texas
	Dennis Bastien, Charleston (W.Va.), South Atlantic
	Bob Beban, Eugene, Northwest
1989	Chuck Domino, Reading, Eastern
	John Baxter, South Bend, Midwest
	Bill Pereira, Boise, Northwest
1990	Joe Preseren, Tulsa, Texas
	Dan Chapman, Stockton, California
	Dave Baggott, Salt Lake City, Pioneer

MINOR LEAGUE EXECUTIVE OF THE YEAR

Year	Executive, Team, League
1993	Todd Vander Woude, Harrisburg, Eastern (AA)
1994	Scott Lane, West Michigan, Midwest (A)
1995	Jack and Mary Cain, Portland, Northwest (A)
1996	Wayne Hodes, Trenton, Eastern (AA)
1997	Andy Milovich, Erie, New York-Pennsylvania (A)
1998	Chuck Domino, Reading, Eastern (AA)
1999	Ben Mondor, Pawtucket, International (AAA)
2000	Art Savage, Sacramento, Pacific Coast (AAA)
2001	Jay Miller, Round Rock, Texas (AA)
2002	Gary Arthur, Sacramento, Pacific Coast (AAA)
2003	Jay Miller, Round Rock, Texas (AA)

1957
MAJORS
P— Bobby Shantz, New York A.L.
C— Sherm Lollar, Chicago A.L.
1B— Gil Hodges, Brooklyn N.L.
2B— Nellie Fox, Chicago A.L.
3B— Frank Malzone, Boston A.L.
SS— Roy McMillan, Cincinnati N.L.
OF— Minnie Minoso, Chicago A.L.
OF— Willie Mays, New York N.L.
OF— Al Kaline, Detroit A.L.

1958
AMERICAN LEAGUE
P— Bobby Shantz, New York
C— Sherm Lollar, Chicago
1B— Vic Power, K.C.-Cle.
2B— Frank Bolling, Detroit
3B— Frank Malzone, Boston
SS— Luis Aparicio, Chicago
OF— Norm Siebern, New York
OF— Jimmy Piersall, Boston
OF— Al Kaline, Detroit

NATIONAL LEAGUE
P— Harvey Haddix, Cincinnati
C— Del Crandall, Milwaukee
1B— Gil Hodges, Los Angeles
2B— Bill Mazeroski, Pittsburgh
3B— Ken Boyer, St. Louis
SS— Roy McMillan, Cincinnati
OF— Frank Robinson, Cincinnati
OF— Willie Mays, San Francisco
OF— Hank Aaron, Milwaukee

1959
AMERICAN LEAGUE
P— Bobby Shantz, New York
C— Sherm Lollar, Chicago
1B— Vic Power, Cleveland
2B— Nellie Fox, Chicago
3B— Frank Malzone, Boston
SS— Luis Aparicio, Chicago
OF— Minnie Minoso, Cleveland
OF— Al Kaline, Detroit
OF— Jackie Jensen, Boston

NATIONAL LEAGUE
P— Harvey Haddix, Pittsburgh
C— Del Crandall, Milwaukee
1B— Gil Hodges, Los Angeles
2B— Charley Neal, Los Angeles
3B— Ken Boyer, St. Louis
SS— Roy McMillan, Cincinnati
OF— Jackie Brandt, San Francisco
OF— Willie Mays, San Francisco
OF— Hank Aaron, Milwaukee

1960
AMERICAN LEAGUE
P— Bobby Shantz, New York
C— Earl Battey, Washington
1B— Vic Power, Cleveland
2B— Nellie Fox, Chicago
3B— Brooks Robinson, Baltimore
SS— Luis Aparicio, Chicago
OF— Minnie Minoso, Chicago
OF— Jim Landis, Chicago
OF— Roger Maris, New York

NATIONAL LEAGUE
P— Harvey Haddix, Pittsburgh
C— Del Crandall, Milwaukee
1B— Bill White, St. Louis
2B— Bill Mazeroski, Pittsburgh
3B— Ken Boyer, St. Louis
SS— Ernie Banks, Chicago
OF— Wally Moon, Los Angeles
OF— Willie Mays, San Francisco
OF— Hank Aaron, Milwaukee

1961
AMERICAN LEAGUE
P— Frank Lary, Detroit
C— Earl Battey, Minnesota
1B— Vic Power, Cleveland
2B— Bobby Richardson, New York
3B— Brooks Robinson, Baltimore
SS— Luis Aparicio, Chicago
OF— Al Kaline, Detroit
OF— Jimmy Piersall, Cleveland
OF— Jim Landis, Chicago

NATIONAL LEAGUE
P— Bobby Shantz, Pittsburgh
C— John Roseboro, Los Angeles
1B— Bill White, St. Louis
2B— Bill Mazeroski, Pittsburgh
3B— Ken Boyer, St. Louis
SS— Maury Wills, Los Angeles
OF— Willie Mays, San Francisco
OF— Roberto Clemente, Pittsburgh
OF— Vada Pinson, Cincinnati

1962
AMERICAN LEAGUE
P— Jim Kaat, Minnesota
C— Earl Battey, Minnesota
1B— Vic Power, Minnesota
2B— Bobby Richardson, New York
3B— Brooks Robinson, Baltimore
SS— Luis Aparicio, Chicago
OF— Jim Landis, Chicago
OF— Mickey Mantle, New York
OF— Al Kaline, Detroit

NATIONAL LEAGUE
P— Bobby Shantz, Hou.-St.L.
C— Del Crandall, Milwaukee
1B— Bill White, St. Louis
2B— Ken Hubbs, Chicago
3B— Jim Davenport, San Francisco
SS— Maury Wills, Los Angeles
OF— Willie Mays, San Francisco
OF— Roberto Clemente, Pittsburgh
OF— Bill Virdon, Pittsburgh

1963
AMERICAN LEAGUE
P— Jim Kaat, Minnesota
C— Elston Howard, New York
1B— Vic Power, Minnesota
2B— Bobby Richardson, New York
3B— Brooks Robinson, Baltimore
SS— Zoilo Versalles, Minnesota
OF— Al Kaline, Detroit
OF— Carl Yastrzemski, Boston
OF— Jim Landis, Chicago

NATIONAL LEAGUE
P— Bobby Shantz, St. Louis
C— Johnny Edwards, Cincinnati
1B— Bill White, St. Louis
2B— Bill Mazeroski, Pittsburgh
3B— Ken Boyer, St. Louis
SS— Bobby Wine, Philadelphia
OF— Willie Mays, San Francisco
OF— Roberto Clemente, Pittsburgh
OF— Curt Flood, St. Louis

1964
AMERICAN LEAGUE
P— Jim Kaat, Minnesota
C— Elston Howard, New York
1B— Vic Power, Min.-L.A.
2B— Bobby Richardson, New York
3B— Brooks Robinson, Baltimore
SS— Luis Aparicio, Baltimore
OF— Al Kaline, Detroit
OF— Jim Landis, Chicago
OF— Vic Davalillo, Cleveland

NATIONAL LEAGUE
P— Bobby Shantz, St.L.-Chi.-Phi.
C— Johnny Edwards, Cincinnati
1B— Bill White, St. Louis
2B— Bill Mazeroski, Pittsburgh
3B— Ron Santo, Chicago
SS— Ruben Amaro, Philadelphia
OF— Willie Mays, San Francisco
OF— Roberto Clemente, Pittsburgh
OF— Curt Flood, St. Louis

1965
AMERICAN LEAGUE
P— Jim Kaat, Minnesota
C— Bill Freehan, Detroit
1B— Joe Pepitone, New York
2B— Bobby Richardson, New York
3B— Brooks Robinson, Baltimore
SS— Zoilo Versalles, Minnesota
OF— Al Kaline, Detroit
OF— Tom Tresh, New York
OF— Carl Yastrzemski, Boston

NATIONAL LEAGUE
P— Bob Gibson, St. Louis
C— Joe Torre, Milwaukee
1B— Bill White, St. Louis
2B— Bill Mazeroski, Pittsburgh
3B— Ron Santo, Chicago
SS— Leo Cardenas, Cincinnati
OF— Willie Mays, San Francisco
OF— Roberto Clemente, Pittsburgh
OF— Curt Flood, St. Louis

1966
AMERICAN LEAGUE
P— Jim Kaat, Minnesota
C— Bill Freehan, Detroit
1B— Joe Pepitone, New York
2B— Bobby Knoop, California
3B— Brooks Robinson, Baltimore
SS— Luis Aparicio, Baltimore
OF— Al Kaline, Detroit
OF— Tommie Agee, Chicago
OF— Tony Oliva, Minnesota

NATIONAL LEAGUE
P— Bob Gibson, St. Louis
C— John Roseboro, Los Angeles
1B— Bill White, Philadelphia
2B— Bill Mazeroski, Pittsburgh
3B— Ron Santo, Chicago
SS— Gene Alley, Pittsburgh
OF— Willie Mays, San Francisco
OF— Curt Flood, St. Louis
OF— Roberto Clemente, Pittsburgh

1967
AMERICAN LEAGUE
P— Jim Kaat, Minnesota
C— Bill Freehan, Detroit
1B— George Scott, Boston
2B— Bobby Knoop, California
3B— Brooks Robinson, Baltimore

SS— Jim Fregosi, California
OF— Carl Yastrzemski, Boston
OF— Paul Blair, Baltimore
OF— Al Kaline, Detroit

NATIONAL LEAGUE
P— Bob Gibson, St. Louis
C— Randy Hundley, Chicago
1B— Wes Parker, Los Angeles
2B— Bill Mazeroski, Pittsburgh
3B— Ron Santo, Chicago
SS— Gene Alley, Pittsburgh
OF— Roberto Clemente, Pittsburgh
OF— Curt Flood, St. Louis
OF— Willie Mays, San Francisco

1968
AMERICAN LEAGUE
P— Jim Kaat, Minnesota
C— Bill Freehan, Detroit
1B— George Scott, Boston
2B— Bobby Knoop, California
3B— Brooks Robinson, Baltimore
SS— Luis Aparicio, Chicago
OF— Mickey Stanley, Detroit
OF— Carl Yastrzemski, Boston
OF— Reggie Smith, Boston

NATIONAL LEAGUE
P— Bob Gibson, St. Louis
C— Johnny Bench, Cincinnati
1B— Wes Parker, Los Angeles
2B— Glenn Beckert, Chicago
3B— Ron Santo, Chicago
SS— Dal Maxvill, St. Louis
OF— Willie Mays, San Francisco
OF— Roberto Clemente, Pittsburgh
OF— Curt Flood, St. Louis

1969
AMERICAN LEAGUE
P— Jim Kaat, Minnesota
C— Bill Freehan, Detroit
1B— Joe Pepitone, New York
2B— Dave Johnson, Baltimore
3B— Brooks Robinson, Baltimore
SS— Mark Belanger, Baltimore
OF— Paul Blair, Baltimore
OF— Mickey Stanley, Detroit
OF— Carl Yastrzemski, Boston

NATIONAL LEAGUE
P— Bob Gibson, St. Louis
C— Johnny Bench, Cincinnati
1B— Wes Parker, Los Angeles
2B— Felix Millan, Atlanta
3B— Clete Boyer, Atlanta
SS— Don Kessinger, Chicago
OF— Roberto Clemente, Pittsburgh
OF— Curt Flood, St. Louis
OF— Pete Rose, Cincinnati

1970
AMERICAN LEAGUE
P— Jim Kaat, Minnesota
C— Ray Fosse, Cleveland
1B— Jim Spencer, California
2B— Dave Johnson, Baltimore
3B— Brooks Robinson, Baltimore
SS— Luis Aparicio, Chicago
OF— Mickey Stanley, Detroit
OF— Paul Blair, Baltimore
OF— Ken Berry, Chicago

NATIONAL LEAGUE
P— Bob Gibson, St. Louis
C— Johnny Bench, Cincinnati
1B— Wes Parker, Los Angeles
2B— Tommy Helms, Cincinnati
3B— Doug Rader, Houston
SS— Don Kessinger, Chicago
OF— Roberto Clemente, Pittsburgh
OF— Tommie Agee, New York
OF— Pete Rose, Cincinnati

1971
AMERICAN LEAGUE
P— Jim Kaat, Minnesota
C— Ray Fosse, Cleveland
1B— George Scott, Boston
2B— Dave Johnson, Baltimore
3B— Brooks Robinson, Baltimore
SS— Mark Belanger, Baltimore
OF— Paul Blair, Baltimore
OF— Amos Otis, Kansas City
OF— Carl Yastrzemski, Boston

NATIONAL LEAGUE
P— Bob Gibson, St. Louis
C— Johnny Bench, Cincinnati
1B— Wes Parker, Los Angeles
2B— Tommy Helms, Cincinnati
3B— Doug Rader, Houston
SS— Bud Harrelson, New York
OF— Roberto Clemente, Pittsburgh
OF— Bobby Bonds, San Francisco
OF— Willie Davis, Los Angeles

1972
AMERICAN LEAGUE
P— Jim Kaat, Minnesota
C— Carlton Fisk, Boston
1B— George Scott, Milwaukee
2B— Doug Griffin, Boston
3B— Brooks Robinson, Baltimore
SS— Ed Brinkman, Detroit
OF— Paul Blair, Baltimore
OF— Bobby Murcer, New York
OF— Ken Berry, California

NATIONAL LEAGUE
P— Bob Gibson, St. Louis
C— Johnny Bench, Cincinnati
1B— Wes Parker, Los Angeles
2B— Felix Millan, Atlanta
3B— Doug Rader, Houston
SS— Larry Bowa, Philadelphia
OF— Roberto Clemente, Pittsburgh
OF— Cesar Cedeno, Houston
OF— Willie Davis, Los Angeles

1973
AMERICAN LEAGUE
P— Jim Kaat, Chicago
C— Thurman Munson, New York
1B— George Scott, Milwaukee
2B— Bobby Grich, Baltimore
3B— Brooks Robinson, Baltimore
SS— Mark Belanger, Baltimore
OF— Paul Blair, Baltimore
OF— Amos Otis, Kansas City
OF— Mickey Stanley, Detroit

NATIONAL LEAGUE
P— Bob Gibson, St. Louis
C— Johnny Bench, Cincinnati
1B— Mike Jorgensen, Montreal
2B— Joe Morgan, Cincinnati
3B— Doug Rader, Houston
SS— Roger Metzger, Houston
OF— Bobby Bonds, San Francisco
OF— Cesar Cedeno, Houston
OF— Willie Davis, Los Angeles

1974
AMERICAN LEAGUE
P— Jim Kaat, Chicago
C— Thurman Munson, New York
1B— George Scott, Milwaukee
2B— Bobby Grich, Baltimore
3B— Brooks Robinson, Baltimore
SS— Mark Belanger, Baltimore
OF— Paul Blair, Baltimore
OF— Amos Otis, Kansas City
OF— Joe Rudi, Oakland

NATIONAL LEAGUE
P— Andy Messersmith, Los Angeles
C— Johnny Bench, Cincinnati
1B— Steve Garvey, Los Angeles
2B— Joe Morgan, Cincinnati
3B— Doug Rader, Houston
SS— Dave Concepcion, Cincinnati
OF— Cesar Cedeno, Houston
OF— Cesar Geronimo, Cincinnati
OF— Bobby Bonds, San Francisco

1975
AMERICAN LEAGUE
P— Jim Kaat, Chicago
C— Thurman Munson, New York
1B— George Scott, Milwaukee
2B— Bobby Grich, Baltimore
3B— Brooks Robinson, Baltimore
SS— Mark Belanger, Baltimore
OF— Paul Blair, Baltimore
OF— Joe Rudi, Oakland
OF— Fred Lynn, Boston

NATIONAL LEAGUE
P— Andy Messersmith, Los Angeles
C— Johnny Bench, Cincinnati
1B— Steve Garvey, Los Angeles
2B— Joe Morgan, Cincinnati
3B— Ken Reitz, St. Louis
SS— Dave Concepcion, Cincinnati
OF— Cesar Cedeno, Houston
OF— Cesar Geronimo, Cincinnati
OF— Garry Maddox, S.F.-Phi.

1976
AMERICAN LEAGUE
P— Jim Palmer, Baltimore
C— Jim Sundberg, Texas
1B— George Scott, Milwaukee
2B— Bobby Grich, Baltimore
3B— Aurelio Rodriguez, Detroit
SS— Mark Belanger, Baltimore
OF— Joe Rudi, Oakland
OF— Dwight Evans, Boston
OF— Rick Manning, Cleveland

NATIONAL LEAGUE
P— Jim Kaat, Philadelphia
C— Johnny Bench, Cincinnati
1B— Steve Garvey, Los Angeles
2B— Joe Morgan, Cincinnati
3B— Mike Schmidt, Philadelphia
SS— Dave Concepcion, Cincinnati
OF— Cesar Cedeno, Houston
OF— Cesar Geronimo, Cincinnati
OF— Garry Maddox, Philadelphia

1977
AMERICAN LEAGUE
P— Jim Palmer, Baltimore
C— Jim Sundberg, Texas
1B— Jim Spencer, Chicago
2B— Frank White, Kansas City
3B— Graig Nettles, New York
SS— Mark Belanger, Baltimore
OF— Juan Beniquez, Texas
OF— Carl Yastrzemski, Boston
OF— Al Cowens, Kansas City

NATIONAL LEAGUE
P— Jim Kaat, Philadelphia
C— Johnny Bench, Cincinnati
1B— Steve Garvey, Los Angeles
2B— Joe Morgan, Cincinnati
3B— Mike Schmidt, Philadelphia
SS— Dave Concepcion, Cincinnati
OF— Cesar Geronimo, Cincinnati
OF— Garry Maddox, Philadelphia
OF— Dave Parker, Pittsburgh

1978
AMERICAN LEAGUE
P— Jim Palmer, Baltimore
C— Jim Sundberg, Texas
1B— Chris Chambliss, New York
2B— Frank White, Kansas City
3B— Graig Nettles, New York
SS— Mark Belanger, Baltimore
OF— Fred Lynn, Boston
OF— Dwight Evans, Boston
OF— Rick Miller, California

NATIONAL LEAGUE
P— Phil Niekro, Atlanta
C— Bob Boone, Philadelphia
1B— Keith Hernandez, St. Louis
2B— Dave Lopes, Los Angeles
3B— Mike Schmidt, Philadelphia
SS— Larry Bowa, Philadelphia
OF— Garry Maddox, Philadelphia
OF— Dave Parker, Pittsburgh
OF— Ellis Valentine, Montreal

1979
AMERICAN LEAGUE
P— Jim Palmer, Baltimore
C— Jim Sundberg, Texas
1B— Cecil Cooper, Milwaukee
2B— Frank White, Kansas City
3B— Buddy Bell, Texas
SS— Rick Burleson, Boston
OF— Dwight Evans, Boston
OF— Sixto Lezcano, Milwaukee
OF— Fred Lynn, Boston

NATIONAL LEAGUE
P— Phil Niekro, Atlanta
C— Bob Boone, Philadelphia
1B— Keith Hernandez, St. Louis
2B— Manny Trillo, Philadelphia
3B— Mike Schmidt, Philadelphia
SS— Dave Concepcion, Cincinnati
OF— Garry Maddox, Philadelphia
OF— Dave Parker, Pittsburgh
OF— Dave Winfield, San Diego

1980
AMERICAN LEAGUE
P— Mike Norris, Oakland
C— Jim Sundberg, Texas
1B— Cecil Cooper, Milwaukee
2B— Frank White, Kansas City
3B— Buddy Bell, Texas
SS— Alan Trammell, Detroit
OF— Fred Lynn, Boston
OF— Dwayne Murphy, Oakland
OF— Willie Wilson, Kansas City

NATIONAL LEAGUE
P— Phil Niekro, Atlanta
C— Gary Carter, Montreal
1B— Keith Hernandez, St. Louis
2B— Doug Flynn, New York
3B— Mike Schmidt, Philadelphia
SS— Ozzie Smith, San Diego
OF— Andre Dawson, Montreal
OF— Garry Maddox, Philadelphia
OF— Dave Winfield, San Diego

1981
AMERICAN LEAGUE
P— Mike Norris, Oakland
C— Jim Sundberg, Texas
1B— Mike Squires, Chicago
2B— Frank White, Kansas City
3B— Buddy Bell, Texas
SS— Alan Trammell, Detroit
OF— Dwayne Murphy, Oakland
OF— Dwight Evans, Boston
OF— Rickey Henderson, Oakland

NATIONAL LEAGUE
P— Steve Carlton, Philadelphia
C— Gary Carter, Montreal
1B— Keith Hernandez, St. Louis
2B— Manny Trillo, Philadelphia
3B— Mike Schmidt, Philadelphia
SS— Ozzie Smith, San Diego
OF— Andre Dawson, Montreal
OF— Garry Maddox, Philadelphia
OF— Dusty Baker, Los Angeles

1982
AMERICAN LEAGUE
P— Ron Guidry, New York
C— Bob Boone, California
1B— Eddie Murray, Baltimore
2B— Frank White, Kansas City
3B— Buddy Bell, Texas
SS— Robin Yount, Milwaukee
OF— Dwight Evans, Boston
OF— Dave Winfield, New York
OF— Dwayne Murphy, Oakland

NATIONAL LEAGUE
P— Phil Niekro, Atlanta
C— Gary Carter, Montreal
1B— Keith Hernandez, St. Louis
2B— Manny Trillo, Philadelphia
3B— Mike Schmidt, Philadelphia
SS— Ozzie Smith, St. Louis
OF— Andre Dawson, Montreal
OF— Dale Murphy, Atlanta
OF— Garry Maddox, Philadelphia

1983
AMERICAN LEAGUE
P— Ron Guidry, New York
C— Lance Parrish, Detroit
1B— Eddie Murray, Baltimore
2B— Lou Whitaker, Detroit
3B— Buddy Bell, Texas
SS— Alan Trammell, Detroit
OF— Dwight Evans, Boston
OF— Dave Winfield, New York
OF— Dwayne Murphy, Oakland

NATIONAL LEAGUE
P— Phil Niekro, Atlanta
C— Tony Pena, Pittsburgh
1B— Keith Hernandez, St.L.-N.Y.
2B— Ryne Sandberg, Chicago
3B— Mike Schmidt, Philadelphia
SS— Ozzie Smith, St. Louis
OF— Andre Dawson, Montreal
OF— Dale Murphy, Atlanta
OF— Willie McGee, St. Louis

1984
AMERICAN LEAGUE
P— Ron Guidry, New York
C— Lance Parrish, Detroit
1B— Eddie Murray, Baltimore
2B— Lou Whitaker, Detroit
3B— Buddy Bell, Texas
SS— Alan Trammell, Detroit
OF— Dwight Evans, Boston
OF— Dave Winfield, New York
OF— Dwayne Murphy, Oakland

NATIONAL LEAGUE
P— Joaquin Andujar, St. Louis
C— Tony Pena, Pittsburgh
1B— Keith Hernandez, New York
2B— Ryne Sandberg, Chicago
3B— Mike Schmidt, Philadelphia
SS— Ozzie Smith, St. Louis
OF— Dale Murphy, Atlanta
OF— Bob Dernier, Chicago
OF— Andre Dawson, Montreal

1985
AMERICAN LEAGUE
P— Ron Guidry, New York
C— Lance Parrish, Detroit
1B— Don Mattingly, New York
2B— Lou Whitaker, Detroit
3B— George Brett, Kansas City
SS— Alfredo Griffin, Oakland
OF— Gary Pettis, California
OF— Dave Winfield, New York
OF— Dwight Evans, Boston (tie)
Dwayne Murphy, Oakland (tie)

NATIONAL LEAGUE
P— Rick Reuschel, Pittsburgh
C— Tony Pena, Pittsburgh
1B— Keith Hernandez, New York
2B— Ryne Sandberg, Chicago
3B— Tim Wallach, Montreal
SS— Ozzie Smith, St. Louis
OF— Willie McGee, St. Louis
OF— Dale Murphy, Atlanta
OF— Andre Dawson, Montreal

1986
AMERICAN LEAGUE
P— Ron Guidry, New York
C— Bob Boone, California
1B— Don Mattingly, New York
2B— Frank White, Kansas City
3B— Gary Gaetti, Minnesota
SS— Tony Fernandez, Toronto
OF— Gary Pettis, California
OF— Jesse Barfield, Toronto
OF— Kirby Puckett, Minnesota

NATIONAL LEAGUE
P— Fernando Valenzuela, Los Angeles
C— Jody Davis, Chicago
1B— Keith Hernandez, New York
2B— Ryne Sandberg, Chicago
3B— Mike Schmidt, Philadelphia
SS— Ozzie Smith, St. Louis
OF— Tony Gwynn, San Diego
OF— Dale Murphy, Atlanta
OF— Willie McGee, St. Louis

1987
AMERICAN LEAGUE
P— Mark Langston, Seattle
C— Bob Boone, California
1B— Don Mattingly, New York
2B— Frank White, Kansas City
3B— Gary Gaetti, Minnesota
SS— Tony Fernandez, Toronto
OF— Jesse Barfield, Toronto
OF— Kirby Puckett, Minnesota
OF— Dave Winfield, New York

NATIONAL LEAGUE
P— Rick Reuschel, Pit.-S.F.
C— Mike LaValliere, Pittsburgh
1B— Keith Hernandez, New York
2B— Ryne Sandberg, Chicago
3B— Terry Pendleton, St. Louis
SS— Ozzie Smith, St. Louis
OF— Eric Davis, Cincinnati
OF— Tony Gwynn, San Diego
OF— Andre Dawson, Chicago

1988

AMERICAN LEAGUE

P— Mark Langston, Seattle
C— Bob Boone, California
1B— Don Mattingly, New York
2B— Harold Reynolds, Seattle
3B— Gary Gaetti, Minnesota
SS— Tony Fernandez, Toronto
OF— Kirby Puckett, Minnesota
OF— Devon White, California
OF— Gary Pettis, Detroit

NATIONAL LEAGUE

P— Orel Hershiser, Los Angeles
C— Benito Santiago, San Diego
1B— Keith Hernandez, New York
2B— Ryne Sandberg, Chicago
3B— Tim Wallach, Montreal
SS— Ozzie Smith, St. Louis
OF— Andy Van Slyke, Pittsburgh
OF— Eric Davis, Cincinnati
OF— Andre Dawson, Chicago

1989

AMERICAN LEAGUE

P— Bret Saberhagen, Kansas City
C— Bob Boone, Kansas City
1B— Don Mattingly, New York
2B— Harold Reynolds, Seattle
3B— Gary Gaetti, Minnesota
SS— Tony Fernandez, Toronto
OF— Kirby Puckett, Minnesota
OF— Devon White, California
OF— Gary Pettis, Detroit

NATIONAL LEAGUE

P— Ron Darling, New York
C— Benito Santiago, San Diego
1B— Andres Galarraga, Montreal
2B— Ryne Sandberg, Chicago
3B— Terry Pendleton, St. Louis
SS— Ozzie Smith, St. Louis
OF— Andy Van Slyke, Pittsburgh
OF— Tony Gwynn, San Diego
OF— Eric Davis, Cincinnati

1990

AMERICAN LEAGUE

P— Mike Boddicker, Boston
C— Sandy Alomar Jr., Cleveland
1B— Mark McGwire, Oakland
2B— Harold Reynolds, Seattle
3B— Kelly Gruber, Toronto
SS— Ozzie Guillen, Chicago
OF— Ken Griffey Jr., Seattle
OF— Ellis Burks, Boston
OF— Gary Pettis, Texas

NATIONAL LEAGUE

P— Greg Maddux, Chicago
C— Benito Santiago, San Diego
1B— Andres Galarraga, Montreal
2B— Ryne Sandberg, Chicago
3B— Tim Wallach, Montreal
SS— Ozzie Smith, St. Louis
OF— Barry Bonds, Pittsburgh
OF— Andy Van Slyke, Pittsburgh
OF— Tony Gwynn, San Diego

1991

AMERICAN LEAGUE

P— Mark Langston, California
C— Tony Pena, Boston
1B— Don Mattingly, New York
2B— Roberto Alomar, Toronto
3B— Robin Ventura, Chicago
SS— Cal Ripken, Baltimore
OF— Ken Griffey Jr., Seattle
OF— Kirby Puckett, Minnesota
OF— Devon White, Toronto

NATIONAL LEAGUE

P— Greg Maddux, Chicago
C— Tom Pagnozzi, St. Louis
1B— Will Clark, San Francisco
2B— Ryne Sandberg, Chicago
3B— Matt Williams, San Francisco
SS— Ozzie Smith, St. Louis
OF— Barry Bonds, Pittsburgh
OF— Andy Van Slyke, Pittsburgh
OF— Tony Gwynn, San Diego

1992

AMERICAN LEAGUE

P— Mark Langston, California
C— Ivan Rodriguez, Texas
1B— Don Mattingly, New York
2B— Roberto Alomar, Toronto
3B— Robin Ventura, Chicago
SS— Cal Ripken, Baltimore
OF— Ken Griffey Jr., Seattle
OF— Kirby Puckett, Minnesota
OF— Devon White, Toronto

NATIONAL LEAGUE

P— Greg Maddux, Chicago
C— Tom Pagnozzi, St. Louis
1B— Mark Grace, Chicago
2B— Jose Lind, Pittsburgh
3B— Terry Pendleton, Atlanta
SS— Ozzie Smith, St. Louis
OF— Barry Bonds, Pittsburgh
OF— Andy Van Slyke, Pittsburgh
OF— Larry Walker, Montreal

1993

AMERICAN LEAGUE

P— Mark Langston, California
C— Ivan Rodriguez, Texas
1B— Don Mattingly, New York
2B— Roberto Alomar, Toronto
3B— Robin Ventura, Chicago
SS— Omar Vizquel, Seattle
OF— Ken Griffey Jr., Seattle
OF— Kenny Lofton, Cleveland
OF— Devon White, Toronto

NATIONAL LEAGUE

P— Greg Maddux, Atlanta
C— Kirt Manwaring, San Francisco
1B— Mark Grace, Chicago
2B— Robby Thompson, San Fran.
3B— Matt Williams, San Francisco
SS— Jay Bell, Pittsburgh
OF— Barry Bonds, San Francisco
OF— Marquis Grissom, Montreal
OF— Larry Walker, Montreal

1994

AMERICAN LEAGUE

P— Mark Langston, California
C— Ivan Rodriguez, Texas
1B— Don Mattingly, New York
2B— Roberto Alomar, Toronto
3B— Wade Boggs, New York
SS— Omar Vizquel, Cleveland
OF— Ken Griffey Jr., Seattle
OF— Kenny Lofton, Cleveland
OF— Devon White, Toronto

NATIONAL LEAGUE

P— Greg Maddux, Atlanta
C— Tom Pagnozzi, St. Louis
1B— Jeff Bagwell, Houston
2B— Craig Biggio, Houston
3B— Matt Williams, San Francisco
SS— Barry Larkin, Cincinnati
OF— Barry Bonds, San Francisco
OF— Marquis Grissom, Montreal
OF— Darren Lewis, San Francisco

1995

AMERICAN LEAGUE

P— Mark Langston, California
C— Ivan Rodriguez, Texas
1B— J.T. Snow, California
2B— Roberto Alomar, Toronto
3B— Wade Boggs, New York
SS— Omar Vizquel, Cleveland
OF— Ken Griffey Jr., Seattle
OF— Kenny Lofton, Cleveland
OF— Devon White, Toronto

NATIONAL LEAGUE

P— Greg Maddux, Atlanta
C— Charles Johnson, Florida
1B— Mark Grace, Chicago
2B— Craig Biggio, Houston
3B— Ken Caminiti, San Diego
SS— Barry Larkin, Cincinnati
OF— Raul Mondesi, Los Angeles
OF— Marquis Grissom, Atlanta
OF— Steve Finley, San Diego

1996

AMERICAN LEAGUE

P— Mike Mussina, Baltimore
C— Ivan Rodriguez, Texas
1B— J.T. Snow, California
2B— Roberto Alomar, Baltimore
3B— Robin Ventura, Chicago
SS— Omar Vizquel, Cleveland
OF— Jay Buhner, Seattle
OF— Ken Griffey Jr., Seattle
OF— Kenny Lofton, Cleveland

NATIONAL LEAGUE

P— Greg Maddux, Atlanta
C— Charles Johnson, Florida
1B— Mark Grace, Chicago
2B— Craig Biggio, Houston
3B— Ken Caminiti, San Diego
SS— Barry Larkin, Cincinnati
OF— Barry Bonds, San Francisco
OF— Marquis Grissom, Atlanta
OF— Steve Finley, San Diego

1997

AMERICAN LEAGUE

P— Mike Mussina, Baltimore
C— Ivan Rodriguez, Texas
1B— Rafael Palmeiro, Baltimore
2B— Chuck Knoblauch, Minnesota
3B— Matt Williams, Cleveland
SS— Omar Vizquel, Cleveland
OF— Jim Edmonds, Anaheim
OF— Ken Griffey Jr., Seattle
OF— Bernie Williams, New York

NATIONAL LEAGUE

P— Greg Maddux, Atlanta
C— Charles Johnson, Florida
1B— J.T. Snow, San Francisco
2B— Craig Biggio, Houston
3B— Ken Caminiti, San Diego
SS— Rey Ordonez, New York
OF— Barry Bonds, San Francisco
OF— Raul Mondesi, Los Angeles
OF— Larry Walker, Colorado

1998

AMERICAN LEAGUE

P— Mike Mussina, Baltimore
C— Ivan Rodriguez, Texas
1B— Rafael Palmeiro, Baltimore
2B— Roberto Alomar, Baltimore
3B— Robin Ventura, White Sox
SS— Omar Vizquel, Cleveland
OF— Jim Edmonds, Anaheim
OF— Ken Griffey Jr., Seattle
OF— Bernie Williams, New York

NATIONAL LEAGUE

P— Greg Maddux, Atlanta
C— Charles Johnson, Fla.-L.A.
1B— J.T. Snow, San Francisco
2B— Bret Boone, Cincinnati
3B— Scott Rolen, Philadelphia
SS— Rey Ordonez, New York
OF— Barry Bonds, San Francisco
OF— Andruw Jones, Atlanta
OF— Larry Walker, Colorado

1999

AMERICAN LEAGUE

P— Mike Mussina, Baltimore
C— Ivan Rodriguez, Texas
1B— Rafael Palmeiro, Texas
2B— Roberto Alomar, Cleveland
3B— Scott Brosius, New York
SS— Omar Vizquel, Cleveland
OF— Shawn Green, Toronto
OF— Ken Griffey Jr., Seattle
OF— Bernie Williams, New York

NATIONAL LEAGUE

P— Greg Maddux, Atlanta
C— Mike Lieberthal, Philadelphia
1B— J.T. Snow, San Francisco
2B— Pokey Reese, Cincinnati
3B— Robin Ventura, New York
SS— Rey Ordonez, New York
OF— Steve Finley, Arizona
OF— Andruw Jones, Atlanta
OF— Larry Walker, Colorado

2000

AMERICAN LEAGUE

P— Kenny Rogers, Texas
C— Ivan Rodriguez, Texas
1B— John Olerud, Seattle
2B— Roberto Alomar, Cleveland
3B— Travis Fryman, Cleveland
SS— Omar Vizquel, Cleveland
OF— Jermaine Dye, Kansas City
OF— Darin Erstad, Anaheim
OF— Bernie Williams, New York

NATIONAL LEAGUE

P— Greg Maddux, Atlanta
C— Mike Matheny, St. Louis
1B— J.T. Snow, San Francisco
2B— Pokey Reese, Cincinnati
3B— Scott Rolen, Philadelphia
SS— Neifi Perez, Colorado
OF— Jim Edmonds, St. Louis
OF— Steve Finley, Arizona
OF— Andruw Jones, Atlanta

2001

AMERICAN LEAGUE

P— Mike Mussina, New York
C— Ivan Rodriguez, Texas
1B— Doug Mientkiewicz, Minnesota
2B— Roberto Alomar, Cleveland
3B— Eric Chavez, Oakland
SS— Omar Vizquel, Cleveland
OF— Mike Cameron, Seattle
OF— Torii Hunter, Minnesota
OF— Ichiro Suzuki, Seattle

NATIONAL LEAGUE

P— Greg Maddux, Atlanta
C— Brad Ausmus, Houston
1B— Todd Helton, Colorado
2B— Fernando Vina, St. Louis
3B— Scott Rolen, Philadelphia
SS— Orlando Cabrera, Montreal
OF— Jim Edmonds, St. Louis
OF— Andruw Jones, Atlanta
OF— Larry Walker, Colorado

2002

AMERICAN LEAGUE

P— Kenny Rogers, Texas
C— Bengie Molina, Anaheim
1B— John Olerud, Seattle
2B— Bret Boone, Seattle
3B— Eric Chavez, Oakland
SS— Alex Rodriguez, Texas
OF— Darin Erstad, Anaheim
OF— Torii Hunter, Minnesota
OF— Ichiro Suzuki, Seattle

NATIONAL LEAGUE

P— Greg Maddux, Atlanta
C— Brad Ausmus, Houston
1B— Todd Helton, Colorado
2B— Fernando Vina, St. Louis
3B— Scott Rolen, Phil.-St.L.
SS— Edgar Renteria, St. Louis
OF— Jim Edmonds, St. Louis
OF— Andruw Jones, Atlanta
OF— Larry Walker, Colorado

2003

AMERICAN LEAGUE

P— Mike Mussina, New York
C— Bengie Molina, Anaheim
1B— John Olerud, Seattle
2B— Bret Boone, Seattle
3B— Eric Chavez, Oakland
SS— Alex Rodriguez, Texas
OF— Mike Cameron, Seattle
OF— Torii Hunter, Minnesota
OF— Ichiro Suzuki, Seattle

NATIONAL LEAGUE

P— Mike Hampton, Atlanta
C— Mike Matheny, St. Louis
1B— Derrek Lee, Florida
2B— Luis Castillo, Florida
3B— Scott Rolen, St. Louis
SS— Edgar Renteria, St. Louis
OF— Jim Edmonds, St. Louis
OF— Andruw Jones, Atlanta
OF— Jose Cruz Jr., San Francisco

HILLERICH & BRADSBY SILVER SLUGGER TEAMS

1980

AMERICAN LEAGUE

1B— Cecil Cooper, Milwaukee
2B— Willie Randolph, New York
3B— George Brett, Kansas City
SS— Robin Yount, Milwaukee
OF— Ben Oglivie, Milwaukee
OF— Al Oliver, Texas
OF— Willie Wilson, Kansas City
C— Lance Parrish, Detroit
DH— Reggie Jackson, New York

NATIONAL LEAGUE

1B— Keith Hernandez, St. Louis
2B— Manny Trillo, Philadelphia
3B— Mike Schmidt, Philadelphia
SS— Garry Templeton, St. Louis
OF— Dusty Baker, Los Angeles
OF— Andre Dawson, Montreal
OF— George Hendrick, St. Louis
C— Ted Simmons, St. Louis
P— Bob Forsch, St. Louis

1981

AMERICAN LEAGUE

1B— Cecil Cooper, Milwaukee
2B— Bobby Grich, California
3B— Carney Lansford, Boston
SS— Rick Burleson, California
OF— Rickey Henderson, Oakland
OF— Dwight Evans, Boston
OF— Dave Winfield, New York
C— Carlton Fisk, Chicago
DH— Al Oliver, Texas

NATIONAL LEAGUE

1B— Pete Rose, Philadelphia
2B— Manny Trillo, Philadelphia
3B— Mike Schmidt, Philadelphia
SS— Dave Concepcion, Cincinnati
OF— Andre Dawson, Montreal
OF— George Foster, Cincinnati
OF— Dusty Baker, Los Angeles
C— Gary Carter, Montreal
P— Fernando Valenzuela, Los Angeles

1982

AMERICAN LEAGUE

1B— Cecil Cooper, Milwaukee
2B— Damaso Garcia, Toronto
3B— Doug DeCinces, California
SS— Robin Yount, Milwaukee
OF— Dave Winfield, New York
OF— Willie Wilson, Kansas City
OF— Reggie Jackson, California
C— Lance Parrish, Detroit
DH— Hal McRae, Kansas City

NATIONAL LEAGUE

1B— Al Oliver, Montreal
2B— Joe Morgan, San Francisco
3B— Mike Schmidt, Philadelphia
SS— Dave Concepcion, Cincinnati
OF— Dale Murphy, Atlanta
OF— Pedro Guerrero, Los Angeles
OF— Leon Durham, Chicago
C— Gary Carter, Montreal
P— Don Robinson, Pittsburgh

1983

AMERICAN LEAGUE

1B— Eddie Murray, Baltimore
2B— Lou Whitaker, Detroit
3B— Wade Boggs, Boston
SS— Cal Ripken Jr., Baltimore
OF— Jim Rice, Boston
OF— Dave Winfield, New York
OF— Lloyd Moseby, Toronto
C— Lance Parrish, Detroit
DH— Don Baylor, New York

NATIONAL LEAGUE

1B— George Hendrick, St. Louis
2B— Johnny Ray, Pittsburgh
3B— Mike Schmidt, Philadelphia
SS— Dickie Thon, Houston
OF— Andre Dawson, Montreal
OF— Dale Murphy, Atlanta
OF— Jose Cruz, Houston
C— Terry Kennedy, San Diego
P— Fernando Valenzuela, Los Angeles

1984

AMERICAN LEAGUE

1B— Eddie Murray, Baltimore
2B— Lou Whitaker, Detroit
3B— Buddy Bell, Texas
SS— Cal Ripken Jr., Baltimore
OF— Tony Armas, Boston
OF— Jim Rice, Boston
OF— Dave Winfield, New York
C— Lance Parrish, Detroit
DH— Andre Thornton, Cleveland

NATIONAL LEAGUE
1B— Keith Hernandez, New York
2B— Ryne Sandberg, Chicago
3B— Mike Schmidt, Philadelphia
SS— Garry Templeton, San Diego
OF— Dale Murphy, Atlanta
OF— Jose Cruz, Houston
OF— Tony Gwynn, San Diego
C— Gary Carter, Montreal
P— Rick Rhoden, Pittsburgh

1985

AMERICAN LEAGUE
1B— Don Mattingly, New York
2B— Lou Whitaker, Detroit
3B— George Brett, Kansas City
SS— Cal Ripken Jr., Baltimore
OF— Rickey Henderson, New York
OF— Dave Winfield, New York
OF— George Bell, Toronto
C— Carlton Fisk, Chicago
DH— Don Baylor, New York

NATIONAL LEAGUE
1B— Jack Clark, St. Louis
2B— Ryne Sandberg, Chicago
3B— Tim Wallach, Montreal
SS— Hubie Brooks, Montreal
OF— Willie McGee, St. Louis
OF— Dale Murphy, Atlanta
OF— Dave Parker, Cincinnati
C— Gary Carter, New York
P— Rick Rhoden, Pittsburgh

1986

AMERICAN LEAGUE
1B— Don Mattingly, New York
2B— Frank White, Kansas City
3B— Wade Boggs, Boston
SS— Cal Ripken Jr., Baltimore
OF— George Bell, Toronto
OF— Kirby Puckett, Minnesota
OF— Jesse Barfield, Toronto
C— Lance Parrish, Detroit
DH— Don Baylor, Boston

NATIONAL LEAGUE
1B— Glenn Davis, Houston
2B— Steve Sax, Los Angeles
3B— Mike Schmidt, Philadelphia
SS— Hubie Brooks, Montreal
OF— Tony Gwynn, San Diego
OF— Tim Raines, Montreal
OF— Dave Parker, Cincinnati
C— Gary Carter, New York
P— Rick Rhoden, Pittsburgh

1987

AMERICAN LEAGUE
1B— Don Mattingly, New York
2B— Lou Whitaker, Detroit
3B— Wade Boggs, Boston
SS— Alan Trammell, Detroit
OF— George Bell, Toronto
OF— Dwight Evans, Boston
OF— Kirby Puckett, Minnesota
C— Matt Nokes, Detroit
DH— Paul Molitor, Milwaukee

NATIONAL LEAGUE
1B— Jack Clark, St. Louis
2B— Juan Samuel, Philadelphia
3B— Tim Wallach, Montreal
SS— Ozzie Smith, St. Louis
OF— Andre Dawson, Chicago
OF— Eric Davis, Cincinnati
OF— Tony Gwynn, San Diego
C— Benito Santiago, San Diego
P— Bob Forsch, St. Louis

1988

AMERICAN LEAGUE
1B— George Brett, Kansas City
2B— Julio Franco, Cleveland
3B— Wade Boggs, Boston
SS— Alan Trammell, Detroit
OF— Kirby Puckett, Minnesota
OF— Jose Canseco, Oakland
OF— Mike Greenwell, Boston
C— Carlton Fisk, Chicago
DH— Paul Molitor, Milwaukee

NATIONAL LEAGUE
1B— Andres Galarraga, Montreal
2B— Ryne Sandberg, Chicago
3B— Bobby Bonilla, Pittsburgh
SS— Barry Larkin, Cincinnati
OF— Darryl Strawberry, New York
OF— Andy Van Slyke, Pittsburgh
OF— Kirk Gibson, Los Angeles
C— Benito Santiago, San Diego
P— Tim Leary, Los Angeles

1989

AMERICAN LEAGUE
1B— Fred McGriff, Toronto
2B— Julio Franco, Texas
3B— Wade Boggs, Boston
SS— Cal Ripken Jr., Baltimore
OF— Kirby Puckett, Minnesota
OF— Ruben Sierra, Texas
OF— Robin Yount, Milwaukee
C— Mickey Tettleton, Baltimore
DH— Harold Baines, Chi.-Tex.

NATIONAL LEAGUE
1B— Will Clark, San Francisco
2B— Ryne Sandberg, Chicago
3B— Howard Johnson, New York
SS— Barry Larkin, Cincinnati
OF— Kevin Mitchell, San Francisco
OF— Tony Gwynn, San Diego
OF— Eric Davis, Cincinnati
C— Craig Biggio, Houston
P— Don Robinson, San Francisco

1990

AMERICAN LEAGUE
1B— Cecil Fielder, Detroit
2B— Julio Franco, Texas
3B— Kelly Gruber, Toronto
SS— Alan Trammell, Detroit
OF— Rickey Henderson, Oakland
OF— Jose Canseco, Oakland
OF— Ellis Burks, Boston
C— Lance Parrish, California
DH— Dave Parker, Milwaukee

NATIONAL LEAGUE
1B— Eddie Murray, Los Angeles
2B— Ryne Sandberg, Chicago
3B— Matt Williams, San Francisco
SS— Barry Larkin, Cincinnati
OF— Barry Bonds, Pittsburgh
OF— Bobby Bonilla, Pittsburgh
OF— Darryl Strawberry, New York
C— Benito Santiago, San Diego
P— Don Robinson, San Francisco

1991

AMERICAN LEAGUE
1B— Cecil Fielder, Detroit
2B— Julio Franco, Texas
3B— Wade Boggs, Boston
SS— Cal Ripken Jr., Baltimore
OF— Jose Canseco, Oakland
OF— Joe Carter, Toronto
OF— Ken Griffey Jr., Seattle
C— Mickey Tettleton, Detroit
DH— Frank Thomas, Chicago

NATIONAL LEAGUE
1B— Will Clark, San Francisco
2B— Ryne Sandberg, Chicago
3B— Howard Johnson, New York
SS— Barry Larkin, Cincinnati
OF— Barry Bonds, Pittsburgh
OF— Bobby Bonilla, Pittsburgh
OF— Ron Gant, Atlanta
C— Benito Santiago, San Diego
P— Tom Glavine, Atlanta

1992

AMERICAN LEAGUE
1B— Mark McGwire, Oakland
2B— Roberto Alomar, Toronto
3B— Edgar Martinez, Seattle
SS— Travis Fryman, Detroit
OF— Joe Carter, Toronto
OF— Juan Gonzalez, Texas
OF— Kirby Puckett, Minnesota
C— Mickey Tettleton, Detroit
DH— Dave Winfield, Toronto

NATIONAL LEAGUE
1B— Fred McGriff, San Diego
2B— Ryne Sandberg, Chicago
3B— Gary Sheffield, San Diego
SS— Barry Larkin, Cincinnati
OF— Barry Bonds, Pittsburgh
OF— Andy Van Slyke, Pittsburgh
OF— Larry Walker, Montreal
C— Darren Daulton, Philadelphia
P— Dwight Gooden, New York

1993

AMERICAN LEAGUE
1B— Frank Thomas, Chicago
2B— Carlos Baerga, Cleveland
3B— Wade Boggs, New York
SS— Cal Ripken Jr., Baltimore
OF— Albert Belle, Cleveland
OF— Juan Gonzalez, Texas
OF— Ken Griffey Jr., Seattle
C— Mike Stanley, New York
DH— Paul Molitor, Toronto

NATIONAL LEAGUE
1B— Fred McGriff, S.D.-Atl.
2B— Robby Thompson, San Fran.
3B— Matt Williams, San Francisco
SS— Jay Bell, Pittsburgh
OF— Barry Bonds, San Francisco
OF— Lenny Dykstra, Philadelphia
OF— David Justice, Atlanta
C— Mike Piazza, Los Angeles
P— Orel Hershiser, Los Angeles

1994

AMERICAN LEAGUE
1B— Frank Thomas, Chicago
2B— Carlos Baerga, Cleveland
3B— Wade Boggs, New York
SS— Cal Ripken Jr., Baltimore
OF— Albert Belle, Cleveland
OF— Ken Griffey Jr., Seattle
OF— Kirby Puckett, Minnesota
C— Ivan Rodriguez, Texas
DH— Julio Franco, Chicago

NATIONAL LEAGUE
1B— Jeff Bagwell, Houston
2B— Craig Biggio, Houston
3B— Matt Williams, San Francisco
SS— Wil Cordero, Montreal
OF— Moises Alou, Montreal
OF— Barry Bonds, San Francisco
OF— Tony Gwynn, San Diego
C— Mike Piazza, Los Angeles
P— Mark Portugal, San Francisco

1995

AMERICAN LEAGUE
1B— Mo Vaughn, Boston
2B— Chuck Knoblauch, Minnesota
3B— Gary Gaetti, Kansas City
SS— John Valentin, Boston
OF— Albert Belle, Cleveland
OF— Tim Salmon, California
OF— Manny Ramirez, Cleveland

C— Ivan Rodriguez, Texas
DH— Edgar Martinez, Seattle

NATIONAL LEAGUE
1B— Eric Karros, Los Angeles
2B— Craig Biggio, Houston
3B— Vinny Castilla, Colorado
SS— Barry Larkin, Cincinnati
OF— Dante Bichette, Colorado
OF— Tony Gwynn, San Diego
OF— Sammy Sosa, Chicago
C— Mike Piazza, Los Angeles
P— Tom Glavine, Atlanta

1996
AMERICAN LEAGUE
1B— Mark McGwire, Oakland
2B— Roberto Alomar, Baltimore
3B— Jim Thome, Cleveland
SS— Alex Rodriguez, Seattle
OF— Albert Belle, Cleveland
OF— Juan Gonzalez, Texas
OF— Ken Griffey Jr., Seattle
C— Ivan Rodriguez, Texas
DH— Paul Molitor, Minnesota

NATIONAL LEAGUE
1B— Andres Galarraga, Colorado
2B— Eric Young, Colorado
3B— Ken Caminiti, San Diego
SS— Barry Larkin, Cincinnati
OF— Barry Bonds, San Francisco
OF— Ellis Burks, Colorado
OF— Gary Sheffield, Florida
C— Mike Piazza, Los Angeles
P— Tom Glavine, Atlanta

1997
AMERICAN LEAGUE
1B— Tino Martinez, New York
2B— Chuck Knoblauch, Minnesota
3B— Matt Williams, Cleveland
SS— Nomar Garciaparra, Boston
OF— Juan Gonzalez, Texas
OF— Ken Griffey Jr., Seattle
OF— David Justice, Cleveland
C— Ivan Rodriguez, Texas
DH— Edgar Martinez, Seattle

NATIONAL LEAGUE
1B— Jeff Bagwell, Houston
2B— Craig Biggio, Houston
3B— Vinny Castilla, Colorado
SS— Jeff Blauser, Atlanta
OF— Barry Bonds, San Francisco
OF— Tony Gwynn, San Diego
OF— Larry Walker, Colorado
C— Mike Piazza, Los Angeles
P— John Smoltz, Atlanta

1998
AMERICAN LEAGUE
1B— Rafael Palmeiro, Baltimore
2B— Damion Easley, Detroit
3B— Dean Palmer, Kansas City
SS— Alex Rodriguez, Seattle
OF— Juan Gonzalez, Texas
OF— Ken Griffey Jr., Seattle
OF— Albert Belle, Chicago
C— Ivan Rodriguez, Texas
DH— Jose Canseco, Toronto

NATIONAL LEAGUE
1B— Mark McGwire, St. Louis
2B— Craig Biggio, Houston
3B— Vinny Castilla, Colorado
SS— Barry Larkin, Cincinnati
OF— Sammy Sosa, Chicago
OF— Moises Alou, Houston
OF— Greg Vaughn, San Diego
C— Mike Piazza, L.A.-Fla.-N.Y.
P— Tom Glavine, Atlanta

1999
AMERICAN LEAGUE
1B— Carlos Delgado, Toronto
2B— Roberto Alomar, Cleveland
3B— Dean Palmer, Detroit
SS— Alex Rodriguez, Seattle
OF— Shawn Green, Toronto
OF— Ken Griffey Jr., Seattle
OF— Manny Ramirez, Cleveland
C— Ivan Rodriguez, Texas
DH— Rafael Palmeiro, Texas

NATIONAL LEAGUE
1B— Jeff Bagwell, Houston
2B— Edgardo Alfonzo, New York
3B— Chipper Jones, Atlanta
SS— Barry Larkin, Cincinnati
OF— Sammy Sosa, Chicago
OF— Vladimir Guerrero, Montreal
OF— Larry Walker, Colorado
C— Mike Piazza, New York
P— Mike Hampton, Houston

2000
AMERICAN LEAGUE
1B— Carlos Delgado, Toronto
2B— Roberto Alomar, Cleveland
3B— Troy Glaus, Anaheim
SS— Alex Rodriguez, Seattle
OF— Darin Erstad, Anaheim
OF— Manny Ramirez, Cleveland
OF— Magglio Ordonez, Chicago
C— Jorge Posada, New York
DH— Frank Thomas, Chicago

NATIONAL LEAGUE
1B— Todd Helton, Colorado
2B— Jeff Kent, San Francisco
3B— Chipper Jones, Atlanta
SS— Edgar Renteria, St. Louis
OF— Sammy Sosa, Chicago
OF— Barry Bonds, San Francisco
OF— Vladimir Guerrero, Montreal
C— Mike Piazza, New York
P— Mike Hampton, New York

2001
AMERICAN LEAGUE
1B— Jason Giambi, Oakland
2B— Bret Boone, Seattle
3B— Troy Glaus, Anaheim
SS— Alex Rodriguez, Texas
OF— Juan Gonzalez, Cleveland
OF— Manny Ramirez, Boston
OF— Ichiro Suzuki, Seattle
C— Jorge Posada, New York
DH— Edgar Martinez, Seattle

NATIONAL LEAGUE
1B— Todd Helton, Colorado
2B— Jeff Kent, San Francisco
3B— Albert Pujols, St. Louis
SS— Rich Aurilia, San Francisco
OF— Barry Bonds, San Francisco
OF— Luis Gonzalez, Arizona
OF— Sammy Sosa, Chicago
C— Mike Piazza, New York
P— Mike Hampton, Colorado

2002
AMERICAN LEAGUE
1B— Jason Giambi, New York
2B— Alfonso Soriano, New York
3B— Eric Chavez, Oakland
SS— Alex Rodriguez, Texas
OF— Garret Anderson, Anaheim
OF— Magglio Ordonez, Chicago
OF— Bernie Williams, New York
C— Jorge Posada, New York
DH— Manny Ramirez, Boston

NATIONAL LEAGUE
1B— Todd Helton, Colorado
2B— Jeff Kent, San Francisco
3B— Scott Rolen, Phi.-St.L.
SS— Edgar Renteria, St. Louis
OF— Barry Bonds, San Francisco
OF— Vladimir Guerrero, Montreal
OF— Sammy Sosa, Chicago
C— Mike Piazza, New York
P— Mike Hampton, Colorado

2003
AMERICAN LEAGUE
1B— Carlos Delgado, Toronto
2B— Bret Boone, Seattle
3B— Bill Mueller, Boston
SS— Alex Rodriguez, Texas
OF— Garret Anderson, Anaheim
OF— Vernon Wells, Toronto
OF— Manny Ramirez, Boston
C— Jorge Posada, New York
DH— Edgar Martinez, Seattle

NATIONAL LEAGUE
1B— Todd Helton, Colorado
2B— Jose Vidro, Montreal
3B— Mike Lowell, Florida
SS— Edgar Renteria, St. Louis
OF— Barry Bonds, San Francisco
OF— Albert Pujols, St. Louis
OF—Gary Sheffield, Atlanta
C— Javy Lopez, Atlanta
P— Mike Hampton, Atlanta

BASEBALL WRITERS' ASSOCIATION OF AMERICA
MOST VALUABLE PLAYER

AMERICAN LEAGUE

Year	Player	Team	Pos.	Points
1931—	Lefty Grove	Philadelphia	P	78
1932—	Jimmie Foxx	Philadelphia	1B	75
1933—	Jimmie Foxx	Philadelphia	1B	74
1934—	Mickey Cochrane	Detroit	C	67
1935—	Hank Greenberg	Detroit	1B	*80
1936—	Lou Gehrig	New York	1B	73
1937—	Charley Gehringer	Detroit	2B	78

NATIONAL LEAGUE

Year	Player	Team	Pos.	Points
1931—	Frank Frisch	St. Louis	2B	65
1932—	Chuck Klein	Philadelphia	OF	78
1933—	Carl Hubbell	New York	P	77
1934—	Dizzy Dean	St. Louis	P	78
1935—	Gabby Hartnett	Chicago	C	75
1936—	Carl Hubbell	New York	P	60
1937—	Joe Medwick	St. Louis	OF	70

AMERICAN LEAGUE

Year	Player	Team	Pos.	Points
1938—	Jimmie Foxx	Boston	1B	305
1939—	Joe DiMaggio	New York	OF	280
1940—	Hank Greenberg	Detroit	OF	292
1941—	Joe DiMaggio	New York	OF	291
1942—	Joe Gordon	New York	2B	270
1943—	Spud Chandler	New York	P	246
1944—	Hal Newhouser	Detroit	P	236
1945—	Hal Newhouser	Detroit	P	236
1946—	Ted Williams	Boston	OF	224
1947—	Joe DiMaggio	New York	OF	202
1948—	Lou Boudreau	Cleveland	SS	324
1949—	Ted Williams	Boston	OF	272
1950—	Phil Rizzuto	New York	SS	284
1951—	Yogi Berra	New York	C	184
1952—	Bobby Shantz	Philadelphia	P	280
1953—	Al Rosen	Cleveland	3B	*336
1954—	Yogi Berra	New York	C	230
1955—	Yogi Berra	New York	C	218
1956—	Mickey Mantle	New York	OF	*336
1957—	Mickey Mantle	New York	OF	233
1958—	Jackie Jensen	Boston	OF	233
1959—	Nellie Fox	Chicago	2B	295
1960—	Roger Maris	New York	OF	225
1961—	Roger Maris	New York	OF	202
1962—	Mickey Mantle	New York	OF	234
1963—	Elston Howard	New York	C	248
1964—	Brooks Robinson	Baltimore	3B	269
1965—	Zoilo Versalles	Minnesota	SS	275
1966—	Frank Robinson	Baltimore	OF	*280
1967—	Carl Yastrzemski	Boston	OF	275
1968—	Denny McLain	Detroit	P	*280
1969—	Harmon Killebrew	Minnesota	1B-3B	294
1970—	Boog Powell	Baltimore	1B	234
1971—	Vida Blue	Oakland	P	268
1972—	Dick Allen	Chicago	1B	321
1973—	Reggie Jackson	Oakland	OF	*336
1974—	Jeff Burroughs	Texas	OF	248
1975—	Fred Lynn	Boston	OF	326
1976—	Thurman Munson	New York	C	304
1977—	Rod Carew	Minnesota	1B	273
1978—	Jim Rice	Boston	OF	352
1979—	Don Baylor	California	OF	347
1980—	George Brett	Kansas City	3B	335
1981—	Rollie Fingers	Milwaukee	P	319
1982—	Robin Yount	Milwaukee	SS	385
1983—	Cal Ripken Jr.	Baltimore	SS	322
1984—	Willie Hernandez	Detroit	P	306
1985—	Don Mattingly	New York	1B	367
1986—	Roger Clemens	Boston	P	339
1987—	George Bell	Toronto	OF	332
1988—	Jose Canseco	Oakland	OF	*392
1989—	Robin Yount	Milwaukee	OF	256
1990—	Rickey Henderson	Oakland	OF	317
1991—	Cal Ripken Jr.	Baltimore	SS	318
1992—	Dennis Eckersley	Oakland	P	306
1993—	Frank Thomas	Chicago	1B	*392
1994—	Frank Thomas	Chicago	1B	372
1995—	Mo Vaughn	Boston	1B	308
1996—	Juan Gonzalez	Texas	OF	290
1997—	Ken Griffey Jr.	Seattle	OF	*392
1998—	Juan Gonzalez	Texas	OF	357
1999—	Ivan Rodriguez	Texas	C	252
2000—	Jason Giambi	Oakland	1B	317
2001—	Ichiro Suzuki	Seattle	OF	289
2002—	Miguel Tejada	Oakland	SS	356
2003—	Alex Rodriguez	Texas	SS	242

NATIONAL LEAGUE

Year	Player	Team	Pos.	Points
1938—	Ernie Lombardi	Cincinnati	C	229
1939—	Bucky Walters	Cincinnati	P	303
1940—	Frank McCormick	Cincinnati	1B	274
1941—	Dolf Camilli	Brooklyn	1B	300
1942—	Mort Cooper	St. Louis	P	263
1943—	Stan Musial	St. Louis	OF	267
1944—	Marty Marion	St. Louis	SS	190
1945—	Phil Cavarretta	Chicago	1B	279
1946—	Stan Musial	St. Louis	1B	319
1947—	Bob Elliott	Boston	3B	205
1948—	Stan Musial	St. Louis	OF	303
1949—	Jackie Robinson	Brooklyn	2B	264
1950—	Jim Konstanty	Philadelphia	P	286
1951—	Roy Campanella	Brooklyn	C	243
1952—	Hank Sauer	Chicago	OF	226
1953—	Roy Campanella	Brooklyn	C	297
1954—	Willie Mays	New York	OF	283
1955—	Roy Campanella	Brooklyn	C	226
1956—	Don Newcombe	Brooklyn	P	223
1957—	Hank Aaron	Milwaukee	OF	239
1958—	Ernie Banks	Chicago	SS	283
1959—	Ernie Banks	Chicago	SS	232 1/2
1960—	Dick Groat	Pittsburgh	SS	276
1961—	Frank Robinson	Cincinnati	OF	219
1962—	Maury Wills	Los Angeles	SS	209
1963—	Sandy Koufax	Los Angeles	P	237
1964—	Ken Boyer	St. Louis	3B	243
1965—	Willie Mays	San Francisco	OF	224
1966—	Roberto Clemente	Pittsburgh	OF	218
1967—	Orlando Cepeda	St. Louis	1B	*280
1968—	Bob Gibson	St. Louis	P	242
1969—	Willie McCovey	San Francisco	1B	265
1970—	Johnny Bench	Cincinnati	C	326
1971—	Joe Torre	St. Louis	3B	318
1972—	Johnny Bench	Cincinnati	C	263
1973—	Pete Rose	Cincinnati	OF	274
1974—	Steve Garvey	Los Angeles	1B	270
1975—	Joe Morgan	Cincinnati	2B	321 1/2
1976—	Joe Morgan	Cincinnati	2B	311
1977—	George Foster	Cincinnati	OF	291
1978—	Dave Parker	Pittsburgh	OF	320
1979—	Willie Stargell	Pittsburgh	1B	216
	Keith Hernandez	St. Louis	1B	216
1980—	Mike Schmidt	Philadelphia	3B	*336
1981—	Mike Schmidt	Philadelphia	3B	321
1982—	Dale Murphy	Atlanta	OF	283
1983—	Dale Murphy	Atlanta	OF	318
1984—	Ryne Sandberg	Chicago	2B	326
1985—	Willie McGee	St. Louis	OF	280
1986—	Mike Schmidt	Philadelphia	3B	287
1987—	Andre Dawson	Chicago	OF	269
1988—	Kirk Gibson	Los Angeles	OF	272
1989—	Kevin Mitchell	San Francisco	OF	314
1990—	Barry Bonds	Pittsburgh	OF	331
1991—	Terry Pendleton	Atlanta	3B	274
1992—	Barry Bonds	Pittsburgh	OF	304
1993—	Barry Bonds	San Francisco	OF	372
1994—	Jeff Bagwell	Houston	1B	*392
1995—	Barry Larkin	Cincinnati	SS	281
1996—	Ken Caminiti	San Diego	3B	*392
1997—	Larry Walker	Colorado	OF	359
1998—	Sammy Sosa	Chicago	OF	438
1999—	Chipper Jones	Atlanta	3B	432
2000—	Jeff Kent	San Francisco	2B	392
2001—	Barry Bonds	San Francisco	OF	438
2002—	Barry Bonds	San Francisco	OF	*448
2003—	Barry Bonds	San Francisco	OF	426

*Unanimous selection.

CY YOUNG MEMORIAL AWARD

Year	Pitcher	Team	Votes
1956—	Don Newcombe	Brooklyn	10
1957—	Warren Spahn	Milwaukee	15
1958—	Bob Turley	New York A.L.	5
1959—	Early Wynn	Chicago A.L.	13
1960—	Vernon Law	Pittsburgh	8
1961—	Whitey Ford	New York A.L.	9
1962—	Don Drysdale	Los Angeles N.L.	14
1963—	Sandy Koufax	Los Angeles N.L.	*20
1964—	Dean Chance	Los Angeles A.L.	17
1965—	Sandy Koufax	Los Angeles N.L.	*20
1966—	Sandy Koufax	Los Angeles N.L.	*20
1967—	A.L.—Jim Lonborg	Boston	18
	N.L.—Mike McCormick	San Francisco	18
1968—	A.L.—Denny McLain	Detroit	*20
	N.L.—Bob Gibson	St. Louis	*20

Year	Pitcher	Team	Votes
1969—A.L.—Denny McLain		Detroit	10
	Mike Cuellar	Baltimore	10
N.L.—Tom Seaver		New York	23
1970—A.L.—Jim Perry		Minnesota	55
N.L.—Bob Gibson		St. Louis	118
1971—A.L.—Vida Blue		Oakland	98
N.L.—Fergie Jenkins		Chicago	97
1972—A.L.—Gaylord Perry		Cleveland	64
N.L.—Steve Carlton		Philadelphia	*120
1973—A.L.—Jim Palmer		Baltimore	88
N.L.—Tom Seaver		New York	71
1974—A.L.—Jim Hunter		Oakland	90
N.L.—Mike Marshall		Los Angeles	96
1975—A.L.—Jim Palmer		Baltimore	98
N.L.—Tom Seaver		New York	98
1976—A.L.—Jim Palmer		Baltimore	108
N.L.—Randy Jones		San Diego	96
1977—A.L.—Sparky Lyle		New York	56½
N.L.—Steve Carlton		Philadelphia	104
1978—A.L.—Ron Guidry		New York	*140
N.L.—Gaylord Perry		San Diego	116
1979—A.L.—Mike Flanagan		Baltimore	136
N.L.—Bruce Sutter		Chicago	72
1980—A.L.—Steve Stone		Baltimore	100
N.L.—Steve Carlton		Philadelphia	118
1981—A.L.—Rollie Fingers		Milwaukee	126
N.L.—Fernando Valenzuela		Los Angeles	70
1982—A.L.—Pete Vuckovich		Milwaukee	87
N.L.—Steve Carlton		Philadelphia	112
1983—A.L.—LaMarr Hoyt		Chicago	116
N.L.—John Denny		Philadelphia	103
1984—A.L.—Willie Hernandez		Detroit	88
N.L.—Rick Sutcliffe		Chicago	*120
1985—A.L.—Bret Saberhagen		Kansas City	127
N.L.—Dwight Gooden		New York	*120
1986—A.L.—Roger Clemens		Boston	*140
N.L.—Mike Scott		Houston	98
1987—A.L.—Roger Clemens		Boston	124
N.L.—Steve Bedrosian		Philadelphia	57
1988—A.L.—Frank Viola		Minnesota	138
N.L.—Orel Hershiser		Los Angeles	*120
1989—A.L.—Bret Saberhagen		Kansas City	138
N.L.—Mark Davis		San Diego	107
1990—A.L.—Bob Welch		Oakland	107
N.L.—Doug Drabek		Pittsburgh	118
1991—A.L.—Roger Clemens		Boston	119
N.L.—Tom Glavine		Atlanta	110
1992—A.L.—Dennis Eckersley		Oakland	107
N.L.—Greg Maddux		Chicago	112
1993—A.L.—Jack McDowell		Chicago	124
N.L.—Greg Maddux		Atlanta	119
1994—A.L.—David Cone		Kansas City	108
N.L.—Greg Maddux		Atlanta	*140
1995—A.L.—Randy Johnson		Seattle	136
N.L.—Greg Maddux		Atlanta	*140
1996—A.L.—Pat Hentgen		Toronto	110
N.L.—John Smoltz		Atlanta	136
1997—A.L.—Roger Clemens		Toronto	134
N.L.—Pedro Martinez		Montreal	134
1998—A.L.—Roger Clemens		Toronto	*140
N.L.—Tom Glavine		Atlanta	99
1999—A.L.—Pedro Martinez		Boston	*140
N.L.—Randy Johnson		Arizona	134
2000—A.L.—Pedro Martinez		Boston	*140
N.L.—Randy Johnson		Arizona	133
2001—A.L.—Roger Clemens		New York	122
N.L.—Randy Johnson		Arizona	156
2002—A.L.—Barry Zito		Oakland	114
N.L.—Randy Johnson		Arizona	*160
2003—A.L.—Roy Halladay		Toronto	136
N.L.—Eric Gagne		Los Angeles	146

*Unanimous selection.

ROOKIE OF THE YEAR

1947—Combined selection—Jackie Robinson, Brooklyn N.L., 1B
1948—Combined selection—Alvin Dark, Boston N.L., SS

AMERICAN LEAGUE

Year	Player	Team	Pos.	Votes
1949—	Roy Sievers	St. Louis	OF	10
1950—	Walt Dropo	Boston	1B	15
1951—	Gil McDougald	New York	3B	13
1952—	Harry Byrd	Philadelphia	P	9
1953—	Harvey Kuenn	Detroit	SS	23
1954—	Bob Grim	New York	P	15
1955—	Herb Score	Cleveland	P	18
1956—	Luis Aparicio	Chicago	SS	22
1957—	Tony Kubek	New York	IF-OF	23
1958—	Albie Pearson	Washington	OF	14
1959—	Bob Allison	Washington	OF	18
1960—	Ron Hansen	Baltimore	SS	22
1961—	Don Schwall	Boston	P	7
1962—	Tom Tresh	New York	OF-SS	13
1963—	Gary Peters	Chicago	P	10
1964—	Tony Oliva	Minnesota	OF	19
1965—	Curt Blefary	Baltimore	OF	12
1966—	Tommie Agee	Chicago	OF	16
1967—	Rod Carew	Minnesota	2B	19
1968—	Stan Bahnsen	New York	P	17
1969—	Lou Piniella	Kansas City	OF	9
1970—	Thurman Munson	New York	C	23
1971—	Chris Chambliss	Cleveland	1B	11
1972—	Carlton Fisk	Boston	C	*24
1973—	Al Bumbry	Baltimore	OF	13½
1974—	Mike Hargrove	Texas	1B	16½
1975—	Fred Lynn	Boston	OF	23½
1976—	Mark Fidrych	Detroit	P	22
1977—	Eddie Murray	Baltimore	DH-1B	12½
1978—	Lou Whitaker	Detroit	2B	21
1979—	John Castino	Minnesota	3B	7
	Alfredo Griffin	Toronto	SS	7

NATIONAL LEAGUE

Year	Player	Team	Pos.	Votes
1949—	Don Newcombe	Brooklyn	P	21
1950—	Sam Jethroe	Boston	OF	11
1951—	Willie Mays	New York	OF	18
1952—	Joe Black	Brooklyn	P	19
1953—	Jim Gilliam	Brooklyn	2B	11
1954—	Wally Moon	St. Louis	OF	17
1955—	Bill Virdon	St. Louis	OF	15
1956—	Frank Robinson	Cincinnati	OF	*24
1957—	Jack Sanford	Philadelphia	P	16
1958—	Orlando Cepeda	San Francisco	1B	*†21
1959—	Willie McCovey	San Francisco	1B	*24
1960—	Frank Howard	Los Angeles	OF	12
1961—	Billy Williams	Chicago	OF	10
1962—	Ken Hubbs	Chicago	2B	19
1963—	Pete Rose	Cincinnati	2B	17
1964—	Dick Allen	Philadelphia	3B	18
1965—	Jim Lefebvre	Los Angeles	2B	13
1966—	Tommy Helms	Cincinnati	3B	12
1967—	Tom Seaver	New York	P	11
1968—	Johnny Bench	Cincinnati	C	10½
1969—	Ted Sizemore	Los Angeles	2B	14
1970—	Carl Morton	Montreal	P	11
1971—	Earl Williams	Atlanta	C	18
1972—	Jon Matlack	New York	P	19
1973—	Gary Matthews	San Francisco	OF	11
1974—	Bake McBride	St. Louis	OF	16
1975—	John Montefusco	San Francisco	P	12
1976—	Butch Metzger	San Diego	P	11
	Pat Zachry	Cincinnati	P	11
1977—	Andre Dawson	Montreal	OF	10
1978—	Bob Horner	Atlanta	3B	12½
1979—	Rick Sutcliffe	Los Angeles	P	20

AMERICAN LEAGUE

Year	Player	Team	Pos.	Votes
1980—	Joe Charboneau	Cleveland	OF	102
1981—	Dave Righetti	New York	P	127
1982—	Cal Ripken	Baltimore	SS-3B	132
1983—	Ron Kittle	Chicago	OF	104
1984—	Alvin Davis	Seattle	1B	134
1985—	Ozzie Guillen	Chicago	SS	101
1986—	Jose Canseco	Oakland	OF	110
1987—	Mark McGwire	Oakland	1B	*140
1988—	Walt Weiss	Oakland	SS	103
1989—	Gregg Olson	Baltimore	P	136
1990—	Sandy Alomar Jr.	Cleveland	C	*140
1991—	Chuck Knoblauch	Minnesota	2B	136
1992—	Pat Listach	Milwaukee	SS	122
1993—	Tim Salmon	California	OF	*140
1994—	Bob Hamelin	Kansas City	DH	134
1995—	Marty Cordova	Minnesota	3B	105
1996—	Derek Jeter	New York	SS	*140
1997—	Nomar Garciaparra	Boston	SS	*140
1998—	Ben Grieve	Oakland	OF	130
1999—	Carlos Beltran	Kansas City	OF	133
2000—	Kazuhiro Sasaki	Seattle	P	104
2001—	Ichiro Suzuki	Seattle	OF	138
2002—	Eric Hinske	Toronto	3B	122
2003—	Angel Berroa	Kansas City	SS	88

*Unanimous selection. †Three writers did not vote.

NATIONAL LEAGUE

Year	Player	Team	Pos.	Votes
1980—	Steve Howe	Los Angeles	P	80
1981—	Fernando Valenzuela	Los Angeles	P	107
1982—	Steve Sax	Los Angeles	2B	63
1983—	Darryl Strawberry	New York	OF	106
1984—	Dwight Gooden	New York	P	118
1985—	Vince Coleman	St. Louis	OF	*120
1986—	Todd Worrell	St. Louis	P	118
1987—	Benito Santiago	San Diego	C	*120
1988—	Chris Sabo	Cincinnati	3B	79
1989—	Jerome Walton	Chicago	OF	116
1990—	Dave Justice	Atlanta	OF	118
1991—	Jeff Bagwell	Houston	1B	118
1992—	Eric Karros	Los Angeles	1B	116
1993—	Mike Piazza	Los Angeles	C	*140
1994—	Raul Mondesi	Los Angeles	OF	*140
1995—	Hideo Nomo	Los Angeles	P	118
1996—	Todd Hollandsworth	Los Angeles	OF	105
1997—	Scott Rolen	Philadelphia	3B	*140
1998—	Kerry Wood	Chicago	P	128
1999—	Scott Williamson	Cincinnati	P	118
2000—	Rafael Furcal	Atlanta	SS-2B	144
2001—	Albert Pujols	St. Louis	OF-3B-1B	*160
2002—	Jason Jennings	Colorado	P	150
2003—	Dontrelle Willis	Florida	P	118

MANAGER OF THE YEAR

AMERICAN LEAGUE

Year	Manager	Team	Points
1983—	Tony La Russa	Chicago	17
1984—	Sparky Anderson	Detroit	96
1985—	Bobby Cox	Toronto	104
1986—	John McNamara	Boston	95
1987—	Sparky Anderson	Detroit	90
1988—	Tony La Russa	Oakland	103
1989—	Frank Robinson	Baltimore	125
1990—	Jeff Torborg	Chicago	128
1991—	Tom Kelly	Minnesota	138
1992—	Tony La Russa	Oakland	132
1993—	Gene Lamont	Chicago	72
1994—	Buck Showalter	New York	132
1995—	Lou Piniella	Seattle	86
1996—	Johnny Oates	Texas	89
	Joe Torre	New York	89
1997—	Dave Johnson	Baltimore	88
1998—	Joe Torre	New York	128
1999—	Jimy Williams	Boston	115
2000—	Jerry Manuel	Chicago	134
2001—	Lou Piniella	Seattle	128
2002—	Mike Scioscia	Anaheim	116
2003—	Tony Pena	Kansas City	130

NATIONAL LEAGUE

Year	Manager	Team	Points
1983—	Tommy Lasorda	Los Angeles	10
1984—	Jim Frey	Chicago	101
1985—	Whitey Herzog	St. Louis	86
1986—	Hal Lanier	Houston	108
1987—	Buck Rodgers	Montreal	92
1988—	Tommy Lasorda	Los Angeles	101
1989—	Don Zimmer	Chicago	118
1990—	Jim Leyland	Pittsburgh	99
1991—	Bobby Cox	Atlanta	96
1992—	Jim Leyland	Pittsburgh	109
1993—	Dusty Baker	San Francisco	105
1994—	Felipe Alou	Montreal	138
1995—	Don Baylor	Colorado	122
1996—	Bruce Bochy	San Diego	76
1997—	Dusty Baker	San Francisco	110
1998—	Larry Dierker	Houston	102
1999—	Jack McKeon	Cincinnati	115
2000—	Dusty Baker	San Francisco	154
2001—	Larry Bowa	Philadelphia	113
2002—	Tony La Russa	St. Louis	129
2003—	Jack McKeon	Florida	116

EARLY MOST VALUABLE PLAYER AWARDS

CHALMERS AWARD

AMERICAN LEAGUE

Year	Player	Team	Pos.	Points
1911—	Ty Cobb	Detroit	OF	64
1912—	Tris Speaker	Boston	OF	59
1913—	Walter Johnson	Washington	P	54
1914—	Eddie Collins	Philadelphia	2B	63

NATIONAL LEAGUE

Year	Player	Team	Pos.	Points
1911—	Frank Schulte	Chicago	OF	29
1912—	Larry Doyle	New York	2B	48
1913—	Jake Daubert	Brooklyn	1B	50
1914—	Johnny Evers	Boston	2B	50

LEAGUE AWARDS

AMERICAN LEAGUE

Year	Player	Team	Pos.	Points
1922—	George Sisler	St. Louis	1B	59
1923—	Babe Ruth	New York	OF	64
1924—	Walter Johnson	Washington	P	55
1925—	Roger Peckinpaugh	Washington	SS	45
1926—	George Burns	Cleveland	1B	63
1927—	Lou Gehrig	New York	1B	56
1928—	Mickey Cochrane	Philadelphia	C	53
1929—	No selection			

NATIONAL LEAGUE

Year	Player	Team	Pos.	Points
1922—	No selection			
1923—	No selection			
1924—	Dazzy Vance	Brooklyn	P	74
1925—	Rogers Hornsby	St. Louis	2B	73
1926—	Bob O'Farrell	St. Louis	C	79
1927—	Paul Waner	Pittsburgh	OF	72
1928—	Jim Bottomley	St. Louis	1B	76
1929—	Rogers Hornsby	Chicago	2B	60

HALL OF FAME

ROSTER OF MEMBERS

Name	Des.*	Elec. year	Votes rec.†	Votes cast‡	% of vote	Teams as player
Aaron, Hank	P	1982	406	415	97.8	Milwaukee NL, Atlanta NL, Milwaukee AL
Alexander, Grover C.	P	1938	212	262	80.9	Philadelphia NL, Chicago NL, St. Louis NL
Alston, Walter	M	1983	CV	—	—	St. Louis NL
Anderson, Sparky	M	2000	CV	—	—	Philadelphia NL
Anson, Cap	P	1939	C1	—	—	Chicago NL
Aparicio, Luis	P	1984	341	403	84.6	Chicago AL, Baltimore AL, Boston AL
Appling, Luke	P	1964	189	225	84.0	Chicago AL
Ashburn, Richie	P	1995	CV	—	—	Philadelphia NL, Chicago NL, New York NL
Averill, Earl	P	1975	CV	—	—	Cleveland AL, Detroit AL, Boston NL
Baker, Home Run	P	1955	CV	—	—	Philadelphia AL, New York AL
Bancroft, Dave	P	1971	CV	—	—	Philadelphia NL, New York NL, Boston NL, Brooklyn NL
Banks, Ernie	P	1977	321	383	83.8	Chicago NL
Barlick, Al	U	1989	CV	—	—	
Barrow, Ed	E	1953	CV	—	—	
Beckley, Jake	P	1971	CV	—	—	Pittsburgh NL, Pittsburgh PL, New York NL, Cincinnati NL, St. Louis NL
Bell, Cool Papa	P	1974	SCNL	—	—	Negro Leagues
Bench, Johnny	P	1989	431	447	96.4	Cincinnati NL
Bender, Chief	P	1953	CV	—	—	Philadelphia AL, Philadelphia NL, Chicago AL
Berra, Yogi	P	1972	339	396	85.6	New York AL, New York NL
Bottomley, Jim	P	1974	CV	—	—	St. Louis NL, Cincinnati NL, St. Louis AL
Boudreau, Lou	P	1970	232	300	77.3	Cleveland AL, Boston AL
Bresnahan, Roger	P	1945	C2	—	—	Washington NL, Chicago NL, Baltimore AL, New York NL, St. Louis NL
Brett, George	P	1999	488	497	98.2	Kansas City AL
Brock, Lou	P	1985	315	395	79.7	Chicago NL, St. Louis NL
Brouthers, Dan	P	1945	C2	—	—	Troy NL, Buffalo NL, Detroit NL, Boston NL, Boston PL, Boston AA,Brooklyn NL, Baltimore NL,Louisville NL, Philadelphia NL, New York NL
Brown, Three Finger	P	1949	C2	—	—	St. Louis NL, Chicago NL, Cincinnati NL
Bulkeley, Morgan	E	1937	CC	—	—	
Bunning, Jim	P	1996	CV	—	—	Detroit AL, Philadelphia NL, Pittsburgh NL, Los Angeles NL
Burkett, Jesse	P	1946	C2	—	—	New York NL, Cleveland NL, St. Louis NL, St. Louis AL, Boston AL
Campanella, Roy	P	1969	270	340	79.4	Brooklyn NL
Carew, Rod	P	1991	401	443	90.5	Minnesota AL, California AL
Carey, Max	P	1961	CV	—	—	Pittsburgh NL, Brooklyn NL
Carlton, Steve	P	1994	436	455	95.8	St. Louis NL, Philadelphia NL, San Francisco NL, Chicago AL, Cleveland AL, Minnesota AL
Carter, Gary	P	2003	387	496	78.0	Montreal NL, New York NL, San Francisco NL, Los Angeles NL
Cartwright, Alexander	O	1938	CC	—	—	
Cepeda, Orlando	P	1999	CV	—	—	San Francisco NL, St. Louis NL, Atlanta NL, Oakland AL, Boston AL, Kansas City AL
Chadwick, Henry	O	1938	CC	—	—	
Chance, Frank	P	1946	C2	—	—	Chicago NL, New York AL
Chandler, Happy	E	1982	CV	—	—	
Charleston, Oscar	P	1976	SCNL	—	—	Negro Leagues
Chesbro, Jack	P	1946	C2	—	—	Pittsburgh NL, New York AL, Boston AL
Chylak, Nestor	U	1999	CV	—	—	
Clarke, Fred	P	1945	C2	—	—	Louisville NL, Pittsburgh NL
Clarkson, John	P	1963	CV	—	—	Worcester NL, Chicago NL, Boston NL, Cleveland NL
Clemente, Roberto	P	1973	393	424	92.7	Pittsburgh NL
Cobb, Ty	P	1936	222	226	98.2	Detroit AL, Philadelphia AL
Cochrane, Mickey	P	1947	128	161	79.5	Philadelphia AL, Detroit AL
Collins, Eddie	P	1939	213	274	77.7	Philadelphia AL, Chicago AL
Collins, Jimmy	P	1945	C2	—	—	Boston NL, Louisville NL, Boston AL, Philadelphia AL
Combs, Earle	P	1970	CV	—	—	New York AL
Comiskey, Charley	F/P	1939	C1	—	—	St. Louis AA, Chicago PL, Cincinnati NL
Conlan, Jocko	U	1974	CV	—	—	Chicago AL
Connolly, Tommy	U	1953	CV	—	—	
Connor, Roger	P	1976	CV	—	—	Troy NL, New York NL, New York PL, Philadelphia NL, St. Louis NL
Coveleski, Stan	P	1969	CV	—	—	Philadelphia AL, Cleveland AL, Washington AL, New York AL
Crawford, Sam	P	1957	CV	—	—	Cincinnati NL, Detroit AL
Cronin, Joe	P	1956	152	193	78.8	Pittsburgh NL, Washington AL, Boston AL

Name	Des.*	Elec. year	Votes rec.†	Votes cast‡	% of vote	Teams as player
Cummings, Candy	P	1939	C1	—	—	Hartford NL, Cincinnati NL
Cuyler, Kiki	P	1968	CV	—	—	Pittsburgh NL, Chicago NL, Cincinnati NL, Brooklyn NL
Dandridge, Ray	P	1987	CV	—	—	Negro Leagues
Davis, George S.	P	1998	CV	—	—	Cleveland NL, New York NL, Chicago AL
Day, Leon	P	1995	CV	—	—	Negro Leagues
Dean, Dizzy	P	1953	209	264	79.2	St. Louis NL, Chicago NL, St. Louis AL
Delahanty, Ed	P	1945	C2	—	—	Philadelphia NL, Cleveland PL, Washington AL
Dickey, Bill	P	1954	202	252	80.2	New York AL
Dihigo, Martin	P	1977	SCNL	—	—	Negro Leagues
DiMaggio, Joe	P	1955	223	251	88.8	New York AL
Doby, Larry	P	1998	CV	—	—	Cleveland AL, Chicago AL, Detroit AL
Doerr, Bobby	P	1986	CV	—	—	Boston AL
Drysdale, Don	P	1984	316	403	78.4	Brooklyn NL, Los Angeles NL
Duffy, Hugh	P	1945	C2	—	—	Chicago NL, Chicago PL, Boston AA, Boston NL, Milwaukee AL, Philadelphia NL
Durocher, Leo	M	1994	CV	—	—	New York AL, Cincinnati NL, St. Louis NL, Brooklyn NL
Eckersley, Dennis	P	2004	421	506	83.2	Cleveland AL, Boston AL, Chicago, NL, Oakland AL, St. Louis NL
Evans, Billy	U	1973	CV	—	—	
Evers, Johnny	P	1946	C2	—	—	Chicago NL, Boston NL, Philadelphia NL, Chicago AL
Ewing, Buck	P	1939	C1	—	—	Troy NL, New York NL, New York PL, Cleveland NL, Cincinnati NL
Faber, Red	P	1964	CV	—	—	Chicago AL
Feller, Bob	P	1962	150	160	93.8	Cleveland AL
Ferrell, Rick	P	1984	CV	—	—	St. Louis AL, Boston AL, Washington AL
Fingers, Rollie	P	1992	349	430	81.2	Oakland AL, San Diego NL, Milwaukee AL
Fisk, Carlton	P	2000	397	499	79.6	Boston AL, Chicago AL
Flick, Elmer	P	1963	CV	—	—	Philadelphia NL, Philadelphia AL, Cleveland AL
Ford, Whitey	P	1974	284	365	77.8	New York AL
Foster, Bill	P	1996	CV	—	—	Negro Leagues
Foster, Rube	P	1981	CV	—	—	Negro Leagues
Fox, Nellie	P	1997	CV	—	—	Philadelphia AL, Chicago AL, Houston NL
Foxx, Jimmie	P	1951	179	226	79.2	Philadelphia AL, Boston AL, Chicago NL, Philadelphia NL
Frick, Ford	E	1970	CV	—	—	
Frisch, Frankie	P	1947	136	161	84.5	New York NL, St. Louis NL
Galvin, Pud	P	1965	CV	—	—	Buffalo NL, Pittsburgh AA, Pittsburgh NL, Pittsburgh PL, St. Louis NL
Gehrig, Lou	P	1939	SE	—	—	New York AL
Gehringer, Charlie	P	1949	159	187	85.0	Detroit AL
Gibson, Bob	P	1981	337	401	84.0	St. Louis NL
Gibson, Josh	P	1972	SCNL	—	—	Negro Leagues
Giles, Warren	E	1979	CV	—	—	
Gomez, Lefty	P	1972	CV	—	—	New York AL, Washington AL
Goslin, Goose	P	1968	CV	—	—	Washington AL, St. Louis AL, Detroit AL
Greenberg, Hank	P	1956	164	193	85.0	Detroit AL, Pittsburgh NL
Griffith, Clark	E	1946	C2	—	—	St. Louis AA, Boston AA, Chicago NL, Chicago AL, New York AL, Cincinnati NL, Washington AL
Grimes, Burleigh	P	1964	CV	—	—	Pittsburgh NL, Brooklyn NL, New York NL, Boston NL, St. Louis NL, Chicago NL, New York AL
Grove, Lefty	P	1947	123	161	76.4	Philadelphia AL, Boston AL
Hafey, Chick	P	1971	CV	—	—	St. Louis NL, Cincinnati NL
Haines, Jesse	P	1970	CV	—	—	Cincinnati NL, St. Louis NL
Hamilton, Billy	P	1961	CV	—	—	Kansas City AA, Philadelphia NL, Boston NL
Hanlon, Ned	M	1996	CV	—	—	Cleveland NL, Detroit NL, Pittsburgh NL, Pittsburgh PL, Baltimore NL
Harridge, Will	E	1972	CV	—	—	
Harris, Bucky	M	1975	CV	—	—	Washington AL, Detroit AL
Hartnett, Gabby	P	1955	195	251	77.7	Chicago NL, New York NL
Heilmann, Harry	P	1952	203	234	86.8	Detroit AL, Cincinnati NL
Herman, Billy	P	1975	CV	—	—	Chicago NL, Brooklyn NL, Boston NL, Pittsburgh NL
Hooper, Harry	P	1971	CV	—	—	Boston AL, Chicago AL
Hornsby, Rogers	P	1942	182	233	78.1	St. Louis NL, New York NL, Boston NL, Chicago NL, St. Louis AL
Hoyt, Waite	P	1969	CV	—	—	New York NL, Boston AL, New York AL, Detroit AL, Philadelphia AL, Brooklyn NL, Pittsburgh NL
Hubbard, Cal	U	1976	CV	—	—	
Hubbell, Carl	P	1947	140	161	87.0	New York NL
Huggins, Miller	M	1964	CV	—	—	Cincinnati NL, St. Louis NL
Hulbert, William	F	1995	CV	—	—	
Hunter, Catfish	P	1987	315	413	76.3	Kansas City AL, Oakland AL, New York AL
Irvin, Monte	P	1973	SCNL	—	—	New York NL, Chicago NL, Negro Leagues
Jackson, Reggie	P	1993	396	423	93.6	Kansas City AL, Oakland AL, Baltimore AL, New York AL, California AL

Name	Des.*	Elec. year	Votes rec.†	Votes cast‡	% of vote	Teams as player
Jackson, Travis	P	1982	CV	—	—	New York NL
Jenkins, Ferguson	P	1991	334	443	75.4	Philadelphia NL, Chicago NL, Texas AL, Boston AL
Jennings, Hugh	P	1945	C2	—	—	Louisville AA, Louisville NL, Baltimore NL, Brooklyn NL, Philadelphia NL, Detroit AL
Johnson, Ban	E	1937	CC	—	—	
Johnson, Judy	P	1975	SCNL	—	—	Negro Leagues
Johnson, Walter	P	1936	189	226	83.6	Washington AL
Joss, Addie	P	1978	CV	—	—	Cleveland AL
Kaline, Al	P	1980	340	385	88.3	Detroit AL
Keefe, Tim	P	1964	CV	—	—	Troy NL, New York AA, New York NL, New York PL, Philadelphia NL
Keeler, Willie	P	1939	207	274	75.5	New York NL, Brooklyn NL, Baltimore NL, New York AL
Kell, George	P	1983	CV	—	—	Philadelphia AL, Detroit AL, Boston AL, Chicago AL, Baltimore AL
Kelley, Joe	P	1971	CV	—	—	Boston NL, Pittsburgh NL, Baltimore NL, Brooklyn NL, Baltimore AL, Cincinnati NL
Kelly, George	P	1973	CV	—	—	New York NL, Pittsburgh NL, Cincinnati NL, Chicago NL, Brooklyn NL
Kelly, King	P	1945	C2	—	—	Cincinnati NL, Chicago NL, Boston NL, Boston PL, Cincinnati AA, Boston AA, New York NL
Killebrew, Harmon	P	1984	335	403	83.1	Washington AL, Minnesota AL, Kansas City AL
Kiner, Ralph	P	1975	273	362	75.4	Pittsburgh NL, Chicago NL, Cleveland AL
Klein, Chuck	P	1980	CV	—	—	Philadelphia NL, Chicago NL, Pittsburgh NL
Klem, Bill	U	1953	CV	—	—	
Koufax, Sandy	P	1972	344	396	86.9	Brooklyn NL, Los Angeles NL
Lajoie, Nap	P	1937	168	201	83.6	Philadelphia NL, Philadelphia AL, Cleveland AL
Landis, Kenesaw M.	E	1944	C2	—	—	
Lasorda, Tommy	M	1997	CV	—	—	Brooklyn NL, Kansas City AL
Lazzeri, Tony	P	1991	CV	—	—	New York AL, Chicago NL, Brooklyn NL, New York NL
Lemon, Bob	P	1976	305	388	78.6	Cleveland AL
Leonard, Buck	P	1972	SCNL	—	—	Negro Leagues
Lindstrom, Fred	P	1976	CV	—	—	New York NL, Pittsburgh NL, Chicago NL, Brooklyn NL
Lloyd, John Henry	P	1977	SCNL	—	—	Negro Leagues
Lombardi, Ernie	P	1986	CV	—	—	Brooklyn NL, Cincinnati NL, Boston NL, New York NL
Lopez, Al	M	1977	CV	—	—	Brooklyn NL, Boston NL, Pittsburgh NL, Cleveland AL
Lyons, Ted	P	1955	217	251	86.5	Chicago AL
Mack, Connie	M	1937	CC	—	—	Washington NL, Buffalo PL, Pittsburgh NL
MacPhail, Larry	E	1978	CV	—	—	
MacPhail, Lee	E	1998	CV	—	—	
Mantle, Mickey	P	1974	322	365	88.2	New York AL
Manush, Heinie	P	1964	CV	—	—	Detroit AL, St. Louis AL, Washington AL, Boston AL, Brooklyn NL, Pittsburgh NL
Maranville, Rabbit	P	1954	209	252	82.9	Boston NL, Pittsburgh NL, Chicago NL, Brooklyn NL, St. Louis NL
Marichal, Juan	P	1983	313	374	83.7	San Francisco NL, Boston AL, Los Angeles NL
Marquard, Rube	P	1971	CV	—	—	New York NL, Brooklyn NL, Cincinnati NL, Boston NL
Mathews, Eddie	P	1978	301	379	79.4	Boston NL, Milwaukee NL, Atlanta NL, Houston NL, Detroit AL
Mathewson, Christy	P	1936	205	226	90.7	New York NL, Cincinnati NL
Mays, Willie	P	1979	409	432	94.7	New York (Giants) NL, San Francisco NL, New York (Mets) NL
Mazeroski, Bill	P	2001	CV	—	—	Pittsburgh NL
McCarthy, Joe	M	1957	CV	—	—	
McCarthy, Tommy	P	1946	C2	—	—	Boston UA, Boston NL, Philadelphia NL, St. Louis AA, Brooklyn NL
McCovey, Willie	P	1986	346	425	81.4	San Francisco NL, San Diego NL, Oakland AL
McGinnity, Joe	P	1946	C2	—	—	Baltimore NL, Brooklyn NL, Baltimore AL, New York NL
McGowan, Bill	U	1992	CV	—	—	
McGraw, John	M	1937	CC	—	—	Baltimore AA, Baltimore NL, St. Louis NL, Baltimore AL, New York NL
McKechnie, Bill	M	1962	CV	—	—	Pittsburgh NL, Boston NL, New York AL, New York NL, Cincinnati NL
McPhee, Bid	P	2000	CV	—	—	Cincinnati AA, Cincinnati NL
Medwick, Joe	P	1968	240	283	84.8	St. Louis NL, Brooklyn NL, New York NL, Boston NL
Mize, Johnny	P	1981	CV	—	—	St. Louis NL, New York NL, New York AL
Molitor, Paul	P	2004	431	506	85.2	Milwaukee AL, Toronto AL, Minnesota AL
Morgan, Joe	P	1990	363	444	81.8	Houston NL, Cincinnati NL, San Francisco NL, Philadelphia NL, Oakland AL
Murray, Eddie	P	2003	423	496	85.3	Baltimore AL, Los Angeles NL, New York NL, Cleveland AL, Anaheim AL
Musial, Stan	P	1969	317	340	93.2	St. Louis NL
Newhouser, Hal	P	1992	CV	—	—	Detroit AL, Cleveland AL

Name	Des.*	Elec. year	Votes rec.†	Votes cast‡	% of vote	Teams as player
Nichols, Kid	P	1949	C2	—	—	Boston NL, St. Louis NL, Philadelphia NL
Niekro, Phil	P	1997	380	473	80.3	Milwaukee NL, Atlanta NL, New York AL, Cleveland AL, Toronto AL
O'Rourke, Jim	P	1945	C2	—	—	Boston NL, Providence NL, Buffalo NL, New York NL, New York PL, Washington NL
Ott, Mel	P	1951	197	226	87.2	New York NL
Paige, Satchel	P	1971	SCNL	—	—	Cleveland AL, St. Louis AL, Kansas City AL, Negro Leagues
Palmer, Jim	P	1990	411	444	92.6	Baltimore AL
Pennock, Herb	P	1948	94	121	77.7	Philadelphia AL, Boston AL, New York AL
Perez, Tony	P	2000	385	499	77.2	Cincinnati NL, Montreal NL, Boston AL, Philadelphia NL
Perry, Gaylord	P	1991	342	443	77.2	San Francisco NL, Cleveland AL, Texas AL, San Diego NL, New York AL, Atlanta NL, Seattle AL, Kansas City AL
Plank, Eddie	P	1946	C2	—	—	Philadelphia AL, St. Louis AL
Puckett, Kirby	P	2001	423	515	82.1	Minnesota AL
Radbourn, Old Hoss	P	1939	C1	—	—	Buffalo NL, Providence NL, Boston NL, Boston PL, Cincinnati NL
Reese, Pee Wee	P	1984	CV	—	—	Brooklyn NL, Los Angeles NL
Rice, Sam	P	1963	CV	—	—	Washington AL, Cleveland AL
Rickey, Branch	E	1967	CV	—	—	St. Louis AL, New York AL
Rixey, Eppa	P	1963	CV	—	—	Philadelphia NL, Cincinnati NL
Rizzuto, Phil	P	1994	CV	—	—	New York AL
Roberts, Robin	P	1976	337	388	86.9	Philadelphia NL, Baltimore AL, Houston NL, Chicago NL
Robinson, Brooks	P	1983	344	374	92.0	Baltimore AL
Robinson, Frank	P	1982	370	415	89.2	Cincinnati NL, Baltimore AL, Los Angeles NL, California AL, Cleveland AL
Robinson, Jackie	P	1962	124	160	77.5	Brooklyn NL
Robinson, Wilbert	M	1945	C2	—	—	Philadelphia AA, Baltimore AA, Baltimore NL, St. Louis NL, Baltimore AL
Rogan, Bullet Joe	P	1998	CV	—	—	Negro Leagues
Roush, Edd	P	1962	CV	—	—	Chicago AL, New York NL, Cincinnati NL
Ruffing, Red	P	1967	266	306	86.9	Boston AL, New York AL, Chicago AL
Rusie, Amos	P	1977	CV	—	—	Indianapolis NL, New York NL, Cincinnati NL
Ruth, Babe	P	1936	215	226	95.1	Boston AL, New York AL, Boston NL
Ryan, Nolan	P	1999	491	497	98.8	New York NL, California AL, Houston NL, Texas AL
Schalk, Ray	P	1955	CV	—	—	Chicago AL, New York NL
Schmidt, Mike	P	1995	444	460	96.5	Philadelphia NL
Schoendienst, Red	P	1989	CV	—	—	St. Louis NL, New York (Giants) NL, Milwaukee NL
Seaver, Tom	P	1992	425	430	98.8	New York NL, Cincinnati NL, Chicago AL, Boston AL
Selee, Frank	M	1999	CV	—	—	
Sewell, Joe	P	1977	CV	—	—	Cleveland AL, New York AL
Simmons, Al	P	1953	199	264	75.4	Philadelphia AL, Chicago AL, Detroit AL, Washington AL, Boston NL, Cincinnati NL, Boston AL
Sisler, George	P	1939	235	274	85.8	St. Louis AL, Washington AL, Boston NL
Slaughter, Enos	P	1985	CV	—	—	St. Louis NL, New York AL, Kansas City AL, Milwaukee NL
Smith, Hilton	P	2001	CV	—	—	Negro Leagues
Smith, Ozzie	P	2002	433	472	91.7	San Diego NL, St. Louis NL
Snider, Duke	P	1980	333	385	86.5	Brooklyn NL, Los Angeles NL, New York NL, San Francisco NL
Spahn, Warren	P	1973	316	380	83.2	Boston NL, Milwaukee NL, New York NL, San Francisco NL
Spalding, Al	P	1939	C1	—	—	Chicago NL
Speaker, Tris	P	1937	165	201	82.1	Boston AL, Cleveland AL, Washington AL, Philadelphia AL
Stargell, Willie	P	1988	352	427	82.4	Pittsburgh NL
Stearnes, Turkey	P	2000	CV	—	—	Negro Leagues
Stengel, Casey	M	1966	CV	—	—	Brooklyn NL, Pittsburgh NL, Philadelphia NL, New York NL, Boston NL
Sutton, Don	P	1998	386	473	81.6	Los Angeles NL, Houston NL, Milwaukee AL, Oakland AL, California AL
Terry, Bill	P	1954	195	252	77.4	New York NL
Thompson, Sam	P	1974	CV	—	—	Detroit NL, Philadelphia NL, Detroit AL
Tinker, Joe	P	1946	C2	—	—	Chicago NL, Cincinnati NL
Traynor, Pie	P	1948	93	121	76.9	Pittsburgh NL
Vance, Dazzy	P	1955	205	251	81.7	Pittsburgh NL, New York AL, Brooklyn NL, St. Louis NL, Cincinnati NL
Vaughan, Arky	P	1985	CV	—	—	Pittsburgh NL, Brooklyn NL
Veeck, Bill	E	1991	CV	—	—	

Name	Des.*	Elec. year	Votes rec.†	Votes cast‡	% of vote	Teams as player
Waddell, Rube	P	1946	C2	—	—	Louisville NL, Pittsburgh NL, Chicago NL, Philadelphia AL, St. Louis AL
Wagner, Honus	P	1936	215	226	95.1	Louisville NL, Pittsburgh NL
Wallace, Bobby	P	1953	CV	—	—	Cleveland NL, St. Louis NL, St. Louis AL
Walsh, Ed	P	1946	C2	—	—	Chicago AL, Boston NL
Waner, Lloyd	P	1967	CV	—	—	Pittsburgh NL, Boston NL, Cincinnati NL, Philadelphia NL, Brooklyn NL
Waner, Paul	P	1952	195	234	83.3	Pittsburgh NL, Brooklyn NL, Boston NL, New York AL
Ward, Monte	P	1964	CV	—	—	Providence NL, New York NL, Brooklyn PL, Brooklyn NL
Weaver, Earl	M	1996	CV	—	—	
Weiss, George	E	1971	CV	—	—	
Welch, Mickey	P	1973	CV	—	—	Troy NL, New York NL
Wells, Willie	P	1997	CV	—	—	Negro Leagues
Wheat, Zack	P	1959	CV	—	—	Brooklyn NL, Philadelphia AL
Wilhelm, Hoyt	P	1985	331	395	83.8	New York NL, St. Louis NL, Cleveland AL, Baltimore AL, Chicago AL, California AL, Atlanta NL, Chicago NL, Los Angeles NL
Williams, Billy	P	1987	354	413	85.7	Chicago NL, Oakland AL
Williams, Smokey Joe	P	1999	CV	—	—	Negro Leagues
Williams, Ted	P	1966	282	302	93.4	Boston AL
Willis, Vic	P	1995	CV	—	—	Boston NL, Pittsburgh NL, St. Louis NL
Wilson, Hack	P	1979	CV	—	—	New York NL, Chicago NL, Brooklyn NL, Philadelphia NL
Winfield, Dave	P	2001	435	515	84.5	San Diego NL, New York AL, California AL, Toronto AL, Minnesota AL, Cleveland AL
Wright, George	P	1937	CC	—	—	Boston NL, Providence NL
Wright, Harry	M	1953	CV	—	—	Boston NL
Wynn, Early	P	1972	301	396	76.0	Washington AL, Cleveland AL, Chicago AL
Yastrzemski, Carl	P	1989	423	447	94.6	Boston AL
Yawkey, Tom	E	1980	CV	—	—	
Young, Cy	P	1937	153	201	76.1	Cleveland NL, St. Louis NL, Boston AL, Cleveland AL, Boston NL
Youngs, Ross	P	1972	CV	—	—	New York NL
Yount, Robin	P	1999	385	497	77.5	Milwaukee AL

*Designation for which he was honored. Abbreviations: E—executive; F—founder; M—manager; O—organizer; P—player; U—umpire.

†Where an abbreviation is listed rather than a vote total, the enshrinee was selected by one of the following groups: Centennial Commission (CC), committee of old-time players and writers (C1), committee on old-timers (C2), Committee on Veterans (CV), special election by Baseball Writers' Association of America (SE) or Special Committee on Negro Leagues (SCNL).

‡Votes cast by eligible members of the Baseball Writers' Association of America.

League abbreviations: AA—American Association; AL—American League; NL—National League; PL—Players League; UA—Union Association.

MINOR LEAGUES

2004 FARM SYSTEMS

AMERICAN LEAGUE

ANAHEIM (6): AAA—Salt Lake. AA—Arkansas. A—Rancho Cucamonga, Cedar Rapids. Rookie—Provo, Mesa Angels.
BALTIMORE (7): AAA—Ottawa. AA—Bowie. A—Frederick, Delmarva, Aberdeen. Rookie—Bluefield, Gulf Coast Orioles.
BOSTON (6): AAA—Pawtucket. AA—Portland (ME). A—Sarasota, Augusta, Lowell. Rookie—Gulf Coast Red Sox.
CHICAGO (6): AAA—Charlotte. AA—Birmingham. A—Winston-Salem, Kannapolis. Rookie—Bristol, Great Falls.
CLEVELAND (6): AAA—Buffalo. AA—Akron. A—Kinston, Lake County, Mahoning Valley. Rookie—Burlington (NC).
DETROIT (6): AAA—Toledo. AA—Erie. A—Lakeland, West Michigan, Oneonta. Rookie—Gulf Coast Tigers.
KANSAS CITY (6): AAA—Omaha. AA—Wichita. A—Wilmington, Burlington (IA). Rookie—Idaho Falls, Arizona Royals.
MINNESOTA (6): AAA—Rochester. AA—New Britain. A—Fort Myers, Quad Cities. Rookie—Elizabethton, Gulf Coast Twins.
NEW YORK (6): AAA—Columbus (OH). AA—Trenton. A—Tampa, Battle Creek, Staten Island. Rookie—Gulf Coast Yankees.
OAKLAND (6): AAA—Sacramento. AA—Midland. A—Modesto, Kane County, Vancouver. Rookie—Scottsdale A's.
SEATTLE (6): AAA—Tacoma. AA—San Antonio. A—San Bernardino, Wisconsin, Everett. Rookie—Peoria (AZ) Mariners.
TAMPA BAY (6): AAA—Durham. AA—Montgomery. A—Bakersfield, Charleston (SC), Hudson Valley. Rookie—Princeton.
TEXAS (6): AAA—Oklahoma. AA—Frisco. A—Stockton, Clinton, Spokane. Rookie—Arizona Rangers.
TORONTO (6): AAA—Syracuse. AA—New Hampshire. A—Dunedin, Charleston (WV), Auburn. Rookie—Pulaski.

NATIONAL LEAGUE

ARIZONA (6): AAA—Tucson. AA—El Paso. A—Lancaster, South Bend, Yakima. Rookie—Missoula.
ATLANTA (6): AAA—Richmond. AA—Greenville. A—Myrtle Beach, Rome. Rookie—Danville, Gulf Coast Braves.
CHICAGO (6): AAA—Iowa. AA—West Tenn. A—Daytona, Lansing, Boise. Rookie—Mesa Cubs.
CINCINNATI (6): AAA—Louisville. AA—Chattanooga. A—Potomac, Dayton. Rookie—Billings, Gulf Coast Reds.
COLORADO (6): AAA—Colorado Springs. AA—Tulsa. A—Visalia, Asheville, Tri-City (WA). Rookie—Casper.
FLORIDA (6): AAA—Albuquerque. AA—Carolina. A—Jupiter, Greensboro, Jamestown. Rookie—Gulf Coast Marlins.
HOUSTON (6): AAA—New Orleans. AA—Round Rock. A—Salem, Lexington, Tri-City (NY). Rookie—Greeneville.
LOS ANGELES (6): AAA—Las Vegas. AA—Jacksonville. A—Vero Beach, South Georgia. Rookie—Ogden, Gulf Coast Dodgers.
MILWAUKEE (6): AAA—Indianapolis. AA—Huntsville. A—High Desert, Beloit. Rookie—Helena, Maryvale.
MONTREAL (6): AAA—Edmonton. AA—Harrisburg. A—Brevard County, Savannah, Vermont. Rookie—Gulf Coast Expos.
NEW YORK (7): AAA—Norfolk. AA—Binghamton. A—St. Lucie, Capital City, Brooklyn. Rookie—Kingsport, Gulf Coast Mets.
PHILADELPHIA (6): AAA—Scranton/Wilkes-Barre. AA—Reading. A—Clearwater, Lakewood, Batavia. Rookie—Gulf Coast Phillies.
PITTSBURGH (6): AAA—Nashville. AA—Altoona. A—Lynchburg, Hickory, Williamsport. Rookie—Gulf Coast Pirates.
ST. LOUIS (6): AAA—Memphis. AA—Tennessee. A—Palm Beach, Peoria (IL), New Jersey. Rookie—Johnson City.
SAN DIEGO (6): AAA—Portland (OR). AA—Mobile. A— Lake Elsinore, Fort Wayne, Eugene. Rookie—Arizona Padres.
SAN FRANCISCO (6): AAA—Fresno. AA—Norwich. A—San Jose, Hagerstown, Salem-Keizer. Rookie—Arizona Giants.

INTERNATIONAL LEAGUE

LEAGUE OFFICE

President
Randy Mobley

Address
55 S. High St., Suite 202
Dublin, OH 43017

Phone
614-791-9300

TEAMS

BUFFALO BISONS

General manager
Mike Buczkowski
Manager
Marty Brown
Ballpark (capacity, surface)
Dunn Tire Park (21,050, grass)
Affiliation
Indians
Address
P.O. Box 450
Buffalo, NY 14205
Phone
716-846-2000

CHARLOTTE KNIGHTS

General manager
Bill Blackwell
Manager
Nick Capra
Ballpark (capacity, surface)
Knights Stadium (10,000, grass)
Affiliation
White Sox
Address
2280 Deerfield Drive
Fort Mill, SC 29715
Phone
704-357-8071

COLUMBUS CLIPPERS

General manager/president
Ken Schnacke
Manager
Bucky Dent
Ballpark (capacity, surface)
Cooper Stadium (15,000, grass)
Affiliation
Yankees
Address
1155 W. Mound St.
Columbus, OH 43223
Phone
614-462-5250

DURHAM BULLS

General manager
Mike Birling
Manager
Bill Evers
Ballpark (capacity, surface)
Durham Bulls Athletic Park
(10,000, grass)
Affiliation
Devil Rays
Address
P.O. Box 507
Durham, NC 27702
Phone
919-687-6500

INDIANAPOLIS INDIANS

General manager
Cal Burleson
Manager
Cecil Cooper
Ballpark (capacity, surface)
Victory Field (15,500, grass)
Affiliation
Brewers
Address
501 W. Maryland St.
Indianapolis, IN 46225
Phone
317-269-3542

LOUISVILLE BATS

President
Gary Ulmer
Manager
Rick Burleson
Ballpark (capacity, surface)
Louisville Slugger Field (13,200, grass)
Affiliation
Reds
Address
401 E. Main Street
Louisville, KY 40202
Phone
502-212-2287

NORFOLK TIDES

General manager
Dave Rosenfield
Manager
John Stearns
Ballpark (capacity, surface)
Harbor Park (12,067, grass)
Affiliation
Mets
Address
150 Park Ave.
Norfolk, VA 23510
Phone
757-622-2222

OTTAWA LYNX

General manager
Kyle Bostwick
Manager
Tim Leiper
Ballpark (capacity, surface)
Lynx Stadium (10,332, grass)
Affiliation
Orioles
Address
300 Coventry Rd.
Ottawa, Ontario K1K 4P5
Phone
613-747-5969

PAWTUCKET RED SOX

President
Mike Tamburro
Manager
Buddy Bailey
Ballpark (capacity, surface)
McCoy Stadium (10,031, grass)
Affiliation
Red Sox
Address
P.O. Box 2365
Pawtucket, RI 02861
Phone
401-724-7303

RICHMOND BRAVES

General manager
Bruce Baldwin
Manager
Pat Kelly
Ballpark (capacity, surface)
The Diamond (12,134, grass)
Affiliation
Braves
Address
P.O. Box 6667
Richmond, VA 23230
Phone
804-359-4444

ROCHESTER RED WINGS

General manager
Dan Mason
Manager
Phil Roof
Ballpark (capacity, surface)
Frontier Field (10,868, grass)
Affiliation
Twins
Address
1 Morrie Silver Way
Rochester, NY 14608
Phone
585-454-1001

SCRANTON/WILKES-BARRE RED BARONS

General manager
To be announced
Manager
Marc Bombard
Ballpark (capacity, surface)
Lackawanna County Multi-Purpose
Stadium (10,982, artificial)
Affiliation
Phillies
Address
P.O. Box 3449
Scranton, PA 18505
Phone
570-969-2255

SYRACUSE SKYCHIEFS

General manager
John Simone
Manager
Marty Pevey
Ballpark (capacity, surface)
P&C Stadium (11,071, artificial)
Affiliation
Blue Jays
Address
One Tex Simone Dr.
Syracuse, NY 13208
Phone
315-474-7833

TOLEDO MUD HENS

General manager
Joe Napoli
Manager
Larry Parrish
Ballpark (capacity, surface)
Fifth Third Field (8,943, grass)
Affiliation
Tigers
Address
406 Washington St.
Toledo, OH 43604
Phone
419-725-4367

2003 FINAL STANDINGS

NORTH DIVISION

Team	W	L	T	Pct.	GB
Pawtucket	83	61	-	.576	...
Ottawa	79	65	-	.549	4.0
Scranton/Wilkes-Barre	73	70	-	.510	9.5
Buffalo	73	70	-	.510	9.5
Rochester	68	75	-	.476	14.5
Syracuse	62	79	-	.440	19.5

SOUTH DIVISION

Team	W	L	T	Pct.	GB
Durham	73	67	-	.521	...
Charlotte	74	70	-	.514	1.0
Norfolk	67	76	-	.469	7.5
Richmond	64	79	-	.448	10.5

WEST DIVISION

Team	W	L	T	Pct.	GB
Louisville	79	64	-	.552	...
Columbus	76	68	-	.528	3.5
Toledo	65	78	-	.455	14.0
Indianapolis	64	78	-	.451	14.5

COMPOSITE

Team	PAW	LOU	OTT	COL	DUR	CHR	SWB	BUF	ROC	NOR	TOL	IND	RMD	SYR	W	L	T	Pct.	GB
Pawtucket (Red Sox)	...	3	8	6	4	6	12	10	9	3	3	2	6	11	83	61	0	.576	...
Louisville (Reds)	5	...	2	11	6	5	2	5	6	7	9	9	7	5	79	64	0	.552	3.5
Ottawa (Orioles)	8	6	...	3	1	4	7	9	10	5	6	4	5	11	79	65	0	.549	4.0
Columbus (Yankees)	2	5	5	...	6	7	5	3	5	5	11	10	6	6	76	68	0	.528	7.0
Durham (Devil Rays)	4	6	7	6	...	6	5	3	5	8	6	7	8	2	73	67	0	.521	8.0
Charlotte (White Sox)	2	7	4	5	10	...	2	4	3	10	7	8	10	2	74	70	0	.514	9.0
Scranton/WB (Phillies)	4	6	9	3	2	6	...	7	8	6	4	5	3	10	73	70	0	.510	9.5
Buffalo (Indians)	6	3	7	5	5	4	9	...	8	7	4	6	3	6	73	70	0	.510	9.5
Rochester (Twins)	7	2	6	3	2	5	8	8	...	3	3	6	6	9	68	75	0	.476	14.5
Norfolk (Mets)	5	5	3	7	8	6	2	1	5	...	9	6	6	4	67	76	0	.469	15.5
Toledo (Tigers)	5	7	2	5	6	5	4	4	5	3	...	8	8	3	65	78	0	.455	17.5
Indianapolis (Brewers)	6	7	4	6	5	4	3	1	2	6	7	...	7	6	64	78	0	.451	18.0
Richmond (Braves)	2	4	3	6	8	6	5	5	2	10	4	5	...	4	64	79	0	.448	18.5
Syracuse (Blue Jays)	5	3	5	2	4	6	6	10	7	3	5	2	4	...	62	79	0	.440	19.5

Major league affiliations in parentheses.

PLAYOFFS: Pawtucket defeated Ottawa, three games to two; Durham defeated Louisville, three games to one; Durham defeated Pawtucket, three games to none, to win league championship.

REGULAR-SEASON ATTENDANCE: Buffalo, 551,916; Charlotte, 268,374; Columbus, 480,445; Durham, 493,138; Indianapolis, 550,319; Louisville, 651,510; Norfolk, 480,963; Ottawa, 176,002; Pawtucket, 550,157; Richmond, 446,882; Rochester, 418,014; Scranton/Wilkes-Barre, 427,445; Syracuse, 356,303; Toledo, 517,331. Total attendance—6,368,799. Playoffs (12 games)—44,992; Class AAA All-Star Game at Memphis—15,214.

MANAGERS: Buffalo, Marty Brown; Charlotte, Nick Capra; Columbus, Bucky Dent; Durham, Bill Evers; Indianapolis, Cecil Cooper; Louisville, Dave Miley (through July 28) and Rick Burleson (July 29 through end of season); Norfolk, Bobby Floyd; Ottawa, Gary Allenson; Pawtucket, Buddy Bailey; Richmond, Pat Kelly; Rochester, Phil Roof; Scranton/Wilkes-Barre, Marc Bombard; Syracuse, Omar Malave; Toledo, Larry Parrish. Managerial record of team with more than one manager: Louisville, Miley (63-47); Burleson (16-17).

ALL-STAR TEAM: 1B—Ross Gload, Charlotte; 2B—Chase Utley, Scranton/Wilkes-Barre; 3B—Brandon Larson, Louisville; SS—Jason Smith, Durham; OF—Andy Abad, Pawtucket; OF—Lou Collier, Pawtucket; OF—Alex Escobar, Buffalo; C—Johnny Estrada, Richmond; DH—Fernando Seguignol, Columbus; Utility—Ryan Jackson, Durham; Starting pitcher—Bronson Arroyo, Pawtucket; Relief pitcher—Fernando Rodney, Toledo; Most Valuable Player—Fernando Seguignol, Columbus; Most Valuable Pitcher—Bronson Arroyo, Pawtucket; Rookie of the Year—Aaron Miles, Charlotte; Manager of the Year—Buddy Bailey, Pawtucket.

2003 BATTING

TEAM

Team	G	TPA	AB	R	H	TB	2B	3B	HR	RBI	SH	SF	HP	BB	IBB	SO	SB	CS	GDP	LOB	ShO	Avg.	OBP	Slg.
Charlotte	144	5251	4748	659	1332	2050	249	26	139	626	61	39	47	356	21	872	72	53	113	921	8	.281	.334	.432
Ottawa	144	5409	4842	666	1363	1912	277	46	60	619	42	38	44	440	20	909	108	58	119	1037	14	.281	.344	.395
Durham	140	5341	4820	652	1312	2083	289	43	132	612	51	38	53	376	31	1016	82	51	95	985	9	.272	.329	.432
Pawtucket	144	5285	4739	689	1282	1968	245	27	129	645	34	43	61	408	23	959	119	54	119	908	9	.271	.333	.415
Columbus	144	5493	4880	697	1304	2028	277	30	129	653	39	40	58	475	19	958	48	44	131	998	11	.267	.337	.416
Buffalo	143	5282	4756	626	1264	1899	257	30	106	593	45	47	65	369	16	902	129	64	110	920	10	.266	.324	.399
Louisville	143	5388	4788	690	1265	1904	256	22	113	628	50	51	52	447	16	937	116	40	101	980	6	.264	.330	.398
Indianapolis	142	5259	4736	553	1244	1815	251	25	90	512	52	41	60	369	20	859	75	55	131	961	6	.263	.321	.383
Rochester	143	5322	4766	607	1250	1922	282	24	114	575	39	42	46	429	32	1049	67	50	102	992	6	.262	.327	.403

Team	G	TPA	AB	R	H	TB	2B	3B	HR	RBI	SH	SF	HP	BB	IBB	SO	SB	CS	GDP	LOB	ShO	Avg.	OBP	Slg.
Norfolk..........	143	5294	4689	581	1218	1792	250	27	90	541	56	52	62	435	21	875	178	50	99	981	10	.260	.327	.382
Richmond	143	5248	4716	544	1228	1858	253	55	89	504	54	46	58	372	12	994	117	45	104	978	10	.260	.319	.394
Syracuse.......	141	5218	4663	598	1213	1847	276	32	98	544	37	37	56	425	22	954	75	30	135	960	7	.260	.327	.396
Scranton/WB.	143	5341	4803	614	1226	1815	272	19	93	570	33	47	59	398	25	868	72	30	101	986	7	.255	.317	.378
Toledo..........	143	5167	4646	577	1154	1840	259	35	119	536	55	41	63	361	10	994	139	60	91	859	10	.248	.309	.396

INDIVIDUAL

TOP QUALIFIERS FOR BATTING CHAMPIONSHIP

Minimum 389 plate appearances. *Lefthanded batter. †Switch-hitter.

Player, Team	G	TPA	AB	R	H	TB	2B	3B	HR	RBI	SH	SF	HP	BB	IBB	SO	SB	CS	GDP	Avg.	OBP	Slg.
Seguignol, Fernando, Col.†....	106	446	402	78	137	251	28	1	28	87	0	2	8	34	3	81	0	0	19	.341	.401	.624
Estrada, Johnny, Richmond †	106	402	354	40	116	175	29	0	10	66	0	6	12	30	5	30	0	0	11	.328	.393	.494
Utley, Chase, Scranton/WB *.	113	490	431	80	139	223	26	2	18	77	0	7	11	41	6	75	10	4	3	.323	.390	.517
Gload, Ross, Charlotte *........	133	549	508	72	160	266	40	6	18	70	5	6	1	29	6	60	6	3	12	.315	.349	.524
Rushford, Jim, Indianapolis *	99	412	373	43	116	155	12	0	9	50	0	2	7	30	4	33	4	3	6	.311	.371	.416
Garcia, Jesse, Richmond	110	449	425	45	130	159	17	3	2	30	5	3	4	12	0	50	29	9	9	.306	.329	.374
Miles, Aaron, Charlotte †	133	595	546	80	166	243	34	5	11	50	5	3	1	40	2	52	8	9	9	.304	.351	.445
Abad, Andy, Pawtucket *	134	573	504	78	153	233	35	3	13	93	3	7	4	55	8	67	0	3	15	.304	.372	.462
Jackson, Ryan, Durham *......	131	553	519	78	157	249	45	4	13	71	2	2	0	30	7	85	2	4	10	.303	.339	.480
Rodriguez, Luis, Rochester †.	131	579	518	65	153	195	35	2	1	44	9	3	3	46	2	46	6	8	15	.295	.354	.376
Brown, Emil, Louisville	97	408	369	58	109	171	20	3	12	63	0	8	4	27	2	76	18	3	7	.295	.343	.463
Smith, Mark, Indianapolis......	103	416	388	46	114	188	25	2	15	62	0	2	5	21	2	58	3	2	14	.294	.337	.485
Collier, Lou, Pawtucket...........	103	438	392	58	115	184	19	4	14	69	0	6	8	32	4	94	8	7	13	.293	.354	.469
LaRocca, Greg, Buffalo	132	553	500	63	145	212	33	2	10	68	1	6	6	40	2	53	5	3	5	.290	.346	.424
Ross, Cody, Toledo	124	520	470	74	135	242	35	6	20	61	4	9	5	32	0	86	15	6	12	.287	.333	.515

DEPARTMENTAL LEADERS: G—Snead, 137; AB—Miles, 546; R—A. Brown, 81; H—Miles, 166; TB—Gload, 266; 2B—Jackson, 45; 3B—J. Smith, 14; HR—Seguignol, 28; RBI—Abad, 93; SH—Guerrero, 19; SF—Henson, Zoccolillo, 10 each; HP—Chapman, 15; BB—Cust, 80; IBB—Abad, 8; SO—Lombard, 143; SB—Snead, 61; CS—French, 12; GIDP—Toca, 21; Slg.—Seguignol, .624; OBP—Cust, .422.

ALL PLAYERS

*Lefthanded batter. †Switch-hitter.

Player, Team	G	TPA	AB	R	H	TB	2B	3B	HR	RBI	SH	SF	HP	BB	IBB	SO	SB	CS	GDP	Avg.	OBP	Slg.
Abad, Andy, Pawtucket *	134	573	504	78	153	233	35	3	13	93	3	7	4	55	8	67	0	3	15	.304	.372	.462
Abernathy, Brent, Durham......	1	5	5	0	3	3	0	0	0	1	0	0	0	0	0	0	0	0	0	.600	.600	.600
Acevas, Jon, Charlotte	8	29	25	3	9	11	2	0	0	4	0	0	2	2	0	5	0	0	1	.360	.448	.440
Acevedo, Jose, Louisville.......	29	4	4	0	0	0	0	0	0	0	0	0	0	0	0	3	0	0	0	.000	.000	.000
Adkins, Tim, Louisville-Col.*..	40	1	1	0	0	0	0	0	0	0	0	0	0	0	0	1	0	0	0	.000	.000	.000
Aguilar, Ray, Richmond †.......	1	3	3	0	0	0	0	0	0	0	0	0	0	0	0	1	0	0	1	.000	.000	.000
Almonte, Erick, Columbus......	48	199	179	26	43	68	11	1	4	26	2	0	1	17	2	46	4	3	5	.240	.310	.380
Alomar, Sandy, Charlotte........	5	16	15	2	4	4	0	0	0	1	0	0	0	1	1	1	0	0	2	.267	.313	.267
Alvarez, Jimmy, Syracuse † ...	99	398	342	45	88	127	13	7	4	25	9	2	0	45	1	92	11	5	4	.257	.342	.371
Alviso, Jerome, Ottawa †	17	59	51	5	7	8	1	0	0	1	1	0	4	3	0	11	2	0	0	.137	.241	.157
Anderson, Jason, Col.-Nor.* ..	16	3	3	1	1	1	0	0	0	0	0	0	0	0	0	1	0	0	0	.333	.333	.333
Anderson, Jimmy, Lou.*........	9	12	12	1	1	1	0	0	0	0	0	0	0	0	0	7	0	0	0	.083	.083	.083
Andrews, Shane, Rochester...	126	498	445	50	114	182	31	2	11	59	1	5	4	43	2	126	2	2	12	.256	.324	.409
Austin, Jeff, Louisville...........	9	7	6	0	0	0	0	0	0	0	0	0	0	1	0	3	0	0	0	.000	.143	.000
Aven, Bruce, Syracuse	56	220	192	21	41	55	5	0	3	17	0	1	1	26	2	44	1	1	5	.214	.309	.286
Bacsik, Mike, Norfolk *	23	15	15	1	1	1	0	0	0	3	0	0	0	0	0	3	0	0	0	.067	.067	.067
Badeaux, Brooks, Durham † ..	73	280	245	27	55	71	13	0	1	13	11	3	4	17	2	46	0	2	4	.224	.283	.290
Baez, Kevin, Louisville............	10	30	29	2	5	5	0	0	0	3	0	0	0	1	0	5	0	0	1	.172	.200	.172
Baldwin, James, Rochester....	6	1	1	0	0	0	0	0	0	0	0	0	0	0	0	0	0	0	0	.000	.000	.000
Bale, John, Norfolk-Lou.*	35	5	5	0	0	0	0	0	0	0	0	0	0	0	0	3	0	0	0	.000	.000	.000
Bard, Josh, Buffalo †	35	130	115	14	38	60	7	0	5	21	0	0	1	14	1	17	1	2	5	.330	.408	.522
Basak, Chris, Norfolk	19	81	71	10	17	23	6	0	0	8	2	0	1	7	0	24	3	3	0	.239	.316	.324
Bates, Fletcher, Ottawa †........	24	79	74	7	16	25	7	1	0	10	1	0	0	4	0	15	1	0	0	.216	.256	.338
Beattie, Andrew, Louisville † ..	9	31	30	5	7	13	1	1	1	6	0	0	0	1	0	4	0	0	3	.233	.258	.433
Belisle, Matt, Rich.-Lou.†......	7	6	5	1	1	1	0	0	0	0	0	0	0	1	0	0	0	0	0	.200	.333	.200
Bell, Heath, Norfolk	40	1	1	0	0	0	0	0	0	0	0	0	0	0	0	1	0	0	0	.000	.000	.000
Berg, Dave, Syracuse	6	22	20	3	5	6	1	0	0	0	0	0	1	1	0	2	0	0	0	.250	.318	.300
Betemit, Wilson, Richmond †	127	521	478	55	125	198	23	13	8	65	3	2	0	38	2	115	8	5	8	.262	.315	.414
Bigbie, Larry, Ottawa *...........	30	133	117	23	41	72	14	4	3	21	0	1	1	14	0	31	0	0	1	.350	.421	.615
Bocachica, Hiram, Toledo.......	95	366	322	48	78	139	19	3	12	37	8	2	10	24	0	57	11	6	5	.242	.313	.432
Borchard, Joe, Charlotte †	114	472	435	62	110	173	20	2	13	53	0	2	8	27	1	103	2	4	14	.253	.307	.398
Boscan, Jean, Richmond	3	13	12	0	3	5	2	0	0	1	0	0	0	1	0	4	0	0	1	.250	.308	.417
Bowen, Rob, Rochester †	30	117	105	14	27	52	7	0	6	17	0	0	1	11	1	25	0	0	3	.257	.333	.495
Branyan, Russell, Louisville *	14	59	49	5	16	24	5	0	1	3	0	0	1	9	0	15	0	0	0	.327	.441	.490
Brazell, Craig, Norfolk *	12	48	46	4	12	15	3	0	0	1	0	0	1	1	1	8	1	0	0	.261	.292	.326
Broussard, Ben, Buffalo *	32	132	120	17	30	43	2	1	3	15	0	2	1	9	0	29	3	0	1	.250	.303	.358
Brown, Adrian, Pawtucket †...	122	533	482	81	136	173	16	3	5	32	3	0	0	48	1	81	34	11	10	.282	.347	.359
Brown, Emil, Louisville	97	408	369	58	109	171	20	3	12	63	0	8	4	27	2	76	18	3	7	.295	.343	.463
Brumbaugh, Cliff, Charlotte....	62	248	223	33	69	113	13	2	9	30	0	2	0	23	3	48	1	3	6	.309	.371	.507
Buddie, Mike, Indianapolis.....	18	2	1	0	0	0	0	0	0	0	1	0	0	0	0	1	0	0	0	.000	.000	.000
Budzinski, Mark, Ind.-Lou.* ...	120	483	418	80	114	150	22	4	2	27	6	2	4	53	0	95	17	6	1	.273	.358	.359
Burba, Dave, Buffalo-Ind........	14	7	7	1	3	4	1	0	0	3	0	0	0	0	0	0	0	0	0	.429	.429	.571
Burke, Jamie, Charlotte..........	94	356	323	47	104	135	13	0	6	50	3	6	4	20	0	39	1	1	9	.322	.363	.418
Burnham, Gary, Syracuse * ...	91	385	349	44	94	148	25	1	9	51	1	3	7	25	4	54	0	1	20	.269	.328	.424
Byrd, Marlon, Scranton/WB ...	1	4	4	1	3	4	1	0	0	0	0	0	0	0	0	1	0	0	0	.750	.750	1.000

Player, Team	G	TPA	AB	R	H	TB	2B	3B	HR	RBI	SH	SF	HP	BB	IBB	SO	SB	CS	GDP	Avg.	OBP	Slg.
Cabrera, Jose, Scranton/WB	25	1	1	0	0	0	0	0	0	0	0	0	0	0	0	1	0	0	0	.000	.000	.000
Caceres, Wilmy, Louisville †	4	7	7	1	0	0	0	0	0	2	0	0	0	0	0	1	0	0	0	.000	.000	.000
Cairns, Troy, Louisville	2	2	1	1	0	0	0	0	0	0	1	0	0	0	0	0	0	0	0	.000	.000	.000
Calzado, Napoleon, Ottawa	51	212	196	30	61	76	7	4	0	15	0	0	2	14	0	30	9	3	1	.311	.363	.388
Camilo, Juan, Scranton/WB *	5	19	18	7	6	8	2	0	0	0	0	0	0	1	0	3	0	0	0	.333	.368	.444
Campos, Francisco, Ind.	8	6	6	0	2	2	0	0	0	1	0	0	0	0	0	0	0	0	1	.333	.333	.333
Canizaro, Jay, Durham	26	103	92	13	22	41	7	0	4	13	0	2	0	9	1	19	2	0	4	.239	.301	.446
Cantu, Jorge, Durham	60	217	200	26	59	89	16	1	4	30	1	6	2	8	1	21	2	1	5	.295	.319	.445
Casanova, Raul, Ottawa †	26	104	91	12	26	40	5	0	3	14	0	1	2	10	2	15	0	0	4	.286	.365	.440
Cash, Kevin, Syracuse	93	360	326	37	88	144	28	2	8	37	0	3	2	29	1	81	1	0	14	.270	.331	.442
Casillas, Uriel, Scranton/WB	13	47	41	4	13	17	4	0	0	3	0	0	1	5	0	3	0	0	2	.317	.404	.415
Castillo, Frank, Richmond	4	1	1	0	0	0	0	0	0	0	0	0	0	0	0	0	0	0	0	.000	.000	.000
Castro, Juan, Louisville	9	35	32	3	7	10	0	0	1	5	0	1	0	2	0	3	0	1	2	.219	.257	.313
Castro, Ramon, Richmond	33	96	84	11	13	15	2	0	0	8	1	1	0	10	0	22	0	0	2	.155	.242	.179
Cerda, Jaime, Norfolk *	22	2	2	0	1	1	0	0	0	0	0	0	0	0	0	1	0	0	0	.500	.500	.500
Chamblee, Jim, Louisville	85	302	263	31	75	111	13	4	5	35	4	1	5	29	0	59	2	0	6	.285	.366	.422
Chapman, Travis, S./WB	134	543	478	62	130	202	36	0	12	82	0	6	15	44	1	97	2	2	12	.272	.348	.423
Charles, Frank, Pawtucket	20	76	72	9	14	26	0	0	4	9	1	1	1	1	0	21	0	0	2	.194	.213	.361
Chevalier, Virgil, Norfolk	42	127	107	8	17	20	0	0	1	11	0	1	0	19	0	16	2	0	0	.159	.283	.187
Chiaffredo, Paul, Syracuse	5	18	15	2	5	7	2	0	0	0	0	0	0	3	0	3	0	0	0	.333	.444	.467
Childers, Matt, Indianapolis	11	1	1	0	1	1	0	0	0	0	0	0	0	0	0	0	0	0	0	1.000	1.000	1.000
Choate, Randy, Columbus *	55	1	1	0	0	0	0	0	0	0	0	0	0	0	0	1	0	0	0	.000	.000	.000
Christensen, McKay, S./WB *	47	200	181	26	43	67	10	1	4	13	3	1	1	14	0	48	7	2	2	.238	.294	.370
Clapinski, Chris, Louisville	7	31	29	8	10	13	0	0	1	3	0	0	0	2	0	9	1	0	0	.345	.387	.448
Clapp, Stubby, Richmond *	105	343	286	43	62	100	11	9	3	23	4	2	5	46	0	66	6	2	6	.217	.333	.350
Clark, Brady, Indianapolis	9	36	34	4	9	12	3	0	0	3	0	0	0	2	0	6	1	0	3	.265	.306	.353
Clark, Howie, Syracuse *	66	285	252	29	65	93	14	1	4	30	3	6	3	21	2	20	1	0	3	.258	.316	.369
Coco, Pasqual, Indianapolis	28	23	23	4	7	7	0	0	0	4	0	0	0	0	0	8	0	0	1	.304	.304	.304
Colangelo, Mike, Syracuse	94	363	310	42	87	128	20	3	5	45	3	2	11	37	1	74	5	2	11	.281	.375	.413
Coleman, Michael, Louisville	18	73	63	12	16	29	4	0	3	19	0	3	1	6	0	12	1	0	1	.254	.315	.460
Collier, Lou, Pawtucket	103	438	392	58	115	184	19	4	14	69	0	6	8	32	4	94	8	7	13	.293	.354	.469
Connacher, Kevin, Rochester	61	162	145	14	32	47	5	2	2	15	2	0	0	15	0	50	4	3	1	.221	.294	.324
Conti, Jason, Indianapolis *	121	498	456	57	113	166	17	3	10	40	6	4	8	24	1	120	13	8	6	.248	.295	.364
Coquillette, Trace, Pawtucket	68	272	233	36	71	107	21	0	5	30	6	4	12	17	0	65	3	3	1	.305	.376	.459
Coste, Chris, Pawtucket	29	102	96	5	18	26	5	0	1	8	1	1	0	4	0	18	0	0	3	.188	.218	.271
Crespo, Cesar, Pawtucket †	132	511	465	69	124	188	31	3	9	58	3	3	0	40	4	93	13	8	14	.267	.323	.404
Crespo, Felipe, Louisville †	107	419	360	43	88	126	20	0	6	48	7	4	5	43	1	54	9	5	9	.244	.330	.350
Crisp, Covelli, Buffalo †	56	267	225	42	81	115	19	6	1	24	9	2	5	26	0	24	20	8	5	.360	.434	.511
Crosby, Bubba, Columbus *	16	71	63	9	19	29	2	1	2	8	0	1	1	6	0	12	3	0	0	.302	.366	.460
Crowell, Jim, Scranton/WB	54	1	0	0	0	0	0	0	0	0	0	0	0	1	0	0	0	0	0	.000	1.000	.000
Cruz, Jacob, Louisville *	36	149	132	25	46	75	8	0	7	29	0	2	1	14	0	22	3	0	5	.348	.409	.568
Cuddyer, Michael, Rochester	53	218	186	25	57	83	17	0	3	34	0	6	1	25	1	49	5	4	4	.306	.381	.446
Cust, Jack, Ottawa *	97	415	333	55	95	142	18	1	9	58	0	2	0	80	1	94	5	2	9	.285	.422	.426
Darula, Bobby, Louisville *	13	45	40	4	12	16	4	0	0	8	1	0	0	4	2	6	1	1	0	.300	.364	.400
Davis, Doug, Indianapolis	5	2	2	0	0	0	0	0	0	0	0	0	0	0	0	1	0	0	0	.000	.000	.000
Davis, Lance, Louisville	28	18	17	2	1	2	1	0	0	2	0	0	0	1	0	7	0	0	1	.059	.111	.118
DeCinces, Tim, Buffalo *	3	11	8	1	1	1	0	0	0	1	0	0	0	3	0	3	1	0	0	.125	.364	.125
Deardorff, Jeff, Rochester	20	72	67	9	20	36	6	2	2	8	1	1	0	3	0	20	2	1	0	.299	.324	.537
Delgado, Alex, Indianapolis	41	142	131	10	39	51	6	0	2	10	4	0	0	7	0	12	2	0	5	.298	.333	.389
DePastino, Joe, Norfolk	84	301	277	26	74	96	16	0	2	22	1	1	2	20	2	51	2	1	8	.267	.320	.347
Diaz, Matt, Durham	67	281	253	35	83	131	18	3	8	45	0	3	8	16	3	45	6	2	8	.328	.382	.518
Dominique, Andy, Pawtucket	79	322	289	42	88	145	18	0	13	57	1	3	7	22	0	45	2	1	10	.304	.364	.502
Dragicevich, Scott, Syracuse	11	41	38	1	11	12	1	0	0	1	0	0	0	3	0	13	0	0	1	.289	.341	.316
Dransfeldt, Kelly, Lou.-Paw.	112	386	354	44	75	125	20	3	8	46	0	3	4	25	0	87	0	2	8	.212	.269	.353
Duckworth, Brandon, S./WB	3	3	2	0	1	1	0	0	0	1	1	0	0	0	0	0	0	0	0	.500	.500	.500
Duncan, Jeff, Norfolk *	4	17	15	2	4	11	1	0	2	4	1	0	0	1	0	7	1	0	0	.267	.313	.733
Elwood, Brad, Columbus	5	16	15	1	2	2	0	0	0	1	1	0	0	0	0	4	0	0	1	.133	.133	.133
Emiliano, Jamie, Richmond	53	1	1	0	0	0	0	0	0	0	0	0	0	0	0	1	0	0	0	.000	.000	.000
Ennis, John, Rich.-Toledo	31	5	4	0	0	0	0	0	0	0	0	0	0	1	0	1	0	0	0	.000	.200	.000
Escalona, Felix, Ottawa	9	33	30	5	7	9	2	0	0	5	0	0	2	1	0	5	2	0	0	.233	.303	.300
Escobar, Alex, Buffalo	118	476	439	63	110	207	21	2	24	78	0	6	7	24	3	133	8	3	11	.251	.296	.472
Estrada, Johnny, Richmond †	106	402	354	40	116	175	29	0	10	66	0	6	12	30	5	30	0	0	11	.328	.393	.494
Etherton, Seth, Louisville	21	14	11	1	0	0	0	0	0	0	2	0	0	1	0	2	0	0	1	.000	.083	.000
Evans, Lee, Richmond †	16	57	53	5	13	13	0	0	0	3	0	0	0	4	0	12	0	0	2	.245	.298	.245
Evans, Tom, Toledo	38	137	118	17	18	33	4	1	3	6	0	0	5	14	0	36	5	0	1	.153	.270	.280
Fabregas, Jorge, Durham *	42	155	140	13	42	55	7	0	2	18	1	3	1	10	1	10	1	0	4	.300	.344	.393
Fagan, Shawn, Syracuse	17	61	58	7	12	15	3	0	0	5	0	1	0	2	0	22	1	0	0	.207	.230	.259
Feliciano, Pedro, Norfolk *	15	1	1	0	0	0	0	0	0	0	0	0	0	0	0	1	0	0	0	.000	.000	.000
Fitzgerald, Jason, Rich.*	13	44	43	2	9	10	1	0	0	1	0	0	1	0	0	10	1	1	0	.209	.227	.233
Ford, Ben, Indianapolis	26	8	6	0	0	0	0	0	0	0	1	0	0	1	0	4	0	0	0	.000	.143	.000
Ford, Lew, Rochester	53	230	211	33	64	95	18	2	3	31	0	1	8	10	1	28	4	5	1	.303	.357	.450
Foreman, JuJu, Louisville *	2	3	3	1	1	1	0	0	0	0	0	0	0	0	0	0	0	0	0	.333	.333	.333
Foster, John, Indianapolis *	27	2	2	0	0	0	0	0	0	0	0	0	0	0	0	1	0	0	0	.000	.000	.000
Francia, Dave, S./WB *	9	18	18	2	2	2	0	0	0	1	0	0	0	0	0	4	1	0	0	.111	.111	.111
Freel, Ryan, Louisville	54	238	215	38	59	81	11	1	3	12	0	2	0	21	0	32	25	6	2	.274	.336	.377
French, Anton, Pawtucket *	98	349	314	51	92	127	9	10	2	22	4	0	1	30	0	61	40	12	4	.293	.357	.404
Fussell, Chris, Richmond	29	24	20	4	8	12	1	0	1	3	4	0	0	0	0	4	0	0	0	.400	.400	.600
Galloway, Mike, Syracuse	3	9	9	2	3	4	1	0	0	0	0	0	0	0	0	3	0	0	0	.333	.333	.444
Garabito, Eddy, Ottawa †	114	505	459	62	129	176	28	5	3	56	7	4	2	31	1	70	14	8	8	.281	.327	.383
Garcia, Daniel, Norfolk	101	427	388	45	102	143	23	3	4	54	2	6	9	22	1	60	11	1	3	.263	.313	.369
Garcia, Jesse, Richmond	110	449	425	45	130	159	17	3	2	30	5	3	4	12	0	50	29	9	9	.306	.329	.374

Player, Team	G	TPA	AB	R	H	TB	2B	3B	HR	RBI	SH	SF	HP	BB	IBB	SO	SB	CS	GDP	Avg.	OBP	Slg.
Garcia, Karim, Buffalo *	14	62	60	6	16	22	6	0	0	7	0	0	0	2	1	17	2	1	1	.267	.290	.367
Garcia, Luis, Buffalo	122	462	432	41	93	143	27	1	7	51	1	2	5	22	0	97	2	4	8	.215	.260	.331
Geary, Geoff, Scranton/WB	46	5	4	0	0	0	0	0	0	0	1	0	0	0	0	1	0	0	0	.000	.000	.000
Gerut, Jody, Buffalo *	17	77	65	13	18	38	5	0	5	19	0	1	0	11	0	11	4	0	1	.277	.377	.585
Giambi, Jeremy, Pawtucket *	10	42	35	6	8	15	4	0	1	4	0	0	0	7	0	15	0	0	0	.229	.357	.429
Gil, Benji, Buffalo	9	36	36	4	5	12	1	0	2	6	0	0	0	0	0	10	0	0	1	.139	.139	.333
Gil, Geronimo, Ottawa	36	148	134	15	47	60	10	0	1	17	3	2	2	7	0	28	0	3	2	.351	.386	.448
Gipson, Charles, Columbus	31	135	120	17	33	41	6	1	0	5	1	0	5	9	0	18	5	6	1	.275	.351	.342
Giron, Roberto, Indianapolis	52	2	2	0	0	0	0	0	0	0	0	0	0	0	0	0	0	0	0	.000	.000	.000
Glavine, Mike, Norfolk *	79	197	169	15	45	71	11	0	5	17	1	2	0	25	4	36	0	0	4	.266	.357	.420
Gload, Ross, Charlotte *	133	549	508	72	160	266	40	6	18	70	5	6	1	29	6	60	6	3	12	.315	.349	.524
Glynn, Ryan, Richmond	16	11	10	2	1	3	0	1	0	1	1	0	0	0	0	2	0	0	0	.100	.100	.300
Goelz, Jim, Pawtucket	8	26	26	1	4	5	1	0	0	1	0	0	0	0	0	7	0	0	1	.154	.154	.192
Gomes, Jonny, Durham	5	23	19	2	6	10	2	1	0	1	0	0	2	2	0	5	0	0	0	.316	.435	.526
Gonzalez, Raul, Norfolk	32	137	120	18	43	57	3	1	3	19	0	1	0	16	1	23	5	2	3	.358	.431	.475
Green, Chad, Rochester †	106	427	397	50	100	157	24	3	9	29	5	1	2	22	0	85	12	7	5	.252	.294	.395
Green, Nick, Richmond	124	440	399	40	99	160	26	1	11	51	2	4	7	26	1	79	7	5	7	.248	.303	.401
Greene, Charlie, Durham	6	16	13	2	1	1	0	0	0	0	0	0	1	2	0	4	0	0	1	.077	.250	.077
Griffiths, Jeremy, Norfolk	21	11	10	0	1	1	0	0	0	0	1	0	0	0	0	3	0	0	0	.100	.100	.100
Grindell, Nate, Buffalo	46	153	130	14	29	44	9	0	2	14	3	1	7	12	0	23	2	4	4	.223	.320	.338
Gross, Gabe, Syracuse *	53	216	182	22	48	83	16	2	5	23	0	0	3	31	3	56	1	1	2	.264	.380	.456
Grummitt, Dan, Durham	15	50	46	3	11	17	3	0	1	5	0	0	2	2	0	16	0	0	1	.239	.300	.370
Guerra, Mark, Indianapolis	5	1	1	0	0	0	0	0	0	0	0	0	0	0	0	1	0	0	0	.000	.000	.000
Guerrero, Wilton, Louisville †	126	524	476	68	132	157	20	1	1	29	19	2	1	26	0	58	30	9	5	.277	.315	.330
Guillen, Jose, Louisville	4	17	15	4	5	6	1	0	0	3	0	1	0	1	0	3	1	0	1	.333	.353	.400
Gutierrez, Ricky, Buffalo	16	71	65	8	19	23	2	1	0	5	0	1	1	4	0	5	4	1	2	.292	.338	.354
Hafner, Travis, Buffalo *	29	126	100	15	27	37	4	0	2	10	0	0	1	25	2	26	2	1	2	.270	.421	.370
Hall, Bill, Indianapolis	89	391	354	57	100	144	25	2	5	32	9	0	1	27	2	79	10	11	7	.282	.335	.407
Hamilton, Joey, Louisville	33	13	13	1	1	2	1	0	0	1	0	0	0	0	0	8	0	0	1	.077	.077	.154
Hammond, Joey, Ottawa	103	400	348	43	95	120	11	7	0	32	5	2	1	44	0	60	2	1	8	.273	.354	.345
Hancock, Josh, Scranton/WB	28	16	15	0	0	0	0	0	0	0	1	0	0	0	0	9	0	0	0	.000	.000	.000
Hanigan, Ryan, Louisville	1	5	3	1	1	1	0	0	0	0	1	0	1	0	0	1	0	0	0	.333	.500	.333
Hankins, Ryan, Charlotte	68	264	239	29	66	100	16	0	6	33	3	4	2	16	0	38	2	4	11	.276	.322	.418
Hansen, Jed, Indianapolis	3	5	5	0	0	0	0	0	0	0	0	0	0	0	0	1	0	0	0	.000	.000	.000
Harnisch, Pete, Louisville	8	4	4	0	1	1	0	0	0	0	0	0	0	0	0	2	0	0	0	.250	.250	.250
Harris, Willie, Charlotte *	28	118	100	22	38	64	6	1	6	13	1	0	0	17	0	20	9	3	0	.380	.470	.640
Haselman, Bill, Pawtucket	79	291	280	37	63	87	6	0	6	24	0	2	0	9	0	46	1	1	15	.225	.247	.311
Haynes, Jimmy, Louisville	2	1	1	0	0	0	0	0	0	0	0	0	0	0	0	0	0	0	0	.000	.000	.000
Headley, Justin, Pawtucket *	12	42	38	4	9	13	1	0	1	4	0	2	2	0	0	6	0	0	1	.237	.262	.342
Heilman, Aaron, Norfolk	16	5	5	0	0	0	0	0	0	0	0	0	0	0	0	2	0	0	1	.000	.000	.000
Helms, Wes, Indianapolis	2	6	5	0	2	2	0	0	0	0	0	0	0	1	0	1	0	0	0	.400	.500	.400
Henson, Drew, Columbus	133	537	483	60	113	199	40	2	14	78	1	10	11	32	3	122	8	4	8	.234	.291	.412
Hernandez, Buddy, Richmond	53	3	3	0	1	2	1	0	0	0	0	0	0	0	0	2	0	0	0	.333	.333	.667
Hernandez, Michel, Col.	89	325	282	39	79	105	14	0	4	30	1	2	3	37	1	35	0	2	9	.280	.367	.372
Hessman, Mike, Richmond	96	395	359	47	89	158	15	3	16	52	0	8	4	24	0	87	3	1	6	.248	.296	.440
Hiles, Cary, Scranton/WB	14	3	2	0	0	0	0	0	0	0	1	0	0	0	0	0	0	0	0	.000	.000	.000
Hill, Jason, Louisville	3	4	3	0	2	3	1	0	0	0	0	0	0	1	0	1	0	0	0	.667	.750	1.000
Hinch, A.J., Toledo	55	205	185	20	48	77	15	1	4	23	2	1	4	13	2	38	0	1	2	.259	.320	.416
Hinske, Eric, Syracuse *	2	8	8	2	4	8	1	0	1	2	0	0	0	0	0	0	0	0	0	.500	.500	1.000
Hitchcox, Brian, S./WB *	15	45	45	2	10	14	1	0	1	2	0	0	0	0	0	3	0	1	1	.222	.222	.311
Hoard, Brent, Rochester	13	3	1	1	0	0	0	0	0	0	1	0	0	1	0	1	0	0	0	.000	.500	.000
Hollins, Damon, Richmond	91	335	307	39	84	148	23	4	11	45	2	2	2	22	0	62	7	2	10	.274	.324	.482
Hollins, Dave, Scranton/WB †	29	113	98	12	20	32	2	2	2	12	0	1	3	11	0	16	1	0	2	.204	.301	.327
Houston, Tyler, S./WB *	6	24	23	2	4	7	1	1	0	0	0	0	0	1	0	1	0	0	0	.174	.208	.304
Hubbard, Mike, Richmond	70	228	206	22	48	66	12	0	2	15	5	2	2	13	0	28	0	0	9	.233	.283	.320
Huckaby, Ken, Syracuse	75	288	267	24	78	101	14	0	3	25	3	3	0	15	2	30	1	1	11	.292	.326	.378
Hummel, Tim, Charlotte	128	541	476	72	135	211	25	3	15	80	10	4	5	46	2	83	9	3	10	.284	.350	.443
Infante, Omar, Toledo	64	257	224	28	50	66	10	0	2	18	6	2	3	22	0	32	22	4	3	.223	.299	.295
Inge, Brandon, Toledo	39	154	142	15	39	63	9	0	5	15	1	0	0	11	1	23	3	1	6	.275	.327	.444
Izturis, Maicer, Buffalo †	85	337	301	43	79	109	16	4	2	29	9	2	1	24	0	28	14	6	14	.262	.317	.362
Jackson, Ryan, Durham *	131	553	519	78	157	249	45	4	13	71	2	2	0	30	7	85	2	4	10	.303	.339	.480
Jennings, Doug, Ind.*	59	199	169	17	44	74	13	1	5	23	0	3	10	17	1	48	1	1	7	.260	.357	.438
Jennings, Robin, Louisville *	64	241	219	23	46	63	12	1	1	15	0	1	3	18	2	43	3	2	10	.210	.278	.288
Jensen, Marcus, Columbus †	66	237	196	20	44	61	8	0	3	15	4	0	1	36	0	53	0	0	4	.224	.348	.311
Johnson, Nick, Columbus *	3	12	10	1	5	10	2	0	1	3	0	0	0	2	0	2	0	0	0	.500	.583	1.000
Johnson, Reed, Syracuse	26	111	101	14	33	45	4	1	2	16	0	2	5	3	0	13	3	1	2	.327	.369	.446
Johnson, Rontrez, Richmond	31	94	81	8	14	15	1	0	0	5	2	1	2	8	0	15	3	1	2	.173	.261	.185
Johnson, Russ, Norfolk	100	403	349	37	99	124	16	0	3	39	0	7	3	44	3	45	6	5	8	.284	.362	.355
Jones, Bobby M., Richmond	37	1	1	0	0	0	0	0	0	0	0	0	0	0	0	1	0	0	0	.000	.000	.000
Jordan, Kevin, Toledo	46	173	160	10	36	49	7	0	2	17	1	1	2	8	0	17	1	1	4	.225	.269	.306
Joseph, Jake, Norfolk	19	7	6	2	1	1	0	0	0	0	0	0	0	1	0	3	0	0	0	.167	.286	.167
Junge, Eric, Scranton/WB	10	4	3	0	0	0	0	0	0	0	1	0	0	0	0	1	0	0	0	.000	.000	.000
Keene, Kurt, Syracuse	42	159	140	20	33	44	6	1	1	14	5	1	0	13	0	28	0	1	7	.236	.299	.314
Kelly, Kenny, Norfolk	30	99	92	15	24	46	6	2	4	8	1	0	0	6	0	25	5	0	1	.261	.306	.500
Kennedy, Bryan, Rochester *	5	14	13	1	4	4	0	0	0	3	0	0	1	0	0	3	0	0	0	.308	.357	.308
Kieschnick, Brooks, Ind.*	11	11	10	0	0	0	0	0	0	0	0	0	0	1	0	4	0	0	0	.000	.091	.000
Kingsale, Eugene, Toledo †	46	178	160	19	39	55	6	5	0	12	3	2	2	11	0	24	9	5	2	.244	.297	.344
Klassen, Danny, Toledo	112	449	407	63	100	160	19	4	11	48	3	4	7	28	1	110	12	5	5	.246	.303	.393
Knox, Ryan, Indianapolis	36	141	131	18	36	44	8	0	0	5	1	0	2	7	0	20	17	3	3	.275	.321	.336
Knupfer, Jason, Scranton/WB	111	452	398	49	85	111	20	0	2	21	5	1	2	46	0	89	13	1	5	.214	.298	.279
Kubes, Greg, Scranton/WB	37	5	5	0	0	0	0	0	0	0	0	0	0	0	0	4	0	0	0	.000	.000	.000

Player, Team	G	TPA	AB	R	H	TB	2B	3B	HR	RBI	SH	SF	HP	BB	IBB	SO	SB	CS	GDP	Avg.	OBP	Slg.
LaForest, Pete, Durham *	61	241	201	40	54	114	14	2	14	38	0	2	2	36	2	56	2	1	2	.269	.382	.567
LaRocca, Greg, Buffalo	132	553	500	63	145	212	33	2	10	68	1	6	6	40	2	53	5	3	5	.290	.346	.424
LaRoche, Adam, Richmond *	72	300	264	33	78	123	21	0	8	35	0	6	3	27	3	58	1	2	6	.295	.360	.466
Lamb, David, Rochester †	120	474	405	45	105	130	15	2	2	31	6	6	8	49	2	60	2	6	10	.259	.346	.321
Langerhans, Ryan, Rich.*	38	146	132	13	37	63	10	2	4	11	1	1	1	11	1	29	2	1	2	.280	.338	.477
Larson, Brandon, Louisville	72	315	282	51	91	174	19	2	20	74	0	3	2	28	1	70	3	0	7	.323	.384	.617
Lawrence, Joe, Indianapolis	43	162	137	19	28	41	7	0	2	8	1	1	0	23	0	33	2	2	3	.204	.317	.299
Lee, Derek, Indianapolis *	15	9	9	0	3	5	0	1	0	1	0	0	0	0	0	2	0	0	0	.333	.333	.556
Lemonis, Chris, Ottawa *	60	214	188	28	44	60	10	0	2	34	3	3	3	17	2	47	1	2	5	.234	.303	.319
Lennon, Pat, Toledo	62	233	203	26	50	89	10	1	9	32	0	4	3	23	0	56	2	1	8	.246	.326	.438
Leon, Donny, Pawtucket †	1	4	4	0	0	0	0	0	0	0	0	0	0	0	0	3	0	0	0	.000	.000	.000
Leon, Jose, Ottawa	79	331	309	33	82	117	19	2	4	39	0	3	4	15	2	47	1	1	12	.265	.305	.379
Levis, Jesse, Scranton/WB *	79	290	265	26	74	90	16	0	0	30	3	2	2	18	4	18	1	0	12	.279	.328	.340
Lewis, Derrick, Richmond	36	2	2	0	0	0	0	0	0	0	0	0	0	0	0	1	0	0	0	.000	.000	.000
Liefer, Jeff, Durham *	44	173	157	20	41	78	10	3	7	24	1	0	1	14	0	49	0	0	2	.261	.326	.497
Little, Mark, Buffalo	45	159	146	20	41	54	5	1	2	16	1	1	6	5	1	45	4	2	1	.281	.329	.370
Littleton, Brandon, Ottawa †	29	126	119	12	30	36	6	0	0	15	2	0	0	5	0	23	3	3	0	.252	.282	.303
Lomasney, Steve, Ottawa	81	289	253	28	61	75	10	2	0	19	6	0	2	28	0	93	2	1	7	.241	.322	.296
Lombard, George, Durham *	112	499	438	57	117	201	25	4	17	64	6	2	6	45	6	143	23	6	6	.267	.342	.459
Lopez, Felipe, Louisville †	35	156	143	22	40	57	11	0	2	18	0	1	0	12	0	38	2	5	0	.280	.333	.399
Lopez, Luis, Ottawa †	52	203	186	23	49	70	6	0	5	32	2	4	5	6	0	24	1	1	3	.263	.299	.376
Lucca, Lou, Buffalo	9	28	27	5	6	9	3	0	0	1	0	0	1	0	0	10	1	1	0	.222	.250	.333
Luuloa, Keith, Indianapolis	109	400	359	50	93	158	26	3	11	54	0	4	1	35	4	45	3	3	12	.259	.323	.440
Machado, Robert, Ottawa	59	242	221	30	74	115	17	0	8	38	1	0	3	17	2	36	0	0	6	.335	.390	.520
Maddox, Garry, S./WB *	18	59	56	4	12	15	3	0	0	8	0	1	1	1	0	12	0	1	0	.214	.237	.268
Madson, Ryan, S./WB *	26	16	13	1	6	6	0	0	0	2	1	0	0	2	0	4	0	0	0	.462	.533	.462
Magee, Wendell, S./WB-Tol.	78	308	285	24	72	102	15	3	3	30	1	3	2	17	1	62	1	6	11	.253	.296	.358
Magruder, Chris, Buffalo †	41	156	137	20	45	65	7	2	3	15	0	3	1	15	1	27	5	1	3	.328	.391	.474
Manning, David, Indianapolis.	23	16	14	0	1	1	0	0	0	0	2	0	0	0	0	5	0	0	0	.071	.071	.071
Manzanillo, Josias, Louisville.	22	1	1	0	0	0	0	0	0	0	0	0	0	0	0	1	0	0	0	.000	.000	.000
Marquez, Rob, Indianapolis	30	3	2	0	1	1	0	0	0	0	1	0	0	0	0	0	0	0	0	.500	.500	.500
Marquis, Jason, Richmond *	16	17	16	0	3	6	1	1	0	1	1	0	0	0	0	2	0	0	0	.188	.188	.375
Marsters, Brandon, Roch.	103	387	359	39	87	141	24	0	10	45	7	3	1	17	1	99	0	2	9	.242	.276	.393
Martinez, Gabby, Durham	12	47	44	5	13	18	2	0	1	2	2	0	0	1	0	6	2	2	0	.295	.311	.409
Martinez, Luis, Indianapolis *	7	7	6	0	0	0	0	0	0	0	0	0	0	1	0	6	0	0	0	.000	.143	.000
Martinez, Victor, Buffalo †	73	314	274	42	90	130	19	0	7	45	0	6	8	26	1	32	3	5	14	.328	.395	.474
Mateo, Ruben, Louisville	57	250	217	36	71	115	15	1	9	50	0	2	5	26	1	34	3	1	3	.327	.408	.530
Matos, Luis, Ottawa	45	194	175	28	53	80	16	4	1	25	1	4	1	13	1	34	6	1	8	.303	.347	.457
Matthews, Lamont, Paw.*	7	21	18	3	3	4	1	0	0	2	0	0	0	3	0	7	1	1	0	.167	.286	.222
Maxwell, Jason, Louisville	103	402	361	52	94	137	17	1	8	46	1	8	3	29	3	57	2	1	8	.260	.314	.380
McConnell, Sam, Rich.*	22	15	11	0	4	4	0	0	0	0	4	0	0	0	0	2	0	0	0	.364	.364	.364
McDonald, Darnell, Ottawa	40	172	152	19	45	54	7	1	0	20	1	0	1	18	0	27	5	7	3	.296	.374	.355
McDonald, Donzell, Rich.†	129	542	464	61	118	160	18	9	2	19	9	3	4	62	0	113	31	10	7	.254	.345	.345
McEwing, Joe, Norfolk	5	23	19	3	6	9	0	0	1	3	0	0	2	2	0	2	3	0	0	.316	.435	.474
McGuire, Ryan, Col.-Roch.*	89	306	267	27	67	91	13	1	3	28	0	3	3	32	3	59	0	1	5	.251	.334	.341
McKay, Cody, Indianapolis *	109	413	371	32	86	121	15	1	6	43	1	6	9	26	2	50	2	2	13	.232	.294	.326
Mears, Chris, Toledo	26	3	3	0	0	0	0	0	0	0	0	0	0	0	0	2	0	0	1	.000	.000	.000
Mendez, Carlos, Ottawa	61	261	248	32	86	124	18	4	4	42	0	1	1	11	5	28	1	2	7	.347	.375	.500
Mendez, Deivi, Columbus	5	15	13	1	0	0	0	0	0	0	1	0	0	1	0	4	0	0	1	.000	.071	.000
Mercado, Hector, S./WB *	14	2	2	0	0	0	0	0	0	0	0	0	0	0	0	1	0	0	0	.000	.000	.000
Michalak, Chris, Louisville *	10	4	3	1	0	0	0	0	0	0	1	0	0	0	0	1	0	0	0	.000	.000	.000
Middlebrook, Jason, Norfolk.	23	15	13	1	1	1	0	0	0	0	2	0	0	0	0	8	0	0	0	.077	.077	.077
Miles, Aaron, Charlotte †	133	595	546	80	166	243	34	5	11	50	5	3	1	40	2	52	8	9	9	.304	.351	.445
Miller, Corky, Louisville	103	400	354	49	88	149	28	0	11	43	1	3	7	35	2	58	0	0	12	.249	.326	.421
Miller, Travis, Louisville-Ind.	20	3	2	1	1	1	0	0	0	0	1	0	0	0	0	1	0	0	0	.500	.500	.500
Minor, Damon, S./WB *	91	367	328	45	76	143	17	1	16	65	0	3	9	27	3	60	1	2	10	.232	.305	.436
Mitchell, Keith, Louisville	18	62	52	5	10	14	2	1	0	5	0	0	0	10	0	16	0	0	1	.192	.323	.269
Molina, Izzy, Ottawa	3	9	9	0	0	0	0	0	0	0	0	0	0	0	0	6	0	0	0	.000	.000	.000
Monroe, Craig, Toledo	14	51	47	14	19	31	4	1	2	6	0	0	0	4	0	10	1	0	0	.404	.451	.660
Moore, Frank, Durham *	13	40	38	0	4	4	0	0	0	2	0	0	0	2	0	11	0	0	2	.105	.150	.105
Morales, Steve, Charlotte †	14	42	37	4	7	11	1	0	1	2	4	0	0	1	0	8	0	0	1	.189	.211	.297
Morgan, Scott, Charlotte	110	405	359	47	95	148	22	2	9	48	4	2	4	36	4	100	5	4	4	.265	.337	.412
Moriarty, Mike, Syracuse	55	201	176	25	41	56	6	0	3	14	2	1	1	21	0	30	4	1	5	.233	.317	.318
Morneau, Justin, Rochester *	71	299	265	39	71	132	11	1	16	42	0	2	4	28	3	56	0	2	2	.268	.344	.498
Morris, Warren, Toledo *	56	229	206	26	57	84	13	4	2	19	5	1	1	16	1	26	4	1	4	.277	.330	.408
Moseley, Dustin, Louisville	8	4	3	0	1	1	0	0	0	0	1	0	0	0	0	0	0	0	0	.333	.333	.333
Mottola, Chad, Dur.-Paw.	77	316	285	35	78	121	10	3	9	46	2	2	2	25	1	47	6	4	5	.274	.334	.425
Mouton, Lyle, Nor.-S./WB-Buf.	106	402	352	48	99	167	22	2	14	58	1	6	6	37	1	93	8	2	15	.281	.354	.474
Munoz, Billy, Toledo *	2	8	6	0	0	0	0	0	0	0	0	0	0	2	0	0	0	0	0	.000	.250	.000
Murphy, Nate, Charlotte *	42	139	126	22	30	58	4	0	8	15	1	1	1	10	0	29	2	0	1	.238	.297	.460
Myette, Aaron, Buf.-S./WB	34	5	5	0	2	2	0	0	0	2	0	0	0	0	0	2	0	0	0	.400	.400	.400
Nance, Shane, Indianapolis *	35	2	2	0	0	0	0	0	0	0	0	0	0	0	0	1	0	0	0	.000	.000	.000
Nelson, Bubba, Richmond	11	1	1	0	0	0	0	0	0	0	0	0	0	0	0	1	0	0	0	.000	.000	.000
Neuberger, Scott, Durham	62	230	205	29	55	82	12	0	5	20	1	1	4	19	1	42	0	4	5	.268	.341	.400
Nicholson, Derek, Toledo *	23	80	67	9	15	23	2	0	2	9	0	1	0	12	1	17	1	0	1	.224	.338	.343
Nicholson, Tommy, Char.*	19	51	43	1	6	7	1	0	0	1	2	0	0	6	0	10	0	1	1	.140	.245	.163
Nieves, Jose, Columbus	44	162	147	20	32	50	2	5	2	16	1	0	4	10	0	22	1	1	6	.218	.286	.340
Nunez, Jorge, Charlotte	112	374	350	35	81	94	8	1	1	26	10	2	0	12	0	80	15	8	12	.231	.255	.269
Nye, Rodney, Norfolk	2	9	7	1	0	0	0	0	0	0	0	0	0	2	0	4	0	0	0	.000	.222	.000
Obermueller, Wes, Ind.	3	2	1	0	0	0	0	0	0	0	1	0	0	0	0	0	0	0	0	.000	.000	.000
Olivares, Teuris, Columbus	5	13	12	0	4	4	0	0	0	1	1	0	0	0	0	1	0	0	0	.333	.333	.333

Player, Team	G	TPA	AB	R	H	TB	2B	3B	HR	RBI	SH	SF	HP	BB	IBB	SO	SB	CS	GDP	Avg.	OBP	Slg.
Olmedo, Rainer, Louisville † ..	9	31	25	4	6	10	1	0	1	4	4	0	0	2	0	6	0	0	0	.240	.296	.400
Ortiz, Hector, Durham	68	249	221	26	54	68	14	0	0	25	7	0	1	20	0	23	0	1	11	.244	.310	.308
Patrick, Brian, Syracuse †	7	26	25	2	2	3	1	0	0	0	0	0	1	0	0	9	0	0	0	.080	.115	.120
Paul, Josh, Charlotte.............	19	72	64	6	12	20	0	1	2	5	2	1	0	5	0	14	1	1	1	.188	.243	.313
Paz, Rich, Indianapolis..........	36	150	131	13	46	54	8	0	0	5	3	0	0	16	0	19	1	2	5	.351	.422	.412
Peeples, Mike, Toledo	23	87	79	4	15	19	4	0	0	11	0	3	0	5	1	14	0	1	2	.190	.230	.241
Pena, Carlos, Toledo *	8	35	30	4	10	16	4	1	0	5	0	0	1	4	1	7	0	0	0	.333	.429	.533
Pena, Wily Mo, Louisville.......	14	60	51	16	19	34	3	0	4	14	0	1	3	5	1	13	0	0	0	.373	.450	.667
Peralta, John, Buffalo............	63	258	237	25	61	78	12	1	1	21	3	0	3	15	0	45	1	3	6	.257	.310	.329
Perez, Antonio, Durham.........	34	149	134	27	38	72	12	2	6	20	1	1	3	10	0	38	3	1	2	.284	.345	.537
Perez, Jhonny, Toledo	72	230	215	22	48	64	8	1	2	17	3	2	3	7	0	37	14	4	0	.223	.256	.298
Perez, Josue, Scranton/WB †	32	133	123	6	27	32	5	0	0	8	1	1	1	7	0	31	2	5	1	.220	.265	.260
Perez, Santiago, Ott.-Lou.†	19	60	51	5	11	16	2	0	1	2	1	0	0	8	0	11	3	2	2	.216	.322	.314
Perez, Timo, Norfolk *	3	10	9	2	2	5	0	0	1	1	0	0	0	1	0	0	0	0	0	.222	.300	.556
Phelps, Josh, Syracuse..........	4	12	11	2	5	11	0	0	2	4	0	0	0	1	0	3	0	0	0	.455	.500	1.000
Phelps, Travis, Richmond	47	4	3	0	0	0	0	0	0	0	1	0	0	0	0	3	0	0	0	.000	.000	.000
Phillips, Andy, Columbus	17	72	67	7	14	24	4	0	2	5	0	0	0	5	0	17	0	0	4	.209	.264	.358
Phillips, Brandon, Buffalo	43	172	154	14	27	43	7	0	3	13	2	1	3	12	0	22	7	3	3	.175	.247	.279
Phillips, Jason, Norfolk..........	22	92	78	13	27	44	5	0	4	20	0	1	2	11	3	9	0	0	4	.346	.435	.564
Piazza, Mike, Norfolk	5	18	17	2	3	6	0	0	1	2	0	0	0	1	0	3	0	0	0	.176	.222	.353
Pickering, Calvin, Louisville *	26	102	81	10	23	38	3	0	4	18	0	1	3	17	1	31	0	0	2	.284	.422	.469
Pond, Simon, Syracuse *	63	266	248	33	76	114	21	1	5	36	0	0	2	16	1	42	1	1	5	.306	.353	.460
Porter, Bo, Richmond............	79	300	267	34	64	102	13	5	5	31	2	3	2	26	0	78	14	4	7	.240	.309	.382
Post, Dave, Columbus............	72	292	248	36	55	83	12	2	4	28	6	3	5	30	0	35	3	3	3	.222	.315	.335
Pratt, Andy, Richmond *	29	15	12	1	3	3	0	0	0	0	2	0	1	0	0	5	0	0	0	.250	.308	.250
Pratt, Scott, Buffalo *	108	383	357	43	88	121	11	5	4	31	8	4	0	14	1	70	18	9	2	.246	.272	.339
Pressley, Josh, Norfolk *	19	73	61	9	9	11	2	0	0	4	0	1	0	11	1	13	0	1	1	.148	.274	.180
Pride, Curtis, Columbus *	55	250	225	44	65	105	11	4	7	34	1	0	4	20	4	48	7	7	7	.289	.357	.467
Prieto, Alex, Rochester	69	252	234	27	62	88	9	1	5	21	4	2	0	12	1	49	6	3	6	.265	.298	.376
Pumphrey, Ken, S./WB...........	17	7	6	1	2	3	1	0	0	0	1	0	0	0	0	2	0	0	0	.333	.333	.500
Punto, Nick, Scranton/WB † ..	25	121	111	19	35	44	7	1	0	9	2	1	0	7	0	13	7	1	0	.315	.353	.396
Quattlebaum, Hugh, Ottawa ...	3	9	8	0	2	3	1	0	0	0	0	0	1	0	0	2	0	0	0	.250	.333	.375
Quevedo, Ruben, Ind.	5	3	2	0	0	0	0	0	0	0	1	0	0	0	0	1	0	0	0	.000	.000	.000
Quinn, Mark, Durham	15	63	60	7	10	15	3	1	0	3	0	0	0	3	0	17	0	0	2	.167	.206	.250
Rabe, Josh, Rochester...........	38	144	131	15	31	52	6	0	5	11	1	0	1	11	0	22	2	1	7	.237	.301	.397
Raines, Tim, Ottawa...............	52	237	214	37	64	94	11	5	3	23	2	1	1	19	0	37	23	9	3	.299	.357	.439
Randall, Scott, Louisville........	31	22	19	2	5	5	0	0	0	0	3	0	0	0	0	3	0	0	1	.263	.263	.263
Redman, Prentice, Norfolk.....	128	483	433	60	110	176	29	2	11	48	2	1	7	40	0	96	24	8	5	.254	.326	.406
Reese, Kevin, Columbus *	15	63	55	11	12	16	1	0	1	3	2	0	0	6	0	8	1	0	0	.218	.295	.291
Reith, Brian, Louisville	16	1	1	1	0	0	0	0	0	0	0	0	0	0	0	0	0	0	0	.000	.000	.000
Restovich, Michael, Roch.	119	508	454	75	125	211	34	2	16	72	0	3	4	47	6	117	10	3	10	.275	.346	.465
Reyes, Jose, Norfolk †	42	181	160	28	43	57	6	4	0	13	4	1	1	15	0	25	26	5	2	.269	.333	.356
Riggan, Jerrod, Buf.-Norfolk..	14	1	1	0	0	0	0	0	0	0	0	0	0	0	0	0	0	0	0	.000	.000	.000
Rios, Armando, Charlotte *	45	176	155	23	50	79	9	1	6	30	1	2	4	14	2	30	5	6	4	.323	.389	.510
Rios, Brian, Ottawa	21	70	65	3	13	21	3	1	1	8	0	2	1	2	0	10	0	0	2	.200	.229	.323
Rivera, Juan, Columbus.........	79	337	308	47	100	142	21	0	7	37	0	3	0	26	1	37	1	3	8	.325	.374	.461
Rivera, Mike, Charlotte..........	68	271	245	38	76	123	11	0	12	52	0	1	9	16	0	50	0	1	4	.310	.373	.502
Rivera, Ruben, Ottawa	14	54	48	12	20	33	3	2	2	7	0	0	2	4	0	12	2	0	1	.417	.481	.688
Roa, Joe, Indianapolis............	5	5	3	0	0	0	0	0	0	0	2	0	0	0	0	2	0	0	0	.000	.000	.000
Roach, Jason, Norfolk	35	21	18	1	3	6	3	0	0	2	1	1	0	1	0	4	0	0	0	.167	.200	.333
Roberge, J.P., Scranton/WB ...	101	370	338	40	90	128	22	2	4	35	1	3	5	23	3	55	3	0	10	.266	.320	.379
Roberts, Brian, Ottawa †	44	211	178	36	56	71	13	1	0	15	4	2	0	27	1	12	19	6	3	.315	.401	.399
Robinson, Bo, Columbus	2	7	7	0	1	1	0	0	0	1	0	0	0	0	0	1	0	0	0	.143	.143	.143
Rodriguez, John, Columbus *	79	261	232	35	61	104	9	2	10	33	3	1	1	24	1	50	6	0	2	.263	.333	.448
Rodriguez, Luis, Rochester †.	131	579	518	65	153	195	35	2	1	44	9	3	3	46	2	46	6	8	15	.295	.354	.376
Rolison, Nate, Columbus *	113	439	385	54	95	164	17	2	16	55	0	4	2	48	2	113	0	3	8	.247	.330	.426
Rolls, Damian, Durham..........	18	83	77	11	19	25	4	1	0	9	2	0	0	4	0	15	4	2	0	.247	.284	.325
Ross, Cody, Toledo	124	520	470	74	135	242	35	6	20	61	4	9	5	32	0	86	15	6	12	.287	.333	.515
Rowand, Aaron, Charlotte	32	139	120	15	29	47	9	0	3	13	6	0	2	11	0	12	0	0	3	.242	.316	.392
Rusch, Glendon, Ind.*	4	2	2	0	0	0	0	0	0	0	0	0	0	0	0	0	0	0	0	.000	.000	.000
Rushford, Jim, Indianapolis *	99	412	373	43	116	155	12	0	9	50	0	2	7	30	4	33	4	3	6	.311	.371	.416
Ryan, Michael, Rochester * ...	115	454	408	56	92	165	20	4	15	60	1	6	1	38	5	89	6	1	8	.225	.289	.404
Ryan, Rob, Syracuse *	50	207	181	30	45	80	17	0	6	20	0	2	3	21	1	24	3	2	5	.249	.333	.442
Salazar, Jeremy, S./WB	71	253	231	16	42	58	7	0	3	25	3	3	1	15	1	51	0	0	5	.182	.232	.251
Sanchez, Freddy, Pawtucket...	58	249	211	46	72	104	17	0	5	25	5	0	2	31	0	36	8	0	7	.341	.430	.493
Sandberg, Jared, Durham	74	305	272	40	63	118	17	1	12	37	1	0	2	30	1	95	1	0	4	.232	.313	.434
Sanders, Anthony, Charlotte ..	76	275	245	32	56	100	10	2	10	40	4	2	3	21	0	65	5	2	5	.229	.295	.408
Santana, Julio, Scranton/WB .	19	3	3	1	2	3	1	0	0	1	0	0	0	0	0	0	0	0	0	.667	.667	1.000
Santos, Angel, Paw.-Buffalo †	83	303	260	35	62	93	10	0	7	28	4	1	1	37	2	58	14	4	6	.238	.334	.358
Sasser, Rob, Ottawa...............	53	193	175	21	33	47	11	0	1	19	1	5	1	10	0	30	3	0	6	.189	.230	.269
Scarborough, Steve, Ind.	127	472	428	46	103	166	25	7	8	43	10	3	3	28	2	115	4	6	9	.241	.290	.388
Schneider, John, Syracuse.....	3	12	12	0	1	1	0	0	0	0	0	0	0	0	0	7	0	0	1	.083	.083	.083
Scobie, Jason, Norfolk...........	8	4	4	1	0	0	0	0	0	0	0	0	0	0	0	2	0	0	0	.000	.000	.000
Scutaro, Marcos, Norfolk.......	70	296	244	42	76	127	18	3	9	32	9	4	6	33	0	34	11	6	6	.311	.401	.520
Seabol, Scott, Indianapolis	25	87	81	6	19	24	1	2	0	9	0	2	0	4	0	18	0	1	4	.235	.264	.296
Sears, Todd, Rochester..........	80	326	283	35	72	107	12	1	7	41	0	2	4	37	6	90	6	1	6	.254	.347	.378
Secrist, Reed, Buffalo *	27	76	69	12	17	32	6	0	3	7	0	0	1	6	2	14	0	1	1	.246	.316	.464
Seestedt, Mike, Ottawa	4	9	8	1	1	1	0	0	0	0	0	0	0	1	0	0	0	0	2	.125	.222	.125
Sefcik, Kevin, Scranton/WB ...	133	542	492	75	138	208	32	4	10	66	1	7	2	40	0	47	10	4	13	.280	.333	.423
Seguignol, Fernando, Col.†	106	446	402	78	137	251	28	1	28	87	0	2	8	34	3	81	0	0	19	.341	.401	.624
Seibel, Phil, Norfolk *	11	8	7	2	3	3	0	0	0	0	0	0	0	1	0	1	0	0	1	.429	.500	.429

Player, Team	G	TPA	AB	R	H	TB	2B	3B	HR	RBI	SH	SF	HP	BB	IBB	SO	SB	CS	GDP	Avg.	OBP	Slg.
Sequea, Jorge, Syracuse	73	311	271	43	69	101	15	4	3	31	3	1	6	30	1	45	7	5	3	.255	.341	.373
Serrano, Jim, Norfolk	27	1	1	0	0	0	0	0	0	0	0	0	0	0	0	0	0	0	0	.000	.000	.000
Shackelford, Brian, Lou.*	13	1	1	0	0	0	0	0	0	0	0	0	0	0	0	0	0	0	0	.000	.000	.000
Shinjo, Tsuyoshi, Norfolk	36	126	111	12	36	54	5	2	3	9	4	1	1	9	1	17	0	1	2	.324	.377	.486
Shipp, Brian, Norfolk	6	22	19	1	5	5	0	0	0	2	0	0	0	3	0	7	0	0	0	.263	.364	.263
Simmons, Brian, S./WB †	42	185	178	26	49	75	9	1	5	13	0	0	0	7	1	45	2	2	6	.275	.303	.421
Smith, Bobby, Columbus	119	515	458	68	129	199	36	5	8	69	5	7	5	40	0	74	4	4	17	.282	.341	.434
Smith, Chuck, Richmond	3	2	2	0	0	0	0	0	0	0	0	0	0	0	0	0	0	0	0	.000	.000	.000
Smith, Jason, Durham *	130	544	515	76	147	240	20	14	15	71	8	5	5	11	0	128	14	9	1	.285	.304	.466
Smith, Mark, Indianapolis	103	416	388	46	114	188	25	2	15	62	0	2	5	21	2	58	3	2	14	.294	.337	.485
Smitherman, Stephen, Lou.	17	69	63	1	8	8	0	0	0	5	0	1	1	4	0	19	0	0	2	.127	.188	.127
Snead, Esix, Norfolk †	137	535	472	64	104	139	14	6	3	31	12	5	5	41	0	83	61	7	8	.220	.287	.294
Snyder, Earl, Pawtucket	130	507	467	61	119	212	25	1	22	71	2	6	8	24	2	113	0	0	6	.255	.299	.454
Sorensen, Zach, Buffalo †	61	269	238	39	57	84	12	3	3	29	5	4	0	22	0	42	12	5	3	.239	.299	.353
Sosa, Juan, Scranton/WB	91	317	298	30	75	97	11	1	3	26	2	2	2	12	0	39	10	2	6	.252	.283	.326
Stefanski, Mike, Louisville	64	219	202	20	44	62	7	1	3	20	1	2	1	13	0	30	1	1	3	.218	.266	.307
Stenson, Dernell, Louisville *	17	65	59	9	14	32	3	0	5	14	0	1	0	5	0	10	0	0	1	.237	.292	.542
Stevens, Lee, Indianapolis *	18	70	64	8	18	26	2	0	2	8	0	0	0	6	0	17	0	0	1	.281	.343	.406
Stewart, Shannon, Syracuse	1	4	3	0	0	0	0	0	0	0	0	0	0	1	0	0	0	0	0	.000	.250	.000
Strange, Pat, Norfolk	31	6	6	0	0	0	0	0	0	0	0	0	0	0	0	4	0	0	0	.000	.000	.000
Swann, Pedro, Ottawa *	121	458	418	62	117	172	21	2	10	53	2	1	2	35	3	73	4	6	17	.280	.338	.411
Sylvester, Billy, Richmond	12	1	0	0	0	0	0	0	0	0	0	0	0	1	0	0	0	0	0	.000	1.000	.000
Taveras, Luis, Toledo	16	44	39	3	5	9	1	0	1	1	1	0	0	4	0	8	0	0	1	.128	.209	.231
Telemaco, Amaury, S./WB	25	15	13	1	2	3	1	0	0	1	1	0	0	1	0	6	0	0	0	.154	.214	.231
Teut, Nate, Indianapolis	18	13	11	2	3	3	0	0	0	0	0	0	0	2	0	1	0	0	0	.273	.385	.273
Thames, Marcus, Columbus	52	217	194	26	54	79	15	2	2	28	0	5	1	17	0	48	3	4	4	.278	.332	.407
Thomas, Juan, Louisville	9	34	31	3	5	6	1	0	0	2	0	0	1	2	0	12	0	0	1	.161	.235	.194
Thompson, Rich, Syracuse *	28	129	112	13	33	37	2	1	0	7	3	0	5	9	0	10	11	1	2	.295	.373	.330
Thompson, Ryan, Durham	2	8	8	0	1	1	0	0	0	0	0	0	0	0	0	3	0	0	1	.125	.125	.125
Toca, Jorge, Norfolk	115	450	424	38	116	167	30	0	7	52	2	5	2	17	1	71	7	1	21	.274	.301	.394
Torres, Andres, Toledo	70	299	271	36	69	94	13	3	2	16	10	0	0	18	0	61	27	11	1	.255	.301	.347
Torres, Gabby, Rochester	21	59	55	4	10	11	1	0	0	2	1	0	1	2	0	8	0	0	0	.182	.224	.200
Truby, Chris, Durham	112	484	430	57	113	188	27	0	16	48	0	3	7	44	4	77	4	6	11	.263	.339	.437
Tyner, Jason, Durham *	65	307	275	34	89	110	11	5	0	24	6	3	1	22	1	25	10	7	5	.324	.372	.400
Umbria, Jose, Syracuse	7	26	23	1	2	2	0	0	0	5	0	2	0	1	0	6	0	0	1	.087	.115	.087
Ust, Brant, Toledo	86	319	296	26	75	119	25	2	5	31	2	2	5	14	0	61	1	3	9	.253	.297	.402
Utley, Chase, Scranton/WB *	113	490	431	80	139	223	26	2	18	77	0	7	11	41	6	75	10	4	3	.323	.390	.517
Valencia, Vic, Buffalo	10	35	35	5	11	16	2	0	1	1	0	0	0	0	0	14	0	0	0	.314	.314	.457
Valent, Eric, Scranton/WB *	134	520	450	62	98	165	27	2	12	51	4	5	1	60	5	102	0	0	5	.218	.308	.367
Valentine, Joe, Louisville	9	1	1	0	1	1	0	0	0	0	0	0	0	0	0	0	0	0	0	1.000	1.000	1.000
Valenzuela, Mario, Charlotte	31	119	114	14	29	43	5	0	3	10	0	1	1	3	0	25	1	0	3	.254	.277	.377
Valera, Yohanny, Toledo	65	207	188	20	37	58	12	0	3	18	5	0	4	10	0	63	1	1	6	.197	.252	.309
Van Poppel, Todd, Louisville	20	6	6	0	0	0	0	0	0	0	0	0	0	0	0	4	0	0	0	.000	.000	.000
Velandia, Jorge, Norfolk	111	427	374	45	88	147	22	2	11	48	6	6	4	37	2	90	2	5	9	.235	.306	.393
Velazquez, Gil, Norfolk	5	16	16	0	4	4	0	0	0	2	0	0	0	0	0	5	0	1	0	.250	.250	.250
Vento, Mike, Columbus	51	201	184	28	56	87	14	1	5	31	0	0	3	14	0	36	1	2	6	.304	.363	.473
Veras, Wilton, Indianapolis	119	434	402	35	89	111	14	1	2	23	3	3	3	23	1	36	2	4	17	.221	.267	.276
Wakeland, Chris, Buffalo *	16	49	45	2	10	14	1	0	1	6	1	1	0	2	0	17	0	0	2	.222	.250	.311
Walbeck, Matt, Toledo †	4	15	12	2	5	5	0	0	0	1	0	0	0	3	0	2	0	0	0	.417	.533	.417
Wathan, Dusty, Buffalo	61	213	188	21	52	65	7	0	2	15	2	0	5	18	0	31	3	0	4	.277	.355	.346
Watson, Mark, Louisville	44	4	3	1	1	1	0	0	0	1	0	0	0	1	0	2	0	0	0	.333	.500	.333
Watson, Matt, Norfolk *	74	291	254	40	75	128	18	1	11	55	1	5	8	23	1	23	2	2	4	.295	.366	.504
Werth, Jayson, Syracuse	64	256	236	37	56	104	19	1	9	34	0	3	2	15	1	68	11	1	7	.237	.285	.441
Wheeler, Dan, Norfolk	22	2	1	0	0	0	0	0	0	0	1	0	0	0	0	1	0	0	0	.000	.000	.000
White, Derrick, Buffalo	10	38	37	3	9	13	1	0	1	7	0	0	1	0	0	13	1	0	1	.243	.263	.351
Williams, Glenn, Syracuse †	59	226	210	27	49	74	10	3	3	24	2	1	1	12	2	56	2	1	6	.233	.277	.352
Wilson, Craig, Columbus	103	452	403	52	107	145	17	0	7	40	9	0	2	38	0	54	1	2	15	.266	.332	.360
Wilson, John, Norfolk	37	112	100	6	19	22	3	0	0	6	2	1	2	7	0	13	0	0	3	.190	.255	.220
Wilson, Travis, Richmond	121	434	409	38	105	157	26	4	6	39	5	3	8	9	0	110	5	2	8	.257	.284	.384
Wise, Dewayne, Syracuse *	80	308	285	37	62	111	11	4	10	37	3	2	1	17	0	72	11	3	10	.218	.262	.389
Witt, Kevin, Toledo *	39	151	133	22	42	79	10	0	9	28	0	1	1	16	1	36	0	0	2	.316	.391	.594
Wright, Ron, Toledo	5	19	17	0	3	3	0	0	0	3	0	0	1	1	0	6	0	0	0	.176	.263	.176
Yates, Tyler, Norfolk	4	3	3	0	0	0	0	0	0	0	0	0	0	0	0	1	0	0	0	.000	.000	.000
Youkilis, Kevin, Pawtucket	32	132	109	9	18	27	3	0	2	15	0	2	3	18	2	21	0	1	2	.165	.295	.248
Young, Ernie, Toledo	128	515	454	56	120	205	22	0	21	84	0	5	6	50	1	119	10	6	10	.264	.342	.452
Young, Kevin, Rochester	4	10	7	0	1	2	1	0	0	1	0	0	0	3	0	3	0	0	1	.143	.400	.286
Zamora, Pete, Norfolk *	56	10	9	2	4	4	0	0	0	0	0	0	1	0	0	0	0	0	1	.444	.500	.444
Zoccolillo, Peter, Ind.*	132	514	443	57	124	198	36	1	12	73	0	10	10	51	1	70	3	5	14	.280	.360	.447
Zuleta, Julio, Pawtucket	55	229	204	28	56	103	11	0	12	49	0	4	8	13	0	47	0	0	3	.275	.336	.505
Zuniga, Tony, Syracuse	71	290	261	33	77	133	20	0	12	41	0	1	1	27	0	47	0	2	10	.295	.362	.510

PLAYERS WITH TWO OR MORE TEAMS

Player, Team	G	TPA	AB	R	H	TB	2B	3B	HR	RBI	SH	SF	HP	BB	IBB	SO	SB	CS	GDP	Avg.	OBP	Slg.
Adkins, Tim, Columbus *	28	0	0	0	0	0	0	0	0	0	0	0	0	0	0	0	0	0	0	.000	.000	.000
Adkins, Tim, Louisville *	12	1	1	0	0	0	0	0	0	0	0	0	0	0	0	1	0	0	0	.000	.000	.000
Anderson, Jason, Col.*	6	0	0	0	0	0	0	0	0	0	0	0	0	0	0	0	0	0	0	.000	.000	.000
Anderson, Jason, Norfolk *	10	3	3	1	1	1	0	0	0	0	0	0	0	0	0	1	0	0	0	.333	.333	.333
Bale, John, Louisville *	27	5	5	0	0	0	0	0	0	0	0	0	0	0	0	3	0	0	0	.000	.000	.000
Bale, John, Norfolk *	8	0	0	0	0	0	0	0	0	0	0	0	0	0	0	0	0	0	0	.000	.000	.000
Belisle, Matt, Richmond †	3	4	3	1	1	1	0	0	0	0	0	0	0	1	0	0	0	0	0	.333	.500	.333
Belisle, Matt, Louisville †	4	2	2	0	0	0	0	0	0	0	0	0	0	0	0	0	0	0	0	.000	.000	.000

Player, Team	G	TPA	AB	R	H	TB	2B	3B	HR	RBI	SH	SF	HP	BB	IBB	SO	SB	CS	GDP	Avg.	OBP	Slg.
Budzinski, Mark, Louisville * .	74	302	259	53	71	95	15	3	1	15	2	1	3	37	0	56	10	4	1	.274	.370	.367
Budzinski, Mark, Ind.*	46	181	159	27	43	55	7	1	1	12	4	1	1	16	0	39	7	2	0	.270	.339	.346
Burba, Dave, Indianapolis	10	7	7	1	3	4	1	0	0	3	0	0	0	0	0	0	0	0	0	.429	.429	.571
Burba, Dave, Buffalo	4	0	0	0	0	0	0	0	0	0	0	0	0	0	0	0	0	0	0	.000	.000	.000
Dransfeldt, Kelly, Louisville	46	152	140	15	30	49	9	2	2	12	0	2	1	9	0	34	0	1	3	.214	.263	.350
Dransfeldt, Kelly, Pawtucket...	66	234	214	29	45	76	11	1	6	34	0	1	3	16	0	53	0	1	5	.210	.274	.355
Ennis, John, Toledo	3	0	0	0	0	0	0	0	0	0	0	0	0	0	0	0	0	0	0	.000	.000	.000
Ennis, John, Richmond	28	5	4	0	0	0	0	0	0	0	0	0	0	1	0	1	0	0	0	.000	.200	.000
Magee, Wendell, Toledo	53	203	192	13	41	58	7	2	2	18	1	1	0	9	0	46	0	3	6	.214	.248	.302
Magee, Wendell, S./WB..........	25	105	93	11	31	44	8	1	1	12	0	2	2	8	1	16	1	3	5	.333	.390	.473
McGuire, Ryan, Columbus * ..	65	218	191	17	44	59	7	1	2	19	0	2	1	23	2	36	0	0	3	.230	.313	.309
McGuire, Ryan, Rochester * ..	24	88	76	10	23	32	6	0	1	9	0	1	2	9	1	23	0	1	2	.303	.386	.421
Miller, Travis, Louisville..........	4	0	0	0	0	0	0	0	0	0	0	0	0	0	0	0	0	0	0	.000	.000	.000
Miller, Travis, Indianapolis......	16	3	2	1	1	1	0	0	0	0	1	0	0	0	0	1	0	0	0	.500	.500	.500
Mottola, Chad, Pawtucket	21	80	72	11	23	39	3	2	3	18	1	0	1	6	0	10	0	1	1	.319	.380	.542
Mottola, Chad, Durham	56	236	213	24	55	82	7	1	6	28	1	2	1	19	1	37	6	3	4	.258	.319	.385
Mouton, Lyle, Scranton/WB ...	10	38	31	3	9	11	2	0	0	4	0	1	0	6	0	8	1	0	1	.290	.395	.355
Mouton, Lyle, Buffalo	49	188	170	21	48	90	10	1	10	30	0	4	1	13	1	36	1	1	10	.282	.330	.529
Mouton, Lyle, Norfolk	47	176	151	24	42	66	10	1	4	24	1	1	5	18	0	49	6	1	4	.278	.371	.437
Myette, Aaron, Buffalo	23	0	0	0	0	0	0	0	0	0	0	0	0	0	0	0	0	0	0	.000	.000	.000
Myette, Aaron, Scranton/WB..	11	5	5	0	2	2	0	0	0	2	0	0	0	0	0	2	0	0	0	.400	.400	.400
Perez, Santiago, Louisville † ..	6	21	16	1	2	5	0	0	1	1	1	0	0	4	0	2	1	0	1	.125	.300	.313
Perez, Santiago, Ottawa †	13	39	35	4	9	11	2	0	0	1	0	0	0	4	0	9	2	2	1	.257	.333	.314
Riggan, Jerrod, Norfolk	5	1	1	0	0	0	0	0	0	0	0	0	0	0	0	0	0	0	0	.000	.000	.000
Riggan, Jerrod, Buffalo	9	0	0	0	0	0	0	0	0	0	0	0	0	0	0	0	0	0	0	.000	.000	.000
Santos, Angel, Pawtucket † ...	70	252	214	25	51	74	8	0	5	20	4	1	1	32	2	50	9	4	6	.238	.339	.346
Santos, Angel, Buffalo †	13	51	46	10	11	19	2	0	2	8	0	0	0	5	0	8	5	0	0	.239	.314	.413

GRAND SLAMS—Restovich, Zuleta, 2 each; Abad, Brumbaugh, Chapman, F. Crespo, Cruz, Dominique, Klassen, Larson, Luuloa, Machado, Miller, Morris, Mottola, Nieves, Peralta, Pride, A. Rios, Rushford, Salazar, Sanders, Sasser, Scarborough, Sefcik, J. Smith, Velandia, Vento, Werth, White, Youkilis, 1 each.

AWARDED FIRST BASE ON CATCHER'S INTERFERENCE—Garabito 2 (DePastino, LaForest); N. Green 2 (Salazar, Stefanski); Lombard 2 (Burke, M. Hernandez); Diaz (Acevas); Jordan (Acevas); McGuire (Salazar); Luuloa (Salazar); Sasser (Bard); Sosa (Wathan).

2003 PITCHING

TEAM

Team	W	L	Pct.	ERA	G	CG	ShO	Sv.	IP	H	TBF	R	ER	HR	SH	SF	HB	BB	IBB	SO	WP	Bk.
Richmond	64	79	.448	3.64	143	4	13	41	1237.0	1191	5331	582	500	87	54	46	63	495	15	1086	58	11
Ottawa..............	79	65	.549	3.66	144	3	6	45	1243.0	1166	5296	579	505	79	43	52	42	482	38	1029	63	8
Toledo	65	78	.455	3.72	143	10	8	37	1241.0	1286	5310	619	513	106	56	38	62	389	39	813	43	8
Scranton/WB.....	73	70	.510	3.79	143	8	15	35	1245.2	1218	5218	597	525	92	45	51	57	334	20	963	30	6
Pawtucket	83	61	.576	3.83	144	3	12	32	1239.0	1225	5251	616	527	113	29	33	52	350	9	993	53	2
Durham	73	67	.521	3.90	140	2	6	41	1237.2	1245	5235	602	536	124	41	35	50	350	14	844	75	4
Indianapolis.......	64	78	.451	3.93	142	3	10	33	1241.1	1273	5324	627	542	115	49	32	66	416	14	974	48	9
Buffalo..............	73	70	.510	4.01	143	5	8	38	1244.2	1242	5367	623	554	110	45	38	63	456	28	969	46	13
Louisville..........	79	64	.552	4.08	143	4	7	38	1243.2	1357	5313	630	564	92	45	53	44	349	9	846	38	7
Norfolk	67	76	.469	4.10	143	3	8	35	1239.0	1277	5274	614	565	106	46	37	62	398	15	943	36	8
Columbus..........	76	68	.528	4.18	144	5	7	34	1269.1	1294	5483	674	589	118	53	40	47	458	17	964	37	8
Rochester..........	68	75	.476	4.26	143	6	5	36	1234.0	1312	5286	653	584	103	56	44	46	367	14	931	68	8
Syracuse	62	79	.440	4.39	141	7	7	29	1216.2	1290	5310	675	594	114	44	51	56	439	27	892	69	1
Charlotte	74	70	.514	4.40	144	8	11	45	1227.2	1279	5300	662	600	142	42	52	74	377	29	899	37	5

INDIVIDUAL

TOP QUALIFIERS FOR EARNED-RUN AVERAGE TITLE

Minimum 115 innings. *Lefthanded pitcher.

Pitcher, Team	W	L	Pct.	ERA	G	GS	CG	ShO	GF	Sv.	IP	H	TBF	R	ER	HR	SH	SF	HB	BB	IBB	SO	WP	Bk.
Griffiths, Jeremy, Norfolk	7	6	.538	2.74	21	19	1	0	1	1	115.0	94	459	43	35	6	1	4	9	26	0	78	5	0
Reyes, Carlos, Durham	10	3	.769	2.86	22	21	1	0	0	0	132.1	124	522	47	42	9	2	1	1	14	1	78	7	0
Loux, Shane, Toledo	11	6	.647	3.02	21	20	2	1	0	0	128.0	129	531	53	43	5	4	5	6	30	0	58	4	0
Robertson, Nathan, Toledo *...	9	7	.563	3.14	24	23	3	1	1	0	155.0	145	640	62	54	14	4	2	6	47	2	102	0	0
Telemaco, Amaury, S./WB.......	10	9	.526	3.24	25	24	3	2	0	0	155.1	125	599	59	56	15	6	4	3	22	1	116	5	0
Towers, Josh, Syracuse	5	7	.417	3.32	21	20	1	1	0	0	132.2	133	545	55	49	10	4	5	2	20	1	76	3	0
Douglass, Sean, Ottawa	10	8	.556	3.40	27	27	0	0	0	0	143.0	142	624	67	54	6	2	5	5	58	4	118	10	0
Pratt, Andy, Richmond *	7	10	.412	3.40	28	27	1	0	0	0	156.0	146	685	77	59	10	5	8	11	77	0	161	14	0
Stanford, Jason, Buffalo *.......	10	4	.714	3.43	20	20	1	0	0	0	126.0	124	515	57	48	13	4	4	5	25	1	108	2	2
Arroyo, Bronson, Pawtucket ...	12	6	.667	3.43	24	24	1	1	0	0	149.2	148	627	66	57	9	5	1	10	23	0	155	8	0
Madson, Ryan, Scranton/WB ..	12	8	.600	3.50	26	26	0	0	0	0	157.0	157	658	70	61	9	2	5	10	42	2	138	6	0
Pulido, Carlos, Rochester *.....	12	5	.706	3.56	25	25	1	0	0	0	149.1	145	611	65	59	13	8	7	2	40	0	87	3	0
Hancock, Josh, Scranton/WB..	10	9	.526	3.86	28	27	2	2	1	0	165.2	147	677	78	71	14	2	6	6	46	1	122	4	0
Adkins, Jon, Charlotte	7	8	.467	3.96	26	19	1	1	2	1	122.2	119	518	65	54	11	2	7	7	34	1	59	2	1
Diaz, Felix, Charlotte	5	7	.417	3.97	27	18	1	0	3	0	115.2	122	497	59	51	12	3	5	4	33	3	83	5	2

DEPARTMENTAL LEADERS: W—Cooper, 15; L—Five pitchers tied with 11; Pct.—Phillips, .909; G—Cubillan, 65; GS—Cooper, 28; CG—De Paula, Marquis, Robertson, Telemaco, 3; ShO—De Paula, Hancock, Telemaco, 2; GF—Gardner, 49; Sv.—Gardner, 30; IP—Cooper, 174.1; H—Cooper, 195; TBF—Cooper, 746; R—Coco, Cooper, James, 91 each; ER—De Paula, 81; HR—De Paula, 22; SH—Ennis, 16; SF—Cooper, 11; HB—Fussell, 19; BB—Pratt, 77; IBB—Brittan, Cassidy, Paronto, 7 each; SO—Pratt, 161; WP—M. Smith, 16; BK—Coco, 6.

ALL PITCHERS

*Lefthanded pitcher.

Pitcher, Team	W	L	Pct.	ERA	G	GS	CG	ShO	GF	Sv.	IP	H	TBF	R	ER	HR	SH	SF	HB	BB	IBB	SO	WP	Bk.
Abbott, David, Syracuse	1	0	1.000	6.00	1	1	0	0	0	0	6.0	7	24	4	4	3	1	0	0	1	0	2	0	0
Acevedo, Jose, Louisville	6	2	.750	3.43	29	3	0	0	9	0	60.1	56	253	26	23	5	1	2	1	20	1	57	2	0
Adkins, Jon, Charlotte	7	8	.467	3.96	26	19	1	1	2	1	122.2	119	518	65	54	11	2	7	7	34	1	59	2	1
Adkins, Tim, Lou.-Columbus *	3	3	.500	4.63	40	1	0	0	11	0	58.1	53	255	30	30	3	3	1	4	35	2	43	3	0
Aguilar, Ray, Richmond *	1	0	1.000	1.80	1	1	0	0	0	0	5.0	2	18	1	1	0	0	0	0	2	0	5	0	0
Ahearne, Pat, Toledo	4	5	.444	3.36	15	15	1	1	0	0	101.2	97	421	43	38	6	4	3	3	26	1	57	2	0
Aldred, Scott, Pawtucket *	2	1	.667	4.63	11	0	0	0	1	0	11.2	10	52	6	6	1	0	0	1	7	0	11	0	0
Almanzar, Carlos, Louisville	2	2	.500	3.50	42	0	0	0	37	23	46.1	47	193	19	18	2	1	1	1	3	0	54	0	0
Almonte, Ed, Char.-Norfolk	3	7	.300	5.40	46	0	0	0	36	20	51.2	61	236	32	31	6	6	4	2	20	4	38	1	0
Almonte, Hector, Pawtucket	3	0	1.000	1.73	21	0	0	0	17	9	26.0	16	97	5	5	2	0	0	0	6	0	28	0	0
Anderson, Jason, Col.-Norfolk	1	3	.250	2.03	16	5	0	0	10	7	31.0	21	120	8	7	3	1	0	0	9	0	22	1	1
Anderson, Jimmy, Louisville *	6	1	.857	3.12	9	9	0	0	0	0	60.2	61	248	26	21	2	3	1	0	14	0	30	4	0
Anderson, Matt, Toledo	1	3	.250	3.79	23	5	0	0	9	3	38.0	50	170	23	16	4	2	0	1	8	1	31	0	0
Andrews, Shane, Rochester	0	0	.000	0.00	1	0	0	0	1	0	1.0	1	3	0	0	0	0	0	0	0	0	0	0	0
Arnold, Jason, Syracuse	4	8	.333	4.33	21	20	1	0	0	0	120.2	121	522	69	58	16	4	6	4	46	2	82	3	0
Arrojo, Rolando, Columbus	1	0	1.000	2.00	4	1	0	0	1	0	9.0	5	37	2	2	0	0	0	1	5	0	10	0	0
Arroyo, Bronson, Pawtucket	12	6	.667	3.43	24	24	1	1	0	0	149.2	148	627	66	57	9	5	1	10	23	0	155	8	0
Austin, Jeff, Louisville	4	2	.667	4.34	9	9	0	0	0	0	45.2	46	196	24	22	5	1	2	1	19	0	37	4	1
Avery, Steve, Toledo *	1	4	.200	3.15	22	2	0	0	4	0	34.1	37	146	16	12	6	2	4	0	10	3	14	1	0
Backe, Brandon, Durham	2	1	.667	4.64	16	2	0	0	4	0	33.0	33	147	21	17	1	0	2	0	13	0	27	1	1
Bacsik, Mike, Norfolk *	2	9	.182	4.97	22	21	0	0	0	0	117.2	129	507	70	65	13	10	6	9	34	1	62	2	1
Baker, Chris, Syracuse	0	1	.000	10.80	2	2	0	0	0	0	6.2	11	34	8	8	1	0	1	1	4	0	4	0	0
Baldwin, James, Rochester	0	2	.000	2.43	5	5	0	0	0	0	29.2	25	114	11	8	2	0	0	0	3	0	18	0	0
Bale, John, Norfolk-Lou.*	4	2	.667	3.30	34	2	0	0	15	4	57.1	47	236	22	21	1	2	3	2	16	0	58	1	0
Balfour, Grant, Rochester	5	2	.714	2.41	21	11	0	0	10	5	71.0	48	276	21	19	6	1	0	3	16	0	87	0	1
Banks, Willie, Columbus	2	3	.400	3.89	31	0	0	0	19	3	39.1	42	171	21	17	5	1	3	0	19	1	26	4	0
Bauer, Rick, Ottawa	3	1	.750	2.45	7	7	0	0	0	0	36.2	31	150	10	10	1	1	1	3	13	0	21	0	0
Beal, Andy, Columbus *	1	6	.143	7.45	8	8	0	0	0	0	38.2	51	176	35	32	8	2	2	1	11	0	25	2	0
Bean, Colter, Columbus	4	2	.667	2.87	50	0	0	0	17	4	69.0	53	289	33	22	5	1	4	5	27	2	70	1	1
Beech, Matt, Columbus *	0	0	.000	0.00	2	0	0	0	0	0	2.2	2	12	0	0	0	1	0	0	2	0	4	0	0
Belisle, Matt, Richmond-Lou.	2	4	.333	3.13	7	7	0	0	0	0	46.0	48	185	21	16	3	0	1	3	5	0	25	0	0
Belitz, Todd, Durham *	2	1	.667	3.38	24	1	0	0	1	0	32.0	27	126	14	12	2	2	2	1	7	1	25	0	0
Bell, Heath, Norfolk	2	3	.400	4.71	40	0	0	0	25	3	49.2	54	206	26	26	4	2	4	2	8	0	54	4	0
Bell, Rob, Durham	6	4	.600	4.02	12	12	0	0	0	0	71.2	72	297	33	32	10	4	1	0	15	1	48	5	0
Beltran, Rigo, Ottawa *	5	4	.556	2.71	31	13	2	1	1	1	103.0	77	412	33	31	3	6	1	3	41	3	69	3	0
Bere, Jason, Buffalo	1	0	1.000	0.61	3	3	0	0	0	0	14.2	9	53	1	1	0	0	0	0	3	1	17	0	0
Betancourt, Rafael, Buffalo	0	0	.000	4.05	4	0	0	0	2	1	6.2	6	27	3	3	1	0	0	0	2	0	6	1	0
Bevel, Bobby, Louisville *	0	0	.000	18.00	2	0	0	0	1	0	1.0	5	7	3	2	1	0	0	0	0	0	0	0	0
Bevis, P.J., Norfolk	1	0	1.000	0.00	4	0	0	0	2	0	8.1	2	29	0	0	0	0	0	0	2	0	8	0	1
Bierbrodt, Nick, Buffalo *	2	2	.500	3.00	16	1	0	0	5	0	27.0	22	121	10	9	1	2	0	2	18	2	31	1	0
Bong, Jung, Richmond *	1	2	.333	5.56	3	3	0	0	0	0	11.1	11	49	7	7	1	0	0	0	3	0	15	0	0
Borrell, Danny, Columbus *	4	2	.667	2.93	10	10	0	0	0	0	55.1	55	241	24	18	4	3	3	1	22	1	30	1	1
Bowers, Cedrick, Durham *	4	3	.571	4.41	32	8	0	0	5	2	83.2	75	364	46	41	6	4	8	6	39	0	80	12	0
Bowles, Brian, Syracuse	2	3	.400	2.66	41	0	0	0	34	14	47.1	47	210	23	14	1	4	0	2	21	3	32	2	0
Boyd, Jason, Buffalo	1	0	1.000	1.23	9	0	0	0	5	3	14.2	12	56	3	2	0	0	0	0	2	0	14	1	0
Brazelton, Dewon, Durham	2	2	.500	4.21	5	5	0	0	0	0	25.2	23	110	14	12	1	0	1	0	11	0	18	0	0
Brittan, Corey, Toledo	5	5	.500	3.73	44	1	0	0	18	1	62.2	74	281	36	26	3	7	4	2	23	7	24	4	2
Brown, Jamie, Buf.-Pawtucket	8	5	.615	2.95	31	13	0	0	6	1	113.0	85	448	43	37	5	7	3	7	22	2	65	2	0
Buddie, Mike, Indianapolis	0	4	.000	3.75	18	2	0	0	3	0	36.0	32	147	16	15	5	2	0	2	12	0	18	1	0
Burba, Dave, Buf.-Ind.	6	7	.462	4.33	14	13	0	0	0	0	72.2	83	311	43	35	6	1	2	2	21	0	44	4	0
Cabrera, Jose, Scranton/WB	3	4	.429	2.76	25	1	0	0	10	1	45.2	45	184	16	14	2	3	1	2	10	2	33	1	0
Cameron, Ryan, Pawtucket	1	3	.250	4.79	27	1	0	0	7	1	56.1	56	258	32	30	6	0	2	4	34	1	46	5	0
Cammack, Eric, Norfolk	0	0	.000	4.50	5	0	0	0	2	1	8.0	6	31	4	4	1	0	0	0	1	0	7	0	0
Campos, Francisco, Ind.	2	4	.333	5.72	8	8	0	0	0	0	39.1	53	184	30	25	8	0	1	6	12	0	28	3	0
Caracciolo, Lance, Buffalo *	4	8	.333	5.10	34	13	0	0	5	2	100.2	123	450	61	57	11	2	7	7	35	2	83	5	2
Carnes, Matt, Rochester	2	7	.222	5.28	25	20	0	0	2	0	119.1	141	510	74	70	13	8	6	0	26	1	70	4	1
Carrasco, Hector, Ottawa	4	2	.667	2.22	33	0	0	0	16	4	44.2	32	181	11	11	2	4	3	0	20	2	47	7	1
Cassidy, Scott, Syracuse	3	4	.429	3.24	57	0	0	0	21	4	80.2	75	354	31	29	3	2	6	3	46	7	75	5	0
Castillo, Carlos, Charlotte	0	1	.000	9.77	6	1	0	0	2	0	15.2	24	79	19	17	4	0	1	1	7	0	9	3	0
Castillo, Frank, Richmond	0	1	.000	1.50	4	3	0	0	0	0	18.0	23	79	5	3	1	0	0	0	4	0	14	0	0
Cerda, Jaime, Norfolk *	3	0	1.000	1.67	22	0	0	0	4	0	32.1	29	131	7	6	3	1	1	1	10	1	35	0	0
Cerros, Juan, Louisville	0	0	.000	4.50	4	0	0	0	1	0	4.0	6	17	2	2	0	0	0	0	0	0	1	0	0
Chen, Bruce, Pawtucket *	5	5	.500	4.24	16	15	1	1	1	1	85.0	80	347	44	40	12	1	1	2	15	1	73	2	0
Chevalier, Virgil, Norfolk	0	0	.000	0.00	1	0	0	0	1	0	1.0	1	4	0	0	0	0	0	0	0	0	1	0	0
Childers, Jason, Indianapolis	5	4	.556	2.29	46	0	0	0	24	10	63.0	50	255	22	16	6	4	0	1	20	2	47	1	0
Childers, Matt, Indianapolis	3	0	1.000	0.47	11	0	0	0	4	0	19.0	15	75	2	1	1	2	0	0	6	2	19	0	0
Choate, Randy, Columbus *	3	5	.375	3.91	54	3	0	0	15	1	71.1	75	312	35	31	4	7	1	3	24	3	56	0	0
Chulk, Vinny, Syracuse	8	10	.444	4.22	23	21	1	0	1	0	119.1	118	524	70	56	14	6	6	5	46	0	90	5	0
Clapp, Stubby, Richmond	0	0	.000	0.00	2	0	0	0	2	0	1.1	2	6	0	0	0	0	0	0	0	0	0	0	0
Claussen, Brandon, Col.-Lou.*	2	2	.500	3.63	14	14	1	0	0	0	84.1	70	340	41	34	7	2	6	1	24	0	55	0	2
Coco, Pasqual, Indianapolis	10	9	.526	4.80	27	27	1	0	0	0	146.1	168	644	91	78	17	6	2	13	46	2	100	11	6
Coggin, Dave, Scranton/WB	0	0	.000	1.50	4	3	0	0	0	0	6.0	4	22	1	1	0	0	0	1	1	0	3	0	0
Colangelo, Mike, Syracuse	0	0	.000	0.00	1	0	0	0	1	0	1.0	2	5	0	0	0	0	0	1	0	0	1	0	0
Contreras, Jose, Columbus	2	0	1.000	1.20	3	3	0	0	0	0	15.0	10	56	2	2	1	0	0	1	2	0	18	0	0
Cooper, Brian, Charlotte	15	9	.625	3.98	28	28	2	0	0	0	174.1	195	746	91	77	18	4	11	12	35	2	106	0	0
Cortes, David, Buffalo	1	0	1.000	2.70	5	0	0	0	2	1	6.2	4	26	3	2	1	0	0	0	0	0	9	0	0
Cortes, Jorge, Louisville	0	0	.000	0.00	1	0	0	0	1	0	1.0	0	3	0	0	0	0	0	0	0	0	0	0	0
Coste, Chris, Pawtucket	0	0	.000	9.00	2	0	0	0	2	0	2.0	2	9	2	2	1	0	0	0	1	0	1	0	0

Pitcher, Team	W	L	Pct.	ERA	G	GS	CG	ShO	GF	Sv.	IP	H	TBF	R	ER	HR	SH	SF	HB	BB	IBB	SO	WP	Bk.
Crain, Jesse, Rochester	3	1	.750	3.12	23	0	0	0	20	10	26.0	24	113	10	9	0	3	1	1	10	1	33	2	0
Cressend, Jack, Buffalo	1	0	1.000	1.23	8	0	0	0	2	0	14.2	7	56	2	2	0	2	1	0	6	0	12	0	0
Croushore, Rick, Ottawa-Lou.	1	0	1.000	2.63	14	0	0	0	5	0	13.2	10	63	4	4	0	1	1	1	14	1	13	1	0
Crowell, Jim, Scranton/WB *	0	8	.000	4.12	54	0	0	0	34	9	54.2	63	251	31	25	5	5	2	2	23	5	42	0	1
Crudale, Mike, Indianapolis	0	0	.000	0.00	2	0	0	0	1	0	2.0	1	7	0	0	0	0	0	0	0	0	1	0	0
Cubillan, Darwin, Ottawa	5	6	.455	3.21	65	0	0	0	39	20	73.0	57	307	29	26	6	2	3	0	34	6	77	7	0
Cunnane, Will, Richmond	1	0	1.000	0.00	15	0	0	0	7	2	21.0	11	74	2	0	0	0	3	0	2	0	19	1	0
Davey, Tom, Pawtucket	1	2	.333	3.45	16	0	0	0	0	0	28.2	28	126	14	11	0	0	0	0	16	0	28	9	0
Davis, Doug, Indianapolis *	1	2	.333	4.15	5	5	0	0	0	0	34.2	33	145	16	16	2	1	0	2	10	0	19	0	0
Davis, Lance, Louisville *	8	9	.471	4.55	26	22	1	1	0	0	138.1	166	609	75	70	14	4	8	1	42	1	62	2	1
Dawley, Joey, Richmond	3	5	.375	3.34	46	4	0	0	35	23	56.2	47	240	25	21	4	0	4	0	23	1	73	5	0
De La Cruz, Fernando, Toledo	0	0	.000	13.50	2	0	0	0	0	0	3.1	6	19	5	5	1	0	0	0	2	0	4	0	0
De La Rosa, Jorge, Paw.*	1	2	.333	3.75	5	5	0	0	0	0	24.0	27	110	14	10	0	1	0	0	12	0	17	2	1
De Los Santos, Luis, Durham	1	3	.250	5.57	4	4	0	0	0	0	21.0	28	92	15	13	2	1	2	3	1	0	3	1	0
De Paula, Jorge, Columbus	10	11	.476	4.35	27	27	3	2	0	0	167.2	168	712	90	81	22	6	2	6	57	2	125	1	0
DePaula, Sean, Louisville	0	0	.000	6.17	10	0	0	0	3	0	11.2	15	57	10	8	1	0	0	2	7	0	8	0	0
Dempster, Ryan, Louisville	1	1	.500	3.29	2	2	1	0	0	0	13.2	13	55	5	5	1	0	1	0	3	0	9	1	0
Denney, Kyle, Buffalo	2	1	.667	5.28	6	6	0	0	0	0	30.2	35	139	18	18	4	1	0	1	10	2	26	0	0
Diaz, Felix, Charlotte	5	7	.417	3.97	27	18	1	0	3	0	115.2	122	497	59	51	12	3	5	4	33	3	83	5	2
Douglass, Sean, Ottawa	10	8	.556	3.40	27	27	0	0	0	0	143.0	142	624	67	54	6	2	5	5	58	4	118	10	0
Driskill, Travis, Ottawa	4	0	1.000	2.84	9	9	0	0	0	0	50.2	46	202	17	16	8	2	1	0	6	0	36	5	0
Drumright, Mike, Ottawa	4	5	.444	5.55	23	15	0	0	1	0	94.0	106	421	65	58	7	2	4	1	41	0	70	4	3
Dubose, Eric, Ottawa *	9	5	.643	3.39	19	19	0	0	0	0	114.0	112	476	49	43	7	5	3	5	34	2	107	2	0
Duckworth, Brandon, S./WB	2	1	.667	3.38	3	3	0	0	0	0	18.2	21	82	11	7	3	1	0	2	4	0	14	0	0
Durbin, Chad, Buffalo	3	6	.333	4.60	10	10	1	0	0	0	58.2	51	241	30	30	9	1	0	5	16	0	64	2	0
Durocher, Jayson, Ind.	0	0	.000	2.57	7	3	0	0	2	0	7.0	7	30	2	2	0	0	0	0	1	0	9	1	0
Duvall, Mike, Rochester *	1	4	.200	5.48	24	6	0	0	6	0	44.1	59	206	32	27	7	1	0	1	15	1	29	1	0
Eason, Clay, Charlotte	0	0	.000	12.23	8	0	0	0	3	0	17.2	30	94	24	24	7	0	0	2	12	1	14	1	0
Ebert, Derrin, Indianapolis *	0	2	.000	4.50	4	1	0	0	0	0	10.0	11	37	5	5	1	0	0	0	3	0	6	0	0
Eckenstahler, Eric, Toledo *	3	6	.333	3.16	39	0	0	0	9	0	42.2	32	186	21	15	2	4	0	7	25	3	40	4	0
Elder, Dave, Buffalo	0	0	.000	0.00	8	0	0	0	6	6	12.2	5	47	0	0	0	0	0	0	6	0	17	0	0
Elmore, Chris, Pawtucket *	2	2	.500	5.24	8	8	0	0	0	0	34.1	37	151	20	20	3	1	1	2	18	0	19	0	0
Emiliano, Jamie, Richmond	0	7	.000	4.07	53	0	0	0	19	1	73.0	80	324	41	33	5	4	2	3	30	4	40	5	0
Ennis, John, Rich.-Toledo	3	11	.214	5.51	31	18	0	0	4	0	116.0	143	533	79	71	11	16	7	9	42	1	85	4	2
Erdos, Todd, Rochester	2	2	.500	4.54	29	0	0	0	18	11	33.2	42	144	20	17	3	0	3	3	5	0	16	4	0
Estrella, Leo, Indianapolis	1	0	1.000	1.20	7	0	0	0	2	0	15.0	9	59	2	2	1	0	0	0	6	0	12	0	0
Etherton, Seth, Louisville	7	7	.500	4.31	21	21	2	1	0	0	123.1	144	523	62	59	11	2	7	3	26	1	69	1	0
Eyre, Willie, Rochester	0	2	.000	6.00	6	5	0	0	1	0	24.0	30	116	18	16	2	0	1	2	16	0	23	2	0
Feliciano, Pedro, Norfolk *	3	2	.600	3.97	15	0	0	0	9	1	22.2	20	91	10	10	3	1	0	0	6	1	18	0	0
File, Bob, Syracuse	0	0	.000	4.22	11	0	0	0	3	0	10.2	10	43	5	5	0	0	0	1	2	0	7	0	0
Fiore, Tony, Rochester	5	6	.455	3.95	16	11	2	0	2	1	84.1	80	349	43	37	5	4	0	2	21	2	48	4	1
Flohr, Adam, Rochester *	0	0	.000	9.39	2	0	0	0	1	0	7.2	12	42	9	8	1	0	2	1	4	1	6	4	1
Ford, Ben, Indianapolis	5	4	.556	3.00	26	9	1	0	10	1	84.0	80	342	32	28	8	2	1	6	18	0	72	0	0
Fortunato, Bartolome, Durham	1	2	.333	3.32	5	4	0	0	1	0	21.2	15	91	11	8	3	1	1	0	11	0	20	1	0
Fossum, Casey, Pawtucket *	1	0	1.000	3.46	5	4	0	0	1	1	13.0	11	53	5	5	1	0	0	1	5	0	14	0	0
Foster, John, Indianapolis *	2	2	.500	3.70	27	0	0	0	7	0	41.1	44	181	21	17	4	3	1	2	13	1	37	0	0
Foster, Kris, Pawtucket	1	1	.500	7.11	4	0	0	0	0	0	6.1	14	33	5	5	0	0	1	0	2	0	3	0	0
Fox, Chad, Pawtucket	0	0	.000	13.50	1	0	0	0	1	0	1.1	3	8	3	2	1	1	0	0	1	0	2	1	0
Franco, John, Norfolk *	0	0	.000	0.00	2	0	0	0	0	0	1.2	1	7	0	0	0	0	0	0	1	0	2	0	0
Frederick, Kevin, Syracuse	1	3	.250	8.06	24	0	0	0	14	2	25.2	40	129	28	23	5	2	2	1	12	3	20	2	0
Fussell, Chris, Richmond	7	11	.389	4.03	29	26	0	0	2	0	152.0	142	663	77	68	12	7	6	19	74	0	130	8	1
Fyhrie, Mike, Buffalo	1	5	.167	5.80	8	8	1	0	0	0	45.0	55	196	30	29	4	0	0	3	12	0	31	1	0
Garcia, Gerardo, Durham	2	2	.500	4.13	6	6	0	0	0	0	28.1	28	124	15	13	4	1	0	2	10	0	15	3	0
Garcia, Mike, Ottawa	2	2	.500	2.55	34	0	0	0	24	13	35.1	30	152	15	10	2	1	2	2	13	0	44	1	0
Gardner, Lee, Durham	3	7	.300	3.73	57	0	0	0	49	30	62.2	68	268	29	26	9	2	0	3	14	2	56	3	0
Gassner, Dave, Syracuse *	1	0	1.000	1.80	1	1	0	0	0	0	5.0	5	21	1	1	0	0	0	0	1	0	4	0	0
Geary, Geoff, Scranton/WB	9	4	.692	2.16	46	3	0	0	18	5	87.2	73	343	26	21	3	2	5	4	13	1	80	1	0
German, Franklyn, Toledo	1	4	.200	2.45	24	0	0	0	10	4	29.1	21	118	9	8	2	3	1	6	9	1	32	6	0
Giese, Dan, Scranton/WB	2	0	1.000	3.17	34	0	0	0	11	0	48.1	37	189	19	17	8	0	2	1	10	0	49	0	0
Gil, Dave, Louisville	0	1	.000	3.38	16	2	0	0	6	0	32.0	33	134	14	12	2	2	0	2	7	0	20	1	0
Ginter, Matt, Charlotte	3	5	.375	3.03	49	0	0	0	27	14	68.1	66	298	27	23	2	5	2	4	22	3	52	1	0
Giron, Roberto, Indianapolis	1	5	.167	4.73	52	0	0	0	36	15	59.0	65	268	37	31	3	5	5	3	28	2	56	1	1
Glaser, Eric, Pawtucket	2	0	1.000	4.82	4	1	0	0	0	0	9.1	9	41	5	5	3	0	0	0	5	0	7	0	0
Glynn, Ryan, Richmond	6	5	.545	2.91	16	16	0	0	0	0	92.2	84	384	31	30	4	3	3	3	31	3	75	2	0
Gomes, Wayne, Scranton/WB	4	2	.667	2.59	46	0	0	0	38	14	48.2	31	202	17	14	1	1	2	3	24	2	43	2	0
Gonzalez, Dicky, Pawtucket	8	8	.500	4.04	27	25	1	0	2	0	151.2	180	654	77	68	13	3	3	9	29	1	104	3	0
Gonzalez, Jeremi, Durham	1	0	1.000	2.53	7	6	0	0	1	0	32.0	24	127	11	9	2	0	1	1	6	0	33	2	0
Gonzalez, Mike, Pawtucket *	0	0	.000	0.00	2	0	0	0	1	1	1.2	2	8	0	0	0	0	0	0	1	0	2	0	0
Graman, Alex, Columbus *	9	10	.474	4.48	26	26	0	0	0	0	142.2	135	612	77	71	14	8	0	1	63	0	110	5	1
Greisinger, Seth, Toledo	6	9	.400	3.97	25	21	2	1	1	0	136.0	154	578	77	60	16	4	3	7	23	3	80	1	2
Griffiths, Jeremy, Norfolk	7	6	.538	2.74	21	19	1	0	1	1	115.0	94	459	43	35	6	1	4	9	26	0	78	5	0
Guerra, Mark, Indianapolis	0	3	.000	5.47	5	4	0	0	0	0	24.2	24	103	16	15	3	0	4	1	6	0	13	0	0
Guthrie, Jeremy, Buffalo	4	9	.308	6.52	18	18	1	0	0	0	96.2	129	444	75	70	15	3	1	7	30	1	62	3	1
Haines, Talley, Durham	5	3	.625	2.53	50	0	0	0	20	2	67.2	57	265	19	19	5	2	0	1	11	1	64	4	1
Hamilton, Joey, Louisville	8	3	.727	3.23	33	8	0	0	7	1	86.1	103	366	38	31	5	2	5	4	18	1	45	0	1
Hancock, Josh, Scranton/WB	10	9	.526	3.86	28	27	2	2	1	0	165.2	147	677	78	71	14	2	6	6	46	1	122	4	0
Hansell, Greg, Columbus	0	0	.000	6.32	9	0	0	0	5	0	15.2	25	72	11	11	1	0	0	0	2	0	12	2	0
Harang, Aaron, Louisville	0	1	.000	15.00	1	1	0	0	0	0	3.0	5	16	5	5	1	0	0	0	2	0	4	0	0
Harikkala, Tim, Ottawa	5	0	1.000	0.81	20	3	0	0	2	2	44.1	27	163	4	4	0	2	0	1	7	1	29	0	0
Harnisch, Pete, Louisville	0	4	.000	10.06	8	8	0	0	0	0	34.0	59	169	39	38	6	2	5	1	11	0	17	0	0
Haynes, Jimmy, Louisville	1	1	.500	2.53	2	2	0	0	0	0	10.2	10	44	4	3	1	0	0	0	3	0	7	0	0

Pitcher, Team	W	L	Pct.	ERA	G	GS	CG	ShO	GF	Sv.	IP	H	TBF	R	ER	HR	SH	SF	HB	BB	IBB	SO	WP	Bk.
Hebson, Bryan, Pawtucket	2	1	.667	2.73	18	0	0	0	7	0	26.1	17	102	9	8	4	0	0	0	6	0	22	0	0
Heilman, Aaron, Norfolk	6	4	.600	3.24	16	16	0	0	0	0	94.1	99	399	37	34	5	3	1	2	32	0	71	1	0
Hendrickson, Mark, Syr.*	0	0	.000	4.50	1	1	0	0	0	0	6.0	8	25	4	3	1	0	0	0	1	0	5	0	0
Hernandez, Adrian, Columbus	8	5	.615	3.21	32	9	0	0	8	1	101.0	92	443	47	36	6	3	4	4	49	4	103	6	3
Hernandez, Buddy, Richmond	4	3	.571	3.42	53	0	0	0	17	4	71.0	65	308	30	27	2	4	2	2	31	1	82	0	3
Hernandez, Roberto, Rich.	1	1	.500	9.45	6	0	0	0	1	0	6.2	11	38	9	7	0	0	0	1	4	0	10	1	0
Hernandez, Yoel, S./WB	0	0	.000	6.00	2	0	0	0	0	0	3.0	5	14	2	2	0	0	0	0	0	0	3	0	0
Herrera, Alex, Buffalo *	4	6	.400	5.30	34	0	0	0	15	1	56.0	51	262	40	33	9	1	2	2	45	1	46	3	5
Hiles, Cary, Scranton/WB	0	1	.000	3.71	13	0	0	0	2	0	26.2	31	116	11	11	3	0	0	1	11	1	11	0	0
Hoard, Brent, Rochester *	3	5	.375	5.35	13	12	0	0	1	0	65.2	88	296	46	39	10	1	3	0	15	0	31	5	0
Howry, Bobby, Pawtucket	2	0	1.000	1.06	13	0	0	0	3	0	17.0	14	67	2	2	1	0	0	1	1	0	10	0	0
Izquierdo, Hansel, Pawtucket	0	1	.000	11.48	4	3	0	0	1	0	13.1	21	67	17	17	2	0	0	2	6	0	4	0	0
Jacquez, Tom, Charlotte *	5	3	.625	4.08	13	1	0	0	3	0	28.2	29	134	14	13	0	3	0	4	16	1	21	0	0
James, Delvin, Durham	5	10	.333	5.23	34	21	0	0	1	0	137.2	172	616	91	80	21	5	6	10	36	2	65	9	2
Jimenez, Jason, Toledo *	1	2	.333	4.04	47	0	0	0	16	2	49.0	42	213	23	22	2	3	1	2	29	3	35	1	1
Johnson, Adam, Rochester	6	11	.353	5.35	28	17	1	0	5	0	114.1	128	510	73	68	7	5	8	11	48	2	78	8	0
Johnson, James, Pawtucket *	0	0	.000	0.00	3	0	0	0	2	0	3.0	0	9	0	0	0	0	0	0	0	0	3	0	0
Jones, Bobby M., Richmond *	1	3	.250	3.12	37	0	0	0	14	5	34.2	29	151	12	12	3	1	1	1	18	1	39	0	0
Joseph, Jake, Norfolk	5	6	.455	5.93	19	11	0	0	3	0	71.1	97	326	51	47	6	2	5	9	21	1	42	4	2
Junge, Eric, Scranton/WB	1	0	1.000	3.06	10	8	0	0	0	0	47.0	38	196	20	16	2	1	0	3	16	1	42	1	0
Kaye, Justin, Pawtucket	2	2	.500	2.49	31	0	0	0	17	4	43.1	37	183	16	12	2	3	3	1	19	0	24	4	0
Keller, Kris, Louisville	0	1	.000	9.00	2	0	0	0	1	0	1.0	1	5	1	1	0	0	0	0	2	0	0	0	0
Kennedy, Joe, Durham *	1	0	1.000	1.42	1	1	0	0	0	0	6.1	6	24	1	1	0	0	0	0	0	0	4	0	0
Kershner, Jason, Syracuse *	6	1	.857	2.36	24	0	0	0	4	0	45.2	42	181	15	12	1	3	4	0	9	1	30	2	0
Kieschnick, Brooks, Ind.	1	0	1.000	8.56	8	0	0	0	4	0	13.2	17	68	15	13	3	0	1	1	10	2	14	0	0
Kingrey, Jarrod, Syracuse	0	0	.000	9.00	3	0	0	0	0	0	3.0	4	15	3	3	0	0	0	2	3	0	3	0	0
Kleine, Victor, Buffalo *	0	0	.000	1.80	1	1	0	0	0	0	5.0	4	24	2	1	0	0	0	0	4	0	4	0	0
Knotts, Gary, Toledo	4	6	.400	5.13	13	13	0	0	0	0	79.0	98	361	54	45	15	4	1	6	28	3	63	5	0
Koch, Billy, Charlotte	0	1	.000	4.91	4	0	0	0	0	0	3.2	5	19	2	2	0	0	0	0	3	0	2	0	0
Kohlmeier, Ryan, Charlotte	7	4	.636	4.71	33	17	1	0	11	0	116.2	129	499	62	61	18	1	4	6	20	6	73	2	0
Kolb, Dan, Indianapolis	0	1	.000	1.37	26	0	0	0	21	4	39.1	26	156	10	6	1	1	0	0	13	0	46	3	0
Kubes, Greg, Scranton/WB *	6	3	.667	4.26	37	10	0	0	8	3	95.0	117	416	49	45	7	9	7	2	16	2	62	2	4
Larrison, Preston, Toledo	0	1	.000	3.38	1	1	0	0	0	0	5.1	3	22	3	2	1	1	0	0	2	0	3	0	0
Lavigne, Tim, Norfolk	0	0	.000	0.00	1	0	0	0	0	0	1.0	1	6	0	0	0	1	0	0	2	0	0	0	0
Lee, Cliff, Buffalo *	6	1	.857	3.27	11	11	0	0	0	0	63.1	62	279	24	23	4	4	2	4	31	0	61	2	1
Lee, Derek, Indianapolis *	2	4	.333	3.75	14	8	0	0	3	0	60.0	55	258	30	25	1	1	2	5	19	0	55	5	1
Lee, Seung, Scranton/WB	0	2	.000	23.63	2	1	0	0	0	0	5.1	18	34	15	14	2	0	1	2	0	0	5	0	0
Lewis, Derrick, Richmond	2	5	.286	7.15	36	5	0	0	11	0	61.2	83	294	53	49	7	3	2	3	29	0	46	11	2
Lidle, Cory, Syracuse	0	0	.000	0.00	1	1	0	0	0	0	4.0	5	16	0	0	0	0	0	0	0	0	3	0	0
Linton, Doug, Syracuse	2	10	.167	5.28	32	13	1	0	8	0	109.0	133	467	67	64	13	2	3	5	19	2	79	5	0
Loux, Shane, Toledo	11	6	.647	3.02	21	20	2	1	0	0	128.0	129	531	53	43	5	4	5	6	30	0	58	4	0
Lyon, Brandon, Pawtucket	0	0	.000	3.24	5	0	0	0	2	0	8.1	7	34	3	3	1	0	0	0	2	0	7	0	1
Madson, Ryan, Scranton/WB	12	8	.600	3.50	26	26	0	0	0	0	157.0	157	658	70	61	9	2	5	10	42	2	138	6	0
Magrane, Jim, Durham	0	1	.000	7.50	2	2	0	0	0	0	12.0	15	52	10	10	6	0	0	0	4	0	4	0	0
Majewski, Gary, Charlotte	6	4	.600	3.96	42	1	0	0	13	4	72.2	62	307	33	32	3	3	1	5	29	2	72	3	0
Malaska, Mark, Durham *	1	1	.500	4.30	15	0	0	0	5	0	23.0	24	99	12	11	1	0	0	1	8	0	22	5	0
Manning, David, Indianapolis	6	8	.429	4.91	23	17	0	0	1	0	99.0	103	455	57	54	7	3	5	3	60	0	76	8	0
Manzanillo, Josias, Louisville	1	1	.500	4.18	22	0	0	0	8	0	28.0	25	119	17	13	0	5	1	2	11	1	16	1	0
Marquez, Rob, Indianapolis	0	2	.000	3.99	30	1	0	0	11	0	56.1	55	248	31	25	6	4	3	8	25	1	44	4	0
Marquis, Jason, Richmond	8	4	.667	3.35	15	15	3	1	0	0	94.0	93	400	40	35	5	3	0	0	34	0	75	4	0
Marsonek, Sam, Columbus	4	4	.500	4.84	54	2	0	0	34	18	83.2	84	370	52	45	9	2	3	8	31	0	57	3	0
Martinez, Anastacio, Paw.	2	1	.667	1.93	8	0	0	0	2	0	14.0	12	56	3	3	2	0	0	0	3	0	15	0	0
Martinez, Luis, Indianapolis *	4	0	1.000	0.99	7	7	0	0	0	0	45.2	37	177	5	5	0	2	0	0	19	0	46	2	0
McConnell, Sam, Richmond *	8	4	.667	2.70	22	13	0	0	1	0	93.1	94	383	31	28	5	6	3	2	17	2	64	1	2
Mears, Chris, Toledo	5	1	.833	2.78	25	5	0	0	7	2	58.1	53	240	20	18	5	0	2	3	19	2	28	0	0
Mendoza, Ramiro, Pawtucket	0	0	.000	2.00	4	0	0	0	1	1	9.0	8	33	2	2	1	0	0	0	0	0	8	0	0
Mercado, Hector, S./WB *	0	3	.000	1.41	14	2	0	0	2	0	32.0	34	136	12	5	2	3	2	0	11	0	20	0	0
Meyer, Jake, Charlotte	1	2	.333	3.42	20	0	0	0	12	0	26.1	26	112	11	10	2	1	2	1	10	1	15	2	0
Miceli, Danny, Buffalo	0	1	.000	3.00	5	0	0	0	3	0	6.0	7	26	2	2	1	0	0	0	1	1	6	0	0
Michalak, Chris, Louisville *	2	1	.667	5.13	9	3	0	0	1	0	26.1	35	111	15	15	3	0	1	1	5	0	18	0	2
Middlebrook, Jason, Norfolk	7	10	.412	4.49	23	23	0	0	0	0	118.1	121	497	64	59	21	5	4	1	33	0	91	3	1
Miller, Travis, Louisville-Ind.*	6	2	.750	4.94	20	8	0	0	3	0	54.2	78	247	32	30	5	1	0	2	10	0	37	2	0
Mills, Ryan, Rochester *	5	1	.833	4.11	32	0	0	0	11	0	61.1	62	269	37	28	4	7	1	2	31	0	51	4	1
Mohler, Mike, Ottawa *	6	5	.545	3.88	50	1	0	0	12	1	72.0	69	321	40	31	4	3	3	2	42	4	50	3	0
Morales, Steve, Charlotte	0	0	.000	0.00	1	0	0	0	1	0	1.0	2	5	0	0	0	0	0	0	0	0	0	0	0
Moreno, Orber, Norfolk	5	1	.833	1.90	38	0	0	0	32	12	52.0	36	206	11	11	1	0	0	1	17	0	58	2	0
Moseley, Dustin, Louisville	2	3	.400	2.70	8	8	0	0	0	0	50.0	46	207	19	15	5	1	3	1	14	0	27	2	1
Mottl, Ryan, Louisville	0	2	.000	5.63	3	3	0	0	0	0	16.0	20	73	10	10	4	1	0	2	8	0	12	0	0
Munoz, Arnaldo, Charlotte *	4	3	.571	4.75	49	0	0	0	17	6	55.0	52	238	35	29	7	3	0	3	27	2	63	7	1
Myette, Aaron, Buf.-S./WB	5	4	.556	4.39	34	11	0	0	10	1	92.1	83	399	49	45	8	5	3	4	43	1	79	7	0
Nakamura, Micheal, Roch.	6	6	.500	2.99	43	0	0	0	16	2	78.1	71	326	28	26	4	4	1	2	28	1	95	7	0
Nance, Shane, Indianapolis *	2	4	.333	1.38	35	1	0	0	7	3	52.1	34	201	10	8	4	2	1	1	13	1	53	1	0
Navarro, Jaime, Louisville	0	1	.000	2.70	2	2	0	0	0	0	10.0	11	40	3	3	0	0	0	0	2	0	4	0	0
Nelson, Bubba, Richmond	0	1	.000	1.88	11	0	0	0	5	0	14.1	10	54	3	3	1	1	1	2	5	0	7	2	0
Nickle, Doug, Charlotte	1	1	.500	2.87	11	0	0	0	5	2	15.2	17	67	5	5	1	0	0	2	3	0	16	0	0
Obermueller, Wes, Ind.	0	2	.000	4.70	3	3	0	0	0	0	15.1	18	66	9	8	1	0	0	0	6	0	11	1	0
Padilla, Juan, Rochester	7	4	.636	3.36	57	0	0	0	29	6	91.0	94	386	40	34	7	8	3	4	17	3	68	5	0
Palki, Jeromy, Rochester	7	6	.538	4.10	47	7	1	0	10	1	101.0	105	441	50	46	6	4	7	8	31	1	91	7	0
Paniagua, Jose, Charlotte	0	0	.000	7.71	3	0	0	0	0	0	2.1	4	12	2	2	0	0	0	0	2	0	2	1	0
Parker, Christian, Columbus	7	6	.538	4.90	19	19	0	0	0	0	108.1	135	487	63	59	4	3	4	5	44	0	41	6	0
Paronto, Chad, Buffalo	3	5	.375	4.34	49	0	0	0	47	18	56.0	64	263	36	27	2	5	0	3	22	7	48	4	0

Pitcher, Team	W	L	Pct.	ERA	G	GS	CG	ShO	GF	Sv.	IP	H	TBF	R	ER	HR	SH	SF	HB	BB	IBB	SO	WP	Bk.
Parque, Jim, Durham *	5	7	.417	4.08	21	21	1	0	0	0	121.1	132	524	62	55	13	3	3	9	47	1	49	5	0
Patterson, Danny, Toledo	1	0	1.000	2.45	10	0	0	0	2	0	11.0	8	45	3	3	0	1	0	1	5	1	6	2	0
Pearson, Terry, Toledo	5	3	.625	4.34	45	0	0	0	19	2	47.2	61	226	36	23	0	2	2	2	20	3	27	5	0
Pena, Juan, Syracuse	0	1	.000	7.56	8	0	0	0	5	3	8.1	7	37	7	7	2	0	0	0	6	0	7	0	0
Perisho, Matt, Durham *	7	4	.636	6.52	34	0	0	0	13	1	38.2	43	173	29	28	5	3	0	2	12	2	41	2	0
Person, Robert, Pawtucket	0	0	.000	4.70	6	1	0	0	3	1	7.2	5	33	4	4	0	0	0	0	5	0	6	2	0
Phelps, Travis, Richmond	9	5	.643	3.47	47	8	0	0	13	4	93.1	77	388	44	36	11	1	2	2	38	1	91	0	0
Phillips, Jason, Buffalo	10	1	.909	2.12	13	12	1	0	0	0	85.0	68	334	24	20	4	3	1	5	19	0	56	0	0
Pina, Rafael, Ottawa	2	5	.286	5.30	7	7	0	0	0	0	37.1	41	173	24	22	3	3	5	3	23	3	20	0	0
Politte, Cliff, Syracuse	0	0	.000	0.00	1	0	0	0	0	0	1.0	0	3	0	0	0	0	0	0	0	0	1	0	0
Porzio, Mike, Charlotte *	8	6	.571	4.24	26	22	1	0	3	0	133.2	124	568	70	63	19	7	6	8	47	1	115	3	0
Powell, Brian, Scranton/WB	2	4	.333	4.61	8	7	2	1	0	0	52.2	57	223	33	27	1	2	2	0	12	2	36	3	0
Pratt, Andy, Richmond *	7	10	.412	3.40	28	27	1	0	0	0	156.0	146	685	77	59	10	5	8	11	77	0	161	14	0
Prinz, Bret, Columbus	0	1	.000	8.03	10	0	0	0	3	0	12.1	20	57	11	11	2	0	1	0	1	0	13	1	0
Proctor, Scott, Columbus	2	0	1.000	1.42	10	0	0	0	1	0	19.0	13	71	3	3	2	1	0	1	3	0	26	0	0
Pulido, Carlos, Rochester *	12	5	.706	3.56	25	25	1	0	0	0	149.1	145	611	65	59	13	8	7	2	40	0	87	3	0
Pulsipher, Bill, Ottawa *	4	5	.444	5.63	51	0	0	0	19	3	54.1	59	254	43	34	3	3	3	4	29	5	43	3	0
Pumphrey, Ken, Scranton/WB	5	7	.417	7.41	17	17	1	0	0	0	81.1	108	389	75	67	9	4	8	9	32	0	46	2	0
Quevedo, Ruben, Indianapolis	2	1	.667	2.10	5	5	0	0	0	0	25.2	24	106	7	6	1	1	1	0	8	1	23	0	0
Rakers, Aaron, Ottawa	2	4	.333	5.13	21	0	0	0	8	1	26.1	19	111	18	15	1	1	3	2	11	2	26	3	1
Rakers, Jason, Buffalo-Ottawa	0	1	.000	8.22	5	1	0	0	1	0	7.2	10	36	7	7	1	1	0	0	3	1	7	0	0
Ramirez, Ramon, Columbus	0	1	.000	4.50	2	1	0	0	0	0	6.0	5	25	5	3	1	0	0	0	1	0	5	0	0
Randall, Scott, Louisville	10	4	.714	4.63	30	20	0	0	3	3	136.0	170	611	76	70	9	3	5	14	39	0	86	9	0
Rauch, Jon, Charlotte	7	1	.875	4.11	24	23	1	0	1	0	124.2	121	517	60	57	16	4	6	2	35	1	94	3	0
Rayborn, Kenny, Buffalo	1	0	1.000	3.00	1	1	0	0	0	0	6.0	6	26	2	2	0	0	0	1	1	0	2	2	0
Reichert, Dan, Syracuse	4	3	.571	3.57	41	0	0	0	10	0	58.0	55	259	26	23	2	5	1	2	35	1	60	7	1
Reith, Brian, Louisville	3	1	.750	1.96	16	0	0	0	6	1	23.0	12	91	9	5	1	1	0	2	9	2	28	1	0
Reitsma, Chris, Louisville	1	2	.333	4.00	4	4	0	0	0	0	18.0	22	80	10	8	1	0	0	0	5	0	11	0	0
Reyes, Al, Columbus	1	1	.500	3.71	15	0	0	0	13	2	17.0	16	72	7	7	1	0	0	0	5	0	21	0	0
Reyes, Carlos, Durham	10	3	.769	2.86	22	21	1	0	0	0	132.1	124	522	47	42	9	2	1	1	14	1	78	7	0
Riggan, Jerrod, Buf.-Norfolk	2	1	.667	2.38	14	0	0	0	8	1	22.2	21	91	7	6	0	0	1	0	6	1	25	0	0
Rijo, Fernando, Ottawa	2	0	1.000	2.25	2	2	0	0	0	0	12.0	11	49	3	3	1	0	2	0	4	0	13	0	1
Riley, Matt, Ottawa *	4	2	.667	3.58	13	13	0	0	0	0	70.1	70	300	30	28	4	0	4	0	28	1	77	4	2
Rincon, Juan, Rochester	0	2	.000	7.56	2	2	0	0	0	0	8.1	12	39	7	7	0	1	0	0	5	0	8	0	0
Rizzo, Todd, Ottawa *	2	4	.333	4.58	47	0	0	0	14	0	59.0	67	272	36	30	5	2	2	2	31	3	36	6	0
Roa, Joe, Indianapolis	2	2	.500	4.74	5	4	0	0	0	0	24.2	32	106	15	13	3	3	0	1	3	0	18	0	0
Roach, Jason, Norfolk	5	11	.313	5.07	31	20	2	0	2	0	120.2	140	528	74	68	12	2	3	7	36	1	98	4	0
Roberts, Grant, Norfolk	0	0	.000	3.52	8	0	0	0	2	0	7.2	7	36	3	3	0	0	0	1	5	0	6	0	0
Robertson, Nathan, Toledo *	9	7	.563	3.14	24	23	3	1	1	0	155.0	145	640	62	54	14	4	2	6	47	2	102	0	0
Rodney, Fernando, Toledo	1	1	.500	1.33	38	0	0	0	35	23	40.2	22	156	6	6	0	1	3	4	13	0	58	3	0
Rodriguez, Jose, Rochester *	0	0	.000	5.87	6	0	0	0	2	0	7.2	9	38	5	5	3	0	0	0	6	1	6	0	0
Rodriguez, Ricardo, Buffalo	0	1	.000	4.32	2	2	0	0	0	0	8.1	6	34	4	4	2	0	0	1	3	0	7	1	0
Rogers, Brian, Columbus	0	0	.000	0.00	2	0	0	0	1	1	7.2	5	29	1	0	0	0	0	0	1	0	5	0	0
Romano, Mike, Richmond	1	0	1.000	0.73	8	0	0	0	3	2	12.1	9	46	1	1	0	1	2	0	3	0	7	0	0
Rupe, Ryan, Pawtucket	8	4	.667	3.26	20	18	0	0	0	0	102.0	93	421	50	37	11	2	4	4	19	1	77	3	0
Rusch, Glendon, Ind.*	1	1	.500	3.86	4	3	1	0	0	0	21.0	17	84	9	9	4	0	0	2	4	0	20	0	0
Rust, Evan, Durham	2	2	.500	3.25	26	0	0	0	6	1	36.0	32	149	13	13	1	3	2	3	10	1	26	4	0
Sadler, Carl, Buffalo *	2	1	.667	6.28	31	0	0	0	14	3	53.0	62	247	41	37	4	1	4	3	31	3	32	3	0
Sanders, Dave, Charlotte *	1	1	.500	3.68	19	0	0	0	10	4	22.0	23	97	9	9	3	0	0	4	6	0	25	1	0
Santana, Julio, Scranton/WB	1	1	.500	3.64	19	0	0	0	8	3	29.2	29	127	12	12	0	2	1	1	12	0	26	0	1
Santiago, Jose, Buffalo	3	3	.500	2.43	25	4	0	0	5	2	66.2	79	291	25	18	1	0	2	2	22	1	33	0	0
Schmitt, Eric, Columbus	6	0	1.000	4.19	13	12	1	0	1	0	68.2	78	293	35	32	8	5	3	0	16	0	45	1	0
Scobie, Jason, Norfolk	1	3	.250	6.83	8	4	0	0	1	0	27.2	37	130	24	21	4	2	1	5	10	0	15	0	0
Seanez, Rudy, Pawtucket	2	2	.500	6.10	17	0	0	0	10	3	20.2	20	90	14	14	5	0	1	0	10	1	24	2	0
Seay, Bobby, Durham *	3	0	1.000	2.10	25	0	0	0	7	0	30.0	23	131	10	7	1	0	1	3	15	0	29	1	0
Secrist, Reed, Buffalo	0	0	.000	4.50	1	0	0	0	1	0	2.0	1	7	1	1	1	0	0	0	0	0	1	0	0
Seibel, Phil, Norfolk *	2	3	.400	6.03	11	5	0	0	0	0	34.1	38	158	25	23	5	1	1	4	17	0	25	0	2
Serrano, Jim, Norfolk	1	2	.333	2.39	27	0	0	0	9	0	49.0	38	193	13	13	2	3	0	1	19	3	47	2	0
Service, Scott, Louisville	0	0	.000	2.45	4	0	0	0	1	0	3.2	3	14	1	1	0	0	0	0	0	0	7	0	0
Shackelford, Brian, Lou.*	1	0	1.000	2.30	12	0	0	0	2	0	15.2	15	69	4	4	0	2	1	1	7	0	10	0	0
Shepard, David, Columbus	0	1	.000	5.74	8	0	0	0	3	0	15.2	19	69	11	10	3	1	0	1	3	0	14	0	0
Shibilo, Andy, Pawtucket	2	1	.667	4.76	38	1	0	0	14	1	45.1	46	202	26	24	3	1	2	1	22	0	49	5	0
Shiell, Jason, Pawtucket	3	2	.600	2.42	20	0	0	0	13	2	26.0	26	107	11	7	0	0	2	0	6	0	22	0	0
Smith, Chuck, Richmond	1	0	1.000	2.00	3	3	0	0	0	0	18.0	13	75	5	4	1	0	0	2	9	0	13	0	1
Smith, Mike, Syracuse	8	9	.471	5.00	26	21	2	0	0	0	131.1	140	583	80	73	13	5	5	11	58	1	89	16	0
Sosa, Jorge, Durham	1	1	.500	5.47	4	4	0	0	0	0	24.2	32	112	15	15	3	0	0	1	9	0	17	3	0
Standridge, Jason, Durham	2	4	.333	4.50	12	10	0	0	2	1	60.0	62	265	32	30	5	3	3	1	28	0	37	1	0
Stanford, Jason, Buffalo *	10	4	.714	3.43	20	20	1	0	0	0	126.0	124	515	57	48	13	4	4	5	25	1	108	2	2
Stephens, John, Ottawa	6	7	.462	3.97	27	27	1	0	0	0	158.2	155	663	76	70	15	3	6	9	39	1	132	4	0
Stewart, Josh, Charlotte *	0	3	.000	6.15	5	5	0	0	0	0	26.1	38	121	18	18	4	1	2	2	6	0	10	0	1
Stewart, Paul, Pawtucket	6	8	.429	4.30	27	24	0	0	1	0	121.1	133	541	79	58	16	4	5	8	42	0	76	1	0
Strange, Pat, Norfolk	5	4	.556	5.74	31	10	0	0	4	1	89.1	111	407	61	57	8	2	4	2	44	1	64	4	0
Stull, Everett, Rochester	4	6	.400	5.97	11	11	1	0	0	0	57.1	68	253	41	38	7	0	1	4	20	0	36	5	1
Sturkie, Scott, Buffalo	0	0	.000	0.00	1	0	0	0	0	0	2.0	1	7	0	0	0	0	0	1	0	0	1	0	0
Switzer, Jon, Durham *	1	0	1.000	1.80	1	1	0	0	0	0	5.0	6	19	1	1	1	0	0	0	0	0	3	0	0
Sylvester, Billy, Richmond	0	0	.000	3.86	12	1	0	0	2	0	18.2	11	87	9	8	1	0	0	2	19	1	27	1	0
Tadano, Kazuhito, Buffalo	0	0	.000	3.86	2	0	0	0	2	0	7.0	6	31	3	3	0	0	1	0	4	1	6	0	1
Takeoka, Kazuhiro, Richmond	0	0	.000	2.31	9	0	0	0	3	0	11.2	10	47	3	3	2	1	0	1	5	0	7	0	0
Tallet, Brian, Buffalo *	4	4	.500	5.14	15	15	0	0	0	0	84.0	89	377	50	48	10	3	5	5	34	1	67	6	0
Tam, Jeff, Syracuse	1	0	1.000	1.53	17	0	0	0	10	4	17.2	16	74	3	3	1	1	0	1	3	0	11	1	0
Telemaco, Amaury, S./WB	10	9	.526	3.24	25	24	3	2	0	0	155.1	125	599	59	56	15	6	4	3	22	1	116	5	0
Teut, Nate, Indianapolis *	3	5	.375	4.41	18	13	0	0	1	0	83.2	92	358	47	41	11	4	3	3	20	0	47	1	1
Thomas, Brad, Rochester *	0	3	.000	3.53	15	11	0	0	2	0	58.2	68	244	23	23	3	1	0	0	10	0	50	3	2
Thomas, Evan, Syracuse	4	8	.333	5.15	20	18	1	0	0	0	94.1	108	413	57	54	11	3	3	2	29	1	63	3	0
Thurman, Corey, Syracuse	6	4	.600	4.27	17	16	0	0	0	0	86.1	90	373	45	41	8	0	5	6	26	0	72	6	0

Pitcher, Team	W	L	Pct.	ERA	G	GS	CG	ShO	GF	Sv.	IP	H	TBF	R	ER	HR	SH	SF	HB	BB	IBB	SO	WP	Bk.
Thurman, Mike, Columbus	7	7	.500	4.79	26	12	0	0	2	1	94.0	115	414	56	50	11	6	3	4	23	2	74	1	0
Tolar, Kevin, Pawtucket *	5	1	.833	2.27	47	0	0	0	17	4	31.2	19	125	9	8	3	0	0	1	17	2	34	1	0
Towers, Josh, Syracuse	5	7	.417	3.32	21	20	1	1	0	0	132.2	133	545	55	49	10	4	5	2	20	1	76	3	0
Truby, Chris, Durham	0	0	.000	27.00	1	0	0	0	1	0	1.0	5	7	3	3	0	0	0	0	0	0	0	0	0
Valentine, Joe, Louisville	1	0	1.000	0.79	9	0	0	0	6	1	11.1	5	41	1	1	0	0	0	0	3	0	8	0	1
Van Hekken, Andy, Toledo *	4	6	.400	5.88	13	12	1	1	0	0	72.0	93	316	47	47	11	4	4	2	18	1	25	1	0
Van Poppel, Todd, Louisville	4	3	.571	3.17	20	5	0	0	6	1	54.0	49	214	23	19	4	4	1	0	11	1	45	4	0
Vargas, Jose, Buffalo	0	0	.000	16.20	1	0	0	0	0	0	1.2	6	13	5	3	0	0	1	0	2	0	2	0	1
Veras, Jose, Durham	0	0	.000	8.44	3	0	0	0	0	0	5.1	9	27	5	5	2	0	0	1	1	0	3	1	0
Waechter, Doug, Durham	3	3	.500	3.33	10	10	0	0	0	0	51.1	51	210	25	19	9	2	1	0	12	0	35	3	0
Wagner, Ryan, Louisville	0	1	.000	4.50	4	0	0	0	0	0	4.0	5	16	2	2	0	0	0	0	0	0	4	0	0
Walker, Pete, Syracuse	0	1	.000	6.75	5	5	0	0	0	0	13.1	15	57	10	10	2	0	0	0	3	0	8	0	0
Walker, Tyler, Toledo	2	9	.182	4.45	26	22	1	0	2	0	131.1	139	569	73	65	13	4	2	2	47	5	117	3	3
Wasdin, John, Syracuse	2	1	.667	5.23	10	1	0	0	3	0	20.2	28	91	13	12	1	1	0	1	1	0	21	2	0
Wathan, Dusty, Buffalo	0	0	.000	0.00	1	0	0	0	1	0	0.1	0	1	0	0	0	0	0	0	0	0	0	0	0
Watson, Mark, Louisville *	4	4	.500	4.36	44	0	0	0	23	4	53.2	53	226	30	26	1	6	7	1	14	1	46	3	0
Wedel, Jeremy, Scranton/WB	1	0	1.000	3.76	17	1	0	0	2	0	26.1	28	115	12	11	2	0	2	1	9	0	18	2	0
West, Brian, Charlotte	1	0	1.000	5.40	1	1	0	0	0	0	5.0	4	22	3	3	0	0	0	1	2	1	2	0	0
Westbrook, Jake, Buffalo	1	0	1.000	0.00	2	2	0	0	0	0	10.0	0	35	0	0	0	1	0	0	4	0	7	1	0
Wheeler, Dan, Norfolk	4	2	.667	3.94	22	5	0	0	10	4	45.2	48	199	20	20	4	1	0	1	16	3	44	0	0
White, Gabe, Louisville *	0	0	.000	9.00	1	1	0	0	0	0	1.0	2	6	1	1	0	0	0	0	1	0	0	0	0
White, Matt, Paw.-Buffalo *	2	3	.400	1.97	21	1	0	0	7	0	45.2	37	189	13	10	3	4	1	0	16	0	39	2	0
Wiggins, Scott, Syracuse *	2	2	.500	6.62	35	0	0	0	15	1	35.1	47	176	29	26	4	1	3	3	22	4	22	1	0
Williams, Glenn, Syracuse	0	0	.000	0.00	1	0	0	0	1	0	0.1	0	1	0	0	0	0	0	0	0	0	0	0	0
Williams, Todd, Durham	3	2	.600	1.55	56	0	0	0	22	4	69.2	55	274	12	12	2	3	0	1	14	2	36	1	0
Wilson, Craig, Columbus	0	0	.000	45.00	1	0	0	0	1	0	1.0	5	11	5	5	1	0	0	0	3	0	0	0	0
Woodard, Steve, Pawtucket	6	7	.462	4.69	31	11	0	0	9	2	94.0	103	393	55	49	9	4	6	3	12	1	58	3	0
Wright, Danny, Charlotte	1	3	.250	4.64	8	7	1	0	0	0	33.0	25	132	18	17	5	0	1	3	10	0	25	0	0
Wright, Jamey, Indianapolis	1	3	.250	7.36	7	4	0	0	0	0	22.0	32	108	21	18	5	1	1	3	10	0	17	1	0
Wunsch, Kelly, Charlotte *	0	1	.000	5.40	3	0	0	0	0	0	3.1	6	17	3	2	1	0	1	2	0	0	4	0	0
Yates, Tyler, Norfolk	1	2	.333	4.05	4	4	0	0	0	0	20.0	22	86	9	9	1	0	0	1	9	0	15	1	0
Yofu, Tetsu, Charlotte	0	1	.000	4.82	3	1	0	0	1	0	9.1	11	42	5	5	3	0	0	0	4	0	13	2	0
Young, Tim, Syracuse *	2	3	.400	6.75	19	0	0	0	4	1	26.2	23	128	22	20	2	0	1	3	25	1	25	6	0
Zambrano, Victor, Durham	0	1	.000	4.50	1	1	0	0	0	0	4.0	4	20	6	2	0	0	0	0	2	0	6	1	0
Zamora, Pete, Norfolk *	5	3	.625	3.49	55	0	0	0	12	1	90.1	94	389	42	35	4	7	1	5	32	3	53	3	0

PITCHERS WITH TWO OR MORE TEAMS

Pitcher, Team	W	L	Pct.	ERA	G	GS	CG	ShO	GF	Sv.	IP	H	TBF	R	ER	HR	SH	SF	HB	BB	IBB	SO	WP	Bk.
Adkins, Tim, Columbus *	3	2	.600	5.57	28	0	0	0	9	0	32.1	30	148	20	20	2	1	1	4	24	2	22	3	0
Adkins, Tim, Louisville *	0	1	.000	3.46	12	1	0	0	2	0	26.0	23	107	10	10	1	2	0	0	11	0	21	0	0
Almonte, Ed, Norfolk	1	1	.500	2.55	16	0	0	0	14	6	17.2	16	77	5	5	0	1	1	1	6	0	14	0	0
Almonte, Ed, Charlotte	2	6	.250	6.88	30	0	0	0	22	14	34.0	45	159	27	26	6	5	3	1	14	4	24	1	0
Anderson, Jason, Columbus	0	0	.000	0.00	6	0	0	0	6	3	7.2	3	29	0	0	0	1	0	0	2	0	13	0	0
Anderson, Jason, Norfolk	1	3	.250	2.70	10	5	0	0	4	4	23.1	18	91	8	7	3	0	0	0	7	0	9	1	1
Bale, John, Louisville *	4	1	.800	3.30	26	2	0	0	14	4	43.2	36	181	17	16	1	1	2	2	13	0	43	1	0
Bale, John, Norfolk *	0	1	.000	3.29	8	0	0	0	1	0	13.2	11	55	5	5	0	1	1	0	3	0	15	0	0
Brown, Jamie, Buffalo	4	4	.500	3.52	13	10	0	0	0	0	61.1	45	246	26	24	4	4	2	5	17	1	26	0	0
Brown, Jamie, Pawtucket	4	1	.800	2.26	18	3	0	0	6	1	51.2	40	202	17	13	1	3	1	2	5	1	39	2	0
Burba, Dave, Indianapolis	5	4	.556	5.33	10	9	0	0	0	0	50.2	65	225	37	30	4	1	1	1	16	0	34	4	0
Burba, Dave, Buffalo	1	3	.250	2.05	4	4	0	0	0	0	22.0	18	86	6	5	2	0	1	1	5	0	10	0	0
Claussen, Brandon, Col.*	2	1	.667	2.75	11	11	1	0	0	0	68.2	53	275	28	21	4	1	6	1	18	0	39	0	2
Claussen, Brandon, Lou.*	0	1	.000	7.47	3	3	0	0	0	0	15.2	17	65	13	13	3	1	0	0	6	0	16	0	0
Croushore, Rick, Ottawa	0	0	.000	3.00	9	0	0	0	5	0	9.0	7	40	3	3	0	1	1	0	7	1	8	1	0
Croushore, Rick, Louisville	1	0	1.000	1.93	5	0	0	0	0	0	4.2	3	23	1	1	0	0	0	1	7	0	5	0	0
Ennis, John, Toledo	1	0	1.000	5.17	3	3	0	0	0	0	15.2	22	72	9	9	0	2	1	2	5	0	9	1	0
Ennis, John, Richmond	2	11	.154	5.56	28	15	0	0	4	0	100.1	121	461	70	62	11	14	6	7	37	1	76	3	2
Miller, Travis, Louisville *	1	0	1.000	0.00	4	0	0	0	1	0	4.0	4	16	0	0	0	0	0	0	1	0	4	2	0
Miller, Travis, Indianapolis *	5	2	.714	5.33	16	8	0	0	2	0	50.2	74	231	32	30	5	1	0	2	9	0	33	0	0
Myette, Aaron, Buffalo	0	0	.000	4.59	23	1	0	0	9	1	33.1	33	154	21	17	4	3	2	0	23	1	25	6	0
Myette, Aaron, Scranton/WB	5	4	.556	4.27	11	10	0	0	1	0	59.0	50	245	28	28	4	2	1	4	20	0	54	1	0
Rakers, Jason, Ottawa	0	0	.000	10.13	2	1	0	0	0	0	5.1	8	25	6	6	1	0	0	0	1	0	6	0	0
Rakers, Jason, Buffalo	0	1	.000	3.86	3	0	0	0	1	0	2.1	2	11	1	1	0	1	0	0	2	1	1	0	0
Riggan, Jerrod, Norfolk	0	0	.000	2.84	5	0	0	0	2	1	6.1	7	26	2	2	0	0	0	0	1	0	11	0	0
Riggan, Jerrod, Buffalo	2	1	.667	2.20	9	0	0	0	6	0	16.1	14	65	5	4	0	0	1	0	5	1	14	0	0
White, Matt, Pawtucket *	0	0	.000	0.00	2	0	0	0	0	0	3.1	1	12	1	0	0	0	0	0	0	0	5	0	0
White, Matt, Buffalo *	2	3	.400	2.13	19	1	0	0	7	0	42.1	36	177	12	10	3	4	1	0	16	0	34	2	0

COMBINATION SHUTOUTS: Buffalo (8)—Brown-Herrera, Bere-Myette-Paronto, Tallet-Herrera-Miceli, Guthrie-Paronto, Lee-Santiago-Sadler, Phillips-Santiago-Paronto, Westbrook-White-Paronto, Guthrie-White-Paronto. Charlotte (10)—Porzio-Ginter-Majewski-Almonte, Cooper-Sanders-Almonte, Porzio-Munoz, Adkins-Ginter-Munoz, Kohlmeier-Adkins, Adkins-Ginter, Cooper-Wunsch-Ginter, Rauch-Ginter, Jacquez-Majewski, Porzio-Meyer. Columbus (5)—Arroyo-Hernandez-Choate, Schmitt-Choate-Adkins, Schmitt-Hernandez-Choate-Marsonek, de paula-Marsonek, Hernandez-Proctor. Durham (6)—Bell-Williams-Perisho, James-Perisho-Williams, James-Williams-Gardner, Parque-Haines-Williams-Gardner, Parque-Seay-Haines, Bowers-Belitz-Rust. Indianapolis (10)—Coco-Kolb-Manning-J. Childers, Manning-Nance-Giron, Miller-J. Childers-Kolb, Miller-Kolb, Martinez-Nance-J. Childers, Lee-Nance, Martinez-J. Childers, Martinez-Nance-J. Childers, Coco-Nance-J. Childers, Teut-M. Childers-J. Childers. Louisville (5)—Etherton-De Paula-Reith-Randall-Watson, Anderson-Manzanillo-Almanzar, Haynes-Acevedo-Adkins, Anderson-Manzanillo, Belisle-Van Poppel-Almanzar. Norfolk (8)—Middlebrook-Zamora, Strange-Feliciano, Heilman-Feliciano-Bell, Roach-Franco-Zamora-Moreno, Griffiths-Strange-Moreno, Yates-Roach-Moreno, Middlebrook-Joseph-Almonte, Griffiths-Moreno. Ottawa (5)—Dubose-Rizzo-Garcia, Beltran-Mohler, Dubose-Beltran-Cubillan, Dubose-Harikkala-Mohler, Douglass-Harikkala-Garcia-Cubillan. Pawtucket (10)—Elmore-Kaye-Howry, Gonzalez-Almonte-Howry, Gonzalez-Shibilo, Stewart-Chen, Arroyo-Tolar-Kaye, Brown-Cameron, Fossum-Tolar-Hebson-Gonzalez, Rupe-Woodard-Shiell, DeLaRosa-Martinez-Stewart, Chen-Hebson-Tolar-Shiell. Richmond (12)—Pratt-Phelps-C. Hernandez-Jones, Sylvester-Phelps-C. Hernandez, Fussell-Phelps-Jones-Dawley, Glynn-Lewis, Pratt-Dawley, Pratt-Emiliano-Jones-Phelps-Dawley, McConnell-Cunnane-Dawley, Phelps-Cunnane, McConnell-Cunnane-Dawley, Belisle-Nelson-Dawley, Bong-C. Hernandez-Romano-Dawley, McConnell-Castillo-Nelson. Rochester (5)—Stull-Nakamura-Erdos, Pulido-Fiore, Balfour-Palki-Padilla, Pulido-Crain, Palki-Mills-Padilla. Scranton-Wilkes Barre (10)—Kubes-Santana-Cabrera, Telemaco-Santana-Crowell-Gomes, Hancock-Kubes-Crowell, Madson-Mercado-Kubes, Hancock-Gomes, Myette-Geary-Gomes, Hancock-Geary-Crowell, Myette-Cabrera-Crowell, Coggin-Powell-Geary, Hancock-Mercado-Geary. Syracuse (6)—Thurman-Reichert-Wiggins-Bowles, Thurman-Young-Cassidy-Bowles, Smith-Kershner-Cassidy-Wiggins, Towers-Linton, Arnold-Bowles, Towers-Tam-Bowles. Toledo (3)—Loux-Jimenez-Brittan-Eckenstahler, Walker-Pearson-Jimenez-Rodney, Mears-Anderson-Eckenstahler-Rodney.

NO-HIT GAMES: Arroyo, Pawtucket, defeated Buffalo, 7-0, August 10.

2003 FIELDING

TEAM

Team	G	PO	A	E	TC	DP	TP	PB	Pct.
Rochester	143	3702	1462	93	5257	144	0	12	.982
Norfolk	143	3717	1486	99	5302	146	0	12	.981
Durham	140	3713	1558	112	5383	129	0	11	.979
Pawtucket	144	3717	1296	113	5126	96	0	16	.978
Charlotte	144	3683	1281	114	5078	105	0	10	.978
Scranton/WB	143	3737	1428	114	5279	124	0	7	.978
Louisville	143	3731	1515	123	5369	152	0	7	.977
Columbus	144	3808	1403	122	5333	133	0	8	.977
Indianapolis	142	3724	1488	122	5334	136	0	18	.977
Buffalo	143	3734	1439	129	5302	138	0	11	.976
Ottawa	144	3729	1395	131	5255	123	0	9	.975
Syracuse	141	3650	1424	135	5209	130	0	20	.974
Richmond	143	3711	1355	138	5204	137	0	11	.973
Toledo	143	3723	1616	154	5493	168	0	10	.972

INDIVIDUAL

FIRST BASEMEN

NOTE: All caps denotes fielding-percentage leader based on 72 games for catchers, 96 for all other non-pitchers and 115 innings for pitchers. *Throws lefthanded.

Player, Team	Pct.	G	PO	A	E	TC	DP
Abad, Andy, Pawtucket *	.995	90	700	36	4	740	54
Alviso, Jerome, Ottawa	.900	1	9	0	1	10	0
Andrews, Shane, Rochester	.977	11	81	4	2	87	8
Bates, Fletcher, Ottawa	1.000	2	3	1	0	4	0
Branyan, Russell, Louisville	.958	2	22	1	1	24	1
Brazell, Craig, Norfolk	1.000	12	105	13	0	118	11
Broussard, Ben, Buffalo *	.990	24	190	18	2	210	22
Burke, Jamie, Charlotte	1.000	6	36	2	0	38	4
Burnham, Gary, Syracuse *	.988	67	551	37	7	595	53
Casanova, Raul, Ottawa	.900	3	18	0	2	20	1
Chamblee, Jim, Louisville	.995	26	185	14	1	200	18
Chevalier, Virgil, Norfolk	1.000	5	26	2	0	28	0
Clark, Howie, Syracuse	1.000	5	43	2	0	45	6
Collier, Lou, Pawtucket	1.000	1	9	1	0	10	3
Coquillette, Trace, Pawtucket	.000	1	0	0	0	0	0
Coste, Chris, Pawtucket	.978	6	44	0	1	45	3
Crespo, Felipe, Louisville	.991	61	494	30	5	529	55
Cruz, Jacob, Louisville *	.945	6	44	8	3	55	4
Cuddyer, Michael, Rochester	1.000	3	28	1	0	29	1
DePastino, Joe, Norfolk	1.000	1	1	0	0	1	0
Dominique, Andy, Pawtucket	1.000	3	17	0	0	17	1
Evans, Tom, Toledo	1.000	2	6	0	0	6	1
Fabregas, Jorge, Durham	1.000	1	5	0	0	5	1
Fagan, Shawn, Syracuse	.995	17	166	16	1	183	19
Garcia, Luis, Buffalo	.984	73	592	38	10	640	57
Gil, Benji, Buffalo	1.000	3	18	3	0	21	3
Gil, Geronimo, Ottawa	1.000	1	11	0	0	11	1
Glavine, Mike, Norfolk *	.990	27	175	17	2	194	21
GLOAD, ROSS, Charlotte *	.990	112	770	58	8	836	63
Grindell, Nate, Buffalo	1.000	2	1	1	0	2	0
Grummitt, Dan, Durham	1.000	9	73	4	0	77	6
Hafner, Travis, Buffalo	.986	24	197	14	3	214	23
Hammond, Joey, Ottawa	1.000	14	100	4	0	104	4
Hankins, Ryan, Charlotte	.994	21	150	13	1	164	21
Hansen, Jed, Indianapolis	1.000	2	12	0	0	12	0
Headley, Justin, Pawtucket *	1.000	3	23	1	0	24	0
Hessman, Mike, Richmond	.995	54	392	28	2	422	33
Hinch, A.J., Toledo	1.000	2	17	0	0	17	2
Hollins, Dave, Scranton-WB	.994	23	169	10	1	180	19
Houston, Tyler, Scranton-WB	1.000	2	14	1	0	15	2
Hubbard, Mike, Richmond	1.000	1	3	0	0	3	2
Huckaby, Ken, Syracuse	.991	23	198	19	2	219	18
Jackson, Ryan, Durham *	.997	91	860	61	3	924	88
Jennings, Doug, Indianapolis *	1.000	12	101	6	0	107	13
Jennings, Robin, Louisville *	.991	37	325	19	3	347	36
Johnson, Nick, Columbus *	.952	2	19	1	1	21	2
Johnson, Russ, Norfolk	1.000	4	23	1	0	24	0
Jordan, Kevin, Toledo	1.000	17	165	14	0	179	15
Knupfer, Jason, Scranton-WB	1.000	14	80	9	0	89	11
LaRocca, Greg, Buffalo	1.000	4	27	1	0	28	3
LaRoche, Adam, Richmond *	.993	72	549	39	4	592	70
Lamb, David, Rochester	.983	7	55	3	1	59	4
Larson, Brandon, Louisville	.800	1	8	0	2	10	1
Lemonis, Chris, Ottawa	.983	32	225	9	4	238	22
Lennon, Pat, Toledo	.985	47	413	35	7	455	49
Leon, Jose, Ottawa	.936	5	41	3	3	47	3
Liefer, Jeff, Durham	1.000	4	34	3	0	37	2
Lomasney, Steve, Ottawa	.000	1	0	0	0	0	0
Lucca, Lou, Buffalo	.900	1	9	0	1	10	0
Luuloa, Keith, Indianapolis	.993	36	286	15	2	303	23
Martinez, Victor, Buffalo	.982	14	104	8	2	114	7
McEwing, Joe, Norfolk	1.000	1	9	0	0	9	0
McGuire, Ryan, Col.-Roch.*	.994	39	305	27	2	334	31
McKay, Cody, Indianapolis	1.000	5	49	4	0	53	7
Mendez, Carlos, Ottawa	.994	58	470	31	3	504	46
Minor, Damon, Scranton-WB *	.991	41	309	34	3	346	34
Morgan, Scott, Charlotte	.991	14	106	4	1	111	5
Morneau, Justin, Rochester	.993	58	488	43	4	535	54
Morris, Warren, Toledo	1.000	1	5	1	0	6	0
Munoz, Billy, Toledo *	1.000	2	19	1	0	20	4
Nicholson, Derek, Toledo	.990	13	94	5	1	100	14
Ortiz, Hector, Durham	.978	5	42	2	1	45	5
Peeples, Mike, Toledo	.990	21	186	10	2	198	21
Pena, Carlos, Toledo *	.986	7	65	5	1	71	9
Perez, Jhonny, Toledo	1.000	2	6	0	0	6	0
Phillips, Jason, Norfolk	1.000	5	33	4	0	37	4
Piazza, Mike, Norfolk	1.000	1	1	0	0	1	1
Pickering, Calvin, Louisville *	.991	14	104	5	1	110	9
Pond, Simon, Syracuse	1.000	16	133	13	0	146	9
Post, Dave, Columbus	1.000	3	16	1	0	17	1
Pressley, Josh, Norfolk	.971	8	64	3	2	69	10
Prieto, Alex, Rochester	1.000	4	34	6	0	40	1
Quattlebaum, Hugh, Ottawa	.960	3	21	3	1	25	1
Rios, Brian, Ottawa	1.000	3	16	1	0	17	3
Rivera, Mike, Charlotte	1.000	4	29	1	0	30	1
Roberge, J.P., Scranton-WB	.990	71	575	46	6	627	51
Robinson, Bo, Columbus	1.000	2	16	1	0	17	2
Rolison, Nate, Columbus	.993	86	659	45	5	709	72
Rushford, Jim, Indianapolis *	.993	67	552	52	4	608	63
Sandberg, Jared, Durham	.959	8	62	9	3	74	3
Sasser, Rob, Ottawa	.991	29	210	14	2	226	22
Seabol, Scott, Indianapolis	.991	11	105	5	1	111	8
Sears, Todd, Rochester	.989	53	413	38	5	456	54
Secrist, Reed, Buffalo	1.000	8	42	1	0	43	4
Seguignol, Fernando, Columbus	.992	26	226	17	2	245	22
Smith, Bobby, Columbus	1.000	2	17	1	0	18	1
Smith, Mark, Indianapolis	1.000	4	30	1	0	31	1
Smitherman, Stephen, Louisville	1.000	1	2	0	0	2	1
Snyder, Earl, Pawtucket	1.000	14	92	14	0	106	5
Stefanski, Mike, Louisville	.965	10	53	2	2	57	10
Stevens, Lee, Indianapolis *	.990	12	99	5	1	105	7
Swann, Pedro, Ottawa	1.000	4	22	5	0	27	3
Thomas, Juan, Louisville	1.000	4	24	3	0	27	6
Toca, Jorge, Norfolk	.991	94	728	75	7	810	91
Truby, Chris, Durham	.992	28	236	15	2	253	17
Ust, Brant, Toledo	1.000	2	8	2	0	10	2
Valent, Eric, Scranton-WB *	1.000	3	7	0	0	7	0
Valera, Yohanny, Toledo	.987	7	72	2	1	75	7
Veras, Wilton, Indianapolis	1.000	1	8	0	0	8	1
Wathan, Dusty, Buffalo	1.000	2	9	1	0	10	1
Williams, Glenn, Syracuse	.979	12	83	12	2	97	7
Wilson, John, Norfolk	1.000	1	1	0	0	1	0
Wilson, Travis, Richmond	.977	24	158	12	4	174	20
Witt, Kevin, Toledo	.983	24	226	9	4	239	27
Young, Ernie, Toledo	.981	7	48	4	1	53	6
Zuleta, Julio, Pawtucket	.979	36	260	22	6	288	23
Zuniga, Tony, Syracuse	1.000	1	6	1	0	7	1

FIRST BASEMEN WITH TWO OR MORE TEAMS

Player, Team	Pct.	G	PO	A	E	TC	DP
McGuire, Ryan, Columbus *	.992	31	228	22	2	252	20
McGuire, Ryan, Rochester *	1.000	8	77	5	0	82	11

SECOND BASEMEN

Player, Team	Pct.	G	PO	A	E	TC	DP
Abernathy, Brent, Durham	.000	1	0	0	0	0	0
Alvarez, Jimmy, Syracuse	.944	27	37	65	6	108	15
Alviso, Jerome, Ottawa	.982	8	22	32	1	55	5
Badeaux, Brooks, Durham	.977	57	114	189	7	310	52
Beattie, Andrew, Louisville	1.000	7	12	23	0	35	8
Berg, Dave, Syracuse	1.000	4	8	14	0	22	1
Bocachica, Hiram, Toledo	.938	20	29	61	6	96	17
Canizaro, Jay, Durham	.952	18	28	32	3	63	4

Player, Team	Pct.	G	PO	A	E	TC	DP
Casillas, Uriel, Scranton-WB	1.000	3	3	9	0	12	3
Castro, Ramon, Richmond	.973	10	16	20	1	37	7
Chamblee, Jim, Louisville	.981	11	27	26	1	54	7
Clapp, Stubby, Richmond	.957	31	50	60	5	115	19
Clark, Howie, Syracuse	.961	53	85	138	9	232	27
Connacher, Kevin, Rochester	.981	13	26	27	1	54	6
Coquillette, Trace, Pawtucket	.984	50	79	106	3	188	22
Crespo, Cesar, Pawtucket	.967	42	77	98	6	181	19
Cuddyer, Michael, Rochester	1.000	8	15	26	0	41	7
Escalona, Felix, Ottawa	.943	8	18	15	2	35	4
Freel, Ryan, Louisville	.989	39	74	110	2	186	31
Garabito, Eddy, Ottawa	.909	5	11	9	2	22	3
Garcia, Daniel, Norfolk	.972	98	196	254	13	463	66
Garcia, Jesse, Richmond	.938	6	4	11	1	16	3
Gil, Benji, Buffalo	1.000	3	4	11	0	15	2
Gipson, Charles, Columbus	1.000	1	2	3	0	5	0
Goelz, Jim, Pawtucket	.857	1	3	3	1	7	1
Green, Nick, Richmond	.967	108	202	261	16	479	72
Guerrero, Wilton, Louisville	.992	30	54	73	1	128	17
Gutierrez, Ricky, Buffalo	1.000	3	7	3	0	10	1
Hall, Bill, Indianapolis	.967	51	118	142	9	269	33
Hammond, Joey, Ottawa	.993	38	58	86	1	145	19
Harris, Willie, Charlotte	1.000	17	43	44	0	87	10
Hitchcox, Brian, Scranton-WB	1.000	12	24	38	0	62	14
Hummel, Tim, Charlotte	1.000	6	11	7	0	18	3
Izturis, Maicer, Buffalo	.991	20	40	65	1	106	19
Johnson, Russ, Norfolk	.929	4	5	8	1	14	3
Jordan, Kevin, Toledo	.978	22	39	51	2	92	14
Keene, Kurt, Syracuse	1.000	3	4	5	0	9	1
Klassen, Danny, Toledo	.989	30	67	106	2	175	35
Knupfer, Jason, Scranton-WB	.929	14	25	40	5	70	6
LaRocca, Greg, Buffalo	.952	12	29	31	3	63	9
Lamb, David, Rochester	.973	8	20	16	1	37	4
Lawrence, Joe, Indianapolis	.973	11	15	21	1	37	2
Lemonis, Chris, Ottawa	1.000	6	6	15	0	21	2
Lopez, Felipe, Louisville	.972	7	20	15	1	36	4
Lopez, Luis, Ottawa	.963	32	66	91	6	163	23
Luuloa, Keith, Indianapolis	1.000	27	41	67	0	108	18
Martinez, Gabby, Durham	1.000	2	0	3	0	3	0
Maxwell, Jason, Louisville	.983	59	105	177	5	287	44
McEwing, Joe, Norfolk	1.000	1	0	2	0	2	0
Mendez, Deivi, Columbus	1.000	1	1	0	0	1	0
Miles, Aaron, Charlotte	.973	121	224	310	15	549	60
Moore, Frank, Durham	1.000	5	8	7	0	15	0
Morris, Warren, Toledo	.983	44	107	125	4	236	49
Nicholson, Tommy, Charlotte	1.000	3	2	2	0	4	1
Nieves, Jose, Columbus	.889	4	6	2	1	9	0
Olivares, Teuris, Columbus	.000	1	0	0	0	0	0
Olmedo, Rainer, Louisville	.958	4	9	14	1	24	6
Paul, Josh, Charlotte	1.000	1	1	0	0	1	0
Paz, Rich, Indianapolis	.983	35	83	93	3	179	25
Perez, Antonio, Durham	.958	33	73	111	8	192	22
Perez, Jhonny, Toledo	.969	32	69	88	5	162	17
Phillips, Andy, Columbus	.955	12	17	25	2	44	6
Phillips, Brandon, Buffalo	.985	43	99	102	3	204	30
Post, Dave, Columbus	.931	29	38	57	7	102	16
Pratt, Scott, Buffalo	.968	28	48	74	4	126	10
Prieto, Alex, Rochester	1.000	5	8	17	0	25	4
Roberts, Brian, Ottawa	.987	38	72	81	2	155	23
Rodriguez, Luis, Rochester	.984	117	235	307	9	551	85
Sanchez, Freddy, Pawtucket	.989	21	36	50	1	87	9
Sandberg, Jared, Durham	1.000	5	3	12	0	15	2
Santos, Angel, Paw.-Buffalo	.976	45	88	111	5	204	25
Sasser, Rob, Ottawa	.981	16	25	27	1	53	8
Scarborough, Steve, Ind.	.962	23	42	60	4	106	17
Scutaro, Marcos, Norfolk	.982	23	46	63	2	111	11
Sequea, Jorge, Syracuse	.955	50	105	130	11	246	29
Shipp, Brian, Norfolk	.967	4	17	12	1	30	5
Smith, Bobby, Columbus	.958	6	8	15	1	24	4
Smith, Jason, Durham	.961	28	52	72	5	129	17
Sorensen, Zach, Buffalo	.973	30	70	74	4	148	25
Sosa, Juan, Scranton-WB	1.000	5	5	9	0	14	0
Ust, Brant, Toledo	1.000	1	2	4	0	6	0
Utley, Chase, Scranton-WB	.978	113	260	326	13	599	67
Velandia, Jorge, Norfolk	1.000	16	27	39	0	66	8
Williams, Glenn, Syracuse	1.000	8	15	22	0	37	8
WILSON, CRAIG, Columbus	.991	102	174	287	4	465	65
Wilson, Travis, Richmond	1.000	1	0	1	0	1	1

SECOND BASEMEN WITH TWO OR MORE TEAMS

Player, Team	Pct.	G	PO	A	E	TC	DP
Santos, Angel, Buffalo	.946	8	17	18	2	37	5
Santos, Angel, Pawtucket	.982	37	71	93	3	167	20

THIRD BASEMEN

Player, Team	Pct.	G	PO	A	E	TC	DP
Almonte, Erick, Columbus	1.000	1	1	1	0	2	1
Alviso, Jerome, Ottawa	1.000	2	1	4	0	5	0
ANDREWS, SHANE, Rochester	.963	108	71	219	11	301	17
Badeaux, Brooks, Durham	.941	4	2	14	1	17	2
Basak, Chris, Norfolk	1.000	7	3	10	0	13	3
Berg, Dave, Syracuse	1.000	1	1	2	0	3	0
Betemit, Wilson, Richmond	.896	107	62	163	26	251	18
Bocachica, Hiram, Toledo	1.000	2	2	3	0	5	0
Branyan, Russell, Louisville	1.000	2	1	3	0	4	0
Brumbaugh, Cliff, Charlotte	1.000	4	2	3	0	5	0
Burke, Jamie, Charlotte	1.000	1	1	1	0	2	0
Calzado, Napoleon, Ottawa	.875	21	20	36	8	64	7
Cantu, Jorge, Durham	1.000	2	0	5	0	5	1
Cash, Kevin, Syracuse	1.000	1	0	1	0	1	0
Casillas, Uriel, Scranton-WB	.500	1	0	1	1	2	0
Castro, Ramon, Richmond	.667	4	2	2	2	6	0
Chamblee, Jim, Louisville	.982	39	18	89	2	109	9
Chapman, Travis, Scranton-WB	.962	131	75	228	12	315	17
Chevalier, Virgil, Norfolk	1.000	3	1	6	0	7	0
Clapp, Stubby, Richmond	.943	19	8	42	3	53	6
Clark, Howie, Syracuse	1.000	1	1	4	0	5	0
Collier, Lou, Pawtucket	1.000	1	1	2	0	3	0
Connacher, Kevin, Rochester	.919	17	10	24	3	37	3
Crespo, Cesar, Pawtucket	.500	2	1	1	2	4	0
Crespo, Felipe, Louisville	.000	1	0	0	0	0	0
Cuddyer, Michael, Rochester	1.000	4	7	6	0	13	0
Deardorff, Jeff, Rochester	1.000	10	6	17	0	23	2
Dragicevich, Scott, Syracuse	1.000	10	9	18	0	27	2
Dransfeldt, Kelly, Louisville	.929	7	4	9	1	14	0
Evans, Tom, Toledo	.960	34	17	102	5	124	14
Freel, Ryan, Louisville	1.000	4	3	9	0	12	0
Garcia, Jesse, Richmond	1.000	3	1	4	0	5	1
Gil, Benji, Buffalo	.667	1	0	2	1	3	0
Gipson, Charles, Columbus	.909	4	4	6	1	11	2
Grindell, Nate, Buffalo	.960	8	4	20	1	25	1
Guerrero, Wilton, Louisville	.853	15	9	20	5	34	2
Gutierrez, Ricky, Buffalo	1.000	7	4	13	0	17	2
Hammond, Joey, Ottawa	.951	20	11	28	2	41	3
Hankins, Ryan, Charlotte	.960	47	29	67	4	100	6
Hansen, Jed, Indianapolis	1.000	1	0	1	0	1	0
Helms, Wes, Indianapolis	1.000	2	2	5	0	7	1
Henson, Drew, Columbus	.918	132	98	216	28	342	16
Hessman, Mike, Richmond	.962	19	12	39	2	53	2
Hinch, A.J., Toledo	.000	1	0	0	0	0	0
Hinske, Eric, Syracuse	1.000	2	1	1	0	2	0
Houston, Tyler, Scranton-WB	1.000	1	0	2	0	2	0
Huckaby, Ken, Syracuse	.750	2	1	2	1	4	0
Hummel, Tim, Charlotte	.955	97	63	150	10	223	17
Johnson, Russ, Norfolk	.948	86	41	158	11	210	18
Keene, Kurt, Syracuse	.500	2	0	1	1	2	0
Klassen, Danny, Toledo	.667	3	0	2	1	3	1
Knupfer, Jason, Scranton-WB	1.000	3	3	6	0	9	2
LaRocca, Greg, Buffalo	.932	106	66	195	19	280	18
Larson, Brandon, Louisville	.942	70	51	175	14	240	19
Lawrence, Joe, Indianapolis	.889	7	3	13	2	18	3
Lemonis, Chris, Ottawa	.889	9	4	12	2	18	3
Leon, Jose, Ottawa	.946	68	51	125	10	186	13
Liefer, Jeff, Durham	.667	1	2	0	1	3	0
Lopez, Luis, Ottawa	1.000	1	2	1	0	3	0
Lucca, Lou, Buffalo	.750	5	3	3	2	8	0
Luuloa, Keith, Indianapolis	.937	31	15	59	5	79	6
Magee, Wendell, Toledo	.000	1	0	0	0	0	0
Maxwell, Jason, Louisville	.941	13	5	27	2	34	1
McEwing, Joe, Norfolk	1.000	1	1	4	0	5	2
McKay, Cody, Indianapolis	1.000	2	2	6	0	8	0
Mendez, Carlos, Ottawa	.000	1	0	0	0	0	0
Miles, Aaron, Charlotte	1.000	2	1	3	0	4	0
Moriarty, Mike, Syracuse	.955	8	4	17	1	22	1
Morris, Warren, Toledo	.920	9	6	17	2	25	0
Nicholson, Tommy, Charlotte	1.000	2	0	2	0	2	0
Nye, Rodney, Norfolk	1.000	2	1	3	0	4	0
Peralta, John, Buffalo	1.000	3	3	7	0	10	1
Perez, Jhonny, Toledo	1.000	3	0	6	0	6	0
Perez, Santiago, Ottawa	.861	9	3	28	5	36	2
Pond, Simon, Syracuse	.962	31	26	50	3	79	7
Post, Dave, Columbus	.833	1	1	4	1	6	0
Pratt, Scott, Buffalo	.868	16	7	26	5	38	3
Prieto, Alex, Rochester	.946	12	10	25	2	37	5
Rios, Brian, Ottawa	.953	16	10	31	2	43	5
Roberge, J.P., Scranton-WB	.960	7	6	18	1	25	1
Sanchez, Freddy, Pawtucket	1.000	2	0	6	0	6	0

Player, Team	Pct.	G	PO	A	E	TC	DP
Sandberg, Jared, Durham	.973	60	48	133	5	186	11
Santos, Angel, Paw.-Buffalo	1.000	11	5	11	0	16	1
Sasser, Rob, Ottawa	.909	8	5	15	2	22	4
Scutaro, Marcos, Norfolk	.947	36	24	65	5	94	5
Seabol, Scott, Indianapolis	1.000	5	7	11	0	18	0
Secrist, Reed, Buffalo	1.000	3	3	0	0	3	0
Sequea, Jorge, Syracuse	.944	10	6	11	1	18	0
Shipp, Brian, Norfolk	1.000	1	1	4	0	5	0
Smith, Bobby, Columbus	1.000	6	2	14	0	16	1
Smith, Jason, Durham	.960	10	4	20	1	25	2
Snyder, Earl, Pawtucket	.957	103	86	161	11	258	17
Sorensen, Zach, Buffalo	.900	4	3	6	1	10	2
Sosa, Juan, Scranton-WB	.500	1	1	0	1	2	0
Truby, Chris, Durham	.959	66	44	164	9	217	12
Ust, Brant, Toledo	.944	83	47	188	14	249	26
Velandia, Jorge, Norfolk	1.000	9	2	19	0	21	4
Velazquez, Gil, Norfolk	1.000	5	6	11	0	17	2
Veras, Wilton, Indianapolis	.936	105	75	204	19	298	15
Williams, Glenn, Syracuse	.966	19	10	46	2	58	5
Wilson, John, Norfolk	1.000	3	1	7	0	8	0
Wilson, Travis, Richmond	1.000	3	0	5	0	5	0
Witt, Kevin, Toledo	.839	13	3	23	5	31	3
Youkilis, Kevin, Pawtucket	.952	29	29	50	4	83	2
Zuleta, Julio, Pawtucket	1.000	1	1	2	0	3	0
Zuniga, Tony, Syracuse	.934	61	46	109	11	166	11

THIRD BASEMEN WITH TWO OR MORE TEAMS

Player, Team	Pct.	G	PO	A	E	TC	DP
Santos, Angel, Buffalo	1.000	2	2	2	0	4	0
Santos, Angel, Pawtucket	1.000	9	3	9	0	12	1

SHORTSTOPS

Player, Team	Pct.	G	PO	A	E	TC	DP
Almonte, Erick, Columbus	.960	46	79	136	9	224	35
Alvarez, Jimmy, Syracuse	.958	64	76	172	11	259	33
Alviso, Jerome, Ottawa	.967	6	9	20	1	30	3
Badeaux, Brooks, Durham	1.000	2	1	6	0	7	2
Baez, Kevin, Louisville	.931	8	11	16	2	29	3
Basak, Chris, Norfolk	.966	11	17	39	2	58	12
Betemit, Wilson, Richmond	.944	9	8	26	2	36	3
Caceres, Wilmy, Louisville	.800	1	2	2	1	5	0
Calzado, Napoleon, Ottawa	.950	8	19	19	2	40	4
Canizaro, Jay, Durham	1.000	2	0	6	0	6	0
Cantu, Jorge, Durham	.948	53	79	141	12	232	22
Casillas, Uriel, Scranton-WB	.875	2	4	3	1	8	1
Castro, Juan, Louisville	.950	9	11	27	2	40	9
Castro, Ramon, Richmond	1.000	11	17	31	0	48	8
Clapinski, Chris, Louisville	1.000	7	6	18	0	24	6
Clapp, Stubby, Richmond	.979	30	59	78	3	140	25
Collier, Lou, Pawtucket	.961	22	25	49	3	77	6
Crespo, Cesar, Pawtucket	1.000	2	2	2	0	4	0
Dragicevich, Scott, Syracuse	1.000	1	1	5	0	6	0
Dransfeldt, Kelly, Lou.-Paw.	.957	102	146	276	19	441	52
Escalona, Felix, Ottawa	1.000	2	3	2	0	5	0
Garabito, Eddy, Ottawa	.942	106	160	280	27	467	53
Garcia, Jesse, Richmond	.955	94	139	226	17	382	55
Gil, Benji, Buffalo	1.000	1	1	2	0	3	0
Goelz, Jim, Pawtucket	1.000	2	3	6	0	9	1
Green, Nick, Richmond	.900	10	15	21	4	40	7
Guerrero, Wilton, Louisville	.988	18	31	54	1	86	14
Gutierrez, Ricky, Buffalo	1.000	4	3	11	0	14	3
Hall, Bill, Indianapolis	.946	36	60	98	9	167	28
Hummel, Tim, Charlotte	.966	31	37	48	3	88	9
Infante, Omar, Toledo	.942	64	101	191	18	310	48
Izturis, Maicer, Buffalo	.959	66	84	195	12	291	37
Johnson, Russ, Norfolk	1.000	6	12	11	0	23	2
Keene, Kurt, Syracuse	.953	17	23	38	3	64	8
Klassen, Danny, Toledo	.949	76	119	237	19	375	57
Knupfer, Jason, Scranton-WB	.948	76	99	209	17	325	38
Lamb, David, Rochester	.965	89	134	252	14	400	58
Lopez, Felipe, Louisville	.930	28	36	70	8	114	19
Lopez, Luis, Ottawa	.984	15	15	46	1	62	8
Luuloa, Keith, Indianapolis	.833	1	1	4	1	6	0
Martinez, Gabby, Durham	1.000	2	0	7	0	7	1
Maxwell, Jason, Louisville	.962	32	42	84	5	131	21
Mendez, Deivi, Columbus	.947	4	7	11	1	19	3
Moriarty, Mike, Syracuse	.960	48	77	138	9	224	37
Nicholson, Tommy, Charlotte	.870	10	12	8	3	23	1
Nieves, Jose, Columbus	.955	40	43	106	7	156	26
Nunez, Jorge, Charlotte	.949	110	170	296	25	491	55
Olivares, Teuris, Columbus	.750	2	1	5	2	8	0
Olmedo, Rainer, Louisville	1.000	6	13	21	0	34	6
Peralta, John, Buffalo	.968	60	98	201	10	309	49
Perez, Jhonny, Toledo	.938	6	11	19	2	32	4
Perez, Santiago, Ott.-Lou.	.936	8	8	21	2	31	3
Post, Dave, Columbus	.917	4	7	4	1	12	2
Pratt, Scott, Buffalo	1.000	1	1	2	0	3	0
Prieto, Alex, Rochester	.970	47	67	128	6	201	31
Punto, Nick, Scranton-WB	.969	25	37	90	4	131	19
Reyes, Jose, Norfolk	.969	40	52	105	5	162	24
Roberge, J.P., Scranton-WB	.857	1	3	3	1	7	0
Roberts, Brian, Ottawa	.941	6	17	15	2	34	2
Rodriguez, Luis, Rochester	.915	13	14	29	4	47	8
Sanchez, Freddy, Pawtucket	.979	35	52	89	3	144	19
Santos, Angel, Paw.-Buffalo	.933	30	30	81	8	119	12
Sasser, Rob, Ottawa	1.000	1	0	4	0	4	1
SCARBOROUGH, STEVE, Ind.	.965	105	158	286	16	460	68
Scutaro, Marcos, Norfolk	1.000	9	7	15	0	22	6
Sequea, Jorge, Syracuse	.926	10	20	30	4	54	7
Smith, Bobby, Columbus	.965	54	81	140	8	229	31
Smith, Jason, Durham	.959	87	128	268	17	413	61
Sorensen, Zach, Buffalo	.917	9	13	20	3	36	3
Sosa, Juan, Scranton-WB	.933	42	59	107	12	178	30
Ust, Brant, Toledo	1.000	1	1	2	0	3	0
Velandia, Jorge, Norfolk	.951	85	117	236	18	371	51
Veras, Wilton, Indianapolis	1.000	4	5	9	0	14	0
Williams, Glenn, Syracuse	1.000	5	4	15	0	19	4

SHORTSTOPS WITH TWO OR MORE TEAMS

Player, Team	Pct.	G	PO	A	E	TC	DP
Dransfeldt, Kelly, Louisville	.948	37	67	98	9	174	21
Dransfeldt, Kelly, Pawtucket	.963	65	79	178	10	267	31
Perez, Santiago, Louisville	.966	6	8	20	1	29	2
Perez, Santiago, Ottawa	.500	2	0	1	1	2	1
Santos, Angel, Pawtucket	.927	27	28	73	8	109	12
Santos, Angel, Buffalo	1.000	3	2	8	0	10	0

OUTFIELDERS

Player, Team	Pct.	G	PO	A	E	TC	DP
Abad, Andy, Pawtucket *	.982	27	53	1	1	55	0
Aven, Bruce, Syracuse	.957	42	65	1	3	69	1
Badeaux, Brooks, Durham	1.000	1	1	0	0	1	0
Bates, Fletcher, Ottawa	.975	20	36	3	1	40	1
Beattie, Andrew, Louisville	1.000	2	5	1	0	6	0
Bigbie, Larry, Ottawa *	.974	22	34	3	1	38	0
Bocachica, Hiram, Toledo	.964	69	129	4	5	138	1
Borchard, Joe, Charlotte	.985	114	316	9	5	330	2
Branyan, Russell, Louisville	1.000	3	3	0	0	3	0
Brown, Adrian, Pawtucket	.983	121	280	4	5	289	1
Brown, Emil, Louisville	.979	91	223	9	5	237	2
Brumbaugh, Cliff, Charlotte	.985	30	61	3	1	65	1
Budzinski, Mark, Ind.-Lou.*	.992	117	239	4	2	245	1
Byrd, Marlon, Scranton-WB	1.000	1	5	1	0	6	0
Calzado, Napoleon, Ottawa	.976	20	40	0	1	41	0
Camilo, Juan, Scranton-WB	.909	4	9	1	1	11	0
Chamblee, Jim, Louisville	1.000	9	17	0	0	17	0
Chevalier, Virgil, Norfolk	1.000	5	7	0	0	7	0
Christensen, McKay, S./WB *	.992	42	119	2	1	122	1
Clapp, Stubby, Richmond	.800	4	4	0	1	5	0
Clark, Brady, Indianapolis	1.000	7	14	0	0	14	0
Clark, Howie, Syracuse	1.000	7	16	0	0	16	0
Colangelo, Mike, Syracuse	.971	59	98	1	3	102	0
Coleman, Michael, Louisville	1.000	16	25	1	0	26	0
Collier, Lou, Pawtucket	.973	72	137	9	4	150	1
Connacher, Kevin, Rochester	.923	15	9	3	1	13	0
Conti, Jason, Indianapolis	.976	116	266	21	7	294	3
Coquillette, Trace, Pawtucket	1.000	11	10	0	0	10	0
Crespo, Cesar, Pawtucket	.959	79	155	7	7	169	0
Crespo, Felipe, Louisville	.975	18	37	2	1	40	0
Crisp, Covelli, Buffalo	.982	56	155	6	3	164	2
Crosby, Bubba, Columbus *	1.000	16	42	1	0	43	0
Cruz, Jacob, Louisville *	.962	25	48	2	2	52	1
Cuddyer, Michael, Rochester	.984	32	59	1	1	61	0
Cust, Jack, Ottawa	.978	77	126	7	3	136	1
Darula, Bobby, Louisville	1.000	7	16	0	0	16	0
Deardorff, Jeff, Rochester	.000	1	0	0	0	0	0
Diaz, Matt, Durham	.993	64	131	8	1	140	2
Duncan, Jeff, Norfolk *	1.000	4	7	0	0	7	0
Escobar, Alex, Buffalo	.975	103	191	8	5	204	1
Evans, Lee, Richmond	1.000	1	1	0	0	1	0
Evans, Tom, Toledo	1.000	2	1	0	0	1	0
Fitzgerald, Jason, Richmond *	1.000	11	22	1	0	23	0
Ford, Lew, Rochester	.990	44	90	6	1	97	3
Foreman, JuJu, Louisville	.000	1	0	0	0	0	0

Player, Team	Pct.	G	PO	A	E	TC	DP
Francia, Dave, Scranton-WB *	1.000	4	11	0	0	11	0
Freel, Ryan, Louisville	1.000	8	10	1	0	11	0
French, Anton, Pawtucket	.978	92	217	3	5	225	0
Galloway, Mike, Syracuse	1.000	3	3	0	0	3	0
Garcia, Jesse, Richmond	1.000	6	9	0	0	9	0
Garcia, Karim, Buffalo *	1.000	12	22	1	0	23	0
Garcia, Luis, Buffalo	.976	22	38	3	1	42	0
Gerut, Jody, Buffalo *	1.000	16	36	1	0	37	0
Gipson, Charles, Columbus	.978	26	83	5	2	90	1
Glavine, Mike, Norfolk *	1.000	3	2	0	0	2	0
Gload, Ross, Charlotte *	1.000	28	50	2	0	52	0
Goelz, Jim, Pawtucket	1.000	5	7	1	0	8	0
Gomes, Jonny, Durham	1.000	3	3	2	0	5	0
Gonzalez, Raul, Norfolk	1.000	30	56	7	0	63	1
GREEN, CHAD, Rochester	.996	101	228	5	1	234	1
Grindell, Nate, Buffalo	1.000	32	47	0	0	47	0
Gross, Gabe, Syracuse	.985	53	129	5	2	136	1
Guerrero, Wilton, Louisville	1.000	55	84	2	0	86	0
Guillen, Jose, Louisville	1.000	4	5	0	0	5	0
Hall, Bill, Indianapolis	.750	3	3	0	1	4	0
Hammond, Joey, Ottawa	1.000	33	56	0	0	56	0
Harris, Willie, Charlotte	1.000	10	14	1	0	15	0
Headley, Justin, Pawtucket *	1.000	9	17	1	0	18	1
Hessman, Mike, Richmond	.975	24	36	3	1	40	0
Hollins, Damon, Richmond *	.981	89	196	11	4	211	4
Jackson, Ryan, Durham *	.983	29	56	1	1	58	0
Jennings, Doug, Indianapolis *	1.000	9	10	2	0	12	0
Jennings, Robin, Louisville *	1.000	25	45	0	0	45	0
Johnson, Reed, Syracuse	1.000	26	60	2	0	62	1
Johnson, Rontrez, Richmond	1.000	25	50	3	0	53	1
Jordan, Kevin, Toledo	.000	1	0	0	0	0	0
Keene, Kurt, Syracuse	.929	15	26	0	2	28	0
Kelly, Kenny, Norfolk	.981	25	47	5	1	53	0
Kingsale, Eugene, Toledo	1.000	46	84	1	0	85	0
Knox, Ryan, Indianapolis	.973	33	67	4	2	73	2
Langerhans, Ryan, Richmond *	.949	37	73	2	4	79	0
Larson, Brandon, Louisville	1.000	1	1	0	0	1	0
Lawrence, Joe, Indianapolis	.889	8	8	0	1	9	0
Lennon, Pat, Toledo	.917	7	11	0	1	12	0
Liefer, Jeff, Durham	1.000	26	43	3	0	46	0
Little, Mark, Buffalo	.982	42	101	6	2	109	2
Littleton, Brandon, Ottawa *	1.000	29	78	1	0	79	1
Lombard, George, Durham	.989	108	246	13	3	262	2
Maddox, Garry, Scranton-WB	.956	13	43	0	2	45	0
Magee, Wendell, S/WB-Toledo	.991	64	111	4	1	116	0
Magruder, Chris, Buffalo	1.000	40	73	2	0	75	0
Martinez, Gabby, Durham	.941	7	16	0	1	17	0
Mateo, Ruben, Louisville	.984	57	117	3	2	122	0
Matos, Luis, Ottawa	.990	45	95	1	1	97	1
Matthews, Lamont, Pawtucket *	1.000	7	13	0	0	13	0
McDonald, Darnell, Ottawa	.968	37	90	2	3	95	0
McDonald, Donzell, Richmond	.993	123	256	9	2	267	0
McEwing, Joe, Norfolk	1.000	2	2	0	0	2	0
McGuire, Ryan, Col.-Roch.*	1.000	36	65	0	0	65	0
Mitchell, Keith, Louisville	1.000	14	26	1	0	27	0
Monroe, Craig, Toledo	1.000	13	24	0	0	24	0
Moore, Frank, Durham	1.000	6	12	1	0	13	0
Morgan, Scott, Charlotte	.980	64	144	1	3	148	1
Mottola, Chad, Durham-Paw.	.982	55	104	3	2	109	0
Mouton, Lyle, Nor.-S/WB-Buff.	.989	53	81	9	1	91	2
Murphy, Nate, Charlotte *	1.000	38	57	2	0	59	1
Neuberger, Scott, Durham	.969	58	93	1	3	97	0
Nicholson, Derek, Toledo	1.000	2	4	0	0	4	0
Patrick, Brian, Syracuse	.933	7	12	2	1	15	0
Peeples, Mike, Toledo	.857	4	6	0	1	7	0
Pena, Wily Mo, Louisville	.933	14	28	0	2	30	0
Perez, Jhonny, Toledo	1.000	21	28	4	0	32	0
Perez, Josue, Scranton-WB	.989	29	87	2	1	90	0
Perez, Timo, Norfolk *	1.000	3	3	1	0	4	0
Pond, Simon, Syracuse	1.000	11	18	0	0	18	0
Porter, Bo, Richmond	.977	74	122	7	3	132	1
Post, Dave, Columbus	.969	37	60	2	2	64	0
Pratt, Scott, Buffalo	.980	54	95	5	2	102	0
Pride, Curtis, Columbus	.991	48	101	4	1	106	0
Quinn, Mark, Durham	1.000	8	15	0	0	15	0
Rabe, Josh, Rochester	.957	34	44	0	2	46	0
Raines, Tim, Ottawa	.993	52	134	3	1	138	1
Redman, Prentice, Norfolk	.978	120	207	12	5	224	3
Reese, Kevin, Columbus *	.963	13	24	2	1	27	0
Restovich, Michael, Rochester	.989	110	248	13	3	264	4
Rios, Armando, Charlotte *	.976	36	80	2	2	84	0
Rivera, Juan, Columbus	.982	79	160	6	3	169	0
Rivera, Ruben, Ottawa	.950	14	37	1	2	40	0
Rodriguez, John, Columbus *	.981	70	150	4	3	157	0
Rolls, Damian, Durham	.913	14	21	0	2	23	0
Ross, Cody, Toledo *	.977	119	243	15	6	264	0
Rowand, Aaron, Charlotte	.950	32	95	1	5	101	0
Rushford, Jim, Indianapolis *	1.000	29	31	0	0	31	0
Ryan, Michael, Rochester	.988	97	154	8	2	164	0
Ryan, Rob, Syracuse *	.964	33	53	1	2	56	0
Sandberg, Jared, Durham	1.000	1	2	0	0	2	0
Sanders, Anthony, Charlotte	.979	74	135	7	3	145	1
Sasser, Rob, Ottawa	1.000	4	2	0	0	2	0
Scutaro, Marcos, Norfolk	1.000	4	7	0	0	7	0
Seabol, Scott, Indianapolis	.875	5	7	0	1	8	0
Secrist, Reed, Buffalo	1.000	11	18	2	0	20	0
Sefcik, Kevin, Scranton-WB	.978	121	162	13	4	179	1
Shinjo, Tsuyoshi, Norfolk	.983	27	58	1	1	60	0
Simmons, Brian, Scranton-WB	.979	40	91	3	2	96	0
Smith, Bobby, Columbus	.953	42	77	5	4	86	0
Smith, Mark, Indianapolis	.982	65	106	3	2	111	2
Smitherman, Stephen, Louisville	.969	15	29	2	1	32	1
Snead, Esix, Norfolk	.989	132	335	9	4	348	1
Snyder, Earl, Pawtucket	1.000	14	16	3	0	19	1
Sorensen, Zach, Buffalo	.951	18	39	0	2	41	0
Sosa, Juan, Scranton-WB	.983	26	57	0	1	58	0
Stenson, Dernell, Louisville *	.960	17	24	0	1	25	0
Stewart, Shannon, Syracuse	1.000	1	2	0	0	2	0
Swann, Pedro, Ottawa	.977	86	165	6	4	175	0
Thames, Marcus, Columbus	.977	52	123	5	3	131	0
Thompson, Rich, Syracuse	.988	28	82	3	1	86	0
Thompson, Ryan, Durham	.500	1	1	0	1	2	0
Toca, Jorge, Norfolk	1.000	13	19	1	0	20	0
Torres, Andres, Toledo	.973	70	181	2	5	188	1
Tyner, Jason, Durham *	.993	64	147	5	1	153	1
Valent, Eric, Scranton-WB *	.973	132	283	10	8	301	2
Valenzuela, Mario, Charlotte	1.000	20	36	2	0	38	0
Vento, Mike, Columbus	.992	49	122	4	1	127	1
Wakeland, Chris, Buffalo *	.941	15	16	0	1	17	0
Watson, Matt, Norfolk	.939	60	119	5	8	132	2
Werth, Jayson, Syracuse	.954	61	136	10	7	153	1
White, Derrick, Buffalo	1.000	7	12	1	0	13	0
Williams, Glenn, Syracuse	1.000	11	14	1	0	15	1
Wilson, Travis, Richmond	.989	59	91	1	1	93	0
Wise, Dewayne, Syracuse *	.974	76	183	2	5	190	0
Young, Ernie, Toledo	.978	51	84	6	2	92	3
Zoccolillo, Peter, Indianapolis	.986	122	200	8	3	211	0

OUTFIELDERS WITH TWO OR MORE TEAMS

Player, Team	Pct.	G	PO	A	E	TC	DP
Budzinski, Mark, Indianapolis *	1.000	45	86	1	0	87	0
Budzinski, Mark, Louisville *	.987	72	153	3	2	158	1
Magee, Wendell, Scranton-WB	1.000	21	38	2	0	40	0
Magee, Wendell, Toledo	.987	43	73	2	1	76	0
McGuire, Ryan, Columbus *	1.000	22	39	0	0	39	0
McGuire, Ryan, Rochester *	1.000	14	26	0	0	26	0
Mottola, Chad, Durham	.988	40	76	3	1	80	0
Mottola, Chad, Pawtucket	.966	15	28	0	1	29	0
Mouton, Lyle, Norfolk	1.000	30	44	4	0	48	1
Mouton, Lyle, Scranton-WB	1.000	5	6	1	0	7	0
Mouton, Lyle, Buffalo	.972	18	31	4	1	36	1

CATCHERS

Player, Team	Pct.	G	PO	A	E	TC	DP	PB
Acevas, Jon, Charlotte	.962	7	45	6	2	53	1	1
Alomar, Sandy, Charlotte	1.000	3	11	2	0	13	0	0
Bard, Josh, Buffalo	.995	30	201	16	1	218	3	2
Boscan, Jean, Richmond	1.000	3	26	3	0	29	1	0
Bowen, Rob, Rochester	.995	26	176	18	1	195	1	4
Burke, Jamie, Charlotte	.989	72	493	34	6	533	5	3
Casanova, Raul, Ottawa	1.000	3	26	4	0	30	0	0
CASH, KEVIN, Syracuse	.998	90	521	77	1	599	12	10
Charles, Frank, Pawtucket	.993	19	130	8	1	139	0	7
Chevalier, Virgil, Norfolk	1.000	23	152	5	0	157	0	2
Chiaffredo, Paul, Syracuse	1.000	5	28	2	0	30	0	1
Coste, Chris, Pawtucket	.961	8	46	3	2	51	1	1
DeCinces, Tim, Buffalo	1.000	2	9	0	0	9	0	0
Delgado, Alex, Indianapolis	.996	37	239	29	1	269	7	3
DePastino, Joe, Norfolk	.995	78	512	53	3	568	6	5
Dominique, Andy, Pawtucket	.992	51	322	30	3	355	1	5
Elwood, Brad, Columbus	1.000	5	24	2	0	26	0	0
Estrada, Johnny, Richmond	.994	83	627	40	4	671	8	7
Evans, Lee, Richmond	.987	11	68	7	1	76	1	3

Player, Team	Pct.	G	PO	A	E	TC	DP	PB
Fabregas, Jorge, Durham	.987	33	202	18	3	223	0	2
Gil, Geronimo, Ottawa	.992	29	220	27	2	249	1	3
Greene, Charlie, Durham	1.000	5	25	0	0	25	0	0
Hanigan, Ryan, Louisville	1.000	1	5	1	0	6	1	0
Haselman, Bill, Pawtucket	.989	72	497	39	6	542	2	3
Hernandez, Michel, Columbus	.993	83	563	43	4	610	6	5
Hill, Jason, Louisville	1.000	1	7	2	0	9	0	0
Hinch, A.J., Toledo	.991	48	299	22	3	324	5	3
Hubbard, Mike, Richmond	.995	55	376	28	2	406	1	1
Huckaby, Ken, Syracuse	.988	46	308	17	4	329	2	9
Inge, Brandon, Toledo	1.000	35	207	28	0	235	2	4
Jensen, Marcus, Columbus	.995	62	411	19	2	432	2	3
Kennedy, Bryan, Rochester	1.000	5	28	1	0	29	0	1
LaForest, Pete, Durham	.990	50	272	19	3	294	5	6
LaRocca, Greg, Buffalo	.000	1	0	0	0	0	0	0
Lawrence, Joe, Indianapolis	1.000	17	89	9	0	98	0	5
Levis, Jesse, Scranton-WB	.996	77	514	41	2	557	3	4
Lomasney, Steve, Ottawa	.992	68	468	47	4	519	3	5
Luuloa, Keith, Indianapolis	1.000	1	4	0	0	4	0	0
Machado, Robert, Ottawa	.994	40	278	40	2	320	6	1
Marsters, Brandon, Rochester	.994	98	649	46	4	699	6	5
Martinez, Victor, Buffalo	.995	56	393	27	2	422	5	5
McKay, Cody, Indianapolis	.986	92	660	62	10	732	6	10
Mendez, Carlos, Ottawa	1.000	1	4	0	0	4	0	0
Miller, Corky, Louisville	.989	98	608	51	7	666	5	5
Molina, Izzy, Ottawa	1.000	3	16	1	0	17	0	0
Morales, Steve, Charlotte	.989	13	87	5	1	93	0	1
Ortiz, Hector, Durham	.993	60	384	21	3	408	0	3
Paul, Josh, Charlotte	.982	17	101	8	2	111	2	0
Phillips, Jason, Norfolk	1.000	16	125	8	0	133	2	1
Piazza, Mike, Norfolk	1.000	4	20	0	0	20	1	1
Rivera, Mike, Charlotte	.991	36	216	15	2	233	1	5
Salazar, Jeremy, Scranton-WB	.984	70	469	32	8	509	1	3
Schneider, John, Syracuse	1.000	3	31	1	0	32	0	0
Secrist, Reed, Buffalo	1.000	1	0	1	0	1	0	0
Seestedt, Mike, Ottawa	1.000	4	16	0	0	16	1	0
Stefanski, Mike, Louisville	.987	50	270	31	4	305	4	2
Taveras, Luis, Toledo	.974	14	68	8	2	78	1	1
Torres, Gabby, Rochester	.991	20	99	9	1	109	1	2
Umbria, Jose, Syracuse	1.000	4	26	2	0	28	0	0
Valencia, Vic, Buffalo	1.000	8	55	3	0	58	0	1
Valera, Yohanny, Toledo	.980	54	265	31	6	302	4	1
Walbeck, Matt, Toledo	1.000	1	7	1	0	8	0	1
Wathan, Dusty, Buffalo	.992	54	336	24	3	363	6	3
Wilson, John, Norfolk	.983	30	164	13	3	180	1	3

PITCHERS

Player, Team	Pct.	G	PO	A	E	TC	DP
Abbott, David, Syracuse	1.000	1	0	2	0	2	0
Acevedo, Jose, Louisville	1.000	29	3	6	0	9	0
Adkins, Jon, Charlotte	.958	26	3	20	1	24	3
Adkins, Tim, Lou.-Columbus *	1.000	40	4	13	0	17	1
Aguilar, Ray, Richmond *	1.000	1	1	2	0	3	0
Ahearne, Pat, Toledo	.974	15	9	29	1	39	1
Aldred, Scott, Pawtucket *	.000	11	0	0	0	0	0
Almanzar, Carlos, Louisville	.889	42	5	3	1	9	0
Almonte, Ed, Charlotte-Norfolk	1.000	46	5	10	0	15	0
Almonte, Hector, Pawtucket	.000	21	0	0	0	0	0
Anderson, Jason, Col.-Norfolk	1.000	16	3	4	0	7	0
Anderson, Jimmy, Louisville *	1.000	9	3	10	0	13	0
Anderson, Matt, Toledo	.500	23	0	1	1	2	0
Andrews, Shane, Rochester	.000	1	0	0	0	0	0
Arnold, Jason, Syracuse	.897	21	11	15	3	29	1
Arrojo, Rolando, Columbus	.000	4	0	0	0	0	0
Arroyo, Bronson, Pawtucket	.933	24	11	17	2	30	2
Austin, Jeff, Louisville	.769	9	3	7	3	13	0
Avery, Steve, Toledo *	.778	22	2	5	2	9	0
Backe, Brandon, Durham	1.000	16	0	7	0	7	0
Bacsik, Mike, Norfolk *	1.000	22	9	25	0	34	1
Baker, Chris, Syracuse	.000	2	0	0	0	0	0
Baldwin, James, Rochester	1.000	5	5	3	0	8	0
Bale, John, Norfolk-Louisville *	.667	34	1	1	1	3	0
Balfour, Grant, Rochester	.833	21	5	5	2	12	0
Banks, Willie, Columbus	1.000	31	4	7	0	11	1
Bauer, Rick, Ottawa	1.000	7	2	8	0	10	1
Beal, Andy, Columbus *	1.000	8	2	6	0	8	0
Bean, Colter, Columbus	.929	50	5	8	1	14	1
Beech, Matt, Columbus *	1.000	2	0	1	0	1	0
Belisle, Matt, Rich.-Louisville	.917	7	3	8	1	12	0
Belitz, Todd, Durham *	.800	24	1	3	1	5	0
Bell, Heath, Norfolk	1.000	40	1	8	0	9	0
Bell, Rob, Durham	1.000	12	4	8	0	12	0
Beltran, Rigo, Ottawa *	1.000	31	5	16	0	21	2
Bere, Jason, Buffalo	1.000	3	0	1	0	1	0
Betancourt, Rafael, Buffalo	1.000	4	1	1	0	2	0
Bevel, Bobby, Louisville *	.000	2	0	0	0	0	0
Bevis, P.J., Norfolk	1.000	4	1	1	0	2	0
Bierbrodt, Nick, Buffalo *	1.000	16	1	3	0	4	0
Bong, Jung, Richmond *	1.000	3	1	0	0	1	0
Borrell, Danny, Columbus *	1.000	10	1	14	0	15	0
Bowers, Cedrick, Durham *	1.000	32	3	12	0	15	1
Bowles, Brian, Syracuse	.895	41	5	12	2	19	1
Boyd, Jason, Buffalo	1.000	9	5	1	0	6	0
Brazelton, Dewon, Durham	.833	5	3	2	1	6	0
Brittan, Corey, Toledo	.923	44	4	8	1	13	0
Brown, Jamie, Buff.-Pawtucket	.880	31	9	13	3	25	1
Buddie, Mike, Indianapolis	.875	18	3	4	1	8	1
Burba, Dave, Buff.-Ind.	1.000	14	4	6	0	10	3
Cabrera, Jose, Scranton-WB	.875	25	5	9	2	16	0
Cameron, Ryan, Pawtucket	.923	27	3	9	1	13	1
Cammack, Eric, Norfolk	.000	5	0	0	0	0	0
Campos, Francisco, Ind.	1.000	8	0	1	0	1	0
Caraccioli, Lance, Buffalo *	.917	34	4	18	2	24	0
Carnes, Matt, Rochester	.963	25	12	14	1	27	1
Carrasco, Hector, Ottawa	.889	33	3	5	1	9	2
Cassidy, Scott, Syracuse	.938	57	4	11	1	16	2
Castillo, Carlos, Charlotte	.667	6	1	1	1	3	0
Castillo, Frank, Richmond	1.000	4	1	2	0	3	0
Cerda, Jaime, Norfolk *	1.000	22	0	3	0	3	0
Cerros, Juan, Louisville	.000	4	0	0	0	0	0
Chen, Bruce, Pawtucket *	1.000	16	5	10	0	15	0
Chevalier, Virgil, Norfolk	.000	1	0	0	0	0	0
Childers, Jason, Indianapolis	.913	46	3	18	2	23	1
Childers, Matt, Indianapolis	1.000	11	0	1	0	1	1
Choate, Randy, Columbus *	1.000	54	6	20	0	26	1
Chulk, Vinny, Syracuse	.875	23	10	18	4	32	4
Clapp, Stubby, Richmond	.000	2	0	0	0	0	0
Claussen, Brandon, Col.-Lou.*	1.000	14	4	9	0	13	0
Coco, Pasqual, Indianapolis	.943	27	10	23	2	35	4
Coggin, Dave, Scranton-WB	1.000	4	0	1	0	1	0
Colangelo, Mike, Syracuse	.000	1	0	0	0	0	0
Contreras, Jose, Columbus	1.000	3	1	0	0	1	0
Cooper, Brian, Charlotte	.971	28	7	26	1	34	3
Cortes, David, Buffalo	.500	5	1	0	1	2	0
Cortes, Jorge, Louisville	.000	1	0	0	0	0	0
Coste, Chris, Pawtucket	1.000	2	1	0	0	1	0
Crain, Jesse, Rochester	1.000	23	1	4	0	5	0
Cressend, Jack, Buffalo	1.000	8	2	2	0	4	0
Croushore, Rick, Ott.-Lou.	1.000	14	1	0	0	1	0
Crowell, Jim, Scranton-WB *	.944	54	4	13	1	18	2
Crudale, Mike, Indianapolis	.000	2	0	0	0	0	0
Cubillan, Darwin, Ottawa	.900	65	1	8	1	10	0
Cunnane, Will, Richmond	1.000	15	1	5	0	6	0
Davey, Tom, Pawtucket	1.000	16	2	1	0	3	0
Davis, Doug, Indianapolis *	.917	5	3	8	1	12	0
Davis, Lance, Louisville *	.875	26	6	15	3	24	1
Dawley, Joey, Richmond	1.000	46	2	3	0	5	0
De La Cruz, Fernando, Toledo	1.000	2	1	1	0	2	0
De La Rosa, Jorge, Pawtucket *	1.000	5	0	4	0	4	0
De Los Santos, Luis, Durham	.800	4	2	2	1	5	0
De Paula, Jorge, Columbus	.926	27	13	12	2	27	3
DePaula, Sean, Louisville	1.000	10	1	0	0	1	0
Dempster, Ryan, Louisville	1.000	2	2	0	0	2	0
Denney, Kyle, Buffalo	1.000	6	2	4	0	6	0
Diaz, Felix, Charlotte	.900	27	7	11	2	20	0
Douglass, Sean, Ottawa	1.000	27	6	9	0	15	0
Driskill, Travis, Ottawa	1.000	9	6	7	0	13	1
Drumright, Mike, Ottawa	.889	23	3	5	1	9	0
Dubose, Eric, Ottawa *	.947	19	5	13	1	19	0
Duckworth, Brandon, S/WB	1.000	3	2	3	0	5	0
Durbin, Chad, Buffalo	.750	10	1	2	1	4	0
Durocher, Jayson, Indianapolis	1.000	7	0	1	0	1	0
Duvall, Mike, Rochester *	1.000	24	1	8	0	9	0
Eason, Clay, Charlotte	1.000	8	2	4	0	6	2
Ebert, Derrin, Indianapolis *	1.000	4	0	2	0	2	1
Eckenstahler, Eric, Toledo *	.833	39	1	4	1	6	0
Elder, Dave, Buffalo	1.000	8	0	2	0	2	0
Elmore, Chris, Pawtucket *	1.000	8	1	5	0	6	0
Emiliano, Jamie, Richmond	.920	53	3	20	2	25	0
Ennis, John, Richmond-Toledo	1.000	31	2	21	0	23	0
Erdos, Todd, Rochester	1.000	29	0	5	0	5	0
Estrella, Leo, Indianapolis	1.000	7	2	3	0	5	0
Etherton, Seth, Louisville	.917	21	6	5	1	12	1
Eyre, Willie, Rochester	1.000	6	1	5	0	6	0

Player, Team	Pct.	G	PO	A	E	TC	DP
Feliciano, Pedro, Norfolk *	.900	15	0	9	1	10	0
File, Bob, Syracuse	1.000	11	1	1	0	2	0
Fiore, Tony, Rochester	.931	16	9	18	2	29	3
Flohr, Adam, Rochester *	1.000	2	1	0	0	1	0
Ford, Ben, Indianapolis	.867	26	6	7	2	15	1
Fortunato, Bartolome, Durham	.800	5	2	2	1	5	0
Fossum, Casey, Pawtucket *	1.000	5	1	3	0	4	0
Foster, John, Indianapolis *	1.000	27	0	12	0	12	1
Foster, Kris, Pawtucket	1.000	4	2	1	0	3	1
Fox, Chad, Pawtucket	1.000	1	0	1	0	1	0
Franco, John, Norfolk *	1.000	2	0	1	0	1	0
Frederick, Kevin, Syracuse	1.000	24	1	4	0	5	0
Fussell, Chris, Richmond	.900	29	4	32	4	40	2
Fyhrie, Mike, Buffalo	1.000	8	1	7	0	8	1
Garcia, Gerardo, Durham	.875	6	1	6	1	8	0
Garcia, Mike, Ottawa	.857	34	4	2	1	7	0
Gardner, Lee, Durham	.833	57	9	6	3	18	0
Gassner, Dave, Syracuse *	1.000	1	1	1	0	2	0
Geary, Geoff, Scranton-WB	1.000	46	1	7	0	8	0
German, Franklyn, Toledo	1.000	24	3	2	0	5	0
Giese, Dan, Scranton-WB	1.000	34	3	3	0	6	1
Gil, Dave, Louisville	1.000	16	1	2	0	3	1
Ginter, Matt, Charlotte	.833	49	1	4	1	6	1
Giron, Roberto, Indianapolis	.813	52	5	8	3	16	0
Glaser, Eric, Pawtucket	1.000	4	1	1	0	2	0
Glynn, Ryan, Richmond	.750	16	2	10	4	16	0
Gomes, Wayne, Scranton-WB	1.000	46	1	3	0	4	0
Gonzalez, Dicky, Pawtucket	1.000	27	9	21	0	30	2
Gonzalez, Jeremi, Durham	1.000	7	1	4	0	5	0
Gonzalez, Mike, Pawtucket *	.000	2	0	0	0	0	0
Graman, Alex, Columbus *	.931	26	6	21	2	29	0
Greisinger, Seth, Toledo	.933	25	5	23	2	30	0
Griffiths, Jeremy, Norfolk	.905	21	6	13	2	21	2
Guerra, Mark, Indianapolis	1.000	5	2	4	0	6	0
Guthrie, Jeremy, Buffalo	.870	18	5	15	3	23	1
Haines, Talley, Durham	1.000	50	6	12	0	18	1
Hamilton, Joey, Louisville	1.000	33	2	11	0	13	3
Hancock, Josh, Scranton-WB	.950	28	10	9	1	20	1
Hansell, Greg, Columbus	.750	9	2	1	1	4	0
Harang, Aaron, Louisville	.000	1	0	0	0	0	0
Harikkala, Tim, Ottawa	1.000	20	4	9	0	13	1
Harnisch, Pete, Louisville	.600	8	1	2	2	5	0
Haynes, Jimmy, Louisville	1.000	2	1	0	0	1	0
Hebson, Bryan, Pawtucket	1.000	18	0	2	0	2	0
Heilman, Aaron, Norfolk	1.000	16	3	16	0	19	1
Hendrickson, Mark, Syracuse *	.000	1	0	0	0	0	0
Hernandez, Adrian, Columbus	.906	32	12	17	3	32	2
Hernandez, Buddy, Richmond	1.000	53	0	9	0	9	0
Hernandez, Roberto, Richmond	.000	6	0	0	0	0	0
Hernandez, Yoel, Scranton-WB	.000	2	0	0	0	0	0
Herrera, Alex, Buffalo *	.833	34	2	3	1	6	0
Hiles, Cary, Scranton-WB	1.000	13	3	2	0	5	0
Hoard, Brent, Rochester *	.875	13	3	4	1	8	0
Howry, Bobby, Pawtucket	1.000	13	0	1	0	1	0
Izquierdo, Hansel, Pawtucket	1.000	4	0	2	0	2	0
Jacquez, Tom, Charlotte *	.833	13	2	3	1	6	0
James, Delvin, Durham	1.000	34	9	22	0	31	1
Jimenez, Jason, Toledo *	.900	47	5	4	1	10	0
Johnson, Adam, Rochester	.889	28	6	10	2	18	2
Johnson, James, Pawtucket *	.000	3	0	0	0	0	0
Jones, Bobby M., Richmond *	1.000	37	1	5	0	6	0
Joseph, Jake, Norfolk	1.000	19	5	13	0	18	1
Junge, Eric, Scranton-WB	1.000	10	5	4	0	9	0
Kaye, Justin, Pawtucket	1.000	31	3	5	0	8	0
Keller, Kris, Louisville	.000	2	0	0	0	0	0
Kennedy, Joe, Durham *	.000	1	0	0	0	0	0
Kershner, Jason, Syracuse *	.933	24	5	9	1	15	2
Kieschnick, Brooks, Indianapolis	.750	8	0	3	1	4	1
Kingrey, Jarrod, Syracuse	1.000	3	1	0	0	1	0
Kleine, Victor, Buffalo *	1.000	1	0	1	0	1	0
Knotts, Gary, Toledo	.778	13	1	6	2	9	0
Koch, Billy, Charlotte	1.000	4	0	1	0	1	0
Kohlmeier, Ryan, Charlotte	1.000	33	7	8	0	15	0
Kolb, Dan, Indianapolis	1.000	26	4	6	0	10	0
Kubes, Greg, Scranton-WB *	1.000	37	3	11	0	14	0
Larrison, Preston, Toledo	.000	1	0	0	0	0	0
Lavigne, Tim, Norfolk	1.000	1	1	0	0	1	0
Lee, Cliff, Buffalo *	.900	11	1	8	1	10	0
Lee, Derek, Indianapolis *	1.000	14	6	6	0	12	1
Lee, Seung, Scranton-WB	1.000	2	0	1	0	1	0
Lewis, Derrick, Richmond	1.000	36	1	6	0	7	1
Lidle, Cory, Syracuse	1.000	1	0	1	0	1	0
Linton, Doug, Syracuse	.967	32	11	18	1	30	2
Loux, Shane, Toledo	1.000	21	11	23	0	34	1
Lyon, Brandon, Pawtucket	1.000	5	1	1	0	2	0
Madson, Ryan, Scranton-WB	1.000	26	10	17	0	27	2
Magrane, Jim, Durham	1.000	2	1	1	0	2	0
Majewski, Gary, Charlotte	1.000	42	3	9	0	12	1
Malaska, Mark, Durham *	1.000	15	0	5	0	5	1
Manning, David, Indianapolis	1.000	23	7	13	0	20	0
Manzanillo, Josias, Louisville	1.000	22	2	4	0	6	0
Marquez, Rob, Indianapolis	1.000	30	2	7	0	9	0
Marquis, Jason, Richmond	.833	15	11	9	4	24	0
Marsonek, Sam, Columbus	1.000	54	3	7	0	10	1
Martinez, Anastacio, Pawtucket	1.000	8	0	2	0	2	0
Martinez, Luis, Indianapolis *	1.000	7	0	7	0	7	1
McConnell, Sam, Richmond *	1.000	22	5	13	0	18	2
Mears, Chris, Toledo	1.000	25	2	8	0	10	1
Mendoza, Ramiro, Pawtucket	1.000	4	0	1	0	1	0
Mercado, Hector, S/WB *	1.000	14	0	3	0	3	0
Meyer, Jake, Charlotte	1.000	20	0	2	0	2	0
Miceli, Danny, Buffalo	1.000	5	2	0	0	2	0
Michalak, Chris, Louisville *	1.000	9	0	12	0	12	0
Middlebrook, Jason, Norfolk	1.000	23	9	14	0	23	2
Miller, Travis, Lou.-Ind.*	1.000	20	1	8	0	9	0
Mills, Ryan, Rochester *	.909	32	2	8	1	11	1
Mohler, Mike, Ottawa *	1.000	50	2	25	0	27	0
Morales, Steve, Charlotte	.000	1	0	0	0	0	0
Moreno, Orber, Norfolk	1.000	38	6	2	0	8	0
Moseley, Dustin, Louisville	.900	8	2	7	1	10	0
Mottl, Ryan, Louisville	1.000	3	0	2	0	2	0
Munoz, Arnaldo, Charlotte *	.875	49	2	12	2	16	0
Myette, Aaron, Buffalo-S/WB	.941	34	9	7	1	17	1
Nakamura, Micheal, Rochester	.913	43	7	14	2	23	1
Nance, Shane, Indianapolis *	1.000	35	1	16	0	17	0
Navarro, Jaime, Louisville	1.000	2	1	2	0	3	0
Nelson, Bubba, Richmond	.857	11	2	4	1	7	1
Nickle, Doug, Charlotte	1.000	11	1	4	0	5	0
Obermueller, Wes, Indianapolis	1.000	3	1	1	0	2	0
Padilla, Juan, Rochester	.926	57	12	13	2	27	0
Palki, Jeromy, Rochester	1.000	47	8	14	0	22	1
Paniagua, Jose, Charlotte	.000	3	0	0	0	0	0
Parker, Christian, Columbus	.964	19	7	20	1	28	3
Paronto, Chad, Buffalo	.900	49	5	4	1	10	1
Parque, Jim, Durham *	.950	21	3	16	1	20	0
Patterson, Danny, Toledo	1.000	10	0	3	0	3	0
Pearson, Terry, Toledo	.833	45	2	3	1	6	0
Pena, Juan, Syracuse	1.000	8	0	1	0	1	1
Perisho, Matt, Durham *	1.000	34	2	3	0	5	0
Person, Robert, Pawtucket	.000	6	0	0	0	0	0
Phelps, Travis, Richmond	.920	47	6	17	2	25	1
Phillips, Jason, Buffalo	.941	13	5	11	1	17	0
Pina, Rafael, Ottawa	1.000	7	1	4	0	5	0
Politte, Cliff, Syracuse	.000	1	0	0	0	0	0
Porzio, Mike, Charlotte *	.958	26	1	22	1	24	0
Powell, Brian, Scranton-WB	1.000	8	5	8	0	13	0
Pratt, Andy, Richmond *	.700	28	6	8	6	20	0
Prinz, Bret, Columbus	1.000	10	0	1	0	1	0
Proctor, Scott, Columbus	1.000	10	2	4	0	6	0
Pulido, Carlos, Rochester *	1.000	25	9	20	0	29	1
Pulsipher, Bill, Ottawa *	.900	51	0	9	1	10	0
Pumphrey, Ken, Scranton-WB	1.000	17	8	9	0	17	1
Quevedo, Ruben, Indianapolis	.000	5	0	0	0	0	0
Rakers, Aaron, Ottawa	.500	21	0	1	1	2	0
Rakers, Jason, Buffalo-Ottawa	1.000	5	0	2	0	2	0
Ramirez, Ramon, Columbus	1.000	2	0	1	0	1	0
Randall, Scott, Louisville	1.000	30	5	21	0	26	2
Rauch, Jon, Charlotte	1.000	24	8	11	0	19	0
Rayborn, Kenny, Buffalo	1.000	1	0	2	0	2	0
Reichert, Dan, Syracuse	.917	41	5	6	1	12	0
Reith, Brian, Louisville	1.000	16	0	2	0	2	0
Reitsma, Chris, Louisville	1.000	4	6	1	0	7	1
Reyes, Al, Columbus	1.000	15	1	0	0	1	0
Reyes, Carlos, Durham	.971	22	12	21	1	34	2
Riggan, Jerrod, Buffalo-Norfolk	1.000	14	1	1	0	2	0
Rijo, Fernando, Ottawa	1.000	2	2	2	0	4	0
Riley, Matt, Ottawa *	.800	13	1	3	1	5	0
Rincon, Juan, Rochester	1.000	2	1	2	0	3	0
Rizzo, Todd, Ottawa *	.889	47	0	8	1	9	0
Roa, Joe, Indianapolis	.857	5	2	4	1	7	1
ROACH, JASON, Norfolk	1.000	31	14	21	0	35	1
Roberts, Grant, Norfolk	1.000	8	1	0	0	1	0
Robertson, Nathan, Toledo *	.833	24	3	22	5	30	1
Rodney, Fernando, Toledo	1.000	38	1	3	0	4	1

Player, Team	Pct.	G	PO	A	E	TC	DP
Rodriguez, Jose, Rochester *	.000	6	0	0	0	0	0
Rodriguez, Ricardo, Buffalo	.000	2	0	0	0	0	0
Rogers, Brian, Columbus	.000	2	0	0	2	2	0
Romano, Mike, Richmond	1.000	8	1	0	0	1	0
Rupe, Ryan, Pawtucket	.857	20	5	7	2	14	0
Rusch, Glendon, Indianapolis *	1.000	4	0	1	0	1	0
Rust, Evan, Durham	1.000	26	2	7	0	9	0
Sadler, Carl, Buffalo *	1.000	31	2	9	0	11	1
Sanders, Dave, Charlotte *	1.000	19	0	5	0	5	0
Santana, Julio, Scranton-WB	1.000	19	1	7	0	8	1
Santiago, Jose, Buffalo	1.000	25	5	12	0	17	0
Schmitt, Eric, Columbus	1.000	13	6	6	0	12	0
Scobie, Jason, Norfolk	.846	8	3	8	2	13	2
Seanez, Rudy, Pawtucket	.000	17	0	0	0	0	0
Seay, Bobby, Durham *	1.000	25	0	3	0	3	0
Secrist, Reed, Buffalo	1.000	1	1	0	0	1	0
Seibel, Phil, Norfolk *	1.000	11	1	7	0	8	0
Serrano, Jim, Norfolk	1.000	27	5	7	0	12	0
Service, Scott, Louisville	1.000	4	1	0	0	1	0
Shackelford, Brian, Louisville *	1.000	12	1	2	0	3	1
Shepard, David, Columbus	1.000	8	0	1	0	1	0
Shibilo, Andy, Pawtucket	.714	38	2	8	4	14	1
Shiell, Jason, Pawtucket	1.000	20	2	3	0	5	0
Smith, Chuck, Richmond	1.000	3	4	1	0	5	0
Smith, Mike, Syracuse	.938	26	14	16	2	32	1
Sosa, Jorge, Durham	1.000	4	0	2	0	2	0
Standridge, Jason, Durham	1.000	12	2	10	0	12	1
Stanford, Jason, Buffalo *	.913	20	8	13	2	23	2
Stephens, John, Ottawa	.966	27	8	20	1	29	1
Stewart, Josh, Charlotte *	1.000	5	1	6	0	7	1
Stewart, Paul, Pawtucket	1.000	27	5	12	0	17	0
Strange, Pat, Norfolk	1.000	31	10	6	0	16	0
Stull, Everett, Rochester	1.000	11	6	5	0	11	2
Sturkie, Scott, Buffalo	1.000	1	0	1	0	1	0
Switzer, Jon, Durham *	.000	1	0	0	0	0	0
Sylvester, Billy, Richmond	1.000	12	0	1	0	1	0
Tadano, Kazuhito, Buffalo	.000	2	0	0	1	1	0
Takeoka, Kazuhiro, Richmond	1.000	9	1	4	0	5	1
Tallet, Brian, Buffalo *	.889	15	1	7	1	9	0
Tam, Jeff, Syracuse	1.000	17	1	3	0	4	0
Telemaco, Amaury, S/WB	1.000	25	13	18	0	31	2
Teut, Nate, Indianapolis *	.842	18	4	12	3	19	1
Thomas, Brad, Rochester *	1.000	15	4	7	0	11	1
Thomas, Evan, Syracuse	1.000	20	7	10	0	17	2
Thurman, Corey, Syracuse	1.000	17	9	6	0	15	0
Thurman, Mike, Columbus	.955	26	1	20	1	22	2
Tolar, Kevin, Pawtucket *	1.000	47	2	5	0	7	0
Towers, Josh, Syracuse	.893	21	8	17	3	28	3
Truby, Chris, Durham	.000	1	0	0	0	0	0
Valentine, Joe, Louisville	1.000	9	1	1	0	2	0
Van Hekken, Andy, Toledo *	1.000	13	2	13	0	15	3
Van Poppel, Todd, Louisville	1.000	20	4	4	0	8	1
Vargas, Jose, Buffalo	.000	1	0	0	0	0	0
Veras, Jose, Durham	.000	3	0	0	0	0	0
Waechter, Doug, Durham	.889	10	1	7	1	9	0
Wagner, Ryan, Louisville	1.000	4	1	0	0	1	0
Walker, Pete, Syracuse	.875	5	3	4	1	8	2
Walker, Tyler, Toledo	.889	26	7	17	3	27	0
Wasdin, John, Syracuse	1.000	10	0	2	0	2	0
Wathan, Dusty, Buffalo	.000	1	0	0	0	0	0
Watson, Mark, Louisville *	.875	44	1	6	1	8	0
Wedel, Jeremy, Scranton-WB	.833	17	3	2	1	6	0
West, Brian, Charlotte	1.000	1	1	0	0	1	0
Westbrook, Jake, Buffalo	1.000	2	2	4	0	6	0
Wheeler, Dan, Norfolk	1.000	22	4	3	0	7	0
White, Gabe, Louisville *	.000	1	0	0	0	0	0
White, Matt, Paw.-Buffalo *	.667	21	0	4	2	6	0
Wiggins, Scott, Syracuse *	1.000	35	2	1	0	3	0
Williams, Glenn, Syracuse	.000	1	0	0	0	0	0
Williams, Todd, Durham	1.000	56	5	18	0	23	1
Wilson, Craig, Columbus	.000	1	0	0	0	0	0
Woodard, Steve, Pawtucket	1.000	31	8	8	0	16	1
Wright, Danny, Charlotte	.857	8	4	2	1	7	0
Wright, Jamey, Indianapolis	.833	7	1	4	1	6	0
Wunsch, Kelly, Charlotte *	.500	3	0	1	1	2	0
Yates, Tyler, Norfolk	1.000	4	1	1	0	2	0
Yofu, Tetsu, Charlotte	1.000	3	1	2	0	3	0
Young, Tim, Syracuse *	1.000	19	0	5	0	5	0
Zambrano, Victor, Durham	.000	1	0	0	0	0	0
Zamora, Pete, Norfolk *	1.000	55	5	12	0	17	1

PITCHERS WITH TWO OR MORE TEAMS

Player, Team	Pct.	G	PO	A	E	TC	DP
Adkins, Tim, Columbus *	1.000	28	1	7	0	8	1
Adkins, Tim, Louisville *	1.000	12	3	6	0	9	0
Almonte, Ed, Norfolk	1.000	16	2	2	0	4	0
Almonte, Ed, Charlotte	1.000	30	3	8	0	11	0
Anderson, Jason, Norfolk	1.000	10	1	3	0	4	0
Anderson, Jason, Columbus	1.000	6	2	1	0	3	0
Bale, John, Louisville *	.667	26	1	1	1	3	0
Bale, John, Norfolk *	.000	8	0	0	0	0	0
Belisle, Matt, Louisville	.857	4	1	5	1	7	0
Belisle, Matt, Richmond	1.000	3	2	3	0	5	0
Brown, Jamie, Buffalo	.933	13	5	9	1	15	0
Brown, Jamie, Pawtucket	.800	18	4	4	2	10	1
Burba, Dave, Indianapolis	1.000	10	2	3	0	5	2
Burba, Dave, Buffalo	1.000	4	2	3	0	5	1
Claussen, Brandon, Columbus *	1.000	11	3	6	0	9	0
Claussen, Brandon, Louisville *	1.000	3	1	3	0	4	0
Croushore, Rick, Louisville	.000	5	0	0	0	0	0
Croushore, Rick, Ottawa	1.000	9	1	0	0	1	0
Ennis, John, Toledo	1.000	3	0	4	0	4	0
Ennis, John, Richmond	1.000	28	2	17	0	19	0
Miller, Travis, Indianapolis *	1.000	16	1	7	0	8	0
Miller, Travis, Louisville *	1.000	4	0	1	0	1	0
Myette, Aaron, Buffalo	1.000	23	1	6	0	7	0
Myette, Aaron, Scranton-WB	.900	11	8	1	1	10	1
Rakers, Jason, Buffalo	1.000	3	0	1	0	1	0
Rakers, Jason, Ottawa	1.000	2	0	1	0	1	0
Riggan, Jerrod, Norfolk	1.000	5	0	1	0	1	0
Riggan, Jerrod, Buffalo	1.000	9	1	0	0	1	0
White, Matt, Buffalo *	.750	19	0	3	1	4	0
White, Matt, Pawtucket *	.500	2	0	1	1	2	0

The following players appeared only as a designated hitter, pinch-hitter or pinch-runner: Cairns, ph; Giambi, dh; Leon, dh; Phelps, dh; Wright, dh; Young, dh, ph.

LEAGUE CHAMPIONS

Year	Team	Pct.
1884—	Trenton	.520
1885—	Syracuse	.584
1886—	Utica	.646
1887—	Toronto	.644
1888—	Syracuse	.723
1889—	Detroit	.649
1890—	Detroit	.617
1891—	Buffalo (reg. season)	.727
	Buffalo (supplemental)	.680
1892—	Providence	.615
	Binghamton*	.667
1893—	Erie	.606
1894—	Providence	.696
1895—	Springfield	.687
1896—	Providence	.602
1897—	Syracuse	.632
1898—	Montreal	.586
1899—	Rochester	.624
1900—	Providence	.616
1901—	Rochester	.642
1902—	Toronto	.669
1903—	Jersey City	.742
1904—	Buffalo	.657
1905—	Providence	.638
1906—	Buffalo	.607
1907—	Toronto	.619
1908—	Baltimore	.593
1909—	Rochester	.596
1910—	Rochester	.601
1911—	Rochester	.645
1912—	Toronto	.595
1913—	Newark	.625
1914—	Providence	.617
1915—	Buffalo	.632
1916—	Buffalo	.586
1917—	Toronto	.604
1918—	Toronto	.693
1919—	Baltimore	.671
1920—	Baltimore	.719
1921—	Baltimore	.717
1922—	Baltimore	.689
1923—	Baltimore	.677
1924—	Baltimore	.709
1925—	Baltimore	.633
1926—	Toronto	.657
1927—	Buffalo	.667
1928—	Rochester	.549
1929—	Rochester	.613
1930—	Rochester	.629
1931—	Rochester	.601
1932—	Newark	.649
1933—	Newark	.622
	Buffalo (4th)†	.494

Year	Team	Pct.
1934—	Newark	.608
	Toronto (3rd)†	.559
1935—	Montreal	.597
	Syracuse (2nd)†	.565
1936—	Buffalo‡	.610
1937—	Newark‡	.717
1938—	Newark‡	.684
1939—	Jersey City	.582
	Rochester (2nd)†	.556
1940—	Rochester	.611
	Newark (2nd)†	.594
1941—	Newark	.649
	Montreal (2nd)†	.584
1942—	Newark	.601
	Syracuse (3rd)†	.513
1943—	Toronto	.625
	Syracuse (3rd)†	.536
1944—	Baltimore‡	.553
1945—	Montreal	.621
	Newark (2nd)†	.582
1946—	Montreal‡	.649
1947—	Jersey City	.610
	Syracuse (3rd)†	.575
1948—	Montreal‡	.614
1949—	Buffalo	.584
	Montreal (3rd)†	.545
1950—	Rochester	.609
	Baltimore (3rd)†	.556
1951—	Montreal‡	.617
1952—	Montreal	.629
	Rochester (3rd)†	.619
1953—	Rochester	.630
	Montreal (2nd)†	.586
1954—	Toronto	.630
	Syracuse (4th)§	.510
1955—	Montreal	.617
	Rochester (4th)†	.497
1956—	Toronto	.566
	Rochester (2nd)†	.553
1957—	Toronto	.575
	Buffalo (2nd)†	.571
1958—	Montreal‡	.588
1959—	Buffalo	.582
	Havana (3rd)†	.523
1960—	Toronto‡	.649
1961—	Columbus	.597
	Buffalo (3rd)†	.559
1962—	Jacksonville	.610
	Atlanta (3rd)†	.539
1963—	Syracuse∞	.533
	Indianapolis‡	.562
1964—	Jacksonville	.589
	Rochester (4th)†	.532
1965—	Columbus	.582
	Toronto (3rd)†	.556
1966—	Rochester	.565
	Toronto (2nd-tied)†	.558
1967—	Richmond	.574
	Toledo (3rd)†	.525
1968—	Toledo	.565
	Jacksonville (4th)†	.514
1969—	Tidewater	.563
	Syracuse (3rd)†	.536
1970—	Syracuse‡	.600
1971—	Rochester‡	.614
1972—	Louisville	.563
	Tidewater (3rd)†	.545
1973—	Charleston	.586
	Pawtuckets†	.534
1974—	Memphis	.613
	Rochester ∞‡	.611
1975—	Tidewater‡	.610
1976—	Rochester	.638
	Syracuse (2nd)†	.590
1977—	Pawtucket	.571
	Charleston (2nd)‡	.557
1978—	Charleston	.607
	Richmond (4th)†	.511
1979—	Columbus‡	.612
1980—	Columbus‡	.593
1981—	Columbus‡	.633
1982—	Richmond	.590
	Tidewater (3rd)†	.540
1983—	Columbus	.593
	Tidewater (4th)†	.511
1984—	Columbus	.590
	Pawtucket (4th)†	.536
1985—	Syracuse	.564
	Tidewater (4th)†	.540
1986—	Richmond‡	.571
1987—	Tidewater	.579
	Columbus†	.550
1988—	Rochester◆	.546
	Tidewater	.546
1989—	Syracuse	.572
	Richmond◆	.555
1990—	Rochester◆	.614
	Columbus	.596
1991—	Columbus◆	.590
	Pawtucket	.552
1992—	Columbus◆	.660
	Scr. W.B.	.592
1993—	Charlotte◆	.610
	Rochester	.525
1994—	Richmond◆	.567
	Pawtucket	.549
1995—	Norfolk	.606
	Ottawa◆	.507
1996—	Columbus◆	.599
	Rochester	.511
1997—	Rochester◆	.589
	Columbus	.556
1998—	Buffalo■	.566
1999—	Columbus	.589
	Charlotte▲	.569
2000—	Buffalo	.593
	Indianapolis▲	.563
2001—	Buffalo	.641
	Louisville▼	.583
2002—	Scranton/Wilkes-Barre	.632
	Durham▲	.556
2003—	Pawtucket	.576
	Durham▲	.521

*Won split-season playoff. †Won four-team playoff. ‡Won championship and four-team playoff. §Defeated Havana in game to decide fourth place, then won four-team playoff. ∞League was divided into Northern, Southern divisions. ◆League divided into Eastern, Western divisions; won playoffs. ■League divided into Eastern, Northern and Southern divisions; won four-team playoff. ▲League divided into North, South and West divisions; won four-team playoff. ▼League divided into North, South and West divisions; was leading final series of four-team playoff and was declared champion when Professional Baseball declared a stoppage of play. (NOTE—Known as Eastern League in 1884, New York State League in 1885, International League in 1886-87, International Association in 1888, International League in 1889-90, Eastern Association in 1891 and Eastern League from 1892 until 1912.)

MEXICAN LEAGUE

2003 FINAL STANDINGS

FIRST HALF

NORTHERN DIVISION

Team	W	L	T	Pct.	GB
Mexico	37	19	-	.661	...
Monterrey	35	21	-	.625	2
Puebla	32	24	-	.571	5
Saltillo	28	28	-	.500	9
Monclova	26	29	-	.473	10.5
Vaqueros	26	30	-	.464	11
Dos Laredos	23	33	-	.411	14
Reynosa	18	37	-	.327	18.5

SOUTHERN DIVISION

Team	W	L	T	Pct.	GB
Tigres	39	16	-	.709	...
Yucatan	33	23	-	.589	6.5
Oaxaca	31	25	-	.554	8.5
Tabasco	27	28	-	.491	12
Cancun	27	29	-	.482	12.5
Campeche	26	30	-	.464	13.5
Veracruz	24	32	-	.429	15.5
Cordoba	14	42	-	.250	25.5

SECOND HALF

NORTHERN DIVISION

Team	W	L	T	Pct.	GB
Saltillo	34	17	-	.667	...
Mexico	31	21	-	.596	3.5
Monterrey	31	22	-	.585	4
Dos Laredos	30	23	-	.566	5
Puebla	30	24	-	.556	5.5
Reynosa	25	26	-	.490	9
Monclova	23	30	-	.434	12
Vaqueros	13	41	-	.241	22.5

SOUTHERN DIVISION

Team	W	L	T	Pct.	GB
Tigres	33	19	-	.635	...
Campeche	29	21	-	.580	3
Yucatan	28	22	-	.560	4
Veracruz	26	22	-	.542	5
Oaxaca	26	27	-	.491	7.5
Tabasco	22	31	-	.415	11.5
Cancun	17	34	-	.333	15.5
Cordoba	15	33	-	.313	16

COMPOSITE

Team	TIG	MXO	MTY	SLT	YUC	PUE	OAX	CAM	LAR	VER	TAB	MVA	CCN	REY	VAQ	COR	W	L	T	Pct.	GB
Tigres	...	1	2	2	9	2	13	8	1	5	9	2	6	3	1	8	72	35	0	.673	...
Mexico	2	...	6	5	2	9	1	2	7	2	0	8	2	9	11	2	68	40	0	.630	4.5
Monterrey	1	6	...	10	2	8	1	0	6	2	2	8	2	8	8	2	66	43	0	.606	7.0
Saltillo	1	6	4	...	1	5	2	3	9	2	2	8	2	8	6	3	62	45	0	.579	10.0
Yucatan	3	1	1	1	...	1	7	7	2	7	8	2	10	2	1	8	61	45	0	.575	10.5
Puebla	1	5	4	7	2	...	3	1	8	2	1	6	3	7	9	3	62	48	0	.564	11.5
Oaxaca	1	2	2	1	5	0	...	4	0	9	8	2	12	1	1	9	57	52	0	.523	16.0
Campeche	3	0	3	0	4	2	7	...	2	6	7	0	9	3	1	8	55	51	0	.519	16.5
Dos Laredos	2	5	6	3	1	4	3	1	...	2	1	8	1	6	8	2	53	56	0	.486	20.0
Veracruz	7	1	1	1	4	1	3	6	0	...	7	1	7	2	2	7	50	54	0	.481	20.5
Tabasco	2	3	1	1	4	2	4	7	2	5	...	1	7	1	1	8	49	59	0	.454	23.5
Monclova	1	4	4	4	1	6	1	3	4	1	2	...	0	6	9	3	49	59	0	.454	23.5
Cancun	5	1	1	1	4	0	0	3	2	4	5	3	...	2	3	10	44	63	0	.411	28.0
Reynosa	0	3	3	3	1	5	2	0	8	1	2	5	1	...	8	1	43	63	0	.406	28.5
Vaqueros	2	1	4	6	2	3	2	2	4	1	2	5	0	4	...	1	39	71	0	.355	34.5
Cordoba	4	1	1	0	3	0	3	4	1	5	3	0	1	1	2	...	29	75	0	.279	41.5

PLAYOFFS: Oaxaca defeated Yucatan, four games to none; Reds defeated Puebla, four games to three; Tigres defeated Campeche, four games to two; Monterrey defeated Saltillo, four games to three; Reds defeated Monterrey, four games to two; Tigres defeated Oaxaca, four games to two; Reds defeated Mexico City Tigres, four games to one, to win league championship.

REGULAR-SEASON ATTENDANCE: Not available.

MANAGERS: Campeche, Francisco Estrada; Cancun, Guadalupe Salinas (through May 27), Ramon Montoya (May 28 through June 15), Enrique Ramirez (June 16 through end of season); Cordoba, Eddie Diaz (through April 30), Guadalupe Jabalera (May 1 through May 12 and May 20 through July 22), Antonio Aguilera (May 13 through May 19 and July 23 through end of season); Dos Laredos, Mario Mendoza (through April 21), Ruben Estrada (April 22 through June 19), Andres Mora (June 20 through end of season); Reds, Bernie Tatis; Tigres, Lee Sigman; Monterrey, Dan Firova; Monclova, Derek Bryant; Oaxaca, Alfonso Jimenez; Puebla, Enrique Reyes; Reynosa, Francisco Rodriguez; Saltillo, Raul Cano (through May 19), Fernando Elizondo (May 20 through end of season); Tabasco, Serbio Borges (through April 12), Gilberto Reyes (April 13 through end of season); Vaqueros, Alex Taveras (through May 13), Roberto Mendez (May 14 through May 27 and July 1 through end of season), Jose Juan Bellazetin (May 28 through June 30), Veracruz, Andres Mora (through April 29), Miguel Angel Ruiz (April 30), Rolando Camarero (May 1 through end of season); Yucatan, Juan Jose Pacho. Managerial record of teams with more than one manager: Cancun, Salinas (27-30), Montoya (3-14), Ramirez (14-19); Cordoba, Diaz (8-29), Jabalera (17-41), Aguilera (4-5); Dos Laredos, Mendoza (11-18), Estrada (27-20), Mora (15-18); Saltillo, Cano (26-27), Elizondo (36-18); Tabasco, Borges (8-14), Reyes (41-45); Vaqueros, Taveras (23-25), Mendez (7-25), Bellazetin (9-21); Veracruz, Mora (15-21), Ruiz (1-0), Camarero (34-33).

ALL-STAR TEAM: 1B—Guillermo Garcia, Tigres; 2B—Jesus Arredondo, Puebla; 3B—Ramon Orantes, Monterrey; SS—Jose Luis Sandoval, Reds; OF—Roberto Carlos Mendez, Oaxaca; OF—Luis Carlos Garcia, Tigres; OF—Lorenzo Buelna, Puebla; C—Noe Munoz, Saltillo; RHP—Pablo Ortega, Puebla; LHP—Jesus Guzman, Tigres; Relief pitcher—Santos Hernandez, Tigres; Manager of the Year—Enrique Reyes, Puebla.

2003 BATTING

TEAM

Team	G	TPA	AB	R	H	TB	2B	3B	HR	RBI	SH	SF	HP	BB	IBB	SO	SB	CS	GDP	LOB	ShO	Avg.	OBP	Slg.
Mexico	108	4355	3728	721	1160	1791	198	26	127	683	19	53	39	513	36	477	76	36	104	853	4	.311	.395	.480
Tigres	108	4194	3704	636	1148	1722	189	26	111	592	25	42	42	381	32	496	112	46	102	800	4	.310	.377	.465
Puebla	110	4374	3778	615	1165	1614	198	16	73	571	74	28	76	417	38	598	54	36	101	926	1	.308	.386	.427
Oaxaca	109	4344	3807	576	1145	1641	178	15	96	533	54	19	36	427	37	514	53	31	117	884	6	.301	.375	.431
Saltillo	107	4286	3669	683	1092	1660	185	10	121	633	25	37	35	518	19	658	102	42	104	844	4	.298	.386	.452
Vaqueros	110	4338	3799	550	1115	1579	155	12	95	506	33	23	33	448	21	571	49	37	137	899	8	.293	.371	.416

Team	G	TPA	AB	R	H	TB	2B	3B	HR	RBI	SH	SF	HP	BB	IBB	SO	SB	CS	GDP	LOB	ShO	Avg.	OBP	Slg.
Monterrey	109	4189	3636	591	1060	1534	185	14	87	539	50	35	62	405	35	542	96	49	95	794	5	.292	.369	.422
Dos Laredos..	110	4290	3748	542	1056	1526	169	14	91	507	30	29	77	406	23	533	54	39	122	849	2	.282	.361	.407
Yucatan	106	3971	3516	445	991	1369	142	13	70	416	71	23	29	332	25	460	81	40	87	787	3	.282	.347	.389
Campeche	106	4034	3542	436	996	1396	137	13	79	394	64	22	46	360	24	491	39	39	113	823	8	.281	.353	.394
Cordoba	104	3786	3416	400	925	1280	139	12	64	377	43	26	42	259	13	491	50	31	100	684	10	.271	.328	.375
Reynosa	107	4039	3594	459	970	1348	174	9	62	421	38	21	45	341	23	618	73	32	105	753	4	.270	.339	.375
Cancun	107	3934	3479	402	936	1286	148	8	62	378	73	27	48	303	25	437	33	39	111	760	13	.269	.334	.370
Veracruz	106	4167	3626	464	972	1374	150	6	80	427	55	29	63	394	37	483	72	42	98	846	4	.268	.348	.379
Monclova	110	4190	3717	470	992	1443	186	11	81	445	40	26	37	370	22	621	45	19	82	840	11	.267	.337	.388
Tabasco	109	4155	3637	413	962	1261	132	16	45	367	58	28	46	385	29	466	72	47	94	841	10	.265	.340	.347

INDIVIDUAL

TOP QUALIFIERS FOR BATTING CHAMPIONSHIP

Minimum 297 plate appearances. *Lefthanded batter. †Switch-hitter.

Player, Team	G	TPA	AB	R	H	TB	2B	3B	HR	RBI	SH	SF	HP	BB	IBB	SO	SB	CS	GDP	Avg.	OBP	Slg.
Jose, Felix, Mexico †	89	403	334	82	126	209	24	1	19	83	0	3	0	66	8	54	10	3	5	.377	.476	.626
Villalobos, Carlos, Puebla	79	330	281	46	104	165	25	0	12	63	2	3	6	38	5	44	0	3	14	.370	.451	.587
Arredondo, Jesus, Puebla * ...	103	415	332	51	117	136	15	2	0	42	18	2	18	45	3	36	3	5	8	.352	.453	.410
Garcia, Luis, Tigres †	103	456	413	70	144	218	21	1	17	68	0	2	0	41	4	48	20	6	13	.349	.406	.528
Sherman, Darrell, Puebla *	87	417	349	82	121	164	20	4	5	39	5	1	6	56	6	32	14	8	5	.347	.444	.470
Buelna, Lorenzo, Puebla	105	446	399	66	138	189	26	2	7	62	9	4	10	24	1	58	7	5	11	.346	.394	.474
Robles, Javier, Tigres	94	383	335	69	115	166	29	2	6	47	0	3	5	40	0	34	11	6	12	.343	.418	.496
Garcia, Cornelio, Mex.-Oax.-Vaq.*	93	418	348	60	119	154	20	3	3	50	2	7	3	58	2	39	8	7	12	.342	.433	.443
Orantes, Ramon, Monterrey...	98	388	360	54	123	155	17	0	5	62	1	2	5	20	1	37	1	1	16	.342	.382	.431
Brinkley, Darryl, Yucatan	98	401	362	62	123	171	12	0	12	57	0	3	5	31	5	39	22	7	9	.340	.397	.472
Rodarte, Raul, Mont.-Rey.......	90	350	315	49	106	152	18	2	8	39	3	3	2	27	1	47	13	2	10	.337	.389	.483
Garcia, Guillermo, Tigres.......	108	473	390	80	131	238	21	1	28	95	0	6	6	71	11	66	3	0	12	.336	.440	.610
Iturbe, Pedro, Puebla *	98	435	385	69	129	179	30	1	6	56	6	5	4	34	7	38	7	4	14	.335	.390	.465
Verdugo, Vincente, Saltillo.....	86	371	341	51	114	140	14	0	4	42	9	1	3	17	0	26	1	4	7	.334	.370	.411
Munoz, Noe, Saltillo	97	406	347	70	114	182	27	1	13	92	1	6	3	49	1	54	0	1	12	.329	.410	.524

DEPARTMENTAL LEADERS: G—D. Castro, C. Rodriguez (Vaqueros), 110; AB—R. Espinosa, 452; R—Bass, 91; H—L. Garcia, 144; TB—G. Garcia, 238; 2B—Davis, 31; 3B—O. Robles, 9; HR—G. Garcia, 28; RBI—G. Garcia, 95; SH—J. Arredondo, 18; SF—Velez, 9; HP—R. Zambrano, 21; BB—R. Mendez, 119; IBB—R. Mendez, 17; SO—E. Jimenez, 96; SB—D. Smith, 53; CS—D. Smith, 18; GIDP—White, 26; Slg.—Jose, .626; OBP—R. Mendez, .478.

ALL PLAYERS

*Lefthanded batter. †Switch-hitter.

Player, Team	G	TPA	AB	R	H	TB	2B	3B	HR	RBI	SH	SF	HP	BB	IBB	SO	SB	CS	GDP	Avg.	OBP	Slg.
Acosta, Francisco, Tabasco....	4	1	1	0	0	0	0	0	0	0	0	0	0	0	0	0	0	0	0	.000	.000	.000
Acuna, Jose, Cancun †	12	19	16	1	2	4	2	0	0	1	1	0	0	2	0	4	0	0	0	.125	.222	.250
Adriana, Sharnol, Cordoba.....	87	360	299	53	90	146	21	1	11	49	0	6	8	47	2	45	9	6	6	.301	.403	.488
Aganza, Ruben, Monc.-Yuc.-Salt.	67	187	164	23	34	66	5	0	9	25	2	3	0	18	1	23	0	1	4	.207	.281	.402
Aguilera, Antonio, Cordoba *.	28	48	43	3	12	15	0	0	1	4	0	0	0	5	0	11	0	0	1	.279	.354	.349
Aguilera, Armando, Vera.-Camp.	47	142	130	9	27	34	4	0	1	13	3	0	1	8	0	21	0	1	5	.208	.259	.262
Ahumada, Alex, Monterrey.....	60	113	95	24	25	33	6	1	0	11	0	2	5	11	0	22	3	1	2	.263	.363	.347
Alcantara, Izzy, Vaqueros	61	272	249	48	85	141	14	0	14	45	0	1	2	20	4	40	2	2	8	.341	.393	.566
Alejos, Fernando, Yucatan.......	2	1	1	0	1	1	0	0	0	1	0	0	0	0	0	0	0	0	0	1.000	1.000	1.000
Almeida, Shammar, Oaxaca *	68	223	189	29	53	85	5	0	9	34	1	2	2	29	2	28	1	2	7	.280	.378	.450
Almonte, Wady, Cordoba	50	193	178	17	59	78	5	1	4	25	1	1	0	13	0	22	5	4	5	.331	.375	.438
Alvarez, Hector, Oaxaca..........	68	237	224	23	66	85	11	1	2	34	3	1	0	9	0	35	1	0	6	.295	.321	.379
Amador, Jose, Vaqueros	78	282	242	34	67	104	17	1	6	31	2	1	2	35	0	40	4	1	11	.277	.371	.430
Amezcua, Adan, Monterrey	81	303	261	40	79	112	16	1	5	43	4	5	8	25	1	33	3	3	11	.303	.375	.429
Arana, Carlos, Cancun............	3	1	1	0	0	0	0	0	0	0	0	0	0	0	0	1	0	0	0	.000	.000	.000
Arano, Eloy, Vaq.-Cordoba † ..	84	271	247	25	55	61	4	1	0	9	7	0	5	12	1	35	3	4	6	.223	.273	.247
Arano, Wilfrido, D.Laredos * .	29	112	101	12	31	42	6	1	1	16	0	2	1	8	0	7	1	1	4	.307	.357	.416
Arauz, Escarcega, Monclova ..	32	64	57	3	12	19	1	0	2	8	3	0	1	3	0	14	0	0	0	.211	.262	.333
Arauz, Leobardo, Monc.-Yuc.†	67	281	238	35	59	100	5	0	12	42	1	2	4	36	0	44	2	1	4	.248	.354	.420
Arias, Francisco, Saltillo.........	83	206	182	34	63	89	13	2	3	41	4	2	4	14	0	27	5	2	5	.346	.401	.489
Armenta, Guillermo, Mex.†	19	40	35	6	8	9	1	0	0	3	0	0	0	5	0	3	0	2	0	.229	.325	.257
Arredondo, Alan, Yucatan † ...	64	87	80	25	25	25	0	0	0	3	3	0	1	3	0	9	2	1	1	.313	.345	.313
Arredondo, Eduardo, Tab.*	92	234	213	32	60	80	13	2	1	23	7	3	0	11	0	25	3	4	1	.282	.313	.376
Arredondo, Hernando, Cord.-Tab.	87	312	289	40	83	134	15	0	12	43	7	1	3	12	1	32	3	2	7	.287	.321	.464
Arredondo, Jesus, Puebla * ...	103	415	332	51	117	136	15	2	0	42	18	2	18	45	3	36	3	5	8	.352	.453	.410
Arredondo, Luis, Yucatan *....	103	468	421	62	128	142	9	1	1	20	7	2	0	38	2	49	23	15	1	.304	.360	.337
Avila, Carlos, Tigres-Puebla *	34	25	24	8	5	5	0	0	0	2	0	0	0	1	0	4	0	0	0	.208	.240	.208
Avila, Ignacio, Cordoba	3	5	4	1	0	0	0	0	0	0	1	0	0	0	0	2	0	0	0	.000	.000	.000
Avila, Rolo, Tabasco..............	4	17	16	5	5	7	2	0	0	2	0	0	0	1	0	2	1	1	0	.313	.353	.438
Baez, Carlos, Tabasco	3	12	11	0	2	3	1	0	0	0	0	0	0	1	0	2	0	0	0	.182	.250	.273
Barajas, Edison, Cordoba *....	63	182	165	14	36	49	4	0	3	16	2	1	2	12	1	48	0	1	4	.218	.278	.297
Barragan, Effrain, Saltillo *	1	3	3	0	1	1	0	0	0	0	0	0	0	0	0	1	0	0	0	.333	.333	.333
Barron, Alejandro, Cordoba....	10	5	5	1	0	0	0	0	0	0	0	0	0	0	0	3	0	0	0	.000	.000	.000
Bass, Jayson, Saltillo *	103	459	382	91	119	197	29	2	15	71	0	3	5	69	2	76	36	5	9	.312	.420	.516
Beltran, Juan, Campeche	64	69	61	13	15	21	1	1	1	4	2	0	0	6	0	22	0	2	3	.246	.313	.344
Bernal, Cosme, Monclova	41	82	79	13	22	33	6	1	1	6	0	0	0	3	0	19	0	1	0	.278	.305	.418
Berroa, Geronimo, Monterrey	25	101	93	19	24	46	4	0	6	18	0	0	0	8	0	18	1	0	3	.258	.317	.495
Bojorquez, Victor, Mexico	105	434	394	58	119	179	17	5	11	68	3	7	6	24	1	39	10	5	10	.302	.346	.454
Borges, Luis, Yucatan *	98	325	298	22	72	80	4	2	0	28	8	1	1	17	1	33	1	0	7	.242	.284	.268
Brena, Jaime, Oaxaca.............	59	247	215	34	71	84	7	0	2	25	8	0	4	20	0	21	4	2	1	.330	.397	.391

Player, Team	G	TPA	AB	R	H	TB	2B	3B	HR	RBI	SH	SF	HP	BB	IBB	SO	SB	CS	GDP	Avg.	OBP	Slg.
Brinkley, Darryl, Yucatan	98	401	362	62	123	171	12	0	12	57	0	3	5	31	5	39	22	7	9	.340	.397	.472
Buelna, Lorenzo, Puebla	105	446	399	66	138	189	26	2	7	62	9	4	10	24	1	58	7	5	11	.346	.394	.474
Bullett, Scott, Reyn.-Mont.*	107	435	372	76	120	184	16	3	14	51	0	5	7	51	7	64	13	7	6	.323	.409	.495
Bustillos, Luis, Reynosa	68	217	199	29	45	63	13	1	1	14	5	0	4	9	0	36	2	2	5	.226	.274	.317
Canales, Joel, Reynosa	4	10	9	1	0	0	0	0	0	0	0	0	0	1	0	2	0	0	0	.000	.100	.000
Canizalez, Juan, Campeche †	50	201	181	22	48	69	10	1	3	20	1	1	2	16	2	28	0	0	3	.265	.330	.381
Carpenter, Bubba, Monc.*	25	104	84	13	23	37	8	0	2	12	0	3	2	15	1	16	2	0	1	.274	.385	.440
Carrasco, Ernesto, Puebla *	79	239	193	31	46	56	6	2	0	22	3	0	6	37	1	28	1	2	1	.238	.377	.290
Carrillo, Jesus, Vaqueros *	16	50	45	1	11	13	2	0	0	3	1	0	2	2	0	6	0	0	1	.244	.306	.289
Carrillo, Matias, Tigres *	102	400	354	70	102	164	15	1	15	58	1	5	4	36	6	22	9	0	9	.288	.356	.463
Carrillo, Oscar, Mexico	11	10	9	2	0	0	0	0	0	0	1	0	0	0	0	3	0	0	0	.000	.000	.000
Castaneda, Hector, Yucatan *	68	242	181	27	57	87	7	1	7	31	2	1	2	56	5	38	0	2	8	.315	.479	.481
Castaneda, Rafael, Reyn.-Mont.	55	182	160	17	46	74	10	0	6	33	0	0	2	20	0	16	2	0	8	.288	.374	.463
Castellano, Pedro, Campeche	93	399	328	37	103	145	18	0	8	52	5	2	13	51	5	52	0	0	8	.314	.424	.442
Castillo, Alberto, Mex.-Vaq.	83	351	303	51	91	140	13	0	12	61	2	2	4	40	2	29	1	2	9	.300	.387	.462
Castro, Arnoldo, Cancun	96	392	323	35	81	95	8	0	2	26	13	2	3	51	1	29	1	3	8	.251	.356	.294
Castro, Domingo, Monclova	110	406	357	33	79	109	13	1	5	43	14	4	3	28	1	55	4	3	3	.221	.281	.305
Cazarin, Manuel, Camp.-Vera.	94	349	309	29	80	118	8	0	10	37	11	4	6	19	1	20	1	2	12	.259	.311	.382
Cervantes, Ivan, Oaxaca	101	389	363	43	113	140	14	2	3	32	10	3	3	10	1	49	4	3	18	.311	.332	.386
Cervantes, Peter, Vera.-Pue.*	39	1	1	0	0	0	0	0	0	0	0	0	0	0	0	0	0	0	0	.000	.000	.000
Cervantes, Refugio, Cancun *	99	394	355	43	105	174	14	2	17	64	3	2	0	34	5	50	0	0	11	.296	.355	.490
Cervera, Francisco, Cancun	68	242	200	25	49	64	6	0	3	13	9	1	7	25	1	33	1	2	13	.245	.348	.320
Cesar, Dionys, Veracruz †	55	253	227	32	75	98	12	1	3	26	2	0	0	24	3	29	11	4	4	.330	.394	.432
Chan, Armando, Monclova *	12	12	10	0	1	1	0	0	0	0	2	0	0	0	0	5	0	0	0	.100	.100	.100
Cisneros, Ventura, Reynosa	9	17	15	3	3	5	2	0	0	1	0	0	0	2	0	2	0	1	0	.200	.294	.333
Clemente, Edgard, Cancun	30	107	96	13	24	39	4	1	3	10	2	0	1	8	1	15	0	2	2	.250	.314	.406
Cobos, Rogelio, Mexico	26	53	50	5	12	19	4	0	1	3	0	0	2	1	0	11	0	0	1	.240	.283	.380
Coleman, Michael, Reynosa	20	87	70	14	19	32	4	0	3	8	0	0	0	17	3	13	3	0	3	.271	.414	.457
Connell, Lino, Oax.-Reynosa	101	454	397	57	117	155	22	2	4	44	4	1	0	52	2	53	18	7	15	.295	.376	.390
Contreras, Albino, Puebla	86	229	195	34	53	76	5	3	4	28	4	0	5	25	4	39	12	2	4	.272	.369	.390
Contreras, Jose, Tabasco	31	59	49	6	11	13	2	0	0	5	1	1	2	6	0	5	0	2	4	.224	.328	.265
Contreras, Sergio, Tigres *	45	130	113	18	37	46	3	3	0	18	1	4	0	12	0	14	14	3	1	.327	.380	.407
Cookson, Brent, Oaxaca	32	135	119	15	34	41	4	0	1	16	0	1	1	14	2	20	0	1	3	.286	.363	.345
Correa, Miguel, Tabasco †	48	189	166	24	47	64	9	1	2	17	1	0	2	20	2	27	9	3	4	.283	.367	.386
Cruz, Fausto, Yucatan	103	421	347	51	100	159	21	1	12	63	6	5	5	58	1	65	18	2	10	.288	.393	.458
Cruz, Marco, Campeche	41	104	99	6	31	34	3	0	0	12	2	0	1	2	0	4	0	0	5	.313	.333	.343
Davis, Jay, Cordoba-Mont.*	104	438	399	66	126	192	31	1	11	71	2	5	0	32	6	74	6	3	12	.316	.362	.481
De La Torre, Francisco, Vaq.	71	189	177	21	40	57	4	2	3	21	0	1	1	10	0	37	0	2	5	.226	.270	.322
Diaz, Alex, Oaxaca †	10	46	42	3	10	11	1	0	0	3	1	1	0	2	0	8	0	1	1	.238	.267	.262
Diaz, Edwin, Veracruz	106	465	394	61	110	194	22	1	20	64	4	4	9	54	3	80	7	5	12	.279	.375	.492
Diaz, Luis, Puebla *	58	132	111	18	28	46	3	0	5	22	0	0	3	18	2	29	3	1	1	.252	.371	.414
Diaz, Pedro, Puebla-Veracruz	28	68	60	4	12	14	2	0	0	3	3	0	2	3	1	17	0	0	2	.200	.262	.233
Diaz, Remigio, Monterrey	76	281	254	26	56	70	10	2	0	25	5	1	1	20	0	19	3	1	7	.220	.279	.276
Espino, Daniel, Tabasco	83	272	245	20	67	85	13	1	1	27	3	2	6	15	0	27	2	2	12	.273	.328	.347
Espino, Omar, Cancun	12	16	13	1	2	2	0	0	0	1	0	1	2	0	0	2	0	0	0	.154	.250	.154
Espinosa, Ramon, Yuc.-D.Lar.	105	485	452	57	138	175	19	3	4	44	7	3	10	13	1	49	18	10	9	.305	.337	.387
Espinoza, Efren, Vaq.-Mex.	46	116	108	16	24	33	3	0	2	10	0	0	1	7	0	20	2	0	1	.222	.276	.306
Espinoza, Jose, D.Laredos †	70	228	206	17	50	57	7	0	0	13	1	0	3	18	1	22	2	5	2	.243	.313	.277
Espinoza, Ramon, Vaqueros	28	71	65	6	9	12	3	0	0	5	3	0	1	2	0	24	1	1	2	.138	.176	.185
Esqueda, Jhonatan, Veracruz	12	17	13	4	2	2	0	0	0	1	0	0	2	2	0	5	0	0	1	.154	.353	.154
Esquer, Ramon, Campeche *	42	69	57	13	19	23	1	0	1	5	4	1	0	7	0	7	0	1	1	.333	.400	.404
Estrada, Hector, Vaq.-Cord.	75	262	241	28	61	94	12	0	7	25	1	0	2	18	1	25	3	0	9	.253	.310	.390
Estrella, Isaac, Dos Laredos	46	26	22	11	6	10	2	1	0	2	1	0	0	3	0	7	1	0	0	.273	.360	.455
Evans, Tom, Tabasco	36	151	119	23	27	45	7	1	3	19	0	1	3	28	2	21	1	1	3	.227	.384	.378
Felix, Alejandro, Vaqueros	10	14	13	3	4	4	0	0	0	0	0	0	0	1	0	2	0	0	0	.308	.357	.308
Felix, Lauro, Tabasco	30	70	57	9	10	17	4	0	1	4	0	0	0	13	0	21	1	0	0	.175	.329	.298
Fentanes, Oscar, Veracruz	95	365	325	30	81	108	15	0	4	32	3	0	15	22	4	34	1	3	9	.249	.326	.332
Fernandez, Dan, Mexico *	98	467	389	70	118	141	14	3	1	45	8	6	4	60	1	26	5	6	11	.303	.397	.362
Flores, Kevin, Puebla	69	190	171	28	43	55	10	1	0	22	5	0	5	9	0	39	0	0	5	.251	.308	.322
Flores, Miguel, Reyn.-Yuc.	85	352	312	37	85	109	13	1	3	33	3	2	6	29	3	56	13	6	6	.272	.344	.349
Fornes, Daniel, Monterrey *	95	350	302	45	90	152	13	2	15	71	3	3	6	36	5	27	2	5	5	.298	.380	.503
Franco, Iker, Tigres	86	261	233	30	61	99	15	4	5	37	3	2	2	21	0	46	3	2	6	.262	.326	.425
Gamez, Miguel, Reynosa	13	30	27	1	8	8	0	0	0	1	1	0	1	1	0	3	0	0	1	.296	.345	.296
Garcia, Amaury, Campeche	102	438	397	50	123	167	16	5	6	31	9	0	4	28	2	50	18	7	6	.310	.361	.421
Garcia, Cornelio, Mex.-Oax.-Vaq.*	93	418	348	60	119	154	20	3	3	50	2	7	3	58	2	39	8	7	12	.342	.433	.443
Garcia, Guillermo, Tigres	108	473	390	80	131	238	21	1	28	95	0	6	6	71	11	66	3	0	12	.336	.440	.610
Garcia, Hector, Tabasco	92	369	338	34	100	112	9	0	1	24	10	2	2	17	0	24	5	5	9	.296	.331	.331
Garcia, Heriberto, Veracruz	69	262	223	34	53	73	11	0	3	22	8	0	5	26	0	27	12	2	4	.238	.331	.327
Garcia, Luis, Tigres †	103	456	413	70	144	218	21	1	17	68	0	2	0	41	4	48	20	6	13	.349	.406	.528
Garcia, Nick, Puebla	74	195	174	32	57	71	8	0	2	20	9	1	0	11	0	33	1	1	2	.328	.366	.408
Garcia, Omar, Vera.-D.Lar.†	75	338	299	49	97	139	16	1	8	45	0	0	2	37	3	29	0	0	13	.324	.402	.465
Garza, Gerardo, Vaqueros	2	6	4	1	1	1	0	0	0	0	0	0	0	2	0	0	0	0	0	.250	.500	.250
Garzon, Eliseo, Saltillo	30	68	58	7	12	17	2	0	1	10	1	2	2	5	0	12	0	0	0	.207	.284	.293
Gastelum, Carlos, Tigres	79	331	303	52	99	118	9	5	0	33	4	1	4	19	1	29	20	8	5	.327	.373	.389
Gastelum, Gato, Tigres	51	84	79	4	17	23	0	0	2	11	3	0	0	2	0	9	0	0	6	.215	.235	.291
Gastelum, Sergio, Tigres	34	134	103	24	31	43	6	0	2	9	2	2	7	20	0	13	6	3	0	.301	.439	.417
Gavia, Jesus, Cancun	35	91	87	8	22	24	2	0	0	5	0	1	0	3	0	15	0	0	0	.253	.275	.276
Gomez, Heber, Monterrey	104	464	388	65	108	145	22	0	5	40	15	2	5	53	0	45	6	8	9	.278	.371	.374
Gonzalez, Fernando, Reynosa	28	78	71	7	13	21	2	0	2	8	1	0	3	3	0	18	1	0	2	.183	.247	.296
Gonzalez, Israel, Campeche	62	123	108	13	22	38	7	0	3	14	2	2	0	11	2	14	0	2	10	.204	.273	.352
Gonzalez, Roman, Cordoba	95	267	242	19	55	68	7	3	0	22	11	2	1	11	0	32	3	3	7	.227	.262	.281

Player, Team	G	TPA	AB	R	H	TB	2B	3B	HR	RBI	SH	SF	HP	BB	IBB	SO	SB	CS	GDP	Avg.	OBP	Slg.
Gonzalez, Santiago, Veracruz.	62	67	59	17	13	15	2	0	0	4	4	0	1	3	0	12	3	2	0	.220	.270	.254
Gracia, Rafael, Oaxaca	3	3	3	0	0	0	0	0	0	0	0	0	0	0	0	3	0	0	0	.000	.000	.000
Grijak, Kevin, Veracruz *	100	427	375	46	120	169	20	1	9	58	0	3	6	43	8	33	3	4	12	.320	.396	.451
Guerrero, Sergio, Campeche..	101	375	329	43	105	154	20	1	9	40	10	4	6	26	0	23	3	3	14	.319	.375	.468
Guizar, Hector, Cordoba	101	402	375	28	103	119	11	1	1	41	9	7	2	9	1	18	8	4	21	.275	.290	.317
Gutierrez, Said, Yucatan	56	170	152	17	34	50	4	0	4	19	4	3	2	9	0	27	1	1	3	.224	.271	.329
Hernandez, Julio, D.Laredos ..	104	468	393	65	117	165	15	3	9	49	4	2	10	59	0	44	2	4	13	.298	.401	.420
Hernandez, Vladimir, Cancun .	102	455	421	51	128	169	22	2	5	41	8	2	6	18	4	19	15	13	18	.304	.340	.401
Herrera, Jose, Yucatan *	66	293	268	28	78	117	10	4	7	36	9	1	2	13	0	25	4	1	11	.291	.327	.437
Hubbard, Trenidad, Oaxaca	12	55	47	6	13	22	3	0	2	5	0	0	1	7	0	10	3	1	0	.277	.382	.468
Hurtado, Hector, D.Laredos....	100	340	319	26	80	111	10	0	7	37	6	1	8	6	0	68	0	2	14	.251	.281	.348
Ibarra, Juvenal, Vaqueros * ...	14	47	44	4	11	13	2	0	0	5	0	1	0	2	0	9	0	0	2	.250	.277	.295
Iturbe, Pedro, Puebla *	98	435	385	69	129	179	30	1	6	56	6	5	4	34	7	38	7	4	14	.335	.390	.465
Jimenez, Eduardo, Saltillo * ...	104	452	338	71	87	170	8	0	25	73	0	1	1	112	5	96	1	0	8	.257	.442	.503
Jones, Chris, Cordoba	20	80	70	9	21	29	3	1	1	6	0	0	0	10	1	8	1	0	6	.300	.388	.414
Jose, Felix, Mexico †	89	403	334	82	126	209	24	1	19	83	0	3	0	66	8	54	10	3	5	.377	.476	.626
Kelly, Roberto, Mexico	85	392	335	79	110	162	20	1	10	57	0	3	5	47	2	42	10	2	11	.328	.415	.484
Lara, Idelfonso, Vaqueros	89	328	307	36	92	135	16	0	9	57	0	3	4	14	0	63	0	1	12	.300	.335	.440
Laurean, Julian, Monclova	1	1	1	0	0	0	0	0	0	0	0	0	0	0	0	1	0	0	0	.000	.000	.000
Laya, Rayner, Tabasco	92	416	378	50	122	139	9	4	0	26	3	2	2	31	2	32	25	13	8	.323	.375	.368
LeBron, Juan, Camp.-Oaxaca.	83	347	320	39	88	147	12	1	15	52	1	1	2	23	0	77	3	2	12	.275	.327	.459
Leach, Jalal, Saltillo *	8	32	28	5	4	8	2	1	0	7	0	0	0	4	0	5	3	0	0	.143	.250	.286
Leyritz, Jim, Oaxaca	4	18	18	4	7	11	1	0	1	6	0	0	0	0	0	2	0	0	1	.389	.389	.611
Leyva, German, Salt.-D.Lar.* .	77	229	186	34	51	65	9	1	1	18	5	2	2	34	1	14	4	0	5	.274	.388	.349
Leyva, Octavio, Tabasco *	20	58	51	4	10	11	1	0	0	2	0	0	3	4	0	6	1	0	4	.196	.293	.216
Lofton, James, Reynosa	83	372	342	37	89	112	17	0	2	28	2	3	1	24	3	55	7	5	10	.260	.308	.327
Lopez, Fabian, Oaxaca *	31	79	73	12	20	26	3	0	1	15	0	0	0	6	1	7	0	0	2	.274	.329	.356
Lopez, Fausto, Mexico	33	24	22	11	8	10	0	1	0	2	0	1	0	1	0	3	2	1	3	.364	.375	.455
Lopez, Gonzalo, Monclova	25	37	36	0	7	7	0	0	0	3	0	0	0	1	0	7	1	0	2	.194	.216	.194
Lopez, Raul, Monclova *	102	406	359	49	99	142	28	0	5	46	1	2	0	44	3	59	1	1	11	.276	.353	.396
Lucca, Lou, Cordoba-Vaq.......	75	306	265	34	84	123	10	1	9	47	0	2	9	30	2	35	3	1	8	.317	.402	.464
Lugo, Roberto, Mont.-Reyn. ..	73	204	191	20	45	56	7	2	0	16	6	1	2	4	0	38	1	0	4	.236	.258	.293
Macias, Roberto, Cancun *	3	3	2	0	0	0	0	0	0	0	0	0	0	1	0	2	0	0	0	.000	.333	.000
Magallanes, Ever, Tabasco * ..	81	337	300	25	86	103	11	0	2	25	5	3	2	27	1	32	2	0	6	.287	.346	.343
Martinez, Abel, Cancun	73	261	237	18	61	73	6	0	2	16	4	1	2	17	1	21	4	4	9	.257	.311	.308
Martinez, Enrique, Reynosa ...	84	318	278	43	83	108	13	0	4	27	3	3	1	33	0	37	5	3	9	.299	.371	.388
Martinez, Felix, Tabasco †	36	154	141	15	39	54	5	5	0	15	2	1	3	7	1	22	1	1	1	.277	.322	.383
Martinez, Gabby, Vaqueros	23	110	101	22	47	56	4	1	1	13	3	0	0	6	0	8	14	9	1	.465	.495	.554
Martinez, Gil, Monclova	11	44	41	4	9	14	2	0	1	3	0	0	2	1	0	6	0	0	1	.220	.273	.341
Martinez, Grimaldo, Cordoba .	84	337	314	35	81	98	9	1	2	17	1	2	4	16	0	26	3	0	7	.258	.301	.312
Martinez, Luis, Saltillo	10	17	15	2	5	6	1	0	0	1	1	0	0	1	0	1	0	0	0	.333	.375	.400
Martinez, Rafael, Veracruz * ..	8	34	31	4	6	10	1	0	1	3	1	1	1	0	0	6	0	0	0	.194	.212	.323
Martinez, Ramon, Mexico	96	400	311	66	94	155	22	0	13	74	0	8	9	72	6	65	8	1	10	.302	.438	.498
Martinez, Raul, Tabasco	8	13	11	2	3	3	0	0	0	1	0	0	0	2	0	1	0	0	0	.273	.385	.273
Martinez, Sandy, Campeche *	34	122	108	12	27	36	1	1	2	16	1	1	2	10	2	23	0	0	3	.250	.322	.333
Mata, Noe, Veracruz	61	171	157	15	32	45	1	0	4	17	4	1	1	8	2	31	3	2	6	.204	.246	.287
Medina, Eric, Mont.-Oaxaca ...	6	10	9	0	0	0	0	0	0	0	0	0	0	1	0	5	0	0	2	.000	.100	.000
Medina, Jose, Reynosa	51	136	126	6	32	35	3	0	0	13	2	0	0	8	0	29	2	0	4	.254	.299	.278
Mejia, Roberto, Oaxaca	51	232	210	37	73	120	9	1	12	36	2	1	1	18	3	31	10	4	6	.348	.400	.571
Melo, Juan, Mexico-Cord.†	26	116	106	15	28	33	2	0	1	9	1	0	1	8	1	17	1	1	5	.264	.322	.311
Mendez, Francisco, Mont.-Reyn.*	91	338	290	36	85	133	15	0	11	45	4	3	1	40	6	50	2	2	8	.293	.377	.459
Mendez, Roberto, Oaxaca * ...	105	463	336	75	98	182	16	1	22	78	3	2	3	119	17	65	5	5	5	.292	.478	.542
Mendoza, Omar, Tab.-Reyn.-Oax.	74	215	187	27	44	61	6	1	3	18	4	5	0	19	1	31	2	2	6	.235	.299	.326
Mercedes, Henry, Vaqueros ...	12	51	39	4	8	9	1	0	0	0	0	0	0	12	0	14	0	0	0	.205	.392	.231
Mere, Carlos, Veracruz	29	17	13	4	2	2	0	0	0	0	1	0	0	3	0	4	0	0	1	.154	.313	.154
Mere, Pedro, Veracruz	75	303	260	28	63	90	12	0	5	32	4	6	3	30	3	30	2	3	4	.242	.321	.346
Meza, Alfredo, Monterrey †	38	134	124	5	30	34	4	0	0	8	4	1	0	5	0	15	0	0	4	.242	.269	.274
Meza, Gonzalo, Vaqueros *	103	429	382	57	115	146	12	2	5	45	3	2	0	42	2	41	6	4	11	.301	.369	.382
Minjarez, Francisco, Puebla ...	61	137	123	16	36	39	1	1	0	12	3	0	1	10	0	22	1	0	1	.293	.351	.317
Montenegro, Jose, Oaxaca	65	210	173	27	45	67	10	0	4	18	6	2	3	26	0	27	1	1	6	.260	.363	.387
Morales, Carlos, Yucatan	3	6	6	1	1	2	1	0	0	0	0	0	0	0	0	2	0	0	0	.167	.167	.333
Morales, Francisco, Cordoba .	11	45	37	6	8	16	2	0	2	6	0	0	1	7	0	12	0	0	0	.216	.356	.432
Morejon, Oswaldo, Yucatan ...	83	359	302	44	94	129	21	1	4	28	15	0	3	39	4	23	3	1	8	.311	.395	.427
Mouton, James, Reynosa	17	73	55	16	13	18	2	0	1	4	3	0	4	11	0	12	0	1	1	.236	.400	.327
Munoz, Adan, Monc.-Tigres *	85	291	257	35	59	90	9	2	6	26	3	3	4	24	3	43	1	1	3	.230	.302	.350
Munoz, Jose, Saltillo *	98	309	262	40	62	80	5	2	3	28	0	1	0	46	0	52	5	3	7	.237	.350	.305
Munoz, Noe, Saltillo	97	406	347	70	114	182	27	1	13	92	1	6	3	49	1	54	0	1	12	.329	.410	.524
Newson, Warren, Tab.-Monc.*	95	399	322	49	96	139	16	0	9	43	0	2	3	72	6	66	12	3	12	.298	.429	.432
Nunez, Reymond, D.Lar.-Reyn.	38	167	152	16	38	49	5	0	2	20	0	2	1	12	0	15	0	0	7	.250	.305	.322
Obando, Sherman, Mexico	53	226	200	35	63	105	16	1	8	47	0	1	1	24	6	22	1	0	6	.315	.389	.525
Ojeda, Miguel, Mexico	43	187	159	30	52	100	14	2	10	41	0	2	2	24	3	23	4	1	7	.327	.417	.629
Orantes, Ramon, Monterrey ...	98	388	360	54	123	155	17	0	5	62	1	2	5	20	1	37	1	1	16	.342	.382	.431
Orrantia, Carlos, Monterrey....	64	170	148	20	42	51	6	0	1	19	5	1	3	13	0	15	4	0	3	.284	.352	.345
Ortega, Antonio, Campeche ...	8	17	14	1	1	1	0	0	0	0	1	0	0	2	0	2	0	0	1	.071	.188	.071
Ortiz, Alex, Vaqueros	75	318	270	33	65	98	3	0	10	38	0	3	2	43	1	40	0	0	7	.241	.346	.363
Pacho, Carlos, Yucatan	41	62	59	7	15	20	2	0	1	4	1	2	0	0	0	10	0	2	2	.254	.246	.339
Paez, Hector, Yucatan *	61	177	166	6	47	69	14	1	2	24	6	2	1	2	0	12	0	1	3	.283	.292	.416
Paez, Raul, Veracruz *	67	221	182	19	55	69	5	0	3	21	1	2	4	32	3	19	1	0	8	.302	.414	.379
Palafox, Sergio, Saltillo	62	126	116	22	38	63	7	0	6	27	0	1	1	8	0	9	3	0	4	.328	.373	.543
Paul, Corey, Saltillo-Tab.*	94	399	330	66	108	163	22	0	11	53	0	4	2	63	10	65	10	0	12	.327	.434	.494
Payro, Edison, Cordoba *	28	50	44	4	9	11	2	0	0	4	0	0	0	6	0	12	1	0	2	.205	.300	.250

Player, Team	G	TPA	AB	R	H	TB	2B	3B	HR	RBI	SH	SF	HP	BB	IBB	SO	SB	CS	GDP	Avg.	OBP	Slg.
Pemberton, Rudy, Monclova..	106	458	417	54	129	185	18	4	10	48	0	0	7	34	4	56	4	2	11	.309	.371	.444
Perez, Alfredo, Campeche......	20	11	10	5	3	4	1	0	0	1	0	0	0	1	0	0	0	0	1	.300	.364	.400
Perez, Antonio, Cordoba........	24	43	43	0	11	13	2	0	0	4	0	0	0	0	0	7	0	0	1	.256	.256	.302
Perez, Francisco, Reynosa * ..	82	264	241	25	57	83	9	1	5	34	0	1	8	14	3	54	0	0	7	.237	.299	.344
Perez, Jose, Reynosa............	48	146	134	20	44	54	7	0	1	14	0	1	2	9	0	26	1	2	3	.328	.377	.403
Perez, Rob, Mexico...............	41	192	181	34	65	108	12	2	9	33	0	2	1	8	0	18	4	0	6	.359	.385	.597
Pickering, Calvin, Vaqueros *	88	370	291	64	94	182	13	0	25	63	0	1	2	75	8	84	1	0	14	.323	.463	.625
Pinto, Placido, Cordoba.........	10	20	18	2	1	1	0	0	0	1	1	0	0	1	0	8	0	0	1	.056	.105	.056
Presichi, Cristian, Saltillo.......	90	273	240	54	67	111	8	0	12	38	4	1	2	26	1	80	9	5	8	.279	.353	.463
Quinones, Ruben, Cordoba....	72	242	225	23	58	78	11	0	3	25	2	1	1	13	2	32	1	1	7	.258	.300	.347
Quintero, Christian, Oaxaca....	105	457	419	67	137	199	24	4	10	54	2	2	3	31	4	31	12	2	13	.327	.376	.475
Quintero, Edgar, Monterrey *.	53	87	78	8	15	27	3	0	3	9	0	1	0	8	3	25	0	2	0	.192	.264	.346
Radmanovich, Ryan, Mont.*..	41	177	156	21	47	69	12	2	2	20	1	1	2	17	0	32	3	0	5	.301	.375	.442
Ramirez, Enrique, Cancun......	19	42	37	2	9	12	3	0	0	6	2	1	0	2	0	4	0	0	0	.243	.275	.324
Ramirez, Jesus, Oaxaca.........	58	196	171	35	53	65	6	0	2	17	6	1	4	14	0	13	2	2	2	.310	.374	.380
Ramirez, Omar, Veracruz........	105	490	420	63	117	176	20	0	13	50	5	5	3	57	4	49	10	8	6	.279	.365	.419
Ramirez, Oscar, Campeche....	105	460	406	58	120	173	16	2	11	45	3	4	6	41	1	55	3	11	9	.296	.365	.426
Raven, Luis, Cancun.............	63	255	244	23	66	99	12	0	7	40	1	0	1	9	1	41	0	0	9	.270	.299	.406
Resendez, Carlos, Monclova..	50	144	128	18	30	52	13	0	3	18	4	2	5	5	1	31	1	0	3	.234	.286	.406
Reyes, Eleazar, Oaxaca *........	16	13	10	3	1	1	0	0	0	1	0	0	0	3	0	3	0	0	0	.100	.308	.100
Rincon, Isaias, Mexico...........	47	123	115	21	30	37	4	0	1	16	0	1	1	6	0	22	4	1	2	.261	.301	.322
Rios, Eduardo, Can.-Oaxaca...	94	398	362	34	102	142	22	0	6	47	2	5	2	27	3	39	1	1	21	.282	.331	.392
Rivera, Francisco, Vera.-D.Lar.	58	104	89	12	23	35	6	0	2	11	0	2	0	13	1	12	0	0	2	.258	.346	.393
Rivera, Jesus, Tabasco *	43	81	70	2	10	10	0	0	0	8	2	2	0	7	0	11	1	0	3	.143	.215	.143
Robles, Javier, Tigres............	94	383	335	69	115	166	29	2	6	47	0	3	5	40	0	34	11	6	12	.343	.418	.496
Robles, Juan, Reynosa-Tab....	33	66	64	5	17	21	1	0	1	7	0	0	1	1	0	16	2	0	3	.266	.288	.328
Robles, Oscar, Mexico *	99	477	398	81	123	178	13	9	8	53	2	8	0	69	1	29	6	3	10	.309	.404	.447
Robles, Ricardo, Monclova *.	56	129	117	14	30	47	5	0	4	29	0	0	3	9	1	17	0	0	3	.256	.326	.402
Robles, Trinidad, Tigres.........	83	253	220	38	59	92	11	2	6	34	4	2	1	26	1	46	5	6	5	.268	.345	.418
Rodarte, Raul, Mont.-Reyn. ...	90	350	315	49	106	152	18	2	8	39	3	3	2	27	1	47	13	2	10	.337	.389	.483
Rodriguez, Armando, Puebla .	30	72	66	10	12	23	2	0	3	13	1	0	1	4	0	13	0	0	2	.182	.239	.348
Rodriguez, Boi, Campeche *..	50	213	168	38	54	83	5	0	8	26	0	1	1	43	5	35	7	2	5	.321	.460	.494
Rodriguez, Carlos, Reynosa...	35	95	82	8	23	35	4	1	2	10	0	0	0	13	1	22	0	0	1	.280	.379	.427
Rodriguez, Carlos, Vaq.†........	110	507	430	73	138	159	19	1	0	23	8	1	3	64	1	23	12	7	15	.321	.412	.370
Rodriguez, Erick, Oaxaca.......	46	123	113	11	29	34	3	1	0	10	0	0	1	8	0	9	1	0	4	.257	.311	.301
Rodriguez, Fernando, Camp...	91	349	311	25	87	123	9	0	9	35	6	1	3	28	2	30	0	0	10	.280	.344	.395
Rodriguez, Leonardo, Mont. ..	9	12	10	1	5	6	1	0	0	3	0	1	1	0	0	0	0	0	0	.500	.500	.600
Rodriguez, Serafin, Tigres......	47	132	124	22	47	60	5	4	0	12	0	1	1	6	0	15	3	2	3	.379	.409	.484
Rodriguez, Victor, Campeche.	16	73	67	7	16	21	2	0	1	3	1	0	0	5	0	5	0	0	5	.239	.292	.313
Rojas, Homar, Oaxaca............	35	148	131	12	40	56	7	0	3	20	2	0	1	14	1	10	2	1	4	.305	.377	.427
Romero, Flavio, Saltillo *.......	85	329	280	51	76	101	11	1	4	25	2	1	1	44	1	57	24	15	7	.271	.371	.361
Romero, Marco, Saltillo.........	79	303	267	44	70	126	11	0	15	62	0	3	3	30	2	49	2	1	12	.262	.340	.472
Romero, Oscar, Reynosa.......	30	123	115	10	31	40	6	0	1	16	1	2	1	4	0	17	3	1	7	.270	.295	.348
Romero, Willie, Salt.-Yuc.......	62	268	233	38	65	89	12	0	4	22	4	1	5	25	1	39	11	4	3	.279	.360	.382
Rosas, Ezequiel, Oaxaca........	7	22	20	1	4	5	1	0	0	2	1	0	0	1	0	3	0	0	3	.200	.238	.250
Rose, Pete, Cordoba *	29	123	106	13	29	44	3	0	4	18	0	1	1	15	0	19	0	0	1	.274	.366	.415
Ruiz, Juan, Monclova.............	98	372	339	49	94	144	20	0	10	36	4	4	2	23	0	38	3	0	9	.277	.323	.425
Saenz, Ricardo, Monc.-Salt....	105	431	383	49	110	155	21	0	8	45	0	1	3	44	2	92	4	1	7	.287	.364	.405
Salas, Heriberto, Cancun........	58	195	168	25	48	74	12	1	4	17	5	2	3	17	1	11	0	0	2	.286	.358	.440
Salazar, Francisco, Mexico *..	4	6	6	1	2	4	2	0	0	2	0	0	0	0	0	1	0	0	0	.333	.333	.667
Salcedo, Eder, Reynosa..........	21	54	50	3	11	16	5	0	0	7	1	0	0	3	0	11	0	0	3	.220	.264	.320
Salinas, Trey, Cancun............	92	366	311	44	83	116	12	0	7	39	8	2	7	38	4	51	6	7	8	.267	.358	.373
Samuels, Scott, Veracruz *....	31	130	108	18	29	34	5	0	0	5	0	0	3	19	1	20	10	4	1	.269	.392	.315
Sanchez, Gerardo, Puebla......	10	15	11	1	2	5	0	0	1	2	1	0	0	3	0	3	0	0	1	.182	.357	.455
Sanchez, Jose, Dos Laredos..	48	101	89	23	23	28	2	0	1	6	0	0	0	12	0	15	2	1	0	.258	.347	.315
Sanchez, Orlando, Reynosa...	31	100	91	7	17	20	3	0	0	5	4	0	3	2	0	15	2	1	5	.187	.229	.220
Sanchez, Raul, Cancun..........	103	402	346	46	100	132	17	0	5	40	5	3	9	35	3	54	4	4	5	.289	.366	.382
Sanchez, Roque, Yucatan.......	45	97	95	7	23	27	4	0	0	8	0	0	1	1	0	7	0	0	4	.242	.258	.284
Sanchez. Wilfredo, Cordoba...	36	87	80	9	16	23	3	2	0	7	0	0	1	6	0	18	0	1	1	.200	.264	.288
Sandoval, Jose, Mexico.........	106	433	367	67	112	195	17	0	22	91	0	5	3	57	8	44	6	7	11	.305	.398	.531
Sandoval, Octavio, Tigres.......	77	136	120	28	33	53	6	1	4	18	3	1	3	9	0	14	7	1	3	.275	.338	.442
Santana, Mario, Tabasco........	103	357	315	21	71	79	5	0	1	28	10	1	1	30	2	36	4	6	7	.225	.294	.251
Santana, Pedro, Cordoba.......	41	169	146	38	55	86	6	2	7	18	2	1	5	15	0	22	7	2	4	.377	.449	.589
Santos, Andres, Dos Laredos	34	50	46	5	11	13	2	0	0	5	1	1	0	2	0	14	0	1	2	.239	.265	.283
Sauceda, Victor, Cancun *.....	64	114	103	13	29	36	3	2	0	4	0	0	1	10	0	14	0	2	2	.282	.351	.350
Saucedo, Robert, Tabasco.....	95	402	329	40	75	124	10	0	13	43	1	1	7	64	10	63	0	1	9	.228	.364	.377
Sherman, Darrell, Puebla *....	87	417	349	82	121	164	20	4	5	39	5	1	6	56	6	32	14	8	5	.347	.444	.470
Sievers, Carlos, Tabasco *.....	87	279	242	25	62	96	11	1	7	37	0	4	4	29	3	24	1	3	10	.256	.341	.397
Smith, Charles, Monterrey.....	101	428	357	66	92	173	15	0	22	70	0	3	10	58	7	66	0	1	9	.258	.374	.485
Smith, Demond, Monterrey †	100	466	384	80	120	174	18	3	10	41	10	3	12	57	5	70	53	18	5	.313	.414	.453
Sojo, Luis, Oaxaca................	22	92	83	17	34	49	6	0	3	16	1	1	0	7	0	5	0	0	1	.410	.451	.590
Soriano, Ricardo, Cordoba *..	66	238	209	25	58	72	11	0	1	16	4	0	4	21	1	31	3	4	4	.278	.355	.344
Soto, Saul, Oaxaca-Mexico....	97	393	345	53	100	159	18	1	13	53	1	4	5	38	1	55	2	0	18	.290	.365	.461
Sotomayor, Gilberto, Monc.*.	71	213	188	25	54	73	9	2	2	19	3	0	0	22	1	25	2	2	4	.287	.362	.388
Suarez, Luis, Tigres *	81	239	213	33	71	104	18	0	5	38	1	3	1	21	5	26	6	2	4	.333	.391	.488
Tellez, Alonso, Yucatan..........	106	434	399	45	106	163	17	2	12	52	0	2	0	33	5	61	0	1	16	.266	.320	.409
Thompson, Ryan, Oaxaca......	27	124	106	20	35	56	6	0	5	14	1	0	3	14	1	18	0	2	2	.330	.423	.528
Timmons, Ozzie, Reynosa......	35	146	121	23	34	52	9	0	3	25	0	0	2	23	2	22	0	0	3	.281	.404	.430
Trapaga, Julio, Puebla...........	19	25	23	3	6	9	3	0	0	4	0	1	1	0	0	3	1	0	0	.261	.280	.391
Tress, Irving, Cordoba...........	6	19	17	0	2	3	1	0	0	0	1	0	0	1	0	6	0	0	0	.118	.167	.176
Valdez, Emmanuel, Tigres......	16	45	38	5	8	12	1	0	1	3	0	0	0	7	0	15	0	1	1	.211	.333	.316

Player, Team	G	TPA	AB	R	H	TB	2B	3B	HR	RBI	SH	SF	HP	BB	IBB	SO	SB	CS	GDP	Avg.	OBP	Slg.
Valdez, Francisco, Vera.-Pue.	69	220	192	20	51	69	3	0	5	23	8	5	3	12	1	21	1	0	6	.266	.311	.359
Valdez, Ramon, Campeche *	93	387	342	36	87	104	9	1	2	23	9	2	6	28	0	35	5	10	4	.254	.320	.304
Valencia, Abraham, D.Lar.	92	364	325	45	102	136	16	0	6	47	2	4	10	23	0	54	5	4	12	.314	.373	.418
Valencia, Carlos, D.Laredos	106	450	412	46	94	156	17	3	13	50	5	4	2	27	4	47	5	3	10	.228	.276	.379
Valenzuela, Irving, Monclova	55	121	110	12	29	34	2	0	1	9	3	0	2	6	0	12	3	2	2	.264	.314	.309
Valle, Cosme, Mexico	12	36	35	1	6	9	1	1	0	4	0	0	0	1	0	7	0	2	1	.171	.194	.257
Valle, Jorge, Vaqueros	87	300	273	22	69	91	10	0	4	38	5	3	3	16	1	46	1	2	17	.253	.298	.333
Vazquez, Gregorio, Tabasco	66	256	216	27	63	74	6	1	1	20	8	1	5	26	1	19	7	4	2	.292	.379	.343
Vazquez, Jorge Alberto, Tig.	80	272	247	35	69	124	11	1	14	60	0	5	1	19	3	65	2	1	11	.279	.327	.502
Vazquez, Ricardo, Tigres	2	1	1	2	0	0	0	0	0	0	0	0	0	0	0	1	0	0	0	.000	.000	.000
Vega, Edgar, Puebla	75	267	240	30	68	86	9	0	3	30	4	4	2	17	0	47	1	4	13	.283	.331	.358
Velazquez, Guillermo, Camp.-Pue.*	109	418	366	38	91	130	15	0	8	51	1	1	0	50	8	82	0	0	13	.249	.338	.355
Velez, Manuel, Saltillo	87	357	316	44	102	131	15	1	4	41	1	9	3	27	1	29	1	4	9	.323	.372	.415
Verdugo, Vincente, Saltillo	86	371	341	51	114	140	14	0	4	42	9	1	3	17	0	26	1	4	7	.334	.370	.411
Villalobos, Carlos, Puebla	79	330	281	46	104	165	25	0	12	63	2	3	6	38	5	44	0	3	14	.370	.451	.587
Villarreal, Alejandro, D.Lar.	79	270	237	23	68	85	11	0	2	26	1	0	3	29	1	31	1	2	9	.287	.372	.359
Villegas, Fernando, Cancun	93	303	263	32	61	82	15	0	2	26	11	5	4	20	1	39	1	1	8	.232	.291	.312
Virgen, Constancio, Mexico	25	52	47	2	9	9	0	0	0	1	3	0	0	2	0	10	0	0	1	.191	.224	.191
Vizcarra, Roberto, Tigres	96	428	387	52	117	155	18	1	6	48	2	5	5	29	0	30	3	4	11	.302	.354	.401
White, Derrick, Dos Laredos	109	466	406	61	124	204	19	2	19	87	0	4	8	48	8	49	12	4	26	.305	.386	.502
Wilson, Craig, Oaxaca	14	59	46	8	12	18	1	1	1	9	2	0	2	9	1	12	1	1	1	.261	.404	.391
Yan, Julian, Puebla	108	486	417	63	124	202	24	0	18	90	1	4	6	58	4	81	3	1	11	.297	.388	.484
Zambrano, Roberto, D.Lar.	105	463	345	77	95	181	23	0	21	75	0	3	21	94	6	93	1	3	2	.275	.454	.525
Zazueta, Juan, Veracruz †	73	262	237	25	53	65	5	2	1	16	2	2	1	20	0	29	7	2	5	.224	.285	.274
Zazueta, Mauricio, Monc.†	79	333	313	31	78	102	16	1	2	20	3	1	0	16	0	36	6	2	8	.249	.285	.326

PLAYERS WITH TWO OR MORE TEAMS

Player, Team	G	TPA	AB	R	H	TB	2B	3B	HR	RBI	SH	SF	HP	BB	IBB	SO	SB	CS	GDP	Avg.	OBP	Slg.
Aganza, Ruben, Yucatan	27	59	50	7	8	16	2	0	2	7	1	0	0	8	1	3	0	0	0	.160	.276	.320
Aganza, Ruben, Saltillo	20	51	46	9	11	16	2	0	1	5	1	1	0	3	0	7	0	0	2	.239	.280	.348
Aganza, Ruben, Monclova	20	77	68	7	15	34	1	0	6	13	0	2	0	7	0	13	0	1	2	.221	.286	.500
Aguilera, Armando, Camp.	24	59	56	5	11	15	1	0	1	2	1	0	0	2	0	9	0	0	1	.196	.224	.268
Aguilera, Armando, Veracruz	23	83	74	4	16	19	3	0	0	11	2	0	1	6	0	12	0	1	4	.216	.284	.257
Arano, Eloy, Vaqueros †	59	184	170	18	36	41	3	1	0	5	5	0	4	5	0	22	0	3	6	.212	.251	.241
Arano, Eloy, Cordoba †	25	87	77	7	19	20	1	0	0	4	2	0	1	7	1	13	3	1	0	.247	.318	.260
Arauz, Leobardo, Yucatan †	18	54	47	5	8	18	1	0	3	7	0	0	1	6	0	6	0	0	2	.170	.278	.383
Arauz, Leobardo, Monclova †	49	227	191	30	51	82	4	0	9	35	1	2	3	30	0	38	2	1	2	.267	.372	.429
Arredondo, Hernando, Tab.	46	148	133	18	35	60	4	0	7	22	3	1	2	9	1	17	2	1	3	.263	.317	.451
Arredondo, Hernando, Cord.	41	164	156	22	48	74	11	0	5	21	4	0	1	3	0	15	1	1	4	.308	.325	.474
Avila, Carlos, Tigres *	1	1	1	0	0	0	0	0	0	0	0	0	0	0	0	1	0	0	0	.000	.000	.000
Avila, Carlos, Puebla *	33	24	23	8	5	5	0	0	0	2	0	0	0	1	0	3	0	0	0	.217	.250	.217
Bullett, Scott, Monterrey *	78	316	268	55	87	124	11	1	8	37	0	5	4	39	7	50	9	7	5	.325	.411	.463
Bullett, Scott, Reynosa *	29	119	104	21	33	60	5	2	6	14	0	0	3	12	0	14	4	0	1	.317	.403	.577
Castaneda, Rafael, Monterrey	4	9	8	1	2	3	1	0	0	1	0	0	0	1	0	1	0	0	1	.250	.333	.375
Castaneda, Rafael, Reynosa	51	173	152	16	44	71	9	0	6	32	0	0	2	19	0	15	2	0	7	.289	.376	.467
Castillo, Alberto, Mexico	17	69	60	13	21	28	4	0	1	14	1	1	1	6	0	7	1	1	1	.350	.412	.467
Castillo, Alberto, Vaqueros	66	282	243	38	70	112	9	0	11	47	1	1	3	34	2	22	0	1	8	.288	.381	.461
Cazarin, Manuel, Veracruz	66	247	221	23	62	93	4	0	9	27	6	2	5	13	1	15	1	2	8	.281	.332	.421
Cazarin, Manuel, Campeche	28	102	88	6	18	25	4	0	1	10	5	2	1	6	0	5	0	0	4	.205	.258	.284
Cervantes, Peter, Veracruz *	12	0	0	0	0	0	0	0	0	0	0	0	0	0	0	0	0	0	0	.000	.000	.000
Cervantes, Peter, Puebla *	27	1	1	0	0	0	0	0	0	0	0	0	0	0	0	0	0	0	0	.000	.000	.000
Connell, Lino, Reynosa	65	287	247	37	75	99	15	0	3	28	2	1	0	37	1	34	16	7	8	.304	.393	.401
Connell, Lino, Oaxaca	36	167	150	20	42	56	7	2	1	16	2	0	0	15	1	19	2	0	7	.280	.345	.373
Davis, Jay, Cordoba *	40	167	157	21	49	80	10	0	7	21	0	2	0	8	0	28	1	1	6	.312	.341	.510
Davis, Jay, Monterrey *	64	271	242	45	77	112	21	1	4	50	2	3	0	24	6	46	5	2	6	.318	.375	.463
Diaz, Pedro, Veracruz	19	50	43	4	7	9	2	0	0	3	3	0	1	3	1	13	0	0	2	.163	.234	.209
Diaz, Pedro, Puebla	9	18	17	0	5	5	0	0	0	0	0	0	1	0	0	4	0	0	0	.294	.333	.294
Espinosa, Ramon, D.Laredos	81	377	352	49	108	141	15	3	4	34	4	3	8	10	1	37	18	9	9	.307	.338	.401
Espinosa, Ramon, Yucatan	24	108	100	8	30	34	4	0	0	10	3	0	2	3	0	12	0	1	0	.300	.333	.340
Espinoza, Efren, Mexico	20	42	38	9	9	12	0	0	1	3	0	0	0	4	0	6	0	0	0	.237	.310	.316
Espinoza, Efren, Vaqueros	26	74	70	7	15	21	3	0	1	7	0	0	1	3	0	14	2	0	1	.214	.257	.300
Estrada, Hector, Cordoba	55	187	170	20	39	60	9	0	4	15	1	0	2	14	1	19	2	0	4	.229	.296	.353
Estrada, Hector, Vaqueros	20	75	71	8	22	34	3	0	3	10	0	0	0	4	0	6	1	0	5	.310	.347	.479
Flores, Miguel, Reynosa	67	286	253	30	71	89	10	1	2	29	0	2	4	27	3	44	12	3	5	.281	.357	.352
Flores, Miguel, Yucatan	18	66	59	7	14	20	3	0	1	4	3	0	2	2	0	12	1	3	1	.237	.286	.339
Garcia, Cornelio, Oaxaca *	24	105	93	12	26	32	3	0	1	9	0	0	1	11	0	18	2	2	3	.280	.362	.344
Garcia, Cornelio, Vaqueros *	58	262	213	38	79	104	13	3	2	34	2	5	1	41	2	19	4	4	6	.371	.465	.488
Garcia, Cornelio, Mexico *	11	51	42	10	14	18	4	0	0	7	0	2	1	6	0	2	2	1	3	.333	.412	.429
Garcia, Omar, Dos Laredos †	33	151	134	27	48	70	7	0	5	23	0	0	2	15	0	10	0	0	5	.358	.430	.522
Garcia, Omar, Veracruz †	42	187	165	22	49	69	9	1	3	22	0	0	0	22	3	19	0	0	8	.297	.380	.418
LeBron, Juan, Oaxaca	27	108	103	15	27	53	5	0	7	20	0	0	1	4	0	26	0	1	0	.262	.296	.515
LeBron, Juan, Campeche	56	239	217	24	61	94	7	1	8	32	1	1	1	19	0	51	3	1	12	.281	.340	.433
Leyva, German, D.Laredos *	53	198	162	31	45	57	7	1	1	14	5	1	1	29	1	13	4	0	5	.278	.389	.352
Leyva, German, Saltillo *	24	31	24	3	6	8	2	0	0	4	0	1	1	5	0	1	0	0	0	.250	.387	.333
Lucca, Lou, Vaqueros	29	117	100	12	37	46	4	1	1	16	0	0	2	15	0	11	1	0	5	.370	.462	.460
Lucca, Lou, Cordoba	46	189	165	22	47	77	6	0	8	31	0	2	7	15	2	24	2	1	3	.285	.365	.467
Lugo, Roberto, Monterrey	2	5	5	1	2	2	0	0	0	2	0	0	0	0	0	1	0	0	0	.400	.400	.400
Lugo, Roberto, Reynosa	71	199	186	19	43	54	7	2	0	14	6	1	2	4	0	37	1	0	4	.231	.254	.290
Medina, Eric, Oaxaca	3	3	3	0	0	0	0	0	0	0	0	0	0	0	0	0	0	0	1	.000	.000	.000
Medina, Eric, Monterrey	3	7	6	0	0	0	0	0	0	0	0	0	0	1	0	5	0	0	1	.000	.143	.000
Melo, Juan, Cordoba †	18	77	71	7	19	20	1	0	0	6	1	0	1	4	1	10	0	1	5	.268	.316	.282

Player, Team	G	TPA	AB	R	H	TB	2B	3B	HR	RBI	SH	SF	HP	BB	IBB	SO	SB	CS	GDP	Avg.	OBP	Slg.
Melo, Juan, Mexico †	8	39	35	8	9	13	1	0	1	3	0	0	0	4	0	7	1	0	0	.257	.333	.371
Mendez, Francisco, Reyn.*	84	324	277	36	81	129	15	0	11	45	4	3	1	39	6	50	2	2	8	.292	.378	.466
Mendez, Francisco, Mont.*	7	14	13	0	4	4	0	0	0	0	0	0	0	1	0	0	0	0	0	.308	.357	.308
Mendoza, Omar, Oaxaca	25	74	62	11	16	24	3	1	1	5	2	0	0	10	1	12	2	0	2	.258	.361	.387
Mendoza, Omar, Tabasco	25	78	69	7	15	21	3	0	1	8	2	3	0	4	0	11	0	0	4	.217	.250	.304
Mendoza, Omar, Reynosa	24	63	56	9	13	16	0	0	1	5	0	2	0	5	0	8	0	2	0	.232	.286	.286
Munoz, Adan, Tigres *	12	35	30	3	7	7	0	0	0	3	1	0	2	2	1	2	0	1	0	.233	.324	.233
Munoz, Adan, Monclova *	73	256	227	32	52	83	9	2	6	23	2	3	2	22	2	41	1	0	3	.229	.299	.366
Newson, Warren, Monclova *	86	361	293	44	88	126	14	0	8	42	0	2	3	63	6	58	11	3	11	.300	.427	.430
Newson, Warren, Tabasco *	9	38	29	5	8	13	2	0	1	1	0	0	0	9	0	8	1	0	1	.276	.447	.448
Nunez, Reymond, D.Laredos	28	125	113	13	32	39	4	0	1	16	0	2	0	10	0	10	0	0	7	.283	.336	.345
Nunez, Reymond, Reynosa	10	42	39	3	6	10	1	0	1	4	0	0	1	2	0	5	0	0	0	.154	.214	.256
Paul, Corey, Saltillo *	66	278	233	51	83	128	18	0	9	45	0	4	1	40	6	46	7	0	11	.356	.446	.549
Paul, Corey, Tabasco *	28	121	97	15	25	35	4	0	2	8	0	0	1	23	4	19	3	0	1	.258	.405	.361
Rios, Eduardo, Cancun	68	276	256	22	66	91	10	0	5	29	1	4	2	13	2	32	1	1	16	.258	.295	.355
Rios, Eduardo, Oaxaca	26	122	106	12	36	51	12	0	1	18	1	1	0	14	1	7	0	0	5	.340	.413	.481
Rivera, Francisco, Veracruz	2	3	3	1	1	4	0	0	1	4	0	0	0	0	0	0	0	0	0	.333	.333	1.333
Rivera, Francisco, D.Laredos	56	101	86	11	22	31	6	0	1	7	0	2	0	13	1	12	0	0	2	.256	.347	.360
Robles, Juan, Tabasco	26	43	41	4	9	13	1	0	1	2	0	0	1	1	0	11	2	0	2	.220	.256	.317
Robles, Juan, Reynosa	7	23	23	1	8	8	0	0	0	5	0	0	0	0	0	5	0	0	1	.348	.348	.348
Rodarte, Raul, Reynosa	66	257	231	34	74	110	13	1	7	30	3	2	2	19	1	32	10	2	7	.320	.374	.476
Rodarte, Raul, Monterrey	24	93	84	15	32	42	5	1	1	9	0	1	0	8	0	15	3	0	3	.381	.430	.500
Romero, Willie, Yucatan	36	141	123	14	27	39	6	0	2	14	3	1	1	13	1	27	6	2	1	.220	.297	.317
Romero, Willie, Saltillo	26	127	110	24	38	50	6	0	2	8	1	0	4	12	0	12	5	2	2	.345	.429	.455
Saenz, Ricardo, Monclova	82	343	302	39	90	119	17	0	4	32	0	1	2	38	2	74	4	1	6	.298	.379	.394
Saenz, Ricardo, Saltillo	23	88	81	10	20	36	4	0	4	13	0	0	1	6	0	18	0	0	1	.247	.307	.444
Soto, Saul, Oaxaca	47	194	179	24	50	68	10	1	2	20	0	1	2	12	1	22	0	0	13	.279	.330	.380
Soto, Saul, Mexico	50	199	166	29	50	91	8	0	11	33	1	3	3	26	0	33	2	0	5	.301	.399	.548
Valdez, Francisco, Veracruz	34	113	96	10	26	30	1	0	1	9	5	3	2	7	1	16	1	0	3	.271	.324	.313
Valdez, Francisco, Puebla	35	107	96	10	25	39	2	0	4	14	3	2	1	5	0	5	0	0	3	.260	.298	.406
Velazquez, Guillermo, Pue.*	54	194	171	16	46	64	9	0	3	28	0	1	0	22	5	41	0	0	5	.269	.351	.374
Velazquez, Guillermo, Camp.*	55	224	195	22	45	66	6	0	5	23	1	0	0	28	3	41	0	0	8	.231	.327	.338

GRAND SLAMS—L. Arauz, Ramon Martinez, R. Mendez, J.L. Sandoval, Velazquez, Yan, 2 each; Amador, Arias, H. Arredondo, Buelna, Canizalez, Castellano, A. Castillo, R. Cervantes, A. Contreras, Davis, E. Diaz, L. Diaz, Fornes, Hurtado, LeBron, Leyritz, Ra. Lopez, Mata, Mejia, N. Munoz, Newson, Ortiz, Palafox, E. Rios, R. Robles, T. Robles, M. Romero, Saenz, Ra. Sanchez, Saucedo, C. Smith, S. Soto, Timmons, J. Vazquez, Vega, D. White, 1 each.

AWARDED FIRST BASE ON CATCHER'S INTERFERENCE—Ra. Sanchez 4 (Esqueda, Garzon, An. Martinez, R. Quinones); Kelly 2 (R. Quinones, A. Rodriguez); D. Espino (Er. Rodriguez); H. Gomez (R. Quinones); Iturbe (S. Soto); Pickering (Esqueda); C. Rodriguez, Vaqueros (F. Valdez); Er. Rodriguez (R. Quinones); F. Romero (A. Meza); J.L. Sandoval (R. Quinones); Velez (R. Quinones).

2003 PITCHING

TEAM

Team	W	L	Pct.	ERA	G	CG	ShO	Sv.	IP	H	TBF	R	ER	HR	SH	SF	HB	BB	IBB	SO	WP	Bk.
Yucatan	61	45	.575	3.53	106	10	11	30	919.0	901	3956	396	360	60	41	30	44	362	19	556	60	1
Tabasco	49	59	.454	3.74	109	2	7	28	959.2	951	4167	444	399	63	67	21	47	393	51	524	38	3
Tigres	72	35	.673	3.77	108	4	8	40	938.1	1027	4064	450	393	73	38	31	36	348	20	497	33	1
Campeche	55	51	.519	3.84	106	16	4	26	923.1	891	4018	450	394	82	60	27	50	430	26	510	32	2
Monterrey	66	43	.606	3.90	109	3	8	28	945.1	985	4105	465	410	78	47	26	42	387	32	596	47	5
Veracruz	50	54	.481	3.97	106	7	7	22	952.0	1041	4156	478	420	88	62	27	69	351	46	442	41	3
Cancun	44	63	.411	4.35	107	13	11	24	913.2	1033	4023	505	442	86	44	29	31	318	21	420	37	1
Oaxaca	57	52	.523	4.51	109	9	4	31	963.1	1123	4299	582	483	63	44	32	37	386	18	579	58	2
Saltillo	62	45	.579	4.59	107	7	2	25	926.0	1014	4113	536	472	82	41	28	40	395	19	619	40	3
Monclova	49	59	.454	4.66	110	5	6	28	957.0	1122	4313	569	496	87	47	29	43	408	13	535	54	5
Dos Laredos	53	56	.486	4.78	110	5	8	24	964.2	1120	4319	560	512	85	50	36	60	414	29	589	42	3
Mexico	68	40	.630	4.81	108	11	2	32	943.2	1158	4211	546	504	87	34	30	45	326	16	552	46	1
Reynosa	43	63	.406	4.89	107	2	5	23	931.2	1021	4185	563	506	72	46	35	41	407	13	498	57	6
Puebla	62	48	.564	4.92	110	10	9	25	949.1	1081	4273	574	519	85	46	30	40	457	41	555	53	2
Cordoba	29	75	.279	5.69	104	7	3	20	884.0	1114	4059	593	559	107	44	27	52	383	34	425	54	3
Vaqueros	39	71	.355	5.95	110	7	2	17	949.0	1103	4385	692	627	146	41	30	79	494	41	559	65	2

INDIVIDUAL

TOP QUALIFIERS FOR EARNED-RUN AVERAGE TITLE

Minimum 88 innings. *Lefthanded pitcher.

Pitcher, Team	W	L	Pct.	ERA	G	GS	CG	ShO	GF	Sv.	IP	H	TBF	R	ER	HR	SH	SF	HB	BB	IBB	SO	WP	Bk.
Serafini, Dan, Monterrey *	10	2	.833	1.59	16	15	0	0	0	0	96.1	70	386	24	17	5	2	0	3	41	1	89	3	0
Moreno, Angel, Veracruz *	8	4	.667	2.27	21	19	3	2	2	1	126.2	121	515	40	32	4	2	0	5	27	0	42	5	0
Manzanillo, Ravelo, Yuc.-Salt.*	10	3	.769	2.36	17	17	1	0	0	0	118.0	81	492	33	31	2	9	4	7	65	2	81	5	0
Campos, Francisco, Cam	6	4	.600	2.40	12	12	3	1	0	0	90.0	85	370	31	24	9	9	1	5	20	2	58	0	0
Vega, Obed, Cancun	9	4	.692	2.67	21	21	1	0	0	0	141.1	135	582	50	42	8	6	5	7	40	0	65	3	0
Vargas, Joel, Tabasco	7	4	.636	2.69	20	20	1	1	0	0	124.0	110	510	42	37	5	8	3	6	41	5	61	1	0
Romano, Mike, Tabasco	5	4	.556	2.72	38	9	0	0	26	13	99.1	100	421	34	30	3	6	4	5	32	3	57	5	0
Campillo, Jorge, Tigres	12	5	.706	2.79	21	21	2	1	0	0	119.1	116	490	47	37	7	4	2	4	30	1	63	4	0
Nunez, Jose, Dos Laredos	11	5	.688	2.89	21	19	4	2	1	1	140.1	148	583	52	45	7	5	4	4	33	2	73	4	0
Guzman, Jesus, Tigres *	10	3	.769	2.92	27	12	0	0	3	0	98.2	100	407	41	32	2	6	2	4	24	0	47	2	0
Rodriguez, Salvador, Yucatan	10	4	.714	3.00	19	19	1	0	0	0	120.0	111	504	45	40	10	7	1	7	37	1	71	3	0
Magee, Bo, Campeche *	10	6	.625	3.06	23	23	8	0	0	0	170.1	118	730	67	58	12	17	4	8	109	3	155	6	0
Ortega, Pablo, Puebla	13	4	.765	3.14	23	23	4	3	0	0	160.2	153	663	61	56	9	14	2	9	46	6	98	2	0
Valdez, Efrain, Tabasco *	3	6	.333	3.15	16	16	0	0	0	0	94.1	96	405	34	33	6	8	1	3	31	3	41	1	1
Esquer, Mercedes, Reynosa *	7	7	.500	3.17	20	20	0	0	0	0	125.0	128	521	51	44	6	6	1	4	17	0	51	0	0

DEPARTMENTAL LEADERS: W—Mercedes, 14; L—J. Acosta, Hurtado, E. Lopez, Quinones, 11; Pct.—Patrick, .867; G—Garibay, 59; GS—Several pitchers tied with 23; CG—Hurtado, 12; ShO—P. Ortega, 3; GF—Alberro, 48; Sv.—S. Hernandez, 36; IP—Hurtado, 175.0; H—O. Alvarez, 202; TBF—Hurtado, 736; R—O. Alvarez, 87; ER—O. Alvarez, 80; HR—Reynoso, 19; SH—Magee, 17; SF—Or. Verdugo, 7; HB—H. Navarro, 17; BB—Magee, 109; IBB—T. Alvarez, Amarillas, 9; SO—Magee, 155; WP—Hurtado, 12; BK—Quintanilla, 3.

ALL PITCHERS

*Lefthanded pitcher.

Pitcher, Team	W	L	Pct.	ERA	G	GS	CG	ShO	GF	Sv.	IP	H	TBF	R	ER	HR	SH	SF	HB	BB	IBB	SO	WP	Bk.
Aceves, Alfredo, Yucatan	1	1	.500	3.35	27	2	0	0	11	1	43.0	49	193	17	16	3	0	1	4	18	2	29	3	0
Acosta, Aaron, Tabasco	1	2	.333	5.06	11	8	0	0	0	0	42.2	49	199	27	24	1	5	1	3	22	0	17	5	0
Acosta, Jasiel, Monclova *	6	11	.353	5.49	23	22	2	1	0	0	116.1	137	528	79	71	10	5	5	1	62	0	56	2	2
Agosto, Stevenson, Tab.-Oax.*	5	4	.556	4.88	16	11	0	0	3	0	72.0	74	318	42	39	9	5	1	3	41	1	63	7	0
Aguilar, Hugo, Monc.-Tigres *	1	1	.500	6.61	21	3	0	0	6	0	31.1	42	157	28	23	4	4	2	2	25	0	21	3	0
Aguilar, Mario, Campeche *	1	0	1.000	1.23	11	0	0	0	2	0	7.1	3	25	1	1	0	1	1	0	1	0	1	0	0
Aguirre, Alejandro, Monclova	0	0	.000	5.85	22	1	0	0	14	1	40.0	52	186	29	26	5	1	4	1	18	2	18	5	0
Aguirre, Gaudencio, Mont.	4	0	1.000	2.42	50	0	0	0	4	0	52.0	42	218	15	14	2	4	1	3	25	6	42	2	0
Alberro, Jose, Monclova	6	5	.545	2.28	52	0	0	0	48	24	71.0	62	289	18	18	7	3	0	5	26	2	55	0	0
Almeida, Rowsell, D.Lar.-Vera.*	0	1	.000	12.27	8	1	0	0	2	0	7.1	13	44	10	10	0	0	1	2	7	2	5	3	0
Alvarez, Antonio, Cordoba	2	3	.400	5.00	33	6	2	0	5	0	66.2	87	307	40	37	8	6	3	6	28	5	28	7	0
Alvarez, Azael, Monc.-Pue.*	2	2	.500	4.26	23	8	0	0	1	0	61.1	58	287	34	29	4	1	1	5	47	0	47	6	1
Alvarez, Juan, Vaqueros	4	6	.400	6.19	16	14	0	0	1	0	72.2	86	337	55	50	11	3	2	9	39	0	31	7	0
Alvarez, Octavio, Mexico	11	8	.579	4.35	23	23	4	0	0	0	165.1	202	709	87	80	10	13	1	9	29	1	88	4	0
Alvarez, Trevor, Vaqueros	5	6	.455	4.13	45	0	0	0	43	17	56.2	51	247	26	26	2	6	2	3	28	9	37	1	0
Amarillas, Asdrubal, Cord.-Vaq.	0	4	.000	7.97	35	1	0	0	5	1	49.2	63	244	46	44	6	1	3	3	37	9	18	11	0
Angulo, Victor, Puebla *	1	1	.500	3.80	21	3	0	0	6	0	23.2	23	112	10	10	1	1	0	0	23	0	10	6	0
Arellano, Salvador, Yucatan	8	3	.727	3.92	17	16	1	0	0	0	78.0	80	337	38	34	7	2	2	5	30	0	52	6	0
Armenta, Alejandro, Tigres *	4	2	.667	4.26	14	4	0	0	1	0	38.0	38	164	19	18	6	0	0	1	19	0	23	3	0
Arroyo, Luis, Monclova *	7	8	.467	4.09	24	22	3	2	0	0	123.1	124	549	61	56	8	8	0	5	63	2	99	2	0
Atondo, Sergio, Yucatan	0	1	.000	21.60	2	1	0	0	0	0	3.1	8	20	8	8	0	0	0	0	3	0	2	2	0
Avalos, Jose, Oaxaca	6	1	.857	3.15	41	0	0	0	12	1	34.1	37	159	16	12	2	4	1	1	21	1	15	7	0
Avila, Mauricio, Cancun	0	0	.000	0.00	2	0	0	0	1	0	1.1	1	7	0	0	0	0	0	0	2	0	0	0	0
Ayala, Ramon, Campeche	0	1	.000	7.36	8	1	0	0	0	0	11.0	10	55	10	9	2	0	1	1	11	0	1	3	0
Baez, Sixto, Oaxaca	2	4	.333	1.73	38	0	0	0	35	25	36.1	29	151	14	7	1	1	0	4	13	3	19	1	0
Banda, Alfredo, Monterrey *	0	0	.000	0.00	1	0	0	0	1	0	0.2	0	2	0	0	0	0	0	0	1	0	0	0	0
Barreras, Juan, Vaqueros	2	1	.667	5.17	34	0	0	0	16	0	55.2	57	251	39	32	8	0	4	2	33	2	28	9	0
Beltran, Alonso, Puebla	3	5	.375	5.97	16	15	0	0	0	0	78.1	101	369	62	52	9	3	4	4	40	4	37	2	0
Bernal, Manuel, Mexico	5	5	.500	6.48	27	9	0	0	5	0	76.1	116	361	59	55	11	3	2	3	20	1	41	5	0
Blancas, Rigoberto, Cord.*	1	9	.100	6.89	29	14	0	0	3	0	78.1	102	361	63	60	12	5	2	1	30	2	30	4	0
Bones, Ricky, Saltillo	0	1	.000	9.45	3	2	0	0	1	1	6.2	7	35	7	7	1	0	0	2	7	0	6	0	0
Bustillos, Oscar, Tigres	0	0	.000	10.20	12	0	0	0	2	0	15.0	22	72	18	17	3	2	1	1	6	1	4	1	0
Cabrales, Gabriel, Pue.-Vera.	1	0	1.000	3.67	27	3	0	0	9	0	49.0	57	207	20	20	6	1	3	3	17	4	23	1	0
Camacho, Daniel, Yucatan	0	0	.000	6.35	3	0	0	0	3	0	5.2	7	26	4	4	1	1	1	0	2	0	1	2	0
Camara, Pedro, Yucatan *	3	2	.600	4.58	32	0	0	0	2	1	19.2	18	92	11	10	1	1	0	1	16	1	21	5	0
Campillo, Jorge, Tigres	12	5	.706	2.79	21	21	2	1	0	0	119.1	116	490	47	37	7	4	2	4	30	1	63	4	0
Campos, Francisco, Camp.	6	4	.600	2.40	12	12	3	1	0	0	90.0	85	370	31	24	9	9	1	5	20	2	58	0	0
Carrasco, Alejandro, Mexico	6	2	.750	3.04	41	1	0	0	8	0	56.1	60	246	22	19	5	1	3	5	21	3	26	0	0
Carrillo, Guillermo, D.Laredos	0	0	.000	6.23	11	0	0	0	4	0	13.0	17	62	10	9	1	0	0	0	8	2	7	0	0
Carrillo, Jose, Reynosa	0	1	.000	5.86	10	1	0	0	2	0	27.2	34	127	18	18	3	1	2	1	13	0	15	2	0
Castaneda, Federico, Vaq.	1	7	.125	4.59	26	6	0	0	5	0	68.2	70	312	40	35	12	2	6	8	36	3	50	7	0
Castellanos, Hugo, D.Laredos	1	1	.500	6.30	12	1	0	0	1	0	20.0	19	94	17	14	1	0	0	4	10	1	18	0	0
Castillo, Ismael, Campeche	0	0	.000	5.87	12	0	0	0	3	0	15.1	19	71	10	10	3	1	0	0	8	1	10	0	0
Castillo, Jorge, Mexico *	0	0	.000	13.50	1	0	0	0	0	0	0.2	1	3	1	1	0	0	0	0	1	0	0	0	0
Castro, Carlos, Saltillo	0	0	.000	0.00	1	0	0	0	0	0	1.1	2	8	1	0	0	0	0	0	2	0	0	1	0
Castro, Luis, Oaxaca	0	0	.000	13.50	2	0	0	0	1	0	1.1	3	10	2	2	0	0	0	0	3	0	0	0	0
Cazares, Juan, Campeche *	0	0	.000	1.80	12	0	0	0	2	0	5.0	5	22	1	1	1	0	1	0	2	0	3	0	0
Cazares, Rosario, Saltillo	2	0	1.000	4.05	31	0	0	0	3	0	33.1	31	139	15	15	5	0	0	3	8	3	15	4	0
Cazares, Tomas, Tabasco *	0	1	.000	6.14	12	0	0	0	2	0	7.1	7	33	5	5	0	0	0	1	4	0	5	2	0
Cerros, Juan, Monterrey	1	1	.500	2.76	51	0	0	0	21	2	49.0	47	210	18	15	2	2	3	4	14	2	24	1	0
Cervantes, Eustorgio, D.Lar.	1	0	1.000	4.15	4	0	0	0	2	0	4.1	2	16	3	2	1	0	0	0	2	0	2	0	0
Cervantes, Peter, Vera.-Puebla	3	4	.429	4.26	39	0	0	0	33	15	50.2	49	205	24	24	6	3	3	2	13	3	40	4	0
Chapa, Javier, Vaqueros	0	1	.000	34.71	2	1	0	0	0	0	2.1	7	17	9	9	1	2	0	0	3	0	0	0	0
Chavarria, Hector, Cord.-Vaq.	6	6	.500	6.02	19	19	0	0	0	0	89.2	107	415	64	60	12	3	3	8	52	1	37	10	0
Chavez, Alejandro, Mexico *	0	0	.000	6.83	18	2	0	0	3	0	27.2	24	133	24	21	3	0	3	2	23	0	34	7	0
Chavez, Carlos, Veracruz	1	2	.333	4.50	8	0	0	0	7	2	10.0	11	46	10	5	1	1	1	0	5	1	5	1	0
Colon, Jose, Saltillo	1	1	.500	4.28	25	0	0	0	22	7	27.1	30	110	14	13	4	0	0	0	3	1	16	0	0
Cordova, Francisco, Mexico	6	5	.545	4.78	28	4	0	0	14	5	43.1	54	200	25	23	6	1	2	3	24	4	23	3	0
Cordova, Francisco, Puebla	0	0	.000	16.20	3	0	0	0	1	0	3.1	9	21	6	6	1	0	0	0	3	0	4	1	0
Cortes, David, Dos Laredos	4	3	.571	2.70	48	0	0	0	42	18	53.1	58	229	17	16	3	5	4	0	18	1	39	2	0
Cortez, Martin, Cancun *	0	0	.000	8.31	6	0	0	0	2	1	4.1	4	18	4	4	1	0	1	0	3	0	1	0	0
Couoh, Enrique, Cancun	0	0	.000	3.72	4	0	0	0	2	0	9.2	9	40	4	4	1	1	0	0	3	1	7	0	0
Cruz, Javier, Mexico	0	1	.000	10.80	4	0	0	0	3	0	5.0	6	25	7	6	0	1	0	1	2	1	6	1	0
Cruz, Luis Manuel, Puebla	0	3	.000	7.90	15	1	0	0	1	0	27.1	41	137	27	24	3	1	2	2	13	2	12	2	0
DeSilva, John, Reynosa	4	3	.571	2.64	10	10	1	1	0	0	64.2	68	281	21	19	3	5	2	4	21	1	36	2	0
Delahoya, Javier, Vera.-Camp.	5	4	.556	3.70	17	17	1	0	0	0	97.1	105	439	41	40	7	8	2	10	43	3	56	5	0
Delfin, Adolpho, Dos Laredos	5	7	.417	5.63	30	12	1	0	2	0	86.1	101	406	60	54	9	5	4	11	49	6	47	5	0
Delgadillo, Juan, Yucatan	6	6	.500	4.11	20	14	0	0	2	0	85.1	85	374	42	39	8	4	3	2	44	1	41	10	0
Diaz, Marco, Saltillo	4	0	1.000	4.99	18	8	0	0	1	0	48.2	57	226	30	27	1	1	2	3	25	0	34	1	0
Diaz, Ralph, Saltillo	4	4	.500	5.27	13	11	0	0	0	0	56.1	61	267	39	33	3	2	2	3	33	3	39	2	0
Dingman, Craig, Yuc.-Cancun	4	7	.364	3.53	42	0	0	0	40	19	43.1	41	183	22	17	2	4	3	3	13	2	37	0	0
Dominguez, Carlos, Salt.-D.Lar.*	6	6	.500	4.70	26	19	0	0	2	0	99.2	113	451	56	52	8	2	2	5	55	2	47	5	0
Dominguez, David, Oaxaca	5	5	.500	7.57	39	2	0	0	9	3	52.1	62	247	50	44	3	4	2	5	24	4	28	6	1
Dorame, Randey, Mex.-Vaq.*	0	2	.000	11.81	16	6	0	0	3	0	26.2	35	131	35	35	6	1	0	3	17	1	16	1	0

Pitcher, Team	W	L	Pct.	ERA	G	GS	CG	ShO	GF	Sv.	IP	H	TBF	R	ER	HR	SH	SF	HB	BB	IBB	SO	WP	Bk.
Duarte, Miguel, Saltillo	4	2	.667	4.58	33	1	0	0	7	0	39.1	39	179	22	20	3	1	0	3	22	1	30	2	0
Elizalde, Carlos, Oaxaca	6	4	.600	5.03	22	12	0	0	1	0	77.0	100	354	54	43	4	2	4	3	32	2	45	9	0
Elvira, Abraham, Cord.-Vaq.*	1	2	.333	7.94	40	3	0	0	7	0	34.0	49	175	32	30	7	2	2	1	25	1	26	4	0
Elvira, Narciso, Campeche *	4	2	.667	1.87	8	8	2	0	0	0	57.2	37	229	17	12	2	3	2	4	24	0	33	2	0
Enriquez, Martin, Reyn.-Can	3	2	.600	4.31	41	0	0	0	17	7	39.2	43	173	19	19	1	6	1	1	13	5	15	2	0
Espadas, Gary, Yucatan	2	0	1.000	2.78	16	3	0	0	3	0	45.1	37	186	17	14	3	1	0	2	15	1	25	0	0
Esquer, Mercedes, Reynosa *	7	7	.500	3.17	20	20	0	0	0	0	125.0	128	521	51	44	6	6	1	4	17	0	51	0	0
Federico, Gustavo, Salt.-Vera.	1	7	.125	9.67	28	0	0	0	6	0	27.0	52	142	33	29	7	2	0	2	16	0	9	0	0
Fernandez, Osvaldo, Mexico	10	4	.714	4.71	19	19	3	1	0	0	126.0	157	566	70	66	12	5	5	7	42	0	77	4	0
Flores, Ignacio, Saltillo	7	6	.538	4.65	24	13	0	0	2	0	89.0	99	380	49	46	11	2	2	1	32	0	70	7	0
Flores, Ignacio, Yucatan	3	3	.500	2.22	39	0	0	0	15	4	44.2	44	186	12	11	4	2	1	1	13	2	29	1	0
Flores, Jorge, Monclova *	4	1	.800	5.14	31	5	0	0	7	0	63.0	89	297	42	36	9	3	0	1	20	1	25	4	1
Flores, Wilfredo, Tabasco	0	0	.000	13.50	1	1	0	0	0	0	2.0	4	13	3	3	0	0	1	1	2	0	1	1	0
Fregoso, Raul, Veracruz	0	0	.000	21.60	1	0	0	0	0	0	1.2	1	9	4	4	1	0	0	0	3	0	2	0	0
Galvez, Randy, Oaxaca	5	8	.385	6.04	21	17	0	0	2	0	95.1	131	440	71	64	11	5	2	3	42	1	45	7	0
Gandarillas, Gus, Tigres	13	5	.722	3.40	21	21	1	0	0	0	127.0	157	539	54	48	7	7	5	3	37	1	45	0	0
Garcia, Adolfo, Camp.-Vera.	5	6	.455	4.88	28	13	0	0	3	0	86.2	113	377	51	47	9	6	1	2	29	3	26	4	0
Garcia, Alfredo, Mexico	8	5	.615	4.66	22	22	2	0	0	0	131.1	156	587	71	68	18	1	4	2	64	0	77	8	0
Garcia, Carlos, Mexico	0	0	.000	3.00	4	0	0	0	1	0	3.0	5	15	1	1	0	0	1	0	1	0	0	0	0
Garcia, Humberto, Reynosa *	0	1	.000	7.36	29	0	0	0	2	0	18.1	28	97	17	15	2	1	1	1	14	1	16	5	0
Garcia, Jose, Saltillo *	1	3	.250	4.81	53	0	0	0	9	2	33.2	25	148	19	18	2	2	1	2	21	6	30	1	0
Garcia, Mike, Yucatan	0	1	.000	1.32	12	0	0	0	12	7	13.2	9	55	2	2	0	1	0	0	5	1	17	1	0
Garcia, Ramon, Mont.-Reyn.	2	0	1.000	6.02	38	0	0	0	13	1	43.1	55	206	34	29	2	0	2	1	24	1	22	3	0
Garibaldi, Cecilio, Tigres	4	0	1.000	2.14	43	0	0	0	7	0	46.1	42	194	13	11	2	3	0	2	16	2	24	3	0
Garibay, Salvador, D.Laredos	3	3	.500	4.62	59	0	0	0	8	1	76.0	81	320	42	39	4	8	2	1	27	1	49	5	0
Garza, Conrado, Tabasco *	1	2	.333	2.70	38	0	0	0	4	0	20.0	14	87	6	6	0	5	1	1	14	3	9	0	0
Giron, Isabel, Vaqueros	9	9	.500	3.76	23	23	5	1	0	0	148.1	150	641	70	62	15	7	2	14	48	2	112	1	0
Gomez, Alejandro, Puebla	2	1	.667	5.60	10	1	0	0	3	0	17.2	20	78	14	11	4	0	0	0	6	0	12	1	2
Gomez, Martin, Vaqueros	6	5	.545	5.56	24	14	1	0	2	0	92.1	115	429	65	57	13	4	3	3	44	5	38	3	0
Gomez, Miguel, Tigres	1	1	.500	5.68	3	3	0	0	0	0	12.2	20	58	11	8	1	0	0	0	2	0	7	1	0
Gonzalez, Arturo, Monterrey	0	0	.000	3.00	1	1	0	0	0	0	3.0	3	13	1	1	0	0	0	0	1	0	1	0	0
Gonzalez, Erubiel, Veracruz	6	5	.545	3.21	49	0	0	0	26	10	56.0	42	232	23	20	4	6	1	6	24	6	31	1	0
Gonzalez, Gilberto, Mont.*	1	0	1.000	3.38	9	0	0	0	1	0	10.2	13	49	6	4	0	0	1	1	3	0	7	0	0
Gonzalez, Leonardo, D.Lar.	4	3	.571	4.27	24	10	0	0	1	0	78.0	88	333	38	37	6	0	2	8	20	1	55	6	0
Gonzalez, Miguel, Saltillo	2	0	1.000	3.86	22	1	0	0	3	0	35.0	44	156	18	15	3	0	1	1	9	0	19	3	0
Gonzalez, Rodolfo, Vaqueros	0	1	.000	6.75	4	4	0	0	0	0	13.1	11	68	12	10	0	0	1	5	13	0	10	1	0
Gonzalez, Vinicio, Tabasco	3	4	.429	4.15	16	8	1	1	3	1	52.0	48	226	28	24	5	2	2	2	19	0	35	0	0
Grajales, Norberto, Campeche	2	2	.500	2.48	24	0	0	0	4	0	29.0	26	122	10	8	0	3	0	2	12	2	6	0	0
Guerra, Pascual, Cordoba	0	0	.000	16.20	3	0	0	0	1	0	1.2	7	15	3	3	1	0	0	1	3	1	0	0	0
Gutierrez, Jorge, Vaqueros	3	5	.375	7.01	28	5	0	0	5	0	51.1	72	242	44	40	11	0	1	3	23	2	25	5	0
Gutierrez, Luis, Dos Laredos	1	0	1.000	13.50	7	0	0	0	2	0	4.2	8	28	7	7	0	1	0	0	7	0	5	0	0
Guzman, Jesus, Tigres *	10	3	.769	2.92	27	12	0	0	3	0	98.2	100	407	41	32	2	6	2	4	24	0	47	2	0
Guzman, Ricardo, Monclova	0	0	.000	5.19	10	0	0	0	7	1	17.1	28	90	17	10	3	0	2	0	9	0	6	2	0
Harikkala, Tim, Oaxaca	3	7	.300	4.63	12	12	2	0	0	0	79.2	98	349	51	41	5	6	1	1	17	0	50	3	0
Hasselhoff, Derek, Tigres	0	1	.000	7.04	10	0	0	0	3	0	7.2	8	36	7	6	0	1	0	0	4	1	2	0	0
Heredia, Julian, Campeche	1	1	.500	3.86	8	0	0	0	4	0	9.1	7	39	4	4	3	1	0	1	3	0	4	0	0
Hernandez, Jose, Veracruz *	4	1	.800	2.48	55	0	0	0	8	1	36.1	41	161	14	10	3	5	2	3	9	2	19	1	0
Hernandez, Martin, Cancun	3	4	.429	5.56	11	11	0	0	0	0	56.2	71	266	42	35	6	1	4	0	26	1	22	2	0
Hernandez, Santos, Tigres	1	1	.500	1.95	50	0	0	0	47	36	50.2	49	211	13	11	3	1	1	1	15	1	29	2	0
Herrera, Enrique, Tabasco	3	1	.750	3.48	45	0	0	0	13	0	44.0	52	190	18	17	0	4	1	1	15	5	14	0	1
Hoil, Nelson, Campeche *	0	0	.000	0.00	4	0	0	0	0	0	2.0	3	10	0	0	0	1	0	0	1	0	0	1	0
Huerta, Edgar, Tigres *	4	2	.667	3.70	31	5	0	0	4	0	56.0	53	265	28	23	1	2	2	6	38	1	69	2	0
Huerta, Luis, Dos Laredos	3	8	.273	4.49	21	20	0	0	1	0	100.1	125	447	52	50	7	10	4	4	39	2	51	6	0
Hurtado, Edwin, Can.-Yucatan.	9	11	.450	3.70	26	23	12	2	3	1	175.0	167	736	80	72	10	10	5	2	71	5	124	12	0
Ibarra, Francisco, Tigres	0	0	.000	1.86	10	0	0	0	4	0	9.2	9	38	2	2	1	0	1	0	4	0	4	1	0
Jacome, Victor, Veracruz *	0	0	.000	0.00	2	0	0	0	1	0	1.1	0	5	0	0	0	0	0	0	1	0	1	0	0
Jean, Domingo, Cancun	3	4	.429	4.69	8	7	3	1	0	0	48.0	59	212	32	25	2	1	1	1	14	2	15	1	0
Jimenez, Isaac, Vaqueros *	0	2	.000	7.04	4	4	0	0	0	0	15.1	18	73	12	12	1	2	0	3	9	0	8	0	0
Jimenez, Jose, Oaxaca *	1	1	.500	3.96	46	0	0	0	4	0	36.1	35	164	20	16	1	3	1	1	20	2	32	3	0
Jimenez, Julio, Vaqueros *	1	6	.143	5.57	48	6	0	0	5	0	53.1	59	259	38	33	5	2	3	4	40	1	41	1	0
Johnson, Aldo, Saltillo	0	0	.000	13.50	3	0	0	0	1	0	3.1	6	18	5	5	0	0	0	1	2	0	3	0	1
Jusaino, Luis, Vaqueros	0	0	.000	2.25	4	0	0	0	3	0	4.0	5	15	1	1	1	0	0	0	0	0	1	0	0
Kamar, Emil, Monclova	6	9	.400	4.66	23	22	0	0	1	0	116.0	139	531	71	60	3	7	6	10	60	0	50	8	0
Kelley, Rich, Puebla *	8	8	.500	4.88	35	15	3	0	4	1	118.0	123	518	67	64	6	9	2	8	51	2	81	6	0
Keppen, Jeffrey, Dos Laredos	4	5	.444	4.73	10	9	0	0	0	0	51.1	59	242	30	27	6	2	3	7	30	1	34	4	0
Lara, Jorge, Cancun	3	6	.333	4.62	28	3	0	0	17	5	39.0	55	185	22	20	6	2	1	0	12	2	20	0	0
Lara, Mauricio, Monterrey *	1	0	1.000	4.58	26	0	0	0	3	0	19.2	24	91	10	10	2	2	2	0	11	2	13	2	0
Leon, Cupertino, Oaxaca	3	0	1.000	2.78	31	1	0	0	9	1	58.1	51	237	20	18	2	1	1	1	24	1	32	1	0
Leon, Juan, Tabasco	6	7	.462	3.70	25	18	0	0	1	1	92.1	82	406	45	38	12	4	2	9	49	2	70	5	1
Leyva, Edgar, Monterrey	11	3	.786	3.28	18	18	0	0	0	0	104.1	105	442	43	38	7	8	3	7	32	0	66	7	1
Lira, Felipe, Oaxaca	8	9	.471	3.19	23	23	5	1	0	0	169.1	188	715	75	60	9	5	6	3	44	0	103	2	1
Loaiza, Sabino, Dos Laredos	4	5	.444	5.04	28	13	0	0	1	0	84.0	107	386	54	47	9	2	6	5	35	1	38	0	0
Lomeli, Israel, Oaxaca	5	4	.556	6.75	20	16	0	0	2	0	74.2	105	371	66	56	7	2	3	3	49	1	48	5	0
Lontayo, Alejandro, Oaxaca *	2	1	.667	2.60	6	6	1	1	0	0	34.2	27	150	14	10	0	4	1	1	23	0	24	5	0
Lopez, Emigdio, Cordoba	3	11	.214	4.95	21	21	3	1	0	0	132.2	175	595	77	73	14	6	4	4	48	4	68	0	0
Lopez, Gilberto, Cordoba	0	2	.000	6.18	40	0	0	0	11	0	39.1	49	192	34	27	7	1	1	2	26	1	14	2	2
Lopez, Jesus, Vaqueros	0	0	.000	13.50	2	0	0	0	1	0	3.1	5	18	5	5	2	0	0	0	5	0	1	1	0
Lopez, Jonas, Tabasco	0	1	.000	8.10	5	0	0	0	1	0	3.1	8	20	3	3	0	0	0	0	2	0	4	0	0
Lopez, Jose, Monterrey	0	5	.000	4.10	26	0	0	0	10	4	26.1	27	110	13	12	3	4	2	0	8	2	12	0	1
Lopez, Mariano, Vera.-Vaq.	0	0	.000	7.11	6	0	0	0	0	0	6.1	15	46	12	5	1	0	0	1	11	0	3	2	0
Lopez, Miguel, Tigres-Puebla	5	1	.833	3.92	44	0	0	0	11	4	43.2	41	191	22	19	2	1	4	5	25	4	24	0	0
Lopez, Nain, Cancun *	4	6	.400	5.55	27	13	1	0	3	2	94.0	118	429	66	58	12	3	3	3	29	1	34	4	0

Pitcher, Team	W	L	Pct.	ERA	G	GS	CG	ShO	GF	Sv.	IP	H	TBF	R	ER	HR	SH	SF	HB	BB	IBB	SO	WP	Bk.
Lopez, Rogelio, Cordoba	0	1	.000	12.60	3	0	0	0	1	0	5.0	9	25	7	7	4	0	0	2	1	0	4	0	0
Loya, Rigoberto, Monterrey	9	6	.600	4.03	22	22	1	0	0	0	118.1	123	521	63	53	11	3	3	6	57	2	63	4	0
Lugo, Javier, Reynosa *	0	0	.000	3.18	3	0	0	0	2	0	5.2	8	28	3	2	0	0	0	0	4	0	2	1	0
Macias, Eduardo, Yucatan	0	0	.000	0.00	1	0	0	0	1	0	1.0	1	3	0	0	0	0	0	0	0	0	0	0	0
Macias, Luis, Monc.-Puebla	0	1	.000	4.30	20	3	0	0	5	1	29.1	37	135	15	14	3	1	1	1	19	2	6	1	0
Madero, Francisco, Mexico	2	1	.667	5.85	18	0	0	0	5	2	32.1	38	144	22	21	4	0	0	5	13	0	24	1	0
Magee, Bo, Campeche *	10	6	.625	3.06	23	23	8	0	0	0	170.1	118	730	67	58	12	17	4	8	109	3	155	6	0
Manrique, Alberto, Monterrey	5	7	.417	4.75	20	17	1	1	0	0	100.1	124	451	61	53	11	5	5	4	40	0	37	5	0
Manzanillo, Ravelo, Yuc.-Salt.*	10	3	.769	2.36	17	17	1	0	0	0	118.0	81	492	33	31	2	9	4	7	65	2	81	5	0
Manzano, Adrian, Tigres	0	0	.000	3.63	43	0	0	0	6	2	44.2	50	187	20	18	1	2	2	1	8	1	14	1	0
Marquez, Isidro, Campeche	8	4	.667	2.34	43	0	0	0	41	25	50.0	44	210	19	13	4	2	0	1	21	3	27	0	0
Martinez, Cesar, Campeche *	2	6	.250	6.17	15	9	0	0	4	0	46.2	57	224	33	32	6	3	1	7	28	1	19	3	0
Martinez, Javier, Saltillo	1	0	1.000	6.75	6	0	0	0	3	0	5.1	10	28	4	4	0	1	0	0	3	0	4	0	1
Martinez, Jesus, Cordoba	0	0	.000	6.00	11	3	0	0	3	0	21.0	25	100	14	14	3	0	1	2	16	0	4	0	0
Martinez, Juan, Vaqueros	0	0	.000	14.29	5	0	0	0	1	0	5.2	11	35	9	9	2	0	1	1	7	0	3	1	0
Martinez, Renan, Puebla *	7	3	.700	4.39	15	14	2	1	0	0	82.0	85	369	43	40	7	2	1	3	56	1	55	5	0
Medina, Roberto, Puebla *	0	0	.000	22.85	12	0	0	0	1	0	4.1	12	32	11	11	1	0	0	0	7	0	2	1	0
Melendez, Nestor, Reynosa *	2	2	.500	4.20	37	5	0	0	9	2	45.0	34	206	24	21	3	1	4	1	37	1	30	7	0
Mendoza, Mario, Saltillo	4	0	1.000	5.57	17	4	0	0	1	0	32.1	35	153	25	20	4	3	1	0	25	1	17	2	0
Mendoza, Omar, Puebla	0	0	.000	21.60	3	0	0	0	2	0	3.1	9	21	8	8	0	0	0	0	3	0	1	1	0
Mercedes, Jose, Saltillo	14	6	.700	3.71	22	22	6	0	0	0	160.0	172	701	78	66	11	8	6	5	53	1	114	5	0
Meza, Jose Luis, D.Laredos *	1	0	1.000	3.67	32	1	0	0	4	0	27.0	33	119	13	11	4	2	0	0	11	1	21	1	0
Montane, Ivan, Cordoba	1	2	.333	10.13	3	0	0	0	3	0	2.2	5	15	3	3	1	1	0	0	2	1	3	2	0
Montemayor, Humberto, Mont.	6	5	.545	5.38	24	19	1	1	1	0	110.1	142	485	70	66	12	5	3	1	28	1	60	6	1
Montoya, Saul, Reynosa	0	2	.000	5.61	7	3	0	0	0	0	25.2	23	107	18	16	2	1	0	3	9	0	16	2	1
Mora, Eleazar, Veracruz *	5	5	.500	4.23	20	18	0	0	0	0	106.1	129	457	52	50	14	12	1	9	22	4	42	1	0
Mora, Sergio, Monterrey	3	0	1.000	4.91	32	0	0	0	4	0	44.0	35	187	25	24	5	2	0	2	22	2	27	4	0
Morales, Alfiero, Yucatan	0	1	.000	10.57	3	1	0	0	0	0	7.2	14	39	9	9	2	0	0	1	2	0	5	1	0
Morales, Fernando, Campeche	0	0	.000	1.59	6	0	0	0	3	0	5.2	3	21	1	1	0	0	0	0	5	0	0	0	0
Morales, Luis, Saltillo *	1	1	.500	5.23	10	3	0	0	0	0	20.2	22	95	12	12	1	1	3	0	16	1	10	0	0
Moreno, Angel, Veracruz *	8	4	.667	2.27	21	19	3	2	2	1	126.2	121	515	40	32	4	2	0	5	27	0	42	5	0
Moreno, Claudio, Mexico	3	3	.500	5.25	45	2	0	0	35	17	58.1	86	277	38	34	4	4	3	2	22	3	30	1	0
Moreno, Edgar, Veracruz	2	1	.667	4.71	27	0	0	0	7	0	28.2	37	136	16	15	2	1	0	0	19	5	18	0	0
Moreno, Leo, Veracruz *	2	4	.333	4.63	12	10	1	0	0	0	58.1	59	253	31	30	6	3	3	4	23	1	32	1	0
Mota, Danny, Campeche	4	2	.667	3.17	14	7	1	0	3	0	54.0	49	223	20	19	6	1	0	1	20	2	26	2	0
Munoz, Leonardo, Mont.*	1	1	.500	6.33	48	0	0	0	7	0	27.0	36	125	21	19	1	2	1	1	12	4	24	2	0
Munoz, Miguel, Veracruz	0	0	.000	3.86	5	0	0	0	0	0	4.2	10	26	2	2	0	2	0	0	2	2	3	0	0
Murguia, Edgar, Saltillo	0	0	.000	40.50	4	0	0	0	1	0	2.0	8	17	9	9	1	0	0	0	3	0	1	1	0
Murillo, Meza, Monclova	2	4	.333	2.74	37	0	0	0	3	0	46.0	62	205	21	14	5	1	1	4	14	1	16	3	1
Navarro, Hector, Veracruz	8	5	.615	3.56	30	18	1	0	2	0	118.2	118	524	57	47	8	8	5	17	52	6	71	7	1
Navarro, Jaime, Oaxaca	1	2	.333	7.85	5	5	0	0	0	0	28.2	46	139	27	25	4	2	0	1	5	1	14	1	0
Navarro, Joel, Oaxaca	6	2	.750	3.97	25	10	1	1	1	0	95.1	99	409	51	42	5	3	2	7	33	0	62	4	0
Navarro, Jose, Tigres-Puebla	3	7	.300	5.26	28	11	0	0	3	0	90.2	124	420	57	53	14	5	2	3	32	3	30	8	0
Neri, Braulio, Cord.-Vaq.*	1	2	.333	4.99	46	0	0	0	7	0	30.2	48	144	18	17	1	4	2	4	7	1	15	3	0
Neri, Eduardo, Oaxaca *	1	1	.500	3.41	54	0	0	0	12	1	29.0	39	137	13	11	2	0	2	1	12	2	21	0	0
Nieblas, Mauro, Monterrey *	5	4	.556	2.69	34	7	0	0	3	2	60.1	52	259	22	18	2	3	1	3	31	2	51	2	2
Nieblas, Omar, Tab.-Vera.*	1	3	.250	6.75	27	1	0	0	9	1	28.0	33	126	21	21	6	4	0	0	15	2	15	4	0
Nina, Elvin, Cordoba	0	3	.000	9.39	5	0	0	0	2	0	7.2	12	40	8	8	0	1	0	0	6	1	6	1	0
Nunez, Javier, Cordoba	2	3	.400	5.65	18	2	1	0	5	0	43.0	49	195	27	27	5	0	1	2	22	0	24	1	0
Nunez, Jose, Dos Laredos	11	5	.688	2.89	21	19	4	2	1	1	140.1	148	583	52	45	7	5	4	4	33	2	73	4	0
Nunez, Jose, Tabasco-Puebla	2	0	1.000	5.16	19	0	0	0	2	0	22.2	33	104	16	13	4	1	0	0	7	2	12	0	0
Ochoa, Pablo, Monterrey	3	5	.375	6.45	11	10	0	0	1	0	51.2	69	244	39	37	9	0	0	6	23	1	30	4	0
Olague, Jesus, Tigres	4	4	.500	7.19	16	9	0	0	3	0	46.1	63	228	41	37	6	3	4	2	33	3	43	2	1
Orea, Flavio, Cordoba	4	3	.571	2.42	22	0	0	0	9	0	26.0	22	106	8	7	1	1	1	2	8	3	13	4	1
Ortega, Pablo, Puebla	13	4	.765	3.14	23	23	4	3	0	0	160.2	153	663	61	56	9	14	2	9	46	6	98	2	0
Ortega, Roberto, Puebla *	0	0	.000	13.50	1	0	0	0	0	0	0.2	1	3	1	1	0	0	0	0	0	0	0	0	0
Ortega, Wilbert, Yucatan *	1	0	1.000	5.23	12	0	0	0	4	0	10.1	11	46	6	6	1	0	0	0	4	1	8	2	0
Osuna, Adrian, Mex.-Vaq.	1	0	1.000	5.79	12	0	0	0	3	0	18.2	19	84	12	12	4	1	1	1	10	0	10	3	0
Osuna, Ricardo, Yuc.-Tabasco	4	6	.400	3.92	18	15	0	0	1	0	80.1	77	350	39	35	5	3	2	4	43	2	45	4	0
Osuna, Ulises, Monterrey	0	0	.000	4.50	3	0	0	0	0	0	4.0	5	18	2	2	0	0	0	0	1	0	1	0	0
Pablos, Rene, Saltillo *	0	0	.000	3.00	2	0	0	0	1	0	3.0	2	10	1	1	1	0	0	0	0	0	3	0	0
Pacheco, Alexander, Puebla	2	3	.400	9.00	21	0	0	0	19	7	22.0	34	115	23	22	4	1	0	0	15	3	26	4	0
Palacios, Joaquin, Veracruz	0	0	.000	27.00	1	0	0	0	1	0	1.0	3	6	3	3	1	0	0	0	0	0	1	0	0
Palacios, Vicente, D.Laredos	0	3	.000	4.43	12	0	0	0	2	0	20.1	25	92	12	10	0	0	0	0	14	1	11	2	0
Palafox, Juan, Yucatan	10	8	.556	3.48	18	18	2	0	0	0	113.2	121	496	51	44	8	4	6	6	34	3	44	5	0
Paniagua, Jose, Veracruz	0	2	.000	9.45	6	0	0	0	3	1	6.2	8	34	9	7	1	1	2	3	5	1	2	0	0
Parra, Jose, Cordoba	1	3	.250	4.38	29	1	0	0	18	7	37.0	37	160	18	18	3	0	1	3	15	2	29	1	0
Parra, Julio, Dos Laredos	4	4	.500	4.50	43	0	0	0	22	4	44.0	40	200	25	22	5	4	2	3	26	3	42	3	0
Patrick, Bronswell, Mexico	13	2	.867	4.04	23	19	2	1	1	0	133.2	153	561	63	60	9	3	3	2	27	0	75	7	1
Pena, Joel, Tabasco	8	3	.727	3.41	43	2	0	0	11	2	71.1	65	305	28	27	4	6	2	1	34	5	31	3	0
Pena, Juan, Vaqueros *	0	0	.000	14.09	5	0	0	0	1	0	7.2	14	41	12	12	4	0	0	1	4	0	6	1	0
Perez, Edgar, Vaqueros	0	3	.000	7.62	22	2	0	0	3	0	39.0	60	194	38	33	6	3	0	6	17	1	20	2	0
Perez, Guadalupe, Veracruz	0	0	.000	2.90	30	1	0	0	9	0	49.2	46	197	17	16	4	3	1	0	11	2	26	0	1
Perez, Leonardo, Cordoba	2	8	.200	6.27	16	9	1	0	0	0	66.0	95	300	47	46	11	5	1	5	15	1	27	1	0
Perez, Sergio, Reynosa	0	1	.000	12.60	3	0	0	0	0	0	5.0	7	26	7	7	0	0	0	2	3	1	6	0	0
Pesqueira, Omar, Can.-Yuc.	6	7	.462	3.50	19	18	0	0	0	0	108.0	116	462	49	42	6	5	2	4	37	1	36	1	0
Pichardo, Hipolito, Saltillo	0	0	.000	1.05	24	0	0	0	24	13	25.2	22	108	6	3	1	1	0	2	10	0	17	0	0
Pimentel, Roberto, Cancun *	1	1	.500	3.00	38	3	0	0	11	2	42.0	54	187	19	14	4	1	2	3	12	3	27	1	1
Pina, Rafael, Veracruz	6	5	.545	3.77	15	15	2	0	0	0	93.0	89	402	48	39	8	3	4	9	34	1	36	9	1
Preston, George, Reynosa	1	4	.200	8.56	6	6	0	0	0	0	27.1	30	140	29	26	0	2	0	1	25	0	23	4	0
Pulido, Raymundo, Campeche	0	3	.000	3.99	13	4	0	0	4	1	29.1	29	138	15	13	2	2	0	0	23	1	13	0	2
Quinones, Enrique, Reynosa	6	11	.353	5.09	21	21	1	0	0	0	122.0	147	531	75	69	11	7	2	7	30	0	46	4	1

Pitcher, Team	W	L	Pct.	ERA	G	GS	CG	ShO	GF	Sv.	IP	H	TBF	R	ER	HR	SH	SF	HB	BB	IBB	SO	WP	Bk.
Quintanilla, Enrique, D.Lar.-Salt.	1	5	.167	7.55	34	7	0	0	9	0	62.0	89	293	54	52	10	5	1	10	17	3	49	3	3
Quiroz, Aaron, Saltillo	4	4	.500	5.00	22	15	0	0	1	0	84.2	107	374	59	47	13	3	4	3	17	0	56	2	0
Ramirez, Adrian, Monclova *	6	8	.429	5.31	31	13	0	0	4	0	101.2	120	440	67	60	9	4	3	0	24	2	56	2	0
Ramirez, Jose, Monclova	0	0	.000	1.74	5	0	0	0	0	0	10.1	8	43	2	2	1	0	0	0	5	0	10	0	0
Ramirez, Roberto, Mexico *	1	1	.500	4.13	6	6	0	0	0	0	32.2	43	146	18	15	1	0	0	1	11	0	15	0	0
Ramirez, Silvio, Campeche *	0	0	.000	8.22	9	0	0	0	3	0	7.2	12	37	7	7	2	0	1	0	3	0	3	0	0
Ramon, Jose, Tabasco	0	0	.000	23.63	2	0	0	0	0	0	2.2	8	17	7	7	0	0	0	0	1	0	1	1	0
Renovato, Nestor, Reynosa	1	6	.143	7.14	19	12	0	0	4	0	58.0	79	275	48	46	8	2	6	2	26	0	33	2	0
Reyes, Nate, Saltillo *	1	6	.143	5.92	24	9	1	1	4	0	59.1	73	259	42	39	7	7	3	1	24	0	32	1	0
Reynoso, Jose, Vaq.-Cordoba	3	9	.250	5.23	23	17	1	0	0	0	113.2	116	487	68	66	19	4	3	3	40	3	57	8	0
Rios, Alejandro, Puebla	0	4	.000	10.69	27	4	0	0	5	1	33.2	58	184	42	40	6	1	2	0	31	2	17	7	0
Rios, Jesus, Tabasco	0	7	.000	4.86	23	12	0	0	0	0	92.2	98	407	55	50	8	2	1	2	38	7	45	4	0
Rivera, Francisco, Cord.-Vaq.	2	8	.200	6.11	33	13	0	0	8	0	95.2	114	440	75	65	14	6	0	4	52	8	39	5	0
Rivera, Lino, Monclova-Tigres	6	3	.667	4.35	16	14	1	0	0	0	78.2	82	338	41	38	11	2	2	6	28	0	21	1	0
Rivera, Oscar, Yucatan *	1	0	1.000	7.24	24	0	0	0	1	0	13.2	14	66	11	11	1	0	1	2	9	1	18	1	1
Rivera, Oscar, Campeche	3	6	.333	5.20	14	12	1	0	1	0	72.2	90	337	48	42	6	0	2	2	38	2	39	6	0
Rivera, Paul, Campeche *	0	0	.000	5.06	11	0	0	0	3	0	10.2	17	53	7	6	2	0	0	1	4	0	3	0	0
Rodriguez, Enoc, Cancun *	4	8	.333	5.04	15	15	0	0	0	0	75.0	78	328	45	42	11	6	1	1	34	1	28	3	0
Rodriguez, Jesus, Monclova	0	0	.000	10.80	3	0	0	0	2	0	6.2	9	35	8	8	0	0	0	0	6	0	2	0	0
Rodriguez, Manuel, Campeche	5	4	.556	6.02	33	3	0	0	4	0	55.1	60	243	40	37	8	2	6	3	25	2	24	1	0
Rodriguez, Salvador, Yucatan	10	4	.714	3.00	19	19	1	0	0	0	120.0	111	504	45	40	10	7	1	7	37	1	71	3	0
Rojas, Mel, Monclova	3	1	.750	3.35	27	0	0	0	8	2	43.0	49	196	17	16	2	6	3	5	18	2	29	10	0
Romano, Mike, Tabasco	5	4	.556	2.72	38	9	0	0	26	13	99.1	100	421	34	30	3	6	4	5	32	3	57	5	0
Romero, Alejandro, Monclova	3	5	.375	5.71	13	13	0	0	0	0	52.0	67	231	37	33	8	1	1	3	14	0	25	4	0
Roque, Rafael, Tigres *	10	6	.625	3.25	20	20	0	0	0	0	116.1	122	509	49	42	7	2	4	2	54	5	68	3	0
Rubio, Miguel, Monterrey	6	4	.600	2.92	44	0	0	0	43	20	52.1	46	217	20	17	5	5	1	0	26	7	40	5	0
Ruelas, Heriberto, Mexico *	3	2	.600	5.16	38	0	0	0	6	0	22.2	16	103	17	13	1	1	0	3	15	1	22	2	0
Ruiz, Arturo, Dos Laredos *	0	0	.000	5.79	9	0	0	0	3	0	4.2	4	20	3	3	1	0	0	1	2	0	5	1	0
Ruiz, Cecilio, Tabasco *	3	3	.500	4.30	47	2	0	0	8	0	37.2	42	170	23	18	4	2	1	2	10	4	23	1	0
Saldana, Jose, Puebla-Vera.	4	1	.800	3.40	14	9	1	0	1	0	47.2	50	218	26	18	2	1	2	0	28	0	31	1	0
Salgado, Eduardo, Vera.-Pue.	5	4	.556	4.18	47	1	0	0	12	1	79.2	92	350	42	37	9	2	5	2	23	7	39	2	0
Sanchez, Alejandro, Cancun	1	1	.500	3.35	36	0	0	0	7	2	43.0	48	187	18	16	5	3	1	1	17	3	17	2	0
Sanchez, Claudio, Oaxaca	1	1	.500	4.28	39	0	0	0	11	0	27.1	34	116	15	13	4	1	5	0	7	0	11	1	0
Sanchez, Efrain, Campeche	4	5	.444	4.27	23	16	0	0	3	0	97.0	103	427	52	46	7	6	3	6	39	3	32	3	0
Sandoval, Guillermo, Tabasco	0	1	.000	15.75	5	0	0	0	3	0	4.0	7	22	7	7	1	0	0	0	3	0	5	0	0
Sangeado, Juan, Cancun	2	2	.500	5.47	30	3	0	0	12	0	54.1	65	241	34	33	5	1	0	3	16	0	29	6	0
Serafini, Dan, Monterrey *	10	2	.833	1.59	16	15	0	0	0	0	96.1	70	386	24	17	5	2	0	3	41	1	89	3	0
Sierra, Abel, Cancun	0	0	.000	6.85	17	0	0	0	2	0	22.1	32	109	18	17	1	2	0	1	10	0	16	1	0
Silva, Doug, Veracruz	0	2	.000	8.59	4	1	0	0	0	0	7.1	12	37	8	7	2	1	1	0	5	0	4	1	0
Silva, Walter, Mont.-Reynosa	0	4	.000	4.86	35	0	0	0	11	2	46.1	40	211	26	25	2	2	2	0	34	0	40	5	0
Sinohui, David, Sal.-Tab.-Cor.	2	3	.400	4.17	43	0	0	0	33	23	41.0	47	185	19	19	2	1	2	2	19	3	26	3	0
Solis, Jesus, Dos Laredos	1	0	1.000	7.76	16	0	0	0	7	0	26.2	34	126	23	23	5	1	1	1	14	1	16	0	1
Solis, Tomas, Tigres-Puebla *	0	1	.000	6.19	30	0	0	0	4	1	16.0	18	71	12	11	3	1	2	0	9	2	4	0	0
Soto, Cruz, Reynosa	1	4	.200	5.80	30	3	0	0	5	1	49.2	47	228	36	32	8	4	1	3	34	3	32	3	0
Strong, Joe, Reynosa	6	4	.600	2.71	46	2	0	0	38	16	66.1	54	286	24	20	5	4	2	6	28	2	44	5	1
Tatis, Ramon, Dos Laredos *	0	0	.000	15.43	1	1	0	0	0	0	2.1	6	15	4	4	1	0	0	0	4	0	2	0	0
Tejeda, Felix, Campeche *	1	1	.500	6.20	25	0	0	0	4	0	20.1	30	96	18	14	1	1	1	2	9	2	10	1	0
Terrazas, J.C., Cancun *	0	3	.000	4.24	20	0	0	0	6	0	17.0	20	78	10	8	3	0	1	1	10	1	8	4	0
Trujillo, Jorge, Veracruz	0	0	.000	15.63	7	0	0	0	3	0	6.1	11	36	11	11	2	0	1	1	6	1	3	0	0
Valdez, Armando, Puebla	3	3	.500	3.84	14	11	0	0	0	0	61.0	66	274	32	26	7	2	1	3	30	3	39	5	0
Valdez, Efrain, Vaqueros-Tab.*	4	7	.364	4.12	20	20	0	0	0	0	111.1	123	482	52	51	10	8	1	3	36	3	52	1	2
Valenzuela, Jose, Tigres	0	1	.000	18.56	7	0	0	0	2	0	5.1	10	31	11	11	3	0	2	0	5	0	2	0	0
Valenzuela, Saul, Cancun	1	3	.250	4.86	13	4	1	0	3	0	37.0	39	162	21	20	6	1	2	1	16	0	12	2	0
Valerio, Julio, Monclova *	3	3	.500	3.13	54	0	0	0	9	0	69.0	74	283	28	24	5	4	2	0	5	1	30	4	0
Vargas, Joel, Tabasco	7	4	.636	2.69	20	20	1	1	0	0	124.0	110	510	42	37	5	8	3	6	41	5	61	1	0
Vazquez, Adrian, Cordoba	3	6	.333	5.52	17	17	0	0	0	0	93.0	123	428	61	57	10	3	2	6	30	1	58	3	0
Vega, Obed, Cancun	9	4	.692	2.67	21	21	1	0	0	0	141.1	135	582	50	42	8	6	5	7	40	0	65	3	0
Verdugo, Hugo, Vaq.-Cordoba	3	5	.375	5.01	33	0	0	0	10	1	41.1	41	185	27	23	7	3	2	4	19	4	26	5	1
Verdugo, Orlando, Reynosa	6	5	.545	4.07	29	13	0	0	6	0	104.0	113	459	57	47	7	0	7	4	40	0	46	4	0
Verdugo, Oswaldo, Yucatan	1	2	.333	3.35	31	0	0	0	11	2	43.0	37	178	17	16	2	3	2	3	10	0	17	3	0
Verdugo, Roberto, Tabasco	2	5	.286	2.08	42	0	0	0	12	1	56.1	49	237	16	13	0	7	1	6	18	7	36	3	0
Villaluna, Juan, Reynosa *	0	1	.000	9.82	20	0	0	0	2	0	11.0	10	50	12	12	1	1	0	0	7	0	6	0	0
Villarreal, Salvador, Reynosa	3	3	.500	5.27	12	8	0	0	0	0	41.0	44	192	25	24	3	2	1	2	29	0	16	5	1
Villegas, Jose, Puebla	1	0	1.000	10.50	14	0	0	0	3	0	18.0	33	89	21	21	2	1	1	0	4	0	6	1	0
Vizcarra, William, Cancun	0	1	.000	9.82	3	0	0	0	0	0	3.2	9	32	5	4	1	0	1	0	0	0	2	0	0
Wallace, Kent, Tabasco	0	1	.000	2.16	7	0	0	0	5	3	8.1	9	38	3	2	0	0	0	0	3	1	8	0	0
Ward, Bryan, Saltillo *	4	3	.571	4.14	7	7	0	0	0	0	37.0	34	157	20	17	2	1	1	2	18	0	21	0	0
Williams, Slim, Cordoba *	0	1	.000	13.50	4	0	0	0	3	3	3.1	5	16	5	5	0	1	0	0	1	0	3	0	0
Yepiz, Heriberto Martinez, Cor.	0	0	.000	13.50	3	0	0	0	1	0	1.1	3	10	2	2	0	0	0	0	3	0	1	1	0
Zambrano, Baudel, Reynosa	2	4	.333	7.40	38	3	0	0	13	1	48.2	77	237	45	40	7	6	1	0	19	1	19	3	2
Zavala, Marcos, Tigres *	3	1	.750	4.74	31	0	0	0	12	2	24.2	31	111	14	13	4	1	0	3	7	2	18	2	0
navarro, Luis, Yucatan	2	1	.667	3.00	32	1	0	0	4	0	42.0	52	184	17	14	1	1	4	2	12	0	20	1	0

PITCHERS WITH TWO OR MORE TEAMS

Pitcher, Team	W	L	Pct.	ERA	G	GS	CG	ShO	GF	Sv.	IP	H	TBF	R	ER	HR	SH	SF	HB	BB	IBB	SO	WP	Bk.
Agosto, Stevenson, Oaxaca *	2	2	.500	5.40	7	5	0	0	1	0	33.1	39	151	23	20	3	1	1	2	17	0	30	3	0
Agosto, Stevenson, Tabasco *	3	2	.600	4.42	9	6	0	0	2	0	38.2	35	167	19	19	6	4	0	1	24	1	33	4	0
Aguilar, Hugo, Monclova *	1	1	.500	10.91	10	2	0	0	0	0	15.2	27	90	23	19	4	3	1	2	15	0	15	0	0
Aguilar, Hugo, Tigres *	0	0	.000	2.30	11	1	0	0	6	0	15.2	15	67	5	4	0	1	1	0	10	0	6	3	0
Almeida, Rowsell, D.Lar.*	0	0	.000	21.60	4	1	0	0	0	0	3.1	9	25	8	8	0	0	1	1	4	0	2	1	0
Almeida, Rowsell, Veracruz *	0	1	.000	4.50	4	0	0	0	2	0	4.0	4	19	2	2	0	0	0	1	3	2	3	2	0
Alvarez, Azael, Puebla *	0	0	.000	4.70	10	0	0	0	1	0	7.2	9	37	6	4	0	0	0	0	6	0	8	0	0
Alvarez, Azael, Monclova *	2	2	.500	4.19	13	8	0	0	0	0	53.2	49	250	28	25	4	1	1	5	41	0	39	6	1
Amarillas, Asdrubal, Vaqueros	0	1	.000	8.22	6	0	0	0	0	0	7.2	14	40	7	7	2	0	0	1	5	2	1	2	0
Amarillas, Asdrubal, Cordoba	0	3	.000	7.93	29	1	0	0	5	1	42.0	49	204	39	37	4	1	3	2	32	7	17	9	0
Cabrales, Gabriel, Puebla	1	0	1.000	2.50	15	0	0	0	7	0	18.0	20	74	5	5	1	1	1	2	6	2	13	1	0

Pitcher, Team	W	L	Pct.	ERA	G	GS	CG	ShO	GF	Sv.	IP	H	TBF	R	ER	HR	SH	SF	HB	BB	IBB	SO	WP	Bk.
Cabrales, Gabriel, Veracruz	0	0	.000	4.35	12	3	0	0	2	0	31.0	37	133	15	15	5	0	2	1	11	2	10	0	0
Cervantes, Peter, Veracruz	0	1	.000	6.06	12	0	0	0	9	6	16.1	18	73	11	11	3	1	1	2	7	1	13	3	0
Cervantes, Peter, Puebla	3	3	.500	3.41	27	0	0	0	24	9	34.1	31	132	13	13	3	2	2	0	6	2	27	1	0
Chavarria, Hector, Cordoba	6	4	.600	5.76	16	16	0	0	0	0	75.0	89	347	52	48	9	3	2	6	43	1	31	8	0
Chavarria, Hector, Vaqueros	0	2	.000	7.36	3	3	0	0	0	0	14.2	18	68	12	12	3	0	1	2	9	0	6	2	0
Delahoya, Javier, Campeche	3	2	.600	3.22	10	10	1	0	0	0	58.2	57	251	22	21	3	5	2	5	20	1	35	3	0
Delahoya, Javier, Veracruz	2	2	.500	4.42	7	7	0	0	0	0	38.2	48	188	19	19	4	3	0	5	23	2	21	2	0
Dingman, Craig, Yucatan	3	2	.600	3.08	27	0	0	0	26	14	26.1	25	109	10	9	1	1	1	1	9	0	20	0	0
Dingman, Craig, Cancun	1	5	.167	4.24	15	0	0	0	14	5	17.0	16	74	12	8	1	3	2	2	4	2	17	0	0
Dominguez, Carlos, Saltillo *	0	1	.000	4.73	3	3	0	0	0	0	13.1	18	63	7	7	1	0	0	0	7	0	6	3	0
Dominguez, Carlos, D.Lar.*	6	5	.545	4.69	23	16	0	0	2	0	86.1	95	388	49	45	7	2	2	5	48	2	41	2	0
Dorame, Randey, Vaqueros *	0	1	.000	12.32	10	5	0	0	2	0	19.0	25	94	26	26	6	0	0	3	12	1	13	0	0
Dorame, Randey, Mexico *	0	1	.000	10.57	6	1	0	0	1	0	7.2	10	37	9	9	0	1	0	0	5	0	3	1	0
Elvira, Abraham, Vaqueros *	0	2	.000	13.85	17	2	0	0	3	0	13.0	21	75	21	20	6	1	0	1	15	1	10	2	0
Elvira, Abraham, Cordoba *	1	0	1.000	4.29	23	1	0	0	4	0	21.0	28	100	11	10	1	1	2	0	10	0	16	2	0
Enriquez, Martin, Reynosa	2	0	1.000	3.75	13	0	0	0	5	0	12.0	17	54	5	5	0	1	1	0	4	2	8	0	0
Enriquez, Martin, Cancun	1	2	.333	4.55	28	0	0	0	12	7	27.2	26	119	14	14	1	5	0	1	9	3	7	2	0
Federico, Gustavo, Saltillo	1	4	.200	9.00	17	0	0	0	4	0	20.0	36	103	24	20	5	1	0	1	13	0	9	0	0
Federico, Gustavo, Veracruz	0	3	.000	11.57	11	0	0	0	2	0	7.0	16	39	9	9	2	1	0	1	3	0	0	0	0
Garcia, Adolfo, Campeche	1	2	.333	7.85	13	1	0	0	2	0	18.1	27	85	17	16	3	2	1	1	4	1	8	1	0
Garcia, Adolfo, Veracruz	4	4	.500	4.08	15	12	0	0	1	0	68.1	86	292	34	31	6	4	0	1	25	2	18	3	0
Garcia, Ramon, Monterrey	0	0	.000	6.59	9	0	0	0	7	0	13.2	18	65	11	10	1	0	0	1	7	0	8	0	0
Garcia, Ramon, Reynosa	2	0	1.000	5.76	29	0	0	0	6	1	29.2	37	141	23	19	1	0	2	0	17	1	14	3	0
Hurtado, Edwin, Yucatan	4	5	.444	3.18	12	11	5	0	1	1	82.0	69	340	32	29	2	7	3	0	39	5	58	7	0
Hurtado, Edwin, Cancun	5	6	.455	4.16	14	12	7	2	2	0	93.0	98	396	48	43	8	3	2	2	32	0	66	5	0
Lopez, Mariano, Veracruz	0	0	.000	0.00	2	0	0	0	0	0	1.0	5	10	5	0	1	0	0	0	1	0	0	0	0
Lopez, Mariano, Vaqueros	0	0	.000	8.44	4	0	0	0	0	0	5.1	10	36	7	5	0	0	0	1	10	0	3	2	0
Lopez, Miguel, Puebla	5	1	.833	3.40	43	0	0	0	11	4	42.1	37	184	19	16	1	1	4	5	25	4	24	0	0
Lopez, Miguel, Tigres	0	0	.000	20.25	1	0	0	0	0	0	1.1	4	7	3	3	1	0	0	0	0	0	0	0	0
Macias, Luis, Monclova	0	0	.000	12.00	7	0	0	0	2	0	6.0	13	32	9	8	2	0	0	0	3	0	1	1	0
Macias, Luis, Puebla	0	1	.000	2.31	13	3	0	0	3	1	23.1	24	103	6	6	1	1	1	1	16	2	5	0	0
Manzanillo, Ravelo, Yucatan *	4	2	.667	2.90	9	9	1	0	0	0	59.0	46	251	19	19	2	4	2	5	30	0	40	4	0
Manzanillo, Ravelo, Saltillo *	6	1	.857	1.83	8	8	0	0	0	0	59.0	35	241	14	12	0	5	2	2	35	2	41	1	0
Navarro, Jose, Puebla	3	6	.333	4.30	13	11	0	0	1	0	67.0	82	295	35	32	6	4	0	2	19	2	20	5	0
Navarro, Jose, Tigres	0	1	.000	7.99	15	0	0	0	2	0	23.2	42	125	22	21	8	1	2	1	13	1	10	3	0
Neri, Braulio, Vaqueros *	0	0	.000	6.75	10	0	0	0	1	0	8.0	16	42	7	6	0	1	0	1	4	1	2	0	0
Neri, Braulio, Cordoba *	1	2	.333	4.37	36	0	0	0	6	0	22.2	32	102	11	11	1	3	2	3	3	0	13	3	0
Nieblas, Omar, Veracruz *	1	3	.250	6.33	21	1	0	0	7	1	21.1	28	99	15	15	4	3	0	0	13	0	13	3	0
Nieblas, Omar, Tabasco *	0	0	.000	8.10	6	0	0	0	2	0	6.2	5	27	6	6	2	1	0	0	2	2	2	1	0
Nunez, Jose, Tabasco	0	0	.000	10.80	5	0	0	0	2	0	5.0	15	29	9	6	2	1	0	0	0	0	1	0	0
Nunez, Jose, Puebla	2	0	1.000	3.57	14	0	0	0	0	0	17.2	18	75	7	7	2	0	0	0	7	2	11	0	0
Osuna, Adrian, Vaqueros	1	0	1.000	4.66	4	0	0	0	0	0	9.2	6	43	5	5	1	1	0	1	8	0	6	2	0
Osuna, Adrian, Mexico	0	0	.000	7.00	8	0	0	0	3	0	9.0	13	41	7	7	3	0	1	0	2	0	4	1	0
Osuna, Ricardo, Tabasco	2	3	.400	3.89	10	7	0	0	1	0	39.1	34	170	19	17	4	1	0	2	21	2	16	1	0
Osuna, Ricardo, Yucatan	2	3	.400	3.95	8	8	0	0	0	0	41.0	43	180	20	18	1	2	2	2	22	0	29	3	0
Pesqueira, Omar, Yucatan	0	0	.000	3.05	4	3	0	0	0	0	20.2	20	91	8	7	2	0	0	0	8	0	9	0	0
Pesqueira, Omar, Cancun	6	7	.462	3.61	15	15	0	0	0	0	87.1	96	371	41	35	4	5	2	4	29	1	27	1	0
Quintanilla, Enrique, D.Lar.	0	4	.000	9.16	10	7	0	0	0	0	38.1	61	188	41	39	8	3	1	5	13	3	31	0	2
Quintanilla, Enrique, Saltillo	1	1	.500	4.94	24	0	0	0	9	0	23.2	28	105	13	13	2	2	0	5	4	0	18	3	1
Reynoso, Jose, Vaqueros	2	7	.222	5.46	19	13	1	0	0	0	89.0	97	387	56	54	13	3	2	2	32	3	48	6	0
Reynoso, Jose, Cordoba	1	2	.333	4.38	4	4	0	0	0	0	24.2	19	100	12	12	6	1	1	1	8	0	9	2	0
Rivera, Francisco, Cordoba	1	4	.200	6.20	9	9	0	0	0	0	49.1	64	227	36	34	4	3	0	3	20	2	15	0	0
Rivera, Francisco, Vaqueros	1	4	.200	6.02	24	4	0	0	8	0	46.1	50	213	39	31	10	3	0	1	32	6	24	5	0
Rivera, Lino, Monclova	0	1	.000	15.00	2	2	0	0	0	0	6.0	13	38	12	10	2	0	0	1	5	0	3	1	0
Rivera, Lino, Tigres	6	2	.750	3.47	14	12	1	0	0	0	72.2	69	300	29	28	9	2	2	5	23	0	18	0	0
Saldana, Jose, Veracruz	0	1	.000	13.50	1	1	0	0	0	0	3.1	7	19	5	5	0	0	0	0	2	0	1	0	0
Saldana, Jose, Puebla	4	0	1.000	2.64	13	8	1	0	1	0	44.1	43	199	21	13	2	1	2	0	26	0	30	1	0
Salgado, Eduardo, Veracruz	1	3	.250	2.79	29	0	0	0	7	0	48.1	54	208	18	15	2	2	2	1	15	5	25	1	0
Salgado, Eduardo, Puebla	4	1	.800	6.32	18	1	0	0	5	1	31.1	38	142	24	22	7	0	3	1	8	2	14	1	0
Silva, Walter, Reynosa	0	4	.000	4.80	32	0	0	0	11	2	45.0	36	199	25	24	2	2	2	0	30	0	39	5	0
Silva, Walter, Monterrey	0	0	.000	6.75	3	0	0	0	0	0	1.1	4	12	1	1	0	0	0	0	4	0	1	0	0
Sinohui, David, Saltillo	0	1	.000	4.50	7	0	0	0	3	2	6.0	11	33	3	3	0	0	0	0	3	0	8	1	0
Sinohui, David, Cordoba	0	1	.000	4.85	12	0	0	0	10	8	13.0	15	60	7	7	2	0	0	1	7	0	10	2	0
Sinohui, David, Mexico	0	0	.000	3.65	13	0	0	0	12	8	12.1	18	57	5	5	0	0	2	0	4	2	7	1	0
Sinohui, David, Tabasco	2	2	.500	4.02	18	0	0	0	11	7	15.2	14	68	7	7	0	1	0	1	8	1	9	0	0
Solis, Tomas, Puebla *	0	1	.000	7.71	21	0	0	0	2	1	9.1	11	46	9	8	2	1	2	0	9	2	3	0	0
Solis, Tomas, Tigres *	0	0	.000	4.05	9	0	0	0	2	0	6.2	7	25	3	3	1	0	0	0	0	0	1	0	0
Valdez, Efrain, Tabasco *	3	6	.333	3.15	16	16	0	0	0	0	94.1	96	405	34	33	6	8	1	3	31	3	41	1	1
Valdez, Efrain, Vaqueros *	1	1	.500	9.53	4	4	0	0	0	0	17.0	27	77	18	18	4	0	0	0	5	0	11	0	1
Verdugo, Hugo, Vaqueros	3	1	.750	5.16	24	0	0	0	3	0	29.2	28	131	19	17	7	1	2	4	13	2	24	4	1
Verdugo, Hugo, Cordoba	0	4	.000	4.63	9	0	0	0	7	1	11.2	13	54	8	6	0	2	0	0	6	2	2	1	0

COMBINATION SHUTOUTS: Campeche (3)—Elvira-Pulido, Campos-Marquez, Magee-Pulido-Marquez. Cancun (8)—Rodriguez-Sanchez-Terrazas-Valenzuela-Lopez, Hernandez-Lopez, Pesqueira-Sanchez-Pimentel, Vega-Lara, Pimentel-Sangeado-Terrazas-Sanchez-Dingman, Sangeado-Enriquez, Sangeado-Enriquez, Vega-Sanchez-Enriquez. Cordoba (2)—Lopez-Orea, Chavarria-Neri-Parra-Sinohui. Dos Laredos (6)—Huerta-Loaiza, Gonzalez-Nunez, Huerta-Garibay-Cortes, Gonzalez-Loaiza-Palacios-Parra-Cortes, Nunez-Cortes, Nunez-Garibay-Cortes. Mexico City Tigres (7)—Gandarillas-Navarro-Manzano-Guzman-Hasselhoff, Campillo-Garibaldi-Hernandez, Campillo-Garibaldi-Hernandez, Roque-Manzano-Zavala, Rivera-Zavala-Olague-Hernandez, Campillo-Aguilar-Huerta, Olague-Huerta-Manzano. Monclova (3)—Acosta-Ramirez, Arroyo-Valerio-Rojas, Romero-Valerio-Alberro. Monterrey (6)—Loya-Garcia, Leyva-Aguirre-Lopez, Serafini-Rubio, Serafini-Aguirre-Lara, Leyva-Cerros-Rubio, Serafini-Aguirre-Munoz-Rubio. Oaxaca (1)—Lomeli-Dominguez. Puebla (5)—Martinez-Kelley-Pacheco, Navarro-Lopez-Cervantes, Ortega-Lopez, Navarro-Lopez-Cervantes, Martinez-Nunez-Solis-Lopez. Reynosa (4)—Preston-Strong, Verdugo-Melendez-Strong, Quinones-Silva-Strong, Esquer-Melendez-Garcia. Saltillo (1)—Ward-Cazares-Gonzalez. Tabasco (5)—Leon-Ruiz-Gonzalez, Valdez-Verdugo-Romano, Vargas-Ruiz-Verdugo, Vargas-Ruiz-Verdugo-Romano, Leon-Gonzalez. Vasqueros (1)—Gomez-Jimenez-Alvarez. Veracruz (5)—Pina-Chavez, Delahoya-Hernandez-Salgado, Moreno-Gonzalez, Mora-Perez-Hernandez-Gonzalez, Garcia-Hernandez-Federico. Yucatan (11)—Palafox-Verdugo-Aceves, Osuna-Camara-Flores-Dingman, Rodriguez-Dingman, Manzanillo-Navarro-Ortega-Dingman, Degadillo-Flores-Dingman, Arellano-Camara-Aceves-Dingman, Delgadillo-Rivera-Navarro-Aceves, Rodriguez-Camara-Aceves, Rodriguez-Verdugo-Flores, Arellano-Camara-Aceves-Flores, Rodriguez-Garcia.

NO-HIT GAMES: None.

2003 FIELDING

TEAM

Team	G	PO	A	E	TC	DP	TP	PB	Pct.
Mexico	108	2831	1299	66	4196	131	0	9	.984
Monterrey	109	2836	1253	83	4172	118	0	7	.980
Yucatan	106	2757	1174	85	4016	100	0	13	.979
Vaqueros	110	2847	1359	100	4306	126	0	8	.977
Tigres	108	2815	1354	99	4268	156	0	6	.977
Dos Laredos	110	2894	1216	100	4210	145	0	17	.976
Monclova	110	2871	1271	102	4244	132	0	14	.976
Puebla	110	2848	1395	104	4347	142	0	5	.976
Veracruz	106	2856	1402	105	4363	119	0	11	.976
Cancun	107	2741	1136	108	3985	97	0	11	.973
Tabasco	109	2879	1293	118	4290	100	0	16	.972
Reynosa	107	2795	1142	116	4053	85	0	8	.971
Saltillo	107	2778	1275	119	4172	113	0	5	.971
Cordoba	104	2652	1202	115	3969	117	0	16	.971
Campeche	106	2770	1271	119	4160	118	0	11	.971
Oaxaca	109	2890	1415	133	4438	138	0	7	.970

INDIVIDUAL

FIRST BASEMEN

NOTE: All caps denotes fielding-percentage leader based on 55 games for catchers, 73 for all other non-pitchers and 88 innings for pitchers. *Throws lefthanded.

Player, Team	Pct.	G	PO	A	E	TC	DP
Adriana, Sharnol, Cordoba	.991	48	395	31	4	430	51
Aganza, Ruben, Monc.-Yuc.-Sal.	.995	47	358	46	2	406	47
Aguilera, Armando, Veracruz	1.000	1	3	1	0	4	1
Almeida, Shammar, Oaxaca	.994	56	473	35	3	511	59
Alvarez, Hector, Oaxaca	1.000	1	1	0	0	1	0
Arredondo, Hernando, Tabasco	1.000	1	4	0	0	4	1
Barajas, Edison, Cordoba *	.989	13	81	7	1	89	7
Beltran, Juan, Campeche	1.000	1	2	0	0	2	0
Bullett, Scott, Reynosa *	1.000	2	3	0	0	3	0
Bustillos, Luis, Reynosa	.800	1	3	1	1	5	0
Carrillo, Jesus, Vaqueros	1.000	1	5	2	0	7	1
Castaneda, Hector, Yucatan	.995	58	544	39	3	586	43
Castaneda, Rafael, Reyn.-Mont.	.992	30	212	31	2	245	17
Castellano, Pedro, Campeche	1.000	25	119	11	0	130	10
Cervantes, Refugio, Cancun	.991	89	799	59	8	866	84
Chan, Armando, Monclova *	1.000	1	1	0	0	1	0
Cisneros, Ventura, Reynosa	1.000	4	8	3	0	11	1
Cobos, Rogelio, Mexico	.987	11	72	3	1	76	10
Connell, Lino, Oaxaca-Reynosa	.983	14	109	7	2	118	8
Contreras, Sergio, Tigres *	1.000	3	14	1	0	15	4
Davis, Jay, Cordoba *	1.000	1	2	0	0	2	0
Diaz, Luis, Puebla *	1.000	1	1	0	0	1	0
Diaz, Pedro, Veracruz	.990	13	94	8	1	103	13
Espino, Daniel, Tabasco	1.000	20	137	23	0	160	14
Espinosa, Ramon, Yuc.-D.L.	.996	26	233	19	1	253	28
Espinoza, Ramon, Vaqueros	1.000	1	3	0	0	3	1
Esquer, Ramon, Campeche	1.000	4	3	3	0	6	0
Estrada, Hector, Vaq.-Cordoba	.980	29	220	24	5	249	17
Evans, Tom, Tabasco	1.000	2	9	2	0	11	1
Fentanes, Oscar, Veracruz	1.000	1	2	0	0	2	0
Fornes, Daniel, Monterrey *	.988	26	214	23	3	240	25
Garcia, Cornelio, Mex.-Oax.-Vaq. *	.990	30	260	22	3	285	33
Garcia, Guillermo, Tigres	.992	97	954	78	8	1040	132
Garcia, Omar, Vera.-D.L.	.997	37	355	17	1	373	43
Gavia, Jesus, Cancun	.947	6	32	4	2	38	2
Gracia, Rafael, Oaxaca	1.000	2	6	0	0	6	1
Grijak, Kevin, Veracruz	1.000	38	338	22	0	360	30
Hernandez, Vladimir, Cancun	1.000	1	7	0	0	7	0
Ibarra, Juvenal, Vaqueros	1.000	2	3	0	0	3	0
Iturbe, Pedro, Puebla *	.984	27	226	24	4	254	33
Lara, Idelfonso, Vaqueros	.992	28	217	32	2	251	32
LeBron, Juan, Oaxaca	.952	3	19	1	1	21	2
Leyva, German, Saltillo-D.L.	.995	36	196	11	1	208	22
Lopez, Fabian, Oaxaca	1.000	1	2	0	0	2	0
Lopez, Gonzalo, Monclova	1.000	2	10	1	0	11	0
LOPEZ, RAUL, Monclova	.998	76	621	33	1	655	80
Macias, Roberto, Cancun	1.000	1	4	1	0	5	0
Magallanes, Ever, Tabasco	1.000	5	13	2	0	15	1
Martinez, Abel, Cancun	1.000	1	0	1	0	1	0
Martinez, Felix, Tabasco	1.000	1	1	0	0	1	0
Martinez, Rafael, Veracruz *	.978	7	81	7	2	90	6
Martinez, Ramon, Mexico	1.000	4	27	5	0	32	1
Mendez, Francisco, Mont.-Reyn.*	.990	75	590	69	7	666	61
Mendez, Roberto, Oaxaca	1.000	2	18	0	0	18	4
Mendoza, Omar, Oaxaca	1.000	2	6	1	0	7	1
Mere, Carlos, Veracruz	.000	1	0	0	0	0	0
Minjarez, Francisco, Puebla	1.000	1	1	0	0	1	0
Montenegro, Jose, Oaxaca	.941	3	16	0	1	17	0
Morales, Carlos, Yucatan	1.000	2	6	0	0	6	1
Munoz, Adan, Monclova-Tigres	1.000	3	16	1	0	17	2
Munoz, Jose, Saltillo *	1.000	8	56	5	0	61	6
Nunez, Reymond, D.L.-Reynosa	.996	26	226	32	1	259	34
Obando, Sherman, Mexico	.990	49	470	28	5	503	48
Ojeda, Miguel, Mexico	.985	15	116	13	2	131	16
Orantes, Ramon, Monterrey	1.000	3	4	2	0	6	2
Ortiz, Alex, Vaqueros	1.000	6	47	6	0	53	4
Paez, Raul, Veracruz *	.996	49	429	24	2	455	42
Paul, Corey, Saltillo *	1.000	5	38	3	0	41	1
Perez, Alfredo, Campeche	1.000	5	12	0	0	12	1
Perez, Antonio, Cordoba	.969	11	58	4	2	64	5
Perez, Francisco, Reynosa *	1.000	2	7	2	0	9	0
Perez, Rob, Mexico	.989	26	263	16	3	282	28
Pickering, Calvin, Vaqueros *	.977	64	574	67	15	656	69
Presichi, Cristian, Saltillo	1.000	16	107	12	0	119	10
Quinones, Ruben, Cordoba	1.000	4	10	0	0	10	4
Ramirez, Enrique, Cancun	1.000	1	1	0	0	1	0
Rios, Eduardo, Cancun-Oaxaca	.989	30	256	22	3	281	30
Rivera, Francisco, Dos Laredos	1.000	3	23	2	0	25	5
Robles, Juan, Tabasco	1.000	1	2	1	0	3	0
Robles, Ricardo, Monclova	.982	29	157	10	3	170	20
Rodarte, Raul, Mont.-Reynosa	.986	7	62	8	1	71	6
Rodriguez, Armando, Puebla	.000	1	0	0	0	0	0
Rodriguez, Boi, Campeche	1.000	4	27	1	0	28	2
Rodriguez, Carlos, Reynosa	.000	1	0	0	0	0	0
Rodriguez, Fernando, Campeche	.990	45	358	30	4	392	35
Rodriguez, Leonardo, Monterrey	1.000	1	6	0	0	6	1
Rojas, Homar, Oaxaca	.909	1	9	1	1	11	1
Romero, Marco, Saltillo	.989	76	669	42	8	719	76
Romero, Oscar, Reynosa	1.000	1	11	0	0	11	1
Romero, Willie, Yucatan	1.000	8	60	1	0	61	6
Rose, Pete, Cordoba	.990	28	276	15	3	294	29
Ruiz, Juan, Monclova	1.000	1	2	0	0	2	0
Salinas, Trey, Cancun	1.000	1	4	0	0	4	0
Samuels, Scott, Veracruz	1.000	1	1	0	0	1	0
Sanchez, Roque, Yucatan	1.000	8	39	4	0	43	2
Santos, Andres, Dos Laredos	.976	8	38	2	1	41	4
Sauceda, Victor, Cancun	1.000	4	2	1	0	3	0
Saucedo, Robert, Tabasco	.990	79	698	68	8	774	64
Sievers, Carlos, Tabasco	.980	18	130	14	3	147	13
Smith, Charles, Monterrey	.993	84	767	57	6	830	76
Sojo, Luis, Oaxaca	1.000	12	117	15	0	132	14
Soto, Saul, Mexico	1.000	6	40	4	0	44	3
Suarez, Luis, Tigres *	.000	1	0	0	1	1	0
Valdez, Francisco, Veracruz	1.000	1	3	0	0	3	0
Valencia, Abraham, Dos Laredos	.983	20	162	15	3	180	17
Valle, Cosme, Mexico	1.000	3	21	1	0	22	1
Valle, Jorge, Vaqueros	1.000	8	36	7	0	43	2
Vazquez, Jorge Alberto, Tigres	1.000	6	5	4	0	9	3
Velazquez, Guillermo, Cam.-Pue.*	.991	76	697	53	7	757	91
Verdugo, Vincente, Saltillo	1.000	4	9	3	0	12	1
Villalobos, Carlos, Puebla	.000	1	0	0	0	0	0
Villarreal, Alejandro, D.L.	1.000	5	15	4	0	19	2
Virgen, Constancio, Mexico	1.000	1	1	0	0	1	1
Vizcarra, Roberto, Tigres	1.000	11	67	15	0	82	12
Yan, Julian, Puebla	.992	62	578	62	5	645	69
Zambrano, Roberto, D.L.	.983	20	165	9	3	177	24
Zazueta, Juan, Veracruz	1.000	1	1	0	0	1	1

FIRST BASEMEN WITH TWO OR MORE TEAMS

Player, Team	Pct.	G	PO	A	E	TC	DP
Aganza, Ruben, Yucatan	.990	13	91	9	1	101	12
Aganza, Ruben, Saltillo	1.000	14	87	12	0	99	11
Aganza, Ruben, Monclova	.995	20	180	25	1	206	24
Castaneda, Rafael, Reynosa	.992	29	212	31	2	245	17
Castaneda, Rafael, Monterrey	.000	1	0	0	0	0	0
Connell, Lino, Reynosa	1.000	2	2	1	0	3	0
Connell, Lino, Oaxaca	.983	12	107	6	2	115	8
Espinosa, Ramon, Dos Laredos	.917	2	9	2	1	12	2
Espinosa, Ramon, Yucatan	1.000	24	224	17	0	241	26
Estrada, Hector, Cordoba	.985	17	119	12	2	133	12
Estrada, Hector, Vaqueros	.974	12	101	12	3	116	5

Player, Team	Pct.	G	PO	A	E	TC	DP
Garcia, Cornelio, Vaqueros *	.962	3	22	3	1	26	5
Garcia, Cornelio, Mexico *	.989	10	85	8	1	94	12
Garcia, Cornelio, Oaxaca *	.994	17	153	11	1	165	16
Garcia, Omar, Veracruz	.994	16	160	6	1	167	15
Garcia, Omar, Dos Laredos	1.000	21	195	11	0	206	28
Leyva, German, Saltillo	1.000	16	58	4	0	62	3
Leyva, German, Dos Laredos	.993	20	138	7	1	146	19
Mendez, Francisco, Reynosa *	.989	73	585	69	7	661	58
Mendez, Francisco, Monterrey *	1.000	2	5	0	0	5	3
Munoz, Adan, Tigres	1.000	1	5	1	0	6	1
Munoz, Adan, Monclova	1.000	2	11	0	0	11	1
Nunez, Reymond, Reynosa	1.000	1	4	1	0	5	1
Nunez, Reymond, Dos Laredos	.996	25	222	31	1	254	33
Rios, Eduardo, Oaxaca	.989	18	157	15	2	174	24
Rios, Eduardo, Cancun	.991	12	99	7	1	107	6
Rodarte, Raul, Reynosa	.983	6	53	6	1	60	4
Rodarte, Raul, Monterrey	1.000	1	9	2	0	11	2
Velazquez, Guillermo, Puebla *	.988	25	234	18	3	255	35
Velazquez, Guillermo, Cam.*	.992	51	463	35	4	502	56

SECOND BASEMEN

Player, Team	Pct.	G	PO	A	E	TC	DP
Acosta, Francisco, Tabasco	.000	1	0	0	0	0	0
Adriana, Sharnol, Cordoba	.958	11	22	24	2	48	4
Ahumada, Alex, Monterrey	1.000	4	6	5	0	11	4
Amador, Jose, Vaqueros	.667	1	1	1	1	3	0
Arias, Francisco, Saltillo	.948	22	25	30	3	58	4
Armenta, Guillermo, Mexico	.963	11	21	31	2	54	3
Arredondo, Alan, Yucatan	1.000	8	9	25	0	34	3
Arredondo, Jesus, Puebla	.979	95	219	305	11	535	94
Barron, Alejandro, Cordoba	1.000	3	2	3	0	5	2
Brena, Jaime, Oaxaca	.983	47	97	131	4	232	41
Buelna, Lorenzo, Puebla	1.000	1	0	1	0	1	0
Carrasco, Ernesto, Puebla	1.000	11	19	19	0	38	6
Carrillo, Oscar, Mexico	.917	4	3	8	1	12	1
Castro, Arnoldo, Cancun	.977	95	256	257	12	525	57
Cervantes, Ivan, Oaxaca	1.000	1	0	1	0	1	1
Cesar, Dionys, Veracruz	.964	7	19	34	2	55	10
Connell, Lino, Oaxaca	.929	3	8	5	1	14	4
Espinoza, Efren, Vaq.-Mexico	.968	20	25	36	2	63	8
Esquer, Ramon, Campeche	1.000	19	37	28	0	65	7
Felix, Alejandro, Vaqueros	1.000	2	0	3	0	3	0
Felix, Lauro, Tabasco	.966	17	42	42	3	87	7
Flores, Kevin, Puebla	1.000	8	12	19	0	31	4
Flores, Miguel, Reynosa-Yucatan	.967	83	214	221	15	450	46
Gamez, Miguel, Reynosa	1.000	11	26	23	0	49	6
Garcia, Nick, Puebla	1.000	1	0	1	0	1	0
GASTELUM, CARLOS, Tigres	.994	74	203	260	3	466	87
Gastelum, Sergio, Tigres	.966	7	11	17	1	29	5
Gomez, Heber, Monterrey	.981	76	178	236	8	422	51
Gonzalez, Israel, Campeche	1.000	3	2	2	0	4	0
Gonzalez, Roman, Cordoba	1.000	1	0	1	0	1	0
Gonzalez, Santiago, Veracruz	1.000	7	7	1	0	8	1
Guerrero, Sergio, Campeche	.978	98	297	284	13	594	82
Guizar, Hector, Cordoba	.833	1	2	3	1	6	1
Hernandez, Vladimir, Cancun	.985	16	27	39	1	67	9
Laya, Rayner, Tabasco	1.000	5	17	12	0	29	5
Leyva, Octavio, Tabasco	.984	17	23	37	1	61	9
Lofton, James, Reynosa	1.000	4	5	6	0	11	2
Lopez, Fabian, Oaxaca	1.000	4	8	8	0	16	4
Lopez, Fausto, Mexico	.000	3	0	0	1	1	0
Lopez, Gonzalo, Monclova	1.000	6	10	12	0	22	5
Magallanes, Ever, Tabasco	.992	21	64	59	1	124	10
Martinez, Abel, Cancun	1.000	2	4	5	0	9	2
Martinez, Felix, Tabasco	.980	33	94	100	4	198	18
Martinez, Grimaldo, Cordoba	.976	83	189	258	11	458	74
Martinez, Luis, Saltillo	1.000	4	3	5	0	8	1
Mejia, Roberto, Oaxaca	.980	32	78	121	4	203	26
Melo, Juan, Mexico-Cordoba	.988	13	43	38	1	82	9
Mendoza, Omar, Tab.-Oaxaca	.984	25	56	68	2	126	16
Mere, Carlos, Veracruz	1.000	2	4	4	0	8	2
Mere, Pedro, Veracruz	.987	68	171	216	5	392	48
Minjarez, Francisco, Puebla	.967	15	9	20	1	30	1
Morejon, Oswaldo, Yucatan	.984	83	210	210	7	427	62
Orrantia, Carlos, Monterrey	.980	43	79	115	4	198	27
Palafox, Sergio, Saltillo	.960	36	34	63	4	101	11
Perez, Jose, Reynosa	1.000	10	20	27	0	47	9
Ramirez, Enrique, Cancun	.000	1	0	0	0	0	0
Ramirez, Jesus, Oaxaca	.950	37	83	127	11	221	29
Rivera, Jesus, Tabasco	.925	14	27	22	4	53	7
Robles, Oscar, Mexico	.983	82	202	272	8	482	72
Robles, Trinidad, Tigres	.989	39	84	96	2	182	31
Rodarte, Raul, Monterrey	1.000	3	9	10	0	19	3
Rodriguez, Carlos, Vaqueros	.987	110	292	322	8	622	97
Rosas, Ezequiel, Oaxaca	.750	1	2	1	1	4	0
Ruiz, Juan, Monclova	1.000	9	15	12	0	27	4
Salas, Heriberto, Cancun	1.000	2	2	1	0	3	0
Salazar, Francisco, Mexico	1.000	1	2	3	0	5	0
Sanchez, Jose, Dos Laredos	.963	28	46	57	4	107	13
Sanchez, Orlando, Reynosa	.957	23	48	62	5	115	11
Sanchez, Roque, Yucatan	1.000	2	3	4	0	7	2
Sanchez. Wilfredo, Cordoba	.963	9	13	13	1	27	4
Santana, Pedro, Cordoba	1.000	4	9	7	0	16	0
Sauceda, Victor, Cancun	.950	9	11	8	1	20	2
Sojo, Luis, Oaxaca	.000	1	0	0	0	0	0
Trapaga, Julio, Puebla	.885	8	11	12	3	26	3
Valencia, Abraham, Dos Laredos	1.000	2	4	7	0	11	3
Valencia, Carlos, Dos Laredos	.972	94	219	294	15	528	95
Valenzuela, Irving, Monclova	.986	33	69	75	2	146	20
Valle, Jorge, Vaqueros	1.000	4	4	1	0	5	1
Verdugo, Vincente, Saltillo	.987	84	185	255	6	446	71
Vizcarra, Roberto, Tigres	1.000	4	4	4	0	8	1
Zazueta, Juan, Veracruz	.970	36	91	106	6	203	28
Zazueta, Mauricio, Monclova	.979	79	229	232	10	471	79

SECOND BASEMEN WITH TWO OR MORE TEAMS

Player, Team	Pct.	G	PO	A	E	TC	DP
Espinoza, Efren, Vaqueros	.000	2	0	0	0	0	0
Espinoza, Efren, Mexico	.968	18	25	36	2	63	8
Flores, Miguel, Reynosa	.970	67	186	173	11	370	38
Flores, Miguel, Yucatan	.950	16	28	48	4	80	8
Melo, Juan, Cordoba	1.000	5	14	15	0	29	3
Melo, Juan, Mexico	.981	8	29	23	1	53	6
Mendoza, Omar, Tabasco	.983	23	54	64	2	120	16
Mendoza, Omar, Oaxaca	1.000	2	2	4	0	6	0

THIRD BASEMEN

Player, Team	Pct.	G	PO	A	E	TC	DP
Adriana, Sharnol, Cordoba	.863	22	17	52	11	80	5
Ahumada, Alex, Monterrey	.934	40	20	51	5	76	8
Alvarez, Hector, Oaxaca	1.000	1	0	5	0	5	0
Amador, Jose, Vaqueros	1.000	1	0	2	0	2	0
Arano, Eloy, Vaqueros-Cordoba	.917	51	38	94	12	144	12
Arias, Francisco, Saltillo	.917	6	4	7	1	12	0
Armenta, Guillermo, Mexico	1.000	2	1	1	0	2	0
Arredondo, Hernando, Tabasco	.909	16	11	29	4	44	1
Beltran, Juan, Campeche	.972	33	7	28	1	36	3
Brena, Jaime, Oaxaca	1.000	1	0	2	0	2	0
Carrasco, Ernesto, Puebla	.958	58	32	126	7	165	13
Carrillo, Oscar, Mexico	1.000	1	0	1	0	1	1
Castaneda, Rafael, Reyn.-Mont.	.894	16	13	29	5	47	2
Castellano, Pedro, Campeche	.960	78	66	174	10	250	22
Cervera, Francisco, Cancun	.924	54	34	99	11	144	7
Cesar, Dionys, Veracruz	1.000	1	0	2	0	2	0
Connell, Lino, Oaxaca-Reynosa	.932	68	59	118	13	190	9
Contreras, Albino, Puebla	.000	1	0	0	0	0	0
Contreras, Jose, Tabasco	.970	29	12	52	2	66	2
Cruz, Fausto, Yucatan	.960	97	62	204	11	277	16
Diaz, Edwin, Veracruz	.961	106	94	255	14	363	25
Diaz, Pedro, Puebla	.875	5	3	4	1	8	0
Espinoza, Efren, Vaq.-Mexico	.857	10	1	17	3	21	2
Esquer, Ramon, Campeche	1.000	5	2	0	0	2	0
Evans, Tom, Tabasco	.929	20	13	39	4	56	3
Felix, Lauro, Tabasco	.833	5	0	5	1	6	0
Flores, Miguel, Yucatan	.500	1	1	0	1	2	0
Garcia, Hector, Tabasco	.000	1	0	0	0	0	0
Gastelum, Carlos, Tigres	1.000	1	0	1	0	1	0
Gastelum, Sergio, Tigres	1.000	3	1	2	0	3	0
Gonzalez, Israel, Campeche	.929	7	5	8	1	14	1
Gonzalez, Roman, Cordoba	.000	1	0	0	0	0	0
Grijak, Kevin, Veracruz	.000	1	0	0	0	0	0
Guerrero, Sergio, Campeche	.857	4	4	2	1	7	0
Guizar, Hector, Cordoba	.980	18	19	30	1	50	2
Lara, Idelfonso, Vaqueros	1.000	2	2	0	0	2	0
Leyva, German, Dos Laredos	.958	31	21	48	3	72	4
Leyva, Octavio, Tabasco	.000	1	0	0	0	0	0
Lopez, Fabian, Oaxaca	.848	12	2	26	5	33	3
Lopez, Gonzalo, Monclova	.643	10	2	7	5	14	0
Lopez, Raul, Monclova	.908	27	15	44	6	65	4
Lucca, Lou, Cordoba-Vaqueros	.958	72	50	177	10	237	14
Magallanes, Ever, Tabasco	.919	56	42	117	14	173	10
Martinez, Abel, Cancun	.955	56	58	89	7	154	9
Martinez, Ramon, Mexico	.969	91	55	192	8	255	16
Mejia, Roberto, Oaxaca	1.000	15	9	37	0	46	5

Player, Team	Pct.	G	PO	A	E	TC	DP
Melo, Juan, Cordoba	.966	9	6	22	1	29	3
Mendoza, Omar, Reyn.-Oaxaca	.986	28	22	50	1	73	5
Mere, Carlos, Veracruz	.000	3	0	0	0	0	0
Minjarez, Francisco, Puebla	.950	22	14	43	3	60	3
Montenegro, Jose, Oaxaca	.857	15	3	27	5	35	3
Nunez, Reymond, Reynosa	1.000	8	4	26	0	30	2
Orantes, Ramon, Monterrey	.957	77	57	143	9	209	12
Orrantia, Carlos, Monterrey	.828	12	7	17	5	29	0
Perez, Alfredo, Campeche	1.000	4	0	2	0	2	0
Perez, Jose, Reynosa	1.000	5	2	3	0	5	0
Presichi, Cristian, Saltillo	.914	18	14	39	5	58	4
Ramirez, Enrique, Cancun	.900	7	5	4	1	10	1
Rios, Eduardo, Cancun-Oaxaca	.919	14	8	26	3	37	2
Rivera, Jesus, Tabasco	1.000	9	1	7	0	8	2
Robles, Oscar, Mexico	.972	27	16	54	2	72	7
Robles, Trinidad, Tigres	.867	25	11	28	6	45	6
Rodarte, Raul, Mont.-Reynosa	.968	21	18	42	2	62	5
Rodriguez, Armando, Puebla	.000	1	0	0	0	0	0
Rodriguez, Victor, Campeche	.969	16	17	46	2	65	6
Romero, Oscar, Reynosa	.942	29	22	59	5	86	2
Rosas, Ezequiel, Oaxaca	.818	5	4	5	2	11	0
Ruiz, Juan, Monclova	.955	90	67	188	12	267	21
Salas, Heriberto, Cancun	1.000	2	1	1	0	2	0
Sanchez, Jose, Dos Laredos	.000	1	0	0	0	0	0
Sanchez, Orlando, Reynosa	1.000	1	1	1	0	2	0
Sanchez, Roque, Yucatan	.982	30	15	40	1	56	3
Sanchez. Wilfredo, Cordoba	.000	1	0	0	0	0	0
Santana, Pedro, Cordoba	1.000	2	0	2	0	2	1
Santos, Andres, Dos Laredos	1.000	2	1	2	0	3	0
Sauceda, Victor, Cancun	1.000	3	0	3	0	3	0
Sievers, Carlos, Tabasco	.000	1	0	0	0	0	0
Sojo, Luis, Oaxaca	.846	8	6	16	4	26	2
Valencia, Carlos, Dos Laredos	.927	23	11	27	3	41	2
Valenzuela, Irving, Monclova	1.000	8	4	7	0	11	0
Valle, Jorge, Vaqueros	.985	54	38	154	3	195	16
Vazquez, Jorge Alberto, Tigres	.906	59	37	117	16	170	16
VELEZ, MANUEL, Saltillo	.980	87	49	241	6	296	29
Verdugo, Vincente, Saltillo	1.000	2	1	3	0	4	0
Villalobos, Carlos, Puebla	.934	50	38	133	12	183	18
Villarreal, Alejandro, D.L.	.962	71	48	128	7	183	16
Vizcarra, Roberto, Tigres	.934	46	20	94	8	122	12
Wilson, Craig, Oaxaca	.958	14	8	38	2	48	3
Zazueta, Juan, Veracruz	.833	5	2	3	1	6	0

THIRD BASEMEN WITH TWO OR MORE TEAMS

Player, Team	Pct.	G	PO	A	E	TC	DP
Arano, Eloy, Cordoba	.891	18	18	23	5	46	4
Arano, Eloy, Vaqueros	.929	33	20	71	7	98	8
Castaneda, Rafael, Reynosa	.895	14	9	25	4	38	1
Castaneda, Rafael, Monterrey	.889	2	4	4	1	9	1
Connell, Lino, Oaxaca	.957	22	22	44	3	69	4
Connell, Lino, Reynosa	.917	46	37	74	10	121	5
Espinoza, Efren, Vaqueros	.889	8	1	15	2	18	1
Espinoza, Efren, Mexico	.667	2	0	2	1	3	1
Lucca, Lou, Cordoba	.943	43	34	114	9	157	10
Lucca, Lou, Vaqueros	.988	29	16	63	1	80	4
Mendoza, Omar, Oaxaca	1.000	22	16	41	0	57	5
Mendoza, Omar, Reynosa	.938	6	6	9	1	16	0
Rios, Eduardo, Cancun	.000	1	0	0	0	0	0
Rios, Eduardo, Oaxaca	.919	13	8	26	3	37	2
Rodarte, Raul, Monterrey	.955	8	3	18	1	22	3
Rodarte, Raul, Reynosa	.975	13	15	24	1	40	2

SHORTSTOPS

Player, Team	Pct.	G	PO	A	E	TC	DP
Ahumada, Alex, Monterrey	.929	8	9	17	2	28	1
Alejos, Fernando, Yucatan	1.000	1	1	0	0	1	0
Amador, Jose, Vaqueros	.958	72	110	213	14	337	48
Arias, Francisco, Saltillo	.935	55	69	132	14	215	27
Armenta, Guillermo, Mexico	.000	1	0	0	0	0	0
Arredondo, Alan, Yucatan	.964	8	13	14	1	28	1
Barragan, Effrain, Saltillo	1.000	1	0	1	0	1	0
Beltran, Juan, Campeche	.889	15	7	25	4	36	3
Borges, Luis, Yucatan	.965	96	131	313	16	460	50
Brena, Jaime, Oaxaca	.961	17	26	47	3	76	10
Bustillos, Luis, Reynosa	.953	55	89	153	12	254	32
Canales, Joel, Reynosa	.000	1	0	0	0	0	0
Carrasco, Ernesto, Puebla	1.000	1	1	1	0	2	1
Carrillo, Oscar, Mexico	.857	5	1	5	1	7	1
Castro, Domingo, Monclova	.961	110	199	394	24	617	85
Cervantes, Ivan, Oaxaca	.954	99	186	354	26	566	85
Cesar, Dionys, Veracruz	.955	49	102	198	14	314	35
Connell, Lino, Reynosa	.942	26	43	55	6	104	9
Cruz, Fausto, Yucatan	.982	19	20	35	1	56	7
Diaz, Remigio, Monterrey	.977	76	104	230	8	342	51
Espinoza, Efren, Vaq.-Mexico	.909	13	20	40	6	66	8
Evans, Tom, Tabasco	.918	16	29	61	8	98	9
Felix, Alejandro, Vaqueros	.944	4	5	12	1	18	3
Felix, Lauro, Tabasco	1.000	2	2	1	0	3	0
Flores, Kevin, Puebla	.964	58	67	150	8	225	41
Garcia, Heriberto, Veracruz	.967	46	84	177	9	270	40
Garcia, Nick, Puebla	.961	71	105	192	12	309	44
Gastelum, Carlos, Tigres	1.000	4	3	5	0	8	1
Gomez, Heber, Monterrey	.981	34	46	111	3	160	22
Guizar, Hector, Cordoba	.961	89	143	274	17	434	65
Hernandez, Julio, Dos Laredos	.978	104	200	324	12	536	102
Hernandez, Vladimir, Cancun	.956	63	82	181	12	275	35
Laya, Rayner, Tabasco	.952	89	168	288	23	479	46
Leyva, German, Saltillo	1.000	1	1	1	0	2	1
Lofton, James, Reynosa	1.000	5	7	7	0	14	3
Lopez, Fausto, Mexico	1.000	13	12	17	0	29	3
Lopez, Gonzalo, Monclova	.667	5	0	4	2	6	2
Lucca, Lou, Cordoba	1.000	2	3	3	0	6	1
Martinez, Abel, Cancun	.800	1	1	3	1	5	1
Martinez, Felix, Tabasco	.750	2	3	3	2	8	2
Martinez, Gabby, Vaqueros	.910	12	18	43	6	67	12
Martinez, Luis, Saltillo	.929	6	6	7	1	14	1
Melo, Juan, Cordoba	1.000	3	7	9	0	16	1
Mendoza, Omar, Reynosa	.878	13	14	29	6	49	4
Mere, Carlos, Veracruz	.958	13	4	19	1	24	2
Meza, Gonzalo, Vaqueros	.000	2	0	0	0	0	0
Minjarez, Francisco, Puebla	.930	16	15	25	3	43	5
Perez, Jose, Reynosa	.969	27	36	58	3	97	9
Ramirez, Enrique, Cancun	.963	8	8	18	1	27	1
Ramirez, Jesus, Oaxaca	.000	1	0	0	0	0	0
Ramirez, Oscar, Campeche	.939	105	159	347	33	539	58
Rivera, Jesus, Tabasco	.966	8	12	16	1	29	5
Robles, Javier, Tigres	.975	94	163	375	14	552	92
Robles, Trinidad, Tigres	.964	19	20	60	3	83	14
Romero, Flavio, Saltillo	.937	73	109	204	21	334	41
Salas, Heriberto, Cancun	.954	51	61	148	10	219	28
Sanchez, Jose, Dos Laredos	.962	10	4	21	1	26	2
Sanchez, Orlando, Reynosa	1.000	5	6	8	0	14	1
Sanchez, Roque, Yucatan	1.000	1	1	0	0	1	0
Sanchez. Wilfredo, Cordoba	.966	23	33	53	3	89	6
SANDOVAL, JOSE, Mexico	.983	106	159	367	9	535	86
Sojo, Luis, Oaxaca	1.000	3	3	7	0	10	3
Trapaga, Julio, Puebla	.929	9	3	10	1	14	3
Valenzuela, Irving, Monclova	1.000	12	3	10	0	13	1
Valle, Jorge, Vaqueros	.959	25	35	58	4	97	14
Zazueta, Juan, Veracruz	.930	13	13	40	4	57	2

SHORTSTOPS WITH TWO OR MORE TEAMS

Player, Team	Pct.	G	PO	A	E	TC	DP
Espinoza, Efren, Mexico	.000	1	0	0	0	0	0
Espinoza, Efren, Vaqueros	.909	12	20	40	6	66	8

OUTFIELDERS

Player, Team	Pct.	G	PO	A	E	TC	DP
Acuna, Jose, Cancun	1.000	11	17	0	0	17	0
Aguilera, Antonio, Cordoba	1.000	3	1	0	0	1	0
Alcantara, Izzy, Vaqueros	.990	59	92	7	1	100	1
Almonte, Wady, Cordoba	.980	48	93	6	2	101	0
Alvarez, Hector, Oaxaca	.964	55	76	4	3	83	0
Amezcua, Adan, Monterrey	1.000	2	2	1	0	3	0
Arano, Eloy, Vaqueros-Cordoba	1.000	28	55	1	0	56	0
Arano, Wilfrido, Dos Laredos	.982	29	52	2	1	55	1
Arauz, Escarcega, Monclova	1.000	5	3	1	0	4	0
Arauz, Leobardo, Monc.-Yuc.	.969	64	118	6	4	128	1
Arredondo, Alan, Yucatan	1.000	15	29	0	0	29	0
Arredondo, Eduardo, Tabasco *	.964	75	103	5	4	112	0
Arredondo, Hernando, Cor.-Tab.	.959	64	110	6	5	121	0
Arredondo, Luis, Yucatan *	.963	103	174	7	7	188	0
Avila, Carlos, Tigres-Puebla *	.889	18	8	0	1	9	0
Avila, Ignacio, Cordoba	1.000	3	1	0	0	1	0
Avila, Rolo, Tabasco	1.000	4	5	0	0	5	0
Barajas, Edison, Cordoba *	1.000	18	25	1	0	26	0
Bass, Jayson, Saltillo *	.917	102	149	6	14	169	0
Beltran, Juan, Campeche	1.000	9	11	0	0	11	0
Bernal, Cosme, Monclova	1.000	37	61	2	0	63	1
Berroa, Geronimo, Monterrey	.964	22	25	2	1	28	0
Bojorquez, Victor, Mexico	.985	105	191	6	3	200	0
Brinkley, Darryl, Yucatan	.982	98	210	8	4	222	4
Buelna, Lorenzo, Puebla	.970	102	185	10	6	201	0

Player, Team	Pct.	G	PO	A	E	TC	DP
Bullett, Scott, Reynosa-Mont.*	.970	97	190	6	6	202	3
Canales, Joel, Reynosa	1.000	2	3	0	0	3	0
Canizalez, Juan, Campeche	1.000	3	3	0	0	3	0
Carpenter, Bubba, Monclova *	.980	25	43	5	1	49	1
Carrillo, Matias, Tigres *	.985	72	124	5	2	131	0
Chan, Armando, Monclova *	1.000	3	1	0	0	1	0
Clemente, Edgard, Cancun	.984	26	60	2	1	63	0
Coleman, Michael, Reynosa	1.000	20	38	3	0	41	1
Connell, Lino, Oaxaca-Reynosa	1.000	5	4	0	0	4	0
Contreras, Albino, Puebla	.979	68	87	5	2	94	0
Contreras, Sergio, Tigres *	.966	38	56	1	2	59	0
Cookson, Brent, Oaxaca	.935	31	41	2	3	46	1
Correa, Miguel, Tabasco	.961	48	98	1	4	103	1
Cruz, Fausto, Yucatan	1.000	2	1	0	0	1	0
Davis, Jay, Cordoba-Monterrey *	.961	96	189	7	8	204	0
De La Torre, Francisco, Vaq.	.981	65	96	8	2	106	1
Diaz, Alex, Oaxaca	.923	10	23	1	2	26	0
Diaz, Luis, Puebla *	1.000	18	23	1	0	24	0
Espino, Daniel, Tabasco	.976	35	37	3	1	41	1
Espino, Omar, Cancun	1.000	11	5	0	0	5	0
Espinosa, Ramon, Yuc.-D.L.	.966	80	218	6	8	232	2
Espinoza, Jose, Dos Laredos	.982	64	101	7	2	110	2
Estrella, Isaac, Dos Laredos	1.000	29	16	0	0	16	0
Fentanes, Oscar, Veracruz	.966	88	156	14	6	176	1
Fernandez, Dan, Mexico *	.986	66	136	1	2	139	0
Fornes, Daniel, Monterrey *	.984	32	56	7	1	64	0
Franco, Iker, Tigres	1.000	1	2	0	0	2	0
Garcia, Amaury, Campeche	.973	101	165	14	5	184	6
Garcia, Cornelio, Oax.-Vaq.*	.970	49	64	1	2	67	0
Garcia, Hector, Tabasco	.979	89	181	10	4	195	1
Garcia, Luis, Tigres	.970	103	216	7	7	230	0
Garcia, Omar, Vera.-D.L.	1.000	3	1	0	0	1	0
Gastelum, Sergio, Tigres	.959	26	45	2	2	49	0
Gonzalez, Israel, Campeche	.943	26	31	2	2	35	0
GONZALEZ, ROMAN, Cordoba	1.000	89	187	8	0	195	0
Gonzalez, Santiago, Veracruz	.955	48	40	2	2	44	0
Grijak, Kevin, Veracruz	.931	57	90	5	7	102	2
Hernandez, Vladimir, Cancun	.935	17	40	3	3	46	1
Herrera, Jose, Yucatan *	.993	66	141	8	1	150	0
Hubbard, Trenidad, Oaxaca	.975	12	37	2	1	40	1
Ibarra, Juvenal, Vaqueros	1.000	14	19	1	0	20	0
Iturbe, Pedro, Puebla *	1.000	70	95	2	0	97	0
Jones, Chris, Cordoba	1.000	3	8	0	0	8	0
Jose, Felix, Mexico	1.000	35	54	5	0	59	1
Kelly, Roberto, Mexico	.982	78	106	3	2	111	0
Lara, Idelfonso, Vaqueros	.968	49	59	2	2	63	0
Laurean, Julian, Monclova	1.000	1	1	0	0	1	0
LeBron, Juan, Cam.-Oaxaca	.954	78	118	6	6	130	1
Leach, Jalal, Saltillo *	.947	8	18	0	1	19	0
Leyritz, Jim, Oaxaca	1.000	4	10	0	0	10	0
Leyva, Octavio, Tabasco	.000	1	0	0	0	0	0
Lofton, James, Reynosa	.979	77	184	5	4	193	0
Lopez, Fausto, Mexico	1.000	1	2	0	0	2	0
Lopez, Gonzalo, Monclova	1.000	1	2	0	0	2	0
Lopez, Raul, Monclova	1.000	8	7	2	0	9	0
Lucca, Lou, Vaqueros	.000	1	0	0	0	0	0
Martinez, Abel, Cancun	.963	12	24	2	1	27	1
Martinez, Enrique, Reynosa	.980	76	192	3	4	199	0
Martinez, Gabby, Vaqueros	.909	10	26	4	3	33	1
Martinez, Gil, Monclova	.938	10	15	0	1	16	0
Mata, Noe, Veracruz	1.000	57	76	4	0	80	1
Medina, Eric, Monterrey	1.000	2	1	0	0	1	0
Medina, Jose, Reynosa	1.000	36	53	5	0	58	2
Mejia, Roberto, Oaxaca	1.000	4	5	0	0	5	0
Melo, Juan, Cordoba	1.000	1	2	0	0	2	0
Mendez, Francisco, Mont.-Reyn.*	1.000	10	10	0	0	10	0
Mendez, Roberto, Oaxaca	.972	66	97	7	3	107	1
Mere, Carlos, Veracruz	.000	1	0	0	0	0	0
Meza, Gonzalo, Vaqueros	.991	100	211	2	2	215	0
Montenegro, Jose, Oaxaca	1.000	2	2	0	0	2	0
Mouton, James, Reynosa	1.000	17	31	0	0	31	0
Munoz, Adan, Tigres	1.000	3	5	1	0	6	0
Munoz, Jose, Saltillo *	.970	82	126	4	4	134	0
Newson, Warren, Tab.-Monc.*	.984	34	61	0	1	62	0
Ojeda, Miguel, Mexico	1.000	4	8	0	0	8	0
Orantes, Ramon, Monterrey	1.000	3	1	0	0	1	0
Orrantia, Carlos, Monterrey	1.000	1	1	0	0	1	0
Pacho, Carlos, Yucatan	.667	1	2	0	1	3	0
Paez, Hector, Yucatan	1.000	5	10	0	0	10	0
Paez, Raul, Veracruz *	1.000	1	1	0	0	1	0
Palafox, Sergio, Saltillo	1.000	13	11	0	0	11	0
Paul, Corey, Saltillo-Tabasco *	.994	89	164	2	1	167	0
Payro, Edison, Cordoba *	.971	26	29	4	1	34	1
Pemberton, Rudy, Monclova	.973	97	175	8	5	188	3
Perez, Alfredo, Campeche	1.000	3	1	0	0	1	0
Perez, Rob, Mexico	1.000	17	32	1	0	33	0
Presichi, Cristian, Saltillo	.946	52	67	3	4	74	0
Quintero, Christian, Oaxaca	.948	105	194	5	11	210	0
Quintero, Edgar, Monterrey *	1.000	20	9	1	0	10	1
Radmanovich, Ryan, Monterrey	.989	40	83	5	1	89	0
Ramirez, Jesus, Oaxaca	1.000	16	15	1	0	16	0
Ramirez, Omar, Veracruz	.974	105	212	16	6	234	0
Resendez, Carlos, Monclova	.000	1	0	0	0	0	0
Reyes, Eleazar, Oaxaca	1.000	6	2	0	0	2	0
Rincon, Isaias, Mexico	1.000	46	53	2	0	55	0
Rios, Eduardo, Cancun	.981	56	103	3	2	108	0
Rivera, Jesus, Tabasco	.000	1	0	0	0	0	0
Rodarte, Raul, Mont.-Reynosa	.989	44	82	4	1	87	0
Rodriguez, Boi, Campeche	.988	48	79	6	1	86	0
Rodriguez, Serafin, Tigres	.977	41	41	2	1	44	0
Romero, Flavio, Saltillo	1.000	10	6	1	0	7	0
Romero, Willie, Saltillo-Yucatan	.979	53	133	4	3	140	0
Saenz, Ricardo, Monc.-Saltillo	.968	71	117	5	4	126	0
Salcedo, Eder, Reynosa	.951	18	37	2	2	41	0
Salinas, Trey, Cancun	1.000	2	4	1	0	5	0
Samuels, Scott, Veracruz	1.000	23	47	2	0	49	0
Sanchez, Raul, Cancun	.969	103	266	17	9	292	1
Sanchez, Roque, Yucatan	1.000	1	1	0	0	1	0
Sandoval, Octavio, Tigres	1.000	74	76	6	0	82	0
Santana, Pedro, Cordoba	.965	32	49	6	2	57	0
Santos, Andres, Dos Laredos	1.000	6	5	0	0	5	0
Sauceda, Victor, Cancun	.983	38	55	2	1	58	0
Sherman, Darrell, Puebla *	.989	86	171	3	2	176	1
Smith, Charles, Monterrey	1.000	1	1	0	0	1	0
Smith, Demond, Monterrey	.995	99	188	4	1	193	0
Soriano, Ricardo, Cordoba *	.962	50	97	5	4	106	0
Sotomayor, Gilberto, Monc.*	1.000	61	120	7	0	127	0
Suarez, Luis, Tigres *	.986	50	70	0	1	71	0
Thompson, Ryan, Oaxaca	.957	15	21	1	1	23	0
Timmons, Ozzie, Reynosa	.956	31	63	2	3	68	0
Tress, Irving, Cordoba	1.000	3	5	0	0	5	0
Valdez, Francisco, Veracruz	.750	2	3	0	1	4	0
Valdez, Ramon, Campeche *	.981	93	194	11	4	209	3
Valencia, Abraham, Dos Laredos	.969	63	119	4	4	127	0
Valenzuela, Irving, Monclova	.000	1	0	0	0	0	0
Vazquez, Gregorio, Tabasco	.975	59	111	6	3	120	1
Villalobos, Carlos, Puebla	1.000	22	46	1	0	47	0
Villegas, Fernando, Cancun	.981	85	152	5	3	160	1
White, Derrick, Dos Laredos	.968	106	178	4	6	188	1
Zazueta, Juan, Veracruz	.000	1	0	0	0	0	0

OUTFIELDERS WITH 2 OR MORE TEAMS

Player, Team	Pct.	G	PO	A	E	TC	DP
Arano, Eloy, Vaqueros	1.000	24	49	1	0	50	0
Arano, Eloy, Cordoba	1.000	4	6	0	0	6	0
Arauz, Leobardo, Yucatan	1.000	16	24	3	0	27	0
Arauz, Leobardo, Monclova	.960	48	94	3	4	101	1
Arredondo, Hernando, Cordoba	.959	37	67	3	3	73	0
Arredondo, Hernando, Tabasco	.958	27	43	3	2	48	0
Avila, Carlos, Puebla *	.889	17	8	0	1	9	0
Avila, Carlos, Tigres *	.000	1	0	0	0	0	0
Bullett, Scott, Reynosa *	.966	26	56	1	2	59	0
Bullett, Scott, Monterrey *	.972	71	134	5	4	143	3
Connell, Lino, Reynosa	1.000	3	2	0	0	2	0
Connell, Lino, Oaxaca	1.000	2	2	0	0	2	0
Davis, Jay, Cordoba *	.955	36	81	3	4	88	0
Davis, Jay, Monterrey *	.966	60	108	4	4	116	0
Espinosa, Ramon, Yucatan	.000	1	0	0	0	0	0
Espinosa, Ramon, Dos Laredos	.966	79	218	6	8	232	2
Garcia, Cornelio, Vaqueros *	.985	47	64	1	1	66	0
Garcia, Cornelio, Oaxaca *	.000	2	0	0	1	1	0
Garcia, Omar, Veracruz	.000	2	0	0	0	0	0
Garcia, Omar, Dos Laredos	1.000	1	1	0	0	1	0
LeBron, Juan, Campeche	.936	56	83	5	6	94	1
LeBron, Juan, Oaxaca	1.000	22	35	1	0	36	0
Mendez, Francisco, Reynosa *	1.000	9	8	0	0	8	0
Mendez, Francisco, Monterrey *	1.000	1	2	0	0	2	0
Newson, Warren, Monclova *	.982	30	56	0	1	57	0
Newson, Warren, Tabasco *	1.000	4	5	0	0	5	0
Paul, Corey, Saltillo *	.990	61	100	2	1	103	0
Paul, Corey, Tabasco *	1.000	28	64	0	0	64	0
Rodarte, Raul, Monterrey	1.000	6	11	0	0	11	0
Rodarte, Raul, Reynosa	.987	38	71	4	1	76	0
Romero, Willie, Yucatan	1.000	27	79	3	0	82	0
Romero, Willie, Saltillo	.948	26	54	1	3	58	0
Saenz, Ricardo, Saltillo	.946	23	33	2	2	37	0
Saenz, Ricardo, Monclova	.978	48	84	3	2	89	0

CATCHERS

Player, Team	Pct.	G	PO	A	E	TC	DP	PB
Aguilera, Armando, Vera.-Cam..	.966	46	186	15	7	208	1	4
Amezcua, Adan, Monterrey	.989	74	420	43	5	468	9	5
Arana, Carlos, Cancun	1.000	3	6	0	0	6	0	0
Arauz, Escarcega, Monclova	1.000	23	64	7	0	71	0	2
Baez, Carlos, Tabasco	1.000	2	8	0	0	8	0	0
Carrillo, Jesus, Vaqueros	.984	15	54	6	1	61	0	0
Castaneda, Rafael, Reynosa	1.000	1	1	1	0	2	0	0
CASTILLO, ALBERTO, Mx.-Vaq.	.996	83	448	50	2	500	5	3
Cazarin, Manuel, Cam.-Vera.	.989	91	381	60	5	446	2	10
Cobos, Rogelio, Mexico	1.000	12	26	2	0	28	1	1
Cordova, Alfredo, Yucatan	1.000	1	1	1	0	2	0	0
Cruz, Marco, Campeche	1.000	39	167	15	0	182	1	4
Espinoza, Ramon, Vaqueros	1.000	24	81	6	0	87	1	1
Esqueda, Jhonatan, Veracruz	.913	11	18	3	2	23	2	2
Estrada, Hector, Vaq.-Cordoba..	.987	35	134	23	2	159	1	3
Franco, Iker, Tigres	.975	85	317	36	9	362	2	2
Garza, Gerardo, Vaqueros	.909	2	8	2	1	11	0	0
Garzon, Eliseo, Saltillo	.991	28	99	6	1	106	1	4
Gastelum, Gato, Tigres	1.000	51	130	13	0	143	0	2
Gavia, Jesus, Cancun	1.000	28	112	9	0	121	1	2
Gonzalez, Fernando, Reynosa	.968	27	116	4	4	124	1	1
Grijak, Kevin, Veracruz	1.000	1	2	1	0	3	0	0
Gutierrez, Said, Yucatan	.968	56	245	24	9	278	4	4
Hurtado, Hector, Dos Laredos	.977	100	522	60	14	596	6	16
Lopez, Fabian, Oaxaca	1.000	2	2	0	0	2	0	0
Lugo, Roberto, Mont.-Rey.	.976	72	293	35	8	336	1	2
Martinez, Raul, Tabasco	.944	8	16	1	1	18	0	0
Martinez, Sandy, Campeche	.941	32	147	13	10	170	2	2
Mercedes, Henry, Vaqueros	.986	12	60	9	1	70	0	4
Meza, Alfredo, Monterrey	.982	38	202	15	4	221	1	2
Montenegro, Jose, Oaxaca	.985	37	173	24	3	200	2	3
Morales, Francisco, Cordoba	.960	4	23	1	1	25	0	0
Munoz, Adan, Monc.-Tigres	.985	78	342	49	6	397	5	8
Munoz, Noe, Saltillo	.980	95	545	42	12	599	5	1
Ojeda, Miguel, Mexico	1.000	31	144	14	0	158	0	1
Ortega, Antonio, Campeche	1.000	8	26	2	0	28	0	0
Pacho, Carlos, Yucatan	.991	36	102	8	1	111	1	3
Paez, Hector, Yucatan	.977	53	237	22	6	265	6	6
Pinto, Placido, Cordoba	1.000	10	30	3	0	33	0	4
Quinones, Ruben, Cordoba	.967	68	316	37	12	365	6	9
Resendez, Carlos, Monclova	.990	48	176	15	2	193	0	4
Rivera, Francisco, Vera.-D.L.	.982	37	101	10	2	113	2	1
Robles, Juan, Reyn.-Tabasco	.976	28	76	4	2	82	1	2
Rodriguez, Armando, Puebla	.981	23	95	8	2	105	1	1
Rodriguez, Carlos, Reynosa	.966	30	103	11	4	118	0	4
Rodriguez, Erick, Oaxaca	.986	42	197	20	3	220	4	2
Rodriguez, Leonardo, Mont.	1.000	7	8	1	0	9	0	0
Salinas, Trey, Cancun	.976	90	363	41	10	414	2	9
Sanchez, Roque, Yucatan	1.000	1	3	0	0	3	0	0
Santana, Mario, Tabasco	.993	102	506	72	4	582	2	15
Santos, Andres, Dos Laredos	1.000	2	5	2	0	7	0	0
Soto, Saul, Oaxaca-Mexico	.991	93	493	44	5	542	4	5
Valdez, Emmanuel, Tigres	.972	16	66	3	2	71	0	2
Valdez, Francisco, Vera.-Puebla	.984	58	224	29	4	257	2	1
Vega, Edgar, Puebla	.988	72	381	37	5	423	1	3
Virgen, Constancio, Mexico	.988	24	78	6	1	85	1	4

CATCHERS WITH TWO OR MORE TEAMS

Player, Team	Pct.	G	PO	A	E	TC	DP	PB
Aguilera, Armando, Veracruz	.972	22	97	7	3	107	0	2
Aguilera, Armando, Campeche..	.960	24	89	8	4	101	1	2
Castillo, Alberto, Mexico	.989	17	87	4	1	92	1	0
Castillo, Alberto, Vaqueros	.998	66	361	46	1	408	4	3
Cazarin, Manuel, Veracruz	.987	64	256	44	4	304	1	7
Cazarin, Manuel, Campeche	.993	27	125	16	1	142	1	3
Estrada, Hector, Vaqueros	1.000	4	26	2	0	28	0	0
Estrada, Hector, Cordoba	.985	31	108	21	2	131	1	3
Lugo, Roberto, Reynosa	.976	71	290	35	8	333	1	2
Lugo, Roberto, Monterrey	1.000	1	3	0	0	3	0	0
Munoz, Adan, Monclova	.984	70	323	46	6	375	5	8
Munoz, Adan, Tigres	1.000	8	19	3	0	22	0	0
Rivera, Francisco, Veracruz	1.000	1	1	0	0	1	0	0
Rivera, Francisco, Dos Laredos	.982	36	100	10	2	112	2	1
Robles, Juan, Reynosa	.968	7	30	0	1	31	0	1
Robles, Juan, Tabasco	.980	21	46	4	1	51	1	1
Soto, Saul, Mexico	.992	47	244	20	2	266	2	3
Soto, Saul, Oaxaca	.989	46	249	24	3	276	2	2
Valdez, Francisco, Veracruz	.983	25	103	11	2	116	1	0
Valdez, Francisco, Puebla	.986	33	121	18	2	141	1	1

PITCHERS

Player, Team	Pct.	G	PO	A	E	TC	DP
Aceves, Alfredo, Yucatan	1.000	27	2	6	0	8	1
Acosta, Aaron, Tabasco	1.000	11	1	6	0	7	0
Acosta, Jasiel, Monclova *	.700	23	2	12	6	20	1
Agosto, Stevenson, Tab.-Oax.*	.913	16	4	17	2	23	1
Aguilar, Hugo, Monc.-Tigres *	1.000	21	0	4	0	4	0
Aguilar, Mario, Campeche *	1.000	11	0	2	0	2	1
Aguirre, Alejandro, Monclova	1.000	22	4	3	0	7	1
Aguirre, Gaudencio, Monterrey	1.000	50	4	11	0	15	1
Alberro, Jose, Monclova	.875	52	2	5	1	8	0
Almeida, Rowsell, D.L.-Vera.*	.500	8	0	1	1	2	0
Alvarez, Antonio, Cordoba	1.000	33	3	12	0	15	1
Alvarez, Azael, Monc.-Puebla *	1.000	23	7	7	0	14	0
Alvarez, Juan, Vaqueros	.900	16	2	7	1	10	0
Alvarez, Octavio, Mexico	.955	23	10	32	2	44	6
Alvarez, Trevor, Vaqueros	1.000	45	11	13	0	24	2
Amarillas, Asdrubal, Cord.-Vaq.	1.000	35	1	6	0	7	0
Angulo, Victor, Puebla *	1.000	21	0	8	0	8	0
Arellano, Salvador, Yucatan	1.000	17	4	7	0	11	0
Armenta, Alejandro, Tigres *	1.000	14	0	7	0	7	0
ARROYO, LUIS, Monclova *	1.000	24	11	26	0	37	0
Atondo, Sergio, Yucatan	.000	2	0	0	0	0	0
Avalos, Jose, Oaxaca	1.000	41	3	6	0	9	0
Avila, Mauricio, Cancun	.000	2	0	0	0	0	0
Ayala, Ramon, Campeche	1.000	8	1	1	0	2	0
Baez, Sixto, Oaxaca	.900	38	0	9	1	10	1
Banda, Alfredo, Monterrey *	1.000	1	0	1	0	1	1
Barreras, Juan, Vaqueros	.750	34	3	3	2	8	0
Beltran, Alonso, Puebla	.909	16	2	8	1	11	0
Bernal, Manuel, Mexico	1.000	27	4	12	0	16	2
Blancas, Rigoberto, Cordoba *	.750	29	2	7	3	12	0
Bones, Ricky, Saltillo	.000	3	0	0	1	1	0
Bustillos, Oscar, Tigres	1.000	12	1	4	0	5	0
Cabrales, Gabriel, Puebla-Vera.	1.000	27	2	6	0	8	1
Camacho, Daniel, Yucatan	.000	3	0	0	0	0	0
Camara, Pedro, Yucatan *	1.000	32	1	3	0	4	0
Campillo, Jorge, Tigres	.875	21	4	10	2	16	3
Campos, Francisco, Campeche	1.000	12	8	14	0	22	0
Carrasco, Alejandro, Mexico	.900	41	2	7	1	10	0
Carrillo, Guillermo, Dos Laredos	1.000	11	3	1	0	4	1
Carrillo, Jose, Reynosa	.800	10	1	3	1	5	0
Castaneda, Federico, Vaqueros	1.000	26	6	15	0	21	1
Castellanos, Hugo, Dos Laredos	.833	12	2	3	1	6	0
Castillo, Ismael, Campeche	.500	12	0	1	1	2	0
Castillo, Jorge, Mexico *	.000	1	0	0	0	0	0
Castro, Carlos, Saltillo	.000	1	0	0	0	0	0
Castro, Luis, Oaxaca	.000	2	0	0	0	0	0
Cazares, Juan, Campeche *	.000	12	0	0	0	0	0
Cazares, Rosario, Saltillo	.929	31	2	11	1	14	0
Cazares, Tomas, Tabasco *	.000	12	0	0	0	0	0
Cerros, Juan, Monterrey	1.000	51	5	5	0	10	0
Cervantes, Eustorgio, D.L.	1.000	4	1	0	0	1	0
Cervantes, Peter, Vera.-Puebla	1.000	39	6	13	0	19	1
Chapa, Javier, Vaqueros	1.000	2	0	1	0	1	0
Chavarria, Hector, Cord.-Vaq.	.923	19	7	5	1	13	0
Chavez, Alejandro, Mexico *	1.000	18	2	0	0	2	0
Chavez, Carlos, Veracruz	1.000	8	0	3	0	3	0
Colon, Jose, Saltillo	.750	25	1	2	1	4	0
Cordova, Francisco, Puebla	.000	3	0	0	0	0	0
Cordova, Francisco, Mexico	.929	28	2	11	1	14	1
Cortes, David, Dos Laredos	1.000	48	3	5	0	8	0
Cortez, Martin, Cancun *	.000	6	0	0	0	0	0
Couoh, Enrique, Cancun	1.000	4	0	1	0	1	0
Cruz, Javier, Mexico	.000	4	0	0	0	0	0
Cruz, Luis Manuel, Puebla	.833	15	1	4	1	6	0
DeSilva, John, Reynosa	1.000	10	6	6	0	12	1
Delahoya, Javier, Vera.-Cam.	.920	17	6	17	2	25	1
Delfin, Adolpho, Dos Laredos	.895	30	7	10	2	19	1
Delgadillo, Juan, Yucatan	1.000	20	4	11	0	15	0
Diaz, Marco, Saltillo	1.000	18	5	6	0	11	1
Diaz, Ralph, Saltillo	.933	13	5	9	1	15	0
Dingman, Craig, Yuc.-Cancun	1.000	42	1	8	0	9	1
Dominguez, Carlos, Sal.-D.L.*	.941	26	2	14	1	17	0
Dominguez, David, Oaxaca	1.000	39	2	5	0	7	0
Dorame, Randey, Mex.-Vaq.*	1.000	16	0	7	0	7	0
Duarte, Miguel, Saltillo	1.000	33	0	5	0	5	0
Elizalde, Carlos, Oaxaca	.962	22	7	18	1	26	2
Elvira, Abraham, Cordoba-Vaq.*	1.000	40	3	6	0	9	0
Elvira, Narciso, Campeche *	.889	8	1	7	1	9	0
Enriquez, Martin, Reyn.-Cancun	1.000	41	1	6	0	7	0
Espadas, Gary, Yucatan	.600	16	0	3	2	5	1
Esquer, Mercedes, Reynosa *	.960	20	3	21	1	25	1

Player, Team	Pct.	G	PO	A	E	TC	DP
Federico, Gustavo, Sal.-Vera.	.900	28	4	5	1	10	3
Fernandez, Osvaldo, Mexico	1.000	19	4	17	0	21	1
Flores, Ignacio, Yucatan	.833	39	3	7	2	12	0
Flores, Ignacio, Saltillo	1.000	24	4	14	0	18	1
Flores, Jorge, Monclova *	1.000	31	4	7	0	11	0
Flores, Wilfredo, Tabasco	.000	1	0	0	0	0	0
Fregoso, Raul, Veracruz	.000	1	0	0	0	0	0
Galvez, Randy, Oaxaca	1.000	21	3	18	0	21	0
Gandarillas, Gus, Tigres	.964	21	10	17	1	28	2
Garcia, Adolfo, Cam.-Veracruz	1.000	28	4	13	0	17	1
Garcia, Alfredo, Mexico	1.000	22	3	17	0	20	1
Garcia, Carlos, Mexico	1.000	4	1	0	0	1	0
Garcia, Humberto, Reynosa *	1.000	29	2	3	0	5	0
Garcia, Jose, Saltillo *	1.000	53	1	3	0	4	0
Garcia, Mike, Yucatan	1.000	12	0	2	0	2	0
Garcia, Ramon, Mont.-Reynosa	1.000	38	7	3	0	10	0
Garibaldi, Cecilio, Tigres	.929	43	5	8	1	14	0
Garibay, Salvador, Dos Laredos	.929	59	2	11	1	14	0
Garza, Conrado, Tabasco *	1.000	38	2	4	0	6	0
Giron, Isabel, Vaqueros	.939	23	15	16	2	33	1
Gomez, Alejandro, Puebla	1.000	10	2	5	0	7	0
Gomez, Martin, Vaqueros	.917	24	7	15	2	24	0
Gomez, Miguel, Tigres	.000	3	0	0	1	1	0
Gonzalez, Arturo, Monterrey	.000	1	0	0	0	0	0
Gonzalez, Erubiel, Veracruz	.941	49	3	13	1	17	1
Gonzalez, Gilberto, Monterrey *	1.000	9	0	1	0	1	0
Gonzalez, Leonardo, D.L.	1.000	24	7	15	0	22	2
Gonzalez, Miguel, Saltillo	1.000	22	8	0	0	8	0
Gonzalez, Rodolfo, Vaqueros	1.000	4	2	1	0	3	0
Gonzalez, Vinicio, Tabasco	1.000	16	1	1	0	2	0
Grajales, Norberto, Campeche	1.000	24	2	5	0	7	1
Guerra, Pascual, Cordoba	.000	3	0	0	0	0	0
Gutierrez, Jorge, Vaqueros	1.000	28	6	4	0	10	0
Gutierrez, Luis, Dos Laredos	1.000	7	0	1	0	1	0
Guzman, Jesus, Tigres *	.889	27	5	19	3	27	2
Guzman, Ricardo, Monclova	.750	10	0	3	1	4	0
Harikkala, Tim, Oaxaca	1.000	12	5	11	0	16	1
Hasselhoff, Derek, Tigres	1.000	10	0	1	0	1	0
Heredia, Julian, Campeche	.000	8	0	0	0	0	0
Hernandez, Jose, Veracruz *	.900	55	2	7	1	10	0
Hernandez, Martin, Cancun	1.000	11	2	2	0	4	0
Hernandez, Santos, Tigres	1.000	50	2	9	0	11	0
Herrera, Enrique, Tabasco	1.000	45	0	10	0	10	0
Higuera, Marcos, Puebla *	.000	1	0	0	0	0	0
Hoil, Nelson, Campeche *	.000	4	0	0	0	0	0
Huerta, Edgar, Tigres *	.833	31	1	4	1	6	0
Huerta, Luis, Dos Laredos	1.000	21	6	15	0	21	2
Hurtado, Edwin, Can.-Yucatan	.971	26	11	23	1	35	3
Ibarra, Francisco, Tigres	1.000	10	1	0	0	1	1
Jacome, Victor, Veracruz *	.000	2	0	0	0	0	0
Jean, Domingo, Cancun	.857	8	5	7	2	14	1
Jimenez, Isaac, Vaqueros *	.500	4	0	1	1	2	0
Jimenez, Jose, Oaxaca *	.900	46	2	7	1	10	1
Jimenez, Julio, Vaqueros *	.917	48	2	9	1	12	0
Johnson, Aldo, Saltillo	1.000	3	0	1	0	1	0
Jusaino, Luis, Vaqueros	.000	4	0	0	0	0	0
Kamar, Emil, Monclova	.852	23	11	12	4	27	0
Kelley, Rich, Puebla *	.935	35	4	25	2	31	3
Keppen, Jeffrey, Dos Laredos	.909	10	3	7	1	11	1
Lara, Jorge, Cancun	.875	28	0	7	1	8	1
Lara, Mauricio, Monterrey *	1.000	26	1	2	0	3	0
Leon, Cupertino, Oaxaca	1.000	31	3	15	0	18	3
Leon, Juan, Tabasco	.933	25	6	8	1	15	1
Leyva, Edgar, Monterrey	.905	18	6	13	2	21	1
Lira, Felipe, Oaxaca	.972	23	11	24	1	36	1
Loaiza, Sabino, Dos Laredos	1.000	28	1	16	0	17	1
Lomeli, Israel, Oaxaca	1.000	20	7	11	0	18	1
Lontayo, Alejandro, Oaxaca *	.813	6	0	13	3	16	0
Lopez, Emigdio, Cordoba	.974	21	10	27	1	38	2
Lopez, Gilberto, Cordoba	.857	40	3	3	1	7	0
Lopez, Jesus, Vaqueros	.000	2	0	0	0	0	0
Lopez, Jonas, Tabasco	.000	5	0	0	0	0	0
Lopez, Jose, Monterrey	1.000	26	1	3	0	4	0
Lopez, Mariano, Vera.-Vaq.	.667	6	0	2	1	3	0
Lopez, Miguel, Tigres-Puebla	1.000	44	1	4	0	5	1
Lopez, Nain, Cancun *	1.000	27	3	12	0	15	0
Lopez, Rogelio, Cordoba	.000	3	0	0	0	0	0
Loya, Rigoberto, Monterrey	.967	22	11	18	1	30	1
Lugo, Javier, Reynosa *	1.000	3	1	0	0	1	0
Macias, Eduardo, Yucatan	.500	1	0	1	1	2	0
Macias, Luis, Monclova-Puebla	1.000	20	2	3	0	5	1
Madero, Francisco, Mexico	1.000	18	1	5	0	6	0
Magee, Bo, Campeche *	.889	23	11	29	5	45	2
Manrique, Alberto, Monterrey	.950	20	6	13	1	20	2
Manzanillo, Ravelo, Yuc.-Sal.*	.957	17	1	21	1	23	0
Manzano, Adrian, Tigres	1.000	43	3	4	0	7	1
Marquez, Isidro, Campeche	.955	43	7	14	1	22	2
Martinez, Cesar, Campeche *	1.000	15	1	9	0	10	0
Martinez, Javier, Saltillo	1.000	6	0	1	0	1	0
Martinez, Jesus, Cordoba	1.000	11	2	4	0	6	2
Martinez, Juan, Vaqueros	1.000	5	0	1	0	1	0
Martinez, Renan, Puebla *	.929	15	3	10	1	14	0
Medina, Roberto, Puebla *	1.000	12	0	1	0	1	0
Melendez, Nestor, Reynosa *	1.000	37	0	3	0	3	0
Mendoza, Mario, Saltillo	.875	17	2	5	1	8	0
Mendoza, Omar, Puebla	.000	3	0	0	0	0	0
Mercedes, Jose, Saltillo	.973	22	8	28	1	37	1
Meza, Jose Luis, Dos Laredos *	.800	32	0	4	1	5	1
Montane, Ivan, Cordoba	.000	3	0	0	0	0	0
Montemayor, Humberto, Mont.	1.000	24	4	13	0	17	2
Montoya, Saul, Reynosa	1.000	7	2	5	0	7	0
Mora, Eleazar, Veracruz *	.950	20	8	30	2	40	1
Mora, Sergio, Monterrey	1.000	32	1	5	0	6	0
Morales, Alfiero, Yucatan	.000	3	0	0	0	0	0
Morales, Fernando, Campeche	1.000	6	0	2	0	2	0
Morales, Luis, Saltillo *	1.000	10	1	4	0	5	0
Moreno, Angel, Veracruz *	1.000	21	5	27	0	32	2
Moreno, Claudio, Mexico	.917	45	6	5	1	12	0
Moreno, Edgar, Veracruz	1.000	27	3	3	0	6	0
Moreno, Leo, Veracruz *	1.000	12	2	11	0	13	2
Mota, Danny, Campeche	1.000	14	1	5	0	6	0
Munoz, Leonardo, Monterrey *	1.000	48	3	8	0	11	0
Munoz, Miguel, Veracruz	1.000	5	0	1	0	1	0
Murguia, Edgar, Saltillo	.000	4	0	0	0	0	0
Murillo, Meza, Monclova	.857	37	0	6	1	7	0
Navarro, Hector, Veracruz	.889	30	3	13	2	18	1
Navarro, Jaime, Oaxaca	1.000	5	1	4	0	5	0
Navarro, Joel, Oaxaca	.842	25	4	12	3	19	1
Navarro, Jose, Tigres-Puebla	1.000	28	6	10	0	16	1
Neri, Braulio, Cor.-Vaqueros *	1.000	46	3	11	0	14	0
Neri, Eduardo, Oaxaca *	.778	54	4	3	2	9	0
Nieblas, Mauro, Monterrey *	1.000	34	2	5	0	7	0
Nieblas, Omar, Tab.-Veracruz *	.917	27	3	8	1	12	0
Nina, Elvin, Cordoba	.500	5	1	1	2	4	0
Nunez, Javier, Cordoba	.900	18	0	9	1	10	2
Nunez, Jose, Tabasco-Puebla	1.000	19	2	7	0	9	0
Nunez, Jose, Dos Laredos	.960	21	9	15	1	25	1
Ochoa, Pablo, Monterrey	.900	11	5	4	1	10	0
Olague, Jesus, Tigres	.818	16	3	6	2	11	0
Orea, Flavio, Cordoba	1.000	22	2	2	0	4	1
Ortega, Pablo, Puebla	.971	23	8	26	1	35	1
Ortega, Roberto, Puebla *	.000	1	0	0	0	0	0
Ortega, Wilbert, Yucatan *	1.000	12	0	2	0	2	0
Osuna, Adrian, Mexico-Vaqueros	1.000	12	0	1	0	1	0
Osuna, Ricardo, Yuc.-Tabasco	1.000	18	4	13	0	17	3
Osuna, Ulises, Monterrey	.000	3	0	0	0	0	0
Pablos, Rene, Saltillo *	.000	2	0	0	0	0	0
Pacheco, Alexander, Puebla	1.000	21	2	0	0	2	0
Palacios, Joaquin, Veracruz	.000	1	0	0	0	0	0
Palacios, Vicente, Dos Laredos	1.000	12	1	0	0	1	1
Palafox, Juan, Yucatan	1.000	18	5	12	0	17	0
Paniagua, Jose, Veracruz	1.000	6	1	1	0	2	0
Parra, Jose, Cordoba	1.000	29	3	2	0	5	0
Parra, Julio, Dos Laredos	1.000	43	5	4	0	9	0
Patrick, Bronswell, Mexico	.976	23	12	28	1	41	2
Pena, Joel, Tabasco	1.000	43	3	5	0	8	0
Pena, Juan, Vaqueros *	1.000	5	1	0	0	1	0
Perez, Edgar, Vaqueros	1.000	22	1	8	0	9	0
Perez, Guadalupe, Veracruz	1.000	30	0	8	0	8	0
Perez, Leonardo, Cordoba	.923	16	4	8	1	13	0
Perez, Sergio, Reynosa	.000	3	0	0	0	0	0
Pesqueira, Omar, Can.-Yucatan	.950	19	5	14	1	20	2
Pichardo, Hipolito, Saltillo	1.000	24	0	3	0	3	0
Pimentel, Roberto, Cancun *	1.000	38	3	7	0	10	1
Pina, Rafael, Veracruz	.955	15	9	12	1	22	0
Preston, George, Reynosa	.667	6	1	3	2	6	1
Pulido, Raymundo, Campeche	.857	13	4	2	1	7	0
Quinones, Enrique, Reynosa	.952	21	6	14	1	21	1
Quintanilla, Enrique, D.L.-Saltillo	1.000	34	5	9	0	14	0
Quiroz, Aaron, Saltillo	1.000	22	2	11	0	13	0
Ramirez, Adrian, Monclova *	.909	31	0	10	1	11	1
Ramirez, Jose, Monclova	1.000	5	2	2	0	4	0
Ramirez, Roberto, Mexico *	.875	6	1	6	1	8	0
Ramirez, Silvio, Campeche *	1.000	9	0	1	0	1	0

Player, Team	Pct.	G	PO	A	E	TC	DP
Ramon, Jose, Tabasco	.000	2	0	0	0	0	0
Renovato, Nestor, Reynosa	1.000	19	1	10	0	11	0
Reyes, Nate, Saltillo *	1.000	24	1	14	0	15	0
Reynoso, Jose, Vaq.-Cordoba	1.000	23	8	16	0	24	2
Rios, Alejandro, Puebla	.667	27	1	3	2	6	0
Rios, Jesus, Tabasco	1.000	23	5	8	0	13	0
Rivera, Francisco, Cor.-Vaqueros	1.000	33	5	19	0	24	4
Rivera, Lino, Monclova-Tigres	1.000	16	5	5	0	10	2
Rivera, Oscar, Yucatan *	.000	24	0	0	0	0	0
Rivera, Oscar, Campeche	1.000	14	6	16	0	22	0
Rivera, Paul, Campeche *	1.000	11	0	2	0	2	0
Rodriguez, Enoc, Cancun *	.789	15	2	13	4	19	1
Rodriguez, Jesus, Monclova	.000	3	0	0	0	0	0
Rodriguez, Manuel, Campeche	.917	33	5	6	1	12	0
Rodriguez, Salvador, Yucatan	.963	19	5	21	1	27	1
Rojas, Mel, Monclova	1.000	27	1	6	0	7	0
Romano, Mike, Tabasco	.950	38	6	13	1	20	2
Romero, Alejandro, Monclova	1.000	13	3	7	0	10	0
Roque, Rafael, Tigres *	1.000	20	4	14	0	18	2
Rubio, Miguel, Monterrey	1.000	44	3	7	0	10	0
Ruelas, Heriberto, Mexico *	1.000	38	1	3	0	4	0
Ruiz, Arturo, Dos Laredos *	1.000	9	1	0	0	1	0
Ruiz, Cecilio, Tabasco *	.889	47	2	6	1	9	0
Saldana, Jose, Puebla-Veracruz	.900	14	5	4	1	10	1
Salgado, Eduardo, Vera.-Puebla	1.000	47	4	12	0	16	0
Sanchez, Alejandro, Cancun	1.000	36	1	7	0	8	0
Sanchez, Claudio, Oaxaca	.500	39	0	1	1	2	0
Sanchez, Efrain, Campeche	.963	23	10	16	1	27	0
Sandoval, Guillermo, Tabasco	.000	5	0	0	0	0	0
Sangeado, Juan, Cancun	.889	30	2	6	1	9	0
Serafini, Dan, Monterrey *	.875	16	1	13	2	16	1
Sierra, Abel, Cancun	1.000	17	0	4	0	4	0
Silva, Doug, Veracruz	1.000	4	1	1	0	2	0
Silva, Walter, Mont.-Reynosa	.933	35	3	11	1	15	2
Sinohui, David, Sal.-Tab.-Cor.-Mx	1.000	50	2	2	0	4	1
Sinohui, David, Mexico	.000	13	0	0	0	0	0
Solis, Jesus, Dos Laredos	1.000	16	0	3	0	3	0
Solis, Tomas, Tigres-Puebla *	1.000	30	1	6	0	7	0
Soto, Cruz, Reynosa	1.000	30	5	9	0	14	0
Strong, Joe, Reynosa	1.000	46	3	9	0	12	0
Tatis, Ramon, Dos Laredos *	1.000	1	0	1	0	1	0
Tejeda, Felix, Campeche *	1.000	25	0	6	0	6	1
Terrazas, J.C., Cancun *	.750	20	1	2	1	4	0
Trujillo, Jorge, Veracruz	.667	7	1	1	1	3	0
Valdez, Armando, Puebla	.917	14	1	10	1	12	0
Valdez, Efrain, Vaq.-Tabasco *	.923	20	6	18	2	26	1
Valenzuela, Jose, Tigres	.000	7	0	0	0	0	0
Valenzuela, Saul, Cancun	1.000	13	2	6	0	8	1
Valerio, Julio, Monclova *	1.000	54	2	10	0	12	0
Vargas, Joel, Tabasco	.920	20	8	15	2	25	1
Vazquez, Adrian, Cordoba	1.000	17	2	15	0	17	0
Vega, Obed, Cancun	1.000	21	7	17	0	24	3
Verdugo, Hugo, Vaq.-Cordoba	.933	33	6	8	1	15	1
Verdugo, Orlando, Reynosa	.913	29	4	17	2	23	0
Verdugo, Oswaldo, Yucatan	.917	31	3	8	1	12	2
Verdugo, Roberto, Tabasco	.933	42	3	11	1	15	2
Villaluna, Juan, Reynosa *	1.000	20	1	2	0	3	0
Villarreal, Salvador, Reynosa	1.000	12	4	2	0	6	0
Villegas, Jose, Puebla	1.000	14	2	3	0	5	0
Vizcarra, William, Cancun	.000	3	0	0	0	0	0
Wallace, Kent, Tabasco	1.000	7	0	1	0	1	0
Ward, Bryan, Saltillo *	.800	7	1	3	1	5	0
Williams, Slim, Cordoba *	.000	4	0	0	0	0	0
Yepiz, Heriberto Martinez, Cor.	.000	3	0	0	0	0	0
Zambrano, Baudel, Reynosa	1.000	38	3	10	0	13	1
Zavala, Marcos, Tigres *	1.000	31	1	2	0	3	1
navarro, Luis, Yucatan	.900	32	2	7	1	10	0

PITCHERS WITH TWO OR MORE TEAMS

Player, Team	Pct.	G	PO	A	E	TC	DP
Agosto, Stevenson, Tabasco *	.917	9	2	9	1	12	0
Agosto, Stevenson, Oaxaca *	.909	7	2	8	1	11	1
Aguilar, Hugo, Monclova *	1.000	10	0	3	0	3	0
Aguilar, Hugo, Tigres *	1.000	11	0	1	0	1	0
Almeida, Rowsell, D.L.*	1.000	4	0	1	0	1	0
Almeida, Rowsell, Veracruz *	.000	4	0	0	1	1	0
Alvarez, Azael, Monclova *	1.000	13	7	6	0	13	0
Alvarez, Azael, Puebla *	1.000	10	0	1	0	1	0
Amarillas, Asdrubal, Cordoba	1.000	29	0	6	0	6	0
Amarillas, Asdrubal, Vaqueros	1.000	6	1	0	0	1	0
Cabrales, Gabriel, Veracruz	1.000	12	0	1	0	1	0
Cabrales, Gabriel, Puebla	1.000	15	2	5	0	7	1
Cervantes, Peter, Puebla	1.000	27	5	5	0	10	0
Cervantes, Peter, Veracruz	1.000	12	1	8	0	9	1
Chavarria, Hector, Cordoba	.917	16	7	4	1	12	0
Chavarria, Hector, Vaqueros	1.000	3	0	1	0	1	0
Delahoya, Javier, Veracruz	1.000	7	1	6	0	7	0
Delahoya, Javier, Campeche	.889	10	5	11	2	18	1
Dingman, Craig, Cancun	1.000	15	0	2	0	2	0
Dingman, Craig, Yucatan	1.000	27	1	6	0	7	1
Dominguez, Carlos, Saltillo *	1.000	3	0	1	0	1	0
Dominguez, Carlos, D.L.*	.938	23	2	13	1	16	0
Dorame, Randey, Mexico *	1.000	6	0	2	0	2	0
Dorame, Randey, Vaqueros *	1.000	10	0	5	0	5	0
Elvira, Abraham, Cordoba *	1.000	23	1	4	0	5	0
Elvira, Abraham, Vaqueros *	1.000	17	2	2	0	4	0
Enriquez, Martin, Cancun	1.000	28	0	5	0	5	0
Enriquez, Martin, Reynosa	1.000	13	1	1	0	2	0
Federico, Gustavo, Saltillo	.857	17	2	4	1	7	2
Federico, Gustavo, Veracruz	1.000	11	2	1	0	3	1
Garcia, Adolfo, Campeche	1.000	13	0	4	0	4	1
Garcia, Adolfo, Veracruz	1.000	15	4	9	0	13	0
Garcia, Ramon, Reynosa	1.000	29	6	2	0	8	0
Garcia, Ramon, Monterrey	1.000	9	1	1	0	2	0
Hurtado, Edwin, Yucatan	1.000	12	7	12	0	19	2
Hurtado, Edwin, Cancun	.938	14	4	11	1	16	1
Lopez, Mariano, Veracruz	.000	2	0	0	0	0	0
Lopez, Mariano, Vaqueros	.667	4	0	2	1	3	0
Lopez, Miguel, Tigres	.000	1	0	0	0	0	0
Lopez, Miguel, Puebla	1.000	43	1	4	0	5	1
Macias, Luis, Puebla	1.000	13	0	3	0	3	0
Macias, Luis, Monclova	1.000	7	2	0	0	2	1
Manzanillo, Ravelo, Yucatan *	.923	9	1	11	1	13	0
Manzanillo, Ravelo, Saltillo *	1.000	8	0	10	0	10	0
Navarro, Jose, Puebla	1.000	13	6	6	0	12	1
Navarro, Jose, Tigres	1.000	15	0	4	0	4	0
Neri, Braulio, Vaqueros *	1.000	10	0	2	0	2	0
Neri, Braulio, Cordoba *	1.000	36	3	9	0	12	0
Nieblas, Omar, Tabasco *	1.000	6	1	2	0	3	0
Nieblas, Omar, Veracruz *	.889	21	2	6	1	9	0
Nunez, Jose, Puebla	1.000	14	2	6	0	8	0
Nunez, Jose, Tabasco	1.000	5	0	1	0	1	0
Osuna, Adrian, Mexico	.000	8	0	0	0	0	0
Osuna, Adrian, Vaqueros	1.000	4	0	1	0	1	0
Osuna, Ricardo, Yucatan	1.000	8	1	7	0	8	2
Osuna, Ricardo, Tabasco	1.000	10	3	6	0	9	1
Pesqueira, Omar, Yucatan	.667	4	1	1	1	3	0
Pesqueira, Omar, Cancun	1.000	15	4	13	0	17	2
Quintanilla, Enrique, Saltillo	1.000	24	2	4	0	6	0
Quintanilla, Enrique, D.L.	1.000	10	3	5	0	8	0
Reynoso, Jose, Vaqueros	1.000	19	6	13	0	19	2
Reynoso, Jose, Cordoba	1.000	4	2	3	0	5	0
Rivera, Francisco, Cordoba	1.000	9	4	12	0	16	2
Rivera, Francisco, Vaqueros	1.000	24	1	7	0	8	2
Rivera, Lino, Tigres	1.000	14	5	5	0	10	2
Rivera, Lino, Monclova	.000	2	0	0	0	0	0
Saldana, Jose, Veracruz	1.000	1	0	1	0	1	0
Saldana, Jose, Puebla	.889	13	5	3	1	9	1
Salgado, Eduardo, Puebla	1.000	18	1	5	0	6	0
Salgado, Eduardo, Veracruz	1.000	29	3	7	0	10	0
Silva, Walter, Monterrey	1.000	3	0	1	0	1	0
Silva, Walter, Reynosa	.929	32	3	10	1	14	2
Sinohui, David, Saltillo	1.000	7	1	1	0	2	0
Sinohui, David, Cordoba	1.000	12	1	0	0	1	0
Sinohui, David, Tabasco	1.000	18	0	1	0	1	1
Sinohui, David, Mexico	.000	13	0	0	0	0	0
Solis, Tomas, Tigres *	1.000	9	1	2	0	3	0
Solis, Tomas, Puebla *	1.000	21	0	4	0	4	0
Valdez, Efrain, Vaqueros *	1.000	4	1	1	0	2	0
Valdez, Efrain, Tabasco *	.917	16	5	17	2	24	1
Verdugo, Hugo, Cordoba	1.000	9	2	1	0	3	0
Verdugo, Hugo, Vaqueros	.917	24	4	7	1	12	1

The following players appeared only as a designated hitter, pinch-hitter or pinch-runner: E. Jimenez, dh; Au. Martinez, pr; Raven, dh, ph; G. Sanchez, dh, ph; Tellez, dh; R. Vazquez, dh, pr.

LEAGUE CHAMPIONS

Year	Team	Pct.
1955—	Mexico City Tigers*	.539
1956—	Mexico City Reds	.692
1957—	Yucatan	.567
	Mex. C. Reds (2nd)†	.550
1958—	Nuevo Laredo	.625
1959—	Poza Rica	.575
	Mex. C. Reds (3rd)†	.507
1960—	Mexico City Tigers	.538
1961—	Veracruz	.575
1962—	Monterrey	.592
1963—	Puebla	.606
1964—	Mexico City Reds	.586
1965—	Mexico City Tigers	.590
1966—	Mexico City Tigers‡	.614
	Mexico City Reds	.571
1967—	Jalisco	.607
1968—	Mexico City Reds	.586
1969—	Reynosa	.591
1970—	Aguila§	.580
	Mexico City Reds	.607
1971—	Jalisco§	.558
	Saltillo	.593
1972—	Saltillo	.636
	Cordoba§	.541
1973—	Saltillo	.656
	Mexico City Reds∞	.590
1974—	Jalisco	.627
	Mexico City Reds∞	.551
1975—	Tampico∞	.541
	Cordoba	.649
1976—	Mexico City Reds∞	.543
	Union Laguna	.547
1977—	Mexico City Reds	.623
	Nuevo Laredo∞	.507
1978—	Aguascalientes∞	.589
	Union Laguna	.523
1979—	Saltillo	.704
	Puebla∞	.628
1980—	No champion▲	
1981—	Mexico City Reds	.615
	Reynosa	.492
1982—	Ciudad Juarez∞	.570
	Mexico City Tigers	.508
1983—	Campeche◆	.614
	Ciudad Juarez	.535
1984—	Yucatan◆	.560
	Ciudad Juarez	.509
1985—	Mexico City Reds◆	.606
	Nuevo Laredo	.5275
1986—	Puebla◆	.682
	Monclova	.598
1987—	Mexico City Reds◆	.605
	Monterrey	.536
1988—	Mexico City Reds◆	.646
	Nuevo Laredo	.602
1989—	Nuevo Laredo◆	.621
	Yucatan	.539
1990—	Nuevo Laredo	.618
	Leon◆	.565
1991—	Monterrey◆	.683
	Mexico City Reds	.627
1992—	Mexico City Tigers◆	.594
	Nuevo Laredo	.538
1993—	Nuevo Laredo	.589
	Tabasco◆	.528
1994—	Mexico City Red Devils◆	.646
	Monterrey Sultans	.608
1995—	Mexico City Red Devils	.708
	Monterrey Sultans◆	.570
1996—	Monterrey Sultans	.713
	Mexico City Reds◆	.619
1997—	Mexico City Red Devils	.686
	Mexico City Tigers■	.658
1998—	Monterrey	.672
	Oaxaca■	.576
1999—	Mexico City Tigers	.664
	Mexico City Reds■	.632
2000—	Saltillo	.647
	Mexico City Tigers■	.627
2001—	Mexico City Tigers■	.632
	Mexico City Reds	.575
2002—	Mexico City Reds▼	.673
2003—	Mexico▼	.630

*Defeated Nuevo Laredo, two games to none, in playoff for pennant. †Won four-team playoff. ‡Won split-season playoff. §League divided into Northern, Southern divisions; won two-team playoff. ∞League divided into Northern, Southern zones; sub-divided into Eastern, Western divisions, won eight-team playoff. ▲ A players strike on July 1 forced the cancellation of the regular season and playoff schedule. ◆ League divided into Northern, Southern zones; four clubs from each zone qualified for postseason play. Won final series for league championship. ■ League divided into Northern, Central and Southern zones; played split season, with top eight teams qualifying for playoffs. Won final series for league championship. ▼ League divided into Northern and Southern divisions; played split season, with top eight teams qualifying for playoffs. Won final series for league championship.

PACIFIC COAST LEAGUE

LEAGUE OFFICE

President
Branch Rickey

Address
1631 Mesa Ave., Suite A
Colorado Springs, CO 80906-2917

Phone
719-636-3399

TEAMS

ALBUQUERQUE ISOTOPES

General manager
John Traub
Manager
Tracy Woodson
Ballpark (capacity, surface)
Isotopes Park (11,124, grass)
Affiliation
Marlins
Address
1601 Avenida Cesar Chavez SE
Albuquerque, NM 87106
Phone
505-924-2255

COLORADO SPRINGS SKY SOX

General manager/president
Robert Goughan
Manager
Marv Foley
Ballpark (capacity, surface)
Sky Sox Stadium (9,000, grass)
Affiliation
Rockies
Address
4385 Tutt Blvd.
Colorado Springs, CO 80922
Phone
719-597-1449

EDMONTON TRAPPERS

President
Hugh Campbell
Manager
Dave Huppert
Ballpark (capacity, surface)
TELUS Field (9,200; artificial infield, grass outfield)
Affiliation
Expos
Address
10233 96th Ave.
Edmonton, Alberta T5K 0A5
Phone
780-414-4450

FRESNO GRIZZLIES

General manager
Bill Gorman
Manager
Bill Hayes
Ballpark (capacity, surface)
Grizzlies Stadium (12,500, grass)
Affiliation
Giants
Address
700 W. Van Ness Avenue
Fresno, CA 93721
Phone
559-442-1994

IOWA CUBS

General manager
Sam Bernabe
Manager
Mike Quade
Ballpark (capacity, surface)
Sec Taylor Stadium (10,500, grass)
Affiliation
Cubs
Address
350 SW First St.
Des Moines, IA 50309
Phone
515-243-6111

LAS VEGAS 51s

General manager/president
Don Logan
Manager
Terry Kennedy
Ballpark (capacity, surface)
Cashman Field (9,370, grass)
Affiliation
Dodgers
Address
850 Las Vegas Blvd. N
Las Vegas, NV 89101
Phone
702-386-7200

MEMPHIS REDBIRDS

President/general manager
Dave Chase
Manager
Danny Sheaffer
Ballpark (capacity, surface)
AutoZone Park (14,200; grass)
Affiliation
Cardinals
Address
175 Toyota Plaza, Suite 300
Memphis, TN 38103
Phone
901-721-6050

NASHVILLE SOUNDS

General manager
Glenn Yaeger
Manager
Trent Jewett
Ballpark (capacity, surface)
Greer Stadium (11,500, grass)
Affiliation
Pirates
Address
534 Chestnut Street
Nashville, TN 37203
Phone
615-242-4371

NEW ORLEANS ZEPHYRS

Vice president/general manager
Dan Rajkowski
Manager
Chris Maloney
Ballpark (capacity, surface)
Zephyr Field (11,000, grass)
Affiliation
Astros
Address
6000 Airline Dr.
Metairie, LA 70003
Phone
504-734-5155

OKLAHOMA REDHAWKS

President/general manager
Tim O'Toole
Manager
Bobby Jones
Ballpark (capacity, surface)
SBC Bricktown Ballpark (13,066, grass)
Affiliation
Rangers
Address
2 South Mickey Mantle Dr.
Oklahoma City, OK 73104
Phone
405-218-1000

OMAHA ROYALS

Vice president/general manager
Doug Stewart
Manager
Mike Jirschele
Ballpark (capacity, surface)
Omaha's Rosenblatt Stadium (23,000, grass)
Affiliation
Royals
Address
1202 Bert Murphy Ave.
Omaha, NE 68107
Phone
402-734-2550

PORTLAND BEAVERS

President/general manager
Mark Schuster
Manager
Craig Colbert
Ballpark (capacity, surface)
PGE Park (20,000, artificial)
Affiliation
Padres
Address
920 SW Sixth Avenue, Mezzanine Level
Portland Ore. 97204

Phone
503-553-5400

SACRAMENTO RIVER CATS

General Manager
Gary Arthur
Manager
Tony DeFrancesco
Ballpark (capacity, surface)
Raley Field (10,500, grass)
Affiliation
Athletics
Address
400 Ballpark Drive
West Sacramento, CA 95691
Phone
916-376-4700

SALT LAKE STINGERS

Vice president/ general manager
Dorsena Picknell
Manager
Mike Brumley
Ballpark (capacity, surface)
Franklin Covey Field (15,500, grass)
Affiliation
Angels
Address
P.O. Box 4108
Salt Lake City, UT 84110
Phone
801-485-3800

TACOMA RAINIERS

General manager
Dave Lewis
Manager
Dan Rohn
Ballpark (capacity, surface)
Cheney Stadium (10,106, grass)
Affiliation
Mariners
Address
P.O. Box 11087
Tacoma, WA 98411
Phone
253-752-7707

TUCSON SIDEWINDERS

General manager
Rick Parr
Manager
Chip Hale
Ballpark (capacity, surface)
Tucson Electric Park (10,000, grass)
Affiliation
Diamondbacks
Address
P.O. Box 27045
Tucson, AZ 85726
Phone
520-434-1021

2003 FINAL STANDINGS

EASTERN DIVISION

Team	W	L	T	Pct.	GB
Nashville	81	62	-	.566	...
New Orleans	71	73	-	.493	10.5
Oklahoma	70	72	-	.493	10.5
Memphis	64	79	-	.448	17.0

CENTRAL DIVISION

Team	W	L	T	Pct.	GB
Albuquerque	74	70	-	.514	...
Colorado Springs	73	70	-	.510	0.5
Iowa	70	72	-	.493	3.0
Omaha	70	73	-	.490	3.5

NORTHERN DIVISION

Team	W	L	T	Pct.	GB
Edmonton	73	69	-	.514	...
Portland	69	75	-	.479	5.0
Salt Lake	68	75	-	.476	5.5
Tacoma	66	78	-	.458	8.0

SOUTHERN DIVISION

Team	W	L	T	Pct.	GB
Sacramento	92	52	-	.639	...
Las Vegas	76	66	-	.535	15.0
Tucson	73	71	-	.507	19.0
Fresno	55	88	-	.385	36.5

COMPOSITE

Team	SCO	NVL	LVG	EDM	ABQ	CSP	TCN	NO	OKL	IWA	OMA	POR	SLK	TAC	MEM	FRN	W	L	T	Pct.	GB
Sacramento (Athletics)	...	3	9	11	2	2	9	2	4	3	2	9	11	10	4	11	92	52	0	.639	...
Nashville (Pirates)	1	...	2	2	10	9	2	11	10	12	8	2	2	0	9	1	81	62	0	.566	10.5
Las Vegas (Dodgers)	7	1	...	10	0	2	6	1	4	2	1	10	9	11	2	10	76	66	0	.535	15.0
Edmonton (Expos)	5	2	5	...	3	0	6	2	2	1	3	10	10	9	2	13	73	69	0	.514	18.0
Albuquerque (Marlins)	2	6	4	1	...	10	1	8	7	9	7	2	2	4	10	1	74	70	0	.514	18.0
Colo. Springs (Rockies)	2	7	2	4	6	...	3	8	8	8	6	2	4	3	9	1	73	70	0	.510	18.5
Tucson (D'backs)	7	2	10	10	3	1	...	4	2	2	2	5	7	7	1	10	73	71	0	.507	19.0
New Orleans (Astros)	2	5	3	2	8	8	0	...	7	10	8	3	2	4	7	2	71	73	0	.493	21.0
Oklahoma (Rangers)	0	6	0	2	9	8	2	9	...	5	11	1	2	3	8	4	70	72	0	.493	21.0
Iowa (Cubs)	1	4	2	3	7	8	2	6	9	...	10	2	1	2	10	3	70	72	0	.493	21.0
Omaha (Royals)	2	8	3	1	9	9	2	8	5	6	...	0	3	0	10	4	70	73	0	.490	21.5
Portland (Padres)	7	2	6	6	2	2	11	1	3	2	4	...	4	8	2	9	69	75	0	.479	23.0
Salt Lake (Angels)	5	2	7	6	2	0	9	2	2	3	1	12	...	9	2	6	68	75	0	.476	23.5
Tacoma (Mariners)	6	4	5	7	0	1	9	0	1	2	4	8	7	...	3	9	66	78	0	.458	26.0
Memphis (Cardinals)	0	7	2	1	6	7	3	9	8	6	6	2	2	1	...	4	64	79	0	.448	27.5
Fresno (Giants)	5	3	6	3	3	3	6	2	0	1	0	7	9	7	0	...	55	88	0	.385	36.5

Major league affiliations in parentheses.

PLAYOFFS: Sacramento defeated Edmonton, three games to none; Nashville defeated Albuquerque, three games to one; Sacramento defeated Nashville, three games to none, to win league championship.

REGULAR-SEASON ATTENDANCE: Albuquerque, 576,867; Colorado Springs, 253,548; Edmonton, 333,792; Fresno, 522,174; Iowa, 490,150; Las Vegas, 326,243; Memphis, 749,446; Nashville, 387,345; New Orleans, 379,819; Oklahoma, 380,051; Omaha, 304,421; Portland, 438,931; Sacramento, 766,326; Salt Lake, 474,647; Tacoma, 327,927; Tucson, 286,657. Total attendance—6,998,344. Playoffs (10 games)—84,839. Class AAA All-Star Game at Memphis—15,214.

MANAGERS: Albuquerque, Dean Treanor; Colorado Springs, Rick Sofield; Edmonton, Dave Huppert; Fresno, Fred Stanley; Iowa, Mike Quade; Las Vegas, John Shoemaker; Memphis, Tom Spencer (through June 10) and Danny Sheaffer (June 11 through end of season); Nashville, Trent Jewett; New Orleans, Chris Maloney; Oklahoma, Bobby Jones; Omaha, Mike Jirschele; Portland, Rick Sweet; Sacramento, Tony DeFrancesco; Salt Lake, Mike Brumley; Tacoma, Dan Rohn; Tucson, Al Pedrique. Managerial record of team with more than one manager: Memphis, Spencer (23-42) and Sheaffer (41-37).

ALL-STAR TEAM: 1B—Graham Koonce, Sacramento; 2B—Bernie Castro, Portland; 3B—Chad Tracy, Tucson; SS—Bobby Crosby, Sacramento; OF—John Barnes, Nashville; OF—Rene Reyes, Colorado Springs; OF—Termel Sledge, Edmonton; C—Koyie Hill, Las Vegas; DH—Rob Stratton, Albuquerque; RHP—Justin Duchscherer, Sacramento; LHP—Chris Capuano, Tucson; Relief pitcher—Mark Corey, Nashville; Most Valuable Player—Graham Koonce, Sacramento; Rookie of the Year—Bobby Crosby, Sacramento; Pitcher of the Year—Justin Duchscherer, Sacramento; Manager of the Year—Tony DeFrancesco, Sacramento.

2003 BATTING

TEAM

Team	G	TPA	AB	R	H	TB	2B	3B	HR	RBI	SH	SF	HP	BB	IBB	SO	SB	CS	GDP	LOB	ShO	Avg.	OBP	Slg.
Edmonton	142	5413	4799	706	1401	2006	261	31	94	654	51	54	46	463	18	834	62	31	132	1073	7	.292	.356	.418
Colo. Springs	143	5394	4856	707	1396	2118	292	32	122	662	51	44	51	392	25	819	72	65	115	989	7	.287	.344	.436
Las Vegas	142	5429	4873	733	1396	2133	287	57	112	693	66	54	61	375	21	838	107	44	99	975	5	.286	.342	.438
Salt Lake	143	5548	4988	725	1417	2133	274	62	106	685	11	60	45	442	16	869	145	50	96	1050	6	.284	.344	.428
Sacramento	144	5675	4843	859	1360	2139	246	37	153	797	38	66	54	673	14	845	97	30	146	1097	5	.281	.370	.442
Tucson	144	5496	4971	721	1380	2108	276	55	114	676	33	39	59	392	20	978	64	50	103	972	7	.278	.335	.424
Albuquerque	144	5522	4884	721	1351	2058	254	42	123	669	75	43	69	449	25	971	178	79	94	1016	9	.277	.343	.421
Fresno	143	5385	4874	607	1333	1878	201	37	90	552	65	35	59	352	11	776	89	45	115	986	10	.273	.328	.385
Tacoma	144	5372	4809	608	1286	1911	247	21	112	551	45	42	69	406	19	859	176	90	101	976	11	.267	.331	.397
Portland	144	5478	4907	651	1310	1992	250	18	132	624	32	46	59	432	17	852	166	46	103	1030	11	.267	.331	.406
Nashville	143	5300	4756	651	1265	1962	275	37	116	585	54	43	53	392	25	880	186	76	89	921	3	.266	.326	.413
Omaha	143	5612	4913	736	1306	2068	281	26	143	689	45	46	91	514	25	873	76	43	115	1043	3	.266	.343	.421
New Orleans	144	5431	4886	609	1294	1886	260	34	88	566	74	42	54	375	27	890	83	41	90	1015	10	.265	.322	.386
Iowa	142	5345	4743	620	1223	1942	249	25	140	589	49	39	62	444	19	928	78	35	115	992	10	.258	.327	.409
Oklahoma	142	5408	4772	646	1230	1904	244	41	116	607	38	47	48	503	18	852	141	40	102	1017	6	.258	.332	.399
Memphis	143	5310	4765	567	1211	1898	228	39	127	544	54	36	45	409	38	882	95	38	103	976	10	.254	.317	.398

INDIVIDUAL

TOP QUALIFIERS FOR BATTING CHAMPIONSHIP

Minimum 389 plate appearances. *Lefthanded batter. †Switch-hitter.

Player, Team	G	TPA	AB	R	H	TB	2B	3B	HR	RBI	SH	SF	HP	BB	IBB	SO	SB	CS	GDP	Avg.	OBP	Slg.
Dallimore, Brian, Fresno	91	390	330	53	116	148	16	2	4	46	8	5	10	37	0	37	6	4	6	.352	.427	.448
Reyes, Rene, Colo. Springs †	98	398	370	60	127	174	23	3	6	50	1	3	2	22	0	56	12	8	11	.343	.380	.470
Sledge, Terrmel, Edmonton *	131	572	497	95	161	271	26	9	22	92	0	9	5	61	3	93	13	5	10	.324	.397	.545
Tracy, Chad, Tucson *	133	576	522	91	169	238	31	4	10	80	0	9	4	41	3	52	0	2	7	.324	.372	.456
Barnes, John, Nashville	120	439	402	61	130	205	32	2	13	69	0	5	4	28	2	41	15	7	4	.323	.369	.510
Atkins, Garrett, Colo. Springs	118	492	439	80	140	211	30	1	13	67	0	5	3	45	2	52	2	4	9	.319	.382	.481
Hubbard, Trenidad, Iowa	91	402	348	65	111	146	16	2	5	27	0	2	5	47	3	29	24	7	13	.319	.405	.420
Figueroa, Luis, Edmonton †	126	530	480	66	152	192	30	2	2	44	5	6	3	36	1	31	7	7	12	.317	.364	.400
Gall, John, Memphis	123	504	461	62	144	218	24	1	16	73	1	1	2	39	0	56	5	2	13	.312	.368	.473
Castro, Bernabel, Portland †	105	456	425	57	132	165	17	5	2	24	3	2	1	25	0	43	49	13	5	.311	.349	.388
Quinlan, Robb, Salt Lake	95	421	393	55	122	175	18	4	9	68	0	2	1	25	2	59	10	3	9	.310	.352	.445
Ruan, Wilkin, Las Vegas	108	429	403	58	124	136	6	3	0	40	7	2	7	10	0	38	41	7	6	.308	.334	.337
Crosby, Bobby, Sacramento	127	543	465	86	143	253	32	6	22	90	4	4	7	63	2	110	24	4	16	.308	.395	.544
German, Esteban, Sac.	115	544	467	86	143	188	20	8	3	51	13	6	2	56	1	64	32	8	17	.306	.379	.403
Durrington, Trent, Salt Lake	117	521	447	81	136	194	27	5	7	54	0	7	6	61	3	75	35	8	6	.304	.390	.434

DEPARTMENTAL LEADERS: G—Koonce, Pascucci, 138 each; AB—Thurston, 538; R—Sledge, 95; H—Tracy, 169; TB—Sledge, 271; 2B—Barmes, Hiatt, A. Riggs, 35; 3B—Figgins, Terrero, 15; HR—Koonce, 34; RBI—Koonce, 115; SH—R. Castillo, German, 13 each; SF—Koonce, 12; HP—Thurston, 18; BB—Pascucci, 101; IBB—Nunnally, 7; SO—Stratton, 175; SB—Castro, 49; CS—Terrero, 19; GIDP—Bozied, 19; Slg.—J. Davis, .554; OBP—Dallimore, .427.

ALL PLAYERS

*Lefthanded batter. †Switch-hitter.

Player, Team	G	TPA	AB	R	H	TB	2B	3B	HR	RBI	SH	SF	HP	BB	IBB	SO	SB	CS	GDP	Avg.	OBP	Slg.
Abbott, Jeff, Tacoma	4	15	15	1	2	3	1	0	0	0	0	0	0	0	0	2	0	0	1	.133	.133	.200
Abbott, Kurt, Memphis	21	68	62	2	14	19	5	0	0	6	0	2	0	4	0	21	0	0	0	.226	.265	.306
Abbott, Paul, Tucson	11	9	8	0	4	5	1	0	0	0	1	0	0	0	0	3	0	0	0	.500	.500	.625
Abernathy, Brent, Omaha	92	416	368	60	107	150	22	0	7	40	6	4	4	34	3	38	13	7	9	.291	.354	.408
Agamennone, Brandon, Edm.	5	1	1	0	0	0	0	0	0	0	0	0	0	0	0	0	0	0	0	.000	.000	.000
Agbayani, Benny, Omaha	88	359	299	49	71	127	8	0	16	45	0	2	5	53	1	61	0	2	10	.237	.359	.425
Alexander, Chad, Iowa	9	15	13	2	1	1	0	0	0	0	0	0	0	2	0	3	0	0	0	.077	.200	.077
Alexander, Manny, Oklahoma	120	490	450	52	116	157	17	6	4	48	4	2	4	30	1	75	27	10	11	.258	.309	.349
Alfaro, Jason, New Orleans	105	400	361	45	107	162	20	4	9	49	4	2	3	30	1	53	2	3	14	.296	.354	.449
Allen, Chad, Albuquerque	91	370	337	45	109	167	30	2	8	53	5	4	6	18	0	48	11	10	10	.323	.364	.496
Allen, Luke, Colo. Springs *	127	494	438	65	120	165	21	3	6	45	0	5	0	51	4	78	9	12	11	.274	.346	.377
Alvarez, Juan, Albuquerque *	51	4	4	1	0	0	0	0	0	0	0	0	0	0	0	2	0	0	0	.000	.000	.000
Alvarez, Tony, Nashville	106	393	349	50	104	164	27	3	9	53	1	5	9	28	1	69	22	9	8	.298	.361	.470
Alvarez, Victor, Las Vegas *	22	11	8	0	0	0	0	0	0	0	2	0	0	1	0	4	0	0	0	.000	.111	.000
Alvarez, Wilson, Las Vegas *	8	8	6	1	2	2	0	0	0	0	2	0	0	0	0	1	0	0	0	.333	.333	.333
Alviso, Jerome, Co.Spr.-Salt Lk.†	54	170	159	16	45	49	4	0	0	11	2	1	1	7	2	13	3	2	0	.283	.315	.308
Amezaga, Alfredo, Salt Lk.†	75	344	317	55	110	149	20	5	3	45	1	2	4	20	2	39	14	8	3	.347	.391	.470
Anderson, Brady, Portland *	23	88	68	15	20	23	1	1	0	7	0	0	2	18	1	15	5	1	0	.294	.455	.338
Anderson, Jimmy, Fresno *	8	8	5	1	0	0	0	0	0	0	2	0	0	1	0	3	0	0	0	.000	.167	.000
Anderson, Keith, Fresno	4	12	11	2	3	7	1	0	1	3	0	1	0	0	0	3	0	0	0	.273	.250	.636
Ardoin, Danny, Oklahoma	74	265	239	35	58	94	11	2	7	35	1	1	3	21	0	58	0	2	9	.243	.311	.393
Arteaga, Joshua, Iowa	30	88	83	14	22	28	6	0	0	9	0	1	2	2	0	11	0	0	8	.265	.295	.337
Ashby, Chris, Albuquerque	20	75	68	9	23	29	3	0	1	11	0	0	0	7	0	10	3	0	2	.338	.400	.426
Atkins, Garrett, Colo. Springs	118	492	439	80	140	211	30	1	13	67	0	5	3	45	2	52	2	4	9	.319	.382	.481
Aybar, Manny, Fresno	52	1	1	0	0	0	0	0	0	0	0	0	0	0	0	1	0	0	0	.000	.000	.000
Bailey, Jeff, Edmonton	5	21	17	5	7	13	3	0	1	6	0	0	1	3	0	5	0	0	1	.412	.524	.765
Balfe, Ryan, Edmonton †	54	205	183	33	54	85	13	0	6	30	1	2	1	18	1	40	0	0	3	.295	.358	.464
Banks, Willie, Iowa	25	1	0	0	0	0	0	0	0	0	0	0	0	1	0	0	0	0	0	.000	1.000	.000
Barajas, Rod, Tucson	4	17	16	3	7	11	1	0	1	4	0	0	0	1	0	1	0	0	0	.438	.471	.688
Barber, Scott, Tucson	5	7	6	0	0	0	0	0	0	0	1	0	0	0	0	3	0	0	0	.000	.000	.000

Player, Team	G	TPA	AB	R	H	TB	2B	3B	HR	RBI	SH	SF	HP	BB	IBB	SO	SB	CS	GDP	Avg.	OBP	Slg.
Barcelo, Lorenzo, Fresno	20	2	2	0	0	0	0	0	0	0	0	0	0	0	0	2	0	0	0	.000	.000	.000
Barker, Kevin, Albuquerque *	10	31	24	1	4	4	0	0	0	1	0	0	0	7	0	5	0	0	1	.167	.355	.167
Barkett, Andy, Tacoma *	112	450	401	40	97	159	21	1	13	60	2	5	4	38	2	81	4	3	4	.242	.310	.397
Barmes, Clint, Colo. Springs	136	533	493	63	136	194	35	1	7	54	4	5	9	22	2	63	12	7	9	.276	.316	.394
Barnes, John, Nashville	120	439	402	61	130	205	32	2	13	69	0	5	4	28	2	41	15	7	4	.323	.369	.510
Barnes, Larry, Las Vegas *	82	331	302	43	83	154	20	3	15	57	0	4	2	23	3	61	4	1	3	.275	.326	.510
Barrett, Michael, Edmonton	2	6	6	2	2	3	1	0	0	0	0	0	0	0	0	2	1	0	0	.333	.333	.500
Barthol, Blake, Nashville	38	119	102	15	23	34	5	0	2	12	2	2	4	9	2	22	1	1	2	.225	.308	.333
Bartosh, Cliff, Portland *	64	5	4	0	0	0	0	0	0	0	0	0	0	1	0	2	0	0	1	.000	.200	.000
Bausher, Andy, Portland	7	1	1	0	0	0	0	0	0	0	0	0	0	0	0	0	0	0	0	.000	.000	.000
Bautista, Danny, Tucson	8	26	24	4	9	15	1	1	1	4	0	0	0	2	0	2	1	1	2	.375	.423	.625
Bay, Jason, Portland	91	373	307	64	93	166	11	1	20	59	0	6	5	55	1	71	23	4	3	.303	.410	.541
Beck, Rod, Iowa	21	1	1	1	1	1	0	0	0	0	0	0	0	0	0	0	0	0	0	1.000	1.000	1.000
Belitz, Todd, Co. Springs-Alb.*	16	1	1	0	1	1	0	0	0	0	0	0	0	0	0	0	0	0	0	1.000	1.000	1.000
Bell, Mike, Tucson	117	456	416	60	109	174	26	3	11	70	3	5	6	26	0	59	1	3	12	.262	.311	.418
Bell, Rick, Las Vegas	91	366	343	49	101	155	25	7	5	49	0	3	4	16	1	44	2	2	11	.294	.331	.452
Bellhorn, Mark, Colo. Spr.†	16	66	54	11	21	40	5	1	4	16	0	1	0	11	0	10	2	0	0	.389	.485	.741
Belliard, Ronnie, Colo. Spr.	6	19	19	2	5	6	1	0	0	0	0	0	0	0	0	1	0	0	0	.263	.263	.316
Bellinger, Clay, Fresno	117	412	377	55	101	173	18	3	16	54	4	2	4	25	0	72	2	2	7	.268	.319	.459
Beltran, Francis, Iowa	31	5	5	0	2	2	0	0	0	1	0	0	0	0	0	1	0	0	0	.400	.400	.400
Benard, Marvin, Fresno *	14	52	50	8	11	17	3	0	1	8	0	0	1	1	0	4	2	0	2	.220	.250	.340
Benes, Alan, Iowa	19	37	35	2	7	11	1	0	1	7	1	1	0	0	0	9	0	0	0	.200	.194	.314
Bennett, Jeff, Nashville	9	4	4	1	0	0	0	0	0	0	0	0	0	0	0	0	0	0	0	.000	.000	.000
Berger, Brandon, Omaha	62	270	226	43	61	119	16	3	12	53	0	4	6	31	1	58	6	1	5	.270	.367	.527
Bergeron, Pete, Edmonton *	110	438	388	62	117	153	19	7	1	32	8	4	1	37	0	64	12	3	3	.302	.360	.394
Bergman, Sean, Albuquerque	29	43	35	2	3	3	0	0	0	0	8	0	0	0	0	16	0	0	1	.086	.086	.086
Bevel, Bobby, Colo. Springs *	26	2	1	1	0	0	0	0	0	0	0	0	0	1	0	1	0	0	0	.000	.500	.000
Blank, Matt, Edm.-Fresno *	13	18	17	2	3	4	1	0	0	1	0	0	0	1	0	2	1	0	1	.176	.222	.235
Bochtler, Doug, Albuquerque	23	10	9	0	2	2	0	0	0	1	1	0	0	0	0	2	0	0	1	.222	.222	.222
Bonser, Boof, Fresno	4	7	7	0	3	3	0	0	0	1	0	0	0	0	0	0	0	0	1	.429	.429	.429
Borders, Pat, Tacoma	79	320	293	36	92	157	27	1	12	51	0	3	4	20	3	54	1	2	12	.314	.363	.536
Bowers, Jason, Memphis	117	456	415	42	102	152	15	7	7	34	8	1	8	24	5	69	7	6	8	.246	.299	.366
Bozied, Tagg, Portland	119	495	450	59	123	194	25	2	14	59	0	4	3	38	1	80	1	0	19	.273	.331	.431
Brito, Juan, Omaha	36	130	122	14	29	37	2	0	2	12	4	0	1	3	0	25	0	2	4	.238	.262	.303
Brock, Tarrik, Las Vegas *	15	38	32	2	4	4	0	0	0	0	0	0	0	6	1	10	0	0	0	.125	.263	.125
Brooks, Frank, Nashville *	17	2	2	0	0	0	0	0	0	0	0	0	0	0	0	0	0	0	0	.000	.000	.000
Brown, Dee, Omaha *	12	53	47	6	13	21	2	0	2	9	0	1	1	4	0	9	1	0	2	.277	.340	.447
Brown, Elliot, Fresno	12	9	8	1	1	1	0	0	0	1	1	0	0	0	0	1	0	0	0	.125	.125	.125
Brown, Jason, Edmonton	4	12	10	2	4	4	0	0	0	2	0	1	1	0	0	4	0	0	0	.400	.417	.400
Bruback, Matt, Ia.-Nash.-Port.	26	42	37	1	1	1	0	0	0	0	5	0	0	0	0	22	0	0	0	.027	.027	.027
Bruntlett, Eric, New Orleans	84	370	324	48	84	100	10	0	2	27	3	5	3	35	0	51	9	4	3	.259	.332	.309
Buck, John, New Orleans	78	293	274	32	70	98	18	2	2	39	1	0	4	14	0	53	1	0	11	.255	.301	.358
Buford, Damon, Edmonton	15	27	20	3	3	4	1	0	0	1	1	1	0	5	0	6	1	2	0	.150	.308	.200
Bullinger, Kirk, New Orleans	55	3	3	0	0	0	0	0	0	0	0	0	0	0	0	1	0	0	0	.000	.000	.000
Bump, Nate, Albuquerque	15	28	25	1	6	7	1	0	0	2	3	0	0	0	0	4	0	0	0	.240	.240	.280
Burkhart, Lance, Oklahoma	3	9	7	1	1	1	0	0	0	0	0	0	0	2	0	4	0	0	0	.143	.333	.143
Burkhart, Morgan, Omaha †	104	451	382	54	96	165	18	0	17	57	0	2	17	50	5	67	2	0	5	.251	.361	.432
Butler, Brent, Colo. Springs	54	228	205	37	68	107	19	1	6	27	0	0	4	19	1	20	0	1	7	.332	.399	.522
Bynum, Mike, Portland *	26	35	28	4	7	13	3	0	1	4	5	0	0	2	0	8	0	0	0	.250	.300	.464
Cairo, Miguel, Memphis	3	13	13	2	3	4	1	0	0	0	0	0	0	0	0	3	0	0	0	.231	.231	.308
Camp, Shawn, Nashville	33	1	1	0	0	0	0	0	0	0	0	0	0	0	0	1	0	0	0	.000	.000	.000
Capuano, Chris, Tucson *	23	35	32	1	3	3	0	0	0	0	2	0	0	1	0	13	0	0	0	.094	.121	.094
Carpenter, Chris, Memphis	3	1	1	0	0	0	0	0	0	0	0	0	0	0	0	1	0	0	0	.000	.000	.000
Carvajal, Jhonny, Tucson	43	142	123	12	25	44	7	0	4	13	2	3	3	11	1	29	0	2	3	.203	.279	.358
Casanova, Raul, Colo. Spr.†	60	210	193	25	58	90	20	0	4	36	1	1	1	14	0	21	0	0	9	.301	.349	.466
Castillo, Alberto, Fresno	12	42	34	2	8	9	1	0	0	7	0	0	0	8	0	8	0	0	1	.235	.381	.265
Castillo, Ruben, Tacoma	111	374	337	34	71	85	14	0	0	15	13	0	2	22	0	71	17	10	8	.211	.263	.252
Castro, Bernabel, Portland †	105	456	425	57	132	165	17	5	2	24	3	2	1	25	0	43	49	13	5	.311	.349	.388
Cepicky, Matt, Edmonton *	122	484	442	61	133	185	23	4	7	64	2	5	4	31	0	82	7	2	12	.301	.349	.419
Cervantes, Chris, Tucson *	11	5	3	0	1	1	0	0	0	0	1	0	0	1	0	1	0	0	1	.333	.500	.333
Cesar, Dionys, Edmonton †	21	63	56	8	17	23	6	0	0	11	1	1	1	4	0	11	0	0	1	.304	.355	.411
Chavez, Raul, New Orleans	101	390	355	47	97	145	28	1	6	47	6	5	11	13	1	43	0	2	11	.273	.315	.408
Chavez, Wilton, Iowa	26	36	31	2	5	5	0	0	0	4	5	0	0	0	0	10	0	0	0	.161	.161	.161
Chen, Chin-Feng, Las Vegas	133	539	474	84	133	251	30	5	26	86	0	4	2	59	1	106	6	4	15	.281	.360	.530
Chiavacci, Ron, Edmonton	23	18	17	0	3	4	1	0	0	2	1	0	0	0	0	3	0	0	0	.176	.176	.235
Choi, Hee Seop, Iowa *	18	77	66	12	17	41	4	1	6	16	0	1	1	9	0	19	0	1	2	.258	.351	.621
Christenson, Ryan, Oklahoma	52	227	195	30	61	93	15	1	5	24	2	1	1	28	0	45	11	1	6	.313	.400	.477
Cintron, Alex, Tucson †	26	115	107	21	42	63	11	2	2	21	0	0	0	8	0	6	1	0	0	.393	.435	.589
Cirillo, Jeff, Tacoma	5	21	17	7	6	15	3	0	2	6	0	0	1	3	0	3	0	0	0	.353	.476	.882
Clapinski, Chris, Las Vegas †	96	312	278	43	88	146	18	5	10	59	2	3	4	25	0	44	5	2	5	.317	.377	.525
Clark, Doug, Fresno *	13	23	21	4	5	5	0	0	0	0	0	0	0	2	0	3	0	1	0	.238	.304	.238
Clark, Jermaine, Port.-Okla.*	99	379	331	51	78	128	8	6	10	34	6	2	2	38	1	50	25	4	4	.236	.316	.387
Clements, Jason, Portland †	1	1	1	0	0	0	0	0	0	0	0	0	0	0	0	1	0	0	0	.000	.000	.000
Clontz, Brad, Colo. Springs	57	1	1	0	0	0	0	0	0	0	0	0	0	0	0	0	0	0	0	.000	.000	.000
Coffie, Ivanon, Memphis *	12	38	34	3	7	14	1	0	2	5	0	1	0	3	1	3	0	0	0	.206	.263	.412
Colbrunn, Greg, Tacoma	3	12	11	3	3	6	0	0	1	2	0	0	0	1	0	1	0	0	0	.273	.333	.545
Cole, Eric, New Orleans	32	85	81	4	17	24	4	0	1	6	1	0	0	3	0	13	1	1	0	.210	.238	.296
Colon, Jose, Edmonton	13	1	1	0	0	0	0	0	0	0	0	0	0	0	0	1	0	0	0	.000	.000	.000
Condrey, Clay, Portland	11	13	13	1	3	5	2	0	0	6	0	0	0	0	0	5	0	0	0	.231	.231	.385
Connelly, Steve, Fresno	38	1	1	0	0	0	0	0	0	0	0	0	0	0	0	1	0	0	0	.000	.000	.000
Connors, Greg, Tacoma	32	119	113	14	27	43	4	0	4	13	0	0	1	5	0	28	0	1	3	.239	.277	.381

Player, Team	G	TPA	AB	R	H	TB	2B	3B	HR	RBI	SH	SF	HP	BB	IBB	SO	SB	CS	GDP	Avg.	OBP	Slg.
Cook, Aaron, Colo. Springs	2	2	2	0	0	0	0	0	0	0	0	0	0	0	0	0	0	0	0	.000	.000	.000
Cook, B.R., Memphis	13	1	1	0	0	0	0	0	0	0	0	0	0	0	0	0	0	0	0	.000	.000	.000
Corey, Bryan, Las Vegas	61	9	9	0	3	3	0	0	0	1	0	0	0	0	0	2	0	0	0	.333	.333	.333
Corey, Mark, Nashville	46	2	1	0	0	0	0	0	0	0	0	0	0	1	0	1	0	0	0	.000	.500	.000
Cormier, Lance, Tucson	5	6	6	0	1	1	0	0	0	0	0	0	0	0	0	4	0	0	0	.167	.167	.167
Correia, Kevin, Fresno	3	7	5	0	0	0	0	0	0	0	1	0	0	1	0	1	0	0	0	.000	.167	.000
Cota, Humberto, Nashville	62	222	200	23	41	74	9	0	8	27	0	0	2	20	1	59	2	0	4	.205	.284	.370
Counsell, Craig, Tucson *	5	25	23	8	10	12	2	0	0	2	0	0	0	1	0	3	0	0	0	.435	.458	.522
Cresse, Brad, Tucson	82	330	306	40	70	123	21	1	10	47	0	1	5	18	0	89	0	0	7	.229	.282	.402
Cromer, Tripp, New Orleans	84	268	242	29	61	94	15	3	4	36	4	3	2	17	0	41	0	0	5	.252	.303	.388
Crosby, Bobby, Sacramento	127	543	465	86	143	253	32	6	22	90	4	4	7	63	2	110	24	4	16	.308	.395	.544
Crosby, Bubba, Las Vegas *	76	313	277	57	100	176	24	8	12	57	1	7	3	25	0	47	8	0	6	.361	.410	.635
Cruz, Juan, Iowa	9	16	14	2	4	4	0	0	0	0	2	0	0	0	0	5	0	0	0	.286	.286	.286
Cruz, Nelson, Colo. Springs	4	4	3	1	1	1	0	0	0	0	1	0	0	0	0	1	0	0	0	.333	.333	.333
Cummings, Jeremy, Mem.	13	19	15	1	0	0	0	0	0	0	3	0	0	1	0	8	0	0	0	.000	.063	.000
Cummings, Midre, Iowa *	114	433	385	53	98	181	22	2	19	54	0	4	4	40	3	86	1	3	10	.255	.328	.470
Cunnane, Will, Iowa	12	1	1	0	0	0	0	0	0	0	0	0	0	0	0	1	0	0	0	.000	.000	.000
DaVanon, Jeff, Salt Lake †	16	72	60	11	18	30	4	1	2	14	2	0	1	9	0	9	4	1	1	.300	.400	.500
Dallimore, Brian, Fresno	91	390	330	53	116	148	16	2	4	46	8	5	10	37	0	37	6	4	6	.352	.427	.448
Darensbourg, Vic, Co. Spr.-Edm.*	31	1	1	0	1	1	0	0	0	1	0	0	0	0	0	0	0	0	0	1.000	1.000	1.000
Davis, J.J., Nashville	122	468	426	68	121	236	29	4	26	67	0	3	4	35	4	85	23	6	11	.284	.342	.554
Davis, Kane, Iowa	22	1	1	0	0	0	0	0	0	0	0	0	0	0	0	1	0	0	0	.000	.000	.000
Dawkins, Gookie, L.V.-Omaha	65	251	227	23	48	67	11	1	2	30	4	3	1	16	1	50	5	4	6	.211	.263	.295
De La Rosa, Tomas, Nashville	101	297	263	33	65	91	12	1	4	30	5	1	3	25	1	38	6	2	6	.247	.318	.346
DeHaan, Kory, Portland *	54	203	183	26	37	52	7	1	2	11	0	1	2	17	1	34	8	1	1	.202	.276	.284
DeJesus, David, Omaha *	59	265	215	49	64	101	16	3	5	23	5	2	9	34	2	30	8	4	9	.298	.412	.470
Delgado, Alex, Memphis	8	29	24	2	9	10	1	0	0	5	1	1	1	2	1	5	0	0	0	.375	.429	.417
Delgado, Wilson, Memphis †	26	96	86	11	20	28	2	0	2	12	0	0	0	10	1	15	2	1	2	.233	.313	.326
Devey, Phil, Las Vegas *	3	1	1	0	0	0	0	0	0	0	0	0	0	0	0	0	0	0	0	.000	.000	.000
Devore, Doug, Tucson *	134	511	462	74	135	220	29	7	14	75	1	1	3	44	5	95	5	7	11	.292	.357	.476
Dingman, Craig, Iowa	11	1	1	0	0	0	0	0	0	0	0	0	0	0	0	1	0	0	0	.000	.000	.000
Donaldson, Bo, Salt Lk.-Edm.	12	3	3	0	1	1	0	0	0	0	0	0	0	0	0	1	0	0	0	.333	.333	.333
Donnels, Chris, Alb.*	42	149	127	23	38	66	7	0	7	21	0	1	1	20	1	24	1	1	5	.299	.396	.520
Donnels, Chris, Tucson *	36	80	62	10	20	27	1	0	2	13	0	0	1	17	2	6	0	0	3	.323	.475	.435
Donnels, Chris, Iowa *	31	93	74	11	18	35	5	0	4	8	0	0	2	17	1	11	0	0	3	.243	.398	.473
Doster, Dave, Nashville	122	488	456	68	126	204	32	5	12	57	2	6	3	20	1	55	4	5	10	.276	.307	.447
Downs, Scott, Edmonton *	21	29	24	3	1	1	0	0	0	1	5	0	0	0	0	3	0	0	0	.042	.042	.042
Drew, Tim, Edmonton	29	26	22	4	7	10	3	0	0	2	2	1	0	1	0	6	0	0	1	.318	.333	.455
Duncan, Courtney, Port.-Salt Lk.*	56	2	2	1	1	1	0	0	0	1	0	0	0	0	0	1	0	0	0	.500	.500	.500
Dunwoody, Todd, Memphis *	102	357	334	39	75	135	26	2	10	39	1	4	0	18	5	77	13	4	6	.225	.261	.404
Durrington, Trent, Salt Lake	117	521	447	81	136	194	27	5	7	54	0	7	6	61	3	75	35	8	6	.304	.390	.434
Dye, Jermaine, Sacramento	13	60	49	9	14	22	2	0	2	9	0	0	0	11	1	11	0	0	1	.286	.417	.449
Dzurilla, Mike, Iowa	7	26	22	4	5	11	3	0	1	5	1	0	0	3	0	1	0	0	0	.227	.320	.500
Ebert, Derrin, Iowa-Tucson	21	1	1	0	0	0	0	0	0	0	0	0	0	0	0	1	0	0	0	.000	.000	.000
Edwards, Mike, Sacramento	125	507	436	78	130	203	23	4	14	95	1	4	6	60	0	78	5	2	17	.298	.387	.466
Elarton, Scott, Colo. Springs	20	31	23	2	5	6	1	0	0	1	6	0	0	2	0	6	0	0	0	.217	.280	.261
Ellison, Jason, Fresno	119	515	461	74	136	184	22	4	6	39	6	3	6	39	1	52	21	13	7	.295	.356	.399
Encarnacion, Mar., Edm.-Mem.	22	76	69	9	18	23	2	0	1	6	0	0	0	7	0	16	0	1	4	.261	.329	.333
Erickson, Matt, Alb.*	98	355	298	43	102	138	22	4	2	35	4	0	10	43	2	42	14	9	7	.342	.442	.463
Erstad, Darin, Salt Lake *	7	29	27	6	11	11	0	0	0	4	0	0	0	2	0	1	1	0	0	.407	.448	.407
Espada, Joe, Memphis	8	26	26	3	7	14	0	2	1	1	0	0	0	0	0	5	0	0	0	.269	.269	.538
Esslinger, Cam, Colo. Springs	6	1	1	0	0	0	0	0	0	0	0	0	0	0	0	1	0	0	0	.000	.000	.000
Estrella, Luis, Fresno	51	10	9	1	2	2	0	0	0	1	0	0	1	0	0	0	0	0	0	.222	.300	.222
Evans, Keith, Edmonton-Iowa	22	4	4	0	1	1	0	0	0	0	0	0	0	0	0	1	0	0	0	.250	.250	.250
Evans, Tom, Iowa-Colo. Spr.	11	20	19	2	3	4	1	0	0	1	0	0	0	1	0	2	0	0	1	.158	.200	.211
Everett, Adam, New Orleans	25	111	100	23	25	36	6	1	1	9	3	0	1	7	0	16	3	1	1	.250	.306	.360
Farmer, Tom, Las Vegas	5	10	8	2	1	1	0	0	0	0	1	0	0	1	0	4	0	0	1	.125	.222	.125
Fatheree, Danny, N.Orleans	19	16	15	1	3	4	1	0	0	0	0	0	0	1	0	5	0	0	2	.200	.250	.267
Febles, Carlos, Omaha	9	37	32	7	10	14	4	0	0	6	1	0	1	3	0	6	0	0	0	.313	.389	.438
Fernandez, Alex, Portland *	105	395	379	49	115	172	23	2	10	52	0	2	1	13	0	53	16	6	10	.303	.327	.454
Fernandez, Jared, N.Orleans	26	28	24	0	1	1	0	0	0	0	4	0	0	0	0	13	0	0	0	.042	.042	.042
Ferrari, Anthony, Edmonton *	28	6	6	0	1	1	0	0	0	0	0	0	0	0	0	1	0	0	0	.167	.167	.167
Fesh, Sean, Albuquerque *	6	1	1	0	0	0	0	0	0	0	0	0	0	0	0	0	0	0	0	.000	.000	.000
Figgins, Chone, Salt Lake †	68	321	285	55	89	145	14	15	4	30	2	2	3	29	1	36	16	6	4	.312	.379	.509
Figueroa, Luis, Edmonton †	126	530	480	66	152	192	30	2	2	44	5	6	3	36	1	31	7	7	12	.317	.364	.400
Figueroa, Luis, Tacoma	123	478	423	40	119	146	18	0	3	50	1	6	3	45	2	35	1	5	16	.281	.350	.345
Figueroa, Nelson, Nashville †	23	45	33	5	6	8	2	0	0	2	9	0	0	3	0	4	0	0	0	.182	.250	.242
Flores, Jose, Sacramento	107	445	370	72	101	123	12	2	2	38	5	5	3	62	1	48	16	2	16	.273	.377	.332
Flores, Randy, Colo. Spr.*	28	38	30	3	3	4	1	0	0	2	5	0	1	2	0	8	0	0	2	.100	.182	.133
Fogg, Josh, Nashville	2	2	2	0	0	0	0	0	0	0	0	0	0	0	0	1	0	0	0	.000	.000	.000
Fordham, Tom, Nashville *	13	9	6	1	1	1	0	0	0	1	1	0	0	2	0	3	0	0	0	.167	.375	.167
Freeman, Choo, Colo. Spr.	103	363	327	44	83	121	9	4	7	36	4	2	7	23	1	71	2	8	7	.254	.315	.370
Frese, Nate, Iowa	99	351	309	37	75	111	14	2	6	32	3	0	1	38	1	64	0	0	5	.243	.328	.359
Fuell, Jerrod, Albuquerque	3	1	1	0	0	0	0	0	0	0	0	0	0	0	0	0	0	0	0	.000	.000	.000
Fyhrie, Mike, Omaha-Alb.	20	1	1	0	0	0	0	0	0	0	0	0	0	0	0	1	0	0	0	.000	.000	.000
Gaal, Bryan, Portland	2	1	1	0	0	0	0	0	0	0	0	0	0	0	0	1	0	0	0	.000	.000	.000
Gall, John, Memphis	123	504	461	62	144	218	24	1	16	73	1	1	2	39	0	56	5	2	13	.312	.368	.473
Gallo, Mike, New Orleans *	16	1	1	0	0	0	0	0	0	0	0	0	0	0	0	0	0	0	0	.000	.000	.000
Gandolfo, Rob, Tacoma *	13	44	38	7	7	9	2	0	0	4	4	0	1	1	0	8	1	0	1	.184	.225	.237

Player, Team	G	TPA	AB	R	H	TB	2B	3B	HR	RBI	SH	SF	HP	BB	IBB	SO	SB	CS	GDP	Avg.	OBP	Slg.
Garcia, James, Fresno	8	6	6	0	2	2	0	0	0	0	0	0	0	0	0	2	0	0	0	.333	.333	.333
German, Esteban, Sac.	115	544	467	86	143	188	20	8	3	51	13	6	2	56	1	64	32	8	17	.306	.379	.403
Giese, Dan, Portland	3	1	1	0	0	0	0	0	0	0	0	0	0	0	0	1	0	0	0	.000	.000	.000
Gilbert, Shawn, Nashville	18	44	39	2	6	7	1	0	0	3	0	2	0	3	0	10	0	2	1	.154	.205	.179
Girardi, Joe, Memphis	18	71	65	3	19	20	1	0	0	4	0	0	1	5	0	6	0	0	4	.292	.352	.308
Gissell, Chris, Colo. Springs	40	29	28	2	6	8	2	0	0	0	1	0	0	0	0	7	0	0	1	.214	.214	.286
Glanville, Doug, Oklahoma	9	40	37	4	6	6	0	0	0	3	0	0	1	2	1	3	1	0	1	.162	.225	.162
Gomez, Alexis, Omaha *	121	490	457	49	123	186	23	8	8	58	2	4	1	26	1	92	4	5	12	.269	.307	.407
Gomez, Rich, Portland	80	251	227	33	69	112	8	1	11	44	0	2	4	18	2	36	21	1	3	.304	.363	.493
Gomez, Rudy, Salt Lake	2	4	3	0	0	0	0	0	0	0	0	0	0	1	0	1	0	0	0	.000	.250	.000
Gonzalez, Adrian, Alb.*	39	154	139	17	30	40	5	1	1	18	0	1	0	14	0	25	1	0	6	.216	.286	.288
Gonzalez, Alfredo, L.V.†	2	3	3	1	1	1	0	0	0	0	0	0	0	0	0	0	0	0	0	.333	.333	.333
Gonzalez, Edgar, Tucson	21	32	31	3	6	6	0	0	0	0	1	0	0	0	0	6	0	0	1	.194	.194	.194
Gonzalez, Mike, Nashville	7	2	1	0	0	0	0	0	0	0	0	0	0	1	0	0	0	0	0	.000	.500	.000
Gonzalez, Wiki, Portland	44	175	149	17	42	64	8	1	4	20	1	1	3	21	0	12	1	0	5	.282	.379	.430
Good, Andrew, Tucson	12	20	17	2	4	4	0	0	0	1	0	1	0	2	0	3	0	0	0	.235	.300	.235
Gordon, Brian, Tucson *	124	489	449	58	119	192	20	7	13	70	2	4	1	33	2	93	1	3	6	.265	.314	.428
Gosling, Mike, Tucson *	26	30	22	0	2	2	0	0	0	1	1	1	0	6	0	12	0	0	0	.091	.276	.091
Grabow, John, Nashville *	17	1	1	0	0	0	0	0	0	0	0	0	0	0	0	1	0	0	0	.000	.000	.000
Grabowski, Jason, Sac.*	67	286	250	44	73	117	13	2	9	40	0	5	0	31	0	46	7	2	6	.292	.364	.468
Greene, Khalil, Portland	76	355	319	42	92	141	19	0	10	47	0	5	11	20	1	52	5	4	3	.288	.346	.442
Gregorio, Tom, Salt Lake	54	200	181	26	40	65	10	0	5	24	0	1	4	14	0	44	0	0	1	.221	.290	.359
Grilli, Jason, Albuquerque	13	17	12	4	3	6	0	0	1	2	4	0	0	1	0	2	0	0	0	.250	.308	.500
Grudzielanek, Mark, Iowa	2	11	10	1	5	5	0	0	0	1	0	0	0	1	0	1	0	0	0	.500	.545	.500
Guerrier, Matt, Nashville	20	25	18	2	2	2	0	0	0	0	3	0	0	4	0	8	0	0	1	.111	.273	.111
Guiel, Aaron, Omaha *	52	233	190	38	53	90	9	2	8	30	0	1	9	33	2	43	3	0	3	.279	.408	.474
Guiel, Jeff, Salt Lake *	94	377	325	48	78	137	16	2	13	48	1	1	1	48	1	80	3	1	2	.240	.339	.422
Guillen, Carlos, Tacoma †	4	15	14	2	5	12	1	0	2	4	0	0	1	0	0	1	0	0	2	.357	.400	.857
Gulan, Mike, Nashville	110	449	417	53	122	187	29	3	10	59	0	4	2	26	1	105	6	4	9	.293	.334	.448
Gulin, Lindsay, Las Vegas *	28	30	23	1	2	2	0	0	0	0	2	0	1	4	0	15	0	0	0	.087	.250	.087
Guzman, Edwards, Edm.*	55	223	213	26	75	98	12	1	3	27	0	2	0	8	1	18	5	1	6	.352	.372	.460
Guzman, Freddy, Portland †	2	10	10	1	3	3	0	0	0	0	0	0	0	0	0	1	3	0	0	.300	.300	.300
Haad, Yamid, Portland	80	277	258	24	60	105	13	1	10	34	0	2	2	15	0	55	3	2	1	.233	.278	.407
Hairston, Scott, Tucson	1	1	0	0	0	0	0	0	0	1	0	1	0	0	0	0	0	0	0	.000	.000	.000
Hammock, Rob, Tucson	33	131	116	14	31	47	6	2	2	17	0	4	0	11	0	24	1	0	2	.267	.321	.405
Hammonds, Jeffrey, Fresno	11	39	36	7	12	19	1	0	2	2	0	0	0	3	0	3	1	0	1	.333	.385	.528
Hampton, Matt, Portland	33	4	4	0	0	0	0	0	0	0	0	0	0	0	0	1	0	0	0	.000	.000	.000
Hanrahan, Joel, Las Vegas	5	5	5	1	2	4	2	0	0	1	0	0	0	0	0	1	0	0	0	.400	.400	.800
Hansen, Jed, Mem.-Omaha	103	425	359	54	89	151	25	2	11	45	2	2	5	57	1	88	9	8	5	.248	.357	.421
Haren, Danny, Memphis	8	7	7	0	0	0	0	0	0	1	0	0	0	0	0	1	0	0	0	.000	.000	.000
Harris, Brian, Omaha †	72	287	243	37	63	91	11	4	3	19	6	2	4	32	1	38	2	2	2	.259	.352	.374
Harris, Lenny, Albuquerque *	8	28	24	3	4	5	1	0	0	1	0	0	0	4	2	3	0	0	1	.167	.286	.208
Harrison, Adonis, Salt Lake *	47	204	178	23	52	64	8	2	0	18	0	4	0	22	0	18	1	2	8	.292	.363	.360
Hart, Bo, Memphis	67	284	266	30	79	118	14	2	7	31	0	3	0	15	1	55	4	2	2	.297	.331	.444
Hart, Jason, Oklahoma	137	581	512	65	129	214	22	0	21	82	2	8	5	54	0	106	2	1	12	.252	.325	.418
Haynes, Dee, Memphis	125	464	441	53	111	195	24	3	18	70	0	4	3	15	2	50	3	1	12	.252	.279	.442
Haynes, Nathan, Salt Lake *	28	132	120	16	26	38	3	3	1	7	0	1	2	9	1	20	6	0	2	.217	.280	.317
Hebson, Bryan, Edmonton	30	5	4	1	0	0	0	0	0	0	0	0	1	0	0	2	0	0	0	.000	.200	.000
Herges, Matt, Portland *	4	1	1	0	0	0	0	0	0	0	0	0	0	0	0	1	0	0	0	.000	.000	.000
Hermansen, Chad, Las Vegas	68	257	235	43	83	127	15	1	9	31	0	1	2	19	0	38	4	1	4	.353	.405	.540
Hermanson, Dustin, Fresno	4	8	5	0	1	1	0	0	0	0	1	0	0	2	0	1	1	0	0	.200	.429	.200
Hermida, Jeremy, Alb.*	1	3	3	0	0	0	0	0	0	0	0	0	0	0	0	3	0	0	0	.000	.000	.000
Hernandez, Carlos, Fres.-N.Orl.	90	286	256	23	54	62	5	0	1	16	9	2	2	17	4	50	4	1	7	.211	.264	.242
Hiatt, Phil, Iowa	134	535	478	72	130	242	35	1	25	89	0	8	4	45	4	110	10	2	16	.272	.335	.506
Hill, Bobby, Iowa-Nashville †	109	486	427	58	115	171	25	5	7	44	4	2	8	45	0	73	9	9	7	.269	.349	.400
Hill, Jason, Salt Lake	11	40	34	5	7	15	0	1	2	5	0	1	0	4	0	3	1	0	2	.206	.282	.441
Hill, Koyie, Las Vegas †	85	331	312	48	98	125	18	0	3	36	1	2	1	15	3	39	5	0	7	.314	.345	.401
Hillenbrand, Shea, Tucson	3	10	10	0	3	4	1	0	0	1	0	0	0	0	0	1	0	0	0	.300	.300	.400
Hodges, Scott, Edmonton *	126	520	482	67	139	202	21	3	12	66	0	7	2	29	2	93	5	2	10	.288	.327	.419
Holbert, Aaron, Nashville	116	435	397	57	107	150	20	7	3	37	8	3	8	19	1	78	29	13	5	.270	.314	.378
Holst, Micah, Fresno	7	3	3	2	1	1	0	0	0	0	0	0	0	0	0	1	0	1	0	.333	.333	.333
Holtz, Mike, Nashville *	45	4	4	0	1	1	0	0	0	1	0	0	0	0	0	2	0	0	0	.250	.250	.250
Hooper, Kevin, Albuquerque	130	551	493	77	131	151	9	4	1	54	9	4	10	35	3	62	25	9	5	.266	.325	.306
Hoover, Paul, Albuquerque	81	279	256	35	69	110	22	2	5	40	2	1	2	18	1	62	10	3	7	.270	.321	.430
Horgan, Joe, Fresno *	56	5	5	0	1	1	0	0	0	0	0	0	0	0	0	1	0	0	0	.200	.200	.200
Horner, Jim, Tacoma	2	8	6	0	1	1	0	0	0	0	0	0	0	2	0	1	0	0	0	.167	.375	.167
Houlton, D.J., New Orleans	11	16	15	1	2	2	0	0	0	1	1	0	0	0	0	5	0	0	0	.133	.133	.133
Howard, Ben, Portland	24	40	35	1	6	8	2	0	0	3	5	0	0	0	0	14	0	0	2	.171	.171	.229
Hubbard, Trenidad, Iowa	91	402	348	65	111	146	16	2	5	27	0	2	5	47	3	29	24	7	13	.319	.405	.420
Huffman, Royce, N.Orleans	128	517	460	49	133	163	20	2	2	60	4	5	5	43	4	68	7	3	7	.289	.353	.354
Hunter, Johnny, Portland	11	3	2	0	0	0	0	0	0	0	1	0	0	0	0	1	0	0	0	.000	.000	.000
Hyzdu, Adam, Nashville	40	156	135	22	38	68	10	1	6	18	0	2	1	18	1	28	2	2	2	.281	.365	.504
Iapoce, Anthony, Alb.	52	152	128	16	29	38	7	1	0	12	3	2	3	16	1	21	6	2	2	.227	.322	.297
Izquierdo, Hansel, Edmonton	17	8	7	0	0	0	0	0	0	0	1	0	0	0	0	3	0	0	0	.000	.000	.000
Jackson, Nic, Iowa *	125	505	458	56	116	176	19	4	11	44	3	2	7	35	1	102	17	9	4	.253	.315	.384
Jarvis, Matt, Fresno	23	2	2	1	1	1	0	0	0	0	0	0	0	0	0	1	0	0	0	.500	.500	.500
Jensen, Ryan, Fresno	27	19	16	1	6	7	1	0	0	5	3	0	0	0	0	4	1	0	0	.375	.375	.438
Johnson, Dan, Sacramento *	1	4	4	0	1	2	1	0	0	0	0	0	0	0	0	0	0	0	0	.250	.250	.500
Johnson, Gary, Salt Lake *	121	518	447	65	114	187	23	7	12	74	0	6	4	61	2	112	4	2	5	.255	.346	.418
Johnson, Jonathan, N.Orl.	14	18	16	0	2	2	0	0	0	2	2	0	0	0	0	4	0	1	0	.125	.125	.125
Johnson, Keith, Salt Lake	117	482	451	51	129	199	33	2	11	64	0	7	5	19	1	70	6	6	14	.286	.317	.441

Player, Team	G	TPA	AB	R	H	TB	2B	3B	HR	RBI	SH	SF	HP	BB	IBB	SO	SB	CS	GDP	Avg.	OBP	Slg.
Johnson, Mark, Sac.*	51	204	162	28	37	59	11	1	3	30	1	3	3	35	0	23	0	1	2	.228	.369	.364
Johnson, Mike, Fresno *	30	6	6	0	0	0	0	0	0	0	0	0	0	0	0	3	0	0	0	.000	.000	.000
Johnson, Randy, Tucson	1	1	1	0	0	0	0	0	0	0	0	0	0	0	0	0	0	0	1	.000	.000	.000
Johnson, Rontrez, Oklahoma	70	271	241	35	54	85	10	3	5	20	1	3	7	19	0	29	14	6	1	.224	.296	.353
Jones, Jason, Oklahoma †	100	429	375	52	108	164	29	0	9	55	1	1	2	50	4	80	7	2	8	.288	.374	.437
Jongejan, Ferenc, Iowa *	29	2	1	0	0	0	0	0	0	0	0	0	0	1	0	0	0	0	0	.000	.500	.000
Joseph, Kevin, Mem.-Edm.	29	12	12	2	4	5	1	0	0	0	0	0	0	0	0	3	0	0	0	.333	.333	.417
Journell, Jimmy, Memphis	40	12	8	0	0	0	0	0	0	0	2	0	1	1	0	3	0	0	0	.000	.200	.000
Judd, Mike, Albuquerque	30	13	11	1	1	2	1	0	0	1	1	0	0	1	0	6	0	0	0	.091	.167	.182
Kapler, Gabe, Colo. Springs	13	45	35	5	6	10	2	1	0	2	0	1	1	8	0	10	4	0	0	.171	.333	.286
Karnuth, Jason, Iowa	13	4	3	0	0	0	0	0	0	0	1	0	0	0	0	1	0	0	0	.000	.000	.000
Kata, Matt, Tucson †	48	214	201	31	58	90	13	5	3	25	0	1	3	9	1	29	2	3	1	.289	.327	.448
Kaye, Justin, Iowa	20	3	3	0	0	0	0	0	0	0	0	0	0	0	0	3	0	0	0	.000	.000	.000
Keagle, Greg, Albuquerque	3	1	1	0	0	0	0	0	0	0	0	0	0	0	0	1	0	0	0	.000	.000	.000
Keisler, Randy, Port.-Okla.-N.Orl.*	23	28	26	0	3	4	1	0	0	2	2	0	0	0	0	4	0	0	0	.115	.115	.154
Keller, Kris, Portland	18	2	2	0	1	1	0	0	0	0	0	0	0	0	0	1	0	0	0	.500	.500	.500
Kellner, Ryan, Las Vegas	48	170	153	9	32	43	11	0	0	14	2	3	4	8	0	49	1	0	4	.209	.262	.281
Kelly, Kenny, Tacoma	96	381	341	42	84	148	15	5	13	37	1	4	6	29	1	79	20	7	4	.246	.313	.434
Kelly, Mike, Omaha	100	430	368	63	109	182	29	1	14	65	1	6	5	50	3	80	6	1	9	.296	.382	.495
Kelton, Dave, Iowa	121	495	442	62	119	197	24	3	16	67	1	4	2	46	1	115	8	2	7	.269	.338	.446
Kida, Masao, Las Vegas	22	23	16	0	3	3	0	0	0	0	6	0	0	1	0	5	0	0	1	.188	.235	.188
Kim, Byung-Hyun, Tucson	3	8	6	1	1	1	0	0	0	0	2	0	0	0	0	2	0	0	0	.167	.167	.167
Kim, Sun-Woo, Edmonton	22	37	34	4	9	11	2	0	0	7	2	0	0	1	0	6	0	0	2	.265	.286	.324
King, Brad, Nashville	79	248	197	27	42	56	8	0	2	21	1	3	5	42	5	45	0	3	3	.213	.360	.284
Knorr, Randy, Edmonton	88	350	316	37	96	138	19	1	7	48	1	2	2	29	3	57	1	0	10	.304	.364	.437
Knott, Eric, Edmonton *	24	19	17	1	1	1	0	0	0	2	1	0	0	1	0	7	0	0	2	.059	.111	.059
Knott, Jon, Portland	7	30	26	5	9	13	1	0	1	5	0	0	0	4	0	3	0	0	1	.346	.433	.500
Koonce, Graham, Sac.*	138	602	480	82	133	260	23	1	34	115	0	12	11	98	3	119	0	0	11	.277	.403	.542
Krause, Scott, Memphis	3	10	10	4	4	4	0	0	0	0	0	0	0	0	0	0	0	0	0	.400	.400	.400
Kuzmic, Craig, Tacoma-Fres.†	101	349	303	41	74	121	12	4	9	40	2	2	2	40	2	94	6	4	6	.244	.334	.399
Laird, Gerald, Oklahoma	99	385	338	50	88	145	20	5	9	42	1	2	7	37	4	61	9	3	7	.260	.344	.429
Lamb, Mike, Oklahoma *	73	323	274	45	79	133	19	4	9	46	2	3	2	42	3	45	1	1	4	.288	.383	.485
Landry, Jacques, Tacoma	44	179	153	24	38	70	11	0	7	24	1	2	6	17	1	46	6	2	2	.248	.343	.458
Lane, Jason, New Orleans	71	287	248	37	74	112	17	0	7	39	1	5	3	30	1	26	2	1	6	.298	.374	.452
Langone, Steve, Las Vegas	6	1	1	0	0	0	0	0	0	0	0	0	0	0	0	1	0	0	0	.000	.000	.000
Layfield, Scotty, Memphis	22	2	1	0	0	0	0	0	0	0	1	0	0	0	0	0	0	0	0	.000	.000	.000
Leach, Jalal, Tacoma *	70	277	250	25	73	103	8	2	6	28	4	0	1	22	1	51	5	5	3	.292	.352	.412
Leon, Donny, Iowa †	90	375	350	45	105	177	26	2	14	55	1	6	3	10	0	51	2	1	8	.300	.320	.506
Lesher, Brian, Memphis	10	34	29	4	8	10	2	0	0	2	1	0	0	4	1	5	0	0	1	.276	.364	.345
Levrault, Allen, Albuquerque	21	1	0	0	0	0	0	0	0	0	0	0	0	1	0	0	0	0	0	.000	1.000	.000
Lewis, Richie, Edmonton	7	1	1	0	0	0	0	0	0	0	0	0	0	0	0	0	0	0	1	.000	.000	.000
Lincoln, Mike, Nashville	8	1	1	0	0	0	0	0	0	0	0	0	0	0	0	0	0	0	0	.000	.000	.000
Linden, Todd, Fresno †	125	532	471	75	131	194	24	3	11	56	4	0	17	40	2	105	14	4	9	.278	.356	.412
Linebrink, Scott, New Orleans	2	1	1	0	0	0	0	0	0	0	0	0	0	0	0	1	0	0	0	.000	.000	.000
Liniak, Cole, Oklahoma	62	232	210	26	52	86	12	2	6	29	5	1	1	15	1	32	2	3	4	.248	.300	.410
Little, Mark, Tucson	31	104	95	13	30	58	5	4	5	13	1	0	5	3	0	18	3	1	0	.316	.369	.611
Lockhart, Keith, Portland *	4	13	11	0	2	2	0	0	0	4	0	0	1	1	0	0	0	0	0	.182	.308	.182
Lockwood, Mike, Sac.*	83	293	263	45	80	121	11	3	8	33	7	2	2	19	0	28	1	2	7	.304	.353	.460
Loeb, Bryan, Tucson	5	17	15	1	5	7	2	0	0	0	0	0	0	2	0	5	0	0	0	.333	.412	.467
Loewer, Carlton, Portland †	23	29	24	2	2	2	0	0	0	1	5	0	0	0	0	11	0	0	0	.083	.083	.083
Logan, Kyle, New Orleans *	134	497	460	43	118	162	25	2	5	44	4	6	5	22	4	88	14	8	3	.257	.294	.352
Looney, Brian, Colo. Spr.*	3	5	4	0	0	0	0	0	0	0	1	0	0	0	0	2	0	0	0	.000	.000	.000
Lopez, Luis, Colo. Springs †	47	152	140	14	29	48	10	0	3	18	1	0	2	9	1	29	0	1	2	.207	.265	.343
Lopez, Luis, Sacramento	131	548	498	67	122	204	28	0	18	72	0	6	4	40	1	68	0	1	17	.245	.303	.410
Lopez, Mickey, Tacoma †	129	519	455	68	125	177	23	4	7	41	5	6	6	47	2	50	20	12	12	.275	.346	.389
Lorraine, Andrew, L.V.*	30	35	30	0	4	4	0	0	0	0	5	0	0	0	0	16	0	0	1	.133	.133	.133
Lowry, Noah, Fresno *	4	4	3	0	1	1	0	0	0	0	0	0	0	1	0	1	0	0	0	.333	.500	.333
Ludwick, Ryan, Oklahoma	81	360	317	51	96	177	24	3	17	63	0	5	5	33	3	71	1	1	9	.303	.372	.558
Lunar, Fernando, Omaha	75	271	251	28	53	80	9	0	6	24	5	0	4	11	0	34	0	0	5	.211	.256	.319
Lunsford, Trey, Fresno	69	230	206	20	59	77	10	1	2	20	4	2	1	17	0	33	0	1	4	.286	.341	.374
Mabry, John, Tacoma *	3	13	11	1	4	4	0	0	0	0	0	0	0	2	1	1	0	0	0	.364	.462	.364
Mackowiak, Rob, Nashville *	59	238	217	21	50	69	11	1	2	23	0	3	0	18	0	51	7	3	3	.230	.286	.318
Maduro, Jorge, Tacoma	5	18	18	0	0	0	0	0	0	0	0	0	0	0	0	5	0	0	0	.000	.000	.000
Magee, Wendell, Colo. Spr.	38	140	134	15	44	63	10	0	3	21	0	0	1	5	1	22	1	2	9	.328	.357	.470
Mahomes, Pat, Nashville	43	11	11	3	3	5	2	0	0	3	0	0	0	0	0	4	0	0	1	.273	.273	.455
Mahoney, Mike, Iowa	65	208	190	19	49	69	12	1	2	18	3	2	2	11	1	32	0	1	9	.258	.302	.363
Mairena, Ozwaldo, Alb.*	61	5	3	0	0	0	0	0	0	0	2	0	0	0	0	2	0	0	0	.000	.000	.000
Malloy, Marty, L.V.-Mem.*	92	299	264	31	67	91	14	2	2	21	9	1	3	22	4	39	7	2	8	.254	.317	.345
Mann, Jim, Nashville	51	4	4	0	0	0	0	0	0	1	0	0	0	0	0	2	0	0	0	.000	.000	.000
Manon, Julio, Edmonton *	35	1	1	0	0	0	0	0	0	0	0	0	0	0	0	1	0	0	0	.000	.000	.000
Marrero, Eli, Memphis	5	14	12	2	3	7	1	0	1	1	0	0	1	1	0	0	0	0	1	.250	.357	.583
Marshall, Lee, Tucson	50	3	2	0	0	0	0	0	0	0	0	0	1	0	0	1	0	0	0	.000	.333	.000
Martin, Billy, Tucson	53	201	179	32	62	116	16	1	12	40	0	2	2	18	0	43	0	0	4	.346	.408	.648
Martinez, Sandy, Omaha *	24	83	73	12	18	28	1	0	3	13	0	2	3	5	0	15	0	1	1	.247	.313	.384
Matos, Julius, Omaha	92	402	370	44	107	147	19	0	7	48	8	3	8	13	0	31	10	5	7	.289	.325	.397
Matos, Pascual, Colo. Spr.	10	29	26	5	6	13	1	0	2	5	0	1	0	2	0	11	0	0	0	.231	.276	.500
Matranga, Dave, New Orleans	102	350	315	34	76	109	16	4	3	25	9	1	4	21	3	71	3	3	3	.241	.296	.346
Mattes, Troy, Edmonton	1	3	3	1	2	2	0	0	0	1	0	0	0	0	0	0	0	0	0	.667	.667	.667
McCarty, Dave, Sacramento	91	404	352	69	95	167	23	2	15	72	0	5	3	44	0	71	4	1	12	.270	.351	.474
McDonald, Keith, Iowa	94	326	280	31	67	124	15	0	14	45	2	2	9	30	1	44	0	0	7	.239	.330	.443
McDougall, Marshall, Okla.	30	126	111	11	30	44	4	2	2	9	0	2	0	13	0	21	1	1	2	.270	.341	.396

Player, Team	G	TPA	AB	R	H	TB	2B	3B	HR	RBI	SH	SF	HP	BB	IBB	SO	SB	CS	GDP	Avg.	OBP	Slg.
McKnight, Tony, Las Vegas *	4	4	1	1	0	0	0	0	0	0	1	0	1	1	0	0	0	0	0	.000	.667	.000
McLeary, Marty, Albuquerque	20	2	2	0	0	0	0	0	0	0	0	0	0	0	0	1	0	0	0	.000	.000	.000
McMillon, Billy, Sac.*	38	172	153	31	51	85	10	0	8	35	0	1	1	17	0	30	1	1	3	.333	.401	.556
Meadows, Brian, Nashville	9	10	9	0	2	2	0	0	0	0	1	0	0	0	0	2	0	0	0	.222	.222	.222
Medrano, Anthony, Edm.	125	495	425	63	104	134	18	3	2	46	8	3	9	50	3	49	5	4	12	.245	.335	.315
Medrano, Jesus, Alb.	31	129	114	22	26	34	3	1	1	12	0	1	0	14	0	26	7	2	2	.228	.310	.298
Melhuse, Adam, Sac.†	45	175	147	26	42	60	9	0	3	17	0	1	1	26	0	32	0	1	5	.286	.394	.408
Meliah, Dave, Oklahoma *	56	198	185	22	46	68	7	0	5	19	1	1	1	10	0	42	0	0	1	.249	.289	.368
Melian, Jackson, Iowa	43	137	129	7	23	36	4	0	3	9	0	0	0	8	0	27	4	0	2	.178	.226	.279
Meluskey, Mitch, Sac.†	4	16	14	0	2	4	2	0	0	4	0	1	0	1	0	3	0	0	0	.143	.188	.286
Mench, Kevin, Oklahoma	29	131	105	16	28	48	8	0	4	21	0	6	1	19	0	15	2	0	1	.267	.366	.457
Mendez, Donaldo, Portland	102	394	358	49	81	116	17	0	6	36	1	3	7	25	1	83	10	7	7	.226	.288	.324
Mendoza, Carlos, Fresno †	9	26	24	3	6	8	2	0	0	0	2	0	0	0	0	4	0	0	1	.250	.250	.333
Meyers, Chad, Tacoma	97	420	377	50	113	151	20	3	4	34	4	1	7	30	0	46	37	12	7	.300	.361	.401
Meyers, Mike, Iowa	30	13	12	0	2	2	0	0	0	0	0	0	0	1	0	5	0	0	0	.167	.231	.167
Michalak, Chris, Colo. Spr.*	25	35	30	1	6	6	0	0	0	2	4	0	0	1	0	9	0	0	0	.200	.226	.200
Miller, Greg, New Orleans *	9	12	11	0	1	1	0	0	0	1	1	0	0	0	0	5	0	0	0	.091	.091	.091
Miller, Matt, Colo. Springs	61	6	4	0	0	0	0	0	0	0	0	0	0	2	0	4	0	0	0	.000	.333	.000
Minor, Damon, Fresno *	37	151	141	16	33	61	2	1	8	21	0	1	3	6	0	29	0	0	3	.234	.278	.433
Molina, Gabe, Memphis	57	2	1	1	0	0	0	0	0	0	0	0	0	1	0	0	0	0	0	.000	.500	.000
Montero, Agustin, Las Vegas	35	2	1	0	0	0	0	0	0	0	1	0	0	0	0	0	0	0	0	.000	.000	.000
Montgomery, Matt, Fresno	24	4	4	0	1	1	0	0	0	0	0	0	0	0	0	2	0	0	0	.250	.250	.250
Morales, Willie, Tuc.-Mem.-Co.Spr.	48	184	174	19	41	81	9	2	9	31	2	1	2	5	0	42	1	1	10	.236	.264	.466
Moriarty, Mike, New Orleans	58	192	172	19	43	69	9	1	5	17	1	1	2	16	3	30	3	1	0	.250	.319	.401
Mosquera, Julio, Tacoma	85	315	291	35	83	113	16	1	4	22	2	1	10	11	1	42	6	4	4	.285	.332	.388
Mullen, Scott, Omaha-L.V.	27	16	12	0	1	1	0	0	0	1	3	0	0	1	0	4	0	0	0	.083	.154	.083
Munro, Pete, New Orleans	5	6	6	0	0	0	0	0	0	0	0	0	0	0	0	2	0	0	0	.000	.000	.000
Murray, Calvin, Las Vegas	102	347	312	45	81	120	18	6	3	40	2	3	3	27	3	50	13	4	5	.260	.322	.385
Myers, Adrian, Tacoma	117	473	428	57	115	161	25	3	5	47	4	5	2	34	0	75	23	11	8	.269	.322	.376
Myers, Rodney, Las Vegas	46	8	6	2	2	3	1	0	0	1	2	0	0	0	0	1	0	0	0	.333	.333	.500
Nady, Xavier, Portland	37	152	136	19	36	64	7	0	7	23	0	2	2	12	0	28	0	0	2	.265	.329	.471
Nagy, Charles, Portland *	3	2	2	0	0	0	0	0	0	0	0	0	0	0	0	1	0	0	0	.000	.000	.000
Neagle, Denny, Colo. Spr.*	4	7	6	0	2	3	1	0	0	2	1	0	0	0	0	0	0	0	0	.333	.333	.500
Neal, Steve, Tucson *	97	312	285	32	70	112	17	2	7	37	1	0	2	23	2	78	0	1	6	.246	.306	.393
Neufeld, Andy, Sacramento *	17	30	25	5	3	4	1	0	0	1	0	0	0	5	0	9	0	0	1	.120	.267	.160
Nevin, Phil, Portland	6	19	18	0	2	2	0	0	0	1	0	0	0	1	0	1	0	0	2	.111	.158	.111
Newhan, David, Colo. Spr.*	72	264	244	43	85	115	17	2	3	28	1	1	2	16	2	36	6	4	6	.348	.392	.471
Niekro, Lance, Fresno	98	405	381	43	115	146	15	2	4	41	1	3	1	19	1	39	3	3	12	.302	.334	.383
Nieves, Jose, Memphis	23	74	70	4	14	18	2	1	0	1	1	0	2	1	0	6	3	0	3	.200	.233	.257
Nieves, Wil, Salt Lake	102	395	361	48	102	134	16	2	4	38	3	5	1	25	3	53	1	2	8	.283	.327	.371
Nivar, Ramon, Oklahoma	23	96	89	11	30	42	2	2	2	12	1	1	0	5	0	5	6	1	4	.337	.368	.472
Norris, Dax, New Orleans	9	21	19	1	3	4	1	0	0	1	1	1	0	0	0	2	0	0	2	.158	.150	.211
Norton, Phil, Iowa	49	2	2	0	0	0	0	0	0	0	0	0	0	0	0	0	0	0	0	.000	.000	.000
Nunez, Abraham, Alb.†	59	246	212	35	66	116	13	2	11	38	0	2	0	32	2	56	9	4	1	.311	.398	.547
Nunez, Vladimir, Albuquerque	46	11	9	1	2	3	1	0	0	0	1	0	0	1	0	3	0	0	0	.222	.300	.333
Nunnally, Jon, Memphis *	134	535	428	81	115	220	20	5	25	53	1	3	5	98	7	126	19	11	0	.269	.408	.514
Ohme, Kevin, Memphis *	49	7	7	0	1	1	0	0	0	1	0	0	0	0	0	2	0	0	0	.143	.143	.143
Ojeda, Augie, Iowa †	106	334	283	42	71	93	10	3	2	23	6	1	10	34	3	25	4	0	6	.251	.351	.329
Olsen, Kevin, Albuquerque	7	9	7	0	0	0	0	0	0	0	2	0	0	0	0	4	0	0	0	.000	.000	.000
Olson, Tim, Tucson	115	439	397	59	104	144	22	0	6	40	3	2	6	31	2	77	11	2	14	.262	.323	.363
Ordaz, Luis, Omaha	49	197	178	15	43	56	13	0	0	21	3	4	1	11	0	19	3	0	8	.242	.284	.315
Ortiz, Luis, Edmonton	59	207	190	30	58	101	13	0	10	39	0	1	2	14	1	26	1	0	10	.305	.357	.532
Ottavinia, Paul, Oklahoma *	50	192	178	13	46	51	5	0	0	13	1	1	0	12	0	23	5	1	3	.258	.304	.287
Overbay, Lyle, Tucson *	35	148	119	24	34	57	11	0	4	16	0	1	0	28	2	19	0	0	2	.286	.419	.479
Ozuna, Pablo, Colo. Springs	56	235	219	30	59	89	13	7	1	17	5	1	1	9	0	23	12	6	3	.269	.300	.406
Paquette, Craig, Memphis	11	52	49	3	13	14	1	0	0	4	0	1	0	2	0	12	0	0	1	.265	.288	.286
Parrott, Rhett, Memphis	7	11	7	2	2	2	0	0	0	0	3	0	0	1	0	0	0	0	1	.286	.375	.286
Pascucci, Val, Edmonton	138	572	459	80	129	205	29	1	15	85	1	2	9	101	1	132	3	2	11	.281	.419	.447
Patterson, Jarrod, Omaha *	123	536	478	74	123	214	33	2	18	91	1	4	2	51	5	92	4	1	9	.257	.329	.448
Patterson, John, Tucson	18	33	28	2	4	4	0	0	0	1	4	0	0	1	0	10	0	0	0	.143	.172	.143
Paul, Josh, Iowa	47	156	146	12	37	47	4	0	2	15	1	0	1	8	0	30	0	2	5	.253	.297	.322
Pavkovich, Adam, Salt Lake	1	5	5	0	1	1	0	0	0	0	0	0	0	0	0	0	0	0	0	.200	.200	.200
Pearce, Josh, Memphis	10	11	10	1	3	3	0	0	0	0	1	0	0	0	0	0	0	0	0	.300	.300	.300
Pearson, Jason, Memphis *	44	1	1	0	0	0	0	0	0	0	0	0	0	0	0	1	0	0	0	.000	.000	.000
Pecci, Jay, Tacoma-Fresno †	25	81	73	7	15	15	0	0	0	5	0	1	3	4	0	5	3	0	3	.205	.272	.205
Peeples, Mike, Memphis	30	93	84	7	18	21	3	0	0	3	1	2	3	3	2	16	1	1	5	.214	.261	.250
Pelaez, Alex, Portland	76	308	292	36	84	121	16	0	7	49	0	4	0	12	1	31	0	0	9	.288	.312	.414
Pellow, Kit, Colorado Springs	89	358	320	48	93	167	15	1	19	57	0	1	12	25	2	75	2	1	5	.291	.363	.522
Perez, Oliver, Portland *	8	12	11	2	1	1	0	0	0	0	1	0	0	0	0	3	0	0	0	.091	.091	.091
Perisho, Matt, Tuc.-Co.Spr.*	12	2	1	1	0	0	0	0	0	0	1	0	0	0	0	1	0	0	0	.000	.000	.000
Pernalete, Marco, Fresno †	4	3	2	0	0	0	0	0	0	0	0	0	0	1	0	1	0	0	0	.000	.333	.000
Perry, Chan, Nashville	11	31	29	1	7	8	1	0	0	1	0	0	0	2	0	4	1	0	3	.241	.290	.276
Petrick, Ben, Colo. Springs	80	258	228	38	59	114	16	3	11	40	0	3	1	26	1	53	4	4	8	.259	.333	.500
Phillips, J.R., Tacoma *	81	335	310	35	92	154	20	0	14	54	0	5	3	17	3	74	4	3	4	.297	.334	.497
Pickford, Kevin, Fresno *	26	35	32	5	10	20	1	0	3	6	1	0	0	2	0	6	0	0	0	.313	.353	.625
Pickler, Jeff, Oklahoma *	125	566	486	68	108	144	20	5	2	36	10	3	3	64	1	74	32	5	10	.222	.315	.296
Porter, Colin, New Orleans *	102	387	356	52	114	182	23	6	11	50	2	4	3	22	3	80	22	6	3	.320	.361	.511
Post, Dave, Colo. Springs	12	30	27	2	7	9	0	1	0	2	0	0	0	3	0	2	1	0	0	.259	.333	.333
Powell, Brian, Fresno	23	25	21	3	4	4	0	0	0	2	3	0	0	1	0	5	0	0	1	.190	.227	.190
Powers, John, Oklahoma *	3	11	11	0	0	0	0	0	0	0	0	0	0	0	0	1	0	0	1	.000	.000	.000
Prieto, Ariel, Nashville	4	5	4	0	1	1	0	0	0	0	1	0	0	0	0	3	0	0	0	.250	.250	.250

Player, Team	G	TPA	AB	R	H	TB	2B	3B	HR	RBI	SH	SF	HP	BB	IBB	SO	SB	CS	GDP	Avg.	OBP	Slg.
Prieto, Chris, Sacramento *	111	455	390	70	110	148	12	7	4	54	4	6	7	48	1	40	5	3	7	.282	.366	.379
Prince, Tom, Omaha	29	110	91	16	28	41	10	0	1	6	0	1	4	14	0	15	0	1	2	.308	.418	.451
Pritchett, Chris, Iowa *	43	119	102	8	16	29	4	0	3	14	1	2	1	13	0	21	0	0	4	.157	.254	.284
Proctor, Scott, Las Vegas	24	5	3	0	0	0	0	0	0	0	0	0	0	2	0	2	0	0	0	.000	.400	.000
Puffer, Brandon, N.Orleans	44	1	1	0	0	0	0	0	0	0	0	0	0	0	0	1	0	0	0	.000	.000	.000
Quinlan, Robb, Salt Lake	95	421	393	55	122	175	18	4	9	68	0	2	1	25	2	59	10	3	9	.310	.352	.445
Quinn, Mark, Portland	55	210	180	28	49	86	13	0	8	29	0	3	3	24	1	36	0	0	5	.272	.362	.478
Raggio, Brady, Tucson	18	8	8	1	1	1	0	0	0	0	0	0	0	0	0	2	0	0	2	.125	.125	.125
Ramirez, Dan, Tucson	73	238	230	23	63	76	4	0	3	22	3	0	0	5	0	43	14	5	5	.274	.289	.330
Ramirez, Julio, Salt Lake	110	424	402	50	112	171	17	6	10	48	0	5	5	12	0	86	16	6	7	.279	.304	.425
Randolph, Steve, Tucson *	7	3	3	0	1	1	0	0	0	0	0	0	0	0	0	0	0	0	0	.333	.333	.333
Ransom, Cody, Fresno	112	450	396	56	100	160	16	4	12	50	3	3	3	45	1	91	14	4	14	.253	.331	.404
Raymundo, G.J., Oklahoma	9	32	25	4	3	4	1	0	0	4	0	2	0	5	0	4	0	0	0	.120	.250	.160
Reames, Britt, Edmonton	27	26	24	3	5	6	1	0	0	1	1	0	1	0	0	6	0	0	0	.208	.240	.250
Reboulet, Jeff, Nashville	17	59	49	6	11	12	1	0	0	2	0	0	0	10	0	11	0	3	1	.224	.356	.245
Redman, Tike, Nashville *	100	401	360	60	106	144	12	7	4	29	3	2	0	36	1	32	42	9	5	.294	.357	.400
Reid, Justin, Nashville	35	15	14	1	2	2	0	0	0	0	0	0	0	1	0	5	0	0	0	.143	.200	.143
Reyes, Dennys, Tucson	33	2	2	0	0	0	0	0	0	0	0	0	0	0	0	1	0	0	0	.000	.000	.000
Reyes, Rene, Colo. Springs †	98	398	370	60	127	174	23	3	6	50	1	3	2	22	0	56	12	8	11	.343	.380	.470
Riggs, Adam, Salt Lake	103	447	394	59	116	193	35	0	14	82	1	10	5	37	0	67	8	2	13	.294	.354	.490
Riggs, Eric, Las Vegas †	125	475	410	70	115	182	31	6	8	58	2	7	7	49	5	73	3	1	8	.280	.362	.444
Risinger, Ben, Portland	86	311	278	32	70	103	18	0	5	35	2	1	6	23	4	30	3	2	13	.252	.321	.371
Rivera, Carlos, Nashville *	72	277	262	28	69	114	18	0	9	31	0	1	1	13	3	38	3	1	2	.263	.300	.435
Rivera, Mike, Portland	13	51	50	0	8	9	1	0	0	2	0	0	0	1	0	21	0	1	1	.160	.176	.180
Roberts, Dave, Las Vegas *	2	6	5	2	0	0	0	0	0	0	0	0	0	1	0	0	0	0	0	.000	.167	.000
Robinson, Kerry, Memphis *	16	63	61	14	21	25	2	1	0	3	1	0	0	1	0	7	5	0	0	.344	.355	.410
Rodriguez, Guillermo, Fresno	78	260	239	31	66	97	8	4	5	36	1	1	5	14	0	25	1	0	9	.276	.328	.406
Rodriguez, Luis, Memphis	75	219	199	19	43	59	6	2	2	9	1	1	1	17	3	46	2	0	6	.216	.280	.296
Rodriguez, Nerio, Memphis	13	20	18	0	0	0	0	0	0	0	1	0	0	1	0	10	0	0	1	.000	.053	.000
Rogelstad, Matt, Tacoma *	5	4	4	1	0	0	0	0	0	0	0	0	0	0	0	0	0	0	0	.000	.000	.000
Rojas, Carlos, Iowa	1	1	1	0	1	1	0	0	0	1	0	0	0	0	0	0	0	0	0	1.000	1.000	1.000
Romano, Jason, Las Vegas	57	234	216	45	66	104	18	4	4	23	5	2	0	11	2	32	10	6	3	.306	.336	.481
Romero, Mandy, Colo. Spr.†	81	277	250	30	74	99	11	1	4	31	1	6	2	18	0	38	0	0	7	.296	.341	.396
Rosario, Rodrigo, N.Orleans	15	17	16	0	3	3	0	0	0	1	1	0	0	0	0	5	0	0	1	.188	.188	.188
Rose, Mike, Sacramento †	70	274	221	44	58	94	10	1	8	30	2	3	4	44	4	50	2	1	6	.262	.390	.425
Ross, David, Las Vegas	24	100	86	12	19	38	4	0	5	16	1	1	1	11	0	27	0	2	0	.221	.313	.442
Rouse, Michael, Sac.*	2	7	7	2	3	3	0	0	0	1	0	0	0	0	0	0	0	0	0	.429	.429	.429
Ruan, Wilkin, Las Vegas	108	429	403	58	124	136	6	3	0	40	7	2	7	10	0	38	41	7	6	.308	.334	.337
Rueter, Kirk, Fresno *	1	2	2	0	0	0	0	0	0	0	0	0	0	0	0	0	0	0	0	.000	.000	.000
Rushford, Jim, Oklahoma *	24	96	84	8	16	22	4	1	0	9	0	2	2	8	0	11	2	0	2	.190	.271	.262
Ryan, Jason, Memphis †	32	48	46	1	5	7	2	0	0	1	2	0	0	0	0	13	0	0	1	.109	.109	.152
Ryan, Rob, Fresno *	49	123	108	15	26	38	5	2	1	14	0	2	0	13	0	22	0	1	1	.241	.317	.352
Saarloos, Kirk, New Orleans	14	15	13	0	2	2	0	0	0	2	2	0	0	0	0	6	0	0	0	.154	.154	.154
Sabel, Erik, Tucson	42	3	2	0	0	0	0	0	0	0	0	0	0	1	0	2	0	0	0	.000	.333	.000
Sadler, Donnie, Oklahoma	19	81	66	14	20	29	4	1	1	6	2	1	2	10	0	9	6	1	1	.303	.405	.439
Saipe, Mike, Las Vegas	23	21	17	1	5	6	1	0	0	4	2	0	0	2	0	2	1	0	2	.294	.368	.353
Sakamoto, Mitsuru, Co.Spr.*	1	1	1	0	0	0	0	0	0	0	0	0	0	0	0	0	0	0	0	.000	.000	.000
Saladin, Miguel, N.Orleans	55	4	4	0	0	0	0	0	0	0	0	0	0	0	0	0	0	0	0	.000	.000	.000
Salazar, Oscar, Salt Lake	7	30	26	5	8	15	2	1	1	4	0	1	0	3	0	4	0	0	1	.308	.367	.577
Sanchez, Duaner, Nashville	41	5	5	1	3	4	1	0	0	2	0	0	0	0	0	1	0	0	0	.600	.600	.800
Sanchez, Freddy, Nashville	1	5	5	1	2	3	1	0	0	0	0	0	0	0	0	1	0	0	0	.400	.400	.600
Sanchez, Jesus, Colo. Spr.*	46	5	3	0	0	0	0	0	0	0	2	0	0	0	0	1	0	0	0	.000	.000	.000
Sanders, Scott, Albuquerque	20	28	24	4	8	11	0	0	1	2	2	0	0	1	0	3	0	0	2	.333	.360	.458
Sandusky, Scott, Edmonton	39	122	109	10	31	36	5	0	0	8	1	1	3	8	0	27	0	1	6	.284	.347	.330
Santos, Francisco, Fresno *	87	314	301	23	72	115	15	5	6	42	0	3	0	10	0	38	1	0	3	.239	.261	.382
Sasser, Rob, Omaha	17	62	61	6	17	25	3	1	1	5	0	0	0	1	0	13	4	1	3	.279	.290	.410
Scales, Bobby, Portland †	11	50	43	8	16	23	7	0	0	2	0	0	0	7	0	6	3	0	0	.372	.460	.535
Scanlan, Bob, New Orleans	32	18	14	0	0	0	0	0	0	0	4	0	0	0	0	4	0	0	1	.000	.000	.000
Seabol, Scott, Memphis	88	351	307	40	92	164	22	1	16	58	0	4	8	32	1	64	2	0	5	.300	.376	.534
Secoda, Jason, Salt Lk.-Alb.	10	1	1	0	0	0	0	0	0	0	0	0	0	0	0	1	0	0	0	.000	.000	.000
Selby, Bill, Memphis *	76	305	279	33	73	124	12	6	9	41	1	1	0	24	1	32	5	1	5	.262	.319	.444
Sellier, Brian, Sacramento *	30	106	90	15	19	22	3	0	0	10	1	2	0	13	0	15	0	1	2	.211	.305	.244
Serafini, Dan, Memphis †	3	2	1	0	0	0	0	0	0	1	1	0	0	0	0	0	0	0	0	.000	.000	.000
Sessions, Doug, New Orleans	31	43	38	0	1	1	0	0	0	1	3	0	0	2	0	12	0	0	0	.026	.075	.026
Shaffar, Ben, Nashville †	4	2	2	0	0	0	0	0	0	0	0	0	0	0	0	2	0	0	0	.000	.000	.000
Silva, Jose, Sac.-Port.-Iowa	24	3	2	0	0	0	0	0	0	0	0	0	0	1	0	0	0	0	0	.000	.333	.000
Simas, Bill, Las Vegas *	26	2	2	0	1	1	0	0	0	0	0	0	0	0	0	0	0	0	0	.500	.500	.500
Simmons, Brian, Portland †	10	22	20	0	2	2	0	0	0	3	0	1	0	1	0	4	0	0	0	.100	.136	.100
Simon, Randall, Nashville *	2	8	8	3	3	7	1	0	1	2	0	0	0	0	0	0	0	0	1	.375	.375	.875
Sinclair, Steve, Iowa *	6	1	1	0	0	0	0	0	0	0	0	0	0	0	0	0	0	0	0	.000	.000	.000
Sledge, Terrmel, Edmonton *	131	572	497	95	161	271	26	9	22	92	0	9	5	61	3	93	13	5	10	.324	.397	.545
Small, Aaron, Albuquerque	14	24	17	1	3	4	1	0	0	3	7	0	0	0	0	6	0	0	0	.176	.176	.235
Smith, Brian, Colo. Springs	9	1	1	0	0	0	0	0	0	1	0	0	0	0	0	0	0	0	0	.000	.000	.000
Smyth, Steve, Iowa *	25	31	26	3	3	3	0	0	0	0	4	0	0	1	0	11	0	0	0	.115	.148	.115
Snelling, Chris, Tacoma *	18	75	67	11	18	29	2	0	3	10	0	1	2	5	0	12	1	0	0	.269	.333	.433
Snusz, Chris, Nashville	6	9	9	2	3	4	1	0	0	2	0	0	0	0	0	1	0	0	1	.333	.333	.444
Sodowsky, Clint, Alb.*	3	6	6	0	0	0	0	0	0	0	0	0	0	0	0	2	0	0	0	.000	.000	.000
Song, Seung, Edmonton	13	13	10	2	3	3	0	0	0	0	2	0	0	1	0	1	0	0	0	.300	.364	.300
Spivey, Junior, Tucson	4	16	15	3	4	6	2	0	0	1	0	0	0	1	0	1	0	0	0	.267	.313	.400
Stairs, Matt, Nashville *	7	27	18	4	3	9	0	0	2	3	0	0	2	7	0	2	0	0	1	.167	.444	.500
Stanifer, Rob, Iowa-N.Orleans	44	4	3	0	0	0	0	0	0	0	1	0	0	0	0	1	0	0	0	.000	.000	.000

Player, Team	G	TPA	AB	R	H	TB	2B	3B	HR	RBI	SH	SF	HP	BB	IBB	SO	SB	CS	GDP	Avg.	OBP	Slg.
Stanley, Henri, N.Orleans *	135	574	506	85	148	225	28	8	11	48	4	2	2	60	2	93	15	7	6	.292	.368	.445
Stark, Dennis, Colo. Springs	4	5	4	0	0	0	0	0	0	0	1	0	0	0	0	2	0	0	0	.000	.000	.000
Stein, Blake, Edmonton	15	9	5	0	2	2	0	0	0	0	4	0	0	0	0	1	0	0	1	.400	.400	.400
Stemle, Steve, Memphis	26	44	41	1	3	3	0	0	0	0	0	0	0	3	0	13	0	0	3	.073	.136	.073
Stockman, Phil, Tucson	2	2	1	0	0	0	0	0	0	0	1	0	0	0	0	0	0	0	0	.000	.000	.000
Stratton, Rob, Albuquerque	110	421	372	63	79	191	12	2	32	82	1	8	4	36	1	175	6	4	2	.212	.283	.513
Strong, Jamal, Tacoma	56	244	210	38	64	78	6	1	2	19	3	1	5	25	0	38	26	11	3	.305	.390	.371
Sullivan, Kevin, Colo. Spr.	4	13	12	1	2	3	1	0	0	2	0	1	0	0	0	5	0	0	0	.167	.154	.250
Sweeney, Mark, Colo. Spr.*	51	205	165	24	49	76	10	1	5	35	1	5	0	34	5	32	1	4	5	.297	.407	.461
Sweeney, Mike, Omaha	2	9	8	3	2	6	1	0	1	1	0	0	0	1	0	1	0	0	0	.250	.333	.750
Swindell, Greg, Tucson *	8	5	5	0	0	0	0	0	0	0	0	0	0	0	0	1	0	0	1	.000	.000	.000
Szuminski, Jason, Iowa	3	2	1	0	0	0	0	0	0	0	1	0	0	0	0	0	0	0	0	.000	.000	.000
Taguchi, So, Memphis	90	288	258	31	66	84	8	2	2	24	5	1	2	22	0	36	14	5	5	.256	.318	.326
Tankersley, Dennis, Portland	29	29	23	1	1	1	0	0	0	0	4	0	0	2	0	7	0	0	0	.043	.120	.043
Terrero, Luis, Tucson	118	512	467	83	134	193	20	15	3	46	2	1	11	31	0	103	23	19	6	.287	.345	.413
Teut, Nate, Alb.-Iowa	5	4	3	0	0	0	0	0	0	0	0	0	0	1	0	2	0	0	0	.000	.250	.000
Thames, Marcus, Oklahoma	18	74	66	9	17	27	4	0	2	7	0	0	0	8	0	12	1	0	2	.258	.338	.409
Theodorou, Nick, L.V.†	23	38	32	6	6	7	1	0	0	4	0	0	0	6	0	11	0	0	1	.188	.316	.219
Thompson, Rich, Nashville *	35	124	109	17	28	35	3	2	0	11	1	1	4	9	0	21	22	3	0	.257	.333	.321
Thrower, Jake, Port.-Edm.†	79	248	226	23	55	77	13	0	3	28	1	6	2	13	1	26	1	1	14	.243	.283	.341
Thurston, Joe, Las Vegas *	132	606	538	77	156	216	27	6	7	68	11	8	18	31	0	48	1	12	10	.290	.345	.401
Toca, Jorge, Nashville	10	36	34	7	10	18	2	0	2	10	0	0	0	2	1	8	0	1	0	.294	.333	.529
Tollberg, Brian, Portland	20	10	9	1	3	4	1	0	0	1	0	0	0	1	0	1	0	0	0	.333	.400	.444
Topolski, Jon, New Orleans *	5	11	11	1	4	7	0	0	1	1	0	0	0	0	0	2	0	0	0	.364	.364	.636
Torcato, Tony, Fresno *	106	440	423	36	125	156	18	2	3	48	2	7	2	6	2	33	4	0	18	.296	.304	.369
Torrealba, Steve, Memphis	46	140	117	16	32	49	9	1	2	18	2	2	3	16	3	20	1	1	3	.274	.370	.419
Torres, Salomon, Nashville	1	2	2	0	0	0	0	0	0	0	0	0	0	0	0	1	0	0	0	.000	.000	.000
Tracy, Chad, Tucson *	133	576	522	91	169	238	31	4	10	80	0	9	4	41	3	52	0	2	7	.324	.372	.456
Treanor, Matt, Albuquerque	98	375	315	45	86	139	18	1	11	40	1	3	17	39	1	44	9	4	8	.273	.380	.441
Trujillo, J.J., Portland	27	2	2	0	0	0	0	0	0	0	0	0	0	0	0	1	0	0	0	.000	.000	.000
Tucker, T.J., Edmonton	4	6	6	0	1	1	0	0	0	0	0	0	0	0	0	0	0	0	0	.167	.167	.167
Ugueto, Luis, Tacoma †	8	32	26	9	8	17	3	0	2	4	1	0	0	5	0	4	2	0	0	.308	.419	.654
Ullery, Dave, Omaha *	2	5	5	1	2	3	1	0	0	1	0	0	0	0	0	1	0	0	0	.400	.400	.600
Urban, Jeff, Fresno	32	36	30	2	5	8	3	0	0	2	3	0	0	3	0	12	0	0	0	.167	.242	.267
Valderrama, Carlos, Fresno	54	221	202	20	56	70	5	0	3	10	5	0	2	12	0	28	7	8	3	.277	.324	.347
Valdez, Mario, Portland *	90	267	226	23	61	92	16	0	5	24	1	3	2	34	2	42	0	0	5	.270	.366	.407
Valdez, Wilson, Albuquerque	90	371	338	45	97	117	12	4	0	18	12	1	1	19	2	37	33	9	10	.287	.326	.346
Vance, Cory, Colo. Spr.*	24	47	40	1	10	12	2	0	0	1	7	0	0	0	0	7	0	0	1	.250	.250	.300
Vargas, Claudio, Edmonton	2	5	3	1	1	2	1	0	0	0	2	0	0	0	0	0	0	0	0	.333	.333	.667
Vaughn, Greg, Colo. Springs	35	134	116	26	35	80	7	1	12	35	0	1	1	16	1	28	1	0	2	.302	.388	.690
Veres, Dave, Iowa	11	3	3	1	1	1	0	0	0	1	0	0	0	0	0	2	0	0	0	.333	.333	.333
Victorino, Shane, L.V.†	11	45	41	6	16	24	1	2	1	9	2	1	0	1	0	5	0	1	1	.390	.395	.585
Villafuerte, Brandon, Portland	37	2	2	0	0	0	0	0	0	0	0	0	0	0	0	1	0	0	0	.000	.000	.000
Villone, Ron, Tucson-N.Orl.*	20	11	10	1	2	2	0	0	0	0	0	0	1	0	0	2	0	0	0	.200	.273	.200
Vina, Fernando, Memphis *	5	20	17	1	3	3	0	0	0	1	0	1	0	2	0	2	0	0	1	.176	.250	.176
Vining, Ken, New Orleans *	41	10	6	2	3	3	0	0	0	0	4	0	0	0	0	2	0	0	0	.500	.500	.500
Vitiello, Joe, Fresno-Edm.	50	191	171	20	42	60	12	0	2	17	0	2	0	18	1	26	0	0	6	.246	.314	.351
Vizcaino, Jose, N.Orleans †	2	9	8	1	2	5	0	0	1	1	0	0	0	1	0	0	0	0	0	.250	.333	.625
Vogelsong, Ryan, Nashville	26	36	29	1	8	10	2	0	0	3	5	0	1	1	0	7	0	0	0	.276	.323	.345
Wakeland, Chris, Alb.*	65	242	219	32	62	99	12	2	7	30	0	2	4	17	1	62	2	2	3	.283	.343	.452
Waldron, Jeff, Tucson *	34	123	101	10	25	29	4	0	0	11	1	1	6	14	0	27	0	1	3	.248	.369	.287
Walker, Kevin, Portland *	34	4	4	1	0	0	0	0	0	0	0	0	0	0	0	1	0	0	0	.000	.000	.000
Walrond, Les, Mem.-Omaha *	28	2	2	0	0	0	0	0	0	0	0	0	0	0	0	0	0	0	0	.000	.000	.000
Ward, Daryle, Las Vegas *	34	140	128	16	38	59	9	0	4	24	0	2	0	10	1	22	0	0	3	.297	.343	.461
Ward, Jeremy, Tucson	25	3	3	1	1	1	0	0	0	0	0	0	0	0	0	1	0	0	0	.333	.333	.333
Ware, Jeremy, Edmonton	12	21	20	3	6	9	0	0	1	1	0	0	0	1	0	4	0	0	1	.300	.333	.450
Wasdin, John, Nashville	20	31	24	1	3	4	1	0	0	0	6	0	0	1	0	5	0	0	2	.125	.160	.167
Washington, Rico, Portland *	17	70	58	11	13	26	2	1	3	10	0	1	1	10	0	14	0	1	1	.224	.343	.448
Wathan, Derek, Alb. †	116	449	409	54	121	171	24	7	4	55	1	3	2	34	3	56	21	8	3	.296	.350	.418
Watkins, Steve, Portland	14	4	4	0	1	2	1	0	0	1	0	0	0	0	0	2	0	0	0	.250	.250	.500
Wayne, Justin, Albuquerque	24	38	34	2	6	8	2	0	0	4	2	1	0	1	0	11	0	0	0	.176	.194	.235
Webb, Brandon, Tucson	3	3	1	0	1	1	0	0	0	1	0	1	0	1	0	0	0	0	0	1.000	.667	1.000
Weibl, Clint, Memphis	20	21	19	2	1	1	0	0	0	1	2	0	0	0	0	13	0	0	0	.053	.053	.053
Wellemeyer, Todd, Iowa	13	18	14	1	1	1	0	0	0	1	3	0	0	1	0	5	0	0	0	.071	.133	.071
Wesson, Barry, Salt Lake	123	521	475	62	133	196	27	6	8	53	0	5	3	38	0	86	17	3	10	.280	.334	.413
Whiteside, Matt, Colo. Spr.	21	2	2	0	0	0	0	0	0	0	0	0	0	0	0	2	0	0	0	.000	.000	.000
Widger, Chris, Memphis	23	80	71	8	17	30	7	0	2	10	1	1	0	7	0	12	1	0	0	.239	.304	.423
Wilkins, Marc, Albuquerque	20	3	2	0	1	1	0	0	0	0	0	0	0	1	0	1	0	0	0	.500	.667	.500
Williams, Dave, Nashville *	16	26	23	1	5	5	0	0	0	1	3	0	0	0	0	11	0	0	1	.217	.217	.217
Williams, Gerald, Alb.	85	359	327	59	99	173	22	5	14	50	1	2	4	24	2	45	15	11	2	.303	.356	.529
Williams, Jerome, Fresno	10	7	7	0	0	0	0	0	0	1	0	0	0	0	0	2	0	0	0	.000	.000	.000
Winchester, Scott, Las Vegas	20	10	9	0	0	0	0	0	0	0	1	0	0	0	0	4	0	0	0	.000	.000	.000
Witasick, Jay, Portland	5	1	0	0	0	0	0	0	0	0	0	0	0	1	0	0	0	0	0	.000	1.000	.000
Wood, Jason, Albuquerque	128	533	473	80	140	222	26	4	16	83	3	7	5	45	3	96	5	1	13	.296	.358	.469
Wright, Jaret, Portland	12	4	4	1	1	4	0	0	1	2	0	0	0	0	0	2	0	0	0	.250	.250	1.000
Wuertz, Mike, Iowa	43	21	16	0	3	4	1	0	0	3	3	1	0	1	0	7	0	0	0	.188	.222	.250
Yennaco, Jay, Memphis	8	8	8	0	1	1	0	0	0	1	0	0	0	0	0	4	0	0	0	.125	.125	.125
Young, Jason, Colo. Spr.	23	29	26	3	7	10	3	0	0	3	1	0	0	2	0	4	0	0	0	.269	.321	.385
Young, Tim, Colo. Spr.	29	2	2	0	0	0	0	0	0	0	0	0	0	0	0	1	0	0	0	.000	.000	.000
Zerbe, Chad, Fresno *	8	4	2	1	1	1	0	0	0	0	1	0	0	1	0	0	0	0	0	.500	.667	.500
Zinter, Alan, New Orleans †	114	384	342	48	87	155	17	0	17	57	0	1	5	36	5	77	1	0	10	.254	.333	.453

PLAYERS WITH TWO OR MORE TEAMS

Player, Team	G	TPA	AB	R	H	TB	2B	3B	HR	RBI	SH	SF	HP	BB	IBB	SO	SB	CS	GDP	Avg.	OBP	Slg.
Alviso, Jerome, Colo. Spr.†	38	109	102	12	32	35	3	0	0	6	1	1	1	4	2	7	1	2	0	.314	.343	.343
Alviso, Jerome, Salt Lake †	16	61	57	4	13	14	1	0	0	5	1	0	0	3	0	6	2	0	0	.228	.267	.246
Belitz, Todd, Albuquerque *	13	1	1	0	1	1	0	0	0	0	0	0	0	0	0	0	0	0	0	1.000	1.000	1.000
Belitz, Todd, Colo. Springs *	3	0	0	0	0	0	0	0	0	0	0	0	0	0	0	0	0	0	0	.000	.000	.000
Blank, Matt, Fresno *	8	11	11	0	1	2	1	0	0	0	0	0	0	0	0	1	0	0	1	.091	.091	.182
Blank, Matt, Edmonton *	5	7	6	2	2	2	0	0	0	1	0	0	0	1	0	1	1	0	0	.333	.429	.333
Bruback, Matt, Iowa	20	33	29	1	1	1	0	0	0	0	4	0	0	0	0	17	0	0	0	.034	.034	.034
Bruback, Matt, Portland	2	2	2	0	0	0	0	0	0	0	0	0	0	0	0	1	0	0	0	.000	.000	.000
Bruback, Matt, Nashville	4	7	6	0	0	0	0	0	0	0	1	0	0	0	0	4	0	0	0	.000	.000	.000
Clark, Jermaine, Portland *	50	186	160	27	40	58	2	2	4	10	2	1	1	22	1	24	14	3	1	.250	.342	.363
Clark, Jermaine, Oklahoma *	49	193	171	24	38	70	6	4	6	24	4	1	1	16	0	26	11	1	3	.222	.291	.409
Darensbourg, Vic, Edm.*	11	0	0	0	0	0	0	0	0	0	0	0	0	0	0	0	0	0	0	.000	.000	.000
Darensbourg, Vic, Colo. Spr.*	20	1	1	0	1	1	0	0	0	1	0	0	0	0	0	0	0	0	0	1.000	1.000	1.000
Dawkins, Gookie, Las Vegas	32	127	115	5	19	26	5	1	0	12	2	1	0	9	1	26	3	1	1	.165	.224	.226
Dawkins, Gookie, Omaha	33	124	112	18	29	41	6	0	2	18	2	2	1	7	0	24	2	3	5	.259	.303	.366
Donaldson, Bo, Salt Lake	3	0	0	0	0	0	0	0	0	0	0	0	0	0	0	0	0	0	0	.000	.000	.000
Donaldson, Bo, Edmonton	9	3	3	0	1	1	0	0	0	0	0	0	0	0	0	1	0	0	0	.333	.333	.333
Duncan, Courtney, Portland *	54	2	2	1	1	1	0	0	0	1	0	0	0	0	0	1	0	0	0	.500	.500	.500
Duncan, Courtney, Salt Lk.*	2	0	0	0	0	0	0	0	0	0	0	0	0	0	0	0	0	0	0	.000	.000	.000
Ebert, Derrin, Tucson	15	0	0	0	0	0	0	0	0	0	0	0	0	0	0	0	0	0	0	.000	.000	.000
Ebert, Derrin, Iowa	6	1	1	0	0	0	0	0	0	0	0	0	0	0	0	1	0	0	0	.000	.000	.000
Encarnacion, Mario, Edm.	16	55	48	8	15	20	2	0	1	6	0	0	0	7	0	11	0	1	3	.313	.400	.417
Encarnacion, Mario, Mem.	6	21	21	1	3	3	0	0	0	0	0	0	0	0	0	5	0	0	1	.143	.143	.143
Evans, Keith, Edmonton	12	3	3	0	0	0	0	0	0	0	0	0	0	0	0	1	0	0	0	.000	.000	.000
Evans, Keith, Iowa	10	1	1	0	1	1	0	0	0	0	0	0	0	0	0	0	0	0	0	1.000	1.000	1.000
Evans, Tom, Iowa	6	11	10	1	2	3	1	0	0	0	0	0	0	1	0	0	0	0	1	.200	.273	.300
Evans, Tom, Colo. Springs	5	9	9	1	1	1	0	0	0	1	0	0	0	0	0	2	0	0	0	.111	.111	.111
Fyhrie, Mike, Omaha	15	0	0	0	0	0	0	0	0	0	0	0	0	0	0	0	0	0	0	.000	.000	.000
Fyhrie, Mike, Albuquerque	5	1	1	0	0	0	0	0	0	0	0	0	0	0	0	1	0	0	0	.000	.000	.000
Hansen, Jed, Omaha	93	392	337	50	85	144	25	2	10	44	1	2	5	47	1	81	8	7	5	.252	.350	.427
Hansen, Jed, Memphis	10	33	22	4	4	7	0	0	1	1	1	0	0	10	0	7	1	1	0	.182	.438	.318
Hernandez, Carlos, Fresno	73	241	216	17	45	51	3	0	1	14	7	1	2	15	4	38	4	1	6	.208	.265	.236
Hernandez, Carlos, N.Orleans	17	45	40	6	9	11	2	0	0	2	2	1	0	2	0	12	0	0	1	.225	.256	.275
Hill, Bobby, Iowa †	92	411	361	53	104	153	23	4	6	40	3	2	8	37	0	65	8	7	5	.288	.365	.424
Hill, Bobby, Nashville †	17	75	66	5	11	18	2	1	1	4	1	0	0	8	0	8	1	2	2	.167	.257	.273
Joseph, Kevin, Edmonton	7	1	1	0	1	1	0	0	0	0	0	0	0	0	0	0	0	0	0	1.000	1.000	1.000
Joseph, Kevin, Memphis	22	11	11	2	3	4	1	0	0	0	0	0	0	0	0	3	0	0	0	.273	.273	.364
Keisler, Randy, N.Orleans *	10	18	17	0	2	2	0	0	0	0	1	0	0	0	0	3	0	0	0	.118	.118	.118
Keisler, Randy, Oklahoma *	5	0	0	0	0	0	0	0	0	0	0	0	0	0	0	0	0	0	0	.000	.000	.000
Keisler, Randy, Portland *	8	10	9	0	1	2	1	0	0	2	1	0	0	0	0	1	0	0	0	.111	.111	.222
Kuzmic, Craig, Tacoma †	54	184	160	25	34	65	7	0	8	23	0	1	1	22	2	48	1	2	5	.213	.310	.406
Kuzmic, Craig, Fresno †	47	165	143	16	40	56	5	4	1	17	2	1	1	18	0	46	5	2	1	.280	.362	.392
Malloy, Marty, Memphis *	85	278	244	28	60	82	12	2	2	19	9	1	2	22	4	33	7	2	7	.246	.312	.336
Malloy, Marty, Las Vegas *	7	21	20	3	7	9	2	0	0	2	0	0	1	0	0	6	0	0	1	.350	.381	.450
Morales, Willie, Tucson	11	43	42	4	12	19	2	1	1	3	0	0	0	1	0	9	1	0	3	.286	.302	.452
Morales, Willie, Memphis	16	64	55	4	13	25	4	1	2	10	2	1	2	4	0	16	0	0	6	.236	.306	.455
Morales, Willie, Colo. Spr.	21	77	77	11	16	37	3	0	6	18	0	0	0	0	0	17	0	1	1	.208	.208	.481
Mullen, Scott, Las Vegas	7	16	12	0	1	1	0	0	0	1	3	0	0	1	0	4	0	0	0	.083	.154	.083
Mullen, Scott, Omaha	20	0	0	0	0	0	0	0	0	0	0	0	0	0	0	0	0	0	0	.000	.000	.000
Pecci, Jay, Fresno †	11	34	33	4	10	10	0	0	0	2	0	0	0	1	0	2	2	0	1	.303	.324	.303
Pecci, Jay, Tacoma †	14	47	40	3	5	5	0	0	0	3	0	1	3	3	0	3	1	0	2	.125	.234	.125
Perisho, Matt, Tucson *	4	0	0	0	0	0	0	0	0	0	0	0	0	0	0	0	0	0	0	.000	.000	.000
Perisho, Matt, Colo. Spr.*	8	2	1	1	0	0	0	0	0	0	1	0	0	0	0	1	0	0	0	.000	.000	.000
Secoda, Jason, Albuquerque	3	1	1	0	0	0	0	0	0	0	0	0	0	0	0	1	0	0	0	.000	.000	.000
Secoda, Jason, Salt Lake	7	0	0	0	0	0	0	0	0	0	0	0	0	0	0	0	0	0	0	.000	.000	.000
Silva, Jose, Sacramento	7	0	0	0	0	0	0	0	0	0	0	0	0	0	0	0	0	0	0	.000	.000	.000
Silva, Jose, Portland	17	3	2	0	0	0	0	0	0	0	0	0	0	1	0	0	0	0	0	.000	.333	.000
Silva, Jose, Iowa	3	0	0	0	0	0	0	0	0	0	0	0	0	0	0	0	0	0	0	.000	.000	.000
Stanifer, Rob, Iowa	3	0	0	0	0	0	0	0	0	0	0	0	0	0	0	0	0	0	0	.000	.000	.000
Stanifer, Rob, New Orleans	41	4	3	0	0	0	0	0	0	0	1	0	0	0	0	1	0	0	0	.000	.000	.000
Teut, Nate, Albuquerque	2	2	2	0	0	0	0	0	0	0	0	0	0	0	0	1	0	0	0	.000	.000	.000
Teut, Nate, Iowa	3	2	1	0	0	0	0	0	0	0	0	0	0	1	0	1	0	0	0	.000	.500	.000
Thrower, Jake, Portland †	28	94	83	11	23	34	8	0	1	13	0	2	2	7	0	8	1	0	3	.277	.340	.410
Thrower, Jake, Edmonton †	51	154	143	12	32	43	5	0	2	15	1	4	0	6	1	18	0	1	11	.224	.248	.301
Villone, Ron, Tucson *	15	2	2	0	0	0	0	0	0	0	0	0	0	0	0	1	0	0	0	.000	.000	.000
Villone, Ron, New Orleans *	5	9	8	1	2	2	0	0	0	0	0	0	1	0	0	1	0	0	0	.250	.333	.250
Vitiello, Joe, Fresno	23	83	75	9	16	21	5	0	0	3	0	0	0	8	0	9	0	0	3	.213	.289	.280
Vitiello, Joe, Edmonton	27	108	96	11	26	39	7	0	2	14	0	2	0	10	1	17	0	0	3	.271	.333	.406
Walrond, Les, Memphis *	10	2	2	0	0	0	0	0	0	0	0	0	0	0	0	0	0	0	0	.000	.000	.000
Walrond, Les, Omaha *	18	0	0	0	0	0	0	0	0	0	0	0	0	0	0	0	0	0	0	.000	.000	.000

GRAND SLAMS—Abernathy, Berger, Hiatt, Sledge, 2 each; Alvarez, Barkett, J. Barnes, Bellinger, DaVanon, Dawkins, DeJesus, Devore, Doster, Edwards, Frese, Ri. Gomez, J. Guiel, B. Hart, J. Hart, K. Johnson, Ma. Johnson, Linden, Luis Lopez (C.S.), Luis Lopez (Sac.), Ludwick, Magee, J. Matos, A. Medrano, Moriarty, Newhan, Ortiz, Pascucci, Pellow, A. Riggs, Risinger, Seabol, Selby, Stratton, Ma. Sweeney, Terrero, Torcato, M. Valdez, Wathan, G. Williams, Zinter, 1 each.

AWARDED FIRST BASE ON CATCHER'S INTERFERENCE—Leon 5 (Ardoin, Cresse, Lunar, Gu. Rodriguez, Treanor); Berger 3 (Laird, Petrick, Treanor); McDonald 3 (Ardoin, Laird, Lunar); A. Alvarez (Laird); Counsell (Rose); Doster (Widger); J. Guiel (Borders); D. Haynes (Romero); Ja. Hill (Haad); Koonce (Waldron); C. Meyers (W. Gonzalez); Neal (Laird); Risinger (K. Hill); Sanders (Petrick); M. Valdez (Lunsford); G. Williams (Romero).

2003 PITCHING

TEAM

Team	W	L	Pct.	ERA	G	CG	ShO	Sv.	IP	H	TBF	R	ER	HR	SH	SF	HB	BB	IBB	SO	WP	Bk.
New Orleans	71	73	.493	3.71	144	7	10	35	1266.2	1247	5370	582	522	101	58	36	66	401	25	766	42	3
Nashville	81	62	.566	3.88	143	9	16	41	1253.1	1198	5337	601	540	111	61	45	53	394	53	1030	40	3
Memphis	64	79	.448	3.89	143	2	10	31	1250.2	1288	5337	593	541	128	60	40	42	388	35	787	55	7

Team	W	L	Pct.	ERA	G	CG	ShO	Sv.	IP	H	TBF	R	ER	HR	SH	SF	HB	BB	IBB	SO	WP	Bk.
Sacramento	92	52	.639	3.90	144	2	10	35	1261.2	1237	5399	618	547	105	31	33	47	439	24	973	71	4
Tacoma	66	78	.458	3.96	144	5	6	41	1257.2	1273	5424	636	553	129	41	39	57	433	7	899	45	4
Tucson	73	71	.507	4.10	144	5	11	32	1268.1	1375	5558	698	578	88	56	53	65	422	13	856	68	3
Las Vegas	76	66	.535	4.17	142	2	9	40	1246.1	1362	5443	672	577	108	43	52	61	424	18	816	41	7
Oklahoma	70	72	.493	4.21	142	7	8	40	1245.2	1328	5388	643	583	100	54	45	48	418	12	838	52	8
Iowa	70	72	.493	4.35	142	4	3	33	1245.1	1280	5436	667	602	125	58	55	62	493	56	945	40	6
Omaha	70	73	.490	4.40	143	6	1	31	1276.2	1303	5506	686	624	132	37	43	56	501	9	859	60	6
Colo. Springs	73	70	.510	4.47	143	6	5	38	1231.1	1332	5489	733	612	130	64	39	77	468	23	956	55	17
Portland	69	75	.479	4.54	144	0	10	46	1262.1	1317	5478	710	637	127	36	50	69	456	9	929	50	2
Salt Lake	68	75	.476	4.66	143	6	5	34	1251.2	1404	5461	747	648	129	35	54	59	420	3	813	53	3
Albuquerque	74	70	.514	4.80	144	6	3	36	1264.0	1402	5526	770	674	134	46	47	66	433	16	893	51	4
Fresno	55	88	.385	4.88	143	1	6	29	1247.2	1421	5553	765	677	122	71	62	56	444	12	810	61	9
Edmonton	73	69	.514	5.08	142	10	7	34	1211.2	1392	5413	746	684	119	30	43	41	479	23	776	49	6

INDIVIDUAL

TOP QUALIFIERS FOR EARNED-RUN AVERAGE TITLE

Minimum 115 innings. *Lefthanded pitcher.

Pitcher, Team	W	L	Pct.	ERA	G	GS	CG	ShO	GF	Sv.	IP	H	TBF	R	ER	HR	SH	SF	HB	BB	IBB	SO	WP	Bk.
Ryan, Jason, Memphis	8	6	.571	2.70	29	28	0	0	0	0	189.2	195	783	63	57	18	9	7	9	45	1	110	2	1
Sessions, Doug, New Orleans	9	5	.643	2.92	31	25	1	1	2	1	157.1	149	653	57	51	16	2	5	2	43	4	92	3	0
Figueroa, Nelson, Nashville	12	5	.706	2.97	23	23	3	1	0	0	151.1	144	627	54	50	11	7	2	8	37	5	121	5	0
Duchscherer, Justin, Sac.	14	2	.875	3.25	24	23	0	0	0	0	155.0	151	623	59	56	12	1	8	2	18	0	117	2	0
Capuano, Chris, Tucson *	9	5	.643	3.34	23	23	0	0	0	0	142.2	133	602	66	53	9	11	4	11	43	2	108	6	1
Stemle, Steve, Memphis	6	11	.353	3.46	26	26	1	0	0	0	156.0	155	652	71	60	12	8	6	5	36	4	89	3	0
Anderson, Craig, Tacoma *	13	11	.542	3.56	28	27	4	1	0	0	177.0	187	751	93	70	27	4	5	2	46	1	67	4	0
Gonzalez, Edgar, Tucson	8	7	.533	3.75	20	19	1	0	1	0	129.2	126	542	65	54	4	6	5	8	28	0	69	5	1
Wright, Jamey, Okla.-Omaha	5	6	.455	3.80	20	19	3	1	0	0	116.0	108	502	53	49	11	4	2	6	59	0	105	4	0
Fernandez, Jared, N. Orleans	7	10	.412	3.81	26	23	2	0	0	0	156.0	164	660	73	66	16	6	3	7	37	1	51	2	0
Sanders, Scott, Albuquerque	7	5	.583	3.92	19	19	2	0	0	0	117.0	124	499	57	51	12	7	2	6	32	1	110	4	0
Young, Jason, Colo. Springs	6	7	.462	3.95	23	21	2	1	0	0	116.1	128	525	63	51	10	6	2	8	37	0	99	3	0
Bruback, Matt, Iowa	6	8	.429	3.96	20	19	1	0	1	0	125.0	120	536	65	55	10	6	7	15	33	4	90	2	0
Bruback, Matt, Ia.-Nash.-Port.	10	10	.500	4.00	26	25	1	0	1	0	157.1	150	682	80	70	14	10	8	19	49	4	112	3	0
Lorraine, Andrew, Las Vegas *	8	9	.471	4.16	30	27	0	0	0	0	158.0	211	718	86	73	17	5	6	7	39	1	77	2	0

DEPARTMENTAL LEADERS: W—Duchscherer, 14; L—Reames, 13; Pct.—Myers, .900; G—Bartosh, 64; GS—Hiljus, 29; CG—C. Anderson, 4; ShO—S. Kim, Patterson, Vance, 2; GF—Clontz, 49; Sv.—Clontz, M. Corey, 30; IP—Ryan, 189.2; H—Lorraine, 211; TBF—Ryan, 783; R—Gosling, Hiljus, 106; ER—Hiljus, 91; HR—Hiljus, 28; SH—Capuano, Jensen, 11; SF—Bootcheck, 12; HB—Bruback, 19; BB—Smyth, 72; IBB—Molina, Reid, Wuertz, 8; SO—Tankersley, 148; WP—Gosling, 13; BK—Vance, 10.

ALL PITCHERS

*Lefthanded pitcher.

Pitcher, Team	W	L	Pct.	ERA	G	GS	CG	ShO	GF	Sv.	IP	H	TBF	R	ER	HR	SH	SF	HB	BB	IBB	SO	WP	Bk.
Abbott, Paul, Tucson	3	4	.429	3.95	11	8	1	1	1	0	54.2	63	242	29	24	3	1	3	4	12	0	50	3	0
Agamennone, Brandon, Edm.	1	2	.333	6.94	5	1	0	0	1	0	11.2	16	55	10	9	3	0	0	0	7	2	9	0	0
Ainsworth, Kurt, Fresno	0	0	.000	4.50	1	1	0	0	0	0	2.0	2	10	1	1	0	0	0	0	2	0	1	0	0
Alfonseca, Antonio, Iowa	0	1	.000	4.91	3	0	0	0	0	0	3.2	6	19	2	2	0	1	0	0	1	0	5	0	0
Alvarez, Juan, Albuquerque *	3	2	.600	5.88	51	0	0	0	15	0	52.0	69	245	38	34	9	4	4	3	24	1	43	2	2
Alvarez, Victor, Las Vegas *	4	4	.500	2.70	22	7	0	0	4	1	63.1	53	256	25	19	2	2	2	1	15	0	47	1	0
Alvarez, Wilson, Las Vegas *	5	1	.833	1.34	8	8	0	0	0	0	47.0	36	181	9	7	1	2	2	4	6	0	33	0	0
Alviso, Jerome, Co. Spr.-Salt Lk.	0	0	.000	9.00	1	0	0	0	1	0	1.0	1	5	1	1	1	0	0	0	1	0	1	0	0
Anderson, Craig, Tacoma *	13	11	.542	3.56	28	27	4	1	0	0	177.0	187	751	93	70	27	4	5	2	46	1	67	4	0
Anderson, Jimmy, Fresno *	1	4	.200	6.44	8	8	0	0	0	0	43.1	65	209	36	31	3	4	2	3	15	0	17	2	1
Atchison, Scott, Tacoma	6	9	.400	4.31	39	7	0	0	10	1	108.2	114	474	57	52	8	7	2	3	37	2	83	2	0
Aybar, Manny, Fresno	2	4	.333	4.08	52	0	0	0	41	17	57.1	55	247	27	26	7	4	2	1	23	0	45	4	1
Baerlocher, Ryan, Omaha	4	7	.364	4.65	19	19	1	0	0	0	120.0	115	501	68	62	17	5	3	5	42	0	73	6	0
Baldwin, James, Omaha	3	2	.600	4.08	8	8	0	0	0	0	46.1	48	200	25	21	3	0	3	3	13	0	24	3	1
Banks, Willie, Iowa	2	0	1.000	2.03	25	0	0	0	22	17	31.0	24	122	7	7	1	1	0	0	7	2	29	2	0
Barber, Scott, Tucson	1	0	1.000	2.05	5	2	1	1	1	0	22.0	19	88	5	5	1	2	0	1	5	0	4	0	0
Barcelo, Lorenzo, Fresno	0	3	.000	6.49	20	0	0	0	8	0	26.1	33	114	19	19	1	2	3	1	4	0	16	2	0
Bartosh, Cliff, Portland *	2	5	.286	4.29	64	0	0	0	29	10	71.1	67	299	36	34	4	4	1	3	22	1	51	4	0
Bausher, Andy, Portland *	1	0	1.000	8.25	7	1	0	0	2	0	12.0	17	57	11	11	2	0	0	1	3	0	6	1	0
Beasley, Ray, Oklahoma *	5	5	.500	4.59	43	0	0	0	23	4	51.0	57	228	28	26	4	6	4	5	20	2	29	0	0
Beck, Rod, Iowa	1	1	.500	0.59	21	0	0	0	9	4	30.2	25	122	3	2	2	4	1	0	7	0	26	1	0
Belitz, Todd, Colo. Spr.-Alb.*	1	0	1.000	7.23	16	0	0	0	4	0	18.2	29	96	18	15	0	2	1	5	6	1	11	0	0
Beltran, Francis, Iowa	6	2	.750	2.96	31	2	0	0	23	4	48.2	46	206	17	16	2	0	0	1	19	3	33	0	0
Benes, Alan, Iowa	7	7	.500	5.37	19	17	2	0	0	0	114.0	129	498	74	68	13	9	5	1	44	1	81	5	0
Bennett, Jeff, Nashville	1	3	.250	6.56	9	5	0	0	1	0	23.1	26	111	21	17	4	2	2	1	12	0	16	1	0
Benoit, Joaquin, Oklahoma	2	1	.667	3.82	6	6	0	0	0	0	33.0	28	134	17	14	3	0	0	2	11	0	31	1	0
Bergman, Dusty, Salt Lake *	0	1	.000	20.25	1	0	0	0	0	0	1.1	5	10	5	3	0	1	1	0	1	0	0	0	0
Bergman, Sean, Albuquerque	8	11	.421	4.69	28	28	2	1	0	0	170.2	193	732	99	89	19	2	7	5	44	2	101	2	1
Bevel, Bobby, Colo. Springs *	1	2	.333	3.60	26	0	0	0	11	0	30.0	31	132	18	12	1	0	3	1	12	0	20	4	0
Bland, Nate, New Orleans *	0	1	.000	2.84	17	0	0	0	5	1	19.0	15	81	6	6	1	1	1	1	9	1	23	0	0
Blank, Matt, Edm.-Fresno *	2	3	.400	4.21	13	13	0	0	0	0	68.1	78	297	36	32	5	2	4	3	21	1	52	2	1
Bochtler, Doug, Albuquerque	5	3	.625	5.37	23	5	0	0	6	1	53.2	61	232	33	32	9	1	0	2	18	2	40	1	0
Bonser, Boof, Fresno	1	2	.333	3.13	4	4	0	0	0	0	23.0	17	97	13	8	4	1	1	0	8	0	28	2	0
Bootcheck, Chris, Salt Lake	8	9	.471	4.25	28	26	3	0	0	0	171.1	194	737	103	81	19	6	12	7	43	1	82	1	0
Borbon, Pedro, Memphis *	0	1	.000	3.12	7	0	0	0	4	1	8.2	6	32	3	3	1	1	0	1	0	0	6	1	0
Borland, Toby, Albuquerque	1	1	.500	3.72	9	0	0	0	9	3	9.2	6	44	5	4	1	1	0	3	6	0	12	4	0
Bottalico, Ricky, Tucson	2	2	.500	3.66	31	0	0	0	6	0	39.1	39	170	24	16	4	0	2	1	16	1	28	2	0

Pitcher, Team	W	L	Pct.	ERA	G	GS	CG	ShO	GF	Sv.	IP	H	TBF	R	ER	HR	SH	SF	HB	BB	IBB	SO	WP	Bk.
Bowie, Micah, Sacramento *	0	0	.000	0.00	5	0	0	0	4	2	4.0	2	16	1	0	0	0	0	0	1	0	3	0	0
Brohawn, Troy, Las Vegas *	1	0	1.000	4.50	1	0	0	0	0	0	4.0	3	16	2	2	1	0	1	0	0	0	1	0	0
Brooks, Frank, Nashville *	2	0	1.000	2.54	16	0	0	0	4	0	28.1	22	113	9	8	2	1	0	0	11	2	22	1	0
Brown, Elliot, Fresno	3	3	.500	4.62	12	5	0	0	3	0	37.0	37	157	21	19	5	4	1	0	13	0	12	2	0
Brown, Eric, Iowa	0	0	.000	0.00	3	0	0	0	2	0	3.2	3	16	0	0	0	0	0	0	1	0	6	0	0
Bruback, Matt, Ia.-Nash.-Port.	10	10	.500	4.00	26	25	1	0	1	0	157.1	150	682	80	70	14	10	8	19	49	4	112	3	0
Bruney, Brian, Tucson	3	1	.750	2.81	32	0	0	0	29	12	32.0	24	139	12	10	0	0	3	2	18	0	32	2	0
Bukvich, Ryan, Omaha	1	2	.333	4.91	34	0	0	0	21	5	36.2	39	171	21	20	2	1	2	0	25	0	44	6	0
Bullinger, Kirk, New Orleans	3	3	.500	1.94	55	0	0	0	45	20	65.0	56	263	18	14	3	1	2	3	14	4	46	0	0
Bump, Nate, Albuquerque	6	5	.545	4.43	15	15	0	0	0	0	85.1	89	368	48	42	4	3	1	7	24	1	52	1	0
Bynum, Mike, Portland *	7	12	.368	4.81	24	23	0	0	0	0	125.1	130	554	76	67	11	2	2	10	60	2	106	6	1
Callaway, Mickey, Salt Lk.-Okla.	3	0	1.000	2.35	11	8	0	0	0	0	38.1	38	154	14	10	1	1	2	0	11	0	19	3	0
Cammack, Eric, New Orleans	0	0	.000	1.93	4	0	0	0	3	0	4.2	4	20	2	1	1	1	0	0	2	0	3	1	0
Camp, Shawn, Nashville	0	1	.000	4.98	33	1	0	0	9	0	43.1	50	193	26	24	2	2	1	2	15	2	36	4	0
Capuano, Chris, Tucson *	9	5	.643	3.34	23	23	0	0	0	0	142.2	133	602	66	53	9	11	4	11	43	2	108	6	1
Carlyle, Buddy, Omaha	0	1	.000	5.40	2	0	0	0	0	0	5.0	5	20	3	3	2	0	0	0	1	0	4	0	0
Carpenter, Chris, Memphis	0	0	.000	5.40	3	3	0	0	0	0	8.1	11	36	5	5	0	0	1	0	2	0	4	0	0
Carrara, Giovanni, Tacoma	1	1	.500	4.23	18	0	0	0	13	5	27.2	28	117	14	13	2	1	1	0	9	0	27	3	0
Castillo, Frank, Sacramento	5	4	.556	4.13	19	16	0	0	2	0	96.0	104	414	47	44	12	1	1	6	34	2	59	1	0
Cate, Troy, Tacoma *	1	0	1.000	1.69	1	1	0	0	0	0	5.1	4	24	3	1	2	0	0	1	2	0	6	0	0
Cervantes, Chris, Tucson *	3	4	.429	4.04	11	7	0	0	1	1	42.1	41	188	22	19	3	4	2	4	24	0	27	1	0
Chacon, Shawn, Colo. Springs	0	0	.000	6.00	1	1	0	0	0	0	3.0	5	13	2	2	1	0	0	0	0	0	2	1	0
Chavez, Wilton, Iowa	11	7	.611	4.24	26	22	1	0	1	0	140.0	144	605	69	66	17	2	5	11	51	6	113	5	0
Chiavacci, Ron, Edmonton	4	6	.400	5.46	23	15	1	0	3	0	97.1	112	439	65	59	10	4	5	5	41	1	81	6	0
Christiansen, Jason, Fresno *	0	0	.000	5.40	4	1	0	0	0	0	5.0	5	22	3	3	0	0	1	1	1	0	2	0	0
Clontz, Brad, Colo. Springs	3	2	.600	3.42	57	0	0	0	49	30	55.1	54	248	31	21	4	2	1	5	26	0	63	2	0
Cloude, Ken, Tacoma	4	4	.500	5.95	21	17	0	0	0	0	75.2	88	351	56	50	15	0	2	9	37	0	39	4	1
Colon, Jose, Edmonton	1	1	.500	5.85	13	0	0	0	5	0	20.0	25	89	13	13	4	0	0	2	6	1	14	0	0
Colyer, Steve, Las Vegas *	2	3	.400	3.21	44	0	0	0	44	23	47.2	44	206	18	17	1	1	1	1	22	0	50	1	0
Condrey, Clay, Portland	3	3	.500	4.14	11	11	0	0	0	0	63.0	64	261	34	29	7	1	4	0	12	0	46	4	0
Connelly, Steve, Fresno	3	4	.429	7.43	38	1	0	0	10	0	59.1	97	295	54	49	10	6	3	4	24	1	29	5	0
Cook, Aaron, Colo. Springs	1	1	.500	2.25	2	2	1	0	0	0	16.0	10	61	4	4	2	0	0	0	4	0	12	0	0
Cook, B.R., Memphis	0	1	.000	9.31	13	0	0	0	3	0	19.1	29	97	20	20	5	0	1	0	14	0	7	2	0
Corcoran, Roy, Edmonton	0	0	.000	0.00	2	0	0	0	1	0	2.0	0	6	0	0	0	0	0	0	0	0	1	0	0
Corey, Bryan, Las Vegas	4	5	.444	2.97	60	0	0	0	24	3	91.0	94	390	40	30	8	3	2	5	29	2	46	2	0
Corey, Mark, Nashville	1	3	.250	4.34	46	0	0	0	40	30	45.2	37	191	23	22	5	0	0	0	18	2	63	1	0
Cormier, Lance, Tucson	1	1	.500	2.60	5	4	0	0	0	0	27.2	26	108	10	8	1	3	0	0	5	0	11	1	0
Correia, Kevin, Fresno	1	0	1.000	2.84	3	3	0	0	0	0	19.0	16	74	8	6	3	0	0	0	2	0	23	2	0
Croushore, Rick, Albuquerque	0	0	.000	0.00	3	0	0	0	0	0	3.0	0	10	0	0	0	0	0	0	1	0	2	0	0
Crudale, Mike, Memphis	5	5	.500	5.52	32	0	0	0	29	6	29.1	34	131	19	18	7	0	0	0	11	1	23	2	0
Crumpton, Chuck, Edmonton	2	1	.667	4.79	19	2	0	0	9	4	47.0	42	197	25	25	5	1	2	1	21	0	19	0	0
Cruz, Juan, Iowa	4	0	1.000	1.95	9	9	0	0	0	0	50.2	37	200	12	11	1	3	3	4	11	0	47	1	1
Cruz, Nelson, Colo. Springs	1	2	.333	7.20	4	4	0	0	0	0	15.0	24	72	18	12	3	1	2	1	3	0	10	0	0
Cumberland, Chris, Portland *	0	0	.000	3.68	4	0	0	0	2	0	7.1	7	31	3	3	0	0	0	0	2	0	5	0	0
Cummings, Jeremy, Memphis	7	3	.700	4.81	13	13	0	0	0	0	73.0	73	305	40	39	14	2	2	0	20	0	37	5	0
Cummings, Ryan, Salt Lake	1	3	.250	8.36	12	0	0	0	5	0	14.0	22	70	14	13	2	3	2	2	7	0	6	0	0
Cunnane, Will, Iowa	0	1	.000	2.20	12	0	0	0	3	0	16.1	17	73	5	4	0	2	1	0	8	3	16	3	0
Darensbourg, Vic, Co.Spr.-Edm.*	3	3	.500	2.97	31	0	0	0	10	0	36.1	36	156	16	12	1	3	0	2	12	1	26	2	0
Darnell, Paul, Colo. Springs *	0	1	.000	0.00	1	0	0	0	1	0	1.2	1	9	1	0	0	1	0	0	2	0	1	0	0
Davis, Doug, Oklahoma *	3	0	1.000	3.25	4	4	0	0	0	0	27.2	29	109	10	10	3	0	0	1	1	0	18	0	1
Davis, Kane, Iowa	2	1	.667	2.35	22	0	0	0	8	2	30.2	21	120	8	8	3	1	1	0	12	1	24	2	0
DeHart, Rick, Omaha *	1	3	.250	4.82	25	0	0	0	12	1	28.0	38	128	15	15	1	2	2	3	7	2	17	1	0
Devey, Phil, Las Vegas *	0	2	.000	9.82	3	1	0	0	0	0	7.1	9	35	8	8	1	0	0	0	6	0	4	1	0
Dickey, R.A., Oklahoma	1	1	.500	1.20	3	2	0	0	0	0	15.0	14	57	3	2	1	0	0	0	3	0	4	0	0
Dingman, Craig, Iowa	1	0	1.000	2.00	11	0	0	0	5	0	18.0	14	74	4	4	0	0	1	0	7	1	12	1	0
Dominguez, Juan, Oklahoma	1	0	1.000	3.50	3	3	0	0	0	0	18.0	15	71	7	7	1	2	0	0	3	0	14	1	0
Donaldson, Bo, Salt Lk.-Edm.	0	0	.000	3.80	12	1	0	0	5	0	23.2	25	111	13	10	3	0	0	0	16	1	17	0	0
Downs, Scott, Edmonton *	8	9	.471	4.29	21	21	3	0	0	0	121.2	119	502	67	58	13	2	7	1	39	0	54	1	0
Drese, Ryan, Oklahoma	8	6	.571	4.65	20	20	0	0	0	0	122.0	143	533	70	63	8	2	7	7	39	1	68	5	1
Drew, Tim, Edmonton	5	9	.357	7.23	27	15	0	0	6	2	93.1	128	429	80	75	10	4	4	3	35	2	54	5	1
Duchscherer, Justin, Sac.	14	2	.875	3.25	24	23	0	0	0	0	155.0	151	623	59	56	12	1	8	2	18	0	117	2	0
Duff, Matt, Memphis	4	2	.667	2.62	32	0	0	0	12	3	34.1	28	145	12	10	4	3	1	0	14	2	33	4	0
Duncan, Courtney, Port.-Salt Lk.	2	6	.250	4.38	56	0	0	0	44	18	63.2	68	298	39	31	4	2	4	8	39	1	54	4	0
Dunn, Scott, Salt Lake	0	0	.000	11.74	6	0	0	0	0	0	7.2	9	43	10	10	1	0	0	0	10	0	11	1	0
Ebert, Derrin, Iowa-Tucson *	1	1	.500	3.92	21	0	0	0	10	0	20.2	30	102	9	9	1	0	2	2	10	2	11	1	0
Elarton, Scott, Colo. Springs	6	8	.429	5.31	20	20	0	0	0	0	118.2	146	546	81	70	15	3	6	8	39	1	92	4	0
Ellis, Robert, Oklahoma	3	10	.231	4.94	27	15	2	0	7	3	118.1	128	516	68	65	12	8	7	7	35	3	49	7	1
Emanuel, Brandon, Salt Lake	6	10	.375	5.14	29	23	1	0	5	2	147.0	186	640	93	84	25	3	7	4	37	1	71	4	0
Enochs, Chris, Sacramento	6	3	.667	5.23	37	4	0	0	6	0	62.0	76	289	40	36	2	2	3	2	30	5	49	9	0
Esslinger, Cam, Colo. Springs	0	1	.000	9.82	6	0	0	0	4	0	7.1	10	44	9	8	0	1	0	2	12	0	8	2	0
Estrella, Luis, Fresno	2	9	.182	5.56	51	6	0	0	21	5	89.0	104	405	62	55	5	4	5	2	41	2	52	7	1
Evans, Keith, Edmonton-Iowa	2	2	.500	5.01	22	1	0	0	6	1	41.1	50	185	25	23	5	0	3	4	13	1	16	0	0
Falkenborg, Brian, Tacoma	4	2	.667	2.94	17	14	0	0	0	0	79.2	66	331	28	26	7	1	3	2	26	0	62	2	0
Farmer, Tom, Las Vegas	2	2	.500	2.54	5	5	0	0	0	0	28.1	30	122	12	8	1	1	0	3	9	0	14	2	0
Ferguson, Ian, Omaha	0	2	.000	6.39	3	3	0	0	0	0	12.2	14	65	9	9	1	0	1	1	13	0	5	0	0
Fernandez, Jared, N.Orleans	7	10	.412	3.81	26	23	2	0	0	0	156.0	164	660	73	66	16	6	3	7	37	1	51	2	0
Ferns, Robert, Tucson	0	0	.000	5.40	1	0	0	0	0	0	1.2	2	8	1	1	1	0	0	0	1	0	1	0	0
Ferrari, Anthony, Edmonton *	5	2	.714	4.89	28	0	0	0	16	0	49.2	63	229	29	27	3	3	3	6	18	4	17	0	0
Fesh, Sean, Albuquerque *	1	0	1.000	10.80	6	0	0	0	3	0	6.2	12	36	9	8	0	0	0	0	5	0	4	0	0
Field, Nathan, Omaha	2	2	.500	3.18	19	0	0	0	15	4	22.2	15	85	8	8	4	0	0	1	4	0	17	3	0
Figueroa, Nelson, Nashville	12	5	.706	2.97	23	23	3	1	0	0	151.1	144	627	54	50	11	7	2	8	37	5	121	5	0
Fikac, Jeremy, Sacramento	3	3	.500	2.25	42	0	0	0	19	4	56.0	40	218	19	14	4	0	2	0	13	1	50	1	0

Pitcher, Team	W	L	Pct.	ERA	G	GS	CG	ShO	GF	Sv.	IP	H	TBF	R	ER	HR	SH	SF	HB	BB	IBB	SO	WP	Bk.
Flores, Randy, Colo.Springs *	10	8	.556	4.98	28	24	0	0	1	0	142.2	156	651	89	79	16	8	4	10	67	4	116	8	1
Flores, Ron, Sacramento *	2	0	1.000	6.59	12	0	0	0	0	0	13.2	16	58	10	10	0	0	2	0	3	1	10	1	0
Flury, Pat, Portland-Omaha	0	0	.000	5.19	14	0	0	0	2	0	17.1	19	87	12	10	3	0	0	3	15	0	16	2	1
Fogg, Josh, Nashville	0	1	.000	5.40	2	2	0	0	0	0	10.0	12	40	6	6	1	1	1	0	1	0	7	0	0
Foppert, Jesse, Fresno	0	0	.000	1.80	1	1	0	0	0	0	5.0	3	19	1	1	0	0	0	1	0	0	9	3	0
Fordham, Tom, Nashville *	2	2	.500	6.87	13	4	1	0	4	0	36.2	51	181	29	28	7	3	2	1	21	2	20	2	0
Fox, Chad, Albuquerque	0	0	.000	3.86	3	0	0	0	0	0	2.1	4	12	1	1	0	0	0	0	1	0	5	0	0
Fruto, Emiliano, Tacoma	1	0	1.000	0.00	1	0	0	0	0	0	4.0	1	14	0	0	0	0	0	0	2	0	2	0	0
Fuell, Jerrod, Albuquerque	0	0	.000	3.60	3	0	0	0	1	0	5.0	6	21	3	2	1	0	0	0	0	0	2	0	0
Fultz, Aaron, Oklahoma *	0	0	.000	27.00	1	0	0	0	0	0	1.0	2	6	3	3	2	0	0	0	1	0	2	0	0
Fyhrie, Mike, Omaha-Alb.	8	4	.667	4.05	20	14	0	0	1	0	109.0	110	461	55	49	10	4	1	5	41	2	72	1	0
Gaal, Bryan, Portland	0	1	.000	4.50	2	0	0	0	0	0	2.0	2	8	1	1	0	0	0	0	0	0	1	0	0
Gallo, Mike, New Orleans *	3	0	1.000	2.08	16	0	0	0	3	0	17.1	13	64	4	4	0	0	0	1	3	0	11	0	0
Garcia, James, Fresno	1	3	.250	4.18	7	4	0	0	2	0	23.2	23	107	12	11	3	1	2	4	12	0	22	0	0
Garcia, Reynaldo, Oklahoma	4	3	.571	3.69	39	3	0	0	24	9	61.0	64	261	27	25	3	1	2	1	19	1	64	6	0
Garcia, Rosman, Oklahoma	1	2	.333	1.91	17	2	0	0	13	10	28.1	20	109	7	6	1	1	0	0	6	0	21	0	0
George, Chris, Omaha *	3	5	.375	7.29	10	10	0	0	0	0	54.1	71	251	49	44	8	0	2	1	22	0	28	2	0
Giese, Dan, Portland	1	0	1.000	13.50	3	0	0	0	1	0	6.0	12	32	9	9	2	0	0	0	3	0	6	0	0
Gilfillan, Jason, Omaha	6	0	1.000	2.05	35	0	0	0	20	7	52.2	46	209	14	12	4	0	3	2	12	0	33	0	0
Gissell, Chris, Colo. Springs	8	4	.667	3.55	38	10	0	0	6	1	109.0	96	467	53	43	8	7	1	11	35	1	82	4	0
Gonzalez, Alfredo, Las Vegas	1	0	1.000	1.13	2	2	0	0	0	0	8.0	6	34	2	1	0	0	0	1	3	0	5	0	0
Gonzalez, Edgar, Tucson	8	7	.533	3.75	20	19	1	0	1	0	129.2	126	542	65	54	4	6	5	8	28	0	69	5	1
Gonzalez, Mike, Nashville *	0	0	.000	4.50	7	0	0	0	2	2	10.0	9	45	5	5	0	0	0	2	4	1	10	0	0
Good, Andrew, Tucson	4	4	.500	5.00	11	11	0	0	0	0	63.0	78	276	36	35	12	1	0	2	13	0	45	1	0
Gosling, Mike, Tucson *	9	12	.429	5.61	26	26	0	0	0	0	136.1	190	645	106	85	13	5	5	3	56	0	89	13	0
Grabow, John, Nashville *	0	2	.000	4.74	17	0	0	0	4	0	24.2	31	112	17	13	0	1	0	0	7	2	26	0	0
Graham, Tom, Oklahoma	3	1	.750	5.27	22	0	0	0	7	1	41.0	39	167	24	24	5	2	2	1	12	1	28	0	0
Green, Steve, Salt Lake	9	5	.643	4.66	21	21	0	0	0	0	110.0	120	481	63	57	6	3	2	6	47	0	70	3	0
Gregg, Kevin, Salt Lake	7	4	.636	4.03	15	15	0	0	0	0	91.2	90	378	47	41	10	0	1	8	18	0	75	4	0
Grilli, Jason, Albuquerque	6	2	.750	3.38	12	12	0	0	0	0	66.2	64	282	30	25	3	0	2	3	30	1	38	3	0
Guerrier, Matt, Nashville	4	6	.400	4.53	20	19	0	0	1	0	105.1	108	442	56	53	15	4	3	4	18	1	78	5	0
Gulin, Lindsay, Las Vegas *	10	10	.500	4.85	28	27	1	1	0	0	154.0	153	678	97	83	16	4	10	9	63	1	127	9	2
Hampton, Matt, Portland *	1	3	.250	5.83	33	0	0	0	6	0	46.1	51	206	32	30	7	3	5	1	22	1	36	2	0
Hamulack, Tim, Tacoma *	1	0	1.000	3.86	10	0	0	0	5	0	14.0	16	62	6	6	1	1	0	0	8	0	12	0	0
Hanrahan, Joel, Las Vegas	1	2	.333	10.08	5	5	0	0	0	0	25.0	36	130	28	28	2	1	2	2	20	1	13	2	0
Harang, Aaron, Sacramento	8	2	.800	2.71	12	12	0	0	0	0	69.2	62	287	24	21	5	1	0	4	17	0	60	1	0
Harden, Rich, Sacramento	9	4	.692	3.15	16	14	0	0	0	0	88.2	72	357	34	31	6	1	1	1	35	0	91	5	0
Haren, Danny, Memphis	2	1	.667	4.93	8	8	0	0	0	0	45.2	50	197	25	25	6	1	0	4	8	1	35	1	1
Harris, Brian, Omaha	0	0	.000	9.00	1	0	0	0	1	0	1.0	1	4	1	1	0	0	1	0	0	0	0	0	0
Harville, Chad, Sacramento	3	5	.375	2.05	48	0	0	0	44	18	57.0	42	232	16	13	5	3	0	0	21	2	57	5	0
Heaverlo, Jeff, Tacoma	5	12	.294	5.39	24	24	0	0	0	0	123.2	150	554	80	74	8	5	8	10	38	0	75	4	2
Hebson, Bryan, Edmonton	6	0	1.000	4.36	30	0	0	0	16	6	43.1	44	200	23	21	3	3	2	4	22	1	44	3	1
Henrie, Matt, Tucson	0	0	.000	3.00	1	1	0	0	0	0	6.0	8	28	3	2	0	0	0	1	2	0	1	0	0
Hensley, Matt, Salt Lake	8	12	.400	4.89	27	27	1	0	0	0	158.1	194	710	105	86	16	4	5	11	49	0	85	4	1
Herges, Matt, Portland	0	0	.000	1.80	4	0	0	0	2	0	5.0	1	18	1	1	0	0	0	0	2	0	5	0	0
Hermanson, Dustin, Fresno	0	1	.000	4.85	4	4	0	0	0	0	26.0	29	109	16	14	2	1	4	1	3	1	17	1	0
Hernandez, Runelvys, Omaha	1	0	1.000	1.80	1	1	0	0	0	0	5.0	3	20	1	1	0	0	0	1	2	0	5	0	0
Hiljus, Erik, Sacramento	11	10	.524	4.69	29	29	2	1	0	0	174.2	174	751	106	91	28	4	6	5	52	1	129	6	0
Hill, Jeremy, Omaha	1	3	.250	7.81	26	1	0	0	7	1	40.1	42	202	38	35	5	2	1	4	42	0	41	9	0
Holtz, Mike, Nashville *	3	2	.600	4.91	45	0	0	0	7	0	44.0	45	193	25	24	7	3	1	1	19	3	49	2	0
Horgan, Joe, Fresno *	7	7	.500	5.67	55	0	0	0	23	3	74.2	80	333	51	47	9	4	4	5	30	1	65	7	1
Houlton, D.J., New Orleans	3	4	.429	5.40	11	11	0	0	0	0	61.2	70	266	39	37	12	1	0	3	19	0	48	3	1
House, Craig, Tacoma-Alb.	0	0	.000	11.85	12	0	0	0	6	0	13.2	20	78	18	18	0	0	1	2	18	0	12	3	0
Howard, Ben, Portland	7	9	.438	4.55	22	22	0	0	0	0	130.2	118	550	69	66	17	6	3	6	49	0	68	7	0
Hughes, Travis, Oklahoma	1	3	.250	5.46	11	11	0	0	0	0	57.2	79	278	41	35	4	3	3	5	27	0	36	1	0
Hunter, Johnny, Portland	2	2	.500	6.29	11	3	0	0	4	1	24.1	31	118	21	17	3	0	3	2	17	0	21	0	0
Iapoce, Anthony, Alb.*	0	0	.000	0.00	2	0	0	0	2	0	2.0	0	6	0	0	0	0	0	0	0	0	1	0	0
Izquierdo, Hansel, Edmonton	2	2	.500	7.41	17	5	0	0	6	3	51.0	73	242	42	42	4	1	2	4	19	0	37	5	0
Jarvis, Matt, Fresno *	1	2	.333	4.35	23	1	0	0	6	0	31.0	42	140	15	15	0	3	1	3	11	0	17	0	0
Jensen, Ryan, Fresno	1	10	.091	5.30	27	18	0	0	1	0	103.2	114	463	70	61	14	11	9	6	36	2	50	4	1
Johnson, Jonathan, N.Orleans	5	4	.556	3.92	13	13	1	0	0	0	78.0	74	333	38	34	4	3	2	2	27	0	62	9	0
Johnson, Keith, Salt Lake	0	0	.000	0.00	1	0	0	0	1	0	0.2	0	2	0	0	0	0	1	0	0	0	1	0	0
Johnson, Mike, Fresno	4	3	.571	3.72	30	4	0	0	7	1	65.1	58	280	31	27	5	2	2	3	26	2	56	7	0
Johnson, Randy, Tucson *	0	0	.000	0.00	1	1	0	0	0	0	4.0	0	12	0	0	0	0	0	0	0	0	4	0	0
Johnson, Rett, Tacoma	5	2	.714	2.15	11	10	1	1	0	0	71.0	63	288	26	17	2	0	3	6	18	0	49	4	0
Jones, Bobby M., Omaha *	1	2	.333	3.65	20	1	0	0	9	1	37.0	28	156	15	15	4	2	1	0	20	1	27	4	0
Jones, Greg, Salt Lake	2	3	.400	4.40	33	0	0	0	14	4	47.0	36	184	24	23	4	0	1	0	9	0	56	2	0
Jongejan, Ferenc, Iowa *	2	1	.667	5.59	29	0	0	0	6	1	29.0	34	138	20	18	3	1	1	4	15	2	23	0	0
Joseph, Kevin, Mem.-Edm.	2	7	.222	5.40	29	6	0	0	11	1	75.0	96	343	50	45	10	4	4	2	28	4	38	8	0
Journell, Jimmy, Memphis	6	6	.500	3.92	40	7	0	0	16	5	78.0	80	343	38	34	3	5	1	6	32	2	70	5	0
Judd, Mike, Albuquerque	4	9	.308	6.05	30	8	0	0	12	4	58.0	58	262	44	39	7	3	4	2	30	1	54	8	0
Karnuth, Jason, Iowa	0	1	.000	4.74	13	0	0	0	4	1	19.0	23	88	12	10	4	1	1	0	12	0	7	0	0
Kaye, Justin, Iowa	1	4	.200	7.20	20	0	0	0	9	0	30.0	33	141	26	24	3	0	2	2	18	1	21	3	2
Keagle, Greg, Albuquerque	0	2	.000	14.85	3	2	0	0	0	0	6.2	14	43	13	11	1	1	1	2	8	0	6	1	0
Keisler, Randy, Port.-Ok.-N.Orl.*	7	6	.538	4.13	22	17	0	0	0	0	102.1	107	437	49	47	11	6	2	1	38	2	60	3	0
Keller, Kris, Portland	1	1	.500	5.63	18	1	0	0	5	0	24.0	34	116	19	15	4	3	3	0	11	0	11	1	0
Kida, Masao, Las Vegas	2	4	.333	5.02	21	12	0	0	2	1	84.1	89	365	53	47	9	2	5	6	23	1	57	6	1
Kim, Byung-Hyun, Tucson	1	1	.500	2.55	3	3	0	0	0	0	17.2	17	69	5	5	2	1	1	3	1	0	8	0	0
Kim, Sun-Woo, Edmonton	10	8	.556	5.03	22	22	3	2	0	0	132.1	147	587	83	74	18	5	2	3	53	1	83	5	0
King, Brad, Nashville	0	0	.000	18.00	3	0	0	0	3	0	3.0	8	19	6	6	2	0	0	0	1	0	0	0	0
Knott, Eric, Edmonton *	6	5	.545	4.32	24	10	1	1	6	0	77.0	102	341	40	37	6	2	1	1	13	4	38	2	2
Koplove, Mike, Tucson	0	1	.000	13.50	3	0	0	0	2	1	2.2	4	15	4	4	1	0	0	0	3	0	2	0	0

Pitcher, Team	W	L	Pct.	ERA	G	GS	CG	ShO	GF	Sv.	IP	H	TBF	R	ER	HR	SH	SF	HB	BB	IBB	SO	WP	Bk.
Kroon, Marc, Salt Lake	2	1	.667	3.86	9	0	0	0	4	2	14.0	10	56	6	6	2	0	0	1	3	0	10	1	0
Kusiewicz, Mike, Sac.*	3	1	.750	4.13	27	0	0	0	6	0	28.1	21	120	16	13	1	2	1	4	10	2	20	3	0
Kuzmic, Craig, Tacoma-Fresno	0	0	.000	3.00	3	0	0	0	3	0	3.0	4	15	1	1	1	0	0	0	2	0	1	0	0
Lambert, Jeremy, Memphis	1	0	1.000	3.86	12	0	0	0	4	0	11.2	11	49	5	5	1	0	0	0	5	1	9	0	0
Landry, Jacques, Tacoma	0	0	.000	0.00	1	0	0	0	1	0	1.0	0	5	0	0	0	0	0	0	2	0	1	0	0
Langone, Steve, Las Vegas	0	0	.000	8.31	6	0	0	0	1	0	8.2	14	40	11	8	2	0	1	0	0	0	9	0	0
Layfield, Scotty, Memphis	0	3	.000	4.33	22	0	0	0	7	2	27.0	29	119	13	13	2	1	1	0	16	1	17	3	2
Lee, Dave, Las Vegas	3	2	.600	3.13	56	0	0	0	30	9	60.1	47	264	22	21	4	1	3	2	36	3	61	0	1
Lehr, Justin, Sacramento	3	2	.600	3.72	53	0	0	0	16	4	75.0	74	320	34	31	3	3	0	4	27	3	64	5	0
Leicester, Jon, Iowa	0	0	.000	7.20	1	1	0	0	0	0	5.0	6	23	4	4	0	0	2	0	2	0	4	0	0
Levrault, Allen, Albuquerque	3	0	1.000	1.40	21	0	0	0	5	0	25.2	12	97	5	4	2	1	1	2	9	1	18	2	0
Lewis, Colby, Oklahoma	5	1	.833	3.02	7	7	0	0	0	0	47.2	36	195	16	16	6	0	1	0	19	0	43	3	2
Lewis, Richie, Edmonton	0	0	.000	6.08	7	0	0	0	4	0	13.1	17	63	9	9	2	0	1	1	7	0	7	1	0
Lincoln, Mike, Nashville	1	1	.500	0.71	8	0	0	0	1	0	12.2	8	52	2	1	1	3	1	1	4	0	9	1	0
Linebrink, Scott, New Orleans	0	2	.000	2.70	2	2	0	0	0	0	10.0	8	41	3	3	1	0	0	0	5	0	6	2	0
Liniak, Cole, Oklahoma	0	0	.000	4.50	1	0	0	0	1	0	2.0	2	10	1	1	0	0	0	2	0	0	1	1	0
Loewer, Carlton, Portland	7	8	.467	5.40	23	23	0	0	0	0	125.0	161	554	84	75	9	5	8	10	28	0	57	1	0
Looney, Brian, Colo. Springs *	2	1	.667	7.53	3	3	0	0	0	0	14.1	23	72	17	12	6	1	0	2	6	0	11	1	0
Looper, Aaron, Tacoma	5	2	.714	3.11	46	0	0	0	20	5	75.1	72	324	27	26	10	3	1	2	26	2	67	2	0
Lopez, Albie, Omaha	0	0	.000	0.00	4	0	0	0	2	0	5.0	3	18	0	0	0	0	0	0	0	0	2	1	0
Lorraine, Andrew, Las Vegas *	8	9	.471	4.16	30	27	0	0	0	0	158.0	211	718	86	73	17	5	6	7	39	1	77	2	0
Lowe, Sean, Omaha	4	0	1.000	3.25	14	7	0	0	1	0	52.2	54	222	22	19	3	1	1	3	19	0	27	1	0
Lowry, Noah, Fresno *	1	0	1.000	2.37	4	4	0	0	0	0	19.0	15	74	5	5	0	2	0	0	6	0	13	0	0
Lukasiewicz, Mark, Salt Lk.*	2	2	.500	6.06	40	4	0	0	10	1	62.1	74	277	47	42	8	1	6	0	18	0	52	1	0
Lundberg, Spike, Oklahoma	1	0	1.000	2.08	2	0	0	0	0	0	4.1	5	19	1	1	0	0	1	0	2	0	2	0	0
Mahay, Ron, Oklahoma *	4	2	.667	4.22	26	0	0	0	12	3	42.2	36	172	21	20	5	0	0	1	10	0	51	1	0
Mahomes, Pat, Nashville	8	4	.667	2.67	38	2	0	0	10	2	64.0	55	262	20	19	4	3	3	1	21	3	28	2	1
Mairena, Ozwaldo, Alb.*	6	4	.600	5.86	61	0	0	0	14	1	86.0	110	383	62	56	11	6	4	2	28	1	55	2	0
Mallette, Brian, Las Vegas	0	0	.000	4.50	1	1	0	0	0	0	4.0	4	16	2	2	1	0	0	1	0	0	1	0	0
Mann, Jim, Nashville	3	2	.600	3.06	51	0	0	0	28	5	61.2	38	241	23	21	8	1	2	1	20	5	48	3	0
Manon, Julio, Edmonton	3	1	.750	2.14	35	0	0	0	32	14	42.0	33	180	12	10	4	0	0	0	19	1	48	2	0
Mantei, Matt, Tucson	0	0	.000	2.25	3	0	0	0	1	0	4.0	2	13	1	1	1	0	0	0	0	0	4	0	0
Marshall, Lee, Tucson	4	6	.400	6.21	50	3	0	0	14	1	66.2	97	315	52	46	5	7	2	2	23	0	43	4	0
Mattes, Troy, Edmonton	1	0	1.000	1.50	1	1	0	0	0	0	6.0	5	27	1	1	0	0	1	0	4	0	3	0	0
McKnight, Tony, Las Vegas	2	0	1.000	3.31	4	3	0	0	0	0	16.1	20	72	7	6	1	0	0	0	5	1	6	0	0
McLeary, Marty, Albuquerque	1	1	.500	4.32	20	1	0	0	4	0	33.1	40	160	22	16	3	1	2	3	18	1	17	3	0
Meadows, Brian, Nashville	7	0	1.000	1.41	9	8	1	1	0	0	51.0	32	185	11	8	2	2	1	2	0	0	40	0	0
Mecir, Jim, Sacramento	0	0	.000	5.40	3	2	0	0	0	0	3.1	5	18	4	2	0	0	0	0	2	0	3	0	0
Meyers, Mike, Iowa	5	2	.714	4.60	30	9	0	0	5	0	74.1	77	327	42	38	9	3	4	0	36	3	45	0	1
Miadich, Bart, Salt Lake	5	5	.500	3.68	46	0	0	0	38	16	51.1	39	234	23	21	4	2	1	4	41	0	65	12	1
Michalak, Chris, Colo. Spr.*	7	9	.438	4.41	24	18	0	0	2	1	120.1	138	535	76	59	22	5	3	6	44	3	72	2	3
Miller, Greg, New Orleans *	0	3	.000	7.02	9	7	0	0	1	0	41.0	59	203	37	32	5	3	4	5	22	0	16	0	0
Miller, Matt, Colorado Springs	5	0	1.000	2.13	61	0	0	0	13	3	63.1	46	260	17	15	0	5	1	6	23	1	83	2	1
Moehler, Brian, New Orleans	0	0	.000	4.50	1	1	0	0	0	0	2.0	3	9	1	1	0	1	0	0	0	0	3	0	0
Molina, Gabe, Memphis	2	9	.182	5.09	57	0	0	0	35	9	63.2	73	288	40	36	9	6	0	1	31	8	47	7	1
Montero, Agustin, Las Vegas	2	2	.500	4.97	35	0	0	0	9	1	50.2	57	233	32	28	4	4	4	3	31	3	30	1	2
Montgomery, Matt, Fresno	2	2	.500	4.58	24	0	0	0	11	1	39.1	40	173	25	20	4	2	4	0	14	0	35	1	1
Mounce, Tony, Oklahoma *	2	4	.333	3.39	11	11	2	0	0	0	66.1	60	274	25	25	6	1	0	0	26	0	51	2	0
Mullen, Scott, Omaha-L.V.*	9	5	.643	3.90	27	16	0	0	6	1	110.2	125	477	57	48	7	6	6	4	36	1	73	2	0
Munro, Pete, New Orleans	0	4	.000	6.04	5	4	0	0	0	0	22.1	28	106	16	15	1	2	1	0	12	1	12	0	0
Murray, Dan, Oklahoma	5	9	.357	5.86	41	6	0	0	13	2	81.1	108	380	56	53	9	5	5	1	35	1	49	5	0
Myers, Rodney, Las Vegas	9	1	.900	3.30	46	1	0	0	10	1	71.0	66	299	32	26	4	2	2	5	22	1	48	3	1
Nagy, Charles, Portland	1	0	1.000	1.23	3	1	0	0	1	1	7.1	8	28	1	1	1	0	0	1	0	0	5	0	0
Neagle, Denny, Colo. Spr.*	3	0	1.000	3.38	4	4	0	0	0	0	24.0	28	101	10	9	2	1	0	0	4	0	16	0	0
Neal, Blaine, Albuquerque	3	2	.600	2.33	40	0	0	0	30	21	46.1	55	202	22	12	1	2	1	2	16	2	32	3	0
Nickle, Doug, Salt Lake	2	2	.500	1.48	34	0	0	0	16	4	48.2	40	197	8	8	1	1	1	0	18	0	23	4	0
Nitkowski, C.J., Oklahoma *	5	4	.556	4.09	33	6	0	0	12	2	81.1	88	356	40	37	6	4	3	5	31	2	53	5	1
Norton, Phil, Iowa *	4	2	.667	3.78	48	1	0	0	17	1	47.2	44	211	26	20	4	3	1	1	24	3	43	3	1
Nunez, Vladimir, Albuquerque	4	1	.800	4.76	46	3	0	0	26	5	68.0	67	290	36	36	13	3	2	6	20	0	54	4	0
O'Brien, Matt, Sacramento *	1	0	1.000	4.82	10	0	0	0	1	0	9.1	10	44	5	5	1	1	0	1	6	1	2	0	0
Obermueller, Wes, Omaha	10	5	.667	4.40	17	17	2	0	0	0	106.1	108	466	61	52	11	3	2	7	42	1	62	0	0
Ohme, Kevin, Memphis *	5	5	.500	4.32	49	0	0	0	13	1	66.2	77	296	34	32	8	0	3	2	21	4	32	4	1
Olsen, Kevin, Albuquerque	2	1	.667	2.11	7	7	0	0	0	0	38.1	36	151	12	9	1	0	2	0	7	1	28	0	0
Oropesa, Eddie, Tucson *	0	1	.000	2.35	15	0	0	0	5	0	15.1	14	63	4	4	0	1	0	1	4	1	9	1	0
Osting, Jimmy, Omaha *	1	4	.200	5.66	9	9	1	0	0	0	49.1	48	218	31	31	10	1	2	3	23	0	26	1	0
Oswalt, Roy, New Orleans	0	0	.000	3.00	1	1	0	0	0	0	3.0	3	12	1	1	0	0	0	0	0	0	2	1	0
Painter, Lance, Memphis *	0	0	.000	0.00	3	0	0	0	0	0	3.0	2	10	0	0	0	0	0	0	0	0	1	0	0
Park, Chan Ho, Oklahoma	1	0	1.000	5.89	3	3	0	0	0	0	18.1	27	87	12	12	4	0	1	0	8	0	12	1	0
Parrott, Rhett, Memphis	2	3	.400	3.54	7	7	0	0	0	0	40.2	39	174	16	16	2	0	1	2	19	1	25	0	1
Patterson, John, Tucson	10	5	.667	2.63	18	18	2	2	0	0	109.1	100	474	48	32	6	3	7	5	43	0	74	6	0
Pearce, Josh, Memphis	3	3	.500	4.08	10	9	0	0	0	0	46.1	51	192	22	21	8	1	1	0	8	1	27	2	0
Pearson, Jason, Memphis *	4	4	.500	3.10	44	0	0	0	8	3	52.1	41	207	21	18	3	0	2	2	9	1	36	1	0
Pelaez, Alex, Portland	0	0	.000	0.00	1	0	0	0	1	0	1.0	0	3	0	0	0	0	0	0	0	0	0	0	0
Pena, Jesus, Colo. Springs *	0	2	.000	4.50	11	1	0	0	2	0	12.0	15	60	8	6	1	0	1	0	9	0	9	0	1
Perez, Oliver, Portland *	3	3	.500	3.02	8	8	0	0	0	0	47.2	44	200	20	16	6	3	2	4	12	0	48	1	1
Perisho, Matt, Tuc.-Colo.Spr.*	1	1	.500	4.28	12	4	0	0	2	0	27.1	29	131	20	13	2	1	2	2	16	2	17	2	1
Phelps, Tommy, Alb.*	0	0	.000	1.17	5	0	0	0	1	0	7.2	5	26	1	1	1	0	0	0	3	0	13	1	0
Pickford, Kevin, Fresno *	9	8	.529	5.09	25	25	0	0	0	0	145.0	169	652	91	82	15	7	7	10	56	0	64	3	1
Powell, Brian, Fresno	7	8	.467	4.19	23	15	0	0	1	0	101.0	118	444	57	47	10	3	3	0	32	2	59	1	0
Prieto, Ariel, Nashville	0	1	.000	2.55	4	4	0	0	0	0	17.2	17	79	6	5	1	1	0	1	8	1	22	0	0
Prinz, Bret, Tucson	0	1	.000	6.00	10	0	0	0	2	0	12.0	19	59	9	8	1	0	1	0	3	0	7	1	0
Proctor, Scott, Las Vegas	4	2	.667	3.66	24	0	0	0	8	1	39.1	35	160	17	16	2	4	1	0	13	3	35	0	0

Pitcher, Team	W	L	Pct.	ERA	G	GS	CG	ShO	GF	Sv.	IP	H	TBF	R	ER	HR	SH	SF	HB	BB	IBB	SO	WP	Bk.
Puffer, Brandon, New Orleans	7	3	.700	2.91	44	0	0	0	20	5	52.2	50	226	23	17	1	1	4	7	16	1	41	1	0
Putz, J.J., Tacoma	0	3	.000	2.51	41	0	0	0	22	11	86.0	69	352	30	24	4	7	1	3	34	0	60	3	0
Raggio, Brady, Tucson	4	4	.500	3.49	18	7	0	0	3	0	56.2	60	235	27	22	4	1	2	0	8	0	32	2	0
Ramirez, Erasmo, Oklahoma *	2	1	.667	1.53	22	0	0	0	11	4	35.1	36	147	8	6	0	4	1	0	2	0	20	0	0
Ramirez, Santiago, N.Orleans	4	0	1.000	4.26	10	0	0	0	4	0	12.2	7	56	7	6	1	3	0	4	9	0	9	0	0
Ramos, Mario, Oklahoma *	0	3	.000	6.40	5	5	0	0	0	0	32.1	39	142	24	23	1	1	1	0	12	0	22	0	1
Ramsay, Rob, Portland *	0	0	.000	12.00	2	0	0	0	0	0	3.0	5	13	4	4	0	0	1	0	0	0	1	0	0
Randolph, Steve, Tucson *	1	0	1.000	3.86	7	0	0	0	2	0	9.1	8	41	5	4	1	0	2	1	3	0	6	2	0
Reames, Britt, Edmonton	5	13	.278	5.42	25	20	0	0	2	0	118.0	146	542	80	71	8	2	3	3	46	1	86	7	1
Reid, Justin, Nashville	3	7	.300	4.81	34	8	0	0	8	1	82.1	90	364	52	44	9	3	7	6	23	8	51	3	0
Reyes, Dennys, Tucson *	2	1	.667	2.84	33	0	0	0	12	2	31.2	24	140	16	10	0	1	0	1	22	2	30	6	0
Rheinecker, John, Sac.*	2	0	1.000	3.79	6	6	0	0	0	0	38.0	47	171	19	16	1	0	2	2	12	1	26	0	1
Risinger, Ben, Portland	0	0	.000	0.00	1	0	0	0	1	0	1.0	0	3	0	0	0	0	0	0	0	0	0	0	0
Rivard, Reggie, Oklahoma	0	1	.000	7.11	4	0	0	0	2	0	6.1	8	34	5	5	0	1	0	1	6	0	7	0	0
Roberts, Rick, Las Vegas *	0	0	.000	13.50	2	0	0	0	1	0	1.1	0	8	2	2	0	0	0	0	5	0	2	0	0
Robertson, Jeriome, N.Orl.*	1	0	1.000	6.75	1	1	0	0	0	0	6.2	7	28	5	5	2	0	0	0	2	0	6	1	0
Robertson, Luke, Sacramento	0	1	.000	12.71	1	1	0	0	0	0	5.2	8	30	8	8	2	1	1	0	3	0	2	1	0
Rodgers, Bobby, Edm.-Iowa	0	1	.000	12.00	13	0	0	0	2	0	15.0	30	93	20	20	0	0	2	1	18	2	15	2	0
Rodriguez, Jose, Edmonton *	0	1	.000	5.32	13	0	0	0	7	1	23.2	26	108	16	14	1	0	2	0	10	1	15	1	1
Rodriguez, Nerio, Memphis	5	1	.833	1.89	11	11	1	1	0	0	76.1	57	299	19	16	3	9	1	2	12	0	54	0	0
Rodriguez, Rich, Salt Lake *	3	2	.600	2.47	34	0	0	0	12	1	43.2	47	181	14	12	3	0	3	0	12	0	18	3	0
Rosario, Rodrigo, N.Orleans	5	7	.417	4.03	15	15	1	1	0	0	87.0	71	364	40	39	7	4	1	7	32	0	68	3	0
Rueter, Kirk, Fresno *	0	0	.000	0.00	1	1	0	0	0	0	4.2	1	16	0	0	0	0	0	0	2	0	6	0	0
Ryan, Jason, Memphis	8	6	.571	2.70	29	28	0	0	0	0	189.2	195	783	63	57	18	9	7	9	45	1	110	2	1
Saarloos, Kirk, New Orleans	5	0	1.000	3.08	13	7	2	1	1	0	61.1	54	239	22	21	4	2	0	3	11	1	34	0	0
Sabel, Erik, Tucson	2	3	.400	4.94	42	2	0	0	9	1	62.0	79	282	38	34	6	0	5	2	18	0	34	3	0
Saipe, Mike, Las Vegas	6	5	.545	4.99	21	18	0	0	1	0	101.0	123	452	67	56	13	4	2	6	35	0	63	6	0
Saladin, Miguel, New Orleans	5	6	.455	2.99	55	0	0	0	18	3	84.1	75	360	35	28	3	3	2	6	33	2	60	3	1
Sanchez, Duaner, Nashville	4	4	.500	3.69	41	1	0	0	11	1	61.0	63	269	28	25	3	1	2	1	27	5	34	1	1
Sanchez, Jesus, Colo. Spr.*	2	0	1.000	3.98	46	3	0	0	12	2	63.1	61	269	28	28	4	2	1	3	26	1	52	6	0
Sanders, Scott, Albuquerque	7	5	.583	3.92	19	19	2	0	0	0	117.0	124	499	57	51	12	7	2	6	32	1	110	4	0
Santos, Victor, Oklahoma	5	4	.556	3.41	20	16	1	1	2	1	108.1	112	470	54	41	6	6	2	2	35	0	65	2	0
Sasaki, Kazuhiro, Tacoma	0	1	.000	9.82	3	2	0	0	1	1	3.2	5	17	4	4	0	0	0	0	1	0	5	0	0
Scanlan, Bob, New Orleans	1	9	.100	3.75	32	14	0	0	3	0	98.1	95	415	47	41	8	6	1	9	34	1	49	4	0
Scarbery, Chad, Tucson	0	0	.000	6.75	2	0	0	0	1	0	5.1	7	25	4	4	1	0	0	0	2	0	7	1	0
Schilling, Curt, Tucson	1	0	1.000	4.50	2	2	0	0	0	0	10.0	10	42	5	5	3	0	0	0	3	0	15	0	0
Seanez, Rudy, Oklahoma-Iowa	1	3	.250	3.12	18	0	0	0	7	2	17.1	15	85	14	6	1	2	1	0	14	2	20	2	1
Secoda, Jason, Salt Lake-Alb.	3	1	.750	10.90	10	0	0	0	0	0	17.1	24	88	22	21	2	2	1	2	17	0	7	2	0
Sedlacek, Shawn, Omaha	4	11	.267	6.45	27	13	0	0	5	0	96.1	137	435	75	69	11	1	3	4	25	0	52	8	1
Sele, Aaron, Salt Lake	1	2	.333	6.43	3	3	0	0	0	0	14.0	16	63	10	10	2	0	0	0	9	0	8	1	0
Serafini, Dan, Memphis *	0	1	.000	9.00	3	2	0	0	0	0	8.0	19	43	9	8	0	0	0	1	2	0	2	0	0
Serrano, Elio, Salt Lake	5	4	.556	4.72	46	1	0	0	13	2	68.2	84	308	43	36	7	4	3	3	22	1	46	1	0
Serrano, Jim, Omaha	3	2	.600	3.21	19	0	0	0	6	3	28.0	25	118	12	10	2	0	4	1	11	0	28	1	0
Service, Scott, Tucson	0	0	.000	0.00	9	0	0	0	7	3	12.1	6	49	2	0	0	0	1	1	2	0	13	1	0
Sessions, Doug, New Orleans	9	5	.643	2.92	31	25	1	1	2	1	157.1	149	653	57	51	16	2	5	2	43	4	92	3	0
Shaffar, Ben, Nashville	0	0	.000	2.31	4	1	0	0	1	0	11.2	11	51	4	3	1	0	1	1	6	0	12	0	0
Shouse, Brian, Oklahoma *	0	1	.000	3.68	6	0	0	0	3	1	7.1	8	32	3	3	0	0	0	1	3	0	2	1	0
Shuey, Paul, Las Vegas	0	1	.000	27.00	1	1	0	0	0	0	1.0	2	6	3	3	1	0	0	0	1	0	1	0	0
Silva, Jose, Sac.-Port.-Iowa	1	5	.167	5.29	24	7	0	0	5	0	51.0	64	233	35	30	2	0	0	3	22	2	32	3	0
Simas, Bill, Las Vegas	4	0	1.000	1.96	26	3	0	0	3	0	46.0	46	184	12	10	3	1	1	1	9	0	25	1	0
Simpson, Allan, Tacoma	2	5	.286	4.16	43	0	0	0	23	1	62.2	60	291	30	29	7	3	1	6	42	1	69	2	0
Sinclair, Steve, Iowa *	0	0	.000	4.00	6	0	0	0	1	0	9.0	6	38	5	4	0	0	0	2	3	0	9	0	0
Small, Aaron, Albuquerque	6	4	.600	4.63	14	14	0	0	0	0	89.1	95	378	50	46	12	2	4	2	18	0	56	2	0
Smith, Brian, Colo. Springs	0	4	.000	10.45	9	0	0	0	2	0	10.1	21	61	16	12	4	1	3	0	5	2	9	2	0
Smith, Roy, Sacramento	7	4	.636	5.23	52	3	0	0	16	3	72.1	77	345	49	42	3	2	3	7	48	1	47	8	1
Smyth, Steve, Iowa *	6	11	.353	5.23	25	24	0	0	1	0	130.2	143	591	85	76	16	9	7	5	72	6	98	6	0
Snare, Ryan, Oklahoma *	4	5	.444	3.46	9	9	0	0	0	0	54.2	59	235	26	21	7	3	3	2	13	0	28	3	0
Snow, Bert, Sacramento	1	0	1.000	5.28	12	0	0	0	3	0	15.1	18	67	9	9	3	0	0	0	4	0	5	4	0
Snyder, John, Salt Lake	3	2	.600	4.88	10	10	0	0	0	0	55.1	60	241	38	30	5	0	3	5	19	0	31	1	0
Snyder, Kyle, Omaha	3	0	1.000	2.79	5	5	0	0	0	0	29.0	28	116	9	9	3	0	1	1	6	0	15	0	0
Sodowsky, Clint, Albuquerque	0	3	.000	11.05	3	3	0	0	0	0	14.2	31	73	18	18	4	2	0	0	1	0	8	2	0
Song, Seung, Edmonton	7	2	.778	3.79	13	13	1	1	0	0	73.2	69	309	34	31	6	2	1	1	33	0	40	5	0
Sonnier, Shawn, Iowa	0	0	.000	13.50	3	0	0	0	1	0	2.0	4	11	3	3	1	0	0	1	1	0	1	0	0
Soriano, Rafael, Tacoma	4	3	.571	3.19	11	10	0	0	0	0	62.0	43	241	24	22	2	0	1	4	12	0	63	0	1
Spradlin, Jerry, Tucson	0	1	.000	19.80	6	0	0	0	1	0	5.0	13	30	12	11	0	0	0	3	1	0	3	0	0
Springer, Russ, Memphis	0	0	.000	1.42	7	0	0	0	0	0	6.1	2	23	1	1	1	0	0	0	4	0	5	0	0
Stamler, Keith, Oklahoma	0	1	.000	4.50	7	0	0	0	3	0	10.0	8	42	5	5	0	1	0	1	3	1	3	1	0
Stanifer, Rob, Iowa-N.Orleans	4	2	.667	3.96	44	0	0	0	15	4	63.2	63	273	30	28	4	8	3	2	17	6	43	1	0
Stark, Dennis, Colo. Springs	0	2	.000	5.95	4	4	0	0	0	0	19.2	22	90	14	13	1	1	0	0	9	0	10	2	0
Steidlmayer, Luke, Portland	1	0	1.000	1.80	1	0	0	0	0	0	5.0	4	17	1	1	1	0	0	0	0	0	3	1	0
Stein, Blake, Edmonton	2	1	.667	5.16	15	5	1	0	5	2	52.1	60	232	32	30	4	0	0	2	18	0	34	1	0
Stemle, Steve, Memphis	6	11	.353	3.46	26	26	1	0	0	0	156.0	155	652	71	60	12	8	6	5	36	4	89	3	0
Stitt, Brian, Tacoma	0	0	.000	2.45	4	0	0	0	0	0	7.1	9	32	3	2	0	0	0	0	1	0	1	1	0
Stockman, Phil, Tucson	1	1	.500	1.00	2	1	0	0	0	0	9.0	8	37	1	1	0	1	0	1	4	0	5	0	1
Stokley, Billy, Salt Lake	0	5	.000	6.46	9	9	1	0	0	0	47.1	69	216	40	34	7	2	2	4	13	0	16	1	1
Sweeney, Brian, Tacoma	11	10	.524	4.28	29	21	0	0	2	0	141.0	165	613	80	67	17	4	3	2	32	0	115	4	0
Swindell, Greg, Tucson *	0	1	.000	6.53	8	3	0	0	1	0	20.2	32	94	15	15	1	2	0	2	5	1	8	0	0
Szuminski, Jason, Iowa	0	0	.000	3.55	3	2	0	0	0	0	12.2	11	49	5	5	0	1	0	0	1	0	5	0	0
Tankersley, Dennis, Portland	8	11	.421	4.65	27	27	0	0	0	0	151.0	149	660	82	78	15	1	4	9	67	0	148	7	0
Taylor, Aaron, Tacoma	1	3	.250	2.45	33	0	0	0	31	16	40.1	30	164	11	11	3	3	2	2	13	1	34	2	0

Pitcher, Team	W	L	Pct.	ERA	G	GS	CG	ShO	GF	Sv.	IP	H	TBF	R	ER	HR	SH	SF	HB	BB	IBB	SO	WP	Bk.
Teut, Nate, Alb.-Iowa*	0	4	.000	9.50	5	5	0	0	0	0	18.0	29	92	23	19	6	0	1	1	9	0	13	0	1
Thompson, Doug, Colo. Spr.	1	1	.500	6.32	10	0	0	0	4	0	15.2	13	72	12	11	1	0	1	1	11	1	11	2	0
Thompson, Eric, Sacramento	0	0	.000	6.23	3	0	0	0	0	0	4.1	2	18	3	3	0	0	0	0	3	0	3	0	0
Thornton, Matt, Tacoma *	0	2	.000	8.00	2	2	0	0	0	0	9.0	14	44	11	8	2	0	2	0	3	0	5	1	0
Tollberg, Brian, Portland	5	3	.625	5.25	20	12	0	0	2	0	82.1	94	353	52	48	12	2	4	2	13	0	45	0	0
Torres, Salomon, Nashville	1	0	1.000	1.80	1	1	0	0	0	0	5.0	2	19	1	1	0	0	0	1	1	0	4	0	0
Trujillo, J.J., Portland	1	1	.500	5.63	27	0	0	0	5	3	32.0	32	136	22	20	6	1	0	2	10	0	22	2	0
Tucker, T.J., Edmonton	1	0	1.000	2.76	3	3	0	0	0	0	16.1	16	68	5	5	2	0	0	0	7	0	6	0	0
Turman, Jason, Omaha	2	5	.286	3.87	31	5	0	0	8	4	74.1	68	308	34	32	8	1	0	0	35	2	45	3	0
Turnbow, Derrick, Salt Lake	1	2	.333	5.73	35	0	0	0	15	2	55.0	68	255	36	35	5	2	1	1	24	0	63	7	0
Ulloa, Enmanuel, Edmonton	0	0	.000	11.05	3	0	0	0	2	0	7.1	14	38	10	9	2	0	0	0	2	0	5	0	0
Urban, Jeff, Fresno *	3	10	.231	5.24	29	19	0	0	2	0	127.0	166	586	83	74	11	7	4	5	47	0	87	4	1
Valentine, Joe, Sacramento	1	3	.250	4.82	40	0	0	0	23	4	52.1	44	239	33	28	5	1	1	2	37	3	53	9	1
Valverde, Jose, Tucson	1	1	.500	3.10	22	0	0	0	14	5	29.0	26	127	11	10	1	1	2	0	14	1	26	3	0
Vance, Cory, Colo. Springs *	9	11	.450	4.63	24	24	3	2	0	0	157.1	179	680	89	81	18	9	6	6	50	2	96	1	10
Vargas, Claudio, Edmonton	0	0	.000	2.79	2	2	0	0	0	0	9.2	7	43	3	3	1	0	0	1	5	2	12	0	0
Venafro, Mike, New Orleans *	2	1	.667	3.54	23	0	0	0	9	0	28.0	35	121	11	11	0	2	0	1	5	1	11	2	0
Vent, Kevin, Fresno	0	0	.000	14.90	6	0	0	0	3	0	9.2	20	55	17	16	1	0	1	0	6	0	7	1	0
Veres, Dave, Iowa	0	1	.000	2.81	11	4	0	0	2	0	16.0	15	63	5	5	2	0	0	0	1	0	13	2	0
Villafuerte, Brandon, Portland	3	1	.750	1.84	37	0	0	0	23	12	44.0	42	183	10	9	1	2	1	3	14	1	40	0	0
Villone, Ron, Tucson-N.Orl.*	4	2	.667	2.30	20	5	0	0	6	1	54.2	44	219	19	14	2	4	3	1	22	1	40	0	0
Vining, Ken, New Orleans *	3	5	.375	5.20	41	6	0	0	9	1	64.0	75	286	41	37	8	5	5	2	22	1	30	5	1
Vogelsong, Ryan, Nashville	12	8	.600	4.29	26	26	1	1	0	0	149.0	142	643	75	71	12	9	5	6	54	5	146	6	0
Voyles, Brad, Omaha	2	2	.500	2.99	29	9	1	0	14	2	81.1	68	326	27	27	5	5	2	1	24	0	69	2	1
Walker, Kevin, Portland *	3	1	.750	4.08	34	1	0	0	7	0	46.1	53	198	24	21	5	1	3	2	10	1	43	2	0
Walrond, Les, Mem.-Omaha *	3	1	.750	1.88	28	1	0	0	7	2	43.0	31	180	11	9	1	1	2	1	16	1	34	4	1
Ward, Bryan, Colo. Springs *	0	1	.000	16.39	9	0	0	0	4	0	9.1	19	53	17	17	3	2	0	0	6	2	6	2	0
Ward, Jeremy, Tucson	1	1	.500	6.51	25	0	0	0	12	5	27.2	37	129	21	20	1	2	0	2	11	3	13	1	0
Wasdin, John, Nashville	8	4	.667	3.04	18	18	3	1	0	0	112.1	101	462	46	38	4	4	7	3	24	4	116	1	0
Watkins, Steve, Portland	1	0	1.000	3.08	14	0	0	0	3	0	26.1	20	109	11	9	1	0	0	0	12	0	23	1	0
Wayne, Justin, Albuquerque	4	12	.250	4.24	23	23	2	0	0	0	136.0	138	573	81	64	10	4	3	6	40	0	82	2	1
Wear, Gregory, Tacoma	0	0	.000	0.00	2	0	0	0	2	0	2.0	1	7	0	0	0	0	0	0	0	0	1	0	0
Webb, Alan, Portland *	0	0	.000	0.00	1	0	0	0	0	0	2.0	0	7	0	0	0	0	0	1	1	0	1	0	0
Webb, Brandon, Tucson	1	1	.500	6.00	3	3	0	0	0	0	18.0	18	84	17	12	0	0	2	3	9	0	17	2	0
Weibl, Clint, Memphis	3	6	.333	4.53	20	16	0	0	1	1	95.1	102	420	56	48	13	5	6	3	33	1	59	4	0
Wellemeyer, Todd, Iowa	5	5	.500	5.18	13	12	0	0	0	0	66.0	68	291	39	38	7	2	4	2	33	4	56	1	0
Whiteside, Matt, Colo. Springs	3	0	1.000	4.66	21	0	0	0	5	1	29.0	26	121	16	15	2	2	2	0	8	2	15	2	0
Wilkins, Marc, Albuquerque	1	1	.500	6.75	20	2	0	0	4	1	36.0	46	171	28	27	6	2	5	6	17	0	27	1	0
Williams, Dave, Nashville *	7	4	.636	4.19	16	16	0	0	0	0	77.1	78	346	44	36	7	6	3	7	30	2	56	1	1
Williams, Jerome, Fresno	4	2	.667	2.68	10	10	1	0	0	0	57.0	52	242	19	17	3	2	1	4	16	0	40	2	0
Williams, Randy, Tacoma *	2	2	.500	5.26	18	0	0	0	4	1	25.2	25	112	17	15	3	0	1	1	11	0	19	1	0
Wilson, Kris, Omaha	0	2	.000	8.03	5	0	0	0	3	0	12.1	21	61	12	11	2	1	1	1	3	0	9	0	1
Winchester, Scott, Las Vegas	2	9	.182	5.95	19	14	1	0	3	0	87.2	134	401	63	58	10	4	6	3	18	1	38	4	0
Witasick, Jay, Portland	0	0	.000	3.00	5	0	0	0	3	1	6.0	4	24	2	2	0	0	1	0	1	0	8	1	0
Wood, Mike, Sacramento	9	3	.750	3.05	16	16	0	0	0	0	91.1	87	373	34	31	5	5	2	4	23	1	59	3	1
Wright, Chris, Tacoma	0	6	.000	6.36	9	9	0	0	0	0	46.2	53	216	33	33	8	2	2	3	27	0	33	4	0
Wright, Jamey, Okla.-Omaha	5	6	.455	3.80	20	19	3	1	0	0	116.0	108	502	53	49	11	4	2	6	59	0	105	4	0
Wright, Jaret, Portland	2	1	.667	1.42	12	1	0	0	1	0	19.0	16	81	7	3	0	0	0	2	7	0	21	2	0
Wuertz, Mike, Iowa	3	9	.250	4.57	43	16	0	0	4	1	124.0	140	536	70	63	16	5	5	5	35	8	92	2	0
Yarnall, Ed, Sacramento *	3	3	.500	3.76	18	13	0	0	1	0	64.2	72	292	28	27	6	3	0	1	30	0	46	4	0
Yennaco, Jay, Memphis	0	3	.000	6.62	8	7	0	0	1	0	34.0	41	159	25	25	3	5	2	2	18	2	15	2	0
Young, Jason, Colo. Springs	6	7	.462	3.95	23	21	2	1	0	0	116.1	128	525	63	51	10	6	2	8	37	0	99	3	0
Young, Tim, Colo. Springs	2	0	1.000	2.49	29	0	0	0	7	0	25.1	21	105	8	7	3	1	1	3	8	0	27	2	0
Zerbe, Chad, Fresno *	1	1	.500	2.61	7	0	0	0	2	2	10.1	11	42	6	3	3	0	1	0	1	0	7	0	0

PITCHERS WITH TWO OR MORE TEAMS

Pitcher, Team	W	L	Pct.	ERA	G	GS	CG	ShO	GF	Sv.	IP	H	TBF	R	ER	HR	SH	SF	HB	BB	IBB	SO	WP	Bk.
Belitz, Todd, Albuquerque *	1	0	1.000	5.93	13	0	0	0	2	0	13.2	20	69	12	9	0	1	1	3	4	1	8	0	0
Belitz, Todd, Colo. Springs *	0	0	.000	10.80	3	0	0	0	2	0	5.0	9	27	6	6	0	1	0	2	2	0	3	0	0
Blank, Matt, Fresno *	1	2	.333	4.19	8	8	0	0	0	0	43.0	49	184	22	20	4	1	1	2	12	1	30	1	1
Blank, Matt, Edmonton *	1	1	.500	4.26	5	5	0	0	0	0	25.1	29	113	14	12	1	1	3	1	9	0	22	1	0
Bruback, Matt, Iowa	6	8	.429	3.96	20	19	1	0	1	0	125.0	120	536	65	55	10	6	7	15	33	4	90	2	0
Bruback, Matt, Portland	2	0	1.000	2.61	2	2	0	0	0	0	10.1	12	49	3	3	1	0	0	1	4	0	6	0	0
Bruback, Matt, Nashville	2	2	.500	4.91	4	4	0	0	0	0	22.0	18	97	12	12	3	4	1	3	12	0	16	1	0
Callaway, Mickey, Oklahoma	2	0	1.000	1.59	4	4	0	0	0	0	17.0	16	69	6	3	0	0	1	0	5	0	9	2	0
Callaway, Mickey, Salt Lake	1	0	1.000	2.95	7	4	0	0	0	0	21.1	22	85	8	7	1	1	1	0	6	0	10	1	0
Darensbourg, Vic, Edm.*	1	1	.500	1.98	11	0	0	0	0	0	13.2	12	60	3	3	0	0	0	2	7	0	11	1	0
Darensbourg, Vic, Colo. Spr.*	2	2	.500	3.57	20	0	0	0	10	0	22.2	24	96	13	9	1	3	0	0	5	1	15	1	0
Donaldson, Bo, Salt Lake	0	0	.000	1.80	3	0	0	0	2	0	5.0	5	21	1	1	1	0	0	0	2	0	5	0	0
Donaldson, Bo, Edmonton	0	0	.000	4.34	9	1	0	0	3	0	18.2	20	90	12	9	2	0	0	0	14	1	12	0	0
Duncan, Courtney, Portland	2	6	.250	4.57	54	0	0	0	42	18	61.0	66	285	39	31	4	2	4	7	37	1	49	3	0
Duncan, Courtney, Salt Lake	0	0	.000	0.00	2	0	0	0	2	0	2.2	2	13	0	0	0	0	0	1	2	0	5	1	0
Ebert, Derrin, Tucson *	0	1	.000	2.63	15	0	0	0	7	0	13.2	21	66	4	4	0	0	1	0	6	1	7	1	0
Ebert, Derrin, Iowa *	1	0	1.000	6.43	6	0	0	0	3	0	7.0	9	36	5	5	1	0	1	2	4	1	4	0	0
Evans, Keith, Edmonton	1	2	.333	6.00	12	0	0	0	2	1	21.0	28	94	15	14	2	0	1	0	6	0	6	0	0
Evans, Keith, Iowa	1	0	1.000	3.98	10	1	0	0	4	0	20.1	22	91	10	9	3	0	2	4	7	1	10	0	0
Flury, Pat, Portland	0	0	.000	6.14	7	0	0	0	0	0	7.1	8	41	7	5	1	0	0	1	12	0	9	2	0
Flury, Pat, Omaha	0	0	.000	4.50	7	0	0	0	2	0	10.0	11	46	5	5	2	0	0	2	3	0	7	0	1
Fyhrie, Mike, Omaha	7	4	.636	4.21	15	14	0	0	0	0	98.1	103	421	52	46	10	4	1	5	38	2	64	1	0
Fyhrie, Mike, Albuquerque	1	0	1.000	2.53	5	0	0	0	1	0	10.2	7	40	3	3	0	0	0	0	3	0	8	0	0
House, Craig, Tacoma	0	0	.000	2.84	5	0	0	0	3	0	6.1	6	29	2	2	0	0	1	1	5	0	4	2	0
House, Craig, Albuquerque	0	0	.000	19.64	7	0	0	0	3	0	7.1	14	49	16	16	0	0	0	1	13	0	8	1	0

Pitcher, Team	W	L	Pct.	ERA	G	GS	CG	ShO	GF	Sv.	IP	H	TBF	R	ER	HR	SH	SF	HB	BB	IBB	SO	WP	Bk.
Joseph, Kevin, Edmonton	1	2	.333	9.39	7	1	0	0	5	1	15.1	25	77	16	16	5	0	1	0	7	1	8	1	0
Joseph, Kevin, Memphis	1	5	.167	4.37	22	5	0	0	6	0	59.2	71	266	34	29	5	4	3	2	21	3	30	7	0
Keisler, Randy, New Orleans *	2	3	.400	4.28	9	9	0	0	0	0	48.1	53	211	24	23	3	5	1	1	21	2	27	1	0
Keisler, Randy, Oklahoma *	0	2	.000	8.53	5	2	0	0	0	0	12.2	21	60	13	12	2	1	0	0	5	0	9	0	0
Keisler, Randy, Portland *	5	1	.833	2.61	8	6	0	0	0	0	41.1	33	166	12	12	6	0	1	0	12	0	24	2	0
Mullen, Scott, Las Vegas *	4	2	.667	3.95	7	7	0	0	0	0	41.0	50	177	22	18	4	2	1	1	14	0	23	0	0
Mullen, Scott, Omaha *	5	3	.625	3.88	20	9	0	0	6	1	69.2	75	300	35	30	3	4	5	3	22	1	50	2	0
Perisho, Matt, Tucson *	0	0	.000	9.82	4	0	0	0	1	0	3.2	4	17	4	4	1	0	1	0	2	0	2	0	0
Perisho, Matt, Colo. Spr.*	1	1	.500	3.42	8	4	0	0	1	0	23.2	25	114	16	9	1	1	1	2	14	2	15	2	1
Rodgers, Bobby, Edmonton	0	0	.000	7.00	8	0	0	0	1	0	9.0	14	53	7	7	0	0	2	0	11	0	10	2	0
Rodgers, Bobby, Iowa	0	1	.000	19.50	5	0	0	0	1	0	6.0	16	40	13	13	0	0	0	1	7	2	5	0	0
Seanez, Rudy, Oklahoma	0	1	.000	2.08	5	0	0	0	2	0	4.1	3	23	4	1	0	1	0	0	5	0	7	2	1
Seanez, Rudy, Iowa	1	2	.333	3.46	13	0	0	0	5	2	13.0	12	62	10	5	1	1	1	0	9	2	13	0	0
Secoda, Jason, Albuquerque	1	0	1.000	29.25	3	0	0	0	0	0	4.0	12	30	13	13	2	0	0	0	8	0	3	2	0
Secoda, Jason, Salt Lake	2	1	.667	5.40	7	0	0	0	0	0	13.1	12	58	9	8	0	2	1	2	9	0	4	0	0
Silva, Jose, Sacramento	1	2	.333	5.04	7	5	0	0	1	0	25.0	32	115	18	14	1	0	0	2	9	0	18	3	0
Silva, Jose, Portland	0	3	.000	5.54	17	2	0	0	4	0	26.0	32	118	17	16	1	0	0	1	13	2	14	0	0
Silva, Jose, Iowa	0	2	.000	7.71	3	0	0	0	0	0	4.2	8	24	4	4	2	0	0	0	4	1	2	1	0
Stanifer, Rob, Iowa	1	0	1.000	3.86	3	0	0	0	1	0	7.0	8	35	3	3	0	3	0	0	4	1	5	0	0
Stanifer, Rob, New Orleans	3	2	.600	3.97	41	0	0	0	14	4	56.2	55	238	27	25	4	5	3	2	13	5	38	1	0
Teut, Nate, Albuquerque *	0	1	.000	7.56	2	2	0	0	0	0	8.1	14	42	9	7	2	0	1	0	5	0	6	0	0
Teut, Nate, Iowa *	0	3	.000	11.17	3	3	0	0	0	0	9.2	15	50	14	12	4	0	0	1	4	0	7	0	1
Villone, Ron, Tucson *	1	1	.500	3.55	15	0	0	0	6	1	25.1	20	104	14	10	2	3	2	1	12	1	22	0	0
Villone, Ron, New Orleans *	3	1	.750	1.23	5	5	0	0	0	0	29.1	24	115	5	4	0	1	1	0	10	0	18	0	0
Walrond, Les, Memphis *	0	0	.000	1.04	10	1	0	0	2	0	17.1	12	71	2	2	0	0	1	0	7	1	14	0	0
Walrond, Les, Omaha *	3	1	.750	2.45	18	0	0	0	5	2	25.2	19	109	9	7	1	1	1	1	9	0	20	4	1
Wright, Jamey, Oklahoma	2	1	.667	4.12	7	7	2	1	0	0	39.1	38	172	18	18	1	1	1	3	21	0	40	2	0
Wright, Jamey, Omaha	3	5	.375	3.64	13	12	1	0	0	0	76.2	70	330	35	31	10	3	1	3	38	0	65	2	0

COMBINATION SHUTOUTS: Albuquerque (2)—Wayne-Phelps-Borland, Olsen-Neal. Colorado Springs (2)—Flores-Gissell-Miller, Gissell-Sanchez. Edmonton (3)—Song-Crumpton, Downs-Ferrari-Crumpton, Stein-Drew. Fresno (6)—Pickford-Johnson-Aybar, Urban-Aybar, Powell-Horgan-Johnson, Powell-Aybar, Rueter-Horgan-Jensen-Aybar, Lowry-Zerbe. Iowa (3)—Wellemeyer-Bruback, Meyers-Norton-Kaye-Seanez-Banks, Chavez-Kaye-Seanez. Las Vegas (8)—Lorraine-Alvarez-Corey, Alvarez-Myers-Corey, Saipe-Alvarez-Colyer, Winchester-McKnight-Lee-Colyer, McKnight-Myers-Alvarez, Alvarez-Montero-Winchester, Kida-Proctor-Myers-Lee, Farmer-Simas-Lee. Memphis (9)—Ryan-Molina, Stemle-Molina, Stemle-Ohme, Rodriguez-Layfield, Pearce-Painter-Molina, Carpenter-Ohme-Cook, Cummings-Ohme-Molina-Pearson, Parrott-Pearson-Crudale, Parrott-Duff. Nashville (12)—Figueroa-Reid-Holtz-Corey, Prieto-Mahomes-Sanchez-Mann, Meadows-Reid-Holtz-Mann, Vogelsong-Sanchez-Corey, Williams-Camp-Holtz-Mann-Corey, Guerrier-Mahomes, Camp-Holtz-Mann-Corey, Williams-Mahomes-Corey, Williams-Sanchez-Mann, Bruback-Corey, Bennett-Brooks-Grabow-Mann, Williams-Holtz-Grabow. New Orleans (7)—Saarloos-Bullinger-Vining-Saladin-Puffer-Ramirez, Rosario-Bland, Johnson-Gallo-Bullinger, Fernandez-Stanifer-Gallo, Sessions-Puffer-Venafro, Keisler-Puffer-Bland-Bullinger, Sessions-Saladin. Oklahoma (6)—Murray-Mahay, Wright-Garcia-Nitkowski-Garcia, Snare-Nitkowski, Drese-Stamler-Garcia, Garcia-Santos, Callaway-Murray-Garcia. Omaha (1)—Baerlocher-Gilfillan-Jones. Portland (10)—Howard-Bartosh-Duncan, Loewer-Flury-Trujillo, Keisler-Nagy, Howard-Bartosh, Perez-Trujillo-Duncan, Tankersley-Witasick, Wright-Villafuerte-Silva-Duncan, Howard-Tollberg-Villafuerte, Bynum-Watkins, Bruback-Hampton-Bartosh. Sacramento (9)—Wood-O'Brien-Enochs-Valentine, Wood-Smith, Duchscherer-Valentine-Bowie, Harden-Harville-Yarnall, Harang-Smith-Fikac-Harville, Harden-Fikac-Harville, Harden-Kusiewicz-Fikac, Castillo-Valentine, Wood-Snow. Salt Lake (5)—Green-Serrano-Nickle-Miadich, Emanuel-Rodriguez-Miadich, Gregg-Turnbow-Lukasiewicz, Gregg-Rodriguez-Turnbow, Hensley-Turnbow. Tacoma (4)—Atchison-Hamulack, Sweeney-Putz-Taylor, Johnson-Putz-Carrara, Heaverlo-Simpson. Tucson (7)—Cervantes-Ward-Service, Kim-Sabel-Oropesa-Valverde, Gosling-Cervantes, Patterson-Gonzalez, Stockman-Sabel-Ward, Capuano-Prinz-Bruney, Capuano-Bruney.

NO-HIT GAMES: Wasdin, Nashville, defeated Albuquerque, 4-0, April 7; Gulin, Las Vegas, defeated Tacoma, 7-0, June 13.

2003 FIELDING

TEAM

Team	G	PO	A	E	TC	DP	TP	PB	Pct.
Memphis	143	3752	1430	104	5286	118	0	8	.980
New Orleans	144	3800	1574	111	5485	140	0	13	.980
Sacramento	144	3785	1442	109	5336	102	0	15	.980
Portland	144	3787	1464	113	5364	134	0	22	.979
Iowa	142	3736	1399	111	5246	133	0	10	.979
Albuquerque	144	3792	1576	120	5488	153	0	13	.978
Nashville	143	3760	1316	113	5189	96	0	10	.978
Omaha	143	3830	1604	124	5558	156	0	10	.978
Edmonton	142	3635	1456	122	5213	147	0	13	.977
Oklahoma	142	3737	1483	125	5345	140	0	10	.977
Tacoma	144	3773	1413	123	5309	127	0	12	.977
Salt Lake	143	3755	1488	132	5375	159	0	13	.975
Las Vegas	142	3739	1483	136	5358	130	0	14	.975
Fresno	143	3743	1443	136	5322	121	0	13	.974
Colo. Springs	143	3694	1537	168	5399	123	0	13	.969
Tucson	144	3805	1564	175	5544	121	0	6	.968

INDIVIDUAL

FIRST BASEMEN

NOTE: All caps denotes fielding-percentage leader based on 72 games for catchers, 96 for all other non-pitchers and 115 innings for pitchers. *Throws lefthanded.

Player, Team	Pct.	G	PO	A	E	TC	DP
Alviso, Jerome, Colo. Springs	1.000	8	35	5	0	40	2
Ashby, Chris, Albuquerque	1.000	1	6	1	0	7	0
Atkins, Garrett, Colo. Springs	1.000	3	22	1	0	23	2
Bailey, Jeff, Edmonton	1.000	2	24	2	0	26	2
Balfe, Ryan, Edmonton	.990	38	281	25	3	309	33
Barker, Kevin, Albuquerque *	.981	7	49	4	1	54	2
Barkett, Andy, Tacoma *	.991	79	607	51	6	664	65
Barnes, Larry, Las Vegas *	.989	65	583	39	7	629	49
Bell, Mike, Tucson	.985	17	126	8	2	136	12
Bell, Rick, Las Vegas	.993	22	141	9	1	151	19
Bellinger, Clay, Fresno	1.000	17	112	9	0	121	11
Berger, Brandon, Omaha	.917	2	22	0	2	24	5
Borders, Pat, Tacoma	1.000	1	2	0	0	2	0
Bozied, Tagg, Portland	.991	111	911	77	9	997	87
Brock, Tarrik, Las Vegas *	.970	10	62	3	2	67	5
Burkhart, Morgan, Omaha *	.997	96	817	63	3	883	89
Butler, Brent, Colorado Springs	.989	12	84	2	1	87	5
Casanova, Raul, Colo. Springs	.980	11	95	3	2	100	9
Cepicky, Matt, Edmonton	.875	2	14	0	2	16	4
Chen, Chin-Feng, Las Vegas	.954	13	92	11	5	108	9
Choi, Hee Seop, Iowa *	1.000	18	125	14	0	139	13
Clapinski, Chris, Las Vegas	1.000	7	56	5	0	61	7
Colbrunn, Greg, Tacoma	1.000	1	8	2	0	10	0
Cromer, Tripp, New Orleans	1.000	3	3	0	0	3	0
Donnels, Chris, Tuc.-Ia.-Alb.	.992	45	337	26	3	366	37
Dunwoody, Todd, Memphis *	.986	9	64	4	1	69	5
Durrington, Trent, Salt Lake	.980	15	138	11	3	152	14
Encarnacion, Mario, Edm.-Mem.	.861	5	29	2	5	36	5
Gall, John, Memphis	.993	120	1010	48	7	1065	81
Gilbert, Shawn, Nashville	.889	2	7	1	1	9	0
Gonzalez, Adrian, Albuquerque *	.997	38	330	28	1	359	40
Grabowski, Jason, Sacramento	1.000	3	26	1	0	27	0
Guiel, Jeff, Salt Lake	.983	35	261	20	5	286	35
Gulan, Mike, Nashville	.959	7	44	3	2	49	2
Guzman, Edwards, Edmonton	.993	16	132	10	1	143	10
Haad, Yamid, Portland	1.000	1	1	0	0	1	0
Hammock, Rob, Tucson	1.000	3	29	5	0	34	3
Hansen, Jed, Omaha	.984	18	161	19	3	183	22
Harris, Lenny, Albuquerque	.977	4	41	2	1	44	2

Player, Team	Pct.	G	PO	A	E	TC	DP
HART, JASON, Oklahoma	.997	130	1102	70	4	1176	107
Hermansen, Chad, Las Vegas	1.000	1	8	0	0	8	1
Hiatt, Phil, Iowa	.993	91	672	60	5	737	82
Hill, Jason, Salt Lake	1.000	3	24	1	0	25	0
Hill, Koyie, Las Vegas	1.000	1	1	0	0	1	0
Hillenbrand, Shea, Tucson	1.000	2	4	0	0	4	0
Hoover, Paul, Albuquerque	.986	10	63	6	1	70	3
Huffman, Royce, New Orleans	.990	92	828	60	9	897	81
Hyzdu, Adam, Nashville	.963	9	51	1	2	54	5
Johnson, Dan, Sacramento	1.000	1	8	1	0	9	0
Johnson, Keith, Salt Lake	1.000	3	26	4	0	30	3
Jones, Jason, Oklahoma	.990	12	97	3	1	101	12
Kelton, Dave, Iowa	1.000	1	9	0	0	9	1
King, Brad, Nashville	1.000	9	55	3	0	58	4
Knorr, Randy, Edmonton	1.000	1	5	0	0	5	0
Knott, Jon, Portland	1.000	7	56	6	0	62	5
Koonce, Graham, Sacramento *	.995	81	683	55	4	742	54
Kuzmic, Craig, Tacoma	.987	19	146	9	2	157	11
Lamb, Mike, Oklahoma	1.000	5	34	1	0	35	7
Lane, Jason, New Orleans *	.987	7	71	6	1	78	7
Leon, Donny, Iowa	1.000	3	15	2	0	17	2
Lopez, Luis, Colorado Springs	1.000	5	20	1	0	21	1
Lopez, Luis, Sacramento	1.000	1	10	0	0	10	0
Mackowiak, Rob, Nashville	.989	41	339	18	4	361	25
Mahoney, Mike, Iowa	1.000	4	22	0	0	22	4
Martin, Billy, Tucson	.992	26	223	14	2	239	15
McCarty, Dave, Sacramento *	.993	62	510	42	4	556	42
Meyers, Chad, Tacoma	1.000	2	10	0	0	10	2
Minor, Damon, Fresno *	.995	20	194	20	1	215	21
Morales, Willie, Tuc.-Colo.Spr.	1.000	4	30	2	0	32	1
Neal, Steve, Tucson *	.994	76	594	42	4	640	64
Nevin, Phil, Portland	1.000	2	12	0	0	12	1
Newhan, David, Colo. Springs	.981	17	143	11	3	157	9
Niekro, Lance, Fresno	.993	17	123	11	1	135	12
Nieves, Wil, Salt Lake	.992	15	127	5	1	133	17
Ortiz, Luis, Edmonton	.997	36	307	15	1	323	21
Overbay, Lyle, Tucson *	.985	33	294	25	5	324	19
Paquette, Craig, Memphis	1.000	2	13	2	0	15	0
Pascucci, Val, Edmonton	.980	29	229	16	5	250	33
Patterson, Jarrod, Omaha	.988	28	240	14	3	257	24
Paul, Josh, Iowa	.900	1	9	0	1	10	0
Peeples, Mike, Memphis	.990	14	95	5	1	101	8
Pelaez, Alex, Portland	1.000	7	38	5	0	43	6
Pellow, Kit, Colorado Springs	.990	55	449	30	5	484	38
Perry, Chan, Nashville	.983	8	54	5	1	60	2
Petrick, Ben, Colorado Springs	.984	23	184	4	3	191	23
Phillips, J.R., Tacoma *	.990	48	380	29	4	413	37
Post, Dave, Colorado Springs	1.000	6	30	1	0	31	2
Pritchett, Chris, Iowa	.978	27	204	17	5	226	14
Quinlan, Robb, Salt Lake	1.000	59	483	46	0	529	58
Riggs, Adam, Salt Lake	.989	20	174	14	2	190	18
Riggs, Eric, Las Vegas	.973	3	31	5	1	37	3
Risinger, Ben, Portland	1.000	1	3	0	0	3	1
Rivera, Carlos, Nashville *	.997	70	544	52	2	598	40
Romero, Mandy, Colo. Springs	1.000	8	37	2	0	39	4
Santos, Francisco, Fresno *	.989	23	175	11	2	188	12
Sasser, Rob, Omaha	1.000	1	12	1	0	13	1
Seabol, Scott, Memphis	.961	6	46	3	2	51	7
Simon, Randall, Nashville *	1.000	2	10	1	0	11	2
Sledge, Terrmel, Edmonton *	1.000	1	5	0	0	5	1
Stairs, Matt, Nashville	1.000	2	12	2	0	14	0
Sweeney, Mark, Colo. Springs *	.976	11	77	3	2	82	9
Theodorou, Nick, Las Vegas	1.000	1	3	2	0	5	0
Thrower, Jake, Edmonton	1.000	4	35	2	0	37	3
Toca, Jorge, Nashville	1.000	7	40	6	0	46	3
Torcato, Tony, Fresno	.983	58	492	36	9	537	46
Valdez, Mario, Portland	1.000	24	196	10	0	206	17
Vaughn, Greg, Colo. Springs	.947	10	68	4	4	76	7
Vitiello, Joe, Fresno-Edmonton	.991	35	302	25	3	330	32
Ward, Daryle, Las Vegas *	.992	30	220	36	2	258	29
Washington, Rico, Portland	1.000	2	12	2	0	14	1
Wathan, Derek, Albuquerque	.986	47	406	28	6	440	49
Widger, Chris, Memphis	1.000	1	5	0	0	5	1
Wood, Jason, Albuquerque	.977	22	160	11	4	175	17
Zinter, Alan, New Orleans	.996	60	429	33	2	464	38

FIRST BASEMEN WITH TWO OR MORE TEAMS

Player, Team	Pct.	G	PO	A	E	TC	DP
Donnels, Chris, Tucson	1.000	4	26	4	0	30	1
Donnels, Chris, Iowa	1.000	11	73	6	0	79	7
Donnels, Chris, Albuquerque	.988	30	238	16	3	257	29
Encarnacion, Mario, Edmonton	.852	4	21	2	4	27	4
Encarnacion, Mario, Memphis	.889	1	8	0	1	9	1
Morales, Willie, Tucson	1.000	1	1	1	0	2	0
Morales, Willie, Colo. Springs	1.000	3	29	1	0	30	1
Vitiello, Joe, Fresno	.986	14	136	7	2	145	11
Vitiello, Joe, Edmonton	.995	21	166	18	1	185	21

SECOND BASEMEN

Player, Team	Pct.	G	PO	A	E	TC	DP
Abbott, Kurt, Memphis	1.000	3	6	5	0	11	0
Abernathy, Brent, Omaha	.981	87	178	241	8	427	66
Alexander, Manny, Oklahoma	.981	11	20	31	1	52	5
Alviso, Jerome, C.S.-S.L.	.984	27	41	83	2	126	19
Amezaga, Alfredo, Salt Lake	.982	10	21	34	1	56	12
Arteaga, Joshua, Iowa	.984	17	29	31	1	61	8
Barmes, Clint, Colorado Springs	.833	2	2	3	1	6	1
Bell, Mike, Tucson	.964	78	150	196	13	359	49
Bellhorn, Mark, Colo. Springs	1.000	4	7	8	0	15	2
Belliard, Ronnie, Colo. Springs	1.000	6	2	15	0	17	1
Bellinger, Clay, Fresno	.941	5	7	9	1	17	0
Bowers, Jason, Memphis	.986	18	31	40	1	72	8
Bruntlett, Eric, New Orleans	.971	30	42	92	4	138	20
Butler, Brent, Colorado Springs	.979	42	78	109	4	191	28
Cairo, Miguel, Memphis	1.000	2	5	3	0	8	1
Carvajal, Jhonny, Tucson	.947	28	27	63	5	95	9
Castro, Bernabel, Portland	.970	95	185	261	14	460	59
Cesar, Dionys, Edmonton	.955	10	17	25	2	44	6
Cintron, Alex, Tucson	1.000	2	8	8	0	16	1
Clapinski, Chris, Las Vegas	.833	2	0	5	1	6	2
Clark, Jermaine, Port.-Okla.	.966	15	19	38	2	59	8
Coffie, Ivanon, Memphis	1.000	2	8	6	0	14	2
Counsell, Craig, Tucson	.889	2	4	4	1	9	2
Cromer, Tripp, New Orleans	.984	49	103	136	4	243	37
Dallimore, Brian, Fresno	.973	68	146	176	9	331	45
De La Rosa, Tomas, Nashville	.972	26	41	62	3	106	12
Delgado, Wilson, Memphis	1.000	1	0	1	0	1	0
Donnels, Chris, Iowa	.967	10	16	13	1	30	3
Doster, Dave, Nashville	.994	85	138	208	2	348	36
Durrington, Trent, Salt Lake	.989	57	97	161	3	261	30
Dzurilla, Mike, Iowa	.972	7	19	16	1	36	5
Erickson, Matt, Albuquerque	.972	33	57	83	4	144	17
Evans, Tom, Iowa	.909	2	4	6	1	11	2
Everett, Adam, New Orleans	.938	3	4	11	1	16	3
Febles, Carlos, Omaha	1.000	5	9	15	0	24	5
Figgins, Chone, Salt Lake	.948	35	54	111	9	174	30
Figueroa, Luis, Tacoma	1.000	13	22	32	0	54	6
Figueroa, Luis, Edmonton	.981	102	213	291	10	514	73
Flores, Jose, Sacramento	.966	27	56	84	5	145	14
Gandolfo, Rob, Tacoma	.978	11	19	25	1	45	4
German, Esteban, Sacramento	.976	115	218	318	13	549	55
Gilbert, Shawn, Nashville	.800	1	3	1	1	5	0
Grudzielanek, Mark, Iowa	1.000	1	2	1	0	3	0
Gulan, Mike, Nashville	1.000	4	5	7	0	12	0
Guzman, Edwards, Edmonton	.965	11	19	36	2	57	7
Hansen, Jed, Omaha	.979	19	42	53	2	97	9
Harris, Brian, Omaha	.970	30	72	88	5	165	24
Harrison, Adonis, Salt Lake	.953	15	31	50	4	85	10
Hart, Bo, Memphis	.979	45	72	113	4	189	25
Hernandez, Carlos, Fresno-N.O.	.970	59	96	163	8	267	37
Hiatt, Phil, Iowa	1.000	6	12	12	0	24	3
Hill, Bobby, Iowa-Nashville	.981	103	224	231	9	464	59
Holbert, Aaron, Nashville	.970	17	25	39	2	66	6
Hooper, Kevin, Albuquerque	.986	79	144	219	5	368	63
Huffman, Royce, New Orleans	.952	15	27	32	3	62	5
Johnson, Keith, Salt Lake	.964	11	26	27	2	55	11
Kata, Matt, Tucson	.958	40	70	112	8	190	23
Kuzmic, Craig, Tacoma-Fresno	.961	28	39	60	4	103	11
Liniak, Cole, Oklahoma	1.000	1	3	0	0	3	0
Lockhart, Keith, Portland	1.000	1	0	1	0	1	0
Lopez, Luis, Colorado Springs	.968	31	61	61	4	126	10
LOPEZ, MICKEY, Tacoma	.987	100	192	270	6	468	63
Mackowiak, Rob, Nashville	1.000	5	6	2	0	8	0
Malloy, Marty, L.V.-Memphis	.993	64	136	153	2	291	39
Matos, Julius, Omaha	1.000	2	4	7	0	11	0
Matranga, Dave, New Orleans	.982	51	122	147	5	274	24
Medrano, Jesus, Albuquerque	.992	29	50	82	1	133	21
Meliah, Dave, Oklahoma	1.000	8	14	21	0	35	3
Mendez, Donaldo, Portland	.977	20	34	51	2	87	11
Mendoza, Carlos, Fresno	.000	1	0	0	1	1	0
Meyers, Chad, Tacoma	.933	13	26	30	4	60	7
Neufeld, Andy, Sacramento	.969	10	11	20	1	32	4
Newhan, David, Colo. Springs	.943	33	72	77	9	158	17

Player, Team	Pct.	G	PO	A	E	TC	DP
Nieves, Jose, Memphis	1.000	2	3	3	0	6	0
Nivar, Ramon, Oklahoma	.944	4	9	8	1	18	0
Ojeda, Augie, Iowa	.983	26	51	66	2	119	17
Olson, Tim, Tucson	1.000	7	15	14	0	29	5
Ordaz, Luis, Omaha	1.000	8	20	21	0	41	8
Ozuna, Pablo, Colorado Springs	.988	21	30	52	1	83	7
Pecci, Jay, Tacoma-Fresno	.975	24	50	66	3	119	16
Pelaez, Alex, Portland	.986	14	23	45	1	69	9
Pickler, Jeff, Oklahoma	.982	112	243	344	11	598	85
Post, Dave, Colorado Springs	1.000	3	5	3	0	8	3
Powers, John, Oklahoma	1.000	1	4	2	0	6	1
Raymundo, G.J., Oklahoma	1.000	2	2	4	0	6	0
Reboulet, Jeff, Nashville	1.000	3	2	1	0	3	0
Riggs, Adam, Salt Lake	.900	8	12	24	4	40	5
Riggs, Eric, Las Vegas	1.000	7	22	17	0	39	5
Rogelstad, Matt, Tacoma	.000	1	0	0	0	0	0
Romano, Jason, Las Vegas	.975	9	18	21	1	40	4
Sadler, Donnie, Oklahoma	1.000	1	2	3	0	5	1
Salazar, Oscar, Salt Lake	.977	7	20	22	1	43	6
Sanchez, Freddy, Nashville	1.000	1	4	2	0	6	2
Scales, Bobby, Portland	1.000	2	5	2	0	7	0
Selby, Bill, Memphis	.980	20	41	56	2	99	15
Spivey, Junior, Tucson	1.000	4	4	13	0	17	3
Theodorou, Nick, Las Vegas	1.000	1	1	2	0	3	1
Thrower, Jake, Port.-Edmonton	.983	42	77	92	3	172	17
Thurston, Joe, Las Vegas	.980	125	277	360	13	650	85
Valdez, Wilson, Albuquerque	.975	6	21	18	1	40	6
Vina, Fernando, Memphis	1.000	4	1	12	0	13	1
Vizcaino, Jose, New Orleans	.889	2	1	7	1	9	0
Wathan, Derek, Albuquerque	1.000	4	2	9	0	11	0

SECOND BASEMEN WITH TWO OR MORE TEAMS

Player, Team	Pct.	G	PO	A	E	TC	DP
Alviso, Jerome, Colo. Springs	.990	23	34	65	1	100	15
Alviso, Jerome, Salt Lake	.962	4	7	18	1	26	4
Clark, Jermaine, Portland	.939	9	11	20	2	33	7
Clark, Jermaine, Oklahoma	1.000	6	8	18	0	26	1
Hernandez, Carlos, New Orleans	.974	9	14	24	1	39	6
Hernandez, Carlos, Fresno	.969	50	82	139	7	228	31
Hill, Bobby, Nashville	1.000	16	37	37	0	74	7
Hill, Bobby, Iowa	.977	87	187	194	9	390	52
Kuzmic, Craig, Tacoma	.967	8	15	14	1	30	2
Kuzmic, Craig, Fresno	.959	20	24	46	3	73	9
Malloy, Marty, Memphis	.993	63	134	151	2	287	38
Malloy, Marty, Las Vegas	1.000	1	2	2	0	4	1
Pecci, Jay, Fresno	.981	11	24	29	1	54	9
Pecci, Jay, Tacoma	.969	13	26	37	2	65	7
Thrower, Jake, Portland	.980	12	19	30	1	50	7
Thrower, Jake, Edmonton	.984	30	58	62	2	122	10

THIRD BASEMEN

Player, Team	Pct.	G	PO	A	E	TC	DP
Abbott, Kurt, Memphis	.881	13	9	28	5	42	4
Abernathy, Brent, Omaha	.750	4	3	6	3	12	1
Alexander, Manny, Oklahoma	1.000	5	1	6	0	7	0
Alfaro, Jason, New Orleans	.947	47	29	79	6	114	11
Alviso, Jerome, Colo. Springs	.000	1	0	0	0	0	0
Ardoin, Danny, Oklahoma	.900	10	11	16	3	30	2
Arteaga, Joshua, Iowa	1.000	3	3	4	0	7	0
Atkins, Garrett, Colo. Springs	.938	110	70	232	20	322	18
Balfe, Ryan, Edmonton	.913	8	6	15	2	23	4
Bell, Mike, Tucson	.857	14	20	16	6	42	4
Bell, Rick, Las Vegas	.905	70	44	118	17	179	8
Bellhorn, Mark, Colo. Springs	.974	12	10	28	1	39	2
Bellinger, Clay, Fresno	.959	37	24	69	4	97	7
Bowers, Jason, Memphis	.905	9	4	15	2	21	0
Carvajal, Jhonny, Tucson	.750	1	1	2	1	4	1
Cesar, Dionys, Edmonton	1.000	2	2	3	0	5	1
Chavez, Raul, New Orleans	.956	40	26	82	5	113	7
Cirillo, Jeff, Tacoma	1.000	3	3	6	0	9	1
Clapinski, Chris, Las Vegas	.938	4	3	12	1	16	0
Clark, Jermaine, Portland	1.000	2	4	1	0	5	0
Coffie, Ivanon, Memphis	.846	7	3	8	2	13	0
Connors, Greg, Tacoma	.941	14	9	23	2	34	3
Counsell, Craig, Tucson	1.000	1	1	4	0	5	0
Cromer, Tripp, New Orleans	.972	13	14	21	1	36	1
Dallimore, Brian, Fresno	.984	20	20	43	1	64	3
Dawkins, Gookie, Omaha	.923	4	2	10	1	13	1
De La Rosa, Tomas, Nashville	.852	15	4	19	4	27	0
Donnels, Chris, Tucson-Iowa	.833	6	3	2	1	6	0
Doster, Dave, Nashville	.941	24	9	39	3	51	3
Durrington, Trent, Salt Lake	.943	28	21	45	4	70	8
Edwards, Mike, Sacramento	.833	3	1	4	1	6	0
Erickson, Matt, Albuquerque	.941	48	25	86	7	118	7
Evans, Tom, Iowa-Colo. Springs	.800	3	0	4	1	5	0
Figgins, Chone, Salt Lake	1.000	2	1	11	0	12	1
Figueroa, Luis, Tacoma	.932	110	82	190	20	292	16
Flores, Jose, Sacramento	.800	12	2	14	4	20	2
Gilbert, Shawn, Nashville	.909	7	3	7	1	11	0
Grabowski, Jason, Sacramento	1.000	1	1	4	0	5	0
Guiel, Jeff, Salt Lake	.936	22	9	35	3	47	5
Guillen, Carlos, Tacoma	1.000	3	3	9	0	12	1
Gulan, Mike, Nashville	.951	96	60	154	11	225	12
Guzman, Edwards, Edmonton	.968	9	11	19	1	31	1
Hammock, Rob, Tucson	1.000	2	1	4	0	5	1
Hansen, Jed, Memphis-Omaha	.924	34	27	58	7	92	12
Harris, Brian, Omaha	1.000	12	7	26	0	33	2
Harris, Lenny, Albuquerque	1.000	1	1	2	0	3	0
Hart, Bo, Memphis	.906	13	5	24	3	32	4
Hernandez, Carlos, New Orleans	1.000	2	0	1	0	1	0
Hiatt, Phil, Iowa	.800	3	2	2	1	5	0
Hill, Bobby, Iowa	.818	6	4	5	2	11	0
Hill, Jason, Salt Lake	.000	1	0	0	0	0	0
Hillenbrand, Shea, Tucson	1.000	2	0	4	0	4	0
Hodges, Scott, Edmonton	.945	122	74	235	18	327	31
Holbert, Aaron, Nashville	1.000	3	1	4	0	5	0
Hoover, Paul, Albuquerque	1.000	4	0	6	0	6	0
Hubbard, Trenidad, Iowa	1.000	9	4	11	0	15	2
Huffman, Royce, New Orleans	1.000	1	0	1	0	1	0
Johnson, Keith, Salt Lake	.953	96	67	137	10	214	17
Kelton, Dave, Iowa	.855	34	23	42	11	76	5
King, Brad, Nashville	.000	1	0	0	0	0	0
Kuzmic, Craig, Tacoma-Fresno	.952	21	12	28	2	42	4
Lamb, Mike, Oklahoma	.944	66	62	124	11	197	16
Leon, Donny, Iowa	.930	83	54	146	15	215	16
Liniak, Cole, Oklahoma	.945	31	27	42	4	73	3
Lopez, Luis, Colorado Springs	1.000	4	1	4	0	5	2
Lopez, Luis, Sacramento	.959	129	72	212	12	296	12
Mackowiak, Rob, Nashville	.853	14	7	22	5	34	3
Malloy, Marty, Las Vegas	1.000	1	1	4	0	5	1
Matos, Julius, Omaha	1.000	1	0	1	0	1	1
Matranga, Dave, New Orleans	.967	15	9	20	1	30	5
McDougall, Marshall, Oklahoma	.909	7	5	15	2	22	1
Melhuse, Adam, Sacramento	1.000	3	2	4	0	6	0
Meliah, Dave, Oklahoma	.851	24	21	42	11	74	4
Mendez, Donaldo, Portland	.950	22	17	40	3	60	8
Morales, Willie, Mem.-C.S.	1.000	6	3	10	0	13	1
Moriarty, Mike, New Orleans	.927	42	37	90	10	137	10
Mosquera, Julio, Tacoma	.931	13	7	20	2	29	0
Neufeld, Andy, Sacramento	1.000	2	0	2	0	2	1
Niekro, Lance, Fresno	.926	76	51	125	14	190	12
Nieves, Jose, Memphis	.500	4	0	1	1	2	0
Ojeda, Augie, Iowa	.975	17	13	26	1	40	0
Ordaz, Luis, Omaha	.936	21	10	34	3	47	1
Ozuna, Pablo, Colorado Springs	.947	7	6	12	1	19	0
Paquette, Craig, Memphis	.870	10	5	15	3	23	2
Patterson, Jarrod, Omaha	.928	71	36	169	16	221	9
Pecci, Jay, Tacoma	1.000	1	0	3	0	3	0
Peeples, Mike, Memphis	.750	1	0	6	2	8	0
Pelaez, Alex, Portland	.966	60	44	97	5	146	14
Pellow, Kit, Colorado Springs	.941	10	2	14	1	17	0
Powers, John, Oklahoma	1.000	2	0	3	0	3	0
Raymundo, G.J., Oklahoma	.864	8	3	16	3	22	1
Reboulet, Jeff, Nashville	.833	2	3	2	1	6	1
Riggs, Eric, Las Vegas	.925	66	42	131	14	187	12
Risinger, Ben, Portland	.973	47	36	73	3	112	4
Rogelstad, Matt, Tacoma	.000	1	0	0	0	0	0
Romano, Jason, Las Vegas	.944	8	8	9	1	18	2
Rouse, Michael, Sacramento	1.000	1	1	1	0	2	0
Sasser, Rob, Omaha	1.000	10	8	16	0	24	1
Scales, Bobby, Portland	1.000	3	3	4	0	7	0
Seabol, Scott, Memphis	.948	81	63	157	12	232	16
Selby, Bill, Memphis	.970	13	6	26	1	33	3
Theodorou, Nick, Las Vegas	1.000	4	2	3	0	5	1
Thrower, Jake, Port.-Edm.	.929	16	8	18	2	28	3
Torcato, Tony, Fresno	.842	6	8	8	3	19	3
Tracy, Chad, Tucson	.951	125	94	292	20	406	17
Valdez, Mario, Portland	1.000	1	0	2	0	2	0
Washington, Rico, Portland	.943	15	12	38	3	53	4
Wathan, Derek, Albuquerque	.889	5	3	5	1	9	0
WOOD, JASON, Albuquerque	.972	101	71	204	8	283	23
Zinter, Alan, New Orleans	.000	1	0	0	1	1	0

THIRD BASEMEN WITH TWO OR MORE TEAMS

Player, Team	Pct.	G	PO	A	E	TC	DP
Donnels, Chris, Iowa	.667	4	1	1	1	3	0
Donnels, Chris, Tucson	1.000	2	2	1	0	3	0
Evans, Tom, Iowa	1.000	1	0	1	0	1	0
Evans, Tom, Colorado Springs	.750	2	0	3	1	4	0
Hansen, Jed, Memphis	.941	8	6	10	1	17	1
Hansen, Jed, Omaha	.920	26	21	48	6	75	11
Kuzmic, Craig, Fresno	.966	12	8	20	1	29	3
Kuzmic, Craig, Tacoma	.923	9	4	8	1	13	1
Morales, Willie, Memphis	1.000	1	0	1	0	1	0
Morales, Willie, Colo. Springs	1.000	5	3	9	0	12	1
Thrower, Jake, Edmonton	.941	9	4	12	1	17	2
Thrower, Jake, Portland	.909	7	4	6	1	11	1

SHORTSTOPS

Player, Team	Pct.	G	PO	A	E	TC	DP
Abernathy, Brent, Omaha	.000	1	0	0	1	1	0
Alexander, Manny, Oklahoma	.972	104	185	305	14	504	80
Alfaro, Jason, New Orleans	.961	44	65	131	8	204	24
Alviso, Jerome, C.S.-Salt Lake	.921	19	17	41	5	63	12
Amezaga, Alfredo, Salt Lake	.982	64	125	206	6	337	46
Arteaga, Joshua, Iowa	.938	7	13	17	2	32	3
Barmes, Clint, Colorado Springs	.953	132	177	385	28	590	70
Bellinger, Clay, Fresno	.942	10	16	33	3	52	7
Bowers, Jason, Memphis	.968	89	129	258	13	400	53
Bruntlett, Eric, New Orleans	.964	47	93	149	9	251	39
Butler, Brent, Colorado Springs	1.000	1	0	2	0	2	0
Carvajal, Jhonny, Tucson	.984	18	20	40	1	61	4
Castillo, Ruben, Tacoma	.950	110	179	295	25	499	66
Cintron, Alex, Tucson	.966	23	43	70	4	117	18
Clapinski, Chris, Las Vegas	.974	62	94	171	7	272	36
Clark, Jermaine, Portland	.917	6	9	13	2	24	3
Coffie, Ivanon, Memphis	1.000	1	1	4	0	5	0
Counsell, Craig, Tucson	1.000	2	6	7	0	13	3
Crosby, Bobby, Sacramento	.973	125	186	349	15	550	59
Dawkins, Gookie, L.V.-Omaha	.958	60	97	174	12	283	40
De La Rosa, Tomas, Nashville	.954	49	67	99	8	174	15
Delgado, Alex, Memphis	1.000	2	2	4	0	6	0
Delgado, Wilson, Memphis	.991	25	43	70	1	114	9
Edwards, Mike, Sacramento	1.000	2	3	3	0	6	0
Espada, Joe, Memphis	1.000	7	8	18	0	26	1
Everett, Adam, New Orleans	.990	22	39	57	1	97	13
Febles, Carlos, Omaha	.933	4	6	8	1	15	3
Figgins, Chone, Salt Lake	.938	27	42	78	8	128	21
Figueroa, Luis, Edmonton	.957	28	43	69	5	117	12
Flores, Jose, Sacramento	.934	20	34	51	6	91	11
Frese, Nate, Iowa	.971	96	136	267	12	415	55
Gandolfo, Rob, Tacoma	1.000	2	0	1	0	1	0
Garcia, James, Fresno	1.000	1	1	0	0	1	0
Gilbert, Shawn, Nashville	1.000	1	1	3	0	4	0
Greene, Khalil, Portland	.967	76	96	230	11	337	42
Gulan, Mike, Nashville	.000	1	0	0	0	0	0
Hansen, Jed, Omaha	1.000	1	2	4	0	6	0
Harris, Brian, Omaha	.958	24	44	70	5	119	14
Harrison, Adonis, Salt Lake	.964	32	51	83	5	139	14
Hart, Bo, Memphis	1.000	9	10	24	0	34	4
Hernandez, Carlos, Fresno	.988	16	27	52	1	80	14
Holbert, Aaron, Nashville	.953	94	126	235	18	379	39
Hooper, Kevin, Albuquerque	.975	48	64	169	6	239	39
Johnson, Keith, Salt Lake	.936	10	16	28	3	47	7
Kata, Matt, Tucson	.957	11	22	22	2	46	9
Liniak, Cole, Oklahoma	.864	6	10	9	3	22	1
Lopez, Luis, Colorado Springs	.897	9	7	19	3	29	5
Lopez, Mickey, Tacoma	.979	35	50	88	3	141	13
Malloy, Marty, L.V.-Memphis	.933	5	8	20	2	30	6
Matos, Julius, Omaha	.949	68	109	207	17	333	45
Matranga, Dave, New Orleans	.976	22	42	40	2	84	14
McDougall, Marshall, Oklahoma	.955	13	18	45	3	66	9
MEDRANO, ANTHONY, Edm.	.975	123	178	358	14	550	80
Meliah, Dave, Oklahoma	.917	7	8	14	2	24	0
Mendez, Donaldo, Portland	.956	58	98	139	11	248	35
Mendoza, Carlos, Fresno	.971	7	12	21	1	34	4
Moriarty, Mike, New Orleans	.981	14	17	35	1	53	6
Neufeld, Andy, Sacramento	.900	4	6	3	1	10	1
Nieves, Jose, Memphis	.944	14	25	26	3	54	5
Ojeda, Augie, Iowa	.975	57	75	161	6	242	36
Olson, Tim, Tucson	.937	104	141	293	29	463	50
Ordaz, Luis, Omaha	.982	23	35	75	2	112	22
Ozuna, Pablo, Colorado Springs	.964	14	20	34	2	56	6
Pavkovich, Adam, Salt Lake	1.000	1	5	6	0	11	2
Ransom, Cody, Fresno	.959	112	155	317	20	492	53
Reboulet, Jeff, Nashville	1.000	9	14	20	0	34	3
Riggs, Eric, Las Vegas	.942	48	62	116	11	189	27
Risinger, Ben, Portland	1.000	2	1	8	0	9	0
Romano, Jason, Las Vegas	1.000	2	4	5	0	9	0
Rouse, Michael, Sacramento	1.000	1	0	1	0	1	0
Sadler, Donnie, Oklahoma	.952	16	32	47	4	83	8
Thrower, Jake, Portland	1.000	6	8	15	0	23	5
Thurston, Joe, Las Vegas	.929	6	8	18	2	28	4
Ugueto, Luis, Tacoma	.936	8	14	30	3	47	12
Valdez, Wilson, Albuquerque	.974	82	143	237	10	390	56
Vizcaino, Jose, New Orleans	.000	1	0	0	0	0	0
Wathan, Derek, Albuquerque	.953	19	18	63	4	85	15
Wood, Jason, Albuquerque	.000	1	0	0	0	0	0

SHORTSTOPS WITH TWO OR MORE TEAMS

Player, Team	Pct.	G	PO	A	E	TC	DP
Alviso, Jerome, Colo. Springs	.833	7	1	9	2	12	0
Alviso, Jerome, Salt Lake	.941	12	16	32	3	51	12
Dawkins, Gookie, Las Vegas	.928	32	43	85	10	138	15
Dawkins, Gookie, Omaha	.986	28	54	89	2	145	25
Malloy, Marty, Las Vegas	.833	2	1	4	1	6	3
Malloy, Marty, Memphis	.958	3	7	16	1	24	3

OUTFIELDERS

Player, Team	Pct.	G	PO	A	E	TC	DP
Agbayani, Benny, Omaha	.984	35	59	1	1	61	0
Alexander, Chad, Iowa	1.000	4	8	0	0	8	0
Alfaro, Jason, New Orleans	1.000	11	21	1	0	22	0
Allen, Chad, Albuquerque	.993	82	145	5	1	151	1
Allen, Luke, Colorado Springs	.971	120	222	11	7	240	2
Alvarez, Tony, Nashville	.984	91	178	10	3	191	2
Alviso, Jerome, Colo. Springs	.000	1	0	0	0	0	0
Anderson, Brady, Portland *	1.000	18	29	1	0	30	0
Ashby, Chris, Albuquerque	.973	16	32	4	1	37	0
Bailey, Jeff, Edmonton	1.000	1	1	0	0	1	0
Balfe, Ryan, Edmonton	1.000	1	1	0	0	1	0
Barkett, Andy, Tacoma *	.964	14	24	3	1	28	1
Barnes, John, Nashville	.973	93	137	5	4	146	1
Barnes, Larry, Las Vegas *	.973	15	36	0	1	37	0
Bautista, Danny, Tucson	1.000	8	8	1	0	9	0
Bay, Jason, Portland	.995	90	195	10	1	206	1
Bell, Mike, Tucson	.923	10	12	0	1	13	0
Bellinger, Clay, Fresno	.978	22	43	1	1	45	0
Benard, Marvin, Fresno *	.967	13	28	1	1	30	1
Berger, Brandon, Omaha	.978	39	85	6	2	93	1
Bergeron, Pete, Edmonton	.981	97	243	10	5	258	2
Bozied, Tagg, Portland	.000	1	0	0	0	0	0
Brock, Tarrik, Las Vegas *	1.000	1	1	0	0	1	0
Brooks, Frank, Nashville *	.000	1	0	0	0	0	0
Brown, Dee, Omaha	.955	9	19	2	1	22	0
Bruntlett, Eric, New Orleans	1.000	3	5	0	0	5	0
Buford, Damon, Edmonton	.889	9	8	0	1	9	0
Cepicky, Matt, Edmonton	.954	93	187	1	9	197	0
Cesar, Dionys, Edmonton	.667	2	2	0	1	3	0
Chen, Chin-Feng, Las Vegas	.969	104	179	8	6	193	0
Christenson, Ryan, Oklahoma	1.000	52	136	2	0	138	0
Clark, Doug, Fresno	1.000	5	5	0	0	5	0
Clark, Jermaine, Port.-Okla.	.986	78	136	6	2	144	1
Cole, Eric, New Orleans	.980	22	49	0	1	50	0
Connors, Greg, Tacoma	1.000	10	21	0	0	21	0
Crosby, Bubba, Las Vegas *	.991	57	108	7	1	116	1
Cummings, Midre, Iowa	.987	89	146	1	2	149	1
DaVanon, Jeff, Salt Lake	.933	15	28	0	2	30	0
Dallimore, Brian, Fresno	1.000	1	1	0	0	1	0
Davis, J.J., Nashville	.964	114	239	3	9	251	1
De La Rosa, Tomas, Nashville	.000	1	0	0	0	0	0
DeHaan, Kory, Portland	.992	51	131	1	1	133	1
DeJesus, David, Omaha *	1.000	56	114	2	0	116	1
Devore, Doug, Tucson *	.967	126	221	13	8	242	1
Doster, Dave, Nashville	.950	11	18	1	1	20	1
Dunwoody, Todd, Memphis *	.987	79	144	5	2	151	1
Durrington, Trent, Salt Lake	1.000	8	6	1	0	7	0
Dye, Jermaine, Sacramento	1.000	6	13	0	0	13	0
Edwards, Mike, Sacramento	.989	98	177	2	2	181	0
Ellison, Jason, Fresno	.974	117	320	16	9	345	3
Encarnacion, Mario, Edm.-Mem.	.955	10	20	1	1	22	0
Erickson, Matt, Albuquerque	1.000	3	3	0	0	3	0
Erstad, Darin, Salt Lake *	1.000	7	16	0	0	16	0
Fernandez, Alex, Portland *	.976	99	185	15	5	205	3
Figgins, Chone, Salt Lake	1.000	5	21	0	0	21	0
Flores, Jose, Sacramento	.964	46	76	4	3	83	0

Player, Team	Pct.	G	PO	A	E	TC	DP
Freeman, Choo, Colo. Springs	.936	92	174	1	12	187	1
Gall, John, Memphis	1.000	6	8	1	0	9	0
Glanville, Doug, Oklahoma	1.000	8	10	0	0	10	0
Gomez, Alexis, Omaha *	.970	120	278	11	9	298	1
Gomez, Rich, Portland	.971	60	99	3	3	105	1
Gordon, Brian, Tucson	.982	113	218	6	4	228	0
Grabowski, Jason, Sacramento	.964	49	78	2	3	83	1
Guiel, Aaron, Omaha	.962	52	121	6	5	132	0
Guiel, Jeff, Salt Lake	.977	18	40	3	1	44	0
Gulan, Mike, Nashville	.000	3	0	0	1	1	0
Guzman, Freddy, Portland	1.000	2	4	0	0	4	0
Hammock, Rob, Tucson	1.000	5	5	2	0	7	0
Hammonds, Jeffrey, Fresno	1.000	9	26	0	0	26	0
Hansen, Jed, Omaha	1.000	31	68	2	0	70	1
Hart, Jason, Oklahoma	1.000	7	6	0	0	6	0
Haynes, Dee, Memphis	.983	113	224	9	4	237	3
Haynes, Nathan, Salt Lake *	.950	26	76	0	4	80	0
Hermansen, Chad, Las Vegas	.988	41	80	1	1	82	0
Hermida, Jeremy, Albuquerque	1.000	1	1	0	0	1	0
Hiatt, Phil, Iowa	1.000	29	48	2	0	50	2
Holst, Micah, Fresno	1.000	2	1	0	0	1	0
Hoover, Paul, Albuquerque	1.000	1	2	0	0	2	0
Hubbard, Trenidad, Iowa	.970	87	181	12	6	199	2
Huffman, Royce, New Orleans	.933	17	26	2	2	30	0
Hyzdu, Adam, Nashville	1.000	32	52	0	0	52	0
Iapoce, Anthony, Albuquerque*	.963	40	70	7	3	80	0
Jackson, Nic, Iowa	.994	122	306	6	2	314	4
Johnson, Gary, Salt Lake *	.985	86	186	9	3	198	2
Johnson, Rontrez, Oklahoma	.981	70	155	2	3	160	0
Jones, Jason, Oklahoma	.990	55	89	6	1	96	1
Kapler, Gabe, Colorado Springs	.955	11	20	1	1	22	0
Kelly, Kenny, Tacoma	.981	85	197	11	4	212	1
Kelly, Mike, Omaha	.986	82	132	5	2	139	1
Kelton, Dave, Iowa	.973	74	138	6	4	148	1
Krause, Scott, Memphis	1.000	2	2	1	0	3	0
Kuzmic, Craig, Tacoma	.000	1	0	0	0	0	0
Landry, Jacques, Tacoma	.986	38	64	4	1	69	1
Lane, Jason, New Orleans *	.966	53	86	0	3	89	0
Leach, Jalal, Tacoma *	.962	51	74	1	3	78	1
Leon, Donny, Iowa	1.000	2	6	1	0	7	1
Lesher, Brian, Memphis *	1.000	6	12	0	0	12	0
Linden, Todd, Fresno	.985	120	251	7	4	262	0
Liniak, Cole, Oklahoma	1.000	14	23	1	0	24	0
Little, Mark, Tucson	.951	21	37	2	2	41	0
Lockwood, Mike, Sacramento *	.986	75	141	2	2	145	0
Logan, Kyle, New Orleans	.979	128	230	6	5	241	0
Lopez, Mickey, Tacoma	1.000	1	2	0	0	2	0
Ludwick, Ryan, Oklahoma *	.975	50	116	3	3	122	2
Lunsford, Trey, Fresno	1.000	1	2	0	0	2	0
Mackowiak, Rob, Nashville	1.000	3	5	0	0	5	0
Magee, Wendell, Colo. Springs	1.000	34	56	4	0	60	1
Marrero, Eli, Memphis	1.000	3	3	0	0	3	0
Martin, Billy, Tucson	.875	5	6	1	1	8	0
Matos, Julius, Omaha	.946	19	33	2	2	37	0
Matranga, Dave, New Orleans	1.000	2	4	0	0	4	0
McCarty, Dave, Sacramento *	1.000	10	18	0	0	18	0
McDougall, Marshall, Oklahoma	.882	7	14	1	2	17	0
McMillon, Billy, Sacramento *	.966	36	55	1	2	58	1
Melhuse, Adam, Sacramento	.944	12	17	0	1	18	0
Meliah, Dave, Oklahoma	1.000	9	8	2	0	10	0
Melian, Jackson, Iowa	1.000	37	69	1	0	70	0
Meluskey, Mitch, Sacramento	1.000	1	2	0	0	2	0
Mench, Kevin, Oklahoma	1.000	29	54	0	0	54	0
Meyers, Chad, Tacoma	.967	74	177	1	6	184	1
Murray, Calvin, Las Vegas	.995	82	201	7	1	209	2
Myers, Adrian, Tacoma	.992	105	235	6	2	243	0
Nady, Xavier, Portland	.954	32	60	2	3	65	1
Nevin, Phil, Portland	1.000	2	4	0	0	4	0
Newhan, David, Colo. Springs	.920	15	21	2	2	25	0
Nivar, Ramon, Oklahoma	1.000	20	56	2	0	58	0
Nunez, Abraham, Albuquerque	.979	57	139	3	3	145	0
Nunnally, Jon, Memphis	.987	119	302	7	4	313	3
Olson, Tim, Tucson	1.000	8	14	1	0	15	0
Ortiz, Luis, Edmonton	1.000	4	4	0	0	4	0
Ottavinia, Paul, Oklahoma *	.979	38	88	4	2	94	1
Ozuna, Pablo, Colorado Springs	.949	20	37	0	2	39	0
Pascucci, Val, Edmonton	.981	109	197	15	4	216	5
Patterson, Jarrod, Omaha	1.000	2	2	1	0	3	1
Paul, Josh, Iowa	1.000	15	17	1	0	18	0
Peeples, Mike, Memphis	1.000	7	13	0	0	13	0
Pellow, Kit, Colorado Springs	1.000	3	1	0	0	1	0
Petrick, Ben, Colorado Springs	.971	33	31	3	1	35	2
Pickler, Jeff, Oklahoma	1.000	2	0	1	0	1	0
Porter, Colin, New Orleans *	.989	97	255	6	3	264	2
Post, Dave, Colorado Springs	.000	3	0	0	0	0	0
PRIETO, CHRIS, Sacramento *	1.000	105	253	7	0	260	3
Quinlan, Robb, Salt Lake	1.000	29	51	3	0	54	1
Quinn, Mark, Portland	.971	37	62	4	2	68	1
Ramirez, Dan, Tucson	.966	59	112	2	4	118	0
Ramirez, Julio, Salt Lake	.975	103	268	8	7	283	2
Redman, Tike, Nashville *	.987	94	226	3	3	232	0
Reid, Justin, Nashville	.000	1	0	0	0	0	0
Reyes, Rene, Colorado Springs	.970	93	153	7	5	165	1
Riggs, Adam, Salt Lake	.971	23	34	0	1	35	0
Risinger, Ben, Portland	1.000	7	3	1	0	4	0
Roberts, Dave, Las Vegas *	.000	2	0	0	0	0	0
Robinson, Kerry, Memphis *	.979	16	46	0	1	47	0
Rodriguez, Luis, Memphis	1.000	1	4	0	0	4	0
Rogelstad, Matt, Tacoma	1.000	3	1	0	0	1	0
Romano, Jason, Las Vegas	.981	39	101	3	2	106	0
Rose, Mike, Sacramento	.000	1	0	0	0	0	0
Ruan, Wilkin, Las Vegas	.992	104	242	11	2	255	2
Rushford, Jim, Oklahoma *	.977	23	40	3	1	44	1
Ryan, Rob, Fresno *	.982	28	54	1	1	56	0
Sadler, Donnie, Oklahoma	1.000	1	2	0	0	2	0
Santos, Francisco, Fresno *	.978	47	84	5	2	91	0
Scales, Bobby, Portland	1.000	6	13	1	0	14	0
Selby, Bill, Memphis	.987	34	69	5	1	75	0
Sellier, Brian, Sacramento	1.000	23	44	1	0	45	0
Simmons, Brian, Portland	1.000	4	8	0	0	8	0
Sledge, Terrmel, Edmonton *	.971	121	258	11	8	277	1
Snelling, Chris, Tacoma *	1.000	13	27	1	0	28	0
Stairs, Matt, Nashville	1.000	4	6	0	0	6	0
Stanley, Henri, New Orleans *	.980	125	235	4	5	244	1
Stratton, Rob, Albuquerque	.973	90	172	6	5	183	0
Strong, Jamal, Tacoma	.958	55	136	2	6	144	1
Sullivan, Kevin, Colo. Springs	1.000	1	2	0	0	2	0
Sweeney, Mark, Colo. Springs *	1.000	37	54	0	0	54	0
Taguchi, So, Memphis	.994	70	170	3	1	174	1
Terrero, Luis, Tucson	.968	117	298	8	10	316	2
Thames, Marcus, Oklahoma	.968	17	30	0	1	31	0
Theodorou, Nick, Las Vegas	1.000	5	5	0	0	5	0
Thompson, Rich, Nashville	1.000	27	59	1	0	60	0
Toca, Jorge, Nashville	1.000	2	7	0	0	7	0
Topolski, Jon, New Orleans	.667	1	4	0	2	6	0
Torcato, Tony, Fresno	1.000	36	75	0	0	75	0
Valderrama, Carlos, Fresno	.969	51	94	1	3	98	0
Valdez, Mario, Portland	1.000	28	33	1	0	34	0
Vaughn, Greg, Colorado Springs	.944	13	17	0	1	18	0
Victorino, Shane, Las Vegas	.966	10	28	0	1	29	0
Vitiello, Joe, Fresno	1.000	4	7	0	0	7	0
Wakeland, Chris, Albuquerque *	.972	52	65	4	2	71	1
Ware, Jeremy, Edmonton	1.000	5	9	2	0	11	1
Wathan, Derek, Albuquerque	.957	34	65	1	3	69	0
Wesson, Barry, Salt Lake	.968	118	253	19	9	281	5
Widger, Chris, Memphis	1.000	2	4	0	0	4	0
Williams, Gerald, Albuquerque	.972	79	200	9	6	215	2

OUTFIELDERS WITH TWO OR MORE TEAMS

Player, Team	Pct.	G	PO	A	E	TC	DP
Clark, Jermaine, Oklahoma	.975	43	73	5	2	80	1
Clark, Jermaine, Portland	1.000	35	63	1	0	64	0
Encarnacion, Mario, Memphis	1.000	3	12	1	0	13	0
Encarnacion, Mario, Edmonton	.889	7	8	0	1	9	0

CATCHERS

Player, Team	Pct.	G	PO	A	E	TC	DP	PB
Anderson, Keith, Fresno	1.000	3	14	1	0	15	0	1
Ardoin, Danny, Oklahoma	.980	52	295	40	7	342	3	2
Ashby, Chris, Albuquerque	1.000	1	1	0	0	1	0	0
Barajas, Rod, Tucson	1.000	3	19	2	0	21	1	0
Barrett, Michael, Edmonton	1.000	2	3	1	0	4	0	0
Barthol, Blake, Nashville	.995	34	196	14	1	211	1	3
Bellinger, Clay, Fresno	1.000	3	17	3	0	20	1	0
Borders, Pat, Tacoma	.987	66	433	31	6	470	4	2
Brito, Juan, Omaha	1.000	36	238	21	0	259	4	5
Brown, Jason, Edmonton	1.000	4	26	1	0	27	1	0
Buck, John, New Orleans	.993	71	385	36	3	424	2	9
Burkhart, Lance, Oklahoma	1.000	3	12	0	0	12	0	0
Casanova, Raul, Colo. Springs	.977	36	231	19	6	256	2	1
Castillo, Alberto, Fresno	1.000	11	100	5	0	105	0	0
Chavez, Raul, New Orleans	.983	58	305	45	6	356	6	2

Player, Team	Pct.	G	PO	A	E	TC	DP	PB
Cota, Humberto, Nashville	1.000	59	417	23	0	440	1	3
Cresse, Brad, Tucson	.987	78	490	46	7	543	1	2
Delgado, Alex, Memphis	1.000	5	36	3	0	39	0	0
Durrington, Trent, Salt Lake	1.000	2	10	1	0	11	0	1
Fatheree, Danny, New Orleans	1.000	6	5	0	0	5	0	0
Girardi, Joe, Memphis	1.000	18	73	14	0	87	3	0
Gonzalez, Wiki, Portland	.987	42	278	19	4	301	3	2
Grabowski, Jason, Sacramento	.958	7	45	1	2	48	0	1
Gregorio, Tom, Salt Lake	1.000	53	271	37	0	308	3	7
Guzman, Edwards, Edmonton	.985	21	124	11	2	137	1	5
Haad, Yamid, Portland	.984	74	463	40	8	511	2	12
Hammock, Rob, Tucson	.962	21	114	14	5	133	2	2
Hill, Jason, Salt Lake	1.000	7	41	3	0	44	0	0
Hill, Koyie, Las Vegas	.982	77	448	36	9	493	1	9
Hoover, Paul, Albuquerque	.986	59	330	29	5	364	4	6
Horner, Jim, Tacoma	1.000	2	15	0	0	15	0	0
Johnson, Mark, Sacramento	.992	50	343	27	3	373	0	9
Kellner, Ryan, Las Vegas	.989	45	245	19	3	267	4	4
King, Brad, Nashville	.983	63	421	30	8	459	4	4
Knorr, Randy, Edmonton	.994	86	465	27	3	495	4	5
Kuzmic, Craig, Tacoma-Fresno	1.000	18	91	11	0	102	0	2
Laird, Gerald, Oklahoma	.983	89	552	71	11	634	5	8
Loeb, Bryan, Tucson	1.000	5	29	1	0	30	0	0
Lunar, Fernando, Omaha	.984	73	423	55	8	486	5	1
Lunsford, Trey, Fresno	.989	65	341	28	4	373	2	9
Maduro, Jorge, Tacoma	1.000	5	35	2	0	37	0	0
Mahoney, Mike, Iowa	.988	51	291	31	4	326	2	3
Martinez, Sandy, Omaha	1.000	15	62	8	0	70	0	3
Matos, Pascual, Colo. Springs	.984	8	56	7	1	64	0	1
MCDONALD, KEITH, Iowa	.997	77	532	43	2	577	4	4
Melhuse, Adam, Sacramento	.996	27	202	21	1	224	4	2
Morales, Willie, Tuc.-Mem.-C.S.	.991	35	215	15	2	232	1	0
Mosquera, Julio, Tacoma	.989	71	421	33	5	459	3	9
Nieves, Wil, Salt Lake	.988	88	510	45	7	562	5	5
Norris, Dax, New Orleans	1.000	9	36	4	0	40	0	1
Paul, Josh, Iowa	1.000	25	146	20	0	166	5	3
Pellow, Kit, Colorado Springs	.994	24	143	15	1	159	1	7
Petrick, Ben, Colorado Springs	.955	20	82	2	4	88	0	0
Prince, Tom, Omaha	1.000	28	174	16	0	190	2	1
Risinger, Ben, Portland	.993	23	133	10	1	144	2	4
Rivera, Mike, Portland	.990	13	96	7	1	104	0	4
Rodriguez, Guillermo, Fresno	.977	60	303	36	8	347	2	2
Rodriguez, Luis, Memphis	.985	67	298	40	5	343	1	5
Romero, Mandy, Colo. Springs	.983	59	386	22	7	415	4	3
Rose, Mike, Sacramento	.982	63	404	35	8	447	0	3
Ross, David, Las Vegas	.989	24	160	14	2	176	2	1
Sandusky, Scott, Edmonton	1.000	36	176	15	0	191	2	3
Snusz, Chris, Nashville	1.000	4	14	1	0	15	1	0
Sullivan, Kevin, Colo. Springs	1.000	2	6	0	0	6	0	1
Torrealba, Steve, Memphis	.996	40	207	15	1	223	0	2
Treanor, Matt, Albuquerque	.984	96	602	54	11	667	3	7
Ullery, Dave, Omaha	1.000	2	9	1	0	10	0	0
Waldron, Jeff, Tucson	.980	34	182	16	4	202	2	2
Widger, Chris, Memphis	.968	19	110	10	4	124	3	1
Zinter, Alan, New Orleans	1.000	20	74	5	0	79	0	1

CATCHERS WITH TWO OR MORE TEAMS

Player, Team	Pct.	G	PO	A	E	TC	DP	PB
Kuzmic, Craig, Fresno	1.000	11	59	7	0	66	0	1
Kuzmic, Craig, Tacoma	1.000	7	32	4	0	36	0	1
Morales, Willie, Memphis	.989	16	89	5	1	95	1	0
Morales, Willie, Colo. Springs	1.000	11	82	5	0	87	0	0
Morales, Willie, Tucson	.980	8	44	5	1	50	0	0

PITCHERS

Player, Team	Pct.	G	PO	A	E	TC	DP
Abbott, Paul, Tucson	.833	11	3	2	1	6	0
Agamennone, Brandon, Edm.	.750	5	2	1	1	4	1
Ainsworth, Kurt, Fresno	.000	1	0	0	0	0	0
Alfonseca, Antonio, Iowa	1.000	3	0	1	0	1	0
Alvarez, Juan, Albuquerque *	1.000	51	2	12	0	14	2
Alvarez, Victor, Las Vegas *	1.000	22	4	5	0	9	0
Alvarez, Wilson, Las Vegas *	1.000	8	1	8	0	9	2
Alviso, Jerome, Colo. Springs	.000	1	0	0	0	0	0
Anderson, Craig, Tacoma *	.971	28	12	21	1	34	0
Anderson, Jimmy, Fresno *	.769	8	5	5	3	13	1
Atchison, Scott, Tacoma	.944	39	6	11	1	18	0
Aybar, Manny, Fresno	.900	52	3	6	1	10	0
Baerlocher, Ryan, Omaha	.935	19	9	20	2	31	1
Baldwin, James, Omaha	.857	8	3	3	1	7	1
Banks, Willie, Iowa	1.000	25	4	3	0	7	0
Barber, Scott, Tucson	1.000	5	1	5	0	6	0
Barcelo, Lorenzo, Fresno	1.000	20	1	3	0	4	1
Bartosh, Cliff, Portland *	1.000	64	4	11	0	15	0
Bausher, Andy, Portland *	1.000	7	0	1	0	1	0
Beasley, Ray, Oklahoma *	1.000	43	3	10	0	13	0
Beck, Rod, Iowa	1.000	21	1	2	0	3	0
Belitz, Todd, Colo. Springs-Alb.*	.571	16	1	3	3	7	1
Beltran, Francis, Iowa	1.000	31	2	5	0	7	1
Benes, Alan, Iowa	.969	19	7	24	1	32	1
Bennett, Jeff, Nashville	.714	9	5	0	2	7	0
Benoit, Joaquin, Oklahoma	1.000	6	1	3	0	4	0
Bergman, Dusty, Salt Lake *	1.000	1	0	1	0	1	0
Bergman, Sean, Albuquerque	.923	28	10	26	3	39	1
Bevel, Bobby, Colo. Springs *	.750	26	1	5	2	8	0
Bland, Nate, New Orleans *	1.000	17	0	2	0	2	0
Blank, Matt, Edmonton-Fresno *	1.000	13	3	12	0	15	2
Bochtler, Doug, Albuquerque	1.000	23	3	9	0	12	0
Bonser, Boof, Fresno	.667	4	2	2	2	6	0
Bootcheck, Chris, Salt Lake	.936	28	17	27	3	47	0
Borbon, Pedro, Memphis *	1.000	7	0	1	0	1	0
Borland, Toby, Albuquerque	1.000	9	1	2	0	3	0
Bottalico, Ricky, Tucson	1.000	31	2	4	0	6	1
Bowie, Micah, Sacramento *	1.000	5	1	0	0	1	0
Brohawn, Troy, Las Vegas *	1.000	1	0	2	0	2	0
Brooks, Frank, Nashville *	1.000	16	0	5	0	5	0
Brown, Elliot, Fresno	.857	12	0	6	1	7	0
Brown, Eric, Iowa	.000	3	0	0	0	0	0
Bruback, Matt, Ia.-Nash.-Port.	.967	26	12	17	1	30	1
Bruney, Brian, Tucson	1.000	32	1	3	0	4	0
Bukvich, Ryan, Omaha	1.000	34	2	4	0	6	1
Bullinger, Kirk, New Orleans	1.000	55	5	17	0	22	2
Bump, Nate, Albuquerque	.958	15	5	18	1	24	0
Bynum, Mike, Portland *	.964	24	9	18	1	28	3
Callaway, Mickey, S.L.-Okla.	1.000	11	4	7	0	11	1
Cammack, Eric, New Orleans	1.000	4	0	1	0	1	0
Camp, Shawn, Nashville	1.000	33	5	4	0	9	0
Capuano, Chris, Tucson *	.865	23	10	35	7	52	1
Carlyle, Buddy, Omaha	1.000	2	0	1	0	1	0
Carpenter, Chris, Memphis	1.000	3	1	2	0	3	0
Carrara, Giovanni, Tacoma	1.000	18	0	1	0	1	0
Castillo, Frank, Sacramento	1.000	19	6	16	0	22	0
Cate, Troy, Tacoma *	.000	1	0	0	0	0	0
Cervantes, Chris, Tucson *	.909	11	1	9	1	11	1
Chacon, Shawn, Colo. Springs	.000	1	0	0	0	0	0
Chavez, Wilton, Iowa	.909	26	8	12	2	22	0
Chiavacci, Ron, Edmonton	1.000	23	5	7	0	12	0
Christiansen, Jason, Fresno *	1.000	4	0	1	0	1	0
Clontz, Brad, Colorado Springs	.917	57	2	9	1	12	1
Cloude, Ken, Tacoma	1.000	21	6	5	0	11	0
Colon, Jose, Edmonton	.500	13	0	1	1	2	0
Colyer, Steve, Las Vegas *	1.000	44	0	5	0	5	0
Condrey, Clay, Portland	1.000	11	7	8	0	15	2
Connelly, Steve, Fresno	.929	38	3	10	1	14	1
Cook, Aaron, Colorado Springs	1.000	2	1	9	0	10	0
Cook, B.R., Memphis	1.000	13	0	1	0	1	0
Corcoran, Roy, Edmonton	.000	2	0	0	0	0	0
Corey, Bryan, Las Vegas	.960	60	10	14	1	25	4
Corey, Mark, Nashville	.750	46	1	2	1	4	0
Cormier, Lance, Tucson	1.000	5	2	3	0	5	0
Correia, Kevin, Fresno	.000	3	0	0	0	0	0
Croushore, Rick, Albuquerque	.000	3	0	0	0	0	0
Crudale, Mike, Memphis	1.000	32	2	3	0	5	0
Crumpton, Chuck, Edmonton	1.000	19	8	4	0	12	1
Cruz, Juan, Iowa	.818	9	3	6	2	11	0
Cruz, Nelson, Colorado Springs	.667	4	0	2	1	3	0
Cumberland, Chris, Portland *	1.000	4	1	0	0	1	0
Cummings, Jeremy, Memphis	1.000	13	3	7	0	10	0
Cummings, Ryan, Salt Lake	.000	12	0	0	0	0	0
Cunnane, Will, Iowa	.600	12	1	2	2	5	1
Darensbourg, Vic, C.S.-Edm.*	.923	31	2	10	1	13	0
Darnell, Paul, Colo. Springs *	.000	1	0	0	0	0	0
Davis, Doug, Oklahoma *	1.000	4	0	5	0	5	0
Davis, Kane, Iowa	1.000	22	2	4	0	6	1
DeHart, Rick, Omaha *	1.000	25	1	6	0	7	0
Devey, Phil, Las Vegas *	1.000	3	0	2	0	2	0
Dickey, R.A., Oklahoma	.833	3	2	3	1	6	0
Dingman, Craig, Iowa	1.000	11	1	2	0	3	0

Player, Team	Pct.	G	PO	A	E	TC	DP
Dominguez, Juan, Oklahoma	.000	3	0	0	0	0	0
Donaldson, Bo, Salt Lake-Edm.	.000	12	0	0	1	1	0
Downs, Scott, Edmonton *	.963	21	7	19	1	27	2
Drese, Ryan, Oklahoma	.909	20	7	13	2	22	3
Drew, Tim, Edmonton	.917	27	6	16	2	24	1
Duchscherer, Justin, Sac.	.967	24	9	20	1	30	1
Duff, Matt, Memphis	.667	32	1	3	2	6	0
Duncan, Courtney, Port.-S.L.	.800	56	6	6	3	15	0
Dunn, Scott, Salt Lake	1.000	6	0	1	0	1	0
Ebert, Derrin, Iowa-Tucson *	1.000	21	2	6	0	8	1
Elarton, Scott, Colo. Springs	1.000	20	5	27	0	32	3
Ellis, Robert, Oklahoma	.900	27	4	14	2	20	0
Emanuel, Brandon, Salt Lake	.958	29	9	14	1	24	2
Enochs, Chris, Sacramento	1.000	37	4	3	0	7	0
Esslinger, Cam, Colo. Springs	1.000	6	0	1	0	1	0
Estrella, Luis, Fresno	1.000	51	12	12	0	24	1
Evans, Keith, Edmonton-Iowa	1.000	22	3	5	0	8	0
Falkenborg, Brian, Tacoma	1.000	17	2	7	0	9	1
Farmer, Tom, Las Vegas	1.000	5	0	1	0	1	0
Ferguson, Ian, Omaha	1.000	3	3	1	0	4	0
FERNANDEZ, JARED, N.O.	1.000	26	8	34	0	42	2
Ferns, Robert, Tucson	.000	1	0	0	0	0	0
Ferrari, Anthony, Edmonton *	1.000	28	6	5	0	11	0
Fesh, Sean, Albuquerque *	1.000	6	1	0	0	1	0
Field, Nathan, Omaha	1.000	19	4	2	0	6	0
Figueroa, Nelson, Nashville	1.000	23	8	26	0	34	4
Fikac, Jeremy, Sacramento	1.000	42	3	3	0	6	1
Flores, Randy, Colo. Springs *	.955	28	9	33	2	44	2
Flores, Ron, Sacramento *	1.000	12	1	3	0	4	0
Flury, Pat, Portland-Omaha	.750	14	3	0	1	4	0
Fogg, Josh, Nashville	1.000	2	0	2	0	2	0
Foppert, Jesse, Fresno	.000	1	0	0	0	0	0
Fordham, Tom, Nashville *	1.000	13	0	7	0	7	0
Fox, Chad, Albuquerque	.000	3	0	0	0	0	0
Fruto, Emiliano, Tacoma	1.000	1	0	1	0	1	0
Fuell, Jerrod, Albuquerque	.000	3	0	0	0	0	0
Fultz, Aaron, Oklahoma *	.000	1	0	0	0	0	0
Fyhrie, Mike, Omaha-Alb.	.963	20	9	17	1	27	5
Gaal, Bryan, Portland	1.000	2	2	0	0	2	0
Gallo, Mike, New Orleans *	1.000	16	0	2	0	2	0
Galva, Claudio, Sacramento *	.000	1	0	0	0	0	0
Garcia, James, Fresno	1.000	7	2	1	0	3	0
Garcia, Reynaldo, Oklahoma	1.000	39	0	5	0	5	1
Garcia, Rosman, Oklahoma	.857	17	2	4	1	7	0
George, Chris, Omaha *	1.000	10	3	5	0	8	0
Giese, Dan, Portland	.000	3	0	0	1	1	0
Gilfillan, Jason, Omaha	.933	35	6	8	1	15	2
Gissell, Chris, Colorado Springs	.750	38	5	7	4	16	1
Gonzalez, Alfredo, Las Vegas	1.000	2	0	1	0	1	0
Gonzalez, Edgar, Tucson	.926	20	10	15	2	27	0
Gonzalez, Mike, Nashville *	1.000	7	0	3	0	3	0
Good, Andrew, Tucson	1.000	11	7	15	0	22	0
Gosling, Mike, Tucson *	.893	26	6	19	3	28	0
Grabow, John, Nashville *	1.000	17	0	4	0	4	0
Graham, Tom, Oklahoma	1.000	22	1	3	0	4	0
Green, Steve, Salt Lake	.917	21	7	15	2	24	3
Gregg, Kevin, Salt Lake	1.000	15	7	9	0	16	2
Grilli, Jason, Albuquerque	.944	12	4	13	1	18	1
Guerrier, Matt, Nashville	.968	20	11	19	1	31	0
Gulin, Lindsay, Las Vegas *	1.000	28	6	33	0	39	1
Hampton, Matt, Portland *	.875	33	1	6	1	8	0
Hamulack, Tim, Tacoma *	1.000	10	0	2	0	2	0
Hanrahan, Joel, Las Vegas	1.000	5	0	2	0	2	1
Harang, Aaron, Sacramento	.889	12	3	5	1	9	0
Harden, Rich, Sacramento	.941	16	7	9	1	17	0
Haren, Danny, Memphis	1.000	8	2	2	0	4	0
Harris, Brian, Omaha	.000	1	0	0	0	0	0
Harville, Chad, Sacramento	.789	48	2	13	4	19	0
Heaverlo, Jeff, Tacoma	.955	24	7	14	1	22	0
Hebson, Bryan, Edmonton	1.000	30	1	6	0	7	1
Henrie, Matt, Tucson	.000	1	0	0	0	0	0
Hensley, Matt, Salt Lake	.833	27	18	17	7	42	1
Herges, Matt, Portland	.000	4	0	0	0	0	0
Hermanson, Dustin, Fresno	.500	4	1	0	1	2	0
Hernandez, Runelvys, Omaha	.000	1	0	0	0	0	0
Hiljus, Erik, Sacramento	.958	29	14	9	1	24	0
Hill, Jeremy, Omaha	1.000	26	3	9	0	12	1
Holtz, Mike, Nashville *	1.000	45	4	6	0	10	0
Horgan, Joe, Fresno *	.917	55	2	9	1	12	0
Houlton, D.J., New Orleans	1.000	11	2	3	0	5	0
House, Craig, Tacoma-Alb.	1.000	12	0	2	0	2	0
Howard, Ben, Portland	.946	22	15	20	2	37	1

Player, Team	Pct.	G	PO	A	E	TC	DP
Hughes, Travis, Oklahoma	1.000	11	2	7	0	9	1
Hunter, Johnny, Portland	1.000	11	0	1	0	1	0
Iapoce, Anthony, Albuquerque *	.000	2	0	0	0	0	0
Izquierdo, Hansel, Edmonton	1.000	17	3	8	0	11	0
Jarvis, Matt, Fresno *	1.000	23	2	6	0	8	0
Jensen, Ryan, Fresno	.882	27	6	9	2	17	0
Johnson, Jonathan, N.Orleans	1.000	13	5	2	0	7	1
Johnson, Keith, Salt Lake	.000	1	0	0	0	0	0
Johnson, Mike, Fresno	.929	30	4	9	1	14	0
Johnson, Randy, Tucson *	.000	1	0	0	0	0	0
Johnson, Rett, Tacoma	.947	11	7	11	1	19	2
Jones, Bobby M., Omaha *	1.000	20	1	3	0	4	0
Jones, Greg, Salt Lake	1.000	33	4	2	0	6	0
Jongejan, Ferenc, Iowa *	.917	29	3	8	1	12	0
Joseph, Kevin, Memphis-Edm.	1.000	29	4	15	0	19	0
Journell, Jimmy, Memphis	.900	40	1	8	1	10	0
Judd, Mike, Albuquerque	1.000	30	4	5	0	9	1
Karnuth, Jason, Iowa	1.000	13	0	5	0	5	0
Kaye, Justin, Iowa	1.000	20	1	3	0	4	0
Keagle, Greg, Albuquerque	1.000	3	0	1	0	1	0
Keisler, Randy, Port.-Okla.-N.O.*	1.000	22	2	14	0	16	1
Keller, Kris, Portland	.800	18	3	1	1	5	0
Kida, Masao, Las Vegas	.952	21	3	17	1	21	2
Kim, Byung-Hyun, Tucson	1.000	3	0	3	0	3	0
Kim, Sun-Woo, Edmonton	.960	22	8	16	1	25	3
King, Brad, Nashville	1.000	3	0	1	0	1	0
Knott, Eric, Edmonton *	.857	24	4	8	2	14	0
Koplove, Mike, Tucson	.000	3	0	0	0	0	0
Kroon, Marc, Salt Lake	1.000	9	0	3	0	3	0
Kusiewicz, Mike, Sacramento *	1.000	27	3	10	0	13	1
Kuzmic, Craig, Tacoma-Fresno	1.000	3	0	0	0	0	0
Lambert, Jeremy, Memphis	1.000	12	0	1	0	1	0
Landry, Jacques, Tacoma	.000	1	0	0	0	0	0
Langone, Steve, Las Vegas	.750	6	1	2	1	4	0
Layfield, Scotty, Memphis	1.000	22	0	2	0	2	0
Lee, Dave, Las Vegas	1.000	56	3	4	0	7	1
Lehr, Justin, Sacramento	.950	53	10	9	1	20	0
Leicester, Jon, Iowa	1.000	1	2	0	0	2	0
Levrault, Allen, Albuquerque	1.000	21	2	4	0	6	0
Lewis, Colby, Oklahoma	1.000	7	2	3	0	5	0
Lewis, Richie, Edmonton	1.000	7	0	2	0	2	0
Lincoln, Mike, Nashville	1.000	8	2	2	0	4	0
Linebrink, Scott, New Orleans	.000	2	0	0	0	0	0
Liniak, Cole, Oklahoma	.000	1	0	0	0	0	0
Loewer, Carlton, Portland	1.000	23	8	17	0	25	2
Looney, Brian, Colo. Springs *	1.000	3	1	1	0	2	0
Looper, Aaron, Tacoma	.938	46	4	11	1	16	2
Lopez, Albie, Omaha	1.000	4	1	4	0	5	0
Lorraine, Andrew, Las Vegas *	.935	30	14	29	3	46	1
Lowe, Sean, Omaha	.941	14	3	13	1	17	0
Lowry, Noah, Fresno *	1.000	4	0	4	0	4	0
Lukasiewicz, Mark, Salt Lake *	.800	40	1	3	1	5	0
Lundberg, Spike, Oklahoma	1.000	2	2	0	0	2	0
Mahay, Ron, Oklahoma *	1.000	26	2	3	0	5	0
Mahomes, Pat, Nashville	1.000	38	5	9	0	14	2
Mairena, Ozwaldo, Alb.*	.889	61	2	6	1	9	0
Mallette, Brian, Las Vegas	1.000	1	0	1	0	1	0
Mann, Jim, Nashville	1.000	51	4	4	0	8	1
Manon, Julio, Edmonton	.800	35	3	1	1	5	0
Mantei, Matt, Tucson	1.000	3	0	1	0	1	0
Marshall, Lee, Tucson	.938	50	5	10	1	16	2
Mattes, Troy, Edmonton	.000	1	0	0	0	0	0
McKnight, Tony, Las Vegas	1.000	4	3	0	0	3	0
McLeary, Marty, Albuquerque	.800	20	0	4	1	5	0
Meadows, Brian, Nashville	.917	9	4	7	1	12	0
Mecir, Jim, Sacramento	1.000	3	0	1	0	1	0
Meyers, Mike, Iowa	1.000	30	3	9	0	12	1
Miadich, Bart, Salt Lake	1.000	46	2	7	0	9	0
Michalak, Chris, Colo. Springs *	.957	24	7	37	2	46	3
Miller, Greg, New Orleans *	.778	9	2	5	2	9	0
Miller, Matt, Colorado Springs	.727	61	2	6	3	11	0
Moehler, Brian, New Orleans	1.000	1	0	1	0	1	0
Molina, Gabe, Memphis	1.000	57	1	9	0	10	0
Montero, Agustin, Las Vegas	.933	35	6	8	1	15	1
Montgomery, Matt, Fresno	.667	24	0	2	1	3	0
Mounce, Tony, Oklahoma *	1.000	11	2	4	0	6	0
Mullen, Scott, Omaha-L.V.*	.875	27	3	18	3	24	1
Munro, Pete, New Orleans	.800	5	1	3	1	5	1
Murray, Dan, Oklahoma	.917	41	2	9	1	12	0
Myers, Rodney, Las Vegas	.950	46	10	9	1	20	0
Nagy, Charles, Portland	1.000	3	0	1	0	1	1
Neagle, Denny, Colo. Springs *	1.000	4	2	4	0	6	0

Player, Team	Pct.	G	PO	A	E	TC	DP
Neal, Blaine, Albuquerque	1.000	40	2	2	0	4	0
Nickle, Doug, Salt Lake	.867	34	4	9	2	15	2
Nitkowski, C.J., Oklahoma *	.955	33	8	13	1	22	1
Norton, Phil, Iowa *	.929	48	3	10	1	14	0
Nunez, Vladimir, Albuquerque	1.000	46	6	5	0	11	1
O'Brien, Matt, Sacramento *	1.000	10	0	1	0	1	0
Obermueller, Wes, Omaha	1.000	17	14	19	0	33	1
Ohme, Kevin, Memphis *	1.000	49	8	8	0	16	0
Olsen, Kevin, Albuquerque	.857	7	2	4	1	7	0
Oropesa, Eddie, Tucson *	1.000	15	1	3	0	4	1
Osting, Jimmy, Omaha *	1.000	9	0	7	0	7	1
Oswalt, Roy, New Orleans	.000	1	0	0	0	0	0
Painter, Lance, Memphis *	.000	3	0	0	0	0	0
Park, Chan Ho, Oklahoma	1.000	3	1	2	0	3	1
Parrott, Rhett, Memphis	1.000	7	3	3	0	6	0
Patterson, John, Tucson	.824	18	5	9	3	17	1
Pearce, Josh, Memphis	1.000	10	1	3	0	4	0
Pearson, Jason, Memphis *	1.000	44	2	9	0	11	1
Pelaez, Alex, Portland	.000	1	0	0	0	0	0
Pena, Jesus, Colo. Springs *	1.000	11	2	2	0	4	0
Peralta, Joel, Salt Lake	.000	1	0	0	0	0	0
Perez, Oliver, Portland *	.824	8	2	12	3	17	0
Perisho, Matt, Tucson-C.S.*	1.000	12	0	6	0	6	1
Phelps, Tommy, Albuquerque *	1.000	5	0	3	0	3	0
Pickford, Kevin, Fresno *	1.000	25	11	16	0	27	1
Powell, Brian, Fresno	.933	23	13	15	2	30	2
Prieto, Ariel, Nashville	.600	4	1	2	2	5	0
Prinz, Bret, Tucson	1.000	10	0	1	0	1	0
Proctor, Scott, Las Vegas	1.000	24	0	5	0	5	1
Puffer, Brandon, New Orleans	.917	44	1	10	1	12	0
Putz, J.J., Tacoma	1.000	41	3	16	0	19	1
Raggio, Brady, Tucson	1.000	18	1	5	0	6	0
Ramirez, Erasmo, Oklahoma *	.889	22	2	6	1	9	0
Ramirez, Santiago, New Orleans	1.000	10	2	3	0	5	0
Ramos, Mario, Oklahoma *	1.000	5	1	5	0	6	0
Ramsay, Rob, Portland *	.000	2	0	0	0	0	0
Randolph, Steve, Tucson *	.000	7	0	0	0	0	0
Reames, Britt, Edmonton	.943	25	7	26	2	35	2
Reid, Justin, Nashville	1.000	34	3	13	0	16	2
Reyes, Dennys, Tucson *	.833	33	1	4	1	6	0
Rheinecker, John, Sacramento *	1.000	6	3	5	0	8	1
Risinger, Ben, Portland	.000	1	0	0	0	0	0
Rivard, Reggie, Oklahoma	1.000	4	0	1	0	1	0
Roberts, Rick, Las Vegas *	.000	2	0	0	0	0	0
Robertson, Jeriome, N.O.*	1.000	1	0	1	0	1	0
Robertson, Luke, Sacramento	.750	1	2	1	1	4	0
Rodgers, Bobby, Edm.-Iowa	1.000	13	2	2	0	4	0
Rodriguez, Jose, Edmonton *	1.000	13	0	5	0	5	0
Rodriguez, Nerio, Memphis	.833	11	0	10	2	12	0
Rodriguez, Rich, Salt Lake *	1.000	34	0	6	0	6	0
Rosario, Rodrigo, New Orleans	1.000	15	3	10	0	13	1
Rueter, Kirk, Fresno *	1.000	1	0	1	0	1	0
Ryan, Jason, Memphis	.969	29	8	23	1	32	1
Saarloos, Kirk, New Orleans	1.000	13	3	23	0	26	2
Sabel, Erik, Tucson	.909	42	4	6	1	11	1
Saipe, Mike, Las Vegas	.867	21	3	10	2	15	2
Saladin, Miguel, New Orleans	1.000	55	7	15	0	22	2
Sanchez, Duaner, Nashville	1.000	41	5	14	0	19	0
Sanchez, Jesus, Colo. Springs *	1.000	46	3	12	0	15	2
Sanders, Scott, Albuquerque	.938	19	11	19	2	32	2
Santos, Victor, Oklahoma	.800	20	6	10	4	20	1
Sasaki, Kazuhiro, Tacoma	.500	3	1	0	1	2	0
Scanlan, Bob, New Orleans	1.000	32	9	22	0	31	1
Scarbery, Chad, Tucson	1.000	2	1	0	0	1	0
Schilling, Curt, Tucson	.000	2	0	0	0	0	0
Seanez, Rudy, Oklahoma-Iowa	1.000	18	0	3	0	3	0
Secoda, Jason, Salt Lake-Alb.	1.000	10	1	2	0	3	1
Sedlacek, Shawn, Omaha	1.000	27	12	10	0	22	2
Sele, Aaron, Salt Lake	1.000	3	0	1	0	1	0
Serafini, Dan, Memphis *	1.000	3	0	3	0	3	0
Serrano, Elio, Salt Lake	.909	46	5	5	1	11	0
Serrano, Jim, Omaha	1.000	19	3	1	0	4	0
Service, Scott, Tucson	1.000	9	1	0	0	1	0
Sessions, Doug, New Orleans	1.000	31	4	20	0	24	0
Shaffar, Ben, Nashville	.000	4	0	0	0	0	0
Shouse, Brian, Oklahoma *	1.000	6	0	3	0	3	1
Shuey, Paul, Las Vegas	1.000	1	1	1	0	2	0
Silva, Jose, Sac.-Port.-Iowa	.900	27	3	6	1	10	0
Simas, Bill, Las Vegas	1.000	26	8	6	0	14	1
Simpson, Allan, Tacoma	1.000	43	0	9	0	9	1
Sinclair, Steve, Iowa *	1.000	6	0	1	0	1	0
Small, Aaron, Albuquerque	.947	14	7	11	1	19	0
Smith, Brian, Colorado Springs	.000	9	0	0	1	1	0
Smith, Roy, Sacramento	.909	52	3	17	2	22	0
Smyth, Steve, Iowa *	1.000	25	6	15	0	21	2
Snare, Ryan, Oklahoma *	.889	9	1	7	1	9	0
Snow, Bert, Sacramento	1.000	12	1	1	0	2	0
Snyder, John, Salt Lake	1.000	10	4	8	0	12	0
Snyder, Kyle, Omaha	1.000	5	2	3	0	5	0
Sodowsky, Clint, Albuquerque	1.000	3	1	3	0	4	0
Song, Seung, Edmonton	.857	13	3	3	1	7	2
Sonnier, Shawn, Iowa	.000	3	0	0	0	0	0
Soriano, Rafael, Tacoma	1.000	11	3	7	0	10	1
Spradlin, Jerry, Tucson	.000	6	0	0	1	1	0
Springer, Russ, Memphis	1.000	7	0	1	0	1	0
Stamler, Keith, Oklahoma	1.000	7	2	4	0	6	0
Stanifer, Rob, Iowa-New Orleans	.895	44	6	11	2	19	0
Stark, Dennis, Colorado Springs	1.000	4	0	5	0	5	0
Steidlmayer, Luke, Portland	.000	1	0	0	0	0	0
Stein, Blake, Edmonton	1.000	15	6	2	0	8	0
Stemle, Steve, Memphis	.917	26	11	22	3	36	0
Stitt, Brian, Tacoma	1.000	4	3	1	0	4	0
Stockman, Phil, Tucson	1.000	2	0	1	0	1	0
Stokley, Billy, Salt Lake	.905	9	6	13	2	21	1
Sweeney, Brian, Tacoma	.952	29	7	13	1	21	0
Swindell, Greg, Tucson *	1.000	8	1	2	0	3	0
Szuminski, Jason, Iowa	1.000	3	1	1	0	2	1
Tankersley, Dennis, Portland	1.000	27	9	24	0	33	2
Taylor, Aaron, Tacoma	1.000	33	4	4	0	8	0
Teut, Nate, Albuquerque-Iowa *	.800	5	1	3	1	5	0
Thompson, Doug, Colo. Springs	1.000	10	0	1	0	1	0
Thompson, Eric, Sacramento	.000	3	0	0	0	0	0
Thornton, Matt, Tacoma *	1.000	2	2	0	0	2	0
Tollberg, Brian, Portland	.867	20	7	6	2	15	1
Torres, Salomon, Nashville	1.000	1	1	0	0	1	0
Trujillo, J.J., Portland	1.000	27	3	8	0	11	0
Tucker, T.J., Edmonton	1.000	3	5	1	0	6	0
Turman, Jason, Omaha	1.000	31	4	7	0	11	1
Turnbow, Derrick, Salt Lake	.857	35	3	3	1	7	0
Ulloa, Enmanuel, Edmonton	.000	3	0	0	0	0	0
Urban, Jeff, Fresno *	.920	29	7	16	2	25	2
Valentine, Joe, Sacramento	1.000	40	2	5	0	7	0
Valverde, Jose, Tucson	.667	22	1	1	1	3	0
Vance, Cory, Colorado Springs *	1.000	24	8	32	0	40	2
Vargas, Claudio, Edmonton	.500	2	1	0	1	2	0
Venafro, Mike, New Orleans *	.889	23	4	4	1	9	0
Vent, Kevin, Fresno	1.000	6	1	0	0	1	0
Veres, Dave, Iowa	1.000	11	0	2	0	2	0
Villafuerte, Brandon, Portland	1.000	37	4	6	0	10	1
Villone, Ron, Tucson-N.O.*	.882	20	5	10	2	17	1
Vining, Ken, New Orleans *	1.000	41	2	10	0	12	1
Vogelsong, Ryan, Nashville	1.000	26	6	18	0	24	0
Voyles, Brad, Omaha	.941	29	4	12	1	17	0
Walker, Kevin, Portland *	.929	34	3	10	1	14	0
Walrond, Les, Mem.-Omaha *	1.000	28	5	7	0	12	0
Ward, Bryan, Colo. Springs *	1.000	9	0	1	0	1	0
Ward, Jeremy, Tucson	1.000	25	0	4	0	4	0
Wasdin, John, Nashville	.750	18	3	9	4	16	0
Watkins, Steve, Portland	.000	14	0	0	0	0	0
Wayne, Justin, Albuquerque	.960	23	8	16	1	25	1
Wear, Gregory, Tacoma	1.000	2	1	0	0	1	0
Webb, Alan, Portland *	.000	1	0	0	0	0	0
Webb, Brandon, Tucson	.909	3	1	9	1	11	0
Weibl, Clint, Memphis	1.000	20	6	6	0	12	1
Wellemeyer, Todd, Iowa	.909	13	4	6	1	11	0
Whiteside, Matt, Colo. Springs	1.000	21	0	4	0	4	0
Wilkins, Marc, Albuquerque	.875	20	0	7	1	8	0
Williams, Dave, Nashville *	.933	16	4	10	1	15	0
Williams, Jerome, Fresno	1.000	10	4	9	0	13	0
Williams, Randy, Tacoma *	1.000	18	3	1	0	4	0
Wilson, Kris, Omaha	1.000	5	0	1	0	1	0
Winchester, Scott, Las Vegas	1.000	19	3	11	0	14	1
Witasick, Jay, Portland	1.000	5	0	1	0	1	0
Wood, Mike, Sacramento	.941	16	8	24	2	34	0
Wright, Chris, Tacoma	1.000	9	4	7	0	11	0
Wright, Jamey, Okla.-Omaha	1.000	20	7	18	0	25	0
Wright, Jaret, Portland	1.000	12	1	4	0	5	0
Wuertz, Mike, Iowa	.895	43	6	11	2	19	2
Yarnall, Ed, Sacramento *	.947	18	4	14	1	19	1
Yennaco, Jay, Memphis	1.000	8	0	7	0	7	0
Young, Jason, Colorado Springs	.952	23	9	11	1	21	0
Young, Tim, Colorado Springs	1.000	29	0	4	0	4	0
Zerbe, Chad, Fresno *	1.000	7	0	2	0	2	0

PITCHERS WITH TWO OR MORE TEAMS

Player, Team	Pct.	G	PO	A	E	TC	DP
Belitz, Todd, Colorado Springs *	.667	3	0	2	1	3	0
Belitz, Todd, Albuquerque *	.500	13	1	1	2	4	1
Blank, Matt, Edmonton *	1.000	5	1	6	0	7	1
Blank, Matt, Fresno *	1.000	8	2	6	0	8	1
Bruback, Matt, Portland	.667	2	1	1	1	3	0
Bruback, Matt, Iowa	1.000	20	10	13	0	23	1
Bruback, Matt, Nashville	1.000	4	1	3	0	4	0
Callaway, Mickey, Salt Lake	1.000	7	2	3	0	5	0
Callaway, Mickey, Oklahoma	1.000	4	2	4	0	6	1
Darensbourg, Vic, C.S.*	.889	20	2	6	1	9	0
Darensbourg, Vic, Edmonton *	1.000	11	0	4	0	4	0
Donaldson, Bo, Edmonton	.000	9	0	0	1	1	0
Donaldson, Bo, Salt Lake	.000	3	0	0	0	0	0
Duncan, Courtney, Portland	.786	54	6	5	3	14	0
Duncan, Courtney, Salt Lake	1.000	2	0	1	0	1	0
Ebert, Derrin, Iowa *	.000	6	0	0	0	0	0
Ebert, Derrin, Tucson *	1.000	15	2	6	0	8	1
Evans, Keith, Iowa	1.000	10	1	3	0	4	0
Evans, Keith, Edmonton	1.000	12	2	2	0	4	0
Flury, Pat, Portland	1.000	7	1	0	0	1	0
Flury, Pat, Omaha	.667	7	2	0	1	3	0
Fyhrie, Mike, Albuquerque	1.000	5	0	1	0	1	0
Fyhrie, Mike, Omaha	.962	15	9	16	1	26	5
House, Craig, Albuquerque	1.000	7	0	2	0	2	0
House, Craig, Tacoma	.000	5	0	0	0	0	0
Joseph, Kevin, Memphis	1.000	22	4	12	0	16	0
Joseph, Kevin, Edmonton	1.000	7	0	3	0	3	0
Keisler, Randy, Oklahoma *	1.000	5	1	1	0	2	0
Keisler, Randy, New Orleans *	1.000	9	0	7	0	7	1
Keisler, Randy, Portland *	1.000	8	1	6	0	7	0
Kuzmic, Craig, Tacoma	.000	2	0	0	0	0	0
Kuzmic, Craig, Fresno	.000	1	0	0	0	0	0
Mullen, Scott, Las Vegas *	1.000	7	0	8	0	8	1
Mullen, Scott, Omaha *	.813	20	3	10	3	16	0
Perisho, Matt, Tucson *	1.000	4	0	1	0	1	0
Perisho, Matt, Colo. Springs *	1.000	8	0	5	0	5	1
Rodgers, Bobby, Iowa	1.000	5	1	1	0	2	0
Rodgers, Bobby, Edmonton	1.000	8	1	1	0	2	0
Seanez, Rudy, Oklahoma	1.000	5	0	1	0	1	0
Seanez, Rudy, Iowa	1.000	13	0	2	0	2	0
Secoda, Jason, Salt Lake	1.000	7	1	2	0	3	1
Secoda, Jason, Albuquerque	.000	3	0	0	0	0	0
Silva, Jose, Portland	1.000	17	2	5	0	7	0
Silva, Jose, Iowa	.000	3	0	0	0	0	0
Silva, Jose, Sacramento	.667	7	1	1	1	3	0
Stanifer, Rob, New Orleans	1.000	41	5	10	0	15	0
Stanifer, Rob, Iowa	.500	3	1	1	2	4	0
Teut, Nate, Iowa *	1.000	3	0	2	0	2	0
Teut, Nate, Albuquerque *	.667	2	1	1	1	3	0
Villone, Ron, Tucson *	.778	15	3	4	2	9	0
Villone, Ron, New Orleans *	1.000	5	2	6	0	8	1
Walrond, Les, Omaha *	1.000	18	1	5	0	6	0
Walrond, Les, Memphis *	1.000	10	4	2	0	6	0
Wright, Jamey, Omaha	1.000	13	6	10	0	16	0
Wright, Jamey, Oklahoma	1.000	7	1	8	0	9	0

The following players appeared only as a designated hitter, pinch-hitter or pinch-runner: J. Abbott, dh; Clements, ph; Ro. Gomez, dh, ph; Hairston, ph; Mabry, dh; Pernalete, ph, pr; Rojas, ph; Sakamoto, ph; Mi. Sweeney, dh.

LEAGUE CHAMPIONS

Year	Team	Pct.
1903—	Los Angeles	.630
1904—	Tacoma	.589
	Tacoma§	.571
	Los Angeles§	.571
1905—	Tacoma	.583
	Los Angeles*	.604
1906—	Portland	.657
1907—	Los Angeles	.608
1908—	Los Angeles	.585
1909—	San Francisco	.623
1910—	Portland	.567
1911—	Portland	.589
1912—	Oakland	.591
1913—	Portland	.559
1914—	Portland	.574
1915—	San Francisco	.570
1916—	Los Angeles	.601
1917—	San Francisco	.561
1918—	Vernon	.569
	Los Angeles (2nd)◆	.548
1919—	Vernon	.613
1920—	Vernon	.556
1921—	Los Angeles	.574
1922—	San Francisco	.638
1923—	San Francisco	.617
1924—	Seattle	.545
1925—	San Francisco	.643
1926—	Los Angeles	.599
1927—	Oakland	.615
1928—	San Francisco*	.630
	Sacramento∞	.626
	San Francisco∞	.626
1929—	Mission	.643
	Hollywood*	.592
1930—	Los Angeles	.576
	Hollywood*	.650
1931—	Hollywood	.626
	San Francisco*	.608
1932—	Portland	.587
1933—	Los Angeles	.610
1934—	Los Angeles▼	.786
	Los Angeles▼	.689
1935—	Los Angeles	.648
	San Francisco*	.608
1936—	Portland‡	.549
1937—	Sacramento	.573
	San Diego (3rd)†	.545
1938—	Los Angeles	.590
	Sacramento (3rd)†	.537
1939—	Seattle	.589
	Sacramento (4th)†	.500
1940—	Seattle‡	.629
1941—	Seattle‡	.598
1942—	Sacramento	.590
	Seattle (3rd)†	.539
1943—	Los Angeles	.710
	S. Francisco (2nd)†	.574
1944—	Los Angeles	.586
	S. Francisco (3rd)†	.509
1945—	Portland	.622
	S. Francisco (4th)†	.525
1946—	San Francisco‡	.628
1947—	Los Angeles▲	.567
1948—	Oakland‡	.606
1949—	Hollywood‡	.583
1950—	Oakland	.590
1951—	Seattle‡	.593
1952—	Hollywood	.606
1953—	Hollywood	.589
1954—	San Diego■	.604
1955—	Seattle	.552
1956—	Los Angeles	.637
1957—	San Francisco	.601
1958—	Phoenix	.578
1959—	Salt Lake City	.552
1960—	Spokane	.601
1961—	Tacoma	.630
1962—	San Diego	.604
1963—	Spokane	.620
	Oklahoma City•	.632
1964—	Arkansas	.609
	San Diego•	.576
1965—	Oklahoma City	.628
	Portland	.547
1966—	Seattle•	.561
	Tulsa	.578
1967—	San Diego•	.574
	Spokane	.541
1968—	Tulsa•	.642
	Spokane	.586
1969—	Tacoma•	.589
	Eugene	.603
1970—	Spokane•	.644
	Hawaii	.671
1971—	Salt Lake City	.534
	Tacoma	.545
1972—	Albuquerque	.622
	Eugene	.534
1973—	Tucson	.583
	Spokane•	.563
1974—	Spokane•	.549
	Albuquerque	.535
1975—	Salt Lake City	.556
	Hawaii•	.611
1976—	Salt Lake City	.625
	Hawaii•	.531
1977—	Phoenix•	.579
	Hawaii	.541
1978—	Tacoma††	.584
	Albuquerque††	.557
1979—	Albuquerque	.581
	Salt Lake City‡‡	.541
1980—	Albuquerque	.578
	Hawaii	.539
1981—	Albuquerque*	.712
	Tacoma	.561
1982—	Albuquerque*	.594
	Spokane	.545
1983—	Albuquerque	.594
	Portland*	.528
1984—	Hawaii	.621
	Edmonton*	.486
1985—	Vancouver*	.522
	Phoenix	.563
1986—	Vancouver	.616
	Las Vegas*	.563
1987—	Calgary	.596
	Albuquerque*	.542
1988—	Vancouver	.599
	Las Vegas*	.529
1989—	Albuquerque	.563
	Vancouver*	.514
1990—	Albuquerque*	.641
	Edmonton	.553

Year	Team	Pct.	Year	Team	Pct.	Year	Team	Pct.
1991—	Albuquerque	.580	1995—	Salt Lake	.549	1999—	Vancouver‡	.592
	Tucson*	.564		Colorado Springs*	.538	2000—	Salt Lake	.629
1992—	Colorado Springs*	.596	1996—	Edmonton*	.592		Memphis‡	.576
	Portland	.576		Phoenix	.479	2001—	Tacoma§§	.590
1993—	Portland	.608	1997—	Phoenix	.615		New Orleans§§	.590
	Tucson*	.580		Edmonton*	.556	2002—	Las Vegas	.590
1994—	Albuquerque*	.597	1998—	Iowa	.590		Edmonton†	.579
	Vancouver	.542		New Orleans†	.535	2003—	Sacramento‡	.639

*Won split-season playoff. †Won four-team playoff. ‡Won pennant and four-team playoff. §Tied for second-half title with Tacoma winning playoff. ∞Tied for second-half title, with Sacramento winning playoff. ▲Ended regular season in tie with San Francisco and won one-game playoff for pennant, then won four-club playoff. ◆Won playoff from first-place Vernon and awarded championship. ■Defeated Hollywood in one-game playoff for pennant. ▼Won both halves, no playoff. •League was divided into Northern, Southern divisions in 1963, 1969-70-71, and Eastern, Western divisions in 1964 through 1968 and 1972 through 1977, won two-team playoff. ††League divided into Eastern and Western divisions, Tacoma and Albuquerque declared co-champions following cancellation of four-team playoff due to continuing rain and wet grounds. ‡‡Won second-half title and defeated Hawaii in four-team playoff. §§Were entering finals of four-team playoff and were declared co-champions when Professional Baseball declared a stoppage of play.

EASTERN LEAGUE

LEAGUE OFFICE

President
Joe McEacharn

Address
P.O. Box 9711
Portland, ME 04104

Phone
207-761-2700

TEAMS

AKRON AEROS

General manager/vice president
Jeff Auman
Manager
Brad Komminsk
Ballpark (capacity, surface)
Canal Park (9,097, grass)
Affiliation
Indians
Address
300 S. Main St.
Akron, OH 44308
Phone
330-253-5151

ALTOONA CURVE

General manager
Todd Parnell
Manager
Dale Sveum
Ballpark (capacity, surface)
Blair County Ballpark (7,200, grass)
Affiliation
Pirates
Address
1000 Park Avenue
Altoona, PA 16602
Phone
814-943-5400

BINGHAMTON METS

General manager
Bill Terlecky
Manager
Ken Oberkfell
Ballpark (capacity, surface)
NYSEG Stadium (6,012, grass)
Affiliation
Mets
Address
211 Henry Street
Binghamton, NY 13901
Phone
607-723-6387

BOWIE BAYSOX

General manager
Mike Munter
Manager
Dave Trembley
Ballpark (capacity, surface)
Prince George's Stadium
(10,000, grass)
Affiliation
Orioles
Address
4101 NE Crain Highway
Bowie, MD 20716
Phone
301-805-6000

ERIE SEAWOLVES

General manager
John Frey
Manager
Rick Sweet
Ballpark (capacity, surface)
Jerry Uht Park (6,000, grass)
Affiliation
Tigers
Address
110 E. 10th Street
Erie, PA 16501
Phone
814-456-1300

HARRISBURG SENATORS

General manager
Todd Vander Woude
Manager
Dave Machemer
Ballpark (capacity, surface)
Commerce Bank Park (6,300, grass)
Affiliation
Expos
Address
RiverSide Stadium/City Island
Harrisburg, PA 17101
Phone
717-231-4444

NEW BRITAIN ROCK CATS

General manager/president
Bill Dowling
Manager
Stan Cliburn
Ballpark (capacity, surface)
New Britain Stadium (6,146, grass)
Affiliation
Twins
Address
230 John Karbonic Way
New Britain, CT 06051
Phone
860-224-8383

NEW HAMPSHIRE FISHER CATS

General manager
Shawn Smith
Manager
Mike Basso
Ballpark (capacity, surface)
Gill Stadium (to be determined)
Affiliation
Blue Jays
Address
P.O. Box 120
(New Hampshire Plaza, 1000 Elm St.)
Manchester, NH 03101
Phone
603-641-2005

NORWICH NAVIGATORS

General manager
Keith Hallal
Manager
Shane Turner
Ballpark (capacity, surface)
Thomas J. Dodd Memorial Stadium
(6,270, grass)
Affiliation
Giants
Address
14 Stott Ave.
Norwich, CT 06360
Phone
860-887-7962

PORTLAND SEA DOGS

General manager/president
Charlie Eshbach
Manager
Ron Johnson
Ballpark (capacity, surface)
Hadlock Field (6,975, grass)
Affiliation
Red Sox
Address
271 Park Avenue
Portland, ME 04102
Phone
207-874-9300

READING PHILLIES

General manager
Chuck Domino
Manager
Greg Legg
Ballpark (capacity, surface)
First Energy Stadium (9,100, grass)
Affiliation
Phillies
Address
Route 61 South/1900 South Centre Ave.
Reading, PA 19605
Phone
610-375-8469

TRENTON THUNDER

General manager
Rick Brenner
Manager
Stump Merrill
Ballpark (capacity, surface)
Samuel J. Plumeri Sr. Field at Mercer County Waterfront Park (6,341, grass)
Affiliation
Yankees
Address
One Thunder Road
Trenton, NJ 08611
Phone
609-394-3300

2003 FINAL STANDINGS

NORTHERN DIVISION

Team	W	L	T	Pct.	GB
New Haven	79	63	-	.556	...
New Britain	73	68	-	.518	5.5
Portland	72	70	-	.507	7.0
Trenton	70	71	-	.496	8.5
Binghamton	63	78	-	.447	15.5
Norwich	62	79	-	.440	16.5

SOUTHERN DIVISION

Team	W	L	T	Pct.	GB
Akron	88	53	-	.624	...
Altoona	78	63	-	.553	10.0
Erie	72	70	-	.507	16.5
Bowie	69	72	1	.489	19.0
Reading	62	79	1	.440	26.0
Harrisburg	60	82	-	.423	28.5

COMPOSITE

Team	AKR	NHV	ALT	NBR	PRT	ERI	TRE	BOW	BNG	REA	NRW	HRB	W	L	T	Pct.	GB
Akron (Indians)	...	4	11	5	3	12	3	13	6	15	5	11	88	53	0	.624	...
New Haven (Blue Jays)	4	...	4	12	10	5	10	2	11	5	12	4	79	63	0	.556	9.5
Altoona (Pirates)	9	4	...	3	3	8	3	11	6	13	5	13	78	63	0	.553	10.0
New Britain (Twins)	2	8	3	...	10	3	10	4	13	5	13	2	73	68	0	.518	15.0
Portland (Red Sox)	3	10	3	10	...	1	11	5	8	5	12	4	72	70	0	.507	16.5
Erie (Tigers)	8	3	12	5	5	...	1	12	2	12	3	9	72	70	0	.507	16.5
Trenton (Yankees)	3	10	3	10	9	5	...	3	10	4	7	6	70	71	0	.496	18.0
Bowie (Orioles)	7	4	9	4	3	8	5	...	5	8	4	12	69	72	1	.489	19.0
Binghamton (Mets)	2	9	2	7	12	6	9	1	...	1	10	4	63	78	0	.447	25.0
Reading (Phillies)	5	1	7	1	3	8	4	11	5	...	4	13	62	79	1	.440	26.0
Norwich (Giants)	1	8	2	7	8	3	13	2	10	4	...	4	62	79	0	.440	26.0
Harrisburg (Expos)	9	2	7	4	4	11	2	8	2	7	4	...	60	82	0	.423	28.5

Major league affiliations in parentheses.

PLAYOFFS: Akron defeated Altoona, three games to one; New Haven defeated New Britain, three games to two; Akron defeated New Haven, three games to none, to win league championship.

REGULAR-SEASON ATTENDANCE: Akron, 445,603; Altoona, 365,376; Binghamton, 211,533; Bowie, 324,813; Erie, 197,656; Harrisburg, 257,898; New Britain, 268,532; New Haven, 140,922; Norwich, 158,622; Portland, 405,021; Reading, 465,717; Trenton, 427,567. Total attendance—3,669,260. Playoffs (12 games)—68,146. All-Star Game at New Britain—7,168.

MANAGERS: Akron, Brad Komminsk; Altoona, Dale Sveum; Binghamton, John Stearns; Bowie, Dave Trembley; Erie, Kevin Bradshaw; Harrisburg, Dave Machemer; New Britain, Stan Cliburn; New Haven, Marty Pevey; Norwich, Shane Turner; Portland, Ron Johnson; Reading, Greg Legg; Trenton, Stump Merrill.

ALL-STAR TEAM: 1B—Craig Brazell, Binghamton; 2B—Mike Fontenot, Bowie; 3B—Terry Tiffee, New Britain; SS—Jason Bartlett, New Britain; OF—Jeff Inglin, Reading; OF—Alexis Rios, New Haven; OF—Grady Sizemore, Akron; C—Guillermo Quiroz, New Haven; DH—Alejandro Freire, Norwich; Utility—Kevin Youkilis, Portland; RHP—Kyle Denney, Akron; LHP—Sean Bennett, Altoona; Relief pitcher—Brian Schmack, Erie; Most Valuable Player—Alexis Rios, New Haven; Pitcher of the Year—Sean Bennett, Altoona; Rookie of the Year—Grady Sizemore, Akron; Manager of the Year—Marty Pevey, New Haven.

2003 BATTING

TEAM

Team	G	TPA	AB	R	H	TB	2B	3B	HR	RBI	SH	SF	HP	BB	IBB	SO	SB	CS	GDP	LOB	ShO	Avg.	OBP	Slg.
New Haven	142	5488	4792	752	1402	2032	267	42	93	682	37	50	74	533	26	862	64	27	148	1098	9	.293	.369	.424
New Britain	141	5299	4717	701	1330	1948	273	33	93	642	40	55	79	408	25	808	115	65	114	985	4	.282	.346	.413
Binghamton	141	5215	4621	637	1292	1923	281	22	102	591	75	54	53	412	15	1010	115	77	83	971	7	.280	.342	.416
Altoona	141	5295	4739	636	1278	1847	274	38	73	583	53	52	54	397	29	811	114	67	119	954	9	.270	.330	.390
Akron	141	5327	4717	672	1259	1912	230	45	111	616	26	48	57	479	14	804	74	41	110	993	6	.267	.339	.405
Trenton	141	5254	4568	664	1219	1831	252	21	106	612	37	51	84	513	25	840	120	48	98	1020	9	.267	.348	.401
Portland	142	5339	4682	660	1240	1870	271	25	103	608	36	43	92	486	15	989	75	49	98	1048	7	.265	.343	.399
Norwich	141	5120	4563	583	1206	1720	229	21	81	537	49	36	70	401	13	834	97	49	115	942	14	.264	.331	.377
Harrisburg	142	5349	4725	653	1225	1792	209	35	96	593	52	61	44	467	22	866	116	54	93	976	7	.259	.328	.379
Erie	142	5305	4695	621	1213	1804	220	37	99	579	62	41	50	456	20	896	79	27	109	987	9	.258	.328	.384
Bowie	142	5165	4640	577	1192	1731	228	22	89	527	53	42	60	368	12	817	142	60	98	934	10	.257	.317	.373
Reading	142	5341	4677	610	1193	1770	198	14	117	560	58	42	64	499	23	900	145	62	139	983	13	.255	.332	.378

INDIVIDUAL

TOP QUALIFIERS FOR BATTING CHAMPIONSHIP

Minimum 383 plate appearances. *Lefthanded batter. †Switch-hitter.

Player, Team	G	TPA	AB	R	H	TB	2B	3B	HR	RBI	SH	SF	HP	BB	IBB	SO	SB	CS	GDP	Avg.	OBP	Slg.
Rios, Alexis, New Haven	127	563	514	86	181	268	32	11	11	82	1	3	6	39	4	85	11	3	22	.352	.402	.521
Jacobs, Mike, Binghamton *	119	450	407	56	134	223	36	1	17	81	0	8	7	28	1	87	0	3	11	.329	.376	.548
Youkilis, Kevin, Portland	94	417	312	74	102	145	23	1	6	37	0	4	15	86	2	40	7	0	7	.327	.487	.465
Fontenot, Mike, Bowie *	126	515	449	63	146	216	24	5	12	66	4	4	8	50	3	89	16	5	6	.325	.399	.481
Watson, Brandon, Har.*	139	621	565	86	180	212	17	6	1	39	11	4	3	38	2	60	18	17	7	.319	.362	.375
Gonzalez, Luis, Akron	116	493	431	72	137	188	22	4	7	62	2	8	6	46	2	41	1	0	17	.318	.385	.436
Deardorff, Jeff, New Britain	108	459	412	66	130	213	28	2	17	73	0	4	2	41	0	110	16	5	9	.316	.377	.517
Tiffee, Terry, New Britain †	139	570	530	77	167	246	31	3	14	93	0	7	2	31	5	49	4	1	13	.315	.351	.464
Fagan, Shawn, New Haven	115	497	421	78	132	167	14	3	5	50	0	8	6	62	4	82	4	2	10	.314	.402	.397
Nye, Rodney, Binghamton	138	546	474	77	148	229	41	5	10	70	3	7	4	58	2	72	3	5	5	.312	.387	.483
Freire, Alejandro, Norwich	137	564	498	71	155	242	31	1	18	80	0	5	13	48	5	87	1	0	21	.311	.383	.486
Hall, Noah, Harrisburg	131	565	449	94	138	199	23	4	10	70	1	8	16	91	1	67	33	9	12	.307	.434	.443
Myrow, Brian, Trenton *	137	591	461	99	141	242	31	8	18	78	1	6	16	107	8	113	6	3	3	.306	.447	.525
Sizemore, Grady, Akron *	128	559	496	96	151	238	26	11	13	78	1	5	11	46	1	73	10	9	5	.304	.373	.480
Acuna, Ron, Binghamton	125	521	474	70	144	184	28	3	2	50	7	4	2	34	1	88	24	12	11	.304	.350	.388

DEPARTMENTAL LEADERS: G—Inglin, 141; AB—B. Watson, 565; R—Myrow, 99; H—A. Rios, 181; TB—A. Rios, 268; 2B—Nye, West, 41; 3B—A. Rios, Sizemore, 11; HR—Inglin, 24; RBI—Inglin, 103; SH—E. Logan, Nieves, 12; SF—Jones, 10; HP—Bartlett, Duffy, 20; BB—An. Machado, 108; IBB—Inglin, Myrow, 8; SO—J. Owens, 161; SB—An. Machado, 49; CS—Bartlett, 24; GIDP—A. Rios, 22; Slg.—Jacobs, .548; OBP—Youkilis, .487.

ALL PLAYERS

*Lefthanded batter. †Switch-hitter.

Player, Team	G	TPA	AB	R	H	TB	2B	3B	HR	RBI	SH	SF	HP	BB	IBB	SO	SB	CS	GDP	Avg.	OBP	Slg.
Ackerman, Scott, Harrisburg	88	316	292	30	65	105	11	4	7	43	0	6	1	17	1	43	0	2	7	.223	.263	.360
Acuna, Ron, Binghamton	125	521	474	70	144	184	28	3	2	50	7	4	2	34	1	88	24	12	11	.304	.350	.388
Adams, Daniel, Reading	10	3	3	0	1	1	0	0	0	0	0	0	0	0	0	2	0	0	0	.333	.333	.333
Adams, Russ, New Haven *	65	305	271	42	75	105	10	4	4	26	4	0	0	30	1	37	8	1	5	.277	.349	.387
Airoso, Kurt, Bowie	41	142	119	17	25	48	5	0	6	19	1	0	3	17	1	33	2	1	2	.210	.324	.403
Alviso, Jerome, Bowie †	9	33	30	4	11	12	1	0	0	0	1	0	0	2	0	2	2	1	0	.367	.406	.400
Anderson, Luke, Norwich	6	1	1	0	0	0	0	0	0	0	0	0	0	0	0	1	0	0	0	.000	.000	.000
Asche, Kirk, Binghamton	19	50	42	7	6	10	1	0	1	8	0	0	1	7	0	20	2	1	0	.143	.280	.238
Athas, Jamie, Norwich *	128	514	444	59	122	149	14	2	3	41	4	3	16	47	2	82	12	10	6	.275	.363	.336
Avila, Rob, Reading	10	25	23	1	4	4	0	0	0	2	0	1	0	0	0	4	0	0	1	.174	.167	.174
Bacani, David, Binghamton	52	134	103	13	25	28	3	0	0	7	6	1	2	22	1	19	5	3	2	.243	.383	.272
Bailey, Jeff, Harrisburg	109	413	362	54	89	152	18	3	13	57	2	6	8	35	2	74	2	1	14	.246	.321	.420
Balfe, Ryan, Harrisburg †	26	92	78	9	23	30	4	0	1	13	0	1	1	12	1	17	0	0	2	.295	.391	.385
Barker, Glen, Bowie †	20	66	59	5	14	17	1	1	0	7	2	0	0	5	0	10	2	2	3	.237	.297	.288
Barns, B.J., Altoona *	22	43	38	3	7	7	0	0	0	2	1	0	0	4	1	11	0	2	2	.184	.262	.184
Baron, Brian, New Britain *	98	307	276	34	70	85	11	2	0	34	4	6	1	20	3	17	1	4	16	.254	.300	.308
Bartlett, Jason, New Britain	139	636	548	96	162	233	31	8	8	48	4	6	20	58	3	67	41	24	7	.296	.380	.425
Basak, Chris, Binghamton	113	460	404	59	110	160	25	2	7	42	8	8	5	35	0	101	18	10	3	.272	.332	.396
Bates, Fletcher, Bowie †	23	84	75	14	18	27	4	1	1	7	0	1	0	8	0	14	0	0	0	.240	.310	.360
Bautista, Rayner, Erie	115	431	398	44	114	173	18	4	11	48	8	3	4	18	0	96	4	3	12	.286	.322	.435
Begg, Chris, Norwich	4	3	2	0	0	0	0	0	0	0	0	0	0	1	0	2	0	0	0	.000	.333	.000
Bennett, Jeff, Altoona	33	3	3	0	0	0	0	0	0	0	0	0	0	0	0	2	0	0	0	.000	.000	.000
Bennett, Steve, Binghamton	28	1	1	0	0	0	0	0	0	0	0	0	0	0	0	1	0	0	0	.000	.000	.000
Bentz, Chad, Harrisburg	52	2	1	0	0	0	0	0	0	0	1	0	0	0	0	0	0	0	0	.000	.000	.000
Bevis, P.J., Binghamton	46	1	1	0	0	0	0	0	0	0	0	0	0	0	0	0	0	0	0	.000	.000	.000
Billingsley, Brent, Reading *	4	1	1	0	0	0	0	0	0	0	0	0	0	0	0	0	0	0	0	.000	.000	.000
Blasi, Blake, Portland †	4	12	11	1	2	2	0	0	0	0	0	0	0	1	0	1	0	0	0	.182	.250	.182
Bonifay, Josh, Altoona	114	432	386	51	110	173	30	0	11	56	1	5	1	39	3	106	1	4	9	.285	.348	.448
Bonilla, Clemente, Bowie	1	1	1	0	0	0	0	0	0	0	0	0	0	0	0	1	0	0	0	.000	.000	.000
Bonser, Boof, Norwich	24	15	13	0	2	3	1	0	0	3	2	0	0	0	0	5	0	0	0	.154	.154	.231
Boone, Doug, Trenton	4	5	5	0	2	3	1	0	0	1	0	0	0	0	0	1	0	0	0	.400	.400	.600
Borner, Brady, Altoona *	17	1	1	0	0	0	0	0	0	0	0	0	0	0	0	1	0	0	0	.000	.000	.000
Borowiak, Zachary, Portland	3	11	11	0	2	2	0	0	0	0	0	0	0	0	0	2	0	0	0	.182	.182	.182
Bowen, Rob, New Britain †	42	150	134	17	41	57	13	0	1	16	1	0	2	13	0	24	0	0	0	.306	.376	.425
Bozanich, Sam, Trenton	30	86	71	13	14	21	5	1	0	7	0	1	1	13	0	21	2	1	1	.197	.326	.296
Brazell, Craig, Binghamton *	111	468	432	58	126	204	23	2	17	76	0	7	6	23	4	97	2	1	4	.292	.331	.472
Brisson, Dustin, Portland *	60	232	211	23	47	74	15	0	4	32	2	3	2	14	0	42	4	1	8	.223	.274	.351
Broadway, Larry, Harris.*	21	89	78	13	25	43	3	0	5	18	0	3	1	7	2	15	0	0	0	.321	.371	.551
Brooks, Frank, Reading-Alt.*	35	1	1	0	0	0	0	0	0	0	0	0	0	0	0	0	0	0	0	.000	.000	.000
Brown, Andy, Trenton *	18	64	58	7	10	18	5	0	1	5	0	0	0	6	0	20	0	0	1	.172	.250	.310
Brown, Elliot, Norwich	4	2	2	0	0	0	0	0	0	0	0	0	0	0	0	1	0	0	0	.000	.000	.000
Brown, Jason, Harrisburg	13	54	50	5	16	32	4	0	4	12	0	2	1	1	0	13	0	0	1	.320	.333	.640
Brown, Tonayne, Port.-Erie	125	502	464	64	119	170	25	7	4	60	2	1	7	28	1	92	4	3	10	.256	.308	.366
Bruso, Greg, Norwich	11	12	10	0	0	0	0	0	0	0	2	0	0	0	0	6	0	0	0	.000	.000	.000
Buchholz, Taylor, Reading	25	28	22	1	3	4	1	0	0	2	5	0	0	1	0	4	0	0	0	.136	.174	.182
Bucktrot, Keith, Reading *	7	6	5	0	1	1	0	0	0	0	1	0	0	0	0	1	0	0	0	.200	.200	.200
Burnett, Sean, Altoona *	27	26	19	0	2	3	1	0	0	0	6	0	0	1	0	7	0	0	0	.105	.150	.158
Burnitz, Jeromy, Bing.*	3	13	13	1	3	6	0	0	1	3	0	0	0	0	0	4	1	0	0	.231	.231	.462
Byrd, Marlon, Reading	3	16	16	3	5	8	0	0	1	3	0	0	0	0	0	3	0	0	1	.313	.313	.500
Calabrese, Tony, Binghamton	43	118	110	9	28	40	6	0	2	16	0	0	0	8	0	28	1	0	6	.255	.305	.364
Calzado, Napoleon, Bowie	40	176	166	16	44	55	6	1	1	11	2	1	2	5	0	14	11	3	4	.265	.293	.331
Camilo, Juan, Reading *	21	71	64	6	11	18	1	0	2	10	0	0	0	7	0	13	1	1	0	.172	.254	.281
Cammack, Eric, Binghamton	10	1	1	0	0	0	0	0	0	0	0	0	0	0	0	0	0	0	0	.000	.000	.000
Camp, Shawn, Altoona	18	1	0	0	0	0	0	0	0	0	0	0	0	1	0	0	0	0	0	.000	1.000	.000
Cannizaro, Andy, Trenton	108	415	369	50	102	130	23	1	1	39	8	2	9	26	1	24	9	4	7	.276	.337	.352
Cano, Robinson, Trenton *	46	181	164	21	46	60	9	1	1	13	2	0	6	9	0	16	0	0	6	.280	.341	.366
Carroll, Wes, Harrisburg	7	24	22	1	7	8	1	0	0	3	0	0	0	2	0	3	0	1	1	.318	.375	.364
Carter, Ryan, Reading *	19	16	11	1	2	2	0	0	0	0	4	0	1	0	0	3	0	0	1	.182	.250	.182
Caruso, Joe, Altoona	83	265	224	28	44	56	6	0	2	29	2	4	7	28	0	43	3	1	4	.196	.300	.250
Casadiego, Gerardo, Harris.	22	7	6	0	2	2	0	0	0	0	1	0	0	0	0	3	0	0	0	.333	.333	.333
Casillas, Uriel, Reading	76	231	200	22	50	63	7	0	2	25	4	3	2	22	0	22	6	1	8	.250	.326	.315
Castillo, Jose, Altoona	126	549	498	68	143	194	24	6	5	66	0	8	3	40	1	81	19	10	18	.287	.339	.390
Castro, Nelson, Portland †	16	71	63	11	14	16	2	0	0	1	0	0	2	6	0	14	6	3	1	.222	.310	.254
Catalanotte, Greg, Portland †	21	72	65	10	13	22	6	0	1	10	0	0	1	6	0	24	1	0	3	.200	.278	.338
Cates, Gary, Bowie	19	57	46	10	13	19	4	1	0	10	2	2	2	5	0	3	2	0	1	.283	.364	.413
Cervenak, Mike, Norwich	137	563	511	74	138	226	26	1	20	91	0	5	11	36	3	80	2	1	19	.270	.329	.442
Chauncey, Clinton, Akron	5	13	13	0	0	0	0	0	0	0	0	0	0	0	0	7	0	0	0	.000	.000	.000
Chevalier, Virgil, Binghamton	50	198	174	22	42	68	14	0	4	18	3	2	1	18	1	26	2	2	4	.241	.313	.391
Chiaffredo, Paul, New Haven	66	232	202	28	54	85	8	1	7	29	3	2	4	21	0	59	1	1	6	.267	.345	.421
Chiavacci, Ron, Harrisburg	8	4	3	0	0	0	0	0	0	0	1	0	0	0	0	2	0	0	0	.000	.000	.000
Christensen, Mike, N. Britain	6	15	15	0	2	3	1	0	0	0	0	0	0	0	0	6	0	0	1	.133	.133	.200
Chrysler, Clint, Altoona *	16	2	1	0	0	0	0	0	0	0	1	0	0	0	0	1	0	0	0	.000	.000	.000
Church, Ryan, Akron *	99	409	371	47	97	159	17	3	13	52	0	2	4	32	1	64	4	3	17	.261	.325	.429
Clark, Doug, Norwich *	113	448	396	47	119	162	23	4	4	49	1	4	2	45	1	67	8	5	9	.301	.371	.409

Player, Team	G	TPA	AB	R	H	TB	2B	3B	HR	RBI	SH	SF	HP	BB	IBB	SO	SB	CS	GDP	Avg.	OBP	Slg.
Clark, Jeff, Norwich	7	6	6	0	0	0	0	0	0	0	0	0	0	0	0	3	0	0	0	.000	.000	.000
Coffie, Ivanon, Bowie *	93	370	319	47	78	140	20	0	14	42	0	4	5	42	2	66	1	4	10	.245	.338	.439
Cole, Joey, Binghamton *	25	12	11	1	0	0	0	0	0	0	1	0	0	0	0	4	0	0	2	.000	.000	.000
Collins, Pat, Harrisburg	25	3	3	0	0	0	0	0	0	0	0	0	0	0	0	3	0	0	0	.000	.000	.000
Connacher, Kevin, N. Britain	6	20	18	2	5	6	1	0	0	0	1	0	0	1	0	4	0	1	1	.278	.316	.333
Connolly, Mike, Altoona *	25	22	21	0	0	0	0	0	0	0	1	0	0	0	0	14	0	0	0	.000	.000	.000
Coquillette, Trace, Portland	48	193	158	23	39	69	7	1	7	21	1	3	9	22	2	46	5	5	1	.247	.365	.437
Corcoran, Roy, Harrisburg	14	1	1	0	0	0	0	0	0	0	0	0	0	0	0	0	0	0	0	.000	.000	.000
Corr, Frank, Binghamton	48	189	170	24	47	72	13	0	4	17	5	2	0	12	1	32	1	6	3	.276	.321	.424
Correia, Kevin, Norwich	16	11	10	0	1	1	0	0	0	0	0	0	0	1	0	5	0	0	0	.100	.182	.100
Cotto, Luis, Akron	1	4	4	0	1	1	0	0	0	0	0	0	0	0	0	2	0	0	0	.250	.250	.250
Cox, Mike, Binghamton *	11	2	2	0	1	1	0	0	0	0	0	0	0	0	0	1	0	0	0	.500	.500	.500
Cox, Ryan, Norwich	26	1	1	0	0	0	0	0	0	0	0	0	0	0	0	0	0	0	0	.000	.000	.000
Cozier, Vance, Norwich	26	10	8	1	0	0	0	0	0	0	2	0	0	0	0	4	0	0	0	.000	.000	.000
Crozier, Eric, Akron *	108	404	347	52	85	158	10	3	19	52	0	3	3	51	3	92	5	3	3	.245	.344	.455
Crumpton, Chuck, Harris.	26	4	3	0	0	0	0	0	0	0	1	0	0	0	0	3	0	0	0	.000	.000	.000
Cruz, Edgar, Reading	62	230	213	18	47	70	11	0	4	23	2	3	1	11	1	37	0	0	12	.221	.259	.329
Curry, Chris, Norwich	73	243	219	23	57	80	11	0	4	19	2	2	7	13	0	50	0	0	9	.260	.320	.365
Daigle, Leo, Erie	118	464	412	59	98	164	25	1	13	54	0	3	8	41	2	82	3	1	13	.238	.317	.398
Davidson, Seth, New Britain	12	41	38	2	10	11	1	0	0	3	1	1	0	1	0	3	0	1	0	.263	.275	.289
Davis, Glenn, Harrisburg †	101	369	333	34	70	117	19	2	8	46	1	2	1	32	1	93	1	2	3	.210	.280	.351
Dawson, Layne, Reading	14	8	7	0	0	0	0	0	0	0	1	0	0	0	0	4	0	0	0	.000	.000	.000
De Renne, Keoni, Trenton	37	102	96	5	23	30	4	0	1	7	0	1	0	5	1	13	0	1	5	.240	.275	.313
Deardorff, Jeff, New Britain	108	459	412	66	130	213	28	2	17	73	0	4	2	41	0	110	16	5	9	.316	.377	.517
Del Rosario, Manny, Bowie †	9	24	24	2	3	3	0	0	0	0	0	0	0	0	0	1	0	0	0	.125	.125	.125
Dequin, Benji, Harrisburg	22	3	2	1	1	1	0	0	0	0	0	0	0	1	0	1	0	0	0	.500	.667	.500
Deschaine, Jim, N.Haven-Read.	83	288	258	36	75	125	11	0	13	46	3	1	2	24	2	30	0	3	8	.291	.354	.484
Deschenes, Pat, Bing*	44	94	80	9	22	23	1	0	0	4	1	0	0	13	1	10	1	1	2	.275	.376	.288
Diaz, Felix, Harrisburg †	57	202	185	17	36	69	4	4	7	19	1	0	2	14	1	79	1	1	1	.195	.259	.373
Diaz, Juan, Bowie	68	279	248	29	68	132	22	0	14	55	0	4	1	26	1	64	1	0	11	.274	.341	.532
Diaz, Victor, Binghamton	45	187	175	29	62	91	11	0	6	23	1	2	1	8	0	32	7	5	3	.354	.382	.520
Dinardo, Lenny, Bing*	7	4	4	0	0	0	0	0	0	0	0	0	0	0	0	4	0	0	0	.000	.000	.000
Dominique, Andy, Portland	32	119	97	18	35	51	7	0	3	21	0	3	3	16	0	15	0	0	1	.361	.454	.526
Duffy, Chris, Altoona *	137	569	494	84	135	173	23	6	1	42	8	3	20	44	6	78	34	12	7	.273	.355	.350
Duncan, Jeff, Binghamton *	76	330	278	49	80	113	11	5	4	23	8	3	5	36	2	59	24	10	0	.288	.376	.406
Erickson, Corey, Norwich	16	60	48	5	11	15	4	0	0	5	3	1	0	8	0	13	0	0	0	.229	.333	.313
Escalona, Felix, Bowie	1	3	3	0	1	1	0	0	0	0	0	0	0	0	0	1	0	0	0	.333	.333	.333
Espy, Nate, Reading	119	409	347	49	84	125	14	0	9	49	1	2	5	54	1	78	10	6	10	.242	.350	.360
Fagan, Shawn, New Haven	115	497	421	78	132	167	14	3	5	50	0	8	6	62	4	82	4	2	10	.314	.402	.397
Fernandez, Alejandro, Tren.	4	6	6	0	2	2	0	0	0	1	0	0	0	0	0	3	0	0	0	.333	.333	.333
Flohr, Adam, New Britain *	43	2	1	0	0	0	0	0	0	0	0	0	0	1	0	1	0	0	0	.000	.500	.000
Fontenot, Mike, Bowie *	126	515	449	63	146	216	24	5	12	66	4	4	8	50	3	89	16	5	6	.325	.399	.481
Fordham, Tom, Altoona *	13	6	6	0	1	1	0	0	0	0	0	0	0	0	0	1	0	0	1	.167	.167	.167
Foster, Quincy, Harrisburg *	88	232	216	34	63	80	7	2	2	18	3	1	0	12	1	26	22	6	1	.292	.328	.370
Franco, Martire, Reading	28	4	3	0	0	0	0	0	0	0	1	0	0	0	0	1	0	0	0	.000	.000	.000
Freire, Alejandro, Norwich	137	564	498	71	155	242	31	1	18	80	0	5	13	48	5	87	1	0	21	.311	.383	.486
Fuentes, Omar, Trenton	84	290	250	29	59	90	16	0	5	27	2	5	6	27	0	39	0	0	11	.236	.319	.360
Garbe, B.J., New Britain	66	245	225	27	40	60	9	1	3	21	0	1	3	16	0	60	5	3	2	.178	.241	.267
Garcia, Daniel, Binghamton	32	134	117	22	39	62	12	1	3	22	1	3	3	10	0	20	2	2	2	.333	.391	.530
Garrett, Shawn, Altoona †	124	515	468	68	135	215	29	6	13	67	3	5	3	36	7	96	20	7	15	.288	.340	.459
Gingrich, Troy, Harrisburg *	20	48	45	5	12	20	2	0	2	4	1	0	0	2	0	5	2	1	0	.267	.298	.444
Glen, William, Reading	31	6	6	0	0	0	0	0	0	0	0	0	0	0	0	4	0	0	0	.000	.000	.000
Godwin, Tyrell, New Haven *	33	129	123	20	38	53	6	3	1	13	1	1	1	3	0	27	6	1	5	.309	.328	.431
Goelz, Jim, Akron-Portland	62	208	196	24	45	52	7	0	0	10	1	1	2	8	0	26	1	2	1	.230	.266	.265
Gonzalez, Luis, Akron	116	493	431	72	137	188	22	4	7	62	2	8	6	46	2	41	1	0	17	.318	.385	.436
Gonzalez, Mike, Altoona	5	1	0	1	0	0	0	0	0	0	0	0	0	1	1	0	0	0	0	.000	1.000	.000
Grabow, John, Altoona *	24	15	11	1	3	3	0	0	0	4	1	1	0	2	0	3	0	0	0	.273	.357	.273
Gredvig, Doug, Bowie	26	107	100	5	22	31	6	0	1	13	0	2	0	5	0	20	1	0	2	.220	.252	.310
Griffin, John-Ford, N.Haven *	104	429	373	48	104	172	23	3	13	75	0	5	2	49	4	85	2	0	8	.279	.361	.461
Grindell, Nate, Akron	42	165	142	24	33	58	12	2	3	22	1	2	0	20	0	24	0	0	7	.232	.323	.408
Gross, Gabe, New Haven *	84	373	310	52	99	149	23	3	7	51	2	2	5	52	1	53	3	2	9	.319	.423	.481
Grove, Jason, Trenton *	76	272	244	28	70	97	12	0	5	28	2	0	3	23	3	48	0	2	5	.287	.356	.398
Gulledge, Kelley, New Britain	33	97	80	12	20	29	6	0	1	7	2	1	5	9	0	23	1	0	0	.250	.358	.363
Gutierrez, Vic, Harrisburg	90	282	262	33	63	77	9	1	1	19	2	1	1	16	0	42	8	2	9	.240	.286	.294
Guy, Brad, Altoona-Reading	39	3	3	0	0	0	0	0	0	0	0	0	0	0	0	1	0	0	0	.000	.000	.000
Hairston, Jerry, Bowie	6	23	20	4	6	10	1	0	1	2	0	0	2	1	0	4	0	0	0	.300	.391	.500
Hall, Noah, Harrisburg	131	565	449	94	138	199	23	4	10	70	1	8	16	91	1	67	33	9	12	.307	.434	.443
Hallmark, Pat, Norwich	135	543	485	55	114	158	22	2	6	58	5	3	10	40	0	88	31	12	5	.235	.305	.326
Hammond, Joey, Bowie	18	70	57	7	19	22	3	0	0	6	1	1	0	11	0	5	3	1	2	.333	.435	.386
Hannahan, Buzz, Reading	117	453	380	61	99	125	15	1	3	26	7	2	8	56	1	74	25	4	11	.261	.365	.329
Hannahan, Jack, Erie *	135	530	471	64	121	166	18	0	9	45	5	2	3	48	6	78	2	0	13	.257	.328	.352
Harvey, Ian, Reading	11	1	1	0	0	0	0	0	0	0	0	0	0	0	0	1	0	0	0	.000	.000	.000
Hattig, John, Portland †	8	34	32	3	7	9	2	0	0	1	0	0	0	2	0	11	0	0	2	.219	.265	.281
Haverbusch, Kevin, Portland	59	231	203	19	48	77	12	1	5	30	2	0	8	18	1	44	0	4	5	.236	.323	.379
Headley, Justin, Portland *	116	510	457	69	118	172	23	2	9	61	1	5	7	40	2	68	6	3	8	.258	.324	.376
Hee, Aaron, Binghamton *	22	4	4	0	0	0	0	0	0	0	0	0	0	0	0	2	0	0	0	.000	.000	.000
Heintz, Chris, Altoona	78	299	271	28	70	96	12	4	2	26	5	1	3	19	2	24	0	0	6	.258	.313	.354
Hernandez, Yoel, Reading	43	2	1	0	0	0	0	0	0	0	1	0	0	0	0	1	0	0	0	.000	.000	.000
Hietpas, Joe, Binghamton	5	10	10	1	1	2	1	0	0	0	0	0	0	0	0	2	0	0	0	.100	.100	.200
Hill, Shawn, Harrisburg	4	2	2	1	1	4	0	0	1	4	0	0	0	0	0	0	0	0	0	.500	.500	2.000
Hitchcox, Brian, Reading *	92	358	304	36	76	112	13	4	5	27	5	1	7	41	2	54	8	5	4	.250	.351	.368

Player, Team	G	TPA	AB	R	H	TB	2B	3B	HR	RBI	SH	SF	HP	BB	IBB	SO	SB	CS	GDP	Avg.	OBP	Slg.
Hoffpauir, Josh, Bowie *	108	403	356	38	103	134	21	2	2	33	10	1	10	26	1	24	13	7	8	.289	.354	.376
House, J.R., Altoona	20	68	63	12	21	33	6	0	2	11	0	0	0	5	0	11	0	0	4	.333	.382	.524
Huber, Justin, Binghamton	55	223	193	16	51	82	13	0	6	36	3	1	7	19	0	54	0	2	4	.264	.350	.425
Inglett, Joe, Akron *	71	322	276	41	78	108	16	1	4	25	1	2	6	37	0	36	1	2	8	.283	.377	.391
Inglin, Jeff, Reading	141	602	539	86	153	254	27	1	24	103	1	7	10	45	8	58	7	3	17	.284	.346	.471
Izturis, Maicer, Akron †	53	251	218	31	61	85	11	5	1	20	6	2	1	24	1	23	14	6	4	.280	.351	.390
Jacobs, Mike, Binghamton *	119	450	407	56	134	223	36	1	17	81	0	8	7	28	1	87	0	3	11	.329	.376	.548
Jacobsen, Landon, Altoona	27	19	15	0	1	1	0	0	0	1	3	0	0	1	0	8	0	0	1	.067	.125	.067
Jacobson, Russ, Reading	37	121	109	9	30	37	4	0	1	5	0	1	4	7	2	16	1	1	6	.275	.339	.339
Jester, Joe, Norwich	40	143	121	19	27	40	7	0	2	11	1	0	3	18	0	26	6	2	4	.223	.338	.331
Jeter, Derek, Trenton	5	22	18	2	8	11	1	1	0	5	0	0	1	3	0	0	0	0	0	.444	.545	.611
Johnson, Nick, Trenton *	4	18	12	3	5	6	1	0	0	1	0	0	1	5	0	0	0	0	1	.417	.611	.500
Johnston, Mike, Altoona *	46	4	4	0	1	2	1	0	0	0	0	0	0	0	0	0	0	0	0	.250	.250	.500
Jones, Mitch, Trenton	136	546	463	76	112	199	18	0	23	91	1	10	14	58	1	131	5	4	6	.242	.338	.430
Joseph, Jake, Binghamton	11	8	6	0	0	0	0	0	0	0	2	0	0	0	0	5	0	0	0	.000	.000	.000
Kapler, Gabe, Portland	1	3	3	1	1	2	1	0	0	0	0	0	0	0	0	1	0	0	0	.333	.333	.667
Karp, Josh, Harrisburg	23	19	18	1	3	3	0	0	0	0	0	0	1	0	0	3	0	1	0	.167	.211	.167
Keene, Kurt, New Haven	43	168	153	18	43	56	7	0	2	23	0	3	2	10	0	12	2	1	4	.281	.327	.366
Kelly, Donald, Erie *	22	101	83	14	22	32	5	1	1	13	3	0	0	15	0	9	0	0	2	.265	.378	.386
Keppel, Bob, Binghamton	18	6	4	2	1	2	1	0	0	1	1	0	0	1	0	0	0	0	0	.250	.400	.500
Knoedler, Jason, Erie †	5	17	14	0	2	2	0	0	0	0	0	0	1	2	0	6	1	0	0	.143	.294	.143
Kratz, Erik, New Haven	1	4	4	0	0	0	0	0	0	0	0	0	0	0	0	1	0	0	0	.000	.000	.000
Kropf, Andy, Erie †	16	45	42	5	8	8	0	0	0	4	1	1	0	1	0	9	0	0	1	.190	.205	.190
LaBarbera, Anthony, Nor.	9	25	23	4	4	4	0	0	0	1	0	0	0	2	0	8	0	0	0	.174	.240	.174
Labandeira, John, Harris.	60	266	238	25	57	85	18	2	2	26	4	3	1	20	0	38	0	2	7	.239	.298	.357
Lane, Rich, Harrisburg *	56	217	207	19	44	63	3	2	4	24	0	2	1	7	0	40	1	0	4	.213	.240	.304
Lavigne, Tim, Binghamton	47	5	5	0	2	4	2	0	0	0	0	0	0	0	0	0	0	0	0	.400	.400	.800
Lawton, Matt, Akron *	5	21	19	1	1	1	0	0	0	1	0	0	0	2	0	6	0	0	1	.053	.143	.053
Lee, Seung, Reading	26	25	22	0	3	3	0	0	0	1	3	0	0	0	0	8	0	0	0	.136	.136	.136
Lemonis, Chris, Bowie *	9	35	34	4	7	9	2	0	0	2	0	1	0	0	0	3	0	0	0	.206	.200	.265
Leon, Carlos, Portland †	75	300	259	45	78	102	10	4	2	23	9	3	8	21	1	34	10	6	4	.301	.368	.394
Littleton, Brandon, Bowie †	52	151	135	24	31	42	9	1	0	12	1	2	0	13	1	22	6	2	1	.230	.293	.311
Lockwood, Luke, Harris.*	26	20	18	3	2	2	0	0	0	1	2	0	0	0	0	7	0	0	1	.111	.111	.111
Logan, Matt, New Haven *	92	348	299	45	80	105	14	1	3	36	1	3	6	39	2	37	3	2	16	.268	.360	.351
Logan, Nook, Erie †	136	584	514	71	129	171	16	7	4	38	12	6	1	51	3	103	37	13	5	.251	.316	.333
Lorenzo, Juan, New Britain †	37	100	83	12	20	27	5	1	0	4	9	1	2	5	0	13	0	0	2	.241	.297	.325
Lowry, Noah, Norwich *	24	19	15	1	6	6	0	0	0	2	3	0	0	1	0	3	0	0	1	.400	.438	.400
Loyd, Brian, Portland	29	109	100	9	29	38	6	0	1	11	1	0	1	7	0	11	1	0	3	.290	.343	.380
Luderer, Brian, Akron	76	282	245	29	59	87	12	2	4	34	1	5	7	24	0	33	0	1	4	.241	.320	.355
Luna, Hector, Akron	127	522	462	87	137	166	19	2	2	38	5	2	5	48	1	64	17	5	10	.297	.368	.359
Machado, Albenis, Harris.†	110	409	339	46	73	86	13	0	0	25	9	7	2	52	1	52	3	3	5	.215	.318	.254
Machado, Andy, Reading †	123	541	423	80	83	125	19	4	5	20	8	1	1	108	0	120	49	15	2	.196	.360	.296
Mack, Tony, Bowie †	21	71	68	4	16	17	1	0	0	4	1	0	0	2	0	12	1	4	2	.235	.257	.250
Maddox, Garry, Reading *	50	205	180	28	52	98	8	1	12	38	0	0	6	19	1	43	3	6	1	.289	.376	.544
Magruder, Chris, Akron †	3	14	13	0	6	6	0	0	0	3	0	0	0	1	0	2	1	0	0	.462	.500	.462
Martinez, Octavio, Bowie	3	5	4	1	0	0	0	0	0	0	0	0	1	0	0	0	0	0	1	.000	.200	.000
Martinez, Raul, Bowie *	1	1	1	0	0	0	0	0	0	0	0	0	0	0	0	0	0	0	0	.000	.000	.000
Martinez, Victor, Akron †	3	12	12	1	4	6	2	0	0	2	0	0	0	0	0	1	0	0	1	.333	.333	.500
Mata, Gustavo, Harrisburg	22	13	10	0	3	3	0	0	0	1	2	0	0	1	0	2	0	0	0	.300	.364	.300
Mattes, Troy, Harrisburg	5	3	3	0	0	0	0	0	0	0	0	0	0	0	0	2	0	0	0	.000	.000	.000
Mattioni, Nick, Binghamton	42	3	1	0	0	0	0	0	0	0	0	0	0	2	0	0	0	0	0	.000	.667	.000
Mattox, David, Binghamton	21	12	9	0	2	2	0	0	0	0	2	0	0	1	0	2	0	0	0	.222	.300	.222
Mauer, Joe, New Britain *	73	310	276	48	94	125	17	1	4	41	0	4	5	25	4	25	0	0	10	.341	.400	.453
Maule, Jason, Trenton *	42	144	117	20	32	35	3	0	0	13	4	0	1	22	1	17	5	1	3	.274	.393	.299
Maust, David, Harrisburg *	17	6	5	0	1	2	1	0	0	0	1	0	0	0	0	2	0	0	0	.200	.200	.400
McDade, Neal, Altoona	38	6	6	1	1	1	0	0	0	0	0	0	0	0	0	4	0	0	0	.167	.167	.167
McGowan, Sean, Portland	79	322	299	41	93	132	21	0	6	39	0	3	0	20	1	38	3	0	12	.311	.351	.441
McKinley, Josh, Harrisburg †	126	528	458	82	132	214	33	2	15	75	2	7	1	60	5	86	17	5	7	.288	.367	.467
McNeal, Aaron, Reading	118	454	421	40	107	168	20	1	13	71	0	9	0	24	0	103	0	1	18	.254	.289	.399
Mendez, Deivi, Trenton	5	12	11	1	1	4	0	0	1	1	0	0	0	1	0	1	1	0	0	.091	.167	.364
Mendoza, Carlos, Norwich †	58	195	180	22	42	67	10	0	5	19	0	2	0	13	0	28	1	1	6	.233	.282	.372
Miller, Josh, Reading	43	6	4	2	2	2	0	0	0	0	0	0	0	2	0	0	0	0	0	.500	.667	.500
Minges, Tyler, Akron	122	457	422	49	94	152	18	5	10	44	1	5	2	27	0	65	6	4	11	.223	.270	.360
Molina, Izzy, Bowie	5	21	16	3	5	6	1	0	0	2	0	0	0	5	0	4	0	1	0	.313	.476	.375
Montes, Albert, Norwich	36	4	4	0	0	0	0	0	0	0	0	0	0	0	0	3	0	0	0	.000	.000	.000
Montgomery, Matt, Norwich	28	1	1	0	0	0	0	0	0	0	0	0	0	0	0	0	0	0	0	.000	.000	.000
Mora, Melvin, Bowie	6	23	21	3	6	12	0	0	2	5	0	0	0	2	0	4	0	0	0	.286	.348	.571
Morneau, Justin, N.Britain *	20	86	79	14	26	49	3	1	6	13	0	0	0	7	2	14	0	0	0	.329	.384	.620
Munoz, Billy, Erie *	110	430	378	49	106	178	15	3	17	61	1	4	2	45	5	83	4	0	5	.280	.357	.471
Musser, Neal, Binghamton *	20	9	6	1	2	3	1	0	0	0	2	0	0	1	0	1	0	0	0	.333	.429	.500
Myrow, Brian, Trenton *	137	591	461	99	141	242	31	8	18	78	1	6	16	107	8	113	6	3	3	.306	.447	.525
Nathans, John, Portland	25	76	72	5	14	17	3	0	0	4	0	0	2	2	0	25	0	0	0	.194	.237	.236
Navarrete, Ray, Altoona	92	305	285	32	73	110	20	1	5	35	2	1	2	15	1	40	1	5	5	.256	.297	.386
Navarro, Dioner, Trenton †	58	233	208	28	71	98	15	0	4	37	1	5	1	18	1	26	2	3	6	.341	.388	.471
Nicholson, Derek, Erie *	80	327	279	35	75	102	16	1	3	31	1	4	4	39	0	56	3	2	6	.269	.362	.366
Nicholson, Kevin, Altoona †	114	456	405	63	119	181	31	5	7	45	1	6	3	41	0	44	8	8	8	.294	.358	.447
Nieves, Raul, Portland †	71	293	253	31	63	73	8	1	0	21	12	2	2	24	0	28	5	6	8	.249	.317	.289
Nonemaker, Karl, Reading *	14	37	34	4	5	6	1	0	0	1	1	0	0	2	0	7	1	1	3	.147	.194	.176
Nunnari, Talmadge, Harris.*	12	43	31	4	6	6	0	0	0	4	0	2	0	10	0	11	0	0	2	.194	.372	.194
Nye, Rodney, Binghamton	138	546	474	77	148	229	41	5	10	70	3	7	4	58	2	72	3	5	5	.312	.387	.483
O'Sullivan, Patrick, Bowie	13	42	40	4	10	17	4	0	1	4	0	0	1	1	0	13	0	0	0	.250	.286	.425

Player, Team	G	TPA	AB	R	H	TB	2B	3B	HR	RBI	SH	SF	HP	BB	IBB	SO	SB	CS	GDP	Avg.	OBP	Slg.
Olivares, Teuris, Trenton	65	237	208	26	48	74	8	0	6	33	6	3	0	20	0	35	3	4	7	.231	.294	.356
Oquendo, Ian, Altoona	6	6	6	0	1	1	0	0	0	0	0	0	0	0	0	3	0	0	0	.167	.167	.167
Otanez, Willis, Bowie	16	63	55	6	13	16	3	0	0	9	0	0	1	7	0	13	0	0	1	.236	.333	.291
Owens, Jeremy, Portland	136	524	471	63	124	228	25	8	21	68	5	3	4	41	2	161	15	7	7	.263	.326	.484
Owens, Ryan, New Britain	96	355	301	49	76	117	16	2	7	39	1	8	4	41	0	74	1	5	8	.252	.342	.389
Ozias, Todd, Altoona	51	5	4	0	0	0	0	0	0	0	1	0	0	0	0	3	0	0	0	.000	.000	.000
Pachot, John, Norwich	90	334	320	31	85	125	28	0	4	36	3	2	0	9	1	42	2	1	9	.266	.284	.391
Padilla, Jorge, Reading	46	193	173	21	51	72	13	1	2	23	0	1	1	18	1	29	11	8	7	.295	.363	.416
Palma, Rick, Altoona *	35	6	5	2	2	2	0	0	0	0	0	0	0	1	0	1	0	0	0	.400	.500	.400
Panther, Nathan, Akron *	3	9	9	0	0	0	0	0	0	1	0	0	0	0	0	3	0	0	0	.000	.000	.000
Parrish, Dave, Trenton	32	116	103	16	23	32	4	1	1	15	1	1	1	10	1	18	2	0	5	.223	.296	.311
Patrick, Brian, New Haven †	14	28	25	1	6	6	0	0	0	1	0	0	1	2	0	5	0	0	0	.240	.321	.240
Paulino, Ronny, Altoona	46	176	159	19	36	62	6	1	6	19	3	1	1	12	1	35	0	2	4	.226	.283	.390
Pautz, Brad, Reading	29	1	1	0	0	0	0	0	0	0	0	0	0	0	0	1	0	0	0	.000	.000	.000
Pecci, Jay, Norwich †	35	129	110	11	26	31	5	0	0	8	3	2	2	11	0	15	1	2	1	.236	.312	.282
Perez, Jhonny, Erie	20	82	68	8	18	29	6	1	1	12	3	1	2	8	0	9	4	0	1	.265	.354	.426
Perez, Josue, Reading †	48	202	183	26	56	69	7	0	2	21	2	3	0	14	1	24	10	4	9	.306	.350	.377
Pernalete, Marco, Norwich †	57	196	173	22	36	59	6	1	5	29	2	2	0	19	0	39	0	0	4	.208	.284	.341
Perry, Chan, Altoona	109	425	386	46	110	157	24	1	7	63	0	9	2	28	2	38	4	2	13	.285	.329	.407
Peterson, Matt, Binghamton	6	2	2	0	2	2	0	0	0	0	0	0	0	0	0	0	0	0	0	1.000	1.000	1.000
Pond, Simon, New Haven *	61	273	228	44	77	117	17	1	7	49	0	2	4	39	6	33	1	1	6	.338	.440	.513
Pressley, Josh, Bing.*	30	104	98	9	26	35	6	0	1	10	0	1	0	5	0	16	0	0	5	.265	.298	.357
Puello, Ignacio, Harrisburg	18	2	2	0	0	0	0	0	0	0	0	0	0	0	0	2	0	0	0	.000	.000	.000
Quiroz, Guillermo, N.Haven	108	434	369	63	104	191	27	0	20	79	1	7	12	45	1	83	0	0	13	.282	.372	.518
Rabe, Josh, New Britain	94	407	366	63	111	163	15	2	11	72	0	5	6	30	1	63	19	3	10	.303	.361	.445
Raines, Tim, Bowie	66	283	247	44	76	111	15	4	4	26	8	2	5	21	0	40	28	6	3	.308	.371	.449
Ramos, Kelly, Bowie †	30	104	97	7	20	33	4	0	3	12	1	1	0	5	1	18	0	1	1	.206	.243	.340
Reed, Keith, Bowie	114	463	419	63	108	151	11	1	10	39	4	4	5	31	1	94	16	9	7	.258	.314	.360
Reese, Kevin, Trenton *	86	342	309	42	84	113	13	2	4	21	4	2	2	25	1	58	27	5	4	.272	.328	.366
Renick, Josh, New Britain	102	377	328	57	79	93	8	3	0	38	10	3	7	29	1	51	13	5	13	.241	.313	.284
Requena, Alex, Akron †	50	166	150	18	27	36	2	2	1	5	3	0	3	10	0	39	6	3	0	.180	.245	.240
Rich, Dominic, New Haven *	108	433	390	49	101	136	22	2	3	46	3	1	9	30	0	48	1	4	16	.259	.326	.349
Richardson, Corey, Erie †	49	142	128	14	22	32	5	1	1	11	5	0	0	9	0	28	2	2	2	.172	.226	.250
Richardson, Juan, Reading	65	274	248	37	67	121	9	0	15	34	2	2	5	17	3	69	2	1	5	.270	.327	.488
Rifkin, Aaron, Trenton *	137	571	510	71	137	225	29	1	19	90	0	7	5	49	4	104	5	6	7	.269	.335	.441
Rios, Alexis, New Haven	127	563	514	86	181	268	32	11	11	82	1	3	6	39	4	85	11	3	22	.352	.402	.521
Rios, Brian, Bowie	6	25	23	2	5	5	0	0	0	3	0	0	0	2	0	6	0	0	0	.217	.280	.217
Rivera, Ruben, Bowie	41	143	128	17	25	50	5	1	6	20	0	1	2	12	0	35	0	1	4	.195	.273	.391
Robinson, Bo, Trenton	76	261	228	29	55	78	17	0	2	19	2	1	7	23	0	42	2	1	8	.241	.328	.342
Rodriguez, Cristobal, Harris.	1	1	1	0	0	0	0	0	0	0	0	0	0	0	0	0	0	0	0	.000	.000	.000
Rogers, Ed, Bowie	97	368	340	48	72	105	13	1	6	35	7	3	6	12	0	64	27	8	7	.212	.249	.309
Romero, Willie, Bowie	20	86	81	9	21	29	3	1	1	7	0	1	1	3	0	10	4	2	4	.259	.291	.358
Romprey, Ed, Erie	17	28	24	2	7	10	3	0	0	2	1	0	0	3	0	3	0	0	0	.292	.370	.417
Roneberg, Brett, Altoona *	125	491	442	60	124	191	29	4	10	61	3	5	1	40	4	56	12	6	13	.281	.338	.432
Ruiz, Carlos, Reading	52	188	169	22	45	57	6	0	2	16	1	3	3	12	0	15	1	1	10	.266	.321	.337
Sadler, Ray, Altoona	14	58	53	8	14	22	5	0	1	7	0	1	1	3	0	16	0	0	0	.264	.310	.415
Saenz, Jason, Binghamton *	32	1	0	1	0	0	0	0	0	0	0	0	0	1	0	0	0	0	0	.000	1.000	.000
Sanchez, Rey, Binghamton	3	12	9	1	1	1	0	0	0	0	2	0	0	1	0	1	0	0	3	.111	.200	.111
Sanders, Anthony, N.Haven	28	116	107	20	30	49	8	1	3	15	0	0	1	8	1	24	0	0	3	.280	.336	.458
Sandusky, Scott, Harrisburg	26	92	83	7	20	30	5	1	1	11	0	0	1	8	1	14	2	0	2	.241	.315	.361
Sasser, Rob, Bowie	12	44	40	7	9	16	4	0	1	4	0	0	0	4	0	8	1	0	0	.225	.295	.400
Scanlon, Matt, New Britain *	115	419	358	45	89	135	22	3	6	43	5	3	12	41	4	71	10	8	9	.249	.343	.377
Schrager, Tony, Portland	117	480	412	48	104	161	28	1	9	54	1	5	5	57	2	85	3	5	3	.252	.347	.391
Schroder, Chris, Harrisburg	49	5	2	1	1	1	0	0	0	1	0	0	0	3	0	1	1	0	0	.500	.800	.500
Scobie, Jason, Binghamton	9	8	5	0	0	0	0	0	0	0	3	0	0	0	0	1	0	0	0	.000	.000	.000
Scott, Luke, Akron *	50	202	183	21	50	86	13	1	7	37	3	3	2	11	0	37	0	1	2	.273	.317	.470
Seale, Dustin, Harrisburg *	26	4	4	0	0	0	0	0	0	0	0	0	0	0	0	2	0	0	0	.000	.000	.000
Seale, Marvin, Binghamton †	120	383	345	36	77	108	12	2	5	30	6	3	1	28	0	102	13	9	3	.223	.281	.313
Seestedt, Mike, Bowie	46	146	123	8	30	33	3	0	0	6	5	3	1	14	0	17	0	1	3	.244	.319	.268
Seibel, Phil, Binghamton *	17	8	8	1	1	1	0	0	0	0	0	0	0	0	0	2	0	0	0	.125	.125	.125
Sequea, Jorge, New Haven	33	128	111	17	38	51	7	0	2	13	3	2	1	11	0	21	0	4	0	.342	.400	.459
Shabala, Adam, Norwich *	132	567	513	71	137	198	22	6	9	54	3	3	2	46	0	99	10	7	11	.267	.328	.386
Shaffar, Ben, Altoona †	13	10	7	1	2	2	0	0	0	1	2	0	0	1	0	2	0	0	0	.286	.375	.286
Shelton, Chris, Altoona	35	133	122	17	34	46	10	1	0	14	0	1	2	8	0	23	0	1	1	.279	.331	.377
Sherrod, Justin, Portland	127	512	448	69	116	193	28	2	15	74	0	3	14	47	0	143	6	5	11	.259	.346	.431
Shier, Peter, Bowie	1	5	5	1	1	1	0	0	0	0	0	0	0	0	0	1	0	0	0	.200	.200	.200
Shipp, Brian, Binghamton	63	179	164	21	31	60	6	1	7	23	2	0	3	10	1	62	5	0	3	.189	.249	.366
Shoppach, Kelly, Portland	92	385	340	45	96	166	30	2	12	60	0	5	5	35	2	83	0	0	10	.282	.353	.488
Singleton, Justin, N.Haven *	84	276	244	41	62	90	11	4	3	31	4	5	1	22	0	73	4	0	4	.254	.313	.369
Sitzman, Jay, Reading *	72	274	249	23	69	85	13	0	1	9	3	0	7	15	2	56	9	1	5	.277	.336	.341
Sizemore, Grady, Akron *	128	559	496	96	151	238	26	11	13	78	1	5	11	46	1	73	10	9	5	.304	.373	.480
Skrehot, Shaun, Altoona	89	346	304	41	84	108	15	3	1	33	9	1	5	27	0	48	12	7	7	.276	.344	.355
Smith, Bud, Reading *	8	6	4	0	0	0	0	0	0	0	2	0	0	0	0	0	0	0	0	.000	.000	.000
Smith, Corey, Akron	127	526	473	51	128	188	27	3	9	64	2	1	0	50	0	99	7	2	9	.271	.340	.397
Smith, Jeff, Portland *	10	36	35	4	10	15	2	0	1	5	0	0	0	1	0	8	0	0	0	.286	.306	.429
Snusz, Chris, Altoona	6	19	19	0	1	1	0	0	0	0	0	0	0	0	0	6	0	0	0	.053	.053	.053
Solano, Danny, New Haven	123	466	396	54	104	148	30	4	2	43	11	5	5	49	0	65	3	2	17	.263	.347	.374
Soler, Ramon, Norwich †	66	210	184	27	47	53	4	1	0	12	7	1	2	16	0	32	10	2	3	.255	.320	.288
Song, Seung, Harrisburg	13	9	7	1	2	2	0	0	0	0	1	0	0	1	0	1	0	0	1	.286	.375	.286
Spiehs, R.D., Norwich	39	4	2	0	0	0	0	0	0	0	0	0	1	1	0	0	0	0	0	.000	.500	.000
St. Pierre, Maxim, Erie	115	447	399	50	94	143	16	0	11	54	5	5	5	33	1	66	2	0	9	.236	.299	.358

Player, Team	G	TPA	AB	R	H	TB	2B	3B	HR	RBI	SH	SF	HP	BB	IBB	SO	SB	CS	GDP	Avg.	OBP	Slg.
Stein, Blake, Ak.-Harris.	6	2	2	0	0	0	0	0	0	0	0	0	0	0	0	0	0	0	0	.000	.000	.000
Taschner, Jack, Norwich *	34	5	4	0	0	0	0	0	0	0	1	0	0	0	0	2	0	0	0	.000	.000	.000
Taveras, Luis, Erie	44	164	146	19	37	54	6	1	3	22	1	1	0	16	0	20	1	0	4	.253	.325	.370
Thompson, Kevin, Trenton	86	374	328	48	74	109	16	2	5	20	3	2	4	37	1	57	47	8	5	.226	.310	.332
Thompson, Rich, N.Haven *	49	203	182	39	57	64	5	1	0	9	2	1	8	10	0	24	15	3	2	.313	.373	.352
Thrower, Jake, Harrisburg †	15	63	53	11	15	20	3	1	0	5	2	0	0	8	2	6	3	1	0	.283	.377	.377
Tiffee, Terry, New Britain †	139	570	530	77	167	246	31	3	14	93	0	7	2	31	5	49	4	1	13	.315	.351	.464
Torres, Gabby, New Britain	48	174	155	26	50	73	14	3	1	18	1	1	5	12	0	23	1	0	4	.323	.387	.471
Tousa, Scott, Erie *	130	533	437	56	107	155	17	8	5	51	9	7	10	70	0	81	10	3	6	.245	.357	.355
Tucker, Mamon, Reading	10	40	38	0	10	12	0	1	0	6	0	0	0	2	0	6	0	0	1	.263	.300	.316
Turco, Anthony, Norwich *	1	1	1	0	0	0	0	0	0	0	0	0	0	0	0	1	0	0	0	.000	.000	.000
Ulloa, Enmanuel, Harrisburg	6	2	2	0	0	0	0	0	0	0	0	0	0	0	0	0	0	0	0	.000	.000	.000
Umbria, Jose, New Haven	7	22	19	3	6	6	0	0	0	5	0	0	0	3	0	0	0	0	1	.316	.409	.316
Urquhart, Derick, Harris.*	4	18	17	2	3	4	1	0	0	3	0	0	0	1	0	3	1	0	0	.176	.222	.235
Ust, Brant, Erie	45	170	161	24	46	76	11	2	5	25	1	0	1	7	1	26	2	0	4	.286	.320	.472
Valderrama, Carlos, Norwich	65	272	240	37	74	98	15	3	1	18	5	1	1	25	1	34	13	6	7	.308	.375	.408
Valencia, Vic, Akron	58	232	207	22	52	92	11	1	9	33	0	3	2	20	2	49	2	1	7	.251	.319	.444
VanBenschoten, John, Alt.	17	12	12	2	4	6	2	0	0	1	0	0	0	0	0	4	0	0	1	.333	.333	.500
Vargas, Claudio, Harrisburg	2	2	2	0	0	0	0	0	0	0	0	0	0	0	0	1	0	0	0	.000	.000	.000
Varner, Noochie, Erie	44	191	175	25	53	72	6	2	3	30	1	1	0	14	0	29	0	0	9	.303	.353	.411
Velazquez, Gil, Binghamton	59	162	141	17	32	47	6	0	3	19	5	1	0	15	0	30	1	3	4	.227	.299	.333
Vent, Kevin, Norwich	37	6	6	0	0	0	0	0	0	0	0	0	0	0	0	5	0	0	0	.000	.000	.000
Vento, Mike, Trenton	81	345	314	46	95	147	19	3	9	56	0	4	5	22	1	52	4	4	6	.303	.354	.468
Walk, Mitch, Norwich *	36	13	12	3	3	3	0	0	0	1	0	0	0	1	0	3	0	0	0	.250	.308	.250
Walker, Matt, Erie	87	322	291	43	78	123	18	0	9	44	4	2	4	21	1	60	2	2	10	.268	.324	.423
Ware, Jeremy, Harrisburg	68	278	254	33	71	119	10	1	12	52	0	6	2	16	1	41	1	0	6	.280	.320	.469
Wathan, Dusty, Akron	9	35	33	3	9	11	2	0	0	4	0	2	0	0	0	4	0	0	1	.273	.257	.333
Watson, Brandon, Harris.*	139	621	565	86	180	212	17	6	1	39	11	4	3	38	2	60	18	17	7	.319	.362	.375
Watson, Matt, Binghamton *	8	31	28	6	11	17	3	0	1	1	0	0	1	2	0	2	1	1	0	.393	.452	.607
West, Kevin, New Britain	136	529	494	54	138	223	41	1	14	79	1	4	3	27	2	110	3	5	9	.279	.318	.451
Whiteside, Eli, Bowie	81	275	265	21	54	72	13	1	1	23	1	0	4	5	0	44	0	0	7	.204	.230	.272
Whittaker, Tim, New Haven	5	11	10	0	0	0	0	0	0	0	0	0	0	1	0	2	0	0	0	.000	.091	.000
Wilken, Kris, Bowie †	116	458	426	40	112	139	19	1	2	43	2	4	0	26	1	58	5	1	8	.263	.303	.326
Williams, Bernie, Trenton †	5	21	15	4	5	7	2	0	0	4	0	1	1	4	1	1	0	1	1	.333	.476	.467
Wilson, John, Binghamton	43	130	108	19	35	43	5	0	1	11	3	1	4	14	0	21	2	1	3	.324	.417	.398
Wilson, Mike, Read.-Nor.	11	11	11	0	0	0	0	0	0	0	0	0	0	0	0	8	0	0	0	.000	.000	.000
Wright, Ron, Akron	50	213	176	25	46	82	9	0	9	38	0	3	5	29	3	39	0	1	3	.261	.376	.466
Yates, Tyler, Binghamton	8	2	2	0	0	0	0	0	0	0	0	0	0	0	0	2	0	0	0	.000	.000	.000
Youkilis, Kevin, Portland	94	417	312	74	102	145	23	1	6	37	0	4	15	86	2	40	7	0	7	.327	.487	.465
Young, Chris, Harrisburg	15	14	11	1	1	1	0	0	0	0	3	0	0	0	0	3	0	0	0	.091	.091	.091
Youngbauer, Scott, Reading †	16	52	42	2	13	17	1	0	1	5	1	2	1	6	0	7	1	0	0	.310	.392	.405

PLAYERS WITH TWO OR MORE TEAMS

Player, Team	G	TPA	AB	R	H	TB	2B	3B	HR	RBI	SH	SF	HP	BB	IBB	SO	SB	CS	GDP	Avg.	OBP	Slg.
Brooks, Frank, Reading *	34	1	1	0	0	0	0	0	0	0	0	0	0	0	0	0	0	0	0	.000	.000	.000
Brooks, Frank, Altoona *	1	0	0	0	0	0	0	0	0	0	0	0	0	0	0	0	0	0	0	.000	.000	.000
Brown, Tonayne, Portland	53	205	189	25	43	56	6	2	1	26	1	0	2	13	0	40	2	2	3	.228	.284	.296
Brown, Tonayne, Erie	72	297	275	39	76	114	19	5	3	34	1	1	5	15	1	52	2	1	7	.276	.324	.415
Deschaine, Jim, Reading	67	238	217	32	64	111	8	0	13	40	2	1	2	16	0	24	0	3	7	.295	.347	.512
Deschaine, Jim, New Haven	16	50	41	4	11	14	3	0	0	6	1	0	0	8	2	6	0	0	1	.268	.388	.341
Goelz, Jim, Akron	6	16	15	2	3	4	1	0	0	1	0	0	0	1	0	1	0	0	0	.200	.250	.267
Goelz, Jim, Portland	56	192	181	22	42	48	6	0	0	9	1	1	2	7	0	25	1	2	1	.232	.267	.265
Guy, Brad, Altoona	8	1	1	0	0	0	0	0	0	0	0	0	0	0	0	1	0	0	0	.000	.000	.000
Guy, Brad, Reading	31	2	2	0	0	0	0	0	0	0	0	0	0	0	0	0	0	0	0	.000	.000	.000
Stein, Blake, Harrisburg	4	2	2	0	0	0	0	0	0	0	0	0	0	0	0	0	0	0	0	.000	.000	.000
Stein, Blake, Akron	2	0	0	0	0	0	0	0	0	0	0	0	0	0	0	0	0	0	0	.000	.000	.000
Wilson, Mike, Reading	9	11	11	0	0	0	0	0	0	0	0	0	0	0	0	8	0	0	0	.000	.000	.000
Wilson, Mike, Norwich	2	0	0	0	0	0	0	0	0	0	0	0	0	0	0	0	0	0	0	.000	.000	.000

GRAND SLAMS—Griffin, Espy, 2 each; Bautista, Brisson, Casillas, Cervenak, Chiaffredo, Church, Daigle, Davis, J. Diaz, Freire, Fuentes, Haverbusch, Hill, Huber, Inglin, Jones, McKinley, McNeal, Minges, Munoz, Pernalete, Perry, Pond, Rifkin, A. Rios, Rogers, Shabala, Sherrod, Tiffee, Walker, Ware, West, 1 each.

AWARDED FIRST BASE ON CATCHER'S INTERFERENCE—Airoso 2 (Avila, Ruiz); Gross 2 (Fuentes, Jacobs); Avila (Seestedt); Cannizaro (Jacobs); J. Hannahan (Fuentes); Pecci (Fuentes).

2003 PITCHING

TEAM

Team	W	L	Pct.	ERA	G	CG	ShO	Sv.	IP	H	TBF	R	ER	HR	SH	SF	HB	BB	IBB	SO	WP	Bk.
Akron	88	53	.624	3.19	141	10	11	46	1238.1	1208	5299	555	439	65	45	43	42	420	11	952	53	12
Altoona	78	63	.553	3.32	141	4	10	35	1240.2	1205	5194	525	457	76	56	40	53	363	18	920	51	5
Bowie	69	72	.489	3.85	142	7	16	33	1214.1	1135	5196	589	519	105	33	37	61	491	27	945	55	4
Portland	72	70	.507	3.98	142	7	7	30	1212.1	1225	5213	644	536	101	44	46	70	408	9	899	76	8
New Haven	79	63	.556	4.02	142	5	5	29	1221.2	1275	5300	633	546	79	44	45	70	422	17	876	63	9
Erie	72	70	.507	4.02	142	6	9	36	1233.1	1283	5278	639	551	123	52	45	72	379	14	761	47	10
New Britain	73	68	.518	4.20	141	8	11	33	1208.0	1269	5251	625	564	94	50	44	72	421	43	830	50	9
Harrisburg	60	82	.423	4.43	142	4	8	35	1234.1	1280	5452	700	608	116	61	52	56	532	22	789	56	7
Binghamton	63	78	.447	4.44	141	3	13	32	1194.2	1207	5291	696	590	88	46	57	80	573	22	936	78	11
Norwich	62	79	.440	4.61	141	9	9	35	1186.1	1277	5256	705	608	82	52	57	72	488	13	797	61	6
Reading	62	79	.440	4.75	142	4	3	29	1240.0	1328	5444	738	654	146	54	56	88	437	25	846	51	2
Trenton	70	71	.496	4.77	141	9	2	29	1189.1	1357	5323	717	630	88	41	53	45	485	18	886	70	9

INDIVIDUAL

TOP QUALIFIERS FOR EARNED-RUN AVERAGE TITLE

Minimum 114 innings. *Lefthanded pitcher.

Pitcher, Team	W	L	Pct.	ERA	G	GS	CG	ShO	GF	Sv.	IP	H	TBF	R	ER	HR	SH	SF	HB	BB	IBB	SO	WP	Bk.
Gassner, Dave, New Haven *	10	4	.714	2.79	35	19	1	0	4	1	145.1	139	587	54	45	10	5	1	4	28	1	92	2	1
Jacobsen, Landon, Altoona	9	11	.450	2.93	27	27	1	0	0	0	162.2	156	669	60	53	11	11	8	10	40	0	80	7	1
Reimers, Cameron, N.H.	10	5	.667	3.08	28	26	0	0	1	0	163.2	170	684	68	56	10	7	3	6	38	0	96	1	1
Cruceta, Francisco, Akron	13	9	.591	3.09	27	25	6	0	1	0	163.1	141	684	70	56	7	3	6	2	66	0	134	3	4
Burnett, Sean, Altoona *	14	6	.700	3.21	27	27	2	1	0	0	159.2	158	649	60	57	2	8	9	7	29	1	86	10	0
Borkowski, Dave, Erie-Bowie	6	8	.429	3.30	30	19	2	0	1	0	128.1	136	530	54	47	11	5	5	1	24	2	70	4	0
Bonilla, Henry, New Britain	9	7	.563	3.36	26	20	1	1	2	0	142.0	143	601	58	53	8	8	5	9	37	5	77	4	2
Forystek, Brian, Bowie *	9	9	.500	3.39	29	21	1	1	0	0	124.2	116	512	57	47	8	3	3	2	42	4	103	3	0
Connolly, Mike, Altoona *	7	8	.467	3.39	25	23	0	0	0	0	127.1	123	540	55	48	10	3	3	9	38	1	90	2	0
Buchholz, Taylor, Reading	9	11	.450	3.55	25	24	1	0	0	0	144.2	136	600	62	57	14	3	7	9	33	0	114	3	0
Evans, Kyle, Akron	9	5	.643	3.59	28	19	0	0	3	1	133.0	140	572	72	53	3	2	4	7	37	0	69	2	1
Kester, Tim, Portland	10	10	.500	3.78	27	27	3	2	0	0	164.1	193	687	88	69	18	4	3	7	21	0	128	4	1
Stevens, Josh, Portland	10	9	.526	3.85	25	24	1	0	0	0	154.1	163	627	76	66	11	6	5	4	19	1	96	2	0
Baker, Chris, New Haven	9	6	.600	3.90	25	25	1	0	0	0	147.2	158	626	74	64	10	4	3	4	37	2	95	3	0

DEPARTMENTAL LEADERS: W—Burnett, 14; L—Walk, 13; Pct.—Schroeder, .818; G—Hodge, E. Rodriguez, 56; GS—Burnett, Jacobsen, Kester, 27; CG—Cruceta, 6; ShO—Five pitchers with 2; GF—Schmack, 48; Sv.—Schmack, 29; IP—Kester, 164.1; H—Kester, 193; TBF—Kester, 687; R—Ortiz, 105; ER—Ortiz, 96; HR—S. Lee, 21; SH—Jacobsen, 11; SF—Burnett, Van Dusen, 9; HB—Walk, 14; BB—Paradis, 81; IBB—Hodge, 11; SO—Cruceta, 134; WP—Van Dusen, 13; BK—Cruceta, 4.

ALL PITCHERS

*Lefthanded pitcher.

Pitcher, Team	W	L	Pct.	ERA	G	GS	CG	ShO	GF	Sv.	IP	H	TBF	R	ER	HR	SH	SF	HB	BB	IBB	SO	WP	Bk.
Abbott, David, New Haven	0	1	.000	9.00	3	1	0	0	1	0	7.0	8	33	8	7	1	1	0	2	4	0	4	0	0
Abbott, Jim, New Britain	4	2	.667	2.60	10	8	1	1	1	0	45.0	44	187	17	13	4	1	2	0	14	0	35	2	1
Adams, Brian, Portland *	0	1	.000	4.76	7	0	0	0	3	0	11.1	8	58	6	6	0	0	2	3	15	0	7	0	0
Adams, Daniel, Reading	1	1	.500	5.40	10	0	0	0	3	0	15.0	17	66	9	9	2	1	1	0	6	1	11	1	0
Agamennone, Brandon, Bowie	2	2	.500	4.79	29	3	0	0	9	1	56.1	65	248	33	30	8	0	3	2	13	3	37	2	0
Ahearne, Pat, Erie	4	1	.800	2.07	12	12	2	0	0	0	82.2	61	324	23	19	6	1	1	2	20	0	53	3	0
Aldred, Scott, Portland *	0	0	.000	0.84	18	0	0	0	15	8	21.1	13	81	3	2	0	0	2	0	6	0	18	1	1
Alvarado, Carlo, Erie	3	2	.600	3.14	37	1	0	0	15	0	66.0	56	283	29	23	4	3	3	4	28	2	55	2	1
Alvarez, Oscar, Akron *	2	2	.500	4.09	13	6	0	0	4	0	33.0	33	144	19	15	2	2	0	1	13	0	20	1	2
Alviso, Jerome, Bowie	0	0	.000	0.00	1	0	0	0	1	0	3.2	3	13	0	0	0	0	0	0	0	0	4	1	0
Anderson, Luke, Norwich	0	0	.000	4.38	6	0	0	0	2	0	12.1	9	48	6	6	0	0	0	1	4	0	13	0	0
Arnold, Jason, New Haven	3	1	.750	1.53	6	6	0	0	0	0	35.1	18	137	7	6	2	2	2	4	11	0	33	6	0
Baker, Chris, New Haven	9	6	.600	3.90	25	25	1	0	0	0	147.2	158	626	74	64	10	4	3	4	37	2	95	3	0
Bauer, Peter, New Haven	5	6	.455	4.96	29	13	1	0	4	0	103.1	116	457	59	57	6	1	5	8	45	3	60	10	3
Baugh, Kenny, Erie	7	9	.438	4.60	19	19	1	0	0	0	109.2	111	473	71	56	16	2	4	12	32	1	58	4	0
Beal, Andy, Trenton *	6	0	1.000	3.51	17	12	2	0	1	0	74.1	76	319	35	29	4	1	2	0	20	0	64	2	0
Bean, Colter, Trenton	0	0	.000	0.00	3	0	0	0	0	0	4.2	2	18	0	0	0	0	0	0	2	0	9	0	0
Begg, Chris, Norwich	2	1	.667	4.38	4	4	0	0	0	0	24.2	31	114	14	12	2	1	4	0	13	0	13	0	0
Bennett, Jeff, Altoona	4	4	.500	2.72	33	2	0	0	9	1	59.2	45	249	22	18	2	0	1	1	23	3	62	0	0
Bennett, Steve, Binghamton	1	3	.250	6.90	28	0	0	0	5	0	45.2	68	233	42	35	7	1	3	5	34	2	42	2	0
Bentz, Chad, Harrisburg *	1	4	.200	2.55	52	0	0	0	28	16	84.2	72	350	31	24	4	8	4	0	39	2	56	7	0
Betancourt, Rafael, Akron	0	0	.000	1.39	31	0	0	0	20	16	45.1	33	183	10	7	0	1	0	0	13	2	75	1	0
Bevis, P.J., Binghamton	4	7	.364	4.18	46	0	0	0	34	6	71.0	55	305	37	33	4	2	6	5	30	1	100	5	0
Billingsley, Brent, Reading *	0	1	.000	10.03	4	2	0	0	0	0	11.2	14	59	14	13	3	2	1	2	8	0	10	4	0
Birtwell, John, Erie	1	0	1.000	3.93	11	0	0	0	2	0	18.1	22	79	8	8	1	1	3	2	3	0	26	0	0
Bonifay, Josh, Altoona	0	0	.000	9.00	1	0	0	0	1	0	1.0	2	5	1	1	0	0	0	0	0	0	0	0	0
Bonilla, Henry, New Britain	9	7	.563	3.36	26	20	1	1	2	0	142.0	143	601	58	53	8	8	5	9	37	5	77	4	2
Bonser, Boof, Norwich	7	10	.412	4.00	24	24	1	1	0	0	135.0	122	579	80	60	11	7	7	0	67	0	103	10	0
Borkowski, Dave, Erie-Bowie	6	8	.429	3.30	30	19	2	0	1	0	128.1	136	530	54	47	11	5	5	1	24	2	70	4	0
Borner, Brady, Altoona *	3	2	.600	3.96	17	0	0	0	6	0	25.0	24	107	11	11	4	1	0	0	10	0	19	0	0
Brazoban, Yhency, Trenton	2	2	.500	7.81	20	0	0	0	16	3	27.2	33	127	25	24	5	3	3	2	14	1	19	4	0
Brooks, Frank, Read.-Alt.*	3	4	.429	2.51	35	0	0	0	20	9	61.0	43	234	18	17	6	2	3	0	13	1	75	2	0
Brown, Elliot, Norwich	1	2	.333	6.85	4	4	0	0	0	0	23.2	29	106	21	18	2	2	1	2	6	0	7	0	0
Bruso, Greg, Norwich	5	4	.556	3.42	11	11	2	0	0	0	76.1	72	307	32	29	6	2	7	4	11	1	45	1	0
Buchholz, Taylor, Reading	9	11	.450	3.55	25	24	1	0	0	0	144.2	136	600	62	57	14	3	7	9	33	0	114	3	0
Bucktrot, Keith, Reading	3	1	.750	2.56	7	7	0	0	0	0	45.2	34	181	17	13	3	1	5	3	15	0	30	2	0
Burnett, Sean, Altoona *	14	6	.700	3.21	27	27	2	1	0	0	159.2	158	649	60	57	2	8	9	7	29	1	86	10	0
Burnside, Adrian, Erie *	2	4	.333	6.28	15	11	0	0	2	2	67.1	81	313	57	47	9	2	3	8	27	0	46	3	1
Bush, David, New Haven	7	3	.700	2.78	14	14	1	0	0	0	81.0	73	333	26	25	4	3	2	4	19	1	73	2	0
Cable, Taft, Reading	0	1	.000	2.51	4	3	0	0	0	0	14.1	8	53	4	4	3	0	0	0	4	0	13	0	0
Cabrera, Fernando, Akron	9	4	.692	2.97	36	15	0	0	14	5	109.0	96	456	41	36	8	6	3	2	40	0	115	3	1
Cameron, Ryan, Portland	2	4	.333	3.14	10	9	1	0	0	0	51.2	49	214	21	18	1	1	0	2	17	0	37	3	0
Cammack, Eric, Binghamton	1	1	.500	4.50	10	0	0	0	2	0	18.0	19	77	10	9	2	0	1	0	4	0	17	0	1
Camp, Shawn, Altoona	0	2	.000	4.34	18	0	0	0	3	0	29.0	26	127	14	14	2	2	0	4	11	0	35	2	0
Candelario, Eddie, Trenton	8	5	.615	4.52	28	13	0	0	4	1	93.2	94	419	51	47	9	4	8	5	47	0	69	0	2
Carmona, Fausto, Akron	0	0	.000	4.50	1	1	0	0	0	0	6.0	8	27	3	3	1	0	0	1	0	0	3	0	0
Carnes, Matt, New Britain	1	3	.250	4.15	6	6	0	0	0	0	30.1	32	135	15	14	3	1	0	4	11	0	26	3	1
Carter, Ryan, Reading *	2	7	.222	6.00	17	17	0	0	0	0	75.0	105	362	61	50	7	5	4	7	32	1	47	5	0
Caruso, Joe, Altoona	0	0	.000	0.00	1	0	0	0	1	0	2.0	1	9	0	0	0	0	0	0	2	0	1	0	0
Casadiego, Gerardo, Harris.	1	4	.200	6.64	22	7	0	0	7	1	61.0	71	288	46	45	10	3	3	4	41	0	31	6	1
Casillas, Uriel, Reading	0	0	.000	0.00	1	0	0	0	1	0	0.2	0	2	0	0	0	0	0	0	0	0	0	0	0
Castellanos, Hugo, N.Haven	3	7	.300	5.13	21	0	0	0	12	0	33.1	41	153	25	19	3	1	3	2	13	2	28	0	0

Pitcher, Team	W	L	Pct.	ERA	G	GS	CG	ShO	GF	Sv.	IP	H	TBF	R	ER	HR	SH	SF	HB	BB	IBB	SO	WP	Bk.
Chacin, Gustavo, N.Haven *	3	4	.429	4.15	46	2	0	0	9	2	69.1	78	314	39	32	1	3	4	2	29	1	55	7	3
Chapman, Jake, Portland *	6	1	.857	3.45	35	0	0	0	14	0	57.1	65	258	35	22	5	3	1	4	21	2	49	4	0
Chiavacci, Ron, Harrisburg	1	4	.200	6.02	8	8	0	0	0	0	40.1	41	181	27	27	5	1	0	3	19	0	38	2	1
Chrysler, Clint, Altoona *	2	1	.667	10.46	16	1	0	0	9	0	26.2	43	136	33	31	4	0	4	0	18	1	14	1	0
Clark, Jeff, Norwich	2	4	.333	4.58	7	7	0	0	0	0	37.1	45	159	25	19	4	1	1	1	5	0	32	1	0
Cole, Joey, Binghamton	8	7	.533	4.83	25	20	0	0	0	0	113.2	122	521	76	61	9	5	5	11	59	1	77	8	1
Collins, Pat, Harrisburg	2	3	.400	7.12	25	0	0	0	7	0	43.0	46	202	37	34	0	0	5	1	31	2	30	4	0
Connolly, Mike, Altoona *	7	8	.467	3.39	25	23	0	0	0	0	127.1	123	540	55	48	10	3	3	9	38	1	90	2	0
Contreras, Jose, Trenton	0	0	.000	0.00	1	1	0	0	0	0	1.2	1	8	0	0	0	0	0	0	2	0	3	0	0
Cooksey, Wes, Trenton	1	2	.333	16.20	3	0	0	0	0	0	5.0	13	29	9	9	1	0	1	1	1	0	5	0	0
Corcoran, Roy, Harrisburg	1	1	.500	0.38	14	0	0	0	11	3	23.2	14	96	4	1	0	1	0	4	7	1	26	0	0
Corcoran, Tim, Bowie	4	1	.800	4.09	26	2	0	0	14	3	44.0	37	184	22	20	1	0	3	2	19	2	33	1	0
Cordova, Jorge, Erie	1	1	.500	4.53	30	0	0	0	8	0	47.2	47	210	28	24	6	3	6	6	16	3	31	1	0
Corona, Ronnie, New Britain	0	1	.000	3.46	4	3	0	0	0	0	13.0	8	60	6	5	0	0	2	2	12	0	12	5	1
Correia, Kevin, Norwich	6	6	.500	3.65	16	14	0	0	0	0	86.1	80	363	38	35	3	4	3	4	30	0	73	4	1
Cox, Mike, Binghamton *	1	0	1.000	4.12	11	1	0	0	4	1	19.2	10	95	9	9	1	2	0	1	25	0	27	3	0
Cox, Ryan, Norwich	1	3	.250	7.46	26	4	0	0	10	0	60.1	89	305	54	50	7	1	4	6	28	0	37	5	0
Cozier, Vance, Norwich	6	7	.462	4.14	26	13	2	1	7	0	100.0	117	451	54	46	5	1	7	6	36	2	36	1	1
Crain, Jesse, New Britain	1	1	.500	0.69	22	0	0	0	15	9	39.0	13	143	4	3	0	1	0	1	10	1	56	2	1
Cressend, Jack, Akron	2	0	1.000	0.00	8	0	0	0	3	1	16.0	15	67	4	0	0	1	0	0	2	0	10	1	0
Crouthers, Dave, Bowie	4	2	.667	3.80	9	9	0	0	0	0	45.0	37	192	20	19	4	0	0	6	18	1	29	1	0
Cruceta, Francisco, Akron	13	9	.591	3.09	27	25	6	0	1	0	163.1	141	684	70	56	7	3	6	2	66	0	134	3	4
Crumpton, Chuck, Harrisburg	4	6	.400	3.57	26	5	0	0	9	3	63.0	72	284	34	25	3	5	3	4	24	2	30	0	0
Currier, Rik, Trenton	1	0	1.000	2.60	7	5	0	0	0	0	34.2	22	136	11	10	1	0	1	0	15	0	33	1	0
Dawson, Layne, Reading	1	9	.100	7.42	14	14	2	0	0	0	74.0	102	349	65	61	12	1	5	4	27	0	45	3	0
De La Cruz, Fernando, Erie	1	0	1.000	8.25	7	0	0	0	2	0	12.0	18	55	12	11	3	0	0	0	3	0	6	1	1
De La Rosa, Jorge, Portland *	6	3	.667	2.80	22	20	0	0	1	1	99.2	87	413	39	31	6	2	2	5	36	0	102	8	1
DeJong, Jordan, New Haven	4	5	.444	3.58	27	0	0	0	11	1	27.2	27	124	16	11	0	1	2	2	17	0	29	3	0
Denney, Kyle, Akron	7	3	.700	2.42	18	18	1	0	0	0	104.0	97	433	34	28	7	2	5	4	24	0	87	1	1
Dequin, Benji, Harrisburg *	2	4	.333	4.69	22	0	0	0	5	0	40.1	47	193	34	21	6	4	1	3	20	1	44	3	0
Dinardo, Lenny, Binghamton *	1	3	.250	3.60	7	7	1	0	0	0	40.0	35	169	19	16	3	1	3	4	13	0	36	0	0
Douglas, Shea, Akron *	0	1	.000	2.70	2	0	0	0	2	0	3.1	3	14	1	1	0	0	0	0	1	1	2	0	0
Drumright, Mike, Bowie	2	1	.667	2.23	6	6	0	0	0	0	32.1	23	134	13	8	3	0	2	2	10	0	39	2	1
Duckworth, Brandon, Reading	0	0	.000	4.50	1	1	0	0	0	0	2.0	1	7	1	1	1	0	0	0	0	0	2	0	0
Durbin, Chad, Akron	2	0	1.000	1.50	3	3	0	0	0	0	12.0	7	46	2	2	1	0	0	2	1	0	11	0	0
Durbin, J.D., New Britain	6	3	.667	3.14	14	14	2	0	0	0	94.2	102	401	39	33	10	1	0	4	29	0	70	1	1
Edwards, Brad, Bowie *	1	0	1.000	10.13	2	0	0	0	0	0	2.2	5	13	4	3	0	0	0	0	1	0	2	0	0
Elliott, Chad, Binghamton *	2	0	1.000	8.71	7	0	0	0	3	0	10.1	14	49	10	10	1	0	0	0	5	0	8	2	0
Elmore, Chris, Portland *	1	1	.500	3.65	3	3	0	0	0	0	12.1	11	59	5	5	0	0	1	2	10	0	7	3	0
Estrada, Horacio, N.Britain *	2	1	.667	3.34	5	5	1	1	0	0	29.2	26	119	14	11	1	1	1	0	5	0	19	1	0
Evans, Kyle, Akron	9	5	.643	3.59	28	19	0	0	3	1	133.0	140	572	72	53	3	2	4	7	37	0	69	2	1
Eyre, Willie, New Britain	6	5	.545	3.46	29	10	1	1	8	0	96.1	93	416	42	37	6	2	2	6	38	4	66	5	0
Farnsworth, Jeff, Erie	3	3	.500	3.21	8	8	2	2	0	0	53.1	59	219	21	19	6	1	0	2	10	0	35	1	2
Ferrari, Anthony, Harrisburg *	2	0	1.000	0.56	14	0	0	0	12	5	16.0	13	66	1	1	0	0	0	2	6	1	9	0	0
Fisher, Pete, New Britain	4	1	.800	4.60	8	8	0	0	0	0	45.0	56	199	23	23	2	2	0	4	11	0	22	4	0
Flohr, Adam, New Britain *	2	1	.667	4.88	43	2	0	0	15	0	62.2	61	284	35	34	6	4	2	9	35	10	41	7	1
Fordham, Tom, Altoona *	5	2	.714	3.17	13	12	0	0	0	0	71.0	71	292	27	25	5	1	2	3	18	0	59	0	0
Forystek, Brian, Bowie *	9	9	.500	3.39	29	21	1	1	0	0	124.2	116	512	57	47	8	3	3	2	42	4	103	3	0
Fossum, Casey, Portland *	0	1	.000	6.75	3	2	0	0	0	0	4.0	5	21	3	3	1	0	0	1	3	0	7	0	0
Fox, Chad, Portland	0	0	.000	0.00	1	0	0	0	0	0	1.1	1	7	0	0	0	0	0	0	2	0	2	0	0
Franco, Martire, Reading	4	7	.364	5.71	28	13	1	0	8	4	86.2	116	403	66	55	9	3	4	5	25	1	47	3	1
Frederick, Kevin, New Haven	2	2	.500	3.38	25	0	0	0	18	7	29.1	32	135	16	11	3	1	2	0	14	2	27	6	0
Freire, Alejandro, Norwich	0	0	.000	9.00	1	0	0	0	1	0	1.0	0	7	1	1	0	0	1	1	3	0	2	0	0
Gamble, Jerome, Portland	2	0	1.000	4.91	2	2	0	0	0	0	11.0	10	45	6	6	0	0	1	1	1	0	11	2	0
Garza, Alberto, Trenton	0	1	.000	4.00	5	0	0	0	1	0	9.0	5	43	6	4	0	0	1	0	11	0	6	4	0
Gassner, Dave, New Haven *	10	4	.714	2.79	35	19	1	0	4	1	145.1	139	587	54	45	10	5	1	4	28	1	92	2	1
Giese, Dan, Reading	2	1	.667	1.46	9	0	0	0	4	1	12.1	8	46	2	2	1	1	0	1	1	0	16	0	0
Glaser, Eric, Portland	3	3	.500	4.10	29	7	0	0	3	0	74.2	65	315	38	34	11	2	5	1	25	2	52	3	0
Glen, William, Reading	3	6	.333	3.83	31	14	0	0	3	0	103.1	100	462	61	44	13	4	5	8	53	2	79	2	1
Glick, David, Trenton *	4	0	1.000	5.31	45	0	0	0	13	0	40.2	58	200	34	24	3	2	1	5	24	2	31	1	0
Gonzalez, Mike, Altoona *	0	0	.000	1.23	5	0	0	0	2	1	7.1	4	28	1	1	1	0	0	0	2	0	10	0	0
Grabow, John, Altoona *	6	1	.857	3.36	24	9	0	0	5	1	83.0	87	341	34	31	9	6	5	1	19	2	73	3	1
Grace, Bryan, Trenton	1	2	.333	8.04	7	6	0	0	0	0	31.1	54	150	29	28	3	0	3	0	10	0	14	2	0
Guthrie, Jeremy, Akron	6	2	.750	1.44	10	9	2	2	0	0	62.2	44	243	11	10	0	3	2	0	14	0	35	2	1
Gutierrez, Vic, Harrisburg	0	0	.000	0.00	2	0	0	0	2	0	2.0	2	11	2	0	0	0	0	0	2	0	0	0	0
Guy, Brad, Altoona-Reading	3	8	.273	5.10	39	4	0	0	21	3	83.0	91	357	52	47	9	4	4	7	20	2	42	3	0
Halsey, Brad, Trenton *	7	5	.583	4.93	15	15	0	0	0	0	91.1	123	410	51	50	4	4	0	5	22	0	78	3	0
Hamann, Rob, New Haven	0	2	.000	11.91	6	0	0	0	2	0	11.1	22	64	17	15	0	2	0	2	5	1	3	1	0
Hansell, Greg, Trenton	0	2	.000	1.89	17	1	0	0	5	1	19.0	19	81	5	4	0	1	1	1	5	1	21	2	0
Harvey, Ian, Reading	4	1	.800	3.75	11	0	0	0	6	1	24.0	22	105	10	10	2	2	0	2	11	0	22	1	0
Hee, Aaron, Binghamton *	2	2	.500	5.85	22	3	0	0	12	0	40.0	27	190	31	26	2	1	3	4	43	2	38	5	3
Henkel, Rob, Erie *	9	3	.750	3.38	16	16	0	0	0	0	82.2	67	335	33	31	7	1	1	1	27	0	70	4	0
Hernandez, Adrian, Trenton	0	0	.000	3.86	1	1	0	0	0	0	4.2	5	23	4	2	0	0	0	0	2	0	7	0	1
Hernandez, Yoel, Reading	6	3	.667	4.26	43	1	0	0	22	2	74.0	100	349	43	35	4	9	4	7	31	3	46	4	0
Herndon, Junior, Portland	9	8	.529	4.85	25	23	2	0	0	0	133.2	154	576	79	72	17	4	5	3	31	0	69	5	0
Hill, Jeremy, Binghamton	0	2	.000	10.38	11	0	0	0	4	0	13.0	14	70	15	15	3	2	0	1	15	2	10	7	0
Hill, Shawn, Harrisburg	3	1	.750	3.54	4	4	0	0	0	0	20.1	23	95	12	8	0	0	1	1	11	1	12	0	0
Hoard, Brent, New Britain *	0	0	.000	0.00	3	2	0	0	1	0	5.0	3	20	0	0	0	1	0	0	3	0	4	0	0
Hodge, Kevin, New Britain	6	8	.429	3.86	56	0	0	0	27	9	93.1	87	393	45	40	9	9	4	4	28	11	66	2	0
Hutchison, Ryan, Reading	3	2	.600	3.76	34	0	0	0	20	5	52.2	54	230	23	22	6	3	1	8	17	5	17	1	0
Isaacson, Charlie, Trenton	1	3	.250	6.12	14	0	0	0	5	1	25.0	37	113	17	17	3	1	0	1	11	0	15	0	0

Pitcher, Team	W	L	Pct.	ERA	G	GS	CG	ShO	GF	Sv.	IP	H	TBF	R	ER	HR	SH	SF	HB	BB	IBB	SO	WP	Bk.
Jackson, Dan, New Haven	5	1	.833	4.02	33	0	0	0	13	2	47.0	46	211	23	21	2	2	3	4	24	1	38	5	0
Jacobsen, Landon, Altoona	9	11	.450	2.93	27	27	1	0	0	0	162.2	156	669	60	53	11	11	8	10	40	0	80	7	1
Johnson, James, Portland *	3	5	.375	3.74	38	0	0	0	16	5	55.1	40	226	24	23	7	4	0	4	20	1	66	2	0
Johnson, Jeremy, Erie	5	3	.625	2.82	10	10	0	0	0	0	60.2	52	245	23	19	5	2	3	3	15	0	31	1	1
Johnson, Mark, Erie	8	3	.727	3.59	48	3	0	0	14	4	87.2	87	361	39	35	6	4	1	5	19	4	54	5	0
Johnston, Mike, Altoona *	6	2	.750	2.12	46	0	0	0	19	7	72.1	49	285	17	17	4	5	2	5	27	3	65	7	1
Joseph, Jake, Binghamton	2	4	.333	5.57	11	11	0	0	0	0	53.1	68	235	40	33	5	1	1	0	15	0	30	5	0
Kaercher, Matthew, Portland	0	0	.000	27.00	1	0	0	0	0	0	0.1	3	4	1	1	0	0	0	0	0	0	0	0	0
Kalita, Tim, Erie *	0	5	.000	7.15	15	10	0	0	0	0	50.1	75	246	43	40	7	2	1	2	23	0	29	5	1
Karp, Josh, Harrisburg	4	10	.286	4.99	23	23	1	0	0	0	122.2	126	543	76	68	12	3	6	11	49	1	77	9	0
Kegley, Chuck, New Haven	0	0	.000	9.00	12	0	0	0	7	0	14.0	12	77	19	14	1	2	3	2	20	2	7	5	0
Kemp, Beau, New Britain	5	6	.455	3.98	36	0	0	0	27	11	52.0	63	239	32	23	1	5	3	2	23	2	38	1	0
Kennard, Jeff, Trenton	1	0	1.000	3.86	10	0	0	0	2	0	18.2	16	82	9	8	2	1	1	0	14	0	8	6	2
Keppel, Bob, Binghamton	7	4	.636	3.04	18	17	2	2	0	0	94.2	92	388	36	32	6	5	1	6	27	0	46	3	1
Kester, Tim, Portland	10	10	.500	3.78	27	27	3	2	0	0	164.1	193	687	88	69	18	4	3	7	21	0	128	4	1
Knowles, Mike, Trenton	0	1	.000	7.59	8	0	0	0	5	0	10.2	16	52	9	9	2	0	2	2	2	0	6	1	0
Kremer, John, Trenton	0	0	.000	13.50	3	0	0	0	1	0	3.1	8	20	6	5	2	0	0	1	0	0	3	0	0
Kumagai, Ryo, Portland	0	0	.000	1.93	3	0	0	0	3	0	4.2	5	21	1	1	0	0	0	0	2	0	4	0	0
Larrison, Preston, Erie	4	12	.250	5.61	24	24	0	0	0	0	126.2	161	583	89	79	10	8	6	10	59	0	53	6	2
Larson, Ryan, Akron	2	6	.250	3.84	40	0	0	0	20	2	63.1	78	281	36	27	8	6	0	3	18	2	29	1	1
Lavigne, Tim, Binghamton	3	5	.375	4.42	46	0	0	0	27	11	71.1	85	321	42	35	6	3	3	2	39	7	50	2	0
Lee, Cliff, Akron *	1	0	1.000	1.50	2	2	0	0	0	0	12.0	7	46	2	2	1	0	0	0	4	0	13	0	0
Lee, Seung, Reading	11	6	.647	4.96	26	25	0	0	0	0	147.0	140	627	85	81	21	8	2	6	47	0	109	4	0
Lira, James, Norwich	1	1	.500	7.04	6	3	0	0	1	0	15.1	21	76	12	12	2	0	1	0	11	0	11	3	0
Lockwood, Luke, Harrisburg *	8	11	.421	5.16	26	26	2	1	0	0	144.2	175	634	89	83	16	8	3	5	41	3	64	2	1
Lopez, Rodrigo, Bowie	1	0	1.000	0.00	1	1	0	0	0	0	6.1	3	21	0	0	0	0	0	0	0	0	13	0	0
Lowry, Noah, Norwich *	9	6	.600	4.72	23	23	2	0	0	0	118.1	127	509	66	62	7	7	5	4	47	0	97	3	2
Maness, Nick, Binghamton	0	1	.000	10.50	8	1	0	0	2	0	12.0	20	61	15	14	2	1	0	3	4	0	4	2	0
Manning, Charlie, Trenton *	0	2	.000	6.26	23	6	0	0	5	0	46.0	53	216	34	32	1	2	3	1	35	2	34	5	0
Markwell, Diego, N.H.*	5	7	.417	7.04	28	19	0	0	2	0	110.0	146	524	96	86	20	5	6	9	54	0	69	4	0
Martin, Kevin, Akron	0	0	.000	4.50	2	0	0	0	2	0	2.0	3	10	1	1	0	0	0	0	2	0	3	0	0
Martinez, Anastacio, Port.-Alt.	3	1	.750	2.25	37	0	0	0	35	14	44.0	37	195	14	11	4	1	4	4	25	0	38	6	0
Mata, Gustavo, Harrisburg	6	8	.429	4.95	22	22	0	0	0	0	107.1	141	490	67	59	9	6	5	0	39	0	42	5	1
Mattes, Troy, Harrisburg	0	1	.000	5.68	5	3	0	0	1	0	19.0	21	82	15	12	1	1	0	0	3	0	8	0	0
Mattioni, Nick, Binghamton	0	3	.000	3.58	42	0	0	0	12	4	75.1	75	341	31	30	1	5	6	9	40	3	68	7	0
Mattox, David, Binghamton	8	7	.533	3.49	21	20	0	0	0	0	113.1	103	474	50	44	7	4	3	9	40	0	86	4	1
Maust, David, Harrisburg *	3	6	.333	2.70	17	9	0	0	4	1	66.2	58	274	24	20	5	0	1	1	21	2	33	1	0
McDade, Neal, Altoona	1	6	.143	2.72	38	0	0	0	20	4	72.2	75	307	32	22	5	2	1	2	18	2	48	3	0
McDonald, Jon, New Britain	0	0	.000	11.30	8	2	0	0	2	0	14.1	26	81	19	18	1	1	2	1	13	1	4	3	0
McGowan, Dustin, New Haven	7	0	1.000	3.17	14	14	1	0	0	0	76.2	78	324	28	27	1	0	2	4	19	0	72	5	1
Mendoza, Marcos, Akron *	1	0	1.000	10.67	9	0	0	0	2	0	14.1	16	77	21	17	0	2	1	1	13	0	14	1	0
Mercado, Hector, Reading *	0	0	.000	0.00	1	1	0	0	0	0	2.0	0	6	0	0	0	0	0	0	1	0	0	0	0
Miller, Josh, Reading	0	3	.000	5.36	43	2	0	0	16	1	84.0	98	366	52	50	9	3	4	7	19	4	40	3	0
Miniel, Rene, Portland	0	1	.000	2.45	15	0	0	0	9	0	25.2	27	116	16	7	2	3	1	0	12	0	20	6	0
Montalbano, Greg, Portland *	2	1	.667	9.39	6	5	0	0	0	0	15.1	25	83	17	16	3	0	1	2	13	0	8	1	1
Montano, Ignacio, Akron *	0	0	.000	9.00	1	0	0	0	1	0	1.0	3	6	1	1	0	0	0	0	0	0	0	0	0
Montes, Albert, Norwich	3	1	.750	4.43	36	0	0	0	18	5	63.0	74	279	40	31	2	4	2	6	18	3	30	6	2
Montgomery, Matt, Norwich	4	3	.571	2.68	28	0	0	0	23	13	37.0	35	161	11	11	3	1	1	1	13	1	39	3	0
Moreno, Orber, Binghamton	2	0	1.000	1.69	4	0	0	0	3	1	5.1	4	21	1	1	1	0	0	0	1	0	7	0	0
Moreno, Victor, New Britain	1	1	.500	6.95	24	0	0	0	11	0	33.2	37	159	27	26	5	2	2	1	22	2	27	4	0
Musser, Neal, Binghamton *	5	9	.357	4.57	20	20	0	0	0	0	100.1	108	436	57	51	9	4	4	6	39	0	76	5	1
Myette, Aaron, Akron	0	0	.000	0.00	3	0	0	0	0	0	5.0	0	18	0	0	0	0	0	0	2	0	7	0	0
Neil, Dan, Akron *	0	0	.000	7.71	5	0	0	0	4	0	7.0	10	32	6	6	1	0	2	1	1	0	4	0	0
Neshek, Pat, New Britain	1	1	.500	5.87	5	1	0	0	2	1	7.2	7	34	5	5	2	0	0	1	3	0	5	0	0
Nicolas, Mike, Portland	4	2	.667	6.06	20	0	0	0	7	0	32.2	20	159	26	22	2	2	1	9	33	0	37	8	3
Nin, Sandy, New Haven	0	1	.000	2.57	1	1	0	0	0	0	7.0	5	26	2	2	1	0	0	1	0	0	9	0	0
Ogiltree, John, New Haven	4	4	.500	3.38	45	0	0	0	21	2	61.1	55	270	29	23	1	0	2	4	31	0	38	1	0
Oquendo, Ian, Altoona	4	0	1.000	1.96	6	6	0	0	0	0	36.2	36	155	13	8	2	0	1	1	10	0	23	2	0
Orloski, Joe, Binghamton	0	3	.000	10.95	10	0	0	0	2	0	12.1	18	63	16	15	2	2	2	1	6	0	5	1	0
Ormond, Rodney, Bowie	7	2	.778	2.86	46	0	0	0	11	1	85.0	70	355	33	27	5	2	1	5	31	4	72	3	0
Ortiz, Javier, Trenton	6	11	.353	5.76	28	26	1	0	0	0	150.0	181	686	105	96	11	1	4	3	71	1	91	8	1
Outlaw, Mark, Reading *	0	0	.000	5.40	12	0	0	0	4	0	11.2	11	56	8	7	1	0	0	0	11	0	9	0	0
Ozias, Todd, Altoona	2	2	.500	1.62	51	0	0	0	43	21	61.0	47	244	14	11	2	4	2	0	17	2	52	3	0
Pahucki, David, Portland	0	0	.000	3.27	2	1	0	0	0	0	11.0	9	45	5	4	0	0	0	0	5	0	3	2	0
Palma, Rick, Altoona *	6	5	.545	3.67	35	5	0	0	9	0	68.2	70	296	35	28	3	5	0	0	24	1	61	4	0
Palmer, Matt, Norwich	0	0	.000	13.50	5	0	0	0	1	0	6.2	12	41	11	10	0	0	1	2	5	0	5	3	0
Paradis, Mike, Bowie	5	10	.333	5.27	25	25	1	0	0	0	124.2	129	571	85	73	13	3	5	9	81	3	82	8	0
Parker, Christian, Trenton	1	2	.333	2.83	5	5	2	1	0	0	28.2	17	114	11	9	1	1	2	1	11	0	9	0	0
Parrish, John, Bowie *	3	3	.500	2.00	49	0	0	0	17	6	76.1	58	310	22	17	5	3	1	2	33	0	85	8	0
Pautz, Brad, Reading	4	5	.444	7.69	29	1	0	0	11	1	48.0	60	222	44	41	6	1	4	5	20	5	34	5	0
Pearson, Terry, Erie	1	0	1.000	3.55	9	0	0	0	3	0	12.2	12	49	5	5	1	1	0	1	0	0	11	0	0
Pena, Juan, New Haven	0	0	.000	2.45	7	0	0	0	5	5	7.1	5	32	2	2	1	0	0	0	5	0	10	1	0
Pennington, Todd, Akron	1	0	1.000	3.60	7	0	0	0	2	0	10.0	8	42	4	4	0	0	1	0	6	0	9	4	0
Perez, Juan, Portland *	3	3	.500	3.82	18	0	0	0	6	0	30.2	37	136	19	13	4	1	3	0	11	1	24	2	0
Peterson, Adam, New Haven	2	2	.500	4.88	24	0	0	0	19	9	24.0	24	105	13	13	1	2	2	2	7	1	24	1	0
Peterson, Matt, Binghamton	1	2	.333	3.45	6	6	0	0	0	0	31.1	29	140	18	12	2	1	2	0	20	0	23	1	0
Pettyjohn, Adam, Erie *	1	4	.200	4.00	19	10	1	0	5	0	81.0	87	340	39	36	9	2	2	3	18	0	49	0	0
Pina, Rafael, Bowie	0	1	.000	4.30	6	0	0	0	2	1	14.2	13	57	7	7	2	1	0	1	1	0	7	1	0
Pinales, Aquiles, Akron	1	1	.500	7.00	6	0	0	0	2	0	9.0	5	42	7	7	0	1	0	1	8	2	8	2	0
Pridie, Jon, New Britain	6	9	.400	5.19	27	17	1	0	4	0	111.0	136	502	72	64	7	4	2	10	35	2	65	1	0
Puello, Ignacio, Harrisburg	1	0	1.000	7.32	18	0	0	0	7	0	35.2	40	176	31	29	6	2	5	3	28	0	21	2	0

Pitcher, Team	W	L	Pct.	ERA	G	GS	CG	ShO	GF	Sv.	IP	H	TBF	R	ER	HR	SH	SF	HB	BB	IBB	SO	WP	Bk.
Rakers, Aaron, Bowie	5	0	1.000	2.75	31	0	0	0	21	8	39.1	27	161	12	12	7	2	0	2	19	1	42	1	0
Rakers, Jason, Akron	1	1	.500	1.08	4	0	0	0	2	1	8.1	7	32	2	1	0	0	1	0	1	0	9	1	0
Ramirez, Enrique, Bowie	1	3	.250	5.64	14	0	0	0	0	0	22.1	20	105	15	14	1	1	1	1	19	2	20	6	0
Ramirez, Ramon, Trenton	1	1	.500	1.69	4	3	0	0	0	0	21.1	18	88	8	4	3	0	1	0	8	1	21	0	1
Ramsey, Keith, Akron *	1	0	1.000	6.35	2	2	0	0	0	0	11.1	15	52	8	8	1	0	1	0	3	0	4	0	0
Rayborn, Kenny, Akron	4	1	.800	2.05	5	4	0	0	0	0	26.1	28	114	7	6	1	2	0	4	5	0	20	0	0
Reimers, Cameron, N.Haven	10	5	.667	3.08	28	26	0	0	1	0	163.2	170	684	68	56	10	7	3	6	38	0	96	1	1
Reynoso, Edison, Trenton	8	8	.500	6.87	22	12	1	0	4	0	77.1	109	362	69	59	7	2	3	3	22	1	43	10	1
Rigdon, Paul, Akron	3	0	1.000	3.23	6	6	0	0	0	0	30.2	27	125	12	11	2	0	1	2	5	0	16	0	0
Rijo, Fernando, Bowie	3	10	.231	5.47	20	19	2	2	0	0	100.1	107	448	65	61	18	0	3	5	46	1	71	1	1
Riley, Matt, Bowie *	5	2	.714	3.11	14	14	1	1	0	0	72.1	56	297	27	25	4	3	3	1	23	1	73	4	2
Ring, Royce, Binghamton *	3	0	1.000	1.66	18	0	0	0	15	7	21.2	13	87	4	4	2	1	0	1	11	0	18	1	0
Rivera, Homero, Erie *	13	4	.765	2.97	54	0	0	0	25	1	72.2	76	308	26	24	8	4	2	7	22	0	36	1	1
Rizzo, Todd, Bowie *	0	0	.000	3.24	7	0	0	0	4	0	8.1	5	35	3	3	0	0	1	0	7	1	6	0	0
Robbins, Jake, Akron	6	3	.667	2.16	34	0	0	0	16	8	58.1	44	234	18	14	1	5	1	2	24	0	38	8	0
Robinson, Bo, Trenton	0	0	.000	0.00	1	0	0	0	1	0	1.0	0	3	0	0	0	0	0	0	0	0	0	0	0
Rodriguez, Cristobal, Harris.	0	0	.000	54.00	1	0	0	0	0	0	1.0	4	9	6	6	2	0	0	0	2	0	1	0	0
Rodriguez, Eddy, Bowie	3	4	.429	2.34	56	0	0	0	43	13	73.0	49	309	26	19	3	4	2	6	35	2	66	3	0
Rogers, Brian, Trenton	1	3	.250	5.97	13	2	1	0	3	0	34.2	40	162	27	23	2	2	6	4	21	1	16	3	0
Roller, Adam, Trenton	4	3	.571	2.90	36	0	0	0	28	10	40.1	49	185	19	13	2	2	1	1	15	1	36	8	0
Romero, Josmir, New Britain	2	5	.286	5.37	27	7	0	0	7	0	63.2	80	293	40	38	4	1	4	6	25	2	50	3	0
Romprey, Ed, Erie	0	1	.000	9.00	1	0	0	0	1	0	1.0	2	7	1	1	0	0	0	0	2	0	1	0	0
Rosario, Juan, Bowie	0	3	.000	8.68	5	5	0	0	0	0	18.2	25	93	19	18	2	0	0	5	10	0	5	0	0
Rudrude, Brett, Portland	1	2	.333	4.26	6	6	0	0	0	0	31.2	39	144	20	15	1	0	1	5	10	0	16	4	1
Saenz, Jason, Binghamton *	4	3	.571	4.30	32	0	0	0	12	2	58.2	58	266	35	28	2	1	2	6	40	3	36	9	2
Schmack, Brian, Erie	3	3	.500	2.05	53	0	0	0	48	29	57.0	53	228	15	13	2	6	2	0	10	2	47	4	0
Schmitt, Eric, Trenton	0	2	.000	2.76	21	1	0	0	7	1	42.1	44	181	17	13	1	2	0	0	15	2	48	4	0
Schoening, Brent, N.Britain	12	6	.667	3.98	26	26	0	0	0	0	147.0	141	610	67	65	15	4	8	5	43	1	105	2	0
Schroder, Chris, Harrisburg	9	2	.818	2.84	49	0	0	0	22	4	82.1	68	353	29	26	5	6	4	2	47	1	81	1	0
Scobie, Jason, Binghamton	2	4	.333	4.14	9	9	0	0	0	0	50.0	50	210	29	23	1	0	3	2	13	1	24	1	1
Seale, Dustin, Harrisburg *	1	2	.333	4.82	26	1	0	0	16	1	46.2	47	208	29	25	10	3	1	2	23	2	23	1	0
Seibel, Phil, Binghamton *	5	5	.500	3.59	17	17	0	0	0	0	82.2	79	358	48	33	6	3	8	3	32	0	71	3	0
Sequea, Jacobo, Bowie	1	3	.250	5.40	12	8	0	0	1	0	40.0	43	189	26	24	5	2	1	4	28	0	24	4	0
Shaffar, Ben, Altoona	1	3	.250	4.48	13	11	0	0	1	0	64.1	68	269	38	32	3	2	1	3	20	0	50	4	0
Shepard, David, Trenton	8	7	.533	2.82	53	0	0	0	29	12	67.0	55	278	22	21	7	3	2	5	18	3	65	3	0
Shibilo, Andy, Portland	1	2	.333	1.33	13	0	0	0	10	1	20.1	14	81	4	3	1	2	1	1	7	1	19	2	0
Shipp, Brian, Binghamton	0	0	.000	13.50	1	0	0	0	1	0	0.2	2	5	1	1	0	0	0	0	1	0	0	0	0
Sims, Kenny, Bowie	0	1	.000	27.00	1	1	0	0	0	0	2.1	10	18	7	7	0	0	0	1	0	0	2	0	0
Smith, Bud, Reading *	1	1	.500	5.35	8	8	0	0	0	0	37.0	40	164	23	22	6	1	0	3	15	0	24	1	0
Smith, Matt, Trenton *	2	3	.400	4.26	9	9	0	0	0	0	50.2	57	226	29	24	6	1	3	2	24	0	36	0	0
Song, Seung, Harrisburg	5	2	.714	2.35	13	13	1	0	0	0	72.2	55	295	26	19	5	3	2	1	24	2	44	4	1
Spencer, Sean, Bowie *	2	1	.667	1.53	12	0	0	0	4	0	17.2	19	78	3	3	0	1	0	0	7	1	12	2	0
Spiegel, Mike, Erie *	0	5	.000	3.07	24	3	0	0	10	0	44.0	43	193	25	15	3	3	2	3	20	1	28	2	0
Spiehs, R.D., Norwich	2	5	.286	3.28	39	0	0	0	13	7	60.1	57	267	31	22	3	5	0	7	29	3	51	5	0
Stanton, Mike, Binghamton *	0	1	.000	9.00	1	1	0	0	0	0	1.0	6	9	3	1	0	0	1	0	0	0	1	0	0
Stein, Blake, Akron-Harrisburg	1	4	.200	9.14	6	3	0	0	0	0	21.2	30	109	23	22	3	3	1	1	15	0	14	1	0
Stevens, Josh, Portland	10	9	.526	3.85	25	24	1	0	0	0	154.1	163	627	76	66	11	6	5	4	19	1	96	2	0
Tadano, Kazuhito, Akron	4	1	.800	1.24	31	0	0	0	9	3	72.2	62	294	15	10	4	2	1	2	15	2	78	4	0
Taschner, Jack, Norwich *	0	6	.000	5.71	34	12	0	0	10	0	75.2	78	347	53	48	7	4	3	5	45	0	46	6	0
Threets, Erick, Norwich *	0	0	.000	15.88	11	0	0	0	4	0	11.1	15	72	20	20	1	0	0	2	21	0	16	6	0
Torres, Luis, Harrisburg	0	4	.000	4.80	11	0	0	0	4	0	15.0	11	67	10	8	3	1	2	2	10	1	20	2	0
Ulloa, Enmanuel, Harrisburg	0	2	.000	10.95	6	1	0	0	3	1	12.1	19	64	15	15	3	0	1	0	9	0	12	1	0
Van Dusen, Derrick, Akron *	10	8	.556	4.92	28	26	1	0	0	0	139.0	183	645	100	76	11	4	9	5	51	0	77	13	1
Van Hekken, Andy, Erie *	5	6	.455	4.02	13	13	0	0	0	0	80.2	89	342	41	36	13	4	2	1	18	0	32	3	0
VanBenschoten, John, Altoona	7	6	.538	3.69	17	17	1	0	0	0	90.1	95	399	46	37	5	4	1	6	34	1	78	2	2
Vargas, Claudio, Harrisburg	1	0	1.000	0.75	2	2	0	0	0	0	12.0	7	46	1	1	0	1	0	1	3	0	13	0	0
Vargas, Jose, Akron	3	2	.600	1.92	37	0	0	0	23	8	51.2	52	233	21	11	4	1	3	1	27	2	52	2	0
Vent, Kevin, Norwich	6	5	.545	3.50	37	0	0	0	13	1	74.2	72	318	36	29	6	2	3	3	30	1	47	1	0
Villegas, Felix, Portland	1	8	.111	6.37	23	5	0	0	7	0	53.2	61	252	41	38	4	4	1	4	28	1	34	4	0
Villegas, Francisco, Trenton	0	0	.000	1.74	6	0	0	0	2	0	10.1	6	48	2	2	0	0	0	0	11	0	10	0	0
Wade, Travis, Norwich	0	2	.000	7.33	19	0	0	0	13	2	23.1	35	111	20	19	1	1	0	3	10	2	13	0	0
Walk, Mitch, Norwich *	6	13	.316	4.12	36	20	2	1	16	7	137.2	147	608	75	63	9	9	6	14	55	0	76	3	0
Walker, Pete, New Haven	0	1	.000	9.00	2	2	0	0	0	0	2.0	3	8	2	2	0	0	0	0	0	0	1	0	0
Wallace, Shane, Akron *	0	2	.000	4.82	10	1	0	0	1	1	18.2	23	89	11	10	1	0	1	1	12	0	3	2	0
Wang, Chien-ming, Trenton	7	6	.538	4.65	21	21	2	1	0	0	122.0	143	534	71	63	7	8	4	2	32	2	84	3	1
Warden, Jim Ed, Akron	0	1	.000	9.00	1	1	0	0	0	0	4.0	6	21	4	4	0	0	1	0	5	0	1	1	0
Weatherby, Charlie, Portland	2	2	.500	5.92	30	1	0	0	8	1	51.2	68	234	41	34	3	3	5	0	20	0	25	2	0
Weaver, Eric, Reading	1	1	.500	6.57	10	0	0	0	5	2	12.1	12	55	9	9	3	1	0	0	10	1	9	3	0
White, Gabe, Trenton *	0	0	.000	7.71	2	2	0	0	0	0	2.1	3	10	2	2	1	0	0	0	0	0	2	0	0
White, Matt, Portland *	0	0	.000	0.00	2	1	0	0	1	0	3.0	1	13	1	0	0	1	0	1	2	0	3	1	0
Wickman, Bob, Akron	0	0	.000	16.20	2	2	0	0	0	0	1.2	3	9	3	3	0	1	0	0	1	0	2	0	0
Wiggins, Scott, New Haven *	0	1	.000	4.00	17	0	0	0	8	0	18.0	19	76	10	8	1	2	0	4	2	0	13	0	0
Wilson, Jeff, Bowie *	5	7	.417	3.78	28	8	0	0	8	0	81.0	84	341	36	34	4	4	4	3	24	0	50	0	0
Wilson, Mike, Read.-Norwich	3	2	.600	4.46	11	8	0	0	0	0	40.1	45	182	25	20	7	1	2	5	21	0	23	1	0
Wohlers, Mark, Akron	0	0	.000	5.40	2	1	0	0	0	0	1.2	5	10	1	1	0	0	0	0	2	0	0	0	0
Wolfe, Brian, New Britain	5	7	.417	6.42	30	10	1	0	11	3	82.2	111	375	65	59	10	2	5	3	24	2	42	0	1
Woodyard, Mark, Erie	1	0	1.000	5.56	2	2	0	0	0	0	11.1	14	50	7	7	1	1	1	0	5	0	6	1	0
Yates, Tyler, Binghamton	1	2	.333	4.35	8	8	0	0	0	0	39.1	33	167	21	19	4	1	0	1	17	0	36	2	0
Young, Chris, Harrisburg	4	4	.500	4.01	15	15	0	0	0	0	83.0	83	354	39	37	9	3	4	5	22	0	64	5	2
Zink, Charlie, Portland	3	2	.600	3.43	6	6	0	0	0	0	39.1	21	159	16	15	1	1	1	7	14	0	18	2	0

PITCHERS WITH TWO OR MORE TEAMS

Pitcher, Team	W	L	Pct.	ERA	G	GS	CG	ShO	GF	Sv.	IP	H	TBF	R	ER	HR	SH	SF	HB	BB	IBB	SO	WP	Bk.
Borkowski, Dave, Erie	0	1	.000	3.38	6	0	0	0	1	0	8.0	10	35	4	3	0	1	2	0	2	1	4	0	0
Borkowski, Dave, Bowie	6	7	.462	3.29	24	19	2	0	0	0	120.1	126	495	50	44	11	4	3	1	22	1	66	4	0
Brooks, Frank, Reading *	3	4	.429	2.30	34	0	0	0	19	9	58.2	40	224	16	15	5	2	3	0	13	1	71	2	0
Brooks, Frank, Altoona *	0	0	.000	7.71	1	0	0	0	1	0	2.1	3	10	2	2	1	0	0	0	0	0	4	0	0
Guy, Brad, Altoona	1	2	.333	5.79	8	1	0	0	5	0	14.0	16	61	9	9	0	2	0	1	2	1	9	0	0
Guy, Brad, Reading	2	6	.250	4.96	31	3	0	0	16	3	69.0	75	296	43	38	9	2	4	6	18	1	33	3	0
Martinez, Anastacio, Portland	3	1	.750	2.25	34	0	0	0	32	14	40.0	31	179	13	10	3	1	4	4	24	0	37	5	0
Martinez, Anastacio, Altoona	0	0	.000	2.25	3	0	0	0	3	0	4.0	6	16	1	1	1	0	0	0	1	0	1	1	0
Stein, Blake, Harrisburg	1	3	.250	6.63	4	3	0	0	0	0	19.0	24	91	15	14	2	2	1	1	11	0	10	1	0
Stein, Blake, Akron	0	1	.000	27.00	2	0	0	0	0	0	2.2	6	18	8	8	1	1	0	0	4	0	4	0	0
Wilson, Mike, Reading	2	2	.500	3.93	9	6	0	0	0	0	34.1	35	154	20	15	6	1	2	5	20	0	18	1	0
Wilson, Mike, Norwich	1	0	1.000	7.50	2	2	0	0	0	0	6.0	10	28	5	5	1	0	0	0	1	0	5	0	0

COMBINATION SHUTOUTS: Akron (9)—Guthrie-Betancourt-Larson, Cabrera-Myette-Vargas, Denney-Wohlers-Cressend, Evans-Tadano-Larson, Evans-Alvarez, Lee-Tadano, Durbin-Alvarez, Evans-Robbins-Pennington, Rayborn-Tadano-Cabrera. Altoona (9)—Jacobsen-Borner, Jacobsen-Guy-Palma-Bennett, Fordham-McDade, Bennett-McDade, Bennett-Johnston-Ozias, Fordham-Ozias, Burnett-Ozias, Connolly-McDade-Ozias, Oquendo-Johnston. Binghamton (11)—Joseph-Cammack-Bevis, Keppel-Saenz-Lavigne, Seibel-Elliott-Hee-Mattioni, Keppel-Saenz, Hee-Moreno-Bevis, Seibel-Lavigne, Musser-Bevis, Mattox-Mattioni-Bevis, Mattox-Bevis, Musser-Saenz, Cole-Bevis. Bowie (12)—Riley-Parrish, Riley-Forystek-Rodriguez, Paradis-Parrish-Rakers, Sequea-Rodriguez-Rakers, Forystek-Borkowski-Parrish-Rakers, Forystek-Sequea-Rodriguez, Riley-Rodriguez, Rijo-Parrish-Rodriguez, Paradis-Ormond-Rodriguez, Wilson-Agamennone-Rodriguez, Drumright-Ormond-Corcoran, Crouthers-Wilson-Corcoran. Erie (7)—Larrison-Spiegel, Ahearne-Johnson-Schmack, Farnsworth-Rivera-Cordova, Henkel-Rivera, Baugh-Pearson-Schmack, Van Hekken-Birtwell-Schmack, Larrison-Cordova-Johnson. Harrisburg (7)—Song-Bentz-Ferrari, Vargas-Collins-Bentz-Ferrari-Casadiego-Dequin, Crumpton-Collins-Bentz, Mata-Bentz, Maust-Schroeder-Bentz, Young-Corcoran, Maust-Bentz. New Britain (7)—Carnes-Hodge-Flohr-Kemp, Schoening-Hodge, Bonilla-Crain, Schoening-Hoard, Hoard-Pridie-Hodge, Estrada-Neshek, Bonilla-Pridie. New Haven (5)—Arnold-Gassner-Ogiltree, Reimers-Peterson, McGowan-Markwell, Bush-Wiggins-DeJong, Gassner-Wiggins-Jackson. Norwich (6)—Lowry-Correia-Montgomery, Lowry-Montgomery, Taschner-Spiehs, Lowry-Spiehs-Wade, Lowry-Walk, Clark-Walk. Portland (5)—Elmore-Weathersby-Martinez, Cameron-Miniel-Johnson, DeLaRosa-Johnson-Martinez, Herndon-Shibilo, Zink-Johnson. Reading (3)—Lee-Brooks-Hernandez, Lee-Giese, Franco-Gien-Hernandez.

NO-HIT GAMES: Song, Harrisburg, defeated Erie, 2-1, April 28; Keppel, Binghamton, defeated Portland, 3-0, August 2; Estrada, New Britain, defeated Reading, 10-0, August 24.

2003 FIELDING

TEAM

Team	G	PO	A	E	TC	DP	TP	PB	Pct.
Reading	142	3720	1361	111	5192	111	0	25	.979
Altoona	141	3722	1558	128	5408	135	0	6	.976
New Britain	141	3624	1410	123	5157	123	0	10	.976
Norwich	141	3559	1410	133	5102	146	0	13	.974
Trenton	141	3568	1424	134	5126	139	0	18	.974
Harrisburg	142	3703	1421	136	5260	127	0	13	.974
Erie	142	3700	1626	140	5466	165	0	16	.974
New Haven	142	3665	1535	137	5337	129	0	16	.974
Bowie	142	3643	1415	139	5197	121	0	19	.973
Binghamton	141	3584	1498	151	5233	142	0	17	.971
Portland	142	3637	1396	152	5185	139	0	13	.971
Akron	141	3715	1384	164	5263	109	0	16	.969

INDIVIDUAL

FIRST BASEMEN

NOTE: All caps denotes fielding-percentage leader based on 72 games for catchers, 96 for all other non-pitchers and 115 innings for pitchers. *Throws lefthanded.

Player, Team	Pct.	G	PO	A	E	TC	DP
Bailey, Jeff, Harrisburg	.988	31	247	8	3	258	24
Balfe, Ryan, Harrisburg	1.000	1	5	0	0	5	0
Bates, Fletcher, Bowie	.962	4	24	1	1	26	1
Brazell, Craig, Binghamton	.989	108	895	78	11	984	104
Brisson, Dustin, Portland	.989	40	329	17	4	350	32
Broadway, Larry, Harrisburg *	.988	20	153	11	2	166	19
Calabrese, Tony, Binghamton	.971	5	28	5	1	34	5
Cervenak, Mike, Norwich	.988	50	371	24	5	400	50
Chiaffredo, Paul, New Haven	1.000	1	1	1	0	2	0
Christensen, Mike, New Britain	.969	3	28	3	1	32	2
Coquillette, Trace, Portland	1.000	3	20	1	0	21	0
Crozier, Eric, Akron *	.986	100	771	66	12	849	62
Curry, Chris, Norwich	1.000	7	57	5	0	62	8
Daigle, Leo, Erie	.991	90	832	46	8	886	92
Davis, Glenn, Harrisburg *	.995	73	568	62	3	633	57
DEARDORFF, JEFF, New Britain	.993	98	791	64	6	861	81
Deschaine, Jim, N.H.-Reading	.987	13	69	5	1	75	7
Deschenes, Pat, Binghamton	1.000	3	11	0	0	11	0
Diaz, Juan, Bowie	.985	40	322	16	5	343	31
Dominique, Andy, Portland	.981	12	93	10	2	105	3
Espy, Nate, Reading	.994	88	611	54	4	669	52
Fagan, Shawn, New Haven	.986	44	385	27	6	418	37
Freire, Alejandro, Norwich	.991	87	687	43	7	737	75
Gonzalez, Luis, Akron	.995	43	362	27	2	391	34
Gredvig, Doug, Bowie	.990	23	181	11	2	194	18
Grindell, Nate, Akron	.889	2	7	1	1	9	1
Headley, Justin, Portland *	.992	44	331	21	3	355	42
Jacobs, Mike, Binghamton	1.000	6	53	4	0	57	5
Johnson, Nick, Trenton *	1.000	4	43	3	0	46	7
Kapler, Gabe, Portland	1.000	1	2	0	0	2	0
Keene, Kurt, New Haven	1.000	2	12	1	0	13	3
Kelly, Donald, Erie	1.000	1	7	0	0	7	1
Lane, Rich, Harrisburg *	.995	23	184	15	1	200	15
Logan, Matt, New Haven	.994	86	732	54	5	791	65
Luderer, Brian, Akron	1.000	1	3	0	0	3	0
McGowan, Sean, Portland	.981	50	387	33	8	428	50
McNeal, Aaron, Reading	.991	68	525	44	5	574	51
Morneau, Justin, New Britain	1.000	20	157	26	0	183	12
Munoz, Billy, Erie *	.986	60	504	45	8	557	58
Navarrete, Ray, Altoona	1.000	6	40	5	0	45	7
Nicholson, Derek, Erie	1.000	2	7	2	0	9	0
Nunnari, Talmadge, Harrisburg *	.947	2	15	3	1	19	0
Nye, Rodney, Binghamton	1.000	8	46	5	0	51	6
O'Sullivan, Patrick, Bowie	1.000	4	34	0	0	34	2
Owens, Ryan, New Britain	.984	17	109	13	2	124	11
Perry, Chan, Altoona	.992	53	435	34	4	473	35
Pond, Simon, New Haven	1.000	6	42	6	0	48	4
Pressley, Josh, Binghamton	.985	17	122	7	2	131	12
Rifkin, Aaron, Trenton *	.989	128	1034	84	12	1130	116
Rios, Brian, Bowie	1.000	1	10	0	0	10	1
Robinson, Bo, Trenton	1.000	10	64	9	0	73	7
Roneberg, Brett, Altoona *	.988	70	611	55	8	674	72
Sasser, Rob, Bowie	1.000	3	23	2	0	25	1
Schrager, Tony, Portland	1.000	1	1	1	0	2	0
Shelton, Chris, Altoona	.995	22	166	29	1	196	13
Tiffee, Terry, New Britain	.972	8	58	12	2	72	8
Velazquez, Gil, Binghamton	1.000	2	4	0	0	4	0
Wilken, Kris, Bowie	.993	66	545	38	4	587	54
Wright, Ron, Akron	1.000	2	12	0	0	12	1

FIRST BASEMEN WITH TWO OR MORE TEAMS

Player, Team	Pct.	G	PO	A	E	TC	DP
Deschaine, Jim, New Haven	.986	12	68	5	1	74	7
Deschaine, Jim, Reading	1.000	1	1	0	0	1	0

SECOND BASEMEN

Player, Team	Pct.	G	PO	A	E	TC	DP
Alviso, Jerome, Bowie	1.000	1	2	7	0	9	0
Athas, Jamie, Norwich	1.000	1	1	0	0	1	0
Bacani, David, Binghamton	.981	32	43	63	2	108	16
Basak, Chris, Binghamton	.923	3	5	7	1	13	3
Bautista, Rayner, Erie	1.000	2	3	3	0	6	3
Blasi, Blake, Portland	1.000	4	8	6	0	14	2
Bonifay, Josh, Altoona	.833	1	2	3	1	6	1

Player, Team	Pct.	G	PO	A	E	TC	DP
Bozanich, Sam, Trenton	.953	26	35	47	4	86	9
Calabrese, Tony, Binghamton	.972	10	14	21	1	36	5
Cannizaro, Andy, Trenton	.971	43	91	113	6	210	42
Cano, Robinson, Trenton	.977	44	100	108	5	213	33
Carroll, Wes, Harrisburg	1.000	5	3	9	0	12	2
Caruso, Joe, Altoona	.961	20	32	66	4	102	16
Casillas, Uriel, Reading	.973	25	42	66	3	111	7
Castillo, Jose, Altoona	.973	74	170	185	10	365	56
Cates, Gary, Bowie	1.000	1	0	5	0	5	0
Connacher, Kevin, New Britain	1.000	4	7	7	0	14	2
Coquillette, Trace, Portland	.980	24	40	59	2	101	18
Cotto, Luis, Akron	.857	1	2	4	1	7	0
Davidson, Seth, New Britain	1.000	11	12	27	0	39	9
De Renne, Keoni, Trenton	1.000	3	3	6	0	9	2
Del Rosario, Manny, Bowie	.944	3	6	11	1	18	2
Diaz, Victor, Binghamton	.968	43	80	104	6	190	30
Escalona, Felix, Bowie	1.000	1	1	3	0	4	1
Fontenot, Mike, Bowie	.968	114	226	317	18	561	69
Garcia, Daniel, Binghamton	.967	29	58	58	4	120	18
Goelz, Jim, Akron-Portland	1.000	11	18	22	0	40	5
Gonzalez, Luis, Akron	.977	32	57	71	3	131	17
Gutierrez, Vic, Harrisburg	.957	16	37	30	3	70	7
Hairston, Jerry, Bowie	.941	4	5	11	1	17	1
Hall, Noah, Harrisburg	.889	3	5	3	1	9	0
Hannahan, Buzz, Reading	.991	27	51	57	1	109	13
Hitchcox, Brian, Reading	.986	89	195	218	6	419	54
Hoffpauir, Josh, Bowie	.977	22	33	53	2	88	10
Inglett, Joe, Akron	.966	66	112	172	10	294	33
Izturis, Maicer, Akron	.951	41	66	110	9	185	19
Jester, Joe, Norwich	.962	38	78	98	7	183	22
Keene, Kurt, New Haven	.973	18	37	36	2	75	9
LaBarbera, Anthony, Norwich	.882	4	7	8	2	17	4
Lemonis, Chris, Bowie	1.000	2	3	5	0	8	2
Leon, Carlos, Portland	.956	70	119	166	13	298	46
Lorenzo, Juan, New Britain	.902	12	18	19	4	41	4
Luna, Hector, Akron	1.000	1	2	3	0	5	0
Machado, Albenis, Harrisburg	.929	6	8	18	2	28	3
Maule, Jason, Trenton	.908	14	35	34	7	76	7
McKinley, Josh, Harrisburg	.967	119	255	325	20	600	76
Mendoza, Carlos, Norwich	.992	29	48	69	1	118	17
Myrow, Brian, Trenton	.956	24	45	63	5	113	11
Navarrete, Ray, Altoona	.989	45	77	111	2	190	20
Nicholson, Kevin, Altoona	.978	11	13	31	1	45	6
Nieves, Raul, Portland	.961	12	16	33	2	51	9
Owens, Ryan, New Britain	.987	40	62	94	2	158	23
Pecci, Jay, Norwich	.975	33	69	88	4	161	19
Perez, Jhonny, Erie	1.000	3	7	11	0	18	1
Pernalete, Marco, Norwich	.976	9	21	19	1	41	6
Renick, Josh, New Britain	.970	85	156	196	11	363	43
Rich, Dominic, New Haven	.981	101	214	289	10	513	75
Schrager, Tony, Portland	.950	37	63	90	8	161	20
Sequea, Jorge, New Haven	.981	11	19	34	1	54	7
Shipp, Brian, Binghamton	.952	28	35	64	5	104	18
Skrehot, Shaun, Altoona	1.000	5	5	9	0	14	2
Solano, Danny, New Haven	.989	17	35	54	1	90	14
Soler, Ramon, Norwich	.987	35	69	85	2	156	35
Thrower, Jake, Harrisburg	1.000	1	2	1	0	3	1
TOUSA, SCOTT, Erie	.986	129	265	388	9	662	118
Ust, Brant, Erie	.981	13	17	35	1	53	8
Velazquez, Gil, Binghamton	1.000	13	12	27	0	39	7
Youngbauer, Scott, Reading	.957	16	19	26	2	47	4

SECOND BASEMEN WITH TWO OR MORE TEAMS

Player, Team	Pct.	G	PO	A	E	TC	DP
Goelz, Jim, Akron	1.000	2	3	4	0	7	0
Goelz, Jim, Portland	1.000	9	15	18	0	33	5

THIRD BASEMEN

Player, Team	Pct.	G	PO	A	E	TC	DP
Alviso, Jerome, Bowie	1.000	1	0	2	0	2	0
Bacani, David, Binghamton	.833	4	0	5	1	6	0
Bailey, Jeff, Harrisburg	.923	5	2	10	1	13	1
Balfe, Ryan, Harrisburg	.875	4	3	4	1	8	0
Calabrese, Tony, Binghamton	1.000	4	1	7	0	8	0
Calzado, Napoleon, Bowie	.950	36	25	70	5	100	8
Carroll, Wes, Harrisburg	1.000	1	3	2	0	5	1
Caruso, Joe, Altoona	.964	42	26	80	4	110	7
Casillas, Uriel, Reading	.940	26	22	41	4	67	6
Cates, Gary, Bowie	1.000	1	1	5	0	6	0
Cervenak, Mike, Norwich	.944	83	53	149	12	214	18
Christensen, Mike, New Britain	.000	1	0	0	0	0	0
Coffie, Ivanon, Bowie	.951	82	43	151	10	204	14
De Renne, Keoni, Trenton	1.000	9	3	12	0	15	1
Deardorff, Jeff, New Britain	.947	10	3	15	1	19	4
Deschaine, Jim, N.H.-Reading	.914	51	38	57	9	104	5
Deschenes, Pat, Binghamton	.857	6	4	2	1	7	1
Diaz, Felix, Harrisburg	.874	50	21	83	15	119	7
Erickson, Corey, Norwich	.895	15	11	23	4	38	1
Fagan, Shawn, New Haven	.915	31	20	55	7	82	4
Goelz, Jim, Portland	1.000	3	1	2	0	3	2
Gonzalez, Luis, Akron	.871	12	9	18	4	31	1
Grindell, Nate, Akron	.950	11	3	16	1	20	2
Gutierrez, Vic, Harrisburg	.921	53	38	67	9	114	9
Hannahan, Buzz, Reading	.950	13	12	7	1	20	2
Hannahan, Jack, Erie	.928	132	103	334	34	471	41
Hattig, John, Portland	.875	8	7	14	3	24	2
Haverbusch, Kevin, Portland	.818	3	4	5	2	11	0
Keene, Kurt, New Haven	.929	22	9	56	5	70	1
Lemonis, Chris, Bowie	.800	2	1	3	1	5	0
Logan, Matt, New Haven	1.000	1	0	1	0	1	1
Lorenzo, Juan, New Britain	.800	12	3	9	3	15	0
Machado, Albenis, Harrisburg	.963	35	26	52	3	81	7
McKinley, Josh, Harrisburg	1.000	2	0	4	0	4	0
Mendez, Deivi, Trenton	1.000	2	0	3	0	3	0
Mendoza, Carlos, Norwich	.951	18	3	36	2	41	1
Myrow, Brian, Trenton	.891	86	50	129	22	201	14
Navarrete, Ray, Altoona	.971	29	20	47	2	69	6
Nicholson, Kevin, Altoona	.934	81	40	173	15	228	17
Nye, Rodney, Binghamton	.935	130	85	276	25	386	30
Otanez, Willis, Bowie	1.000	1	1	0	0	1	0
Perez, Jhonny, Erie	.857	4	1	5	1	7	0
Pernalete, Marco, Norwich	.927	29	24	52	6	82	4
Pond, Simon, New Haven	.890	53	34	127	20	181	12
Richardson, Juan, Reading	.916	63	63	112	16	191	11
Robinson, Bo, Trenton	.981	52	27	75	2	104	7
Romprey, Ed, Erie	.857	5	1	5	1	7	1
Sasser, Rob, Bowie	1.000	3	0	6	0	6	1
Schrager, Tony, Portland	.913	37	33	72	10	115	8
Sequea, Jorge, New Haven	.875	8	3	11	2	16	1
Shipp, Brian, Binghamton	.857	7	1	11	2	14	1
Smith, Corey, Akron	.865	122	77	204	44	325	9
Solano, Danny, New Haven	.978	34	17	71	2	90	9
Thrower, Jake, Harrisburg	1.000	7	4	10	0	14	0
TIFFEE, TERRY, New Britain	.947	126	89	252	19	360	28
Ust, Brant, Erie	.947	5	0	18	1	19	2
Velazquez, Gil, Binghamton	1.000	4	1	9	0	10	1
Wilken, Kris, Bowie	.852	21	12	34	8	54	2
Youkilis, Kevin, Portland	.925	93	66	182	20	268	19

THIRD BASEMEN WITH TWO OR MORE TEAMS

Player, Team	Pct.	G	PO	A	E	TC	DP
Deschaine, Jim, Reading	.912	50	36	57	9	102	5
Deschaine, Jim, New Haven	1.000	1	2	0	0	2	0

SHORTSTOPS

Player, Team	Pct.	G	PO	A	E	TC	DP
Adams, Russ, New Haven	.944	64	95	175	16	286	36
Alviso, Jerome, Bowie	.889	7	8	16	3	27	3
Athas, Jamie, Norwich	.938	127	210	365	38	613	101
Bacani, David, Binghamton	.800	5	0	4	1	5	0
BARTLETT, JASON, New Britain	.969	139	249	380	20	649	74
Basak, Chris, Binghamton	.969	112	160	306	15	481	75
Bautista, Rayner, Erie	.954	107	140	300	21	461	69
Borowiak, Zachary, Portland	.842	3	5	11	3	19	4
Calabrese, Tony, Binghamton	.944	8	6	11	1	18	1
Calzado, Napoleon, Bowie	.833	1	2	3	1	6	0
Cannizaro, Andy, Trenton	.959	65	81	179	11	271	36
Cano, Robinson, Trenton	1.000	1	0	1	0	1	0
Caruso, Joe, Altoona	.833	5	2	3	1	6	0
Casillas, Uriel, Reading	.913	8	8	13	2	23	2
Castillo, Jose, Altoona	.949	52	82	162	13	257	40
Castro, Nelson, Portland	.924	15	23	38	5	66	10
Cates, Gary, Bowie	.882	9	5	10	2	17	2
Coffie, Ivanon, Bowie	.978	10	14	30	1	45	4
Coquillette, Trace, Portland	.889	5	2	6	1	9	0
De Renne, Keoni, Trenton	.962	15	18	32	2	52	7
Del Rosario, Manny, Bowie	.917	6	4	7	1	12	1
Goelz, Jim, Akron-Portland	.969	28	33	62	3	98	13
Gonzalez, Luis, Akron	1.000	6	8	15	0	23	3
Gutierrez, Vic, Harrisburg	.931	12	11	16	2	29	2
Hammond, Joey, Bowie	.961	18	22	51	3	76	10
Hannahan, Buzz, Reading	1.000	19	25	43	0	68	9
Hoffpauir, Josh, Bowie	.000	1	0	0	1	1	0
Izturis, Maicer, Akron	.921	9	15	20	3	38	0
Jeter, Derek, Trenton	.957	5	9	13	1	23	5
Keene, Kurt, New Haven	1.000	1	2	1	0	3	0
Kelly, Donald, Erie	.959	20	28	66	4	98	14
LaBarbera, Anthony, Norwich	.917	4	3	8	1	12	2

Player, Team	Pct.	G	PO	A	E	TC	DP
Labandeira, John, Harrisburg	.953	60	91	175	13	279	34
Leon, Carlos, Portland	1.000	3	0	1	0	1	0
Lorenzo, Juan, New Britain	1.000	3	5	6	0	11	3
Luna, Hector, Akron	.935	126	188	319	35	542	73
Machado, Albenis, Harrisburg	.975	69	100	209	8	317	49
Machado, Andy, Reading	.951	122	186	318	26	530	60
Mendez, Deivi, Trenton	.800	3	0	4	1	5	0
Mendoza, Carlos, Norwich	.956	12	18	25	2	45	3
Navarrete, Ray, Altoona	.000	1	0	0	0	0	0
Nicholson, Kevin, Altoona	.976	10	13	27	1	41	4
Nieves, Raul, Portland	.974	60	98	162	7	267	44
Olivares, Teuris, Trenton	.963	64	110	201	12	323	55
Perez, Jhonny, Erie	.909	5	4	16	2	22	2
Pernalete, Marco, Norwich	1.000	1	3	2	0	5	1
Rogers, Ed, Bowie	.957	97	139	242	17	398	58
Romprey, Ed, Erie	.955	5	10	11	1	22	8
Sanchez, Rey, Binghamton	.900	3	6	3	1	10	1
Schrager, Tony, Portland	.959	43	61	102	7	170	18
Sequea, Jorge, New Haven	.911	13	14	27	4	45	7
Shier, Peter, Bowie	1.000	1	0	5	0	5	1
Skrehot, Shaun, Altoona	.972	81	115	228	10	353	44
Smith, Corey, Akron	.000	1	0	0	1	1	0
Solano, Danny, New Haven	.961	69	98	225	13	336	43
Thrower, Jake, Harrisburg	.957	8	6	16	1	23	2
Ust, Brant, Erie	.911	14	16	35	5	56	9
Velazquez, Gil, Binghamton	.956	32	47	84	6	137	19

SHORTSTOPS WITH TWO OR MORE TEAMS

Player, Team	Pct.	G	PO	A	E	TC	DP
Goelz, Jim, Akron	1.000	1	1	4	0	5	1
Goelz, Jim, Portland	.968	27	32	58	3	93	12

OUTFIELDERS

Player, Team	Pct.	G	PO	A	E	TC	DP
Acuna, Ron, Binghamton	.986	124	256	21	4	281	4
Airoso, Kurt, Bowie	.971	40	65	1	2	68	0
Asche, Kirk, Binghamton	1.000	9	12	0	0	12	0
Bailey, Jeff, Harrisburg	.977	23	41	2	1	44	0
Balfe, Ryan, Harrisburg	1.000	2	1	0	0	1	0
Barker, Glen, Bowie	1.000	18	33	3	0	36	0
Barns, B.J., Altoona *	.933	13	14	0	1	15	0
Baron, Brian, New Britain	.982	37	53	3	1	57	0
Bates, Fletcher, Bowie	.923	10	11	1	1	13	0
Bonifay, Josh, Altoona	.964	103	155	7	6	168	1
Brown, Andy, Trenton *	.975	17	37	2	1	40	0
Brown, Tonayne, Portland-Erie *	.983	125	221	4	4	229	1
Burnitz, Jeromy, Binghamton	1.000	3	2	1	0	3	0
Byrd, Marlon, Reading	.800	3	4	0	1	5	0
Calabrese, Tony, Binghamton	.947	10	18	0	1	19	0
Calzado, Napoleon, Bowie	1.000	2	5	0	0	5	0
Camilo, Juan, Reading	1.000	20	37	0	0	37	0
Carroll, Wes, Harrisburg	1.000	1	2	0	0	2	0
Caruso, Joe, Altoona	1.000	10	14	0	0	14	0
Casillas, Uriel, Reading	1.000	7	8	0	0	8	0
Catalanotte, Greg, Portland	.971	20	31	2	1	34	1
Cates, Gary, Bowie	1.000	8	9	0	0	9	0
Chevalier, Virgil, Binghamton	.977	50	81	4	2	87	0
Church, Ryan, Akron *	.977	98	245	11	6	262	2
Clark, Doug, Norwich	1.000	89	194	9	0	203	1
Coquillette, Trace, Portland	1.000	14	22	0	0	22	0
Corr, Frank, Binghamton	.949	48	85	8	5	98	1
Crozier, Eric, Akron *	1.000	2	3	0	0	3	0
Curry, Chris, Norwich	.000	1	0	0	0	0	0
De Renne, Keoni, Trenton	1.000	3	7	0	0	7	0
Deschaine, Jim, Reading	1.000	11	12	1	0	13	0
Deschenes, Pat, Binghamton	1.000	6	3	0	0	3	0
Diaz, Felix, Harrisburg	.000	1	0	0	0	0	0
Duffy, Chris, Altoona *	.987	135	305	8	4	317	1
Duncan, Jeff, Binghamton *	.987	76	150	6	2	158	1
Espy, Nate, Reading	.000	1	0	0	0	0	0
Fagan, Shawn, New Haven	.962	14	23	2	1	26	0
Foster, Quincy, Harrisburg	.973	62	104	5	3	112	0
Freire, Alejandro, Norwich	1.000	3	1	0	0	1	0
Garbe, B.J., New Britain	.995	66	201	3	1	205	0
Garrett, Shawn, Altoona	.979	120	229	6	5	240	4
Gingrich, Troy, Harrisburg *	.935	19	28	1	2	31	0
Godwin, Tyrell, New Haven	.940	32	46	1	3	50	0
Goelz, Jim, Akron-Portland	.919	21	33	1	3	37	0
Gonzalez, Luis, Akron	1.000	15	21	1	0	22	0
Griffin, John-Ford, New Haven *	.977	66	125	3	3	131	0
Grindell, Nate, Akron	.974	21	33	4	1	38	0
Gross, Gabe, New Haven	.980	77	139	10	3	152	2
Grove, Jason, Trenton *	1.000	23	34	1	0	35	0
Gutierrez, Vic, Harrisburg	.800	4	3	1	1	5	0
Hall, Noah, Harrisburg	.989	120	253	5	3	261	1
Hallmark, Pat, Norwich	.985	134	326	7	5	338	1
Hannahan, Buzz, Reading	.993	64	135	8	1	144	0
Haverbusch, Kevin, Portland	1.000	36	63	2	0	65	0
Headley, Justin, Portland *	1.000	27	45	3	0	48	0
Hoffpauir, Josh, Bowie	.977	66	123	4	3	130	0
Inglett, Joe, Akron	1.000	2	2	0	0	2	0
INGLIN, JEFF, Reading	1.000	122	249	12	0	261	1
Jones, Mitch, Trenton	.991	116	209	9	2	220	2
Kapler, Gabe, Portland	1.000	1	2	0	0	2	0
Keene, Kurt, New Haven	1.000	3	2	1	0	3	0
Knoedler, Jason, Erie	1.000	5	8	0	0	8	0
Kropf, Andy, Erie	.000	2	0	0	0	0	0
Lane, Rich, Harrisburg *	1.000	18	31	1	0	32	0
Lemonis, Chris, Bowie	1.000	1	1	0	0	1	0
Littleton, Brandon, Bowie *	.978	45	90	1	2	93	0
Logan, Matt, New Haven	.000	1	0	0	0	0	0
Logan, Nook, Erie	.991	134	340	9	3	352	2
Mack, Tony, Bowie	1.000	21	45	1	0	46	0
Maddox, Garry, Reading	1.000	46	123	4	0	127	0
Magruder, Chris, Akron	1.000	1	5	0	0	5	0
Maule, Jason, Trenton	.941	24	32	0	2	34	0
McGowan, Sean, Portland	1.000	12	11	3	0	14	0
Minges, Tyler, Akron	.979	118	268	18	6	292	5
Mora, Melvin, Bowie	1.000	6	10	0	0	10	0
Munoz, Billy, Erie *	1.000	2	2	0	0	2	0
Myrow, Brian, Trenton	.972	16	32	3	1	36	0
Nathans, John, Portland	1.000	1	1	0	0	1	0
Nicholson, Derek, Erie	.952	59	96	4	5	105	0
Nonemaker, Karl, Reading *	1.000	12	30	0	0	30	0
Nunnari, Talmadge, Harrisburg *	.933	8	14	0	1	15	0
Otanez, Willis, Bowie	1.000	1	1	0	0	1	0
Owens, Jeremy, Portland	.976	136	352	10	9	371	1
Owens, Ryan, New Britain	.951	24	37	2	2	41	0
Pachot, John, Norwich	.000	1	0	0	0	0	0
Padilla, Jorge, Reading	.990	44	94	2	1	97	0
Panther, Nathan, Akron *	1.000	2	6	1	0	7	0
Patrick, Brian, New Haven	.765	11	12	1	4	17	0
Perez, Jhonny, Erie	1.000	7	12	0	0	12	0
Perez, Josue, Reading	.981	48	100	5	2	107	1
Pernalete, Marco, Norwich	.944	6	17	0	1	18	0
Pressley, Josh, Binghamton	.833	9	5	0	1	6	0
Rabe, Josh, New Britain	.982	94	221	3	4	228	0
Raines, Tim, Bowie	.976	56	120	3	3	126	0
Reed, Keith, Bowie	.979	112	224	11	5	240	3
Reese, Kevin, Trenton *	.980	82	191	3	4	198	0
Requena, Alex, Akron	.984	35	57	3	1	61	2
Richardson, Corey, Erie	.987	44	75	2	1	78	0
Rios, Alexis, New Haven	.990	123	277	8	3	288	1
Rios, Brian, Bowie	1.000	3	8	0	0	8	0
Rivera, Ruben, Bowie	1.000	37	86	6	0	92	1
Romero, Willie, Bowie	1.000	20	34	1	0	35	0
Romprey, Ed, Erie	.000	1	0	0	0	0	0
Roneberg, Brett, Altoona *	.989	49	83	7	1	91	1
Ruiz, Carlos, Reading	1.000	2	1	1	0	2	0
Sadler, Ray, Altoona	1.000	13	29	2	0	31	0
Sanders, Anthony, New Haven	1.000	25	47	2	0	49	0
Sasser, Rob, Bowie	1.000	4	5	1	0	6	0
Scanlon, Matt, New Britain	.965	81	135	3	5	143	0
Scott, Luke, Akron	.947	17	34	2	2	38	0
Seale, Marvin, Binghamton	.975	113	181	11	5	197	1
Shabala, Adam, Norwich	.990	129	283	16	3	302	4
Sherrod, Justin, Portland	.973	123	235	17	7	259	5
Singleton, Justin, New Haven	.953	72	114	7	6	127	2
Sitzman, Jay, Reading *	.975	67	152	5	4	161	2
Sizemore, Grady, Akron *	.986	125	283	6	4	293	0
Skrehot, Shaun, Altoona	1.000	1	1	0	0	1	0
Solano, Danny, New Haven	1.000	1	1	0	0	1	0
Soler, Ramon, Norwich	1.000	3	3	0	0	3	0
Thompson, Kevin, Trenton	.963	84	151	6	6	163	0
Thompson, Rich, New Haven	.952	29	56	4	3	63	1
Thrower, Jake, Harrisburg	1.000	1	1	0	0	1	0
Tucker, Mamon, Reading	1.000	9	16	2	0	18	1
Urquhart, Derick, Harrisburg *	1.000	2	3	0	0	3	0
Ust, Brant, Erie	1.000	8	10	0	0	10	0
Valderrama, Carlos, Norwich	.983	64	115	2	2	119	0
Varner, Noochie, Erie	1.000	44	80	6	0	86	1
Vento, Mike, Trenton	.966	69	138	5	5	148	2
Walker, Matt, Erie	.974	75	147	3	4	154	0
Ware, Jeremy, Harrisburg	.994	60	148	6	1	155	3
Watson, Brandon, Harrisburg	.983	139	389	8	7	404	2
Watson, Matt, Binghamton	1.000	6	8	0	0	8	0
West, Kevin, New Britain	.964	135	283	13	11	307	4
Wilken, Kris, Bowie	1.000	7	11	0	0	11	0
Williams, Bernie, Trenton	1.000	4	6	0	0	6	0

OUTFIELDERS WITH TWO OR MORE TEAMS

Player, Team	Pct.	G	PO	A	E	TC	DP
Brown, Tonayne, Portland *	.969	53	93	0	3	96	0
Brown, Tonayne, Erie *	.992	72	128	4	1	133	1
Goelz, Jim, Akron	1.000	2	1	0	0	1	0
Goelz, Jim, Portland	.917	19	32	1	3	36	0

CATCHERS

Player, Team	Pct.	G	PO	A	E	TC	DP	PB
Ackerman, Scott, Harrisburg	.994	77	416	53	3	472	7	8
Avila, Rob, Reading	.980	10	45	5	1	51	1	0
Bailey, Jeff, Harrisburg	.981	28	141	11	3	155	0	3
Balfe, Ryan, Harrisburg	1.000	8	34	1	0	35	0	1
Boone, Doug, Trenton	1.000	4	12	0	0	12	0	0
Bowen, Rob, New Britain	.992	41	222	28	2	252	3	5
Brown, Jason, Harrisburg	.962	13	92	8	4	104	1	0
Cano, Robinson, Trenton	1.000	1	1	0	0	1	0	0
Chauncey, Clinton, Akron	1.000	5	26	2	0	28	0	0
Chevalier, Virgil, Binghamton	1.000	3	6	0	0	6	0	0
Chiaffredo, Paul, New Haven	1.000	38	233	16	0	249	1	4
Cruz, Edgar, Reading	.990	61	360	42	4	406	1	15
Curry, Chris, Norwich	.970	59	326	34	11	371	2	5
Dominique, Andy, Portland	.986	10	64	4	1	69	0	1
Fernandez, Alejandro, Trenton	1.000	4	3	0	0	3	0	0
Fuentes, Omar, Trenton	.988	75	449	52	6	507	3	9
Gulledge, Kelley, New Britain	.975	25	147	10	4	161	1	1
Heintz, Chris, Altoona	.991	76	508	37	5	550	0	3
Hietpas, Joe, Binghamton	1.000	5	26	2	0	28	0	1
House, J.R., Altoona	.983	9	57	0	1	58	0	1
Huber, Justin, Binghamton	.979	43	259	23	6	288	4	5
Jacobs, Mike, Binghamton	.986	65	449	34	7	490	1	6
Jacobson, Russ, Reading	.986	32	201	18	3	222	1	4
Kratz, Erik, New Haven	1.000	1	5	1	0	6	0	0
Kropf, Andy, Erie	.980	12	46	2	1	49	0	3
Loyd, Brian, Portland	.994	26	161	8	1	170	2	6
LUDERER, BRIAN, Akron	.996	73	462	41	2	505	5	11
Martinez, Octavio, Bowie	1.000	3	13	3	0	16	0	1
Martinez, Victor, Akron	1.000	1	5	0	0	5	0	0
Mauer, Joe, New Britain	.992	60	351	29	3	383	3	2
Molina, Izzy, Bowie	1.000	2	14	0	0	14	0	0
Nathans, John, Portland	.991	22	104	6	1	111	0	1
Navarro, Dioner, Trenton	.986	41	260	23	4	287	3	3
Pachot, John, Norwich	.993	85	494	66	4	564	6	8
Parrish, Dave, Trenton	.991	30	189	29	2	220	2	6
Paulino, Ronny, Altoona	.988	43	285	35	4	324	1	2
Quiroz, Guillermo, New Haven	.994	100	605	57	4	666	6	10
Ramos, Kelly, Bowie	.982	29	199	21	4	224	2	1
Ruiz, Carlos, Reading	.994	49	279	33	2	314	1	6
Sandusky, Scott, Harrisburg	.987	23	140	7	2	149	0	1
Seestedt, Mike, Bowie	.996	45	254	24	1	279	1	3
Shelton, Chris, Altoona	.987	10	66	8	1	75	0	0
Shoppach, Kelly, Portland	.982	82	547	64	11	622	8	3
Smith, Jeff, Portland	1.000	10	53	3	0	56	0	2
Snusz, Chris, Altoona	1.000	6	29	9	0	38	1	0
St. Pierre, Maxim, Erie	.984	104	545	76	10	631	7	5
Taveras, Luis, Erie	.981	35	193	18	4	215	2	8
Torres, Gabby, New Britain	.993	24	131	3	1	135	0	2
Umbria, Jose, New Haven	.981	7	45	8	1	54	0	1
Ust, Brant, Erie	1.000	1	1	0	0	1	0	0
Valencia, Vic, Akron	.994	57	441	30	3	474	3	5
Wathan, Dusty, Akron	1.000	9	59	9	0	68	1	0
Whiteside, Eli, Bowie	.989	78	489	55	6	550	8	14
Whittaker, Tim, New Haven	1.000	4	16	2	0	18	2	1
Wilson, John, Binghamton	.985	41	240	24	4	268	0	5

PITCHERS

Player, Team	Pct.	G	PO	A	E	TC	DP
Abbott, David, New Haven	.000	3	0	0	0	0	0
Abbott, Jim, New Britain	1.000	10	5	2	0	7	0
Adams, Brian, Portland *	1.000	7	1	2	0	3	0
Adams, Daniel, Reading	1.000	10	1	6	0	7	0
Agamennone, Brandon, Bowie	1.000	29	3	5	0	8	2
Ahearne, Pat, Erie	.960	12	5	19	1	25	1
Aldred, Scott, Portland *	1.000	18	2	0	0	2	0
Alvarado, Carlo, Erie	1.000	37	6	7	0	13	0
Alvarez, Oscar, Akron *	1.000	13	0	11	0	11	0
Alviso, Jerome, Bowie	.000	1	0	0	0	0	0
Anderson, Luke, Norwich	1.000	6	0	2	0	2	0
Arnold, Jason, New Haven	.875	6	3	4	1	8	0
Baker, Chris, New Haven	1.000	25	7	19	0	26	0
Bauer, Peter, New Haven	1.000	29	5	8	0	13	0
Baugh, Kenny, Erie	.842	19	8	8	3	19	1
Beal, Andy, Trenton *	.824	17	1	13	3	17	0
Bean, Colter, Trenton	.000	3	0	0	0	0	0
Begg, Chris, Norwich	1.000	4	0	3	0	3	0
Bennett, Jeff, Altoona	.750	33	3	9	4	16	0
Bennett, Steve, Binghamton	.900	28	3	6	1	10	1
Bentz, Chad, Harrisburg *	1.000	52	5	15	0	20	0
Betancourt, Rafael, Akron	1.000	31	1	3	0	4	0
Bevis, P.J., Binghamton	.800	46	2	6	2	10	0
Billingsley, Brent, Reading *	.667	4	0	2	1	3	0
Birtwell, John, Erie	1.000	11	0	2	0	2	0
Bonifay, Josh, Altoona	.000	1	0	0	0	0	0
Bonilla, Henry, New Britain	.955	26	5	16	1	22	1
Bonser, Boof, Norwich	.960	24	7	17	1	25	2
Borkowski, Dave, Erie-Bowie	1.000	30	11	17	0	28	3
Borner, Brady, Altoona *	1.000	17	0	2	0	2	0
Brazoban, Yhency, Trenton	1.000	20	1	7	0	8	0
Brooks, Frank, Reading-Alt. *	1.000	35	0	6	0	6	1
Brown, Elliot, Norwich	1.000	4	1	3	0	4	1
Bruso, Greg, Norwich	1.000	11	3	5	0	8	1
Buchholz, Taylor, Reading	.929	25	11	15	2	28	0
Bucktrot, Keith, Reading	1.000	7	1	6	0	7	0
Burnett, Sean, Altoona *	.960	27	11	37	2	50	5
Burnside, Adrian, Erie *	.813	15	5	8	3	16	0
Bush, David, New Haven	.909	14	5	5	1	11	0
Cable, Taft, Reading	1.000	4	0	1	0	1	0
Cabrera, Fernando, Akron	.944	36	4	13	1	18	1
Cameron, Ryan, Portland	1.000	10	4	7	0	11	0
Cammack, Eric, Binghamton	.667	10	1	3	2	6	0
Camp, Shawn, Altoona	1.000	18	2	6	0	8	0
Candelario, Eddie, Trenton	.929	28	8	5	1	14	0
Carmona, Fausto, Akron	1.000	1	1	0	0	1	0
Carnes, Matt, New Britain	1.000	6	4	4	0	8	0
Carter, Ryan, Reading *	1.000	17	4	8	0	12	0
Caruso, Joe, Altoona	1.000	1	0	1	0	1	0
Casadiego, Gerardo, Harrisburg	.824	22	5	9	3	17	3
Casillas, Uriel, Reading	.000	1	0	0	0	0	0
Castellanos, Hugo, New Haven	.938	21	3	12	1	16	2
Chacin, Gustavo, New Haven *	.889	46	3	5	1	9	2
Chapman, Jake, Portland *	1.000	35	0	10	0	10	1
Chiavacci, Ron, Harrisburg	1.000	8	0	3	0	3	0
Chrysler, Clint, Altoona *	1.000	16	2	7	0	9	1
Clark, Jeff, Norwich	1.000	7	3	4	0	7	1
Cole, Joey, Binghamton	.886	25	10	21	4	35	1
Collins, Pat, Harrisburg	1.000	25	1	11	0	12	0
Connolly, Mike, Altoona *	.917	25	10	12	2	24	1
Contreras, Jose, Trenton	.000	1	0	0	0	0	0
Cooksey, Wes, Trenton	.000	3	0	0	0	0	0
Corcoran, Roy, Harrisburg	1.000	14	2	1	0	3	0
Corcoran, Tim, Bowie	1.000	26	1	1	0	2	0
Cordova, Jorge, Erie	1.000	30	4	4	0	8	0
Corona, Ronnie, New Britain	1.000	4	2	0	0	2	0
Correia, Kevin, Norwich	.923	16	8	16	2	26	1
Cox, Mike, Binghamton *	.667	11	1	1	1	3	0
Cox, Ryan, Norwich	.867	26	6	7	2	15	0
Cozier, Vance, Norwich	1.000	26	7	19	0	26	1
Crain, Jesse, New Britain	1.000	22	2	3	0	5	0
Cressend, Jack, Akron	1.000	8	1	1	0	2	0
Crouthers, Dave, Bowie	1.000	9	1	3	0	4	0
Cruceta, Francisco, Akron	.972	27	10	25	1	36	2
Crumpton, Chuck, Harrisburg	1.000	26	4	17	0	21	1
Currier, Rik, Trenton	.857	7	3	3	1	7	0
Daal, Omar, Bowie *	.000	1	0	0	0	0	0
Dawson, Layne, Reading	.923	14	6	6	1	13	2
De La Cruz, Fernando, Erie	.750	7	1	2	1	4	0
De La Rosa, Jorge, Portland *	.929	22	1	12	1	14	0
DeJong, Jordan, New Haven	1.000	27	3	4	0	7	0
Denney, Kyle, Akron	.944	18	6	11	1	18	0
Dequin, Benji, Harrisburg *	.857	22	2	10	2	14	0
Dinardo, Lenny, Binghamton *	1.000	7	5	9	0	14	0
Douglas, Shea, Akron *	.000	2	0	0	0	0	0
Drumright, Mike, Bowie	.400	6	2	0	3	5	0
Duckworth, Brandon, Reading	.000	1	0	0	0	0	0
Durbin, Chad, Akron	1.000	3	1	2	0	3	0
Durbin, J.D., New Britain	.889	14	4	20	3	27	2
Edwards, Brad, Bowie *	1.000	2	0	1	0	1	0
Elliott, Chad, Binghamton *	1.000	7	0	3	0	3	0
Elmore, Chris, Portland *	1.000	3	0	1	0	1	0
Estrada, Horacio, New Britain *	.889	5	2	6	1	9	2
Evans, Kyle, Akron	.952	28	15	25	2	42	2
Eyre, Willie, New Britain	.971	29	14	20	1	35	2
Farnsworth, Jeff, Erie	1.000	8	3	9	0	12	0
Ferrari, Anthony, Harrisburg *	1.000	14	2	0	0	2	0
Fisher, Pete, New Britain	.938	8	8	7	1	16	0
Flohr, Adam, New Britain *	.957	43	6	16	1	23	0

Player, Team	Pct.	G	PO	A	E	TC	DP
Fordham, Tom, Altoona *	.909	13	2	8	1	11	0
Forystek, Brian, Bowie *	1.000	29	4	17	0	21	0
Fossum, Casey, Portland *	.000	3	0	0	0	0	0
Fox, Chad, Portland	1.000	1	1	0	0	1	0
Franco, Martire, Reading	1.000	28	6	8	0	14	0
Frederick, Kevin, New Haven	1.000	25	0	1	0	1	0
Freire, Alejandro, Norwich	.000	1	0	0	0	0	0
Gamble, Jerome, Portland	1.000	2	1	2	0	3	0
Garza, Alberto, Trenton	1.000	5	0	2	0	2	0
Gassner, Dave, New Haven *	1.000	35	9	20	0	29	2
Giese, Dan, Reading	.000	9	0	0	0	0	0
Glaser, Eric, Portland	.800	29	2	2	1	5	0
Glen, William, Reading	.813	31	4	9	3	16	0
Glick, David, Trenton *	.929	45	5	8	1	14	1
Gonzalez, Mike, Altoona *	.500	5	0	1	1	2	0
Grabow, John, Altoona *	1.000	24	3	13	0	16	0
Grace, Bryan, Trenton	.929	7	2	11	1	14	1
Guthrie, Jeremy, Akron	.947	10	3	15	1	19	1
Gutierrez, Vic, Harrisburg	1.000	2	1	0	0	1	0
Guy, Brad, Altoona-Reading	.952	39	9	11	1	21	0
Halsey, Brad, Trenton *	1.000	15	4	16	0	20	0
Hamann, Rob, New Haven	.800	6	0	4	1	5	0
Hansell, Greg, Trenton	1.000	17	1	5	0	6	1
Harvey, Ian, Reading	.800	11	1	3	1	5	0
Hee, Aaron, Binghamton *	.889	22	2	6	1	9	0
Henkel, Rob, Erie *	1.000	16	4	10	0	14	0
Hernandez, Adrian, Trenton	.000	1	0	0	0	0	0
Hernandez, Yoel, Reading	.960	43	6	18	1	25	0
HERNDON, JUNIOR, Portland	1.000	25	7	27	0	34	4
Hill, Jeremy, Binghamton	.000	11	0	0	0	0	0
Hill, Shawn, Harrisburg	1.000	4	1	3	0	4	0
Hoard, Brent, New Britain *	.500	3	1	0	1	2	0
Hodge, Kevin, New Britain	1.000	56	6	18	0	24	0
Hutchison, Ryan, Reading	.882	34	7	8	2	17	0
Isaacson, Charlie, Trenton	1.000	14	2	2	0	4	0
Jackson, Dan, New Haven	1.000	33	4	2	0	6	0
Jacobsen, Landon, Altoona	.913	27	14	28	4	46	3
Johnson, James, Portland *	1.000	38	5	4	0	9	0
Johnson, Jeremy, Erie	1.000	10	4	8	0	12	0
Johnson, Mark, Erie	.958	48	10	13	1	24	2
Johnston, Mike, Altoona *	1.000	46	7	14	0	21	0
Joseph, Jake, Binghamton	.938	11	4	11	1	16	0
Kaercher, Matthew, Portland	.000	1	0	0	0	0	0
Kalita, Tim, Erie *	1.000	15	0	2	0	2	0
Karp, Josh, Harrisburg	.862	23	10	15	4	29	1
Kegley, Chuck, New Haven	1.000	12	0	3	0	3	0
Kemp, Beau, New Britain	.750	36	2	4	2	8	0
Kennard, Jeff, Trenton	1.000	10	1	1	0	2	0
Keppel, Bob, Binghamton	.946	18	10	25	2	37	3
Kester, Tim, Portland	1.000	27	7	26	0	33	2
Knowles, Mike, Trenton	.000	8	0	0	0	0	0
Kremer, John, Trenton	.000	3	0	0	0	0	0
Kumagai, Ryo, Portland	1.000	3	0	1	0	1	0
Larrison, Preston, Erie	.929	24	4	22	2	28	0
Larson, Ryan, Akron	.952	40	5	15	1	21	0
Lavigne, Tim, Binghamton	.957	46	7	15	1	23	0
Lee, Cliff, Akron *	1.000	2	0	1	0	1	1
Lee, Seung, Reading	.970	26	13	19	1	33	0
Lira, James, Norwich	1.000	6	3	1	0	4	0
Lockwood, Luke, Harrisburg *	.968	26	7	23	1	31	1
Lopez, Rodrigo, Bowie	.000	1	0	0	0	0	0
Lowry, Noah, Norwich *	.920	23	3	20	2	25	2
Maness, Nick, Binghamton	1.000	8	1	2	0	3	0
Manning, Charlie, Trenton *	1.000	23	2	9	0	11	1
Markwell, Diego, New Haven *	.919	28	13	21	3	37	3
Martin, Kevin, Akron	1.000	2	0	1	0	1	0
Martinez, Anastacio, Port.-Alt.	.900	37	2	7	1	10	0
Mata, Gustavo, Harrisburg	.971	22	12	22	1	35	1
Mattes, Troy, Harrisburg	.833	5	1	4	1	6	0
Mattioni, Nick, Binghamton	.905	42	5	14	2	21	2
Mattox, David, Binghamton	.857	21	5	13	3	21	1
Maust, David, Harrisburg *	.917	17	3	8	1	12	0
McDade, Neal, Altoona	.864	38	9	10	3	22	1
McDonald, Jon, New Britain	.800	8	2	2	1	5	0
McGowan, Dustin, New Haven	.909	14	4	6	1	11	1
Mendoza, Marcos, Akron *	1.000	9	0	2	0	2	0
Mercado, Hector, Reading *	1.000	1	0	2	0	2	0
Miller, Josh, Reading	1.000	43	6	15	0	21	2
Miniel, Rene, Portland	.667	15	1	1	1	3	1
Montalbano, Greg, Portland *	1.000	6	0	2	0	2	0
Montano, Ignacio, Akron *	.000	1	0	0	0	0	0
Montes, Albert, Norwich	1.000	36	2	13	0	15	1
Montgomery, Matt, Norwich	.833	28	3	2	1	6	0
Moreno, Orber, Binghamton	.000	4	0	0	0	0	0
Moreno, Victor, New Britain	1.000	24	2	1	0	3	0

Player, Team	Pct.	G	PO	A	E	TC	DP
Musser, Neal, Binghamton *	.931	20	8	19	2	29	3
Myette, Aaron, Akron	1.000	3	1	0	0	1	0
Neil, Dan, Akron *	.000	5	0	0	1	1	0
Neshek, Pat, New Britain	1.000	5	1	1	0	2	1
Nicolas, Mike, Portland	.667	20	0	2	1	3	0
Nin, Sandy, New Haven	1.000	1	1	0	0	1	0
Ogiltree, John, New Haven	.913	45	7	14	2	23	0
Oquendo, Ian, Altoona	1.000	6	4	3	0	7	0
Orloski, Joe, Binghamton	1.000	10	0	2	0	2	0
Ormond, Rodney, Bowie	.870	46	4	16	3	23	1
Ortiz, Javier, Trenton	.967	28	11	18	1	30	2
Outlaw, Mark, Reading *	1.000	12	2	0	0	2	0
Ozias, Todd, Altoona	.933	51	6	8	1	15	1
Pahucki, David, Portland	1.000	2	3	1	0	4	0
Palma, Rick, Altoona *	.900	35	6	12	2	20	0
Palmer, Matt, Norwich	.000	5	0	0	0	0	0
Paradis, Mike, Bowie	.912	25	11	20	3	34	0
Parker, Christian, Trenton	1.000	5	5	10	0	15	0
Parrish, John, Bowie *	.838	49	7	24	6	37	0
Pautz, Brad, Reading	1.000	29	1	8	0	9	0
Pearson, Terry, Erie	1.000	9	1	1	0	2	0
Pena, Juan, New Haven	1.000	7	1	1	0	2	0
Pennington, Todd, Akron	1.000	7	0	1	0	1	0
Perez, Juan, Portland *	.600	18	1	2	2	5	0
Peterson, Adam, New Haven	1.000	24	0	7	0	7	0
Peterson, Matt, Binghamton	.889	6	3	5	1	9	0
Pettyjohn, Adam, Erie *	1.000	19	1	12	0	13	0
Pina, Rafael, Bowie	1.000	6	1	0	0	1	0
Pinales, Aquiles, Akron	1.000	6	1	0	0	1	1
Pridie, Jon, New Britain	.857	27	8	22	5	35	2
Puello, Ignacio, Harrisburg	1.000	18	1	5	0	6	0
Rakers, Aaron, Bowie	1.000	31	1	9	0	10	0
Rakers, Jason, Akron	.000	4	0	0	0	0	0
Ramirez, Enrique, Bowie	.667	14	3	1	2	6	0
Ramirez, Ramon, Trenton	1.000	4	1	2	0	3	0
Ramsey, Keith, Akron *	1.000	2	0	3	0	3	0
Rayborn, Kenny, Akron	1.000	5	1	3	0	4	0
Reimers, Cameron, New Haven	1.000	28	11	19	0	30	0
Reynoso, Edison, Trenton	1.000	22	4	8	0	12	0
Rigdon, Paul, Akron	1.000	6	2	8	0	10	0
Rijo, Fernando, Bowie	.810	20	8	9	4	21	0
Riley, Matt, Bowie *	1.000	14	3	9	0	12	0
Ring, Royce, Binghamton *	1.000	18	1	4	0	5	0
Rivera, Homero, Erie *	1.000	54	5	15	0	20	4
Rizzo, Todd, Bowie *	1.000	7	1	0	0	1	0
Robbins, Jake, Akron	.917	34	4	18	2	24	5
Robinson, Bo, Trenton	.000	1	0	0	0	0	0
Rodriguez, Cristobal, Harrisburg	.000	1	0	0	0	0	0
Rodriguez, Eddy, Bowie	.889	56	3	5	1	9	0
Rogers, Brian, Trenton	1.000	13	1	5	0	6	0
Roller, Adam, Trenton	1.000	36	4	5	0	9	0
Romero, Josmir, New Britain	1.000	27	4	14	0	18	0
Romprey, Ed, Erie	1.000	1	1	0	0	1	0
Rosario, Juan, Bowie	1.000	5	2	5	0	7	0
Rudrude, Brett, Portland	1.000	6	3	6	0	9	0
Saenz, Jason, Binghamton *	.813	32	6	7	3	16	1
Schmack, Brian, Erie	1.000	53	2	15	0	17	0
Schmitt, Eric, Trenton	1.000	21	5	3	0	8	0
Schoening, Brent, New Britain	1.000	26	10	15	0	25	2
Schroder, Chris, Harrisburg	1.000	49	3	11	0	14	0
Scobie, Jason, Binghamton	1.000	9	5	7	0	12	1
Seale, Dustin, Harrisburg *	.857	26	1	5	1	7	0
Seibel, Phil, Binghamton *	.952	17	4	16	1	21	1
Sequea, Jacobo, Bowie	.750	12	2	4	2	8	0
Shaffar, Ben, Altoona	.917	13	5	6	1	12	0
Shepard, David, Trenton	1.000	53	5	9	0	14	1
Shibilo, Andy, Portland	1.000	13	0	4	0	4	0
Shipp, Brian, Binghamton	.000	1	0	0	0	0	0
Sims, Kenny, Bowie	.000	1	0	0	1	1	0
Smith, Bud, Reading *	1.000	8	2	8	0	10	0
Smith, Matt, Trenton *	.875	9	3	4	1	8	0
Song, Seung, Harrisburg	.889	13	6	10	2	18	0
Spencer, Sean, Bowie *	1.000	12	2	4	0	6	0
Spiegel, Mike, Erie *	.714	24	1	9	4	14	0
Spiehs, R.D., Norwich	1.000	39	2	11	0	13	1
Stanton, Mike, Binghamton *	.000	1	0	0	0	0	0
Stein, Blake, Akron-Harrisburg	1.000	6	1	0	0	1	0
Stevens, Josh, Portland	.976	25	14	26	1	41	3
Tadano, Kazuhito, Akron	1.000	31	2	13	0	15	0
Taschner, Jack, Norwich *	.875	34	4	10	2	16	0
Threets, Erick, Norwich *	1.000	11	1	4	0	5	0
Torres, Luis, Harrisburg	1.000	11	2	0	0	2	0
Ulloa, Enmanuel, Harrisburg	.000	6	0	0	0	0	0
Van Dusen, Derrick, Akron *	.885	28	5	18	3	26	1
Van Hekken, Andy, Erie *	1.000	13	4	13	0	17	0

Player, Team	Pct.	G	PO	A	E	TC	DP
VanBenschoten, John, Altoona	.923	17	12	12	2	26	0
Vargas, Claudio, Harrisburg	.000	2	0	0	0	0	0
Vargas, Jose, Akron	1.000	37	1	7	0	8	0
Vent, Kevin, Norwich	1.000	37	4	11	0	15	2
Villegas, Felix, Portland	.800	23	6	6	3	15	0
Villegas, Francisco, Trenton	1.000	6	0	1	0	1	0
Wade, Travis, Norwich	.833	19	2	3	1	6	1
Walk, Mitch, Norwich *	.944	36	8	26	2	36	4
Walker, Pete, New Haven	.000	2	0	0	0	0	0
Wallace, Shane, Akron *	1.000	10	0	4	0	4	0
Wang, Chien-ming, Trenton	.933	21	0	28	2	30	1
Warden, Jim Ed, Akron	1.000	1	2	2	0	4	0
Weatherby, Charlie, Portland	1.000	30	3	12	0	15	0
Weaver, Eric, Reading	1.000	10	0	2	0	2	0
White, Gabe, Trenton *	.000	2	0	0	0	0	0
White, Matt, Portland *	.000	2	0	0	0	0	0
Wickman, Bob, Akron	1.000	2	0	1	0	1	0
Wiggins, Scott, New Haven *	1.000	17	1	1	0	2	0
Wilson, Jeff, Bowie *	1.000	28	1	10	0	11	0
Wilson, Mike, Reading-Norwich	1.000	11	0	7	0	7	1
Wohlers, Mark, Akron	.000	2	0	0	0	0	0
Wolfe, Brian, New Britain	.964	30	8	19	1	28	0
Woodyard, Mark, Erie	1.000	2	2	2	0	4	0
Yates, Tyler, Binghamton	.917	8	3	8	1	12	0
Young, Chris, Harrisburg	1.000	15	5	7	0	12	0
Zink, Charlie, Portland	.800	6	1	3	1	5	0

PITCHERS WITH TWO OR MORE TEAMS

Player, Team	Pct.	G	PO	A	E	TC	DP
Borkowski, Dave, Bowie	1.000	24	10	16	0	26	3
Borkowski, Dave, Erie	1.000	6	1	1	0	2	0
Brooks, Frank, Altoona *	.000	1	0	0	0	0	0
Brooks, Frank, Reading *	1.000	34	0	6	0	6	1
Guy, Brad, Altoona	1.000	8	2	1	0	3	0
Guy, Brad, Reading	.944	31	7	10	1	18	0
Martinez, Anastacio, Altoona	1.000	3	0	1	0	1	0
Martinez, Anastacio, Portland	.889	34	2	6	1	9	0
Stein, Blake, Akron	.000	2	0	0	0	0	0
Stein, Blake, Harrisburg	1.000	4	1	0	0	1	0
Wilson, Mike, Norwich	.000	2	0	0	0	0	0
Wilson, Mike, Reading	1.000	9	0	7	0	7	1

The following players appeared only as a designated hitter, pinch-hitter or pinch-runner: C. Bonilla, ph; Lawton, dh; R. Martinez, ph; Turco, ph.

LEAGUE CHAMPIONS

Year	Team	Pct.
1923—	Williamsport	.661
1924—	Williamsport	.654
1925—	York§	.583
	Williamsport§	.583
1926—	Scranton	.627
1927—	Harrisburg	.630
1928—	Harrisburg	.603
1929—	Binghamton	.597
1930—	Wilkes-Barre	.572
1931—	Harrisburg	.597
1932—	Wilkes-Barre	.561
1933—	Binghamton	.690
1934—	Binghamton	.694
	Williamsport*	.603
1935—	Scranton	.657
	Binghamton*	.580
1936—	Scranton*	.609
	Elmira	.629
1937—	Elmira†	.622
1938—	Binghamton	.622
	Elmira (3rd)‡	.522
1939—	Scranton†	.571
1940—	Scranton	.568
	Binghamton (2nd)‡	.554
1941—	Wilkes-Barre	.630
	Elmira (3rd)‡	.514
1942—	Albany	.600
	Scranton (2nd)‡	.593
1943—	Scranton	.630
	Elmira (2nd)‡	.568
1944—	Hartford	.723
	Binghamton (4th)‡	.474
1945—	Utica	.615
	Albany (3rd)‡	.564
1946—	Scranton†	.691
1947—	Utica†	.652
1948—	Scranton†	.636
1949—	Albany	.664
	Binghamton (4th)‡	.500
1950—	Wilkes-Barre‡	.652
1951—	Wilkes-Barre‡	.612
	Scranton (2nd)†	.562
1952—	Albany	.603
	Binghamton (2nd)‡	.562
1953—	Reading	.682
	Binghamton (2nd)‡	.636
1954—	Wilkes-Barre	.576
	Albany (3rd)‡	.540
1955—	Reading	.613
	Allentown (2nd)‡	.565
1956—	Schenectady†	.609
1957—	Binghamton	.607
	Reading (3rd)‡	.529
1958—	Lancaster∞	.568
	Binghamton (6th)‡	.493
1959—	Springfield†	.607
1960—	Williamsport▲	.551
	Springfield (3rd)▲	.496
1961—	Springfield	.612
1962—	Williamsport	.593
	Elmira (2nd)‡	.514
1963—	Charleston	.593
1964—	Elmira	.586
1965—	Pittsfield	.607
1966—	Elmira	.633
1967—	Binghamton◆	.586
	Elmira	.532
1968—	Pittsfield	.604
	Reading (2nd)‡	.579
1969—	York	.640
1970—	Waterbury■	.560
	Reading■	.553
1971—	Three Rivers	.569
	Elmira▼	.561
1972—	West Haven▼	.600
	Three Rivers	.559
1973—	Reading▼	.551
	Pittsfield	.551
1974—	Thetford Miners (2nd)•	.536
	Pittsfield (2nd)	.496
1975—	Reading	.613
	Bristol*	.587
1976—	Three Rivers	.601
	West Haven††	.576
1977—	West Haven‡‡	.623
	Three Rivers	.551
1978—	Reading	.642
	Bristol*	.580
1979—	West Haven§§	.597
1980—	Holyoke*	.561
	Waterbury	.540
1981—	Glens Falls	.615
	Bristol*	.577
1982—	West Haven*	.614
	Lynn	.590
1983—	Lynn	.554
	New Britain‡	.518
1984—	Waterbury	.543
	Vermont‡	.536
1985—	Albany	.540
	Vermont‡	.514
1986—	Reading	.566
	Vermont‡	.554
1987—	Pittsfield	.630
	Harrisburg‡	.550
1988—	Glens Falls	.584
	Albany‡	.522
1989—	Albany‡	.657
	Harrisburg	.522
1990—	Albany	.568
	London‡	.547
1991—	Harrisburg	.621
	Albany‡	.543
1992—	Canton/Akron	.580
	Binghamton‡	.572
1993—	Harrisburg‡	.681
	Canton/Akron	.543
1994—	Harrisburg	.633
	Binghamton‡	.582
1995—	New Haven	.556
	Reading‡	.514
1996—	Portland	.589
	Harrisburg‡	.521
1997—	Harrisburg‡	.606
	Portland	.556
1998—	New Britain	.585
	Harrisburg‡	.514
1999—	Trenton	.648
	Harrisburg‡	.535
2000—	Reading	.599
	New Haven‡	.577
2001—	New Britain∞∞	.613
	Reading∞∞	.542
2002—	Akron	.660
	Norwich‡	.543
2003—	Akron†	.624

*Won split-season playoff. †Won championship and four-team playoff. ‡Won four-team playoff. §Tied for pennant, York winning playoff. ∞League was divided into Northern, Southern divisions and played a split season; Lancaster was overall season leader. ▲Playoff finals canceled after one game because of rain with Williamsport and Springfield declared playoff co-champions. ◆League was divided into Eastern, Western divisions; Binghamton won playoff. ■Tied for pennant, Waterbury winning playoff. ▼League was divided into American, National divisions; won playoff. •League was divided into American and National divisions; won four-team playoff. ††League was divided into Northern, Southern divisions, won playoff. ‡‡League was divided into New England and Canadian-American divisions; won playoff. §§Won both halves of split season (no playoffs). ∞∞Were entering finals of four-team playoff and were declared co-champions when Professional Baseball declared a stoppage of play. (NOTE—Known as New York-Pennsylvania League prior to 1938.)

SOUTHERN LEAGUE

LEAGUE OFFICE

President
Don Mincher
Vice president/operations
Lori Webb

Media coordinator
Joey Elger
Address
2551 Roswell Road, Suite 330
Marietta, GA 30062

Phone
770-321-0400

TEAMS

BIRMINGHAM BARONS

General manager
Tony Ensor
Manager
Razor Shines
Ballpark (capacity, surface)
Hoover Metropolitan Stadium (10,800, grass)
Affiliation
White Sox
Address
P.O. Box 360007
Birmingham, AL 35236
Phone
205-988-3200

CAROLINA MUDCATS

General manager
Joe Kremer
Manager
Ron Hassey
Ballpark (capacity, surface)
Five County Stadium (6,500, grass)
Affiliation
Marlins
Address
P.O. Drawer 1218
Zebulon, NC 27597
Phone
919-269-2287

CHATTANOOGA LOOKOUTS

President/general manager
J. Frank Burke
Manager
Jayhawk Owens
Ballpark (capacity, surface)
BellSouth Park (6,100, grass)
Affiliation
Reds
Address
201 Power Alley
Chattanooga, TN 37402
Phone
423-267-2208

GREENVILLE BRAVES

General manager
Steve DeSalvo
Manager
Brian Snitker
Ballpark (capacity, surface)
Greenville Municipal Stadium (7,027, grass)
Affiliation
Braves
Address
P.O. Box 16683
Greenville, SC 29606
Phone
864-299-3456

HUNTSVILLE STARS

President/general manager
Bryan Dingo
Manager
Frank Kremblas
Ballpark (capacity, surface)
Joe W. Davis Stadium (10,400, grass)
Affiliation
Brewers
Address
3125 Leeman Ferry Road
Huntsville, AL 35801
Phone
256-882-2562

JACKSONVILLE SUNS

Vice president/general manager
Peter Bragan Jr.
Manager
Dino Ebel
Ballpark (capacity, surface)
Baseball Grounds of Jacksonville (11,000, grass)
Affiliation
Dodgers
Address
301 A. Philip Randolph Blvd.
Jacksonville FL 32202
Phone
904-358-2846

MOBILE BAYBEARS

Vice president/general manager
Bill Shanahan
Manager
Gary Jones
Ballpark (capacity, surface)
Hank Aaron Stadium (6,000, grass)
Affiliation
Padres
Address
755 Bolling Brothers Blvd.
Mobile, AL 36606
Phone
251-479-2327

MONTGOMERY BISCUITS

General manager/operations
Greg Rauch
Manager
Charlie Montoyo
Ballpark (capacity, surface)
Montgomery Riverwalk Stadium (7,000, grass)
Affiliation
Devil Rays
Address
Union Station, 300 Water St.
Montgomery, AL 36104
Phone
334-323-2255

TENNESSEE SMOKIES

General manager
Brian Cox
Manager
Mark DeJohn
Ballpark (capacity, surface)
Smokies Park (6,000, grass)
Affiliation
Cardinals
Address
3540 Line Drive
Kodak, TN 37764
Phone
865-637-9494

WEST TENN DIAMOND JAXX

General manager
Jeff Parker
Manager
Bobby Dickerson
Ballpark (capacity, surface)
Pringles Park (6,000, grass)
Affiliation
Cubs
Address
4 Fun Place
Jackson, TN 38305
Phone
901-664-2020

2003 FINAL STANDINGS

FIRST HALF

EAST DIVISION

Team	W	L	T	Pct.	GB
Carolina	42	26	-	.618	...
Greenville	36	32	-	.529	6.0
Tennessee	35	35	-	.500	8.0
Orlando	32	37	-	.464	10.5
Jacksonville	31	38	-	.449	11.5

WEST DIVISION

Team	W	L	T	Pct.	GB
Huntsville	40	28	-	.588	...
West Tenn	34	36	-	.486	7.0
Birmingham	33	35	-	.485	7.0
Chattanooga	32	38	-	.457	9.0
Mobile	29	39	-	.426	11.0

SECOND HALF

EAST DIVISION

Team	W	L	T	Pct.	GB
Carolina	38	32	-	.543	...
Tennessee	37	32	-	.536	.5
Jacksonville	35	35	-	.500	3.0
Orlando	33	35	-	.485	4.0
Greenville	32	38	-	.457	6.0

WEST DIVISION

Team	W	L	T	Pct.	GB
Birmingham	40	29	-	.580	...
Huntsville	35	35	-	.500	5.5
Chattanooga	34	36	-	.486	6.5
Mobile	32	38	-	.457	8.5
West Tenn	31	37	-	.456	8.5

COMPOSITE

Team	CAR	HVL	BIR	TEN	GRV	JAX	ORL	CNG	WTE	MOB	W	L	T	Pct.	GB
Carolina (Marlins)	...	5	3	13	10	13	11	10	6	9	80	58	0	.580	...
Huntsville (Brewers)	2	...	11	5	6	4	3	19	11	14	75	63	0	.543	5.0
Birmingham (White Sox)	3	14	...	4	3	10	8	10	9	12	73	64	0	.533	6.5
Tennessee (Cardinals)	11	7	3	...	14	13	11	3	5	5	72	67	0	.518	8.5
Greenville (Braves)	14	4	5	12	...	12	11	2	4	4	68	70	0	.493	12.0
Jacksonville (Dodgers)	7	3	8	10	12	...	13	5	4	4	66	73	0	.475	14.5
Orlando (Devil Rays)	11	4	4	12	9	11	...	4	5	5	65	72	0	.474	14.5
Chattanooga (Reds)	2	8	10	5	5	3	4	...	18	11	66	74	0	.471	15.0
West Tenn (Cubs)	6	9	10	3	8	4	4	8	...	13	65	73	0	.471	15.0
Mobile (Padres)	2	9	10	3	3	3	7	13	11	...	61	77	0	.442	19.0

Major league affiliations in parentheses.

PLAYOFFS: Carolina defeated Tennessee, three games to one; Huntsville defeated Birmingham, three games to two; Carolina defeated Huntsville, three games to two, to win league championship.

REGULAR-SEASON ATTENDANCE: Birmingham, 276,717; Carolina, 204,867; Chattanooga, 237,235; Greenville, 183,564; Huntsville, 198,416; Jacksonville, 359,979; Mobile, 219,007; Orlando, 150,051; Tennessee, 256,597; West Tenn, 197,226. Total attendance—2,283,659. Playoffs (14 games)—22,878. All-Star Game at Jacksonville—7,552.

MANAGERS: Birmingham, Wally Backman; Carolina, Tracy Woodson; Chattanooga, Phillip Wellman; Greenville, Brian Snitker; Huntsville, Frank Kremblas; Jacksonville, Dino Ebel; Mobile, Craig Colbert; Orlando, Charlie Montoyo; Tennessee, Mark DeJohn; West Tenn, Bobby Dickerson.

ALL-STAR TEAM: 1B—Bucky Jacobsen, Tennessee; 2B—Caonabo Cosme, Tennessee; 3B—Corey Hart, Huntsville; SS—J.J. Hardy, Huntsville; OF—Matt Diaz, Orlando; OF—Jon Knott, Mobile; OF—Dave Krynzel, Huntsville; OF—Stephen Smitherman, Chattanooga; C—Humberto Quintero, Mobile; DH—Dernell Stenson, Chattanooga; Utility—Gabe Alvarez, Birmingham; RHP—Joel Hanrahan, Jacksonville; LHP—Neal Cotts, Birmingham; Relief pitcher—Rusty Tucker, Mobile; Most Valuable Player—Corey Hart, Huntsville; Most Outstanding Pitcher—Joel Hanrahan, Jacksonville; Hustler of the Year—Pete Orr, Greenville; Manager of the Year—Frank Kremblas, Huntsville.

2003 BATTING

TEAM

Team	G	TPA	AB	R	H	TB	2B	3B	HR	RBI	SH	SF	HP	BB	IBB	SO	SB	CS	GDP	LOB	ShO	Avg.	OBP	Slg.
Birmingham	137	5121	4451	567	1202	1667	227	23	64	531	93	54	57	466	16	852	110	81	99	1001	8	.270	.343	.375
Carolina	138	5236	4596	654	1225	1814	264	38	83	601	54	56	33	496	33	906	126	46	86	1006	10	.267	.339	.395
Orlando	137	5104	4522	552	1199	1713	253	21	73	520	51	42	86	402	19	941	84	37	96	1043	15	.265	.334	.379
Chattanooga	140	5242	4624	660	1209	1834	265	24	104	598	55	48	44	471	26	1042	123	69	76	929	5	.261	.332	.397
Tennessee	139	5167	4595	564	1178	1734	233	22	93	522	47	34	59	432	31	924	94	48	102	985	8	.256	.326	.377
West Tenn	138	5077	4478	517	1125	1629	232	31	70	480	59	45	61	434	19	900	98	64	97	974	11	.251	.323	.364
Greenville	138	5106	4478	571	1116	1651	230	31	81	526	43	40	41	503	27	1044	109	53	71	993	10	.249	.328	.369
Jacksonville	139	5134	4527	554	1113	1680	213	36	94	498	74	39	56	438	19	1081	124	73	88	925	14	.246	.318	.371
Huntsville	138	5203	4556	596	1117	1597	225	24	69	527	46	43	65	493	26	1033	174	79	74	955	9	.245	.325	.351
Mobile	138	5213	4564	547	1085	1636	227	18	96	514	47	26	69	507	18	1076	111	40	76	1036	10	.238	.322	.358

INDIVIDUAL

TOP QUALIFIERS FOR BATTING CHAMPIONSHIP

Minimum 378 plate appearances. *Lefthanded batter. †Switch-hitter.

Player, Team	G	TPA	AB	R	H	TB	2B	3B	HR	RBI	SH	SF	HP	BB	IBB	SO	SB	CS	GDP	Avg.	OBP	Slg.
Aguila, Chris, Carolina	93	382	337	58	108	168	21	3	11	55	2	5	2	36	5	67	6	2	6	.320	.384	.499
Bikowski, Scott, Birm.*	118	462	394	53	123	161	23	3	3	49	9	5	4	50	4	65	3	7	9	.312	.391	.409
Smitherman, Stephen, Chat.	105	430	365	60	113	195	21	2	19	73	0	5	6	54	6	95	11	3	7	.310	.402	.534
Alvarez, Gabe, Birmingham	118	484	410	60	127	194	34	0	11	78	3	5	8	58	0	87	2	5	13	.310	.401	.473
Stenson, Dernell, Chat.*	101	405	356	51	109	179	28	0	14	76	1	7	2	39	4	74	4	5	10	.306	.371	.503
Hart, Corey, Huntsville	130	535	493	70	149	230	40	1	13	94	0	9	5	28	5	101	25	8	7	.302	.340	.467
Quintero, Humberto, Mobile	110	421	386	37	115	150	26	0	3	52	4	3	9	19	5	41	0	0	17	.298	.343	.389
Jacobsen, Bucky, Tennessee	131	521	447	84	133	252	24	1	31	84	0	5	13	56	8	91	3	1	7	.298	.388	.564

Player, Team	G	TPA	AB	R	H	TB	2B	3B	HR	RBI	SH	SF	HP	BB	IBB	SO	SB	CS	GDP	Avg.	OBP	Slg.
Piniella, Juan, Birmingham	115	393	346	45	101	141	24	2	4	27	12	2	5	28	0	82	12	5	4	.292	.352	.408
Sadler, Ray, West Tenn	110	457	412	56	120	179	31	5	6	42	2	3	7	33	4	81	17	7	8	.291	.352	.434
Sandoval, Danny, Birm.†	130	547	478	62	137	180	30	2	3	49	14	9	3	43	2	67	21	11	10	.287	.343	.377
Jurries, James, Greenville	129	522	465	73	132	202	35	4	9	54	2	3	4	48	1	108	4	2	10	.284	.354	.434
Harris, Brendan, West Tenn	120	502	435	56	122	185	34	7	5	52	5	3	8	51	1	72	6	7	10	.280	.364	.425
Hardy, J.J., Huntsville	114	485	416	67	116	178	26	0	12	62	4	4	3	58	4	54	6	4	11	.279	.368	.428
Bolivar, Papo, Tennessee	133	529	474	56	132	174	24	3	4	52	3	3	3	46	4	73	30	11	18	.278	.344	.367

DEPARTMENTAL LEADERS: G—J. Nelson, 136; AB—J. Nelson, 506; R—Jacobsen, 84; H—Hart, 149; TB—Jacobsen, 252; 2B—Hart, 40; 3B—Krynzel, 11; HR—Jacobsen, 31; RBI—Hart, 94; SH—Sandoval, 14; SF—Wilson, 10; HP—Grummitt, 22; BB—Knott, 82; IBB—Jacobsen, 8; SO—Abercrombie, 164; SB—W. Hall, 45; CS—Krynzel, 21; GIDP—Bolivar, 18; Slg.—Jacobsen, .564; OBP—Smitherman, .402.

ALL PLAYERS

*Lefthanded batter. †Switch-hitter.

Player, Team	G	TPA	AB	R	H	TB	2B	3B	HR	RBI	SH	SF	HP	BB	IBB	SO	SB	CS	GDP	Avg.	OBP	Slg.
Abercrombie, Reggie, Jack.	116	479	448	59	117	201	25	7	15	54	3	3	9	16	2	164	28	9	3	.261	.298	.449
Abreu, Dennis, Tennessee	18	59	52	6	13	19	1	1	1	8	2	1	0	4	1	13	2	2	0	.250	.298	.365
Acevas, Jon, Birmingham	51	151	126	17	29	45	7	0	3	16	3	2	6	14	0	35	0	2	5	.230	.331	.357
Adams, Brian, Huntsville *	32	7	6	0	0	0	0	0	0	0	0	0	0	1	0	5	0	0	0	.000	.143	.000
Adams, Mike, Huntsville	45	8	7	0	0	0	0	0	0	0	0	0	0	1	0	4	0	0	0	.000	.125	.000
Aguila, Chris, Carolina	93	382	337	58	108	168	21	3	11	55	2	5	2	36	5	67	6	2	6	.320	.384	.499
Aguilar, Ray, Greenville †	35	22	21	3	4	7	0	0	1	4	0	0	0	1	0	3	0	0	1	.190	.227	.333
Aldridge, Cory, Greenville *	127	494	448	55	105	177	20	2	16	49	0	4	5	37	4	134	11	3	5	.234	.298	.395
Alvarado, Joel, Huntsville	14	48	39	1	6	6	0	0	0	5	0	1	1	7	0	7	0	4	4	.154	.292	.154
Alvarez, Gabe, Birmingham	118	484	410	60	127	194	34	0	11	78	3	5	8	58	0	87	2	5	13	.310	.401	.473
Alvarez, Nick, Jacksonville	101	322	292	39	80	115	16	2	5	46	2	4	3	21	4	47	19	10	9	.274	.325	.394
Ambres, Chip, Carolina	127	457	380	75	98	167	23	8	10	55	0	3	2	72	1	81	9	6	3	.258	.376	.439
Anderson, Bryan, Chat.	44	121	101	12	21	32	8	0	1	14	1	2	4	13	0	30	0	1	2	.208	.317	.317
Anderson, Dennis, Carolina †	15	45	39	2	11	17	6	0	0	8	1	0	1	4	1	5	1	0	0	.282	.364	.436
Anderson, Travis, West Tenn.	14	7	7	0	0	0	0	0	0	0	0	0	0	0	0	5	0	0	0	.000	.000	.000
Andrews, Clayton, Chat.	2	3	2	0	1	1	0	0	0	0	1	0	0	0	0	1	0	0	0	.500	.500	.500
Ankiel, Rick, Tennessee *	30	26	25	2	6	10	1	0	1	5	0	0	0	1	0	2	0	0	0	.240	.269	.400
Arteaga, Joshua, West Tenn	59	156	147	20	36	46	7	0	1	8	0	1	1	7	0	27	1	1	4	.245	.282	.313
Ashby, Chris, Carolina	72	252	240	21	63	89	12	1	4	31	2	2	2	6	0	34	4	2	6	.263	.284	.371
Axelson, Josh, Tennessee	27	15	10	3	1	1	0	0	0	0	3	0	1	1	0	2	0	0	0	.100	.250	.100
Bacon, Dwaine, West Tenn †	12	51	47	7	7	9	2	0	0	2	1	0	0	3	0	11	3	0	0	.149	.200	.191
Badeaux, Brooks, Orlando †	13	53	42	7	12	20	1	2	1	3	2	0	0	9	0	6	2	1	1	.286	.412	.476
Baker, Brad, Mobile	17	11	10	0	0	0	0	0	0	0	1	0	0	0	0	7	0	0	0	.000	.000	.000
Baker, Ryan, Carolina	44	9	9	2	3	3	0	0	0	1	0	0	0	0	0	2	0	0	1	.333	.333	.333
Bannon, Jeff, Chattanooga	13	53	48	4	5	6	1	0	0	2	0	0	0	5	0	8	0	0	4	.104	.189	.125
Barbier, Blair, West Tenn	50	160	137	8	31	36	2	0	1	16	0	4	3	16	2	19	0	3	4	.226	.313	.263
Barnett, Marty, Carolina	5	4	3	0	0	0	0	0	0	0	1	0	0	0	0	1	0	0	0	.000	.000	.000
Barns, B.J., Orlando *	54	196	164	21	40	49	9	0	0	22	1	2	2	27	0	41	0	1	1	.244	.354	.299
Barnwell, Chris, Huntsville	102	355	313	39	77	93	7	0	3	25	4	2	9	27	2	47	6	6	12	.246	.322	.297
Barreto, Joel, Chattanooga	15	2	1	0	0	0	0	0	0	0	1	0	0	0	0	0	0	0	0	.000	.000	.000
Barry, Kevin, Greenville	51	3	3	0	0	0	0	0	0	0	0	0	0	0	0	2	0	0	0	.000	.000	.000
Basham, Bobby, Chattanooga	17	28	23	2	3	3	0	0	0	0	4	0	0	1	0	9	0	0	0	.130	.167	.130
Battersby, Eric, Birmingham	24	56	46	4	8	10	2	0	0	3	0	1	3	6	0	11	2	0	0	.174	.304	.217
Bauer, Greg, Jacksonville	46	10	8	1	0	0	0	0	0	0	1	0	0	1	0	7	0	0	0	.000	.111	.000
Bautista, Denny, Carolina	11	15	15	0	4	5	1	0	0	3	0	0	0	0	0	5	0	0	0	.267	.267	.333
Beattie, Andrew, Chat.†	116	482	423	52	106	152	28	0	6	38	9	1	1	48	3	87	5	9	6	.251	.328	.359
Beckett, Josh, Carolina	1	1	0	0	0	0	0	0	0	0	0	0	0	1	0	0	0	0	0	.000	1.000	.000
Belisle, Matt, Greenville †	21	36	30	2	6	7	1	0	0	3	4	0	0	2	0	8	0	0	2	.200	.250	.233
Bellorin, Edwin, Jacksonville	17	60	57	2	11	15	2	1	0	3	1	0	0	2	0	13	0	0	0	.193	.220	.263
Benick, Jon, Mobile †	37	132	123	11	25	35	7	0	1	9	0	0	1	8	0	32	0	1	3	.203	.258	.285
Benik, Brett, West Tenn	3	1	1	0	0	0	0	0	0	0	0	0	0	0	0	1	0	0	0	.000	.000	.000
Benjamin, Al, Tennessee	33	84	79	10	14	27	4	0	3	11	1	2	2	0	0	11	1	2	1	.177	.193	.342
Bevel, Bobby, Chattanooga *	16	6	5	0	1	1	0	0	0	0	1	0	0	0	0	1	0	0	0	.200	.200	.200
Bikowski, Scott, Birm.*	118	462	394	53	123	161	23	3	3	49	9	5	4	50	4	65	3	7	9	.312	.391	.409
Bolivar, Papo, Tennessee	133	529	474	56	132	174	24	3	4	52	3	3	3	46	4	73	30	11	18	.278	.344	.367
Boscan, Jean, Greenville	41	148	130	13	24	35	5	0	2	15	1	3	0	14	0	35	0	1	2	.185	.259	.269
Bost, Tom, Carolina *	47	151	126	15	27	41	2	3	2	11	2	4	2	17	1	31	2	1	2	.214	.309	.325
Boyd, Shaun, Tennessee	27	97	88	9	24	30	6	0	0	6	2	2	1	4	0	12	2	2	3	.273	.305	.341
Bravo, Danny, Mobile †	113	416	365	41	84	109	16	0	3	38	3	0	0	48	0	52	0	1	5	.230	.320	.299
Brewer, Jace, Orlando	86	302	281	25	62	93	17	1	4	19	7	2	0	12	1	60	1	1	9	.221	.251	.331
Bridges, Donnie, Carolina	44	59	53	4	20	28	8	0	0	7	2	0	0	4	0	14	0	0	0	.377	.421	.528
Brock, Tarrik, Jacksonville *	98	365	305	52	83	151	23	6	11	57	0	2	2	56	4	96	4	7	1	.272	.386	.495
Brown, Andrew, Jacksonville	1	1	1	0	0	0	0	0	0	0	0	0	0	0	0	1	0	0	0	.000	.000	.000
Brown, Eric, West Tenn	44	2	2	1	1	1	0	0	0	0	0	0	0	0	0	1	0	0	0	.500	.500	.500
Bruso, Greg, Huntsville	2	3	3	0	1	1	0	0	0	1	0	0	0	0	0	0	0	0	0	.333	.333	.333
Bullard, Jim, Birmingham *	53	1	1	0	0	0	0	0	0	0	0	0	0	0	0	1	0	0	0	.000	.000	.000
Bumstead, Mike, Mobile	37	10	7	0	1	1	0	0	0	0	1	0	0	2	0	4	0	0	0	.143	.333	.143
Burns, Kevan, Tennessee *	87	300	272	39	78	113	14	6	3	29	2	1	1	24	2	66	8	2	2	.287	.346	.415
Cabrera, Miguel, Carolina	69	303	266	46	97	162	29	3	10	59	0	4	2	31	7	49	9	4	8	.365	.429	.609
Caceres, Wilmy, Chat.†	108	388	357	56	98	126	12	2	4	27	3	2	0	26	1	39	22	9	1	.275	.322	.353
Cairns, Troy, Chattanooga	19	50	42	4	8	14	3	0	1	5	0	1	0	7	0	10	0	0	0	.190	.300	.333
Cantu, Jorge, Orlando	43	173	158	15	34	53	10	0	3	17	3	2	1	9	0	27	0	3	3	.215	.259	.335
Cardona, Javier, West Tenn	10	36	33	4	5	9	1	0	1	2	1	0	1	1	0	5	0	1	0	.152	.200	.273
Carpenter, Chris, Tennessee	1	1	1	0	0	0	0	0	0	0	0	0	0	0	0	0	0	0	0	.000	.000	.000
Cash, David, West Tenn	50	4	3	1	1	1	0	0	0	0	0	0	0	1	0	1	0	0	0	.333	.500	.333
Castro, Ramon, Greenville	66	237	204	33	59	85	9	1	5	20	3	1	2	27	0	39	4	5	1	.289	.376	.417

Player, Team	G	TPA	AB	R	H	TB	2B	3B	HR	RBI	SH	SF	HP	BB	IBB	SO	SB	CS	GDP	Avg.	OBP	Slg.
Cesar, Dionys, Chattanooga †	12	50	46	7	19	23	4	0	0	8	0	0	0	4	1	2	1	1	2	.413	.460	.500
Chamblee, Jim, Chattanooga	28	116	102	16	34	53	7	0	4	16	0	0	5	9	0	27	3	1	1	.333	.414	.520
Chavez, Wilton, West Tenn	2	2	2	0	0	0	0	0	0	0	0	0	0	0	0	1	0	0	0	.000	.000	.000
Childers, Matt, Huntsville	37	12	12	0	2	2	0	0	0	2	0	0	0	0	0	3	0	0	0	.167	.167	.167
Childress, Daylan, Chat.	9	9	8	0	0	0	0	0	0	0	1	0	0	0	0	3	0	0	0	.000	.000	.000
Clark, Daryl, Huntsville *	72	245	202	27	47	66	11	1	2	17	0	1	2	40	2	62	6	1	3	.233	.363	.327
Clements, Jason, Mobile †	18	49	42	1	7	7	0	0	0	2	1	0	1	5	0	11	1	0	1	.167	.271	.167
Clute, Kris, Carolina	4	10	7	1	1	1	0	0	0	0	0	0	0	3	1	2	0	0	0	.143	.400	.143
Collazo, William, Greenville *	39	4	4	0	0	0	0	0	0	0	0	0	0	0	0	0	0	0	0	.000	.000	.000
Collins, Mike, Jacksonville	83	303	279	19	66	71	5	0	0	24	4	3	1	16	1	28	1	4	9	.237	.278	.254
Collins, Pat, Tennessee	5	7	7	0	0	0	0	0	0	0	0	0	0	0	0	5	0	0	0	.000	.000	.000
Colon, Roman, Greenville	39	28	25	1	6	6	0	0	0	3	1	0	0	2	0	11	0	0	1	.240	.296	.240
Conley, Evan, Chattanooga	8	19	17	2	3	4	1	0	0	2	0	0	0	2	0	5	0	0	0	.176	.263	.235
Cook, B.R., Tennessee	30	2	2	0	0	0	0	0	0	0	0	0	0	0	0	2	0	0	0	.000	.000	.000
Cook, Jeremy, Tennessee	10	4	2	0	0	0	0	0	0	0	1	0	0	1	0	1	0	0	0	.000	.333	.000
Correll, Brad, Chattanooga	22	78	74	8	17	28	1	2	2	11	2	1	0	1	0	12	3	3	4	.230	.237	.378
Cortez, Fernando, Orlando *	30	118	114	15	36	44	3	1	1	6	1	0	0	3	0	22	1	2	2	.316	.333	.386
Cosbey, Chris, Huntsville *	33	90	70	9	12	16	4	0	0	6	4	1	2	13	1	21	9	1	0	.171	.314	.229
Cosme, Caonabo, Tennessee	132	538	495	63	135	194	35	3	6	45	4	3	4	32	3	112	9	6	13	.273	.320	.392
Crabtree, Tim, Huntsville	6	1	0	0	0	0	0	0	0	0	0	0	0	1	0	0	0	0	0	.000	1.000	.000
Creighton, Matt, West Tenn	28	82	68	8	15	23	5	0	1	10	1	2	1	10	1	7	0	2	2	.221	.321	.338
Cueto, Jose, Carolina	39	8	5	1	0	0	0	0	0	0	3	0	0	0	0	3	0	1	0	.000	.000	.000
Cummings, Jeremy, Tenn	15	30	24	0	1	1	0	0	0	0	2	0	0	4	0	4	0	0	1	.042	.179	.042
Curtis, Daniel, Greenville	17	22	21	1	4	4	0	0	0	4	0	0	0	1	0	4	0	0	1	.190	.227	.190
Darnell, Paul, Chattanooga	15	2	2	0	0	0	0	0	0	0	0	0	0	0	0	2	0	0	0	.000	.000	.000
Darula, Bobby, Chattanooga *	1	3	3	1	1	4	0	0	1	2	0	0	0	0	0	0	0	0	0	.333	.333	1.333
Davis, Doug, Huntsville	1	3	2	0	0	0	0	0	0	1	0	1	0	0	0	1	0	0	0	.000	.000	.000
Davis, John-Paul, Orlando	34	131	110	21	27	39	9	0	1	17	0	1	5	15	0	28	0	0	3	.245	.359	.355
Dawkins, Gookie, Jack.	35	133	113	12	30	48	6	0	4	20	7	1	2	10	0	12	3	2	2	.265	.333	.425
De Renne, Keoni, Greenville	23	49	41	3	6	6	0	0	0	0	0	0	1	7	0	11	0	0	1	.146	.286	.146
DeHart, Casey, Chattanooga *	41	15	13	3	5	12	2	1	1	6	1	0	0	1	0	2	0	0	0	.385	.429	.923
DeMent, Dan, Orlando	96	396	349	41	89	122	22	1	3	34	3	3	2	39	3	62	2	2	9	.255	.331	.350
Deago, Roger, Mobile	27	39	31	2	7	8	1	0	0	5	6	0	0	2	0	4	0	0	0	.226	.273	.258
Deck, Ronnie, Orlando	3	7	7	0	1	1	0	0	0	0	0	0	0	0	0	4	0	0	0	.143	.143	.143
Dellaero, Jason, Chat.	22	72	65	7	15	27	4	1	2	13	0	2	0	5	0	20	2	0	1	.231	.278	.415
Detienne, Dave, Jacksonville	32	110	94	14	18	24	6	0	0	3	6	1	1	8	0	29	3	1	1	.191	.260	.255
Devey, Phil, Chattanooga *	12	2	1	0	0	0	0	0	0	0	0	0	0	1	0	0	0	0	0	.000	.500	.000
Diaz, Alejandro, Chat.	105	390	360	44	97	133	18	3	4	33	5	5	1	19	2	56	16	10	3	.269	.304	.369
Diaz, Matt, Orlando	60	258	227	32	87	123	21	0	5	41	1	3	8	19	6	24	9	5	7	.383	.444	.542
Diaz, Victor, Jacksonville	85	355	316	42	92	146	20	2	10	55	1	5	6	27	1	60	8	10	10	.291	.353	.462
Digby, Bryan, Greenville	9	1	1	0	0	0	0	0	0	0	0	0	0	0	0	1	0	0	0	.000	.000	.000
Diggins, Ben, Huntsville	8	8	8	1	2	2	0	0	0	0	0	0	0	0	0	2	0	0	1	.250	.250	.250
Dingman, Craig, West Tenn	4	1	1	0	0	0	0	0	0	0	0	0	0	0	0	0	0	0	0	.000	.000	.000
Dodson, Jeremy, Tenn.*	41	130	112	14	25	40	6	0	3	10	0	2	3	13	2	30	6	2	2	.223	.315	.357
Donovan, Todd, Mobile	112	472	420	61	85	134	11	7	8	32	0	1	4	47	0	80	31	11	5	.202	.288	.319
Dubois, Jason, West Tenn	130	521	443	57	119	203	31	4	15	73	0	6	15	57	3	118	2	4	12	.269	.367	.458
Duncan, Chris, Tennessee *	10	25	25	1	5	9	1	0	1	3	0	0	0	0	0	6	0	0	1	.200	.200	.360
Dunn, Scott, Chat.-Birm.	39	4	3	1	0	0	0	0	0	0	0	0	0	1	0	1	0	0	0	.000	.250	.000
Duplissea, Bill, Jacksonville	7	20	14	0	1	1	0	0	0	2	1	0	0	5	0	5	0	1	0	.071	.316	.071
Durham, Chad, Birmingham	119	463	408	59	110	130	13	2	1	37	11	3	2	39	0	81	15	16	7	.270	.334	.319
Dzurilla, Mike, West Tenn	104	368	337	50	89	150	22	3	11	44	1	4	4	22	1	66	4	3	7	.264	.313	.445
Encarnacion, Edwin, Chat.	67	284	254	40	69	99	13	1	5	36	0	5	3	22	0	44	8	3	3	.272	.331	.390
Ennis, John, Greenville	1	1	1	0	0	0	0	0	0	0	0	0	0	0	0	0	0	0	0	.000	.000	.000
Erickson, Corey, Tennessee	100	359	311	45	64	133	21	0	16	50	1	4	4	39	2	82	5	1	5	.206	.299	.428
Escalona, Felix, Orlando	22	103	90	11	22	32	7	0	1	8	3	0	5	5	0	14	0	0	3	.244	.320	.356
Evans, Lee, Greenville †	55	210	183	21	42	64	9	2	3	16	1	2	2	22	2	44	3	0	2	.230	.316	.350
Evert, Brett, Greenville *	34	28	25	3	7	8	1	0	0	4	1	0	0	2	0	10	0	0	2	.280	.333	.320
Faison, Vince, Mobile *	119	448	392	41	90	117	15	0	4	28	2	2	5	47	2	116	13	2	4	.230	.318	.298
Farmer, Tom, Jacksonville	20	25	24	1	4	5	1	0	0	2	1	0	0	0	0	11	0	0	1	.167	.167	.208
Feliciano, Jesus, Jack.-Orl.*	109	370	332	38	82	99	11	0	2	25	6	2	4	26	3	41	9	4	10	.247	.308	.298
Fernandez, Alex, Mobile *	21	79	75	7	23	33	5	1	1	10	0	0	0	4	0	16	2	3	0	.307	.342	.440
Fesh, Sean, Carolina *	49	6	4	0	1	1	0	0	0	0	1	0	0	1	0	2	0	1	0	.250	.400	.250
Fitzgerald, Jason, Green.*	110	431	386	45	100	138	14	3	6	44	0	2	1	41	2	72	19	7	9	.259	.330	.358
Flannery, Mike, Carolina	56	2	2	0	0	0	0	0	0	0	0	0	0	0	0	2	0	0	0	.000	.000	.000
Frasor, Jason, Jacksonville	35	1	1	0	0	0	0	0	0	0	0	0	0	0	0	0	0	0	0	.000	.000	.000
Fuell, Jerrod, Carolina	6	2	2	0	1	2	1	0	0	0	0	0	0	0	0	1	0	0	0	.500	.500	1.000
Furmaniak, J.J., Mobile	31	117	103	10	27	42	4	1	3	11	1	1	4	8	0	27	0	0	0	.262	.336	.408
Gaal, Bryan, Mobile	62	3	3	0	0	0	0	0	0	0	0	0	0	0	0	2	0	0	0	.000	.000	.000
Gall, John, Tennessee	12	56	52	6	17	27	1	0	3	12	0	1	0	3	0	4	0	1	0	.327	.357	.519
Gathright, Joey, Orlando *	22	93	85	12	32	33	1	0	0	5	0	1	2	5	0	15	12	3	0	.376	.419	.388
Gautreau, Jake, Mobile *	122	494	438	48	106	172	24	0	14	55	0	2	4	50	2	131	1	4	9	.242	.324	.393
Gemoll, Brandon, Hunt.*	128	515	456	52	124	195	32	3	11	65	0	6	3	50	2	105	7	9	2	.272	.344	.428
Gerber, Joseph, Mobile *	24	79	69	9	15	28	4	0	3	10	1	1	0	8	0	34	0	0	1	.217	.295	.406
German, Amado, Orlando †	111	438	395	40	107	150	25	3	4	48	3	4	3	33	1	83	5	5	14	.271	.329	.380
Germano, Justin, Mobile	9	16	15	0	0	0	0	0	0	0	0	0	1	0	0	9	0	0	0	.000	.063	.000
Gil, Dave, Chattanooga	32	9	7	1	2	2	0	0	0	0	1	0	0	1	0	2	0	0	0	.286	.375	.286
Girardi, Joe, Tennessee	3	11	10	0	4	4	0	0	0	1	0	0	1	0	0	0	0	1	0	.400	.455	.400
Gomes, Jonny, Orlando	120	515	442	68	110	195	28	3	17	56	0	4	16	53	1	148	23	2	5	.249	.348	.441
Gomez, Rich, Mobile	30	105	93	15	23	39	4	0	4	14	0	0	2	10	0	22	8	0	1	.247	.333	.419
Gonzalez, Adrian, Carolina *	36	152	137	15	42	56	9	1	1	16	0	1	0	14	0	25	1	1	6	.307	.368	.409
Gonzalez, Alfredo, Jack.	10	11	10	0	1	1	0	0	0	0	1	0	0	0	0	4	0	0	0	.100	.100	.100

Player, Team	G	TPA	AB	R	H	TB	2B	3B	HR	RBI	SH	SF	HP	BB	IBB	SO	SB	CS	GDP	Avg.	OBP	Slg.
Gracesqui, Frank, Carolina † ..	44	6	6	3	4	5	1	0	0	0	0	0	0	0	0	0	0	0	1	.667	.667	.833
Gray, Brett, Chattanooga	44	6	5	2	0	0	0	0	0	0	1	0	0	0	0	1	0	0	0	.000	.000	.000
Greene, Khalil, Mobile	59	248	229	20	63	93	17	2	3	20	0	1	2	16	0	55	2	3	7	.275	.327	.406
Gripp, Ryan, Huntsville	67	169	144	22	41	61	5	0	5	22	0	0	3	22	0	36	1	0	4	.285	.391	.424
Grummitt, Dan, Orlando	93	360	303	33	75	128	18	1	11	51	0	4	22	30	3	95	1	2	5	.248	.354	.422
Gubanich, Creighton, Chat.	42	128	119	13	27	40	7	0	2	14	0	1	1	7	0	26	0	0	6	.227	.273	.336
Guerrero, Cristian, Huntsville .	32	127	123	8	24	30	6	0	0	7	0	0	0	4	0	29	3	1	2	.195	.220	.244
Gutierrez, Franklin, Jack.	18	75	67	12	21	40	3	2	4	12	0	0	1	7	0	20	3	3	1	.313	.387	.597
Gutierrez, Jesse, Chat.	27	118	107	12	23	45	8	1	4	20	0	0	2	9	0	16	0	0	2	.215	.288	.421
Guzman, Angel, West Tenn	15	24	22	1	2	2	0	0	0	0	2	0	0	0	0	5	0	0	1	.091	.091	.091
Guzman, Freddy, Mobile †	46	205	177	30	48	60	5	2	1	11	1	0	1	26	2	34	38	7	0	.271	.368	.339
Haad, Yamid, Mobile	9	32	29	3	8	13	2	0	1	5	0	0	0	3	0	4	0	0	2	.276	.344	.448
Haas, Chris, Chattanooga *	32	107	90	12	23	38	8	2	1	14	0	1	1	15	0	33	1	1	2	.256	.364	.422
Hall, Billy, Carolina †	114	412	367	59	90	115	10	3	3	33	6	2	3	34	3	47	45	4	5	.245	.313	.313
Hall, Josh, Chattanooga	26	42	37	3	7	10	1	1	0	1	4	0	0	1	0	15	0	0	0	.189	.211	.270
Hamilton, Jon, W.Tenn-Birm.*	122	468	411	51	99	144	20	2	7	45	9	2	2	44	3	78	22	10	9	.241	.316	.350
Hammons, Matt, Huntsville....	13	2	1	0	0	0	0	0	0	0	0	0	0	1	0	1	0	0	0	.000	.500	.000
Hankins, Ryan, Birmingham ..	67	278	243	34	70	113	20	1	7	36	0	2	3	30	0	39	5	3	8	.288	.371	.465
Hanrahan, Joel, Jacksonville ..	23	33	30	3	3	5	2	0	0	0	2	0	0	1	0	6	0	0	0	.100	.129	.167
Hardy, J.J., Huntsville	114	485	416	67	116	178	26	0	12	62	4	4	3	58	4	54	6	4	11	.279	.368	.428
Haren, Danny, Tennessee	9	16	14	1	3	6	0	0	1	1	1	0	0	1	0	4	0	0	1	.214	.267	.429
Harper, Brandon, Carolina	67	224	195	18	47	65	12	0	2	20	1	2	2	24	3	34	2	0	6	.241	.327	.333
Harris, Brendan, West Tenn ...	120	502	435	56	122	185	34	7	5	52	5	3	8	51	1	72	6	7	10	.280	.364	.425
Hart, Corey, Huntsville	130	535	493	70	149	230	40	1	13	94	0	9	5	28	5	101	25	8	7	.302	.340	.467
Harvey, Ian, Mobile	6	3	3	1	0	0	0	0	0	0	0	0	0	0	0	2	0	0	0	.000	.000	.000
Hastings, Joseph, Mobile *	4	14	12	0	1	2	1	0	0	1	0	0	0	2	0	6	0	0	0	.083	.214	.167
Hendrickson, Ben, Huntsville .	17	18	15	0	4	4	0	0	0	2	3	0	0	0	0	6	0	0	0	.267	.267	.267
Herndon, Eric, Greenville *	7	1	1	0	0	0	0	0	0	0	0	0	0	0	0	0	0	0	0	.000	.000	.000
Hill, Jason, Chattanooga	6	18	15	0	1	1	0	0	0	2	0	0	1	2	0	2	0	0	1	.067	.222	.067
Hill, Koyie, Jacksonville †	25	107	101	9	23	30	7	0	0	7	0	0	0	6	2	19	2	1	3	.228	.271	.297
Holt, Daylan, Birmingham	5	15	13	1	0	0	0	0	0	0	0	0	0	2	0	7	0	0	0	.000	.133	.000
Hood, Donnie, West Tenn	48	164	154	16	42	63	16	1	1	12	0	2	2	6	0	41	3	0	2	.273	.305	.409
House, Craig, Carolina	8	2	2	0	1	1	0	0	0	0	0	0	0	0	0	0	0	0	0	.500	.500	.500
Housman, Jeff, Huntsville * ...	9	14	12	3	3	3	0	0	0	0	0	0	0	2	0	5	0	0	0	.250	.357	.250
Howington, Ty, Chat.†	4	5	4	0	0	0	0	0	0	0	0	0	0	1	0	4	0	0	0	.000	.200	.000
Hundley, Jeff, Huntsville *	11	5	3	1	1	1	0	0	0	0	1	0	0	1	0	1	0	0	0	.333	.500	.333
Hunter, Johnny, Mobile	1	1	1	0	0	0	0	0	0	0	0	0	0	0	0	1	0	0	0	.000	.000	.000
Hutchinson, Trevor, Carolina ..	8	8	6	1	0	0	0	0	0	0	0	0	0	2	0	6	0	0	0	.000	.250	.000
Ingram, Darron, Birmingham .	65	256	227	27	47	81	3	2	9	28	0	3	3	23	3	79	2	1	2	.207	.285	.357
Isenia, Chairon, Orlando	46	157	142	13	31	36	5	0	0	11	3	0	4	8	1	11	0	0	7	.218	.279	.254
Jackson, Edwin, Jacksonville .	27	31	29	2	4	4	0	0	0	3	1	0	0	1	0	12	0	0	0	.138	.167	.138
Jacobsen, Bucky, Tennessee ..	131	521	447	84	133	252	24	1	31	84	0	5	13	56	8	91	3	1	7	.298	.388	.564
Janke, Cheyenne, Tennessee ..	9	6	6	1	3	4	1	0	0	0	0	0	0	0	0	2	0	0	0	.500	.500	.667
Jeffcoat, Bryon, Greenville	37	124	100	15	26	31	5	0	0	11	3	3	1	17	0	24	1	0	1	.260	.364	.310
Jenkins, Geoff, Huntsville * ...	6	21	20	6	5	11	0	0	2	3	0	0	0	1	0	7	1	0	0	.250	.286	.550
Jennings, Robin, Chat.*	8	33	30	5	10	18	3	1	1	2	0	0	0	3	0	7	0	0	2	.333	.394	.600
Johnson, Ben, Mobile	44	140	127	8	23	31	5	0	1	7	1	0	2	10	0	36	0	1	0	.181	.252	.244
Johnson, Kade, Huntsville......	65	241	213	26	41	63	8	1	4	31	1	3	3	21	1	65	5	3	3	.192	.271	.296
Johnson, Kelly, Greenville * ...	98	377	334	46	92	142	22	5	6	45	3	5	0	35	3	81	10	3	4	.275	.340	.425
Johnson, Tyler, Tennessee † ..	20	2	2	0	0	0	0	0	0	0	0	0	0	0	0	2	0	0	0	.000	.000	.000
Jones, Mike, Huntsville	17	27	25	1	3	4	1	0	0	1	2	0	0	0	0	6	0	0	0	.120	.120	.160
Jorgensen, Ryan, Carolina	67	246	211	28	51	85	16	0	6	34	0	3	2	30	2	53	1	0	2	.242	.337	.403
Jurries, James, Greenville	129	522	465	73	132	202	35	4	9	54	2	3	4	48	1	108	4	2	10	.284	.354	.434
Karnuth, Jason, West Tenn	45	2	2	0	0	0	0	0	0	0	0	0	0	0	0	2	0	0	0	.000	.000	.000
Kearns, Austin, Chattanooga ..	3	8	5	2	1	1	0	0	0	1	0	0	1	2	0	2	0	0	0	.200	.500	.200
Keller, Kris, Chattanooga	35	3	3	1	0	0	0	0	0	0	0	0	0	0	0	1	0	0	1	.000	.000	.000
Kelly, Heath, Orlando	14	47	45	7	12	19	1	0	2	8	0	0	0	2	0	15	0	0	1	.267	.298	.422
Kelly, Steve, Chattanooga	6	9	8	0	0	0	0	0	0	0	0	0	0	1	0	7	0	0	0	.000	.111	.000
Kent, Steve, Carolina *	39	10	10	2	3	3	0	0	0	0	0	0	0	0	0	1	0	0	1	.300	.300	.300
King, Brennan, Jacksonville ...	124	491	434	47	105	149	15	1	9	43	2	6	5	44	2	92	0	3	13	.242	.315	.343
Knott, Jon, Mobile	127	537	432	83	109	222	32	0	27	82	0	6	17	82	1	117	5	3	1	.252	.387	.514
Knox, Ryan, Huntsville	96	377	340	58	81	113	18	4	2	21	5	3	5	24	0	76	29	9	4	.238	.296	.332
Kopitzke, Casey, West Tenn....	106	359	318	27	83	95	10	1	0	25	4	1	7	29	2	45	3	5	8	.261	.335	.299
Koronka, John, Chat.-W.Tenn.*	26	40	36	2	4	4	0	0	0	0	4	0	0	0	0	14	0	0	2	.111	.111	.111
Krause, Scott, Tennessee	73	231	201	30	59	95	17	2	5	23	2	1	8	19	0	36	5	3	6	.294	.376	.473
Krawiec, Aaron, West Tenn * .	8	9	8	0	0	0	0	0	0	0	0	0	0	1	0	8	0	0	0	.000	.111	.000
Kremblas, Mike, Huntsville	68	239	198	23	38	57	7	0	4	19	2	1	12	26	1	53	5	3	6	.192	.321	.288
Krynzel, Dave, Huntsville *	124	531	457	72	122	163	13	11	2	34	5	3	6	60	4	119	43	21	3	.267	.357	.357
LaForest, Pete, Orlando *	21	91	72	9	18	35	8	0	3	15	0	2	1	16	1	17	0	0	1	.250	.385	.486
LaRoche, Adam, Greenville * .	61	260	219	42	62	112	12	1	12	37	0	4	3	34	3	53	1	2	6	.283	.381	.511
Lambert, Jeremy, Tennessee ..	33	2	2	0	0	0	0	0	0	0	0	0	0	0	0	2	0	0	0	.000	.000	.000
Langerhans, Ryan, Green.*	94	387	336	42	85	130	23	2	6	38	2	0	3	46	3	85	10	10	6	.253	.348	.387
Langone, Steve, Jacksonville .	22	4	3	1	1	2	1	0	0	0	1	0	0	0	0	0	0	0	0	.333	.333	.667
Lee, Derek, Huntsville *	20	18	16	1	1	1	0	0	0	0	2	0	0	0	0	6	0	0	0	.063	.063	.063
Leicester, Jon, West Tenn	48	27	20	1	4	4	0	0	0	0	6	0	0	1	0	4	0	0	0	.200	.238	.200
Lemanczyk, Matt, Tennessee .	7	14	12	1	2	2	0	0	0	0	1	0	1	0	0	1	1	1	0	.167	.231	.167
Leon, Donny, West Tenn †	23	85	77	11	23	34	8	0	1	8	0	1	0	7	0	16	0	0	3	.299	.353	.442
Lewis, Derrick, Greenville	3	1	1	0	0	0	0	0	0	0	0	0	0	0	0	1	0	0	0	.000	.000	.000
Lewis, Kenneth, Chat.*	6	23	17	4	2	3	1	0	0	0	1	0	1	4	0	9	3	2	0	.118	.318	.176
Lewis, Richard, Greenville......	129	515	460	59	110	157	23	3	6	47	3	6	2	44	3	101	19	9	6	.239	.305	.341
Liriano, Pedro, West Tenn......	10	41	37	4	12	15	1	1	0	4	1	1	0	2	0	6	4	2	0	.324	.350	.405

Player, Team	G	TPA	AB	R	H	TB	2B	3B	HR	RBI	SH	SF	HP	BB	IBB	SO	SB	CS	GDP	Avg.	OBP	Slg.
Liriano, Pedro, Huntsville	27	42	38	3	3	3	0	0	0	1	2	1	0	1	0	16	2	0	1	.079	.100	.079
Lorenzana, Luis, Mobile	18	55	43	6	8	8	0	0	0	3	2	1	0	9	0	7	0	0	2	.186	.321	.186
Lyons, Mike, Tennessee	57	1	1	0	0	0	0	0	0	0	0	0	0	0	0	1	0	0	0	.000	.000	.000
Machado, Alejandro, Hunt.	45	177	155	14	35	41	4	1	0	13	5	0	2	15	1	24	11	1	0	.226	.302	.265
Magness, Pat, Carolina *	52	160	132	10	30	46	7	0	3	18	0	2	2	24	0	36	0	1	7	.227	.350	.348
Maldonado, Carlos, Birm.	120	469	408	50	107	151	24	1	6	63	3	9	6	43	1	50	1	1	13	.262	.335	.370
Martinez, Gabby, Orlando	25	115	108	16	39	50	5	0	2	7	2	0	0	5	0	9	6	0	1	.361	.389	.463
Martinez, Luis, Huntsville *	20	32	25	1	1	1	0	0	0	1	4	0	0	3	0	21	0	0	0	.040	.143	.040
Massiatte, Danny, Orlando	58	194	169	18	36	49	7	0	2	14	6	2	1	16	0	37	0	1	5	.213	.282	.290
Matthews, Lamont, Jack.*	12	36	30	2	6	10	2	1	0	3	1	0	1	4	0	12	0	0	0	.200	.314	.333
McAdoo, Duncan, Mobile	31	40	35	1	4	5	1	0	0	3	3	1	0	1	0	9	0	0	3	.114	.135	.143
McCarthy, Bill, Greenville	86	326	276	35	69	110	19	2	6	47	2	2	5	41	1	59	5	1	3	.250	.355	.399
McConnell, Sam, Greenville *	16	1	0	0	0	0	0	0	0	0	1	0	0	0	0	0	0	0	0	.000	.000	.000
McCrotty, Will, Jacksonville	32	20	14	2	2	2	0	0	0	0	2	0	0	4	0	6	0	0	0	.143	.333	.143
McKnight, Lukas, W.Tenn *	42	129	112	7	22	23	1	0	0	11	1	4	2	10	0	26	2	0	2	.196	.266	.205
McLeary, Marty, Carolina	11	8	5	0	1	2	1	0	0	1	1	0	0	2	0	3	0	0	0	.200	.429	.400
Medrano, Jesus, Carolina	73	301	251	36	63	88	15	2	2	28	3	4	2	41	1	48	18	6	1	.251	.356	.351
Melian, Jackson, West Tenn	79	274	252	28	65	100	8	3	7	28	0	0	2	20	1	47	8	7	3	.258	.318	.397
Merritt, Graig, Orlando	26	82	71	9	14	15	1	0	0	4	3	0	0	8	0	16	0	0	1	.197	.278	.211
Messenger, Randy, Carolina	29	31	29	1	2	2	0	0	0	1	1	0	0	1	0	10	0	0	0	.069	.100	.069
Michaelis, Derek, Jack.*	120	437	378	56	101	172	28	2	13	50	1	3	4	51	0	123	9	0	7	.267	.358	.455
Miller, Greg, Greenville	16	48	42	6	9	12	0	0	1	6	0	0	0	6	1	6	2	1	0	.214	.313	.286
Miller, Greg, Jacksonville *	4	9	8	0	0	0	0	0	0	0	1	0	0	0	0	3	0	0	0	.000	.000	.000
Miller, Ryan, Huntsville	51	14	14	3	4	5	1	0	0	2	0	0	0	0	0	5	0	0	0	.286	.286	.357
Minor, Ryan, Jacksonville	16	1	1	0	0	0	0	0	0	0	0	0	0	0	0	1	0	0	0	.000	.000	.000
Mitchell, Keith, Chattanooga	20	69	55	11	16	28	4	1	2	8	0	0	0	14	0	8	1	0	0	.291	.435	.509
Mitchell, Nathan, West Tenn	4	1	1	0	0	0	0	0	0	0	0	0	0	0	0	0	0	0	0	.000	.000	.000
Mitre, Sergio, West Tenn.	25	42	27	2	5	8	0	0	1	4	6	0	0	9	0	9	0	0	0	.185	.389	.296
Molina, Yadier, Tennessee	104	397	364	32	100	121	13	1	2	51	0	3	5	25	2	45	0	1	11	.275	.327	.332
Montero, Agustin, Jack.	16	2	2	0	0	0	0	0	0	0	0	0	0	0	0	1	0	0	0	.000	.000	.000
Moon, Brian, Huntsville †	6	23	22	3	5	11	3	0	1	3	1	0	0	0	0	1	0	0	0	.227	.227	.500
Moore, Frank, Orlando *	100	387	354	38	98	141	16	6	5	34	4	3	1	25	0	78	9	1	2	.277	.324	.398
Morales, Steve, Birmingham	31	98	86	6	21	30	1	1	2	12	4	2	1	5	0	12	0	0	0	.244	.287	.349
Moseley, Dustin, Chat.	19	39	37	6	13	17	1	0	1	9	1	0	0	1	0	6	1	0	1	.351	.368	.459
Moser, Todd, Carolina *	18	32	28	0	3	4	1	0	0	1	4	0	0	0	0	7	0	0	2	.107	.107	.143
Mottl, Ryan, Chattanooga †	23	31	28	4	7	7	0	0	0	0	2	0	0	1	0	10	0	0	0	.250	.276	.250
Moylan, Dan, Tennessee *	64	214	182	21	50	61	3	1	2	23	2	0	1	29	1	28	1	0	5	.275	.377	.335
Nannini, Mike, West Tenn	31	48	44	5	9	9	0	0	0	3	4	0	0	0	0	9	0	0	1	.205	.205	.205
Narveson, Chris, Tennessee *	10	15	10	2	2	2	0	0	0	0	2	0	0	3	0	2	0	0	0	.200	.385	.200
Nelson, Brad, Huntsville *	39	157	143	15	30	45	12	0	1	14	0	1	2	11	2	34	2	2	4	.210	.274	.315
Nelson, Bubba, Greenville	23	37	33	2	3	3	0	0	0	1	3	0	0	1	0	7	0	0	1	.091	.118	.091
Nelson, John, Tennessee	136	556	506	60	120	159	22	1	5	42	2	1	3	44	3	117	10	5	14	.237	.301	.314
Netwall, Chris, Tennessee	3	12	10	0	2	2	0	0	0	3	1	0	0	1	0	2	0	0	0	.200	.273	.200
Nicholson, Tommy, Birm.*	47	149	125	14	35	48	8	1	1	11	4	1	3	16	0	20	2	1	0	.280	.372	.384
Niles, Drew, Carolina †	118	439	390	64	102	134	17	3	3	37	8	1	2	38	2	79	1	3	7	.262	.329	.344
Nina, Elvin, Jacksonville	8	3	3	0	0	0	0	0	0	0	0	0	0	0	0	1	0	0	0	.000	.000	.000
Nolasco, Dave, Huntsville	9	8	8	0	1	1	0	0	0	1	0	0	0	0	0	5	0	0	0	.125	.125	.125
Novinsky, John, Tennessee	18	1	1	0	0	0	0	0	0	0	0	0	0	0	0	0	0	0	0	.000	.000	.000
Nunez, Jose, Mobile *	9	1	1	0	0	0	0	0	0	0	0	0	0	0	0	1	0	0	0	.000	.000	.000
Olmedo, Rainer, Chat.†	49	182	160	23	47	64	11	0	2	15	7	1	0	14	1	29	3	3	3	.294	.349	.400
Orr, Pete, Greenville *	98	292	257	22	58	78	10	2	2	31	4	3	3	25	3	48	14	5	3	.226	.299	.304
Ortiz, Nick, West Tenn	43	164	148	18	44	63	10	0	3	17	2	1	0	13	0	30	0	1	5	.297	.352	.426
Ortiz, Omar, Carolina †	8	2	2	0	0	0	0	0	0	0	0	0	0	0	0	1	0	0	0	.000	.000	.000
Owens, Ryan, Chattanooga	20	55	50	6	10	19	3	0	2	4	0	1	1	3	0	18	0	0	0	.200	.255	.380
Oxspring, Chris, Mobile *	40	39	27	3	3	4	1	0	0	3	5	0	0	7	0	11	0	0	1	.111	.294	.148
Padgett, Matt, Carolina *	129	516	462	65	128	210	29	1	17	76	0	8	3	43	3	104	2	3	9	.277	.337	.455
Parker, Matt, Huntsville	42	13	11	0	0	0	0	0	0	0	0	0	0	2	0	8	0	0	0	.000	.154	.000
Parrott, Rhett, Tennessee	24	49	43	1	7	7	0	0	0	1	5	0	0	1	0	11	0	0	0	.163	.182	.163
Paz, Rich, Huntsville	73	293	228	39	56	73	14	0	1	24	0	2	5	58	0	36	6	3	4	.246	.406	.320
Pearce, Josh, Tennessee	5	9	8	0	0	0	0	0	0	0	1	0	0	0	0	3	0	0	0	.000	.000	.000
Pena, Juan, Tennessee *	29	23	19	0	2	2	0	0	0	0	4	0	0	0	0	11	0	0	0	.105	.105	.105
Perez, Antonio, Orlando	24	105	81	16	22	35	5	1	2	10	1	1	4	18	0	18	3	1	0	.272	.423	.432
Perez, Santiago, Chat.†	62	268	234	45	71	105	12	5	4	30	1	2	0	31	0	68	19	9	5	.303	.382	.449
Peterson, Brian, Chattanooga	36	111	100	15	24	31	7	0	0	4	0	0	1	10	1	22	3	1	2	.240	.315	.310
Pignatiello, Carmen, W.Tenn	1	3	1	0	0	0	0	0	0	0	0	0	0	2	0	0	0	0	0	.000	.667	.000
Pilkington, Brian, Jack.	5	12	10	2	1	1	0	0	0	0	2	0	0	0	0	3	0	0	0	.100	.100	.100
Pineda, Luis, Jacksonville	9	1	1	0	0	0	0	0	0	0	0	0	0	0	0	0	0	0	0	.000	.000	.000
Piniella, Juan, Birmingham	115	393	346	45	101	141	24	2	4	27	12	2	5	28	0	82	12	5	4	.292	.352	.408
Polcovich, Kevin, Carolina	13	47	42	4	6	6	0	0	0	5	4	0	1	0	0	7	2	1	1	.143	.163	.143
Powers, John, West Tenn *	34	124	102	11	24	29	3	1	0	10	0	0	0	22	0	18	3	0	1	.235	.371	.284
Proctor, Scott, Jacksonville	17	2	2	1	0	0	0	0	0	0	0	0	0	0	0	1	0	0	0	.000	.000	.000
Quintero, Humberto, Mobile	110	421	386	37	115	150	26	0	3	52	4	3	9	19	5	41	0	0	17	.298	.343	.389
Ramirez, Emmanuel, W.Tenn	22	1	1	0	0	0	0	0	0	0	0	0	0	0	0	1	0	0	0	.000	.000	.000
Ray, Ken, Huntsville	31	9	8	1	0	0	0	0	0	0	0	0	0	1	0	3	0	0	1	.000	.111	.000
Reed, Jeremy, Birmingham *	66	281	242	51	99	143	17	3	7	43	7	1	2	29	5	19	18	13	7	.409	.474	.591
Reinking, Kevin, Mobile	14	47	40	5	5	9	1	0	1	6	0	1	3	3	0	20	0	0	1	.125	.234	.225
Repko, Jason, Jacksonville	119	476	416	62	100	154	14	5	10	23	9	3	6	42	0	89	21	8	1	.240	.317	.370
Reyes, Guillermo, Birm.†	116	429	376	40	79	105	10	2	4	34	11	6	4	32	0	71	15	8	7	.210	.275	.279
Rico, Matt, Orlando	2	8	7	2	1	2	1	0	0	0	0	0	1	0	0	2	0	0	1	.143	.250	.286
Riggans, Shawn, Orlando	22	69	62	7	17	26	6	0	1	11	0	2	1	4	0	14	0	0	0	.274	.319	.419
Roat, Kyle, Greenville	1	1	1	0	0	0	0	0	0	0	0	0	0	0	0	1	0	0	0	.000	.000	.000

Player, Team	G	TPA	AB	R	H	TB	2B	3B	HR	RBI	SH	SF	HP	BB	IBB	SO	SB	CS	GDP	Avg.	OBP	Slg.
Robinson, Jeff, Huntsville	3	2	2	0	1	1	0	0	0	0	0	0	0	0	0	0	0	0	0	.500	.500	.500
Rodriguez, Orlando, Jack.*	11	2	2	0	0	0	0	0	0	0	0	0	0	0	0	2	0	0	0	.000	.000	.000
Rodriguez, Victor, Jack.	45	165	154	12	39	56	8	0	3	17	3	1	1	6	0	19	1	1	7	.253	.284	.364
Rogers, Brandon, Jack.	6	14	10	2	4	8	1	0	1	1	0	0	0	4	0	3	0	0	0	.400	.571	.800
Rohlicek, Russ, West Tenn	13	3	3	0	0	0	0	0	0	0	0	0	0	0	0	1	0	0	0	.000	.000	.000
Rojas, Chris, Mobile	34	33	25	0	3	4	1	0	0	0	5	0	1	2	0	9	0	0	1	.120	.214	.160
Roman, Jesse, Tennessee *	16	52	48	3	8	13	2	0	1	4	0	0	1	3	1	16	0	0	0	.167	.231	.271
Ryu, Jae-kuk, West Tenn	11	19	16	1	3	4	1	0	0	0	2	0	0	1	0	4	0	0	1	.188	.235	.250
Sadler, Ray, West Tenn	110	457	412	56	120	179	31	5	6	42	2	3	7	33	4	81	17	7	8	.291	.352	.434
Saenz, Chris, Huntsville	1	2	2	0	0	0	0	0	0	0	0	0	0	0	0	1	0	0	0	.000	.000	.000
Salas, Juan, Orlando	75	293	279	30	76	97	8	2	3	41	0	3	1	10	0	43	1	2	7	.272	.297	.348
Salmon, Brad, Chattanooga	11	8	6	2	0	0	0	0	0	0	1	0	0	1	0	2	0	0	0	.000	.143	.000
Sanchez, Felix, West Tenn	30	14	14	1	0	0	0	0	0	0	0	0	0	0	0	11	0	0	0	.000	.000	.000
Sandoval, Danny, Birm.†	130	547	478	62	137	180	30	2	3	49	14	9	3	43	2	67	21	11	10	.287	.343	.377
Sardinha, Dane, Chattanooga	72	275	246	21	63	87	15	0	3	32	0	6	1	22	3	61	5	3	1	.256	.313	.354
Saunders, Chris, Birmingham	17	58	47	4	9	9	0	0	0	6	0	0	0	11	0	15	1	0	2	.191	.345	.191
Scales, Bobby, Mobile †	100	342	301	41	85	122	22	3	3	37	1	2	2	36	2	63	8	2	4	.282	.361	.405
Schrager, Tony, West Tenn	18	57	49	1	8	11	1	1	0	3	3	0	0	5	0	11	1	1	1	.163	.241	.224
Schramek, Mark, Chat.*	42	153	141	14	25	34	9	0	0	10	0	0	4	8	1	55	2	1	0	.177	.242	.241
Schumaker, Skip, Tenn.*	91	387	342	43	86	118	20	3	2	22	2	2	4	37	2	54	6	6	4	.251	.330	.345
Secrist, Reed, Chattanooga*	17	63	54	9	13	25	3	0	3	9	0	2	2	5	0	14	1	1	0	.241	.317	.463
Senjem, Guye, Chattanooga*	123	418	351	75	93	161	21	1	15	61	2	3	6	56	3	81	9	3	4	.265	.373	.459
Shackelford, Brian, Chat.*	13	3	2	1	0	0	0	0	0	0	0	0	0	1	0	1	0	0	0	.000	.333	.000
Shaffer, Josh, Birmingham*	98	332	304	17	62	73	7	2	0	21	7	1	3	17	0	70	1	2	6	.204	.252	.240
Shelley, Jason, Huntsville	9	15	13	0	2	3	1	0	0	3	1	1	0	0	0	5	0	0	0	.154	.143	.231
Shumpert, Terry, Orlando	2	10	9	1	2	2	0	0	0	1	0	0	1	0	0	2	0	0	0	.222	.300	.222
Sing, Brandon, West Tenn	42	157	139	15	29	51	7	0	5	23	1	6	1	10	0	39	2	1	4	.209	.256	.367
Small, Aaron, Carolina	8	10	9	0	1	1	0	0	0	0	1	0	0	0	0	2	0	0	0	.111	.111	.111
Smith, Chuck, Greenville	3	6	6	0	1	1	0	0	0	1	0	0	0	0	0	2	0	0	0	.167	.167	.167
Smith, Matt, Birmingham	52	1	1	0	0	0	0	0	0	0	0	0	0	0	0	0	0	0	0	.000	.000	.000
Smith, Ryan, Mobile	11	37	33	1	5	8	0	0	1	3	0	0	1	3	0	11	0	0	0	.152	.243	.242
Smith, Will, Carolina *	34	136	123	23	36	46	5	1	1	13	0	2	0	11	0	23	1	0	1	.293	.346	.374
Smitherman, Stephen, Chat.	105	430	365	60	113	195	21	2	19	73	0	5	6	54	6	95	11	3	7	.310	.402	.534
Snare, Ryan, Carolina *	18	28	26	1	2	2	0	0	0	2	1	1	0	0	0	6	0	0	0	.077	.074	.077
Socarras, Tony, Jacksonville*	66	215	182	22	37	64	8	2	5	31	5	4	6	18	1	50	1	0	4	.203	.290	.352
Sodowsky, Clint, Carolina *	5	9	8	0	1	1	0	0	0	0	1	0	0	0	0	4	0	0	0	.125	.125	.125
Sonnier, Shawn, West Tenn	12	2	2	0	1	1	0	0	0	0	0	0	0	0	0	0	0	0	0	.500	.500	.500
Spearman, Jemel, West Tenn.	15	64	57	11	20	27	2	1	1	9	1	0	0	6	0	6	5	2	2	.351	.413	.474
Spiehs, R.D., Mobile	15	1	1	0	0	0	0	0	0	0	0	0	0	0	0	1	0	0	0	.000	.000	.000
Sprague, Kevin, Tennessee *	53	3	2	0	0	0	0	0	0	1	0	0	0	1	0	0	0	0	0	.000	.333	.000
Steffek, Brian, Jacksonville	24	1	1	0	0	0	0	0	0	0	0	0	0	0	0	1	0	0	0	.000	.000	.000
Stenson, Dernell, Chat.*	101	405	356	51	109	179	28	0	14	76	1	7	2	39	4	74	4	5	10	.306	.371	.503
Stewart, Cory, Mobile *	25	44	38	1	5	7	2	0	0	3	5	0	0	1	0	14	0	0	1	.132	.154	.184
Stocks, Nick, Tennessee	28	42	41	4	10	14	4	0	0	4	1	0	0	0	0	15	0	0	2	.244	.244	.341
Stults, Eric, Jacksonville *	9	9	8	2	3	6	1	1	0	3	0	0	0	1	0	2	0	0	0	.375	.444	.750
Sylvester, Billy, Greenville	41	1	1	0	0	0	0	0	0	0	0	0	0	0	0	1	0	0	0	.000	.000	.000
Szuminski, Jason, W.Tenn	29	8	6	0	0	0	0	0	0	0	1	0	0	1	0	2	0	0	0	.000	.143	.000
Takeoka, Kazuhiro, Greenville.	20	2	2	0	0	0	0	0	0	0	0	0	0	0	0	1	0	0	0	.000	.000	.000
Terveen, Bryce, Greenville *	61	218	178	17	35	42	7	0	0	16	2	2	6	30	1	49	1	0	2	.197	.329	.236
Theodorou, Nick, Jack.†	36	148	119	18	35	42	7	0	0	7	3	1	3	22	0	19	1	2	2	.294	.414	.353
Theriot, Ryan, West Tenn †	53	215	178	20	42	48	3	0	1	9	4	1	3	29	1	21	9	8	6	.236	.351	.270
Thomas, Charles, Green.*	47	197	176	29	57	79	14	4	0	23	0	0	3	18	0	25	5	4	1	.324	.396	.449
Thompson, Travis, Chat.	9	8	8	1	2	2	0	0	0	0	0	0	0	0	0	2	0	0	0	.250	.250	.250
Totten, Heath, Jacksonville	28	40	33	4	5	5	0	0	0	1	7	0	0	0	0	11	0	0	1	.152	.152	.152
Trujillo, J.J., Mobile	28	5	4	0	1	1	0	0	0	0	1	0	0	0	0	2	0	0	0	.250	.250	.250
Tucker, Rusty, Mobile	51	2	1	0	0	0	0	0	0	0	0	0	0	1	0	0	0	0	0	.000	.500	.000
Ungs, Nic, Carolina	10	13	12	1	1	1	0	0	0	0	0	0	0	1	0	4	0	0	0	.083	.154	.083
Upton, B.J., Orlando	29	127	105	14	29	40	8	0	1	16	2	2	2	16	0	25	2	4	1	.276	.376	.381
Urdaneta, Lino, Jacksonville	44	4	2	0	0	0	0	0	0	0	1	0	0	1	0	2	0	0	0	.000	.333	.000
Valdez, Wilson, Carolina	37	169	144	28	45	55	6	2	0	14	7	2	0	15	1	17	16	5	2	.313	.373	.382
Van Buizen, Rodney, Jack.	20	54	46	3	10	10	0	0	0	2	2	0	1	5	0	11	1	0	3	.217	.308	.217
Varner, Noochie, Huntsville	80	312	293	30	79	113	12	2	6	47	0	3	2	14	1	52	7	3	2	.270	.304	.386
Velazquez, Jose, West Tenn *	54	163	138	11	33	39	3	0	1	22	0	4	0	21	1	22	1	1	3	.239	.331	.283
Victorino, Shane, Jack.†	66	293	266	37	75	98	9	4	2	15	2	1	3	21	1	41	16	7	3	.282	.340	.368
Villalon, Julio, Tennessee	12	16	14	0	1	1	0	0	0	0	0	0	1	1	0	3	0	0	0	.071	.188	.071
Wainwright, Adam, Green.	27	47	42	2	9	10	1	0	0	5	5	0	0	0	0	13	0	0	0	.214	.214	.238
Waligora, T.P., West Tenn	11	1	1	0	0	0	0	0	0	0	0	0	0	0	0	0	0	0	0	.000	.000	.000
Ward, Daryle, Jacksonville *	4	16	16	0	2	2	0	0	0	1	0	0	0	0	0	3	0	0	0	.125	.125	.125
Washington, Rico, Mobile *	111	459	402	60	98	163	19	2	14	60	0	4	9	44	4	73	2	2	7	.244	.329	.405
Waszgis, B.J., Jacksonville	40	144	116	7	21	27	3	0	1	9	1	0	0	27	0	35	1	1	4	.181	.336	.233
Waters, Chris, Greenville *	18	24	22	1	3	3	0	0	0	1	2	0	0	0	0	5	0	0	1	.136	.136	.136
Watkins, Steve, Mobile	18	23	17	0	5	6	1	0	0	4	3	0	0	3	0	6	0	0	0	.294	.400	.353
Webb, Alan, Mobile *	58	14	14	1	3	3	0	0	0	0	0	0	0	0	0	6	0	0	0	.214	.214	.214
Webb, John, West Tenn	30	37	34	2	8	12	1	0	1	2	2	0	0	1	0	7	0	0	0	.235	.257	.353
Weekly, Chris, Tennessee *	111	325	279	27	71	93	13	0	3	31	2	3	2	39	0	53	5	1	6	.254	.347	.333
Wellemeyer, Todd, W.Tenn	4	4	3	0	0	0	0	0	0	0	1	0	0	0	0	1	0	0	0	.000	.000	.000
Weston, Aron, West Tenn *	56	214	194	27	39	58	6	2	3	14	3	1	3	13	0	54	12	4	4	.201	.261	.299
Willingham, Josh, Carolina	22	83	67	15	20	39	2	1	5	14	0	0	3	13	2	20	0	0	0	.299	.434	.582
Willis, Dontrelle, Carolina *	6	11	10	2	2	2	0	0	0	0	0	0	0	1	0	0	0	0	0	.200	.273	.200
Wilson, Josh, Carolina	118	475	434	53	110	161	30	6	3	58	2	10	2	27	0	70	6	5	9	.253	.294	.371
Winkelsas, Joe, Greenville	23	2	1	0	1	1	0	0	0	1	0	0	0	1	0	0	0	0	0	1.000	1.000	1.000
Zumwalt, Alec, Greenville	11	3	2	0	1	1	0	0	0	0	0	0	0	1	0	0	0	0	0	.500	.667	.500

PLAYERS WITH TWO OR MORE TEAMS

Player, Team	G	TPA	AB	R	H	TB	2B	3B	HR	RBI	SH	SF	HP	BB	IBB	SO	SB	CS	GDP	Avg.	OBP	Slg.
Dunn, Scott, Birmingham	8	0	0	0	0	0	0	0	0	0	0	0	0	0	0	0	0	0	0	.000	.000	.000
Dunn, Scott, Chattanooga......	31	4	3	1	0	0	0	0	0	0	0	0	0	1	0	1	0	0	0	.000	.250	.000
Feliciano, Jesus, Jack.*	37	94	81	7	12	15	0	0	1	4	0	1	1	11	1	16	2	3	3	.148	.255	.185
Feliciano, Jesus, Orlando *	72	276	251	31	70	84	11	0	1	21	6	1	3	15	2	25	7	1	7	.279	.326	.335
Hamilton, Jon, Birmingham *	51	198	170	22	38	53	4	1	3	18	5	2	1	20	1	41	10	6	6	.224	.306	.312
Hamilton, Jon, West Tenn * ...	71	270	241	29	61	91	16	1	4	27	4	0	1	24	2	37	12	4	3	.253	.323	.378
Koronka, John, West Tenn * ..	1	2	2	0	0	0	0	0	0	0	0	0	0	0	0	2	0	0	0	.000	.000	.000
Koronka, John, Chat.*	25	38	34	2	4	4	0	0	0	0	4	0	0	0	0	12	0	0	2	.118	.118	.118

GRAND SLAMS—Hart, 3; Erickson, 2; Abercrombie, Boscan, Brock, Burns, Cabrera, Correll, Dawkins, Gemoll, Gerber, Grummitt, F. Gutierrez, J. Gutierrez, Jurries, Moseley, Orr, Reed, Senjem, 1 each.

AWARDED FIRST BASE ON CATCHER'S INTERFERENCE—Fitzgerald (Jorgensen); Grummitt (Socarras); Valdez (R. Smith).

2003 PITCHING

TEAM

Team	W	L	Pct.	ERA	G	CG	ShO	Sv.	IP	H	TBF	R	ER	HR	SH	SF	HB	BB	IBB	SO	WP	Bk.
Huntsville	75	63	.543	3.17	138	4	12	41	1225.1	1143	5249	542	431	77	75	35	51	522	9	952	59	9
Carolina.............	80	58	.580	3.45	138	2	12	41	1198.1	1085	5157	546	460	60	61	44	70	524	21	957	76	7
Jacksonville.......	66	73	.475	3.50	139	3	8	29	1217.2	1185	5171	557	473	78	56	38	48	405	36	997	44	6
Tennessee	72	67	.518	3.58	139	2	13	43	1209.0	1122	5164	561	481	106	55	37	62	475	31	1047	52	5
Greenville	68	70	.493	3.62	138	6	18	30	1175.0	1140	4986	549	472	83	63	52	57	399	15	903	41	9
Birmingham	73	64	.533	3.76	137	3	7	45	1185.1	1158	5175	580	495	64	37	50	57	506	42	965	63	9
Orlando	65	72	.474	3.77	137	6	9	28	1170.2	1163	5048	604	491	89	40	41	46	400	15	870	42	6
West Tenn	65	73	.471	3.83	138	3	9	35	1190.0	1186	5157	586	507	86	54	35	67	454	17	1064	46	9
Mobile...............	61	77	.442	3.88	138	3	6	37	1206.0	1093	5172	595	520	88	54	51	52	499	31	1102	33	0
Chattanooga......	66	74	.471	4.08	140	2	6	41	1214.0	1294	5324	662	550	96	74	44	61	458	17	942	56	11

INDIVIDUAL

TOP QUALIFIERS FOR EARNED-RUN AVERAGE TITLE

Minimum 112 innings. *Lefthanded pitcher.

Pitcher, Team	W	L	Pct.	ERA	G	GS	CG	ShO	GF	Sv.	IP	H	TBF	R	ER	HR	SH	SF	HB	BB	IBB	SO	WP	Bk.
Hanrahan, Joel, Jacksonville...	10	4	.714	2.43	23	23	1	0	0	0	133.1	117	556	44	36	5	4	2	7	53	2	130	4	0
Pacheco, Enemencio, Birm.	12	2	.857	2.56	30	24	0	0	0	0	151.1	131	632	51	43	5	3	8	9	51	1	116	5	0
Martinez, Luis, Huntsville *	8	5	.615	2.58	20	20	1	0	0	0	115.0	93	489	46	33	4	11	1	7	54	0	116	6	1
Bridges, Donnie, Carolina........	10	2	.833	2.81	31	19	1	1	3	0	134.2	85	550	47	42	6	8	3	11	70	1	109	11	1
Oxspring, Chris, Mobile..........	10	6	.625	2.92	40	18	1	0	8	0	135.2	106	572	47	44	6	1	5	1	62	3	129	1	0
Nelson, Bubba, Greenville	8	10	.444	3.18	23	20	0	0	1	0	119.0	106	496	47	42	7	3	4	4	45	0	77	4	0
Magrane, Jim, Orlando............	10	6	.625	3.26	25	24	0	0	0	0	143.2	147	626	69	52	9	1	4	6	51	1	87	5	1
Parrott, Rhett, Tennessee........	8	9	.471	3.27	21	21	1	0	0	0	124.0	122	519	52	45	11	2	3	3	40	3	112	7	1
Mitre, Sergio, West Tenn.........	7	9	.438	3.34	25	24	0	0	0	0	145.2	162	639	75	54	6	9	3	12	41	0	128	6	0
Wainwright, Adam, Greenville .	10	8	.556	3.37	27	27	1	0	0	0	149.2	133	599	59	56	9	2	3	7	37	0	128	4	2
Totten, Heath, Jacksonville......	11	12	.478	3.42	28	28	2	1	0	0	181.1	196	751	83	69	15	7	5	5	17	3	114	1	0
Switzer, Jon, Orlando *	8	8	.500	3.43	22	22	2	0	0	0	126.0	117	522	63	48	10	5	4	5	32	1	100	9	1
Farmer, Tom, Jacksonville.......	5	8	.385	3.45	20	19	0	0	0	0	117.1	116	486	51	45	9	5	4	5	26	0	69	6	0
Veras, Jose, Orlando	6	9	.400	3.45	27	22	1	1	1	0	130.1	108	551	59	50	11	3	3	6	53	0	118	8	1
Hall, Josh, Chattanooga	8	10	.444	3.47	26	25	2	0	0	0	153.0	152	655	73	59	9	8	6	3	53	1	114	10	1

DEPARTMENTAL LEADERS: W—Pacheco, Stewart, 12; L—Koronka, Liriano, 13; Pct.—Fesh, .900; G—Gaal, 62; GS—Totten, 28; CG—Five pitchers with 2; ShO—Several pitchers with 1; GF—Lyons, 49; Sv.—Lyons, 31; IP—Totten, 181.1; H—Totten, 196; TBF—Totten, 751; R—Koronka, 88; ER—Stocks, 80; HR—Stocks, 17; SH—Koronka, 15; SF—McAdoo, 11; HB—Stocks, 13; BB—Bridges, 70; IBB—Bauer, 8; SO—Nannini, 158; WP—Bridges, Gracesqui, 11; BK—Koronka, 5.

ALL PITCHERS

*Lefthanded pitcher.

Pitcher, Team	W	L	Pct.	ERA	G	GS	CG	ShO	GF	Sv.	IP	H	TBF	R	ER	HR	SH	SF	HB	BB	IBB	SO	WP	Bk.
Adams, Brian, Huntsville *	3	1	.750	2.95	32	0	0	0	14	3	61.0	57	270	30	20	1	3	2	3	36	0	32	4	0
Adams, Mike, Huntsville..........	3	7	.300	3.15	45	2	0	0	34	14	74.1	58	318	30	26	6	4	0	2	33	1	83	3	2
Adkins, Tim, Chattanooga *	0	2	.000	1.86	9	0	0	0	1	0	9.2	8	42	5	2	0	0	1	1	4	1	11	0	0
Aguilar, Ray, Greenville *	3	4	.429	2.71	35	7	0	0	6	1	93.0	81	378	39	28	8	8	4	2	20	0	91	2	0
An, Byeong, Birmingham *	5	3	.625	3.94	16	14	0	0	0	0	80.0	76	346	38	35	4	2	4	0	34	3	45	3	0
Andersen, Derek, Orlando *	2	1	.667	4.29	22	0	0	0	2	0	21.0	22	89	12	10	1	1	0	2	3	0	13	0	0
Anderson, Travis, West Tenn...	2	3	.400	4.37	14	5	0	0	3	0	35.0	37	153	17	17	5	0	1	3	13	1	25	4	0
Andrews, Clayton, Chat.*	0	1	.000	3.48	2	2	0	0	0	0	10.1	14	47	8	4	0	2	1	2	3	0	3	0	0
Ankiel, Rick, Tennessee *	2	6	.250	6.29	20	10	1	0	1	0	54.1	45	253	42	38	5	2	2	6	49	1	64	10	0
Arteaga, Joshua, West Tenn....	0	0	.000	3.86	3	0	0	0	3	1	2.1	3	11	1	1	0	0	0	0	2	0	0	0	0
Ashby, Chris, Carolina.............	0	1	.000	2.21	9	0	0	0	9	0	20.1	15	86	6	5	1	0	0	1	11	1	12	1	0
Autrey, Scott, Orlando............	5	4	.556	2.99	12	12	2	0	0	0	78.1	79	330	31	26	9	3	3	2	15	0	37	1	0
Axelson, Josh, Tennessee	4	2	.667	2.76	27	8	0	0	6	0	75.0	68	301	26	23	7	2	1	4	19	1	58	6	0
Bajenaru, Jeff, Birmingham.....	4	2	.667	3.20	50	0	0	0	27	14	64.2	53	271	29	23	2	2	5	0	28	3	62	8	0
Baker, Brad, Mobile	1	6	.143	5.68	17	9	0	0	5	0	50.2	50	234	34	32	3	3	1	3	36	1	53	3	0
Baker, Ryan, Carolina	5	2	.714	2.95	44	1	0	0	17	4	64.0	54	279	28	21	1	3	5	1	38	3	56	4	0
Barnett, Marty, Carolina...........	0	2	.000	5.68	5	5	0	0	0	0	19.0	29	91	20	12	4	1	3	2	5	0	12	0	0
Barreto, Joel, Chattanooga	0	1	.000	3.70	15	0	0	0	3	0	24.1	19	97	10	10	2	2	0	0	9	2	15	0	0
Barry, Kevin, Greenville	4	4	.500	4.95	51	0	0	0	19	5	56.1	54	257	36	31	1	2	3	3	32	0	68	3	0
Basham, Bobby, Chattanooga .	5	10	.333	5.17	17	17	0	0	0	0	94.0	133	436	72	54	16	6	3	1	24	1	56	8	0
Battersby, Eric, Birmingham *.	0	0	.000	4.50	1	0	0	0	1	0	2.0	2	13	2	1	0	0	0	1	3	0	1	0	0

Pitcher, Team	W	L	Pct.	ERA	G	GS	CG	ShO	GF	Sv.	IP	H	TBF	R	ER	HR	SH	SF	HB	BB	IBB	SO	WP	Bk.
Bauer, Greg, Jacksonville	6	6	.500	2.93	46	3	0	0	17	2	86.0	92	381	34	28	2	7	2	3	41	8	61	2	0
Bautista, Denny, Carolina	4	5	.444	3.71	11	11	0	0	0	0	53.1	45	239	33	22	5	3	1	1	35	0	61	8	0
Beckett, Josh, Carolina	0	0	.000	4.50	1	1	0	0	0	0	4.0	4	15	2	2	1	0	0	0	0	0	7	0	0
Belisle, Matt, Greenville	6	8	.429	3.52	21	21	1	0	0	0	125.1	128	532	59	49	5	8	5	6	42	2	94	3	2
Benedetti, John, Orlando	5	5	.500	3.72	42	1	0	0	19	3	65.1	69	287	28	27	6	5	2	4	25	3	51	5	0
Benik, Brett, West Tenn	0	1	.000	1.42	3	0	0	0	1	0	6.1	6	26	1	1	0	0	0	0	3	0	4	0	0
Bevel, Bobby, Chattanooga *	2	1	.667	1.63	16	1	0	0	7	1	27.2	20	118	12	5	1	2	1	3	9	1	28	1	0
Blank, Matt, Greenville *	0	0	.000	0.00	2	0	0	0	1	0	2.0	0	6	0	0	0	0	0	0	0	0	0	0	0
Bludau, Frank, Chattanooga	0	1	.000	12.00	3	0	0	0	3	0	3.0	7	21	4	4	2	0	0	0	5	0	2	0	0
Brazelton, Dewon, Orlando	2	0	1.000	2.53	2	2	0	0	0	0	10.2	8	50	6	3	0	0	0	2	8	0	5	0	0
Bridges, Donnie, Carolina	10	2	.833	2.81	31	19	1	1	3	0	134.2	85	550	47	42	6	8	3	11	70	1	109	11	1
Brock, Tarrik, Jacksonville *	0	0	.000	0.00	1	0	0	0	1	0	0.1	0	1	0	0	0	0	0	0	0	0	1	0	0
Brown, Andrew, Jacksonville	0	0	.000	0.00	1	1	0	0	0	0	1.0	0	3	0	0	0	0	0	0	0	0	1	0	0
Brown, Eric, West Tenn	6	1	.857	3.71	44	0	0	0	10	1	51.0	59	225	25	21	2	3	2	2	14	2	40	2	0
Bruso, Greg, Huntsville	1	1	.500	3.60	2	2	0	0	0	0	10.0	13	44	5	4	1	0	1	0	6	0	5	0	1
Bullard, Jim, Birmingham *	5	3	.625	3.69	53	6	0	0	10	3	90.1	103	413	51	37	6	1	7	6	42	4	61	4	0
Bumstead, Mike, Mobile	1	2	.333	2.88	37	1	0	0	12	0	68.2	65	288	23	22	1	2	0	3	28	0	44	0	0
Byrd, Paul, Greenville	0	0	.000	8.31	1	1	0	0	0	0	4.1	8	23	6	4	1	0	0	0	1	0	3	0	0
Campbell, Jarrett, Orlando	0	1	.000	7.71	4	0	0	0	2	0	4.2	6	24	4	4	0	0	0	0	3	0	2	0	0
Carpenter, Chris, Tennessee	0	1	.000	13.50	1	1	0	0	0	0	3.1	7	19	5	5	1	1	0	0	2	0	2	0	0
Cash, David, West Tenn	2	5	.286	4.98	50	0	0	0	28	11	59.2	64	270	37	33	8	2	1	2	27	1	80	3	0
Castillo, Carlos, Birmingham	3	1	.750	3.96	5	4	0	0	0	0	25.0	23	103	11	11	2	0	2	0	6	0	19	1	0
Chavez, Wilton, West Tenn	0	0	.000	2.25	2	1	0	0	0	0	8.0	5	34	2	2	0	1	0	2	2	0	15	1	0
Childers, Matt, Huntsville	1	0	1.000	2.93	36	1	0	0	20	8	73.2	67	316	32	24	3	3	4	5	24	0	44	2	1
Childress, Daylan, Chat.	2	4	.333	6.75	9	9	0	0	0	0	48.0	53	222	41	36	4	6	3	6	26	0	35	0	0
Collazo, William, Greenville *	6	2	.750	3.66	39	0	0	0	11	0	46.2	41	202	22	19	3	7	3	1	21	1	34	3	2
Collins, Pat, Tennessee	1	2	.333	5.96	5	5	0	0	0	0	22.2	26	115	20	15	3	2	2	1	18	0	14	1	0
Colon, Roman, Greenville	11	3	.786	3.36	39	12	1	0	8	2	107.0	104	448	48	40	9	9	3	4	33	3	58	3	0
Cook, B.R., Tennessee	1	0	1.000	2.43	29	0	0	0	10	1	33.1	26	142	15	9	0	4	3	0	18	1	23	2	0
Cook, Jeremy, Tennessee	0	3	.000	4.74	10	2	0	0	1	0	24.2	28	108	14	13	4	1	1	3	3	0	14	1	0
Coose, Austin, Orlando	0	0	.000	1.80	3	0	0	0	1	0	5.0	2	18	1	1	1	0	0	0	1	0	4	0	0
Cortes, Jorge, Chattanooga	1	2	.333	5.84	9	0	0	0	4	0	12.1	15	56	8	8	2	1	0	2	4	0	9	1	0
Cotton, Nathan, Chattanooga	0	0	.000	0.00	1	0	0	0	1	0	1.0	2	6	0	0	0	0	0	0	1	0	1	0	0
Cotts, Neal, Birmingham *	9	7	.563	2.16	21	21	0	0	0	0	108.1	67	440	32	26	2	2	2	3	56	1	133	0	0
Crabtree, Tim, Huntsville	0	0	.000	9.82	6	0	0	0	1	0	7.1	11	36	8	8	0	0	0	1	4	0	3	0	0
Cromer, Jason, Orlando *	1	5	.167	5.71	6	6	0	0	0	0	34.2	39	157	27	22	3	0	2	2	14	1	16	0	0
Cueto, Jose, Carolina	5	3	.625	3.22	35	2	0	0	3	1	58.2	49	262	23	21	2	6	7	5	35	2	43	6	1
Cummings, Jeremy, Tenn.	8	6	.571	3.34	15	14	0	0	0	0	89.0	69	354	36	33	8	4	4	6	22	1	63	3	0
Curtis, Daniel, Greenville	6	4	.600	2.87	17	12	2	1	1	0	78.1	72	321	29	25	4	2	5	2	15	0	47	3	0
Cyr, Eric, Chattanooga *	0	0	.000	13.50	1	0	0	0	0	0	2.0	6	12	3	3	0	0	0	0	0	0	0	0	0
Darnell, Paul, Chattanooga *	0	0	.000	6.50	15	0	0	0	7	2	18.0	25	90	17	13	2	1	1	0	13	1	14	2	0
Davis, Doug, Huntsville *	1	0	1.000	3.00	1	1	0	0	0	0	6.0	5	26	2	2	0	0	0	1	3	0	6	2	0
De Renne, Keoni, Greenville	0	0	.000	18.00	1	0	0	0	1	0	1.0	2	5	2	2	1	0	0	0	0	0	0	0	0
DeHart, Casey, Chattanooga *	3	2	.600	3.86	41	4	0	0	13	2	74.2	78	332	35	32	2	5	0	2	43	3	50	1	1
DeMent, Dan, Orlando	0	0	.000	36.00	1	0	0	0	1	0	1.0	5	9	4	4	1	0	0	0	1	0	0	0	0
Deago, Roger, Mobile *	8	7	.533	4.03	26	20	0	0	1	0	118.1	127	517	64	53	9	6	5	3	51	1	109	3	0
Deck, Ronnie, Orlando	0	0	.000	18.00	1	0	0	0	1	0	1.0	3	6	2	2	1	0	0	0	0	0	1	0	0
Devey, Phil, Chattanooga *	1	0	1.000	5.06	12	0	0	0	4	1	16.0	15	69	10	9	2	1	1	2	2	0	11	0	0
Diaz, Joselo, Jacksonville	1	0	1.000	0.00	5	0	0	0	1	0	7.2	5	30	1	0	0	0	0	0	3	0	7	1	0
Digby, Bryan, Greenville	0	1	.000	5.40	9	1	0	0	3	0	11.2	12	52	8	7	1	0	0	1	7	0	6	0	0
Diggins, Ben, Huntsville	3	2	.600	2.36	8	8	0	0	0	0	45.2	41	191	18	12	2	0	0	1	16	0	32	1	0
Dingman, Craig, West Tenn	0	1	.000	6.00	4	0	0	0	1	0	6.0	6	28	4	4	2	1	0	0	5	1	5	0	0
Dunn, Scott, Chat.-Birm.	6	3	.667	3.35	39	0	0	0	22	9	51.0	39	209	23	19	3	3	1	0	21	4	68	6	0
Eason, Clay, Birmingham	1	3	.250	3.72	17	1	0	0	5	1	36.1	47	167	23	15	5	3	1	0	13	2	38	0	0
Ennis, John, Greenville	0	0	.000	2.45	1	1	0	0	0	0	3.2	4	16	1	1	1	0	0	0	2	0	3	0	0
Evert, Brett, Greenville	4	9	.308	4.02	33	15	1	0	5	1	116.1	126	516	57	52	12	8	7	12	44	4	103	7	0
Farmer, Tom, Jacksonville	5	8	.385	3.45	20	19	0	0	0	0	117.1	116	486	51	45	9	5	4	5	26	0	69	6	0
Fesh, Sean, Carolina *	9	1	.900	1.87	49	0	0	0	20	7	77.0	58	305	20	16	1	4	0	4	21	1	71	2	0
Figueroa, Juan, Tennessee	5	2	.714	2.92	34	0	0	0	16	2	37.0	30	158	15	12	5	1	1	4	15	4	44	0	1
Flannery, Mike, Carolina	7	3	.700	2.31	56	0	0	0	46	23	58.1	42	245	20	15	1	4	1	2	26	2	50	2	0
Flinn, Chris, Orlando	1	2	.333	2.57	7	4	0	0	1	0	21.0	15	84	11	6	0	0	1	0	6	0	16	1	0
Fortunato, Bartolome, Orlando	4	2	.667	3.06	35	1	0	0	8	1	53.0	48	227	25	18	4	5	2	2	20	1	63	1	0
Frasor, Jason, Jacksonville	1	0	1.000	2.95	35	0	0	0	32	17	36.2	33	154	14	12	2	2	0	1	14	0	50	1	0
Fuell, Jerrod, Carolina	1	0	1.000	3.38	6	0	0	0	3	0	10.2	12	48	4	4	0	1	1	3	2	0	7	0	0
Gaal, Bryan, Mobile	3	5	.375	3.10	62	0	0	0	30	3	72.2	64	306	26	25	7	3	3	0	29	5	78	6	0
Garcia, Gerardo, Orlando	0	0	.000	3.00	4	3	0	0	0	0	12.0	13	52	4	4	0	0	0	0	3	0	8	1	0
Gaudin, Chad, Orlando	2	0	1.000	0.47	3	3	1	1	0	0	19.0	8	64	1	1	0	0	0	0	3	0	23	0	0
Germano, Justin, Mobile	2	5	.286	4.34	9	9	1	0	0	0	58.0	60	246	34	28	6	3	1	5	13	3	44	0	0
Giese, Dan, Mobile	1	0	1.000	2.25	2	0	0	0	0	0	4.0	1	15	1	1	1	0	0	2	0	0	4	0	0
Gil, Dave, Chattanooga	1	2	.333	3.14	30	4	0	0	24	11	48.2	45	212	22	17	5	3	3	2	16	1	39	1	0
Gonzalez, Alfredo, Jack.	4	4	.500	5.47	10	10	0	0	0	0	49.1	65	225	33	30	6	1	0	1	17	0	37	2	0
Gracesqui, Frank, Carolina *	3	3	.500	2.48	44	0	0	0	14	5	58.0	44	259	19	16	0	2	3	2	43	1	75	11	1
Gray, Brett, Chattanooga	5	3	.625	3.94	43	2	0	0	16	1	64.0	76	275	34	28	8	4	4	2	14	0	57	2	1
Guillory, Dan, Orlando	2	2	.500	3.92	23	0	0	0	15	0	41.1	39	183	21	18	0	2	3	5	18	2	30	0	0
Guzman, Angel, West Tenn	3	3	.500	2.81	15	15	0	0	0	0	89.2	83	366	30	28	8	3	2	2	26	0	87	3	1
Hall, Josh, Chattanooga	8	10	.444	3.47	26	25	2	0	0	0	153.0	152	655	73	59	9	8	6	3	53	1	114	10	1
Hammons, Matt, Huntsville	0	1	.000	4.30	13	0	0	0	7	0	14.2	14	67	9	7	2	3	0	0	11	0	16	3	0
Hanrahan, Joel, Jacksonville	10	4	.714	2.43	23	23	1	0	0	0	133.1	117	556	44	36	5	4	2	7	53	2	130	4	0
Haren, Danny, Tennessee	6	0	1.000	0.82	8	8	0	0	0	0	55.0	36	209	8	5	2	3	0	1	6	0	49	1	0
Harvey, Ian, Mobile	2	0	1.000	4.66	6	0	0	0	0	0	9.2	13	45	6	5	3	1	0	2	1	0	10	0	0
Hendrickson, Ben, Huntsville	7	6	.538	3.45	17	16	0	0	0	0	78.1	82	327	35	30	6	3	1	0	28	0	56	3	0
Herndon, Eric, Greenville	0	0	.000	6.23	7	0	0	0	2	0	8.2	14	42	9	6	1	1	1	1	2	0	9	0	0
Hines, Carlos, Orlando	0	1	.000	9.00	2	0	0	0	0	0	3.0	5	14	3	3	0	1	0	0	1	0	2	0	0
Honel, Kris, Birmingham	1	0	1.000	3.75	2	2	0	0	0	0	12.0	9	52	6	5	2	0	0	2	6	0	13	0	0
House, Craig, Carolina	1	1	.500	4.35	8	0	0	0	3	1	10.1	7	42	5	5	0	1	0	0	6	1	8	3	0
Housman, Jeff, Huntsville *	3	2	.600	3.30	8	8	1	0	0	0	46.1	49	198	21	17	4	1	1	0	17	0	26	0	0
Howington, Ty, Chattanooga *	0	2	.000	6.91	4	4	0	0	0	0	14.1	15	78	12	11	1	1	1	1	20	0	16	2	0

Pitcher, Team	W	L	Pct.	ERA	G	GS	CG	ShO	GF	Sv.	IP	H	TBF	R	ER	HR	SH	SF	HB	BB	IBB	SO	WP	Bk.
Hundley, Jeff, Huntsville *	1	1	.500	1.59	9	1	0	0	5	2	17.0	15	74	3	3	0	1	0	2	4	0	11	0	2
Hunter, Johnny, Mobile	0	1	.000	9.00	1	1	0	0	0	0	4.0	5	20	5	4	2	0	0	0	3	0	5	1	0
Hutchinson, Trevor, Carolina	3	3	.500	3.86	8	6	0	0	1	0	35.0	32	151	21	15	1	2	2	3	13	0	18	1	0
Isenia, Chairon, Orlando	0	0	.000	9.00	1	0	0	0	1	0	1.0	2	6	1	1	0	0	0	0	0	0	0	0	0
Isringhausen, Jason, Tenn.	0	0	.000	0.00	2	2	0	0	0	0	2.0	1	7	0	0	0	0	0	0	0	0	3	0	0
Jackson, Edwin, Jacksonville	7	7	.500	3.70	27	27	0	0	0	0	148.1	121	619	68	61	9	4	3	8	53	0	157	9	1
Janke, Cheyenne, Tennessee	0	1	.000	4.34	9	1	0	0	2	0	18.2	15	81	10	9	3	0	0	1	7	0	21	0	0
Jeffcoat, Bryon, Greenville	0	0	.000	9.00	1	0	0	0	1	0	1.0	1	7	1	1	0	0	0	1	2	0	1	0	0
Johnson, Tyler, Tennessee *	1	0	1.000	1.65	20	0	0	0	6	0	27.1	16	116	7	5	1	2	1	3	15	1	39	0	0
Jones, Mike, Huntsville	7	2	.778	2.40	17	17	0	0	0	0	97.2	87	424	35	26	4	4	4	4	47	0	63	4	0
Karnuth, Jason, West Tenn	3	5	.375	3.35	45	0	0	0	36	13	48.1	53	208	21	18	3	1	2	2	11	2	36	0	0
Keller, Kris, Chattanooga	2	1	.667	2.35	35	0	0	0	20	12	38.1	34	166	11	10	1	1	2	4	15	0	28	3	0
Kelly, Steve, Chattanooga	4	2	.667	2.09	6	6	0	0	0	0	38.2	34	152	11	9	0	2	0	4	12	0	30	2	0
Kennedy, Joe, Orlando *	0	0	.000	8.10	1	1	0	0	0	0	3.1	6	17	3	3	0	0	1	0	1	0	3	0	0
Kent, Steve, Carolina *	4	5	.444	5.37	37	2	0	0	10	0	58.2	58	265	36	35	3	2	0	4	36	3	30	3	1
Key, Chris, Carolina *	0	0	.000	0.00	1	0	0	0	1	0	2.0	3	8	0	0	0	0	0	1	0	0	1	0	0
Kinney, Josh, Tennessee	2	1	.667	0.68	29	0	0	0	12	2	39.2	19	147	4	3	2	1	0	0	12	0	48	1	0
Koronka, John, Chat.-W.Tenn*	7	13	.350	4.20	26	26	0	0	0	0	162.2	180	705	88	76	8	15	9	5	61	1	118	7	5
Krawiec, Aaron, West Tenn *	3	4	.429	3.25	8	8	0	0	0	0	44.1	50	191	19	16	6	0	3	4	9	0	24	2	0
Kremblas, Mike, Huntsville	0	0	.000	0.00	1	0	0	0	1	0	1.0	0	4	0	0	0	0	0	0	1	0	0	0	0
LaRoche, Adam, Greenville *	0	0	.000	0.00	1	0	0	0	1	0	0.2	0	2	0	0	0	0	0	0	0	0	1	0	0
Lambert, Jeremy, Tennessee	0	2	.000	2.18	33	0	0	0	10	2	41.1	31	167	14	10	5	4	1	1	15	3	56	0	0
Langone, Steve, Jacksonville	3	0	1.000	1.98	22	0	0	0	8	1	50.0	38	204	15	11	0	1	1	6	12	2	51	2	0
Lee, Derek, Huntsville *	11	3	.786	3.30	20	13	1	0	2	0	87.1	85	358	36	32	6	6	3	3	28	0	59	4	1
Leicester, Jon, West Tenn	6	7	.462	3.89	45	9	1	1	13	6	106.1	89	455	54	46	7	5	1	4	53	0	106	4	1
Lewis, Derrick, Greenville	0	0	.000	7.56	3	1	0	0	0	0	8.1	12	39	7	7	1	0	1	0	4	0	6	0	0
Liriano, Pedro, Huntsville	9	13	.409	3.79	27	26	0	0	0	0	142.2	138	621	77	60	12	7	5	7	62	2	116	9	1
Lyons, Mike, Tennessee	3	4	.429	3.38	57	0	0	0	49	31	53.1	50	240	27	20	2	1	2	1	23	2	63	1	0
Magrane, Jim, Orlando	10	6	.625	3.26	25	24	0	0	0	0	143.2	147	626	69	52	9	1	4	6	51	1	87	5	1
Malaska, Mark, Orlando *	1	1	.500	2.16	19	0	0	0	5	1	25.0	21	96	6	6	2	2	1	0	4	1	22	0	0
Malone, Corwin, Birm.*	4	2	.667	5.40	8	8	0	0	0	0	40.0	50	194	26	24	2	0	1	1	28	1	28	3	0
Marchbanks, David, Carolina *	0	1	.000	3.00	1	1	1	0	0	0	6.0	4	25	2	2	0	1	0	1	5	0	3	2	0
Martinez, Luis, Huntsville *	8	5	.615	2.58	20	20	1	0	0	0	115.0	93	489	46	33	4	11	1	7	54	0	116	6	1
McAdoo, Duncan, Mobile	6	8	.429	4.14	30	19	0	0	2	0	130.1	128	536	70	60	9	4	11	5	31	2	110	3	0
McConnell, Sam, Greenville *	1	0	1.000	4.11	16	0	0	0	4	0	15.1	18	65	7	7	0	0	1	0	4	0	8	0	2
McCrotty, Will, Jacksonville	3	5	.375	4.06	32	11	0	0	11	1	93.0	88	406	52	42	6	4	4	4	41	2	67	4	2
McLeary, Marty, Carolina	1	1	.500	1.80	11	2	0	0	1	0	30.0	22	124	8	6	1	0	0	3	15	0	22	3	0
McNutt, Mike, Carolina	0	1	.000	9.00	1	1	0	0	0	0	5.0	8	25	5	5	1	0	1	0	2	0	6	0	0
McWhirter, Kris, Birmingham	3	8	.273	5.64	25	5	1	0	8	0	60.2	60	283	44	38	2	3	2	4	44	5	42	1	3
Meaux, Ryan, Birmingham *	1	2	.333	2.13	26	0	0	0	9	2	38.0	39	149	11	9	0	2	1	2	3	1	29	0	2
Messenger, Randy, Carolina	5	7	.417	5.46	29	23	0	0	3	0	113.2	137	532	83	69	7	10	5	3	51	1	78	9	0
Meyer, Jake, Birmingham	1	1	.500	3.20	17	0	0	0	5	1	25.1	22	109	10	9	0	2	0	2	10	3	20	2	0
Miller, Greg, Jacksonville *	1	1	.500	1.01	4	4	0	0	0	0	26.2	15	103	5	3	1	0	0	0	7	0	40	2	0
Miller, Ryan, Huntsville	1	8	.111	3.84	50	1	0	0	18	4	86.2	80	383	46	37	3	9	3	2	46	4	82	4	0
Miller, Travis, Chattanooga *	0	1	.000	40.50	1	0	0	0	0	0	0.2	3	6	4	3	0	0	0	0	0	0	1	0	0
Miniel, Rene, Mobile	0	0	.000	0.00	1	0	0	0	0	0	1.0	0	3	0	0	0	0	0	0	0	0	2	0	0
Minix, Travis, Orlando	5	3	.625	3.86	44	6	0	0	9	0	79.1	86	333	40	34	7	3	1	1	14	1	70	1	0
Minor, Ryan, Jacksonville	1	2	.333	5.19	15	0	0	0	7	0	17.1	21	74	12	10	4	1	2	0	4	3	9	3	0
Mitchell, Nathan, West Tenn	0	0	.000	3.18	4	0	0	0	1	0	5.2	5	24	2	2	1	0	0	0	2	0	4	1	0
Mitre, Sergio, West Tenn	7	9	.438	3.34	25	24	0	0	0	0	145.2	162	639	75	54	6	9	3	12	41	0	128	6	0
Montero, Agustin, Jack.	2	1	.667	3.04	16	0	0	0	5	0	26.2	24	113	10	9	1	1	2	0	13	1	22	2	0
Moore, Frank, Orlando	0	0	.000	0.00	1	0	0	0	1	0	1.0	0	5	0	0	0	0	0	0	2	0	1	0	0
Moseley, Dustin, Chattanooga	5	6	.455	3.83	18	18	0	0	0	0	112.2	116	480	55	48	10	3	3	7	28	0	73	2	0
Moser, Todd, Carolina *	6	4	.600	3.41	18	18	0	0	0	0	97.2	107	425	42	37	8	1	0	5	29	2	78	1	2
Mottl, Ryan, Chattanooga	6	5	.545	3.94	23	19	0	0	1	0	114.1	116	505	57	50	10	4	3	11	47	1	101	6	0
Murray, Brad, Birmingham *	0	0	.000	5.40	5	0	0	0	3	0	5.0	7	25	3	3	0	0	0	0	4	0	1	0	0
Nannini, Mike, West Tenn	10	9	.526	3.62	31	24	1	0	4	0	154.0	155	654	70	62	12	10	3	3	47	1	158	3	0
Narveson, Chris, Tennessee *	4	3	.571	3.00	10	10	0	0	0	0	57.0	56	247	21	19	6	4	3	0	26	2	34	4	1
Nelson, Bubba, Greenville	8	10	.444	3.18	23	20	0	0	1	0	119.0	106	496	47	42	7	3	4	4	45	0	77	4	0
Nicolas, Mike, Mobile	0	1	.000	8.10	5	0	0	0	1	1	6.2	6	33	6	6	1	0	1	0	7	0	11	1	0
Niles, Drew, Carolina	0	0	.000	0.00	1	0	0	0	1	0	1.0	1	5	0	0	0	0	0	0	1	0	0	0	0
Nina, Elvin, Jacksonville	1	0	1.000	2.77	8	1	0	0	3	0	13.0	7	54	4	4	1	0	1	1	10	0	10	1	0
Nolasco, Dave, Huntsville	3	2	.600	3.58	9	5	0	0	1	0	32.2	34	140	17	13	1	4	2	2	13	0	15	0	0
Novinsky, John, Tennessee	2	0	1.000	4.38	18	0	0	0	8	3	24.2	32	119	13	12	1	1	1	4	13	0	15	1	0
Nunez, Jose, Mobile *	1	2	.333	6.00	9	0	0	0	5	0	12.0	11	54	10	8	1	1	2	0	4	1	11	1	0
O'Connor, Brian, Orlando *	0	1	.000	5.19	8	0	0	0	5	0	8.2	14	44	6	5	1	0	0	0	4	0	5	1	0
O'Neal, Brandon, Birmingham	0	0	.000	7.20	5	0	0	0	3	0	5.0	6	26	4	4	0	0	0	3	4	0	2	0	0
Ortiz, Omar, Carolina	0	1	.000	6.08	8	0	0	0	1	0	13.1	16	64	9	9	1	2	2	2	8	2	12	2	0
Oxspring, Chris, Mobile	10	6	.625	2.92	40	18	1	0	8	0	135.2	106	572	47	44	6	1	5	1	62	3	129	1	0
Pacheco, Enemencio, Birm.	12	2	.857	2.56	30	24	0	0	0	0	151.1	131	632	51	43	5	3	8	9	51	1	116	5	0
Parker, Josh, Orlando	0	3	.000	3.10	24	0	0	0	22	12	29.0	29	123	13	10	0	1	2	0	7	0	19	2	1
Parker, Matt, Huntsville	8	6	.571	3.10	42	5	0	0	15	6	95.2	96	412	40	33	9	7	3	2	36	1	72	6	0
Parrott, Rhett, Tennessee	8	9	.471	3.27	21	21	1	0	0	0	124.0	122	519	52	45	11	2	3	3	40	3	112	7	1
Pearce, Josh, Tennessee	2	1	.667	4.09	5	5	0	0	0	0	33.0	34	134	15	15	3	2	0	3	3	0	20	0	0
Pearson, Jason, Tennessee *	0	0	.000	0.00	9	0	0	0	0	0	11.0	7	43	0	0	0	1	0	1	2	0	11	0	0
Pena, Juan, Tennessee *	6	5	.545	3.49	29	14	0	0	3	0	95.1	101	416	47	37	7	6	2	1	44	3	69	3	0
Phillips, Mike, Birmingham *	0	1	.000	10.50	1	1	0	0	0	0	6.0	14	31	8	7	1	0	0	0	1	0	5	0	0
Pignatiello, Carmen, W.Tenn*	1	0	1.000	1.50	1	1	0	0	0	0	6.0	3	22	1	1	1	0	0	0	2	0	11	0	0
Pilkington, Brian, Jacksonville	3	0	1.000	3.34	5	5	0	0	0	0	32.1	31	127	13	12	3	1	0	0	2	0	24	0	1
Pineda, Luis, Jacksonville	1	1	.500	4.09	9	0	0	0	1	0	11.0	13	50	5	5	0	2	0	1	6	2	11	0	0
Proctor, Scott, Jacksonville	1	2	.333	1.00	17	0	0	0	12	0	27.0	20	108	6	3	0	2	3	0	7	3	24	1	1
Purvis, Rob, Birmingham	0	0	.000	9.47	13	0	0	0	5	0	19.0	27	100	24	20	2	0	2	1	14	0	15	3	2
Ramirez, Emmanuel, W.Tenn	3	1	.750	2.01	22	0	0	0	9	0	31.1	25	137	9	7	0	1	0	2	20	2	34	2	0
Ray, Ken, Huntsville	2	1	.667	2.93	31	0	0	0	15	4	61.1	65	262	25	20	6	5	2	3	25	0	49	1	0
Reina, Dimas, Jacksonville	0	0	.000	9.64	4	0	0	0	2	0	4.2	9	29	10	5	1	0	0	0	6	0	4	1	0
Rice, Leonard, Chattanooga *	0	0	.000	0.00	2	0	0	0	2	0	5.0	4	17	0	0	0	0	0	0	0	0	4	0	0
Ring, Royce, Birmingham *	1	4	.200	2.52	36	0	0	0	32	19	35.2	33	159	11	10	1	2	1	3	14	1	44	3	0

Pitcher, Team	W	L	Pct.	ERA	G	GS	CG	ShO	GF	Sv.	IP	H	TBF	R	ER	HR	SH	SF	HB	BB	IBB	SO	WP	Bk.
Robinson, Jeff, Huntsville	0	0	.000	6.10	3	3	0	0	0	0	10.1	11	46	7	7	2	0	1	0	4	0	7	0	0
Rocker, John, Orlando *	0	1	.000	9.15	17	0	0	0	4	0	19.2	23	105	23	20	4	0	0	1	26	0	20	2	1
Rodriguez, Orlando, Jack.*	1	2	.333	3.75	11	0	0	0	2	0	12.0	10	52	5	5	1	2	0	0	7	1	14	0	0
Rohlicek, Russ, West Tenn *	2	3	.400	9.77	13	2	0	0	3	0	15.2	22	80	17	17	0	0	1	2	13	1	12	2	0
Rojas, Chris, Mobile	5	10	.333	4.27	32	19	1	0	5	0	109.2	94	477	62	52	6	3	2	11	53	1	92	3	0
Ruhl, Nathan, Jacksonville	0	1	.000	4.00	5	0	0	0	1	0	9.0	9	41	4	4	0	2	1	0	6	2	7	1	1
Rust, Evan, Orlando	1	3	.250	2.65	30	0	0	0	26	11	34.0	28	149	13	10	0	0	1	1	15	2	35	0	0
Ryu, Jae-kuk, West Tenn	2	5	.286	5.43	11	11	1	0	0	0	58.0	63	261	37	35	3	4	2	5	25	0	45	2	1
Saenz, Chris, Huntsville	0	0	.000	1.50	1	0	0	0	1	0	6.0	4	23	2	1	0	0	0	0	3	0	6	0	0
Salmon, Brad, Chattanooga	4	0	1.000	5.11	10	1	0	0	5	1	24.2	27	107	14	14	2	0	0	1	9	0	21	0	1
Sanchez, Felix, West Tenn *	2	2	.500	3.23	30	8	0	0	4	0	64.0	57	284	30	23	3	3	3	4	31	0	55	5	2
Santos, Alex, Orlando	3	2	.600	6.02	25	1	0	0	7	0	40.1	52	184	29	27	3	2	4	0	15	1	23	0	0
Saucedo, Matthew, Carolina	0	0	.000	0.00	1	0	0	0	0	0	2.0	1	9	0	0	0	0	0	2	0	0	1	0	0
Saunders, Chris, Birmingham	0	0	.000	0.00	1	0	0	0	1	0	0.1	0	1	0	0	0	0	0	0	0	0	1	0	0
Shackelford, Brian, Chat.*	3	2	.600	6.30	13	1	0	0	4	1	20.0	26	100	18	14	3	2	0	1	14	2	19	2	1
Shelley, Jason, Huntsville	3	2	.600	2.63	9	9	1	1	0	0	54.2	38	220	18	16	5	4	2	6	21	1	53	7	0
Small, Aaron, Carolina	3	4	.429	4.83	8	7	0	0	0	0	41.0	47	184	23	22	5	2	4	2	14	0	24	1	0
Smith, Chuck, Greenville	1	2	.333	3.38	3	3	0	0	0	0	18.2	14	73	8	7	1	1	1	1	5	0	12	0	0
Smith, Matt, Birmingham	4	1	.800	3.89	52	0	0	0	15	2	69.1	74	313	33	30	7	3	2	2	31	4	44	9	0
Snare, Ryan, Carolina *	5	4	.556	3.67	18	18	0	0	0	0	103.0	98	436	46	42	4	3	2	7	37	0	77	4	1
Sodowsky, Clint, Carolina	1	0	1.000	2.70	5	5	0	0	0	0	26.2	22	106	8	8	1	1	0	1	4	1	27	1	0
Sonnier, Shawn, West Tenn	0	0	.000	3.44	12	0	0	0	1	0	18.1	11	73	8	7	2	1	2	0	11	2	16	0	0
Spiehs, R.D., Mobile	0	2	.000	5.30	15	0	0	0	5	0	18.2	17	80	12	11	2	3	1	1	7	1	17	0	0
Sprague, Kevin, Tennessee *	3	4	.429	5.26	53	0	0	0	13	2	63.1	67	291	43	37	4	3	1	1	38	7	61	5	2
Steffek, Brian, Jacksonville	1	5	.167	7.92	24	0	0	0	7	1	30.2	41	156	28	27	3	3	1	3	23	2	31	1	0
Stewart, Cory, Mobile *	12	7	.632	3.72	24	24	0	0	0	0	125.2	104	537	60	52	10	9	4	6	50	1	133	0	0
Stocks, Nick, Tennessee	10	8	.556	4.77	27	26	0	0	0	0	151.0	160	663	86	80	17	5	6	13	58	2	109	4	0
Stokes, Brian, Orlando	2	5	.286	3.20	10	10	0	0	0	0	50.2	55	220	26	18	2	0	2	4	13	0	33	1	1
Stults, Eric, Jacksonville *	3	4	.429	4.97	9	7	0	0	1	1	38.0	46	169	23	21	5	2	3	0	13	0	14	0	0
Stumm, Jason, Birmingham	0	0	.000	4.50	7	0	0	0	2	0	8.0	8	38	4	4	1	0	2	0	6	0	8	0	0
Switzer, Jon, Orlando *	8	8	.500	3.43	22	22	2	0	0	0	126.0	117	522	63	48	10	5	4	5	32	1	100	9	1
Sylvester, Billy, Greenville	1	2	.333	1.51	41	0	0	0	39	18	41.2	22	171	7	7	0	2	0	3	25	1	55	2	0
Szuminski, Jason, West Tenn.	7	4	.636	2.26	29	3	0	0	8	2	59.2	51	246	19	15	1	3	2	3	19	2	45	1	0
Takeoka, Kazuhiro, Greenville	2	1	.667	6.00	20	0	0	0	11	1	27.0	32	119	19	18	3	2	1	4	7	2	9	1	0
Therneau, Dave, Chattanooga	1	0	1.000	3.72	9	0	0	0	2	0	9.2	13	42	4	4	2	1	0	0	4	0	8	0	1
Thompson, Travis, Chat.	2	0	1.000	2.89	9	2	0	0	2	1	28.0	27	113	11	9	1	2	1	0	5	0	21	0	0
Tillery, Josh, Greenville	0	2	.000	11.57	8	0	0	0	6	0	7.0	13	40	11	9	2	0	1	1	5	0	3	2	0
Totten, Heath, Jacksonville	11	12	.478	3.42	28	28	2	1	0	0	181.1	196	751	83	69	15	7	5	5	17	3	114	1	0
Trujillo, J.J., Mobile	1	2	.333	3.70	28	0	0	0	8	3	41.1	35	172	20	17	1	3	5	2	12	1	33	0	0
Tucker, Rusty, Mobile *	2	6	.250	3.74	51	0	0	0	42	28	53.0	49	244	26	22	4	4	2	3	31	4	63	5	0
Ulacia, Dennis, Birmingham *	1	5	.167	4.53	11	10	0	0	0	0	49.2	59	223	27	25	4	2	2	2	21	5	31	2	0
Ungs, Nic, Carolina	3	4	.429	3.53	10	10	0	0	0	0	58.2	61	244	30	23	4	4	4	4	8	0	37	0	0
Urdaneta, Lino, Jacksonville	0	8	.000	4.29	44	0	0	0	25	6	65.0	68	279	37	31	4	5	4	3	24	5	42	0	0
Velazquez, Jose, West Tenn *	0	1	.000	0.00	1	0	0	0	1	0	0.2	2	5	1	0	0	0	0	0	2	0	0	0	1
Veras, Jose, Orlando	6	9	.400	3.45	27	22	1	1	1	0	130.1	108	551	59	50	11	3	3	6	53	0	118	8	1
Villalon, Julio, Tennessee	4	7	.364	4.61	12	12	0	0	0	0	66.1	72	287	39	34	8	3	3	5	23	0	48	2	0
Waechter, Doug, Orlando	5	3	.625	4.13	13	12	0	0	0	0	76.1	74	314	39	35	6	3	3	1	19	0	45	1	0
Wagner, Ryan, Chattanooga	1	0	1.000	0.00	5	0	0	0	1	0	5.0	2	19	1	0	0	1	0	0	2	0	6	0	0
Wainwright, Adam, Greenville	10	8	.556	3.37	27	27	1	0	0	0	149.2	133	599	59	56	9	2	3	7	37	0	128	4	2
Waligora, T.P., West Tenn	0	0	.000	10.54	11	0	0	0	4	0	13.2	18	71	17	16	4	0	0	2	11	1	12	0	2
Walrond, Les, Tennessee *	0	0	.000	2.70	4	0	0	0	0	0	6.2	4	28	2	2	1	0	0	0	4	0	7	0	0
Waters, Chris, Greenville *	3	8	.273	4.41	17	17	0	0	0	0	85.2	104	381	53	42	11	7	6	1	26	1	54	2	1
Watkins, Steve, Mobile	5	4	.556	4.17	18	18	0	0	0	0	101.1	100	430	50	47	8	6	5	0	34	1	75	1	0
Webb, Alan, Mobile *	1	3	.250	3.30	58	0	0	0	11	2	84.2	58	363	39	31	8	2	3	5	47	6	79	5	0
Webb, John, West Tenn	5	8	.385	4.50	30	22	0	0	5	1	132.0	135	573	74	66	11	6	5	10	52	1	85	4	1
Wellemeyer, Todd, West Tenn	1	1	.500	5.48	4	4	0	0	0	0	21.1	19	95	13	13	1	0	2	3	10	0	34	0	0
West, Brian, Birmingham	3	5	.375	5.80	12	11	1	0	0	0	54.1	70	257	39	35	6	2	1	2	28	2	37	10	0
White, Matt, Orlando	0	4	.000	7.47	7	7	0	0	0	0	31.1	40	159	34	26	8	3	2	2	23	1	18	3	0
Willis, Dontrelle, Carolina *	4	0	1.000	1.49	6	6	0	0	0	0	36.1	24	133	6	6	2	0	0	0	9	0	32	1	0
Winkelsas, Joe, Greenville	1	1	.500	2.93	23	0	0	0	8	2	27.2	26	115	11	9	2	0	3	3	8	0	14	0	0
Wylie, Mitch, Birmingham	3	5	.375	4.40	14	10	1	0	0	0	57.1	53	239	33	28	2	1	4	2	17	0	42	2	0
Yofu, Tetsu, Birmingham	9	8	.529	3.50	29	20	0	0	3	2	131.0	117	548	58	51	8	6	3	12	37	4	114	7	2
Zumwalt, Alec, Greenville	1	1	.500	1.42	11	0	0	0	4	0	19.0	13	81	3	3	0	1	0	0	12	1	19	2	0

PITCHERS WITH TWO OR MORE TEAMS

Pitcher, Team	W	L	Pct.	ERA	G	GS	CG	ShO	GF	Sv.	IP	H	TBF	R	ER	HR	SH	SF	HB	BB	IBB	SO	WP	Bk.
Dunn, Scott, Birmingham	3	1	.750	1.69	8	0	0	0	5	1	10.2	8	43	2	2	0	1	0	0	5	2	14	0	0
Dunn, Scott, Chattanooga	3	2	.600	3.79	31	0	0	0	17	8	40.1	31	166	21	17	3	2	1	0	16	2	54	6	0
Koronka, John, West Tenn *	0	0	.000	0.00	1	1	0	0	0	0	7.0	3	24	0	0	0	1	0	0	1	0	3	0	0
Koronka, John, Chattanooga *	7	13	.350	4.39	25	25	0	0	0	0	155.2	177	681	88	76	8	14	9	5	60	1	115	7	5

COMBINATION SHUTOUTS: Birmingham (7)—Cotts-Smith-Ring, Pacheco-Meyer-Ring, Cotts-Bajenaru-Smith, Wylie-Bajenaru-Ring, Cotts-Purvis-Smith, Yofu-Meaux, Cotts-Smith-Meaux. Carolina (11)—Sodowski-Fesh-Flannery, Snare-Kent-Baker, Snare-Baker, Bridges-Cueto-Baker, Bridges-McLeary-Flannery, Snare-Fesh, Moser-Cueto-Flannery, Moser-Cueto-Flannery, Small-Cueto-Fesh-Flannery, Bautista-Gracesqui-Messenger, Bridges-Fesh-Flannery. Chattanooga (6)—Koronka-Dunn, Hall-Keller-Devey, Andrews-Bevel-Dunn, Thompson-Keller, Salmon-Bevel-Keller, Childress-Gray. Greenville (17)—Belisle-Herndon-Winkelsas, Nelson-Curtis-Winkelsas-Barry, Colon-Aguilar, Waters-Takeoka, Smith-Evert-Takeoka-Barry-Sylvester, Nelson-Colon, Nelson-Collazo-Barry-Sylvester, Belisle-Colon, Evert-Zumwalt-Sylvester, Evert-Nelson-Collazo, Aguilar-Colon-Sylvester, Aguilar-Blank, Aguilar-Barry-Sylvester, Evert-Lewis-Colon-Collazo-Sylvester, Wainright-Barry-Digby, Wainwright-Digby-Colon-Barry, Curtis-Collazo-Colon-Zumwalt. Huntsville (11)—Lee-Childers, Martinez-Parker-Lee-Adams, Jones-Crabtree-Childers, Lee-Parker, Martinez-Hammons-Miller, Jones-Hammons-Childers, Liriano-Parker, Liriano-Ray-Adams, Childers-Parker-Ray, Housman-Parker, Liriano-Childers. Jacksonville (7)—Jackson-Langone-Urdaneta, Farmer-Montero-Urdaneta, Hanrahan-Montero-McCrotty, Jackson-McCrotty, Gonzalez-Langone-Montero, Miller-Bauer-Frasor, McCrotty-Pineda-Nina. Mobile (6)—Baker-Harvey-Webb-Oxspring, Stewart-Gaal-Tucker, Watkins-Gaal-Tucker, Stewart-Gaal-Tucker, Oxspring-Bumstead-Gaal, Stewart-Webb-Bumstead. Orlando (7)—Veras-Magrane-Benedetti-Fortunato, Veras-Rust, Magrane-Benedetti, Magrane-Anderson-Parker, Gaudin-Minix-Benedetti, Veras-Guillory, Magrane-Parker. Tennessee (13)—Haren-Ankiel-Lambert, Haren-Cook, Cummings-Sprague, Stocks-Figueroa-Lyons, Haren-Lambert-Lyons, Cummings-Walrond-Lyons, Cummings-Figueroa, Villalon-Axelson, Parrott-Cook-Pena, Ankiel-Cook-Lyons, Narveson-Kinney-Lyons, Cook-Johnson-Novinsky, Axelson-Kinney-Lyons. West Tenn (8)—Nannini-Anderson-Leicester, Guzman-Leicester-Cash, Anderson-Szuminski-Waligora-Brown-Sanchez-Leicester, Sanchez-Brown-Cash, Guzman-Karnuth-Cash, Szuminski-Mitchell-Karnuth-Cash, Szyminski-Dingman-Karnuth, Koronka-Mitre-Sanchez.

NO-HIT GAMES: Gaudin, Orlando, defeated Jacksonville, 1-0 (first game), July 15.

2003 FIELDING

TEAM

Team	G	PO	A	E	TC	DP	TP	PB	Pct.
Tennessee	139	3627	1452	123	5202	113	0	20	.976
West Tenn	138	3570	1301	127	4998	101	0	6	.975
Greenville	138	3525	1416	128	5069	98	0	13	.975
Carolina	138	3595	1370	131	5096	117	0	9	.974
Jacksonville	139	3653	1415	145	5213	128	1	18	.972
Mobile	138	3618	1300	150	5068	101	0	9	.970
Chattanooga	140	3642	1441	159	5242	105	0	10	.970
Huntsville	138	3676	1517	165	5358	131	0	30	.969
Birmingham	137	3556	1235	153	4944	104	0	10	.969
Orlando	137	3512	1330	164	5006	97	0	22	.967

INDIVIDUAL

FIRST BASEMEN

NOTE: All caps denotes fielding-percentage leader based on 70 games for catchers, 93 for all other non-pitchers and 112 innings for pitchers. *Throws lefthanded.

Player, Team	Pct.	G	PO	A	E	TC	DP
Acevas, Jon, Birmingham	.980	17	98	1	2	101	7
Alvarez, Gabe, Birmingham	.985	87	583	53	10	646	59
Alvarez, Nick, Jacksonville	1.000	30	232	31	0	263	24
Arteaga, Joshua, West Tenn	1.000	1	10	1	0	11	0
Ashby, Chris, Carolina	.988	52	374	37	5	416	44
Barnwell, Chris, Huntsville	.944	2	17	0	1	18	2
Battersby, Eric, Birmingham *	.979	20	90	3	2	95	4
Benick, Jon, Mobile	.986	32	257	18	4	279	27
Bravo, Danny, Mobile	.992	35	218	23	2	243	11
Brewer, Jace, Orlando	1.000	6	48	1	0	49	5
Brock, Tarrik, Jacksonville *	1.000	9	64	9	0	73	4
Castro, Ramon, Greenville	.900	1	7	2	1	10	0
Chamblee, Jim, Chattanooga	1.000	3	26	1	0	27	3
Conley, Evan, Chattanooga	1.000	3	30	1	0	31	2
Creighton, Matt, West Tenn	1.000	2	20	1	0	21	0
Davis, John-Paul, Orlando	.991	26	208	14	2	224	14
Dellaero, Jason, Chattanooga	1.000	1	9	1	0	10	0
Dubois, Jason, West Tenn	.972	16	103	3	3	109	6
Dzurilla, Mike, West Tenn	.995	50	366	25	2	393	31
Evans, Lee, Greenville	.969	9	57	5	2	64	7
Fitzgerald, Jason, Greenville *	1.000	20	164	15	0	179	13
Gall, John, Tennessee	1.000	2	17	0	0	17	1
GEMOLL, BRANDON, Hunt.*	.990	118	1025	77	11	1113	100
Gerber, Joseph, Mobile *	.992	16	125	7	1	133	8
Gonzalez, Adrian, Carolina *	.987	36	291	21	4	316	24
Gripp, Ryan, Huntsville	.984	15	115	10	2	127	11
Grummitt, Dan, Orlando	.994	81	625	47	4	676	52
Gubanich, Creighton, Chat.	.935	8	55	3	4	62	2
Gutierrez, Jesse, Chattanooga	.995	24	190	17	1	208	21
Haad, Yamid, Mobile	.952	5	39	1	2	42	5
Haas, Chris, Chattanooga	.994	21	146	10	1	157	13
Hamilton, Jon, Birmingham *	.988	13	77	5	1	83	3
Hankins, Ryan, Birmingham	1.000	21	130	18	0	148	16
Harper, Brandon, Carolina	.000	1	0	0	0	0	0
Hastings, Joseph, Mobile	1.000	3	23	0	0	23	1
Hood, Donnie, West Tenn	.985	20	122	13	2	137	10
Jacobsen, Bucky, Tennessee	.985	114	963	58	16	1037	80
Jeffcoat, Bryon, Greenville	.990	23	178	20	2	200	9
Jennings, Robin, Chattanooga *	.984	8	56	5	1	62	2
Jurries, James, Greenville	.988	32	234	14	3	251	15
Knott, Jon, Mobile	.983	53	394	23	7	424	40
Krause, Scott, Tennessee	1.000	14	112	3	0	115	6
LaRoche, Adam, Greenville *	.996	60	496	39	2	537	46
Leon, Donny, West Tenn	1.000	2	16	1	0	17	1
Magness, Pat, Carolina	.975	39	252	24	7	283	17
Maldonado, Carlos, Birmingham	1.000	2	10	0	0	10	2
Michaelis, Derek, Jacksonville *	.982	106	789	64	16	869	80
Moore, Frank, Orlando	.989	30	257	21	3	281	21
Moylan, Dan, Tennessee	.964	3	26	1	1	28	5
Nelson, Brad, Huntsville	1.000	6	36	3	0	39	6
Niles, Drew, Carolina	.988	17	77	6	1	84	8
Owens, Ryan, Chattanooga	.989	9	79	7	1	87	4
Padgett, Matt, Carolina *	.976	7	33	7	1	41	4
Peterson, Brian, Chattanooga	.000	1	0	0	0	0	0
Powers, John, West Tenn	1.000	2	6	0	0	6	0
Roat, Kyle, Greenville	1.000	1	2	0	0	2	0
Roman, Jesse, Tennessee *	1.000	10	79	6	0	85	5
Sandoval, Danny, Birmingham	1.000	2	3	0	0	3	1
Saunders, Chris, Birmingham	1.000	3	23	2	0	25	4
Sing, Brandon, West Tenn	.993	38	284	18	2	304	29
Smitherman, Stephen, Chat.	.974	5	36	2	1	39	3
Stenson, Dernell, Chattanooga *	.983	64	535	29	10	574	42
Velazquez, Jose, West Tenn *	1.000	20	149	17	0	166	13
Ward, Daryle, Jacksonville *	1.000	2	13	4	0	17	1
Washington, Rico, Mobile	1.000	5	36	2	0	38	2
Weekly, Chris, Tennessee	.974	5	35	2	1	38	5
Willingham, Josh, Carolina	1.000	9	51	4	0	55	4

SECOND BASEMEN

Player, Team	Pct.	G	PO	A	E	TC	DP
Abreu, Dennis, Tennessee	.714	2	1	4	2	7	0
Anderson, Bryan, Chattanooga	1.000	3	12	8	0	20	3
Arteaga, Joshua, West Tenn	1.000	17	22	30	0	52	8
Badeaux, Brooks, Orlando	1.000	2	7	3	0	10	1
Barbier, Blair, West Tenn	1.000	12	19	17	0	36	2
Barnwell, Chris, Huntsville	.946	35	72	102	10	184	23
BEATTIE, ANDREW, Chattanooga	.981	104	192	264	9	465	54
Bravo, Danny, Mobile	1.000	1	1	3	0	4	1
Brewer, Jace, Orlando	1.000	2	5	9	0	14	2
Caceres, Wilmy, Chattanooga	1.000	11	18	30	0	48	4
Cairns, Troy, Chattanooga	.962	7	12	13	1	26	0
Cantu, Jorge, Orlando	1.000	2	3	4	0	7	0
Castro, Ramon, Greenville	.931	8	10	17	2	29	5
Cesar, Dionys, Chattanooga	.966	11	21	36	2	59	6
Clements, Jason, Mobile	.909	2	5	5	1	11	2
Clute, Kris, Carolina	1.000	2	2	5	0	7	0
Collins, Mike, Jacksonville	.975	27	55	63	3	121	16
Cortez, Fernando, Orlando	.963	28	37	67	4	108	8
Cosme, Caonabo, Tennessee	.978	129	253	373	14	640	79
Creighton, Matt, West Tenn	.932	20	28	41	5	74	7
De Renne, Keoni, Greenville	1.000	4	6	10	0	16	2
DeMent, Dan, Orlando	.972	28	33	71	3	107	8
Dellaero, Jason, Chattanooga	1.000	1	2	0	0	2	0
Diaz, Alejandro, Chattanooga	1.000	1	3	1	0	4	0
Diaz, Victor, Jacksonville	.962	77	145	207	14	366	51
Donovan, Todd, Mobile	1.000	1	1	2	0	3	1
Dzurilla, Mike, West Tenn	.993	33	57	79	1	137	11
Escalona, Felix, Orlando	.974	6	16	21	1	38	6
Gautreau, Jake, Mobile	.968	112	167	257	14	438	50
Hall, Billy, Carolina	.967	16	23	35	2	60	11
Hankins, Ryan, Birmingham	1.000	7	15	14	0	29	5
Harris, Brendan, West Tenn	1.000	20	22	39	0	61	3
Hood, Donnie, West Tenn	1.000	1	2	1	0	3	0
Kopitzke, Casey, West Tenn	1.000	1	1	0	0	1	0
Kremblas, Mike, Huntsville	1.000	1	1	0	0	1	0
Lewis, Richard, Greenville	.979	120	217	302	11	530	60
Liriano, Pedro, West Tenn	.875	3	3	4	1	8	0
Lorenzana, Luis, Mobile	1.000	7	18	21	0	39	5
Machado, Alejandro, Huntsville	.985	40	94	105	3	202	30
Martinez, Gabby, Orlando	.977	9	18	24	1	43	5
Medrano, Jesus, Carolina	.955	72	139	180	15	334	37
Moore, Frank, Orlando	.972	40	83	92	5	180	22
Nicholson, Tommy, Birmingham	.933	20	33	51	6	90	10
Niles, Drew, Carolina	.982	30	47	60	2	109	11
Olmedo, Rainer, Chattanooga	1.000	1	1	1	0	2	0
Orr, Pete, Greenville	1.000	13	27	29	0	56	6
Owens, Ryan, Chattanooga	.800	1	1	3	1	5	0
Paz, Rich, Huntsville	.976	67	145	187	8	340	37
Perez, Antonio, Orlando	.967	21	40	49	3	92	13
Perez, Santiago, Chattanooga	.971	7	19	15	1	35	2
Powers, John, West Tenn	.985	27	50	84	2	136	17
Reyes, Guillermo, Birmingham	1.000	13	28	29	0	57	7
Rodriguez, Victor, Jacksonville	.989	22	38	50	1	89	13
Sandoval, Danny, Birmingham	.975	108	194	227	11	432	45
Scales, Bobby, Mobile	.957	19	28	38	3	69	14
Schrager, Tony, West Tenn	1.000	11	18	16	0	34	1
Shaffer, Josh, Birmingham	.896	8	19	24	5	48	4
Shumpert, Terry, Orlando	1.000	1	1	3	0	4	0
Spearman, Jemel, West Tenn	.984	14	26	37	1	64	5
Theodorou, Nick, Jacksonville	1.000	7	15	18	0	33	5
Valdez, Wilson, Carolina	.981	32	82	74	3	159	26
Van Buizen, Rodney, Jack.	.949	11	18	19	2	39	6
Washington, Rico, Mobile	1.000	1	0	1	0	1	0
Weekly, Chris, Tennessee	.988	22	30	49	1	80	8
Wilson, Josh, Carolina	1.000	1	4	3	0	7	3

THIRD BASEMEN

Player, Team	Pct.	G	PO	A	E	TC	DP
Abreu, Dennis, Tennessee	.833	7	1	9	2	12	0
Alvarez, Gabe, Birmingham	.875	16	6	15	3	24	2
Anderson, Bryan, Chattanooga	1.000	1	0	1	0	1	0

Player, Team	Pct.	G	PO	A	E	TC	DP
Anderson, Dennis, Carolina	.000	1	0	0	0	0	0
Badeaux, Brooks, Orlando	.955	10	6	15	1	22	0
Barbier, Blair, West Tenn	.900	25	14	40	6	60	1
Barnwell, Chris, Huntsville	.929	18	17	48	5	70	3
Bravo, Danny, Mobile	.852	23	10	42	9	61	3
Brewer, Jace, Orlando	.500	2	1	0	1	2	0
Cabrera, Miguel, Carolina	.924	64	45	137	15	197	22
Caceres, Wilmy, Chattanooga	.947	7	3	15	1	19	1
Cairns, Troy, Chattanooga	.800	2	2	6	2	10	0
Cantu, Jorge, Orlando	.924	36	19	54	6	79	5
Castro, Ramon, Greenville	.941	34	27	68	6	101	4
Chamblee, Jim, Chattanooga	.973	13	10	26	1	37	3
Clements, Jason, Mobile	1.000	1	1	2	0	3	0
Collins, Mike, Jacksonville	.871	11	8	19	4	31	1
Conley, Evan, Chattanooga	1.000	1	2	2	0	4	0
Creighton, Matt, West Tenn	1.000	1	0	1	0	1	0
De Renne, Keoni, Greenville	1.000	2	0	2	0	2	0
DeMent, Dan, Orlando	.846	22	5	39	8	52	3
Detienne, Dave, Jacksonville	.941	7	5	11	1	17	1
Dzurilla, Mike, West Tenn	.667	2	1	3	2	6	0
Encarnacion, Edwin, Chat.	.897	62	63	119	21	203	8
ERICKSON, COREY, Tennessee	.940	94	53	151	13	217	16
Escalona, Felix, Orlando	.864	6	4	15	3	22	2
Gripp, Ryan, Huntsville	.808	6	3	18	5	26	1
Haas, Chris, Chattanooga	1.000	5	3	12	0	15	0
Hall, Billy, Carolina	.864	25	10	28	6	44	3
Hankins, Ryan, Birmingham	.908	32	16	43	6	65	1
Harris, Brendan, West Tenn	.921	103	60	138	17	215	13
Hart, Corey, Huntsville	.897	119	74	206	32	312	23
Hood, Donnie, West Tenn	.923	4	5	7	1	13	0
Jeffcoat, Bryon, Greenville	1.000	8	5	16	0	21	2
Jurries, James, Greenville	.926	88	55	146	16	217	13
King, Brennan, Jacksonville	.924	120	67	223	24	314	27
Krause, Scott, Tennessee	.765	8	1	12	4	17	1
LaForest, Pete, Orlando	.000	1	0	0	0	0	0
Leon, Donny, West Tenn	.962	13	7	18	1	26	1
Lorenzana, Luis, Mobile	1.000	1	1	1	0	2	0
Moore, Frank, Orlando	.667	3	1	1	1	3	0
Nicholson, Tommy, Birmingham	.931	31	21	33	4	58	3
Niles, Drew, Carolina	.932	55	33	104	10	147	17
Orr, Pete, Greenville	.932	19	19	22	3	44	1
Owens, Ryan, Chattanooga	1.000	2	0	4	0	4	0
Perez, Santiago, Chattanooga	.852	7	14	9	4	27	0
Salas, Juan, Orlando	.924	64	55	127	15	197	4
Sandoval, Danny, Birmingham	.903	12	7	21	3	31	3
Saunders, Chris, Birmingham	.963	12	4	22	1	27	1
Scales, Bobby, Mobile	.878	29	23	42	9	74	3
Schramek, Mark, Chattanooga	.947	41	22	68	5	95	7
Shaffer, Josh, Birmingham	.870	63	36	84	18	138	14
Spearman, Jemel, West Tenn	.667	1	0	4	2	6	0
Van Buizen, Rodney, Jack.	.846	4	3	8	2	13	0
Washington, Rico, Mobile	.932	91	52	153	15	220	7
Weekly, Chris, Tennessee	.933	50	19	78	7	104	7
Willingham, Josh, Carolina	1.000	3	3	6	0	9	0

SHORTSTOPS

Player, Team	Pct.	G	PO	A	E	TC	DP
Abreu, Dennis, Tennessee	1.000	3	6	6	0	12	1
Acevas, Jon, Birmingham	1.000	1	0	1	0	1	1
Anderson, Bryan, Chattanooga	.954	17	27	35	3	65	9
Arteaga, Joshua, West Tenn	.951	26	37	60	5	102	15
Badeaux, Brooks, Orlando	1.000	2	2	3	0	5	0
Bannon, Jeff, Chattanooga	.955	13	29	35	3	67	12
Barnwell, Chris, Huntsville	.967	34	70	78	5	153	17
Benick, Jon, Mobile	1.000	1	1	1	0	2	0
Bravo, Danny, Mobile	.959	52	71	138	9	218	33
Brewer, Jace, Orlando	.940	73	83	199	18	300	34
Caceres, Wilmy, Chattanooga	.919	41	64	106	15	185	16
Cantu, Jorge, Orlando	1.000	5	7	7	0	14	1
Castro, Ramon, Greenville	.938	11	16	29	3	48	7
Clements, Jason, Mobile	.909	1	4	6	1	11	1
Collins, Mike, Jacksonville	.969	38	50	104	5	159	18
Cosme, Caonabo, Tennessee	1.000	7	10	13	0	23	0
Dawkins, Gookie, Jacksonville	.953	34	54	89	7	150	23
Dellaero, Jason, Chattanooga	.979	11	23	24	1	48	6
Detienne, Dave, Jacksonville	.941	20	26	54	5	85	13
Encarnacion, Edwin, Chat.	.667	2	2	2	2	6	0
Escalona, Felix, Orlando	.848	9	11	28	7	46	5
Furmaniak, J.J., Mobile	.929	31	48	69	9	126	10
Greene, Khalil, Mobile	.949	54	50	119	9	178	30
HARDY, J.J., Huntsville	.970	108	167	321	15	503	58
Harris, Brendan, West Tenn	1.000	1	0	1	0	1	0
Hood, Donnie, West Tenn	.910	16	25	36	6	67	7
Johnson, Kelly, Greenville	.959	91	122	249	16	387	40

Player, Team	Pct.	G	PO	A	E	TC	DP
Kelly, Heath, Orlando	.882	14	15	30	6	51	9
Liriano, Pedro, West Tenn	.929	8	6	20	2	28	4
Lorenzana, Luis, Mobile	.960	7	8	16	1	25	1
Martinez, Gabby, Orlando	1.000	1	1	3	0	4	0
Moore, Frank, Orlando	.906	14	26	32	6	64	4
Nelson, John, Tennessee	.960	134	159	391	23	573	67
Niles, Drew, Carolina	.932	14	19	22	3	44	5
Olmedo, Rainer, Chattanooga	.950	45	66	125	10	201	29
Orr, Pete, Greenville	.948	49	53	130	10	193	21
Ortiz, Nick, West Tenn	.940	41	67	105	11	183	20
Perez, Santiago, Chattanooga	.907	20	29	39	7	75	5
Polcovich, Kevin, Carolina	.927	13	13	38	4	55	5
Reyes, Guillermo, Birmingham	.940	104	135	227	23	385	40
Rodriguez, Victor, Jacksonville	1.000	23	23	75	0	98	14
Sandoval, Danny, Birmingham	.985	21	24	40	1	65	12
Schrager, Tony, West Tenn	.931	7	13	14	2	29	5
Shaffer, Josh, Birmingham	.911	28	40	52	9	101	9
Theodorou, Nick, Jacksonville	.950	29	33	62	5	100	13
Theriot, Ryan, West Tenn	.953	50	83	121	10	214	19
Upton, B.J., Orlando	.879	27	41	61	14	116	11
Valdez, Wilson, Carolina	.947	5	3	15	1	19	3
Wilson, Josh, Carolina	.952	114	150	290	22	462	47

OUTFIELDERS

Player, Team	Pct.	G	PO	A	E	TC	DP
Abercrombie, Reggie, Jack.	.939	115	256	7	17	280	1
Abreu, Dennis, Tennessee	.833	2	4	1	1	6	0
Aguila, Chris, Carolina	.989	88	161	11	2	174	1
Aldridge, Cory, Greenville	.971	121	198	3	6	207	0
Alvarez, Nick, Jacksonville	.962	29	47	3	2	52	1
AMBRES, CHIP, Carolina	1.000	117	265	4	0	269	0
Anderson, Bryan, Chattanooga	1.000	9	18	0	0	18	0
Ashby, Chris, Carolina	1.000	6	11	1	0	12	0
Bacon, Dwaine, West Tenn	.920	12	22	1	2	25	1
Barbier, Blair, West Tenn	.000	1	0	0	0	0	0
Barns, B.J., Orlando *	1.000	28	50	0	0	50	0
Barnwell, Chris, Huntsville	.500	1	1	0	1	2	0
Battersby, Eric, Birmingham *	.846	5	10	1	2	13	0
Beattie, Andrew, Chattanooga	1.000	5	10	1	0	11	0
Benjamin, Al, Tennessee	.975	23	36	3	1	40	1
Bikowski, Scott, Birmingham *	.977	84	167	5	4	176	0
Bolivar, Papo, Tennessee	.985	128	187	7	3	197	0
Bost, Tom, Carolina	1.000	35	70	2	0	72	0
Boyd, Shaun, Tennessee	.983	26	56	2	1	59	0
Brock, Tarrik, Jacksonville *	.976	60	119	4	3	126	1
Burns, Kevan, Tennessee *	.992	70	117	3	1	121	0
Cabrera, Miguel, Carolina	1.000	3	7	0	0	7	0
Caceres, Wilmy, Chattanooga	.972	31	67	3	2	72	0
Chamblee, Jim, Chattanooga	1.000	11	20	1	0	21	0
Clark, Daryl, Huntsville	.946	55	82	5	5	92	1
Clements, Jason, Mobile	1.000	6	6	0	0	6	0
Correll, Brad, Chattanooga	.927	21	34	4	3	41	0
Cosbey, Chris, Huntsville *	1.000	17	27	0	0	27	0
Darula, Bobby, Chattanooga	1.000	1	3	0	0	3	0
DeMent, Dan, Orlando	1.000	2	1	1	0	2	0
Diaz, Alejandro, Chattanooga	.996	93	224	5	1	230	1
Diaz, Matt, Orlando	.994	60	147	7	1	155	3
Dodson, Jeremy, Tennessee	.981	33	50	3	1	54	0
Donovan, Todd, Mobile	.982	107	262	8	5	275	1
Dubois, Jason, West Tenn	.969	108	177	12	6	195	2
Duncan, Chris, Tennessee	.889	5	8	0	1	9	0
Durham, Chad, Birmingham	.982	115	260	8	5	273	4
Dzurilla, Mike, West Tenn	1.000	8	12	1	0	13	0
Faison, Vince, Mobile	.952	111	184	16	10	210	1
Feliciano, Jesus, Jack.-Orl.*	.983	90	171	5	3	179	2
Fernandez, Alex, Mobile *	.970	19	32	0	1	33	0
Fitzgerald, Jason, Greenville *	.963	86	147	9	6	162	0
Gall, John, Tennessee	1.000	10	12	0	0	12	0
Gathright, Joey, Orlando	.983	18	56	2	1	59	0
Gerber, Joseph, Mobile *	1.000	3	7	0	0	7	0
German, Amado, Orlando	.981	107	294	8	6	308	1
Gomes, Jonny, Orlando	.977	105	167	6	4	177	1
Gomez, Rich, Mobile	.977	27	41	2	1	44	0
Gripp, Ryan, Huntsville	1.000	5	8	0	0	8	0
Guerrero, Cristian, Huntsville	.984	31	57	3	1	61	1
Gutierrez, Franklin, Jacksonville	1.000	18	31	1	0	32	0
Guzman, Freddy, Mobile	.984	46	120	2	2	124	0
Hall, Billy, Carolina	1.000	58	89	5	0	94	1
Hamilton, Jon, W.Tenn-Birm.*	.975	103	189	4	5	198	1
Hart, Corey, Huntsville	.000	1	0	0	0	0	0
Holt, Daylan, Birmingham	1.000	4	4	0	0	4	0
Ingram, Darron, Birmingham	1.000	36	58	2	0	60	0
Jenkins, Geoff, Huntsville	1.000	6	7	0	0	7	0
Johnson, Ben, Mobile	.984	35	60	0	1	61	0

Player, Team	Pct.	G	PO	A	E	TC	DP
Kearns, Austin, Chattanooga	1.000	2	2	1	0	3	0
Knott, Jon, Mobile	.968	72	116	4	4	124	0
Knox, Ryan, Huntsville	.973	88	176	7	5	188	2
Krause, Scott, Tennessee	1.000	39	59	5	0	64	2
Kremblas, Mike, Huntsville	1.000	1	2	0	0	2	0
Krynzel, Dave, Huntsville *	.963	120	273	14	11	298	3
Langerhans, Ryan, Greenville *	.991	89	204	9	2	215	1
Lemanczyk, Matt, Tennessee	.600	4	2	1	2	5	0
Leon, Donny, West Tenn	1.000	9	8	1	0	9	0
Lewis, Kenneth, Chattanooga *	1.000	5	6	1	0	7	0
Martinez, Gabby, Orlando	1.000	7	9	0	0	9	0
Massiatte, Danny, Orlando	.000	1	0	0	0	0	0
Matthews, Lamont, Jack.*	.944	10	17	0	1	18	0
McCarthy, Bill, Greenville	1.000	78	123	3	0	126	1
Melian, Jackson, West Tenn	.990	64	96	4	1	101	0
Miller, Greg, Greenville	1.000	11	23	0	0	23	0
Minor, Ryan, Jacksonville	.000	1	0	0	0	0	0
Mitchell, Keith, Chattanooga	.870	17	20	0	3	23	0
Moore, Frank, Orlando	.947	14	18	0	1	19	0
Moylan, Dan, Tennessee	.875	4	7	0	1	8	0
Nelson, Brad, Huntsville	.956	32	42	1	2	45	0
Orr, Pete, Greenville	1.000	4	3	0	0	3	0
Owens, Ryan, Chattanooga	1.000	1	2	0	0	2	0
Padgett, Matt, Carolina *	.987	111	221	12	3	236	2
Paz, Rich, Huntsville	.667	3	2	0	1	3	0
Perez, Santiago, Chattanooga	.929	24	51	1	4	56	0
Piniella, Juan, Birmingham	.979	103	181	4	4	189	0
Reed, Jeremy, Birmingham *	1.000	60	150	5	0	155	0
Repko, Jason, Jacksonville	.980	109	229	12	5	246	3
Rico, Matt, Orlando	1.000	2	3	0	0	3	0
Roman, Jesse, Tennessee *	1.000	3	4	1	0	5	0
Sadler, Ray, West Tenn	.988	107	231	8	3	242	2
Salas, Juan, Orlando	1.000	11	15	1	0	16	0
Scales, Bobby, Mobile	.957	18	21	1	1	23	0
Schumaker, Skip, Tennessee	.994	88	171	5	1	177	1
Senjem, Guye, Chattanooga	.970	88	151	13	5	169	3
Smith, Will, Carolina	1.000	30	44	2	0	46	0
Smitherman, Stephen, Chat.	.994	98	166	7	1	174	2
Stenson, Dernell, Chattanooga *	.957	32	43	1	2	46	0
Thomas, Charles, Greenville *	.983	44	109	4	2	115	0
Varner, Noochie, Huntsville	.965	77	125	11	5	141	3
Velazquez, Jose, West Tenn *	.933	14	14	0	1	15	0
Victorino, Shane, Jacksonville	.978	65	172	7	4	183	3
Ward, Daryle, Jacksonville *	.667	2	2	0	1	3	0
Weekly, Chris, Tennessee	.966	29	26	2	1	29	0
Weston, Aron, West Tenn *	.982	53	104	5	2	111	1
Willingham, Josh, Carolina	1.000	3	9	0	0	9	0

OUTFIELDERS WITH TWO OR MORE TEAMS

Player, Team	Pct.	G	PO	A	E	TC	DP
Feliciano, Jesus, Orlando *	.980	71	143	3	3	149	2
Feliciano, Jesus, Jacksonville *	1.000	19	28	2	0	30	0
Hamilton, Jon, Birmingham *	.966	38	85	1	3	89	0
Hamilton, Jon, West Tenn *	.982	65	104	3	2	109	1

CATCHERS

Player, Team	Pct.	G	PO	A	E	TC	DP	PB
Acevas, Jon, Birmingham	.984	23	171	9	3	183	0	3
Alvarado, Joel, Huntsville	.992	14	116	16	1	133	1	5
Anderson, Dennis, Carolina	.988	12	80	5	1	86	1	2
Ashby, Chris, Carolina	1.000	5	11	3	0	14	1	0
Bellorin, Edwin, Jacksonville	.981	17	137	19	3	159	5	0
Boscan, Jean, Greenville	.997	40	286	27	1	314	2	2
Cardona, Javier, West Tenn	.979	10	84	9	2	95	2	0
Deck, Ronnie, Orlando	1.000	3	10	0	0	10	0	1
Duplissea, Bill, Jacksonville	.977	7	33	9	1	43	0	2
Evans, Lee, Greenville	.988	42	298	24	4	326	1	10
Girardi, Joe, Tennessee	1.000	3	17	2	0	19	1	1
Gubanich, Creighton, Chat.	1.000	23	126	15	0	141	1	2
Gutierrez, Jesse, Chattanooga	.960	4	21	3	1	25	0	1
Haad, Yamid, Mobile	.944	3	16	1	1	18	0	0
Hankins, Ryan, Birmingham	1.000	1	2	1	0	3	0	0
Harper, Brandon, Carolina	.994	64	437	26	3	466	4	4
Hill, Jason, Chattanooga	.933	3	10	4	1	15	1	0
Hill, Koyie, Jacksonville	.989	24	170	17	2	189	5	3
Isenia, Chairon, Orlando	.972	37	221	23	7	251	1	3
Johnson, Kade, Huntsville	.987	63	401	40	6	447	3	9
Jorgensen, Ryan, Carolina	.988	65	439	42	6	487	6	3
Kopitzke, Casey, West Tenn	.993	100	761	92	6	859	2	3
Kremblas, Mike, Huntsville	.987	62	412	54	6	472	4	13
LaForest, Pete, Orlando	.981	9	48	4	1	53	1	3
Maldonado, Carlos, Birm.	.988	94	632	51	8	691	5	6
Massiatte, Danny, Orlando	.990	56	346	50	4	400	2	7
McKnight, Lukas, West Tenn	.992	34	240	14	2	256	1	3
Merritt, Graig, Orlando	.981	23	145	14	3	162	2	5
Molina, Yadier, Tennessee	.991	100	775	72	8	855	8	11
Moon, Brian, Huntsville	.961	6	36	13	2	51	1	3
Morales, Steve, Birmingham	.975	29	181	18	5	204	2	1
Moylan, Dan, Tennessee	.993	40	259	20	2	281	2	7
Netwall, Chris, Tennessee	1.000	3	14	3	0	17	0	1
Peterson, Brian, Chattanooga	.991	28	204	25	2	231	0	2
QUINTERO, HUMBERTO, Mob.	.995	109	857	93	5	955	5	6
Reinking, Kevin, Mobile	.991	13	104	2	1	107	0	1
Riggans, Shawn, Orlando	1.000	21	117	7	0	124	0	3
Rogers, Brandon, Jacksonville	.957	4	22	0	1	23	0	0
Sardinha, Dane, Chattanooga	.985	70	476	67	8	551	8	2
Secrist, Reed, Chattanooga	.993	16	133	10	1	144	1	3
Smith, Ryan, Mobile	.988	11	79	6	1	86	2	0
Socarras, Tony, Jacksonville	.994	60	422	37	3	462	3	4
Terveen, Bryce, Greenville	.987	58	355	35	5	395	3	1
Washington, Rico, Mobile	.985	10	61	6	1	68	0	2
Waszgis, B.J., Jacksonville	1.000	37	241	18	0	259	1	9
Willingham, Josh, Carolina	1.000	4	24	3	0	27	0	0

PITCHERS

Player, Team	Pct.	G	PO	A	E	TC	DP
Adams, Brian, Huntsville *	.929	32	3	10	1	14	3
Adams, Mike, Huntsville	1.000	45	9	7	0	16	0
Adkins, Tim, Chattanooga *	1.000	9	1	0	0	1	0
Aguilar, Ray, Greenville *	.900	35	5	22	3	30	2
An, Byeong, Birmingham *	.933	16	4	10	1	15	0
Andersen, Derek, Orlando *	1.000	22	1	6	0	7	0
Anderson, Bryan, Chattanooga	.000	1	0	0	0	0	0
Anderson, Travis, West Tenn	1.000	14	2	2	0	4	0
Andrews, Clayton, Chat.*	.800	2	1	3	1	5	0
Ankiel, Rick, Tennessee *	.818	20	3	6	2	11	0
Arteaga, Joshua, West Tenn	.000	3	0	0	0	0	0
Ashby, Chris, Carolina	1.000	9	4	1	0	5	0
Autrey, Scott, Orlando	1.000	12	4	11	0	15	0
Axelson, Josh, Tennessee	.909	27	5	15	2	22	1
Bajenaru, Jeff, Birmingham	1.000	50	4	8	0	12	1
Baker, Brad, Mobile	.909	17	1	9	1	11	0
Baker, Ryan, Carolina	.857	44	5	7	2	14	1
Barnett, Marty, Carolina	.800	5	1	3	1	5	1
Barreto, Joel, Chattanooga	1.000	15	3	2	0	5	1
Barry, Kevin, Greenville	.889	51	2	6	1	9	0
Basham, Bobby, Chattanooga	.905	17	6	13	2	21	0
Battersby, Eric, Birmingham *	.000	1	0	0	0	0	0
Bauer, Greg, Jacksonville	.964	46	5	22	1	28	2
Bautista, Denny, Carolina	.818	11	2	7	2	11	0
Beckett, Josh, Carolina	.000	1	0	0	0	0	0
Belisle, Matt, Greenville	.897	21	8	18	3	29	2
Benedetti, John, Orlando	.941	42	3	13	1	17	1
Benik, Brett, West Tenn	.000	3	0	0	0	0	0
Bevel, Bobby, Chattanooga *	1.000	16	3	2	0	5	1
Blank, Matt, Greenville *	1.000	2	1	0	0	1	0
Bludau, Frank, Chattanooga	.000	3	0	0	0	0	0
Brazelton, Dewon, Orlando	.000	2	0	0	0	0	0
Bridges, Donnie, Carolina	1.000	31	9	10	0	19	0
Brock, Tarrik, Jacksonville *	.000	1	0	0	0	0	0
Brown, Andrew, Jacksonville	1.000	1	1	0	0	1	0
Brown, Eric, West Tenn	.889	44	3	5	1	9	0
Bruso, Greg, Huntsville	.750	2	0	3	1	4	1
Bullard, Jim, Birmingham *	.750	53	3	9	4	16	2
Bumstead, Mike, Mobile	.938	37	4	11	1	16	1
Byrd, Paul, Greenville	1.000	1	0	1	0	1	0
Campbell, Jarrett, Orlando	.000	4	0	0	0	0	0
Carpenter, Chris, Tennessee	1.000	1	1	1	0	2	0
Cash, David, West Tenn	1.000	50	7	6	0	13	0
Castillo, Carlos, Birmingham	1.000	5	0	3	0	3	0
Chavez, Wilton, West Tenn	.500	2	1	0	1	2	0
Childers, Matt, Huntsville	.900	36	7	11	2	20	0
Childress, Daylan, Chattanooga	1.000	9	1	10	0	11	1
Collazo, William, Greenville *	1.000	39	4	12	0	16	0
Collins, Pat, Tennessee	.600	5	2	1	2	5	0
Colon, Roman, Greenville	.957	39	8	14	1	23	1
Cook, B.R., Tennessee	.875	29	3	4	1	8	0
Cook, Jeremy, Tennessee	1.000	10	2	6	0	8	0
Coose, Austin, Orlando	.000	3	0	0	0	0	0
Cortes, Jorge, Chattanooga	1.000	9	1	3	0	4	0
Cotton, Nathan, Chattanooga	.000	1	0	0	0	0	0
Cotts, Neal, Birmingham *	.952	21	7	13	1	21	2
Crabtree, Tim, Huntsville	1.000	6	1	0	0	1	0
Cromer, Jason, Orlando *	1.000	6	4	4	0	8	0
Cueto, Jose, Carolina	.846	35	1	10	2	13	1
Cummings, Jeremy, Tennessee	1.000	15	4	15	0	19	1
Curtis, Daniel, Greenville	.963	17	12	14	1	27	2
Cyr, Eric, Chattanooga *	1.000	1	0	1	0	1	0

Player, Team	Pct.	G	PO	A	E	TC	DP
Darnell, Paul, Chattanooga *	1.000	15	3	1	0	4	0
Davis, Doug, Huntsville *	1.000	1	0	1	0	1	1
De Renne, Keoni, Greenville	.000	1	0	0	0	0	0
DeHart, Casey, Chattanooga *	1.000	41	6	17	0	23	2
DeMent, Dan, Orlando	1.000	1	0	1	0	1	0
Deago, Roger, Mobile *	.963	26	8	18	1	27	2
Deck, Ronnie, Orlando	1.000	1	1	0	0	1	0
Devey, Phil, Chattanooga *	1.000	12	1	5	0	6	0
Diaz, Joselo, Jacksonville	1.000	5	0	1	0	1	0
Digby, Bryan, Greenville	1.000	9	0	2	0	2	0
Diggins, Ben, Huntsville	.938	8	5	10	1	16	1
Dingman, Craig, West Tenn	1.000	4	0	1	0	1	0
Dunn, Scott, Chat.-Birmingham	.833	39	3	7	2	12	0
Eason, Clay, Birmingham	1.000	17	1	7	0	8	1
Ennis, John, Greenville	1.000	1	0	1	0	1	0
Evert, Brett, Greenville	.969	33	8	23	1	32	1
Farmer, Tom, Jacksonville	.964	20	10	17	1	28	1
Fesh, Sean, Carolina *	1.000	49	6	9	0	15	0
Figueroa, Juan, Tennessee	1.000	34	1	3	0	4	1
Flannery, Mike, Carolina	1.000	56	3	9	0	12	0
Flinn, Chris, Orlando	.750	7	1	2	1	4	0
Fortunato, Bartolome, Orlando	.727	35	1	7	3	11	0
Frasor, Jason, Jacksonville	1.000	35	3	1	0	4	0
Fuell, Jerrod, Carolina	1.000	6	2	1	0	3	0
Gaal, Bryan, Mobile	1.000	62	4	9	0	13	1
Garcia, Gerardo, Orlando	.500	4	0	1	1	2	0
Gaudin, Chad, Orlando	1.000	3	3	2	0	5	0
Germano, Justin, Mobile	.933	9	3	11	1	15	0
Giese, Dan, Mobile	.000	2	0	0	0	0	0
Gil, Dave, Chattanooga	.800	30	1	3	1	5	0
Gonzalez, Alfredo, Jacksonville	1.000	10	4	8	0	12	0
Gracesqui, Frank, Carolina *	.917	44	1	10	1	12	1
Gray, Brett, Chattanooga	1.000	43	1	15	0	16	0
Guillory, Dan, Orlando	1.000	23	1	7	0	8	2
Guzman, Angel, West Tenn	.900	15	5	13	2	20	2
Hall, Josh, Chattanooga	.884	26	8	30	5	43	1
Hamilton, Jon, West Tenn *	.000	1	0	0	0	0	0
Hammons, Matt, Huntsville	1.000	13	0	1	0	1	0
Hanrahan, Joel, Jacksonville	.897	23	9	17	3	29	1
Haren, Danny, Tennessee	.875	8	3	4	1	8	0
Harvey, Ian, Mobile	1.000	6	0	3	0	3	0
Hendrickson, Ben, Huntsville	.952	17	7	13	1	21	0
Herndon, Eric, Greenville	1.000	7	1	1	0	2	0
Hines, Carlos, Orlando	1.000	2	0	1	0	1	0
Honel, Kris, Birmingham	1.000	2	1	2	0	3	0
House, Craig, Carolina	1.000	8	0	1	0	1	0
Housman, Jeff, Huntsville *	1.000	8	0	5	0	5	0
Howington, Ty, Chattanooga *	1.000	4	0	1	0	1	0
Hundley, Jeff, Huntsville *	1.000	9	0	2	0	2	0
Hunter, Johnny, Mobile	.000	1	0	0	0	0	0
Hutchinson, Trevor, Carolina	1.000	8	5	3	0	8	0
Isenia, Chairon, Orlando	.000	1	0	0	0	0	0
Isringhausen, Jason, Tennessee	1.000	2	0	2	0	2	0
Jackson, Edwin, Jacksonville	.929	27	11	15	2	28	1
Janke, Cheyenne, Tennessee	1.000	9	2	1	0	3	0
Jeffcoat, Bryon, Greenville	.000	1	0	0	0	0	0
Johnson, Tyler, Tennessee *	1.000	20	1	4	0	5	0
Jones, Mike, Huntsville	.960	17	10	14	1	25	1
Karnuth, Jason, West Tenn	1.000	45	2	6	0	8	2
Keller, Kris, Chattanooga	.667	35	0	2	1	3	0
Kelly, Steve, Chattanooga	1.000	6	2	4	0	6	0
Kennedy, Joe, Orlando *	1.000	1	0	1	0	1	0
Kent, Steve, Carolina *	1.000	37	1	6	0	7	1
Key, Chris, Carolina *	1.000	1	0	3	0	3	2
Kinney, Josh, Tennessee	1.000	29	1	7	0	8	1
Koronka, John, Chat.-W.Tenn *	.961	26	5	44	2	51	0
Krawiec, Aaron, West Tenn *	1.000	8	1	3	0	4	2
Kremblas, Mike, Huntsville	.000	1	0	0	0	0	0
LaRoche, Adam, Greenville *	.000	1	0	0	0	0	0
Lambert, Jeremy, Tennessee	.750	33	1	2	1	4	0
Langone, Steve, Jacksonville	.929	22	4	9	1	14	0
Lee, Derek, Huntsville *	.933	20	3	25	2	30	5
Leicester, Jon, West Tenn	.960	45	5	19	1	25	3
Lewis, Derrick, Greenville	1.000	3	2	1	0	3	0
Liriano, Pedro, Huntsville	.900	27	10	26	4	40	0
Lyons, Mike, Tennessee	1.000	57	2	4	0	6	0
Magrane, Jim, Orlando	.913	25	12	30	4	46	1
Malaska, Mark, Orlando *	1.000	19	4	1	0	5	0
Malone, Corwin, Birmingham *	1.000	8	2	4	0	6	0
Marchbanks, David, Carolina *	1.000	1	1	3	0	4	0
Martinez, Luis, Huntsville *	.909	20	2	18	2	22	1
McAdoo, Duncan, Mobile	.909	30	8	12	2	22	1
McConnell, Sam, Greenville *	1.000	16	1	3	0	4	0
McCrotty, Will, Jacksonville	.941	32	10	6	1	17	0
McLeary, Marty, Carolina	.714	11	2	3	2	7	0

Player, Team	Pct.	G	PO	A	E	TC	DP
McNutt, Mike, Carolina	.000	1	0	0	0	0	0
McWhirter, Kris, Birmingham	1.000	25	0	11	0	11	0
Meaux, Ryan, Birmingham *	1.000	26	4	10	0	14	1
Messenger, Randy, Carolina	.957	29	6	16	1	23	0
Meyer, Jake, Birmingham	.857	17	1	5	1	7	0
Miller, Greg, Jacksonville *	1.000	4	2	3	0	5	0
Miller, Ryan, Huntsville	.900	50	8	19	3	30	2
Miller, Travis, Chattanooga *	.000	1	0	0	0	0	0
Miniel, Rene, Mobile	.000	1	0	0	0	0	0
Minix, Travis, Orlando	.875	44	4	3	1	8	0
Minor, Ryan, Jacksonville	1.000	15	2	4	0	6	0
Mitchell, Nathan, West Tenn	1.000	4	1	1	0	2	0
Mitre, Sergio, West Tenn	.932	25	14	27	3	44	2
Montero, Agustin, Jacksonville	1.000	16	3	4	0	7	0
Moore, Frank, Orlando	1.000	1	0	1	0	1	0
Moseley, Dustin, Chattanooga	.957	18	3	19	1	23	0
Moser, Todd, Carolina *	.786	18	4	7	3	14	0
Mottl, Ryan, Chattanooga	.889	23	5	11	2	18	0
Murray, Brad, Birmingham *	.000	5	0	0	0	0	0
Nannini, Mike, West Tenn	.952	31	8	12	1	21	2
Narveson, Chris, Tennessee *	.923	10	2	10	1	13	1
Nelson, Bubba, Greenville	.857	23	6	18	4	28	0
Nicolas, Mike, Mobile	.000	5	0	0	0	0	0
Niles, Drew, Carolina	.000	1	0	0	0	0	0
Nina, Elvin, Jacksonville	.000	8	0	0	1	1	0
Nolasco, Dave, Huntsville	.833	9	0	5	1	6	1
Novinsky, John, Tennessee	.833	18	0	5	1	6	0
Nunez, Jose, Mobile *	.750	9	1	2	1	4	0
O'Connor, Brian, Orlando *	.667	8	2	0	1	3	0
O'Neal, Brandon, Birmingham	1.000	5	1	1	0	2	1
Ortiz, Omar, Carolina	1.000	8	0	3	0	3	0
Oxspring, Chris, Mobile	.931	40	8	19	2	29	1
Pacheco, Enemencio, Birm.	.933	30	8	20	2	30	2
Parker, Josh, Orlando	1.000	24	1	8	0	9	0
Parker, Matt, Huntsville	.933	42	3	11	1	15	0
Parrott, Rhett, Tennessee	1.000	21	7	17	0	24	1
Pearce, Josh, Tennessee	1.000	5	2	4	0	6	0
Pearson, Jason, Tennessee *	1.000	9	1	1	0	2	0
Pena, Juan, Tennessee *	1.000	29	1	16	0	17	2
Phillips, Mike, Birmingham *	.000	1	0	0	0	0	0
Pignatiello, Carmen, W.Tenn *	.000	1	0	0	0	0	0
Pilkington, Brian, Jacksonville	1.000	5	3	5	0	8	0
Pineda, Luis, Jacksonville	1.000	9	2	4	0	6	1
Proctor, Scott, Jacksonville	1.000	17	2	2	0	4	0
Purvis, Rob, Birmingham	1.000	13	1	4	0	5	0
Ramirez, Emmanuel, West Tenn	1.000	22	2	2	0	4	0
Ray, Ken, Huntsville	.867	31	3	10	2	15	1
Reina, Dimas, Jacksonville	.000	4	0	0	0	0	0
Rice, Leonard, Chattanooga *	1.000	2	0	1	0	1	0
Ring, Royce, Birmingham *	1.000	36	1	3	0	4	0
Robinson, Jeff, Huntsville	1.000	3	0	1	0	1	0
Rocker, John, Orlando *	.000	17	0	0	0	0	0
Rodriguez, Orlando, Jack.*	1.000	11	0	3	0	3	0
Rohlicek, Russ, West Tenn *	.750	13	1	2	1	4	0
Rojas, Chris, Mobile	.833	32	6	19	5	30	3
Ruhl, Nathan, Jacksonville	1.000	5	0	1	0	1	0
Rust, Evan, Orlando	.750	30	3	9	4	16	0
Ryu, Jae-kuk, West Tenn	1.000	11	5	9	0	14	0
Saenz, Chris, Huntsville	.000	1	0	0	0	0	0
Salmon, Brad, Chattanooga	1.000	10	0	2	0	2	0
Sanchez, Felix, West Tenn *	.429	30	0	3	4	7	0
Santos, Alex, Orlando	.833	25	2	3	1	6	0
Saucedo, Matthew, Carolina	.000	1	0	0	0	0	0
Saunders, Chris, Birmingham	.000	1	0	0	0	0	0
Shackelford, Brian, Chat.*	1.000	13	0	6	0	6	0
Shelley, Jason, Huntsville	1.000	9	2	6	0	8	0
Small, Aaron, Carolina	1.000	8	0	5	0	5	0
Smith, Chuck, Greenville	1.000	3	1	2	0	3	0
Smith, Matt, Birmingham	1.000	52	2	8	0	10	0
SNARE, RYAN, Carolina *	1.000	18	10	20	0	30	1
Sodowsky, Clint, Carolina	1.000	5	1	3	0	4	0
Sonnier, Shawn, West Tenn	1.000	12	1	2	0	3	0
Spiehs, R.D., Mobile	1.000	15	1	2	0	3	0
Sprague, Kevin, Tennessee *	.889	53	1	7	1	9	0
Steffek, Brian, Jacksonville	1.000	24	2	4	0	6	1
Stewart, Cory, Mobile *	.824	24	4	10	3	17	0
Stocks, Nick, Tennessee	.885	27	8	15	3	26	0
Stokes, Brian, Orlando	1.000	10	3	12	0	15	0
Stults, Eric, Jacksonville *	.909	9	2	8	1	11	0
Stumm, Jason, Birmingham	.000	7	0	0	0	0	0
Switzer, Jon, Orlando *	.957	22	6	16	1	23	0
Sylvester, Billy, Greenville	1.000	41	5	5	0	10	1
Szuminski, Jason, West Tenn	1.000	29	6	18	0	24	1
Takeoka, Kazuhiro, Greenville	.857	20	3	3	1	7	1
Therneau, Dave, Chattanooga	1.000	9	0	1	0	1	0

Player, Team	Pct.	G	PO	A	E	TC	DP
Thompson, Travis, Chattanooga	1.000	9	0	5	0	5	1
Tillery, Josh, Greenville	.500	8	0	1	1	2	0
Totten, Heath, Jacksonville	.944	28	10	24	2	36	2
Trujillo, J.J., Mobile	1.000	28	7	14	0	21	2
Tucker, Rusty, Mobile *	1.000	51	3	7	0	10	1
Ulacia, Dennis, Birmingham *	1.000	11	4	9	0	13	1
Ungs, Nic, Carolina	.933	10	5	9	1	15	1
Urdaneta, Lino, Jacksonville	1.000	44	4	11	0	15	1
Velazquez, Jose, West Tenn *	.000	1	0	0	0	0	0
Veras, Jose, Orlando	.917	27	5	17	2	24	0
Villalon, Julio, Tennessee	1.000	12	4	16	0	20	1
Waechter, Doug, Orlando	.875	13	2	5	1	8	0
Wagner, Ryan, Chattanooga	.000	5	0	0	0	0	0
Wainwright, Adam, Greenville	.882	27	9	21	4	34	0
Waligora, T.P., West Tenn	1.000	11	2	0	0	2	0
Walrond, Les, Tennessee *	1.000	4	1	0	0	1	0
Waters, Chris, Greenville *	.800	17	5	15	5	25	0
Watkins, Steve, Mobile	.962	18	9	16	1	26	0
Webb, Alan, Mobile *	.833	58	3	7	2	12	0
Webb, John, West Tenn	.941	30	9	23	2	34	3
Wellemeyer, Todd, West Tenn	1.000	4	0	2	0	2	0
West, Brian, Birmingham	1.000	12	5	6	0	11	0
White, Matt, Orlando	1.000	7	1	3	0	4	0
Willis, Dontrelle, Carolina *	1.000	6	7	9	0	16	0
Winkelsas, Joe, Greenville	1.000	23	1	4	0	5	0
Wylie, Mitch, Birmingham	.700	14	3	4	3	10	1
Yofu, Tetsu, Birmingham	.944	29	10	24	2	36	1
Zumwalt, Alec, Greenville	1.000	11	2	0	0	2	0

PITCHERS WITH TWO OR MORE TEAMS

Player, Team	Pct.	G	PO	A	E	TC	DP
Dunn, Scott, Birmingham	1.000	8	1	4	0	5	0
Dunn, Scott, Chattanooga	.714	31	2	3	2	7	0
Koronka, John, West Tenn *	.000	1	0	0	0	0	0
Koronka, John, Chattanooga *	.961	25	5	44	2	51	0

LEAGUE CHAMPIONS

Year	Team	Pct.
1904—	Macon	.598
1905—	Macon	.625
1906—	Savannah	.637
1907—	Charleston	.620
1908—	Jackonsville	.694
1909—	Chattanooga*	.738
	Augusta	.702
1910—	Columbus	.588
1911—	Columbus*	.681
	Columbia	.710
1912—	Jacksonville*	.679
	Columbus	.632
1913—	Savannah	.754
	Savannah	.593
1914—	Savannah*	.667
	Albany	.650
1915—	Macon	.588
	Columbus*	.686
1916—	Augusta*	.617
	Columbia	.631
1917—	Charleston	.741
	Columbia*	.667
1918—	Did not operate.	
1919—	Columbia	.585
1920—	Columbia	.633
1921—	Columbia	.642
1922—	Charleston	.625
1923—	Charlotte*	.653
	Macon	.580
1924—	Augusta	.612
1925—	Spartanburg	.620
1926—	Greenville	.662
1927—	Greenville	.622
1928—	Asheville	.664
1929—	Asheville	.605
	Knoxville*	.634
1930—	Greenville*	.620
	Macon	.643
1931-35—	Did not operate.	
1936—	Jacksonville	.652
	Columbus*	.650
1937—	Columbus	.572
	Savannah (3rd)†	.565
1938—	Savannah	.574
	Macon (2nd)†	.570
1939—	Columbus	.601
	Augusta (2nd)†	.597
1940—	Savannah	.627
	Columbus (2nd)†	.583
1941—	Macon	.643
	Columbia (2nd)†	.636
1942—	Charleston	.620
	Macon (2nd)†	.585
1943-45—	Did not operate.	
1946—	Columbus	.568
	Augusta (4th)†	.547
1947—	Columbus	.575
	Savannah (2nd)†	.563
1948—	Charleston	.572
	Greenville (3rd)†	.549
1949—	Macon‡	.623
1950—	Macon‡	.588
1951—	Montgomery	.607
1952—	Columbia	.649
	Montgomery (3rd)†	.558
1953—	Jacksonville	.679
	Savannah (2nd)†	.571
1954—	Jacksonville	.593
	Savannah (2nd)†	.571
1955—	Columbia	.636
	Augusta (3rd)†	.543
1956—	Jacksonville‡	.621
1957—	Augusta	.636
	Charlotte (2nd)†	.562
1958—	Augusta	.550
	Macon (3rd)†	.500
1959—	Knoxville	.557
	Gastonia (4th)†	.504
1960—	Columbia	.597
	Savannah (3rd)†	.561
1961—	Asheville	.635
1962—	Savannah	.662
	Macon (3rd)†	.576
1963—	Augusta*	.661
	Lynchburg	.662
1964—	Lynchburg	.579
1965—	Columbus	.572
1966—	Mobile	.629
1967—	Birmingham	.604
1968—	Asheville	.614
1969—	Charlotte	.579
1970—	Columbus	.569
1971—	Did not operate as league—clubs were members of Dixie Association.	
1972—	Asheville	.583
	Montgomery§	.561
1973—	Montgomery§	.580
	Jacksonville	.559
1974—	Jacksonville	.565
	Knoxville§	.533
1975—	Orlando	.587
	Montgomery§	.545
1976—	Montgomery∞	.591
	Orlando	.540
1977—	Montgomery∞	.628
	Jacksonville	.522
1978—	Knoxville∞	.611
	Savannah	.500
1979—	Columbus	.587
	Nashville∞	.576
1980—	Memphis	.576
	Charlotte∞	.500
1981—	Nashville	.566
	Orlando∞	.556
1982—	Jacksonville	.576
	Nashville∞	.535
1983—	Birmingham∞	.628
	Jacksonville	.531
1984—	Charlotte∞	.510
	Knoxville	.483
1985—	Charlotte	.545
	Huntsville∞	.542
1986—	Huntsville	.553
	Columbus∞	.500
1987—	Charlotte	.586
	Birmingham∞	.476
1988—	Greenville	.604
	Chattanooga∞	.566
1989—	Birmingham∞	.615
	Greenville	.504
1990—	Orlando	.590
	Memphis∞	.507
1991—	Greenville	.611
	Orlando∞	.535
1992—	Greenville∞	.699
	Chattanooga	.629
1993—	Birmingham∞	.549
	Knoxville	.500
1994—	Huntsville∞	.587
	Carolina	.529
1995—	Carolina∞	.618
	Chattanooga	.580
1996—	Chattanooga	.579
	Jacksonville∞	.543
1997—	Huntsville	.554
	Greenville∞	.529
1998—	Mobile∞	.614
	Jacksonville	.614
1999—	West Tenn	.596
	Orlando∞	.507
2000—	West Tenn∞	.580
	Jacksonville	.493
2001—	Jacksonville▲	.597
	Huntsville▲	.543
2002—	Birmingham∞	.564
2003—	Carolina∞	.580

*Won split season playoff. †Won four-club playoff. ‡Won championship and four-club playoff. §League was divided into Eastern and Western divisions; won playoff. ∞League was divided into Eastern and Western divisions and played split season; won playoff. ▲Were entering finals of four-team playoff and were declared co-champions when Professional Baseball declared a stoppage of play.

TEXAS LEAGUE

LEAGUE OFFICE

President/treasurer
Tom Kayser

Address
2442 Facet Oak
San Antonio, TX 78232

Phone
210-545-5297

TEAMS

ARKANSAS TRAVELERS

Vice president/general manager
Bill Valentine
Manager
Tyrone Boykin
Ballpark (capacity, surface)
Ray Winder Field (6,083, grass)
Affiliation
Angels
Address
P.O. Box 55066
Little Rock, AR 72215
Phone
501-664-1555

EL PASO DIABLOS

General manager
Andrew Wheeler
Manager
Scott Coolbaugh
Ballpark (capacity, surface)
Cohen Stadium (9,765, grass)
Affiliation
Diamondbacks
Address
9700 Gateway Blvd. N.
El Paso, TX 79924
Phone
915-755-2000

FRISCO ROUGHRIDERS

General manager/president
Mike McCall
Manager
Tim Ireland
Ballpark (capacity, surface)
Dr Pepper/7 Up Ballpark (9,000, grass)
Affiliation
Rangers
Address
7300 Roughriders Trail
Frisco, TX 75034
Phone
972-731-9200

MIDLAND ROCKHOUNDS

General manager
Monty Hoppel
Manager
Webster Garrison
Ballpark (capacity, surface)
First American Bank Ballpark (5,000, grass)
Affiliation
Athletics
Address
5514 Champions Dr.
Midland, TX 79706
Phone
915-520-2255

ROUND ROCK EXPRESS

General manager/vice president
Jay Miller
Manager
Jackie Moore
Ballpark (capacity, surface)
The Dell Diamond (7,500, grass)
Affiliation
Astros
Address
P.O. Box 5309
Round Rock, TX 78683
Phone
512-255-2255

SAN ANTONIO MISSIONS

President
To be announced
Manager
Dave Brundage
Ballpark (capacity, surface)
Nelson Wolff Stadium (6,300, grass)
Affiliation
Mariners
Address
5757 Highway 90 West
San Antonio, TX 78227
Phone
210-675-7275

TULSA DRILLERS

Executive v.p./general manager
Chuck Lamson
Manager
Tom Runnells
Ballpark (capacity, surface)
Drillers Stadium (10,842, grass)
Affiliation
Rockies
Address
4802 E. 15th St.
Tulsa, OK 74112
Phone
918-744-5998

WICHITA WRANGLERS

General manager
To be announced
Manager
Frank White
Ballpark (capacity, surface)
Lawrence-Dumont Stadium (6,111, artificial infield, grass outfield)
Affiliation
Royals
Address
P.O. Box 1420
Wichita, KS 67201
Phone
316-267-3372

2003 FINAL STANDINGS

FIRST HALF

EAST DIVISION

Team	W	L	T	Pct.	GB
Frisco	40	30	-	.571	...
Tulsa	34	34	1	.500	5.0
Arkansas	33	37	-	.471	7.0
Wichita	31	39	-	.443	9.0

WEST DIVISION

Team	W	L	T	Pct.	GB
San Antonio	47	22	-	.681	...
El Paso	38	32	-	.543	9.5
Midland	35	34	1	.507	12.5
Round Rock	20	50	-	.286	27.5

SECOND HALF

EAST DIVISION

Team	W	L	T	Pct.	GB
Wichita	40	30	-	.571	...
Tulsa	40	30	-	.571	...
Arkansas	37	33	-	.529	3.0
Frisco	33	37	-	.471	7.0

WEST DIVISION

Team	W	L	T	Pct.	GB
San Antonio	41	29	-	.586	...
Midland	34	36	-	.486	7.0
El Paso	29	41	-	.414	12.0
Round Rock	26	44	-	.371	15.0

COMPOSITE

Team	SAN	TUL	FRI	WCH	ARK	MDL	ELP	ROU	W	L	T	Pct.	GB
San Antonio (Mariners)	...	11	12	10	11	12	14	18	88	51	0	.633	...
Tulsa (Rockies)	4	...	16	10	11	11	9	13	74	64	1	.536	13.5
Frisco (Rangers)	4	10	...	14	15	10	10	10	73	67	0	.521	15.5
Wichita (Royals)	6	14	12	...	12	9	7	11	71	69	0	.507	17.5
Arkansas (Angels)	5	15	9	14	...	5	11	11	70	70	0	.500	18.5
Midland (Athletics)	12	4	6	7	11	...	12	17	69	70	1	.496	19.0
El Paso (Diamondbacks)	14	7	6	9	5	12	...	14	67	73	0	.479	21.5
Round Rock (Astros)	6	3	6	5	5	11	10	...	46	94	0	.329	42.5

Major league affiliations in parentheses.

PLAYOFFS: Frisco defeated Wichita, three games to none; San Antonio defeated Frisco, four games to one, to win league championship.

REGULAR-SEASON ATTENDANCE: Arkansas, 187,401; El Paso, 224,821; Frisco, 666,977; Midland, 270,627; Round Rock, 685,973; San Antonio, 305,235; Tulsa, 273,155; Wichita, 153,665. Total attendance—2,767,854. Playoffs (8 games)—46,750. All-Star Game at Wichita—2,583.

MANAGERS: Arkansas, Tyrone Boykin; El Paso, Scott Coolbaugh; Frisco, Tim Ireland; Midland, Greg Sparks; Round Rock, Jackie Moore; San Antonio, Dave Brundage; Tulsa, Marv Foley; Wichita, Keith Bodie.

ALL-STAR TEAM: 1B—Dan Johnson, Midland; 2B—Ramon Nivar, Frisco; 3B—Justin Leone, San Antonio; SS—Jose Lopez, San Antonio; OF—Mike Curry, San Antonio; OF—Byron Gettis, Wichita; OF—Tydus Meadows, Wichita; OF—Jake Weber, Arkansas; C—J.D. Closser, Tulsa; DH—A.J. Zapp, San Antonio; Utility—Chris Burke, Round Rock; LHP—Travis Blackley, San Antonio; LHP—Jimmy Gobble, Wichita; LHP—Bobby Madritsch, San Antonio; LHP—A.J. Murray, Frisco; RHP—Clint Nageoette, San Antonio; RHP—Phil Stockman, El Paso; RHP—Chin-Hui Tsao, Tulsa; Player of the Year—Justin Leone, San Antonio; Pitcher of the Year—Travis Blackley, San Antonio; Manager of the Year—Dave Brundage, San Antonio.

2003 BATTING

TEAM

Team	G	TPA	AB	R	H	TB	2B	3B	HR	RBI	SH	SF	HP	BB	IBB	SO	SB	CS	GDP	LOB	ShO	Avg.	OBP	Slg.
El Paso	140	5469	4888	689	1364	1978	283	44	81	636	43	39	79	419	24	962	91	68	122	1015	10	.279	.343	.405
Wichita	140	5332	4701	665	1304	1817	229	25	78	595	59	48	83	441	23	866	137	74	120	1009	8	.277	.347	.387
San Antonio	139	5308	4765	701	1317	1940	261	46	90	629	30	50	60	403	30	977	210	85	82	953	7	.276	.337	.407
Midland	140	5530	4780	710	1293	1853	231	34	87	660	52	57	66	574	34	1059	87	36	100	1147	15	.271	.353	.388
Arkansas	140	5364	4774	636	1285	1870	244	43	85	585	59	42	67	421	42	882	123	62	95	1020	5	.269	.334	.392
Tulsa	139	5230	4707	668	1245	1989	264	39	134	628	32	50	51	390	27	882	82	42	82	926	9	.264	.324	.423
Round Rock	140	5280	4744	575	1216	1733	186	29	91	532	47	35	47	407	19	944	106	60	115	966	9	.256	.319	.365
Frisco	140	5262	4654	619	1184	1771	202	38	103	552	42	42	45	475	19	942	123	61	102	955	8	.254	.327	.381

INDIVIDUAL

TOP QUALIFIERS FOR BATTING CHAMPIONSHIP

Minimum 378 plate appearances. *Lefthanded batter. †Switch-hitter.

Player, Team	G	TPA	AB	R	H	TB	2B	3B	HR	RBI	SH	SF	HP	BB	IBB	SO	SB	CS	GDP	Avg.	OBP	Slg.
Weber, Jake R., Arkansas *	136	611	539	67	163	215	31	3	5	66	6	9	10	47	9	45	12	5	16	.302	.364	.399
Gettis, Byron E., Wichita	140	591	510	80	154	241	31	4	16	103	2	11	13	55	5	110	15	11	11	.302	.377	.473
Green, Andrew M., El Paso	126	555	490	70	148	196	38	2	2	51	11	3	13	38	1	51	17	9	6	.302	.366	.400
Burke, Christopher A., R.R.	137	633	549	88	165	213	23	8	3	41	11	2	14	57	1	57	34	10	8	.301	.379	.388
Hopper, Norris S., Wichita	115	472	424	56	127	145	14	2	0	40	16	1	4	27	1	58	24	10	10	.300	.346	.342
Hall, Victor O., El Paso *	124	555	490	76	147	184	13	12	0	45	6	3	5	51	1	88	23	19	7	.300	.370	.376
Sullivan, Cory, Tulsa *	135	610	557	81	167	232	34	8	5	61	5	5	4	39	3	83	17	13	4	.300	.347	.417
Rouse, Michael G., Midland *	129	546	457	75	137	185	33	3	3	53	13	4	9	63	2	83	7	2	16	.300	.392	.405
Tracy, Andrew M., Tulsa *	106	432	384	75	115	216	24	1	25	62	1	2	4	41	4	116	3	3	1	.299	.371	.563
Haynes, Nathan R., Ark.*	91	414	372	59	110	161	16	10	5	42	4	2	2	34	3	74	27	9	6	.296	.356	.433
Stanley, Stephen V., Mid.*	124	550	479	68	142	158	10	3	0	39	12	2	1	56	1	65	13	7	11	.296	.370	.330
Salazar, Oscar E., Ark.-Wich.	117	481	430	56	127	189	21	4	11	64	1	5	2	43	5	68	6	5	8	.295	.358	.440
Myers, Corey C., El Paso	124	480	428	63	124	184	27	3	9	60	0	6	4	42	5	78	3	3	12	.290	.354	.430
Johnson, Daniel R., Mid.*	139	619	538	90	156	271	26	4	27	114	0	11	2	68	16	82	7	4	14	.290	.365	.504
Meadows, Tydus L., Wichita	114	478	421	60	122	208	27	4	17	79	0	3	13	41	3	75	14	8	10	.290	.368	.494

DEPARTMENTAL LEADERS: G—Gettis, 140; AB—C. Sullivan, 557; R—Leone, 103; H—C. Sullivan, 167; TB—Johnson, 271; 2B—Green, Leone, 38; 3B—Hall, 12; HR—Johnson, 27; RBI—Johnson, 114; SH—Hopper, 16; SF—Gettis, Johnson, 11; HP—Cunningham, 17; BB—Leone, 92; IBB—Johnson, 16; SO—Zapp, 178; SB—Curry, 58; CS—Hall, 19; GIDP—Cota, 22; Slg.—Tracy, .563; OBP—Leone, .405.

ALL PLAYERS

*Lefthanded batter. †Switch-hitter.

Player, Team	G	TPA	AB	R	H	TB	2B	3B	HR	RBI	SH	SF	HP	BB	IBB	SO	SB	CS	GDP	Avg.	OBP	Slg.
Acevedo, Anthony J., R.R. *	130	525	459	62	130	189	22	2	11	56	1	5	4	56	5	101	10	4	9	.283	.363	.412
Airoso, A. Kurt, Frisco	76	279	235	36	58	106	9	3	11	38	1	4	3	33	1	68	2	2	4	.247	.342	.451
Alfaro, Jason, Round Rock	22	86	81	6	12	15	3	0	0	9	0	0	0	5	0	20	0	1	1	.148	.198	.185
Allegra, Matthew J., Midland	128	497	452	55	108	176	22	2	14	69	1	5	6	33	2	156	5	2	1	.239	.296	.389
Alviso, Jerome B., Ark. †	2	9	8	0	0	0	0	0	0	0	0	0	0	1	0	1	0	0	0	.000	.111	.000
Anderson, Travis J., Tulsa	17	3	3	0	1	1	0	0	0	0	0	0	0	0	0	2	0	0	0	.333	.333	.333
Ansman, Craig M., El Paso	63	252	213	46	69	133	17	1	15	49	0	2	6	31	2	58	5	3	6	.324	.421	.624
Aquino, Gregori E., El Paso	20	9	9	0	2	2	0	0	0	0	0	0	0	0	0	2	0	0	0	.222	.222	.222
Arnerich, Anthony J., Wichita	3	11	10	1	2	2	0	0	0	0	0	0	0	1	0	1	0	0	1	.200	.273	.200
Baker, John D., Midland *	43	171	150	16	36	42	3	0	1	21	0	3	4	14	0	46	0	0	2	.240	.316	.280
Barden, Brian, El Paso	109	426	383	50	110	153	24	5	3	57	3	3	8	29	0	78	10	4	8	.287	.348	.399
Bautista, Daniel, El Paso	2	8	7	1	1	1	0	0	0	1	0	0	0	1	0	2	0	0	0	.143	.250	.143
Beinbrink, Andrew B., Frisco	133	536	451	67	120	176	24	1	10	65	11	6	8	60	1	90	26	11	14	.266	.358	.390

Player, Team	G	TPA	AB	R	H	TB	2B	3B	HR	RBI	SH	SF	HP	BB	IBB	SO	SB	CS	GDP	Avg.	OBP	Slg.
Belflower, James B., El Paso..	53	2	2	0	0	0	0	0	0	0	0	0	0	0	0	0	0	0	0	.000	.000	.000
Beltran, Carlos I., Wichita † ...	3	11	9	3	3	5	2	0	0	1	0	0	0	2	0	3	1	0	0	.333	.455	.556
Bledsoe, M. Hunter, Wichita...	31	123	110	16	28	37	3	0	2	10	1	4	2	6	0	18	1	1	4	.255	.295	.336
Botts, Jason, Frisco †	55	220	194	26	51	76	11	1	4	27	0	2	3	21	1	45	6	1	6	.263	.341	.392
Bouknight, Kip M., Tulsa........	26	16	14	1	3	3	0	0	0	0	2	0	0	0	0	9	0	0	0	.214	.214	.214
Bourgeois, Jason J., Frisco....	55	228	202	28	51	76	5	4	4	21	4	4	2	16	0	45	3	1	4	.252	.308	.376
Boyd, Patrick F., Frisco †	46	182	160	21	31	51	5	3	3	9	2	1	3	16	0	39	9	3	1	.194	.278	.319
Brown, Jeremy S., Midland....	66	278	233	37	64	91	10	1	5	37	0	1	3	41	1	38	3	0	11	.275	.388	.391
Bruney, Brian A., El Paso	28	2	1	0	0	0	0	0	0	0	1	0	0	0	0	1	0	0	0	.000	.000	.000
Bubela, Jaime L., S.A. *	128	516	473	60	131	186	29	7	4	61	5	4	3	31	3	108	26	11	4	.277	.323	.393
Budde, Ryan D., Arkansas	96	382	342	45	73	114	9	1	10	41	1	2	2	35	1	76	1	1	5	.213	.289	.333
Buglovsky, Christopher, Tul.*.	28	16	14	1	1	1	0	0	0	0	2	0	0	0	0	3	0	0	0	.071	.071	.071
Bumatay, Michael J., Tulsa *..	40	1	1	0	1	1	0	0	0	1	0	0	0	0	0	0	0	0	0	1.000	1.000	1.000
Burford, Kevin J., Tulsa *.......	90	323	271	39	70	108	15	1	7	35	0	2	5	45	2	48	5	1	5	.258	.372	.399
Burke, Christopher A., R.R.....	137	633	549	88	165	213	23	8	3	41	11	2	14	57	1	57	34	10	8	.301	.379	.388
Burkhart, Lance E., Frisco......	40	130	109	12	22	42	6	1	4	12	0	1	3	17	0	42	0	1	5	.202	.323	.385
Burns, Kevan C., El Paso *	12	45	40	5	12	19	2	1	1	8	0	0	0	5	0	9	0	1	0	.300	.378	.475
Burns, Michael J., R.R.	38	8	5	0	0	0	0	0	0	0	0	0	1	2	0	2	0	0	1	.000	.375	.000
Bynum, Freddie L., Midland *	132	588	510	84	134	185	18	9	5	58	12	2	8	56	4	135	22	8	6	.263	.344	.363
Cahill, Jonathan E., Arkansas.	1	4	2	0	0	0	0	0	0	0	0	0	0	2	0	0	0	0	1	.000	.500	.000
Campo, Michael C., Mid.*......	100	362	304	45	80	109	10	2	5	38	3	5	16	34	0	71	7	4	6	.263	.362	.359
Carvajal, Jhonny R., El Paso..	35	144	131	14	35	51	8	1	2	17	1	3	0	9	1	16	2	3	2	.267	.308	.389
Castellano, John S., S.A.........	6	16	15	1	2	2	0	0	0	2	0	0	0	1	0	4	0	0	0	.133	.188	.133
Ceriani, Matthew S., El Paso..	9	34	34	4	5	6	1	0	0	0	0	0	0	0	0	11	0	0	1	.147	.147	.176
Closser, Jeffrey D., Tulsa †.....	118	463	410	62	116	193	28	5	13	54	0	3	3	47	3	79	3	2	10	.283	.359	.471
Cole, Eric S., Round Rock......	87	347	327	43	87	121	14	1	6	33	0	1	2	17	0	52	17	7	12	.266	.305	.370
Colina, Javier J., Tulsa	95	413	388	61	108	189	26	2	17	61	0	8	4	13	0	59	7	0	12	.278	.303	.487
Coolbaugh, Michael R., R.R...	42	175	147	24	38	65	6	0	7	29	0	5	1	22	1	43	1	0	5	.259	.349	.442
Cormier, Lance R., El Paso	9	2	1	0	0	0	0	0	0	0	1	0	0	0	0	0	0	0	0	.000	.000	.000
Cota, Jesus E., El Paso *	98	396	364	51	99	124	16	3	1	37	2	2	1	27	2	57	2	5	22	.272	.322	.341
Coughenour, Jory E., R.R.	34	2	2	1	1	2	1	0	0	0	0	0	0	0	0	1	0	0	0	.500	.500	1.000
Craig, Beau J., Midland †.......	2	6	6	0	0	0	0	0	0	0	0	0	0	0	0	3	0	0	0	.000	.000	.000
Cunningham, Marco A., Wich.	104	373	319	60	88	122	12	2	6	35	5	3	17	29	0	50	13	9	8	.276	.364	.382
Curry, Michael T., S.A. *	134	600	518	89	143	202	30	10	3	52	2	7	6	67	0	116	58	11	4	.276	.361	.390
Daigle, S. Casey, El Paso	29	26	26	2	6	10	1	0	1	2	0	0	0	0	0	8	0	0	0	.231	.231	.385
Dejesus, David C., Wichita *..	17	83	71	14	24	34	4	0	2	10	0	1	2	9	0	8	1	3	3	.338	.422	.479
Del Chiaro, Brenton M., Ark...	46	170	154	18	25	43	11	2	1	10	3	1	3	9	0	56	0	0	4	.162	.222	.279
Dellaero, Jason C., Wichita....	1	4	4	0	0	0	0	0	0	0	0	0	0	0	0	0	0	0	0	.000	.000	.000
Dewey, Jason M., Frisco........	81	247	225	25	44	72	8	1	6	20	1	2	0	19	0	81	0	2	8	.196	.256	.320
Difelice, Mark A., Tulsa	21	15	11	1	1	1	0	0	0	1	2	0	1	1	0	5	0	0	0	.091	.231	.091
Dobbs, Greg S., S.A. *...........	2	6	6	0	2	4	2	0	0	0	0	0	0	0	0	1	0	0	0	.333	.333	.667
Dohmann, C. Scott, Tulsa	50	3	1	0	1	1	0	0	0	0	1	0	0	1	0	0	0	0	0	1.000	1.000	1.000
Duncan, J. Carlos, Arkansas..	87	324	303	33	74	114	19	3	5	28	1	3	5	12	0	94	25	4	3	.244	.282	.376
Espada, Josue, Frisco	13	44	41	4	9	9	0	0	0	1	0	0	0	3	0	7	0	0	3	.220	.273	.220
Fatheree, Danny W., R.R.	1	2	2	0	0	0	0	0	0	0	0	0	0	0	0	0	0	0	0	.000	.000	.000
Fenster, Darren J., Wichita.....	5	17	15	2	2	3	1	0	0	2	1	0	0	1	0	3	0	0	1	.133	.188	.200
Firlit, Daniel J., El Paso..........	46	156	147	10	30	37	2	1	1	12	0	2	3	4	0	46	3	1	2	.204	.237	.252
Fleming, Ryan T., Frisco *......	119	474	423	60	114	147	23	5	0	24	4	1	3	42	3	50	14	12	7	.270	.339	.348
Freed, Mark A., El Paso *.......	67	3	2	0	1	1	0	0	0	1	1	0	0	0	0	1	0	0	0	.500	.500	.500
Gallo, Michael D., R.R. *........	17	3	2	0	0	0	0	0	0	0	0	0	0	1	0	0	0	0	0	.000	.333	.000
Gandolfo, Robert, S.A. *........	54	172	157	18	46	54	6	1	0	12	1	2	3	9	1	25	10	5	3	.293	.339	.344
Gemoll, Justin M., Wichita.....	117	444	382	52	105	127	19	0	1	34	8	2	6	46	0	58	15	5	12	.275	.360	.332
German, Ramon N., R.R. †....	35	130	115	5	25	29	1	0	1	8	3	0	0	12	0	26	0	1	8	.217	.291	.252
Gettis, Byron E., Wichita.......	140	591	510	80	154	241	31	4	16	103	2	11	13	55	5	110	15	11	11	.302	.377	.473
Glanville, Douglas M., Frisco .	4	16	15	2	2	2	0	0	0	0	0	0	0	1	0	4	0	0	0	.133	.188	.133
Goldbach, Jeffrey M., Frisco..	36	82	73	10	13	21	2	0	2	7	1	0	0	8	0	24	0	0	1	.178	.259	.288
Gonzalez, Adrian, Frisco *......	45	187	173	16	49	68	6	2	3	17	0	2	1	11	2	27	0	0	6	.283	.326	.393
Gonzalez, Edgar G., El Paso...	6	2	2	0	0	0	0	0	0	0	0	0	0	0	0	0	0	0	0	.000	.000	.000
Gorneault, Nicholas A., Ark....	29	121	110	19	38	58	6	4	2	19	2	0	1	8	0	25	2	0	3	.345	.395	.527
Green, Andrew M., El Paso	126	555	490	70	148	196	38	2	2	51	11	3	13	38	1	51	17	9	6	.302	.366	.400
Greene, Todd A., Frisco..........	3	11	9	3	3	9	0	0	2	4	0	0	0	2	0	2	0	0	1	.333	.455	1.000
Guzman, Elpidio, S.A. *	129	506	475	60	131	172	13	8	4	53	6	3	1	21	2	66	28	10	10	.276	.306	.362
Guzman, Jacob P., Wichita.....	1	1	1	0	0	0	0	0	0	0	0	0	0	0	0	0	0	0	0	.000	.000	.000
Hairston, Scott A., El Paso.....	88	374	337	53	93	158	21	7	10	47	0	1	6	30	1	80	6	2	10	.276	.345	.469
Hall, Victor O., El Paso *........	124	555	490	76	147	184	13	12	0	45	6	3	5	51	1	88	23	19	7	.300	.370	.376
Harris, Brian N., Wichita †	37	169	145	16	37	53	6	2	2	16	5	2	2	15	0	28	5	4	2	.255	.329	.366
Harrison, Adonis M., Ark. * ...	46	163	139	18	43	66	9	4	2	15	2	1	1	20	4	20	3	5	3	.309	.398	.475
Hart, Corey D., Wichita †	93	391	334	40	92	113	9	0	4	47	3	3	2	49	4	69	12	4	5	.275	.369	.338
Hawpe, Bradley B., Tulsa *	93	379	346	52	96	174	27	0	17	68	0	1	1	31	1	84	1	3	5	.277	.338	.503
Haynes, Nathan R., Ark. *......	91	414	372	59	110	161	16	10	5	42	4	2	2	34	3	74	27	9	6	.296	.356	.433
Henrie, Matthew S., El Paso*.	14	10	8	1	2	3	1	0	0	3	2	0	0	0	0	3	0	0	0	.250	.250	.375
Hernandez, Carlos E., R.R......	16	68	62	9	16	20	1	0	1	9	1	1	1	3	0	8	4	0	0	.258	.299	.323
Hill, Jason A., Arkansas	67	256	247	21	59	81	10	0	4	27	1	1	3	3	0	27	4	1	3	.239	.256	.328
Hill, Michael G., Round Rock.	45	169	159	16	39	56	4	2	3	21	0	1	1	8	0	36	2	1	5	.245	.284	.352
Holliday, Matthew T., Tulsa.....	135	578	522	65	132	206	28	5	12	72	0	7	6	43	4	74	15	9	9	.253	.313	.395
Holsten, Ryan W., El Paso......	38	9	9	0	0	0	0	0	0	0	0	0	0	0	0	3	0	0	0	.000	.000	.000
Hopper, Norris S., Wichita	115	472	424	56	127	145	14	2	0	40	16	1	4	27	1	58	24	10	10	.300	.346	.342
Horner, James P., S.A.	71	277	254	37	79	107	11	1	5	43	1	5	5	12	1	37	4	1	6	.311	.348	.421
Houlton, Dennis S., R.R.........	18	12	10	3	2	4	2	0	0	1	2	0	0	0	0	3	0	0	0	.200	.200	.400
Huisman, Justin R., Tulsa	57	1	1	0	1	1	0	0	0	1	0	0	0	0	0	0	0	0	0	1.000	1.000	1.000
Ireland, Eric W., Round Rock.	32	4	3	2	1	1	0	0	0	0	0	0	0	1	0	1	0	0	0	.333	.500	.333

Player, Team	G	TPA	AB	R	H	TB	2B	3B	HR	RBI	SH	SF	HP	BB	IBB	SO	SB	CS	GDP	Avg.	OBP	Slg.
Jackson, Steve W., Midland	81	307	274	36	73	117	13	2	9	48	0	2	4	27	0	73	1	1	4	.266	.339	.427
Jacobs, Gregory P., S.A. *	34	134	126	11	39	49	7	0	1	14	0	0	0	8	0	14	1	3	3	.310	.351	.389
James, Kennouth L., Ark. †	125	501	447	60	127	163	23	2	3	46	9	4	7	34	5	63	13	7	5	.284	.341	.365
Janke, Cheyenne L., R.R.	28	3	2	0	0	0	0	0	0	0	1	0	0	0	0	1	0	0	0	.000	.000	.000
Joffrion, Jack R., Tulsa	38	131	124	16	31	45	5	0	3	13	2	0	1	4	0	35	2	0	5	.250	.279	.363
Johnson, Daniel R., Midl.*	139	619	538	90	156	271	26	4	27	114	0	11	2	68	16	82	7	4	14	.290	.365	.504
Jones, James P., El Paso *	10	33	31	3	10	10	0	0	0	2	0	0	0	2	0	7	0	0	1	.323	.364	.323
Kent, Jeffrey F., Round Rock	3	12	10	1	3	6	0	0	1	6	0	1	0	1	0	1	0	1	1	.300	.333	.600
Krawczyk, Jack B., Mid.-E.P.	21	2	2	0	0	0	0	0	0	0	0	0	0	0	0	0	0	0	0	.000	.000	.000
Kroeger, Joshua J., El Paso *	54	224	208	26	57	79	9	2	3	22	2	1	3	10	2	54	3	5	7	.274	.315	.380
Landry, Jacques Y., R.R.	68	282	259	34	64	112	15	3	9	31	0	0	6	17	2	75	5	2	1	.247	.309	.432
Lentini, Fehlandt A., R.R.	17	25	23	4	5	8	1	1	0	1	0	0	0	2	0	8	0	0	1	.217	.280	.348
Leone, Justin P., S.A.	135	558	455	103	131	246	38	7	21	92	0	8	3	92	10	104	20	6	7	.288	.405	.541
Lindsey, John W., S.A.	88	344	307	40	91	139	22	1	8	43	2	2	11	22	1	81	9	1	5	.296	.363	.453
Liniak, Cole E., Frisco	19	64	56	7	12	14	2	0	0	8	2	2	1	3	1	10	1	2	1	.214	.258	.250
Lira, James C., Round Rock	18	1	1	0	0	0	0	0	0	0	0	0	0	0	0	0	0	0	0	.000	.000	.000
Lockwood, Michael F., Mid.*	28	114	93	11	23	34	8	0	1	7	4	2	0	15	2	17	0	1	0	.247	.345	.366
Loeb, Bryan A., El Paso	63	203	182	29	52	78	10	2	4	27	2	2	11	6	0	34	3	1	4	.286	.343	.429
Loggins, Joshua M., Tulsa	9	28	27	0	4	5	1	0	0	2	0	0	0	1	0	12	0	0	1	.148	.179	.185
Lopez, Chuck N., S.A. *	13	44	40	1	11	11	0	0	0	7	0	1	0	3	0	1	1	1	1	.275	.318	.275
Lopez, Jose C., S.A.	132	588	538	82	139	217	35	2	13	69	7	6	10	27	3	56	18	8	12	.258	.303	.403
Lora, Thomas, Wichita †	16	49	43	6	10	12	2	0	0	2	1	0	0	5	0	7	2	1	0	.233	.313	.279
Lugo, Ruddy J., Round Rock	41	14	13	0	5	5	0	0	0	0	1	0	0	0	0	0	0	0	0	.385	.385	.385
Macha, Erick M., El Paso	19	47	43	5	12	15	3	0	0	2	3	0	0	1	0	12	0	1	1	.279	.295	.349
Machado, Alejandro J., Wich.†	78	334	289	59	83	109	13	5	1	31	5	2	4	34	2	45	19	9	4	.287	.368	.377
Mann, Derek R., Arkansas *	9	25	19	2	4	5	1	0	0	1	2	0	0	4	0	1	0	1	0	.211	.348	.263
Martin, Billy J., El Paso	44	186	160	27	56	83	16	1	3	27	0	0	4	22	0	40	1	0	1	.350	.441	.519
Martin, Tyler D., Frisco †	43	141	121	13	23	36	2	1	3	10	2	0	2	16	0	30	2	1	0	.190	.295	.298
Mathis, Jeffery S., Arkansas	24	111	95	19	27	44	11	0	2	14	1	2	1	12	1	16	1	2	2	.284	.364	.463
Maynard, Scott A., S.A.	71	259	237	28	49	62	6	2	1	18	2	0	0	20	1	63	0	2	5	.207	.268	.262
Mcclaskey, Timothy K., R.R.	15	4	4	1	0	0	0	0	0	0	0	0	0	0	0	3	0	0	0	.000	.000	.000
Mcdougall, Marshall J., Frisco	110	467	418	61	108	169	16	3	13	69	0	4	2	43	0	68	18	3	12	.258	.328	.404
Mcpherson, Dallas L., Ark. *	28	122	102	22	32	58	9	1	5	27	0	0	1	19	4	25	4	0	4	.314	.426	.569
Meadows, Tydus L., Wichita	114	478	421	60	122	208	27	4	17	79	0	3	13	41	3	75	14	8	10	.290	.368	.494
Medders, Brandon E., E.P.	56	4	3	0	1	1	0	0	0	0	0	0	0	1	0	2	0	0	0	.333	.500	.333
Medrano, Steve, Wichita †	10	30	28	4	9	10	1	0	0	3	0	0	1	1	0	6	1	0	2	.321	.367	.357
Meluskey, Mitchell W., R.R. †	13	55	49	5	13	18	2	0	1	6	0	1	0	5	0	9	1	0	1	.265	.327	.367
Mench, Kevin F., Frisco	3	12	11	1	1	1	0	0	0	0	0	0	0	1	0	2	0	0	1	.091	.167	.091
Mensik, Todd L., Frisco *	70	224	197	20	41	59	9	0	3	14	0	0	3	24	0	46	2	2	4	.208	.304	.299
Merrill, Ronald G., Tulsa †	62	226	199	32	36	58	8	4	2	20	4	2	2	19	0	40	2	2	6	.181	.257	.291
Merritt, Timothy L., S.A.	13	49	44	7	9	15	2	2	0	5	1	0	1	3	0	6	2	0	1	.205	.271	.341
Meyer, Drew E., Frisco *	26	111	98	14	31	34	1	1	0	6	2	0	0	11	1	23	9	1	1	.316	.385	.347
Miller, Gregory T., R.R. *	27	7	6	0	1	2	1	0	0	0	1	0	0	0	0	3	0	0	0	.167	.167	.333
Morales, William A., El Paso	26	99	89	15	28	37	6	0	1	11	0	1	2	7	0	14	0	0	4	.315	.374	.416
Morrissey, Adam, Midland	125	531	469	66	125	171	27	2	5	65	3	7	2	50	2	99	9	1	13	.267	.335	.365
Murphy, Nathan L., El Paso *	79	331	289	52	84	133	23	1	8	48	2	1	6	32	3	68	8	6	5	.291	.372	.460
Myers, Corey C., El Paso	124	480	428	63	124	184	27	3	9	60	0	6	4	42	5	78	3	3	12	.290	.354	.430
Nivar, Ramon A., Frisco	79	349	317	53	110	147	17	4	4	37	8	2	2	20	0	23	9	9	5	.347	.387	.464
Nix, Laynce M., Frisco *	87	375	335	52	95	163	23	0	15	63	0	6	0	34	6	68	9	2	4	.284	.344	.487
Norris, S. Dax, Round Rock	77	290	265	22	65	95	12	0	6	45	1	2	1	21	2	35	0	0	8	.245	.301	.358
O'Keefe, Michael D., Ark. *	122	519	444	52	116	173	25	1	10	71	1	5	7	62	6	71	6	9	20	.261	.357	.390
Olson, Timothy L., El Paso	14	62	56	5	11	19	2	0	2	8	0	1	0	5	0	19	0	2	1	.196	.258	.339
Ortiz, Nicolas Y., Wichita	35	136	126	15	29	36	4	0	1	7	0	0	1	9	0	32	1	2	3	.230	.287	.286
Ottavinia, Paul T., Frisco *	75	285	255	29	68	96	9	5	3	36	0	1	2	27	0	36	12	5	5	.267	.340	.376
Ozuna, Pablo J., Tulsa	12	61	59	4	15	18	3	0	0	4	0	0	0	2	1	5	4	2	0	.254	.279	.305
Parrish, Wade R., Tulsa *	24	5	4	0	0	0	0	0	0	0	1	0	0	0	0	0	0	0	0	.000	.000	.000
Pecci, Jay M., S.A. †	10	44	40	3	12	13	1	0	0	1	0	0	0	4	0	7	0	1	2	.300	.364	.325
Perez, Beltran O., El Paso	29	17	14	1	1	4	0	0	1	2	2	1	0	0	0	5	0	0	0	.071	.067	.286
Perry, Herbert E., Frisco	9	39	34	5	11	16	2	0	1	6	0	0	2	3	1	3	0	0	2	.324	.410	.471
Pichardo, Maximo A., Ark.	25	98	88	9	18	24	6	0	0	8	1	0	5	4	0	13	3	1	1	.205	.278	.273
Piedra, Jorge M., Tulsa *	96	401	357	56	98	183	17	7	18	53	0	5	8	31	4	50	5	2	6	.275	.342	.513
Polanco, Enohel, Tulsa	42	147	135	16	34	49	10	1	1	16	1	3	2	6	0	29	1	1	2	.252	.288	.363
Powell, Greg S., Round Rock	36	12	10	0	0	0	0	0	0	0	2	0	0	0	0	7	0	0	0	.000	.000	.000
Powers, John M., Frisco *	13	31	27	4	4	5	1	0	0	0	1	0	0	3	0	5	0	2	1	.148	.233	.185
Qualls, Chad M., R.R.	28	20	17	1	2	2	0	0	0	0	3	0	0	0	0	6	0	0	0	.118	.118	.118
Quintero, Edgar, Arkansas *	3	9	8	1	0	0	0	0	0	0	0	0	0	1	0	3	0	0	0	.000	.111	.000
Ramirez, Daniel E., El Paso	9	26	24	3	1	2	1	0	0	2	0	0	1	1	1	6	0	0	1	.042	.115	.083
Roberts, Nick E., R.R.	13	6	6	1	2	2	0	0	0	1	0	0	0	0	0	1	0	0	0	.333	.333	.333
Rodriguez, Victor A., Wichita	47	209	184	32	60	74	11	0	1	26	2	6	3	14	0	13	2	1	6	.326	.372	.402
Rosamond, G. Michael, R.R.	127	489	455	55	124	185	24	2	11	43	2	0	1	31	0	124	7	8	7	.273	.320	.407
Rouse, Michael G., Midland *	129	546	457	75	137	185	33	3	3	53	13	4	9	63	2	83	7	2	16	.300	.392	.405
Salazar, Oscar E., Ark.-Wich.	117	481	430	56	127	189	21	4	11	64	1	5	2	43	5	68	6	5	8	.295	.358	.440
Sampson, Benjamin D., Tulsa	18	11	9	0	2	2	0	0	0	0	1	0	0	1	0	3	0	0	0	.222	.300	.222
Sanchez, Agustin A., Tulsa †	96	351	313	33	73	95	12	2	2	35	2	7	3	26	3	31	4	1	4	.233	.292	.304
Santos, Chad R., Wichita *	111	438	396	48	107	167	21	3	11	49	1	3	3	35	2	116	3	0	14	.270	.332	.422
Santos, Sergio J., El Paso	37	148	137	13	35	50	7	1	2	16	1	2	0	8	0	25	0	0	4	.255	.293	.365
Schneidmiller, Gary L., Mid.	31	102	81	16	13	18	2	0	1	10	0	1	1	19	0	20	0	0	3	.160	.324	.222
Sellier, Brian S., Midland *	72	320	271	51	82	125	17	4	6	44	0	4	1	43	2	54	9	3	4	.303	.395	.461
Silva, Jesus R., El Paso	55	2	2	0	0	0	0	0	0	0	0	0	0	0	0	1	0	0	0	.000	.000	.000
Smith, Jeffrey H., Frisco *	31	112	102	5	26	33	2	1	1	10	1	0	3	6	0	14	1	0	2	.255	.315	.324
Smith, S. Casey, Arkansas	82	361	324	46	92	118	10	2	4	32	11	3	4	19	0	44	5	7	5	.284	.329	.364

Player, Team	G	TPA	AB	R	H	TB	2B	3B	HR	RBI	SH	SF	HP	BB	IBB	SO	SB	CS	GDP	Avg.	OBP	Slg.
Smith, William H., Frisco *	37	137	130	11	26	46	6	1	4	15	0	2	0	5	0	28	0	0	1	.200	.226	.354
Snelling, Christopher D., S.A.*	47	202	186	24	62	87	12	2	3	25	0	3	5	8	0	30	1	7	0	.333	.371	.468
Snyder, Christopher R., E.P....	53	213	188	21	38	64	14	0	4	26	0	2	4	19	1	29	0	0	9	.202	.286	.340
Soules, Ryan M., Frisco *	73	262	229	33	61	97	13	1	7	33	1	2	2	28	2	61	0	1	3	.266	.349	.424
Specht, Brian J., Arkansas †..	128	526	458	62	116	184	18	4	14	63	9	6	7	46	7	112	12	8	3	.253	.327	.402
Spivey, Ernest L., El Paso	4	15	11	2	5	6	1	0	0	1	0	1	1	2	1	1	2	0	1	.455	.533	.545
Stanley, Stephen V., Mid.*	124	550	479	68	142	158	10	3	0	39	12	2	1	56	1	65	13	7	11	.296	.370	.330
Stark, Dennis J., Tulsa	1	1	1	0	0	0	0	0	0	0	0	0	0	0	0	0	0	0	0	.000	.000	.000
Stockman, Phillip M., El Paso	26	14	13	0	1	2	1	0	0	0	1	0	0	0	0	3	0	0	0	.077	.077	.154
Stotts, Jarrett A., Midland......	46	203	176	24	54	62	8	0	0	14	4	2	3	18	1	41	4	2	1	.307	.377	.352
Sullivan, Cory, Tulsa *...........	135	610	557	81	167	232	34	8	5	61	5	5	4	39	3	83	17	13	4	.300	.347	.417
Sullivan, Kevin L., Tulsa.........	52	152	142	9	34	39	5	0	0	12	1	1	2	6	0	34	2	0	5	.239	.278	.275
Swisher, Nicholas T., Mid.†....	76	336	287	36	66	109	24	2	5	43	0	6	6	37	1	76	0	1	8	.230	.324	.380
Tamargo, John F., R.R. *.......	83	331	288	25	65	77	4	1	2	27	6	1	2	34	2	38	5	2	7	.226	.311	.267
Taylor, T. Seth, Tulsa	90	355	322	50	84	136	16	3	10	50	6	1	4	22	2	55	10	2	6	.261	.315	.422
Thompson, Douglas W., Tul...	29	4	4	1	1	1	0	0	0	0	0	0	0	0	0	3	0	0	0	.250	.250	.250
Timmons, Osborne L., E.P.	63	242	216	31	66	103	17	1	6	40	1	2	1	22	1	31	0	3	6	.306	.369	.477
Tonis, Michael T., Wichita	87	342	307	34	73	97	18	0	2	24	7	2	3	23	1	52	3	1	14	.238	.296	.316
Topolski, Jon P., R.R. *.........	82	238	207	31	47	78	6	5	5	31	1	1	0	29	3	53	9	6	2	.227	.321	.377
Tracy, Andrew M., Tulsa *......	106	432	384	75	115	216	24	1	25	62	1	2	4	41	4	116	3	3	1	.299	.371	.563
Tremblay, Max B., R.R. *	41	1	1	0	0	0	0	0	0	0	0	0	0	0	0	0	0	0	0	.000	.000	.000
Tremie, Christopher J., R.R....	93	339	301	33	73	113	11	1	9	35	2	5	5	26	1	50	0	1	10	.243	.309	.375
Tsao, Chin-Hui, Tulsa	18	9	8	1	4	5	1	0	0	1	0	1	0	0	0	1	0	1	0	.500	.444	.625
Udy, Nicholas A., S.A. *	6	10	9	0	2	2	0	0	0	0	0	0	0	1	0	2	0	0	1	.222	.300	.222
Ugueto, Luis E., S.A. †..........	89	384	350	53	91	110	12	2	1	40	3	3	1	27	0	75	25	10	7	.260	.312	.314
Ullery, David D., Wichita *	37	129	119	12	24	27	3	0	0	12	1	1	0	8	0	30	0	0	0	.202	.250	.227
Uribe, Juan C., Tulsa..............	5	21	20	3	5	10	2	0	1	4	0	1	0	0	0	2	0	0	0	.250	.238	.500
Vaz, Roberto R., Frisco *	8	17	14	1	0	0	0	0	0	0	1	0	0	2	0	1	0	0	0	.000	.125	.000
Waldron, Jeffrey M., E.P.*......	27	88	75	7	17	25	2	0	2	10	1	0	0	12	1	17	0	0	1	.227	.333	.333
Walter, Scott A., Wichita	48	183	167	21	45	75	13	1	5	21	1	1	7	7	1	36	1	1	3	.269	.324	.449
Warren, A. Chris, Tulsa	21	74	60	9	11	16	2	0	1	2	1	1	1	11	0	20	1	0	1	.183	.315	.267
Weber, Jake R., Arkansas * ...	136	611	539	67	163	215	31	3	5	66	6	9	10	47	9	45	12	5	16	.302	.364	.399
White, William C., El Paso * ..	15	4	4	0	0	0	0	0	0	0	0	0	0	0	0	0	0	0	0	.000	.000	.000
Whiteman, Thomas, R.R.	133	578	532	65	139	200	18	2	13	70	1	5	5	35	0	102	3	8	19	.261	.310	.376
Wilson, Daniel A., S.A.	2	7	7	0	0	0	0	0	0	0	0	0	0	0	0	3	0	0	0	.000	.000	.000
Womack, Anthony D., E.P.* ...	4	19	17	3	5	5	0	0	0	2	0	0	0	2	1	2	3	0	0	.294	.368	.294
Wright, Gavin M., R.R.	111	409	372	38	92	115	15	1	2	29	8	4	3	22	2	78	8	8	9	.247	.292	.309
Zamora, Junior, Arkansas	115	471	430	61	121	180	24	4	9	54	4	1	6	30	1	96	3	1	10	.281	.336	.419
Zapp, Andrew J., S.A. *	137	592	528	84	147	262	35	1	26	92	0	6	11	47	8	178	7	8	11	.278	.346	.496

PLAYERS WITH TWO OR MORE TEAMS

Player, Team	G	TPA	AB	R	H	TB	2B	3B	HR	RBI	SH	SF	HP	BB	IBB	SO	SB	CS	GDP	Avg.	OBP	Slg.
Krawczyk, Jack B., El Paso	12	2	2	0	0	0	0	0	0	0	0	0	0	0	0	0	0	0	0	.000	.000	.000
Krawczyk, Jack B., Midland ...	9	0	0	0	0	0	0	0	0	0	0	0	0	0	0	0	0	0	0	.000	.000	.000
Salazar, Oscar E., Arkansas....	39	167	143	22	47	69	6	2	4	21	1	2	2	19	1	20	2	1	1	.329	.410	.483
Salazar, Oscar E., Wichita	78	314	287	34	80	120	15	2	7	43	0	3	0	24	4	48	4	4	7	.279	.331	.418

GRAND SLAMS—Allegra, Budde, Burke, Cole, Colina, Firlit, Hawpe, Hernandez, Leone, Myers, Nix, O'Keefe, Piedra, Soules, Topolski, 1 each.

AWARDED FIRST BASE ON CATCHER'S INTERFERENCE—Airoso 3 (Closser, Sanchez, Walter); Fleming (Jackson); Ja. Hill (Closser); Murphy (Jackson); Sellier (Maynard).

2003 PITCHING

TEAM

Team	W	L	Pct.	ERA	G	CG	ShO	Sv.	IP	H	TBF	R	ER	HR	SH	SF	HB	BB	IBB	SO	WP	Bk.
San Antonio	88	51	.633	3.03	139	5	14	45	1238.2	1071	5214	503	417	75	44	30	60	491	18	1131	56	5
Tulsa.................	74	64	.536	3.85	139	2	8	35	1214.0	1242	5224	625	519	102	44	39	59	417	15	916	64	12
Arkansas	70	70	.500	3.99	140	6	10	37	1233.1	1172	5303	654	547	96	36	46	76	462	13	987	67	2
Wichita.............	71	69	.507	4.11	140	4	9	39	1218.2	1290	5254	629	557	118	32	46	73	401	28	838	72	10
Frisco	73	67	.521	4.16	140	1	7	43	1237.1	1267	5373	660	572	95	44	56	62	455	36	892	56	8
Midland	69	70	.496	4.41	140	6	11	38	1225.0	1348	5328	681	600	77	50	40	47	377	35	882	48	10
El Paso.............	67	73	.479	4.69	140	4	5	27	1249.2	1476	5656	758	651	81	59	57	61	476	32	887	76	7
Round Rock......	46	94	.329	4.76	140	7	7	18	1223.2	1342	5423	753	647	105	55	49	60	451	41	981	42	4

INDIVIDUAL

TOP QUALIFIERS FOR EARNED-RUN AVERAGE TITLE

Minimum 112 innings.*Lefthanded pitcher.

Pitcher, Team	W	L	Pct.	ERA	G	GS	CG	ShO	GF	Sv.	IP	H	TBF	R	ER	HR	SH	SF	HB	BB	IBB	SO	WP	Bk.
Tsao, Chin-Hui, Tulsa...............	11	4	.733	2.46	18	18	0	0	0	0	113.1	88	446	34	31	7	2	2	5	26	0	125	3	3
Blackley, Travis J., S.A.*	17	3	.850	2.61	27	27	0	0	0	0	162.1	125	658	55	47	11	5	4	6	62	0	144	9	2
Nageotte, Clinton S., S.A........	11	7	.611	3.10	27	27	2	1	0	0	154.0	127	653	60	53	6	2	3	14	67	1	157	8	1
Gobble, B. James, Wichita * ...	12	8	.600	3.19	22	22	2	1	0	0	132.2	128	559	57	47	11	5	5	5	40	1	100	5	0
Moreno, Edwin A., Frisco	6	5	.545	3.29	29	15	0	0	9	0	112.0	105	465	50	41	7	2	4	3	33	0	74	4	2
Murray, Arlington J., Frisco *..	10	4	.714	3.63	27	25	0	0	1	0	144.0	134	611	68	58	13	5	12	4	63	2	90	9	0
Madritsch, Robert A., S.A.*	13	7	.650	3.63	27	27	2	1	0	0	158.2	133	668	75	64	11	6	5	2	67	0	154	5	2
Difelice, Mark A., Tulsa...........	7	6	.538	3.72	21	21	0	0	0	0	113.2	121	479	61	47	16	4	2	4	24	2	75	7	0
Qualls, Chad M., Round Rock.	8	11	.421	3.85	28	28	3	2	0	0	175.1	174	744	85	75	12	6	8	10	61	0	132	8	0
Ramos, Mario M., Frisco *......	8	7	.533	3.86	19	19	0	0	0	0	121.1	130	509	59	52	9	4	5	2	28	1	103	1	3

Pitcher, Team	W	L	Pct.	ERA	G	GS	CG	ShO	GF	Sv.	IP	H	TBF	R	ER	HR	SH	SF	HB	BB	IBB	SO	WP	Bk.
Powell, Greg S., Round Rock..	7	9	.438	3.89	36	18	1	1	7	0	141.0	155	609	75	61	7	6	6	6	39	5	80	4	0
Stockman, Phillip M., El Paso.	11	7	.611	3.96	26	26	0	0	0	0	147.2	137	648	75	65	9	8	6	9	64	0	146	2	0
Ziegler, Michael D., Midland....	12	9	.571	4.04	27	25	2	1	0	0	165.0	185	692	81	74	6	4	5	6	29	3	105	6	3
Bouknight, Kip M., Tulsa.........	10	7	.588	4.04	26	26	1	0	0	0	158.1	153	671	84	71	16	9	3	5	57	1	101	6	1
Tamayo, I. Daniel, Wichita.......	11	14	.440	4.56	27	26	1	0	0	0	154.0	159	667	84	78	16	5	1	8	56	1	95	13	1

DEPARTMENTAL LEADERS: W—Blackley, 17; L—Lugo, 15; Pct.—Blackley, .850; G—Freed, 67; GS—Buglovsky, Qualls, 28; CG—Qualls, 3; ShO—Qualls, 2; GF—Hoerman, Huisman, 52; Sv.—Hoerman, 36; IP—Daigle, 176.1; H—Daigle, 219; TBF—Daigle, 793; R—Buglovsky, 111; ER—Daigle, 90; HR—Lee, 17; SH—Bouknight, 9; SF—Murray, 12; HB—Nageotte, 14; BB—Madritsch, Nageotte, 67; IBB—Freed, 8; SO—Nageotte, 157; WP—Daigle, 14; BK—Several players tied with 3.

ALL PITCHERS

*Lefthanded pitcher.

Pitcher, Team	W	L	Pct.	ERA	G	GS	CG	ShO	GF	Sv.	IP	H	TBF	R	ER	HR	SH	SF	HB	BB	IBB	SO	WP	Bk.
Anderson, Travis J., Tulsa.......	1	5	.167	4.56	17	8	0	0	6	0	51.1	50	226	30	26	6	1	1	2	23	0	46	7	0
Andrade, Stephen M., Ark.......	5	1	.833	2.65	36	0	0	0	13	7	51.0	26	199	16	15	2	2	0	1	19	1	74	4	0
Aquino, Gregori E., El Paso.....	7	3	.700	3.46	20	20	0	0	0	0	106.2	115	458	43	41	5	3	0	4	38	1	91	7	3
Asencio, Miguel D., Wichita....	0	0	.000	0.00	1	1	0	0	0	0	4.0	1	14	0	0	0	0	0	0	1	0	3	0	0
Baek, Cha-Seung, S.A.	3	3	.500	2.57	9	9	0	0	0	0	56.0	49	229	18	16	2	2	0	4	17	1	46	0	0
Baerlocher, Ryan L., Wichita...	2	1	.667	4.93	12	2	0	0	1	0	34.2	40	161	25	19	1	1	3	2	14	2	36	2	0
Bazzell, Shane A., Midland......	3	6	.333	4.61	34	1	0	0	4	1	56.2	57	252	36	29	4	6	0	4	25	3	42	0	0
Beasley, Raymond E., Frisco *	0	0	.000	2.25	3	0	0	0	3	3	4.0	4	16	1	1	0	0	0	0	0	0	5	1	0
Belflower, James B., El Paso...	4	2	.667	5.14	53	0	0	0	21	2	70.0	105	335	51	40	6	5	4	4	24	5	35	5	0
Bergman, Dustin M., Ark. *.....	6	5	.545	3.79	50	10	0	0	13	0	109.1	116	472	54	46	7	5	6	3	33	3	82	3	0
Blackley, Travis J., S.A. *	17	3	.850	2.61	27	27	0	0	0	0	162.1	125	658	55	47	11	5	4	6	62	0	144	9	2
Blanton, Joseph M., Midland ..	3	1	.750	1.26	7	5	1	0	2	1	35.2	21	129	6	5	1	1	0	0	7	0	30	0	0
Bouknight, Kip M., Tulsa.........	10	7	.588	4.04	26	26	1	0	0	0	158.1	153	671	84	71	16	9	3	5	57	1	101	6	1
Brink, James W., Frisco...........	0	0	.000	32.40	4	0	0	0	0	0	3.1	14	30	13	12	1	0	1	1	4	0	0	0	0
Brunet, Michael A., Arkansas ..	6	8	.429	4.69	32	19	2	1	2	0	126.2	133	554	78	66	16	0	8	8	43	0	87	5	0
Bruney, Brian A., El Paso	0	2	.000	2.59	28	0	0	0	25	14	31.1	29	140	17	9	1	1	1	1	13	2	28	0	1
Buglovsky, Christopher, Tulsa .	10	10	.500	4.83	28	28	0	0	0	0	158.1	204	723	111	85	10	7	9	10	60	1	75	12	1
Bumatay, Michael J., Tulsa *...	4	1	.800	2.60	40	0	0	0	11	1	55.1	42	237	20	16	4	2	2	3	29	1	69	2	3
Burke, Erick L., Frisco *	4	4	.500	2.59	64	0	0	0	18	3	59.0	51	251	22	17	3	5	0	3	27	5	51	8	0
Burns, Michael J., R.R.	2	13	.133	6.13	38	14	0	0	9	0	105.2	129	477	80	72	15	4	4	4	30	3	89	4	2
Cabaniel, Tomas E., Midland...	1	0	1.000	0.79	3	2	0	0	1	0	11.1	5	38	1	1	0	0	1	1	1	0	5	0	0
Cammack, Eric W., R.R.	0	1	.000	0.59	26	0	0	0	16	5	30.1	21	126	6	2	0	2	1	1	13	1	27	1	0
Campos, Juan C., R.R.	0	0	.000	8.53	9	0	0	0	1	0	12.2	19	61	12	12	1	1	0	0	3	1	17	0	0
Carlyle, Earl L., Wichita...........	3	2	.600	1.98	15	0	0	0	9	3	27.1	19	107	6	6	0	1	0	0	7	0	41	1	0
Cormier, Lance R., El Paso......	2	3	.400	6.10	9	8	0	0	0	0	41.1	59	201	33	28	3	3	1	0	22	0	26	4	0
Coughenour, Jory E., R.R........	2	5	.286	7.09	34	1	0	0	13	3	53.1	71	260	46	42	3	4	2	5	30	5	34	0	0
Cramblitt, S. Joseph, El Paso..	1	0	1.000	0.00	1	0	0	0	0	0	2.0	2	8	0	0	0	0	0	0	0	0	0	0	0
Crowell, Kyle R., Midland........	0	1	.000	3.12	9	0	0	0	4	1	17.1	17	72	8	6	1	1	1	2	5	1	12	1	0
Cullen, Ryan M., Midland *.....	2	1	.667	3.38	30	1	0	0	12	2	45.1	54	198	19	17	1	4	2	1	13	4	25	1	1
Cummings, Ryan M., Ark.	1	5	.167	5.26	37	2	0	0	8	0	65.0	86	297	48	38	4	5	1	7	23	0	22	6	0
Cyr, Eric, Arkansas *	6	6	.500	4.96	20	20	0	0	0	0	103.1	91	445	61	57	9	3	1	4	52	1	78	2	1
Daigle, S. Casey, El Paso.........	11	11	.500	4.59	29	27	1	0	0	0	176.1	219	793	108	90	9	7	8	6	51	1	115	14	0
Del Chiaro, Brenton M., Ark. ...	0	0	.000	0.00	1	0	0	0	1	0	1.0	0	3	0	0	0	0	0	0	0	0	1	0	0
Difelice, Mark A., Tulsa...........	7	6	.538	3.72	21	21	0	0	0	0	113.2	121	479	61	47	16	4	2	4	24	2	75	7	0
Dohmann, C. Scott, Tulsa........	9	4	.692	4.13	50	4	0	0	17	4	93.2	94	403	47	43	11	4	2	5	29	2	102	6	0
Dominguez, Juan R., Frisco....	5	0	1.000	2.60	9	9	0	0	0	0	55.1	35	220	17	16	2	0	1	1	21	0	54	1	0
Dotel, Melido, Tulsa................	4	6	.400	4.46	49	0	0	0	23	1	66.2	71	303	39	33	6	4	3	4	37	0	59	7	0
Douglass, Ryan L., Wichita.....	0	3	.000	4.77	28	7	0	0	11	1	66.0	94	304	43	35	8	0	2	7	16	1	38	6	2
Drese, Ryan T., Frisco	1	1	.500	4.00	2	2	0	0	0	0	9.0	10	38	4	4	1	0	0	2	0	0	8	0	0
Dunn, Scott A., Arkansas........	1	0	1.000	0.00	3	0	0	0	2	0	5.0	2	16	0	0	0	0	0	0	0	0	7	1	0
Echols, Justin K., Frisco..........	1	3	.250	4.91	8	8	0	0	0	0	44.0	32	189	25	24	5	3	3	1	26	1	33	3	0
Espada, Josue, Frisco	0	0	.000	9.00	1	0	0	0	1	0	1.0	1	4	1	1	1	0	0	0	0	0	0	0	0
Esslinger, Cameron S., Tulsa...	0	0	.000	2.61	15	0	0	0	3	0	20.2	21	87	9	6	0	0	1	1	8	0	11	2	0
Ferguson, Ian M., Wichita.......	2	1	.667	7.52	13	3	0	0	2	0	26.1	37	133	23	22	2	2	1	2	17	0	15	3	0
Field, Nathan P., Wichita..........	1	0	1.000	3.60	15	0	0	0	14	3	20.0	20	87	9	8	2	0	0	1	8	1	20	2	1
Fischer, Richard D., Arkansas .	5	11	.313	4.61	26	26	2	0	0	0	154.1	159	661	91	79	14	4	9	12	43	0	123	7	0
Fischer, Stephen R., Midland...	0	0	.000	5.40	10	1	0	0	2	0	15.0	20	72	10	9	0	1	1	0	11	0	3	0	0
Flores, Ronald J., Midland * ...	3	2	.600	2.88	39	0	0	0	17	6	59.1	44	235	19	19	6	3	0	1	15	3	66	4	0
Flury, Patrick S., Wichita.........	2	0	1.000	3.04	17	0	0	0	5	0	26.2	24	113	11	9	1	0	2	2	12	1	25	3	0
Francisco, Franklin, Frisco.......	2	3	.400	8.41	7	6	0	0	0	0	35.1	43	167	33	33	5	0	4	4	18	1	22	0	0
Freed, Mark A., El Paso *........	4	3	.571	4.81	67	0	0	0	8	1	63.2	75	310	38	34	4	2	3	5	37	8	43	4	0
Frick, Michael T., Midland........	1	2	.333	5.05	28	0	0	0	13	0	35.2	47	159	22	20	5	3	0	2	9	1	21	1	0
Fultz, R. Aaron, Frisco *..........	0	0	.000	9.00	1	0	0	0	0	0	1.0	2	6	1	1	0	0	0	0	0	0	0	0	0
Gallo, Michael D., R.R. *.........	1	1	.500	1.37	17	0	0	0	8	2	19.2	17	78	3	3	1	2	1	0	6	2	22	0	0
Gandolfo, Robert, S.A.	0	0	.000	0.00	1	0	0	0	1	0	1.0	0	3	0	0	0	0	0	0	0	0	0	0	0
Garcia, Jose A., Arkansas........	2	2	.500	4.54	6	6	0	0	0	0	33.2	39	148	17	17	4	2	0	2	15	1	25	2	0
Garcia, Sonny C., Midland.......	3	5	.375	6.79	10	10	0	0	0	0	50.1	76	241	44	38	5	0	1	4	20	1	26	1	0
Gardner, Hayden B., Frisco......	4	1	.800	4.50	33	0	0	0	9	0	52.0	63	243	28	26	7	4	2	2	25	2	29	3	0
Gobble, B. James, Wichita * ...	12	8	.600	3.19	22	22	2	1	0	0	132.2	128	559	57	47	11	5	5	5	40	1	100	5	0
Gonzalez, Edgar G., El Paso	2	2	.500	3.50	6	6	0	0	0	0	36.0	40	155	18	14	1	1	0	1	11	0	30	3	0
Graham, Thomas M., Frisco....	2	1	.667	4.84	16	0	0	0	7	2	22.1	23	94	12	12	1	0	1	1	8	1	21	1	0
Gregg, Kevin M., Arkansas......	4	3	.571	3.53	15	11	2	0	0	0	66.1	60	279	29	26	2	2	5	4	19	0	60	2	0
Greinke, D. Zackary, Wichita ...	4	3	.571	3.23	9	9	0	0	0	0	53.0	58	214	20	19	5	0	3	3	5	2	34	0	0
Griffith, Dustin A., Arkansas....	1	0	1.000	9.00	1	0	0	0	1	0	1.0	2	5	1	1	0	1	0	0	0	0	0	0	0
Gwyn, Marcus E., Midland	1	1	.500	5.00	9	0	0	0	0	0	9.0	9	36	5	5	1	0	0	0	2	0	12	0	0
Hampson, Justin M., Tulsa *...	0	1	.000	13.50	1	1	0	0	0	0	4.0	8	22	6	6	0	0	0	0	3	0	0	0	0
Hamulack, Timothy W., S.A. *.	0	1	.000	2.09	40	0	0	0	11	1	47.1	32	186	13	11	0	0	1	3	15	2	54	2	0
Harden, J. Richard, Midland....	2	0	1.000	0.00	2	2	0	0	0	0	13.0	0	39	0	0	0	0	0	0	0	0	17	0	0
Hart, Corey D., Wichita...........	0	0	.000	0.00	1	0	0	0	1	0	1.0	0	3	0	0	0	0	0	0	0	0	1	0	0

Pitcher, Team	W	L	Pct.	ERA	G	GS	CG	ShO	GF	Sv.	IP	H	TBF	R	ER	HR	SH	SF	HB	BB	IBB	SO	WP	Bk.
Henrie, Matthew S., El Paso....	5	7	.417	4.13	14	14	2	1	0	0	89.1	112	393	45	41	3	4	6	4	17	0	44	1	0
Hernandez, Runelvys A., Wich.	0	2	.000	3.86	2	2	0	0	0	0	9.1	9	40	4	4	0	0	0	0	5	0	5	0	0
Hill, Jeremy D., Wichita..........	0	0	.000	0.00	2	0	0	0	1	0	2.0	0	10	1	0	0	0	1	0	3	0	3	3	0
Hoerman, Jared J., S.A.	3	6	.333	3.84	56	0	0	0	52	36	58.2	62	259	32	25	4	1	1	3	23	0	56	3	0
Holsten, Ryan W., El Paso.......	2	8	.200	6.93	38	12	1	1	7	0	101.1	139	497	89	78	9	4	7	6	54	1	41	6	0
Hooten, David W., Midland......	7	8	.467	4.43	39	14	0	0	3	0	111.2	122	485	59	55	9	3	3	4	32	2	76	8	0
Houlton, Dennis S., R.R.	5	4	.556	3.47	18	18	1	1	0	0	109.0	93	449	45	42	11	4	2	3	28	1	101	2	0
House, Craig M., S.A..............	1	0	1.000	2.75	14	0	0	0	4	1	19.2	14	87	7	6	0	1	1	3	16	1	17	3	0
Hughes, Travis W., Frisco.........	4	8	.333	4.99	24	10	1	1	3	0	74.0	81	330	47	41	6	2	5	5	26	1	58	0	0
Huisman, Justin R., Tulsa	7	2	.778	1.75	57	0	0	0	52	26	61.2	55	250	22	12	1	4	0	4	7	1	46	2	1
Ireland, Eric W., Round Rock..	1	5	.167	5.21	32	6	0	0	10	0	67.1	85	319	51	39	6	2	4	6	30	6	55	4	0
Jackson, Steve W., Midland	0	0	.000	0.00	1	0	0	0	1	0	2.0	2	9	0	0	0	0	0	0	1	0	1	0	0
Janke, Cheyenne L., R.R.	2	4	.333	4.45	28	3	0	0	9	1	54.2	63	248	29	27	3	2	1	2	22	0	42	5	0
Jenks, Robert S., Arkansas	7	2	.778	2.17	16	16	0	0	0	0	83.0	56	350	23	20	2	2	2	2	51	0	103	6	0
Johnson, Everrett T., S.A.........	6	2	.750	3.04	14	14	1	1	0	0	83.0	74	345	31	28	7	6	0	6	21	1	63	3	0
Johnson, Randall D., E.P.*	0	0	.000	0.00	1	1	0	0	0	0	4.0	3	18	2	0	0	0	2	2	1	0	5	0	0
Komine, Shane K., Midland.....	4	6	.400	3.75	19	18	1	1	0	0	103.1	108	442	51	43	6	5	6	1	30	2	75	4	1
Kozlowski, Benjamin A., Fris.*	3	2	.600	5.43	11	10	0	0	0	0	54.2	71	261	38	33	4	3	1	3	27	0	29	2	1
Krawczyk, Jack B., Mid.-E.P. ...	1	3	.250	6.80	21	0	0	0	6	0	41.0	56	190	32	31	3	6	3	3	11	3	27	2	0
Kroon, Marc J., Arkansas........	3	3	.500	3.00	37	1	0	0	17	4	45.0	28	198	20	15	1	0	1	6	31	0	60	8	0
Kusiewicz, Michael E., Mid.* ...	0	1	.000	4.30	18	0	0	0	8	1	23.0	25	106	14	11	1	1	1	1	8	1	21	1	0
Lamber, Justin D., S.A. *	3	2	.600	3.39	39	0	0	0	17	0	58.1	65	253	35	22	2	6	1	3	15	1	36	4	0
Leclair, Aric A., El Paso *	1	0	1.000	0.00	11	0	0	0	2	0	12.1	9	49	1	0	0	1	0	0	6	1	10	1	0
Lee, W. Garrett, Wichita	5	9	.357	5.02	30	13	1	0	6	1	118.1	146	525	72	66	17	7	6	10	33	5	74	5	1
Lira, James C., Round Rock....	0	5	.000	6.04	18	5	0	0	6	1	47.2	67	224	33	32	4	1	1	2	18	2	39	4	0
Lugo, Ruddy J., Round Rock..	4	15	.211	6.01	41	15	1	0	10	1	118.1	133	539	93	79	12	6	6	5	53	5	112	3	0
Luna, Brandon M., Frisco........	0	0	.000	36.00	1	0	0	0	0	0	1.0	1	8	4	4	1	0	0	1	3	0	1	0	0
Lundberg, David D., Frisco......	3	5	.375	2.48	57	0	0	0	51	31	65.1	63	268	21	18	4	3	4	4	15	6	57	1	1
Luque, Roger E., Wichita *	0	1	.000	9.64	5	0	0	0	1	0	4.2	10	28	5	5	1	0	0	1	2	2	2	0	0
Mabeus, Christopher E., Mid...	1	3	.250	3.52	32	0	0	0	26	13	38.1	37	162	20	15	1	4	4	0	9	2	40	1	0
Macha, Erick M., El Paso.........	0	0	.000	0.00	1	0	0	0	1	0	1.0	1	6	0	0	0	0	0	0	2	0	0	0	0
Madritsch, Robert A., S.A. * ...	13	7	.650	3.63	27	27	2	1	0	0	158.2	133	668	75	64	11	6	5	2	67	0	154	5	2
Marshall, C. Lee, El Paso.........	1	0	1.000	4.15	5	0	0	0	1	0	4.1	7	22	3	2	0	1	0	0	2	0	6	0	0
Martin, Chandler J., Tulsa	0	0	.000	3.93	5	2	0	0	1	0	18.1	17	77	10	8	1	0	0	2	4	0	12	0	0
Martinez, Gustavo A., S.A.	7	6	.538	3.13	35	9	0	0	6	0	92.0	76	407	36	32	8	3	3	12	50	3	74	4	0
Matos, Josue, San Antonio	7	2	.778	2.24	48	0	0	0	13	4	88.1	58	353	23	22	8	3	1	2	37	3	104	6	0
Mcclaskey, Timothy K., R.R. ...	5	4	.556	4.66	15	9	0	0	4	1	65.2	69	276	39	34	6	1	2	0	15	0	56	1	1
Medders, Brandon E., El Paso.	5	3	.625	4.41	56	0	0	0	37	7	69.1	65	297	37	34	3	3	2	0	26	6	72	3	1
Mendoza, Mario, Arkansas......	0	1	.000	11.32	6	0	0	0	4	0	10.1	20	58	13	13	2	1	0	2	8	1	4	1	0
Mensik, Todd L., Frisco *	0	0	.000	27.00	1	0	0	0	0	0	1.0	2	7	3	3	1	0	0	0	2	0	1	0	0
Meyer, Jake M., El Paso	0	1	.000	6.75	3	0	0	0	1	0	2.2	3	12	2	2	0	0	0	0	1	0	2	1	0
Miller, Gregory T., R.R. *.........	3	4	.429	5.49	27	10	1	0	3	0	77.0	80	347	56	47	11	3	3	9	38	2	63	1	1
Moore, Darin K., Frisco	0	3	.000	5.94	22	1	0	0	10	1	36.1	37	170	31	24	1	3	3	3	24	3	26	6	0
Moreno, Edwin A., Frisco	6	5	.545	3.29	29	15	0	0	9	0	112.0	105	465	50	41	7	2	4	3	33	0	74	4	2
Mounce, Anthony D., Frisco *.	7	1	.875	1.43	9	7	0	0	2	0	50.1	41	197	13	8	2	3	0	1	12	0	31	0	1
Murphy, William R., Midland *	3	3	.500	4.09	11	11	0	0	0	0	55.0	44	233	25	25	4	1	3	3	26	1	34	1	3
Murray, Arlington J., Frisco *..	10	4	.714	3.63	27	25	0	0	1	0	144.0	134	611	68	58	13	5	12	4	63	2	90	9	0
Nageotte, Clinton S., S.A.........	11	7	.611	3.10	27	27	2	1	0	0	154.0	127	653	60	53	6	2	3	14	67	1	157	8	1
Natale, Michael J., Wichita	1	2	.333	2.79	20	0	0	0	8	4	38.2	32	163	12	12	2	2	2	1	19	1	28	5	0
Nickoli, Michael J., Arkansas...	1	2	.333	7.56	4	4	0	0	0	0	16.2	23	86	19	14	1	0	1	2	10	0	11	1	0
O'Brien, Matthew T., Mid.*......	6	1	.857	4.92	36	0	0	0	13	0	53.0	56	229	31	29	3	1	1	1	23	4	55	2	0
Olore, Kevin L., San Antonio ...	0	2	.000	5.67	13	5	0	0	1	0	39.2	52	187	26	25	4	1	2	0	17	1	39	3	0
Park, Chan H., Frisco	1	0	1.000	2.45	2	2	0	0	0	0	11.0	10	52	5	3	0	0	2	4	4	0	6	1	0
Parrish, Wade R., Tulsa *........	4	6	.400	5.52	24	10	0	0	4	0	73.1	91	333	49	45	5	2	5	2	37	2	33	3	1
Peralta, Joel G., Arkansas	5	4	.556	2.24	47	0	0	0	43	20	52.1	39	209	13	13	3	1	1	5	12	2	48	3	0
Perez, Beltran O., El Paso........	2	11	.154	5.30	29	20	0	0	2	0	147.2	180	656	94	87	13	7	8	6	54	1	88	11	0
Pine, Christopher C., Arkansas	2	0	1.000	5.11	9	0	0	0	1	0	12.1	12	56	11	7	3	0	1	0	7	0	6	0	0
Powell, Greg S., Round Rock..	7	9	.438	3.89	36	18	1	1	7	0	141.0	155	609	75	61	7	6	6	6	39	5	80	4	0
Powell, James W., Frisco	0	0	.000	2.70	4	0	0	0	1	1	6.2	5	30	2	2	0	0	1	0	5	0	8	0	0
Prinz, Bret R., El Paso............	0	0	.000	4.50	2	0	0	0	0	0	2.0	3	10	1	1	0	0	0	0	1	0	2	0	0
Qualls, Chad M., Round Rock.	8	11	.421	3.85	28	28	3	2	0	0	175.1	174	744	85	75	12	6	8	10	61	0	132	8	0
Ramirez, Emmanuel, Tulsa......	0	0	.000	0.00	4	0	0	0	0	0	6.0	2	22	0	0	0	0	0	0	4	0	7	2	0
Ramirez, Erasmo, Frisco *	1	0	1.000	6.00	3	0	0	0	2	0	3.0	4	15	2	2	1	0	0	0	1	0	4	1	0
Ramirez, Santiago, R.R.	0	0	.000	0.00	6	1	0	0	2	1	4.2	5	22	0	0	0	0	0	0	4	0	3	1	0
Ramos, Mario M., Frisco *......	8	7	.533	3.86	19	19	0	0	0	0	121.1	130	509	59	52	9	4	5	2	28	1	103	1	3
Regilio, Nicholas D., Frisco	0	1	.000	21.60	1	0	0	0	0	0	1.2	5	10	4	4	0	0	0	0	1	0	2	1	0
Rheinecker, John P., Mid.*......	9	6	.600	4.74	23	23	1	1	0	0	142.1	186	640	90	75	13	3	4	7	32	1	89	3	1
Rivard, Rejean L., Frisco	0	1	.000	4.86	31	0	0	0	12	1	53.2	76	252	39	29	5	1	0	1	22	4	40	5	0
Roberts, Nick E., R.R.	2	8	.200	4.95	13	12	0	0	0	0	72.2	77	316	47	40	7	4	5	1	26	2	51	0	0
Rogers, Brian, Arkansas..........	2	1	.667	3.97	25	2	0	0	5	0	34.0	38	154	19	15	3	2	1	5	14	2	27	3	1
Rose, Brian L., Wichita............	0	4	.000	5.40	7	5	0	0	1	0	25.0	27	110	17	15	5	1	2	1	12	1	11	0	0
Sampson, Benjamin D., Tulsa*	5	6	.455	3.68	18	18	1	0	0	0	107.2	117	455	49	44	10	2	4	3	25	0	61	1	1
Sanches, Brian L., Wichita	1	5	.167	3.16	38	6	0	0	13	2	85.1	84	351	38	30	8	4	4	3	17	2	73	3	2
Santana, Ervin R., Arkansas....	1	1	.500	3.94	6	6	0	0	0	0	29.2	23	125	15	13	4	0	1	3	12	0	23	1	0
Santillan, Manuel, R.R............	0	0	.000	15.00	4	0	0	0	1	0	3.0	6	21	5	5	2	1	1	1	5	1	2	0	0
Scanlan, Robert G., R.R.	0	0	.000	0.00	4	0	0	0	3	0	3.0	2	13	1	0	0	1	0	0	1	0	4	0	0
Schneider, Scott B., Arkansas .	8	4	.667	4.06	33	2	0	0	8	0	71.0	63	309	39	32	7	2	2	4	25	1	51	4	0
Sedlacek, Shawn P., Wichita ...	1	2	.333	5.60	5	5	0	0	0	0	27.1	32	118	17	17	3	0	1	2	7	1	15	1	0
Sherrill, George F., S.A. *	3	0	1.000	0.33	16	0	0	0	6	0	27.1	19	111	2	1	1	2	1	0	12	1	31	0	0
Shiery, Shaun A., Wichita *.....	0	1	.000	9.00	3	0	0	0	1	0	3.0	3	13	3	3	0	0	0	0	2	1	3	0	0
Silva, Jesus R., El Paso...........	5	4	.556	5.02	55	0	0	0	23	3	66.1	84	304	44	37	7	3	3	2	20	4	56	8	1
Smith, H. Clifford, Arkansas....	1	0	1.000	2.60	13	1	0	0	5	0	27.2	20	113	9	8	2	1	1	0	15	1	10	1	0

Pitcher, Team	W	L	Pct.	ERA	G	GS	CG	ShO	GF	Sv.	IP	H	TBF	R	ER	HR	SH	SF	HB	BB	IBB	SO	WP	Bk.
Snow, Robert B., Midland	1	5	.167	6.08	32	0	0	0	25	13	37.0	34	174	27	25	2	3	0	2	27	3	41	6	1
Snyder, Kyle E., Wichita	0	0	.000	0.00	1	1	0	0	0	0	5.0	2	17	0	0	0	0	0	1	0	0	2	0	0
Stamler, Keith P., Frisco	4	6	.400	3.75	44	0	0	0	10	1	69.2	69	297	31	29	4	3	3	7	18	6	37	2	0
Stark, Dennis J., Tulsa	0	1	.000	6.23	1	1	0	0	0	0	4.1	4	23	5	3	0	0	2	1	4	0	3	0	0
Stiles, Brad A., Wichita *	0	0	.000	10.64	8	0	0	0	6	0	11.0	21	59	14	13	1	1	2	1	7	2	7	1	0
Stockman, Phillip M., El Paso	11	7	.611	3.96	26	26	0	0	0	0	147.2	137	648	75	65	9	8	6	9	64	0	146	2	0
Stokley, William R., Arkansas	2	9	.182	3.57	26	14	0	0	3	1	111.0	115	467	66	44	7	2	5	6	23	0	58	6	0
Strelitz, Brian J., San Antonio	0	2	.000	3.32	11	1	0	0	7	1	19.0	18	82	10	7	1	1	2	0	7	1	11	0	0
Sullivan, Kevin L., Tulsa	0	0	.000	0.00	1	0	0	0	1	0	1.0	0	3	0	0	0	0	0	0	0	0	0	0	0
Tamayo, I. Daniel, Wichita	11	14	.440	4.56	27	26	1	0	0	0	154.0	159	667	84	78	16	5	1	8	56	1	95	13	1
Thompson, Douglas W., Tulsa	0	3	.000	4.55	29	2	0	0	4	1	61.1	68	271	34	31	8	1	1	4	21	4	47	2	0
Thompson, Eric B., Mid.-Wich.	11	3	.786	2.92	25	18	0	0	4	1	108.0	93	442	40	35	9	1	6	3	41	0	65	3	0
Thornton, Matthew J., S.A. *	3	0	1.000	0.36	4	4	0	0	0	0	25.1	8	87	3	1	0	0	1	0	9	0	18	0	0
Tremblay, Max B., R.R. *	2	3	.400	5.91	41	0	0	0	9	0	32.0	37	151	27	21	2	4	2	2	14	2	35	3	0
Tsao, Chin-Hui, Tulsa	11	4	.733	2.46	18	18	0	0	0	0	113.1	88	446	34	31	7	2	2	5	26	0	125	3	3
Turnbow, T. Derrick, Arkansas	1	0	1.000	0.00	7	0	0	0	5	3	14.0	4	51	0	0	0	0	0	0	5	0	19	1	0
Ulloa, Enmanuel, San Antonio	0	1	.000	9.28	8	0	0	0	4	0	10.2	14	57	12	11	0	1	0	0	11	1	9	1	0
Valdes, Ismael, Frisco	1	2	.333	2.03	3	3	0	0	0	0	13.1	12	55	5	3	0	1	1	0	2	0	6	0	0
Van Poppel, Todd M., Frisco	0	0	.000	2.00	2	2	0	0	0	0	9.0	8	37	2	2	0	0	0	1	2	0	7	0	0
Vasquez, Jorge, Wichita	3	1	.750	1.92	36	0	0	0	32	22	51.2	39	211	12	11	3	2	2	5	18	2	52	8	1
Wade, Travis, Round Rock	2	2	.500	4.70	28	0	0	0	22	3	30.2	39	143	20	16	2	1	0	3	15	3	17	1	0
Walrond, Leslie D., Wichita *	2	0	1.000	3.27	2	2	0	0	0	0	11.0	7	43	4	4	2	0	0	0	2	0	9	2	0
Wells, Carlton E., El Paso *	2	2	.500	10.29	10	0	0	0	3	0	7.0	13	43	14	8	1	0	1	2	5	2	4	0	0
White, William C., El Paso *	1	3	.250	6.23	15	6	0	0	2	0	39.0	42	179	27	27	4	1	2	8	22	0	25	5	1
Wilhite, Matthew T., Arkansas	0	2	.000	8.38	5	0	0	0	2	2	9.2	17	47	12	9	3	1	0	0	1	0	8	0	0
Wilkerson, G. Wesley, Wichita	6	6	.500	4.80	32	13	0	0	12	1	105.0	117	466	65	56	8	1	1	8	46	1	35	1	1
Williams, Randall D., S.A. *	4	1	.800	1.73	29	0	0	0	11	2	41.2	33	165	9	8	2	2	1	0	7	0	38	0	0
Wilson, Christopher J., Fris.*	6	9	.400	5.05	22	21	0	0	0	0	123.0	135	541	79	69	11	2	3	8	38	3	89	6	0
Withers, Darvin T., Midland	7	4	.636	5.45	23	22	1	0	0	0	119.0	160	547	83	72	6	4	6	5	34	0	69	6	0
Wright, Christopher B., S.A.	7	6	.538	3.76	20	16	0	0	1	0	95.2	112	424	56	40	8	2	3	2	38	1	80	5	0
Wrightsman, Dustin L., Wich.	4	4	.500	6.07	20	10	0	0	6	1	75.2	98	338	55	51	14	0	2	7	17	1	51	4	1
Young, Colin M., Tulsa *	2	2	.500	2.40	40	0	0	0	15	2	45.0	36	193	15	12	1	2	2	4	19	1	44	2	1
Young, Douglas W., Wichita	0	0	.000	9.00	6	0	0	0	2	0	6.0	7	28	6	6	1	0	1	0	6	0	3	2	0
Ziegler, Michael D., Midland	12	9	.571	4.04	27	25	2	1	0	0	165.0	185	692	81	74	6	4	5	6	29	3	105	6	3

PITCHERS WITH TWO OR MORE TEAMS

Pitcher, Team	W	L	Pct.	ERA	G	GS	CG	ShO	GF	Sv.	IP	H	TBF	R	ER	HR	SH	SF	HB	BB	IBB	SO	WP	Bk.
Krawczyk, Jack B., El Paso	1	1	.500	5.08	12	0	0	0	3	0	28.1	34	122	16	16	3	5	3	1	5	0	18	1	0
Krawczyk, Jack B., Midland	0	2	.000	10.66	9	0	0	0	3	0	12.2	22	68	16	15	0	1	0	2	6	3	9	1	0
Thompson, Eric B., Wichita	11	0	1.000	2.11	20	13	0	0	4	1	94.0	76	372	26	22	7	0	5	3	29	0	57	2	0
Thompson, Eric B., Midland	0	3	.000	8.36	5	5	0	0	0	0	14.0	17	70	14	13	2	1	1	0	12	0	8	1	0

COMBINATION SHUTOUTS: Arkansas (9)—Jenks-Pine-Turnbow, Cyr-Turnbow, Stokley-Andrade, Cyr-Rogers-Schneider-Kroon, Santana-Kroon-Peralta, Jenks-Rogers-Cummings-Kroon-Peralta, Jenks-Schneider-Andrade, Jenks-Wilhite, Cyr-Mendoza. El Paso (3)—Gonzalez-Holsten-Freed, Aquino-Silva-Bruney, Daigle-Freed-Medders. Frisco (6)—Wilson-Stamler-Lundberg, Wilson-Moreno, Mounce-Burke, Dominguez-Stamler-Burke-Lundberg, Dominguez-Burke-Lundberg, Valdes-Murray-Burke. Midland (8)—Harden-Krawszyk-Snow, Rheinecker-Krawczyk-Flores-Kusiewicz, Komine-O'Brien-Crowell-Gwyn-Mabeus, Komine-O'Brien-Cullen-Mabeus, Murphy-Frick-Hooten-Crowell, Ziegler-Cullen-Frick, Murphy-Cullen-Blanton, Ziegler-Mabeus. Round Rock (3)—Houlton-Ireland-Tremblay-Wade, Houlton-Tremblay-Burns-Lugo, Qualls-Cammack. San Antonio (11)—Olore-Matos-Martinez, Nageotte-Williams-Hoerman, Nageotte-House, Thornton-Matos-Williams, Thornton-Matos-Lamber, Nageotte-Hamulack, Blackley-Hamulack-Lamber, Baek-Hoerman, Baek-Lamber-Matos, Nageotte-Sherrill-Lamber-Hoerman, Baek-Hoerman. Tulsa (8)—Bouknight-Dotel-Young, Buglovsky-Esslinger-Huisman, DiFelice-Dotel, Bouknight-Dotel-Huisman, Sampson-Thompson, Buglovsky-Dotel, Sampson-Huisman, Sampson-Dohmann. Wichita (8)—Gobble-Carlyle, Tamayo-Thompson, Wilkerson-Thompson, Gobble-Wilkerson-Douglass, Snyder-Tamayo-Vasquez, Greinke-Carlyle-Flury-Vasquez, Sanches-Carlyle-Hill, Greinke-Flury-Vasquez.

NO-HIT GAMES: None.

2003 FIELDING

TEAM

Team	G	PO	A	E	TC	DP	TP	PB	Pct.
Wichita	140	3656	1404	114	5174	133	0	13	.978
Frisco	140	3712	1552	133	5397	113	0	15	.975
San Antonio	139	3716	1465	147	5328	123	0	13	.972
Midland	140	3675	1581	149	5405	134	0	11	.972
Arkansas	140	3700	1392	163	5255	121	0	24	.969
Round Rock	140	3671	1363	159	5193	123	0	13	.969
Tulsa	139	3642	1421	166	5229	126	1	11	.968
El Paso	140	3749	1502	182	5433	112	0	29	.967

INDIVIDUAL

FIRST BASEMEN

NOTE: All caps denotes fielding-percentage leader based on 70 games for catchers, 93 for all other non-pitchers and 112 innings for pitchers. *Throws lefthanded.

Player, Team	Pct.	G	PO	A	E	TC	DP
Acevedo, Anthony, R.R.*	1.000	1	11	0	0	11	2
Allegra, Matt, Midland	1.000	1	1	0	0	1	0
Beinbrink, Andrew, Frisco	1.000	2	13	1	0	14	5
Bledsoe, Hunter, Wichita	.971	8	62	5	2	69	7
Botts, Jason, Frisco	.983	10	114	3	2	119	8
Burford, Kevin, Tulsa *	.994	77	612	44	4	660	58
Cole, Eric, Round Rock	.977	44	323	21	8	352	30
Coolbaugh, Mike, Round Rock	.978	12	81	7	2	90	15
Del Chiaro, Brent, Arkansas	1.000	1	5	0	0	5	0
German, Ramon, Round Rock	1.000	4	33	1	0	34	4
Gonzalez, Adrian, Frisco *	.983	45	364	53	7	424	35
Greene, Todd, Frisco	1.000	1	5	2	0	7	1
Hart, Corey, Wichita	.959	20	154	10	7	171	13
Hawpe, Brad, Tulsa *	.980	18	140	10	3	153	11
Hill, Jason, Arkansas	.992	25	226	12	2	240	21
Jackson, Steve, Midland	.993	31	274	26	2	302	24
JOHNSON, DAN, Midland	.992	111	952	100	8	1060	94
Jones, Jaime, El Paso *	1.000	1	2	1	0	3	0
Landry, Jacques, Round Rock	.973	28	199	16	6	221	21
Leone, Justin, San Antonio	1.000	2	11	0	0	11	0
Lindsey, John, San Antonio	.959	7	38	9	2	49	4
Lockwood, Mike, Midland *	1.000	2	1	0	0	1	1
Loeb, Bryan, El Paso	1.000	7	70	4	0	74	2
Loggins, Josh, Tulsa	.987	8	74	0	1	75	13
Martin, Billy, El Paso	.993	17	129	9	1	139	12
Martin, Tyler, Frisco	.981	12	92	11	2	105	7
Mensik, Todd, Frisco *	.966	4	26	2	1	29	3
Morales, Willie, El Paso	.974	8	73	2	2	77	5
Morrissey, Adam, Midland	1.000	1	4	0	0	4	1
Myers, Corey, El Paso	.985	112	930	86	15	1031	81

Player, Team	Pct.	G	PO	A	E	TC	DP
Norris, Dax, Round Rock	1.000	3	21	2	0	23	1
O'Keefe, Mike, Arkansas *	.984	95	748	68	13	829	91
Ottavinia, Paul, Frisco *	.990	15	94	8	1	103	5
Perry, Herbert, Frisco	1.000	1	4	0	0	4	0
Sanchez, Tino, Tulsa	.953	6	36	5	2	43	3
Santos, Chad, Wichita *	.986	107	861	63	13	937	92
Schneidmiller, Gary, Midland	1.000	1	2	0	0	2	0
Soules, Ryan, Frisco	.997	65	533	42	2	577	39
Sullivan, Kevin, Tulsa	.965	15	98	12	4	114	12
Swisher, Nick, Midland *	1.000	2	13	0	0	13	3
Timmons, Ozzie, El Paso	.900	1	9	0	1	10	0
Topolski, Jon, Round Rock	.990	47	362	23	4	389	27
Tracy, Andy, Tulsa	.989	23	170	17	2	189	18
Tremie, Chris, Round Rock	.972	12	94	11	3	108	11
Ullery, Dave, Wichita	.976	10	78	5	2	85	9
Zamora, Junior, Arkansas	.995	25	165	20	1	186	4
Zapp, A.J., San Antonio	.988	133	1082	113	15	1210	107

SECOND BASEMEN

Player, Team	Pct.	G	PO	A	E	TC	DP
Alviso, Jerome, Arkansas	1.000	1	4	1	0	5	0
Barden, Brian, El Paso	1.000	2	1	2	0	3	0
Beinbrink, Andrew, Frisco	.978	33	54	79	3	136	8
Bourgeois, Jason, Frisco	.965	54	101	149	9	259	33
BURKE, CHRIS, Round Rock	.983	93	205	269	8	482	50
Bynum, Freddie, Midland	.954	116	249	367	30	646	75
Carvajal, Jhonny, El Paso	.900	3	6	3	1	10	1
Colina, Javier, Tulsa	.963	71	178	210	15	403	57
Coolbaugh, Mike, Round Rock	1.000	8	8	21	0	29	3
Duncan, Carlos, Arkansas	.958	19	24	45	3	72	4
Espada, Joe, Frisco	1.000	2	3	7	0	10	1
Fenster, Darren, Wichita	1.000	4	9	5	0	14	0
Gandolfo, Rob, San Antonio	.976	38	69	97	4	170	18
Green, Andy, El Paso	.983	64	102	188	5	295	28
Hairston, Scott, El Paso	.960	74	131	227	15	373	38
Harris, Brian, Wichita	.984	36	69	113	3	185	25
Harrison, Adonis, Arkansas	.955	20	22	41	3	66	11
Hart, Corey, Wichita	1.000	6	14	16	0	30	4
Hernandez, Carlos, Round Rock	1.000	9	20	17	0	37	8
Hill, Jason, Arkansas	.000	1	0	0	0	0	0
Hopper, Norris, Wichita	.000	1	0	0	0	0	0
Joffrion, Jack, Tulsa	.848	13	19	20	7	46	0
Kent, Jeff, Round Rock	.875	2	2	5	1	8	0
Leone, Justin, San Antonio	1.000	1	3	3	0	6	0
Lopez, Jose, San Antonio	.978	34	81	97	4	182	23
Lora, Tom, Wichita	1.000	2	2	1	0	3	1
Macha, Erick, El Paso	1.000	5	4	9	0	13	1
Machado, Alejandro, Wichita	.990	75	167	214	4	385	51
Mann, Derek, Arkansas	1.000	6	7	23	0	30	2
McDougall, Marshall, Frisco	1.000	1	0	2	0	2	0
Medrano, Steve, Wichita	1.000	1	3	1	0	4	0
Merritt, Tim, San Antonio	.980	13	19	29	1	49	10
Morrissey, Adam, Midland	.922	20	31	52	7	90	11
Nivar, Ramon, Frisco	.989	54	108	162	3	273	37
Ozuna, Pablo, Tulsa	.923	7	12	12	2	26	1
Pecci, Jay, San Antonio	.979	10	18	28	1	47	10
Pichardo, Maximo, Arkansas	.933	3	6	8	1	15	3
Powers, John, Frisco	.900	2	4	5	1	10	0
Rodriguez, Victor, Wichita	1.000	1	1	3	0	4	1
Salazar, Oscar, Arkansas-Wichita	.973	46	88	124	6	218	33
Smith, Casey, Arkansas	.955	64	92	186	13	291	36
Specht, Brian, Arkansas	.957	9	14	30	2	46	8
Spivey, Junior, El Paso	.909	4	7	3	1	11	0
Stotts, J.T., Midland	.964	13	18	35	2	55	9
Tamargo, John, Round Rock	.981	32	66	87	3	156	26
Taylor, Seth, Tulsa	.974	37	77	109	5	191	26
Ugueto, Luis, San Antonio	.980	45	82	118	4	204	24
Uribe, Juan, Tulsa	1.000	2	4	3	0	7	2
Warren, Chris, Tulsa	.891	17	27	55	10	92	9

SECOND BASEMEN WITH TWO OR MORE TEAMS

Player, Team	Pct.	G	PO	A	E	TC	DP
Salazar, Oscar, Wichita	1.000	21	42	53	0	95	12
Salazar, Oscar, Arkansas	.951	25	46	71	6	123	21

THIRD BASEMEN

Player, Team	Pct.	G	PO	A	E	TC	DP
Alfaro, Jason, Round Rock	.882	22	9	36	6	51	2
Allegra, Matt, Midland	.833	5	2	3	1	6	0
Barden, Brian, El Paso	.931	101	80	178	19	277	12
Beinbrink, Andrew, Frisco	.921	100	54	180	20	254	16
Bynum, Freddie, Midland	1.000	2	0	2	0	2	0
Cahill, Jonathan, Arkansas	1.000	1	0	1	0	1	0
Carvajal, Jhonny, El Paso	.929	17	13	26	3	42	2
Castellano, John, San Antonio	1.000	1	0	2	0	2	0
Colina, Javier, Tulsa	.939	30	23	39	4	66	4
Coolbaugh, Mike, Round Rock	.919	13	6	28	3	37	3
Dobbs, Greg, San Antonio	1.000	2	0	6	0	6	1
Duncan, Carlos, Arkansas	.800	4	1	7	2	10	1
Espada, Joe, Frisco	1.000	3	1	3	0	4	0
Fenster, Darren, Wichita	1.000	1	0	2	0	2	0
Firlit, Dan, El Paso	.750	2	0	3	1	4	1
Gandolfo, Rob, San Antonio	.909	5	3	7	1	11	0
GEMOLL, JUSTIN, Wichita	.952	108	78	178	13	269	16
German, Ramon, Round Rock	.905	30	25	51	8	84	5
Green, Andy, El Paso	.957	10	8	14	1	23	1
Harrison, Adonis, Arkansas	.950	8	7	12	1	20	0
Hart, Corey, Wichita	.960	18	14	34	2	50	4
Hernandez, Carlos, Round Rock	.909	6	8	12	2	22	2
Hill, Jason, Arkansas	.750	5	0	9	3	12	1
Horner, Jim, San Antonio	1.000	1	0	1	0	1	0
Landry, Jacques, Round Rock	.923	4	2	10	1	13	0
Leone, Justin, San Antonio	.942	123	74	251	20	345	18
Liniak, Cole, Frisco	.900	14	8	28	4	40	4
Loggins, Josh, Tulsa	.000	1	0	0	0	0	0
Lopez, Jose, San Antonio	.926	10	4	21	2	27	0
Macha, Erick, El Paso	.882	9	3	12	2	17	0
Mann, Derek, Arkansas	1.000	1	0	1	0	1	0
Martin, Tyler, Frisco	.947	15	15	21	2	38	2
McDougall, Marshall, Frisco	.936	16	10	34	3	47	6
McPherson, Dallas, Arkansas	.955	21	17	25	2	44	2
Medrano, Steve, Wichita	.000	2	0	0	0	0	0
Morales, Willie, El Paso	1.000	10	3	15	0	18	0
Morrissey, Adam, Midland	.929	105	62	211	21	294	12
Myers, Corey, El Paso	.800	3	1	3	1	5	0
Ozuna, Pablo, Tulsa	1.000	3	1	3	0	4	0
Pichardo, Maximo, Arkansas	.946	16	12	23	2	37	2
Polanco, Enohel, Tulsa	.800	7	0	4	1	5	0
Powers, John, Frisco	1.000	5	2	8	0	10	0
Salazar, Oscar, Arkansas-Wichita	.886	22	10	29	5	44	2
Sanchez, Tino, Tulsa	1.000	6	1	13	0	14	1
Schneidmiller, Gary, Midland	.926	26	15	35	4	54	3
Smith, Casey, Arkansas	.933	18	8	34	3	45	3
Smith, Will, Frisco	1.000	1	0	1	0	1	0
Stotts, J.T., Midland	.947	11	5	13	1	19	1
Tamargo, John, Round Rock	.944	35	21	47	4	72	1
Taylor, Seth, Tulsa	.910	28	17	44	6	67	3
Tracy, Andy, Tulsa	.940	75	46	125	11	182	12
Tremie, Chris, Round Rock	1.000	5	0	2	0	2	0
Ugueto, Luis, San Antonio	1.000	1	1	1	0	2	0
Uribe, Juan, Tulsa	1.000	1	0	2	0	2	0
Whiteman, Tommy, Round Rock	.905	34	21	55	8	84	10
Zamora, Junior, Arkansas	.902	69	44	121	18	183	10
Zapp, A.J., San Antonio	1.000	1	1	1	0	2	0

THIRD BASEMEN WITH TWO OR MORE TEAMS

Player, Team	Pct.	G	PO	A	E	TC	DP
Salazar, Oscar, Wichita	.919	16	8	26	3	37	2
Salazar, Oscar, Arkansas	.714	6	2	3	2	7	0

SHORTSTOPS

Player, Team	Pct.	G	PO	A	E	TC	DP
Alviso, Jerome, Arkansas	1.000	1	3	3	0	6	1
Burke, Chris, Round Rock	.932	42	79	98	13	190	28
Bynum, Freddie, Midland	.917	8	11	22	3	36	6
Carvajal, Jhonny, El Paso	.919	16	22	46	6	74	10
Dellaero, Jason, Wichita	1.000	1	1	2	0	3	0
Espada, Joe, Frisco	1.000	5	10	20	0	30	3
Firlit, Dan, El Paso	.966	42	64	108	6	178	14
Green, Andy, El Paso	.925	39	79	107	15	201	23
Harrison, Adonis, Arkansas	.958	16	27	41	3	71	9
Hart, Corey, Wichita	.956	36	53	98	7	158	19
Joffrion, Jack, Tulsa	.920	23	29	63	8	100	13
Leone, Justin, San Antonio	.972	9	12	23	1	36	3
Lopez, Jose, San Antonio	.946	88	147	235	22	404	55
Lora, Tom, Wichita	.956	13	16	27	2	45	10
Machado, Alejandro, Wichita	.000	1	0	0	0	0	0
McDougall, Marshall, Frisco	.965	94	135	275	15	425	45
Medrano, Steve, Wichita	.941	7	15	17	2	34	5
Merrill, Ronnie, Tulsa	.933	62	101	162	19	282	37
Meyer, Drew, Frisco	.966	26	48	93	5	146	20
Morrissey, Adam, Midland	1.000	1	0	1	0	1	0
Nivar, Ramon, Frisco	.920	17	23	69	8	100	3
Olson, Tim, El Paso	.949	12	28	28	3	59	8
Ortiz, Nick, Wichita	.971	33	50	86	4	140	24
Ozuna, Pablo, Tulsa	.957	4	9	13	1	23	6
Polanco, Enohel, Tulsa	.938	35	36	99	9	144	16
Powers, John, Frisco	1.000	2	2	4	0	6	1

Player, Team	Pct.	G	PO	A	E	TC	DP
Rodriguez, Victor, Wichita	.968	43	63	117	6	186	22
ROUSE, MICHAEL, Midland	.967	122	179	374	19	572	81
Salazar, Oscar, Arkansas-Wichita	.970	24	47	51	3	101	16
Santos, Sergio, El Paso	.924	37	60	98	13	171	26
Specht, Brian, Arkansas	.936	119	204	294	34	532	77
Stotts, J.T., Midland	.983	13	17	41	1	59	9
Taylor, Seth, Tulsa	.961	20	27	47	3	77	12
Ugueto, Luis, San Antonio	.925	44	55	131	15	201	26
Uribe, Juan, Tulsa	1.000	1	4	5	0	9	2
Warren, Chris, Tulsa	1.000	1	1	0	0	1	0
Whiteman, Tommy, Round Rock	.932	100	136	249	28	413	52
Womack, Tony, El Paso	.923	4	4	8	1	13	2

SHORTSTOPS WITH TWO OR MORE TEAMS

Player, Team	Pct.	G	PO	A	E	TC	DP
Salazar, Oscar, Arkansas	.969	7	14	17	1	32	4
Salazar, Oscar, Wichita	.971	17	33	34	2	69	12

OUTFIELDERS

Player, Team	Pct.	G	PO	A	E	TC	DP
Acevedo, Anthony, R.R.*	.965	114	185	6	7	198	3
Airoso, Kurt, Frisco	.966	63	110	5	4	119	2
Alfaro, Jason, Round Rock	.000	1	0	0	0	0	0
Allegra, Matt, Midland	.951	123	210	22	12	244	3
Bautista, Danny, El Paso	1.000	2	4	0	0	4	0
Beltran, Carlos, Wichita	1.000	2	3	0	0	3	0
Botts, Jason, Frisco	.951	27	57	1	3	61	0
Boyd, Patrick, Frisco	.993	46	136	3	1	140	0
Bubela, Jaime, San Antonio	.971	119	217	15	7	239	3
Burford, Kevin, Tulsa *	.000	1	0	0	0	0	0
Burke, Chris, Round Rock	1.000	1	4	0	0	4	0
Burns, Kevan, El Paso *	.957	9	22	0	1	23	0
Campo, Mike, Midland	1.000	50	77	3	0	80	1
Castellano, John, San Antonio	1.000	3	3	0	0	3	0
Closser, J.D., Tulsa	.000	1	0	0	1	1	0
Cole, Eric, Round Rock	.990	41	94	3	1	98	1
Cota, Jesus, El Paso	.976	89	154	6	4	164	0
CUNNINGHAM, MARCO, Wichita	.995	100	213	8	1	222	3
Curry, Mike, San Antonio	.974	130	263	3	7	273	1
DeJesus, David, Wichita *	.980	17	48	0	1	49	0
Duncan, Carlos, Arkansas	.932	47	64	4	5	73	1
Fleming, Ryan, Frisco *	.982	113	211	10	4	225	1
Gandolfo, Rob, San Antonio	1.000	4	6	0	0	6	0
Gettis, Byron, Wichita	.980	135	289	5	6	300	1
Glanville, Doug, Frisco	.875	4	7	0	1	8	0
Gorneault, Nick, Arkansas	.988	29	75	4	1	80	0
Green, Andy, El Paso	1.000	14	25	2	0	27	0
Guzman, Elpidio, San Antonio *	.965	121	216	6	8	230	2
Hall, Victor, El Paso *	.964	121	287	7	11	305	2
Hart, Corey, Wichita	.000	1	0	0	0	0	0
Hawpe, Brad, Tulsa *	.970	49	93	3	3	99	0
Haynes, Nathan, Arkansas *	.976	90	240	8	6	254	4
Hill, Jason, Arkansas	.000	1	0	0	0	0	0
Hill, Mike, Round Rock	1.000	7	14	0	0	14	0
Holliday, Matt, Tulsa	.991	126	211	15	2	228	0
Hopper, Norris, Wichita	.981	112	250	8	5	263	1
Jacobs, Greg, San Antonio *	.895	13	15	2	2	19	0
James, Kenny, Arkansas	.980	124	282	7	6	295	2
Johnson, Dan, Midland	.000	1	0	0	0	0	0
Jones, Jaime, El Paso *	.909	8	10	0	1	11	0
Kroeger, Josh, El Paso *	.984	54	118	6	2	126	1
Landry, Jacques, Round Rock	.957	28	64	2	3	69	0
Lentini, Fehlandt, Round Rock	1.000	6	6	0	0	6	0
Liniak, Cole, Frisco	.000	1	0	0	0	0	0
Lockwood, Mike, Midland *	1.000	22	37	4	0	41	2
Loeb, Bryan, El Paso	.906	17	27	2	3	32	0
Lopez, Chuck, San Antonio *	1.000	9	9	0	0	9	0
Macha, Erick, El Paso	.000	1	0	0	0	0	0
Martin, Billy, El Paso	.833	5	5	0	1	6	0
Meadows, Tydus, Wichita	.965	63	133	5	5	143	1
Meluskey, Mitch, Round Rock	.667	1	2	0	1	3	0
Mench, Kevin, Frisco	1.000	3	4	1	0	5	0
Mensik, Todd, Frisco *	.905	16	18	1	2	21	0
Morrissey, Adam, Midland	.000	1	0	0	0	0	0
Murphy, Nate, El Paso *	.990	76	184	14	2	200	2
Nivar, Ramon, Frisco	.962	8	24	1	1	26	0
Nix, Laynce, Frisco *	.984	81	186	3	3	192	1
O'Keefe, Mike, Arkansas *	1.000	9	14	0	0	14	0
Olson, Tim, El Paso	.875	2	6	1	1	8	0
Ottavinia, Paul, Frisco *	.960	47	70	2	3	75	0
Piedra, Jorge, Tulsa *	.973	78	170	10	5	185	1
Quintero, Edgar, Arkansas *	.000	1	0	0	0	0	0
Ramirez, Dan, El Paso	1.000	8	16	2	0	18	0
Rosamond, Mike, Round Rock	.967	123	255	9	9	273	0
Salazar, Oscar, Arkansas-Wichita	.944	12	15	2	1	18	0
Sanchez, Tino, Tulsa	1.000	20	37	4	0	41	0
Sellier, Brian, Midland	1.000	59	88	1	0	89	0
Smith, Will, Frisco	1.000	33	62	2	0	64	0
Snelling, Chris, San Antonio *	1.000	28	41	2	0	43	0
Stanley, Steve, Midland *	.985	117	254	13	4	271	1
Sullivan, Cory, Tulsa *	.994	133	328	13	2	343	2
Sullivan, Kevin, Tulsa	1.000	12	26	0	0	26	0
Swisher, Nick, Midland *	.969	65	154	3	5	162	0
Timmons, Ozzie, El Paso	.965	37	54	1	2	57	1
Topolski, Jon, Round Rock	1.000	13	12	2	0	14	0
Uribe, Juan, Tulsa	1.000	1	3	0	0	3	0
Warren, Chris, Tulsa	1.000	1	1	0	0	1	0
Weber, Jake, Arkansas	.980	125	237	10	5	252	1
Wright, Gavin, Round Rock	.968	103	237	6	8	251	2

OUTFIELDERS WITH TWO OR MORE TEAMS

Player, Team	Pct.	G	PO	A	E	TC	DP
Salazar, Oscar, Arkansas	1.000	3	6	2	0	8	0
Salazar, Oscar, Wichita	.900	9	9	0	1	10	0

CATCHERS

Player, Team	Pct.	G	PO	A	E	TC	DP	PB
Ansman, Craig, El Paso	.979	49	306	23	7	336	0	4
Arnerich, Tony, Wichita	.889	3	16	0	2	18	0	3
Baker, John, Midland	.997	42	275	17	1	293	2	3
Brown, Jeremy, Midland	.983	63	388	28	7	423	3	6
Budde, Ryan, Arkansas	.985	73	515	60	9	584	2	7
Burkhart, Lance, Frisco	1.000	29	172	16	0	188	0	3
Castellano, John, San Antonio	1.000	2	6	2	0	8	0	0
Ceriani, Matt, El Paso	.977	5	35	8	1	44	2	1
Closser, J.D., Tulsa	.978	94	670	69	17	756	7	8
Craig, Beau, Midland	.929	2	11	2	1	14	0	0
Del Chiaro, Brent, Arkansas	.982	33	193	28	4	225	0	9
Dewey, Jason, Frisco	.984	79	454	49	8	511	4	7
Fatheree, Danny, Round Rock	1.000	1	2	0	0	2	0	0
Goldbach, Jeff, Frisco	.994	29	135	18	1	154	3	4
Greene, Todd, Frisco	1.000	2	7	0	0	7	0	0
Guzman, Jacob, Wichita	1.000	1	1	0	0	1	0	0
Hill, Jason, Arkansas	.981	18	95	11	2	108	0	3
Horner, Jim, San Antonio	.997	66	575	39	2	616	6	5
Jackson, Steve, Midland	.980	37	224	19	5	248	1	2
Loeb, Bryan, El Paso	.976	28	149	14	4	167	2	4
Mathis, Jeff, Arkansas	.995	23	176	16	1	193	0	5
MAYNARD, SCOTT, S.A.	.993	71	541	45	4	590	6	8
Meluskey, Mitch, Round Rock	1.000	8	62	3	0	65	0	2
Morales, Willie, El Paso	1.000	3	28	0	0	28	0	0
Norris, Dax, Round Rock	.989	65	422	39	5	466	3	8
Sanchez, Tino, Tulsa	.986	43	250	24	4	278	1	2
Smith, Jeff, Frisco	.988	26	148	14	2	164	1	1
Snyder, Chris, El Paso	.991	49	308	35	3	346	2	16
Sullivan, Kevin, Tulsa	.931	5	25	2	2	29	0	1
Tonis, Mike, Wichita	.987	83	482	60	7	549	4	4
Tremie, Chris, Round Rock	.991	75	508	54	5	567	8	3
Udy, Nicholas, San Antonio	1.000	6	15	1	0	16	0	0
Ullery, Dave, Wichita	.994	24	147	22	1	170	0	2
Waldron, Jeff, El Paso	.983	18	105	10	2	117	1	4
Walter, Scott, Wichita	.991	35	200	18	2	220	1	4
Wilson, Dan, San Antonio	.941	2	15	1	1	17	0	0

PITCHERS

Player, Team	Pct.	G	PO	A	E	TC	DP
Anderson, Travis, Tulsa	.800	17	1	7	2	10	1
Andrade, Stephen, Arkansas	1.000	36	7	3	0	10	1
Aquino, Greg, El Paso	1.000	20	11	18	0	29	2
Asencio, Miguel, Wichita	1.000	1	1	1	0	2	0
Baek, Cha-Sueng, San Antonio	1.000	9	4	5	0	9	0
Baerlocher, Ryan, Wichita	.857	12	3	3	1	7	0
Bazzell, Shane, Midland	.933	34	3	11	1	15	0
Beasley, Ray, Frisco *	1.000	3	1	1	0	2	0
Belflower, Jay, El Paso	1.000	53	4	5	0	9	0
Bergman, Dusty, Arkansas *	1.000	50	6	10	0	16	1
Blackley, Travis, San Antonio *	.978	27	7	38	1	46	1
Blanton, Joe, Midland	1.000	7	0	3	0	3	0
Bouknight, Kip, Tulsa	.941	26	13	19	2	34	1
Brink, Jim, Frisco	1.000	4	2	1	0	3	0
Brunet, Mike, Arkansas	.880	32	9	13	3	25	1
Bruney, Brian, El Paso	1.000	28	1	3	0	4	0
Buglovsky, Chris, Tulsa	.949	28	6	31	2	39	4
Bumatay, Mike, Tulsa *	1.000	40	6	7	0	13	1
Burke, Erick, Frisco *	.867	64	3	10	2	15	0
Burns, Mike, Round Rock	1.000	38	10	8	0	18	1
Cabaniel, Tomas, Midland	1.000	3	1	1	0	2	0
Cammack, Eric, Round Rock	.875	26	2	5	1	8	0

Player, Team	Pct.	G	PO	A	E	TC	DP
Campos, Juan, Round Rock	1.000	9	0	1	0	1	0
Carlyle, Buddy, Wichita	1.000	15	0	1	0	1	0
Cormier, Lance, El Paso	1.000	9	5	12	0	17	1
Coughenour, Jory, Round Rock	.941	34	4	12	1	17	0
Cramblitt, Joey, El Paso	.000	1	0	0	0	0	0
Crowell, Kyle, Midland	1.000	9	3	1	0	4	0
Cullen, Ryan, Midland *	.923	30	1	11	1	13	1
Cummings, Ryan, Arkansas	1.000	37	11	18	0	29	2
Cyr, Eric, Arkansas *	1.000	20	5	14	0	19	1
Daigle, Casey, El Paso	.838	29	9	22	6	37	3
Del Chiaro, Brent, Arkansas	.000	1	0	0	0	0	0
DiFelice, Mark, Tulsa	.957	21	8	14	1	23	0
Dohmann, Scott, Tulsa	1.000	50	6	7	0	13	0
Dominguez, Juan, Frisco	.889	9	1	7	1	9	0
Dotel, Melido, Tulsa	.895	49	9	8	2	19	0
Douglass, Ryan, Wichita	.938	28	7	8	1	16	1
Drese, Ryan, Frisco	1.000	2	1	2	0	3	0
Duncan, Carlos, Arkansas	.000	1	0	0	0	0	0
Dunn, Scott, Arkansas	.000	3	0	0	0	0	0
Echols, Justin, Frisco	.889	8	4	4	1	9	0
Espada, Joe, Frisco	.000	1	0	0	0	0	0
Esslinger, Cam, Tulsa	.500	15	3	1	4	8	0
Ferguson, Ian, Wichita	1.000	13	1	5	0	6	0
Field, Nathan, Wichita	1.000	15	2	2	0	4	1
Fischer, Rich, Arkansas	.929	26	12	14	2	28	0
Fischer, Steve, Midland	1.000	10	1	1	0	2	0
Flores, Ron, Midland *	1.000	39	5	7	0	12	2
Flury, Pat, Wichita	1.000	17	2	3	0	5	0
Francisco, Frank, Frisco	.833	7	2	3	1	6	0
Freed, Mark, El Paso *	1.000	67	3	16	0	19	0
Frick, Mike, Midland	1.000	28	1	4	0	5	0
Fultz, Aaron, Frisco *	.000	1	0	0	0	0	0
Gallo, Mike, Round Rock *	1.000	17	0	3	0	3	1
Gandolfo, Rob, San Antonio	.000	1	0	0	0	0	0
Garcia, Jose, Arkansas	1.000	6	2	7	0	9	0
Garcia, Sonny, Midland	.875	10	4	10	2	16	2
Gardner, Hayden, Frisco	1.000	33	5	8	0	13	0
Gobble, Jimmy, Wichita *	1.000	22	6	17	0	23	1
Gonzalez, Edgar, El Paso	1.000	6	2	11	0	13	0
Graham, Tom, Frisco	1.000	16	1	3	0	4	0
Gregg, Kevin, Arkansas	1.000	15	4	5	0	9	0
Greinke, Zack, Wichita	1.000	9	2	11	0	13	2
Griffith, Dustin, Arkansas	.000	1	0	0	0	0	0
Gwyn, Marc, Midland	1.000	9	1	1	0	2	0
Hampson, Justin, Tulsa *	1.000	1	0	1	0	1	0
Hamulack, Tim, San Antonio *	.800	40	1	3	1	5	0
Harden, Rich, Midland	1.000	2	0	1	0	1	0
Hart, Corey, Wichita	.000	1	0	0	0	0	0
Henrie, Matt, El Paso	.829	14	10	19	6	35	2
Hernandez, Runelvys, Wichita	1.000	2	0	1	0	1	0
Hill, Jeremy, Wichita	1.000	2	1	1	0	2	0
Hoerman, Jared, San Antonio	.857	56	3	3	1	7	1
Holsten, Ryan, El Paso	.900	38	1	17	2	20	1
Hooten, Dave, Midland	.976	39	23	18	1	42	0
Houlton, D.J., Round Rock	1.000	18	7	15	0	22	0
House, Craig, San Antonio	.750	14	2	1	1	4	0
Hughes, Travis, Frisco	1.000	24	7	9	0	16	2
Huisman, Justin, Tulsa	1.000	57	2	14	0	16	0
Ireland, Eric, Round Rock	.857	32	3	15	3	21	4
Jackson, Steve, Midland	.000	1	0	0	0	0	0
Janke, Cheyenne, Round Rock	1.000	28	1	8	0	9	0
Jenks, Bobby, Arkansas	1.000	16	5	5	0	10	0
Johnson, Randy, El Paso *	1.000	1	0	1	0	1	1
Johnson, Rett, San Antonio	.970	14	9	23	1	33	1
Komine, Shane, Midland	.947	19	23	13	2	38	2
Kozlowski, Ben, Frisco *	.857	11	0	6	1	7	0
Krawczyk, Jack, Midland-El Paso	1.000	21	6	8	0	14	0
Kroon, Marc, Arkansas	1.000	37	2	3	0	5	0
Kusiewicz, Mike, Midland *	.813	18	5	8	3	16	0
Lamber, Justin, San Antonio *	.964	39	10	17	1	28	4
Leclair, Aric, El Paso *	1.000	11	0	6	0	6	1
Lee, Garrett, Wichita	1.000	30	12	18	0	30	0
Lira, James, Round Rock	1.000	18	2	7	0	9	1
Lugo, Ruddy, Round Rock	1.000	41	5	14	0	19	0
Luna, Brandon, Frisco	.000	1	0	0	0	0	0
Lundberg, Spike, Frisco	1.000	57	7	11	0	18	3
Luque, Roger, Wichita *	1.000	5	1	2	0	3	0
Mabeus, Chris, Midland	.857	32	1	5	1	7	0
Macha, Erick, El Paso	.000	1	0	0	0	0	0
Madritsch, Bobby, S.A.*	.958	27	8	15	1	24	0
Marshall, Lee, El Paso	.000	5	0	0	0	0	0
Martin, Chandler, Tulsa	1.000	5	4	2	0	6	0
Martinez, Gustavo, San Antonio	1.000	35	10	15	0	25	0
Matos, Josue, San Antonio	.857	48	6	6	2	14	1
McClaskey, Tim, Round Rock	.818	15	3	6	2	11	1
Medders, Brandon, El Paso	1.000	56	3	8	0	11	0
Mendoza, Mario, Arkansas	1.000	6	1	5	0	6	1
Mensik, Todd, Frisco *	.000	1	0	0	0	0	0
Meyer, Jake, El Paso	.000	3	0	0	0	0	0
Miller, Greg, Round Rock *	.889	27	4	12	2	18	1
Moore, Darin, Frisco	1.000	22	4	7	0	11	2
Moreno, Edwin, Frisco	1.000	29	7	13	0	20	1
Mounce, Tony, Frisco *	1.000	9	0	7	0	7	0
Murphy, Bill, Midland *	.917	11	4	7	1	12	0
Murray, A.J., Frisco *	.964	27	10	17	1	28	2
Nageotte, Clint, San Antonio	.846	27	15	18	6	39	1
Natale, Mike, Wichita	1.000	20	4	9	0	13	1
Nickoli, Mike, Arkansas	1.000	4	4	2	0	6	1
O'Brien, Matt, Midland *	1.000	36	1	9	0	10	0
Olore, Kevin, San Antonio	.714	13	5	5	4	14	0
Park, Chan Ho, Frisco	.000	2	0	0	0	0	0
Parrish, Wade, Tulsa *	1.000	24	3	16	0	19	1
Peralta, Joel, Arkansas	.938	47	6	9	1	16	0
Perez, Beltran, El Paso	.872	29	15	19	5	39	0
Pine, Chris, Arkansas	1.000	9	1	1	0	2	0
Powell, Greg, Round Rock	1.000	36	7	22	0	29	4
Powell, Jay, Frisco	1.000	4	0	1	0	1	0
Prinz, Bret, El Paso	.000	2	0	0	0	0	0
Qualls, Chad, Round Rock	.976	28	17	24	1	42	2
Ramirez, Emmanuel, Tulsa	1.000	4	1	0	0	1	0
Ramirez, Erasmo, Frisco *	.000	3	0	0	1	1	0
Ramirez, Santiago, Round Rock	1.000	6	0	1	0	1	0
Ramos, Mario, Frisco *	.969	19	9	22	1	32	1
Regilio, Nick, Frisco	1.000	1	1	1	0	2	0
RHEINECKER, JOHN, Midland *	1.000	23	8	33	0	41	2
Rivard, Reggie, Frisco	.909	31	6	4	1	11	0
Roberts, Nick, Round Rock	1.000	13	3	5	0	8	1
Rogers, Brian, Arkansas	1.000	25	6	4	0	10	1
Rose, Brian, Wichita	1.000	7	2	5	0	7	1
Sampson, Benj, Tulsa *	1.000	18	10	18	0	28	0
Sanches, Brian, Wichita	1.000	38	5	7	0	12	0
Santana, Ervin, Arkansas	1.000	6	4	2	0	6	0
Santillan, Manny, Round Rock	1.000	4	0	1	0	1	0
Scanlan, Bob, Round Rock	.000	4	0	0	0	0	0
Schneider, Scott, Arkansas	.909	33	6	4	1	11	0
Sedlacek, Shawn, Wichita	1.000	5	1	1	0	2	0
Sherrill, George, San Antonio *	1.000	16	1	2	0	3	1
Shiery, Shaun, Wichita *	1.000	3	0	2	0	2	1
Silva, Jesus, El Paso	.929	55	3	10	1	14	0
Smith, Cliff, Arkansas	1.000	13	2	0	0	2	0
Snow, Bert, Midland	1.000	32	6	3	0	9	0
Snyder, Kyle, Wichita	1.000	1	1	1	0	2	1
Stamler, Keith, Frisco	1.000	44	6	12	0	18	1
Stark, Dennis, Tulsa	.000	1	0	0	0	0	0
Stiles, Brad, Wichita *	.750	8	0	3	1	4	0
Stockman, Phil, El Paso	.875	26	3	11	2	16	0
Stokley, Billy, Arkansas	.970	26	11	21	1	33	1
Strelitz, Brian, San Antonio	1.000	11	4	0	0	4	0
Sullivan, Kevin, Tulsa	.000	1	0	0	0	0	0
Tamayo, Danny, Wichita	.833	27	6	19	5	30	0
Thompson, Doug, Tulsa	1.000	29	7	6	0	13	1
Thompson, Eric, Mid.-Wichita	.917	25	3	8	1	12	0
Thornton, Matt, San Antonio *	1.000	4	0	2	0	2	0
Tremblay, Max, Round Rock *	.889	41	3	5	1	9	1
Tsao, Chin-hui, Tulsa	1.000	18	7	11	0	18	1
Turnbow, Derrick, Arkansas	1.000	7	1	4	0	5	1
Ulloa, Enmanuel, San Antonio	.000	8	0	0	0	0	0
Valdes, Ismael, Frisco	1.000	3	3	1	0	4	0
Van Poppel, Todd, Frisco	1.000	2	0	1	0	1	0
Vasquez, Jorge, Wichita	1.000	36	3	6	0	9	0
Wade, Travis, Round Rock	.889	28	1	7	1	9	0
Walrond, Les, Wichita *	.000	2	0	0	0	0	0
Wells, Carlton, El Paso *	.714	10	4	1	2	7	0
White, Bill, El Paso *	.875	15	1	6	1	8	0
Wilhite, Matt, Arkansas	.667	5	0	2	1	3	1
Wilkerson, Wes, Wichita	.931	32	8	19	2	29	3
Williams, Randy, San Antonio *	1.000	29	1	7	0	8	0
Wilson, C.J., Frisco *	.913	22	8	13	2	23	0
Withers, Darvin, Midland	.903	23	10	18	3	31	1
Wright, Chris, San Antonio	.828	20	8	16	5	29	1
Wrightsman, Dusty, Wichita	1.000	20	4	13	0	17	0
Young, Colin, Tulsa *	1.000	40	0	4	0	4	0
Young, Doug, Wichita	1.000	6	0	2	0	2	0
Ziegler, Mike, Midland	1.000	27	13	20	0	33	3

PITCHERS WITH TWO OR MORE TEAMS

Player, Team	Pct.	G	PO	A	E	TC	DP
Krawczyk, Jack, Midland	1.000	9	4	2	0	6	0
Krawczyk, Jack, El Paso	1.000	12	2	6	0	8	0
Thompson, Eric, Wichita	.889	20	0	8	1	9	0
Thompson, Eric, Midland	1.000	5	3	0	0	3	0

The following players appeared only as a designated hitter, pinch-hitter or pinch-runner: Vaz, dh, ph.

LEAGUE CHAMPIONS

Year	Team	Pct.
1888—	Dallas	.671
1889—	Houston	.551
1890—	Galveston	.705
1892—	Houston	.741
	Houston	.613
1895—	Dallas	.754
	Fort Worth*	.750
1896—	Fort Worth	.757
	Houston*	.679
	Galveston	.548
1897—	San Antonio†	.657
	Galveston†	.717
1898—League disbanded.		
1899—	Galveston	.632
	Galveston	.762
1900-01—Did not operate.		
1902—	Corsicana	.866
	Corsicana	.682
1903—	Paris-Waco	.615
	Dallas*	.648
1904—	Corsicana*	.615
	Fort Worth	.800
1905—	Fort Worth	.545
1906—	Fort Worth	.677
	Cleburne∞	.609
1907—	Austin	.629
1908—	San Antonio	.664
1909—	Houston	.601
1910—	Dallas†	.586
	Houston†	.586
1911—	Austin	.575
1912—	Houston	.626
1913—	Houston	.620
1914—	Houston†	.671
	Waco†	.671
1915—	Waco	.592
1916—	Waco	.587
1917—	Dallas	.600
1918—	Dallas	.584
1919—	Shreveport*	.677
	Fort Worth	.651
1920—	Fort Worth	.703
	Fort Worth	.750
1921—	Fort Worth	.691
	Fort Worth	.662
1922—	Fort Worth	.694
	Fort Worth	.711
1923—	Fort Worth	.632
1924—	Fort Worth	.689
	Fort Worth	.763
1925—	Fort Worth	.711
	Fort Worth▲	.653
1926—	Dallas	.574
1927—	Wichita Falls	.654
1928—	Houston*	.679
	Wichita Falls	.731
1929—	Dallas*	.588
	Wichita Falls	.620
1930—	Wichita Falls	.697
	Fort Worth*	.632
1931—	Houston◆	.625
	Houston	.734
1932—	Beaumont*	.640
	Dallas	.727
1933—	Houston	.623
	San Antonio (4th)§	.523
1934—	Galveston‡	.579
1935—	Oklahoma City‡	.590
1936—	Dallas	.604
	Tulsa (3rd)§	.519
1937—	Oklahoma City	.635
	Fort Worth (3rd)§	.535
1938—	Beaumont	.635
1939—	Houston	.606
	Fort Worth (4th)§	.540
1940—	Houston‡	.652
1941—	Houston	.673
	Dallas (4th)§	.519
1942—	Beaumont	.605
	Shreveport (2nd)§	.576
1943-44-45—Did not operate.		
1946—	Fort Worth	.656
	Dallas (2nd)§	.591
1947—	Houston‡	.623
1948—	Fort Worth‡	.601
1949—	Fort Worth	.649
	Tulsa (2nd)§	.584
1950—	Beaumont	.595
	San Antonio (4th)§	.513
1951—	Houston‡	.619
1952—	Dallas	.571
	Shreveport (3rd)§	.522
1953—	Dallas‡	.571
1954—	Shreveport	.559
	Houston (2nd)§	.553
1955—	Dallas	.581
	Shreveport (3rd)§	.540
1956—	Houston‡	.623
1957—	Dallas	.662
	Houston (2nd)§	.630
1958—	Fort Worth	.582
	Cor. Christi (3rd)§	.507
1959—	Victoria	.589
	Austin (2nd)§	.548
1960—	Rio Grande Valley	.590
	Tulsa (3rd)	.528
1961—	Amarillo	.643
	San Antonio (3rd)§	.532
1962—	El Paso	.571
	Tulsa (2nd)§	.550
1963—	San Antonio	.564
	Tulsa (3rd)§	.529
1964—	San Antonio‡	.607
1965—	Tulsa	.574
	Albuquerque■	.550
1966—	Arkansas	.579
1967—	Albuquerque	.557
1968—	Arkansas	.586
	El Paso■	.562
1969—	Amarillo	.593
	Memphis■	.504
1970—	Albuquerque◆	.615
	Memphis	.507
1971—	Did not operate as league—clubs were members of Dixie Association.	
1972—	Alexandria	.600
	El Paso■	.557
1973—	San Antonio	.590
	Memphis■	.558
1974—	Victoria■	.581
	El Paso	.555
1975—	Lafayette▼	.558
	Midland▼	.604
1976—	Amarillo■	.600
	Shreveport	.515
1977—	El Paso	.600
	Arkansas•	.485
1978—	El Paso•	.593
	Jackson	.567
1979—	Arkansas•	.571
	Midland	.563
1980—	Arkansas•	.596
	San Antonio	.544
1981—	San Antonio	.571
	Jackson•	.507
1982—	El Paso	.559
	Tulsa•	.515
1983—	Jackson	.507
	Beaumont•	.500
1984—	Beaumont	.654
	Jackson•	.610
1985—	El Paso	.632
	Jackson•	.537
1986—	El Paso•	.630
	Jackson	.533
1987—	Wichita•	.515
	Jackson	.515
1988—	El Paso	.552
	Tulsa•	.522
1989—	Arkansas•	.585
	Wichita	.537
1990—	San Antonio	.582
	Shreveport•	.489
1991—	Shreveport•	.632
	El Paso	.596
1992—	Shreveport	.566
	Wichita•	.515
1993—	El Paso	.563
	Jackson•	.541
1994—	El Paso•	.647
	Jackson	.548
1995—	Shreveport•	.652
	Midland	.485
1996—	Jackson•	.547
	Wichita	.500
1997—	San Antonio•	.604
	Shreveport	.551
1998—	Arkansas	.571
	Tulsa•	.557
1999—	Wichita•	.593
2000—	Round Rock*	.593
2001—	Round Rock	.614
	Arkansas††	.485
2002—	Wichita	.576
	San Antonio§	.486
2003—	San Antonio§§	.633

*Won split-season playoff. †Won playoff for title. ‡Finished first and won four-club playoff. §Won four-club playoff. §§Won both halves of split season, received a bye into playoffs and won three-team playoff. ∞Title to Cleburne by default. ▲Tied with Dallas in second half and won playoff for championship. ◆Tied with Beaumont at end of first half and won title in best-of-five series played as part of second-half schedule. ■League divided into Eastern, Western divisions; won two-team playoff. ▼League divided into Eastern, Western divisions; declared co-champions when playoffs were not completed. •League divided into Eastern and Western divisions and played split-season; won playoffs. NOTE—Championship awarded to winner of four-team playoff, 1933-51; first-place team and playoff winner co-champions, 1952-64. ††Was leading final round of split-season playoff, two games to none, and was declared champion when Professional Baseball declared a stoppage of play.

CALIFORNIA LEAGUE

LEAGUE OFFICE

President
Joe Gagliardi
Address
2380 S. Bascom Ave., Suite 200
Campbell, CA 95008
Phone
408-369-8038

Teams (affiliation)
Bakersfield Blaze (Devil Rays)
High Desert Mavericks (Brewers)
Inland Empire 66ers of San Bernardino (Mariners)
Lake Elsinore Storm (Padres)
Lancaster Jethawks (Diamondbacks)
Modesto A's (A's)
Rancho Cucamonga Quakes (Angels)
San Jose Giants (Giants)
Stockton Ports (Rangers)
Visalia Oaks (Rockies)

2003 FINAL STANDINGS

FIRST HALF

NORTHERN DIVISION

Team	W	L	T	Pct.	GB
Stockton	41	29	-	.586	...
Bakersfield	38	32	-	.543	3.0
Visalia	35	35	-	.500	6.0
Modesto	32	38	-	.457	9.0
San Jose	28	42	-	.400	13.0

SOUTHERN DIVISION

Team	W	L	T	Pct.	GB
Rancho Cucamonga	40	30	-	.571	...
Lancaster	39	31	-	.557	1.0
Inland Empire	36	34	-	.514	4.0
Lake Elsinore	36	34	-	.514	4.0
High Desert	25	45	-	.357	15.0

SECOND HALF

NORTHERN DIVISION

Team	W	L	T	Pct.	GB
Visalia	44	26	-	.629	...
Modesto	42	28	-	.600	2.0
Stockton	36	34	-	.514	8.0
Bakersfield	32	38	-	.457	12.0
San Jose	30	40	-	.429	14.0

SOUTHERN DIVISION

Team	W	L	T	Pct.	GB
Inland Empire	42	28	-	.600	...
Lake Elsinore	39	31	-	.557	3.0
Rancho Cucamonga	34	36	-	.486	8.0
Lancaster	34	36	-	.486	8.0
High Desert	17	53	-	.243	25.0

COMPOSITE

Team	VIS	INL	STK	LKE	RC	MOD	LNC	BAK	SJ	HD	W	L	T	Pct.	GB
Visalia (Rockies)	...	3	14	2	5	13	4	17	15	6	79	61	0	.564	...
Inland Empire (Mariners)	3	...	4	14	16	2	12	4	4	19	78	62	0	.557	1.0
Stockton (Rangers)	13	2	...	4	5	12	3	18	18	2	77	63	0	.550	2.0
Lake Elsinore (Padres)	4	13	2	...	10	3	18	2	4	19	75	65	0	.536	4.0
Rancho Cucamonga (Angels)	1	12	1	17	...	5	13	3	5	17	74	66	0	.529	5.0
Modesto (Athletics)	15	4	16	3	2	...	2	12	15	5	74	66	0	.529	5.0
Lancaster (Diamondbacks	2	15	3	10	15	4	...	3	1	20	73	67	0	.521	6.0
Bakersfield (Devil Rays)	10	2	10	4	3	15	3	...	18	5	70	70	0	.500	9.0
San Jose (Giants)	13	2	9	2	1	11	5	10	...	5	58	82	0	.414	21.0
High Desert (Brewers)	0	9	4	9	9	1	7	1	2	...	42	98	0	.300	37.0

Major league affiliations in parentheses.

PLAYOFFS: Visalia defeated Modesto, two games to none; Inland Empire defeated Lake Elsinore, two games to none; Inland Empire defeated Rancho Cucamonga, three games to one; Stockton defeated Visalia, three games to two; Inland Empire defeated Stockton, three games to none, to win league championship.

REGULAR-SEASON ATTENDANCE: Bakersfield, 90,099; High Desert, 126,705; Lake Elsinore, 240,171; Lancaster, 151,616; Modesto, 148,194; Rancho Cucamonga, 296,118; Inland Empire, 217,876; San Jose, 154,927; Stockton, 75,609; Visalia, 62,863. Total attendance—1,564,178. Playoffs (16 games)—24,588. California-Carolina League All-Star Game at Rancho Cucamonga—5,737.

MANAGERS: Bakersfield, Omar Munoz; High Desert, Tim Blackwell; Lake Elsinore, Jeff Gardner; Lancaster, Mike Aldrete; Modesto, Rick Rodriguez; Rancho Cucamonga, Bobby Meacham; Inland Empire, Steve Roadcap; San Jose, Jack Lind; Stockton, Arnie Beyeler; Visalia, Stu Cole.

ALL-STAR TEAM: 1B—Kyle Nichols, Lancaster; 2B—Josh Barfield, Lake Elsinore; 3B—Dallas McPherson, Rancho Cucamonga; SS—J.J. Furmaniak, Lake Elsinore; OF—Joey Gathright, Bakersfield; OF—Greg Jacobs, Inland Empire; OF—Gary Thomas, Modesto; C—Jeff Mathis, Rancho Cucamonga; DH—Corey Slavik, Visalia; RHP—Ervin Santana, Rancho Cucamonga; LHP—Ryan Ketchner, Inland Empire; LHP—Brad Weis, Modesto; LHP—Justin Hampson, Visalia; Most Valuable Player—Josh Barfield, Lake Elsinore; Rookie of the Year—Joey Gathright, Bakersfield; Pitcher of the Year—Ervin Santana, Rancho Cucamonga; Manager of the Year—Stu Cole, Visalia.

2003 BATTING

TEAM

Team	G	TPA	AB	R	H	TB	2B	3B	HR	RBI	SH	SF	HP	BB	IBB	SO	SB	CS	GDP	LOB	ShO	Avg.	OBP	Slg.
Lancaster	140	5608	4975	810	1420	2190	280	41	136	739	53	45	70	464	14	1052	121	48	92	1047	3	.285	.352	.440
Lake Elsinore	140	5553	4874	821	1363	2087	288	41	118	763	32	55	72	518	8	1104	162	47	94	1040	8	.280	.354	.428
Inland Empire	140	5372	4759	700	1330	1962	280	50	84	620	32	50	81	447	13	752	121	64	129	1006	4	.279	.348	.412
Stockton	140	5501	4791	736	1319	1911	260	40	84	679	50	55	48	556	10	1016	130	56	100	1068	11	.275	.353	.399
Rancho Cuca.	140	5368	4841	685	1330	2054	278	40	122	624	36	34	75	382	15	1018	108	72	66	999	6	.275	.335	.424
Modesto	140	5631	4871	759	1332	1926	273	30	87	687	33	58	88	581	8	1007	68	21	136	1149	3	.273	.357	.395
Bakersfield	140	5288	4772	668	1292	1862	256	19	92	614	23	32	74	386	6	1183	150	59	80	978	7	.271	.333	.390
High Desert	140	5403	4860	687	1314	1898	243	49	81	626	55	46	55	386	5	903	191	84	75	958	3	.270	.328	.391
Visalia	140	5436	4782	720	1250	1948	283	32	117	641	36	58	95	464	7	1087	87	55	79	1041	4	.261	.335	.407
San Jose	140	5280	4737	620	1224	1830	257	38	91	565	29	46	99	368	9	977	132	67	96	975	7	.258	.322	.386

INDIVIDUAL

TOP QUALIFIERS FOR BATTING CHAMPIONSHIP

Minimum 378 plate appearances. *Lefthanded batter. †Switch-hitter.

Player, Team	G	TPA	AB	R	H	TB	2B	3B	HR	RBI	SH	SF	HP	BB	IBB	SO	SB	CS	GDP	Avg.	OBP	Slg.
Jacobs, Greg, Inland Emp.*	95	401	347	67	124	200	35	7	9	64	1	4	7	42	4	43	4	5	5	.357	.433	.576
Barfield, Josh, Lake Elsinore	135	615	549	99	185	291	46	6	16	128	1	11	4	50	3	122	16	4	11	.337	.389	.530
Gathright, Joey, Bakersfield *	89	389	340	65	110	122	6	3	0	23	2	0	6	41	0	54	57	13	3	.324	.406	.359
Mathis, Jeff, Rancho Cuca.	97	422	378	73	122	189	28	3	11	54	0	4	5	35	0	74	5	3	4	.323	.384	.500
Slavik, Corey, Visalia *	109	449	392	66	126	197	27	1	14	75	0	8	9	40	0	67	1	5	5	.321	.390	.503
Gorneault, Nick, Rancho Cuca.	97	400	374	67	120	202	36	2	14	72	0	1	5	20	3	82	11	6	3	.321	.363	.540
Belcher, Jason, High Desert *	91	385	350	43	112	156	23	3	5	54	1	4	4	26	0	35	4	6	7	.320	.370	.446
Nichols, Kyle, Lancaster	130	547	484	82	151	278	34	0	31	108	0	7	5	51	6	118	0	0	13	.312	.378	.574
Castellano, John, In. Emp.	114	500	461	61	141	215	34	2	12	80	0	3	4	32	0	50	11	3	17	.306	.354	.466
Richar, Danny, Lancaster	123	433	405	51	123	163	19	9	1	42	10	1	3	14	0	70	6	3	10	.304	.331	.402
Ortmeier, Daniel, San Jose †	115	460	408	62	124	192	32	6	8	56	0	2	11	39	4	89	13	6	13	.304	.378	.471
Raymundo, G.J., Stockton	103	461	396	64	120	179	34	5	5	67	3	10	7	44	5	68	3	3	9	.303	.374	.452
Thomas, Gary, Modesto	117	566	498	95	151	223	30	3	12	68	4	5	18	41	0	83	22	7	6	.303	.374	.448
Carter, Josh, Lake Elsinore	96	399	357	58	107	149	18	3	6	56	0	4	5	32	0	53	8	3	7	.300	.362	.417
Shealy, Ryan, Visalia	93	404	341	70	102	177	31	1	14	73	0	7	14	42	0	72	0	0	5	.299	.391	.519

DEPARTMENTAL LEADERS: G—Nix, 137; AB—Murphy, 565; R—Nix, 107; H—Barfield, 185; TB—Barfield, 291; 2B—Barfield, Nix, 46; 3B—Choo, 13; HR—Nichols, 31; RBI—Barfield, 128; SH—R. Santana, 13; SF—Sain, 12; HP—B. Carter, 26; BB—Kiger, 77; IBB—Nichols, 6; SO—Lincoln, 151; SB—C. Morris, 67; CS—C. Morris, 18; GIDP—Teahen, 19; Slg.—Jacobs, .576; OBP—Jacobs, .433.

ALL PLAYERS

*Lefthanded batter. †Switch-hitter.

Player, Team	G	TPA	AB	R	H	TB	2B	3B	HR	RBI	SH	SF	HP	BB	IBB	SO	SB	CS	GDP	Avg.	OBP	Slg.
Alvarado, Joel, High Desert	67	222	198	23	32	42	10	0	0	20	3	2	2	17	0	32	1	0	6	.162	.233	.212
Anderson, Keith, San Jose	56	197	173	24	38	46	5	0	1	22	1	2	1	20	0	44	1	2	1	.220	.301	.266
Arhart, Josh, Bakersfield	88	322	286	43	73	102	15	1	4	28	0	2	7	26	0	70	1	3	8	.255	.330	.357
Asadoorian, Rick, Stockton	31	117	108	14	20	38	2	2	4	17	2	0	2	5	0	31	3	1	4	.185	.235	.352
Aspito, Jason, R.C. *	117	492	449	57	116	191	31	4	12	61	2	5	14	22	0	94	7	8	8	.258	.310	.425
Ayala, Odannys, Stockton	24	97	81	15	16	21	3	1	0	9	1	1	2	12	0	16	0	2	3	.198	.313	.259
Balet, Pichi, Inland Empire	21	94	84	14	26	37	3	1	2	14	0	1	4	5	0	12	1	0	6	.310	.372	.440
Barajas, Rod, Lancaster	3	13	12	2	5	5	0	0	0	3	0	0	0	1	0	2	0	0	0	.417	.462	.417
Barfield, Josh, Lake Elsinore	135	615	549	99	185	291	46	6	16	128	1	11	4	50	3	122	16	4	11	.337	.389	.530
Barker, Sean, Visalia	104	415	378	61	106	168	24	4	10	41	1	3	7	25	0	71	6	3	3	.280	.334	.444
Barre, Brian, Visalia *	39	154	123	21	30	60	4	4	6	18	2	0	0	29	0	31	2	2	3	.244	.388	.488
Bastida-Martinez, Evel, In.E.*	87	316	288	44	79	112	14	2	5	32	1	2	2	23	0	31	6	6	6	.274	.330	.389
Belcher, Jason, High Desert *	91	385	350	43	112	156	23	3	5	54	1	4	4	26	0	35	4	6	7	.320	.370	.446
Benard, Marvin, San Jose *	3	10	9	2	2	2	0	0	0	0	0	0	1	0	0	2	0	0	0	.222	.300	.222
Benavidez, Julian, San Jose	58	220	200	18	41	62	8	2	3	22	0	2	2	16	0	57	1	1	9	.205	.268	.310
Benick, Jon, Lake Elsinore †	82	360	327	50	98	151	24	1	9	47	0	3	3	27	0	53	1	0	8	.300	.356	.462
Bernier, Doug, Visalia †	84	341	268	50	54	59	5	0	0	21	6	1	2	64	1	63	12	2	3	.201	.358	.220
Bone, Blake, Inland Empire *	27	94	83	11	19	38	7	0	4	16	0	2	1	8	0	24	0	1	3	.229	.298	.458
Bonner, Adam, Bakersfield *	23	98	85	20	24	51	7	1	6	19	0	0	0	13	0	30	1	2	0	.282	.378	.600
Botts, Jason, Stockton †	76	330	283	58	89	134	14	2	9	61	0	1	1	45	1	59	12	3	8	.314	.409	.473
Bourgeois, Jason, Stockton	69	325	277	75	91	131	22	3	4	34	3	2	7	36	0	33	16	3	4	.329	.416	.473
Bowser, Matt, Modesto *	112	497	429	60	126	186	29	5	7	57	0	4	7	57	2	83	1	1	11	.294	.382	.434
Boyd, Dan, High Desert	37	164	143	30	42	61	16	0	1	14	1	0	4	16	0	29	3	2	1	.294	.380	.427
Boyd, Patrick, Stockton †	58	261	221	48	65	121	17	0	13	50	1	5	5	29	0	68	11	1	5	.294	.381	.548
Bravo, Danny, L.E. †	15	65	55	13	16	31	4	1	3	17	1	1	0	8	0	7	2	1	0	.291	.375	.564
Brown, Hunter, Inland Empire	126	542	452	84	112	197	34	3	15	68	3	8	11	67	0	102	9	6	7	.248	.353	.436
Budde, Ryan, R.C.	14	54	50	6	12	20	3	1	1	6	0	2	0	2	1	10	0	0	1	.240	.259	.400
Candelaria, Scott, H.D.	115	485	455	54	131	178	28	5	3	52	4	4	8	14	0	65	5	3	12	.288	.318	.391
Carter, Bryan, San Jose *	131	542	471	68	119	175	26	3	8	66	2	6	26	37	4	114	28	11	8	.253	.337	.372
Carter, Josh, Lake Elsinore	96	399	357	58	107	149	18	3	6	56	0	4	5	32	0	53	8	3	7	.300	.362	.417
Castellano, John, In. E.	114	500	461	61	141	215	34	2	12	80	0	3	4	32	0	50	11	3	17	.306	.354	.466
Castro, Ismael, In. E. †	98	347	327	46	90	122	19	2	3	25	0	1	7	12	0	33	9	7	7	.275	.314	.373
Centeno, Irwin, Bakersfield	71	242	218	28	51	57	6	0	0	12	2	0	6	16	0	61	9	2	4	.234	.304	.261
Chavez, Angel, San Jose	120	512	478	69	134	199	23	6	10	58	2	6	4	22	0	60	20	11	13	.280	.314	.416
Chavez, Ozzie, High Desert †	81	301	272	29	61	84	2	6	3	25	4	2	0	23	0	52	5	9	3	.224	.283	.309
Choo, Shin-soo, In. E. *	110	471	412	62	118	189	18	13	9	55	2	4	9	44	1	84	18	10	8	.286	.365	.459
Christy, Jeff, Modesto *	79	338	282	48	70	91	12	3	1	24	4	1	3	48	1	50	9	3	6	.248	.362	.323
Cirillo, Jeff, Inland Empire	5	18	15	1	3	4	1	0	0	1	0	0	0	3	0	1	0	0	1	.200	.333	.267
Clark, Aaron, Bakersfield *	136	577	527	57	134	207	26	1	15	83	0	2	5	43	1	146	6	4	1	.254	.315	.393
Clark, Daryl, High Desert *	50	226	191	38	60	118	6	5	14	35	0	2	1	32	1	51	1	2	4	.314	.412	.618
Clements, Jason, L.E. †	55	198	174	28	52	77	7	3	4	31	3	0	2	19	0	30	2	2	3	.299	.374	.443
Collins, Chris, Inland Empire	70	229	199	16	56	71	12	0	1	29	3	4	3	20	1	24	0	1	5	.281	.350	.357
Conway, Dan, Visalia	86	351	319	42	93	131	17	3	5	43	0	1	8	23	1	59	1	2	9	.292	.353	.411
Corbeil, Azarias, R.C. *	76	265	244	22	62	84	13	0	3	38	1	2	4	14	0	53	0	1	4	.254	.303	.344
Cordido, Julio, San Jose	122	500	464	49	123	166	20	7	3	43	5	6	5	20	1	75	6	5	9	.265	.299	.358
Cortez, Fernando, Bak. *	102	438	384	53	108	130	19	0	1	53	2	9	2	41	2	61	32	9	7	.281	.346	.339
Coulie, Jason, R.C.	38	161	148	22	36	52	11	1	1	13	0	0	1	12	1	32	3	5	2	.243	.304	.351
Craig, Beau, Modesto †	4	17	16	4	6	8	2	0	0	1	0	0	0	1	0	5	0	0	0	.375	.412	.500
De Paula, Luis, Bakersfield	119	456	419	50	108	137	20	0	3	46	7	3	4	23	0	99	9	8	6	.258	.301	.327
Deck, Ronnie, Bakersfield	5	10	9	1	2	2	0	0	0	0	0	0	0	1	0	2	1	0	0	.222	.300	.222
Del Chiaro, Brent, R.C.	7	27	22	2	5	5	0	0	0	3	0	0	2	3	0	9	0	0	0	.227	.370	.227
Delgado, Gabriel, Stockton †	41	171	144	13	44	52	8	0	0	18	10	2	0	15	0	17	8	7	5	.306	.366	.361

Player, Team	G	TPA	AB	R	H	TB	2B	3B	HR	RBI	SH	SF	HP	BB	IBB	SO	SB	CS	GDP	Avg.	OBP	Slg.
Delucchi, Dustin, In. E. *	77	361	312	61	102	140	19	5	3	32	7	1	3	36	3	35	15	2	6	.327	.401	.449
DiRosa, Michael, Lancaster	77	295	257	22	58	93	17	0	6	37	1	3	4	30	1	85	0	2	5	.226	.313	.362
Dill, Jason, Stockton *	87	335	286	34	74	107	11	2	6	35	1	3	0	45	0	80	3	0	2	.259	.356	.374
Duenas, Tommy, R.C.	5	16	14	0	1	1	0	0	0	1	1	0	0	1	0	6	0	0	0	.071	.133	.071
Eldridge, Rashad, Stockton †	130	531	462	74	133	189	23	6	7	69	6	5	2	56	1	110	20	9	7	.288	.364	.409
Ernster, Mark, High Desert	46	185	163	28	47	69	12	2	2	29	1	5	1	14	2	31	6	1	2	.288	.339	.423
Esposito, Brian, R.C.	9	33	32	2	11	13	2	0	0	2	1	0	0	0	0	5	0	0	1	.344	.344	.406
Eylward, Mike, R.C.	109	435	389	51	113	183	27	2	13	61	1	4	6	35	1	67	1	4	6	.290	.355	.470
Firlit, Dan, Lancaster	21	79	69	5	15	21	1	1	1	10	3	1	2	4	0	15	1	0	1	.217	.276	.304
Florence, Branden, San Jose	101	429	405	46	119	180	26	7	7	58	0	5	7	12	0	34	8	3	10	.294	.322	.444
Foster, Brian, High Desert	88	323	294	47	56	125	12	3	17	46	2	2	5	20	0	108	2	2	6	.190	.252	.425
Frome, Jason, Visalia *	35	138	126	18	29	45	8	1	2	16	0	3	0	9	0	47	1	2	2	.230	.275	.357
Frost, Jeremy, High Desert	55	217	195	27	47	91	14	0	10	35	2	7	1	12	0	58	2	1	4	.241	.279	.467
Fuller, Casey, Visalia *	1	3	3	0	0	0	0	0	0	0	0	0	0	0	0	3	0	0	0	.000	.000	.000
Fulse, Sheldon, In. E. †	49	188	157	19	44	64	10	2	2	14	1	0	4	26	0	35	16	5	3	.280	.396	.408
Furmaniak, J.J., L.E.	78	358	309	65	97	162	22	8	9	54	3	2	8	36	1	55	10	4	5	.314	.397	.524
Garcia, Isaac, Modesto	84	338	307	36	74	98	10	1	4	41	2	5	0	24	1	80	3	1	6	.241	.292	.319
Garthwaite, Jay, Lancaster	113	479	437	82	130	233	33	2	22	87	1	3	8	30	0	97	3	5	6	.297	.351	.533
Gates, David, R.C.	75	287	264	35	62	111	17	1	10	42	1	2	3	17	1	78	3	3	3	.235	.287	.420
Gathright, Joey, Bakersfield *	89	389	340	65	110	122	6	3	0	23	2	0	6	41	0	54	57	13	3	.324	.406	.359
Gerber, Joseph, L.E. *	76	319	284	47	79	134	20	1	11	56	0	2	6	27	1	81	0	2	7	.278	.351	.472
Glaus, Troy, R.C.	2	9	6	1	2	2	0	0	0	1	0	0	0	3	0	2	0	0	0	.333	.556	.333
Gomes, Joey, Bakersfield	105	452	401	67	108	165	26	2	9	55	0	1	9	41	1	88	2	4	9	.269	.350	.411
Gonzalez, Edgar, Bakersfield	100	405	349	51	104	162	34	3	6	62	1	5	5	45	0	82	8	7	7	.298	.381	.464
Gorman, Jason, Lancaster	42	146	125	19	29	48	6	2	3	18	1	2	2	16	0	34	0	1	4	.232	.324	.384
Gorneault, Nick, R.C.	97	400	374	67	120	202	36	2	14	72	0	1	5	20	3	82	11	6	3	.321	.363	.540
Guerrero, Cristian, H.D.-In. E.	86	337	311	55	87	138	10	7	9	40	0	2	4	20	2	62	12	7	9	.280	.329	.444
Gulledge, Kelley, Stockton	26	106	97	15	27	44	6	1	3	14	1	0	3	5	0	22	1	0	2	.278	.333	.454
Guzman, Freddy, L.E. †	70	326	281	64	80	104	12	3	2	22	1	2	2	40	1	60	49	10	1	.285	.375	.370
Harriman, David, Modesto	33	131	119	14	29	38	3	0	2	12	5	1	0	6	1	26	0	0	3	.244	.278	.319
Hastings, Joseph, L.E. *	79	292	267	34	63	103	16	0	8	51	0	4	4	17	0	69	1	1	6	.236	.288	.386
Heard, Scott, Stockton *	79	312	267	30	65	87	10	0	4	28	0	4	1	40	0	56	1	2	4	.243	.340	.326
Heath, Matt, Lancaster †	12	48	43	6	7	13	3	0	1	3	0	0	1	4	0	14	1	0	0	.163	.250	.302
Holst, Micah, San Jose	99	409	366	58	98	127	24	1	1	32	2	4	17	20	0	51	17	5	11	.268	.332	.347
Isenia, Chairon, Bakersfield	24	108	92	16	25	40	9	0	2	11	1	2	4	9	0	19	0	0	4	.272	.355	.435
Jacobo, Kervin, L.E. †	4	17	16	2	5	7	2	0	0	0	0	0	0	1	0	2	0	0	0	.313	.353	.438
Jacobs, Greg, In. E. *	95	401	347	67	124	200	35	7	9	64	1	4	7	42	4	43	4	5	5	.357	.433	.576
Johnson, Ben, Lake Elsinore	52	210	184	30	49	82	9	0	8	29	1	0	5	20	0	49	6	1	5	.266	.354	.446
Johnson, Bryan, Lancaster †	35	90	78	7	17	21	4	0	0	7	1	1	1	9	0	16	0	0	2	.218	.303	.269
Johnson, Kade, High Desert	32	146	134	28	43	83	11	1	9	31	1	0	5	6	0	28	3	0	7	.321	.372	.619
Johnson, Michael, L.E. *	46	198	178	22	49	83	17	1	5	24	0	1	2	17	0	48	0	1	3	.275	.343	.466
Jones, Jaime, Lancaster *	97	396	351	62	101	156	15	2	12	53	0	5	6	34	1	62	4	3	3	.288	.356	.444
Jones, Kennard, L.E. *	17	81	76	16	19	26	3	2	0	5	1	0	0	4	0	11	3	2	4	.250	.288	.342
Kelly, Heath, Bakersfield	31	127	118	12	19	26	1	0	2	10	2	1	4	2	0	47	0	0	2	.161	.200	.220
Kennedy, Adam, R.C. *	3	12	11	3	3	7	1	0	1	1	0	0	1	0	0	2	0	0	0	.273	.333	.636
Kiger, Mark, Modesto	131	614	526	95	148	216	38	3	8	73	3	4	4	77	0	106	3	0	17	.281	.375	.411
Kimpton, Nick, R.C. *	109	384	342	27	78	93	8	2	1	18	9	1	3	29	0	63	20	7	6	.228	.293	.272
Knoedler, Justin, San Jose	101	399	354	48	91	150	25	2	10	43	2	4	3	35	0	78	13	3	5	.257	.326	.424
Knowlton, Jay, San Jose	24	96	83	10	22	31	6	0	1	8	0	0	6	7	0	18	2	0	1	.265	.365	.373
Kotchman, Casey, R.C. *	57	245	206	42	72	108	12	0	8	28	0	3	6	30	5	16	2	0	4	.350	.441	.524
Kroeger, Josh, Lancaster *	78	345	305	50	104	161	30	6	5	55	0	3	2	35	4	58	6	6	9	.341	.409	.528
Lambert, Casey, Visalia	1	4	4	0	1	1	0	0	0	0	0	0	0	0	0	0	0	0	1	.250	.250	.250
Lima, Joseph, Lake Elsinore	17	50	46	6	10	12	2	0	0	1	1	0	1	2	0	19	1	0	3	.217	.265	.261
Lincoln, Justin, Visalia	121	483	428	47	96	161	22	5	11	59	1	7	11	36	2	151	0	3	7	.224	.297	.376
Lozada, Charlie, High Desert	7	31	27	3	10	11	1	0	0	4	1	0	0	3	0	6	1	0	0	.370	.433	.407
Lunsford, Trey, San Jose	2	7	7	1	2	5	0	0	1	1	0	0	0	0	0	4	0	0	0	.286	.286	.714
Macha, Erick, Lancaster	16	33	31	7	8	11	3	0	0	3	0	0	0	2	0	6	1	0	0	.258	.303	.355
Maduro, Jorge, Bakersfield	11	36	36	3	8	12	1	0	1	2	0	0	0	0	0	10	0	0	1	.222	.222	.333
Mann, Derek, R.C. *	11	41	39	5	11	12	1	0	0	3	1	0	0	1	0	4	0	1	0	.282	.300	.308
Martin, Brian, Bakersfield	129	531	478	73	132	199	26	4	11	65	1	3	14	35	1	147	19	3	5	.276	.342	.416
Mateo, Luis, Bakersfield	107	412	400	45	112	171	26	0	11	46	1	0	3	8	0	130	1	3	9	.280	.299	.428
Mathis, Jeff, R.C.	97	422	378	73	122	189	28	3	11	54	0	4	5	35	0	74	5	3	4	.323	.384	.500
McAndrews, Travis, Lan.*	37	107	96	12	24	30	3	0	1	11	4	0	1	6	0	18	1	0	0	.250	.301	.313
McBeth, Marcus, Modesto	15	62	54	7	7	7	0	0	0	5	0	2	1	5	0	20	2	0	4	.130	.210	.130
McMains, Derin, San Jose †	25	120	109	14	27	34	2	1	1	12	1	1	2	7	0	8	3	2	0	.248	.303	.312
McPherson, Dallas, R.C. *	77	339	292	65	90	177	21	6	18	59	0	0	6	41	2	79	12	6	4	.308	.404	.606
Melgarejo, Ransel, R.C.	29	126	111	15	29	37	3	1	1	10	2	1	1	11	0	14	4	2	1	.261	.331	.333
Menchaca, Eriberto, In. E.	116	368	331	28	76	88	8	2	0	33	10	7	4	16	0	60	3	1	12	.230	.268	.266
Merloni, Lou, Lake Elsinore	5	21	19	3	9	15	3	0	1	7	0	1	0	1	0	0	0	0	0	.474	.476	.789
Merritt, Graig, Bakersfield	24	86	78	4	17	20	3	0	0	7	3	1	0	4	0	12	0	1	1	.218	.253	.256
Merritt, Tim, Inland Empire	11	41	37	4	3	3	0	0	0	3	0	0	0	4	0	13	1	0	2	.081	.171	.081
Meyer, Drew, Stockton *	94	446	398	59	112	161	16	9	5	53	9	7	0	32	1	92	24	10	6	.281	.330	.405
Miller, Tony, Visalia	67	316	266	47	66	102	14	5	4	31	4	3	3	40	0	58	11	7	6	.248	.349	.383
Mirizzi, Marc, Stockton †	29	129	114	17	35	56	7	1	4	18	0	0	1	14	0	17	2	0	1	.307	.388	.491
Moore, Jason, Stockton †	67	263	221	32	43	59	11	1	1	18	4	2	2	34	0	52	4	1	4	.195	.305	.267
Morris, Chris, High Desert †	128	558	486	81	129	169	26	4	2	52	8	3	6	55	0	107	67	18	2	.265	.345	.348
Morris, Jed, Modesto *	101	423	367	57	103	170	26	1	13	75	0	4	5	47	1	58	1	0	13	.281	.366	.463
Murphy, Tommy, R.C.	132	614	565	74	151	221	25	6	11	43	7	3	8	31	0	138	24	12	7	.267	.313	.391
Myers, Casey, Modesto	45	191	166	21	50	58	5	0	1	25	2	2	5	16	0	18	0	0	8	.301	.376	.349
Napoli, Michael, R.C.	47	195	165	28	44	68	10	1	4	26	0	3	4	23	1	32	5	0	3	.267	.364	.412
Neal, Steve, Lancaster *	12	48	40	2	12	16	4	0	0	8	0	0	0	8	0	11	0	0	1	.300	.417	.400

Player, Team	G	TPA	AB	R	H	TB	2B	3B	HR	RBI	SH	SF	HP	BB	IBB	SO	SB	CS	GDP	Avg.	OBP	Slg.
Nelson, Brad, High Desert *	41	182	167	23	52	66	9	1	1	18	0	1	2	12	0	22	2	2	3	.311	.363	.395
Nettles, Marcus, L.E. *	120	495	423	71	98	124	9	7	1	30	12	2	7	50	0	122	32	10	4	.232	.322	.293
Neufeld, Andy, Modesto *	63	263	218	38	51	78	13	1	4	30	5	4	6	30	0	50	4	1	6	.234	.337	.358
Nevin, Phil, Lake Elsinore	5	20	15	1	4	5	1	0	0	5	0	3	0	2	0	2	0	0	1	.267	.300	.333
Nichols, Kyle, Lancaster	130	547	484	82	151	278	34	0	31	108	0	7	5	51	6	118	0	0	13	.312	.378	.574
Nix, Jayson, Visalia	137	635	562	107	158	267	46	0	21	86	3	6	10	54	2	131	24	8	3	.281	.351	.475
Oliveros, Luis, Inland Empire	93	353	322	43	92	126	19	0	5	41	2	4	7	18	1	24	2	3	13	.286	.333	.391
Ortmeier, Daniel, San Jose †	115	460	408	62	124	192	32	6	8	56	0	2	11	39	4	89	13	6	13	.304	.378	.471
Ozuna, Pablo, Visalia	2	9	8	1	5	5	0	0	0	1	0	0	0	1	0	1	1	1	0	.625	.667	.625
Pack, Branden, Stockton †	45	168	148	14	32	48	6	2	2	18	2	1	0	17	1	44	1	2	1	.216	.295	.324
Pagan, Carlos, Inland Empire	6	19	18	5	4	9	2	0	1	4	0	0	0	1	0	4	0	0	0	.222	.263	.500
Pecci, Jay, Inland Empire †	10	42	37	4	11	12	1	0	0	4	0	0	1	4	0	0	0	0	1	.297	.381	.324
Peck, Bryan, Visalia	35	144	116	15	30	47	9	1	2	24	0	4	2	22	1	24	3	0	0	.259	.375	.405
Perry, Jason, Modesto *	50	219	190	28	58	81	9	1	4	26	0	1	7	21	0	46	0	1	5	.305	.393	.426
Phillips, Dan, Visalia	119	525	484	68	127	219	32	3	18	73	2	6	13	20	0	115	13	8	9	.262	.306	.452
Pichardo, Maximo, R.C.	34	103	94	11	21	26	5	0	0	6	0	0	1	8	0	11	2	1	3	.223	.291	.277
Pohle, Richard, In. E. *	48	168	148	15	38	55	15	1	0	19	0	3	3	14	0	20	2	1	5	.257	.327	.372
Quero, Pedro, Stockton	41	175	168	19	44	57	6	2	1	15	0	1	0	6	0	26	7	1	8	.262	.286	.339
Quintanilla, Omar, Modesto *	8	39	36	9	15	24	3	0	2	6	0	0	0	3	0	6	0	0	1	.417	.462	.667
Quintero, Cesar, In. E.	3	10	10	3	3	3	0	0	0	1	0	0	0	0	0	2	0	0	0	.300	.300	.300
Raburn, Johnny, H.D. †	121	513	448	68	129	153	12	6	0	42	5	2	0	58	0	71	26	12	2	.288	.368	.342
Raymundo, G.J., Stockton	103	461	396	64	120	179	34	5	5	67	3	10	7	44	5	68	3	3	9	.303	.374	.452
Reece, Eric, Bakersfield *	90	351	324	44	90	163	22	3	15	52	0	2	1	24	1	75	1	0	7	.278	.328	.503
Reinking, Kevin, L.E.	18	68	57	7	11	18	4	0	1	10	0	1	4	6	1	20	0	0	0	.193	.309	.316
Richar, Danny, Lancaster	123	433	405	51	123	163	19	9	1	42	10	1	3	14	0	70	6	3	10	.304	.331	.402
Richardson, Mike, L.E.	71	244	206	27	50	85	14	3	5	29	1	2	1	34	0	60	1	0	5	.243	.350	.413
Riera, Zack, R.C. †	3	12	10	1	0	0	0	0	0	0	0	0	1	1	0	4	0	0	0	.000	.167	.000
Riley, Ryan, Bakersfield	24	91	82	10	21	24	3	0	0	9	1	0	1	7	0	15	2	0	3	.256	.322	.293
Rodriguez, Javy, R.C.	32	128	122	17	32	45	5	1	2	6	1	0	0	5	0	21	6	4	1	.262	.291	.369
Rogelstad, Matt, In. E. *	9	38	38	8	15	21	4	1	0	1	0	0	0	0	0	0	2	1	0	.395	.395	.553
Roper, Zach, Stockton	111	464	412	55	105	158	32	0	7	68	1	4	7	40	1	101	3	2	12	.255	.328	.383
Rosario, Melvin, Visalia *	97	380	338	36	79	98	13	3	0	24	8	4	2	28	0	87	7	7	3	.234	.293	.290
Saenz, Olmedo, Modesto	1	5	4	0	0	0	0	0	0	1	0	0	1	0	0	1	0	0	0	.000	.200	.000
Sain, Greg, Lake Elsinore	123	529	467	74	128	220	35	0	19	100	0	12	7	43	1	119	3	1	9	.274	.336	.471
Salas, Juan, Bakersfield	37	148	137	26	44	70	6	1	6	30	0	1	3	7	0	30	1	0	3	.321	.365	.511
Salazar, Jeff, Visalia *	1	5	5	1	0	0	0	0	0	0	0	0	0	0	0	0	0	0	0	.000	.000	.000
Sandel, George, In. E. *	3	8	7	1	2	2	0	0	0	2	0	0	0	1	0	0	0	0	1	.286	.375	.286
Santana, Mayobanex, Lan.	54	180	162	30	45	59	9	1	1	18	1	0	1	16	0	25	0	0	7	.278	.346	.364
Santana, Ralph, H.D. *	112	466	419	60	120	145	11	4	2	41	13	1	4	29	0	58	42	16	2	.286	.338	.346
Santora, Jack, L.E. †	47	209	174	38	56	73	10	2	1	11	4	0	3	28	0	24	10	0	1	.322	.424	.420
Santos, Sergio, Lancaster	93	392	341	55	98	139	13	2	8	49	3	3	4	41	0	64	5	4	7	.287	.368	.408
Schneidmiller, Gary, Modesto	60	236	205	31	52	71	14	1	1	25	1	3	3	24	0	38	4	0	11	.254	.336	.346
Serrano, Eddie, Lake Elsinore	5	16	14	3	2	2	0	0	0	0	0	0	0	2	0	5	0	0	0	.143	.250	.143
Shealy, Ryan, Visalia	93	404	341	70	102	177	31	1	14	73	0	7	14	42	0	72	0	0	5	.299	.391	.519
Sinisi, Vincent, Stockton *	14	67	62	9	16	20	1	0	1	5	1	1	0	3	0	8	1	1	0	.258	.288	.323
Slavik, Corey, Visalia *	109	449	392	66	126	197	27	1	14	75	0	8	9	40	0	67	1	5	5	.321	.390	.503
Smith, Casey, R.C.	37	147	130	12	37	48	2	0	3	15	4	0	3	10	0	11	1	2	2	.285	.350	.369
Smith, Dustin, Stockton	41	154	129	17	39	51	9	0	1	18	2	3	5	15	0	21	1	1	7	.302	.388	.395
Snyder, Chris, Lancaster	69	290	245	53	77	127	16	2	10	53	0	2	8	35	2	43	0	1	4	.314	.414	.518
Sobieraj, Aaron, San Jose	17	74	64	10	14	21	4	0	1	5	1	0	1	8	0	13	1	0	1	.219	.315	.328
Soler, Ramon, San Jose †	46	191	164	24	46	60	4	2	2	13	7	1	5	14	0	35	15	6	0	.280	.353	.366
Soto, Jorge, Modesto	35	132	116	12	17	30	4	0	3	8	1	1	3	11	0	56	0	0	0	.147	.237	.259
Soules, Ryan, Stockton *	25	111	101	15	28	47	7	0	4	18	0	0	1	9	0	23	0	0	2	.277	.342	.465
Stanek, Jeff, Lancaster *	20	64	56	8	13	19	6	0	0	2	1	0	0	7	0	21	0	0	0	.232	.317	.339
Stonard, Peter, L.E. *	1	5	5	1	1	1	0	0	0	1	0	0	0	0	0	2	0	0	0	.200	.200	.200
Stotts, J.T., Modesto	75	335	292	34	83	107	16	1	2	37	4	2	6	31	0	37	11	4	6	.284	.363	.366
Stringfellow, Christopher, Sto.	116	478	416	59	121	151	15	3	3	46	3	3	2	54	0	72	9	7	6	.291	.373	.363
Strong, Zach, San Jose †	115	436	361	40	87	120	22	1	3	35	4	1	2	68	0	91	1	6	2	.241	.363	.332
Sullivan, Kevin, Visalia	4	12	12	1	4	7	0	0	1	2	0	0	0	0	0	1	0	0	0	.333	.333	.583
Swisher, Nick, Modesto †	51	237	189	38	56	104	14	2	10	43	0	5	2	41	1	49	0	2	4	.296	.418	.550
Teahen, Mark, Modesto *	121	530	453	68	128	172	27	4	3	71	0	5	6	66	1	113	4	0	19	.283	.377	.380
Tena, Hector, Visalia	84	328	298	32	63	80	12	1	1	16	8	2	4	16	0	55	4	2	12	.211	.259	.268
Thiessen, Mike, Lancaster	85	321	281	42	78	111	10	4	5	29	3	2	2	33	0	55	11	5	3	.278	.355	.395
Thomas, Gary, Modesto	117	566	498	95	151	223	30	3	12	68	4	5	18	41	0	83	22	7	6	.303	.374	.448
Toner, John, High Desert	20	83	78	9	17	32	5	2	2	9	0	0	0	5	0	18	4	0	4	.218	.265	.410
Tritle, Chris, Modesto	42	171	153	16	31	46	6	0	3	16	1	3	3	11	0	47	2	0	7	.203	.265	.301
Trumble, Dan, San Jose	97	334	296	45	61	136	12	0	21	43	1	1	5	31	0	120	3	6	5	.206	.291	.459
Trzesniak, Nick, Lake Elsinore	109	438	375	59	92	126	10	0	8	45	3	4	7	49	0	88	17	4	10	.245	.340	.336
Turco, Anthony, San Jose *	24	60	57	3	11	12	1	0	0	2	0	0	0	3	0	21	0	0	1	.193	.233	.211
Turner, Justin, R.C. *	106	421	384	46	100	159	17	9	8	55	5	3	1	28	0	111	2	7	3	.260	.310	.414
Turner, Lloyd, Modesto	30	122	104	20	24	26	2	0	0	5	1	0	5	12	0	9	0	1	2	.231	.339	.250
Uggla, Dan, Lancaster	134	609	534	104	155	269	31	7	23	90	11	6	11	46	0	105	24	9	7	.290	.355	.504
Uribe, Juan, Visalia	2	10	9	4	5	6	1	0	0	1	0	0	0	1	0	0	0	0	1	.556	.600	.667
Van Meetren, Jason, In. E.	100	340	290	40	70	94	14	2	2	32	2	3	7	38	0	74	9	4	10	.241	.340	.324
Varela, Edgar, Lancaster *	40	153	143	16	34	48	4	2	2	16	1	1	4	4	0	19	0	1	5	.238	.276	.336
Vazquez, Ramon, L.E. *	5	20	16	3	3	6	0	0	1	4	0	0	1	3	0	3	0	1	1	.188	.350	.375
Villanueva, Froilan, H.D.	112	471	439	46	129	190	23	4	10	76	2	4	11	15	1	66	4	3	5	.294	.330	.433
Von Schell, Tyler, San Jose	70	284	268	29	65	112	17	0	10	46	1	5	1	9	0	63	0	0	7	.243	.265	.418
Weber, Jon, Modesto *	35	165	147	28	53	92	10	4	7	38	0	6	3	9	0	26	2	0	1	.361	.394	.626
Wells, Carlton, Lancaster *	46	1	1	0	0	0	0	0	0	0	0	0	0	0	0	0	0	0	0	.000	.000	.000
West, Todd, High Desert	109	432	389	47	93	118	21	2	0	41	7	7	1	28	1	62	13	7	4	.239	.287	.303

Player, Team	G	TPA	AB	R	H	TB	2B	3B	HR	RBI	SH	SF	HP	BB	IBB	SO	SB	CS	GDP	Avg.	OBP	Slg.
Wilkins, Joe, Lancaster †	16	56	46	5	11	13	2	0	0	5	2	1	0	7	0	14	0	1	1	.239	.333	.283
Williams, Brady, Bakersfield	5	9	9	0	2	2	0	0	0	1	0	0	0	0	0	5	0	0	0	.222	.222	.222
Williams, Marland, Lancaster	102	475	425	85	122	151	15	1	4	30	10	4	5	31	0	99	57	7	4	.287	.340	.355
Williamson, John, In. E. †	22	69	57	7	13	20	2	1	1	9	0	1	0	11	1	14	0	1	3	.228	.348	.351
Willingham, Phil, In. E. *	11	31	28	3	6	9	0	0	1	3	0	0	0	3	0	9	1	0	0	.214	.290	.321
Wilson, Andy, Lancaster	3	8	8	3	3	5	2	0	0	2	0	0	0	0	0	1	1	0	0	.375	.375	.625
Winchester, Jeff, Visalia	83	330	302	33	76	118	18	0	8	37	1	3	10	14	0	51	1	3	7	.252	.304	.391

PLAYERS WITH TWO OR MORE TEAMS

Player, Team	G	TPA	AB	R	H	TB	2B	3B	HR	RBI	SH	SF	HP	BB	IBB	SO	SB	CS	GDP	Avg.	OBP	Slg.
Guerrero, Cristian, In.E.	83	324	299	52	83	131	9	6	9	38	0	2	4	19	2	58	12	7	8	.278	.327	.438
Guerrero, Cristian, H.D.	3	13	12	3	4	7	1	1	0	2	0	0	0	1	0	4	0	0	1	.333	.385	.583

GRAND SLAMS—B. Carter, Gorneault, 2 each; Asadoorian, Belcher, Botts, Bourgeois, Bowser, Frost, Garcia, Lincoln, Martin, Mateo, Napoli, Neufeld, Nichols, Raymundo, Sain, M. Santana, Snyder, Uggla, Varela, Von Schell, Winchester, 1 each.

AWARDED FIRST BASE ON CATCHER'S INTERFERENCE—Delucchi 2 (Alvarado, Trzesniak); Arhart (Heard); Barker (Knoedler); Brown (Del Chiaro); J. Carter (Knoedler); Ernster (Heard); Knoedler (Heath); Nettles (Alvarado); Raymundo (Anderson); Uggla (Collins).

2003 PITCHING

TEAM

Team	W	L	Pct.	ERA	G	CG	ShO	Sv.	IP	H	TBF	R	ER	HR	SH	SF	HB	BB	IBB	SO	WP	Bk.
Inland Empire	78	62	.557	3.77	140	2	8	39	1229.2	1140	5212	583	515	88	45	39	75	396	13	1180	56	12
Stockton	77	63	.550	3.99	140	0	5	37	1241.1	1229	5445	684	551	93	30	62	99	480	6	1022	80	10
Visalia	79	61	.564	4.04	140	6	11	31	1231.0	1280	5329	628	553	84	32	40	84	410	10	1021	58	13
Bakersfield	70	70	.500	4.06	140	4	9	32	1216.1	1329	5357	665	549	100	41	31	79	404	1	957	77	10
Modesto	74	66	.529	4.22	140	4	4	33	1243.1	1312	5503	720	583	89	36	49	69	458	10	1067	75	12
Lake Elsinore	75	65	.536	4.35	140	2	3	32	1232.2	1375	5424	714	596	67	38	49	46	389	19	889	73	8
Rancho Cuca.	74	66	.529	4.49	140	6	7	42	1233.2	1287	5425	736	616	112	41	53	69	469	4	951	113	8
San Jose	58	82	.414	4.68	140	3	7	29	1216.1	1304	5443	740	633	93	41	47	78	498	11	1070	74	10
Lancaster	73	67	.521	4.69	140	4	0	38	1254.0	1427	5615	777	654	118	42	46	72	492	16	904	84	9
High Desert	42	98	.300	6.34	140	2	2	28	1226.0	1491	5687	959	864	168	33	63	86	556	5	1038	92	13

INDIVIDUAL

TOP QUALIFIERS FOR EARNED-RUN AVERAGE TITLE

Minimum 112 innings. *Lefthanded pitcher.

Pitcher, Team	W	L	Pct.	ERA	G	GS	CG	ShO	GF	Sv.	IP	H	TBF	R	ER	HR	SH	SF	HB	BB	IBB	SO	WP	Bk.
Santana, Ervin, Rancho Cuca.	10	2	.833	2.53	20	20	1	0	0	0	124.2	98	510	44	35	9	3	1	7	36	0	130	14	0
Weis, Brad, Modesto *	15	7	.682	2.82	30	24	3	0	1	0	159.2	132	670	66	50	3	2	5	15	60	1	145	5	2
Bott, Glenn, Inland Empire *	7	7	.500	3.16	31	21	0	0	4	1	142.1	131	591	55	50	8	2	4	3	38	1	143	6	1
Ketchner, Ryan, In. Emp.*	14	7	.667	3.45	31	22	2	2	3	1	156.2	133	628	63	60	10	3	4	4	33	0	159	6	0
Thomas, J.T., San Jose *	5	12	.294	3.45	33	19	0	0	8	3	125.1	134	555	64	48	6	6	5	5	35	1	104	6	2
Francis, Jeff, Visalia *	12	9	.571	3.47	27	27	2	2	0	0	160.2	135	648	66	62	8	4	5	5	45	1	153	6	0
Andrew, Jason, Stockton	8	7	.533	3.51	31	15	0	0	4	1	118.0	127	508	66	46	9	1	8	8	31	0	94	4	0
Pavon, Julio, San Jose	5	4	.556	3.54	41	8	0	0	14	2	112.0	106	456	48	44	7	4	0	1	26	1	103	9	1
Hampson, Justin, Visalia *	14	7	.667	3.68	26	26	1	0	0	0	159.0	153	684	73	65	12	3	3	21	51	1	150	2	2
Esposito, Michael, Visalia	12	6	.667	3.75	27	27	1	0	0	0	161.0	173	697	83	67	14	5	7	5	55	0	116	10	2
Woods, Jake, Rancho Cuca.*	12	7	.632	3.99	28	28	2	1	0	0	171.1	178	737	90	76	9	7	8	8	54	0	109	2	2
Matthews, Jarod, Bakersfield	8	7	.533	4.02	23	21	1	0	0	0	121.0	131	526	62	54	12	2	2	9	27	0	109	5	0
Cate, Troy, Inland Empire *	9	11	.450	4.11	27	25	0	0	0	0	160.0	165	680	79	73	10	6	3	10	37	1	153	7	2
Treadway, Brion, San Jose	8	7	.533	4.11	29	22	0	0	4	2	133.2	136	580	66	61	14	3	5	11	53	0	100	7	2
Shell, Steven, Rancho Cuca.	6	8	.429	4.24	22	21	1	1	0	0	127.1	123	540	66	60	13	4	3	12	26	0	100	3	1

DEPARTMENTAL LEADERS: W—Weis, 15; L—Barnett, Hall, 14; Pct.—Santana, .883; G—Cassel, 64; GS—Woods, 28; CG—Weis, 3; ShO—Francis, Ketchner, 2; GF—Speier, 43; Sv.—Sikaras, 23; IP—Woods, 171.1; H—Kolb, 194; TBF—Woods, 737; R—Kolb, 118; ER—Kolb, 107; HR—Kolb, 24; SH—McMachen, 9; SF—Abraham, Barnett, 9; HB—Hampson, 21; BB—Wechsler, 64; IBB—Fruto, 5; SO—Ketchner, 159; WP—Bruksch, 19; BK—Shields, Simpson, Webb, 3.

ALL PITCHERS

*Lefthanded pitcher.

Pitcher, Team	W	L	Pct.	ERA	G	GS	CG	ShO	GF	Sv.	IP	H	TBF	R	ER	HR	SH	SF	HB	BB	IBB	SO	WP	Bk.
Aardsma, David, San Jose	1	1	.500	1.96	18	0	0	0	12	8	18.1	14	74	4	4	2	1	0	0	7	0	28	0	0
Abraham, Paul, Stockton	6	1	.857	4.06	47	0	0	0	24	2	57.2	60	260	33	26	4	1	9	1	33	1	41	9	0
Alvarez, Tim, San Jose *	0	2	.000	7.36	8	0	0	0	5	0	11.0	13	54	9	9	2	1	0	4	6	1	7	2	0
Andersen, Derek, Bak. *	1	1	.500	2.82	17	0	0	0	8	1	22.1	18	88	7	7	1	2	2	1	5	0	13	1	0
Anderson, Keith, San Jose	0	0	.000	3.86	4	0	0	0	4	0	4.2	6	22	2	2	1	0	0	0	0	0	4	0	0
Andrade, Stephen, R.C.	0	0	.000	0.00	3	0	0	0	2	1	3.0	0	13	0	0	0	0	0	1	3	0	7	2	0
Andrew, Jason, Stockton	8	7	.533	3.51	31	15	0	0	4	1	118.0	127	508	66	46	9	1	8	8	31	0	94	4	0
Avendano, Elvis, Modesto	2	2	.500	5.19	6	3	0	0	2	0	26.0	37	130	25	15	6	0	2	2	9	0	20	1	0
Backsmeyer, Justin, H.D.	1	9	.100	6.33	40	0	0	0	20	4	69.2	77	315	52	49	12	2	7	6	24	0	55	3	0
Baek, Cha-Sueng, Inland Emp.	5	1	.833	3.65	13	10	0	0	2	1	56.2	55	236	27	23	3	4	0	2	9	0	50	1	1
Baker, Brad, Lake Elsinore	3	0	1.000	2.01	27	4	0	0	21	12	44.2	31	182	13	10	2	1	0	1	14	1	69	8	0
Barber, Scott, Lancaster	10	7	.588	5.31	23	23	0	0	0	0	134.0	165	592	86	79	19	7	2	6	39	1	89	5	1
Barnett, John, Stockton	4	14	.222	4.95	34	18	0	0	6	4	123.2	149	567	82	68	12	8	9	8	36	1	102	3	2
Bazzell, Shane, Modesto	1	0	1.000	2.79	9	0	0	0	7	1	19.1	17	80	7	6	0	1	0	0	4	1	23	1	0
Beavers, Kevin, L.E. *	4	3	.571	3.66	42	2	0	0	10	0	64.0	74	282	32	26	3	2	4	0	21	3	42	3	0
Begg, Chris, San Jose	4	1	.800	1.15	7	5	1	1	0	0	39.0	30	145	5	5	3	0	0	0	4	0	21	1	0
Bengochea, Kiki, Stockton	10	8	.556	5.51	34	18	0	0	6	1	119.1	127	544	84	73	14	2	8	9	60	0	94	5	0
Biggs, Billy, Lancaster	2	5	.286	3.73	54	0	0	0	25	8	60.1	57	265	38	25	5	3	3	4	28	3	46	6	0
Bilke, Austin, R.C.	2	1	.667	7.25	14	0	0	0	2	0	22.1	35	112	22	18	3	2	4	0	10	0	16	2	0
Bittner, Tim, R.C. *	5	0	1.000	0.28	6	6	1	1	0	0	32.2	18	128	5	1	0	0	1	1	14	0	28	0	1

Pitcher, Team	W	L	Pct.	ERA	G	GS	CG	ShO	GF	Sv.	IP	H	TBF	R	ER	HR	SH	SF	HB	BB	IBB	SO	WP	Bk.
Blood, Justin, Inland Empire *	5	2	.714	3.07	50	0	0	0	18	2	58.2	48	256	20	20	2	2	1	6	27	0	77	4	0
Bott, Glenn, Inland Empire *	7	7	.500	3.16	31	21	0	0	4	1	142.1	131	591	55	50	8	2	4	3	38	1	143	6	1
Bowie, Micah, Modesto *	0	0	.000	0.00	2	2	0	0	0	0	2.0	0	6	0	0	0	0	0	0	0	0	3	0	0
Brazelton, Dewon, Bakersfield	1	5	.167	5.26	9	9	0	0	0	0	49.2	62	230	33	29	4	0	0	3	19	0	42	4	1
Brown, Elliot, San Jose	2	7	.222	6.53	15	12	0	0	2	1	60.2	84	300	57	44	5	1	4	8	21	1	32	2	1
Bruksch, Jeffrey, Modesto	10	8	.556	5.13	23	23	0	0	0	0	126.1	144	559	84	72	14	1	8	4	54	0	87	19	1
Bruso, Greg, San Jose	7	5	.583	3.11	14	13	1	0	0	0	84.0	69	332	34	29	5	0	4	1	11	0	77	1	0
Buckley, Allen, R.C.	1	0	1.000	6.50	6	4	0	0	0	0	18.0	20	83	13	13	3	0	1	1	7	0	22	3	0
Bukowski, Stan, R.C.	0	0	.000	0.57	6	0	0	0	3	0	15.2	8	60	2	1	0	2	0	1	4	0	9	2	0
Bulger, Jason, Lancaster	2	1	.667	6.75	4	4	0	0	0	0	17.1	23	79	13	13	3	0	0	0	5	0	20	0	0
Bumatay, Mike, Visalia *	0	0	.000	0.00	8	0	0	0	3	2	9.0	1	32	0	0	0	0	0	0	5	0	16	0	0
Bumstead, Mike, L.E.	1	1	.500	5.55	5	5	0	0	0	0	24.1	31	117	19	15	2	1	1	1	13	0	19	0	0
Burres, Brian, San Jose *	3	3	.500	3.86	39	0	0	0	16	1	60.2	55	276	33	26	4	2	4	3	36	3	64	7	0
Bystrowski, Bobby, H.D.	0	4	.000	5.53	48	0	0	0	37	13	53.2	56	239	35	33	6	3	1	5	21	0	41	5	2
Camp, Rusty, R.C.	3	1	.750	8.34	17	0	0	0	6	0	22.2	34	113	25	21	1	1	0	3	14	0	21	8	0
Campbell, Jarrett, Bakersfield	5	4	.556	2.65	32	4	0	0	4	1	78.0	79	333	32	23	6	1	1	4	21	0	64	8	0
Candelaria, Scott, High Desert	0	0	.000	22.50	2	0	0	0	1	0	2.0	7	13	5	5	0	0	0	1	1	0	1	0	0
Cassel, Jack, Lake Elsinore	5	4	.556	3.59	64	0	0	0	22	3	72.2	69	300	34	29	0	4	0	4	18	1	52	7	0
Castellanos, Jonathan, Lan.	7	3	.700	4.63	30	13	1	0	3	0	116.2	138	519	67	60	13	3	5	4	41	2	66	2	0
Cate, Troy, Inland Empire *	9	11	.450	4.11	27	25	0	0	0	0	160.0	165	680	79	73	10	6	3	10	37	1	153	7	2
Christiansen, Jason, S.J.*	0	0	.000	1.93	5	1	0	0	0	0	4.2	5	20	1	1	0	0	1	0	3	0	2	0	0
Clark, Jeff, San Jose	2	2	.500	3.04	9	9	0	0	0	0	53.1	49	220	23	18	4	2	2	2	11	0	43	1	0
Coleman, Jeff, Modesto	2	2	.500	5.00	37	0	0	0	17	5	66.2	72	301	40	37	3	2	0	5	26	0	86	2	0
Coose, Austin, Bakersfield	5	5	.500	3.44	50	0	0	0	13	2	65.1	69	304	30	25	4	5	3	2	41	1	66	7	0
Cormier, Lance, Lancaster	6	5	.545	3.82	15	15	0	0	0	0	94.1	102	390	55	40	6	5	3	2	16	1	59	4	1
Cortez, Renee, Inland Empire	0	1	.000	1.66	15	0	0	0	10	3	21.2	10	83	5	4	0	0	1	1	6	1	16	2	0
Craker, Justin, Lake Elsinore	4	1	.800	5.08	50	0	0	0	7	0	67.1	70	314	41	38	3	4	4	1	45	2	56	4	0
Cram, Josh, San Jose	2	4	.333	3.92	31	0	0	0	13	1	57.1	55	249	30	25	3	3	1	9	27	0	29	3	0
Cramblitt, Joey, Lancaster	0	1	.000	1.98	10	0	0	0	3	0	13.2	14	60	10	3	2	0	0	2	5	0	8	1	0
Cramer, Bob, Bakersfield *	0	0	.000	3.55	5	0	0	0	0	0	12.2	10	52	6	5	1	1	0	0	5	0	10	0	0
Crawford, Chris, Bakersfield *	6	6	.500	4.16	47	0	0	0	15	2	88.2	96	398	53	41	6	5	1	7	36	0	59	5	0
Crockett, Ben, Visalia	2	3	.400	4.50	5	5	0	0	0	0	32.0	35	138	18	16	5	1	2	2	7	0	26	0	0
Crowell, Kyle, Modesto	2	2	.500	1.93	30	0	0	0	12	4	60.2	46	250	16	13	3	4	5	2	19	0	61	3	0
Cullen, Ryan, Modesto *	1	0	1.000	2.83	15	0	0	0	6	3	28.2	21	119	10	9	2	0	2	0	11	1	24	1	0
D'Amico, Leonardo, R.C.	0	1	.000	7.00	6	1	0	0	1	0	9.0	8	39	7	7	3	0	1	1	3	0	5	3	0
Darnell, Paul, Visalia *	1	1	.500	4.63	23	1	0	0	10	1	35.0	40	152	21	18	3	2	0	1	11	0	30	0	0
Dean, Aaron, High Desert	5	5	.500	6.87	38	1	0	0	9	1	90.1	108	436	72	69	10	2	8	3	54	0	82	12	0
Dominguez, Juan, Stockton	4	0	1.000	2.84	16	9	0	0	1	1	63.1	55	266	27	20	3	0	1	6	16	0	72	3	1
Done, Juan, Inland Empire	3	4	.429	4.85	30	11	0	0	5	2	68.2	77	315	50	37	6	3	4	6	31	0	46	3	2
Dorman, Rich, Inland Empire	5	0	1.000	2.65	13	5	0	0	3	1	37.1	29	162	11	11	1	2	3	3	21	0	40	3	0
Dukeman, Greg, Bakersfield	3	4	.429	4.50	28	5	0	0	9	0	76.0	94	341	44	38	5	5	4	4	25	0	47	8	0
Ebert, Derrin, High Desert *	2	1	.667	6.19	3	3	0	0	0	0	16.0	20	68	11	11	4	0	0	2	1	0	11	0	0
Echols, Justin, Stockton	4	6	.400	2.85	25	13	0	0	6	0	98.0	74	417	42	31	4	6	3	5	43	0	98	10	1
Edwards, John, Visalia	0	0	.000	0.00	1	0	0	0	0	0	1.0	1	3	0	0	0	0	0	0	0	0	1	0	0
Ellis, Rob, Bakersfield *	0	0	.000	15.00	2	0	0	0	0	0	3.0	4	17	5	5	0	0	0	0	5	0	0	0	1
Esposito, Michael, Visalia	12	6	.667	3.75	27	27	1	0	0	0	161.0	173	697	83	67	14	5	7	5	55	0	116	10	2
Esslinger, Cam, Visalia	2	1	.667	5.52	11	0	0	0	0	0	14.2	16	65	9	9	0	1	1	0	10	0	13	2	0
Firlit, Dan, Lancaster	0	0	.000	0.00	1	0	0	0	1	0	1.0	2	5	0	0	0	0	0	0	0	0	1	0	0
Fischer, Steve, Modesto	7	5	.583	3.39	24	13	0	0	8	5	98.1	109	428	47	37	5	2	2	5	24	0	73	6	0
Flinn, Chris, Bakersfield	8	6	.571	4.57	24	17	2	0	1	0	100.1	116	452	65	51	8	6	5	6	35	0	79	7	1
Foppert, Jesse, San Jose	0	1	.000	9.00	1	1	0	0	0	0	3.0	5	14	3	3	0	0	1	0	0	0	3	0	0
France, Ryan, Modesto	0	0	.000	18.00	1	0	0	0	0	0	2.0	6	14	4	4	1	0	0	0	2	0	0	0	0
Francis, Jeff, Visalia *	12	9	.571	3.47	27	27	2	2	0	0	160.2	135	648	66	62	8	4	5	5	45	1	153	6	0
Fritz, Ben, Modesto	4	7	.364	4.91	15	15	0	0	0	0	77.0	83	345	49	42	3	2	2	8	34	0	77	4	2
Fruto, Emiliano, Inland Empire	7	8	.467	3.78	42	4	0	0	25	7	78.2	80	347	43	33	5	3	3	3	38	5	83	4	1
Garcia, James, San Jose	5	4	.556	4.16	33	3	0	0	14	7	71.1	67	319	37	33	4	2	1	6	35	2	105	6	1
Gardner, Hayden, Stockton	1	0	1.000	0.00	4	0	0	0	4	2	6.2	4	23	0	0	0	0	0	0	1	0	6	0	0
Garvin, Robert, Lake Elsinore	3	5	.375	4.24	61	0	0	0	17	1	68.0	75	297	36	32	3	1	5	3	19	1	43	2	0
Gaudin, Chad, Bakersfield	5	3	.625	2.13	14	14	1	0	0	0	80.1	63	323	23	19	2	3	1	1	23	0	70	0	2
George, Christopher, San Jose	1	0	1.000	7.00	4	0	0	0	2	0	9.0	12	41	7	7	0	0	0	1	2	0	6	0	0
Germano, Justin, L.E.	9	5	.643	4.23	19	19	1	0	0	0	110.2	127	482	61	52	4	3	2	9	25	1	78	2	0
Gilbert, Rich, Stockton *	6	2	.750	4.26	51	0	0	0	18	5	61.1	63	289	34	29	3	3	1	7	36	1	52	8	0
Gold, J.M., High Desert	1	1	.500	6.65	11	3	0	0	1	0	23.0	29	104	20	17	3	0	2	0	5	0	21	4	0
Gonzalez, Cristian, Modesto	5	2	.714	3.29	8	7	0	0	0	0	52.0	37	212	27	19	4	0	2	2	15	0	26	4	3
Gordon, Justin, High Desert *	1	4	.200	5.51	38	1	0	0	15	5	83.1	90	399	63	51	12	2	1	8	56	3	72	15	2
Gorman, Jason, Lancaster	0	0	.000	9.00	1	0	0	0	0	0	1.0	3	6	1	1	0	0	0	0	0	0	2	0	0
Gray, Rusty, Inland Empire	0	0	.000	12.27	3	0	0	0	1	0	3.2	5	19	5	5	1	0	0	1	1	0	0	1	0
Green, Sean, Visalia	3	4	.429	4.84	46	2	0	0	17	0	80.0	90	370	54	43	2	3	1	8	38	2	56	4	0
Griffin, Charles, Lancaster	0	0	.000	5.56	20	2	0	0	5	0	34.0	37	155	25	21	7	0	5	2	18	2	27	8	1
Griffith, Dustin, R.C.	3	2	.600	3.89	36	2	0	0	12	2	71.2	76	308	33	31	12	2	5	4	19	0	53	4	0
Gross, Kyle, San Jose	0	0	.000	4.50	2	0	0	0	1	0	2.0	2	12	1	1	0	0	0	0	4	0	3	2	0
Gwyn, Marc, Modesto	1	1	.500	3.18	32	1	0	0	21	7	51.0	46	218	20	18	2	5	1	3	24	4	61	3	0
Hall, Dan, High Desert	6	14	.300	7.10	26	26	0	0	0	0	123.0	169	578	116	97	19	5	8	6	47	0	79	6	3
Hampson, Justin, Visalia *	14	7	.667	3.68	26	26	1	0	0	0	159.0	153	684	73	65	12	3	3	21	51	1	150	2	2
Hannaman, Ryan, San Jose *	4	4	.500	4.71	13	13	1	0	0	0	63.0	66	292	41	33	7	2	0	4	32	0	77	4	2
Henrie, Matt, Lancaster	5	7	.417	3.30	14	14	2	0	0	0	90.0	92	371	39	33	5	1	4	1	16	0	60	2	0
Hensley, Clay, San Jose-L.E.	5	7	.417	4.40	13	13	0	0	0	0	73.2	88	321	44	36	4	4	5	1	23	0	65	3	0
Hines, Carlos, Bakersfield	1	1	.500	2.77	25	0	0	0	24	8	26.0	22	117	10	8	0	0	0	4	13	0	23	5	0
Hoffman, Trevor, L.E.	0	0	.000	0.00	3	0	0	0	0	0	3.0	2	12	0	0	0	0	0	1	0	0	4	0	0
Holsten, Ryan, Lancaster	1	0	1.000	4.66	2	1	0	0	0	0	9.2	10	39	5	5	1	0	0	0	3	0	3	0	0
Huber, Jon, Lake Elsinore	3	5	.375	5.18	12	11	0	0	0	0	57.1	69	265	41	33	2	1	2	1	31	1	43	2	1
Hundley, Jeff, High Desert *	0	1	.000	4.29	23	1	0	0	11	1	35.2	32	151	18	17	1	0	4	2	12	1	34	1	1
Hutchison, Wes, San Jose	3	6	.333	7.04	39	2	0	0	14	3	53.2	78	267	50	42	6	3	2	3	36	1	48	1	0
Jarvis, Kevin, Lake Elsinore	2	1	.667	4.09	3	3	0	0	0	0	22.0	18	85	11	10	1	0	0	0	4	0	19	0	0
Jimenez, Kelvin, Stockton	6	5	.545	4.73	34	18	0	0	4	2	131.1	135	565	81	69	14	2	3	9	43	1	101	11	2

Pitcher, Team	W	L	Pct.	ERA	G	GS	CG	ShO	GF	Sv.	IP	H	TBF	R	ER	HR	SH	SF	HB	BB	IBB	SO	WP	Bk.
Jimenez, Ubaldo, Visalia	1	0	1.000	0.00	1	0	0	0	1	0	5.0	3	18	0	0	0	0	0	0	1	0	7	0	0
Johnson, Randy, Lancaster *	0	1	.000	6.00	1	1	0	0	0	0	6.0	11	32	5	4	1	0	0	2	0	0	6	0	0
Jones, Geoffrey, L.E. *	2	2	.500	3.89	25	2	0	0	5	0	34.2	29	151	18	15	0	0	1	5	13	1	32	3	0
Keiter, Ben, Stockton	1	6	.143	5.96	25	13	0	0	4	3	83.0	92	388	64	55	6	0	5	11	44	0	53	6	1
Kerbs, Reuben, Lancaster *	1	0	1.000	11.05	9	0	0	0	2	0	14.2	20	84	21	18	5	0	1	2	14	0	14	2	1
Ketchner, Ryan, Inland Emp.*	14	7	.667	3.45	31	22	2	2	3	1	156.2	133	628	63	60	10	3	4	4	33	0	159	6	0
Kolb, Dan, High Desert	6	12	.333	6.42	27	27	0	0	0	0	150.0	194	682	118	107	24	3	2	3	51	0	110	9	1
Kozol, Anthony, Lake Elsinore	2	0	1.000	4.24	15	0	0	0	6	1	17.0	19	75	8	8	2	1	0	3	1	0	9	1	0
Kranawetter, Josh, Lancaster	2	2	.500	4.85	17	0	0	0	8	0	29.2	36	140	19	16	2	1	0	4	14	0	15	2	0
Krawczyk, Jack, Lancaster	0	0	.000	2.08	3	0	0	0	1	0	4.1	7	20	1	1	0	1	0	1	0	0	6	0	0
Lipari, Thomas, L.E. *	0	4	.000	6.32	12	7	0	0	2	0	37.0	55	189	37	26	3	2	4	2	19	0	28	4	3
Liriano, Francisco, San Jose *	0	1	.000	54.00	1	1	0	0	0	0	0.2	5	9	4	4	0	0	0	0	2	0	0	1	0
Little, Joe, Bakersfield *	0	1	.000	4.82	2	2	0	0	0	0	9.1	10	40	5	5	2	0	1	0	4	0	8	0	0
Lockwood, Brian, Bakersfield	6	6	.500	4.97	27	17	0	0	5	0	117.2	152	524	79	65	15	3	1	13	31	0	72	8	0
Loe, Kameron, Stockton	3	0	1.000	0.96	9	4	0	0	2	1	37.2	26	152	7	4	1	0	1	3	6	0	31	3	0
Mabeus, Chris, Modesto	2	0	1.000	1.52	18	0	0	0	15	2	23.2	19	99	6	4	1	0	1	0	6	0	30	1	0
Markert, Jackson, San Jose	0	2	.000	4.18	13	4	0	0	7	1	28.0	31	127	15	13	2	1	1	1	12	0	23	0	0
Martin, Sean, San Jose	0	0	.000	3.09	5	0	0	0	1	0	11.2	13	50	6	4	0	0	1	0	2	0	14	3	0
Martinez, Javier, Lake Elsinore	6	3	.667	3.23	16	16	0	0	0	0	83.2	76	351	35	30	7	0	2	1	23	0	70	3	1
Marx, Tommy, High Desert *	0	5	.000	12.15	21	4	0	0	6	0	33.1	43	189	48	45	3	3	1	5	49	0	21	11	0
Matthews, Jarod, Bakersfield	8	7	.533	4.02	23	21	1	0	0	0	121.0	131	526	62	54	12	2	2	9	27	0	109	5	0
Mazone, Brian, High Desert *	0	7	.000	9.31	13	13	0	0	0	0	59.0	97	299	66	61	11	0	8	1	27	0	49	4	0
McCall, Derell, Modesto	3	12	.200	5.87	19	19	0	0	0	0	102.2	127	480	80	67	11	1	4	5	46	0	64	10	3
McMachen, Clifford, Lan.*	7	4	.636	3.61	33	5	0	0	13	1	84.2	69	366	41	34	7	9	3	5	42	2	86	5	0
Mead, David, Stockton	1	3	.250	7.18	24	0	0	0	6	0	26.1	29	140	23	21	2	0	2	11	23	2	29	4	0
Medlin, Corbey, Lancaster	2	2	.500	6.27	33	0	0	0	10	0	51.2	62	247	42	36	5	1	1	8	27	0	36	12	1
Menchaca, Eriberto, In. Emp.	1	0	1.000	0.00	1	0	0	0	1	0	2.0	1	9	0	0	0	0	0	0	2	0	0	0	0
Mendoza, Mario, R.C.	1	0	1.000	11.57	4	0	0	0	1	0	7.0	14	37	9	9	1	0	1	0	3	0	6	4	0
Moore, Darin, Stockton	0	4	.000	4.26	21	5	0	0	4	0	44.1	44	211	28	21	2	2	1	3	33	0	30	4	1
Morel, Eudy, Lake Elsinore	0	0	.000	4.00	5	0	0	0	5	0	9.0	12	43	5	4	0	0	0	0	4	2	7	0	0
Morgan, Russ, Inland Emp.*	1	1	.500	8.10	15	0	0	0	1	0	20.0	36	105	22	18	6	1	0	3	10	0	17	1	2
Mowday, Chris, Modesto	2	1	.667	8.00	9	0	0	0	3	0	9.0	13	46	8	8	1	0	0	1	5	0	18	1	0
Mozingo, Dan, R.C. *	6	7	.462	6.04	20	16	1	0	2	0	92.1	110	416	72	62	18	3	6	3	39	1	55	9	0
Narron, Sam, Stockton *	10	4	.714	3.48	26	14	0	0	4	0	103.1	107	417	48	40	8	3	4	3	19	0	75	2	0
Neagle, Denny, Visalia *	1	0	1.000	0.00	2	2	0	0	0	0	10.0	4	37	0	0	0	0	0	1	2	0	13	1	0
Nickoli, Mike, R.C.	1	0	1.000	3.32	4	3	0	0	0	0	19.0	19	77	8	7	2	0	0	1	5	0	8	1	0
Nolasco, Dave, High Desert	3	5	.375	5.44	21	7	0	0	4	0	81.0	103	368	56	49	8	0	6	8	28	0	63	0	1
Nunez, Jose, Lake Elsinore *	0	0	.000	1.04	8	0	0	0	2	0	8.2	7	36	2	1	0	0	0	0	2	0	3	0	0
O'Connor, Brian, Bakersfield *	0	0	.000	4.91	2	1	0	0	0	0	7.1	9	33	4	4	0	1	1	0	2	0	4	3	0
O'Sullivan, Mark, R.C.	3	2	.600	3.70	52	0	0	0	13	2	75.1	59	317	34	31	3	2	2	1	33	0	56	10	1
Obenchain, Stephen, Modesto	3	4	.429	5.15	9	9	0	0	0	0	43.2	56	206	36	25	3	1	3	1	20	0	19	4	0
Olore, Kevin, Inland Empire	1	2	.333	5.03	8	8	0	0	0	0	39.1	37	174	24	22	2	3	0	2	18	0	37	2	0
Padgett, Daniel, San Jose *	0	1	.000	18.47	11	0	0	0	6	0	12.2	22	80	29	26	1	4	1	3	16	0	7	1	0
Pannone, Anthony, San Jose	3	10	.231	5.45	22	19	0	0	0	0	110.2	118	495	73	67	8	3	5	6	51	0	89	9	0
Parker, Josh, Bakersfield	0	0	.000	1.38	31	0	0	0	30	16	32.2	32	132	6	5	0	1	0	1	4	0	42	0	0
Parker, Zach, Visalia *	5	5	.500	3.69	16	16	1	1	0	0	90.1	85	379	38	37	10	2	3	7	27	0	52	1	0
Pavlik, Isaac, Visalia *	3	3	.500	4.94	51	0	0	0	20	1	54.2	65	254	33	30	1	3	2	5	19	0	50	3	1
Pavon, Julio, San Jose	5	4	.556	3.54	41	8	0	0	14	2	112.0	106	456	48	44	7	4	0	1	26	1	103	9	1
Perez, Elvis, Inland Empire	5	5	.500	3.72	13	12	0	0	1	0	65.1	55	266	30	27	6	1	1	3	16	0	58	1	0
Perez, Jeffrey, Inland Empire	1	1	.500	7.65	12	0	0	0	2	0	20.0	23	103	18	17	1	1	2	4	15	1	15	5	0
Petke, Tim, R.C.	2	7	.222	4.39	10	10	0	0	0	0	55.1	60	233	31	27	3	7	3	2	17	0	35	5	1
Petty, Chad, High Desert *	0	10	.000	7.41	17	16	1	0	0	0	81.1	112	391	76	67	14	4	5	9	38	0	55	3	1
Price, Brett, Modesto *	2	1	.667	2.98	41	0	0	0	13	1	54.1	41	245	25	18	2	2	1	4	38	1	64	2	0
Price, Ryan, Visalia	0	0	.000	7.47	7	0	0	0	1	0	15.2	20	76	13	13	1	1	1	3	10	0	13	4	0
Prinz, Bret, Lancaster	0	0	.000	0.00	1	1	0	0	0	0	1.0	0	3	0	0	0	0	0	0	0	0	2	0	0
Pruett, Hubert, High Desert	1	0	1.000	7.20	1	1	0	0	0	0	5.0	8	23	4	4	1	0	0	0	3	0	2	0	1
Pruett, Jason, Bakersfield *	2	0	1.000	3.78	48	0	0	0	24	1	47.2	54	215	23	20	3	1	1	5	16	0	34	3	0
Raburn, Johnny, High Desert	0	0	.000	0.00	2	0	0	0	2	0	0.2	0	6	0	0	0	0	0	2	1	0	1	0	0
Rall, Tim, Inland Empire *	2	3	.400	3.65	10	4	0	0	2	0	37.0	34	151	16	15	5	2	0	4	9	0	30	0	1
Ramirez, Edward, R.C.	0	2	.000	8.10	4	4	0	0	0	0	16.2	29	83	16	15	5	1	0	0	7	0	9	1	0
Ramsay, Rob, Lake Elsinore *	3	1	.750	3.57	27	4	0	0	4	0	68.0	77	293	37	27	5	3	4	1	19	1	44	6	1
Ray, Ken, High Desert	1	1	.500	7.71	7	0	0	0	2	0	14.0	22	70	13	12	4	0	1	0	6	0	18	0	0
Reece, Eric, Bakersfield	0	0	.000	0.00	1	0	0	0	1	0	1.0	0	4	0	0	0	0	0	0	0	0	1	0	0
Reyes, Ramon, R.C.	0	0	.000	22.50	1	0	0	0	1	0	2.0	5	16	5	5	1	0	0	0	5	0	2	3	0
Reynolds, Josh, Lake Elsinore	0	0	.000	8.22	3	1	0	0	0	0	7.2	13	40	10	7	2	0	0	0	4	0	5	1	0
Ribas, Gabe, Lake Elsinore	4	5	.444	5.81	9	9	0	0	0	0	48.0	63	222	35	31	4	2	3	2	14	1	36	6	0
Richards, John, L.E. *	0	0	.000	10.54	10	0	0	0	3	0	13.2	26	70	16	16	2	0	0	1	4	0	8	2	1
Richardson, Mike, L.E.	1	0	1.000	5.40	2	0	0	0	2	0	1.2	2	8	1	1	0	0	0	0	2	0	0	1	0
Rigueiro, Rafael, San Jose	0	2	.000	13.19	17	0	0	0	7	0	29.1	55	183	50	43	2	0	1	8	34	0	26	5	1
Robertson, Luke, Modesto	7	7	.500	6.39	29	17	0	0	5	0	119.2	167	566	104	85	14	3	4	7	33	2	83	7	1
Robinson, Jeff, High Desert	1	1	.500	2.16	7	4	0	0	2	1	25.0	26	110	8	6	1	2	1	2	9	0	20	0	0
Rosario, Melvin, Visalia *	0	0	.000	0.00	1	0	0	0	1	0	1.0	0	3	0	0	0	0	0	0	0	0	1	0	0
Rouwenhorst, Jonathon, R.C.*	1	5	.167	1.73	52	0	0	0	34	20	62.1	58	260	27	12	0	2	4	3	14	1	52	4	0
Rowe, Steven, Stockton	5	0	1.000	1.28	48	0	0	0	40	15	63.1	42	261	18	9	3	1	0	7	23	0	63	3	1
Rowland-Smith, Ryan, In.E.*	0	1	.000	3.20	15	0	0	0	3	0	19.2	12	80	9	7	0	0	3	3	8	0	15	0	1
Saenz, Chris, High Desert	9	9	.500	5.20	26	26	1	0	0	0	128.0	121	559	80	74	20	3	2	15	56	0	136	7	0
Sanchez, Adiel, Modesto *	0	0	.000	4.50	4	0	0	0	2	0	4.0	4	16	2	2	1	0	0	0	1	0	2	0	0
Santana, Ervin, R.C.	10	2	.833	2.53	20	20	1	0	0	0	124.2	98	510	44	35	9	3	1	7	36	0	130	14	0
Sasaki, Kazuhiro, Inland Emp.	0	0	.000	0.00	1	1	0	0	0	0	1.0	0	4	0	0	0	0	0	0	1	0	2	0	0
Sauer, Marc, Modesto	4	3	.571	3.94	22	7	1	0	7	2	75.1	86	328	43	33	9	6	4	3	15	0	58	1	0
Schaub, Greg, High Desert	0	1	.000	2.08	8	0	0	0	1	0	17.1	19	79	4	4	1	0	0	0	9	0	21	0	0
Schmidt, Jeremy, San Jose	0	0	.000	6.52	5	0	0	0	3	0	9.2	10	47	9	7	0	1	0	0	8	1	14	2	0
Schneider, Scott, R.C.	3	2	.600	5.19	17	0	0	0	10	3	26.0	27	122	17	15	0	1	0	2	18	0	21	2	0
Schultz, Mike, Lancaster	2	2	.500	4.67	9	9	0	0	0	0	44.1	57	198	27	23	5	2	3	2	20	0	32	2	0
Seddon, Chris, Bakersfield *	9	11	.450	5.00	26	26	0	0	0	0	133.1	147	595	93	74	12	2	6	7	54	0	95	7	1

Pitcher, Team	W	L	Pct.	ERA	G	GS	CG	ShO	GF	Sv.	IP	H	TBF	R	ER	HR	SH	SF	HB	BB	IBB	SO	WP	Bk.
Sele, Aaron, R.C.	0	0	.000	4.50	3	2	0	0	0	0	8.0	12	35	4	4	0	0	0	0	3	0	7	0	0
Serrano, Alex, Visalia	4	5	.444	3.09	49	0	0	0	20	4	75.2	74	314	34	26	4	0	3	6	13	3	71	1	0
Shank, Chris, Modesto	1	2	.333	4.14	26	0	0	0	17	3	41.1	49	185	21	19	1	4	3	2	12	0	43	0	0
Shell, Steven, R.C.	6	8	.429	4.24	22	21	1	1	0	0	127.1	123	540	66	60	13	4	3	12	26	0	100	3	1
Shields, Jamie, Bakersfield	10	10	.500	4.45	26	24	0	0	1	1	143.2	161	632	85	71	19	3	2	12	38	0	119	6	4
Sikaras, Pete, Lancaster	3	1	.750	2.83	46	0	0	0	41	23	47.2	44	210	21	15	2	0	1	3	27	0	56	7	0
Simpson, Gerrit, Visalia	11	10	.524	5.37	27	27	1	1	0	0	157.2	188	701	103	94	10	3	6	11	56	0	84	11	4
Slaten, Doug, Lancaster *	6	7	.462	6.03	32	19	0	0	3	0	119.1	156	555	94	80	13	3	1	10	47	0	78	4	3
Smart, Pete, High Desert *	1	3	.250	9.00	5	5	0	0	0	0	22.0	33	102	22	22	4	3	0	0	9	0	23	2	1
Smith, Cliff, R.C.	2	2	.500	5.79	15	5	0	0	6	2	32.2	38	142	23	21	3	0	2	1	9	0	25	1	0
Smith, Jesse, R.C.	0	4	.000	7.13	5	5	0	0	0	0	24.0	26	110	19	19	3	0	1	4	12	0	7	1	0
Songster, Judd, Visalia	0	1	.000	5.40	9	0	0	0	7	3	8.1	13	40	5	5	1	1	0	0	3	0	9	3	0
Speier, Ryan, Visalia	4	2	.667	1.53	56	0	0	0	43	18	58.2	50	248	14	10	2	1	3	6	17	2	73	2	0
Stanton, Kyle, Visalia	1	1	.500	6.05	14	0	0	0	3	0	19.1	24	87	13	13	2	1	0	0	7	1	14	1	0
Stark, Dennis, Visalia	0	0	.000	0.00	1	1	0	0	0	0	4.0	2	15	0	0	0	0	0	0	1	0	5	0	0
Stavros, Tony, High Desert	2	3	.400	4.46	46	1	0	0	25	3	84.2	87	377	49	42	7	1	6	5	39	1	101	7	0
Steele, Mike, Inland Empire	2	2	.500	2.56	33	0	0	0	31	16	38.2	29	152	14	11	3	3	2	2	8	1	26	3	0
Stout, Danny, High Desert	2	2	.500	7.07	12	1	0	0	2	0	28.0	38	129	23	22	3	0	0	3	10	0	22	3	0
Strelitz, Brian, Inland Empire	4	2	.667	3.48	29	1	0	0	10	1	54.1	51	221	25	21	9	2	2	3	11	1	29	1	0
Thomas, J.T., San Jose *	5	12	.294	3.45	33	19	0	0	8	3	125.1	134	555	64	48	6	6	5	5	35	1	104	6	2
Thomas, Jared, Inland Emp.*	5	3	.625	3.61	41	7	0	0	15	3	87.1	67	373	39	35	7	4	4	6	46	0	108	2	0
Thompson, Erik, Stockton	8	3	.727	2.91	19	9	0	0	5	0	80.1	74	326	28	26	6	0	4	4	13	0	62	2	1
Thompson, Mike, L.E.	10	11	.476	4.42	28	22	0	0	1	0	136.1	163	590	78	67	8	4	6	2	31	0	75	7	0
Thompson, Richard, R.C.	2	2	.500	4.91	24	0	0	0	18	8	29.1	28	135	19	16	4	0	1	2	18	1	33	5	0
Thornton, Matt, Inland Emp.*	0	0	.000	4.00	2	2	0	0	0	0	9.0	9	40	4	4	2	0	1	1	4	0	14	0	0
Tierney, Chris, Lake Elsinore *	1	0	1.000	1.50	1	1	0	0	0	0	6.0	4	23	1	1	0	1	0	0	3	0	4	1	0
Torres, Joe, R.C. *	3	3	.500	5.88	8	7	0	0	1	0	33.2	47	160	28	22	1	0	2	2	20	0	17	1	1
Treadway, Brion, San Jose	8	7	.533	4.11	29	22	0	0	4	2	133.2	136	580	66	61	14	3	5	11	53	0	100	7	2
Trejo, Francisco, Lancaster *	1	1	.500	5.02	16	1	0	0	2	0	28.2	38	140	20	16	3	0	2	3	13	0	36	4	0
Turco, Anthony, San Jose	0	0	.000	0.00	1	0	0	0	1	0	0.2	0	2	0	0	0	0	0	0	0	0	0	0	0
Ulloa, Enmanuel, Inland Emp.	1	1	.500	3.20	17	7	0	0	1	1	50.2	49	208	20	18	1	3	1	4	6	2	61	3	1
Valdez, Domingo, Stockton	0	0	.000	4.94	9	4	0	0	2	0	23.2	21	111	19	13	2	1	3	4	20	0	19	3	0
Vent, Kevin, San Jose	1	0	1.000	11.05	4	1	0	0	1	0	7.1	14	42	11	9	1	1	1	0	5	0	7	1	0
Vicente, Ruben, Lancaster	0	1	.000	5.19	3	3	0	0	0	0	17.1	22	82	12	10	0	0	2	1	5	1	10	1	0
Villafuerte, Brandon, L.E.	0	0	.000	0.00	2	0	0	0	2	2	2.0	1	8	0	0	0	0	0	0	1	0	2	0	0
Walker, Kevin, Lake Elsinore *	0	0	.000	13.50	4	0	0	0	0	0	4.0	6	21	6	6	1	0	0	1	2	0	3	0	0
Washburn, Ben, San Jose	0	0	.000	8.10	4	0	0	0	2	0	6.2	9	37	6	6	2	0	2	1	8	0	8	0	0
Wear, Gregory, Inland Empire	0	0	.000	36.00	1	0	0	0	0	0	1.0	4	9	4	4	0	0	0	1	1	0	1	1	0
Webb, Nick, Visalia *	3	2	.600	4.81	25	6	0	0	4	1	73.0	98	341	45	39	7	1	3	2	29	0	65	7	4
Wechsler, Justin, Lancaster	9	11	.450	5.61	27	21	0	0	2	0	112.1	129	525	79	70	10	1	7	7	64	2	88	13	1
Weis, Brad, Modesto *	15	7	.682	2.82	30	24	3	0	1	0	159.2	132	670	66	50	3	2	5	15	60	1	145	5	2
Wells, Carlton, Lancaster *	4	3	.571	2.95	46	0	0	0	17	6	73.1	80	323	27	24	1	4	1	0	27	2	41	4	0
Whatley, Keith, Lancaster *	3	3	.500	5.17	8	8	1	0	0	0	47.0	53	209	29	27	3	1	2	3	21	0	17	0	0
Wiedmeyer, Jason, L.E. *	7	3	.700	5.38	14	13	0	0	0	0	72.0	99	318	49	43	5	2	3	1	13	2	32	0	0
Williams, Brady, Bakersfield	0	0	.000	0.00	1	0	0	0	1	0	0.1	0	1	0	0	0	0	0	0	0	0	0	0	0
Williams, Bryan, R.C.	3	3	.500	6.80	19	2	0	0	5	0	42.1	55	205	40	32	9	0	0	2	27	0	20	6	0
Wilson, Phil, R.C.	1	1	.500	3.72	2	2	0	0	0	0	9.2	13	49	13	4	0	0	0	1	3	0	6	1	0
Witasick, Jay, Lake Elsinore	0	0	.000	5.79	4	0	0	0	0	0	4.2	6	20	4	3	0	0	0	0	0	0	7	0	0
Wodnicki, Mike, Lake Elsinore	2	5	.286	3.90	43	10	1	0	29	13	87.2	81	371	45	38	8	3	5	6	20	2	53	5	0
Wolensky, Dave, R.C.	4	4	.500	5.87	46	2	0	0	17	4	79.2	89	385	64	52	6	4	7	6	46	1	92	16	1
Woods, Jake, R.C. *	12	7	.632	3.99	28	28	2	1	0	0	171.1	178	737	90	76	9	7	8	8	54	0	109	2	2
Wrigley, Jase, Visalia	0	1	.000	10.13	5	0	0	0	4	1	5.1	10	27	6	6	2	0	0	1	3	0	3	0	0
Yoshida, Nobuaki, L.E. *	0	2	.000	7.11	3	3	0	0	0	0	12.2	20	66	15	10	0	0	2	0	10	0	6	2	1
Zerbe, Chad, San Jose *	0	0	.000	0.00	2	2	0	0	0	0	3.0	3	15	2	0	0	0	1	0	2	0	1	0	0

PITCHERS WITH TWO OR MORE TEAMS

Pitcher, Team	W	L	Pct.	ERA	G	GS	CG	ShO	GF	Sv.	IP	H	TBF	R	ER	HR	SH	SF	HB	BB	IBB	SO	WP	Bk.
Hensley, Clay, San Jose	2	3	.400	5.83	5	5	0	0	0	0	29.1	38	128	20	19	4	1	4	1	9	0	25	0	0
Hensley, Clay, Lake Elsinore	3	4	.429	3.45	8	8	0	0	0	0	44.1	50	193	24	17	0	3	1	0	14	0	40	3	0

COMBINATION SHUTOUTS: Bakersfield (9)—Lockwood-Shields-Andersen, O'Connor-Crawford-Parker, Seddon-Coose-Pruett-Parker, Lockwood-Parker, Flinn-Dukeman-Pruett-Parker, Matthews-Coose, Shields-Dukeman, Matthews-Coose-Pruett-Hines, Brazelton-Crawford. High Desert (2)—Saenz-Robinson-Bystrowski, Saenz-Stavros. Inland Empire (6)—Done-Strelitz-Blood-Steele, Cate-Thomas, Bott—Dorman—Rowland-Smith, Perez-Fruto, Perez-Blood, Perez-Rall-Done-Blood-Cortez-Fruto. Lake Elsinore (3)—Bumstead-Cassel-Garvin-Wodnicki, Martinez-Beavers-Cassel-Baker, Wodnicki-Garvin-Beavers-Cassel. Modesto (4)—Bruksch-Gwyn-Weis-Fischer, Robertson-Price-Crowell, Weis-Mabeus, Weis-Price-Gwyn. Rancho Cucamonga (4)—Santana-Wolensky, Petke-Rouwenhorst-Thompson, Bittner-O'Sullivan-Bukowski, Woods-Thompson-O'Sullivan-Rouwenhorst. San Jose (6)—Hannaman-Schmidt, Pannone-Garcia, Pannone-Thomas, Thomas-Cram-Burres, Pavon-Cram-Markert, Thomas-Cram. Stockton (5)—Jimenez-Barnett, Andrew-Abraham-Moore-Rowe, Dominguez-Keiter, Jimenez-Barnett-Rowe, Thompson-Keiter. Visalia (7)—Francis-Green-Webb, Esposito-Songster-Serrano, Parker-Wrigley, Francis-Bumatay, Simpson-Pavlik, Green-Esslinger-Stanton-Serrano-Speier, Hampson-Pavlik-Darnell.

NO-HIT GAMES: Francis, Visalia, defeated Modesto, 6-0, July 6.

2003 FIELDING

TEAM

Team	G	PO	A	E	TC	DP	TP	PB	Pct.
Inland Empire	140	3689	1214	130	5033	84	0	21	.974
Visalia	140	3693	1565	146	5404	155	0	26	.973
High Desert	140	3678	1384	153	5215	107	0	33	.971
Lancaster	140	3762	1674	168	5604	125	0	26	.970
San Jose	140	3649	1331	167	5147	114	0	29	.968
Stockton	140	3724	1475	185	5384	120	0	29	.966
Rancho Cuca.	140	3701	1401	180	5282	119	0	19	.966
Bakersfield	140	3649	1369	192	5210	126	0	33	.963
Lake Elsinore	140	3698	1532	202	5432	120	0	13	.963
Modesto	140	3730	1322	202	5254	89	0	35	.962

INDIVIDUAL

FIRST BASEMEN

NOTE: All caps denotes fielding-percentage leader based on 70 games for catchers, 93 for all other non-pitchers and 112 innings for pitchers. *Throws lefthanded.

Player, Team	Pct.	G	PO	A	E	TC	DP
Alvarado, Joel, High Desert	1.000	1	13	0	0	13	0
Anderson, Keith, San Jose	1.000	13	98	9	0	107	8
Arhart, Josh, Bakersfield	1.000	1	4	1	0	5	1
Balet, Pichi, Inland Empire	1.000	9	59	8	0	67	3
Benavidez, Julian, San Jose	.979	56	403	23	9	435	34
Benick, Jon, Lake Elsinore	.985	66	572	39	9	620	55

Player, Team	Pct.	G	PO	A	E	TC	DP
Bone, Blake, Inland Empire	.988	12	73	12	1	86	7
Botts, Jason, Stockton	.977	73	656	34	16	706	51
Bowser, Matt, Modesto *	.980	94	713	56	16	785	43
Brown, Hunter, Inland Empire	.750	1	3	0	1	4	0
Candelaria, Scott, High Desert	.986	44	314	27	5	346	25
Castellano, John, Inland Empire	.990	87	629	44	7	680	48
CLARK, AARON, Bakersfield *	.993	113	883	73	7	963	84
Corbeil, Azarias, R.C.	.980	45	314	26	7	347	23
Cordido, Julio, San Jose	1.000	5	29	1	0	30	2
Dill, Jason, Stockton *	.975	11	71	7	2	80	7
Ernster, Mark, High Desert	.970	6	29	3	1	33	1
Eylward, Mike, R.C.	.991	52	431	27	4	462	44
Frost, Jeremy, High Desert	.989	22	168	20	2	190	19
Garcia, Isaac, Modesto	1.000	2	16	2	0	18	0
Gerber, Joseph, Lake Elsinore *	.983	23	215	10	4	229	16
Gomes, Joey, Bakersfield	.882	6	30	0	4	34	4
Hastings, Joseph, Lake Elsinore	.953	12	94	7	5	106	9
Heath, Matt, Lancaster	1.000	2	16	1	0	17	1
Johnson, Bryan, Lancaster	.982	20	147	21	3	171	9
Johnson, Michael, Lake Elsinore	.970	34	281	12	9	302	26
Jones, Jaime, Lancaster *	.500	1	1	0	1	2	0
Kotchman, Casey, R.C.*	.988	48	388	23	5	416	36
Lincoln, Justin, Visalia	.991	12	108	4	1	113	17
Moore, Jason, Stockton	1.000	1	2	1	0	3	0
Myers, Casey, Modesto	.971	13	92	7	3	102	5
Napoli, Michael, R.C.	1.000	6	51	3	0	54	7
Neal, Steve, Lancaster *	1.000	9	76	7	0	83	3
Nelson, Brad, High Desert	.988	31	239	15	3	257	21
Nichols, Kyle, Lancaster	.984	66	570	43	10	623	62
Oliveros, Luis, Inland Empire	1.000	1	8	0	0	8	0
Pack, Branden, Stockton	.978	4	41	4	1	46	9
Peck, Bryan, Visalia	.982	20	154	11	3	168	12
Quero, Pedro, Stockton	.994	34	287	29	2	318	30
Raburn, Johnny, High Desert	1.000	1	1	0	0	1	0
Reece, Eric, Bakersfield	.995	25	182	11	1	194	20
Roper, Zach, Stockton	1.000	2	19	1	0	20	3
Sain, Greg, Lake Elsinore	.964	9	50	4	2	56	2
Santana, Mayobanex, Lancaster	.988	28	155	9	2	166	17
Santana, Ralph, High Desert	1.000	2	3	0	0	3	1
Schneidmiller, Gary, Modesto	.972	18	128	9	4	141	13
Shealy, Ryan, Visalia	.993	76	677	54	5	736	79
Sinisi, Vincent, Stockton *	1.000	2	17	1	0	18	3
Slavik, Corey, Visalia	.997	34	318	21	1	340	32
Soto, Jorge, Modesto	1.000	16	106	5	0	111	14
Soules, Ryan, Stockton	.983	18	166	10	3	179	12
Stanek, Jeff, Lancaster	.982	17	146	15	3	164	9
Strong, Zach, San Jose	.969	4	29	2	1	32	5
Swisher, Nick, Modesto *	1.000	3	19	2	0	21	4
Thiessen, Mike, Lancaster	1.000	1	8	0	0	8	0
Van Meetren, Jason, I.E.	.989	36	238	22	3	263	16
Varela, Edgar, Lancaster	.980	25	217	28	5	250	19
Villanueva, Froilan, High Desert	.997	44	323	25	1	349	27
Von Schell, Tyler, San Jose	.992	67	558	30	5	593	52
Williams, Brady, Bakersfield	1.000	1	2	0	0	2	0

SECOND BASEMEN

Player, Team	Pct.	G	PO	A	E	TC	DP
Barfield, Josh, Lake Elsinore	.971	130	304	368	20	692	83
Bastida-Martinez, Evel, I.E.	.968	75	131	138	9	278	30
Bernier, Doug, Visalia	1.000	3	5	12	0	17	2
Bone, Blake, Inland Empire	.000	1	0	0	0	0	0
Bourgeois, Jason, Stockton	.943	51	97	150	15	262	32
Candelaria, Scott, High Desert	1.000	5	8	10	0	18	4
Castro, Ismael, Inland Empire	.962	77	94	131	9	234	30
Centeno, Irwin, Bakersfield	.750	3	2	1	1	4	0
Clements, Jason, Lake Elsinore	1.000	5	10	10	0	20	3
Cordido, Julio, San Jose	.970	36	63	100	5	168	22
Cortez, Fernando, Bakersfield	.955	100	234	235	22	491	59
De Paula, Luis, Bakersfield	.959	23	52	66	5	123	19
Delgado, Gabriel, Stockton	.970	39	70	92	5	167	22
Ernster, Mark, High Desert	1.000	1	0	2	0	2	0
Garcia, Isaac, Modesto	.960	34	51	94	6	151	13
Gonzalez, Edgar, Bakersfield	.953	10	18	23	2	43	3
Gorman, Jason, Lancaster	.965	36	57	81	5	143	25
Jacobo, Kervin, Lake Elsinore	1.000	1	3	5	0	8	1
Kelly, Heath, Bakersfield	1.000	1	1	2	0	3	1
Kennedy, Adam, R.C.	.923	3	8	4	1	13	2
Kiger, Mark, Modesto	.958	75	170	197	16	383	38
Knowlton, Jay, San Jose	.962	23	34	42	3	79	12
Lima, Joseph, Lake Elsinore	1.000	5	11	10	0	21	1
Macha, Erick, Lancaster	.667	1	1	1	1	3	0
Mann, Derek, R.C.	1.000	6	6	13	0	19	2
McMains, Derin, San Jose	1.000	25	44	69	0	113	17
Merloni, Lou, Lake Elsinore	1.000	2	3	3	0	6	1
Merritt, Tim, Inland Empire	1.000	8	10	11	0	21	2
Meyer, Drew, Stockton	1.000	2	6	4	0	10	2
Moore, Jason, Stockton	.964	35	56	105	6	167	22
Neufeld, Andy, Modesto	.915	19	36	50	8	94	11
NIX, JAYSON, Visalia	.972	135	273	460	21	754	120
Ozuna, Pablo, Visalia	1.000	1	1	4	0	5	1
Pichardo, Maximo, R.C.	.950	9	9	10	1	20	3
Pohle, Richard, Inland Empire	.857	3	6	0	1	7	0
Raburn, Johnny, High Desert	.981	25	45	57	2	104	11
Raymundo, G.J., Stockton	.959	19	28	42	3	73	7
Richar, Danny, Lancaster	.968	87	152	238	13	403	42
Riley, Ryan, Bakersfield	.966	6	8	20	1	29	2
Rodriguez, Javy, R.C.	.925	23	41	57	8	106	15
Rogelstad, Matt, Inland Empire	1.000	6	12	14	0	26	3
Sandel, George, Inland Empire	1.000	3	6	1	0	7	0
Santana, Mayobanex, Lancaster	.000	1	0	0	0	0	0
Santana, Ralph, High Desert	.976	62	138	145	7	290	29
Serrano, Eddie, Lake Elsinore	1.000	1	1	0	0	1	0
Smith, Casey, R.C.	.985	13	29	36	1	66	11
Sobieraj, Aaron, San Jose	.949	16	30	26	3	59	11
Soler, Ramon, San Jose	.948	46	63	102	9	174	20
Stotts, J.T., Modesto	1.000	2	2	2	0	4	1
Turner, Justin, R.C.	.952	93	157	203	18	378	46
Turner, Lloyd, Modesto	.938	10	23	22	3	48	3
Uggla, Dan, Lancaster	.977	45	86	127	5	218	23
Uribe, Juan, Visalia	1.000	1	4	2	0	6	0
Varela, Edgar, Lancaster	1.000	1	0	1	0	1	0
West, Todd, High Desert	1.000	55	102	124	0	226	34
Williams, Brady, Bakersfield	.875	2	3	4	1	8	1

THIRD BASEMEN

Player, Team	Pct.	G	PO	A	E	TC	DP
Bastida-Martinez, Evel, I.E.	.824	4	6	8	3	17	0
Benavidez, Julian, San Jose	.857	2	1	5	1	7	1
Benick, Jon, Lake Elsinore	1.000	1	0	1	0	1	0
Bernier, Doug, Visalia	.955	16	7	35	2	44	6
Bone, Blake, Inland Empire	.800	3	2	2	1	5	0
Bourgeois, Jason, Stockton	1.000	1	0	1	0	1	0
Bravo, Danny, Lake Elsinore	.968	11	4	26	1	31	1
Brown, Hunter, Inland Empire	.925	122	88	207	24	319	14
Candelaria, Scott, High Desert	.929	51	31	99	10	140	4
Castellano, John, Inland Empire	.875	3	2	5	1	8	0
Castro, Ismael, Inland Empire	.333	3	0	1	2	3	0
Centeno, Irwin, Bakersfield	.500	1	0	1	1	2	0
Cirillo, Jeff, Inland Empire	.833	3	2	3	1	6	0
Clements, Jason, Lake Elsinore	.887	28	11	36	6	53	3
Collins, Chris, Inland Empire	1.000	4	1	3	0	4	0
Cordido, Julio, San Jose	.920	51	32	95	11	138	7
Ernster, Mark, High Desert	.904	28	12	35	5	52	1
Eylward, Mike, R.C.	.884	31	17	44	8	69	2
Firlit, Dan, Lancaster	.500	1	1	0	1	2	0
Furmaniak, J.J., Lake Elsinore	1.000	1	1	3	0	4	0
Garcia, Isaac, Modesto	.922	20	16	31	4	51	4
Gonzalez, Edgar, Bakersfield	.897	79	42	166	24	232	10
Gorman, Jason, Lancaster	.923	5	4	8	1	13	0
Jacobo, Kervin, Lake Elsinore	.857	2	1	5	1	7	0
Johnson, Bryan, Lancaster	1.000	3	0	1	0	1	0
Kiger, Mark, Modesto	1.000	2	0	3	0	3	0
Lambert, Casey, Visalia	1.000	1	1	1	0	2	0
Lima, Joseph, Lake Elsinore	.905	6	5	14	2	21	0
Lincoln, Justin, Visalia	.923	92	49	180	19	248	20
Mann, Derek, R.C.	.900	6	5	13	2	20	1
McPherson, Dallas, R.C.	.926	67	37	137	14	188	16
Menchaca, Eriberto, I.E.	.000	1	0	0	0	0	0
Merloni, Lou, Lake Elsinore	1.000	2	0	7	0	7	0
Merritt, Tim, Inland Empire	1.000	2	1	3	0	4	0
Moore, Jason, Stockton	.952	25	17	42	3	62	2
Neufeld, Andy, Modesto	.786	5	1	10	3	14	2
Pack, Branden, Stockton	.750	1	1	2	1	4	0
Pichardo, Maximo, R.C. 848	18	7	32	7	46	5	
Raburn, Johnny, High Desert	.875	31	15	48	9	72	4
Raymundo, G.J., Stockton	.972	51	33	104	4	141	7
Reece, Eric, Bakersfield	.905	36	19	57	8	84	5
Riley, Ryan, Bakersfield	.857	5	1	5	1	7	0
Rodriguez, Javy, R.C.	.833	3	1	4	1	6	0
Roper, Zach, Stockton	.860	70	35	106	23	164	5
Sain, Greg, Lake Elsinore	.882	94	68	194	35	297	20
Salas, Juan, Bakersfield	.930	27	20	33	4	57	3
Santana, Mayobanex, Lancaster	.990	33	23	73	1	97	9
Santana, Ralph, High Desert	.714	3	1	4	2	7	0

Player, Team	Pct.	G	PO	A	E	TC	DP
Serrano, Eddie, Lake Elsinore	1.000	2	0	4	0	4	0
Slavik, Corey, Visalia	.901	35	11	62	8	81	8
Smith, Casey, R.C.	.923	22	18	42	5	65	2
Stonard, Peter, Lake Elsinore	.000	1	0	0	0	0	0
Strong, Zach, San Jose	.883	95	44	144	25	213	14
Teahen, Mark, Modesto	.931	116	100	197	22	319	11
UGGLA, DAN, Lancaster	.941	102	76	212	18	306	18
Varela, Edgar, Lancaster	.973	16	7	29	1	37	1
Villanueva, Froilan, High Desert	.929	40	36	68	8	112	7
Williams, Brady, Bakersfield	1.000	1	0	3	0	3	0

SHORTSTOPS

Player, Team	Pct.	G	PO	A	E	TC	DP
Bastida-Martinez, Evel, I.E.	.000	1	0	0	0	0	0
Bernier, Doug, Visalia	.948	61	92	182	15	289	46
Bourgeois, Jason, Stockton	.923	14	25	35	5	65	6
Bravo, Danny, Lake Elsinore	1.000	1	2	2	0	4	0
Brown, Hunter, Inland Empire	.800	2	2	2	1	5	0
Candelaria, Scott, High Desert	.833	2	2	3	1	6	0
Castro, Ismael, Inland Empire	.990	33	35	65	1	101	14
Chavez, Angel, San Jose	.957	117	213	344	25	582	66
Chavez, Ozzie, High Desert	.955	79	124	219	16	359	44
Clements, Jason, Lake Elsinore	.893	11	16	34	6	56	7
Cordido, Julio, San Jose	.942	28	32	65	6	103	10
Cortez, Fernando, Bakersfield	.900	3	3	6	1	10	0
De Paula, Luis, Bakersfield	.923	95	128	234	30	392	62
Delgado, Gabriel, Stockton	1.000	2	1	3	0	4	0
Ernster, Mark, High Desert	1.000	1	1	0	0	1	0
Firlit, Dan, Lancaster	.980	20	37	60	2	99	15
Furmaniak, J.J., Lake Elsinore	.945	76	127	250	22	399	47
Garcia, Isaac, Modesto	.926	17	29	46	6	81	10
Gorman, Jason, Lancaster	1.000	1	1	1	0	2	0
Jacobo, Kervin, Lake Elsinore	1.000	1	1	2	0	3	0
Kelly, Heath, Bakersfield	.909	30	55	94	15	164	22
Kiger, Mark, Modesto	.968	48	85	124	7	216	24
Lima, Joseph, Lake Elsinore	.625	3	0	5	3	8	0
Macha, Erick, Lancaster	1.000	5	4	2	0	6	0
MENCHACA, ERIBERTO, I.E.	.970	115	147	246	12	405	44
Merloni, Lou, Lake Elsinore	1.000	1	2	1	0	3	0
Merritt, Tim, Inland Empire	1.000	2	1	1	0	2	0
Meyer, Drew, Stockton	.944	92	137	336	28	501	69
Mirizzi, Marc, Stockton	.953	29	46	96	7	149	18
Moore, Jason, Stockton	1.000	5	9	16	0	25	3
Murphy, Tommy, R.C.	.942	131	212	375	36	623	69
Ozuna, Pablo, Visalia	1.000	1	1	5	0	6	2
Pack, Branden, Stockton	.000	1	0	0	0	0	0
Pecci, Jay, Inland Empire	.963	10	12	14	1	27	3
Pichardo, Maximo, R.C.	.944	3	10	7	1	18	3
Quintanilla, Omar, Modesto	.902	8	15	22	4	41	5
Raburn, Johnny, High Desert	.968	9	9	21	1	31	4
Richar, Danny, Lancaster	.948	41	53	110	9	172	21
Riley, Ryan, Bakersfield	.943	13	26	40	4	70	12
Rodriguez, Javy, R.C.	1.000	4	5	12	0	17	3
Rogelstad, Matt, Inland Empire	.923	3	5	7	1	13	0
Santora, Jack, Lake Elsinore	.935	46	68	147	15	230	18
Santos, Sergio, Lancaster	.951	91	133	271	21	425	58
Serrano, Eddie, Lake Elsinore	1.000	1	1	0	0	1	0
Smith, Casey, R.C.	1.000	2	5	6	0	11	0
Stotts, J.T., Modesto	.916	68	88	162	23	273	21
Tena, Hector, Visalia	.935	83	127	246	26	399	54
Uribe, Juan, Visalia	1.000	1	0	1	0	1	0
Vazquez, Ramon, Lake Elsinore	.950	5	6	13	1	20	3
West, Todd, High Desert	.980	53	96	143	5	244	25
Wilson, Andy, Lancaster	1.000	3	1	4	0	5	0

OUTFIELDERS

Player, Team	Pct.	G	PO	A	E	TC	DP
Asadoorian, Rick, Stockton	.988	30	77	3	1	81	1
Aspito, Jason, R.C.	.975	111	184	8	5	197	2
Ayala, Odannys, Stockton	.957	21	43	2	2	47	0
Balet, Pichi, Inland Empire	.667	4	2	0	1	3	0
Barker, Sean, Visalia	.971	92	125	10	4	139	1
Barre, Brian, Visalia *	.976	30	36	4	1	41	1
Belcher, Jason, High Desert	.938	77	127	9	9	145	2
Benard, Marvin, San Jose *	1.000	2	4	0	0	4	0
Bernier, Doug, Visalia	1.000	4	3	0	0	3	0
Bone, Blake, Inland Empire	.000	1	0	0	0	0	0
Bonner, Adam, Bakersfield	.981	23	49	4	1	54	0
Bowser, Matt, Modesto *	.900	7	9	0	1	10	0
Boyd, Dan, High Desert	1.000	34	50	0	0	50	0
Boyd, Patrick, Stockton	.984	57	122	5	2	129	2
Candelaria, Scott, High Desert	.944	12	16	1	1	18	0
Carter, Bryan, San Jose *	.987	130	298	6	4	308	3
Carter, Josh, Lake Elsinore	.985	94	195	7	3	205	1
Castro, Ismael, Inland Empire	1.000	2	2	0	0	2	0
Centeno, Irwin, Bakersfield	.955	63	97	9	5	111	0
Choo, Shin-soo, Inland Empire *	.980	104	183	9	4	196	1
Christy, Jeff, Modesto	.983	79	170	4	3	177	0
Clark, Aaron, Bakersfield *	.980	26	47	2	1	50	1
Clark, Daryl, High Desert	.974	45	69	5	2	76	3
Clements, Jason, Lake Elsinore	.929	12	23	3	2	28	0
Corbeil, Azarias, R.C.	.000	1	0	0	0	0	0
Cordido, Julio, San Jose	1.000	11	15	1	0	16	0
Coulie, Jason, R.C.	.981	34	52	1	1	54	0
Delucchi, Dustin, I.E. *	1.000	77	182	2	0	184	1
Dill, Jason, Stockton *	.976	56	82	1	2	85	0
Eldridge, Rashad, Stockton	.975	128	234	4	6	244	0
Ernster, Mark, High Desert	1.000	1	1	0	0	1	0
Eylward, Mike, R.C.	.875	8	14	0	2	16	0
Florence, Branden, San Jose	.990	62	103	1	1	105	0
Foster, Brian, High Desert	1.000	2	2	0	0	2	0
Frome, Jason, Visalia *	.980	32	48	0	1	49	0
Frost, Jeremy, High Desert	.929	9	12	1	1	14	0
Fulse, Sheldon, Inland Empire	.983	48	108	5	2	115	2
Garthwaite, Jay, Lancaster	.973	105	213	5	6	224	1
Gates, David, R.C.	.951	55	93	4	5	102	0
Gathright, Joey, Bakersfield	.981	63	150	7	3	160	1
Gerber, Joseph, Lake Elsinore *	.968	37	57	4	2	63	1
Gomes, Joey, Bakersfield	.984	30	58	3	1	62	2
Gorman, Jason, Lancaster	1.000	2	2	0	0	2	0
Gorneault, Nick, R.C.	.972	94	237	8	7	252	1
Guerrero, Cristian, H.D.-I.E.	.968	74	148	3	5	156	2
Guzman, Freddy, Lake Elsinore	.962	48	121	5	5	131	4
Hastings, Joseph, Lake Elsinore	.833	16	14	1	3	18	0
Heath, Matt, Lancaster	1.000	2	1	0	0	1	0
Holst, Micah, San Jose	.959	81	129	11	6	146	1
Jacobs, Greg, Inland Empire *	.969	88	153	5	5	163	2
Johnson, Ben, Lake Elsinore	.969	48	122	4	4	130	0
Jones, Jaime, Lancaster *	.934	80	106	7	8	121	0
Jones, Kennard, Lake Elsinore *	.957	17	44	0	2	46	0
Kimpton, Nick, R.C. *	.983	108	286	9	5	300	3
Kroeger, Josh, Lancaster *	.953	74	118	5	6	129	0
Lima, Joseph, Lake Elsinore	1.000	2	1	0	0	1	0
Macha, Erick, Lancaster	1.000	4	2	0	0	2	0
Martin, Brian, Bakersfield	.987	128	285	11	4	300	3
Mateo, Luis, Bakersfield	.934	96	173	11	13	197	2
McAndrews, Travis, Lancaster *	.944	30	33	1	2	36	0
McBeth, Marcus, Modesto	.973	15	35	1	1	37	0
Melgarejo, Ransel, R.C.	.984	29	61	2	1	64	1
Miller, Tony, Visalia	.961	67	144	3	6	153	0
Morris, Chris, High Desert	.974	124	324	9	9	342	3
Nelson, Brad, High Desert	1.000	10	13	0	0	13	0
Nettles, Marcus, Lake Elsinore *	.959	115	206	5	9	220	0
Neufeld, Andy, Modesto	1.000	7	14	0	0	14	0
Ortmeier, Daniel, San Jose *	.979	72	138	2	3	143	2
Perry, Jason, Modesto	.942	38	60	5	4	69	0
Phillips, Dan, Visalia	.965	115	188	6	7	201	0
Quero, Pedro, Stockton	.000	1	0	0	1	1	0
Raburn, Johnny, High Desert	.918	53	84	5	8	97	0
Richardson, Mike, Lake Elsinore	.965	52	76	7	3	86	0
Roper, Zach, Stockton	1.000	13	22	1	0	23	0
ROSARIO, MELVIN, Visalia *	1.000	95	208	15	0	223	5
Salas, Juan, Bakersfield	.895	12	16	1	2	19	0
Salazar, Jeff, Visalia *	1.000	1	2	0	0	2	0
Santana, Ralph, High Desert	.961	46	110	12	5	127	2
Schneidmiller, Gary, Modesto	.960	36	47	1	2	50	1
Sinisi, Vincent, Stockton *	.857	8	18	0	3	21	0
Stringfellow, Christopher, Stock.	.987	112	217	5	3	225	0
Sugden, Jason, R.C.	.000	1	0	0	0	0	0
Sullivan, Kevin, Visalia	1.000	1	2	0	0	2	0
Swisher, Nick, Modesto *	.964	43	104	2	4	110	0
Thiessen, Mike, Lancaster	.961	63	98	1	4	103	0
Thomas, Gary, Modesto	.969	112	274	8	9	291	2
Toner, John, High Desert	.939	19	28	3	2	33	0
Tritle, Chris, Modesto	.947	38	89	1	5	95	0
Trumble, Dan, San Jose	.950	83	128	6	7	141	1
Turner, Lloyd, Modesto	.935	18	24	5	2	31	0
Van Meetren, Jason, I.E.	1.000	26	37	0	0	37	0
Villanueva, Froilan, High Desert	1.000	2	1	0	0	1	0
Weber, Jon, Modesto *	1.000	35	61	2	0	63	0
Williams, Marland, Lancaster	.981	95	207	2	4	213	0
Williamson, John, Inland Empire	1.000	17	28	1	0	29	0
Willingham, Phil, Inland Empire	1.000	4	5	0	0	5	0

OUTFIELDERS WITH TWO OR MORE TEAMS

Player, Team	Pct.	G	PO	A	E	TC	DP
Guerrero, Cristian, High Desert	1.000	3	6	0	0	6	0
Guerrero, Cristian, I.E.	.967	71	142	3	5	150	2

CATCHERS

Player, Team	Pct.	G	PO	A	E	TC	DP	PB
Alvarado, Joel, High Desert	.982	64	456	47	9	512	6	12
Anderson, Keith, San Jose	.985	38	296	28	5	329	1	10
Arhart, Josh, Bakersfield	.992	70	461	37	4	502	4	17
Barajas, Rod, Lancaster	1.000	2	16	1	0	17	0	1
Budde, Ryan, R.C.	.967	12	76	13	3	92	0	0
Candelaria, Scott, High Desert	.000	1	0	0	0	0	0	0
Castellano, John, I.E.	1.000	2	12	1	0	13	0	0
Collins, Chris, Inland Empire	.993	59	402	30	3	435	2	11
Conway, Dan, Visalia	.991	76	529	38	5	572	4	15
Corbeil, Azarias, R.C.	.957	10	40	4	2	46	0	0
Craig, Beau, Modesto	.964	4	21	6	1	28	0	0
Deck, Ronnie, Bakersfield	1.000	4	14	1	0	15	0	0
Del Chiaro, Brent, R.C.	.982	7	52	3	1	56	1	0
DiRosa, Michael, Lancaster	.979	72	416	48	10	474	0	12
Duenas, Tommy, R.C.	.976	5	37	3	1	41	0	2
Esposito, Brian, R.C.	1.000	7	52	5	0	57	0	0
Foster, Brian, High Desert	.984	51	279	37	5	321	2	14
Frost, Jeremy, High Desert	.981	7	48	5	1	54	0	4
Gulledge, Kelley, Stockton	.991	15	98	11	1	110	0	1
Harriman, David, Modesto	.985	33	248	16	4	268	1	7
Heard, Scott, Stockton	.982	68	453	38	9	500	0	18
Heath, Matt, Lancaster	.941	4	13	3	1	17	0	1
Isenia, Chairon, Bakersfield	.995	24	180	19	1	200	2	1
Johnson, Kade, High Desert	.972	20	153	23	5	181	1	1
Knoedler, Justin, San Jose	.989	98	755	60	9	824	6	16
Lozada, Charlie, High Desert	.976	4	39	2	1	42	0	0
Lunsford, Trey, San Jose	1.000	1	7	1	0	8	0	0
Maduro, Jorge, Bakersfield	.982	9	51	5	1	57	0	3
Mathis, Jeff, R.C.	.991	82	562	67	6	635	6	14
Merritt, Graig, Bakersfield	.977	24	150	20	4	174	0	4
Morris, Jed, Modesto	.984	74	580	51	10	641	2	22
Myers, Casey, Modesto	.968	17	118	3	4	125	1	1
Napoli, Michael, R.C.	.986	20	119	20	2	141	0	2
OLIVEROS, LUIS, I.E.	.994	89	770	52	5	827	2	10
Pack, Branden, Stockton	.968	23	184	26	7	217	1	3
Pagan, Carlos, Inland Empire	.941	3	14	2	1	17	0	0
Raburn, Johnny, High Desert	1.000	1	0	1	0	1	0	0
Reece, Eric, Bakersfield	.993	20	124	9	1	134	0	8
Reinking, Kevin, Lake Elsinore	.992	18	119	10	1	130	2	1
Richardson, Mike, L.E.	.962	10	43	8	2	53	0	1
Riera, Zack, R.C.	.960	3	23	1	1	25	0	1
Sain, Greg, Lake Elsinore	.989	15	83	11	1	95	0	1
Smith, Dustin, Stockton	.990	40	280	27	3	310	2	7
Snyder, Chris, Lancaster	.984	56	365	54	7	426	1	11
Soto, Jorge, Modesto	.979	18	130	9	3	142	1	5
Sullivan, Kevin, Visalia	1.000	2	8	0	0	8	0	1
Trzesniak, Nick, Lake Elsinore	.991	104	672	75	7	754	7	10
Turco, Anthony, San Jose	.920	10	41	5	4	50	0	3
Villanueva, Froilan, H.D.	1.000	14	76	9	0	85	0	2
Wilkins, Joe, Lancaster	.980	15	92	8	2	102	0	1
Winchester, Jeff, Visalia	.994	63	493	40	3	536	7	10

PITCHERS

Player, Team	Pct.	G	PO	A	E	TC	DP
Aardsma, David, San Jose	1.000	18	1	0	0	1	0
Abraham, Paul, Stockton	.778	47	2	5	2	9	0
Alvarez, Tim, San Jose *	1.000	8	2	2	0	4	0
Andersen, Derek, Bakersfield *	1.000	17	2	4	0	6	0
Anderson, Keith, San Jose	.000	4	0	0	0	0	0
Andrade, Stephen, R.C.	.000	3	0	0	0	0	0
Andrew, Jason, Stockton	1.000	31	3	12	0	15	1
Avendano, Elvis, Modesto	1.000	6	0	5	0	5	1
Backsmeyer, Justin, High Desert	.941	40	7	9	1	17	1
Baek, Cha-Sueng, Inland Empire	.952	13	9	11	1	21	0
Baker, Brad, Lake Elsinore	1.000	27	1	3	0	4	0
Barber, Scott, Lancaster	.971	23	13	20	1	34	2
Barnett, John, Stockton	.880	34	11	11	3	25	1
Bazzell, Shane, Modesto	1.000	9	0	3	0	3	0
Beavers, Kevin, Lake Elsinore *	.750	42	4	8	4	16	0
Begg, Chris, San Jose	1.000	7	3	4	0	7	1
Bengochea, Kiki, Stockton	.722	34	4	9	5	18	0
Biggs, Billy, Lancaster	1.000	54	6	12	0	18	1
Bilke, Austin, R.C.	.800	14	0	4	1	5	0
Bittner, Tim, R.C.*	.889	6	1	7	1	9	1
Blood, Justin, Inland Empire *	.929	50	4	9	1	14	0
Bott, Glenn, Inland Empire *	.781	31	6	19	7	32	1
Bowie, Micah, Modesto *	.000	2	0	0	0	0	0
Brazelton, Dewon, Bakersfield	.917	9	7	4	1	12	0
Brown, Elliot, San Jose	.833	15	4	6	2	12	0
Bruksch, Jeffrey, Modesto	.905	23	3	16	2	21	1
Bruso, Greg, San Jose	.958	14	9	14	1	24	2
Buckley, Allen, R.C.	1.000	6	2	1	0	3	0
Bukowski, Stan, R.C.	1.000	6	1	4	0	5	1
Bulger, Jason, Lancaster	1.000	4	2	4	0	6	0
Bumatay, Mike, Visalia *	1.000	8	1	0	0	1	0
Bumstead, Mike, Lake Elsinore	.857	5	2	4	1	7	0
Burres, Brian, San Jose *	.800	39	1	7	2	10	0
Bystrowski, Bobby, High Desert	1.000	48	4	6	0	10	0
Camp, Rusty, R.C.	.750	17	0	3	1	4	0
Campbell, Jarrett, Bakersfield	1.000	32	6	11	0	17	1
Candelaria, Scott, High Desert	.000	2	0	0	0	0	0
Cassel, Jack, Lake Elsinore	.885	64	7	16	3	26	0
Castellanos, Jonathan, Lan.	1.000	30	12	9	0	21	2
Cate, Troy, Inland Empire *	.857	27	8	22	5	35	0
Christiansen, Jason, San Jose *	1.000	5	1	0	0	1	0
Clark, Jeff, San Jose	.875	9	3	4	1	8	0
Coleman, Jeff, Modesto	.933	37	6	8	1	15	2
Coose, Austin, Bakersfield	.900	50	1	8	1	10	1
Cormier, Lance, Lancaster	.968	15	13	17	1	31	1
Cortez, Renee, Inland Empire	1.000	15	2	3	0	5	0
Craker, Justin, Lake Elsinore	.941	50	4	12	1	17	1
Cram, Josh, San Jose	1.000	31	3	9	0	12	2
Cramblitt, Joey, Lancaster	.000	10	0	0	1	1	0
Cramer, Bob, Bakersfield *	1.000	5	0	3	0	3	0
Crawford, Chris, Bakersfield *	.963	47	2	24	1	27	3
Crockett, Ben, Visalia	1.000	5	1	6	0	7	0
Crowell, Kyle, Modesto	1.000	30	2	3	0	5	0
Cullen, Ryan, Modesto *	1.000	15	1	3	0	4	0
D'Amico, Leonardo, R.C.	1.000	6	0	1	0	1	0
Darnell, Paul, Visalia *	.000	23	0	0	0	0	0
Dean, Aaron, High Desert	1.000	38	7	3	0	10	0
Dominguez, Juan, Stockton	1.000	16	3	3	0	6	0
Done, Juan, Inland Empire	.929	30	4	9	1	14	0
Dorman, Rich, Inland Empire	1.000	13	3	7	0	10	0
Dukeman, Greg, Bakersfield	1.000	28	5	11	0	16	2
Ebert, Derrin, High Desert *	.000	3	0	0	0	0	0
Echols, Justin, Stockton	.800	25	4	8	3	15	0
Edwards, John, Visalia	.000	1	0	0	0	0	0
Ellis, Rob, Bakersfield *	1.000	2	0	1	0	1	0
Esposito, Michael, Visalia	.914	27	12	20	3	35	3
Esslinger, Cam, Visalia	1.000	11	2	4	0	6	1
Firlit, Dan, Lancaster	.000	1	0	0	0	0	0
Fischer, Steve, Modesto	.875	24	4	10	2	16	1
Flinn, Chris, Bakersfield	.926	24	13	12	2	27	2
Foppert, Jesse, San Jose	.000	1	0	0	0	0	0
France, Ryan, Modesto	1.000	1	0	1	0	1	0
Francis, Jeff, Visalia *	1.000	27	10	18	0	28	1
Fritz, Ben, Modesto	.875	15	6	8	2	16	0
Fruto, Emiliano, Inland Empire	.889	42	4	12	2	18	1
Garcia, James, San Jose	1.000	33	3	5	0	8	0
Gardner, Hayden, Stockton	.000	4	0	0	0	0	0
Garvin, Robert, Lake Elsinore	.857	61	4	8	2	14	0
Gaudin, Chad, Bakersfield	.857	14	7	11	3	21	0
George, Christopher, San Jose	.000	4	0	0	0	0	0
Germano, Justin, Lake Elsinore	1.000	19	4	19	0	23	0
Gilbert, Rich, Stockton *	.857	51	3	9	2	14	2
Gold, J.M., High Desert	1.000	11	1	2	0	3	1
Gonzalez, Cristian, Modesto	1.000	8	6	6	0	12	0
Gordon, Justin, High Desert *	.944	38	5	12	1	18	0
Gorman, Jason, Lancaster	.000	1	0	0	0	0	0
Gray, Rusty, Inland Empire	1.000	3	2	0	0	2	0
Green, Sean, Visalia	.875	46	9	19	4	32	2
Griffin, Charles, Lancaster	.889	20	4	4	1	9	1
Griffith, Dustin, R.C.	1.000	36	2	9	0	11	0
Gross, Kyle, San Jose	1.000	2	1	0	0	1	0
Gwyn, Marc, Modesto	.909	32	1	9	1	11	2
Hall, Dan, High Desert	.974	26	13	25	1	39	2
Hampson, Justin, Visalia *	.941	26	4	28	2	34	1
Hannaman, Ryan, San Jose *	.800	13	2	6	2	10	0
Henrie, Matt, Lancaster	.919	14	10	24	3	37	2
Hensley, Clay, S.J.-Lake Elsinore	.722	13	3	10	5	18	1

Player, Team	Pct.	G	PO	A	E	TC	DP
Hines, Carlos, Bakersfield	.750	25	2	1	1	4	0
Hoffman, Trevor, Lake Elsinore	.000	3	0	0	0	0	0
Holsten, Ryan, Lancaster	1.000	2	1	0	0	1	0
Huber, Jon, Lake Elsinore	1.000	12	2	4	0	6	0
Hundley, Jeff, High Desert *	1.000	23	2	7	0	9	0
Hutchison, Wes, San Jose	.769	39	2	8	3	13	0
Jarvis, Kevin, Lake Elsinore	1.000	3	3	1	0	4	0
Jimenez, Kelvin, Stockton	1.000	34	10	14	0	24	1
Jimenez, Ubaldo, Visalia	.000	1	0	0	0	0	0
Johnson, Randy, Lancaster *	.000	1	0	0	0	0	0
Jones, Geoffrey, Lake Elsinore *	.909	25	3	7	1	11	0
Keiter, Ben, Stockton	1.000	25	6	8	0	14	1
Kerbs, Reuben, Lancaster *	1.000	9	1	1	0	2	0
Ketchner, Ryan, Inland Empire *	1.000	31	9	16	0	25	0
Kolb, Dan, High Desert	.967	27	12	17	1	30	1
Kozol, Anthony, Lake Elsinore	1.000	15	0	4	0	4	0
Kranawetter, Josh, Lancaster	1.000	17	1	4	0	5	0
Krawczyk, Jack, Lancaster	.000	3	0	0	0	0	0
Lipari, Thomas, Lake Elsinore *	.833	12	0	5	1	6	0
Liriano, Francisco, San Jose *	.000	1	0	0	0	0	0
Little, Joe, Bakersfield *	1.000	2	0	1	0	1	0
Lockwood, Brian, Bakersfield	.935	27	12	17	2	31	1
Loe, Kameron, Stockton	.875	9	4	3	1	8	0
Mabeus, Chris, Modesto	.667	18	0	2	1	3	0
Markert, Jackson, San Jose	.750	13	0	3	1	4	0
Martin, Sean, San Jose	1.000	5	1	4	0	5	1
Martinez, Javier, Lake Elsinore	1.000	16	2	10	0	12	1
Marx, Tommy, High Desert *	.857	21	0	6	1	7	1
Matthews, Jarod, Bakersfield	1.000	23	5	7	0	12	0
Mazone, Brian, High Desert *	.727	13	2	6	3	11	0
McCall, Derell, Modesto	.923	19	4	20	2	26	0
McMachen, Clifford, Lancaster *	1.000	33	4	13	0	17	0
Mead, David, Stockton	1.000	24	2	2	0	4	0
Medlin, Corbey, Lancaster	.909	33	4	6	1	11	0
Menchaca, Eriberto, I.E.	.000	1	0	0	0	0	0
Mendoza, Mario, R.C.	1.000	4	0	3	0	3	0
Moore, Darin, Stockton	1.000	21	3	9	0	12	0
Morel, Eudy, Lake Elsinore	.000	5	0	0	0	0	0
Morgan, Russ, Inland Empire *	.500	15	1	1	2	4	0
Mowday, Chris, Modesto	.000	9	0	0	0	0	0
Mozingo, Dan, R.C. *	.944	20	4	13	1	18	2
Narron, Sam, Stockton *	.971	26	9	25	1	35	4
Neagle, Denny, Visalia *	1.000	2	0	1	0	1	0
Nickoli, Mike, R.C.	.667	4	0	2	1	3	0
Nolasco, Dave, High Desert	.889	21	1	7	1	9	0
Nunez, Jose, Lake Elsinore *	1.000	8	2	1	0	3	0
O'Connor, Brian, Bakersfield *	.000	2	0	0	0	0	0
O'Sullivan, Mark, R.C.	1.000	52	7	10	0	17	0
Obenchain, Stephen, Modesto	1.000	9	6	5	0	11	0
Olore, Kevin, Inland Empire	.714	8	2	3	2	7	1
Padgett, Daniel, San Jose *	.800	11	0	4	1	5	0
Pannone, Anthony, San Jose	.929	22	3	10	1	14	0
Parker, Josh, Bakersfield	.800	31	2	2	1	5	1
Parker, Zach, Visalia *	.957	16	5	17	1	23	0
Pavlik, Isaac, Visalia *	.750	51	1	5	2	8	0
Pavon, Julio, San Jose	.903	41	6	22	3	31	1
Perez, Elvis, Inland Empire	.909	13	5	5	1	11	1
Perez, Jeffrey, Inland Empire	1.000	12	1	4	0	5	0
Petke, Tim, Rancho Cucamonga	1.000	10	4	9	0	13	1
Petty, Chad, High Desert *	.857	17	2	10	2	14	1
Price, Brett, Modesto *	.778	41	3	4	2	9	0
Price, Ryan, Visalia	.500	7	1	0	1	2	0
Prinz, Bret, Lancaster	.000	1	0	0	0	0	0
Pruett, Hubert, High Desert	.000	1	0	0	0	0	0
Pruett, Jason, Bakersfield *	.900	48	4	5	1	10	0
Raburn, Johnny, High Desert	.000	2	0	0	0	0	0
Rall, Tim, Inland Empire *	1.000	10	5	4	0	9	0
Ramirez, Edward, R.C.	.500	4	1	1	2	4	0
Ramsay, Rob, Lake Elsinore *	1.000	27	0	4	0	4	0
Ray, Ken, High Desert	.333	7	0	1	2	3	0
Reece, Eric, Bakersfield	.000	1	0	0	0	0	0
Reyes, Ramon, R.C.	.000	1	0	0	0	0	0
Reynolds, Josh, Lake Elsinore	1.000	3	2	1	0	3	0
Ribas, Gabe, Lake Elsinore	1.000	9	2	7	0	9	0
Richards, John, Lake Elsinore *	1.000	10	0	3	0	3	1
Richardson, Mike, Lake Elsinore	.000	2	0	0	0	0	0
Rigueiro, Rafael, San Jose	.600	17	0	3	2	5	0
Robertson, Luke, Modesto	.857	29	6	18	4	28	1

Player, Team	Pct.	G	PO	A	E	TC	DP
Robinson, Jeff, High Desert	.833	7	3	2	1	6	0
Rosario, Melvin, Visalia *	.000	1	0	0	0	0	0
Rouwenhorst, Jonathon, R.C. *	.909	52	3	17	2	22	1
Rowe, Steven, Stockton	.833	48	3	7	2	12	2
Rowland-Smith, Ryan, I.E.*	1.000	15	1	2	0	3	0
Saenz, Chris, High Desert	.850	26	5	12	3	20	1
Sanchez, Adiel, Modesto *	1.000	4	0	1	0	1	0
Santana, Ervin, R.C.	.917	20	9	13	2	24	0
Sasaki, Kazuhiro, Inland Empire	.000	1	0	0	0	0	0
Sauer, Marc, Modesto	.833	22	3	7	2	12	0
Schaub, Greg, High Desert	1.000	8	0	2	0	2	0
Schmidt, Jeremy, San Jose	1.000	5	1	1	0	2	0
Schneider, Scott, R.C.	.778	17	0	7	2	9	1
Schultz, Mike, Lancaster	1.000	9	4	10	0	14	1
Seddon, Chris, Bakersfield *	.867	26	5	21	4	30	3
Sele, Aaron, Rancho Cucamonga	1.000	3	0	1	0	1	0
Serrano, Alex, Visalia	1.000	49	6	13	0	19	0
Shank, Chris, Modesto	1.000	26	1	3	0	4	0
Shell, Steven, R.C.	.963	22	6	20	1	27	0
Shields, Jamie, Bakersfield	.909	26	8	12	2	22	1
Sikaras, Pete, Lancaster	1.000	46	2	3	0	5	0
Simpson, Gerrit, Visalia	.957	27	19	26	2	47	3
Slaten, Doug, Lancaster *	.889	32	6	26	4	36	1
Smart, Pete, High Desert *	1.000	5	1	7	0	8	2
Smith, Cliff, Rancho Cucamonga	.800	15	2	2	1	5	0
Smith, Jesse, R.C.	1.000	5	1	7	0	8	0
Songster, Judd, Visalia	1.000	9	0	1	0	1	0
Speier, Ryan, Visalia	.714	56	3	2	2	7	0
Stanton, Kyle, Visalia	1.000	14	1	2	0	3	0
Stark, Dennis, Visalia	.000	1	0	0	0	0	0
Stavros, Tony, High Desert	1.000	46	6	9	0	15	2
Steele, Mike, Inland Empire	1.000	33	2	7	0	9	0
Stout, Danny, High Desert	1.000	12	3	4	0	7	0
Strelitz, Brian, Inland Empire	1.000	29	3	13	0	16	0
Thomas, J.T., San Jose *	.914	33	6	26	3	35	0
Thomas, Jared, Inland Empire *	.600	41	0	3	2	5	0
Thompson, Erik, Stockton	.923	19	7	5	1	13	0
THOMPSON, MIKE, L.E.	1.000	28	12	22	0	34	2
Thompson, Richard, R.C.	.800	24	2	2	1	5	1
Thornton, Matt, Inland Empire *	.000	2	0	0	0	0	0
Tierney, Chris, Lake Elsinore *	1.000	1	0	1	0	1	0
Torres, Joe, R.C. *	.917	8	5	6	1	12	0
Treadway, Brion, San Jose	.950	29	7	12	1	20	0
Trejo, Francisco, Lancaster *	1.000	16	2	1	0	3	0
Turco, Anthony, San Jose	.000	1	0	0	0	0	0
Ulloa, Enmanuel, Inland Empire	.909	17	4	6	1	11	0
Valdez, Domingo, Stockton	.500	9	0	1	1	2	0
Vent, Kevin, San Jose	.000	4	0	0	0	0	0
Vicente, Ruben, Lancaster	.833	3	5	0	1	6	0
Villafuerte, Brandon, L.E.	.000	2	0	0	0	0	0
Walker, Kevin, Lake Elsinore *	.000	4	0	0	0	0	0
Washburn, Ben, San Jose	.000	4	0	0	0	0	0
Wear, Gregory, Inland Empire	1.000	1	1	0	0	1	0
Webb, Nick, Visalia *	.917	25	4	7	1	12	0
Wechsler, Justin, Lancaster	.944	27	7	10	1	18	1
Weis, Brad, Modesto *	.886	30	4	35	5	44	1
Wells, Carlton, Lancaster *	.929	46	10	16	2	28	0
Whatley, Keith, Lancaster *	1.000	8	1	16	0	17	0
Wiedmeyer, Jason, L.E. *	.950	14	5	14	1	20	1
Williams, Brady, Bakersfield	.000	1	0	0	0	0	0
Williams, Bryan, R.C.	.889	19	2	6	1	9	1
Wilson, Phil, R.C.	1.000	2	0	1	0	1	0
Witasick, Jay, Lake Elsinore	.000	4	0	0	0	0	0
Wodnicki, Mike, Lake Elsinore	1.000	43	5	13	0	18	0
Wolensky, Dave, R.C.	.857	46	3	9	2	14	1
Woods, Jake, R.C. *	1.000	28	7	21	0	28	1
Wrigley, Jase, Visalia	.000	5	0	0	0	0	0
Yoshida, Nobuaki, L.E. *	1.000	3	0	5	0	5	0
Zerbe, Chad, San Jose *	1.000	2	1	1	0	2	0

PITCHERS WITH TWO OR MORE TEAMS

Player, Team	Pct.	G	PO	A	E	TC	DP
Hensley, Clay, Lake Elsinore	.750	8	1	8	3	12	1
Hensley, Clay, San Jose	.667	5	2	2	2	6	0

The following players appeared only as a designated hitter, pinch-hitter or pinch-runner: Fuller, dh; Glaus, dh; Nevin, dh; Quintero, dh, ph; O. Saenz, dh.

LEAGUE CHAMPIONS

Year	Team	Pct.
1914—	Fresno	.571
1915—	Modesto	.857
1916-40—Did not operate.		
1941—	Fresno	.643
	Santa Barbara (2nd)*	.597
1942—	Santa Barbara†	.642
1943-44-45—Did not operate.		
1946—	Stockton‡	.600
1947—	Stockton‡	.679
1948—	Fresno	.607
	Santa Barbara (3rd)*	.529
1949—	Bakersfield	.612
	San Jose (4th)*	.543
1950—	Ventura	.607
	Modesto (2nd)*	.586
1951—	Santa Barbara‡	.599
1952—	Fresno‡	.629
1953—	San Jose‡	.664
1954—	Modesto‡	.623
1955—	Stockton	.733
	Fresno§	.718
1956—	Fresno§	.650
1957—	Visalia∞	.622
	Salinas (4th)*	.504
1958—	Fresno*	.639
	Bakersfield	.672
1959—	Bakersfield	.592
	Modesto§	.643
1960—	Reno	.614
	Reno	.657
1961—	Reno	.743
	Reno	.643
1962—	San Jose§	.686
	Reno	.587
1963—	Modesto	.589
	Stockton§	.687
1964—	Fresno	.638
	Fresno	.600
1965—	San Jose	.586
	Stockton§	.614
1966—	Modesto	.577
	Modesto	.671
1967—	San Jose§	.676
	Modesto	.586
1968—	San Jose	.629
	Fresno§	.623
1969—	Stockton§	.600
	Visalia	.614
1970—	Bakersfield	.667
	Bakersfield	.671
1971—	Visalia§	.583
	Fresno	.500
1972—	Modesto§	.547
	Bakersfield	.629
1973—	Lodi§	.657
	Bakersfield	.571
1974—	Fresno§	.607
	San Jose	.579
1975—	Reno	.614
	Reno	.614
1976—	Salinas	.650
	Reno§	.547
1977—	Salinas	.564
	Lodi§	.579
1978—	Visalia§	.698
	Lodi	.607
1979—	San Jose§	.636
	Reno	.525
1980—	Stockton§	.638
	Visalia	.507
1981—	Visalia	.621
	Lodi§	.521
1982—	Modesto§	.671
	Visalia	.586
1983—	Visalia	.621
	Redwood§	.529
1984—	Modesto§	.597
	Bakersfield	.486
1985—	Fresno§	.575
	Stockton	.566
1986—	Palm Springs	.613
	Stockton§	.585
1987—	Fresno§	.559
	Reno	.535
1988—	Stockton	.657
	Riverside§	.599
1989—	Stockton	.627
	Bakersfield§	.577
1990—	Visalia	.638
	Stockton§	.582
1991—	San Jose	.676
	High Desert§	.537
1992—	Stockton§	.610
	Visalia	.551
1993—	High Desert§	.620
	Modesto	.529
1994—	Modesto	.706
	Rancho Cucamonga§	.566
1995—	San Bernardino§	.612
	San Jose	.550
1996—	San Jose	.636
	Lake Elsinore‡	.550
1997—	High Desert▲	.593
	San Bernardino	.486
1998—	San Jose▲	.593
	Rancho Cucamonga	.550
1999—	Modesto	.629
	San Bernardino▲	.567
Year	**Team**	**Pct.**
2000—	Lancaster	.636
	San Bernardino▲	.550
2001—	Lake Elsinore◆	.650
	San Jose◆	.550
2002—	Stockton▲	.636
2003—	Inland Empire▲	.557

*Won four-club playoff. †League disbanded June 28. ‡Won championship and four-club playoff. §Won split-season playoff. ∞Won both halves of split season. ▲Played split season and won six-club playoff. ◆Played split season and were in midst of six-club playoff and declared co-champions when Professional Baseball declared a stoppage of play.

CAROLINA LEAGUE

LEAGUE OFFICE

President/treasurer
John Hopkins
Address
P.O. Box 9503
Greensboro, NC 27429
Phone
336-691-9030

Teams (affiliation)
Frederick Keys (Orioles)
Kinston Indians (Indians)
Lynchburg Hillcats (Pirates)
Myrtle Beach Pelicans (Braves)
Potomac Cannons (Reds)
Salem Avalanche (Astros)
Wilmington (Del.) Blue Rocks (Royals)
Winston-Salem Warthogs (White Sox)

2003 FINAL STANDINGS

FIRST HALF

NORTHERN DIVISION

Team	W	L	T	Pct.	GB
Lynchburg	37	28	-	.569	...
Wilmington	38	32	-	.543	1.5
Potomac	30	39	-	.435	9.0
Frederick	26	40	-	.394	11.5

SOUTHERN DIVISION

Team	W	L	T	Pct.	GB
Winston-Salem	39	29	-	.574	...
Salem	35	33	-	.515	4.0
Kinston	34	35	-	.493	5.5
Myrtle Beach	33	36	-	.478	6.5

SECOND HALF

NORTHERN DIVISION

Team	W	L	T	Pct.	GB
Wilmington	42	28	-	.600	...
Lynchburg	39	31	-	.557	3.0
Frederick	34	35	-	.493	7.5
Potomac	32	38	-	.457	10.0

SOUTHERN DIVISION

Team	W	L	T	Pct.	GB
Kinston	39	31	-	.557	...
Salem	38	32	-	.543	1.0
Winston-Salem	32	38	-	.457	7.0
Myrtle Beach	23	46	-	.333	15.5

COMPOSITE

Team	WIL	LYN	SAL	KIN	W-S	POT	FRE	MYR	W	L	T	Pct.	GB
Wilmington (Royals)	...	12	9	14	13	12	11	9	80	60	0	.571	...
Lynchburg (Pirates)	8	...	11	13	11	10	10	13	76	59	0	.563	1.5
Salem (Astros)	11	7	...	10	8	14	13	10	73	65	0	.529	6.0
Kinston (Indians)	6	7	10	...	8	13	12	17	73	66	0	.525	6.5
Winston-Salem (White Sox)	7	8	12	12	...	12	10	10	71	67	0	.514	8.0
Potomac (Reds)	8	10	6	7	8	...	10	13	62	77	0	.446	17.5
Frederick (Orioles)	9	8	7	7	9	10	...	10	60	75	0	.444	17.5
Myrtle Beach (Braves)	11	7	10	3	10	6	9	...	56	82	0	.406	23.0

Major league affiliations in parentheses.

PLAYOFFS: Lynchburg defeated Wilmington, two games to none; Winston-Salem defeated Kinston, two games to none; Winston-Salem defeated Lynchburg, three games to none, to win league championship.

REGULAR-SEASON ATTENDANCE: Frederick, 285,048; Kinston, 103,433; Lynchburg, 91,935; Myrtle Beach, 203,443; Potomac, 160,238; Salem, 175,155; Wilmington, 315,134; Winston-Salem, 124,454. Total attendance—1,458,840. Playoffs (7 games)—9,093. Carolina-California League All-Star Game at Rancho Cucamonga, Calif.—5,737.

MANAGERS: Frederick, Tom Lawless; Kinston, Torey Lovullo; Lynchburg, Dave Clark; Myrtle Beach, Randy Ingle; Potomac, Jayhawk Owens; Salem, John Massarelli; Wilmington, Billy Gardner Jr.; Winston-Salem, Razor Shines.

ALL-STAR TEAM: 1B—Walter Young, Lynchburg; 2B—Ruddy Yan, Winston-Salem; 3B—Andy Marte, Myrtle Beach; SS—(tie) Jeff Bannon, Potomac and Andres Blanco, Wilmington; Utility INF—Todd Self, Salem; OF—Nate McLouth, Lynchburg; OF—Trey Dyson, Wilmington-Kinston; OF—Willy Taveras, Kinston; Utility OF—Woody Cliffords, Frederick; C—Ryan Doumit, Lynchburg; DH—Chris Shelton, Lynchburg; Starting pitcher—Zack Greinke, Wilmington; Relief pitcher—Lee Gronkiewicz, Kinston; Most Valuable Player—Chris Shelton, Lynchburg; Pitcher of the Year—Zack Greinke, Wilmington; Manager of the Year—Dave Clark, Lynchburg.

2003 BATTING

TEAM

Team	G	TPA	AB	R	H	TB	2B	3B	HR	RBI	SH	SF	HP	BB	IBB	SO	SB	CS	GDP	LOB	ShO	Avg.	OBP	Slg.
Lynchburg	135	4972	4391	670	1190	1766	247	25	93	602	48	35	67	431	19	837	109	46	87	913	5	.271	.343	.402
Frederick	135	4967	4413	541	1144	1654	237	18	79	486	47	39	54	414	19	908	59	51	114	923	13	.259	.328	.375
Wilmington	140	5295	4577	589	1173	1597	211	21	57	530	58	45	85	529	22	839	73	32	101	1131	12	.256	.341	.349
Win.-Salem	138	4930	4328	574	1107	1652	237	22	88	523	66	46	47	443	23	824	196	55	83	898	11	.256	.328	.382
Potomac	139	5050	4475	543	1136	1636	233	21	75	503	58	53	45	418	17	909	122	56	103	930	12	.254	.320	.366
Myrtle Beach	138	5028	4494	506	1142	1605	209	25	68	446	48	39	57	389	23	914	109	77	113	913	17	.254	.319	.357
Kinston	139	5076	4448	570	1121	1580	205	25	68	518	52	41	76	459	21	991	183	72	66	959	12	.252	.330	.355
Salem	138	5116	4477	611	1115	1598	220	31	67	559	58	46	55	480	25	904	114	41	87	945	4	.249	.326	.357

INDIVIDUAL

TOP QUALIFIERS FOR BATTING CHAMPIONSHIP

Minimum 378 plate appearances. *Lefthanded batter. †Switch-hitter.

Player, Team	G	TPA	AB	R	H	TB	2B	3B	HR	RBI	SH	SF	HP	BB	IBB	SO	SB	CS	GDP	Avg.	OBP	Slg.
Shelton, Chris, Lynchburg	95	389	315	71	113	202	24	1	21	69	0	1	5	68	8	67	1	4	6	.359	.478	.641
Self, Todd, Salem *	126	531	431	84	137	186	27	2	6	57	2	6	5	87	5	93	2	1	9	.318	.433	.432
Cates, Gary, Frederick	92	389	355	50	112	150	23	3	3	35	7	1	5	21	1	40	11	12	5	.315	.361	.423
Shanks, James, Wilmington	85	380	346	54	104	129	15	2	2	23	1	1	4	28	2	71	21	8	3	.301	.359	.373
McLouth, Nathan, Lynch.*	117	508	440	85	132	181	27	2	6	33	5	1	7	55	2	68	40	4	4	.300	.386	.411
Bannon, Jeff, Potomac	104	415	366	45	108	162	26	2	8	42	4	5	5	35	1	67	7	8	10	.295	.360	.443
Huggins, Mike, Frederick	126	520	454	66	133	204	32	0	13	74	0	8	3	55	5	93	3	3	14	.293	.367	.449
Rogers, Omar, Frederick	99	411	356	49	104	137	24	0	3	28	5	2	6	42	1	70	4	5	11	.292	.374	.385
Buttler, Vic, Lynchburg *	117	437	382	49	109	146	18	5	3	44	9	1	8	37	1	47	22	5	7	.285	.360	.382
Marte, Andy, Myrtle Beach	130	541	463	69	132	217	35	1	16	63	0	9	2	67	8	109	5	2	13	.285	.372	.469
Conrad, Brooks, Salem †	99	401	345	50	98	161	24	3	11	61	5	3	6	42	3	60	4	2	7	.284	.369	.467
Cliffords, Woody, Frederick *	124	531	440	70	124	179	29	1	8	44	5	5	10	71	4	77	16	10	15	.282	.390	.407
Taveras, Willy, Kinston	113	468	397	64	112	139	9	6	2	35	6	1	12	52	1	68	57	12	4	.282	.381	.350
Lentini, Fehlandt, Salem	100	403	369	45	103	141	21	4	3	48	4	3	2	25	1	58	19	7	11	.279	.326	.382
Dyson, Trey, Wilm.-Kinston *	135	564	480	69	134	211	32	0	15	75	1	7	10	66	9	98	7	2	8	.279	.373	.440

DEPARTMENTAL LEADERS: G—Dyson, Fallon, 135; AB—Bergolla, 523; R—McLouth, Yan, 85; H—Bergolla, 142; TB—Marte, 217; 2B—Doumit, 38; 3B—Rodriguez, 8; HR—Shelton, 21; RBI—Young, 87; SH—A. Blanco, 21; SF—Becker, 11; HP—Cowan, 16; BB—Self, 87; IBB—Dyson, 9; SO—G. Blanco, 114; SB—Yan, 76; CS—Bergolla, 18; GIDP—Salas, 16; Slg.—Shelton, .641; OBP—Shelton, .478.

ALL PLAYERS

*Lefthanded batter. †Switch-hitter.

Player, Team	G	TPA	AB	R	H	TB	2B	3B	HR	RBI	SH	SF	HP	BB	IBB	SO	SB	CS	GDP	Avg.	OBP	Slg.
Alleva, J.D., Wilmington *	58	208	184	20	46	59	7	0	2	17	2	4	2	16	0	28	0	4	6	.250	.311	.321
Amador, Chris, Win.-Salem	26	72	66	6	13	16	1	1	0	3	0	1	1	4	0	18	8	0	0	.197	.250	.242
Anderson, Bryan, Potomac	60	237	200	20	49	72	17	0	2	26	8	9	3	17	0	41	3	0	8	.245	.301	.360
Arko, Tommy, Frederick	34	123	113	13	21	42	3	0	6	15	0	1	1	8	0	40	0	0	5	.186	.244	.372
Arnerich, Tony, Wilmington	53	181	148	13	29	42	8	1	1	20	3	1	5	24	1	28	0	0	6	.196	.326	.284
Asprilla, Avelino, Lynchburg	33	117	106	12	22	28	6	0	0	17	6	2	0	3	0	24	0	2	3	.208	.225	.264
Bannon, Jeff, Potomac	104	415	366	45	108	162	26	2	8	42	4	5	5	35	1	67	7	8	10	.295	.360	.443
Barnett, Dan, Win.-Salem	9	20	18	1	2	3	1	0	0	1	0	1	0	1	0	6	0	0	0	.111	.150	.167
Bautista, Jose, Lynchburg	51	195	165	28	40	70	14	2	4	20	0	0	3	27	0	48	1	5	1	.242	.359	.424
Becker, Brian, Winston-Salem	115	449	408	47	105	188	24	1	19	72	1	11	2	27	4	98	3	3	12	.257	.299	.461
Bergolla, William, Potomac	128	572	523	77	142	179	25	3	2	31	15	4	1	29	1	59	52	18	13	.272	.309	.342
Bernard, Miguel, M.B.	1	2	2	0	0	0	0	0	0	0	0	0	0	0	0	1	0	0	0	.000	.000	.000
Berroa, Cristian, Lynchburg †	39	126	123	11	27	33	4	1	0	10	0	1	0	2	0	18	1	0	4	.220	.230	.268
Blanco, Andres, Wil.†	113	469	394	61	96	113	11	3	0	25	21	2	8	44	1	50	13	7	9	.244	.330	.287
Blanco, Gregor, M.B.*	126	527	461	66	125	173	19	7	5	36	3	1	8	54	0	114	34	16	4	.271	.357	.375
Blanco, Tony, Potomac	69	278	241	33	64	115	17	2	10	49	0	7	4	26	2	62	0	0	5	.266	.338	.477
Boruff, Gabriel, Wilmington †	1	4	4	0	0	0	0	0	0	0	0	0	0	0	0	1	0	0	0	.000	.000	.000
Boscan, Jean, Myrtle Beach	28	100	87	9	18	25	4	0	1	11	2	0	0	11	0	33	2	0	1	.207	.296	.287
Bozanich, Sam, Lynchburg	40	139	117	15	27	39	6	0	2	12	2	1	3	16	1	32	2	0	3	.231	.336	.333
Burrows, Angelo, M.B.*	41	138	127	14	32	41	7	1	0	10	5	0	1	5	0	18	3	4	3	.252	.286	.323
Buttler, Vic, Lynchburg *	117	437	382	49	109	146	18	5	3	44	9	1	8	37	1	47	22	5	7	.285	.360	.382
Calitri, Mike, Potomac	55	196	171	22	38	68	10	1	6	26	1	2	1	21	0	48	3	1	7	.222	.308	.398
Camacaro, Armando, Kinston	58	207	182	19	43	56	7	0	2	17	3	4	9	9	0	29	2	3	9	.236	.299	.308
Campana, Wandel, Potomac	5	15	12	2	1	4	0	0	1	1	2	0	0	1	0	2	0	0	0	.083	.154	.333
Canales, Josh, Salem	71	165	142	18	23	23	0	0	0	3	3	0	0	20	1	42	3	1	2	.162	.265	.162
Caraway, Brandon, Salem †	123	499	436	74	110	141	21	2	2	50	4	5	5	49	1	65	17	9	7	.252	.331	.323
Cates, Gary, Frederick	92	389	355	50	112	150	23	3	3	35	7	1	5	21	1	40	11	12	5	.315	.361	.423
Chaves, Brandon, Lynch.†	121	498	443	62	116	160	23	6	3	49	9	2	4	40	0	82	13	8	6	.262	.327	.361
Checksfield, Steven, Salem	79	277	252	29	60	101	16	2	7	37	1	1	2	21	0	54	2	0	8	.238	.301	.401
Choy Foo, Rodney, Kinston †	125	507	444	57	114	168	17	2	11	65	1	3	6	53	4	95	22	8	5	.257	.342	.378
Ciraco, Darren, Win.-Salem	2	7	7	0	2	3	1	0	0	0	0	0	0	0	0	1	0	0	0	.286	.286	.429
Cliffords, Woody, Frederick *	124	531	440	70	124	179	29	1	8	44	5	5	10	71	4	77	16	10	15	.282	.390	.407
Cockrell, Michael, Lynchburg	7	26	24	3	11	14	3	0	0	3	0	0	0	2	0	1	0	0	3	.458	.500	.583
Conrad, Brooks, Salem †	99	401	345	50	98	161	24	3	11	61	5	3	6	42	3	60	4	2	7	.284	.369	.467
Cooper, Jason, Kinston *	61	250	218	36	67	115	17	2	9	36	0	4	3	25	4	46	3	0	3	.307	.380	.528
Correll, Brad, Potomac	38	159	143	19	41	69	11	1	5	24	0	0	1	15	0	22	2	1	3	.287	.358	.483
Cortes, Jorge, Lynchburg *	37	145	129	17	34	43	6	0	1	15	2	3	0	11	0	25	1	1	2	.264	.315	.333
Costa, Shane, Wilmington *	3	10	7	1	1	2	1	0	0	0	0	0	1	2	0	1	0	0	0	.143	.400	.286
Cotto, Luis, Wil.-Kinston	56	193	163	14	26	30	4	0	0	11	8	1	5	16	0	52	1	1	2	.160	.254	.184
Cowan, Justin, Wilmington	119	484	438	52	120	176	23	6	7	52	2	3	16	25	0	66	2	0	10	.274	.334	.402
Davies, Gregg, Frederick *	14	44	37	1	10	12	2	0	0	3	0	1	1	5	0	4	0	0	2	.270	.364	.324
Davis, Justin, Potomac *	30	79	67	6	10	12	2	0	0	3	0	0	0	12	0	15	0	1	1	.149	.278	.179
De Caster, Yurendell, Lynch.	97	361	330	50	76	141	24	1	13	56	0	5	4	22	1	86	3	2	9	.230	.283	.427
Denorfia, Chris, Potomac	128	541	470	60	111	143	10	5	4	39	11	3	3	54	0	106	20	7	10	.236	.317	.304
Dorsey, Ryan, Wilmington	2	5	2	1	0	0	0	0	0	0	0	0	0	3	0	0	0	0	0	.000	.600	.000
Doumit, Ryan, Lynchburg †	127	524	458	75	126	199	38	1	11	77	0	8	13	45	3	79	4	0	7	.275	.351	.434
Draper, John, Wilmington	127	510	441	42	103	126	15	1	2	47	11	4	12	41	3	80	9	2	8	.234	.313	.286
Duran, Carlos, M.B.*	118	448	415	45	93	134	20	6	3	35	3	8	4	17	3	60	11	10	8	.224	.257	.323
Dyson, Trey, Wil.-Kinston *	135	564	480	69	134	211	32	0	15	75	1	7	10	66	9	98	7	2	8	.279	.373	.440
Elder, Rick, Kinston *	42	160	136	15	30	55	7	0	6	21	0	3	1	20	0	55	0	1	2	.221	.319	.404
Encarnacion, Edwin, Potomac	58	244	215	40	69	104	15	1	6	29	1	3	1	24	1	32	7	1	2	.321	.387	.484
Fahey, Brandon, Frederick *	107	404	365	41	85	105	11	3	1	22	13	2	2	22	0	56	4	2	7	.233	.279	.288

Player, Team	G	TPA	AB	R	H	TB	2B	3B	HR	RBI	SH	SF	HP	BB	IBB	SO	SB	CS	GDP	Avg.	OBP	Slg.
Fallon, Chris, Wilmington *	135	570	471	69	128	189	28	0	11	79	0	7	8	84	4	99	4	2	11	.272	.386	.401
Fenster, Darren, Wilmington	88	372	312	39	74	84	10	0	0	33	3	2	4	51	0	40	0	2	8	.237	.350	.269
Gimenez, Hector, Salem †	109	419	381	41	94	134	17	1	7	54	1	4	4	29	1	75	2	0	7	.247	.304	.352
Gordon, Alex, Frederick *	69	258	235	29	52	78	11	3	3	29	1	3	1	18	1	85	0	0	5	.221	.276	.332
Gotay, Ruben, Wilmington †	134	582	502	68	131	193	31	2	9	72	4	9	7	60	1	97	8	1	7	.261	.343	.384
Gredvig, Doug, Frederick	12	47	40	8	11	17	3	0	1	6	0	0	1	6	0	6	0	0	2	.275	.383	.425
Groves, Brett, Wilmington	66	214	180	28	46	58	7	1	1	14	2	1	5	26	2	41	1	2	5	.256	.363	.322
Guerrero, Henry, Frederick	6	23	21	1	6	7	1	0	0	0	0	0	0	2	0	2	0	0	0	.286	.348	.333
Gutierrez, Jesse, Potomac	108	437	400	52	111	185	26	0	16	76	0	6	9	22	3	52	1	2	12	.278	.325	.463
Hanson, Mike, Myrtle Beach	5	15	15	0	3	4	1	0	0	0	0	0	0	0	0	1	0	0	0	.200	.200	.267
Harts, Jeremy, Lynchburg †	91	297	272	31	60	90	11	2	5	39	5	2	3	15	0	74	4	2	3	.221	.267	.331
Hawes, B.J., Potomac	59	185	172	14	42	50	6	1	0	9	2	1	1	9	0	36	3	3	4	.244	.284	.291
Helquist, Jon, Salem	28	108	93	14	17	28	3	1	2	11	2	2	1	10	1	25	1	1	2	.183	.264	.301
Hernandez, Habelito, Pot.	8	30	28	2	7	7	0	0	0	1	0	1	0	1	0	7	0	0	0	.250	.267	.250
Hernandez, Jose, Lynchburg	3	4	4	0	2	2	0	0	0	0	0	0	0	0	0	1	0	0	0	.500	.500	.500
Herr, Aaron, Myrtle Beach	113	446	416	40	111	169	17	1	13	46	2	3	6	19	0	99	5	8	9	.267	.306	.406
Holt, Daylan, Winston-Salem	112	384	340	50	88	149	28	0	11	58	0	7	2	35	5	68	8	4	4	.259	.326	.438
Honeycutt, Heath, Potomac	57	218	197	22	51	76	15	2	2	22	0	1	2	18	0	42	1	3	3	.259	.326	.386
Hubele, Ryan, Frederick	26	102	92	11	23	32	6	0	1	12	3	1	1	5	1	14	0	1	2	.250	.293	.348
Huggins, Mike, Frederick	126	520	454	66	133	204	32	0	13	74	0	8	3	55	5	93	3	3	14	.293	.367	.449
Inglett, Joe, Kinston *	28	108	85	21	28	40	10	1	0	15	0	2	1	20	0	14	1	0	2	.329	.454	.471
Iorg, Isaac, Myrtle Beach	89	308	280	34	75	99	14	2	2	32	3	1	3	21	0	55	4	6	9	.268	.325	.354
Jeffcoat, Bryon, Myrtle Beach	37	115	96	12	23	30	4	0	1	9	1	1	2	15	0	25	1	1	3	.240	.351	.313
Jenkins, Brian, Kinston	27	115	105	15	27	38	6	1	1	16	1	3	0	6	0	17	0	3	4	.257	.289	.362
Jimerson, Charlton, Salem	97	367	336	53	89	150	19	3	12	55	1	3	2	25	1	109	27	4	4	.265	.317	.446
Johnson, Tripper, Frederick	123	474	417	43	114	160	25	3	5	50	0	1	10	46	4	92	7	8	6	.273	.359	.384
Keim, Adam, Wilmington	63	237	213	13	48	67	9	2	2	12	3	1	0	20	1	46	1	0	5	.225	.291	.315
Keppinger, Jeff, Lynchburg	92	373	342	55	111	145	21	2	3	51	3	4	1	23	0	28	3	2	10	.325	.365	.424
Keylor, Cory, Frederick *	79	304	270	38	66	106	15	2	7	39	2	3	1	28	1	65	2	3	7	.244	.315	.393
Kirby, Brian, Kinston *	40	113	103	6	19	29	1	0	3	7	1	1	2	6	0	39	0	0	2	.184	.241	.282
Knox, Matt, Kinston	61	244	230	26	57	81	10	1	4	27	1	2	2	9	1	41	0	2	6	.248	.280	.352
Lackaff, John, Win.-Salem	28	90	80	14	21	32	5	0	2	11	0	0	6	4	0	11	3	0	4	.263	.344	.400
Lentini, Fehlandt, Salem	100	403	369	45	103	141	21	4	3	48	4	3	2	25	1	58	19	7	11	.279	.326	.382
Likely, Cameron, Salem	11	33	31	1	3	3	0	0	0	1	0	1	0	1	0	13	1	2	2	.097	.121	.097
Lopez, Pedro, Winston-Salem	4	14	13	1	3	3	0	0	0	0	0	0	0	1	0	0	0	0	0	.231	.286	.231
Lucas, Matt, Salem	7	17	15	1	2	3	1	0	0	1	1	0	0	1	0	4	0	0	0	.133	.188	.200
Lydic, Joe, Salem	58	169	153	11	31	43	6	0	2	12	3	2	2	9	0	40	0	0	1	.203	.253	.281
Lytle, Derrik, Wilmington *	43	156	132	20	36	45	2	2	1	11	1	0	2	21	0	39	3	1	2	.273	.381	.341
Majewski, Val, Frederick *	41	168	159	15	46	81	18	1	5	20	0	1	1	7	0	23	0	0	2	.289	.321	.509
Malave, Dennis, Kinston *	41	128	112	6	20	21	1	0	0	12	2	4	2	8	0	31	3	3	0	.179	.238	.188
Manley, Adam, Frederick *	82	297	275	28	54	91	7	0	10	34	2	1	3	16	0	82	3	1	11	.196	.247	.331
Margalski, Ben, Kinston *	41	142	117	11	18	22	4	0	0	6	2	1	1	21	0	40	2	1	0	.154	.286	.188
Marte, Andy, Myrtle Beach	130	541	463	69	132	217	35	1	16	63	0	9	2	67	8	109	5	2	13	.285	.372	.469
Martel, Normand, Win.-Salem*	117	382	348	36	95	125	13	4	3	36	11	0	1	22	0	32	9	5	6	.273	.318	.359
Martin, Kyle, Frederick	19	65	54	7	12	15	3	0	0	3	1	0	1	9	0	6	0	0	1	.222	.344	.278
Martinez, Candido, Potomac	13	37	31	3	4	6	2	0	0	0	1	0	0	5	0	9	2	2	0	.129	.250	.194
Martinez, Octavio, Frederick	42	142	133	12	33	37	4	0	0	6	1	0	4	4	1	19	0	0	2	.248	.291	.278
Martinez, Raul, Frederick *	5	12	12	0	3	3	0	0	0	0	0	0	0	0	0	5	0	0	1	.250	.250	.250
McLouth, Nathan, Lynch.*	117	508	440	85	132	181	27	2	6	33	5	1	7	55	2	68	40	4	4	.300	.386	.411
Meath, Matt, Lynchburg †	12	33	28	1	3	3	0	0	0	0	0	0	0	5	0	8	0	1	0	.107	.242	.107
Miller, Greg, Myrtle Beach	85	341	297	30	78	92	12	1	0	37	8	5	5	26	0	57	11	6	8	.263	.327	.310
Morse, Michael, Win.-Salem	122	468	432	45	106	170	30	2	10	55	2	2	7	25	0	91	4	4	12	.245	.296	.394
Mote, Trevor, Salem †	125	499	426	55	100	130	20	2	2	50	7	8	3	55	6	81	6	1	14	.235	.321	.305
Motooka, Rafael, Potomac	14	41	35	3	6	6	0	0	0	4	0	2	0	4	0	12	0	0	1	.171	.244	.171
Nicholson, Tommy, Win.-Salem*	26	101	90	16	26	41	7	1	2	9	4	0	2	5	0	18	1	1	0	.289	.340	.456
O'Sullivan, Patrick, Frederick	27	95	90	6	16	29	2	1	3	12	0	2	1	2	0	31	1	0	1	.178	.200	.322
Ochoa, Ivan, Kinston	82	340	296	42	75	93	12	3	0	23	7	0	6	31	1	67	28	10	2	.253	.336	.314
Osborn, Pat, Kinston	60	234	205	24	52	71	16	0	1	24	0	3	3	23	1	42	1	2	4	.254	.333	.346
Patchett, Gary, Potomac	47	130	113	11	27	31	1	0	1	6	3	0	4	10	1	24	0	2	6	.239	.323	.274
Paulino, Ronny, Lynchburg	23	91	81	8	19	25	3	0	1	12	0	1	1	8	0	8	1	0	6	.235	.308	.309
Peavey, Bill, Kinston *	42	166	140	14	32	44	9	0	1	23	0	1	3	22	1	30	0	0	1	.229	.343	.314
Pena, Brayan, Myrtle Beach †	82	306	286	24	84	106	14	1	2	27	6	2	1	11	0	28	2	5	8	.294	.320	.371
Pena, Rodolfo, Lynchburg	12	31	30	0	4	6	2	0	0	2	0	0	0	1	0	7	0	0	1	.133	.161	.200
Pena, Tony, Myrtle Beach	120	438	405	43	105	133	14	1	4	30	7	0	2	24	1	82	17	12	9	.259	.304	.328
Peters, Yaron, Myrtle Beach	35	135	112	9	19	30	3	1	2	5	0	1	7	15	1	30	0	0	3	.170	.304	.268
Peterson, Brian, Potomac	49	160	142	16	38	46	6	1	0	8	4	1	1	12	1	30	4	0	2	.268	.327	.324
Phillips, Paul, Wilmington	13	48	46	1	11	12	1	0	0	6	0	0	1	1	0	6	0	1	3	.239	.271	.261
Prince, Bryan, Potomac	47	168	145	14	36	51	3	0	4	15	2	0	1	20	2	30	0	0	3	.248	.343	.352
Quattlebaum, Hugh, Frederick	30	92	79	5	14	15	1	0	0	4	0	1	0	12	0	11	0	1	5	.177	.283	.190
Quintana, Miguel, Kinston *	99	366	343	33	97	131	18	2	4	35	1	3	2	17	3	71	3	6	6	.283	.318	.382
Ravelo, Manny, Lynchburg	57	198	171	21	38	40	2	0	0	6	7	1	3	16	0	46	11	6	2	.222	.298	.234
Reed, Jeremy, Win.-Salem *	65	274	222	37	74	106	18	1	4	52	5	5	1	41	3	17	27	6	5	.333	.431	.477
Rios, Fernando, Potomac	36	149	125	13	34	44	5	1	1	21	0	2	0	21	0	17	4	4	2	.272	.372	.352
Roat, Kyle, Myrtle Beach	14	49	42	6	9	11	2	0	0	5	0	1	1	5	0	10	0	0	0	.214	.306	.262
Rodriguez, Mike, Salem *	113	503	443	78	123	176	22	8	5	42	3	2	5	50	4	50	23	9	4	.278	.356	.397
Rogers, Omar, Frederick	99	411	356	49	104	137	24	0	3	28	5	2	6	42	1	70	4	5	11	.292	.374	.385
Rogowski, Casey, Win.-Salem*	116	424	357	46	88	131	20	1	7	38	3	3	8	53	4	73	18	4	8	.246	.354	.367
Rosa, Wally, Winston-Salem	69	223	199	17	42	52	7	0	1	13	4	2	3	15	0	40	1	2	1	.211	.274	.261
Ruiz, Junior, Potomac *	41	163	139	22	39	54	10	1	1	17	3	0	2	19	1	17	12	1	4	.281	.375	.388
Ruiz, Randy, Frederick	17	73	68	7	17	26	4	1	1	8	0	0	1	4	0	24	0	0	1	.250	.301	.382
Ruiz, Reinaldo, Salem	53	165	147	13	25	39	8	0	2	20	4	2	3	9	0	26	0	0	3	.170	.230	.265

Player, Team	G	TPA	AB	R	H	TB	2B	3B	HR	RBI	SH	SF	HP	BB	IBB	SO	SB	CS	GDP	Avg.	OBP	Slg.
Salas, Jose, Myrtle Beach †	73	255	235	20	57	79	7	0	5	23	0	2	3	15	2	38	1	2	16	.243	.294	.336
Salvo, Andrew, Win.-Salem *	5	16	14	1	2	2	0	0	0	0	0	0	0	2	0	1	0	0	0	.143	.250	.143
Schramek, Mark, Potomac *	36	138	128	9	26	36	4	0	2	12	0	0	4	6	0	42	0	0	2	.203	.261	.281
Scott, Luke, Kinston *	67	272	241	37	67	120	12	1	13	44	0	0	4	27	0	62	6	3	0	.278	.360	.498
Seestedt, Mike, Frederick	13	38	35	1	8	10	2	0	0	5	0	0	0	3	0	6	0	0	0	.229	.289	.286
Segui, David, Frederick †	1	4	4	0	1	1	0	0	0	0	0	0	0	0	0	1	0	0	0	.250	.250	.250
Self, Todd, Salem *	126	531	431	84	137	186	27	2	6	57	2	6	5	87	5	93	2	1	9	.318	.433	.432
Shanks, Eric, Frederick-Pot.	18	53	47	4	13	19	3	0	1	3	2	1	0	3	0	5	0	2	0	.277	.314	.404
Shanks, James, Wilmington	85	380	346	54	104	129	15	2	2	23	1	1	4	28	2	71	21	8	3	.301	.359	.373
Shelton, Chris, Lynchburg	95	389	315	71	113	202	24	1	21	69	0	1	5	68	8	67	1	4	6	.359	.478	.641
Sherrill, J.J., Kinston †	46	194	173	21	43	67	7	4	3	22	3	2	0	16	1	50	5	1	2	.249	.309	.387
Shier, Peter, Frederick	74	290	255	36	68	100	8	0	8	31	6	4	1	24	0	51	8	5	7	.267	.327	.392
Soto, T.J., Salem	30	119	111	8	17	32	4	1	3	21	1	1	0	6	0	37	2	1	2	.153	.195	.288
Spidale, Mike, Win.-Salem	120	476	393	61	103	137	21	5	1	42	12	6	8	57	2	76	25	7	8	.262	.362	.349
Stegall, Ryan, Salem	128	441	366	36	83	107	11	2	3	36	16	3	15	41	1	72	5	3	4	.227	.327	.292
Stern, Adam, Myrtle Beach *	28	121	103	11	20	22	2	0	0	6	4	1	0	13	0	21	7	3	1	.194	.282	.214
Stewart, Chris, Win.-Salem	76	252	217	18	45	63	8	2	2	27	7	1	0	27	1	29	1	0	6	.207	.294	.290
Stocker, Mel, Wilmington †	20	61	56	6	13	15	0	1	0	8	1	1	0	3	0	12	5	0	0	.232	.267	.268
Storey, Eric, Winston-Salem	111	385	331	48	90	144	25	1	9	31	3	0	2	49	0	98	10	5	6	.272	.369	.435
Sulbaran, Orlando, Potomac	2	3	3	0	1	1	0	0	0	0	0	0	0	0	0	2	0	0	0	.333	.333	.333
Taveras, Willy, Kinston	113	468	397	64	112	139	9	6	2	35	6	1	12	52	1	68	57	12	4	.282	.381	.350
Thomas, Charles, M.B.*	66	248	207	30	50	66	8	1	2	15	4	0	8	29	2	54	6	2	5	.242	.357	.319
Thorman, Scott, M.B.*	124	495	445	44	108	174	26	2	12	56	0	4	4	42	6	79	0	0	13	.243	.311	.391
Torres, Eider, Kinston †	124	507	447	63	111	127	13	0	1	39	16	1	4	39	1	73	43	14	4	.248	.314	.284
Wallace, David, Kinston	44	168	147	20	33	52	13	0	2	14	0	0	5	16	0	43	1	0	6	.224	.321	.354
Walter, Scott, Wilmington	52	209	191	29	52	79	12	0	5	34	2	1	2	13	0	27	0	0	8	.272	.324	.414
Welsh, Eric, Win.-Salem *	96	346	308	45	74	136	17	0	15	51	1	5	4	28	4	74	2	1	5	.240	.307	.442
Wilken, Kris, Frederick †	9	23	21	0	3	3	0	0	0	3	0	1	0	1	0	1	0	0	2	.143	.174	.143
Williamson, Chris, Potomac *	102	357	319	31	63	89	20	0	2	30	0	4	1	33	4	113	1	0	4	.197	.272	.279
Wong, Travis, Potomac	21	83	76	7	13	21	2	0	2	12	0	2	1	4	0	21	0	0	1	.171	.217	.276
Wright, Brian, Kinston *	54	225	194	29	51	78	11	2	4	28	1	3	3	24	1	35	4	2	4	.263	.348	.402
Yan, Ruddy, Win.-Salem †	130	547	485	85	128	151	11	3	2	24	13	2	0	47	0	73	76	13	6	.264	.328	.311
Young, Walter, Lynchburg *	117	480	431	76	120	199	15	2	20	87	0	2	12	35	3	88	2	4	10	.278	.348	.462

BATTERS WITH TWO OR MORE TEAMS

Player, Team	G	TPA	AB	R	H	TB	2B	3B	HR	RBI	SH	SF	HP	BB	IBB	SO	SB	CS	GDP	Avg.	OBP	Slg.
Cotto, Luis, Wilmington	17	61	52	8	9	9	0	0	0	5	1	1	0	7	0	15	0	0	2	.173	.267	.173
Cotto, Luis, Kinston	39	132	111	6	17	21	4	0	0	6	7	0	5	9	0	37	1	1	0	.153	.248	.189
Dyson, Trey, Kinston *	7	30	22	5	8	12	1	0	1	3	0	0	2	6	2	6	1	0	0	.364	.533	.545
Dyson, Trey, Wilmington *	128	534	458	64	126	199	31	0	14	72	1	7	8	60	7	92	6	2	8	.275	.364	.434
Shanks, Eric, Frederick	14	38	33	4	8	14	3	0	1	3	1	1	0	3	0	4	0	0	0	.242	.297	.424
Shanks, Eric, Potomac	4	15	14	0	5	5	0	0	0	0	1	0	0	0	0	1	0	2	0	.357	.357	.357

GRAND SLAMS—Buttler, Choy Foo, Conrad, Correll, Fallon, Majewski, Morse, Shelton, Stegall, Walter, 1 each.

AWARDED FIRST BASE ON CATCHER'S INTERFERENCE—Draper (Salas); Duran (Stewart); Rios (Salas).

2003 PITCHING

TEAM

Team	W	L	Pct.	ERA	G	CG	ShO	Sv.	IP	H	TBF	R	ER	HR	SH	SF	HB	BB	IBB	SO	WP	Bk.
Wilmington	80	60	.571	2.92	140	7	16	38	1204.1	1072	4995	477	391	65	45	42	34	386	28	950	55	2
Win.-Salem	71	67	.514	3.32	138	5	13	36	1152.2	1049	4932	542	425	75	59	47	71	491	32	856	78	7
Myrtle Beach	56	82	.406	3.63	138	4	11	20	1190.2	1147	5141	580	480	75	57	42	48	493	14	946	70	5
Kinston	73	66	.525	3.65	139	5	7	43	1187.1	1170	5090	561	482	78	46	37	61	440	20	825	65	1
Potomac	62	77	.446	3.72	139	5	9	38	1181.2	1161	5053	579	489	64	59	47	59	415	11	955	68	3
Lynchburg	76	59	.563	3.80	135	5	8	38	1140.1	1110	4918	585	481	66	62	50	60	416	13	909	53	3
Salem	73	65	.529	4.05	138	6	11	35	1184.2	1223	5145	612	533	74	66	36	76	419	18	782	52	2
Frederick	60	75	.444	4.40	135	2	11	40	1164.1	1196	5160	668	569	98	41	43	77	503	33	903	79	3

INDIVIDUAL

TOP QUALIFIERS FOR EARNED-RUN AVERAGE TITLE

Minimum 112 innings. *Lefthanded pitcher.

Pitcher, Team	W	L	Pct.	ERA	G	GS	CG	ShO	GF	Sv.	IP	H	TBF	R	ER	HR	SH	SF	HB	BB	IBB	SO	WP	Bk.
Middleton, Kyle, Wilmington	11	8	.579	2.41	27	27	1	0	0	0	160.1	155	661	59	43	6	9	5	7	35	2	75	10	0
Kleine, Victor, Kinston *	6	5	.545	2.56	28	16	0	0	4	1	116.0	114	483	42	33	6	5	1	5	35	2	79	8	0
Gothreaux, Jared, Salem	13	4	.765	2.82	29	22	1	1	4	1	146.2	144	602	54	46	4	11	5	3	26	0	85	3	0
Bass, Brian, Wilmington	9	8	.529	2.84	26	26	2	0	0	0	152.1	129	625	59	48	7	5	7	7	43	1	119	7	0
McClellan, Zach, Wilmington	8	8	.500	2.84	30	23	1	1	0	0	133.0	101	529	51	42	6	4	5	5	39	1	100	5	0
McBride, Macay, M.B.*	9	8	.529	2.95	27	27	1	0	0	0	164.2	164	692	63	54	5	10	2	4	49	0	139	4	0
Wing, Ryan, Winston-Salem *	9	7	.563	2.98	26	26	0	0	0	0	145.0	116	588	62	48	9	4	3	4	67	2	107	11	1
Honel, Kris, Winston-Salem	9	7	.563	3.11	24	24	3	1	0	0	133.0	122	550	51	46	7	5	3	8	42	3	122	3	0
Oquendo, Ian, Lynchburg	10	3	.769	3.33	20	20	1	1	0	0	116.1	105	477	46	43	3	8	3	3	33	1	122	4	2
Lewis, Rommie, Frederick *	4	9	.308	3.34	26	20	1	0	2	0	113.1	108	503	54	42	9	2	4	6	60	1	69	6	0
Miner, Zach, Myrtle Beach	6	10	.375	3.69	27	27	2	0	0	0	153.2	150	652	74	63	10	6	5	7	61	1	88	4	1
Foley, Travis, Kinston	10	10	.500	3.69	24	24	1	0	0	0	126.2	115	524	54	52	7	5	5	7	54	0	96	4	1
Roberson, Brandon, Salem	8	5	.615	3.72	38	18	2	0	8	0	125.2	134	527	58	52	6	8	4	9	24	0	78	7	0
Coenen, Matt, Myrtle Beach *	8	10	.444	3.86	28	28	0	0	0	0	147.0	145	634	74	63	4	8	7	6	62	0	90	11	0
Rodaway, Brian, Salem *	5	9	.357	3.99	26	25	2	2	0	0	140.0	156	593	68	62	16	6	4	5	35	0	82	5	0

DEPARTMENTAL LEADERS: W—Gothreaux, 13; L—Birkins, Tierney, 11; Pct.—Greinke, .917; G—Mitchell, 60; GS—Coenen, 28; CG—Greinke, Honel, 3; ShO—Rodaway, 2; GF—Gronkiewicz, 47; Sv.—Gronkiewicz, 37; IP—McBride, 164.2; H—McBride, 164; TBF—McBride, 692; R—Barrett, 87; ER—Barrett, 82; HR—Rodaway, 16; SH—Gothreaux, 11; SF—Allen, 11; HB—Birkins, 13; BB—Allen, 89; IBB—Fields, Rleal, 7; SO—McBride, 139; WP—Allen, 21; BK—Meaux, 3.

ALL PITCHERS

*Lefthanded pitcher.

Pitcher, Team	W	L	Pct.	ERA	G	GS	CG	ShO	GF	Sv.	IP	H	TBF	R	ER	HR	SH	SF	HB	BB	IBB	SO	WP	Bk.
Acosta, Manuel, Myrtle Beach	2	0	1.000	6.39	8	0	0	0	3	1	12.2	19	70	14	9	1	1	0	0	11	1	10	1	0
Agamennone, Brandon, Fred	0	0	.000	6.75	2	1	0	0	0	0	4.0	5	18	3	3	1	0	0	0	1	0	2	0	0
Alcala, Jason, Lynchburg	2	0	1.000	3.81	15	0	0	0	6	1	28.1	29	120	13	12	1	0	1	1	9	1	22	0	0
Allen, Wyatt, Winston-Salem	6	8	.429	4.39	28	25	0	0	1	0	139.1	128	626	79	68	12	8	11	10	89	2	86	21	1
Alvarez, Oscar, Kinston *	1	1	.500	2.78	4	3	0	0	0	0	22.2	18	92	7	7	1	1	0	1	7	1	19	1	0
An, Byeong, Winston-Salem *	8	4	.667	3.16	12	12	1	0	0	0	68.1	66	291	29	24	5	6	3	4	27	1	45	1	0
Andrews, Clayton, Potomac *	5	6	.455	4.62	18	18	1	1	0	0	101.1	95	439	66	52	11	6	8	8	43	0	46	5	0
Armitage, Barry, Wilmington	0	2	.000	6.27	30	0	0	0	9	0	37.1	44	179	29	26	6	3	1	1	24	0	36	2	0
Arthurs, Shane, Kinston	1	0	1.000	4.58	12	0	0	0	5	0	19.2	19	85	10	10	0	2	2	0	7	2	15	0	0
Astacio, Andres, Salem	0	1	.000	13.00	3	3	0	0	0	0	9.0	15	52	15	13	1	0	1	2	8	0	3	0	0
Babula, Shaun, Frederick *	7	1	.875	2.68	37	0	0	0	9	1	50.1	45	214	20	15	1	1	1	4	16	3	46	3	0
Barreto, Joel, Potomac	0	0	.000	0.00	3	0	0	0	0	0	8.0	5	30	0	0	0	0	0	0	2	0	15	0	0
Barrett, Jimmy, Salem	7	10	.412	5.33	26	26	0	0	0	0	138.1	160	622	87	82	13	5	1	12	56	0	75	6	0
Bartlett, Richard, Frederick	1	2	.333	9.12	9	6	0	0	2	1	25.2	38	134	31	26	6	1	0	0	22	1	17	2	0
Barzilla, Philip, Salem *	8	3	.727	3.10	52	0	0	0	18	5	93.0	86	395	39	32	1	8	2	5	41	5	51	4	0
Basham, Bobby, Potomac	0	1	.000	2.70	1	1	0	0	0	0	6.2	5	27	3	2	0	0	0	1	1	0	1	0	0
Bass, Brian, Wilmington	9	8	.529	2.84	26	26	2	0	0	0	152.1	129	625	59	48	7	5	7	7	43	1	119	7	0
Bedard, Erik, Frederick *	0	1	.000	7.36	1	1	0	0	0	0	3.2	5	16	3	3	1	0	1	0	1	0	2	0	0
Berube, Martin, Frederick	0	0	.000	3.38	3	0	0	0	1	0	5.1	5	24	2	2	0	0	1	0	4	0	3	1	0
Birkins, Kurt, Frederick *	8	11	.421	4.70	25	25	0	0	0	0	126.1	152	576	82	66	10	5	6	13	40	0	79	12	0
Bittner, Tim, Winston-Salem *	3	3	.500	3.60	17	0	0	0	3	1	30.0	18	117	13	12	3	1	0	2	12	1	23	1	0
Borner, Brady, Lynchburg *	4	1	.800	1.68	20	6	0	0	4	0	75.0	63	300	21	14	2	5	2	3	12	0	62	0	0
Boughner, Anthony, Fred.*	3	3	.500	7.71	18	2	0	0	4	0	28.0	41	136	26	24	2	1	1	1	10	2	21	2	1
Bradley, Bobby, Lynchburg	3	2	.600	3.40	12	12	0	0	0	0	50.1	43	222	21	19	1	3	1	5	28	0	36	7	0
Brannon, Nick, Potomac *	4	5	.444	3.29	40	0	0	0	15	0	52.0	53	235	21	19	0	3	4	3	30	0	55	1	0
Bruksch, Jeffrey, Potomac	1	3	.250	4.50	6	6	0	0	0	0	30.0	29	137	16	15	1	1	1	1	21	0	16	5	0
Bullington, Bryan, Lynchburg	8	4	.667	3.05	17	17	2	1	0	0	97.1	101	420	39	33	5	7	4	8	27	0	67	3	0
Burch, Matt, Wilmington	1	2	.333	2.70	13	1	0	0	5	1	23.1	24	102	8	7	2	1	2	1	10	2	16	0	0
Bush, Paul, Myrtle Beach	4	4	.500	3.63	34	2	0	0	13	0	62.0	49	268	32	25	7	3	1	1	30	1	64	1	0
Butler, Matt, Myrtle Beach	1	4	.200	9.00	10	5	0	0	2	0	22.0	27	113	23	22	4	0	1	2	21	1	14	1	1
Campos, Juan, Salem	3	0	1.000	1.84	45	0	0	0	37	24	68.1	51	271	15	14	1	4	3	3	16	3	68	5	0
Capps, Matt, Lynchburg	0	0	.000	5.40	1	1	0	0	0	0	5.0	3	22	3	3	0	0	0	0	4	0	5	0	0
Casey, Reid, Kinston	0	0	.000	27.00	1	0	0	0	0	0	1.0	4	7	3	3	0	0	0	0	0	0	1	0	0
Castillo, Carlos, Win.-Salem	0	2	.000	7.20	2	2	0	0	0	0	10.0	15	49	8	8	2	1	2	2	3	0	4	1	0
Castro, Julio, Winston-Salem	3	1	.750	1.01	26	0	0	0	10	2	35.2	25	146	7	4	2	1	0	4	13	1	26	1	0
Cedeno, Blas, Lynchburg	0	2	.000	5.79	4	4	0	0	0	0	23.1	24	104	17	15	4	1	2	4	7	0	14	1	1
Childress, Daylan, Potomac	5	9	.357	3.00	17	16	2	0	0	0	96.0	78	407	44	32	3	5	6	4	45	1	89	8	0
Chrysler, Clint, Lynchburg *	1	0	1.000	2.08	7	0	0	0	2	1	8.2	11	39	3	2	0	2	0	1	3	0	6	0	0
Coenen, Matt, Myrtle Beach *	8	10	.444	3.86	28	28	0	0	0	0	147.0	145	634	74	63	4	8	7	6	62	0	90	11	0
Coffey, Todd, Potomac	0	2	.000	1.96	11	0	0	0	5	2	23.0	16	83	6	5	0	0	2	1	3	0	21	1	0
Collazo, William, M.B.*	0	1	.000	3.07	11	0	0	0	2	1	14.2	12	59	5	5	1	0	0	1	4	0	15	0	0
Cooper, Chris, Kinston *	2	4	.333	3.71	40	0	0	0	20	2	68.0	67	291	30	28	8	1	2	4	23	3	51	4	0
Coppinger, Joe, Frederick	1	0	1.000	3.38	1	1	0	0	0	0	5.1	5	23	2	2	1	0	0	1	1	0	6	0	0
Corcoran, Tim, Frederick	2	5	.286	5.74	22	3	0	0	4	0	47.0	57	227	38	30	3	4	2	0	27	2	41	6	0
Cortes, Jorge, Potomac	0	0	.000	6.43	5	0	0	0	3	0	7.0	7	32	5	5	0	0	1	1	6	0	4	0	0
Cotton, Nathan, Potomac	2	4	.333	4.24	48	0	0	0	43	28	46.2	39	192	26	22	3	3	1	5	7	0	51	1	0
Coughenour, Jory, Salem	1	0	1.000	2.08	10	0	0	0	4	1	17.1	20	78	8	4	0	2	2	0	7	0	11	0	0
Cressend, Jack, Kinston	0	1	.000	12.46	2	0	0	0	0	0	4.1	9	21	6	6	1	0	0	0	0	0	4	0	0
Crouthers, Dave, Frederick	7	5	.583	3.59	18	18	0	0	0	0	92.2	83	401	47	37	1	4	4	8	43	0	82	12	1
Culp, Brandon, Potomac	3	6	.333	3.56	31	11	0	0	10	0	98.2	92	424	48	39	8	5	3	5	38	2	74	12	1
Curtis, Daniel, Myrtle Beach	3	4	.429	4.04	12	11	1	1	0	0	64.2	77	293	41	29	5	2	3	2	23	0	55	2	0
David, Brad, Myrtle Beach *	0	0	.000	4.57	17	0	0	0	9	0	21.2	24	99	11	11	1	0	1	2	11	1	13	1	0
Daws, Josh, Potomac	0	2	.000	7.71	18	0	0	0	11	1	18.2	35	90	16	16	1	2	1	1	5	2	13	0	0
DeHart, Casey, Potomac *	0	1	.000	5.06	6	0	0	0	3	0	10.2	11	46	7	6	2	1	0	0	3	0	6	2	0
De los Santos, Carlos, Lynch.	0	1	.000	8.36	10	0	0	0	6	0	14.0	13	72	13	13	2	0	1	1	18	0	17	2	0
Denham, Dan, Kinston	5	5	.500	4.50	14	14	1	0	0	0	72.0	82	321	42	36	2	6	4	9	27	0	39	8	0
Deza, Fredy, Frederick	0	0	.000	27.00	1	0	0	0	0	0	1.1	4	12	5	4	0	0	0	0	3	0	2	0	0
Digby, Bryan, Myrtle Beach	0	1	.000	4.45	21	0	0	0	3	0	32.1	31	146	20	16	0	2	1	4	17	0	21	10	1
Dittler, Jake, Kinston	5	1	.833	2.40	8	8	1	1	0	0	48.2	47	198	17	13	2	2	1	1	11	0	32	1	0
Douglass, Ryan, Wilmington	4	0	1.000	1.93	8	5	0	0	1	0	32.2	22	123	8	7	1	0	1	0	5	1	28	0	0
Dumatrait, Phillip, Potomac *	4	1	.800	3.35	7	7	1	0	0	0	37.2	36	162	17	14	2	2	0	1	14	0	32	3	0
Edens, Kyle, Potomac	0	5	.000	4.91	28	2	0	0	11	3	55.0	73	252	39	30	2	6	3	0	16	1	45	1	0
Edwards, Brad, Frederick *	0	0	.000	14.73	3	0	0	0	0	0	3.2	5	21	6	6	0	0	0	2	2	0	4	1	0
Farren, Dave, Frederick	0	4	.000	5.71	18	10	0	0	2	1	69.1	73	307	45	44	12	0	3	7	29	1	52	4	0
Fernley, Nathan, Kinston	1	1	.500	3.57	15	0	0	0	9	0	22.2	24	107	12	9	1	4	1	2	14	2	6	1	0
Fields, Josh, Winston-Salem	6	7	.462	3.10	58	0	0	0	44	20	72.2	54	303	29	25	5	6	0	6	25	7	68	0	0
Fitch, Steve, Lynchburg	2	3	.400	5.26	12	1	0	0	1	0	25.2	26	110	17	15	2	4	0	0	9	2	9	0	0
Foley, Travis, Kinston	10	10	.500	3.69	24	24	1	0	0	0	126.2	115	524	54	52	7	5	5	7	54	0	96	4	1
Francisco, Frank, Win.-Salem	7	3	.700	3.56	16	16	1	1	0	0	78.1	59	332	40	31	7	1	4	6	36	0	67	4	1
Garza, Rolando, Win.-Salem	1	0	1.000	5.93	17	0	0	0	3	0	13.2	12	72	10	9	0	0	1	0	21	0	14	6	0

Pitcher, Team	W	L	Pct.	ERA	G	GS	CG	ShO	GF	Sv.	IP	H	TBF	R	ER	HR	SH	SF	HB	BB	IBB	SO	WP	Bk.
Gomez, Mariano, Kinston *	6	4	.600	3.67	18	18	1	0	0	0	100.2	91	424	49	41	11	4	3	4	38	0	69	2	0
Gonzalez, Mike, Lynchburg *	0	1	.000	5.14	5	0	0	0	0	0	7.0	7	32	9	4	0	1	0	0	5	0	9	0	0
Gothreaux, Jared, Salem	13	4	.765	2.82	29	22	1	1	4	1	146.2	144	602	54	46	4	11	5	3	26	0	85	3	0
Granado, Jan, Potomac *	3	6	.333	4.66	15	11	0	0	3	1	67.2	76	305	37	35	4	3	1	3	33	0	46	3	0
Gray, Brett, Potomac	1	0	1.000	0.96	2	2	0	0	0	0	9.1	12	36	2	1	0	0	0	0	0	0	9	0	0
Greinke, Zack, Wilmington	11	1	.917	1.14	14	14	3	1	0	0	87.0	56	330	16	11	5	1	0	2	13	0	78	1	0
Griffin, Colt, Wilmington	1	0	1.000	0.00	1	1	0	0	0	0	6.0	3	21	1	0	0	0	0	0	0	0	5	0	0
Gronkiewicz, Lee, Kinston	2	3	.400	2.41	51	0	0	0	47	37	56.0	50	226	19	15	4	2	1	0	14	0	46	3	0
Guerrero, Julio, Lynchburg	4	1	.800	3.90	16	0	0	0	4	0	32.1	37	143	17	14	2	1	1	0	6	0	20	2	0
Hamilton, Mark, Salem *	0	4	.000	5.13	34	2	0	0	8	1	59.2	57	261	37	34	9	3	1	5	25	0	47	1	0
Hannaman, Ryan, Frederick *	1	3	.250	3.79	5	5	0	0	0	0	19.0	14	88	9	8	2	1	0	2	17	0	22	1	0
Hart, Alex, Lynchburg	4	5	.444	4.60	11	11	1	0	0	0	58.2	55	255	34	30	2	1	4	1	24	0	44	2	0
Harts, Jeremy, Lynchburg *	0	0	.000	6.75	3	2	0	0	1	1	2.2	3	15	2	2	0	0	0	0	4	0	3	2	0
Hernandez, Michael, Kinston *	6	3	.667	3.73	19	0	0	0	7	0	31.1	31	133	17	13	1	1	1	2	8	2	37	7	0
Higgins, Joshua, Lynchburg	7	2	.778	2.37	37	0	0	0	13	0	60.2	56	244	19	16	2	2	5	2	12	3	48	2	0
Honel, Kris, Winston-Salem	9	7	.563	3.11	24	24	3	1	0	0	133.0	122	550	51	46	7	5	3	8	42	3	122	3	0
Howington, Ty, Potomac *	7	7	.500	3.53	19	19	0	0	0	0	99.1	103	425	44	39	4	2	3	6	34	0	86	5	0
Hummel, Rick, Win.-Salem	1	1	.500	3.27	19	0	0	0	7	1	22.0	30	99	12	8	0	2	0	1	4	1	9	0	0
Ireland, Eric, Salem	1	0	1.000	0.00	1	0	0	0	1	0	4.0	3	16	0	0	0	0	0	0	1	0	5	1	0
Kelly, Steve, Potomac	7	5	.583	3.87	17	17	0	0	0	0	95.1	105	416	52	41	3	6	6	5	28	1	69	10	1
Keppinger, Billy, Wilmington *	6	2	.750	2.25	34	0	0	0	17	2	52.0	41	206	16	13	3	1	5	0	16	4	34	4	0
Kirkland, Aaron, Win.-Salem	1	0	1.000	4.07	16	0	0	0	6	0	24.1	32	119	17	11	0	0	3	2	16	0	16	0	0
Kleine, Victor, Kinston *	6	5	.545	2.56	28	16	0	0	4	1	116.0	114	483	42	33	6	5	1	5	35	2	79	8	0
Knapp, Ben, Frederick	0	3	.000	9.24	9	5	0	0	1	0	25.1	37	120	28	26	5	3	2	2	9	0	15	1	0
Knox, Matt, Kinston	1	0	1.000	0.00	1	0	0	0	1	0	1.0	0	4	0	0	0	1	0	0	1	0	1	0	0
LaMura, B.J., Winston-Salem	0	2	.000	9.00	4	2	0	0	2	0	13.0	19	61	14	13	3	0	3	1	6	0	8	0	0
Lantz, Doug, Kinston	3	3	.500	3.66	27	0	0	0	11	1	51.2	53	227	27	21	4	1	1	4	19	1	32	1	0
Leclair, Aric, Wilmington *	1	2	.333	3.03	32	0	0	0	13	5	38.2	32	175	17	13	1	2	1	0	30	3	53	4	0
Lee, Cliff, Kinston *	0	0	.000	0.00	1	1	0	0	0	0	4.1	0	17	1	0	0	1	0	0	3	0	4	0	0
Lewis, Rommie, Frederick *	4	9	.308	3.34	26	20	1	0	2	0	113.1	108	503	54	42	9	2	4	6	60	1	69	6	0
Lopez, Gonzalo, Myrtle Beach	0	2	.000	9.00	3	2	0	0	0	0	10.0	12	46	10	10	4	0	0	1	4	0	10	0	0
Lopez, Jose, Lynchburg	5	6	.455	3.48	20	19	0	0	0	0	106.0	99	450	55	41	7	4	5	5	42	0	46	5	0
Lord, Justin, Wilmington	0	2	.000	4.09	13	1	0	0	5	0	22.0	17	90	10	10	1	1	0	4	5	1	18	1	0
Lubisich, Nik, Win.-Salem *	1	0	1.000	3.18	3	0	0	0	1	0	5.2	6	26	3	2	1	2	0	0	2	2	2	0	0
Mabry, Barry, Myrtle Beach	0	0	.000	0.00	1	0	0	0	0	0	3.0	3	12	0	0	0	0	0	0	0	0	2	0	0
Maine, John, Frederick	6	1	.857	3.07	12	12	1	1	0	0	70.1	48	276	27	24	5	2	1	1	20	0	77	0	0
Makowsky, Carl, Frederick	2	2	.500	4.02	29	0	0	0	14	3	40.1	31	177	21	18	5	3	0	5	24	2	34	3	0
Manning, Charlie, Potomac *	5	0	1.000	1.19	6	6	0	0	0	0	37.2	24	145	7	5	1	1	0	1	11	0	31	1	0
Mansfield, Monte, Salem	1	1	.500	4.30	13	0	0	0	3	0	23.0	24	107	16	11	0	1	1	3	12	2	24	3	0
Martin, J.D., Kinston	5	3	.625	4.27	16	16	0	0	0	0	86.1	95	375	50	41	7	3	1	3	30	0	57	3	0
Martin, Kevin, Kinston	0	1	.000	2.70	1	0	0	0	0	0	3.1	5	15	1	1	0	1	0	0	1	1	1	0	0
Mattison, Kieran, Wil.-Kinston	3	1	.750	3.86	9	7	0	0	0	0	37.1	41	156	18	16	5	1	0	0	11	1	32	0	0
McBride, Macay, M.B.*	9	8	.529	2.95	27	27	1	0	0	0	164.2	164	692	63	54	5	10	2	4	49	0	139	4	0
McClellan, Robbie, Wil.	0	0	.000	0.00	1	0	0	0	1	1	1.0	1	4	0	0	0	0	0	0	0	0	1	0	0
McClellan, Zach, Wilmington	8	8	.500	2.84	30	23	1	1	0	0	133.0	101	529	51	42	6	4	5	5	39	1	100	5	0
McCurdy, Nick, Frederick	1	6	.143	4.89	19	18	0	0	0	0	92.0	125	426	58	50	9	1	4	7	28	2	76	4	0
McDaniel, Denny, M.B.-Salem*	6	1	.857	3.86	45	0	0	0	18	2	56.0	66	249	28	24	1	2	3	3	12	1	52	5	0
McGill, Trae, Wilmington	0	0	.000	1.35	6	0	0	0	3	0	13.1	10	48	2	2	0	0	0	0	2	0	7	0	0
McWhirter, Kris, Win.-Salem	0	3	.000	3.27	11	5	0	0	2	1	33.0	21	139	14	12	4	1	2	1	18	1	36	2	0
Meaux, Ryan, Win.-Salem *	1	3	.250	1.15	32	0	0	0	19	10	55.0	49	216	14	7	2	5	2	1	3	1	43	3	3
Mendez, David, M.B.*	0	0	.000	6.75	3	0	0	0	0	0	4.0	5	22	3	3	1	0	0	0	5	0	3	1	0
Mendoza, Marcos, Kinston *	2	3	.400	3.25	28	2	0	0	11	0	52.2	51	232	24	19	3	1	4	2	26	1	34	3	0
Merricks, Matt, Myrtle Beach*	1	8	.111	3.23	11	8	0	0	1	0	47.1	45	211	29	17	5	4	3	2	23	1	37	3	1
Meyer, Dan, Myrtle Beach *	3	6	.333	2.87	13	13	0	0	0	0	78.1	69	315	29	25	7	1	2	3	17	1	63	1	0
Middleton, Kyle, Wilmington	11	8	.579	2.41	27	27	1	0	0	0	160.1	155	661	59	43	6	9	5	7	35	2	75	10	0
Miller, Jeff, Lynchburg	5	6	.455	4.88	27	7	1	0	9	0	75.2	89	339	51	41	4	4	10	5	25	1	59	7	0
Miller, Matt, Myrtle Beach *	0	0	.000	7.20	4	0	0	0	2	0	5.0	6	25	4	4	0	0	1	0	4	0	3	0	0
Miner, Zach, Myrtle Beach	6	10	.375	3.69	27	27	2	0	0	0	153.2	150	652	74	63	10	6	5	7	61	1	88	4	1
Mitchell, Andy, Frederick	5	4	.556	3.46	60	0	0	0	8	1	91.0	84	385	41	35	1	5	1	7	36	3	49	4	0
Moran, Nick, Kinston	4	0	1.000	3.55	6	6	0	0	0	0	33.0	32	140	14	13	4	0	0	2	7	0	20	1	0
Morris, Cory, Frederick	3	2	.600	2.61	7	7	0	0	0	0	38.0	32	159	15	11	2	1	3	1	16	0	28	0	0
Morrison, Robbie, Wilmington	4	3	.571	3.54	42	0	0	0	26	11	53.1	39	215	22	21	3	1	3	0	18	1	65	4	1
Natale, Mike, Wilmington	2	2	.500	2.79	27	0	0	0	18	7	38.2	35	167	14	12	2	1	0	1	13	3	57	2	0
Navarro, Rodolfo, Kinston	0	1	.000	6.23	2	0	0	0	1	0	4.1	5	23	5	3	0	1	1	0	2	1	4	0	0
O'Brien, Patrick, Lynchburg	2	6	.250	5.47	12	10	0	0	0	0	49.1	64	228	38	30	7	7	6	1	18	0	16	3	0
O'Neal, Brandon, Win.-Salem	2	3	.400	3.47	35	5	0	0	17	1	62.1	58	288	40	24	1	4	3	9	42	3	28	19	0
Oquendo, Ian, Lynchburg	10	3	.769	3.33	20	20	1	1	0	0	116.1	105	477	46	43	3	8	3	3	33	1	122	4	2
Owens, Henry, Lynchburg	1	2	.333	2.45	13	0	0	0	11	5	14.2	9	65	6	4	0	2	0	1	11	0	21	0	0
Patchett, Gary, Potomac	0	0	.000	0.00	1	0	0	0	1	0	0.2	0	2	0	0	0	0	0	0	0	0	1	0	0
Patten, Scott, Winston-Salem	1	1	.500	4.82	10	1	0	0	3	0	18.2	29	98	17	10	1	1	0	3	10	1	14	0	0
Pena, Francisco, Salem	5	9	.357	3.80	33	12	0	0	10	0	94.2	89	415	51	40	4	5	2	12	44	1	64	5	1
Pena, Rodolfo, Lynchburg	0	0	.000	0.00	1	0	0	0	1	0	1.0	1	4	0	0	0	0	0	0	0	0	1	0	0
Phillips, Mike, Win.-Salem *	2	7	.222	3.58	13	13	0	0	0	0	75.1	84	311	37	30	6	7	6	0	7	0	51	1	1
Pluta, Tony, Salem	0	1	.000	5.84	3	3	0	0	0	0	12.1	13	57	8	8	1	0	0	1	8	0	14	2	0
Pollok, Dwayne, Win.-Salem	0	1	.000	3.92	14	0	0	0	4	0	20.2	25	88	12	9	1	0	0	2	2	0	14	0	0
Prahm, Ryan, Kinston	1	3	.250	4.21	9	2	0	0	2	0	25.2	23	111	12	12	1	1	0	2	14	1	16	2	0

Pitcher, Team	W	L	Pct.	ERA	G	GS	CG	ShO	GF	Sv.	IP	H	TBF	R	ER	HR	SH	SF	HB	BB	IBB	SO	WP	Bk.
Purvis, Rob, Winston-Salem	4	3	.571	2.14	12	7	0	0	0	0	42.0	34	176	15	10	2	2	0	1	20	4	30	1	0
Quattlebaum, Hugh, Frederick	0	0	.000	0.00	1	0	0	0	1	0	1.0	4	8	3	0	0	0	1	0	0	0	0	0	0
Quintana, Miguel, Kinston	0	0	.000	9.00	1	0	0	0	1	0	1.0	2	6	1	1	0	0	1	0	1	0	0	0	0
Ramirez, Enrique, Frederick	2	0	1.000	4.56	13	0	0	0	5	0	23.2	24	106	12	12	2	0	1	1	15	0	17	1	0
Reed, Chris, Potomac	0	0	.000	2.08	8	0	0	0	3	0	13.0	12	57	4	3	0	1	0	0	6	0	13	2	0
Rice, Scott, Frederick *	1	3	.250	3.19	25	0	0	0	5	0	31.0	34	136	12	11	1	0	0	3	14	2	27	3	0
Rleal, Sendy, Frederick	3	5	.375	3.16	44	0	0	0	27	11	57.0	35	228	20	20	8	4	2	1	23	7	59	6	1
Roberson, Brandon, Salem	8	5	.615	3.72	38	18	2	0	8	0	125.2	134	527	58	52	6	8	4	9	24	0	78	7	0
Roberts, Nick, Salem	0	2	.000	9.00	3	3	0	0	0	0	12.0	18	55	12	12	4	1	0	2	2	0	8	0	0
Roberts, Ralph, Myrtle Beach	3	5	.375	2.92	44	0	0	0	40	8	61.2	50	260	27	20	4	8	1	0	23	2	68	0	0
Rodaway, Brian, Salem *	5	9	.357	3.99	26	25	2	2	0	0	140.0	156	593	68	62	16	6	4	5	35	0	82	5	0
Rodriguez, Jose, Myrtle Beach	0	0	.000	1.08	5	0	0	0	2	0	8.1	7	36	2	1	0	0	2	1	3	0	6	1	0
Rodriguez, Wandy, Salem *	8	7	.533	3.49	20	20	1	1	0	0	111.0	102	480	51	43	9	3	4	6	41	1	72	1	1
Salazar, Richard, Frederick *	0	0	.000	10.38	6	0	0	0	0	0	8.2	8	39	11	10	2	1	0	0	8	0	4	0	0
Salmon, Brad, Potomac	3	2	.600	4.56	32	1	0	0	12	1	49.1	55	221	27	25	4	8	1	0	18	4	53	3	0
Sampson, Christopher, Salem	1	1	.500	5.91	9	0	0	0	5	1	10.2	14	51	8	7	0	2	0	1	5	2	6	0	0
Santillan, Manny, Salem	3	5	.375	6.00	36	4	0	0	10	0	51.0	56	248	39	34	3	6	2	4	41	2	33	0	0
Sequea, Jacobo, Frederick	1	0	1.000	2.87	32	0	0	0	29	20	31.1	27	130	11	10	2	0	1	0	11	3	26	0	0
Shackelford, Brian, Potomac *	0	1	.000	1.98	18	0	0	0	6	1	27.1	17	106	6	6	1	0	0	4	8	0	20	1	0
Sharber, Jason, Lynchburg	5	6	.455	4.74	21	16	0	0	2	1	95.0	97	422	63	50	13	4	3	5	38	0	88	3	0
Shumaker, Casey, Lynchburg	1	3	.250	3.65	33	0	0	0	19	4	44.1	34	187	22	18	3	3	1	5	20	1	45	5	0
Sims, Kenny, Frederick	1	1	.500	5.29	11	0	0	0	4	0	17.0	22	76	10	10	1	1	0	2	5	1	6	3	0
Sinclair, Ernnie, Salem	0	0	.000	12.38	6	0	0	0	1	0	8.0	15	45	12	11	0	0	1	0	5	0	4	3	0
Slocum, Brian, Kinston	6	7	.462	4.46	22	21	0	0	1	1	107.0	112	469	61	53	7	0	2	5	41	0	66	1	0
Sobkowiak, Scott, Potomac	1	2	.333	5.91	4	4	0	0	0	0	21.1	19	97	19	14	1	1	2	4	9	0	21	2	0
Sperring, Jayme, Frederick	0	3	.000	5.64	15	0	0	0	10	2	22.1	30	116	20	14	3	1	4	2	15	3	21	4	0
Stanton, Kyle, Potomac	1	3	.250	3.38	20	0	0	0	5	1	34.2	32	139	15	13	2	0	2	0	6	0	35	1	0
Stiles, Brad, Wilmington *	2	2	.500	2.41	26	0	0	0	9	2	37.1	32	163	12	10	1	4	0	0	18	2	40	3	1
Stodolka, Mike, Wilmington *	2	1	.667	3.00	5	5	0	0	0	0	21.0	15	84	8	7	0	0	3	0	9	0	10	0	0
Stumm, Jason, Win.-Salem	1	0	1.000	3.60	20	0	0	0	7	0	25.0	28	111	10	10	1	2	1	2	11	1	23	0	0
Sturkie, Scott, Kinston	4	2	.667	2.76	40	0	0	0	12	1	78.1	73	334	27	24	4	2	5	3	27	3	44	7	0
Sutton, Zach, Frederick	0	1	.000	1.29	5	0	0	0	4	0	7.0	5	26	1	1	1	0	0	0	0	0	4	0	0
Tadano, Kazuhito, Kinston	2	1	.667	1.89	7	1	0	0	2	0	19.0	13	73	5	4	0	1	0	1	3	0	28	2	0
Thompson, Travis, Potomac	5	4	.556	3.30	17	11	1	0	2	0	79.0	77	319	30	29	6	2	2	1	17	0	62	0	1
Tierney, Chris, Wilmington *	5	11	.313	4.38	26	26	0	0	0	0	127.1	160	571	77	62	11	5	4	2	48	0	73	5	0
Tiller, James, Frederick	0	0	.000	6.23	1	1	0	0	0	0	4.1	4	18	3	3	1	0	0	1	0	0	3	0	0
Tillery, Josh, Myrtle Beach	2	2	.500	2.98	26	0	0	0	10	0	45.1	47	192	16	15	2	2	1	2	13	0	32	3	0
Torres, Melqui, Lynchburg	2	5	.286	4.23	47	0	0	0	40	25	55.1	55	250	31	26	3	2	0	4	25	2	57	1	0
Tremblay, Max, Salem *	4	2	.667	3.44	13	0	0	0	9	1	18.1	20	84	11	7	1	0	0	0	11	1	13	2	0
Ulacia, Dennis, Win.-Salem *	3	1	.750	0.42	12	0	0	0	3	0	21.2	12	93	6	1	0	0	0	2	12	1	13	3	0
Valdez, Edward, Potomac	5	2	.714	3.40	8	7	0	0	1	0	55.2	55	229	22	21	5	1	0	4	11	0	41	1	0
VanBenschoten, John, Lynch.	6	0	1.000	2.22	9	9	0	0	0	0	48.2	33	192	14	12	1	1	0	1	18	0	49	1	0
Vasquez, Jorge, Wilmington	1	2	.333	1.96	17	0	0	0	12	7	23.0	19	102	7	5	1	3	0	0	14	3	31	1	0
Vianna, Marcel, Myrtle Beach	5	4	.556	2.96	26	0	0	0	6	0	51.2	36	220	20	17	3	3	1	6	29	3	42	2	0
Villacis, Eduardo, Wilmington	6	2	.750	2.82	42	4	0	0	12	2	92.2	78	379	36	29	4	1	4	2	28	3	64	6	0
Waligora, T.P., Lynchburg	3	0	1.000	3.93	21	0	0	0	9	0	34.1	36	150	19	15	2	0	0	3	11	0	36	3	0
Warden, Jim Ed, Kinston	0	4	.000	7.52	7	7	1	0	0	0	26.1	32	136	23	22	4	0	1	4	25	0	21	6	0
Waters, Chris, Myrtle Beach *	1	1	.500	2.89	2	2	0	0	0	0	9.1	7	43	7	3	0	1	3	1	6	0	6	3	0
Watkins, Dave, Myrtle Beach	0	3	.000	1.92	25	0	0	0	12	3	51.2	31	197	13	11	2	0	2	1	18	0	51	5	0
Wilson, Jeff, Frederick *	1	0	1.000	2.00	7	0	0	0	1	0	9.0	6	34	2	2	1	0	0	0	3	0	9	0	0
Wing, Ryan, Winston-Salem *	9	7	.563	2.98	26	26	0	0	0	0	145.0	116	588	62	48	9	4	3	4	67	2	107	11	1
Withelder, Greg, Lynchburg *	1	0	1.000	7.59	7	0	0	0	2	0	10.2	17	56	12	9	0	0	1	1	7	2	7	0	0
Wright, Matt, Myrtle Beach	2	7	.222	6.38	13	13	0	0	0	0	60.2	82	299	47	43	7	1	3	2	42	0	58	12	1
Wrightsman, Dusty, Wil.	3	1	.750	4.42	10	0	0	0	2	0	18.1	21	81	9	9	0	2	1	2	7	0	11	0	0
Wylie, Mitch, Winston-Salem	2	0	1.000	3.38	4	0	0	0	1	0	8.0	7	33	3	3	1	0	0	0	3	0	7	0	0
Zumwalt, Alec, Myrtle Beach	5	2	.714	2.22	30	0	0	0	25	6	44.2	29	174	11	11	2	4	2	0	16	2	43	3	0

PITCHERS WITH TWO OR MORE TEAMS

Pitcher, Team	W	L	Pct.	ERA	G	GS	CG	ShO	GF	Sv.	IP	H	TBF	R	ER	HR	SH	SF	HB	BB	IBB	SO	WP	Bk.
Mattison, Kieran, Kinston	0	0	.000	4.91	2	0	0	0	0	0	3.2	3	16	2	2	0	0	0	0	2	0	3	0	0
Mattison, Kieran, Wilmington	3	1	.750	3.74	7	7	0	0	0	0	33.2	38	140	16	14	5	1	0	0	9	1	29	0	0
McDaniel, Denny, M.B.*	1	0	1.000	1.88	11	0	0	0	4	1	14.1	20	63	5	3	0	1	0	0	1	0	13	1	0
McDaniel, Denny, Salem *	5	1	.833	4.54	34	0	0	0	14	1	41.2	46	186	23	21	1	1	3	3	11	1	39	4	0

COMBINATION SHUTOUTS: Frederick (10)—Birkins-Farren, Boughner-Mitchell-Rleal, Lewis-Makowsky, Crouthers-Makowsky-Wilson-Sequea, Lewis-Mitchell-Wilson-Sequea, McCurdy-Babula-Sequea, Lewis-Mitchell-Rice-Sequea, Birkins-Babula-Rice-Sequea, Maine-Rice-Sequea, Birkins-Babula-Rice-Sequea. Kinston (6)—Gomez-Tadano, Martin-Sturkle-Gronkiewicz, Dittler-Hernandez-Gronkiewicz, Foley-Sturkie-Gronkiewicz, Denham-Cooper, Denham-Cooper-Mattison-Gronkiewicz. Lynchburg (6)—Bradley-Higgins-Torres, Sharber-Higgins-Torres, Lopez-Borner-Torres, Borner-Alcala, Lopez-Owens-Chrysler, Miller-Chrysler-Torres. Myrtle Beach (10)—Miner-Rodriguez-Zumwalt, Coenen-Bush-Zumwalt, Coenen-Bush, McBride-Zumwalt, Wright-Collazo-Watkins, Coenen-Watkins-Roberts, Miner-Watkins, Butler-Digby-David-Roberts, Merricks-Watkins, McBride-Acosta. Potomac (8)—Howington-Culp-Brannon-Cotton, Thompson-Shackelford-Cotton, Howington-Stanton-Cotton, Andrews-Cotton, Childress-Brannon-Salmon-Culp-Cotton, Culp-Barreto-Cotton, Manning-Brannon, Valdez-Granado. Salem (7)—Rodriguez-Campos-Barzilla, Pena-McDaniel, Rodaway-Coughenour, Barrett-McDaniel, Barrett-Santillan, Barrett-Barzilla-Hamilton, Rodriguez-Rodaway-Hamilton-Roberson-Barzilla. Wilmington (14)—Middleton-Natale-Villacis, Middleton-Morrison, Middleton-Morrison-Vasquez, Z. McClellan-Armitage-Leclair-Natale, Greinke-Keppinger, Villacis-Stiles-Leclair, Greinke-Armitage-Keppinger-Lord, Greinke-Leclair-Morrison, Bass-Lord-Leclair, Mattison-Villacis-Keppinger, Middleton-Stiles, Middleton-Villacis-McGill, Douglass-Morrison, Middleton-Keppinger-Morrison. Winston-Salem (11)—Wing-McWhirter-Meaux-Fields, Wing-Meaux, Francisco-Patten-Fields, An-Garza-Kirkland, Francisco-McWhirter-O'Neal-Stumm, Francisco-Stumm-Fields, Wing-Meaux-Fields, Purvis-Bittner-Hummel, Phillips-Pollok-Hummel, O'Neal-Ulacia-Castro, O'Neal-Ulacia-Castro-Lubisich-Fields.

NO-HIT GAMES: Maine, Frederick, defeated Winston-Salem, 3-0 (second game), July 3.

2003 FIELDING

TEAM

Team	G	PO	A	E	TC	DP	TP	PB	Pct.
Kinston	139	3562	1467	128	5157	117	0	30	.975
Salem	138	3554	1577	134	5265	104	0	23	.975
Wilmington	140	3613	1523	132	5268	129	0	15	.975
Frederick	135	3493	1407	137	5037	116	0	40	.973
Myrtle Beach	138	3572	1423	144	5139	117	0	23	.972
Winston-Salem	138	3458	1360	144	4962	93	0	22	.971
Lynchburg	135	3421	1313	146	4880	100	0	35	.970
Potomac	139	3545	1453	174	5172	134	0	15	.966

INDIVIDUAL

FIRST BASEMEN

NOTE: All caps denotes fielding-percentage leader based on 70 games for catchers, 93 for all other non-pitchers and 112 innings for pitchers. *Throws lefthanded.

Player, Team	Pct.	G	PO	A	E	TC	DP
Alleva, J.D., Wilmington	1.000	1	2	0	0	2	1
Becker, Brian, Winston-Salem	.995	23	172	19	1	192	13
Blanco, Tony, Potomac	.971	15	129	7	4	140	8
Calitri, Mike, Potomac	1.000	30	231	29	0	260	23
Checksfield, Steven, Salem	.971	22	184	15	6	205	6
Correll, Brad, Potomac	1.000	5	49	2	0	51	4
Cowan, Justin, Wilmington	.957	2	22	0	1	23	0
De Caster, Yurendell, Lynchburg	.995	23	169	15	1	185	10
Dyson, Trey, Wilm.-Kinston *	.989	27	231	27	3	261	19
Elder, Rick, Kinston *	.987	28	218	18	3	239	17
Fallon, Chris, Wilmington	.990	114	988	82	11	1081	98
Gredvig, Doug, Frederick	1.000	3	26	3	0	29	1
Gutierrez, Jesse, Potomac	.973	19	168	11	5	184	14
Huggins, Mike, Frederick	.990	115	967	75	10	1052	92
Iorg, Isaac, Myrtle Beach	1.000	4	35	0	0	35	4
Jeffcoat, Bryon, Myrtle Beach	1.000	5	32	1	0	33	1
Keppinger, Jeff, Lynchburg	1.000	1	2	0	0	2	0
Kirby, Brian, Kinston	1.000	18	134	8	0	142	15
Knox, Matt, Kinston	.988	55	469	33	6	508	42
Lydic, Joe, Salem	.977	32	239	17	6	262	18
Manley, Adam, Frederick *	.973	5	35	1	1	37	0
Mote, Trevor, Salem	1.000	2	12	0	0	12	1
O'Sullivan, Patrick, Frederick	1.000	5	45	4	0	49	6
Peavey, Bill, Kinston *	.982	42	361	27	7	395	33
Peters, Yaron, Myrtle Beach	1.000	11	68	6	0	74	10
Quattlebaum, Hugh, Frederick	1.000	9	69	13	0	82	6
ROGOWSKI, CASEY, W.S.*	.997	104	826	62	3	891	66
Ruiz, Randy, Frederick	1.000	1	10	0	0	10	2
Salas, Jose, Myrtle Beach	.963	6	49	3	2	54	3
Self, Todd, Salem	.994	95	839	60	5	904	64
Shelton, Chris, Lynchburg	.997	41	323	23	1	347	34
Soto, T.J., Salem	.960	2	22	2	1	25	3
Storey, Eric, Winston-Salem	1.000	2	5	3	0	8	0
Thorman, Scott, Myrtle Beach	.992	120	999	49	8	1056	96
Welsh, Eric, Winston-Salem *	.992	16	109	12	1	122	12
Wilken, Kris, Frederick	1.000	1	4	1	0	5	0
Williamson, Chris, Potomac *	.985	55	434	38	7	479	56
Wong, Travis, Potomac	.995	19	175	8	1	184	16
Young, Walter, Lynchburg	.977	77	570	74	15	659	44

FIRST BASEMEN WITH TWO OR MORE TEAMS

Player, Team	Pct.	G	PO	A	E	TC	DP
Dyson, Trey, Wilmington *	.992	26	217	25	2	244	19
Dyson, Trey, Kinston *	.941	1	14	2	1	17	0

SECOND BASEMEN

Player, Team	Pct.	G	PO	A	E	TC	DP
Amador, Chris, Winston-Salem	.963	6	10	16	1	27	1
Anderson, Bryan, Potomac	1.000	4	6	4	0	10	1
Asprilla, Avelino, Lynchburg	.957	6	11	11	1	23	3
Bautista, Jose, Lynchburg	.889	7	12	12	3	27	3
Bergolla, William, Potomac	.959	127	244	380	27	651	76
Berroa, Cristian, Lynchburg	.966	8	13	15	1	29	4
Bozanich, Sam, Lynchburg	.967	30	34	54	3	91	6
Campana, Wandel, Potomac	1.000	1	6	3	0	9	1
Canales, Josh, Salem	.964	13	22	31	2	55	6
Cates, Gary, Frederick	.962	39	59	117	7	183	22
Choy Foo, Rodney, Kinston	.986	43	91	126	3	220	31
Cockrell, Michael, Lynchburg	.962	5	11	14	1	26	1
Conrad, Brooks, Salem	.970	97	170	315	15	500	50
Cotto, Luis, Wilmington-Kinston	1.000	4	9	13	0	22	4
Fenster, Darren, Wilmington	.933	3	5	9	1	15	0
Gotay, Ruben, Wilmington	.973	128	199	379	16	594	82
Groves, Brett, Wilmington	1.000	11	22	31	0	53	6
Hanson, Mike, Myrtle Beach	1.000	5	9	8	0	17	4
Helquist, Jon, Salem	.960	28	56	111	7	174	16
Hernandez, Habelito, Potomac	.944	4	5	12	1	18	3
HERR, AARON, Myrtle Beach	.976	105	170	272	11	453	70
Inglett, Joe, Kinston	.979	17	37	58	2	97	10
Iorg, Isaac, Myrtle Beach	.955	31	51	76	6	133	15
Jeffcoat, Bryon, Myrtle Beach	1.000	2	3	5	0	8	0
Keppinger, Jeff, Lynchburg	.971	87	148	224	11	383	47
Lopez, Pedro, Winston-Salem	1.000	2	4	6	0	10	0
Mote, Trevor, Salem	.900	2	4	5	1	10	2
Nicholson, Tommy, W.S.	1.000	4	6	6	0	12	1
Patchett, Gary, Potomac	.889	3	2	6	1	9	0
Rogers, Omar, Frederick	.971	88	161	237	12	410	41
Ruiz, Junior, Potomac	1.000	2	1	3	0	4	1
Salvo, Andrew, Winston-Salem	1.000	1	0	2	0	2	0
Shanks, Eric, Frederick-Potomac	.913	5	7	14	2	23	4
Shier, Peter, Frederick	.925	9	17	20	3	40	3
Soto, T.J., Salem	.933	2	6	8	1	15	1
Storey, Eric, Winston-Salem	1.000	2	4	4	0	8	1
Torres, Eider, Kinston	.987	84	139	240	5	384	42
Wilken, Kris, Frederick	1.000	1	1	0	0	1	0
Yan, Ruddy, Winston-Salem	.975	129	250	326	15	591	65

SECOND BASEMEN WITH TWO OR MORE TEAMS

Player, Team	Pct.	G	PO	A	E	TC	DP
Cotto, Luis, Wilmington	1.000	3	9	13	0	22	4
Cotto, Luis, Kinston	.000	1	0	0	0	0	0
Shanks, Eric, Potomac	.875	2	3	4	1	8	1
Shanks, Eric, Frederick	.933	3	4	10	1	15	3

THIRD BASEMEN

Player, Team	Pct.	G	PO	A	E	TC	DP
Amador, Chris, Winston-Salem	.909	12	11	9	2	22	0
Anderson, Bryan, Potomac	.889	15	13	19	4	36	4
Asprilla, Avelino, Lynchburg	.906	11	6	23	3	32	2
Bannon, Jeff, Potomac	1.000	3	2	7	0	9	1
Bautista, Jose, Lynchburg	.946	44	36	86	7	129	8
Berroa, Cristian, Lynchburg	.875	16	6	29	5	40	1
Bozanich, Sam, Lynchburg	.750	12	6	9	5	20	0
Calitri, Mike, Potomac	.929	25	18	47	5	70	4
Canales, Josh, Salem	.979	28	14	33	1	48	4
Cates, Gary, Frederick	.000	1	0	0	0	0	0
Choy Foo, Rodney, Kinston	.932	60	39	99	10	148	8
Correll, Brad, Potomac	1.000	1	1	0	0	1	0
Cotto, Luis, Wilmington-Kinston	.938	21	13	47	4	64	7
De Caster, Yurendell, Lynchburg	.953	63	49	94	7	150	8
Encarnacion, Edwin, Potomac	.879	57	34	89	17	140	4
Fenster, Darren, Wilmington	.959	74	47	142	8	197	14
Groves, Brett, Wilmington	.976	18	10	30	1	41	3
Herr, Aaron, Myrtle Beach	1.000	3	0	4	0	4	0
Honeycutt, Heath, Potomac	.867	3	4	9	2	15	0
Iorg, Isaac, Myrtle Beach	.944	16	9	25	2	36	3
Jeffcoat, Bryon, Myrtle Beach	.923	9	5	7	1	13	0
JOHNSON, TRIPPER, Frederick	.940	118	98	202	19	319	21
Keim, Adam, Wilmington	.970	56	37	93	4	134	13
Keppinger, Jeff, Lynchburg	1.000	3	2	5	0	7	0
Kirby, Brian, Kinston	1.000	3	1	6	0	7	0
Knox, Matt, Kinston	.000	2	0	0	0	0	0
Lackaff, John, Winston-Salem	.948	27	18	37	3	58	4
Lydic, Joe, Salem	1.000	14	9	17	0	26	2
Marte, Andy, Myrtle Beach	.911	117	71	215	28	314	20
Mote, Trevor, Salem	.932	116	75	211	21	307	15
Nicholson, Tommy, W.S.	.905	19	11	27	4	42	2
Osborn, Pat, Kinston	.940	60	45	111	10	166	8
Quattlebaum, Hugh, Frederick	1.000	3	1	4	0	5	1
Schramek, Mark, Potomac	.928	36	24	66	7	97	6
Shier, Peter, Frederick	.929	15	15	37	4	56	8
Soto, T.J., Salem	.909	5	1	9	1	11	2
Spidale, Mike, Winston-Salem	.000	1	0	0	1	1	0
Storey, Eric, Winston-Salem	.896	91	62	153	25	240	13
Wilken, Kris, Frederick	1.000	1	1	2	0	3	1

THIRD BASEMEN WITH TWO OR MORE TEAMS

Player, Team	Pct.	G	PO	A	E	TC	DP
Cotto, Luis, Wilmington	1.000	1	0	2	0	2	0
Cotto, Luis, Kinston	.935	20	13	45	4	62	7

SHORTSTOPS

Player, Team	Pct.	G	PO	A	E	TC	DP
Amador, Chris, Winston-Salem	.792	6	7	12	5	24	3
Anderson, Bryan, Potomac	.950	3	8	11	1	20	5
Asprilla, Avelino, Lynchburg	.914	9	10	22	3	35	3
Bannon, Jeff, Potomac	.950	99	168	247	22	437	58
Bergolla, William, Potomac	1.000	2	0	1	0	1	0
Berroa, Cristian, Lynchburg	.944	12	13	21	2	36	9
Blanco, Andres, Wilmington	.947	110	157	305	26	488	65
Canales, Josh, Salem	.976	25	24	57	2	83	7
Cates, Gary, Frederick	.700	4	4	3	3	10	0
Chaves, Brandon, Lynchburg	.952	118	183	291	24	498	54
Choy Foo, Rodney, Kinston	1.000	4	6	10	0	16	1
Cockrell, Michael, Lynchburg	1.000	2	0	1	0	1	0
Cotto, Luis, Wilmington-Kinston	.922	20	31	52	7	90	12
Fahey, Brandon, Frederick	.962	106	175	307	19	501	64
Fenster, Darren, Wilmington	.977	9	15	28	1	44	9
Groves, Brett, Wilmington	.899	26	33	65	11	109	12
Hernandez, Habelito, Potomac	1.000	4	5	12	0	17	3
Iorg, Isaac, Myrtle Beach	.941	8	8	24	2	34	4
Jeffcoat, Bryon, Myrtle Beach	.958	19	22	47	3	72	8
Lopez, Pedro, Winston-Salem	.867	2	5	8	2	15	3
Morse, Michael, Winston-Salem	.959	120	164	285	19	468	51
Mote, Trevor, Salem	.000	1	0	0	0	0	0
Nicholson, Tommy, W.S.	1.000	4	8	14	0	22	3
Ochoa, Ivan, Kinston	.968	81	134	225	12	371	40
Patchett, Gary, Potomac	.939	35	44	79	8	131	24
PENA, TONY, Myrtle Beach	.965	116	186	336	19	541	76
Salvo, Andrew, Winston-Salem	1.000	4	6	7	0	13	1
Shanks, Eric, Frederick-Potomac	.933	4	8	6	1	15	1
Shier, Peter, Frederick	.939	25	41	67	7	115	11
Stegall, Ryan, Salem	.959	127	203	354	24	581	65
Storey, Eric, Winston-Salem	.833	4	5	10	3	18	1
Torres, Eider, Kinston	.927	39	51	114	13	178	26
Wilken, Kris, Frederick	1.000	1	0	1	0	1	1

SHORTSTOPS WITH TWO OR MORE TEAMS

Player, Team	Pct.	G	PO	A	E	TC	DP
Cotto, Luis, Wilmington	.875	2	1	6	1	8	1
Cotto, Luis, Kinston	.927	18	30	46	6	82	11
Shanks, Eric, Frederick	.900	2	4	5	1	10	1
Shanks, Eric, Potomac	1.000	2	4	1	0	5	0

OUTFIELDERS

Player, Team	Pct.	G	PO	A	E	TC	DP
Anderson, Bryan, Potomac	.985	41	62	3	1	66	1
Asprilla, Avelino, Lynchburg	1.000	7	17	1	0	18	0
Blanco, Gregor, Myrtle Beach *	.967	123	260	6	9	275	0
Burrows, Angelo, Myrtle Beach	.961	34	72	2	3	77	0
Buttler, Vic, Lynchburg *	.988	114	242	7	3	252	2
Canales, Josh, Salem	1.000	1	2	0	0	2	0
Caraway, Brandon, Salem	.987	113	206	19	3	228	1
Cates, Gary, Frederick	.982	36	53	2	1	56	0
Checksfield, Steven, Salem	1.000	3	4	0	0	4	0
Ciraco, Darren, Winston-Salem	1.000	2	3	0	0	3	0
Cliffords, Woody, Frederick	.989	117	261	9	3	273	0
Cooper, Jason, Kinston *	1.000	36	67	1	0	68	0
Correll, Brad, Potomac	.944	33	48	3	3	54	0
Cortes, Jorge, Lynchburg *	.957	36	58	8	3	69	1
Costa, Shane, Wilmington	1.000	3	3	0	0	3	0
Cowan, Justin, Wilmington	.981	70	100	4	2	106	0
Davies, Gregg, Frederick *	1.000	14	26	1	0	27	0
Davis, Justin, Potomac *	.909	13	10	0	1	11	0
De Caster, Yurendell, Lynchburg	.938	10	14	1	1	16	0
Denorfia, Chris, Potomac	.982	126	263	15	5	283	2
Draper, John, Wilmington	.974	126	258	7	7	272	1
Duran, Carlos, Myrtle Beach *	.983	111	222	16	4	242	0
DYSON, TREY, Wilm.-Kinston *	.989	104	171	8	2	181	1
Gordon, Alex, Frederick *	.985	38	62	5	1	68	1
Harts, Jeremy, Lynchburg *	.920	88	121	5	11	137	2
Hawes, B.J., Potomac	.991	58	104	5	1	110	2
Holt, Daylan, Winston-Salem	.977	106	165	8	4	177	0
Honeycutt, Heath, Potomac	.984	46	60	3	1	64	0
Iorg, Isaac, Myrtle Beach	1.000	1	1	0	0	1	0
Jeffcoat, Bryon, Myrtle Beach	1.000	2	4	0	0	4	0
Jenkins, Brian, Kinston	.947	20	34	2	2	38	0
Jimerson, Charlton, Salem	.985	91	196	4	3	203	1
Keylor, Cory, Frederick	.962	74	123	3	5	131	1
Lentini, Fehlandt, Salem	.987	72	145	8	2	155	3
Likely, Cameron, Salem	1.000	10	18	0	0	18	0
Lytle, Derrik, Wilmington *	.962	29	49	1	2	52	0
Majewski, Val, Frederick *	.938	35	60	1	4	65	0
Malave, Dennis, Kinston *	1.000	39	60	12	0	72	1
Manley, Adam, Frederick *	.991	65	102	4	1	107	1
Martel, Normand, W.S.	.979	112	184	6	4	194	0
Martinez, Candido, Potomac	.800	11	12	0	3	15	0
McLouth, Nathan, Lynchburg	.979	116	228	4	5	237	1
Meath, Matt, Lynchburg	1.000	12	21	0	0	21	0
Miller, Greg, Myrtle Beach	.982	66	105	2	2	109	0
O'Sullivan, Patrick, Frederick	1.000	4	6	0	0	6	0
Quintana, Miguel, Kinston	.977	83	152	16	4	172	1
Ravelo, Manny, Lynchburg	.979	53	89	4	2	95	0
Reed, Jeremy, Winston-Salem *	.979	64	135	6	3	144	0
Rios, Fernando, Potomac	.955	36	60	3	3	66	1
Rodriguez, Mike, Salem *	.972	101	163	8	5	176	0
Ruiz, Junior, Potomac	.985	39	65	1	1	67	0
Ruiz, Randy, Frederick	1.000	4	8	0	0	8	0
Scott, Luke, Kinston	.989	45	85	2	1	88	0
Self, Todd, Salem	.976	26	41	0	1	42	0
Shanks, Eric, Frederick	1.000	6	8	0	0	8	0
Shanks, James, Wilmington	.967	84	176	2	6	184	0
Sherrill, J.J., Kinston	.970	46	92	5	3	100	1
Shier, Peter, Frederick	.972	27	34	1	1	36	0
Soto, T.J., Salem	1.000	15	22	0	0	22	0
Spidale, Mike, Winston-Salem	.989	120	272	1	3	276	1
Spidale, Mike, Winston-Salem	.989	120	272	1	3	276	1
Stern, Adam, Myrtle Beach	1.000	26	66	1	0	67	0
Stocker, Mel, Wilmington	.976	18	40	0	1	41	0
Taveras, Willy, Kinston	.978	109	267	5	6	278	0
Thomas, Charles, M.B.*	.969	60	121	5	4	130	0
Welsh, Eric, Winston-Salem *	.958	51	67	2	3	72	0
Wilken, Kris, Frederick	.667	4	1	1	1	3	0
Williamson, Chris, Potomac *	.957	36	43	1	2	46	0
Wright, Brian, Kinston	1.000	51	70	5	0	75	0

OUTFIELDERS WITH TWO OR MORE TEAMS

Player, Team	Pct.	G	PO	A	E	TC	DP
Dyson, Trey, Kinston *	1.000	4	9	1	0	10	0
Dyson, Trey, Wilmington *	.988	100	162	7	2	171	1

CATCHERS

Player, Team	Pct.	G	PO	A	E	TC	DP	PB
Alleva, J.D., Wilmington	.993	48	269	24	2	295	0	3
Arko, Tommy, Frederick	.981	34	242	19	5	266	1	8
Arnerich, Tony, Wilmington	.990	45	282	23	3	308	1	7
Barnett, Dan, Winston-Salem	1.000	2	2	0	0	2	0	0
Bernard, Miguel, Myrtle Beach	1.000	1	5	0	0	5	0	0
Boscan, Jean, Myrtle Beach	.977	27	189	26	5	220	0	4
Camacaro, Armando, Kinston	.990	58	358	30	4	392	3	7
Doumit, Ryan, Lynchburg	.985	86	526	65	9	600	5	23
GIMENEZ, HECTOR, Salem	.991	101	574	77	6	657	7	19
Guerrero, Henry, Frederick	1.000	6	36	9	0	45	1	3
Gutierrez, Jesse, Potomac	.988	37	221	26	3	250	2	2
Hernandez, Jose, Lynchburg	1.000	3	10	0	0	10	0	0
Hubele, Ryan, Frederick	.973	26	170	12	5	187	1	13
Kirby, Brian, Kinston	1.000	5	10	0	0	10	0	2
Lucas, Matt, Salem	.952	7	19	1	1	21	0	2
Margalski, Ben, Kinston	.985	41	237	26	4	267	3	7
Martin, Kyle, Frederick	.960	19	132	13	6	151	0	8
Martinez, Octavio, Frederick	.976	38	258	30	7	295	3	3
Martinez, Raul, Frederick	1.000	5	20	1	0	21	0	1
Motooka, Rafael, Potomac	.964	14	72	9	3	84	0	4
Paulino, Ronny, Lynchburg	.983	14	105	11	2	118	1	4
Pena, Brayan, Myrtle Beach	.996	62	408	46	2	456	2	7
Pena, Rodolfo, Lynchburg	.974	11	69	5	2	76	0	3
Peterson, Brian, Potomac	.965	49	313	49	13	375	7	7
Phillips, Paul, Wilmington	.988	11	77	8	1	86	0	1
Prince, Bryan, Potomac	.992	47	347	40	3	390	2	1
Roat, Kyle, Myrtle Beach	.986	13	68	4	1	73	1	2
Rosa, Wally, Winston-Salem	.982	69	379	46	8	433	0	13
Ruiz, Reinaldo, Salem	1.000	45	210	14	0	224	2	2
Salas, Jose, Myrtle Beach	.982	45	284	45	6	335	1	10
Seestedt, Mike, Frederick	1.000	13	67	10	0	77	0	4
Shelton, Chris, Lynchburg	.987	28	208	19	3	230	0	5
Stewart, Chris, Winston-Salem	.976	76	500	68	14	582	3	8
Storey, Eric, Winston-Salem	1.000	1	1	0	0	1	0	1
Sulbaran, Orlando, Potomac	1.000	2	5	1	0	6	0	1
Wallace, David, Kinston	.986	43	261	22	4	287	1	14
Walter, Scott, Wilmington	.986	44	338	23	5	366	4	4

PITCHERS

Player, Team	Pct.	G	PO	A	E	TC	DP
Acosta, Manuel, Myrtle Beach	1.000	8	1	5	0	6	0
Agamennone, Brandon, Fred.	.000	2	0	0	1	1	0
Alcala, Jason, Lynchburg	1.000	15	5	3	0	8	1
Allen, Wyatt, Winston-Salem	.844	28	10	17	5	32	1
Alvarez, Oscar, Kinston *	1.000	4	1	3	0	4	0
An, Byeong, Winston-Salem *	.952	12	2	18	1	21	1
ANDREWS, CLAYTON, Pot.*	1.000	18	7	25	0	32	4
Armitage, Barry, Wilmington	1.000	30	2	2	0	4	0
Arthurs, Shane, Kinston	1.000	12	1	2	0	3	0
Astacio, Andres, Salem	.600	3	0	3	2	5	0
Babula, Shaun, Frederick *	1.000	37	7	10	0	17	0
Barreto, Joel, Potomac	.000	3	0	0	0	0	0
Barrett, Jimmy, Salem	.909	26	14	26	4	44	2
Bartlett, Richard, Frederick	1.000	9	4	6	0	10	0
BARZILLA, PHILIP, Salem *	1.000	52	9	23	0	32	0
Basham, Bobby, Potomac	.000	1	0	0	0	0	0
Bass, Brian, Wilmington	.963	26	21	31	2	54	5
Bedard, Erik, Frederick *	1.000	1	0	1	0	1	0
Berube, Martin, Frederick	1.000	3	1	0	0	1	0
BIRKINS, KURT, Frederick *	1.000	25	8	24	0	32	3
Bittner, Tim, Winston-Salem *	1.000	17	0	9	0	9	0
Borner, Brady, Lynchburg *	.933	20	5	9	1	15	2
Boughner, Anthony, Frederick *	1.000	18	2	5	0	7	0
Bradley, Bobby, Lynchburg	.944	12	5	12	1	18	2
Brannon, Nick, Potomac *	.889	40	2	6	1	9	0
Bruksch, Jeffrey, Potomac	.818	6	3	6	2	11	1
Bullington, Bryan, Lynchburg	.920	17	9	14	2	25	0
Burch, Matt, Wilmington	.857	13	1	5	1	7	0
Bush, Paul, Myrtle Beach	.889	34	1	7	1	9	0
Butler, Matt, Myrtle Beach	1.000	10	0	1	0	1	0
Campos, Juan, Salem	1.000	45	5	8	0	13	0
Capps, Matt, Lynchburg	1.000	1	0	1	0	1	0
Casey, Reid, Kinston	.000	1	0	0	0	0	0
Castillo, Carlos, Winston-Salem	1.000	2	1	3	0	4	0
Castro, Julio, Winston-Salem	1.000	26	2	3	0	5	0
Cedeno, Blas, Lynchburg	1.000	4	0	3	0	3	0
Childress, Daylan, Potomac	.917	17	11	22	3	36	5
Chrysler, Clint, Lynchburg *	1.000	7	0	3	0	3	1
Coenen, Matt, Myrtle Beach *	.759	28	3	19	7	29	0
Coffey, Todd, Potomac	1.000	11	1	3	0	4	0
Collazo, William, Myrtle Beach *	1.000	11	0	2	0	2	0
Cooper, Chris, Kinston *	1.000	40	3	9	0	12	0
Coppinger, Joe, Frederick	.000	1	0	0	0	0	0
Corcoran, Tim, Frederick	.929	22	5	8	1	14	1
Cortes, Jorge, Potomac	.000	5	0	0	1	1	0
Cotton, Nathan, Potomac	.929	48	4	9	1	14	0
Coughenour, Jory, Salem	.667	10	1	1	1	3	0
Cressend, Jack, Kinston	1.000	2	1	0	0	1	0
Crouthers, Dave, Frederick	1.000	18	4	7	0	11	1
Culp, Brandon, Potomac	.960	31	8	16	1	25	2
Curtis, Daniel, Myrtle Beach	1.000	12	2	12	0	14	0
David, Brad, Myrtle Beach *	1.000	17	0	1	0	1	0
Daws, Josh, Potomac	1.000	18	1	4	0	5	0
DeHart, Casey, Potomac *	.000	6	0	0	0	0	0
De los Santos, Carlos, Lynch.	1.000	10	1	3	0	4	0
Denham, Dan, Kinston	1.000	14	6	11	0	17	0
Deza, Fredy, Frederick	.000	1	0	0	0	0	0
Digby, Bryan, Myrtle Beach	.900	21	2	7	1	10	0
Dittler, Jake, Kinston	1.000	8	4	10	0	14	1
Douglass, Ryan, Wilmington	1.000	8	2	9	0	11	2
Dumatrait, Phillip, Potomac *	.900	7	4	5	1	10	0
Edens, Kyle, Potomac	.875	28	7	7	2	16	0
Edwards, Brad, Frederick *	.000	3	0	0	0	0	0
Farren, Dave, Frederick	.909	18	4	6	1	11	1
Fernley, Nathan, Kinston	.889	15	2	6	1	9	0
Fields, Josh, Winston-Salem	.920	58	6	17	2	25	2
Fitch, Steve, Lynchburg	1.000	12	5	3	0	8	0
Foley, Travis, Kinston	.952	24	12	8	1	21	0
Francisco, Frank, W.S.	.833	16	3	2	1	6	0
Garza, Rolando, Winston-Salem	1.000	17	1	1	0	2	0
Gomez, Mariano, Kinston *	.957	18	4	18	1	23	2
Gonzalez, Mike, Lynchburg *	1.000	5	0	1	0	1	0
Gothreaux, Jared, Salem	.923	29	5	19	2	26	0
Granado, Jan, Potomac *	1.000	15	0	9	0	9	1
Gray, Brett, Potomac	1.000	2	1	1	0	2	0
Greinke, Zack, Wilmington	1.000	14	9	16	0	25	0
Griffin, Colt, Wilmington	.000	1	0	0	0	0	0
Gronkiewicz, Lee, Kinston	1.000	51	6	6	0	12	0
Guerrero, Julio, Lynchburg	1.000	16	2	6	0	8	0
Hamilton, Mark, Salem *	1.000	34	2	13	0	15	1
Hannaman, Ryan, Frederick *	1.000	5	0	1	0	1	0
Hart, Alex, Lynchburg	1.000	11	13	6	0	19	0
Harts, Jeremy, Lynchburg *	.000	3	0	0	0	0	0
Hernandez, Michael, Kinston *	.500	19	0	1	1	2	0
Higgins, Joshua, Lynchburg	1.000	37	3	13	0	16	1
Honel, Kris, Winston-Salem	1.000	24	5	20	0	25	1
Howington, Ty, Potomac *	.905	19	6	13	2	21	2
Hummel, Rick, Winston-Salem	1.000	19	3	4	0	7	1
Ireland, Eric, Salem	1.000	1	0	1	0	1	0
Kelly, Steve, Potomac	1.000	17	6	17	0	23	2
Keppinger, Billy, Wilmington *	1.000	34	3	6	0	9	1
Kirkland, Aaron, Winston-Salem	1.000	16	1	3	0	4	0
Kleine, Victor, Kinston *	1.000	28	7	20	0	27	1
Knapp, Ben, Frederick	1.000	9	3	8	0	11	0
Knox, Matt, Kinston	1.000	1	0	1	0	1	0
LaMura, B.J., Winston-Salem	.500	4	1	0	1	2	0
Lantz, Doug, Kinston	.941	27	6	10	1	17	2
Leclair, Aric, Wilmington *	1.000	32	0	9	0	9	0
Lee, Cliff, Kinston *	.333	1	0	1	2	3	0
Lewis, Rommie, Frederick *	.905	26	3	16	2	21	2
Lopez, Gonzalo, Myrtle Beach	.000	3	0	0	0	0	0
Lopez, Jose, Lynchburg	.885	20	13	10	3	26	0
Lord, Justin, Wilmington	1.000	13	2	2	0	4	0
Lubisich, Nik, Winston-Salem *	1.000	3	0	2	0	2	0
Mabry, Barry, Myrtle Beach	.000	1	0	0	0	0	0
Maine, John, Frederick	1.000	12	4	7	0	11	0
Makowsky, Carl, Frederick	.900	29	3	6	1	10	0
Manning, Charlie, Potomac *	.933	6	2	12	1	15	1
Mansfield, Monte, Salem	1.000	13	0	1	0	1	0
Martin, J.D., Kinston	.926	16	6	19	2	27	4
Martin, Kevin, Kinston	1.000	1	0	2	0	2	0
Mattison, Kieran, Wilm.-Kinston	.750	9	1	2	1	4	0
McBride, Macay, Myrtle Beach *	.907	27	5	34	4	43	3
McClellan, Robbie, Wilmington	.000	1	0	0	0	0	0
McClellan, Zach, Wilmington	.978	30	14	31	1	46	5
McCurdy, Nick, Frederick	1.000	19	7	9	0	16	0
McDaniel, Denny, M.B.-Salem*	.917	45	3	8	1	12	0
McGill, Trae, Wilmington	1.000	6	1	1	0	2	0
McWhirter, Kris, Winston-Salem	.600	11	0	3	2	5	0
Meaux, Ryan, Winston-Salem *	.947	32	3	15	1	19	0
Mendez, David, Myrtle Beach *	1.000	3	0	2	0	2	0
Mendoza, Marcos, Kinston *	.700	28	1	6	3	10	1
Merricks, Matt, Myrtle Beach *	.800	11	4	12	4	20	0
Meyer, Dan, Myrtle Beach *	1.000	13	6	12	0	18	1
Middleton, Kyle, Wilmington	.902	27	11	35	5	51	2
Miller, Jeff, Lynchburg	.960	27	11	13	1	25	0
Miller, Matt, Myrtle Beach *	1.000	4	0	2	0	2	0
Miner, Zach, Myrtle Beach	.931	27	7	20	2	29	1
Mitchell, Andy, Frederick	.955	60	11	31	2	44	3
Moran, Nick, Kinston	.889	6	0	8	1	9	0
Morris, Cory, Frederick	1.000	7	3	2	0	5	2
Morrison, Robbie, Wilmington	1.000	42	6	11	0	17	0
Natale, Mike, Wilmington	.857	27	2	4	1	7	0
Navarro, Rodolfo, Kinston	.000	2	0	0	1	1	0
O'Brien, Patrick, Lynchburg	1.000	12	1	13	0	14	1
O'Neal, Brandon, Winston-Salem	.944	35	6	11	1	18	2
Oquendo, Ian, Lynchburg	1.000	20	10	13	0	23	0
Owens, Henry, Lynchburg	1.000	13	1	1	0	2	0
Patchett, Gary, Potomac	.000	1	0	0	0	0	0
Patten, Scott, Winston-Salem	.600	10	2	1	2	5	0
Pena, Francisco, Salem	.875	33	7	14	3	24	1
Pena, Rodolfo, Lynchburg	.000	1	0	0	0	0	0
Phillips, Mike, Winston-Salem *	.944	13	1	16	1	18	0
Pluta, Tony, Salem	.000	3	0	0	0	0	0
Pollok, Dwayne, Winston-Salem	1.000	14	1	3	0	4	0
Prahm, Ryan, Kinston	1.000	9	1	3	0	4	0
Purvis, Rob, Winston-Salem	.929	12	2	11	1	14	1
Quattlebaum, Hugh, Frederick	.000	1	0	0	0	0	0
Quintana, Miguel, Kinston	.000	1	0	0	0	0	0
Ramirez, Enrique, Frederick	1.000	13	4	1	0	5	0
Reed, Chris, Potomac	1.000	8	3	1	0	4	0
Rice, Scott, Frederick *	1.000	25	2	6	0	8	0
Rleal, Sendy, Frederick	1.000	44	5	12	0	17	0
Roberson, Brandon, Salem	.971	38	11	22	1	34	3
Roberts, Nick, Salem	1.000	3	1	0	0	1	0
Roberts, Ralph, Myrtle Beach	.810	44	4	13	4	21	0
Rodaway, Brian, Salem *	.952	26	9	31	2	42	2
Rodriguez, Jose, Myrtle Beach	.000	5	0	0	0	0	0
Rodriguez, Wandy, Salem *	.917	20	4	18	2	24	0
Salazar, Richard, Frederick *	1.000	6	1	5	0	6	2

Player, Team	Pct.	G	PO	A	E	TC	DP
Salmon, Brad, Potomac	1.000	32	2	13	0	15	0
Sampson, Christopher, Salem	.833	9	0	5	1	6	0
Santillan, Manny, Salem	.929	36	3	10	1	14	1
Sequea, Jacobo, Frederick	.500	32	1	0	1	2	0
Shackelford, Brian, Potomac *	.917	18	4	7	1	12	0
Sharber, Jason, Lynchburg	.952	21	9	11	1	21	1
Shumaker, Casey, Lynchburg	.909	33	5	5	1	11	0
Sims, Kenny, Frederick	1.000	11	3	4	0	7	1
Sinclair, Ernnie, Salem	1.000	6	1	1	0	2	0
Slocum, Brian, Kinston	.909	22	9	11	2	22	0
Sobkowiak, Scott, Potomac	1.000	4	0	5	0	5	0
Sperring, Jayme, Frederick	.750	15	2	1	1	4	0
Stanton, Kyle, Potomac	1.000	20	2	1	0	3	0
Stiles, Brad, Wilmington *	.750	26	4	2	2	8	1
Stodolka, Mike, Wilmington *	1.000	5	0	2	0	2	0
Stumm, Jason, Winston-Salem	1.000	20	1	4	0	5	1
Sturkie, Scott, Kinston	1.000	40	6	14	0	20	1
Sutton, Zach, Frederick	.000	5	0	0	0	0	0
Tadano, Kazuhito, Kinston	1.000	7	0	1	0	1	0
Thompson, Travis, Potomac	1.000	17	3	12	0	15	4
Tierney, Chris, Wilmington *	.861	26	5	26	5	36	1
Tiller, James, Frederick	1.000	1	0	1	0	1	0
Tillery, Josh, Myrtle Beach	1.000	26	1	3	0	4	0
Torres, Melqui, Lynchburg	.833	47	5	5	2	12	1
Tremblay, Max, Salem *	.000	13	0	0	0	0	0
Ulacia, Dennis, Winston-Salem *	1.000	12	2	2	0	4	0
Valdez, Edward, Potomac	.833	8	5	5	2	12	1
VanBenschoten, John, Lynch.	1.000	9	3	9	0	12	3
Vasquez, Jorge, Wilmington	1.000	17	1	3	0	4	0
Vianna, Marcel, Myrtle Beach	1.000	26	1	9	0	10	0
Villacis, Eduardo, Wilmington	1.000	42	8	13	0	21	1
Waligora, T.P., Lynchburg	1.000	21	3	1	0	4	0
Warden, Jim Ed, Kinston	.667	7	2	2	2	6	0
Waters, Chris, Myrtle Beach *	1.000	2	2	0	0	2	0
Watkins, Dave, Myrtle Beach	.909	25	4	6	1	11	2
Wilson, Jeff, Frederick *	.000	7	0	0	0	0	0
Wing, Ryan, Winston-Salem *	.963	26	14	38	2	54	1
Withelder, Greg, Lynchburg *	1.000	7	0	2	0	2	0
Wright, Matt, Myrtle Beach	.889	13	3	13	2	18	1
Wrightsman, Dusty, Wilmington	1.000	10	2	4	0	6	0
Wylie, Mitch, Winston-Salem	1.000	4	0	2	0	2	0
Zumwalt, Alec, Myrtle Beach	1.000	30	3	9	0	12	0

PITCHERS WITH TWO OR MORE TEAMS

Player, Team	Pct.	G	PO	A	E	TC	DP
Mattison, Kieran, Wilmington	.750	7	1	2	1	4	0
Mattison, Kieran, Kinston	.000	2	0	0	0	0	0
McDaniel, Denny, M.B.*	1.000	11	1	3	0	4	0
McDaniel, Denny, Salem *	.875	34	2	5	1	8	0

The following players appeared only as a designated hitter, pinch-hitter or pinch-runner: Boruff, dh; Dorsey, dh, pr; Segui, dh.

LEAGUE CHAMPIONS

Year	Team	Pct.
1945—	Danville	.681
1946—	Greensboro	.599
	Raleigh (2nd)†	.563
1947—	Burlington	.613
	Raleigh (3rd)†	.574
1948—	Raleigh	.592
	Martinsville (2nd)†	.570
1949—	Danville	.601
	Burlington (4th)†	.500
1950—	Winston-Salem*	.693
1951—	Durham	.600
	Winston-Salem (2nd)†	.583
1952—	Raleigh	.581
	Reidsville (4th)†	.536
1953—	Raleigh	.593
	Danville (2nd)†	.572
1954—	Fayetteville*	.628
1955—	HP-Thomasville	.580
	Danville (2nd)†	.533
1956—	HP-Thomasville	.591
	Fayetteville (4th)§	.523
1957—	Durham	.632
	HP-Thomasville	.622
1958—	Danville	.576
	Burlington (4th)†	.511
1959—	Raleigh	.600
	Wilson (2nd)†	.550
1960—	Greensboro‡	.636
	Burlington	.586
1961—	Wilson	.594
1962—	Durham	.636
	Wilson	.600
	Kinston (2nd)†	.593
1963—	Kinston§	.538
	Greensboro§	.590
	Wilson (2nd)†	.535
1964—	Kinston§	.572
	Winston-Salem§†	.590
1965—	Peninsula§	.597
	Durham§	.580
	Tidewater†	.528
1966—	Kinston§	.547
	Winston-Salem§	.586
	Rocky Mount†	.533
1967—	Durham∞(West.)	.536
	Raleigh (East.)	.542
1968—	Salem (West.)	.607
	Ral-Dur (East.)	.597
	HP-Thom.▲(W.)	.493
1969—	Rocky M (East.)	.569
	Salem (West.)	.542
	Ral-Dur◆(East.)	.560
1970—	Winston-Salem‡	.586
	Burlington	.597
1971—	Peninsula‡	.647
	Kinston	.623
1972—	Salem‡	.657
	Burlington	.632
1973—	Lynchburg	.588
	Winston-Salem‡	.557
1974—	Salem	.671
	Salem	.582
1975—	Rocky Mount	.667
	Rocky Mount	.614
1976—	Winston-Salem	.618
	Winston-Salem	.551
1977—	Lynchburg	.591
	Peninsula‡	.556
1978—	Peninsula	.696
	Lynchburg‡	.614
1979—	Winston-Salem■	.607
1980—	Peninsula‡	.714
	Durham	.600
1981—	Peninsula	.522
	Hagerstown‡	.507
1982—	Alexandria‡	.597
	Durham	.588
1983—	Lynchburg‡	.691
	Winston-Salem	.529
1984—	Lynchburg‡	.645
	Durham	.486
1985—	Lynchburg	.679
	Winston-Salem‡	.417
1986—	Hagerstown	.655
	Winston-Salem‡	.594
1987—	Salem‡	.576
	Kinston	.536
1988—	Kinston§	.629
	Lynchburg	.486
1989—	Durham	.609
	Prince William‡	.522
1990—	Kinston	.652
	Frederick‡	.544
1991—	Kinston‡	.645
	Lynchburg	.482
1992—	Lynchburg	.570
	Peninsula‡	.536
1993—	Wilmington	.532
	Winston-Salem‡	.514
1994—	Wilmington‡	.681
	Winston-Salem	.555
1995—	Wilmington	.601
	Kinston‡	.591
1996—	Wilmington▼	.571
	Kinston	.551
1997—	Kinston	.621
	Lynchburg†	.586
1998—	Wilmington▼	.614
	Winston-Salem	.568
1999—	Kinston	.577
	Myrtle Beach•	.568
	Wilmington•	.568
2000—	Myrtle Beach▼	.629
2001—	Kinston	.636
	Salem▼	.507
2002—	Wilmington	.636
	Lynchburg▼	.621
2003—	Wilmington	.571
	Winston-Salem▼	.514

*Won championship and four-club playoff. †Won four-club playoff. ‡Won split-season playoff. §League was divided into Eastern, Western divisions. ∞Won eight-club, two-division playoff. ▲Won eight-club, two-division playoff against Raleigh-Durham. ◆Won eight-club, two-division playoff against Burlington. ■Won both halves of split season (no playoffs). ▼League divided into Northern and Southern divisions and played a split-season, won playoffs. •Declared co-champions after final series cancelled due to hurricane.

FLORIDA STATE LEAGUE

LEAGUE OFFICE

President
Chuck Murphy
Address
P.O. Box 349
Daytona Beach, FL 32115
Phone
386-252-7479

Teams (affiliation)
Brevard County Manatees (Expos)
Clearwater Threshers (Phillies)
Daytona Cubs (Cubs)
Dunedin Blue Jays (Blue Jays)
Fort Myers Miracle (Twins)
Jupiter Hammerheads (Marlins)
Lakeland Tigers (Tigers)
Palm Beach Cardinals (Cardinals)
St. Lucie Mets (Mets)
Sarasota Red Sox (Red Sox)
Tampa Yankees (Yankees)
Vero Beach Dodgers (Dodgers)

2003 FINAL STANDINGS

FIRST HALF

EAST DIVISION

Team	W	L	T	Pct.	GB
Jupiter	42	28	-	.600	...
Vero Beach	36	31	-	.537	4.5
Brevard County	35	33	-	.515	6.0
St. Lucie	33	37	-	.471	9.0
Daytona	32	38	-	.457	10.0
Palm Beach	25	43	-	.368	16.0

WEST DIVISION

Team	W	L	T	Pct.	GB
Fort Myers	44	26	-	.629	...
Clearwater	37	31	-	.544	6.0
Tampa	38	32	-	.543	6.0
Dunedin	38	32	-	.543	6.0
Sarasota	31	38	-	.449	12.5
Lakeland	24	46	-	.343	20.0

SECOND HALF

EAST DIVISION

Team	W	L	T	Pct.	GB
St. Lucie	44	25	-	.638	...
Daytona	34	33	-	.507	9.0
Jupiter	34	34	-	.500	9.5
Brevard County	30	33	-	.476	11.0
Palm Beach	29	41	-	.414	15.5
Vero Beach	26	38	-	.406	15.5

WEST DIVISION

Team	W	L	T	Pct.	GB
Dunedin	40	30	-	.571	...
Clearwater	35	30	-	.538	2.5
Sarasota	32	29	-	.525	3.5
Lakeland	31	32	-	.492	5.5
Tampa	30	32	-	.484	6.0
Fort Myers	29	37	-	.439	9.0

COMPOSITE

Team	DUN	SLU	JUP	CLW	FTM	TAM	BRE	SAR	DAY	VB	LAK	PLM	W	L	T	Pct.	GB
Dunedin (Blue Jays)	...	5	5	13	9	10	4	10	6	6	6	4	78	62	0	.557	...
St. Lucie (Mets)	3	...	10	5	6	6	11	3	8	5	6	14	77	62	0	.554	0.5
Jupiter (Marlins)	3	10	...	4	4	3	11	6	8	7	5	15	76	62	0	.551	1.0
Clearwater (Phillies)	11	3	4	...	12	8	3	10	5	5	9	2	72	61	0	.541	2.5
Fort Myers (Twins)	7	2	4	4	...	8	5	13	5	6	13	6	73	63	0	.537	3.0
Tampa (Yankees)	10	2	5	8	7	...	5	7	4	3	13	4	68	64	0	.515	6.0
Brevard County (Expos)	4	9	5	5	3	2	...	5	9	11	2	10	65	66	0	.496	8.5
Sarasota (Red Sox)	6	5	2	5	8	8	3	...	3	5	12	6	63	67	0	.485	10.0
Daytona (Cubs)	2	8	6	3	3	4	8	5	...	13	4	10	66	71	0	.482	10.5
Vero Beach (Dodgers)	2	10	6	3	2	4	6	3	13	...	6	7	62	69	0	.473	11.5
Lakeland (Tigers)	10	2	2	6	7	7	6	3	4	2	...	6	55	78	0	.414	19.5
Palm Beach (Cardinals)	4	6	13	5	2	4	4	2	6	6	2	...	54	84	0	.391	23.0

Major league affiliations in parentheses.

PLAYOFFS: St. Lucie defeated Jupiter, two games to none; Dunedin defeated Fort Myers, two games to one; St. Lucie defeated Dunedin, three games to one, to win league championship.

REGULAR-SEASON ATTENDANCE: Brevard County, 83,314; Clearwater, 63,655; Daytona, 97,362; Dunedin, 42,752; Fort Myers, 110,356; Jupiter, 90,080; Lakeland, 30,832; Palm Beach, 68,210; St. Lucie, 81,154; Sarasota, 49,684; Tampa, 67,565; Vero Beach, 57,339. Total attendance—842,303. Playoffs (9 games)—7,496. All-Star Game at Fort Myers—4,629.

MANAGERS: Brevard County, Doug Sisson; Clearwater, Roly DeArmas; Daytona, Rick Kranitz; Dunedin, Mike Basso; Fort Myers, Jose Marzan; Jupiter, Luis Dorante; Lakeland, Gary Green; Palm Beach, Tom Nieto; St. Lucie, Ken Oberkfell; Sarasota, Tim Leiper; Tampa, Billy Masse; Vero Beach, Scott Little.

ALL-STAR TEAM: 1B—Ryan Howard, Clearwater; 2B—Luis Maza, Fort Myers; 3B—David Wright, St. Lucie; SS—Don Kelly, Lakeland; Utility INF—Chase Lambin, St. Lucie; LF—Wayne Lydon, St. Lucie; CF—Franklin Gutierrez, Vero Beach; RF—Jason Kubel, Fort Myers; Utility OF—Eric Reed, Jupiter; C—(tie) Jared Blasdell, Daytona and Joe Mauer, Fort Myers; DH—Jason Stokes, Jupiter; RHP—Ezequiel Astacio, Clearwater; RHP—Chad Blasko, Daytona; LHP—Greg Miller, Vero Beach; RHP—Nic Ungs, Jupiter; RHP—Jared Blasdell, Daytona; RHP—Kevin Cave, Jupiter; Most Valuable Player—Ryan Howard, Clearwater; Most Valuable Pitcher—Nic Ungs, Jupiter; Manager of the Year—Mike Basso, Dunedin; Coach of the Year—(tie) Luis Dorante, Jupiter and Ken Oberfell, St. Lucie.

2003 BATTING

TEAM

Team	G	TPA	AB	R	H	TB	2B	3B	HR	RBI	SH	SF	HP	BB	IBB	SO	SB	CS	GDP	LOB	ShO	Avg.	OBP	Slg.
Fort Myers	136	5135	4516	607	1211	1600	180	31	49	541	61	55	80	421	24	727	91	48	111	999	13	.268	.338	.354
Dunedin	140	5121	4549	573	1199	1626	239	16	52	514	53	38	58	422	17	793	64	42	131	999	9	.264	.331	.357
Tampa	132	4882	4377	562	1126	1607	233	40	56	510	14	43	50	398	8	885	83	32	97	936	6	.257	.323	.367
Clearwater	133	4915	4368	529	1118	1556	227	26	53	487	27	33	59	426	17	845	75	41	117	958	8	.256	.328	.356
Daytona	137	5174	4521	574	1149	1629	227	26	67	516	54	45	70	478	18	955	184	60	105	997	8	.254	.332	.360

Team	G	TPA	AB	R	H	TB	2B	3B	HR	RBI	SH	SF	HP	BB	IBB	SO	SB	CS	GDP	LOB	ShO	Avg.	OBP	Slg.
Jupiter	138	5032	4420	549	1104	1566	194	32	68	494	92	33	70	416	17	959	128	65	87	933	11	.250	.322	.354
Lakeland	133	4922	4340	540	1085	1596	215	43	70	507	40	44	39	457	11	963	81	46	69	958	7	.250	.324	.368
St. Lucie	139	5033	4415	566	1104	1560	226	25	60	510	52	49	73	441	15	861	216	81	84	935	14	.250	.325	.353
Vero Beach	131	4851	4294	551	1074	1563	213	15	82	498	59	32	69	395	13	858	109	79	88	863	12	.250	.321	.364
Sarasota	130	4741	4107	480	971	1369	194	30	48	425	39	39	54	501	8	901	148	70	97	888	12	.236	.325	.333
Brevard Co.	131	4719	4177	466	978	1372	187	30	49	420	39	26	54	423	16	938	90	56	85	879	11	.234	.311	.328
Palm Beach	138	5115	4477	449	1011	1375	185	16	49	394	42	35	70	489	15	1010	82	54	103	1018	18	.226	.310	.307

INDIVIDUAL

TOP QUALIFIERS FOR BATTING CHAMPIONSHIP

Minimum 378 plate appearances. *Lefthanded batter. †Switch-hitter.

Player, Team	G	TPA	AB	R	H	TB	2B	3B	HR	RBI	SH	SF	HP	BB	IBB	SO	SB	CS	GDP	Avg.	OBP	Slg.
Howard, Ryan, Clearwater *	130	553	490	67	149	252	32	1	23	82	0	5	8	50	9	151	0	0	12	.304	.374	.514
Tomlin, James, Fort Myers	122	557	498	88	151	178	17	2	2	42	13	6	4	36	1	51	24	10	8	.303	.351	.357
Reed, Eric, Jupiter *	134	588	514	86	154	185	15	8	0	25	19	0	3	52	4	83	53	18	4	.300	.367	.360
Kubel, Jason, Fort Myers *	116	482	420	56	125	168	20	4	5	82	0	13	1	48	8	54	4	6	11	.298	.361	.400
Hattig, John, Sarasota †	114	466	400	51	118	169	29	2	6	70	1	4	2	59	3	70	9	7	15	.295	.385	.423
Maza, Luis, Fort Myers	111	477	410	70	119	164	18	6	5	61	9	5	19	34	0	79	1	1	6	.290	.368	.400
Lambin, Chase, St. Lucie †	118	459	401	58	116	162	27	2	5	49	5	3	4	46	4	81	13	8	7	.289	.366	.404
Granderson, Curtis, Lake.*	127	545	476	71	136	218	29	10	11	51	5	3	12	49	2	91	10	7	5	.286	.365	.458
Craig, Matt, Daytona †	119	498	442	56	126	188	25	2	11	66	2	3	5	46	2	87	4	4	14	.285	.357	.425
Roman, Jesse, Palm Beach *	99	414	364	24	103	155	27	2	7	53	2	7	5	36	3	62	1	5	8	.283	.350	.426
Gutierrez, Franklin, V.B.	110	474	425	65	120	218	28	5	20	68	4	3	3	39	4	111	17	5	9	.282	.345	.513
Tucker, Mamon, Clearwater	109	458	418	62	117	148	21	2	2	45	1	2	2	35	0	66	14	4	14	.280	.337	.354
Tejeda, Juan, Lakeland	125	528	461	63	129	195	28	4	10	76	0	6	5	56	6	68	6	3	10	.280	.360	.423
Mauer, Jake, Fort Myers	109	386	340	39	95	103	8	0	0	17	5	2	11	28	2	32	11	5	12	.279	.352	.303
Cosby, Rob, Dunedin	133	531	476	53	132	182	34	2	4	52	3	3	3	46	1	61	3	5	15	.277	.343	.382

DEPARTMENTAL LEADERS: G—Snyder, 137; AB—Reed, 514; R—Tomlin, 88; H—Reed, 154; TB—Howard, 252; 2B—Wright, 39; 3B—Granderson, 10; HR—Howard, 23; RBI—Stokes, 89; SH—DeMarco, 20; SF—Kubel, 13; HP—Maza, Walsh, 19; BB—Wright, 72; IBB—Howard, 9; SO—Howard, 151; SB—Lydon, 75; CS—Lydon, 20; GIDP—Vukovich, 16; Slg.—Howard, .514; OBP—Bacon, .392.

ALL PLAYERS

*Lefthanded batter. †Switch-hitter.

Player, Team	G	TPA	AB	R	H	TB	2B	3B	HR	RBI	SH	SF	HP	BB	IBB	SO	SB	CS	GDP	Avg.	OBP	Slg.
Abreu, Dennis, Palm Beach	32	125	116	12	25	38	5	1	2	8	0	1	2	6	0	21	3	1	3	.216	.264	.328
Abreu, Etanislao, Vero Beach	3	11	10	0	0	0	0	0	0	0	0	0	0	1	0	2	0	0	0	.000	.091	.000
Acevedo, Carlos, Clearwater	15	50	45	4	7	9	2	0	0	1	0	0	0	5	0	9	1	1	3	.156	.240	.200
Adams, Russ, Dunedin *	68	310	258	50	72	100	9	5	3	16	5	3	6	38	1	27	9	2	5	.279	.380	.388
Alvarez, Renyel, Fort Myers *	92	323	293	28	76	90	9	1	1	24	0	3	5	22	3	42	1	2	12	.259	.319	.307
Ambrosini, Anthony, B.C.	52	156	143	13	34	38	4	0	0	6	2	0	2	9	0	23	2	1	4	.238	.292	.266
Ambrosini, Dominick, B.C. *	114	411	383	35	100	147	26	3	5	45	1	1	1	25	4	98	7	2	6	.261	.307	.384
Anderson, Dennis, Jupiter †	68	241	197	22	47	55	6	1	0	18	5	3	12	24	0	20	2	5	4	.239	.352	.279
Apodaca, Luis, B.C.	2	3	3	0	1	1	0	0	0	0	0	0	0	0	0	0	0	0	0	.333	.333	.333
Aponte, Jose, Jupiter *	13	31	29	3	6	9	1	1	0	3	1	0	0	1	0	8	2	0	1	.207	.233	.310
Asadoorian, Rick, P.B.	44	147	130	11	25	33	3	1	1	10	2	2	3	10	0	35	3	1	4	.192	.262	.254
Asche, Kirk, Palm Beach	14	50	41	5	4	7	3	0	0	2	0	0	4	5	0	15	1	0	0	.098	.260	.171
Avila, Rob, Clearwater	51	177	160	11	36	45	6	0	1	14	1	2	1	11	0	19	0	1	7	.225	.276	.281
Aybar, Willy, Vero Beach †	119	495	445	47	122	190	29	3	11	74	1	5	3	41	1	70	9	9	3	.274	.336	.427
Bacani, David, St. Lucie	44	158	131	14	34	38	4	0	0	12	2	2	2	21	0	16	6	2	5	.260	.365	.290
Bacon, Dwaine, Daytona †	106	428	350	65	94	130	12	6	4	22	5	1	9	63	3	100	71	12	3	.269	.392	.371
Bailie, Stefan, Sarasota	75	294	267	27	67	92	14	1	3	29	1	5	5	16	1	70	7	2	9	.251	.300	.345
Balfe, Ryan, B.C. †	30	123	110	10	32	54	10	0	4	27	0	2	4	7	0	27	0	1	1	.291	.350	.491
Barclay, Mike, Sarasota	31	89	79	8	21	25	1	0	1	5	0	1	0	9	0	18	4	1	3	.266	.337	.316
Bellorin, Edwin, Vero Beach	67	253	233	19	57	75	9	0	3	28	2	3	5	10	0	32	0	2	8	.245	.287	.322
Benjamin, Al, Palm Beach	24	101	91	13	25	35	7	0	1	12	1	1	1	7	0	18	2	0	3	.275	.330	.385
Bernhardt, Joe, Dunedin	9	37	34	2	4	5	1	0	0	1	1	0	0	2	0	8	0	0	1	.118	.167	.147
Berroa, Cristian, B.C. †	9	31	29	6	9	12	1	1	0	2	0	0	1	1	0	3	1	0	0	.310	.355	.414
Blasi, Blake, Sarasota-P.B. †	109	469	398	57	97	125	18	2	2	37	7	4	5	55	1	65	13	8	3	.244	.340	.314
Bledsoe, Hunter, Tampa	61	251	222	29	69	87	16	1	0	17	0	0	4	25	0	16	1	1	7	.311	.390	.392
Blum, Greg, Fort Myers	76	268	230	25	48	76	11	1	5	21	1	5	7	25	1	45	1	0	7	.209	.300	.330
Boran, Patrick, Sarasota †	29	109	95	10	22	28	4	1	0	3	1	0	1	11	0	24	1	0	2	.232	.318	.295
Borowiak, Zachary, Sarasota	27	106	93	2	17	21	4	0	0	2	5	0	1	7	1	13	0	2	0	.183	.248	.226
Bost, Tom, Jupiter *	59	229	200	26	51	67	7	3	1	16	3	2	3	21	2	53	10	5	2	.255	.332	.335
Bouras, Brad, Daytona	62	260	233	21	60	85	10	0	5	26	0	3	5	19	1	31	0	1	4	.258	.323	.365
Boyd, Shaun, Palm Beach	110	479	416	59	107	143	17	2	5	35	4	3	2	54	2	70	28	14	8	.257	.343	.344
Broadway, Larry, B.C. *	25	98	76	8	17	29	7	1	1	7	0	3	1	18	0	20	0	1	0	.224	.367	.382
Brown, Andy, Tampa *	85	313	285	29	68	112	17	3	7	37	0	0	0	28	0	89	7	1	3	.239	.307	.393
Brown, Jason, B.C.	44	126	111	5	19	27	3	1	1	9	3	2	1	9	0	31	0	0	6	.171	.236	.243
Brown, Kevin, Palm Beach	7	28	25	2	7	11	1	0	1	1	0	0	0	3	0	4	0	0	1	.280	.357	.440
Buckley, James, Sarasota	17	63	55	5	13	21	2	0	2	7	1	0	0	7	0	12	0	0	1	.236	.323	.382
Cabrera, Ruben, Vero Beach	6	15	15	0	3	3	0	0	0	1	0	0	0	0	0	4	0	0	1	.200	.200	.200
Calabrese, Tony, St. Lucie	26	92	76	7	16	22	1	1	1	8	1	1	1	13	0	25	2	1	1	.211	.330	.289
Calitri, Mike, Sarasota	61	244	201	32	53	80	10	4	3	23	1	2	2	38	0	62	1	4	5	.264	.383	.398
Callahan, Dave, Sarasota *	20	83	69	6	16	23	7	0	0	7	0	1	0	13	0	12	2	4	1	.232	.349	.333
Camilo, Juan, Clearwater *	103	429	387	45	99	146	17	6	6	49	2	1	3	36	2	91	11	5	14	.256	.323	.377
Cano, Robinson, Tampa *	90	390	366	50	101	138	16	3	5	50	0	3	4	17	1	49	1	1	5	.276	.313	.377
Carroll, Wes, Brevard County	99	370	338	29	78	93	12	0	1	36	1	3	2	26	0	50	6	3	6	.231	.287	.275

Player, Team	G	TPA	AB	R	H	TB	2B	3B	HR	RBI	SH	SF	HP	BB	IBB	SO	SB	CS	GDP	Avg.	OBP	Slg.
Carter, Shannon, Dunedin *	32	107	101	18	23	27	4	0	0	7	2	0	0	4	0	13	3	1	3	.228	.257	.267
Castillo, Osmar, Sarasota †	31	133	103	14	16	16	0	0	0	7	2	1	3	24	0	20	4	2	2	.155	.328	.155
Castro, Nelson, Vero Beach †	25	92	85	14	12	25	4	0	3	8	2	0	3	2	0	23	1	0	1	.141	.189	.294
Catalanotte, Greg, Sarasota †	102	391	342	41	73	130	14	5	11	40	1	3	0	45	1	110	16	6	7	.213	.303	.380
Cavin, Jonathan, B.C. *	11	34	30	5	3	5	2	0	0	1	0	0	1	3	0	11	1	0	1	.100	.206	.167
Cedeno, Ronny, Daytona	107	420	380	43	80	112	18	1	4	36	12	3	4	21	0	82	19	6	5	.211	.257	.295
Chavez, Ender, St. Lucie *	29	121	105	9	21	23	2	0	0	8	4	0	2	10	0	14	5	4	0	.200	.282	.219
Christensen, Mike, Ft. Myers	21	89	79	10	17	27	4	0	2	16	1	2	1	6	0	16	1	0	3	.215	.273	.342
Clark, Tony, St. Lucie †	1	4	4	0	1	1	0	0	0	0	0	0	0	0	0	1	0	0	0	.250	.250	.250
Cleveland, Russ, Lakeland	20	76	73	6	14	17	3	0	0	6	0	0	0	3	0	18	0	0	1	.192	.224	.233
Clute, Kris, Jupiter	15	41	34	1	5	6	1	0	0	3	2	0	1	4	0	12	2	1	1	.147	.256	.176
Comfort, Geoff, Vero Beach	4	18	17	2	4	6	2	0	0	0	0	0	0	1	0	5	0	1	0	.235	.278	.353
Concepcion, Alberto, Sara.	56	187	156	16	34	39	5	0	0	5	9	1	6	15	0	40	2	0	3	.218	.309	.250
Coomer, Ron, Vero Beach	3	11	10	1	5	6	1	0	0	2	0	1	0	0	0	1	0	0	0	.500	.455	.600
Cooper, Matt, Sarasota	44	161	131	11	23	39	4	0	4	12	0	1	9	20	0	53	0	2	2	.176	.323	.298
Corporan, Elvis, Tampa †	116	471	410	48	101	136	15	4	4	47	0	6	1	54	1	91	9	3	10	.246	.331	.332
Corr, Frank, St. Lucie	85	345	318	31	75	113	18	1	6	41	1	4	5	16	0	50	5	4	6	.236	.280	.355
Cosbey, Chris, Clearwater *	65	273	240	31	59	72	9	2	0	16	5	1	1	26	0	27	8	7	3	.246	.321	.300
Cosby, Rob, Dunedin	133	531	476	53	132	182	34	2	4	52	3	3	3	46	1	61	3	5	15	.277	.343	.382
Coulie, Jason, Palm Beach	28	83	72	5	9	12	0	0	1	3	3	0	3	5	0	18	2	0	2	.125	.213	.167
Craig, Matt, Daytona †	119	498	442	56	126	188	25	2	11	66	2	3	5	46	2	87	4	4	14	.285	.357	.425
Creighton, Matt, Daytona	16	56	48	9	17	28	5	0	2	7	0	0	2	6	0	5	0	0	1	.354	.446	.583
Cruz, Edgar, Clearwater	11	43	37	3	6	9	3	0	0	3	2	1	0	3	0	5	0	0	0	.162	.220	.243
Davenport, Ron, Dunedin *	119	460	421	39	116	162	27	2	5	57	0	3	4	32	4	74	6	7	10	.276	.330	.385
Davis, Stockton, B.C. *	42	1	1	0	0	0	0	0	0	0	0	0	0	0	0	1	0	0	0	.000	.000	.000
Delfino, Lee, Dunedin	62	182	161	13	25	31	3	0	1	11	1	1	3	16	1	38	2	0	11	.155	.243	.193
DeMarco, Matt, Jupiter *	114	430	375	36	90	110	10	2	2	43	20	5	6	24	0	44	4	7	7	.240	.293	.293
Deschaine, Jim, Clearwater	27	111	96	13	30	39	9	0	0	15	0	1	1	13	0	11	0	1	2	.313	.396	.406
Detienne, Dave, Vero Beach	30	123	106	14	28	34	4	1	0	8	6	0	1	10	0	24	5	3	2	.264	.333	.321
Devarez, Noel, St. Lucie	3	13	12	1	2	5	1	1	0	1	1	0	0	0	0	4	0	0	1	.167	.167	.417
Diaz, Felix, Brevard County †	21	72	66	3	8	11	0	0	1	3	0	0	3	3	0	29	0	0	0	.121	.194	.167
Dodson, Jeremy, P.B. *	53	193	170	11	32	51	8	1	3	12	4	1	1	16	1	49	0	1	1	.188	.261	.300
Dorta, Melvin, Sarasota	93	374	324	36	70	79	7	1	0	27	9	6	7	28	0	46	20	9	9	.216	.288	.244
Drew, J.D., Palm Beach *	8	27	19	4	7	10	0	0	1	3	0	0	1	7	2	4	0	0	0	.368	.556	.526
Duncan, Chris, Palm Beach *	121	476	425	26	108	134	20	0	2	42	1	5	1	44	1	115	4	4	12	.254	.322	.315
Duncan, Shelley, Tampa	91	375	330	42	87	134	19	2	8	47	0	6	4	35	0	83	5	1	8	.264	.336	.406
Durazo, William, Sarasota †	23	78	73	6	13	17	1	0	1	7	0	0	1	4	0	18	2	1	1	.178	.231	.233
Easterday, Matt, Jupiter	78	243	213	23	44	53	4	1	1	15	6	1	3	20	0	35	2	3	6	.207	.283	.249
Eickhorst, Chris, Palm Beach	64	236	194	14	38	47	6	0	1	17	4	1	10	27	0	59	0	1	6	.196	.323	.242
Ellerson, Brian, B.C.	12	36	32	4	7	12	2	0	1	2	1	0	1	2	0	6	0	0	0	.219	.286	.375
Emmerick, Josh, B.C.	6	14	13	1	3	6	0	0	1	4	1	0	0	0	0	6	0	0	0	.231	.231	.462
Espada, Joe, Palm Beach	47	200	178	17	42	49	7	0	0	9	1	0	1	20	0	13	10	4	8	.236	.317	.275
Espinosa, David, Lakeland †	92	409	350	57	95	139	18	7	4	46	2	6	1	50	0	78	13	10	1	.271	.359	.397
Esposito, Brian, Sarasota	2	7	7	0	0	0	0	0	0	0	0	0	0	0	0	0	0	0	0	.000	.000	.000
Fernandez, Alejandro, Tampa	42	164	157	11	38	48	7	0	1	9	1	0	4	2	0	45	0	0	6	.242	.270	.306
Ferrer, Simon, Vero Beach †	20	60	49	4	10	14	2	1	0	4	4	0	2	5	0	14	1	3	0	.204	.304	.286
Fowler, Maleke, Tampa	45	187	158	24	43	60	9	1	2	9	2	1	1	25	0	39	7	2	4	.272	.373	.380
Frazier, Charles, Jupiter	63	221	194	25	41	53	5	2	1	17	7	1	4	15	0	43	17	5	1	.211	.280	.273
Fulse, Sheldon, Sarasota †	22	95	81	14	22	37	7	1	2	5	0	1	0	13	0	18	13	2	1	.272	.368	.457
Galante, Matt, St. Lucie	20	70	61	6	10	12	2	0	0	4	2	0	0	7	0	11	1	1	3	.164	.250	.197
Galloway, Mike, Dunedin	1	3	3	1	1	2	1	0	0	1	0	0	0	0	0	2	0	0	0	.333	.333	.667
Garcia, Sergio, Vero Beach	64	230	188	27	41	50	6	0	1	19	8	4	6	24	0	25	8	3	5	.218	.320	.266
Garcia, Tony, Palm Beach	110	439	377	41	81	100	13	0	2	30	2	1	11	48	1	62	5	4	13	.215	.320	.265
Gillitzer, Scott, Vero Beach	107	418	379	41	87	118	16	0	5	42	6	4	7	22	1	41	9	6	12	.230	.282	.311
Gingrich, Troy, B.C. *	94	364	318	45	69	92	14	3	1	14	4	0	4	38	4	63	16	6	4	.217	.308	.289
Godwin, Tyrell, Dunedin *	97	366	322	52	88	107	16	0	1	33	7	0	8	29	2	39	20	7	6	.273	.348	.332
Goelz, Jim, Sarasota	21	93	83	9	24	31	4	0	1	8	1	0	1	8	0	16	1	1	1	.289	.359	.373
Gonzalez, Daniel, Clear.†	113	496	436	62	118	150	22	5	0	34	7	1	3	49	1	56	5	2	7	.271	.348	.344
Granderson, Curtis, Lake.*	127	545	476	71	136	218	29	10	11	51	5	3	12	49	2	91	10	7	5	.286	.365	.458
Greenberg, Adam, Daytona *	72	320	271	42	81	111	11	5	3	27	2	2	2	38	0	46	26	9	1	.299	.387	.410
Grove, Jason, Tampa *	18	70	63	7	17	24	7	0	0	13	0	1	0	6	0	17	1	0	0	.270	.329	.381
Grzecka, Casey, Jupiter	14	42	38	1	5	6	1	0	0	2	0	0	1	3	0	9	0	0	1	.132	.214	.158
Guerrero, Vladimir, B.C.	3	7	6	2	3	6	0	0	1	1	0	0	1	0	0	0	0	0	0	.500	.571	1.000
Gulledge, Kelley, Fort Myers	8	32	31	0	3	4	1	0	0	2	0	0	0	1	0	9	0	0	2	.097	.125	.129
Gutierrez, Franklin, V.B.	110	474	425	65	120	218	28	5	20	68	4	3	3	39	4	111	17	5	9	.282	.345	.513
Guzman, Joel, Vero Beach	62	252	240	30	59	89	13	1	5	24	1	0	0	11	0	60	0	4	7	.246	.279	.371
Hamill, Ryan, Palm Beach	12	48	44	0	7	7	0	0	0	2	0	0	0	4	0	9	0	0	1	.159	.229	.159
Harper, Brett, St. Lucie *	13	52	44	5	9	11	2	0	0	4	0	1	2	5	0	13	1	0	0	.205	.308	.250
Hattig, John, Sarasota †	114	466	400	51	118	169	29	2	6	70	1	4	2	59	3	70	9	7	15	.295	.385	.423
Hermansen, Chad, V.B.	17	71	63	12	15	22	4	0	1	7	0	2	0	6	0	7	0	1	2	.238	.296	.349
Hernandez, Anderson, Lake.†	106	424	380	47	87	112	11	4	2	28	14	3	0	27	0	69	15	7	10	.229	.278	.295
Hernandez, Johnny, P.B. †	14	48	42	4	7	10	3	0	0	2	0	0	0	6	1	7	0	0	1	.167	.271	.238
Herrera, Christian, V.B.	40	142	126	12	26	29	3	0	0	9	4	0	0	12	0	18	0	4	2	.206	.275	.230
Hicks, Scott, Jupiter *	56	183	150	20	31	41	5	1	1	14	6	1	3	23	0	53	0	4	2	.207	.322	.273
Hietpas, Joe, St. Lucie	63	215	195	12	31	44	8	1	1	19	1	3	2	14	0	60	3	1	6	.159	.220	.226
Hileman, Jutt, Palm Beach	25	106	89	17	26	34	5	0	1	7	1	1	3	12	1	23	0	1	1	.292	.390	.382
Hill, Aaron, Dunedin	32	134	119	26	34	41	7	0	0	11	0	3	1	11	0	10	1	0	3	.286	.343	.345
Hoffpauir, Micah, Daytona *	124	533	477	59	121	182	33	2	8	58	0	5	7	44	7	96	2	1	11	.254	.323	.382
Holdzkom, Lincoln, Jupiter	14	3	2	0	0	0	0	0	0	0	1	0	0	0	0	1	0	0	1	.000	.000	.000
Hoorelbeke, Jesse, V.B.	57	215	200	27	56	92	6	0	10	29	1	0	3	11	0	43	1	3	2	.280	.327	.460
Housel, David, St. Lucie †	17	48	44	4	11	12	1	0	0	1	1	0	1	2	0	16	3	1	1	.250	.298	.273

Player, Team	G	TPA	AB	R	H	TB	2B	3B	HR	RBI	SH	SF	HP	BB	IBB	SO	SB	CS	GDP	Avg.	OBP	Slg.
Howard, Ryan, Clearwater * ..	130	553	490	67	149	252	32	1	23	82	0	5	8	50	9	151	0	0	12	.304	.374	.514
Huber, Justin, St. Lucie..........	50	211	183	26	52	94	15	0	9	36	0	2	9	17	0	30	1	1	9	.284	.370	.514
Hundley, Todd, Vero Beach †.	7	28	24	2	2	2	0	0	0	1	0	0	1	3	0	5	0	0	0	.083	.214	.083
Jaramillo, Milko, P.B. †	35	133	121	11	23	29	4	1	0	5	1	0	1	10	0	24	0	1	4	.190	.258	.240
Jarvis, Andrew, Clearwater * .	3	10	9	0	3	4	1	0	0	2	0	0	0	1	0	1	0	0	0	.333	.400	.444
Jenkins, Neil, Lakeland	88	345	321	28	71	136	21	1	14	55	0	2	0	22	0	150	1	0	5	.221	.270	.424
Jiannetti, Joe, St. Lucie..........	56	209	188	23	39	60	10	1	3	20	0	3	1	17	0	33	6	1	2	.207	.273	.319
Johnson, Gabe, Palm Beach ..	107	448	385	50	82	124	12	3	8	40	3	5	3	52	1	104	5	3	10	.213	.308	.322
Johnson, Gary, Palm Beach ...	23	98	90	6	17	22	2	0	1	9	0	0	3	5	0	16	0	1	2	.189	.255	.244
Jones, Garrett, Fort Myers * ..	117	443	404	52	89	165	12	5	18	67	3	2	2	32	1	98	5	4	8	.220	.280	.408
Jova, Maikel, Dunedin............	64	248	240	34	65	92	12	0	5	24	0	0	1	6	0	42	0	1	10	.271	.291	.383
Kavourias, Jim, Jupiter	108	427	389	54	96	177	19	1	20	65	0	3	1	34	1	97	10	1	12	.247	.307	.455
Kay, Brett, St. Lucie	64	228	195	25	49	72	14	0	3	19	4	4	3	21	0	30	5	1	5	.251	.327	.369
Keene, Kurt, Dunedin	36	151	135	20	46	63	9	1	2	16	4	1	4	7	0	19	2	2	3	.341	.388	.467
Kelly, Donald, Lakeland *	87	355	303	48	96	124	17	4	1	38	1	5	1	45	1	25	15	2	4	.317	.401	.409
Kennedy, Bryan, Fort Myers *	25	100	89	9	19	23	4	0	0	5	2	2	2	5	0	19	0	0	2	.213	.265	.258
Kirkpatrick, Michael, P.B. *	14	35	30	1	4	4	0	0	0	4	1	1	1	2	0	8	1	0	2	.133	.206	.133
Koutnik, Jared, Tampa	87	311	282	38	76	104	14	1	4	29	2	1	7	19	0	62	1	1	5	.270	.330	.369
Kropf, Andy, Lakeland †	44	172	148	16	42	49	5	1	0	13	1	3	0	19	0	32	0	2	5	.284	.359	.331
Kubel, Jason, Fort Myers *	116	482	420	56	125	168	20	4	5	82	0	13	1	48	8	54	4	6	11	.298	.361	.400
Kuhaulua, Kaulana, Ft. Myers.	33	121	108	13	27	34	7	0	0	8	5	0	1	7	0	19	10	1	5	.250	.302	.315
Labandeira, John, B.C.	62	266	238	41	77	98	13	4	0	25	2	1	1	24	0	35	6	5	6	.324	.386	.412
Lafferty, Will, Palm Beach	2	3	3	0	0	0	0	0	0	0	0	0	0	0	0	1	0	0	0	.000	.000	.000
Lambin, Chase, St. Lucie †	118	459	401	58	116	162	27	2	5	49	5	3	4	46	4	81	13	8	7	.289	.366	.404
Lane, Rich, Brevard County *	67	284	247	39	74	109	8	3	7	44	0	2	6	29	1	40	7	0	4	.300	.384	.441
Langill, Eric, Vero Beach	27	74	69	5	17	19	2	0	0	9	1	0	3	1	0	11	0	1	4	.246	.288	.275
Langs, Ronte, Vero Beach......	60	250	203	35	44	60	8	1	2	21	3	2	7	35	1	58	5	3	3	.217	.348	.296
Lawson, Forrest, St. Lucie	57	218	186	17	51	64	5	1	2	15	4	2	6	20	0	38	6	3	6	.274	.360	.344
Lemon, Tim, Palm Beach	54	183	168	17	25	48	9	1	4	10	2	1	3	9	0	66	0	2	1	.149	.204	.286
Loney, James, Vero Beach * ..	125	516	468	64	129	187	31	3	7	46	3	1	1	43	5	80	9	4	13	.276	.337	.400
Lopez, Angel, Jupiter	43	144	132	9	33	49	6	2	2	14	0	1	2	9	1	40	0	1	4	.250	.306	.371
Lugo, Alfredo, Lakeland	88	325	287	34	73	92	11	1	2	19	4	2	3	28	0	63	2	2	6	.254	.325	.321
Lydon, Wayne, St. Lucie	133	562	488	83	129	169	14	7	4	44	9	5	8	52	1	96	75	20	2	.264	.342	.346
Lynam, Guy, Jupiter	6	15	13	2	3	4	1	0	0	2	0	0	0	2	0	3	0	0	0	.231	.333	.308
Macha, Erick, Tampa	19	57	53	7	9	11	2	0	0	3	1	1	0	2	0	5	1	2	3	.170	.196	.208
Maddox, Garry, Clearwater * .	7	28	22	3	6	11	2	0	1	7	0	1	1	4	0	6	0	1	0	.273	.393	.500
Madera, Sandy, Tampa...........	7	21	20	2	5	10	2	0	1	3	0	1	0	0	0	7	0	0	0	.250	.238	.500
Malek, Bobby, St. Lucie *	79	322	286	45	80	108	20	1	2	36	0	2	4	30	3	50	17	7	4	.280	.354	.378
Mallory, Mike, Daytona	122	489	411	59	94	156	29	0	11	50	4	5	14	55	0	136	15	3	15	.229	.336	.380
Martinez, Casey, Clearwater ...	7	21	21	1	4	4	0	0	0	0	0	0	0	0	0	7	0	0	2	.190	.190	.190
Martinez, Edgar, Sarasota	66	217	199	17	40	46	6	0	0	11	0	1	4	13	0	24	6	3	8	.201	.263	.231
Matthews, Lamont, Sara.*	57	233	192	29	51	88	14	4	5	31	0	2	1	38	1	59	5	1	1	.266	.386	.458
Mattle, David, Lakeland *	102	395	365	41	83	129	16	3	8	52	1	3	1	25	1	69	6	3	3	.227	.277	.353
Mauer, Jake, Fort Myers.........	109	386	340	39	95	103	8	0	0	17	5	2	11	28	2	32	11	5	12	.279	.352	.303
Mauer, Joe, Fort Myers *	62	261	233	25	78	96	13	1	1	44	0	3	1	24	3	24	3	0	11	.335	.395	.412
Mayorson, Manuel, Dunedin ..	106	406	363	39	83	97	14	0	0	30	9	5	4	25	0	36	6	7	9	.229	.282	.267
Maza, Luis, Fort Myers	111	477	410	70	119	164	18	6	5	61	9	5	19	34	0	79	1	1	6	.290	.368	.400
McDonald, Kevin, Lakeland *.	5	15	15	1	2	2	0	0	0	0	0	0	0	0	0	6	0	0	0	.133	.133	.133
McEachran, Aaron, Dune.*	61	215	182	18	42	57	9	0	2	17	4	1	2	26	1	40	0	0	3	.231	.332	.313
McGowan, Sean, Sarasota	18	73	67	12	24	34	5	1	1	11	0	0	0	6	0	7	3	2	3	.358	.411	.507
McGriff, Fred, Vero Beach * ...	2	7	6	0	1	1	0	0	0	0	0	0	0	1	0	2	0	0	0	.167	.286	.167
McIntyre, Robert, St. Lucie	85	314	271	31	67	94	12	0	5	47	4	7	12	19	1	68	8	5	4	.247	.317	.347
McKnight, Lukas, Daytona * ..	6	26	24	0	5	10	5	0	0	6	1	0	0	1	0	5	0	0	0	.208	.240	.417
McMillan, Drew, B.C.	53	180	157	8	30	40	7	0	1	16	3	1	6	13	0	50	1	1	3	.191	.277	.255
Medina, Rodney, Dunedin † ...	2	8	8	1	2	6	1	0	1	3	0	0	0	0	0	0	0	0	0	.250	.250	.750
Mendez, Deivi, Tampa	30	97	92	7	21	26	5	0	0	8	1	1	0	3	0	16	0	0	2	.228	.250	.283
Mendez, Jose, Fort Myers......	8	30	30	3	8	11	0	0	1	3	0	0	0	0	0	2	0	0	0	.267	.267	.367
Michaels, Jason, Clearwater ..	4	16	14	1	0	0	0	0	0	0	0	0	0	2	0	4	0	0	0	.000	.125	.000
Miller, Chris, Daytona.............	49	195	180	17	45	69	12	0	4	23	1	3	2	9	0	22	0	1	9	.250	.289	.383
Monahan, Joey, Daytona........	27	111	90	10	18	24	3	0	1	15	4	0	0	17	1	23	4	2	3	.200	.327	.267
Money, Freddie, Sarasota.......	16	47	45	7	9	18	3	0	2	5	0	0	1	1	0	9	4	1	1	.200	.234	.400
Montanez, Luis, Daytona........	126	537	486	51	123	162	18	3	5	38	6	6	6	33	0	89	11	4	11	.253	.305	.333
Moore, Jason, Palm Beach †.	25	110	94	14	27	36	3	0	2	10	0	1	0	15	0	24	6	2	1	.287	.382	.383
Morales, Jose, Fort Myers † ..	12	43	42	6	15	20	3	1	0	2	0	0	0	1	1	5	0	2	1	.357	.372	.476
Morrow, Alvin, Palm Beach....	4	14	13	3	2	3	1	0	0	0	0	0	0	1	0	5	0	0	0	.154	.214	.231
Murphy, David, Sarasota *	45	173	153	18	37	47	5	1	1	18	0	0	0	20	1	33	6	2	3	.242	.329	.307
Navarro, Dioner, Tampa †	52	221	197	28	59	92	16	4	3	28	1	2	4	17	0	27	1	0	4	.299	.364	.467
Netwall, Chris, Palm Beach	65	210	178	10	30	38	3	1	1	7	4	0	4	24	1	57	4	2	2	.169	.282	.213
Norris, Shawn, B.C. *	57	236	194	28	38	55	9	1	2	14	0	2	3	37	0	49	1	2	3	.196	.331	.284
Nunez, Abraham, Jupiter †	8	33	29	6	8	11	3	0	0	2	0	0	0	4	0	9	1	0	1	.276	.364	.379
O'Toole, Paul, Daytona *	49	153	124	11	23	27	4	0	0	11	7	0	3	19	3	25	3	0	4	.185	.308	.218
Pagan, Angel, St. Lucie †.......	113	490	441	64	110	138	15	5	1	33	11	1	2	35	1	80	35	15	5	.249	.307	.313
Parrish, Dave, Tampa	18	64	57	7	13	16	3	0	0	3	0	0	3	4	0	10	0	0	2	.228	.313	.281
Perez, Josue, Clearwater †.....	13	61	56	8	16	20	4	0	0	7	0	0	0	5	0	12	3	1	0	.286	.344	.357
Perez, Kenny, Sarasota †	65	252	230	32	64	95	17	4	2	39	1	5	1	15	0	24	11	4	8	.278	.319	.413
Perry, Jason, Dunedin *	39	151	135	17	41	57	11	1	1	17	2	2	2	10	0	32	1	0	5	.304	.356	.422
Perry, Rod, Clearwater...........	9	34	30	3	4	4	0	0	0	0	1	0	1	2	0	5	1	0	0	.133	.212	.133
Phelps, Jeff, Clearwater	85	334	297	39	78	115	20	1	5	33	0	3	3	31	0	55	1	2	7	.263	.335	.387
Phillips, Kyle, Fort Myers *	1	2	2	0	1	1	0	0	0	0	0	0	0	0	0	0	0	0	0	.500	.500	.500
Pierce, Sean, Vero Beach	22	79	60	9	15	17	2	0	0	4	0	0	3	16	0	18	2	2	0	.250	.430	.283
Pratt, Trent, Clearwater	78	285	253	31	55	70	13	1	0	25	2	1	3	26	0	50	1	0	7	.217	.297	.277

Player, Team	G	TPA	AB	R	H	TB	2B	3B	HR	RBI	SH	SF	HP	BB	IBB	SO	SB	CS	GDP	Avg.	OBP	Slg.
Pressley, Josh, St. Lucie *	61	254	234	27	60	81	13	1	2	30	0	2	3	15	0	34	3	0	7	.256	.307	.346
Price, Jared, Vero Beach	32	119	105	21	19	38	4	0	5	13	3	0	3	8	0	38	3	0	1	.181	.259	.362
Raburn, Ryan, Lakeland	95	382	325	52	72	128	14	3	12	56	0	2	10	45	0	89	2	1	5	.222	.332	.394
Ramos, Jason, Sarasota †	6	16	10	2	3	3	0	0	0	0	0	0	0	6	0	3	0	0	0	.300	.563	.300
Reed, Eric, Jupiter *	134	588	514	86	154	185	15	8	0	25	19	0	3	52	4	83	53	18	4	.300	.367	.360
Rico, Erik, Dunedin *	13	38	35	1	10	10	0	0	0	2	1	0	0	2	0	3	2	1	1	.286	.324	.286
Rigsby, Randy, Jupiter *	40	141	131	11	36	49	8	1	1	12	4	1	0	5	0	28	1	2	2	.275	.299	.374
Rodgers, Albert, Palm Beach	26	102	94	5	20	27	1	0	2	7	0	1	1	6	0	25	0	1	2	.213	.265	.287
Rodriguez, Eladio, Sarasota	57	189	172	18	39	57	12	0	2	20	0	0	2	15	0	36	11	1	2	.227	.296	.331
Rodriguez, Robert, B.C.	11	29	21	3	5	6	1	0	0	1	2	0	0	6	0	9	0	1	0	.238	.407	.286
Rogers, Brandon, Vero Beach	20	61	54	4	13	16	3	0	0	1	2	0	0	5	0	11	1	1	2	.241	.305	.296
Rohan, Jimmy, Vero Beach	7	24	24	3	6	7	1	0	0	0	0	0	0	0	0	0	0	0	1	.250	.250	.292
Rojas, Tommy, Tampa	11	31	24	2	7	12	2	0	1	6	0	0	2	5	0	6	0	1	0	.292	.452	.500
Roman, Jesse, Palm Beach *	99	414	364	24	103	155	27	2	7	53	2	7	5	36	3	62	1	5	8	.283	.350	.426
Rombley, Danny, B.C.	107	425	376	52	90	116	16	5	0	23	5	0	7	37	0	95	22	15	8	.239	.319	.309
Rooi, Vince, Brevard County	97	366	319	34	81	121	19	0	7	52	1	5	5	36	2	70	3	9	11	.254	.334	.379
Roughton, Jody, Lakeland *	14	60	51	4	10	11	1	0	0	3	0	0	2	7	0	10	0	0	1	.196	.317	.216
Ruiz, Carlos, Clearwater	15	56	54	5	17	23	0	0	2	9	0	0	0	2	0	5	2	2	5	.315	.339	.426
Rundgren, Rex, Jupiter	119	451	415	44	96	115	15	2	0	31	13	0	3	19	0	76	5	2	13	.231	.270	.277
Sanchez, Danilo, Lakeland	12	44	38	4	4	5	1	0	0	3	0	0	1	5	0	13	0	0	1	.105	.227	.132
Sandoval, Michael, Ft. Myers	74	287	248	34	73	93	14	0	2	34	0	1	6	31	0	37	2	4	2	.294	.385	.375
Santos, Jose, Jupiter	94	372	314	31	81	114	16	1	5	36	3	2	11	42	4	74	2	3	7	.258	.363	.363
Sardinha, Bronson, Tampa *	59	240	212	23	41	56	8	2	1	17	0	2	2	24	0	57	8	2	3	.193	.279	.264
Schnabel, Nick, B.C.	61	169	147	11	25	28	3	0	0	12	7	0	3	12	0	25	2	0	3	.170	.247	.190
Schrager, Tony, Sarasota	4	19	17	1	5	7	2	0	0	2	0	0	0	2	0	1	1	0	1	.294	.368	.412
Schutzenhofer, Andy, P.B. *	13	57	46	11	15	20	3	1	0	10	0	0	0	11	0	5	0	0	2	.326	.456	.435
Segar, Jeff, Tampa	111	440	403	49	90	139	29	1	6	59	0	4	4	29	0	66	10	2	12	.223	.280	.345
Seguignol, Fernando, Tampa†	3	13	13	1	5	5	0	0	0	1	0	0	0	0	0	2	0	0	1	.385	.385	.385
Seiber, Antron, Sarasota	29	117	106	10	21	33	1	4	1	6	0	1	0	10	0	37	6	2	0	.198	.265	.311
Shanks, Eric, Sarasota	33	138	113	18	25	32	7	0	0	9	1	2	3	19	0	19	2	4	2	.221	.343	.283
Sing, Brandon, Daytona	39	154	136	20	32	50	6	0	4	23	0	1	0	17	0	29	0	3	4	.235	.318	.368
Smith, Will, Sarasota	8	30	25	2	3	4	1	0	0	2	0	0	0	5	0	7	1	2	2	.120	.267	.160
Smith, Will, Jupiter *	3	12	12	0	1	2	1	0	0	2	0	0	0	0	0	2	0	0	1	.083	.083	.167
Snyder, Mike, Dunedin *	137	569	496	70	133	184	24	0	9	75	1	3	3	66	4	113	6	0	15	.268	.356	.371
Soto, Geovany, Daytona	89	340	297	26	72	94	12	2	2	38	4	6	2	31	0	58	0	0	10	.242	.313	.316
Spearman, Jemel, Daytona	100	420	365	53	100	121	13	1	2	47	4	6	6	39	0	71	15	11	9	.274	.349	.332
Sterner, George, Tampa	17	49	44	6	8	9	1	0	0	3	0	0	1	4	0	13	0	0	2	.182	.265	.205
Stokes, Jason, Jupiter	121	509	462	67	119	207	31	3	17	89	0	7	4	36	1	135	6	4	6	.258	.312	.448
Stone, Greg, Sarasota *	17	72	65	9	15	18	3	0	0	1	1	0	0	6	0	11	4	1	2	.231	.296	.277
Story-Harden, Thomari, V.B.	51	188	165	21	42	67	10	0	5	14	0	0	8	15	1	47	2	3	1	.255	.346	.406
Sucre, Antonio, B.C.	1	2	2	0	0	0	0	0	0	0	0	0	0	0	0	2	0	0	0	.000	.000	.000
Tablado, Raul, Dunedin	54	202	182	27	47	77	9	3	5	19	1	0	2	17	1	47	1	2	1	.258	.328	.423
Tamburrino, Brett, Ft. Myers†	75	282	238	36	61	85	8	5	2	28	5	2	4	33	1	42	15	3	5	.256	.354	.357
Tejeda, Ferdin, Tampa	51	230	217	33	64	83	9	5	0	20	2	2	3	6	2	38	4	3	6	.295	.320	.382
Tejeda, Juan, Lakeland	125	528	461	63	129	195	28	4	10	76	0	6	5	56	6	68	6	3	10	.280	.360	.423
Tempesta, Nick, Clearwater	11	34	30	0	2	2	0	0	0	2	0	1	2	1	0	6	0	0	0	.067	.147	.067
Thissen, Greg, B.C.	89	315	275	33	49	59	6	2	0	13	6	0	0	34	0	65	10	4	6	.178	.269	.215
Thomas, Charles, Vero Beach	108	417	338	53	80	111	19	0	4	37	5	5	6	61	0	84	30	15	5	.237	.359	.328
Thompson, Kevin, Tampa	44	203	163	42	54	90	13	4	5	25	0	6	2	32	2	27	16	5	3	.331	.433	.552
Tomlin, James, Fort Myers	122	557	498	88	151	178	17	2	2	42	13	6	4	36	1	51	24	10	8	.303	.351	.357
Toner, John, St. Lucie	7	26	22	1	1	1	0	0	0	0	0	0	2	2	0	6	1	1	0	.045	.192	.045
Tope, Stephen, Fort Myers	93	347	302	42	78	113	19	2	4	33	1	4	9	31	3	73	0	3	9	.258	.341	.374
Tosca, Daniel, Tampa *	22	77	64	10	18	21	3	0	0	13	1	1	0	11	0	11	0	0	1	.281	.382	.328
Tress, Irving, Lakeland	3	6	5	0	1	1	0	0	0	0	0	0	0	1	0	2	0	0	0	.200	.333	.200
Trezza, Alex, Lakeland *	74	288	267	16	71	101	19	1	3	27	0	3	0	18	0	65	0	1	6	.266	.309	.378
Tucker, Mamon, Clearwater	109	458	418	62	117	148	21	2	2	45	1	2	2	35	0	66	14	4	14	.280	.337	.354
Tucker, Michael, Jupiter	107	425	384	36	106	147	22	2	5	51	2	3	4	32	1	92	2	2	8	.276	.336	.383
Turner, Jason, Tampa *	21	78	65	7	14	19	0	1	1	9	0	0	1	12	1	9	0	2	0	.215	.346	.292
Umbria, Jose, Dunedin	42	146	127	3	28	33	5	0	0	15	5	2	2	10	0	26	0	0	2	.220	.284	.260
Urquhart, Derick, B.C. *	58	181	160	13	34	46	5	2	1	12	0	0	1	20	2	24	2	4	6	.213	.304	.288
Urueta, Luis, Palm Beach †	8	21	15	4	1	1	0	0	0	0	3	0	2	1	0	4	0	0	0	.067	.222	.067
Van Buizen, Rodney, V.B.	52	208	187	19	61	67	6	0	0	29	3	2	4	12	0	24	6	6	4	.326	.376	.358
Vasquez, Willie, Tampa †	21	86	73	7	17	21	4	0	0	7	1	2	1	9	0	20	0	2	2	.233	.318	.288
Velazquez, Gil, St. Lucie	19	64	57	6	12	18	3	0	1	6	1	0	0	6	0	5	0	0	2	.211	.286	.316
Velazquez, Juan, Ft. Myers†	60	207	172	18	38	43	3	1	0	17	8	2	2	23	0	36	2	2	2	.221	.317	.250
Veracierto, Fernando, Sara.	6	23	19	2	4	5	1	0	0	0	0	0	1	3	0	4	0	0	0	.211	.348	.263
Voshell, Chase, Palm Beach	42	166	155	9	39	51	7	1	1	18	0	0	1	9	0	32	0	2	4	.252	.297	.329
Vukovich, Vince, Clearwater *	106	400	361	31	93	112	14	1	1	42	2	4	1	32	1	56	7	5	16	.258	.317	.310
Walsh, Sean, Clearwater	106	425	359	58	95	144	29	1	6	47	0	4	19	43	3	81	11	2	8	.265	.369	.401
Wardinsky, Ryan, Clear.†	61	224	195	15	39	47	5	0	1	18	0	4	4	21	0	52	3	3	4	.200	.286	.241
Watkins, Tommy, Fort Myers	104	398	347	53	90	106	9	2	1	35	8	3	5	34	0	44	11	5	5	.259	.332	.305
Watson, Matt, St. Lucie *	2	9	7	2	2	4	0	1	0	2	0	1	0	1	0	2	1	0	0	.286	.333	.571
Watson, Rob, Lakeland	31	125	114	14	25	43	9	0	3	7	2	2	2	5	0	23	1	0	1	.219	.260	.377
Waugh, Jason, Dunedin	79	329	286	32	78	117	14	2	7	38	3	6	2	32	2	61	0	5	11	.273	.344	.409
Werth, Jayson, Dunedin	18	67	62	10	23	40	5	0	4	18	0	2	0	3	0	14	1	0	2	.371	.388	.645
Weston, Aron, Daytona *	58	234	207	32	58	80	11	4	1	23	2	1	3	20	1	50	14	3	1	.280	.351	.386
Whittaker, Tim, Dunedin	86	326	287	34	81	106	22	0	1	41	3	3	5	28	0	65	1	2	10	.282	.353	.369
Williams, Clyde, B.C. *	118	420	382	38	92	161	19	4	14	51	0	4	0	34	3	106	3	1	7	.241	.300	.421
Williams, Matt, Palm Beach	9	35	29	1	5	6	1	0	0	2	0	1	1	4	0	15	0	0	0	.172	.286	.207
Willingham, Josh, Jupiter	59	251	193	46	51	106	17	1	12	34	0	3	9	46	3	42	9	2	3	.264	.422	.549
Winrow, Gary, Tampa *	111	443	407	53	101	154	16	8	7	47	2	3	2	29	1	80	11	3	8	.248	.299	.378

Player, Team	G	TPA	AB	R	H	TB	2B	3B	HR	RBI	SH	SF	HP	BB	IBB	SO	SB	CS	GDP	Avg.	OBP	Slg.
Woods, Michael, Lakeland	116	428	361	38	74	94	12	4	0	27	10	4	1	52	1	92	10	8	5	.205	.304	.260
Wright, David, St. Lucie	133	549	466	69	126	214	39	2	15	75	1	6	4	72	5	98	19	5	8	.270	.369	.459
Yepez, Jose, Dunedin	40	135	116	13	25	30	2	0	1	10	1	0	6	12	0	23	0	0	5	.216	.321	.259
Youngbauer, Scott, Clear.†	97	397	358	36	85	130	18	6	5	36	4	1	6	28	1	70	7	4	6	.237	.303	.363

PLAYERS WITH TWO OR MORE TEAMS

Player, Team	G	TPA	AB	R	H	TB	2B	3B	HR	RBI	SH	SF	HP	BB	IBB	SO	SB	CS	GDP	Avg.	OBP	Slg.
Blasi, Blake, Sarasota †	41	169	135	15	29	35	4	1	0	13	4	2	3	25	0	25	6	4	2	.215	.345	.259
Blasi, Blake, Palm Beach †	68	300	263	42	68	90	14	1	2	24	3	2	2	30	1	40	7	4	1	.259	.337	.342

GRAND SLAMS—Craig, Stokes, 2 each; DeMarco, Emmerick, Hoorelbeke, Howard, Gabe Johnson, Matthews, Navarro, Segar, 1 each.

AWARDED FIRST BASE ON CATCHER'S INTERFERENCE—Greenberg 5 (Cabrera 2, Huber, Langill, E. Martinez); Avila 2 (Bellorin, Trezza); Thomas 2 (Hietpas, Soto); Boran (Huber); Corr (J. Brown); Dodson (Whittaker); Jova (Trezza); Kay (Kennedy); Kropf (E. Martinez); Lugo (Kay); McIntyre (E. Martinez); Rundgren (Emmerick); Sandoval (E. Martinez); Voshell (McMillan); Watkins (E. Martinez); Weston (Yepez).

2003 PITCHING

TEAM

Team	W	L	Pct.	ERA	G	CG	ShO	Sv.	IP	H	TBF	R	ER	HR	SH	SF	HB	BB	IBB	SO	WP	Bk.
St. Lucie	77	62	.554	3.09	139	4	10	46	1186.0	998	5001	505	407	53	47	32	63	490	7	1050	69	9
Jupiter	76	62	.551	3.09	138	5	13	42	1193.1	1112	5046	500	410	36	42	32	76	414	13	890	83	7
Clearwater	72	61	.541	3.25	133	6	13	44	1148.2	1130	4817	498	415	56	44	39	47	319	6	782	41	10
Brevard Co.	65	66	.496	3.35	131	5	15	34	1117.2	1065	4747	490	416	47	57	43	66	347	8	745	51	5
Dunedin	78	62	.557	3.37	140	3	12	41	1187.2	1081	5072	518	445	58	49	39	71	471	13	953	85	3
Daytona	66	71	.482	3.45	137	4	12	30	1198.2	1075	5152	549	460	61	53	38	81	473	21	1105	69	8
Vero Beach	62	69	.473	3.49	131	7	7	37	1145.1	1049	4889	530	444	81	49	32	46	443	10	918	68	12
Sarasota	63	67	.485	3.49	130	3	10	41	1125.2	1084	4849	535	437	59	42	51	72	439	12	783	53	7
Tampa	68	64	.515	3.55	132	2	8	35	1127.0	1023	4830	535	444	45	39	47	47	480	21	879	77	7
Fort Myers	73	63	.537	3.72	136	3	13	34	1181.0	1123	5052	560	488	71	44	28	52	483	22	887	80	6
Palm Beach	54	84	.391	3.93	138	3	8	34	1205.0	1189	5230	606	526	65	66	41	64	465	34	873	82	11
Lakeland	55	78	.414	4.17	133	5	8	31	1127.2	1203	4955	621	522	71	40	50	61	443	12	830	77	7

INDIVIDUAL

TOP QUALIFIERS FOR EARNED-RUN AVERAGE TITLE

Minimum 112 innings. *Lefthanded pitcher.

Pitcher, Team	W	L	Pct.	ERA	G	GS	CG	ShO	GF	Sv.	IP	H	TBF	R	ER	HR	SH	SF	HB	BB	IBB	SO	WP	Bk.
Blasko, Chadd, Daytona	10	5	.667	1.98	24	24	1	1	0	0	136.1	100	545	33	30	3	6	2	6	43	0	131	5	0
Ungs, Nic, Jupiter	8	3	.727	1.99	18	17	1	0	1	0	113.1	92	437	28	25	5	4	1	3	14	0	80	0	0
Miller, Greg, Vero Beach *	11	4	.733	2.49	21	21	1	0	0	0	115.2	103	478	40	32	5	6	1	0	41	0	111	3	0
Harper, Jesse, Dunedin	13	4	.765	2.54	26	24	1	0	1	0	131.0	112	531	41	37	4	2	2	7	31	1	100	2	0
Hill, Shawn, Brevard County	9	4	.692	2.56	22	21	2	1	0	0	126.2	118	525	47	36	3	6	7	10	26	0	66	1	0
Stevenson, Jason, Brev. Co.*	9	6	.600	2.62	36	11	0	0	6	0	113.1	88	455	36	33	4	6	3	4	33	1	60	4	0
Miller, Colby, Fort Myers	9	6	.600	2.71	26	26	1	1	0	0	156.0	139	637	58	47	10	6	4	8	43	3	114	10	3
Nolasco, Ricky, Daytona	11	5	.688	2.96	26	26	1	0	0	0	149.0	129	620	58	49	7	5	4	8	48	0	136	12	1
Floyd, Gavin, Clearwater	7	8	.467	3.00	24	20	1	1	0	0	138.0	128	577	61	46	9	4	3	7	45	0	115	6	0
Pinto, Renyel, Daytona *	3	8	.273	3.22	20	19	0	0	0	0	114.2	91	476	47	41	4	6	4	9	45	1	104	6	3
Astacio, Ezequiel, Clearwater	15	5	.750	3.29	25	22	2	1	2	0	147.2	140	609	60	54	9	3	4	7	29	0	83	2	2
Pleiness, Chad, Dunedin	7	8	.467	3.41	25	24	0	0	0	0	129.1	124	563	60	49	9	9	3	9	60	0	89	15	0
Nall, T.J., Vero Beach	6	7	.462	3.42	29	16	2	0	4	1	115.2	118	491	56	44	9	5	2	2	23	1	73	7	0
Ramirez, Elizardo, Clearwater	13	9	.591	3.78	27	25	1	0	0	0	157.1	181	668	85	66	4	4	2	4	33	0	101	4	2
Pilkington, Brian, Vero Beach	10	6	.625	3.88	21	21	1	0	0	0	125.1	136	521	55	54	9	3	4	5	16	0	74	1	1

DEPARTMENTAL LEADERS: W—E. Astacio, 15; L—McDowell, Rodney, 12; Pct.—McGinley, .900; G—Cali, 62; GS—C. Miller, Nolasco, Pignatiello, 26; CG—Several pitchers tied with 2; ShO—Several pitchers tied with 1; GF—Blasdell, 47; Sv.—Blasdell, 27; IP—El. Ramirez, 157.1; H—El. Ramirez, 181; TBF—Pignatiello, 674; R—Pignatiello, 87; ER—Pignatiello, 76; HR—McDowell, Pignatiello, 13; SH—Pleiness, 9; SF—Caputo, 8; HB—Caple, 19; BB—J. Diaz, 73; IBB—Cali, Novinsky, 6; SO—Pignatiello, 140; WP—Levinski, D. Martinez, 16; BK—J. Diaz, 6.

ALL PITCHERS

*Lefthanded pitcher.

Pitcher, Team	W	L	Pct.	ERA	G	GS	CG	ShO	GF	Sv.	IP	H	TBF	R	ER	HR	SH	SF	HB	BB	IBB	SO	WP	Bk.
Abbott, David, Dunedin	1	2	.333	5.87	8	3	0	0	0	0	23.0	34	104	16	15	3	0	1	1	5	0	11	0	0
Abbott, Jim, Fort Myers	5	3	.625	2.31	17	8	0	0	1	0	58.1	43	231	15	15	3	2	1	1	19	0	52	2	0
Akens, Phil, Jupiter	6	3	.667	2.88	11	11	1	1	0	0	65.2	67	269	24	21	0	0	2	6	14	0	45	6	0
Alvarado, Carlo, Lakeland	0	0	.000	3.68	4	0	0	0	1	0	7.1	5	34	3	3	0	1	0	0	6	2	12	1	0
Anderson, Travis, Daytona	2	0	1.000	0.00	12	0	0	0	4	2	22.2	10	82	1	0	0	1	1	2	1	0	23	4	0
Artiles, Carlos, Tampa *	2	3	.400	3.86	24	0	0	0	9	1	46.2	48	215	29	20	5	2	2	1	26	3	39	5	1
Asahina, Jonathan, Jupiter	1	2	.333	2.70	12	4	0	0	2	0	36.2	36	156	16	11	0	2	1	2	18	0	21	8	0
Astacio, Ezequiel, Clearwater	15	5	.750	3.29	25	22	2	1	2	0	147.2	140	609	60	54	9	3	4	7	29	0	83	2	2
Astacio, Pedro, St. Lucie	0	2	.000	2.08	4	4	0	0	0	0	17.1	15	70	6	4	0	1	0	1	3	0	15	0	0
Axelson, Josh, Palm Beach	0	2	.000	3.12	9	1	0	0	1	0	26.0	21	104	9	9	1	1	1	2	4	2	23	2	0
Baez, Benito, Jupiter *	1	0	1.000	1.42	3	2	0	0	0	0	6.1	3	22	1	1	1	0	0	1	1	0	6	0	0
Baisley, Brad, Clearwater	0	1	.000	0.00	1	1	0	0	0	0	2.0	1	7	1	0	0	1	0	0	0	0	1	0	0
Baugh, Kenny, Lakeland	3	0	1.000	3.86	4	4	0	0	0	0	21.0	21	93	14	9	2	0	1	1	11	0	12	2	0
Bautista, Denny, Jupiter	8	4	.667	3.21	14	14	0	0	0	0	84.0	68	353	32	30	2	1	2	5	35	0	77	7	1
Beckett, Josh, Jupiter	0	0	.000	0.00	1	1	0	0	0	0	3.0	2	11	0	0	0	0	0	0	0	0	5	0	0
Belizario, Ronald, Jupiter	1	2	.333	4.91	6	4	0	0	2	0	18.1	20	82	10	10	0	1	0	1	8	0	13	0	0
Bell, Gary, Tampa *	3	3	.500	4.04	22	7	0	0	2	0	62.1	58	267	31	28	5	0	0	3	31	0	52	2	0
Benik, Brett, Daytona	4	2	.667	3.61	25	2	0	0	12	0	47.1	59	210	25	19	3	3	3	0	14	2	32	0	0
Bennett, Steve, St. Lucie	0	0	.000	0.00	3	0	0	0	3	1	2.1	1	9	0	0	0	0	0	0	1	0	2	0	0

Pitcher, Team	W	L	Pct.	ERA	G	GS	CG	ShO	GF	Sv.	IP	H	TBF	R	ER	HR	SH	SF	HB	BB	IBB	SO	WP	Bk.
Bicondoa, Ryan, Tampa-St.L....	4	3	.571	3.50	20	9	0	0	4	1	74.2	78	324	35	29	1	4	2	3	30	1	46	2	2
Birtwell, John, Lakeland..........	3	3	.500	1.74	35	0	0	0	13	3	41.1	35	164	11	8	0	2	0	1	11	2	41	3	1
Blalock, Casey, Jupiter............	1	0	1.000	0.00	2	0	0	0	2	1	3.0	0	10	0	0	0	0	0	0	1	0	1	0	0
Blankenship, Jon, Tampa *	0	0	.000	1.35	10	0	0	0	6	3	20.0	13	79	3	3	0	1	0	0	5	0	12	1	0
Blasdell, Jared, Daytona..........	3	4	.429	3.20	56	0	0	0	47	27	59.0	52	266	25	21	1	2	0	3	34	4	84	5	0
Blasko, Chadd, Daytona	10	5	.667	1.98	24	24	1	1	0	0	136.1	100	545	33	30	3	6	2	6	43	0	131	5	0
Bonilla, Henry, Fort Myers.......	1	2	.333	4.91	10	0	0	0	9	3	11.0	14	48	6	6	2	0	0	0	3	0	11	0	0
Bowyer, Travis, Fort Myers......	5	2	.714	3.83	45	0	0	0	10	1	80.0	68	349	43	34	1	7	6	1	56	2	70	9	0
Brazoban, Yhency, Tampa	0	2	.000	2.83	24	0	0	0	22	15	28.2	27	124	13	9	0	0	1	1	12	2	34	2	0
Brito, Eude, Clearwater *.........	4	3	.571	3.09	36	0	0	0	19	6	58.1	50	248	21	20	3	4	1	0	27	1	54	7	2
Brownlie, Bobby, Daytona	5	4	.556	3.00	13	13	1	1	0	0	66.0	48	268	26	22	2	2	2	1	24	0	59	4	0
Brumit, Matt, Tampa................	0	2	.000	4.15	9	0	0	0	7	1	13.0	11	60	9	6	0	1	2	1	6	2	5	0	0
Bucktrot, Keith, Clearwater......	7	7	.500	3.33	19	17	0	0	0	0	110.2	104	460	50	41	8	3	3	9	29	0	68	3	0
Bush, David, Dunedin..............	7	3	.700	2.81	14	14	0	0	0	0	77.0	64	310	29	24	6	3	3	7	9	0	75	4	0
Byard, David, St. Lucie............	1	1	.500	1.46	27	0	0	0	16	4	37.0	20	154	8	6	1	1	0	2	24	1	32	1	1
Byron, Terry, Sarasota.............	0	1	.000	2.17	32	0	0	0	18	9	45.2	41	191	13	11	1	2	1	2	20	0	39	4	1
Cable, Taft, Clearwater.............	4	3	.571	3.41	31	5	0	0	12	1	71.1	61	295	29	27	8	7	5	5	25	0	42	1	0
Cali, Carmen, Palm Beach *....	2	1	.667	4.99	62	0	0	0	23	3	70.1	72	321	49	39	2	7	4	6	32	6	70	2	0
Campbell, Dayle, Vero Beach ..	0	0	.000	0.00	1	0	0	0	1	0	1.1	0	5	0	0	0	0	0	0	1	0	0	0	0
Caple, Chance, Palm Beach.....	2	6	.250	4.85	20	17	1	0	0	0	91.0	83	429	53	49	5	8	3	19	63	1	45	13	1
Caputo, Rob, Brevard County..	4	6	.400	4.31	21	20	0	0	0	0	94.0	110	440	62	45	8	3	8	8	42	0	57	2	1
Carbajal, Alex, Sarasota *.......	2	3	.400	4.17	22	1	0	0	9	0	36.2	40	160	17	17	3	1	5	2	16	0	22	3	0
Cardwell, Brian, Dunedin.........	1	0	1.000	3.60	8	0	0	0	3	0	10.0	6	48	6	4	0	0	1	3	8	0	5	3	0
Carpenter, Chris, Palm Beach..	0	1	.000	1.29	4	4	0	0	0	0	7.0	6	28	3	1	1	0	0	0	1	0	6	0	0
Carter, Mark, Daytona *	0	1	.000	5.60	16	0	0	0	6	0	17.2	20	80	12	11	1	0	2	1	8	0	17	1	1
Casadiego, Gerardo, B.C.	0	3	.000	3.20	7	2	0	0	4	0	19.2	23	83	7	7	1	0	0	1	4	0	12	0	0
Castro, Rafael, St. Lucie..........	1	0	1.000	1.42	2	0	0	0	1	0	6.1	5	27	1	1	0	0	0	0	5	0	5	0	0
Cave, Kevin, Jupiter.................	2	2	.500	1.60	39	0	0	0	37	23	45.0	36	185	11	8	0	4	0	1	14	1	43	4	1
Cerezo, Hector, B.C.*	0	0	.000	27.00	1	0	0	0	1	0	0.1	2	3	1	1	0	0	0	0	0	0	0	0	0
Chenard, Ken, St. Lucie...........	7	4	.636	4.04	17	16	0	0	1	0	75.2	65	321	36	34	5	2	2	4	32	0	83	6	0
Christensen, Ben, Daytona	0	2	.000	5.27	14	3	0	0	2	0	27.1	32	125	18	16	3	1	1	3	11	0	21	2	0
Clark, Ray, Tampa....................	2	1	.667	3.76	5	5	0	0	0	0	26.1	37	125	15	11	1	0	0	1	8	0	15	1	0
Claussen, Brandon, Tampa *...	2	0	1.000	1.64	4	4	0	0	0	0	22.0	16	86	5	4	0	0	2	0	3	0	26	0	1
Clelland, James, Sarasota	4	2	.667	3.57	11	10	1	0	1	0	58.0	67	244	27	23	4	3	3	3	12	1	36	0	1
Coggin, Dave, Clearwater	0	0	.000	2.25	3	3	0	0	0	0	4.0	3	17	1	1	0	0	0	1	2	0	2	0	0
Collins, Pat, Palm Beach	1	2	.333	2.17	10	3	0	0	1	0	29.0	20	128	9	7	1	0	1	3	18	1	27	2	0
Comolli, Mark, Dunedin...........	1	3	.250	3.43	21	0	0	0	19	11	21.0	16	94	9	8	1	4	1	2	13	2	24	1	0
Cone, David, St. Lucie.............	0	1	.000	2.84	3	3	0	0	0	0	12.2	10	51	4	4	1	0	1	0	3	0	6	3	0
Contreras, Jean, Fort Myers *.	0	2	.000	6.23	14	3	0	0	2	1	21.2	29	107	17	15	3	1	0	3	12	1	19	1	0
Contreras, Jose, Tampa...........	0	0	.000	4.50	1	1	0	0	0	0	4.0	4	18	2	2	0	0	0	1	3	0	5	1	0
Cook, Jeremy, Palm Beach......	4	3	.571	3.62	45	0	0	0	18	2	59.2	52	233	24	24	4	2	3	0	10	1	33	2	2
Cooksey, Wes, Tampa	2	1	.667	4.34	18	0	0	0	8	0	29.0	29	128	14	14	2	1	3	1	14	1	8	1	0
Corcoran, Roy, B.C..................	5	3	.625	1.91	28	0	0	0	25	12	33.0	19	131	8	7	1	6	1	2	11	1	35	0	0
Cordero, Chad, B.C..................	1	1	.500	2.05	19	0	0	0	13	6	26.1	17	103	8	6	1	4	2	1	10	0	17	0	0
Correa, Cristobal, Palm Beach.	4	9	.308	5.19	21	18	0	0	0	0	95.1	100	424	64	55	9	2	5	4	49	0	49	5	4
Cosby, Rob, Dunedin...............	1	0	1.000	0.00	1	0	0	0	1	0	1.0	1	6	0	0	0	1	0	0	2	2	0	0	0
Cox, Mike, St. Lucie *	6	0	1.000	3.32	27	2	0	0	12	4	57.0	35	239	22	21	4	2	4	3	38	0	72	5	0
Crain, Jesse, Fort Myers..........	2	1	.667	2.84	10	0	0	0	3	0	19.0	10	70	6	6	0	0	0	0	5	0	25	0	0
Cuello, Felix, Lakeland............	0	1	.000	6.23	14	2	0	0	3	0	26.0	31	139	21	18	3	0	2	5	27	0	17	4	0
Currier, Rik, Tampa.................	4	3	.571	1.95	29	5	0	0	9	1	73.2	53	303	22	16	1	1	2	2	30	3	86	4	0
Davis, Stockton, B.C...............	3	2	.600	3.82	42	0	0	0	12	1	68.1	74	307	36	29	4	0	5	4	28	0	51	7	0
Daws, Josh, Fort Myers	0	1	.000	3.86	11	0	0	0	11	5	14.0	11	59	7	6	0	3	1	1	6	1	11	1	0
Dawson, Layne, Clearwater.....	6	3	.667	3.24	14	10	1	1	4	2	66.2	77	290	33	24	2	1	5	4	13	0	31	1	0
Day, Zach, Brevard County......	0	0	.000	1.69	1	1	0	0	0	0	5.1	3	19	1	1	0	0	0	0	1	0	3	0	0
DeJong, Jordan, Dunedin........	2	3	.400	2.79	28	0	0	0	25	17	29.0	23	129	10	9	2	2	0	1	18	2	30	2	0
Dejesus, Elvis, Sarasota	0	0	.000	3.79	27	0	0	0	9	0	40.1	42	182	20	17	2	1	2	2	18	0	21	2	1
Delcarmen, Manny, Sarasota...	1	1	.500	3.13	4	3	0	0	0	0	23.0	16	91	9	8	1	0	1	3	7	0	16	0	0
Demontel, Jimmy, Jupiter	0	1	.000	1.93	2	0	0	0	1	0	4.2	5	22	3	1	0	0	0	1	2	0	4	0	0
Dennison, Michael, Sarasota...	0	1	.000	2.84	4	0	0	0	4	2	6.1	5	25	2	2	0	0	0	0	1	0	5	0	0
Dequin, Benji, B.C.*	6	3	.667	2.63	17	2	0	0	5	0	41.0	34	175	13	12	3	5	0	3	18	0	38	2	0
Diaz, Felix, Brevard County......	0	0	.000	0.00	1	0	0	0	1	0	1.0	1	5	0	0	0	0	0	1	0	0	2	0	0
Diaz, Joselo, V.B.-St. Lucie......	7	4	.636	3.33	26	13	0	0	4	2	92.0	55	404	37	34	2	5	1	10	73	1	110	9	6
Diaz, Luis, Lakeland	2	1	.667	4.12	10	0	0	0	4	0	19.2	16	80	11	9	4	0	2	0	7	1	13	3	0
Dinardo, Lenny, St. Lucie *.....	3	8	.273	2.01	19	13	1	0	2	1	85.0	64	325	27	19	1	3	1	3	14	0	93	5	0
Doble, Clemente, Clearwater ...	0	1	.000	6.75	1	1	0	0	0	0	4.0	5	19	3	3	0	0	1	0	3	0	1	1	0
Dodson, Jeremy, Palm Beach .	0	0	.000	0.00	2	0	0	0	2	0	2.0	1	8	0	0	0	0	0	0	2	0	2	1	0
Dougherty, Kevin, V.B.*..........	0	0	.000	3.52	7	0	0	0	1	0	7.2	13	43	5	3	0	0	0	0	7	1	5	0	0
Duckworth, Brandon, Clear......	0	0	.000	1.00	2	2	0	0	0	0	9.0	3	32	1	1	1	0	0	0	2	0	11	0	0
Dumatrait, Phillip, Sarasota * .	7	5	.583	3.02	21	20	0	0	1	1	104.1	74	429	41	35	4	2	2	4	59	0	74	4	0
Durbin, J.D., Fort Myers..........	9	2	.818	3.09	14	14	0	0	0	0	87.1	73	355	35	30	3	1	3	3	22	0	69	3	1
Easterday, Matt, Jupiter...........	0	0	.000	0.00	1	0	0	0	1	0	1.0	1	4	0	0	0	0	0	0	0	0	2	0	0
Eckert, Harold, St. Lucie..........	7	3	.700	2.93	17	13	0	0	0	0	76.2	72	331	30	25	5	4	3	4	38	0	50	2	0
Elliott, Chad, St. Lucie *..........	4	5	.444	3.03	22	3	1	0	11	3	71.1	64	295	30	24	2	7	4	2	26	1	46	1	0
Elmore, Chris, Sarasota *	0	0	.000	1.93	1	1	0	0	0	0	4.2	3	24	4	1	0	0	1	1	4	0	2	1	0
Embree, Alan, Sarasota *.......	0	0	.000	13.50	1	1	0	0	0	0	0.2	2	4	1	1	0	0	0	0	0	0	2	0	0
Encarnacion, Luis, Clearwater.	0	0	.000	0.00	1	0	0	0	1	0	1.0	1	4	0	0	0	0	0	0	0	0	1	0	0
Esarey, Brad, Dunedin *..........	0	0	.000	11.81	6	0	0	0	2	0	5.1	8	31	8	7	2	0	1	2	5	0	8	0	0
Estes, Jonathan, Palm Beach ..	1	0	1.000	3.31	15	0	0	0	1	0	32.2	36	142	13	12	2	2	1	0	7	1	15	0	0
Fahrner, Evan, Daytona............	1	2	.333	0.46	13	0	0	0	4	0	19.2	13	80	4	1	1	1	0	1	7	1	28	1	0
Fernley, Nathan, Daytona..........	2	2	.500	5.76	17	0	0	0	4	0	29.2	40	141	20	19	2	1	1	3	10	2	29	1	0
Ferreras, Yorkin, Daytona *.....	0	2	.000	6.86	11	0	0	0	2	0	21.0	26	104	16	16	2	0	0	0	15	1	19	0	0
File, Bob, Dunedin...................	0	0	.000	3.00	3	2	0	0	0	0	3.0	3	11	1	1	1	0	0	0	0	0	0	0	0
Flores, Neomar, Dunedin.........	7	8	.467	4.78	29	18	1	0	4	0	111.0	108	482	61	59	8	3	5	5	44	2	78	6	0
Florian, Frailyn, Jupiter *.........	3	3	.500	4.95	10	5	0	0	1	0	36.1	37	155	24	20	2	1	4	1	15	0	17	4	1

Pitcher, Team	W	L	Pct.	ERA	G	GS	CG	ShO	GF	Sv.	IP	H	TBF	R	ER	HR	SH	SF	HB	BB	IBB	SO	WP	Bk.
Floyd, Gavin, Clearwater	7	8	.467	3.00	24	20	1	1	0	0	138.0	128	577	61	46	9	4	3	7	45	0	115	6	0
Flynn, Brian, Palm Beach	2	1	.667	5.91	7	0	0	0	2	0	10.2	18	53	10	7	1	1	0	0	3	0	5	0	0
Foli, Daniel, Daytona	1	1	.500	8.10	6	0	0	0	1	0	10.0	12	52	11	9	1	2	1	1	8	0	7	1	0
Foote, Joe, Fort Myers	0	3	.000	9.37	5	4	0	0	0	0	16.1	31	83	17	17	3	2	0	1	5	1	4	1	0
Fox, Chad, Sarasota	0	0	.000	4.50	2	1	0	0	0	0	2.0	2	9	1	1	0	0	0	0	1	0	1	0	0
Franco, John, St. Lucie *	0	1	.000	6.23	4	3	0	0	0	0	4.1	6	20	3	3	1	0	0	0	1	0	5	0	0
Franco, Martire, Clearwater	0	0	.000	2.25	1	1	0	0	0	0	4.0	4	19	3	1	0	1	1	0	1	0	3	0	1
Frasor, Jason, Vero Beach	1	0	1.000	1.85	15	0	0	0	9	6	24.1	16	94	7	5	0	1	1	0	4	0	36	0	1
Fuell, Jerrod, Jupiter	3	1	.750	2.68	46	0	0	0	22	6	50.1	48	207	19	15	1	1	1	2	10	0	43	2	0
Fulchino, Jeff, Jupiter	2	4	.333	4.04	17	16	1	0	0	0	78.0	76	341	41	35	1	1	3	10	32	0	47	5	0
Gabbard, Kason, Sarasota *	0	1	.000	10.29	2	2	0	0	0	0	7.0	13	34	8	8	0	2	1	0	3	0	4	0	0
Galbraith, Jason, P.B.*	0	1	.000	4.70	5	0	0	0	3	0	7.2	6	33	5	4	0	0	0	0	5	0	5	0	1
Gamble, Jerome, Sarasota	6	4	.600	3.66	17	14	0	0	0	0	76.1	68	320	36	31	2	2	3	10	21	0	51	5	0
Garcia, Jose, Tampa	1	0	1.000	1.74	4	4	0	0	0	0	20.2	13	79	4	4	0	0	0	0	4	0	14	0	0
Glen, William, Clearwater	1	2	.333	1.29	7	0	0	0	4	1	14.0	13	59	4	2	0	1	0	1	5	1	8	1	0
Gonzalez, Luis, Vero Beach *	2	3	.400	1.48	21	0	0	0	13	3	30.1	25	124	6	5	0	2	1	2	11	1	19	5	0
Graves, Don, Palm Beach	1	0	1.000	4.26	3	3	0	0	0	0	19.0	23	82	9	9	1	2	0	0	3	0	8	1	0
Greusel, Evan, Jupiter	4	3	.571	3.95	24	0	0	0	6	1	41.0	39	180	21	18	3	1	1	1	17	1	36	5	0
Grilli, Jason, Jupiter	4	2	.667	2.53	7	7	0	0	0	0	42.2	38	173	13	12	1	0	0	6	6	0	30	1	1
Gutierrez, Jannio, Fort Myers	2	3	.400	3.53	40	0	0	0	23	10	51.0	46	224	23	20	2	0	1	0	26	4	56	7	1
Halsey, Brad, Tampa *	10	4	.714	3.43	14	13	1	0	0	0	84.0	96	354	36	32	3	3	2	1	14	0	56	4	0
Hamann, Rob, Dunedin	1	0	1.000	2.08	4	0	0	0	1	0	8.2	7	34	2	2	0	1	0	0	3	0	4	0	0
Hamels, Cole, Clearwater *	0	2	.000	2.73	5	5	0	0	0	0	26.1	29	115	9	8	0	1	2	1	14	0	32	2	0
Hamilton, Jamaal, V.B.*	0	0	.000	0.00	4	0	0	0	1	0	9.1	3	31	0	0	0	0	0	1	2	0	7	0	0
Hamman, Corey, Lakeland *	6	5	.545	3.32	46	0	0	0	15	1	59.2	63	254	30	22	2	2	1	1	21	3	46	4	0
Hammons, Matt, Palm Beach	2	2	.500	1.25	21	0	0	0	17	8	21.2	11	85	4	3	0	1	2	0	9	3	32	5	0
Harper, Jesse, Dunedin	13	4	.765	2.54	26	24	1	0	1	0	131.0	112	531	41	37	4	2	2	7	31	1	100	2	0
Hawksworth, Blake, P.B.	1	3	.250	3.94	6	6	0	0	0	0	32.0	28	132	14	14	2	0	1	1	11	0	32	2	0
Haynes, Brad, Jupiter	0	0	.000	7.79	13	0	0	0	2	0	17.1	20	90	17	15	0	1	1	2	18	0	10	2	0
Hee, Aaron, Vero Beach *	0	0	.000	4.91	9	0	0	0	2	0	11.0	8	60	6	6	1	1	1	1	18	0	7	2	0
Hendrickson, Mark, Dunedin *	1	0	1.000	1.59	1	1	0	0	0	0	5.2	5	28	2	1	0	1	0	1	4	0	3	0	0
Henn, Sean, Tampa *	4	3	.571	3.61	16	16	0	0	0	0	72.1	69	314	31	29	3	5	5	1	37	0	52	7	0
Hernandez, Adrian, Tampa	0	0	.000	0.00	1	0	0	0	0	0	2.0	1	6	0	0	0	0	0	0	0	0	4	0	0
Hernandez, Orlando, B.C.	0	1	.000	10.80	2	2	0	0	0	0	5.0	5	25	6	6	0	1	0	0	4	0	7	0	0
Hill, Shawn, Brevard County	9	4	.692	2.56	22	21	2	1	0	0	126.2	118	525	47	36	3	6	7	10	26	0	66	1	0
Hinckley, Michael, B.C.*	4	0	1.000	0.72	4	4	1	0	0	0	25.0	14	89	2	2	1	0	0	0	1	0	23	2	0
Hoffpauir, Micah, Daytona *	0	0	.000	0.00	1	0	0	0	1	0	0.1	1	1	0	0	0	0	0	0	0	0	0	0	0
Holdzkom, Lincoln, Jupiter	0	2	.000	3.07	13	0	0	0	9	2	14.2	9	63	6	5	0	1	0	1	7	2	20	0	0
Holubec, Ken, Fort Myers *	4	5	.444	4.59	26	11	2	1	2	0	82.1	96	363	44	42	3	5	3	3	35	0	49	2	0
Hosford, Clint, Vero Beach	1	5	.167	5.48	8	8	0	0	0	0	42.2	57	199	31	26	9	0	3	3	12	0	30	4	0
Houston, Ryan, Dunedin	1	2	.333	2.66	26	4	0	0	10	3	50.2	36	214	15	15	2	0	0	3	30	0	54	7	0
Howell, Jason, Sarasota *	9	4	.692	2.99	48	0	0	0	19	5	75.1	71	320	29	25	7	3	3	3	24	2	59	5	0
Howell, Michael, Lakeland	0	4	.000	5.57	5	5	0	0	0	0	21.0	27	99	19	13	1	1	3	0	10	0	13	2	0
Huang, Kevin, Sarasota	1	0	1.000	3.97	4	1	0	0	1	1	11.1	13	52	8	5	1	0	0	0	6	0	9	1	0
Hull, Eric, Vero Beach	3	5	.375	2.68	31	14	1	0	3	1	110.2	82	440	37	33	9	4	7	1	40	0	105	7	0
Hutchinson, Trevor, Jupiter	9	2	.818	2.77	14	13	2	1	1	0	84.1	77	342	30	26	3	1	4	4	16	0	58	1	0
Hutchison, Ryan, Clearwater	0	0	.000	0.96	8	0	0	0	7	5	9.1	7	34	1	1	0	1	0	0	0	0	9	0	0
Isaacson, Charlie, Tampa	0	0	.000	2.53	7	0	0	0	5	4	10.2	9	44	3	3	0	1	0	1	5	0	4	1	0
Jackson, Dan, Dunedin	1	0	1.000	1.88	9	0	0	0	3	0	14.1	12	59	4	3	1	0	1	1	4	0	17	1	0
Johnson, Tyler, Palm Beach *	5	5	.500	3.08	22	10	0	0	3	0	79.0	79	346	29	27	2	4	1	1	38	2	81	8	0
Kaercher, Matthew, Sarasota	0	2	.000	3.38	8	0	0	0	3	0	10.2	7	44	6	4	0	0	1	2	3	2	4	1	0
Kazmir, Scott, St. Lucie *	1	2	.333	3.27	7	7	0	0	0	0	33.0	29	141	15	12	0	1	1	2	16	0	40	2	0
Kegley, Chuck, Dunedin	5	0	1.000	3.20	19	0	0	0	3	0	25.1	26	111	9	9	0	0	0	1	12	0	23	3	0
Keirstead, Mike, Vero Beach	4	5	.444	3.84	10	10	1	0	0	0	58.2	53	247	29	25	2	2	0	2	18	0	34	4	0
Kemlo, Chris, Tampa	3	0	1.000	1.74	4	0	0	0	1	0	10.1	6	39	3	2	0	0	2	1	2	0	8	2	0
Kemp, Beau, Fort Myers	1	2	.333	3.76	22	0	0	0	19	11	26.1	30	117	14	11	3	0	0	1	7	0	16	0	0
Kennard, Jeff, Tampa	6	3	.667	2.15	26	1	0	0	13	2	54.1	34	223	17	13	0	3	2	5	29	1	34	1	0
Kennedy, Casey, Vero Beach	0	3	.000	6.18	8	5	0	0	2	0	27.2	31	129	23	19	1	2	3	3	10	0	8	0	1
Kent, Steve, Jupiter *	2	2	.500	2.93	5	4	0	0	0	0	27.2	25	117	9	9	0	1	0	2	10	1	13	1	0
Key, Chris, Jupiter *	4	2	.667	1.70	45	0	0	0	15	2	74.0	78	314	27	14	1	4	1	0	15	2	40	4	0
Kieninger, Billy, Lakeland	0	2	.000	7.46	21	0	0	0	7	0	35.0	56	168	33	29	1	0	7	1	7	0	20	3	0
King, Jeremy, Tampa	0	7	.000	4.50	11	9	0	0	0	0	52.0	45	225	33	26	3	2	2	5	19	0	45	8	0
Kinney, Josh, Palm Beach	3	0	1.000	1.52	31	0	0	0	10	3	41.1	38	167	7	7	0	2	0	0	10	4	35	5	0
Kirsten, Rick, Lakeland	1	1	.500	3.60	2	2	0	0	0	0	10.0	11	42	4	4	0	0	1	1	2	0	8	0	0
Knowles, Mike, Tampa	0	0	.000	3.52	4	0	0	0	1	1	7.2	8	34	3	3	0	0	0	0	3	0	4	0	0
Knox, Michael, Tampa	1	1	.500	3.72	3	1	0	0	0	0	9.2	8	43	6	4	1	1	1	1	6	0	5	3	0
Kobow, Mike, Lakeland	5	1	.833	1.05	32	0	0	0	27	15	34.1	24	142	8	4	0	2	1	1	14	0	28	4	0
Korecky, Bobby, Clearwater	5	4	.556	2.26	49	0	0	0	44	25	59.2	52	234	19	15	3	3	0	2	9	1	46	2	0
Kremer, John, Tampa	2	2	.500	2.98	20	0	0	0	17	1	42.1	29	170	18	14	0	1	3	3	13	4	38	1	0
Kumagai, Ryo, Sarasota	0	0	.000	4.50	1	0	0	0	0	0	2.0	2	8	1	1	0	1	1	0	0	0	1	0	0
Lambert, Jeremy, Palm Beach	0	0	.000	2.57	7	0	0	0	2	0	7.0	8	31	4	2	2	0	0	0	0	0	8	0	0
League, Brandon, Dunedin	4	3	.571	4.75	13	12	0	0	0	0	66.1	76	296	40	35	3	5	1	6	20	0	34	8	1
Leu, Trevor, Lakeland *	5	6	.455	3.24	33	14	0	0	4	0	108.1	121	481	54	39	5	7	1	5	42	0	84	9	1
Levinski, Donald, Jupiter	4	11	.267	4.03	21	21	0	0	0	0	87.0	75	405	48	39	1	3	2	11	70	0	77	16	0
Lieber, Jon, Tampa	0	0	.000	13.50	1	1	0	0	0	0	2.0	5	12	3	3	0	1	0	0	0	0	4	1	0
Lincoln, Jeff, Fort Myers	0	0	.000	1.17	6	0	0	0	1	0	7.2	8	36	2	1	0	0	0	0	5	1	4	1	0
Lohse, Eric, Fort Myers	0	2	.000	4.05	15	0	0	0	4	0	26.2	28	119	12	12	4	2	1	2	9	2	22	0	0
Lopez, Arturo, Vero Beach *	1	1	.500	4.32	11	0	0	0	5	0	16.2	11	61	8	8	0	0	0	0	3	0	16	1	0
Lopez, Rafael, St. Lucie	4	4	.500	3.13	37	0	0	0	22	10	60.1	52	261	25	21	0	3	1	3	29	3	50	4	0
Madson, Ryan, Clearwater	0	0	.000	5.63	2	2	0	0	0	0	8.0	11	36	5	5	0	0	0	0	2	0	9	0	0
Maness, Nick, St. Lucie	0	0	.000	4.26	7	0	0	0	4	0	12.2	10	56	8	6	0	0	0	0	6	0	8	1	0
Manning, Charlie, Tampa *	2	4	.333	3.45	6	6	0	0	0	0	31.1	27	134	14	12	2	1	1	1	15	1	25	2	0
Martin, Greg, B.C.*	0	0	.000	6.35	7	0	0	0	2	0	5.2	9	28	4	4	0	0	0	0	4	0	1	0	0
Martin, Nick, Daytona *	6	10	.375	4.20	33	17	0	0	6	0	115.2	121	510	71	54	11	1	7	4	41	1	85	9	1

Pitcher, Team	W	L	Pct.	ERA	G	GS	CG	ShO	GF	Sv.	IP	H	TBF	R	ER	HR	SH	SF	HB	BB	IBB	SO	WP	Bk.
Martinez, Dave, Tampa *	5	4	.556	4.79	14	12	1	0	1	0	56.1	64	271	40	30	3	1	2	3	34	0	41	16	0
Martinez, Miguel, Palm Beach	1	1	.500	4.50	8	5	0	0	1	0	30.0	43	135	17	15	0	2	1	2	8	1	17	1	0
Mata, Gustavo, B.C.	2	0	1.000	0.60	5	5	0	0	0	0	30.0	20	112	3	2	0	0	1	3	4	0	15	2	0
Maureau, Justin, Dunedin *	3	4	.429	4.84	38	3	0	0	9	0	48.1	55	226	34	26	0	5	2	2	28	0	35	2	0
Maust, David, B.C.*	1	2	.333	1.31	31	0	0	0	11	4	48.0	36	189	12	7	1	1	1	2	8	2	41	1	0
Mayfield, Brandon, Clearwater	3	5	.375	5.33	25	0	0	0	6	0	52.1	67	236	32	31	2	1	6	2	15	1	24	1	0
McAdam, Scott, B.C.	0	0	.000	36.00	1	0	0	0	0	0	1.0	5	11	4	4	0	0	0	1	2	0	1	0	0
McCracken, Vance, V.B.	0	1	.000	6.75	8	0	0	0	4	0	16.0	15	73	17	12	4	1	1	2	7	0	11	0	0
McCrotty, Will, Vero Beach	1	1	.500	3.98	4	4	0	0	0	0	20.1	19	86	10	9	3	1	2	0	11	0	13	1	0
McDowell, Kevin, Lakeland *	5	12	.294	4.99	24	22	0	0	1	0	126.1	139	553	77	70	13	4	7	10	47	0	75	8	1
McEachran, Aaron, Dunedin	0	0	.000	0.00	1	0	0	0	1	0	1.0	0	3	0	0	0	0	0	0	0	0	0	0	0
McGinley, Blake, St. Lucie *	9	1	.900	1.02	37	0	0	0	22	7	79.1	51	303	11	9	0	0	3	1	20	0	86	2	1
McGowan, Dustin, Dunedin	5	6	.455	2.85	14	14	1	1	0	0	75.2	62	313	29	24	1	1	5	4	25	0	66	9	0
McNutt, Mike, Jupiter	7	4	.636	2.45	33	8	0	0	5	1	95.2	80	390	35	26	6	4	6	5	22	0	83	5	1
Mejia, Anderson, Daytona	0	0	.000	4.50	1	0	0	0	0	0	2.0	2	9	1	1	0	0	0	0	2	0	1	0	0
Mejia, Juan, Palm Beach	3	0	1.000	5.68	8	5	0	0	0	0	31.2	39	147	21	20	3	2	1	4	13	0	14	5	0
Mendoza, Cristian, Tampa	0	1	.000	2.82	10	1	0	0	4	0	22.1	16	99	12	7	1	0	1	0	18	1	14	1	0
Mendoza, Ramiro, Sarasota	1	0	1.000	0.00	1	1	0	0	0	0	5.0	2	17	0	0	0	1	0	0	1	0	4	0	0
Meyer, Todd, Brevard County	0	0	.000	40.50	1	0	0	0	0	0	0.2	3	7	3	3	0	1	0	0	2	0	0	0	0
Miller, Colby, Fort Myers	9	6	.600	2.71	26	26	1	1	0	0	156.0	139	637	58	47	10	6	4	8	43	3	114	10	3
Miller, Greg, Vero Beach *	11	4	.733	2.49	21	21	1	0	0	0	115.2	103	478	40	32	5	6	1	0	41	0	111	3	0
Miller, Jason, Fort Myers *	3	4	.429	4.24	13	10	0	0	1	0	51.0	60	224	30	24	3	1	1	1	21	0	39	3	0
Miller, Josh, Clearwater	0	0	.000	0.00	1	0	0	0	1	0	1.0	0	3	0	0	0	0	0	0	0	0	0	0	0
Miller, Justin, Dunedin	0	1	.000	4.50	1	1	0	0	0	0	6.0	3	22	3	3	0	1	0	1	2	0	5	0	0
Miniel, Rene, Sarasota	3	4	.429	3.34	19	7	0	0	3	0	64.2	62	283	27	24	2	7	2	8	27	0	47	2	0
Minor, Ryan, Vero Beach	0	0	.000	1.59	6	0	0	0	3	0	5.2	7	24	3	1	1	0	1	0	0	0	2	1	0
Mitchell, Nathan, Daytona	3	4	.429	3.21	42	3	0	0	11	0	70.0	66	312	29	25	3	6	2	6	33	4	66	4	0
Moates, Jason, Lakeland	4	6	.400	3.61	31	13	2	0	4	2	92.1	83	396	41	37	5	2	4	4	50	1	84	4	0
Monahan, Joey, Daytona	0	0	.000	0.00	1	0	0	0	1	0	0.2	0	2	0	0	0	0	0	0	0	0	1	1	0
Moore, Benjamin, Tampa	0	0	.000	5.52	12	0	0	0	9	3	14.2	17	63	10	9	0	1	0	1	5	0	13	4	0
Morales, Alex, Brevard County	0	0	.000	0.00	2	0	0	0	2	1	5.1	3	22	0	0	0	0	0	0	3	0	8	0	0
Moreno, Victor, Fort Myers	3	1	.750	2.03	16	0	0	0	6	0	26.2	21	115	9	6	1	1	0	1	14	1	32	2	0
Moser, Todd, Jupiter *	3	0	1.000	1.50	5	5	0	0	0	0	30.0	25	116	5	5	2	4	0	1	7	0	24	2	0
Musser, Neal, St. Lucie *	3	0	1.000	4.67	7	6	0	0	0	0	34.2	41	155	20	18	5	1	1	3	9	0	16	1	1
Myers, Damien, Lakeland *	2	3	.400	2.93	26	0	0	0	10	3	43.0	40	176	15	14	1	2	0	1	14	1	35	1	1
Nall, T.J., Vero Beach	6	7	.462	3.42	29	16	2	0	4	1	115.2	118	491	56	44	9	5	2	2	23	1	73	7	0
Narveson, Chris, P.B.*	7	7	.500	2.86	15	14	1	0	0	0	91.1	83	369	34	29	4	3	2	2	19	0	65	4	0
Nelson, Steve, Vero Beach	0	2	.000	2.08	4	3	1	0	0	0	17.1	12	68	4	4	1	0	1	1	5	0	20	0	0
Neshek, Pat, Fort Myers	4	1	.800	2.15	20	0	0	0	15	2	29.1	22	117	8	7	2	1	0	1	6	1	29	0	1
Nicolas, Mike, Brevard County	0	2	.000	3.65	8	0	0	0	3	1	12.1	8	54	5	5	0	3	0	4	4	1	12	3	0
Nina, Elvin, Vero Beach	0	0	.000	3.60	4	0	0	0	0	0	5.0	6	23	5	2	0	0	0	1	1	0	7	0	0
Nolasco, Ricky, Daytona	11	5	.688	2.96	26	26	1	0	0	0	149.0	129	620	58	49	7	5	4	8	48	0	136	12	1
Norderum, Jason, B.C.*	4	11	.267	5.29	25	18	0	0	2	0	98.2	117	444	66	58	5	5	7	4	33	0	59	5	1
Novinsky, John, Palm Beach	2	3	.400	3.18	37	0	0	0	31	16	45.1	41	189	16	16	5	2	2	1	16	6	36	1	0
Novoa, Roberto, Lakeland	4	5	.444	3.73	19	15	2	0	1	0	99.0	93	414	45	41	8	1	0	5	25	0	71	2	2
Nunley, Derrick, Dunedin	3	2	.600	2.20	42	0	0	0	18	1	57.1	41	246	17	14	1	2	1	2	36	1	64	12	2
O'Flaherty, Liam, V.B.*	0	1	.000	0.00	1	0	0	0	0	0	1.1	0	6	1	0	0	0	0	0	2	0	0	0	0
Obispo, Jose, Vero Beach	0	0	.000	2.40	4	4	0	0	0	0	15.0	7	72	4	4	1	1	0	0	20	0	17	2	0
Ojeda, Alvis, Vero Beach	0	1	.000	12.00	1	1	0	0	0	0	3.0	5	17	4	4	0	0	0	0	4	0	1	0	0
Olson, Justin, Fort Myers	2	0	1.000	2.25	6	0	0	0	5	1	8.0	9	37	2	2	0	1	0	0	5	0	6	0	0
Osoria, Franquelis, V.B.	3	6	.333	3.00	33	3	0	0	20	6	75.0	69	316	34	25	4	7	2	5	19	5	53	5	1
Ostlund, Ian, Lakeland *	0	1	.000	8.59	17	0	0	0	5	0	22.0	35	107	21	21	6	1	1	0	5	0	17	1	0
Osuna, Antonio, Tampa	0	0	.000	0.00	2	2	0	0	0	0	4.0	1	13	0	0	0	0	0	0	1	0	5	0	0
Ough, Wayne, St. Lucie	7	5	.583	2.86	22	14	1	0	3	1	103.2	84	424	37	33	3	5	1	2	37	0	97	6	0
Overman, Matt, Jupiter	0	2	.000	3.38	11	2	0	0	2	0	26.2	35	117	10	10	1	1	2	0	11	2	15	2	0
Ozuna, Francisco, Dunedin *	0	0	.000	5.79	11	0	0	0	0	0	14.0	16	69	13	9	1	1	2	3	8	0	8	0	0
Paddock, Josh, Clearwater	0	1	.000	5.55	20	1	0	0	6	1	35.2	45	167	30	22	2	1	2	1	13	1	17	2	0
Pahucki, David, Sarasota	3	8	.273	4.68	18	17	0	0	0	0	84.2	103	396	57	44	6	3	7	5	46	1	42	2	0
Painter, Lance, Palm Beach *	0	0	.000	0.00	1	1	0	0	0	0	1.0	0	3	0	0	0	0	0	0	0	0	1	0	0
Parker, Christian, Tampa	0	0	.000	1.80	1	1	0	0	0	0	5.0	6	19	1	1	0	0	0	1	1	0	6	0	0
Paulk, Robert, St. Lucie	1	1	.500	13.50	2	0	0	0	2	0	2.0	3	13	5	3	0	1	0	0	2	0	3	0	0
Pearce, Josh, Palm Beach	1	4	.200	3.21	6	5	0	0	0	0	28.0	28	108	10	10	2	2	1	1	2	0	15	1	0
Peeples, Ross, St. Lucie *	1	5	.167	5.31	14	7	0	0	4	1	57.2	69	267	43	34	7	4	2	2	21	0	30	2	0
Perez, Juan, Sarasota *	3	4	.429	2.37	33	0	0	0	24	18	38.0	34	165	15	10	0	2	3	0	12	2	37	4	0
Perkins, Vince, Dunedin	7	6	.538	2.45	18	17	0	0	0	0	84.1	58	351	32	23	1	2	3	4	53	0	69	7	0
Person, Robert, Sarasota	1	1	.500	2.92	7	7	0	0	0	0	24.2	27	102	12	8	1	0	0	0	6	0	17	0	0
Peterson, Adam, Dunedin	1	0	1.000	0.71	9	0	0	0	3	1	12.2	5	44	1	1	1	0	0	1	0	0	13	0	0
Peterson, Matt, St. Lucie	9	2	.818	1.71	15	15	1	0	0	0	84.0	65	337	24	16	2	3	0	3	24	0	73	5	1
Petty, Chad, Lakeland *	3	4	.429	4.40	10	10	0	0	0	0	57.1	66	252	35	28	3	3	4	5	10	0	36	4	0
Phelps, Tommy, Jupiter *	0	0	.000	6.00	2	1	0	0	0	0	3.0	5	14	2	2	0	0	0	0	0	0	3	0	0
Phillips, Mark, Tampa *	6	6	.500	5.76	16	13	0	0	1	0	70.1	63	316	48	45	2	3	5	4	51	0	50	3	1
Pignatiello, Carmen, Daytona*	8	11	.421	4.38	26	26	1	0	0	0	156.1	144	674	87	76	13	5	3	13	55	0	140	7	2
Pilkington, Brian, Vero Beach	10	6	.625	3.88	21	21	1	0	0	0	125.1	136	521	55	54	9	3	4	5	16	0	74	1	1
Pinto, Renyel, Daytona *	3	8	.273	3.22	20	19	0	0	0	0	114.2	91	476	47	41	4	6	4	9	45	1	104	6	3
Pleiness, Chad, Dunedin	7	8	.467	3.41	25	24	0	0	0	0	129.1	124	563	60	49	9	9	3	9	60	0	89	15	0
Pope, Justin, P.B.-Tampa	6	11	.353	4.60	22	18	1	1	1	0	115.1	130	502	71	59	9	5	0	5	34	0	72	5	0
Portobanco, Luz, St. Lucie	2	5	.286	5.69	16	10	0	0	1	1	61.2	63	287	47	39	5	3	1	9	36	0	38	7	2
Puello, Ignacio, B.C.	2	5	.286	6.45	18	9	0	0	5	1	53.0	57	242	40	38	2	3	2	7	24	1	27	5	1
Ramirez, Elizardo, Clearwater	13	9	.591	3.78	27	25	1	0	0	0	157.1	181	668	85	66	4	4	2	4	33	0	101	4	2
Ramirez, Emmanuel, Daytona	2	0	1.000	3.14	11	0	0	0	3	0	14.1	11	62	5	5	0	1	0	2	6	0	13	0	0
Ramirez, Ramon, Tampa	2	8	.200	5.21	14	14	0	0	0	0	74.1	88	327	47	43	7	1	2	2	20	2	70	3	1
Randazzo, Jeff, Fort Myers *	5	6	.455	4.66	20	17	0	0	0	0	87.0	95	383	53	45	6	4	2	4	40	1	35	5	0
Rawson, Anthony, P.B.*	0	4	.000	3.78	25	0	0	0	5	0	33.1	34	152	16	14	0	2	1	0	19	2	26	3	0
Reina, Dimas, Vero Beach	1	0	1.000	6.88	15	0	0	0	4	0	17.0	23	84	13	13	5	1	0	1	9	0	16	3	0

Pitcher, Team	W	L	Pct.	ERA	G	GS	CG	ShO	GF	Sv.	IP	H	TBF	R	ER	HR	SH	SF	HB	BB	IBB	SO	WP	Bk.
Reynolds, Josh, Sarasota	3	1	.750	3.53	23	7	0	0	9	2	58.2	61	247	27	23	3	2	1	7	8	1	49	1	1
Rhodes, Shane, Sarasota *	3	4	.429	3.39	39	0	0	0	14	1	61.0	61	281	36	23	4	3	2	7	29	1	43	10	1
Richardson, Jason, Ft. Myers	4	2	.667	3.78	46	2	0	0	9	0	88.0	77	373	38	37	3	3	3	9	42	2	60	11	0
Roberts, Grant, St. Lucie	1	0	1.000	0.00	5	2	0	0	0	0	9.0	5	36	4	0	0	0	1	0	3	0	5	0	0
Rodney, Lee, Lakeland	6	12	.333	4.26	27	23	0	0	0	0	133.0	150	579	69	63	7	2	6	9	44	0	103	2	0
Rodriguez, Cristobal, B.C.	0	0	.000	3.86	2	0	0	0	2	0	2.1	2	9	1	1	0	0	0	0	0	0	3	0	0
Rodriguez, Jose, B.C.*	0	0	.000	0.00	1	0	0	0	1	1	1.0	0	3	0	0	0	0	0	0	0	0	1	0	0
Rodriguez, Osvaldo, V.B.	0	1	.000	4.50	1	1	0	0	0	0	4.0	3	16	2	2	0	0	0	0	3	0	3	1	0
Rohlicek, Russ, Daytona *	2	3	.400	2.40	41	0	0	0	14	0	48.2	34	203	13	13	1	1	1	7	21	2	50	1	0
Rojas, Jose, Vero Beach	3	4	.429	5.00	14	6	0	0	2	0	36.0	34	167	23	20	4	0	1	5	27	0	29	3	1
Roman, Orlando, St. Lucie	3	5	.375	3.94	28	0	0	0	13	1	61.2	56	275	41	27	5	1	1	8	30	1	53	6	0
Romero, Josmir, Fort Myers	2	2	.500	2.40	5	2	0	0	0	0	15.0	12	60	8	4	1	0	0	0	4	0	6	2	0
Rudrude, Brett, Sarasota	4	7	.364	4.22	22	12	0	0	5	1	79.0	82	337	42	37	7	2	3	7	18	1	59	2	1
Rundles, Rich, B.C.*	5	6	.455	2.95	19	19	2	1	0	0	106.2	111	446	44	35	2	4	2	2	24	0	76	4	1
Runyon, Bob, Palm Beach	0	2	.000	9.00	5	1	0	0	3	0	11.0	19	58	12	11	1	1	2	0	5	1	3	0	0
Russ, James, Jupiter	0	1	.000	3.60	1	1	0	0	0	0	5.0	6	23	4	2	0	0	0	1	3	0	4	0	0
Russelburg, Aaron, P.B.	1	3	.250	6.52	6	4	0	0	0	0	19.1	19	88	19	14	0	2	2	3	7	0	12	0	0
Russell, Eddie, Jupiter	1	1	.500	3.78	10	0	0	0	3	1	16.2	19	79	10	7	0	1	0	2	15	0	9	4	2
Ryu, Jae-kuk, Daytona	0	1	.000	3.05	4	4	0	0	0	0	20.2	14	90	14	7	1	1	1	2	11	0	22	2	0
Sandoval, Marcos, Dunedin	0	0	.000	0.00	1	0	0	0	0	0	1.0	1	6	0	0	0	1	0	2	1	0	0	0	0
Santiago, Victor, Vero Beach	2	2	.500	6.56	10	2	0	0	1	1	23.1	28	116	23	17	3	2	0	1	17	0	15	7	2
Scalamandre, Rich, P.B.	1	0	1.000	2.45	4	0	0	0	1	0	3.2	6	17	1	1	0	0	0	0	0	0	2	0	0
Schultz, Cory, Clearwater	0	1	.000	4.41	9	0	0	0	5	1	16.1	21	70	8	8	0	3	1	1	2	0	13	0	1
Scobie, Jason, St. Lucie	2	1	.667	1.31	4	4	0	0	0	0	20.2	19	88	4	3	0	1	1	4	4	0	20	1	0
Seale, Dustin, B.C.*	1	0	1.000	4.12	9	1	0	0	7	2	19.2	24	87	11	9	1	0	1	1	7	1	9	0	0
Searles, Jon, Brevard County	2	3	.400	2.93	18	0	0	0	8	2	27.2	28	122	9	9	1	4	0	2	15	1	17	2	0
Silva, Efrain, Vero Beach	0	1	.000	2.54	16	0	0	0	3	0	28.1	19	118	8	8	1	1	0	0	17	0	37	2	1
Sloan, Brandon, Jupiter	2	5	.286	5.38	41	0	0	0	21	5	72.0	83	332	54	43	6	5	1	6	33	4	57	4	0
Smith, Bud, Clearwater *	1	0	1.000	1.47	4	2	0	0	0	0	18.1	10	67	3	3	0	0	1	0	4	0	12	0	0
Smith, Chris, Sarasota	2	0	1.000	0.00	2	2	0	0	0	0	12.0	8	47	2	0	0	0	0	1	2	0	9	0	0
Smith, Jared, Palm Beach	2	3	.400	3.09	45	5	0	0	10	1	75.2	63	323	28	26	1	6	1	3	44	2	70	8	0
Smith, Jason, Tampa	0	0	.000	2.19	6	1	0	0	1	0	12.1	7	49	4	3	1	2	0	1	7	0	4	0	0
Smith, Matt, Tampa *	2	3	.400	2.23	6	6	0	0	0	0	32.1	20	131	11	8	0	0	4	1	12	0	25	1	0
Squires, Matt, Clearwater *	4	2	.667	1.86	41	0	0	0	16	2	63.0	61	263	14	13	1	3	2	0	23	1	52	5	2
Steffek, Brian, Vero Beach	0	1	.000	0.99	23	0	0	0	16	10	27.1	16	110	6	3	1	1	0	2	13	1	32	2	0
Stevenson, Jason, B.C.*	9	6	.600	2.62	36	11	0	0	6	0	113.1	88	455	36	33	4	6	3	4	33	1	60	4	0
Stewart, James, Vero Beach	0	0	.000	11.57	4	0	0	0	1	0	4.2	7	22	6	6	2	1	0	0	2	0	2	0	0
Stewart, Scott, B.C.*	0	0	.000	0.00	2	2	0	0	0	0	3.2	1	13	0	0	0	0	0	0	1	0	4	0	0
Stockman, Landon, Lakeland	2	3	.400	5.20	44	0	0	0	33	7	53.2	54	256	41	31	3	6	7	7	37	0	31	10	1
Strayhorn, Kole, V.B.-St. Lucie	6	3	.667	2.49	46	0	0	0	32	17	61.1	49	256	19	17	2	3	1	2	22	1	60	4	0
Stults, Eric, Vero Beach *	0	1	.000	6.00	1	1	0	0	0	0	3.0	6	13	2	2	0	0	0	0	1	0	1	0	0
Szuminski, Jason, Daytona	2	1	.667	3.65	13	0	0	0	5	0	24.2	29	111	12	10	0	2	1	1	9	1	23	0	0
Teekel, Josh, Palm Beach	0	0	.000	13.50	1	0	0	0	0	0	0.2	2	4	2	1	0	1	0	0	0	0	0	0	0
Tejada, Manny, Fort Myers	1	0	1.000	1.88	8	6	0	0	1	0	24.0	9	98	5	5	1	0	0	2	20	0	20	0	0
Tejeda, Rob, Clearwater	2	4	.333	3.20	11	11	1	0	0	0	64.2	53	267	25	23	4	2	0	2	23	0	42	3	0
Tequida, Mauricio, Vero Beach	0	0	.000	0.00	3	0	0	0	1	0	9.1	4	35	0	0	0	0	0	0	3	0	3	0	0
Thompson, Bradley, P.B.	1	0	1.000	0.00	2	1	0	0	0	0	6.0	3	20	0	0	0	1	0	0	0	0	4	0	0
Thompson, Matt, Sarasota	2	3	.400	4.70	20	0	0	0	4	1	30.2	32	146	21	16	1	4	2	0	19	1	19	3	0
Torres, Andy, Dunedin	4	3	.571	2.16	43	0	0	0	16	5	75.0	62	299	24	18	4	2	2	0	23	1	67	1	0
Torres, Luis, Brevard County	1	3	.250	5.55	30	3	0	0	12	3	58.1	71	267	36	36	6	2	2	2	24	0	40	9	0
Ulloa, Enmanuel, B.C.	0	2	.000	2.21	5	3	0	0	0	0	20.1	17	85	6	5	0	2	1	2	6	0	15	1	0
Ungs, Nic, Jupiter	8	3	.727	1.99	18	17	1	0	1	0	113.1	92	437	28	25	5	4	1	3	14	0	80	0	0
Urquhart, Derick, B.C.*	0	0	.000	13.50	2	0	0	0	2	0	1.1	2	7	2	2	0	0	0	1	0	0	1	0	0
Valdez, Jose, Tampa	1	1	.500	4.02	3	3	0	0	0	0	15.2	11	61	7	7	2	1	1	0	4	0	9	1	0
Valdez, Santo, Dunedin	2	2	.500	4.90	41	3	0	0	15	1	79.0	96	356	46	43	6	3	5	2	25	1	46	1	0
Vermilyea, Jamie, Dunedin	0	2	.000	2.49	9	0	0	0	3	2	21.2	21	86	6	6	1	0	0	1	2	1	25	1	0
Villalon, Julio, Palm Beach	1	0	1.000	1.50	1	1	0	0	0	0	6.0	3	22	1	1	0	0	0	0	1	0	7	0	0
Villegas, Felix, Sarasota	1	2	.333	1.23	10	2	0	0	3	0	22.0	17	93	3	3	0	1	1	1	11	0	15	0	0
Villegas, Francisco, Tampa	3	0	1.000	3.22	22	0	0	0	10	3	36.1	28	156	15	13	3	3	0	1	21	0	34	0	2
Vorwald, Matt, Fort Myers	3	1	.750	5.40	15	0	0	0	9	0	15.0	16	70	14	9	2	1	0	3	6	1	13	3	0
Washburn, Ben, B.C.	1	1	.500	2.77	8	0	0	0	2	0	13.0	15	59	7	4	0	0	0	0	3	0	5	1	1
Watkins, Tommy, Fort Myers	0	0	.000	0.00	2	0	0	0	2	0	2.0	0	6	0	0	0	0	0	0	0	0	1	0	0
Wayne, Justin, Jupiter	0	0	.000	0.00	1	1	0	0	0	0	6.0	6	24	0	0	0	0	0	0	0	0	4	0	0
Wendell, Turk, Clearwater	0	0	.000	0.00	5	5	0	0	0	0	6.0	3	21	0	0	0	0	0	0	0	0	5	0	0
White, Gabe, Tampa *	0	0	.000	0.00	1	1	0	0	0	0	0.2	1	3	0	0	0	0	0	0	0	0	0	0	0
White, Matt, Sarasota *	0	0	.000	0.00	2	2	0	0	0	0	5.0	6	22	1	0	0	0	0	0	1	0	2	0	0
Williams, Blake, Palm Beach	2	10	.167	4.36	20	16	0	0	1	1	84.2	81	382	55	41	7	6	6	7	33	1	56	6	3
Williams, Ryan, Vero Beach	3	4	.429	4.03	19	0	0	0	9	1	29.0	32	132	20	13	2	1	1	1	15	0	18	0	0
Wolfe, Brian, Fort Myers	2	1	.667	2.53	7	7	0	0	0	0	46.1	41	185	15	13	3	0	1	1	6	0	22	2	0
Woodyard, Mark, Lakeland	4	8	.333	4.53	23	23	1	0	0	0	117.1	133	526	69	59	7	4	2	4	53	2	84	10	0
Wynegar, Adam, Daytona *	1	3	.250	5.40	19	0	0	0	10	1	25.0	21	129	21	15	2	6	2	8	27	2	14	3	0
Yates, Tyler, St. Lucie	1	2	.333	4.31	14	11	0	0	0	0	48.0	41	205	28	23	5	0	2	2	24	0	49	2	0
Yeatman, Matt, Fort Myers	6	11	.353	5.16	25	25	0	0	0	0	129.0	134	577	79	74	12	3	1	6	64	1	100	15	0
Young, Chris, Brevard County	5	2	.714	1.62	8	8	0	0	0	0	50.0	26	180	9	9	3	1	0	1	5	0	39	0	0
Zink, Charlie, Sarasota	7	9	.438	3.90	24	19	2	0	0	0	136.0	123	576	69	59	10	0	6	4	64	0	94	3	1

PITCHERS WITH TWO OR MORE TEAMS

Pitcher, Team	W	L	Pct.	ERA	G	GS	CG	ShO	GF	Sv.	IP	H	TBF	R	ER	HR	SH	SF	HB	BB	IBB	SO	WP	Bk.
Bicondoa, Ryan, St. Lucie	1	1	.500	3.42	5	4	0	0	1	1	26.1	30	119	12	10	1	2	0	0	10	0	16	1	1
Bicondoa, Ryan, Tampa	3	2	.600	3.54	15	5	0	0	3	0	48.1	48	205	23	19	0	2	2	3	20	1	30	1	1
Diaz, Joselo, St. Lucie	2	2	.500	2.97	11	2	0	0	2	1	30.1	16	131	12	10	0	1	1	5	25	0	41	5	2
Diaz, Joselo, Vero Beach	5	2	.714	3.50	15	11	0	0	2	1	61.2	39	273	25	24	2	4	0	5	48	1	69	4	4
Strayhorn, Kole, Vero Beach	5	2	.714	2.93	30	0	0	0	17	7	46.0	42	195	17	15	2	2	0	2	13	0	44	3	0
Strayhorn, Kole, St. Lucie	1	1	.500	1.17	16	0	0	0	15	10	15.1	7	61	2	2	0	1	1	0	9	1	16	1	0

COMBINATION SHUTOUTS: Brevard County (13)—Caputo-Torres-Maust-Norderum, Puello-Stevenson-Davis-Maust, Mata-Puello, Young-Davis-Maust-Corcoran, Young-Corcoran, Young-Stevenson-Corcoran, Stevenson-Dequin-Davis, Hill-Davis-Torres, Hill-Davis-Cordero, Hill-Dequin, Stevenson-Cordero, Rundles-Ulloa-Caputo-Cordero, Hinckley-Cordero. Clearwater (10)—Ramirez-Korecky, Floyd-Miller, Coggin-Astacio, Ramirez-Brito, Astacio-Paddock-Squires-Korecky, Bucktrot-Korecky, Cable-Brito, Ramirez-Squires, Astacio-Brito-Korecky, Ramirez-Squires. Daytona (10)—Benik-Anderson-Rohlicek-Blasdell, Ryu-Mitchell-Anderson, Blasko-Ferreras-Blasdell, Blasko-Martin-Blasdell, Brownlie-Rohlicek-Wynegar-Benik, Nolasco-Martin-Wynegar, Blasko-Rohlicek, Pignatiello-Blasdell, Mitchell-Fernley-Blasdell, Blasko-Christensen. Dunedin (11)—McGowan-Harper-Esarey-Valdez, Pleiness-Cardwell, Pleiness-Torres-Nunley-DeJong, Perkins-Torres, Bush-Peterson-Maureau, McGowan-Peterson-Cardwell-DeJong, Pleiness-Torres-Peterson, Harper-Ozuna-Nunley, League-Maureau-Valdez, File-Perkins-Nunley-Torres, Flores-Vermilyea. Fort Myers (11)—Wolfe-Bowyer-Daws, Miller-Crain, Wolfe-Crain, Durbin-Richardson-Vorwald, Abbott-Holubec-Gutierrez, Durbin-Richardson-Kemp, Miller-Kemp, Yeatman-Miller-Kemp, Miller-Richardson-Neshek-Kemp, Miller-Gutierrez, Holubec-Romero-Gutierrez. Jupiter (11)—Wayne-Hutchinson, Levinski-Key-Fuell, Ungs-Fuell, Hutchinson-McNutt-Haynes-Sloan, Ungs-Fuell-Cave, Bautista-McNutt, Florian-Key-Cave, Beckett-Ungs, Ungs-Fuell-Cave, Fulchino-Greusel, Olsen-Phelps-Key-Blalock. Lakeland (8)—Woodyard-Moates-Ostlund-Stockman, Rodney-Ostlund-Stockman, Petty-Moates-Hamman-Ostlund, McDowell-Hamman-Stockman, Moates-Birtwell, Leu-Hamman-Birtwell-Kobow, Leu-Kobow, Novoa-Myers-Kobow. Palm Beach (7)—Narveson-Lambert-Kinney, Pope-Cook-Kinney-Novinsky, Narveson-Novinsky, Williams-Cook-Johnson-Smith-Novinsky, Correa-Cali, Correa-Thompson-Scalamandre-Estes, Thompson-Estes-Cali. St. Lucie (10)—Scobie-Roman-Eckert-Lopez, Ough-Cox, Peeples-Bennett, Peterson-Dinardo, Yates-Elliott, Chenard-Cox, Peterson-Elliott, Peterson-Cox, Portobanco-Dinardo-Lopez, Dinardo-Lopez-Strayhorn. Sarasota (10)—Miniel-Thompson-Howell, Delcarmen-Rudrude-Thompson, Rudrude-Rhodes-Howell-Perez, Dumatrait-Thompson-Reynolds, Dumatrait-Thompson-DeJesus-Perez, Reynolds-Howell-Perez, Mendoza-Dumatrait, Clelland-Byron, Gamble-Reynolds, Reynolds-Howell. Tampa (8)—Martinez-Cooksey-Brumit-Mendoza, Bell-Cooksey-Brumit, Halsey-Artiles-Brazoban, Claussen-Kennard, Henn-Kremer, Smith-Kennard-Blankenship, Garcia-Moore-Blankenship, Garcia-Kennard. Vero Beach (7)—Miller-Frasor-Lopez-Steffek, Osoria-Diaz-Hull-Steffek, Pilkington-Reina-Steffek, Pilkington-Reina, Diaz-Minor-Strayhorn-Frasor, Nall-Strayhorn-Reina-Minor, Miller-Hull-Strayhorn.

NO-HIT GAMES: None.

2003 FIELDING

TEAM

Team	G	PO	A	E	TC	DP	TP	PB	Pct.
Fort Myers	136	3543	1382	106	5031	121	0	23	.979
Dunedin	140	3563	1364	117	5044	104	0	23	.977
Clearwater	133	3446	1432	126	5004	126	0	21	.975
Jupiter	138	3580	1509	143	5232	141	0	29	.973
Lakeland	133	3383	1391	143	4917	140	0	15	.971
Sarasota	130	3377	1364	143	4884	131	0	34	.971
Tampa	132	3381	1363	141	4885	108	0	20	.971
Vero Beach	131	3436	1334	149	4919	119	0	14	.970
Brevard Co.	131	3353	1400	150	4903	103	0	17	.969
St. Lucie	139	3558	1399	159	5116	124	0	12	.969
Palm Beach	138	3615	1459	167	5241	123	0	24	.968
Daytona	137	3596	1329	180	5105	106	0	14	.965

INDIVIDUAL

FIRST BASEMEN

NOTE: All caps denotes fielding-percentage leader based on 70 games for catchers, 93 for all other non-pitchers and 112 innings for pitchers. *Throws lefthanded.

Player, Team	Pct.	G	PO	A	E	TC	DP
Abreu, Dennis, Palm Beach	1.000	2	11	2	0	13	1
Ambrosini, Dominick, B.C.*	.973	7	64	7	2	73	7
Anderson, Dennis, Jupiter	1.000	1	10	1	0	11	4
Avila, Rob, Clearwater	1.000	2	17	2	0	19	2
Bailie, Stefan, Sarasota	.974	52	448	33	13	494	50
Bernhardt, Joe, Dunedin	1.000	4	44	6	0	50	1
Bledsoe, Hunter, Tampa	.992	42	339	19	3	361	26
Blum, Greg, Fort Myers	1.000	1	10	0	0	10	2
Bouras, Brad, Daytona	.978	29	209	9	5	223	16
Broadway, Larry, B.C.*	1.000	20	178	17	0	195	19
Calabrese, Tony, St. Lucie	1.000	8	50	2	0	52	8
Calitri, Mike, Sarasota	.987	60	486	38	7	531	56
Callahan, Dave, Sarasota *	1.000	1	15	0	0	15	2
Carroll, Wes, Brevard County	1.000	1	2	0	0	2	0
Clark, Tony, St. Lucie	1.000	1	8	2	0	10	0
Coomer, Ron, Vero Beach	1.000	2	19	0	0	19	4
Corr, Frank, St. Lucie	.977	61	520	28	13	561	47
Creighton, Matt, Daytona	1.000	10	70	3	0	73	7
Deschaine, Jim, Clearwater	1.000	1	7	0	0	7	1
Duncan, Chris, Palm Beach	.987	116	984	63	14	1061	87
Durazo, William, Sarasota	1.000	11	82	4	0	86	6
Esposito, Brian, Sarasota	1.000	1	3	1	0	4	0
Fernandez, Alejandro, Tampa	.889	1	8	0	1	9	1
Gillitzer, Scott, Vero Beach	1.000	4	12	2	0	14	2
Harper, Brett, St. Lucie	.989	11	83	8	1	92	5
Hattig, John, Sarasota	.900	1	8	1	1	10	0
Hicks, Scott, Jupiter	.989	12	82	8	1	91	6
Hoffpauir, Micah, Daytona *	.993	95	775	44	6	825	68
Hoorelbeke, Jesse, Vero Beach	.979	11	88	4	2	94	2
Howard, Ryan, Clearwater *	.991	116	1044	89	10	1143	102
Jarvis, Andrew, Clearwater *	1.000	3	26	9	0	35	5
Jones, Garrett, Fort Myers *	.994	110	889	84	6	979	95
Jones, Garrett, Fort Myers *	.994	110	889	84	6	979	95
Kay, Brett, St. Lucie	1.000	8	57	6	0	63	3
Keene, Kurt, Dunedin	1.000	2	20	1	0	21	0
Kelly, Donald, Lakeland	1.000	15	135	17	0	152	18
Kropf, Andy, Lakeland	1.000	4	25	3	0	28	3
Lambin, Chase, St. Lucie	1.000	1	7	1	0	8	1
Lane, Rich, Brevard County *	.986	32	255	20	4	279	14
LONEY, JAMES, Vero Beach *	.994	110	871	89	6	966	80
Lugo, Alfredo, Lakeland	1.000	1	5	1	0	6	1
Mauer, Jake, Fort Myers	1.000	4	28	3	0	31	3
Mauer, Joe, Fort Myers	1.000	1	1	0	0	1	1
McEachran, Aaron, Dunedin	1.000	3	25	2	0	27	0
McGowan, Sean, Sarasota	.986	8	63	5	1	69	9
McGriff, Fred, Vero Beach *	1.000	1	1	1	0	2	0
O'Toole, Paul, Daytona	1.000	6	45	2	0	47	1
Phelps, Jeff, Clearwater	1.000	2	7	0	0	7	0
Pressley, Josh, St. Lucie	.987	55	446	26	6	478	46
Roman, Jesse, Palm Beach *	1.000	14	83	8	0	91	9
Roughton, Jody, Lakeland	1.000	5	36	0	0	36	4
Schutzenhofer, Andy, P.B.*	.992	13	117	8	1	126	10
Segar, Jeff, Tampa	.986	76	656	41	10	707	59
Seguignol, Fernando, Tampa	1.000	2	18	2	0	20	2
Sing, Brandon, Daytona	1.000	2	16	0	0	16	1
Snyder, Mike, Dunedin	.983	131	1055	82	20	1157	96
Stokes, Jason, Jupiter	.987	101	878	68	12	958	93
Story-Harden, Thomari, V.B.	1.000	10	90	5	0	95	10
Tablado, Raul, Dunedin	1.000	2	12	1	0	13	0
Tejeda, Juan, Lakeland	.985	110	895	67	15	977	102
Tope, Stephen, Fort Myers	1.000	19	127	20	0	147	8
Tucker, Michael, Jupiter	1.000	21	174	11	0	185	21
Turner, Jason, Tampa *	.985	13	127	8	2	137	12
Walsh, Sean, Clearwater	1.000	14	119	8	0	127	10
Watkins, Tommy, Fort Myers	1.000	8	51	6	0	57	3
Williams, Clyde, B.C.*	.990	79	673	55	7	735	55
Williams, Matt, Palm Beach	1.000	1	8	0	0	8	0
Willingham, Josh, Jupiter	.976	9	72	8	2	82	5

SECOND BASEMEN

Player, Team	Pct.	G	PO	A	E	TC	DP
Abreu, Dennis, Palm Beach	1.000	1	1	0	0	1	0
Abreu, Etanislao, Vero Beach	1.000	3	2	5	0	7	0
Aybar, Willy, Vero Beach	1.000	1	4	7	0	11	2
Bacani, David, St. Lucie	1.000	2	2	1	0	3	0
Blasi, Blake, Sarasota-P.B.	.950	74	127	216	18	361	43
Borowiak, Zachary, Sarasota	1.000	1	4	6	0	10	2
Boyd, Shaun, Palm Beach	.918	42	94	107	18	219	23
Calabrese, Tony, St. Lucie	1.000	1	2	3	0	5	1
Cano, Robinson, Tampa	.970	88	165	250	13	428	54
Carroll, Wes, Brevard County	.865	13	21	24	7	52	4
Castillo, Osmar, Sarasota	1.000	2	6	4	0	10	0
Castro, Nelson, Vero Beach	.966	13	19	38	2	59	6
Cedeno, Ronny, Daytona	.935	28	53	77	9	139	13
Clute, Kris, Jupiter	1.000	14	21	32	0	53	5
Creighton, Matt, Daytona	.923	2	6	6	1	13	1
Delfino, Lee, Dunedin	.971	40	66	104	5	175	17
DeMarco, Matt, Jupiter	.980	78	142	248	8	398	69
Deschaine, Jim, Clearwater	.957	5	9	13	1	23	3
Detienne, Dave, Vero Beach	1.000	3	8	4	0	12	3
Dorta, Melvin, Sarasota	.971	86	176	260	13	449	61
Easterday, Matt, Jupiter	.976	60	96	144	6	246	28
Ferrer, Simon, Vero Beach	.974	17	27	48	2	77	5
Galante, Matt, St. Lucie	.958	20	26	65	4	95	11
Garcia, Sergio, Vero Beach	.963	45	83	124	8	215	24

Player, Team	Pct.	G	PO	A	E	TC	DP
Garcia, Tony, Palm Beach	.984	37	76	110	3	189	30
Gillitzer, Scott, Vero Beach	.975	57	108	122	6	236	35
Goelz, Jim, Sarasota	1.000	1	3	1	0	4	1
Housel, David, St. Lucie	.981	12	26	26	1	53	10
Jiannetti, Joe, St. Lucie	.933	45	66	128	14	208	20
Keene, Kurt, Dunedin	1.000	5	7	15	0	22	0
Kelly, Donald, Lakeland	1.000	2	1	5	0	6	2
Koutnik, Jared, Tampa	.959	15	27	43	3	73	6
Kuhaulua, Kaulana, Fort Myers	.963	7	12	14	1	27	5
Lambin, Chase, St. Lucie	.960	55	112	152	11	275	37
Lugo, Alfredo, Lakeland	.983	12	26	33	1	60	10
Macha, Erick, Tampa	.980	11	16	32	1	49	2
Mauer, Jake, Fort Myers	.978	17	12	32	1	45	7
Mayorson, Manuel, Dunedin	.990	87	139	262	4	405	45
MAZA, LUIS, Fort Myers	.973	104	194	269	13	476	66
McIntyre, Robert, St. Lucie	.956	7	16	27	2	45	6
Mendez, Deivi, Tampa	.955	4	10	11	1	22	1
Monahan, Joey, Daytona	.966	7	10	18	1	29	3
Montanez, Luis, Daytona	.952	82	163	213	19	395	50
Norris, Shawn, Brevard County	.987	30	63	84	2	149	16
Phelps, Jeff, Clearwater	.000	1	0	0	0	0	0
Schnabel, Nick, Brevard County	.975	39	63	90	4	157	19
Shanks, Eric, Sarasota	.965	23	44	65	4	113	17
Spearman, Jemel, Daytona	.968	19	36	54	3	93	14
Sterner, George, Tampa	.917	14	19	25	4	48	13
Stone, Greg, Sarasota	1.000	4	8	12	0	20	1
Tablado, Raul, Dunedin	1.000	13	19	41	0	60	11
Tamburrino, Brett, Fort Myers	1.000	9	12	20	0	32	4
Tempesta, Nick, Clearwater	1.000	5	1	7	0	8	0
Thissen, Greg, Brevard County	.959	68	114	188	13	315	37
Van Buizen, Rodney, Vero Beach	.957	12	20	24	2	46	7
Vasquez, Willie, Tampa	.889	3	4	12	2	18	1
Walsh, Sean, Clearwater	1.000	3	3	5	0	8	0
Wardinsky, Ryan, Clearwater	.970	34	51	113	5	169	25
Watkins, Tommy, Fort Myers	.980	9	20	28	1	49	6
Watson, Rob, Lakeland	.982	9	22	32	1	55	10
Woods, Michael, Lakeland	.964	114	232	309	20	561	74
Youngbauer, Scott, Clearwater	.964	90	147	279	16	442	56

SECOND BASEMEN WITH TWO OR MORE TEAMS

Player, Team	Pct.	G	PO	A	E	TC	DP
Blasi, Blake, Sarasota	.918	15	18	38	5	61	8
Blasi, Blake, Palm Beach	.957	59	109	178	13	300	35

THIRD BASEMEN

Player, Team	Pct.	G	PO	A	E	TC	DP
Abreu, Dennis, Palm Beach	1.000	9	8	23	0	31	2
Avila, Rob, Clearwater	.875	3	2	5	1	8	0
Aybar, Willy, Vero Beach	.944	110	87	199	17	303	29
Bernhardt, Joe, Dunedin	.667	1	0	2	1	3	0
Berroa, Cristian, Brevard County	1.000	4	5	9	0	14	0
Blasi, Blake, Sarasota	1.000	9	5	17	0	22	2
Boran, Patrick, Sarasota	.846	8	8	14	4	26	1
Calabrese, Tony, St. Lucie	.875	5	1	6	1	8	0
Calitri, Mike, Sarasota	.500	1	0	1	1	2	0
Carroll, Wes, Brevard County	.902	19	16	39	6	61	2
Castillo, Osmar, Sarasota	.926	10	6	19	2	27	3
Christensen, Mike, Fort Myers	.982	21	15	40	1	56	4
Concepcion, Alberto, Sarasota	.000	1	0	0	0	0	0
Coomer, Ron, Vero Beach	1.000	1	1	1	0	2	0
Corporan, Elvis, Tampa	.913	114	63	198	25	286	6
COSBY, ROB, Dunedin	.957	122	82	185	12	279	18
Craig, Matt, Daytona	.917	105	70	194	24	288	20
Delfino, Lee, Dunedin	.941	12	5	11	1	17	2
DeMarco, Matt, Jupiter	1.000	20	8	32	0	40	5
Detienne, Dave, Vero Beach	1.000	6	3	8	0	11	0
Diaz, Felix, Brevard County	.778	2	2	5	2	9	0
Dorta, Melvin, Sarasota	.667	2	1	1	1	3	0
Ellerson, Brian, Brevard County	.800	1	0	4	1	5	0
Ferrer, Simon, Vero Beach	.500	2	1	0	1	2	0
Garcia, Tony, Palm Beach	.951	12	8	31	2	41	5
Gillitzer, Scott, Vero Beach	.824	9	6	8	3	17	0
Goelz, Jim, Sarasota	1.000	1	0	2	0	2	0
Hattig, John, Sarasota	.925	97	71	199	22	292	21
Hoorelbeke, Jesse, Vero Beach	.900	3	0	9	1	10	2
Johnson, Gabe, Palm Beach	.918	99	82	163	22	267	17
Keene, Kurt, Dunedin	.929	6	6	7	1	14	0
Kelly, Donald, Lakeland	.957	34	30	58	4	92	9
Koutnik, Jared, Tampa	.941	18	9	39	3	51	0
Kuhaulua, Kaulana, Fort Myers	.000	1	0	0	0	0	0
Lugo, Alfredo, Lakeland	.942	19	6	43	3	52	6
Macha, Erick, Tampa	.667	1	0	2	1	3	0
Mauer, Jake, Fort Myers	1.000	16	9	21	0	30	2
McIntyre, Robert, St. Lucie	.900	6	3	6	1	10	0
Monahan, Joey, Daytona	.750	5	1	8	3	12	2
Morales, Jose, Fort Myers	.800	3	2	2	1	5	0
Norris, Shawn, Brevard County	.909	20	11	49	6	66	5
O'Toole, Paul, Daytona	.667	1	2	0	1	3	0
Phelps, Jeff, Clearwater	.894	71	50	136	22	208	12
Raburn, Ryan, Lakeland	.911	84	53	163	21	237	20
Rodgers, Albert, Palm Beach	.824	13	6	22	6	34	3
Rohan, Jimmy, Vero Beach	.933	5	3	11	1	15	1
Rooi, Vince, Brevard County	.920	90	55	176	20	251	13
Sandoval, Michael, Fort Myers	.924	69	48	98	12	158	6
Santos, Jose, Jupiter	.943	42	19	80	6	105	7
Schnabel, Nick, Brevard County	.000	2	0	0	0	0	0
Soto, Geovany, Daytona	1.000	1	0	2	0	2	0
Spearman, Jemel, Daytona	.921	30	12	58	6	76	3
Sterner, George, Tampa	.000	1	0	0	0	0	0
Stone, Greg, Sarasota	.889	4	0	8	1	9	0
Tablado, Raul, Dunedin	1.000	3	3	4	0	7	1
Tamburrino, Brett, Fort Myers	1.000	8	7	16	0	23	2
Tempesta, Nick, Clearwater	.000	1	0	0	0	0	0
Thissen, Greg, Brevard County	1.000	2	1	7	0	8	2
Tucker, Michael, Jupiter	.922	86	50	152	17	219	14
Van Buizen, Rodney, Vero Beach	.875	2	1	6	1	8	1
Voshell, Chase, Palm Beach	.667	1	0	2	1	3	0
Walsh, Sean, Clearwater	.935	60	40	89	9	138	6
Wardinsky, Ryan, Clearwater	1.000	2	0	2	0	2	0
Watkins, Tommy, Fort Myers	.887	28	17	46	8	71	4
Watson, Rob, Lakeland	1.000	1	1	3	0	4	0
Whittaker, Tim, Dunedin	.000	1	0	0	0	0	0
Williams, Matt, Palm Beach	.917	7	10	12	2	24	4
Willingham, Josh, Jupiter	1.000	2	3	1	0	4	0
Wright, David, St. Lucie	.951	130	70	243	16	329	17

SHORTSTOPS

Player, Team	Pct.	G	PO	A	E	TC	DP
Adams, Russ, Dunedin	.941	66	114	187	19	320	34
Aybar, Willy, Vero Beach	1.000	1	1	3	0	4	0
Bacani, David, St. Lucie	.976	22	22	58	2	82	7
Berroa, Cristian, Brevard County	1.000	4	10	9	0	19	3
Blasi, Blake, Sarasota	.921	11	13	22	3	38	9
Boran, Patrick, Sarasota	.867	10	15	24	6	45	9
Borowiak, Zachary, Sarasota	.967	26	56	63	4	123	20
Calabrese, Tony, St. Lucie	.917	4	6	5	1	12	1
Carroll, Wes, Brevard County	.954	44	47	118	8	173	21
Castillo, Osmar, Sarasota	.962	5	11	14	1	26	5
Castro, Nelson, Vero Beach	1.000	3	8	4	0	12	1
Cedeno, Ronny, Daytona	.944	77	121	217	20	358	46
Craig, Matt, Daytona	1.000	1	1	3	0	4	0
DeMarco, Matt, Jupiter	.976	23	27	55	2	84	14
Detienne, Dave, Vero Beach	.875	15	14	35	7	56	8
Dorta, Melvin, Sarasota	1.000	1	1	3	0	4	0
Espada, Joe, Palm Beach	.946	46	81	145	13	239	28
Ferrer, Simon, Vero Beach	.000	1	0	0	0	0	0
Garcia, Sergio, Vero Beach	.947	17	24	47	4	75	5
Garcia, Tony, Palm Beach	.936	38	62	98	11	171	22
Goelz, Jim, Sarasota	1.000	4	7	13	0	20	7
GONZALEZ, DANIEL, Clearwater	.964	113	175	358	20	553	85
Guzman, Joel, Vero Beach	.921	60	77	155	20	252	34
Hernandez, Anderson, Lakeland	.947	102	160	304	26	490	62
Herrera, Christian, Vero Beach	.926	40	72	102	14	188	22
Hill, Aaron, Dunedin	.930	30	41	65	8	114	16
Jaramillo, Milko, Palm Beach	.954	35	43	101	7	151	18
Jiannetti, Joe, St. Lucie	1.000	1	1	1	0	2	1
Keene, Kurt, Dunedin	1.000	1	3	0	0	3	0
Kelly, Donald, Lakeland	.967	20	32	56	3	91	18
Koutnik, Jared, Tampa	.960	46	52	114	7	173	26
Kuhaulua, Kaulana, Fort Myers	1.000	1	2	5	0	7	1
Labandeira, John, B.C.	.949	57	77	146	12	235	23
Lambin, Chase, St. Lucie	.927	49	73	131	16	220	38
Mauer, Jake, Fort Myers	.983	68	111	185	5	301	36
Mayorson, Manuel, Dunedin	.959	20	25	45	3	73	8
McIntyre, Robert, St. Lucie	.917	50	74	126	18	218	36
Mendez, Deivi, Tampa	.976	26	45	77	3	125	13
Monahan, Joey, Daytona	.867	11	8	18	4	30	2
Montanez, Luis, Daytona	.921	33	44	84	11	139	12
Moore, Jason, Palm Beach	.954	19	22	61	4	87	13
Norris, Shawn, Brevard County	.947	5	5	13	1	19	4
Perez, Kenny, Sarasota	.972	62	86	155	7	248	22
Ramos, Jason, Sarasota	.960	6	8	16	1	25	6
Rundgren, Rex, Jupiter	.956	119	204	387	27	618	84
Schnabel, Nick, Brevard County	.929	18	23	42	5	70	9

Player, Team	Pct.	G	PO	A	E	TC	DP
Schrager, Tony, Sarasota	.900	4	7	11	2	20	5
Spearman, Jemel, Daytona	.909	19	31	39	7	77	7
Sterner, George, Tampa	1.000	2	0	1	0	1	0
Stone, Greg, Sarasota	1.000	2	5	1	0	6	0
Tablado, Raul, Dunedin	.920	25	34	70	9	113	12
Tejeda, Ferdin, Tampa	.956	48	67	174	11	252	34
Tempesta, Nick, Clearwater	1.000	4	5	12	0	17	1
Thissen, Greg, Brevard County	.938	9	16	29	3	48	7
Vasquez, Willie, Tampa	.905	16	17	40	6	63	7
Velazquez, Gil, St. Lucie	.948	19	27	46	4	77	8
Velazquez, Juan, Fort Myers	.956	59	102	138	11	251	35
Veracierto, Fernando, Sarasota	.958	6	12	11	1	24	2
Wardinsky, Ryan, Clearwater	.933	20	28	42	5	75	9
Watkins, Tommy, Fort Myers	.914	17	20	54	7	81	9
Watson, Rob, Lakeland	.968	16	31	61	3	95	10

OUTFIELDERS

Player, Team	Pct.	G	PO	A	E	TC	DP
Abreu, Dennis, Palm Beach	1.000	1	1	0	0	1	0
Acevedo, Carlos, Clearwater	.963	11	23	3	1	27	1
Alvarez, Renyel, Fort Myers *	.979	29	44	2	1	47	0
Ambrosini, Dominick, B.C.*	.971	92	160	5	5	170	1
Aponte, Jose, Jupiter	.958	12	22	1	1	24	0
Asadoorian, Rick, Palm Beach	.979	42	90	4	2	96	0
Asche, Kirk, Palm Beach	.967	14	27	2	1	30	0
Avila, Rob, Clearwater	1.000	1	1	0	0	1	0
Bacon, Dwaine, Daytona	.969	101	185	5	6	196	1
Bailie, Stefan, Sarasota	.667	1	2	0	1	3	0
Barclay, Mike, Sarasota	1.000	28	39	4	0	43	0
Benjamin, Al, Palm Beach	.981	24	50	2	1	53	0
Blasi, Blake, Sarasota	1.000	1	2	0	0	2	0
Boran, Patrick, Sarasota	1.000	2	2	0	0	2	0
Bost, Tom, Jupiter	.934	50	80	5	6	91	0
Bouras, Brad, Daytona	1.000	1	1	0	0	1	0
Boyd, Shaun, Palm Beach	.979	50	137	3	3	143	0
Brown, Andy, Tampa *	.980	80	136	8	3	147	3
Calabrese, Tony, St. Lucie	1.000	8	10	0	0	10	0
Callahan, Dave, Sarasota *	1.000	11	22	0	0	22	0
Camilo, Juan, Clearwater	.957	90	167	10	8	185	4
Carroll, Wes, Brevard County	1.000	21	35	1	0	36	0
Carter, Shannon, Dunedin *	.954	30	60	2	3	65	0
Castillo, Osmar, Sarasota	1.000	13	18	2	0	20	0
Castro, Nelson, Vero Beach	1.000	11	12	1	0	13	0
Catalanotte, Greg, Sarasota	.975	92	143	10	4	157	1
Cavin, Jonathan, Brevard County	.938	9	14	1	1	16	0
Chavez, Ender, St. Lucie *	1.000	29	43	3	0	46	0
Comfort, Geoff, Vero Beach	1.000	2	2	0	0	2	0
Cooper, Matt, Sarasota	.956	33	64	1	3	68	0
Corr, Frank, St. Lucie	1.000	5	12	2	0	14	1
Cosbey, Chris, Clearwater *	.985	64	134	1	2	137	0
Cosby, Rob, Dunedin	.938	11	14	1	1	16	0
Coulie, Jason, Palm Beach	.971	24	30	3	1	34	2
Creighton, Matt, Daytona	.000	1	0	0	0	0	0
DAVENPORT, RON, Dunedin	1.000	109	184	4	0	188	0
Deschaine, Jim, Clearwater	.963	11	26	0	1	27	0
Detienne, Dave, Vero Beach	.900	5	9	0	1	10	0
Diaz, Felix, Brevard County	1.000	7	18	0	0	18	0
Dodson, Jeremy, Palm Beach	1.000	42	86	3	0	89	1
Dorta, Melvin, Sarasota	.000	1	0	0	0	0	0
Drew, J.D., Palm Beach	1.000	6	2	1	0	3	1
Duncan, Shelley, Tampa	1.000	3	3	0	0	3	0
Easterday, Matt, Jupiter	.941	12	15	1	1	17	0
Ellerson, Brian, Brevard County	.900	6	8	1	1	10	0
Espinosa, David, Lakeland	.984	91	188	2	3	193	1
Ferrer, Simon, Vero Beach	1.000	1	2	1	0	3	0
Fowler, Maleke, Tampa	1.000	44	94	3	0	97	0
Frazier, Charles, Jupiter	.965	48	79	4	3	86	1
Fulse, Sheldon, Sarasota	.955	22	60	3	3	66	1
Galloway, Mike, Dunedin	.000	1	0	0	0	0	0
Garcia, Sergio, Vero Beach	1.000	4	5	0	0	5	0
Garcia, Tony, Palm Beach	.000	1	0	0	0	0	0
Gillitzer, Scott, Vero Beach	1.000	50	68	5	0	73	2
Gingrich, Troy, Brevard County *	.989	90	171	4	2	177	0
Godwin, Tyrell, Dunedin	.982	94	216	4	4	224	1
Goelz, Jim, Sarasota	.975	16	37	2	1	40	0
Granderson, Curtis, Lakeland	.984	126	292	15	5	312	3
Greenberg, Adam, Daytona *	1.000	69	127	6	0	133	1
Grove, Jason, Tampa *	1.000	17	28	1	0	29	0
Guerrero, Vladimir, B.C.	1.000	2	5	0	0	5	0
Gutierrez, Franklin, Vero Beach	.984	106	240	4	4	248	1
Hermansen, Chad, Vero Beach	.952	13	19	1	1	21	0
Hernandez, Johnny, P.B.*	1.000	11	19	1	0	20	0
Hicks, Scott, Jupiter	.983	42	55	3	1	59	0
Hileman, Jutt, Palm Beach	.940	25	47	0	3	50	0
Hoffpauir, Micah, Daytona *	.853	24	28	1	5	34	0
Holdzkom, Lincoln, Jupiter	1.000	1	1	1	0	2	1
Hoorelbeke, Jesse, Vero Beach	1.000	4	4	0	0	4	0
Housel, David, St. Lucie	1.000	2	3	0	0	3	0
Jenkins, Neil, Lakeland	.976	33	40	0	1	41	0
Johnson, Gary, Palm Beach	1.000	23	51	4	0	55	0
Jones, Garrett, Fort Myers *	1.000	1	2	0	0	2	0
Jova, Maikel, Dunedin	.981	57	100	6	2	108	0
Kavourias, Jim, Jupiter	.988	100	149	12	2	163	3
Keene, Kurt, Dunedin	.964	14	26	1	1	28	0
Kirkpatrick, Michael, P.B.*	1.000	3	5	0	0	5	0
Koutnik, Jared, Tampa	.933	7	13	1	1	15	0
Kropf, Andy, Lakeland	1.000	1	4	1	0	5	0
Kubel, Jason, Fort Myers	.991	109	207	15	2	224	1
Kuhaulua, Kaulana, Fort Myers	1.000	19	36	1	0	37	0
Lane, Rich, Brevard County *	.983	31	56	2	1	59	0
Langs, Ronte, Vero Beach	.992	55	117	2	1	120	1
Lawson, Forrest, St. Lucie	.957	54	84	6	4	94	1
Lemon, Tim, Palm Beach	.979	49	89	4	2	95	1
Loney, James, Vero Beach *	.833	2	5	0	1	6	0
Lugo, Alfredo, Lakeland	.989	53	83	5	1	89	0
Lydon, Wayne, St. Lucie	.974	132	220	9	6	235	0
Macha, Erick, Tampa	1.000	5	8	0	0	8	0
Maddox, Garry, Clearwater	1.000	7	14	1	0	15	0
Malek, Bobby, St. Lucie	1.000	75	125	7	0	132	2
Mallory, Mike, Daytona	.992	121	248	9	2	259	1
Matthews, Lamont, Sarasota *	.993	57	141	2	1	144	1
Mattle, David, Lakeland	.965	99	183	12	7	202	0
Mauer, Jake, Fort Myers	1.000	2	1	0	0	1	0
McEachran, Aaron, Dunedin	1.000	1	1	0	0	1	0
Medina, Rodney, Dunedin	.875	2	7	0	1	8	0
Michaels, Jason, Clearwater	1.000	4	10	0	0	10	0
Money, Freddie, Sarasota	.971	13	31	2	1	34	0
Murphy, David, Sarasota *	.990	43	93	2	1	96	1
Nunez, Abraham, Jupiter	1.000	5	12	0	0	12	0
O'Toole, Paul, Daytona	1.000	6	7	1	0	8	0
Pagan, Angel, St. Lucie	.967	112	221	10	8	239	1
Perez, Josue, Clearwater	1.000	13	24	0	0	24	0
Perry, Jason, Dunedin	1.000	15	15	0	0	15	0
Perry, Rod, Clearwater	.900	7	17	1	2	20	0
Pierce, Sean, Vero Beach	.950	22	37	1	2	40	0
Pressley, Josh, St. Lucie	.000	2	0	0	0	0	0
Reed, Eric, Jupiter *	.986	129	335	10	5	350	2
Rico, Erik, Dunedin *	1.000	13	12	0	0	12	0
Rigsby, Randy, Jupiter *	.966	27	55	1	2	58	0
Rodgers, Albert, Palm Beach	.968	14	29	1	1	31	1
Rodriguez, Eladio, Sarasota	.920	25	43	3	4	50	0
Rogers, Brandon, Vero Beach	1.000	1	4	0	0	4	0
Rohan, Jimmy, Vero Beach	.750	3	3	0	1	4	0
Roman, Jesse, Palm Beach *	.992	74	119	8	1	128	0
Rombley, Danny, B.C.	.992	105	228	10	2	240	2
Sardinha, Bronson, Tampa	.971	58	131	3	4	138	1
Segar, Jeff, Tampa	.983	34	54	3	1	58	0
Seiber, Antron, Sarasota	.971	28	65	1	2	68	1
Shanks, Eric, Sarasota	1.000	6	8	1	0	9	0
Sing, Brandon, Daytona	.945	32	49	3	3	55	0
Smith, Will, Jupiter	.000	2	0	0	0	0	0
Smith, Will, Sarasota	1.000	7	20	0	0	20	0
Spearman, Jemel, Daytona	1.000	9	13	0	0	13	0
Stone, Greg, Sarasota	1.000	7	16	0	0	16	0
Sucre, Antonio, Brevard County	1.000	1	1	0	0	1	0
Tamburrino, Brett, Fort Myers	.979	55	94	0	2	96	0
Thissen, Greg, Brevard County	.818	6	8	1	2	11	0
Thomas, Charles, Vero Beach	.957	100	174	4	8	186	0
Thompson, Kevin, Tampa	1.000	44	91	4	0	95	0
Tomlin, James, Fort Myers	.986	120	269	8	4	281	4
Toner, John, St. Lucie	1.000	3	6	0	0	6	0
Tope, Stephen, Fort Myers	1.000	63	115	5	0	120	1
Tress, Irving, Lakeland	.500	3	1	0	1	2	0
Tucker, Mamon, Clearwater	.984	92	179	2	3	184	0
Turner, Jason, Tampa *	1.000	6	9	1	0	10	0
Urquhart, Derick, B.C.*	1.000	52	90	1	0	91	0
Urueta, Luis, Palm Beach	.941	7	16	0	1	17	0
Van Buizen, Rodney, Vero Beach	.985	40	64	1	1	66	0
Vasquez, Willie, Tampa	1.000	2	3	0	0	3	0
Voshell, Chase, Palm Beach	.983	31	53	5	1	59	0
Vukovich, Vince, Clearwater	.984	87	174	8	3	185	0
Walsh, Sean, Clearwater	1.000	18	33	3	0	36	0
Watkins, Tommy, Fort Myers	.951	38	73	5	4	82	2
Watson, Matt, St. Lucie	1.000	2	2	0	0	2	0
Waugh, Jason, Dunedin	.979	78	135	8	3	146	3
Werth, Jayson, Dunedin	1.000	16	26	1	0	27	0
Weston, Aron, Daytona *	.964	56	103	4	4	111	2
Willingham, Josh, Jupiter	1.000	3	4	0	0	4	0
Winrow, Gary, Tampa *	.978	108	215	5	5	225	2

CATCHERS

Player, Team	Pct.	G	PO	A	E	TC	DP	PB
Ambrosini, Anthony, B.C.	.996	45	230	20	1	251	4	6
Anderson, Dennis, Jupiter	.988	62	373	39	5	417	2	9
Apodaca, Luis, B.C.	1.000	1	1	0	0	1	0	0
Avila, Rob, Clearwater	.990	32	187	11	2	200	0	9
Balfe, Ryan, Brevard County	1.000	7	37	4	0	41	0	0
Bellorin, Edwin, Vero Beach	.980	61	430	48	10	488	6	4
Blum, Greg, Fort Myers	.990	64	355	38	4	397	4	10
Brown, Jason, Brevard County	.987	31	142	11	2	155	0	1
Brown, Kevin, Palm Beach	1.000	4	32	9	0	41	1	1
Buckley, James, Sarasota	.989	14	79	8	1	88	1	3
Cabrera, Ruben, Vero Beach	.917	6	28	5	3	36	0	3
Cleveland, Russ, Lakeland	.992	20	113	13	1	127	1	2
Concepcion, Alberto, Sarasota	.996	46	246	19	1	266	3	9
Cruz, Edgar, Clearwater	1.000	9	43	7	0	50	1	3
Durazo, William, Sarasota	1.000	5	18	1	0	19	0	1
Eickhorst, Chris, Palm Beach	.991	64	405	34	4	443	1	12
Ellerson, Brian, Brevard County	.000	1	0	0	0	0	0	0
Emmerick, Josh, B.C.	.979	6	39	7	1	47	1	3
Esposito, Brian, Sarasota	.900	1	8	1	1	10	0	1
Fernandez, Alejandro, Tampa	.993	38	239	28	2	269	2	10
Grzecka, Casey, Jupiter	.988	13	81	4	1	86	0	0
Gulledge, Kelley, Fort Myers	1.000	5	38	3	0	41	1	1
Hamill, Ryan, Palm Beach	.977	12	75	11	2	88	1	2
Hietpas, Joe, St. Lucie	.981	63	454	53	10	517	6	4
Huber, Justin, St. Lucie	.982	34	256	24	5	285	0	4
Hundley, Todd, Vero Beach	1.000	2	8	0	0	8	0	0
Kay, Brett, St. Lucie	.995	47	352	30	2	384	3	4
Kennedy, Bryan, Fort Myers	.981	21	141	13	3	157	1	4
Kropf, Andy, Lakeland	.982	25	152	12	3	167	2	1
Lafferty, Will, Palm Beach	.900	2	8	1	1	10	1	0
Langill, Eric, Vero Beach	.986	24	125	14	2	141	3	1
Lopez, Angel, Jupiter	.987	32	205	20	3	228	3	1
Lynam, Guy, Jupiter	.962	5	21	4	1	26	0	0
Martinez, Casey, Clearwater	.972	7	33	2	1	36	0	1
Martinez, Edgar, Sarasota	.984	62	378	54	7	439	1	9
Mauer, Jake, Fort Myers	1.000	1	5	0	0	5	0	0
Mauer, Joe, Fort Myers	1.000	39	294	29	0	323	3	3
McDonald, Kevin, Lakeland	1.000	5	26	4	0	30	1	1
McEachran, Aaron, Dunedin	1.000	11	57	3	0	60	0	2
McKnight, Lukas, Daytona	.983	6	53	4	1	58	2	1
McMillan, Drew, B.C.	.983	51	264	30	5	299	3	2
Mendez, Jose, Fort Myers	1.000	8	54	3	0	57	0	3
Miller, Chris, Daytona	.980	38	325	17	7	349	3	3
Morales, Jose, Fort Myers	.957	5	22	0	1	23	0	2
Navarro, Dioner, Tampa	.992	50	344	28	3	375	2	6
Netwall, Chris, Palm Beach	.988	64	370	56	5	431	6	9
O'Toole, Paul, Daytona	.986	20	126	15	2	143	2	3
Parrish, Dave, Tampa	.992	18	110	17	1	128	1	1
Phillips, Kyle, Fort Myers	1.000	1	5	0	0	5	0	0
Pratt, Trent, Clearwater	.991	78	493	45	5	543	4	7
Price, Jared, Vero Beach	.988	32	237	17	3	257	1	3
Rodriguez, Eladio, Sarasota	.990	17	93	10	1	104	2	11
Rodriguez, Robert, B.C.	.982	10	49	5	1	55	0	5
Rogers, Brandon, Vero Beach	.991	18	100	14	1	115	2	3
Rojas, Tommy, Tampa	1.000	11	51	5	0	56	1	1
Ruiz, Carlos, Clearwater	1.000	10	62	6	0	68	0	1
Sanchez, Danilo, Lakeland	1.000	12	95	5	0	100	1	3
Soto, Geovany, Daytona	.987	79	617	61	9	687	5	7
Tosca, Daniel, Tampa	.977	21	156	15	4	175	1	2
Trezza, Alex, Lakeland	.980	74	456	44	10	510	5	8
Umbria, Jose, Dunedin	.988	36	229	16	3	248	0	4
WHITTAKER, TIM, Dunedin	.996	71	473	42	2	517	2	13
Willingham, Josh, Jupiter	1.000	36	232	27	0	259	3	19
Yepez, Jose, Dunedin	.992	31	214	21	2	237	3	4

PITCHERS

Player, Team	Pct.	G	PO	A	E	TC	DP
Abbott, David, Dunedin	1.000	8	4	1	0	5	1
Abbott, Jim, Fort Myers	.917	17	4	7	1	12	0
Akens, Phil, Jupiter	.917	11	5	6	1	12	0
Alvarado, Carlo, Lakeland	1.000	4	0	1	0	1	0
Anderson, Travis, Daytona	1.000	12	2	4	0	6	1
Artiles, Carlos, Tampa *	.833	24	2	8	2	12	0
Asahina, Jonathan, Jupiter	.857	12	3	9	2	14	1
Astacio, Ezequiel, Clearwater	1.000	25	17	12	0	29	0
Astacio, Pedro, St. Lucie	1.000	4	1	0	0	1	0
Axelson, Josh, Palm Beach	1.000	9	1	4	0	5	1
Baez, Benito, Jupiter *	.000	3	0	0	0	0	0
Baisley, Brad, Clearwater	1.000	1	0	1	0	1	0
Baugh, Kenny, Lakeland	.667	4	1	1	1	3	1
Bautista, Denny, Jupiter	.909	14	7	13	2	22	0
Beckett, Josh, Jupiter	1.000	1	0	1	0	1	0
Belizario, Ronald, Jupiter	1.000	6	2	1	0	3	0
Bell, Gary, Tampa *	.938	22	5	10	1	16	2
Benik, Brett, Daytona	.917	25	2	9	1	12	0
Bennett, Steve, St. Lucie	.000	3	0	0	0	0	0
Bicondoa, Ryan, Tampa-St.L.	.957	20	10	12	1	23	0
Birtwell, John, Lakeland	1.000	35	1	1	0	2	0
Blalock, Casey, Jupiter	1.000	2	0	2	0	2	0
Blankenship, Jon, Tampa *	1.000	10	1	2	0	3	0
Blasdell, Jared, Daytona	1.000	56	0	10	0	10	1
Blasko, Chadd, Daytona	.963	24	5	21	1	27	0
Bonilla, Henry, Fort Myers	1.000	10	1	1	0	2	0
Bowyer, Travis, Fort Myers	.962	45	7	18	1	26	2
Brazoban, Yhency, Tampa	1.000	24	1	4	0	5	1
Brito, Eude, Clearwater *	1.000	36	10	13	0	23	0
Brownlie, Bobby, Daytona	.900	13	4	5	1	10	0
Brumit, Matt, Tampa	1.000	9	1	0	0	1	0
Bucktrot, Keith, Clearwater	1.000	19	6	15	0	21	2
Bush, David, Dunedin	.929	14	7	6	1	14	0
Byard, David, St. Lucie	.909	27	2	8	1	11	0
Byron, Terry, Sarasota	1.000	32	7	3	0	10	1
Cable, Taft, Clearwater	1.000	31	3	7	0	10	0
Cali, Carmen, Palm Beach *	.810	62	6	11	4	21	0
Campbell, Dayle, Vero Beach	1.000	1	0	1	0	1	0
Caple, Chance, Palm Beach	.963	20	9	17	1	27	0
Caputo, Rob, Brevard County	.800	21	5	7	3	15	1
Carbajal, Alex, Sarasota *	1.000	22	3	7	0	10	1
Cardwell, Brian, Dunedin	1.000	8	2	1	0	3	0
Carpenter, Chris, Palm Beach	1.000	4	2	1	0	3	0
Carter, Mark, Daytona *	.750	16	0	3	1	4	0
Casadiego, Gerardo, B.C.	1.000	7	0	1	0	1	0
Castro, Rafael, St. Lucie	.000	2	0	0	0	0	0
Cave, Kevin, Jupiter	1.000	39	3	7	0	10	1
Cerezo, Hector, B.C.*	.000	1	0	0	0	0	0
Chenard, Ken, St. Lucie	1.000	17	5	9	0	14	1
Christensen, Ben, Daytona	1.000	14	1	5	0	6	0
Clark, Ray, Tampa	1.000	5	1	2	0	3	0
Claussen, Brandon, Tampa *	1.000	4	1	2	0	3	0
Clelland, James, Sarasota	1.000	11	4	5	0	9	1
Coggin, Dave, Clearwater	.000	3	0	0	1	1	0
Collins, Pat, Palm Beach	.500	10	0	1	1	2	0
Comolli, Mark, Dunedin	1.000	21	3	5	0	8	0
Cone, David, St. Lucie	1.000	3	0	1	0	1	0
Contreras, Jean, Fort Myers *	1.000	14	0	1	0	1	0
Contreras, Jose, Tampa	.000	1	0	0	0	0	0
Cook, Jeremy, Palm Beach	.882	45	4	11	2	17	2
Cooksey, Wes, Tampa	1.000	18	1	7	0	8	0
Corcoran, Roy, Brevard County	.923	28	4	8	1	13	0
Cordero, Chad, Brevard County	.917	19	5	6	1	12	1
Correa, Cristobal, Palm Beach	1.000	21	14	5	0	19	0
Cosby, Rob, Dunedin	1.000	1	0	1	0	1	0
Cox, Mike, St. Lucie *	.818	27	3	6	2	11	2
Crain, Jesse, Fort Myers	1.000	10	1	2	0	3	0
Cuello, Felix, Lakeland	.750	14	2	1	1	4	0
Currier, Rik, Tampa	.667	29	1	3	2	6	0
Davis, Stockton, Brevard County	1.000	42	4	8	0	12	0
Daws, Josh, Fort Myers	.750	11	1	2	1	4	0
Dawson, Layne, Clearwater	1.000	14	6	4	0	10	0
Day, Zach, Brevard County	1.000	1	1	0	0	1	0
DeJong, Jordan, Dunedin	1.000	28	2	4	0	6	0
Dejesus, Elvis, Sarasota	1.000	27	3	5	0	8	0
Delcarmen, Manny, Sarasota	1.000	4	2	3	0	5	0
Demontel, Jimmy, Jupiter	.000	2	0	0	0	0	0
Dennison, Michael, Sarasota	.000	4	0	0	0	0	0
Dequin, Benji, Brevard County *	.800	17	1	7	2	10	0
Diaz, Felix, Brevard County	.000	1	0	0	0	0	0
Diaz, Joselo, V.B.-St. Lucie	.944	26	8	9	1	18	0
Diaz, Luis, Lakeland	1.000	10	1	0	0	1	1
Dinardo, Lenny, St. Lucie *	1.000	19	3	15	0	18	0
Doble, Clemente, Clearwater	.000	1	0	0	0	0	0
Dodson, Jeremy, Palm Beach	.000	2	0	0	0	0	0
Dougherty, Kevin, Vero Beach *	1.000	7	0	1	0	1	0
Duckworth, Brandon, Clearwater	1.000	2	0	2	0	2	0
Dumatrait, Phillip, Sarasota *	1.000	21	7	17	0	24	1
Durbin, J.D., Fort Myers	.923	14	6	18	2	26	1
Easterday, Matt, Jupiter	.000	1	0	0	0	0	0
Eckert, Harold, St. Lucie	.944	17	9	8	1	18	0
Elliott, Chad, St. Lucie *	.895	22	9	8	2	19	0
Elmore, Chris, Sarasota *	.000	1	0	0	0	0	0
Embree, Alan, Sarasota *	.000	1	0	0	0	0	0
Encarnacion, Luis, Clearwater	1.000	1	0	1	0	1	0
Esarey, Brad, Dunedin *	.500	6	0	1	1	2	0
Estes, Jonathan, Palm Beach	1.000	15	2	6	0	8	0
Fahrner, Evan, Daytona	.667	13	1	1	1	3	0
Fernley, Nathan, Daytona	1.000	17	4	5	0	9	0
Ferreras, Yorkin, Daytona *	.500	11	0	1	1	2	0
File, Bob, Dunedin	1.000	3	0	1	0	1	0

Player, Team	Pct.	G	PO	A	E	TC	DP
Flores, Neomar, Dunedin	1.000	29	5	12	0	17	1
Florian, Frailyn, Jupiter *	.750	10	0	6	2	8	0
Floyd, Gavin, Clearwater	.900	24	16	29	5	50	3
Flynn, Brian, Palm Beach	.000	7	0	0	0	0	0
Foli, Daniel, Daytona	1.000	6	0	1	0	1	0
Foote, Joe, Fort Myers	1.000	5	1	4	0	5	0
Fox, Chad, Sarasota	.500	2	0	1	1	2	0
Franco, John, St. Lucie *	.000	4	0	0	1	1	0
Franco, Martire, Clearwater	.000	1	0	0	0	0	0
Frasor, Jason, Vero Beach	1.000	15	4	1	0	5	0
Fuell, Jerrod, Jupiter	1.000	46	4	2	0	6	0
Fulchino, Jeff, Jupiter	.909	17	2	8	1	11	0
Gabbard, Kason, Sarasota *	.000	2	0	0	0	0	0
Galbraith, Jason, Palm Beach *	.000	5	0	0	0	0	0
Gamble, Jerome, Sarasota	1.000	17	8	6	0	14	0
Garcia, Jose, Tampa	1.000	4	3	2	0	5	1
Glen, William, Clearwater	.800	7	1	3	1	5	0
Gonzalez, Luis, Vero Beach *	1.000	21	5	4	0	9	0
Graves, Don, Palm Beach	.667	3	0	2	1	3	0
Greusel, Evan, Jupiter	1.000	24	0	5	0	5	0
Grilli, Jason, Jupiter	.889	7	2	6	1	9	0
Gutierrez, Jannio, Fort Myers	1.000	40	5	4	0	9	0
Halsey, Brad, Tampa *	1.000	14	1	21	0	22	0
Hamann, Rob, Dunedin	1.000	4	2	2	0	4	0
Hamels, Cole, Clearwater *	1.000	5	1	5	0	6	2
Hamilton, Jamaal, Vero Beach *	1.000	4	0	1	0	1	0
Hamman, Corey, Lakeland *	.941	46	6	10	1	17	0
Hammons, Matt, Palm Beach	1.000	21	0	2	0	2	0
Harper, Jesse, Dunedin	1.000	26	12	13	0	25	3
Hawksworth, Blake, Palm Beach	1.000	6	1	2	0	3	0
Haynes, Brad, Jupiter	1.000	13	1	1	0	2	0
Hee, Aaron, Vero Beach *	1.000	9	1	3	0	4	0
Hendrickson, Mark, Dunedin *	.000	1	0	0	0	0	0
Henn, Sean, Tampa *	.800	16	1	11	3	15	0
Hernandez, Adrian, Tampa	.000	1	0	0	0	0	0
Hernandez, Orlando, B.C.	1.000	2	1	1	0	2	0
Hill, Shawn, Brevard County	.914	22	14	39	5	58	2
Hinckley, Michael, B.C.*	1.000	4	4	4	0	8	0
Hoffpauir, Micah, Daytona *	.000	1	0	0	0	0	0
Holdzkom, Lincoln, Jupiter	.000	13	0	0	0	0	0
Holubec, Ken, Fort Myers *	.926	26	8	17	2	27	2
Hosford, Clint, Vero Beach	.917	8	5	6	1	12	0
Houston, Ryan, Dunedin	1.000	26	3	7	0	10	0
Howell, Jason, Sarasota *	.913	48	2	19	2	23	0
Howell, Michael, Lakeland	1.000	5	0	3	0	3	0
Huang, Kevin, Sarasota	.000	4	0	0	0	0	0
Hull, Eric, Vero Beach	1.000	31	4	8	0	12	0
Hutchinson, Trevor, Jupiter	.882	14	9	6	2	17	0
Hutchison, Ryan, Clearwater	1.000	8	1	2	0	3	0
Isaacson, Charlie, Tampa	1.000	7	0	4	0	4	1
Jackson, Dan, Dunedin	1.000	9	0	2	0	2	0
Johnson, Tyler, Palm Beach *	1.000	22	5	11	0	16	0
Kaercher, Matthew, Sarasota	1.000	8	1	2	0	3	0
Kazmir, Scott, St. Lucie *	.750	7	0	3	1	4	1
Kegley, Chuck, Dunedin	1.000	19	3	4	0	7	1
Keirstead, Mike, Vero Beach	.909	10	8	12	2	22	0
Kemlo, Chris, Tampa	.000	4	0	0	0	0	0
Kemp, Beau, Fort Myers	1.000	22	4	4	0	8	0
Kennard, Jeff, Tampa	1.000	26	3	7	0	10	0
Kennedy, Casey, Vero Beach	.750	8	3	3	2	8	0
Kent, Steve, Jupiter *	.833	5	1	4	1	6	0
Key, Chris, Jupiter *	.906	45	7	22	3	32	3
Kieninger, Billy, Lakeland	.800	21	1	7	2	10	1
King, Jeremy, Tampa	.700	11	4	3	3	10	0
Kinney, Josh, Palm Beach	1.000	31	1	11	0	12	2
Kirsten, Rick, Lakeland	1.000	2	0	1	0	1	0
Knowles, Mike, Tampa	1.000	4	0	1	0	1	0
Knox, Michael, Tampa	.667	3	0	2	1	3	0
Kobow, Mike, Lakeland	.750	32	0	3	1	4	0
Korecky, Bobby, Clearwater	.938	49	4	11	1	16	1
Kremer, John, Tampa	1.000	20	2	6	0	8	0
Kumagai, Ryo, Sarasota	1.000	1	0	1	0	1	0
Lambert, Jeremy, Palm Beach	.000	7	0	0	0	0	0
League, Brandon, Dunedin	1.000	13	6	15	0	21	0
Leu, Trevor, Lakeland *	1.000	33	4	20	0	24	1
Levinski, Donald, Jupiter	.778	21	9	12	6	27	1
Lieber, Jon, Tampa	.000	1	0	0	0	0	0
Lincoln, Jeff, Fort Myers	1.000	6	0	1	0	1	0
Lohse, Eric, Fort Myers	1.000	15	0	3	0	3	0
Lopez, Arturo, Vero Beach *	1.000	11	1	2	0	3	0
Lopez, Rafael, St. Lucie	1.000	37	3	8	0	11	0
Madson, Ryan, Clearwater	1.000	2	0	1	0	1	0

Player, Team	Pct.	G	PO	A	E	TC	DP
Maness, Nick, St. Lucie	1.000	7	0	1	0	1	0
Manning, Charlie, Tampa *	.857	6	0	6	1	7	0
Martin, Greg, Brevard County *	.000	7	0	0	0	0	0
Martin, Nick, Daytona *	.733	33	1	10	4	15	0
Martinez, Dave, Tampa *	.818	14	4	5	2	11	1
Martinez, Miguel, Palm Beach	.857	8	1	5	1	7	1
Mata, Gustavo, Brevard County	1.000	5	4	4	0	8	0
Maureau, Justin, Dunedin *	1.000	38	1	12	0	13	1
Maust, David, Brevard County *	1.000	31	4	6	0	10	0
Mayfield, Brandon, Clearwater	1.000	25	6	6	0	12	1
McAdam, Scott, Brevard County	.000	1	0	0	0	0	0
McCracken, Vance, Vero Beach	1.000	8	1	1	0	2	0
McCrotty, Will, Vero Beach	1.000	4	2	2	0	4	0
MCDOWELL, KEVIN, Lakeland *	1.000	24	12	18	0	30	1
McEachran, Aaron, Dunedin	.000	1	0	0	0	0	0
McGinley, Blake, St. Lucie *	1.000	37	4	4	0	8	1
McGowan, Dustin, Dunedin	.818	14	11	7	4	22	1
McNutt, Mike, Jupiter	.722	33	2	11	5	18	0
Mejia, Anderson, Daytona	1.000	1	0	1	0	1	0
Mejia, Juan, Palm Beach	.833	8	0	5	1	6	1
Mendoza, Cristian, Tampa	.667	10	2	2	2	6	0
Mendoza, Ramiro, Sarasota	1.000	1	0	3	0	3	0
Meyer, Todd, Brevard County	1.000	1	0	1	0	1	0
Miller, Colby, Fort Myers	.914	26	13	19	3	35	3
Miller, Greg, Vero Beach *	1.000	21	3	14	0	17	0
Miller, Jason, Fort Myers *	1.000	13	0	6	0	6	0
Miller, Josh, Clearwater	1.000	1	0	1	0	1	0
Miller, Justin, Dunedin	1.000	1	1	0	0	1	0
Milton, Eric, Fort Myers *	.000	1	0	0	0	0	0
Miniel, Rene, Sarasota	.889	19	2	14	2	18	0
Minor, Ryan, Vero Beach	1.000	6	2	0	0	2	0
Mitchell, Nathan, Daytona	.938	42	5	10	1	16	0
Moates, Jason, Lakeland	.889	31	4	4	1	9	0
Monahan, Joey, Daytona	.000	1	0	0	0	0	0
Moore, Benjamin, Tampa	1.000	12	0	2	0	2	0
Morales, Alex, Brevard County	.500	2	1	0	1	2	0
Moreno, Victor, Fort Myers	1.000	16	3	2	0	5	0
Moser, Todd, Jupiter *	.800	5	1	3	1	5	0
Musser, Neal, St. Lucie *	1.000	7	3	6	0	9	0
Myers, Damien, Lakeland *	.900	26	4	5	1	10	2
Nall, T.J., Vero Beach	.974	29	18	19	1	38	1
Narveson, Chris, Palm Beach *	.958	15	6	17	1	24	0
Nelson, Steve, Vero Beach	1.000	4	0	3	0	3	0
Neshek, Pat, Fort Myers	.900	20	6	3	1	10	0
Nicolas, Mike, Brevard County	.000	8	0	0	0	0	0
Nina, Elvin, Vero Beach	1.000	4	1	0	0	1	0
Nolasco, Ricky, Daytona	.750	26	2	10	4	16	0
Norderum, Jason, B.C.*	.926	25	14	11	2	27	1
Novinsky, John, Palm Beach	.889	37	1	7	1	9	0
Novoa, Roberto, Lakeland	1.000	19	6	13	0	19	1
Nunley, Derrick, Dunedin	.889	42	4	4	1	9	0
O'Flaherty, Liam, Vero Beach *	.000	1	0	0	0	0	0
Obispo, Jose, Vero Beach	.833	4	2	3	1	6	0
Ojeda, Alvis, Vero Beach	.000	1	0	0	0	0	0
Olsen, Kevin, Jupiter	.000	1	0	0	0	0	0
Olson, Justin, Fort Myers	1.000	6	0	1	0	1	0
Osoria, Franquelis, Vero Beach	.870	33	6	14	3	23	1
Ostlund, Ian, Lakeland *	1.000	17	1	4	0	5	0
Osuna, Antonio, Tampa	1.000	2	0	1	0	1	0
Ough, Wayne, St. Lucie	.909	22	4	16	2	22	1
Overman, Matt, Jupiter	1.000	11	2	4	0	6	1
Ozuna, Francisco, Dunedin *	1.000	11	1	2	0	3	0
Paddock, Josh, Clearwater	1.000	20	1	7	0	8	0
Pahucki, David, Sarasota	.920	18	8	15	2	25	4
Painter, Lance, Palm Beach *	.000	1	0	0	0	0	0
Parker, Christian, Tampa	1.000	1	0	1	0	1	0
Paulk, Robert, St. Lucie	.000	2	0	0	0	0	0
Pearce, Josh, Palm Beach	1.000	6	0	6	0	6	0
Peeples, Ross, St. Lucie *	1.000	14	4	13	0	17	0
Perez, Juan, Sarasota *	1.000	33	1	4	0	5	0
Perkins, Vince, Dunedin	.882	18	3	12	2	17	1
Person, Robert, Sarasota	1.000	7	0	1	0	1	0
Peterson, Adam, Dunedin	1.000	9	1	3	0	4	0
Peterson, Matt, St. Lucie	1.000	15	8	10	0	18	0
Petty, Chad, Lakeland *	.800	10	1	7	2	10	0
Phelps, Tommy, Jupiter *	1.000	2	1	0	0	1	0
Phillips, Mark, Tampa *	.947	16	5	13	1	19	0
Pignatiello, Carmen, Daytona *	.844	26	6	21	5	32	0
Pilkington, Brian, Vero Beach	1.000	21	13	16	0	29	2
Pinto, Renyel, Daytona *	.929	20	1	12	1	14	0
Pleiness, Chad, Dunedin	.970	25	12	20	1	33	2

Player, Team	Pct.	G	PO	A	E	TC	DP
Pope, Justin, P.B.-Tampa	.964	22	7	20	1	28	3
Portobanco, Luz, St. Lucie	.909	16	4	6	1	11	0
Puello, Ignacio, Brevard County	.923	18	5	7	1	13	1
Ramirez, Elizardo, Clearwater	.975	27	20	19	1	40	5
Ramirez, Emmanuel, Daytona	1.000	11	1	1	0	2	0
Ramirez, Ramon, Tampa	1.000	14	3	5	0	8	0
Randazzo, Jeff, Fort Myers *	.971	20	8	25	1	34	1
Rawson, Anthony, Palm Beach *	.571	25	0	4	3	7	0
Reina, Dimas, Vero Beach	.750	15	0	3	1	4	0
Reynolds, Josh, Sarasota	1.000	23	2	14	0	16	0
Rhodes, Shane, Sarasota *	1.000	39	4	8	0	12	0
Richardson, Jason, Fort Myers	.966	46	11	17	1	29	0
Roberts, Grant, St. Lucie	.800	5	2	2	1	5	0
Rodney, Lee, Lakeland	1.000	27	6	9	0	15	2
Rodriguez, Cristobal, B.C.	.000	2	0	0	0	0	0
Rodriguez, Jose, B.C.*	.000	1	0	0	0	0	0
Rodriguez, Osvaldo, Vero Beach	1.000	1	0	1	0	1	0
Rohlicek, Russ, Daytona *	1.000	41	3	11	0	14	0
Rojas, Jose, Vero Beach	1.000	14	2	7	0	9	2
Roman, Orlando, St. Lucie	1.000	28	1	10	0	11	3
Romero, Josmir, Fort Myers	1.000	5	0	1	0	1	0
Rudrude, Brett, Sarasota	.955	22	7	14	1	22	1
Rundles, Rich, Brevard County *	.967	19	6	23	1	30	1
Runyon, Bob, Palm Beach	1.000	5	1	1	0	2	0
Russ, James, Jupiter	1.000	1	1	0	0	1	0
Russelburg, Aaron, Palm Beach	1.000	6	1	3	0	4	0
Russell, Eddie, Jupiter	1.000	10	1	2	0	3	1
Ryu, Jae-kuk, Daytona	1.000	4	0	2	0	2	0
Sandoval, Marcos, Dunedin	1.000	1	0	1	0	1	0
Santiago, Victor, Vero Beach	1.000	10	3	5	0	8	1
Scalamandre, Rich, Palm Beach	.000	4	0	0	0	0	0
Schultz, Cory, Clearwater	1.000	9	0	3	0	3	0
Scobie, Jason, St. Lucie	.889	4	1	7	1	9	0
Seale, Dustin, Brevard County *	.667	9	0	2	1	3	0
Searles, Jon, Brevard County	1.000	18	2	7	0	9	1
Silva, Efrain, Vero Beach	1.000	16	1	2	0	3	0
Sloan, Brandon, Jupiter	.938	41	3	12	1	16	1
Smith, Bud, Clearwater *	1.000	4	1	2	0	3	0
Smith, Chris, Sarasota	1.000	2	0	1	0	1	0
Smith, Jared, Palm Beach	1.000	45	2	7	0	9	0
Smith, Jason, Tampa	1.000	6	1	3	0	4	0
Smith, Matt, Tampa *	.714	6	1	4	2	7	0
Squires, Matt, Clearwater *	1.000	41	2	9	0	11	0
Steffek, Brian, Vero Beach	1.000	23	1	5	0	6	0
Stevenson, Jason, B.C.*	.903	36	10	18	3	31	2
Stewart, James, Vero Beach	1.000	4	0	1	0	1	0
Stewart, Scott, Brevard County *	.000	2	0	0	0	0	0
Stockman, Landon, Lakeland	.800	44	1	3	1	5	0
Strayhorn, Kole, V.B.-St. Lucie	1.000	46	1	8	0	9	0
Stults, Eric, Vero Beach *	.000	1	0	0	0	0	0
Szuminski, Jason, Daytona	1.000	13	3	5	0	8	0
Teekel, Josh, Palm Beach	1.000	1	0	1	0	1	0
Tejada, Manny, Fort Myers	1.000	8	1	0	0	1	0
Tejeda, Rob, Clearwater	1.000	11	0	8	0	8	1
Tequida, Mauricio, Vero Beach	.000	3	0	0	0	0	0
Thompson, Bradley, Palm Beach	1.000	2	1	0	0	1	0
Thompson, Matt, Sarasota	1.000	20	1	10	0	11	0
Torres, Andy, Dunedin	.957	43	5	17	1	23	1
Torres, Luis, Brevard County	.846	30	6	5	2	13	0
Ulloa, Enmanuel, B.C.	1.000	5	1	0	0	1	0
Ungs, Nic, Jupiter	.842	18	9	7	3	19	1
Urquhart, Derick, B.C.*	.000	2	0	0	0	0	0
Valdez, Jose, Tampa	1.000	3	0	1	0	1	0
Valdez, Santo, Dunedin	.941	41	6	10	1	17	1
Vermilyea, Jamie, Dunedin	1.000	9	0	2	0	2	0
Villalon, Julio, Palm Beach	1.000	1	1	0	0	1	0
Villegas, Felix, Sarasota	.750	10	1	5	2	8	0
Villegas, Francisco, Tampa	1.000	22	1	5	0	6	0
Vorwald, Matt, Fort Myers	.900	15	5	4	1	10	0
Washburn, Ben, Brevard County	.000	8	0	0	0	0	0
Watkins, Tommy, Fort Myers	1.000	2	1	0	0	1	0
Wayne, Justin, Jupiter	.000	1	0	0	0	0	0
Wendell, Turk, Clearwater	1.000	5	0	2	0	2	0
White, Gabe, Tampa *	.000	1	0	0	0	0	0
White, Matt, Sarasota *	.000	2	0	0	0	0	0
Williams, Blake, Palm Beach	.826	20	4	15	4	23	1
Williams, Ryan, Vero Beach	.750	19	0	3	1	4	0
Wolfe, Brian, Fort Myers	1.000	7	4	8	0	12	0
Woodyard, Mark, Lakeland	.875	23	9	12	3	24	2
Wynegar, Adam, Daytona *	1.000	19	0	6	0	6	0
Yates, Tyler, St. Lucie	1.000	14	2	10	0	12	2
Yeatman, Matt, Fort Myers	.833	25	9	11	4	24	2
Young, Chris, Brevard County	1.000	8	4	2	0	6	0
Zink, Charlie, Sarasota	.966	24	10	18	1	29	1

PITCHERS WITH TWO OR MORE TEAMS

Player, Team	Pct.	G	PO	A	E	TC	DP
Bicondoa, Ryan, St. Lucie	1.000	5	2	4	0	6	0
Bicondoa, Ryan, Tampa	.941	15	8	8	1	17	0
Diaz, Joselo, St. Lucie	1.000	11	1	2	0	3	0
Diaz, Joselo, Vero Beach	.933	15	7	7	1	15	0
Pope, Justin, Palm Beach	.960	20	6	18	1	25	3
Pope, Justin, Tampa	1.000	2	1	2	0	3	0
Strayhorn, Kole, Vero Beach	1.000	30	0	7	0	7	0
Strayhorn, Kole, St. Lucie	1.000	16	1	1	0	2	0

The following players appeared only as a designated hitter, pinch-hitter or pinch-runner: Devarez, dh; Madera, dh, ph; Morrow, dh.

LEAGUE CHAMPIONS

Year	Team	Pct.
1919—	Sanford*	.605
	Orlando*	.703
1920—	Tampa	.654
	Tampa	.722
1921—	Orlando	.635
1922—	St. Petersburg	.503
	St. Petersburg	.618
1923—	Orlando	.667
	Orlando	.678
1924—	Lakeland	.695
	Lakeland	.683
1925—	St. Petersburg	.667
	Tampa†	.696
1926—	Sanford	.647
	Sanford	.623
1927—	Orlando†	.600
	Miami	.661
1928-35—	Did not operate.	
1936—	Gainesville	.542
	St. Augustine (4th)†	.492
1937—	Gainesville§	.616
1938—	Leesburg	.626
	Gainesville (2nd)‡	.615
1939—	Sanford§	.787
1940—	Daytona Beach	.619
	Orlando (4th)‡	.507
1941—	St. Augustine	.659
	Leesburg (4th)‡	.488
1942-45—	Did not operate.	
1946—	Orlando§	.681
1947—	St. Augustine	.625
	Gainesville (2nd)‡	.584
1948—	Orlando	.643
	Daytona Beach (2nd)‡	.616
1949—	Gainesville	.635
	St. Augustine (3rd)‡	.556
1950—	Orlando	.629
	DeLand (3rd)‡	.590
1951—	DeLand§	.643
1952—	DeLand∞	.704
	Palatka (3rd)‡	.569
1953—	Daytona Beach†	.657
	DeLand	.703
1954—	Jacksonville Beach	.629
	Lakeland†	.594
1955—	Orlando	.671
	Orlando	.643
1956—	Cocoa	.614
	Cocoa	.671
1957—	Palatka	.629
	Tampa†	.681
1958—	St. Petersburg	.732
	St. Petersburg	.681
1959—	Tampa	.591
	St. Petersburg†	.612
1960—	Lakeland	.731
	Palatka†	.614
1961—	Tampa†	.710
	Sarasota	.696
1962—	Sarasota	.689
	Fort Lauderdale†	.623
1963—	Sarasota	.645
	Sarasota	.667
1964—	Fort Lauderdale†	.629
	St. Petersburg	.594
1965—	Fort Lauderdale	.627
	Fort Lauderdale	.634
1966—	Leesburg†	.781
	St. Petersburg	.700
1967—	St. Petersburg▲	.691
	Orlando	.638
1968—	Miami	.613
	Orlando◆	.579
1969—	Miami■	.606
	Orlando	.606
1970—	Miami▼	.662
	St. Petersburg	.600
1971—	Miami▼	.667
	Daytona Beach	.586
1972—	Miami•	.562
	Daytona Beach	.606
1973—	St. Petersburg††	.575
	West Palm Beach	.580
1974—	West Palm Beach††	.598
	Fort Lauderdale	.626

Year	Team	Pct.
1975—	St. Petersburg††	.652
	Miami	.581
1976—	Tampa	.559
	Lakeland††	.536
1977—	Lakeland††	.616
	West Palm Beach	.583
1978—	Lakeland	.565
	Miami§	.539
1979—	Fort Lauderdale	.643
	Winter Haven‡‡	.577
1980—	Daytona Beach	.628
	Fort Lauderdale††	.606
1981—	Fort Myers	.554
	Daytona Beach§§	.504
1982—	Fort Lauderdale§§	.621
	Tampa	.546
1983—	Daytona Beach	.634
	Vero Beach§§	.515
1984—	Tampa	.532
	Fort Lauderdale§§	.521
1985—	Fort Myers∞∞	.590
	Fort Lauderdale	.550
1986—	St. Petersburg∞∞	.647
	West Palm Beach	.593
1987—	Fort Lauderdale∞∞	.616
	Osceola	.576
1988—	Osceola	.606
	St. Lucie▲▲	.532
1989—	Port Charlotte▲▲	.540
	St. Petersburg	.540
1990—	West Palm Beach	.697
	Vero Beach▲▲	.585
1991—	Clearwater	.623
	West Palm Beach▲▲	.550
1992—	Sarasota	.639
	Lakeland◆◆	.530
1993—	St. Lucie	.600
	Clearwater§§	.556
1994—	Tampa§§	.606
	Brevard County	.561
1995—	Daytona§§	.644
	Fort Myers	.577
1996—	Tampa	.627
	St. Lucie§§	.534
1997—	St. Petersburg■■	.591
	Vero Beach	.511
1998—	Charlotte	.594
	St. Lucie■■	.515
1999—	Dunedin	.628
	Kissimmee■■	.578
2000—	Dunedin	.609
	Daytona■■	.547
2001—	Brevard County▼▼	.593
	Tampa▼▼	.554
2002—	Charlotte■■	.600
2003—	St. Lucie■■	.554

*Split-season playoff abandoned after each team won three games. †Won split-season playoff. ‡Won four-club playoff. §Won championship and four-club playoff. ∞Won both halves of split season. ▲League divided into Eastern and Western divisions with split season. St. Petersburg and Orlando won both halves of split season; St. Petersburg won playoff. ◆League divided into Eastern and Western divisions. Miami won regular-season pennant on basis of highest won-lost percentage. Orlando won four-club playoff involving first two teams in each division. ■ League divided into Southern and Central divisions. Miami won playoff between division leaders. (NOTE—Pennant awarded to playoff winner in 1936.) ▼League divided into Eastern and Western divisions. Miami won regular-season pennant on basis of highest won-loss percentage, and also won four-club playoff involving first two teams in each division. •League divided into Eastern and Western divisions. Won four-club playoff involving first two teams in each division. ††League divided into Northern and Southern divisions. Won four-club playoff involving first two teams in each division. ‡‡League divided into Northern and Southern divisions. Same two clubs won both halves; won playoffs. §§Won split-season playoff. ∞∞League divided into Western, Central and Southern divisions. Won four-club playoff. ▲▲League divided into Eastern, Western and Central divisions; played split-season. Won six-club playoff. ◆◆League divided into Eastern, Western and Central divisions; played split-season. Won eight-club playoff. ■■ League divided into East and West divisions and played split season; won four-club playoff. ▼▼League divided into East and West divisions and played split season; teams were about to start final round of playoffs, but were declared co-champions when Professional Baseball declared a stoppage of play.

MIDWEST LEAGUE

LEAGUE OFFICE

President
George H. Spelius

Address
P.O. Box 936
Beloit, WI 53512

Phone
608-364-1188

Teams (affiliation)
Battle Creek Yankees (Yankees)
Beloit Snappers (Brewers)
Burlington Bees (Royals)
Cedar Rapids Kernels (Angels)
Clinton Lumber Kings (Rangers)
Dayton Dragons (Reds)
Fort Wayne Wizards (Padres)
Kane County Cougars (A's)
Lansing Lugnuts (Cubs)
Peoria Chiefs (Cardinals)
Swing of the Quad Cities (Twins)
South Bend Silver Hawks (Diamondbacks)
West Michigan Whitecaps (Tigers)
Wisconsin Timber Rattlers (Mariners)

2003 FINAL STANDINGS

FIRST HALF

EASTERN DIVISION

Team	W	L	T	Pct.	GB
Fort Wayne	40	28	-	.588	...
Lansing	38	27	-	.585	0.5
West Michigan	37	33	-	.529	4.0
Dayton	35	35	-	.500	6.0
Battle Creek	33	35	-	.485	7.0
South Bend	28	38	-	.424	11.0

WESTERN DIVISION

Team	W	L	T	Pct.	GB
Kane County	41	29	-	.586	...
Wisconsin	38	28	-	.576	1.0
Beloit	32	35	-	.478	7.5
Quad City	32	36	-	.471	8.0
Cedar Rapids	32	37	-	.464	8.5
Clinton	30	36	-	.455	9.0
Peoria	30	39	-	.435	10.5
Burlington	29	39	-	.426	11.0

SECOND HALF

EASTERN DIVISION

Team	W	L	T	Pct.	GB
South Bend	44	26	-	.629	...
Battle Creek	40	29	-	.580	3.5
Fort Wayne	31	38	-	.449	12.5
Lansing	31	39	-	.443	13.0
West Michigan	30	40	-	.429	14.0
Dayton	26	43	-	.377	17.5

WESTERN DIVISION

Team	W	L	T	Pct.	GB
Beloit	43	26	-	.623	...
Kane County	39	30	-	.565	4.0
Clinton	39	30	-	.565	4.0
Peoria	35	34	-	.507	8.0
Burlington	35	35	-	.500	8.5
Cedar Rapids	34	35	-	.493	9.0
Wisconsin	31	38	-	.449	12.0
Quad City	27	42	-	.391	16.0

COMPOSITE

Team	KNC	BLT	BTC	SBN	FTW	WIS	LAN	CLN	WMI	CR	PEO	BUR	DTN	QC	W	L	T	Pct.	GB
Kane County (Athletics)	...	10	4	5	6	5	5	5	3	7	9	8	6	7	80	59	0	.576	...
Beloit (Brewers)	5	...	6	3	4	9	3	7	5	4	9	9	6	5	75	61	0	.551	3.5
Battle Creek (Yankees)	4	2	...	8	7	5	6	4	10	5	5	2	9	6	73	64	0	.533	6.0
South Bend (Diamondbacks)	3	5	8	...	3	2	11	4	8	5	3	4	12	4	72	64	0	.529	6.5
Fort Wayne (Padres)	2	4	8	8	...	3	7	4	10	2	8	3	9	3	71	66	0	.518	8.0
Wisconsin (Mariners)	7	5	3	6	4	...	5	4	6	6	7	5	3	8	69	66	0	.511	9.0
Lansing (Cubs)	3	5	5	3	9	3	...	4	8	4	5	6	10	4	69	66	0	.511	9.0
Clinton (Rangers)	7	5	4	3	4	7	3	...	4	8	7	8	3	6	69	66	0	.511	9.0
West Michigan (Tigers)	5	3	6	8	6	2	8	4	...	6	5	6	3	5	67	73	0	.479	13.5
Cedar Rapids (Angels)	5	8	3	3	6	6	4	7	2	...	3	7	3	9	66	72	0	.478	13.5
Peoria (Cardinals)	3	3	3	5	0	9	3	5	3	8	...	8	6	9	65	73	0	.471	14.5
Burlington (Royals)	4	3	5	4	5	7	1	8	2	9	4	...	4	8	64	74	0	.464	15.5
Dayton (Reds)	2	2	7	4	7	4	6	5	9	5	2	4	...	4	61	78	0	.439	19.0
Quad City (Twins)	9	6	2	4	5	4	4	5	3	3	6	4	4	...	59	78	0	.431	20.0

Major league affiliations in parentheses.

PLAYOFFS: Battle Creek defeated Fort Wayne, two games to none; Beloit defeated Wisconsin, two games to none; Lansing defeated South Bend, two games to none; Clinton defeated Kane County, two games to one; Lansing defeated Battle Creek, two games to none; Beloit defeated Clinton, two games to one; Lansing defeated Beloit, three games to none, to win league championship.

REGULAR-SEASON ATTENDANCE: Battle Creek, 93,314; Beloit, 96,431; Burlington, 59,427; Cedar Rapids, 174,451; Clinton, 81,535; Dayton, 590,382; Fort Wayne, 257,013; Kane County, 516,133; Lansing, 364,623; Peoria, 246,370; Quad City, 132,983; South Bend, 203,690; West Michigan, 361,545; Wisconsin, 198,001. Total attendance—3,375,898. Playoffs (17 games)—20,928. All-Star Game at Comstock, Park, Mich.—10,037.

MANAGERS: Battle Creek, Mitch Seoane; Beloit, Don Money; Burlington, Joe Szekely; Cedar Rapids, Todd Claus; Clinton, Carlos Subero; Dayton, Donnie Scott; Fort Wayne, Gary Jones; Kane County, Webster Garrison; Lansing, Julio Garcia; Peoria, Joe Cunningham; Quad City, Jeff Carter; South Bend, Von Hayes; West Michigan, Phil Regan; Wisconsin, Daren Brown.

ALL-STAR TEAM: 1B—Prince Fielder, Beloit; 2B—Alberto Callaspo, Cedar Rapids; 3B—Travis Hanson, Peoria; SS—Erick Aybar, Cedar Rapids; OF—Felix Pie, Lansing; OF—Kennard Jones, Fort Wayne; OF—Rudy Guillen, Battle Creek; C—Jon Mark Sprowl, South Bend-Battle Creek; DH—(tie) Jayson Drobiak, Battle Creek and Brian Stavisky, Kane County; RHP—Gabe Ribas, Fort Wayne; LHP—Jon Connolly, West Michigan; RH Reliever—Dale Thayer, Fort Wayne; LH Reliever—Ian Ostlund, West Michigan; Most Valuable Player—Prince Fielder, Beloit; Prospect of the Year—Prince Fielder, Beloit; Manager of the Year—Webster Garrison, Kane County.

2003 BATTING

TEAM

Team	G	TPA	AB	R	H	TB	2B	3B	HR	RBI	SH	SF	HP	BB	IBB	SO	SB	CS	GDP	LOB	ShO	Avg.	OBP	Slg.
Cedar Rapids.	138	5202	4678	634	1238	1707	202	36	65	559	27	47	66	384	5	855	118	58	76	970	9	.265	.326	.365
Battle Creek...	137	5120	4544	628	1185	1765	230	28	98	560	32	55	64	425	16	808	76	40	93	957	10	.261	.329	.388
South Bend...	136	5133	4546	597	1186	1656	224	30	62	534	41	43	70	429	17	822	143	65	82	960	7	.261	.331	.364
Beloit............	137	5248	4560	639	1185	1630	192	26	67	563	104	39	73	472	22	877	172	59	85	1007	9	.260	.336	.357
Quad City......	138	5114	4690	573	1215	1635	200	29	54	510	54	37	5	327	13	763	94	55	94	980	14	.259	.306	.349
Wisconsin.....	136	5197	4635	618	1187	1698	226	27	77	538	29	39	66	427	13	1014	158	66	85	972	11	.256	.325	.366
Lansing.........	135	5012	4481	554	1133	1651	236	30	74	507	34	39	64	394	18	899	131	64	87	911	11	.253	.320	.368
Burlington.....	138	5329	4623	628	1168	1560	181	35	47	549	54	57	80	515	4	856	123	48	87	1051	13	.253	.334	.337
Kane County..	139	5394	4708	636	1188	1696	231	17	81	569	48	43	91	504	13	1029	123	51	84	1052	10	.252	.334	.360
Peoria...........	138	5099	4549	571	1133	1602	194	31	71	504	56	36	63	393	15	954	171	72	76	925	15	.249	.315	.352
Clinton..........	135	5056	4343	584	1073	1534	208	29	65	525	48	44	60	560	8	966	187	68	77	994	9	.247	.338	.353
W. Michigan..	140	5160	4527	570	1100	1583	188	50	65	495	54	28	55	496	12	965	119	63	100	978	9	.243	.323	.350
Dayton..........	139	5173	4593	580	1116	1555	195	17	70	525	39	35	79	426	15	1050	93	46	86	973	12	.243	.316	.339
Fort Wayne....	138	5073	4468	520	1043	1404	182	19	47	455	29	54	42	480	15	932	75	58	95	952	16	.233	.310	.314

INDIVIDUAL

TOP QUALIFIERS FOR BATTING CHAMPIONSHIP

Minimum 378 plate appearances. *Lefthanded batter. †Switch-hitter.

Player, Team	G	TPA	AB	R	H	TB	2B	3B	HR	RBI	SH	SF	HP	BB	IBB	SO	SB	CS	GDP	Avg.	OBP	Slg.
Callaspo, Alberto, C.R.†	133	565	514	86	168	220	38	4	2	67	0	6	3	42	4	28	20	6	8	.327	.377	.428
Sprowl, Jon-Mark, S.B.-B.C.*	124	505	418	77	134	185	30	3	5	62	2	5	9	71	0	39	5	5	7	.321	.425	.443
Murphy, Donald R., Burl.	132	588	504	77	158	214	29	6	5	98	3	7	9	65	1	78	15	6	8	.313	.397	.425
Fielder, Prince S., Beloit *	137	594	502	81	157	264	22	2	27	112	0	6	15	71	16	80	2	1	14	.313	.409	.526
Aybar, Erick J., C.R.†	125	535	496	83	153	221	30	10	6	57	6	3	13	17	0	54	32	9	6	.308	.346	.446
Lebron, Hector, Clinton *	91	379	351	40	107	147	17	4	5	45	0	4	0	24	0	56	6	5	9	.305	.346	.419
Bibbs, Kennard V., Beloit *.....	124	564	497	87	150	166	14	1	0	40	14	0	1	52	0	63	55	18	4	.302	.369	.334
Oeltjen, Trent C., Quad City *.	123	532	466	73	139	179	12	8	4	44	4	5	20	37	1	57	29	14	3	.298	.371	.384
Sprowl, Jon-Mark, S.B.*.......	95	385	321	56	95	135	22	3	4	42	2	3	5	54	0	31	5	4	6	.296	.402	.421
Merchan, Jesus D., Quad City	101	439	392	60	116	153	16	3	5	53	2	3	11	31	1	18	8	6	5	.296	.362	.390
Romero, Alexander R., Q.C.†.	120	476	423	50	125	159	16	3	4	40	5	4	1	43	3	43	11	8	10	.296	.359	.376
Drobiak, Jayson E., B.C.*.......	128	545	499	83	146	279	35	4	30	86	0	2	2	42	3	120	18	6	6	.293	.349	.559
Luellwitz, Sean P., S.B...........	128	533	475	59	138	228	34	1	18	79	0	1	7	49	5	82	5	2	8	.291	.365	.480
Pie, Felix, Lansing *	124	555	505	72	144	196	22	9	4	47	3	0	6	41	2	98	19	13	3	.285	.346	.388
Espino, Damaso M., Burl. † ...	130	569	480	58	137	177	25	3	3	88	6	8	6	69	1	76	8	4	15	.285	.377	.369

DEPARTMENTAL LEADERS: G—Clevlen, 138; AB—Nelson, 537; R—Bibbs, 87; H—Callaspo, 168; TB—Drobiak, 279; 2B—Callaspo, Nelson, 38; 3B—V. Mendez, 11; HR—Drobiak, 30; RBI—Fielder, 112; SH—Crabbe, 18; SF—Biernbaum, Dvorsky, Fransz, McAnulty, 9; HP—Oeltjen, 20; BB—Ringe, 82; IBB—Fielder, 16; SO—Nelson, 168; SB—Lemanczyk, 56; CS—K. Jones, 19; GIDP—Guillen, 16; Slg.—Drobiak, .559; OBP—Sprowl, .425.

ALL PLAYERS

*Lefthanded batter. †Switch-hitter.

Player, Team	G	TPA	AB	R	H	TB	2B	3B	HR	RBI	SH	SF	HP	BB	IBB	SO	SB	CS	GDP	Avg.	OBP	Slg.
Abram, Matthew J., C.R........	41	144	132	19	26	54	7	0	7	24	0	0	1	11	0	35	1	0	2	.197	.264	.409
Abruzzo, Jared A., C.R. †.......	130	534	468	64	127	198	30	1	13	73	0	5	2	59	0	99	1	0	7	.271	.352	.423
Agosto, Rolando, Fort Wayne	9	26	24	1	4	5	1	0	0	1	0	0	0	2	0	5	2	0	1	.167	.231	.208
Agustin, Hugo, Clinton..........	17	65	58	8	14	21	4	0	1	6	1	2	0	4	0	22	1	2	0	.241	.281	.362
Alexander, Alexis G., Burl.......	16	55	50	2	7	9	0	1	0	7	0	2	1	2	0	24	1	0	0	.140	.182	.180
Andrus, Erold E., B.C. †	35	147	140	20	40	50	5	1	1	6	1	0	0	6	0	20	1	2	3	.286	.315	.357
Aoki, Tomoshi, Wis.	53	157	134	21	30	43	8	1	1	10	3	0	2	19	0	40	2	1	3	.218	.325	.308
Araque, M. Tulio, Dayton........	12	39	35	2	3	4	1	0	0	1	1	0	2	1	0	12	0	0	0	.086	.158	.114
Arias, Joaquin, Battle Creek...	130	520	481	60	128	165	12	8	3	48	7	3	3	26	0	44	12	5	7	.266	.306	.343
Arroyo, Carlos F., Wis. *	101	401	359	47	98	122	11	2	3	40	6	2	0	34	1	49	18	8	4	.273	.334	.340
Asadoorian, Eric A., Clinton ...	45	195	176	35	48	72	7	1	5	22	0	0	1	18	0	43	12	6	3	.273	.344	.409
Avlas, A. Phil, South Bend	47	154	133	14	27	37	7	0	1	15	2	3	0	16	0	17	4	1	5	.203	.283	.278
Ayala, Odannys, Clinton	3	12	11	1	1	1	0	0	0	0	0	0	0	1	0	4	0	0	1	.091	.167	.091
Aybar, Erick J., C.R. †	125	535	496	83	153	221	30	10	6	57	6	3	13	17	0	54	32	9	6	.308	.346	.446
Baez, Fleming, Clinton...........	2	2	2	0	0	0	0	0	0	0	0	0	0	0	0	2	0	0	0	.000	.000	.000
Baker, John D., K.C. *	82	365	304	42	94	139	23	2	6	49	0	4	10	47	2	77	1	0	4	.309	.414	.457
Baker, Steve A., Fort Wayne...	127	510	464	53	112	158	16	3	8	51	0	2	12	32	2	117	11	8	10	.241	.306	.341
Ball, Jarred A., South Bend †.	125	518	463	62	130	169	23	2	4	52	2	5	5	41	2	84	32	11	11	.281	.342	.365
Barrett, Richard T., S.B.	47	92	82	6	17	20	3	0	0	9	1	2	1	6	0	20	12	2	1	.207	.264	.244
Basil, Jason M., Kane County	105	401	343	37	83	107	13	1	3	36	2	2	4	50	1	64	4	1	8	.242	.343	.312
Bassett, Michael H., Dayton *	28	91	82	9	24	34	4	0	2	19	0	2	0	7	1	21	1	0	1	.293	.341	.415
Belz, Timothy E., Peoria.........	9	16	15	0	0	0	0	0	0	1	0	0	1	0	0	6	0	1	1	.000	.063	.000
Bibbs, Kennard V., Beloit *.....	124	564	497	87	150	166	14	1	0	40	14	0	1	52	0	63	55	18	4	.302	.369	.334
Biernbaum, Leonard J., F.W. *	124	511	444	55	105	163	16	6	10	66	0	9	2	56	2	91	3	2	9	.236	.319	.367
Blase, Blake R., B.C. *	8	21	16	2	1	1	0	0	0	0	0	0	0	5	0	12	0	0	0	.063	.286	.063
Bohanan, Keith, Beloit...........	38	109	94	9	17	17	0	0	0	6	5	0	2	8	0	32	3	0	1	.181	.260	.181
Bohn, Thomas J., Wisconsin.	128	556	471	75	128	202	31	2	13	70	1	6	8	70	1	131	16	8	5	.272	.371	.429
Bolivar, Luis E., Dayton †.......	57	207	183	26	42	58	8	1	2	14	3	1	3	17	0	42	6	5	1	.230	.304	.317
Bone, J. Blake, Wisconsin *...	12	44	35	5	8	12	4	0	0	4	0	1	2	6	0	7	0	0	2	.229	.364	.343
Boone, Matthew J., Dayton....	55	231	210	21	41	56	9	0	2	16	0	1	2	17	0	70	2	0	3	.195	.261	.267
Booth, Steven W., Dayton	4	13	10	0	2	3	1	0	0	3	0	1	2	0	0	7	0	0	0	.200	.308	.300

Player, Team	G	TPA	AB	R	H	TB	2B	3B	HR	RBI	SH	SF	HP	BB	IBB	SO	SB	CS	GDP	Avg.	OBP	Slg.
Boyer, J. Kyle, Peoria	36	137	121	18	21	28	5	1	0	8	2	2	2	10	0	28	7	1	4	.174	.244	.231
Brito, Angel S., W. Mich.	9	24	23	0	2	2	0	0	0	0	0	0	1	0	0	4	0	0	1	.087	.125	.087
Brooks, Cedric B., F.W.-S.B.	111	440	390	62	102	155	26	6	5	48	0	4	10	36	1	104	1	7	6	.262	.336	.397
Brown, Matthew B., C.R.	49	189	164	22	34	51	6	1	3	15	0	1	5	19	0	36	1	0	4	.207	.307	.311
Brown, Nebasett W., S.B. *	133	557	491	74	127	182	24	5	7	42	5	5	9	47	0	59	19	10	6	.259	.332	.371
Burgamy, Brian R., F.W. †	130	539	455	69	101	137	20	2	4	35	2	3	1	78	2	98	17	4	6	.222	.335	.301
Burgos, J. Omar, Quad City	127	506	456	45	102	123	13	1	2	33	3	4	12	31	1	99	4	1	9	.224	.288	.270
Burkhart, Lance E., Clinton	3	12	9	0	2	2	0	0	0	1	0	1	1	1	0	4	0	0	0	.222	.333	.222
Butler, Keith I., Lansing	121	485	432	47	108	150	27	0	5	56	3	8	4	38	3	51	21	4	11	.250	.311	.347
Cairns, Troy M., Dayton	18	77	72	8	15	18	3	0	0	7	2	0	0	3	0	8	0	0	3	.208	.240	.250
Callahan, Daniel T., S.B. *	22	72	66	7	13	15	2	0	0	4	0	0	0	6	0	8	2	0	3	.197	.264	.227
Callaspo, Alberto, C.R. †	133	565	514	86	168	220	38	4	2	67	0	6	3	42	4	28	20	6	8	.327	.377	.428
Camacho, Juan P., B.C. †	78	297	273	16	60	81	12	0	3	37	2	5	5	12	3	39	1	0	10	.220	.261	.297
Campos, Tiago, Dayton	64	225	211	18	41	64	9	1	4	11	4	1	2	7	0	56	2	1	3	.194	.226	.303
Carlin, Luke C., Fort Wayne †	17	54	50	2	12	12	0	0	0	4	0	0	0	4	0	11	0	1	2	.240	.296	.240
Carson, Matthew R., B.C.	119	482	432	61	112	167	20	1	11	52	0	7	6	37	3	100	1	1	5	.259	.322	.387
Carter, Nicholas A., Beloit	62	219	200	17	29	34	3	1	0	18	5	2	0	12	1	50	6	4	5	.145	.192	.170
Chauncey, Clinton R., Peoria	15	43	34	5	10	13	3	0	0	7	2	0	1	6	0	12	2	0	0	.294	.415	.382
Chirinos, Robinson D., Lan.	108	403	362	51	84	134	27	1	7	39	4	2	7	28	0	82	10	2	11	.232	.298	.370
Clevlen, Brent A., W. Mich.	138	560	481	67	125	197	22	7	12	63	0	3	4	72	0	111	6	3	16	.260	.359	.410
Coats, Buck, Lansing *	132	564	488	64	135	177	25	7	1	59	6	2	4	64	5	93	32	15	13	.277	.364	.363
Colamarino, Brant A., K.C. *	133	576	498	68	129	212	26	0	19	80	1	5	13	59	4	101	1	0	2	.259	.350	.426
Collins, Kevin C., Lansing *	89	350	306	40	69	132	19	1	14	43	0	3	2	39	4	116	1	3	1	.225	.314	.431
Contreras, Sergio A., C.R. *	12	42	34	6	6	7	1	0	0	3	0	0	2	6	0	7	3	1	1	.176	.333	.206
Cook, Jeff, South Bend *	65	269	233	30	65	86	12	3	1	18	4	2	4	26	4	33	10	2	4	.279	.358	.369
Cordova, Roman L., Wis. †	23	78	75	10	17	18	1	0	0	5	1	0	0	2	0	10	1	1	3	.227	.247	.240
Correll, Richard B., Dayton	78	314	276	50	78	124	20	1	8	48	1	3	4	30	0	44	9	2	3	.283	.358	.449
Cosby, Quantwan J., C.R. †	104	419	370	55	92	98	4	1	0	21	7	4	2	36	0	79	17	9	7	.249	.316	.265
Coughlan, Cameron B., Clin.†	113	428	352	67	96	119	9	7	0	24	9	1	0	66	0	88	47	13	4	.273	.387	.338
Crabbe, Callix S., Beloit †	129	557	465	79	121	161	25	6	1	46	18	3	3	68	0	52	25	9	12	.260	.356	.346
Craig, Beau J., K.C. †	25	93	76	9	16	24	2	0	2	11	1	0	0	16	0	21	0	0	3	.211	.348	.316
Creighton, Matthew D., Lan.	43	148	135	21	31	56	7	3	4	15	0	0	3	10	0	28	4	2	2	.230	.297	.415
Cruz, Luis A., Fort Wayne	129	529	481	55	111	161	24	1	8	53	5	8	5	30	1	55	2	2	15	.231	.279	.335
Cruz, Nelson R., Kane County	119	515	470	65	112	202	26	2	20	85	1	6	9	29	2	128	10	5	7	.238	.292	.430
Cruz, Orlando O., Clinton	51	140	117	19	26	29	3	0	0	11	2	2	4	15	0	32	4	1	1	.222	.326	.248
Davidson, Seth A., Quad City	109	470	428	52	114	154	26	1	4	58	4	5	15	18	1	32	7	6	7	.266	.315	.360
Davis, Justin L., Dayton *	38	146	120	14	29	44	6	0	3	24	0	2	1	23	2	19	1	1	4	.242	.363	.367
De Leon, Virgilio, Fort Wayne	49	181	166	21	39	50	8	0	1	8	1	0	2	12	1	54	5	2	2	.235	.294	.301
Dean, Erik M., Burlington *	64	261	223	35	59	79	9	1	3	42	2	7	5	24	0	37	3	1	4	.265	.340	.354
Delgado, Gabriel, Clinton †	42	163	142	17	35	46	7	2	0	14	5	1	0	15	0	13	4	4	1	.246	.316	.324
Delucchi, Dustin J., Wis. *	43	177	143	22	38	53	9	0	2	15	3	0	1	29	3	28	2	2	2	.266	.393	.371
Dibetta, John M., Fort Wayne	14	56	48	8	9	12	3	0	0	6	0	2	0	6	0	15	0	1	1	.188	.268	.250
Dopirak, Brian A., Lansing	19	82	78	8	21	30	3	0	2	10	0	0	2	2	0	22	0	0	0	.269	.305	.385
Drobiak, Jayson E., B.C. *	128	545	499	83	146	279	35	4	30	86	0	2	2	42	3	120	18	6	6	.293	.349	.559
Duenas, Tomas J., C.R.	22	53	51	4	11	19	2	0	2	10	0	0	1	1	0	15	0	1	2	.216	.245	.373
Durham, Tyler R., Peoria	55	148	133	10	30	44	2	0	4	17	2	0	0	13	1	32	1	1	5	.226	.295	.331
Dvorsky, Alexander M., C.R.	96	356	302	42	76	113	10	3	7	36	0	9	10	35	0	52	2	2	2	.252	.340	.374
Ehrnsberger, Chad, Wis.-Peo.	46	191	167	24	48	76	8	1	6	28	0	3	2	19	0	36	3	3	2	.287	.361	.455
Eickhorst, Chris E., Peoria	10	37	30	7	6	10	2	1	0	2	0	0	0	7	0	10	0	0	0	.200	.351	.333
Ernster, Mark T., Beloit	9	37	35	7	8	13	2	0	1	5	0	0	0	2	0	11	1	0	0	.229	.270	.371
Esparragoza, Pedro, Beloit	75	293	254	36	62	79	9	1	2	23	13	3	2	21	2	48	14	3	6	.244	.304	.311
Espino, Damaso M., Burl. †	130	569	480	58	137	177	25	3	3	88	6	8	6	69	1	76	8	4	15	.285	.377	.369
Ethier, Andre E., K.C. *	40	183	162	23	44	54	10	0	0	11	0	0	2	19	2	25	2	2	4	.272	.355	.333
Eure, Jeffrey R., Beloit	123	527	475	69	116	178	21	4	11	53	3	1	13	35	0	128	29	4	7	.244	.313	.375
Evans, Michael T., Peoria	104	410	382	35	94	154	28	1	10	41	4	2	3	19	0	86	13	6	8	.246	.286	.403
Falcon, Omar E., Fort Wayne	12	44	33	5	6	8	2	0	0	4	1	0	0	10	0	15	0	0	0	.182	.372	.242
Fielder, Prince S., Beloit *	137	594	502	81	157	264	22	2	27	112	0	6	15	71	16	80	2	1	14	.313	.409	.526
Firlit, Daniel J., South Bend	7	22	21	2	3	4	1	0	0	0	1	0	0	0	0	9	0	0	0	.143	.143	.190
Foreman, Julius L., Dayton *	12	57	50	6	11	12	1	0	0	2	1	0	0	6	0	9	0	1	0	.220	.304	.240
Fox, Jacob, Lansing	29	112	100	13	26	49	8	0	5	12	0	1	3	8	0	19	0	0	3	.260	.330	.490
Francia, Juan C., W. Mich. †	118	460	405	49	97	116	7	6	0	27	10	0	3	42	0	78	31	14	3	.240	.316	.286
Fransz, Jason A., Lan.-Clin.	89	353	306	32	80	125	13	1	10	46	0	9	8	30	0	73	4	4	3	.261	.334	.408
Frend, Timothy J., Burl.	120	504	453	57	121	182	22	3	11	55	4	4	4	39	0	75	8	5	13	.267	.328	.402
Fry, Ryan J., Dayton	59	232	214	30	50	101	4	1	15	42	1	0	4	13	0	80	1	0	1	.234	.290	.472
Garcia, Alexander, F.W. †	23	68	59	8	9	13	2	1	0	1	2	1	0	6	0	14	2	2	0	.153	.227	.220
Garcia, Cipriano T., Wis.	20	55	50	4	12	17	2	0	1	8	1	1	1	2	0	19	0	0	1	.240	.278	.340
Garciaparra, Michael R., Wis.	122	493	440	55	107	127	12	1	2	38	3	3	9	38	0	80	14	4	7	.243	.314	.289
Gates, J. David, C.R.	25	96	88	11	22	40	1	1	5	19	1	1	1	5	0	24	1	1	0	.250	.295	.455
Geiger, Kyle Z., Quad City	11	39	36	4	5	6	1	0	0	1	1	0	0	2	0	7	0	0	1	.139	.184	.167
Gil, Jerry B., South Bend	116	457	429	52	111	151	16	6	4	58	10	6	2	10	0	90	19	10	7	.259	.275	.352
Ginther, Andrew M., Peoria	3	9	8	1	2	2	0	0	0	1	0	0	0	1	0	3	0	0	0	.250	.333	.250
Girardi, Joseph E., Peoria	3	10	9	0	1	1	0	0	0	1	0	0	1	0	0	2	0	0	0	.111	.200	.111
Gold, Nathan G., Clinton	107	442	369	58	99	176	35	3	12	71	2	7	5	59	2	76	4	2	6	.268	.370	.477
Gomez, Francis J., K.C.	128	547	483	65	128	167	18	3	5	53	15	5	15	29	0	74	21	9	13	.265	.323	.346
Gomon, Dusty A., Quad City	42	165	150	19	23	38	9	0	2	18	0	2	2	11	0	45	2	1	3	.153	.218	.253
Gonzalez, Jose L., Clinton †	27	99	82	9	16	18	2	0	0	4	1	0	2	14	0	17	4	3	1	.195	.327	.220
Gonzalez, Juan M., W. Mich.†	126	535	453	65	113	153	16	6	4	39	9	4	4	65	2	81	24	10	7	.249	.346	.338
Gonzalez, Luis E., Burlington	64	236	210	15	36	48	3	0	3	15	1	2	11	12	0	58	0	1	7	.171	.251	.229
Gorecki, Reid E., Peoria	128	542	480	77	128	208	19	8	15	61	4	4	3	51	4	90	23	11	5	.267	.338	.433
Graham, Bryan P., Burl. *	15	64	60	7	14	16	2	0	0	3	0	0	0	4	0	11	0	0	1	.233	.281	.267
Grayson, Larry O., Clinton	75	242	208	29	43	76	14	2	5	28	2	2	1	29	1	71	6	3	7	.207	.304	.365

Player, Team	G	TPA	AB	R	H	TB	2B	3B	HR	RBI	SH	SF	HP	BB	IBB	SO	SB	CS	GDP	Avg.	OBP	Slg.
Griffin, Brock C., Wisconsin *	1	3	3	0	0	0	0	0	0	0	0	0	0	0	0	1	0	0	0	.000	.000	.000
Guillen, Rodolfo D., B.C.	133	537	493	64	128	204	29	4	13	79	0	5	7	32	0	87	13	6	16	.260	.311	.414
Guzman, Garrett J., Q.C.*	82	332	298	44	84	119	18	4	3	33	5	1	5	23	3	22	2	1	7	.282	.343	.399
Guzman, Jacob P., Burlington	1	6	6	0	1	1	0	0	0	0	0	0	0	0	0	1	0	0	0	.167	.167	.167
Gwynn, Anthony K., Beloit * ..	61	279	236	35	66	77	8	0	1	33	4	5	2	32	0	31	14	2	3	.280	.364	.326
Hagen, Matthew M., Wis.	126	515	450	65	99	190	28	0	21	65	0	5	4	56	2	129	8	6	7	.220	.309	.422
Haley, Adam J., S.B. *	18	46	40	2	5	6	1	0	0	1	1	0	2	3	0	11	0	1	0	.125	.222	.150
Hamblen, Christopher W., Clin.†	8	30	27	3	7	11	2	1	0	3	0	0	0	3	0	5	0	2	0	.259	.333	.407
Hancock, Justin K., C.R.	23	69	62	3	10	13	3	0	0	2	0	0	1	6	0	24	0	0	1	.161	.246	.210
Hanigan, Ryan M., Dayton	92	359	311	43	86	101	12	0	1	31	1	3	4	40	1	44	3	4	8	.277	.363	.325
Hanson, Travis O., Peoria *....	136	574	527	70	146	214	31	5	9	78	1	6	5	35	7	104	3	4	11	.277	.325	.406
Harrington, Corey M., Wis.	93	398	353	55	91	129	18	7	2	31	1	3	12	29	0	69	20	9	6	.258	.332	.365
Harris, E. Garrison, Wis. *	127	577	525	80	149	200	25	7	4	52	2	5	8	36	2	75	36	13	12	.285	.337	.384
Hawes, Bobby, Dayton	11	44	44	6	10	18	2	0	2	4	0	0	0	0	0	8	1	0	0	.227	.227	.409
Heath, Demetrius M., W.Mich.	73	228	195	34	50	63	6	2	1	24	1	3	3	26	0	39	5	3	3	.256	.348	.323
Heether, Adam R., Beloit	47	196	171	28	39	59	12	1	2	22	4	0	3	18	0	28	4	4	4	.228	.313	.345
Hickman, Charles J., Lansing.	9	31	30	3	6	7	1	0	0	1	1	0	0	0	0	7	1	0	0	.200	.200	.233
Hileman, Justin J., Peoria	37	139	120	20	30	37	4	0	1	11	1	1	1	16	0	24	3	2	4	.250	.341	.308
Hinton, Travis C., Beloit *	103	418	372	37	86	136	21	1	9	58	8	5	6	27	1	72	1	1	10	.231	.290	.366
Hood, Donald G., Lansing	49	205	186	36	59	104	16	1	9	32	0	2	2	15	2	46	0	2	2	.317	.371	.559
Howard, Kevin C., Dayton * ...	134	578	509	80	145	204	26	3	9	75	6	5	8	50	4	67	12	5	15	.285	.355	.401
Huether, John D., Quad City...	35	137	125	11	31	35	4	0	0	14	0	1	1	10	1	11	0	1	6	.248	.307	.280
Hutchinson, Burnell F., S.B. *	10	30	25	4	4	5	1	0	0	2	0	0	0	5	0	7	2	0	0	.160	.300	.200
Jacobo, Kervin M., S.B.-F.W.†	75	265	239	15	49	61	9	0	1	21	3	2	1	20	0	76	4	4	7	.205	.267	.255
Jaile, Christopher A., Clinton .	90	342	289	29	69	90	12	0	3	30	1	3	2	47	0	60	1	2	10	.239	.346	.311
Jaramillo, Milko A., Peoria †..	96	368	329	37	75	100	10	3	3	16	11	0	9	18	0	53	7	6	9	.228	.287	.304
Jenkins, Kevin D., C.R. *	50	141	123	9	21	26	0	1	1	9	3	1	2	12	0	37	6	2	2	.171	.254	.211
Jensen, David C., Burl. *........	105	425	371	32	76	91	10	1	1	21	1	4	3	46	0	90	3	2	3	.205	.295	.245
Johnson, Bryan D., S.B. †......	20	66	58	6	15	22	2	1	1	5	0	0	1	7	0	11	0	0	1	.259	.348	.379
Johnson, Jonathan J., Lan.....	104	397	361	40	87	110	10	2	3	41	0	2	1	33	1	55	6	2	14	.241	.305	.305
Johnson, Joshua N., Q.C.	12	37	34	2	6	6	0	0	0	0	0	0	0	3	1	9	0	0	1	.176	.243	.176
Jones, Kennard D., F.W. *	81	364	306	61	94	118	13	4	1	30	3	2	3	50	2	52	20	19	5	.307	.407	.386
Jones, Nick, Lansing	42	126	119	11	23	31	6	1	0	6	0	1	4	2	0	19	3	2	2	.193	.230	.261
Kaaihue, M. Kila, Burl. *	114	482	395	53	94	150	21	1	11	63	6	6	8	67	1	87	1	3	13	.238	.355	.380
Kennedy, Bryan R., Q.C.*	63	264	223	26	66	95	10	2	5	36	1	2	10	28	0	33	0	0	1	.296	.395	.426
Kennedy, Jason, W. Mich.	19	47	39	2	4	7	1	1	0	2	0	0	0	8	0	11	0	0	0	.103	.255	.179
Keown, Clinton W., Dayton	17	65	55	6	14	14	0	0	0	0	2	0	0	8	0	15	1	2	1	.255	.349	.255
Knoedler, Jason A., W.Mich.†	91	287	248	36	52	74	10	0	4	25	5	2	3	29	0	75	14	2	4	.210	.298	.298
Kuhaulua, Kaulana K., Q.C.	57	217	196	24	45	62	12	1	1	21	3	0	2	16	0	38	5	2	9	.230	.294	.316
Lafferty, William C., Peoria.....	17	51	46	4	8	11	0	0	1	4	1	0	2	2	0	13	0	0	1	.174	.240	.239
Lebron, Edgardo J., Q.C.†......	53	202	195	16	38	48	4	0	2	12	4	1	0	2	0	57	0	0	5	.195	.202	.246
Lebron, Hector, Clinton *	91	379	351	40	107	147	17	4	5	45	0	4	0	24	0	56	6	5	9	.305	.346	.419
Lemanczyk, Matthew J., Peo.	125	536	477	74	130	147	12	1	1	32	10	4	4	41	1	83	56	13	5	.273	.333	.308
Lemon, Timothy, Peoria	48	172	156	15	29	41	6	0	2	12	0	1	2	13	0	46	9	2	2	.186	.256	.263
Lewis, Domonique A., Dayton	46	171	155	25	44	55	8	0	1	19	0	2	5	9	0	31	10	2	3	.284	.339	.355
Lima, Joseph W., F.W.	20	69	63	6	13	19	3	0	1	5	0	0	0	6	0	15	0	0	0	.206	.275	.302
Liz, Jose R., Quad City	34	106	101	5	22	25	3	0	0	6	1	1	1	2	0	24	1	1	1	.218	.238	.248
Lonnquist, Eric M., Burl.	55	215	175	30	38	41	3	0	0	8	5	0	6	29	0	29	6	0	0	.217	.348	.234
Lopaze, Daniel M., Lansing *.	10	37	31	2	7	10	3	0	0	2	1	1	0	4	0	11	0	0	1	.226	.306	.323
Lopez, Gabe, Battle Creek	121	501	426	58	115	155	21	2	5	41	11	7	10	47	0	52	7	3	12	.270	.351	.364
Luellwitz, Sean P., S.B.	128	533	475	59	138	228	34	1	18	79	0	1	7	49	5	82	5	2	8	.291	.365	.480
Lytle, Derrik T., Burlington * ..	47	185	157	27	35	46	6	1	1	9	7	3	2	16	0	43	3	2	3	.223	.298	.293
Macias, Andres A., F.W. *	1	3	2	0	0	0	0	0	0	0	1	0	0	0	0	1	0	0	1	.000	.000	.000
Madera, Sandy M., B.C.	48	163	144	25	43	66	8	0	5	23	0	0	1	18	1	30	0	0	2	.299	.380	.458
Maher, Caleb C., C.R.	92	361	335	36	78	118	13	3	7	46	0	4	6	16	0	71	2	1	7	.233	.277	.352
Majewski, Dustin C., K.C. *....	4	19	18	2	3	4	1	0	0	2	0	0	0	1	0	9	0	0	0	.167	.211	.222
Maples, Christopher D., W.Mich.	85	260	235	23	44	67	11	0	4	27	0	2	2	21	0	47	1	2	1	.187	.258	.285
Martinez, Domingo, F.W.	8	19	17	1	3	4	1	0	0	1	1	0	0	1	0	6	0	0	0	.176	.222	.235
Martinez, Freddy, Dayton	4	13	13	2	2	4	2	0	0	1	0	0	0	0	0	3	0	0	0	.154	.154	.308
Mathis, Jacob D., C.R. *	104	386	354	32	81	104	9	1	4	40	3	1	3	25	0	104	5	5	4	.229	.285	.294
Matienzo, Daniel, Quad City ...	90	381	349	45	96	167	20	3	15	59	5	1	4	22	0	77	1	0	7	.275	.324	.479
McAnulty, Paul M., F.W. *	133	542	455	48	124	172	27	0	7	73	2	9	9	67	2	82	5	3	7	.273	.370	.378
McBeth, Marcus A., K.C.	68	272	234	30	60	87	9	3	4	26	3	1	6	28	0	57	8	4	3	.256	.349	.372
McCoy, Michael H., Peoria	131	544	464	67	117	158	16	5	5	46	10	3	16	51	0	77	24	10	2	.252	.345	.341
McCurdy, John C., K.C.	130	575	515	64	141	188	33	1	4	52	7	6	13	34	0	86	22	5	14	.274	.331	.365
McGehee, Casey M., Lansing.	64	258	243	24	66	95	18	1	3	23	0	3	2	10	0	46	2	3	8	.272	.302	.391
McNulty, Joseph S., Wis. *....	11	25	23	3	5	6	1	0	0	1	0	0	0	2	0	1	0	0	0	.217	.280	.261
Medlin, Clifton J., Lansing	12	33	30	2	3	4	1	0	0	0	1	0	1	1	0	12	0	0	0	.100	.156	.133
Mejia, Gilberto, W. Mich. †.....	34	126	115	14	23	30	2	1	1	9	3	0	0	8	0	31	0	1	3	.200	.252	.261
Melgarejo, Ransel A., C.R.	85	327	290	43	76	98	11	1	3	28	3	2	4	28	0	40	9	5	8	.262	.333	.338
Mendez, Mario A., Beloit	111	386	350	38	86	113	13	4	2	30	9	2	1	24	0	81	6	5	9	.246	.294	.323
Mendez, Victor M., W. Mich.†	137	531	471	64	111	180	20	11	9	63	10	1	2	47	3	85	14	8	15	.236	.307	.382
Merchan, Jesus D., Quad City	101	439	392	60	116	153	16	3	5	53	2	3	11	31	1	18	8	6	5	.296	.362	.390
Merritt, Timothy L., Wis.	84	371	339	44	87	113	12	4	2	26	6	2	2	22	1	62	24	6	8	.257	.304	.333
Metheny, Brenton E., Wis. * ..	24	96	86	7	19	20	1	0	0	7	1	0	0	9	0	17	1	1	3	.221	.295	.233
Miller, Christopher J., Lan......	5	16	12	2	3	4	1	0	0	3	0	1	2	1	0	2	0	1	0	.250	.375	.333
Molina, Felix N., Quad City †..	79	297	268	33	65	82	11	0	2	31	3	3	4	19	1	33	3	6	10	.243	.299	.306
Monahan, Joseph P., Lansing	5	20	18	3	2	2	0	0	0	3	0	0	0	2	0	1	1	1	2	.111	.200	.111
Monette, Daylon, Peoria †......	23	65	61	4	11	13	2	0	0	4	0	0	1	3	0	8	0	0	0	.180	.231	.213
Moore, Scott A., W. Mich. *...	107	421	372	40	89	135	16	6	6	45	0	1	7	41	0	110	2	4	9	.239	.325	.363
Morales, Jose G., Quad City †	48	182	170	14	46	64	10	1	2	25	3	1	3	5	0	32	0	1	6	.271	.302	.376

Player, Team	G	TPA	AB	R	H	TB	2B	3B	HR	RBI	SH	SF	HP	BB	IBB	SO	SB	CS	GDP	Avg.	OBP	Slg.
Morgan, Matthew D., S.B.	16	54	48	6	10	11	1	0	0	4	1	0	1	4	0	10	0	0	0	.208	.283	.229
Morton, K. Colt, Fort Wayne	22	81	76	5	13	23	4	0	2	7	0	0	0	5	1	28	0	0	2	.171	.222	.303
Moss, Steve J., Beloit	57	228	186	25	54	71	8	3	1	22	2	4	4	32	1	44	7	5	0	.290	.398	.382
Motte, Jason L., Peoria	48	148	133	8	27	28	1	0	0	10	4	1	0	10	0	44	1	1	4	.203	.257	.211
Murphy, Donald R., Burl.	132	588	504	77	158	214	29	6	5	98	3	7	9	65	1	78	15	6	8	.313	.397	.425
Murray, Joshua A., Beloit	10	37	32	4	6	8	2	0	0	4	1	0	2	2	0	11	0	0	0	.188	.278	.250
Nelson, Jonathan R., Wis.	134	565	537	71	142	232	38	2	16	91	0	5	7	16	1	168	13	3	11	.264	.292	.432
Nordness, Kirk T., K.C.	38	145	129	17	28	34	6	0	0	15	1	2	1	12	0	25	1	1	3	.217	.285	.264
Nunez, Andres A., B.C.	41	119	113	5	20	24	2	1	0	6	1	1	1	3	0	22	0	0	4	.177	.203	.212
O'Riordan, Chris, Clinton	48	205	172	26	56	71	10	1	1	26	0	1	6	26	0	21	8	3	6	.326	.429	.413
O'Toole, Paul J., Lansing *	8	28	25	3	9	10	1	0	0	3	0	0	0	3	0	3	2	0	0	.360	.429	.400
Oakes, Matt D., W. Mich.	42	94	87	8	20	26	3	0	1	7	3	0	1	3	0	17	0	2	3	.230	.264	.299
Oeltjen, Trent C., Quad City *	123	532	466	73	139	179	12	8	4	44	4	5	20	37	1	57	29	14	3	.298	.371	.384
Pagan, Andres A., F.W.	95	342	315	28	59	61	2	0	0	15	2	2	1	22	0	66	1	0	11	.187	.241	.194
Parker, Tyler K., Peoria	55	209	189	16	42	66	8	2	4	35	1	4	3	12	0	54	9	2	2	.222	.274	.349
Pattee, Benjamin, Quad City	5	17	14	0	4	4	0	0	0	2	1	0	1	1	0	3	0	1	0	.286	.375	.286
Paula, Manuel A., Dayton	48	180	162	16	28	31	1	1	0	9	2	1	4	11	0	61	7	2	1	.173	.242	.191
Pavkovich, Adam W., C.R.	35	147	125	20	40	49	6	0	1	18	3	4	2	13	0	19	1	1	2	.320	.382	.392
Perez, Miguel A., Dayton	20	68	58	3	10	10	0	0	0	3	2	0	4	4	0	19	1	0	2	.172	.273	.172
Perodin, Ronald J., Q.C.*	35	104	92	16	25	27	2	0	0	4	4	1	0	7	0	27	8	4	2	.272	.320	.293
Phillips, Christopher R., Wis.	32	97	92	4	23	27	4	0	0	12	0	0	1	4	0	19	0	1	4	.250	.289	.293
Pie, Felix, Lansing *	124	555	505	72	144	196	22	9	4	47	3	0	6	41	2	98	19	13	3	.285	.346	.388
Porter, Gregory A., C.R. *	79	318	279	48	85	124	17	5	4	52	0	3	6	30	1	52	1	2	6	.305	.381	.444
Quero, Pedro J., Clinton	81	336	303	45	78	120	13	1	9	47	0	4	3	26	2	47	14	3	6	.257	.318	.396
Rabelo, Michael G., W.Mich.†	123	438	394	41	108	139	16	0	5	40	5	5	3	31	3	62	9	4	13	.274	.328	.353
Raburn, Ryan N., W. Mich.	16	65	57	14	20	36	7	0	3	12	0	0	2	6	0	14	1	1	0	.351	.431	.632
Reyes, Ivan, Dayton	26	83	76	8	11	15	1	0	1	3	1	0	0	6	0	25	1	0	1	.145	.207	.197
Reyes, Jose R., Lansing †	70	256	234	18	56	65	9	0	0	20	2	1	3	16	0	37	2	1	3	.239	.295	.278
Reynolds, Lagatila M., S.B.	23	70	61	9	16	18	0	1	0	6	3	0	1	5	0	11	1	1	1	.262	.328	.295
Reynolds, Wilton E., W. Mich.	102	401	359	39	96	149	17	6	8	44	2	1	6	33	3	86	7	6	5	.267	.338	.415
Richardson, Kevin G., Clinton	22	81	67	4	11	11	0	0	0	4	0	1	3	10	1	22	0	1	1	.164	.296	.164
Richardson, Michael L., F.W.	7	22	16	6	3	3	0	0	0	1	0	0	0	6	0	4	0	0	1	.188	.409	.188
Richie, Anthony J., Lansing	21	66	57	6	10	12	2	0	0	4	2	0	1	6	0	12	0	0	2	.175	.266	.211
Ringe, Craig D., Clinton	119	531	419	62	91	125	19	3	3	36	12	4	14	82	0	102	16	7	4	.217	.360	.298
Rivera, Rene, Wisconsin	116	458	407	39	112	158	19	0	9	54	1	5	7	38	2	81	2	2	6	.275	.344	.388
Rodriguez, Marcos A., Peo.*	16	63	60	8	16	22	2	2	0	6	0	0	0	3	0	14	0	0	2	.267	.302	.367
Rogers, Nicholas W., K.C.	89	347	307	42	74	103	12	1	5	34	1	3	2	34	0	82	15	12	6	.241	.318	.336
Rojas, Thomas R., B.C.	52	192	162	13	34	48	9	1	1	18	1	4	4	21	0	43	0	1	3	.210	.309	.296
Romero, Alexander R., Q.C.†	120	476	423	50	125	159	16	3	4	40	5	4	1	43	3	43	11	8	10	.296	.359	.376
Romprey, Edward L., W.Mich.	9	23	22	1	1	2	1	0	0	0	1	0	0	0	0	4	0	0	0	.045	.045	.091
Roughton, Jody S., W.Mich.*	106	418	380	41	97	145	28	4	4	46	3	1	2	32	0	72	0	2	10	.255	.316	.382
Ruiz, Alvaro E., Dayton *	71	299	250	38	69	93	10	4	2	22	1	3	7	38	3	32	2	4	4	.276	.383	.372
Salas, Francisco I., Lansing	52	200	175	27	47	84	12	2	7	28	3	3	9	10	0	24	2	4	2	.269	.335	.480
Sanchez, Angel L., Burlington	106	449	408	54	110	126	8	1	2	35	6	3	4	28	0	52	14	5	10	.270	.321	.309
Santa, Alexander, B.C. *	31	107	103	12	26	31	3	1	0	7	0	0	1	3	0	19	3	5	1	.252	.280	.301
Santana, Emmanuel A., Clin.*	75	286	255	24	64	87	8	0	5	33	3	1	2	24	1	47	4	0	4	.251	.319	.341
Santana, Mayobanex A., S.B.	66	281	248	36	75	104	11	0	6	33	4	1	4	24	0	33	4	0	6	.302	.372	.419
Santiago, Rudy, S.B. *	73	230	215	16	44	52	6	1	0	13	2	2	1	10	0	48	6	7	5	.205	.241	.242
Santor, Johnathon A., Peo.†	133	539	474	57	127	186	28	2	9	71	1	4	6	54	2	105	4	5	4	.268	.348	.392
Santos, Omir, Battle Creek	82	319	277	35	65	82	11	0	2	30	6	8	3	25	0	36	0	0	8	.235	.297	.296
Sardinha, Bronson K., B.C. *	71	318	269	54	74	114	16	0	8	41	0	4	5	40	2	40	5	3	5	.275	.374	.424
Schmidt, Jarrod S., Dayton	69	281	254	28	72	107	15	1	6	33	1	2	3	21	1	61	3	1	4	.283	.343	.421
Schmidt, Jon-Paul, K.C. *	44	158	137	21	21	26	5	0	0	11	2	1	1	17	0	32	8	0	4	.153	.250	.190
Schramek, Mark E., Dayton *	57	232	206	29	61	92	18	2	3	37	1	1	5	19	1	58	2	1	4	.296	.368	.447
Senreiso, Juan, Clinton	121	515	473	48	102	143	18	4	5	58	5	4	3	30	0	117	45	8	7	.216	.265	.302
Serrano, Eddie, F.W.	38	122	110	11	25	27	2	0	0	3	1	0	2	9	0	28	0	5	5	.227	.298	.245
Shelley, J. Randall, Clinton	114	425	348	44	78	123	18	0	9	49	4	4	10	59	1	103	7	2	6	.224	.349	.353
Shirley, Steve, Fort Wayne	60	206	190	17	37	51	8	0	2	19	1	5	2	8	0	32	0	1	4	.195	.229	.268
Shorsher, J. Adam, F.W.	1	3	2	0	0	0	0	0	0	0	0	0	0	1	0	0	0	0	0	.000	.333	.000
Simon, Brandon D., S.B. *	17	43	36	6	7	8	1	0	0	3	0	0	6	1	1	2	7	1	0	.194	.326	.222
Smith, Rashad B., F.W. *	35	117	106	11	22	27	5	0	0	5	2	2	0	7	1	23	3	0	2	.208	.252	.255
Sprowl, Jon-Mark, S.B.-B.C. *	124	505	418	77	134	185	30	3	5	62	2	5	9	71	0	39	5	5	7	.321	.425	.443
Stanek, Jeffrey A., S.B. *	83	300	245	31	62	84	13	0	3	37	0	7	0	48	3	68	2	2	2	.253	.367	.343
Stavisky, Brian S., K.C. *	98	407	331	54	88	130	20	2	6	35	5	0	9	62	0	74	4	1	5	.266	.396	.393
Stephens, L. Bernard, Burl. *	121	483	432	64	106	137	15	5	2	34	5	2	3	41	0	106	24	12	6	.245	.314	.317
Stocker, M. Romel, Burl. †	103	474	403	85	110	153	16	9	3	33	8	2	15	46	0	48	36	5	0	.273	.367	.380
Stonard, Peter M., F.W. *	64	263	239	22	70	80	10	0	0	27	3	3	0	18	1	25	4	5	5	.293	.338	.335
Sugden, Jason A., C.R. †	21	64	56	6	17	19	0	1	0	7	1	0	0	7	0	21	0	1	1	.304	.381	.339
Sulbaran, Orlando L., Dayton	11	42	39	1	8	8	0	0	0	1	1	0	2	0	0	7	1	0	1	.205	.244	.205
Summerville, Kaazim F., B.C.	23	45	32	11	6	10	1	0	1	2	2	0	1	10	0	9	6	3	1	.188	.395	.313
Suomi, John Richard, K.C. *	69	263	241	29	62	86	19	1	1	28	1	5	2	14	1	34	4	2	1	.257	.298	.357
Teilon, Nilson, South Bend	105	389	358	50	99	140	16	2	7	55	1	1	10	19	0	61	7	3	5	.277	.330	.391
Terni, Charles A., Beloit	106	412	352	37	84	104	12	1	2	36	15	3	9	33	0	81	1	1	5	.239	.317	.295
Theriot, Ryan S., Lansing †	58	257	220	29	57	70	8	1	1	17	5	0	1	31	1	34	21	5	4	.259	.353	.318
Tiburcio, Hector A., Dayton †	114	455	407	53	93	106	9	2	0	22	7	2	3	36	2	90	22	8	11	.229	.295	.260
Tosca, Daniel S., S.B. *	19	59	46	4	12	14	2	0	0	4	1	0	1	11	1	9	0	0	2	.261	.414	.304
Tranum, Josh, Fort Wayne *	36	144	119	13	26	42	5	1	3	19	0	3	1	21	0	21	0	0	1	.218	.333	.353
Tritle, Christopher J., K.C.	42	141	132	11	23	30	2	1	1	10	2	1	0	6	0	48	6	2	4	.174	.209	.227
Tupman, Mathew D., Burl. *	81	333	296	32	66	90	12	3	2	38	0	7	3	27	1	41	1	2	4	.223	.288	.304
Turner, Lloyd S., K.C.	4	12	12	2	4	4	0	0	0	1	0	0	0	0	0	0	0	0	0	.333	.333	.333
Udy, Nicholas A., Wis. *	10	27	23	3	3	3	0	0	0	0	0	0	0	4	0	5	0	0	0	.130	.259	.130

Player, Team	G	TPA	AB	R	H	TB	2B	3B	HR	RBI	SH	SF	HP	BB	IBB	SO	SB	CS	GDP	Avg.	OBP	Slg.
Vanden Berg, John A., Beloit	76	305	276	37	82	115	12	0	7	39	3	2	4	20	1	56	2	2	4	.297	.351	.417
Vasquez, Wuillians M., B.C. †	66	266	229	29	51	84	16	1	5	26	1	4	2	30	0	64	3	3	5	.223	.313	.367
Vavao, Jason M., Dayton	60	242	219	25	49	73	9	0	5	32	1	1	3	18	0	49	3	2	4	.224	.290	.333
Verbryke, Eric E., B.C. *	113	421	358	59	97	154	22	4	9	38	0	3	9	51	4	63	6	1	4	.271	.373	.430
Voshell, Chase R., Peoria	68	244	217	22	52	67	9	0	2	21	2	2	3	19	0	45	7	5	6	.240	.307	.309
Votto, Joseph D., Dayton *	60	233	195	19	45	56	8	0	1	20	0	2	2	34	0	64	2	5	3	.231	.348	.287
Watson, Robert L., W. Mich.	58	242	191	32	48	62	5	0	3	22	2	5	12	32	1	38	5	1	7	.251	.383	.325
Wayment, Kory M., K.C.	115	375	316	55	78	99	6	0	5	30	6	2	4	47	1	92	16	7	3	.247	.350	.313
Webster, Anthony G., Clin.*	18	78	74	11	20	30	7	0	1	9	1	1	2	0	0	8	4	1	0	.270	.286	.405
Weed, James D., C.R. *	116	456	435	45	115	135	14	3	0	32	0	3	2	16	0	58	16	12	6	.264	.292	.310
Wells, Randy D., Lansing	24	78	67	5	10	10	0	0	0	1	3	1	0	7	0	14	0	0	0	.149	.227	.149
Whitrock, Scott R., Quad City	91	311	274	34	63	89	13	2	3	20	5	2	13	16	0	96	13	2	1	.230	.302	.325
Wilkins, Joseph E., S.B. †	19	59	52	3	7	8	1	0	0	4	0	2	1	4	0	12	1	0	1	.135	.203	.154
Williams, Matthew B., Peoria	2	8	7	0	2	2	0	0	0	0	0	0	0	1	0	2	0	0	0	.286	.375	.286
Wong, Travis K., Dayton	48	196	177	14	33	50	8	0	3	26	0	2	9	8	0	48	0	0	5	.186	.255	.282

PLAYERS WITH TWO OR MORE TEAMS

Player, Team	G	TPA	AB	R	H	TB	2B	3B	HR	RBI	SH	SF	HP	BB	IBB	SO	SB	CS	GDP	Avg.	OBP	Slg.
Brooks, Cedric B., S.B.	82	326	289	53	78	123	20	5	5	38	0	3	9	25	1	67	1	7	5	.270	.344	.426
Brooks, Cedric B., F.W.	29	114	101	9	24	32	6	1	0	10	0	1	1	11	0	37	0	0	1	.238	.316	.317
Ehrnsberger, Chad, Wis.	25	104	90	8	19	26	2	1	1	9	0	1	2	11	0	23	1	1	1	.211	.308	.289
Ehrnsberger, Chad, Peoria	21	87	77	16	29	50	6	0	5	19	0	2	0	8	0	13	2	2	1	.377	.425	.649
Fransz, Jason A., Clinton	12	48	39	5	10	16	3	0	1	4	0	1	1	7	0	6	0	0	0	.256	.375	.410
Fransz, Jason A., Lansing	77	305	267	27	70	109	10	1	9	42	0	8	7	23	0	67	4	4	3	.262	.328	.408
Jacobo, Kervin M., S.B. †	35	121	111	9	26	34	5	0	1	10	1	0	0	8	0	39	4	1	3	.241	.292	.313
Jacobo, Kervin M., F.W. †	40	144	127	5	22	26	4	0	0	11	2	2	1	12	0	37	0	3	4	.173	.246	.205
Sprowl, Jon-Mark, B.C. *	29	120	97	21	39	50	8	0	1	20	0	2	4	17	0	8	0	1	1	.402	.500	.515
Sprowl, Jon-Mark, S.B. *	95	385	321	56	95	135	22	3	4	42	2	3	5	54	0	31	5	4	6	.296	.402	.421

GRAND SLAMS—Luellwitz, 3; S. Baker, Biernbaum, Shelley, 2 each; Abram, Collins, L. Cruz, N. Cruz, Davis, Ehrnsberger, Espino, Fielder, Fransz, Fry, Gil, Ju. Gonzalez, Hagen, Harris, Maher, Merchan, Nelson, Salas, Santor, Schramek, Vanden Berg, Vavao, 1 each.

AWARDED FIRST BASE ON CATCHER'S INTERFERENCE—Ball 2 (Hanigan, Santos); Boone (Pagan); Delucchi (L. Gonzalez); Jaramillo (Geiger); Luellwitz (Madera); E. Santana (Santos); Voshell (Dvorsky); Whitrock (Wells).

2003 PITCHING

TEAM

Team	W	L	Pct.	ERA	G	CG	ShO	Sv.	IP	H	TBF	R	ER	HR	SH	SF	HB	BB	IBB	SO	WP	Bk.
Fort Wayne	71	66	.518	3.02	138	3	12	43	1203.2	1081	5070	529	404	62	34	44	59	373	9	1064	68	5
Lansing	69	66	.511	3.18	135	5	15	31	1180.1	1052	5042	536	417	43	45	27	85	427	10	1018	98	6
Kane County	80	59	.576	3.22	139	13	21	35	1239.2	1144	5196	519	444	49	46	38	64	348	10	966	67	9
South Bend	72	64	.529	3.29	136	7	16	35	1195.1	1097	5085	553	437	51	45	27	61	455	36	863	76	11
Wisconsin	69	66	.511	3.34	136	7	9	31	1198.1	1216	5161	569	445	51	58	45	63	403	8	889	71	11
Peoria	65	73	.471	3.48	138	5	8	36	1200.0	1185	5092	558	464	64	44	38	53	396	14	779	74	11
W. Michigan	67	73	.479	3.54	140	7	12	35	1201.0	1146	5192	583	472	52	51	48	68	472	21	933	80	9
Beloit	75	61	.551	3.65	137	3	10	34	1209.2	1195	5269	643	490	77	55	39	69	470	6	996	80	12
Battle Creek	73	64	.533	3.80	137	6	12	33	1184.1	1118	5076	598	500	72	38	56	66	448	13	884	62	11
Clinton	69	66	.511	3.94	135	1	8	39	1160.1	1217	5113	636	508	76	45	48	0	394	6	769	72	13
Cedar Rapids	66	72	.478	3.98	138	2	11	31	1199.2	1139	5307	656	530	69	50	59	84	551	20	864	117	6
Burlington	64	74	.464	4.05	138	5	10	30	1214.2	1149	5239	631	547	94	45	33	63	492	0	864	93	2
Dayton	61	78	.439	4.05	139	0	5	39	1203.0	1196	5225	639	541	85	39	47	63	484	19	923	101	9
Quad City	59	78	.431	4.45	138	3	6	29	1208.1	1215	5342	682	597	98	54	47	80	519	14	978	106	6

INDIVIDUAL

TOP QUALIFIERS FOR EARNED-RUN AVERAGE TITLE

Minimum 112 innings.*Lefthanded pitcher.

Pitcher, Team	W	L	Pct.	ERA	G	GS	CG	ShO	GF	Sv.	IP	H	TBF	R	ER	HR	SH	SF	HB	BB	IBB	SO	WP	Bk.
Connolly, Jonathan J., W.M.*	16	3	.842	1.41	25	25	5	2	0	0	166.0	128	658	37	26	4	7	6	2	38	2	104	2	1
Whitaker, Brian G., Ft Wayne	7	6	.538	2.09	26	26	3	1	0	0	164.0	149	657	60	38	5	3	5	7	20	0	121	8	0
Ribas, Gabriel A., Fort Wayne	13	3	.813	2.25	19	19	0	0	0	0	116.0	86	461	36	29	3	1	3	4	26	0	116	6	1
Teekel, Joshua B., Peoria	6	6	.500	2.36	26	16	0	0	3	1	118.1	107	503	43	31	1	7	2	14	39	1	85	11	1
Edwards, Bryan K., Ft Wayne	4	7	.364	2.40	39	10	0	0	11	2	112.1	104	459	41	30	4	0	3	2	29	0	79	9	0
Toledo, Jean C., Cedar Rapids	12	7	.632	2.44	24	24	0	0	0	0	136.1	132	577	60	37	6	4	7	14	50	1	58	9	1
Blanton, Joseph M., Kane Co.	8	7	.533	2.57	21	21	2	2	0	0	133.0	110	531	47	38	6	2	3	5	19	0	144	1	0
Fulmer, Thomas A., Wisconsin	9	8	.529	2.58	27	27	5	0	0	0	167.2	154	685	60	48	5	8	2	5	37	0	130	4	0
Garcia, Jose I., Battle Creek	9	8	.529	2.64	21	21	4	0	0	0	136.1	111	540	46	40	10	5	2	3	33	0	90	4	0
Livingston, Robert J., Wis.*	15	7	.682	2.73	26	26	1	0	0	0	178.0	176	733	72	54	10	7	7	12	28	0	105	1	3
Parra, Manuel A., Beloit *	11	2	.846	2.73	23	23	1	0	0	0	138.2	127	551	50	42	9	5	0	0	24	0	117	5	3
Doyle, Jared M., S.B.*	12	8	.600	2.78	27	26	3	2	1	0	148.2	124	621	64	46	6	7	2	6	65	1	93	5	3
Sarfate, Dennis S., Beloit	12	2	.857	2.84	26	26	0	0	0	0	139.2	114	581	50	44	11	4	5	3	66	0	140	5	2
Rosario, Adriano, South Bend	9	5	.643	2.86	27	27	0	0	0	0	160.1	149	652	69	51	3	6	5	7	30	0	119	8	4
Jimenez, Cesar E., Wis.*	8	11	.421	2.94	28	20	0	0	3	0	125.2	134	552	61	41	7	8	6	2	46	2	76	10	0

DEPARTMENTAL LEADERS: W—Connolly, S. Smith, 16; L—Vasquez, 13; Pct.—Sarfate, .857; G—Wylie, 57; GS—Dickinson, 28; CG—Connolly, Dickinson, Fulmer, 5; ShO—Dickinson, S. Smith, 3; GF—Wylie, 49; Sv.—Wilkinson, 30; IP—Dickinson, 191.1; H—Sandoval, 190; TBF—Dickinson, 766; R—Sandoval, 97; ER—Ackerman, Sandoval, 78; HR—Adamczyk, 15; SH—Dickinson, Sandoval, 9; SF—Cimorelli, 11; HB—Griffin, Hogan, O'Brien, T. Watson, 15; BB—Griffin, 97; IBB—McWilliams, 7; SO—Blanton, 144; WP—Griffin, 23; BK—J. Rodriguez, Rosario, J. Valdez, T. Watson, 4.

ALL PITCHERS

*Lefthanded pitcher.

Pitcher, Team	W	L	Pct.	ERA	G	GS	CG	ShO	GF	Sv.	IP	H	TBF	R	ER	HR	SH	SF	HB	BB	IBB	SO	WP	Bk.
Ackerman, Eric C., Burl. *	9	5	.643	4.69	26	25	0	0	0	0	149.2	156	652	87	78	10	7	7	6	62	0	74	4	0
Acosta, Manuel A., B.C.	0	8	.000	6.64	15	11	0	0	3	0	61.0	80	290	58	45	3	3	7	3	29	0	45	4	0
Adamczyk, Tyler F., Peoria	7	12	.368	4.49	26	26	1	0	0	0	140.1	158	614	81	70	15	6	3	8	48	1	93	8	0
Alliston, Joshua W., Beloit	4	6	.400	3.33	52	0	0	0	35	10	70.1	67	299	34	26	4	2	3	6	18	1	75	8	0
Arias, Daniel, Cedar Rapids	2	2	.500	4.39	29	0	0	0	12	0	41.0	41	186	22	20	1	1	5	4	21	1	37	2	0
Armitage, Barry P., Burlington	0	1	.000	6.52	8	0	0	0	4	1	9.2	14	45	7	7	1	0	1	1	4	0	5	0	0
Astacio, Hector B., C.R.	2	2	.500	4.18	6	6	0	0	0	0	28.0	32	120	18	13	1	1	1	1	6	0	19	1	0
Atencio, A. Gregory, Burl.	0	1	.000	12.38	2	0	0	0	0	0	8.0	15	46	12	11	3	0	0	2	5	0	7	4	0
Baez, Federico B., Lansing	4	3	.571	3.38	51	0	0	0	15	1	66.2	72	297	39	25	1	3	1	2	20	3	46	8	1
Baker, Jason L., Beloit	5	4	.556	4.08	21	6	0	0	3	0	57.1	70	264	35	26	5	1	1	7	18	0	35	3	0
Baker, T. Scott, Q.C.	3	1	.750	2.49	11	11	0	0	0	0	50.2	45	204	16	14	4	1	1	2	8	0	47	4	0
Ballouli, Khalid W., Beloit	5	4	.556	4.15	15	8	0	0	2	2	56.1	60	244	34	26	1	0	3	3	14	0	45	4	1
Barreto, Joel A., Dayton	4	3	.571	1.93	29	0	0	0	13	4	56.0	28	223	17	12	2	1	0	1	32	1	72	5	0
Barrett, Richard T., S.B.	0	0	.000	0.00	1	0	0	0	1	0	1.0	1	4	0	0	0	0	0	0	1	0	0	0	0
Barrett, William D., Q.C. *	0	1	.000	3.29	3	3	0	0	0	0	13.2	13	64	5	5	2	0	1	1	11	0	4	0	0
Batista, Gorky, Dayton	1	3	.250	3.69	8	8	0	0	0	0	46.1	46	189	25	19	3	2	4	2	11	0	30	2	0
Batista, Roberto, Peoria	3	1	.750	9.19	13	0	0	0	6	2	15.2	23	80	16	16	1	0	1	1	10	0	5	1	0
Bausher, Timothy M., Beloit	1	2	.333	3.33	19	0	0	0	9	3	27.0	19	112	12	10	3	2	0	0	12	0	39	2	1
Bayliss, Jonah J., Burlington	7	12	.368	3.86	26	26	2	1	0	0	140.0	129	624	78	60	11	4	8	10	69	0	133	9	0
Beam, Theodore L., B.C.	2	1	.667	5.82	5	5	0	0	0	0	21.2	27	100	16	14	3	0	0	2	8	0	19	0	0
Beavers, Kevin E., F.W. *	1	0	1.000	0.00	10	0	0	0	1	0	18.2	4	62	0	0	0	1	0	1	3	0	12	2	0
Bechtel, Charles A., F.W.	2	0	1.000	1.48	17	0	0	0	4	0	24.1	21	111	14	4	0	4	3	2	12	0	28	1	0
Bell, Gary D., Battle Creek *	1	3	.250	3.08	10	6	0	0	3	0	38.0	31	165	17	13	3	1	1	4	20	1	27	0	0
Beltre, Omar, Clinton	3	3	.500	2.39	16	5	0	0	7	1	49.0	46	198	19	13	4	1	1	1	11	0	27	5	1
Benik, Brett J., Lansing	2	0	1.000	3.20	18	0	0	0	4	1	25.1	25	109	10	9	0	0	0	1	8	0	30	0	1
Berry, Jonathan W., Dayton	2	2	.500	5.79	12	0	0	0	7	0	18.2	24	90	13	12	1	2	0	0	9	2	20	2	0
Bilke, Austin N., C.R.	1	3	.250	5.91	19	0	0	0	15	4	21.1	26	102	15	14	2	1	0	3	6	1	25	0	0
Blackburn, R. Nicholas, Q.C.	2	9	.182	4.86	16	10	2	1	4	1	76.0	78	320	44	41	13	4	3	4	18	0	40	5	0
Blair, Thomas C., Peoria *	2	2	.500	1.66	7	6	0	0	0	0	43.1	35	169	9	8	1	0	0	1	11	0	17	0	0
Blanton, Joseph M., K.C.	8	7	.533	2.57	21	21	2	2	0	0	133.0	110	531	47	38	6	2	3	5	19	0	144	1	0
Blasko, Chadd E., Lansing	0	1	.000	1.64	2	2	0	0	0	0	11.0	10	47	3	2	0	1	0	2	5	0	6	0	0
Bohanan, Keith, Beloit	0	0	.000	0.00	3	0	0	0	3	0	2.0	0	4	0	0	0	0	1	0	0	0	0	0	0
Booker, Christopher S., Day.	0	0	.000	9.00	5	0	0	0	1	0	5.0	4	23	5	5	3	0	0	0	4	0	6	0	0
Breslow, Craig A., Beloit *	3	4	.429	5.12	33	0	0	0	12	2	65.0	64	286	43	37	4	4	2	1	27	0	80	1	0
Bright, Nathan A., Clinton	2	1	.667	6.75	5	0	0	0	0	0	4.0	7	22	7	3	0	1	0	0	2	0	3	0	0
Brumit, Matthew J., B.C.	5	3	.625	2.47	43	0	0	0	40	23	47.1	48	204	15	13	2	3	2	4	13	2	29	1	0
Burch, Matthew D., Burlington	0	1	.000	2.20	8	0	0	0	6	1	16.1	16	68	4	4	0	1	0	0	5	0	13	5	0
Burch, Robert J., Peoria	0	2	.000	4.85	13	0	0	0	6	2	13.0	13	54	7	7	1	0	0	0	3	0	9	0	0
Burgos, Ambiorix, Burlington	0	1	.000	5.40	2	2	0	0	0	0	5.0	3	21	3	3	1	0	0	0	6	0	4	1	0
Burton, L. Jared, Kane County	2	1	.667	2.27	15	2	0	0	3	1	31.2	19	120	9	8	2	2	0	2	7	0	33	4	0
Cameron, Kevin J., Quad City	1	5	.167	3.92	39	0	0	0	16	2	62.0	57	281	30	27	2	5	1	2	33	5	58	13	0
Carpenter, Calvin R., Beloit	3	6	.333	3.86	16	12	0	0	1	0	60.2	53	289	40	26	4	0	2	4	50	0	46	5	0
Carroll, James C., C.R.	1	2	.333	2.56	23	0	0	0	12	5	31.2	25	131	12	9	4	1	2	2	10	1	19	2	0
Carter, Mark S., Lansing *	4	1	.800	2.25	45	0	0	0	15	0	52.0	32	204	14	13	2	5	0	4	11	1	54	3	0
Carter, Ramsey M., Burlington	0	0	.000	1.29	2	0	0	0	0	0	7.0	5	28	2	1	0	0	1	0	2	0	6	0	0
Cavazos, Andres, Peoria	5	4	.556	3.99	36	13	0	0	16	10	103.2	106	445	51	46	9	3	6	1	40	2	56	7	2
Cedeno, Jovanny R., Clinton	1	0	1.000	2.00	8	0	0	0	4	1	18.0	7	71	4	4	1	0	1	1	6	0	20	3	0
Chamberlain, Stephen G., Burl.	3	7	.300	3.38	33	0	0	0	23	10	74.2	54	302	29	28	5	3	0	4	23	0	57	6	1
Cherry, Rocky T., Lansing	2	0	1.000	2.76	8	4	0	0	2	0	29.1	23	119	10	9	1	2	0	4	7	0	18	3	0
Christensen, Daniel J., Burl. *	1	12	.077	5.92	17	16	0	0	1	0	79.0	83	353	62	52	11	1	5	7	31	0	46	2	0
Cimorelli, Brett M., C.R.	1	2	.333	7.57	31	5	0	0	10	0	69.0	89	351	68	58	8	4	11	11	54	1	31	6	1
Ciprian, Wilson, Peoria	0	1	.000	2.45	5	0	0	0	2	1	7.1	6	32	2	2	0	0	0	0	3	0	2	0	0
Clark, Raymond M., B.C.	8	7	.533	3.55	22	19	1	1	3	0	126.2	127	528	57	50	5	4	7	7	26	2	92	6	0
Coffey, J. Todd, Dayton	3	3	.500	2.25	39	0	0	0	26	9	56.0	61	235	20	14	1	3	4	2	14	0	53	3	0
Coffin, Ryan M., South Bend	3	9	.250	4.18	29	17	0	0	3	0	116.1	120	516	72	54	8	3	2	13	37	2	58	7	1
Colton, Kyle C., Burlington	0	0	.000	6.35	2	0	0	0	0	0	5.2	5	27	4	4	0	0	1	0	6	0	3	1	0
Connolly, Jonathan J., W.M.*	16	3	.842	1.41	25	25	5	2	0	0	166.0	128	658	37	26	4	7	6	2	38	2	104	2	1
Coonrod, Aaron J., F.W.	0	0	.000	0.00	4	0	0	0	1	0	7.0	6	31	1	0	0	0	0	0	3	0	9	0	0
Corona, Andrew, Fort Wayne	3	3	.500	4.94	21	1	0	0	8	0	31.0	37	151	20	17	1	1	2	6	15	0	22	4	0
Corrado, Robert P., Clinton	2	2	.500	6.86	6	4	0	0	0	0	21.0	33	103	18	16	4	0	1	3	6	1	17	0	0
Cortez, Renee A., Wisconsin	4	2	.667	2.91	28	0	0	0	18	4	46.1	40	193	20	15	3	1	3	4	16	0	51	2	0
Crawford, Tristan G., Q.C.	2	2	.500	5.45	19	0	0	0	9	1	34.2	45	168	27	21	5	1	0	3	17	1	17	5	0
Creighton, Matthew D., Lan.	0	1	.000	10.80	1	0	0	0	1	0	1.2	2	11	2	2	0	0	1	1	4	0	1	1	0
D'Amico, Leonardo S., C.R.	1	2	.333	5.90	12	5	0	0	3	1	29.0	33	131	20	19	5	3	2	2	7	1	16	2	1
Davis, Mikael J., South Bend	0	4	.000	6.55	23	0	0	0	7	1	34.1	44	171	34	25	2	3	1	1	25	5	20	3	0
Daws, Joshua L., Dayton	0	1	.000	1.74	18	0	0	0	17	11	20.2	11	89	7	4	1	2	1	2	12	0	24	2	0
Dejaynes, Brandon M., Peoria	0	0	.000	0.00	2	0	0	0	0	0	3.0	3	11	0	0	0	0	0	1	0	0	2	1	0
De la Cruz, Andres, Burlington	2	0	1.000	4.60	21	0	0	0	13	0	29.1	23	136	18	15	1	0	2	3	21	0	9	6	0
Delgado, Daniel, Wisconsin	0	0	.000	4.50	4	0	0	0	3	0	4.0	4	18	2	2	0	0	0	0	3	0	5	0	1
Delgado, Oscar H., Wis.*	3	3	.500	3.88	40	0	0	0	21	3	58.0	55	251	26	25	3	2	4	2	28	2	47	1	0
Desalvo, Matthew T., B.C.	2	0	1.000	0.82	3	3	0	0	0	0	22.0	15	82	5	2	0	0	0	0	5	1	21	0	0
Devenney, Nicholas R., Clin.	0	2	.000	8.36	6	2	0	0	0	0	14.0	13	74	18	13	0	0	2	2	16	0	13	3	0
Diaz, Luis J., West Michigan	0	0	.000	3.97	4	2	0	0	2	0	11.1	12	47	5	5	0	0	0	0	2	0	5	0	1
Dickinson, Andrew H., K.C.*	11	11	.500	3.15	28	28	5	3	0	0	191.1	168	766	75	67	4	9	5	1	42	1	114	4	1
Dorman, Richard E., Wis.	1	2	.333	2.80	25	1	0	0	12	4	45.0	36	187	19	14	1	1	0	0	24	0	62	10	0
Dowdy, Justin S., Wisconsin *	2	3	.400	5.92	10	1	0	0	1	0	24.1	25	105	18	16	1	2	1	1	7	1	23	2	0
Doyle, Jared M., S.B. *	12	8	.600	2.78	27	26	3	2	1	0	148.2	124	621	64	46	6	7	2	6	65	1	93	5	3
Doyne, M. Cory, Fort Wayne	4	6	.400	4.21	12	12	0	0	0	0	47.0	44	214	31	22	2	1	1	4	29	0	37	4	1

Pitcher, Team	W	L	Pct.	ERA	G	GS	CG	ShO	GF	Sv.	IP	H	TBF	R	ER	HR	SH	SF	HB	BB	IBB	SO	WP	Bk.
Drown, Erik L., Peoria	1	2	.333	4.74	5	5	0	0	0	0	24.2	27	109	16	13	0	0	0	2	12	0	15	3	0
Dulkowski, Marc A., F.W.	2	2	.500	6.66	16	0	0	0	8	3	24.1	29	122	22	18	2	1	1	1	17	0	14	5	0
Dunwell, Christopher J., K.C.	4	0	1.000	3.21	30	0	0	0	12	2	53.1	44	228	23	19	2	3	1	3	21	0	53	5	0
Edens, Kyle O., Dayton	0	0	.000	1.80	6	0	0	0	5	1	10.0	9	41	2	2	1	0	0	0	3	0	6	2	0
Edwards, Bryan K., F.W.	4	7	.364	2.40	39	10	0	0	11	2	112.1	104	459	41	30	4	0	3	2	29	0	79	9	0
Endicott, Drew D., Burlington	7	5	.583	3.73	32	11	1	1	14	5	115.2	125	490	55	48	6	8	1	2	29	0	60	6	0
Estes, Jonathan A., Peoria	2	2	.500	3.93	26	0	0	0	10	1	36.2	38	159	21	16	0	1	3	2	13	1	19	1	0
Farfan, Alexander E., Dayton	5	3	.625	3.73	40	0	0	0	18	4	79.2	73	335	35	33	2	2	3	3	30	2	43	10	2
Ferreras, Yorkin F., Lansing *	4	1	.800	3.56	10	9	1	0	0	0	55.2	50	230	22	22	3	1	2	1	15	0	62	3	2
Figueroa, Juan A., W. Mich.	2	5	.286	6.44	55	0	0	0	36	13	50.1	51	247	43	36	3	5	4	6	38	4	55	9	0
Fischer, Eric M., Quad City *	2	5	.286	5.02	11	11	0	0	0	0	57.1	57	253	36	32	9	3	4	2	28	0	42	2	1
Flynn, Brian J., Peoria	2	5	.286	4.24	30	0	0	0	12	2	34.0	30	147	18	16	4	2	2	0	17	3	19	4	0
Foli, Daniel J., Lansing	6	9	.400	4.08	34	13	0	0	4	0	103.2	93	463	57	47	5	3	3	7	64	2	84	7	0
Frias, Juan C., Dayton *	10	10	.500	3.54	25	25	0	0	0	0	140.0	140	594	68	55	9	4	4	7	53	1	94	6	0
Fulmer, Thomas A., Wisconsin	9	8	.529	2.58	27	27	5	0	0	0	167.2	154	685	60	48	5	8	2	5	37	0	130	4	0
Gabriel, Justin K., Beloit *	2	0	1.000	4.23	21	0	0	0	4	1	44.2	54	210	25	21	2	7	1	4	19	1	44	4	0
Galbraith, Jason W., Peoria *	0	0	.000	21.60	2	0	0	0	0	0	1.2	4	11	4	4	0	0	0	0	2	0	1	0	0
Garber, Michael A., S.B. *	0	0	.000	6.14	6	0	0	0	1	0	7.1	12	40	6	5	0	0	0	0	6	0	4	0	0
Garcia, Anderson, B.C.	3	6	.333	3.32	16	11	1	0	2	0	76.0	57	317	35	28	2	1	2	4	36	0	62	5	3
Garcia, Jairo, Kane County	0	1	.000	2.55	14	9	0	0	1	0	42.1	40	183	14	12	0	1	0	3	19	0	28	5	0
Garcia, Jose I., Battle Creek	9	8	.529	2.64	21	21	4	0	0	0	136.1	111	540	46	40	10	5	2	3	33	0	90	4	0
Gemmell, Donald S., Dayton	1	2	.333	5.24	22	2	0	0	9	0	44.2	53	197	26	26	3	1	4	2	12	1	33	9	2
George, Bradley M., Dayton	2	2	.500	3.38	24	1	0	0	5	1	50.2	42	219	22	19	4	2	1	8	21	0	39	1	0
Gerk, Jordan A., W. Mich. *	2	5	.286	3.07	55	1	0	0	10	2	67.1	69	287	26	23	4	1	5	4	12	0	68	0	0
Gillman, Justin P., Dayton	0	3	.000	3.96	7	7	0	0	0	0	36.1	33	160	23	16	4	0	3	0	16	0	22	3	0
Gliemmo, R. Hayden, C.R. *	7	3	.700	3.73	42	0	0	0	2	0	62.2	55	277	32	26	2	3	2	2	33	3	53	8	0
Goas, Adrian J., C.R.	0	0	.000	5.06	18	0	0	0	5	1	26.2	28	128	21	15	0	1	1	4	17	1	12	3	0
Gonzalez, Cristian J., K.C.	7	8	.467	4.47	19	14	3	1	3	0	92.2	99	403	51	46	5	7	3	7	26	0	52	7	0
Gonzalez, Enrique C., S.B.	4	3	.571	2.13	55	0	0	0	18	3	72.0	58	300	22	17	5	3	0	2	29	3	63	3	0
Graham, Jason M., W. Mich.	2	1	.667	4.23	28	0	0	0	8	0	44.2	51	204	24	21	2	2	4	2	25	1	20	8	0
Granado, Jan C., Dayton *	4	4	.500	4.39	13	13	0	0	0	0	69.2	77	310	38	34	5	3	6	4	20	0	45	6	2
Graves, Donovan D., Peoria	8	7	.533	3.22	22	22	2	0	0	0	128.2	137	540	56	46	8	3	3	5	24	0	59	6	0
Gray, Joshua M., Quad City *	3	3	.500	4.19	10	10	0	0	0	0	53.2	59	233	27	25	2	2	3	2	15	0	29	3	0
Green, Craig J., Lansing	0	0	.000	7.94	6	0	0	0	2	0	11.1	14	60	14	10	1	0	1	1	7	0	5	4	0
Gregg, Grant J., Fort Wayne *	0	0	.000	0.00	5	0	0	0	1	0	8.0	4	30	1	0	0	1	0	0	2	0	5	0	0
Griffin, J. Colt, Burlington	9	11	.450	3.91	27	27	0	0	0	0	149.2	127	663	80	65	7	4	3	15	97	0	107	23	1
Griffith, Dustin A., C.R.	0	0	.000	5.68	4	0	0	0	0	0	6.1	10	31	4	4	1	0	0	1	2	0	3	0	0
Gruler, Christopher R., Dayton	0	2	.000	27.00	3	3	0	0	0	0	5.2	10	42	19	17	0	0	1	2	12	0	6	3	0
Guevara, Jose C., Dayton	0	1	.000	3.43	12	3	0	0	3	0	39.1	37	171	17	15	4	4	0	3	14	1	39	6	0
Hall, Jeremy C., Beloit	8	4	.667	2.59	46	0	0	0	32	11	73.0	52	301	27	21	3	3	6	3	29	4	76	4	1
Harben, Adam B., Quad City	5	6	.455	4.33	16	15	0	0	0	0	87.1	91	395	54	42	5	0	1	7	35	0	77	11	1
Harmsen, Brandon G., B.C.	1	3	.250	4.71	8	7	0	0	0	0	36.1	55	181	30	19	2	1	3	1	18	0	17	3	0
Hawksworth, Blake E., Peoria	5	1	.833	2.30	10	10	0	0	0	0	54.2	37	213	16	14	0	1	1	1	12	0	57	1	1
Haynes, Jimmy W., Dayton	1	0	1.000	0.00	1	1	0	0	0	0	7.0	2	25	1	0	0	0	0	0	2	0	6	0	0
Heaston, Bryan W., Wisconsin	2	2	.500	2.87	41	0	0	0	30	8	53.1	53	230	20	17	0	3	2	1	26	1	21	5	1
Heiberger, Heath E., S.B. *	4	5	.444	3.61	39	2	0	0	11	0	52.1	53	238	30	21	1	3	2	2	26	2	37	6	1
Henderson, Eric B., Beloit *	4	2	.667	4.53	10	10	0	0	0	0	53.2	61	228	29	27	3	4	0	3	23	0	23	3	1
Hernandez, Felix A., Wis.	0	0	.000	1.93	2	2	0	0	0	0	14.0	9	54	4	3	1	0	0	0	3	0	18	0	0
Herrera, Cesar, Clinton	10	9	.526	4.20	31	19	0	0	7	1	128.2	145	564	72	60	3	7	6	6	41	1	70	5	0
Hill, Joshua J., Quad City	7	4	.636	3.95	26	21	1	0	1	0	136.2	135	597	63	60	7	3	5	13	57	0	132	12	1
Hill, Richard J., Lansing *	0	1	.000	2.76	15	4	0	0	2	0	29.1	14	139	12	9	0	1	0	3	36	0	50	9	0
Hintz, Beau W., Wisconsin *	0	4	.000	8.39	6	6	0	0	0	0	24.2	37	117	24	23	3	2	2	0	6	0	21	0	0
Hoelscher, Nathan G., Burl. *	2	4	.333	4.22	34	0	0	0	21	3	59.2	68	264	33	28	4	3	0	3	16	0	53	1	0
Hogan, Gary R., Clinton	6	5	.545	4.03	32	17	0	0	9	4	116.0	121	527	63	52	3	2	4	15	53	0	64	10	1
Holcomb, James R., C.R.	2	6	.250	3.91	14	14	0	0	0	0	71.1	68	317	37	31	4	3	2	3	36	0	61	9	0
Housman, Jeff D., Beloit *	2	7	.222	1.81	20	15	0	0	1	0	89.1	79	378	40	18	5	3	2	5	26	0	50	1	1
Howell, Michael E., W. Mich.	7	3	.700	2.09	11	9	1	1	1	0	77.2	52	293	22	18	3	3	0	2	12	0	50	2	0
Huber, Jonathon L., F.W.	1	1	.500	3.76	7	7	0	0	0	0	38.1	31	157	18	16	2	1	4	4	11	0	34	0	0
Hudgins, John M., Clinton	0	0	.000	0.00	1	0	0	0	0	0	2.0	1	7	0	0	0	0	0	0	0	0	4	0	0
Huizinga, Jon, Beloit	4	0	1.000	4.32	23	0	0	0	10	2	41.2	56	198	34	20	3	2	1	2	13	0	30	9	0
Incinelli, Matthew J., S.B.	0	1	.000	4.50	2	1	0	0	0	0	4.0	4	15	2	2	0	0	0	0	2	0	2	0	0
Isaacson, Charlie C., B.C.	3	0	1.000	0.54	27	0	0	0	15	4	33.1	18	126	4	2	0	0	0	0	13	0	33	2	0
Jepsen, Kevin M., C.R.	6	3	.667	2.65	10	10	0	0	0	0	51.0	32	211	24	15	2	1	2	2	28	0	42	0	0
Jimenez, Cesar E., Wis.*	8	11	.421	2.94	28	20	0	0	3	0	125.2	134	552	61	41	7	8	6	2	46	2	76	10	0
Jones, Justin W., Lansing *	3	5	.375	2.28	16	16	0	0	0	0	71.0	56	302	29	18	1	2	0	7	32	0	87	2	0
Jordan, Robert B., Peoria *	0	1	.000	6.00	2	0	0	0	1	0	3.0	4	12	2	2	0	1	0	0	0	0	3	0	0
Julianel, Benjamin P., Peo.-B.C.*	4	2	.667	1.11	55	0	0	0	26	9	57.0	47	247	12	7	1	5	2	0	27	0	88	5	2
Jumelles, Edduar A., Dayton	2	2	.500	6.56	16	0	0	0	6	1	23.1	22	116	20	17	1	0	2	5	21	0	15	8	0
Kaanoi, Jason K., Burlington	2	3	.400	6.06	31	0	0	0	17	2	52.0	58	242	38	35	5	2	1	0	29	0	30	5	0
Keeling, Justin A., Quad City *	0	1	.000	6.75	4	0	0	0	2	0	5.1	5	21	4	4	0	0	0	1	3	0	3	1	1
Keiter, Benjamin R., Clinton	1	0	1.000	1.71	5	2	0	0	3	1	21.0	14	84	5	4	0	1	0	2	7	0	14	4	0
Keppinger, William G., Burl. *	0	0	.000	0.00	3	0	0	0	1	0	5.0	2	17	0	0	0	1	0	0	1	0	5	0	0
Kieninger, William A., W.Mich.	2	2	.500	3.00	26	0	0	0	6	0	48.0	63	218	25	16	2	1	1	1	17	1	31	3	0
King, Jeremy P., Battle Creek	4	6	.400	3.36	14	14	0	0	0	0	83.0	73	340	35	31	9	4	1	5	24	0	75	5	0
King, Ocfuske J., Dayton	0	1	.000	3.55	4	4	0	0	0	0	12.2	10	51	5	5	2	0	0	0	6	0	9	1	0
Kinsey, Christopher C., S.B.	0	0	.000	6.94	10	0	0	0	1	0	11.2	10	57	12	9	1	0	1	0	15	0	5	5	0
Kirsten, Joel D., Clinton *	2	2	.500	5.79	9	5	0	0	2	1	28.0	42	134	23	18	1	0	2	3	7	0	13	1	0
Koenig, J. Ross, W. Mich.	0	1	.000	7.83	20	0	0	0	7	0	23.0	25	119	24	20	3	0	2	4	20	2	22	4	0
Kohn, Shawn A., Kane County	6	4	.600	2.54	45	4	0	0	16	2	88.2	71	352	27	25	5	2	2	6	15	2	69	1	3

Pitcher, Team	W	L	Pct.	ERA	G	GS	CG	ShO	GF	Sv.	IP	H	TBF	R	ER	HR	SH	SF	HB	BB	IBB	SO	WP	Bk.
Komine, Shane K., K.C.	6	0	1.000	1.82	8	8	1	1	0	0	54.1	45	216	12	11	1	0	3	2	9	0	50	0	1
Kranawetter, Joshua R., S.B.	1	3	.250	6.96	24	0	0	0	10	0	32.1	43	162	30	25	1	2	1	7	20	0	23	5	1
Krawczyk, Jack B., S.B.	3	1	.750	1.59	16	0	0	0	5	0	28.1	23	110	7	5	1	1	2	0	6	1	40	1	0
Kuhaulua, Kaulana K., Q.C.	0	0	.000	0.00	2	0	0	0	2	0	2.0	2	8	0	0	0	0	0	0	1	0	0	0	0
Landeros, Leonard L., K.C.*	1	0	1.000	1.48	15	0	0	0	6	0	24.1	25	103	7	4	0	1	2	3	4	0	12	1	0
Leon, Brigmer J., K.C.	2	1	.667	3.82	30	5	0	0	12	2	63.2	71	279	31	27	1	2	1	5	20	0	44	6	1
Lewis, Lavon J., W. Mich.	0	1	.000	13.50	1	1	0	0	0	0	2.0	2	13	4	3	0	0	1	0	5	0	1	1	0
Lincoln, Matthew R., C.R. *	1	1	.500	3.55	10	0	0	0	3	1	12.2	12	56	5	5	0	1	0	0	5	0	14	3	0
Lipari, Thomas M., F.W. *	7	6	.538	2.52	19	15	0	0	2	0	96.1	89	401	33	27	5	2	1	4	21	0	59	0	0
Livingston, Robert J., Wis.*	15	7	.682	2.73	26	26	1	0	0	0	178.0	176	733	72	54	10	7	7	12	28	0	105	1	3
Lizarraga, Sergio O., S.B.	9	2	.818	1.78	42	9	0	0	15	1	96.0	71	383	22	19	6	3	3	2	29	5	85	2	1
Loe, Kameron D., Clinton	4	3	.571	1.95	23	11	0	0	5	2	97.0	78	388	34	21	3	5	1	4	19	0	94	1	0
Lohse, Eric K., Quad City	6	5	.545	3.32	28	1	0	0	11	1	62.1	65	261	31	23	4	4	4	4	15	0	51	1	1
Lord, Justin D., Burlington	3	1	.750	3.92	19	0	0	0	13	1	43.2	36	174	20	19	6	2	0	2	8	0	33	3	0
Lowery, Devon E., Burlington	6	4	.600	3.36	26	10	0	0	11	5	96.1	78	394	39	36	9	4	2	3	34	0	74	4	0
Lucas, Christopher K., Dayton	4	9	.308	4.53	25	15	0	0	4	2	115.1	140	498	69	58	10	1	2	0	33	1	79	5	0
Lugo, Osvaldo, Cedar Rapids	1	2	.333	2.63	52	0	0	0	30	10	65.0	40	268	20	19	4	2	2	6	29	0	79	9	1
Luna, Brandon M., Clinton	2	1	.667	3.30	20	0	0	0	5	0	30.0	29	134	16	11	3	2	1	1	18	0	13	1	1
Lynch, Matthew J., K.C.*	4	4	.500	4.53	13	11	0	0	0	0	59.2	84	267	33	30	1	3	4	2	11	0	43	3	0
Marcano, Luis, Clinton	2	2	.500	1.88	39	0	0	0	26	13	52.2	46	225	15	11	1	2	1	6	17	0	27	4	3
Markray, Thaddius A., B.C.	4	4	.500	2.91	34	0	0	0	10	0	58.2	56	250	22	19	3	2	4	3	16	0	49	1	1
Marquez, Jeffrey, C.R.	3	4	.429	5.23	45	2	0	0	14	0	82.2	93	392	60	48	3	4	4	2	43	3	51	9	0
Marshall, Sean C., Lansing *	1	0	1.000	0.00	1	1	0	0	0	0	7.0	5	26	1	0	0	0	0	0	0	0	11	0	0
Martin, Forrest K., Beloit	0	0	.000	6.48	4	0	0	0	1	0	8.1	12	36	6	6	1	0	0	2	0	0	3	0	0
Martinez, Domingo, F.W.	1	0	1.000	0.00	1	0	0	0	1	0	4.0	1	12	0	0	0	0	0	0	1	0	1	0	0
Martinez, Miguel, Peoria	6	6	.500	3.39	20	20	1	0	0	0	116.2	112	480	55	44	5	3	5	3	32	1	60	4	2
Martinez, Miguel A., Wis.*	2	1	.667	1.13	24	3	0	0	4	2	55.2	41	218	9	7	1	2	2	1	17	0	69	2	2
Masset, Nicholas A., Clinton	7	7	.500	4.08	30	20	0	0	6	2	123.2	144	557	75	56	7	6	6	9	43	0	63	8	3
Mattison, Kieran Y., Burlington	8	5	.615	2.50	17	17	2	1	0	0	108.0	82	424	32	30	10	3	1	3	26	0	89	9	0
Mauer, William M., Quad City	0	0	.000	3.52	4	0	0	0	1	0	7.2	6	34	6	3	0	0	0	0	4	0	2	2	0
McCall, L. Derell, Kane County	3	1	.750	2.66	8	7	1	0	1	1	47.1	47	197	18	14	3	0	1	1	7	0	24	1	0
McGill, Trae B., Burlington	3	1	.750	3.27	16	2	0	0	8	2	44.0	46	188	17	16	3	2	0	0	10	0	49	4	0
McWilliams, Matthew W., Day.*	5	3	.625	2.48	36	0	0	0	12	2	54.1	38	228	18	15	2	5	2	1	31	7	49	5	0
Mead, M. David, Clinton	0	2	.000	10.57	3	2	0	0	0	0	7.2	14	41	9	9	2	1	0	2	4	0	0	0	0
Medina, Julio C., Dayton	0	1	.000	6.23	1	1	0	0	0	0	4.1	5	17	3	3	0	0	0	0	1	0	2	0	0
Mejia, Juan L., Peoria	2	3	.400	3.88	30	0	0	0	12	0	53.1	50	226	24	23	5	3	4	3	25	2	27	3	1
Mendez, Adalberto, Lansing	0	0	.000	4.38	9	1	0	0	3	0	12.1	15	59	9	6	1	0	1	0	6	0	11	0	0
Mendez, Mario A., Beloit	0	0	.000	29.45	5	0	0	0	2	0	3.2	10	29	12	12	0	0	1	1	8	0	3	1	0
Mendoza, Cristian E., B.C.	4	0	1.000	3.80	32	0	0	0	9	2	47.1	33	201	23	20	1	2	4	2	28	1	28	1	1
Mendoza, Gabriel A., Beloit *	1	2	.333	4.13	18	0	0	0	7	2	32.2	34	158	24	15	2	4	2	3	16	0	38	6	0
Metzger, Jonathan P., Burl. *	0	0	.000	16.88	3	0	0	0	1	0	2.2	8	20	5	5	1	0	0	1	5	0	0	0	0
Miller, Jason D., Quad City *	5	1	.833	2.36	13	12	0	0	0	0	68.2	67	285	25	18	4	4	2	4	21	0	50	4	0
Moorhead, Michael B., Wis.	0	2	.000	9.00	5	0	0	0	5	3	4.0	7	24	4	4	0	0	0	0	5	0	5	0	0
Morban, Carlos M., C.R.	0	0	.000	5.59	9	0	0	0	3	0	9.2	14	48	6	6	1	1	0	0	6	0	13	6	0
Morel, Eudy, Fort Wayne	4	4	.500	4.65	40	0	0	0	16	1	60.0	63	257	34	31	3	3	4	2	18	0	64	6	0
Moreno, Abel, Cedar Rapids	1	1	.500	1.62	3	3	0	0	0	0	16.2	13	67	3	3	0	2	2	3	3	0	15	0	0
Morrow, David W., Wisconsin	0	0	.000	6.48	6	0	0	0	5	0	8.1	7	38	7	6	2	0	1	0	7	0	9	4	0
Mosley, Eric J., Battle Creek	0	0	.000	10.29	4	0	0	0	0	0	7.0	14	39	8	8	0	0	1	1	4	0	6	1	0
Mowday, Christopher R., K.C.	4	3	.571	6.49	21	8	0	0	2	0	51.1	60	258	45	37	3	2	1	6	42	0	48	4	0
Muessig, Jeffrey G., K.C.	0	1	.000	2.60	22	0	0	0	16	10	27.2	26	117	9	8	1	0	1	1	8	0	37	1	0
Murphy, William R., K.C.*	7	4	.636	2.25	14	14	1	1	0	0	92.0	61	363	27	23	5	1	4	2	32	0	87	1	3
Murray, Steven R., Q.C. *	3	1	.750	4.57	47	0	0	0	13	1	61.0	56	251	33	31	6	2	1	6	11	1	54	3	0
Neitz, Joshua R., B.C.	2	1	.667	7.94	31	0	0	0	14	1	45.1	63	220	44	40	4	2	5	6	17	1	31	3	0
Neshek, Patrick J., Quad City	3	2	.600	0.52	28	0	0	0	24	14	34.1	20	136	3	2	0	3	0	1	11	2	53	1	0
Nippert, Dustin D., S.B.	6	4	.600	2.82	17	17	0	0	0	0	95.2	66	383	32	30	4	1	1	4	32	3	96	5	0
O'Brien, Weston C., Lansing	1	5	.167	3.20	55	0	0	0	20	0	64.2	48	286	32	23	3	2	1	15	32	2	77	9	0
O'Malley, Ryan J., Lansing *	6	4	.600	2.88	40	3	0	0	10	0	81.1	85	342	34	26	3	6	0	3	17	1	55	5	0
Oakes, Gerard A., Quad City	2	5	.286	9.45	24	5	0	0	11	1	53.1	61	282	62	56	8	4	4	5	60	0	33	14	0
Obenchain, Stephen H., K.C.	3	5	.375	2.57	11	8	0	0	1	0	49.0	48	203	16	14	3	0	2	0	13	0	30	2	0
Olson, Justin M., Quad City	1	0	1.000	2.33	14	0	0	0	11	5	19.1	17	80	5	5	0	1	0	1	8	1	23	0	0
Ortiz, Omar, Clinton	1	1	.500	2.03	9	0	0	0	4	0	13.1	13	62	5	3	0	0	4	1	8	1	7	2	0
Ostlund, Ian S., W. Mich. *	3	0	1.000	1.59	44	0	0	0	40	19	45.1	31	181	10	8	1	3	1	2	14	5	56	0	0
Ovalles, Juan C., Wisconsin	0	0	.000	3.00	2	0	0	0	0	0	3.0	3	12	1	1	0	0	0	0	1	0	4	0	0
Parra, Manuel A., Beloit *	11	2	.846	2.73	23	23	1	0	0	0	138.2	127	551	50	42	9	5	0	0	24	0	117	5	3
Parris, Matthew M., W. Mich.	6	6	.500	3.21	32	15	0	0	6	0	126.0	127	536	56	45	9	1	5	5	38	0	80	6	0
Pauley, David W., Fort Wayne	7	7	.500	3.29	22	21	0	0	1	1	117.2	109	495	51	43	9	2	2	8	38	0	117	5	0
Pauly, Thomas E., Dayton	2	5	.286	4.02	12	12	0	0	0	0	47.0	45	197	26	21	5	3	1	1	10	0	36	1	0
Pena, Luismar A., Beloit	2	6	.250	3.90	23	18	1	0	2	0	90.0	92	406	51	39	6	8	1	7	46	0	53	9	0
Pender, Matthew A., W. Mich.	2	10	.167	5.65	17	17	0	0	0	0	86.0	95	389	60	54	4	6	4	10	42	1	51	10	0
Pezely, Franco, Clinton *	4	4	.500	3.16	44	0	0	0	29	8	62.2	64	274	32	22	7	6	0	5	19	0	51	2	2
Pickford, Troy M., W. Mich.	5	7	.417	2.66	16	16	1	0	0	0	98.0	97	415	41	29	1	6	6	6	26	1	71	7	0
Plancich, Nicholas C., Peoria	0	0	.000	0.00	2	0	0	0	1	0	1.1	2	9	4	0	0	0	0	0	2	0	1	1	0
Posey, Micah B., C.R. *	8	6	.571	3.34	20	20	0	0	0	0	110.1	100	482	48	41	5	5	3	9	51	2	68	2	0
Prunty, Thomas J., Quad City	4	10	.286	4.97	30	19	0	0	4	0	126.2	142	558	82	70	14	7	7	6	46	0	81	4	0
Quezada, Elvys, Battle Creek	2	0	1.000	1.38	2	2	0	0	0	0	13.0	5	46	2	2	1	0	0	1	3	0	10	1	0
Ramirez, Edward R., C.R.	1	1	.500	3.32	6	1	0	0	0	0	19.0	17	83	7	7	2	0	1	1	8	0	15	1	0
Rapada, Clayton A., Lansing *	1	2	.333	5.31	21	4	0	0	2	0	42.1	46	193	29	25	3	0	3	3	19	0	24	1	0
Rawson, Anthony P., Peoria *	0	2	.000	4.09	20	0	0	0	13	6	22.0	22	92	11	10	1	1	1	0	7	0	17	3	0
Ray, Ronald A., Cedar Rapids	3	11	.214	5.13	20	20	0	0	0	0	100.0	109	459	65	57	6	6	3	6	46	3	60	13	1

Pitcher, Team	W	L	Pct.	ERA	G	GS	CG	ShO	GF	Sv.	IP	H	TBF	R	ER	HR	SH	SF	HB	BB	IBB	SO	WP	Bk.
Reyes, E. Ramon, C.R.	2	0	1.000	0.00	4	0	0	0	2	0	5.1	2	22	2	0	0	0	0	0	3	0	4	1	0
Ribas, Gabriel A., Fort Wayne	13	3	.813	2.25	19	19	0	0	0	0	116.0	86	461	36	29	3	1	3	4	26	0	116	6	1
Richards, John A., F.W. *	0	3	.000	4.50	9	6	0	0	1	0	34.0	40	151	25	17	3	0	0	0	10	0	22	2	0
Rodriguez, Jermy, W. Mich.	3	6	.333	3.81	41	0	0	0	8	0	52.0	54	238	30	22	3	5	3	1	28	2	32	7	4
Rodriguez, Luis A., Clinton	2	0	1.000	6.75	14	2	0	0	2	0	26.2	38	126	20	20	5	0	2	1	9	0	20	2	0
Rodriguez, Manuel, K.C.	3	3	.500	7.42	33	0	0	0	15	0	43.2	56	214	41	36	3	2	1	5	20	2	22	8	0
Rodriguez, Rafael, C.R.	10	11	.476	4.31	26	26	1	1	0	0	144.0	129	623	85	69	7	4	6	7	59	2	100	19	1
Rogers, Joseph R., Peoria *	2	1	.667	2.30	37	0	0	0	8	0	43.0	30	165	15	11	0	0	0	1	12	0	46	1	0
Rosario, Adriano, S.B.	9	5	.643	2.86	27	27	0	0	0	0	160.1	149	652	69	51	3	6	5	7	30	0	119	8	4
Rowland-Smith, Ryan B., Wis.*	3	0	1.000	1.11	13	0	0	0	5	1	32.1	22	141	13	4	0	2	1	3	14	0	37	0	0
Runyon, Robert, Peoria	4	6	.400	4.23	11	11	1	0	0	0	61.2	68	275	43	29	7	2	3	1	20	0	23	7	1
Rupe, Joshua M., Clinton	4	1	.800	3.90	6	5	0	0	0	0	27.2	29	122	14	12	1	1	2	3	7	0	23	2	0
Russelburg, Aaron G., Peoria	1	2	.333	4.05	6	5	0	0	1	0	26.2	31	119	13	12	1	2	1	2	14	0	13	0	0
Ryu, Jae-Kuk, Lansing	6	1	.857	1.75	11	11	0	0	0	0	72.0	59	292	19	14	2	2	4	5	19	0	57	10	1
Saldana, Jaime, B.C. *	4	1	.800	3.65	41	0	0	0	10	1	49.1	42	215	22	20	1	2	3	1	22	1	43	5	0
Sanchez, Humberto A., W.M.	7	7	.500	4.42	23	23	0	0	0	0	116.0	107	525	71	57	3	6	1	11	78	2	96	9	3
Sandoval, Juan F., Wisconsin	11	10	.524	4.46	27	27	0	0	0	0	157.1	190	718	97	78	8	9	5	12	58	0	73	12	0
Sarfate, Dennis S., Beloit	12	2	.857	2.84	26	26	0	0	0	0	139.2	114	581	50	44	11	4	5	3	66	0	140	5	2
Scalamandre, Richard, Peoria	0	0	.000	1.88	18	0	0	0	9	2	24.0	18	92	5	5	2	1	0	1	9	1	23	1	0
Schara, Zackary K., Clinton	1	1	.500	7.47	12	0	0	0	3	0	15.2	21	74	13	13	2	0	1	1	4	0	12	3	1
Scheffel, Dustin R., Clinton	0	7	.000	6.66	15	9	0	0	3	0	48.2	66	235	42	36	8	1	3	8	19	0	24	4	0
Schweitzer, Stephen S., Peo.*	0	1	.000	13.50	10	0	0	0	0	0	6.2	11	34	10	10	0	2	0	0	4	0	6	3	0
Seibert, Kevin, Fort Wayne	1	2	.333	3.72	19	3	0	0	3	0	46.0	52	209	22	19	4	2	4	0	21	0	42	4	0
Shank, Christopher D., K.C.	5	0	1.000	2.86	12	0	0	0	4	0	22.0	15	82	7	7	1	1	2	2	2	0	15	0	0
Shiery, Shaun A., Burl. *	2	0	1.000	1.32	2	2	0	0	0	0	13.2	16	61	6	2	0	0	0	1	3	0	7	0	0
Sierra, Edwardo, Kane County	3	5	.375	2.09	51	0	0	0	34	17	60.1	46	264	23	14	2	5	2	8	24	4	52	11	0
Sisco, Andrew F., Lansing *	6	8	.429	3.54	19	19	3	0	0	0	94.0	76	388	44	37	3	3	4	5	31	0	99	8	0
Skaggs, Jon S., Battle Creek	4	3	.571	5.25	14	14	0	0	0	0	72.0	65	321	49	42	6	4	6	6	40	1	55	5	0
Smiley, Gerald W., Clinton	4	2	.667	3.74	13	6	0	0	2	0	45.2	40	189	20	19	1	1	1	2	17	1	23	1	0
Smith, Cody, Clinton	1	0	1.000	0.00	2	1	0	0	0	0	8.0	5	29	1	0	0	0	0	0	1	0	1	1	0
Smith, Daniel L., W. Mich.	1	1	.500	4.91	12	0	0	0	6	1	14.2	17	71	10	8	0	0	1	2	9	0	16	6	0
Smith, Dustin M., W. Mich.	1	4	.200	5.35	7	7	0	0	0	0	38.2	34	166	23	23	2	2	0	5	14	0	30	1	0
Smith, Ryan J., Quad City	0	0	.000	3.86	11	0	0	0	4	0	16.1	20	78	9	7	1	3	0	0	7	0	17	0	0
Smith, Samuel M., S.B.	16	6	.727	3.83	27	27	4	3	0	0	167.0	185	708	77	71	7	2	2	2	38	3	77	10	0
Soto, Darwin S., Fort Wayne	7	1	.875	2.64	53	0	0	0	24	9	64.2	53	279	24	19	4	3	4	3	26	5	72	1	2
Steidlmayer, Luke P., F.W.	2	5	.286	4.20	11	11	0	0	0	0	55.2	51	235	32	26	4	1	2	5	12	0	43	3	1
Steinborn, Christopher E., W.M.*	1	6	.143	6.39	18	5	0	0	3	0	43.2	62	209	37	31	5	0	2	2	16	0	19	1	0
Steitz, Jonathan G., Beloit	0	1	.000	5.79	4	0	0	0	0	0	9.1	12	47	9	6	2	1	0	1	5	0	5	0	0
Sullivan, Bradley K., K.C.	1	0	1.000	3.18	6	0	0	0	0	0	11.1	9	50	4	4	1	3	0	0	7	1	9	2	0
Taulli, Sam S., S.B. *	1	4	.200	5.66	23	6	0	0	6	0	41.1	51	193	33	26	4	1	2	3	24	1	26	0	0
Tautor, Peter J., Quad City	4	5	.444	4.60	43	0	0	0	17	3	62.2	64	288	36	32	3	5	4	8	27	3	48	6	0
Tavares, Anderson J., Lansing	12	9	.571	3.24	26	25	1	1	0	0	152.2	154	626	69	55	9	2	5	7	25	0	100	10	0
Teekel, Joshua B., Peoria	6	6	.500	2.36	26	16	0	0	3	1	118.1	107	503	43	31	1	7	2	14	39	1	85	11	1
Thayer, Dale, Fort Wayne	1	3	.250	2.06	45	0	0	0	35	25	48.0	31	194	15	11	2	5	2	2	15	1	72	1	0
Thigpen, Joshua N., Dayton	3	9	.250	5.10	28	14	0	0	6	2	84.2	96	397	53	48	5	2	3	4	50	0	66	6	1
Thompson, Bradley J., Peoria	5	3	.625	2.91	30	4	0	0	7	0	65.0	70	274	23	21	2	1	1	6	10	2	43	4	2
Thompson, Erik M., Clinton	5	2	.714	2.81	14	7	0	0	4	2	57.2	49	230	24	18	6	2	2	3	5	1	52	1	0
Thompson, Richard G., C.R.	1	2	.333	0.24	31	0	0	0	23	9	37.2	18	145	5	1	1	2	1	0	13	0	54	6	0
Toledo, Jean C., C.R.	12	7	.632	2.44	24	24	0	0	0	0	136.1	132	577	60	37	6	4	7	14	50	1	58	9	1
Truselo, Randy J., Clinton	0	0	.000	9.00	2	1	0	0	0	0	4.0	6	19	4	4	0	0	0	1	1	0	5	0	0
Trytten, Ryan G., Beloit	3	4	.429	6.33	28	4	0	0	10	1	58.1	81	287	53	41	3	2	5	10	29	0	31	8	2
Tyler, Scott R., Quad City	6	12	.333	5.50	30	20	0	0	4	0	106.1	93	495	70	65	7	2	5	7	82	1	110	14	1
Urena, Sixto M., Clinton	3	5	.375	5.00	38	8	0	0	9	1	81.0	89	365	54	45	12	5	5	6	30	0	59	4	1
Ursin, Damian J., Dayton	0	2	.000	7.50	13	0	0	0	7	2	18.0	25	86	16	15	0	1	0	1	11	0	15	4	0
Valdez, Domingo, Clinton	2	4	.333	4.20	14	9	1	1	3	2	55.2	57	254	29	26	2	1	2	14	23	1	49	4	0
Valdez, Edward E., Dayton	11	3	.786	3.72	19	19	0	0	0	0	113.2	111	477	54	47	11	1	4	12	28	2	67	5	1
Valdez, Jose, Battle Creek	11	7	.611	3.64	22	22	0	0	0	0	133.2	132	568	67	54	14	3	5	8	42	1	76	8	4
Van, Robert M., S.B. *	1	2	.333	3.91	21	0	0	0	3	0	25.1	12	113	12	11	0	2	0	7	25	1	12	10	0
Vasquez, Carlos A., Lansing *	10	13	.435	3.74	24	23	0	0	0	0	137.1	136	605	74	57	5	8	1	9	47	0	87	9	1
Vazquez, Camilo T., Dayton *	1	4	.200	5.93	13	11	0	0	0	0	44.0	54	215	37	29	6	0	2	3	28	1	47	6	1
Viane, David C., Wisconsin	3	4	.429	3.12	34	0	0	0	16	6	60.2	59	254	24	21	1	5	2	3	18	2	45	8	0
Villatoro, Wilmer A., F.W.	3	2	.600	2.62	39	0	0	0	15	2	55.0	31	223	20	16	7	1	2	3	28	2	77	3	0
Villegas, Francisco J., B.C.	1	1	.500	3.00	6	0	0	0	6	1	6.0	2	24	2	2	1	0	0	0	4	0	8	0	0
Watson, Michael J., S.B.	0	0	.000	0.78	16	1	0	0	0	0	23.0	15	94	3	2	0	2	0	1	14	3	17	0	0
Watson, Tanner J., Wisconsin	6	7	.462	4.58	23	23	1	0	0	0	116.0	142	544	79	59	5	6	6	15	53	0	80	10	4
Watts, Joldy C., Clinton	0	0	.000	0.00	1	0	0	0	1	0	1.0	0	5	0	0	0	0	0	0	1	0	1	1	0
Wear, Gregory M., Wisconsin	0	0	.000	3.15	17	0	0	0	6	0	20.0	22	87	9	7	0	0	1	2	6	0	8	0	0
Wells, Randy D., Lansing	0	0	.000	0.00	1	0	0	0	1	0	1.0	1	3	0	0	0	0	0	0	0	0	0	0	0
Whatley, J. Keith, S.B. *	0	1	.000	2.93	3	3	0	0	0	0	15.1	18	63	5	5	0	1	0	1	3	0	6	0	0
Whitaker, Brian G., F.W.	7	6	.538	2.09	26	26	3	1	0	0	164.0	149	657	60	38	5	3	5	7	20	0	121	8	0
Wilhelmsen, Thomas M., Bel.	5	5	.500	2.76	15	15	1	0	0	0	88.0	78	361	35	27	6	3	3	4	27	0	63	2	0
Wilkinson, Matthew J., S.B.	3	6	.333	2.29	55	0	0	0	47	30	63.0	38	262	21	16	2	5	3	3	28	6	80	6	0
Williams, Aaron L., Q.C.	0	0	.000	12.19	5	0	0	0	1	0	10.1	17	50	14	14	2	0	1	1	1	0	7	1	0
Williams, J. Bryan, C.R.	0	0	.000	7.94	7	0	0	0	2	0	11.1	11	57	11	10	2	0	2	1	12	0	9	6	0
Wilson, Philip, C.R.	0	1	.000	4.09	2	2	1	0	0	0	11.0	10	43	6	5	2	0	0	0	3	0	6	0	0
Wiseman, Steven A., B.C.	2	1	.667	4.41	35	0	0	0	14	1	51.0	46	224	29	25	1	1	3	3	29	2	48	3	0
Wright, S. Chase, B.C. *	1	1	.500	6.43	7	2	0	0	2	0	14.0	12	71	11	10	1	0	0	2	16	0	10	3	1
Wylie, Jason A., Lansing	1	2	.333	1.38	57	0	0	0	49	29	58.2	36	241	13	9	0	4	0	5	22	1	54	6	0
Yoshida, Nobuaki, F.W. *	1	5	.167	6.03	10	7	0	0	3	0	31.1	46	159	29	21	2	1	1	1	16	1	18	4	0
Zumaya, Joel M., W. Mich.	7	5	.583	2.79	19	19	0	0	0	0	90.1	69	376	35	28	3	3	2	3	38	0	126	4	0

COMBINATION SHUTOUTS: Battle Creek (11)—Garcia-Saldana-Villegas, Garcia-Saldana-Isaacson, Garcia-Saldana, Garcia-Saldana-Isaacson, King-Isaacson-Brumit-Mendoza, Garcia-Neitz, Valdez-Mendoza, Clark-Saldana, DeSalvo-Brumit, DeSalvo-Mendoza-Neitz, Skaggs-Julianel-Brumit. Beloit (10)—Housman-Breslow-Hall, Wilhelmsen-Gabriel, Sarfate-Trytten, Housman-Breslow, Housman-Trytten-Gabriel, Housman-Carpenter-Ballouli-Alliston, Sarfate-Breslow-Trytten, Carpenter-Ballouli-Hall, Parra-Hall, Carpenter-Ballouli. Burlington (7)—Bayliss-Endicott, Endicott-Burch, Mattison-Hoelscher, Endicott-Kaanoi, Griffin-Hoelscher, McGill-Hoelscher, Shiery-Lord-Hoelscher. Cedar Rapids (10)—Jepsen-Gliemmo-Bilke, Toledo-Gliemmo-Bilke, Astacio-Gliemmo-Arias, Jepsen-Lugo-Thompson, Toledo-Gliemmo-Bilke, Posey-Lugo-Gliemmo-Bilke, Posey-Carroll, D'Amico-Gliemmo-Lugo, Posey-Goas, Moreno-Carroll-Lincoln. Clinton (7)—Loe-Kirsten, Masset-Loe, Hogan-Valdez, Smiley-Luna-Urena-Rodriguez, Valdez-Rodriguez-Hogan, Masset-Cedeno, Hogan-Cedeno. Dayton (5)—Thigpen-Farfan, Frias-Lucas, Pauly-George-Thigpen-Jumelles-Barreto, Lucas-Thigpen, Pauly-Edens. Fort Wayne (11)—Ribas-Soto, Ribas-Edwards-Thayer, Steidlmayer-Richards-Villatoro, Whitaker-Thayer, Seibert-Corona-Villatoro-Morel, Lipari-Soto-Thayer, Edwards-Villatoro-Soto-Thayer, Lipari-Morel, Lipari-Villatoro-Thayer, Pauley-Corona-Soto, Doyne-Bechtel-Soto. Kane County (13)—Dickinson-Kohn, Blanton-Shank, Komine-Muessig, Blanton-Leon, Komine-Gonzalez, Murphy-Leon, Blanton-Kohn-Sierra, Blanton-Lynch-Dunwell-Sierra, Obenchain-Kohn, Garcia-Lynch-Dunwell-Mowday-Rodriguez, Blanton-Kohn-Sierra, Leon-Garcia-Kohn, Obenchain-Garcia-Sierra. Lansing (14)—Sisco-Wylie, Jones-O'Brien-Carter, Vasquez-Wylie, Vasquez-Baez-O'Brien, Ferreras-Foli-Wylie, Tavarez-Hill-Baez, Vasquez-Carter-Wylie, Jones-Baez-Carter-Wylie, Foli-Baez-Carter-Wylie, Sisco-Baez-Carter-Wylie, Foli-O'Malley-Wylie, Tavarez-O'Malley, Vasquez-Baez-O'Malley, Cherry-Benik-Wylie. Peoria (8)—Cavazos-Julianel-Batista, Martinez-Rogers-Plancich, Adamczyk-Ciprian, Hawksworth-Rawson, Martinez-Rawson, Cavazos-Thompson-Julianel-Rawson, Martinez-Flynn-Julianel-Cavazos, Adamczyk-Thompson-Julianel-Cavazos. Quad City (5)—Hill-Tautor, Prunty-Tautor-Neshek, Hill-Lohse, Miller-Neshek, Hill-Tautor-Cameron-Blackburn. South Bend (11)—Whatley-Lizarraga, Nippert-Kranawetter-Wilkinson, Smith-Gonzalez, Coffin-Gonzalez-Wilkinson, Doyle-Lizarraga, Coffin-Gonzalez-Wilkinson, Doyle-Heiberger-Gonzalez-Wilkinson, Smith-Heiberger-Van, Nippert-Krawczyk-Van-Watson-Gonzalez-Wilkinson, Lizarraga-Gonzalez-Wilkinson, Lizarraga-Coffin-Heiberger. West Michigan (9)—Connolly-Gerk-Koenig, Pickford-Rodriguez-Ostlund, Connolly-Ostlund, Zumaya-Gerk-Ostlund, Zumaya-Parris-Gerk-Figueroa-Ostlund, Howell-Ostlund-Figueroa, Connolly-Howell, Parris-Kieninger-Gerk-Ostlund, Steinborn-Kieninger. Wisconsin (9)—Livingston—Rowland-Smith, Watson-Dorman-Heaston-Jimenez, Fulmer-Delgado-Dorman, Fulmer-Delgado-Heaston, Fulmer-Heaston, Livingston-Viane, Fulmer-Delgado, Hernandez-Viane-Moorhead, Jimenez-Heaston-Ovalles-Moorhead.

NO-HIT GAMES: Murphy, Kane County, defeated West Michigan, 6-0, June 10; Valdez, Clinton, defeated Kane County, 4-0 (second game), July 9; Bayliss, Burlington, defeated Peoria, 1-0, August 5.

2003 FIELDING

TEAM

Team	G	PO	A	E	TC	DP	TP	PB	Pct.
Kane County	139	3719	1456	145	5320	83	1	16	.973
Peoria	138	3600	1670	157	5427	123	0	15	.971
Burlington	138	3644	1464	151	5259	116	0	32	.971
Quad City	138	3625	1426	158	5209	107	0	33	.970
Battle Creek	137	3553	1351	167	5071	124	0	22	.967
South Bend	136	3586	1451	172	5209	105	0	27	.967
West Michigan	140	3603	1391	173	5167	93	0	15	.967
Cedar Rapids	138	3599	1377	177	5153	108	0	21	.966
Dayton	139	3609	1477	184	5270	127	0	19	.965
Lansing	135	3541	1469	193	5203	104	1	25	.963
Beloit	137	3629	1387	199	5215	96	0	28	.962
Wisconsin	136	3595	1514	204	5313	118	0	21	.962
Clinton	135	3481	1383	200	5064	100	0	18	.961
Fort Wayne	138	3611	1404	209	5224	108	0	19	.960

INDIVIDUAL

FIRST BASEMEN

NOTE: All caps denotes fielding-percentage leader based on 70 games for catchers, 93 for all other non-pitchers and 112 innings for pitchers. *Throws lefthanded.

Player, Team	Pct.	G	PO	A	E	TC	DP
Abram, Matt, Cedar Rapids	.988	28	233	17	3	253	22
Basil, Jason, Kane County	1.000	11	73	6	0	79	3
Blase, Blake, Battle Creek	.000	1	0	0	0	0	0
Bohanan, Keith, Beloit	1.000	2	16	1	0	17	3
Bone, Blake, Wisconsin	.952	2	19	1	1	21	2
Brito, Angel, West Michigan	1.000	9	44	5	0	49	5
Brown, Matt, Cedar Rapids	1.000	1	7	0	0	7	2
Burgos, Omar, Quad City	.989	25	168	14	2	184	19
Colamarino, Brant, Kane Co.*	.991	133	1184	66	11	1261	74
Collins, Kevin, Lansing *	.979	71	626	38	14	678	45
Contreras, Sergio, C.R.*	1.000	8	74	7	0	81	3
Creighton, Matt, Lansing	.984	24	172	13	3	188	15
Dopirak, Brian, Lansing	.992	13	119	4	1	124	7
Drobiak, Jayson, Battle Creek	.984	93	768	48	13	829	64
Durham, Tyler, Peoria	.976	11	75	5	2	82	8
Eure, Jeffrey, Beloit	.989	10	86	2	1	89	5
Evans, Terry, Peoria	1.000	1	8	1	0	9	0
Fielder, Prince, Beloit	.984	126	1030	67	18	1115	83
Fry, Ryan, Dayton	1.000	1	7	0	0	7	2
Garcia, Cip, Wisconsin	1.000	2	3	0	0	3	0
Gold, Nate, Clinton	.990	87	697	65	8	770	63
Gomon, Dusty, Quad City	.992	40	330	28	3	361	28
Hagen, Matt, Wisconsin	1.000	1	2	0	0	2	1
Hancock, Justin, Cedar Rapids	.975	10	71	6	2	79	9
Hood, Donnie, Lansing	.966	15	138	6	5	149	13
Huether, J.D., Quad City	1.000	19	156	16	0	172	17
Jaile, Chris, Clinton	.938	2	14	1	1	16	3
Jenkins, Kevin, Cedar Rapids *	.932	10	64	4	5	73	5
Jensen, Dave, Burlington *	.989	67	582	52	7	641	47
Johnson, Bryan, South Bend	1.000	3	20	2	0	22	2
Kaaihue, Kila, Burlington	.985	72	669	31	11	711	53
Kennedy, Bryan, Quad City	1.000	3	22	3	0	25	2
Lebron, Edgardo, Quad City	.988	20	158	12	2	172	12
Lebron, Hector, Clinton	.991	29	207	15	2	224	17
Liz, Jose, Quad City	1.000	2	5	1	0	6	1
Lopaze, Daniel, Lansing	1.000	10	82	5	0	87	5
LUELLWITZ, SEAN, South Bend	.996	110	912	70	4	986	75
Madera, Sandy, Battle Creek	.980	12	91	5	2	98	6
Maples, Chris, West Michigan	.980	51	319	19	7	345	23
Mathis, Jake, Cedar Rapids	.984	94	729	52	13	794	55
Matienzo, Danny, Quad City	.982	37	321	14	6	341	23
McAnulty, Paul, Fort Wayne	.986	123	1039	56	16	1111	92
McNulty, Josh, Wisconsin	1.000	4	30	4	0	34	2
Metheny, Brenton, Wisconsin	.981	22	184	21	4	209	11
Nelson, Jon, Wisconsin	.980	111	957	70	21	1048	81
Nunez, Andres, Battle Creek	1.000	3	10	0	0	10	1
Quero, Pedro, Clinton	.989	20	169	16	2	187	10
Reyes, Ivan, Dayton	.967	9	56	2	2	60	5
Richardson, Kevin, Clinton	.983	6	56	2	1	59	1
Rodriguez, Marcos, Peoria *	1.000	1	1	1	0	2	0
Rojas, Tommy, Battle Creek	1.000	3	17	1	0	18	1
Roughton, Jody, West Michigan	.990	99	750	58	8	816	56
Ruiz, Junior, Dayton	.929	3	13	0	1	14	2
Salas, Francisco, Lansing	1.000	11	61	13	0	74	9
Santana, Mayobanex, S.B.	1.000	1	2	0	0	2	0
Santor, John, Peoria	.991	133	1277	98	13	1388	104
Shirley, Steve, Fort Wayne	.959	18	155	10	7	172	10
Stanek, Jeff, South Bend	.978	30	256	17	6	279	22
Suomi, John, Kane County	1.000	1	2	0	0	2	0
Tranum, Josh, Fort Wayne *	1.000	3	14	1	0	15	0
Vasquez, Willie, Battle Creek	1.000	1	7	2	0	9	1
Vavao, Jason, Dayton	.991	48	402	36	4	442	40
Verbryke, Eric, Battle Creek *	.982	34	262	12	5	279	36
Votto, Joey, Dayton	.980	48	404	40	9	453	37
Wells, Randy, Lansing	1.000	2	2	0	0	2	1
Wong, Travis, Dayton	.988	36	313	18	4	335	36

SECOND BASEMEN

Player, Team	Pct.	G	PO	A	E	TC	DP
Agosto, Rolando, Fort Wayne	.857	4	4	8	2	14	0
Agustin, Hugo, Clinton	.900	10	16	29	5	50	6
Bohanan, Keith, Beloit	.875	9	10	18	4	32	3
Bolivar, Luis, Dayton	.964	9	18	35	2	55	11
Boyer, Kyle, Peoria	.000	2	0	0	0	0	0
Brooks, Doc, South Bend	1.000	1	3	2	0	5	0
Brown, Neb, South Bend	.969	107	211	288	16	515	58
Burgamy, Brian, Fort Wayne	.966	27	50	64	4	118	9
Cairns, Troy, Dayton	1.000	2	4	6	0	10	0
Callaspo, Alberto, Cedar Rapids	.969	124	234	332	18	584	68
Chirinos, Robinson, Lansing	.978	54	115	153	6	274	42
Cordova, Roman, Wisconsin	.956	22	43	65	5	113	17
Coughlan, Cameron, Clinton	.964	39	80	134	8	222	26
Crabbe, Callix, Beloit	.946	113	232	328	32	592	64
Creighton, Matt, Lansing	.976	10	13	27	1	41	1
Cruz, Luis, Fort Wayne	.981	18	33	69	2	104	12
Davidson, Seth, Quad City	.973	8	16	20	1	37	5
Dean, Erik, Burlington	.967	29	45	74	4	123	14

Player, Team	Pct.	G	PO	A	E	TC	DP
Delgado, Gabriel, Clinton	.944	38	66	102	10	178	17
Durham, Tyler, Peoria	.986	18	24	47	1	72	7
Ehrnsberger, Chad, Wis.-Peoria	.940	12	24	39	4	67	6
Ernster, Mark, Beloit	1.000	1	2	3	0	5	1
Espino, Damaso, Burlington	.000	1	0	0	0	0	0
Francia, Juan, West Michigan	.948	70	129	162	16	307	36
GOMEZ, FRANCIS, Kane County	.977	118	237	354	14	605	44
Gonzalez, Jose, Clinton	.947	12	36	35	4	75	11
Haley, Adam, South Bend	.957	10	20	25	2	47	1
Harrington, Corey, Wisconsin	.960	43	84	110	8	202	24
Heath, Demetrius, W. Michigan	1.000	3	7	2	0	9	0
Heether, Adam, Beloit	1.000	2	1	4	0	5	0
Hickman, Charles, Lansing	.955	9	19	23	2	44	3
Howard, Kevin, Dayton	.970	126	249	369	19	637	69
Jones, Nick, Lansing	.892	11	12	21	4	37	2
Kuhaulua, Kaulana, Quad City	.970	27	60	71	4	135	17
Lewis, Domonique, Dayton	1.000	2	2	4	0	6	2
Lima, Joseph, Fort Wayne	.945	18	42	44	5	91	12
Lonnquist, Eric, Burlington	.989	19	39	51	1	91	10
Lopez, Gabe, Battle Creek	.969	119	256	341	19	616	90
Maples, Chris, West Michigan	1.000	12	11	23	0	34	4
McCoy, Mike, Peoria	.966	125	252	382	22	656	74
Mejia, Gilberto, West Michigan	.970	25	39	58	3	100	14
Merchan, Jesus, Quad City	.979	36	71	72	3	146	18
Merritt, Tim, Wisconsin	.969	71	153	186	11	350	45
Molina, Felix, Quad City	.955	67	103	197	14	314	34
Monahan, Joey, Lansing	1.000	4	10	12	0	22	3
Morales, Jose, Quad City	1.000	4	9	7	0	16	0
Morgan, Matt, South Bend	1.000	1	1	1	0	2	0
Murphy, Donald, Burlington	.984	82	172	250	7	429	55
Nunez, Andres, Battle Creek	.889	11	17	23	5	45	2
O'Riordan, Chris, Clinton	.973	38	67	110	5	182	14
Pattee, Benjamin, Quad City	.882	3	10	5	2	17	1
Pavkovich, Adam, Cedar Rapids	1.000	1	1	0	0	1	0
Reyes, Ivan, Dayton	1.000	4	10	14	0	24	5
Romprey, Ed, West Michigan	.938	6	4	11	1	16	3
Salas, Francisco, Lansing	.964	7	10	17	1	28	2
Sanchez, Angel, Burlington	.957	9	18	27	2	47	3
Schmidt, J.P., Kane County	.889	3	3	5	1	9	0
Serrano, Eddie, Fort Wayne	.944	16	18	33	3	54	7
Stonard, Peter, Fort Wayne	.967	63	128	199	11	338	41
Teilon, Nilson, South Bend	.935	32	51	79	9	139	12
Theriot, Ryan, Lansing	.967	51	111	152	9	272	22
Turner, Lloyd, Kane County	.857	2	3	3	1	7	1
Vasquez, Willie, Battle Creek	.967	15	23	36	2	61	6
Watson, Rob, West Michigan	.965	42	94	98	7	199	21
Wayment, Kory, Kane County	.965	25	49	61	4	114	9
Weed, B.J., Cedar Rapids	.975	29	34	45	2	81	10
Weeks, Rickie, Beloit	.923	19	31	53	7	91	6

SECOND BASEMEN WITH TWO OR MORE TEAMS

Player, Team	Pct.	G	PO	A	E	TC	DP
Ehrnsberger, Chad, Wisconsin	1.000	5	10	15	0	25	0
Ehrnsberger, Chad, Peoria	.905	7	14	24	4	42	6

THIRD BASEMEN

Player, Team	Pct.	G	PO	A	E	TC	DP
Abram, Matt, Cedar Rapids	.667	3	1	1	1	3	1
Agustin, Hugo, Clinton	.818	5	1	8	2	11	0
Basil, Jason, Kane County	.895	73	46	99	17	162	4
Bohanan, Keith, Beloit	1.000	3	0	1	0	1	0
Bolivar, Luis, Dayton	.875	21	16	26	6	48	3
Boone, Matt, Dayton	.924	51	25	97	10	132	8
Brown, Matt, Cedar Rapids	.896	48	37	92	15	144	8
Brown, Neb, South Bend	.971	26	14	54	2	70	2
Burgamy, Brian, Fort Wayne	.888	61	35	92	16	143	5
Burgos, Omar, Quad City	.930	101	61	164	17	242	18
Cairns, Troy, Dayton	.950	7	5	14	1	20	2
Camacho, Juan, Battle Creek	.943	73	42	91	8	141	6
Carlin, Luke, Fort Wayne	.667	1	1	1	1	3	0
Chirinos, Robinson, Lansing	.917	43	23	88	10	121	5
Cordova, Roman, Wisconsin	1.000	1	1	0	0	1	0
Correll, Brad, Dayton	1.000	2	1	2	0	3	0
Creighton, Matt, Lansing	.667	2	0	2	1	3	1
Dean, Erik, Burlington	.860	19	14	35	8	57	3
Dibetta, John, Fort Wayne	.914	14	7	25	3	35	1
Drobiak, Jayson, Battle Creek	.880	35	19	62	11	92	9
Durham, Tyler, Peoria	.917	6	4	7	1	12	1
Ernster, Mark, Beloit	.900	5	3	6	1	10	0
Espino, Damaso, Burlington	.899	115	71	188	29	288	19
EURE, JEFFREY, Beloit	.951	93	63	171	12	246	7
Gold, Nate, Clinton	.870	23	16	24	6	46	2
Gonzalez, Jose, Clinton	.000	2	0	0	0	0	0
Gonzalez, Juan, West Michigan	.867	13	8	18	4	30	2
Hagen, Matt, Wisconsin	.905	126	92	241	35	368	21
Hancock, Justin, Cedar Rapids	.857	8	9	9	3	21	1
Hanson, Travis, Peoria	.940	135	92	268	23	383	21
Harrington, Corey, Wisconsin	.895	12	9	25	4	38	4
Heether, Adam, Beloit	.869	38	23	50	11	84	2
Hood, Donnie, Lansing	.882	6	2	13	2	17	1
Jacobo, Kervin, S.B.-Fort Wayne	.887	73	43	129	22	194	10
Jones, Nick, Lansing	1.000	3	0	2	0	2	0
Kuhaulua, Kaulana, Quad City	.947	14	12	24	2	38	1
Lebron, Edgardo, Quad City	.667	5	4	4	4	12	0
Lonnquist, Eric, Burlington	.818	5	2	7	2	11	0
Maples, Chris, West Michigan	.895	17	5	29	4	38	3
Mathis, Jake, Cedar Rapids	.923	12	5	19	2	26	1
McGehee, Casey, Lansing	.944	64	40	130	10	180	6
Merchan, Jesus, Quad City	.960	21	12	36	2	50	3
Metheny, Brenton, Wisconsin	1.000	1	1	6	0	7	1
Moore, Scott, West Michigan	.887	102	64	156	28	248	11
Morales, Jose, Quad City	1.000	1	0	1	0	1	0
Morgan, Matt, South Bend	.833	13	9	16	5	30	1
Nunez, Andres, Battle Creek	.933	20	9	19	2	30	4
Pavkovich, Adam, Cedar Rapids	.937	26	19	55	5	79	8
Porter, Greg, Cedar Rapids	.938	48	47	88	9	144	7
Raburn, Ryan, West Michigan	.889	7	4	12	2	18	1
Reyes, Ivan, Dayton	.846	6	3	8	2	13	1
Reynolds, Lagatila, South Bend	1.000	7	2	15	0	17	1
Richardson, Mike, Fort Wayne	1.000	1	3	1	0	4	0
Ringe, Craig, Clinton	.833	1	2	3	1	6	0
Salas, Francisco, Lansing	.917	24	15	51	6	72	4
Santana, Mayobanex, S.B.	.944	66	49	138	11	198	13
Schmidt, J.P., Kane County	.875	5	2	5	1	8	0
Schramek, Mark, Dayton	.927	56	28	111	11	150	6
Serrano, Eddie, Fort Wayne	.917	10	4	18	2	24	0
Shelley, Randall, Clinton	.934	114	104	177	20	301	12
Shirley, Steve, Fort Wayne	.781	15	6	19	7	32	2
Teilon, Nilson, South Bend	1.000	4	2	3	0	5	0
Turner, Lloyd, Kane County	.000	1	0	0	0	0	0
Vasquez, Willie, Battle Creek	.939	21	7	24	2	33	3
Voshell, Chase, Peoria	.000	1	0	0	0	0	0
Watson, Rob, West Michigan	.903	15	8	20	3	31	0
Wayment, Kory, Kane County	.936	90	45	144	13	202	6
Weed, B.J., Cedar Rapids	.667	2	0	2	1	3	0

THIRD BASEMEN WITH TWO OR MORE TEAMS

Player, Team	Pct.	G	PO	A	E	TC	DP
Jacobo, Kervin, Fort Wayne	.857	40	26	70	16	112	7
Jacobo, Kervin, South Bend	.927	33	17	59	6	82	3

SHORTSTOPS

Player, Team	Pct.	G	PO	A	E	TC	DP
Agosto, Rolando, Fort Wayne	.909	4	3	7	1	11	1
Agustin, Hugo, Clinton	1.000	2	7	2	0	9	0
Arias, Joaquin, Battle Creek	.946	130	183	415	34	632	78
Aybar, Erick, Cedar Rapids	.944	124	212	324	32	568	64
Bohanan, Keith, Beloit	.889	13	16	32	6	54	8
Bolivar, Luis, Dayton	.949	29	43	68	6	117	17
Boyer, Kyle, Peoria	.903	35	43	106	16	165	19
Cairns, Troy, Dayton	.750	1	1	2	1	4	0
Callaspo, Alberto, Cedar Rapids	.966	7	13	15	1	29	3
Chirinos, Robinson, Lansing	.906	9	7	22	3	32	0
Coats, Buck, Lansing	.912	122	206	323	51	580	59
Crabbe, Callix, Beloit	.846	6	11	11	4	26	3
Cruz, Luis, Fort Wayne	.927	111	160	345	40	545	61
Davidson, Seth, Quad City	.964	99	158	291	17	466	60
Dean, Erik, Burlington	1.000	1	1	3	0	4	1
Delgado, Gabriel, Clinton	1.000	2	2	3	0	5	0
Durham, Tyler, Peoria	1.000	2	1	8	0	9	0
Eure, Jeffrey, Beloit	.833	8	10	20	6	36	5
Firlit, Dan, South Bend	1.000	6	4	17	0	21	4
Francia, Juan, West Michigan	.921	30	33	83	10	126	13
Garcia, Alex, Fort Wayne	.914	20	25	60	8	93	11
Garciaparra, Michael, Wisconsin	.915	122	178	358	50	586	67
Gil, Jerry, South Bend	.947	115	225	348	32	605	58
Gomez, Francis, Kane County	.941	9	12	20	2	34	4
Gonzalez, Jose, Clinton	.925	13	23	39	5	67	9
GONZALEZ, JUAN, W. Michigan	.972	116	165	326	14	505	51
Haley, Adam, South Bend	.900	6	8	10	2	20	1
Hancock, Justin, Cedar Rapids	.833	6	1	4	1	6	0
Harrington, Corey, Wisconsin	1.000	5	3	4	0	7	1
Hickman, Charles, Lansing	1.000	1	3	1	0	4	1
Jaramillo, Milko, Peoria	.966	96	174	343	18	535	63

Player, Team	Pct.	G	PO	A	E	TC	DP
Kuhaulua, Kaulana, Quad City	.929	3	3	10	1	14	3
Lonnquist, Eric, Burlington	1.000	1	1	3	0	4	1
McCoy, Mike, Peoria	.942	11	17	32	3	52	3
McCurdy, John, Kane County	.950	130	182	371	29	582	59
Merchan, Jesus, Quad City	.934	41	61	109	12	182	12
Merritt, Tim, Wisconsin	.980	12	12	36	1	49	7
Molina, Felix, Quad City	.917	2	4	7	1	12	2
Morgan, Matt, South Bend	.900	2	2	7	1	10	1
Murphy, Donald, Burlington	.963	41	64	116	7	187	19
Murray, Joshua, Beloit	.868	10	16	17	5	38	4
Nunez, Andres, Battle Creek	1.000	4	3	3	0	6	0
Pavkovich, Adam, Cedar Rapids	.905	10	12	26	4	42	4
Porter, Greg, Cedar Rapids	1.000	4	3	1	0	4	0
Reyes, Ivan, Dayton	.929	3	7	6	1	14	0
Reynolds, Lagatila, South Bend	.979	12	22	24	1	47	6
Ringe, Craig, Clinton	.928	118	191	338	41	570	66
Romprey, Ed, West Michigan	1.000	3	3	5	0	8	2
Salas, Francisco, Lansing	1.000	1	0	1	0	1	0
Sanchez, Angel, Burlington	.953	97	138	286	21	445	53
Serrano, Eddie, Fort Wayne	.958	6	7	16	1	24	3
Stonard, Peter, Fort Wayne	1.000	1	1	0	0	1	0
Terni, Chas, Beloit	.932	105	188	279	34	501	51
Theriot, Ryan, Lansing	.909	7	7	23	3	33	4
Tiburcio, Hector, Dayton	.932	113	203	317	38	558	70
Vasquez, Willie, Battle Creek	.885	8	7	16	3	26	4

OUTFIELDERS

Player, Team	Pct.	G	PO	A	E	TC	DP
Alexander, Alexis, Burlington	1.000	16	29	1	0	30	0
Andrus, Erold, Battle Creek *	1.000	29	62	1	0	63	1
Aoki, Tomoshi, Wisconsin	1.000	35	51	0	0	51	0
Araque, Tulio, Dayton	1.000	11	18	0	0	18	0
Arroyo, Carlos, Wisconsin *	.983	68	108	6	2	116	2
Asadoorian, Rick, Clinton	.991	45	109	3	1	113	2
Ayala, Odannys, Clinton	.000	1	0	0	0	0	0
Baker, Steve, Fort Wayne	.984	126	243	7	4	254	2
Ball, Jarred, South Bend	.976	125	277	2	7	286	0
Barrett, Rich, South Bend	.983	40	57	2	1	60	1
Basil, Jason, Kane County	.933	8	13	1	1	15	1
Bassett, Mike, Dayton *	.900	7	9	0	1	10	0
Belz, Tim, Peoria	.000	1	0	0	0	0	0
Bibbs, Kennard, Beloit *	.991	122	216	12	2	230	1
Biernbaum, L.J., Fort Wayne *	.964	118	175	12	7	194	1
Bohn, T.J., Wisconsin	.980	117	270	20	6	296	5
Brooks, Doc, Fort Wayne-S.B.	.938	90	149	3	10	162	0
Burgamy, Brian, Fort Wayne	1.000	37	58	4	0	62	0
Butler, Keith, Lansing	.981	110	153	3	3	159	1
Callahan, Dan, South Bend *	.958	16	22	1	1	24	0
Campos, Tiago, Dayton	.985	60	131	4	2	137	0
Carson, Matt, Battle Creek	.985	114	253	5	4	262	0
Carter, Nic, Beloit	.950	62	73	3	4	80	0
Clevlen, Brent, West Michigan	.966	134	271	16	10	297	3
Contreras, Sergio, C.R.*	1.000	4	5	0	0	5	0
Cook, Jeff, South Bend	.974	65	108	5	3	116	0
Correll, Brad, Dayton	.963	71	96	9	4	109	2
Cosby, Quan, Cedar Rapids	.981	101	246	6	5	257	1
Coughlan, Cameron, Clinton	.962	69	126	0	5	131	0
Cruz, Nelson, Kane County	.979	119	271	8	6	285	1
Cruz, Orlando, Clinton	1.000	51	79	5	0	84	0
Davis, Justin, Dayton *	.925	38	47	2	4	53	0
De Leon, Virgilio, Fort Wayne	.892	31	56	2	7	65	0
Delucchi, Dustin, Wisconsin *	.949	26	51	5	3	59	0
Ehrnsberger, Chad, Wis.-Peoria	1.000	15	21	1	0	22	0
Ethier, Andre, Kane County *	.973	40	109	0	3	112	0
Evans, Terry, Peoria	.977	82	120	10	3	133	1
Foreman, JuJu, Dayton	1.000	12	24	3	0	27	0
Fransz, Jason, Lansing-Clinton	.967	68	84	4	3	91	0
Frend, Tim, Burlington	.981	111	199	4	4	207	1
Fry, Ryan, Dayton	.941	39	58	6	4	68	0
Gates, David, Cedar Rapids	1.000	18	28	2	0	30	0
Gorecki, Reid, Peoria	.957	128	271	17	13	301	4
Graham, Bryan, Burlington *	.909	15	17	3	2	22	0
Grayson, Larry, Clinton	.940	71	118	7	8	133	1
Guillen, Rudy, Battle Creek	.966	130	272	12	10	294	3
Guzman, Garrett, Quad City *	.979	73	132	5	3	140	0
Gwynn, Anthony, Beloit	.988	61	158	6	2	166	3
Haley, Adam, South Bend	.000	1	0	0	0	0	0
Hancock, Justin, Cedar Rapids	.000	1	0	0	0	0	0
Harrington, Corey, Wisconsin	.887	34	50	5	7	62	0
Harris, Gary, Wisconsin	.976	118	229	12	6	247	2
Hawes, B.J., Dayton	.941	11	15	1	1	17	0
Heath, Demetrius, W. Michigan	.973	23	35	1	1	37	0
Hileman, Jutt, Peoria	.952	32	57	3	3	63	1
Hinton, Travis, Beloit *	.952	36	58	1	3	62	0
Hutchinson, Burnell, South Bend	.667	3	2	0	1	3	0
Jenkins, Kevin, Cedar Rapids *	.959	32	46	1	2	49	0
Johnson, J.J., Lansing	.941	103	162	14	11	187	3
Jones, Kennard, Fort Wayne *	.954	80	158	8	8	174	2
Jones, Nick, Lansing	1.000	18	22	0	0	22	0
Kennedy, Jason, West Michigan	1.000	4	1	0	0	1	0
Keown, Clint, Dayton	1.000	17	31	2	0	33	0
Knoedler, Jason, West Michigan	.975	72	112	7	3	122	1
Kuhaulua, Kaulana, Quad City	1.000	8	11	0	0	11	0
Lebron, Hector, Clinton	.933	44	83	1	6	90	0
Lemanczyk, Matt, Peoria	.979	125	228	5	5	238	1
Lemon, Tim, Peoria	.980	25	43	6	1	50	1
Lewis, Domonique, Dayton	.963	40	74	3	3	80	0
Lima, Joseph, Fort Wayne	.000	5	0	0	0	0	0
Liz, Jose, Quad City	.964	19	26	1	1	28	0
Lonnquist, Eric, Burlington	.944	9	16	1	1	18	0
Lytle, Derrik, Burlington *	1.000	46	96	4	0	100	1
Macias, Andres, Fort Wayne *	.000	1	0	0	0	0	0
Maher, Caleb, Cedar Rapids	.950	69	110	5	6	121	1
Majewski, Dustin, Kane Co.*	.875	4	7	0	1	8	0
McAnulty, Paul, Fort Wayne	1.000	4	1	0	0	1	0
McBeth, Marcus, Kane County	.986	67	141	2	2	145	2
Melgarejo, Ransel, Cedar Rapids	.994	80	164	1	1	166	0
Mendez, Mario, Beloit	.969	100	182	4	6	192	1
Mendez, Victor, West Michigan	.977	135	329	7	8	344	2
Monette, Daylon, Peoria *	1.000	6	7	0	0	7	0
Moss, Steve, Beloit	1.000	57	125	9	0	134	0
Nelson, Jon, Wisconsin	1.000	12	19	0	0	19	0
Nordness, Kirk, Kane County	.960	33	46	2	2	50	0
Nunez, Andres, Battle Creek	1.000	3	6	0	0	6	0
O'Toole, Paul, Lansing	1.000	6	4	0	0	4	0
Oeltjen, Trent, Quad City *	.968	114	240	4	8	252	1
Paula, Manuel, Dayton	.983	48	112	5	2	119	0
Perodin, Ron, Quad City *	.962	25	48	2	2	52	0
Pie, Felix, Lansing *	.981	123	257	5	5	267	1
Porter, Greg, Cedar Rapids	.980	29	47	3	1	51	1
Reyes, Jose, Lansing	.000	1	0	0	0	0	0
Reynolds, Wilton, W. Michigan	.943	77	138	10	9	157	1
Richardson, Kevin, Clinton	.909	11	10	0	1	11	0
Richardson, Mike, Fort Wayne	1.000	2	3	0	0	3	0
Rodriguez, Marcos, Peoria *	.905	14	18	1	2	21	0
Rogers, Nick, Kane County	.977	77	128	2	3	133	0
Romero, Alex, Quad City	.982	115	271	8	5	284	1
Ruiz, Junior, Dayton	.992	53	118	5	1	124	1
Santa, Alexander, Battle Creek *	1.000	28	55	4	0	59	1
Santiago, Rudy, South Bend	.972	70	131	7	4	142	0
Sardinha, Bronson, Battle Creek	.955	60	102	5	5	112	0
Schmidt, J.P., Kane County	.949	33	55	1	3	59	0
Schmidt, Jarrod, Dayton	1.000	26	44	4	0	48	0
Senreiso, Juan, Clinton	.955	121	278	20	14	312	5
Simon, Brandon, South Bend *	.895	12	16	1	2	19	0
Sprowl, Jon-Mark, South Bend	.909	8	10	0	1	11	0
Stavisky, Brian, Kane County	.958	16	22	1	1	24	0
Stephens, Bernard, Burlington	.973	121	235	17	7	259	2
STOCKER, MEL, Burlington	.992	101	250	6	2	258	1
Sugden, Jason, Cedar Rapids	.963	20	23	3	1	27	1
Summerville, Kaazim, B.C.	.885	13	23	0	3	26	0
Teilon, Nilson, South Bend	.973	47	71	1	2	74	0
Tranum, Josh, Fort Wayne *	1.000	3	3	0	0	3	0
Tritle, Chris, Kane County	.959	36	70	1	3	74	0
Vasquez, Willie, Battle Creek	1.000	12	22	2	0	24	0
Verbryke, Eric, Battle Creek *	.961	34	71	3	3	77	1
Voshell, Chase, Peoria	1.000	3	4	0	0	4	0
Webster, Anthony, Clinton	.923	15	33	3	3	39	0
Weed, B.J., Cedar Rapids	.966	94	163	7	6	176	2
Whitrock, Scott, Quad City	.957	71	124	8	6	138	0
Williams, Matt, Peoria	1.000	2	3	0	0	3	0

OUTFIELDERS WITH TWO OR MORE TEAMS

Player, Team	Pct.	G	PO	A	E	TC	DP
Brooks, Doc, Fort Wayne	.967	20	29	0	1	30	0
Brooks, Doc, South Bend	.932	70	120	3	9	132	0
Ehrnsberger, Chad, Peoria	1.000	2	1	0	0	1	0
Ehrnsberger, Chad, Wisconsin	1.000	13	20	1	0	21	0
Fransz, Jason, Lansing	.959	60	67	4	3	74	0
Fransz, Jason, Clinton	1.000	8	17	0	0	17	0

CATCHERS

Player, Team	Pct.	G	PO	A	E	TC	DP	PB
Abram, Matt, Cedar Rapids	1.000	4	5	0	0	5	0	0
Abruzzo, Jared, Cedar Rapids	.978	94	572	54	14	640	3	18
Avlas, Phil, South Bend	.991	46	311	35	3	349	1	7
Baker, John, Kane County	.985	60	417	30	7	454	2	4
Basil, Jason, Kane County	1.000	12	78	15	0	93	0	3
Belz, Tim, Peoria	1.000	8	28	5	0	33	0	1
Booth, Steve, Dayton	1.000	4	20	3	0	23	0	0
Brooks, Doc, Fort Wayne	1.000	1	6	1	0	7	0	2
Burkhart, Lance, Clinton	1.000	2	11	1	0	12	0	0
Carlin, Luke, Fort Wayne	.989	15	81	13	1	95	1	2
Chauncey, Clinton, Peoria	.987	15	62	14	1	77	2	3
Craig, Beau, Kane County	.985	18	117	12	2	131	1	1
Duenas, Tommy, Cedar Rapids	1.000	20	86	8	0	94	0	1
Durham, Tyler, Peoria	1.000	1	2	0	0	2	0	0
Dvorsky, Alex, Cedar Rapids	.996	38	224	31	1	256	1	2
Eickhorst, Chris, Peoria	1.000	10	54	7	0	61	0	1
Esparragoza, Pedro, Beloit	.977	75	528	77	14	619	2	10
Falcon, Omar, Fort Wayne	1.000	12	107	5	0	112	0	2
Fox, Jacob, Lansing	.981	22	133	22	3	158	1	5
Fry, Ryan, Dayton	1.000	2	13	2	0	15	0	0
Garcia, Cip, Wisconsin	1.000	5	26	1	0	27	0	0
Geiger, Kyle, Quad City	.976	10	77	5	2	84	0	3
Ginther, Andy, Peoria	.875	3	14	0	2	16	0	1
Girardi, Joe, Peoria	1.000	2	8	1	0	9	0	0
Gonzalez, Luis, Burlington	.987	64	397	46	6	449	8	18
Griffin, Brock, Wisconsin	1.000	1	13	2	0	15	1	0
Guzman, Jacob, Burlington	1.000	1	17	2	0	19	0	0
Hanigan, Ryan, Dayton	.987	82	580	48	8	636	3	8
Huether, J.D., Quad City	.974	12	66	8	2	76	0	6
Jaile, Chris, Clinton	.984	87	499	69	9	577	0	12
Johnson, Josh, Quad City	.984	11	55	8	1	64	0	2
Kennedy, Bryan, Quad City	.988	54	367	45	5	417	2	7
Lafferty, Will, Peoria	1.000	17	72	12	0	84	0	0
Madera, Sandy, Battle Creek	.973	11	65	6	2	73	0	1
Martinez, Domingo, F.W.	1.000	5	22	2	0	24	0	0
Martinez, Freddy, Dayton	1.000	3	15	4	0	19	1	2
Matienzo, Danny, Quad City	.988	31	210	27	3	240	0	5
Medlin, C.J., Lansing	.957	12	84	4	4	92	0	2
Miller, Chris, Lansing	1.000	4	25	4	0	29	0	0
Morales, Jose, Quad City	.976	28	181	20	5	206	0	10
Morgan, Matt, South Bend	1.000	1	1	0	0	1	0	0
Morton, Colt, Fort Wayne	.992	17	117	15	1	133	0	2
Motte, Jason, Peoria	.987	48	262	47	4	313	4	5
O'Toole, Paul, Lansing	.968	3	29	1	1	31	0	2
Oakes, Matt, West Michigan	.980	42	186	12	4	202	0	8
Pagan, Andres, Fort Wayne	.987	95	722	61	10	793	5	11
Parker, Tyler, Peoria	.973	51	287	35	9	331	2	4
Perez, Miguel, Dayton	.950	18	121	12	7	140	0	3
Phillips, Christopher, Wis.	.972	24	134	7	4	145	1	6
RABELO, MIKE, West Michigan	.994	118	773	84	5	862	4	7
Reyes, Jose, Lansing	.990	64	443	60	5	508	1	10
Richardson, Mike, Fort Wayne	1.000	1	9	2	0	11	1	0
Richie, Tony, Lansing	.987	19	138	11	2	151	0	3
Rivera, Rene, Wisconsin	.987	109	727	114	11	852	6	15
Rogers, Nick, Kane County	.000	1	0	0	0	0	0	0
Rojas, Tommy, Battle Creek	.994	42	282	24	2	308	3	13
Santana, Manny, Clinton	.984	52	280	25	5	310	2	6
Santos, Omir, Battle Creek	.984	71	436	50	8	494	4	5
Schmidt, Jarrod, Dayton	.960	24	134	9	6	149	0	4
Sprowl, Jon-Mark, S.B.-B.C.	.977	93	505	49	13	567	1	18
Sulbaran, Orlando, Dayton	.987	11	66	8	1	75	0	2
Suomi, John, Kane County	.982	55	354	34	7	395	1	8
Tosca, Daniel, South Bend	.978	15	87	4	2	93	0	1
Tupman, Matt, Burlington	.984	78	478	63	9	550	8	14
Udy, Nicholas, Wisconsin	1.000	7	25	2	0	27	0	0
Vanden Berg, John, Beloit	.987	65	492	33	7	532	2	18
Wells, Randy, Lansing	.989	20	162	19	2	183	0	3
Wilkins, Joe, South Bend	.969	17	83	10	3	96	2	4

CATCHERS WITH TWO OR MORE TEAMS

Player, Team	Pct.	G	PO	A	E	TC	DP	PB
Sprowl, Jon-Mark, Battle Creek	.992	18	119	7	1	127	1	3
Sprowl, Jon-Mark, South Bend	.973	75	386	42	12	440	0	15

PITCHERS

Player, Team	Pct.	G	PO	A	E	TC	DP
Ackerman, Eric, Burlington *	.909	26	11	39	5	55	2
Acosta, Manuel, Battle Creek	.846	15	1	10	2	13	0
Adamczyk, Tyler, Peoria	.970	26	14	18	1	33	3
Alliston, Josh, Beloit	.917	52	5	6	1	12	0
Arias, Daniel, Cedar Rapids	1.000	29	2	4	0	6	0
Armitage, Barry, Burlington	1.000	8	1	5	0	6	1
Astacio, Hector, Cedar Rapids	1.000	6	3	2	0	5	0
Atencio, Greg, Burlington	.750	2	1	2	1	4	0
Baez, Federico, Lansing	.889	51	4	12	2	18	0
Baker, Jason, Beloit	1.000	21	1	7	0	8	0
Baker, Scott, Quad City	1.000	11	7	7	0	14	1
Ballouli, Khalid, Beloit	.846	15	4	7	2	13	0
Barreto, Joel, Dayton	1.000	29	1	3	0	4	0
Barrett, Rich, South Bend	.000	1	0	0	0	0	0
Barrett, Ricky, Quad City *	1.000	3	0	1	0	1	0
Batista, Gorky, Dayton	.875	8	2	5	1	8	0
Batista, Roberto, Peoria	1.000	13	0	4	0	4	0
Bausher, Tim, Beloit	.500	19	0	1	1	2	0
Bayliss, Jonah, Burlington	.935	26	11	18	2	31	0
Beam, T.J., Battle Creek	.000	5	0	0	2	2	0
Beavers, Kevin, Fort Wayne *	1.000	10	1	1	0	2	0
Bechtel, Charles, Fort Wayne	1.000	17	1	2	0	3	0
Bell, Gary, Battle Creek *	1.000	10	2	4	0	6	1
Beltre, Omar, Clinton	1.000	16	4	7	0	11	1
Benik, Brett, Lansing	1.000	18	1	4	0	5	0
Berry, Jon, Dayton	.857	12	3	3	1	7	1
Bilke, Austin, Cedar Rapids	1.000	19	2	3	0	5	0
Blackburn, Nick, Quad City	1.000	16	9	12	0	21	1
Blair, Tom, Peoria *	1.000	7	1	12	0	13	0
Blanton, Joe, Kane County	.905	21	4	15	2	21	0
Blasko, Chadd, Lansing	1.000	2	1	4	0	5	1
Bohanan, Keith, Beloit	.000	3	0	0	0	0	0
Booker, Chris, Dayton	1.000	5	0	1	0	1	0
Breslow, Craig, Beloit *	.938	33	2	13	1	16	0
Bright, Nathan, Clinton	1.000	5	0	1	0	1	0
Brumit, Matt, Battle Creek	1.000	43	6	6	0	12	0
Burch, Jason, Peoria	1.000	13	1	1	0	2	0
Burch, Matt, Burlington	1.000	8	3	3	0	6	0
Burgos, Ambiorix, Burlington	.667	2	0	2	1	3	1
Burton, Jared, Kane County	1.000	15	2	3	0	5	1
Cameron, Kevin, Quad City	.926	39	4	21	2	27	0
Carpenter, Calvin, Beloit	.917	16	5	6	1	12	0
Carroll, James, Cedar Rapids	1.000	23	1	6	0	7	0
Carter, Mark, Lansing *	1.000	45	1	7	0	8	0
Carter, Ramsey, Burlington	1.000	2	0	1	0	1	0
Cavazos, Andy, Peoria	.933	36	10	18	2	30	0
Cedeno, Jovanny, Clinton	1.000	8	1	0	0	1	0
Chamberlain, Steve, Burlington	.895	33	9	8	2	19	0
Cherry, Rocky, Lansing	1.000	8	3	6	0	9	0
Christensen, Danny, Burl.*	.923	17	2	10	1	13	0
Cimorelli, Brett, Cedar Rapids	.700	31	4	3	3	10	0
Ciprian, Wilson, Peoria	.000	5	0	0	0	0	0
Clark, Ray, Battle Creek	.900	22	8	10	2	20	1
Coffey, Todd, Dayton	.857	39	1	11	2	14	2
Coffin, Ryan, South Bend	.800	29	4	12	4	20	1
Colton, Kyle, Burlington	.000	2	0	0	0	0	0
Connolly, Jon, West Michigan *	.973	25	5	31	1	37	1
Coonrod, Aaron, Fort Wayne	1.000	4	1	0	0	1	0
Corona, Andrew, Fort Wayne	.600	21	1	2	2	5	0
Corrado, Rob, Clinton	.857	6	1	5	1	7	0
Cortez, Renee, Wisconsin	1.000	28	7	7	0	14	1
Crawford, Tristan, Quad City	.500	19	1	1	2	4	0
Creighton, Matt, Lansing	.000	1	0	0	0	0	0
D'Amico, Leonardo, C.R.	.667	12	0	2	1	3	0
Davis, Mike, South Bend	1.000	23	4	4	0	8	1
Daws, Josh, Dayton	1.000	18	2	2	0	4	0
DeJaynes, Brandon, Peoria	.000	2	0	0	0	0	0
De la Cruz, Andres, Burlington	1.000	21	4	1	0	5	0
Delgado, Danny, Wisconsin	1.000	4	0	1	0	1	0
Delgado, Oscar, Wisconsin *	.882	40	4	11	2	17	0
Desalvo, Matthew, Battle Creek	1.000	3	1	5	0	6	0
Devenney, Nick, Clinton	.500	6	2	1	3	6	0
Diaz, Luis, West Michigan	1.000	4	2	1	0	3	0
Dickinson, Drew, Kane County *	.985	28	12	55	1	68	3
Dorman, Rich, Wisconsin	1.000	25	2	1	0	3	1
Dowdy, Justin, Wisconsin *	.727	10	1	7	3	11	0
Doyle, Jared, South Bend *	.806	27	9	20	7	36	2
Doyne, Cory, Fort Wayne	.909	12	1	9	1	11	0
Drown, Erik, Peoria	.750	5	0	3	1	4	0
Dulkowski, Marc, Fort Wayne	.875	16	2	5	1	8	0
Dunwell, Chris, Kane County	.923	30	2	10	1	13	0
Edens, Kyle, Dayton	1.000	6	1	3	0	4	1
Edwards, Bryan, Fort Wayne	.885	39	7	16	3	26	1
Endicott, Drew, Burlington	.939	32	13	18	2	33	1
Estes, Jonathan, Peoria	1.000	26	3	5	0	8	0
Farfan, Alexander, Dayton	.960	40	11	13	1	25	1

Player, Team	Pct.	G	PO	A	E	TC	DP
Ferreras, Yorkin, Lansing *	.909	10	1	9	1	11	0
Figueroa, Juan, West Michigan	.667	55	3	3	3	9	0
Fischer, Eric, Quad City *	1.000	11	3	16	0	19	0
Flynn, Brian, Peoria	.857	30	2	4	1	7	1
Foli, Daniel, Lansing	.941	34	5	11	1	17	0
Frias, Juan, Dayton *	.936	25	9	35	3	47	2
Fulmer, T.A., Wisconsin	.944	27	9	25	2	36	0
Gabriel, Justin, Beloit *	1.000	21	1	10	0	11	1
Galbraith, Jason, Peoria *	1.000	2	1	0	0	1	0
Garber, Mike, South Bend *	1.000	6	0	1	0	1	0
Garcia, Anderson, Battle Creek	.882	16	0	15	2	17	0
Garcia, Jairo, Kane County	1.000	14	0	6	0	6	0
Garcia, Jose, Battle Creek	.971	21	13	21	1	35	1
Gemmell, Don, Dayton	1.000	22	1	5	0	6	0
George, Brad, Dayton	.875	24	4	3	1	8	0
Gerk, Jordan, West Michigan *	.952	55	6	14	1	21	0
Gillman, Justin, Dayton	.600	7	1	2	2	5	0
Gliemmo, Hayden, C.R.*	.923	42	6	6	1	13	0
Goas, Adrian, Cedar Rapids	1.000	18	0	3	0	3	0
Gonzalez, Cristian, Kane County	1.000	19	7	16	0	23	1
Gonzalez, Enrique, South Bend	.963	55	7	19	1	27	1
Graham, Jason, West Michigan	.800	28	1	7	2	10	0
Granado, Jan, Dayton *	.938	13	4	11	1	16	0
Graves, Don, Peoria	.967	22	7	22	1	30	0
Gray, Joshua, Quad City *	.889	10	3	5	1	9	0
Green, Craig, Lansing	.857	6	4	2	1	7	0
Gregg, Grant, Fort Wayne *	1.000	5	0	4	0	4	1
Griffin, Colt, Burlington	.878	27	10	26	5	41	1
Griffith, Dustin, Cedar Rapids	1.000	4	2	1	0	3	1
Gruler, Chris, Dayton	.000	3	0	0	1	1	0
Guevara, Jose, Dayton	.889	12	4	4	1	9	0
Hall, Bo, Beloit	1.000	46	1	6	0	7	0
Harben, Adam, Quad City	.867	16	7	6	2	15	0
Harmsen, Brandon, Battle Creek	.929	8	4	9	1	14	0
Hawksworth, Blake, Peoria	1.000	10	1	8	0	9	1
Haynes, Jimmy, Dayton	1.000	1	0	2	0	2	1
Heaston, Bryan, Wisconsin	1.000	41	3	12	0	15	2
Heiberger, Heath, South Bend *	.875	39	1	6	1	8	0
Henderson, Eric, Beloit *	.926	10	3	22	2	27	0
Hernandez, Felix, Wisconsin	1.000	2	2	1	0	3	0
Herrera, Cesar, Clinton	.909	31	13	17	3	33	1
Hill, Josh, Quad City	.833	26	12	18	6	36	0
Hill, Richard, Lansing *	.750	15	0	3	1	4	0
Hintz, Beau, Wisconsin *	1.000	6	2	5	0	7	0
Hoelscher, Nate, Burlington *	1.000	34	7	4	0	11	0
Hogan, Gary, Clinton	.833	32	11	14	5	30	0
Holcomb, James, Cedar Rapids	.789	14	8	7	4	19	1
Housman, Jeff, Beloit *	.950	20	4	15	1	20	2
Howell, Michael, West Michigan	.941	11	8	8	1	17	0
Huber, Jon, Fort Wayne	.500	7	1	3	4	8	0
Hudgins, John, Clinton	.000	1	0	0	0	0	0
Huizinga, Jon, Beloit	.714	23	2	3	2	7	0
Incinelli, Matt, South Bend	1.000	2	0	2	0	2	0
Isaacson, Charlie, Battle Creek	1.000	27	3	5	0	8	1
Jepsen, Kevin, Cedar Rapids	.750	10	4	5	3	12	0
Jimenez, Cesar, Wisconsin *	.931	28	7	20	2	29	1
Jones, Justin, Lansing *	.923	16	7	17	2	26	2
Jordan, B.J., Peoria *	.000	2	0	0	0	0	0
Julianel, Ben, Peoria-B.C.*	1.000	55	1	7	0	8	0
Jumelles, Edduar, Dayton	1.000	16	1	3	0	4	1
Kaanoi, Jason, Burlington	1.000	31	3	10	0	13	1
Keeling, Justin, Quad City *	.000	4	0	0	0	0	0
Keiter, Ben, Clinton	1.000	5	1	2	0	3	0
Keppinger, Billy, Burlington *	1.000	3	0	2	0	2	0
Kieninger, Billy, West Michigan	.933	26	6	8	1	15	1
King, Jeremy, Battle Creek	.833	14	5	5	2	12	0
King, O.J., Dayton	.667	4	1	1	1	3	0
Kinsey, Christopher, South Bend	1.000	10	1	0	0	1	0
Kirsten, Joel, Clinton *	1.000	9	3	3	0	6	0
Knowles, Mike, Peoria	.000	1	0	0	0	0	0
Koenig, Ross, West Michigan	.800	20	0	4	1	5	0
Kohn, Shawn, Kane County	.947	45	2	16	1	19	1
Komine, Shane, Kane County	1.000	8	2	10	0	12	0
Kranawetter, Josh, South Bend	1.000	24	2	5	0	7	0
Krawczyk, Jack, South Bend	.800	16	0	4	1	5	0
Kuhaulua, Kaulana, Quad City	.000	2	0	0	0	0	0
Landeros, Leonard, Kane Co.*	1.000	15	1	6	0	7	2
Leon, Brigmer, Kane County	.818	30	4	5	2	11	1
Lewis, Lavon, West Michigan	.000	1	0	0	1	1	0
Lincoln, Matthew, C.R.*	.667	10	0	4	2	6	0
Lipari, Thomas, Fort Wayne *	1.000	19	2	6	0	8	0
Livingston, Bobby, Wisconsin *	.909	26	12	38	5	55	2
Lizarraga, Sergio, South Bend	.923	42	12	12	2	26	1
Loe, Kameron, Clinton	.931	23	7	20	2	29	0
Lohse, Eric, Quad City	.917	28	1	10	1	12	0
Lord, Justin, Burlington	1.000	19	1	2	0	3	0
Lowery, Devon, Burlington	.941	26	4	12	1	17	3
Lucas, Kyle, Dayton	.929	25	4	9	1	14	1
Lugo, Ozzie, Cedar Rapids	1.000	52	3	6	0	9	0
Luna, Brandon, Clinton	1.000	20	2	4	0	6	2
Lynch, Matt, Kane County *	1.000	13	1	11	0	12	0
Marcano, Luis, Clinton	.909	39	6	4	1	11	0
Markray, Thad, Battle Creek	1.000	34	2	4	0	6	0
Marquez, Jeff, Cedar Rapids	.905	45	7	12	2	21	1
Marshall, Sean, Lansing *	1.000	1	1	0	0	1	0
Martin, Forrest, Beloit	1.000	4	0	2	0	2	0
Martinez, Domingo, Fort Wayne	1.000	1	0	1	0	1	0
Martinez, Miguel, Wisconsin *	1.000	24	3	4	0	7	0
Martinez, Miguel, Peoria	.958	20	8	15	1	24	0
Masset, Nicholas, Clinton	.808	30	9	12	5	26	0
Mattison, Kieran, Burlington	.947	17	6	12	1	19	0
Mauer, William, Quad City	1.000	4	1	3	0	4	0
McCall, Derell, Kane County	1.000	8	4	6	0	10	0
McGill, Trae, Burlington	1.000	16	8	11	0	19	1
McWilliams, Matt, Dayton *	1.000	36	1	10	0	11	1
Mead, David, Clinton	1.000	3	0	3	0	3	0
Medina, Julio, Dayton	.000	1	0	0	1	1	0
Mejia, Juan, Peoria	1.000	30	3	8	0	11	1
Mendez, Adalberto, Lansing	.000	9	0	0	0	0	0
Mendez, Mario, Beloit	1.000	5	0	1	0	1	0
Mendoza, Cristian, Battle Creek	.800	32	3	5	2	10	2
Mendoza, Gabriel, Beloit *	1.000	18	0	6	0	6	1
Metzger, Jon, Burlington *	.000	3	0	0	0	0	0
Miller, Jason, Quad City *	.875	13	1	6	1	8	0
Moorhead, Michael, Wisconsin	.000	5	0	0	0	0	0
Morban, Carlos, Cedar Rapids	1.000	9	0	3	0	3	0
Morel, Eudy, Fort Wayne	.857	40	6	6	2	14	2
Moreno, Abel, Cedar Rapids	1.000	3	1	3	0	4	0
Morrow, David, Wisconsin	1.000	6	1	0	0	1	0
Mosley, Eric, Battle Creek	.000	4	0	0	0	0	0
Mowday, Chris, Kane County	.923	21	3	9	1	13	0
Muessig, Jeff, Kane County	1.000	22	1	2	0	3	0
Murphy, Bill, Kane County *	.952	14	2	18	1	21	0
Murray, Steve, Quad City *	1.000	47	2	13	0	15	0
Neitz, Josh, Battle Creek	.833	31	4	6	2	12	2
Neshek, Pat, Quad City	.800	28	2	2	1	5	0
Nippert, Dustin, South Bend	.941	17	5	11	1	17	0
O'Brien, Wes, Lansing	.929	55	2	11	1	14	0
O'Malley, Ryan, Lansing *	.963	40	7	19	1	27	1
Oakes, Gerry, Quad City	.889	24	4	12	2	18	0
Obenchain, Stephen, Kane Co.	1.000	11	1	8	0	9	0
Olson, Justin, Quad City	1.000	14	2	1	0	3	0
Ortiz, Omar, Clinton	1.000	9	1	1	0	2	0
Ostlund, Ian, West Michigan *	1.000	44	1	2	0	3	0
Ovalles, Juan, Wisconsin	.000	2	0	0	0	0	0
PARRA, MANNY, Beloit *	1.000	23	4	22	0	26	0
Parris, Matt, West Michigan	.939	32	14	17	2	33	2
Pauley, David, Fort Wayne	1.000	22	7	12	0	19	2
Pauly, Thomas, Dayton	.889	12	1	7	1	9	0
Pena, Luismar, Beloit	.905	23	8	11	2	21	1
Pender, Matthew, West Michigan	.900	17	6	12	2	20	0
Pezely, Franco, Clinton *	.944	44	5	12	1	18	1
Pickford, Troy, West Michigan	1.000	16	7	16	0	23	0
Plancich, Nick, Peoria	1.000	2	0	1	0	1	0
Posey, Micah, Cedar Rapids *	.960	20	2	22	1	25	3
Prunty, T.J., Quad City	1.000	30	5	15	0	20	0
Quezada, Elvys, Battle Creek	1.000	2	1	1	0	2	0
Ramirez, Edward, Cedar Rapids	1.000	6	0	1	0	1	0
Rapada, Clayton, Lansing *	.889	21	3	5	1	9	0
Rawson, Anthony, Peoria *	.917	20	4	7	1	12	0
Ray, Ronnie, Cedar Rapids	1.000	20	6	19	0	25	1
Reyes, Ramon, Cedar Rapids	1.000	4	1	1	0	2	0
Ribas, Gabe, Fort Wayne	.833	19	5	10	3	18	0
Richards, John, Fort Wayne *	.500	9	0	3	3	6	0
Rodriguez , Rafael, C.R.	.967	26	12	17	1	30	0
Rodriguez, Jermy, W. Michigan	.778	41	2	5	2	9	0
Rodriguez, Luis, Clinton	1.000	14	0	3	0	3	0
Rodriguez, Manuel, Kane County	1.000	33	0	6	0	6	0
Rogers, Joe, Peoria *	1.000	37	4	2	0	6	0
Rosario, Adriano, South Bend	.881	27	13	24	5	42	0
Rowland-Smith, Ryan, Wis.*	.818	13	3	6	2	11	0
Runyon, Bob, Peoria	1.000	11	5	7	0	12	0
Rupe, Josh, Clinton	.857	6	1	5	1	7	0

Player, Team	Pct.	G	PO	A	E	TC	DP
Russelburg, Aaron, Peoria	1.000	6	1	2	0	3	0
Ryu, Jae-kuk, Lansing	1.000	11	7	4	0	11	3
Saldana, Jaime, Battle Creek *	.857	41	1	5	1	7	0
Sanchez, Humberto, W. Mich.	.838	23	5	26	6	37	0
Sandoval, Juan, Wisconsin	.889	27	21	19	5	45	3
Sarfate, Dennis, Beloit	.864	26	4	15	3	22	0
Scalamandre, Rich, Peoria	1.000	18	1	4	0	5	0
Schara, Zackary, Clinton	1.000	12	0	1	0	1	0
Scheffel, Dustin, Clinton	.600	15	2	4	4	10	0
Schweitzer, Scott, Peoria *	.000	10	0	0	1	1	0
Seibert, Kevin, Fort Wayne	1.000	19	1	4	0	5	0
Shank, Chris, Kane County	.500	12	0	1	1	2	0
Shiery, Shaun, Burlington *	1.000	2	0	8	0	8	0
Sierra, Edwardo, Kane County	.909	51	4	6	1	11	1
Sisco, Andy, Lansing *	.667	19	0	12	6	18	0
Skaggs, Jon, Battle Creek	.714	14	3	7	4	14	0
Smiley, Gerald, Clinton	1.000	13	4	6	0	10	0
Smith, Cody, Clinton	1.000	2	2	0	0	2	0
Smith, Dan, West Michigan	1.000	12	0	3	0	3	0
Smith, Dustin, West Michigan	.800	7	2	2	1	5	0
Smith, Ryan, Quad City	1.000	11	0	5	0	5	0
Smith, Sam, South Bend	1.000	27	8	10	0	18	0
Soto, Darwin, Fort Wayne	1.000	53	3	5	0	8	0
Steidlmayer, Luke, Fort Wayne	.933	11	4	10	1	15	0
Steinborn, Chris, W. Michigan *	1.000	18	0	5	0	5	0
Steitz, Jon, Beloit	.667	4	0	2	1	3	0
Sullivan, Bradley, Kane County	1.000	6	1	4	0	5	0
Taulli, Sam, South Bend *	.923	23	5	7	1	13	0
Tautor, Peter, Quad City	.789	43	3	12	4	19	0
Tavares, Anderson, Lansing	.912	26	14	17	3	34	1
Teekel, Josh, Peoria	.931	26	3	24	2	29	1
Thayer, Dale, Fort Wayne	.778	45	4	3	2	9	0
Thigpen, Josh, Dayton	.923	28	7	5	1	13	1
Thompson, Bradley, Peoria	1.000	30	7	13	0	20	1
Thompson, Erik, Clinton	1.000	14	3	10	0	13	0
Thompson, Richard, C.R.	.800	31	2	2	1	5	0
Toledo, Jean, Cedar Rapids	.912	24	8	23	3	34	2
Truselo, Randy, Clinton	.000	2	0	0	0	0	0
Trytten, Ryan, Beloit	.941	28	7	9	1	17	0
Tyler, Scott, Quad City	1.000	30	5	13	0	18	1
Urena, Sixto, Clinton	1.000	38	3	6	0	9	0
Ursin, Damian, Dayton	.833	13	2	3	1	6	0
Valdez, Domingo, Clinton	.889	14	3	5	1	9	0
Valdez, Edward, Dayton	.914	19	12	20	3	35	1
Valdez, Jose, Battle Creek	.923	22	3	9	1	13	1
Van, Robert, South Bend *	.923	21	0	12	1	13	0
Vasquez, Carlos, Lansing *	.944	24	2	32	2	36	1
Vazquez, Camilo, Dayton *	1.000	13	0	11	0	11	0
Viane, David, Wisconsin	1.000	34	5	16	0	21	1
Villatoro, Wilmer, Fort Wayne	.875	39	4	3	1	8	1
Villegas, Francisco, Battle Creek	1.000	6	1	0	0	1	0
Watson, Mike, South Bend	1.000	16	0	1	0	1	0
Watson, Tanner, Wisconsin	.852	23	6	17	4	27	0
Watts, Joldy, Clinton	.000	1	0	0	0	0	0
Wear, Gregory, Wisconsin	1.000	17	3	7	0	10	0
Wells, Randy, Lansing	.000	1	0	0	0	0	0
Whatley, Keith, South Bend *	1.000	3	0	4	0	4	0
Whitaker, Brian, Fort Wayne	.944	26	9	25	2	36	1
Wilhelmsen, Tom, Beloit	.920	15	8	15	2	25	1
Wilkinson, Matty, South Bend	1.000	55	3	9	0	12	0
Williams, Aaron, Quad City	1.000	5	1	0	0	1	0
Williams, Bryan, Cedar Rapids	1.000	7	0	1	0	1	0
Wilson, Phil, Cedar Rapids	.500	2	0	1	1	2	1
Wiseman, Steven, Battle Creek	.900	35	3	6	1	10	0
Wright, Chase, Battle Creek *	1.000	7	0	1	0	1	0
Wylie, Jason, Lansing	1.000	57	6	7	0	13	0
Yoshida, Nobuaki, Fort Wayne *	1.000	10	0	4	0	4	0
Zumaya, Joel, West Michigan	.800	19	3	5	2	10	0

PITCHERS WITH TWO OR MORE TEAMS

Player, Team	Pct.	G	PO	A	E	TC	DP
Julianel, Ben, Battle Creek *	.000	4	0	0	0	0	0
Julianel, Ben, Peoria *	1.000	51	1	7	0	8	0

The following players appeared only as a designated hitter, pinch-hitter or pinch-runner: Hamblen, dh, ph; Shorsher, dh; Ra. Smith, dh, ph, pr.

LEAGUE CHAMPIONS

Year	Team	Pct.
1947—	Belleville	.667
	Belleville	.672
1948—	West Frankfort*	.708
1949—	Centralia	.627
	Paducah (4th)†	.454
1950—	Centralia‡	.675
1951—	Paris§	.700
	Danville (4th)†	.432
1952—	Danville∞	.685
	Decatur (3rd)†	.584
1953—	Decatur*	.576
1954—	Decatur	.587
	Danville (2nd)‡	.528
1955—	Dubuque*	.587
1956—	Paris▲	.656
	Dubuque	.603
1957—	Decatur▲	.683
	Clinton	.623
1958—	Michigan City	.623
	Waterloo◆	.613
1959—	Waterloo	.613
	Waterloo	.613
1960—	Waterloo	.629
	Waterloo	.677
1961—	Waterloo	.613
	Quincy◆	.594
1962—	Dubuque◆	.667
	Waterloo	.625
1963—	Clinton	.710
	Clinton	.629
1964—	Clinton	.667
	Fox Cities◆	.667
1965—	Burlington	.667
	Burlington	.677
1966—	Fox Cities◆	.689
	Cedar Rapids	.762
1967—	Wisconsin Rapids	.685
	Appleton◆	.587
1968—	Decatur	.656
	Quad Cities◆	.648
1969—	Appleton	.648
	Appleton	.690
1970—	Quincy◆	.691
	Quad Cities	.581
1971—	Appleton	.642
	Quad Cities■	.548
1972—	Appleton	.598
	Danville■	.584
1973—	Wisconsin Rapids■	.562
	Danville	.537
1974—	Appleton	.593
	Danville■	.517
1975—	Waterloo■	.727
	Quad Cities	.624
1976—	Waterloo■	.600
	Cedar Rapids	.595
1977—	Waterloo	.580
	Burlington■	.511
1978—	Appleton■	.708
	Burlington	.500
1979—	Waterloo	.600
	Quad Cities■	.579
1980—	Waterloo■	.610
	Quad Cities	.532
1981—	Wausau■	.636
	Quad Cities	.570
1982—	Madison	.626
	Appleton▼	.579
1983—	Appleton•	.635
	Springfield	.576
1984—	Appleton•	.640
	Springfield	.504
1985—	Kenosha▼	.568
	Peoria	.536
1986—	Springfield	.621
	Waterloo▼	.557
1987—	Springfield	.671
	Kenosha▼	.586
1988—	Cedar Rapids■	.621
	Kenosha	.579
1989—	South Bend■	.644
	Springfield	.541
1990—	Cedar Rapids	.657
	Quad City■	.579
1991—	Clinton■	.583
	Madison	.558
1992—	Quad City	.664
	Cedar Rapids■	.594
1993—	Clinton	.597
	South Bend■	.566
1994—	Rockford	.640
	Cedar Rapids■	.554
1995—	Beloit††	.633
	Michigan	.543
1996—	Wisconsin	.570
	West Michigan††	.558
1997—	Kane County	.507
	Lansing**	.504
1998—	West Michigan††	.593
1999—	Kane County	.569
	Burlington**	.511
2000—	West Michigan	.629
	Michigan‡‡	.594
2001—	Kane County▲▲	.638
2002—	Peoria‡‡	.616
2003—	Lansing‡‡	.511

*Won championship and four-club playoff. †Won four-club playoff. ‡Playoff finals canceled because of bad weather. §Won both halves of split season. ∞Won first half of split season and tied Paris for second-half title. ▲Won first-half title and four-team playoff. ◆Won split season playoff. ■League divided into Northern and Southern divisions and played split season. Playoff winner. ▼League divided into Northern, Central and Southern divisions. Playoff winner. •League divided into Northern, Central and Southern divisions; regular season and playoff winner. ††League divided into Eastern, Central and Western divisions; regular season and playoff winner. **League divided into Eastern, Central and Western divisions, playoff winner. ‡‡League divided into Eastern and Western divisions and played split season. Playoff winner. (NOTE—Known as Illinois State League in 1947-48 and Mississippi-Ohio Valley League from 1949 through 1955.) ▲▲League divided into Eastern and Western divisions and played split season; was leading final series of four-team playoff and was declared champion when Professional Baseball declared a stoppage of play.

SOUTH ATLANTIC LEAGUE

LEAGUE OFFICE

President/secretary-treasurer
John Moss

Address
P.O. Box 38
504 Crescent Hill
Kings Mountain, NC 28086

Phone
704-739-3466

Teams (affiliation)
Asheville Tourists (Rockies)
Augusta GreenJackets (Red Sox)
Capital City Bombers (Mets)
Charleston (S.C.) RiverDogs (Devil Rays)
Charleston (W.Va.) Alley Cats (Blue Jays)
Delmarva Shorebirds (Orioles)
Greensboro Bats (Marlins)
Hagerstown Suns (Giants)
Hickory Crawdads (Pirates)
Kannapolis Intimidators (White Sox)
Lake County Captains (Indians)
Lakewood BlueClaws (Phillies)
Lexington Legends (Astros)
Rome Braves (Braves)
Savannah Sand Gnats (Expos)
South Georgia Waves (Dodgers)

2003 FINAL STANDINGS

FIRST HALF

NORTHERN DIVISION

Team	W	L	T	Pct.	GB
Lake County	48	22	-	.686	...
Delmarva	36	32	-	.529	11.0
Greensboro	36	33	-	.522	11.5
Hagerstown	35	32	-	.522	11.5
Lexington	32	36	-	.471	15.0
Kannapolis	32	36	-	.471	15.0
Charleston-WV	27	36	-	.429	17.5
Lakewood	22	47	-	.319	25.5

SOUTHERN DIVISION

Team	W	L	T	Pct.	GB
Hickory	42	25	-	.627	...
Capital City	39	29	-	.574	3.5
Charleston-SC	39	30	-	.565	4.0
Rome	36	33	-	.522	7.0
Asheville	36	33	-	.522	7.0
Savannah	31	38	-	.449	12.0
South Georgia	28	38	-	.424	13.5
Augusta	24	43	-	.358	18.0

SECOND HALF

NORTHERN DIVISION

Team	W	L	T	Pct.	GB
Lake County	49	21	-	.700	...
Lexington	43	27	-	.614	6.0
Lakewood	35	34	-	.507	13.5
Hagerstown	33	35	-	.485	15.0
Greensboro	31	36	-	.463	16.5
Delmarva	31	39	-	.443	18.0
Charleston-WV	30	40	-	.429	19.0
Kannapolis	23	46	-	.333	25.5

SOUTHERN DIVISION

Team	W	L	T	Pct.	GB
Rome	42	28	-	.600	...
Hickory	40	29	-	.580	1.5
Charleston-SC	38	32	-	.543	4.0
Asheville	38	32	-	.543	4.0
South Georgia	36	34	-	.514	6.0
Capital City	34	36	-	.486	8.0
Savannah	27	42	-	.391	14.5
Augusta	25	44	-	.362	16.5

COMPOSITE

Team	LCO	HCK	ROM	CSC	LEX	ASH	CAP	HAG	GBO	DEL	SGA	CWV	SAV	LWD	KAN	AUG	W	L	T	Pct.	GB
Lake County (Indians)	...	2	1	2	9	2	4	13	9	11	4	10	2	11	13	4	97	43	0	.693	...
Hickory (Pirates)	2	...	10	7	4	13	7	1	2	2	8	3	7	2	2	12	82	54	0	.603	13.0
Rome (Braves)	3	3	...	11	3	7	7	1	2	2	13	3	9	4	3	7	78	61	0	.561	18.5
Charl.-SC (Devil Rays)	2	6	10	...	1	8	3	3	3	1	10	2	13	3	4	8	77	62	0	.554	19.5
Lexington (Astros)	6	0	1	3	...	2	2	9	8	9	3	6	4	7	14	1	75	63	0	.543	21.0
Asheville (Rockies)	2	13	6	5	2	...	6	3	2	2	6	2	8	1	3	13	74	65	0	.532	22.5
Capital City (Mets)	0	8	5	9	2	10	...	1	1	2	7	1	6	4	3	14	73	65	0	.529	23.0
Hagerstown (Giants)	3	2	3	1	7	1	3	...	7	10	1	10	2	7	9	2	68	67	0	.504	26.5
Greensboro (Marlins)	2	2	2	1	7	1	3	8	...	7	2	9	1	11	9	2	67	69	0	.493	28.0
Delmarva (Orioles)	5	2	2	3	5	2	2	4	8	...	2	10	4	10	7	1	67	71	0	.486	29.0
S. Georgia (Dodgers)	0	3	7	6	1	6	6	1	2	2	...	4	11	3	2	10	64	72	0	.471	31.0
Charl.-WV (Blue Jays)	6	1	1	2	8	2	2	4	7	6	0	...	2	8	7	1	57	76	0	.429	36.5
Savannah (Expos)	2	5	7	7	0	4	7	2	2	0	10	2	...	2	1	7	58	80	0	.420	38.0
Lakewood (Phillies)	7	2	0	1	5	3	0	9	9	6	1	6	2	...	5	1	57	81	0	.413	39.0
Kannapolis (White Sox)	3	1	1	0	6	1	1	6	5	8	2	8	3	6	...	4	55	82	0	.401	40.5
Augusta (Red Sox)	0	4	5	4	3	3	12	2	2	3	3	0	6	2	0	...	49	87	0	.360	46.0

Major league affiliations in parentheses.

PLAYOFFS: Lake County defeated Lexington, two games to none; Rome defeated Hickory, two games to one; Rome defeated Lake County, three games to one, to win league championship.

REGULAR-SEASON ATTENDANCE: Asheville, 143,596; Augusta, 131,650; Capital City, 102,149; Charleston (S.C.), 259,007; Charleston (W.Va.), 95,590; Delmarva, 228,344; Greensboro, 164,589; Hagerstown, 100,865; Hickory, 176,366; Kannapolis, 92,321; Lake County, 437,515; Lakewood, 445,838; Lexington, 370,656; Rome, 246,718; Savannah, 103,443; South Georgia, 30,565. Total attendance—3,129,212. Playoffs (9 games)—42,834. All-Star Game at Lexington—8,122.

MANAGERS: Asheville, Joe Mikulik; Augusta, Russ Morman; Capital City, Tony Tijerina; Charleston (S.C.), Mako Oliveras; Charleston (W.Va.), Mark Meleski; Delmarva, Stan Hough; Greensboro, Steve Phillips; Hagerstown, Mike Ramsey; Hickory, Tony Beasley; Kannapolis, John Orton; Lake County, Luis Rivera; Lakewood, Buddy Biancalana; Lexington, Russ Nixon; Rome, Rocket Wheeler; Savannah, Joey Cora; South Georgia, Dann Bilardello.

ALL-STAR TEAM: 1B—Larry Broadway, Savannah; 2B—Delwyn Young, South Georgia; 3B—Aaron Baldiris, Capital City; SS—B.J. Upton, Charleston (S.C.); Utility INF—Chad Spann, Augusta; OF—Jeff Salazar, Asheville; OF—Jorge Cortes, Hickory; OF—Jeff Francoeur, Rome; DH—Chad Chop, Savannah; Utility OF—Rajai Davis, Hickory; C—Brian McCann, Rome; RHP—Fausto Carmona, Lake County; LHP—Josh Habel, Hagerstown; Manager—Luis Rivera, Lake County; Coach—Tony Arnold, Lake County; Most Valuable Player—Jorge Cortes, Hickory; Most Valuable Pitcher—Fausto Carmona, Lake County; Most Outstanding Major League Prospect—B.J. Upton, Charleston (S.C.).

2003 BATTING

TEAM

Team	G	TPA	AB	R	H	TB	2B	3B	HR	RBI	SH	SF	HP	BB	IBB	SO	SB	CS	GDP	LOB	ShO	Avg.	OBP	Slg.
Hickory	136	5007	4419	622	1182	1737	202	37	93	559	47	44	69	426	19	846	143	62	64	942	5	.267	.338	.393
Asheville	139	5370	4710	707	1246	1937	259	27	126	650	33	37	79	511	16	962	170	89	92	981	7	.265	.344	.411
Rome	139	5041	4523	577	1192	1680	205	35	71	505	42	37	60	379	16	783	150	66	99	940	12	.264	.326	.371
S. Georgia	136	5073	4493	623	1179	1700	211	29	84	568	47	33	82	417	14	1003	136	80	70	936	9	.262	.334	.378
Charl.-SC	139	5184	4496	657	1161	1761	227	32	103	576	31	46	61	549	12	1020	190	90	88	963	6	.258	.344	.392
Lake County	140	5218	4527	689	1147	1808	238	39	115	608	31	61	74	525	10	966	152	65	58	965	2	.253	.337	.399
Augusta	136	4908	4290	530	1074	1453	207	23	42	478	31	45	95	446	8	879	137	53	96	965	11	.250	.331	.339
Savannah	138	4930	4427	568	1101	1577	203	42	63	511	29	35	68	369	18	970	153	68	81	855	9	.249	.314	.356
Capital City	138	5086	4411	612	1098	1551	223	25	60	540	69	40	98	464	14	1116	203	84	55	957	9	.249	.331	.352
Delmarva	138	5077	4443	562	1079	1613	236	38	74	508	39	34	86	474	14	1029	107	57	77	947	7	.243	.325	.363
Kannapolis	137	4925	4358	524	1048	1407	218	12	39	468	54	30	49	432	11	859	120	65	58	887	16	.240	.314	.323
Lexington	138	5197	4492	587	1068	1631	222	25	97	518	78	32	89	501	14	986	98	38	93	992	6	.238	.324	.363
Hagerstown	135	5004	4368	505	1038	1432	194	34	44	447	39	27	67	502	14	1008	109	52	81	1002	11	.238	.324	.328
Greensboro	136	4977	4366	542	1011	1477	205	27	69	480	42	33	60	471	15	1064	128	45	70	911	15	.232	.313	.338
Charl.-WV	133	4913	4338	490	1003	1419	220	23	50	429	31	25	53	461	7	963	57	29	89	967	14	.231	.311	.327
Lakewood	138	4836	4219	464	916	1326	186	31	54	394	45	41	74	455	13	1159	196	90	92	838	17	.217	.302	.314

INDIVIDUAL

TOP QUALIFIERS FOR BATTING CHAMPIONSHIP

Minimum 378 plate appearances. *Lefthanded batter. †Switch-hitter.

Player, Team	G	TPA	AB	R	H	TB	2B	3B	HR	RBI	SH	SF	HP	BB	IBB	SO	SB	CS	GDP	Avg.	OBP	Slg.
Lytle, Chaz, Hickory *	101	409	364	55	122	139	11	3	0	42	9	2	6	26	0	39	22	2	5	.335	.387	.382
Cortes, Jorge, Hickory *	98	418	345	55	112	164	24	2	8	66	1	6	10	56	7	47	9	5	1	.325	.427	.475
Young, Delwyn, S. Georgia †	119	493	443	67	143	240	38	7	15	73	2	4	8	36	1	87	5	2	2	.323	.381	.542
Chop, Chad, Savannah *	131	527	485	55	156	225	26	5	11	77	0	4	6	32	5	75	10	8	10	.322	.368	.464
Baldiris, Aaron, Capital City	107	459	393	55	123	168	19	4	6	68	4	5	6	51	2	55	13	5	6	.313	.396	.427
Spann, Chad, Augusta	116	467	414	55	129	171	21	3	5	63	0	5	8	40	1	64	9	5	14	.312	.379	.413
Davis, Rajai, Hickory †	125	549	478	84	146	199	21	7	6	54	8	2	6	55	0	65	40	13	7	.305	.383	.416
Upton, B.J., Charleston-SC	101	453	384	70	116	171	22	6	7	46	1	6	5	57	0	80	38	17	8	.302	.394	.445
Davis, John-Paul, Char.-SC	97	408	355	65	105	176	24	1	15	52	0	1	5	47	2	59	14	2	12	.296	.385	.496
Joseph, Onil, Rome	120	530	483	66	143	183	16	6	4	47	6	1	3	37	2	89	32	22	8	.296	.349	.379
McCann, Brian, Rome *	115	453	424	40	123	196	31	3	12	71	0	3	2	24	2	73	7	4	5	.290	.329	.462
Webster, Anthony, Kan.*	94	405	363	68	105	131	18	1	2	33	3	2	6	31	1	58	20	12	3	.289	.353	.361
Panther, Nathan, Lake Co.*	108	487	428	88	122	195	22	6	13	52	4	5	5	45	0	75	38	11	5	.285	.356	.456
Mercedes, Victor, Hickory	126	511	456	76	130	183	22	5	7	53	12	3	4	36	0	87	22	15	2	.285	.341	.401
Gonzalez, Bernie, Asheville	129	562	504	70	143	222	38	4	11	81	0	4	11	43	0	100	17	9	13	.284	.351	.440

DEPARTMENTAL LEADERS: G—Schuerholz, 135; AB—Pridie, 530; R—Salazar, 109; H—Chop, 156; TB—Salazar, 256; 2B—B. Gonzalez, D. Young, 38; 3B—Pridie, 10; HR—Salazar, 29; RBI—Salazar, 98; SH—Fernando, 21; SF—C. Bass, 10; HP—Ontiveros, 20; BB—Hermida, 80; IBB—Salazar, 8; SO—Eldred, 142; SB—Roberson, 59; CS—Joseph, 22; GIDP—Francoeur, 21; Slg.—D. Young, .542; OBP—Cortes, .427.

ALL PLAYERS

*Lefthanded batter. †Switch-hitter.

Player, Team	G	TPA	AB	R	H	TB	2B	3B	HR	RBI	SH	SF	HP	BB	IBB	SO	SB	CS	GDP	Avg.	OBP	Slg.
Acevas, Jon, Kannapolis	24	94	81	14	23	47	9	0	5	15	2	1	1	9	0	15	0	0	0	.284	.359	.580
Acevedo, Freddy, Lexington	110	450	405	51	96	162	28	4	10	46	0	3	8	34	0	132	11	6	11	.237	.307	.400
Alcala, Arian, Augusta	2	8	7	0	0	0	0	0	0	0	0	0	0	1	0	1	0	0	0	.000	.125	.000
Alexander, Kevin, Hagerstown	72	302	255	37	69	88	14	1	1	25	0	0	2	45	0	38	6	5	7	.271	.384	.345
Alvarez, Gera, Delmarva	100	397	331	47	86	126	21	2	5	43	10	2	8	46	1	48	18	9	6	.260	.362	.381
Alvarez, Wilner, Lexington	91	302	260	27	56	78	13	0	3	14	11	0	7	24	0	51	9	4	2	.215	.299	.300
Amador, Chris, Kannapolis	5	17	16	1	4	5	1	0	0	1	0	0	0	1	0	3	2	0	0	.250	.294	.313
Anderson, Jimmy, C.C.	38	132	116	19	32	50	9	0	3	17	0	1	11	4	0	22	3	0	2	.276	.356	.431
Anderson, Scott, Asheville	20	72	63	5	7	10	3	0	0	6	1	0	4	4	0	8	0	1	0	.111	.211	.159
Andino, Robert, Greensboro	119	474	416	45	78	105	17	2	2	27	7	5	0	46	0	128	6	5	6	.188	.266	.252
Aponte, Jose, Greensboro *	53	239	218	28	65	84	10	3	1	19	4	1	2	14	0	45	9	9	2	.298	.345	.385
Arko, Tommy, Delmarva	47	178	152	19	31	48	5	0	4	12	1	0	5	20	0	50	1	2	3	.204	.316	.316
Arlis, Patrick, Greensboro	74	271	246	26	50	63	8	1	1	21	4	1	3	17	0	61	10	3	1	.203	.262	.256
Arnold, Eric, Charleston-WV	39	139	126	15	26	45	10	0	3	16	0	0	0	13	0	43	1	2	3	.206	.281	.357
Arroyo, William, Gre. †	7	25	20	4	4	6	2	0	0	2	0	0	0	5	0	4	0	1	2	.200	.360	.300
Asprilla, Avelino, Hickory	10	36	32	5	11	19	5	0	1	4	0	0	1	3	0	8	1	1	1	.344	.417	.594
Aubrey, Michael, Lake Co. *	38	154	138	22	48	76	13	0	5	19	0	1	1	14	0	22	0	0	2	.348	.409	.551
Bagley, David, South Georgia	60	245	204	33	54	71	8	0	3	19	2	1	10	28	1	44	3	1	9	.265	.379	.348
Baker, Jeffrey, Asheville	70	305	263	44	76	126	17	0	11	44	0	3	9	30	2	79	4	2	2	.289	.377	.479
Baldiris, Aaron, Capital City	107	459	393	55	123	168	19	4	6	68	4	5	6	51	2	55	13	5	6	.313	.396	.427
Bankston, Wes, Char.-SC	103	436	375	46	96	152	18	1	12	60	0	6	2	53	3	94	2	3	11	.256	.346	.405
Barnett, Dan, Kannapolis	23	80	68	9	18	26	5	0	1	11	2	0	1	7	0	22	0	0	0	.265	.342	.382
Barthel, Cole, Rome	10	35	32	1	8	9	1	0	0	4	0	1	0	2	0	3	0	0	0	.250	.286	.281
Barthelemy, Ryan, Lak.*	90	343	312	23	69	88	14	1	1	26	1	6	3	21	1	88	4	3	6	.221	.272	.282
Bass, Bryan, Delmarva †	60	235	205	23	42	64	8	7	0	21	3	3	3	21	1	58	7	4	4	.205	.284	.312
Bass, Chris, Hickory	123	509	456	59	121	198	23	3	16	79	2	10	7	34	2	81	4	1	10	.265	.320	.434
Bastardo, Angel, Lake County	8	23	17	3	5	9	1	0	1	1	0	0	1	5	0	3	0	0	0	.294	.478	.529
Benavidez, Julian, Hag.	66	262	227	25	54	78	11	2	3	24	0	1	3	31	0	42	0	1	3	.238	.336	.344
Bernadina, Rogearvin, Sav.*	77	308	278	36	66	96	12	3	4	39	3	4	4	19	1	53	11	4	3	.237	.292	.345
Bernard, Miguel, Rome	35	119	107	17	33	45	10	1	0	17	0	2	2	8	0	9	2	2	2	.308	.361	.421

Player, Team	G	TPA	AB	R	H	TB	2B	3B	HR	RBI	SH	SF	HP	BB	IBB	SO	SB	CS	GDP	Avg.	OBP	Slg.
Berroa, Cristian, Savannah †..	5	20	19	1	4	9	2	0	1	1	0	0	1	0	0	4	1	0	1	.211	.250	.474
Bibee, Hal, Asheville..............	26	98	88	5	21	28	4	0	1	12	2	0	2	6	0	14	0	1	6	.239	.302	.318
Bocchino, Anthony, Hickory *	15	52	49	5	8	10	2	0	0	4	0	0	0	2	0	6	0	0	1	.163	.196	.204
Bok, Matt, South Georgia *....	31	96	77	11	15	23	3	1	1	8	1	1	6	11	0	23	1	2	2	.195	.337	.299
Bonilla, Clemente, Delmarva..	3	4	4	0	0	0	0	0	0	0	0	0	0	0	0	0	0	0	0	.000	.000	.000
Bonner, Adam, Char.-SC *.....	69	270	216	41	50	90	14	1	8	38	0	6	2	46	0	74	4	2	3	.231	.363	.417
Bonvechio, Brett, Augusta * ..	75	294	263	21	50	76	12	1	4	34	0	5	2	24	1	54	1	2	5	.190	.259	.289
Borgo, Alex, Lakewood.........	17	58	50	3	10	13	3	0	0	1	0	0	1	7	0	19	0	0	1	.200	.310	.260
Bowman, Addison, Augusta...	88	344	298	23	78	99	14	2	1	32	1	6	14	25	0	64	3	2	6	.262	.341	.332
Bramasco, Omar, Lakewood..	24	76	58	3	8	9	1	0	0	4	2	1	5	10	0	23	3	0	0	.138	.311	.155
Brand, Kevin, Asheville †.......	12	33	31	2	2	5	0	0	1	4	0	0	0	2	0	8	0	1	2	.065	.121	.161
Brewer, Anthony, Greensboro	87	289	248	30	49	69	6	4	2	18	7	2	2	28	0	92	11	1	3	.198	.282	.278
Brice, Thomas, Kannapolis * .	120	451	397	50	111	139	21	2	1	49	3	3	5	43	3	63	8	7	1	.280	.355	.350
Brisson, Dustin, Augusta *....	34	136	117	23	32	54	7	0	5	21	0	2	2	15	0	22	1	1	4	.274	.360	.462
Broadway, Larry, Savannah *.	83	340	290	56	89	164	25	4	14	51	0	3	3	44	4	70	3	4	5	.307	.400	.566
Brown, Dusty, Augusta.........	87	333	285	27	75	110	17	6	2	41	1	3	7	37	2	69	7	1	4	.263	.358	.386
Brown, Tony, Savannah *.......	34	133	126	11	28	31	1	1	0	4	0	0	1	6	0	38	6	2	0	.222	.263	.246
Bryan, Jason, Augusta..........	11	42	38	3	4	7	3	0	0	3	0	0	1	3	0	15	3	0	1	.105	.190	.184
Buller, Dayton, Hagerstown....	11	37	30	2	6	10	1	0	1	3	0	0	2	5	0	8	1	0	1	.200	.351	.333
Burrows, Angelo, Rome *......	22	57	49	6	10	18	3	1	1	5	2	2	0	4	0	8	3	2	0	.204	.255	.367
Burrus, Josh, Rome..............	16	49	45	4	8	13	2	0	1	2	0	0	3	1	0	12	2	1	0	.178	.245	.289
Buscher, Brian, Hagerstown *	54	217	200	19	55	64	7	1	0	26	0	3	4	10	0	25	0	0	4	.275	.318	.320
Bushey, Andrew, Asheville * ..	4	11	8	2	0	0	0	0	0	1	0	0	0	3	0	1	0	0	0	.000	.273	.000
Carter, Chris, Delmarva.........	26	107	92	18	26	40	4	2	2	11	0	0	3	12	0	15	6	1	2	.283	.383	.435
Castillo, Osmar, Augusta †.....	25	85	66	12	22	24	0	1	0	6	1	0	1	17	0	20	3	1	1	.333	.476	.364
Cavin, Jonathan, Kan.-Sav.* ..	59	204	172	21	36	43	4	0	1	15	3	1	2	26	0	59	1	2	2	.209	.318	.250
Cespedes, Robinson, Lex.......	88	367	310	41	71	93	11	1	3	33	9	1	9	38	0	46	7	2	5	.229	.330	.300
Chapman, Travis, Hickory......	64	242	217	23	51	77	12	1	4	19	4	3	1	17	0	34	0	3	3	.235	.290	.355
Chavez, Ender, Capital City *..	34	150	139	20	42	43	1	0	0	14	0	1	1	9	0	25	10	8	1	.302	.347	.309
Checksfield, Steven, Lex.	32	132	116	19	28	57	4	2	7	21	0	1	1	14	1	35	1	1	1	.241	.326	.491
Chop, Chad, Savannah *........	131	527	485	55	156	225	26	5	11	77	0	4	6	32	5	75	10	8	10	.322	.368	.464
Chourio, Junior, Char.-WV.....	11	44	42	3	7	8	1	0	0	2	1	0	1	0	0	11	0	0	1	.167	.186	.190
Christensen, Mike, Kan.	70	268	243	34	57	94	16	0	7	36	0	1	2	22	0	58	0	0	2	.235	.302	.387
Ciraco, Darren, Kannapolis....	100	375	338	32	77	116	19	4	4	54	2	9	2	24	1	69	7	1	5	.228	.276	.343
Clanton, Ja'Mar, Savannah.....	37	121	104	9	21	23	2	0	0	10	1	1	0	12	0	36	1	1	3	.202	.282	.221
Clements, Zachary, C.C..........	50	149	121	13	23	27	2	1	0	16	3	4	2	19	0	29	7	3	2	.190	.301	.223
Clendenin, Morgan, Del.*.......	11	28	22	2	3	4	1	0	0	4	0	1	0	5	0	13	0	0	1	.136	.286	.182
Clute, Kris, Greensboro..........	65	224	198	19	40	44	4	0	0	19	4	1	4	17	1	46	9	7	4	.202	.277	.222
Coffey, David, Augusta *........	63	240	216	26	52	63	9	1	0	23	0	3	2	19	0	25	11	0	3	.241	.304	.292
Colina, Alvin, Asheville..........	72	281	256	26	68	102	20	1	4	23	1	0	4	20	0	53	5	4	5	.266	.329	.398
Collum, Mike, Hickory...........	10	27	26	5	7	11	1	0	1	2	0	0	1	0	0	3	1	0	0	.269	.296	.423
Colmenter, Jesus, Lake Co. †.	19	61	51	6	8	8	0	0	0	4	0	2	0	8	0	14	1	0	0	.157	.262	.157
Columbus, Jason, Hag..........	64	258	232	26	49	76	12	0	5	27	0	1	4	21	1	72	0	0	5	.211	.287	.328
Conlisk, Jason, Savannah †...	92	344	306	30	61	79	13	1	1	29	1	2	3	32	0	70	8	3	6	.199	.280	.258
Conrad, Brooks, Lexington † .	38	161	140	20	26	44	5	2	3	11	1	0	3	17	0	25	7	1	2	.186	.288	.314
Cook, David, Kannapolis........	40	150	136	14	22	27	5	0	0	7	0	1	0	13	0	36	4	0	1	.162	.233	.199
Cooper, Jason, Lake Co. *.....	69	301	263	50	78	145	17	7	12	36	0	0	6	32	3	52	3	2	2	.297	.385	.551
Cooper, Matt, Augusta..........	57	232	188	24	55	79	15	0	3	30	0	1	9	34	2	51	1	1	2	.293	.422	.420
Cordell, Brent, Char.-SC †......	97	387	323	42	74	132	20	1	12	48	1	1	13	49	4	74	1	2	11	.229	.352	.409
Corrente, David, Char.-WV.....	67	251	224	19	48	62	8	0	2	18	1	0	7	19	0	55	2	1	6	.214	.296	.277
Cortes, Jorge, Hickory *.......	98	418	345	55	112	164	24	2	8	66	1	6	10	56	7	47	9	5	1	.325	.427	.475
Curtis, Lee, Augusta..............	57	199	179	14	46	60	8	0	2	10	0	1	3	15	0	32	2	6	5	.257	.323	.335
Davidson, Kevin, Lexington....	1	3	3	1	1	4	0	0	1	2	0	0	0	0	0	1	0	0	0	.333	.333	1.333
Davies, Gregg, Delmarva *....	43	163	141	17	31	41	4	0	2	18	1	2	2	17	0	34	5	1	2	.220	.309	.291
Davis, John-Paul, Char.-SC....	97	408	355	65	105	176	24	1	15	52	0	1	5	47	2	59	14	2	12	.296	.385	.496
Davis, Rajai, Hickory †.........	125	549	478	84	146	199	21	7	6	54	8	2	6	55	0	65	40	13	7	.305	.383	.416
De La Cruz, Christopher, Lk.Co.†	108	452	402	44	106	119	9	2	0	49	2	7	4	37	1	55	6	7	5	.264	.327	.296
De La Cruz, Miguel, Hickory..	78	290	266	24	67	88	10	1	3	26	0	2	2	20	2	54	1	3	2	.252	.307	.331
Deck, Ronnie, Char.-SC..........	17	49	45	6	7	8	1	0	0	4	0	0	0	4	0	12	0	0	1	.156	.224	.178
Delos Santos, Esteban, Lak.†.	9	32	31	1	5	7	0	1	0	1	0	0	0	1	0	10	0	4	1	.161	.188	.226
Denker, Travis, South Georgia	8	24	22	2	5	7	2	0	0	1	0	0	0	2	0	6	0	1	0	.227	.292	.318
Devarez, Noel, Capital City.....	7	1	1	0	1	1	0	0	0	0	0	0	0	0	0	0	0	0	0	1.000	1.000	1.000
Diaz, Frank, Savannah...........	122	468	440	63	119	176	28	4	7	49	1	7	5	15	1	73	19	4	9	.270	.298	.400
Dion, Nate, Charleston-SC.....	39	133	124	16	35	49	3	1	3	14	2	1	1	5	0	34	9	3	2	.282	.313	.395
Donato, Greg, Rome.............	10	31	29	4	8	12	1	0	1	3	0	0	1	1	0	4	0	0	0	.276	.323	.414
Done, Mike, Delmarva †.........	85	341	298	37	75	111	22	1	4	32	3	3	4	33	1	78	2	1	3	.252	.331	.372
Dragicevich, Scott, Char.-WV.	108	439	382	56	94	120	23	0	1	37	3	2	9	43	1	88	3	4	8	.246	.335	.314
Dukes, Elijah, Char.-SC †.......	117	445	383	51	94	140	17	4	7	53	4	3	10	45	1	130	33	11	5	.245	.338	.366
Duncan, Trey, Charleston-SC .	62	219	199	22	44	74	9	0	7	22	0	2	0	18	0	47	3	1	1	.221	.283	.372
Durazo, William, Augusta †....	23	73	62	4	12	14	2	0	0	4	0	0	3	8	0	13	0	0	2	.194	.315	.226
Durbin, Chris, Augusta...........	29	110	96	10	22	38	4	0	4	10	0	3	2	9	0	19	1	2	3	.229	.300	.396
Eldred, Brad, Hickory............	115	472	420	62	105	211	22	0	28	80	0	3	11	38	2	142	7	1	5	.250	.326	.502
Ellerson, Brian, Savannah......	61	232	202	35	56	80	5	2	5	23	2	0	6	22	1	27	7	3	5	.277	.365	.396
Ellis, Andrew, South Georgia..	3	7	6	0	0	0	0	0	0	0	0	0	1	0	0	0	0	1	0	.000	.143	.000
Emmerick, Josh, Savannah....	46	178	152	20	34	50	7	0	3	23	0	1	5	20	0	23	2	2	6	.224	.331	.329
Encarnacion, Henry, Sav.†	4	13	12	1	2	2	0	0	0	2	0	0	0	1	0	0	0	1	1	.167	.231	.167
Ezi, Travis, South Georgia †...	120	499	451	51	117	156	10	4	7	42	7	3	4	33	0	136	33	14	2	.259	.314	.346
Fagan, John, Lexington..........	116	425	346	53	87	160	17	1	18	57	0	3	16	52	3	115	0	0	6	.251	.372	.462
Fernando, Osvaldo, Lex.†.......	129	520	451	58	102	124	17	1	1	36	21	4	9	33	0	81	17	7	10	.226	.290	.275
Fitzpatrick, Reggie, Sav.*.......	113	467	430	48	96	122	9	7	1	26	5	2	7	23	0	101	36	11	3	.223	.273	.284
Francisco, Ben, Lake Co.........	80	330	289	57	83	139	21	1	11	48	1	5	4	31	1	50	15	6	7	.287	.359	.481

Player, Team	G	TPA	AB	R	H	TB	2B	3B	HR	RBI	SH	SF	HP	BB	IBB	SO	SB	CS	GDP	Avg.	OBP	Slg.
Francoeur, Jeff, Rome	134	567	524	78	147	233	26	9	14	68	0	6	7	30	5	68	14	6	21	.281	.325	.445
Freeman, Ashley, Asheville	89	366	333	41	83	120	20	1	5	32	0	1	4	28	1	53	5	10	9	.249	.314	.360
Frome, Jason, Asheville *	36	154	131	33	44	71	7	1	6	26	0	1	1	21	2	37	10	1	2	.336	.429	.542
Galante, Matt, Capital City	38	117	105	7	18	20	2	0	0	7	2	1	0	9	0	26	1	0	2	.171	.235	.190
Garcia, Julio, Lake County †	4	14	13	2	3	3	0	0	0	1	1	0	0	0	0	5	0	0	0	.231	.231	.231
Garcia, Sergio, South Georgia	49	214	177	23	46	55	4	1	1	18	0	3	8	26	0	20	10	9	1	.260	.374	.311
Garcia, Travis, Capital City	17	66	59	14	17	21	4	0	0	2	0	1	0	6	0	12	2	0	0	.288	.348	.356
Gentry, Garett, Asheville *	44	194	175	29	57	94	8	4	7	34	0	2	4	13	0	18	3	2	2	.326	.381	.537
George, Trey, Asheville	25	94	83	9	16	21	3	1	0	9	0	1	2	8	0	16	0	1	6	.193	.277	.253
Gillikin, Joey, Kannapolis	35	131	104	14	21	36	9	0	2	14	0	1	0	26	0	34	3	0	2	.202	.359	.346
Goelz, Bryan, S. Georgia *	110	424	367	54	100	124	14	2	2	42	4	2	4	47	1	61	14	9	6	.272	.360	.338
Gomes, Joey, Charleston-SC	26	103	86	12	30	47	9	1	2	10	0	0	0	17	0	15	6	2	4	.349	.456	.547
Gonzalez, Andy, Kannapolis	123	509	429	58	99	121	17	1	1	39	4	0	7	69	1	82	22	10	8	.231	.347	.282
Gonzalez, Bernie, Asheville	129	562	504	70	143	222	38	4	11	81	0	4	11	43	0	100	17	9	13	.284	.351	.440
Gonzalez, Patrick, Delmarva	24	74	60	9	8	9	1	0	0	3	1	0	1	12	0	19	3	0	1	.133	.288	.150
Gordon, Alex, Delmarva *	8	29	25	3	5	11	3	0	1	3	0	0	2	2	0	13	0	0	1	.200	.310	.440
Goss, Michael, Augusta *	100	366	319	45	78	94	9	2	1	28	8	0	5	34	0	71	29	7	10	.245	.327	.295
Gradoville, Tim, Lakewood	64	217	193	17	38	42	4	0	0	6	6	0	3	15	0	58	13	5	3	.197	.265	.218
Grasso, Mike, Rome	36	82	76	14	20	25	3	1	0	7	2	1	0	3	0	21	6	0	2	.263	.288	.329
Gretz, Nick, Asheville *	87	365	327	33	89	152	16	1	15	62	0	4	2	32	2	70	1	2	15	.272	.337	.465
Griffin, Daniel, Greensboro	36	1	0	0	0	0	0	0	0	1	0	0	0	1	0	0	0	0	0	.000	1.000	.000
Grzecka, Casey, Greensboro	27	91	76	13	21	29	5	0	1	12	1	1	3	10	0	15	0	0	3	.276	.378	.382
Guance, Walkill, Asheville	108	424	369	47	89	133	18	4	6	37	7	6	4	38	0	93	21	11	7	.241	.314	.360
Guzman, Carlos, Rome	99	354	314	40	72	123	15	3	10	44	1	4	8	27	1	105	11	3	2	.229	.303	.392
Guzman, Joel, South Georgia	58	229	217	33	51	88	13	0	8	29	1	2	0	9	0	62	4	4	4	.235	.263	.406
Hansen, Bryan, Lakewood *	55	203	175	11	35	47	6	0	2	12	0	4	4	20	1	44	5	3	3	.200	.291	.269
Harper, Brett, Capital City *	23	85	79	5	26	35	6	0	1	9	0	0	2	4	1	20	1	1	0	.329	.376	.443
Harris, Cory, Delmarva	37	162	139	15	40	62	11	1	3	22	1	3	6	13	2	11	6	4	3	.288	.366	.446
Harrison, Vince, Char.-SC	132	553	488	75	134	219	20	4	19	79	2	5	5	53	0	90	16	7	9	.275	.348	.449
Harvey, Ryan, Capital City	38	138	119	15	33	35	2	0	0	15	3	0	6	10	0	20	3	3	1	.277	.363	.294
Hassey, Brad, Charleston-WV	98	385	338	34	64	81	17	0	0	25	3	1	7	32	0	62	2	1	6	.189	.272	.240
Hawkins, Dustin, Lexington *	95	394	336	40	66	83	11	3	0	26	9	1	0	48	1	72	7	3	6	.196	.296	.247
Heitzman, Aaron, Lexington *	28	1	0	0	0	0	0	0	0	0	0	0	0	1	0	0	0	0	0	.000	1.000	.000
Hendricks, K.J., Asheville †	106	438	376	69	95	121	11	3	3	20	8	1	1	52	1	53	50	11	3	.253	.344	.322
Hermida, Jeremy, Gre. *	133	560	468	73	133	184	23	5	6	49	4	6	2	80	3	100	28	2	3	.284	.387	.393
Hernandez, Jose, Hickory	61	240	227	15	58	71	5	1	2	18	1	1	3	8	1	37	2	3	3	.256	.289	.313
Hernandez, Luis, Rome †	111	381	337	27	78	90	4	1	2	25	18	0	2	24	2	42	7	3	7	.231	.287	.267
Herrera, Christian, S. Georgia	17	67	58	8	9	10	1	0	0	2	2	0	3	4	0	8	2	0	3	.155	.246	.172
Herrera, Javier, Lake County	46	183	154	15	37	54	14	0	1	22	1	6	5	17	0	32	0	2	4	.240	.324	.351
Hickman, Brian, Kannapolis	9	21	16	1	2	2	0	0	0	1	0	1	0	4	0	7	0	0	1	.125	.286	.125
Hill, Jamar, Capital City	8	22	20	0	6	7	1	0	0	1	0	0	1	1	0	6	0	2	1	.300	.364	.350
Holm, Steve, Hagerstown	55	187	173	12	38	53	10	1	1	17	2	1	3	8	0	32	3	1	5	.220	.265	.306
Hoorelbeke, Jesse, S. Geo.	52	216	190	35	62	109	11	0	12	39	0	1	3	22	0	44	4	1	3	.326	.403	.574
Hopper, Matthew, Lakewood	32	117	96	9	18	26	3	1	1	5	0	0	2	19	0	34	0	1	5	.188	.333	.271
Hornostaj, Aaron, Hag. *	50	209	184	19	38	47	4	1	1	18	2	3	2	18	0	39	2	1	8	.207	.280	.255
Hubele, Ryan, Delmarva	56	218	195	25	49	74	6	2	5	22	2	1	6	14	1	31	0	1	2	.251	.319	.379
Hudnall, Joshua, Hickory	11	31	27	5	6	10	2	1	0	2	0	0	0	4	0	9	1	0	0	.222	.323	.370
Hudson, William, C.C. †	32	94	82	10	15	19	4	0	0	4	1	0	0	11	0	13	3	1	0	.183	.280	.232
Humphries, Justin, Lexington	102	405	338	39	91	158	21	2	14	50	1	5	7	54	5	83	0	1	5	.269	.376	.467
Isenhower, Jeremy, Lak. *	102	387	326	43	80	114	17	4	3	39	1	5	13	40	0	84	14	4	8	.245	.346	.350
Ishikawa, Travis, Hag. *	57	232	194	20	40	54	5	0	3	22	1	1	3	33	5	69	3	4	7	.206	.329	.278
Italiano, Nicholas, Lak. *	3	10	9	1	2	4	0	1	0	1	0	1	0	0	0	1	0	0	1	.222	.200	.444
Ivy, Bjorn, Kannapolis	42	131	115	10	20	23	1	1	0	6	0	0	2	14	0	25	10	5	1	.174	.275	.200
James, Willie, Rome †	30	76	59	14	14	16	2	0	0	3	0	0	1	16	0	10	10	1	3	.237	.408	.271
Jansen, Ardley, Rome	97	405	373	53	97	123	13	2	3	29	3	2	2	25	1	84	18	6	5	.260	.308	.330
Jarvis, Andrew, Lakewood *	21	84	75	10	20	31	2	0	3	11	0	1	0	8	2	22	0	2	3	.267	.333	.413
Jernigan, Karl, Hagerstown	70	254	223	28	44	57	4	3	1	18	3	2	11	15	0	40	12	0	5	.197	.279	.256
Jiannetti, Joe, Capital City	38	145	137	16	39	60	8	2	3	19	2	0	1	5	0	20	6	1	1	.285	.315	.438
Johnson, Elliot, Char.-SC †	54	189	151	22	32	36	4	0	0	15	0	0	0	38	0	32	8	5	2	.212	.370	.238
Johnson, Eric, Lake County	45	185	167	23	36	58	3	2	5	17	0	3	0	15	0	41	9	4	0	.216	.276	.347
Johnston, Clint, Char.-WV *	23	85	74	10	15	33	3	0	5	14	0	1	0	10	0	23	0	0	2	.203	.294	.446
Jones, Terry, Lakewood	129	502	454	57	109	177	27	4	11	66	2	2	1	43	2	111	11	9	14	.240	.306	.390
Joseph, Onil, Rome	120	530	483	66	143	183	16	6	4	47	6	1	3	37	2	89	32	22	8	.296	.349	.379
Jova, Maikel, Char.-WV	53	228	216	19	63	85	15	2	1	28	0	2	2	8	1	21	6	2	6	.292	.320	.394
Joyce, Tom, Delmarva *	41	172	150	19	35	57	11	1	3	12	0	0	3	19	0	57	5	1	0	.233	.331	.380
Kelly, Kevin, Hagerstown	86	348	324	39	80	112	14	0	6	33	1	1	2	20	2	75	0	1	4	.247	.294	.346
Kent, Bryan, Lake County	85	306	274	33	59	82	11	0	4	33	6	5	2	19	1	53	7	0	6	.215	.267	.299
Kingsbury, Bobby, Hickory *	108	418	367	44	82	143	16	6	11	48	5	4	5	37	3	87	15	9	5	.223	.300	.390
Kirby, Brian, Lake County *	17	67	61	10	13	30	5	0	4	6	0	0	0	6	0	22	0	0	0	.213	.284	.492
Knicely, Jeremy, Char.-WV	7	21	19	4	6	8	2	0	0	1	0	0	0	2	0	7	0	0	0	.316	.381	.421
Knowlton, Jay, Hagerstown	12	45	38	4	10	11	1	0	0	4	0	0	2	5	0	10	1	1	1	.263	.378	.289
Knox, Matt, Lake County	68	274	237	33	58	109	17	2	10	43	0	4	8	25	0	35	0	2	7	.245	.332	.460
Kochen, Ryan, Lexington	123	519	475	65	118	181	28	1	11	53	3	1	10	30	0	96	5	2	9	.248	.306	.381
Kratz, Erik, Charleston-WV	8	22	19	0	6	9	3	0	0	2	0	0	2	1	0	7	0	0	1	.316	.409	.474
LaBarbera, Anthony, Hag.	22	98	88	13	21	31	3	2	1	6	0	0	1	9	1	12	2	0	1	.239	.316	.352
Lackaff, John, Kannapolis	19	74	61	9	11	21	4	0	2	8	0	1	2	10	0	10	1	0	2	.180	.311	.344
Larkin, Shaun, Lake County *	128	534	448	79	119	211	26	3	20	80	0	6	7	73	2	70	5	3	6	.266	.373	.471
Lawson, Forrest, Capital City	37	153	133	14	34	46	7	1	1	20	1	0	4	15	1	30	4	5	0	.256	.349	.346
Lebron, Freddie, Kan. †	15	54	48	4	11	11	0	0	0	4	2	0	0	4	0	11	3	1	0	.229	.288	.229
Lee, Taber, Hickory †	115	421	356	59	88	126	19	5	3	29	3	4	7	51	1	62	7	3	7	.247	.349	.354
Lewis, Fred, Hagerstown *	114	502	420	61	105	141	17	8	1	27	6	2	6	68	1	112	30	15	5	.250	.361	.336

Player, Team	G	TPA	AB	R	H	TB	2B	3B	HR	RBI	SH	SF	HP	BB	IBB	SO	SB	CS	GDP	Avg.	OBP	Slg.
Likely, Cameron, Lexington	46	190	164	26	43	54	4	2	1	17	5	2	0	19	0	26	11	2	1	.262	.335	.329
Lisk, Charlie, Kannapolis	42	147	126	20	24	43	8	1	3	17	1	0	2	18	0	41	0	2	1	.190	.301	.341
Littleton, Brandon, Del.†	34	138	119	21	35	45	2	4	0	12	2	1	1	15	0	19	12	2	1	.294	.375	.378
Lopez, Pedro, Kannapolis	109	437	390	40	103	126	23	0	0	33	16	2	3	26	1	43	24	14	8	.264	.314	.323
Louisa, Lorvin, Savannah	12	32	29	2	1	1	0	0	0	1	1	0	1	1	0	13	0	1	0	.034	.097	.034
Luna, Leonardo, Kannapolis	19	67	62	4	11	16	2	0	1	6	1	0	1	3	0	9	0	0	0	.177	.227	.258
Lynam, Guy, Greensboro	3	8	7	1	0	0	0	0	0	0	1	0	0	0	0	4	0	0	0	.000	.000	.000
Lytle, Chaz, Hickory *	101	409	364	55	122	139	11	3	0	42	9	2	6	26	0	39	22	2	5	.335	.387	.382
Majewski, Val, Delmarva *	56	240	208	38	63	115	15	8	7	48	0	3	1	28	2	20	10	1	3	.303	.383	.553
Malek, Bobby, Capital City *	43	176	149	20	39	53	11	0	1	26	0	1	0	26	0	22	11	3	2	.262	.369	.356
Maniscalco, Matthew, Char.-SC	62	238	205	31	53	65	10	1	0	18	5	2	3	23	0	46	9	7	2	.259	.339	.317
Manriquez, Salomon, Sav.	37	126	117	14	28	49	12	0	3	22	1	1	3	4	1	25	0	0	3	.239	.280	.419
Margalski, Ben, Savannah *	37	138	110	15	28	41	5	1	2	14	0	0	2	26	1	30	3	2	4	.255	.406	.373
Marshall, Andre, Lakewood †	98	319	273	35	49	71	7	3	3	18	4	3	2	37	1	116	12	6	5	.179	.279	.260
Martin, Kyle, Delmarva	13	43	40	10	10	13	1	1	0	2	0	0	0	3	0	9	0	0	1	.250	.302	.325
Martin, Russell, S. Georgia	25	109	98	15	28	43	4	1	3	14	1	1	0	9	0	11	5	2	1	.286	.343	.439
Martinez, Casey, Lakewood	32	97	87	8	22	32	8	1	0	11	1	2	2	5	0	20	0	2	3	.253	.302	.368
Materano, Oscar, Asheville	82	367	339	48	85	113	14	1	4	30	7	1	3	17	0	78	8	3	2	.251	.292	.333
McCann, Brian, Rome *	115	453	424	40	123	196	31	3	12	71	0	3	2	24	2	73	7	4	5	.290	.329	.462
McCullough, Clayton, Lk.Co.*	45	131	109	6	18	19	1	0	0	6	3	1	1	17	0	25	0	1	1	.165	.281	.174
McCurdy, Joshua, Delmarva	7	25	23	0	2	3	1	0	0	0	1	0	0	1	0	2	2	0	1	.087	.125	.130
McDonald, John, Lake Co.	1	3	3	0	0	0	0	0	0	0	0	0	0	0	0	0	0	0	0	.000	.000	.000
McMains, Derin, Hag. †	54	234	194	31	56	76	14	3	0	27	0	1	0	39	2	21	18	2	3	.289	.406	.392
McRoberts, Mark, Lakewood	103	379	322	40	57	124	14	1	17	38	2	1	3	51	0	120	7	4	5	.177	.294	.385
Meath, Matt, Hickory †	48	177	143	27	37	54	7	2	2	17	1	3	2	28	1	39	10	2	0	.259	.381	.378
Medina, Rodney, Char.-WV †	119	506	452	69	128	200	23	8	11	45	4	2	2	45	1	44	6	4	4	.283	.349	.442
Melendez, German, Lex.	59	209	179	16	39	45	6	0	0	16	8	2	5	15	1	35	3	0	4	.218	.294	.251
Mercedes, Victor, Hickory	126	511	456	76	130	183	22	5	7	53	12	3	4	36	0	87	22	15	2	.285	.341	.401
Merkle, Tom, Greensboro	88	339	295	39	82	127	14	2	9	35	0	1	3	40	3	75	0	1	8	.278	.369	.431
Merritt, Graig, Char.-SC	23	81	70	6	11	14	0	0	1	6	1	0	1	9	0	17	1	2	0	.157	.263	.200
Mills, Rock, Asheville	21	74	56	11	13	22	6	0	1	13	1	1	4	12	0	10	2	1	2	.232	.397	.393
Miranda, Miguel, Hag. †	15	54	47	2	8	8	0	0	0	4	1	0	0	6	0	6	1	0	0	.170	.264	.170
Mitchell, Lee, Greensboro	23	85	79	7	18	28	4	0	2	7	0	0	0	6	0	17	1	1	0	.228	.282	.354
Molina, Angel, Greensboro	79	286	258	34	65	111	16	3	8	48	0	1	2	25	1	72	3	0	9	.252	.322	.430
Molina, Gustavo, Kannapolis	96	350	315	30	72	104	15	1	5	41	8	1	9	17	0	56	5	3	4	.229	.287	.330
Montague, Ed, S. Georgia *	113	415	377	52	87	125	19	2	5	48	4	2	6	26	3	75	5	9	7	.231	.290	.332
Munhall, Brian, Hagerstown	89	340	293	32	73	96	16	2	1	30	5	2	2	38	0	59	3	3	5	.249	.337	.328
Myers, Kenton, Augusta	21	75	67	4	11	13	2	0	0	7	0	0	0	8	0	19	0	0	1	.164	.253	.194
Negron, Miguel, Char.-WV *	30	116	109	13	33	46	8	1	1	11	1	1	3	2	0	16	6	2	1	.303	.330	.422
Newman, Ryan, Hickory	50	155	142	16	27	27	0	0	0	13	1	1	1	10	0	36	1	1	7	.190	.247	.190
Nikolic, Adam, Char.-SC *	14	39	39	2	8	10	0	1	0	5	0	0	0	0	0	7	1	0	0	.205	.205	.256
Nino, Denny, Hickory	1	4	4	0	0	0	0	0	0	0	0	0	0	0	0	1	0	0	1	.000	.000	.000
Nixon, Mike, South Georgia	102	433	390	58	107	132	20	1	1	38	5	2	3	33	0	76	13	5	9	.274	.334	.338
Noboa, Joel, Savannah	32	109	96	14	17	35	2	5	2	10	1	2	2	8	0	47	1	0	1	.177	.250	.365
Nonemaker, Karl, Lak. *	48	166	141	20	30	35	5	0	0	9	6	1	0	18	1	25	12	2	5	.213	.300	.248
Norris, Shawn, Savannah *	67	260	223	38	64	93	19	2	2	35	1	3	2	31	2	42	4	2	4	.287	.375	.417
Nulton, Kevin, Lakewood	26	78	73	4	9	12	0	0	1	4	0	1	0	4	0	18	3	1	1	.123	.167	.164
O'Sullivan, Patrick, Delmarva	10	43	41	4	13	21	5	0	1	7	0	0	0	2	0	12	2	0	0	.317	.349	.512
Obradovich, Mark, Lex.†	84	328	275	28	60	81	13	1	2	25	9	2	3	39	0	51	4	2	12	.218	.320	.295
Oliva, Chad, Lakewood	30	117	100	11	24	33	3	0	2	12	0	0	1	16	0	43	5	2	3	.240	.350	.330
Ontiveros, Jeff, Augusta	104	400	344	44	83	122	24	0	5	50	0	2	20	34	0	79	1	0	10	.241	.343	.355
Ordorica, Eric, Greensboro	105	411	371	35	80	106	21	1	1	43	3	2	6	29	1	54	9	4	10	.216	.282	.286
Ortiz, Juan, Greensboro	9	22	20	2	4	5	1	0	0	2	0	0	0	2	0	7	0	0	0	.200	.273	.250
Owen, Ryan, South Georgia	24	77	65	9	16	22	3	0	1	8	3	0	4	5	0	19	2	1	0	.246	.338	.338
Owens, Justin, Char.-WV *	111	443	373	41	88	126	16	5	4	52	0	4	4	62	1	106	6	3	4	.236	.348	.338
Panther, Nathan, Lake Co. *	108	487	428	88	122	195	22	6	13	52	4	5	5	45	0	75	38	11	5	.285	.356	.456
Parker, Rashad, Capital City	18	79	61	15	12	17	2	0	1	8	2	1	2	13	0	24	9	1	0	.197	.351	.279
Paulk, Barry, Capital City *	2	5	3	2	0	0	0	0	0	0	1	0	0	1	0	1	2	0	0	.000	.250	.000
Peavey, Bill, Lake County *	22	93	77	10	20	36	1	0	5	14	0	1	0	15	0	19	0	0	1	.260	.376	.468
Peavey, Pat, Lexington	104	429	369	43	88	140	19	0	11	49	1	5	9	45	0	60	0	2	12	.238	.332	.379
Pedrique, Franmig, Lexington	1	1	0	0	0	0	0	0	0	0	0	0	0	1	0	0	0	0	0	.000	1.000	.000
Pellow, Kit, Asheville	6	28	20	3	9	14	2	0	1	8	0	1	2	5	0	5	0	0	0	.450	.571	.700
Pena, Rodolfo, Hickory	3	13	11	2	1	1	0	0	0	2	0	0	2	0	0	0	0	0	2	.091	.231	.091
Perozo, Hector, S. Georgia	108	404	353	43	83	118	15	1	6	49	9	4	7	31	1	109	10	6	2	.235	.306	.334
Perry, Rod, Lakewood	23	60	53	8	13	18	1	2	0	3	0	0	0	7	0	10	2	2	1	.245	.333	.340
Peters, Yaron, Rome	86	348	318	46	91	153	27	1	11	47	0	1	2	27	0	70	0	3	4	.286	.345	.481
Pierce, Sean, South Georgia	33	151	124	15	30	42	6	3	0	12	0	0	1	26	0	25	11	3	1	.242	.377	.339
Pinckney, Brandon, Lake Co.	3	10	7	2	3	3	0	0	0	1	0	0	1	2	0	1	0	0	0	.429	.600	.429
Pridie, Jason, Char.-SC *	128	572	530	75	138	207	28	10	7	48	3	5	4	30	1	113	26	17	2	.260	.302	.391
Ragsdale, Corey, Capital City	105	430	355	50	64	92	11	4	3	27	10	3	14	46	0	133	31	8	7	.180	.297	.259
Ramirez, Hanley, Augusta †	111	464	422	69	116	170	24	3	8	50	5	3	2	32	0	73	36	13	12	.275	.327	.403
Ramos, Kelly, Delmarva †	34	128	113	14	27	46	4	0	5	15	1	1	4	9	0	12	1	0	3	.239	.315	.407
Randel, Kevin, Greensboro *	124	533	449	66	97	163	21	3	13	54	5	1	15	63	1	96	30	7	6	.216	.331	.363
Reames, Joe Don, Char.-SC	13	21	17	3	0	0	0	0	0	1	0	0	1	3	0	8	0	1	2	.000	.190	.000
Resop, Chris, Greensboro	37	91	89	6	17	26	4	1	1	8	0	0	1	1	0	29	0	0	3	.191	.209	.292
Reyes, Julio, Kannapolis *	90	350	336	35	86	111	17	1	2	32	1	2	2	9	1	75	1	1	7	.256	.278	.330
Reyes, Milver, Hickory	11	34	33	1	3	6	0	0	1	1	0	0	0	1	0	9	0	0	2	.091	.118	.182
Rico, Erik, Charleston-WV *	49	178	158	18	36	43	5	1	0	7	0	0	0	20	0	36	3	3	2	.228	.315	.272
Rico, Matt, Charleston-SC	10	28	25	3	4	4	0	0	0	2	0	1	0	2	0	11	1	0	2	.160	.214	.160
Riggans, Shawn, Char.-SC	68	260	232	33	65	91	17	0	3	34	1	4	4	19	0	35	3	4	8	.280	.340	.392
Rijo, Carlos, Delmarva	111	424	403	26	107	123	13	0	1	38	1	2	4	14	0	60	2	5	15	.266	.296	.305

Player, Team	G	TPA	AB	R	H	TB	2B	3B	HR	RBI	SH	SF	HP	BB	IBB	SO	SB	CS	GDP	Avg.	OBP	Slg.
Riley, Ryan, Charleston-SC	64	229	187	29	51	58	7	0	0	12	8	1	5	26	1	35	13	4	3	.273	.374	.310
Rivas, Arturo, Delmarva	44	181	163	16	31	47	11	1	1	11	0	0	2	16	1	42	2	2	2	.190	.271	.288
Rivera, Willie, Char.-WV *	116	482	409	51	99	128	15	1	4	37	8	4	4	57	0	86	8	2	10	.242	.338	.313
Roat, Kyle, Rome	61	210	187	17	41	55	5	0	3	15	0	1	1	21	1	30	1	1	8	.219	.300	.294
Roberson, Chris, Lakewood ...	132	548	470	64	110	145	19	5	2	32	8	1	12	57	1	108	59	16	9	.234	.331	.309
Robinson, Levi, Delmarva	97	338	281	51	68	92	18	3	0	17	6	0	8	43	1	53	12	9	5	.242	.358	.327
Robinson-Pierce, Whit, Del. ...	10	33	32	1	6	6	0	0	0	1	0	0	0	1	0	12	0	0	1	.188	.212	.188
Rodriguez, Andres, C.C.	127	494	461	54	119	164	26	2	5	54	2	3	6	22	3	94	6	5	12	.258	.299	.356
Rodriguez, Carlos, Lak. †	93	365	322	27	63	79	10	3	0	24	6	3	4	30	0	63	18	10	4	.196	.270	.245
Rodriguez, Edgar, C.C.	80	267	251	39	66	117	30	0	7	32	3	3	3	7	1	67	7	5	3	.263	.288	.466
Rodriguez, Robert, Savannah	40	127	115	9	21	23	2	0	0	8	1	0	5	6	0	32	3	0	3	.183	.254	.200
Rogers, Brandon, S. Georgia .	15	53	50	5	13	20	1	0	2	6	0	0	1	2	0	12	0	2	1	.260	.302	.400
Rohleder, Andy, Greensboro ..	128	534	457	64	114	177	22	1	13	64	1	4	11	61	1	93	11	3	2	.249	.349	.387
Rojas, Ricardo, Lake County ..	105	410	379	48	88	132	19	5	5	42	2	4	2	23	1	98	29	11	2	.232	.277	.348
Roy, Angus, Augusta *	30	1	1	0	0	0	0	0	0	0	0	0	0	0	0	1	0	0	0	.000	.000	.000
Ruelas, Alonzo, Rome	64	230	215	18	48	58	7	0	1	18	0	3	1	11	0	30	2	1	9	.223	.261	.270
Ruiz, Daniel, Rome	48	134	122	13	30	39	6	0	1	12	2	2	1	7	0	26	0	0	5	.246	.288	.320
Ruiz, Randy, Delmarva	67	276	239	33	74	129	18	2	11	51	0	3	5	29	1	70	3	3	4	.310	.391	.540
Russell, Mike, Delmarva	27	83	74	10	13	21	5	0	1	3	1	0	3	5	0	31	0	1	2	.176	.256	.284
Salas, Jose, Charleston-WV †	8	23	20	1	3	4	1	0	0	3	0	0	0	1	0	6	0	0	0	.150	.190	.200
Salazar, Jeff, Asheville *	129	578	486	109	138	256	23	4	29	98	4	4	7	77	8	74	28	14	5	.284	.387	.527
Salvo, Andrew, Kan.-C.C. *	77	248	202	30	50	62	6	0	2	17	5	0	0	40	1	44	7	6	1	.248	.372	.307
Santiago, Rudy, Asheville *	5	15	15	0	2	3	1	0	0	2	0	0	0	0	0	5	0	0	0	.133	.133	.200
Santora, Jack, Lakewood †	17	68	53	7	13	18	2	0	1	2	3	0	2	10	0	7	5	2	2	.245	.385	.340
Sardinha, Duke, Asheville	42	177	158	23	45	78	18	0	5	27	0	1	3	15	0	36	0	1	4	.285	.356	.494
Sato, G.G., Lakewood	96	350	312	40	77	129	28	3	6	42	1	4	10	22	2	90	19	5	4	.247	.313	.413
Schilling, Micah, Lake Co. * ...	109	425	360	53	83	108	15	5	0	43	2	4	4	55	1	92	6	6	4	.231	.336	.300
Schneider, John, Char.-WV	56	208	174	10	34	45	11	0	0	14	1	0	1	32	0	42	3	0	5	.195	.324	.259
Schuerholz, Jon, Rome †	135	486	407	52	102	122	14	3	0	39	6	4	10	59	1	68	25	7	6	.251	.356	.300
Serrano, Ray, Charleston-SC ..	13	45	35	6	10	14	4	0	0	6	3	2	0	5	0	4	1	0	0	.286	.357	.400
Sherrill, J.J., Lake County † ...	60	268	216	44	56	104	20	2	8	31	6	4	6	36	0	59	12	4	1	.259	.374	.481
Siriveaw, Nom, Char.-WV †	15	58	52	4	6	8	2	0	0	4	1	0	0	5	0	17	0	0	3	.115	.193	.154
Slack, Jonathan, C.C. *	69	293	238	47	65	87	9	2	3	27	6	3	4	42	0	60	21	6	2	.273	.387	.366
Smallwood, Erik, Delmarva * .	6	17	14	1	3	3	0	0	0	2	0	0	0	3	0	5	0	0	0	.214	.353	.214
Smith, David, Char.-WV	86	381	342	44	83	124	13	2	8	29	1	0	6	32	1	67	7	1	11	.243	.318	.363
Sosa, Carlos, Hagerstown * ...	125	525	460	51	108	162	16	4	10	63	5	4	4	52	1	134	9	3	8	.235	.315	.352
Soto, Jose, Augusta †	55	187	176	22	42	58	6	2	2	11	3	1	2	5	0	48	8	2	1	.239	.266	.330
Soto, T.J., Lexington	86	366	325	60	96	167	25	5	12	62	0	2	2	37	3	77	16	5	7	.295	.369	.514
Spann, Chad, Augusta	116	467	414	55	129	171	21	3	5	63	0	5	8	40	1	64	9	5	14	.312	.379	.413
Spilborghs, Ryan, Asheville ...	119	510	434	78	122	193	22	2	15	61	1	4	8	63	0	96	10	11	4	.281	.379	.445
St. Clair, Jason, Char.-SC	9	27	27	1	4	4	0	0	0	3	0	0	0	0	0	3	1	0	0	.148	.148	.148
St. Martine, Michael, Sav.*	32	113	104	6	18	23	2	0	1	11	1	1	0	7	0	28	2	2	3	.173	.223	.221
Stephenson, Neal, Del.*	124	489	437	56	99	158	23	3	10	48	3	2	5	42	1	137	6	5	5	.227	.300	.362
Stone, Greg, Augusta *	97	405	346	59	91	105	10	2	0	25	5	4	4	46	1	60	13	7	5	.263	.353	.303
Story-Harden, Thomari, S.Geo.	51	194	165	23	33	56	9	1	4	22	1	0	4	24	0	55	2	1	8	.200	.316	.339
Street, Dan, Asheville	12	46	42	7	16	22	6	0	0	9	0	0	1	3	0	5	2	0	1	.381	.435	.524
Sultemeier, Eric, Delmarva	7	26	23	2	4	7	3	0	0	1	0	0	1	2	0	3	1	0	0	.174	.269	.304
Sweeney, James, Asheville	21	77	67	5	10	15	2	0	1	7	0	1	1	8	0	20	3	1	1	.149	.247	.224
Sweeney, Tim, Savannah	24	80	75	8	17	19	2	0	0	4	0	0	0	5	0	13	1	2	0	.227	.275	.253
Tablado, Raul, Char.-WV	61	256	226	29	43	73	10	1	6	26	2	2	1	25	1	69	2	1	5	.190	.272	.323
Tempesta, Nick, Lakewood	39	152	136	11	35	42	4	0	1	21	0	5	4	7	2	18	2	6	2	.257	.303	.309
Terrell, Jim, Kannapolis *	52	198	172	18	47	58	8	0	1	12	5	2	0	19	1	31	8	3	3	.273	.342	.337
Testa, Chris, South Georgia *	113	430	387	56	107	170	22	4	11	69	2	5	7	29	6	72	4	3	4	.276	.334	.439
Thede, Matt, Savannah	14	53	51	4	11	13	2	0	0	3	0	0	0	2	0	14	0	1	0	.216	.245	.255
Timmons, Wes, Rome	124	494	422	67	119	167	19	4	7	49	2	4	14	52	1	31	10	4	12	.282	.376	.396
Todd, Jeremy, Asheville *	7	25	23	0	2	2	0	0	0	0	0	0	0	2	0	12	0	0	0	.087	.160	.087
Toner, John, Capital City	34	129	114	15	25	37	6	0	2	13	0	1	1	13	0	24	3	1	0	.219	.302	.325
Tucker, Michael, Greensboro ..	17	74	63	9	16	24	8	0	0	7	1	1	0	9	0	6	0	0	2	.254	.342	.381
Tugwell, Marc, Lakewood	27	88	80	7	17	24	7	0	0	5	2	0	2	4	0	23	0	1	3	.213	.267	.300
Turay, Alhaji, Capital City	85	363	314	44	74	117	19	3	6	45	3	0	13	28	2	94	14	6	7	.236	.324	.373
Upton, B.J., Char.-SC	101	453	384	70	116	171	22	6	7	46	1	6	5	57	0	80	38	17	8	.302	.394	.445
Van Every, Jon, Lake Co. *	59	221	197	22	38	66	9	2	5	24	3	2	7	12	0	89	15	5	0	.193	.261	.335
Varela, Edgar, Kannapolis *	72	272	248	17	57	72	12	0	1	29	0	2	3	19	1	37	0	0	4	.230	.290	.290
Veracierto, Fernando, Aug.	61	174	155	16	31	36	5	0	0	8	4	1	3	11	0	28	4	0	2	.200	.265	.232
Vizquel, Omar, Lake Co. †	4	15	14	0	1	1	0	0	0	0	0	0	0	1	0	2	1	0	0	.071	.133	.071
Wald, Jake, Hagerstown	114	452	391	39	85	120	19	2	4	27	12	1	7	41	1	123	7	6	4	.217	.302	.307
Wallace, David, Lake County ..	64	271	223	39	65	101	14	2	6	36	0	1	10	37	0	52	5	1	5	.291	.413	.453
Walsh, Sean, Lakewood	6	16	14	3	3	6	1	1	0	1	0	0	0	2	0	1	2	0	0	.214	.313	.429
Walter, Randy, Hagerstown	121	449	395	45	99	148	26	4	5	46	1	4	9	38	0	91	11	9	5	.251	.327	.375
Wardinsky, Ryan, Lak. †	2	5	4	1	0	0	0	0	0	0	0	0	0	1	0	3	0	0	0	.000	.200	.000
Watts, Derran, Capital City	111	471	395	64	96	136	22	3	4	45	15	4	13	44	2	136	30	11	3	.243	.336	.344
Waugh, Jason, Char.-WV	36	152	139	18	29	41	7	1	1	8	3	0	0	10	0	30	2	0	2	.209	.262	.295
Wayne, Brett, South Georgia ..	88	293	272	30	73	89	8	1	2	29	3	2	2	14	1	58	8	4	5	.268	.307	.327
Webb, Trey, Savannah	58	230	214	32	51	74	13	2	2	20	3	1	2	10	0	29	6	4	4	.238	.278	.346
Webster, Anthony, Kan.*	94	405	363	68	105	131	18	1	2	33	3	2	6	31	1	58	20	12	3	.289	.353	.361
Welsch, Travis, Asheville	20	76	63	8	14	14	0	0	0	4	1	1	2	9	0	18	1	2	1	.222	.333	.222
West, Eric, Augusta	70	273	231	29	45	60	15	0	0	22	3	5	5	29	1	51	4	3	5	.195	.293	.260
Whealy, Blake, Capital City	71	285	241	47	62	117	13	3	12	41	1	5	4	34	2	85	9	4	2	.257	.352	.485
Wilson, Brandon, Capital City	70	257	221	16	40	50	7	0	1	19	6	3	4	23	0	71	1	1	1	.181	.267	.226
Word, Robert, Greensboro * ..	112	421	388	41	78	126	19	1	9	44	0	6	6	17	4	120	1	1	6	.201	.242	.325
Yepez, Jose, Charleston-WV ..	21	76	66	4	15	23	5	0	1	7	0	3	1	6	1	12	0	0	3	.227	.289	.348

Player, Team	G	TPA	AB	R	H	TB	2B	3B	HR	RBI	SH	SF	HP	BB	IBB	SO	SB	CS	GDP	Avg.	OBP	Slg.
Yepez, Marcos, Savannah †	108	454	401	56	106	138	13	5	3	41	6	3	9	35	2	113	28	10	6	.264	.335	.344
York, Larry, Savannah †	2	9	7	0	0	0	0	0	0	0	0	0	0	2	0	2	0	0	0	.000	.222	.000
Young, Delwyn, S. Georgia †	119	493	443	67	143	240	38	7	15	73	2	4	8	36	1	87	5	2	2	.323	.381	.542
Young, Eddie, Kannapolis	22	71	65	7	15	16	1	0	0	7	1	0	0	5	0	10	1	3	3	.231	.286	.246
Yount, Dustin, Delmarva *	122	485	419	45	93	137	20	0	8	49	2	7	9	47	2	115	1	5	6	.222	.309	.327
Zinsman, Zeph, Char.-WV *	110	422	378	28	77	107	22	1	2	43	2	3	3	36	0	115	0	3	6	.204	.276	.283

PLAYERS WITH TWO OR MORE TEAMS

Player, Team	G	TPA	AB	R	H	TB	2B	3B	HR	RBI	SH	SF	HP	BB	IBB	SO	SB	CS	GDP	Avg.	OBP	Slg.
Cavin, Jonathan, Savannah *	14	49	41	5	7	11	1	0	1	8	1	0	1	6	0	12	1	1	1	.171	.292	.268
Cavin, Jonathan, Kan.*	45	155	131	16	29	32	3	0	0	7	2	1	1	20	0	47	0	1	1	.221	.327	.244
Salvo, Andrew, Kannapolis *	37	119	98	19	23	30	4	0	1	6	1	0	0	19	1	17	1	2	1	.235	.359	.306
Salvo, Andrew, C.C. *	40	129	104	11	27	32	2	0	1	11	4	0	0	21	0	27	6	4	0	.260	.384	.308

GRAND SLAMS—Knox, 2; Acevedo, Baker, Bankston, Benavidez, Broadway, Cavin, Checksfield, Columbus, Cortes, Eldred, Francisco, Gretz, C. Guzman, Harrison, Kent, Larkin, Majewski, Manriquez, D. Ruiz, J. Salazar, Tempesta, Testa, Turay, 1 each.

AWARDED FIRST BASE ON CATCHER'S INTERFERENCE—Fagan 4 (Corrente, J. Herrera, Munhall, Myers); Word 4 (Kyle Martin 2, Sato, Wilson); Hassey 3 (Holm, McCullough, Melendez); Turay 3 (Emmerick, Gradoville, Lisk); Clanton 2 (Gradoville, McCann); Barnett (Melendez); Bocchino (J. Sweeney); Brewer (Corrente); Curtis (J. Anderson); Ezi (Bowman); Fernando (J. Anderson); Isenhower (Chapman); Lytle (Bowman); Medina (Obradovich); Ragsdale (Martinez); Riley (Emmerick); Salas (Munhall); Salvo (J. Anderson); Sato (Wilson); Walter (Corrente); Yount (Melendez).

2003 PITCHING

TEAM

Team	W	L	Pct.	ERA	G	CG	ShO	Sv.	IP	H	TBF	R	ER	HR	SH	SF	HB	BB	IBB	SO	WP	Bk.
Lake County	97	43	.693	2.67	140	5	22	52	1215.2	1033	5027	440	360	82	42	22	58	362	7	1098	47	9
Rome	78	61	.561	2.95	139	4	16	41	1179.1	1042	4951	471	387	56	42	29	50	460	18	1107	62	13
Hagerstown	68	67	.504	3.09	135	9	16	34	1167.0	956	4819	487	401	97	38	25	57	409	6	1064	57	8
Lexington	75	63	.543	3.41	138	1	8	42	1210.2	1054	5152	555	459	76	36	45	57	513	17	1026	59	9
Greensboro	67	69	.493	3.43	136	7	10	29	1169.0	1051	5028	563	445	60	46	43	89	448	5	954	65	14
Delmarva	67	71	.486	3.47	138	4	10	46	1190.2	1057	5088	586	459	72	31	23	62	460	5	1148	53	14
Hickory	82	54	.603	3.52	136	9	13	47	1161.0	1051	4845	532	454	78	58	35	50	388	13	923	64	4
Capital City	73	65	.529	3.53	138	5	7	31	1179.0	1092	5036	560	463	74	34	33	74	463	13	1078	111	14
Charl.-WV	57	76	.429	3.58	133	4	10	30	1141.0	1059	4870	545	454	51	40	39	75	480	22	950	80	12
Charl.-SC	77	62	.554	3.61	139	3	7	47	1198.2	1228	5139	591	481	60	50	46	74	361	15	838	89	11
Kannapolis	55	82	.401	3.81	137	9	7	28	1158.2	1052	5063	616	490	64	51	35	87	577	22	957	89	20
Lakewood	57	81	.413	3.82	138	5	8	33	1169.1	1082	5075	599	496	64	58	42	66	532	24	911	86	10
Asheville	74	65	.532	3.83	139	3	4	42	1233.2	1219	5338	643	525	104	37	33	2	436	12	966	75	10
Savannah	58	80	.420	4.52	138	7	6	31	1153.2	1175	5101	672	579	83	45	47	97	509	13	871	97	12
Augusta	49	87	.360	4.55	136	0	10	24	1122.2	1196	4995	673	568	74	37	52	88	448	4	825	89	12
S. Georgia	64	72	.471	4.66	136	0	2	33	1163.0	1196	5219	726	602	89	43	51	78	536	19	897	92	7

INDIVIDUAL

TOP QUALIFIERS FOR EARNED-RUN AVERAGE TITLE

Minimum 112 innings.*Lefthanded pitcher.

Pitcher, Team	W	L	Pct.	ERA	G	GS	CG	ShO	GF	Sv.	IP	H	TBF	R	ER	HR	SH	SF	HB	BB	IBB	SO	WP	Bk.
Carmona, Fausto, Lake Co.	17	4	.810	2.06	24	24	1	0	0	0	148.1	117	573	48	34	10	7	2	3	14	0	83	3	0
Valdez, Merkin, Hagerstown	9	5	.643	2.25	26	26	2	1	0	0	156.0	119	617	42	39	11	2	1	5	49	0	166	4	0
Habel, Josh, Hagerstown *	11	7	.611	2.36	37	16	1	0	7	2	122.0	90	489	36	32	9	4	0	6	35	0	127	2	1
Lerew, Anthony, Rome	7	6	.538	2.38	25	25	0	0	0	0	143.2	112	575	45	38	7	5	3	3	43	2	127	0	0
Crockett, Ben, Asheville	10	9	.526	2.49	23	23	2	0	0	0	151.2	152	638	60	42	11	5	2	13	32	0	117	1	0
Hanson, D.J., Charleston-WV	10	10	.500	2.54	25	25	2	1	0	0	138.1	110	557	51	39	4	1	3	8	56	2	113	5	1
Olsen, Scott, Greensboro *	7	9	.438	2.81	25	24	0	0	1	0	128.1	101	534	51	40	4	4	5	7	59	0	129	7	0
Davies, Kyle, Rome	8	8	.500	2.89	27	27	1	0	0	0	146.1	128	611	52	47	9	8	6	6	53	0	148	7	0
Nin, Sandy, Charleston-WV	7	8	.467	2.89	23	23	1	0	0	0	131.0	124	526	50	42	4	2	5	4	19	2	87	3	0
Prochaska, Mike, Char.-SC *	9	7	.563	2.98	29	20	0	0	2	0	124.0	111	508	49	41	10	4	4	8	35	0	76	6	0
Ramsey, Keith, Lake County *	13	6	.684	2.99	24	24	3	1	0	0	144.2	146	590	54	48	10	4	1	5	15	0	108	1	2
Ramirez, Ismael, Char.-WV	6	5	.545	3.02	24	22	1	0	1	0	119.1	110	494	51	40	6	1	5	4	31	1	70	1	1
Butto, Francisco, Lakewood	10	12	.455	3.03	27	25	2	1	1	0	148.2	134	629	65	50	8	9	4	6	59	2	104	10	1
Gwaltney, Lee, Lakewood	8	8	.500	3.06	22	22	1	0	0	0	117.2	92	482	48	40	5	6	2	7	49	1	72	13	1
Albaladejo, Jonathan, Hickory	12	5	.706	3.11	29	20	5	0	2	1	139.0	114	536	53	48	14	2	4	4	19	1	110	5	1

DEPARTMENTAL LEADERS: W—Carmona, 17; L—Peguero, 13; Pct.—Hart, .900; G—Beckstead, 63; GS—Heitzman, D. Johnson, Nieve, 28; CG—Albaladejo, 5; ShO—Bazardo, Hensley, 2; GF—Beckstead, 54; Sv.—Beckstead, 29; IP—D. Johnson, 167.1; H—D. Johnson, 182; TBF—D. Johnson, 727; R—Hammes, 91; ER—Heitzman, D. Johnson, 76; HR—Clarke, 22; SH—Butto, Hammes, Hart, 9; SF—Mildren, 10; HB—Cartier, D. Johnson, 16; BB—D. Cabrera, 78; IBB—Richardson, 7; SO—Valdez, 166; WP—Anez, Bulger, 22; BK—Reynoso, 5.

ALL PITCHERS

*Lefthanded pitcher.

Pitcher, Team	W	L	Pct.	ERA	G	GS	CG	ShO	GF	Sv.	IP	H	TBF	R	ER	HR	SH	SF	HB	BB	IBB	SO	WP	Bk.
Acosta, Anthony, Capital City	3	3	.500	2.50	32	0	0	0	12	3	68.1	61	279	25	19	2	4	1	2	22	0	51	5	0
Akens, Phil, Greensboro	7	6	.538	3.15	16	16	2	0	0	0	100.0	89	418	38	35	4	3	5	11	28	0	70	1	1
Albaladejo, Jonathan, Hickory	12	5	.706	3.11	29	20	5	0	2	1	139.0	114	536	53	48	14	2	4	4	19	1	110	5	1
Allen, Blake, Lake County *	6	3	.667	2.24	36	0	0	0	11	5	76.1	65	317	23	19	3	3	1	3	25	2	74	3	0
Allen, Brian, Charleston-SC	6	5	.545	2.89	50	0	0	0	22	3	71.2	63	283	28	23	2	1	6	1	12	2	53	2	0
Almeida, Brian, Rome	0	0	.000	0.93	6	0	0	0	3	0	9.2	4	43	1	1	0	0	0	2	9	0	6	0	2
Alvarez, Gabriel, S. Georgia	0	1	.000	8.31	8	0	0	0	3	2	8.2	12	45	8	8	3	0	1	0	6	0	12	2	0
Alvarez, Gera, Delmarva	0	0	.000	0.00	1	0	0	0	0	0	1.0	0	3	0	0	0	0	0	0	0	0	1	0	0

Pitcher, Team	W	L	Pct.	ERA	G	GS	CG	ShO	GF	Sv.	IP	H	TBF	R	ER	HR	SH	SF	HB	BB	IBB	SO	WP	Bk.
Anez, Omar, Capital City	7	7	.500	3.83	26	18	1	0	3	2	127.0	113	553	72	54	8	2	3	13	52	2	105	22	1
Arellan, Felix, Kannapolis *	1	3	.250	5.03	31	0	0	0	13	0	53.2	55	253	34	30	1	3	3	6	42	1	45	10	1
Arteaga, Francisco, Rome	1	0	1.000	7.36	4	0	0	0	2	0	7.1	11	37	6	6	0	0	0	1	3	0	7	0	0
Asahina, Jonathan, Gre.	1	0	1.000	0.00	5	0	0	0	2	0	8.0	4	33	0	0	0	1	0	2	2	0	11	1	0
Autrey, Scott, Charleston-SC	9	3	.750	2.61	14	14	0	0	0	0	93.0	77	366	29	27	6	1	1	3	10	0	54	3	2
Baisley, Brad, Lakewood	0	2	.000	6.91	6	6	0	0	0	0	14.1	18	70	15	11	1	0	0	1	5	0	8	2	0
Barlow, Chris, Savannah	6	10	.375	3.99	29	20	1	0	7	3	133.0	146	580	78	59	5	7	6	11	38	0	65	9	2
Barrios, Angel, Lexington	0	0	.000	4.50	3	0	0	0	3	0	6.0	6	30	5	3	0	2	0	1	6	0	4	2	1
Bartlett, Richard, Delmarva	1	5	.167	4.33	12	12	0	0	0	0	60.1	58	268	38	29	5	1	0	3	26	0	47	4	1
Bartz, Jason, Charleston-SC	3	0	1.000	4.74	13	0	0	0	2	0	19.0	17	87	13	10	2	1	4	1	10	1	15	5	0
Bayer, Russ, Hickory *	1	0	1.000	3.60	3	0	0	0	1	0	5.0	6	19	2	2	2	0	0	0	0	0	2	0	0
Bazardo, Yorman, Greensboro	9	8	.529	3.12	21	21	4	2	0	0	130.0	132	550	56	45	8	6	3	9	26	0	70	4	2
Beckstead, Jentry, Asheville	3	5	.375	4.09	63	0	0	0	54	29	61.2	52	275	31	28	5	2	3	11	37	4	66	12	2
Beigh, David, Hickory	0	0	.000	3.38	14	0	0	0	10	2	26.2	26	113	12	10	1	0	0	0	11	0	20	2	0
Belizario, Ronald, Greensboro	5	1	.833	3.00	10	8	1	0	1	0	48.0	41	207	23	16	3	1	1	8	18	0	45	2	0
Bere, Jason, Lake County	0	0	.000	6.75	1	1	0	0	0	0	4.0	7	18	3	3	1	0	0	0	0	0	1	0	0
Bergmann, Jason, Savannah	6	11	.353	4.29	23	22	1	1	0	0	109.0	108	480	57	52	8	5	2	11	53	0	82	10	0
Berry, Jon, Hickory	2	0	1.000	4.11	22	0	0	0	10	3	30.2	27	126	15	14	1	0	0	0	14	0	21	3	0
Bittner, Tim, Kannapolis *	4	4	.500	3.40	10	10	1	0	0	0	50.1	45	223	24	19	4	2	2	7	26	1	45	2	0
Blalock, Casey, Greensboro	5	3	.625	1.75	56	0	0	0	47	18	67.0	47	270	17	13	0	5	1	2	15	1	75	3	1
Blaney, Matt, Augusta	1	2	.333	4.78	16	0	0	0	6	0	26.1	33	136	17	14	2	2	3	7	18	0	10	4	0
Bostick, Adam, Greensboro *	0	1	.000	3.77	7	1	0	0	3	0	14.1	12	66	6	6	1	2	0	0	12	0	15	1	1
Bourgeois, Nick, Lakewood *	7	10	.412	4.42	26	24	0	0	1	0	110.0	92	482	64	54	7	3	6	9	61	0	108	10	3
Bowen, Chad, Capital City	0	1	.000	5.59	13	0	0	0	2	0	19.1	22	94	17	12	1	0	1	0	16	0	14	1	1
Boyer, Blaine, Rome	12	8	.600	3.69	30	26	1	0	0	0	136.2	146	604	70	56	5	1	2	4	58	0	115	10	1
Brice, Thomas, Kannapolis *	0	0	.000	0.00	1	0	0	0	1	0	1.0	1	4	0	0	0	0	0	0	0	0	1	0	0
Broxton, Jonathan, S. Georgia	4	2	.667	3.13	9	8	0	0	0	0	37.1	27	157	15	13	1	1	2	2	22	0	30	2	0
Bulger, Brian, Charleston-SC	11	9	.550	5.21	25	25	0	0	0	0	129.2	145	582	86	75	5	4	8	10	53	2	94	22	2
Bullington, Bryan, Hickory	5	1	.833	1.39	8	7	0	0	1	0	45.1	25	173	10	7	3	0	1	0	11	0	46	1	0
Butto, Francisco, Lakewood	10	12	.455	3.03	27	25	2	1	1	0	148.2	134	629	65	50	8	9	4	6	59	2	104	10	1
Cabrera, Daniel, Delmarva	5	9	.357	4.24	26	26	1	0	0	0	125.1	105	556	74	59	6	2	6	3	78	0	120	5	3
Cabrera, Yunior, Capital City *	3	5	.375	3.16	18	15	0	0	3	1	85.1	76	358	40	30	6	2	6	6	36	2	81	9	3
Cain, Matthew, Hagerstown	4	4	.500	2.55	14	14	0	0	0	0	74.0	57	303	24	21	5	1	0	5	24	0	90	1	1
Campbell, Dayle, S. Georgia	3	0	1.000	3.98	21	0	0	0	15	8	43.0	40	181	22	19	3	0	2	2	13	0	36	4	0
Capellan, Jose, Rome	1	2	.333	3.80	14	12	1	0	0	0	47.1	43	194	23	20	2	3	2	0	19	0	32	2	1
Carlson, Jesse, Lexington *	3	0	1.000	1.56	53	0	0	0	27	13	63.1	37	241	11	11	2	3	0	2	16	3	84	1	0
Carmona, Fausto, Lake Co.	17	4	.810	2.06	24	24	1	0	0	0	148.1	117	573	48	34	10	7	2	3	14	0	83	3	0
Cartier, Richard, Asheville	12	5	.706	4.11	30	20	0	0	3	0	140.0	132	608	81	64	8	4	2	16	43	0	104	10	1
Casey, Reid, Lake County	1	0	1.000	3.00	7	0	0	0	6	1	9.0	9	37	3	3	0	0	0	1	3	0	10	0	0
Castillo, Osmar, Augusta	0	0	.000	0.00	1	0	0	0	1	0	0.2	1	2	0	0	0	0	0	0	0	0	0	0	0
Castro, Fabio, Kannapolis *	0	2	.000	3.27	2	2	0	0	0	0	11.0	8	45	5	4	0	0	0	0	5	0	16	0	0
Castro, Julio, Kannapolis	1	3	.250	3.38	14	0	0	0	3	0	29.1	26	124	11	11	5	0	2	1	11	0	44	1	0
Cedeno, Blas, Hickory	0	0	.000	6.75	4	0	0	0	1	0	4.0	6	20	5	3	0	1	0	2	0	0	3	1	0
Cedeno, Juan, Augusta *	7	9	.438	3.02	23	21	0	0	1	0	101.1	87	425	38	34	8	0	8	2	44	0	87	10	0
Cerrato, Justin, Lakewood	0	1	.000	4.42	9	0	0	0	4	0	18.1	22	83	10	9	1	1	1	0	7	0	15	1	0
Clarke, Darren, Asheville	8	6	.571	3.83	27	25	1	0	0	0	157.1	155	676	80	67	22	5	8	6	59	0	107	5	2
Clelland, James, Augusta	0	0	.000	3.00	2	0	0	0	0	0	3.0	3	15	4	1	0	0	0	0	1	0	3	0	0
Comolli, Mark, Charleston-WV	1	0	1.000	2.51	26	0	0	0	21	13	28.2	20	107	8	8	2	0	1	1	8	2	25	1	0
Cooney, Jim, Delmarva *	0	0	.000	11.25	6	0	0	0	2	0	8.0	14	42	11	10	2	0	1	1	6	0	4	0	0
Coppinger, Joe, Delmarva	2	1	.667	3.94	13	3	0	0	0	0	29.2	31	136	15	13	1	0	0	0	14	0	26	1	0
Costello, Ryan, Char.-WV *	4	4	.500	4.29	45	0	0	0	22	3	65.0	67	291	34	31	2	6	1	3	32	1	60	4	0
Cozier, Vance, Hagerstown	0	2	.000	3.38	4	1	0	0	0	0	10.2	13	51	9	4	1	2	0	1	5	0	3	0	0
Cram, Josh, Hagerstown	1	2	.333	4.02	13	0	0	0	6	1	31.1	25	127	15	14	1	2	0	2	6	1	18	0	0
Crockett, Ben, Asheville	10	9	.526	2.49	23	23	2	0	0	0	151.2	152	638	60	42	11	5	2	13	32	0	117	1	0
Cromer, Jason, Char.-SC *	2	9	.182	3.32	21	21	0	0	0	0	119.1	164	542	67	44	4	7	6	4	30	0	62	9	0
Cromer, Nathan, Char.-SC *	3	2	.600	3.47	43	1	0	0	10	3	62.1	71	271	29	24	1	1	0	4	17	1	54	3	1
Cuen, David, South Georgia *	2	2	.500	4.11	9	7	0	0	0	0	35.0	38	162	22	16	1	1	2	4	18	0	23	7	0
Dannemiller, Beau, Asheville	4	3	.571	4.58	42	0	0	0	16	1	55.0	52	238	33	28	6	1	0	5	18	0	42	2	0
David, Brad, Rome *	2	1	.667	2.90	28	0	0	0	27	15	31.0	33	128	12	10	3	0	0	0	5	0	28	0	0
Davies, Kyle, Rome	8	8	.500	2.89	27	27	1	0	0	0	146.1	128	611	52	47	9	8	6	6	53	0	148	7	0
Davies, Michael, Asheville *	1	5	.167	3.92	10	10	0	0	0	0	57.1	61	245	30	25	7	4	0	3	12	0	34	0	2
Davila, Marcus, Hickory	6	7	.462	1.94	36	0	0	0	6	1	65.0	65	276	25	14	2	6	1	3	17	2	47	3	0
Davis, Brendon, Lexington	1	0	1.000	3.78	10	0	0	0	4	0	16.2	15	78	10	7	2	0	0	1	10	0	13	0	0
De La Cruz, Carlos, Lake Co.	8	1	.889	3.66	32	3	0	0	10	3	76.1	67	329	34	31	3	2	2	4	30	0	94	4	0
De Leon, Juan, Lexington	2	0	1.000	1.83	26	0	0	0	9	2	39.1	24	159	11	8	3	2	2	0	22	1	45	2	0
De Los Santos, Omar, S.Geo.	1	2	.333	6.16	22	1	0	0	7	1	49.2	40	222	37	34	10	0	3	8	32	1	39	11	2
DeBarr, Nick, Charleston-SC	11	7	.611	4.15	27	20	2	0	1	0	138.2	149	607	77	64	8	7	3	10	40	2	105	10	3
DeChristofaro, Vinny, Lak.*	0	2	.000	6.65	6	4	0	0	1	0	23.0	24	112	19	17	1	0	2	0	23	1	17	4	0
DeLeon, Maikel, Capital City	1	0	1.000	0.00	2	0	0	0	2	0	4.0	2	14	0	0	0	0	0	0	0	0	3	0	0
Deaton, Kevin, Capital City	7	5	.583	3.86	26	25	0	0	0	0	135.1	128	577	66	58	8	7	3	5	56	2	121	11	1
Deck, Ronnie, Charleston-SC	0	0	.000	0.00	2	0	0	0	2	0	1.1	1	5	0	0	0	0	0	0	0	0	1	0	0
Deininger, Todd, Kannapolis	6	4	.600	3.65	32	14	0	0	6	0	111.0	90	485	63	45	10	3	3	10	56	2	103	5	0
Delossantos, Carlos, Hickory	2	2	.500	2.04	24	0	0	0	19	13	39.2	23	161	10	9	1	2	0	3	15	3	47	4	0
Demontel, Jimmy, Greensboro	1	2	.333	5.73	31	1	0	0	10	2	37.2	46	174	26	24	4	3	3	4	15	0	29	3	0
Denham, Dan, Lake County	5	2	.714	3.08	14	14	0	0	0	0	73.0	75	316	28	25	4	4	0	5	22	0	63	1	1
Dennison, Michael, Augusta	1	1	.500	1.35	18	0	0	0	15	5	20.0	16	86	5	3	0	0	0	3	8	0	15	0	0
Devarez, Noel, Capital City	0	0	.000	5.40	6	0	0	0	3	0	6.2	8	31	4	4	0	0	1	0	5	0	5	1	0
Diaz, Eddie, Savannah	0	0	.000	6.52	7	0	0	0	3	0	9.2	8	51	10	7	0	0	0	4	10	0	17	1	1
Diaz, Jose, South Georgia	0	1	.000	7.04	5	5	0	0	0	0	15.1	21	75	14	12	1	0	0	2	6	0	8	0	0
Dischiavo, John, Char.-SC	1	0	1.000	9.00	4	0	0	0	2	0	9.0	14	49	11	9	3	0	0	1	6	1	4	0	0
Dittler, Jake, Lake County	6	4	.600	2.63	17	17	1	0	0	0	89.0	86	379	39	26	4	2	0	3	20	0	82	0	0
Done, Mike, Delmarva	0	0	.000	40.50	1	0	0	0	0	0	0.2	4	7	3	3	0	0	0	0	1	0	1	0	0

Pitcher, Team	W	L	Pct.	ERA	G	GS	CG	ShO	GF	Sv.	IP	H	TBF	R	ER	HR	SH	SF	HB	BB	IBB	SO	WP	Bk.
Dooley, Jason, Asheville..........	0	2	.000	11.08	11	0	0	0	2	0	13.0	27	75	19	16	3	1	1	1	9	1	10	2	0
Douglas, Shea, Lake County *	5	3	.625	1.37	34	0	0	0	13	10	85.2	46	334	14	13	2	3	1	5	30	3	104	4	0
Doyne, Cory, Lexington...........	3	1	.750	2.14	9	9	0	0	0	0	54.2	34	220	18	13	4	2	1	6	19	0	48	2	0
Duke, Zach, Hickory *............	8	7	.533	3.11	26	26	1	1	0	0	141.2	124	589	66	49	7	8	6	5	46	0	113	2	2
Dunkle, Peter, Asheville...........	0	0	.000	22.50	4	0	0	0	3	0	4.0	8	30	11	10	0	0	1	2	9	0	1	1	0
Eazor, Kyle, Greensboro *.......	0	0	.000	3.97	9	0	0	0	3	0	11.1	22	68	16	5	0	0	1	2	10	0	6	1	0
Eisentrager, Dan, Lake Co.	12	3	.800	1.72	32	6	0	0	12	6	104.2	79	411	20	20	4	3	3	11	19	0	99	2	2
Ellis, Rob, Charleston-SC *.....	1	0	1.000	3.52	8	0	0	0	3	0	15.1	15	64	7	6	1	0	0	2	2	0	14	0	0
Esarey, Brad, Char.-WV *........	0	5	.000	3.77	31	0	0	0	21	7	45.1	47	212	24	19	2	1	1	8	28	1	37	3	1
Escobar, Rodrigo, Lexington ...	1	0	1.000	5.63	25	0	0	0	14	1	46.1	49	210	32	29	9	2	1	4	22	1	41	2	1
Esposito, Brian, Augusta.........	1	2	.333	5.33	13	0	0	0	7	0	25.1	27	122	22	15	1	2	3	4	13	2	11	1	0
Esquivia, Manuel, Greensboro.	10	5	.667	4.24	42	13	0	0	5	0	114.2	113	498	60	54	14	5	2	3	40	0	91	7	0
Everts, Clint, Savannah	0	3	.000	3.46	5	5	0	0	0	0	26.0	23	114	13	10	1	1	1	2	10	0	21	2	0
Ewin, Ryan, Rome..................	5	4	.556	2.38	16	7	0	0	2	0	64.1	55	258	22	17	4	1	1	1	20	0	61	5	1
Farren, Dave, Delmarva...........	0	0	.000	4.22	7	0	0	0	2	1	10.2	9	47	7	5	0	0	0	0	6	0	10	0	0
Fiedler, Erik, Savannah	1	5	.167	4.56	35	0	0	0	14	0	53.1	56	245	41	27	5	4	5	5	27	5	36	10	1
Figueroa, Jonathan, S.Geo.* ...	1	8	.111	4.94	17	17	0	0	0	0	78.1	79	354	60	43	4	3	5	5	42	0	74	3	1
Florian, Frailyn, Greensboro *.	0	0	.000	4.73	14	1	0	0	0	0	26.2	29	124	18	14	1	0	0	0	16	0	19	1	1
Freeman, Daniel, Lexington.....	4	2	.667	1.64	44	0	0	0	39	21	55.0	46	235	17	10	1	2	0	5	18	0	63	1	0
Friske, Parker, Augusta *	1	2	.333	6.75	14	0	0	0	8	0	22.2	22	106	19	17	2	0	1	5	14	0	18	1	0
Fryson, Andrew, Kannapolis....	1	4	.200	3.24	21	5	1	0	8	0	58.1	52	258	30	21	3	5	1	5	27	3	37	1	0
Fulchino, Jeff, Greensboro	1	2	.333	4.01	5	4	0	0	0	0	24.2	28	113	14	11	1	1	1	3	7	0	16	0	2
Fuller, Brendan, Char.-WV	2	3	.400	8.56	41	0	0	0	12	0	54.2	51	272	53	52	2	2	4	6	59	1	61	19	0
Gallagher, Buddy, Asheville * ..	0	1	.000	3.21	11	0	0	0	3	0	14.0	16	65	8	5	2	2	0	1	6	1	9	4	0
Galvez, Willy, Augusta............	0	2	.000	7.71	13	0	0	0	5	1	21.0	28	100	19	18	3	0	0	1	10	0	14	4	0
Garber, Mike, Augusta *..........	2	4	.333	4.40	35	2	0	0	12	5	57.1	66	270	40	28	2	3	3	2	23	2	44	4	0
Garcia, Anderson, Capital City.	0	1	.000	4.26	5	2	0	0	0	0	12.2	10	50	6	6	1	1	0	1	2	0	12	1	0
Garza, Rolando, Kannapolis	1	1	.500	2.89	21	0	0	0	11	1	28.0	20	130	11	9	0	2	1	2	30	2	30	11	2
Generelli, Daniel, Augusta	2	3	.400	7.71	17	1	0	0	6	0	32.2	42	165	35	28	4	1	2	1	22	0	23	11	0
Girdley, Josh, Savannah *.......	2	5	.286	4.76	12	11	0	0	1	0	51.0	49	232	32	27	4	3	2	6	27	1	38	4	0
Gonzalez, Luis, S. Georgia * ...	2	2	.500	3.30	19	0	0	0	9	3	30.0	25	130	13	11	2	3	0	3	11	1	31	2	1
Gravelle, Nick, Hickory *.........	11	5	.688	3.38	26	26	2	0	0	0	149.0	121	599	61	56	12	7	5	2	47	1	103	8	1
Greusel, Evan, Greensboro......	2	0	1.000	1.52	12	1	0	0	7	2	29.2	24	118	6	5	0	0	0	2	3	0	31	2	0
Griffin, Daniel, Greensboro......	3	1	.750	6.13	36	0	0	0	13	0	47.0	53	242	45	32	4	0	4	5	45	0	31	10	2
Grigsby, Derick, Lexington	2	2	.500	4.79	12	9	0	0	0	0	35.2	40	156	19	19	2	2	1	3	14	0	21	1	1
Guerrero, Julio, Hickory	5	3	.625	3.42	18	3	0	0	6	1	50.0	46	200	21	19	2	0	1	0	9	0	25	2	0
Guzman, Juan, Delmarva	3	2	.600	3.25	31	2	0	0	9	1	63.2	55	268	25	23	3	3	2	0	27	1	52	1	2
Gwaltney, Lee, Lakewood........	8	8	.500	3.06	22	22	1	0	0	0	117.2	92	482	48	40	5	6	2	7	49	1	72	13	1
Habel, Josh, Hagerstown *	11	7	.611	2.36	37	16	1	0	7	2	122.0	90	489	36	32	9	4	0	6	35	0	127	2	1
Hamels, Cole, Lakewood *......	6	1	.857	0.84	13	13	1	1	0	0	74.2	32	268	8	7	0	3	1	3	25	0	115	3	0
Hamilton, Jamaal, S. Georgia*	4	4	.500	3.82	14	14	0	0	0	0	73.0	84	312	37	31	8	2	2	3	11	0	46	2	0
Hamilton, Mark, Lexington * ...	0	0	.000	0.96	4	0	0	0	1	0	9.1	5	39	2	1	0	0	0	1	3	0	17	1	0
Hammel, Jason, Char.-SC	6	2	.750	3.40	14	12	1	0	1	0	76.2	70	320	32	29	2	3	3	2	27	1	50	4	1
Hammes, Zach, S. Georgia......	7	11	.389	5.54	25	24	0	0	0	0	117.0	138	548	91	72	11	9	3	3	65	0	75	6	1
Hansack, Devern, Lexington....	10	6	.625	4.52	22	16	0	0	0	0	91.2	100	397	53	46	10	1	3	1	32	0	76	6	1
Hanson, D.J., Charleston-WV..	10	10	.500	2.54	25	25	2	1	0	0	138.1	110	557	51	39	4	1	3	8	56	2	113	5	1
Hart, Alex, Hickory	9	1	.900	2.66	15	15	0	0	0	0	81.1	50	328	27	24	5	9	2	6	38	1	68	4	0
Hawley, Ross, South Georgia..	0	1	.000	23.14	3	0	0	0	1	0	2.1	6	19	8	6	0	0	2	0	4	0	3	2	0
Heitzman, Aaron, Lexington *.	12	10	.545	4.35	28	28	0	0	0	0	157.1	165	678	87	76	12	2	8	6	60	1	75	8	1
Henderson, Brian, Char.-SC * .	2	0	1.000	2.51	24	0	0	0	7	2	32.1	31	140	11	9	2	0	1	3	12	0	27	4	1
Hennessey, Brad, Hagerstown.	3	9	.250	4.20	15	15	1	0	0	0	79.1	81	346	49	37	6	3	4	5	27	0	44	4	0
Henry, Paul, Delmarva............	4	4	.500	2.76	42	0	0	0	17	4	84.2	70	355	40	26	10	4	3	3	18	0	99	5	0
Hensley, Clay, Hagerstown	4	3	.571	3.18	12	12	3	2	0	0	68.0	56	276	26	24	4	3	0	1	20	0	74	4	0
Hertzler, Barry, Augusta..........	1	0	1.000	0.84	8	0	0	0	6	1	10.2	6	39	2	1	0	0	0	0	3	0	5	1	0
Hinckley, Michael, Savannah *	9	5	.643	3.64	23	23	2	1	0	0	121.0	124	515	54	49	4	2	6	9	41	1	111	8	2
Hines, Carlos, Charleston-SC ..	1	0	1.000	1.46	30	0	0	0	29	16	37.0	25	141	6	6	2	3	0	1	9	1	25	4	0
Hiraldo, Nelson, Lake County..	1	1	.500	3.14	3	2	0	0	0	0	14.1	11	56	5	5	3	0	0	2	2	0	14	0	0
Hodges, Daniel, Lakewood * ...	2	0	1.000	0.82	14	0	0	0	8	3	22.0	16	86	2	2	0	1	0	0	7	0	13	0	0
Holdzkom, Lincoln, Gre...........	1	4	.200	2.84	43	0	0	0	21	4	57.0	36	239	24	18	0	4	2	8	27	2	74	11	2
Hosford, Clint, South Georgia .	1	3	.250	5.56	4	4	0	0	0	0	22.2	21	99	16	14	1	0	2	1	9	1	10	0	0
Houston, Ryan, Char.-WV	2	4	.333	2.67	13	3	0	0	5	2	30.1	22	125	14	9	1	1	2	1	12	0	38	1	0
Huang, Kevin, Augusta............	2	5	.286	3.86	22	12	0	0	7	2	72.1	72	312	38	31	3	2	4	4	26	0	77	4	1
Hudson, Jeremy, Kannapolis...	0	0	.000	0.00	1	0	0	0	1	0	1.0	1	4	0	0	0	0	0	0	0	0	0	0	0
Hummel, Rick, Kannapolis	2	3	.400	1.47	27	0	0	0	25	10	36.2	27	155	13	6	0	2	1	2	16	1	33	0	0
Jarvis, Andrew, Lakewood * ...	0	0	.000	0.00	1	0	0	0	1	0	1.0	2	5	0	0	0	0	0	0	0	0	1	0	0
Jimenez, Ubaldo, Asheville......	10	6	.625	3.46	27	27	0	0	0	0	153.2	129	646	67	59	11	2	1	14	67	0	138	9	0
Johnson, Blair, Hickory...........	1	1	.500	8.71	2	2	0	0	0	0	10.1	11	44	10	10	0	1	1	0	3	0	7	0	0
Johnson, Doug, Asheville........	12	8	.600	4.09	29	28	0	0	0	0	167.1	182	727	85	76	11	4	7	16	45	0	88	6	0
Johnson, Josh, Greensboro	4	7	.364	3.61	17	17	0	0	0	0	82.1	69	349	44	33	5	1	1	9	29	0	59	2	0
Johnston, Rikki, Asheville *	4	3	.571	5.03	29	2	0	0	6	0	48.1	45	219	32	27	3	1	2	3	31	1	46	2	1
Jones, Chris, Asheville *........	0	1	.000	5.40	16	0	0	0	5	0	18.1	22	84	13	11	2	1	0	1	6	0	26	1	0
Jung, Sung, Rome	1	4	.200	2.16	53	0	0	0	35	18	66.2	56	277	21	16	3	2	0	4	26	3	83	2	1
Kazmir, Scott, Capital City *	4	4	.500	2.36	18	18	0	0	0	0	76.1	50	304	26	20	6	3	0	3	28	0	105	12	1
Keefer, Ryan, Delmarva..........	7	12	.368	4.36	26	26	1	0	0	0	148.2	162	634	88	72	11	1	5	10	34	0	94	6	1
Keirstead, Mike, Hickory	0	5	.000	6.75	13	12	0	0	0	0	61.1	87	295	53	46	6	8	3	4	32	1	38	6	0
Kennedy, Casey, S. Georgia.....	5	1	.833	2.11	23	2	0	0	9	2	59.2	58	250	17	14	3	2	1	5	15	3	26	6	0
Kensing, Logan, Greensboro...	0	2	.000	4.50	4	4	0	0	0	0	20.0	18	82	10	10	2	1	1	1	5	0	11	0	0
Kentner, Brandon, Capital City.	1	0	1.000	6.92	9	0	0	0	3	0	13.0	15	57	10	10	0	1	0	2	4	0	11	2	1
King, Bryan, Capital City..........	3	4	.429	3.74	23	0	0	0	16	3	43.1	39	188	18	18	6	1	0	2	24	0	44	11	1
Knapp, Ben, Delmarva............	5	0	1.000	2.53	15	4	0	0	4	3	46.1	39	197	14	13	2	4	1	7	14	0	48	1	0
Krause, Lukas, Capital City *...	0	2	.000	6.45	10	0	0	0	4	0	22.1	28	111	18	16	1	1	1	4	15	2	11	3	0
Kumagai, Ryo, Augusta...........	0	3	.000	7.47	20	0	0	0	8	0	31.1	43	166	31	26	4	1	2	6	20	0	33	6	0

Pitcher, Team	W	L	Pct.	ERA	G	GS	CG	ShO	GF	Sv.	IP	H	TBF	R	ER	HR	SH	SF	HB	BB	IBB	SO	WP	Bk.
LaMura, B.J., Kannapolis	6	10	.375	3.58	24	21	2	0	2	0	128.1	125	553	69	51	3	1	8	7	62	2	101	10	1
LaSalle, Julio, South Georgia	2	4	.333	6.34	34	1	0	0	6	1	61.0	71	292	51	43	7	4	1	2	36	1	66	6	0
Lara, Juan, Lake County *	1	4	.200	5.00	16	3	0	0	6	1	45.0	51	215	31	25	7	1	2	3	26	0	37	6	1
Larson, Adam, Kannapolis	2	4	.333	3.62	39	1	0	0	21	7	74.2	74	310	35	30	4	3	0	3	13	2	66	4	4
Lawson, Jarrod, Lakewood	1	0	1.000	2.60	12	0	0	0	7	4	27.2	13	113	8	8	2	1	0	1	17	1	29	1	0
League, Brandon, Char.-WV	2	3	.400	1.91	12	12	0	0	0	0	70.2	58	277	15	15	1	2	1	4	18	0	61	3	0
Lerew, Anthony, Rome	7	6	.538	2.38	25	25	0	0	0	0	143.2	112	575	45	38	7	5	3	3	43	2	127	0	0
Lester, Jonathan, Augusta *	6	9	.400	3.65	24	21	0	0	2	0	106.0	102	452	54	43	7	6	4	8	44	0	71	2	0
Lindstrom, Matthew, C.C.	2	3	.400	2.86	12	11	0	0	0	0	56.2	46	237	21	18	2	0	1	1	33	0	50	6	3
Lissir, Alexander, Hickory	1	2	.333	4.55	18	0	0	0	8	3	29.2	37	129	15	15	2	2	4	1	8	1	20	1	0
Long, Nick, Savannah	2	7	.222	3.92	15	12	0	0	1	0	59.2	53	260	29	26	7	1	1	5	29	0	43	5	0
Lopez, Aleurys, Charleston-SC	1	1	.500	6.91	8	1	0	0	2	1	14.1	17	63	12	11	0	0	0	0	6	0	7	4	0
Lopez, Arturo, South Georgia	1	4	.200	8.68	20	4	0	0	8	0	37.1	48	177	40	36	5	0	1	4	15	0	27	1	1
Lubisich, Nik, Kannapolis *	2	2	.500	3.09	16	7	0	0	3	1	67.0	68	283	27	23	8	4	1	5	17	2	31	1	1
Lundgren, Wayne, Augusta	0	0	.000	9.00	3	0	0	0	2	1	5.0	6	25	7	5	0	0	2	3	0	0	3	0	0
Mabry, Barry, Rome	1	1	.500	2.96	14	0	0	0	6	0	24.1	18	101	9	8	2	0	2	1	7	1	19	1	0
MacLane, Thomas, Augusta *	1	3	.250	4.37	21	0	0	0	10	1	35.0	41	158	19	17	2	0	2	3	11	0	28	0	2
Maine, John, Delmarva	7	3	.700	1.53	14	14	1	0	0	0	76.1	43	283	16	13	1	2	0	2	18	0	108	1	1
Makowsky, Carl, Delmarva	2	2	.500	1.73	22	0	0	0	8	3	26.0	24	112	6	5	1	0	0	0	10	0	28	0	0
Malone, Corwin, Kannapolis *	0	3	.000	5.11	5	5	1	0	0	0	24.2	27	111	19	14	2	1	1	0	10	0	29	4	1
Marceau, Pierre-Luc, Sav.*	5	4	.556	4.30	36	5	0	0	13	3	92.0	99	397	50	44	5	4	3	8	27	0	65	3	0
Marchbanks, David, Gre.*	0	1	.000	2.12	3	3	0	0	0	0	17.0	16	68	5	4	0	1	1	1	1	0	15	0	0
Martin, Greg, Savannah *	1	1	.500	5.65	20	0	0	0	2	0	28.2	32	131	18	18	3	3	0	1	19	0	17	4	1
Martin, Kevin, Lake County	1	1	.500	1.07	28	0	0	0	25	4	33.2	27	135	5	4	0	2	0	1	7	1	29	0	0
Martinez, Carlos, Greensboro	0	3	.000	2.95	15	0	0	0	5	1	18.1	18	80	7	6	1	1	1	2	4	0	15	0	0
Martinez, Roberto, Savannah	1	1	.500	8.03	17	0	0	0	7	0	24.2	33	130	23	22	4	0	0	4	18	0	14	5	1
Martinez, Samuel, Savannah	2	6	.250	5.81	12	11	0	0	0	0	48.0	41	211	34	31	3	2	2	6	30	1	34	5	0
Maruffi, Joseph, Savannah	0	0	.000	7.88	4	0	0	0	2	1	8.0	15	43	7	7	1	0	0	2	4	0	4	0	0
Mateo, Aneudis, Augusta	0	5	.000	4.89	13	11	0	0	1	0	53.1	62	231	33	29	2	0	1	2	16	0	34	3	0
McCally, Ryan, Charleston-SC	0	0	.000	4.50	2	0	0	0	0	0	4.0	4	16	2	2	0	0	0	0	1	0	5	0	0
McCracken, Vance, S. Georgia	1	2	.333	3.28	21	0	0	0	10	0	46.2	56	217	22	17	2	3	0	6	19	3	31	4	0
McCurdy, Nick, Delmarva	2	4	.333	3.38	6	6	0	0	0	0	32.0	30	132	17	12	5	0	0	3	3	0	27	1	0
McLemore, Mark, Lexington *	2	11	.154	4.58	36	7	0	0	9	0	92.1	84	420	57	47	4	6	8	6	55	5	101	6	0
McNab, Tim, Capital City	9	9	.500	3.16	43	0	0	0	32	11	74.0	63	310	30	26	3	2	3	5	23	1	56	5	0
Mendoza, Luis, Augusta	3	3	.500	2.26	13	11	0	0	0	0	59.2	46	241	19	15	1	2	1	5	14	0	29	2	0
Menocal, Victor, Lakewood	2	7	.222	4.69	22	4	0	0	10	3	78.2	95	365	50	41	5	6	5	8	39	4	37	7	0
Merricks, Matt, Rome *	5	7	.417	2.82	14	10	0	0	2	0	67.0	58	278	27	21	1	2	1	6	19	0	60	9	1
Meyer, Dan, Rome *	4	4	.500	2.87	15	15	0	0	0	0	81.2	76	330	35	26	6	2	1	6	15	1	95	7	0
Meyer, Todd, Savannah	1	5	.167	6.05	25	1	0	0	10	1	38.2	45	189	28	26	4	2	2	2	26	3	24	5	0
Mildren, Paul, Greensboro *	4	10	.286	4.43	27	21	0	0	1	0	101.2	94	451	70	50	4	3	10	6	54	0	83	7	1
Miller, Brian, Kannapolis	8	12	.400	5.30	25	25	1	1	0	0	125.2	124	560	85	74	7	6	2	11	61	1	93	10	2
Minor, Zach, Lakewood	2	3	.400	5.09	25	0	0	0	15	1	40.2	46	182	24	23	2	2	1	3	14	2	28	0	0
Mitchell, Jay, Asheville	0	1	.000	7.71	2	2	0	0	0	0	7.0	6	38	7	6	0	0	1	0	14	0	3	6	0
Mitchell, Tom, Savannah	1	1	.500	7.79	19	0	0	0	8	2	34.2	46	174	34	30	5	0	3	1	33	0	9	4	0
Montague, Ed, South Georgia	0	0	.000	9.00	1	0	0	0	1	0	1.0	2	5	1	1	0	0	0	0	0	0	2	0	0
Montani, Jeff, Delmarva	4	5	.444	3.17	58	0	0	0	47	23	59.2	53	263	29	21	3	3	0	5	30	1	49	2	0
Montano, Ignacio, Lake Co.*	2	0	1.000	3.38	21	0	0	0	13	2	40.0	45	171	20	15	5	1	1	1	8	1	36	1	0
Mora, Ramon, Charleston-WV	4	4	.500	3.92	36	6	0	0	13	4	78.0	85	340	38	34	7	3	1	5	28	1	73	6	2
Morle, Carlos, Augusta *	2	2	.500	5.40	28	0	0	0	17	7	40.0	33	173	25	24	3	2	0	2	22	0	37	2	4
Morris, Cory, Delmarva	5	4	.556	3.19	19	19	1	1	0	0	96.0	74	406	42	34	2	0	1	3	45	0	110	3	0
Mueller, Mike, Rome	0	2	.000	5.08	24	4	0	0	4	0	44.1	42	200	26	25	2	1	3	3	29	0	40	4	1
Munter, Scott, Hagerstown	3	5	.375	2.36	40	0	0	0	18	5	68.2	61	300	28	18	3	3	2	2	28	0	47	7	1
Murray, Brad, Kannapolis *	1	1	.500	0.54	11	0	0	0	7	3	16.2	13	69	2	1	0	3	0	2	8	1	12	0	0
Navaroli, Michael, Char.-SC	0	1	.000	2.67	21	0	0	0	7	0	27.0	38	127	16	8	0	3	1	1	5	1	26	3	0
Nelson, Steve, South Georgia	4	8	.333	4.33	22	15	0	0	1	0	87.1	85	394	56	42	5	3	4	3	45	0	58	6	0
Neuage, Leigh, South Georgia	1	5	.167	6.69	9	9	0	0	0	0	35.0	44	162	27	26	5	0	2	1	14	0	37	2	0
Nickerson, Jon-Michael, Gre.*	0	0	.000	1.80	1	1	0	0	0	0	5.0	3	18	1	1	1	0	0	1	1	0	2	0	0
Nieve, Fernando, Lexington	14	9	.609	3.65	28	28	1	0	0	0	150.1	133	638	69	61	10	4	8	0	65	0	144	7	1
Nin, Sandy, Charleston-WV	7	8	.467	2.89	23	23	1	0	0	0	131.0	124	526	50	42	4	2	5	4	19	2	87	3	0
Nunez, Leo, Hickory	2	1	.667	5.59	13	7	0	0	4	0	48.1	59	216	34	30	6	3	1	4	14	0	37	4	0
O'Brien, Patrick, Hickory	6	4	.600	2.59	12	12	1	0	0	0	73.0	69	308	26	21	5	2	1	5	28	1	58	2	0
O'Connor, Michael, Sav.*	8	3	.727	3.86	42	0	0	0	24	1	70.0	56	301	36	30	6	2	1	3	35	1	83	6	1
Ochoa, Javier, Capital City	0	1	.000	3.15	14	0	0	0	9	0	20.0	9	86	8	7	0	0	1	2	15	1	24	2	1
Olsen, Scott, Greensboro *	7	9	.438	2.81	25	24	0	0	1	0	128.1	101	534	51	40	4	4	5	7	59	0	129	7	0
Olson, Ryan, Capital City *	7	2	.778	2.89	36	1	0	0	16	2	74.2	60	309	30	24	1	4	1	5	26	1	94	11	0
Ontiveros, Jeff, Augusta	0	0	.000	0.00	1	0	0	0	1	0	1.0	0	3	0	0	0	0	0	0	0	0	0	0	0
Owens, Henry, Hickory	2	1	.667	2.91	22	0	0	0	17	9	34.0	21	143	14	11	1	1	0	6	17	0	52	7	0
Ozuna, Francisco, Char.-WV *	2	2	.500	4.88	5	5	0	0	0	0	24.0	36	107	13	13	1	1	1	0	9	0	7	2	0
Pahucki, David, Augusta	1	1	.500	1.89	5	4	0	0	1	0	19.0	7	74	4	4	1	0	0	0	9	0	17	2	0
Palmer, Matt, Hagerstown	5	0	1.000	1.20	44	0	0	0	41	25	52.1	21	195	7	7	3	2	0	4	15	0	56	3	1
Patitucci, Mike, Delmarva *	0	0	.000	10.80	2	0	0	0	1	0	1.2	4	10	4	2	0	0	0	0	1	0	3	0	0
Paulk, Robert, Capital City	2	1	.667	1.55	18	0	0	0	17	7	29.0	22	127	9	5	1	0	0	1	17	1	23	1	0
Peeples, Ross, Capital City *	1	4	.200	6.35	11	3	0	0	3	0	39.2	51	184	31	28	7	1	2	1	14	0	32	2	0
Peguero, Jailen, Lexington	5	13	.278	3.64	31	21	0	0	5	1	146.0	110	609	74	59	11	2	6	8	69	1	111	10	0
Pennington, Todd, Lake Co.	2	1	.667	0.72	36	0	0	0	35	20	37.1	14	145	3	3	1	2	0	1	17	0	65	5	0
Peralta, Efigenio, Rome	4	2	.667	2.52	20	0	0	0	6	0	39.1	33	155	12	11	2	1	1	2	11	0	36	2	1
Perez, Armando, Kannapolis *	4	6	.400	4.41	34	5	0	0	11	0	81.2	82	365	51	40	5	2	4	6	40	0	56	2	1
Perez, Randy, Lake County *	1	2	.333	4.05	5	4	0	0	0	0	26.2	31	112	15	12	3	1	0	1	6	0	17	0	0
Perkins, Vince, Char.-WV	3	1	.750	1.83	8	8	0	0	0	0	44.1	19	168	9	9	1	2	2	2	22	1	60	3	0
Peterson, Adam, Char.-WV	2	4	.333	2.19	10	0	0	0	6	1	24.2	15	99	8	6	1	5	0	2	13	2	19	3	1
Phillips, Mike, Kannapolis *	2	0	1.000	1.71	3	3	0	0	0	0	21.0	13	79	4	4	1	1	0	0	5	0	11	0	0
Pinango, Miguel, Capital City	13	6	.684	3.47	24	23	3	0	1	0	132.1	140	561	62	51	8	3	4	7	25	1	106	1	1

Pitcher, Team	W	L	Pct.	ERA	G	GS	CG	ShO	GF	Sv.	IP	H	TBF	R	ER	HR	SH	SF	HB	BB	IBB	SO	WP	Bk.
Plummer, Jarod, S. Georgia	1	2	.333	4.34	9	0	0	0	5	2	18.2	12	79	10	9	2	0	4	1	10	0	21	1	1
Portorreal, Daniel, Hag.	1	4	.200	3.16	6	6	0	0	0	0	25.2	21	115	18	9	0	0	2	4	19	0	20	3	1
Prahm, Ryan, Lake County	1	1	.500	1.32	5	1	0	0	2	0	13.2	5	54	3	2	0	0	1	0	7	0	14	0	1
Priola, John, Augusta	0	1	.000	4.09	5	0	0	0	2	0	11.0	13	50	6	5	2	1	0	2	5	0	7	0	0
Prochaska, Mike, Char.-SC *	9	7	.563	2.98	29	20	0	0	2	0	124.0	111	508	49	41	10	4	4	8	35	0	76	6	0
Ramirez, Ismael, Char.-WV	6	5	.545	3.02	24	22	1	0	1	0	119.1	110	494	51	40	6	1	5	4	31	1	70	1	1
Ramsey, Keith, Lake County *	13	6	.684	2.99	24	24	3	1	0	0	144.2	146	590	54	48	10	4	1	5	15	0	108	1	2
Ransom, Troy, Hagerstown	3	0	1.000	5.40	29	0	0	0	13	0	48.1	57	205	34	29	12	3	1	0	8	0	22	2	0
Rasner, Darrell, Savannah	7	7	.500	4.19	22	22	2	0	0	0	105.1	106	450	53	49	8	6	6	7	36	0	90	9	1
Read, Robby, Lakewood	2	4	.333	5.61	33	2	0	0	16	2	77.0	79	368	63	48	3	3	2	3	51	2	73	7	0
Reba, Steve, Asheville	6	3	.667	2.66	47	2	0	0	10	3	81.1	81	336	31	24	6	1	2	4	15	1	81	6	1
Reina, Dimas, South Georgia	8	0	1.000	3.02	23	0	0	0	16	4	50.2	37	207	19	17	4	0	3	3	22	3	42	2	0
Rengel, Orlando, Capital City	0	0	.000	4.50	1	0	0	0	0	0	2.0	3	9	1	1	0	0	1	0	1	0	1	0	0
Resop, Chris, Greensboro	0	1	.000	4.97	11	0	0	0	2	0	12.2	11	54	7	7	1	0	0	0	5	0	15	1	1
Reynolds, Eric, Greensboro *	0	1	.000	3.00	3	0	0	0	0	0	3.0	1	12	1	1	0	0	0	0	2	0	1	0	0
Reynoso, Paulino, Kan.*	5	7	.417	3.16	22	21	1	0	0	0	108.1	81	446	46	38	7	4	2	5	55	1	86	8	5
Rice, Scott, Delmarva *	4	1	.800	0.94	32	0	0	0	17	5	47.2	21	178	7	5	0	1	0	4	12	1	53	2	1
Richardson, Beau, Lak.*	6	5	.545	2.66	47	0	0	0	39	16	91.1	82	376	34	27	4	7	0	4	29	7	55	2	1
Ridgway, Jeff, Charl.-SC *	5	8	.385	4.17	24	19	0	0	1	0	99.1	102	444	63	46	2	7	4	12	41	0	74	5	1
Rigueiro, Rafael, Hagerstown	0	1	.000	1.35	5	0	0	0	1	0	6.2	3	26	3	1	1	0	0	0	2	0	12	4	0
Rodriguez, Jose, Rome	4	1	.800	4.20	37	0	0	0	8	0	55.2	61	254	34	26	4	2	3	2	30	4	41	3	3
Rodriguez, Jose, Savannah	0	1	.000	6.75	7	0	0	0	1	0	13.1	15	66	10	10	1	1	0	3	11	0	5	2	1
Rodriguez, Juan, Hickory	0	0	.000	2.08	2	0	0	0	1	0	4.1	5	21	2	1	0	0	0	1	2	0	5	1	0
Rodriguez, Mike, S. Georgia	1	4	.200	10.61	9	5	0	0	2	0	18.2	23	107	26	22	1	2	2	2	25	0	19	4	0
Rodriguez, Osvaldo, S. Geo.	3	0	1.000	1.80	10	7	0	0	2	0	40.0	30	165	9	8	0	1	1	2	23	0	30	4	0
Rodriguez, Ricardo, Rome	8	4	.667	3.45	33	0	0	0	11	1	60.0	51	269	30	23	2	6	1	5	38	3	52	4	0
Roman, Orlando, Capital City	2	2	.500	3.34	7	6	0	0	1	0	29.2	29	130	14	11	2	0	0	3	20	0	35	3	0
Romero, Felix, Charleston-WV	2	3	.400	3.89	42	0	0	0	15	0	69.1	63	298	37	30	2	2	2	6	25	3	77	4	0
Roy, Angus, Augusta	3	7	.300	5.54	29	3	0	0	6	0	66.2	77	305	44	41	6	5	5	7	33	0	37	6	0
Rueckel, Danny, Savannah	1	3	.250	4.06	40	1	0	0	26	14	68.2	68	286	38	31	4	1	5	2	16	1	64	3	1
Rupe, Josh, Kannapolis	5	5	.500	3.02	26	7	2	0	11	6	65.2	50	277	27	22	0	2	1	2	36	2	69	2	0
Rupert, Chris, Lakewood *	1	2	.333	5.59	23	0	0	0	13	0	37.0	39	170	27	23	3	1	3	4	16	0	27	3	0
Russell, Eddie, Greensboro	1	1	.500	3.77	9	0	0	0	2	0	14.1	12	68	8	6	0	0	0	1	14	0	15	1	0
Russell, Mike, Delmarva	0	0	.000	0.00	1	0	0	0	1	0	0.1	0	1	0	0	0	0	0	0	0	0	0	0	0
Sadler, William, Hagerstown	0	0	.000	4.80	12	0	0	0	6	1	15.0	15	72	8	8	4	0	0	2	13	0	10	0	0
Salazar, Julio, Lexington *	1	0	1.000	2.81	8	0	0	0	2	1	16.0	7	65	6	5	0	0	1	1	9	1	11	0	2
Salazar, Richard, Delmarva *	5	3	.625	1.85	41	0	0	0	14	3	63.1	44	253	17	13	2	3	0	3	21	0	65	4	1
Sampson, Christopher, Lex.	4	3	.571	1.39	22	14	0	0	2	1	84.0	66	332	17	13	2	1	0	5	14	0	66	0	0
Sanchez, Emilio, Lakewood	0	3	.000	4.98	11	0	0	0	4	1	21.2	29	102	17	12	2	2	1	2	5	1	18	2	0
Sandoval, Marcos, Char.-WV	1	4	.200	5.34	16	3	0	0	7	0	28.2	34	143	23	17	3	1	4	5	17	1	17	3	0
Santiago, Victor, S. Georgia	4	0	1.000	3.35	23	2	0	0	10	3	51.0	45	212	22	19	4	1	3	7	14	1	52	3	0
Schmidt, Jeremy, Hagerstown	1	4	.200	5.85	24	0	0	0	12	0	32.1	43	157	29	21	4	3	2	2	19	3	26	2	0
Seale, Dustin, Savannah *	2	0	1.000	3.66	4	3	1	0	1	1	19.2	17	79	8	8	2	0	1	1	7	0	13	0	0
Searles, Jon, Savannah	3	2	.600	3.66	20	2	0	0	11	5	39.1	35	167	19	16	3	1	1	4	12	0	36	2	0
Segovia, Zach, Lakewood	1	5	.167	3.99	11	10	0	0	0	0	49.2	63	225	25	22	2	2	2	2	14	1	27	2	0
Serrato, Juan, Hagerstown	0	2	.000	3.71	6	3	0	0	0	0	17.0	12	68	8	7	2	0	2	2	6	0	21	1	1
Shafer, Kurt, Hickory	3	1	.750	3.80	19	0	0	0	7	2	42.2	46	176	19	18	5	1	1	0	5	0	22	1	0
Sheffield, Christopher, Char.-WV	0	0	.000	2.08	7	0	0	0	1	0	8.2	7	45	4	2	1	3	0	2	11	0	7	3	0
Shipman, Andrew, Augusta	0	1	.000	11.12	4	1	0	0	1	0	5.2	13	37	10	7	1	0	1	1	5	0	6	1	0
Shortslef, Josh, Hickory *	0	5	.000	7.50	5	5	0	0	0	0	18.0	21	81	15	15	0	1	2	1	6	0	14	1	0
Silva, Efrain, South Georgia	1	0	1.000	2.31	7	0	0	0	3	0	11.2	9	52	4	3	0	0	0	1	7	0	13	1	0
Simon, Alfredo, Lakewood	5	0	1.000	3.79	14	7	0	0	4	2	71.1	59	298	32	30	4	4	3	3	25	0	66	5	1
Sinclair, Ernnie, Lexington	5	3	.625	3.15	21	6	0	0	8	0	54.1	45	232	22	19	1	1	2	2	28	0	47	5	1
Smith, Brandon, Augusta	0	5	.000	9.87	16	4	0	0	2	0	34.2	61	179	41	38	2	1	1	3	14	0	30	6	2
Smith, Chris, Augusta	3	3	.500	4.27	8	8	0	0	0	0	46.1	48	188	22	22	4	1	3	3	5	0	25	3	1
Smith, Sean, Lake County	11	4	.733	3.71	26	26	0	0	0	0	121.1	100	520	62	50	17	5	5	6	67	0	101	7	2
Soto, T.J., Lexington	0	1	.000	3.86	1	0	0	0	1	0	2.1	4	13	1	1	0	1	0	1	3	0	0	0	0
Southerland, Chip, Lake Co.	0	0	.000	0.00	1	0	0	0	1	0	1.1	2	7	0	0	0	0	0	0	0	0	2	0	0
Sperring, Jayme, Delmarva	7	7	.500	4.19	25	12	0	0	5	1	81.2	77	343	39	38	10	2	1	4	30	0	92	6	2
Stahl, Richard, Delmarva *	1	3	.250	5.48	28	1	0	0	3	1	47.2	47	242	41	29	4	4	2	6	50	2	46	4	2
Stephenson, Eric, Char.-WV *	4	4	.500	4.38	18	8	0	0	2	0	61.2	67	281	43	30	4	6	2	3	36	1	47	4	2
Stirm, Brian, Hagerstown	8	5	.615	2.86	17	15	0	0	1	0	85.0	63	334	30	27	10	0	3	1	23	0	80	2	1
Sturge, Justin, Augusta *	2	0	1.000	0.56	11	0	0	0	4	1	16.0	13	61	3	1	0	1	0	2	5	0	8	2	0
Sweeney, Matt, Lakewood	4	12	.250	4.00	26	17	1	0	4	0	114.2	116	514	66	51	10	5	8	6	61	2	74	10	3
Tadefa, Fernando, Rome *	3	5	.375	2.88	45	0	0	0	21	5	50.0	43	217	19	16	2	3	0	2	30	3	44	1	0
Talanoa, Charles, Char.-WV	2	5	.286	3.71	9	9	0	0	0	0	43.2	49	200	23	18	0	0	1	2	21	1	37	5	2
Tavarez, Milton, Augusta	1	1	.500	2.86	18	3	0	0	5	0	44.0	43	186	18	14	3	0	2	2	13	0	36	5	1
Teeter, Travis, Delmarva	0	0	.000	5.68	8	0	0	0	4	1	12.2	15	56	9	8	0	0	0	0	3	0	13	0	0
Tejeda, Rob, Lakewood	0	3	.000	5.30	5	4	0	0	0	0	18.2	17	88	11	11	4	2	0	1	16	0	20	1	0
Testa, Chris, South Georgia *	0	0	.000	0.53	14	0	0	0	9	2	17.0	9	71	1	1	1	1	0	3	11	1	19	1	0
Thompson, Matt, Augusta	2	2	.500	4.78	11	10	0	0	0	0	43.1	45	196	23	23	2	2	1	6	19	0	35	3	0
Thorpe, Tracy, Charleston-WV	1	2	.333	6.68	20	1	0	0	2	0	32.1	37	156	26	24	5	0	2	4	22	0	21	5	0
Threets, Erick, Hagerstown *	2	3	.400	3.26	22	0	0	0	3	0	49.2	26	215	20	18	2	0	2	7	42	0	47	9	1
Tiller, James, Delmarva	3	6	.333	3.51	13	13	0	0	0	0	66.2	78	296	44	26	4	1	1	5	13	0	52	7	0
Tisch, Tim, Kannapolis *	1	0	1.000	1.93	3	2	0	0	0	0	14.0	11	62	5	3	0	0	1	1	8	0	11	1	1
Tracey, Sean, Kannapolis	2	7	.222	9.50	14	9	0	0	0	0	41.2	51	231	54	44	4	5	2	11	46	0	28	16	1
Urrutia, Carlos, Lakewood	0	1	.000	7.94	9	0	0	0	5	1	11.1	12	57	11	10	0	0	1	3	9	0	4	3	0
Valdez, Merkin, Hagerstown	9	5	.643	2.25	26	26	2	1	0	0	156.0	119	617	42	39	11	2	1	5	49	0	166	4	0
Vandermeer, Scott, Char.-SC	3	2	.600	4.55	6	6	0	0	0	0	31.2	34	141	16	16	5	1	1	4	15	0	18	0	0
Vazquez, Will, Asheville	0	0	.000	0.00	3	0	0	0	0	0	5.2	9	31	11	0	0	0	2	1	1	1	2	2	0
Villarreal, Luis, Augusta *	7	11	.389	5.17	25	24	0	0	0	0	111.1	140	492	75	64	9	5	3	4	31	0	82	6	1
Volquez, Bolivar, Char.-SC	0	0	.000	6.53	10	0	0	0	3	0	20.2	28	96	16	15	0	0	2	2	10	1	5	2	0

Pitcher, Team	W	L	Pct.	ERA	G	GS	CG	ShO	GF	Sv.	IP	H	TBF	R	ER	HR	SH	SF	HB	BB	IBB	SO	WP	Bk.
Waddell, Jason, Hagerstown *	4	2	.667	3.52	36	2	0	0	13	0	61.1	52	256	32	24	7	3	3	4	21	1	54	2	0
Walker, Brian, Capital City *	8	5	.615	3.77	24	16	1	0	6	2	107.1	117	467	52	45	11	2	4	11	29	0	94	2	0
Warden, Jim Ed, Lake County	4	3	.571	2.86	14	13	0	0	1	0	69.1	49	301	30	22	5	2	3	3	44	0	61	10	0
Warriax, Brandon, S. Georgia	6	5	.545	5.13	30	11	0	0	6	0	100.0	124	458	70	57	5	7	4	4	31	4	53	9	0
Washburn, Ben, Hagerstown	1	0	1.000	2.75	11	0	0	0	4	0	19.2	15	79	6	6	2	2	0	1	4	1	12	1	0
Wasserman, Ehren, Kan.	1	1	.500	1.00	6	0	0	0	5	0	9.0	8	36	1	1	0	2	0	1	3	1	10	1	0
Watkins, Dave, Rome	0	0	.000	0.00	1	0	0	0	0	0	1.0	2	4	0	0	0	0	0	0	0	0	0	0	0
Watson, Mike, Asheville	1	3	.250	5.02	17	0	0	0	7	0	28.2	31	123	18	16	3	1	1	1	11	0	29	1	0
Wayne, Brett, South Georgia	1	0	1.000	10.80	5	0	0	0	3	0	3.1	5	21	4	4	0	0	1	1	5	0	3	0	0
Weichard, Paul, Rome *	2	0	1.000	2.14	22	0	0	0	8	2	21.0	17	97	8	5	0	3	1	2	13	1	15	1	0
Wesley, John, Charleston-WV	2	5	.286	3.48	8	8	0	0	0	0	41.1	38	169	21	16	2	1	1	5	13	2	32	2	2
Westhoff, Billy, Lexington	6	2	.750	3.10	45	0	0	0	13	2	90.0	84	400	44	31	3	3	4	4	48	4	59	5	0
Wickman, Bob, Lake County	0	0	.000	0.00	2	2	0	0	0	0	2.0	1	7	0	0	0	0	0	0	0	0	4	0	0
Williams, Ryan, South Georgia	0	0	.000	3.09	11	0	0	0	10	5	11.2	7	46	4	4	0	0	0	0	5	0	11	1	0
Withelder, Greg, Hickory *	0	0	.000	4.63	12	0	0	0	6	0	11.2	11	56	6	6	1	0	1	1	11	0	7	1	0
Wolf, Ross, Greensboro	6	1	.857	1.61	27	0	0	0	6	2	50.1	32	192	10	9	2	4	1	2	10	2	26	0	0
Woolard, Glenn, Hagerstown	8	9	.471	3.44	26	25	2	1	1	0	144.0	126	588	63	55	10	5	3	3	43	0	135	6	0
Wright, Matt, Rome	10	2	.833	1.65	14	13	1	1	0	0	82.0	53	319	19	15	2	2	2	0	32	0	98	4	1
Yarbrough, Joe, Char.-SC *	3	6	.333	1.99	56	0	0	0	42	22	72.1	52	287	21	16	5	7	2	5	20	2	69	3	0
Youman, Shane, Hickory *	6	3	.667	4.65	40	1	0	0	28	12	50.1	51	236	31	26	2	4	1	2	35	2	58	5	0
Young, Chris, Asheville	3	4	.429	2.73	59	0	0	0	27	9	69.1	59	284	26	21	4	3	0	4	21	3	63	5	1
Zinsman, Zeph, Char.-WV *	0	0	.000	0.00	1	0	0	0	1	0	1.0	0	3	0	0	0	0	0	0	0	0	1	0	0

COMBINATION SHUTOUTS: Asheville (4)—Jimenez-Young-Beckstead, Reba-Johnston-Young, Cartier-Beckstead, Cartier-Young. Augusta (10)—Lester-Roy-Esposito, Pahucki-Cedeno-Esposito, Cedeno-Generelli-Huang-Friske, Cedeno-Huang, Villarreal-Roy, Huang-Cedeno, Huang-Tavarez-Garber, Lester-Garber, Lester-Sturge-Morle, Mendoza-Lundgren. Capital City (7)—Pinango-McNab-Paulk, Lindstrom-Bowen-McNab, Deaton-Acosta-McNab, Kazmir-Anez, Kazmir-McNab, Kazmir-Olson-McNab, Pinango-Devarez-Olson. Charleston (S.C.) (7)—Autrey-Bartz-Hines, Autrey-Bartz, Autrey-Hines, Prochaska-Henderson-Ellis, Prochaska-Cromer, Prochaska-Allen-Yarbrough, Bulger-Cromer-Yarbrough. Charleston (W.Va.) (9)—League-Houston-Comolli, Nin-Peterson, Houston-Costello-Comolli, Hanson-Romero-Mora, Hanson-Romero-Costello, Ramirez-Romero-Mora, Hanson-Sandoval-Esarey, Hanson-Esarey, Nin-Romero. Delmarva (9)—Maine-Rice-Farren, Keefer-Henry, Maine-Rice-Montani, Maine-Stahl-Henry-Montani, Maine-Rice, Morris-Montani-Sperring, Maine-Stahl, Cabrera-Salazar-Henry-Montani, Keefer-Salazar. Greensboro (8)—Belizario-Holdzkom, Akens-Esquivia-Asahina, Olsen-Demontel-Holdzkom-Blalock, Olsen-Demontel, Johnson-Demontel-Holdzkom-Blalock, Olsen-Russell-Demontel, Kensing-Mildred-Martinez, Johnson-Olsen. Hagerstown (12)—Portorreal-Waddell-Palmer, Cain-Munter-Palmer, Valdez-Habel-Woolard, Valdez-Palmer, Woolard-Cram, Cain-Habel-Palmer, Valdez-Munter-Habel-Palmer, Cain-Threets-Palmer, Valdez-Munter-Habel-Washburn-Palmer, Stirm-Waddell-Palmer, Habel-Sadler-Palmer, Stirm-Threets-Munter-Palmer. Hickory (12)—Hart-Shafer, Bullington-Bayer, Gravelle-Albaladejo-Shafer-Owens, Bullington-Shafer, Hart-Owens, Albaladejo-Davila-Bullington, Gravelle-Owens, Hart-Davila, Keirstead-Davila-DeLosSantos-Berry, Duke-Owens, O'Brien-Withelder-Berry, Guerrero-DeLosSantos. Kannapolis (6)—Reynoso-Castro-Fryson, Bittner-Fryson, Phillips-Castro, Reynoso-Arellan-Lubisich, Lubisich-Larson-Arellan, Lubisich-Larson. Lake County (21)—Smith-Montano, Carmona-Eisentrager, Denham-Allen-Pennington, Carmona-DeLaCruz, Carmona-Pennington, Smith-Douglas, Smith-Allen-Pennington, DeLaCruz-Eisentrager, Smith-Pennington, Denham-Allen-Eisentrager, Ramsey-Eisentrager, Warden-DeLaCruz-Martin, Smith-Eisentrager-Pennington, Carmona-Allen, Ramsey-Eisentrager, Dittler-Allen-Martin, Prahm-Douglas-Eisentrager, Eisentrager-Allen-Montano, Ramsey-Montano-Martin, Wickman-Hiraldo-Montano-Casey, Warden-Montano. Lakewood (6)—Butto-Richardson, Sweeney-Richardson, Bourgeois-Cabrera, Butto-Richardson, Gwaltney-Richardson, Bourgeois-Lawson. Lexington (8)—Heitzman-Westhoff-Carlson, Heitzman-Westhoff, Heitzman-DeLeon-Carlson, Nieve-Sinclair-Carlson-Freeman, Hansack-DeLeon-Carlson-Freeman, Nieve-Carlson, Sampson-Salazar, Sampson-Peguero. Rome (15)—Merricks-Jung, Davies-Tadefa-Jung, Meyer-Rodriguez-Jung, Davies-Mueller-Tadefa-David, Lerew-Tadefa-David, Capellan-Rodriguez-David, Mueller-Rodriguez-Jung-Tadefa, Merricks-Rodriguez, Lerew-Boyer-Rodriguez-Mabry-Ewin-Jung, Ewin-Peralta-Jung, Wright-Capellan-Jung-Weichard, Boyer-Weichard-Jung, Lerew-Rodriguez-Jung, Ewin-Peralta-Weichard, Wright-Weichard-Mueller. Savannah (4)—Girdley-Barlow, Long-Searles, Hinckley-Meyer-Fieldler-Martin-Martinez, Barlow-O'Connor-Rueckel. South Georgia (2)—Hammes-LaSalle-Warriax, Figueroa-DeLosSantos-Plummer.

NO-HIT GAMES: Hensley, Hagerstown, defeated Kannapolis, 2-0 (second game), May 3; Miller, Kannapolis, defeated Greensboro, 2-0 (first game), June 10.

2003 FIELDING

TEAM

Team	G	PO	A	E	TC	DP	TP	PB	Pct.
Lake County	140	3647	1456	143	5246	84	0	32	.973
Rome	139	3538	1260	136	4934	101	0	24	.972
Charleston-Wv.	133	3423	1434	138	4995	131	0	21	.972
Hagerstown	135	3501	1363	144	5008	81	0	16	.971
Lexington	138	3632	1480	159	5271	110	0	47	.970
Hickory	136	3483	1385	152	5020	105	0	19	.970
Asheville	139	3701	1529	166	5396	115	0	24	.969
Kannapolis	137	3476	1386	154	5016	52	0	52	.969
Lakewood	138	3508	1337	160	5005	102	0	45	.968
Savannah	138	3461	1394	159	5014	111	0	26	.968
Charleston-Sc.	139	3596	1507	176	5279	125	0	26	.967
Capital City	138	3537	1509	178	5224	79	0	23	.966
Delmarva	138	3572	1322	174	5068	74	0	26	.966
Greensboro	136	3507	1344	174	5025	87	0	25	.965
Augusta	136	3368	1332	179	4879	97	0	26	.963
South Georgia	136	3489	1385	194	5068	108	0	27	.962

INDIVIDUAL

FIRST BASEMEN

NOTE: All caps denotes fielding-percentage leader based on 70 games for catchers, 93 for all other non-pitchers and 112 innings for pitchers. *Throws lefthanded.

Player, Team	Pct.	G	PO	A	E	TC	DP
Acevas, Jon, Kannapolis	.986	8	66	4	1	71	3
Alexander, Kevin, Hagerstown	1.000	6	50	4	0	54	3
Arnold, Eric, Charleston-WV	1.000	1	1	0	0	1	0
Aubrey, Michael, Lake County *	.994	37	331	30	2	363	30
Bagley, David, South Georgia	1.000	1	1	0	0	1	0
Baldiris, Aaron, Capital City	.990	15	96	6	1	103	4
Bankston, Wes, Charleston-SC	1.000	5	41	2	0	43	0
Barthelemy, Ryan, Lakewood	.994	63	486	43	3	532	40
Bass, Chris, Hickory	.993	17	133	14	1	148	13
Bastardo, Angel, Lake County	.971	5	32	2	1	35	2
Benavidez, Julian, Hagerstown	.987	60	487	34	7	528	41
Bok, Matt, South Georgia	.983	8	54	5	1	60	9
Bonvechio, Brett, Augusta	.988	42	314	27	4	345	34
Bowman, Addison, Augusta	1.000	1	7	0	0	7	0
Brand, Kevin, Asheville	.986	9	64	5	1	70	7
Brice, Thomas, Kannapolis *	.971	15	97	5	3	105	7
Brisson, Dustin, Augusta	.992	29	229	14	2	245	21
Broadway, Larry, Savannah *	.993	80	688	57	5	750	70
Bushey, Andrew, Asheville	1.000	1	8	0	0	8	0
Checksfield, Steven, Lexington	1.000	1	9	0	0	9	1
Chop, Chad, Savannah *	.986	43	330	19	5	354	25
Christensen, Mike, Kannapolis	1.000	6	32	2	0	34	3
Clute, Kris, Greensboro	.976	5	37	4	1	42	1
Colmenter, Jesus, Lake County	.986	9	66	4	1	71	6
Columbus, Jason, Hagerstown	.970	12	91	6	3	100	9
Cordell, Brent, Charleston-SC	.994	38	322	36	2	360	36
Davis, John-Paul, Charleston-SC	.990	84	720	65	8	793	60
De La Cruz, Miguel, Hickory	.977	17	123	6	3	132	14
Donato, Greg, Rome	1.000	10	68	3	0	71	8
Dragicevich, Scott, Charl.-WV	.987	19	145	12	2	159	12
Duncan, Trey, Charleston-SC	1.000	14	109	4	0	113	11
Durazo, William, Augusta	1.000	1	7	0	0	7	1
ELDRED, BRAD, Hickory	.990	105	851	62	9	922	62
Ellis, Andrew, South Georgia	1.000	1	1	1	0	2	0
Fagan, John, Lexington	.985	114	867	79	14	960	75
Freeman, Ashley, Asheville	.995	42	344	27	2	373	21
Gretz, Nick, Asheville	.986	46	398	24	6	428	36

Player, Team	Pct.	G	PO	A	E	TC	DP
Grzecka, Casey, Greensboro	1.000	1	3	0	0	3	3
Hansen, Bryan, Lakewood *	.967	34	262	29	10	301	28
Harper, Brett, Capital City	1.000	8	52	3	0	55	3
Harrison, Vince, Charleston-SC	.923	2	9	3	1	13	0
Holm, Steve, Hagerstown	1.000	1	2	0	0	2	0
Hoorelbeke, Jesse, S. Georgia	.991	46	412	20	4	436	33
Hopper, Matthew, Lakewood	.987	20	141	14	2	157	14
Hudson, William, Capital City	1.000	1	1	0	0	1	1
Humphries, Justin, Lexington	.997	39	307	16	1	324	24
Ishikawa, Travis, Hagerstown *	.990	57	481	38	5	524	22
Jarvis, Andrew, Lakewood *	.984	21	175	7	3	185	10
Johnston, Clint, Charl.-WV *	.972	5	31	4	1	36	7
Kent, Bryan, Lake County	.991	12	105	6	1	112	11
Kirby, Brian, Lake County	.991	12	99	6	1	106	4
Knowlton, Jay, Hagerstown	.962	3	23	2	1	26	2
Knox, Matt, Lake County	.986	64	574	39	9	622	26
Kratz, Erik, Charleston-WV	1.000	4	41	1	0	42	3
Luna, Leonardo, Kannapolis	.000	1	0	0	0	0	0
Manriquez, Salomon, Savannah	1.000	1	2	0	0	2	1
Margalski, Ben, Savannah	1.000	1	3	0	0	3	1
McRoberts, Mark, Lakewood	1.000	3	14	2	0	16	1
Merkle, Tom, Greensboro	.988	75	632	33	8	673	49
Mills, Rock, Asheville	1.000	2	15	1	0	16	3
Molina, Gustavo, Kannapolis	1.000	26	176	21	0	197	9
Nixon, Mike, South Georgia	1.000	2	1	0	0	1	0
Noboa, Joel, Savannah	.992	18	122	3	1	126	8
O'Sullivan, Patrick, Delmarva	.975	4	36	3	1	40	5
Ontiveros, Jeff, Augusta	.991	68	517	41	5	563	32
Ordorica, Eric, Greensboro	1.000	2	9	0	0	9	1
Peavey, Bill, Lake County *	1.000	6	31	5	0	36	2
Pellow, Kit, Asheville	1.000	3	24	2	0	26	4
Peters, Yaron, Rome	.983	84	589	40	11	640	43
Ragsdale, Corey, Capital City	1.000	1	3	0	0	3	0
Ramos, Kelly, Delmarva	.972	4	34	1	1	36	3
Randel, Kevin, Greensboro	1.000	1	3	0	0	3	0
Reyes, Julio, Kannapolis	.990	73	539	33	6	578	20
Roat, Kyle, Rome	.980	20	139	9	3	151	15
Rodriguez, Andres, Capital City	.989	122	1054	72	12	1138	67
Rodriguez, Edgar, Capital City	1.000	2	15	0	0	15	0
Ruelas, Alonzo, Rome	.986	10	66	6	1	73	6
Ruiz, Daniel, Rome	.994	31	156	3	1	160	15
Ruiz, Randy, Delmarva	1.000	12	93	8	0	101	3
Russell, Mike, Delmarva	.983	7	54	3	1	58	2
Sardinha, Duke, Asheville	.974	33	281	19	8	308	24
Siriveaw, Nom, Charleston-WV	1.000	5	32	4	0	36	8
Story-Harden, Thomari, S.Ga.	.982	51	404	29	8	441	27
Street, Dan, Asheville	1.000	4	42	0	0	42	4
Tempesta, Nick, Lakewood	1.000	1	10	1	0	11	0
Terrell, Jim, Kannapolis	.984	8	58	5	1	64	5
Testa, Chris, South Georgia *	.988	41	314	25	4	343	33
Todd, Jeremy, Asheville	1.000	7	57	5	0	62	5
Tucker, Michael, Greensboro	1.000	7	41	2	0	43	2
Varela, Edgar, Kannapolis	1.000	17	95	7	0	102	2
Walsh, Sean, Lakewood	.000	1	0	0	0	0	0
Word, Robert, Greensboro *	.974	54	426	27	12	465	27
Yepez, Jose, Charleston-WV	1.000	2	8	2	0	10	0
Yepez, Marcos, Savannah	1.000	4	33	0	0	33	3
Yount, Dustin, Delmarva	.980	112	911	59	20	990	55
Zinsman, Zeph, Charl.-WV *	.984	106	856	76	15	947	91

SECOND BASEMEN

Player, Team	Pct.	G	PO	A	E	TC	DP
Alcala, Arian, Augusta	1.000	1	1	1	0	2	0
Alexander, Kevin, Hagerstown	1.000	3	5	10	0	15	1
Alvarez, Gera, Delmarva	.971	17	22	45	2	69	10
Amador, Chris, Kannapolis	1.000	2	4	5	0	9	1
Anderson, Scott, Asheville	.952	9	22	18	2	42	5
Arnold, Eric, Charleston-WV	1.000	8	10	19	0	29	3
Arroyo, William, Greensboro	.875	6	7	14	3	24	2
Asprilla, Avelino, Hickory	1.000	2	2	1	0	3	0
Bramasco, Omar, Lakewood	1.000	9	25	21	0	46	2
Brand, Kevin, Asheville	1.000	1	0	1	0	1	0
Castillo, Osmar, Augusta	1.000	20	33	50	0	83	15
Clute, Kris, Greensboro	.967	14	22	37	2	61	10
Colmenter, Jesus, Lake County	1.000	6	9	17	0	26	2
Conlisk, Jason, Savannah	.969	91	158	252	13	423	55
Conrad, Brooks, Lexington	.966	38	74	126	7	207	27
Curtis, Lee, Augusta	.941	47	81	94	11	186	17
Denker, Travis, South Georgia	.947	5	8	10	1	19	5
Donato, Greg, Rome	.000	1	0	0	0	0	0
Done, Mike, Delmarva	.971	43	67	99	5	171	11
Encarnacion, Henry, Savannah	.846	3	2	9	2	13	2
Freeman, Ashley, Asheville	.923	2	3	9	1	13	2
Galante, Matt, Capital City	.987	38	61	94	2	157	21
Garcia, Julio, Lake County	.941	4	9	7	1	17	3
Gonzalez, Patrick, Delmarva	1.000	3	4	5	0	9	1
Grasso, Mike, Rome	.952	26	40	59	5	104	10
Guance, Walkill, Asheville	.955	106	192	317	24	533	53
Harrison, Vince, Charleston-SC	.960	17	30	42	3	75	7
Hassey, Brad, Charleston-WV	.960	15	25	47	3	75	14
Hendricks, K.J., Asheville	.982	13	23	33	1	57	8
Hornostaj, Aaron, Hagerstown	.949	43	70	98	9	177	15
Hudnall, Joshua, Hickory	1.000	1	2	4	0	6	1
Hudson, William, Capital City	1.000	11	22	32	0	54	4
Isenhower, Jeremy, Lakewood	.960	71	125	161	12	298	36
Italiano, Nicholas, Lakewood	1.000	1	1	3	0	4	0
James, Willie, Rome	.968	15	23	38	2	63	9
Johnson, Elliot, Charleston-SC	.971	49	84	117	6	207	34
Kelly, Kevin, Hagerstown	.974	46	79	106	5	190	23
Kent, Bryan, Lake County	1.000	23	41	54	0	95	14
Knowlton, Jay, Hagerstown	1.000	1	1	6	0	7	2
LaBarbera, Anthony, Hagerstown	.974	8	12	26	1	39	6
Lebron, Freddie, Kannapolis	.947	14	23	31	3	57	8
Lopez, Pedro, Kannapolis	.974	92	171	211	10	392	19
Luna, Leonardo, Kannapolis	.974	14	35	40	2	77	6
Maniscalco, Matthew, Charl.-SC	.985	26	52	79	2	133	22
McMains, Derin, Hagerstown	1.000	23	38	59	0	97	7
Mercedes, Victor, Hickory	.971	125	278	329	18	625	78
Miranda, Miguel, Hagerstown	1.000	11	17	18	0	35	1
Molina, Gustavo, Kannapolis	.000	1	0	0	0	0	0
Newman, Ryan, Hickory	.954	16	27	35	3	65	6
Nulton, Kevin, Lakewood	.982	15	30	25	1	56	6
Ordorica, Eric, Greensboro	.979	22	33	60	2	95	10
Peavey, Pat, Lexington	.979	26	30	62	2	94	7
Pedrique, Franmig, Lexington	.000	1	0	0	0	0	0
Pierce, Sean, South Georgia	.000	1	0	0	0	0	0
Pinckney, Brandon, Lake County	.900	2	6	3	1	10	0
Randel, Kevin, Greensboro	.954	96	200	255	22	477	40
Riley, Ryan, Charleston-SC	.976	51	94	153	6	253	21
RIVERA, WILLIE, Charleston-WV	.984	112	222	317	9	548	85
Robinson, Levi, Delmarva	.957	85	127	203	15	345	30
Salvo, Andrew, Kan.-Capital City	.950	51	82	90	9	181	10
Sardinha, Duke, Asheville	.897	5	9	17	3	29	5
Schilling, Micah, Lake County	.948	109	159	275	24	458	44
Schuerholz, Jon, Rome	.975	103	170	264	11	445	45
Soto, T.J., Lexington	.956	75	132	192	15	339	35
St. Clair, Jason, Charleston-SC	.903	8	10	18	3	31	4
Stone, Greg, Augusta	.982	13	23	33	1	57	9
Sweeney, Tim, Savannah	.968	7	16	14	1	31	5
Tempesta, Nick, Lakewood	.965	24	34	49	3	86	12
Timmons, Wes, Rome	1.000	3	5	5	0	10	2
Tugwell, Marc, Lakewood	.991	26	48	58	1	107	14
Veracierto, Fernando, Augusta	.963	19	39	40	3	82	7
Wardinsky, Ryan, Lakewood	1.000	1	1	0	0	1	0
Wayne, Brett, South Georgia	.941	29	39	56	6	101	5
Welsch, Travis, Asheville	.974	7	16	22	1	39	6
West, Eric, Augusta	.955	44	87	124	10	221	23
Whealy, Blake, Capital City	.937	68	119	165	19	303	24
Yepez, Marcos, Savannah	.974	39	65	85	4	154	17
Young, Delwyn, South Georgia	.942	110	206	315	32	553	54

SECOND BASEMEN WITH TWO OR MORE TEAMS

Player, Team	Pct.	G	PO	A	E	TC	DP
Salvo, Andrew, Capital City	.934	29	54	60	8	122	9
Salvo, Andrew, Kannapolis	.983	22	28	30	1	59	1

THIRD BASEMEN

Player, Team	Pct.	G	PO	A	E	TC	DP
Alcala, Arian, Augusta	1.000	2	1	4	0	5	0
Alexander, Kevin, Hagerstown	.871	14	6	21	4	31	1
Alvarez, Gera, Delmarva	.866	26	14	44	9	67	4
Amador, Chris, Kannapolis	1.000	3	0	4	0	4	0
Arnold, Eric, Charleston-WV	.917	27	26	40	6	72	2
Arroyo, William, Greensboro	1.000	1	1	2	0	3	0
Asprilla, Avelino, Hickory	1.000	4	3	7	0	10	0
Baker, Jeffrey, Asheville	.902	61	43	104	16	163	6
Baldiris, Aaron, Capital City	.949	85	60	181	13	254	12
Barthel, Cole, Rome	.667	10	3	5	4	12	0
Barthelemy, Ryan, Lakewood	.000	1	0	0	0	0	0
Bass, Chris, Hickory	.945	68	50	106	9	165	11
Berroa, Cristian, Savannah	.000	1	0	0	0	0	0
Bonvechio, Brett, Augusta	.939	21	14	32	3	49	4
Bramasco, Omar, Lakewood	1.000	1	0	2	0	2	0
Brand, Kevin, Asheville	1.000	1	0	4	0	4	0
Buscher, Brian, Hagerstown	.964	53	30	104	5	139	9
Castillo, Osmar, Augusta	1.000	4	5	4	0	9	0
Christensen, Mike, Kannapolis	.957	49	34	98	6	138	3
Clute, Kris, Greensboro	.926	43	39	87	10	136	7

Player, Team	Pct.	G	PO	A	E	TC	DP
Collum, Mike, Hickory	1.000	4	3	7	0	10	1
Colmenter, Jesus, Lake County	.714	2	2	3	2	7	0
Curtis, Lee, Augusta	.857	8	5	13	3	21	1
De La Cruz, Miguel, Hickory	.853	50	29	99	22	150	16
Denker, Travis, South Georgia	1.000	2	1	2	0	3	0
Done, Mike, Delmarva	.873	27	17	45	9	71	6
Dragicevich, Scott, Charl.-WV	.958	92	62	167	10	239	17
Duncan, Trey, Charleston-SC	.854	28	27	43	12	82	6
Ellerson, Brian, Savannah	.908	55	29	79	11	119	3
Freeman, Ashley, Asheville	.922	42	38	81	10	129	7
Garcia, Travis, Capital City	.885	8	6	17	3	26	0
Gonzalez, Andy, Kannapolis	.000	1	0	0	0	0	0
Gonzalez, Patrick, Delmarva	.952	14	8	32	2	42	3
Grasso, Mike, Rome	.000	1	0	0	0	0	0
Guzman, Joel, South Georgia	1.000	1	1	3	0	4	0
Harrison, Vince, Charleston-SC	.936	113	81	226	21	328	21
Hassey, Brad, Charleston-WV	1.000	8	3	14	0	17	2
Hendricks, K.J., Asheville	.944	22	14	37	3	54	6
Holm, Steve, Hagerstown	1.000	10	7	7	0	14	1
Hudnall, Joshua, Hickory	1.000	1	0	1	0	1	0
James, Willie, Rome	.833	5	1	4	1	6	0
Jones, Terry, Lakewood	.944	123	82	188	16	286	15
Kelly, Kevin, Hagerstown	.878	34	21	51	10	82	3
Kent, Bryan, Lake County	.962	19	12	39	2	53	2
Knowlton, Jay, Hagerstown	1.000	1	0	3	0	3	0
Kochen, Ryan, Lexington	.912	81	43	155	19	217	21
Lackaff, John, Kannapolis	.954	18	14	48	3	65	3
Larkin, Shaun, Lake County	.924	120	55	200	21	276	7
Lebron, Freddie, Kannapolis	.000	1	0	0	0	0	0
Lopez, Pedro, Kannapolis	1.000	1	1	0	0	1	0
Luna, Leonardo, Kannapolis	1.000	2	1	2	0	3	0
Martin, Russell, South Georgia	.500	1	1	0	1	2	0
McMains, Derin, Hagerstown	.937	27	20	54	5	79	3
Merkle, Tom, Greensboro	.795	13	6	25	8	39	2
Mitchell, Lee, Greensboro	.958	23	19	49	3	71	5
Molina, Gustavo, Kannapolis	.000	1	0	0	0	0	0
Montague, Ed, South Georgia	.000	1	0	0	0	0	0
Newman, Ryan, Hickory	.957	18	12	33	2	47	3
Noboa, Joel, Savannah	.906	10	7	22	3	32	3
Norris, Shawn, Savannah	.950	64	40	113	8	161	11
Nulton, Kevin, Lakewood	1.000	6	5	7	0	12	1
Ordorica, Eric, Greensboro	.952	49	28	112	7	147	11
Peavey, Pat, Lexington	.925	59	31	130	13	174	12
Pellow, Kit, Asheville	.750	2	1	2	1	4	0
Perozo, Hector, South Georgia	.910	103	70	184	25	279	15
Pridie, Jason, Charleston-SC	.667	2	0	2	1	3	0
Rijo, Carlos, Delmarva	.897	79	46	120	19	185	2
Riley, Ryan, Charleston-SC	.800	3	0	8	2	10	1
Rodriguez, Edgar, Capital City	.915	50	28	112	13	153	8
Ruiz, Daniel, Rome	.792	14	5	14	5	24	0
Russell, Mike, Delmarva	.500	2	0	1	1	2	0
Salas, Jose, Charleston-WV	.846	6	4	7	2	13	0
Salvo, Andrew, Kan.-Capital City	.900	16	5	13	2	20	0
Schneider, John, Charl.-WV	1.000	1	1	1	0	2	0
Siriveaw, Nom, Charleston-WV	.750	4	3	6	3	12	0
Spann, Chad, Augusta	.937	102	79	174	17	270	21
Stone, Greg, Augusta	1.000	1	0	2	0	2	0
Street, Dan, Asheville	.833	3	5	5	2	12	2
Sweeney, Tim, Savannah	.950	8	4	15	1	20	2
Tempesta, Nick, Lakewood	1.000	7	2	17	0	19	3
Thede, Matt, Savannah	1.000	3	8	5	0	13	1
TIMMONS, WES, Rome	.960	121	88	152	10	250	13
Tucker, Michael, Greensboro	.960	11	5	19	1	25	1
Tugwell, Marc, Lakewood	1.000	1	0	3	0	3	1
Varela, Edgar, Kannapolis	.950	58	46	126	9	181	2
Veracierto, Fernando, Augusta	1.000	5	1	9	0	10	1
Walsh, Sean, Lakewood	1.000	3	0	3	0	3	0
Wayne, Brett, South Georgia	.910	32	14	57	7	78	7
Welsch, Travis, Asheville	.968	9	9	21	1	31	1
Yepez, Marcos, Savannah	.714	3	1	4	2	7	0

THIRD BASEMEN WITH TWO OR MORE TEAMS

Player, Team	Pct.	G	PO	A	E	TC	DP
Salvo, Andrew, Capital City	.000	1	0	0	0	0	0
Salvo, Andrew, Kannapolis	.900	15	5	13	2	20	0

SHORTSTOPS

Player, Team	Pct.	G	PO	A	E	TC	DP
Alexander, Kevin, Hagerstown	1.000	1	1	3	0	4	2
Alvarez, Gera, Delmarva	.956	44	48	103	7	158	17
Anderson, Scott, Asheville	.925	10	13	36	4	53	7
Andino, Robert, Greensboro	.945	119	164	315	28	507	49
Asprilla, Avelino, Hickory	.900	3	8	10	2	20	3
Bass, Bryan, Delmarva	.880	58	84	135	30	249	21
Bonilla, Clemente, Delmarva	1.000	1	2	1	0	3	0
Bramasco, Omar, Lakewood	.982	14	16	40	1	57	11
Castillo, Osmar, Augusta	1.000	1	0	1	0	1	1
Clanton, Ja'Mar, Savannah	.916	36	52	101	14	167	16
Collum, Mike, Hickory	1.000	2	0	1	0	1	0
Colmenter, Jesus, Lake County	.000	1	0	0	0	0	0
De La Cruz, Christopher, Lake Co.	.943	106	148	285	26	459	46
Delos Santos, Esteban, Lak.	.838	9	16	15	6	37	3
Fernando, Osvaldo, Lexington	.951	129	205	355	29	589	56
Garcia, Sergio, South Georgia	.923	48	69	135	17	221	25
Garcia, Travis, Capital City	.979	9	16	31	1	48	6
Gonzalez, Andy, Kannapolis	.935	121	236	307	38	581	37
Gonzalez, Patrick, Delmarva	1.000	5	8	14	0	22	3
Guzman, Joel, South Georgia	.928	57	75	170	19	264	27
Hassey, Brad, Charleston-WV	.971	69	125	207	10	342	40
Hendricks, K.J., Asheville	.975	55	77	153	6	236	28
HERNANDEZ, LUIS, Rome	.958	110	165	288	20	473	58
Herrera, Christian, S. Georgia	.944	17	25	43	4	72	6
Hornostaj, Aaron, Hagerstown	1.000	6	6	18	0	24	1
Hudnall, Joshua, Hickory	.867	5	6	7	2	15	1
Hudson, William, Capital City	.914	18	16	37	5	58	1
James, Willie, Rome	.947	4	8	10	1	19	2
Johnson, Elliot, Charleston-SC	.800	1	2	2	1	5	0
Jones, Terry, Lakewood	.000	1	0	0	0	0	0
Kent, Bryan, Lake County	.963	33	43	87	5	135	11
Knowlton, Jay, Hagerstown	1.000	1	1	1	0	2	0
Kochen, Ryan, Lexington	.897	10	18	34	6	58	5
LaBarbera, Anthony, Hagerstown	.963	6	6	20	1	27	4
Lee, Taber, Hickory	.939	115	121	308	28	457	44
Lopez, Pedro, Kannapolis	.955	16	22	42	3	67	4
Luna, Leonardo, Kannapolis	1.000	3	0	5	0	5	0
Maniscalco, Matthew, Charl.-SC	.975	36	51	103	4	158	24
Materano, Oscar, Asheville	.930	73	113	230	26	369	44
McDonald, John, Lake County	1.000	1	2	1	0	3	0
McMains, Derin, Hagerstown	1.000	4	3	10	0	13	2
Miranda, Miguel, Hagerstown	.955	4	10	11	1	22	1
Molina, Gustavo, Kannapolis	1.000	1	0	1	0	1	0
Newman, Ryan, Hickory	.959	15	13	34	2	49	8
Nulton, Kevin, Lakewood	.900	3	7	11	2	20	5
Ordorica, Eric, Greensboro	.955	18	26	37	3	66	6
Perozo, Hector, South Georgia	1.000	2	3	4	0	7	1
Pinckney, Brandon, Lake County	1.000	1	0	1	0	1	1
Ragsdale, Corey, Capital City	.946	104	134	336	27	497	38
Ramirez, Hanley, Augusta	.926	102	162	286	36	484	37
Rijo, Carlos, Delmarva	.950	33	40	75	6	121	7
Riley, Ryan, Charleston-SC	.962	10	22	29	2	53	3
Rivera, Willie, Charleston-WV	.706	4	6	6	5	17	1
Robinson, Levi, Delmarva	1.000	3	1	4	0	5	0
Rodriguez, Carlos, Lakewood	.929	92	116	252	28	396	39
Salvo, Andrew, Kan.-Capital City	.923	13	10	26	3	39	5
Santora, Jack, Lakewood	.952	17	32	27	3	62	6
Schuerholz, Jon, Rome	.972	30	48	58	3	109	14
Stone, Greg, Augusta	.935	14	16	42	4	62	5
Sweeney, Tim, Savannah	.944	4	6	11	1	18	2
Tablado, Raul, Charleston-WV	.950	61	113	190	16	319	51
Tempesta, Nick, Lakewood	1.000	9	12	17	0	29	4
Upton, B.J., Charleston-SC	.907	95	154	255	42	451	55
Veracierto, Fernando, Augusta	.600	4	1	5	4	10	1
Vizquel, Omar, Lake County	1.000	4	4	16	0	20	4
Wald, Jake, Hagerstown	.944	113	177	330	30	537	41
Wardinsky, Ryan, Lakewood	1.000	1	0	3	0	3	1
Wayne, Brett, South Georgia	.953	16	17	44	3	64	6
Webb, Trey, Savannah	.930	54	71	155	17	243	25
Welsch, Travis, Asheville	.957	4	7	15	1	23	2
West, Eric, Augusta	.910	20	32	39	7	78	9
Yepez, Marcos, Savannah	.970	48	74	152	7	233	33

SHORTSTOPS WITH TWO OR MORE TEAMS

Player, Team	Pct.	G	PO	A	E	TC	DP
Salvo, Andrew, Capital City	.917	12	8	25	3	36	5
Salvo, Andrew, Kannapolis	1.000	1	2	1	0	3	0

OUTFIELDERS

Player, Team	Pct.	G	PO	A	E	TC	DP
Acevedo, Freddy, Lexington	.951	110	201	11	11	223	1
Alexander, Kevin, Hagerstown	.971	21	29	4	1	34	1
Alvarez, Gera, Delmarva	1.000	13	17	0	0	17	0
Alvarez, Wilner, Lexington	.974	84	179	9	5	193	3
Aponte, Jose, Greensboro	.957	51	84	6	4	94	1
Bankston, Wes, Charleston-SC	.976	88	163	3	4	170	0
Bernadina, Rogearvin, Sav.*	.979	67	90	3	2	95	0
Bocchino, Anthony, Hickory *	1.000	2	2	1	0	3	0
Bok, Matt, South Georgia	.950	18	18	1	1	20	0
Bonner, Adam, Charleston-SC	.985	44	65	2	1	68	0

Player, Team	Pct.	G	PO	A	E	TC	DP
Borgo, Alex, Lakewood	.963	17	26	0	1	27	0
Bowman, Addison, Augusta	.973	45	70	3	2	75	0
Brewer, Anthony, Greensboro	.991	86	222	1	2	225	0
Brice, Thomas, Kannapolis *	.968	94	142	8	5	155	0
Brown, Dusty, Augusta	1.000	9	15	1	0	16	0
Brown, Tony, Savannah	.943	30	65	1	4	70	0
Bryan, Jason, Augusta	.913	11	21	0	2	23	0
Burrows, Angelo, Rome	1.000	20	33	5	0	38	2
Burrus, Josh, Rome	.938	15	14	1	1	16	0
Carter, Chris, Delmarva	.971	23	32	2	1	35	1
Cavin, Jonathan, Kan.-Sav.	.943	50	81	2	5	88	0
Cespedes, Robinson, Lexington	.965	84	159	8	6	173	0
Chavez, Ender, Capital City *	.961	33	43	6	2	51	0
Checksfield, Steven, Lexington	1.000	19	35	0	0	35	0
Chop, Chad, Savannah *	.984	80	118	4	2	124	0
Chourio, Junior, Charleston-WV	.941	11	16	0	1	17	0
Ciraco, Darren, Kannapolis	.945	94	143	11	9	163	0
Coffey, David, Augusta	.973	61	108	2	3	113	1
Cook, David, Kannapolis	.980	37	95	2	2	99	0
Cooper, Jason, Lake County *	.966	58	85	1	3	89	0
Cooper, Matt, Augusta	.952	36	59	1	3	63	0
Cortes, Jorge, Hickory *	.970	93	179	13	6	198	1
Davies, Gregg, Delmarva *	.987	42	71	6	1	78	0
Davis, Rajai, Hickory	.975	117	260	15	7	282	2
Diaz, Frank, Savannah	.980	119	218	21	5	244	2
Dion, Nate, Charleston-SC	.949	32	72	3	4	79	0
Donato, Greg, Rome	1.000	1	1	0	0	1	0
Dukes, Elijah, Charleston-SC	.966	110	190	7	7	204	1
Durbin, Chris, Augusta	.984	29	61	2	1	64	0
Ezi, Travis, South Georgia *	.966	118	304	9	11	324	3
Fagan, John, Lexington	.000	1	0	0	0	0	0
Fitzpatrick, Reggie, Savannah *	.967	109	260	3	9	272	0
Francisco, Ben, Lake County	.993	65	131	4	1	136	0
Francoeur, Jeff, Rome	.986	127	276	10	4	290	1
Freeman, Ashley, Asheville	1.000	4	7	0	0	7	0
Frome, Jason, Asheville *	.976	24	39	1	1	41	1
George, Trey, Asheville	1.000	22	38	2	0	40	1
Goelz, Bryan, South Georgia *	.985	106	186	11	3	200	1
Gomes, Joey, Charleston-SC	.938	7	15	0	1	16	0
Gonzalez, Bernie, Asheville	.967	120	227	7	8	242	1
Goss, Michael, Augusta *	.955	95	210	4	10	224	1
Guzman, Carlos, Rome	.975	56	76	3	2	81	1
Harris, Cory, Delmarva	.987	36	73	3	1	77	0
Harvey, Ryan, Capital City	.923	28	34	2	3	39	0
Hawkins, Dustin, Lexington *	.981	90	151	8	3	162	1
Hendricks, K.J., Asheville	.750	3	3	0	1	4	0
Hermida, Jeremy, Greensboro	.964	129	209	7	8	224	0
Hill, Jamar, Capital City	1.000	7	12	0	0	12	0
Hudnall, Joshua, Hickory	1.000	2	3	0	0	3	0
Isenhower, Jeremy, Lakewood	1.000	18	25	0	0	25	0
Ivy, Bjorn, Kannapolis	.981	37	50	3	1	54	0
Jansen, Ardley, Rome	.975	95	151	7	4	162	2
Jernigan, Karl, Hagerstown	.966	65	111	3	4	118	0
Jiannetti, Joe, Capital City	.974	22	34	4	1	39	0
Johnson, Elliot, Charleston-SC	.000	1	0	0	0	0	0
Johnson, Eric, Lake County	.981	32	49	3	1	53	0
Johnston, Clint, Charl.-WV *	.943	19	30	3	2	35	1
Joseph, Onil, Rome	.971	116	225	12	7	244	1
Jova, Maikel, Charleston-WV	1.000	53	82	4	0	86	0
Joyce, Tom, Delmarva *	1.000	40	64	1	0	65	1
Kingsbury, Bobby, Hickory *	.982	97	209	6	4	219	2
Knicely, Jeremy, Charleston-WV	.000	1	0	0	0	0	0
Knowlton, Jay, Hagerstown	1.000	5	2	1	0	3	0
Lawson, Forrest, Capital City	1.000	33	45	2	0	47	1
Lewis, Fred, Hagerstown	.986	111	206	5	3	214	1
Likely, Cameron, Lexington	.986	39	69	2	1	72	1
Littleton, Brandon, Delmarva *	1.000	30	51	2	0	53	1
Louisa, Lorvin, Savannah	1.000	10	20	2	0	22	1
Lytle, Chaz, Hickory *	.992	69	120	3	1	124	0
Majewski, Val, Delmarva *	.980	56	98	2	2	102	0
Malek, Bobby, Capital City	.974	25	33	4	1	38	0
Marshall, Andre, Lakewood	.972	95	198	10	6	214	2
Martin, Russell, South Georgia	1.000	2	0	1	0	1	0
McCurdy, Joshua, Delmarva	1.000	7	9	1	0	10	0
McRoberts, Mark, Lakewood	.950	81	132	2	7	141	0
Meath, Matt, Hickory	.952	35	59	1	3	63	0
Medina, Rodney, Charleston-WV	.935	119	193	9	14	216	1
Molina, Gustavo, Kannapolis	1.000	1	2	0	0	2	0
Montague, Ed, South Georgia	.930	91	140	7	11	158	4
Negron, Miguel, Charl.-WV *	1.000	27	47	3	0	50	0
Nikolic, Adam, Charleston-SC *	1.000	8	7	0	0	7	0
Nixon, Mike, South Georgia	1.000	8	2	0	0	2	0
Noboa, Joel, Savannah	.000	1	0	0	0	0	0
Nonemaker, Karl, Lakewood *	.989	43	82	4	1	87	0
O'Sullivan, Patrick, Delmarva	1.000	4	8	1	0	9	0
Oliva, Chad, Lakewood	.960	26	46	2	2	50	0
Ordorica, Eric, Greensboro	.800	4	3	1	1	5	0
Ortiz, Juan, Greensboro	1.000	8	9	0	0	9	0
Panther, Nathan, Lake County *	.973	96	173	9	5	187	0
Parker, Rashad, Capital City	1.000	17	40	0	0	40	0
Paulk, Barry, Capital City	1.000	2	2	0	0	2	0
Perry, Rod, Lakewood	.903	20	25	3	3	31	0
Pierce, Sean, South Georgia	.974	29	33	4	1	38	0
Pridie, Jason, Charleston-SC	.987	122	305	10	4	319	2
Randel, Kevin, Greensboro	1.000	1	1	0	0	1	0
Reames, Joe Don, Charl.-SC	1.000	12	13	1	0	14	0
Resop, Chris, Greensboro	.933	21	27	1	2	30	0
Reyes, Julio, Kannapolis	1.000	7	7	0	0	7	0
Rico, Erik, Charleston-WV *	.959	48	67	4	3	74	0
Rico, Matt, Charleston-SC	.917	8	11	0	1	12	0
Rivas, Arturo, Delmarva	.970	44	92	4	3	99	0
Roberson, Chris, Lakewood	.980	132	323	20	7	350	3
Rodriguez, Edgar, Capital City	.667	7	3	1	2	6	0
Rodriguez, Robert, Savannah	.000	1	0	0	0	0	0
ROHLEDER, ANDY, Greensboro	.991	124	222	2	2	226	1
Rojas, Ricardo, Lake County	.971	94	192	6	6	204	1
Roy, Angus, Augusta	.000	1	0	0	0	0	0
Ruiz, Randy, Delmarva	1.000	4	1	0	0	1	0
Russell, Mike, Delmarva	.000	1	0	0	1	1	0
Salazar, Jeff, Asheville *	.987	126	292	21	4	317	4
Salvo, Andrew, Kannapolis	.000	1	0	0	0	0	0
Santiago, Rudy, Asheville	1.000	4	7	1	0	8	0
Sardinha, Duke, Asheville	1.000	2	2	0	0	2	0
Sherrill, J.J., Lake County	.971	37	67	0	2	69	0
Siriveaw, Nom, Charleston-WV	1.000	4	6	0	0	6	0
Slack, Jonathan, Capital City *	1.000	67	93	9	0	102	1
Smallwood, Erik, Delmarva	1.000	5	5	0	0	5	0
Smith, David, Charleston-WV	.963	86	153	4	6	163	1
Sosa, Carlos, Hagerstown *	.965	100	159	5	6	170	0
Soto, Jose, Augusta	.960	47	93	4	4	101	1
Spilborghs, Ryan, Asheville	.982	116	211	12	4	227	1
Stephenson, Neal, Delmarva	.989	118	179	7	2	188	2
Stone, Greg, Augusta	.993	70	143	3	1	147	2
Street, Dan, Asheville	1.000	1	3	0	0	3	0
Sultemeier, Eric, Delmarva	1.000	7	10	1	0	11	0
Terrell, Jim, Kannapolis	.906	13	29	0	3	32	0
Testa, Chris, South Georgia *	.955	56	80	5	4	89	0
Timmons, Wes, Rome	1.000	1	1	0	0	1	0
Toner, John, Capital City	1.000	20	39	2	0	41	0
Turay, Alhaji, Capital City	.957	65	104	8	5	117	0
Van Every, Jon, Lake County *	.964	41	53	1	2	56	0
Veracierto, Fernando, Augusta	.950	30	36	2	2	40	0
Wald, Jake, Hagerstown	.000	1	0	0	0	0	0
Walsh, Sean, Lakewood	1.000	2	2	2	0	4	0
Walter, Randy, Hagerstown	.981	117	200	8	4	212	2
Watts, Derran, Capital City	.969	106	147	9	5	161	0
Waugh, Jason, Charleston-WV	.985	35	63	4	1	68	0
Wayne, Brett, South Georgia	1.000	10	8	0	0	8	0
Webster, Anthony, Kannapolis	.984	91	185	3	3	191	0
Young, Eddie, Kannapolis	.971	19	34	0	1	35	0

OUTFIELDERS WITH TWO OR MORE TEAMS

Player, Team	Pct.	G	PO	A	E	TC	DP
Cavin, Jonathan, Savannah	.957	10	20	2	1	23	0
Cavin, Jonathan, Kannapolis	.938	40	61	0	4	65	0

CATCHERS

Player, Team	Pct.	G	PO	A	E	TC	DP	PB
Acevas, Jon, Kannapolis	.991	15	89	17	1	107	1	3
Anderson, Jimmy, Capital City	.973	34	208	11	6	225	0	6
Arko, Tommy, Delmarva	.987	46	402	39	6	447	0	6
Arlis, Patrick, Greensboro	.987	74	486	57	7	550	3	10
Barnett, Dan, Kannapolis	.994	22	139	19	1	159	0	10
Bastardo, Angel, Lake County	1.000	2	6	0	0	6	0	2
Bernard, Miguel, Rome	.976	34	216	32	6	254	1	8
Bibee, Hal, Asheville	1.000	26	190	18	0	208	2	6
Bok, Matt, South Georgia	1.000	1	2	0	0	2	0	0
Bowman, Addison, Augusta	.973	41	258	35	8	301	1	3
Brown, Dusty, Augusta	.972	66	351	64	12	427	3	20
Buller, Dayton, Hagerstown	.977	11	76	9	2	87	0	4
Bushey, Andrew, Asheville	1.000	3	12	2	0	14	0	1
Chapman, Travis, Hickory	.990	64	431	46	5	482	4	8
Clements, Zachary, Capital City	.991	47	285	29	3	317	2	7
Clendenin, Morgan, Delmarva	.948	11	60	13	4	77	0	1
Colina, Alvin, Asheville	.987	70	483	64	7	554	4	10
Cordell, Brent, Charleston-SC	.989	44	241	34	3	278	3	6
Corrente, David, Charl.-WV	.977	67	450	59	12	521	4	14
Davidson, Kevin, Lexington	1.000	1	9	0	0	9	0	1
Deck, Ronnie, Charleston-SC	.985	14	60	6	1	67	0	3
Devarez, Noel, Capital City	1.000	1	5	1	0	6	0	0

Player, Team	Pct.	G	PO	A	E	TC	DP	PB
Durazo, William, Augusta	.985	19	116	14	2	132	0	2
Ellis, Andrew, South Georgia	.929	2	12	1	1	14	1	0
Emmerick, Josh, Savannah	.978	39	236	32	6	274	1	8
Gentry, Garett, Asheville	1.000	13	82	6	0	88	0	1
Gradoville, Tim, Lakewood	.992	61	424	43	4	471	5	13
Grzecka, Casey, Greensboro	.974	19	135	17	4	156	0	2
Hernandez, Jose, Hickory	.993	61	390	48	3	441	3	9
Herrera, Javier, Lake County	.983	44	323	25	6	354	1	7
Hickman, Brian, Kannapolis	1.000	8	40	5	0	45	0	1
Holm, Steve, Hagerstown	.991	39	281	32	3	316	1	2
Hubele, Ryan, Delmarva	.986	43	331	23	5	359	0	9
Hudson, William, Capital City	1.000	1	0	1	0	1	0	0
Knicely, Jeremy, Charl.-WV	1.000	4	17	0	0	17	0	0
Kratz, Erik, Charleston-WV	1.000	3	15	1	0	16	0	1
Lisk, Charlie, Kannapolis	.976	31	257	22	7	286	0	21
Lynam, Guy, Greensboro	1.000	3	20	1	0	21	0	1
Manriquez, Salomon, Savannah	.990	27	166	26	2	194	1	3
Margalski, Ben, Savannah	.979	25	175	16	4	195	1	6
Martin, Kyle, Delmarva	.960	13	93	3	4	100	0	5
Martin, Russell, South Georgia	.964	14	101	7	4	112	0	4
Martinez, Casey, Lakewood	.986	31	199	18	3	220	1	10
McCann, Brian, Rome	.995	64	529	47	3	579	5	10
McCullough, Clayton, Lake Co.	.991	42	279	37	3	319	1	5
McRoberts, Mark, Lakewood	1.000	9	44	4	0	48	0	3
Melendez, German, Lexington	.988	58	435	51	6	492	6	19
Merritt, Graig, Charleston-SC	.985	23	172	20	3	195	2	7
Mills, Rock, Asheville	1.000	13	80	9	0	89	0	0
Molina, Angel, Greensboro	.989	48	318	29	4	351	0	12
Molina, Gustavo, Kannapolis	.983	71	465	55	9	529	1	17
Munhall, Brian, Hagerstown	.978	88	724	69	18	811	2	10
Myers, Kenton, Augusta	.979	21	125	12	3	140	2	1
Nino, Denny, Hickory	1.000	1	9	0	0	9	0	1
Nixon, Mike, South Georgia	.994	89	607	49	4	660	4	14
Nixon, Mike, South Georgia	.994	89	607	49	4	660	4	14
OBRADOVICH, MARK, Lex.	.994	84	593	61	4	658	2	27
Owen, Ryan, South Georgia	.994	23	139	15	1	155	0	6
Pena, Rodolfo, Hickory	1.000	3	19	0	0	19	0	0
Ramos, Kelly, Delmarva	.986	22	189	19	3	211	0	4
Reyes, Julio, Kannapolis	1.000	1	1	0	0	1	0	0
Reyes, Milver, Hickory	.977	11	77	8	2	87	0	1
Riggans, Shawn, Charl.-SC	.988	55	294	35	4	333	4	9
Roat, Kyle, Rome	.982	27	155	12	3	170	2	5
Robinson-Pierce, Whit, Del.	.981	10	97	6	2	105	0	1
Rodriguez, Robert, Savannah	.978	22	121	14	3	138	0	2
Rogers, Brandon, S. Georgia	.974	12	68	8	2	78	1	3
Ruelas, Alonzo, Rome	1.000	32	229	20	0	249	2	1
Sato, G.G., Lakewood	.982	49	276	49	6	331	1	19
Schneider, John, Charl.-WV	.989	51	409	29	5	443	0	6
Serrano, Ray, Charleston-SC	1.000	12	83	4	0	87	1	1
St. Martine, Michael, Savannah	.975	28	185	13	5	203	0	7
Sweeney, James, Asheville	.973	21	133	12	4	149	2	6
Thede, Matt, Savannah	1.000	2	10	3	0	13	0	0
Wallace, David, Lake County	.998	60	486	46	1	533	1	18
Wilson, Brandon, Capital City	.982	70	596	51	12	659	1	10
Yepez, Jose, Charleston-WV	.988	12	77	8	1	86	0	0

PITCHERS

Player, Team	Pct.	G	PO	A	E	TC	DP
Acosta, Anthony, Capital City	.833	32	5	10	3	18	1
Akens, Phil, Greensboro	1.000	16	8	7	0	15	0
Albaladejo, Jonathan, Hickory	.889	29	4	12	2	18	1
Allen, Blake, Lake County *	.889	36	2	22	3	27	0
Allen, Brian, Charleston-SC	1.000	50	4	13	0	17	0
Almeida, Brian, Rome	.000	6	0	0	0	0	0
Alvarez, Gabriel, South Georgia	.500	8	1	0	1	2	0
Alvarez, Gera, Delmarva	.000	1	0	0	0	0	0
Anez, Omar, Capital City	.912	26	12	19	3	34	2
Arellan, Felix, Kannapolis *	.933	31	3	11	1	15	1
Arteaga, Francisco, Rome	1.000	4	1	0	0	1	0
Asahina, Jonathan, Greensboro	.500	5	1	1	2	4	0
Autrey, Scott, Charleston-SC	1.000	14	7	12	0	19	0
Baisley, Brad, Lakewood	1.000	6	0	3	0	3	0
Barlow, Chris, Savannah	.906	29	14	15	3	32	1
Barrios, Angel, Lexington	1.000	3	1	2	0	3	0
Bartlett, Richard, Delmarva	.900	12	2	7	1	10	0
Bartz, Jason, Charleston-SC	.750	13	3	3	2	8	0
Bayer, Russ, Hickory *	1.000	3	0	1	0	1	0
Bazardo, Yorman, Greensboro	.958	21	17	29	2	48	3
Beckstead, Jentry, Asheville	.923	63	4	8	1	13	0
Beigh, David, Hickory	1.000	14	4	3	0	7	1
Belizario, Ronald, Greensboro	.625	10	4	1	3	8	0
Bere, Jason, Lake County	.000	1	0	0	0	0	0
Bergmann, Jason, Savannah	.667	23	4	8	6	18	0
Berry, Jon, Hickory	.667	22	0	2	1	3	0
Bittner, Tim, Kannapolis *	.917	10	1	10	1	12	0
Blalock, Casey, Greensboro	.833	56	3	12	3	18	0
Blaney, Matt, Augusta	1.000	16	2	7	0	9	0
Bostick, Adam, Greensboro *	1.000	7	0	5	0	5	1
Bourgeois, Nick, Lakewood *	.909	26	7	13	2	22	0
Bowen, Chad, Capital City	1.000	13	0	1	0	1	0
Boyer, Blaine, Rome	.967	30	11	18	1	30	0
Brice, Thomas, Kannapolis *	.000	1	0	0	0	0	0
Broxton, Jonathan, S. Georgia	1.000	9	1	5	0	6	0
Bulger, Brian, Charleston-SC	.854	25	21	14	6	41	1
Bullington, Bryan, Hickory	1.000	8	3	5	0	8	1
Butto, Francisco, Lakewood	.884	27	10	28	5	43	1
Cabrera, Daniel, Delmarva	.933	26	7	7	1	15	1
Cabrera, Yunior, Capital City *	.900	18	0	18	2	20	0
Cain, Matthew, Hagerstown	1.000	14	1	4	0	5	0
Campbell, Dayle, South Georgia	1.000	21	2	4	0	6	2
Capellan, Jose, Rome	.889	14	0	8	1	9	1
Carlson, Jesse, Lexington *	1.000	53	6	9	0	15	1
Carmona, Fausto, Lake County	.981	24	11	42	1	54	2
Cartier, Richard, Asheville	.939	30	15	16	2	33	0
Casey, Reid, Lake County	1.000	7	0	2	0	2	0
Castillo, Osmar, Augusta	.000	1	0	0	0	0	0
Castro, Fabio, Kannapolis *	1.000	2	0	1	0	1	0
Castro, Julio, Kannapolis	1.000	14	1	3	0	4	0
Cedeno, Blas, Hickory	1.000	4	0	2	0	2	0
Cedeno, Juan, Augusta *	.929	23	3	10	1	14	0
Cerrato, Justin, Lakewood	.333	9	0	1	2	3	1
Clarke, Darren, Asheville	1.000	27	7	27	0	34	1
Clelland, James, Augusta	.000	2	0	0	0	0	0
Comolli, Mark, Charleston-WV	.875	26	3	4	1	8	0
Cooney, Jim, Delmarva *	1.000	6	0	2	0	2	0
Coppinger, Joe, Delmarva	1.000	13	3	2	0	5	0
Costello, Ryan, Charleston-WV *	1.000	45	1	11	0	12	0
Cozier, Vance, Hagerstown	1.000	4	1	5	0	6	2
Cram, Josh, Hagerstown	1.000	13	2	5	0	7	0
Crockett, Ben, Asheville	.912	23	8	23	3	34	1
Cromer, Jason, Charleston-SC *	.917	21	10	34	4	48	2
Cromer, Nathan, Charl.-SC *	.857	43	5	7	2	14	0
Cuen, David, South Georgia *	1.000	9	3	4	0	7	0
Dannemiller, Beau, Asheville	.875	42	0	14	2	16	1
David, Brad, Rome *	.750	28	2	1	1	4	0
Davies, Kyle, Rome	.955	27	4	17	1	22	1
Davies, Michael, Asheville *	.867	10	2	11	2	15	0
Davila, Marcus, Hickory	.950	36	5	14	1	20	0
Davis, Brendon, Lexington	1.000	10	4	0	0	4	1
De La Cruz, Carlos, Lake County	1.000	32	3	12	0	15	0
De Leon, Juan, Lexington	.923	26	6	6	1	13	0
De Los Santos, Omar, S. Ga.	.900	22	3	6	1	10	2
DeBarr, Nick, Charleston-SC	.893	27	5	20	3	28	1
DeChristofaro, Vinny, Lak.*	.750	6	1	2	1	4	0
DeLeon, Maikel, Capital City	1.000	2	1	1	0	2	0
Deaton, Kevin, Capital City	.962	26	8	17	1	26	1
Deck, Ronnie, Charleston-SC	.000	2	0	0	0	0	0
Deininger, Todd, Kannapolis	.931	32	13	14	2	29	0
Delossantos, Carlos, Hickory	.778	24	5	2	2	9	1
Demontel, Jimmy, Greensboro	.889	31	1	7	1	9	0
Denham, Dan, Lake County	.765	14	4	9	4	17	0
Dennison, Michael, Augusta	.667	18	0	2	1	3	0
Devarez, Noel, Capital City	1.000	6	1	1	0	2	1
Diaz, Eddie, Savannah	1.000	7	0	1	0	1	0
Diaz, Jose, South Georgia	1.000	5	1	0	0	1	0
Dischiavo, John, Charleston-SC	.000	4	0	0	0	0	0
Dittler, Jake, Lake County	.909	17	6	14	2	22	0
Done, Mike, Delmarva	.000	1	0	0	0	0	0
Dooley, Jason, Asheville	.500	11	0	2	2	4	0
Douglas, Shea, Lake County *	1.000	34	8	14	0	22	0
Doyne, Cory, Lexington	.933	9	3	11	1	15	0
Duke, Zach, Hickory *	.921	26	7	28	3	38	1
Dunkle, Peter, Asheville	1.000	4	1	0	0	1	0
Eazor, Kyle, Greensboro *	.667	9	1	3	2	6	0
Eisentrager, Dan, Lake County	.968	32	11	19	1	31	0
Ellis, Rob, Charleston-SC *	1.000	8	3	2	0	5	1
Esarey, Brad, Charleston-WV *	1.000	31	2	3	0	5	0
Escobar, Rodrigo, Lexington	.923	25	6	6	1	13	2
Esposito, Brian, Augusta	1.000	13	1	6	0	7	1
Esquivia, Manuel, Greensboro	.824	42	7	7	3	17	0
Everts, Clint, Savannah	1.000	5	0	4	0	4	0
Ewin, Ryan, Rome	.889	16	3	5	1	9	1
Farren, Dave, Delmarva	.000	7	0	0	0	0	0
Fiedler, Erik, Savannah	1.000	35	3	10	0	13	0
Figueroa, Jonathan, S. Georgia *	.846	17	2	9	2	13	0
Florian, Frailyn, Greensboro *	.500	14	2	1	3	6	0
Freeman, Daniel, Lexington	.889	44	1	7	1	9	0
Friske, Parker, Augusta *	1.000	14	1	4	0	5	0
Fryson, Andrew, Kannapolis	.636	21	0	7	4	11	0
Fulchino, Jeff, Greensboro	1.000	5	1	2	0	3	0

Player, Team	Pct.	G	PO	A	E	TC	DP
Fuller, Brendan, Charleston-WV..	1.000	41	2	9	0	11	1
Gallagher, Buddy, Asheville *	1.000	11	0	2	0	2	0
Galvez, Willy, Augusta	1.000	13	1	2	0	3	0
Garber, Mike, Augusta *	.727	35	2	6	3	11	0
Garcia, Anderson, Capital City	.000	5	0	0	1	1	0
Garza, Rolando, Kannapolis	1.000	21	0	6	0	6	0
Generelli, Daniel, Augusta	.750	17	0	3	1	4	0
Girdley, Josh, Savannah *	.941	12	6	10	1	17	1
Gonzalez, Luis, South Georgia*	.833	19	1	4	1	6	0
Gravelle, Nick, Hickory *	.950	26	7	31	2	40	0
Greusel, Evan, Greensboro	.800	12	1	3	1	5	0
Griffin, Daniel, Greensboro	.900	36	5	4	1	10	0
Grigsby, Derick, Lexington	1.000	12	1	4	0	5	0
Guerrero, Julio, Hickory	.857	18	3	9	2	14	0
Guzman, Juan, Delmarva	.929	31	4	9	1	14	0
Gwaltney, Lee, Lakewood	.938	22	5	25	2	32	0
Habel, Josh, Hagerstown *	.875	37	3	11	2	16	0
Hamels, Cole, Lakewood *	.889	13	5	11	2	18	2
Hamilton, Jamaal, S. Georgia *	.944	14	4	13	1	18	0
Hamilton, Mark, Lexington *	1.000	4	1	2	0	3	0
Hammel, Jason, Charleston-SC	.833	14	7	13	4	24	0
Hammes, Zach, South Georgia	.900	25	6	12	2	20	1
Hansack, Devern, Lexington	.842	22	3	13	3	19	0
Hanson, D.J., Charleston-WV	.947	25	19	17	2	38	4
Hart, Alex, Hickory	.933	15	3	11	1	15	0
Hawley, Ross, South Georgia	.000	3	0	0	0	0	0
Heitzman, Aaron, Lexington *	.917	28	13	31	4	48	3
Henderson, Brian, Charl.-SC *	1.000	24	1	6	0	7	0
Hennessey, Brad, Hagerstown	1.000	15	5	9	0	14	1
Henry, Paul, Delmarva	1.000	42	4	12	0	16	0
Hensley, Clay, Hagerstown	.913	12	4	17	2	23	3
Hertzler, Barry, Augusta	1.000	8	1	2	0	3	0
Hinckley, Michael, Savannah *	.935	23	5	24	2	31	2
Hines, Carlos, Charleston-SC	1.000	30	6	5	0	11	0
Hiraldo, Nelson, Lake County	1.000	3	2	0	0	2	0
Hodges, Daniel, Lakewood *	1.000	14	0	2	0	2	0
Holdzkom, Lincoln, Greensboro	.813	43	1	12	3	16	0
Hosford, Clint, South Georgia	1.000	4	2	1	0	3	0
Houston, Ryan, Charleston-WV	1.000	13	2	0	0	2	0
Huang, Kevin, Augusta	.929	22	4	9	1	14	0
Hudson, Jeremy, Kannapolis	.000	1	0	0	0	0	0
Hummel, Rick, Kannapolis	1.000	27	2	10	0	12	0
Jarvis, Andrew, Lakewood *	.000	1	0	0	0	0	0
Jimenez, Ubaldo, Asheville	.926	27	9	16	2	27	1
Johnson, Blair, Hickory	1.000	2	0	2	0	2	0
Johnson, Doug, Asheville	.967	29	9	20	1	30	0
Johnson, Josh, Greensboro	.938	17	7	8	1	16	1
Johnston, Rikki, Asheville *	.889	29	6	10	2	18	0
Jones, Chris, Asheville *	1.000	16	0	3	0	3	0
Jung, Sung, Rome	.923	53	2	10	1	13	0
Kazmir, Scott, Capital City *	.900	18	3	15	2	20	0
Keefer, Ryan, Delmarva	.979	26	15	31	1	47	1
Keirstead, Mike, Hickory	.913	13	8	13	2	23	1
Kennedy, Casey, South Georgia	.947	23	8	10	1	19	1
Kensing, Logan, Greensboro	1.000	4	0	3	0	3	0
Kentner, Brandon, Capital City	1.000	9	1	1	0	2	0
King, Bryan, Capital City	1.000	23	1	3	0	4	0
Knapp, Ben, Delmarva	1.000	15	3	10	0	13	0
Krause, Lukas, Capital City *	1.000	10	2	2	0	4	0
Kumagai, Ryo, Augusta	.667	20	0	2	1	3	1
LaMura, B.J., Kannapolis	.906	24	5	24	3	32	2
LaSalle, Julio, South Georgia	.778	34	1	6	2	9	1
Lara, Juan, Lake County *	1.000	16	1	11	0	12	1
Larson, Adam, Kannapolis	1.000	39	4	12	0	16	0
Lawson, Jarrod, Lakewood	.000	12	0	0	1	1	0
League, Brandon, Charl.-WV	1.000	12	8	16	0	24	3
Lerew, Anthony, Rome	.886	25	13	18	4	35	1
Lester, Jonathan, Augusta *	1.000	24	4	14	0	18	0
Lindstrom, Matthew, Capital City	.760	12	2	17	6	25	0
Lissir, Alexander, Hickory	1.000	18	1	4	0	5	0
Long, Nick, Savannah	1.000	15	3	7	0	10	1
Lopez, Aleurys, Charleston-SC	1.000	8	3	1	0	4	0
Lopez, Arturo, South Georgia	1.000	20	5	8	0	13	0
Lubisich, Nik, Kannapolis *	1.000	16	3	6	0	9	1
Lundgren, Wayne, Augusta	1.000	3	1	2	0	3	0
Mabry, Barry, Rome	1.000	14	3	1	0	4	0
MacLane, Thomas, Augusta *	.667	21	0	2	1	3	0
Maine, John, Delmarva	.917	14	4	7	1	12	0
Makowsky, Carl, Delmarva	1.000	22	2	9	0	11	0
Malone, Corwin, Kannapolis *	1.000	5	0	3	0	3	0
Marceau, Pierre-Luc, Sav.*	.905	36	6	13	2	21	2
Marchbanks, David, Green.*	1.000	3	1	2	0	3	1
Martin, Greg, Savannah *	1.000	20	1	3	0	4	0
Martin, Kevin, Lake County	1.000	28	0	9	0	9	0
Martinez, Carlos, Greensboro	.000	15	0	0	0	0	0
Martinez, Roberto, Savannah	1.000	17	0	2	0	2	0
Martinez, Samuel, Savannah	.800	12	1	11	3	15	0
Maruffi, Joseph, Savannah	.000	4	0	0	0	0	0
Mateo, Aneudis, Augusta	.875	13	2	5	1	8	0
McCally, Ryan, Charleston-SC	.000	2	0	0	0	0	0
McCracken, Vance, S. Georgia	1.000	21	3	4	0	7	0
McCurdy, Nick, Delmarva	1.000	6	4	4	0	8	0
McLemore, Mark, Lexington *	.900	36	3	15	2	20	1
McNab, Tim, Capital City	.933	43	9	19	2	30	1
Mendoza, Luis, Augusta	.944	13	1	16	1	18	0
Menocal, Victor, Lakewood	.900	22	8	10	2	20	0
Merricks, Matt, Rome *	.750	14	2	10	4	16	0
Meyer, Dan, Rome *	.947	15	4	14	1	19	1
Meyer, Todd, Savannah	1.000	25	7	10	0	17	1
Mildren, Paul, Greensboro *	.889	27	4	12	2	18	0
Miller, Brian, Kannapolis	1.000	25	8	14	0	22	0
Minor, Zach, Lakewood	.917	25	6	5	1	12	0
Mitchell, Jay, Asheville	.500	2	0	1	1	2	0
Mitchell, Tom, Savannah	1.000	19	2	2	0	4	1
Montague, Ed, South Georgia	.000	1	0	0	0	0	0
Montani, Jeff, Delmarva	.960	58	7	17	1	25	0
Montano, Ignacio, Lake Co.*	1.000	21	0	9	0	9	0
Mora, Ramon, Charleston-WV	.955	36	8	13	1	22	1
Morla, Carlos, Augusta *	1.000	28	2	2	0	4	0
Morris, Cory, Delmarva	.893	19	9	16	3	28	0
Mueller, Mike, Rome	.600	24	0	3	2	5	0
Munter, Scott, Hagerstown	.870	40	3	17	3	23	0
Murray, Brad, Kannapolis *	.833	11	1	4	1	6	0
Navaroli, Michael, Charleston-SC	.600	21	1	2	2	5	0
Nelson, Steve, South Georgia	.923	22	7	17	2	26	1
Neuage, Leigh, South Georgia	.833	9	1	4	1	6	0
Nickerson, Jon-Michael, Green.*	1.000	1	1	1	0	2	0
Nieve, Fernando, Lexington	.909	28	9	11	2	22	1
Nin, Sandy, Charleston-WV	.962	23	11	14	1	26	0
Nunez, Leo, Hickory	.923	13	4	8	1	13	0
O'Brien, Patrick, Hickory	.941	12	4	12	1	17	0
O'Connor, Michael, Savannah *	1.000	42	2	4	0	6	0
Ochoa, Javier, Capital City	1.000	14	1	2	0	3	0
Olsen, Scott, Greensboro *	.944	25	3	14	1	18	1
Olson, Ryan, Capital City *	1.000	36	1	7	0	8	0
Ontiveros, Jeff, Augusta	.000	1	0	0	0	0	0
Owens, Henry, Hickory	1.000	22	0	4	0	4	1
Ozuna, Francisco, Charl.-WV *	.889	5	3	5	1	9	1
Pahucki, David, Augusta	1.000	5	0	4	0	4	0
Palmer, Matt, Hagerstown	1.000	44	4	12	0	16	0
Patitucci, Mike, Delmarva *	.500	2	0	1	1	2	0
Paulk, Robert, Capital City	.667	18	1	3	2	6	0
Peeples, Ross, Capital City *	.917	11	3	8	1	12	0
Peguero, Jailen, Lexington	.941	31	17	15	2	34	2
Pennington, Todd, Lake County	1.000	36	1	5	0	6	0
Peralta, Efigenio, Rome	.750	20	1	5	2	8	0
Perez, Armando, Kannapolis *	1.000	34	1	19	0	20	0
Perez, Randy, Lake County *	1.000	5	2	8	0	10	1
Perkins, Vince, Charleston-WV	1.000	8	1	6	0	7	0
Peterson, Adam, Charleston-WV	.923	10	2	10	1	13	0
Phillips, Mike, Kannapolis *	1.000	3	1	2	0	3	0
Pinango, Miguel, Capital City	.895	24	12	22	4	38	1
Plummer, Jarod, South Georgia	.800	9	1	3	1	5	0
Portorreal, Daniel, Hagerstown	.500	6	1	0	1	2	0
Prahm, Ryan, Lake County	1.000	5	1	1	0	2	0
Priola, John, Augusta	1.000	5	2	2	0	4	0
Prochaska, Mike, Charl.-SC *	1.000	29	7	23	0	30	1
Ramirez, Ismael, Charleston-WV	1.000	24	7	13	0	20	1
RAMSEY, KEITH, Lake County *	1.000	24	8	35	0	43	3
Ransom, Troy, Hagerstown	1.000	29	7	13	0	20	0
Rasner, Darrell, Savannah	1.000	22	7	19	0	26	1
Read, Robby, Lakewood	.750	33	3	3	2	8	0
Reba, Steve, Asheville	1.000	47	6	14	0	20	1
Reina, Dimas, South Georgia	1.000	23	2	5	0	7	0
Rengel, Orlando, Capital City	.000	1	0	0	0	0	0
Resop, Chris, Greensboro	.667	11	1	1	1	3	0
Reynolds, Eric, Greensboro *	.000	3	0	0	0	0	0
Reynoso, Paulino, Kannapolis *	.879	22	2	27	4	33	1
Rice, Scott, Delmarva *	1.000	32	4	13	0	17	0
Richardson, Beau, Lakewood *	.968	47	3	27	1	31	0
Ridgway, Jeff, Charleston-SC *	.917	24	5	17	2	24	0
Rigueiro, Rafael, Hagerstown	.000	5	0	0	0	0	0
Rodriguez, Jose, Savannah	.000	7	0	0	2	2	0
Rodriguez, Jose, Rome	.889	37	1	7	1	9	1
Rodriguez, Juan, Hickory	1.000	2	0	2	0	2	0
Rodriguez, Mike, S. Georgia	.667	9	1	1	1	3	0
Rodriguez, Osvaldo, S. Georgia	.909	10	3	7	1	11	3
Rodriguez, Ricardo, Rome	.765	33	6	7	4	17	0
Roman, Orlando, Capital City	.933	7	5	9	1	15	1

Player, Team	Pct.	G	PO	A	E	TC	DP
Romero, Felix, Charleston-WV	.944	42	6	11	1	18	2
Roy, Angus, Augusta	.923	29	7	5	1	13	0
Rueckel, Danny, Savannah	.750	40	3	3	2	8	0
Rupe, Josh, Kannapolis	.824	26	4	10	3	17	1
Rupert, Chris, Lakewood *	.929	23	3	10	1	14	0
Russell, Eddie, Greensboro	1.000	9	0	3	0	3	0
Russell, Mike, Delmarva	.000	1	0	0	0	0	0
Sadler, William, Hagerstown	1.000	12	2	3	0	5	0
Salazar, Julio, Lexington *	1.000	8	0	4	0	4	0
Salazar, Richard, Delmarva *	1.000	41	3	13	0	16	1
Sampson, Christopher, Lex.	1.000	22	5	24	0	29	2
Sanchez, Emilio, Lakewood	1.000	11	2	4	0	6	0
Sandoval, Marcos, Charl.-WV	1.000	16	0	5	0	5	0
Santiago, Victor, South Georgia	1.000	23	2	7	0	9	1
Schmidt, Jeremy, Hagerstown	.909	24	5	5	1	11	1
Seale, Dustin, Savannah *	1.000	4	1	2	0	3	0
Searles, Jon, Savannah	1.000	20	1	10	0	11	0
Segovia, Zach, Lakewood	1.000	11	3	8	0	11	1
Serrato, Juan, Hagerstown	1.000	6	1	2	0	3	0
Shafer, Kurt, Hickory	.750	19	1	5	2	8	0
Sheffield, Christopher, Charl.-WV	1.000	7	1	2	0	3	0
Shipman, Andrew, Augusta	1.000	4	1	0	0	1	0
Shortslef, Josh, Hickory *	1.000	5	1	2	0	3	0
Silva, Efrain, South Georgia	1.000	7	1	4	0	5	0
Simon, Alfredo, Lakewood	.947	14	1	17	1	19	1
Sinclair, Ernnie, Lexington	1.000	21	1	8	0	9	0
Smith, Brandon, Augusta	.857	16	3	3	1	7	0
Smith, Chris, Augusta	1.000	8	2	8	0	10	0
Smith, Sean, Lake County	.912	26	10	21	3	34	3
Soto, T.J., Lexington	1.000	1	0	2	0	2	1
Southerland, Chip, Lake County	.000	1	0	0	0	0	0
Sperring, Jayme, Delmarva	1.000	25	1	10	0	11	0
Stahl, Richard, Delmarva *	.923	28	1	11	1	13	0
Stephenson, Eric, Charl.-WV *	.957	18	2	20	1	23	1
Stirm, Brian, Hagerstown	1.000	17	4	7	0	11	0
Sturge, Justin, Augusta *	.833	11	1	4	1	6	0
Sweeney, Matt, Lakewood	.818	26	7	11	4	22	1
Tadefa, Fernando, Rome *	1.000	45	1	11	0	12	0
Talanoa, Charles, Charl.-WV	.900	9	1	8	1	10	0
Tavarez, Milton, Augusta	.667	18	2	2	2	6	0
Teeter, Travis, Delmarva	1.000	8	0	1	0	1	0
Tejeda, Rob, Lakewood	.667	5	1	1	1	3	0
Testa, Chris, South Georgia *	1.000	14	2	1	0	3	0
Thompson, Matt, Augusta	1.000	11	3	8	0	11	0
Thorpe, Tracy, Charleston-WV	1.000	20	2	8	0	10	0
Threets, Erick, Hagerstown *	.933	22	4	10	1	15	1
Tiller, James, Delmarva	1.000	13	1	7	0	8	1
Tisch, Tim, Kannapolis *	1.000	3	0	1	0	1	0
Tracey, Sean, Kannapolis	.941	14	2	14	1	17	0
Urrutia, Carlos, Lakewood	.667	9	1	1	1	3	0
Valdez, Merkin, Hagerstown	.950	26	9	29	2	40	1
Vandermeer, Scott, Charl.-SC	1.000	6	4	4	0	8	0
Vazquez, Will, Asheville	1.000	3	0	1	0	1	0
Villarreal, Luis, Augusta *	1.000	25	2	20	0	22	0
Volquez, Bolivar, Charleston-SC	1.000	10	1	2	0	3	0
Waddell, Jason, Hagerstown *	1.000	36	2	15	0	17	1
Walker, Brian, Capital City *	.889	24	1	23	3	27	0
Warden, Jim Ed, Lake County	.889	14	5	11	2	18	0
Warriax, Brandon, S. Georgia	.951	30	10	29	2	41	0
Washburn, Ben, Hagerstown	.857	11	3	3	1	7	0
Wasserman, Ehren, Kannapolis	1.000	6	1	2	0	3	1
Watkins, Dave, Rome	.000	1	0	0	0	0	0
Watson, Mike, Asheville	1.000	17	1	5	0	6	0
Wayne, Brett, South Georgia	.000	5	0	0	0	0	0
Weichard, Paul, Rome *	.500	22	0	3	3	6	0
Wesley, John, Charleston-WV	.933	8	3	11	1	15	0
Westhoff, Billy, Lexington	1.000	45	5	11	0	16	2
Wickman, Bob, Lake County	.000	2	0	0	0	0	0
Williams, Ryan, South Georgia	.000	11	0	0	0	0	0
Withelder, Greg, Hickory *	1.000	12	1	1	0	2	0
Wolf, Ross, Greensboro	.875	27	1	6	1	8	0
Woolard, Glenn, Hagerstown	.903	26	8	20	3	31	1
Wright, Matt, Rome	.950	14	4	15	1	20	0
Yarbrough, Joe, Charleston-SC *	.913	56	4	17	2	23	0
Youman, Shane, Hickory *	1.000	40	3	7	0	10	0
Young, Chris, Asheville	1.000	59	6	13	0	19	2
Zinsman, Zeph, Charl.-WV *	.000	1	0	0	0	0	0

The following players appeared only as a designated hitter, pinch-hitter or pinch-runner: Gillikin, dh, ph; Gordon, dh; J. Owens, dh, pr; York, dh.

LEAGUE CHAMPIONS

Year	Team	Pct.
1948	Lincolnton*	.627
1949	Newton-Conover	.667
	Rutherford Co. (2nd)†	.627
1950	Newton-Conover	.627
	Lenoir (2nd)†	.626
1951	Morganton	.645
	Shelby (2nd)†	.604
1952	Lincolnton	.649
	Shelby (2nd)†	.645
1953-59	League inactive.	
1960	Lexington	.707
	Salisbury (2nd)†	.650
1961	Salisbury	.627
	Shelby (4th)†	.481
1962	Statesville	.563
	Statesville	.700
1963	Greenville†	.576
	Salisbury	.631
1964	Rock Hill	.672
	Salisbury‡	.631
1965	Salisbury	.641
	Rock Hill‡	.603
1966	Spartanburg	.682
	Spartanburg	.767
1967	Spartanburg	.730
	Spartanburg	.567
1968	Spartanburg	.597
	Greenwood‡	.597
1969	Greenwood‡	.587
	Shelby	.565
1970	Greenville	.576
	Greenville	.619
1971	Greenwood	.631
	Greenwood	.759
1972	Spartanburg‡	.788
	Greenville	.652
1973	Spartanburg‡	.646
	Gastonia	.619
1974	Gastonia	.606
	Gastonia	.672
1975	Spartanburg	.543
	Spartanburg	.614
1976	Asheville	.544
	Greenwood‡	.600
1977	Greenwood	.557
	Gastonia‡	.590
1978	Greenwood	.614
	Greenwood	.565
1979	Greenwood‡	.565
	Spartanburg	.525
1980	Greensboro	.590
	Charleston	.561
1981	Greensboro‡	.695
	Greenwood	.549
1982	Greensboro‡	.681
	Florence	.546
1983	Columbia	.620
	Gastonia‡	.587
1984	Charleston	.549
	Asheville‡	.510
1985	Florence‡	.599
	Greensboro	.540
1986	Columbia‡	.682
	Asheville	.643
1987	Asheville	.655
	Myrtle Beach‡	.597
1988	Charleston (S.C.)	.616
	Spartanburg‡	.500
1989	Gastonia	.657
	Augusta‡	.535
1990	Columbia	.580
	Charleston (W.Va.)‡	.538
1991	Charleston (W.Va.)	.648
	Columbia‡	.614
1992	Columbia	.572
	Myrtle Beach‡	.522
1993	Savannah‡	.662
	Greensboro	.603
1994	Columbus	.630
	Savannah‡	.599
1995	Piedmont	.586
	Augusta‡	.551
1996	Delmarva	.585
	Savannah†	.511
1997	Delmarva§	.543
	Greensboro	.536
1998	Columbia§	.638
	Hagerstown	.574
1999	Hagerstown	.600
	Augusta§	.496
2000	Piedmont	.657
	Delmarva∞	.544
2001	Lexington††	.657
2002	Hickory∞	.597
2003	Rome∞	.561

*Won championship and four-club playoff. †Won four-club playoff. ‡Won split-season playoff. §Won split season, eight-club playoff. ∞Won split season, four-club playoff. ††Was leading final series of split-season, four-club playoff and was declared champion when Professional Baseball declared a stoppage of play. (NOTE—Known as Western Carolina League from 1948 through 1962 and known as Western Carolinas League through 1979.)

NEW YORK-PENN LEAGUE

LEAGUE OFFICE

President
Ben Hayes
Address
9410 International Court North
St. Petersburg, FL 33716
Phone
727-576-6300

Teams (affiliation)
Aberdeen IronBirds (Orioles)
Auburn Doubledays (Blue Jays)
Batavia Muckdogs (Phillies)
Brooklyn Cyclones (Mets)
Hudson Valley Renegades (Devil Rays)
Jamestown Jammers (Marlins)
Lowell Spinners (Red Sox)
Mahoning Valley Scrappers (Indians)
New Jersey Cardinals (Cardinals)
Oneonta Tigers (Tigers)
Staten Island Yankees (Yankees)
Tri-City ValleyCats (Astros)
Vermont Expos (Expos)
Williamsport Crosscutters (Pirates)

2003 FINAL STANDINGS

McNAMARA DIVISION

Team	W	L	T	Pct.	GB
Brooklyn	47	28	-	.627	...
Williamsport	46	30	-	.605	1.5
Hudson Valley	37	37	-	.500	9.5
Aberdeen	38	38	-	.500	9.5
New Jersey	31	42	-	.425	15.0
Staten Island	29	43	-	.403	16.5

PINCKNEY DIVISION

Team	W	L	T	Pct.	GB
Auburn	56	18	-	.757	...
Mahoning Valley	38	36	-	.514	18.0
Batavia	30	45	-	.400	26.5
Jamestown	22	51	-	.301	33.5

STEDLER DIVISION

Team	W	L	T	Pct.	GB
Oneonta	45	30	-	.600	...
Tri-City	44	32	-	.579	1.5
Lowell	39	35	-	.527	5.5
Vermont	19	56	-	.253	26.0

COMPOSITE

Team	AUB	BRK	WPT	ONE	TRC	LOW	MHV	HDV	ABD	NJY	STA	BAT	JAM	VMT	W	L	T	Pct.	GB
Auburn (Blue Jays)	...	2	2	2	2	2	8	3	1	2	2	12	15	3	56	18	0	.757	...
Brooklyn (Mets)	1	...	6	2	1	1	1	6	7	6	8	3	2	3	47	28	0	.627	9.5
Williamsport (Pirates)	1	4	...	2	1	1	1	6	7	8	8	1	3	3	46	30	0	.605	11.0
Oneonta (Tigers)	0	1	1	...	10	8	1	2	2	1	2	2	3	12	45	30	0	.600	11.5
Tri-City (Astros)	1	2	2	6	...	9	2	2	1	2	2	1	1	13	44	32	0	.579	13.0
Lowell (Red Sox)	1	1	2	7	6	...	2	1	1	1	2	2	2	11	39	35	0	.527	17.0
Mahoning Valley (Indians)	7	2	2	2	1	1	...	1	3	1	2	9	6	1	38	36	0	.514	18.0
Hudson Valley (Devil Rays)	0	4	4	1	1	1	2	...	4	8	6	2	2	2	37	37	0	.500	19.0
Aberdeen (Orioles)	2	3	5	1	2	2	0	6	...	6	4	3	3	1	38	38	0	.500	19.0
New Jersey (Cardinals)	1	4	2	2	1	2	2	3	4	...	3	1	3	3	31	42	0	.425	24.5
Staten Island (Yankees)	1	4	2	1	1	1	1	4	6	5	...	1	1	1	29	43	0	.403	26.0
Batavia (Phillies)	3	0	2	1	2	1	6	1	0	2	2	...	8	2	30	45	0	.400	26.5
Jamestown (Marlins)	0	1	0	0	2	1	8	1	0	0	1	7	...	1	22	51	0	.301	33.5
Vermont (Expos)	0	0	0	3	2	5	2	1	2	0	1	1	2	...	19	56	0	.253	37.5

Major league affiliations in parentheses.

PLAYOFFS: Williamsport defeated Auburn, two games to none; Brooklyn defeated Oneonta, two games to one; Williamsport defeated Brooklyn, two games to none, to win league championship.

REGULAR-SEASON ATTENDANCE: Aberdeen, 234,143; Auburn, 65,047; Batavia, 42,801; Brooklyn, 307,383; Hudson Valley, 146,613; Jamestown, 53,469; Lowell, 175,000; Mahoning Valley, 141,889; New Jersey, 117,220; Oneonta, 48,905; Staten Island, 163,432; Tri-City, 103,984; Vermont, 101,431; Williamsport, 83,346. Total attendance—1,784,663. Playoffs (7 games)—24,601.

MANAGERS: Aberdeen, Joe Almaraz; Auburn, Dennis Holmberg; Batavia, Luis Melendez; Brooklyn, Tim Teufel; Hudson Valley, Dave Howard; Jamestown, Benny Castillo; Lowell, John Deeble (through August 26), Lynn Jones (August 27 through end of season); Mahoning Valley, Ted Kubiak; New Jersey, Tommy Shields; Oneonta, Randy Ready; Staten Island, Andy Stankiewicz; Tri-City, Ivan DeJesus; Vermont, Dave Barnett; Williamsport, Andy Stewart. Managerial record of team with more than one manager: Lowell, Deeble (36-30); Jones (3-5).

ALL-STAR TEAM: 1B—Vito Chiaravolloti, Auburn; 2B—Eric Rodland, Oneonta; 3B—Kody Kirkland, Oneonta; SS—Aaron Hill, Auburn; Reserve INF—Tony Giarrantano, Oneonta; OF—Nyjer Morgan, Williamsport; OF—AJ Porfirio, Auburn; OF—Ryan Goleski, Mahoning Valley; OF—Josh Anderson, Tri-City; C—Paul Richmond, Auburn; C—Danilo Sanchez, Oneonta; RHP—Matt Lindstrom, Brooklyn; RHP—Brian Bannister, Brooklyn; LHP—Kurt Isenberg, Auburn; LHP—Aaron Gangi, Hudson Valley; DH—Mike Madrid, Williamsport; Most Valuable Player—Vito Chiaravolloti, Auburn; Manager of the Year—Dennis Holmberg, Auburn.

2003 BATTING

TEAM

Team	G	TPA	AB	R	H	TB	2B	3B	HR	RBI	SH	SF	HP	BB	IBB	SO	SB	CS	GDP	LOB	ShO	Avg.	OBP	Slg.
Auburn	74	2937	2485	454	703	1050	141	19	56	420	19	30	40	361	4	583	46	21	56	590	2	.283	.379	.423
Mahoning Val.	74	2797	2471	365	659	986	137	23	48	324	18	31	35	242	9	541	61	30	46	510	3	.267	.337	.399
Williamsport	76	2863	2539	354	673	922	129	30	20	312	39	23	74	188	8	427	65	38	36	544	4	.265	.331	.363
Oneonta	75	2842	2529	352	661	945	117	46	25	302	14	25	50	224	5	515	73	30	55	547	3	.261	.331	.374
Tri-City	76	2851	2501	349	629	902	138	21	31	301	39	34	57	217	8	463	70	27	40	533	4	.251	.321	.361
Lowell	74	2783	2400	348	594	859	132	20	31	309	16	32	44	290	4	597	96	42	38	511	5	.248	.336	.358
Brooklyn	75	2745	2401	291	579	789	105	15	25	254	26	27	45	246	2	563	103	54	33	509	5	.241	.320	.329
New Jersey	73	2752	2426	282	579	788	106	29	15	255	18	28	51	227	4	498	81	28	47	518	6	.239	.314	.325

Team	G	TPA	AB	R	H	TB	2B	3B	HR	RBI	SH	SF	HP	BB	IBB	SO	SB	CS	GDP	LOB	ShO	Avg.	OBP	Slg.
Jamestown....	73	2680	2376	282	561	790	98	19	31	241	14	21	52	217	5	618	87	29	48	490	5	.236	.311	.332
Staten Island.	72	2769	2456	281	576	808	101	22	29	247	18	14	47	233	5	585	83	27	43	515	7	.235	.311	.329
Hudson Val....	74	2729	2440	281	572	815	106	25	29	244	15	15	41	218	13	607	49	23	31	516	5	.234	.306	.334
Aberdeen.......	76	2833	2476	294	562	808	111	27	27	238	40	18	32	267	14	537	113	52	33	498	10	.227	.308	.326
Batavia..........	75	2827	2497	266	568	812	107	28	27	239	24	18	51	237	6	615	107	54	43	502	5	.227	.305	.325
Vermont........	75	2705	2392	215	515	686	81	12	22	193	32	14	38	229	3	574	55	24	52	514	9	.215	.293	.287

INDIVIDUAL

TOP QUALIFIERS FOR BATTING CHAMPIONSHIP

Minimum 205 plate appearances. *Lefthanded batter. †Switch-hitter.

Player, Team	G	TPA	AB	R	H	TB	2B	3B	HR	RBI	SH	SF	HP	BB	IBB	SO	SB	CS	GDP	Avg.	OBP	Slg.
Chiaravolloti, Vito, Auburn.....	68	290	228	47	80	138	20	1	12	67	0	4	7	47	1	48	0	0	6	.351	.469	.605
Morgan, Nyjer, Wil.*.............	72	324	268	49	92	107	7	4	0	23	10	0	13	33	1	44	26	17	2	.343	.439	.399
Rodland, Eric, Oneonta *.......	57	267	244	43	80	111	15	8	0	27	2	1	3	17	0	25	13	2	4	.328	.377	.455
Giarratano, Tony, Oneonta †...	47	206	189	31	62	90	11	4	3	27	0	3	2	12	0	22	9	4	3	.328	.369	.476
Bocchino, Anthony, Wil.*.......	59	240	215	26	70	95	13	6	0	29	4	4	2	15	2	28	5	2	1	.326	.369	.442
Cota, Carlo, Auburn................	51	206	169	31	54	88	13	3	5	34	4	3	3	27	0	45	3	2	3	.320	.416	.521
Ryan, Brendan, New Jersey...	53	213	193	20	60	82	14	4	0	13	1	2	3	14	1	25	11	3	4	.311	.363	.425
Robinson, Christopher, Tri-City*	58	227	209	36	64	85	8	2	3	29	7	2	0	9	1	28	4	2	2	.306	.332	.407
Kirkland, Kody, Oneonta........	67	295	254	46	77	126	15	11	4	49	0	3	13	25	1	60	14	5	6	.303	.390	.496
Goleski, Ryan, M.V................	64	268	243	39	72	115	15	2	8	37	0	1	3	21	0	66	3	5	6	.296	.358	.473
Bear, Ryan, Jamestown..........	70	271	240	42	71	111	12	5	6	37	1	2	4	24	3	36	15	2	3	.296	.367	.463
Estrada, Kevin, New Jersey †.	64	268	236	42	69	85	9	2	1	24	1	3	1	25	0	33	21	6	5	.292	.358	.360
Conroy, Mike, M.V.*...............	73	311	288	34	84	129	12	6	7	44	2	3	1	17	2	47	4	3	5	.292	.330	.448
Martinez, Gabriel, H.V.*.........	70	269	243	27	71	102	21	2	2	43	1	1	2	22	4	52	0	1	6	.292	.354	.420
Blue, Vincent, Oneonta *........	70	275	233	47	67	96	7	8	2	26	2	1	1	38	1	56	13	3	0	.288	.388	.412

DEPARTMENTAL LEADERS: G—Anderson, Bladergroe, 74; AB—Anderson, 297; R—Peralta, 62; H—Morgan, 92; TB—Chiaravolloti, 138; 2B—Koman, Mulhern, 25; 3B—Kirkland, 11; HR—Chiaravolloti, 12; RBI—Chiaravolloti, 67; SH—Morgan, 10; SF—Murton, 7; HP—Dierks, 18; BB—Jordan, 49; IBB—Hansen, 5; SO—Snyder, 82; SB—Moran, 27; CS—Morgan, 17; GIDP—Roberts, 10; Slg.—Chiaravolloti, .605; OBP—Chiaravolloti, .469.

ALL PLAYERS

*Lefthanded batter. †Switch-hitter.

Player, Team	G	TPA	AB	R	H	TB	2B	3B	HR	RBI	SH	SF	HP	BB	IBB	SO	SB	CS	GDP	Avg.	OBP	Slg.
Alen, Luis, Jamestown...........	25	59	54	3	15	21	3	0	1	6	2	1	0	2	0	13	0	1	1	.278	.298	.389
Allan, Joshua, Jamestown.....	24	78	69	12	17	33	7	0	3	12	0	1	0	8	0	13	1	0	1	.246	.321	.478
Anderson, Joshua, Tri-City *..	74	329	297	44	85	113	11	4	3	30	2	4	10	16	2	53	26	9	2	.286	.339	.380
Arbinger, Mike, Wil.*.............	41	158	141	21	35	54	7	3	2	23	2	4	4	7	0	25	1	0	4	.248	.295	.383
Arias, Claudio, Lowell............	49	198	187	29	49	75	9	1	5	33	0	2	2	7	0	55	3	3	2	.262	.293	.401
Arko, Tommy, Aberdeen.........	14	50	43	7	11	28	3	1	4	7	0	0	1	6	0	19	0	0	0	.256	.360	.651
Arnold, Eric, Auburn..............	4	16	12	2	2	2	0	0	0	4	0	0	0	4	0	5	1	0	1	.167	.375	.167
Arroyo, Xavier, Jamestown †.	35	149	132	15	21	26	5	0	0	5	1	0	2	14	0	47	13	3	4	.159	.250	.197
Ascencion, Quincy, Aberdeen.	9	32	30	2	3	5	2	0	0	3	0	1	0	1	0	6	0	0	0	.100	.125	.167
Ayala, Abraham, H.V..............	38	141	130	9	26	29	3	0	0	10	0	2	3	6	0	13	0	0	3	.200	.248	.223
Baldiris, Aaron, Brooklyn.......	26	102	88	20	32	41	5	2	0	18	0	0	0	14	0	13	2	2	1	.364	.451	.466
Barnowski, Bryan, Lowell.......	4	15	13	1	1	1	0	0	0	0	0	0	1	1	0	4	0	0	0	.077	.200	.077
Bass, Bryan, Aberdeen †........	70	286	254	26	49	68	11	1	2	14	4	0	4	24	4	75	11	11	3	.193	.273	.268
Bastardo, Frederick, Jam........	15	51	45	6	10	11	1	0	0	0	0	0	1	5	0	11	1	1	1	.222	.314	.244
Batista, Wilson, Brooklyn †....	3	6	6	0	0	0	0	0	0	0	0	0	0	0	0	3	0	0	0	.000	.000	.000
Bear, Ryan, Jamestown..........	70	271	240	42	71	111	12	5	6	37	1	2	4	24	3	36	15	2	3	.296	.367	.463
Beck, Alan, Aberdeen............	18	53	48	3	4	8	1	0	1	3	1	1	0	3	0	12	1	1	2	.083	.135	.167
Bennett, Charles, Brooklyn *..	35	101	88	10	19	28	6	0	1	9	1	0	1	11	0	33	3	3	0	.216	.310	.318
Bernazard, Oscar, Vermont †.	32	113	91	9	18	22	4	0	0	7	0	1	2	19	0	30	0	1	0	.198	.345	.242
Blackburn, Alex, Auburn........	23	36	34	3	6	7	1	0	0	3	0	1	1	0	0	8	0	0	0	.176	.194	.206
Bladergroen, Ian, Brooklyn *.	74	305	274	33	78	114	12	3	6	36	0	1	9	21	2	51	0	2	4	.285	.354	.416
Blake, Ryan, Jamestown........	46	162	137	22	39	71	7	2	7	18	1	1	8	15	0	40	4	1	3	.285	.385	.518
Blalock, Jake, Batavia............	72	299	261	36	64	116	23	7	5	31	2	4	2	30	0	81	9	4	2	.245	.323	.444
Blanco, Luis, Vermont...........	12	42	42	3	7	15	2	0	2	4	0	0	0	0	0	17	0	0	1	.167	.167	.357
Blue, Vincent, Oneonta *........	70	275	233	47	67	96	7	8	2	26	2	1	1	38	1	56	13	3	0	.288	.388	.412
Bocchino, Anthony, Wil.*.......	59	240	215	26	70	95	13	6	0	29	4	4	2	15	2	28	5	2	1	.326	.369	.442
Bock, Brian, Aberdeen...........	43	141	126	15	28	30	2	0	0	9	3	1	2	9	0	19	4	2	4	.222	.283	.238
Boeve, Adam, Williamsport....	39	159	132	20	33	53	9	1	3	16	3	2	7	15	1	39	6	1	1	.250	.353	.402
Bonvechio, Brett, Lowell *.....	34	122	105	14	20	34	5	0	3	9	1	0	3	13	0	27	0	0	1	.190	.298	.324
Borgo, Alex, Batavia..............	14	59	47	8	12	24	3	0	3	5	0	0	5	7	0	18	1	0	0	.255	.407	.511
Borowiak, Zachary, Lowell.....	35	149	125	13	34	41	5	1	0	7	4	0	4	16	0	18	12	4	0	.272	.372	.328
Boudon, Chad, Aberdeen.......	34	99	87	11	17	30	5	1	2	10	3	3	1	5	0	21	1	2	3	.195	.240	.345
Bourn, Michael, Batavia *......	35	153	125	12	35	37	0	1	0	4	2	0	3	23	0	28	23	5	2	.280	.404	.296
Bowman, Shawn, Brooklyn....	42	151	138	10	28	37	7	1	0	5	1	1	1	10	0	49	2	1	1	.203	.260	.268
Bramasco, Omar, Batavia.......	48	180	148	19	32	55	7	2	4	10	0	0	5	27	0	57	3	2	1	.216	.356	.372
Bridges, Josh, New Jersey.....	3	8	7	0	1	1	0	0	0	1	1	0	0	0	0	1	0	0	0	.143	.143	.143
Brito, Henry, Batavia.............	15	53	51	3	6	6	0	0	0	1	0	0	1	1	0	13	0	2	2	.118	.151	.118
Brown, Curtis, Oneonta *.......	45	184	169	18	45	61	5	4	1	10	3	0	4	8	0	19	5	1	7	.266	.315	.361
Brown, Gregory, Jamestown..	13	22	19	2	4	4	0	0	0	1	0	0	2	1	0	4	0	0	0	.211	.318	.211
Brown, Tim, Williamsport *...	50	192	158	24	40	56	10	0	2	16	0	0	13	21	0	44	0	1	1	.253	.385	.354
Brown, Tony, Vermont *........	9	27	26	4	4	4	0	0	0	1	0	0	0	1	0	4	0	0	1	.154	.185	.154
Brunink, Joseph, Batavia *....	42	173	154	16	30	44	6	1	2	14	0	2	2	15	0	50	5	3	2	.195	.272	.286
Buckley, James, Lowell..........	37	127	114	15	18	33	9	0	2	13	1	1	1	10	1	46	1	0	2	.158	.230	.289
Burgos, Richard, Oneonta......	34	141	125	11	36	54	4	4	2	22	0	5	1	10	1	31	0	1	1	.288	.333	.432

Player, Team	G	TPA	AB	R	H	TB	2B	3B	HR	RBI	SH	SF	HP	BB	IBB	SO	SB	CS	GDP	Avg.	OBP	Slg.
Cabrera, Melky, Staten Is.†	67	311	279	34	79	99	10	2	2	31	4	1	4	23	1	36	13	5	6	.283	.345	.355
Calzado, Napoleon, Aberdeen	4	18	16	5	3	3	0	0	0	0	0	0	0	2	0	0	3	0	0	.188	.278	.188
Caradonna, Troy, Staten Is.†	7	14	14	0	1	1	0	0	0	0	0	0	0	0	0	4	0	0	1	.071	.071	.071
Casto, Kory, Vermont *	71	292	259	26	62	92	14	2	4	28	0	1	2	30	1	47	1	1	3	.239	.322	.355
Cenate, Josh, Aberdeen *	1	1	1	0	0	0	0	0	0	0	0	0	0	0	0	0	0	0	0	.000	.000	.000
Chance, Andrew, Wil.	43	163	149	22	33	53	4	2	4	20	1	1	4	8	0	42	2	1	3	.221	.278	.356
Chauncey, Clinton, M.V.	24	97	83	16	20	22	2	0	0	6	0	2	3	9	1	18	3	0	2	.241	.330	.265
Chavez, Ender, Brooklyn *	40	140	122	14	22	26	2	1	0	9	2	1	1	14	0	17	9	6	2	.180	.268	.213
Chiaravolloti, Vito, Auburn	68	290	228	47	80	138	20	1	12	67	0	4	7	47	1	48	0	0	6	.351	.469	.605
Clanton, Ja'Mar, Vermont	58	202	176	13	31	36	3	1	0	11	8	1	3	14	0	44	11	3	5	.176	.247	.205
Clements, Zachary, Brooklyn	5	16	15	1	3	3	0	0	0	1	0	0	0	1	0	3	2	0	0	.200	.250	.200
Clendenin, Morgan, Aber.*	17	52	45	6	12	25	6	2	1	8	0	1	0	6	0	20	2	2	1	.267	.346	.556
Cloar, Jason, Vermont	5	20	17	1	2	2	0	0	0	1	0	0	0	3	0	4	0	0	0	.118	.250	.118
Cloninger, Erich, Lowell	24	49	38	4	10	13	3	0	0	1	0	1	0	8	0	16	3	0	3	.263	.383	.342
Cockrell, Michael, Wil.	70	306	274	47	76	118	23	5	3	41	5	3	9	15	0	25	7	6	6	.277	.332	.431
Colbert, Eddie, Aberdeen †	10	20	18	1	5	6	1	0	0	0	1	0	0	1	0	7	1	0	0	.278	.316	.333
Coles, Corey, Brooklyn *	15	39	36	5	6	8	0	1	0	3	0	0	0	3	0	4	3	3	2	.167	.231	.222
Collum, Mike, Williamsport	12	42	38	5	7	11	2	1	0	6	1	0	1	2	0	9	1	0	0	.184	.244	.289
Colmenter, Jesus, M.V.†	65	276	249	25	62	76	9	1	1	29	4	4	1	18	0	39	2	3	3	.249	.298	.305
Conroy, Mike, M.V.*	73	311	288	34	84	129	12	6	7	44	2	3	1	17	2	47	4	3	5	.292	.330	.448
Cooper, Chad, Hudson Valley	8	31	28	2	6	8	0	1	0	3	0	0	1	2	0	6	2	0	0	.214	.290	.286
Cortez, Jose, Batavia †	41	157	142	9	24	29	2	0	1	17	1	1	1	12	0	34	0	1	4	.169	.237	.204
Cota, Carlo, Auburn	51	206	169	31	54	88	13	3	5	34	4	3	3	27	0	45	3	2	3	.320	.416	.521
Cotto, Luis, Mahoning Valley	9	32	25	3	3	3	0	0	0	0	0	0	1	6	0	7	0	0	1	.120	.313	.120
Cotto, Pedro, Oneonta *	30	105	99	11	27	32	5	0	0	3	0	0	1	5	0	7	1	3	3	.273	.314	.323
Covarrubias, Nic, Staten Is.	24	89	79	9	21	26	3	1	0	8	0	0	2	8	1	18	3	1	1	.266	.348	.329
Cruz, Enrique, Staten Island	32	150	130	23	37	50	7	3	0	14	2	0	2	14	0	20	4	2	2	.285	.363	.385
Cucinotta, Robert, Lowell	24	69	67	7	15	19	2	1	0	8	0	0	1	1	0	15	2	1	4	.224	.246	.284
Cuevas, Aneudi, H.V.	68	248	223	31	58	99	17	6	4	25	0	0	2	23	0	77	5	2	3	.260	.335	.444
Davidson, Tyler, Brooklyn	15	49	46	7	14	19	2	0	1	5	0	0	1	2	0	14	4	2	0	.304	.347	.413
Davis, Morrin, Auburn	36	89	81	7	19	23	4	0	0	8	1	0	0	7	0	34	2	1	0	.235	.295	.284
DeVries, Jonathan, Lowell	35	121	99	9	18	24	3	0	1	9	0	0	5	17	0	47	0	0	4	.182	.331	.242
Del Rosario, Manny, Aber.†	60	196	175	21	42	45	3	0	0	7	6	0	0	15	0	17	18	5	0	.240	.300	.257
Delos Santos, Esteban, Bat.	47	169	153	15	28	37	4	1	1	8	0	0	7	9	0	52	5	4	3	.183	.260	.242
Diaz, Jeury, Batavia †	15	53	43	4	9	11	2	0	0	3	2	1	0	7	0	16	1	1	0	.209	.314	.256
Dierks, Scott, Jamestown	60	219	180	33	38	63	7	0	6	18	0	2	18	19	0	60	6	4	4	.211	.342	.350
Dion, Nate, Hudson Valley	39	160	144	21	35	59	4	10	0	8	0	0	4	12	0	43	7	0	3	.243	.319	.410
Ditter, Brad, Vermont *	64	247	214	27	58	74	7	3	1	16	1	0	4	28	0	41	6	0	8	.271	.366	.346
Doyle, Nate, Oneonta	29	97	79	16	15	20	5	0	0	12	0	2	4	12	0	27	2	1	2	.190	.320	.253
Dufner, Kris, Hudson Valley †	59	248	218	27	47	69	5	1	5	14	2	0	3	25	0	74	1	4	2	.216	.305	.317
Duncan, Eric, Staten Island *	14	63	59	11	22	41	5	4	2	13	0	0	2	2	0	11	1	0	1	.373	.413	.695
Duncan, Jacob, Aberdeen *	43	133	118	13	19	29	3	2	1	7	6	0	1	8	0	29	3	2	1	.161	.220	.246
Encarnacion, Henry, Ver.†	22	88	73	5	11	15	2	1	0	4	2	1	1	11	0	20	0	3	2	.151	.267	.205
Estrada, Kevin, New Jersey †	64	268	236	42	69	85	9	2	1	24	1	3	1	25	0	33	21	6	5	.292	.358	.360
Evans, Robert, Lowell *	58	211	181	33	48	87	13	4	6	33	3	3	4	20	0	43	5	4	0	.265	.346	.481
Ewen, Nicholas, Jam.*	25	108	94	9	20	34	3	1	3	9	0	1	0	13	0	20	4	0	2	.213	.306	.362
Fair, Kerry, Tri-City	57	141	119	21	22	25	3	0	0	10	6	3	5	8	0	20	9	2	0	.185	.259	.210
Falu, Melvin, New Jersey †	57	236	213	25	53	87	9	5	5	28	2	5	4	12	0	22	6	0	3	.249	.295	.408
Fisher, Kiel, Batavia *	26	112	97	12	33	44	4	2	1	11	0	1	1	13	1	26	3	1	3	.340	.420	.454
Flowers, Bo, Oneonta	37	135	124	17	22	27	1	2	0	9	0	0	2	9	0	42	5	1	4	.177	.244	.218
Ford, Jake, Oneonta	28	108	97	8	21	34	7	0	2	14	0	2	3	6	0	18	0	0	1	.216	.278	.351
Foust, Justin, Batavia	37	142	128	13	29	34	5	0	0	16	2	1	2	9	0	31	4	1	3	.227	.286	.266
Frank, Kyle, Staten Island *	15	33	30	2	5	5	0	0	0	1	0	0	1	2	0	4	0	1	0	.167	.242	.167
Frisella, Paul, New Jersey	7	24	22	3	3	5	0	1	0	0	0	0	1	1	0	8	1	0	1	.136	.208	.227
Galloway, Mike, Auburn	52	198	172	36	52	82	12	3	4	33	0	3	3	20	1	47	3	1	5	.302	.379	.477
Garcia, Julio, M.V.†	1	4	4	0	0	0	0	0	0	0	0	0	0	0	0	3	0	0	0	.000	.000	.000
Garcia, Travis, Brooklyn	12	36	36	4	7	7	0	0	0	1	0	0	0	0	0	6	3	0	0	.194	.194	.194
Garcia, Yunir, Brooklyn	37	118	96	11	17	25	5	0	1	12	3	1	0	18	0	33	1	0	3	.177	.304	.260
Garko, Ryan, M.V.	45	183	165	23	45	67	8	1	4	16	2	0	4	12	0	19	1	1	5	.273	.337	.406
Giarratano, Tony, Oneonta †	47	206	189	31	62	90	11	4	3	27	0	3	2	12	0	22	9	4	3	.328	.369	.476
Ginther, Andy, New Jersey	15	37	34	4	8	12	4	0	0	3	1	0	0	2	0	10	0	0	1	.235	.278	.353
Goldfield, Josh, M.V.*	2	4	3	0	0	0	0	0	0	0	0	0	0	1	0	1	0	0	0	.000	.250	.000
Goleski, Ryan, M.V.	64	268	243	39	72	115	15	2	8	37	0	1	3	21	0	66	3	5	6	.296	.358	.473
Gonzalez, Edwar, Staten Is.	61	248	231	25	53	77	12	3	2	22	1	1	5	10	0	72	4	0	5	.229	.275	.333
Gonzalez, Humberto, Brook.	24	29	22	4	5	5	0	0	0	3	1	0	1	5	0	4	1	1	1	.227	.393	.227
Gonzalez, Patrick, Aberdeen	9	25	22	0	2	2	0	0	0	0	0	0	1	2	0	4	1	0	1	.091	.200	.091
Graham, Andrew, Oneonta	20	62	55	6	10	13	3	0	0	8	2	1	1	3	1	11	0	0	1	.182	.233	.236
Grimm, Casey, New Jersey *	68	268	224	29	64	84	9	4	1	33	1	3	13	25	3	36	1	1	5	.286	.385	.375
Grimm, Eric, Aberdeen †	56	198	165	22	45	59	11	0	1	18	0	0	1	32	3	40	2	2	1	.273	.394	.358
Guzman, Javier, Williamsport	47	190	173	19	42	61	9	2	2	24	6	1	0	10	0	26	4	3	2	.243	.283	.353
Hairston, Jerry, Aberdeen	2	6	3	2	1	1	0	0	0	0	0	0	0	3	0	0	1	0	0	.333	.667	.333
Hanish, Tyson, Staten Island	25	79	66	6	9	12	3	0	0	2	0	1	2	10	0	18	2	0	1	.136	.266	.182
Hansen, Bryan, Batavia *	67	288	248	29	53	88	18	4	3	33	2	4	4	30	5	45	4	2	4	.214	.304	.355
Harper, Brett, Brooklyn *	28	96	87	5	26	37	8	0	1	18	1	2	1	5	0	12	1	0	3	.299	.337	.425
Harris, Justin, Williamsport	50	179	171	18	40	46	6	0	0	18	2	2	1	3	0	15	1	2	1	.234	.249	.269
Harvey, Ryan, Brooklyn	16	52	46	5	14	19	2	0	1	2	0	0	2	4	0	5	3	0	0	.304	.385	.413
Headley, Jack, Batavia	48	206	180	19	49	66	6	4	1	22	6	1	7	12	0	13	10	10	6	.272	.340	.367
Hearod, Beau, Tri-City	52	183	162	17	37	65	9	2	5	20	0	0	8	13	0	44	0	0	2	.228	.317	.401
Herrera, Javier, M.V.	12	51	45	9	13	16	3	0	0	8	0	1	0	5	0	11	0	0	0	.289	.353	.356
Hill, Aaron, Auburn	33	148	122	22	44	60	4	0	4	34	0	4	6	16	2	20	1	1	2	.361	.446	.492
Hoffpauir, Josh, Aberdeen *	3	13	12	2	4	5	1	0	0	1	0	0	0	1	0	1	1	0	0	.333	.385	.417

Player, Team	G	TPA	AB	R	H	TB	2B	3B	HR	RBI	SH	SF	HP	BB	IBB	SO	SB	CS	GDP	Avg.	OBP	Slg.
Holmes, Brett, Williamsport...	34	93	87	16	22	27	3	1	0	6	0	1	1	4	0	21	3	0	1	.253	.290	.310
Housel, David, Brooklyn †......	11	34	31	3	8	11	3	0	0	4	1	1	0	1	0	8	0	0	1	.258	.273	.355
Hubele, Ryan, Aberdeen.........	3	14	13	1	5	7	2	0	0	2	1	0	0	0	0	2	0	0	0	.385	.385	.538
Huddleston, Bobby, Oneonta..	38	136	120	10	25	29	4	0	0	10	1	1	5	9	0	18	0	0	3	.208	.289	.242
Hunt, Kelly, Oneonta	47	200	179	18	46	65	13	0	2	21	1	2	2	16	0	42	0	0	8	.257	.322	.363
Jaso, John, Hudson Valley *..	47	188	154	20	35	48	7	0	2	20	2	3	4	25	3	26	2	0	2	.227	.344	.312
Jimenez, Franklyn, Vermont...	58	238	217	23	55	68	7	0	2	17	7	1	3	10	0	43	8	2	6	.253	.294	.313
Jimenez, Luis, Aberdeen *.....	53	197	168	17	41	53	9	0	1	21	2	0	1	26	0	40	7	4	2	.244	.349	.315
Johnson, Eric, M.V................	14	68	57	14	16	27	3	1	2	7	0	0	5	6	1	16	10	1	0	.281	.397	.474
Johnston, Clint, Auburn *......	23	80	66	17	21	32	8	0	1	6	0	0	0	14	0	12	0	0	3	.318	.438	.485
Jones, Mitch, Hudson Valley..	71	308	273	37	53	65	10	1	0	16	2	3	4	26	0	78	13	4	3	.194	.271	.238
Jordan, Kevin, Lowell *..........	63	273	217	46	57	67	4	3	0	22	3	1	3	49	0	50	24	10	1	.263	.404	.309
Joyce, Tom, Aberdeen *.........	38	123	99	12	22	34	2	2	2	10	1	1	0	22	2	29	5	2	1	.222	.361	.343
Kahr, Danny, Vermont †.........	27	91	82	6	6	11	2	0	1	1	3	0	5	1	0	41	0	1	1	.073	.136	.134
Kapler, Gabe, Lowell..............	1	4	3	2	2	2	0	0	0	0	0	0	0	1	0	0	1	0	1	.667	.750	.667
Kartler, Bryce, Staten Island *	42	128	110	16	32	50	5	2	3	10	0	0	0	18	0	31	5	0	0	.291	.391	.455
Kendrick, Josh, H.V................	63	238	219	22	51	76	13	0	4	24	0	3	8	8	0	68	2	3	6	.233	.282	.347
Kirkland, Kody, Oneonta.........	67	295	254	46	77	126	15	11	4	49	0	3	13	25	1	60	14	5	6	.303	.390	.496
Knicely, Jeremy, Auburn	8	17	15	0	0	0	0	0	0	0	0	0	1	1	0	9	0	0	0	.000	.118	.000
Koman, Brock, Tri-City...........	72	297	266	30	71	111	25	3	3	39	3	3	9	16	2	32	3	0	8	.267	.327	.417
Kouzmanoff, Kevin, M.V.........	54	234	206	31	56	90	8	1	8	33	0	4	3	21	1	36	2	1	6	.272	.342	.437
Kratz, Erik, Auburn.................	49	185	157	25	49	79	15	0	5	26	0	1	6	21	0	31	0	1	2	.312	.411	.503
Lawrence, Horace, Staten Is.*	26	80	71	4	15	19	4	0	0	12	0	1	1	7	0	13	0	1	0	.211	.288	.268
Linares, Jesus, Brooklyn †.....	28	61	52	4	9	16	2	1	1	6	2	1	0	6	0	21	0	1	0	.173	.254	.308
Louisa, Lorvin, Vermont	62	236	218	17	45	67	5	1	5	24	0	2	2	14	0	73	2	0	7	.206	.258	.307
Lunetta, Anthony, M.V...........	58	229	201	31	50	75	16	0	3	29	4	5	3	16	0	38	1	1	5	.249	.307	.373
Lutz, David, Vermont *	13	40	32	2	5	7	2	0	0	1	1	0	1	6	0	5	0	0	1	.156	.308	.219
Mackor, Jeff, Tri-City.............	40	144	132	22	33	49	11	1	1	14	1	1	1	9	0	21	1	2	2	.250	.301	.371
Made, Hector, Staten Island...	7	27	27	4	7	11	1	0	1	1	0	0	0	0	0	5	3	0	0	.259	.259	.407
Madrid, Mike, Williamsport *.	57	225	198	24	54	70	10	0	2	34	0	3	6	18	3	20	2	1	4	.273	.347	.354
Magruder, Chris, M.V.†	3	14	11	5	2	4	2	0	0	0	0	0	1	2	0	1	2	0	0	.182	.357	.364
Majewski, Val, Aberdeen *.....	4	17	16	2	6	12	2	2	0	3	0	0	0	1	0	2	1	0	0	.375	.412	.750
Mangioni, Jarad, Auburn........	42	126	106	12	24	33	9	0	0	19	2	3	1	14	0	32	0	0	1	.226	.315	.311
Manriquez, Salomon, Ver.	45	181	168	14	33	43	4	0	2	11	0	2	1	10	0	41	0	0	7	.196	.243	.256
Markakis, Nicholas, Aber.*.....	59	240	205	22	58	81	14	3	1	28	1	3	1	30	1	33	13	5	6	.283	.372	.395
Martinez, Gabriel, H.V.*	70	269	243	27	71	102	21	2	2	43	1	1	2	22	4	52	0	1	6	.292	.354	.420
Mather, Joe, New Jersey........	65	223	196	23	45	65	12	1	2	22	3	0	6	18	0	38	4	4	4	.230	.314	.332
Mattison, Justin, Jam.*	52	181	161	16	34	48	7	2	1	9	3	0	4	13	0	46	3	2	7	.211	.287	.298
Maysonet, Edwin, Tri-City	45	178	138	30	38	50	7	1	1	13	3	3	5	29	0	28	9	1	0	.275	.411	.362
Mazzuca, Joe, Jamestown	16	54	48	7	8	14	3	0	1	6	0	1	1	4	1	14	1	0	2	.167	.241	.292
McCuistion, Mike, Wil.*	41	154	136	19	28	33	3	1	0	10	0	1	2	15	0	24	1	0	1	.206	.292	.243
McCurdy, Joshua, Aberdeen ..	29	90	87	17	24	30	2	2	0	11	1	0	0	2	0	12	7	3	2	.276	.292	.345
McDonald, John, M.V............	1	3	2	1	0	0	0	0	0	0	0	0	0	1	0	0	0	0	0	.000	.333	.000
McGarvey, Randy, Tri-City *...	36	107	84	8	20	27	2	1	1	7	2	0	2	19	1	14	1	2	2	.238	.390	.321
McGorty, John, Oneonta *	32	104	93	10	16	18	2	0	0	5	0	1	1	9	0	24	0	1	3	.172	.250	.194
McIntyre, Nick, Oneonta †	33	115	102	12	25	28	3	0	0	9	1	0	1	11	0	24	4	5	3	.245	.325	.275
McKinney, Garth, Oneonta	54	214	196	27	44	70	6	4	4	19	0	1	5	12	0	61	6	1	2	.224	.285	.357
Mejia, Gilberto, Oneonta †	6	25	21	4	5	8	1	1	0	5	1	0	0	3	0	3	1	1	0	.238	.333	.381
Miller, Jai, Jamestown	11	48	43	5	10	13	3	0	0	6	0	1	1	3	0	15	1	1	0	.233	.292	.302
Mitchell, Lee, Jamestown	46	192	169	21	52	67	5	2	2	19	0	5	2	16	0	39	3	0	3	.308	.365	.396
Molina, Izzy, Aberdeen	19	72	59	6	12	23	3	1	2	4	0	0	1	12	2	10	2	1	1	.203	.347	.390
Monette, Daylon, N.J.†	52	196	176	19	41	55	9	1	1	32	0	3	1	16	0	49	4	2	6	.233	.296	.313
Moran, Javon, Batavia............	60	272	250	33	71	89	9	3	1	12	5	1	0	16	0	32	27	11	1	.284	.326	.356
Morgan, Nyjer, Wil.*	72	324	268	49	92	107	7	4	0	23	10	0	13	33	1	44	26	17	2	.343	.439	.399
Moss, Brandon, Lowell *	65	252	228	29	54	98	15	4	7	34	0	5	4	15	0	53	7	5	1	.237	.290	.430
Moss, Timothy, Batavia †.......	43	178	160	10	24	36	5	2	1	11	1	2	4	11	0	47	5	5	3	.150	.220	.225
Mulhern, Ryan, M.V.	59	254	229	32	64	106	25	1	5	30	1	2	3	19	2	68	6	2	3	.279	.340	.463
Murphy, David, Lowell *	21	95	78	13	27	31	4	0	0	13	0	1	0	16	2	9	4	1	1	.346	.453	.397
Murton, Matthew, Lowell	53	227	189	30	54	75	11	2	2	29	0	7	4	27	0	39	9	3	5	.286	.374	.397
Nikolic, Adam, H.V.*	40	155	143	14	30	40	2	1	2	9	2	1	1	8	1	32	6	2	1	.210	.255	.280
Noboa, Joel, Vermont	9	25	23	0	2	2	0	0	0	0	0	0	2	0	0	12	0	0	0	.087	.160	.087
Norman, Zachary, Batavia	31	120	110	8	17	28	2	0	3	14	0	0	3	7	0	27	3	0	2	.155	.225	.255
Noviskey, Josh, M.V.†	38	144	125	17	32	49	7	2	2	20	1	1	1	16	1	28	0	1	2	.256	.343	.392
O'Brien, Patrick, Tri-City.........	26	85	74	6	15	16	1	0	0	7	3	2	0	6	0	19	0	0	1	.203	.256	.216
Obrey, Kainoa, New Jersey	41	139	120	4	26	29	3	0	0	11	0	2	2	15	0	39	1	1	1	.217	.309	.242
Ohtsuka, Yoshiyuki, Wil.	16	48	43	4	9	12	3	0	0	5	2	0	2	1	0	5	0	1	1	.209	.261	.279
Olsen, Mikela, Jamestown * ..	47	170	155	14	32	39	5	1	0	21	1	1	0	13	0	45	1	2	2	.206	.266	.252
Osborn, Pat, Mahoning Valley	2	11	8	1	5	6	1	0	0	0	0	0	1	2	0	0	1	0	0	.625	.727	.750
Owens, Jerry, Vermont *	2	8	8	0	1	1	0	0	0	0	0	0	0	0	0	2	1	0	0	.125	.125	.125
Pagnozzi, Matt, New Jersey....	59	185	152	13	27	36	4	1	1	19	3	2	5	23	0	42	3	2	1	.178	.302	.237
Parker, Brett, M.V..................	7	29	27	3	5	8	0	0	1	3	0	0	0	2	0	7	1	0	0	.185	.241	.296
Parker, Rashad, Brooklyn........	60	236	208	36	60	76	8	1	2	17	5	2	7	14	0	46	16	4	2	.288	.351	.365
Parrish, Dave, Staten Island...	6	19	16	1	0	0	0	0	0	0	1	0	1	1	1	6	0	0	0	.000	.111	.000
Patrick, Brian, Auburn †.........	28	93	83	17	25	31	3	0	1	16	0	1	2	7	0	14	2	0	2	.301	.366	.373
Pedrique, Franmig, Tri-City	17	48	44	6	10	14	1	0	1	9	0	0	3	1	0	13	1	0	2	.227	.292	.318
Pena, Omar, New Jersey........	63	229	212	21	50	64	12	1	0	13	0	1	3	13	0	55	6	0	2	.236	.288	.302
Peralta, Juan, Auburn †	71	341	288	62	71	96	14	1	3	30	6	2	2	43	0	50	14	7	4	.247	.346	.333
Piantek, Kurtis, Oneonta	1	2	1	0	1	1	0	0	0	0	0	0	0	1	0	0	0	0	0	1.000	1.000	1.000
Piazza, Tony, Brooklyn	53	188	162	13	34	48	6	1	2	19	1	4	2	19	0	46	3	0	2	.210	.294	.296
Pietsch, Seth, Brooklyn..........	42	140	120	18	22	33	2	0	3	9	3	0	5	12	0	22	7	4	1	.183	.285	.275
Pignatiello, Bret, Vermont * ...	9	34	31	4	8	11	1	1	0	3	0	0	0	3	0	8	0	0	1	.258	.324	.355

Player, Team	G	TPA	AB	R	H	TB	2B	3B	HR	RBI	SH	SF	HP	BB	IBB	SO	SB	CS	GDP	Avg.	OBP	Slg.
Porfirio, A.J., Auburn	71	310	273	49	78	115	8	4	7	40	2	3	2	30	0	63	4	2	9	.286	.357	.421
Prosser, Chad, Tri-City	45	170	144	22	35	47	10	1	0	16	5	4	4	13	1	28	7	1	2	.243	.315	.326
Puebla, Fernando, H.V.	56	193	164	16	32	35	3	0	0	9	3	1	0	25	2	25	3	2	1	.195	.300	.213
Ramos, Jason, Lowell †	28	96	79	10	15	18	3	0	0	10	0	2	1	14	0	17	4	2	1	.190	.313	.228
Ramos, Kelly, Aberdeen †	6	25	24	4	5	12	1	0	2	6	0	0	0	1	0	5	1	0	0	.208	.240	.500
Ramos, Victor, Wil.*	8	16	14	1	4	5	1	0	0	2	0	0	0	2	0	2	0	0	1	.286	.375	.357
Randolph, Andre, Staten Is.*	11	25	23	0	4	4	0	0	0	1	0	0	0	2	0	6	0	1	0	.174	.240	.174
Reames, Joe Don, H.V.	10	26	21	1	2	2	0	0	0	2	2	0	0	3	0	6	0	0	0	.095	.208	.095
Reaver, David, Brooklyn	64	232	205	15	48	58	8	1	0	25	4	4	6	13	0	34	11	8	3	.234	.294	.283
Reuss, Jason, Tri-City	12	47	41	3	4	7	1	1	0	3	0	1	0	5	0	19	0	0	1	.098	.191	.171
Reyes, Melvin, Lowell †	57	212	193	28	50	75	16	3	1	25	2	4	1	12	1	60	8	2	3	.259	.300	.389
Reyes, Milver, Williamsport	40	131	125	13	27	33	6	0	0	12	0	0	3	3	0	22	0	0	5	.216	.252	.264
Richmond, Paul, Auburn *	48	211	169	37	45	72	8	2	5	34	0	1	0	41	0	36	3	1	3	.266	.408	.426
Rico, Matt, Hudson Valley	72	299	278	35	78	119	12	1	9	47	0	0	3	18	1	70	2	2	1	.281	.331	.428
Riley, Justin, Batavia	8	25	23	1	6	8	2	0	0	1	0	0	1	1	0	5	0	2	0	.261	.320	.348
Rine, Jarod, Aberdeen *	67	256	230	36	58	82	8	5	2	14	4	1	6	15	2	44	20	7	3	.252	.313	.357
Roberts, Ryan, Auburn	66	289	248	52	69	109	10	3	8	36	0	2	4	35	0	63	7	3	10	.278	.374	.440
Robinson, Christopher, Tri-City*	58	227	209	36	64	85	8	2	3	29	7	2	0	9	1	28	4	2	2	.306	.332	.407
Robinson, Scott, Tri-City *	73	304	277	36	70	105	23	0	4	36	1	4	2	17	0	32	4	4	4	.253	.297	.379
Robinson-Pierce, Whit, Aber.	10	38	30	3	7	10	1	1	0	4	0	2	2	4	0	8	0	0	0	.233	.342	.333
Robles, Luis, Staten Island	30	96	82	8	19	25	3	0	1	12	2	3	1	8	0	13	2	0	2	.232	.298	.305
Rodland, Eric, Oneonta *	57	267	244	43	80	111	15	8	0	27	2	1	3	17	0	25	13	2	4	.328	.377	.455
Rogers, Ed, Aberdeen	3	15	14	2	5	10	2	0	1	6	0	1	0	0	0	2	0	0	0	.357	.333	.714
Romprey, Ed, Oneonta	8	32	28	1	5	6	1	0	0	3	0	1	0	3	1	9	0	0	0	.179	.250	.214
Rosario, Carlos, Staten Is.	57	212	204	19	32	48	3	2	3	16	1	0	1	6	0	60	3	0	2	.157	.185	.235
Russell, Mike, Aberdeen	58	212	185	19	30	53	7	2	4	22	2	2	4	19	0	49	1	1	0	.162	.252	.286
Ryan, Brendan, New Jersey	53	213	193	20	60	82	14	4	0	13	1	2	3	14	1	25	11	3	4	.311	.363	.425
Salmela, Andy, Tri-City	41	142	124	16	25	40	4	1	3	18	1	2	3	12	1	34	2	0	1	.202	.284	.323
Sanchez, Danilo, Oneonta	38	139	121	16	32	56	9	0	5	23	1	1	1	15	0	16	0	1	4	.264	.348	.463
Santa, Alexander, Staten Is.*	33	127	114	10	22	28	4	1	0	10	2	1	1	9	0	32	7	1	3	.193	.256	.246
Schade, Ryan, Jamestown	47	141	125	11	38	46	3	1	1	15	0	1	2	13	0	21	8	2	2	.304	.376	.368
Schartz, Lance, Lowell	7	14	13	1	2	2	0	0	0	1	0	0	1	0	0	3	0	0	0	.154	.214	.154
Schleicher, Mark, H.V.	12	46	40	5	9	12	0	0	1	3	0	0	2	4	0	10	1	1	0	.225	.326	.300
Schmitt, Billy, New Jersey	42	141	131	15	25	37	5	2	1	10	2	1	1	6	0	31	1	0	2	.191	.230	.282
Schroeder, Benjamin, Jam.*	55	220	200	17	41	50	7	1	0	13	2	1	1	16	0	70	11	6	2	.205	.266	.250
Seifrig, Cole, Jamestown	11	49	46	3	12	15	3	0	0	8	0	1	0	2	0	12	2	0	1	.261	.286	.326
Serrano, Ray, Hudson Valley	23	86	77	4	14	17	3	0	0	5	1	1	1	6	2	10	0	1	0	.182	.247	.221
Seuss, Adam, Tri-City *	73	298	255	34	71	108	17	1	6	40	2	4	5	32	0	50	3	1	5	.278	.365	.424
Shorts, Adam, Staten Island	55	233	202	22	42	63	12	0	3	27	0	1	4	26	1	55	10	3	3	.208	.309	.312
Siriveaw, Nom, Auburn †	4	13	7	3	1	1	0	0	0	0	0	0	1	5	0	2	0	0	0	.143	.538	.143
Skaug, Brian, Tri-City	14	38	36	5	10	14	2	1	0	4	1	0	0	1	0	10	0	2	1	.278	.297	.389
Slack, Jonathan, Brooklyn *	59	253	211	30	54	63	7	1	0	13	1	4	2	35	0	47	17	10	2	.256	.361	.299
Slevin, David, Staten Island	44	158	144	20	32	43	6	1	1	6	1	1	2	10	0	33	3	0	0	.222	.280	.299
Smith, John, Williamsport *	1	4	3	1	0	0	0	0	0	0	0	0	0	1	0	1	0	0	0	.000	.250	.000
Smith, Sean, Williamsport	16	52	48	6	10	16	4	1	0	6	0	0	2	2	0	10	1	0	0	.208	.269	.333
Smithlin, Zach, New Jersey †	44	78	67	5	11	11	0	0	0	2	2	0	0	9	0	17	3	2	2	.164	.263	.164
Snavely, Christian, Auburn *	64	239	208	25	53	66	9	2	0	22	4	2	1	24	0	54	6	2	4	.255	.332	.317
Snyder, Brad, M.V.*	62	271	225	52	64	105	11	6	6	31	1	3	1	41	1	82	14	5	2	.284	.393	.467
Sosa, Pablo, Jamestown	35	141	136	10	33	44	7	2	0	8	0	1	2	2	1	27	1	2	2	.243	.262	.324
St. Clair, Jason, H.V.	25	87	79	9	23	32	5	2	0	6	0	0	3	5	0	14	5	1	0	.291	.356	.405
St. Martine, Michael, Ver.*	3	11	10	1	3	4	1	0	0	1	0	0	0	1	0	1	0	0	1	.300	.364	.400
Stansberry, Craig, Wil.	45	187	166	19	51	72	9	3	2	21	3	1	4	13	1	25	5	3	2	.307	.370	.434
Suarez, Cesar, M.V.	48	176	165	10	39	47	6	1	0	19	2	2	0	7	0	22	4	3	3	.236	.264	.285
Suarez, Ignacio, Lowell	58	244	207	32	46	59	13	0	0	19	2	2	1	32	0	43	12	4	4	.222	.326	.285
Sultemeier, Eric, Aberdeen	4	19	16	3	1	1	0	0	0	1	1	0	2	0	0	3	0	0	0	.063	.167	.063
Sweeney, Tim, Vermont	36	136	114	10	23	28	5	0	0	12	1	1	3	17	0	26	1	1	3	.202	.319	.246
Thedorf, Chris, Jamestown *	34	103	90	10	13	15	0	1	0	7	1	0	2	10	0	31	6	0	1	.144	.245	.167
Thomas, Tee, New Jersey	6	23	20	4	4	5	1	0	0	0	0	0	3	0	0	7	2	1	1	.200	.304	.250
Threinen, Scott, M.V.	17	59	45	6	10	13	3	0	0	3	1	1	1	11	0	9	0	0	2	.222	.379	.289
Tingler, Jayce, Auburn *	7	25	21	5	5	6	1	0	0	1	0	0	0	4	0	0	0	0	1	.238	.360	.286
Tolotti, Jeff, New Jersey *	4	15	13	0	0	0	0	0	0	1	0	0	0	2	0	6	0	0	1	.000	.133	.000
Treadway, Jared, Staten Is.	52	183	164	20	45	63	4	1	4	18	2	0	7	10	0	56	16	7	1	.274	.343	.384
Tugwell, Marc, Batavia	28	126	121	13	30	41	6	1	1	20	0	0	2	3	0	27	3	0	5	.248	.278	.339
Tuttle, Chris, New Jersey *	47	179	153	25	34	39	3	1	0	6	1	2	2	21	0	26	4	5	3	.222	.320	.255
Tuttle, Jason, Vermont *	51	223	203	23	57	66	7	1	0	17	1	2	2	15	0	19	17	4	2	.281	.333	.325
Urick, John, Staten Island *	59	226	186	18	42	51	9	0	0	16	0	4	0	36	1	36	2	2	7	.226	.345	.274
Urueta, Luis, New Jersey †	4	15	15	0	2	2	0	0	0	1	0	0	0	0	0	6	2	0	1	.133	.133	.133
Van Every, Jon, M.V.*	22	79	65	13	17	28	6	1	1	9	0	2	3	9	0	23	7	4	1	.262	.367	.431
Vancamper, Eugenio, Aub.†	7	27	26	2	5	10	2	0	1	7	0	0	0	1	0	10	0	0	0	.192	.222	.385
Virgil, Jose, New Jersey †	66	277	242	30	56	89	12	6	3	36	0	4	6	25	0	47	11	1	4	.231	.314	.368
VonTungeln, Cory, Batavia	18	62	56	6	16	19	3	0	0	6	1	0	1	4	0	13	1	0	0	.286	.344	.339
Vroman, Douglas, Vermont	29	86	72	7	11	14	1	1	0	4	2	1	1	10	0	26	2	2	1	.153	.262	.194
Walls, Michael, Tri-City	34	113	99	13	19	26	3	2	0	6	2	1	0	11	0	18	0	1	5	.192	.270	.263
Wareham, Landon, Aberdeen	1	3	3	0	0	0	0	0	0	0	0	0	0	0	0	1	0	0	0	.000	.000	.000
Watson, Matt, Brooklyn *	4	17	14	0	2	3	1	0	0	0	0	0	1	2	0	3	2	1	0	.143	.294	.214
Watts, Derran, Brooklyn	9	23	20	4	2	2	0	0	0	0	0	0	0	3	0	7	4	0	0	.100	.217	.100
Webb, Trey, Vermont	6	26	24	2	6	7	1	0	0	1	1	0	0	1	0	2	2	0	0	.250	.280	.292
West, Jeremy, Lowell	72	306	264	32	74	105	17	1	4	43	0	3	8	31	0	52	1	3	5	.280	.369	.398
Whealy, Blake, Brooklyn	55	210	182	24	45	66	11	2	2	26	0	4	4	20	0	63	7	6	4	.247	.329	.363
Whitesell, Josh, Vermont *	49	200	167	13	41	68	10	1	5	19	0	1	4	28	2	53	0	0	2	.246	.365	.407
Whiteside, Eli, Aberdeen	2	10	10	0	7	10	3	0	0	4	0	0	0	0	0	1	1	0	0	.700	.700	1.000

Player, Team	G	TPA	AB	R	H	TB	2B	3B	HR	RBI	SH	SF	HP	BB	IBB	SO	SB	CS	GDP	Avg.	OBP	Slg.
Wilson, Andrew, Brooklyn......	31	111	96	15	24	44	8	0	4	13	0	1	1	13	0	19	2	0	1	.250	.342	.458
Woodruff, Ernest, H.V.	3	6	6	1	2	3	1	0	0	0	0	0	0	0	0	3	0	0	0	.333	.333	.500
Wyman, Spencer, Jam.*	26	88	73	8	14	21	5	1	0	7	0	0	1	14	0	29	0	0	1	.192	.330	.288
Wyrick, Dennis, Aberdeen......	57	179	154	14	36	46	6	2	0	15	3	1	4	17	0	26	6	2	2	.234	.324	.299
York, Larry, Vermont †...........	32	139	125	5	26	29	3	0	0	10	5	0	2	7	0	15	4	6	0	.208	.261	.232
Young, Dustin, Jamestown	50	174	160	16	39	44	5	0	0	16	2	1	1	10	0	25	6	2	6	.244	.291	.275
Zamora, Hector, Staten Is.* ...	63	269	225	29	57	92	10	2	7	27	2	0	11	31	0	56	5	3	8	.253	.371	.409

GRAND SLAMS—Alen, Evans, Giarratano, Madrid, Mather, B. Moss, Rico, Roberts, Snyder, Tugwell, 1 each.

AWARDED FIRST BASE ON CATCHER'S INTERFERENCE—S. Robinson 3 (Alen, Pignatiello, Sanchez); Chiaravolloti 2 (Pierce, Schmitt); Cloninger (Riley); Cruz (Clendenin); Estrada (Piazza); C. Grimm (Y. Garcia).

2003 PITCHING

TEAM

Team	W	L	Pct.	ERA	G	CG	ShO	Sv.	IP	H	TBF	R	ER	HR	SH	SF	HB	BB	IBB	SO	WP	Bk.
Auburn	56	18	.757	2.52	74	0	10	25	650.0	493	2616	217	182	20	10	19	36	188	3	698	42	2
Williamsport......	46	30	.605	2.64	76	1	8	21	661.2	545	2754	244	194	30	19	21	51	225	7	550	38	4
Brooklyn............	47	28	.627	2.97	75	0	11	37	658.1	547	2723	244	217	25	28	21	47	214	16	561	39	6
Staten Island.....	29	43	.403	3.12	72	2	4	14	651.1	613	2825	327	226	24	34	27	45	251	4	544	53	10
Hudson Val..........	37	37	.500	3.17	74	1	10	21	645.0	605	2711	286	227	28	20	24	31	198	8	487	36	4
Lowell	39	35	.527	3.21	74	0	6	17	645.2	644	2741	313	230	36	24	19	49	143	10	482	33	4
Aberdeen...........	38	38	.500	3.29	76	1	1	25	680.1	615	2894	308	249	26	26	18	62	234	9	636	27	7
Tri-City	44	32	.579	3.41	76	0	7	21	661.2	546	2820	292	251	32	21	23	60	290	3	631	38	3
Batavia	30	45	.400	3.50	75	1	2	15	678.0	626	2859	333	264	38	25	22	36	230	4	513	37	4
Oneonta.............	45	30	.600	3.68	75	0	4	22	652.2	610	2795	318	267	29	25	28	37	245	8	532	45	8
New Jersey	31	42	.425	3.75	73	0	4	17	645.0	638	2798	331	269	20	25	29	48	263	8	509	75	9
Mahoning Val....	38	36	.514	3.75	74	0	4	15	640.2	628	2772	330	267	29	28	21	47	229	8	536	40	5
Vermont	19	56	.253	4.60	75	1	1	11	640.0	625	2922	427	327	33	36	28	63	338	0	478	87	7
Jamestown.........	22	51	.301	5.61	73	0	1	14	623.2	696	2883	444	389	46	11	30	45	348	2	566	65	10

INDIVIDUAL

TOP QUALIFIERS FOR EARNED-RUN AVERAGE TITLE

Minimum 61 innings. *Lefthanded pitcher.

Pitcher, Team	W	L	Pct.	ERA	G	GS	CG	ShO	GF	Sv.	IP	H	TBF	R	ER	HR	SH	SF	HB	BB	IBB	SO	WP	Bk.
Torrealba, Yoann, Wil.	6	1	.857	2.04	14	14	0	0	0	0	75.0	61	302	24	17	2	1	2	9	15	0	60	2	1
Mastny, Thomas, Auburn	8	0	1.000	2.26	14	14	0	0	0	0	63.2	56	251	19	16	1	0	0	3	12	0	68	2	1
Banks, Joshua, Auburn	7	2	.778	2.43	15	15	0	0	0	0	66.2	58	264	21	18	1	0	4	1	10	0	81	5	0
DeLeon, Joey, Tri-City	5	3	.625	2.47	17	14	0	0	1	0	87.1	67	354	30	24	6	3	3	9	26	0	68	1	0
Karstens, Jeffrey, Staten Is.	4	2	.667	2.54	14	10	0	0	2	0	67.1	63	275	22	19	2	6	5	2	16	1	53	3	0
Tata, Jordan, Oneonta	4	3	.571	2.58	16	12	0	0	2	1	73.1	64	306	32	21	1	5	4	6	20	0	60	4	1
Gangi, Aaron, Hudson Valley *	5	2	.714	2.63	14	14	0	0	0	0	75.1	75	309	33	22	2	1	5	1	10	0	59	4	0
Plexico, Gerald, Vermont *......	3	3	.500	2.69	17	9	0	0	2	1	70.1	59	292	26	21	3	7	3	7	16	0	49	0	1
Libey, Justin, Batavia...............	4	4	.500	2.78	17	9	0	0	1	1	68.0	68	292	31	21	4	1	2	5	24	0	63	4	1
Dixon, Zachary, Aberdeen *	4	3	.571	2.91	14	14	0	0	0	0	68.0	65	290	26	22	3	2	0	10	18	0	70	4	0
Albers, Matt, Tri-City	5	4	.556	2.92	15	14	0	0	0	0	86.1	69	355	37	28	1	3	0	5	25	0	94	4	1
Harmsen, Brandon, Staten Is..	3	6	.333	3.14	15	15	0	0	0	0	86.0	95	377	47	30	1	0	3	2	23	0	54	3	3
Shafer, Kurt, Williamsport	7	3	.700	3.15	14	9	1	0	3	2	65.2	54	267	29	23	3	1	2	5	18	0	35	1	1
Deza, Fredy, Aberdeen..............	3	5	.375	3.25	15	14	1	0	0	0	74.2	75	317	32	27	1	0	2	3	20	2	69	0	3
Coppinger, Joe, Aberdeen	6	4	.600	3.29	14	12	0	0	0	0	63.0	56	265	29	23	2	1	3	4	17	0	59	1	1

DEPARTMENTAL LEADERS: W—Mastny, 8; L—Pearson, 11; Pct.—Mastny, 1.000; G—Buzachero, Morales, Romero, 30; GS—Banks, Bostick, Grigsby, Harmsen, 15; CG—Several pitchers tied with 1; ShO—Several pitchers tied with 1; GF—Buzachero, 26; Sv.—Homer, Paulk, 15; IP—DeLeon, 87.1; H—Harmsen, 95; TBF—Harmsen, 377; R—Long, 65; ER—Long, 56; HR—Bostick, Diefenderf, 9; SH—Plexico, 7; SF—Tomey, 7; HB—Penny, 11; BB—Pearson, 54; IBB—Lopez, 5; SO—Albers, 94; WP—Pearson, 16; BK—Bostick, Deza, Harmsen, Maldonado, 3.

ALL PITCHERS

*Lefthanded pitcher.

Pitcher, Team	W	L	Pct.	ERA	G	GS	CG	ShO	GF	Sv.	IP	H	TBF	R	ER	HR	SH	SF	HB	BB	IBB	SO	WP	Bk.
Aguero, Miguel, New Jersey ...	1	0	1.000	6.75	1	1	0	0	0	0	5.1	7	24	4	4	0	0	0	1	2	0	4	0	0
Albers, Matt, Tri-City	5	4	.556	2.92	15	14	0	0	0	0	86.1	69	355	37	28	1	3	0	5	25	0	94	4	1
Alvarez, Abraham, Lowell *.....	0	0	.000	0.00	9	9	0	0	0	0	19.0	9	68	2	0	0	0	1	0	2	1	19	0	0
Anderson, Wes, Lowell............	0	0	.000	0.00	3	3	0	0	0	0	2.1	1	10	0	0	0	0	0	0	2	0	1	0	0
Astacio, Andres, Tri-City..........	0	1	.000	5.68	3	1	0	0	0	0	6.1	7	28	4	4	1	0	0	0	4	0	6	0	0
Baez, William, Oneonta	0	1	.000	7.20	5	0	0	0	3	0	5.0	5	25	4	4	1	0	0	2	5	0	0	2	0
Baldwin, Andy, Oneonta	4	2	.667	2.76	9	9	0	0	0	0	42.1	41	178	16	13	1	1	0	3	16	0	27	1	0
Banks, Joshua, Auburn	7	2	.778	2.43	15	15	0	0	0	0	66.2	58	264	21	18	1	0	4	1	10	0	81	5	0
Bannister, Brian, Brooklyn........	4	1	.800	2.15	12	9	0	0	1	1	46.0	27	179	12	11	0	3	1	1	18	0	42	4	2
Basch, Zachary, Lowell............	3	2	.600	4.08	24	0	0	0	19	6	28.2	30	137	19	13	0	3	2	2	18	3	25	2	0
Basilio, Manuel, H.V.	1	0	1.000	1.69	15	0	0	0	8	2	21.1	17	89	4	4	2	1	0	3	8	0	16	1	0
Batista, Roberto, New Jersey ..	3	1	.750	0.88	26	0	0	0	20	11	30.2	23	127	8	3	0	1	3	0	11	2	22	1	2
Bayer, Russ, Williamsport *	1	3	.250	2.21	21	2	0	0	7	0	57.0	51	236	18	14	2	1	4	3	21	0	46	2	0
Beam, T.J., Staten Island.........	2	1	.667	2.70	9	5	0	0	1	1	33.1	25	137	14	10	4	1	2	0	9	0	31	1	0
Bedard, Erik, Aberdeen *.........	0	0	.000	2.35	2	2	0	0	0	0	7.2	7	31	2	2	0	0	0	0	1	0	13	1	0
Beltre, Jonathan, Tri-City *......	2	1	.667	3.43	21	0	0	0	8	3	44.2	32	184	18	17	6	2	2	1	20	0	51	1	0
Berube, Martin, Aberdeen	3	3	.500	4.01	18	3	0	0	5	2	51.2	50	230	27	23	5	0	2	5	21	0	48	0	1
Bimeal, Matt, Williamsport......	4	2	.667	1.91	27	0	0	0	16	1	47.0	35	189	13	10	1	2	1	5	13	1	37	6	1
Blackwell, Brad, Staten Island .	0	3	.000	4.79	13	0	0	0	2	0	20.2	20	98	14	11	0	2	0	2	13	1	22	3	0

Pitcher, Team	W	L	Pct.	ERA	G	GS	CG	ShO	GF	Sv.	IP	H	TBF	R	ER	HR	SH	SF	HB	BB	IBB	SO	WP	Bk.
Blair, Tom, New Jersey *	1	2	.333	3.58	8	6	0	0	1	0	37.2	30	148	18	15	0	3	1	1	11	0	32	1	1
Blaney, Matt, Lowell	0	0	.000	2.08	5	0	0	0	3	0	8.2	6	36	3	2	1	0	0	1	4	0	5	1	0
Blanton, Matt, New Jersey *	0	0	.000	3.00	2	2	0	0	0	0	12.0	14	50	4	4	1	1	1	1	2	0	11	2	0
Bonnell, Jared, New Jersey	1	0	1.000	5.91	6	0	0	0	2	0	10.2	10	44	7	7	0	0	0	1	2	0	7	0	0
Bostick, Adam, Jamestown *	4	6	.400	5.12	15	15	0	0	0	0	77.1	77	345	49	44	9	2	4	7	39	0	76	5	3
Boughner, Anthony, Aber.*	1	2	.333	1.90	24	0	0	0	10	6	47.1	40	189	11	10	0	5	0	1	15	1	36	0	0
Brandenburg, Adam, M.V.*	1	4	.200	5.13	11	11	0	0	0	0	47.1	58	211	29	27	3	2	3	2	11	1	26	4	1
Brey, Josh, New Jersey *	3	3	.500	3.24	14	9	0	0	2	1	58.1	59	247	27	21	5	3	2	3	18	0	36	5	0
Burton, T.J., Mahoning Valley	4	2	.667	6.79	14	14	0	0	0	0	63.2	83	294	52	48	7	2	0	2	28	0	39	5	1
Buzachero, Bubbie, Auburn	1	1	.500	1.54	30	0	0	0	26	13	35.0	25	136	8	6	1	2	0	2	7	0	47	2	0
Caceres, Carlos, Vermont	0	2	.000	5.12	12	3	0	0	5	1	31.2	28	144	22	18	5	1	2	4	15	0	15	3	1
Canizal, Joaquin, Auburn	0	1	.000	2.08	3	0	0	0	0	0	4.1	1	17	1	1	0	0	0	1	2	1	4	0	0
Caraballo, Angel, Staten Is.	0	0	.000	18.00	1	0	0	0	0	0	1.0	2	6	2	2	1	1	0	0	1	0	0	1	0
Casey, Reid, Mahoning Valley	1	2	.333	3.06	16	0	0	0	16	7	17.2	18	75	6	6	1	1	0	2	5	0	20	3	0
Castle, Heath, Staten Island *	2	2	.500	6.75	13	0	0	0	7	0	13.1	20	70	14	10	1	2	1	3	5	0	11	1	0
Castro, Rafael, Brooklyn	3	2	.600	2.17	20	1	0	0	3	0	37.1	25	148	9	9	0	1	1	2	11	1	40	2	0
Cevette, Dan, M.V.*	0	2	.000	8.22	2	2	0	0	0	0	7.2	14	44	11	7	1	0	0	1	5	0	3	3	0
Chick, Travis, Jamestown	1	2	.333	5.71	13	10	0	0	0	0	52.0	63	241	41	33	3	1	2	2	26	0	48	3	0
Cierlik, Jason, Aberdeen *	3	1	.750	3.29	22	0	0	0	7	3	38.1	37	177	18	14	2	5	0	4	25	1	39	1	0
Cillo, Cody, Jamestown	3	1	.750	2.86	17	0	0	0	12	1	22.0	23	96	8	7	0	1	2	1	9	0	27	2	0
Cochran, Robert, Lowell *	2	3	.400	4.86	20	0	0	0	12	2	33.1	40	140	26	18	5	0	2	1	4	0	20	0	1
Collar, Michael, Tri-City	2	3	.400	4.11	14	3	0	0	8	5	35.0	29	148	18	16	3	0	2	3	9	0	26	2	0
Colson, Jason, Auburn	0	0	.000	0.00	3	0	0	0	0	0	6.0	3	25	1	0	0	0	0	0	4	0	6	1	0
Contreras, Jose, Staten Island	0	0	.000	0.00	1	1	0	0	0	0	7.0	2	23	0	0	0	0	0	0	0	0	15	0	0
Contreras, Manuel, Oneonta	3	0	1.000	3.28	17	0	0	0	8	1	24.2	29	118	12	9	2	0	1	1	14	0	16	1	1
Cooper, Dexter, Lowell	0	0	.000	5.40	3	0	0	0	0	0	5.0	7	25	4	3	0	0	1	0	3	0	5	1	0
Coppinger, Joe, Aberdeen	6	4	.600	3.29	14	12	0	0	0	0	63.0	56	265	29	23	2	1	3	4	17	0	59	1	1
Cordova, Vincent, Brooklyn	3	2	.600	2.65	9	8	0	0	0	0	37.1	38	158	13	11	3	1	0	4	7	2	41	2	0
Core, Danny, Auburn	6	2	.750	3.14	16	4	0	0	2	1	51.2	41	210	22	18	5	1	2	6	17	0	34	5	0
Corn, Jessie, Lowell	0	0	.000	0.00	4	0	0	0	0	0	4.1	2	20	5	0	0	0	0	0	3	0	4	1	0
Correa, Stephen, Brooklyn *	1	1	.500	7.16	13	0	0	0	1	0	16.1	18	83	13	13	2	1	0	2	13	2	19	2	0
Cramer, Bob, Hudson Valley *	0	1	.000	1.69	5	2	0	0	2	1	10.2	9	41	2	2	1	1	0	0	1	0	6	0	0
Danly, Ryan, Brooklyn *	2	2	.500	3.29	13	11	0	0	0	0	54.2	51	229	24	20	2	5	3	2	15	0	29	1	0
Davis, Brendon, Tri-City	1	1	.500	2.19	12	0	0	0	4	1	24.2	25	111	12	6	0	1	0	1	10	0	23	3	0
Davis, Matt, Mahoning Valley	4	4	.500	1.54	23	0	0	0	5	0	46.2	34	190	17	8	0	1	1	6	11	0	40	2	0
Day, Dewon, Auburn	0	0	.000	0.00	2	0	0	0	1	0	1.1	1	5	0	0	0	0	0	0	0	0	1	0	0
De Maria, Chris, Williamsport	6	3	.667	2.68	25	1	0	0	9	3	47.0	36	189	15	14	3	1	0	6	10	1	48	3	0
De la Cruz, Eulogio, Oneonta	0	0	.000	10.80	2	0	0	0	0	0	3.1	6	17	4	4	0	0	0	1	1	0	4	1	0
De la Cruz, Julio, Batavia	1	6	.143	4.37	12	12	0	0	0	0	55.2	44	234	33	27	7	3	1	2	22	0	50	2	0
DeChristofaro, Vinny, Bat.*	4	0	1.000	4.62	15	3	0	0	5	0	37.0	36	165	21	19	2	0	2	0	20	0	32	1	0
DeLeon, Joey, Tri-City	5	3	.625	2.47	17	14	0	0	1	0	87.1	67	354	30	24	6	3	3	9	26	0	68	1	0
Dean, Herman, Oneonta	0	0	.000	6.75	1	0	0	0	0	0	1.1	1	7	2	1	0	0	1	0	1	0	1	2	1
Desalvo, Matthew, Staten Is.	3	3	.500	1.84	10	10	1	0	0	0	49.0	42	205	18	10	2	1	0	4	19	1	52	2	2
Deza, Fredy, Aberdeen	3	5	.375	3.25	15	14	1	0	0	0	74.2	75	317	32	27	1	0	2	3	20	2	69	0	3
Diaz, Eddie, Vermont	1	2	.333	3.38	13	1	0	0	5	2	26.2	22	119	13	10	0	0	2	1	17	0	32	6	0
Diaz, Luis, Oneonta	1	0	1.000	2.70	2	2	0	0	0	0	10.0	11	44	3	3	0	0	0	3	3	0	12	0	0
Diefenderfer, Joseph, Bat.*	6	8	.429	5.50	16	13	1	0	2	0	73.2	85	315	49	45	9	3	1	1	14	1	58	3	1
Dischiavo, John, H.V.	1	4	.200	6.56	7	6	0	0	0	0	23.1	29	110	21	17	3	1	2	3	10	0	15	2	0
Dixon, Jeffrey, Vermont	1	1	.500	1.69	7	1	0	0	3	0	10.2	7	42	3	2	1	0	0	2	2	0	9	0	0
Dixon, Zachary, Aberdeen *	4	3	.571	2.91	14	14	0	0	0	0	68.0	65	290	26	22	3	2	0	10	18	0	70	4	0
Dove, Dennis, New Jersey	1	3	.250	3.51	7	7	0	0	0	0	25.2	29	120	15	10	1	0	2	1	15	0	15	4	0
Drown, Erik, New Jersey	3	2	.600	2.96	10	8	0	0	0	0	45.2	26	181	19	15	2	3	0	3	22	0	34	9	0
Durbin, Chad, M.V.	1	1	.500	2.25	2	2	0	0	0	0	12.0	9	46	4	3	1	0	0	2	3	0	8	0	0
Eazor, Kyle, Jamestown *	0	0	.000	11.25	2	0	0	0	0	0	4.0	6	21	6	5	2	0	0	0	5	0	2	0	0
Echarry, Nelson, Batavia	0	0	.000	4.50	2	0	0	0	2	0	4.0	4	20	3	2	0	0	1	0	4	0	4	0	0
Edmiston, Robert, Tri-City	3	2	.600	4.61	18	0	0	0	6	1	27.1	29	132	17	14	2	3	4	4	21	1	21	3	2
Ellis, Rob, Hudson Valley *	1	0	1.000	1.29	11	0	0	0	1	1	28.0	22	105	8	4	1	0	0	0	2	0	21	0	0
Escobar, Rodrigo, Tri-City	4	1	.800	2.97	15	1	0	0	7	1	36.1	35	151	13	12	1	1	2	1	8	0	38	3	0
Everts, Clint, Vermont	2	4	.333	4.17	10	10	0	0	0	0	54.0	49	240	26	25	4	2	1	4	35	0	50	7	0
Farley, Chris, Lowell	1	3	.250	4.70	18	0	0	0	5	0	30.2	30	130	17	16	1	2	2	2	9	1	29	1	0
Farrell, Jarrod, Hudson Valley	3	3	.500	3.70	13	12	1	1	0	0	73.0	71	299	32	30	5	1	0	1	13	1	44	3	0
Fernandez, Carlos, H.V.	1	3	.250	3.12	23	0	0	0	8	0	34.2	31	151	15	12	2	3	1	0	14	1	24	4	0
Finch, Brian, Aberdeen	1	3	.250	1.93	8	5	0	0	0	0	28.0	19	111	9	6	0	0	0	2	5	0	29	0	0
Fischer, Sam, Tri-City	2	3	.400	3.94	22	0	0	0	15	2	29.2	19	138	15	13	0	1	1	5	28	1	43	3	0
Galbraith, Jason, N.J.*	1	1	.500	1.86	17	0	0	0	5	2	19.1	8	77	6	4	0	1	0	3	8	0	17	5	0
Gangi, Aaron, Hudson Valley *	5	2	.714	2.63	14	14	0	0	0	0	75.1	75	309	33	22	2	1	5	1	10	0	59	4	0
Gardner, Jarrett, Lowell	5	3	.625	4.20	14	7	0	0	2	0	60.0	69	254	34	28	6	5	4	2	2	0	29	3	0
Gardner, Michael, Staten Isl.	1	4	.200	1.93	23	0	0	0	18	5	37.1	31	155	14	8	2	2	0	1	11	0	29	6	0
Garza, Alberto, M.V.	0	0	.000	0.00	1	0	0	0	0	0	1.0	0	3	0	0	0	0	0	0	0	0	2	0	0
Garza, Justin, New Jersey	0	0	.000	0.00	2	0	0	0	2	1	3.0	1	11	0	0	0	0	0	0	0	0	5	0	0
Generelli, Daniel, Vermont	0	3	.000	10.18	13	3	0	0	9	1	20.1	34	113	29	23	2	1	4	3	15	0	8	6	1
George, Taylor, Brooklyn	5	3	.625	1.40	26	0	0	0	9	3	38.2	23	147	7	6	1	3	0	3	9	2	29	2	1
Gomez, Warmar, Vermont	1	2	.333	1.82	16	0	0	0	5	2	29.2	19	122	11	6	1	2	1	2	10	0	13	0	0
Gonzalez, Jino, H.V.*	0	1	.000	4.50	3	3	0	0	0	0	12.0	11	53	7	6	0	0	2	0	6	0	11	0	0
Goodman, Chris, Vermont	3	0	1.000	0.84	6	3	0	0	1	0	32.0	18	118	3	3	1	5	1	1	5	0	23	2	0
Gorzelanny, Thomas, Wil.*	1	2	.333	1.78	8	8	0	0	0	0	30.1	23	120	6	6	1	1	1	1	10	0	22	1	0
Gosch, Kirk, Hudson Valley *	0	1	.000	3.86	8	0	0	0	5	0	14.0	13	62	9	6	0	0	0	0	7	0	15	2	0
Graham, Jason, Oneonta	0	1	.000	9.82	7	0	0	0	3	0	11.0	15	59	12	12	2	0	1	2	8	0	7	2	0
Grigsby, Derick, Tri-City	5	5	.500	4.86	15	15	0	0	0	0	76.0	73	334	44	41	7	2	3	7	32	0	62	3	0
Hacker, Eric, Staten Island	0	0	.000	1.00	2	2	0	0	0	0	9.0	10	40	2	1	0	0	0	1	1	0	5	0	0
Hanson, Adam, M.V.	3	2	.600	2.45	21	0	0	0	1	0	40.1	38	166	15	11	1	2	1	3	6	0	33	0	1
Harmsen, Brandon, Staten Is.	3	6	.333	3.14	15	15	0	0	0	0	86.0	95	377	47	30	1	0	3	2	23	0	54	3	3
Harper, Jeremy, Auburn	5	1	.833	3.79	19	1	0	0	2	0	40.1	28	166	18	17	2	0	4	3	18	0	36	2	0

Pitcher, Team	W	L	Pct.	ERA	G	GS	CG	ShO	GF	Sv.	IP	H	TBF	R	ER	HR	SH	SF	HB	BB	IBB	SO	WP	Bk.
Harris, Mark, Mahoning Valley	2	2	.500	4.22	16	0	0	0	7	0	21.1	21	95	10	10	1	1	1	1	10	0	9	4	0
Haught, Dallas, Hudson Valley	0	0	.000	9.00	5	0	0	0	2	0	6.0	11	35	7	6	1	0	0	1	5	0	3	1	0
Hawk, Shane, Brooklyn *	0	0	.000	0.00	6	3	0	0	2	0	12.2	6	47	1	0	0	0	0	1	4	0	12	0	0
Henderson, Jim, Vermont	1	1	.500	6.93	15	0	0	0	4	0	24.2	32	126	28	19	1	3	0	3	15	0	13	2	0
Hernandez, Christopher, Wil.	1	2	.333	1.64	20	0	0	0	6	3	38.1	28	161	8	7	0	5	1	2	16	3	41	3	0
Hernandez, Michael, M.V.*	3	0	1.000	0.00	4	0	0	0	0	0	10.1	2	38	0	0	0	0	0	2	3	0	14	1	0
Hertzler, Barry, Lowell	2	2	.500	3.77	12	0	0	0	6	1	14.1	22	74	9	6	0	0	0	3	5	1	8	2	0
Hirsh, Jason, Tri-City	3	1	.750	1.95	10	8	0	0	0	0	32.1	22	126	10	7	0	0	1	2	7	0	33	1	0
Hodges, Daniel, Batavia *	0	0	.000	1.26	8	0	0	0	5	1	14.1	12	58	3	2	0	2	0	1	3	1	13	3	0
Homer, Chris, Oneonta	2	1	.667	2.60	26	0	0	0	24	15	27.2	17	108	9	8	2	2	1	0	10	1	30	4	0
Howell, Michael, Oneonta	2	0	1.000	1.35	4	3	0	0	0	0	20.0	13	78	4	3	2	0	0	0	4	0	12	0	0
Humen, David, Jamestown	1	1	.500	11.57	7	0	0	0	4	0	9.1	15	51	13	12	4	0	0	1	11	0	10	2	0
Iehl, Jason, Jamestown	1	2	.333	9.00	4	4	0	0	0	0	18.0	22	83	18	18	1	0	2	4	5	0	16	2	1
Isenberg, Kurt, Auburn *	7	2	.778	1.63	13	13	0	0	0	0	60.2	40	244	17	11	1	1	2	4	19	0	57	1	0
Jackson, Kyle, Lowell	1	1	.500	0.93	2	2	0	0	0	0	9.2	7	39	6	1	0	0	0	2	2	0	2	0	0
James, Justin, Auburn	2	1	.667	3.20	13	8	0	0	0	0	39.1	34	159	14	14	2	2	2	1	11	0	42	7	0
John, Jason, New Jersey	1	3	.250	5.84	21	3	0	0	5	0	49.1	81	240	41	32	2	2	2	1	23	0	39	8	1
Jordan, B.J., New Jersey *	4	1	.800	2.08	27	0	0	0	11	1	30.1	30	131	12	7	0	0	1	3	11	1	27	2	0
Karstens, Jeffrey, Staten Is.	4	2	.667	2.54	14	10	0	0	2	0	67.1	63	275	22	19	2	6	5	2	16	1	53	3	0
Kartler, Bryce, Staten Island *.	0	3	.000	5.89	14	0	0	0	9	1	18.1	20	89	15	12	1	3	1	5	11	0	19	4	0
Kensing, Logan, Jamestown	2	4	.333	5.73	8	6	0	0	0	0	33.0	48	155	23	21	1	0	2	3	6	0	20	2	0
Keppel, Bob, Brooklyn	2	0	1.000	2.51	3	3	0	0	0	0	14.1	10	57	5	4	0	0	0	2	2	0	13	0	0
Kerschen, Joshua, Staten Is.	0	2	.000	5.56	8	0	0	0	1	0	11.1	17	55	15	7	2	1	1	1	3	0	7	0	0
Kiley, Jason, Williamsport	0	1	.000	4.73	10	1	0	0	4	0	13.1	16	64	10	7	1	0	2	0	8	0	8	4	0
King, Bryan, Brooklyn	2	2	.500	2.67	17	0	0	0	5	3	30.1	25	124	10	9	2	2	1	2	7	1	30	0	0
Kirkman, Ty, Vermont *	0	3	.000	7.66	21	0	0	0	5	0	24.2	39	135	31	21	1	1	3	3	21	0	9	5	2
Knapp, Ben, Aberdeen	0	0	.000	7.71	2	2	0	0	0	0	4.2	5	24	4	4	0	0	0	1	4	0	2	1	0
Kupper, Dustin, Jamestown	3	6	.333	5.43	14	8	0	0	2	0	56.1	57	258	35	34	1	2	6	7	32	0	49	4	0
Lara, Juan, Mahoning Valley *	3	3	.500	3.50	12	12	0	0	0	0	61.2	54	261	29	24	4	4	1	8	18	1	54	6	0
Libey, Justin, Batavia	4	4	.500	2.78	17	9	0	0	1	1	68.0	68	292	31	21	4	1	2	5	24	0	63	4	1
Lincoln, Roger, M.V.*	3	0	1.000	2.64	17	4	0	0	3	0	44.1	43	183	13	13	0	1	1	1	11	1	41	2	1
Lindstrom, Matthew, Brooklyn	7	3	.700	3.44	14	14	0	0	0	0	65.1	61	280	28	25	2	0	2	7	27	0	52	6	0
Lissir, Alexander, Wil.	5	4	.556	3.72	15	14	0	0	0	0	72.2	77	320	40	30	7	3	4	5	24	0	49	2	0
Little, Chris, Vermont	0	4	.000	5.88	21	0	0	0	12	2	33.2	41	178	38	22	3	3	2	8	25	0	28	7	0
Little, Joe, Hudson Valley *	4	0	1.000	0.29	5	5	0	0	0	0	31.0	17	115	1	1	0	1	0	1	10	0	25	2	0
Loewen, Adam, Aberdeen *	0	2	.000	2.70	7	7	0	0	0	0	23.1	13	91	7	7	0	0	0	4	9	0	25	2	0
Long, Nick, Vermont	3	9	.250	7.34	14	14	1	0	0	0	68.2	77	323	65	56	2	4	1	6	36	0	63	10	0
Lopez, Aleurys, Hudson Valley	5	1	.833	2.50	11	2	0	0	5	1	39.2	28	161	15	11	2	1	1	0	17	5	22	1	1
Lovato, Nicholas, Jam.*	2	6	.250	8.06	20	0	0	0	1	0	25.2	37	136	28	23	1	1	4	2	18	0	21	3	1
Lundgren, Wayne, Lowell	1	2	.333	3.46	15	2	0	0	1	0	39.0	39	160	22	15	0	1	0	1	3	0	17	1	0
Lyons, Tom, Oneonta	2	5	.286	4.41	12	4	0	0	2	0	34.2	38	152	20	17	2	2	2	1	10	0	22	8	0
MacLane, Evan, Brooklyn *	1	0	1.000	0.00	1	1	0	0	0	0	6.0	3	23	0	0	0	0	0	0	1	0	5	0	0
Machi, Jean, Batavia	2	4	.333	4.78	8	8	0	0	0	0	32.0	30	139	21	17	1	1	2	7	13	0	19	2	0
Maholm, Paul, Williamsport *.	2	1	.667	1.83	8	8	0	0	0	0	34.1	25	138	11	7	1	0	1	0	10	0	32	1	0
Maldonado, Ivan, Brooklyn	5	2	.714	4.06	18	4	0	0	2	1	51.0	50	214	23	23	4	1	2	3	12	1	34	0	3
Mann, Brandon, H.V.*	0	2	.000	6.97	2	2	0	0	0	0	10.1	8	39	8	8	0	0	0	0	5	0	7	0	1
Mansfield, Monte, Tri-City	1	1	.500	2.79	10	0	0	0	9	4	9.2	6	46	3	3	0	1	0	3	9	0	11	0	0
Marchbanks, David, Jam.*	0	0	.000	1.23	5	3	0	0	0	0	14.2	11	57	2	2	1	0	0	0	3	0	12	1	1
Marcum, Shaun, Auburn	1	0	1.000	1.32	21	0	0	0	13	8	34.0	15	124	6	5	1	0	0	1	7	0	47	2	0
Marshall, Brian, Lowell *	1	1	.500	1.08	15	0	0	0	13	6	16.2	10	63	3	2	1	1	0	1	2	1	15	0	0
Martin, Greg, Vermont *	0	1	.000	7.94	3	0	0	0	0	0	5.2	6	28	5	5	0	0	0	0	4	0	3	5	0
Martinez, Carlos, Jamestown	0	1	.000	5.40	1	0	0	0	1	0	1.2	2	9	1	1	0	0	0	0	1	0	4	1	0
Martinez, Roberto, Vermont	0	0	.000	4.63	8	0	0	0	7	1	11.2	13	54	8	6	0	0	3	1	3	0	7	2	0
Maruffi, Joseph, Vermont	0	0	.000	4.91	3	0	0	0	2	0	3.2	4	17	4	2	0	0	0	0	1	0	1	0	0
Mastny, Thomas, Auburn	8	0	1.000	2.26	14	14	0	0	0	0	63.2	56	251	19	16	1	0	0	3	12	0	68	2	1
Mathieson, Scott, Batavia	0	0	.000	0.00	2	0	0	0	1	1	6.0	0	18	0	0	0	0	0	0	0	0	7	0	0
McCally, Ryan, Hudson Valley	1	2	.333	3.35	9	8	0	0	0	0	45.2	47	193	21	17	3	1	1	3	11	0	31	0	0
McConnell, Caleb, Batavia	0	4	.000	4.08	23	0	0	0	10	2	46.1	54	201	22	21	0	2	1	1	13	0	32	2	1
McCormack, Zach, Jam.*	0	2	.000	4.56	17	0	0	0	8	4	25.2	24	124	18	13	0	1	0	2	26	0	35	4	0
Meccage, Justin, Staten Island	0	0	.000	108.00	1	0	0	0	0	0	0.1	6	8	4	4	0	0	1	0	1	0	0	1	0
Menocal, Victor, Batavia	3	0	1.000	1.61	5	5	0	0	0	0	28.0	14	105	7	5	0	1	1	1	12	0	14	1	0
Merchant, Jamie, Tri-City	5	1	.833	3.44	16	8	0	0	5	1	55.0	36	226	22	21	1	0	1	5	25	0	56	3	0
Michael, Mark, New Jersey	1	2	.333	3.17	11	10	0	0	0	0	54.0	50	226	23	19	0	0	1	4	20	0	56	4	1
Mincey, T.W., Aberdeen *	1	1	.500	3.52	9	0	0	0	6	0	7.2	7	36	3	3	0	0	0	3	4	2	6	3	0
Minor, Zach, Batavia	0	2	.000	1.25	15	0	0	0	3	1	36.0	22	140	10	5	0	2	0	3	14	0	15	4	0
Miramontes, Matthew, Brook.	0	0	.000	18.00	1	1	0	0	0	0	1.0	0	8	2	2	0	0	0	0	5	0	1	1	0
Mondesir, James, New Jersey.	0	4	.000	6.66	7	7	0	0	0	0	24.1	34	116	22	18	1	3	2	3	10	0	19	1	1
Montano, Ignacio, M.V.*	0	1	.000	15.43	5	0	0	0	2	0	4.2	9	27	8	8	1	0	0	1	3	0	3	0	0
Morales, Juan, New Jersey	1	2	.333	2.09	30	0	0	0	10	1	38.2	22	153	10	9	1	1	2	4	13	2	38	3	0
Muecke, Joshua, Tri-City *	3	3	.500	4.14	14	11	0	0	0	0	54.1	58	233	28	25	2	2	1	1	25	0	43	5	0
Mulholland, Chad, Auburn	1	0	1.000	2.78	8	5	0	0	0	0	22.2	23	97	10	7	1	1	1	1	7	0	14	1	0
Muniz, Carlos, Brooklyn	0	0	.000	0.45	19	0	0	0	15	13	20.0	12	73	1	1	1	1	0	0	5	2	23	3	0
Naatjes, Darin, Batavia	1	3	.250	3.62	8	7	0	0	0	0	27.1	23	117	15	11	0	0	1	1	10	0	24	1	0
Navaroli, Michael, H.V.	1	0	1.000	0.73	8	0	0	0	2	1	12.1	9	47	3	1	0	0	0	0	4	0	11	0	0
Neal, Tony, Aberdeen	2	1	.667	1.94	19	0	0	0	6	1	41.2	30	169	15	9	1	3	2	4	19	0	43	2	0
Nowicki, Nathan, Jamestown	0	2	.000	5.46	18	0	0	0	10	3	28.0	32	125	18	17	1	1	2	2	13	2	18	4	1
Nunez, Franklin, Brooklyn	0	0	.000	5.06	7	0	0	0	3	0	5.1	5	26	4	3	0	0	1	1	4	0	8	1	0
Nunez, Leo, Williamsport	4	3	.571	3.05	8	8	0	0	0	0	38.1	31	163	14	13	0	1	1	2	12	0	41	0	0
Nyquist, Brett, Vermont *	0	3	.000	3.15	5	5	0	0	0	0	20.0	16	82	8	7	1	0	0	0	6	0	19	1	0
O'Connor, Shaun, Jamestown.	0	0	.000	11.25	3	0	0	0	3	0	4.0	7	22	6	5	0	0	0	0	5	0	3	3	1
Ochoa, Javier, Brooklyn	3	1	.750	6.23	6	0	0	0	0	0	8.2	10	45	8	6	0	0	0	0	11	1	7	1	0
Ochoa, Nehomar, Vermont	2	1	.667	1.80	5	5	0	0	0	0	30.0	26	123	8	6	1	0	0	2	8	0	13	1	0
Ohalek, Corey, Jamestown *	1	0	1.000	5.68	3	0	0	0	1	0	6.1	9	30	5	4	2	0	0	0	2	0	6	1	0

Pitcher, Team	W	L	Pct.	ERA	G	GS	CG	ShO	GF	Sv.	IP	H	TBF	R	ER	HR	SH	SF	HB	BB	IBB	SO	WP	Bk.
Ool, Kevin, Lowell *	3	1	.750	2.56	25	0	0	0	8	1	38.2	37	157	14	11	2	4	0	1	5	1	33	0	0
Orloski, Joe, Brooklyn	3	0	1.000	1.08	11	0	0	0	2	0	16.2	12	65	3	2	0	0	0	2	4	0	14	1	0
Orozco, Antonio, Jamestown	0	1	.000	9.00	1	0	0	0	0	0	4.0	9	20	4	4	1	0	1	0	0	0	2	0	0
Orvella, Chad, Hudson Valley	0	0	.000	0.00	10	0	0	0	9	8	12.1	6	44	0	0	0	0	0	0	1	0	15	0	0
Osberg, Tanner, Brooklyn	1	3	.250	3.00	8	6	0	0	0	0	33.0	30	134	13	11	1	1	2	1	6	0	17	0	0
Osentowski, Chris, Aberdeen	4	5	.444	5.05	19	1	0	0	8	0	41.0	43	182	30	23	2	3	2	4	11	1	33	2	1
Overton, Brad, Batavia	2	1	.667	3.19	19	0	0	0	11	2	42.1	37	183	20	15	1	3	3	3	19	1	25	2	1
Padilla, Matthew, Batavia	1	2	.333	2.70	25	0	0	0	10	2	43.1	44	196	27	13	5	4	1	2	21	1	33	4	0
Pals, Jordan, New Jersey	2	4	.333	6.93	6	5	0	0	1	0	24.2	34	116	23	19	1	1	3	1	8	2	13	1	0
Papelbon, Jonathan, Lowell	1	2	.333	6.34	13	6	0	0	1	0	32.2	43	152	23	23	2	1	0	4	9	0	36	3	0
Parcus, William, Batavia *	2	4	.333	4.01	13	11	0	0	0	0	60.2	59	250	28	27	3	1	4	0	13	0	36	2	0
Patitucci, Mike, Aberdeen *	0	1	.000	3.75	18	0	0	0	11	6	24.0	21	101	12	10	0	1	0	2	9	0	25	0	0
Paulk, Robert, Brooklyn	1	1	.500	2.53	27	0	0	0	22	15	32.0	18	130	12	9	1	4	2	5	10	1	38	3	0
Pawelk, Reed, Jamestown	0	0	.000	7.11	18	0	0	0	8	0	25.1	34	121	23	20	4	0	0	2	10	0	21	2	2
Pearson, Anthony, Vermont	0	11	.000	6.90	15	10	0	0	0	0	58.2	57	290	52	45	3	1	2	6	54	0	48	16	0
Peguero, Tony, Hudson Valley	4	6	.400	3.34	12	12	0	0	0	0	56.2	60	245	26	21	0	0	4	7	15	0	55	4	2
Pender, Matthew, Oneonta	0	2	.000	3.47	7	4	0	0	1	0	23.1	16	92	10	9	1	0	1	2	8	0	19	2	0
Penny, David, Lowell	4	1	.800	2.68	12	10	0	0	0	0	53.2	43	228	22	16	3	1	2	11	14	0	36	2	0
Pereyra, Honeudis, M.V.	1	1	.500	2.59	21	0	0	0	4	1	41.2	32	183	16	12	0	3	2	4	27	1	51	3	0
Perez, Antonio, H.V.*	4	7	.364	5.23	28	0	0	0	16	3	31.0	32	137	19	18	2	6	1	2	14	1	30	2	0
Perez, Ezequiel, Oneonta	2	2	.500	2.64	21	0	0	0	8	1	44.1	37	184	15	13	0	2	1	1	13	3	27	4	1
Perez, Randy, M.V.*	1	1	.500	4.26	7	5	0	0	0	0	31.2	34	140	21	15	1	0	3	2	12	0	20	0	1
Perrin, Devin, Vermont	2	4	.333	3.27	11	11	0	0	0	0	52.1	47	221	23	19	3	4	2	5	23	0	36	4	1
Petit, Yusmeiro, Brooklyn	1	0	1.000	2.19	2	2	0	0	0	0	12.1	5	45	3	3	0	0	0	1	2	0	20	0	0
Picco, John, Staten Island *	4	3	.571	6.75	15	0	0	0	7	0	18.2	13	96	17	14	0	0	1	5	21	0	12	3	0
Pillsbury, Christopher, Jam.	1	4	.200	4.97	18	8	0	0	3	0	54.1	56	245	35	30	7	0	0	1	26	0	54	4	0
Plexico, Gerald, Vermont *	3	3	.500	2.69	17	9	0	0	2	1	70.1	59	292	26	21	3	7	3	7	16	0	49	0	1
Prahm, Ryan, M.V.	2	0	1.000	2.89	3	1	0	0	0	0	9.1	5	38	4	3	0	1	0	0	4	0	14	0	0
Prieto, Victor, Jamestown	0	6	.000	5.52	13	11	0	0	1	0	45.2	40	213	29	28	0	0	2	6	40	0	45	13	0
Primus, Carl, Jamestown	2	3	.400	6.25	18	4	0	0	3	0	40.1	40	182	29	28	5	1	0	4	20	0	35	0	0
Quezada, Elvys, Staten Island	3	0	1.000	1.83	8	8	0	0	0	0	39.1	23	161	10	8	2	3	2	5	20	0	39	2	0
Ramirez, Greg, Brooklyn	1	3	.250	2.96	18	5	0	0	2	1	51.2	51	226	19	17	1	2	1	6	17	1	48	5	0
Ramsey, Robert, Tri-City	3	2	.600	1.38	20	0	0	0	6	3	39.0	21	168	6	6	2	1	1	9	27	1	47	2	0
Ray, Christopher, Aberdeen	2	0	1.000	2.82	9	8	0	0	0	0	38.1	32	158	15	12	0	1	1	4	10	0	44	0	0
Reed, Brian, Auburn	1	2	.333	1.99	28	0	0	0	13	1	40.2	29	164	14	9	0	1	0	1	11	0	53	2	0
Reid, Brett, Vermont	0	2	.000	4.76	19	0	0	0	12	1	22.2	24	111	15	12	1	2	1	3	16	0	35	10	1
Rich, Dan, Mahoning Valley *	1	1	.500	1.61	18	0	0	0	13	4	22.1	15	87	5	4	0	2	1	1	5	0	20	2	0
Rickert, Brandon, M.V.	0	1	.000	6.35	5	0	0	0	3	0	5.2	8	32	4	4	0	0	0	0	7	0	4	1	0
Rigdon, Paul, M.V.	0	0	.000	3.60	3	3	0	0	0	0	10.0	11	40	4	4	0	0	0	0	3	0	8	0	0
Rijo, Fernando, Aberdeen	0	0	.000	0.00	2	0	0	0	1	0	3.0	1	9	0	0	0	0	0	0	1	0	4	0	0
Roehl, Scott, Mahoning Valley	5	6	.455	3.64	14	14	0	0	0	0	64.1	63	276	35	26	2	3	3	4	28	0	50	2	0
Roga, Mike, Auburn	0	0	.000	6.75	2	0	0	0	1	0	4.0	6	22	3	3	2	0	0	2	2	0	3	0	0
Rogers, Brian, Oneonta	3	2	.600	3.34	12	12	0	0	0	0	56.2	49	237	23	21	2	2	2	3	18	0	66	1	0
Rohr, Charles, Hudson Valley	4	0	1.000	3.33	16	0	0	0	3	1	27.0	30	124	14	10	1	2	3	1	13	0	25	7	0
Romero, Davis, Auburn *	4	1	.800	2.38	30	0	0	0	10	2	41.2	31	165	13	11	1	0	1	0	8	1	53	5	0
Ronz, Kenon, Oneonta *	4	1	.800	2.10	25	0	0	0	9	3	30.0	19	119	11	7	1	3	0	0	8	1	44	0	0
Roper, Derek, New Jersey	3	3	.500	3.32	17	8	0	0	0	0	65.0	70	277	26	24	2	1	2	5	18	0	43	2	2
Runyon, Bob, New Jersey	0	2	.000	3.72	4	1	0	0	1	0	9.2	15	42	4	4	0	0	0	0	2	0	8	0	1
Rupert, Chris, Batavia *	0	4	.000	3.38	17	0	0	0	14	3	29.1	26	127	15	11	2	0	2	3	16	0	29	1	0
Russell, Eddie, Jamestown	0	1	.000	2.08	4	0	0	0	1	0	8.2	8	34	2	2	0	0	0	0	5	0	6	0	0
Russell, James, Vermont	0	0	.000	3.24	5	0	0	0	2	0	8.1	7	44	9	3	0	0	0	2	11	0	4	0	0
Sanders, David, Lowell *	0	1	.000	2.41	9	0	0	0	2	1	18.2	22	82	11	5	3	1	0	0	5	2	14	1	0
Sandoval, Marcos, Auburn	2	1	.667	2.55	4	4	0	0	0	0	17.2	8	69	5	5	0	0	1	3	7	0	13	2	0
Santo, Brian, Oneonta	4	0	1.000	2.20	23	0	0	0	8	0	41.0	32	166	14	10	1	2	0	3	16	2	35	0	1
Santos, Arthur, Lowell	3	4	.429	1.99	14	13	0	0	0	0	58.2	65	244	24	13	3	0	1	2	7	0	35	3	1
Saucedo, Matthew, Jam.	1	1	.500	4.71	17	0	0	0	10	4	28.2	32	130	18	15	1	0	0	0	18	0	24	3	0
Scalamandre, Rich, N.J.	1	0	1.000	2.25	8	0	0	0	0	0	12.0	8	46	4	3	0	0	1	0	2	0	12	3	0
Schmitt, Billy, New Jersey	0	0	.000	0.00	2	0	0	0	2	0	3.0	0	10	0	0	0	0	0	0	2	0	1	0	0
Schneider, Jonathan, Wil.	1	0	1.000	0.00	12	0	0	0	11	6	12.0	7	52	1	0	0	1	0	1	6	2	4	0	0
Scobie, Jason, Brooklyn	0	0	.000	0.00	1	1	0	0	0	0	1.0	0	3	0	0	0	0	0	0	0	0	0	0	0
Shafer, Kurt, Williamsport	7	3	.700	3.15	14	9	1	0	3	2	65.2	54	267	29	23	3	1	2	5	18	0	35	1	1
Sharpless, Joshua, Wil.	1	1	.500	2.59	22	0	0	0	9	5	31.1	19	130	9	9	2	1	0	2	17	0	45	0	0
Shortell, Rory, Tri-City	0	0	.000	9.00	1	0	0	0	0	0	1.0	2	5	1	1	0	0	1	0	0	0	0	0	0
Silva, Sergio, Williamsport	6	3	.667	2.17	12	11	0	0	0	0	58.0	45	236	18	14	5	0	1	5	19	0	49	6	0
Smith, Brandon, Lowell	2	5	.286	4.14	10	6	0	0	1	0	41.1	50	191	26	19	4	0	4	9	13	0	21	5	1
Smith, David, Brooklyn *	0	0	.000	7.71	8	0	0	0	1	0	9.1	15	47	9	8	1	0	4	0	5	1	2	1	0
Smith, Joshua, Staten Island	1	2	.333	4.55	11	0	0	0	6	1	31.2	31	144	23	16	2	2	1	2	16	1	31	3	1
Sopko, Mark, Auburn	3	0	1.000	2.10	18	0	0	0	3	0	34.1	20	133	8	8	2	0	1	1	14	1	29	2	0
Soteropoulos, Peter, N.J.*	1	1	.500	4.37	15	0	0	0	2	0	22.2	29	104	13	11	0	1	2	1	11	1	16	5	0
Southerland, Chip, M.V.	0	0	.000	4.09	8	0	0	0	6	3	11.0	6	44	5	5	1	0	1	0	4	1	20	1	0
Spillers, Brandon, Aberdeen	0	2	.000	2.57	17	0	0	0	9	7	14.0	13	69	12	4	2	0	0	2	14	0	10	1	1
Spring, Daniel, Oneonta	4	2	.667	4.89	23	0	0	0	7	1	38.2	37	168	24	21	1	3	4	1	19	1	21	5	2
Stanton, Mike, Brooklyn *	0	0	.000	0.00	1	1	0	0	0	0	2.0	1	6	0	0	0	0	0	0	0	0	1	0	0
Steinborn, Chris, Oneonta *	3	0	1.000	0.64	6	3	0	0	0	0	28.0	26	113	4	2	0	0	1	0	9	0	19	1	0
Stiehl, Rob, Tri-City	0	0	.000	16.88	4	1	0	0	0	0	2.2	7	15	5	5	0	0	0	0	1	0	1	2	0
Sturge, Justin, Lowell *	2	0	1.000	1.40	12	0	0	0	1	0	25.2	18	97	5	4	0	0	0	1	1	0	28	1	1
Talanoa, Charles, Auburn	2	2	.500	4.22	5	5	0	0	0	0	21.1	19	91	11	10	0	0	0	1	8	0	25	1	0
Tamulionis, Mike, New Jersey	2	1	.667	2.30	18	1	0	0	7	0	27.1	23	116	8	7	1	1	3	2	11	0	22	2	0
Tata, Jordan, Oneonta	4	3	.571	2.58	16	12	0	0	2	1	73.1	64	306	32	21	1	5	4	6	20	0	60	4	1
Tate, Matt, Aberdeen	1	1	.500	3.78	10	0	0	0	7	0	16.2	18	74	9	7	2	1	3	0	7	2	12	1	0
Teeter, Travis, Aberdeen	3	2	.600	3.43	12	6	0	0	0	0	44.2	34	181	19	17	3	3	2	7	9	0	42	1	0
Templet, Jordy, Auburn	1	0	1.000	1.04	8	3	0	0	1	0	17.1	15	74	3	2	0	0	0	1	8	0	13	0	0
Thorp, Paul, Staten Island	1	2	.333	1.98	20	0	0	0	11	6	36.1	29	145	10	8	2	1	1	1	9	0	23	0	2

Pitcher, Team	W	L	Pct.	ERA	G	GS	CG	ShO	GF	Sv.	IP	H	TBF	R	ER	HR	SH	SF	HB	BB	IBB	SO	WP	Bk.
Tiller, James, Aberdeen	1	0	1.000	2.08	2	2	0	0	0	0	8.2	7	32	2	2	0	0	0	0	1	0	9	0	0
Tomey, Anthony, Oneonta	3	2	.600	5.43	20	7	0	0	0	0	53.0	46	241	38	32	4	2	7	4	34	0	56	4	1
Torrealba, Yoann, Wil.	6	1	.857	2.04	14	14	0	0	0	0	75.0	61	302	24	17	2	1	2	9	15	0	60	2	1
Torres, Carlos, Aberdeen	3	2	.600	6.35	16	0	0	0	5	0	34.0	42	158	26	24	3	1	1	2	14	0	18	7	0
Tower, Scott, Williamsport *	1	1	.500	5.20	15	0	0	0	3	0	27.2	25	126	20	16	1	1	1	4	17	0	29	5	1
Travis, Matt, Hudson Valley *	0	0	.000	0.00	3	0	0	0	1	1	3.0	2	12	0	0	0	1	0	0	1	0	2	0	0
Tribe, Phillip, Staten Island	1	0	1.000	2.32	17	0	0	0	4	0	31.0	35	135	17	8	0	2	1	3	7	0	32	5	0
Urrutia, Carlos, Batavia	0	0	.000	9.00	1	0	0	0	0	0	1.0	1	6	1	1	0	0	0	2	1	0	0	0	0
Van Gorder, Joe, N.J.*	0	2	.000	6.32	8	1	0	0	1	0	15.2	20	74	11	11	2	0	0	1	7	0	16	2	0
Vandermeer, Scott, H.V.	2	2	.500	3.05	8	8	0	0	0	0	41.1	36	181	20	14	2	0	2	7	20	0	21	3	0
Vaquedano, Jose, Lowell	7	4	.636	3.30	14	10	0	0	0	0	73.2	67	303	30	27	4	4	0	6	15	0	70	5	0
Vasquez, Matt, Oneonta	3	4	.429	6.92	11	11	0	0	0	0	53.1	76	245	43	41	5	0	1	2	10	0	35	1	0
Vaughan, Beau, Lowell	1	0	1.000	2.32	11	6	0	0	0	0	31.0	27	131	8	8	1	1	0	0	15	0	30	1	0
Vermilyea, Jamie, Auburn	5	1	.833	2.37	9	2	0	0	1	0	30.1	22	119	10	8	0	2	1	3	5	0	53	0	0
Walker, Adam, Brooklyn *	0	2	.000	4.86	8	4	0	0	3	0	16.2	12	70	9	9	1	1	0	1	9	0	10	3	0
Wallace, Shane, M.V.*	1	2	.333	5.40	8	0	0	0	5	0	11.2	12	56	9	7	1	1	1	3	5	1	13	0	0
Weaver, Joe, Mahoning Valley	1	0	1.000	2.91	13	6	0	0	2	0	34.0	36	150	20	11	2	2	1	2	11	0	21	0	0
Weeden, Brandon, Staten Is.	0	2	.000	3.72	5	5	0	0	0	0	19.1	14	90	13	8	0	0	0	3	14	0	17	1	0
Weimer, Andrew, H.V.	0	2	.000	4.21	23	0	0	0	11	2	36.1	41	159	21	17	1	0	2	1	11	0	29	0	0
Wheeler, Adam, Staten Island	1	3	.250	1.80	14	2	0	0	2	0	40.0	33	174	14	8	0	3	6	3	21	0	24	3	1
Wheeler, William, Auburn	0	1	.000	6.88	10	0	0	0	1	0	17.0	18	81	13	13	0	0	0	1	11	0	19	2	1
White, Brian, Williamsport	0	0	.000	4.61	11	0	0	0	7	1	13.2	12	61	8	7	1	0	0	1	9	0	4	2	0
White, Chris, M.V.*	1	1	.500	4.87	14	0	0	0	7	0	20.1	23	93	13	11	2	2	1	0	9	2	23	1	0
Williamson, Willie, N.J.*	1	5	.167	9.90	17	4	0	0	1	0	20.0	15	118	26	22	1	3	1	9	34	0	16	15	0
Wilson, Joseph, Batavia *	1	1	.500	2.40	3	2	0	0	1	0	15.0	11	60	4	4	0	0	0	1	7	0	14	2	0
Wood, Timothy, Jamestown	0	2	.000	5.35	16	4	0	0	5	2	38.2	44	185	33	23	2	1	3	1	28	0	32	6	0
Woodrow, Christopher, Bat.	2	2	.500	2.94	17	5	0	0	8	2	52.0	51	210	22	17	4	2	0	3	3	0	39	3	0
Worthington, Timothy, Brook.	2	0	1.000	3.49	17	1	0	0	4	0	38.2	39	156	16	15	3	2	1	1	10	1	26	1	0
Wright, Chase, Staten Is.*	3	5	.375	3.56	14	14	1	0	0	0	81.0	82	342	42	32	2	4	1	2	30	0	68	11	1
Yurek, Ryan, Tri-City	0	0	.000	5.14	12	0	0	0	7	0	14.0	9	66	9	8	0	1	1	4	13	0	8	2	0
Zell, Danny, Oneonta *	1	2	.333	4.65	8	8	0	0	0	0	31.0	32	138	18	16	1	1	1	2	18	0	19	2	0
Ziegler, Brad, Batavia	1	0	1.000	1.50	3	0	0	0	1	0	6.0	5	23	1	1	0	0	0	0	1	0	6	0	0

COMBINATION SHUTOUTS: Aberdeen (1)—Coppinger-Boughner-Patitucci-Spillers. Auburn (10)—Talanoa-Colson-Sopko-Reed, Isenberg-Vermilyea-Reed-Buzachero, Mastny-Harper-Buzachero, Isenberg-Core, Mastny-Romero-Buzachero, Core-Romero-Buzachero, Mastny-Romero-Reed-Buzachero, James-Sopko-Marcum, Mastny-Reed-Marcum, Banks-Core-Sopko-Reed-Romero-Marcum-Buzachero. Batavia (2)—Machi-Padilla, Diefenderfer-Woodrow. Brooklyn (11)—Keppel-Bannister, Lindstrom-Orloski-Paulk, Danly-George-Paulk, Lindstrom-George-Worthington-Muniz, Stanton-Danly-Paulk, Maldonado-George-Castro, Bannister-Castro-George, Cordova-Castro-Smith-Walker, Maclane-George, Petit-Paulk, Cordova-King-George. Hudson Valley (9)—Peguero-Navaroli-Weimer, Peguero-Fernandez-Orvella, Gangi-Weimer-Perez-Orvella, Little-Rohr-Perez, Peguero-Basilio, Gangi-Rohr-Perez-Lopez, Little-Rohr-Perez-Basilio, Little-Cramer, Little-Rohr. Jamestown (1)—Iehl-Lobatto-Nowicki. Lowell (6)—Santos-Farley-Sturge-Cochran, Vaquedano-Farley-Cochran, Gardner-Papelbon-Hertzler, Anderson-Vaquedano-Marshall, Vaquedano-Sanders-Marshall, Santos-Cochran-Basch-Marshall. Mahoning Valley (4)—Roehl-Hernandez-Hanson-Rich, Lara-Davis-Rich, Weaver-Pereyra, Roehl-Hanson-White. New Jersey (4)—Brey-Scalamandre-Batista, Drown-Jordan-Roper-Batista, Roper-Morales-Galbraith, Roper-Jordan-Morales. Oneonta (4)—Zell-Tomey-Spring-Ronz-Homer, Steinborn-Perez-Spring-Ronz-Santo, Tomey-Perez, Tata-Homer. Staten Island (4)—Quezada-Beam-Gardner, Harmsen-Blackwell-Gardner-Picco, Quezada-Gardner, Karstens-Smith. Tri-City (7)—Grigsby-Ramsey-Fischer, Grigsby-Ramsey-Escobar, Hirsh-Merchant, Hirsh-Collar, Albers-Yurek, DeLeon-Merchant, Hirsh-Beltre-Collar. Vermont (1)—Perrin-Gomez-Little. Williamsport (8)—Shafer-Tower-Bimeal, Nunez-Hernandez-Kiley-White, Silva-Bayer, Shafer-Hernandez-Sharpless, Torrealba-Sharpless-Bimeal-Schneider, Lissir-Sharpless-Schneider, Torrealba-DeMaria, Maholm-Sharpless.

NO-HIT GAMES: None.

2003 FIELDING

TEAM

Team	G	PO	A	E	TC	DP	TP	PB	Pct.
Auburn	74	1950	727	68	2745	50	0	15	.975
Williamsport	76	1985	794	86	2865	55	1	12	.970
Brooklyn	75	1975	751	85	2811	55	0	5	.970
New Jersey	73	1935	820	88	2843	62	0	7	.969
Oneonta	75	1958	789	87	2834	62	0	13	.969
Tri-City	76	1985	769	89	2843	60	0	13	.969
Batavia	75	2034	855	95	2984	66	0	19	.968
Mahoning Val.	74	1922	783	89	2794	65	0	11	.968
Jamestown	73	1871	705	89	2665	59	0	20	.967
Aberdeen	76	2041	742	94	2877	40	0	23	.967
Lowell	74	1937	794	105	2836	68	0	8	.963
Hudson Valley	74	1935	803	112	2850	64	1	11	.961
Staten Island	72	1954	792	121	2867	48	0	20	.958
Vermont	75	1920	770	126	2816	52	0	33	.955

INDIVIDUAL

FIRST BASEMEN

NOTE: All caps denotes fielding-percentage leader based on 38 games for catchers, 51 for all other non-pitchers and 61 innings for pitchers. *Throws lefthanded.

Player, Team	Pct.	G	PO	A	E	TC	DP
Ayala, Abraham, Hudson Valley	1.000	2	6	0	0	6	0
Barnowski, Bryan, Lowell	1.000	2	15	0	0	15	0
Bastardo, Frederick, Jamestown	1.000	1	8	0	0	8	1
Bear, Ryan, Jamestown	.990	65	541	29	6	576	48
Bladergroen, Ian, Brooklyn *	.984	72	571	48	10	629	48
Blanco, Luis, Vermont	.972	8	62	7	2	71	4
Bonvechio, Brett, Lowell	1.000	12	104	5	0	109	10
Boudon, Chad, Aberdeen	.986	18	130	8	2	140	8
Brown, Tim, Williamsport *	.990	45	378	25	4	407	30
Brunink, Joseph, Batavia	.975	17	143	11	4	158	15
Burgos, Richard, Oneonta	.968	24	196	15	7	218	19
Chiaravolloti, Vito, Auburn	.990	58	456	22	5	483	29
Colmenter, Jesus, M.V.	1.000	5	40	4	0	44	5
Cucinotta, Robert, Lowell	.980	18	137	7	3	147	12
Davidson, Tyler, Brooklyn	.750	1	3	0	1	4	0
Goldfield, Josh, Mahoning Valley	1.000	1	6	0	0	6	2
Hansen, Bryan, Batavia *	.991	59	499	56	5	560	42
Harper, Brett, Brooklyn	1.000	4	22	2	0	24	2
Hunt, Kelly, Oneonta	.987	32	289	23	4	316	26
Jimenez, Franklyn, Vermont	1.000	8	60	7	0	67	5
Jimenez, Luis, Aberdeen *	.988	21	153	8	2	163	7
Johnston, Clint, Auburn *	1.000	13	87	7	0	94	8
Kendrick, Josh, Hudson Valley	.962	16	116	9	5	130	10
Kratz, Erik, Auburn	.989	12	88	2	1	91	9
Lutz, David, Vermont	.966	7	51	6	2	59	4
Madrid, Mike, Williamsport *	.993	36	259	37	2	298	21
Martinez, Gabriel, Hudson Valley	.981	63	545	36	11	592	47
MATHER, JOE, New Jersey	.994	63	493	38	3	534	40
McGorty, John, Oneonta *	.990	23	177	13	2	192	11
Mulhern, Ryan, Mahoning Valley	.977	47	399	22	10	431	32
Noboa, Joel, Vermont	.917	1	8	3	1	12	1
Noviskey, Josh, Mahoning Valley	.975	15	112	5	3	120	11
Obrey, Kainoa, New Jersey	.975	14	107	9	3	119	9
Olsen, Mikela, Jamestown *	.985	10	60	5	1	66	5
Piantek, Kurtis, Oneonta	1.000	1	5	1	0	6	2
Piazza, Tony, Brooklyn	1.000	1	9	1	0	10	0
Pignatiello, Bret, Vermont	1.000	1	5	0	0	5	0
Rico, Matt, Hudson Valley	1.000	1	5	0	0	5	0

Player, Team	Pct.	G	PO	A	E	TC	DP
Robinson, Scott, Tri-City	.985	55	476	34	8	518	37
Robles, Luis, Staten Island	.978	12	85	6	2	93	6
Russell, Mike, Aberdeen	.983	44	328	27	6	361	21
Salmela, Andy, Tri-City	.985	22	183	17	3	203	16
Schmitt, Billy, New Jersey	.983	7	53	4	1	58	3
Shorts, Adam, Staten Island	.985	8	59	7	1	67	4
Suarez, Cesar, Mahoning Valley	1.000	6	57	2	0	59	9
Sweeney, Tim, Vermont	.957	5	40	4	2	46	6
Threinen, Scott, M.V.	1.000	3	22	4	0	26	0
Urick, John, Staten Island *	.983	59	468	43	9	520	31
West, Jeremy, Lowell	.986	46	412	22	6	440	41
Whealy, Blake, Brooklyn	1.000	1	1	0	0	1	0
Whitesell, Josh, Vermont *	.984	46	377	42	7	426	21
Wyrick, Dennis, Aberdeen	.900	1	9	0	1	10	1

SECOND BASEMEN

Player, Team	Pct.	G	PO	A	E	TC	DP
Arnold, Eric, Auburn	1.000	3	4	7	0	11	0
Bastardo, Frederick, Jamestown	.950	4	7	12	1	20	1
Bernazard, Oscar, Vermont	.935	7	9	20	2	31	3
Bramasco, Omar, Batavia	1.000	11	20	43	0	63	9
Clanton, Ja'Mar, Vermont	.000	1	0	0	0	0	0
Cockrell, Michael, Williamsport	.945	59	95	161	15	271	28
Colmenter, Jesus, M.V.	.985	30	59	72	2	133	14
Cooper, Chad, Hudson Valley	.946	8	12	23	2	37	3
Cota, Carlo, Auburn	.993	37	43	98	1	142	18
Cotto, Luis, Mahoning Valley	1.000	1	0	2	0	2	0
Cruz, Enrique, Staten Island	.959	30	42	74	5	121	11
Del Rosario, Manny, Aberdeen	.969	37	48	75	4	127	9
Dierks, Scott, Jamestown	.965	43	90	103	7	200	22
Ditter, Brad, Vermont	.966	24	35	51	3	89	8
Dufner, Kris, Hudson Valley	.926	6	10	15	2	27	1
Encarnacion, Henry, Vermont	.964	13	20	33	2	55	6
Estrada, Kevin, New Jersey	.974	50	123	138	7	268	34
Falu, Melvin, New Jersey	1.000	3	9	7	0	16	3
Gonzalez, Humberto, Brooklyn	.971	12	17	16	1	34	5
Grimm, Eric, Aberdeen	.967	50	74	103	6	183	15
Guzman, Javier, Williamsport	.875	5	0	7	1	8	0
Hairston, Jerry, Aberdeen	1.000	1	0	1	0	1	0
Harris, Justin, Williamsport	.982	13	26	29	1	56	7
Headley, Jack, Batavia	1.000	6	13	6	0	19	1
Hoffpauir, Josh, Aberdeen	1.000	3	6	10	0	16	2
Housel, David, Brooklyn	.925	10	17	20	3	40	5
Jimenez, Franklyn, Vermont	1.000	3	4	7	0	11	1
Linares, Jesus, Brooklyn	1.000	10	14	13	0	27	5
Lunetta, Anthony, M.V.	.991	26	45	70	1	116	14
Maysonet, Edwin, Tri-City	.950	32	50	102	8	160	19
McIntyre, Nick, Oneonta	.962	19	33	42	3	78	8
Mejia, Gilberto, Oneonta	1.000	3	8	7	0	15	2
Moss, Timothy, Batavia	.955	43	82	130	10	222	31
Ohtsuka, Yoshiyuki, Wil.	1.000	3	0	5	0	5	0
Patrick, Brian, Auburn	.950	5	6	13	1	20	2
Pedrique, Franmig, Tri-City	.909	7	6	14	2	22	1
Pena, Omar, New Jersey	.947	21	37	52	5	94	9
Peralta, Juan, Auburn	.967	31	40	77	4	121	16
Prosser, Chad, Tri-City	.989	42	57	115	2	174	18
Puebla, Fernando, H.V.	.970	43	75	116	6	197	21
Ramos, Jason, Lowell	.957	11	17	28	2	47	9
Randolph, Andre, Staten Island	.923	8	10	14	2	26	1
Reyes, Melvin, Lowell	.943	55	100	167	16	283	25
RODLAND, ERIC, Oneonta	.970	55	94	165	8	267	35
Schade, Ryan, Jamestown	.942	11	16	33	3	52	6
Seifrig, Cole, Jamestown	.984	11	29	34	1	64	7
Shorts, Adam, Staten Island	.934	35	69	87	11	167	15
Slevin, David, Staten Island	1.000	5	6	9	0	15	0
Smith, John, Williamsport	1.000	1	2	1	0	3	0
St. Clair, Jason, Hudson Valley	.916	22	35	63	9	107	12
Suarez, Cesar, Mahoning Valley	.961	24	58	65	5	128	13
Suarez, Ignacio, Lowell	.969	11	24	39	2	65	10
Sweeney, Tim, Vermont	1.000	2	4	3	0	7	1
Thomas, Tee, New Jersey	.800	2	1	3	1	5	1
Tugwell, Marc, Batavia	.975	15	33	45	2	80	10
Vancamper, Eugenio, Auburn	.900	5	10	8	2	20	1
Whealy, Blake, Brooklyn	.965	51	94	128	8	230	23
Wilson, Andrew, Brooklyn	.885	4	15	8	3	26	1
York, Larry, Vermont	.965	29	53	85	5	143	14
Young, Dustin, Jamestown	1.000	8	12	18	0	30	4

THIRD BASEMEN

Player, Team	Pct.	G	PO	A	E	TC	DP
Arias, Claudio, Lowell	.826	46	24	85	23	132	9
Arnold, Eric, Auburn	.000	1	0	0	0	0	0
Baldiris, Aaron, Brooklyn	.970	25	23	42	2	67	1
Bass, Bryan, Aberdeen	1.000	3	2	5	0	7	0
Bastardo, Frederick, Jamestown	.600	2	3	0	2	5	0
Bennett, Charles, Brooklyn	1.000	2	1	4	0	5	1
Blalock, Jake, Batavia	.913	7	3	18	2	23	1
Bonvechio, Brett, Lowell	.867	12	5	21	4	30	1
Borowiak, Zachary, Lowell	.889	11	10	22	4	36	3
Boudon, Chad, Aberdeen	.000	1	0	0	0	0	0
Bowman, Shawn, Brooklyn	.934	42	31	68	7	106	5
Bramasco, Omar, Batavia	.929	5	3	10	1	14	0
Cockrell, Michael, Williamsport	.952	11	11	29	2	42	1
Collum, Mike, Williamsport	.923	9	6	18	2	26	2
Cota, Carlo, Auburn	.885	13	6	17	3	26	2
Covarrubias, Nic, Staten Island	.914	9	11	21	3	35	3
Del Rosario, Manny, Aberdeen	1.000	10	3	8	0	11	0
Dierks, Scott, Jamestown	.800	9	4	8	3	15	0
Ditter, Brad, Vermont	.842	31	21	43	12	76	6
Doyle, Nate, Oneonta	1.000	2	2	2	0	4	0
Dufner, Kris, Hudson Valley	.910	53	39	72	11	122	4
Duncan, Eric, Staten Island	.837	13	11	25	7	43	2
Estrada, Kevin, New Jersey	1.000	4	5	10	0	15	0
Falu, Melvin, New Jersey	.917	48	29	82	10	121	5
Fisher, Kiel, Batavia	.947	25	11	43	3	57	4
Ford, Jake, Oneonta	.800	9	0	12	3	15	0
Gonzalez, Patrick, Aberdeen	.900	9	5	13	2	20	0
Grimm, Eric, Aberdeen	.750	4	1	5	2	8	0
Harper, Brett, Brooklyn	.000	3	0	0	0	0	0
Harris, Justin, Williamsport	1.000	1	0	1	0	1	0
Jimenez, Franklyn, Vermont	.852	19	13	33	8	54	2
Kirkland, Kody, Oneonta	.913	65	46	111	15	172	11
Koman, Brock, Tri-City	.961	69	41	108	6	155	15
KOUZMANOFF, KEVIN, M.V.	.964	52	35	126	6	167	11
Linares, Jesus, Brooklyn	1.000	6	5	6	0	11	1
Mangioni, Jarad, Auburn	.333	2	1	0	2	3	0
Martinez, Gabriel, Hudson Valley	1.000	9	4	14	0	18	0
Mather, Joe, New Jersey	1.000	3	0	5	0	5	1
McIntyre, Nick, Oneonta	.875	3	4	3	1	8	0
Mitchell, Lee, Jamestown	.932	27	13	42	4	59	5
Noboa, Joel, Vermont	.905	5	6	13	2	21	1
Norman, Zachary, Batavia	.918	29	27	63	8	98	5
Noviskey, Josh, Mahoning Valley	.000	1	0	0	0	0	0
Obrey, Kainoa, New Jersey	.957	12	5	17	1	23	3
Ohtsuka, Yoshiyuki, Wil.	.844	12	7	20	5	32	2
Osborn, Pat, Mahoning Valley	1.000	1	0	5	0	5	0
Pedrique, Franmig, Tri-City	.909	7	1	9	1	11	1
Pena, Omar, New Jersey	.000	1	0	0	0	0	0
Puebla, Fernando, H.V.	.889	4	2	6	1	9	0
Ramos, Jason, Lowell	.900	7	2	7	1	10	1
Roberts, Ryan, Auburn	.945	62	32	105	8	145	2
Romprey, Ed, Oneonta	1.000	1	1	2	0	3	0
Russell, Mike, Aberdeen	.842	10	2	14	3	19	1
Ryan, Brendan, New Jersey	1.000	1	0	1	0	1	0
Schade, Ryan, Jamestown	1.000	5	1	5	0	6	0
Schleicher, Mark, Hudson Valley	.846	12	10	23	6	39	4
Schmitt, Billy, New Jersey	.912	12	8	23	3	34	3
Shorts, Adam, Staten Island	.500	1	0	1	1	2	0
Siriveaw, Nom, Auburn	.714	2	3	7	4	14	0
Skaug, Brian, Tri-City	.857	3	1	5	1	7	0
Sosa, Pablo, Jamestown	.865	35	16	48	10	74	1
Stansberry, Craig, Williamsport	.966	45	38	106	5	149	6
Suarez, Cesar, Mahoning Valley	.886	16	15	24	5	44	1
Sweeney, Tim, Vermont	.873	24	19	36	8	63	3
Threinen, Scott, M.V.	.852	7	10	13	4	27	1
Tugwell, Marc, Batavia	.927	11	8	30	3	41	4
Walls, Michael, Tri-City	.833	3	2	3	1	6	0
Wilson, Andrew, Brooklyn	1.000	6	3	4	0	7	0
Wyrick, Dennis, Aberdeen	.931	55	39	69	8	116	4
Young, Dustin, Jamestown	.000	1	0	0	0	0	0
Zamora, Hector, Staten Island	.931	52	49	100	11	160	10

SHORTSTOPS

Player, Team	Pct.	G	PO	A	E	TC	DP
Bass, Bryan, Aberdeen	.926	66	106	168	22	296	23
Batista, Wilson, Brooklyn	1.000	1	3	2	0	5	0
Borowiak, Zachary, Lowell	.954	21	37	67	5	109	13
Bramasco, Omar, Batavia	.976	31	59	106	4	169	22
Clanton, Ja'Mar, Vermont	.937	56	96	156	17	269	22
Cockrell, Michael, Williamsport	.000	1	0	0	0	0	0
Collum, Mike, Williamsport	.800	2	3	1	1	5	1
Colmenter, Jesus, M.V.	.934	32	37	77	8	122	15
Cota, Carlo, Auburn	1.000	1	2	2	0	4	1
Cotto, Luis, Mahoning Valley	.912	8	10	21	3	34	1

Player, Team	Pct.	G	PO	A	E	TC	DP
Cruz, Enrique, Staten Island	.333	1	1	0	2	3	0
Cuevas, Aneudi, Hudson Valley	.944	68	106	197	18	321	40
Del Rosario, Manny, Aberdeen	1.000	12	11	19	0	30	4
Delos Santos, Esteban, Batavia	.927	45	64	138	16	218	26
Doyle, Nate, Oneonta	.981	23	33	72	2	107	18
Encarnacion, Henry, Vermont	.902	10	19	27	5	51	4
Estrada, Kevin, New Jersey	.966	5	15	13	1	29	3
Falu, Melvin, New Jersey	.867	5	6	7	2	15	1
Garcia, Julio, Mahoning Valley	1.000	1	1	4	0	5	1
Garcia, Travis, Brooklyn	.914	8	16	16	3	35	2
Giarratano, Tony, Oneonta	.959	47	65	120	8	193	21
Gonzalez, Humberto, Brooklyn	1.000	1	1	1	0	2	1
Guzman, Javier, Williamsport	.922	42	57	97	13	167	16
Hanish, Tyson, Staten Island	.947	22	35	55	5	95	8
Harris, Justin, Williamsport	.947	37	55	87	8	150	17
Hill, Aaron, Auburn	.934	32	37	77	8	122	14
Linares, Jesus, Brooklyn	1.000	4	0	5	0	5	1
Lunetta, Anthony, M.V.	.953	32	39	82	6	127	14
Made, Hector, Staten Island	.897	7	7	19	3	29	2
Maysonet, Edwin, Tri-City	1.000	13	14	24	0	38	5
Mazzuca, Joe, Jamestown	.903	5	13	15	3	31	3
McDonald, John, M.V.	1.000	1	3	3	0	6	2
McIntyre, Nick, Oneonta	.800	2	1	3	1	5	0
Mitchell, Lee, Jamestown	.976	19	27	54	2	83	13
Parker, Brett, Mahoning Valley	.966	7	12	16	1	29	5
Patrick, Brian, Auburn	.000	1	0	0	0	0	0
Pedrique, Franmig, Tri-City	.667	2	2	4	3	9	0
Pena, Omar, New Jersey	.933	38	57	111	12	180	20
Peralta, Juan, Auburn	.970	41	54	108	5	167	24
Puebla, Fernando, H.V.	.911	11	18	23	4	45	4
Ramos, Jason, Lowell	.952	10	14	26	2	42	4
REAVER, DAVID, Brooklyn	.961	64	93	175	11	279	28
Roberts, Ryan, Auburn	.667	1	1	3	2	6	1
Robinson, Christopher, Tri-City	.934	58	81	145	16	242	28
Rogers, Ed, Aberdeen	.929	3	4	9	1	14	2
Romprey, Ed, Oneonta	.967	7	11	18	1	30	5
Ryan, Brendan, New Jersey	.908	31	49	89	14	152	15
Schade, Ryan, Jamestown	.944	12	14	20	2	36	5
Shorts, Adam, Staten Island	.720	6	9	9	7	25	1
Skaug, Brian, Tri-City	1.000	8	7	19	0	26	4
Slevin, David, Staten Island	.936	41	72	103	12	187	14
Suarez, Ignacio, Lowell	.955	45	81	130	10	221	27
Sweeney, Tim, Vermont	1.000	5	9	5	0	14	1
Vancamper, Eugenio, Auburn	1.000	2	2	5	0	7	0
Webb, Trey, Vermont	.951	6	17	22	2	41	3
Wilson, Andrew, Brooklyn	1.000	3	3	4	0	7	0
York, Larry, Vermont	1.000	1	2	1	0	3	1
Young, Dustin, Jamestown	.938	41	42	124	11	177	21
Zamora, Hector, Staten Island	.750	1	0	3	1	4	0

OUTFIELDERS

Player, Team	Pct.	G	PO	A	E	TC	DP
Allan, Joshua, Jamestown	1.000	2	1	0	0	1	0
Anderson, Joshua, Tri-City	.962	74	148	3	6	157	2
Arbinger, Mike, Williamsport	1.000	26	42	2	0	44	1
Arroyo, Xavier, Jamestown	.968	27	58	2	2	62	1
Ascencion, Quincy, Aberdeen	.929	9	13	0	1	14	0
Bastardo, Frederick, Jamestown	1.000	7	8	0	0	8	0
Beck, Alan, Aberdeen	1.000	14	14	2	0	16	0
Bennett, Charles, Brooklyn	1.000	7	11	0	0	11	0
Blalock, Jake, Batavia	.962	54	94	8	4	106	0
Blue, Vincent, Oneonta	.994	70	150	6	1	157	2
Bocchino, Anthony, Wil.*	.987	48	74	3	1	78	0
Boeve, Adam, Williamsport	.963	25	51	1	2	54	0
Borgo, Alex, Batavia	.964	9	26	1	1	28	0
Boudon, Chad, Aberdeen	1.000	7	4	0	0	4	0
Bourn, Michael, Batavia	.973	34	70	2	2	74	0
Brito, Henry, Batavia	1.000	15	32	3	0	35	0
Brown, Curtis, Oneonta	.985	42	62	4	1	67	0
Brown, Tony, Vermont	.952	9	20	0	1	21	0
Brunink, Joseph, Batavia	1.000	4	8	0	0	8	0
Cabrera, Melky, Staten Island *	.979	67	137	5	3	145	1
Calzado, Napoleon, Aberdeen	1.000	4	13	0	0	13	0
Casto, Kory, Vermont	.972	65	129	8	4	141	3
Chance, Andrew, Williamsport	1.000	28	41	2	0	43	0
Chavez, Ender, Brooklyn *	.964	38	49	5	2	56	1
Cloar, Jason, Vermont *	1.000	1	1	0	0	1	0
Colbert, Eddie, Aberdeen	.933	8	14	0	1	15	0
Coles, Corey, Brooklyn *	1.000	12	10	0	0	10	0
Conroy, Mike, M.V.*	.951	71	93	4	5	102	2
Cota, Carlo, Auburn	.000	1	0	0	0	0	0
Cotto, Pedro, Oneonta *	.976	26	38	2	1	41	1
Covarrubias, Nic, Staten Island	1.000	6	9	0	0	9	0
Davidson, Tyler, Brooklyn	1.000	12	19	0	0	19	0
Davis, Morrin, Auburn	.931	31	27	0	2	29	0
Dierks, Scott, Jamestown	.000	1	0	0	0	0	0
Dion, Nate, Hudson Valley	.947	38	85	4	5	94	1
Duncan, Jacob, Aberdeen *	.967	38	56	3	2	61	2
Evans, Robert, Lowell *	.989	50	81	6	1	88	0
Ewen, Nicholas, Jamestown	.955	25	40	2	2	44	0
Fair, Kerry, Tri-City	.986	55	67	3	1	71	0
Falu, Melvin, New Jersey	.875	4	7	0	1	8	0
Flowers, Bo, Oneonta	.932	35	67	1	5	73	0
Foust, Justin, Batavia	.936	23	41	3	3	47	0
Frank, Kyle, Staten Island *	1.000	10	16	1	0	17	0
Frisella, Paul, New Jersey	1.000	7	10	0	0	10	0
Galloway, Mike, Auburn	.984	43	59	2	1	62	1
Goleski, Ryan, Mahoning Valley	.972	58	100	4	3	107	0
Gonzalez, Edwar, Staten Island	.960	55	93	2	4	99	0
Gonzalez, Humberto, Brooklyn	.000	3	0	0	0	0	0
Grimm, Casey, New Jersey *	.981	41	49	3	1	53	0
Harvey, Ryan, Brooklyn	1.000	7	9	0	0	9	0
Headley, Jack, Batavia	.987	31	74	3	1	78	0
Hearod, Beau, Tri-City	.893	22	24	1	3	28	0
Holmes, Brett, Williamsport	1.000	25	40	4	0	44	0
Jimenez, Franklyn, Vermont	.964	21	51	2	2	55	0
Johnson, Eric, Mahoning Valley	.941	11	16	0	1	17	0
Jones, Mitch, Hudson Valley	.983	70	162	9	3	174	2
Jordan, Kevin, Lowell	.983	51	114	3	2	119	1
Joyce, Tom, Aberdeen *	.968	35	58	3	2	63	0
Kapler, Gabe, Lowell	.000	1	0	0	0	0	0
Kartler, Bryce, Staten Island *	1.000	12	23	0	0	23	0
Kendrick, Josh, Hudson Valley	1.000	17	29	1	0	30	0
Lawrence, Horace, Staten Is.*	.875	6	7	0	1	8	0
Louisa, Lorvin, Vermont	.930	58	104	3	8	115	1
Magruder, Chris, M.V.	1.000	2	4	0	0	4	0
Majewski, Val, Aberdeen *	1.000	3	3	1	0	4	0
Mangioni, Jarad, Auburn	.955	26	21	0	1	22	0
Markakis, Nicholas, Aberdeen *	.991	55	99	6	1	106	0
Martinez, Gabriel, Hudson Valley	.000	1	0	0	0	0	0
Mattison, Justin, Jamestown *	.961	46	68	5	3	76	2
McCurdy, Joshua, Aberdeen	.969	21	31	0	1	32	0
McGorty, John, Oneonta *	.857	7	6	0	1	7	0
McKinney, Garth, Oneonta	.989	51	89	5	1	95	1
Miller, Jai, Jamestown	1.000	11	23	0	0	23	0
Monette, Daylon, New Jersey *	1.000	39	59	2	0	61	1
Moran, Javon, Batavia	.955	60	143	5	7	155	1
Morgan, Nyjer, Williamsport *	.987	71	150	1	2	153	0
Moss, Brandon, Lowell	.973	60	106	4	3	113	0
Mulhern, Ryan, Mahoning Valley	1.000	2	4	0	0	4	0
Murphy, David, Lowell *	.949	20	56	0	3	59	0
Murton, Matthew, Lowell	.976	47	82	1	2	85	0
Nikolic, Adam, Hudson Valley *	.963	33	49	3	2	54	1
Noviskey, Josh, Mahoning Valley	1.000	1	2	0	0	2	0
Olsen, Mikela, Jamestown *	.976	29	39	2	1	42	1
Owens, Jerry, Vermont *	1.000	2	2	0	0	2	0
Parker, Rashad, Brooklyn	.971	58	99	3	3	105	0
Patrick, Brian, Auburn	.958	12	21	2	1	24	0
Piazza, Tony, Brooklyn	1.000	1	3	0	0	3	0
Pietsch, Seth, Brooklyn	.935	37	56	2	4	62	0
Porfirio, A.J., Auburn	.978	71	131	1	3	135	0
Reames, Joe Don, H.V.	1.000	7	6	1	0	7	0
Reuss, Jason, Tri-City	.800	10	8	0	2	10	0
Rico, Matt, Hudson Valley	.990	66	94	10	1	105	1
RINE, JAROD, Aberdeen	1.000	63	127	4	0	131	0
Santa, Alexander, Staten Is.*	.954	31	55	7	3	65	1
Schade, Ryan, Jamestown	1.000	12	14	0	0	14	0
Schroeder, Benjamin, Jam.	.956	54	81	6	4	91	1
Seuss, Adam, Tri-City	.974	71	109	5	3	117	2
Shorts, Adam, Staten Island	1.000	1	2	0	0	2	0
Siriveaw, Nom, Auburn	.000	1	0	0	0	0	0
Slack, Jonathan, Brooklyn *	.993	59	144	4	1	149	0
Smith, Sean, Williamsport	.870	15	20	0	3	23	0
Smithlin, Zach, New Jersey	1.000	39	42	3	0	45	0
Snavely, Christian, Auburn	.977	59	77	7	2	86	1
Snyder, Brad, Mahoning Valley *	.969	62	123	0	4	127	0
Suarez, Cesar, Mahoning Valley	1.000	1	2	0	0	2	0
Sultemeier, Eric, Aberdeen	1.000	4	10	0	0	10	0
Sweeney, Tim, Vermont	.000	1	0	0	0	0	0
Thedorf, Chris, Jamestown *	.950	26	35	3	2	40	0
Thomas, Tee, New Jersey	1.000	4	5	1	0	6	0
Tingler, Jayce, Auburn *	1.000	7	9	0	0	9	0
Tolotti, Jeff, New Jersey *	1.000	3	5	0	0	5	0
Treadway, Jared, Staten Island	1.000	44	81	6	0	87	1

Player, Team	Pct.	G	PO	A	E	TC	DP
Tuttle, Chris, New Jersey	.986	44	68	2	1	71	1
Tuttle, Jason, Vermont *	.967	51	116	3	4	123	2
Urueta, Luis, New Jersey	1.000	3	7	0	0	7	0
Van Every, Jon, M.V.	.974	15	36	2	1	39	1
Virgil, Jose, New Jersey	.977	63	123	7	3	133	2
Vroman, Douglas, Vermont	.967	25	28	1	1	30	0
Walls, Michael, Tri-City	.943	22	30	3	2	35	1
Watson, Matt, Brooklyn	1.000	3	5	0	0	5	0
Watts, Derran, Brooklyn	1.000	7	6	0	0	6	0
Wilson, Andrew, Brooklyn	.938	9	15	0	1	16	0

CATCHERS

Player, Team	Pct.	G	PO	A	E	TC	DP	PB
Alen, Luis, Jamestown	.987	22	133	16	2	151	2	4
Allan, Joshua, Jamestown	1.000	10	58	5	0	63	1	1
Arko, Tommy, Aberdeen	.992	14	112	14	1	127	1	3
Ayala, Abraham, Hudson Valley	.983	31	195	31	4	230	2	3
Bennett, Charles, Brooklyn	1.000	1	1	0	0	1	0	0
Bernazard, Oscar, Vermont	1.000	1	1	0	0	1	0	0
Blackburn, Alex, Auburn	.990	22	92	4	1	97	0	1
Blake, Ryan, Jamestown	.982	35	188	28	4	220	1	10
Bock, Brian, Aberdeen	.987	37	275	33	4	312	0	4
Bridges, Josh, New Jersey	1.000	3	10	1	0	11	0	0
Brown, Gregory, Jamestown	1.000	12	44	7	0	51	1	2
Buckley, James, Lowell	1.000	36	187	16	0	203	1	4
Caradonna, Troy, Staten Island	1.000	3	8	0	0	8	0	0
Chauncey, Clinton, M.V.	.989	23	160	22	2	184	1	2
Clements, Zachary, Brooklyn	1.000	5	39	7	0	46	0	1
Clendenin, Morgan, Aberdeen	.981	7	47	5	1	53	0	3
Cloninger, Erich, Lowell	.957	19	66	0	3	69	0	0
Cortez, Jose, Batavia	.987	41	278	24	4	306	2	11
DeVries, Jonathan, Lowell	.987	34	199	29	3	231	2	3
Diaz, Jeury, Batavia	1.000	15	110	7	0	117	1	4
Garcia, Yunir, Brooklyn	.985	36	235	23	4	262	2	2
Garko, Ryan, Mahoning Valley	.982	34	255	21	5	281	3	3
Ginther, Andy, New Jersey	.988	15	77	8	1	86	1	0
Graham, Andrew, Oneonta	1.000	20	108	13	0	121	1	3
Herrera, Javier, M.V.	.974	12	104	7	3	114	0	4
Hubele, Ryan, Aberdeen	1.000	2	22	2	0	24	0	0
Huddleston, Bobby, Oneonta	.961	27	175	23	8	206	1	4
Jaso, John, Hudson Valley	.969	38	229	25	8	262	3	8
Kahr, Danny, Vermont	.960	24	144	26	7	177	2	10
Knicely, Jeremy, Auburn	.955	5	21	0	1	22	0	1
Kratz, Erik, Auburn	1.000	33	290	38	0	328	2	6
Lutz, David, Vermont	.958	4	18	5	1	24	1	3
MACKOR, JEFF, Tri-City	.994	39	326	28	2	356	4	3
Manriquez, Salomon, Vermont	.990	42	261	35	3	299	4	16
McCuistion, Mike, Williamsport	.987	37	276	31	4	311	1	5
McGarvey, Randy, Tri-City	.994	21	143	12	1	156	0	4
Molina, Izzy, Aberdeen	1.000	8	65	2	0	67	0	2
Noviskey, Josh, M.V.	1.000	5	31	2	0	33	1	2
O'Brien, Patrick, Tri-City	.979	26	164	21	4	189	3	6
Pagnozzi, Matt, New Jersey	.993	58	365	66	3	434	1	5
Parrish, Dave, Staten Island	1.000	5	39	1	0	40	0	0
Piazza, Tony, Brooklyn	.978	44	286	27	7	320	2	2
Pignatiello, Bret, Vermont	.923	4	22	2	2	26	0	3
Ramos, Kelly, Aberdeen	1.000	5	47	7	0	54	1	0
Ramos, Victor, Williamsport	.968	8	27	3	1	31	0	1
Reyes, Milver, Williamsport	.993	40	259	31	2	292	3	6
Richmond, Paul, Auburn	.994	36	288	31	2	321	1	7
Riley, Justin, Batavia	.960	7	44	4	2	50	0	1
Robinson-Pierce, Whit, Aber.	.963	10	74	5	3	82	0	11
Robles, Luis, Staten Island	.990	16	98	5	1	104	0	5
Rosario, Carlos, Staten Island	.979	57	405	65	10	480	4	15
Sanchez, Danilo, Oneonta	.989	38	247	33	3	283	2	6
Schartz, Lance, Lowell	1.000	7	36	1	0	37	1	1
Schmitt, Billy, New Jersey	.964	14	68	12	3	83	2	2
Serrano, Ray, Hudson Valley	1.000	10	67	7	0	74	0	0
St. Martine, Michael, Vermont	1.000	3	28	2	0	30	0	1
VonTungeln, Cory, Batavia	.964	17	98	10	4	112	1	3
Whiteside, Eli, Aberdeen	.917	2	9	2	1	12	0	0
Woodruff, Ernest, H.V.	1.000	1	2	0	0	2	0	0
Wyman, Spencer, Jamestown	.982	18	152	13	3	168	0	3

PITCHERS

Player, Team	Pct.	G	PO	A	E	TC	DP
Aguero, Miguel, New Jersey	1.000	1	0	1	0	1	0
Albers, Matt, Tri-City	.955	15	6	15	1	22	0
Alvarez, Abraham, Lowell *	.833	9	0	5	1	6	0
Anderson, Wes, Lowell	.000	3	0	0	0	0	0
Astacio, Andres, Tri-City	1.000	3	1	1	0	2	0
Baez, William, Oneonta	.000	5	0	0	0	0	0
Baldwin, Andy, Oneonta	.882	9	3	12	2	17	3
Banks, Joshua, Auburn	1.000	15	4	6	0	10	0
Bannister, Brian, Brooklyn	.800	12	3	9	3	15	1
Basch, Zachary, Lowell	1.000	24	0	7	0	7	1
Basilio, Manuel, Hudson Valley	1.000	15	1	2	0	3	0
Batista, Roberto, New Jersey	.900	26	1	8	1	10	0
Bayer, Russ, Williamsport *	.900	21	2	7	1	10	0
Beam, T.J., Staten Island	1.000	9	0	2	0	2	0
Bedard, Erik, Aberdeen *	1.000	2	0	1	0	1	0
Beltre, Jonathan, Tri-City*	.714	21	1	4	2	7	0
Berube, Martin, Aberdeen	.889	18	2	6	1	9	0
Bimeal, Matt, Williamsport	1.000	27	7	8	0	15	3
Blackwell, Brad, Staten Island	.600	13	1	2	2	5	0
Blair, Tom, New Jersey *	.938	8	2	13	1	16	0
Blaney, Matt, Lowell	.000	5	0	0	0	0	0
Blanton, Matt, New Jersey *	1.000	2	2	2	0	4	0
Bonnell, Jared, New Jersey	.000	6	0	0	0	0	0
Bostick, Adam, Jamestown *	.857	15	3	9	2	14	0
Boughner, Anthony, Aberdeen *	1.000	24	2	10	0	12	0
Brandenburg, Adam, M.V.*	1.000	11	0	10	0	10	0
Brey, Josh, New Jersey *	.917	14	3	8	1	12	1
Burton, T.J., Mahoning Valley	1.000	14	6	10	0	16	0
Buzachero, Bubbie, Auburn	.714	30	2	3	2	7	1
Caceres, Carlos, Vermont	1.000	12	3	4	0	7	0
Canizal, Joaquin, Auburn	1.000	3	2	1	0	3	0
Caraballo, Angel, Staten Island	.000	1	0	0	0	0	0
Casey, Reid, Mahoning Valley	1.000	16	2	3	0	5	2
Castle, Heath, Staten Island *	1.000	13	0	2	0	2	0
Castro, Rafael, Brooklyn	.875	20	1	6	1	8	0
Cevette, Dan, Mahoning Valley *	.000	2	0	0	0	0	0
Chick, Travis, Jamestown	1.000	13	1	8	0	9	1
Cierlik, Jason, Aberdeen *	.929	22	3	10	1	14	0
Cillo, Cody, Jamestown	1.000	17	0	4	0	4	0
Cochran, Robert, Lowell *	1.000	20	3	3	0	6	1
Collar, Michael, Tri-City	.909	14	5	5	1	11	0
Colson, Jason, Auburn	1.000	3	0	1	0	1	0
Contreras, Jose, Staten Island	1.000	1	2	0	0	2	0
Contreras, Manuel, Oneonta	1.000	17	2	1	0	3	0
Cooper, Dexter, Lowell	.000	3	0	0	0	0	0
Coppinger, Joe, Aberdeen	.909	14	4	6	1	11	0
Cordova, Vincent, Brooklyn	.833	9	0	5	1	6	0
Core, Danny, Auburn	1.000	16	2	7	0	9	0
Corn, Jessie, Lowell	.800	4	0	4	1	5	0
Correa, Stephen, Brooklyn *	1.000	13	0	2	0	2	0
Cramer, Bob, Hudson Valley *	.750	5	1	2	1	4	1
Danly, Ryan, Brooklyn *	1.000	13	5	13	0	18	0
Davis, Brendon, Tri-City	.800	12	0	4	1	5	0
Davis, Matt, Mahoning Valley	.833	23	2	8	2	12	1
Day, Dewon, Auburn	.000	2	0	0	0	0	0
De Maria, Chris, Williamsport	.900	25	5	4	1	10	0
De la Cruz, Julio, Batavia	.750	12	6	3	3	12	0
DeChristofaro, Vinny, Batavia *	1.000	15	2	3	0	5	0
DeLeon, Joey, Tri-City	.933	17	5	9	1	15	1
Dean, Herman, Oneonta	1.000	1	1	0	0	1	0
Delacruz, Eulogio, Oneonta	.000	2	0	0	0	0	0
Desalvo, Matthew, Staten Island	.889	10	2	14	2	18	1
Deza, Fredy, Aberdeen	.923	15	3	9	1	13	0
Diaz, Eddie, Vermont	1.000	13	4	6	0	10	0
Diaz, Luis, Oneonta	1.000	2	2	0	0	2	1
Diefenderfer, Joseph, Batavia *	1.000	16	4	9	0	13	1
Dischiavo, John, Hudson Valley	.750	7	1	2	1	4	0
Dixon, Jeffrey, Vermont	1.000	7	1	0	0	1	0
Dixon, Zachary, Aberdeen *	.900	14	1	17	2	20	0
Dove, Dennis, New Jersey	1.000	7	2	1	0	3	0
Drown, Erik, New Jersey	1.000	10	1	5	0	6	0
Durbin, Chad, Mahoning Valley	1.000	2	0	3	0	3	1
Eazor, Kyle, Jamestown *	1.000	2	0	2	0	2	0
Echarry, Nelson, Batavia	1.000	2	0	1	0	1	0
Edmiston, Robert, Tri-City	.833	18	2	3	1	6	0
Ellis, Rob, Hudson Valley *	1.000	11	0	4	0	4	1
Escobar, Rodrigo, Tri-City	1.000	15	2	7	0	9	0
Everts, Clint, Vermont	.786	10	8	3	3	14	0
Farley, Chris, Lowell	1.000	18	2	4	0	6	1
Farrell, Jarrod, Hudson Valley	1.000	13	4	9	0	13	0
Fernandez, Carlos, H.V.	.875	23	3	11	2	16	0
Finch, Brian, Aberdeen	1.000	8	0	4	0	4	0
Fischer, Sam, Tri-City	.750	22	2	1	1	4	1
Galbraith, Jason, New Jersey *	1.000	17	0	5	0	5	0
Gangi, Aaron, Hudson Valley *	.800	14	4	8	3	15	0
Gardner, Jarrett, Lowell	.947	14	3	15	1	19	0
Gardner, Michael, Staten Island	.938	23	3	12	1	16	0

Player, Team	Pct.	G	PO	A	E	TC	DP
Garza, Alberto, Mahoning Valley	1.000	1	1	0	0	1	0
Garza, Justin, New Jersey	1.000	2	0	1	0	1	0
Generelli, Daniel, Vermont	.875	13	4	3	1	8	0
George, Taylor, Brooklyn	1.000	26	1	7	0	8	0
Gomez, Warmar, Vermont	.933	16	8	6	1	15	0
Gonzalez, Jino, Hudson Valley *	.000	3	0	0	2	2	0
Goodman, Chris, Vermont	.875	6	3	4	1	8	0
Gorzelanny, Thomas, Wil.*	.909	8	3	7	1	11	1
Gosch, Kirk, Hudson Valley *	1.000	8	0	4	0	4	1
Graham, Jason, Oneonta	1.000	7	1	0	0	1	0
Grigsby, Derick, Tri-City	.889	15	4	12	2	18	0
Hacker, Eric, Staten Island	.500	2	0	1	1	2	0
Hanson, Adam, Mahoning Valley	.667	21	1	3	2	6	0
Harmsen, Brandon, Staten Is.	.871	15	10	17	4	31	1
Harper, Jeremy, Auburn	1.000	19	1	4	0	5	0
Harris, Mark, Mahoning Valley	1.000	16	0	2	0	2	0
Haught, Dallas, Hudson Valley	1.000	5	1	4	0	5	0
Hawk, Shane, Brooklyn *	1.000	6	3	5	0	8	0
Henderson, Jim, Vermont	1.000	15	1	5	0	6	1
Hernandez, Christopher, Wil.	.846	20	2	9	2	13	0
Hernandez, Michael, M.V.*	1.000	4	0	2	0	2	0
Hertzler, Barry, Lowell	1.000	12	0	3	0	3	0
Hirsh, Jason, Tri-City	1.000	10	2	7	0	9	1
Hodges, Daniel, Batavia *	.833	8	1	4	1	6	0
Homer, Chris, Oneonta	1.000	26	1	2	0	3	0
Howell, Michael, Oneonta	1.000	4	6	2	0	8	0
Humen, David, Jamestown	1.000	7	2	0	0	2	0
Iehl, Jason, Jamestown	.000	4	0	0	0	0	0
Isenberg, Kurt, Auburn *	.857	13	3	3	1	7	0
Jackson, Kyle, Lowell	.500	2	1	0	1	2	1
James, Justin, Auburn	1.000	13	2	2	0	4	0
John, Jason, New Jersey	.875	21	2	5	1	8	0
Jordan, B.J., New Jersey *	1.000	27	2	2	0	4	0
Karstens, Jeffrey, Staten Island	.857	14	7	11	3	21	1
Kartler, Bryce, Staten Island *	.857	14	1	5	1	7	0
Kensing, Logan, Jamestown	.833	8	2	3	1	6	2
Keppel, Bob, Brooklyn	.833	3	3	2	1	6	0
Kerschen, Joshua, Staten Island	.750	8	2	1	1	4	0
Kiley, Jason, Williamsport	1.000	10	0	1	0	1	0
King, Bryan, Brooklyn	1.000	17	1	5	0	6	0
Kirkman, Ty, Vermont *	.800	21	1	3	1	5	0
Knapp, Ben, Aberdeen	.000	2	0	0	0	0	0
Kupper, Dustin, Jamestown	1.000	14	7	4	0	11	0
Lara, Juan, Mahoning Valley *	.950	12	4	15	1	20	0
Libey, Justin, Batavia	1.000	17	2	5	0	7	0
Lincoln, Roger, M.V.*	1.000	17	2	5	0	7	0
Lindstrom, Matthew, Brooklyn	.800	14	9	19	7	35	1
Lissir, Alexander, Williamsport	1.000	15	11	8	0	19	0
Little, Chris, Vermont	1.000	21	3	3	0	6	0
Little, Joe, Hudson Valley *	1.000	5	0	7	0	7	1
Loewen, Adam, Aberdeen *	1.000	7	1	8	0	9	0
Long, Nick, Vermont	1.000	14	6	11	0	17	0
Lopez, Aleurys, Hudson Valley	1.000	11	0	6	0	6	0
Lovato, Nicholas, Jamestown *	1.000	20	0	4	0	4	0
Lundgren, Wayne, Lowell	1.000	15	3	8	0	11	0
Lyons, Tom, Oneonta	1.000	12	5	2	0	7	0
MacLane, Evan, Brooklyn *	.000	1	0	0	0	0	0
Machi, Jean, Batavia	.909	8	2	8	1	11	0
Maholm, Paul, Williamsport *	1.000	8	6	2	0	8	0
Maldonado, Ivan, Brooklyn	1.000	18	5	11	0	16	1
Mann, Brandon, H.V.*	1.000	2	0	2	0	2	0
Mansfield, Monte, Tri-City	.500	10	0	1	1	2	0
Marchbanks, David, Jam.*	1.000	5	1	3	0	4	1
Marcum, Shaun, Auburn	1.000	21	3	4	0	7	0
Marshall, Brian, Lowell *	1.000	15	0	3	0	3	0
Martin, Greg, Vermont *	1.000	3	1	1	0	2	0
Martinez, Carlos, Jamestown	.000	1	0	0	0	0	0
Martinez, Roberto, Vermont	1.000	8	1	1	0	2	0
Maruffi, Joseph, Vermont	.000	3	0	0	0	0	0
Mastny, Thomas, Auburn	.926	14	6	19	2	27	1
Mathieson, Scott, Batavia	.000	2	0	0	0	0	0
McCally, Ryan, Hudson Valley	.909	9	5	5	1	11	1
McConnell, Caleb, Batavia	1.000	23	4	6	0	10	1
McCormack, Zach, Jamestown *	1.000	17	1	1	0	2	0
Meccage, Justin, Staten Island	.000	1	0	0	0	0	0
Menocal, Victor, Batavia	1.000	5	3	5	0	8	0
Merchant, Jamie, Tri-City	.846	16	6	5	2	13	0
Michael, Mark, New Jersey	.824	11	7	7	3	17	2
Mincey, T.W., Aberdeen *	1.000	9	0	1	0	1	0
Minor, Zach, Batavia	1.000	15	7	11	0	18	2
Miramontes, Matthew, Brooklyn	.000	1	0	0	0	0	0
Mondesir, James, New Jersey	.700	7	2	5	3	10	0

Player, Team	Pct.	G	PO	A	E	TC	DP
Montano, Ignacio, M.V.*	1.000	5	1	1	0	2	0
Morales, Juan, New Jersey	.929	30	3	10	1	14	0
MUECKE, JOSHUA, Tri-City*	1.000	14	5	15	0	20	0
Mulholland, Chad, Auburn	1.000	8	1	1	0	2	0
Muniz, Carlos, Brooklyn	1.000	19	1	3	0	4	0
Naatjes, Darin, Batavia	1.000	8	1	3	0	4	0
Navaroli, Michael, Hudson Valley	1.000	8	2	3	0	5	0
Neal, Tony, Aberdeen	.875	19	2	5	1	8	1
Nowicki, Nathan, Jamestown	1.000	18	1	3	0	4	0
Nunez, Franklin, Brooklyn	1.000	7	1	0	0	1	0
Nunez, Leo, Williamsport	.833	8	3	2	1	6	0
Nyquist, Brett, Vermont *	.800	5	1	3	1	5	0
O'Connor, Shaun, Jamestown	.000	3	0	0	0	0	0
Ochoa, Javier, Brooklyn	1.000	6	1	0	0	1	0
Ochoa, Nehomar, Vermont	.875	5	3	4	1	8	0
Ohalek, Corey, Jamestown *	1.000	3	0	1	0	1	0
Ool, Kevin, Lowell *	1.000	25	1	5	0	6	0
Orloski, Joe, Brooklyn	1.000	11	3	2	0	5	0
Orozco, Antonio, Jamestown	.000	1	0	0	0	0	0
Orvella, Chad, Hudson Valley	.667	10	0	2	1	3	1
Osberg, Tanner, Brooklyn	1.000	8	2	5	0	7	2
Osentowski, Chris, Aberdeen	.455	19	2	3	6	11	0
Overton, Brad, Batavia	1.000	19	6	8	0	14	2
Padilla, Matthew, Batavia	.750	25	1	5	2	8	0
Pals, Jordan, New Jersey	.917	6	4	7	1	12	0
Papelbon, Jonathan, Lowell	1.000	13	2	5	0	7	0
Parcus, William, Batavia *	.900	13	5	4	1	10	0
Patitucci, Mike, Aberdeen *	.667	18	0	4	2	6	0
Paulk, Robert, Brooklyn	.857	27	1	5	1	7	0
Pawelk, Reed, Jamestown	.857	18	1	5	1	7	0
Pearson, Anthony, Vermont	.800	15	7	1	2	10	0
Peguero, Tony, Hudson Valley	1.000	12	3	10	0	13	0
Pender, Matthew, Oneonta	.750	7	1	2	1	4	0
Penny, David, Lowell	.938	12	3	12	1	16	2
Pereyra, Honeudis, M.V.	.857	21	0	6	1	7	0
Perez, Antonio, Hudson Valley *	1.000	28	1	12	0	13	2
Perez, Ezequiel, Oneonta	.933	21	3	11	1	15	0
Perez, Randy, Mahoning Valley *	.714	7	2	3	2	7	0
Perrin, Devin, Vermont	1.000	11	3	8	0	11	0
Petit, Yusmeiro, Brooklyn	.000	2	0	0	0	0	0
Picco, John, Staten Island *	1.000	15	2	4	0	6	0
Pillsbury, Christopher, Jam.	.750	18	3	3	2	8	0
Plexico, Gerald, Vermont *	.944	17	6	11	1	18	0
Prahm, Ryan, Mahoning Valley	1.000	3	0	2	0	2	0
Prieto, Victor, Jamestown	.636	13	3	4	4	11	0
Primus, Carl, Jamestown	1.000	18	1	5	0	6	0
Quezada, Elvys, Staten Island	.857	8	2	4	1	7	0
Ramirez, Greg, Brooklyn	1.000	18	4	9	0	13	1
Ramsey, Robert, Tri-City	.833	20	2	3	1	6	0
Ray, Christopher, Aberdeen	.923	9	2	10	1	13	0
Reed, Brian, Auburn	.889	28	3	5	1	9	0
Reid, Brett, Vermont	.750	19	1	2	1	4	0
Rich, Dan, Mahoning Valley *	.667	18	0	2	1	3	0
Rickert, Brandon, M.V.	1.000	5	1	4	0	5	0
Rigdon, Paul, Mahoning Valley	1.000	3	1	3	0	4	1
Rijo, Fernando, Aberdeen	1.000	2	0	2	0	2	0
Roehl, Scott, Mahoning Valley	.941	14	5	11	1	17	1
Roga, Mike, Auburn	.000	2	0	0	0	0	0
Rogers, Brian, Oneonta	.667	12	1	5	3	9	0
Rohr, Charles, Hudson Valley	1.000	16	2	3	0	5	0
Romero, Davis, Auburn *	1.000	30	4	8	0	12	0
Ronz, Kenon, Oneonta *	1.000	25	0	6	0	6	0
Roper, Derek, New Jersey	1.000	17	4	11	0	15	2
Runyon, Bob, New Jersey	1.000	4	0	1	0	1	0
Rupert, Chris, Batavia *	1.000	17	1	6	0	7	0
Russell, Eddie, Jamestown	1.000	4	2	0	0	2	0
Russell, James, Vermont	.000	5	0	0	0	0	0
Sanders, David, Lowell *	1.000	9	0	3	0	3	0
Sandoval, Marcos, Auburn	1.000	4	1	3	0	4	0
Santo, Brian, Oneonta	1.000	23	4	3	0	7	0
Santos, Arthur, Lowell	.909	14	5	5	1	11	2
Saucedo, Matthew, Jamestown	1.000	17	0	4	0	4	1
Scalamandre, Rich, New Jersey	.000	8	0	0	0	0	0
Schmitt, Billy, New Jersey	1.000	2	1	1	0	2	0
Schneider, Jonathan, Wil.	.800	12	2	2	1	5	0
Scobie, Jason, Brooklyn	1.000	1	0	1	0	1	0
Shafer, Kurt, Williamsport	.909	14	8	12	2	22	0
Sharpless, Joshua, Williamsport	.667	22	1	1	1	3	0
Shortell, Rory, Tri-City	1.000	1	0	1	0	1	0
Silva, Sergio, Williamsport	1.000	12	6	11	0	17	0
Smith, Brandon, Lowell	1.000	10	1	6	0	7	1

Player, Team	Pct.	G	PO	A	E	TC	DP
Smith, David, Brooklyn *	1.000	8	0	1	0	1	0
Smith, Joshua, Staten Island	1.000	11	2	4	0	6	0
Sopko, Mark, Auburn	1.000	18	4	3	0	7	0
Soteropoulos, Peter, N.J.*	1.000	15	0	5	0	5	0
Southerland, Chip, M.V.	.000	8	0	0	0	0	0
Spillers, Brandon, Aberdeen	1.000	17	2	3	0	5	0
Spring, Daniel, Oneonta	1.000	23	2	4	0	6	1
Stanton, Mike, Brooklyn *	1.000	1	1	1	0	2	0
Steinborn, Chris, Oneonta *	1.000	6	1	5	0	6	0
Stiehl, Rob, Tri-City	.000	4	0	0	0	0	0
Sturge, Justin, Lowell *	.909	12	2	8	1	11	0
Talanoa, Charles, Auburn	1.000	5	1	3	0	4	0
Tamulionis, Mike, New Jersey	1.000	18	3	1	0	4	0
Tata, Jordan, Oneonta	.968	16	10	20	1	31	1
Tate, Matt, Aberdeen	1.000	10	0	1	0	1	0
Teeter, Travis, Aberdeen	1.000	12	1	6	0	7	0
Templet, Jordy, Auburn	1.000	8	1	2	0	3	0
Thorp, Paul, Staten Island	1.000	20	4	4	0	8	1
Tiller, James, Aberdeen	1.000	2	1	1	0	2	0
Tomey, Anthony, Oneonta	.800	20	0	4	1	5	0
TORREALBA, YOANN, Wil.	1.000	14	7	13	0	20	2
Torres, Carlos, Aberdeen	.833	16	1	4	1	6	1
Tower, Scott, Williamsport *	.750	15	3	3	2	8	0
Travis, Matt, Hudson Valley *	1.000	3	0	1	0	1	0
Tribe, Phillip, Staten Island	1.000	17	0	4	0	4	0
Urrutia, Carlos, Batavia	.000	1	0	0	0	0	0
Van Gorder, Joe, New Jersey *	1.000	8	0	2	0	2	0
Vandermeer, Scott, H.V.	.929	8	6	7	1	14	2
Vaquedano, Jose, Lowell	.769	14	2	8	3	13	0
Vasquez, Matt, Oneonta	.917	11	6	5	1	12	0
Vaughan, Beau, Lowell	1.000	11	0	4	0	4	0
Vermilyea, Jamie, Auburn	.667	9	0	4	2	6	0
Walker, Adam, Brooklyn *	1.000	8	1	2	0	3	0
Wallace, Shane, M.V.*	1.000	8	0	2	0	2	0
Weaver, Joe, Mahoning Valley	.889	13	3	5	1	9	0
Weeden, Brandon, Staten Island	1.000	5	1	1	0	2	0
Weimer, Andrew, Hudson Valley	.846	23	0	11	2	13	0
Wheeler, Adam, Staten Island	1.000	14	1	5	0	6	0
Wheeler, William, Auburn	1.000	10	2	5	0	7	0
White, Brian, Williamsport	1.000	11	2	2	0	4	0
White, Chris, Mahoning Valley *	1.000	14	1	4	0	5	0
Williamson, Willie, New Jersey *	1.000	17	4	5	0	9	0
Wilson, Joseph, Batavia *	.000	3	0	0	1	1	0
Wood, Timothy, Jamestown	1.000	16	5	3	0	8	0
Woodrow, Christopher, Batavia	1.000	17	4	4	0	8	0
Worthington, Timothy, Brooklyn	1.000	17	0	4	0	4	1
Wright, Chase, Staten Island *	.974	14	7	31	1	39	3
Yurek, Ryan, Tri-City	1.000	12	2	1	0	3	0
Zell, Danny, Oneonta *	.917	8	2	9	1	12	0
Ziegler, Brad, Batavia	1.000	3	2	1	0	3	0

The following players appeared only as a designated hitter, pinch-hitter or pinch-runner: Cenate, ph; Wareham, dh, pr.

LEAGUE CHAMPIONS

Year	Team	Pct.
1939—	Olean*	.631
1940—	Olean*	.625
1941—	Jamestown	.618
	Bradford (2nd)†	.549
1942—	Jamestown*	.672
1943—	Lockport	.591
	Wellsville (3rd)†	.532
1944—	Lockport	.608
	Jamestown (2nd)†	.565
1945—	Batavia*	.677
1946—	Jamestown‡	.672
	Batavia‡	.672
1947—	Jamestown*	.690
1948—	Lockport*	.603
1949—	Bradford*	.635
1950—	Hornell	.653
	Olean (2nd)†	.568
1951—	Olean	.622
	Hornell (3rd)†	.568
1952—	Hamilton	.659
	Jamestown (2nd)†	.643
1953—	Jamestown*	.704
1954—	Corning*	.621
1955—	Hamilton*	.656
1956—	Wellsville*	.617
1957—	Wellsville	.632
	Erie (2nd)†	.598
1958—	Wellsville	.556
	Geneva (2nd)†	.548
1959—	Wellsville†	.635
1960—	Erie	.643
	Wellsville (2nd)†	.535
1961—	Geneva	.616
	Olean (4th)†	.512
1962—	Jamestown	.580
	Auburn (3rd)†	.521
1963—	Auburn	.585
	Batavia (3rd)†	.485
1964—	Auburn§	.622
1965—	Binghamton	.677
	Binghamton	.607
1966—	Auburn∞	.620
	Binghamton	.646
1967—	Auburn	.667
1968—	Auburn	.645
	Oneonta (2nd)*	.558
1969—	Oneonta	.662
1970—	Auburn	.623
1971—	Oneonta	.662
1972—	Niagara Falls	.686
1973—	Auburn	.667
1974—	Oneonta	.768
1975—	Newark	.688
	Newark	.714
1976—	Elmira	.727
	Elmira	.703
1977—	Oneonta▲	.671
	Batavia	.600
1978—	Oneonta	.729
	Geneva◆	.718
1979—	Geneva	.725
	Oneonta◆	.618
1980—	Oneonta▲	.662
	Geneva	.649
1981—	Oneonta▲	.658
	Jamestown	.649
1982—	Oneonta	.566
	Niagara Falls▲	.553
1983—	Utica▲	.649
	Newark	.649
1984—	Newark	.622
	Little Falls▲	.587
1985—	Oneonta*	.705
	Auburn	.603
1986—	Oneonta	.766
	St. Catharines◆	.632
1987—	Geneva▲	.632
	Watertown	.579
1988—	Oneonta▲	.632
	Jamestown	.618
1989—	Pittsfield	.697
	Jamestown▲	.579
1990—	Oneonta■	.667
	Geneva	.662
1991—	Pittsfield	.662
	Jamestown■	.654
1992—	Hamilton	.737
	Geneva▼	.547
1993—	Niagara Falls▼	.603
	Pittsfield	.533
1994—	Auburn	.592
	New Jersey▼	.573
1995—	Vermont	.645
	Watertown▼	.630
1996—	Vermont▼	.649
	St. Catharines	.579
1997—	Batavia	.635
	Pittsfield▼	.568
1998—	Hudson Valley	.658
	Oneonta††	.592
	Auburn††	.573
1999—	Mahoning Valley	.566
	Hudson Valley‡‡	.553
2000—	Mahoning Valley	.632
	Staten Island§§	.622
2001—	Brooklyn∞∞	.684
	Williamsport∞∞	.649
2002—	Staten Island▲▲	.649
2003—	Williamsport▲▲	.605

*Won championship and four-club playoff. †Won four-club playoff. ‡Jamestown and Batavia declared co-champions; Batavia defeated Jamestown in final of four-club playoff. §Won championship and two-club playoff. ∞Won split-season playoff. ▲League divided into Eastern and Western divisions; won playoff. League divided into Wrigley and Yawkey divisions; won playoff. ■League divided into Eastern, Western and Stedler divisions; won playoff. ▼League divided into McNamara, Pinckney and Stedler divisions; won playoff. ††Named co-champions due to final series being rained out. ‡‡League divided into McNamara and Pinckney divisions; won playoff. §§League divided into McNamara and Stedler divisions; won playoff. ∞∞League divided into McNamara and Stedler divisions; Brooklyn was leading final series of four-team playoff over Williamsport, but both teams were declared co-champions when Professional Baseball declared a stoppage of play. (NOTE—Known as Pennsylvania-Ontario-New York League from 1939 through 1956.) ▲▲League divided into McNamara, Pinckney and Stedler divisions; won playoff.

NORTHWEST LEAGUE

LEAGUE OFFICE

President/treasurer
Bob Richmond
Address
P.O. Box 1645
Boise, ID 83701
Phone
208-429-1511

Teams (affiliation)
Boise Hawks (Cubs)
Eugene Emeralds (Padres)
Everett AquaSox (Mariners)
Salem-Keizer Volcanoes (Giants)
Spokane Indians (Rangers)
Tri-City Dust Devils (Rockies)
Vancouver Canadians (A's)
Yakima Bears (Diamondbacks)

2003 FINAL STANDINGS

EAST DIVISION

Team	W	L	T	Pct.	GB
Spokane	50	26	-	.658	...
Yakima	45	31	-	.592	5.0
Tri-City	33	43	-	.434	17.0
Boise	27	49	-	.355	23.0

WEST DIVISION

Team	W	L	T	Pct.	GB
Salem-Keizer	43	33	-	.566	...
Eugene	39	37	-	.513	4.0
Vancouver	35	41	-	.461	8.0
Everett	32	44	-	.421	11.0

COMPOSITE

Team	SPO	YAK	S-K	EUG	VAN	TRI	EVR	BOI	W	L	T	Pct.	GB
Spokane (Rangers)	...	5	7	8	7	8	7	8	50	26	0	.658	...
Yakima (Diamondbacks)	7	...	4	6	7	5	9	7	45	31	0	.592	5.0
Salem-Keizer (Giants)	3	6	...	8	7	7	6	6	43	33	0	.566	7.0
Eugene (Padres)	2	4	4	...	7	7	9	6	39	37	0	.513	11.0
Vancouver (Athletics)	3	3	5	5	...	5	6	8	35	41	0	.461	15.0
Tri-City (Rockies)	4	7	3	3	5	...	4	7	33	43	0	.434	17.0
Everett (Mariners)	3	1	6	3	6	6	...	7	32	44	0	.421	18.0
Boise (Cubs)	4	5	4	4	2	5	3	...	27	49	0	.355	23.0

Major league affiliations in parentheses.

PLAYOFFS: Spokane defeated Salem-Keizer, three games to none, to win league championship.

REGULAR-SEASON ATTENDANCE: Boise, 104,156; Eugene, 130,657; Everett, 110,043; Salem-Keizer, 119,556; Spokane, 170,640; Tri-City, 58,976; Vancouver, 137,026; Yakima, 60,037. Total attendance—891,091. Playoffs (3 games)—5,453.

MANAGERS: Boise, Steve McFarland; Eugene, Roy Howell; Everett, Pedro Gritol; Salem-Keizer, Joe Strain; Spokane, Darryl Kennedy; Tri-City, Ron Gideon; Vancouver, Dennis Rogers; Yakima, Bill Plummer.

ALL-STAR TEAM: 1B—Brian Dopirak, Boise; 2B—Nick Orlandos, Everett; 3B—Jamie D'Antona, Yakima; SS—Omar Quintanilla, Vancouver; OF—Jeremy Cleveland, Spokane; OF—Brian Wahlbrink, Eugene; OF—Conor Jackson, Yakima; C—Todd Jennings, Salem-Keizer; DH—Brad Vericker, Salem-Keizer; LHP—Sean Thompson, Eugene; RHP—Felix Hernandez, Everett; LH reliever—Clint Goocher, Yakima; RH reliever—(tie) Eddie Bonine, Eugene, and Dustin Glant, Yakima; Most Valuable Player—Conor Jackson, Yakima; Manager of the Year—Darryl Kennedy, Spokane.

2003 BATTING

TEAM

Team	G	TPA	AB	R	H	TB	2B	3B	HR	RBI	SH	SF	HP	BB	IBB	SO	SB	CS	GDP	LOB	ShO	Avg.	OBP	Slg.
Spokane	76	3072	2597	454	694	1014	138	25	44	400	10	34	56	375	5	551	45	23	49	624	2	.267	.367	.390
Salem-Keizer	76	3052	2638	397	705	994	126	20	41	357	37	32	54	291	5	505	51	18	59	630	7	.267	.348	.377
Everett	76	2894	2565	361	666	918	109	19	35	307	21	24	40	244	4	537	117	48	54	529	4	.260	.331	.358
Yakima	76	3022	2588	402	664	978	153	22	39	357	37	21	74	301	9	580	96	23	48	609	1	.257	.348	.378
Vancouver	76	2987	2553	326	654	884	136	14	22	294	29	21	37	347	5	505	54	33	69	642	4	.256	.351	.346
Eugene	76	2935	2588	346	636	892	104	22	36	299	20	18	57	251	6	610	99	29	50	554	5	.246	.324	.345
Boise	76	2800	2534	269	590	889	99	19	54	244	22	19	50	175	4	636	73	40	41	492	9	.233	.293	.351
Tri-City	76	2868	2526	289	575	843	120	20	36	254	37	15	39	251	6	631	42	26	41	535	6	.228	.306	.334

INDIVIDUAL

TOP QUALIFIERS FOR BATTING CHAMPIONSHIP

Minimum 205 plate appearances. *Lefthanded batter. †Switch-hitter.

Player, Team	G	TPA	AB	R	H	TB	2B	3B	HR	RBI	SH	SF	HP	BB	IBB	SO	SB	CS	GDP	Avg.	OBP	Slg.
Bubela, Dane, Spokane *	62	280	229	51	74	114	18	5	4	35	0	3	2	46	2	62	7	4	5	.323	.436	.498
Cleveland, Jeremy, Spokane	64	303	245	64	79	126	20	3	7	53	0	6	12	40	1	50	5	1	3	.322	.432	.514
Jackson, Conor, Yakima	68	300	257	44	82	137	35	1	6	60	0	2	5	36	4	41	3	0	7	.319	.410	.533
Orlandos, Nick, Everett	69	296	265	41	84	111	13	4	2	31	8	3	8	12	0	22	14	7	5	.317	.361	.419
Hornostaj, Aaron, S.-K.*	64	295	257	38	80	97	9	1	2	33	11	5	3	19	1	30	10	3	7	.311	.359	.377
Kim, Edward, Vancouver *	65	279	239	26	73	102	17	0	4	39	0	3	2	35	1	52	1	0	7	.305	.394	.427
Blakeley, Eric, Everett	59	223	195	31	59	81	9	2	3	24	2	3	4	19	0	36	13	2	5	.303	.371	.415
Coutlangus, Jonathan, S.-K.*	51	208	176	34	53	69	7	3	1	24	5	0	2	25	0	31	7	4	1	.301	.394	.392
Wahlbrink, Brian, Eugene	69	306	270	45	81	118	17	4	4	34	0	0	8	28	2	82	19	4	2	.300	.382	.437
Jennings, Jeffery, S.-K.	59	258	233	27	69	91	9	2	3	32	1	4	5	15	0	36	5	3	9	.296	.346	.391
Majewski, Dustin, Van.*	46	205	175	33	51	77	13	2	3	19	0	1	1	28	0	35	6	5	7	.291	.390	.440
Sandoval, Abigail, Spokane	67	281	253	32	72	81	6	0	1	39	1	3	1	23	0	38	7	5	6	.285	.343	.320
Wishy, Andrew, Spokane *	72	320	260	46	74	120	14	7	6	55	0	1	5	54	2	58	3	2	3	.285	.416	.462
Vericker, Brad, S.-K.*	70	297	243	47	69	133	19	0	15	47	0	3	3	48	2	58	0	1	6	.284	.404	.547
Smyres, Justin, Eugene	53	206	186	27	52	61	7	1	0	14	2	2	8	8	0	42	11	4	1	.280	.333	.328

DEPARTMENTAL LEADERS: G—Ramos, 74; AB—Ramos, 290; R—Cleveland, 64; H—Orlandos, 84; TB—D'Antona, 140; 2B—Jackson, 35; 3B—Almonte, 9; HR—D'Antona, Vericker, 15; RBI—Jackson, 60; SH—Hornostaj, 11; SF—Cleveland, Kreuzer, 6; HP—Rose, 16; BB—Wishy, 54; IBB—Jackson, 4; SO—R. Fox, Wahlbrink, 82; SB—Garabrants, 30; CS—Colton, Walker, 9; GIDP—Cornejo, 13; Slg.—Vericker, .547; OBP—Bubela, .436.

ALL PLAYERS

*Lefthanded batter. †Switch-hitter.

Player, Team	G	TPA	AB	R	H	TB	2B	3B	HR	RBI	SH	SF	HP	BB	IBB	SO	SB	CS	GDP	Avg.	OBP	Slg.
Alexander, Christopher, Spo...	55	234	206	24	52	81	14	0	5	30	0	1	7	20	0	59	0	0	5	.252	.338	.393
Almonte, Sandy, Tri-City †	68	296	270	28	57	94	10	9	3	20	5	0	3	18	0	72	9	5	5	.211	.268	.348
Anderson, Scott, Tri-City	13	48	35	4	5	5	0	0	0	2	0	0	0	13	0	10	0	3	1	.143	.375	.143
Appert, Luke, Vancouver *	58	249	192	25	37	44	4	0	1	16	1	4	3	49	1	29	3	7	3	.193	.359	.229
Avlas, Phil, Yakima	17	52	45	7	15	21	4	1	0	4	1	0	0	6	0	11	0	1	1	.333	.412	.467
Ayala, Odannys, Spokane	3	13	9	3	2	4	0	1	0	0	0	0	0	4	0	1	0	0	1	.222	.462	.444
Baker, Casey, Eugene	43	143	128	21	33	45	4	4	0	14	5	0	2	8	0	25	11	1	4	.258	.312	.352
Banks, Gary, Boise †	28	89	81	8	20	22	0	1	0	8	0	1	2	5	0	25	2	1	2	.247	.303	.272
Barrett, Rich, Yakima	37	135	114	21	25	29	2	1	0	12	2	3	6	10	0	25	16	1	3	.219	.308	.254
Barrows, Derek, Salem-Keizer	33	124	109	17	23	32	3	0	2	12	1	1	1	12	0	14	1	1	0	.211	.293	.294
Benjamin, Casey, Spokane *	32	123	103	19	28	35	4	0	1	14	1	0	1	18	0	26	0	0	0	.272	.385	.340
Blakeley, Eric, Everett	59	223	195	31	59	81	9	2	3	24	2	3	4	19	0	36	13	2	5	.303	.371	.415
Blood, Randy, Tri-City *	68	298	265	28	68	93	12	2	3	35	3	4	3	23	1	69	2	2	0	.257	.319	.351
Bochy, Greg, Eugene	31	116	105	11	17	18	1	0	0	5	2	1	4	4	0	37	1	0	5	.162	.219	.171
Bourassa, Adam, Spokane *	59	259	205	40	45	53	6	1	0	22	5	3	1	45	0	31	6	5	2	.220	.358	.259
Boyer, Brett, Salem-Keizer	47	112	100	16	27	36	5	2	0	9	2	1	1	8	0	29	3	1	4	.270	.327	.360
Boyer, Kyle, Boise	47	194	170	28	46	89	6	5	9	27	2	2	3	17	2	57	2	1	2	.271	.344	.524
Bradford, Samuel, Everett †	55	213	184	36	44	69	6	2	5	21	1	0	1	27	1	57	13	6	3	.239	.340	.375
Brinson, Matt, Tri-City *	37	158	144	15	26	40	5	0	3	18	0	1	0	13	1	43	0	0	2	.181	.247	.278
Bubalo, Ty, Vancouver	7	25	23	3	6	10	2	1	0	1	0	0	0	2	0	8	0	0	1	.261	.320	.435
Bubela, Dane, Spokane *	62	280	229	51	74	114	18	5	4	35	0	3	2	46	2	62	7	4	5	.323	.436	.498
Buchanan, Todd, Yakima *	63	253	214	36	56	79	15	1	2	19	0	1	2	36	1	42	0	0	4	.262	.372	.369
Bushey, Andrew, Tri-City *	39	165	147	18	33	37	4	0	0	9	1	0	1	16	2	16	2	1	6	.224	.305	.252
Carlin, Luke, Eugene †	28	116	100	14	25	32	7	0	0	7	0	0	2	14	0	25	1	0	2	.250	.353	.320
Castillo, David, Vancouver	51	176	144	25	37	49	9	0	1	14	2	1	0	29	0	14	0	2	3	.257	.379	.340
Ciesluk, Chris, Salem-Keizer	4	13	12	1	2	5	0	0	1	2	1	0	0	0	0	4	0	0	0	.167	.167	.417
Clark, Douglas, Spokane	38	143	129	22	27	40	7	0	2	12	0	0	5	9	0	21	0	0	1	.209	.287	.310
Cleveland, Jeremy, Spokane	64	303	245	64	79	126	20	3	7	53	0	6	12	40	1	50	5	1	3	.322	.432	.514
Colbrunn, Greg, Everett	1	4	3	0	2	3	1	0	0	0	0	0	0	1	0	0	0	0	0	.667	.750	1.000
Colonel, Christian, Tri-City	56	237	208	21	51	64	8	1	1	21	1	1	8	19	0	31	9	3	3	.245	.331	.308
Colton, Chris, Everett	71	295	250	33	65	94	12	1	5	32	0	4	3	38	0	60	16	9	6	.260	.359	.376
Corder, Gordon, Vancouver	44	155	135	14	33	49	7	0	3	14	1	1	7	11	0	24	0	0	3	.244	.331	.363
Cordova, Roman, Everett †	16	58	53	2	11	13	2	0	0	2	0	0	3	2	0	5	2	0	2	.208	.276	.245
Cornejo, Eduardo, Van.*	41	166	141	15	32	42	8	1	0	16	3	2	1	19	0	13	4	4	13	.227	.319	.298
Coutlangus, Jonathan, S.K.*	51	208	176	34	53	69	7	3	1	24	5	0	2	25	0	31	7	4	1	.301	.394	.392
Cox, Michael, Everett	55	202	175	22	34	55	9	0	4	20	0	2	2	23	1	55	3	2	4	.194	.292	.314
Cruz, Elvis, Everett	7	26	26	1	3	3	0	0	0	3	0	0	0	0	0	10	0	0	1	.115	.115	.115
Czarniecki, Jordan, Tri-City	51	209	184	19	45	57	9	0	1	16	5	3	3	14	0	38	4	4	3	.245	.304	.310
D'Antona, Jamie, Yakima	70	312	271	46	75	140	18	1	15	57	0	5	1	35	1	60	0	0	5	.277	.356	.517
D'Jesus, Francisco, S.K.	23	70	64	5	15	15	0	0	0	2	3	0	1	2	0	9	0	0	2	.234	.269	.234
Dawkins, Lance, Boise	32	109	95	9	15	20	5	0	0	3	0	1	3	10	0	32	2	2	1	.158	.257	.211
Diaz, Randor, Salem-Keizer	2	6	4	1	0	0	0	0	0	0	0	0	2	0	0	3	0	0	0	.000	.333	.000
Dobson, Patrick, S.K.	15	59	52	2	12	18	4	1	0	3	0	0	1	6	0	18	2	0	0	.231	.322	.346
Dopirak, Brian, Boise	52	218	192	25	46	89	4	0	13	37	0	0	2	24	1	58	0	2	4	.240	.330	.464
Dutton, Jeremy, Everett *	66	283	245	29	66	82	6	2	2	32	2	3	2	31	1	37	11	4	6	.269	.352	.335
Ellison, Josh, Everett	49	207	182	26	49	69	4	2	4	26	5	1	3	16	0	42	12	4	2	.269	.337	.379
Ethier, Andre, Vancouver *	10	45	41	7	16	25	4	1	1	7	0	0	1	3	1	3	2	1	3	.390	.444	.610
Fabrizio, Thomas, Eugene *	11	35	33	5	8	8	0	0	0	2	0	0	1	1	0	8	1	0	1	.242	.286	.242
Falcon, Omar, Eugene	32	123	110	16	21	38	2	0	5	14	0	1	3	9	0	37	2	2	4	.191	.268	.345
Farrell, Sean, Vancouver	59	250	215	24	48	68	17	0	1	28	2	2	3	28	0	55	3	1	7	.223	.319	.316
Fox, Adam, Spokane	65	271	235	35	51	78	13	1	4	38	2	4	3	27	0	45	3	2	5	.217	.301	.332
Fox, Ryan, Tri-City	58	225	194	26	34	68	8	1	8	26	1	1	7	22	0	82	1	1	1	.175	.281	.351
Francisco, Alfredo, Boise	14	54	52	3	8	10	2	0	0	0	1	0	1	0	0	15	0	0	3	.154	.170	.192
Francois, Francisco, Van.	47	157	134	21	35	40	2	0	1	16	7	0	4	12	0	29	4	2	3	.261	.340	.299
Frazier, Alex, Yakima	70	307	276	45	73	120	15	4	8	39	0	1	13	17	0	58	1	3	4	.264	.336	.435
Furtado, Micah, Spokane *	2	9	8	1	2	2	0	0	0	1	0	1	0	0	0	1	0	0	0	.250	.222	.250
Gaetti, Joe, Tri-City	34	134	116	15	32	55	7	2	4	9	2	2	0	14	0	38	1	2	3	.276	.348	.474
Garabrants, Steve, Yakima	55	247	199	41	55	77	11	4	1	22	3	0	6	39	2	58	30	5	3	.276	.410	.387
Garcia, Alberto, Boise	5	21	19	3	5	7	2	0	0	3	0	0	2	0	0	3	0	0	0	.263	.333	.368
Garcia, Alex, Eugene †	51	218	192	25	52	59	3	2	0	15	2	2	6	16	0	45	14	8	3	.271	.343	.307
Garcia, Lino, Yakima	49	177	154	24	34	42	6	1	0	18	3	3	1	16	0	34	13	3	1	.221	.293	.273
Garrido, Tomas, Salem-Keizer	37	140	124	7	28	35	5	1	0	11	6	3	1	6	0	23	5	0	2	.226	.261	.282
George, Trey, Tri-City	60	243	219	23	50	78	16	0	4	23	1	1	2	20	1	50	3	0	2	.228	.298	.356
Gibbons, Danny, Vancouver *	63	245	221	28	53	75	13	0	3	27	0	2	3	19	1	51	2	0	1	.240	.306	.339
Gonzalez, Jose, Spokane †	9	30	29	4	7	8	1	0	0	2	0	0	0	1	0	5	0	0	0	.241	.267	.276
Grayson, Larry, Spokane	8	33	29	4	9	11	0	1	0	4	0	1	0	3	0	7	1	0	0	.310	.364	.379
Gresky, David, Boise *	49	188	167	16	36	57	6	3	3	11	0	0	4	17	1	53	3	1	2	.216	.303	.341
Griffin, Brock, Everett *	23	63	52	6	7	10	0	0	1	7	0	1	0	10	0	25	0	1	3	.135	.270	.192
Guarno, Rick, Tri-City	37	155	137	16	32	47	8	2	1	9	5	1	1	11	0	29	3	0	2	.234	.293	.343
Haley, Adam, Yakima *	69	271	237	32	55	74	11	1	2	30	8	2	4	19	0	42	2	2	6	.232	.298	.312
Harriman, David, Vancouver	19	57	47	3	8	8	0	0	0	1	2	0	1	7	0	15	0	0	0	.170	.291	.170
Heath, Matt, Yakima †	3	9	7	3	2	3	1	0	0	1	0	0	0	2	0	2	0	0	0	.286	.444	.429
Hickman, Charles, Boise	45	172	158	16	36	55	10	3	1	14	3	3	1	7	0	29	9	2	2	.228	.260	.348
Hogan, William, Eugene	22	87	78	6	20	30	7	0	1	10	0	0	1	8	0	21	0	0	3	.256	.333	.385
Hornostaj, Aaron, S.K.*	64	295	257	38	80	97	9	1	2	33	11	5	3	19	1	30	10	3	7	.311	.359	.377
Hutting, Timothy, S.K.	64	286	248	29	54	64	7	0	1	31	3	4	6	25	0	32	4	2	6	.218	.300	.258
Ingram, Brian, Vancouver *	43	127	104	15	23	30	5	1	0	13	2	2	1	18	0	28	0	1	1	.221	.336	.288

Player, Team	G	TPA	AB	R	H	TB	2B	3B	HR	RBI	SH	SF	HP	BB	IBB	SO	SB	CS	GDP	Avg.	OBP	Slg.
Ishikawa, Travis, S.K.*	66	298	248	53	63	97	17	4	3	31	0	1	5	44	0	77	0	0	2	.254	.376	.391
Jackson, Conor, Yakima	68	300	257	44	82	137	35	1	6	60	0	2	5	36	4	41	3	0	7	.319	.410	.533
Jacobo, Kervin, Eugene †	21	89	79	6	15	21	3	0	1	8	1	1	0	8	0	21	2	0	3	.190	.261	.266
Jennings, Jeffery, S.K.	59	258	233	27	69	91	9	2	3	32	1	4	5	15	0	36	5	3	9	.296	.346	.391
Johanning, Ben, Eugene *	7	21	18	1	2	3	1	0	0	0	0	0	0	3	0	6	0	0	1	.111	.238	.167
Johnson, Ryan, Eugene *	41	168	149	18	41	60	5	1	4	20	1	2	3	13	1	26	1	2	1	.275	.341	.403
Jones, Adamq, Everett	3	15	13	2	6	7	1	0	0	4	0	1	0	1	0	3	0	0	1	.462	.467	.538
Kim, Edward, Vancouver *	65	279	239	26	73	102	17	0	4	39	0	3	2	35	1	52	1	0	7	.305	.394	.427
Kinsler, Ian, Spokane	51	216	188	32	52	77	10	6	1	15	0	4	4	20	0	34	11	3	5	.277	.352	.410
Klippenstein, Tyler, Van.	4	12	11	1	4	7	0	0	1	1	0	0	0	1	0	2	0	0	0	.364	.417	.636
Knowlton, Jay, Salem-Keizer	8	32	29	4	9	9	0	0	0	3	0	0	1	2	0	5	1	0	0	.310	.375	.310
Kreuzer, Josh, Spokane	55	246	199	35	45	71	8	0	6	40	0	6	12	29	0	35	1	0	4	.226	.350	.357
Kroski, Chris, Everett *	14	45	37	3	7	11	2	1	0	2	0	0	0	8	0	10	0	1	0	.189	.333	.297
LaBarbera, Anthony, S.K.	11	44	37	6	8	11	3	0	0	2	0	1	1	5	1	5	3	0	1	.216	.318	.297
Lahair, Bryan, Everett *	57	213	201	26	49	69	14	0	2	20	0	0	1	11	1	40	4	3	3	.244	.286	.343
Larsen, Andrew, Boise	69	287	266	29	69	101	12	1	6	23	0	3	7	11	0	64	10	3	7	.259	.303	.380
Lauderdale, Matthew, Eugene	12	50	39	7	9	15	3	0	1	7	0	0	4	7	0	15	0	0	0	.231	.400	.385
Leise, Jeff, Eugene *	60	212	185	26	39	49	3	2	1	16	1	4	4	18	0	25	8	3	4	.211	.289	.265
Lentz, Brian, Everett	35	122	106	15	23	30	4	0	1	12	1	2	4	9	0	19	3	1	4	.217	.298	.283
Lopaze, Daniel, Boise *	44	165	148	12	31	48	6	1	3	9	1	1	2	13	0	37	0	2	7	.209	.280	.324
Lunsford, Trey, Salem-Keizer	3	14	10	0	3	3	0	0	0	3	0	1	1	2	0	1	0	0	0	.300	.429	.300
Lynam, Guy, Tri-City	3	11	10	3	4	4	0	0	0	0	0	0	0	1	0	2	1	0	0	.400	.455	.400
Maduro, Jorge, Everett	15	62	56	5	14	21	1	0	2	9	0	2	0	4	0	15	0	0	1	.250	.290	.375
Majewski, Dustin, Van.*	46	205	175	33	51	77	13	2	3	19	0	1	1	28	0	35	6	5	7	.291	.390	.440
Mann, Jason, Spokane *	1	4	4	1	1	2	1	0	0	0	0	0	0	0	0	1	0	0	0	.250	.250	.500
Marquez, Uriak, Boise †	52	218	201	21	48	78	10	1	6	19	1	4	2	10	0	38	2	4	3	.239	.276	.388
Martinez, Domingo, Eugene	7	25	22	0	0	0	0	0	0	0	1	0	0	2	0	11	0	0	0	.000	.083	.000
Mathis, Gregory, Yakima	37	144	128	20	38	60	7	3	3	20	4	0	2	10	0	40	3	2	1	.297	.357	.469
McIntyre, Patrick, Boise	14	45	39	2	6	7	1	0	0	2	0	0	1	5	0	12	0	1	1	.154	.267	.179
McQuade, Anthony, Boise †	52	214	190	19	44	72	8	1	6	25	2	2	5	15	0	40	4	2	4	.232	.302	.379
Medlin, C.J., Boise	29	93	87	7	17	26	6	0	1	7	0	1	2	3	0	22	0	0	1	.195	.237	.299
Mejia, Jorge, Vancouver	7	23	20	1	3	3	0	0	0	1	0	0	1	2	0	11	1	1	0	.150	.261	.150
Monahan, Joey, Boise	23	95	85	9	21	26	5	0	0	11	2	1	4	3	0	19	8	2	0	.247	.301	.306
Mora, Ruben, Eugene †	19	73	63	10	14	17	3	0	0	6	1	0	0	9	0	12	4	0	2	.222	.319	.270
Moreno, Juan J., Yakima *	33	76	71	6	12	19	4	0	1	5	2	1	0	2	0	24	0	0	2	.169	.189	.268
Morgan, Matt, Yakima	58	252	214	27	53	70	13	2	0	23	7	2	3	26	1	36	1	1	3	.248	.335	.327
Morton, Colt, Eugene	25	107	97	14	27	54	6	0	7	20	0	0	0	10	0	29	0	0	1	.278	.346	.557
Navarro, Oswaldo, Everett †	61	248	233	42	60	74	12	1	0	23	0	0	5	10	0	39	16	3	4	.258	.302	.318
Nordness, Kirk, Vancouver	12	44	38	1	4	8	1	0	1	4	2	0	1	3	0	8	0	0	1	.105	.190	.211
Orlandos, Nick, Everett	69	296	265	41	84	111	13	4	2	31	8	3	8	12	0	22	14	7	5	.317	.361	.419
Perez, Luis, Vancouver	66	274	245	31	67	90	14	3	1	24	1	1	4	23	0	30	11	5	7	.273	.344	.367
Pickens, Jordan, Eugene	29	120	107	16	30	55	10	0	5	20	0	0	0	13	2	31	2	0	2	.280	.358	.514
Quintanilla, Omar, Van.*	32	143	129	22	44	57	5	4	0	14	1	0	1	12	0	20	7	1	3	.341	.401	.442
Ramirez, Juan, Vancouver	10	30	27	2	5	7	2	0	0	3	2	0	0	1	0	6	0	0	1	.185	.214	.259
Ramos, Peeter, Eugene	74	319	290	34	67	90	8	6	1	36	4	3	0	22	0	55	16	5	3	.231	.283	.310
Reyes, Jose, Boise †	11	38	36	4	10	10	0	0	0	5	1	0	0	1	0	4	0	1	0	.278	.297	.278
Reynolds, Lagatila, Yakima	8	28	23	3	3	3	0	0	0	2	0	0	2	3	0	8	1	1	1	.130	.286	.130
Richardson, Kevin, Spokane	32	131	112	19	34	62	10	0	6	26	0	0	1	18	0	34	0	0	4	.304	.405	.554
Rick, Alan, Boise *	50	193	171	20	44	69	7	0	6	20	1	0	3	18	0	47	2	1	1	.257	.339	.404
Rogelstad, Matt, Everett *	16	61	58	7	16	18	2	0	0	13	0	0	3	0	0	9	1	0	1	.276	.311	.310
Rosario, Samuel, Boise	30	124	111	13	29	37	4	2	0	6	3	0	3	7	0	23	4	6	1	.261	.322	.333
Rose, Brian, Yakima	53	216	179	17	41	53	7	1	1	25	1	0	16	20	0	43	2	0	5	.229	.358	.296
Ruchti, Justin, Everett	21	82	76	9	21	26	2	0	1	8	0	2	1	3	0	13	1	0	1	.276	.305	.342
Sakamoto, Mitsuru, Tri-City *	16	68	56	7	11	13	2	0	0	5	5	0	0	7	0	11	0	0	0	.196	.286	.232
Sandoval, Abigail, Spokane	67	281	253	32	72	81	6	0	1	39	1	3	1	23	0	38	7	5	6	.285	.343	.320
Sardinha, Duke, Tri-City	26	112	98	11	23	42	7	0	4	16	1	0	1	12	1	23	2	2	1	.235	.324	.429
Schierholtz, Nathan, S.K.*	35	144	124	23	38	57	6	2	3	29	0	3	5	12	1	15	0	1	1	.306	.382	.460
Schmidt, Jesse, S.K.†	64	247	211	31	55	81	11	0	5	27	4	1	2	29	0	50	8	2	4	.261	.354	.384
Shields, Nick, Spokane	29	116	104	18	29	36	4	0	1	11	0	0	2	10	0	30	0	1	4	.279	.353	.346
Shorsher, Adam, Eugene	10	32	30	1	4	6	2	0	0	0	0	0	0	2	0	6	0	0	1	.133	.188	.200
Simon, Brandon, Yakima *	39	178	147	28	41	46	3	1	0	15	5	0	11	15	0	31	24	4	1	.279	.387	.313
Smith, Rashad, Eugene *	11	51	45	7	14	22	1	2	1	5	0	0	1	5	0	4	5	0	1	.311	.392	.489
Smyres, Justin, Eugene	53	206	186	27	52	61	7	1	0	14	2	2	8	8	0	42	11	4	1	.280	.333	.328
Snyder, Brian, Vancouver	44	186	146	14	37	46	6	0	1	17	0	1	0	39	1	36	9	2	2	.253	.409	.315
Spivey, Brett, Tri-City *	14	56	47	7	13	23	3	2	1	12	2	0	0	7	0	12	0	1	1	.277	.370	.489
Street, Dan, Tri-City	33	141	123	12	40	52	10	1	0	16	4	1	1	12	0	22	0	1	3	.325	.387	.423
Sutton, Don, Vancouver	13	46	43	4	13	16	3	0	0	7	0	0	1	2	0	16	0	0	1	.302	.348	.372
Swearingen, Jonathan, Tri-City	20	76	70	9	13	16	3	0	0	2	0	0	3	3	0	13	0	0	2	.186	.250	.229
Sweeney, James, Tri-City	59	236	203	27	38	55	8	0	3	15	1	0	6	26	0	70	5	1	6	.187	.298	.271
Symonds, Grady, Yakima	10	10	8	0	1	1	0	0	0	1	0	1	0	1	0	1	0	0	0	.125	.200	.125
Tidball, Adam, Boise	8	20	19	0	1	1	0	0	0	0	0	0	0	1	0	7	0	0	0	.053	.100	.053
Turner, Lloyd, Vancouver	23	93	83	11	25	31	4	1	0	12	3	1	2	4	0	20	1	1	2	.301	.344	.373
Valenzuela, Fernando, Eug.*	73	318	262	36	65	91	11	0	5	46	0	2	10	43	1	47	1	0	6	.248	.372	.347
Vericker, Brad, S.K.*	70	297	243	47	69	133	19	0	15	47	0	3	3	48	2	58	0	1	6	.284	.404	.547
Viafore, Brian, Yakima	19	55	44	2	3	4	1	0	0	4	1	0	2	8	0	24	0	0	1	.068	.241	.091
Wagner, Michael, S.K.	64	290	257	42	71	108	14	4	5	44	0	3	13	17	0	46	2	0	10	.276	.348	.420
Wahlbrink, Brian, Eugene	69	306	270	45	81	118	17	4	4	34	0	0	8	28	2	82	19	4	2	.300	.382	.437
Walker, Chris, Boise	68	263	247	25	58	65	5	1	0	14	5	0	3	8	0	51	25	9	0	.235	.267	.263
Welch, Scott, Spokane *	16	60	50	4	11	13	2	0	0	3	1	1	0	8	0	13	1	0	1	.220	.322	.260
Williams, Jonny, S.K.*	35	115	100	14	26	33	7	0	0	12	0	1	0	14	0	19	0	0	4	.260	.348	.330
Wishy, Andrew, Spokane *	72	320	260	46	74	120	14	7	6	55	0	1	5	54	2	58	3	2	3	.285	.416	.462
Womack, Josh, Everett *	41	176	155	25	46	72	9	4	3	18	2	0	0	19	0	40	8	5	2	.297	.374	.465

GRAND SLAMS—Cox, D'Antona, R. Fox, Kreuzer, Schierholtz, Schmidt, 1 each.

AWARDED FIRST BASE ON CATCHER'S INTERFERENCE—Haley (Rick); Valenzuela (Rick).

2003 PITCHING

TEAM

Team	W	L	Pct.	ERA	G	CG	ShO	Sv.	IP	H	TBF	R	ER	HR	SH	SF	HB	BB	IBB	SO	WP	Bk.
Spokane	50	26	.658	3.38	76	0	7	26	676.2	609	2861	289	254	26	26	20	53	258	5	513	51	4
Eugene	39	37	.513	3.70	76	0	3	20	679.1	605	2961	339	279	44	23	17	60	307	3	654	46	9
Yakima	45	31	.592	3.74	76	0	7	22	676.1	650	2956	355	281	47	31	22	41	267	3	559	60	12
Salem-Keizer	43	33	.566	3.76	76	0	5	23	679.2	670	2954	343	284	49	30	25	43	268	5	552	44	3
Tri-City	33	43	.434	3.84	76	0	5	19	675.2	667	2916	348	288	22	23	37	56	237	4	439	56	4
Vancouver	35	41	.461	4.04	76	0	3	18	671.0	690	2975	373	301	36	28	23	41	240	6	585	53	8
Boise	27	49	.355	4.06	76	0	6	18	669.0	625	2999	401	302	33	33	20	56	319	14	634	59	7
Everett	32	44	.421	4.45	76	0	2	19	662.2	668	3008	396	328	50	19	20	57	339	4	619	70	8

INDIVIDUAL

TOP QUALIFIERS FOR EARNED-RUN AVERAGE TITLE

Minimum 61 innings. *Lefthanded pitcher.

Pitcher, Team	W	L	Pct.	ERA	G	GS	CG	ShO	GF	Sv.	IP	H	TBF	R	ER	HR	SH	SF	HB	BB	IBB	SO	WP	Bk.
Floyd, Jesse, Salem-Keizer	6	4	.600	1.73	14	14	0	0	0	0	83.1	67	337	18	16	5	3	0	4	19	1	76	3	1
Knox, Brad, Vancouver	6	3	.667	2.06	15	12	0	0	2	0	70.0	55	294	21	16	2	3	3	6	18	1	63	8	1
Misch, Patrick, Salem-Keizer *	7	5	.583	2.18	14	14	0	0	0	0	86.2	78	350	33	21	3	3	4	7	20	0	61	1	0
Farnum, Matt, Spokane	5	1	.833	2.39	17	13	0	0	2	0	75.1	70	307	22	20	2	1	2	7	17	0	57	6	0
Thompson, Sean, Eugene *	7	1	.875	2.48	15	15	0	0	0	0	80.0	58	328	28	22	5	0	1	3	39	0	97	1	2
Marshall, Sean, Boise *	5	6	.455	2.57	14	14	0	0	0	0	73.2	66	315	31	21	1	3	5	5	23	0	88	8	0
Wells, Jared, Eugene	4	6	.400	2.75	14	14	0	0	0	0	78.2	77	341	34	24	6	3	2	3	32	1	53	2	0
Marsden, Aaron, Tri-City *	4	3	.571	2.79	13	10	0	0	1	1	61.1	49	249	21	19	2	2	2	1	18	0	46	3	0
Lynch, Brian, Tri-City	4	3	.571	2.84	14	14	0	0	0	0	69.2	66	287	30	22	1	0	0	4	20	0	48	2	0
Lo, Ching-Lung, Tri-City	3	7	.300	2.85	14	14	0	0	0	0	75.2	66	314	27	24	1	2	2	5	27	0	48	6	0
Oldham, Thomas, Everett *	5	3	.625	2.86	13	11	0	0	0	0	63.0	48	258	27	20	2	2	0	4	23	0	63	0	1
Liebeck, Jered, Yakima	5	3	.625	2.95	12	10	0	0	0	0	64.0	57	258	25	21	3	2	0	1	11	1	50	2	2
Juarez, William, Yakima	5	3	.625	2.95	15	15	0	0	0	0	85.1	87	379	48	28	7	2	3	3	31	0	72	5	4
Peterson, John, Vancouver *	3	4	.429	3.25	14	9	0	0	2	1	61.0	64	258	26	22	0	0	0	1	15	0	55	1	0
Frydendall, Craig, Spokane *	5	4	.556	3.36	17	13	0	0	1	0	64.1	52	268	34	24	1	7	1	0	23	0	41	0	0

DEPARTMENTAL LEADERS: W—Corrado, 8; L—Hintz, Lo, Victor M. Ramirez, Salas, 7; Pct.—S. Thompson, .875; G—Rosales, 36; GS—McGirr, 16; CG—none; ShO—none; GF—Glant, 32; Sv.—Glant, 18; IP—Misch, 86.2; H—Corpas, 98; TBF—Juarez, 379; R—Corpas, 61; ER—Corpas, 54; HR—Alcantara, Corpas, Moore, H. Perez, Victor M. Ramirez, 7; SH—Frydendall, 7; SF—Corpas, Portorreal, 6; HB—Alcantara, Santiago, 11; BB—Portorreal, 48; IBB—Several pitchers tied with 2; SO—Hill, 99; WP—Schilsky, 11; BK—H. Perez, 5.

ALL PITCHERS

*Lefthanded pitcher.

Pitcher, Team	W	L	Pct.	ERA	G	GS	CG	ShO	GF	Sv.	IP	H	TBF	R	ER	HR	SH	SF	HB	BB	IBB	SO	WP	Bk.
Abrams, Casey, Everett *	0	0	.000	7.11	4	0	0	0	0	0	6.1	5	29	5	5	1	0	0	0	7	0	7	1	0
Acosta, Nibaldo, Everett	0	0	.000	3.60	10	0	0	0	1	0	15.0	14	65	6	6	1	0	0	0	6	0	10	1	0
Alcantara, Audy, Everett	0	4	.000	8.67	19	4	0	0	8	0	36.1	40	181	37	35	7	0	2	11	26	0	34	8	0
Alvarez, Tim, Salem-Keizer *	2	1	.667	2.38	14	0	0	0	2	1	22.2	20	96	8	6	1	1	0	4	8	0	18	2	0
Anderson, Luke, Salem-Keizer	1	0	1.000	1.59	3	0	0	0	0	0	5.2	4	25	1	1	0	0	0	0	4	1	8	0	0
Arakawa, Yusuke, Tri-City	3	1	.750	3.18	30	0	0	0	14	2	34.0	31	147	13	12	1	2	1	1	11	0	38	5	1
Barnett, Danny, Vancouver	0	0	.000	5.06	15	0	0	0	8	0	21.1	28	108	20	12	2	0	3	1	14	0	14	1	0
Barrett, Rich, Yakima	0	1	.000	4.91	4	0	0	0	1	0	3.2	5	23	5	2	0	1	0	0	5	0	6	0	0
Bass, Adam, Yakima	0	0	.000	0.80	27	0	0	0	9	3	33.2	26	142	4	3	2	2	0	2	14	0	34	1	0
Bateman, Jamie, Salem-Keizer	3	2	.600	6.63	26	2	0	0	12	4	38.0	47	172	31	28	6	3	2	3	10	1	30	1	0
Bay, Ronald, Boise	1	2	.333	3.74	4	4	0	0	0	0	21.2	17	89	9	9	1	1	0	1	7	0	24	3	0
Bechtel, Charles, Eugene	0	0	.000	1.80	4	0	0	0	3	1	5.0	4	26	1	1	0	0	0	1	5	1	9	3	0
Bondurant, Steven, Van.*	0	4	.000	3.53	14	8	0	0	4	2	58.2	51	249	30	23	5	0	1	3	20	0	54	3	0
Bonine, Eddie, Eugene	1	2	.333	3.78	31	0	0	0	26	14	33.1	32	143	15	14	2	1	1	3	10	0	33	1	0
Bowman, Charles, Spokane	0	0	.000	5.40	4	0	0	0	3	0	3.1	4	21	4	2	0	0	0	2	4	0	0	0	0
Burris, Robert, Vancouver	1	3	.250	1.89	15	0	0	0	10	1	33.1	24	140	12	7	2	3	2	1	12	0	47	2	0
Carque, Joseph, Yakima	0	1	.000	5.91	26	0	0	0	8	0	32.0	35	142	26	21	6	3	0	3	7	0	14	6	0
Carter, Brian, Boise *	2	4	.333	5.35	26	0	0	0	11	2	38.2	47	191	31	23	2	4	0	3	23	1	21	0	0
Castleman, Stephen, Tri-City	0	2	.000	4.55	18	0	0	0	5	0	27.2	30	130	19	14	0	0	3	2	16	1	20	2	0
Chang, Kenly, Everett	0	0	.000	2.97	24	0	0	0	9	1	36.1	37	162	13	12	4	1	2	1	16	0	37	6	0
Chavez, Jesse, Spokane	2	2	.500	4.55	17	8	0	0	1	1	55.1	63	259	30	28	5	0	1	7	31	0	48	4	0
Cherry, Rocky, Boise	5	2	.714	2.17	10	10	0	0	0	0	54.0	36	222	21	13	1	1	1	2	18	0	55	2	0
Chico, Matthew, Yakima *	7	4	.636	3.53	17	13	0	0	0	0	71.1	75	309	28	28	4	3	2	5	25	1	71	9	1
Clark, Chad, Yakima	1	1	.500	4.99	24	0	0	0	5	1	30.2	19	139	19	17	0	2	2	5	29	0	30	5	1
Coonrod, Aaron, Eugene	3	3	.500	5.37	13	10	0	0	0	0	52.0	48	235	32	31	3	1	3	10	33	0	45	3	0
Corchado, Jose, Vancouver	0	1	.000	5.93	19	2	0	0	5	2	44.0	49	204	36	29	3	3	0	2	16	1	50	5	1
Corley, Klent, Yakima	2	1	.667	4.79	5	5	0	0	0	0	20.2	19	95	12	11	2	1	1	1	15	0	12	3	0
Corpas, Manuel, Tri-City	5	6	.455	5.79	15	15	0	0	0	0	84.0	98	375	61	54	7	4	6	7	22	1	47	3	0
Corrado, Rob, Spokane	8	2	.800	3.52	23	0	0	0	7	0	53.2	47	220	21	21	4	4	2	7	11	1	34	6	2
Cuevas, Alvin, Boise	1	1	.500	3.97	19	0	0	0	10	4	22.2	13	99	12	10	1	2	1	2	15	2	17	1	0
Cunningham, Tim, Spokane *	0	4	.000	8.14	9	5	0	0	1	1	21.0	27	105	22	19	1	1	1	0	21	0	17	7	0
Danks, John, Spokane *	0	2	.000	8.53	5	5	0	0	0	0	12.2	12	55	12	12	0	1	2	0	7	0	13	0	0
Darby, James, Eugene	2	4	.333	3.34	33	0	0	0	5	0	35.0	33	162	21	13	0	1	0	10	18	0	36	7	0
Davis, Mike, Yakima	4	0	1.000	0.92	23	0	0	0	1	0	29.1	15	119	3	3	0	2	4	1	14	0	22	2	1
Dawkins, Lance, Boise	0	0	.000	0.00	1	0	0	0	1	0	1.2	0	7	0	0	0	0	0	0	2	0	0	0	0
Devenney, Nick, Spokane	1	3	.250	3.29	23	0	0	0	6	0	38.1	32	174	19	14	1	1	2	6	23	0	26	5	0
Dunkle, Peter, Tri-City	2	1	.667	3.21	22	0	0	0	7	0	33.2	31	154	17	12	1	1	1	4	17	0	22	9	0
Edwards, John, Tri-City	3	2	.600	3.06	22	0	0	0	8	0	35.1	32	145	15	12	3	1	4	1	13	1	27	6	0
Farnum, Matt, Spokane	5	1	.833	2.39	17	13	0	0	2	0	75.1	70	307	22	20	2	1	2	7	17	0	57	6	0
Ferns, Robert, Yakima	1	1	.500	27.00	3	0	0	0	1	0	2.1	10	18	7	7	0	0	0	0	2	0	2	0	0
Floyd, Jesse, Salem-Keizer	6	4	.600	1.73	14	14	0	0	0	0	83.1	67	337	18	16	5	3	0	4	19	1	76	3	1
Forbes, Terry, Everett	0	0	.000	3.52	6	0	0	0	3	0	7.2	14	37	7	3	0	0	0	1	3	1	2	2	0
Frydendall, Craig, Spokane *	5	4	.556	3.36	17	13	0	0	1	0	64.1	52	268	34	24	1	7	1	0	23	0	41	0	0
Frye, Randall, Everett	5	4	.556	4.79	13	12	0	0	0	0	62.0	73	296	40	33	4	2	2	3	33	0	53	6	1
Fyvie, Dan, Vancouver	4	2	.667	2.45	26	0	0	0	13	4	40.1	33	176	15	11	0	3	1	4	17	2	35	4	0
Gagne, J.P., Tri-City	1	2	.333	3.63	32	0	0	0	29	16	34.2	35	144	16	14	1	3	5	1	8	0	21	2	0

Pitcher, Team	W	L	Pct.	ERA	G	GS	CG	ShO	GF	Sv.	IP	H	TBF	R	ER	HR	SH	SF	HB	BB	IBB	SO	WP	Bk.
Gallagher, Buddy, Tri-City *	0	0	.000	0.00	2	0	0	0	0	0	2.0	0	7	0	0	0	0	0	0	1	0	1	0	0
George, Christopher, S.K.	0	0	.000	8.24	13	0	0	0	3	0	19.2	25	99	20	18	3	2	0	0	14	0	24	3	0
Girardeau, Clark, Eugene	4	2	.667	3.74	20	7	0	0	3	0	53.0	47	235	23	22	1	3	1	3	27	1	53	6	0
Glant, Dustin, Yakima	1	2	.333	1.85	34	0	0	0	32	18	34.0	19	133	9	7	2	1	0	2	9	0	31	1	0
Goocher, Clint, Yakima *	3	1	.750	2.73	31	0	0	0	8	0	33.0	28	137	10	10	1	3	2	2	6	0	33	5	0
Green, Craig, Boise	0	1	.000	2.70	11	0	0	0	4	0	13.1	15	67	11	4	0	2	0	0	6	1	8	4	0
Gregg, Grant, Eugene *	0	0	.000	4.76	15	0	0	0	5	0	17.0	15	77	15	9	2	0	0	2	6	0	17	0	0
Gross, Kris, Boise	1	1	.500	3.04	13	0	0	0	2	0	23.2	19	100	10	8	3	0	0	2	7	1	23	1	1
Guerrero, Aneury, Boise *	0	1	.000	9.72	5	0	0	0	0	0	8.1	10	43	9	9	1	0	0	3	7	1	10	3	0
Haley, Adam, Yakima	0	0	.000	54.00	1	0	0	0	1	0	1.0	4	10	6	6	1	0	0	1	2	0	1	0	0
Hayhurst, Dirk, Eugene	4	3	.571	3.82	25	1	0	0	5	0	37.2	38	168	23	16	3	1	0	4	12	0	49	0	0
Hays, Sam, Everett *	2	3	.400	4.89	18	7	0	0	2	0	42.1	44	209	29	23	1	1	1	7	37	1	31	10	1
Hernandez, Felix, Everett	7	2	.778	2.29	11	7	0	0	0	0	55.0	43	232	17	14	2	1	2	8	24	0	73	7	0
Hill, Richard, Boise *	1	6	.143	4.35	14	14	0	0	0	0	68.1	57	296	40	33	5	5	5	9	32	0	99	5	1
Hines, Matthew, Boise	1	3	.250	4.89	24	0	0	0	7	1	38.2	43	188	23	21	0	1	1	4	26	2	44	6	0
Hintz, Beau, Everett *	5	7	.417	4.20	14	14	0	0	0	0	81.1	75	360	43	38	4	2	0	7	35	0	62	6	2
Howay, Chris, Vancouver	2	2	.500	5.32	19	0	0	0	2	2	44.0	55	212	31	26	3	2	2	3	20	0	37	4	1
Jefferson, Drew, S.K.*	1	3	.250	4.38	26	0	0	0	23	13	24.2	24	109	13	12	3	1	0	4	6	0	26	3	0
Juarez, William, Yakima	5	3	.625	2.95	15	15	0	0	0	0	85.1	87	379	48	28	7	2	3	3	31	0	72	5	4
Kaiser, Marc, Tri-City	3	3	.500	0.49	7	7	0	0	0	0	37.0	30	150	10	2	0	3	0	3	8	0	16	2	1
Kerbs, Reuben, Yakima *	1	0	1.000	3.54	15	0	0	0	4	0	20.1	17	91	8	8	1	1	1	1	12	1	23	4	0
Kinsey, Christopher, Yakima	3	3	.500	4.00	9	9	0	0	0	0	45.0	45	194	34	20	6	0	0	3	16	0	23	2	1
Kirsten, Joel, Spokane *	4	0	1.000	1.44	15	0	0	0	7	1	31.1	27	134	7	5	1	0	1	2	8	1	25	1	0
Knox, Brad, Vancouver	6	3	.667	2.06	15	12	0	0	2	0	70.0	55	294	21	16	2	3	3	6	18	1	63	8	1
Kunes, Michael, S.K.*	1	0	1.000	4.60	18	0	0	0	2	1	31.1	31	133	16	16	6	0	1	2	7	1	23	1	0
Landeros, Leonard, Van.*	0	2	.000	9.64	8	0	0	0	3	1	9.1	13	43	11	10	0	1	0	0	2	1	11	0	0
Liebeck, Jered, Yakima	5	3	.625	2.95	12	10	0	0	0	0	64.0	57	258	25	21	3	2	0	1	11	1	50	2	2
Littleton, Wes, Spokane	6	0	1.000	1.56	12	8	0	0	2	0	52.0	36	192	9	9	2	1	0	1	8	0	47	2	1
Lo, Ching-Lung, Tri-City	3	7	.300	2.85	14	14	0	0	0	0	75.2	66	314	27	24	1	2	2	5	27	0	48	6	0
Lorenzo, Matt, Spokane	5	1	.833	2.53	16	12	0	0	1	0	57.0	43	226	19	16	2	2	1	2	22	0	54	2	0
Ludwig, Kellen, Salem-Keizer	1	1	.500	3.38	17	0	0	0	8	0	21.1	21	94	9	8	1	0	0	2	10	0	24	2	0
Lynch, Brian, Tri-City	4	3	.571	2.84	14	14	0	0	0	0	69.2	66	287	30	22	1	0	0	4	20	0	48	2	0
Marsden, Aaron, Tri-City *	4	3	.571	2.79	13	10	0	0	1	1	61.1	49	249	21	19	2	2	2	1	18	0	46	3	0
Marshall, Sean, Boise *	5	6	.455	2.57	14	14	0	0	0	0	73.2	66	315	31	21	1	3	5	5	23	0	88	8	0
Martin, Sean, Salem-Keizer	0	0	.000	3.46	10	0	0	0	4	0	13.0	8	55	5	5	1	0	0	1	8	1	12	1	0
Mattoon, Brian, Spokane *	1	2	.333	5.81	9	6	0	0	0	0	26.1	35	115	17	17	1	1	1	1	9	0	16	2	0
Mazurek, David, Spokane	1	3	.250	2.03	25	0	0	0	20	10	31.0	25	120	11	7	2	1	2	3	8	1	20	3	0
McGirr, Mike, Vancouver	7	5	.583	4.40	16	16	0	0	0	0	75.2	86	331	44	37	3	3	2	4	21	0	58	4	3
McNiven, Brooks, S.K.	7	5	.583	3.62	16	11	0	0	2	0	69.2	74	295	40	28	1	4	1	3	16	0	45	2	0
Mejia, Anderson, Boise	1	5	.167	5.23	19	10	0	0	4	1	63.2	64	295	42	37	1	4	1	2	47	0	22	7	2
Mendez, Adalberto, Boise	0	4	.000	4.09	15	5	0	0	9	7	33.0	29	143	18	15	4	2	1	3	15	1	33	3	2
Misch, Patrick, Salem-Keizer *	7	5	.583	2.18	14	14	0	0	0	0	86.2	78	350	33	21	3	3	4	7	20	0	61	1	0
Moore, Daniel, Eugene *	2	3	.400	6.14	12	8	0	0	0	0	48.1	63	225	35	33	7	0	1	6	14	0	43	4	1
Moorhead, Michael, Everett	0	1	.000	1.57	21	0	0	0	21	13	23.0	27	100	7	4	0	1	0	2	6	1	28	4	0
Moreno, Anthony, S.K.	0	1	.000	7.94	4	4	0	0	0	0	17.0	27	86	18	15	1	0	2	4	8	0	6	1	1
Morrow, David, Everett	0	2	.000	10.03	5	4	0	0	0	0	11.2	12	61	13	13	0	0	0	2	15	0	9	1	0
Muegge, Danny, Yakima	2	3	.400	4.63	21	0	0	0	4	0	23.1	31	105	13	12	2	1	1	1	6	0	22	1	1
Musgrave, Mike, Salem-Keizer	1	2	.333	3.51	15	9	0	0	1	1	48.2	51	216	26	19	4	3	4	0	19	0	54	2	0
Nesmith, Travis, S.K.*	1	0	1.000	4.08	14	0	0	0	3	0	17.2	16	84	10	8	2	2	1	0	17	0	21	4	0
O'Flaherty, Eric, Everett *	1	0	1.000	3.38	3	1	0	0	0	0	10.2	8	41	5	4	1	0	2	2	3	0	7	1	0
Ockerman, Justin, Everett	1	2	.333	4.88	22	0	0	0	11	0	31.1	24	153	25	17	1	3	1	2	31	0	24	7	0
Oldham, Thomas, Everett *	5	3	.625	2.86	13	11	0	0	0	0	63.0	48	258	27	20	2	2	0	4	23	0	63	0	1
Ovalles, Juan, Everett	1	2	.333	5.40	21	0	0	0	12	3	26.2	29	118	18	16	4	1	3	1	10	0	40	1	0
Overholt, Sean, Boise	3	1	.750	0.49	10	0	0	0	4	0	18.1	18	82	9	1	0	0	0	2	7	0	17	2	0
Oyervidez, Jose, Eugene	1	4	.200	3.07	31	0	0	0	11	1	41.0	25	168	15	14	2	3	1	4	17	0	55	1	0
Pence, Howard, Eugene	0	0	.000	54.00	1	0	0	0	0	0	0.1	3	4	2	2	0	0	0	0	0	0	1	0	0
Perez, Elvis, Everett	0	0	.000	1.29	2	2	0	0	0	0	7.0	5	26	1	1	0	0	0	0	0	0	10	0	0
Perez, Henry, Eugene	4	2	.667	4.25	15	15	0	0	0	0	72.0	61	311	40	34	7	5	2	5	31	0	54	5	5
Perry, Brandon, Everett *	0	2	.000	1.29	3	0	0	0	2	0	7.0	4	35	3	1	0	1	1	0	6	0	11	1	0
Petersen, Jeffrey, S.K.	2	1	.667	4.19	17	1	0	0	8	1	34.1	36	155	18	16	4	2	2	0	11	0	26	3	0
Peterson, John, Vancouver *	3	4	.429	3.25	14	9	0	0	2	1	61.0	64	258	26	22	0	0	0	1	15	0	55	1	0
Petrick, Billy, Boise	2	5	.286	4.76	14	14	0	0	0	0	64.1	60	286	49	34	4	1	1	6	27	2	64	1	0
Pickens, J.R., Vancouver	6	2	.750	3.07	23	4	0	0	19	5	44.0	40	187	19	15	2	0	1	4	14	1	40	4	1
Portorreal, Daniel, S.K.	4	4	.500	5.60	12	12	0	0	0	0	53.0	61	257	37	33	4	2	6	5	48	0	16	7	1
Prensa, Carlos, Eugene	0	0	.000	4.09	9	0	0	0	2	0	11.0	8	51	6	5	0	0	1	1	9	0	9	3	0
Ramirez, Victor, Spokane	4	0	1.000	3.44	11	0	0	0	4	2	18.1	14	79	7	7	1	0	2	3	7	0	20	5	0
Ramirez, Victor, Everett *	4	7	.364	5.29	16	10	0	0	2	0	68.0	79	316	49	40	7	3	3	2	31	0	70	4	2
Rapada, Clayton, Boise *	0	0	.000	0.00	1	0	0	0	0	0	3.0	2	12	0	0	0	1	0	0	1	0	3	0	0
Reina, Jesus, Salem-Keizer *	0	1	.000	9.82	3	0	0	0	1	0	3.2	5	20	5	4	0	3	0	1	4	0	2	0	0
Reynolds, Grant, Vancouver	1	3	.250	5.47	11	4	0	0	2	0	26.1	28	122	18	16	3	0	2	1	15	0	23	2	1
Rio, Gabriele, Yakima *	0	0	.000	15.00	5	0	0	0	0	0	6.0	14	40	11	10	0	0	0	0	7	0	5	1	0
Robinson, Ronnie, Eugene	2	6	.250	4.71	19	5	0	0	2	1	49.2	44	214	30	26	2	3	2	4	21	0	35	5	1
Rosales, Leonel, Eugene	3	1	.750	2.09	36	0	0	0	11	3	43.0	32	178	13	10	4	0	2	1	16	0	58	1	0
Rose, Brad, Everett	0	3	.000	5.11	20	2	0	0	3	0	44.0	54	202	32	25	5	0	1	4	17	0	24	2	0
Rosen, Mark, Yakima *	1	1	.500	14.09	2	2	0	0	0	0	7.2	14	44	12	12	1	0	0	3	5	0	8	1	0
Sadowski, Ryan, Salem-Keizer	1	2	.333	3.16	15	3	0	0	4	0	31.1	22	133	11	11	2	0	1	2	22	0	26	3	0
Salas, Pedro, Tri-City	2	7	.222	5.56	11	11	0	0	0	0	56.2	67	254	42	35	1	2	5	7	21	0	20	5	2
Sanchez, Jose, Salem-Keizer	0	1	.000	12.15	4	0	0	0	0	0	6.2	9	36	9	9	1	0	0	0	8	0	9	3	0
Santiago, Tomas, Tri-City	1	4	.200	4.50	21	3	0	0	5	0	46.0	44	205	28	23	2	1	2	11	19	0	32	5	0
Sasaki, Kazuhiro, Everett	0	1	.000	22.50	2	2	0	0	0	0	2.0	5	11	5	5	3	0	0	0	0	0	5	0	0
Scarbery, Chad, Yakima	7	6	.538	4.04	15	15	0	0	0	0	82.1	86	362	47	37	5	4	4	4	33	0	59	10	0
Schara, Zackary, Spokane	1	1	.500	9.82	4	0	0	0	2	0	7.1	12	42	8	8	0	1	0	2	7	1	5	1	0
Scheffel, Dustin, Spokane	0	0	.000	4.50	1	0	0	0	0	0	2.0	3	9	1	1	0	0	0	1	1	0	3	1	0
Schilsky, Stephen, Vancouver	0	2	.000	7.43	16	0	0	0	4	0	26.2	40	143	24	22	0	2	2	3	17	0	23	11	0
Schultz, Mike, Yakima	1	0	1.000	4.71	5	5	0	0	0	0	28.2	21	120	16	15	2	1	2	2	10	0	27	0	1
Shartzer, Bryan, Tri-City	2	1	.667	3.68	24	0	0	0	6	0	36.2	33	166	17	15	1	2	3	8	18	1	23	4	0
Smith, Brandon, Tri-City	0	0	.000	31.50	2	0	0	0	0	0	2.0	7	15	7	7	1	0	0	0	2	0	2	0	0
Sonnier, Shawn, Boise	0	1	.000	7.16	8	0	0	0	4	2	16.1	20	76	13	13	1	1	0	0	8	2	15	2	0
Stitt, Brian, Everett	1	1	.500	4.50	15	0	0	0	2	2	26.0	28	116	14	13	3	1	0	0	10	1	19	2	1
Thompson, Justin, Spokane *	2	0	1.000	1.24	23	0	0	0	0	0	29.0	15	110	5	4	0	2	1	1	8	0	21	0	0
Thompson, Sean, Eugene *	7	1	.875	2.48	15	15	0	0	0	0	80.0	58	328	28	22	5	0	1	3	39	0	97	1	2
Thurmond, J.B., Salem-Keizer	5	0	1.000	1.93	14	6	0	0	3	2	51.1	44	202	15	11	1	1	1	1	9	0	45	2	0

Pitcher, Team	W	L	Pct.	ERA	G	GS	CG	ShO	GF	Sv.	IP	H	TBF	R	ER	HR	SH	SF	HB	BB	IBB	SO	WP	Bk.
Trout, Jared, Vancouver	4	4	.500	3.50	16	13	0	0	2	0	79.2	87	345	39	31	6	6	2	5	24	0	49	3	0
Truselo, Randy, Spokane	3	0	1.000	3.40	15	6	0	0	3	2	50.1	48	214	19	19	1	1	0	4	22	0	27	3	0
Valcarcel, Jonathan, Tri-City *	0	0	.000	0.00	1	0	0	0	0	0	1.0	1	3	0	0	0	0	0	0	0	0	1	0	0
Valdez, Richard, Boise	0	0	.000	6.34	22	0	0	0	10	0	32.2	43	161	34	23	5	1	3	5	15	0	32	4	0
Van, Robert, Yakima *	0	0	.000	0.00	1	0	0	0	0	0	1.0	0	3	0	0	0	0	0	0	1	0	0	0	0
Vargas, Reynaldo, Tri-City	0	1	.000	5.40	17	2	0	0	1	0	38.1	47	171	25	23	0	0	3	1	16	0	27	2	0
Vicente, Ruben, Yakima	1	0	1.000	3.00	10	2	0	0	2	0	21.0	23	93	12	7	2	2	0	1	7	0	14	2	0
Watts, Joldy, Spokane	2	1	.667	3.94	25	0	0	0	16	9	48.0	44	211	22	21	2	2	1	4	21	1	39	3	1
Wells, Jared, Eugene	4	6	.400	2.75	14	14	0	0	0	0	78.2	77	341	34	24	6	3	2	3	32	1	53	2	0
Willett, Reid, Boise	4	5	.444	4.63	20	5	0	0	1	1	56.1	54	248	31	29	2	3	0	3	23	0	49	5	1
Wynegar, Adam, Boise *	0	1	.000	2.16	21	0	0	0	9	0	16.2	12	79	8	4	1	1	1	4	10	1	10	2	0
Yoshida, Nobuaki, Eugene *	2	0	1.000	1.21	17	1	0	0	3	0	22.1	17	95	6	3	0	2	0	0	17	0	7	4	0
Zambotti, Anthony, Vancouver	1	4	.200	5.89	10	8	0	0	0	0	36.2	37	163	27	24	5	2	2	3	15	0	26	0	0

COMBINATION SHUTOUTS: Boise (6)—Hill-Willett-Hines, Mendez-Overholt-Carter, Hill-Sonnier, Cherry-Hines-Carter-Mendez, Marshall-Carter-Cuevas-Mendez, Marshall-Wynegar-Cuevas-Mendez. Eugene (3)—Robinson-Rosales-Bonine, Thompson-Darby-Rosales-Bonine, Perez-Darby-Rosales-Bonine. Everett (2)—Oldham-Acosta-Moorhead, Hays-Ockerman-Chang-Rose. Salem-Keizer (5)—Musgrave-Alvarez, Floyd-NeSmith-Jefferson, Portorreal-Petersen, Floyd-Kunes, Floyd-Bateman-Jefferson. Spokane (7)—Frydendall-Thompson-Corrado-Mazurek, Chavez-Kirsten-Devenney, Lorenzo-Frydendall-Watts, Lorenzo-Frydendall-Mazurek, Farnum-Thompson-Watts, Danks-Thompson-Chavez, Littleton-Kirsten. Tri-City (5)—Kaiser-Marsden-Santiago, Lo-Marsden, Marsden-Dunkle-Gagne, Marsden-Vargas-Shartzer, Marsden-Dunkle-Gagne. Vancouver (3)—McGirr-Howay-Pickens, Knox-Fyvie, Peterson-Pickens. Yakima (7)—Schultz-Goocher-Clark-Glant, Scarbery-Goocher, Liebeck-Bass, Chico-Muegge-Goocher-Glant, Kinsey-Davis-Clark-Bass, Liebeck-Goocher-Bass-Glant, Chico-Clark-Glant.

NO-HIT GAMES: None.

2003 FIELDING

TEAM

Team	G	PO	A	E	TC	DP	TP	PB	Pct.
Spokane	76	2030	865	69	2964	70	0	10	.977
Salem-Keizer	76	2039	853	93	2985	79	0	12	.969
Tri-City	76	2027	874	97	2998	77	0	10	.968
Everett	76	1988	740	95	2823	53	0	12	.966
Eugene	76	2038	719	107	2864	64	0	12	.963
Vancouver	76	2013	742	105	2860	31	0	13	.963
Yakima	76	2029	778	120	2927	62	0	12	.959
Boise	76	2007	770	128	2905	60	0	19	.956

INDIVIDUAL

FIRST BASEMEN

NOTE: All caps denotes fielding-percentage leader based on 38 games for catchers, 51 for all other non-pitchers and 61 innings for pitchers. *Throws lefthanded.

Player, Team	Pct.	G	PO	A	E	TC	DP
ALEXANDER, CHRISTOPHER, Spo.	.992	54	464	26	4	494	35
Appert, Luke, Vancouver	1.000	1	1	0	0	1	0
Blakeley, Eric, Everett	.972	34	197	11	6	214	15
Brinson, Matt, Tri-City *	.994	35	324	20	2	346	37
Buchanan, Todd, Yakima *	.981	58	450	26	9	485	37
Bushey, Andrew, Tri-City	.982	22	200	23	4	227	17
Cleveland, Jeremy, Spokane	1.000	1	3	0	0	3	0
Colonel, Christian, Tri-City	.000	1	0	0	0	0	0
Corder, Gordon, Vancouver	.981	25	199	8	4	211	7
Cornejo, Eduardo, Vancouver	1.000	2	3	1	0	4	0
Cox, Michael, Everett	1.000	6	31	0	0	31	2
D'Antona, Jamie, Yakima	.946	7	50	3	3	56	7
Dopirak, Brian, Boise	.984	41	344	33	6	383	28
Griffin, Brock, Everett *	1.000	1	5	0	0	5	0
Ishikawa, Travis, Salem-Keizer *	.983	66	589	55	11	655	67
Johanning, Ben, Eugene *	1.000	3	8	2	0	10	1
Kim, Edward, Vancouver	.983	48	371	24	7	402	20
Klippenstein, Tyler, Vancouver	.952	2	19	1	1	21	0
Kreuzer, Josh, Spokane	.989	20	176	8	2	186	20
Kroski, Chris, Everett	1.000	6	20	5	0	25	2
Lahair, Bryan, Everett	.991	44	318	20	3	341	30
Larsen, Andrew, Boise	.917	2	10	1	1	12	1
Lopaze, Daniel, Boise	.977	24	190	18	5	213	19
Maduro, Jorge, Everett	.800	1	11	1	3	15	0
McIntyre, Patrick, Boise	.968	11	87	3	3	93	4
Medlin, C.J., Boise	1.000	1	2	0	0	2	1
Morgan, Matt, Yakima	1.000	5	39	2	0	41	5
Pickens, Jordan, Eugene	1.000	4	27	1	0	28	2
Richardson, Kevin, Spokane	1.000	7	62	8	0	70	9
Sardinha, Duke, Tri-City	.978	8	85	4	2	91	7
Street, Dan, Tri-City	.990	11	96	6	1	103	14
Sutton, Don, Vancouver	1.000	1	8	0	0	8	1
Turner, Lloyd, Vancouver	.955	3	20	1	1	22	0
Valenzuela, Fernando, Eugene *	.982	72	575	40	11	626	58
Vericker, Brad, Salem-Keizer *	.990	11	91	4	1	96	10
Viafore, Brian, Yakima	.973	15	97	10	3	110	9

SECOND BASEMEN

Player, Team	Pct.	G	PO	A	E	TC	DP
Almonte, Sandy, Tri-City	.990	19	38	65	1	104	16
Anderson, Scott, Tri-City	1.000	3	8	14	0	22	4
Appert, Luke, Vancouver	.957	51	82	140	10	232	12
Baker, Casey, Eugene	1.000	1	1	0	0	1	0
Benjamin, Casey, Spokane	1.000	6	7	16	0	23	1
Blakeley, Eric, Everett	.955	16	29	55	4	88	16
Blood, Randy, Tri-City	.971	48	86	147	7	240	30
Boyer, Brett, Salem-Keizer	.833	1	3	2	1	6	0
Cordova, Roman, Everett	1.000	5	5	13	0	18	0
Cornejo, Eduardo, Vancouver	1.000	9	9	19	0	28	2
Cox, Michael, Everett	.000	1	0	0	0	0	0
Dutton, Jeremy, Everett	.936	19	37	36	5	78	6
Francois, Francisco, Vancouver	.952	11	17	23	2	42	3
Furtado, Micah, Spokane	1.000	1	3	2	0	5	0
Garabrants, Steve, Yakima	.946	54	98	149	14	261	33
Haley, Adam, Yakima	1.000	4	2	4	0	6	0
Hickman, Charles, Boise	1.000	9	13	28	0	41	8
Hornostaj, Aaron, Salem-Keizer	.956	61	129	195	15	339	48
Hutting, Timothy, Salem-Keizer	.980	12	19	29	1	49	8
Ingram, Brian, Vancouver	.952	12	15	25	2	42	6
LaBarbera, Anthony, S.K.	.964	5	14	13	1	28	6
Marquez, Uriak, Boise	.961	39	68	106	7	181	17
Mejia, Jorge, Vancouver	1.000	2	3	3	0	6	0
Monahan, Joey, Boise	.970	23	37	60	3	100	14
Moreno, Juan J., Yakima	1.000	1	2	4	0	6	1
Morgan, Matt, Yakima	.983	22	38	81	2	121	12
Orlandos, Nick, Everett	.939	37	66	88	10	164	18
Ramos, Peeter, Eugene	.943	74	134	215	21	370	48
Rogelstad, Matt, Everett	1.000	3	7	7	0	14	0
Rosario, Samuel, Boise	.898	12	17	27	5	49	2
SANDOVAL, ABIGAIL, Spokane	.980	61	119	174	6	299	44
Sardinha, Duke, Tri-City	.961	8	19	30	2	51	8
Smyres, Justin, Eugene	1.000	3	8	7	0	15	3
Welch, Scott, Spokane	.938	13	28	33	4	65	8

THIRD BASEMEN

Player, Team	Pct.	G	PO	A	E	TC	DP
Anderson, Scott, Tri-City	1.000	1	1	2	0	3	0
Baker, Casey, Eugene	.000	1	0	0	0	0	0
Barrows, Derek, Salem-Keizer	.875	30	27	50	11	88	8
Benjamin, Casey, Spokane	1.000	8	5	11	0	16	1
Blood, Randy, Tri-City	.800	8	5	7	3	15	2
Bochy, Greg, Eugene	.891	24	20	37	7	64	4
Bushey, Andrew, Tri-City	1.000	8	3	9	0	12	1
Ciesluk, Chris, Salem-Keizer	1.000	4	2	9	0	11	0
Colonel, Christian, Tri-City	.902	43	45	75	13	133	9
Cordova, Roman, Everett	1.000	1	0	1	0	1	0
Cornejo, Eduardo, Vancouver	.934	19	12	45	4	61	4
Cox, Michael, Everett	.917	44	28	72	9	109	2
D'Antona, Jamie, Yakima	.881	58	34	77	15	126	7
Dawkins, Lance, Boise	.882	10	4	11	2	17	1
Dutton, Jeremy, Everett	.949	30	5	51	3	59	3
FOX, ADAM, Spokane	.962	65	45	160	8	213	18
Francisco, Alfredo, Boise	.816	14	9	22	7	38	3
Francois, Francisco, Vancouver	.826	11	7	12	4	23	1
Furtado, Micah, Spokane	.333	1	0	1	2	3	0

Player, Team	Pct.	G	PO	A	E	TC	DP
Garrido, Tomas, Salem-Keizer	.947	10	4	14	1	19	0
Hogan, William, Eugene	.877	22	12	45	8	65	6
Ingram, Brian, Vancouver	1.000	5	5	14	0	19	1
Jacobo, Kervin, Eugene	.893	15	9	16	3	28	2
Knowlton, Jay, Salem-Keizer	.875	5	3	4	1	8	1
LaBarbera, Anthony, S.K.	1.000	1	0	1	0	1	0
Larsen, Andrew, Boise	.924	48	38	96	11	145	8
Lopaze, Daniel, Boise	.909	2	5	5	1	11	1
Mejia, Jorge, Vancouver	1.000	1	0	1	0	1	0
Moreno, Juan J., Yakima	.600	11	6	6	8	20	1
Morgan, Matt, Yakima	.914	15	10	22	3	35	5
Orlandos, Nick, Everett	1.000	3	1	6	0	7	1
Perez, Luis, Vancouver	.000	1	0	0	0	0	0
Rogelstad, Matt, Everett	1.000	1	1	0	0	1	0
Rosario, Samuel, Boise	1.000	2	1	4	0	5	0
Sandoval, Abigail, Spokane	1.000	5	6	13	0	19	0
Sardinha, Duke, Tri-City	.765	8	5	8	4	17	1
Schierholtz, Nathan, S.K.	.930	33	26	54	6	86	6
Smyres, Justin, Eugene	.904	23	20	27	5	52	4
Snyder, Brian, Vancouver	.896	36	21	48	8	77	3
Street, Dan, Tri-City	.957	8	5	17	1	23	2
Swearingen, Jonathan, Tri-City	.000	1	0	0	0	0	0
Turner, Lloyd, Vancouver	.833	14	9	21	6	36	0

SHORTSTOPS

Player, Team	Pct.	G	PO	A	E	TC	DP
Almonte, Sandy, Tri-City	.928	50	115	169	22	306	39
Anderson, Scott, Tri-City	1.000	9	11	32	0	43	4
Baker, Casey, Eugene	1.000	4	7	4	0	11	0
Benjamin, Casey, Spokane	.968	18	32	58	3	93	15
Blakeley, Eric, Everett	.895	4	8	9	2	19	5
Blood, Randy, Tri-City	1.000	5	10	14	0	24	2
Cordova, Roman, Everett	1.000	7	12	13	0	25	1
Cornejo, Eduardo, Vancouver	.909	15	19	31	5	55	2
Cox, Michael, Everett	.900	1	5	4	1	10	0
Dawkins, Lance, Boise	.863	19	21	42	10	73	8
Francois, Francisco, Vancouver	.902	20	21	53	8	82	5
Garcia, Alex, Eugene	.938	49	65	100	11	176	21
Garrido, Tomas, Salem-Keizer	.978	27	41	94	3	138	14
Gonzalez, Jose, Spokane	.947	7	15	21	2	38	6
Haley, Adam, Yakima	.924	65	99	194	24	317	37
Hickman, Charles, Boise	.905	32	43	90	14	147	14
Hutting, Timothy, Salem-Keizer	.955	50	94	162	12	268	41
Ingram, Brian, Vancouver	.929	19	20	19	3	42	1
Jacobo, Kervin, Eugene	1.000	1	2	0	0	2	0
Jones, Adamq, Everett	.857	3	5	7	2	14	1
Kinsler, Ian, Spokane	.969	50	82	138	7	227	18
Larsen, Andrew, Boise	1.000	4	1	6	0	7	1
Marquez, Uriak, Boise	.911	12	19	32	5	56	8
Mejia, Jorge, Vancouver	.600	2	2	1	2	5	0
Moreno, Juan J., Yakima	1.000	1	2	0	0	2	0
Morgan, Matt, Yakima	.906	7	10	19	3	32	6
NAVARRO, OSWALDO, Everett	.937	61	118	164	19	301	33
Orlandos, Nick, Everett	.875	1	1	6	1	8	1
Quintanilla, Omar, Vancouver	.983	29	47	72	2	121	12
Reynolds, Lagatila, Yakima	1.000	8	11	17	0	28	4
Rogelstad, Matt, Everett	1.000	4	7	1	0	8	0
Rosario, Samuel, Boise	.915	15	17	37	5	59	9
Smyres, Justin, Eugene	.931	27	35	59	7	101	17
Swearingen, Jonathan, Tri-City	.901	14	26	47	8	81	13
Welch, Scott, Spokane	.917	3	4	7	1	12	2

OUTFIELDERS

Player, Team	Pct.	G	PO	A	E	TC	DP
Ayala, Odannys, Spokane	1.000	3	5	0	0	5	0
Baker, Casey, Eugene	.972	35	63	6	2	71	0
Banks, Gary, Boise	.978	27	41	4	1	46	0
Barrett, Rich, Yakima	.983	32	56	3	1	60	1
Blakeley, Eric, Everett	1.000	2	3	0	0	3	0
BOURASSA, ADAM, Spokane *	.994	59	146	9	1	156	2
Boyer, Brett, Salem-Keizer	.933	46	55	1	4	60	0
Boyer, Kyle, Boise	.954	40	58	4	3	65	0
Bradford, Samuel, Everett	.991	53	97	9	1	107	1
Bubela, Dane, Spokane	.967	50	79	8	3	90	1
Cleveland, Jeremy, Spokane	.978	56	82	5	2	89	0
Colton, Chris, Everett	.973	69	137	6	4	147	1
Coutlangus, Jonathan, S.K.*	.990	48	92	4	1	97	1
Cruz, Elvis, Everett	1.000	6	9	2	0	11	0
Czarniecki, Jordan, Tri-City	.990	49	95	2	1	98	0
Diaz, Randor, Salem-Keizer	1.000	1	0	1	0	1	0
Dobson, Patrick, Salem-Keizer	.964	15	27	0	1	28	0
Dutton, Jeremy, Everett	1.000	3	1	0	0	1	0
Ellison, Josh, Everett	.923	38	58	2	5	65	0
Ethier, Andre, Vancouver *	1.000	10	28	2	0	30	0
Farrell, Sean, Vancouver	.974	38	73	1	2	76	1
Fox, Ryan, Tri-City	.971	53	96	6	3	105	1
Francois, Francisco, Vancouver	.857	5	6	0	1	7	0
Frazier, Alex, Yakima	.990	56	89	8	1	98	0
Gaetti, Joe, Tri-City	1.000	31	56	3	0	59	0
Garcia, Alex, Eugene	.750	2	3	0	1	4	0
Garcia, Lino, Yakima	.983	49	116	1	2	119	0
George, Trey, Tri-City	.946	58	100	5	6	111	0
Gibbons, Danny, Vancouver	.982	55	107	2	2	111	0
Grayson, Larry, Spokane	.938	8	15	0	1	16	0
Gresky, David, Boise *	.986	45	68	2	1	71	1
Hickman, Charles, Boise	1.000	4	6	0	0	6	0
Ingram, Brian, Vancouver	1.000	1	0	1	0	1	0
Jackson, Conor, Yakima	1.000	29	57	4	0	61	0
Jacobo, Kervin, Eugene	.875	7	7	0	1	8	0
Johnson, Ryan, Eugene *	1.000	41	61	1	0	62	0
Lahair, Bryan, Everett	1.000	3	6	0	0	6	0
Leise, Jeff, Eugene *	.990	56	95	4	1	100	1
Lopaze, Daniel, Boise	1.000	7	8	0	0	8	0
Majewski, Dustin, Vancouver *	1.000	45	101	0	0	101	0
Marquez, Uriak, Boise	.000	1	0	0	0	0	0
Mathis, Gregory, Yakima	.965	36	55	0	2	57	0
McQuade, Anthony, Boise	.951	42	77	1	4	82	0
Mejia, Jorge, Vancouver	.500	1	2	0	2	4	0
Mora, Ruben, Eugene	1.000	19	36	3	0	39	0
Moreno, Juan J., Yakima	1.000	5	3	0	0	3	0
Nordness, Kirk, Vancouver	1.000	12	22	1	0	23	0
Orlandos, Nick, Everett	1.000	23	34	1	0	35	0
Perez, Luis, Vancouver	.968	60	113	7	4	124	0
Pickens, Jordan, Eugene	1.000	1	1	0	0	1	0
Rogelstad, Matt, Everett	1.000	3	8	0	0	8	0
Rosario, Samuel, Boise	.000	1	0	0	0	0	0
Sakamoto, Mitsuru, Tri-City	1.000	13	28	0	0	28	0
Schmidt, Jesse, Salem-Keizer	.984	62	122	5	2	129	2
Simon, Brandon, Yakima *	.964	38	80	1	3	84	0
Smith, Rashad, Eugene	.957	11	21	1	1	23	1
Spivey, Brett, Tri-City	.974	14	38	0	1	39	0
Street, Dan, Tri-City	1.000	14	27	4	0	31	0
Turner, Lloyd, Vancouver	1.000	8	16	1	0	17	0
Vericker, Brad, Salem-Keizer *	.966	26	28	0	1	29	0
Wagner, Michael, Salem-Keizer	.988	61	83	2	1	86	0
Wahlbrink, Brian, Eugene	.978	69	132	3	3	138	0
Walker, Chris, Boise	.973	67	139	5	4	148	2
Wishy, Andrew, Spokane	.987	61	75	3	1	79	1
Womack, Josh, Everett *	.951	37	58	0	3	61	0

CATCHERS

Player, Team	Pct.	G	PO	A	E	TC	DP	PB
Avlas, Phil, Yakima	.981	17	98	7	2	107	0	3
Bubalo, Ty, Vancouver	1.000	3	23	1	0	24	0	2
Bushey, Andrew, Tri-City	.959	8	41	6	2	49	0	1
Carlin, Luke, Eugene	.988	28	233	22	3	258	1	4
Castillo, David, Vancouver	.982	50	344	38	7	389	0	8
Clark, Douglas, Spokane	.989	38	239	27	3	269	3	7
Corder, Gordon, Vancouver	1.000	7	43	1	0	44	0	1
D'Jesus, Francisco, S.K.	1.000	16	92	9	0	101	0	0
Falcon, Omar, Eugene	.995	20	183	17	1	201	1	5
Garcia, Alberto, Boise	1.000	3	26	0	0	26	1	0
Griffin, Brock, Everett	1.000	20	127	16	0	143	0	4
Guarno, Rick, Tri-City	.985	9	58	8	1	67	0	2
Harriman, David, Vancouver	1.000	19	124	11	0	135	1	2
Heath, Matt, Yakima	1.000	1	4	0	0	4	0	0
Jennings, Jeffery, Salem-Keizer	.986	48	327	35	5	367	2	8
Kroski, Chris, Everett	.978	5	40	5	1	46	1	1
Lauderdale, Matthew, Eugene	.986	9	66	7	1	74	0	1
Lentz, Brian, Everett	.996	34	243	30	1	274	2	3
Lunsford, Trey, Salem-Keizer	.960	3	23	1	1	25	1	1
Lynam, Guy, Tri-City	.941	3	15	1	1	17	0	1
Maduro, Jorge, Everett	.988	8	80	4	1	85	1	0
Mann, Jason, Spokane	1.000	1	9	2	0	11	0	0
Martinez, Domingo, Eugene	.986	7	67	2	1	70	0	2
McIntyre, Patrick, Boise	1.000	3	22	0	0	22	0	1
Medlin, C.J., Boise	1.000	24	172	10	0	182	1	2
Morgan, Matt, Yakima	.967	14	107	12	4	123	0	5
Morton, Colt, Eugene	.970	15	115	15	4	134	0	0
Ramirez, Juan, Vancouver	.952	10	53	7	3	63	0	0
Reyes, Jose, Boise	.984	9	56	4	1	61	0	2
Richardson, Kevin, Spokane	.991	16	99	9	1	109	0	1
Rick, Alan, Boise	.977	39	320	24	8	352	3	14
ROSE, BRIAN, Yakima	.992	50	355	31	3	389	0	4
Ruchti, Justin, Everett	.986	18	135	8	2	145	1	4
Shields, Nick, Spokane	.985	28	190	9	3	202	1	2
Sweeney, James, Tri-City	.990	56	334	47	4	385	0	6
Symonds, Grady, Yakima	1.000	6	11	1	0	12	0	0
Tidball, Adam, Boise	1.000	7	48	4	0	52	1	0
Williams, Jonny, Salem-Keizer	.992	19	113	12	1	126	0	3

PITCHERS

Player, Team	Pct.	G	PO	A	E	TC	DP
Abrams, Casey, Everett *	1.000	4	1	0	0	1	0
Acosta, Nibaldo, Everett	1.000	10	2	2	0	4	0
Alcantara, Audy, Everett	1.000	19	3	4	0	7	1
Alvarez, Tim, Salem-Keizer *	.889	14	1	7	1	9	0
Anderson, Luke, Salem-Keizer	1.000	3	0	1	0	1	0
Arakawa, Yusuke, Tri-City	1.000	30	1	4	0	5	1
Barnett, Danny, Vancouver	1.000	15	4	2	0	6	0
Barrett, Rich, Yakima	.000	4	0	0	0	0	0
Bass, Adam, Yakima	1.000	27	3	2	0	5	0
Bateman, Jamie, Salem-Keizer	.909	26	2	8	1	11	0
Bay, Ronald, Boise	1.000	4	1	2	0	3	0
Bechtel, Charles, Eugene	.000	4	0	0	0	0	0
Bondurant, Steven, Vancouver *	.909	14	2	8	1	11	0
Bonine, Eddie, Eugene	1.000	31	2	6	0	8	0
Bowman, Charles, Spokane	1.000	4	1	1	0	2	0
Burris, Robert, Vancouver	.889	15	2	6	1	9	0
Carque, Joseph, Yakima	.929	26	1	12	1	14	0
Carter, Brian, Boise *	.850	26	9	8	3	20	0
Castleman, Stephen, Tri-City	.833	18	1	4	1	6	0
Chang, Kenly, Everett	.833	24	2	3	1	6	0
Chavez, Jesse, Spokane	.929	17	3	10	1	14	0
Cherry, Rocky, Boise	.813	10	4	9	3	16	2
Chico, Matthew, Yakima *	1.000	17	5	11	0	16	0
Clark, Chad, Yakima	.833	24	2	3	1	6	1
Coonrod, Aaron, Eugene	1.000	13	3	7	0	10	0
Corchado, Jose, Vancouver	.933	19	6	8	1	15	0
Corley, Klent, Yakima	.857	5	4	2	1	7	0
Corpas, Manuel, Tri-City	.952	15	11	9	1	21	1
Corrado, Rob, Spokane	1.000	23	3	14	0	17	0
Cuevas, Alvin, Boise	1.000	19	2	4	0	6	0
Cunningham, Tim, Spokane *	.900	9	5	4	1	10	0
Danks, John, Spokane *	1.000	5	0	2	0	2	0
Darby, James, Eugene	.700	33	1	6	3	10	0
Davis, Mike, Yakima	.900	23	2	7	1	10	0
Dawkins, Lance, Boise	1.000	1	0	1	0	1	0
Devenney, Nick, Spokane	.667	23	1	7	4	12	0
Dunkle, Peter, Tri-City	1.000	22	1	7	0	8	0
Edwards, John, Tri-City	1.000	22	4	7	0	11	1
Farnum, Matt, Spokane	.889	17	2	6	1	9	0
Ferns, Robert, Yakima	1.000	3	1	0	0	1	1
Floyd, Jesse, Salem-Keizer	.929	14	3	10	1	14	0
Forbes, Terry, Everett	.500	6	1	0	1	2	0
Frydendall, Craig, Spokane *	.960	17	3	21	1	25	1
Frye, Randall, Everett	.778	13	1	6	2	9	0
Fyvie, Dan, Vancouver	.895	26	7	10	2	19	0
Gagne, J.P., Tri-City	1.000	32	5	4	0	9	1
Gallagher, Buddy, Tri-City *	.000	2	0	0	0	0	0
George, Christopher, S.K.	1.000	13	1	4	0	5	2
Girardeau, Clark, Eugene	1.000	20	4	13	0	17	1
Glant, Dustin, Yakima	1.000	34	1	6	0	7	2
Goocher, Clint, Yakima *	1.000	31	1	7	0	8	1
Green, Craig, Boise	1.000	11	0	3	0	3	0
Gregg, Grant, Eugene *	.500	15	0	1	1	2	0
Gross, Kris, Boise	.750	13	1	2	1	4	0
Guerrero, Aneury, Boise *	1.000	5	0	3	0	3	0
Haley, Adam, Yakima	.000	1	0	0	0	0	0
Hayhurst, Dirk, Eugene	1.000	25	0	3	0	3	0
Hays, Sam, Everett *	.900	18	2	7	1	10	1
Hernandez, Felix, Everett	1.000	11	2	11	0	13	0
Hill, Richard, Boise *	.824	14	2	12	3	17	1
Hines, Matthew, Boise	1.000	24	2	2	0	4	0
HINTZ, BEAU, Everett *	1.000	14	11	13	0	24	0
Howay, Chris, Vancouver	1.000	19	3	4	0	7	0
Jefferson, Drew, Salem-Keizer *	.800	26	1	3	1	5	0
Juarez, William, Yakima	.750	15	9	9	6	24	0
Kaiser, Marc, Tri-City	.923	7	3	9	1	13	1
Kerbs, Reuben, Yakima *	1.000	15	1	2	0	3	1
Kinsey, Christopher, Yakima	1.000	9	6	7	0	13	0
Kirsten, Joel, Spokane *	1.000	15	0	4	0	4	0
Knox, Brad, Vancouver	.938	15	3	12	1	16	0
Kunes, Michael, Salem-Keizer *	1.000	18	1	4	0	5	1
Landeros, Leonard, Vancouver *	1.000	8	2	4	0	6	0
Liebeck, Jered, Yakima	.917	12	7	4	1	12	0
Littleton, Wes, Spokane	.944	12	3	14	1	18	0
Lo, Ching-Lung, Tri-City	1.000	14	0	14	0	14	1
Lorenzo, Matt, Spokane	.818	16	4	5	2	11	0
Ludwig, Kellen, Salem-Keizer	1.000	17	3	1	0	4	0
Lynch, Brian, Tri-City	1.000	14	8	13	0	21	2
Marsden, Aaron, Tri-City *	.895	13	5	12	2	19	0
Marshall, Sean, Boise *	.786	14	3	8	3	14	2
Martin, Sean, Salem-Keizer	1.000	10	0	4	0	4	0
Mattoon, Brian, Spokane *	1.000	9	1	5	0	6	0
Mazurek, David, Spokane	.857	25	2	4	1	7	1
McGirr, Mike, Vancouver	1.000	16	2	11	0	13	0
McNiven, Brooks, Salem-Keizer	1.000	16	4	8	0	12	0
Mejia, Anderson, Boise	.875	19	4	10	2	16	1
Mendez, Adalberto, Boise	1.000	15	1	6	0	7	0
Misch, Patrick, Salem-Keizer *	1.000	14	4	17	0	21	2
Moore, Daniel, Eugene *	1.000	12	2	4	0	6	0
Moorhead, Michael, Everett	.750	21	0	3	1	4	0
Moreno, Anthony, Salem-Keizer	1.000	4	1	2	0	3	0
Morrow, David, Everett	1.000	5	0	1	0	1	0
Muegge, Danny, Yakima	1.000	21	0	5	0	5	0
Musgrave, Mike, Salem-Keizer	.625	15	3	2	3	8	0
Nesmith, Travis, Salem-Keizer *	.500	14	0	1	1	2	0
O'Flaherty, Eric, Everett *	.000	3	0	0	1	1	0
Ockerman, Justin, Everett	1.000	22	2	3	0	5	0
Oldham, Thomas, Everett *	.889	13	1	7	1	9	0
Ovalles, Juan, Everett	1.000	21	1	3	0	4	0
Overholt, Sean, Boise	.000	10	0	0	0	0	0
Oyervidez, Jose, Eugene	.889	31	3	5	1	9	1
Pence, Howard, Eugene	.000	1	0	0	0	0	0
Perez, Elvis, Everett	.000	2	0	0	0	0	0
Perez, Henry, Eugene	.714	15	3	2	2	7	0
Perry, Brandon, Everett *	1.000	3	1	1	0	2	0
Petersen, Jeffrey, Salem-Keizer	1.000	17	2	3	0	5	0
Peterson, John, Vancouver *	.889	14	4	4	1	9	0
Petrick, Billy, Boise	.667	14	1	1	1	3	0
Pickens, J.R., Vancouver	.900	23	1	8	1	10	0
Portorreal, Daniel, Salem-Keizer	.909	12	2	8	1	11	0
Prensa, Carlos, Eugene	1.000	9	0	1	0	1	0
Ramirez, Victor, Everett *	1.000	16	1	11	0	12	0
Ramirez, Victor, Spokane	1.000	11	1	2	0	3	0
Rapada, Clayton, Boise *	1.000	1	0	1	0	1	0
Reina, Jesus, Salem-Keizer *	.750	3	0	3	1	4	0
Reynolds, Grant, Vancouver	.667	11	1	1	1	3	0
Rio, Gabriele, Yakima *	1.000	5	0	2	0	2	0
Robinson, Ronnie, Eugene	.818	19	2	7	2	11	1
Rosales, Leonel, Eugene	1.000	36	1	1	0	2	0
Rose, Brad, Everett	1.000	20	4	7	0	11	0
Rosen, Mark, Yakima *	1.000	2	0	2	0	2	0
Sadowski, Ryan, Salem-Keizer	.833	15	3	2	1	6	1
Salas, Pedro, Tri-City	.933	11	7	7	1	15	1
Sanchez, Jose, Salem-Keizer	.000	4	0	0	0	0	0
Santiago, Tomas, Tri-City	.900	21	3	6	1	10	0
Sasaki, Kazuhiro, Everett	.000	2	0	0	0	0	0
Scarbery, Chad, Yakima	.800	15	4	8	3	15	0
Schara, Zackary, Spokane	.500	4	0	1	1	2	0
Scheffel, Dustin, Spokane	.000	1	0	0	0	0	0
Schilsky, Stephen, Vancouver	1.000	16	2	4	0	6	0
Schultz, Mike, Yakima	.667	5	0	2	1	3	0
Shartzer, Bryan, Tri-City	.875	24	3	4	1	8	0
Smith, Brandon, Tri-City	.000	2	0	0	0	0	0
Sonnier, Shawn, Boise	1.000	8	2	0	0	2	0
Stitt, Brian, Everett	.833	15	0	5	1	6	0
Thompson, Justin, Spokane *	.833	23	1	4	1	6	1
Thompson, Sean, Eugene *	.870	15	5	15	3	23	0
Thurmond, J.B., Salem-Keizer	.929	14	4	9	1	14	1
Trout, Jared, Vancouver	.818	16	7	20	6	33	1
Truselo, Randy, Spokane	1.000	15	7	8	0	15	1
Valcarcel, Jonathan, Tri-City *	.000	1	0	0	0	0	0
Valdez, Richard, Boise	.778	22	4	3	2	9	0
Van, Robert, Yakima *	1.000	1	0	1	0	1	0
Vargas, Reynaldo, Tri-City	1.000	17	5	3	0	8	0
Vicente, Ruben, Yakima	.700	10	3	4	3	10	1
Watts, Joldy, Spokane	.889	25	3	5	1	9	1
Wells, Jared, Eugene	.786	14	4	7	3	14	0
Willett, Reid, Boise	.882	20	2	13	2	17	0
Wynegar, Adam, Boise *	.833	21	2	3	1	6	0
Yoshida, Nobuaki, Eugene *	1.000	17	2	7	0	9	0
Zambotti, Anthony, Vancouver	1.000	10	2	5	0	7	0

The following players appeared only as a designated hitter, pinch-hitter or pinch-runner: Colbrunn, dh; Fabrizio, dh, ph, pr; Shorsher, dh, ph.

LEAGUE CHAMPIONS

Year	Team	Pct.
1901—	Portland	.675
1902—	Butte	.608
1903—	Butte	.578
1904—	Boise	.625
1905—	Vancouver	.586
	Everett*	.667
1906—	Tacoma	.600
1907—	Aberdeen	.625
1908—	Vancouver	.578
1909—	Seattle	.653
1910—	Spokane	.596
1911—	Vancouver	.628
1912—	Seattle	.600
1913—	Vancouver	.600
1914—	Vancouver	.632
1915—	Seattle	.564
1916—	Spokane	.622
1917—	Great Falls	.592
1918—	Seattle	.588
1919—	Seattle	.590
1920—	Victoria	.600
1921—	Yakima	.710
	Yakima	.660
1922—	Calgary‡	.600
1923-36—	Did not operate.	
1937—	Wenatchee	.603
	Tacoma*	.627
1938—	Yakima	.583
	Bellingham (2nd)†	.511
1939—	Wenatchee	.601
	Tacoma (2nd)†	.533
1940—	Spokane	.587
	Tacoma (4th)†	.500
1941—	Spokane	.669
1942—	Vancouver	.594
1943-45—	Did not operate.	
1946—	Wenatchee	.622
1947—	Vancouver	.566
1948—	Spokane	.614
1949—	Yakima	.660
	Vancouver (2nd)†	.615
1950—	Yakima	.613
1951—	Spokane	.655
1952—	Victoria	.631
1953—	Salem	.635
	Spokane*	.590
1954—	Vancouver*	.636
	Lewiston	.629
1955—	Salem	.646
	Eugene*	.639
1956—	Yakima	.691
	Yakima	.619
1957—	Eugene	.576
	Wenatchee*	.647
1958—	Lewiston	.621
	Yakima*	.594
1959—	Salem	.623
	Yakima*	.563
1960—	Yakima	.638
	Yakima	.562
1961—	Lewiston*	.621
	Yakima	.600
1962—	Wenatchee*	.574
	Tri-City	.580
1963—	Lewiston	.594
	Yakima*	.613
1964—	Eugene	.636
	Yakima*	.611
1965—	Lewiston	.667
	Tri-City*	.681
1966—	Tri-City	.679
1967—	Medford	.607
1968—	Tri-City	.600
1969—	Rogue Valley	.633
1970—	Lewiston§	.538
	Coos Bay-No. Bend	.563
1971—	Tri-City§	.625
	Bend	.538
1972—	Lewiston§	.675
	Walla Walla	.513
1973—	Walla Walla∞	.638
	Portland	.563
1974—	Bellingham	.619
	Eugene▲	.571
1975—	Portland	.545
	Eugene◆	.684
1976—	Portland	.556
	Walla Walla◆	.639
1977—	Bellingham■	.618
	Portland	.667
1978—	Grays Harbor▼	.671
	Eugene	.514
1979—	Central Oregon◆	.606
	Walla Walla	.571
1980—	Bellingham•	.643
	Eugene•	.529
1981—	Medford◆	.600
	Bellingham	.557
1982—	Medford	.757
	Salem◆	.486
1983—	Medford††	.735
	Bellingham	.588
1984—	Tri-Cities††	.622
	Medford	.608
1985—	Everett††	.541
	Eugene	.541
1986—	Bellingham††	.608
	Eugene	.608
1987—	Spokane▲	.711
	Everett	.653
1988—	Southern Oregon	.605
	Spokane◆	.553
1989—	Southern Oregon	.600
	Spokane◆	.547
1990—	Boise	.697
	Spokane◆	.645
1991—	Boise◆	.658
	Yakima	.579
1992—	Bellingham◆	.566
	Bend	.566
1993—	Bellingham	.579
	Boise◆	.539
1994—	Yakima	.645
	Boise◆	.579
1995—	Boise◆	.640
	Bellingham	.566
1996—	Eugene	.645
	Yakima§	.526
1997—	Boise	.671
	Portland◆	.579
1998—	Spokane	.618
	Boise	.618
	Salem-Keizer◆	.566
1999—	Spokane◆	.579
2000—	Yakima◆	.539
	Boise	.539
2001—	Boise	.693
	Salem-Keizer◆	.671
2002—	Boise▲	.645
2003—	Spokane▲	.658

*Won split-season playoff. †Won four-club playoff. ‡League disbanded June 18. §League divided into Northern and Southern divisions, declared champion under league rules. ∞League divided into Eastern and Western divisions, declared champion under league rules. ▲League divided into Eastern and Western divisions; won two-team playoff. ◆League divided into North and South divisions; won two-team playoff. ■League divided into Affiliate and Independent divisions; won two-team playoff. ▼Declared league champion after winning one-game playoff. Balance of playoff canceled due to rain and wet grounds. •Declared co-champion after winning one game. Balance of playoff canceled due to rain and wet grounds. ††League divided into Washington and Oregon divisions; won two-team playoff. (NOTE—Known as Pacific Northwest League 1901-02, Pacific National League 1903-04, Northwestern League 1905-18, Pacific Coast International League 1919-22 and Western International League 1937-54.)

APPALACHIAN LEAGUE

LEAGUE OFFICE

President
Lee Landers

Address
283 Deerchase Circle
Statesville, NC 28625

Phone
704-873-5300

Teams (affiliation)
Bluefield Orioles (Orioles)
Bristol White Sox (White Sox)
Burlington Indians (Indians)
Danville Braves (Braves)
Elizabethton Twins (Twins)
Greeneville Astros (Astros)
Johnson City Cardinals (Cardinals)
Kingsport Mets (Mets)
Princeton Devil Rays (Devil Rays)
Pulaski Blue Jays (Blue Jays)

2003 FINAL STANDINGS

EASTERN DIVISION

Team	W	L	T	Pct.	GB
Martinsville	42	23	-	.646	...
Danville	36	30	-	.545	6.5
Burlington	37	31	-	.544	6.5
Bluefield	23	40	-	.365	18.0
Princeton	23	41	-	.359	18.5

WESTERN DIVISION

Team	W	L	T	Pct.	GB
Elizabethton	42	24	-	.636	...
Pulaski	38	29	-	.567	4.5
Bristol	33	33	-	.500	9.0
Johnson City	27	36	-	.429	13.5
Kingsport	25	39	-	.391	16.0

COMPOSITE

Team	MAR	ELZ	PUL	DAN	BRL	BRS	JCY	KPT	BLU	PRI	W	L	T	Pct.	GB
Martinsville (Astros)	...	2	8	6	6	3	3	5	6	3	42	23	0	.646	...
Elizabethton (Twins)	4	...	4	4	3	6	5	7	5	4	42	24	0	.636	0.5
Pulaski (Blue Jays)	4	2	...	3	2	3	4	4	8	8	38	29	0	.567	5.0
Danville (Braves)	4	1	3	...	6	2	3	4	7	6	36	30	0	.545	6.5
Burlington (Indians)	4	3	4	6	...	3	3	3	5	6	37	31	0	.544	6.5
Bristol (White Sox)	1	4	3	4	3	...	5	6	3	4	33	33	0	.500	9.5
Johnson City (Cardinals)	3	6	1	2	3	5	...	5	0	2	27	36	0	.429	14.0
Kingsport (Mets)	1	3	2	2	3	6	3	...	1	4	25	39	0	.391	16.5
Bluefield (Orioles)	0	1	2	3	1	3	6	3	...	4	23	40	0	.365	18.0
Princeton (Devil Rays)	2	2	2	0	4	2	4	2	5	...	23	41	0	.359	18.5

Major league affiliations in parentheses.

PLAYOFFS: Elizabethton defeated Martinsville, two games to one, to win league championship.

REGULAR-SEASON ATTENDANCE: Bluefield, 22,853; Bristol, 19,770; Burlington, 37,380; Danville, 35,621; Elizabethton, 24,004; Johnson City, 31,261; Kingsport, 19,108; Martinsville, 27,821; Princeton, 26,339; Pulaski, 21,828. Total attendance—265,985. Playoffs (3 games)—2,802.

MANAGERS: Bluefield, Don Buford; Bristol, Jerry Hairston; Burlington, Rouglas Odor; Danville, Kevin McMullan; Elizabethton, Ray Smith; Johnson City, Ron Warner; Kingsport, Mookie Wilson; Martinsville, Jorge Orta; Princeton, Jamie Nelson; Pulaski, Paul Elliott.

ALL-STAR TEAM: 1B—Dusty Gomon, Elizabethton; 2B—(tie) Jermy Acey, Pulaski and Mike Hanson, Danville; 3B—Saul Torres, Martinsville; SS—Rob Valido, Bristol; Utility INF—Brandon Pinckney, Burlington; OF—Ervin Alcantara, Martinsville; OF—Matt Esquivel, Danville; OF—Chris Young, Bristol; Utility OF—Sal Frisella, Johnson City; C—Robinson Diaz, Pulaski; DH—Tyler Davidson, Kingsport; RHP—Chris Schutt, Elizabethton; LHP—Rafael Perez, Burlington; Relief pitcher—Celso Rondon, Kingsport; Player of the Year—Tyler Davidson, Kingsport; Pitcher of the Year—Rafael Perez, Burlington; Manager of the Year—Jorge Orta, Martinsville.

2003 BATTING

TEAM

Team	G	TPA	AB	R	H	TB	2B	3B	HR	RBI	SH	SF	HP	BB	IBB	SO	SB	CS	GDP	LOB	ShO	Avg.	OBP	Slg.
Martinsville	65	2460	2172	335	622	882	146	12	30	303	19	17	27	225	7	440	43	21	52	483	4	.286	.358	.406
Pulaski	68	2596	2226	372	614	877	143	15	30	339	12	25	66	267	4	491	34	26	45	523	3	.276	.366	.394
Elizabethton	66	2544	2204	385	585	859	101	16	47	325	4	20	42	274	4	494	83	26	24	523	3	.265	.355	.390
Johnson City	64	2400	2116	316	555	816	99	15	44	282	14	17	36	217	4	508	32	21	35	464	5	.262	.339	.386
Bristol	66	2346	2106	303	533	822	126	20	41	263	35	20	35	149	2	491	76	39	28	393	2	.253	.310	.390
Kingsport	64	2323	2060	259	515	769	119	21	31	231	19	19	35	189	7	482	72	33	35	436	5	.250	.321	.373
Princeton	64	2298	2011	281	501	652	76	18	13	228	14	12	51	209	1	504	99	45	47	426	6	.249	.333	.324
Danville	66	2426	2138	266	522	723	107	14	22	231	19	29	33	202	4	500	93	45	34	434	3	.244	.315	.338
Burlington	68	2606	2314	316	565	786	95	18	30	273	14	23	41	214	4	485	70	23	44	484	2	.244	.316	.340
Bluefield	63	2305	2037	263	484	693	90	7	35	214	18	14	35	201	2	484	59	32	45	413	6	.238	.315	.340

INDIVIDUAL

TOP QUALIFIERS FOR BATTING CHAMPIONSHIP

Minimum 184 plate appearances. *Lefthanded batter. †Switch-hitter.

Player, Team	G	TPA	AB	R	H	TB	2B	3B	HR	RBI	SH	SF	HP	BB	IBB	SO	SB	CS	GDP	Avg.	OBP	Slg.
Diaz, Robinzon, Pulaski	48	199	182	33	68	95	20	2	1	44	0	4	3	10	1	14	1	4	5	.374	.407	.522
Alcantara, Ervin, Martinsville	54	218	195	25	67	91	18	0	2	33	2	0	2	19	1	39	1	4	7	.344	.407	.467
Frisella, Paul, Johnson City	60	207	175	36	59	96	13	0	8	37	2	0	6	24	0	51	1	5	2	.337	.434	.549
Davidson, Tyler, Kingsport	50	193	172	29	58	115	11	8	10	35	0	3	3	15	3	36	3	0	2	.337	.394	.669
Perodin, Ron, Elizabethton *	50	190	170	35	57	71	8	3	0	23	0	0	1	19	0	34	15	3	3	.335	.405	.418
Haerther, Cody, J.C.*	63	249	226	31	75	108	12	6	3	39	0	1	0	22	0	30	2	1	7	.332	.390	.478
Torres, Saul, Martinsville	57	251	214	40	68	93	19	3	0	25	2	2	6	27	0	33	3	1	4	.318	.406	.435
Brown, Travis, Bluefield	48	186	165	27	52	66	11	0	1	15	3	0	3	15	0	27	15	5	0	.315	.383	.400

Player, Team	G	TPA	AB	R	H	TB	2B	3B	HR	RBI	SH	SF	HP	BB	IBB	SO	SB	CS	GDP	Avg.	OBP	Slg.
Valido, Robert, Bristol	58	245	215	39	66	103	15	2	6	31	3	5	5	17	0	28	17	6	3	.307	.364	.479
Reiman, Joey, Pulaski	59	251	206	47	62	87	18	2	1	35	1	2	10	32	1	46	1	3	3	.301	.416	.422
Barton, Daric, Johnson City *	54	212	170	29	50	72	10	0	4	29	0	3	2	37	0	48	0	3	2	.294	.420	.424
Acey, Jermy, Pulaski †	56	263	214	45	63	88	16	0	3	28	2	2	14	31	0	32	11	3	2	.294	.414	.411
Thomas, Nicholas, Pulaski *	50	222	186	36	54	91	14	1	7	39	1	3	2	30	1	47	0	0	1	.290	.389	.489
Young, Chris, Bristol	64	273	238	47	69	114	18	3	7	28	3	4	4	23	0	40	21	7	0	.290	.357	.479
Peterson, Brock, Elizabethton	61	250	207	53	60	98	9	1	9	31	0	2	9	32	0	48	5	1	2	.290	.404	.473

DEPARTMENTAL LEADERS: G—B. Thomas, 66; AB—Pinckney, 257; R—Peterson, 53; H—Haerther, 75; TB—Gomon, 120; 2B—Ro. Diaz, 20; 3B—T. Davidson, 8; HR—Gomon, 15; RBI—Phillips, 49; SH—Tingler, 7; SF—Valido, 5; HP—Acey, 14; BB—Tingler, 46; IBB—T. Davidson, 3; SO—Gomon, 85; SB—Cooper, 25; CS—James, 10; GIDP—Simmons, 10; Slg.—T. Davidson, .669; OBP—Frisella, .434.

ALL PLAYERS

*Lefthanded batter. †Switch-hitter.

Player, Team	G	TPA	AB	R	H	TB	2B	3B	HR	RBI	SH	SF	HP	BB	IBB	SO	SB	CS	GDP	Avg.	OBP	Slg.
Acey, Jermy, Pulaski †	56	263	214	45	63	88	16	0	3	28	2	2	14	31	0	32	11	3	2	.294	.414	.411
Acosta, Jose, Martinsville	27	107	100	15	26	45	11	1	2	20	0	1	1	5	0	21	0	0	2	.260	.299	.450
Alcantara, Ervin, Martinsville	54	218	195	25	67	91	18	0	2	33	2	0	2	19	1	39	1	4	7	.344	.407	.467
Anderson, Jimmy, Kingsport	15	52	50	9	15	31	10	0	2	7	0	0	0	2	1	10	0	0	0	.300	.327	.620
Arias, Angel, Bristol	30	99	92	6	22	30	6	1	0	5	3	0	0	4	0	12	1	2	1	.239	.271	.326
Arneson, Justin, Elizabethton	49	189	160	31	41	59	5	2	3	29	0	0	5	24	0	45	10	3	1	.256	.370	.369
Ascencion, Quincy, Bluefield	39	140	131	20	37	48	8	0	1	18	0	1	3	5	1	14	5	3	7	.282	.321	.366
Babilonia, Edgar, Martinsville	40	152	146	19	37	48	6	1	1	13	3	0	0	3	0	28	5	2	3	.253	.268	.329
Barden, Andy, Danville	29	94	83	3	11	16	5	0	0	5	0	1	2	7	0	39	0	1	1	.133	.215	.193
Barthel, Cole, Danville	7	27	21	1	5	6	1	0	0	2	1	1	0	4	0	7	0	1	0	.238	.346	.286
Barton, Daric, Johnson City *	54	212	170	29	50	72	10	0	4	29	0	3	2	37	0	48	0	3	2	.294	.420	.424
Batista, Ariel, Martinsville	10	32	31	4	8	11	0	0	1	4	0	0	0	1	0	8	0	0	3	.258	.281	.355
Batista, Wilson, Kingsport †	19	76	62	6	16	21	3	1	0	7	3	0	0	11	0	10	2	1	2	.258	.370	.339
Beck, Alan, Bluefield	16	58	46	7	11	17	3	0	1	9	0	0	4	8	0	11	3	0	0	.239	.397	.370
Beech, Travis, Princeton *	48	177	166	21	36	50	6	1	2	16	1	2	1	7	0	32	6	2	3	.217	.250	.301
Bennett, Charles, Kingsport *	4	16	15	2	5	5	0	0	0	3	0	1	0	0	0	4	0	0	0	.333	.313	.333
Blanton, Stephen, Bluefield *	23	57	48	3	7	10	1	1	0	4	0	1	2	6	0	15	0	1	1	.146	.263	.208
Bohlander, Michael, Bristol *	41	110	98	18	22	34	5	2	1	9	1	0	0	11	1	20	1	0	1	.224	.303	.347
Bolen, Josh, Princeton	43	157	126	24	27	38	5	0	2	13	0	1	8	22	0	37	8	2	6	.214	.363	.302
Bowman, Shawn, Kingsport	10	37	33	2	4	5	1	0	0	3	0	0	3	1	0	13	0	0	0	.121	.216	.152
Braun, Randy, Pulaski *	40	153	144	13	26	37	4	2	1	18	0	1	0	8	0	26	0	3	3	.181	.222	.257
Brinkley, Dante, Kingsport	44	171	142	23	43	56	7	3	0	17	3	2	8	16	0	28	9	7	0	.303	.399	.394
Brock, Caleb, Burlington	33	133	118	19	34	44	3	2	1	15	0	1	4	10	0	13	3	1	0	.288	.361	.373
Brown, Travis, Bluefield	48	186	165	27	52	66	11	0	1	15	3	0	3	15	0	27	15	5	0	.315	.383	.400
Burrus, Josh, Danville	53	211	189	25	48	64	11	1	1	16	0	3	4	15	0	48	10	4	1	.254	.318	.339
Cabral, Marcos, Kingsport	43	160	131	15	26	33	5	1	0	9	5	1	2	21	0	25	4	2	0	.198	.316	.252
Camacho, Johan, Kingsport †	51	198	177	15	43	56	8	1	1	16	0	2	3	15	1	44	1	0	2	.243	.310	.316
Capellan, Domingo, J.C.	14	39	35	5	10	20	4	0	2	4	0	0	2	2	0	9	0	0	2	.286	.359	.571
Caraballo, Francisco, Mar.	52	223	206	28	59	95	18	3	4	31	0	3	0	14	0	55	1	2	5	.286	.327	.461
Casillas, Omar, Burlington	17	56	46	6	8	12	1	0	1	4	1	0	1	8	0	6	0	2	0	.174	.309	.261
Castillo, Cesar, Bristol	41	119	99	10	22	28	3	0	1	8	3	0	3	14	0	19	0	2	2	.222	.336	.283
Cenate, Josh, Bluefield *	1	1	1	0	0	0	0	0	0	0	0	0	0	0	0	1	0	0	0	.000	.000	.000
Chourio, Junior, Pulaski	20	76	74	4	13	16	3	0	0	8	0	2	0	0	0	26	0	0	2	.176	.171	.216
Clem, Chris, Burlington	48	184	154	22	42	56	11	0	1	18	0	1	6	23	0	27	6	4	2	.273	.386	.364
Colbert, Eddie, Bluefield †	27	72	64	7	12	13	1	0	0	3	1	0	1	6	0	21	2	0	0	.188	.268	.203
Coles, Corey, Kingsport *	27	107	96	19	32	39	5	1	0	6	1	0	2	8	0	17	6	0	0	.333	.396	.406
Colin, Matt, Burlington	27	100	79	10	18	25	1	0	2	15	0	1	6	14	0	16	0	1	1	.228	.380	.316
Colina, Luis, Johnson City	53	174	158	15	29	35	3	0	1	13	2	2	2	10	1	50	0	1	1	.184	.238	.222
Collaro, Thomas, Bristol	45	155	146	17	33	68	9	1	8	28	0	3	2	4	0	46	1	0	5	.226	.252	.466
Collins, Jesse, Elizabethton †	31	130	107	15	23	35	9	0	1	16	0	0	2	21	0	25	1	0	3	.215	.354	.327
Cooper, Chad, Princeton	55	235	201	38	53	65	5	2	1	22	3	1	9	21	0	35	25	5	3	.264	.358	.323
Corapci, Jason, Martinsville	11	44	41	3	9	10	1	0	0	2	0	0	1	2	0	4	0	0	0	.220	.273	.244
Costello, Michael, Bluefield	8	28	23	1	5	7	0	1	0	7	0	1	0	4	0	8	0	0	0	.217	.321	.304
Cruz, Jose, Burlington †	48	193	166	26	42	69	10	4	3	27	0	0	3	24	0	25	7	2	8	.253	.358	.416
Cumberland, Shaun, Prin.*	62	243	218	28	55	79	11	5	1	32	0	3	2	19	0	41	12	3	4	.252	.314	.362
Dalton, Matthew, Pulaski	19	1	1	0	0	0	0	0	0	0	0	0	0	0	0	0	0	0	0	.000	.000	.000
Davidson, Kevin, Martinsville	39	163	130	23	43	68	11	1	4	29	0	2	1	30	0	25	6	2	4	.331	.454	.523
Davidson, Tyler, Kingsport	50	193	172	29	58	115	11	8	10	35	0	3	3	15	3	36	3	0	2	.337	.394	.669
Davie, Andrew, J.C.*	50	188	169	28	44	79	11	0	8	24	0	1	1	17	1	48	1	1	3	.260	.330	.467
Diaz, Robinzon, Pulaski	48	199	182	33	68	95	20	2	1	44	0	4	3	10	1	14	1	4	5	.374	.407	.522
Diaz, Sandy, Johnson City	12	28	24	2	1	1	0	0	0	0	0	0	2	2	0	10	0	0	0	.042	.179	.042
Donato, Greg \, Danville	24	90	80	12	20	29	3	0	2	12	0	3	0	7	0	13	2	1	0	.250	.300	.363
Dufner, Kris, Princeton †	13	54	47	4	10	17	2	1	1	10	0	0	1	6	0	14	2	1	0	.213	.315	.362
Dulaney, Todd, Kingsport	35	123	99	18	24	26	2	0	0	5	2	1	1	20	0	10	7	5	3	.242	.372	.263
Encarnacion, Teodoro, Burl.	54	208	184	24	50	70	8	0	4	28	2	4	4	14	0	44	1	2	3	.272	.330	.380
Esposito, Vincent, Pulaski *	39	153	127	20	38	58	11	0	3	23	0	2	4	20	0	36	2	1	2	.299	.405	.457
Esquivel, Matt, Danville	61	250	220	41	62	113	10	4	11	42	0	4	6	20	1	72	7	4	4	.282	.352	.514
Estrada, Robert, Bluefield	18	69	59	8	10	17	1	0	2	5	0	0	1	9	0	10	1	1	2	.169	.290	.288
Fermin, Angelo, Eliz.†	42	161	131	22	36	52	7	3	1	15	1	4	2	23	0	36	14	1	0	.275	.381	.397
Foskey, Will, Danville	3	9	8	0	2	2	0	0	0	3	0	0	0	1	0	3	0	0	1	.250	.333	.250
Frias, Fernando, Princeton	41	139	127	20	33	51	7	4	1	14	0	0	0	12	0	47	5	3	0	.260	.324	.402
Frisella, Paul, Johnson City	60	207	175	36	59	96	13	0	8	37	2	0	6	24	0	51	1	5	2	.337	.434	.549
Gamero, Jesus, Kingsport	13	53	46	6	9	12	3	0	0	3	1	0	0	6	1	8	1	0	2	.196	.288	.261
Garcia, Antonio, Mar.†	28	108	95	12	28	42	5	0	3	22	0	0	0	13	2	21	2	1	4	.295	.380	.442
Garcia, Julio, Burlington †	30	113	100	11	22	26	2	1	0	7	2	0	0	11	0	24	5	0	2	.220	.297	.260
Garcia, Junior, Burlington	37	137	129	21	33	54	4	4	3	17	1	0	1	6	1	44	11	2	1	.256	.294	.419

Player, Team	G	TPA	AB	R	H	TB	2B	3B	HR	RBI	SH	SF	HP	BB	IBB	SO	SB	CS	GDP	Avg.	OBP	Slg.
Garcia, Miguel, Kingsport *	15	42	37	3	7	8	1	0	0	2	0	1	1	3	0	13	1	0	0	.189	.262	.216
Garcia, Travis, Kingsport	22	88	77	11	16	23	2	1	1	9	2	1	2	6	0	13	0	2	0	.208	.279	.299
Garcia, Winfield, Martinsville	49	227	210	37	57	68	9	1	0	16	1	1	4	11	0	19	6	1	4	.271	.319	.324
Gary, Tavaris, Johnson City *	38	114	102	14	23	33	4	0	2	7	2	0	1	9	1	22	2	2	2	.225	.295	.324
Garza, Mario, Martinsville *	24	97	78	19	23	44	6	0	5	16	0	2	2	15	1	18	2	0	1	.295	.412	.564
Geiger, Kyle, Elizabethton	9	35	33	1	7	9	2	0	0	4	0	0	0	2	0	6	0	0	0	.212	.257	.273
George, Kyle, Bluefield	53	211	168	25	35	54	7	0	4	16	1	0	2	40	0	47	3	3	5	.208	.367	.321
Gilhooly, Tim, Bluefield	46	172	157	18	33	60	12	0	5	14	0	0	1	14	0	71	3	1	2	.210	.279	.382
Gomon, Dusty, Elizabethton	61	266	233	36	61	120	14	0	15	46	0	3	3	27	2	85	0	1	1	.262	.342	.515
Gonzalez, Humberto, King.	12	33	31	2	4	4	0	0	0	0	0	0	0	2	0	7	0	1	1	.129	.182	.129
Guerrero, Francisco, Bluefield	39	137	128	13	32	44	4	1	2	10	2	2	2	3	0	23	4	2	3	.250	.274	.344
Guerrero, Henry, Bluefield	31	106	97	13	21	26	2	0	1	10	0	1	0	8	0	25	0	0	2	.216	.274	.268
Gustafson, Chris, Princeton *	24	61	53	4	8	8	0	0	0	4	0	1	2	5	0	19	3	0	1	.151	.246	.151
Hadad, Jorge, Bluefield	29	86	80	8	13	16	0	0	1	5	1	0	0	5	0	14	0	0	3	.163	.212	.200
Haerther, Cody, J.C.*	63	249	226	31	75	108	12	6	3	39	0	1	0	22	0	30	2	1	7	.332	.390	.478
Hanson, Mike, Danville	57	238	213	27	59	88	15	4	2	20	4	3	3	15	0	32	9	4	2	.277	.329	.413
Harper, Brett, Kingsport *	11	40	35	6	15	29	8	0	2	10	0	0	2	3	0	9	0	0	3	.429	.500	.829
Hayes, Calvin, Johnson City	35	142	125	25	38	49	5	0	2	11	0	0	3	14	0	20	16	2	2	.304	.387	.392
Hemingway, Jamie, Danville	51	213	191	25	52	70	13	1	1	19	0	2	7	13	0	35	15	5	5	.272	.338	.366
Herring, Matt, Bristol *	46	147	128	17	30	50	4	2	4	22	1	1	1	16	1	41	0	0	3	.234	.322	.391
Hessman, Mike, Danville	5	20	15	1	1	1	0	0	0	2	0	2	1	2	0	2	0	0	0	.067	.200	.067
Hetherington, Luke, Pulaski	46	172	143	27	38	59	8	5	1	24	0	1	6	22	0	50	2	1	5	.266	.384	.413
Hill, Jamar, Kingsport	44	182	170	22	41	71	12	0	6	26	0	2	0	10	1	45	14	4	1	.241	.280	.418
Hodge, Luis, Burlington	51	212	196	23	46	71	7	3	4	29	0	2	4	10	0	46	2	2	2	.235	.283	.362
House, Kevin, Johnson City	33	107	91	14	19	24	3	1	0	10	2	1	0	13	0	21	1	1	2	.209	.305	.264
Houston, Matthew, Bluefield	31	111	100	9	28	35	4	0	1	6	0	1	5	5	0	19	1	1	4	.280	.342	.350
Hudgson, Maximiliano, Mar.†	35	134	116	10	27	38	8	0	1	15	6	3	1	8	0	34	2	1	5	.233	.281	.328
Irvin, Blair, Princeton *	34	87	75	13	23	23	0	0	0	6	3	0	0	9	0	20	4	1	2	.307	.381	.307
James, Willie, Danville †	48	173	148	21	28	31	3	0	0	5	1	0	0	24	1	33	10	10	3	.189	.302	.209
Johnson, Josh, Elizabethton	27	79	67	7	11	15	1	0	1	12	0	1	5	6	0	25	0	1	1	.164	.278	.224
Koenig, Lance, Martinsville	44	153	131	21	36	49	11	1	0	13	1	0	3	18	0	30	4	2	2	.275	.375	.374
Krga, Mike, Princeton	7	16	13	1	2	2	0	0	0	0	1	0	0	2	0	3	0	0	1	.154	.267	.154
Lebron, Freddie, Bristol †	37	131	116	19	29	43	6	1	2	13	4	1	2	8	0	17	10	4	0	.250	.307	.371
Lenderman, Matthew, Bristol	22	51	49	5	10	14	1	0	1	6	0	0	0	2	0	29	0	0	0	.204	.235	.286
Longworth, Chad, Burlington	35	122	107	25	22	41	4	3	3	7	0	1	0	14	0	29	7	0	4	.206	.295	.383
Luna, Leonardo, Bristol	26	120	109	21	35	46	8	0	1	12	5	1	1	4	0	19	1	0	2	.321	.348	.422
Mannix, Brendan, King.†	19	69	64	6	16	24	3	1	1	12	0	0	0	5	0	18	0	1	2	.250	.304	.375
Martin, Scott, Bristol	43	117	108	13	20	34	6	1	2	14	3	1	3	2	0	31	0	0	3	.185	.219	.315
Martinez, Edwin, Danville	27	84	70	7	17	20	3	0	0	6	2	0	1	11	1	15	1	1	2	.243	.354	.286
Mendez, Valentin, Mar.	11	41	38	7	15	20	2	0	1	6	0	0	2	1	0	7	1	0	2	.395	.439	.526
Milledge, Lastings, Kingsport	7	31	26	4	6	8	2	0	0	2	0	1	1	3	0	4	5	1	0	.231	.323	.308
Molina, Felix, Elizabethton †	20	95	88	15	31	47	10	3	0	14	1	1	2	3	0	10	3	1	0	.352	.383	.534
Morel, Elvis, Bluefield	58	248	225	34	60	85	10	3	3	20	4	0	3	16	0	30	14	5	4	.267	.324	.378
Motte, Jason, Johnson City	9	30	29	2	9	12	3	0	0	5	0	1	0	0	0	9	1	1	0	.310	.300	.414
Munsey, Tanner, Burlington	9	13	9	0	1	1	0	0	0	1	0	0	1	3	0	4	0	0	0	.111	.385	.111
Nichols, Thomas, Princeton	55	223	203	21	54	71	12	1	1	34	1	0	2	17	0	55	7	2	7	.266	.329	.350
Pacheco, Fernando, Burl.*	53	202	183	19	38	60	13	0	3	19	0	2	2	15	0	60	0	0	5	.208	.272	.328
Paredes, Salvador, Princeton	63	221	199	33	48	58	4	0	2	19	1	2	4	15	0	61	7	8	1	.241	.305	.291
Partridge, Dominique, Dan.	58	225	208	22	52	73	8	2	3	30	0	1	1	15	0	40	10	2	6	.250	.302	.351
Perez, Angel, Johnson City †	28	87	70	11	13	14	1	0	0	5	3	0	4	10	0	23	1	0	0	.186	.321	.200
Perez, Melvin, Bristol	62	242	221	27	58	91	16	4	3	33	2	2	4	13	0	64	2	3	1	.262	.313	.412
Perodin, Ron, Elizabethton *	50	190	170	35	57	71	8	3	0	23	0	0	1	19	0	34	15	3	3	.335	.405	.418
Peterson, Brock, Elizabethton	61	250	207	53	60	98	9	1	9	31	0	2	9	32	0	48	5	1	2	.290	.404	.473
Phillips, Kyle, Elizabethton *	63	279	246	36	71	107	12	0	8	49	0	4	3	26	2	34	1	0	4	.289	.358	.435
Pietsch, Seth, Kingsport	10	44	40	3	8	10	2	0	0	5	0	0	1	3	0	10	4	0	0	.200	.273	.250
Pinckney, Brandon, Burl.	62	285	257	41	71	85	11	0	1	27	0	3	2	23	1	23	8	2	3	.276	.337	.331
Ponce, Arnoldo, Pulaski †	39	136	117	18	30	37	4	0	1	11	0	1	6	12	0	31	3	2	4	.256	.353	.316
Pospishil, Jason, Eliz.†	29	92	86	13	18	24	4	1	0	12	0	1	2	3	0	26	0	1	0	.209	.250	.279
Purkey, Bryan, Kingsport	3	6	3	2	1	2	1	0	0	1	0	0	0	3	0	1	0	0	0	.333	.667	.667
Pyzik, Steve, Danville	34	105	93	5	20	22	2	0	0	8	2	1	0	9	0	8	0	1	3	.215	.282	.237
Ramirez, Estevinson, Bris.†	29	58	50	9	14	17	3	0	0	5	1	0	0	7	0	16	1	6	0	.280	.368	.340
Reiman, Joey, Pulaski	59	251	206	47	62	87	18	2	1	35	1	2	10	32	1	46	1	3	3	.301	.416	.422
Reyes, Argenis, Burlington †	39	163	151	26	42	44	2	0	0	9	1	1	3	7	1	23	14	1	3	.278	.321	.291
Reynoso, Danilo, Kingsport	39	140	131	8	32	57	11	1	4	13	0	2	1	6	0	46	0	1	1	.244	.279	.435
Rios, Kevin, Kingsport	34	115	108	6	25	31	6	0	0	6	1	0	1	5	0	28	1	1	2	.231	.272	.287
Rivas, Arturo, Bluefield	9	36	32	7	11	15	4	0	0	7	0	1	0	3	0	6	3	0	0	.344	.389	.469
Rivera, Jhonny, Bristol	49	149	139	19	36	49	11	1	0	13	3	1	4	2	0	41	13	5	3	.259	.288	.353
Rodriguez, Manuel, Bristol	29	86	78	8	12	23	3	1	2	10	2	0	2	4	0	30	0	1	3	.154	.214	.295
Rodriguez, Marcos, J.C.*	28	79	74	8	22	31	2	2	1	9	1	0	1	3	0	14	2	0	1	.297	.333	.419
Rodriquez, Yuber, Pulaski †	41	142	131	18	37	54	11	0	2	15	1	0	5	5	0	41	1	1	2	.282	.333	.412
Saccomanno, Mark, Mar.	34	148	136	25	44	60	5	1	3	21	1	1	1	9	0	18	1	1	3	.324	.367	.441
Salas, Jose, Pulaski †	19	60	54	7	15	19	4	0	0	7	0	2	1	3	0	20	0	0	0	.278	.317	.352
Saltalamacchia, Justin, Dan.	9	30	28	3	6	8	2	0	0	3	0	0	0	2	0	1	0	0	0	.214	.267	.286
Sarabia, Hamilton, Mar.*	47	170	150	22	39	46	4	0	1	15	2	0	1	17	1	31	6	4	0	.260	.339	.307
Schade, Scott, Danville	53	197	176	20	45	64	11	1	2	22	4	1	0	16	0	56	6	2	3	.256	.316	.364
Schlichting, Travis, Princeton.	46	163	146	18	33	39	2	2	0	9	2	0	1	14	0	38	6	4	7	.226	.298	.267
Schmidt, Jeffrey, Bristol	26	74	70	5	14	18	4	0	0	10	0	1	0	3	0	15	0	1	0	.200	.230	.257
Schutzenhofer, Andy, J.C.*	41	154	136	28	43	62	11	1	2	19	0	0	3	15	1	12	1	1	5	.316	.396	.456
Sena, Emmanuel, Pulaski †	45	157	136	15	26	33	4	0	1	12	0	0	2	19	0	38	4	1	1	.191	.299	.243
Shafer, Corey, Bluefield *	60	249	218	32	48	80	11	0	7	34	0	4	1	26	1	60	3	4	5	.220	.301	.367
Shelley, Shane, Princeton †	39	112	93	18	27	34	2	1	1	13	1	0	5	13	0	28	7	3	0	.290	.405	.366

Player, Team	G	TPA	AB	R	H	TB	2B	3B	HR	RBI	SH	SF	HP	BB	IBB	SO	SB	CS	GDP	Avg.	OBP	Slg.
Simmons, Colt, Princeton	50	184	146	19	40	51	9	1	0	15	0	0	10	28	1	18	4	5	10	.274	.424	.349
Sims, Justin, Elizabethton *	25	83	76	10	15	22	1	0	2	8	0	2	1	4	0	18	1	1	0	.197	.241	.289
Solano, Roberto, Kingsport	45	181	168	22	36	50	8	3	0	19	1	2	1	9	0	35	10	4	8	.214	.256	.298
Span, Denard, Elizabethton *	50	234	207	34	56	66	5	1	1	18	0	0	4	23	0	34	14	5	2	.271	.355	.319
Spataro, Ryan, Elizabethton *	57	242	205	42	49	66	5	0	4	22	1	1	1	34	0	42	12	3	5	.239	.349	.322
Speigner, Brent, Princeton	37	112	96	6	28	35	7	0	0	9	1	0	6	9	0	27	2	5	1	.292	.387	.365
Sultemeier, Eric, Bluefield	6	22	20	1	4	6	2	0	0	2	0	0	1	1	0	6	0	1	0	.200	.273	.300
Sweeney, Ryan, Bristol *	19	76	67	11	21	30	3	0	2	5	1	0	1	7	0	10	3	0	1	.313	.387	.448
Taylor, Sam, Elizabethton †	52	219	188	35	49	68	9	2	2	26	1	1	2	27	0	26	7	5	2	.261	.358	.362
Thomas, Ben, Danville *	66	266	223	29	55	69	14	0	0	25	2	4	4	29	1	40	7	3	2	.247	.338	.309
Thomas, Nicholas, Pulaski *	50	222	186	36	54	91	14	1	7	39	1	3	2	30	1	47	0	0	1	.290	.389	.489
Thomas, Tee, Johnson City	36	141	125	21	24	42	1	4	3	9	1	1	8	6	0	37	3	0	0	.192	.271	.336
Thurman, Tim, Bluefield	52	205	180	18	45	68	6	1	5	27	0	2	5	18	0	48	0	4	6	.250	.332	.378
Tingler, Jayce, Pulaski *	62	286	223	49	64	82	13	1	1	23	7	4	6	46	0	14	6	2	7	.287	.416	.368
Torres, Saul, Martinsville	57	251	214	40	68	93	19	3	0	25	2	2	6	27	0	33	3	1	4	.318	.406	.435
Valdes, Juan, Burlington †	39	148	130	14	29	37	3	1	1	14	6	2	0	10	0	33	5	3	3	.223	.275	.285
Valido, Robert, Bristol	58	245	215	39	66	103	15	2	6	31	3	5	5	17	0	28	17	6	3	.307	.364	.479
Vancamper, Eugenio, Pul.†	50	196	186	20	48	65	7	2	2	24	0	1	1	8	0	49	3	4	7	.258	.291	.349
Vasquez, Domingo, Burl.	60	244	221	18	49	65	10	0	2	29	0	4	2	17	1	44	0	1	5	.222	.279	.294
Vital, Kevin, Martinsville *	46	192	155	25	36	54	12	0	2	22	1	2	2	32	2	49	3	0	3	.232	.366	.348
Wallace, James, Kingsport	21	76	65	8	13	25	3	0	3	5	0	0	1	10	0	30	0	0	2	.200	.316	.385
Wareham, Landon, Bluefield	32	111	95	12	20	26	3	0	1	2	6	0	1	9	0	28	2	1	1	.211	.286	.274
Webber, Levi, Johnson City	47	181	160	19	30	48	6	0	4	23	0	3	1	17	0	48	1	0	4	.188	.265	.300
Wells, Cory, Kingsport	15	40	36	5	5	6	1	0	0	2	0	0	0	4	0	8	4	2	2	.139	.225	.167
White, Dean, Danville	54	194	172	24	39	47	6	1	0	11	3	3	4	12	0	56	16	6	1	.227	.288	.273
Wilson, Andrew, Kingsport	10	38	35	5	12	18	3	0	1	7	0	0	1	2	0	5	0	1	2	.343	.395	.514
Wilson, Laron, Kingsport	3	12	11	2	3	4	1	0	0	1	0	0	1	0	0	5	0	0	0	.273	.333	.364
Wolfe, Joey, Pulaski *	32	129	102	20	32	56	6	0	6	28	0	0	6	21	1	21	0	1	1	.314	.457	.549
Woodruff, Ernest, Princeton	34	114	102	13	24	31	4	0	1	12	0	2	0	10	0	29	1	1	1	.235	.298	.304
Woodson, Mike, Burlington	26	93	84	11	18	26	5	0	1	7	1	1	2	5	0	24	1	0	2	.214	.272	.310
Wootan, Tanner, J.C.†	53	226	207	27	56	76	8	0	4	28	1	4	0	14	0	39	0	3	2	.271	.311	.367
Yarbrough, Brandon, J.C.*	13	44	42	1	10	14	2	1	0	10	0	0	0	2	0	17	0	0	0	.238	.273	.333
Young, Chris, Bristol	64	273	238	47	69	114	18	3	7	28	3	4	4	23	0	40	21	7	0	.290	.357	.479
Young, Eddie, Bristol	26	94	83	12	20	30	5	1	1	11	0	0	3	8	0	13	5	2	0	.241	.330	.361

GRAND SLAMS—Colin, Frisella, Gilhooly, Shafer, N. Thomas, 1 each.

AWARDED FIRST BASE ON CATCHER'S INTERFERENCE—B. Thomas 4 (H. Guerrero, Reynoso, Simmons, B. Speigner); Barden (Purkey); Camacho (Arias); Cumberland (H. Guerrero); C. Young (Barden).

2003 PITCHING

TEAM

Team	W	L	Pct.	ERA	G	CG	ShO	Sv.	IP	H	TBF	R	ER	HR	SH	SF	HB	BB	IBB	SO	WP	Bk.
Elizabethton	42	24	.636	3.13	66	0	8	12	554.2	470	2347	244	193	25	7	14	25	219	6	581	53	5
Danville	36	30	.545	3.29	66	0	2	19	576.1	535	2463	276	211	20	21	19	31	212	3	514	47	8
Martinsville	42	23	.646	3.54	65	0	2	25	556.1	512	2407	274	219	25	20	17	50	215	2	507	55	6
Burlington	37	31	.544	3.71	68	0	6	15	602.1	562	2602	293	248	23	16	12	54	229	0	592	50	6
Bristol	33	33	.500	3.99	66	1	8	13	550.1	536	2393	291	244	31	15	16	27	218	15	524	44	18
Bluefield	23	40	.365	4.00	63	0	4	10	535.1	540	2354	286	238	32	19	15	42	196	1	467	54	8
Princeton	23	41	.359	4.43	64	1	2	10	524.2	549	2385	350	258	36	19	36	43	250	4	415	84	8
Kingsport	25	39	.391	4.47	64	0	2	16	536.0	549	2354	329	266	38	16	25	48	190	0	489	54	10
Johnson City	27	36	.429	4.70	64	3	3	15	535.2	601	2420	367	280	48	15	26	38	200	3	377	46	4
Pulaski	38	29	.567	4.74	68	1	2	19	572.0	642	2581	386	301	45	20	16	43	218	5	413	60	6

INDIVIDUAL

TOP QUALIFIERS FOR EARNED-RUN AVERAGE TITLE

Minimum 54 innings.*Lefthanded pitcher.

Pitcher, Team	W	L	Pct.	ERA	G	GS	CG	ShO	GF	Sv.	IP	H	TBF	R	ER	HR	SH	SF	HB	BB	IBB	SO	WP	Bk.
Perez, Rafael, Burlington *	9	3	.750	1.70	13	12	0	0	0	0	69.0	56	277	23	13	1	2	0	5	16	0	63	4	0
Pesco, Nick, Burlington	3	1	.750	1.82	13	13	0	0	0	0	54.1	36	221	16	11	0	0	2	5	22	0	55	3	1
Schutt, Christopher, Eliz.	5	2	.714	1.98	11	10	0	0	0	0	54.2	37	225	23	12	0	1	1	1	21	0	72	15	1
Perez, Carlos, Bluefield *	5	5	.500	2.01	12	11	0	0	1	0	58.1	52	240	23	13	4	2	3	0	11	0	58	4	0
Petit, Yusmeiro, Kingsport	3	3	.500	2.32	12	12	0	0	0	0	62.0	47	230	19	16	2	1	2	4	8	0	65	1	0
Douglass, Chance, Mar.	5	1	.833	2.34	10	10	0	0	0	0	57.2	50	222	17	15	1	0	0	5	10	0	48	3	0
Martinez, Ronnie, Martinsville	6	4	.600	2.39	12	12	0	0	0	0	64.0	61	269	29	17	3	1	3	4	11	0	56	2	0
Talbot, Mitch, Martinsville	4	4	.500	2.83	12	12	0	0	0	0	54.0	45	223	26	17	1	4	1	6	11	0	46	1	0
Collins, Danny, Danville *	1	6	.143	2.87	14	14	0	0	0	0	62.2	63	264	32	20	1	1	3	1	19	0	47	0	0
MacLane, Evan, Kingsport *	4	1	.800	2.88	14	6	0	0	4	0	56.1	59	231	20	18	4	2	2	1	8	0	57	5	1
Tisch, Tim, Bristol *	3	5	.375	3.13	11	11	1	1	0	0	60.1	52	246	21	21	4	3	0	1	21	1	44	3	0
Cevette, Dan, Burlington *	2	5	.286	3.45	13	13	0	0	0	0	57.1	58	255	27	22	3	0	1	3	29	0	48	4	1
Aguero, Miguel, Johnson City	4	5	.444	3.69	12	12	1	1	0	0	70.2	76	301	39	29	3	2	1	1	25	0	46	4	0
Suarez, Sony, Bristol	2	4	.333	3.70	16	6	0	0	3	1	56.0	49	234	26	23	4	1	1	3	16	1	59	1	5
Berroa, Yesson, Pulaski	6	2	.750	3.86	13	13	0	0	0	0	63.0	72	274	36	27	2	0	2	6	20	0	39	6	0

DEPARTMENTAL LEADERS: W—R. Perez, 9; L—Caughey, 7; Pct.—Meek, .875; G—Acosta, 28; GS—Collins, 14; CG—Several pitchers tied with 1; ShO—Aguero, Tisch, 1; GF—Day, 24; Sv.—Day, 12; IP—Aguero, 70.2; H—Aguero, 76; TBF—Aguero, 301; R—Rengel, 42; ER—Blanton, J. Perez, Rengel, 32; HR—Neylan, 9; SH—Acosta, 5; SF—Blanton, Van Gorder, 5; HB—Canizal, Chavez, Paulino, 8; BB—Mead, 31; IBB—Several pitchers tied with 2; SO—Schutt, 72; WP—Schutt, 15; BK—Morton, Novoa, Suarez, 5.

ALL PITCHERS

*Lefthanded pitcher.

Pitcher, Team	W	L	Pct.	ERA	G	GS	CG	ShO	GF	Sv.	IP	H	TBF	R	ER	HR	SH	SF	HB	BB	IBB	SO	WP	Bk.
Acosta, Richal, Bluefield	2	6	.250	4.06	28	1	0	0	23	6	31.0	32	132	17	14	2	5	2	1	7	0	30	2	2
Aguero, Miguel, Johnson City	4	5	.444	3.69	12	12	1	1	0	0	70.2	76	301	39	29	3	2	1	1	25	0	46	4	0
Alfonzo, Edgar, Kingsport *	0	0	.000	3.48	8	0	0	0	4	0	10.1	12	46	4	4	1	0	0	0	3	0	4	0	0
Almenar, Aristides, Kingsport	3	5	.375	4.59	13	9	0	0	3	0	49.0	56	220	30	25	4	3	3	5	18	0	34	5	0
Amador, Jonathan, Burlington	0	0	.000	4.26	16	0	0	0	10	0	19.0	16	90	10	9	0	0	1	3	14	0	22	6	0
Arguello, Douglas, Mar.*	4	0	1.000	5.26	17	0	0	0	7	2	25.2	25	112	16	15	2	0	0	3	10	0	17	1	0
Ashabraner, Robert, Burl.	2	1	.667	6.06	17	0	0	0	10	2	16.1	20	79	11	11	2	1	0	3	7	0	18	2	1
Azze, Justin, Bluefield *	0	2	.000	3.07	20	1	0	0	8	1	29.1	21	121	11	10	1	2	2	2	12	0	23	2	1
Banks, Demetrius, Bristol *	1	1	.500	6.85	15	0	0	0	4	0	22.1	25	116	22	17	2	1	0	3	18	2	28	5	3
Barthmaier, James, Mar.	1	1	.500	2.49	8	3	0	0	0	0	21.2	19	93	9	6	0	0	0	2	7	0	18	2	0
Basner, Ryan, Danville	4	1	.800	1.83	19	0	0	0	3	1	44.1	29	176	15	9	0	2	1	2	11	0	50	1	0
Beltre, Elvin, Kingsport	0	0	.000	8.31	4	0	0	0	1	0	4.1	5	24	4	4	0	0	0	1	5	0	2	0	0
Berroa, Yesson, Pulaski	6	2	.750	3.86	13	13	0	0	0	0	63.0	72	274	36	27	2	0	2	6	20	0	39	6	0
Blackmon, Cory, Danville *	3	2	.600	4.11	21	0	0	0	2	0	35.0	29	153	25	16	2	1	1	2	19	0	27	3	1
Blakeney, Jacob, Danville	3	1	.750	1.24	24	0	0	0	15	9	36.1	25	137	6	5	0	3	3	2	5	0	37	4	0
Blanton, Matt, Johnson City *	5	5	.500	5.14	13	10	0	0	1	0	56.0	65	249	38	32	7	4	5	2	14	0	44	2	0
Bonnell, Jared, Johnson City	0	0	.000	6.23	4	0	0	0	0	0	4.1	5	19	4	3	0	0	2	0	3	0	3	0	0
Brandon, Eric, Elizabethton	1	1	.500	2.14	20	0	0	0	4	0	33.2	28	135	10	8	2	1	0	0	8	1	31	1	0
Brewer, Jeff, Kingsport	0	2	.000	7.71	5	0	0	0	1	0	4.2	6	24	4	4	1	1	0	0	4	0	4	0	1
Brown, Darrius, Bluefield *	0	0	.000	27.00	4	0	0	0	0	0	2.0	6	17	6	6	0	0	0	0	6	0	3	6	0
Brubaker, Douglas, Bluefield	4	3	.571	5.52	22	0	0	0	6	0	31.0	29	148	20	19	3	2	0	7	19	0	33	3	0
Burch, Jason, Johnson City	0	1	.000	1.53	17	0	0	0	16	10	17.2	13	71	7	3	2	0	0	1	1	0	25	2	0
Cahill, Casey, Bluefield	0	0	.000	9.00	2	0	0	0	0	0	1.0	2	6	1	1	0	0	0	0	1	0	3	1	0
Canizal, Joaquin, Pulaski	2	3	.400	4.38	27	0	0	0	12	2	39.0	39	183	30	19	4	2	3	8	19	1	32	4	0
Casey, James, Bristol	2	2	.500	4.28	10	6	0	0	1	1	40.0	35	164	19	19	1	1	1	1	15	2	41	1	0
Castro, Fabio, Bristol *	6	2	.750	1.72	19	0	0	0	10	2	47.0	29	190	14	9	1	1	1	1	19	1	59	6	2
Caughey, Trevor, Bluefield *	1	7	.125	4.84	13	12	0	0	0	0	57.2	67	264	41	31	5	1	1	4	20	0	64	8	2
Cevette, Dan, Burlington *	2	5	.286	3.45	13	13	0	0	0	0	57.1	58	255	27	22	3	0	1	3	29	0	48	4	1
Chavez, Miguel, Johnson City	0	3	.000	7.71	17	3	0	0	2	1	30.1	45	159	32	26	5	2	3	8	16	0	14	2	1
Cobb, Matt, Princeton *	2	1	.667	3.34	18	1	0	0	8	1	35.0	34	155	15	13	5	0	4	3	15	1	39	5	1
Collins, Danny, Danville *	1	6	.143	2.87	14	14	0	0	0	0	62.2	63	264	32	20	1	1	3	1	19	0	47	0	0
Culpepper, Kevin, Eliz.*	4	1	.800	3.86	16	5	0	0	2	0	42.0	37	177	19	18	3	0	2	6	18	1	44	1	0
Curreri, Joe, Bristol	0	0	.000	12.27	3	0	0	0	0	0	3.2	6	18	5	5	1	0	1	0	2	0	3	0	0
Dalton, Matthew, Pulaski	3	1	.750	3.00	18	0	0	0	9	1	27.0	36	123	10	9	0	2	2	2	5	1	27	1	0
Davis, Cliff, Martinsville	1	0	1.000	7.50	12	1	0	0	0	0	18.0	13	79	15	15	1	1	0	0	17	0	13	2	0
Day, Dewon, Pulaski	2	0	1.000	1.80	26	0	0	0	24	12	30.0	21	127	8	6	0	1	0	3	9	0	26	1	0
De Aza, Fernando, Bristol	2	2	.500	3.42	12	9	0	0	1	0	47.1	51	201	22	18	4	1	3	0	16	0	28	6	0
De La Cruz, Eduardo, Prin.	1	3	.250	5.66	9	4	0	0	0	0	20.2	22	94	15	13	3	1	1	2	13	0	14	2	0
De La Cruz, Jose, Princeton	0	2	.000	1.33	15	1	0	0	7	1	27.0	25	115	8	4	1	2	2	1	9	0	15	4	0
De Los Santos, Richard, Burl.	3	4	.429	6.41	12	0	0	0	4	1	39.1	45	173	32	28	3	1	1	3	10	0	40	4	0
DeJaynes, Brandon, J.C.	5	1	.833	1.10	25	0	0	0	10	1	32.2	24	139	9	4	0	1	2	4	13	1	27	2	1
DePaula, Julio, Elizabethton	2	3	.400	1.71	22	0	0	0	17	5	26.1	19	106	7	5	1	0	2	1	8	2	24	2	0
Diaz, Raymar, Martinsville	4	0	1.000	0.90	19	0	0	0	12	5	30.0	17	124	4	3	1	3	1	2	13	0	29	7	0
Douglass, Chance, Mar.	5	1	.833	2.34	10	10	0	0	0	0	57.2	50	222	17	15	1	0	0	5	10	0	48	3	0
Dupas, Greg, Princeton	2	2	.500	5.06	10	2	0	0	3	0	21.1	20	95	14	12	3	1	3	1	13	0	22	5	0
Elliott, Adam, Kingsport	1	0	1.000	15.75	5	0	0	0	0	0	8.0	16	45	14	14	3	0	1	1	6	0	9	2	0
Estrada, Paul, Martinsville	1	0	1.000	5.48	12	1	0	0	1	1	21.1	19	107	17	13	2	1	1	2	22	0	25	4	0
Farr, Whitt, Danville	4	0	1.000	2.19	23	1	0	0	5	0	49.1	46	204	16	12	0	2	3	3	10	0	42	2	1
Flores, Rafael, Bristol	3	5	.375	3.27	16	5	0	0	4	0	41.1	49	191	27	15	1	0	0	1	12	2	34	2	1
Foster, Matt, Pulaski *	1	0	1.000	4.05	3	0	0	0	0	0	6.2	3	28	3	3	1	0	0	0	3	0	10	0	0
Freites, Julio, Kingsport	2	2	.500	3.54	13	0	0	0	4	1	20.1	23	95	12	8	1	1	0	1	10	0	22	5	4
Fry, Troy, Kingsport	2	1	.667	4.00	16	0	0	0	7	1	27.0	34	127	20	12	2	0	0	4	8	0	22	2	0
Garay, Kelvin, Kingsport *	0	0	.000	3.60	5	0	0	0	3	0	5.0	5	24	3	2	0	0	0	1	4	0	4	2	0
Garcia, Angel, Elizabethton	2	1	.667	2.89	9	9	0	0	0	0	37.1	37	165	18	12	5	1	1	1	18	0	44	2	0
Garza, Justin, Johnson City	3	0	1.000	1.71	21	0	0	0	9	2	26.1	21	101	10	5	0	0	2	0	6	0	25	0	0
Geddes, Michael, Princeton	1	0	1.000	4.91	8	0	0	0	3	1	11.0	8	51	10	6	0	0	1	2	5	0	15	5	0
Gomez, Jose, Kingsport	0	4	.000	5.10	11	7	0	0	1	0	30.0	28	136	21	17	5	1	1	4	18	0	34	5	1
Gomez, Luis, Johnson City	0	1	.000	11.37	17	0	0	0	7	1	19.0	31	103	34	24	7	0	2	1	12	0	15	4	1
Gonzalez, Jino, Princeton *	2	1	.667	2.00	3	1	0	0	0	0	9.0	5	37	6	2	0	0	0	1	1	0	10	2	0
Gonzalez, Marino, Kingsport	0	2	.000	8.56	8	2	0	0	2	0	13.2	19	67	15	13	1	0	1	0	10	0	17	2	1
Grant, Brian, Pulaski	2	5	.286	4.80	13	13	0	0	0	0	54.1	64	258	40	29	3	3	1	4	27	1	40	7	3
Gray, Joshua, Elizabethton *	0	0	.000	0.00	6	0	0	0	0	0	10.2	3	37	1	0	0	0	0	0	2	0	10	2	0
Grimes, Sean, Pulaski *	0	0	.000	2.70	4	0	0	0	2	0	3.1	4	13	1	1	0	0	0	0	0	0	0	0	0
Gutierrez, Juan, Martinsville	1	2	.333	4.76	16	3	0	0	4	2	34.0	42	162	22	18	2	1	4	5	13	1	30	7	1
Guzman, Angel, Burlington	1	1	.500	3.00	17	0	0	0	9	1	30.0	26	138	11	10	2	1	1	3	17	0	36	1	0
Guzman, Henry, Princeton *	0	0	.000	23.14	2	0	0	0	1	0	2.1	3	15	6	6	1	0	0	1	5	0	0	1	0
Hader, Ryan, Elizabethton *	1	2	.333	2.89	19	0	0	0	2	0	28.0	15	124	11	9	1	1	0	2	24	1	39	5	1
Harrison, Benjamin, Pulaski *	1	0	1.000	10.80	12	0	0	0	3	1	16.2	17	91	23	20	3	0	0	1	21	0	13	8	0
Haynes, Matt, Burlington	1	0	1.000	2.50	17	0	0	0	3	2	36.0	25	165	11	10	1	1	0	4	29	0	57	5	0
Henkenjohann, Tim, Eliz.	0	0	.000	8.22	8	0	0	0	3	0	7.2	6	40	7	7	2	0	0	1	10	0	11	2	1
Hiraldo, Nelson, Burlington	6	1	.857	3.81	12	6	0	0	2	0	52.0	48	216	23	22	3	1	2	3	11	0	52	6	1
Hoey, James, Bluefield	2	3	.400	2.79	11	8	0	0	0	0	42.0	33	177	19	13	3	0	0	6	19	0	20	2	0
Hoffmann, Brett, Johnson City	0	4	.000	5.32	15	6	1	0	1	0	47.1	59	217	36	28	5	2	1	2	17	0	24	5	0
Houser, James, Princeton *	0	4	.000	3.73	10	10	0	0	0	0	41.0	43	182	23	17	1	1	2	2	13	0	44	5	0
Huchingson, Jamin, Bristol	0	1	.000	16.43	7	0	0	0	4	0	7.2	14	52	16	14	0	0	1	3	11	0	2	3	0
Iida, Hiroyuki, Elizabethton	1	0	1.000	4.80	18	1	0	0	3	0	30.0	36	140	22	16	2	0	2	2	9	1	25	1	0
James, Chuck, Danville *	2	1	.667	1.25	11	11	0	0	0	0	50.1	26	193	9	7	1	2	0	0	19	0	68	2	0
Johnson, James, Bluefield	3	2	.600	3.68	11	11	0	0	0	0	51.1	62	237	24	21	2	0	2	4	18	0	46	4	1

Pitcher, Team	W	L	Pct.	ERA	G	GS	CG	ShO	GF	Sv.	IP	H	TBF	R	ER	HR	SH	SF	HB	BB	IBB	SO	WP	Bk.
King, Timothy, Princeton *	0	5	.000	5.65	14	5	0	0	3	0	36.2	37	174	31	23	1	1	3	6	25	0	30	1	1
Kopszywa, Nate, Johnson City	1	1	.500	5.94	12	2	0	0	0	0	16.2	20	83	13	11	0	1	0	2	11	0	6	2	0
Krause, Lukas, Kingsport *	0	0	.000	0.00	3	0	0	0	0	0	5.0	4	22	3	0	0	0	1	0	2	0	6	0	0
Laffey, Aaron, Burlington *	3	1	.750	2.91	9	4	0	0	1	0	34.0	22	143	13	11	0	0	1	7	15	0	46	4	1
Lavergne, Jarrad, Princeton *	4	2	.667	4.28	11	10	0	0	0	0	54.2	69	246	35	26	4	3	3	2	19	0	23	5	1
Little, Jeffrey, Bristol	1	1	.500	12.60	3	0	0	0	1	0	5.0	9	27	8	7	1	0	0	0	3	1	9	2	0
Lopez, Orionny, Bristol	5	3	.625	2.37	17	0	0	0	7	2	49.1	38	203	18	13	2	4	2	1	18	2	53	3	1
Lopez, Romelio, Princeton	2	6	.250	4.37	11	11	0	0	0	0	57.2	63	260	40	28	6	2	3	5	21	0	48	10	1
Lynch, John, Elizabethton *	0	2	.000	3.22	18	0	0	0	8	2	22.1	21	94	11	8	2	1	3	1	5	0	21	1	0
MacLane, Evan, Kingsport *	4	1	.800	2.88	14	6	0	0	4	0	56.1	59	231	20	18	4	2	2	1	8	0	57	5	1
Malone, Corwin, Bristol *	0	0	.000	5.14	4	4	0	0	0	0	14.0	17	63	8	8	2	0	1	2	3	0	15	0	0
Mann, Brandon, Princeton *	4	2	.667	4.29	11	11	1	0	0	0	63.0	61	276	34	30	2	2	2	3	28	0	46	11	2
Marini, Christopher, Eliz.*	3	1	.750	3.21	13	7	0	0	0	0	33.2	34	149	15	12	1	0	1	0	17	0	27	1	1
Markham, Josh, J.C.*	1	0	1.000	6.94	10	0	0	0	3	0	11.2	19	65	19	9	4	0	1	1	6	0	8	1	1
Marshall, Jay, Bristol *	2	0	1.000	2.61	10	10	0	0	0	0	41.1	38	173	15	12	3	0	0	4	13	0	42	2	0
Marte, Violenny, Martinsville	0	2	.000	5.06	12	0	0	0	9	2	16.0	18	76	9	9	3	2	0	1	6	0	19	2	0
Martinez, Ronnie, Martinsville	6	4	.600	2.39	12	12	0	0	0	0	64.0	61	269	29	17	3	1	3	4	11	0	56	2	0
McClellan, Kyle, Johnson City	3	6	.333	3.99	12	12	0	0	0	0	67.2	74	298	34	30	4	1	1	5	16	1	44	5	0
McGary, Gerron, Bristol *	1	0	1.000	4.82	11	0	0	0	8	0	9.1	4	39	6	5	0	0	1	1	6	0	9	2	0
McKeller, Ryan, Martinsville	3	0	1.000	3.58	15	4	0	0	3	3	37.2	33	161	16	15	4	1	0	4	19	0	46	7	1
McKernan, Richard, Bluefield	0	0	.000	27.00	1	0	0	0	0	0	1.0	2	9	4	3	0	0	0	0	3	0	1	0	0
Mead, Dan, Danville *	0	1	.000	7.43	24	0	0	0	11	0	26.2	28	136	26	22	0	0	2	2	31	1	21	9	0
Medina, Dennis, Elizabethton	3	2	.600	5.88	10	7	0	0	1	0	33.2	30	142	23	22	2	1	1	3	12	0	33	2	0
Meek, Evan, Elizabethton	7	1	.875	2.47	14	8	0	0	3	1	51.0	33	209	15	14	2	0	0	0	24	0	47	6	0
Mendez, Orlin, Johnson City	1	1	.500	4.50	17	0	0	0	8	0	24.0	25	117	17	12	2	1	1	4	18	0	15	5	0
Meyers, Ryan, Kingsport	1	0	1.000	4.50	15	0	0	0	2	0	24.0	29	102	15	12	1	0	1	2	4	0	12	2	0
Miller, Adam, Burlington	0	4	.000	4.96	10	10	0	0	0	0	32.2	30	135	20	18	2	0	1	5	9	0	23	1	0
Mincey, T.W., Bluefield *	0	1	.000	8.10	5	0	0	0	0	0	10.0	15	48	9	9	0	0	1	1	3	0	9	2	0
Miramontes, Matthew, King.	1	4	.200	8.44	6	5	0	0	0	0	21.1	23	102	22	20	1	0	2	5	13	0	16	6	0
Morales, Ruddy, Bristol	1	0	1.000	3.46	5	0	0	0	3	2	13.0	9	53	6	5	1	1	1	1	5	0	9	0	0
Morton, Charles, Danville	2	5	.286	4.67	14	13	0	0	0	0	54.0	65	246	32	28	3	2	3	1	25	0	46	9	5
Mujica, Edward, Burlington	2	6	.250	4.37	14	10	0	0	3	0	55.2	57	231	31	27	3	2	1	1	20	0	41	2	1
Mumma, Brad, Pulaski *	2	1	.667	5.06	5	4	0	0	0	0	21.1	25	95	14	12	1	1	0	1	7	0	21	0	0
Murray, Brad, Bristol *	0	0	.000	1.69	5	0	0	0	1	1	5.1	4	19	1	1	0	0	0	0	0	0	4	0	0
Mutch, Paul, Elizabethton	0	1	.000	3.33	18	1	0	0	2	0	24.1	26	119	16	9	0	0	0	1	18	0	19	2	1
Navarro, Rodolfo, Burlington	3	2	.600	5.79	14	0	0	0	7	1	23.1	36	110	20	15	1	3	0	2	3	0	10	0	0
Nelson, Brad, Danville	8	3	.727	4.15	24	0	0	0	11	2	39.0	47	181	23	18	2	1	0	4	9	2	23	4	1
Neylan, Chris, Pulaski *	5	2	.714	4.25	12	8	0	0	0	0	53.0	67	233	32	25	9	2	2	0	13	0	45	1	0
Nieves, Roberto, Danville	0	2	.000	5.21	14	7	0	0	2	0	38.0	39	171	25	22	4	1	1	1	22	0	51	5	0
Novoa, Yunior, Bristol *	4	4	.500	5.49	11	11	0	0	0	0	41.0	48	184	27	25	4	2	1	2	16	2	35	0	5
Olson, Jordan, Princeton *	2	1	.667	3.18	17	0	0	0	2	0	28.1	20	124	14	10	0	1	3	7	20	0	32	6	0
Ortiz, Dario, Bristol	0	0	.000	5.40	7	0	0	0	4	1	8.1	10	41	6	5	0	0	0	0	4	0	8	0	1
Pals, Jordan, Johnson City	2	2	.500	2.16	8	8	1	0	0	0	41.2	35	167	13	10	3	0	0	2	9	0	24	5	0
Paulino, Felipe, Martinsville	2	2	.500	5.61	16	0	0	0	6	1	25.2	23	126	20	16	0	0	1	8	19	0	27	8	0
Penn, Hayden, Bluefield	1	4	.200	4.30	12	11	0	0	0	0	52.1	58	230	27	25	4	2	0	4	19	0	38	3	0
Peralta, Efigenio, Danville	0	0	.000	1.13	2	2	0	0	0	0	8.0	4	29	3	1	1	0	0	1	2	0	6	0	0
Perez, Carlos, Bluefield *	5	5	.500	2.01	12	11	0	0	1	0	58.1	52	240	23	13	4	2	3	0	11	0	58	4	0
Perez, Juan, Pulaski	4	6	.400	4.48	13	13	0	0	0	0	64.1	71	266	37	32	7	1	2	4	12	0	35	0	1
Perez, Rafael, Burlington *	9	3	.750	1.70	13	12	0	0	0	0	69.0	56	277	23	13	1	2	0	5	16	0	63	4	0
Pesco, Nick, Burlington	3	1	.750	1.82	13	13	0	0	0	0	54.1	36	221	16	11	0	0	2	5	22	0	55	3	1
Petit, Yusmeiro, Kingsport	3	3	.500	2.32	12	12	0	0	0	0	62.0	47	230	19	16	2	1	2	4	8	0	65	1	0
Petrick, Russell, Bluefield *	2	0	1.000	2.81	22	0	0	0	3	0	25.2	23	121	13	8	0	1	1	3	15	0	27	2	0
Pidutti, James, Pulaski *	1	3	.250	5.61	16	1	0	0	6	0	25.2	40	123	23	16	1	2	0	0	9	0	8	7	0
Pollok, Dwayne, Bristol	0	0	.000	3.12	11	0	0	0	10	3	8.2	8	36	3	3	0	0	2	0	4	0	8	0	0
Pomeranz, Stuart, J.C.	1	1	.500	6.14	4	3	0	0	0	0	14.2	13	62	10	10	2	0	0	3	4	0	14	0	0
Potter, Josh, Bluefield	1	4	.200	3.11	18	1	0	0	3	0	37.2	35	159	13	13	2	0	1	1	16	1	27	4	0
Redfern, Chad, Danville	0	1	.000	10.38	4	0	0	0	2	0	4.1	7	21	5	5	1	0	0	0	2	0	2	1	0
Reedy, Shane, Johnson City	1	0	1.000	2.70	2	2	0	0	0	0	10.0	9	44	3	3	0	0	0	0	9	0	3	1	0
Reilly, Christopher, Bluefield	1	1	.500	4.25	16	7	0	0	2	0	42.1	38	175	21	20	3	1	1	3	15	0	35	6	0
Rengel, Orlando, Kingsport	1	5	.167	5.76	12	12	0	0	0	0	50.0	57	231	42	32	6	0	4	2	22	0	38	6	1
Rider, Michael, Pulaski	4	0	1.000	6.52	22	0	0	0	5	2	38.2	44	176	30	28	3	2	0	3	14	2	28	4	0
Rodriguez, Claudio, Princeton	0	1	.000	8.36	15	1	0	0	6	0	14.0	13	73	15	13	0	1	0	2	20	1	12	5	2
Rodriguez, Jayson, Pulaski	1	1	.500	5.94	17	3	0	0	5	1	36.1	42	168	28	24	4	2	0	2	19	0	29	10	0
Rodriguez, Joan, Princeton	0	0	.000	5.51	10	0	0	0	5	0	16.1	16	80	18	10	2	0	1	0	14	0	4	5	0
Rohr, Charles, Princeton	2	1	.667	3.46	6	0	0	0	5	2	13.0	14	56	7	5	0	0	2	0	5	0	10	5	0
Romero, Levi, Martinsville	2	2	.500	4.66	16	0	0	0	8	3	29.0	29	128	16	15	1	2	0	1	14	1	24	0	3
Rondon, Celso, Kingsport	2	2	.500	4.10	19	0	0	0	16	11	26.1	19	112	13	12	1	1	1	3	11	0	44	3	0
Russell, Steve, Danville	3	2	.600	3.71	8	8	0	0	0	0	34.0	25	144	17	14	2	1	2	5	13	0	27	1	0
Sager, Brian, Bristol	0	1	.000	9.00	1	1	0	0	0	0	3.0	3	16	5	3	0	0	0	1	2	0	4	1	0
Salas, Marino, Bluefield	1	2	.333	4.89	23	0	0	0	5	0	35.0	36	150	22	19	1	3	1	4	9	0	27	4	2
Salazar, Julio, Martinsville *	5	2	.714	1.83	10	9	0	0	1	0	44.1	42	191	18	9	1	1	1	2	18	0	34	2	0
Sanchez , Raymon, Pulaski *	1	2	.333	5.68	17	1	0	0	1	0	38.0	45	177	31	24	3	0	3	3	18	0	21	5	2
Santana, Hector, Burlington	0	2	.000	7.40	13	0	0	0	2	1	20.2	23	100	19	17	1	2	0	4	11	0	18	3	0
Santos, Reid, Burlington *	1	0	1.000	4.40	14	0	0	0	5	2	28.2	29	120	15	14	1	1	0	3	6	0	25	4	0
Savickas, Russell, Pulaski	3	3	.500	4.28	12	12	1	0	0	0	54.2	52	246	40	26	4	2	1	6	22	0	39	6	0
Schultz, Jimmy, Burlington	1	0	1.000	4.76	13	0	0	0	5	1	17.0	25	84	10	9	0	0	1	0	7	0	14	1	0
Schutt, Christopher, Eliz.	5	2	.714	1.98	11	10	0	0	0	0	54.2	37	225	23	12	0	1	1	1	21	0	72	15	1
Sides, Andrew, Kingsport	0	3	.000	3.61	10	10	0	0	0	0	42.1	32	170	21	17	3	3	2	1	9	0	39	1	0
Simonitsch, Errol, Eliz.*	5	1	.833	1.76	10	8	0	0	1	0	46.0	39	185	13	9	1	0	0	2	6	0	57	6	0
Smith, Cole, Princeton	1	6	.143	5.57	8	7	0	0	0	0	32.1	34	152	28	20	2	2	4	4	17	0	23	2	0
Smith, Dan, Danville *	0	0	.000	5.40	2	0	0	0	0	0	1.2	3	11	1	1	0	1	0	0	3	0	2	1	0

Pitcher, Team	W	L	Pct.	ERA	G	GS	CG	ShO	GF	Sv.	IP	H	TBF	R	ER	HR	SH	SF	HB	BB	IBB	SO	WP	Bk.
Smith, David, Kingsport *	0	1	.000	4.15	5	0	0	0	3	0	4.1	2	17	2	2	0	0	0	1	2	0	5	0	0
Soler, Jose, Martinsville	0	0	.000	4.12	14	0	0	0	9	2	19.2	17	94	10	9	0	1	3	2	15	0	21	3	1
Soteropoulos, Peter, J.C.*	0	1	.000	0.00	9	0	0	0	2	0	9.2	9	37	2	0	0	0	0	0	1	0	5	1	0
Southerland, Chip, Burlington	0	0	.000	0.53	12	0	0	0	7	4	17.0	10	65	1	1	0	1	0	0	3	0	24	0	0
Speigner, Brent, Princeton	0	0	.000	0.00	1	0	0	0	1	0	0.2	0	4	0	0	0	0	0	0	2	0	0	3	0
Speigner, Jimmy, Elizabethton	5	2	.714	3.94	22	0	0	0	19	4	29.2	31	122	13	13	1	0	0	1	4	0	35	2	0
Spivey, Melvin, Bluefield	0	0	.000	3.38	5	0	0	0	1	1	8.0	8	35	4	3	1	0	0	1	1	0	9	1	0
Stefano, Frank, Kingsport *	4	2	.667	4.98	15	0	0	0	3	0	21.2	28	108	18	12	0	2	1	3	8	0	14	3	0
Stewart, Josh, Bristol *	0	0	.000	0.00	2	2	0	0	0	0	6.0	5	24	0	0	0	0	0	0	2	0	5	1	0
Suarez, Sony, Bristol	2	4	.333	3.70	16	6	0	0	3	1	56.0	49	234	26	23	4	1	1	3	16	1	59	1	5
Sutton, Zach, Bluefield	0	0	.000	4.58	18	0	0	0	11	2	19.2	21	85	11	10	1	0	0	1	2	0	14	0	0
Talbot, Mitch, Martinsville	4	4	.500	2.83	12	12	0	0	0	0	54.0	45	223	26	17	1	4	1	6	11	0	46	1	0
Thompson, Sean, Bristol *	0	1	.000	3.24	6	1	0	0	2	0	16.2	21	77	6	6	0	0	0	2	8	0	21	3	0
Tisch, Tim, Bristol *	3	5	.375	3.13	11	11	1	1	0	0	60.1	52	246	21	21	4	3	0	1	21	1	44	3	0
Torres, David, Kingsport	1	2	.333	3.33	15	0	0	0	3	1	27.0	26	117	13	10	1	0	0	2	7	0	25	1	1
Travis, Matt, Princeton *	0	4	.000	2.94	20	0	0	0	19	5	33.2	48	160	22	11	1	2	2	0	4	2	24	1	0
Tucker, Glen, Danville	3	2	.600	3.47	25	0	0	0	13	6	36.1	41	155	18	14	2	3	0	1	3	0	30	1	0
Uhl, Jon, Elizabethton	3	4	.429	3.92	11	10	0	0	1	0	43.2	38	178	20	19	0	1	1	3	15	0	42	2	0
Van Gorder, Joe, J.C.*	0	3	.000	10.21	11	4	0	0	2	0	27.1	43	143	37	31	4	1	5	2	14	0	30	5	0
Van Ruiten, Danny, Princeton	0	0	.000	11.57	5	0	0	0	0	0	7.0	14	36	9	9	4	0	0	1	1	0	4	1	0
Vergara, Alan, Martinsville	3	3	.500	4.21	15	10	0	0	5	4	57.2	59	240	30	27	3	2	2	3	10	0	54	4	0
Wasserman, Ehren, Bristol	0	1	.000	14.73	4	0	0	0	2	0	3.2	9	22	6	6	0	0	0	0	3	1	4	3	0
Weagle, Matt, Johnson City	0	1	.000	11.25	5	2	0	0	0	0	8.0	15	45	10	10	0	0	0	0	5	1	5	0	0
Weichard, Paul, Danville *	0	0	.000	0.00	4	0	0	0	0	0	5.0	5	23	1	0	0	0	0	1	3	0	3	0	0
Weitzman, William, Kingsport	0	0	.000	4.63	17	1	0	0	7	2	23.1	19	104	14	12	1	1	3	7	10	0	16	3	0
White, Sean, Danville	3	3	.500	2.98	14	10	0	0	2	1	51.1	53	219	22	17	1	1	0	5	16	0	32	4	0

COMBINATION SHUTOUTS: Bluefield (4)—Penn-Brubaker-Sutton, Perez-Petrick-Acosta, Hoey-Azze-Acosta, Perez-Brubaker-Potter. Bristol (7)—DeAza-Suarez-Lopez, Casey-Lopez-Murray-McGary, Suarez-McGary-Castro, Novoa-Castro, Tisch-McGary, Thompson-Castro, Suarez-Banks-Lopez. Burlington (6)—Mujica-Santana-Guzman, Mujica-Haynes-Guzman, Pesco-DeLosSantos, Cevette-Guzman-Amador-Schultz, Perez-Santos, Perez-Haynes-Guzman. Danville (2)—James-Farr-Tucker, Nieves-Blackmon-Blakeney. Elizabethton (8)—Schutt-Gray-Brandon, Medina-Mutch-Hader-Speigner, Simonitsch-Iida-Hader-Mutch-Lynch, Simonitsch-Brandon-Speigner-Hader, Medina-DePaula-Lynch, Meek-Lynch-Speigner, Schutt-Hader-Mutch-Culpepper, Meek-Brandon-DePaula-Speigner. Johnson City (2)—McClellan-Garza-Burch, Weagle-Blanton-Markham. Kingsport (2)—Gomez-Fry-Rondon, Petit-Freites-Rondon. Martinsville (2)—Salazar-Diaz, Martinez-Romero-Diaz. Princeton (2)—Houser-Cobb, DeLaCruz-Dupas-Van Ruiten-Travis. Pulaski (2)—Berroa-Harrison-Day, Grant-Canizal-Rodriguez.

NO-HIT GAMES: Tisch, Bristol, defeated Johnson City, 2-0 (first game), July 10.

2003 FIELDING

TEAM

Team	G	PO	A	E	TC	DP	TP	PB	Pct.
Bristol	66	1651	647	86	2384	46	0	21	.964
Burlington	68	1807	709	93	2609	41	0	17	.964
Danville	66	1729	683	93	2505	51	0	15	.963
Kingsport	64	1608	543	90	2241	41	0	19	.960
Elizabethton	66	1664	675	103	2442	47	0	15	.958
Pulaski	68	1716	784	110	2610	63	0	15	.958
Bluefield	63	1606	636	101	2343	49	0	10	.957
Martinsville	65	1669	699	109	2477	58	0	13	.956
Johnson City	64	1604	702	117	2423	62	0	21	.952
Princeton	64	1574	632	127	2333	49	0	18	.946

INDIVIDUAL

FIRST BASEMEN

NOTE: All caps denotes fielding-percentage leader based on 34 games for catchers, 45 for all other non-pitchers and 54 innings for pitchers. *Throws lefthanded.

Player, Team	Pct.	G	PO	A	E	TC	DP
Barthel, Cole, Danville	1.000	1	8	0	0	8	0
Beech, Travis, Princeton	1.000	1	2	0	0	2	0
Blanton, Stephen, Bluefield	.989	11	87	6	1	94	6
Bohlander, Michael, Bristol	.996	34	211	18	1	230	20
Bolen, Josh, Princeton	.967	5	29	0	1	30	1
Camacho, Johan, Kingsport	.992	51	354	30	3	387	33
Castillo, Cesar, Bristol	1.000	1	1	0	0	1	0
Collaro, Thomas, Bristol	.989	23	171	9	2	182	18
Costello, Michael, Bluefield	1.000	3	21	3	0	24	3
Davidson, Tyler, Kingsport	1.000	7	49	3	0	52	2
Davie, Andrew, Johnson City	.983	24	218	11	4	233	20
Donato, Greg, Danville	.991	11	111	4	1	116	2
Garcia, Antonio, Martinsville	.990	26	181	16	2	199	13
George, Kyle, Bluefield	1.000	3	8	0	0	8	0
Gomon, Dusty, Elizabethton	.993	49	405	32	3	440	33
Gomon, Dusty, Elizabethton	.993	49	405	32	3	440	33
Harper, Brett, Kingsport	1.000	2	4	0	0	4	0
Herring, Matt, Bristol *	1.000	1	2	0	0	2	0
Mannix, Brendan, Kingsport	1.000	2	10	2	0	12	1
Nichols, Thomas, Princeton	.981	49	394	21	8	423	37
Pacheco, Fernando, Burlington *	.985	53	426	28	7	461	30
Perez, Melvin, Bristol	.969	9	51	11	2	64	2
Peterson, Brock, Elizabethton	1.000	1	6	3	0	9	1
Phillips, Kyle, Elizabethton	.980	17	136	11	3	150	8
Ponce, Arnoldo, Pulaski	.992	14	113	6	1	120	12
Pyzik, Steve, Danville	1.000	1	5	0	0	5	0
Reiman, Joey, Pulaski	.997	38	359	30	1	390	35
Rios, Kevin, Kingsport	1.000	1	7	3	0	10	0
Rodriguez, Manuel, Bristol	1.000	10	72	8	0	80	1
Saltalamacchia, Justin, Danville	.980	5	46	3	1	50	8
SCHADE, SCOTT, Danville	.993	51	395	16	3	414	35
Schutzenhofer, Andy, J.C.*	.994	37	312	31	2	345	34
Simmons, Colt, Princeton	1.000	5	33	1	0	34	0
Speigner, Brent, Princeton	.987	8	69	5	1	75	5
Thomas, Nicholas, Pulaski	.971	18	159	9	5	173	12
Thurman, Tim, Bluefield	.972	52	441	13	13	467	34
Vasquez, Domingo, Burlington	.994	19	151	17	1	169	9
Vital, Kevin, Martinsville	.990	41	354	24	4	382	38
Webber, Levi, Johnson City	1.000	6	45	5	0	50	5
Wilson, Laron, Kingsport	1.000	2	20	0	0	20	1

SECOND BASEMEN

Player, Team	Pct.	G	PO	A	E	TC	DP
Acey, Jermy, Pulaski	.938	26	40	80	8	128	18
Arneson, Justin, Elizabethton	.943	39	58	90	9	157	13
Babilonia, Edgar, Martinsville	.990	21	44	57	1	102	14
Beech, Travis, Princeton	.943	14	22	28	3	53	7
Brown, Travis, Bluefield	1.000	2	1	0	0	1	0
Cabral, Marcos, Kingsport	.934	17	23	34	4	61	8
Clem, Chris, Burlington	1.000	16	27	31	0	58	7
Colina, Luis, Johnson City	.975	42	65	128	5	198	26
COOPER, CHAD, Princeton	.967	51	82	120	7	209	25
Corapci, Jason, Martinsville	.933	3	4	10	1	15	1
Dulaney, Todd, Kingsport	.925	33	50	74	10	134	14
Fermin, Angelo, Elizabethton	.971	16	27	41	2	70	13
Garcia, Julio, Burlington	.965	20	40	43	3	86	7
Garcia, Travis, Kingsport	.882	5	6	9	2	17	4
George, Kyle, Bluefield	1.000	3	4	3	0	7	3
Gonzalez, Humberto, Kingsport	.958	8	9	14	1	24	1
Guerrero, Francisco, Bluefield	.895	3	9	8	2	19	2
Hanson, Mike, Danville	.961	46	95	125	9	229	27
James, Willie, Danville	.955	22	50	55	5	110	13
Koenig, Lance, Martinsville	.929	43	79	103	14	196	24

Player, Team	Pct.	G	PO	A	E	TC	DP
Lebron, Freddie, Bristol	.973	29	50	58	3	111	17
Luna, Leonardo, Bristol	.947	22	27	63	5	95	8
Mannix, Brendan, Kingsport	1.000	3	3	3	0	6	0
Mendez, Valentin, Martinsville	1.000	2	2	3	0	5	0
Molina, Felix, Elizabethton	.959	11	18	29	2	49	4
Morel, Elvis, Bluefield	.951	33	56	98	8	162	16
Paredes, Salvador, Princeton	1.000	1	3	4	0	7	1
Perez, Angel, Johnson City	.935	12	18	25	3	46	6
Perez, Melvin, Bristol	1.000	2	7	3	0	10	1
Ramirez, Estevinson, Bristol	.949	18	16	40	3	59	5
Reyes, Argenis, Burlington	.946	39	61	96	9	166	11
Rios, Kevin, Kingsport	1.000	4	9	12	0	21	4
Schade, Scott, Danville	1.000	1	1	1	0	2	0
Schlichting, Travis, Princeton	1.000	1	2	0	0	2	1
Sena, Emmanuel, Pulaski	.968	39	68	112	6	186	27
Thomas, Tee, Johnson City	.897	13	11	24	4	39	3
Vancamper, Eugenio, Pulaski	.938	4	6	9	1	16	2
Wareham, Landon, Bluefield	.967	26	44	73	4	121	13
Wootan, Tanner, Johnson City	.964	10	21	32	2	55	7

THIRD BASEMEN

Player, Team	Pct.	G	PO	A	E	TC	DP
Babilonia, Edgar, Martinsville	.833	3	3	7	2	12	1
Barthel, Cole, Danville	.800	3	2	2	1	5	0
Barton, Daric, Johnson City	1.000	6	5	11	0	16	1
Beech, Travis, Princeton	.877	17	14	36	7	57	5
Bowman, Shawn, Kingsport	.966	10	11	17	1	29	3
Clem, Chris, Burlington	.879	30	13	45	8	66	0
Colina, Luis, Johnson City	.912	12	9	22	3	34	1
Corapci, Jason, Martinsville	.867	6	4	9	2	15	0
Dufner, Kris, Princeton	.806	11	9	20	7	36	3
Esposito, Vincent, Pulaski	.857	32	21	63	14	98	4
Fermin, Angelo, Elizabethton	.900	5	1	8	1	10	0
Garcia, Julio, Burlington	1.000	4	1	3	0	4	0
Garcia, Travis, Kingsport	1.000	7	7	9	0	16	0
George, Kyle, Bluefield	.890	44	28	69	12	109	1
Guerrero, Francisco, Bluefield	.915	23	9	45	5	59	1
Haerther, Cody, Johnson City	.829	12	8	21	6	35	3
Harper, Brett, Kingsport	1.000	8	5	10	0	15	1
James, Willie, Danville	.500	1	0	1	1	2	0
Krga, Mike, Princeton	.833	4	1	4	1	6	0
Lebron, Freddie, Bristol	1.000	2	0	2	0	2	0
Luna, Leonardo, Bristol	.333	1	1	0	2	3	0
Mannix, Brendan, Kingsport	.848	13	7	21	5	33	3
Molina, Felix, Elizabethton	.818	8	3	15	4	22	1
Perez, Melvin, Bristol	.920	49	40	86	11	137	7
Peterson, Brock, Elizabethton	.822	53	22	89	24	135	2
Ponce, Arnoldo, Pulaski	.935	24	11	61	5	77	5
Rios, Kevin, Kingsport	.864	21	13	25	6	44	3
Salas, Jose, Pulaski	.855	18	14	33	8	55	2
Schade, Scott, Danville	.333	1	0	1	2	3	0
Schlichting, Travis, Princeton	.862	37	19	62	13	94	3
Schmidt, Jeffrey, Bristol	.846	17	10	23	6	39	0
Taylor, Sam, Elizabethton	.750	1	0	3	1	4	0
THOMAS, BEN, Danville	.942	62	35	111	9	155	8
Torres, Saul, Martinsville	.896	56	37	118	18	173	6
Vasquez, Domingo, Burlington	.926	41	32	81	9	122	6
Wilson, Andrew, Kingsport	.952	9	7	13	1	21	2
Wootan, Tanner, Johnson City	.856	40	40	73	19	132	6

SHORTSTOPS

Player, Team	Pct.	G	PO	A	E	TC	DP
Acey, Jermy, Pulaski	.929	17	34	58	7	99	8
Babilonia, Edgar, Martinsville	.910	15	21	40	6	67	10
Batista, Wilson, Kingsport	.955	19	19	45	3	67	5
Beech, Travis, Princeton	.848	7	15	13	5	33	5
Brown, Travis, Bluefield	.961	44	62	109	7	178	16
Cabral, Marcos, Kingsport	.901	26	36	46	9	91	9
Clem, Chris, Burlington	1.000	1	3	2	0	5	2
Colina, Luis, Johnson City	.900	1	2	7	1	10	3
Corapci, Jason, Martinsville	.909	2	3	7	1	11	1
Fermin, Angelo, Elizabethton	.929	18	31	48	6	85	10
Garcia, Julio, Burlington	.931	6	13	14	2	29	3
Garcia, Travis, Kingsport	.857	11	19	23	7	49	7
Garcia, Winfield, Martinsville	.925	49	94	153	20	267	32
Gonzalez, Humberto, Kingsport	.923	2	3	9	1	13	2
Hayes, Calvin, Johnson City	.883	32	56	88	19	163	21
James, Willie, Danville	.920	22	37	78	10	125	11
Lebron, Freddie, Bristol	.958	7	9	14	1	24	2
Luna, Leonardo, Bristol	1.000	3	0	8	0	8	0
Morel, Elvis, Bluefield	.945	21	36	68	6	110	17
Paredes, Salvador, Princeton	.941	61	81	158	15	254	26
Perez, Angel, Johnson City	.885	17	25	44	9	78	10
PINCKNEY, BRANDON, Burl.	.953	62	75	170	12	257	21
Ponce, Arnoldo, Pulaski	.750	1	4	2	2	8	1
Rios, Kevin, Kingsport	.957	8	9	13	1	23	1
Salas, Jose, Pulaski	.667	1	0	2	1	3	0
Sena, Emmanuel, Pulaski	.950	5	4	15	1	20	4
Taylor, Sam, Elizabethton	.931	49	60	128	14	202	25
Thomas, Tee, Johnson City	.876	20	28	50	11	89	12
Valido, Robert, Bristol	.940	58	80	156	15	251	29
Vancamper, Eugenio, Pulaski	.936	45	72	133	14	219	25
White, Dean, Danville	.925	46	62	123	15	200	18

OUTFIELDERS

Player, Team	Pct.	G	PO	A	E	TC	DP
Acey, Jermy, Pulaski	1.000	1	2	0	0	2	0
Alcantara, Ervin, Martinsville	.966	54	83	2	3	88	0
Arneson, Justin, Elizabethton	.929	8	12	1	1	14	0
Ascencion, Quincy, Bluefield	.987	35	74	1	1	76	0
Batista, Ariel, Martinsville	1.000	9	14	1	0	15	0
Beck, Alan, Bluefield	.833	7	4	1	1	6	0
Bolen, Josh, Princeton	.953	39	54	7	3	64	1
Braun, Randy, Pulaski *	.969	22	29	2	1	32	0
Brinkley, Dante, Kingsport	.986	39	70	2	1	73	1
Burrus, Josh, Danville	.913	49	67	6	7	80	0
Caraballo, Francisco, Mart.	.953	52	98	3	5	106	0
Chourio, Junior, Pulaski	.970	19	31	1	1	33	0
Colbert, Eddie, Bluefield	1.000	21	37	0	0	37	0
Coles, Corey, Kingsport *	1.000	26	58	2	0	60	0
Colin, Matt, Burlington	1.000	6	6	0	0	6	0
Collaro, Thomas, Bristol	1.000	19	26	2	0	28	0
Cruz, Jose, Burlington	1.000	39	52	0	0	52	0
Cumberland, Shaun, Princeton	.982	55	108	4	2	114	2
Davidson, Tyler, Kingsport	1.000	9	11	1	0	12	0
Davie, Andrew, Johnson City	.889	4	7	1	1	9	0
Donato, Greg, Danville	1.000	6	7	0	0	7	0
Encarnacion, Teodoro, Burl.	.947	40	68	3	4	75	0
Esquivel, Matt, Danville	.974	60	111	3	3	117	3
Estrada, Robert, Bluefield	1.000	6	4	0	0	4	0
Frias, Fernando, Princeton	.911	38	72	0	7	79	0
FRISELLA, SAL, Johnson City	1.000	56	83	3	0	86	1
Gamero, Jesus, Kingsport	.957	11	18	4	1	23	0
Garcia, Julio, Burlington	1.000	1	1	0	0	1	0
Garcia, Junior, Burlington	.952	31	58	1	3	62	0
Garcia, Miguel, Kingsport *	1.000	12	16	0	0	16	0
Gary, Tavaris, Johnson City *	.968	35	60	0	2	62	0
Garza, Mario, Martinsville	1.000	4	5	0	0	5	0
Gilhooly, Tim, Bluefield	.935	42	69	3	5	77	1
Guerrero, Francisco, Bluefield	.947	10	18	0	1	19	0
Gustafson, Chris, Princeton	.958	16	23	0	1	24	0
Haerther, Cody, Johnson City	.928	45	58	6	5	69	1
Hemingway, Jamie, Danville	1.000	37	63	2	0	65	1
Hessman, Mike, Danville	1.000	3	3	0	0	3	0
Hetherington, Luke, Pulaski	.963	45	72	6	3	81	2
Hill, Jamar, Kingsport	1.000	38	69	1	0	70	0
Hodge, Luis, Burlington	.962	44	70	5	3	78	1
House, Kevin, Johnson City	.982	31	52	2	1	55	0
Hudgson, Maximiliano, Mart.	.950	35	53	4	3	60	1
Irvin, Blair, Princeton	.920	29	45	1	4	50	0
Longworth, Chad, Burlington	.885	23	23	0	3	26	0
Martin, Scott, Bristol	.941	28	32	0	2	34	0
Morel, Elvis, Bluefield	1.000	4	7	0	0	7	0
Partridge, Dominique, Danville	.978	48	78	10	2	90	2
Perodin, Ron, Elizabethton *	.938	45	56	4	4	64	0
Pietsch, Seth, Kingsport	1.000	9	19	0	0	19	0
Pospishil, Jason, Elizabethton	.962	23	24	1	1	26	1
Rivas, Arturo, Bluefield	1.000	9	12	1	0	13	1
Rivera, Jhonny, Bristol	.968	49	56	5	2	63	2
Rodriguez, Manuel, Bristol	1.000	17	16	1	0	17	0
Rodriguez, Marcos, J.C.*	.967	23	26	3	1	30	0
Rodriquez, Yuber, Pulaski	.929	40	61	4	5	70	1
Saltalamacchia, Justin, Danville	1.000	2	2	0	0	2	0
Sarabia, Hamilton, Martinsville	.986	45	68	0	1	69	0
Shafer, Corey, Bluefield *	.951	58	69	8	4	81	3
Shelley, Shane, Princeton	.919	34	65	3	6	74	0
Sims, Justin, Elizabethton	.895	18	15	2	2	19	0
Solano, Roberto, Kingsport	.919	44	118	7	11	136	1
Span, Denard, Elizabethton *	.980	50	93	3	2	98	0
Spataro, Ryan, Elizabethton	.972	57	97	8	3	108	0
Sultemeier, Eric, Bluefield	.938	6	15	0	1	16	0
Sweeney, Ryan, Bristol *	.871	13	27	0	4	31	0
Taylor, Sam, Elizabethton	.667	1	2	0	1	3	0

Player, Team	Pct.	G	PO	A	E	TC	DP
Thomas, Nicholas, Pulaski	.973	25	33	3	1	37	1
Tingler, Jayce, Pulaski *	.992	62	124	5	1	130	3
Valdes, Juan, Burlington	.984	34	60	3	1	64	0
Webber, Levi, Johnson City	.972	23	33	2	1	36	1
Wells, Cory, Kingsport	.952	11	19	1	1	21	0
Young, Chris, Bristol	.992	64	117	0	1	118	0
Young, Eddie, Bristol	.962	26	48	2	2	52	0

CATCHERS

Player, Team	Pct.	G	PO	A	E	TC	DP	PB
Acosta, Jose, Martinsville	.978	27	199	26	5	230	4	6
Anderson, Jimmy, Kingsport	1.000	12	85	5	0	90	0	3
Arias, Angel, Bristol	.974	25	173	13	5	191	0	9
Barden, Andy, Danville	.977	29	189	27	5	221	1	8
Barton, Daric, Johnson City	.983	37	210	26	4	240	0	9
Bennett, Charles, Kingsport	1.000	3	24	7	0	31	0	1
Brock, Caleb, Burlington	.997	32	262	33	1	296	0	1
Capellan, Domingo, J.C.	1.000	7	24	1	0	25	0	1
Casillas, Omar, Burlington	.989	13	86	4	1	91	0	6
CASTILLO, CESAR, Bristol	.993	39	273	25	2	300	4	5
Collins, Jesse, Elizabethton	.978	25	194	26	5	225	0	5
Davidson, Kevin, Martinsville	.982	39	291	44	6	341	0	7
Diaz, Robinzon, Pulaski	.964	33	183	33	8	224	3	7
Diaz, Sandy, Johnson City	.949	8	32	5	2	39	0	3
Garza, Mario, Martinsville	1.000	1	5	0	0	5	0	0
Geiger, Kyle, Elizabethton	.955	4	37	5	2	44	1	2
Guerrero, Henry, Bluefield	.976	31	213	31	6	250	2	5
Hadad, Jorge, Bluefield	.966	14	80	6	3	89	1	1
Houston, Matthew, Bluefield	.989	26	172	15	2	189	1	4
Johnson, Josh, Elizabethton	.995	25	169	27	1	197	0	5
Lenderman, Matthew, Bristol	.990	18	93	10	1	104	0	7
Martinez, Edwin, Danville	.991	14	110	6	1	117	0	4
Motte, Jason, Johnson City	1.000	9	44	10	0	54	0	2
Munsey, Tanner, Burlington	.913	7	18	3	2	23	0	1
Phillips, Kyle, Elizabethton	.994	18	162	12	1	175	1	3
Purkey, Bryan, Kingsport	.857	2	6	0	1	7	0	0
Pyzik, Steve, Danville	1.000	33	228	18	0	246	1	3
Reiman, Joey, Pulaski	.980	14	91	6	2	99	0	3
Reynoso, Danilo, Kingsport	.966	39	275	38	11	324	1	10
Schlichting, Travis, Princeton	1.000	1	1	0	0	1	0	0
Simmons, Colt, Princeton	.965	27	143	24	6	173	1	6
Speigner, Brent, Princeton	.961	13	66	7	3	76	1	3
Wallace, James, Kingsport	.982	15	106	6	2	114	1	5
Wolfe, Joey, Pulaski	.994	24	146	11	1	158	0	5
Woodruff, Ernest, Princeton	.952	34	198	19	11	228	2	9
Woodson, Mike, Burlington	.992	26	229	27	2	258	1	9
Yarbrough, Brandon, J.C.	.976	13	78	3	2	83	0	6

PITCHERS

Player, Team	Pct.	G	PO	A	E	TC	DP
Acosta, Richal, Bluefield	.875	28	1	6	1	8	0
Aguero, Miguel, Johnson City	.941	12	6	10	1	17	0
Alfonzo, Edgar, Kingsport *	1.000	8	0	4	0	4	0
Almenar, Aristides, Kingsport	.846	13	2	9	2	13	0
Amador, Jonathan, Burlington	.500	16	0	2	2	4	0
Arguello, Douglas, Martinsville *	.818	17	2	7	2	11	2
Ashabraner, Robert, Burlington	.857	17	4	2	1	7	0
Azze, Justin, Bluefield *	.909	20	2	8	1	11	0
Banks, Demetrius, Bristol *	.500	15	0	1	1	2	0
Barthmaier, James, Martinsville	1.000	8	1	0	0	1	0
Basner, Ryan, Danville	.929	19	2	11	1	14	0
Berroa, Yesson, Pulaski	1.000	13	2	14	0	16	0
Blackmon, Cory, Danville *	.750	21	4	5	3	12	0
Blakeney, Jacob, Danville	.857	24	4	2	1	7	0
Blanton, Matt, Johnson City *	1.000	13	1	6	0	7	0
Bonnell, Jared, Johnson City	.000	4	0	0	1	1	0
Brandon, Eric, Elizabethton	.889	20	2	6	1	9	1
Brewer, Jeff, Kingsport	1.000	5	1	0	0	1	0
Brown, Darrius, Bluefield *	.000	4	0	0	1	1	0
Brubaker, Douglas, Bluefield	.750	22	1	5	2	8	0
Canizal, Joaquin, Pulaski	1.000	27	2	4	0	6	0
Casey, James, Bristol	.818	10	2	7	2	11	1
Castro, Fabio, Bristol *	1.000	19	3	15	0	18	1
Caughey, Trevor, Bluefield *	1.000	13	4	10	0	14	0
Cevette, Dan, Burlington *	.778	13	1	6	2	9	1
Chavez, Miguel, Johnson City	.700	17	0	7	3	10	0
Cobb, Matt, Princeton *	1.000	18	1	5	0	6	1
Collins, Danny, Danville *	.800	14	1	7	2	10	0
Culpepper, Kevin, Elizabethton *	.867	16	2	11	2	15	0
Curreri, Joe, Bristol	.500	3	0	1	1	2	0
Dalton, Matthew, Pulaski	.889	18	3	5	1	9	0
Davis, Cliff, Martinsville	.500	12	0	1	1	2	0
Day, Dewon, Pulaski	.625	26	2	3	3	8	0
De Aza, Fernando, Bristol	.813	12	7	6	3	16	1
De La Cruz, Jose, Princeton	.889	15	2	6	1	9	0
De Los Santos, Richard, Burl.	.786	12	4	7	3	14	0
DeJaynes, Brandon, J.C.	1.000	25	4	3	0	7	1
DePaula, Julio, Elizabethton	1.000	22	2	1	0	3	0
Delacruz, Eduardo, Princeton	.875	9	2	5	1	8	0
Diaz, Raymar, Martinsville	.833	19	2	3	1	6	0
Douglass, Chance, Martinsville	.800	10	4	4	2	10	0
Dupas, Greg, Princeton	.750	10	1	2	1	4	0
Elliott, Adam, Kingsport	1.000	5	0	1	0	1	0
Estrada, Paul, Martinsville	.750	12	1	2	1	4	0
Farr, Whitt, Danville	.833	23	3	7	2	12	0
Flores, Rafael, Bristol	1.000	16	7	2	0	9	0
Freites, Julio, Kingsport	1.000	13	0	3	0	3	1
Fry, Troy, Kingsport	.875	16	4	3	1	8	0
Garay, Kelvin, Kingsport *	1.000	5	2	0	0	2	0
Garcia, Angel, Elizabethton	.857	9	2	4	1	7	0
Garza, Justin, Johnson City	1.000	21	1	3	0	4	0
Geddes, Michael, Princeton	1.000	8	1	0	0	1	0
Gomez, Jose, Kingsport	1.000	11	0	1	0	1	0
Gomez, Luis, Johnson City	.750	17	2	1	1	4	0
Gonzalez, Jino, Princeton *	.500	3	0	1	1	2	0
Gonzalez, Marino, Kingsport	1.000	8	1	1	0	2	0
Grant, Brian, Pulaski	.947	13	9	9	1	19	0
Gray, Joshua, Elizabethton *	1.000	6	1	1	0	2	0
Gutierrez, Juan, Martinsville	1.000	16	1	5	0	6	1
Guzman, Angel, Burlington	1.000	17	0	3	0	3	0
Hader, Ryan, Elizabethton *	1.000	19	1	1	0	2	0
Harrison, Benjamin, Pulaski *	.667	12	0	4	2	6	0
Haynes, Matt, Burlington	.625	17	2	3	3	8	0
Henkenjohann, Tim, Elizabethton	1.000	8	0	1	0	1	0
Hiraldo, Nelson, Burlington	.800	12	0	8	2	10	0
Hoey, James, Bluefield	.733	11	2	9	4	15	1
Hoffmann, Brett, Johnson City	.769	15	4	6	3	13	0
Houser, James, Princeton *	.778	10	2	5	2	9	1
Huchingson, Jamin, Bristol	.000	7	0	0	1	1	0
Iida, Hiroyuki, Elizabethton	.833	18	2	3	1	6	1
James, Chuck, Danville *	1.000	11	1	7	0	8	1
Johnson, James, Bluefield	.769	11	5	5	3	13	0
King, Timothy, Princeton *	.867	14	2	11	2	15	1
Kopszywa, Nate, Johnson City	1.000	12	1	3	0	4	0
Krause, Lukas, Kingsport *	1.000	3	0	1	0	1	0
Laffey, Aaron, Burlington *	1.000	9	4	4	0	8	0
Lavergne, Jarrad, Princeton *	1.000	11	1	12	0	13	0
Little, Jeffrey, Bristol	1.000	3	1	1	0	2	0
Lopez, Orionny, Bristol	.857	17	3	9	2	14	1
Lopez, Romelio, Princeton	.864	11	7	12	3	22	0
Lynch, John, Elizabethton *	.800	18	3	1	1	5	0
MacLane, Evan, Kingsport *	1.000	14	3	4	0	7	0
Malone, Corwin, Bristol *	1.000	4	0	1	0	1	0
Mann, Brandon, Princeton *	1.000	11	0	9	0	9	0
Marini, Christopher, Eliz.*	1.000	13	2	5	0	7	0
Markham, Josh, Johnson City *	1.000	10	0	1	0	1	0
Marshall, Jay, Bristol *	.818	10	1	8	2	11	0
Marte, Violenny, Martinsville	1.000	12	1	3	0	4	0
Martinez, Ronnie, Martinsville	.941	12	1	15	1	17	0
McClellan, Kyle, Johnson City	.947	12	8	10	1	19	0
McGary, Gerron, Bristol *	1.000	11	1	1	0	2	0
McKeller, Ryan, Martinsville	.833	15	2	3	1	6	0
Mead, Dan, Danville *	1.000	24	1	1	0	2	0
Medina, Dennis, Elizabethton	1.000	10	2	6	0	8	1
Meek, Evan, Elizabethton	.938	14	7	8	1	16	0
Mendez, Orlin, Johnson City	1.000	17	0	4	0	4	0
Meyers, Ryan, Kingsport	1.000	15	1	2	0	3	0
Miller, Adam, Burlington	.889	10	3	5	1	9	0
Mincey, T.W., Bluefield *	.667	5	1	1	1	3	1
Miramontes, Matthew, Kingsport	1.000	6	2	1	0	3	0
Morales, Ruddy, Bristol	1.000	5	0	2	0	2	1
Morton, Charles, Danville	.875	14	0	7	1	8	1
Mujica, Edward, Burlington	.909	14	1	9	1	11	0
Mumma, Brad, Pulaski *	1.000	5	0	7	0	7	1
Murray, Brad, Bristol *	1.000	5	1	0	0	1	0
Mutch, Paul, Elizabethton	.800	18	2	6	2	10	0
Navarro, Rodolfo, Burlington	.929	14	4	9	1	14	2
Nelson, Brad, Danville	.769	24	1	9	3	13	0
Neylan, Chris, Pulaski *	.714	12	2	3	2	7	0
Nieves, Roberto, Danville	.667	14	0	4	2	6	0
Novoa, Yunior, Bristol *	1.000	11	1	8	0	9	0
Olson, Jordan, Princeton *	.875	17	1	6	1	8	0
Ortiz, Dario, Bristol	1.000	7	1	0	0	1	0
Pals, Jordan, Johnson City	1.000	8	5	6	0	11	0
Paulino, Felipe, Martinsville	.800	16	0	4	1	5	1

Player, Team	Pct.	G	PO	A	E	TC	DP
Penn, Hayden, Bluefield	.800	12	2	6	2	10	0
Peralta, Efigenio, Danville	1.000	2	0	1	0	1	0
Perez, Carlos, Bluefield *	.750	12	1	5	2	8	0
Perez, Juan, Pulaski	.923	13	3	9	1	13	0
Perez, Rafael, Burlington *	.826	13	3	16	4	23	2
Pesco, Nick, Burlington	1.000	13	2	12	0	14	0
Petit, Yusmeiro, Kingsport	1.000	12	4	10	0	14	0
Petrick, Russell, Bluefield *	1.000	22	3	2	0	5	0
Pidutti, James, Pulaski *	1.000	16	3	9	0	12	1
Pollok, Dwayne, Bristol	1.000	11	1	1	0	2	0
Pomeranz, Stuart, Johnson City	1.000	4	0	1	0	1	0
Potter, Josh, Bluefield	.833	18	1	4	1	6	1
Reedy, Shane, Johnson City	1.000	2	0	1	0	1	0
Reilly, Christopher, Bluefield	.900	16	1	8	1	10	0
Rengel, Orlando, Kingsport	.875	12	5	2	1	8	0
Rider, Michael, Pulaski	.900	22	3	6	1	10	1
Rodriguez, Claudio, Princeton	.833	15	0	5	1	6	0
Rodriguez, Jayson, Pulaski	1.000	17	2	9	0	11	1
Rodriguez, Joan, Princeton	1.000	10	1	1	0	2	0
Rohr, Charles, Princeton	1.000	6	0	4	0	4	1
Romero, Levi, Martinsville	1.000	16	3	5	0	8	0
Rondon, Celso, Kingsport	1.000	19	0	3	0	3	0
Russell, Steve, Danville	1.000	8	1	4	0	5	0
Sager, Brian, Bristol	.500	1	0	1	1	2	0
Salas, Marino, Bluefield	1.000	23	1	3	0	4	0
Salazar, Julio, Martinsville *	.900	10	1	8	1	10	0
Sanchez , Raymon, Pulaski *	.714	17	1	4	2	7	0
Santana, Hector, Burlington	.750	13	2	4	2	8	0
Santos, Reid, Burlington *	1.000	14	0	5	0	5	0
Savickas, Russell, Pulaski	1.000	12	7	14	0	21	1
Schultz, Jimmy, Burlington	1.000	13	2	3	0	5	0
Schutt, Christopher, Elizabethton	1.000	11	3	9	0	12	0
Sides, Andrew, Kingsport	.889	10	4	4	1	9	0
Simonitsch, Errol, Elizabethton *	.917	10	0	11	1	12	0
Smith, Cole, Princeton	.500	8	0	1	1	2	0
Soler, Jose, Martinsville	1.000	14	2	1	0	3	0
Southerland, Chip, Burlington	1.000	12	0	2	0	2	0
Speigner, Brent, Princeton	1.000	1	1	0	0	1	0
Speigner, Jimmy, Elizabethton	1.000	22	4	7	0	11	0
Spivey, Melvin, Bluefield	1.000	5	0	1	0	1	0
Stefano, Frank, Kingsport *	.750	15	2	1	1	4	0
Stewart, Josh, Bristol *	1.000	2	0	2	0	2	0
Suarez, Sony, Bristol	.846	16	2	9	2	13	0
Sutton, Zach, Bluefield	1.000	18	1	2	0	3	0
Talbot, Mitch, Martinsville	1.000	12	4	4	0	8	1
Thompson, Sean, Bristol *	.750	6	1	2	1	4	0
TISCH, TIM, Bristol *	1.000	11	9	13	0	22	1
Torres, David, Kingsport	.800	15	2	2	1	5	1
Travis, Matt, Princeton *	.818	20	1	8	2	11	1
Tucker, Glenn, Danville	.818	25	1	8	2	11	0
Uhl, Jon, Elizabethton	.900	11	1	8	1	10	1
Van Gorder, Joe, Johnson City *	1.000	11	2	5	0	7	1
Van Ruiten, Danny, Princeton	1.000	5	1	2	0	3	0
Vergara, Alan, Martinsville	.692	15	2	7	4	13	0
Wasserman, Ehren, Bristol	1.000	4	1	0	0	1	0
Weagle, Matt, Johnson City	1.000	5	3	1	0	4	0
Weichard, Paul, Danville *	1.000	4	0	2	0	2	1
Weitzman, William, Kingsport	.750	17	1	2	1	4	0
White, Sean, Danville	.955	14	5	16	1	22	1

The following players appeared only as a designated hitter, pinch-hitter or pinch-runner: Cenate, ph; Foskey, dh; Milledge, ph; Saccomanno, dh, ph.

LEAGUE CHAMPIONS

Year	Team	Pct.
1921—	Greenville	.608
	Johnson City*	.627
1922—	Bristol	.557
1923—	Knoxville	.635
1924—	Knoxville*	.642
	Bristol	.607
1925—	Greenville	.667
1926-36—	Did not operate.	
1937—	Elizabethton	.559
	Pennington Gap*	.580
1938—	Elizabethton	.664
	Greenville (3rd)†	.571
1939—	Elizabethton‡	.597
1940—	Johnson City§	.726
	Elizabethton	.750
1941—	Johnson City	.614
	Elizabethton*	.661
1942—	Bristol	.667
	Bristol∞	.660
1943—	Bristol	.755
	Bristol▲	.617
1944—	Kingsport‡	.575
1945—	Kingsport‡	.670
1946—	New River‡	.675
1947—	Pulaski	.648
	New River (3rd)†	.516
1948—	Pulaski‡	.680
1949—	Bluefield‡	.721
1950—	Bluefield	.600
	Bluefield◆	.745
1951—	Kingsport‡	.659
1952—	Johnson City	.595
	Welch (3rd)†	.509
1953—	Welch*	.705
	Johnson City	.672
1954—	Bluefield‡	.619
1955—	Salem■	.689
1956—	Did not operate.	
1957—	Bluefield	.701
1958—	Johnson City	.662
1959—	Morristown	.603
1960—	Wytheville	.614
1961—	Middlesboro	.591
1962—	Bluefield	.671
1963—	Bluefield	.652
1964—	Johnson City	.662
1965—	Salem	.614
1966—	Marion	.623
1967—	Bluefield	.627
1968—	Marion	.583
1969—	Pulaski▼	.576
	Johnson City	.544
1970—	Bluefield	.638
1971—	Bluefield▼	.609
	Kingsport	.559
1972—	Bristol▼	.588
	Covington	.586
1973—	Kingsport	.757
1974—	Bristol▼	.754
	Bluefield	.536
1975—	Marion	.515
	Johnson City▼	.603
1976—	Johnson City▼	.714
	Bluefield	.600
1977—	Kingsport	.623
1978—	Elizabethton	.594
1979—	Paintsville	.800
1980—	Paintsville	.657
1981—	Paintsville	.657
1982—	Bluefield▼	.681
	Johnson City	.478
1983—	Paintsville	.653
1984—	Elizabethton•	.580
	Pulaski	.536
1985—	Bristol††	.638
1986—	Johnson City	.667
	Pulaski•	.621
1987—	Burlington•	.729
	Johnson City	.609
1988—	Kingsport•	.644
	Burlington	.529
1989—	Elizabethton•	.691
	Pulaski	.618
1990—	Elizabethton	.761
1991—	Pulaski•	.662
	Burlington	.597
1992—	Elizabethton	.742
	Bluefield•	.597
1993—	Burlington•	.647
	Elizabethton	.552
1994—	Princeton•	.621
	Johnson City	.618
1995—	Bluefield	.754
	Kingsport•	.727
1996—	Kingsport	.716
	Bluefield▼	.618
1997—	Pulaski	.632
	Bluefield•	.580
1998—	Bristol•	.636
	Princeton	.559
1999—	Pulaski	.696
	Martinsville•	.586
2000—	Elizabethton•	.719
2001—	Elizabethton	.651
	Bluefield•	.500
2002—	Bluefield	.662
	Bristol•	.632
2003—	Martinsville	.646
	Elizabethton•	.636

*Won split-season playoff. †Won four-team playoff. ‡Won championship and four-team playoff. §Johnson City, first-half winner, won playoff involving six clubs. ∞Won both halves and defeated second-place Elizabethton in playoff. ▲Won both halves, but Erwin won four-team playoff. ◆Won both halves, but Bristol won two-club playoff. ■Salem and Johnson City declared playoff co-champions when weather forced cancellation of final series. ▼League was divided into Northern, Southern divisions; declared league champion based on highest won-lost percentage. •League was divided into divisions; won playoff. ††Bristol declared league champion based on regular-season record.

PIONEER LEAGUE

LEAGUE OFFICE

President
Jim McCurdy
Address
P.O. Box 2564
Spokane, WA 99220
Phone
509-456-7615

Teams (affiliation)
Billings Mustangs (Reds)
Casper Rockies (Rockies)
Great Falls White Sox (White Sox)
Helena Brewers (Brewers)
Idaho Falls Chukars (Royals)
Missoula Osprey (Diamondbacks)
Ogden Raptors (Dodgers)
Provo Angels (Angels)

2003 FINAL STANDINGS

FIRST HALF

NORTHERN DIVISION

Team	W	L	T	Pct.	GB
Helena	25	13	-	.658	...
Billings	24	14	-	.632	1.0
Great Falls	20	18	-	.526	5.0
Missoula	18	20	-	.474	7.0

SOUTHERN DIVISION

Team	W	L	T	Pct.	GB
Provo	24	14	-	.632	...
Ogden	18	20	-	.474	6.0
Casper	12	26	-	.316	12.0
Idaho Falls	11	27	-	.289	13.0

SECOND HALF

NORTHERN DIVISION

Team	W	L	T	Pct.	GB
Helena	23	15	-	.605	...
Missoula	18	20	-	.474	5.0
Great Falls	18	20	-	.474	5.0
Billings	17	21	-	.447	6.0

SOUTHERN DIVISION

Team	W	L	T	Pct.	GB
Provo	30	8	-	.789	...
Ogden	17	21	-	.447	13.0
Casper	16	22	-	.421	14.0
Idaho Falls	13	25	-	.342	17.0

COMPOSITE

Team	PRV	HEL	BIL	GRF	MSO	OGD	CAS	IDF	W	L	T	Pct.	GB
Provo (Angels)	...	4	5	0	4	12	14	15	54	22	0	.711	...
Helena (Brewers)	3	...	10	11	9	4	5	6	48	28	0	.632	6.0
Billings (Reds)	2	6	...	12	11	5	3	2	41	35	0	.539	13.0
Great Falls (Dodgers)	7	5	4	...	7	6	3	6	38	38	0	.500	16.0
Missoula (Diamondbacks)	3	7	5	9	...	4	3	5	36	40	0	.474	18.0
Ogden (Brewers)	4	3	2	1	3	...	11	11	35	41	0	.461	19.0
Casper (Rockies)	2	2	4	4	4	5	...	7	28	48	0	.368	26.0
Idaho Falls (Padres)	1	1	5	1	2	5	9	...	24	52	0	.316	30.0

Major league affiliations in parentheses.

PLAYOFFS: Provo defeated Ogden, two games to one; Billings defeated Helena, two games to one; Billings defeated Provo, two games to none, to win league championship.

REGULAR-SEASON ATTENDANCE: Billings, 122,090; Casper, 51,427; Great Falls, 114,603; Helena, 47,493; Idaho Falls, 57,854; Missoula, 51,236; Ogden, 126,706; Provo, 56,856. Total attendance—628,265. Playoffs (8 games)—16,179.

MANAGERS: Billings, Rick Burleson; Casper, P.J. Carey; Great Falls, Chris Cron; Helena, Ed Sedar; Idaho Falls, Carlos Lezcano; Missoula, Tony Perezchica; Ogden, Travis Barbary; Provo, Tom Kotchman.

ALL-STAR TEAM: 1B—Brandon Bounds, Great Falls; 2B—Habelito Hernandez, Billings; 3B—Ian Stewart, Casper; SS—Luis Bolivar, Billings; OF—Ricardo Nanita, Great Falls; OF—Warner Madrigal, Provo; OF—Terry Trofholz, Helena; C—Louis Palmisano, Helena; DH—Billy Hogan, Idaho Falls; RHP—Abel Moreno, Provo; LHP—Daniel Davidson, Provo; Relief pitcher—Dana Eveland, Helena; Most Valuable Player—Louis Palmisano, Helena; Pitcher of the Year—Abel Moreno, Provo; Manager of the Year—Ed Sedar, Helena.

2003 BATTING

TEAM

Team	G	TPA	AB	R	H	TB	2B	3B	HR	RBI	SH	SF	HP	BB	IBB	SO	SB	CS	GDP	LOB	ShO	Avg.	OBP	Slg.
Provo	76	3077	2691	538	817	1269	198	22	70	473	11	28	52	294	4	598	44	18	52	607	2	.304	.379	.472
Great Falls	76	3052	2670	468	778	1165	151	25	62	419	31	28	54	269	8	636	63	37	49	579	3	.291	.364	.436
Helena	76	3000	2617	456	755	1015	125	18	33	368	31	29	49	273	4	492	142	37	36	585	1	.288	.363	.388
Billings	76	2982	2640	451	742	1148	143	28	69	409	15	21	50	256	6	724	51	30	33	560	5	.281	.353	.435
Casper	76	2967	2684	389	739	1061	119	31	47	333	15	15	32	220	5	643	96	47	36	555	3	.275	.336	.395
Ogden	76	2958	2603	416	709	1043	144	35	40	355	26	31	50	246	3	614	66	29	42	557	1	.272	.343	.401
Idaho Falls	76	2893	2583	341	655	934	138	21	33	293	19	21	41	227	7	545	68	20	53	556	4	.254	.321	.362
Missoula	76	2827	2537	347	639	927	111	21	45	293	20	18	67	184	6	513	82	31	50	515	3	.252	.317	.365

INDIVIDUAL

TOP QUALIFIERS FOR BATTING CHAMPIONSHIP

Minimum 205 plate appearances. *Lefthanded batter. †Switch-hitter.

Player, Team	G	TPA	AB	R	H	TB	2B	3B	HR	RBI	SH	SF	HP	BB	IBB	SO	SB	CS	GDP	Avg.	OBP	Slg.
Nanita, Ricardo, Great Falls *	47	212	185	38	71	101	7	4	5	37	1	3	6	17	2	28	11	6	2	.384	.445	.546
Madrigal, Warner, Provo	70	297	279	75	103	162	28	2	9	51	0	4	2	12	0	58	2	0	10	.369	.394	.581
Kendrick, Howie, Provo	63	270	234	65	86	121	20	3	3	36	3	3	6	24	1	28	8	3	5	.368	.434	.517
Bolivar, Luis, Billings †	55	259	235	57	82	135	20	3	9	42	0	1	6	17	1	32	12	6	2	.349	.405	.574
Trofholz, Terry, Helena	68	291	261	60	91	107	10	3	0	22	6	2	3	19	0	39	39	6	1	.349	.396	.410
Perez, Miguel, Billings	60	257	227	46	77	95	11	2	1	25	1	1	10	18	1	27	1	1	3	.339	.410	.419
Ramirez, Manuel, Helena	63	250	218	36	72	126	19	1	11	52	0	4	5	23	0	48	0	1	5	.330	.400	.578
Pali, Matt, Provo *	64	263	223	47	73	118	15	3	8	43	0	2	6	32	0	44	2	1	3	.327	.422	.529
Bounds, Brandon, Gr. Falls *	72	301	279	51	91	148	20	5	9	47	0	4	0	18	1	58	3	3	2	.326	.362	.530
Deevers, Robby, Helena	64	247	221	49	72	104	14	3	4	41	2	2	5	17	1	51	9	3	1	.326	.384	.471
Anderson, Drew, Helena *	61	259	214	33	68	91	11	3	2	38	4	2	4	35	1	39	9	5	4	.318	.420	.425
Votto, Joey, Billings *	70	301	240	47	76	117	17	3	6	38	0	1	4	56	3	80	4	0	4	.317	.452	.488
Himes, Benjamin, Billings	62	272	246	40	78	112	11	1	7	42	1	3	3	19	0	87	4	3	4	.317	.369	.455
Stewart, Ian, Casper *	57	257	224	40	71	125	14	5	10	43	0	1	3	29	3	54	4	1	5	.317	.401	.558
Underwood, Daniel, Casper	67	284	266	54	84	120	15	0	7	40	0	0	3	15	0	78	12	3	4	.316	.359	.451

DEPARTMENTAL LEADERS: G—Murillo, 74; AB—Bounds, Madrigal, 279; R—Madrigal, 75; H—Madrigal, 103; TB—Madrigal, 162; 2B—Madrigal, 28; 3B—Kaplan, Nunez, Paul, 6; HR—Fuller, Olmstead, 12; RBI—R. Wilson, 62; SH—Haggerty, 14; SF—Several players tied with 5; HP—R. Carter, 12; BB—Votto, 56; IBB—Several players tied with 5; SO—Himes, 87; SB—Trofholz, 39; CS—Myers, 9; GIDP—R. Wilson, 11; Slg.—Palmisano, .592; OBP—Palmisano, .458.

ALL PLAYERS

*Lefthanded batter. †Switch-hitter.

Player, Team	G	TPA	AB	R	H	TB	2B	3B	HR	RBI	SH	SF	HP	BB	IBB	SO	SB	CS	GDP	Avg.	OBP	Slg.
Acevedo, Juan, Billings †	24	93	88	15	26	41	5	2	2	12	0	0	0	5	0	38	1	0	0	.295	.333	.466
Acosta, Johe, Missoula	65	250	223	35	56	100	10	2	10	30	0	3	11	13	1	75	7	1	2	.251	.320	.448
Almonte, Aneury, Provo	26	69	54	13	14	15	1	0	0	2	2	0	1	12	0	14	6	3	2	.259	.403	.278
Anderson, Brian, Great Falls	13	59	49	6	19	29	2	1	2	13	0	0	1	9	1	10	3	1	1	.388	.492	.592
Anderson, Drew, Helena *	61	259	214	33	68	91	11	3	2	38	4	2	4	35	1	39	9	5	4	.318	.420	.425
Baker, Casey, Idaho Falls	9	34	27	6	4	7	0	0	1	5	0	1	1	5	0	11	2	0	0	.148	.294	.259
Balkcom, Blake, Provo	36	145	131	20	38	56	12	0	2	28	0	2	2	10	0	26	0	0	2	.290	.345	.427
Barnes, Justin, Helena	56	214	195	29	47	74	10	1	5	34	2	4	1	12	0	49	3	2	5	.241	.283	.379
Beale, David, Billings	58	216	191	28	40	52	5	2	1	23	2	1	1	21	0	46	5	3	6	.209	.290	.272
Belz, Tim, Missoula	1	2	2	0	0	0	0	0	0	0	0	0	0	0	0	0	0	0	0	.000	.000	.000
Blanco, Gregory, Provo	4	4	3	0	1	1	0	0	0	0	0	0	1	0	0	2	0	0	0	.333	.500	.333
Bok, Matt, Ogden *	4	10	8	2	3	4	1	0	0	2	0	1	0	1	0	1	0	0	0	.375	.400	.500
Bolivar, Luis, Billings †	55	259	235	57	82	135	20	3	9	42	0	1	6	17	1	32	12	6	2	.349	.405	.574
Bonifacio, Emilio, Missoula	54	172	146	20	29	32	1	1	0	16	4	1	3	18	0	43	15	3	1	.199	.298	.219
Bounds, Brandon, Gr. Falls *	72	301	279	51	91	148	20	5	9	47	0	4	0	18	1	58	3	3	2	.326	.362	.530
Brinson, Matt, Casper *	9	41	35	3	9	14	2	0	1	8	0	0	0	6	0	5	0	1	1	.257	.366	.400
Brito, Javier, Missoula	38	109	97	11	25	31	3	0	1	7	1	1	4	6	0	27	2	1	3	.258	.324	.320
Brown, Matt, Provo	65	290	233	58	68	120	19	0	11	52	0	5	9	42	2	56	2	3	1	.292	.412	.515
Burnham, Brett, Idaho Falls	50	208	176	24	51	70	17	1	0	20	3	2	2	25	0	25	2	2	4	.290	.380	.398
Cairns, Troy, Billings	34	148	132	17	39	47	5	0	1	11	4	2	2	8	0	17	2	2	1	.295	.340	.356
Campos, Tiago, Billings	7	28	28	6	7	21	2	0	4	10	0	0	0	0	0	10	0	1	1	.250	.250	.750
Cardona, Dave, Ogden	38	147	137	15	40	51	8	0	1	14	0	1	5	4	0	39	2	2	1	.292	.333	.372
Carter, Nic, Helena	24	53	50	5	13	14	1	0	0	1	0	0	0	3	0	14	4	2	0	.260	.302	.280
Carter, Ryan, Ogden	49	209	179	32	56	100	13	5	7	35	1	3	12	14	1	49	8	1	2	.313	.394	.559
Castillo, Luis, Ogden	67	289	260	46	74	121	22	2	7	48	0	2	3	24	0	69	0	0	4	.285	.349	.465
Ciriaco, Juan, Idaho Falls	49	172	157	21	35	49	6	4	0	19	0	4	2	9	0	39	8	0	1	.223	.267	.312
Cleveland, Clay, Billings	9	39	34	3	4	4	0	0	0	6	0	0	1	4	0	14	0	0	1	.118	.231	.118
Collins, Mike, Provo	37	139	132	20	44	59	8	2	1	15	0	2	2	3	0	19	0	0	2	.333	.353	.447
Comfort, Geoff, Ogden	49	202	172	36	44	72	12	2	4	21	0	2	4	24	0	46	5	2	3	.256	.356	.419
Cook, David, Great Falls	6	25	22	5	6	6	0	0	0	2	1	0	0	2	0	8	0	0	0	.273	.333	.273
Corporan, Carlos, Helena †	10	34	27	4	6	7	1	0	0	4	0	1	2	4	0	7	0	0	2	.222	.353	.259
Crissotomo, Miguel, Ogden †	33	107	93	16	22	30	4	2	0	9	2	1	1	10	0	20	2	0	1	.237	.314	.323
Cruceta, Julio, Idaho Falls	46	182	171	26	40	51	7	2	0	15	1	3	1	6	0	22	4	2	2	.234	.260	.298
Dale, Lachlan, Idaho Falls	41	147	132	20	33	51	10	1	2	20	1	2	2	10	0	44	0	1	4	.250	.308	.386
De Aza, Alejandro, Ogden *	55	247	208	36	48	67	11	1	2	24	5	0	10	23	0	34	15	6	2	.231	.336	.322
Deevers, Robby, Helena	64	247	221	49	72	104	14	3	4	41	2	2	5	17	1	51	9	3	1	.326	.384	.471
Deuchler, Matthew, Gr. Falls	27	87	80	14	24	35	5	0	2	9	0	0	0	7	0	24	1	0	4	.300	.356	.438
Dickerson, Christopher, Bil.*	58	250	201	36	49	81	6	4	6	38	5	1	4	39	0	66	9	4	0	.244	.376	.403
Dowdy, Brett, Ogden	29	117	105	11	29	39	4	3	0	11	2	1	3	6	0	27	1	0	2	.276	.330	.371
Duenas, Tommy, Provo	14	57	45	10	12	21	3	0	2	7	0	0	0	12	0	11	0	0	1	.267	.421	.467
Edwards, Brian, Idaho Falls	49	209	185	21	48	59	7	2	0	10	1	2	2	19	0	23	11	0	4	.259	.332	.319
Esposito, Brian, Provo	3	11	11	0	1	1	0	0	0	0	0	0	0	0	0	4	0	0	1	.091	.091	.091
Etheridge, Chad, Id. Falls †	10	31	29	3	2	4	2	0	0	0	0	0	0	2	0	13	0	0	1	.069	.129	.138
Ferrer, Simon, Ogden †	8	31	28	4	7	10	3	0	0	2	0	1	0	2	0	9	0	0	1	.250	.290	.357
Figueroa, Baudilio, Id. Falls †	40	123	111	13	27	30	1	1	0	6	3	0	1	8	0	30	2	0	3	.243	.300	.270
Frost, Jeremy, Helena	7	25	25	2	5	6	1	0	0	2	0	0	0	0	0	7	1	0	0	.200	.200	.240
Fuller, Casey, Casper *	49	194	183	27	53	100	5	3	12	43	0	1	1	9	1	61	5	1	2	.290	.325	.546
Garay, Ernesto, Idaho Falls *	46	176	156	17	41	54	4	3	1	13	1	0	2	17	0	28	5	2	1	.263	.343	.346
Gentry, Philip, Billings *	56	200	186	21	42	61	14	1	1	22	0	1	0	13	1	50	1	3	1	.226	.275	.328
Ghutzman, Stephen, Casper †	28	115	102	11	31	44	8	1	1	14	0	0	0	13	0	25	1	2	1	.304	.383	.431
Gomez, Andri, Helena †	52	157	151	23	34	47	7	0	2	13	1	0	3	2	0	20	8	5	2	.225	.250	.311
Gonzalez, Carlos, Missoula *	72	299	275	45	71	111	14	4	6	25	0	3	5	16	1	61	12	7	3	.258	.308	.404

Player, Team	G	TPA	AB	R	H	TB	2B	3B	HR	RBI	SH	SF	HP	BB	IBB	SO	SB	CS	GDP	Avg.	OBP	Slg.
Gonzalez, Juan, Ogden	38	150	135	20	33	39	1	1	1	11	2	2	1	10	0	26	2	4	4	.244	.297	.289
Gray, Antoin, Great Falls	69	337	277	63	81	125	20	0	8	43	2	3	6	49	0	62	4	1	4	.292	.406	.451
Guerrero, Michael, Missoula	25	67	60	3	11	15	4	0	0	9	1	1	1	4	0	16	1	0	1	.183	.242	.250
Gutierrez, Tonys, Billings *	3	10	10	1	2	3	1	0	0	1	0	0	0	0	0	1	0	0	0	.200	.200	.300
Guzman, Jose, Provo †	34	107	94	19	26	42	7	3	1	14	2	0	1	10	0	32	3	0	0	.277	.352	.447
Haggerty, Cory, Great Falls *	60	204	156	35	38	56	9	3	1	16	14	2	7	25	0	40	4	6	3	.244	.368	.359
Hauseman, Chad, Provo	23	70	65	7	13	15	2	0	0	11	0	0	0	5	0	16	1	0	2	.200	.257	.231
Hernandez, Habelito, Billings	36	166	162	42	61	109	14	5	8	32	0	0	3	1	0	22	5	0	2	.377	.392	.673
Herrera, Jonathan, Casper †	39	176	159	27	49	61	7	1	1	25	4	1	2	10	0	25	12	3	2	.308	.355	.384
Hess, Samuel, Provo	3	9	7	1	1	2	1	0	0	1	0	0	0	2	0	1	0	0	0	.143	.333	.286
Himes, Benjamin, Billings	62	272	246	40	78	112	11	1	7	42	1	3	3	19	0	87	4	3	4	.317	.369	.455
Hodges, Brent, Great Falls	9	19	18	1	1	1	0	0	0	0	0	0	1	0	0	5	0	1	1	.056	.105	.056
Hogan, William, Idaho Falls	45	186	163	22	56	84	17	1	3	33	0	1	7	15	2	36	3	3	5	.344	.419	.515
Hu, Chin-lung, Ogden	53	240	220	34	67	95	9	5	3	23	4	2	0	14	0	33	5	4	2	.305	.343	.432
Hudson, William, Billings †	19	66	52	6	10	14	2	1	0	7	1	1	1	11	0	12	1	3	1	.192	.338	.269
Huson, Tim, Great Falls *	5	15	13	1	2	2	0	0	0	0	0	0	0	2	0	5	0	0	2	.154	.267	.154
Ivy, Bjorn, Great Falls	4	10	9	1	2	2	0	0	0	0	0	0	0	1	0	6	1	0	0	.222	.300	.222
Johnson, Ryan, Idaho Falls *	20	88	75	10	21	31	7	0	1	12	0	0	0	13	0	12	0	0	1	.280	.386	.413
Kaplan, Jonathan, Missoula	69	282	257	28	71	110	15	6	4	32	2	0	5	18	0	34	11	5	4	.276	.336	.428
Kaye, Brandon, Idaho Falls *	52	180	161	25	44	84	10	0	10	30	0	2	8	8	1	30	0	0	4	.273	.335	.522
Kelly, Christopher, Great Falls	54	217	200	25	49	78	15	1	4	40	1	2	3	11	0	44	3	0	1	.245	.292	.390
Kendrick, Howie, Provo	63	270	234	65	86	121	20	3	3	36	3	3	6	24	1	28	8	3	5	.368	.434	.517
Kenning, Ryan, Provo *	55	213	184	31	48	98	18	1	10	38	0	1	4	24	0	70	2	0	2	.261	.357	.533
King, Clinton, Great Falls *	59	255	223	41	68	95	10	4	3	29	0	2	4	26	3	55	6	5	3	.305	.384	.426
Kottaras, George, Id. Falls *	42	164	143	27	37	68	8	1	7	24	0	1	1	19	1	36	1	1	2	.259	.348	.476
Laroche, Andy, Ogden	6	21	19	1	4	5	1	0	0	5	0	1	0	1	0	4	0	0	0	.211	.238	.263
Lauderdale, Matthew, Id. Falls	18	64	53	6	9	13	4	0	0	3	0	0	2	8	0	20	1	0	1	.170	.302	.245
Laurin, Dominique, Ogden	30	112	93	12	19	32	6	2	1	11	0	1	3	15	0	35	1	1	3	.204	.330	.344
Lee, Carlos, Great Falls	47	198	180	25	54	76	11	1	3	33	3	2	3	10	0	22	1	0	5	.300	.344	.422
Lewis, William, Helena	1	3	3	0	0	0	0	0	0	0	0	0	0	0	0	0	0	0	0	.000	.000	.000
Lisk, Charlie, Great Falls	54	224	203	40	55	95	11	1	9	34	0	1	4	16	0	63	5	0	5	.271	.335	.468
Lobaton, Jose, Idaho Falls †	56	217	191	22	52	70	15	0	1	32	1	1	2	22	2	50	0	1	4	.272	.352	.366
Lopez, Luis, Idaho Falls	2	5	5	0	0	0	0	0	0	0	0	0	0	0	0	2	0	0	0	.000	.000	.000
Lozada, Charlie, Helena	8	23	22	1	4	5	1	0	0	4	0	0	0	1	0	4	0	0	1	.182	.217	.227
Ludwig, Michael, Ogden	28	109	104	9	28	34	4	1	0	9	0	0	1	4	0	26	0	1	3	.269	.303	.327
Lynch, Michael, Ogden	28	116	102	8	19	22	3	0	0	12	1	2	0	11	0	29	0	0	3	.186	.261	.216
Macias, Andres, Idaho Falls *	61	270	239	41	60	84	10	4	2	13	6	1	5	19	1	32	15	4	8	.251	.318	.351
Madrigal, Warner, Provo	70	297	279	75	103	162	28	2	9	51	0	4	2	12	0	58	2	0	10	.369	.394	.581
Martin, Russell, Ogden	52	222	188	25	51	82	13	0	6	36	2	2	4	26	1	26	3	1	6	.271	.368	.436
Martinez, Domingo, Id. Falls	8	22	22	0	4	6	2	0	0	2	0	0	0	0	0	6	0	0	0	.182	.182	.273
Martinez, Thomas, Id. Falls	25	93	92	8	27	37	2	1	2	12	0	0	1	0	0	10	1	0	3	.293	.301	.402
McCreery, John, Missoula	42	144	125	23	35	52	5	0	4	13	0	1	3	15	0	16	4	2	5	.280	.368	.416
McStoots, Jason, Missoula *	59	238	200	33	45	58	6	2	1	17	5	0	2	31	1	42	8	5	3	.225	.335	.290
Melendez, Cristobal, Mis.	45	140	122	14	28	31	3	0	0	9	6	0	6	6	0	31	5	2	1	.230	.299	.254
Melo, Manuel, Helena †	46	157	141	26	36	42	4	1	0	11	4	0	0	12	0	28	11	3	0	.255	.314	.298
Mercado, Orlando, Missoula	23	51	47	3	10	13	3	0	0	4	0	0	1	3	0	12	0	0	1	.213	.275	.277
Milons, Jereme, Ogden	51	219	195	37	60	80	7	5	1	23	2	2	1	19	0	47	10	3	3	.308	.369	.410
Montero, Miguel, Missoula *	59	216	196	24	59	85	10	2	4	32	0	3	8	9	2	15	2	3	6	.301	.352	.434
Moore, Mewelde, Idaho Falls	4	12	11	0	1	1	0	0	0	0	0	0	0	1	0	4	0	0	0	.091	.167	.091
Morris, Seth, Great Falls	53	226	204	31	51	90	12	0	9	29	1	2	1	18	0	79	3	2	4	.250	.311	.441
Mosby, Robert, Billings	55	203	179	24	40	76	7	1	9	34	0	3	1	20	0	76	0	0	3	.223	.300	.425
Mosqueda, Juan, Casper	51	192	172	20	47	63	5	4	1	19	3	0	0	17	1	60	7	6	2	.273	.339	.366
Motooka, Rafael, Billings	3	6	4	1	0	0	0	0	0	0	0	0	0	2	0	1	0	0	0	.000	.333	.000
Mottram, Allen, Missoula	68	268	244	29	65	96	8	1	7	35	0	3	5	16	0	34	4	0	7	.266	.321	.393
Murillo, Agustin, Missoula	74	305	278	48	84	125	22	2	5	39	0	2	8	17	0	34	2	2	5	.302	.357	.450
Myers, Michael, Great Falls	69	307	249	38	75	103	11	4	3	47	7	3	11	37	0	59	18	9	4	.301	.410	.414
Nanita, Ricardo, Great Falls *	47	212	185	38	71	101	7	4	5	37	1	3	6	17	2	28	11	6	2	.384	.445	.546
Nunez, Florentino, Casper †	55	230	209	34	55	82	12	6	1	27	0	2	3	16	0	37	6	6	2	.263	.322	.392
Olivares, Juan, Missoula	54	187	180	21	40	58	7	1	3	21	0	0	2	5	1	45	8	0	6	.222	.251	.322
Olmstead, Walter, Billings †	70	291	264	42	73	127	14	2	12	48	1	5	8	13	0	82	2	3	3	.277	.324	.481
Pali, Matt, Provo *	64	263	223	47	73	118	15	3	8	43	0	2	6	32	0	44	2	1	3	.327	.422	.529
Palmisano, Louis, Helena	47	203	174	32	68	103	13	2	6	43	0	4	7	18	1	29	13	2	3	.391	.458	.592
Paul, Xavier, Ogden *	69	308	264	60	81	129	15	6	7	47	3	5	2	34	1	58	11	4	2	.307	.384	.489
Paula, Manuel, Billings	7	29	28	2	9	11	0	1	0	3	0	0	0	1	0	10	3	0	0	.321	.345	.393
Pavkovich, Adam, Provo	27	126	106	17	30	39	6	0	1	11	0	2	4	14	0	21	2	1	2	.283	.381	.368
Peel, Aaron, Provo	65	270	242	39	73	113	18	2	6	39	1	2	6	19	1	57	1	2	4	.302	.364	.467
Perez, Miguel, Billings	60	257	227	46	77	95	11	2	1	25	1	1	10	18	1	27	1	1	3	.339	.410	.419
Piazza, Thomas, Ogden *	6	24	23	1	2	3	1	0	0	3	1	0	0	0	0	15	0	0	0	.087	.087	.130
Ramirez, Manuel, Helena	63	250	218	36	72	126	19	1	11	52	0	4	5	23	0	48	0	1	5	.330	.400	.578
Ramirez, Yordany, Idaho Falls	22	83	79	7	21	24	3	0	0	5	0	0	1	3	0	17	7	0	3	.266	.301	.304
Renz, Jordan, Provo †	5	22	20	2	5	9	1	0	1	5	0	0	0	2	0	8	0	0	0	.250	.318	.450
Restrepo, John, Casper *	54	246	222	37	70	96	14	3	2	13	0	1	5	18	0	53	13	8	1	.315	.378	.432
Reyes, Ivan, Billings	9	18	15	1	2	2	0	0	0	0	0	0	0	3	0	6	0	0	0	.133	.278	.133
Reynolds, Henry, Casper	50	224	204	33	62	73	6	1	1	10	4	3	0	13	0	31	15	4	1	.304	.341	.358
Roberts, Dave, Ogden *	3	12	10	4	4	4	0	0	0	0	1	0	0	1	0	0	1	0	0	.400	.455	.400
Robledo, Nelson, Casper	54	223	203	23	49	69	9	1	3	29	0	1	6	13	0	43	3	2	5	.241	.305	.340
Rodriguez, Guilder, Helena †	69	309	255	51	57	60	1	1	0	25	4	1	1	47	0	35	29	3	1	.224	.345	.235
Ronda, Jose, Billings †	1	4	3	2	2	2	0	0	0	0	0	0	0	1	0	1	1	0	0	.667	.750	.667
Rottino, Vinny, Helena	64	261	222	42	69	82	10	0	1	20	1	2	8	28	1	25	5	2	4	.311	.404	.369
Santiago, Jayson, Missoula *	23	40	38	2	5	5	0	0	0	0	1	0	0	1	0	16	0	0	1	.132	.154	.132
Schnurstein, Micah, Gr. Falls	50	209	193	35	51	65	9	1	1	16	1	1	3	11	0	39	0	1	7	.264	.313	.337

Player, Team	G	TPA	AB	R	H	TB	2B	3B	HR	RBI	SH	SF	HP	BB	IBB	SO	SB	CS	GDP	Avg.	OBP	Slg.
Segura Cornier, Alberto, Hel...	28	91	80	10	26	32	1	1	1	11	0	0	4	7	0	11	3	0	1	.325	.407	.400
Sencion, Henry, Idaho Falls....	31	108	95	10	20	23	3	0	0	8	2	1	0	10	0	20	3	2	2	.211	.283	.242
Septimo, Agustin, Helena †....	56	213	182	29	39	44	3	1	0	19	2	3	4	22	0	51	8	2	1	.214	.308	.242
Slimak, Taylor, Ogden *	20	65	60	7	18	24	6	0	0	9	0	2	0	3	0	21	0	0	0	.300	.323	.400
Smith, Kyle, Billings..............	13	44	42	3	11	21	4	0	2	9	0	1	0	1	0	18	0	0	0	.262	.273	.500
Stewart, Ian, Casper *...........	57	257	224	40	71	125	14	5	10	43	0	1	3	29	3	54	4	1	5	.317	.401	.558
Strop, Pedro, Casper..............	40	149	128	13	22	31	4	1	1	11	1	0	5	15	0	43	1	3	1	.172	.284	.242
Sweeney, Ryan, Great Falls *.	10	36	34	0	12	14	2	0	0	4	0	0	0	2	0	3	0	2	1	.353	.389	.412
Tejeda, Francisco, Casper.......	43	152	148	17	30	37	3	2	0	6	1	1	0	2	0	25	5	3	3	.203	.212	.250
Trofholz, Terry, Helena	68	291	261	60	91	107	10	3	0	22	6	2	3	19	0	39	39	6	1	.349	.396	.410
Underwood, Daniel, Casper....	67	284	266	54	84	120	15	0	7	40	0	0	3	15	0	78	12	3	4	.316	.359	.451
Urgelles, Jeff, Billings	7	24	23	2	3	3	0	0	0	2	0	0	1	0	0	8	0	0	1	.130	.167	.130
Valdez, Angel, Casper.............	52	191	177	19	42	48	3	0	1	15	2	2	1	9	0	50	7	1	3	.237	.275	.271
Valdez, Jose, Casper *	39	160	142	16	36	53	4	2	3	15	0	2	0	15	0	20	2	3	2	.254	.321	.373
Valenzuela, Mario, Great Falls	17	76	62	13	22	35	4	0	3	20	0	3	4	7	1	16	0	0	1	.355	.434	.565
Vanzile, Travis, Missoula	36	57	47	8	5	5	0	0	0	4	0	0	3	6	0	12	1	0	1	.106	.250	.106
Vasquez, Jose, Casper *	8	34	31	2	6	8	2	0	0	3	0	0	2	1	0	17	0	0	0	.194	.265	.258
Vincent, Tom, Idaho Falls *....	36	119	110	12	22	34	3	0	3	11	0	0	1	8	0	35	3	2	0	.200	.261	.309
Votto, Joey, Billings *	70	301	240	47	76	117	17	3	6	38	0	1	4	56	3	80	4	0	4	.317	.452	.488
Watchko, Jeff, Casper............	31	1	1	0	0	0	0	0	0	0	0	0	0	0	0	1	0	0	0	.000	.000	.000
Whitney, Barrett, Helena *	56	210	176	24	48	71	18	1	1	28	5	4	2	23	0	35	0	1	5	.273	.356	.403
Willits, Reggie, Provo †	59	276	230	53	69	103	14	4	4	27	3	0	6	37	0	52	14	4	2	.300	.410	.448
Wilson, Neil, Casper...............	23	98	78	13	23	37	6	1	2	12	0	0	1	19	0	15	3	0	1	.295	.439	.474
Wilson, Robert, Provo †	57	258	236	36	67	97	12	0	6	62	0	4	0	18	0	31	0	0	11	.284	.329	.411
Wood, Brandon, Provo...........	42	181	162	25	45	77	13	2	5	31	0	1	2	16	0	48	1	1	2	.278	.348	.475
Young, Chris, Great Falls........	10	35	34	5	6	9	3	0	0	0	0	0	0	1	0	10	0	0	0	.176	.200	.265
Ziemendorf, Chad, Billings.....	22	58	50	9	9	14	5	0	0	4	0	0	5	3	0	20	0	1	0	.180	.293	.280

GRAND SLAMS—Nanita, M. Ramirez, 2 each; Bolivar, R. Carter, Dickerson, Madrigal, Martin, Morris, Mottram, Olivares, Strop, R. Wilson, 1 each.

AWARDED FIRST BASE ON CATCHER'S INTERFERENCE—De Aza 2 (D. Martinez, Robledo); Brown (Perez); Kaye (Underwood); Lauderdale (Underwood); G. Rodriguez (Perez); J. Valdez (Martin); Vanzile (Martin).

2003 PITCHING

TEAM

Team	W	L	Pct.	ERA	G	CG	ShO	Sv.	IP	H	TBF	R	ER	HR	SH	SF	HB	BB	IBB	SO	WP	Bk.
Billings	41	35	.539	3.22	76	0	4	25	662.1	655	2911	343	237	28	23	14	44	251	6	579	70	13
Provo	54	22	.711	3.62	76	0	4	26	661.1	693	2892	344	266	33	21	21	45	196	9	591	53	2
Helena..............	48	28	.632	3.93	76	1	5	27	662.1	711	2905	373	289	51	21	31	55	208	7	600	89	6
Ogden	35	41	.461	4.59	76	0	1	15	657.0	715	2982	449	335	51	21	25	52	275	1	690	104	8
Great Falls.........	38	38	.500	4.89	76	2	3	15	666.0	759	3007	443	362	52	25	25	61	228	5	599	98	5
Casper...............	28	48	.368	5.12	76	1	1	15	665.0	799	3086	513	378	58	19	28	45	267	8	544	53	9
Missoula	36	40	.474	5.13	76	3	3	19	653.0	733	2957	445	372	54	24	21	42	262	4	554	80	10
Idaho Falls.........	24	52	.316	5.55	76	0	1	16	651.2	769	3016	496	402	72	14	26	51	282	3	608	74	6

INDIVIDUAL

TOP QUALIFIERS FOR EARNED-RUN AVERAGE TITLE

Minimum 61 innings.*Lefthanded pitcher.

Pitcher, Team	W	L	Pct.	ERA	G	GS	CG	ShO	GF	Sv.	IP	H	TBF	R	ER	HR	SH	SF	HB	BB	IBB	SO	WP	Bk.
Davidson, Daniel, Provo *	8	2	.800	1.64	15	13	0	0	0	0	71.1	65	294	17	13	3	4	1	3	15	0	50	3	0
Paduch, James, Billings	7	1	.875	1.94	15	15	0	0	0	0	78.2	72	328	28	17	1	0	2	8	20	0	65	5	0
Moreno, Abel, Provo	10	0	1.000	2.38	13	10	0	0	0	0	68.0	58	271	23	18	3	0	1	0	10	0	79	6	1
Knoff, Justin, Billings	7	4	.636	2.83	14	11	0	0	1	0	76.1	76	319	32	24	4	3	0	4	19	1	53	7	0
Hawk, Derek, Billings	5	3	.625	2.97	14	12	0	0	1	1	69.2	70	288	30	23	6	0	1	2	16	0	53	6	0
Rocha, Angel, Missoula *	5	8	.385	3.12	15	15	1	0	0	0	92.1	79	381	43	32	7	7	1	2	26	0	82	5	3
Kloosterman, Gregory, Hel.* ...	6	1	.857	3.28	14	14	0	0	0	0	68.2	68	289	28	25	4	1	1	0	23	0	76	5	0
Megrew, Mike, Ogden *	5	3	.625	3.40	14	14	0	0	0	0	76.2	64	321	40	29	6	2	3	4	24	0	99	9	2
Ramirez, Carlos, Helena *	7	3	.700	3.46	15	15	1	0	0	0	78.0	78	328	34	30	1	6	1	6	17	0	60	5	0
Arias, Alberto, Casper	4	4	.500	3.58	13	13	1	0	0	0	73.0	69	313	45	29	4	2	2	3	23	0	64	5	1
McCarthy, Brandon, Gr. Falls...	9	4	.692	3.65	16	15	1	0	0	0	101.0	105	425	49	41	7	4	3	3	15	0	125	3	3
Tracey, Sean, Great Falls	8	5	.615	3.69	16	12	1	0	1	0	92.2	90	394	45	38	5	5	5	14	22	0	74	5	0
Conden, Gregory, Idaho Falls..	4	3	.571	3.94	15	15	0	0	0	0	80.0	78	342	37	35	3	2	1	9	29	0	96	5	1
Mora, Yency, Idaho Falls	4	3	.571	4.50	19	9	0	0	1	0	72.0	76	321	44	36	9	0	2	5	31	1	58	6	1
Yamaguchi, Tetsuya, Miss.*....	6	7	.462	4.54	15	15	1	0	0	0	83.1	89	365	47	42	3	4	3	7	28	0	63	9	1

DEPARTMENTAL LEADERS: W—Moreno, 10; L—Ponce, 11; Pct.—Moreno, 1.000; G—Bright, 33; GS—Robles, 16; CG—Several pitchers tied with 1; ShO—none; GF—Klatt, 31; Sv.—Cremidan, 15; IP—McCarthy, 101.0; H—Robles, 114; TBF—McCarthy, 425; R—Morillo, 73; ER—Cuen, 58; HR—Cuen, Santo, 12; SH—Rocha, 7; SF—Ponce, 7; HB—Tracey, 14; BB—Allender, 42; IBB—Several pitchers tied with 2; SO—McCarthy, 125; WP—Pratt, 15; BK—Cabrera, 4.

ALL PITCHERS

*Lefthanded pitcher.

Pitcher, Team	W	L	Pct.	ERA	G	GS	CG	ShO	GF	Sv.	IP	H	TBF	R	ER	HR	SH	SF	HB	BB	IBB	SO	WP	Bk.
Ahumada, Edgar, Ogden *	1	5	.167	4.91	12	8	0	0	3	0	44.0	56	213	36	24	2	3	0	4	23	0	33	7	1
Allender, John, Missoula	1	4	.200	11.12	17	8	0	0	4	0	39.2	49	213	57	49	4	0	0	5	42	0	38	15	0
Alvarez, Gabriel, Ogden..........	3	2	.600	4.25	19	0	0	0	2	1	42.1	44	195	26	20	5	0	0	3	22	1	58	8	2
Arias, Alberto, Casper	4	4	.500	3.58	13	13	1	0	0	0	73.0	69	313	45	29	4	2	2	3	23	0	64	5	1
Astacio, Hector, Provo............	0	3	.000	11.39	14	3	0	0	6	0	27.2	50	151	42	35	5	2	1	5	15	1	21	4	1
Austen, David, Provo..............	4	2	.667	1.85	23	3	0	0	12	8	43.2	46	183	12	9	0	0	2	3	7	0	49	3	0
Baca, Daniel, Idaho Falls	0	1	.000	6.30	5	0	0	0	2	0	10.0	14	57	12	7	2	0	1	1	9	0	9	0	0
Bailey, Chad, Ogden *	1	2	.333	2.57	14	2	0	0	4	2	42.0	38	176	17	12	1	0	0	4	19	0	43	8	0

Pitcher, Team	W	L	Pct.	ERA	G	GS	CG	ShO	GF	Sv.	IP	H	TBF	R	ER	HR	SH	SF	HB	BB	IBB	SO	WP	Bk.
Beerer, Scott, Casper	0	2	.000	7.71	5	3	0	0	1	1	14.0	23	70	13	12	3	0	0	1	5	0	10	0	0
Beresford, Simon, Helena	2	4	.333	5.28	17	0	0	0	7	1	29.0	32	139	28	17	3	2	4	6	14	2	19	7	0
Billingsley, Chad, Ogden	5	4	.556	2.83	11	11	0	0	0	0	54.0	49	225	24	17	0	3	2	3	15	0	62	8	0
Bohorquez, Carlos, Billings	1	3	.250	3.41	19	0	0	0	3	1	37.0	34	169	27	14	0	6	2	2	16	0	46	7	2
Bright, Adam, Casper *	2	2	.500	4.29	33	0	0	0	8	0	42.0	46	190	27	20	3	0	0	1	22	0	25	5	0
Cabrera, Walin, Billings	4	5	.444	5.00	16	9	0	0	0	0	54.0	58	248	40	30	3	2	0	4	27	0	36	5	4
Carroll, James, Provo	0	1	.000	3.24	4	0	0	0	2	0	8.1	9	35	3	3	0	0	0	0	2	2	9	1	0
Carter, Nic, Helena	1	0	1.000	4.97	8	0	0	0	2	0	12.2	15	60	12	7	0	0	0	1	10	0	11	7	1
Carvajal, Marcos, Ogden	2	1	.667	3.08	23	0	0	0	21	2	38.0	32	173	16	13	1	2	2	4	22	0	50	6	1
Colbert, Henry, Idaho Falls	0	1	.000	4.15	16	0	0	0	5	1	30.1	38	142	23	14	6	1	1	2	12	0	37	2	0
Conden, Gregory, Idaho Falls	4	3	.571	3.94	15	15	0	0	0	0	80.0	78	342	37	35	3	2	1	9	29	0	96	5	1
Cox, Jason, Provo	1	1	.500	6.39	9	0	0	0	6	1	12.2	17	64	12	9	2	0	1	3	4	0	7	0	0
Cremidan, Alexander, Mis.	2	1	.667	1.40	24	0	0	0	21	15	25.2	17	110	6	4	0	0	1	1	12	1	30	3	1
Cuen, David, Ogden *	3	8	.273	8.11	15	15	0	0	0	0	64.1	102	313	68	58	12	3	4	4	20	0	44	12	0
Cuevas, Manuel, Missoula	0	0	.000	8.07	16	1	0	0	3	0	29.0	49	145	32	26	5	3	0	2	8	0	16	4	2
Davidson, Daniel, Provo *	8	2	.800	1.64	15	13	0	0	0	0	71.1	65	294	17	13	3	4	1	3	15	0	50	3	0
De La O, Danny, Idaho Falls *	3	1	.750	4.50	31	2	0	0	6	3	48.0	47	206	26	24	2	4	0	0	14	1	56	8	0
De Los Santos, Omar, Ogden	0	0	.000	0.00	5	2	0	0	0	0	12.2	7	51	0	0	0	0	0	2	5	0	13	0	0
De Montigny, Mat, Idaho Falls.	0	1	.000	9.00	18	0	0	0	4	0	23.0	39	122	32	23	3	0	2	0	11	0	23	8	0
Diangelo, Jason, Casper	2	3	.400	4.71	17	9	0	0	1	0	65.0	82	289	41	34	5	0	5	4	13	0	47	3	0
Diaz, Jose, Ogden	0	0	.000	3.86	2	0	0	0	0	0	2.1	2	11	1	1	0	0	0	0	1	0	2	0	0
Dillard, Timothy, Helena	0	0	.000	0.00	3	0	0	0	1	0	5.0	5	22	0	0	0	0	0	0	2	0	6	2	0
Dizard, Fraser, Great Falls *	3	0	1.000	4.02	12	6	0	0	2	0	40.1	49	182	22	18	2	0	1	3	16	1	30	7	0
Dove, Shane, Missoula *	1	1	.500	4.19	19	1	0	0	3	1	38.2	40	162	23	18	6	1	1	2	7	1	34	2	0
Dumesnil, Bryan, Ogden *	1	0	1.000	8.05	16	0	0	0	8	0	19.0	17	97	17	17	1	0	0	2	21	0	24	5	0
Durost, Kenneth, Helena	3	5	.375	5.26	17	8	0	0	1	0	51.1	67	233	34	30	9	2	2	4	16	1	42	10	0
Escorcha, Orlando, Billings *	5	1	.833	2.20	17	2	0	0	1	0	41.0	39	180	15	10	1	2	0	1	19	2	44	7	2
Eveland, Dana, Helena *	2	1	.667	2.08	19	0	0	0	18	14	26.0	30	117	9	6	1	1	1	2	8	1	41	5	1
Fernandez, Alfredo, Id. Falls	0	5	.000	6.25	11	11	0	0	0	0	44.2	61	213	37	31	7	1	2	3	23	0	38	9	1
Garcia, Geivy, Idaho Falls	0	2	.000	4.41	24	3	0	0	7	0	49.0	52	232	29	24	4	1	2	9	24	1	53	5	1
Gelatka, Todd, Helena	0	0	.000	3.00	3	0	0	0	1	0	6.0	5	24	2	2	0	0	0	0	1	0	5	1	0
George, Jon, Billings	2	2	.500	3.77	6	6	0	0	0	0	28.2	38	138	19	12	1	0	1	1	13	0	25	4	2
Geraldo, Jose, Idaho Falls	1	3	.250	5.97	21	2	0	0	4	0	34.2	47	163	33	23	1	0	2	2	10	0	25	4	0
Goas, Adrian, Provo	1	0	1.000	3.12	7	0	0	0	7	4	8.2	9	40	3	3	0	1	0	2	2	0	4	0	0
Groeger, Jeff, Billings	1	2	.333	7.33	12	2	0	0	3	2	27.0	34	131	25	22	3	1	2	4	17	1	23	0	1
Grybash, Daniel, Helena	2	1	.667	2.82	17	6	0	0	2	0	38.1	37	162	19	12	1	1	2	5	12	0	31	4	0
Guerrero, Hipolito, Missoula *	0	0	.000	5.40	23	0	0	0	7	0	25.0	27	107	16	15	2	0	0	2	6	0	21	0	0
Guevara, Jose, Billings	1	0	1.000	0.82	2	2	0	0	0	0	11.0	4	40	1	1	0	0	0	0	3	0	14	2	0
Guzman, Carlos, Casper	0	1	.000	14.73	4	1	0	0	0	0	7.1	11	45	12	12	2	1	0	3	11	0	6	3	0
Harrelson, Paul, Casper	1	0	1.000	1.69	5	0	0	0	0	0	10.2	13	47	8	2	0	0	0	0	3	0	14	0	0
Hawk, Derek, Billings	5	3	.625	2.97	14	12	0	0	1	1	69.2	70	288	30	23	6	0	1	2	16	0	53	6	0
Hedden, Wayne, Provo	2	0	1.000	2.76	17	0	0	0	3	1	32.2	33	147	15	10	1	4	2	4	14	1	20	6	0
Henderson, Eric, Helena *	3	0	1.000	3.26	4	2	0	0	0	0	19.1	14	72	8	7	3	0	1	1	2	0	14	0	1
Hendley, Blake, Billings	1	4	.200	4.97	6	6	0	0	0	0	29.0	37	141	22	16	0	1	0	1	11	0	18	2	0
Hendrix, Phillip, Helena	2	1	.667	6.38	16	0	0	0	5	0	24.0	34	114	18	17	4	0	2	1	7	0	23	4	0
Hernandez, Fernando, Gr. Falls	1	3	.250	2.70	24	0	0	0	23	7	23.1	23	101	10	7	0	1	1	1	10	0	14	7	0
Hindman, Scott, Provo *	3	0	1.000	4.13	6	4	0	0	0	0	24.0	21	106	13	11	0	1	1	3	13	0	17	5	0
Hudson, Jeremy, Great Falls	1	0	1.000	5.14	2	1	0	0	0	0	7.0	11	33	4	4	1	1	0	2	1	0	2	2	0
Hurd, John, Great Falls	0	0	.000	13.50	7	0	0	0	4	0	6.0	11	32	10	9	1	0	0	0	4	0	6	3	0
Huson, Tim, Great Falls	0	0	.000	0.00	1	0	0	0	1	0	1.0	1	7	2	0	0	0	0	0	2	0	0	0	0
Ion, Mark, Casper	1	3	.250	3.00	27	0	0	0	27	11	27.0	26	127	15	9	2	2	1	4	13	2	25	4	0
Jacquez, Tom, Great Falls *	0	0	.000	2.45	6	4	0	0	0	0	11.0	12	44	3	3	0	0	0	0	3	0	9	3	0
Johnson, J.D., Great Falls	2	4	.333	4.46	19	0	0	0	3	0	42.1	47	189	25	21	4	4	1	3	10	1	47	9	1
Julio, Donald, Missoula	3	3	.500	7.68	18	5	0	0	2	0	43.1	69	208	41	37	6	1	4	4	9	0	36	8	0
Kane, Kyle, Great Falls	0	1	.000	5.14	5	5	0	0	0	0	7.0	6	30	4	4	0	0	1	1	2	0	3	1	0
Kaye, Brandon, Idaho Falls *	0	0	.000	0.00	1	0	0	0	1	0	1.0	0	4	0	0	0	0	0	1	0	0	0	0	0
Kerschen, Joshua, Casper	0	1	.000	5.40	4	0	0	0	0	0	6.2	8	30	4	4	0	1	0	2	2	2	6	0	0
Klatt, Ryan, Idaho Falls	2	3	.400	2.12	32	0	0	0	31	12	29.2	24	117	9	7	4	0	0	1	3	0	51	2	0
Kloosterman, Gregory, Hel.*	6	1	.857	3.28	14	14	0	0	0	0	68.2	68	289	28	25	4	1	1	0	23	0	76	5	0
Knoff, Justin, Billings	7	4	.636	2.83	14	11	0	0	1	0	76.1	76	319	32	24	4	3	0	4	19	1	53	7	0
Krantz, Ben, Missoula	1	2	.333	5.98	17	8	0	0	2	0	46.2	50	213	36	31	6	1	1	2	23	0	32	6	0
Larson, Brett, Idaho Falls	2	5	.286	6.57	26	0	0	0	6	0	38.1	40	176	32	28	4	2	1	2	26	0	26	13	1
Liebeck, Jered, Missoula	0	0	.000	3.38	5	0	0	0	1	0	8.0	10	37	5	3	0	0	0	1	3	1	11	0	0
Little, Jeffrey, Great Falls	1	0	1.000	3.66	12	0	0	0	2	0	19.2	26	93	11	8	1	0	1	1	7	0	23	4	0
Logan, Boone, Great Falls *	3	3	.500	6.58	16	14	0	0	0	0	67.0	76	321	60	49	4	3	4	11	31	0	48	8	1
McCarthy, Brandon, Gr. Falls	9	4	.692	3.65	16	15	1	0	0	0	101.0	105	425	49	41	7	4	3	3	15	0	125	3	3
McGary, Gerron, Great Falls *	0	0	.000	13.50	2	0	0	0	1	0	4.0	5	22	6	6	1	0	1	0	5	0	8	6	0
McKenna, Daniel, Helena	1	1	.500	5.60	13	0	0	0	3	0	17.2	20	83	12	11	1	1	0	2	7	0	21	4	1
Medina, Julio, Billings	0	0	.000	1.69	4	0	0	0	1	0	5.1	1	24	2	1	0	0	0	1	5	0	1	1	0
Medlock, Calvin, Billings	1	0	1.000	1.88	19	0	0	0	8	1	28.2	25	119	7	6	1	1	2	0	9	0	31	2	0
Megrew, Mike, Ogden *	5	3	.625	3.40	14	14	0	0	0	0	76.2	64	321	40	29	6	2	3	4	24	0	99	9	2
Mendoza, Gabriel, Helena *	0	1	.000	12.46	5	0	0	0	3	0	4.1	9	28	6	6	0	0	0	0	5	2	4	0	1
Merino, Joshua, Casper	0	2	.000	7.50	3	3	0	0	0	0	12.0	17	61	15	10	1	0	0	3	4	0	10	1	2
Merrell, Darric, Casper	4	4	.500	5.10	13	11	0	0	0	0	60.0	77	266	40	34	8	0	2	3	14	0	39	3	2
Mitchell, Jay, Casper	2	3	.400	9.35	22	5	0	0	2	0	42.1	56	219	49	44	5	0	2	2	33	0	33	7	0
Moat, Michael, Great Falls	2	0	1.000	3.99	18	0	0	0	8	2	38.1	34	163	20	17	7	1	1	3	10	1	28	3	0
Montalbo, Brian, Helena	2	1	.667	3.18	13	4	0	0	2	1	45.1	51	200	26	16	4	0	3	2	12	0	30	7	0
Mora, Yency, Idaho Falls	4	3	.571	4.50	19	9	0	0	1	0	72.0	76	321	44	36	9	0	2	5	31	1	58	6	1
Morban, Carlos, Provo	2	1	.667	3.18	21	0	0	0	15	5	22.2	20	97	8	8	1	3	1	1	8	0	26	5	0
Moreira, Greg, Helena	2	2	.500	4.33	17	7	0	0	3	0	43.2	57	204	33	21	4	1	5	7	14	0	22	5	0
Moreno, Abel, Provo	10	0	1.000	2.38	13	10	0	0	0	0	68.0	58	271	23	18	3	0	1	0	10	0	79	6	1
Morillo, Juan, Casper	1	6	.143	5.91	15	15	0	0	0	0	64.0	85	320	73	42	6	4	4	5	40	0	44	7	0
Moviel, Paul, Great Falls	0	3	.000	7.48	14	0	0	0	3	0	21.2	31	109	22	18	0	1	3	1	8	0	20	12	0
Nachreiner, Matthew, Gr. Falls.	2	4	.333	11.25	13	5	0	0	0	0	28.0	50	163	45	35	7	3	0	6	20	1	23	7	0
Nippert, Derik, Missoula	0	0	.000	4.96	13	0	0	0	8	0	16.1	20	76	14	9	1	0	1	2	6	0	9	5	1
Novosel, Walt, Missoula *	4	1	.800	0.30	25	0	0	0	6	1	30.1	21	123	4	1	0	0	1	0	13	0	33	5	0
Paduch, James, Billings	7	1	.875	1.94	15	15	0	0	0	0	78.2	72	328	28	17	1	0	2	8	20	0	65	5	0

Pitcher, Team	W	L	Pct.	ERA	G	GS	CG	ShO	GF	Sv.	IP	H	TBF	R	ER	HR	SH	SF	HB	BB	IBB	SO	WP	Bk.
Parker, David, Ogden	2	1	.667	3.76	18	0	0	0	4	1	40.2	38	175	20	17	3	0	4	2	15	0	47	6	0
Pawelczyk, Kyle, Provo *	3	2	.600	4.03	5	4	0	0	0	0	22.1	19	95	13	10	1	0	2	3	8	0	20	3	0
Payne, Matt, Great Falls	0	0	.000	0.00	4	0	0	0	1	1	3.1	0	14	0	0	0	0	0	0	5	0	4	0	0
Pence, Howard, Idaho Falls	2	2	.500	5.91	27	0	0	0	8	0	35.0	46	162	26	23	2	0	0	3	15	0	19	1	0
Perrault, Josh, Missoula	3	1	.750	3.47	24	1	0	0	8	2	36.1	38	158	15	14	1	2	1	2	11	0	33	2	0
Ponce, William, Idaho Falls	1	11	.083	7.07	15	15	0	0	0	0	70.0	98	338	65	55	8	0	7	7	34	0	54	5	0
Pratt, Jordan, Ogden	0	9	.000	7.69	16	8	0	0	1	0	45.2	65	230	54	39	4	2	4	6	18	0	31	15	0
Pullin, Aaron, Provo	5	1	.833	3.42	23	0	0	0	2	0	47.1	54	199	23	18	0	1	2	3	5	1	32	2	0
Ramirez, Carlos, Helena *	7	3	.700	3.46	15	15	1	0	0	0	78.0	78	328	34	30	1	6	1	6	17	0	60	5	0
Reed, Rylan, Great Falls	1	3	.250	5.75	14	2	0	0	2	0	36.0	47	163	24	23	2	1	2	1	18	0	26	12	0
Requena, Ricardo, Provo	2	2	.500	9.35	9	1	0	0	2	0	17.1	28	94	28	18	3	0	2	3	6	1	14	1	0
Reyes, Ramon, Provo	0	1	.000	7.88	6	0	0	0	6	1	8.0	12	43	7	7	0	0	2	0	6	0	8	3	0
Richardson, Judd, Helena	2	1	.667	5.18	14	12	0	0	0	0	40.0	49	188	27	23	5	0	2	4	22	0	30	2	0
Riley, Kenny, Casper	0	1	.000	7.43	23	0	0	0	3	0	36.1	61	186	37	30	3	0	1	2	17	0	29	3	0
Robles, Larry, Casper	3	7	.300	5.87	16	16	0	0	0	0	79.2	114	378	68	52	9	3	5	5	21	0	58	1	2
Rocha, Angel, Missoula *	5	8	.385	3.12	15	15	1	0	0	0	92.1	79	381	43	32	7	7	1	2	26	0	82	5	3
Rodriguez, Fernando, Provo	0	0	.000	1.50	4	0	0	0	3	1	6.0	9	28	4	1	1	0	0	0	1	0	9	1	0
Rodriguez, Mike, Ogden	1	0	1.000	3.27	2	2	0	0	0	0	11.0	13	46	4	4	0	0	0	0	2	0	6	0	0
Rogers, Nathan, Idaho Falls *	0	6	.000	10.31	9	8	0	0	0	0	29.2	43	154	38	34	5	2	1	5	18	0	19	2	0
Rosen, Mark, Missoula *	5	5	.500	5.81	13	12	0	0	0	0	62.0	76	298	48	40	4	2	3	6	38	0	56	8	0
Russ, John, Great Falls	0	3	.000	4.58	16	2	0	0	8	4	35.1	43	157	25	18	5	0	0	1	13	0	29	4	0
Santo, Joel, Idaho Falls	5	5	.500	6.71	16	11	0	0	1	0	56.1	66	267	53	42	12	1	4	1	23	0	44	4	1
Schmoll, Stephen, Ogden	3	1	.750	3.68	24	1	0	0	22	7	36.2	27	160	23	15	2	0	2	7	15	0	53	4	0
Shafer, David, Billings	0	3	.000	3.04	25	0	0	0	24	13	23.2	25	104	13	8	1	0	1	1	3	1	32	0	0
Silva, Doug, Casper	2	5	.286	2.85	27	0	0	0	8	0	41.0	27	165	15	13	3	2	2	1	12	1	52	0	0
Silva, Erick, Missoula	3	3	.500	6.82	7	7	1	0	0	0	31.2	50	153	26	24	5	1	2	2	10	0	25	4	0
Simard, Michel, Provo	4	1	.800	2.08	12	10	0	0	0	0	52.0	42	209	15	12	2	1	0	3	12	0	53	2	0
Slack, Nicholas, Helena	1	1	.500	2.19	19	0	0	0	18	10	24.2	13	95	6	6	3	0	0	1	6	0	37	5	0
Smith, Jesse, Provo	0	1	.000	2.41	5	3	0	0	0	0	18.2	19	82	8	5	2	0	0	2	6	0	20	1	0
Sobkow, Philip, Ogden	5	3	.625	6.08	14	12	0	0	2	1	53.1	70	255	49	36	7	1	3	4	30	0	48	9	1
Stertzbach, Von, Provo	1	1	.500	4.82	22	5	0	0	5	0	46.2	55	213	31	25	2	0	0	1	14	2	51	1	0
Stetter, Mitchel, Helena *	6	2	.750	3.95	15	8	0	0	0	0	54.2	55	239	34	24	3	1	2	6	12	0	63	7	0
Stewart, James, Ogden	2	1	.667	3.65	18	1	0	0	4	0	44.1	56	194	28	18	7	4	0	0	8	0	34	0	0
Stover, Ricky, Helena *	0	2	.000	6.56	16	0	0	0	7	0	23.1	25	112	24	17	2	1	5	5	15	1	21	7	0
Suarez, Sony, Great Falls	0	1	.000	18.90	2	1	0	0	0	0	3.1	7	18	7	7	1	0	0	1	2	0	4	0	0
Surratt, Randy, Great Falls *	4	1	.800	2.25	23	0	0	0	12	1	36.0	32	149	15	9	2	0	1	3	13	0	34	0	0
Talamantez, David, Billings	2	1	.667	5.35	16	1	0	0	3	0	33.2	35	147	22	20	3	3	1	7	7	0	30	5	0
Taubenheim, Ty, Helena	6	1	.857	2.15	14	0	0	0	2	1	50.1	47	196	13	12	3	4	0	2	3	0	44	2	1
Thompson, Sean, Gr. Falls *	1	1	.500	5.90	10	5	0	0	3	0	29.0	40	140	24	19	2	0	0	4	8	1	28	2	0
Tiffany, Charles, Ogden *	0	0	.000	10.13	3	0	0	0	0	0	2.2	4	15	4	3	0	0	1	1	2	0	4	0	0
Till, Brock, Billings	1	1	.500	2.48	18	0	0	0	9	2	29.0	23	136	16	8	0	2	0	3	21	1	23	4	1
Touchstone, Nick, Provo *	2	1	.667	3.56	14	10	0	0	1	0	48.0	47	219	27	19	2	0	1	4	35	0	48	5	0
Tracey, Sean, Great Falls	8	5	.615	3.69	16	12	1	0	1	0	92.2	90	394	45	38	5	5	5	14	22	0	74	5	0
Trepkowski, Matthew, Bil.*	0	0	.000	5.14	9	0	0	0	4	0	7.0	4	43	5	4	0	0	0	2	17	0	5	3	0
Ulacia, Dennis, Great Falls *	0	2	.000	6.39	4	4	0	0	0	0	12.2	13	58	10	9	0	1	0	2	3	0	14	0	0
Ursin, Damian, Billings	0	0	.000	0.00	7	0	0	0	6	4	9.0	3	32	0	0	0	0	0	0	1	0	13	0	0
Vaillancourt, Tim, Missoula	0	3	.000	6.41	22	0	0	0	8	0	26.2	33	130	21	19	3	1	2	1	16	0	22	4	0
Vazquez, Camilo, Billings *	2	3	.400	3.03	9	8	0	0	0	0	35.2	35	157	20	12	2	1	2	1	15	0	33	5	0
Vicente, Ruben, Missoula	2	1	.667	5.00	3	3	0	0	0	0	18.0	16	78	11	10	1	1	0	1	4	1	13	0	2
Wachman, Corey, Billings	0	1	.000	7.50	2	2	0	0	0	0	6.0	11	32	5	5	1	0	0	0	5	0	5	3	0
Watchko, Jeff, Casper	5	3	.625	1.75	31	0	0	0	13	3	46.1	38	190	17	9	2	3	3	3	11	2	41	3	2
Wells, Mark, Billings	1	1	.500	1.97	23	0	0	0	12	1	32.0	31	135	14	7	1	1	0	2	7	0	29	2	1
White, Michael, Ogden *	1	1	.500	3.95	19	0	0	0	5	1	27.1	31	132	22	12	0	1	0	2	13	0	39	7	1
Wiley, Mike, Casper *	1	1	.500	5.26	32	0	0	0	12	0	37.2	46	190	34	22	2	1	1	3	23	1	41	8	0
Wilhite, Matt, Provo	2	0	1.000	2.63	12	0	0	0	6	5	27.1	23	109	11	8	1	2	1	0	5	0	17	0	0
Yamaguchi, Tetsuya, Mis.*	6	7	.462	4.54	15	15	1	0	0	0	83.1	89	365	47	42	3	4	3	7	28	0	63	9	1
Zimmermann, Bob, Provo	4	2	.667	4.50	11	10	0	0	0	0	48.0	57	213	29	24	4	2	1	2	8	1	37	1	0

COMBINATION SHUTOUTS: Billings (4)—Vazquez-Bohorquez-Wells, Paduch-Till-Trepkowski, Paduch-Medlock, Escorcha-Talamantez-Shafer. Casper (1)—Merrell-Beerer-Bright-Ion. Great Falls (3)—Jacquez-Tracey, Nachreiner-Johnson-Reed, McCarthy-Moat. Helena (5)—Ramirez-McKenna-Gelatka, Grybash-Stover-Durost-McKenna-Mendoza, Richardson-McKenna-Moreira, Durost-Montalbo, Kloosterman-Hendrix-McKenna. Idaho Falls (1)—Mora-Pence-De la O-Klatt. Missoula (3)—Yamaguchi-Novosel-Perrault-Cremidan, Rosen-Julio-Novosel-Cremidan, Rocha-Novosel-Cremidan. Ogden (1)—Billingsley-De Los Santos-White-Schmoll. Provo (4)—Davidson-Hedden-Goas, Simard-Austen-Hedden, Zimmermann-Austen, Moreno-Hedden-Morban.

NO-HIT GAMES: None.

2003 FIELDING

TEAM

Team	G	PO	A	E	TC	DP	TP	PB	Pct.
Missoula	76	1959	818	107	2884	55	0	13	.963
Helena	76	1987	780	115	2882	66	1	23	.960
Provo	76	1984	822	121	2927	64	0	11	.959
Idaho Falls	76	1955	735	129	2819	67	0	25	.954
Ogden	76	1971	785	134	2890	57	0	45	.954
Great Falls	76	1998	788	142	2928	69	0	25	.952
Casper	76	1995	852	160	3007	51	1	44	.947
Billings	76	1987	794	162	2943	66	0	24	.945

INDIVIDUAL

FIRST BASEMEN

NOTE: All caps denotes fielding-percentage leader based on 38 games for catchers, 51 for all other non-pitchers and 61 innings for pitchers. *Throws lefthanded.

Player, Team	Pct.	G	PO	A	E	TC	DP
Bounds, Brandon, Great Falls	.975	60	489	27	13	529	45
Brinson, Matt, Casper *	.958	9	87	5	4	96	5
Brito, Javier, Missoula	.988	34	219	20	3	242	19
Burnham, Brett, Idaho Falls	1.000	5	42	2	0	44	4

Player, Team	Pct.	G	PO	A	E	TC	DP
Comfort, Geoff, Ogden	.979	46	405	23	9	437	36
Dale, Lachlan, Idaho Falls	.967	23	142	5	5	152	15
Fuller, Casey, Casper *	1.000	2	19	0	0	19	2
Ghutzman, Stephen, Casper	.986	8	67	3	1	71	5
Guerrero, Michael, Missoula	1.000	1	0	1	0	1	1
Gutierrez, Tonys, Billings *	1.000	1	5	1	0	6	1
Huson, Tim, Great Falls	.889	1	8	0	1	9	0
Kaye, Brandon, Idaho Falls *	.977	45	321	21	8	350	26
Kelly, Christopher, Great Falls	.982	21	154	7	3	164	11
Kenning, Ryan, Provo *	.983	49	423	28	8	459	27
Kottaras, George, Idaho Falls	1.000	5	30	4	0	34	0
Lee, Carlos, Great Falls	1.000	2	13	1	0	14	1
Ludwig, Michael, Ogden	.992	28	214	24	2	240	16
Lynch, Michael, Ogden	.971	4	31	2	1	34	1
Martinez, Domingo, Idaho Falls	1.000	2	5	1	0	6	0
Martinez, Thomas, Idaho Falls	.969	7	59	4	2	65	7
McCreery, John, Missoula	1.000	26	214	10	0	224	13
Mosby, Robert, Billings	.942	11	62	3	4	69	4
Mottram, Allen, Missoula	.984	28	232	18	4	254	16
Olmstead, Walter, Billings	.982	7	53	2	1	56	1
Pali, Matt, Provo *	.983	35	272	25	5	302	30
Ramirez, Manuel, Helena	.978	18	124	9	3	136	13
Robledo, Nelson, Casper	.990	11	93	6	1	100	1
Rottino, Vinny, Helena	.995	30	201	18	1	220	18
Underwood, Daniel, Casper	.977	33	276	25	7	308	18
Valdez, Jose, Casper	.983	19	153	17	3	173	13
VOTTO, JOEY, Billings	.979	64	517	36	12	565	48
Whitney, Barrett, Helena	.990	38	277	19	3	299	25

SECOND BASEMEN

Player, Team	Pct.	G	PO	A	E	TC	DP
Almonte, Aneury, Provo	.973	23	32	40	2	74	8
Baker, Casey, Idaho Falls	.800	2	3	1	1	5	1
Beale, David, Billings	.972	35	58	81	4	143	19
Bolivar, Luis, Billings	.982	10	24	32	1	57	9
Bonifacio, Emilio, Missoula	.949	51	84	122	11	217	22
Burnham, Brett, Idaho Falls	.986	37	56	84	2	142	17
Cairns, Troy, Billings	1.000	2	1	5	0	6	0
Crissotomo, Miguel, Ogden	.908	19	38	41	8	87	10
Cruceta, Julio, Idaho Falls	.939	14	23	39	4	66	6
Dowdy, Brett, Ogden	.943	16	22	44	4	70	10
Ferrer, Simon, Ogden	.973	8	16	20	1	37	6
Figueroa, Baudilio, Idaho Falls	1.000	1	3	4	0	7	2
Gomez, Andri, Helena	.941	16	23	25	3	51	5
Gonzalez, Juan, Ogden	.982	16	18	37	1	56	5
Gray, Antoin, Great Falls	.935	49	94	121	15	230	23
Guzman, Jose, Provo	.857	4	5	1	1	7	0
Haggerty, Cory, Great Falls	.956	26	44	64	5	113	18
Hernandez, Habelito, Billings	.917	29	55	78	12	145	20
Herrera, Jonathan, Casper	.949	39	76	129	11	216	17
Hodges, Brent, Great Falls	.882	8	6	9	2	17	4
Hudson, William, Billings	.818	2	2	7	2	11	1
Kendrick, Howie, Provo	.944	63	105	183	17	305	36
Laurin, Dominique, Ogden	.989	20	35	57	1	93	9
Lewis, William, Helena	1.000	1	1	1	0	2	1
McStoots, Jason, Missoula	.957	23	33	56	4	93	10
Murillo, Agustin, Missoula	.971	10	12	21	1	34	4
Reyes, Ivan, Billings	.800	2	2	2	1	5	0
Reynolds, Henry, Casper	.963	8	8	18	1	27	3
RODRIGUEZ, GUILDER, Helena	.972	69	146	168	9	323	43
Sencion, Henry, Idaho Falls	.964	28	49	59	4	112	17
Tejeda, Francisco, Casper	.948	30	54	91	8	153	17
Valdez, Jose, Casper	.947	4	8	10	1	19	1

THIRD BASEMEN

Player, Team	Pct.	G	PO	A	E	TC	DP
Barnes, Justin, Helena	.921	54	32	108	12	152	10
Bolivar, Luis, Billings	.783	10	3	15	5	23	2
Brown, Matt, Provo	.901	63	32	131	18	181	13
Cairns, Troy, Billings	.906	31	23	54	8	85	4
Castillo, Luis, Ogden	.868	55	28	104	20	152	7
Ciriaco, Juan, Idaho Falls	1.000	1	1	1	0	2	0
Cruceta, Julio, Idaho Falls	.889	27	11	53	8	72	7
Dale, Lachlan, Idaho Falls	.887	19	10	37	6	53	4
Dowdy, Brett, Ogden	.905	9	8	11	2	21	1
Figueroa, Baudilio, Idaho Falls	.600	3	1	2	2	5	0
Frost, Jeremy, Helena	1.000	2	1	4	0	5	0
Gonzalez, Juan, Ogden	.857	14	7	17	4	28	0
Gray, Antoin, Great Falls	.942	20	16	33	3	52	6
Hernandez, Habelito, Billings	.864	8	6	13	3	22	3
Hogan, William, Idaho Falls	.889	30	19	45	8	72	7
Hudson, William, Billings	1.000	2	2	1	0	3	0
Kelly, Christopher, Great Falls	.810	10	6	11	4	21	2
McCreery, John, Missoula	.892	16	8	25	4	37	1
McStoots, Jason, Missoula	.846	8	4	7	2	13	3
MURILLO, AGUSTIN, Missoula	.948	64	43	121	9	173	11
Olmstead, Walter, Billings	.831	28	25	49	15	89	7
Pavkovich, Adam, Provo	.667	3	0	2	1	3	0
Reyes, Ivan, Billings	.750	4	0	6	2	8	1
Reynolds, Henry, Casper	1.000	1	2	4	0	6	0
Robledo, Nelson, Casper	1.000	1	0	3	0	3	0
Rottino, Vinny, Helena	.839	25	17	30	9	56	4
Schnurstein, Micah, Great Falls	.957	49	31	102	6	139	3
Stewart, Ian, Casper	.917	51	43	100	13	156	7
Strop, Pedro, Casper	.667	1	0	2	1	3	0
Tejeda, Francisco, Casper	.818	8	5	13	4	22	0
Valdez, Jose, Casper	.897	15	10	25	4	39	2
Vanzile, Travis, Missoula	1.000	1	0	1	0	1	0
Vincent, Tom, Idaho Falls	1.000	4	1	4	0	5	0
Wilson, Robert, Provo	1.000	7	4	14	0	18	4
Wood, Brandon, Provo	.850	10	4	13	3	20	0

SHORTSTOPS

Player, Team	Pct.	G	PO	A	E	TC	DP
Beale, David, Billings	.919	25	37	65	9	111	12
Bolivar, Luis, Billings	.886	39	53	95	19	167	18
Burnham, Brett, Idaho Falls	1.000	1	2	4	0	6	0
Ciriaco, Juan, Idaho Falls	.897	45	69	97	19	185	16
Crissotomo, Miguel, Ogden	.714	5	6	9	6	21	2
Dowdy, Brett, Ogden	1.000	2	4	4	0	8	1
Figueroa, Baudilio, Idaho Falls	.925	33	56	93	12	161	20
Gomez, Andri, Helena	.934	29	39	75	8	122	16
Gonzalez, Juan, Ogden	.978	8	18	27	1	46	9
Guzman, Jose, Provo	.859	22	15	46	10	71	6
Haggerty, Cory, Great Falls	.884	30	36	63	13	112	12
Hu, Chin-lung, Ogden	.928	53	67	165	18	250	21
Hudson, William, Billings	.887	14	21	34	7	62	6
Laurin, Dominique, Ogden	.970	10	9	23	1	33	4
McStoots, Jason, Missoula	.943	28	44	72	7	123	13
MYERS, MICHAEL, Great Falls	.935	53	101	156	18	275	34
Olivares, Juan, Missoula	.906	54	60	162	23	245	20
Pavkovich, Adam, Provo	.924	26	54	68	10	132	14
Reyes, Ivan, Billings	.833	3	2	3	1	6	0
Reynolds, Henry, Casper	.975	42	60	134	5	199	20
Ronda, Jose, Billings	1.000	1	2	3	0	5	2
Rottino, Vinny, Helena	.857	2	4	8	2	14	5
Septimo, Agustin, Helena	.894	51	68	125	23	216	18
Strop, Pedro, Casper	.828	36	37	103	29	169	15
Wood, Brandon, Provo	.917	35	46	87	12	145	21

OUTFIELDERS

Player, Team	Pct.	G	PO	A	E	TC	DP
Acevedo, Juan, Billings	.885	17	21	2	3	26	0
Acosta, Johe, Missoula	1.000	29	45	1	0	46	0
Anderson, Brian, Great Falls	1.000	13	23	3	0	26	2
Anderson, Drew, Helena	.938	54	72	3	5	80	0
Baker, Casey, Idaho Falls	.833	5	4	1	1	6	0
Balkcom, Blake, Provo	.935	35	38	5	3	46	3
Campos, Tiago, Billings	1.000	6	6	0	0	6	0
Cardona, Dave, Ogden	.952	34	57	2	3	62	0
Carter, Nic, Helena	.964	17	23	4	1	28	1
Carter, Ryan, Ogden	.889	41	50	6	7	63	0
Cook, David, Great Falls	1.000	5	5	0	0	5	0
De Aza, Alejandro, Ogden *	.979	52	91	4	2	97	1
Deevers, Robby, Helena	.955	63	95	11	5	111	3
Dickerson, Christopher, Bil.*	.978	57	129	4	3	136	0
Edwards, Brian, Idaho Falls	.966	48	79	5	3	87	1
Etheridge, Chad, Idaho Falls	.909	9	8	2	1	11	0
Frost, Jeremy, Helena	1.000	5	6	0	0	6	0
Fuller, Casey, Casper *	.964	30	49	4	2	55	0
Garay, Ernesto, Idaho Falls *	.960	45	70	2	3	75	1
Gentry, Philip, Billings	.960	44	71	1	3	75	0
Gonzalez, Carlos, Missoula *	.942	70	107	6	7	120	1
Guerrero, Michael, Missoula	1.000	17	19	0	0	19	0
Guzman, Jose, Provo	1.000	7	4	0	0	4	0
Hauseman, Chad, Provo	.938	12	15	0	1	16	0
Himes, Benjamin, Billings	.960	62	108	11	5	124	2
Ivy, Bjorn, Great Falls	.750	3	3	0	1	4	0
Johnson, Ryan, Idaho Falls *	.955	17	20	1	1	22	0
Kaplan, Jonathan, Missoula	.964	69	120	12	5	137	1
Kelly, Christopher, Great Falls	.906	25	26	3	3	32	0
Kenning, Ryan, Provo *	1.000	2	2	0	0	2	0
King, Clinton, Great Falls	.918	57	85	4	8	97	0
Macias, Andres, Idaho Falls *	.966	60	135	9	5	149	3

Player, Team	Pct.	G	PO	A	E	TC	DP
Madrigal, Warner, Provo	.950	70	107	6	6	119	1
Melendez, Cristobal, Missoula	.984	44	58	3	1	62	0
Melo, Manuel, Helena	.947	41	66	6	4	76	2
Milons, Jereme, Ogden	.973	48	68	3	2	73	1
Moore, Mewelde, Idaho Falls	1.000	4	3	0	0	3	0
Morris, Seth, Great Falls	.974	44	68	6	2	76	1
Mosqueda, Juan, Casper	.887	50	90	4	12	106	1
Myers, Michael, Great Falls	.971	20	34	0	1	35	0
Nanita, Ricardo, Great Falls *	.948	46	89	3	5	97	2
Nunez, Florentino, Casper	.909	46	67	3	7	77	0
Olmstead, Walter, Billings	.932	34	49	6	4	59	1
Pali, Matt, Provo *	1.000	26	32	1	0	33	1
Paul, Xavier, Ogden	.905	55	71	5	8	84	0
Paula, Manuel, Billings	1.000	7	7	1	0	8	0
Peel, Aaron, Provo	.982	34	49	5	1	55	1
Ramirez, Yordany, Idaho Falls	.900	22	45	0	5	50	0
Renz, Jordan, Provo	.800	5	4	0	1	5	0
Restrepo, John, Casper *	.980	54	97	2	2	101	0
Roberts, Dave, Ogden *	1.000	3	4	0	0	4	0
Rottino, Vinny, Helena	1.000	5	12	1	0	13	0
Santiago, Jayson, Missoula *	1.000	21	21	0	0	21	0
Smith, Kyle, Billings	1.000	11	16	0	0	16	0
Sweeney, Ryan, Great Falls *	.900	10	9	0	1	10	0
TROFHOLZ, TERRY, Helena	.989	67	165	9	2	176	2
Underwood, Daniel, Casper	1.000	4	9	0	0	9	0
Valdez, Angel, Casper	.941	51	89	6	6	101	0
Valenzuela, Mario, Great Falls	.875	12	18	3	3	24	1
Vanzile, Travis, Missoula	.933	33	28	0	2	30	0
Vasquez, Jose, Casper *	.667	4	2	0	1	3	0
Vincent, Tom, Idaho Falls	.930	28	37	3	3	43	2
Willits, Reggie, Provo	.984	58	123	2	2	127	0
Young, Chris, Great Falls	1.000	10	10	0	0	10	0

CATCHERS

Player, Team	Pct.	G	PO	A	E	TC	DP	PB
Belz, Tim, Missoula	1.000	1	5	0	0	5	0	0
Collins, Mike, Provo	.988	22	145	15	2	162	1	5
Corporan, Carlos, Helena	.973	9	60	12	2	74	2	5
Deuchler, Matthew, Great Falls	.994	24	163	16	1	180	3	4
Duenas, Tommy, Provo	.984	13	108	15	2	125	0	1
Esposito, Brian, Provo	.963	3	25	1	1	27	0	1
Ghutzman, Stephen, Casper	.966	12	79	6	3	88	0	6
Hess, Samuel, Provo	1.000	2	13	1	0	14	0	2
Kottaras, George, Idaho Falls	1.000	26	209	17	0	226	0	2
Lauderdale, Matthew, Id. Falls	.950	15	118	15	7	140	2	5
Lee, Carlos, Great Falls	1.000	15	103	6	0	109	0	5
Lisk, Charlie, Great Falls	.969	44	336	33	12	381	4	16
Lobaton, Jose, Idaho Falls	.990	22	169	22	2	193	2	10
Lopez, Luis, Idaho Falls	1.000	2	5	0	0	5	0	1
Lozada, Charlie, Helena	.976	7	37	4	1	42	0	1
Lynch, Michael, Ogden	.985	21	187	15	3	205	1	11
Martin, Russell, Ogden	.974	49	418	63	13	494	0	27
Martinez, Domingo, Idaho Falls	.974	6	35	2	1	38	0	2
Martinez, Thomas, Idaho Falls	.989	11	89	5	1	95	1	5
Mercado, Orlando, Missoula	.990	22	91	6	1	98	0	3
Montero, Miguel, Missoula	.984	52	343	37	6	386	3	7
Motooka, Rafael, Billings	1.000	3	14	3	0	17	0	0
Mottram, Allen, Missoula	.992	19	120	10	1	131	1	3
Palmisano, Louis, Helena	.978	40	285	33	7	325	3	6
Perez, Miguel, Billings	.967	60	445	59	17	521	7	16
Ramirez, Manuel, Helena	1.000	1	2	0	0	2	0	2
Robledo, Nelson, Casper	.974	31	207	19	6	232	1	13
Rottino, Vinny, Helena	.985	11	59	7	1	67	1	1
Segura Cornier, Alberto, Helena	.975	23	141	16	4	161	1	8
Slimak, Taylor, Ogden	.983	9	53	5	1	59	1	7
Underwood, Daniel, Casper	.967	28	155	22	6	183	1	19
Urgelles, Jeff, Billings	.962	3	22	3	1	26	1	3
Valdez, Jose, Casper	1.000	1	5	0	0	5	0	0
Wilson, Neil, Casper	.939	15	100	7	7	114	0	6
WILSON, ROBERT, Provo	.985	40	292	36	5	333	3	2
Ziemendorf, Chad, Billings	.961	20	105	18	5	128	2	5

PITCHERS

Player, Team	Pct.	G	PO	A	E	TC	DP
Ahumada, Edgar, Ogden *	.857	12	1	5	1	7	0
Allender, John, Missoula	.833	17	3	2	1	6	0
Alvarez, Gabriel, Ogden	.889	19	3	5	1	9	0
Arias, Alberto, Casper	.882	13	5	10	2	17	1
Astacio, Hector, Provo	1.000	14	0	5	0	5	0
Austen, David, Provo	.800	23	1	3	1	5	1
Baca, Daniel, Idaho Falls	1.000	5	0	2	0	2	0
Bailey, Chad, Ogden *	.857	14	1	11	2	14	1
Beresford, Simon, Helena	1.000	17	1	2	0	3	0
Billingsley, Chad, Ogden	.750	11	2	7	3	12	1
Bohorquez, Carlos, Billings	.857	19	4	8	2	14	0
Bright, Adam, Casper *	.824	33	2	12	3	17	0
Cabrera, Walin, Billings	.769	16	4	6	3	13	2
Carroll, James, Provo	1.000	4	0	1	0	1	1
Carvajal, Marcos, Ogden	1.000	23	5	4	0	9	0
Colbert, Henry, Idaho Falls	1.000	16	1	4	0	5	0
Conden, Gregory, Idaho Falls	.692	15	1	8	4	13	0
Cox, Jason, Provo	1.000	9	0	2	0	2	0
Cremidan, Alexander, Missoula	.750	24	1	2	1	4	0
Cuen, David, Ogden *	.882	15	6	9	2	17	1
Cuevas, Manuel, Missoula	.818	16	2	7	2	11	1
Davidson, Daniel, Provo *	1.000	15	5	12	0	17	0
De La O, Danny, Idaho Falls *	.923	31	2	10	1	13	1
De Los Santos, Omar, Ogden	1.000	5	0	1	0	1	0
De Montigny, Mat, Idaho Falls	.833	18	2	3	1	6	0
Diangelo, Jason, Casper	.917	17	6	5	1	12	0
Diaz, Jose, Ogden	1.000	2	1	0	0	1	0
Dillard, Timothy, Helena	1.000	3	0	1	0	1	0
Dizard, Fraser, Great Falls *	1.000	12	0	5	0	5	0
Dove, Shane, Missoula *	.889	19	3	5	1	9	0
Dumesnil, Bryan, Ogden *	.667	16	1	1	1	3	1
Durost, Kenneth, Helena	1.000	17	2	7	0	9	0
Escorcha, Orlando, Billings *	.833	17	2	8	2	12	1
Eveland, Dana, Helena *	1.000	19	0	4	0	4	0
Fernandez, Alfredo, Idaho Falls	.750	11	3	9	4	16	0
Garcia, Geivy, Idaho Falls	.857	24	0	6	1	7	0
George, Jon, Billings	1.000	6	2	1	0	3	0
Geraldo, Jose, Idaho Falls	1.000	21	0	5	0	5	0
Goas, Adrian, Provo	1.000	7	1	0	0	1	0
Groeger, Jeff, Billings	1.000	12	2	4	0	6	1
Grybash, Daniel, Helena	.889	17	4	4	1	9	0
Guerrero, Hipolito, Missoula *	1.000	23	1	3	0	4	0
Guevara, Jose, Billings	1.000	2	0	1	0	1	0
Guzman, Carlos, Casper	1.000	4	0	3	0	3	1
Harrelson, Paul, Casper	1.000	5	1	1	0	2	0
Hawk, Derek, Billings	1.000	14	4	6	0	10	2
Hedden, Wayne, Provo	.800	17	1	3	1	5	0
Henderson, Eric, Helena *	.750	4	1	2	1	4	0
Hendley, Blake, Billings	.867	6	3	10	2	15	0
Hendrix, Phillip, Helena	.750	16	0	3	1	4	1
Hernandez, Fernando, Gr. Falls	.750	24	2	4	2	8	0
Hindman, Scott, Provo *	1.000	6	2	5	0	7	1
Hurd, John, Great Falls	1.000	7	0	2	0	2	1
Ion, Mark, Casper	1.000	27	3	1	0	4	0
Jacquez, Tom, Great Falls *	1.000	6	0	3	0	3	1
Johnson, J.D., Great Falls	.923	19	3	9	1	13	0
Julio, Donald, Missoula	1.000	18	4	5	0	9	0
Kane, Kyle, Great Falls	1.000	5	0	1	0	1	0
Kerschen, Joshua, Casper	1.000	4	1	1	0	2	0
Klatt, Ryan, Idaho Falls	1.000	32	1	3	0	4	0
Kloosterman, Gregory, Helena *	1.000	14	1	8	0	9	0
Knoff, Justin, Billings	.889	14	2	14	2	18	0
Krantz, Ben, Missoula	.870	17	5	15	3	23	1
Larson, Brett, Idaho Falls	1.000	26	0	14	0	14	1
Liebeck, Jered, Missoula	1.000	5	0	2	0	2	0
Little, Jeffrey, Great Falls	1.000	12	2	3	0	5	1
Logan, Boone, Great Falls *	.733	16	1	10	4	15	0
McCarthy, Brandon, Great Falls	.864	16	6	13	3	22	0
McKenna, Daniel, Helena	1.000	13	2	1	0	3	0
Medina, Julio, Billings	1.000	4	2	1	0	3	0
Medlock, Calvin, Billings	.800	19	2	2	1	5	1
Megrew, Mike, Ogden *	.917	14	3	8	1	12	1
Mendoza, Gabriel, Helena *	1.000	5	0	1	0	1	0
Merino, Joshua, Casper	.800	3	3	1	1	5	0
Merrell, Darric, Casper	.842	13	3	13	3	19	2
Mitchell, Jay, Casper	.875	22	5	2	1	8	0
Moat, Michael, Great Falls	1.000	18	2	5	0	7	0
Montalbo, Brian, Helena	1.000	13	4	2	0	6	0
Mora, Yency, Idaho Falls	.875	19	3	4	1	8	0
Morban, Carlos, Provo	1.000	21	1	5	0	6	0
Moreira, Greg, Helena	.900	17	2	7	1	10	0
Moreno, Abel, Provo	.769	13	4	6	3	13	0
Morillo, Juan, Casper	.714	15	0	5	2	7	0
Moviel, Paul, Great Falls	.857	14	0	6	1	7	0
Nachreiner, Matthew, Great Falls	.875	13	2	5	1	8	0
Nippert, Derik, Missoula	1.000	13	3	2	0	5	0
Novosel, Walt, Missoula *	1.000	25	2	4	0	6	0
Paduch, James, Billings	1.000	15	2	17	0	19	1
Parker, David, Ogden	1.000	18	0	1	0	1	0
Pawelczyk, Kyle, Provo *	1.000	5	0	4	0	4	0
Payne, Matt, Great Falls	1.000	4	1	1	0	2	0
Pence, Howard, Idaho Falls	.917	27	4	7	1	12	1
Perrault, Josh, Missoula	1.000	24	4	5	0	9	1

Player, Team	Pct.	G	PO	A	E	TC	DP
Ponce, William, Idaho Falls	.923	15	5	7	1	13	3
Pratt, Jordan, Ogden	.909	16	2	8	1	11	0
Pullin, Aaron, Provo	.923	23	6	6	1	13	0
Ramirez, Carlos, Helena *	.833	15	2	13	3	18	1
Reed, Rylan, Great Falls	1.000	14	0	6	0	6	0
Requena, Ricardo, Provo	1.000	9	0	2	0	2	0
Reyes, Ramon, Provo	1.000	6	1	1	0	2	0
Richardson, Judd, Helena	1.000	14	2	5	0	7	1
Riley, Kenny, Casper	1.000	23	3	3	0	6	0
ROBLES, LARRY, Casper	1.000	16	7	13	0	20	0
Rocha, Angel, Missoula *	.733	15	2	9	4	15	0
Rodriguez, Mike, Ogden	1.000	2	3	2	0	5	0
Rogers, Nathan, Idaho Falls *	.857	9	1	5	1	7	0
Rosen, Mark, Missoula *	.938	13	5	10	1	16	0
Russ, John, Great Falls	.909	16	3	7	1	11	0
Santo, Joel, Idaho Falls	1.000	16	3	4	0	7	1
Schmoll, Stephen, Ogden	1.000	24	4	1	0	5	0
Shafer, David, Billings	.000	25	0	0	1	1	0
Silva, Doug, Casper	1.000	27	4	8	0	12	0
Silva, Erick, Missoula	1.000	7	4	11	0	15	2
Simard, Michel, Provo	1.000	12	2	8	0	10	0
Slack, Nicholas, Helena	1.000	19	0	1	0	1	0
Smith, Jesse, Provo	.500	5	0	1	1	2	0
Sobkow, Philip, Ogden	1.000	14	6	2	0	8	0
Stertzbach, Von, Provo	1.000	22	2	5	0	7	2
Stetter, Mitchel, Helena *	.882	15	4	11	2	17	1
Stewart, James, Ogden	.867	18	6	7	2	15	0
Stover, Ricky, Helena *	.857	16	0	6	1	7	0
Surratt, Randy, Great Falls *	.882	23	2	13	2	17	0
Talamantez, David, Billings	1.000	16	1	4	0	5	0
Taubenheim, Ty, Helena	1.000	14	6	6	0	12	1
Thompson, Sean, Great Falls *	.636	10	1	6	4	11	0
Till, Brock, Billings	.917	18	7	4	1	12	2
Touchstone, Nick, Provo *	.941	14	4	12	1	17	0
Tracey, Sean, Great Falls	.900	16	3	15	2	20	2
Ulacia, Dennis, Great Falls *	.750	4	0	3	1	4	0
Ursin, Damian, Billings	1.000	7	2	0	0	2	0
Vaillancourt, Tim, Missoula	.833	22	1	4	1	6	0
Vazquez, Camilo, Billings *	.857	9	0	6	1	7	0
Vicente, Ruben, Missoula	.867	3	5	8	2	15	1
Wachman, Corey, Billings	1.000	2	1	1	0	2	0
Watchko, Jeff, Casper	.909	31	3	7	1	11	0
Wells, Mark, Billings	1.000	23	1	8	0	9	1
White, Michael, Ogden *	.667	19	2	2	2	6	0
Wiley, Mike, Casper *	.889	32	2	6	1	9	0
Wilhite, Matt, Provo	.857	12	1	5	1	7	1
Yamaguchi, Tetsuya, Missoula *	1.000	15	4	13	0	17	0
Zimmermann, Bob, Provo	.938	11	4	11	1	16	0

The following players appeared only as a designated hitter, pinch-hitter or pinch-runner: Blanco, ph; Bok, dh, ph; Cleveland, dh; Laroche, dh, ph; Piazza, dh, ph.

LEAGUE CHAMPIONS

Year	Team	Pct.
1939—	Twin Falls*	.581
1940—	Salt Lake City	.608
	Ogden (4th)*	.492
1941—	Boise	.623
	Ogden (2nd)*	.598
1942—	Pocatello†	.690
	Boise	.683
1943-44-45—	Did not operate.	
1946—	Twin Falls‡	.585
	Salt Lake City†	.585
1947—	Salt Lake City	.618
	Twin Falls†	.600
1948—	Pocatello	.611
	Twin Falls (2nd)*	.595
1949—	Twin Falls	.624
	Pocatello (3rd)*	.595
1950—	Pocatello	.635
	Billings (3rd)*	.571
1951—	Salt Lake City	.618
	Great Falls (3rd)*	.559
1952—	Pocatello	.595
	Idaho Falls (2nd)*	.573
1953—	Ogden	.679
	Salt Lake City (4th)*	.527
1954—	Salt Lake City	.595
	Great Falls (4th)*	.530
1955—	Boise	.588
	Magic Valley (4th)*	.489
1956—	Boise	.561
1957—	Salt Lake City	.650
	Billings†	.582
1958—	Great Falls	.582
	Boise†	.615
1959—	Boise	.633
	Billings (2nd)*	.523
1960—	Boise†	.686
	Idaho Falls	.650
1961—	Boise	.638
	Great Falls*	.571
1962—	Boise§	.565
	Billings†	.706
1963—	Idaho Falls	.702
	Magic Valley†	.643
1964—	Treasure Valley	.615
1965—	Treasure Valley	.530
1966—	Ogden	.591
1967—	Ogden	.621
1968—	Ogden	.609
1969—	Ogden	.620
1970—	Idaho Falls	.629
1971—	Great Falls	.643
1972—	Billings	.694
1973—	Billings	.629
1974—	Idaho Falls	.569
1975—	Great Falls	.577
1976—	Great Falls	.577
1977—	Lethbridge	.629
1978—	Billings∞	.735
1979—	Helena	.623
	Lethbridge▲	.559
1980—	Lethbridge▲	.743
	Billings	.629
1981—	Calgary	.657
	Butte▲	.557
1982—	Medicine Hat▲	.629
	Idaho Falls	.600
1983—	Billings▲	.614
	Calgary	.600
1984—	Billings	.691
	Helena▲	.647
1985—	Great Falls	.771
	Salt Lake City▲	.657
1986—	Salt Lake City◆	.643
	Great Falls	.571
1987—	Salt Lake City◆	.700
	Helena	.657
1988—	Great Falls◆	.754
	Butte	.629
1989—	Great Falls◆	.791
	Butte	.621
1990—	Great Falls◆	.706
	Salt Lake	.618
1991—	Salt Lake City◆	.700
	Great Falls	.657
1992—	Salt Lake	.697
	Billings◆	.697
1993—	Billings◆	.653
	Helena	.589
1994—	Billings◆	.694
	Helena	.611
1995—	Billings	.710
	Helena■	.690
1996—	Helena■	.597
	Ogden	.583
1997—	Great Falls	.556
	Billings■	.549
1998—	Medicine Hat	.622
	Idaho Falls■	.618
1999—	Idaho Falls	.640
	Missoula■	.592
2000—	Idaho Falls■	.608
2001—	Provo	.697
	Billings■	.613
2002—	Great Falls■	.627
2003—	Billings■	.539

*Won four-club playoff. †Won split-season playoff. ‡Ended first half in tie with Salt Lake City and won one-game playoff. §Ended first half in tie with Billings and Great Falls and won playoff. ∞Billings (first place) defeated Idaho Falls (second place) in first place-second place playoff. ▲League divided into Northern and Southern divisions; won two-club playoff. ◆Won two-club playoff. ■League divided into Northern and Southern divisions; won four-club playoff.

ARIZONA LEAGUE

LEAGUE OFFICE

President/treasurer
Bob Richmond
Address
P.O. Box 1645
Boise, ID 83701
Phone
208-429-1511

Teams*
Angels
Athletics
Brewers
Cubs
Giants
Padres
Mariners
Rangers
Royals

*Teams play their games in Maryvale, Mesa, Peoria, Phoenix, Scottsdale and Surprise, Ariz.

ROOKIE *Arizona League*

2003 FINAL STANDINGS

FIRST HALF

Team	W	L	T	Pct.	GB
Royals-1	17	7	-	.708	...
Cubs	15	9	-	.625	2.0
Rangers	16	10	-	.615	2.0
Mariners	14	10	-	.583	3.0
Giants	14	10	-	.583	3.0
Royals-2	15	13	-	.536	4.0
Angels	9	16	-	.360	8.5
Athletics	8	16	-	.333	9.0
Brewers	5	20	-	.200	12.5

SECOND HALF

Team	W	L	T	Pct.	GB
Rangers	19	4	-	.826	...
Royals-2	17	9	-	.654	3.5
Mariners	15	9	-	.625	4.5
Royals-1	14	11	-	.560	6.0
Angels	11	13	-	.458	8.5
Giants	11	14	-	.440	9.0
Brewers	10	14	-	.417	9.5
Cubs	10	15	-	.400	10.0
Athletics	7	17	-	.292	12.5

COMPOSITE

Team	RNG	RY1	MRN	RY2	GIA	CUB	ANG	ATH	BRR	W	L	T	Pct.	GB
Rangers (Rangers)	...	5	5	3	4	3	5	7	6	35	14	0	.714	...
Royals-1 (Royals)	2	...	2	5	6	6	5	5	5	31	18	0	.633	4.0
Mariners (Mariners)	2	5	...	1	3	5	4	6	4	29	19	0	.604	5.5
Royals-2 (Royals)	4	1	6	...	4	5	6	3	3	32	22	0	.593	5.5
Giants (Giants)	3	1	4	3	...	3	3	5	6	25	24	0	.510	10.0
Cubs (Cubs)	4	1	2	2	4	...	5	4	5	25	24	0	.510	10.0
Angels (Angels)	2	2	3	1	4	2	...	3	4	20	29	0	.408	15.0
Athletics (Athletics)	0	2	0	4	2	3	4	...	4	15	33	0	.313	19.5
Brewers (Brewers)	1	2	3	3	1	2	3	3	...	15	34	0	.306	20.0

Club names are major league affiliations.

Games played in Mesa, Peoria, Phoenix and Tucson.

PLAYOFFS: Royals-1 defeated Rangers, one game to none, to win league championship.

REGULAR-SEASON ATTENDANCE: No total attendance figures reported.

MANAGERS: Angels, Brian Harper; Athletics, Ruben Escalera; Brewers, Hector Torres; Cubs, Carmelo Martinez; Giants, Burt Hunter; Mariners, Scott Steinmann; Rangers, Pedro Lopez; Royals-1, Lloyd Simmons; Royals-2, Kevin Boles.

ALL-STAR TEAM: 1B—Donald Sutton, Athletics; 2B—Jorge Mejia, Athletics; 3B—Alexander Batista, Royals-1; SS—Michael Aviles, Royals-1; OF—Ryan Fitzgerald, Cubs; OF—Lizanio Baez, Rangers; OF—Wladimir Balentien, Mariners; C—Mitch Maier, Royals-1; DH—Wladimir Balentien, Mariners; LHP—Dustin Hughes, Royals-1; RHP—Ronald Bay, Cubs; LH reliever—John Gragg, Royals-2; RH reliever—Leslie Nacar, Giants; Most Valuable Player—Michael Aviles, Royals-1; Manager of the Year—Pedro Lopez, Rangers.

2003 BATTING

TEAM

Team	G	TPA	AB	R	H	TB	2B	3B	HR	RBI	SH	SF	HP	BB	IBB	SO	SB	CS	GDP	LOB	ShO	Avg.	OBP	Slg.
Royals-1	55	2211	1979	398	608	946	114	46	44	340	7	22	35	168	0	398	71	39	35	376	0	.307	.368	.478
Mariners	55	2234	1939	341	561	818	100	32	31	283	11	25	44	215	2	409	71	30	36	432	1	.289	.369	.422
Rangers	56	2275	1930	357	552	788	108	31	22	291	12	33	59	238	2	440	117	48	43	428	0	.286	.376	.408
Royals-2	54	2191	1875	310	528	757	113	25	22	261	20	16	41	239	3	406	66	25	37	456	2	.282	.372	.404
Athletics	55	2216	1942	333	545	804	104	19	39	290	10	25	38	201	1	416	32	32	40	415	1	.281	.355	.414
Cubs	56	2206	1981	306	546	796	105	50	15	265	15	17	36	152	1	377	44	32	46	396	2	.276	.336	.402
Brewers	55	2133	1911	284	511	697	96	27	12	238	8	14	30	170	0	447	79	32	30	394	1	.267	.335	.365
Giants	56	2159	1896	281	505	718	89	41	14	233	26	13	33	190	2	466	81	33	39	412	3	.266	.341	.379
Angels	56	2175	1944	288	508	734	86	40	20	242	6	17	26	182	5	509	58	29	34	390	2	.261	.330	.378

INDIVIDUAL

TOP QUALIFIERS FOR BATTING CHAMPIONSHIP

Minimum 151 plate appearances. *Lefthanded batter. †Switch-hitter.

Player, Team	G	TPA	AB	R	H	TB	2B	3B	HR	RBI	SH	SF	HP	BB	IBB	SO	SB	CS	GDP	Avg.	OBP	Slg.
Fitzgerald, Ryan, Cubs	54	226	202	37	77	128	14	8	7	44	1	3	2	18	0	43	9	3	4	.381	.431	.634
Mejia, Jorge, Athletics	50	243	223	48	84	134	17	6	7	30	1	4	0	15	0	46	7	9	4	.377	.409	.601
Batista, Alexander, Royals-1	48	190	180	37	66	83	10	2	1	21	2	0	1	7	0	30	6	4	3	.367	.394	.461
Aviles, Mike, Royals-1	52	237	212	51	77	124	19	5	6	39	2	5	5	13	0	28	11	5	2	.363	.404	.585

Player, Team	G	TPA	AB	R	H	TB	2B	3B	HR	RBI	SH	SF	HP	BB	IBB	SO	SB	CS	GDP	Avg.	OBP	Slg.
Maier, Mitch, Royals-1 *	51	226	203	41	71	103	14	6	2	45	0	3	2	18	0	25	7	3	4	.350	.403	.507
Acosta, Gilberto, Brewers †	50	215	189	43	66	85	8	4	1	26	2	2	2	20	0	30	30	3	3	.349	.413	.450
Springer, Kenard, Royals-1	49	201	182	35	63	89	15	1	3	39	0	4	5	10	0	20	7	4	5	.346	.388	.489
Furtado, Micah, Rangers *	49	235	193	44	66	83	9	4	0	23	1	2	5	33	1	33	17	9	0	.342	.446	.430
Ogando, Alexi, Athletics	48	206	190	33	65	101	13	1	7	36	0	3	6	7	0	42	5	6	4	.342	.379	.532
Sutton, Don, Athletics	40	179	156	33	52	89	16	0	7	35	0	2	3	18	0	31	1	1	2	.333	.408	.571
Craig, Casey, Mariners *	35	157	142	27	47	65	11	2	1	21	1	1	0	13	1	27	10	2	2	.331	.385	.458
Baez, Lizahio, Rangers †	53	252	223	36	73	113	17	1	7	55	0	5	4	20	0	31	4	5	4	.327	.385	.507
Powell, Brandon, Royals-1 *	52	250	215	47	70	124	12	15	4	46	2	4	2	27	0	39	15	6	3	.326	.399	.577
Lubanski, Christopher, Roy.-1*	53	241	221	41	72	100	4	6	4	27	0	0	2	18	0	50	9	10	4	.326	.382	.452
Valdez, Jesus, Cubs	48	188	175	20	56	74	8	5	0	29	0	0	5	7	0	31	7	2	4	.320	.364	.423

DEPARTMENTAL LEADERS: G—Mooney, 56; AB—Baez, J. Mejia, 223; R—Aviles, 51; H—J. Mejia, 84; TB—J. Mejia, 134; 2B—Aviles, 19; 3B—Powell, 15; HR—Balentien, 16; RBI—Baez, 55; SH—Abreu, 9; SF—Aviles, Baez, Baldwin, Hatcher, 5; HP—Cashman, 21; BB—Strain, 41; IBB—Boyer, 2; SO—Walston, 88; SB—Acosta, 30; CS—Lubanski, 10; GIDP—B. Martinez, 7; Slg.—Balentien, .658; OBP—Furtado, .446.

ALL PLAYERS

*Lefthanded batter. †Switch-hitter.

Player, Team	G	TPA	AB	R	H	TB	2B	3B	HR	RBI	SH	SF	HP	BB	IBB	SO	SB	CS	GDP	Avg.	OBP	Slg.
Abreu, Johany, Giants †	50	224	198	32	63	85	10	6	0	27	9	2	2	13	0	33	18	5	3	.318	.363	.429
Acosta, Gilberto, Brewers †	50	215	189	43	66	85	8	4	1	26	2	2	2	20	0	30	30	3	3	.349	.413	.450
Acosta, Jesse, Athletics	46	205	178	28	43	47	4	0	0	15	1	2	1	23	0	33	2	0	1	.242	.328	.264
Alexander, Alexis, Royals-2	25	87	73	17	21	43	4	3	4	10	1	0	2	11	0	26	6	0	0	.288	.395	.589
Alexander, Kevin, Giants	3	14	11	6	5	7	0	1	0	4	0	0	0	3	0	3	1	0	0	.455	.571	.636
Almonte, Aneury, Angels	9	39	30	3	6	6	0	0	0	2	2	0	1	6	0	8	3	0	0	.200	.351	.200
Arias, Roberto, Athletics	12	42	33	8	8	11	1	1	0	1	0	0	0	9	0	9	0	0	1	.242	.405	.333
Aviles, Mike, Royals-1	52	237	212	51	77	124	19	5	6	39	2	5	5	13	0	28	11	5	2	.363	.404	.585
Baez, Lizahio, Rangers †	53	252	223	36	73	113	17	1	7	55	0	5	4	20	0	31	4	5	4	.327	.385	.507
Balcom, Jasha, Cubs *	24	102	85	17	28	33	1	2	0	6	1	1	1	12	0	21	2	2	0	.329	.414	.388
Baldwin, Ryan, Rangers	18	80	64	13	18	20	2	0	0	17	0	5	2	9	0	13	3	0	1	.281	.363	.313
Balentien, Wladimir, Mariners	50	216	187	42	53	123	12	5	16	52	1	3	3	22	0	55	4	2	4	.283	.363	.658
Barry, Jeff, Royals-2	46	220	183	38	56	70	7	2	1	12	5	0	5	27	1	45	15	4	2	.306	.409	.383
Bates, Dallas, Brewers *	38	169	148	17	37	45	8	0	0	15	1	0	2	18	0	35	2	4	2	.250	.339	.304
Bates, Nicholas, Brewers	3	9	7	2	1	1	0	0	0	2	0	0	0	2	0	1	0	0	0	.143	.333	.143
Batista, Alexander, Royals-1	48	190	180	37	66	83	10	2	1	21	2	0	1	7	0	30	6	4	3	.367	.394	.461
Beauregard, Joshua, Ath.*	48	205	177	32	50	72	10	3	2	30	1	4	3	20	1	26	4	3	3	.282	.358	.407
Bernard, Oscar, Cubs	26	91	84	15	19	26	5	1	0	9	1	0	0	6	0	11	1	2	2	.226	.278	.310
Bilezikjian, Charlie, Rangers	3	13	11	0	2	2	0	0	0	2	0	1	0	1	0	2	1	0	0	.182	.231	.182
Blanco, Gregory, Angels	10	30	24	5	7	8	1	0	0	1	0	0	0	6	0	6	0	0	1	.292	.433	.333
Boruff, Gabriel, Royals-2 †	21	77	64	11	15	19	4	0	0	10	0	1	1	11	0	24	0	0	1	.234	.351	.297
Boyer, William, Angels †	41	181	165	24	48	61	3	5	0	18	0	3	0	13	2	40	3	3	1	.291	.337	.370
Bozarth, Dustin, Giants *	2	5	4	1	0	0	0	0	0	0	0	0	0	1	0	3	1	0	0	.000	.200	.000
Bradford, Samuel, Mariners †	4	18	16	2	4	6	2	0	0	3	0	0	1	1	0	3	0	0	0	.250	.333	.375
Brown, Dee, Royals-1 *	2	8	7	4	5	7	2	0	0	3	0	0	1	0	0	2	0	0	0	.714	.750	1.000
Bubalo, Ty, Athletics	8	35	32	4	8	17	1	1	2	9	0	0	0	3	0	9	0	0	2	.250	.314	.531
Buller, Dayton, Giants	36	134	125	14	32	49	3	4	2	15	2	0	2	5	0	40	0	0	3	.256	.295	.392
Caballero, Carlos, Royals-1	30	79	64	17	13	18	2	0	1	6	1	1	6	7	0	18	5	2	1	.203	.333	.281
Cashman, Brandon, Rangers	50	217	169	39	47	76	11	6	2	28	2	4	21	20	0	36	24	4	2	.278	.411	.450
Charles, Larry, Rangers	34	137	120	23	35	54	13	0	2	13	0	1	1	15	0	31	7	6	1	.292	.372	.450
Christianson, Ryan, Mariners	4	12	10	0	2	2	0	0	0	2	0	0	0	2	0	3	0	0	1	.200	.333	.200
Cirillo, Jeff, Mariners	6	25	20	2	6	6	0	0	0	0	0	0	1	4	0	1	0	1	1	.300	.440	.300
Collins, Mike, Angels	11	44	38	9	14	21	5	1	0	6	0	2	2	2	0	5	0	0	0	.368	.409	.553
Connors, Greg, Mariners	7	31	27	7	7	9	2	0	0	6	0	0	0	4	0	2	0	0	0	.259	.355	.333
Conte, Nick, Giants	18	56	45	3	10	11	1	0	0	0	3	0	0	8	0	15	1	2	2	.222	.340	.244
Corporan, Carlos, Brewers †	34	126	120	13	30	42	6	0	2	9	0	1	2	3	0	22	0	1	5	.250	.278	.350
Costa, Shane, Royals-2 *	23	99	88	22	34	51	6	4	1	24	0	1	4	6	0	7	4	3	2	.386	.444	.580
Cowles, Joshua, Angels	47	184	154	16	32	49	8	3	1	18	0	1	4	25	0	66	2	2	1	.208	.332	.318
Craig, Casey, Mariners *	35	157	142	27	47	65	11	2	1	21	1	1	0	13	1	27	10	2	2	.331	.385	.458
Cruz, Elvis, Mariners	40	172	156	20	36	49	3	2	2	19	0	1	0	15	1	33	4	1	2	.231	.297	.314
Davidson, Matthew, Cubs *	12	34	29	2	6	7	1	0	0	1	1	0	1	3	0	5	0	0	1	.207	.303	.241
DePaula, Bartolo, Brewers †	37	124	115	20	25	32	5	1	0	11	1	0	1	7	0	26	6	4	2	.217	.268	.278
Del Orbe, Samuel, Angels	46	165	151	28	43	63	6	4	2	19	1	2	0	11	0	42	6	4	3	.285	.329	.417
Del Rosario, Felipe, Royals-2	34	138	117	18	29	40	9	1	0	7	0	2	4	15	0	29	0	1	5	.248	.348	.342
Denny, John, Mariners *	3	14	12	3	5	9	2	1	0	2	0	0	0	2	0	0	0	2	0	.417	.500	.750
Disla, Lisandro, Giants	49	199	169	28	43	60	11	3	0	19	3	1	5	21	0	39	6	3	3	.254	.352	.355
Donachie, Adam, Ro.-2-Ro.-1	22	84	72	11	18	24	4	1	0	7	0	0	2	10	0	16	0	1	2	.250	.357	.333
Dorsey, Ryan, Royals-2	1	4	3	2	1	1	0	0	0	0	0	0	0	1	0	1	0	0	0	.333	.500	.333
Eusebio, Juan, Royals-2	11	35	28	4	8	10	0	1	0	2	0	0	1	6	0	7	3	0	1	.286	.429	.357
Falu, Irving, Royals-2	36	172	139	26	36	49	6	2	1	11	4	0	5	24	0	22	8	6	1	.259	.387	.353
Felix, Maximo, Giants	29	109	89	16	18	34	4	0	4	10	0	1	8	11	0	28	3	0	2	.202	.339	.382
Fermaint, Charlie, Brewers	25	104	100	16	30	42	3	3	1	9	0	0	1	3	0	19	6	3	0	.300	.327	.420
Ferrara, Matt, Royals-2	40	163	143	15	31	51	7	2	3	23	2	1	4	13	0	52	3	2	1	.217	.298	.357
Figuereo, Anibal, Royals-2	25	110	102	18	29	44	4	1	3	18	0	0	1	7	0	15	3	1	3	.284	.336	.431
Fitzgerald, Ryan, Cubs	54	226	202	37	77	128	14	8	7	44	1	3	2	18	0	43	9	3	4	.381	.431	.634
Fox, Jacob, Cubs	15	56	50	4	12	20	5	0	1	6	0	0	1	5	0	14	0	1	0	.240	.321	.400
Francisco, Alfredo, Cubs	41	168	160	14	42	58	9	2	1	19	2	0	2	4	0	42	1	4	1	.263	.289	.363
Furtado, Micah, Rangers *	49	235	193	44	66	83	9	4	0	23	1	2	5	33	1	33	17	9	0	.342	.446	.430
Gac, Ian, Rangers	46	206	182	22	44	61	8	0	3	19	1	0	6	16	0	59	2	3	7	.242	.324	.335
Gaffney, Michael, Royals-2	39	171	149	15	41	49	6	1	0	25	0	0	1	21	0	17	4	2	2	.275	.368	.329
Garcia, Alberto, Cubs	48	208	182	34	58	93	15	10	0	34	1	2	8	13	0	30	5	3	5	.319	.385	.511
Garcia, Jose, Athletics	44	191	151	37	44	71	11	5	2	31	0	3	8	29	0	40	2	0	1	.291	.424	.470

Player, Team	G	TPA	AB	R	H	TB	2B	3B	HR	RBI	SH	SF	HP	BB	IBB	SO	SB	CS	GDP	Avg.	OBP	Slg.
German, Carlos, Giants	43	163	152	20	25	36	5	3	0	16	0	0	1	9	0	62	4	3	2	.164	.216	.237
Grabowski, Jason, Athletics *	2	9	6	1	2	3	1	0	0	1	0	0	0	3	0	0	0	0	0	.333	.556	.500
Graham, Bryan, Royals-2 *	28	127	113	19	41	68	11	2	4	28	0	0	1	13	0	17	0	0	4	.363	.433	.602
Grana, Robert, Royals-1	6	25	21	3	7	10	1	1	0	3	0	0	1	3	0	8	2	0	1	.333	.440	.476
Grayson, Larry, Rangers	7	30	27	3	12	16	4	0	0	6	0	0	0	3	0	4	2	0	1	.444	.500	.593
Guerra, Alex, Rangers †	20	94	80	16	24	29	5	0	0	17	1	2	0	11	0	16	10	2	2	.300	.376	.363
Guhring, Simon, Brewers	21	64	57	7	16	19	1	1	0	8	0	0	2	5	0	11	2	0	2	.281	.359	.333
Guzman, Jacob, Royals-2	18	72	60	6	13	20	4	0	1	13	1	4	0	7	0	16	0	0	3	.217	.282	.333
Guzman, Juan, Rangers †	22	83	77	9	14	21	4	0	1	9	0	1	2	3	0	36	1	2	1	.182	.229	.273
Hamblen, Chris, Rangers †	15	69	60	11	21	32	3	4	0	15	1	1	1	6	0	10	2	1	2	.350	.412	.533
Hammonds, Jeffrey, Giants	4	11	10	4	5	17	1	1	3	6	0	0	0	1	0	1	0	0	2	.500	.545	1.700
Harrison, Adonis, Angels	1	4	3	0	1	1	0	0	0	0	0	0	0	1	1	0	0	0	0	.333	.500	.333
Harvey, Ryan, Cubs	14	59	51	9	12	22	3	2	1	7	0	0	2	6	0	21	0	0	3	.235	.339	.431
Hatcher, Justin, Rangers	30	120	97	17	26	33	5	1	0	8	2	5	5	11	0	21	5	4	7	.268	.356	.340
Heether, Adam, Brewers	3	14	11	1	0	0	0	0	0	0	0	0	1	2	0	1	0	0	0	.000	.214	.000
Hern, Craig, Mariners	3	11	9	1	2	2	0	0	0	0	0	0	2	0	0	1	2	1	0	.222	.364	.222
Herrera, Javier, Athletics	17	70	61	12	14	25	3	1	2	13	0	0	2	7	0	19	3	1	1	.230	.329	.410
Hess, Samuel, Angels	7	23	21	2	4	5	1	0	0	0	1	0	0	1	0	5	0	0	1	.190	.227	.238
Hrynio, Mike, Mariners	15	1	1	1	1	1	0	0	0	0	0	0	0	0	0	0	0	0	0	1.000	1.000	1.000
Hymon, James, Mariners	38	144	118	17	18	23	1	2	0	8	1	2	3	20	0	52	8	2	3	.153	.287	.195
Jackson, Noah, Cubs	31	121	106	9	22	28	4	1	0	8	1	1	2	11	1	22	0	1	3	.208	.292	.264
Jacobsen, Brock, Rangers †	24	114	91	18	34	51	1	5	2	18	0	0	1	22	0	23	9	1	4	.374	.500	.560
Johnston, Trey, Cubs	28	94	81	10	15	21	3	0	1	9	0	1	1	11	0	27	1	3	6	.185	.287	.259
Jones, Adamq, Mariners	28	128	109	18	31	38	5	1	0	8	3	1	10	5	0	19	5	1	1	.284	.368	.349
Jones, J.J., Angels	29	107	102	13	24	29	5	0	0	14	0	0	2	3	0	21	4	1	0	.235	.271	.284
Jones, Nick, Cubs	6	28	26	5	7	10	3	0	0	3	0	0	2	0	0	5	0	0	0	.269	.321	.385
Klippenstein, Tyler, Athletics	42	180	163	17	39	49	8	1	0	26	1	3	2	11	0	37	0	2	3	.239	.291	.301
Kotchman, Casey, Angels *	7	29	27	5	9	16	1	0	2	6	0	0	0	2	1	3	0	0	1	.333	.379	.593
LePage, Patrice, Angels *	32	105	89	18	19	28	5	2	0	8	0	1	1	14	0	31	1	2	2	.213	.324	.315
Lewis, William, Brewers	25	114	99	16	24	35	5	3	0	19	1	1	6	7	0	16	3	4	2	.242	.327	.354
Liniak, Cole, Rangers	2	7	7	2	3	5	2	0	0	0	0	0	0	0	0	2	0	0	0	.429	.429	.714
Lopez, Baltazar, Angels *	44	189	173	26	52	76	12	3	2	23	0	0	0	16	1	46	3	0	3	.301	.360	.439
Lopez, Mendy, Royals-1	7	25	20	9	5	15	1	0	3	6	0	0	1	4	0	5	0	0	0	.250	.400	.750
Lozada, Charlie, Brewers	24	75	67	10	24	30	4	1	0	10	0	2	0	6	0	10	0	1	0	.358	.400	.448
Lubanski, Christopher, Roy.-1*	53	241	221	41	72	100	4	6	4	27	0	0	2	18	0	50	9	10	4	.326	.382	.452
Lunsford, Trey, Giants	5	21	13	5	6	8	0	1	0	3	0	1	0	7	0	3	1	1	0	.462	.619	.615
Macha, Eric, Athletics	43	168	148	18	24	25	1	0	0	9	1	1	4	14	0	28	0	1	5	.162	.251	.169
Maier, Mitch, Royals-1 *	51	226	203	41	71	103	14	6	2	45	0	3	2	18	0	25	7	3	4	.350	.403	.507
Maldonado, Pedro, Athletics	25	87	77	8	17	21	1	0	1	11	1	1	2	6	0	26	2	3	2	.221	.291	.273
Mann, Jason, Rangers *	30	122	101	13	17	24	2	1	1	10	2	2	3	14	0	24	4	0	2	.168	.283	.238
Mannon, Adam, Brewers	47	204	179	26	49	79	13	4	3	37	0	2	2	21	0	53	6	2	2	.274	.353	.441
Martinez, Brett, Angels	46	170	148	16	37	44	1	3	0	15	1	1	1	19	0	22	9	5	7	.250	.337	.297
Martinez, Eduardo, Rangers	34	150	134	25	38	58	6	4	2	12	1	0	2	13	0	34	11	5	4	.284	.356	.433
McCormack, Taylor, Brewers	42	165	146	24	38	55	9	1	2	19	0	2	3	14	0	41	1	2	3	.260	.333	.377
McDonald, Chamar, Ro.-2-Ro.-1	29	123	106	24	32	49	8	0	3	17	0	1	2	14	0	36	1	0	2	.302	.390	.462
McFall, Brian, Royals-1	51	213	191	34	42	77	9	4	6	36	0	1	4	17	0	50	1	0	1	.220	.296	.403
McIntyre, Patrick, Cubs	18	64	53	7	7	9	0	1	0	3	1	0	2	8	0	14	0	0	3	.132	.270	.170
Mejia, Carlos, Cubs	49	210	202	27	53	92	11	8	4	30	0	3	3	2	0	32	1	3	5	.262	.276	.455
Mejia, Fausto, Brewers	32	114	107	12	33	41	6	1	0	13	1	0	1	5	0	19	3	1	3	.308	.345	.383
Mejia, Jorge, Athletics	50	243	223	48	84	134	17	6	7	30	1	4	0	15	0	46	7	9	4	.377	.409	.601
Metheny, Brenton, Mariners *	24	114	95	21	36	59	7	5	2	22	0	2	1	16	0	16	7	3	1	.379	.465	.621
Mooney, Michael, Giants	56	247	221	30	64	94	15	6	1	39	1	4	3	18	0	55	9	2	7	.290	.346	.425
Morillo, Roberto, Giants †	37	137	120	17	34	46	5	2	1	16	1	3	3	10	0	26	6	2	3	.283	.346	.383
Nunez, Felix, Angels	30	136	123	23	41	51	6	2	0	10	0	1	3	9	0	15	8	6	1	.333	.390	.415
O'Riordan, Chris, Rangers	7	27	19	7	9	15	1	1	1	3	0	0	1	7	0	2	0	1	0	.474	.630	.789
O'Sullivan, Steve, Rangers	2	8	8	1	1	2	1	0	0	0	0	0	0	0	0	2	0	0	0	.125	.125	.250
Ogando, Alexi, Athletics	48	206	190	33	65	101	13	1	7	36	0	3	6	7	0	42	5	6	4	.342	.379	.532
Olayemi, Gbenga, Brewers	24	58	53	7	9	10	1	0	0	3	0	1	1	3	0	17	1	0	2	.170	.224	.189
Opdyke, Bryan, Brewers *	32	121	103	16	28	40	8	2	0	10	0	2	0	16	0	25	1	0	0	.272	.364	.388
Oriental, Rene, Royals-1	47	182	166	27	41	66	4	3	5	27	0	2	0	14	0	40	6	4	3	.247	.302	.398
Ozoria, Pedro, Mariners	39	160	141	17	37	51	7	2	1	12	0	2	3	14	0	34	1	2	6	.262	.338	.362
Paulino, Adalberto, Giants	13	48	46	4	12	18	2	2	0	6	1	0	0	1	0	7	3	1	0	.261	.277	.391
Pena, Antonio, Rangers	43	180	157	36	36	49	7	3	0	23	1	2	2	18	1	39	9	3	3	.229	.313	.312
Perez, Keith, Athletics	17	1	1	0	0	0	0	0	0	0	0	0	0	0	0	1	0	0	0	.000	.000	.000
Petit, Gregorio, Athletics	32	129	117	13	31	37	6	0	0	12	2	0	0	10	0	22	3	5	5	.265	.323	.316
Phillips, Jonathan, Brewers	26	78	68	7	13	14	1	0	0	7	1	0	1	8	0	12	0	1	1	.191	.286	.206
Phillips, Paul, Royals-1	4	14	13	3	6	11	2	0	1	2	0	0	0	1	0	0	0	0	0	.462	.500	.846
Pijuan, Ricky, Brewers *	41	158	145	16	29	43	5	3	1	12	1	0	2	10	0	62	1	0	0	.200	.261	.297
Plasencia, Francisco, Brew.*	47	208	187	30	53	76	11	3	2	21	0	0	2	19	0	43	14	6	3	.283	.356	.406
Powell, Brandon, Royals-1 *	52	250	215	47	70	124	12	15	4	46	2	4	2	27	0	39	15	6	3	.326	.399	.577
Quintero, Cesar, Mariners	28	106	96	16	31	42	6	1	1	16	0	1	2	7	0	23	1	1	2	.323	.377	.438
Ramirez, Juan, Athletics	29	104	90	13	23	41	6	0	4	12	2	1	3	8	0	21	0	0	3	.256	.333	.456
Renz, Jordan, Angels †	52	224	204	31	53	91	9	7	5	28	0	1	2	17	0	59	4	1	2	.260	.321	.446
Rios, Jose, Cubs	38	175	165	27	46	55	5	2	0	17	3	2	0	5	0	16	0	2	3	.279	.297	.333
Rodriguez, Sean, Angels	54	239	216	30	58	82	8	5	2	25	1	1	7	14	0	37	11	4	6	.269	.332	.380
Rogelstad, Matt, Mariners *	15	64	61	11	24	30	4	1	0	11	2	0	0	1	0	5	1	0	1	.393	.403	.492
Rojas, Carlos, Cubs	47	210	187	38	44	57	7	3	0	15	2	1	2	18	0	20	9	3	4	.235	.308	.305
Rosario, Samuel, Cubs	22	95	76	21	23	35	6	3	0	14	1	0	1	17	0	14	8	2	1	.303	.436	.461
Saenz, Olmedo, Athletics	13	55	45	13	15	23	2	0	2	8	0	0	2	8	0	6	1	0	1	.333	.455	.511
Salazar, Darwinson, Royals-2	44	168	141	21	37	51	7	2	1	18	2	3	4	18	1	45	5	4	0	.262	.355	.362
Sandel, George, Mariners *	50	246	205	36	54	67	11	1	0	20	2	3	2	34	0	27	14	5	2	.263	.369	.327

Player, Team	G	TPA	AB	R	H	TB	2B	3B	HR	RBI	SH	SF	HP	BB	IBB	SO	SB	CS	GDP	Avg.	OBP	Slg.
Saunches, Mike, Royals-2 *	44	192	161	15	41	58	14	0	1	23	1	2	1	27	1	35	1	0	5	.255	.361	.360
Schierholtz, Nathan, Giants *	11	49	45	5	18	22	0	2	0	5	0	0	1	3	0	8	4	0	0	.400	.449	.489
Schweiger, Brian, Mariners	42	155	129	21	37	51	9	1	1	15	1	4	3	18	0	24	0	0	4	.287	.377	.395
Sevilla, Walter, Royals-2	40	171	148	28	38	52	8	3	0	10	1	0	4	18	0	22	11	0	4	.257	.353	.351
Solis, Eddie, Royals-1	27	65	58	12	15	33	5	2	3	9	0	0	1	6	0	14	1	0	1	.259	.338	.569
Soto, Luis, Mariners	32	133	118	22	36	53	6	1	3	24	0	2	6	7	0	18	1	1	3	.305	.368	.449
Spanos, Vasili, Athletics	5	20	18	3	5	5	0	0	0	2	0	0	1	1	0	2	1	1	1	.278	.350	.278
Springer, Kenard, Royals-1	49	201	182	35	63	89	15	1	3	39	0	4	5	10	0	20	7	4	5	.346	.388	.489
Strain, Ryan, Giants †	49	228	182	39	55	69	10	2	0	15	2	1	2	41	0	26	7	7	5	.302	.434	.379
Strong, Jamal, Mariners	2	13	7	5	5	7	0	1	0	4	0	2	1	3	0	1	3	0	0	.714	.692	1.000
Sutton, Don, Athletics	40	179	156	33	52	89	16	0	7	35	0	2	3	18	0	31	1	1	2	.333	.408	.571
Swope, Tobin, Rangers	14	56	47	11	18	25	5	1	0	5	0	0	2	7	0	7	2	0	0	.383	.482	.532
Tidball, Adam, Cubs	12	41	37	5	12	17	3	1	0	3	0	1	1	2	0	4	0	1	0	.324	.366	.459
Udy, Nicholas, Mariners *	1	4	2	2	2	2	0	0	0	0	0	0	1	1	0	0	1	0	0	1.000	1.000	1.000
Valdez, Jesus, Cubs	48	188	175	20	56	74	8	5	0	29	0	0	5	7	0	31	7	2	4	.320	.364	.423
Valentin, Geraldo, Royals-2	32	141	122	25	43	63	12	1	2	23	3	2	3	11	0	16	3	2	3	.352	.413	.516
Vega, Miguel, Royals-1	25	84	81	12	18	29	5	0	2	11	0	1	0	2	0	25	0	0	3	.222	.238	.358
Ventura, Robert, Giants	41	145	127	13	23	30	7	0	0	10	2	0	1	15	0	44	7	0	0	.181	.273	.236
Walston, Chris, Angels	52	220	198	25	36	67	7	3	6	36	0	2	1	19	0	88	1	1	3	.182	.255	.338
Ware, Matthew, Mariners	5	16	15	5	8	10	0	1	0	2	0	0	0	1	0	1	2	0	0	.533	.563	.667
Washington, Johnny, Ran.	21	75	63	11	14	19	2	0	1	8	0	2	1	9	0	15	4	2	2	.222	.320	.302
Weeks, Rickie, Brewers	1	5	4	0	2	2	0	0	0	4	0	0	1	0	0	2	1	0	0	.500	.600	.500
Weitz, Konrad, Royals-1	7	8	8	0	1	2	1	0	0	0	0	0	0	0	0	2	0	0	0	.125	.125	.250
Welsch, Travis, Cubs	9	36	30	5	7	11	2	1	0	8	0	2	0	4	0	5	0	0	1	.233	.306	.367
Willis, Lendon, Brewers	2	8	6	1	4	6	2	0	0	3	0	1	0	1	0	2	2	0	0	.667	.625	1.000
Wilson, Michael, Mariners †	48	202	177	33	55	79	9	3	3	25	0	1	4	20	0	46	6	6	1	.311	.391	.446
Winslow, Benjamin, Athletics	27	86	75	12	21	33	3	0	3	9	0	1	1	9	0	17	1	0	1	.280	.360	.440
Wood, Brandon, Angels	19	86	78	14	24	36	8	2	0	13	0	2	2	4	0	15	3	0	2	.308	.349	.462
Wu, Chao, Mariners *	29	92	86	12	24	34	3	2	1	11	0	0	1	5	0	18	1	0	2	.279	.326	.395
Yens, Jose, Giants	53	218	208	32	65	94	10	8	1	26	2	0	4	4	1	37	9	5	4	.313	.338	.452
Zbacnik, William, Giants *	34	151	131	12	27	38	5	0	2	16	0	0	1	19	1	36	1	2	3	.206	.311	.290
Zorrilla, Junior, Athletics	17	1	1	0	0	0	0	0	0	0	0	0	0	0	0	1	0	0	0	.000	.000	.000

BATTERS WITH TWO OR MORE TEAMS

Player, Team	G	TPA	AB	R	H	TB	2B	3B	HR	RBI	SH	SF	HP	BB	IBB	SO	SB	CS	GDP	Avg.	OBP	Slg.
Donachie, Adam, Royals-1	20	74	63	8	14	19	3	1	0	7	0	0	2	9	0	12	0	1	2	.222	.338	.302
Donachie, Adam, Royals-2	2	10	9	3	4	5	1	0	0	0	0	0	0	1	0	4	0	0	0	.444	.500	.556
McDonald, Chamar, Royals-2	7	34	32	7	10	13	3	0	0	4	0	0	0	2	0	6	0	0	0	.313	.353	.406
McDonald, Chamar, Royals-1	22	89	74	17	22	36	5	0	3	13	0	1	2	12	0	30	1	0	2	.297	.404	.486

GRAND SLAMS—Balentien, B. Lopez, Mannon, Plasencia, Quintaro, Renz, Valentin, Zbacnik, 1 each.

AWARDED FIRST BASE ON CATCHER'S INTERFERENCE—Balcom 2 (Hatcher, Sutton); A. Garcia 2 (Felix, Lozada); Cashman (Blanco); Furtado (Bernard); Gac (Blanco); German (Olayemi); Valdez (LePage).

2003 PITCHING

TEAM

Team	W	L	Pct.	ERA	G	CG	ShO	Sv.	IP	H	TBF	R	ER	HR	SH	SF	HB	BB	IBB	SO	WP	Bk.
Royals-1	36	19	.655	3.98	55	0	2	9	488.0	507	2096	260	216	28	10	10	20	146	2	433	36	6
Rangers	38	18	.679	4.05	56	0	1	16	506.1	532	2221	294	228	26	11	13	41	151	3	396	41	8
Giants	28	28	.500	4.33	56	0	3	13	488.2	496	2159	284	235	14	12	17	30	222	1	503	55	6
Royals-2	32	22	.593	4.42	54	0	1	16	478.2	508	2090	286	235	28	11	22	26	150	0	459	36	3
Cubs	27	29	.482	4.74	56	0	0	13	499.2	544	2275	343	263	24	15	25	43	228	4	463	65	5
Mariners	30	25	.545	4.87	55	0	2	12	488.1	530	2219	329	264	22	13	21	47	213	2	381	70	9
Brewers	18	37	.327	5.24	55	0	0	7	474.0	556	2185	348	276	23	18	24	42	202	0	389	58	7
Angels	21	35	.375	5.41	56	0	1	8	493.2	547	2275	366	297	26	15	28	48	256	3	441	64	9
Athletics	19	36	.345	5.73	55	0	2	11	483.2	644	2281	388	308	28	10	22	45	187	1	403	39	8

INDIVIDUAL

TOP QUALIFIERS FOR EARNED-RUN AVERAGE TITLE

Minimum 45 innings. *Lefthanded pitcher.

Pitcher, Team	W	L	Pct.	ERA	G	GS	CG	ShO	GF	Sv.	IP	H	TBF	R	ER	HR	SH	SF	HB	BB	IBB	SO	WP	Bk.
Hawk, Tommy, Brewers	2	1	.667	2.31	12	6	0	0	1	0	46.2	47	203	17	12	3	1	0	5	17	0	30	3	1
Millikan, Bryan, Giants	5	1	.833	2.35	11	10	0	0	0	0	46.0	42	195	16	12	1	0	0	4	22	0	32	4	0
Bay, Ronald, Cubs	7	1	.875	2.50	10	6	0	0	0	0	57.2	51	227	18	16	2	1	0	2	9	0	69	4	0
Hughes, Dustin, Royals-1 *	5	2	.714	2.84	11	6	0	0	1	0	50.2	38	202	21	16	4	0	0	0	18	0	54	4	1
Gragg, John, Royals-2 *	3	2	.600	3.45	13	13	0	0	0	0	60.0	63	258	27	23	4	1	1	2	10	0	55	3	0
Palmer, Lucas, Royals-1	6	0	1.000	3.62	14	7	0	0	3	1	54.2	55	235	28	22	4	1	1	3	17	0	50	1	0
Rosa, Carlos, Royals-1	5	3	.625	3.63	15	11	0	0	0	0	69.1	79	297	36	28	4	1	0	4	18	1	54	9	1
Cox, Jason, Angels	3	3	.500	3.81	10	10	0	0	0	0	49.2	58	208	28	21	6	1	2	2	11	0	37	2	2
Mullis, Jacob, Royals-2	4	3	.571	3.82	13	13	0	0	0	0	63.2	75	270	34	27	5	1	4	6	7	0	57	3	0
Atencio, Greg, Royals-2	2	5	.286	3.91	12	12	0	0	0	0	71.1	62	292	40	31	4	3	3	6	17	0	62	1	3
Villanueva, Carlos, Giants	3	6	.333	3.97	12	10	0	0	0	0	59.0	64	247	31	26	1	0	1	2	13	0	67	5	0
McClellan, Robbie, Royals-2	4	3	.571	4.00	18	0	0	0	4	2	45.0	44	185	24	20	4	0	0	0	7	0	51	4	0
Marmol, Carlos, Cubs	3	5	.375	4.19	14	9	0	0	0	0	62.1	54	288	38	29	5	2	2	7	37	0	74	6	2
Figuereo, Victor, Rangers	4	3	.571	4.29	14	5	0	0	3	0	50.1	64	238	37	24	6	3	1	9	13	0	35	6	1
Sarmiento, Williams, Rangers	6	1	.857	4.36	14	7	0	0	4	2	53.2	61	240	31	26	2	0	1	5	14	0	46	5	0

DEPARTMENTAL LEADERS: W—Bay, 7; L—A. Sanchez, Villanueva, 6; Pct.—Bay, .875; G—Arnold, Dossett, 21; GS—Gragg, Mullis, B. Santana, 13; CG—none; ShO—none; GF—Arnold, 20; Sv.—Nacar, 9; IP—B. Santana, 74.0; H—B. Santana, 88; TBF—B. Santana, 323; R—M. Garcia, P. Rodriguez, 46; ER—P. Rodriguez, 38; HR—Bello, 8; SH—Several pitchers tied with 3; SF—Bannister, 7; HB—Gelinas, 10; BB—I. Brown, 50; IBB—Laird, 2; SO—Marmol, 74; WP—I. Brown, 12; BK—Ramos, 4.

ALL PITCHERS

*Lefthanded pitcher.

Pitcher, Team	W	L	Pct.	ERA	G	GS	CG	ShO	GF	Sv.	IP	H	TBF	R	ER	HR	SH	SF	HB	BB	IBB	SO	WP	Bk.
Acevedo, Danielin, Athletics	0	5	.000	5.94	10	8	0	0	1	0	36.1	46	175	36	24	1	1	1	6	20	0	22	6	0
Acosta, Kelyn, Giants	3	4	.429	4.40	10	8	0	0	0	0	45.0	56	200	28	22	0	1	2	3	16	0	35	1	0
Alleva, Jeff, Royals-1	1	1	.500	3.00	11	0	0	0	1	0	18.0	20	77	6	6	0	0	0	2	3	1	15	2	0
Altman, Kevin, Rangers	3	0	1.000	3.86	11	4	0	0	3	0	35.0	27	146	18	15	2	0	0	0	14	0	26	2	0
Alvarez, Jose, Cubs	1	1	.500	6.04	14	0	0	0	3	0	28.1	34	136	21	19	4	1	4	7	13	0	10	7	1
Anderson, Luke, Giants	0	0	.000	6.75	5	0	0	0	0	0	5.1	8	24	4	4	0	0	0	0	0	0	7	1	0
Arnold, Mitchell, Angels	1	3	.250	3.86	21	0	0	0	20	4	23.1	17	106	14	10	0	0	3	1	19	0	19	3	0
Asencio, Miguel, Royals-1	0	0	.000	2.84	3	3	0	0	0	0	6.1	11	32	3	2	0	1	0	0	1	0	3	0	0
Atencio, Greg, Royals-2	2	5	.286	3.91	12	12	0	0	0	0	71.1	62	292	40	31	4	3	3	6	17	0	62	1	3
Avendano, Elvis, Athletics	1	3	.250	5.45	7	6	0	0	1	1	33.0	44	142	25	20	6	0	2	1	5	0	33	1	0
Bannister, John, Rangers	2	4	.333	4.22	13	7	0	0	3	1	42.2	47	193	31	20	2	0	7	4	16	0	28	2	2
Bates, Nicholas, Brewers	0	0	.000	4.50	1	0	0	0	0	0	2.0	2	9	1	1	0	0	0	0	0	0	3	0	0
Bay, Ronald, Cubs	7	1	.875	2.50	10	6	0	0	0	0	57.2	51	227	18	16	2	1	0	2	9	0	69	4	0
Bello, Cibney, Mariners	1	1	.500	6.56	11	5	0	0	1	0	35.2	42	165	27	26	8	1	1	4	19	0	27	3	0
Benoit, Hector, Angels	0	0	.000	27.00	5	0	0	0	2	0	4.2	10	34	14	14	0	0	1	2	9	0	4	2	1
Bergdall, Kendall, Mariners *	3	4	.429	5.87	9	8	0	0	0	0	30.2	40	148	25	20	1	0	0	1	20	0	27	8	2
Bernat, David, Mariners	1	2	.333	9.89	14	0	0	0	4	0	23.2	35	119	28	26	2	1	2	2	12	0	17	5	0
Blanco, Carlos, Ro.-1-Ro.-2 *	0	1	.000	16.20	9	0	0	0	4	0	8.1	15	48	15	15	0	0	0	0	8	0	10	4	0
Blanton, Jason, Cubs	0	1	.000	2.70	6	3	0	0	0	0	6.2	7	34	4	2	0	0	0	0	9	0	8	7	0
Bost, Heath, Athletics	0	0	.000	9.00	1	0	0	0	0	0	1.0	3	5	1	1	0	0	0	0	0	0	1	0	0
Bowman, Charles, Rangers	0	2	.000	5.00	12	0	0	0	7	1	18.0	24	81	12	10	2	0	3	2	4	1	6	1	0
Braun, Ryan, Royals-1	0	0	.000	2.95	18	0	0	0	13	3	21.1	15	90	9	7	0	0	0	0	10	0	25	0	0
Bray, Stephen, Royals-2	4	2	.667	3.38	14	0	0	0	9	3	40.0	41	156	17	15	2	2	3	0	7	0	32	1	0
Bright, Nathan, Rangers	0	1	.000	1.93	3	0	0	0	2	0	4.2	5	21	5	1	0	0	0	0	1	0	3	0	0
Brito, Jose, Angels *	0	0	.000	4.42	13	0	0	0	5	0	18.1	22	89	15	9	4	0	0	1	11	0	12	3	0
Brito, Luis, Cubs	1	0	1.000	5.17	5	1	0	0	0	0	15.2	16	65	13	9	2	0	1	0	2	0	15	1	0
Brown, Brent, Angels *	2	2	.500	7.71	14	2	0	0	0	0	30.1	38	142	29	26	1	0	4	1	19	0	28	4	0
Brown, Ira, Royals-2	4	2	.667	4.96	15	11	0	0	0	0	61.2	57	288	45	34	2	0	2	3	50	0	66	12	0
Bryan, Bobby, Royals-2	0	1	.000	10.72	15	0	0	0	5	1	22.2	40	123	28	27	2	0	3	3	12	0	17	0	0
Buckley, Allen, Angels	2	0	1.000	0.59	10	0	0	0	2	0	15.1	11	60	3	1	0	3	0	3	4	0	12	1	0
Bukowski, Stan, Angels	1	0	1.000	13.50	4	0	0	0	1	0	4.0	11	25	10	6	0	0	1	0	1	0	1	1	0
Burgos, Ambiorix, Royals-1	3	2	.600	4.00	9	7	0	0	1	0	36.0	37	161	22	16	1	0	0	3	16	0	43	8	1
Cabaniel, Tomas, Athletics	4	3	.571	4.53	11	9	0	0	0	0	47.2	62	224	31	24	5	2	4	2	14	0	33	5	2
Campusano, Emmanuel, Cubs*	1	1	.500	4.91	6	3	0	0	1	0	22.0	30	104	12	12	0	0	1	1	9	1	14	1	1
Carpenter, Calvin, Brewers	0	0	.000	0.00	1	0	0	0	0	0	3.0	3	12	1	0	0	0	0	0	0	0	1	1	0
Castillo, Ruben, Brewers	0	2	.000	13.50	6	0	0	0	2	0	8.0	10	49	14	12	0	2	0	2	13	0	7	2	1
Cedeno , Jonathan, Brewers	0	4	.000	8.75	14	0	0	0	9	0	23.2	39	131	26	23	5	3	4	3	17	0	23	6	1
Cedeno, Jovanny, Rangers	3	0	1.000	1.84	8	0	0	0	3	0	14.2	9	57	3	3	0	0	0	0	4	0	14	4	0
Chiasson, Scott, Cubs	0	0	.000	3.38	2	2	0	0	0	0	2.2	3	10	1	1	0	0	0	0	0	0	5	0	0
Christensen, Ben, Cubs	0	0	.000	2.70	2	0	0	0	0	0	3.1	3	14	2	1	0	0	0	0	1	0	4	1	0
Christensen, Danny, Roy.-1 *	0	0	.000	2.25	4	2	0	0	0	0	12.0	8	50	4	3	0	0	0	0	5	0	12	0	0
Clanton, Matt, Cubs	0	0	.000	0.00	1	1	0	0	0	0	2.0	2	9	0	0	0	0	0	0	2	0	0	0	0
Colton, Kyle, Royals-2	2	1	.667	8.00	5	0	0	0	1	0	9.0	12	52	10	8	1	0	0	1	9	0	8	0	0
Corbett, Jason, Angels	1	2	.333	7.77	20	0	0	0	6	0	22.0	27	117	21	19	0	1	2	1	22	0	29	6	0
Cordeiro, Christopher, Ran.	4	0	1.000	5.87	12	4	0	0	1	0	38.1	63	185	28	25	3	1	0	2	9	1	19	2	0
Correa, Alexander, Brewers *	0	0	.000	12.46	9	0	0	0	6	1	13.0	28	85	26	18	4	0	0	3	13	0	10	4	0
Coughlin, Chris, Royals-1	1	3	.250	6.75	12	0	0	0	6	1	16.0	28	76	15	12	1	0	1	0	2	0	16	2	0
Cox, Jason, Angels	3	3	.500	3.81	10	10	0	0	0	0	49.2	58	208	28	21	6	1	2	2	11	0	37	2	2
Cuevas, Alvin, Mariners	0	0	.000	4.50	1	0	0	0	1	0	2.0	3	8	1	1	0	0	0	0	0	0	1	0	0
Cunningham, Tim, Rangers *	0	0	.000	0.00	3	2	0	0	1	1	7.0	2	26	0	0	0	0	0	0	5	0	7	0	0
D'Amico, Leonardo, Angels	0	0	.000	0.00	1	0	0	0	0	0	1.1	1	7	0	0	0	0	0	0	2	0	2	0	0
Damico, Vovany, Royals-1	2	1	.667	3.32	11	0	0	0	5	0	19.0	25	84	8	7	1	1	1	1	3	0	20	1	1
Danks, John, Rangers *	1	0	1.000	0.69	5	3	0	0	0	0	13.0	6	48	3	1	0	0	0	0	4	0	22	1	0
Dillard, Timothy, Brewers	1	2	.333	3.79	11	4	0	0	3	0	35.2	36	154	19	15	1	1	1	9	5	0	32	1	0
Dorn, Timothy, Mariners	0	0	.000	9.00	6	1	0	0	2	0	11.0	17	52	11	11	0	1	0	0	6	0	8	5	0
Dossett, Dusty, Royals-2	2	1	.667	1.80	21	0	0	0	18	6	25.0	30	111	12	5	0	0	3	1	3	0	23	3	0
Downs, Darin, Cubs *	0	2	.000	6.57	13	11	0	0	0	0	38.1	48	172	30	28	2	0	1	3	17	0	32	5	0
Durocher, Jayson, Brewers	0	0	.000	0.00	2	2	0	0	0	0	2.0	0	6	0	0	0	0	0	0	0	0	3	0	0
Encarnacion, Alexis, Royals-1	2	0	1.000	1.71	14	0	0	0	12	1	21.0	17	81	4	4	1	0	1	1	2	0	19	0	0
English, Jesse, Giants *	0	1	.000	3.98	7	6	0	0	0	0	20.1	11	88	11	9	0	0	0	1	19	0	31	3	0
Espinal, Willy, Rangers	5	2	.714	5.06	14	7	0	0	4	1	53.1	57	230	32	30	2	1	1	5	12	1	38	1	1
Fagan, Robert, Mariners *	1	2	.333	4.36	9	7	0	0	0	0	33.0	40	145	22	16	0	0	1	0	6	0	24	5	0
Falconer, Kenny, Mariners	1	1	.500	8.64	7	0	0	0	2	0	8.1	8	44	8	8	0	0	2	2	11	0	4	2	0
Feierabend, Ryan, Mariners *	2	3	.400	2.61	6	5	0	0	1	1	20.2	23	89	11	6	0	1	1	1	6	0	12	1	1
Feldman, Scott, Rangers	1	1	.500	4.26	3	1	0	0	0	0	6.1	4	31	6	3	0	0	0	1	1	0	7	0	0
Ferguson, Ian, Royals-2	3	1	.750	2.70	5	5	0	0	0	0	23.1	16	94	9	7	2	0	0	2	6	0	26	2	0
Figuereo, Victor, Rangers	4	3	.571	4.29	14	5	0	0	3	0	50.1	64	238	37	24	6	3	1	9	13	0	35	6	1
Fingers, Jason, Royals-1	0	0	.000	6.00	2	0	0	0	0	0	3.0	2	12	2	2	1	0	0	0	1	0	1	0	0
Fitzgerald, Ryan, Cubs	0	0	.000	0.00	1	0	0	0	1	0	0.1	0	1	0	0	0	0	0	0	0	0	0	0	0
Flandes, Wington, Brewers	0	1	.000	4.50	11	0	0	0	11	1	20.0	26	90	13	10	0	0	1	0	1	0	7	2	0
Flores, Ruben, Mariners	2	2	.500	3.73	9	7	0	0	0	0	31.1	28	141	18	13	1	0	2	7	12	0	26	3	1
Forbes, Terry, Mariners	4	0	1.000	5.18	11	6	0	0	0	0	40.0	42	183	29	23	2	0	2	6	14	0	20	2	0
France, Ryan, Athletics	0	0	.000	9.82	3	0	0	0	1	1	7.1	12	36	9	8	0	0	0	1	3	0	7	0	0
Gamboa, Felix, Angels	0	2	.000	9.95	10	2	0	0	2	1	12.2	15	73	15	14	1	0	2	4	17	0	10	6	0
Garcia, Miguel, Brewers	1	5	.167	7.59	12	7	0	0	0	0	42.2	65	208	46	36	0	0	1	2	21	0	27	11	1
Gelinas, Karl, Angels	0	4	.000	6.04	12	7	0	0	0	0	44.2	51	202	35	30	3	2	4	10	9	1	38	2	0
Gittings, Christopher, Brewers	2	2	.500	4.84	13	0	0	0	7	1	22.1	22	90	14	12	1	3	1	2	5	0	10	1	0
Goodman, Chris, Royals-1	3	1	.750	4.09	11	7	0	0	1	0	44.0	48	191	24	20	2	2	2	2	11	0	42	2	0
Gragg, John, Royals-2 *	3	2	.600	3.45	13	13	0	0	0	0	60.0	63	258	27	23	4	1	1	2	10	0	55	3	0
Granado, Julian, Athletics *	0	1	.000	8.15	15	0	0	0	8	0	17.2	28	95	18	16	0	0	0	3	13	1	13	3	1
Green, Craig, Cubs	0	2	.000	10.80	4	0	0	0	2	0	5.0	9	28	7	6	0	1	1	0	2	1	5	1	0
Green, Steve, Angels	1	1	.500	1.29	2	2	0	0	0	0	7.0	4	27	2	1	0	0	1	0	2	0	7	0	0

Pitcher, Team	W	L	Pct.	ERA	G	GS	CG	ShO	GF	Sv.	IP	H	TBF	R	ER	HR	SH	SF	HB	BB	IBB	SO	WP	Bk.
Gross, Kris, Cubs	1	1	.500	2.91	9	0	0	0	6	1	21.2	19	83	7	7	0	1	2	0	6	0	16	2	0
Gross, Kyle, Giants	0	0	.000	31.50	5	0	0	0	1	0	4.0	5	34	16	14	0	0	1	2	15	0	6	5	0
Guzman, Jonathan, Royals-1	1	2	.333	5.09	10	0	0	0	4	1	17.2	22	80	11	10	2	2	0	0	4	0	9	0	0
Hall, Vance, Mariners *	2	2	.500	4.89	9	9	0	0	0	0	46.0	42	193	26	25	4	0	2	2	20	0	31	2	1
Hannaman, Ryan, Giants *	1	1	.500	4.38	4	4	0	0	0	0	12.1	8	53	6	6	0	1	1	2	7	0	14	0	0
Hartnett, Christopher, Angels*	1	0	1.000	6.75	7	0	0	0	1	1	10.2	16	53	9	8	0	0	0	3	2	0	9	1	0
Hawk, Tommy, Brewers	2	1	.667	2.31	12	6	0	0	1	0	46.2	47	203	17	12	3	1	0	5	17	0	30	3	1
Hernandez, Armando, Giants	0	1	.000	4.24	17	0	0	0	0	0	34.0	38	150	16	16	0	1	2	2	12	0	27	0	0
Herrera, Marcos, Rangers	1	1	.500	4.63	11	1	0	0	3	0	23.1	28	108	16	12	0	1	0	1	9	0	13	3	0
Heuser, James, Athletics *	0	1	.000	10.54	14	0	0	0	6	2	13.2	19	70	17	16	1	1	1	3	13	0	16	1	0
Hill, Andrew, Angels	2	2	.500	2.79	6	5	0	0	0	0	19.1	17	87	7	6	0	0	1	4	12	0	18	5	0
Hill, Seth, Rangers *	1	2	.333	2.66	10	0	0	0	4	3	20.1	16	82	9	6	0	1	0	1	4	0	27	1	0
Hindman, Scott, Angels *	2	1	.667	3.13	6	6	0	0	0	0	23.0	22	98	10	8	0	0	1	1	8	0	23	5	2
Hrynio, Mike, Mariners	2	3	.400	4.07	14	0	0	0	5	0	24.1	31	112	20	11	0	1	1	1	9	1	20	1	0
Hughes, Dustin, Royals-1 *	5	2	.714	2.84	11	6	0	0	1	0	50.2	38	202	21	16	4	0	0	0	18	0	54	4	1
James, Craig, Mariners	2	0	1.000	3.81	14	0	0	0	5	2	26.0	28	110	12	11	0	1	1	3	4	0	19	3	1
Jenks, Bobby, Angels	0	0	.000	0.00	1	1	0	0	0	0	4.0	2	13	0	0	0	0	0	0	0	0	5	0	0
Kalita, Ryan, Cubs	0	0	.000	40.50	1	0	0	0	0	0	0.2	5	8	3	3	0	0	0	0	1	0	0	0	0
Laird, Matthew, Cubs	2	0	1.000	0.45	14	0	0	0	9	5	20.0	13	80	3	1	0	0	1	0	7	2	25	5	0
Leaist, Ryan, Mariners	1	1	.500	5.14	11	0	0	0	4	0	14.0	12	68	12	8	0	0	1	1	12	0	19	8	2
Lincoln, Matthew, Angels *	0	0	.000	1.08	6	0	0	0	3	2	8.1	2	32	2	1	0	0	1	0	6	0	14	1	0
Liriano, Francisco, Giants *	0	1	.000	4.32	4	4	0	0	0	0	8.1	5	34	4	4	1	1	1	0	6	0	9	1	1
Lundwall, Todd, Giants	1	1	.500	6.35	12	0	0	0	7	3	11.1	8	58	10	8	1	1	0	1	14	1	12	6	0
Marion, William, Brewers	2	1	.667	4.55	9	4	0	0	1	0	27.2	28	118	18	14	3	0	1	2	9	0	29	1	0
Markert, Jackson, Giants	1	0	1.000	1.59	4	0	0	0	0	0	5.2	3	20	1	1	0	0	1	0	0	0	6	0	0
Marmol, Carlos, Cubs	3	5	.375	4.19	14	9	0	0	0	0	62.1	54	288	38	29	5	2	2	7	37	0	74	6	2
Martin, Forrest, Brewers	2	1	.667	2.78	11	0	0	0	10	2	22.2	25	109	13	7	0	1	2	0	12	0	34	2	0
Martinez Sosa, Alvaro, Brew.	1	5	.167	5.54	12	6	0	0	2	1	39.0	38	193	29	24	1	3	1	3	35	0	47	8	2
Martinez, Roman, Mariners	0	1	.000	6.86	12	0	0	0	2	0	21.0	34	110	20	16	1	1	1	1	12	0	24	7	0
Mateo, Juan, Cubs	4	1	.800	4.46	18	0	0	0	11	2	36.1	42	167	25	18	2	3	2	2	14	0	35	0	0
Matos, Osiris, Giants	2	2	.500	4.67	9	6	0	0	0	0	34.2	35	151	21	18	1	1	4	2	10	0	28	3	0
McCleland, Bruce, Royals-1	2	2	.500	6.04	10	3	0	0	1	0	22.1	24	101	17	15	3	1	1	1	11	0	15	1	2
McClellan, Robbie, Royals-2	4	3	.571	4.00	18	0	0	0	4	2	45.0	44	185	24	20	4	0	0	0	7	0	51	4	0
McConiga, Jacob, Royals-2 *	1	0	1.000	4.15	9	0	0	0	4	1	8.2	9	42	5	4	0	1	1	0	5	0	11	1	0
McGovern, Ryan, Giants *	0	0	.000	6.26	14	0	0	0	3	0	23.0	36	118	21	16	2	0	2	1	8	0	18	2	2
Mendoza, Jorge, Rangers	0	0	.000	7.88	5	0	0	0	3	0	8.0	13	34	7	7	1	0	0	0	1	0	2	1	0
Millikan, Bryan, Giants	5	1	.833	2.35	11	10	0	0	0	0	46.0	42	195	16	12	1	0	0	4	22	0	32	4	0
Mola, Heydin, Athletics	1	3	.250	6.59	14	0	0	0	8	3	27.1	40	130	26	20	2	1	2	1	8	0	22	3	0
Montas, Ipolito, Athletics	1	2	.333	5.15	16	0	0	0	7	0	36.2	50	168	23	21	2	0	1	5	10	0	25	4	2
Moreno, Anthony, Giants	6	1	.857	2.83	10	4	0	0	1	0	35.0	27	143	11	11	1	1	2	1	12	0	39	4	0
Morrison, Tyler, Brewers	1	4	.200	6.02	10	8	0	0	0	0	40.1	58	180	34	27	2	1	3	3	9	0	30	3	0
Morrow, David, Mariners	1	2	.333	2.19	8	4	0	0	0	0	24.2	18	109	8	6	0	1	0	3	16	0	19	6	0
Moye, Jeffrey, Rangers	0	0	.000	9.00	1	0	0	0	0	0	2.0	4	11	2	2	0	0	0	0	1	0	1	0	0
Mullis, Jacob, Royals-2	4	3	.571	3.82	13	13	0	0	0	0	63.2	75	270	34	27	5	1	4	6	7	0	57	3	0
Nacar, Leslie, Giants	0	1	.000	0.95	20	0	0	0	18	9	19.0	9	72	4	2	1	1	0	2	3	0	31	1	1
Nendza, Brian, Royals-2 *	3	0	1.000	3.41	16	0	0	0	6	2	31.2	31	134	13	12	2	1	1	1	6	0	36	2	0
Nottingham, Shawn, Mar.*	1	0	1.000	3.72	12	0	0	0	0	0	19.1	17	85	10	8	2	0	0	2	8	0	17	0	0
O'Flaherty, Eric, Mariners *	3	0	1.000	1.95	13	1	0	0	5	0	27.2	17	110	10	6	1	2	1	2	7	1	20	0	0
Ortiz, Jose, Cubs	1	1	.500	1.52	7	3	0	0	0	0	23.2	19	102	9	4	0	0	1	1	10	0	16	2	0
Overholt, Sean, Cubs	1	0	1.000	5.40	9	1	0	0	4	0	16.2	19	77	15	10	1	0	1	1	6	0	15	4	0
Palmer, Lucas, Royals-1	6	0	1.000	3.62	14	7	0	0	3	1	54.2	55	235	28	22	4	1	1	3	17	0	50	1	0
Pawelczyk, Kyle, Angels *	0	2	.000	6.49	7	5	0	0	0	0	26.1	32	132	25	19	1	0	0	2	19	0	24	4	1
Perez, Keith, Athletics	1	5	.167	5.80	17	4	0	0	7	2	35.2	61	200	38	23	0	0	0	4	23	0	34	5	0
Perry, Brandon, Mariners *	1	0	1.000	2.55	17	0	0	0	17	8	17.2	15	75	8	5	0	0	0	2	4	0	24	2	0
Petke, Tim, Angels	1	0	1.000	1.69	4	1	0	0	1	0	16.0	11	61	4	3	0	0	1	0	5	0	22	0	0
Polanco, Alfredo, Cubs	1	1	.500	7.80	6	5	0	0	0	0	15.0	18	70	14	13	3	0	0	1	8	0	19	1	1
Pruett, Hubert, Brewers	2	3	.400	5.85	10	5	0	0	1	0	40.0	46	182	30	26	2	1	3	0	17	0	31	6	0
Ramirez, Victor, Rangers	1	0	1.000	4.26	10	0	0	0	7	3	12.2	18	61	8	6	2	0	0	0	2	0	19	2	0
Ramos, Jonathan, Rangers	1	0	1.000	5.17	11	0	0	0	2	0	15.2	17	80	13	9	0	2	0	3	13	0	9	4	4
Rauch, Brian, Brewers	2	3	.400	4.01	11	3	0	0	1	1	33.2	30	140	20	15	0	1	2	3	8	0	21	4	0
Regilio, Nick, Rangers	0	0	.000	0.00	2	2	0	0	0	0	5.0	4	19	2	0	0	0	0	1	1	0	7	0	0
Reina, Jesus, Giants *	1	1	.500	3.38	11	0	0	0	5	0	16.0	18	75	9	6	0	1	0	0	11	0	22	0	1
Requena, Ricardo, Angels	0	2	.000	5.85	4	4	0	0	0	0	20.0	25	92	15	13	2	2	0	2	6	1	16	3	0
Reyes, Ramon, Angels	1	3	.250	9.39	9	2	0	0	1	0	15.1	23	78	21	16	4	0	0	0	8	0	10	2	0
Reynolds, Grant, Athletics	0	0	.000	6.57	4	2	0	0	1	0	12.1	15	50	10	9	1	0	0	0	0	0	13	0	1
Rodriguez, Fernando, Angels	0	2	.000	6.48	15	0	0	0	5	0	25.0	29	121	24	18	2	2	1	2	14	1	27	1	1
Rodriguez, Luis, Rangers	0	0	.000	0.00	4	0	0	0	2	1	3.1	3	16	0	0	0	0	0	0	1	0	6	0	0
Rodriguez, Pedro, Cubs	2	4	.333	8.84	14	6	0	0	2	0	38.2	58	199	46	38	2	1	1	7	19	0	31	6	0
Rondon, Yosy, Giants *	2	2	.500	8.46	16	0	0	0	7	0	22.1	32	116	25	21	0	2	0	2	16	0	23	6	0
Roque, Christopher, Angels	0	3	.000	6.66	17	0	0	0	2	0	24.1	35	120	21	18	1	1	0	2	14	0	16	3	1
Rosa, Carlos, Royals-1	5	3	.625	3.63	15	11	0	0	0	0	69.1	79	297	36	28	4	1	0	4	18	1	54	9	1
Rosario, Julio, Royals-1	1	0	1.000	11.49	13	0	0	0	4	0	15.2	18	80	24	20	3	0	1	2	13	0	8	2	0
Rosario, Samuel, Cubs	1	0	1.000	9.00	1	0	0	0	1	0	1.0	2	6	1	1	0	0	0	1	0	0	0	0	0
Rose, Brian, Royals-1	1	0	1.000	0.00	2	0	0	0	0	0	6.0	3	20	0	0	0	0	0	0	0	0	5	0	0
Russ, Christopher, Rangers *	1	0	1.000	3.38	5	0	0	0	0	0	5.1	5	22	2	2	0	0	0	1	1	0	4	0	0
Saladin, John, Angels	1	0	1.000	3.92	13	0	0	0	4	0	20.2	23	92	12	9	0	2	1	3	8	0	16	4	0
Sanchez, Adiel, Athletics *	2	6	.250	5.68	11	9	0	0	0	0	52.1	64	231	37	33	3	1	3	4	11	0	49	2	1
Sanchez, Felix, Cubs *	0	0	.000	0.00	1	1	0	0	0	0	2.0	2	8	0	0	0	0	0	0	0	0	3	0	0
Sanchez, Jose, Giants	2	0	1.000	2.04	12	0	0	0	2	0	35.1	28	144	13	8	2	0	0	4	12	0	35	2	1
Santana, Andy, Cubs *	1	5	.167	5.89	13	4	0	0	3	0	36.2	47	179	41	24	1	2	3	3	27	0	25	4	0
Santana, Braulio, Athletics	6	1	.857	4.50	15	13	0	0	0	0	74.0	88	323	40	37	1	3	4	7	12	0	57	4	0
Santana, Roberto, Athletics *	2	1	.667	5.33	16	1	0	0	2	0	27.0	38	138	28	16	2	0	1	2	20	0	24	2	0
Sarmiento, Williams, Rangers	6	1	.857	4.36	14	7	0	0	4	2	53.2	61	240	31	26	2	0	1	5	14	0	46	5	0
Sherman, Justin, Royals-1	3	2	.600	4.41	12	8	0	0	2	1	49.0	51	203	24	24	1	1	2	1	10	0	40	3	0
Smiley, Jermaine, Giants *	0	0	.000	2.57	10	0	0	0	3	0	14.0	12	66	6	4	0	0	0	0	14	0	20	6	0

Pitcher, Team	W	L	Pct.	ERA	G	GS	CG	ShO	GF	Sv.	IP	H	TBF	R	ER	HR	SH	SF	HB	BB	IBB	SO	WP	Bk.
Smith, Cody, Rangers	2	0	1.000	2.91	12	6	0	0	3	2	43.1	31	171	15	14	3	1	0	4	10	0	27	2	0
Smith, Jesse, Angels	0	0	.000	5.40	3	1	0	0	0	0	6.2	7	29	4	4	0	0	0	1	5	0	7	0	1
Smith, Michael, Royals-2 *	0	0	.000	6.75	5	0	0	0	3	1	9.1	14	41	7	7	0	2	1	1	3	0	6	0	0
Snyder, Kyle, Royals-1	0	0	.000	4.50	1	1	0	0	0	0	2.0	3	8	1	1	0	0	0	0	0	0	1	0	0
Solis, Hairo, Giants	1	4	.200	7.16	15	3	0	0	9	1	32.2	49	147	29	26	3	1	0	0	8	0	33	4	0
Sundstrom, Mathew, Mariners	0	0	.000	9.00	1	0	0	0	1	0	1.0	1	7	1	1	0	0	0	0	3	0	1	0	0
Taveras, Nelson, Royals-1	0	0	.000	3.00	1	0	0	0	1	1	3.0	2	11	1	1	0	0	0	0	1	0	0	1	0
Torres, Joe, Angels *	2	0	1.000	0.56	3	3	0	0	0	0	16.0	7	59	2	1	0	0	1	1	6	0	15	0	0
Tovar, Miguel, Athletics	0	2	.000	9.86	14	0	0	0	7	1	21.0	37	116	26	23	2	0	3	3	15	0	15	2	0
Tucker, Cordoza, Mariners	1	1	.500	5.50	12	1	0	0	4	1	18.0	20	85	16	11	0	2	3	2	7	0	11	5	1
Urena, Jose, Cubs	0	1	.000	4.74	16	0	0	0	10	4	24.2	24	122	21	13	0	2	3	4	22	0	25	6	0
Villanueva, Carlos, Giants	3	6	.333	3.97	12	10	0	0	0	0	59.0	64	247	31	26	1	0	1	2	13	0	67	5	0
Volquez, Edison, Rangers	2	1	.667	4.00	10	4	0	0	1	1	27.0	24	112	14	12	1	1	0	2	11	0	28	4	0
Walker, Edwin, Brewers *	0	2	.000	5.54	9	5	0	0	0	0	26.0	27	112	17	16	1	0	2	2	9	0	22	1	1
Wang, Chao, Mariners	0	0	.000	0.00	1	0	0	0	0	0	1.2	3	8	0	0	0	0	0	0	0	0	1	0	0
Weber, Matthew, Cubs	0	2	.000	4.05	7	0	0	0	3	1	13.1	14	61	10	6	0	0	1	3	3	0	13	2	0
Wells, Randy, Cubs	0	0	.000	3.60	3	0	0	0	0	0	5.0	5	25	2	2	0	1	0	0	4	0	4	0	0
Whitaker, Roger, Giants	0	1	.000	1.69	3	1	0	0	0	0	5.1	2	24	2	1	0	0	0	1	4	0	8	1	0
Whittington, Anthony, Ang.*	0	3	.000	8.03	9	5	0	0	1	0	24.2	31	118	24	22	1	1	1	2	17	0	20	5	0
Wilhelmsen, Tom, Brewers	0	1	.000	4.50	2	2	0	0	0	0	4.0	5	22	2	2	0	0	1	1	4	0	4	0	0
Woerman, Joseph, Mariners	1	0	1.000	5.06	7	1	0	0	1	0	10.2	14	53	6	6	0	1	0	5	5	0	9	2	0
Wooley, Robert, Brewers	2	0	1.000	2.49	7	3	0	0	1	0	21.2	21	92	8	6	0	1	1	2	7	0	18	2	0
Zimmerman, Jeff, Rangers	0	0	.000	0.00	3	3	0	0	0	0	3.0	0	9	0	0	0	0	0	0	0	0	2	0	0
Zorrilla, Junior, Athletics	1	3	.250	3.76	17	3	0	0	6	1	40.2	37	178	23	17	2	1	0	3	20	0	39	1	1

PITCHERS WITH TWO OR MORE TEAMS

Pitcher, Team	W	L	Pct.	ERA	G	GS	CG	ShO	GF	Sv.	IP	H	TBF	R	ER	HR	SH	SF	HB	BB	IBB	SO	WP	Bk.
Blanco, Carlos, Royals-2 *	0	1	.000	18.41	8	0	0	0	4	0	7.1	14	44	15	15	0	0	0	0	8	0	9	4	0
Blanco, Carlos, Royals-1 *	0	0	.000	0.00	1	0	0	0	0	0	1.0	1	4	0	0	0	0	0	0	0	0	1	0	0

COMBINATION SHUTOUTS: Angels (1)—Pawelczyk-Buckley-Corbett-Lincoln-Arnold. Athletics (2)—Santana-Tovar-Houser, Santana-Zorrilla. Giants (3)—Solis-Moreno-Lundwell, Millikan-Hernandez-Solis, Acosta-Hernandez-McGovern. Mariners (2)—Hall-Tucker-Perry, Fagan-Nottingham-Hrynio. Rangers (1)—Espinal-Hill-Herrera. Royals-1 (2)—Burgos-Palmer, Ascencio-Hughes. Royals-2 (1)—Gragg-McClellan-Dossett.

NO-HIT GAMES: None.

2003 FIELDING

TEAM

Team	G	PO	A	E	TC	DP	TP	PB	Pct.
Royals-1	55	1464	609	81	2154	47	0	13	.962
Rangers	56	1519	609	89	2217	54	0	12	.960
Royals-2	54	1436	535	88	2059	39	1	10	.957
Giants	56	1466	560	98	2124	50	0	10	.954
Mariners	55	1465	655	104	2224	40	0	16	.953
Athletics	55	1451	549	98	2098	44	0	18	.953
Brewers	55	1422	568	105	2095	43	0	28	.950
Angels	56	1481	576	109	2166	49	0	16	.950
Cubs	56	1499	574	112	2185	37	0	33	.949

INDIVIDUAL

FIRST BASEMEN

NOTE: All caps denotes fielding-percentage leader based on 28 games for catchers, 37 for all other non-pitchers and 45 innings for pitchers. *Throws lefthanded.

Player, Team	Pct.	G	PO	A	E	TC	DP
Baez, Lizahio, Rangers	.974	4	37	1	1	39	2
Bernard, Oscar, Cubs	1.000	1	3	1	0	4	0
Blanco, Gregory, Angels	1.000	1	8	1	0	9	1
Bubalo, Ty, Athletics	.900	1	9	0	1	10	1
Connors, Greg, Mariners	1.000	2	22	2	0	24	4
Corporan, Carlos, Brewers	.971	15	120	15	4	139	9
Cruz, Elvis, Mariners	.951	5	37	2	2	41	2
Davidson, Matthew, Cubs	1.000	1	1	0	0	1	0
Denny, John, Mariners	1.000	2	14	2	0	16	0
Figuereo, Anibal, Royals-2	.993	19	126	21	1	148	11
Francisco, Alfredo, Cubs	1.000	3	6	0	0	6	1
Gac, Ian, Rangers	.986	44	396	23	6	425	33
Gaffney, Michael, Royals-2	1.000	1	3	0	0	3	0
Garcia, Alberto, Cubs	.974	31	241	17	7	265	20
Guhring, Simon, Brewers	1.000	3	9	0	0	9	1
Hamblen, Chris, Rangers	.977	4	39	3	1	43	4
Jackson, Noah, Cubs	.959	16	132	7	6	145	8
Jacobsen, Brock, Rangers	1.000	4	38	2	0	40	1
Klippenstein, Tyler, Athletics	.992	14	116	4	1	121	12
Kotchman, Casey, Angels *	1.000	4	31	2	0	33	1
Lopez, Baltazar, Angels *	.981	27	195	13	4	212	16
Macha, Eric, Athletics	.943	10	61	5	4	70	4
Maldonado, Pedro, Athletics	1.000	1	2	0	0	2	0
Mann, Jason, Rangers	1.000	1	7	0	0	7	2
Martinez, Brett, Angels	.909	2	10	0	1	11	1
McDonald, Chamar, R.-2-R.-1	.994	21	150	14	1	165	12
MCFALL, BRIAN, Royals-1	.988	41	376	21	5	402	33
McIntyre, Patrick, Cubs	1.000	5	28	3	0	31	1
Metheny, Brenton, Mariners	.960	6	65	7	3	75	2
Pijuan, Ricky, Brewers *	.975	39	321	29	9	359	25
Quintero, Cesar, Mariners	.985	6	61	6	1	68	2
Ramirez, Juan, Athletics	1.000	2	7	0	0	7	0
Saenz, Olmedo, Athletics	1.000	5	29	0	0	29	0
Saunches, Mike, Royals-2 *	.986	33	270	17	4	291	20
Schierholtz, Nathan, Giants	1.000	1	5	0	0	5	1
Schweiger, Brian, Mariners	.976	8	77	4	2	83	5
Soto, Luis, Mariners	.982	24	207	12	4	223	18
Sutton, Don, Athletics	.988	30	242	10	3	255	23
Tidball, Adam, Cubs	1.000	1	7	0	0	7	0
Ventura, Robert, Giants	.960	22	184	8	8	200	17
Walston, Chris, Angels	.987	26	213	8	3	224	27
Welsch, Travis, Cubs	1.000	6	41	2	0	43	4
Wu, Chao, Mariners	.962	5	48	2	2	52	3
Zbacnik, William, Giants *	.962	34	255	20	11	286	28

FIRST BASEMEN WITH TWO OR MORE TEAMS

Player, Team	Pct.	G	PO	A	E	TC	DP
McDonald, Chamar, Royals-1	.993	18	126	13	1	140	11
McDonald, Chamar, Royals-2	1.000	3	24	1	0	25	1

SECOND BASEMEN

Player, Team	Pct.	G	PO	A	E	TC	DP
Abreu, Johany, Giants	.923	3	6	6	1	13	3
Acosta, Jesse, Athletics	1.000	5	8	10	0	18	2
Almonte, Aneury, Angels	.939	8	16	15	2	33	4
Balcom, Jasha, Cubs	.875	5	7	7	2	16	2
Batista, Alexander, Royals-1	1.000	4	6	4	0	10	2
Boyer, William, Angels	.953	41	90	92	9	191	20
Craig, Casey, Mariners	.889	3	4	4	1	9	1
DePaula, Bartolo, Brewers	.939	27	43	64	7	114	14
Del Orbe, Samuel, Angels	.933	8	9	19	2	30	7
Disla, Lisandro, Giants	1.000	6	9	11	0	20	3
Falu, Irving, Royals-2	.977	19	38	46	2	86	8
Furtado, Micah, Rangers	.968	36	70	112	6	188	19
Hymon, James, Mariners	.909	5	4	6	1	11	0
Johnston, Trey, Cubs	.925	8	11	26	3	40	2
Jones, Nick, Cubs	1.000	5	11	10	0	21	2
Lewis, William, Brewers	.990	22	49	46	1	96	13

Player, Team	Pct.	G	PO	A	E	TC	DP
Lopez, Mendy, Royals-1	1.000	3	2	11	0	13	1
MEJIA, JORGE, Athletics	.970	48	84	108	6	198	19
Metheny, Brenton, Mariners	.868	7	14	19	5	38	3
Morillo, Roberto, Giants	.907	13	14	25	4	43	4
O'Riordan, Chris, Rangers	.958	7	7	16	1	24	1
Petit, Gregorio, Athletics	.923	3	7	5	1	13	2
Phillips, Jonathan, Brewers	.977	13	21	21	1	43	3
Powell, Brandon, Royals-1	.957	48	80	143	10	233	30
Rios, Jose, Cubs	.957	24	45	66	5	116	16
Rodriguez, Sean, Angels	1.000	4	7	7	0	14	3
Rogelstad, Matt, Mariners	1.000	2	2	4	0	6	0
Rojas, Carlos, Cubs	.905	6	9	10	2	21	2
Rosario, Samuel, Cubs	.923	7	12	12	2	26	0
Sandel, George, Mariners	.958	42	98	106	9	213	23
Sevilla, Walter, Royals-2	.945	34	72	82	9	163	18
Solis, Eddie, Royals-1	1.000	3	4	7	0	11	2
Strain, Ryan, Giants	.947	35	65	97	9	171	20
Swope, Tobin, Rangers	1.000	1	0	1	0	1	0
Valentin, Geraldo, Royals-2	.800	1	2	2	1	5	0
Washington, Johnny, Rangers	.933	18	34	36	5	75	11
Welsch, Travis, Cubs	1.000	3	2	9	0	11	2
Winslow, Benjamin, Athletics	1.000	4	3	3	0	6	1

THIRD BASEMEN

Player, Team	Pct.	G	PO	A	E	TC	DP
Abreu, Johany, Giants	1.000	4	3	8	0	11	1
Acosta, Jesse, Athletics	.947	9	7	29	2	38	2
Alexander, Kevin, Giants	1.000	1	1	1	0	2	0
Almonte, Aneury, Angels	.667	2	0	2	1	3	0
Batista, Alexander, Royals-1	.881	25	9	50	8	67	2
Cirillo, Jeff, Mariners	1.000	2	0	4	0	4	0
Connors, Greg, Mariners	.750	1	1	2	1	4	0
DePaula, Bartolo, Brewers	.000	2	0	0	1	1	0
Del Orbe, Samuel, Angels	.892	31	22	61	10	93	8
DISLA, LISANDRO, Giants	.929	37	16	62	6	84	4
Ferrara, Matt, Royals-2	.915	39	33	64	9	106	4
Figuereo, Anibal, Royals-2	.500	1	0	2	2	4	0
Francisco, Alfredo, Cubs	.877	40	27	66	13	106	5
Furtado, Micah, Rangers	.828	9	4	20	5	29	1
Gaffney, Michael, Royals-2	.911	16	9	32	4	45	4
Garcia, Alberto, Cubs	.786	6	3	8	3	14	1
Guerra, Alex, Rangers	.894	20	9	50	7	66	1
Heether, Adam, Brewers	.875	2	1	6	1	8	1
Hern, Craig, Mariners	1.000	2	1	2	0	3	0
Hymon, James, Mariners	.867	9	3	10	2	15	3
Johnston, Trey, Cubs	.727	9	3	5	3	11	0
Jones, Nick, Cubs	.500	1	1	0	1	2	0
Liniak, Cole, Rangers	.800	2	1	3	1	5	0
Lopez, Mendy, Royals-1	1.000	2	1	2	0	3	0
Lozada, Charlie, Brewers	.722	6	6	7	5	18	0
Macha, Eric, Athletics	.800	23	15	29	11	55	2
Martinez, Brett, Angels	.882	10	10	20	4	34	1
Martinez, Eduardo, Rangers	.855	23	16	43	10	69	5
McCormack, Taylor, Brewers	.927	40	32	82	9	123	7
Metheny, Brenton, Mariners	.935	7	7	22	2	31	3
Morillo, Roberto, Giants	.941	7	3	13	1	17	1
Nunez, Felix, Angels	1.000	1	1	1	0	2	0
Ozoria, Pedro, Mariners	.958	36	35	101	6	142	10
Petit, Gregorio, Athletics	.846	5	3	8	2	13	1
Phillips, Jonathan, Brewers	.826	8	8	11	4	23	3
Rodriguez, Sean, Angels	.875	12	5	30	5	40	4
Rosario, Samuel, Cubs	.857	6	5	7	2	14	0
Saenz, Olmedo, Athletics	.900	4	2	7	1	10	0
Schierholtz, Nathan, Giants	.950	10	8	11	1	20	2
Solis, Eddie, Royals-1	.949	18	9	28	2	39	8
Spanos, Vasili, Athletics	.875	4	1	6	1	8	0
Swope, Tobin, Rangers	1.000	6	5	13	0	18	2
Vega, Miguel, Royals-1	.881	25	10	42	7	59	3
Welsch, Travis, Cubs	.500	1	0	1	1	2	0
Winslow, Benjamin, Athletics	.841	19	11	26	7	44	3
Wood, Brandon, Angels	.889	4	3	5	1	9	1

SHORTSTOPS

Player, Team	Pct.	G	PO	A	E	TC	DP
Abreu, Johany, Giants	.953	28	37	85	6	128	12
Acosta, Gilberto, Brewers	.960	48	61	130	8	199	26
Acosta, Jesse, Athletics	.949	35	55	95	8	158	10
Almonte, Aneury, Angels	1.000	1	1	0	0	1	0
Aviles, Mike, Royals-1	.953	52	82	141	11	234	26
DePaula, Bartolo, Brewers	.960	11	6	18	1	25	1
Del Orbe, Samuel, Angels	.950	6	6	13	1	20	1
Disla, Lisandro, Giants	.958	6	7	16	1	24	0
Dorsey, Ryan, Royals-2	1.000	1	2	0	0	2	0
Falu, Irving, Royals-2	.957	16	20	46	3	69	9
Gaffney, Michael, Royals-2	.925	22	26	60	7	93	6
Harrison, Adonis, Angels	1.000	1	1	4	0	5	1
Heether, Adam, Brewers	1.000	1	1	0	0	1	0
Hern, Craig, Mariners	.778	1	3	4	2	9	0
Hymon, James, Mariners	.932	12	13	28	3	44	9
Jones, Adamq, Mariners	.921	27	36	80	10	126	6
Lopez, Mendy, Royals-1	1.000	2	5	3	0	8	0
Martinez, Eduardo, Rangers	.982	10	23	32	1	56	6
McCormack, Taylor, Brewers	.800	2	1	3	1	5	0
Morillo, Roberto, Giants	.872	7	18	16	5	39	5
O'Sullivan, Steve, Rangers	1.000	2	4	7	0	11	0
Pena, Antonio, Rangers	.925	43	71	139	17	227	26
Petit, Gregorio, Athletics	.955	22	37	68	5	110	15
Phillips, Jonathan, Brewers	.600	2	3	0	2	5	0
Rios, Jose, Cubs	.948	15	21	34	3	58	7
Rodriguez, Sean, Angels	.909	37	62	98	16	176	18
Rogelstad, Matt, Mariners	.903	12	16	40	6	62	2
ROJAS, CARLOS, Cubs	.979	41	64	122	4	190	20
Rosario, Samuel, Cubs	.833	1	4	1	1	6	0
Sandel, George, Mariners	.970	5	13	19	1	33	4
Sevilla, Walter, Royals-2	1.000	3	1	4	0	5	3
Solis, Eddie, Royals-1	1.000	4	5	11	0	16	3
Swope, Tobin, Rangers	1.000	2	7	5	0	12	3
Valentin, Geraldo, Royals-2	.952	15	21	38	3	62	9
Ventura, Robert, Giants	.954	17	30	53	4	87	18
Winslow, Benjamin, Athletics	.500	2	0	2	2	4	0
Wood, Brandon, Angels	.919	14	19	38	5	62	11

OUTFIELDERS

Player, Team	Pct.	G	PO	A	E	TC	DP
Abreu, Johany, Giants	.964	15	25	2	1	28	1
Alexander, Alexis, Royals-2	.891	24	41	0	5	46	0
Alexander, Kevin, Giants	1.000	1	1	1	0	2	0
Baez, Lizahio, Rangers	.990	45	89	8	1	98	2
Balcom, Jasha, Cubs	.966	16	27	1	1	29	0
Balentien, Wladimir, Mariners	.940	44	59	4	4	67	0
Barry, Jeff, Royals-2	.989	46	91	0	1	92	0
Bates, Dallas, Brewers *	1.000	36	55	2	0	57	0
Bates, Nicholas, Brewers	1.000	1	2	0	0	2	0
Batista, Alexander, Royals-1	.867	13	12	1	2	15	0
Beauregard, Joshua, Athletics *	.959	47	88	6	4	98	1
Bilezikjian, Charlie, Rangers	1.000	3	9	1	0	10	1
Boruff, Gabriel, Royals-2	1.000	9	7	0	0	7	0
Bradford, Samuel, Mariners	1.000	4	12	0	0	12	0
Brown, Dee, Royals-1	1.000	2	1	0	0	1	0
Bubalo, Ty, Athletics	1.000	5	10	1	0	11	0
Caballero, Carlos, Royals-1	.875	26	28	0	4	32	0
Cashman, Brandon, Rangers	.976	50	120	2	3	125	2
Charles, Larry, Rangers	.946	29	35	0	2	37	0
Connors, Greg, Mariners	1.000	1	1	0	0	1	0
Costa, Shane, Royals-2	.889	19	32	0	4	36	0
Cowles, Joshua, Angels	.919	43	89	2	8	99	0
Craig, Casey, Mariners	.912	24	30	1	3	34	0
Cruz, Elvis, Mariners	.930	31	51	2	4	57	0
Eusebio, Juan, Royals-2	.957	10	22	0	1	23	0
Fermaint, Charlie, Brewers	.889	22	48	0	6	54	0
FITZGERALD, RYAN, Cubs	.992	50	115	4	1	120	0
Garcia, Alberto, Cubs	1.000	3	2	1	0	3	0
Garcia, Jose, Athletics	.949	41	86	7	5	98	2
German, Carlos, Giants	.953	38	59	2	3	64	0
Graham, Bryan, Royals-2 *	.935	25	42	1	3	46	0
Grayson, Larry, Rangers	1.000	7	13	1	0	14	0
Guzman, Juan, Rangers	.865	21	29	3	5	37	1
Hammonds, Jeffrey, Giants	1.000	4	5	0	0	5	0
Harvey, Ryan, Cubs	1.000	8	23	0	0	23	0
Herrera, Javier, Athletics	1.000	16	33	4	0	37	1
Hymon, James, Mariners	.935	18	27	2	2	31	0
Jackson, Noah, Cubs	1.000	7	7	1	0	8	0
Jacobsen, Brock, Rangers	1.000	17	23	0	0	23	0
Jones, J.J., Angels	.955	29	38	4	2	44	0
Klippenstein, Tyler, Athletics	.950	16	19	0	1	20	0
LePage, Patrice, Angels	.889	6	16	0	2	18	0
Lubanski, Christopher, R.-1 *	.967	53	83	4	3	90	1
Mannon, Adam, Brewers	.921	45	75	7	7	89	3
Martinez, Brett, Angels	.000	1	0	0	1	1	0
Mejia, Carlos, Cubs	.906	43	71	6	8	85	1
Mejia, Fausto, Brewers	.900	25	34	2	4	40	0
Mooney, Michael, Giants	.967	54	82	5	3	90	1
Nunez, Felix, Angels	1.000	25	42	3	0	45	0
Ogando, Alexi, Athletics	.980	47	96	3	2	101	1

Player, Team	Pct.	G	PO	A	E	TC	DP
Oriental, Rene, Royals-1	.959	46	89	5	4	98	1
Ozoria, Pedro, Mariners	1.000	1	6	0	0	6	0
Paulino, Adalberto, Giants	.958	12	20	3	1	24	0
Plasencia, Francisco, Brewers *	.953	44	95	6	5	106	0
Renz, Jordan, Angels	.964	45	50	3	2	55	1
Rodriguez, Sean, Angels	1.000	4	13	0	0	13	0
Rosario, Samuel, Cubs	1.000	6	14	1	0	15	0
Salazar, Darwinson, Royals-2	.936	44	68	5	5	78	1
Springer, Kenard, Royals-1	.917	42	56	10	6	72	0
Strong, Jamal, Mariners	.889	2	8	0	1	9	0
Valdez, Jesus, Cubs	.904	44	81	4	9	94	1
Walston, Chris, Angels	.959	22	43	4	2	49	1
Ware, Matthew, Mariners	1.000	5	3	0	0	3	0
Wilson, Michael, Mariners	.939	45	73	4	5	82	0
Yens, Jose, Giants	.890	52	79	2	10	91	1

CATCHERS

Player, Team	Pct.	G	PO	A	E	TC	DP	PB
Arias, Roberto, Athletics	.988	12	70	9	1	80	3	5
Baldwin, Ryan, Rangers	.976	10	77	6	2	85	2	3
Bernard, Oscar, Cubs	.965	22	173	21	7	201	2	14
Blanco, Gregory, Angels	.923	6	22	2	2	26	0	0
Boruff, Gabriel, Royals-2	.941	3	27	5	2	34	0	2
Bubalo, Ty, Athletics	1.000	2	15	0	0	15	0	1
BULLER, DAYTON, Giants	.992	30	222	30	2	254	1	3
Christianson, Ryan, Mariners	.962	4	22	3	1	26	0	1
Collins, Mike, Angels	.958	8	60	8	3	71	1	1
Connors, Greg, Mariners	1.000	1	1	0	0	1	0	0
Conte, Nick, Giants	1.000	11	65	4	0	69	0	2
Corporan, Carlos, Brewers	.959	16	97	21	5	123	1	9
Davidson, Matthew, Cubs	.857	4	6	0	1	7	0	1
Del Rosario, Felipe, Royals-2	.970	34	289	36	10	335	3	5
Donachie, Adam, R.-2-R.-1	.988	20	140	18	2	160	0	3
Felix, Maximo, Giants	.955	24	214	22	11	247	1	4
Fox, Jacob, Cubs	.928	8	55	9	5	69	0	2
Garcia, Alberto, Cubs	.989	10	76	12	1	89	0	6
Grana, Robert, Royals-1	1.000	4	27	4	0	31	1	0
Guhring, Simon, Brewers	.958	15	83	8	4	95	1	4
Guzman, Jacob, Royals-2	.971	17	122	12	4	138	1	3
Hatcher, Justin, Rangers	.974	21	135	14	4	153	1	4
Hess, Samuel, Angels	.976	6	35	6	1	42	0	1
LePage, Patrice, Angels	.921	17	85	8	8	101	0	5
Lozada, Charlie, Brewers	.975	10	33	6	1	40	1	2
Lunsford, Trey, Giants	1.000	2	7	1	0	8	0	1
Maier, Mitch, Royals-1	.980	32	272	25	6	303	1	10
Maldonado, Pedro, Athletics	.961	14	88	11	4	103	1	3
Mann, Jason, Rangers	.982	27	194	19	4	217	0	5
Martinez, Brett, Angels	.974	36	255	41	8	304	4	9
McIntyre, Patrick, Cubs	.980	12	82	15	2	99	0	4
Olayemi, Gbenga, Brewers	.975	16	71	6	2	79	2	4
Opdyke, Bryan, Brewers	.977	21	111	19	3	133	1	9
Phillips, Paul, Royals-1	.967	3	28	1	1	30	0	0
Quintero, Cesar, Mariners	.971	16	84	16	3	103	1	3
Ramirez, Juan, Athletics	.972	27	184	27	6	217	0	3
Schweiger, Brian, Mariners	.981	32	182	21	4	207	0	5
Soto, Luis, Mariners	1.000	6	22	2	0	24	0	3
Sutton, Don, Athletics	.920	8	46	0	4	50	0	6
Tidball, Adam, Cubs	.971	9	58	8	2	68	0	6
Udy, Nicholas, Mariners	.667	1	2	0	1	3	0	0
Weitz, Konrad, Royals-1	1.000	5	9	0	0	9	0	0
Wu, Chao, Mariners	.977	17	72	13	2	87	0	4

CATCHERS WITH TWO OR MORE TEAMS

Player, Team	Pct.	G	PO	A	E	TC	DP	PB
Donachie, Adam, Royals-2	.952	2	18	2	1	21	0	0
Donachie, Adam, Royals-1	.993	18	122	16	1	139	0	3

PITCHERS

Player, Team	Pct.	G	PO	A	E	TC	DP
Acevedo, Danielin, Athletics	.667	10	0	4	2	6	0
Acosta, Kelyn, Giants	1.000	10	2	5	0	7	0
Alleva, Jeff, Royals-1	1.000	11	1	3	0	4	0
Altman, Kevin, Rangers	1.000	11	3	1	0	4	0
Alvarez, Jose, Cubs	.833	14	1	4	1	6	0
Anderson, Luke, Giants	.750	5	0	3	1	4	0
Arnold, Mitchell, Angels	.833	21	1	4	1	6	0
Asencio, Miguel, Royals-1	1.000	3	2	1	0	3	0
Atencio, Greg, Royals-2	.960	12	8	16	1	25	1
Avendano, Elvis, Athletics	.889	7	3	5	1	9	1
Bannister, John, Rangers	1.000	13	3	6	0	9	0
Bay, Ronald, Cubs	.750	10	6	6	4	16	1
Bello, Cibney, Mariners	1.000	11	1	8	0	9	1
Benoit, Hector, Angels	1.000	5	1	0	0	1	0
Bergdall, Kendall, Mariners *	1.000	9	3	8	0	11	0
Bernat, David, Mariners	1.000	14	2	4	0	6	0
Blanco, Carlos, R.-1-R.-2 *	1.000	9	0	2	0	2	1
Blanton, Jason, Cubs	1.000	6	0	1	0	1	0
Bowman, Charles, Rangers	.500	12	1	1	2	4	0
Braun, Ryan, Royals-1	1.000	18	1	2	0	3	0
Bray, Stephen, Royals-2	1.000	14	0	6	0	6	0
Bright, Nathan, Rangers	1.000	3	0	1	0	1	0
Brito, Jose, Angels *	1.000	13	0	1	0	1	0
Brito, Luis, Cubs	.750	5	1	2	1	4	0
Brown, Brent, Angels *	.750	14	1	2	1	4	0
Brown, Ira, Royals-2	.813	15	7	6	3	16	1
Bryan, Bobby, Royals-2	1.000	15	0	3	0	3	0
Buckley, Allen, Angels	1.000	10	1	2	0	3	0
Bukowski, Stan, Angels	1.000	4	1	1	0	2	0
Burgos, Ambiorix, Royals-1	.500	9	1	3	4	8	0
Cabaniel, Tomas, Athletics	.600	11	2	4	4	10	0
Campusano, Emmanuel, Cubs *	1.000	6	1	5	0	6	0
Castillo, Ruben, Brewers	.000	6	0	0	1	1	0
Cedeno , Jonathan, Brewers	1.000	14	2	3	0	5	0
Cedeno, Jovanny, Rangers	1.000	8	1	0	0	1	0
Christensen, Danny, Royals-1 *	1.000	4	0	1	0	1	0
Corbett, Jason, Angels	1.000	20	0	1	0	1	0
Cordeiro, Christopher, Rangers	1.000	12	5	7	0	12	1
Correa, Alexander, Brewers *	.667	9	1	1	1	3	0
Coughlin, Chris, Royals-1	.800	12	0	4	1	5	1
Cox, Jason, Angels	1.000	10	5	10	0	15	0
Cunningham, Tim, Rangers *	1.000	3	0	2	0	2	0
D'Amico, Leonardo, Angels	1.000	1	0	1	0	1	0
Damico, Vovany, Royals-1	.750	11	1	2	1	4	1
Danks, John, Rangers *	.000	5	0	0	1	1	0
Dillard, Timothy, Brewers	.778	11	1	6	2	9	0
Dorn, Timothy, Mariners	1.000	6	0	3	0	3	0
Dossett, Dusty, Royals-2	1.000	21	1	1	0	2	0
Downs, Darin, Cubs *	1.000	13	0	12	0	12	0
Encarnacion, Alexis, Royals-1	1.000	14	2	0	0	2	0
English, Jesse, Giants *	1.000	7	1	1	0	2	0
Espinal, Willy, Rangers	1.000	14	1	5	0	6	0
Fagan, Robert, Mariners *	.769	9	2	8	3	13	0
Falconer, Kenny, Mariners	1.000	7	0	3	0	3	0
Feierabend, Ryan, Mariners *	1.000	6	1	9	0	10	0
Feldman, Scott, Rangers	.667	3	0	2	1	3	0
Ferguson, Ian, Royals-2	1.000	5	1	2	0	3	0
Figuereo, Victor, Rangers	.857	14	2	4	1	7	0
Flandes, Wington, Brewers	.000	11	0	0	2	2	0
Flores, Ruben, Mariners	1.000	9	2	4	0	6	0
Forbes, Terry, Mariners	1.000	11	5	10	0	15	0
France, Ryan, Athletics	1.000	3	0	3	0	3	1
Gamboa, Felix, Angels	1.000	10	2	1	0	3	0
Garcia, Miguel, Brewers	1.000	12	3	3	0	6	0
Gelinas, Karl, Angels	.917	12	2	9	1	12	0
Gittings, Christopher, Brewers	1.000	13	5	4	0	9	0
Goodman, Chris, Royals-1	1.000	11	4	7	0	11	0
Gragg, John, Royals-2 *	.950	13	9	10	1	20	2
Granado, Julian, Athletics *	.500	15	0	1	1	2	0
Green, Craig, Cubs	1.000	4	0	2	0	2	0
Green, Steve, Angels	1.000	2	0	1	0	1	0
Gross, Kris, Cubs	1.000	9	2	3	0	5	0
Gross, Kyle, Giants	1.000	5	0	1	0	1	0
Guzman, Jonathan, Royals-1	.500	10	0	1	1	2	0
Hall, Vance, Mariners *	1.000	9	1	5	0	6	0
Hartnett, Christopher, Angels *	1.000	7	0	1	0	1	1
Hawk, Tommy, Brewers	1.000	12	3	7	0	10	1
Hernandez, Armando, Giants	1.000	17	0	3	0	3	0
Herrera, Marcos, Rangers	1.000	11	0	2	0	2	0
Heuser, James, Athletics *	.778	14	1	6	2	9	0
Hill, Andrew, Angels	1.000	6	1	1	0	2	0
Hill, Seth, Rangers *	1.000	10	1	2	0	3	0
Hindman, Scott, Angels *	.667	6	2	2	2	6	0
Hrynio, Mike, Mariners	.667	14	0	2	1	3	0
HUGHES, DUSTIN, Royals-1 *	1.000	11	2	16	0	18	0
James, Craig, Mariners	.929	14	2	11	1	14	1
Jenks, Bobby, Angels	1.000	1	1	1	0	2	0
Laird, Matthew, Cubs	.833	14	1	4	1	6	0
Leaist, Ryan, Mariners	.333	11	0	1	2	3	0
Lincoln, Matthew, Angels *	1.000	6	0	2	0	2	0
Liriano, Francisco, Giants *	1.000	4	0	1	0	1	0
Lundwall, Todd, Giants	.667	12	0	2	1	3	0
Marion, William, Brewers	.750	9	1	2	1	4	0
Markert, Jackson, Giants	1.000	4	0	1	0	1	0
Marmol, Carlos, Cubs	.875	14	4	10	2	16	0
Martin, Forrest, Brewers	1.000	11	3	1	0	4	0

Player, Team	Pct.	G	PO	A	E	TC	DP
Martinez Sosa, Alvaro, Brewers	.625	12	1	4	3	8	0
Martinez, Roman, Mariners	.833	12	0	5	1	6	0
Mateo, Juan, Cubs	.800	18	0	4	1	5	0
Matos, Osiris, Giants	1.000	9	4	0	0	4	0
McCleland, Bruce, Royals-1	1.000	10	1	2	0	3	0
McClellan, Robbie, Royals-2	.750	18	0	3	1	4	0
McConiga, Jacob, Royals-2 *	1.000	9	0	2	0	2	0
McGovern, Ryan, Giants *	1.000	14	1	3	0	4	0
Mendoza, Jorge, Rangers	1.000	5	0	1	0	1	0
Millikan, Bryan, Giants	1.000	11	1	7	0	8	0
Mola, Heydin, Athletics	.600	14	1	2	2	5	0
Montas, Ipolito, Athletics	.833	16	0	5	1	6	0
Moreno, Anthony, Giants	.900	10	2	7	1	10	0
Morrison, Tyler, Brewers	.833	10	7	8	3	18	1
Morrow, David, Mariners	.909	8	6	4	1	11	0
Moye, Jeffrey, Rangers	1.000	1	0	1	0	1	0
Mullis, Jacob, Royals-2	1.000	13	2	7	0	9	1
Nacar, Leslie, Giants	1.000	20	1	3	0	4	0
Nendza, Brian, Royals-2 *	.667	16	1	1	1	3	0
Nottingham, Shawn, Mariners *	1.000	12	2	2	0	4	0
O'Flaherty, Eric, Mariners *	1.000	13	0	3	0	3	0
Ortiz, Jose, Cubs	.833	7	2	3	1	6	0
Overholt, Sean, Cubs	.000	9	0	0	2	2	0
Palmer, Lucas, Royals-1	.786	14	3	8	3	14	0
Pawelczyk, Kyle, Angels *	.800	7	3	1	1	5	1
Perez, Keith, Athletics	.727	17	2	6	3	11	0
Perry, Brandon, Mariners *	1.000	17	1	2	0	3	0
Petke, Tim, Angels	1.000	4	1	3	0	4	0
Polanco, Alfredo, Cubs	1.000	6	1	2	0	3	0
Pruett, Hubert, Brewers	1.000	10	2	2	0	4	0
Ramirez, Victor, Rangers	1.000	10	3	1	0	4	0
Ramos, Jonathan, Rangers	1.000	11	2	1	0	3	0
Rauch, Brian, Brewers	.900	11	4	5	1	10	1
Regilio, Nick, Rangers	1.000	2	0	1	0	1	0
Reina, Jesus, Giants *	1.000	11	1	1	0	2	0
Requena, Ricardo, Angels	1.000	4	0	2	0	2	0
Reyes, Ramon, Angels	1.000	9	0	2	0	2	0
Rodriguez, Fernando, Angels	1.000	15	0	4	0	4	0
Rodriguez, Pedro, Cubs	.818	14	3	6	2	11	0
Rondon, Yosy, Giants *	.667	16	0	2	1	3	0
Roque, Christopher, Angels	1.000	17	0	5	0	5	1
Rosa, Carlos, Royals-1	1.000	15	3	8	0	11	0
Rosario, Julio, Royals-1	1.000	13	1	3	0	4	0
Rosario, Samuel, Cubs	1.000	1	1	0	0	1	0
Russ, Christopher, Rangers *	1.000	5	1	2	0	3	0
Saladin, John, Angels	1.000	13	2	2	0	4	0
Sanchez, Adiel, Athletics *	1.000	11	2	7	0	9	1
Sanchez, Felix, Cubs *	1.000	1	0	1	0	1	0
Sanchez, Jose, Giants	.800	12	6	2	2	10	0
Santana, Andy, Cubs *	.800	13	0	4	1	5	0
Santana, Braulio, Athletics	1.000	15	2	7	0	9	0
Santana, Roberto, Athletics *	1.000	16	1	4	0	5	1
Sarmiento, Williams, Rangers	.600	14	0	3	2	5	0
Sherman, Justin, Royals-1	1.000	12	0	4	0	4	0
Smiley, Jermaine, Giants *	1.000	10	0	2	0	2	0
Smith, Cody, Rangers	1.000	12	4	4	0	8	1
Smith, Michael, Royals-2 *	1.000	5	1	1	0	2	0
Solis, Hairo, Giants	1.000	15	3	4	0	7	0
Taveras, Nelson, Royals-1	1.000	1	0	1	0	1	0
Torres, Joe, Angels *	1.000	3	0	3	0	3	1
Tovar, Miguel, Athletics	1.000	14	1	5	0	6	0
Tucker, Cordoza, Mariners	.714	12	0	5	2	7	0
Urena, Jose, Cubs	.833	16	1	4	1	6	1
Villanueva, Carlos, Giants	.846	12	4	7	2	13	3
Volquez, Edison, Rangers	1.000	10	0	2	0	2	0
Walker, Edwin, Brewers *	1.000	9	2	8	0	10	0
Weber, Matthew, Cubs	1.000	7	0	4	0	4	0
Wells, Randy, Cubs	1.000	3	1	0	0	1	0
Whitaker, Roger, Giants	.333	3	0	1	2	3	0
Whittington, Anthony, Angels *	1.000	9	0	4	0	4	0
Woerman, Joseph, Mariners	1.000	7	1	2	0	3	0
Wooley, Robert, Brewers	1.000	7	1	5	0	6	0
Zorrilla, Junior, Athletics	1.000	17	2	7	0	9	0

PITCHERS WITH TWO OR MORE TEAMS

Player, Team	Pct.	G	PO	A	E	TC	DP
Blanco, Carlos, Royals-2 *	1.000	8	0	1	0	1	0
Blanco, Carlos, Royals-1 *	1.000	1	0	1	0	1	1

The following players appeared only as a designated hitter, pinch-hitter or pinch-runner: Bozarth, dh, ph; Grabowski, dh; Weeks, dh; Willis, dh.

LEAGUE CHAMPIONS

Year	Team	Pct.
1988—	Peoria Brewers	.690
1989—	Peoria Brewers	.732
1990—	Peoria Brewers	.679
1991—	Scottsdale A's	.650
1992—	Scottsdale A's	.607
1993—	Scottsdale A's	.636
1994—	Chandler Cardinals	.607
1995—	Scottsdale A's	.661
1996—	Padres	.643
1997—	Cubs	.618
1998—	Rockies	.750
1999—	Athletics	.696
2000—	Mariners	.709
2001—	Athletics	.625
2002—	Cubs	.625
2003—	Royals-1	.633

GULF COAST LEAGUE

LEAGUE OFFICE

President
Tom Saffell

Address
1503 Clower Creek Dr., H-262
Sarasota, FL 34231

Phone
941-966-6407

Teams*
Braves
Dodgers
Expos
Marlins
Mets
Phillies
Pirates
Reds
Red Sox
Tigers
Twins
Yankees

*Teams play their games in Bradenton, Clearwater, Fort Myers, Jupiter, Kissimmee, Lakeland, Melbourne, Orlando, St. Lucie, Sarasota, Tampa and Vero Beach.

2003 FINAL STANDINGS

EASTERN DIVISION

Team	W	L	T	Pct.	GB
Braves	38	22	-	.633	...
Dodgers	29	31	-	.483	9.0
Marlins	26	32	-	.448	11.0
Expos	25	33	-	.431	12.0

NORTHERN DIVISION

Team	W	L	T	Pct.	GB
Pirates	36	20	-	.643	...
Tigers	28	29	-	.491	8.5
Yankees	26	31	-	.456	10.5
Phillies	23	33	-	.411	13.0

SOUTHERN DIVISION

Team	W	L	T	Pct.	GB
Red Sox	33	26	-	.559	...
Orioles	32	28	-	.533	1.5
Twins	28	31	-	.475	5.0
Reds	26	34	-	.433	7.5

COMPOSITE

Team	PIR	BRV	RSX	ORI	TGR	DGR	TWI	YAN	MRL	RDS	EXP	PHI	W	L	T	Pct.	GB
Pirates	...	0	0	0	11	0	0	11	0	0	0	14	36	20	0	.643	...
Braves	0	...	0	0	0	13	0	0	13	0	12	0	38	22	0	.633	...
Red Sox	0	0	...	12	0	0	12	0	0	9	0	0	33	26	0	.559	4.5
Orioles	0	0	8	...	0	0	12	0	0	12	0	0	32	28	0	.533	6.0
Tigers	7	0	0	0	...	0	0	12	0	0	0	9	28	29	0	.491	8.5
Dodgers	0	7	0	0	0	...	0	0	8	0	14	0	29	31	0	.483	9.0
Twins	0	0	7	8	0	0	...	0	0	13	0	0	28	31	0	.475	9.5
Yankees	9	0	0	0	7	0	0	...	0	0	0	10	26	31	0	.456	10.5
Marlins (Marlins)	0	7	0	0	0	12	0	0	...	0	7	0	26	32	0	.448	11.0
Reds (Reds)	0	0	11	8	0	0	7	0	0	...	0	0	26	34	0	.433	12.0
Expos (Expos)	0	8	0	0	0	6	0	0	11	0	...	0	25	33	0	.431	12.0
Phillies (Phillies)	4	0	0	0	11	0	0	8	0	0	0	...	23	33	0	.411	13.0

Club names are major league affiliations.

PLAYOFFS: Braves defeated Red Sox, one game to none; Braves defeated Pirates, two games to none, to win league championship.

REGULAR-SEASON ATTENDANCE: No total attendance figures reported.

MANAGERS: Braves, Ralph Henriquez; Dodgers, Luis Salazar; Expos, Bobby Henley; Marlins, Tim Cossins; Orioles, Jesus Alfaro; Phillies, Ruben Amaro, Sr.; Pirates, Woody Huyke; Reds, Edgar Caceres; Red Sox, Ralph Treuel; Tigers, Howard Bushong; Twins, Rudy Hernandez; Yankees, Dan Radison.

ALL-STAR TEAM: 1B—Brad Rea, Pirates; 2B—Paul Rutgers, Twins; 3B—Luke Hughes, Twins; SS—Gilberto Mejia, Tigers; OF—Steve Doetsch, Braves; OF—Carl Loadenthal, Braves; OF—Chris Klemm, Phillies; C—Juan Gutierrez, Orioles; Starting pitcher—Matt Capps, Pirates; Relief pitcher—Argimiro Guanchez, Red Sox; Manager of the Year—Woody Huyke, Pirates.

2003 BATTING

TEAM

Team	G	TPA	AB	R	H	TB	2B	3B	HR	RBI	SH	SF	HP	BB	IBB	SO	SB	CS	GDP	LOB	ShO	Avg.	OBP	Slg.
Braves	60	2270	2011	291	538	767	93	20	32	248	14	12	39	194	5	398	54	38	43	416	4	.268	.342	.381
Twins	59	2151	1941	244	516	681	84	27	9	214	18	14	29	149	8	318	68	32	34	401	8	.266	.325	.351
Pirates	56	2110	1896	286	498	689	84	19	23	251	15	23	29	147	6	354	56	23	41	384	5	.263	.322	.363
Red Sox	59	2147	1886	251	478	674	92	25	18	224	19	14	28	199	6	403	47	29	34	407	3	.253	.331	.357
Reds	60	2191	1929	257	485	688	118	17	17	205	15	21	46	180	6	432	77	34	28	419	8	.251	.327	.357
Dodgers	60	2202	1956	223	488	641	81	18	12	187	12	12	45	176	3	402	79	32	40	431	7	.249	.324	.328
Phillies	56	2069	1799	241	447	650	86	24	23	206	17	16	48	189	6	496	55	25	23	423	5	.248	.333	.361
Tigers	57	2062	1833	296	447	677	78	31	30	244	11	13	23	181	3	443	103	26	23	353	2	.244	.318	.369
Orioles	60	2213	1840	282	448	613	81	18	16	234	27	28	33	284	8	434	79	21	49	441	6	.243	.350	.333
Yankees	57	2131	1845	241	434	616	85	11	25	210	6	19	33	222	3	428	39	17	50	428	5	.235	.325	.334
Marlins	58	2052	1825	193	419	560	71	11	16	154	8	18	26	174	2	443	57	30	48	361	5	.230	.303	.307
Expos	58	2041	1787	205	409	541	69	9	15	165	19	18	35	182	1	399	26	26	38	380	6	.229	.310	.303

INDIVIDUAL

TOP QUALIFIERS FOR BATTING CHAMPIONSHIP

Minimum 162 plate appearances. *Lefthanded batter. †Switch-hitter.

Player, Team	G	TPA	AB	R	H	TB	2B	3B	HR	RBI	SH	SF	HP	BB	IBB	SO	SB	CS	GDP	Avg.	OBP	Slg.
Mejia, Gilberto, Tigers †	44	191	175	36	63	107	11	9	5	29	1	2	0	13	0	29	23	5	1	.360	.400	.611
Rutgers, Paul, Twins	56	214	201	35	71	89	12	3	0	21	0	1	3	9	0	15	16	7	3	.353	.388	.443
Apodaca, Luis, Expos	43	180	156	20	53	64	7	2	0	19	1	3	5	15	0	18	1	2	5	.340	.408	.410
Klemm, Christopher, Phillies*	42	165	143	20	48	66	8	2	2	23	1	1	2	18	1	43	3	3	1	.336	.415	.462
Gutierrez, Juan, Orioles †	55	233	194	29	65	96	11	4	4	40	3	4	5	27	5	27	5	2	4	.335	.422	.495
Doetsch, Steve, Braves	60	260	228	39	73	114	11	3	8	37	0	0	7	25	4	49	8	9	5	.320	.404	.500
Solano, Solamdi, Pirates	44	192	166	38	53	68	4	1	3	20	3	3	2	18	0	27	12	4	3	.319	.386	.410
Loadenthal, Carl, Braves	58	253	216	41	67	81	9	1	1	24	2	1	3	31	0	38	21	9	3	.310	.402	.375
Patterson, Tarrence, Twins	49	183	169	32	52	77	9	5	2	23	2	2	1	9	2	19	15	7	1	.308	.343	.456
Hughes, Luke, Twins	54	212	190	22	58	81	9	4	2	25	4	1	2	15	1	22	5	5	5	.305	.361	.426
Gutierrez, Tonys, Reds *	46	183	155	21	47	76	12	4	3	18	0	2	6	20	1	22	1	4	0	.303	.399	.490
Ronda, Jose, Reds †	47	190	173	25	52	78	16	2	2	26	0	2	2	13	0	40	5	2	2	.301	.353	.451
Abreu, Etanislao, Dodgers	44	179	163	30	48	65	7	5	0	20	0	0	5	11	1	24	9	3	3	.294	.358	.399
Macia, Wanell, Pirates	52	199	191	25	56	75	8	4	1	28	0	3	0	5	0	40	6	2	0	.293	.307	.393
Moreta, Carlos, Braves	60	249	225	35	65	105	14	1	8	39	1	1	7	15	0	56	1	1	3	.289	.351	.467

DEPARTMENTAL LEADERS: G—Doetsch, Moreta, 60; AB—Doetsch, 228; R—Loadenthal, 41; H—Doetsch, 73; TB—Doetsch, 114; 2B—Urgelles, 20; 3B—Mejia, 9; HR—Doetsch, Moreta, 8; RBI—J. Gutierrez, 40; SH—Jos. Fulton, Prado, 5; SF—Costello, 5; HP—Gray, Sapp, Sucre, 8; BB—Spears, 40; IBB—J. Gutierrez, 5; SO—Lewis, 66; SB—Lewis, 37; CS—Doetsch, Loadenthal, Prado, 9; GIDP—O. Castro, Ovalles, 7; Slg.—Mejia, .611; OBP—Costello, .436.

ALL PLAYERS

*Lefthanded batter. †Switch-hitter.

Player, Team	G	TPA	AB	R	H	TB	2B	3B	HR	RBI	SH	SF	HP	BB	IBB	SO	SB	CS	GDP	Avg.	OBP	Slg.
Abreu, Etanislao, Dodgers	44	179	163	30	48	65	7	5	0	20	0	0	5	11	1	24	9	3	3	.294	.358	.399
Aguila, Chris, Marlins	1	4	4	1	3	6	0	0	1	2	0	0	0	0	0	1	0	0	0	.750	.750	1.500
Aguilar, Trino, Phillies	24	87	79	14	19	30	7	2	0	8	1	2	2	3	0	20	2	1	2	.241	.279	.380
Alcala, Arian, Red Sox	6	20	19	3	6	8	2	0	0	4	0	0	0	1	0	3	0	0	1	.316	.350	.421
Alen, Luis, Marlins	6	19	18	1	2	3	1	0	0	2	0	0	1	0	0	3	0	0	0	.111	.158	.167
Almonte, Erick, Yankees	6	26	21	4	6	6	0	0	0	0	0	0	0	5	1	9	0	0	0	.286	.423	.286
Alvarado, Wellington, Phillies.	43	152	129	13	24	35	6	1	1	8	1	0	6	16	0	49	1	0	5	.186	.305	.271
Amador, Anderson, Yankees	19	73	66	7	4	6	2	0	0	4	1	1	2	3	0	34	1	0	2	.061	.125	.091
Anderson, Heath, Twins	30	100	82	6	20	26	3	0	1	5	2	1	3	12	0	11	1	0	2	.244	.357	.317
Andrus, Erold, Yankees †	5	25	21	3	7	11	2	1	0	6	0	1	1	2	0	4	0	0	1	.333	.400	.524
Apodaca, Luis, Expos	43	180	156	20	53	64	7	2	0	19	1	3	5	15	0	18	1	2	5	.340	.408	.410
Araque, Tulio, Reds	6	20	18	1	3	3	0	0	0	0	0	0	2	0	0	4	0	2	0	.167	.250	.167
Arias, Garvi, Pirates	23	69	61	9	9	13	1	0	1	7	0	0	2	6	0	12	5	2	0	.148	.246	.213
Arias, Hector, Dodgers	38	138	126	10	28	34	4	1	0	15	1	1	1	9	0	33	11	0	1	.222	.277	.270
Armstrong, Cole, Braves *	9	19	17	0	2	2	0	0	0	0	1	0	0	1	0	2	0	0	2	.118	.167	.118
Arroyo, Xavier, Marlins †	20	79	71	12	20	30	4	3	0	6	0	0	0	8	0	15	5	0	2	.282	.354	.423
Asprilla, Avelino, Pirates	9	39	35	11	15	25	2	1	2	11	0	1	1	2	0	5	3	1	0	.429	.462	.714
Avila, Denny, Reds	27	59	52	5	10	10	0	0	0	1	2	0	1	4	0	13	1	1	0	.192	.263	.192
Aybar, Francisco, Phillies	41	138	122	15	26	36	5	1	1	12	3	1	7	5	0	37	7	2	2	.213	.281	.295
Baez, Edgardo, Expos	34	127	117	12	32	50	7	1	3	15	0	1	0	9	0	31	1	1	2	.274	.323	.427
Baez, Welinson, Phillies	41	161	142	20	35	52	6	1	3	17	1	2	4	12	0	37	3	1	1	.246	.319	.366
Bailie, Stefan, Red Sox	5	23	22	4	9	14	0	1	1	7	0	0	0	1	0	4	0	0	1	.409	.435	.636
Baker, Jordan, Marlins *	46	176	141	12	29	37	6	1	0	11	0	0	3	32	0	42	8	3	2	.206	.364	.262
Barnes, Justin, Tigers	31	80	71	6	17	19	2	0	0	9	0	0	2	7	0	17	0	0	0	.239	.325	.268
Barnett, Toby, Phillies	18	58	52	2	9	11	2	0	0	4	1	0	3	2	0	19	1	1	0	.173	.246	.212
Barthel, Cole, Braves	13	40	35	2	8	8	0	0	0	0	0	0	1	4	0	7	0	0	1	.229	.325	.229
Bastardo, Frederick, Marlins	31	110	95	14	19	29	4	0	2	10	0	1	1	12	0	18	10	1	3	.200	.294	.305
Batista, Rafael, Expos †	30	82	74	10	14	15	1	0	0	9	3	0	0	5	0	20	1	3	0	.189	.241	.203
Battle, Timothy, Yankees	27	116	106	14	22	27	5	0	0	5	1	0	2	7	0	33	5	1	1	.208	.270	.255
Bautista, Jose, Pirates	7	28	23	5	8	12	1	0	1	3	0	1	0	4	1	7	0	0	0	.348	.429	.522
Bawden, Thomas, Red Sox	16	48	42	6	9	11	2	0	0	3	1	0	0	5	0	11	0	1	3	.214	.298	.262
Belcher, Jordan, Reds	53	213	190	23	52	65	11	1	0	17	3	3	0	17	0	27	6	1	1	.274	.329	.342
Berger, Garrett, Marlins	15	1	1	0	0	0	0	0	0	0	0	0	0	0	0	1	0	0	0	.000	.000	.000
Berkenbosch, Kenny, Marlins.	43	144	127	12	31	37	6	0	0	13	0	1	0	16	0	22	3	4	2	.244	.326	.291
Bianucci, Anthony, Red Sox †	22	76	73	10	19	25	2	2	0	6	0	0	0	3	0	31	1	0	1	.260	.289	.342
Bigbie, Larry, Orioles *	2	6	6	1	2	3	1	0	0	0	0	0	0	0	0	1	0	0	0	.333	.333	.500
Billmaier, Kris, Tigers	32	96	78	13	16	22	3	0	1	11	1	0	4	13	0	14	2	2	3	.205	.347	.282
Blanton, Stephen, Orioles *	4	14	13	1	1	1	0	0	0	0	0	0	0	1	0	5	0	0	0	.077	.143	.077
Boitel, Edwin, Red Sox	29	96	87	10	27	34	5	1	0	9	0	1	2	6	0	13	4	2	1	.310	.365	.391
Boone, Doug, Yankees	20	68	57	7	16	25	6	0	1	12	0	1	1	9	0	21	0	0	0	.281	.382	.439
Boone, Matt, Reds	5	22	21	2	6	8	2	0	0	2	0	1	0	0	0	6	0	0	0	.286	.273	.381
Boran, Patrick, Red Sox	2	5	4	0	0	0	0	0	0	0	0	0	0	1	0	1	0	0	0	.000	.200	.000
Brown, Gregory, Marlins	12	43	36	0	7	7	0	0	0	1	1	1	0	5	0	6	1	0	2	.194	.286	.194
Cabrera, Edwin, Yankees †	50	199	175	31	43	67	9	0	5	26	0	2	4	18	1	39	3	2	6	.246	.327	.383
Cabrera, Ruben, Dodgers	28	90	77	2	12	12	0	0	0	3	4	1	2	6	0	17	0	2	5	.156	.233	.156
Campusano, Luis, Twins	16	41	38	6	9	11	0	1	0	2	1	0	0	2	0	8	1	1	0	.237	.275	.289
Cardy, Edwal, Orioles	22	76	65	7	14	20	4	1	0	6	4	0	1	6	0	16	4	0	1	.215	.292	.308
Carlin, Michael, Pirates	34	131	113	14	21	34	2	4	1	15	1	1	1	15	1	14	2	1	6	.186	.285	.301
Castillo, Osmar, Red Sox †	5	16	13	0	6	6	0	0	0	2	1	1	0	1	0	1	0	0	1	.462	.467	.462
Castro, Francisco, Tigers †	47	202	173	33	45	60	6	3	1	21	1	2	1	25	0	34	15	1	1	.260	.353	.347
Castro, Nelson, Red Sox †	4	16	15	4	2	5	0	0	1	3	0	0	0	1	0	3	0	0	0	.133	.188	.333
Castro, Ofilio, Expos	39	139	125	8	19	22	3	0	0	6	2	0	1	11	0	29	0	1	7	.152	.226	.176

Player, Team	G	TPA	AB	R	H	TB	2B	3B	HR	RBI	SH	SF	HP	BB	IBB	SO	SB	CS	GDP	Avg.	OBP	Slg.
Cespedes, Osvaldo, Phillies †	45	140	118	18	21	34	3	2	2	11	2	0	3	17	0	39	7	3	0	.178	.297	.288
Chavez, Dirimo, Red Sox	36	129	111	17	38	42	4	0	0	7	3	1	3	11	1	8	4	3	1	.342	.413	.378
Ciofrone, Peter, Red Sox *	38	147	123	14	34	45	7	2	0	17	0	2	0	22	0	13	0	6	3	.276	.381	.366
Cobb, Maurice, Expos	41	135	128	17	27	37	10	0	0	6	0	0	3	4	1	42	3	2	3	.211	.252	.289
Coffey, Josh, Reds	7	19	15	1	2	3	1	0	0	6	0	3	0	1	0	5	0	0	0	.133	.158	.200
Concepcion, Alberto, R. Sox	5	19	15	0	3	3	0	0	0	3	0	0	1	3	0	3	0	0	0	.200	.368	.200
Conley, Evan, Reds	57	222	194	25	55	79	14	2	2	21	0	1	4	23	1	45	1	2	6	.284	.369	.407
Contreras, Jose, Expos †	47	162	137	19	27	32	3	1	0	7	4	0	3	18	0	42	6	5	1	.197	.304	.234
Corro, Abdiel, Expos	29	91	81	4	13	17	4	0	0	4	1	0	4	5	0	26	0	0	1	.160	.244	.210
Coste, Chris, Red Sox	11	37	30	3	7	14	2	1	1	6	0	0	0	7	1	5	0	0	2	.233	.378	.467
Costello, Michael, Orioles	42	164	120	18	33	48	6	0	3	26	1	5	4	34	1	28	1	0	4	.275	.436	.400
Cronkhite, Ian, Red Sox *	33	129	106	22	26	39	8	1	1	16	0	4	2	17	1	21	9	0	0	.245	.349	.368
Crosland, Jason, Phillies	44	172	152	20	40	68	6	2	6	22	0	2	6	12	1	43	4	3	0	.263	.337	.447
Cruz, Ramon, Braves	18	36	35	0	5	5	0	0	0	2	0	0	1	0	0	9	0	1	3	.143	.167	.143
Cucinotta, Robert, Red Sox	8	29	22	4	3	3	0	0	0	2	0	0	0	7	0	6	0	0	2	.136	.345	.136
Cuddyer, Michael, Twins	2	7	5	1	4	7	0	0	1	3	0	0	1	1	1	0	0	1	0	.800	.857	1.400
Cuevas, Phillip, Phillies	22	83	77	7	16	20	2	1	0	1	0	0	2	4	0	23	0	2	0	.208	.265	.260
Davis, Zach, Orioles *	48	180	153	21	34	41	5	1	0	18	3	3	0	21	1	40	8	4	6	.222	.311	.268
De La Cruz, Carlos, R. Sox †	44	168	148	22	40	53	3	5	0	12	2	1	3	13	0	24	15	4	1	.270	.339	.358
De Los Santos, Edinson, Yan.	28	104	93	14	24	39	7	1	2	11	0	1	1	9	0	25	4	0	3	.258	.327	.419
Deeds, Doug, Twins *	5	16	15	1	5	5	0	0	0	4	0	0	0	1	0	2	1	0	0	.333	.375	.333
Del Carmen, Jose, Orioles	27	77	72	4	16	19	3	0	0	7	2	1	0	2	0	15	0	0	5	.222	.240	.264
Denker, Travis, Dodgers	38	144	122	17	33	52	8	1	3	13	0	0	2	20	0	16	2	0	4	.270	.382	.426
Dennis, Billy, Reds *	3	7	7	0	1	1	0	0	0	0	0	0	0	0	0	1	0	0	0	.143	.143	.143
Desena, Francis, Expos	9	31	25	7	7	10	1	1	0	0	0	0	1	5	0	5	1	1	0	.280	.419	.400
Doetsch, Steve, Braves	60	260	228	39	73	114	11	3	8	37	0	0	7	25	4	49	8	9	5	.320	.404	.500
Duncan, Eric, Yankees *	47	201	180	24	50	72	12	2	2	28	0	1	2	18	0	33	0	2	7	.278	.348	.400
Durand, Alexander, Phillies	32	125	109	13	28	36	4	2	0	9	3	0	2	11	0	33	1	1	2	.257	.336	.330
Eichas, Keith, Braves	40	133	119	18	41	65	9	0	5	22	0	1	4	9	0	28	0	0	6	.345	.406	.546
Ellis, Jason, Reds	21	53	45	7	12	16	4	0	0	5	1	0	5	2	0	6	0	0	1	.267	.365	.356
Encarnacion, Salvador, Mar.	11	31	29	1	3	4	1	0	0	2	0	0	1	1	0	11	0	1	1	.103	.161	.138
Esparragoza, Eyoxy, Reds	44	152	138	21	30	49	10	0	3	14	2	2	6	4	0	44	10	4	3	.217	.267	.355
Ewen, Nicholas, Marlins *	27	113	104	8	23	32	2	2	1	8	0	2	1	6	0	24	2	3	6	.221	.265	.308
Fisher, Kiel, Phillies *	29	119	96	16	31	46	6	3	1	13	0	3	2	18	3	21	4	1	1	.323	.429	.479
Flowers, Bo, Tigers	15	47	44	3	8	13	3	1	0	2	0	0	1	2	0	12	2	1	1	.182	.234	.295
Fox, Chad, Expos	23	85	70	8	13	21	2	0	2	9	0	1	5	9	0	21	0	0	1	.186	.318	.300
Franco, Ambiorix, Reds	19	64	61	1	11	14	3	0	0	6	0	0	0	3	0	21	0	0	1	.180	.219	.230
Franco, Luis, Marlins †	14	38	29	4	7	7	0	0	0	2	2	0	1	6	0	5	1	0	0	.241	.389	.241
Frank, Kyle, Yankees *	16	67	62	7	16	18	2	0	0	4	0	0	1	4	0	8	3	1	4	.258	.313	.290
Fulse, Sheldon, Red Sox †	3	13	9	0	2	3	1	0	0	3	0	0	0	4	0	0	0	0	0	.222	.462	.333
Fulton, Jonathan, Marlins	46	184	168	9	33	45	9	0	1	13	2	2	3	9	1	51	0	3	3	.196	.247	.268
Fulton, Joshua, Pirates †	41	185	161	39	38	47	6	0	1	13	5	0	5	14	0	22	8	2	2	.236	.317	.292
Garbe, B.J., Twins	8	36	34	1	7	9	2	0	0	4	0	0	1	1	0	7	1	1	1	.206	.250	.265
Gil, Luis, Tigers	36	113	105	15	21	31	4	3	0	10	0	0	2	6	0	26	6	1	3	.200	.257	.295
Golindano, Jesus, Dodgers †	28	80	71	11	17	20	3	0	0	8	1	0	1	7	0	12	1	1	3	.239	.316	.282
Gonzalez, Hector, Yankees †	28	99	87	8	28	32	2	1	0	6	0	0	1	10	0	15	1	2	2	.322	.398	.368
Gray, Matthew, Reds *	55	219	186	25	35	52	5	3	2	21	2	2	8	21	2	32	6	6	6	.188	.295	.280
Gredvig, Doug, Orioles	6	26	21	2	5	6	1	0	0	3	0	1	0	4	0	4	1	0	2	.238	.346	.286
Guerra, Junior, Braves	28	60	57	5	11	19	5	0	1	9	0	0	3	0	0	19	0	0	1	.193	.233	.333
Guerrero, Francisco, Orioles	5	17	15	4	6	7	1	0	0	1	0	1	0	1	0	0	0	0	0	.400	.412	.467
Gutierrez, Juan, Orioles †	55	233	194	29	65	96	11	4	4	40	3	4	5	27	5	27	5	2	4	.335	.422	.495
Gutierrez, Tonys, Reds *	46	183	155	21	47	76	12	4	3	18	0	2	6	20	1	22	1	4	0	.303	.399	.490
Guzman, Heriberto, Red Sox	46	172	153	26	38	78	9	5	7	29	1	1	3	14	1	43	3	4	0	.248	.322	.510
Hall, Mickey, Red Sox *	21	85	66	7	15	21	6	0	0	9	0	0	0	19	0	24	1	3	0	.227	.400	.318
Hamisevicz, Victor, Expos *	47	168	146	11	33	48	10	1	1	17	0	3	2	17	0	27	0	0	2	.226	.310	.329
Harris, Estee, Yankees *	27	117	101	18	28	55	7	1	6	18	0	1	1	14	0	28	4	0	1	.277	.368	.545
Hart, Randall, Pirates	7	23	22	2	4	5	1	0	0	3	1	0	0	0	0	6	0	0	1	.182	.182	.227
Hawes, Don, Reds	12	41	39	3	5	9	1	0	1	2	0	0	0	2	0	12	0	0	0	.128	.171	.231
Hernandez, Diory, Braves	54	210	190	26	42	58	9	2	1	12	1	1	4	14	0	24	2	4	3	.221	.287	.305
Hernandez, Habelito, Reds	3	10	10	1	2	2	0	0	0	0	0	0	0	0	0	2	0	0	1	.200	.200	.200
Hicks, Joe, Pirates	44	183	168	19	43	71	6	5	4	25	1	2	3	9	0	48	2	2	4	.256	.302	.423
House, J.R., Pirates	20	82	65	16	26	47	9	0	4	23	0	4	1	12	1	5	0	0	1	.400	.476	.723
Howerton, Matt, Orioles	42	160	139	15	24	33	3	0	2	12	0	3	4	14	0	45	3	3	2	.173	.263	.237
Hughes, Luke, Twins	54	212	190	22	58	81	9	4	2	25	4	1	2	15	1	22	5	5	5	.305	.361	.426
Hummel, Richard, Orioles †	27	71	59	11	8	8	0	0	0	3	0	1	0	11	0	24	4	1	2	.136	.268	.136
Italiano, Nicholas, Phillies *	37	149	129	28	45	60	9	3	0	21	1	3	0	16	1	22	5	3	1	.349	.412	.465
Jarvis, Andrew, Phillies *	35	134	115	13	30	51	4	1	5	20	0	0	0	19	0	18	2	0	2	.261	.366	.443
Johnson, Kelly, Braves *	6	30	26	10	10	16	1	1	1	3	0	0	1	3	1	4	1	1	2	.385	.467	.615
Jones, Larry, Twins	28	81	71	10	17	22	5	0	0	5	0	0	2	8	0	21	1	0	2	.239	.333	.310
Kalin, Travis, Twins	23	51	47	5	11	14	3	0	0	7	0	1	1	2	0	10	1	0	2	.234	.275	.298
Karlsen, Grant, Phillies	23	77	67	5	9	11	2	0	0	10	1	1	1	7	0	23	0	0	2	.134	.224	.164
Katotakis, James, Orioles *	19	42	33	3	8	8	0	0	0	5	2	1	0	5	0	10	0	1	2	.242	.333	.242
Kemp, Matthew, Dodgers	42	169	159	11	43	55	5	2	1	17	0	2	0	7	1	25	2	1	1	.270	.298	.346
Keown, Clint, Reds	5	18	16	1	3	3	0	0	0	1	1	0	0	1	0	2	2	0	0	.188	.235	.188
Klemm, Christopher, Phil. *	42	165	143	20	48	66	8	2	2	23	1	1	2	18	1	43	3	3	1	.336	.415	.462
Lambis, Alberto, Marlins	23	77	74	7	16	18	2	0	0	4	0	0	1	2	0	11	0	1	0	.216	.247	.243
Laster, Jeramy, Tigers	42	132	121	27	29	38	4	1	1	17	0	1	0	10	0	35	9	2	2	.240	.295	.314
Laurin, Dominique, Dodgers	9	35	25	4	4	6	0	1	0	2	0	1	3	6	0	7	1	1	0	.160	.371	.240
Lebron, Edgardo, Twins †	11	41	39	6	6	9	3	0	0	3	1	0	0	1	0	11	0	0	0	.154	.175	.231
Lee, Jonathan, Tigers	13	27	20	1	4	6	2	0	0	1	1	0	0	6	0	8	1	0	0	.200	.385	.300
Lewis, Kenneth, Reds *	55	233	194	40	47	63	8	4	0	14	4	3	3	29	0	66	37	8	0	.242	.345	.325

Player, Team	G	TPA	AB	R	H	TB	2B	3B	HR	RBI	SH	SF	HP	BB	IBB	SO	SB	CS	GDP	Avg.	OBP	Slg.
Lindesey, Juan, Marlins	36	123	117	12	23	26	3	0	0	8	1	1	0	4	0	28	3	0	6	.197	.221	.222
Loadenthal, Carl, Braves	58	253	216	41	67	81	9	1	1	24	2	1	3	31	0	38	21	9	3	.310	.402	.375
Lopez, Javier, Twins	53	214	197	25	46	52	2	2	0	18	1	0	5	11	3	33	8	3	4	.234	.291	.264
Lopez, Mauber, Phillies	25	77	71	2	20	25	5	0	0	6	1	0	0	5	0	5	1	0	4	.282	.329	.352
Loyd, Brian, Red Sox	6	20	20	2	4	6	2	0	0	3	0	0	0	0	0	5	0	0	0	.200	.200	.300
Macia, Wanell, Pirates	52	199	191	25	56	75	8	4	1	28	0	3	0	5	0	40	6	2	0	.293	.307	.393
Made, Hector, Yankees	52	205	178	28	42	67	6	2	5	18	1	4	2	20	1	19	8	4	2	.236	.314	.376
Magness, Pat, Marlins *	1	3	1	0	0	0	0	0	0	0	0	0	0	2	0	0	0	0	0	.000	.667	.000
Majewski, Val, Orioles *	1	4	3	0	1	1	0	0	0	0	0	0	0	1	0	0	0	0	0	.333	.500	.333
Marcos, Emilio, Dodgers	45	165	154	20	37	54	8	0	3	16	0	1	3	7	0	35	9	5	3	.240	.285	.351
Marin, Daniel, Twins	1	4	4	0	0	0	0	0	0	0	0	0	0	0	0	1	0	0	0	.000	.000	.000
Marmolejos, Hector, Orioles	33	112	95	11	19	26	4	0	1	8	2	1	2	12	0	27	4	2	2	.200	.300	.274
Martinez, Edwin, Braves †	7	22	21	3	3	3	0	0	0	1	0	0	0	1	0	4	2	0	0	.143	.182	.143
Mattingly, Taylor, Yankees	24	78	58	4	13	13	0	0	0	7	1	1	4	12	0	10	0	0	5	.224	.387	.224
May, Lucas, Dodgers	48	184	159	19	40	48	8	0	0	10	1	0	5	19	0	38	11	1	5	.252	.350	.302
Mazzuca, Joe, Marlins	20	69	56	13	18	25	5	1	0	5	0	0	1	12	1	18	0	2	0	.321	.449	.446
McDonald, Kevin, Tigers *	5	18	17	1	4	4	0	0	0	2	0	1	0	0	0	4	0	0	0	.235	.222	.235
McGriff, Fred, Dodgers *	1	3	3	1	2	3	1	0	0	0	0	0	0	0	0	0	0	0	0	.667	.667	1.000
McRae, Aaron, Tigers *	7	17	14	2	4	4	0	0	0	0	0	0	0	3	0	7	1	0	0	.286	.412	.286
Medina, Julio, Reds	12	1	1	0	1	1	0	0	0	1	0	0	0	0	0	0	0	0	0	1.000	1.000	1.000
Mejia, Gilberto, Tigers †	44	191	175	36	63	107	11	9	5	29	1	2	0	13	0	29	23	5	1	.360	.400	.611
Melendez, Alcides, Orioles *	38	122	100	16	22	27	5	0	0	4	0	0	0	22	0	20	6	1	4	.220	.361	.270
Mendez, Deivi, Yankees	4	17	14	0	0	0	0	0	0	1	0	1	0	2	0	5	0	0	0	.000	.118	.000
Mendez, Jose, Twins	26	65	60	4	12	18	3	0	1	7	0	0	0	5	0	6	0	1	1	.200	.262	.300
Mendez, Rafael, Tigers	47	181	150	27	31	61	5	2	7	25	0	1	3	27	0	56	8	3	0	.207	.337	.407
Michelsen, Ross, Yankees *	10	36	30	2	3	3	0	0	0	0	0	0	1	5	0	11	1	0	1	.100	.250	.100
Miller, Jai, Marlins	45	166	146	17	29	38	4	1	1	15	1	2	2	15	0	45	9	3	4	.199	.279	.260
Mitchell, Russell, Dodgers	26	94	77	13	26	39	8	1	1	9	1	1	3	12	0	5	2	1	1	.338	.441	.506
Moni-Erigbali, Timi, Phillies	44	181	155	27	35	57	10	3	2	18	1	1	7	17	0	47	12	3	0	.226	.328	.368
Montz, Luke, Expos	32	113	103	8	23	29	0	0	2	9	1	0	0	9	0	21	1	1	2	.223	.286	.282
Morales, Leonardo, Pirates	6	20	18	1	3	3	0	0	0	1	0	0	0	2	0	4	0	0	1	.167	.250	.167
Moreta, Carlos, Braves	60	249	225	35	65	105	14	1	8	39	1	1	7	15	0	56	1	1	3	.289	.351	.467
Moses, Matthew, Twins *	18	72	65	6	25	32	5	1	0	11	0	2	0	5	0	9	0	1	1	.385	.417	.492
Najac, Gregory, Twins *	25	71	63	8	12	15	1	1	0	6	0	0	1	7	0	15	0	0	2	.190	.282	.238
Ndungidi, Sambu, Dodgers †	32	121	109	11	27	41	6	1	2	15	0	0	3	9	1	35	8	1	0	.248	.322	.376
Nelson, Kevin, Yankees	18	53	44	4	7	10	3	0	0	4	1	0	2	6	0	12	0	0	3	.159	.288	.227
Nieves, Raul, Red Sox †	6	23	23	2	3	6	3	0	0	1	0	0	0	0	0	5	0	0	1	.130	.130	.261
Nino, Denny, Pirates	24	84	79	9	25	32	5	1	0	9	0	1	0	4	0	16	1	1	1	.316	.345	.405
Nowak, David, Dodgers *	31	128	103	17	26	34	6	1	0	7	1	0	4	20	0	34	5	4	1	.252	.394	.330
Nunez, Eduardo, Expos	33	115	99	17	27	31	1	0	1	5	3	0	1	12	0	15	8	2	1	.273	.357	.313
Nunez, Tirzon, Expos	26	99	87	7	20	27	5	1	0	10	4	2	0	6	0	10	0	3	1	.230	.274	.310
Ortega, Raul, Braves †	50	139	121	15	28	43	8	2	1	17	1	4	0	13	0	27	1	0	3	.231	.297	.355
Ortiz, Patrick, Twins †	31	87	77	11	16	19	3	0	0	5	4	0	0	6	0	16	3	0	2	.208	.265	.247
Ovalles, Jose, Expos	36	118	101	9	21	22	1	0	0	7	0	3	1	13	0	17	2	2	7	.208	.297	.218
Owen, Ryan, Dodgers	4	7	7	1	1	4	0	0	1	1	0	0	0	0	0	4	0	0	1	.143	.143	.571
Paniagua, Salvador, Red Sox	39	139	130	17	40	58	9	0	3	19	0	1	1	7	2	20	0	0	6	.308	.345	.446
Patino, Jorge, Tigers	29	69	65	7	14	14	0	0	0	1	1	0	1	2	0	8	3	1	2	.215	.250	.215
Patrick, Sean, Orioles	31	101	86	9	21	33	7	1	1	16	4	1	1	9	0	15	1	0	6	.244	.320	.384
Pattee, Benjamin, Twins	36	126	117	12	36	45	7	1	0	17	1	1	3	4	0	9	6	1	1	.308	.344	.385
Patterson, Tarrence, Twins	49	183	169	32	52	77	9	5	2	23	2	2	1	9	2	19	15	7	1	.308	.343	.456
Penalo, Alexander, Red Sox †	32	96	82	12	25	33	5	0	1	9	4	1	1	8	0	15	4	0	2	.305	.370	.402
Perez, Jose, Yankees *	41	155	118	16	22	25	3	0	0	9	0	2	2	30	0	40	5	2	1	.186	.355	.212
Perez, Kenny, Red Sox †	7	23	22	4	6	9	1	1	0	2	0	0	0	1	0	3	0	0	0	.273	.304	.409
Perez, Koby, Red Sox	16	54	52	7	13	18	5	0	0	3	0	0	0	2	0	17	0	0	1	.250	.278	.346
Perry, Rod, Phillies	1	3	2	0	0	0	0	0	0	0	0	0	0	1	0	0	0	1	0	.000	.333	.000
Petersen, Ryan, Red Sox	2	5	4	0	0	0	0	0	0	0	0	0	1	0	0	1	0	0	0	.000	.200	.000
Piantek, Kurtis, Tigers	32	122	111	16	31	53	10	0	4	22	0	1	2	8	0	16	1	0	0	.279	.336	.477
Piazza, Thomas, Dodgers *	3	11	11	1	0	0	0	0	0	0	0	0	0	0	0	8	0	0	0	.000	.000	.000
Pierce, Sean, Dodgers	7	22	16	2	4	4	0	0	0	2	0	1	0	5	0	5	0	2	0	.250	.409	.250
Pignatiello, Bret, Expos *	22	79	63	10	17	24	1	0	2	6	0	0	1	15	0	18	1	0	1	.270	.418	.381
Piste, Carlos, Orioles †	38	113	93	18	13	20	1	0	2	7	0	1	6	13	0	27	7	1	1	.140	.283	.215
Ponce, Angel, Braves	42	145	137	18	32	45	5	1	2	16	1	3	2	2	0	31	5	0	3	.234	.250	.328
Poni, Francis, Pirates	23	86	80	7	7	8	1	0	0	6	0	1	3	2	0	26	0	1	4	.088	.140	.100
Powell, Pedro, Pirates	26	91	79	13	23	26	3	0	0	5	3	0	4	5	0	10	5	3	0	.291	.364	.329
Prado, Martin, Braves	59	251	220	28	63	77	2	6	0	23	5	1	1	24	0	30	9	9	4	.286	.358	.350
Pulley, Matthew, Orioles *	48	207	178	30	49	68	11	1	2	28	2	1	2	24	1	51	0	0	1	.275	.366	.382
Ramirez, Rafael, Pirates	17	59	56	5	8	15	1	0	2	5	0	1	0	2	0	21	0	0	2	.143	.169	.268
Ramirez, Wilkin, Tigers	54	216	200	34	55	90	6	7	5	35	1	1	1	13	2	51	6	1	4	.275	.321	.450
Ramos, Jason, Red Sox †	5	18	15	4	3	3	0	0	0	2	0	0	1	2	0	1	0	0	0	.200	.333	.200
Rea, Brad, Pirates	36	145	134	18	49	62	7	0	2	24	0	1	0	10	1	15	0	1	4	.366	.407	.463
Restko, J.T., Marlins	48	198	177	15	44	62	6	0	4	19	1	1	3	16	0	43	0	2	6	.249	.320	.350
Rigsby, Randy, Marlins *	3	14	13	5	7	11	1	0	1	7	0	0	0	1	0	2	0	0	0	.538	.571	.846
Roa, Joel, Tigers	34	103	90	14	24	34	10	0	0	12	2	0	3	8	0	28	1	1	0	.267	.347	.378
Rodriguez, Rafael, Yankees	51	200	190	23	49	78	11	3	4	29	0	0	2	8	0	27	2	1	7	.258	.295	.411
Rogers, Tanner, Marlins	32	106	94	5	17	25	2	0	2	8	0	2	0	10	0	29	1	1	1	.181	.255	.266
Rohan, Jimmy, Dodgers	47	189	171	17	44	52	4	2	0	15	1	3	4	10	0	12	5	5	4	.257	.309	.304
Rohena, Angel, Dodgers	24	69	62	11	18	25	2	1	1	7	1	1	1	4	0	22	2	0	2	.290	.338	.403
Romak, Jamie, Braves	19	60	51	5	9	11	2	0	0	4	0	0	0	9	0	10	0	0	0	.176	.300	.216
Romero, Luis, Yankees †	34	129	102	9	22	25	3	0	0	8	0	1	3	23	0	21	0	0	2	.216	.372	.245
Ronda, Jose, Reds †	47	190	173	25	52	78	16	2	2	26	0	2	2	13	0	40	5	2	2	.301	.353	.451
Rumsey, John, Twins	50	189	161	26	42	64	7	6	1	25	2	4	2	20	0	31	8	1	2	.261	.342	.398

Player, Team	G	TPA	AB	R	H	TB	2B	3B	HR	RBI	SH	SF	HP	BB	IBB	SO	SB	CS	GDP	Avg.	OBP	Slg.
Rutgers, Paul, Twins	56	214	201	35	71	89	12	3	0	21	0	1	3	9	0	15	16	7	3	.353	.388	.443
Sabino, Luis, Tigers	52	195	171	27	41	69	5	4	5	28	0	2	0	22	1	39	11	2	2	.240	.323	.404
Saltalamacchia, Jarrod, Bra.†	46	165	134	23	32	53	11	2	2	14	0	0	3	28	0	33	0	0	0	.239	.382	.396
Saltalamacchia, Justin, Bra.	24	39	36	3	7	9	2	0	0	6	0	0	1	2	0	5	0	0	1	.194	.256	.250
Sanchez, Carlos, Reds	36	104	94	15	21	23	2	0	0	7	0	0	4	6	0	25	3	2	0	.223	.298	.245
Sandora, Robert, Expos *	22	65	55	4	12	14	2	0	0	5	0	1	0	9	0	10	0	0	1	.218	.323	.255
Sandoval, Mayker, Reds	14	59	54	8	17	22	3	1	0	4	0	0	1	4	1	9	3	1	1	.315	.373	.407
Santiago, John, Pirates	37	152	140	22	39	52	9	2	0	16	0	1	2	9	0	23	1	1	6	.279	.329	.371
Sapp, Steven, Dodgers	38	137	121	12	30	38	6	1	0	7	0	0	8	8	0	38	10	3	1	.248	.336	.314
Schartz, Lance, Red Sox	9	29	25	3	6	9	0	0	1	4	1	0	1	2	0	4	0	0	0	.240	.321	.360
Schwab, Daniel, Yankees *	23	77	67	8	11	14	3	0	0	7	0	2	1	7	0	17	0	0	2	.164	.247	.209
Scott, Lorenzo, Orioles *	33	143	116	30	37	53	8	4	0	24	0	1	1	25	0	28	11	1	1	.319	.441	.457
Seifrig, Cole, Marlins	49	203	186	27	53	70	7	2	2	7	0	2	5	10	0	44	11	3	5	.285	.335	.376
Smith, Jeff, Red Sox *	7	24	22	2	4	4	0	0	0	2	0	0	0	2	0	2	0	0	0	.182	.250	.182
Smith, John, Pirates *	41	171	147	21	41	57	11	1	1	20	0	3	0	21	2	14	3	1	4	.279	.363	.388
Solano, Solamdi, Pirates	44	192	166	38	53	68	4	1	3	20	3	3	2	18	0	27	12	4	3	.319	.386	.410
Sosa, Pablo, Marlins	21	78	71	10	21	25	2	1	0	5	0	2	1	4	0	9	2	3	2	.296	.333	.352
Sovie, Robbie, Tigers	41	142	130	23	26	36	5	1	1	13	0	1	3	7	0	33	9	2	0	.200	.255	.277
Spears, Nathaniel, Orioles	56	231	180	38	52	72	7	5	1	19	4	2	5	40	0	32	18	5	2	.289	.427	.400
Stern, Adam, Braves *	7	36	29	6	10	14	1	0	1	6	1	0	0	6	0	3	2	2	1	.345	.457	.483
Sterner, George, Yankees	6	23	20	3	6	6	0	0	0	2	0	0	0	3	0	4	1	1	0	.300	.391	.300
Stevens, Anthony, Pirates	17	44	41	4	3	5	2	0	0	2	0	0	2	1	0	14	1	0	1	.073	.136	.122
Stoecklein, Brian, Braves	44	123	114	14	30	39	4	1	1	13	1	0	1	7	0	19	2	2	2	.263	.311	.342
Sucre, Antonio, Expos	48	191	166	28	38	64	10	2	4	28	0	4	8	13	0	45	1	3	2	.229	.309	.386
Sulbaran, Orlando, Reds	10	43	38	5	13	16	3	0	0	5	0	0	0	5	0	5	1	0	0	.342	.419	.421
Summerville, Kaazim, Yan.	3	4	3	1	2	2	0	0	0	2	0	0	0	1	0	1	0	0	0	.667	.750	.667
Sutherland, David, Dodgers *	51	203	191	12	45	52	5	1	0	20	0	0	0	12	0	19	1	2	5	.236	.281	.272
Tatum, John, Dodgers	10	34	29	1	3	3	0	0	0	0	1	0	0	4	0	13	0	0	0	.103	.212	.103
Tejeda, Ferdin, Yankees	8	31	28	4	11	13	2	0	0	3	1	0	0	2	0	4	1	0	0	.393	.433	.464
Tintor, Eli, Twins	25	71	64	4	17	20	3	0	0	5	0	0	1	6	1	14	0	2	0	.266	.338	.313
Torborg, Jesse, Phillies	13	48	41	8	11	12	1	0	0	3	0	0	1	6	0	17	2	0	0	.268	.375	.293
Turner, Christopher, Red Sox	35	142	126	18	32	51	8	4	1	15	0	0	5	11	0	36	3	2	3	.254	.338	.405
Unger, Adam, Yankees †	16	28	24	2	2	2	0	0	0	0	0	0	0	4	0	8	0	1	0	.083	.214	.083
Urgelles, Jeff, Reds	56	213	185	21	50	76	20	0	2	28	0	2	4	22	1	32	0	1	5	.270	.357	.411
Vankirk, Robert, Red Sox	9	34	32	0	6	6	0	0	0	5	0	0	0	2	0	11	0	0	0	.188	.235	.188
Veloz, Vladimil, Marlins	23	65	60	5	11	16	5	0	0	3	0	1	2	2	0	13	1	0	3	.183	.231	.267
West, Eric, Red Sox	6	22	20	1	5	7	2	0	0	2	2	0	0	0	0	5	0	0	0	.250	.250	.350
White, Scott, Red Sox	38	146	131	9	22	23	1	0	0	11	1	1	2	11	0	16	0	0	4	.168	.241	.176
Whiteside, Eli, Orioles	1	4	3	0	1	2	1	0	0	0	0	0	0	1	0	1	0	0	0	.333	.500	.667
Williams, Devoris, Red Sox †	35	144	124	18	25	37	5	2	1	8	3	0	2	15	0	48	3	4	0	.202	.298	.298
Williams, Matt, Tigers †	42	111	98	11	14	16	2	0	0	6	3	1	0	9	0	26	5	4	4	.143	.213	.163
Willingham, Josh, Marlins	2	8	7	3	3	7	1	0	1	3	0	0	0	1	0	2	0	0	0	.429	.500	1.000
Winfree, David, Twins	23	73	70	4	9	14	1	2	0	3	0	0	1	2	0	16	0	0	2	.129	.164	.200
Wong, Ivanosky, Expos	16	61	54	6	13	14	1	0	0	3	0	0	0	7	0	2	0	0	1	.241	.328	.259
Wong, Travis, Reds	11	46	43	6	10	18	2	0	2	6	0	0	0	3	0	13	0	0	1	.233	.283	.419
Woodard, Johnny, Twins *	52	197	172	19	41	52	6	1	1	15	0	1	2	22	0	42	1	1	3	.238	.330	.302
Wulf, Kent, Pirates	31	127	117	8	27	32	5	0	0	15	1	0	3	6	0	25	7	1	1	.231	.286	.274
Zapata, Jose, Orioles	40	110	96	14	17	21	2	1	0	7	0	1	2	11	0	18	6	0	4	.177	.273	.219

GRAND SLAMS—Cronkhite, Howerton, Marcos, Moreta, 1 each.

AWARDED FIRST BASE ON CATCHER'S INTERFERENCE—J. Perez 3 (Roa 3); Mattingly 2 (Poni, Roa); Bastardo (Ju. Saltalamacchia); DeLaCruz (J. Mendez); Gonzalez (M. Lopez); Katotakis (Urgelles); Kemp (Cruz); Sovie (Nino).

2003 PITCHING

TEAM

Team	W	L	Pct.	ERA	G	CG	ShO	Sv.	IP	H	TBF	R	ER	HR	SH	SF	HB	BB	IBB	SO	WP	Bk.
Dodgers	29	31	.483	2.85	60	0	5	16	514.0	437	2152	217	163	18	16	18	37	199	2	418	61	6
Red Sox	33	26	.559	3.04	59	0	9	19	497.2	453	2109	223	168	14	26	20	33	172	4	370	39	4
Braves	38	22	.633	3.09	60	1	7	10	528.0	492	2220	220	181	21	12	15	26	174	3	467	39	4
Yankees	26	31	.456	3.22	57	2	5	7	484.0	438	2059	224	173	17	16	14	27	173	8	494	48	10
Orioles	32	28	.533	3.25	60	1	8	12	498.1	471	2136	243	180	10	11	13	21	196	12	408	49	6
Marlins	26	32	.448	3.28	58	2	6	12	496.0	441	2122	223	181	19	16	14	33	197	3	434	53	7
Expos	25	33	.431	3.52	58	0	4	16	483.2	484	2071	252	189	17	9	13	49	156	3	323	37	9
Pirates	36	20	.643	3.56	56	4	3	17	485.1	441	2071	229	192	25	6	16	37	157	2	440	17	4
Reds	26	34	.433	4.04	60	0	4	11	503.0	508	2208	272	226	13	22	20	40	198	10	408	34	9
Phillies	23	33	.411	4.20	56	2	5	15	463.0	482	2079	294	216	19	15	21	30	175	4	368	43	0
Twins	28	31	.475	4.22	59	0	4	16	501.0	495	2249	296	235	23	20	24	42	246	2	401	59	8
Tigers	28	29	.491	4.53	57	3	4	10	474.2	465	2163	317	239	40	12	20	39	234	4	419	36	4

INDIVIDUAL

TOP QUALIFIERS FOR EARNED-RUN AVERAGE TITLE

Minimum 48 innings. *Lefthanded pitcher.

Pitcher, Team	W	L	Pct.	ERA	G	GS	CG	ShO	GF	Sv.	IP	H	TBF	R	ER	HR	SH	SF	HB	BB	IBB	SO	WP	Bk.
Mendez, Wimer, Orioles	5	1	.833	1.52	12	9	0	0	3	0	53.1	42	215	13	9	0	2	0	0	17	0	41	2	1
Russ, James, Marlins	1	2	.333	1.63	11	7	0	0	2	1	49.2	33	190	12	9	2	0	0	2	15	0	46	1	1
Jackson, Kyle, Red Sox	5	2	.714	1.85	12	12	0	0	0	0	58.1	40	224	14	12	3	1	2	5	11	0	37	2	0
Capps, Matt, Pirates	5	1	.833	1.87	10	10	1	0	0	0	62.2	40	240	16	13	1	0	1	5	9	0	54	1	0
Nickerson, Jon-Michael, Mar.*	5	1	.833	1.87	12	12	1	1	0	0	53.0	36	218	15	11	1	0	3	4	23	0	50	4	0

Pitcher, Team	W	L	Pct.	ERA	G	GS	CG	ShO	GF	Sv.	IP	H	TBF	R	ER	HR	SH	SF	HB	BB	IBB	SO	WP	Bk.
Childs, Ryan, Orioles	5	1	.833	1.99	12	7	0	0	2	0	54.1	46	214	15	12	1	1	2	1	11	1	40	7	0
Martinez, Javier, Twins *	3	3	.500	2.03	12	10	0	0	0	0	62.0	43	252	19	14	2	2	0	5	21	0	54	5	2
Ramirez, Luis, Orioles	6	4	.600	2.12	12	11	0	0	1	0	59.1	45	233	17	14	2	1	1	1	14	1	76	1	1
Ochoa, Nehomar, Expos	2	2	.500	2.19	9	9	0	0	0	0	49.1	37	203	15	12	3	0	0	5	19	1	29	2	0
Wilson, Joseph, Phillies *	4	2	.667	2.24	11	9	0	0	0	0	52.1	44	220	20	13	1	0	2	3	17	0	58	2	0
Garcia, Javier, Dodgers	4	5	.444	2.34	14	11	0	0	2	0	61.2	61	251	21	16	2	3	2	7	8	0	41	4	0
Brocato, Russell, Orioles	3	3	.500	2.41	13	7	0	0	3	1	52.1	45	212	19	14	0	1	1	0	14	1	30	3	0
Potoczny, Robert, Dodgers	2	5	.286	2.79	16	7	0	0	2	1	51.2	45	224	25	16	1	2	5	3	26	0	29	4	0
Doble, Clemente, Phillies	5	4	.556	3.00	10	9	1	1	0	0	57.0	57	240	27	19	2	0	3	7	9	0	44	6	0
Lewis, Lavon, Tigers	3	3	.500	3.17	11	8	0	0	1	0	54.0	53	233	29	19	2	2	5	1	18	0	37	1	0

DEPARTMENTAL LEADERS: W—Borland, L. Ramirez, Da. Smith, 6; L—Mathieson, 7; Pct.—Jackson, .714; G—Alvarez, Delacruz, 22; GS—Atilano, Jackson, Nickerson, 12; CG—Munoz, 2; ShO—Several pitchers tied with 1; GF—Delacruz, 18; Sv.—Galvez, 9; IP—Capps, 62.2; H—F. Garcia, 66; TBF—F. Garcia, 275; R—Mathieson, 42; ER—Mathieson, 36; HR—Cr. Martinez, 9; SH—Several pitchers tied with 4; SF—Duguay, Lewis, Potoczny, 5; HB—I. Wright, 11; BB—Merricks, 37; IBB—Quijada, 3; SO—L. Ramirez, 76; WP—Merricks, 14; BK—Sosa, 6.

ALL PITCHERS

*Lefthanded pitcher.

Pitcher, Team	W	L	Pct.	ERA	G	GS	CG	ShO	GF	Sv.	IP	H	TBF	R	ER	HR	SH	SF	HB	BB	IBB	SO	WP	Bk.
Aguero, Miguel, Yankees	1	3	.250	3.38	10	4	0	0	1	0	34.2	33	155	14	13	0	1	1	8	14	1	36	7	1
Alcala, Jason, Pirates	0	0	.000	7.20	2	0	0	0	0	0	5.0	9	24	4	4	0	0	0	0	1	0	4	0	0
Allison, Jeffrey, Marlins	0	2	.000	1.00	3	3	0	0	0	0	9.0	7	38	2	1	0	0	0	0	4	0	11	1	0
Alvarez, Carlos, Dodgers *	2	2	.500	2.05	22	0	0	0	17	3	26.1	19	108	11	6	3	1	2	0	12	1	26	2	1
Anderson, Devin, Braves *	0	1	.000	2.48	18	0	0	0	8	3	29.0	26	118	8	8	0	1	1	0	6	1	30	2	0
Antigua, Erick, Yankees	0	0	.000	3.00	2	1	0	0	0	0	6.0	4	24	2	2	0	0	0	0	2	0	9	0	0
Ascanio, Jose, Braves	4	0	1.000	1.37	8	0	0	0	0	0	26.1	26	104	4	4	0	0	1	2	5	0	17	4	0
Atilano, Luis, Braves	3	2	.600	3.83	12	12	1	1	0	0	54.0	61	225	25	23	5	3	0	3	7	0	24	3	1
Ayala, Luis, Expos	0	0	.000	0.00	2	2	0	0	0	0	3.2	2	15	0	0	0	0	0	0	2	0	2	0	0
Aybar, Ismael, Red Sox *	0	0	.000	8.27	10	0	0	0	5	0	16.1	18	82	15	15	1	3	1	5	15	1	11	2	0
Azze, Justin, Orioles *	0	0	.000	6.00	2	0	0	0	0	0	3.0	4	13	3	2	1	0	0	1	0	0	1	1	0
Bacot, Paul, Braves	4	0	1.000	0.95	9	6	0	0	1	0	38.0	23	147	6	4	0	3	0	3	4	0	26	0	0
Bale, Manuel, Braves	2	0	1.000	3.00	19	0	0	0	14	2	27.0	20	104	10	9	0	0	1	2	8	0	13	1	1
Barrett, Ricky, Twins *	0	1	.000	1.29	5	1	0	0	0	0	7.0	10	35	1	1	0	0	0	0	3	0	5	0	0
Bartlett, Greg, Marlins *	1	1	.500	6.45	15	0	0	0	5	1	22.1	29	104	17	16	2	4	0	3	5	0	17	5	0
Bartlett, Richard, Orioles	0	0	.000	0.00	1	1	0	0	0	0	3.0	3	13	0	0	0	0	0	2	0	0	3	1	0
Batista, Gorky, Reds	2	2	.500	4.05	5	4	0	0	0	0	26.2	26	112	13	12	1	0	2	3	6	0	12	1	1
Bedard, Erik, Orioles *	0	0	.000	1.13	3	3	0	0	0	0	8.0	4	28	1	1	0	0	0	0	2	0	11	1	0
Berger, Garrett, Marlins	1	2	.333	9.15	14	0	0	0	6	0	19.2	27	109	23	20	3	0	2	3	24	0	14	8	1
Bernal, Christian, Reds	0	0	.000	8.10	2	0	0	0	0	0	3.1	6	18	3	3	0	0	1	1	1	0	4	0	0
Blackley, Adam, Red Sox *	0	0	.000	0.73	7	0	0	0	2	1	24.2	13	92	3	2	0	1	1	2	5	0	24	2	0
Blanco, Julio, Red Sox	0	0	.000	0.00	2	0	0	0	0	0	2.0	2	9	1	0	0	0	0	0	1	0	2	0	0
Blankenship, Jon, Yankees *	0	1	.000	3.86	7	0	0	0	2	0	7.0	11	33	4	3	0	1	0	1	2	0	9	0	0
Bolander, Matt, Orioles	0	2	.000	9.00	6	3	0	0	0	0	11.0	16	59	17	11	2	0	0	0	10	1	12	1	0
Bonecio, Ryan, Yankees *	1	0	1.000	6.59	10	0	0	0	6	0	13.2	16	58	10	10	1	0	0	0	1	0	11	4	0
Booker, Chris, Reds	0	2	.000	8.49	12	0	0	0	9	2	11.2	17	61	11	11	1	0	1	0	8	0	11	1	0
Borland, Curt, Red Sox	6	0	1.000	0.83	13	1	0	0	7	1	43.1	42	176	11	4	1	2	0	1	7	0	38	5	0
Borsa, Robert, Reds	1	1	.500	2.74	18	0	0	0	11	2	23.0	22	92	7	7	0	1	2	0	4	0	16	1	0
Bowlin, Jason, Twins	1	0	1.000	2.28	20	0	0	0	14	6	23.2	18	97	10	6	1	1	0	1	6	0	14	0	0
Bradley, Bobby, Pirates	0	0	.000	0.00	1	1	0	0	0	0	3.0	1	10	0	0	0	0	0	0	1	0	4	0	0
Brazoban, Yhency, Yankees	0	0	.000	6.00	3	0	0	0	0	0	3.0	5	15	3	2	0	1	0	0	1	1	5	0	0
Brito, Joel, Marlins	2	4	.333	2.89	12	8	0	0	1	1	46.2	36	196	20	15	1	1	1	2	20	0	50	4	0
Brnardic, Ryan, Orioles	1	1	.500	4.64	12	1	0	0	5	1	21.1	26	97	12	11	0	0	0	0	9	0	17	3	0
Brocato, Russell, Orioles	3	3	.500	2.41	13	7	0	0	3	1	52.1	45	212	19	14	0	1	1	0	14	1	30	3	0
Bryant, Michael, Reds	0	3	.000	3.86	13	0	0	0	5	1	23.1	25	100	13	10	0	2	1	3	5	1	18	1	0
Burch, Kevin, Orioles	0	1	.000	4.05	15	0	0	0	11	1	20.0	19	87	10	9	0	0	0	1	8	0	9	2	0
Cabrera, Nathan, Phillies	0	1	.000	5.56	5	3	1	0	0	0	11.1	9	50	8	7	0	0	0	0	5	0	9	1	0
Caceres, Carlos, Expos	2	0	1.000	0.75	2	2	0	0	0	0	12.0	8	43	2	1	0	0	1	2	0	0	7	1	0
Camacho, Gustavo, Orioles	1	6	.143	5.73	10	9	1	1	0	0	37.2	42	170	32	24	2	2	3	2	16	0	27	3	0
Candelario, Alexis, Braves	1	0	1.000	0.00	3	0	0	0	3	0	4.0	1	14	0	0	0	0	0	0	1	0	4	1	0
Capellan, Jose, Braves	0	1	.000	2.65	5	5	0	0	0	0	17.0	18	75	7	5	0	1	0	1	8	0	17	0	0
Capps, Matt, Pirates	5	1	.833	1.87	10	10	1	0	0	0	62.2	40	240	16	13	1	0	1	5	9	0	54	1	0
Caraballo, Angel, Yankees	1	1	.500	3.86	6	1	0	0	0	0	9.1	11	42	5	4	1	0	0	0	3	0	12	0	0
Caraballo, Jesse, Tigers	1	3	.250	9.67	16	0	0	0	5	0	22.1	27	125	31	24	5	2	1	7	22	1	15	2	0
Castillo, Albenis, Dodgers	2	1	.667	2.72	19	1	0	0	7	0	36.1	35	155	13	11	0	0	3	3	8	0	35	5	0
Castro, Randy, Reds	0	1	.000	9.60	9	1	0	0	2	0	15.0	20	80	16	16	0	0	0	1	16	0	11	3	0
Cedeno, Blas, Pirates	1	0	1.000	0.00	9	0	0	0	9	6	11.2	7	44	0	0	0	0	0	1	3	0	11	0	0
Cerezo, Hector, Expos *	1	1	.500	1.73	14	1	0	0	7	2	26.0	23	101	6	5	0	0	0	3	5	0	18	1	1
Cerrato, Justin, Phillies	0	0	.000	3.00	2	1	0	0	0	0	3.0	2	12	1	1	0	0	0	0	1	0	2	0	0
Cespedes, Osvaldo, Phillies	0	1	.000	3.00	2	0	0	0	2	0	3.0	5	15	1	1	0	0	0	0	2	1	3	0	0
Childs, Ryan, Orioles	5	1	.833	1.99	12	7	0	0	2	0	54.1	46	214	15	12	1	1	2	1	11	1	40	7	0
Chrysler, Clint, Pirates *	1	1	.500	3.00	2	1	0	0	0	0	6.0	6	26	3	2	0	0	0	0	2	0	7	0	0
Cillo, Cody, Marlins	0	0	.000	0.00	3	0	0	0	3	3	5.2	2	20	0	0	0	0	0	1	0	0	9	0	0
Clark, Ryan, Yankees *	0	0	.000	4.50	2	0	0	0	0	0	2.0	3	11	3	1	0	0	0	0	0	0	2	0	0
Clippard, Tyler, Yankees	3	3	.500	2.89	11	5	0	0	2	0	43.2	33	168	16	14	3	1	1	5	5	0	56	4	0
Coke, Phillip, Yankees *	0	0	.000	3.75	10	0	0	0	3	0	12.0	13	53	7	5	0	0	1	0	3	0	5	3	0
Contreras, Jean, Twins *	0	0	.000	0.00	1	0	0	0	0	0	2.0	1	7	0	0	0	0	0	0	0	0	2	1	0
Contreras, Manuel, Tigers	1	1	.500	5.06	4	2	0	0	2	1	16.0	15	67	12	9	3	0	1	0	1	0	11	1	0
Contreras, Omar, Pirates	0	0	.000	10.13	2	0	0	0	2	0	2.2	4	15	4	3	0	0	0	0	1	0	5	1	0
Cordova, Jorge, Tigers	0	0	.000	0.00	3	1	0	0	1	0	3.0	1	10	0	0	0	0	0	0	0	0	3	0	0
Cortes, Jorge, Reds	0	1	.000	0.00	2	1	0	0	1	0	7.0	6	28	4	0	0	0	0	1	1	0	6	0	0
Cowan, Richard, Yankees	1	2	.333	5.71	13	0	0	0	7	1	17.1	19	79	14	11	0	1	0	1	7	0	11	4	1
Craig, Jonathan, Reds	1	1	.500	8.53	5	0	0	0	2	0	6.1	14	39	7	6	1	1	1	2	4	1	5	1	0
Croushore, Rick, Orioles	0	0	.000	0.00	1	1	0	0	0	0	2.0	2	11	0	0	0	0	0	0	2	0	1	0	0
Cruz, Juan, Yankees	2	1	.667	1.23	12	0	0	0	8	0	22.0	9	87	6	3	0	2	1	0	11	0	27	1	0
Cuffman, Jacob, Pirates	2	1	.667	4.98	8	3	0	0	0	0	21.2	29	112	17	12	1	0	0	6	16	0	27	2	0
Davidson, David, Pirates *	0	2	.000	12.91	7	0	0	0	2	0	7.2	10	41	12	11	0	0	2	4	7	0	8	1	0
Davis, Lance, Marlins	0	0	.000	0.00	1	0	0	0	1	0	1.0	0	4	0	0	0	0	0	1	0	0	0	0	0

Pitcher, Team	W	L	Pct.	ERA	G	GS	CG	ShO	GF	Sv.	IP	H	TBF	R	ER	HR	SH	SF	HB	BB	IBB	SO	WP	Bk.
Day, Zach, Expos	0	0	.000	3.86	1	1	0	0	0	0	2.1	3	12	3	1	0	0	1	0	1	0	3	1	0
De La Rosa, Dane, Yankees	0	0	.000	3.00	5	1	0	0	2	0	9.0	5	37	3	3	0	0	0	0	6	0	12	3	1
Dean, Herman, Tigers	2	0	1.000	2.45	7	0	0	0	0	0	14.2	11	68	7	4	1	1	0	0	15	0	10	1	0
Delacruz, Eulogio, Tigers	2	2	.500	2.59	22	0	0	0	18	7	24.1	18	105	10	7	0	1	0	1	15	0	30	4	0
Demme, Asher, Braves	0	1	.000	5.63	4	0	0	0	1	0	8.0	8	37	8	5	1	0	2	0	5	0	3	1	0
Dewar, Andrew, Braves *	2	2	.500	6.00	14	0	0	0	7	0	18.0	19	80	12	12	1	1	0	1	9	1	16	1	0
Doble, Clemente, Phillies	5	4	.556	3.00	10	9	1	1	0	0	57.0	57	240	27	19	2	0	3	7	9	0	44	6	0
Dolsi, Freddy, Tigers	1	1	.500	4.70	8	2	0	0	0	0	23.0	27	114	20	12	1	1	1	2	12	0	19	3	1
Duguay, Steven, Twins	1	4	.200	4.79	16	8	0	0	6	4	47.0	45	194	26	25	3	3	5	5	7	1	36	2	0
Echarry, Nelson, Phillies	1	0	1.000	3.65	6	1	0	0	1	1	12.1	11	56	8	5	0	0	0	2	9	0	10	1	0
Elfeldt, Matthew, Red Sox	0	2	.000	5.63	8	0	0	0	3	0	16.0	18	73	13	10	2	2	1	0	8	2	12	0	0
Encarnacion, Luis, Phillies	1	2	.333	5.50	12	6	0	0	1	0	37.2	41	176	29	23	4	3	2	4	19	0	19	4	0
Eugenio, Mario, Tigers	0	2	.000	8.54	17	0	0	0	12	1	26.1	33	147	32	25	1	1	2	4	30	1	23	6	0
Felix, Wilkin, Orioles	3	2	.600	5.22	16	1	0	0	6	1	29.1	32	140	20	17	0	3	2	2	25	2	30	3	0
Feliz, Ranier, Reds	2	2	.500	3.20	10	10	0	0	0	0	45.0	39	181	17	16	0	3	1	0	13	1	36	1	1
Fernandez, Rodney, Marlins	0	0	.000	13.50	2	0	0	0	1	0	2.0	4	12	3	3	0	0	0	0	2	0	2	2	0
Fink, Douglas, Red Sox	0	1	.000	9.00	1	0	0	0	0	0	1.0	2	5	1	1	1	0	0	0	0	0	2	0	0
Fischer, Eric, Twins *	0	1	.000	16.88	2	1	0	0	0	0	2.2	5	17	5	5	0	1	1	1	3	0	4	1	0
Fisher, Pete, Twins	0	0	.000	16.20	1	1	0	0	0	0	1.2	6	13	6	3	0	0	1	0	1	0	2	1	0
Fleming, Travis, Orioles	0	0	.000	4.35	9	0	0	0	6	5	10.1	13	46	7	5	1	0	0	0	2	0	6	1	0
Frias, Junior, Red Sox	2	4	.333	6.06	10	8	0	0	0	0	32.2	35	156	27	22	1	4	2	3	19	0	17	2	0
Friesen, Roy, Marlins	0	0	.000	108.00	1	0	0	0	0	0	0.1	2	5	4	4	0	0	0	0	2	0	0	2	1
Furrow, Jason, Orioles *	1	1	.500	2.33	15	0	0	0	6	2	27.0	28	122	14	7	0	0	0	2	10	2	21	2	1
Galarraga, Armando, Expos	1	1	.500	1.80	5	5	0	0	0	0	15.0	13	60	5	3	0	0	0	1	5	0	7	1	0
Galvez, Willy, Red Sox	0	2	.000	5.50	16	0	0	0	13	9	18.0	26	85	14	11	0	1	2	0	7	1	13	1	1
Garavito, Jean, Pirates	0	1	.000	7.88	7	0	0	0	5	0	8.0	12	41	7	7	0	0	0	0	3	0	6	0	0
Garcia, Felipe, Tigers	3	4	.429	4.77	11	10	1	0	1	0	60.1	66	275	40	32	3	0	2	3	28	1	43	4	0
Garcia, Harvey, Red Sox	3	0	1.000	1.89	9	8	0	0	0	0	33.1	21	132	11	7	2	0	2	1	12	0	32	4	0
Garcia, Javier, Dodgers	4	5	.444	2.34	14	11	0	0	2	0	61.2	61	251	21	16	2	3	2	7	8	0	41	4	0
Garrison, Kale, Dodgers *	2	2	.500	7.04	15	1	0	0	3	0	23.0	23	110	22	18	0	1	0	2	18	0	24	6	1
Gault, Joe, Twins	2	1	.667	3.66	14	0	0	0	1	1	19.2	17	92	12	8	0	1	1	3	12	0	13	3	0
George, Jon, Reds	4	2	.667	4.91	7	7	0	0	0	0	33.0	40	145	19	18	1	1	1	1	8	0	22	0	1
Gillman, Justin, Reds	1	0	1.000	0.00	3	3	0	0	0	0	18.0	7	63	0	0	0	0	0	1	3	0	16	1	0
Glynn, Josh, Marlins	0	3	.000	1.29	10	2	0	0	3	0	35.0	22	134	7	5	1	0	2	0	7	0	20	0	0
Golden, Michael, Reds	0	1	.000	9.53	6	0	0	0	4	0	5.2	6	26	6	6	0	0	0	1	2	0	5	1	0
Gomez, Abel, Yankees *	2	2	.500	2.63	11	7	1	0	1	0	37.2	19	154	14	11	1	3	2	2	26	0	43	4	2
Gonzalez, Jose, Tigers	1	0	1.000	7.50	8	0	0	0	0	0	6.0	5	36	7	5	0	0	1	1	11	0	8	0	0
Goodman, Chris, Expos	3	1	.750	4.23	10	2	0	0	5	2	27.2	31	117	15	13	2	1	0	1	3	0	14	1	0
Guanchez, Argimiro, R. Sox *	5	0	1.000	1.95	18	0	0	0	12	8	32.1	34	139	11	7	0	1	0	4	9	0	29	0	0
Gwaltney, Lee, Phillies	0	0	.000	0.00	1	1	0	0	0	0	2.0	3	11	2	0	0	0	0	0	0	0	1	0	0
Hacker, Eric, Yankees	3	2	.600	2.86	7	5	0	0	1	0	28.1	25	114	9	9	1	0	0	0	7	0	26	1	0
Harrand, Rob, Phillies	0	0	.000	3.60	2	1	0	0	0	0	5.0	7	23	2	2	0	0	1	1	0	0	7	0	0
Harrison, Matt, Braves *	3	1	.750	3.69	11	6	0	0	1	1	39.0	40	161	18	16	2	0	0	0	9	0	33	3	0
Hayes, Alvin, Dodgers	1	1	.500	4.05	6	2	0	0	0	0	13.1	11	65	8	6	0	0	0	2	16	0	9	8	1
Henderson, Jim, Expos	0	0	.000	2.25	4	0	0	0	1	1	8.0	6	33	3	2	0	0	0	1	1	0	3	1	0
Henn, Sean, Yankees *	1	1	.500	2.25	2	1	0	0	0	0	8.0	5	33	3	2	1	0	0	0	3	0	10	1	0
Hernandez, Moises, Orioles	2	1	.667	4.15	8	4	0	0	1	0	21.2	19	95	13	10	0	0	1	2	13	1	22	3	1
Herrera, Jose, Tigers	2	3	.400	3.05	15	2	1	1	6	1	38.1	39	170	24	13	3	0	4	0	16	0	24	3	1
Hilario, Elpidio, Red Sox	3	3	.500	3.76	14	2	0	0	2	0	38.1	41	167	21	16	0	3	2	1	15	0	21	6	1
Hlebovy, Gus, Expos	1	2	.333	2.60	12	0	0	0	6	1	27.2	26	114	11	8	1	1	1	0	8	0	20	1	0
Holliday, Brian, Pirates *	3	2	.600	3.83	10	10	1	0	0	0	51.2	50	225	24	22	1	1	2	4	22	0	52	1	2
Honsa, Chris, Phillies	1	2	.333	3.00	11	0	0	0	5	4	24.0	24	108	17	8	0	1	0	1	9	0	17	4	0
Humen, David, Marlins	1	0	1.000	1.08	12	0	0	0	8	3	16.2	7	67	2	2	0	1	0	1	14	1	19	8	0
Hummel, John, Pirates *	3	3	.500	3.18	10	0	0	0	6	1	34.0	26	142	16	12	1	1	2	3	9	0	15	1	0
Iehl, Jason, Marlins	3	2	.600	3.22	7	7	1	1	0	0	36.1	38	155	17	13	2	1	1	2	11	0	27	0	0
Jackson, Kyle, Red Sox	5	2	.714	1.85	12	12	0	0	0	0	58.1	40	224	14	12	3	1	2	5	11	0	37	2	0
Jarvis, Andrew, Phillies *	1	0	1.000	2.25	2	0	0	0	1	0	4.0	2	15	1	1	0	0	0	0	1	0	0	1	0
Jenkins, Clyde, Expos	2	1	.667	4.85	14	2	0	0	9	3	26.0	30	117	20	14	2	1	0	0	8	0	30	1	0
Jimenez, Elvis, Phillies	0	1	.000	5.45	16	2	0	0	9	1	34.2	44	170	31	21	1	3	2	4	19	0	19	7	0
Jimenez, Rodny, Braves	1	0	1.000	3.94	16	0	0	0	1	0	32.0	25	146	17	14	1	0	2	5	24	1	38	3	0
Johnson, Blair, Pirates	4	1	.800	1.34	9	9	0	0	0	0	47.0	32	184	9	7	2	1	0	2	11	1	42	0	0
Johnson, Russell, Pirates	0	0	.000	0.00	1	1	0	0	0	0	3.0	0	9	0	0	0	0	0	0	0	0	4	0	0
Jones, K.C., Twins	0	3	.000	7.22	15	4	0	0	1	0	33.2	50	169	31	27	5	0	2	1	23	0	15	4	2
Jumelles, Edduar, Reds	0	0	.000	6.00	3	0	0	0	1	0	6.0	3	25	4	4	1	0	0	1	3	0	7	0	0
Jurrjens, Jair, Tigers	2	1	.667	3.21	7	2	0	0	3	0	28.0	33	121	16	10	3	1	0	4	3	0	20	0	0
Kaercher, Matthew, Red Sox	0	1	.000	2.70	6	0	0	0	2	0	13.1	7	52	4	4	0	2	0	1	3	0	10	0	0
Kamimura, Soichi, Marlins	2	0	1.000	3.07	5	0	0	0	1	0	14.2	13	64	5	5	2	1	0	0	5	0	8	0	0
Kemlo, Chris, Yankees	1	2	.333	2.79	13	0	0	0	8	3	19.1	18	80	6	6	0	4	1	0	6	2	27	4	0
Kendrick, Kyle, Phillies	0	4	.000	5.46	9	5	0	0	0	0	31.1	40	145	24	19	3	1	1	0	12	0	26	2	0
Killion, Terry, Twins	0	1	.000	9.60	16	0	0	0	0	0	15.0	18	88	21	16	0	0	1	4	22	0	7	4	0
Kirsten, Rick, Tigers	1	1	.500	2.00	4	3	0	0	0	0	9.0	7	35	2	2	0	0	0	1	1	0	11	0	0
Knox, Michael, Yankees	2	2	.500	1.48	10	1	0	0	7	2	24.1	13	93	6	4	0	0	1	1	7	0	16	4	0
Koch, Jonathon, Twins	2	3	.400	2.73	12	2	0	0	7	3	26.1	29	105	8	8	1	0	0	1	6	0	18	1	0
Langone, Steve, Dodgers	0	0	.000	3.00	2	1	0	0	0	0	3.0	4	12	1	1	0	0	0	0	0	0	2	0	0
Lankford, Kristofer, Twins	3	1	.750	3.99	15	4	0	0	4	0	29.1	32	126	15	13	1	1	3	0	12	0	22	2	0
Lara, Toni, Yankees *	2	4	.333	3.57	11	6	0	0	0	0	40.1	45	185	24	16	3	0	2	0	22	1	42	4	3
Lawson, Jarrod, Phillies	0	1	.000	9.00	4	0	0	0	1	1	5.0	3	31	11	5	0	0	1	0	11	0	6	2	0
Lehman, James, Expos	1	3	.250	10.19	12	0	0	0	2	0	17.2	34	104	30	20	1	0	2	4	12	0	6	4	0
Lewis, Lavon, Tigers	3	3	.500	3.17	11	8	0	0	1	0	54.0	53	233	29	19	2	2	5	1	18	0	37	1	0
Lieber, Jon, Yankees	0	0	.000	4.50	2	2	0	0	0	0	6.0	8	26	3	3	0	0	0	0	0	0	6	0	0
Linder, Matthew, Phillies	0	0	.000	3.60	3	0	0	0	2	0	5.0	4	23	2	2	0	0	0	0	6	0	4	1	0
Lozado, Henry, Orioles	1	3	.250	3.38	14	1	0	0	6	0	29.1	32	134	16	11	0	1	0	2	15	1	24	6	1
Lugo, Jorge, Dodgers *	0	0	.000	9.00	1	0	0	0	0	0	1.0	1	4	1	1	0	0	1	0	0	0	1	0	1
Lybarger, Craig, Marlins *	2	1	.667	5.73	7	0	0	0	3	0	11.0	15	53	8	7	0	1	0	1	3	0	15	0	0
Mallett, Justin, Reds	0	2	.000	8.35	12	1	0	0	4	0	18.1	26	103	21	17	0	1	3	3	16	2	20	0	1
Marquetti, Agustin, Pirates	0	1	.000	8.25	8	0	0	0	2	0	12.0	13	62	14	11	0	1	1	0	12	0	9	0	0
Martinez, Carlos, Marlins	1	0	1.000	0.00	3	0	0	0	3	1	6.1	1	20	0	0	0	0	0	0	1	0	2	0	0

Pitcher, Team	W	L	Pct.	ERA	G	GS	CG	ShO	GF	Sv.	IP	H	TBF	R	ER	HR	SH	SF	HB	BB	IBB	SO	WP	Bk.
Martinez, Cristhian, Tigers	3	2	.600	5.86	9	5	0	0	2	0	35.1	34	155	25	23	9	0	1	3	11	0	39	1	0
Martinez, Javier, Twins *	3	3	.500	2.03	12	10	0	0	0	0	62.0	43	252	19	14	2	2	0	5	21	0	54	5	2
Martinez, Samuel, Expos	0	1	.000	10.80	3	0	0	0	2	1	3.1	2	16	4	4	0	0	0	1	3	0	3	1	0
Maruffi, Joseph, Expos	0	0	.000	0.00	3	0	0	0	3	2	3.0	0	9	0	0	0	0	0	0	0	0	4	0	0
Mason, Robert, Braves *	0	0	.000	0.00	1	1	0	0	0	0	1.0	1	5	2	0	0	0	0	0	0	0	2	2	0
Mateo, Aneudis, Red Sox	0	0	.000	1.80	2	2	0	0	0	0	5.0	4	18	1	1	0	0	0	0	0	0	6	0	0
Mathieson, Scott, Phillies	2	7	.222	5.52	11	11	0	0	0	0	58.2	59	257	42	36	5	1	3	1	13	0	51	4	0
Mauer, William, Twins	3	1	.750	1.71	15	0	0	0	4	0	21.0	13	89	6	4	0	1	1	0	10	0	18	0	0
McAdam, Scott, Expos	3	2	.600	4.76	16	1	0	0	9	0	22.2	29	106	18	12	2	2	1	5	9	0	12	2	0
McClendon, Matt, Braves	0	0	.000	4.15	3	3	0	0	0	0	4.1	4	20	2	2	1	0	0	0	4	0	3	0	0
McConnell, Brandon, Twins	3	3	.500	4.60	11	9	0	0	1	0	43.0	53	206	31	22	2	4	2	4	22	0	40	6	1
McCormack, Zach, Marlins *	0	0	.000	0.00	4	0	0	0	2	0	6.1	1	21	1	0	0	0	1	0	1	0	6	0	0
McDonald, James, Dodgers	2	4	.333	3.33	12	9	0	0	0	0	48.2	39	199	20	18	3	1	0	6	15	0	47	3	0
Medina, Julio, Reds	2	2	.500	2.84	12	1	0	0	5	2	31.2	24	131	12	10	0	1	0	3	9	1	27	0	1
Medlock, Calvin, Reds	0	0	.000	0.00	3	0	0	0	0	0	5.0	5	21	1	0	0	2	0	0	0	0	3	1	0
Mendez, Wimer, Orioles	5	1	.833	1.52	12	9	0	0	3	0	53.1	42	215	13	9	0	2	0	0	17	0	41	2	1
Mendoza, Luis, Red Sox	0	0	.000	0.00	2	2	0	0	0	0	5.0	4	19	0	0	0	0	0	1	0	0	3	0	0
Mendoza, Ramiro, Red Sox	0	0	.000	0.00	2	2	0	0	0	0	7.0	3	24	0	0	0	0	0	1	0	0	4	0	0
Meque, Jacobo, Reds *	0	0	.000	2.25	2	2	0	0	0	0	4.0	2	15	1	1	0	0	0	0	2	0	3	0	0
Merricks, Alexander, Twins *	0	2	.000	10.80	15	1	0	0	6	0	15.0	13	95	21	18	0	0	0	2	37	0	14	14	1
Michael, Mark, Pirates	1	0	1.000	2.10	13	0	0	0	11	6	25.2	14	93	7	6	2	0	0	2	7	0	32	1	0
Miner, Josh, Marlins	0	3	.000	7.58	11	1	0	0	2	1	19.0	32	96	18	16	1	2	2	1	9	2	11	2	0
Molleken, Dustin, Pirates	0	0	.000	5.68	3	1	0	0	1	0	6.1	6	24	4	4	1	0	2	0	1	0	1	1	0
Montalbano, Greg, Red Sox *	0	0	.000	3.09	3	3	0	0	0	0	11.2	8	49	4	4	0	0	1	1	7	0	6	0	0
Moore, Benjamin, Yankees	1	0	1.000	1.42	4	0	0	0	2	0	6.1	4	26	2	1	1	0	0	1	2	1	9	0	0
Morales, Alex, Expos	1	1	.500	0.90	6	0	0	0	2	1	10.0	10	40	4	1	0	0	0	0	1	0	10	1	1
Munoz, Luis, Pirates	2	1	.667	4.89	9	5	2	0	1	0	38.2	38	167	23	21	5	0	1	1	11	0	29	3	2
Nestor, Scott, Marlins	4	1	.800	2.49	12	0	0	0	4	0	25.1	20	115	11	7	0	2	0	2	16	0	27	3	0
Nickerson, Jon-Michael, Mar.*	5	1	.833	1.87	12	12	1	1	0	0	53.0	36	218	15	11	1	0	3	4	23	0	50	4	0
Nieves, Roberto, Braves	1	0	1.000	0.00	1	0	0	0	0	0	2.0	1	8	0	0	0	0	0	0	1	0	2	0	0
Noriega, Luis, Reds	3	4	.429	3.24	9	9	0	0	0	0	41.2	30	172	17	15	1	1	1	5	20	0	42	2	1
Nunez, Francisco, Twins	5	1	.833	0.31	20	0	0	0	8	1	28.2	21	110	4	1	0	1	0	3	3	0	28	2	0
O'Flaherty, Liam, Dodgers *	3	1	.750	1.55	15	2	0	0	4	2	40.2	33	164	13	7	1	2	2	3	12	0	24	0	0
Obispo, Jose, Dodgers	2	3	.400	3.83	9	8	0	0	0	0	40.0	32	171	23	17	2	0	0	3	21	0	42	10	0
Ochoa, Harry, Phillies *	4	2	.667	2.65	15	1	0	0	8	0	37.1	35	163	15	11	0	2	2	1	14	0	29	2	0
Ochoa, Nehomar, Expos	2	2	.500	2.19	9	9	0	0	0	0	49.1	37	203	15	12	3	0	0	5	19	1	29	2	0
Ohalek, Corey, Marlins *	0	1	.000	5.32	14	0	0	0	7	1	22.0	28	97	15	13	0	0	0	2	2	0	22	2	0
Ojeda, Alvis, Dodgers	4	0	1.000	1.81	21	1	0	0	12	2	44.2	39	180	14	9	3	2	2	2	10	0	35	5	0
Orozco, Antonio, Marlins	0	2	.000	1.57	4	4	0	0	0	0	23.0	16	85	4	4	0	0	1	0	3	0	16	0	1
Orozco, Dernier, Red Sox	4	2	.667	6.07	14	0	0	0	4	0	29.2	42	136	25	20	1	2	1	3	4	0	21	7	2
Ortega, Joel, Pirates	4	1	.800	1.54	10	0	0	0	3	0	23.1	19	100	5	4	2	0	1	1	7	1	22	0	0
Osuna, Antonio, Yankees	0	0	.000	0.00	1	1	0	0	0	0	1.0	1	4	0	0	0	0	0	0	0	0	2	0	0
Overman, Matt, Marlins	1	1	.500	1.71	6	3	0	0	2	0	21.0	13	80	5	4	1	0	0	0	5	0	21	5	0
Pascual, Juan, Orioles	1	2	.333	3.81	14	1	0	0	3	0	28.1	31	133	21	12	0	0	1	3	15	2	19	5	1
Payano, Nelson, Braves *	0	0	.000	6.75	13	0	0	0	4	0	13.1	15	64	10	10	1	0	0	0	10	0	17	4	0
Pearson, Kyle, Pirates	3	2	.600	2.05	7	4	0	0	1	0	26.1	26	113	9	6	0	0	0	0	10	0	25	1	0
Pelland, Tyler, R. Sox-Reds *	3	4	.429	1.51	12	9	0	0	0	0	41.2	29	176	12	7	0	1	3	3	18	0	35	1	0
Penn, Hayden, Orioles	0	0	.000	2.70	1	1	0	0	0	0	3.1	3	13	1	1	0	0	1	0	1	0	4	0	0
Perez, Aneudy A., Reds	3	1	.750	5.06	13	0	0	0	1	0	26.2	36	133	23	15	2	0	2	4	17	1	17	4	3
Person, Robert, Red Sox	0	0	.000	0.00	1	1	0	0	0	0	3.0	2	12	0	0	0	1	0	0	2	0	4	1	0
Petrick, Russell, Orioles *	0	0	.000	11.57	2	0	0	0	0	0	2.1	3	13	4	3	0	0	0	0	2	0	2	2	0
Plummer, Jarod, Dodgers	0	0	.000	2.25	2	2	0	0	0	0	4.0	3	16	2	1	0	0	0	0	1	0	4	1	1
Polanco, Dionicio, Yankees	0	1	.000	81.00	1	0	0	0	0	0	0.1	3	7	4	3	0	0	0	0	3	1	1	1	0
Potoczny, Robert, Dodgers	2	5	.286	2.79	16	7	0	0	2	1	51.2	45	224	25	16	1	2	5	3	26	0	29	4	0
Quijada, Fernando, Phillies	2	4	.333	6.23	17	0	0	0	13	3	34.2	48	172	29	24	2	4	3	3	18	3	33	2	0
Rainwater, Josh, Tigers	1	2	.333	4.78	10	9	0	0	1	0	37.2	41	177	23	20	4	1	1	5	20	0	40	1	1
Ramirez, Luis, Orioles	6	4	.600	2.12	12	11	0	0	1	0	59.1	45	233	17	14	2	1	1	1	14	1	76	1	1
Ramirez, Wandar, Twins	1	0	1.000	6.43	17	0	0	0	3	1	21.0	20	101	17	15	4	1	0	6	14	0	20	4	0
Reyes, Jojo, Braves *	5	3	.625	2.56	11	10	0	0	0	0	45.2	34	181	16	13	1	0	0	1	14	0	55	3	0
Reynolds, Eric, Marlins *	0	0	.000	2.45	4	1	0	0	2	0	7.1	6	32	2	2	0	0	0	1	4	0	10	2	0
Rice, Leonard, Reds *	2	3	.400	2.61	13	6	0	0	3	1	41.1	36	168	15	12	2	2	0	0	11	1	45	3	0
Rodriguez, Cristobal, Expos	0	0	.000	0.00	2	0	0	0	1	0	3.0	1	9	0	0	0	0	0	0	0	0	3	0	0
Rodriguez, Jose, Expos	0	1	.000	4.50	3	0	0	0	0	0	6.0	6	24	3	3	1	0	0	0	0	0	9	0	0
Rodriguez, Juan, Pirates	1	0	1.000	0.96	5	0	0	0	5	3	9.1	3	35	1	1	1	1	0	0	2	0	15	0	0
Rodriguez, Osvaldo, Dodgers	0	0	.000	1.17	6	6	0	0	0	0	23.0	12	92	5	3	0	2	1	2	7	0	27	4	1
Rosario, Eduardo, Braves *	2	5	.286	3.97	12	11	0	0	0	0	45.1	51	190	25	20	2	1	1	2	14	0	37	1	0
Russ, James, Marlins	1	2	.333	1.63	11	7	0	0	2	1	49.2	33	190	12	9	2	0	0	2	15	0	46	1	1
Russell, Eddie, Marlins	0	0	.000	2.25	2	0	0	0	0	0	4.0	4	17	2	1	1	0	0	0	1	0	1	0	0
Russell, James, Expos	0	1	.000	6.00	9	0	0	0	4	0	15.0	17	70	12	10	0	0	0	2	9	1	15	1	0
Samuels, Matthew, Twins	0	0	.000	6.41	18	0	0	0	4	0	19.2	30	99	19	14	3	0	2	2	7	0	10	1	0
Sandoval, Francisco, Expos	3	3	.500	4.20	13	3	0	0	4	1	40.2	43	180	22	19	1	1	3	5	15	0	23	0	0
Santander, Nelson, Phillies	1	0	1.000	6.00	5	2	0	0	1	0	18.0	27	88	15	12	1	0	1	1	6	0	11	2	0
Santiago, Jose, Braves	0	2	.000	1.52	16	0	0	0	9	3	23.2	13	92	5	4	0	0	2	3	6	0	28	2	1
Sborz, Jay, Tigers	0	2	.000	4.85	8	7	0	0	0	0	26.0	20	117	18	14	2	0	1	4	14	0	35	6	0
Schultz, Cory, Phillies	1	1	.500	1.04	11	0	0	0	9	5	17.1	9	64	4	2	0	0	0	1	2	0	13	2	0
Segovia, Omar, Reds *	3	1	.750	3.83	10	10	0	0	0	0	44.2	44	205	29	19	1	2	3	6	19	1	34	5	0
Segovia, Zach, Phillies	0	1	.000	4.00	5	4	0	0	0	0	9.0	8	35	5	4	0	0	0	1	0	0	6	0	0
Shaffar, Ben, Pirates	1	0	1.000	3.27	5	0	0	0	0	0	11.0	12	48	5	4	0	0	0	1	1	0	12	1	0
Shinskie, David, Twins	1	4	.200	7.41	5	5	0	0	0	0	17.0	20	84	18	14	0	1	4	1	10	0	13	0	2
Simas, Bill, Dodgers	0	0	.000	4.50	1	1	0	0	0	0	2.0	1	8	1	1	0	0	0	0	1	0	1	1	0
Skinner, Andrew, Reds	1	2	.333	4.86	13	0	0	0	4	1	16.2	27	79	10	9	1	2	1	0	8	0	8	3	0
Smit, Alexander, Twins *	3	0	1.000	1.18	8	7	0	0	0	0	38.0	19	146	8	5	0	1	0	3	20	0	40	4	0
Smith, Chris, Red Sox	0	2	.000	6.48	3	2	0	0	0	0	8.1	11	39	8	6	0	0	0	0	4	0	3	1	0
Smith, Dan, Braves *	6	0	1.000	1.91	13	0	0	0	7	1	28.1	22	117	7	6	2	0	2	2	8	0	35	2	0
Smith, Dustin, Tigers	3	0	1.000	1.82	6	5	1	1	0	0	34.2	17	131	8	7	3	0	0	1	6	0	39	0	0
Smith, Jason, Yankees	1	0	1.000	0.00	3	0	0	0	1	0	4.0	2	14	0	0	0	0	0	0	1	0	5	0	0
Smith, Jason, Red Sox	0	0	.000	3.86	1	1	0	0	0	0	2.1	2	11	1	1	0	0	0	1	1	0	2	1	0

Pitcher, Team	W	L	Pct.	ERA	G	GS	CG	ShO	GF	Sv.	IP	H	TBF	R	ER	HR	SH	SF	HB	BB	IBB	SO	WP	Bk.
Soriano, Alexander, Red Sox *	2	1	.667	4.07	14	0	0	0	8	0	24.1	19	103	12	11	1	2	1	0	14	0	20	2	0
Soriano, Wally, Reds	0	0	.000	0.00	3	0	0	0	2	0	4.1	2	17	0	0	0	0	0	0	4	0	3	0	0
Sosa, Gabriel, Expos *	1	4	.200	3.80	12	6	0	0	0	0	45.0	38	193	26	19	1	0	0	2	19	0	38	3	6
Soto, Edgar, Yankees *	1	2	.333	3.31	10	7	0	0	0	0	35.1	35	154	18	13	3	1	0	0	13	0	40	0	2
Soto, Reyes, Dodgers	2	2	.500	2.80	14	3	0	0	3	2	35.1	20	145	15	11	1	0	0	2	23	0	29	3	0
Stanley, Adam, Braves *	1	0	1.000	3.96	16	0	0	0	2	0	25.0	35	123	15	11	2	0	0	0	15	0	20	2	0
Starling, Wardell, Pirates	4	1	.800	3.94	11	11	0	0	0	0	48.0	47	210	23	21	5	0	1	6	13	0	52	1	0
Stephens, Jason, Yankees	0	2	.000	4.55	10	3	1	0	3	1	31.2	42	142	20	16	1	1	3	3	9	0	25	1	0
Stevens, Jake, Braves *	3	4	.429	2.87	14	6	0	0	1	0	47.0	49	209	23	15	2	2	3	1	16	0	47	4	1
Stuart, Cory, Yankees	0	0	.000	0.00	1	1	0	0	0	0	2.0	2	8	0	0	0	0	0	0	0	0	3	0	0
Sulbaran, Orlando, Reds	0	0	.000	9.00	1	0	0	0	1	0	1.0	1	5	1	1	0	0	0	0	1	0	1	0	0
Sutton, Zach, Orioles	0	0	.000	0.00	2	0	0	0	2	0	2.0	2	8	1	0	0	0	0	0	0	0	2	0	0
Tate, Matt, Orioles	3	0	1.000	3.26	9	0	0	0	4	1	19.1	14	80	7	7	1	0	1	2	10	0	10	2	0
Tejada, Luis, Pirates	1	2	.333	9.15	7	0	0	0	4	1	20.2	37	106	26	21	3	1	3	1	8	0	4	2	0
Tequida, Mauricio, Dodgers	0	4	.000	2.49	13	0	0	0	9	6	21.2	22	91	7	6	1	2	0	1	2	1	16	1	0
Thomas, Brad, Twins *	0	0	.000	0.00	2	2	0	0	0	0	10.0	6	38	0	0	0	1	0	0	1	0	12	0	0
Thompson, Daryl, Expos	1	2	.333	2.15	12	10	0	0	1	0	46.0	49	185	16	11	1	2	0	2	11	0	18	2	0
Torborg, Jesse, Phillies	0	0	.000	0.00	1	0	0	0	1	0	0.1	0	5	0	0	0	0	0	0	2	0	0	0	0
Valdez, Argelis, Red Sox	0	0	.000	4.50	2	0	0	0	1	0	2.0	3	10	2	1	0	0	0	0	0	0	1	2	0
Valera, Luis, Reds	0	1	.000	0.00	7	0	0	0	3	1	8.0	10	35	1	0	0	0	0	1	3	0	7	0	0
Vanden Hurk, Henricus, Mar.	2	6	.250	5.35	11	10	0	0	0	0	38.2	49	190	30	23	2	3	1	7	20	0	30	4	3
Vasquez, Sendy, Tigers	2	2	.500	7.47	11	1	0	0	2	0	15.2	18	77	13	13	0	2	0	2	11	1	12	3	1
Villalona, Guillermo, Yankees	1	2	.333	3.94	8	5	0	0	0	0	29.2	35	136	18	13	1	0	0	1	9	1	20	0	0
Wang, Chien-ming, Yankees	0	0	.000	0.00	1	1	0	0	0	0	3.0	2	11	0	0	0	0	0	0	0	0	2	0	0
Weeden, Brandon, Yankees	2	0	1.000	1.73	7	4	0	0	1	0	26.0	17	106	10	5	0	0	1	4	9	0	21	2	0
Wheldon, Rhys, Twins	0	2	.000	8.15	5	4	0	0	0	0	17.2	26	86	18	16	1	1	1	0	6	1	14	4	0
White, Gabe, Yankees *	0	0	.000	0.00	1	1	0	0	0	0	1.0	0	4	0	0	0	0	0	0	1	0	1	0	0
White, Scott, Reds	1	2	.333	4.91	12	4	0	0	2	1	33.0	31	143	21	18	1	3	0	3	14	1	28	4	0
Wideman, Aaron, Expos *	2	4	.333	2.01	10	8	0	0	1	1	40.1	37	163	13	9	1	0	3	4	7	0	37	2	0
Wilson, Jonathan, Red Sox	0	2	.000	1.76	10	7	0	0	0	0	30.2	30	131	12	6	1	0	1	0	10	0	18	1	0
Wilson, Joseph, Phillies *	4	2	.667	2.24	11	9	0	0	0	0	52.1	44	220	20	13	1	0	2	3	17	0	58	2	0
Wright, Dequam, Dodgers *	3	1	.750	3.58	14	5	0	0	1	0	37.2	37	157	15	15	1	0	0	1	19	0	26	4	0
Wright, Isaiah, Expos	1	3	.250	5.40	11	6	0	0	1	1	33.1	38	154	22	20	1	1	1	11	16	1	12	10	1

PITCHERS WITH TWO OR MORE TEAMS

Pitcher, Team	W	L	Pct.	ERA	G	GS	CG	ShO	GF	Sv.	IP	H	TBF	R	ER	HR	SH	SF	HB	BB	IBB	SO	WP	Bk.
Pelland, Tyler, Reds *	0	0	.000	0.00	1	1	0	0	0	0	2.2	3	11	0	0	0	0	0	0	0	0	1	1	0
Pelland, Tyler, Red Sox *	3	4	.429	1.62	11	8	0	0	0	0	39.0	26	165	12	7	0	1	3	3	18	0	34	0	0

COMBINATION SHUTOUTS: Braves (6)—Reyes-Dewar-Smith-Anderson-Candelario, Rosario-Smith-Stanley-Anderson, Bacot-Harrison-Anderson, Capellan-Payano-Smith, Harrison-Bacot-Smith, Stevens-Stanley-Anderson-Bale. Dodgers (5)—McDonald-Ojeda-Garrison-Tequida, McDonald-Castillo-Tequida, Garcia-O'Flaherty-Tequida, Rodriguez-McDonald-Garcia, Castillo-Soto-Potoczny. Expos (4)—Goodman-C. Rodriguez, Ochoa-Henderson-Wideman, Ochoa-Jenkins, Sosa-Wright. Marlins (4)—Vanden Hurk-Lybarger-Bartlett-Cillo, Orozco-Nestor-Brito, Overman-Russ, Iehl-Humen-Martinez. Orioles (7)—Bartlett-Ramirez, Lozado-Tate-Burch, Bedard-Childs-Lozado, Bedard-Mendez, Ramirez-Brnardic, Brocato-Fleming, Ramirez-Hernandez-Mendez. Phillies (3)—Doble-Jimenez, Wilson-Honsa, Doble-Honsa. Pirates (4)—Nunez-Arias, Johnson-Hummel, Starling-Ortega-Rodriguez, Starling-Cedeno. Reds (4)—George-White, Noriega-Valera, White-Valera-Mallett-Medina-Borsa, Rice-Skinner-Valera. Red Sox (9)—R. Mendoza-Pelland-Hilario-Galvez, Garcia-Orozco, Montalbano-Guanchez-Galvez, Frias-Wilson-Elfeldt, Pelland-Orozco, Wilson-Borland-Aybar, Hilario-Kaercher-Guanchez, Jackson-Elfeldt-Guanchez, Mendoza-Frias-Blackley. Tigers (2)—Martinez-Rainwater, Kirsten-Herrera-Delacruz. Twins (4)—Smit-Koch-Bowlin-Nunez-Ramirez, Martinez-Ramirez-Nunez-Lankford-Killion-Bowlin, Martinez-Jones-Bowlin, Smit-Koch. Yankees (5)—Villalona-DeLaRosa-Bonecio-Kemlo, Gomez-Cowan, Wang-Henn-Knox, Weeden-Clippard, Soto-Knox.

NO-HIT GAMES: Nickerson, Marlins, defeated Braves, 6-0 (second game), August 15.

2003 FIELDING

TEAM

Team	G	PO	A	E	TC	DP	TP	PB	Pct.
Braves	60	1584	612	77	2273	49	0	11	.966
Expos	58	1451	632	76	2159	57	0	13	.965
Orioles	60	1495	574	78	2147	47	0	16	.964
Red Sox	59	1493	662	82	2237	54	0	14	.963
Yankees	57	1452	548	78	2078	41	0	6	.962
Reds	60	1509	635	90	2234	48	0	8	.960
Dodgers	60	1542	679	94	2315	63	0	19	.959
Twins	59	1503	560	91	2154	49	0	18	.958
Marlins	58	1488	562	92	2142	50	0	7	.957
Pirates	56	1456	523	91	2070	57	0	4	.956
Tigers	57	1424	552	112	2088	38	0	17	.946
Phillies	56	1389	517	111	2017	34	0	12	.945

INDIVIDUAL

FIRST BASEMEN

NOTE: All caps denotes fielding-percentage leader based on 30 games for catchers, 40 for all other non-pitchers and 48 innings for pitchers. *Throws lefthanded.

Player, Team	Pct.	G	PO	A	E	TC	DP
Alcala, Arian, Red Sox	.941	3	15	1	1	17	0
Alvarado, Wellington, Phillies	.985	39	319	8	5	332	24
Araque, Tulio, Reds	1.000	1	13	0	0	13	2
Avila, Denny, Reds	1.000	1	0	1	0	1	0
Baker, Jordan, Marlins *	.983	39	333	14	6	353	33
Blanton, Stephen, Orioles	.968	4	29	1	1	31	0
Boone, Doug, Yankees	1.000	1	1	0	0	1	0
Carlin, Michael, Pirates	.977	27	200	14	5	219	22
Chavez, Dirimo, Red Sox	1.000	3	26	2	0	28	1
Ciofrone, Peter, Red Sox	.973	11	97	12	3	112	8
Concepcion, Alberto, Red Sox	1.000	2	10	0	0	10	0
Conley, Evan, Reds	1.000	3	24	1	0	25	3
Corro, Abdiel, Expos	1.000	4	22	2	0	24	1
Coste, Chris, Red Sox	1.000	4	42	7	0	49	3
Costello, Michael, Orioles	.989	33	247	18	3	268	25
Crosland, Jason, Phillies	.962	6	24	1	1	26	1
Cucinotta, Robert, Red Sox	.974	8	70	4	2	76	6
Eichas, Keith, Braves	1.000	16	132	7	0	139	7
Fox, Chad, Expos	.980	6	44	5	1	50	7
Gredvig, Doug, Orioles	.867	2	12	1	2	15	1
Gutierrez, Juan, Orioles	1.000	18	134	5	0	139	7
Gutierrez, Tonys, Reds *	.987	40	366	25	5	396	21
Guzman, Heriberto, Red Sox	.973	14	100	7	3	110	10
Hamisevicz, Victor, Expos *	.990	46	395	21	4	420	37
Jarvis, Andrew, Phillies *	1.000	17	141	8	0	149	7
Lopez, Javier, Twins	1.000	9	66	4	0	70	9
Magness, Pat, Marlins	1.000	1	4	0	0	4	0
Mattingly, Taylor, Yankees	1.000	12	69	1	0	70	5
McGriff, Fred, Dodgers *	1.000	1	7	0	0	7	1
Mendez, Rafael, Tigers	.983	43	376	18	7	401	22
Michelsen, Ross, Yankees *	.983	9	55	3	1	59	2
MORETA, CARLOS, Braves	.991	49	403	21	4	428	31
Patrick, Sean, Orioles	.939	4	28	3	2	33	3
Perez, Koby, Red Sox	.971	7	63	3	2	68	6
Piantek, Kurtis, Tigers	.984	16	113	8	2	123	10
Pignatiello, Bret, Expos	1.000	6	59	5	0	64	2
Pulley, Matthew, Orioles	.857	4	11	1	2	14	1

Player, Team	Pct.	G	PO	A	E	TC	DP
Rea, Brad, Pirates	.975	31	264	13	7	284	29
Restko, J.T., Marlins	.982	22	148	17	3	168	15
Rohan, Jimmy, Dodgers	1.000	11	76	10	0	86	9
Romero, Luis, Yankees	.984	30	244	9	4	257	19
Sanchez, Carlos, Reds	1.000	4	14	0	0	14	1
Schwab, Daniel, Yankees *	.979	15	85	7	2	94	10
Sulbaran, Orlando, Reds	.988	9	71	9	1	81	6
Sutherland, David, Dodgers *	.988	51	470	26	6	502	47
Urgelles, Jeff, Reds	.913	3	17	4	2	23	4
White, Scott, Red Sox	1.000	14	128	4	0	132	11
Winfree, David, Twins	.983	17	109	8	2	119	3
Wong, Travis, Reds	.980	5	43	5	1	49	6
Woodard, Johnny, Twins	.962	36	319	13	13	345	29
Zapata, Jose, Orioles	.857	3	6	0	1	7	0

SECOND BASEMEN

Player, Team	Pct.	G	PO	A	E	TC	DP
Abreu, Etanislao, Dodgers	.944	36	89	95	11	195	27
Aguilar, Trino, Phillies	.962	18	32	43	3	78	10
Alcala, Arian, Red Sox	1.000	2	0	10	0	10	0
Avila, Denny, Reds	.951	24	35	42	4	81	13
Bastardo, Frederick, Marlins	1.000	4	2	3	0	5	0
Bawden, Thomas, Red Sox	.978	13	16	29	1	46	5
Castillo, Osmar, Red Sox	1.000	4	10	6	0	16	1
Castro, Francisco, Tigers	.949	43	74	95	9	178	20
Castro, Ofilio, Expos	1.000	3	8	9	0	17	2
Chavez, Dirimo, Red Sox	.989	19	32	57	1	90	14
Ciofrone, Peter, Red Sox	.936	21	35	38	5	78	10
Conley, Evan, Reds	.969	33	54	72	4	130	13
Contreras, Jose, Expos	.889	6	7	9	2	18	2
Cuevas, Phillip, Phillies	.947	17	22	50	4	76	3
Denker, Travis, Dodgers	.988	15	34	46	1	81	8
Franco, Luis, Marlins	.864	9	11	8	3	22	1
Golindano, Jesus, Dodgers	1.000	2	0	2	0	2	0
Gonzalez, Hector, Yankees	.929	8	10	16	2	28	1
Guerrero, Francisco, Orioles	.714	1	1	4	2	7	0
Italiano, Nicholas, Phillies	.946	29	44	62	6	112	9
Kalin, Travis, Twins	.912	21	25	27	5	57	10
Keown, Clint, Reds	1.000	1	1	1	0	2	0
Laurin, Dominique, Dodgers	1.000	3	10	6	0	16	3
Made, Hector, Yankees	.933	2	7	7	1	15	3
Mejia, Gilberto, Tigers	.932	8	22	33	4	59	2
Melendez, Alcides, Orioles	.964	35	56	78	5	139	18
Mitchell, Russell, Dodgers	.977	10	22	21	1	44	6
Nieves, Raul, Red Sox	1.000	1	1	3	0	4	1
Nunez, Eduardo, Expos	.950	19	37	39	4	80	13
Nunez, Tirzon, Expos	1.000	2	6	6	0	12	2
Ovalles, Jose, Expos	.942	32	66	81	9	156	15
Patino, Jorge, Tigers	.975	7	17	22	1	40	6
Pattee, Benjamin, Twins	.939	11	13	18	2	33	5
Petersen, Ryan, Red Sox	1.000	2	2	5	0	7	1
Piste, Carlos, Orioles	.967	19	26	33	2	61	4
Prado, Martin, Braves	.986	47	105	112	3	220	28
Ramos, Jason, Red Sox	1.000	2	1	5	0	6	0
Rodriguez, Rafael, Yankees	.965	44	75	92	6	173	20
Rogers, Tanner, Marlins	1.000	5	6	10	0	16	1
Rohan, Jimmy, Dodgers	1.000	2	2	2	0	4	0
Rutgers, Paul, Twins	.958	44	56	80	6	142	14
Sanchez, Carlos, Reds	.941	4	9	7	1	17	1
Sandoval, Mayker, Reds	.956	14	22	43	3	68	3
SEIFRIG, COLE, Marlins	.991	48	96	127	2	225	33
Smith, John, Pirates	.940	21	41	53	6	100	14
Solano, Solamdi, Pirates	.963	35	61	93	6	160	24
Sterner, George, Yankees	1.000	2	2	8	0	10	2
Stoecklein, Brian, Braves	.959	19	38	32	3	73	9
Unger, Adam, Yankees	.952	9	9	11	1	21	2
West, Eric, Red Sox	.917	5	9	13	2	24	2
Zapata, Jose, Orioles	1.000	15	18	20	0	38	6

THIRD BASEMEN

Player, Team	Pct.	G	PO	A	E	TC	DP
Almonte, Erick, Yankees	.833	2	1	4	1	6	1
Asprilla, Avelino, Pirates	1.000	4	4	11	0	15	1
Baez, Welinson, Phillies	.856	32	26	51	13	90	3
Barthel, Cole, Braves	1.000	9	3	10	0	13	0
Bastardo, Frederick, Marlins	.882	22	13	32	6	51	2
Bautista, Jose, Pirates	.929	5	5	8	1	14	2
Boone, Matt, Reds	.818	4	2	7	2	11	1
Boran, Patrick, Red Sox	.800	2	1	3	1	5	0
Castro, Francisco, Tigers	.200	2	0	1	4	5	0
Castro, Ofilio, Expos	.974	26	20	54	2	76	5
Chavez, Dirimo, Red Sox	.917	3	4	7	1	12	1
Conley, Evan, Reds	.938	7	4	11	1	16	0
Corro, Abdiel, Expos	1.000	2	1	2	0	3	1
Costello, Michael, Orioles	1.000	1	5	0	0	5	0
Crosland, Jason, Phillies	.947	6	4	14	1	19	2
Denker, Travis, Dodgers	.875	19	8	34	6	48	5
Duncan, Eric, Yankees	.898	40	23	65	10	98	4
Duncan, Eric, Yankees	.898	40	23	65	10	98	4
Durand, Alexander, Phillies	.500	1	0	1	1	2	0
Esparragoza, Eyoxy, Reds	.857	9	5	7	2	14	0
Fisher, Kiel, Phillies	.780	22	14	25	11	50	4
Franco, Ambiorix, Reds	.887	19	14	33	6	53	5
Franco, Luis, Marlins	.750	2	1	2	1	4	0
Gonzalez, Hector, Yankees	.889	15	3	29	4	36	2
Guerrero, Francisco, Orioles	1.000	2	1	1	0	2	0
Guzman, Heriberto, Red Sox	.935	32	18	68	6	92	4
Hernandez, Diory, Braves	.946	34	8	62	4	74	5
Hernandez, Habelito, Reds	.900	2	0	9	1	10	0
Hughes, Luke, Twins	.938	23	20	41	4	65	1
Laurin, Dominique, Dodgers	.895	6	3	14	2	19	4
Lebron, Edgardo, Twins	.941	10	9	7	1	17	1
Lopez, Javier, Twins	.886	11	7	24	4	35	1
Made, Hector, Yankees	1.000	2	0	1	0	1	0
Mejia, Gilberto, Tigers	1.000	2	1	6	0	7	2
Mitchell, Russell, Dodgers	.880	9	7	15	3	25	1
Moses, Matthew, Twins	.818	14	6	21	6	33	1
Nunez, Eduardo, Expos	.500	4	1	0	1	2	0
Nunez, Tirzon, Expos	.971	24	14	53	2	69	5
Piste, Carlos, Orioles	.933	13	14	14	2	30	3
Prado, Martin, Braves	.923	14	11	25	3	39	3
PULLEY, MATTHEW, Orioles	.898	45	22	66	10	98	6
Ramirez, Rafael, Pirates	.921	17	8	27	3	38	5
Ramirez, Wilkin, Tigers	.838	48	23	86	21	130	3
Restko, J.T., Marlins	.848	17	13	26	7	46	0
Rohan, Jimmy, Dodgers	.931	27	23	72	7	102	14
Romak, Jamie, Braves	.809	16	13	25	9	47	2
Rutgers, Paul, Twins	1.000	6	2	11	0	13	2
Saltalamacchia, Jarrod, Braves	1.000	1	0	1	0	1	1
Saltalamacchia, Justin, Braves	.800	5	1	3	1	5	0
Sanchez, Carlos, Reds	.931	27	10	44	4	58	6
Sandora, Robert, Expos	.923	5	2	10	1	13	0
Santiago, John, Pirates	.899	31	31	67	11	109	5
Seifrig, Cole, Marlins	.875	2	2	5	1	8	0
Solano, Solamdi, Pirates	1.000	3	3	9	0	12	0
Sosa, Pablo, Marlins	.889	19	13	27	5	45	6
Sterner, George, Yankees	1.000	2	1	3	0	4	0
Stevens, Anthony, Pirates	1.000	1	0	1	0	1	0
White, Scott, Red Sox	.984	25	18	44	1	63	7
Williams, Matt, Tigers	.700	10	3	11	6	20	1
Zapata, Jose, Orioles	.941	8	5	11	1	17	1

SHORTSTOPS

Player, Team	Pct.	G	PO	A	E	TC	DP
Abreu, Etanislao, Dodgers	1.000	7	3	19	0	22	2
Aguilar, Trino, Phillies	.917	7	9	13	2	24	1
Almonte, Erick, Yankees	.714	2	3	2	2	7	0
Alvarado, Wellington, Phillies	1.000	1	2	1	0	3	1
Asprilla, Avelino, Pirates	1.000	3	3	9	0	12	0
Aybar, Francisco, Phillies	.860	41	33	96	21	150	12
Baez, Welinson, Phillies	.926	6	8	17	2	27	5
Bastardo, Frederick, Marlins	1.000	4	6	7	0	13	3
Bawden, Thomas, Red Sox	.917	3	1	10	1	12	2
Castillo, Osmar, Red Sox	1.000	1	1	2	0	3	0
Castro, Nelson, Red Sox	.947	4	4	14	1	19	2
Castro, Ofilio, Expos	.952	11	18	41	3	62	3
Chavez, Dirimo, Red Sox	.927	12	11	40	4	55	4
Ciofrone, Peter, Red Sox	1.000	2	5	6	0	11	1
Conley, Evan, Reds	.951	21	17	60	4	81	9
Contreras, Jose, Expos	.940	38	47	111	10	168	24
Corro, Abdiel, Expos	1.000	1	1	1	0	2	1
Cuevas, Phillip, Phillies	.850	7	5	12	3	20	3
Desena, Francis, Expos	.886	9	10	21	4	35	2
Franco, Luis, Marlins	.750	4	2	7	3	12	0
Fulton, Jonathan, Marlins	.909	46	79	141	22	242	29
Fulton, Joshua, Pirates	.897	41	57	91	17	165	24
Gil, Luis, Tigers	.929	27	16	63	6	85	10
Gonzalez, Hector, Yankees	.833	1	1	4	1	6	0
Hernandez, Diory, Braves	.927	29	26	63	7	96	9
Hughes, Luke, Twins	.933	32	40	72	8	120	13
Johnson, Kelly, Braves	1.000	2	2	8	0	10	3
Kalin, Travis, Twins	1.000	1	1	0	0	1	0
Made, Hector, Yankees	.910	49	72	110	18	200	17
May, Lucas, Dodgers	.919	46	62	143	18	223	26

Player, Team	Pct.	G	PO	A	E	TC	DP
Mejia, Gilberto, Tigers	.909	23	30	50	8	88	8
Mendez, Deivi, Yankees	.958	4	7	16	1	24	4
Mitchell, Russell, Dodgers	1.000	2	2	4	0	6	0
Nieves, Raul, Red Sox	.900	5	6	12	2	20	3
Nunez, Eduardo, Expos	.900	8	13	32	5	50	3
Ortega, Raul, Braves	.900	43	41	85	14	140	11
Ortiz, Patrick, Twins	.915	28	38	59	9	106	13
Patino, Jorge, Tigers	.896	21	20	40	7	67	7
Penalo, Alexander, Red Sox	.881	32	41	70	15	126	13
Perez, Kenny, Red Sox	.765	7	6	20	8	34	2
Perez, Koby, Red Sox	.909	2	6	4	1	11	2
Piste, Carlos, Orioles	.950	7	14	24	2	40	5
Ramos, Jason, Red Sox	1.000	3	1	5	0	6	0
Rogers, Tanner, Marlins	.833	4	5	10	3	18	3
Rohan, Jimmy, Dodgers	.889	7	11	13	3	27	3
Ronda, Jose, Reds	.904	42	45	105	16	166	13
Rutgers, Paul, Twins	.917	9	14	19	3	36	6
Sanchez, Carlos, Reds	.875	2	2	5	1	8	0
Santiago, John, Pirates	1.000	1	1	4	0	5	2
Solano, Solamdi, Pirates	.917	3	4	7	1	12	3
SPEARS, NATHANIEL, Orioles	.934	49	75	124	14	213	22
Sterner, George, Yankees	.917	3	4	7	1	12	5
Stevens, Anthony, Pirates	.973	12	17	19	1	37	5
Tejeda, Ferdin, Yankees	.947	5	3	15	1	19	6
Zapata, Jose, Orioles	.929	11	12	27	3	42	4

OUTFIELDERS

Player, Team	Pct.	G	PO	A	E	TC	DP
Amador, Anderson, Yankees	.963	17	25	1	1	27	0
Andrus, Erold, Yankees *	1.000	3	6	0	0	6	0
Araque, Tulio, Reds	1.000	4	6	0	0	6	0
Arias, Garvi, Pirates	.974	22	37	0	1	38	0
Arias, Hector, Dodgers	.968	29	30	0	1	31	0
Arroyo, Xavier, Marlins	1.000	19	34	2	0	36	0
Baez, Edgardo, Expos	.963	32	48	4	2	54	2
Baker, Jordan, Marlins *	1.000	4	4	0	0	4	0
Barnes, Justin, Tigers	1.000	1	1	0	0	1	0
Barthel, Cole, Braves	1.000	5	8	0	0	8	0
Batista, Rafael, Expos	.960	25	42	6	2	50	3
Battle, Timothy, Yankees	.977	27	38	4	1	43	1
Belcher, Jordan, Reds	1.000	52	72	8	0	80	0
Berkenbosch, Kenny, Marlins	1.000	37	46	4	0	50	1
Bianucci, Anthony, Red Sox	.889	16	22	2	3	27	1
Bigbie, Larry, Orioles *	1.000	2	1	0	0	1	0
Billmaier, Kris, Tigers	.918	30	42	3	4	49	2
Boitel, Edwin, Red Sox	1.000	18	22	0	0	22	0
Cabrera, Edwin, Yankees	.968	45	58	2	2	62	0
Campusano, Luis, Twins	.944	14	16	1	1	18	1
Cardy, Edwal, Orioles	1.000	20	35	3	0	38	2
Carlin, Michael, Pirates	1.000	4	3	0	0	3	0
Cespedes, Osvaldo, Phillies	.984	40	59	1	1	61	0
Cobb, Maurice, Expos	.946	39	68	2	4	74	0
Corro, Abdiel, Expos	.972	22	32	3	1	36	0
Cronkhite, Ian, Red Sox *	.982	33	51	4	1	56	2
Crosland, Jason, Phillies	.936	23	43	1	3	47	0
Cuddyer, Michael, Twins	1.000	1	3	0	0	3	0
Davis, Zach, Orioles *	.989	42	84	5	1	90	3
De La Cruz, Carlos, Red Sox *	.984	38	63	0	1	64	0
Deeds, Doug, Twins *	1.000	3	11	0	0	11	0
Doetsch, Steve, Braves	1.000	59	139	4	0	143	1
Doetsch, Steve, Braves	1.000	59	139	4	0	143	1
Durand, Alexander, Phillies	.962	30	48	3	2	53	0
Eichas, Keith, Braves	1.000	1	1	0	0	1	0
Encarnacion, Salvador, Marlins	.800	5	4	0	1	5	0
Esparragoza, Eyoxy, Reds	.933	25	28	0	2	30	0
Ewen, Nicholas, Marlins	.958	25	45	1	2	48	0
Flowers, Bo, Tigers	.900	9	8	1	1	10	0
Fox, Chad, Expos	.800	5	3	1	1	5	0
Frank, Kyle, Yankees *	.941	15	31	1	2	34	0
Fulse, Sheldon, Red Sox	1.000	3	4	0	0	4	0
Garbe, B.J., Twins	1.000	8	13	2	0	15	0
Gray, Matthew, Reds *	1.000	53	95	4	0	99	3
Guerrero, Francisco, Orioles	1.000	2	2	1	0	3	1
Gutierrez, Tonys, Reds *	1.000	3	3	0	0	3	0
Hall, Mickey, Red Sox *	.938	16	30	0	2	32	0
Harris, Estee, Yankees	.960	21	21	3	1	25	0
Hawes, Don, Reds	1.000	1	1	0	0	1	0
Hicks, Joe, Pirates	.941	44	63	1	4	68	0
Howerton, Matt, Orioles	.978	41	86	3	2	91	0
Hummel, Richard, Orioles	.972	25	32	3	1	36	3
Jones, Larry, Twins	.978	26	42	3	1	46	1
Kemp, Matthew, Dodgers	.985	37	59	7	1	67	2
Keown, Clint, Reds	1.000	2	3	0	0	3	0
Klemm, Christopher, Phillies *	.941	38	45	3	3	51	0
Laster, Jeramy, Tigers	.952	37	59	1	3	63	1
Lewis, Kenneth, Reds *	.934	48	81	4	6	91	1
Lindesey, Juan, Marlins	.970	33	62	2	2	66	0
LOADENTHAL, CARL, Braves	1.000	58	96	5	0	101	2
Lopez, Javier, Twins	.929	34	64	1	5	70	1
Macia, Wanell, Pirates	.949	52	85	9	5	99	2
Majewski, Val, Orioles *	1.000	1	1	0	0	1	0
Marcos, Emilio, Dodgers	.953	42	78	3	4	85	1
Marmolejos, Hector, Orioles	.917	30	32	1	3	36	0
Mattingly, Taylor, Yankees	1.000	1	1	0	0	1	0
Miller, Jai, Marlins	.988	43	81	3	1	85	0
Moni-Erigbali, Timi, Phillies	.911	41	91	1	9	101	1
Morales, Leonardo, Pirates	.833	6	5	0	1	6	0
Moreta, Carlos, Braves	1.000	11	20	3	0	23	0
Ndungidi, Sambu, Dodgers	1.000	21	19	1	0	20	0
Nowak, David, Dodgers *	.960	22	24	0	1	25	0
Pattee, Benjamin, Twins	1.000	17	31	0	0	31	0
Patterson, Tarrence, Twins	1.000	45	93	2	0	95	1
Perez, Jose, Yankees *	.968	41	86	4	3	93	0
Perry, Rod, Phillies	1.000	1	2	0	0	2	0
Pierce, Sean, Dodgers	1.000	6	6	1	0	7	0
Ponce, Angel, Braves	.935	40	42	1	3	46	0
Powell, Pedro, Pirates	.961	22	47	2	2	51	1
Rigsby, Randy, Marlins *	1.000	1	2	0	0	2	0
Rodriguez, Rafael, Yankees	1.000	3	5	1	0	6	0
Rumsey, John, Twins	.985	40	61	3	1	65	0
Sabino, Luis, Tigers	.945	50	82	4	5	91	1
Saltalamacchia, Justin, Braves	1.000	9	7	0	0	7	0
Sandora, Robert, Expos	1.000	17	18	1	0	19	0
Sapp, Steven, Dodgers	.932	36	54	1	4	59	1
Scott, Lorenzo, Orioles *	.986	32	67	3	1	71	1
Sovie, Robbie, Tigers	.955	38	61	3	3	67	0
Stern, Adam, Braves	1.000	7	18	1	0	19	0
Stoecklein, Brian, Braves	1.000	1	1	0	0	1	0
Sucre, Antonio, Expos	.974	47	105	6	3	114	0
Summerville, Kaazim, Yankees	1.000	2	2	0	0	2	0
Torborg, Jesse, Phillies	.960	11	24	0	1	25	0
Turner, Christopher, Red Sox	.980	29	47	1	1	49	0
Unger, Adam, Yankees	1.000	2	1	1	0	2	0
Veloz, Vladimil, Marlins	.857	20	17	1	3	21	0
Williams, Devoris, Red Sox	.985	33	63	4	1	68	1
Williams, Matt, Tigers	.957	30	41	3	2	46	1
Winfree, David, Twins	.000	1	0	0	1	1	0
Woodard, Johnny, Twins	1.000	5	4	0	0	4	0
Wulf, Kent, Pirates	.980	30	48	0	1	49	0

CATCHERS

Player, Team	Pct.	G	PO	A	E	TC	DP	PB
Alen, Luis, Marlins	.949	6	53	3	3	59	1	0
Anderson, Heath, Twins	1.000	20	106	11	0	117	4	3
Apodaca, Luis, Expos	.980	32	164	31	4	199	4	4
Armstrong, Cole, Braves	.952	6	19	1	1	21	0	1
Barnes, Justin, Tigers	.988	28	151	16	2	169	2	10
Barnett, Toby, Phillies	.981	18	96	9	2	107	2	5
Boone, Doug, Yankees	.992	16	108	14	1	123	0	0
Brown, Gregory, Marlins	1.000	12	88	13	0	101	0	1
Cabrera, Ruben, Dodgers	.977	27	190	27	5	222	1	8
Coffey, Josh, Reds	1.000	5	18	0	0	18	0	2
Concepcion, Alberto, Red Sox	1.000	4	26	2	0	28	0	2
Coste, Chris, Red Sox	1.000	5	30	4	0	34	1	1
Cruz, Ramon, Braves	.982	14	45	9	1	55	1	1
De Los Santos, Edinson, Yank.	.991	26	194	29	2	225	0	2
Del Carmen, Jose, Orioles	.983	21	101	14	2	117	1	3
Ellis, Jason, Reds	.979	16	86	8	2	96	2	0
Golindano, Jesus, Dodgers	.973	25	92	18	3	113	0	4
Guerra, Junior, Braves	.966	26	96	19	4	119	2	2
Gutierrez, Juan, Orioles	.980	22	129	16	3	148	0	9
Hart, Randall, Pirates	.976	7	40	0	1	41	0	0
Hawes, Don, Reds	.961	8	64	9	3	76	1	3
House, J.R., Pirates	.984	9	60	1	1	62	1	0
Karlsen, Grant, Phillies	.982	23	149	15	3	167	1	1
Katotakis, James, Orioles	.950	8	19	0	1	20	0	1
Lambis, Alberto, Marlins	.969	23	169	19	6	194	0	4
Lee, Jonathan, Tigers	.970	11	28	4	1	33	0	3
Lopez, Mauber, Phillies	.981	25	133	25	3	161	1	6
Loyd, Brian, Red Sox	1.000	6	26	6	0	32	0	0
Marin, Daniel, Twins	1.000	1	5	4	0	9	0	0
Martinez, Edwin, Braves	1.000	7	34	6	0	40	0	2
McDonald, Kevin, Tigers	1.000	4	17	4	0	21	0	0
Mendez, Jose, Twins	.993	26	133	18	1	152	0	0
Montz, Luke, Expos	.967	17	83	6	3	92	3	5
Najac, Gregory, Twins	.952	15	73	7	4	84	4	11

Player, Team	Pct.	G	PO	A	E	TC	DP	PB
Nelson, Kevin, Yankees	.972	18	128	12	4	144	1	3
Nino, Denny, Pirates	.982	24	205	19	4	228	2	3
Owen, Ryan, Dodgers	1.000	3	12	0	0	12	0	0
Paniagua, Salvador, Red Sox	.982	26	150	16	3	169	1	4
Patrick, Sean, Orioles	.983	23	158	14	3	175	1	2
Perez, Koby, Red Sox	1.000	8	34	1	0	35	1	4
Pignatiello, Bret, Expos	.979	10	45	2	1	48	0	1
Poni, Francis, Pirates	.955	20	142	8	7	157	0	1
Roa, Joel, Tigers	.972	34	214	27	7	248	0	4
Rogers, Tanner, Marlins	.985	19	119	14	2	135	0	2
Rohena, Angel, Dodgers	.966	22	118	23	5	146	1	7
Romero, Luis, Yankees	1.000	4	52	2	0	54	1	1
Saltalamacchia, Jarrod, Braves	.971	36	237	35	8	280	1	5
Schartz, Lance, Red Sox	.977	8	35	8	1	44	1	0
Smith, Jeff, Red Sox	.978	7	40	4	1	45	1	1
Tintor, Eli, Twins	.964	18	99	8	4	111	2	4
URGELLES, JEFF, Reds	.993	40	250	29	2	281	1	3
Vankirk, Robert, Red Sox	1.000	8	39	5	0	44	1	2
Whiteside, Eli, Orioles	1.000	1	7	1	0	8	0	1
Wong, Ivanosky, Expos	1.000	7	36	4	0	40	1	3

PITCHERS

Player, Team	Pct.	G	PO	A	E	TC	DP
Aguero, Miguel, Yankees	.800	10	2	2	1	5	0
Alcala, Jason, Pirates	1.000	2	1	1	0	2	0
Allison, Jeffrey, Marlins	1.000	3	0	1	0	1	0
Alvarez, Carlos, Dodgers *	.889	22	2	6	1	9	2
Anderson, Devin, Braves *	1.000	18	4	4	0	8	0
Antigua, Erick, Yankees	1.000	2	1	2	0	3	0
Ascanio, Jose, Braves	.800	8	1	3	1	5	0
Atilano, Luis, Braves	1.000	12	5	11	0	16	0
Ayala, Luis, Expos	1.000	2	0	1	0	1	0
Aybar, Ismael, Red Sox *	1.000	10	0	4	0	4	0
Azze, Justin, Orioles *	1.000	2	1	0	0	1	0
Bacot, Paul, Braves	.889	9	2	6	1	9	0
Bale, Manuel, Braves	.875	19	0	7	1	8	0
Barrett, Ricky, Twins *	1.000	5	0	2	0	2	0
Bartlett, Greg, Marlins *	.800	15	1	3	1	5	0
Bartlett, Richard, Orioles	1.000	1	0	1	0	1	0
Batista, Gorky, Reds	.875	5	3	4	1	8	1
Bedard, Erik, Orioles *	1.000	3	1	1	0	2	0
Berger, Garrett, Marlins	1.000	14	1	0	0	1	0
Bernal, Christian, Reds	.500	2	0	1	1	2	0
Blackley, Adam, Red Sox *	1.000	7	2	7	0	9	0
Blankenship, Jon, Yankees *	1.000	7	1	1	0	2	0
Bolander, Matt, Orioles	1.000	6	0	1	0	1	0
Bonecio, Ryan, Yankees *	1.000	10	1	0	0	1	0
Booker, Chris, Reds	1.000	12	0	2	0	2	0
Borland, Curt, Red Sox	.875	13	2	5	1	8	0
Borsa, Robert, Reds	1.000	18	2	3	0	5	0
Bowlin, Jason, Twins	.875	20	3	4	1	8	1
Brazoban, Yhency, Yankees	1.000	3	1	1	0	2	0
Brito, Joel, Marlins	.941	12	8	8	1	17	0
Brnardic, Ryan, Orioles	.714	12	3	2	2	7	0
Brocato, Russell, Orioles	1.000	13	4	5	0	9	0
Bryant, Michael, Reds	1.000	13	2	2	0	4	0
Burch, Kevin, Orioles	.800	15	0	4	1	5	0
Cabrera, Nathan, Phillies	.500	5	0	1	1	2	0
Caceres, Carlos, Expos	1.000	2	2	4	0	6	1
Camacho, Gustavo, Orioles	1.000	10	1	5	0	6	0
Capellan, Jose, Braves	.917	5	5	6	1	12	0
Capps, Matt, Pirates	1.000	10	2	5	0	7	2
Caraballo, Angel, Yankees	1.000	6	1	2	0	3	0
Caraballo, Jesse, Tigers	1.000	16	1	5	0	6	0
Castillo, Albenis, Dodgers	.833	19	0	5	1	6	0
Castro, Randy, Reds	1.000	9	1	1	0	2	0
Cedeno, Blas, Pirates	1.000	9	1	1	0	2	0
Cerezo, Hector, Expos *	.900	14	2	7	1	10	1
Cerrato, Justin, Phillies	1.000	2	0	1	0	1	0
Childs, Ryan, Orioles	.941	12	4	12	1	17	0
Chrysler, Clint, Pirates *	.500	2	0	1	1	2	0
Cillo, Cody, Marlins	1.000	3	1	3	0	4	0
Clippard, Tyler, Yankees	.750	11	1	2	1	4	0
Coke, Phillip, Yankees *	1.000	10	1	2	0	3	0
Cortes, Jorge, Reds	1.000	2	0	2	0	2	0
Cowan, Richard, Yankees	1.000	13	0	3	0	3	0
Craig, Jonathan, Reds	.333	5	0	1	2	3	0
Cruz, Juan, Yankees	1.000	12	0	2	0	2	0
Cuffman, Jacob, Pirates	1.000	8	1	1	0	2	0
Davis, Lance, Marlins	1.000	1	1	0	0	1	0
Dean, Herman, Tigers	1.000	7	0	3	0	3	0
Delacruz, Eulogio, Tigers	.667	22	1	3	2	6	0
Dewar, Andrew, Braves *	.800	14	0	4	1	5	0
Doble, Clemente, Phillies	.750	10	2	4	2	8	1
Dolsi, Freddy, Tigers	.875	8	0	7	1	8	0
Duguay, Steven, Twins	1.000	16	5	8	0	13	0
Echarry, Nelson, Phillies	1.000	6	0	1	0	1	0
Elfeldt, Matthew, Red Sox	.500	8	1	1	2	4	0
Encarnacion, Luis, Phillies	.750	12	2	4	2	8	0
Eugenio, Mario, Tigers	1.000	17	3	4	0	7	0
Felix, Wilkin, Orioles	.750	16	0	3	1	4	0
Feliz, Ranier, Reds	1.000	10	3	12	0	15	0
Fischer, Eric, Twins *	1.000	2	0	1	0	1	0
Fleming, Travis, Orioles	1.000	9	0	1	0	1	0
Frias, Junior, Red Sox	1.000	10	3	6	0	9	0
Furrow, Jason, Orioles *	1.000	15	1	4	0	5	0
Galarraga, Armando, Expos	1.000	5	0	3	0	3	0
Galvez, Willy, Red Sox	.833	16	1	4	1	6	0
Garavito, Jean, Pirates	1.000	7	1	1	0	2	0
Garcia, Felipe, Tigers	1.000	11	5	3	0	8	0
Garcia, Harvey, Red Sox	.833	9	1	4	1	6	0
Garcia, Javier, Dodgers	1.000	14	3	6	0	9	0
Garrison, Kale, Dodgers *	.857	15	1	5	1	7	0
Gault, Joe, Twins	1.000	14	0	1	0	1	0
George, Jon, Reds	1.000	7	4	3	0	7	0
Gillman, Justin, Reds	1.000	3	2	1	0	3	0
Glynn, Josh, Marlins	.750	10	2	1	1	4	0
Golden, Michael, Reds	1.000	6	0	1	0	1	0
Gomez, Abel, Yankees *	1.000	11	1	6	0	7	0
Goodman, Chris, Expos	1.000	10	2	5	0	7	0
Guanchez, Argimiro, Red Sox *	1.000	18	3	4	0	7	0
Hacker, Eric, Yankees	1.000	7	2	5	0	7	0
Harrand, Rob, Phillies	1.000	2	0	1	0	1	0
Harrison, Matt, Braves *	.800	11	0	4	1	5	0
Hayes, Alvin, Dodgers	1.000	6	2	1	0	3	0
Henderson, Jim, Expos	1.000	4	1	1	0	2	0
Henn, Sean, Yankees *	1.000	2	0	3	0	3	0
Hernandez, Moises, Orioles	.667	8	3	1	2	6	0
Herrera, Jose, Tigers	.800	15	2	2	1	5	0
Hilario, Elpidio, Red Sox	.929	14	4	9	1	14	1
Hlebovy, Gus, Expos	1.000	12	2	2	0	4	0
Holliday, Brian, Pirates *	1.000	10	3	9	0	12	0
Honsa, Chris, Phillies	1.000	11	1	6	0	7	0
Humen, David, Marlins	1.000	12	1	4	0	5	0
Hummel, John, Pirates *	1.000	10	0	8	0	8	0
Iehl, Jason, Marlins	.833	7	0	5	1	6	0
Jackson, Kyle, Red Sox	1.000	12	2	10	0	12	0
Jenkins, Clyde, Expos	1.000	14	1	4	0	5	1
Jimenez, Elvis, Phillies	.889	16	2	6	1	9	0
Jimenez, Rodny, Braves	.778	16	4	3	2	9	0
Johnson, Blair, Pirates	1.000	9	1	3	0	4	0
Jones, K.C., Twins	1.000	15	1	6	0	7	2
Jumelles, Edduar, Reds	1.000	3	0	1	0	1	0
Jurrjens, Jair, Tigers	1.000	7	2	4	0	6	0
Kaercher, Matthew, Red Sox	1.000	6	2	3	0	5	0
Kamimura, Soichi, Marlins	1.000	5	1	2	0	3	0
Kemlo, Chris, Yankees	1.000	13	0	2	0	2	0
Kendrick, Kyle, Phillies	.875	9	3	4	1	8	1
Killion, Terry, Twins	1.000	16	1	2	0	3	0
Knox, Michael, Yankees	.000	10	0	0	1	1	0
Koch, Jonathon, Twins	1.000	12	1	5	0	6	2
Lankford, Kristofer, Twins	.667	15	1	3	2	6	0
Lara, Toni, Yankees *	.800	11	0	4	1	5	0
Lawson, Jarrod, Phillies	.500	4	0	1	1	2	0
Lehman, James, Expos	.667	12	0	2	1	3	0
Lewis, Lavon, Tigers	.889	11	2	6	1	9	0
Lieber, Jon, Yankees	1.000	2	2	1	0	3	0
Lozado, Henry, Orioles	1.000	14	3	8	0	11	0
Lybarger, Craig, Marlins *	1.000	7	1	2	0	3	0
Mallett, Justin, Reds	1.000	12	0	5	0	5	0
Marquetti, Agustin, Pirates	.800	8	2	2	1	5	0
Martinez, Carlos, Marlins	1.000	3	1	1	0	2	0
Martinez, Cristhian, Tigers	.857	9	4	2	1	7	0
Martinez, Javier, Twins *	.905	12	4	15	2	21	0
Martinez, Samuel, Expos	.500	3	0	1	1	2	0
Maruffi, Joseph, Expos	1.000	3	2	1	0	3	0
Mathieson, Scott, Phillies	.750	12	2	4	2	8	0
Mauer, William, Twins	1.000	15	0	4	0	4	0
McAdam, Scott, Expos	1.000	16	1	5	0	6	0
McConnell, Brandon, Twins	.846	11	0	11	2	13	1
McCormack, Zach, Marlins *	1.000	4	3	3	0	6	1
McDonald, James, Dodgers	1.000	12	5	8	0	13	1
Medina, Julio, Reds	.857	12	3	9	2	14	1
Medlock, Calvin, Reds	.500	3	1	0	1	2	0
MENDEZ, WIMER, Orioles	1.000	12	1	16	0	17	0

Player, Team	Pct.	G	PO	A	E	TC	DP
Mendoza, Ramiro, Red Sox	1.000	2	2	1	0	3	0
Meque, Jacobo, Reds *	1.000	2	1	2	0	3	0
Merricks, Alexander, Twins *	1.000	15	0	1	0	1	0
Michael, Mark, Pirates	1.000	13	1	4	0	5	0
Miner, Josh, Marlins	.714	11	0	5	2	7	0
Moore, Benjamin, Yankees	1.000	4	2	0	0	2	0
Morales, Alex, Expos	1.000	6	1	2	0	3	0
Munoz, Luis, Pirates	1.000	9	3	8	0	11	0
Nestor, Scott, Marlins	1.000	12	1	3	0	4	0
Nickerson, Jon-Michael, Marl.*	.833	12	1	4	1	6	0
Noriega, Luis, Reds	.889	9	4	4	1	9	0
Nunez, Francisco, Twins	.750	20	0	3	1	4	0
O'Flaherty, Liam, Dodgers *	1.000	15	3	4	0	7	0
Obispo, Jose, Dodgers	.857	9	3	3	1	7	0
Ochoa, Harry, Phillies *	1.000	15	2	7	0	9	0
Ochoa, Nehomar, Expos	.950	9	10	9	1	20	1
Ohalek, Corey, Marlins *	1.000	14	2	4	0	6	0
Ojeda, Alvis, Dodgers	.938	21	5	10	1	16	1
Orozco, Antonio, Marlins	1.000	4	1	3	0	4	1
Orozco, Dernier, Red Sox	1.000	14	2	6	0	8	0
Ortega, Joel, Pirates	1.000	10	0	1	0	1	0
Osuna, Antonio, Yankees	1.000	1	0	1	0	1	0
Overman, Matt, Marlins	.750	6	1	2	1	4	0
Pascual, Juan, Orioles	.750	14	0	3	1	4	0
Payano, Nelson, Braves *	1.000	13	1	2	0	3	0
Pearson, Kyle, Pirates	.714	7	2	3	2	7	1
Pelland, Tyler, Red Sox-Reds *	1.000	12	2	14	0	16	1
Penn, Hayden, Orioles	.500	1	1	0	1	2	0
Perez, Aneudy A., Reds	.750	13	3	6	3	12	1
Person, Robert, Red Sox	1.000	1	0	1	0	1	1
Potoczny, Robert, Dodgers	.833	16	3	7	2	12	0
Quijada, Fernando, Phillies	.800	17	0	4	1	5	0
Rainwater, Josh, Tigers	.700	10	3	4	3	10	0
Ramirez, Luis, Orioles	1.000	12	2	10	0	12	1
Ramirez, Wandar, Twins	1.000	17	2	5	0	7	1
Reyes, Jojo, Braves *	1.000	11	0	4	0	4	0
Reynolds, Eric, Marlins *	1.000	4	0	2	0	2	1
Rice, Leonard, Reds *	.889	13	0	8	1	9	0
Rodriguez, Juan, Pirates	1.000	5	0	1	0	1	0
Rodriguez, Osvaldo, Dodgers	.800	6	2	6	2	10	1
Rosario, Eduardo, Braves *	.938	12	5	10	1	16	2
Russ, James, Marlins	.833	11	2	3	1	6	0
Russell, Eddie, Marlins	1.000	2	1	0	0	1	0
Russell, James, Expos	1.000	9	2	0	0	2	0
Samuels, Matthew, Twins	1.000	18	2	7	0	9	0
Sandoval, Francisco, Expos	1.000	13	4	2	0	6	0
Santiago, Jose, Braves	1.000	16	1	1	0	2	0
Sborz, Jay, Tigers	1.000	8	0	5	0	5	0
Schultz, Cory, Phillies	1.000	11	2	2	0	4	0
Segovia, Omar, Reds *	.667	10	2	4	3	9	0
Segovia, Zach, Phillies	1.000	5	0	3	0	3	0
Shaffar, Ben, Pirates	1.000	5	1	0	0	1	0
Shinskie, David, Twins	.800	5	2	2	1	5	1
Skinner, Andrew, Reds	1.000	13	2	4	0	6	0
Smit, Alexander, Twins *	.923	8	2	10	1	13	0
Smith, Chris, Red Sox	.750	3	1	2	1	4	0
Smith, Dan, Braves *	1.000	13	5	1	0	6	0
Smith, Dustin, Tigers	1.000	6	2	4	0	6	0
Smith, Jason, Red Sox	1.000	1	0	1	0	1	0
Soriano, Alexander, Red Sox *	1.000	14	2	5	0	7	1
Sosa, Gabriel, Expos *	.800	12	1	3	1	5	0
Soto, Edgar, Yankees *	1.000	10	1	11	0	12	0
Soto, Reyes, Dodgers	.571	14	0	4	3	7	0
Stanley, Adam, Braves *	.800	16	2	2	1	5	0
Starling, Wardell, Pirates	.875	11	0	7	1	8	0
Stephens, Jason, Yankees	1.000	10	1	9	0	10	1
Stevens, Jake, Braves *	.818	14	3	6	2	11	1
Sulbaran, Orlando, Reds	1.000	1	1	0	0	1	0
Tate, Matt, Orioles	1.000	9	0	2	0	2	0
Tejada, Luis, Pirates	.800	7	3	1	1	5	1
Tequida, Mauricio, Dodgers	1.000	13	0	6	0	6	0
Thomas, Brad, Twins *	1.000	2	0	3	0	3	0
Thompson, Daryl, Expos	1.000	12	1	2	0	3	0
Vanden Hurk, Henricus, Marlins	.833	11	0	5	1	6	1
Vasquez, Sendy, Tigers	1.000	11	0	1	0	1	0
Villalona, Guillermo, Yankees	1.000	8	1	3	0	4	0
Wang, Chien-ming, Yankees	1.000	1	0	2	0	2	0
Weeden, Brandon, Yankees	.667	7	2	0	1	3	0
Wheldon, Rhys, Twins	1.000	5	0	3	0	3	0
White, Scott, Reds	.750	12	0	6	2	8	0
Wideman, Aaron, Expos *	.833	10	2	3	1	6	0
Wilson, Jonathan, Red Sox	1.000	10	1	7	0	8	0
Wilson, Joseph, Phillies *	1.000	11	0	8	0	8	0
Wright, Dequam, Dodgers *	1.000	14	2	5	0	7	1
Wright, Isaiah, Expos	.900	11	2	7	1	10	0

PITCHERS WITH TWO OR MORE TEAMS

Player, Team	Pct.	G	PO	A	E	TC	DP
Pelland, Tyler, Reds*	.000	1	0	0	0	0	0
Pelland, Tyler, Red Sox*	1.000	11	2	14	0	16	1

The following players appeared only as a designated hitter, pinch-hitter or pinch-runner: Bailie, dh; Dennis, dh, ph; Mazzuca, dh, ph; McRae, dh, ph; Piazza, dh; Santos, dh, pr; Tatum, dh, ph; Willingham, dh.

LEAGUE CHAMPIONS

Year	Team	Pct.
1964—	Sarasota Braves	.610
1965—	Bradenton Astros	.632
1966—	New York AL	.667
1967—	Kansas City	.614
1968—	Oakland	.650
1969—	Montreal	.585
1970—	Chicago AL	.600
1971—	Kansas City	.755
1972—	Chicago NL*	.651
	Kansas City*	.651
1973—	Texas	.732
1974—	Chicago NL	.702
1975—	Texas	.774
1976—	Texas	.704
1977—	Chicago AL	.731
1978—	Texas	.600
1979—	Houston	.635
1980—	Kansas City-Blue	.635
1981—	Kansas City-Gold	.688
1982—	New York AL	.667
1983—	Texas	.645
	Los Angeles†	.617
1984—	White Sox	.651
	Rangers†	.571
1985—	Yankees§	.705
	Rangers	.532
1986—	Reds	.548
	Dodgers†	.541
1987—	Dodgers†	.683
	Royals	.635
1988—	Yankees†	.714
	Royals	.619
1989—	Yankees‡	.651
	Dodgers	.635
1990—	Expos	.635
	Dodgers‡	.603
1991—	Orioles	.593
	Expos∞	.533
1992—	Royals∞	.695
	Expos	.593
1993—	Rangers▲	.667
	Astros	.593
1994—	Royals◆	.797
	Astros	.695
1995—	Royals■	.649
	Tigers	.579
1996—	Yankees◆	.638
	Rangers	.617
1997—	Mets▼	.700
	Rangers	.567
1998—	Marlins	.633
	Rangers◆	.567
1999—	Mets◆	.650
2000—	Rangers◆	.679
2001—	Dodgers	.683
	Yankees◆	.583
2002—	Phillies◆	.650
2003—	Braves◆	.633

*Declared co-champions; no playoff. †League divided into Northern and Southern divisions; won one-game playoff for league championship. ‡League divided into Northern and Southern divisions; won best-of-three playoff for league championship. §Yankees declared champion based on winning percentage when one-game playoff against Rangers was rained out. ∞League divided into Northern, Southern and Central divisions; won best-of-three playoff for league championship. ▲League divided into Eastern, Central and Western divisions; won three-team playoff. ◆League divided into Eastern, Northern and Southern divisions; won three-team playoff. ■League divided into Eastern, Northern, Northwest and Southwest divisions; won four-team playoff. ▼League divided into Eastern, Western and Northwest divisions; won four-club playoff. (Note—Known as Sarasota Rookie League in 1964 and Florida Rookie League in 1965.)

MINOR LEAGUE INDEX

TEAMS AND CITIES